The World Book Encyclopedia

WORLD BOOK

a Scott Fetzer company
Chicago
www.worldbookonline.com

The World Book Encyclopedia

For information on other World Book publications, visit our website at **http://www.worldbookonline.com** or call **1-800-WORLDBK (967-5325).** For information about sales to schools and libraries call **1-800-975-3250 (United States); 1-800-837-5365 (Canada).**

World Book, Inc.
233 North Michigan Avenue
Chicago, IL 60601
U.S.A.

About the SPINESCAPE®

The SPINESCAPE design for the 2012 edition—*Swifter, Higher, Stronger*—salutes the athletic activities that help keep people healthy and fit. Men and women take part in sports for personal enjoyment, for love of competition, and for physical conditioning. Played individually or in teams, sports help develop the speed, strength, and flexibility that people need to remain active throughout their lives. Just as athletes strive to do their personal best, the editors and staff of *The World Book Encyclopedia* work to help readers achieve their personal best in learning.

Photo credit:
© Mark Nolan, Getty Images; © Koji Aoki, Alfo/Corbis; © Blend Images/SuperStock; © image100/SuperStock; © Belinda Images/SuperStock; © Grant Faint, Getty Images; © Roy Ooms, Masterfile; © James Oliver, Getty Images; © Chris Graythen, Getty Images; © Ron Dahlquist, SuperStock.

Library of Congress Cataloging-in-Publication Data

The World Book encyclopedia.
   p. cm.
  Includes index.
  Summary: "A 22-volume, highly illustrated, A-Z general encyclopedia for all ages, featuring sections on how to use World Book, other research aids, pronunciation key, a student guide to better writing, speaking, and research skills, and comprehensive index"--Provided by publisher.
  ISBN 978-0-7166-0112-8 (set)
  1. Encyclopedias and dictionaries. I. World Book, Inc.
AE5.W54 2012
030--dc23

2011031621

Printed in the United States of America by RR Donnelley, Willard, Ohio
1st printing November 2011

SUSTAINABLE FORESTRY INITIATIVE

Certified Chain of Custody
Promoting Sustainable
Forest Management

www.sfiprogram.org

Nn

N is the 14th letter of the alphabet used for the modern English language. It is also used in a number of other languages, including French, German, and Spanish.

The sound of the letter *N* occurs in such words as *new, enter, can,* and *funny.* At the end of a word, the *N* sound can be spelled *GN,* as in *sign.* The sound represented by the combination *NG* cannot occur in English at the beginning of a word, but it often occurs at the end of a word, as in *sing.*

Scholars believe the letter *N* evolved from an Egyptian *hieroglyph* (pictorial symbol) that represented a viper (a type of snake). Hieroglyphs were adapted to be used for a Semitic language by around 1500 B.C. The alphabet for this Semitic language—the earliest known alphabet—is called Proto-Sinaitic. By 1100 B.C., an alphabet for another Semitic language, Phoenician, had evolved from Proto-Sinaitic. See **Semitic languages.**

The Phoenician letter that can be traced to the Egyptian viper hieroglyph is the 14th letter of the Phoenician alphabet, *nun.* The Phoenicians used the letter to represent the beginning *N* sound of *nun,* which was their word for *fish.* Around 800 B.C., when the Greeks adapted the Phoenician alphabet, *nun* became *nu,* which was used for the same sound. The Etruscans adopted the Greek alphabet about 700 B.C. By around 650 B.C., the Romans adopted the alphabet from the Etruscans.

Peter T. Daniels

See also **Alphabet.**

Development of the letter *N*

Seafarers and traders aided the transmission of letters along the coast of the Mediterranean Sea.

The Latin alphabet was adopted from the Etruscan alphabet by the Romans around 650 B.C. The Roman letter *N* lengthened the other parts of the letter to equal the "tail" section that the letter had featured in Greek and Etruscan.

The Etruscan alphabet was adopted from the Greek about 700 B.C. The Etruscans wrote from right to left, so the direction of their version of *nu* is reversed from the Greek.

Faster ways of writing letters developed during Roman times. Curved, connected lines were faster to write than imitations of the *inscriptional* (carved) Roman letters. The inscriptional forms of the letters developed into capital letters. The curved forms developed into small letters. The form of most small letters, including *n,* was set by around A.D. 800.

A.D. 300   1500   Today

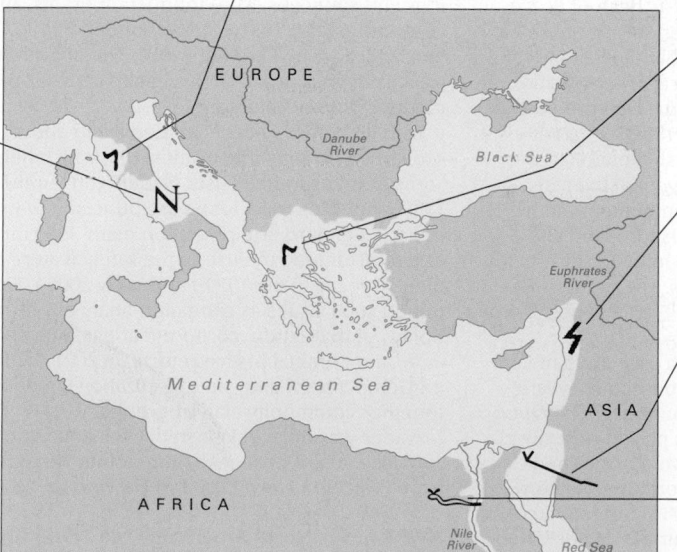

The Greek alphabet evolved from the Phoenician by around 800 B.C. The Greek letter *nu,* which was adapted from *nun,* simplified the Phoenician symbol. By 500 B.C., Greek was written from left to right.

The Phoenician alphabet had evolved from the Proto-Sinaitic by around 1100 B.C. The Phoenician letter *nun* looked like a snake slithering on the ground, but the Phoenician word *nun* meant fish.

A Proto-Sinaitic alphabet for a Semitic language evolved from Egyptian hieroglyphs by around 1500 B.C. The Proto-Sinaitic letter that came from the viper hieroglyph still featured a snake with small horns.

The Egyptians, about 3000 B.C., drew a hieroglyph representing a viper.

NAACP. See National Association for the Advancement of Colored People.

Nabokov, *NAH boh kawf,* **Vladimir,** *VLAH duh meer* (1899-1977), was a Russian-born author. His novels are noted for their complicated plots and the complex attitudes they express toward their subjects. Critics praised Nabokov's novels for their wit, intricate word use, and rich language. His novels, often satirical, include *Invitation to a Beheading* (published in the Soviet Union, 1938; United States, 1959), *The Real Life of Sebastian Knight* (1941), *Lolita* (published in France, 1955; United States, 1958), *Pnin* (1957), *Pale Fire* (1962), and *Ada* (1969). An unfinished novel, *The Original of Laura,* was published in 2009. Nabokov also wrote stories and poetry and translated several Russian literary classics into English. *Speak, Memory* (1951, expanded 1966) is his autobiography. A collection of his lectures at Cornell University in the 1950's was published as *Lectures on Literature* (1980). *The Stories of Vladimir Nabokov* was published in 1995.

Nabokov was born in St. Petersburg, Russia, on April 22, 1899. The family fled to Western Europe in 1919 because of the Bolshevik Revolution. Nabokov attended Cambridge University in England from 1919 to 1922. From 1922 to 1940, he lived in Berlin and Paris among other Russians who had left their country. He wrote his novels in Russian. Most were later translated into English. In 1940, he settled in the United States and began to write in English. Nabokov returned to Europe to live in 1959. He died on July 2, 1977.   Marcus Klein

Nabrit, James Madison, Jr. (1900-1997), won fame as a civil rights lawyer, university president, and diplomat. From 1960 to 1969, he was president of Howard University. He was a deputy United States representative to the United Nations in 1966 and 1967.

Nabrit was born in Atlanta on Sept. 4, 1900. He graduated from Morehouse College and Northwestern University Law School. In 1936, he joined the faculty of Howard University. At his suggestion, the university established—and he taught—the first civil rights course in an American law school. Nabrit served as secretary of the university from 1939 to 1960 and as dean of its law school from 1958 to 1960. As a lawyer, he specialized in school desegregation cases. Nabrit handled a number of cases for the National Association for the Advancement of Colored People (NAACP) Legal Defense and Educational Fund. He died on Dec. 27, 1997.   Robert A. Pratt

Nadal, Rafael (1986-   ), a Spanish tennis star, became one of the most dominant players of the early 2000's. Nadal is known as a fierce competitor who hits with tremendous topspin off both his forehand and backhand. Nadal is the seventh man in tennis history to win all four grand slam tournaments. The grand slam consists of the Australian Open, the French Open, Wimbledon, and the US Open.

Nadal first established himself as a clay court specialist, winning the French Open four consecutive years from 2005 through 2008. He also won the French Open in 2010 and 2011. The tournament is played on a slow clay surface. Nadal's four consecutive victories and six total French Open titles tied the records set by Björn Borg of Sweden. Nadal won the 2008 Wimbledon championship, played on a faster grass surface. He defeated Roger Federer in one of the greatest finals matches in tennis history. Nadal also defeated Federer to win the 2009 Australian Open. Nadal won his second Wimbledon title and his first US Open championship in 2010.

Nadal was born on June 3, 1986, in Manacor on the island of Majorca. He turned professional in 2001. Nadal won the gold medal in men's singles at the 2008 Summer Olympic Games.   James Martin

Nader, *NAY duhr,* **Ralph** (1934-   ), is an American lawyer who became famous for fighting business and government practices he felt endangered public health and safety. He also is an outspoken critic of the influence of large corporations on the American political system. Nader ran for president of the United States in 1996, 2000, 2004, and 2008. However, he won only a small percentage of the votes in each election. Nader was the first Arab American to campaign for president. In the 1996 and 2000 elections, he represented the Green Party. The Green Party's platform stresses community leadership, environmental responsibility, respect for diversity, improved health care, and social justice. In 2004 and 2008, Nader ran for president as an independent candidate.

UPI/Bettmann Newsphotos
Ralph Nader

In his book *Unsafe at Any Speed* (1965), Nader argued that the U.S. automobile industry emphasized profits and style over safety. The National Traffic and Motor Vehicle Safety Act of 1966, which established safety standards for new cars, resulted largely from his work. Nader's studies of the meat and poultry industries, coal mines, and natural gas pipelines also resulted in stricter health and safety laws. He publicized what he felt were the dangers of pesticides, food additives, radiation from color TV sets, and excessive use of X rays.

Nader's operating funds come mainly from his writings and speeches, from foundation grants, and from contributions. In 1971, Nader founded Public Citizen, Inc., which he headed until 1980. The organization specializes in energy problems, health care, tax reform, and other consumer issues.

In 1988, Nader's efforts helped bring about the passage of California's Proposition 103, which helped lower some auto insurance costs. Nader won another battle in 1989 when General Motors announced it would make airbags standard equipment on many 1990 models. Nader had promoted the use of the safety feature for more than 10 years. In the 1990's and early 2000's, Nader spoke out on such issues as campaign finance reform, trade policy, globalization, corporate abuse, universal health care, and criminal justice reform. In 2001, Nader founded Democracy Rising, an organization aimed at bringing together community activist groups.

Nader was born in Winsted, Connecticut, on Feb. 27, 1934, the son of Lebanese immigrants. He graduated from Princeton University and Harvard Law School.

Frederick E. Webster, Jr.

NAFTA. See North American Free Trade Agreement.

Nagasaki, *NAH guh SAH kee* (pop. 442,699), is the Japanese city with which Westerners have had the longest contact. Its harbor was opened to foreign trade in 1571. After 1637, it was the only Japanese port where Westerners were allowed to trade. Dutch traders were permitted to set up a trading post on an island in the harbor, and one Dutch ship each year was allowed to call at the post. In 1857, it was one of the six Japanese ports opened to foreign trade.

Nagasaki is on the west coast of the island of Kyushu. It is the Japanese port city closest to the mainland of China. Nearby coal fields provide soft coal for export. Nagasaki is on a landlocked bay, deep and large enough for many ships. For location, see **Japan** (political map).

Because Nagasaki has a large steel rolling mill, it is an important shipbuilding center. The second atomic bomb used in warfare destroyed many of its factories on Aug. 9, 1945 (see **Nuclear weapon** [picture]). The blast destroyed 1.8 square miles (4.7 square kilometers) in the heart of the city. It injured 40,000 people, and 40,000 were killed or missing. Since World War II (1939-1945), most of Nagasaki has been rebuilt.   Kenneth B. Pyle

See **World, History of the** (picture: The United States dropped an atomic bomb).

Nagoya, *nuh GOY uh* (pop. 2,215,062), is one of the largest cities in Japan. It is the capital of Aichi prefecture on the island of Honshu. It stands on Nobi Plain, facing Ise Bay (see **Japan** [political map]).

Nagoya was once the seat of the powerful *daimyo* (baron) of Owari, a province of early Japan. In 1610, the powerful feudal lord Tokugawa Ieyasu built a great castle in Nagoya. The castle was destroyed during World War II (1939-1945) but was rebuilt in 1959.

Nagoya is famous as a manufacturing center. It has an important textile industry. It also manufactures machines, pottery, porcelain, lacquerware, clocks, fans, and embroidery. Nagoya's industries and its population are crowded into a closely packed area. Nagoya is also one of Japan's major port cities.   Kenneth B. Pyle

Nahum, *NAY uhm,* **Book of,** is a book of the Hebrew Bible (also called the Old Testament) named for an Israelite prophet. Nahum lived in the kingdom of Judah during the second half of the 600's B.C. The book has three chapters. Chapter 1, a hymn, is a vision of God that may be the work of another author. In chapters 2 and 3, Nahum praises the capture and destruction in 612 B.C. of Nineveh, the capital of the hated and feared Assyrian empire. Nahum's description of Nineveh is so vivid that some people believe he actually witnessed the city's fall. The poetic style of the book is among the most elegant in the Bible. Nahum's striking images of God's anger and the safety God can offer lend great power and immediacy to the prophet's words.   Eric M. Meyers

Nail is the most widely used fastener for attaching one piece of wood to another. Nails also join wood and such materials as cloth, sheet metal, and wire. Special nails hold wood and other materials to brick and concrete.

Most nails are made of steel, but some are made of aluminum, brass, copper, or stainless steel. Steel nails may be coated with zinc or plated with aluminum, copper, or nickel to resist rust. Some nails have a coating of *resin,* an adhesive that makes them hold more tightly.

Carpenters generally use a *claw hammer* to drive nails. This kind of hammer has a *claw* for removing nails. Many carpenters who build or remodel houses use power tools to drive nails.

Some types of nails

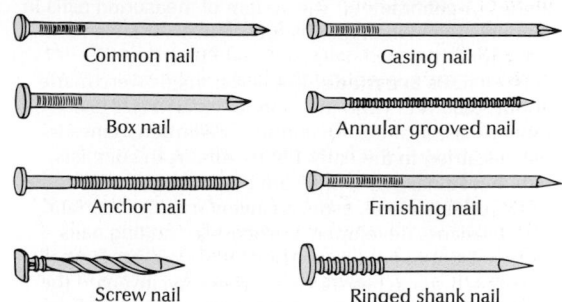

Nails have various shapes, depending on the purposes for which they are used. The different types of nails can be distinguished by their head, *shank* (body), and point.

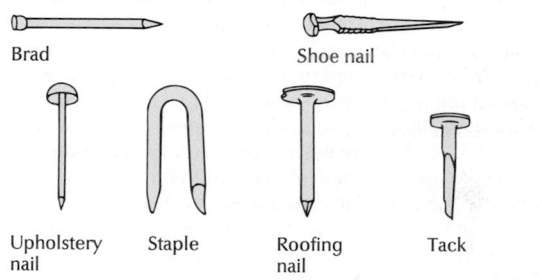

WORLD BOOK illustration

Specialty nails and other metal fasteners are made for specific jobs. For example, they may be used in making shoes, in upholstering furniture, or to hold roofing materials.

The parts of a nail. A nail has three main parts: (1) the point; (2) the *shank,* or body; and (3) the head. The point acts as a wedge that separates the fibers of wood as the nail is driven. After the nail is in place, the fibers grip the shank and keep the nail from loosening. The head covers the hole made by the nail and prevents the wood from springing back.

The most common type of nail point is the *diamond point,* a sharp point that works well in most kinds of wood. A *blunt point* works better in some hardwoods, such as maple and oak. This point breaks off some of the wood fibers and helps keep the wood from splitting.

Most nails have a smooth, round shank. Nails with a twisted, threaded, or ringed shank hold better but cost more. A narrow, flat, or barbed shank helps prevent hardwood from splitting. Nails with a square shank are used to attach wood flooring to concrete.

Most kinds of nails have a broad, flat head. A nail with a narrow head can be hidden in the wood by driving it completely below the surface with a punchlike tool called a *nailset.* The hole left by the nail can be filled with putty and then painted. Roofers use a nail with an extra wide head to install shingles. Upholsterers use tacks with decorative heads if the tacks can be seen.

Sizes of nails. Most countries use the metric system to identify nails, describing both their length and shank diameter in millimeters. In the United States, nails are usually measured in units called *pennies,* designated by the letter *d.* Nails measured in this way range in size from 2-penny nails that are 1 inch (2.5 centimeters) long to 60-penny nails 6 inches (15 centimeters) long. Nails that are shorter or longer than those are measured in inches or centimeters. The system of measuring nails in pennies began in England and originally referred to the price for a hundred nails.

How nails are made. The earliest nails were made about 5,000 years ago in Mesopotamia. Artists used them to fasten sheets of copper to wooden frames to make statues. In the early 1700's, American colonists hammered nails by hand from a bar of hot iron. About 1775, Jeremiah Wilkinson, an inventor in Cumberland, Rhode Island, developed a process for cutting nails from a sheet of cold iron. About 1851, William Hassall (or Hersel), a machinist in New York City, invented the first machine for making nails from wire. Today, almost all nails are made from wire fed into a machine that can produce hundreds per minute. A set of cutters trims off a length of wire and forms the point of the nail at one end. A hammer shapes the head at the other end. The nails are polished, plated, or coated.   Simon Lekakh

Nail is a tough plate that covers the upper surface at the end of each finger and toe. It is a special growth of the *epidermis* (outer portion of the skin) and is made up of hardened cells. It grows from the *matrix,* the skin below the nail. Near the root of the nail, where growth begins, the blood flow in the cells is less visible. The white, crescent-shaped spot indicating this area is the *lunula.*

If a nail is torn off, it will regrow if the matrix has not been severely injured. White spots on the nail are due to bruises or other injuries. They will grow out as the nail grows. The state of a person's health is often indicated by the nails. Illness often affects their growth.

The horns, claws, talons, and hoofs of birds and animals are made of the same materials as the nails on the fingers and toes of the human body. Deer antlers are a different kind of growth.   Paul R. Bergstresser

Naipaul, *ny PAWL,* **V. S.** (1932-   ), is a Trinidad-born novelist, travel writer, and social commentator. He writes about many cultures and societies. Naipaul's recurrent theme is the clash of older traditions and practices with the raw aggressiveness of modern political life. Naipaul won the 2001 Nobel Prize in literature.

Vidiadhar Surajprasad Naipaul was born on Aug. 17, 1932, in Chaguanas on the island of Trinidad to descendants of immigrants from India. He was educated in the Caribbean and at Oxford University in England. After completing his studies, he settled in England. His early fiction tended toward the lightly comic. Naipaul first gained fame with his satirical novel *A House for Mr. Biswas* (1961). The novels *Guerrillas* (1975), *A Bend in the River* (1979), *A Way in the World* (1994), and *Half a Life* (2001) and its sequel *Magic Seeds* (2004) have political themes. Naipaul's many travel books include *The Middle Passage* (1962), about the Caribbean; *An Area of Darkness* (1965), about India; *Among the Believers: An Islamic Journey* (1981), about the Middle East; *A Turn in the South* (1989), about the Southern United States; and *The Masque of Africa* (2010), about Africa. His short stories were collected in *A Flag on the Island* (1967). His nonfiction was published in *The Writer and the World* (2002), *Literary Occasions* (2004), and *A Writer's People: Ways of Looking and Feeling* (2008).   Michael Seidel

Nairobi, *ny ROH bee* (pop. 2,143,254), is the capital of Kenya and the most important commercial center in eastern Africa. The city lies on a high plateau in south-

central Kenya (for the city's location, see **Kenya** [map]).

The central area of Nairobi has many modern hotels and commercial buildings. Its main streets are lined with trees. This area includes the parliament buildings, Kenyatta International Conference Center, Holy Family Cathedral, and Jamia Mosque. The National Museum and the University of Nairobi are north of the central area. Rail yards and an industrial area lie to the south. About 5 miles (8 kilometers) farther south, but still within the city, is Nairobi National Park. It covers 45 square miles (117 square kilometers) of open land where lions, gazelles, wildebeests, zebras, and other wild animals live.

Many of Nairobi's people live in large, low-cost apartments called *estates.* Others live in single-family homes.

The Kenyan government is a major employer in Nairobi. Industries in Nairobi produce beverages, cement, chemicals, foods, metal products, and textiles. Tourism is an important part of the city's economy. Many people visit Nairobi National Park and take trips to other Kenyan game reserves. Nairobi is a center for banking, trade, and commerce. Nairobi was originally the site of a water hole called *Enkare Nairobi,* which means *cold water.* It became a railroad hub in the early 1900's. In 1963, when Kenya became independent from the United Kingdom, the area of Nairobi expanded from about 35 square miles (91 square kilometers) to 266 square miles (689 square kilometers).   Stephen K. Commins

See also **Kenya** (pictures).

Naismith, *NAY smihth,* **James** (1861-1939), invented the game of basketball in 1891 (see **Basketball**). He wanted to develop a game that could be played indoors during the winter months. He tacked up two peach baskets and used a soccer ball for the first game. He invented the game when he was a physical-education teacher at the International YMCA Training School (now Springfield College) in Springfield, Massachusetts.

Naismith was born in Almonte, Ontario, on Nov. 6, 1861. He graduated from McGill University in Montreal. Naismith was one of Canada's greatest rugby and lacrosse players. He studied for the ministry but became a physical-education teacher. He was director of physical education at the University of Kansas from 1898 to 1937. He became a United States citizen in 1925. Naismith died on Nov 28, 1939.   Bob Logan

Naked mole-rat is a burrowing rodent of East Africa known for its unusual appearance and social behavior. Its tubelike body is nearly hairless, with wrinkled pink

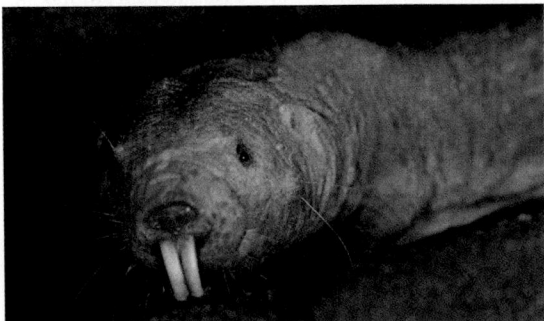

© Frans Lanting Studio/Alamy Images

The naked mole-rat is a burrowing rodent with wrinkled pink skin. It digs using its sharp, chisellike front teeth.

skin. An adult may reach about 3 to 5 inches (8 to 13 centimeters) long and weigh 1 to 3 ounces (28 to 84 grams). The naked mole-rat spends its entire life underground. It lives in burrows with many tunnels and rooms. It digs using its strong jaws and sharp, chisellike front teeth.

The social behavior of naked mole-rats is like that of ants and honey bees. Naked mole-rats live in colonies that usually have about 75 to 80 members, though large colonies have up to 300 members. Only one female, called the *queen,* and one to three males breed. No other members of the colony breed. Instead, they work for the well-being of the colony. This form of social behavior is called *eusociality.* Only one other species of mammal, the Damaraland mole-rat, is known to be eusocial.

A naked mole-rat queen is larger than the other members of the colony. She usually bears 12 pups in a litter, though a litter may have as many as 28 pups. She can bear four to five litters and more than 100 pups in a year. She *harasses* (bullies) nonbreeding females and males. The harassment prevents them from breeding. If the queen dies, another female develops into a queen, grows larger, and begins to breed.

Nonbreeding naked mole-rats do a variety of work for the colony. This work includes caring for the young, maintaining tunnels, finding food, and attacking *predators* (hunting animals). Naked mole-rats feed mainly on tubers and other underground parts of plants. Smaller, younger workers do most of the maintenance work. Larger, older individuals work together to drive off snakes, as well as naked mole-rats from other colonies.

Naked mole-rats are unusual in many other ways. For example, their body temperature varies with the surrounding temperature more than that of any other mammal. Also, naked mole-rats can tolerate stagnant air, with high levels of carbon dioxide.   Paul W. Sherman

Scientific classification. The scientific name of the naked mole-rat is *Heterocephalus glaber.*

See also **Mole-rat.**

Namath, *NAY muhth,* **Joe** (1943-   ), became one of professional football's most successful and colorful quarterbacks while playing for the New York Jets from 1965 to 1976. He was known for his accurate passing and skillful play selections. He passed for 27,663 yards and 173 touchdowns during his pro career. In 1967, Namath became the first pro quarterback ever to pass for more than 4,000 yards in a single season.

Joe William Namath was born in Beaver Falls, Pennsylvania, on May 31, 1943. He starred at quarterback at the University of Alabama, which he attended from 1961 to 1965. Namath was drafted by the Jets when the team was a member of the five-year-old American Football League (AFL). His success helped lead to the merging of the AFL and the established National Football League in 1970. In 1969, Namath led the Jets to a 16-7 upset over the Baltimore Colts in Super Bowl III. Namath played his last season in 1977 with the Los Angeles Rams. He was voted into the Pro Football Hall of Fame in 1985. He became a TV sports commentator and actor.   Carlton Stowers

Name is a word or series of words by which a person, animal, place, or thing is known. Every person has a name. In Western nations, most people have three names—two *given* names and a *family* name. The two given names are the *first name* and the *middle name.* The family name—also called the *surname* or *last*

name—is the name traditionally shared by all the members of a family. All three names together make up the *legal name*—that is, the complete name by which a person is officially known. A title, such as *Mr.,* or a suffix, such as *Jr.,* is not part of one's legal name.

This article discusses the origins and cultural characteristics of personal names. For information about proper etiquette in the use of names, see **Address, Forms of.**

Given names

Many given names have long histories and original meanings, though people today may not be aware of them. In Western nations, many parents choose names for their children without considering the original meanings. But in African and Asian countries, most names have meanings that are widely understood by the community. For instance, in Nigeria, the name *Daren,* which means *night,* is often given to children born at night.

Many given names that are popular in Western nations come from Hebrew, Greek, Latin, Teutonic, or Celtic languages. Others have roots in the languages of Africa, Asia, or elsewhere. A given name is sometimes called a *Christian* name.

Hebrew names taken from the Bible have been an important source of given names in the United States and throughout Europe. Some of the most common names derived from Hebrew are *John* (gracious gift of God), *Mary* (wished for), and *Michael* (who is like God?). Others include *Anna, Anne,* and *Hannah* (gracious); *Elizabeth* (oath of God); *Jacob* and *James* (may God protect, or one who takes the place of another); *Joshua* (God is salvation); *Matthew* (gift of God); *Sarah* (princess); and *Zachary* (God has remembered).

Greek and Latin names. Common given names derived from Greek include *Alexander* (defender of humanity), *Anthony* (flourishing), *Christopher* (Christ bearer), *Doris* (mother of sea gods), *Nicholas* and *Nicole* (victory of the people), and *Sophia* (wisdom). Names derived from Latin include *Diana* (moon goddess), *Emily* (industrious), *Justin* (just or fair), *Olivia* (olive tree), *Patrick* (noble), and *Victor* and *Victoria* (victory).

Teutonic names have origins in the Teutonic, or Germanic, languages. Teutonic languages include Dutch, English, German, and the Scandinavian languages. Teutonic names usually consist of two elements joined together without regard to their relationship. For example, *William* is composed of two name elements: *Wille* (will, or resolution) and *helm* (helmet). But the name's meaning is not *helmet of will* or *resolute helmet.* Instead, it means *will, helmet.* Other names with Teutonic roots include *Audrey* (noble, strength); *Emma* (greatness); *Richard* (power, brave); and *Roger* (famous warrior).

Celtic names are derived from the Breton, Irish, Welsh, and Scottish Gaelic languages. Popular Celtic names include *Brian* and *Brianna* (noble, strong), *Connor* (wise or lover of hounds), *Dylan* (of the sea), *Erin* (Ireland), and *Kevin* (handsome or gentle). Celtic versions of Hebrew, Greek, or Latin names also appear in countries with a Celtic tradition. For instance, *Sean* and *Ian* are the Irish and Scottish forms of *John.*

Black names. Black parents in the United States and other countries often give their children names with European origins. But since the 1960's, many black parents have chosen names that reflect their African heritage, their religious beliefs, or other cultural identities. Some common black names are derived from such African languages as Igbo, Kikuyu (also called Kikikuyu), Swahili (also called Kiswahili), or Yoruba. Examples include *Aba* (born on Thursday), *Aduke* (much loved), *Marjani* (coral), and *Dakarai* (happiness). Other names may have roots in the religion of Islam. For instance, the boxer Cassius Marcellus Clay changed his name to *Muhammad Ali* when he adopted the Black Muslim religion. Various other Muslim names, such as *Malik* and *Khadijah,* have gained popularity among blacks.

Many black parents today create new names that are based on sound patterns that are common in black communities. Examples of such names include *Deshone, Jalen, Montell,* and *Trayvon* for boys, and *Aunjuane, Denisha, Lakeisha,* and *Trinique* for girls.

Hispanic names. Traditionally, the most common given names in Spanish-speaking cultures have been Spanish versions of Hebrew, Greek, Latin, and Teutonic names. *José, Juan, Carlos, María, Isabel, Luisa,* and *Sofía,* for example, are Spanish versions of *Joseph, John, Charles, Mary, Elizabeth, Louise,* and *Sophie,* respectively. Many popular Hispanic names have roots in religion. For instance, the names *Araceli* (altar of heaven), *Mercedes* (mercies), and *Pilar* (pillar) are based on titles given to the Virgin Mary in Roman Catholic tradition. Various other names have been taken from Hispanic novels or adopted from the Native American cultures of Mexico and Central America.

Asian names. In China, Japan, and other East Asian countries, most parents choose names from words that have a clear meaning in their native language. For instance, a Korean family might name a daughter *Joo-eun,* meaning *silver pearl.*

Parents from India, Pakistan, and other South Asian countries often take names from Hindu or Islamic tradition. Some Hindu names include *Kiran* (ray of light) and *Rohan* (ascending) for boys, and *Priya* (beloved) and *Jaya* (victory) for girls. Some Muslim names include *Abdullah* (servant of God) and *Farid* (unique) for boys, and *A'isha* (life or woman) and *Latifah* (kind, gentle) for girls.

Asian parents living in the United States and Canada commonly give their children Western names, or names that can be easily pronounced by English speakers.

Native American names reflect the culture of a particular tribe. Names are often symbolic, though each group has its own naming traditions. For instance, in many groups, a child traditionally had one name at birth and moved on to other names in later stages of life. In other groups, a person's name was related to the *clan* (group of relatives with a common ancestor) within the tribe to which the person belonged.

Today, many Native Americans have "Americanized" names for legal identification purposes, in addition to Native American names that they use within their own families and communities. For instance, the actor Rodney Grant, a member of the Omaha nation, also bears the name *Mon-ga-ska* (white breast of a deer), a traditional name for men of the Deer clan.

Other given names. In many countries, including the United Kingdom and the United States, family names are often used as given names. For instance, the given names *Ashley, Logan, Mackenzie, Madison, Ryan, Scott,* and *Taylor* originated as family names. Other sources of given names include gems *(Amber, Jade)* and place names *(Brittany, Savannah).* Many people have as their middle name the *maiden name* of the mother—that is, the family name that the mother had before marriage.

Family names

Family names have developed in a variety of ways. Common sources of family names include locations, surroundings, occupations, and family background.

The classification of family names is difficult, largely because of changes and inconsistencies in spelling and pronunciation over the years. For many years, the spelling of a name could vary from one writer to another. In some cases, the same name would be spelled in different ways within the same document. Names that immigrants bring into a country are sometimes altered into more familiar-sounding names. For instance, in the United States, the Dutch *Roggenfelder* (dweller in or near a rye field) became the American *Rockefeller.*

Locations. Many family names have origins in a person's surroundings or place of residence. For example, if a man lived on or near a hill or mountain, he might have as his family name *Maki,* if from Finland; *Dumont* or *Depew* in France; *Zola* in Italy; *Jurek* in Poland; or *Hill* in England. Many other family names—including such English names as *Wood, Lake, Brook, Stone,* or *Ford*—are based on natural surroundings. Some family names come from the names of towns, such as *Middleton* or *Kronenberg.* Many English place names have the endings *-ham, -thorp, -ton, -wic,* and *-worth,* which mean a *homestead* or *dwelling.*

Occupations. Family names have also come from people's jobs. Such names as *Baker, Carpenter, Clarke* (the British pronunciation of *clerk*), *Cook, Miller,* and *Taylor* are quite common. The most common surname in the English language is *Smith* (metalworker). The name *Smith* takes the form of *Schmidt* in Germany, *Lefevre* in France, *Ferraro* in Italy, and *Kuznetzvo* in Russia.

Ancestors. Many family names come from the given names of ancestors. Nearly every language has a suffix or prefix that means *son of.* Some names with the term *son of* include Irish names starting with *Mc* or *Mac,* German names ending in *-sohn* or *-son,* and Scandinavian names ending in *-sen* or *-son.* Russian and Serbian names ending in *-ovitch* and Romanian names ending in *-escu* have the same meaning. Family names describing a person as the *son of John* include *Johnson* and *Jackson* in England; *Johns* and *Jones* in Wales; *Jensen, Jansen,* and *Hansen* in Denmark; *Jonsson* and *Johanson* in Sweden; *Janowicz* in Poland; *Ivanov* in Russia and Bulgaria; *Janosfi* in Hungary; and *MacEoin* in Ireland. Irish names beginning with *O'* originally signified a grandson.

Many family names have roots in words that were used to describe an ancestor. In the Middle Ages, which lasted from about the 400's through the 1400's, most Europeans lived in small villages and needed only a single name. But when a village clerk needed to record that a villager named Robert had paid a tax, he often had to add descriptive words to distinguish the villager from others with the same name. For example, the clerk might call the man *Robert, the small,* which would eventually lead to the family name *Small.* The names *Gross* and *Groth* come from the German word for a fat or large person. Names like *Reid, Reed,* and *Read* are early spellings of the word *red* and were originally used to refer to a person with red hair.

Other family names. Many Jewish family names come from combinations of such words as *gold, silver, rosen* (rose), *berg* (mountain), *stein* (stone), and *thal* (valley). Examples of such names include *Goldberg, Silverstein,* and *Rosenthal.* Other Jewish names come from the names of cities, such as *London* and *Modena.* Still others have religious meanings. The name *Katz,* for instance, is an abbreviation of *kohen tzedek,* Hebrew for *priest of righteousness.*

In Spain and other Spanish-speaking countries, a child traditionally takes the surname of both the father and the mother. These names were formerly joined by *y,* the Spanish word for *and.* For example, Julio, the son of Rodrigo Ruiz y Gonzalez and María Lopez y Chavez, would be known as *Julio Ruiz y Lopez.* Among Spanish-speaking people today, a hyphen may join the two names, as in *Julio Ruiz-Lopez.* The name may also be shortened to *Julio Ruiz.*

Many family names have more than one origin. For example, the family name *Lee* may indicate that an ancestor lived near a meadow or forest clearing, or in an English town named *Lee* or *Leigh.* The same name could also be a modernized spelling of the Irish name *Laoidhigh,* meaning *poet,* or the Norwegian word *Li,* meaning *mountain slope.* For families of Chinese descent, the name could come from the word *Li,* meaning *plum.*

Other names

Nicknames are informal names that are used in addition to, or instead of, legal names. Nicknames are often based on a person's prominent characteristics. *Happy* and *Gabby,* for instance, might describe someone's personality. Other nicknames, such as *Tiny* or *Slim,* might be based on physical characteristics.

Sometimes a nickname results from a child's attempt to pronounce a word or name, such as *Lilibet* for *Elizabeth.* In other instances, a nickname is a translation of the person's real name. Many people called New York City mayor Fiorello H. La Guardia *The Little Flower,* a literal translation of his Italian first name. In other cases, a nickname consists of a person's initials. For instance, U.S. President Franklin Delano Roosevelt was widely known as *FDR.*

Pet names, or *nursery names,* often consist of abbreviations of given names, such as *Bob* for *Robert,* or *Liz* for *Elizabeth.* They may also represent family names, such as *Smitty* for *Smith.*

Pseudonyms are fictitious names used by people who wish to conceal their identities or who want to be known by another name. Some celebrities use pseudonyms to avoid being recognized. An *alias* usually refers to a false name taken by a criminal to disguise his or her identity. *Stage names* are names that some entertainers assume in their professions. For instance, the American actor Thomas Cruise Mapother IV gained fame as *Tom Cruise.* Similarly, Frances Gumm, an American singer and actress, was better known as *Judy Garland.*

A *pen name,* or *nom de plume,* is a writer's pseudonym. Many authors have assumed pen names. For example, *Voltaire* was the pen name of François Marie Arouet. Eric Blair, an English writer, wrote under the pen name of *George Orwell.* See **Pen name; Pseudonym.**

The history of names

The Chinese were the first known people to use more than one name. The Emperor Fuxi is said to have decreed the use of family names about 2852 B.C. The Chinese customarily had three names: a family name, placed first; a *generation name;* and a *milk name,* which corresponded to a person's given name.

In early times, Roman citizens used only one name, or sometimes two. But as the republic grew, they developed a system of three names. The *praenomen* stood first as the person's given name. Next came the *nomen,* which indicated the person's *gens,* or clan. The last name, the *cognomen,* designated the family. A person could add a fourth name, the *agnomen,* to commemorate a remarkable action or event. But after the fall of the West Roman Empire in the 300's and 400's, single names again became customary.

Family names came into use again in northern Italy about the late A.D. 900's and became common about the 1200's. Nobles first adopted family names to set them apart from the common people. They made these family names hereditary, and the names descended from father to child. A family name became the mark of a well-bred person, so the common people began to adopt the practice as well. After the Crusaders passed through Italy on their return from the Holy Land, they carried the custom of family names to other European countries.

Middle names appeared in parts of Europe during the Middle Ages, which began about A.D. 400. But middle names did not become common in North America until the late 1700's.   Cleveland Kent Evans

NAMI. See National Alliance on Mental Illness.

Namibia, *nuh MIHB ee uh,* is a country in southwestern Africa. It was formerly named South West Africa. Windhoek is the capital and largest city of the country.

Most of Namibia's people are blacks of African descent. But the territory was held by neighboring South Africa from 1916 to 1990—a period when whites of European descent fully controlled South Africa's govern-

© Gerald Cubitt

Namibia is a country in southwestern Africa. Windhoek, the capital city, has modern downtown buildings.

ment. In March 1990, after many years of negotiations, Namibia gained full independence from South Africa.

Much of Namibia's land is dry and unfertile. But it is rich in mineral deposits, such as diamonds and uranium.

Government. Namibia's government is headed by a president. The people elect the president to a five-year term. Namibia's legislature consists of two groups—the National Assembly and the National Council. The National Assembly writes the nation's laws, and the National Council reviews them. The National Assembly has 72 members, elected by the people to five-year terms. The National Council has 26 members. Each of the country's 13 regional councils elects 2 members of the National Council to six-year terms. Regional council members are elected by the people. The president of Namibia appoints a prime minister from among the members of the National Assembly. The prime minister leads the Assembly and assists the president in carrying out the functions of government.

Namibia's most powerful political party is the South West Africa People's Organization (SWAPO). The main opposition party is the Democratic Turnhalle Alliance (DTA).

Namibia's army is the Namibia Defense Force. Service in the nation's army is voluntary.

People. Namibians belong to a number of ethnic groups. The Ovambo (also spelled Owambo) form the largest group. They comprise over half of the population. The Ovambo live in the north, near the Angolan border. This region is called Ovamboland or Ovambo. Other northerners include the Kavango, who live near the Okavango River; and the Caprivians, who inhabit the eastern end of the narrow strip of land called the Caprivi Strip. The Damara and the Herero occupy central Namibia. San and Tswana people live along the country's eastern border. Two groups of people of mixed ancestry live south of Windhoek—the Basters, who live in or near Rehoboth; and the Nama, who inhabit the far south.

People of Dutch, English, German, and other European ancestry live mainly in or near cities or towns. People of mixed European and African ancestry called Coloureds also live primarily in urban areas.

Facts in brief

Capital: Windhoek.
Official language: English.
Official name: Republic of Namibia.
Area: 318,261 mi² (824,292 km²). *Greatest distances*—east-west, about 880 mi (1,420 km); north-south, about 820 mi (1,320 km). *Coastline*—925 mi (1,489 km).
Elevation: *Highest*—Brandberg, 8,465 ft (2,580 m) above sea level. *Lowest*—sea level, along the coast.
Population: *Estimated 2012 population*—2,286,000; density, 7 per mi² (3 per km²); distribution, 63 percent rural, 37 percent urban. *2001 census*—1,830,330.
Chief products: *Agriculture*—cattle, corn, fish, grapes, millet, sheep, vegetables. *Mining*—copper, diamonds, lead, uranium, zinc.
Flag: A large blue triangle is in the upper left corner, and a large green triangle is in the lower right corner. A sun appears on the blue triangle. The triangles are separated by a red diagonal stripe bordered by white. Adopted 1990. See **Flag** (picture: Flags of Africa).
Money: *Basic units*—Namibian dollar and South African rand. One hundred cents equal one dollar. One hundred cents equal one rand.

Namibia

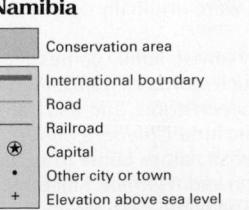
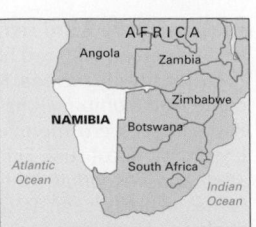
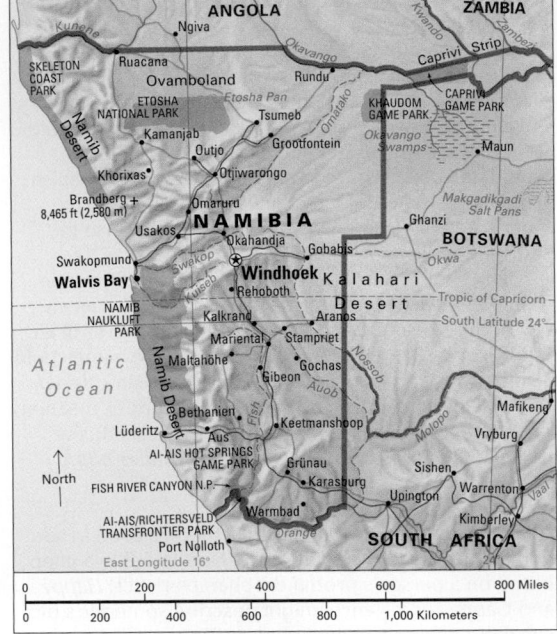

WORLD BOOK maps

Most people of northern Namibia fish, grow crops, and raise livestock for a living. Many Ovambo and Kavango men also work in copper mines at Tsumeb or in diamond mines near the southern border. Most of the rural people south of Ovamboland farm and raise livestock. Many Namibians of European descent hold administrative jobs in urban areas. The standard of living among Namibia's African ethnic groups varies, but most people of African descent must struggle to make a living. People of European ethnicity generally have higher incomes than people of African ethnicity.

Namibia's official language is English. But most Namibians speak local African languages. About 15 such languages are spoken. About 90 percent of the people are Christians. Lutherans form the largest Christian group. Other Christian groups include Roman Catholics, Anglicans, and members of Dutch Reformed Churches.

Public schools provide Namibians with free education. The University of Namibia (formerly the Academy for Tertiary Education) offers postsecondary education.

Land and climate. Namibia is bordered on the north by two large rivers, the Kunene and the Okavango. The Kwando River cuts through the Caprivi Strip. The Zambezi River flows along the northeastern border, and the Orange River forms Namibia's southern border. Otherwise, Namibia is a dry land. Droughts often occur.

The western border of Namibia stretches 950 miles (1,500 kilometers) along the Atlantic Ocean. Huge sand dunes of the Namib Desert lie near the coast. The Kalahari Desert occupies eastern Namibia. The inland territory is mostly a rolling plain about 4,000 feet (1,200 meters) above sea level. This area has stubby trees and enough grassland for grazing cattle and growing corn.

Large antelope live on the interior plain of Namibia. Elephants adapted to desert conditions inhabit the northwest corner of the country. Etosha National Park, which is a huge reserve in north-central Namibia, has a variety of animals, including antelopes, cheetahs, elephants, giraffes, lions, rhinoceroses, and zebras.

Daytime temperatures in Namibia average 75 °F (24 °C) in January and 68 °F (20 °C) in June. Namibia receives most of its rain between December and March. The average annual rainfall totals about 20 inches (50 centimeters) in the north and about 8 to 16 inches (20 to 40 centimeters) in the center. The south gets only about 1 to 6 inches (2.5 to 15 centimeters) of rain a year.

Economy. Mining ranks as one of Namibia's most important economic activities. Diamonds are the chief mined product. Other minerals include copper, lead, uranium, and zinc. Traditionally, farming, livestock raising, and fishing have also been important economic activities. But drought and other problems have reduced farming and livestock activities, and overfishing has reduced fishing in the Atlantic. Most farmers grow only enough food crops for their own use. The chief farm crops include corn, grapes, millet, and vegetables. Cattle and sheep are the most important livestock. The fishing industry yields anchovies, mackerel, and sardines. Little manufacturing takes place in Namibia.

Namibia's leading exports include beverages, fish, and gem diamonds. The country imports machinery, petroleum and petroleum products, transportation equipment, and wheat and other foods. The chief trading partners include Angola, South Africa, Spain, the United States, and the United Kingdom.

Walvis Bay is the chief port. Namibia's railroads connect its major urban areas with one another and with South Africa. Most of Namibia's roads are unpaved. An international airport is near Windhoek.

History. Both the Damara and the San people claim to be the original inhabitants of Namibia. Through the years, large numbers of Herero and Ovambo people moved to Namibia from the north. By the 1800's, the Damara, Herero, and Ovambo were the largest groups, and the Kavango and the Caprivians had settled where they now live. Other groups arrived in the 1800's.

Beginning in 1868, German settlers, missionaries, and soldiers colonized Namibia's coast. Germany annexed the land in 1884, calling it German Southwest Africa. In the 1890's, the Germans brutally forced the Herero and Damara out of the Windhoek area. The Herero began to revolt in 1904. By the time the Germans put down the revolt in 1907, they had killed about 65,000 Herero.

In 1915, during World War I, South African troops attacked the Germans and took over Namibia. The South Africans wanted to make Namibia part of their country. But the United States and other allied nations objected to that plan. In 1920, the newly formed League of Nations gave South Africa a mandate to manage Namibia's government and affairs. Yet, the South Africans governed Namibia as if it were a province of their nation.

The United Nations (UN) replaced the League of Nations in 1945. But South Africa refused to accept the authority of the UN and rejected its request to place Namibia under UN trusteeship. The UN took steps to try to bring Namibia under UN control. In 1966, the UN voted to end South Africa's mandate. In 1971, the International Court of Justice declared South Africa's control of Namibia illegal.

Black Namibians formed a political organization called the South West Africa People's Organization (SWAPO) in 1960. At first, SWAPO tried to persuade South Africa to grant Namibia independence. But beginning in the mid-1960's, it used guerrilla tactics to further its goal. In turn, South Africa set up armed forces along Namibia's borders with Angola and Zambia. Fighting occurred between SWAPO and South Africa until 1989.

In 1977, South Africa was preparing to grant Namibia independence under a plan that would give local political leadership to an assembly dominated by white Namibians. The UN strongly opposed such white domination. Representatives of the United States, the United Kingdom, West Germany, France, and Canada persuaded South Africa to negotiate a new plan that would meet the UN objection. Negotiations for independence were held at various times in the late 1970's and the 1980's.

Finally, in late 1988, South Africa agreed to a plan under which Namibia would gain full independence by April 1990. In April 1989, SWAPO and South Africa agreed to a cease-fire. Elections for a Constituent Assembly in Namibia were held in November 1989. In February 1990, the Assembly approved a constitution and elected Sam Nujoma, the leader of SWAPO, as Namibia's first president. Future presidents were to be elected by the people. Namibia gained independence on March 21, 1990. The Constituent Assembly was then renamed the National Assembly.

When Namibia became independent, South Africa kept the district of Walvis Bay, which included the port of Walvis Bay. Namibian leaders said Walvis Bay should be part of Namibia. In March 1994, South Africa turned over control of Walvis Bay to Namibia. In 1994 and 1999, Namibia's voters reelected Nujoma as president. In 2004, Hifikepunye Pohamba, the SWAPO candidate, was elected president of Namibia.　　Robert I. Rotberg

See also **South Africa; United Nations** (Working for self-government); **Windhoek.**

Nan-ching. See Nanjing.

Nanjing, *nahn jihng* (pop. 3,624,234), also spelled *Nanching* or *Nanking,* is an important center of industry, transportation, government, and culture in east-central China. The city lies on the Yangtze River, about 200 miles (320 kilometers) from the East China Sea. For location, see **China** (political map). Nanjing is the capital of Jiangsu Province and was once the capital of all China.

The city. Government office buildings, museums, and two stadiums are in the center of Nanjing. Commercial and residential areas lie outside the central area. Most of Nanjing's people live in apartment buildings or in apartments above shops. The remains of an ancient defensive wall surround the built-up areas of Nanjing.

Most of Nanjing's people travel by bicycle or public bus. But some people drive cars to and from work.

Wharves that can handle oceangoing ships line the banks of the Yangtze River, which borders Nanjing on the west. East of the city are Xuanwu Lake, a tourist attraction with several islands; and Zijin Mountain, the site of an astronomical observatory. The tomb of Sun Yat-sen, who helped establish the Republic of China in 1912, lies on the mountain. Nanjing's educational institutions include Nanjing University, engineering colleges, and a medical school.

Economy. Nanjing has hundreds of manufacturing plants. Leading products include cement, fertilizers, iron and steel, porcelain, textiles, and trucks. Nearby mines provide iron ore for the iron and steel plants. Many farming families live in towns and villages near Nanjing. The farmers raise cotton, rice, wheat, and other crops.

Railroads connect Nanjing to Beijing, the capital of China, in the north and to Shanghai in the east. Numerous ships dock at the wharves of the city. A double-deck bridge that extends 3 miles (5 kilometers) across the Yangtze River serves both trains and motor vehicles.

History. People have lived in what is now the Nanjing area since about the 400's B.C. Early settlers chose the site because of its location near a river and some roads. During several periods in the A.D. 200's to 500's, the city served as the capital of various local Chinese *dynasties* (series of rulers of the same family). The Ming dynasty gained control of most of China in 1368. The first Ming ruler made Nanjing—which means *southern capital*—the seat of the dynasty. In the early 1400's, the Mings moved the capital to Beijing—which means *northern capital.*

In 1853, rebels called the Taipings seized Nanjing from the Manchus, who ruled China at that time. The Taipings made the city the capital of their empire. The Manchus regained Nanjing in 1864.

In 1912, Chinese revolutionaries overthrew the Manchus. The new rulers met in Nanjing and founded the Republic of China. From 1928 to 1937, the city served as the capital of the republic. Japanese forces captured Nanjing in 1937 and burned much of the city. They murdered or raped many of the city's residents in what became known as the Nanking Massacre or the Rape of Nanking (see **Nanking Massacre**). Nanjing again became China's capital in 1946, the year after Japan's surrender ended World War II. The Chinese Communists took over China in 1949. They made Beijing the capital, but Nanjing remained a center of regional government. During the 1950's, 1960's, and 1970's, the Communists built hundreds of manufacturing plants in Nanjing. The city quickly grew into a major industrial center.   Mingzheng Shi

Nanking. See Nanjing.

Nanking Massacre is a name for the brutality committed by Japanese troops against the people of Nanking (Nanjing), China, in 1937, during the Sino-Japanese War of 1937-1945. This war led into, and became part of, World War II (1939-1945). Also called the Rape of Nanking, the massacre began on December 13—the day after the Japanese entered Nanking, at that time the capital of Nationalist China—and lasted for six weeks. During that period, Japanese forces engaged in widespread arson, cruelty, looting, murder, and rape of unarmed Chinese. Sometimes acting on orders, and often marauding in small groups, Japanese troops burst into businesses, private homes, and even areas under foreign protection to search for Chinese men of military age and for young women. Many men, and prisoners of war captured earlier, were gathered together and murdered. Many women were raped by Japanese soldiers.

Experts disagree about the number of Chinese injured or killed during the Nanking Massacre. The full extent of this atrocity can never be determined precisely. At the time, the Japanese had no interest in counting the dead, and the Chinese had no way of accurately totaling their losses. Neutral observers of many nationalities recorded the horrifying details in reports, letters, photos, and even motion pictures. The death toll probably exceeded 100,000 at Nanking, though some estimates place the figure as high as 300,000. Rapes of women may have numbered 20,000 or more. Many of these victims were then killed or died from their assaults.

The Nanking Massacre occupied a central place in Chinese efforts to win international support for their cause in the war against Japan. The Chinese stressed the cruel behavior of the Japanese invaders. The wartime Japanese government, in contrast, told its people only that the capture of Nanking was a grand achievement.

After the war, many Japanese were charged with war crimes and punished for the massacre after Chinese military trials were held. The International Military Tribunal for the Far East sentenced the Japanese commander at Nanking, General Matsui Iwane, to death. He was hanged on Dec. 23, 1948.   Theodore F. Cook, Jr.

See also **Sino-Japanese War of 1937-1945**.

Nanotechnology, *NAN oh tehk NAHL uh jee,* is the systematic production of structures that are slightly larger than atoms and molecules. Nanotechnology relies on scientific and engineering disciplines, along with manufacturing technologies, to design and produce useful products. It involves working on the *nanometer* scale, or *nanoscale. Nano* means *billionth.* A nanometer is 0.000000001 meter ($\frac{1}{25,400,000}$ inch)—approximately $\frac{1}{100,000}$ the width of a human hair or 3 to 5 times the diameter of a single atom. The nanoscale is considered to cover dimensions between 1 and 100 nanometers. Nanoscale materials, and the objects made from them, display fundamentally different properties and behavior than the same materials at larger scales.

Richard Feynman, an American physicist, outlined the concept of nanotechnology in a 1959 lecture called "There's Plenty of Room at the Bottom." Practical demonstrations of nanotechnology began appearing in the 1980's and 1990's.

Applications of nanotechnology include nanoparticles, nanocrystals, nanocomposites, nanotubes, and nanodevices. Common compounds used in nanoparticles include alumina, zinc oxide, magnesium oxide, silica, and titanium dioxide. Nanoparticles are used in sunscreen to scatter ultraviolet rays, in food packaging to reduce spoilage, and in fabrics to resist stains and to destroy bacteria. Nanoparticles are also used in coatings, pigments, and flame retardants, and as *photocatalysts,* substances that use light to speed a chemical reaction. Photocatalysts are often used to render harmless certain dangerous substances, such as mold or air pollutants.

Nanocrystals are nanoparticles whose atoms are arranged in *crystalline* (orderly) patterns. Nanocrystals can have unusual optical, electronic, and magnetic properties. For example, certain types of nanocrystals emit light when they absorb energy. But the color of the light depends on the crystal's size and shape.

Scientists have produced nanocomposites by combining nanoparticles or other nanoscale objects within metal, plastic, or ceramic structures. Nanocomposites can be stronger, lighter, and longer-lasting than the original materials. For example, exterior car parts made with plastic nanocomposites may be more resistant to scratches and dents than conventional parts.

Nanotubes are tubular structures of carbon atoms several nanometers in diameter and several thousand nanometers in length. Each nanotube is actually a single carbon molecule (see **Carbon** [Forms of carbon]). Nanotubes are about 100 times stronger than steel. Some serve as conductors of electric current.

Nanodevices involve nanoscale machines. For example, scientists are developing "smart dust" in which nanoscale sensors can be spread through the air much like common dust particles. Nanodevices may be similar to microelectromechanical systems (see **Microelectromechanical systems**) but on an even smaller scale.

Making nanoscale objects. There are two approaches to creating nanoscale objects: (1) top-down and (2) bottom-up. The top-down approach involves removing material, much as a sculptor does, to produce nanoscale objects. One top-down method, called *electron beam lithography,* uses a beam of electrons to etch such objects from tiny masses of materials. The bottom-up approach involves the use of biological or chemical methods to build structures and devices from atoms or molecules. Scientists first achieved this kind of assembly by using sensitive probes to manipulate individual atoms or molecules—a time-consuming task.

A bottom-up process called *self-assembly* may be a more effective method of creating nanoscale objects. Self-assembly is common in nature. It is the process by which, for example, an acorn grows into an oak tree rather than another plant. Organic or biological molecules have the potential to direct the self-assembly of nanostructures.　　James F. Shackelford

See also **Carbon** (Fullerenes)

Nansen, *NAN suhn* or *NAHN suhn,* **Fridtjof,** *FRIHT yahf* (1861-1930), was a famous Norwegian polar explorer. He was also a *humanitarian* (person devoted to others' welfare), a statesman, a marine zoologist, and a pioneer oceanographer.

Nansen made his first Arctic cruise in 1882 as a zoological collector aboard a whaler. In the summer of 1888, he and five other men made the first east-to-west crossing of the huge ice sheet that covers Greenland, a feat experts had declared impossible.

Nansen hoped to obtain valuable scientific information by exploring the North Polar Basin. For this expedition, he had a ship built to withstand the grinding *ice floes* (sheets of floating ice). This ship was named the *Fram* (Forward). Nansen left Norway in the *Fram* on June 24, 1893. He deliberately let the ship become jammed in ice north of Siberia. For the next three years, the ice drift carried the ship across the Arctic Ocean to waters near Svalbard. In the second year, Nansen and Hjalmar Johansen left the *Fram* and tried to reach the North Pole with kayaks and sleds. They came within 272 miles (438 kilometers) of the pole, nearer than anyone before them. After meeting many dangers, they boarded a British ship at Franz Josef Land in 1896 and went to Norway. See **Arctic Ocean** (maps).

Nansen played a prominent part in the separation of Norway from Sweden in 1905. From 1906 to 1908, he

served as Norwegian minister to the United Kingdom. When he returned to Norway, he became a professor at the University of Christiania. He went on ocean voyages in 1910, 1912, 1913, and 1914, and published his results in many books. His writings include *Farthest North* (1897) and *In Northern Mists* (1911).

After World War I (1914-1918), Nansen was Norway's delegate to the League of Nations. He aided Soviet refugees in Asia Minor (now part of Turkey) and directed the return of German and Soviet war prisoners to their homelands. He devised the *Nansen passport*—an identification certificate for refugees. He received the 1922 Nobel Peace Prize for his services. Oceanographers use a metal container, called a Nansen bottle in honor of him, to trap seawater.

Nansen was born on Oct. 10, 1861, in Christiania (now Oslo). He died on May 13, 1930.　　William Barr

Nantes, *nants* or *nahnt* (pop. 282,853; met. area pop. 568,743), is a port city in western France, near the mouth of the Loire River (see **France** [political map]). A ship canal connects the city with the port of St.-Nazaire on the Bay of Biscay, an arm of the Atlantic Ocean. Shipping and shipbuilding are the major industries of Nantes. Other economic activities include food processing and the production of copper, steel, and aviation and railroad equipment. The city is the capital of the Pays de la Loire region and the Loire-Atlantique *department* (administrative district). Landmarks include a castle, built in its present form in the 1400's, and the Cathedral of St. Peter and St. Paul, which also dates from the 1400's.

Gauls built a town on the site of what is now Nantes many years before Roman soldiers established a settlement nearby in the 50's B.C. In A.D. 1598, King Henry IV of France signed the famous Edict of Nantes in the city's castle. The edict granted limited religious liberty to Protestants (see **Nantes, Edict of**).　　Mark Kesselman

Nantes, *nants* or *nahnt,* **Edict of,** was the first official recognition of religious tolerance by a major European country. King Henry IV of France signed the *edict* (public order) in the city of Nantes on April 13, 1598. France had suffered 50 years of internal warfare and religious division before Henry signed the edict.

The edict gave French Protestants, called Huguenots, control of about 100 fortified towns for eight years. It also gave them *freedom of conscience* (freedom of beliefs), social and political equality with the Roman Catholic majority, and a certain degree of freedom of worship. Authorities seriously enforced the edict only until Henry's death in 1610. King Louis XIV canceled the edict in 1685. As a result, about 200,000 Huguenots left France.　　Dale A. Johnson

See also **Henry IV** (of France); **Huguenots.**

Nantucket, *nan TUHK uht* (pop. 10,172), is a summer resort on Nantucket Island, off the coast of Cape Cod, Massachusetts (see **Massachusetts** [political map]). The name was taken from the Indian word *Nanticut,* meaning *The Faraway Land.* Because of the scenery and mild climate, there are many summer homes in Nantucket. Its beaches, bike paths, shops, and restaurants also attract tourists. During the late 1700's, Nantucket became one of the greatest whaling centers in the world. As many as 125 whaling ships had their home port there. King Charles I of England granted Nantucket Island to his brother the Duke of York in 1641. The island belonged to the province of New York from 1660 to 1692, when it became a part of Massachusetts.   Laurence A. Lewis

Napalm, *NAY pahm,* is a powder used to thicken gasoline for use in war. When napalm is added to gasoline, the result—a jellylike explosive—is also often called *napalm.* Dropped from the air, a napalm bomb bursts, ignites, and splatters burning napalm over a wide area. The jellied gasoline clings to everything it touches and burns violently. Napalm causes death from burns or suffocation. Napalm is also used in flame throwers carried by ground troops (see **Flame thrower**). Napalm was used in World War II (1939-1945), the Korean War (1950-1953), the Vietnam War (1957-1975), and the Persian Gulf War of 1991.   Frances M. Lussier

Napier, *NAY pee uhr* or *nuh PEER,* **John** (1550-1617), Laird of Merchiston, was a Scottish mathematician. He developed methods of rapid calculation, which he sought to apply to astronomy, trigonometry, navigation, mapmaking, and surveying. Napier discovered how to multiply numbers by doing the easier task of adding other, corresponding numbers that he called *logarithms* (see **Logarithms**). Logarithms are used to describe mathematically many natural phenomena. Napier also invented a set of "rods" or "bones" that could be arranged for arithmetical calculations. He was born near Edinburgh, Scotland. He died on April 4, 1617.   Judith V. Grabiner

Naples, *NAY puhlz* (pop. 1,004,500), is the third largest city of Italy. Only Rome and Milan are larger. Naples lies at the foot of a range of low hills on the west coast of southern Italy. For location, see **Italy** (political map).

Naples ranks as a major manufacturing center, and the Bay of Naples makes it an important seaport. Tourists come from all parts of the world to see the many places of scenic and historical interest in the Naples area. The city's name in Italian is *Napoli.*

About 600 B.C., Greek colonists from Cumae, 14 miles (23 kilometers) to the west, founded a town near the site of present-day Naples. They called the town Parthenope and later renamed it *Neapolis* (New City). The people of Naples are still called Neapolitans. During much of the period from the 1100's until 1860, Naples was the capital of a kingdom. This kingdom included most of southern Italy and the island of Sicily. Since 1861, the city has been the capital of Campania, a political region of Italy.

The city. In the eastern section, church spires rise above old tenement buildings and factories. The Spac-

ca-Napoli district, with its crowded, narrow streets, forms the heart of old Naples. The newer western part of the city lies along the Riviera di Chiaia, a broad drive that runs along the Bay of Naples. A hilly, densely populated modern section called the Vomero lies inland.

The Cathedral of St. Januarius, completed in 1323, honors Naples's patron saint. Castles in the city now house museum collections or government offices. The oldest of these structures, the Castel dell'Ovo (Castle of the Egg), takes its name from its shape. The Castel Sant'Elmo, built in the 1300's and enlarged in the 1500's, served as a prison for many years. The city's attractions also include a botanical garden and a public park. The park has one of Europe's finest aquariums.

Naples lies amid some of the most spectacular scenery in Europe. Artists from many countries go there to paint the landscape or the people. Mount Vesuvius, the only active volcano on the mainland of Europe, rises 7 miles (11 kilometers) southeast of the city. It erupted in A.D. 79, burying the ancient Roman cities of Pompeii and Herculaneum, which are within 20 miles (32 kilometers) of Naples. The ruins of these cities are important archaeological sites for the study of life in Roman times. Capri and Ischia, islands famous for their pleasant climate and scenic beauty, lie to the south across the Bay of Naples. Vineyards and citrus groves dot the hillsides on the bay's eastern shore. Just west of Naples, the Posillipo district offers a lovely view of the Bay of Naples.

Way of life. Music plays an important part in Neapolitan life. Such songs as "Santa Lucia" (1849), "Funiculi, Funicula" (1880), and "O Sole Mio" (1898) have made the city's music familiar in many parts of the world. At the Piedigrotta, an annual music festival, the people hold an outdoor competition to choose the best of the new popular songs. The Teatro San Carlo, one of the largest opera houses in Italy, has presented the first performance of many famous operas.

Neapolitan food includes many varieties of dishes made with spaghetti, macaroni, or other pasta. Naples is the birthplace of pizza, which a baker invented in 1889 to honor the queen of Italy. Neapolitans also eat much fish and other seafood.

The National Archaeological Museum in Naples displays one of the world's largest collections of ancient art. The collection includes glassware, mosaics, paintings, pottery, and statues from Herculaneum and Pompeii;

G. Barone from Madeline Grimoldi

Naples lies at the foot of low hills along the beautiful Bay of Naples. Volcanic Mount Vesuvius, *rear,* adds to the city's scenic beauty. Naples is a leading Italian port and manufacturing center.

and ancient Greek sculpture. The royal palace of Capodimonte, built in the 1700's for the kings of Naples, houses the National Gallery. The gallery owns a collection of paintings, porcelain, sculpture, and tapestries. The National Library is the largest of the city's several libraries. It holds thousands of rare manuscripts. The Carthusian monastery of St. Martin, which adjoins the Castel Sant'Elmo, features a museum collection devoted to the art and history of Naples. The University of Naples Federico II, the best known of the city's many schools and colleges, was founded in 1224 by Emperor Frederick II.

Economy. Products manufactured in Naples include automobiles, cement, chemical products, locomotives, office machinery, ships, and textiles. The highly industrialized area in and around the city has the greatest concentration of factories in southern Italy. Ships from every part of the world use Naples's harbor. Naples still produces many traditional wares for which it became known through the years. They include kidskin gloves, wine, and articles made of coral and tortoise shell, such as combs and jewelry. Despite its industries, Naples suffers from a high rate of unemployment.

History. After more than a century as a Greek colony, Naples came under Roman control about 326 B.C. The city's beauty and mild climate made it a favorite resort of wealthy Romans. The poet Virgil lived in Naples for more than 20 years and is buried on a nearby hill.

After the fall of the West Roman Empire in the A.D. 400's, people fought for control of Naples and the rest of southern Italy. The Byzantines, Franks, Lombards, Normans, and Germans controlled the city for periods during the Middle Ages, from about the 400's through the 1400's. Naples came under Spanish rule in 1442, and Spain held it for most of the next 250 years.

Austria ruled Naples in the early 1700's. During this period, Naples was Italy's largest city and one of the largest cities of Europe. In 1734, the city became the capital of an independent kingdom, which was also called Naples. A Spanish branch of the royal Bourbon family governed this kingdom and Sicily. During the Napoleonic Wars (1796-1814), Naples had a series of French rulers, including Napoleon's brother Joseph Bonaparte. The Bourbons regained power in 1815. In 1816, they formally combined Naples and Sicily to form the Kingdom of the Two Sicilies, which they ruled until 1860. In 1861, the Kingdom of the Two Sicilies became part of the newly formed kingdom of Italy.

During World War II (1939-1945), bombs destroyed many buildings in central Naples and the port area. The damaged areas were rebuilt, but a housing shortage remained. In the 1970's, the Italian government began working to relieve the shortage. In 1980, however, a severe earthquake destroyed many buildings in Naples. During the 1980's, the government provided new housing outside the city. In the 1990's, the city administration helped to modernize Naples by enlarging the airport, improving public transportation, and extending hours at museums and galleries.   John A. Davis

See also **Capri; Herculaneum; Pompeii; Sicilies, Kingdom of the Two; Vesuvius.**

Napoleon I (1769-1821), also known as Napoleon Bonaparte, crowned himself emperor of the French. He was the greatest military genius of his time and perhaps the greatest general in history. Napoleon created an empire that covered most of western and central Europe.

Napoleon was also an excellent administrator. He introduced many reforms, including the creation of a strong central government and the revision and organization of French laws into collections called *codes.* Many of his reforms are evident today in the institutions of France and of areas once under its control.

Napoleon stood 5 feet 2 inches (157 centimeters) tall, about average for Frenchmen of his time, though most French generals and statesmen were taller. He earned the nickname *le Petit Caporal* (the little corporal) in 1796 at the Battle of Lodi, near Milan, Italy. In the battle, General Bonaparte startled his troops by personally aiming the cannon, a risky job usually performed by a corporal.

Napoleon was an inspirational and dramatic leader. He could also be cynical and demanding, though this side of his character was usually hidden from the public. In addition, Napoleon had great energy and ambition. He personally directed complex military maneuvers and at the same time controlled France's press, police system, foreign policy, and domestic affairs. He chose capable subordinates and rewarded them generously with medals, wealth, military rank, and titles of nobility.

Napoleon's ambition ultimately led him to overextend his power. His downfall also resulted in part from feel-

Napoleon I posed in his study for French painter Jacques Louis David in 1812. David served as court painter to the emperor.

ings of nationalism in areas invaded by French troops and from economic hardship brought on by Napoleon's attempts to exclude British goods from continental Europe. Other factors that contributed to his downfall included bitter reaction to the taxes and conscription (the draft) that he imposed across his empire and opposition to Napoleon of many of Europe's royal rulers.

Boyhood. Napoleon was born on Aug. 15, 1769, in Ajaccio, on the island of Corsica in the Mediterranean Sea. In 1768, France had bought Corsica from the Italian city-state of Genoa. Napoleon was the fourth child and second son of Carlo and Letizia Ramolino Buonaparte (later given the French spelling Bonaparte). Napoleon's parents came from noble Italian families. His father was an eloquent lawyer and a prominent citizen of Corsica. Napoleon's mother was beautiful and strong-willed.

In 1779, at the age of 9, Napoleon entered a French military school at Brienne (now known as Brienne-le-Château), a town in France near Troyes. An average student in most subjects, Napoleon excelled in mathematics. In 1784, he was chosen for the elite military academy École Militaire in Paris. He graduated a year later.

Early military career. In January 1785, at the age of 16, Napoleon received a commission in the French Army, as a second lieutenant of artillery. He joined an artillery regiment and briefly attended the royal artillery school in Auxonne, near Dole. He was promoted to first lieutenant in 1791 and to captain in 1792.

The French Revolution broke out in 1789 (see **French Revolution**). During the early 1790's, Napoleon spent many months in Corsica on leave from the French Army. While there, he served in the Corsican National Guard. Napoleon also joined the Jacobins, a radical political society in France. Many Jacobins wanted to make France a democratic republic. Napoleon's membership in the society brought him into conflict with the governor of Corsica, Pasquale Paoli, who was a *royalist* (supporter of the French monarchy). After the revolutionary French government executed King Louis XVI in January 1793, Paoli declared the Bonapartes outlaws. The family fled to France, where Napoleon returned to the French Army.

In June 1793, a group of Jacobins led by Maximilien Robespierre gained control of the French government (see **Robespierre**). Several French cities revolted against the new regime. At Toulon, a British naval fleet aided the

Important dates in Napoleon's life

rebels. After the French artillery commander at Toulon was wounded, Napoleon was sent to replace him. In December 1793, Napoleon positioned the artillery on high ground overlooking Toulon's harbor and fired down on the British ships. The fleet withdrew and French troops gained control of Toulon. For his role in the victory, Napoleon was named brigadier general at the age of 24.

Napoleon's star had risen but soon seemed about to set. In July 1794, Robespierre fell from power and was executed. In August, Napoleon was imprisoned for about a week. After his release, he returned to the Army.

The "whiff of grapeshot." In 1795, Napoleon was in Paris when angry mobs there tried to attack the ruling National Convention at the royal palace called the Tuileries. Royalists who hoped to destroy the convention before it could put a new constitution into effect had encouraged the mobs. Vicomte Paul de Barras, whose troops were guarding the palace, had seen Napoleon in action at Toulon and sent for him. Napoleon defended the palace with cannon fire that killed or wounded hundreds of people and quickly cleared the streets. This cannon fire later became known as the "whiff of grapeshot." Hailed as a hero, Napoleon was promoted to major general. A new government, called the Directory, was installed with Barras as one of its five directors.

Marriage. In 1796, Napoleon married Josephine de Beauharnais, a beautiful woman of French descent from the Caribbean island of Martinique. Josephine's first husband, Vicomte Alexandre de Beauharnais, had been sent to the guillotine during the Reign of Terror (see **French Revolution** [Terror and equality]). When Napoleon met her, Josephine was a leader of fashionable French society. She was six years older than Napoleon and had two children by her previous marriage.

Rise to power

Victories in Italy. From 1792 to 1795, France was at war with much of Europe. By 1796, Austria had become France's chief enemy. Days after marrying Josephine, Napoleon left Paris to take command of a French army on the Italian-French border—an underfed, ill-equipped force of about 38,000 men. The Directory hoped that he could tie up Austrian forces in Italy while larger French armies won the war by marching through Germany and attacking Vienna, Austria's capital. Instead, Napoleon won the war. In less than a year, he defeated four armies, each larger than his own. He won a final victory by marching over the Alps and threatening Vienna in early 1797. In October, France and Austria signed the Treaty of Campo Formio, which enlarged France's territory.

Egypt invaded. Napoleon returned to Paris, where once again he was hailed as a hero. Napoleon had political ambitions, but he felt that he still lacked enough influence to gain control of the government. Therefore, he concentrated on strengthening his military reputation. Late in 1797, the Directory offered to put Napoleon at the head of an invasion of England. But he declined the offer. Instead, he proposed that he invade Egypt to destroy British trade with the Middle East. The Directory agreed to the plan. In May 1798, Napoleon sailed for Egypt with about 38,000 men.

Napoleon reached Egypt in July. There, he defeated the Mamluks, Egypt's military rulers, in the Battle of the Pyramids near Cairo (see **Mamluks**). But on August 1, the

French fleet anchored in Abu Qir Bay was destroyed in the Battle of the Nile by a British fleet commanded by Admiral Horatio Nelson. As a result, Napoleon's army was stranded in Egypt. The Ottoman Empire then formed an alliance with Britain (later also called the United Kingdom) and Russia and declared war on France. In 1799, Napoleon's troops invaded Ottoman Syria and advanced as far as the fortress Acre (now Akko, Israel), which Napoleon failed to capture. Meanwhile, he learned that an Ottoman army was preparing to invade Egypt. He retreated to Egypt, where he met and defeated the Ottomans at Abu Qir, near Abu Qir Bay. About this time, Napoleon learned that Austria, Britain, and Russia had formed a coalition against France and had defeated the French army in Italy. He left his army in the command of General Jean Kléber and sailed for France.

First consul of France

News of Napoleon's victory at Abu Qir arrived with him in Paris. Napoleon formed key political alliances and seized control of the government on Nov. 9, 1799, in a bold move known as the *Coup d' État of Eighteenth Brumaire*. A new constitution, approved by the French people, replaced the Directory with a three-member Consulate. Napoleon became first consul. The other consuls served as his advisers. After 10 years of revolution and civil disorder, the French wanted a strong leader.

Peacemaking. As first consul, Napoleon sought peace through victory over other nations. In May 1800, he led a famous march across the Alps, through the Great St. Bernard Pass and into the Po Valley of northern Italy. In June, his army surprised and defeated the Austrians in the Battle of Marengo. In 1801, Austria signed the Treaty of Lunéville, which reaffirmed the Treaty of Campo Formio. With Austria defeated, the war-weary British agreed to peace in 1802 in the Treaty of Amiens. Russia had dropped out of the coalition against France in 1799. For the first time in 10 years, Europe was at peace.

Administrator and lawmaker. Napoleon proved to be a superb civil administrator. One of his greatest achievements was his supervision of the revision and collection of French law into codes. The new law codes—seven in number—incorporated some of the freedoms gained by the people of France during the French Revolution, including religious toleration and the abolition of serfdom. The most famous of the codes, the Code Napoléon or Code Civil, still forms the basis of French civil law (see **Code Napoléon**). Napoleon also centralized France's government by appointing *prefects* to administer regions called *departments,* into which France had been divided in 1790.

The Napoleonic empire

French aggression. Napoleon was not content simply to govern France. His thoughts soon turned to conquest. At first, he sought to extend French influence in the Western Hemisphere. In 1800, Napoleon forced Spain to cede to France the Louisiana Territory in North America. But the army that he sent to take possession of the territory was destroyed trying to restore French rule over the former colony of Saint-Domingue (present-day Haiti). Frustrated, Napoleon abandoned his plans for the Western Hemisphere and turned his attention to Europe. By 1803, France had annexed the Piedmont region

of northwestern Italy, and Napoleon had become president of the Italian Republic, which bordered Piedmont on the east. Also, fearful of the United Kingdom's naval power, Napoleon had tried to stop British trade with the rest of Europe. He anticipated war with the United Kingdom and in 1803 sold the Louisiana Territory to the United States to raise money for the war. War with the United Kingdom began later that year.

Crowned emperor. In 1802, the French people had approved a constitutional amendment that made Napoleon first consul for life. In May 1804, the French Senate and people voted him their emperor. Napoleon crowned himself emperor on December 2 in ceremonies at the Cathedral of Notre Dame in Paris.

Dominates Europe. By 1805, Austria, Russia, and Sweden had joined the United Kingdom in a new coalition against France. In September 1805, Napoleon led his troops into Germany. In October, he captured an Austrian army at Ulm. In December, he demolished the Austrian and Russian armies at Austerlitz. But earlier that year, Admiral Nelson had destroyed the fleets of France and Spain, France's ally, near Trafalgar, a cape on Spain's southern coast. This victory gave the United Kingdom control of the seas and ended any chance of Napoleon's invading that country.

In 1806, Prussia joined Russia in mounting a new campaign against France. In October, Napoleon's forces overwhelmed the Prussian army at Jena and at nearby Auerstädt. In June 1807, Napoleon demolished Russian armies at Friedland. In 1809, he defeated the Austrians again at Wagram, near Vienna.

After each victory, Napoleon enlarged his empire. In 1806, he set up the Confederation of the Rhine, made up of a number of western German states, and placed it under his protection. He also carved provinces of Germany and Italy into principalities and dukedoms, and gave them to friends and relatives. In 1806, he made his brother Joseph king of Naples, and his brother Louis king of Holland. In 1807, Napoleon made his brother Jerome king of Westphalia and added to France the Grand Duchy of Warsaw. In 1809, he gave his sister Elisa the Grand Duchy of Tuscany and annexed to France the Illyrian Provinces, which covered much of what are now Slovenia and Croatia. In 1810, he brought his empire to its height by annexing Holland and much of Germany.

Divorce and remarriage. By 1809, Napoleon had grown concerned about what would become of his vast empire after his death. Josephine, who was now 46 years old, had no children by him, and Napoleon had no heirs. In December, he divorced Josephine to marry a younger woman. In April 1810, he married the 18-year-old Archduchess Marie Louise, daughter of Emperor Francis I of Austria. In 1811, the couple had a son, also named Napoleon, who was given the title king of Rome.

Fall from power

In 1806, Napoleon had issued the Berlin Decree, which barred British ships from ports under French control. The decree was aimed at destroying British trade with continental Europe. In 1807, Napoleon issued the Milan Decree, which was intended to prevent the ships of neutral nations from carrying British goods to continental Europe. Such ships were attacked by French vessels. The system established by the Berlin and Milan decrees for blocking British trade was known as the Continental System.

Portugal, which had long been friendly with the United Kingdom, refused to follow the Berlin Decree. In 1807, the French gained control of Portugal and occupied parts of Spain. In 1808, French forces under Marshal Joachim Murat seized control of Madrid, Spain's capital. Napoleon removed King Ferdinand VII from the Spanish throne and appointed his brother Joseph king of Spain. Murat took Joseph's place as king of Naples.

The Peninsular War began in 1808 when Spanish and Portuguese forces rebelled against French rule. Soon after the war began, British troops joined the fight against France on the peninsula that consisted of Portugal and Spain. By April 1814, all French forces had been driven from the peninsula. Tens of thousands of French soldiers died in the war, and the loss of Spain and Portugal greatly damaged Napoleon's prestige.

Disaster in Russia. On Dec. 31, 1810, Czar Alexander I of Russia withdrew from the Continental System. Napoleon felt that the czar's withdrawal threatened France, so he assembled a new army to attack Russia. Many years of war had weakened France, but Napoleon raised about 600,000 troops. His allies and subject nations furnished by conscription many of these soldiers. The Russian army had about 200,000 troops.

In June 1812, Napoleon's army crossed the Niemen River (now known as the Neman River) into Russia. The Russians retreated, denying Napoleon a decisive battle. In September, Napoleon fought the Russians at Borodino, near Moscow. The bloody battle resulted in a narrow French victory, and the Russians withdrew.

Napoleon pushed on to Moscow only to find the city nearly deserted. Soon after the French army entered Moscow, fires set by the retreating Russians destroyed large parts of the city. With the bitter Russian winter approaching, Napoleon waited in Moscow for Alexander to offer peace. However, no such offer came. In mid-October, Napoleon, unable to supply his troops, began the long retreat from Moscow. His soldiers struggled against snowstorms and freezing temperatures. Soldiers and horses died of starvation and exposure. Russian soldiers called Cossacks killed many of the stragglers. About 500,000 of Napoleon's troops died, deserted, or were captured during the campaign and the retreat from Russia. After Napoleon returned to Paris, he admitted the disaster. The French continued to support him, but news of the devastating campaign encouraged his enemies throughout Europe.

The enemy alliance. After Napoleon's return from Moscow, he faced a hostile alliance of Austria, Prussia, Russia, Sweden, and the United Kingdom. In April 1813, Napoleon arrived in Germany with a new army and took the offensive against the allies. He won initial victories at Lützen, Bautzen, and Dresden, but his forces were vastly outnumbered. In October, the two sides fought at Leipzig in the Battle of the Nations. In the battle, Napoleon was defeated, and he retreated into France. The allies pursued him and captured Paris in March 1814.

Exile to Elba. On April 6, 1814, Napoleon *abdicated* (gave up) the imperial throne. The allies called for the return of a king of the Bourbon family and placed Louis XVIII, the brother of Louis XVI, on the French throne (see **Louis XVIII**). Napoleon was exiled from France and made

ruler of the tiny island of Elba off the northwest coast of Italy. His wife and son were sent to his wife's father, the emperor of Austria. Napoleon never saw them again.

On Elba, Napoleon planned his return to France. In February 1815, he sailed from the island with about 1,100 followers who had shared his exile. He landed at Cannes on March 1 and began marching to Paris, gathering supporters along the way. Troops led by Marshal Michel Ney were dispatched from Paris to arrest Napoleon. But when they saw their old leader, the soldiers gladly joined him and hailed him as their emperor. Louis XVIII fled from Paris as Napoleon approached. On March 20, Napoleon entered Paris and was carried on the shoulders of cheering crowds into the Tuileries.

The Hundred Days and Waterloo. Napoleon immediately proclaimed a new constitution that limited his powers. He promised the allies that he would not make war. But the allied leaders considered Napoleon an "enemy and disturber of the peace of the world." Once again, both sides prepared for battle.

Napoleon advanced into Belgium with about 125,000 troops, hoping to defeat the separate armies of the British Duke of Wellington and the Prussian Marshal Gebhard von Blücher. On June 16, Napoleon defeated Blücher at Ligny, near Fleurus. On June 18, Napoleon attacked Wellington at Waterloo in what has become one of history's most famous battles. It featured spectacular charges by thousands of French cavalry. But just as it seemed the British forces would collapse, Blücher's troops arrived to reinforce Wellington. Badly outnumbered, the French army suffered a crushing defeat.

Napoleon fled to Paris and abdicated for the second time, on June 22. The period from Napoleon's return to Paris from Elba to his second abdication is known as the Hundred Days. Napoleon surrendered at Rochefort to Frederick Lewis Maitland, the captain of the British battleship *Bellerophon*. Shortly afterward, Napoleon was sent to the barren British island of St. Helena, in the South Atlantic Ocean (see **Atlantic Ocean** [map]).

On St. Helena, Napoleon spent much of his remaining years dictating to friends his version of the events that occurred during his lifetime. He died on May 5, 1821, and was buried on the island. In his will, he had asked to be buried "on the banks of the Seine, among the French people I have loved so much." In 1840, the British and French governments had his remains brought to Paris. There, at the Église du Dôme (Church of the Dome), which is part of the Hôtel des Invalides (Home for Disabled Soldiers), the body of Napoleon was laid to rest.

Napoleon's place in history

Napoleon is both a historical figure and a legend— and it is sometimes difficult to separate the two. The events of his life have fired the imaginations of great writers, filmmakers, and playwrights whose works have done much to create the Napoleonic legend.

Napoleon was one of the greatest military commanders in history. But he has also been portrayed as a power-hungry conqueror. He denied being such a conqueror. He argued that he had tried to build a federation of free peoples in a Europe united under a liberal government. He did intend, though, to achieve this goal by concentrating power in his own hands. But in the states he created, he granted constitutions; introduced law codes;

abolished a political and military system called *feudalism;* created efficient governments; and fostered education, science, literature, and the arts. Rafe Blaufarb

Related articles in *World Book* include:

Biographies

Alexander I (czar)
Bernadotte, Jean B. J.
Blücher, Gebhard
  Leberecht von
Josephine
Louis XVIII
Marie Louise

Metternich
Napoleon II
Nelson, Horatio
Ney, Michel
Talleyrand
Wellington, Duke of

Other related articles

Austerlitz, Battle of
Austria (History)
Code Napoléon
Continental
  System
Corsica
Egypt (History)
Elba
France (History)

French Revolution
Germany (History)
Italy (History)
Louisiana
  Purchase
Milan Decree
Napoleonic Wars
Prussia
Russia (History)

Saint Helena
Spain (History)
Sweden (History)
Trafalgar, Battle of
United Kingdom
  (History)
Vienna, Congress
  of
Waterloo, Battle of

Napoleon II (1811-1832), Duke of Reichstadt, *RYKE shtaht,* was the son of Emperor Napoleon I of France and his second wife, Marie Louise of Austria. Napoleon I had long hoped for a son to inherit his empire, and he gave his newborn son the title of king of Rome.

When Napoleon I was overthrown in 1814, he gave up the throne in favor of his young son. But the French Senate did not recognize Napoleon II as emperor, and Louis XVIII, a member of the Bourbon royal family, became king of France that year. Marie Louise then took her son to live at the court of her father, Emperor Francis I of Austria. After Napoleon I was defeated at the Battle of Waterloo in 1815, he again proclaimed his son emperor of France. But the French refused to give the boy the throne, and he remained in Austria. His mother's family gave him the title of Duke of Reichstadt in 1818.

Napoleon II was never strong. He died of tuberculosis on July 22, 1832, at the age of 21 and was buried in the Habsburg (or Hapsburg) family's church tomb in Vienna. In 1940, Adolf Hitler, dictator of Germany, had the body placed near that of Napoleon I in the Église du Dôme (Church of the Dome) at the Hôtel des Invalides (Home for Disabled Soldiers) in Paris. Napoleon II was born on March 12, 1811, in Paris. Peter N. Stearns

Napoleon III (1808-1873) was emperor of France from 1852 to 1870. His public works programs transformed Paris, but failures in foreign policy became his undoing.

Early life. Napoleon was born on April 20, 1808, in Paris, the son of Louis Bonaparte, king of Holland, and brother of the French Emperor Napoleon I. His full name was Charles Louis Napoleon Bonaparte, but he was usually called Louis Napoleon. A French law of 1816 exiled the Bonapartes from France, and Louis Napoleon spent his youth in Italy, Germany, and Switzerland. He became the head of his family in 1832.

Louis Napoleon was linked with such revolutionary groups as the Carbonari in Italy. He tried to overthrow the French monarchy of Louis Philippe in 1836 and in 1840. Following the 1840 attempt, he was imprisoned in the French fortress of Ham. Louis Napoleon escaped to England in 1846. During these years, he wrote *Napoleonic Ideas* (1839), idealizing the career of his famous uncle, and *The Extinction of Poverty* (1844), proposing that the government act to end poverty and suffering.

Becomes emperor. After the Revolution of 1848 led to the Second Republic in France, Louis Napoleon returned and was elected to the Assembly. In December, benefiting by the glamour of his name, he was elected president by a large margin. He swore an oath to the republic, but in December 1851, he managed to concentrate all power in his hands. He abolished the republic and proclaimed himself emperor in 1852.

Napoleon's domestic policies were conflicting. He ruled as a dictator and was surrounded by dishonest adventurers. Although all men could vote, the legislature was powerless and the press could not publish legislative debates. When, after 1860, Napoleon moved in the direction of a liberal empire, it was too late. Liberal opponents continued to urge the overthrow of his government. Yet Napoleon keenly realized the problems of the industrial age. He favored state help for industries, banks, railroads, and the poor. He also backed major construction projects in Paris to modernize the city and to limit uprisings by the French people.

Foreign affairs. Napoleon tried to settle disputes through international conferences, and he sympathized with claims of nationalism. He helped with independence for Romania, unification for Italy, and, unwittingly, unification for Germany.

Napoleon announced when he became emperor, "The Empire means peace," yet he led France into a long series of unfortunate adventures in other countries. In 1849, he helped overthrow the Roman Republic and restore the pope. He joined the United Kingdom and the Ottoman Empire in 1854 in the Crimean War (1853-1856) against Russia. He secretly promised in 1859 to help the Count di Cavour drive the Austrians from Italy, in return for the promise of Nice and Savoy. But Napoleon withdrew from the war when he saw that Italy, instead of forming a weak confederation, would unite. He supported a scheme making Maximilian, the Archduke of Austria, emperor of Mexico in 1864. Napoleon hoped to increase French prestige, but pressure from the United States in 1867 forced him to withdraw his troops and leave Maximilian to be shot. Napoleon also supported French expeditions in central Africa and in Vietnam.

His defeat. Otto von Bismarck, the prime minister of Prussia, wanted to unite Prussia and all the other German states into one country. Napoleon feared that a unified Germany would weaken France's power in Europe, and he hoped to keep Germany divided. Tensions between France and Prussia grew until they exploded in the Franco-Prussian war of 1870. France, however, was not prepared for war. The Germans easily defeated the French, seized territory in eastern France, and created the German Empire. Napoleon surrendered to the Germans at Sedan, France, on Sept. 2, 1870. Two days later, supporters of a new French republic overthrew his empire. He died on Jan. 9, 1873. Peter N. Stearns

See also **Franco-Prussian War; Maximilian.**

Napoleonic Code. See Code Napoléon.

Napoleonic Wars (1796-1815) were a series of military campaigns led by Napoleon Bonaparte, a French general who became Emperor Napoleon I of France. From the late 1700's to the early 1800's, Napoleon conquered much of Europe and created an extensive empire. However, a number of factors, including his endless ambition and rising nationalism in the areas he conquered, finally led to his downfall.

Background. During the French Revolution (1789-1799), a series of elected legislatures took control of the French government, replacing the king. Beginning in 1792, France fought against several European nations, including Austria, Britain (later also called the United Kingdom), and Prussia. These nations opposed the democratic ideals of the French Revolution and wished to restore King Louis XVI to power. These conflicts between France and the rest of Europe set the stage for Napoleon's eventual conquest of the continent.

The Army of Italy. In 1796, the French government, called the Directory, gave Napoleon command of a small French force that became known as the Army of Italy. The Directory sent Napoleon, then an army general, to Italy to fight against Austrian forces there. At the time, Austria's ruling Habsburg family controlled parts of northern Italy. Napoleon's army drove the Austrians out of northern Italy. It then marched toward Vienna, Austria's capital, and stopped less than 100 miles (160 kilometers) away. On Oct. 17, 1797, Austria and France signed the Treaty of Campo Formio, by which France acquired Belgium and lands west of the Rhine River.

The Egyptian campaign. In July 1798, Napoleon led an invasion of Egypt. His goal was to disrupt British trade with India and other areas and to establish a French presence in Egypt. On July 21, his army defeated the Mamluks, Egypt's military leaders, in the Battle of the Pyramids, near Cairo. But the French became stranded when a British fleet, commanded by Admiral Horatio Nelson, destroyed the French fleet anchored at Abu Qir Bay on August 1. The sultan of the Ottoman Empire, who ruled Egypt, declared war on France. Napoleon's men marched to meet the Ottomans in Syria, where they had limited success. They retreated to Egypt and defeated an Ottoman army at Abu Qir on July 25, 1799. Soon afterward, Napoleon learned that a coalition of Austrian, British, and Russian forces had defeated a French army in Italy. Worried about the situation in Europe, he left for home in August 1799. His army remained in Egypt and surrendered to Britain in 1801.

A brief peace. On Nov. 9-10, 1799, a new government called the Consulate replaced the Directory. Napoleon was named head of the Consulate in December. In 1800, he led an army into northern Italy. On June 14, he defeated Austrian forces at Marengo. On Feb. 9, 1801, France and Austria signed the Treaty of Lunéville, which reconfirmed the Treaty of Campo Formio. Britain, with no remaining allies, and France signed the Treaty of Amiens on March 25, 1802. Britain gave up the West Indies and withdrew from Egypt, and French forces left the Papal States, a territory in Italy controlled by the pope.

During the peace that followed the Treaty of Amiens, Napoleon continued his push to expand French power. By 1803, Napoleon had annexed the Piedmont region of northwestern Italy to France and made himself president of the Italian Republic, east of the Piedmont. His aggression angered the British. A dispute arose in May 1803 over Malta, an island colony that Britain refused to give up.

Renewed hostilities. In 1803, Napoleon began preparations to invade Britain. He assembled a vast and powerful army, called the Grand Army, on the northern coast of France. Worried by Napoleon's growing might, Austria, Britain, Russia, and Sweden formed a coalition in 1805. When Napoleon learned of this alliance, he decided to march against Austria rather than attack Britain. On Oct. 20, 1805, the Grand Army defeated the Austrians at Ulm, in present-day Germany. The next day, however, a British fleet led by Admiral Nelson defeated an allied French and Spanish fleet at the Battle of Trafalgar, off Spain's southwest coast. Nelson died during the battle, but the British forces crippled French naval power.

On Dec. 2, 1805, the Grand Army fought Austrian and Russian forces at Austerlitz, Austria. Although outnumbered, the French were victorious. On December 26, Austria signed the Treaty of Pressburg, by which it gave territory in Italy and southern Germany to France and France's allies. Russia refused peace terms with France.

The alliance of Prussia and Russia. In July 1806, Napoleon created the Confederation of the Rhine, which joined the southern and western states of the former Holy Roman Empire under French control. That same summer, Prussia formed an alliance with Russia. In late September, King Frederick William III of Prussia ordered Napoleon to remove his forces from Germany. Napoleon then attacked Prussian troops in Germany before Russia could send help. On October 14, France defeated Prussia at the Battles of Jena and Auerstädt.

On Feb. 8, 1807, French and Russian armies fought at Eylau, East Prussia. Neither side won a clear victory. On June 14, the French defeated a Russian army at Friedland, East Prussia. Czar Alexander I of Russia then decided to make peace with France. On July 7, he and Napoleon signed the Treaty of Tilsit, in northern Prussia. The czar pledged to take economic measures against Britain, France's enemy. On July 9, Prussia also signed a peace treaty at Tilsit and granted about one-third of its territory to Napoleon's allies.

The Peninsular War. France lacked the naval might to attack Britain, so Napoleon aimed to destroy the British economy. By the Berlin and Milan decrees of 1806 and 1807, he established the Continental System, which banned trade between Britain and the rest of Europe. Portugal failed to heed the ban, and Spain barely enforced it. In November 1807, French troops led by General Andoche Junot marched through Spain, which shares the Iberian Peninsula with Portugal, and occupied Lisbon, the Portuguese capital.

In May 1808, the Spanish, once France's allies, revolted against French occupation. Napoleon proclaimed his brother Joseph king of Spain several days later. Aided by British troops, the Portuguese resisted the French as well. Napoleon then moved troops from Germany to Spain. He entered Madrid, Spain's capital, on Dec. 4, 1808. A long and fierce war against the French followed. British, Portuguese, and Spanish troops, plus thousands of guerrilla fighters, defeated the French by 1813. By the time the French left Iberia in early 1814, over 300,000 French troops had been killed or wounded.

The Austrian war. In April 1809, encouraged by Spanish resistance and German nationalist feeling, Austrian troops led by Archduke Charles attacked French forces in Bavaria, a Confederation state west of Austria. Napoleon retaliated by invading Austria. He captured Vienna on May 13. Two battles along the Danube River followed. On May 21-22, Napoleon's army was repulsed at

The empire of Napoleon I
Napoleon became the ruler of France in 1799. By 1812, his empire covered most of Europe. Napoleon was defeated at Leipzig in 1813 and was forced to give up the French throne in 1814. He later formed another army but was defeated at Waterloo in 1815. The map shows his major battles.

WORLD BOOK map

the first of these battles, the Battle of Aspern-Essling. However, Napoleon defeated an Austrian army at Wagram on July 5-6. On October 14, France and Austria signed the Treaty of Schönbrunn. Austria lost much territory, including its coastline on the Adriatic Sea, to France and its allies. The treaty also forced Austria to join the Continental System.

The invasion of Russia. The Continental System had hurt Russia's economy. In 1810, Czar Alexander decided to resume trade with Britain. Napoleon then assembled nearly 600,000 troops to invade Russia. As French soldiers moved into Russia in the summer of 1812, hunger, fatigue, and harsh weather reduced their numbers.

On Sept. 7, 1812, French and Russian armies fought at Borodino, near Moscow. The bloody battle resulted in a narrow French victory, and the Russians withdrew. Napoleon took control of Moscow a week later. Fires broke out in the city, probably set by retreating Russians to rob the French of shelter. Napoleon and his men stayed in Moscow for about a month, awaiting an offer

of peace. But as winter neared, Napoleon realized he would have to retreat to better quarters. During the retreat, which began in October, cold and starvation killed thousands of French troops. Independent Russian horsemen called Cossacks also killed French stragglers, while Russian army units attacked the retreating French troops. Only 100,000 of Napoleon's men survived.

Napoleon's downfall. Prussia and Russia formed a secret alliance in February 1813 and declared war on France in March. Napoleon scraped together a new army and attacked the allies in Germany. The French won victories at Lützen on May 2 and Bautzen on May 20-21, but the exhaustion of the French and the allies made both sides desire peace. On June 4, France and the allies signed an *armistice* (agreement to stop fighting). Napoleon would not agree to the terms of a peace agreement. Austria and Sweden then joined the alliance, while Britain supplied it with money.

The French army won a victory at Dresden, Germany, on Aug. 26-27, 1813, but eventually it was outnumbered.

At its height, Napoleon's army at this time totaled only 400,000 troops against the allies' 600,000. From October 16 to 19, the two sides fought the Battle of the Nations, also called the Battle of Leipzig, at Leipzig. The French suffered heavy losses and retreated into France. The allies offered a peace settlement that Napoleon rejected, and the allies invaded France. Although Napoleon mounted a brilliant defense, the allies won control of Paris on March 31, 1814. Napoleon *abdicated* (gave up) his throne unconditionally at Fontainebleau on April 6, 1814. He was exiled to the island of Elba in the Mediterranean Sea. Signed May 30, 1814, the Treaty of Paris forced France to return to the territory it had occupied, with a few exceptions, on Nov. 1, 1792.

The Hundred Days. In April 1814, the French Senate invited the brother of King Louis XVI, who had been executed during the French Revolution, to rule France. In May, he took the throne as Louis XVIII. In March 1815, Napoleon returned to France with about 1,100 supporters. Many of the troops sent to stop Napoleon joined him instead. On March 19, Louis XVIII fled. On March 20, Napoleon took over the government without violence.

Since 1814, Austrian, British, Prussian, and Russian representatives had attended the Congress of Vienna, a series of meetings called to decide how Europe should be divided and governed following Napoleon's defeat. The congress had restored European rulers whom Napoleon had ousted. When the representatives heard of Napoleon's return, they formed a military coalition.

Napoleon attacked the coalition armies in Belgium before they could unite. He drove back a Prussian army at Ligny, Belgium, on June 16, 1815. On June 18, he attacked an army led by the Duke of Wellington at Waterloo. Prussian troops arrived late in the battle to aid Wellington, and the combined force beat back the French. Overwhelmed, the French retreated. Napoleon failed to gather a new army. He abdicated again on June 22 and was exiled to the South Atlantic island of St. Helena.

King Louis XVIII returned to France 100 days after he had fled. France and the allies signed the second Treaty of Paris on Nov. 20, 1815, ending the Napoleonic Wars. France had to pay *indemnities* (payments for war damages) and return to its borders as of 1790. In addition, thousands of allied soldiers occupied France. Napoleon died on St. Helena on May 5, 1821.   Rafe Blaufarb

See also the related articles for **Napoleon I.**

Narcissus, *nahr SIHS uhs,* is a large group of early spring flowers with lovely blossoms. Narcissuses are often called *daffodils.* Certain narcissuses are also sometimes called *jonquils.* Narcissuses were named for the legendary Greek youth Narcissus. Narcissuses are native to Europe and Asia, but many are cultivated in North America. In Europe, in the springtime, fragrant masses of wild narcissuses cover the Alpine meadows. People like them because they have fragrant and delicately fashioned blossoms of yellow, white, or sometimes pink or orange. The narcissus is a special flower of December.

Narcissuses grow from brown-coated bulbs. The bulbs are poisonous. Gardeners usually plant narcissus bulbs in the fall. Narcissuses are perennial.

There are various types of narcissuses. All of the plants send up shoots with sword-shaped leaves. The flowers have six petals surrounding a trumpet- or cup-shaped tube, which may be long or short.

A short-trumpet *species* (kind) is the poet's narcissus. It produces a single, wide-open blossom on each stalk. Generally, the blossom has white petals surrounding a short, yellowish cup with a crinkled red edge.

The paperwhite narcissus, also called the cream narcissus, is a short-trumpet species that can be grown indoors in winter from bulbs placed on pebbles. Most cultivated types have large clusters of pure white, heavily scented flowers. When breeders cross the paperwhite narcissus with the poet's narcissus, they get improved varieties, including types with flowers of two different colors on the same plant. People value these beautiful hybrid narcissuses.

August A. De Hertogh

Scientific classification. Narcissuses make up the genus *Narcissus.* The poet's narcissus is *N. poeticus;* the paperwhite is *N. tazetta.*

See also **Bulb; Daffodil; Jonquil.**

WORLD BOOK illustration
by Robert Hynes
Poet's narcissus

Narcissus, *nahr SIHS uhs,* in Greek mythology, was a handsome youth who was courted by many lovers for his beauty. He, however, haughtily rejected all of them, including the nymph Echo. As punishment for his cruelty, the gods condemned Narcissus to contemplate his beauty reflected in a pond on Mount Helicon in Greece. Day after day he lay beside the pond, gazing lovingly at his reflection until he wasted away and died. When searchers looked for him, they found only a flower, now called the narcissus. Echo also wasted away from her love for Narcissus, finally becoming nothing more than a voice in the woods. The best-known version of the Narcissus story appears in the *Metamorphoses,* a collection of tales by the Roman poet Ovid.   Jon D. Mikalson

Narcolepsy, *NAHR kuh LEHP see,* is a disease that causes excessive sleepiness. People with narcolepsy tend to fall asleep several times a day. They also often have trouble staying asleep at night. The disease is a lifelong condition that generally first appears during adolescence. Physicians can treat narcolepsy with medications, but it cannot be cured.

In addition to excessive sleepiness, narcoleptics experience episodes in which their muscles suddenly collapse though they remain awake. This condition, called *cataplexy,* is brought on by strong emotions, especially laughter and anger. Cataplectic episodes last two minutes or less. Narcoleptics may also experience *sleep paralysis* and *hypnagogic hallucinations.* In sleep paralysis, a person suddenly becomes unable to move while falling asleep or waking up. As they fall asleep, people with hypnagogic hallucinations experience vivid, realistic sights and sounds that do not really exist.

Scientists believe the symptoms of narcolepsy are related to REM (rapid eye movement) sleep, the phase of sleep during which people dream. The eyes move rapidly in this phase, and the body is paralyzed while dreaming occurs. Narcoleptics experience this same sort of paralysis during cataplectic episodes. Most cases of narcolepsy are caused by the lack of a brain chemical called *hypocretin.* Scientists believe the loss of hypocretin may be due to an *autoimmune* disorder in which the cells that contain the chemical are attacked by the body's own immune system. Normally, the immune system fights infections. Emmanuel Mignot

See also **Amphetamine** (Medical uses); **Cataplexy; Sleep.**

Narcotic is a substance that has a strong depressant effect upon the human nervous system. Narcotic substances cause insensibility to pain, stupor, sleep, or coma, according to the amount taken. The term *narcotic* comes from a Greek word meaning *to make numb.*

Narcotics include opium, codeine, morphine, and heroin. When a narcotic is given in doses large enough to cause sleep or coma, it is called a *hypnotic.* The term *analgesic* describes a drug that relieves pain without causing unconsciousness. The same narcotic may be an analgesic or a hypnotic, depending on the dosage.

Narcotics produce an analgesic effect by interacting with specific nerve cells called *receptors* in the central nervous system. Several chemicals that occur naturally in the body, including *endorphins* and *enkephalins,* interact with the same receptors. Scientists believe these naturally occurring chemicals control the brain's perception of pain. See **Endorphin.**

Narcotic drugs are extremely useful in medicine, but they also have dangerous effects. Large doses of narcotics may cause death. The careless use of opium and substances made from it to relieve pain has frequently caused a drug habit. No one should use these and other narcotics except under the direction of a physician.

The United States carefully regulates the importation of narcotics as well as the manufacture and distribution of narcotic by-products. Physicians must state certain facts on narcotic prescriptions, and druggists must keep records of them. The Drug Enforcement Administration in the United States Department of Justice oversees all narcotics laws. Barbara M. Bayer

Related articles in *World Book* include:

Analgesic	Cocaine	Hallucino-	Morphine
Barbiturate	Drug abuse	genic drug	Opium
Belladonna		Heroin	

Nard. See Spikenard.

Narragansett Indians, *NAR uh GAN siht,* were a tribe that lived on the west side of Narragansett Bay, in what is now Rhode Island. The Narragansett spoke an Algonquian language. They made their living by hunting, fishing, and farming and by gathering edible plant foods. The tribe's name is also spelled Narraganset.

At first, the Narragansett were friendly to the English colonists who settled in the area. But relations gradually grew worse. In 1675, more than 4,000 Narragansett joined forces with Wampanoag Indian chief King Philip to drive out white settlers. But colonial troops killed all but about 100 warriors. In 1676, English settlers took over the Narragansett lands. Conrad E. Heidenreich

Narváez, *nahr VAH ayth,* **Pánfilo de,** *PAHM fee loh thay* (1470?-1528), was a Spanish soldier and explorer. He helped conquer Cuba in 1511 and lost an eye trying to arrest the Spanish explorer Hernán Cortés in Mexico in 1521. Holy Roman Emperor Charles V granted Narváez the unexplored land of Florida in 1526, and Narváez led an expedition there in 1528. Landing near Tampa Bay, he marched inland and lost many of his men in storms and attacks by American Indians. Having been cut off from

their ships, Narváez and his men built five crude barges. They sailed along the coast to what is now south Texas. In November 1528, winds and currents forced Narváez's boat out into the Gulf of Mexico, and he was drowned. Narváez was born in Valladolid, Spain. Helen Delpar

Narwhal, *NAHR hwuhl,* is an Arctic whale known for its unusual tusk. The male has a spiral ivory tusk typically about 8 feet (2.4 meters) long that juts out of the left side of the upper jaw. The tusk is actually a tooth. Some males have two tusks. Most females have none. Narwhals may reach 15 feet (4.6 meters) long, not including the tusk, and can weigh 3.5 tons (3.2 metric tons). Adults are gray or white on top and whitish underneath. They are covered in dark spots. Newborns are typically gray.

People have long been intrigued by narwhal tusks, once selling them as unicorn horns. Scientists have proposed many explanations for the tusk's purpose. Most scientists think the tusk plays a role in selecting mates. Research also indicates that the tusk is a sensory organ, detecting water temperature, pressure, and other sensations. Tiny tubes connect millions of nerve endings inside the tusk to the water outside. Martin T. Nweeia

Scientific classification. The narwhal's scientific name is *Monodon monoceros.*

See also **Whale** (picture: Some kinds of whales).

NASA. See **National Aeronautics and Space Administration.**

NASCAR is the organization that governs the most popular form of stock car automobile racing in the United States. The full name of the organization is the National Association for Stock Car Auto Racing. Stock cars are large, late-model sedans that resemble ordinary passenger cars but have been built especially for racing.

NASCAR supervises the annual Sprint Cup Series (called the Winston Cup from 1972 to 2003 and the Nextel Cup from 2004 to 2007). The Sprint Cup is considered the premier championship series of stock car racing. NASCAR also governs the Nationwide Series for stock cars and the Camping World Truck Series. In each of these series, drivers compete in a schedule of races, earning points for their performance in each race. The driver with the most points at the end of the season is the champion.

NASCAR was founded in 1947 under the leadership of Bill France, Sr., a gas station owner and amateur stock car racer. The first true NASCAR race was held in Charlotte, North Carolina, in 1949. The NASCAR Hall of Fame opened in 2010 in Charlotte, North Carolina. The first group named to the Hall of Fame consisted of drivers Dale Earnhardt, Junior Johnson, and Richard Petty, plus NASCAR founder Bill France, Sr., and Bill France, Jr., his son and successor as head of NASCAR.

Critically reviewed by NASCAR

See also **Automobile racing** (Stock car racing; table: NASCAR Sprint Cup champions); **Earnhardt, Dale; Gordon, Jeff; Petty, Richard.**

Nasdaq, *NAZ dak,* is the oldest electronic stock market in the world. Its headquarters are in New York City. Originally, its name was an acronym for the National Association of Securities Dealers Automated Quotations System (Nasdaq®). On the Nasdaq market, brokers buy and sell stocks through a vast computer network instead of on a trading floor. Participants around the world receive trading information over this computer network. Nasdaq lists many stocks of high-technology companies, such as computer manufacturers and software developers.

The National Association of Securities Dealers (now part of the Financial Industry Regulatory Authority) created the Nasdaq network in 1971. This network automated the selling of over-the-counter (OTC) stocks, which are stocks not listed on any stock market or exchange. Nasdaq became a stock market in 1975 when it began listing stocks. In 1990, Nasdaq stopped dealing in OTC stocks and changed its name to the Nasdaq Stock Market.

Critically reviewed by Nasdaq.

See also **American Stock Exchange.**

Nash, Charles William (1864-1948), was a pioneer in the United States automobile industry. He became president of the Buick Motor Company in 1910, reorganized the company, and made it financially successful. Nash was elected president of General Motors Company in 1912 when it was close to bankruptcy. The company prospered under Nash's leadership. Nash resigned from General Motors in 1916. He then bought the Thomas B. Jeffery Company, an automobile firm from which he formed Nash Motors Company. He was company president until 1932 and board chairman until he died on June 6, 1948. His firm merged with Hudson Motors in 1954 to form American Motors. Nash was born on Jan. 28, 1864, in De Kalb County, Illinois.   William L. Bailey

Nash, John Forbes, Jr. (1928-   ), is an American mathematician. He contributed to the development of *game theory*—a method of studying strategic decision-making situations in which the participants' choices influence one another. Nash proposed a solution for game situations in which no participant will benefit by changing strategy, thereby creating a stable state of the system. This concept, known as *Nash equilibrium,* has influenced many fields, including biology, economics, and political science. Nash also developed important concepts used in conflict resolution and negotiations.

Nash was born in Bluefield, West Virginia, on June 13, 1928. He received a Ph.D. degree from Princeton University in 1950. He taught at the Massachusetts Institute of Technology from 1951 until 1959, when his career was interrupted by periodic struggles with *schizophrenia,* a severe mental disease. He later returned to Princeton. Nash shared the 1994 Nobel Prize in economic sciences with the Hungarian-born American economist John C. Harsanyi and the German economist Reinhard Selten. A biography of Nash—*A Beautiful Mind* (1998), by the German-born author Sylvia Nasar—was made into a motion picture in 2001.   Roberto Serrano

See also **Game theory.**

Nash, Ogden (1902-1971), was a famous American writer of humorous and satirical poetry. He created a unique poetic style in his light-hearted verses.

Most of Nash's poems have lines of unequal length. He often stretched sentences over several lines to produce surprising and comical rhymes. In "The Terrible People" (1938), for example, Nash wrote:

> People who have what they want are very
> fond of telling people who haven't what
> they want that they really don't want it,
>
> And I wish I could afford to gather all
> such people into a gloomy castle on
> the Danube and hire half a dozen
> capable Draculas to haunt it.

Nash also used many puns and frequently made clever comparisons of apparently unrelated subjects. He sometimes invented words or misspelled real words to produce a carefully planned effect.

Although Nash wrote in a comic style, many of his poems make a serious point. He made satirical comments about American society and ridiculed what he considered foolish behavior, including his own. Nash described people as bewildered by all the complications of modern life. He regarded humor as the best means of surviving in a difficult world.

The first collection of Nash's verses, *Hard Lines,* was published in 1931. His other collections include *Many Long Years Ago* (1945) and *You Can't Get There from Here* (1957). *I Wouldn't Have Missed It* (1975) appeared after his death.

Frederic Ogden Nash was born on Aug. 19, 1902, in Rye, New York. Many of Nash's poems were first published in *The New Yorker* magazine. He died on May 19, 1971.   William Harmon

Nash, Steve (1974-   ), is a star player in the National Basketball Association (NBA). Nash stands 6 feet 3 inches (191 centimeters) tall and plays guard. He was named the NBA's Most Valuable Player for the 2004-2005 and 2005-2006 seasons. Nash is one of the NBA's outstanding playmakers, leading the league in assists for five seasons—2004-2005, 2005-2006, 2006-2007, 2009-2010, and 2010-2011.

Stephen John Nash was born on Feb. 7, 1974, in Johannesburg, South Africa, where his father was a professional soccer player. His family moved to Canada when Nash was a baby, and he grew up in Victoria, British Columbia. Nash played college basketball at Santa Clara University in California, graduating in 1996.

The Phoenix Suns selected Nash as the 15th player chosen in the 1996 NBA draft. Phoenix traded him to the Dallas Mavericks in 1998, and he played in Dallas until he signed as a free agent to play in Phoenix again in 2004. Nash was voted Canadian male athlete of the year in 2005 and 2006.   Neil Milbert

Nashe, Thomas (1567-1601), was an author who wrote some of the first works of prose fiction in English literature. He is remembered chiefly for *The Unfortunate Traveller; or, The Life of Jack Wilton* (1594), a forerunner of the English novel. This energetic narrative combines colorful fictional characters with references to actual people and events. *Pierce Penniless, His Supplication to the Devil* (1592) is a satire on Elizabethan society.

Nashe was born in Lowestoft, England, in November 1657. His name is also spelled Nash. He studied at Cambridge University and was one of the group of playwrights known as the "University Wits."

Nashe's racy style and gift for rough language lent themselves to the pamphlet warfare that was widespread in Elizabethan literary life. In one famous series of pamphlets, Nashe attacked scholar Gabriel Harvey. Nashe also wrote several pamphlets in 1589 and 1590 that defended the bishops of the Church of England against attacks by the Puritans. This heated exchange of pamphlets became known as the Martin Marprelate controversy. Nashe died in unknown circumstances in 1601.   John N. King

Nashua, *NASH oo uh* (pop. 86,494), is New Hampshire's second largest city. Only Manchester has more people.

Nashua and Manchester form a metropolitan area with 400,721 people. Nashua lies at the junction of the Merrimack and Nashua rivers (see **New Hampshire** [political map]). Its products include computers, electronic equipment for the military, and fabricated metal products. The first permanent settlement was made there between 1665 and 1670. A town charter was granted in 1673 under the name of Dunstable. The town was renamed Nashua in 1837. Early settlers referred to the American Indians who lived in the area as the Nashaways. Nashua was incorporated as a city in 1853. It is the home of Rivier and Daniel Webster colleges. A mayor and board of aldermen head the city government.   Claudette Durocher

Nashville (pop. 601,222; met. area pop. 1,589,934) is the capital and second largest city of Tennessee. Only Memphis has more people. Nashville lies in the north-central part of the state (see **Tennessee** [political map]). It is often called the *Athens of the South* because of its many educational institutions and its buildings in the Greek classical style. Nashville is also called *Music City, U.S.A.* because it is a major music recording center and the home of the "Grand Ole Opry" radio show.

Nashville was founded in 1779 by settlers from North Carolina looking for fertile farmland. The settlers built a log stockade on a bluff overlooking the west bank of the Cumberland River. They called the settlement Fort Nashborough after Brigadier General Francis Nash, who was a hero during the American Revolution (1775-1783). The settlement was renamed Nashville in 1784.

The city. Nashville covers 497 square miles (1,287 square kilometers), nearly all of Davidson County. The Nashville-Davidson-Murfreesboro-Franklin metropolitan area covers 5,687 square miles (14,729 square kilometers) and consists of 13 counties.

The Cumberland River flows through downtown Nashville. The State Capitol overlooks Memorial Square. The 33-story AT&T Building in downtown Nashville is the tallest structure in Tennessee.

Most of the people of Nashville were born in the United States. The city's largest ethnic groups include those of English, German, or Irish ancestry. African Americans form about a fourth of Nashville's population. About one-tenth of the city's people are Hispanics.

Economy. Large numbers of Nashville's people work for the state government. Many others have jobs with agencies of the federal or city government. Vanderbilt University combined with its medical center ranks as one of the city's largest employers.

Nashville is the headquarters for a number of major companies. The city also has hundreds of industrial plants. Its chief products include aircraft parts, automobiles, food products, glass, heating and cooking equipment, printed materials, recordings of music, and tires. Nashville's economy received a big boost during the 1950's, when the city became a major music recording center. Hundreds of recording companies, recording studios, and song-publishing firms operate in the city.

Three interstate highways reach Nashville. Freight railroads and Nashville International Airport serve the city. Barge lines connect the city with ports on the Cumberland River. *The Tennessean* is the daily newspaper.

Education. The nine elected members of the Metropolitan Board of Public Education supervise the public school system in metropolitan Nashville. The city also

State of Tennessee

Nashville is the capital of Tennessee and a music recording center. This photo shows the State Capitol, *right,* and the War Memorial Building, *left.*

has many private and parochial schools. Vanderbilt University is the largest of the city's institutions of higher education. Other colleges and universities in the city include Belmont University, Fisk University, Lipscomb University, Meharry Medical College, Tennessee State University, and Trevecca Nazarene University. Middle Tennessee State University is in nearby Murfreesboro.

Cultural life and recreation. The city's arts groups include the Nashville Symphony, the Nashville Ballet, and theater groups. The Tennessee State Museum is in Nashville. An exact replica of the Parthenon of Athens stands in Centennial Park. The Tennessee Centennial of 1897 was held in the park.

Other attractions include the Country Music Hall of Fame and Museum, Frist Center for the Visual Arts, Adventure Science Center, Nashville Zoo at Grassmere, and Cheekwood Botanical Garden and Museum of Art. The Grand Ole Opry House and downtown's historic Ryman Auditorium host the "Grand Ole Opry" and its weekly radio program. The program, which began in Nashville in 1925, features country music. The Hermitage, the home of President Andrew Jackson, lies about 10 miles (16 kilometers) east of Nashville. Jackson and his wife are buried on the grounds of the mansion.

Nashville is the home of the Nashville Predators of the National Hockey League and the Tennessee Titans of the National Football League. The nearby Nashville Superspeedway hosts Indy and stock car races.

Government. Nashville has a mayor-council form of government. The voters elect the mayor and the 40 council members to four-year terms.

History. The first white people who came to what is now the Nashville area found Shawnee Indians living along the Cumberland River. More settlers arrived after the establishment of Fort Nashborough in 1779. By 1780, the settlement consisted of seven forts with a total population of 300. Tennessee became a state in 1796, and Nashville was chartered as a city in 1806.

The first steamboat arrived in Nashville about 1818, and a brisk trade developed between Nashville and ports along the Ohio and Mississippi rivers. Nashville became the permanent capital of Tennessee in 1843. By the time of the 1850 census, the city's population had reached 10,165.

During the American Civil War, Union troops held Nashville from 1862 until the fighting ended in 1865. Confederate General John B. Hood tried to recapture the city in 1864 but was defeated by Union General George H. Thomas. In 1900, Nashville had a population of 80,865. The busy river trade, plus income from the fertile farmlands surrounding the city, contributed to Nashville's prosperity. From 1920 to 1930, the city's population increased from 118,342 to 153,866.

In 1962, Nashville and Davidson County adopted a metropolitan form of government. This government combines city and county functions under one administration and provides services for the entire county.

An urban renewal project for downtown Nashville, completed in 1980, included the widening and landscaping of city streets and the construction of office buildings. Also in the late 1900's, the Nashville Convention Center and Riverfront Park were completed.

In 2010, 10 people died and many buildings were damaged after heavy rains pushed the Cumberland River over its banks. Nashville landmarks suffering damage in the flood included the Grand Ole Opry House and the Country Music Hall of Fame.   Patrick S. "Pat" Embry

For the monthly weather in Nashville, see **Tennessee** (Climate). See also **Tennessee** (pictures).

Naskapi Indians. See Innu Indians.

Nasmyth, *NAY smihth,* **James** (1808-1890), a Scottish engineer, invented the steam hammer in 1839. His steam hammer was able to forge large parts for steamships and railroads. He also developed the *self-acting principle* in machine-tool design, by which a mechanically held tool moves along a track and works on a stationary workpiece. Using this principle, Nasmyth invented a planing mill and a nut-shaping machine.

Nasmyth was born on Aug. 19, 1808, in Edinburgh, Scotland. In 1829, he became assistant to a tool designer and manufacturer. In 1834, Nasmyth started the Bridgewater Foundry at Manchester, which gained fame for machine-tool and steam-engine construction. He retired in 1856 and devoted his time to studying astronomy. Nasmyth died on May 7, 1890.   David F. Channell

Nassau, *NAS aw* (pop. 200,000), is the capital and largest city of the Bahamas. The city borders an excellent harbor on the northeast coast of New Providence Island. For location, see **Bahamas** (map). The city's warm, sunny climate has made it a major tourist center.

Near Nassau's harbor are beautiful beaches and luxurious hotels. Nassau also features fine restaurants, colorful markets, and casinos. Most major banks, stores, and government buildings are on Bay Street, which runs along the harbor. Nassau has several historic buildings, including three forts built in the 1700's. The nation's only college, the College of the Bahamas, also is in Nassau.

Many of Nassau's people work in the tourist industry and are prosperous. The city has few manufacturing industries, and unemployment is high. Some Nassau residents live in charming, pastel houses. In the city's older, poorer neighborhoods, people live in run-down houses, some of which have no running water.

Nassau's busy harbor serves as a port for cruise ships that carry tourists to the city. Smaller ships called *mailboats* move freight and passengers between Nassau and the many islands that make up the Bahamas. Such products as fish, oil, and rum are shipped through Nassau.

English seafarers founded a settlement named Charles Towne at what is now Nassau in the 1660's. The settlement was renamed Nassau in 1695. During the late 1600's, many pirates used Nassau as a base to attack Spanish ships sailing from Cuba or Mexico. The Bahamas became a British colony in 1717, with Nassau as the capital. Nassau became prosperous during the American Civil War (1861-1865), when ships carried goods from the city to the Confederate States. It also prospered during the early 1900's as a distribution center for the illegal shipment of alcoholic beverages to the United States. Tourism has been Nassau's principal industry since 1929. That year, commercial airline flights began operating between the United States and Nassau. In 1973, the Bahamas gained independence from the United Kingdom.   Stephen Small

See also **Bahamas** (picture).

Nasser, *NAH sehr,* **Gamal Abdel,** *gah MAHL AHB duhl* (1918-1970), led the revolt that overthrew King Faruk in 1952 and made Egypt a republic. Nasser served as Egypt's prime minister from 1954 until he was elected president in 1956. Later in 1956, a world crisis occurred after Egypt *nationalized* (took control of) the Suez Canal, then under British and French control. Nasser wanted to use the money generated by the canal to build the Aswan High Dam. When Syria and Egypt formed the United Arab Republic (U.A.R.) in 1958, Nasser served as its president. Syria withdrew from the U.A.R. in 1961.

Nasser resigned after Egypt lost the Sinai Peninsula in the Arab-Israeli War of 1967. But the Egyptian people and the National Assembly refused to accept his resignation. He became both president and prime minister. Fighting between the Arab countries and Israel continued into the 1970's. In August 1970, Nasser agreed to a 90-day cease-fire with Israel. He died on Sept. 28, 1970.

Nasser's book *Egypt's Liberation: The Philosophy of the Revolution* (1955) stated his aims to unite all Arabs under Egyptian leadership and to liberate Egypt from colonialism and underdevelopment. He was unable to unite the Arab world, but he did become one of its most influential leaders. Nasser favored a neutral foreign policy and emphasized nationalism and economic reform. He redistributed land to farmers and also advanced education. However, his efforts to develop Egypt's economy were hampered by overpopulation and poverty.

Nasser was born on Jan. 15, 1918, in Alexandria, Egypt. He graduated from the Royal Military Academy in Cairo in 1938. He fought in the Arab war against Israel in 1948 and 1949.   Imad Harb

See also **Egypt** (Republic).

Nasser, Lake. See Lake Nasser.

Nast, Thomas (1840-1902), was an American political cartoonist. He popularized the famous political symbol of the Democratic donkey and originated the Republican elephant and the Tammany Tiger. His caricatures of the Tammany Tiger from 1869 to1871 helped break up the notorious political organization headed by William "Boss" Tweed in New York City (see **Tweed, William Marcy**).

Nast's cartoons appeared in the magazine *Harper's Weekly* from 1862 to 1886. He did his best work during the American Civil War (1861-1865), when his cartoons

Nast drew the Tammany Tiger to symbolize the corrupt Tammany political machine in New York City. This cartoon appeared after the machine defeated its Republican opponents in 1871.

influenced public opinion in favor of the North. In the presidential campaign of 1872, Nast's barbed cartoons helped bring about the defeat of Horace Greeley (see **Greeley, Horace**). Nast is also credited with creating the present-day image of Santa Claus in sketches that appeared in *Harper's Weekly* in the 1860's.

Nast was only an average draftsman. But he excelled at inventing concepts for cartoons and at arranging the elements of his designs. In most cases, he drew sketches from which other artists made engravings in blocks of wood. The engravings were used to print cartoons.

Nast was born on Sept. 27, 1840, in Landau, Bavaria, and came with his mother to the United States in 1846. He worked as a draftsman on *Frank Leslie's Illustrated Newspaper* and sketched warfare in Italy for New York City, London, and Paris newspapers. Nast died on Dec. 7, 1902.   Charles P. Green

For other pictures by Thomas Nast, see **Carpetbaggers** and **New York City**.

Nasturtium, *nuh STUR shuhm,* is the common name of a group of perennial plants native to tropical America. Nasturtium is a favorite garden flower of North America. There, it is a trailing or climbing annual that may reach about 10 feet (3 meters). Its blossoms are yellow, orange, or red. Dwarf nasturtiums are also grown.

The nasturtium flower has an interesting structure. There are five small *sepals* (outer "petals"). The three upper ones form a long *spur* (hollow projection) that holds the nectar. There are also five petals inside the sepals. The three lower petals are set a little apart from the upper two and have long, fringed claws that reach into the spur. The long-stalked leaves are shaped like an umbrella. They have a spicy taste and are used in salads. The leaves also make an attractive light green background for the bright flowers.

The nasturtium is a North American garden plant. It has umbrella-shaped leaves and orange, red, or yellow blossoms.

Nasturtiums grow well from seeds sown outdoors in spring. They can also be potted in the early spring and transplanted in May. The plants cannot stand frost, but may be grown indoors in winter. Nasturtiums are easy to grow. They thrive best in bright sunlight. Small insects, called black aphids, often attack the plants and live on the underside of the leaves. The insects will destroy the nasturtium unless they are controlled with an insecticide. The name *nasturtium* is also given to the genus of the water cress (see **Cress**).   Daniel F. Austin

Scientific classification. Nasturtiums belong to the nasturtium family, Tropaeolaceae. The scientific name for the garden flower is *Tropaeolum majus.*

Natal, *nuh TAL,* is a historic region on the east coast of South Africa. The region has been the home of Zulu people for centuries. The region's full name is *Terra do Natal,* which means *Land of Christ's Birth* in Portuguese. The name was chosen by the Portuguese explorer Vasco da Gama when he sighted the region on Christmas Day, 1497.

Between 1818 and 1828, a Zulu leader named Shaka established a powerful state known as KwaZulu (Zululand) in northern Natal. The southern part of Natal became a British colony in 1843. White settlers opened sugar plantations and encouraged workers to come from India to Natal. In 1879, after two bloody wars between the Zulu and the Natal colonial authorities, Zululand was made part of the British colony of Natal.

The British gave the government of Natal to the white minority in the region even though more Zulu and Indians lived there. In 1910, Natal became one of the four provinces in the new Union of South Africa. The three other provinces were Cape Province, Orange Free State, and Transvaal. In 1994, black people took over the South African government. That same year, South Africa increased the number of its provinces to nine. The Natal area remained a province, but the province's name was changed to KwaZulu-Natal. The province of KwaZulu-Natal covers about 35,000 square miles (91,000 square kilometers). Pietermaritzburg is its capital. The port city of Durban is its largest city.   Bruce Fetter

See also **Bantu; Durban; Pietermaritzburg; Zulu.**

Natchez, *NACH ihz,* Mississippi (pop. 15,792), is the oldest city on the Mississippi River. It lies on the state's southwestern border (see **Mississippi** [political map]).

Jean Baptiste Le Moyne, Sieur de Bienville, a French governor of Louisiana, built Fort Rosalie on the site in 1716. The settlement around the fort took the name Natchez from a local American Indian tribe. In 1729, the Natchez Indians destroyed the fort, but settlement of the area continued. Britain gained control of the territory in 1763. Spain controlled it from 1779 until it became part of the United States in 1798. The growth of the cotton industry made Natchez Mississippi's center of wealth and culture before the American Civil War (1861-1865).

Natchez attracts many tourists because it has the largest concentration of *antebellum* (pre-Civil War) houses in the nation. The city is also a retail and manufacturing center. Products include lumber, oil, and pecans. Natchez has a mayor-council government. It is the seat of Adams County.   Joan W. Gandy

Natchez Indians, *NACH ihz,* were a tribe in North America whose important chiefs had total power over their subjects' lives and property. The tribe once lived near the city along the Mississippi River that was named after them. They were farmers, and they made excellent fabrics and pottery. Each tribe member inherited a place in a society of rigid class distinctions. There were three classes of nobility, as well as a large group of common people. The Natchez had a highly developed religious life based on sun worship. They believed that their chief was descended from the sun. Servants carried him about in a special litter, so that his feet would not touch the ground. When an important Natchez chief died, tribe members paid considerable respect to the leader and performed sacrifices.

The name of the Natchez first occurs in the reports of Sieur de La Salle's descent of the Mississippi River in 1682. The tribe, which probably included about 6,000 people, was the largest and strongest on the lower Mississippi at that time. They fought three major wars with the French but were so soundly defeated in 1729 that the tribe did not recover. The survivors joined other tribes.   Donald L. Fixico

Natchez Trace was an important commercial and military route between Nashville, Tennessee, and Natchez, Mississippi, in the early 1800's. Pioneers who floated their goods on flatboats down the Mississippi River to New Orleans often returned on horseback along this route. Settlers moving into Alabama, Florida, Louisiana, Mississippi, or Texas frequently traveled south on the trace. In 1800, Congress made it a *post road* (mail route). In 1938, the Natchez Trace National Parkway was established.   William E. Foley

See also **National Park System** (table: Parkways).

Nation is a large group of people united by a common language, ancestry, history, or culture. People often feel great loyalty to their nation and pride in their national characteristics. Such feelings of loyalty and pride are often referred to as *nationalism.* See **Nationalism.**

In international law, *nation* means a group of people exercising self-government within a defined territory with the *recognition* of other nations. Recognition is shown by other nations through the exchange of ambassadors. When a new nation is recognized by other nations, it acquires certain rights and duties. Its rights include the right to navigate freely on the high seas. Its duties include the obligation not to threaten or use military force against other nations. Sometimes in international law, a nation is called a *country* or *state.* See **Country; International law.**   Anthony D'Amato

Nation, Carry Amelia Moore (1846-1911), was an American activist known for her militant efforts to stop the sale of alcoholic liquors. She was arrested often, and some people considered her intolerant. However, she impressed many with her sincerity, courage, and strong beliefs. She carried the temperance movement from the level of education to that of action. She helped bring on national prohibition, which was adopted in 1919, after her death (see **Prohibition**).

Carrie Amelia Moore was born on Nov. 25, 1846, in Garrard County, Kentucky. In 1867, she married Charles Gloyd, a physician suffering from alcoholism, who died in 1869. In the following years, she taught in schools and ran a hotel. From 1877 to 1901, she was married to David Nation, a lawyer and minister. During this time, her strong religious interests intensified, and she began to see visions. She believed that she was divinely protected and thought that her name (Carry A. Nation) had been preordained.

The Nations moved to Kansas in 1889. In 1880, a state law had banned liquor sales there, but the law was not

Brown Bros.

Carry Nation led a crusade against alcoholic beverages in the early 1900's. She used a hatchet often in her violent saloon-wrecking campaign. The Bible was her text for many lectures.

enforced. Carry Nation began in 1890 to pray outside saloons. Later, she began to violently destroy them. A tall and strong woman, she did much damage, first with stones and other implements, and later with hatchets. She closed the saloons of her town, Medicine Lodge, and destroyed saloons in other Kansas cities. She was arrested many times, usually for disturbing the peace.

Nation was an eloquent speaker, and she lectured frequently in support of her cause. She sometimes sold miniature hatchets inscribed with the words *Carry Nation, Joint Smasher.* She brought publicity to the temperance movement and supported the temperance work of others. Nation died on June 9, 1911.   Melanie S. Gustafson

Nation of Islam is a religious group in the United States that preaches black nationalism. The Nation of Islam (also called Black Muslims) was originally founded in Detroit in 1930 by a salesman named Wallace D. Fard (also known as Wali Farad). Elijah Muhammad (formerly Elijah Poole) led the group from 1934 until his death in 1975. He taught that Fard was Allah and that he himself was Allah's messenger. Muhammad also taught that white people were "devils" who sought to harm and oppress blacks. He said that whites would eventually be destroyed and blacks would emerge victorious.

Muhammad's son Warith Deen Mohammed (sometimes spelled Muhammad) succeeded him. Instead of continuing his father's teachings, Warith dismantled the Nation of Islam. He led his followers to Sunni Islam, a traditional branch of Islam practiced by many Africans.

In 1977, the American minister Louis Farrakhan and other discontented followers resurrected the Nation of Islam but rejected the name Black Muslims. Farrakhan also stopped preaching that whites would eventually be destroyed. He based the organization on the teachings of Elijah Muhammad and continued Muhammad's teachings about the need for self-knowledge, the acceptance of black identity, and economic independence.

Farrakhan's Nation of Islam is headquartered in Chicago. Its members are urged to eat only one meal a day and to avoid the use of tobacco and alcohol. Women are expected to focus on housework and child rearing, though some women serve as ministers. The key groups in the organization are the Fruit of Islam and Muslim Girls Training (MGT). Members of the Fruit of Islam provide security in *mosques* (places of worship) and public places. Members of the MGT learn domestic skills.

In 1997, Farrakhan began to move closer to traditional Sunni Islam. He adopted the orthodox Friday worship service, prayer posture, and fasting. These measures helped end 25 years of separation and hostilities between Farrakhan and Mohammed. The two men declared their unity at the second International Islamic Conference in Chicago in February 2000. But they continued to lead separate movements.

Lawrence H. Mamiya

See also **African Americans** (Black militancy); **Black Muslims; Farrakhan, Louis; Mohammed, Warith Deen; Muhammad, Elijah.**

National Academies are a group of organizations in the United States that promote research in the sciences, medicine, and engineering. The academies consist of the National Academy of Sciences (NAS) and three organizations created under its charter—the National Academy of Engineering, the Institute of Medicine, and the National Research Council. The National Academies advise the United States government on scientific and technical matters, but they are not government agencies. All four organizations have headquarters in Washington, D.C. The academies publish many of their findings through the National Academies Press.

The NAS advises the government on matters related to the behavioral, biological, physical, and social sciences. Scientists are elected to the organization in recognition of their achievements in research. The National Academy of Engineering consists of engineers elected on the basis of professional achievement. Members of the Institute of Medicine are chosen for their interest in problems of health and medicine. Many come from fields other than health and medicine.

The National Research Council enables other scientists to work with members of the National Academy of Engineering, the Institute of Medicine, and the NAS. Thousands of scientists and engineers belong to committees and other groups organized by the council to give advice on scientific and technological matters.

Critically reviewed by the National Academies

See also **National Academy of Sciences; National Research Council.**

National Academy of Sciences (NAS) is an organization that promotes research in the behavioral, biological, physical, and social sciences in the United States. The NAS advises the U.S. government on scientific matters, but it is not a government agency. The NAS consists of about 2,000 U.S. scientists elected for life for their achievements in research. The NAS also includes about 350 scientists from other countries elected as foreign associates. Members of the NAS elect new members and foreign associates each year. The NAS has its headquarters in Washington, D.C.

The NAS was established in 1863 by an act of Congress. The NAS charter requires the organization to provide free advice to the government on scientific matters in addition to engaging in other scientific activities. The NAS created the National Research Council in 1916, the National Academy of Engineering in 1964, and the Institute of Medicine in 1970. Together with the NAS, these organizations are known as the National Academies.

Critically reviewed by the National Academy of Sciences

See also **National Academies; National Research Council.**

National Aeronautic Association, also called NAA, promotes the advancement of aviation and space flight in the United States. It is the U.S. representative to the Fédération Aéronautique Internationale (FAI). As such, the NAA is the only U.S. organization that can approve and certify flight records by U.S. civilian and military aircraft. The NAA also sponsors U.S. teams in sport aviation championships. The NAA was chartered in 1922. Its full name is National Aeronautic Association of the U.S.A. Its headquarters are in Washington, D.C.

Critically reviewed by the National Aeronautic Association of the U.S.A.

National Aeronautics and Space Administration (NASA) is a United States government agency that manages the nation's nonmilitary space program and conducts research in aircraft flight. NASA employs thousands of government workers and tens of thousands of additional workers through contracts with private businesses. NASA has headquarters in Washington, D.C., and operates 10 field centers and many smaller facilities across the United States. Its programs advance scientific knowledge and stimulate the development of new technology. NASA also promotes international cooperation through such projects as the International Space Station (ISS) and provides educational programs for the public. NASA's Web site at http://www.nasa.gov presents information on the agency's activities.

NASA's history began with the National Advisory Committee for Aeronautics (NACA), a federal aviation research group founded in 1915. Soon after the Soviet Union launched the first artificial satellite in 1957, U.S. President Dwight D. Eisenhower placed NACA in charge of U.S. nonmilitary space exploration. An act of Congress reorganized the group as NASA in 1958.

The new agency retained NACA's laboratories in

Hampton, Virginia; Cleveland, Ohio; and Moffett Field, California. In addition, it took control of a missile development complex (now the George C. Marshall Space Flight Center) in Huntsville, Alabama; the Jet Propulsion Laboratory in Pasadena, California; and military facilities at Cape Canaveral in Florida, Edwards Air Force Base in California, and White Sands Missile Range in New Mexico. NASA also built new facilities, including an astronaut training and flight control headquarters (now the Johnson Space Center) in Houston and the Goddard Space Flight Center, a space communications and satellite development facility in Greenbelt, Maryland.

In the 1960's, NASA added hundreds of thousands of workers as part of the Apollo program. The program carried astronauts to the first landing on the moon in 1969. Notable later missions include the Voyager space probes, launched in 1977; the space shuttles, the first of which was launched in 1981; the Hubble Space Telescope, which began making observations in 1991; the ISS, begun in 1998; and the Mars Exploration Rover Mission, two rovers that landed on the planet in 2004.

Space exploration is by its nature expensive and risky. Some experts, though, have criticized NASA leaders for errors in judgment that contributed to major disasters. Two space shuttle accidents, the loss of Challenger in 1986 and of Columbia in 2003, each resulted in the deaths of seven crew members. Investigators concluded that faulty management and safety practices played a part in both accidents, leading NASA to adopt some reforms. Experts have also criticized the agency for excessive costs and delays in major projects, such as the ISS. In 2011, NASA retired the remaining space shuttles after two final missions to the ISS.   James Oberg

Related articles in *World Book* include:
Astronaut
Hubble Space Telescope
International Space Station
Jet Propulsion Laboratory
Johnson Space Center
Kennedy Space Center
Space exploration

National Air and Space Museum, in Washington, D.C., features exhibits on aviation and space flight. It is part of the Smithsonian Institution. The museum has more than 20 galleries, a theater, and a planetarium. The displays include the Wright brothers' 1903 *Flyer;* Charles A. Lindbergh's *Spirit of St. Louis;* X-1 and X-15 aircraft; and Mercury, Gemini, and Apollo spacecraft.

Congress created the National Air Museum in 1946 and gave it its present name in 1966. The museum's main building, on the National Mall, opened in 1976. In 2003, the museum opened the Steven F. Udvar-Hazy Center at Washington Dulles International Airport in Virginia. Exhibits there include several craft too large to fit in the museum's main building.

Critically reviewed by the National Air and Space Museum

National Alliance of Business (NAB) was a nonprofit organization committed to building a quality work force for the United States. The NAB helped private businesses, state and local governments, education organizations, and labor groups form partnerships to improve education, training, and employment programs.

The NAB helped state and local partnerships (1) develop learning programs in the workplace, (2) involve business in the restructuring and reform of public educa-

tion, and (3) create job training for unskilled and unemployed individuals. It provided guidance and information on these efforts through publications, conferences, seminars, and an information center.

President Lyndon B. Johnson established the NAB in 1968. The organization closed in 2002.

National Alliance on Mental Illness (NAMI) is a private, nonprofit organization that works to improve the quality of life of all people affected by serious mental illness. It serves not only the mentally ill themselves, but also their families, caregivers, and friends. NAMI was founded in 1979. Today, it has more than 1,000 local and state affiliates throughout the United States.

NAMI affiliates provide support and education through more than 150 programs. NAMI offers information on mental illnesses and available treatments. It helps patients and families access social and mental health services. Local affiliates provide a forum for people to share information and provide encouragement to one another. NAMI also addresses public policy concerns that relate to mental illness, including insurance coverage, fair housing and employment regulations, and issues of discrimination that affect the mentally ill.

Critically reviewed by the National Alliance on Mental Illness

See also **Mental illness** (Recent developments).

National anthem is the official patriotic song of a nation. National anthems are intended to stir a sense of patriotism and loyalty among citizens of a country. They are performed at official and ceremonial public occasions, international gatherings, and athletic events. They are also played to honor a head of state.

Most national anthems are composed as marches, hymns, and anthems. The words of some commemorate the ideals of the nation. Others celebrate a country's natural beauty or honor a national hero. Some recall a na-

© Tom Benoit, Superstock

The National Air and Space Museum in Washington, D.C., features exhibits on aviation and space flight.

tional crisis or important event in a country's history.

Many countries have adapted existing music and words for their anthems. For example, John Stafford Smith, an English composer, wrote "To Anacreon in Heaven" (1760's). The song became the music for "The Star-Spangled Banner," the national anthem of the United States. The words of the anthem are a poem written by Francis Scott Key in 1814.

The idea of an official national anthem dates from about 1825. At that time, the United Kingdom's patriotic song "God Save the King" (or "Queen") was called "the national anthem." However, the song had been performed as early as 1745 and ranks as the oldest official national anthem in the world. The Dutch national anthem "Wilhelmus van Nassouwe" ("William of Nassau") was written between 1568 and 1572, but it did not become the country's official national anthem until 1932.   Don B. Wilmeth

Related articles. For the national anthem of many countries, see the *Facts in brief* section of the country article. See also:

Deutschland über Alles	O Canada
God Save the Queen	Star-Spangled Banner
Marseillaise	

National Archives and Records Administration, *AHR kyvz,* is an independent federal agency that

preserves and makes available for public use the permanently valuable records of the United States government. The archives, established in 1934, include most U.S. presidential libraries (see **Presidential libraries**).

The National Archives and Records Administration stores millions of records, including maps, sound recordings, still pictures, and motion pictures. These records date from 1774 to the present. Many of the records are kept in the National Archives Building in Washington, D.C. The temperature and humidity of the building's many stack areas are carefully controlled. Millions of people have visited the Exhibition Hall to see such historic documents as the Declaration of Independence, the Constitution of the United States, and the Bill of Rights. These charters of American freedom are displayed in airtight cases filled with argon gas.

Critically reviewed by the National Archives and Records Administration

See also **Declaration of Independence** (picture: The original Declaration of Independence).

National Assessment of Educational Progress

is a government program designed to evaluate the quality and progress of education in the United States. It is sometimes referred to as NAEP or "the Nation's Report Card." The program was created by Congress in 1964. It is directed and funded by the U.S. Department of Education's National Center for Education Statistics. NAEP conducted its first evaluation in 1969. Since then, it has issued hundreds of reports.

The program's staff surveys students at three age and grade levels: 9-year-olds and 4th-graders, 13-year-olds and 8th-graders, and 17-year-olds and 12th-graders. The assessment presents profiles based on nationally representative samples of these students. The tests eventually will cover 12 subject areas—the arts, civics, economics, foreign language. geography, world history, United States history, mathematics, reading, science, technology and engineering literacy, and writing. Educational Testing Service, a private, nonprofit company, works with the Education Department to design and administer NAEP.   Critically reviewed by Educational Testing Service

National Association for the Advancement of Colored People (NAACP) is a civil rights organization

in the United States. It works to end discrimination against blacks and other minority groups.

The NAACP achieves many goals through legal action. It played an important part in the 1954 ruling of the Supreme Court of the United States that segregation of blacks in public schools is unconstitutional. Thurgood Marshall, a lawyer from the NAACP Legal Defense and Educational Fund, presented the argument in the case, known as *Brown v. Board of Education of Topeka.*

The organization also achieves its goals through legislative action. It played a leading role in obtaining passage of the Civil Rights Act of 1957, which protects the right to vote. This act established the Civil Rights Division of the Department of Justice and the Commission on Civil Rights. The NAACP worked for passage of the Civil Rights Act of 1964, which forbids discrimination in public places. This law established the Equal Employment Opportunity Commission (EEOC). The association also helped bring into law the Voting Rights Act of 1965, which protects voter registration.

Activities. The NAACP has worked successfully to fight discrimination in housing and to strengthen the penalties for violations of civil rights. In the 1970's and 1980's, it helped win extensions of the Voting Rights Act of 1965. The NAACP also led successful efforts in 1972 to increase the power of the EEOC. In 1986, the NAACP successfully campaigned for the United States to impose economic sanctions against South Africa because of its system of racial segregation, called *apartheid.* The NAACP helped obtain passage of an amendment in 1988 that strengthened the Fair Housing Act of 1968.

The organization strives to protect the rights of prison inmates. Its investigation of problems facing black military personnel led to changes in the system of military assignments and promotions. The NAACP sponsors a program of voter education and registration. It works for desegregation of public schools and fights dismissals and demotions of black teachers and administrators that it considers discriminatory. It urges publishers to produce textbooks that provide an accurate account of the achievements and activities of blacks. The NAACP also seeks to reduce the number of students who drop out of school and to encourage and reward academic, scientific, and artistic excellence among black students.

The NAACP also acts to reduce poverty and hunger. In 1968, it established the Mississippi Emergency Relief Fund to feed poor blacks in the Mississippi Delta area.

History. The NAACP was founded in 1909 by 60 black and white citizens. In 1910, the organization began to publish *The Crisis,* a magazine about blacks who have achieved success in the arts, business, and other fields.

During the NAACP's first 30 years, it worked to prevent violence against blacks, unjust legal penalties, and job discrimination. Much of its activity centered on passage and enforcement of antilynching laws. During World War II (1939-1945), the NAACP tried to obtain equal rights for black military personnel and more job opportunities for black civilians. After the war, the association stepped up its long struggle against the policy that treated blacks as "separate but equal." This policy had been established in 1896 by the Supreme Court's ruling in the case of *Plessy v. Ferguson.*

The NAACP has hundreds of thousands of members and hundreds of youth councils. It receives funds from membership fees and from private donations. It has headquarters in Baltimore and a legislative bureau in Washington, D.C. The NAACP Legal Defense and Educational Fund, which has been an independent organization since 1957, is headquartered in New York City.

Critically reviewed by the National Association for the Advancement of Colored People

Related articles in *World Book* include:
Brown v. Board of Education of Topeka
Du Bois, W. E. B.
Evers, Medgar
Evers-Williams, Myrlie
Hooks, Benjamin L.
Marshall, Thurgood
Mfume, Kweisi
Plessy v. Ferguson
White, Walter F.
Wilkins, Roy

National Association for Stock Car Auto Racing. See NASCAR.

National Association of Congregational Christian Churches is a Protestant religious fellowship. It was founded in 1955 by a number of Congregational Christian Churches. It stresses cooperation among member churches but has no authority over them.

The association operates domestic and international missions, provides financial support to seminary students, and conducts its own educational programs for clergy and lay leaders. It also has various commissions and committees to deal with such issues as youth ministry, interfaith relations, and communication between member churches. In addition, it publishes a magazine called *The Congregationalist*. The national office is in Oak Creek, Wisconsin.   Critically reviewed by the National Association of Congregational Christian Churches

National Association of Manufacturers (NAM) is an organization of American manufacturing companies. It is the largest broad-based manufacturing *advocacy* (support) group in the United States. NAM serves as a policymaking body for the manufacturing industry on industrial and economic matters, and other public issues. It also interprets industry's policies to the federal government and the public. The organization has thousands of member companies. Representatives from NAM's member companies form policymaking committees that make recommendations to its board of directors. The board and an executive committee meet several times a year to determine policies. NAM was founded in 1895. It has headquarters in Washington, D.C.

Critically reviewed by the National Association of Manufacturers

National Association of Securities Dealers Automated Quotation System. See Nasdaq.

National Baptist Convention, USA, Inc., is the oldest and largest African American religious organization and the one to which most African American Baptists belong. The convention is not a single church but an organization of thousands of Baptist churches. The convention promotes home and foreign missions, encourages and supports Christian education, and publishes and distributes Sunday school and other religious literature.

The convention was organized in 1880 in Montgomery, Alabama, as the Foreign Mission Convention and in-

corporated under its present name in 1915. It has headquarters in Nashville.

Critically reviewed by the National Baptist Convention, USA, Inc.

See also **Baptists; National Baptist Convention of America, Inc.**

National Baptist Convention of America, Inc., is an organization of African American Baptists. It originated with the founding of the Foreign Mission Baptist Convention in 1880. The National Baptist Convention was formed in 1895, when the Foreign Mission Baptist Convention merged with two other Baptist conventions. In 1915, this group split into the National Baptist Convention of America and the National Baptist Convention, USA, Inc. The National Baptist Convention of America, Inc., is an agency of Christian education and missionary work. It combines the efforts of Baptist churches and organizations in missionary activity nationally and internationally. It supports foreign missions in Ghana, Haiti, Jamaica, Panama, and the Virgin Islands.

Critically reviewed by the National Baptist Convention of America, Inc.

National Baseball League. See Baseball.
National Basketball Association. See Basketball.
National Battlefield. See National Park System.
National budget is the financial plan for a nation's government. The budget forecasts the government's income and expenditures for one *fiscal year* (from October 1 to September 30 in the United States). It forecasts how much money the government will collect from taxes and other sources, and suggests how much money each government department should spend.

In the United States, the Office of Management and Budget prepares the federal budget, and the congressional budget committees review and amend it. The government gets most of its income from individual and corporation income taxes and payroll taxes for social insurance. Most government expenditures are for social insurance benefits, national defense, and interest on the national debt (see **National debt**).   Thomas F. Dernburg

See also **Budget** (Government budgets); **Congressional Budget Office; Management and Budget, Office of; Taxation** (illustration: The federal government dollar).

National Bureau of Economic Research is a private nonprofit corporation that conducts research on economic issues. It provides universities, professional associations, corporations, and the United States government with information and objective analyses of economic problems. The bureau is not affiliated with any university, government agency, or other organization.

The bureau is perhaps best known for its studies of *business cycles,* the rises and falls in economic activity. For example, it determines when U.S. *recessions* (periods of reduced economic activity) begin and end. The bureau also researches such matters as international trade, taxation, investment, and labor markets. Other projects deal with private pensions and social security, and with the historical development of the economy.

Researchers at the bureau have developed important statistical methods now used to measure economic performance. For example, they devised ways to estimate national income and studied the rate of *capital formation* (growth in the stock of machinery, buildings, and other productive goods). Business people, economists, and government officials use these figures to determine economic conditions and to plan for the future.

The National Bureau of Economic Research was founded in 1920. It is governed by a board of directors, which includes industrial leaders, bankers, financial experts, university economists, and accountants. The bureau's offices are in Cambridge, Massachusetts; New York City; and Stanford, California.

Critically reviewed by the National Bureau of Economic Research

National Bureau of Standards. See National Institute of Standards and Technology.

National Cathedral. See Washington National Cathedral.

National Catholic Educational Association is an organization that encourages cooperation and mutual helpfulness among Catholic educators. It also promotes—by study, conference, and discussion—Catholic educational work in the United States. The organization was founded as the Catholic Educational Association in 1904 in St. Louis. In 1927, it became the National Catholic Educational Association. Various departments carry on its work. They include departments for Catholic educational administrators, for elementary schools, for religious education, for secondary schools, for seminaries, and for boards and councils of Catholic education. The organization's headquarters are in Arlington, Virginia.

Critically reviewed by the National Catholic Educational Association

National cemetery is a burial place for men and women who served in the armed forces of the United States. Veterans are eligible to be buried in a national cemetery unless they received a dishonorable discharge. The spouses and dependent children of these veterans may also be buried in national cemeteries. The U.S. government maintains 147 national cemeteries throughout the United States and Puerto Rico, as well as 24 military cemeteries in other countries.

Four government agencies operate the national cemeteries. The Department of Veterans Affairs maintains 131 of the cemeteries. The National Park Service is responsible for 14 national cemeteries that are part of historic sites. The Department of the Army operates 2 cemeteries—Arlington National Cemetery in Arlington, Virginia, and Soldiers' and Airmen's Home National Cemetery in Washington, D.C. The American Battle Monuments Commission maintains all U.S. military cemeteries that are outside the United States and its possessions.

The Department of Veterans Affairs provides headstones and markers for all graves in national cemeteries and for all graves of veterans that do not have them. These graves include those of soldiers who fought in the American Civil War (1861-1865).

The national cemetery system was established in 1862, during the Civil War. That year, Congress granted President Abraham Lincoln permission to establish cemeteries for Union Army veterans.

One of the best-known national cemeteries operated by the National Park Service is in Gettysburg, Pennsylvania. A crucial battle of the Civil War was fought in Gettysburg in July 1863. On November 19 that year, Lincoln delivered his Gettysburg Address at a ceremony dedicating part of the battlefield as a cemetery. The other historic cemeteries operated by the National Park Service are Andersonville in Georgia; Andrew Johnson, Fort Donelson, Shiloh, and Stones River in Tennessee; Antietam in Maryland; Battleground in Washington, D.C.;

Chalmette in Louisiana; Custer at Little Bighorn Battlefield National Monument in Montana; Fredericksburg, Poplar Grove, and Yorktown in Virginia; and Vicksburg in Mississippi.

Critically reviewed by the National Cemetery System of the Department of the Army

See also Arlington National Cemetery; Little Bighorn Battlefield National Monument.

National Collegiate Athletic Association (NCAA) is an organization that establishes athletic standards and official playing rules for college sports. It conducts national championships in three divisions in sports for men and women and keeps the official national statistics and records of selected college sports.

The National Collegiate Athletic Association also conducts studies on issues in athletics, and it maintains a large film and video library covering play in championship events. The association also sponsors a postgraduate scholarship program and a degree-completion program for student-athletes who have exhausted their intercollegiate athletics eligibility.

The NCAA was founded in 1906. The association's membership today includes colleges and universities, athletic conferences, and coaches' associations. The headquarters of the NCAA are in Indianapolis.

Critically reviewed by the National Collegiate Athletic Association

National Conference for Community and Justice (NCCJ) is an American human relations organization that works to fight racism and other forms of prejudice. It tries to foster understanding and respect among all cultural, racial, and religious groups. The NCCJ works with students and teachers and religious, business, and government leaders. Its programs include youth camps and workshops, community discussions, race relations and interreligious dialogues, and workplace consulting. It also produces educational materials for young children and provides support for youths working to improve their communities. The NCCJ was founded in 1927 as the National Conference of Christians and Jews in response to anti-Roman Catholic sentiment. It later expanded to address issues of class, race, gender, sexual orientation, and the rights of people with disabilities. It took its present name in 1998. For additional information, see its website at http://www.nccj.org.

Critically reviewed by the National Conference for Community and Justice

National Congress of American Indians is the oldest, largest, and most representative national American Indian organization in the United States. It represents hundreds of tribes.

The National Congress of American Indians (NCAI) is organized as a representative congress to reach agreement on issues of national importance. It evaluates and monitors policies of the federal government on Indian affairs and promotes government initiatives and programs to improve the economic well-being, educational opportunities, and health of American Indians and Alaskan natives. The NCAI works to persuade members of the U.S. Congress to support laws that benefit Native Americans.

The NCAI is governed by a president and by an executive council of members democratically elected from 12 geographic areas of the United States. The organization operates under an executive director. The NCAI publishes a newsletter called the *Sentinel*.

The NCAI was founded in 1944. Its national office is in Washington, D.C.   Leon F. Cook

National Congress of Parents and Teachers is a volunteer organization that unites the forces of home, school, and community to promote the education, health, and safety of children. The National Congress is commonly called the National PTA. Local units of the organization, known as Parent-Teacher Associations (PTA's), operate in individual schools from the elementary to the high school level and in other community locations. In many high schools, the local groups are called Parent-Teacher-Student Associations (PTSA's) because students also take part in their activities. PTA's and PTSA's urge their members to become fully informed about education and to take an active interest in school programs. The units conduct regularly scheduled meetings and organize workshops and community service programs to benefit children, teenagers, and families.

PTA's and PTSA's design their programs to fit both their own needs and the goals of the National PTA. One of the National PTA's goals is to provide students with the best possible mental and physical education. The group also calls for adequate laws to protect children and young people. In addition, the PTA promotes the welfare of youth in the community, home, and school.

The National PTA conducts programs at the national, state, and local levels. At the national level, projects have dealt with parent education and the prevention of alcohol and drug abuse. The National PTA issues an award-winning print magazine, *Our Children,* as well as an online edition, *The PTA Magazine.* The organization also offers planning kits, videos, and pamphlets for use by local units.

State branches of the National PTA are in all 50 states, in Washington, D.C., and in Europe for U.S. military personnel there. Membership in local units is open to anyone who wants to help the association achieve its goals. A person who joins a local PTA or PTSA automatically becomes a member of the state branch and the national organization.

The National Congress of Parents and Teachers was founded as the National Congress of Mothers in 1897. State branches were organized the same year. Headquarters of the National PTA are in Chicago.

Critically reviewed by the National Congress of Parents and Teachers

See also **Parent-teacher organizations** (Parent-Teacher Associations).

National Consumers League is an organization founded in 1899 to develop a sense of responsibility for the promotion of safety, health, and economic welfare of consumers and workers. The league worked for child labor laws, the elimination of sweatshops, the 8-hour day for women, social insurance, and national health insurance for the elderly under Social Security. The league introduced the idea of minimum wage laws in the United States. It also worked for the establishment of the Food and Drug Administration, meat inspection, and other consumer protection legislation.

Today, the National Consumers League works to promote affordable health care, awareness of hazardous chemicals used in jobs and in the community, food and drug safety, fair tax policies, child labor laws, and consumer protection. Its headquarters are in Washington, D.C.   Critically reviewed by the National Consumers League

National Council of Churches is an organization of Christian churches in the United States. It includes Anglican, Protestant, and Orthodox denominations. Its members promote Christian unity, working together on programs that serve the churches and wider society. The council carries out many ministries, including education, social justice, theological dialogue, and interfaith relations.

About 300 representatives form the council's General Assembly, which meets regularly to set council policy. A little over half its members are clergy of member churches. The others are lay leaders.

The council was formed in 1950 by 29 member denominations and through the merger of 14 interdenominational agencies. Its full name is the National Council of the Churches of Christ in the U.S.A. The council publishes a monthly electronic newsletter called *EcuLink.* The council has offices in New York City and Washington, D.C.   Critically reviewed by the National Council of Churches

National Council of La Raza is an organization that aims to improve life opportunities for Hispanic Americans. The council addresses such issues as poverty, discrimination, health, and education. It is the largest Hispanic organization in the United States. The organization began in 1968.

The National Council of La Raza uses two main approaches. First, it provides *capacity-building assistance* to community-based Hispanic organizations. Its help in management, programming, and resource development enables smaller programs to reach greater numbers of people. Second, the council conducts research and analysis on matters of government policy and public concern. It publishes many materials and holds frequent media activities to raise awareness of Hispanic issues.

The council takes its name from the writings of Mexican scholar José Vasconcelos. Vasconcelos originally used the term *La Raza Cósmica,* which roughly translates into English as *The Cosmic People.* The phrase reflects the diversity of races and cultures in the Hispanic community.   Critically reviewed by the National Council of La Raza

See also **Hispanic Americans.**

National debt is the total amount that the federal government owes because of money it has borrowed by selling bonds or other securities. In Canada, this debt is commonly known as the *federal government debt.* The national debt exists because the government's expenses frequently exceed its income from taxes. In such situations, the government sells bonds to get the extra money that it needs. The government must repay the amount of the bonds on a specified date. In addition, it must pay interest on this indebtedness.

Government debt differs from private debt because the government is not required to post any *collateral* (pledge of security) to guarantee payment of a loan. However, the United States government has always repaid its loans.

Causes of national debt. The U.S. debt originated in the 1790's, when the newly established federal government assumed debts that the states had run up during the American Revolution (1775-1783). Until the 1980's, wars were by far the most common cause of increases in the national debt. For example, the debt was only $1 billion before World War I (1914-1918). The war raised the debt to about $25 billion. By the end of World War II

(1939-1945), the national debt had risen to about $259 billion.

The Korean War (1950-1953) and the Vietnam War (1957-1975) caused the national debt to rise sharply again. Between 1980 and 1985, major reductions in taxes and increases in defense spending also contributed to a sharp rise in the debt. By 2010, the U.S. national debt was about $13 ½ trillion.

Wars have also been responsible for high national debts in other countries. In 1867, the newly formed Dominion of Canada assumed the Canadian debt of $93 million. After increases caused chiefly by Canada's participation in two world wars, the debt totaled about $19 billion in the mid-1940's. By 2008, the Canadian national debt had risen to nearly $595 billion.

Public improvements also increase the national debt. These include such long-lasting improvements as canals, highways, and dams. Some of these works yield enough income to pay the principal and interest on the bonds issued to finance them. Others, such as roads, benefit the nation but generally do not yield income.

Ownership of the debt. About 35 percent of the national debt is held by government agencies. But banks and private individuals are the largest owners of the debt. Banks and insurance companies buy government bonds as a safe investment and to earn interest on funds not used for other purposes. Individuals also buy bonds for family security and for patriotic reasons. During World War II, millions of Americans bought war bonds. Also, businesses buy government bonds when they have extra cash that they wish to keep in a safe place while it earns interest. For those who wish to invest for a short time only, the government issues securities known as *Treasury bills* that mature after 13, 26, or 52 weeks. These securities must be repaid out of income from taxes or from sales of newly issued bills to other investors. Banks and businesses buy most Treasury bills.

Debt policy. It is important to consider the national debt in relation to the nation's total economic strength. One way of doing this is to compare the national debt to the *gross domestic product* (GDP). The GDP is the total value of goods and services produced within a country

United States gross national debt and economic growth since the Civil War (1861-1865)

The gross national debt of the United States is about 5,060 times as large today as it was in 1865. But the U.S. population is only about 8 ½ times as large. As a result, the debt per person is about 585 times as great as it was in 1865. In 1945, the year World War II ended, the national debt exceeded the U.S. gross domestic product (GDP). The GDP is the total value of goods and services produced within a country in a year. Today, the debt is about 93 percent of the GDP.

Year	Gross national debt	Debt per person	Gross national debt as percentage of gross domestic product*	Year	Gross national debt	Debt per person	Gross national debt as percentage of gross domestic product*
1865	$ 2,681,000,000	$ 75	—	**1950**	$ 257,357,000,000	$ 1,701	88
1870	2,481,000,000	64	33	**1960**	286,331,000,000	1,597	54
1880	2,120,000,000	42	19	**1970**	370,919,000,000	1,824	36
1890	1,552,000,000	25	12	**1980**	907,701,000,000	4,006	33
1900	2,137,000,000	28	11	**1985**	1,823,103,000,000	7,672	43
1910	2,653,000,000	29	8	**1990**	3,233,313,000,000	13,000	56
1920	25,952,000,000	245	28	**1995**	4,973,980,000,000	18,739	67
1930	16,185,000,000	131	18	**2000**	5,674,178,000,000	20,109	57
1940	42,967,000,000	325	42	**2005**	7,932,710,000,000	26,822	63
1945	258,682,000,000	1,825	116	**2010**	13,561,623,000,000	43,925	93

U.S. gross national debt

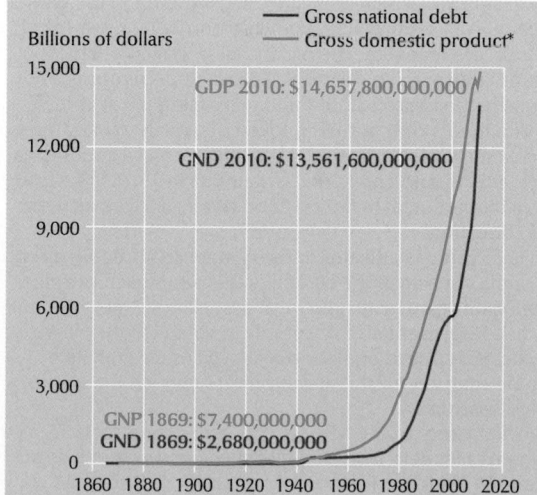

*Figures prior to 1929 are gross national product.
Sources: U.S. Department of Commerce; U.S. Department of the Treasury.

U.S. gross national debt as a percentage of GDP

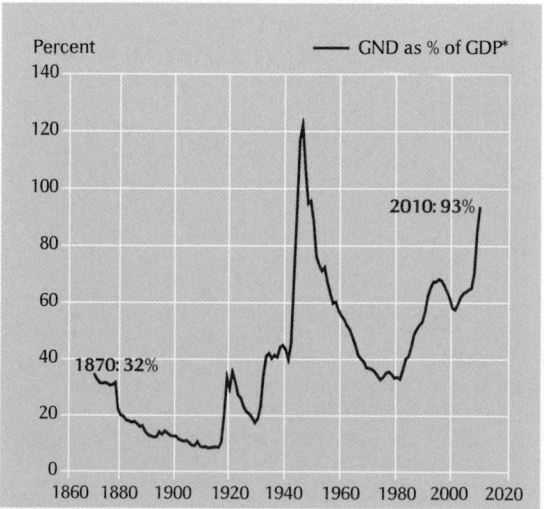

*Figures prior to 1929 are gross national product.
Sources: U.S. Department of Commerce; U.S. Department of the Treasury.

in a year. For example, the United States national debt rose from about $259 billion in 1945 to about $13 ½ trillion in 2010. But the 1945 debt amounted to 116 percent of that year's GDP, while the 2010 debt was 93 percent of the 2010 GDP.

Some people argue that, just as in a family or business, federal government spending should be kept equal to or below its income. Others declare that this comparison is misleading. They point out that, except for the small portion of the debt held by people in other countries, the debt's size is not as important as the effects that increasing or reducing the debt might have on the economy. Both groups usually agree that taxes in prosperous times should be high enough to cover government spending and to reduce the debt.

Those who call for a balanced budget would not favor

Canada national debt and economic growth since Confederation in 1867

Canada's national debt, like that of the United States, generally has increased because the government has borrowed huge sums to develop the country and to fight wars.

Year	Gross national debt (in Canadian dollars)*	Debt per person	Gross national debt as percentage of gross domestic product†
1867	$ 93,046,000	$ 27	—
1870	115,994,000	32	25
1880	194,634,000	46	33
1890	286,112,000	60	36
1900	346,207,000	65	33
1910	470,663,000	67	21
1920	3,041,530,000	355	55
1930	2,544,586,000	249	42
1940	4,028,729,000	354	57
1950	16,750,756,000	1,222	88
1960	19,918,000,000	1,119	53
1970	33,858,000,000	1,594	43
1980	84,672,000,000	3,497	27
1990	386,785,000,000	14,718	58
2000	648,212,000,000	21,122	60
2008	594,390,000,000	17,843	37

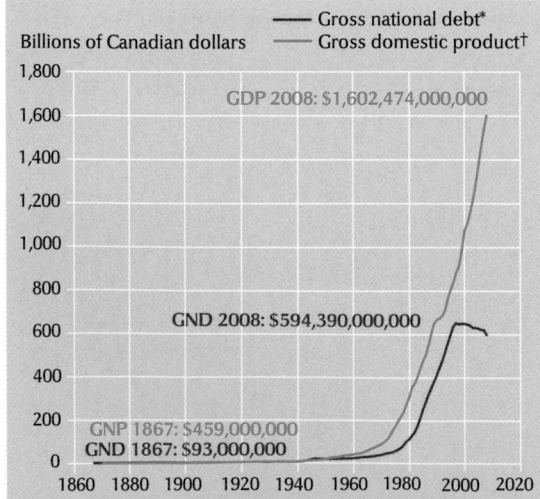

Billions of Canadian dollars — Gross national debt* — Gross domestic product†

GDP 2008: $1,602,474,000,000

GND 2008: $594,390,000,000

GNP 1867: $459,000,000
GND 1867: $93,000,000

*Figures are for the 12-month period beginning April 1 of the year indicated.
†The GDP figure is for the 12-month period ending December 31 of the year indicated; figures prior to 1926 are gross national product.
Source: Statistics Canada. Canada is revising how it calculates its national debt, and so data after 2008 are currently unavailable.

measures that would increase the national debt if a recession occurred or threatened to occur. But members of the second group would urge government borrowing to pay for public improvements as a sound way to prevent or end recession. They believe it is the government's responsibility to take such action to stimulate business activity, thereby creating more jobs to reduce unemployment.   Thomas F. Dernburg

See also **Gross domestic product; Keynes, John Maynard; National budget; Savings bond.**

National defense. See Defense, Department of; Government (Defense); Homeland Security, Department of.

National Defense Education Act (NDEA) was a law enacted by the United States Congress in 1958. It was one of the most significant education bills in the history of the United States.

The 1957 launch by the Soviet Union of the first successful artificial space satellite, Sputnik 1, created concern in the United States that the nation's students were falling behind in education, especially in science and technology. The NDEA was one response to this concern. It provided financial aid to states, educational institutions, and individuals to improve educational programs in the United States.

The NDEA provided federal loans to students who showed financial need. Repayment began after the student left school. A borrower who entered certain fields of teaching or who taught in certain schools might have part of the debt canceled.

The NDEA also provided funds for states to buy teaching equipment in science, mathematics, language, English, reading, history, civics, and geography. Private schools also could borrow money for that purpose. The NDEA was administered by the United States Department of Education. Over time, as certain sections of the NDEA were repealed and other sections were replaced by new laws, the importance of the NDEA ended. Some of the laws that replaced the NDEA included the Elementary and Secondary Education Act (1965) and the Higher Education Act (1965).   Douglas Sloan

National Education Association (NEA) is the largest professional education organization in the world. The NEA has more than 3 million members, most of whom are teachers. The organization's main goals include improving public education and classroom conditions in the United States, and increasing the salaries and benefits of school employees. It works toward these goals through professional activities, judicial and legislative efforts, and collective bargaining. In 1979, the NEA was instrumental in the creation of the U.S. Department of Education.

The NEA has affiliates in every state. In addition, it represents citizens of the United States who teach overseas. Delegates from state and local associations meet annually in a Representative Assembly to establish the NEA's policies. A board of directors as well as an executive committee act for the organization between the Assembly's sessions.

The history of the NEA can be traced back to 1857, when 43 leaders from state teachers' associations organized the National Teachers Association. In 1870, this group merged with the Association of School Superintendents, the Central College Association, and the

American Normal School Association to form the National Educational Association. For many years, school administrators provided much of the NEA leadership. However, by the mid-1960's, classroom teachers held almost all offices in the NEA.

The NEA sponsors American Education Week. The NEA's headquarters are in Washington, D.C.

See also **Education Week, American; Teaching** (Teachers organizations); **Utah** (The mid-1900's).

National Farmers Organization (NFO) is an organization set up by farmers and ranchers to negotiate prices and other terms of sale for their *commodities* (products). The NFO's main form of negotiation is *collective bargaining,* in which it negotiates on behalf of many farmers and ranchers at once.

The National Farmers Organization also uses *risk management* techniques to decrease the chance that its members will lose money. For example, the organization helps farmers negotiate contracts that ensure buyers will pay a certain price for an agricultural commodity in the future. Such agreements occur well before the farmers produce the commodity. They protect farmers against loss if the market price of the product falls after the contract is signed.

The National Farmers Organization collects payments from buyers and distributes shares of the money to its members. In addition, the organization provides reserve funds to protect members in case a buyer does not pay. The group also checks the credit quality of potential buyers.

The National Farmers Organization was set up in 1955. National headquarters are in Ames, Iowa.

National Farmers Union is a national federation of state Farmers Union organizations. It is dedicated to preserving and improving the family farm system of agriculture. The union represents approximately 200,000 farm families. It promotes legislation and education that benefits farmers. In addition, the union develops cooperative buying and selling methods and businesses.

The National Farmers Union was founded in Texas in 1902. Its official name is the Farmers' Educational and Cooperative Union of America. The union has national headquarters in Denver. Stephen Jones

National Federation of Music Clubs. See Music Clubs, National Federation of.

National Football League. See Football (Professional competition; The rise of professional football).

National forest is an area set aside by the United States Congress to be protected and managed by the federal government. The Forest Service, which is a part of the United States Department of Agriculture, manages 155 national forests in the United States and Puerto Rico. The forests and grasslands managed by the Forest Service cover an area of about 193 million acres (78 million hectares). This area is larger than the states of California and Nevada combined. Many of the forests are named for Indian tribes or for famous people in American history.

Uses. Originally, the national forests served primarily as a source of timber and water. Today, the Forest Service manages these areas, along with the country's national grasslands, to maintain a continuous supply of a wide variety of resources. These resources include wood, water, and such minerals as lead and uranium; grazing land for cattle and sheep; and recreational areas. The lands also serve as a home for much of the nation's wildlife.

Managing the national forests is challenging because of the many competing uses for the nation's woodlands. Through public involvement, partnerships linking the U.S. Forest Service with environmental groups and industry groups, and volun-

U.S. Forest Service
National forest symbol

Bob and Ira Spring

Wenatchee National Forest in western Washington has many scenic trails for horseback riders and hikers.

teer programs, citizens can participate in caring for and managing these areas.

Administration. A *forest supervisor* administers each national forest. The forests are divided into *ranger districts,* each headed by a *district ranger.* A ranger's first duty is to manage all forest uses and services. These include production of wood, water, forage, wildlife, and resources for outdoor recreation. The ranger is also responsible for protecting the forests from such threats as fire, harmful insects, and disease.

United States national forests are grouped into nine regions. Regional foresters head each region. They direct the work of the forest supervisors in their regions. The regional foresters, in turn, report to the chief of the Forest Service in Washington, D.C.

History. Early settlers in the United States adopted the first conservation laws. Nevertheless, destruction of forests became widespread during the settlement of the United States. In 1891, Congress established the first national forest-conservation policy. In that year, Congress authorized the president to set aside areas known as *forest reserves.* The first one was established in Wyoming. In 1907, the name was changed to national forests.

Critically reviewed by the Forest Service

See also **Forest Service.**

National Foundation-March of Dimes. See March of Dimes Foundation.

National Foundation on the Arts and the Humanities is an independent agency of the federal government. The foundation develops and promotes a national policy of support for the humanities and the arts.

The foundation is administered by a National Endowment for the Arts and a National Endowment for the Humanities. Each endowment is guided by a council composed of 26 private citizens distinguished for their knowledge and experience in the two allied cultural areas, the arts and the humanities. A Federal Council on the Arts and the Humanities coordinates the foundation's activities with related federal agencies.

The Arts Endowment is authorized to assist individuals and nonprofit organizations in a wide range of artistic endeavors. Additional funds are authorized to aid activities in the arts that are sponsored by the states. The Humanities Endowment also makes grants to its state councils. It directly supports projects in education, public programs, preservation, research, and scholarship in the humanities.

Each endowment is headed by a chairperson, who serves on the federal council, along with representatives of federal agencies whose programs are related to the arts and humanities. The foundation was established in 1965. It is in Washington, D.C.

Critically reviewed by the National Foundation on the Arts and the Humanities

National Gallery of Art, in Washington, D.C., is one of the world's leading art museums. Its collections begin with works from the 1100's and represent some of the Western world's greatest achievements in painting, sculpture, and the graphic arts. The collections are especially rich in European Old Master paintings and American, British, French, Italian, and Spanish paintings of the 1700's and 1800's. The museum also displays sculptures from the late 1100's to the present, medals and bronzes from the early 1400's to the early 1900's, and porcelain

© Lee Snider, Corbis

The National Gallery of Art East Building was designed by the Chinese American architect I. M. Pei. A sculpture group by the American sculptor Tony Smith stands in front of the building.

from China. In addition, it has almost 100,000 works of graphic art from the 1100's to the present.

The National Gallery of Art was established in 1937, when American financier Andrew W. Mellon gave most of his magnificent art collection to the government. He also provided money to construct the museum's original building, now called the West Building. American architect John Russell Pope designed the marble Neoclassical structure. It opened in 1941. The East Building, designed by Chinese American architect I. M. Pei, was completed in 1978. It houses the museum's growing collection of art from the 1900's. It also includes offices, a library, a sculpture garden, space for temporary exhibitions, and the Center for Advanced Study in the Visual Arts.

All the works in the gallery have been donated or bought with private funds. Major donations include the collections of Samuel H. Kress, Rush H. Kress, Joseph Widener, Chester Dale, Ailsa Mellon Bruce, Lessing J. Rosenwald, Edgar William and Bernice Chrysler Garbisch, Paul Mellon, and the Mark Rothko Foundation.

The National Gallery of Art is affiliated with the Smithsonian Institution, but it is governed by its own board of trustees. The museum receives operating funds from Congress. Critically reviewed by the National Gallery of Art

National Gallery of Canada, in Ottawa, Ontario, exhibits the most important collection of Canadian art in Canada. The gallery also has important collections of American, Asian, and European art. It houses more than 45,000 works, including paintings, sculptures, prints, drawings, photographs, videotapes, and films.

Major donations to the gallery include the Massey Collection of English Painting, the Henry Birks Collection of Canadian Silver, the Bronfman Gift of Drawings, and the Heeramaneck Collection of Southeast Asian Art. The gallery also includes a fine arts reference library. In addition, the gallery provides guided tours and lectures on its collections and exhibitions.

The National Gallery was founded in 1880 to display a collection of works by members of the Royal Canadian Academy of Arts. Before moving to its present location, the gallery had been housed at a series of temporary sites, none of which was designed for the gallery's special needs. Today, the gallery is housed in a three-story

Fiona Spalding-Smith, National Gallery of Canada

The National Gallery of Canada, in Ottawa, occupies a modern building designed by Canadian architect Moshe Safdie.

building of stainless steel, glass, and rose-colored granite. This building, designed by the Israeli-born Canadian architect Moshe Safdie, opened in 1988.

Critically reviewed by the National Gallery of Canada

National Geographic Society is one of the world's largest nonprofit scientific and educational organizations. It was formed in 1888 to gather and spread geographic information throughout the world. It has millions of members all over the world. The society has sponsored and supported a wide variety of expeditions and research projects.

The society distributes information through *National Geographic Magazine,* a monthly journal; *National Geographic Kids,* a magazine for children; *National Geographic Traveler,* a travel magazine; authoritative books; and an information service for the press, radio, and television. It produces atlases, globes, maps, computer and videodisc programs for schools, and television programs. The society also sponsors a program to train geography teachers and promote the teaching of geography in classrooms.

Among the projects the National Geographic Society has helped sponsor are the historic polar expeditions by Richard E. Byrd and Robert E. Peary. The society also helped back the first successful United States expedition to the top of Mount Everest and aided in the discovery of the wreckage of the sunken *Titanic.* It also sponsored excavations in east Africa that uncovered fossils of primitive human beings who lived about 2 million years ago. The National Geographic Society's headquarters are in Washington, D.C.

Critically reviewed by the National Geographic Society

National Guard is one of the organizations of the United States Army and Air Force. An outgrowth of the volunteer militia that was first authorized in 1792, the National Guard is a reserve group. Other civilian reserves, such as the Army, Air Force, and Navy reserves, have no connection with the National Guard.

Each state, each territory, and the District of Columbia has its own National Guard. The National Guard Bureau of the Department of the Army directs Army units. The Department of the Air Force supervises Air National

National Guard Bureau emblem

Guard units. About 360,000 men and women serve in Army units of the National Guard. About 105,000 serve in the Air National Guard.

Members of the National Guard enlist voluntarily and are formed into distinctive units. The Army and Air Force supervise the training of the National Guard. State funds provide armories and other storage facilities. Federal funds provide clothing, weapons, and equipment.

During peacetime, National Guard personnel attend one weekend of training each month. They also receive two weeks of field training every year. The federal government pays members of the National Guard for the time they spend training. About 92,000 members serve full-time to help organize, administer, recruit, and train the National Guard.

Guard members have a *dual status* because they take an oath of allegiance to their state and to the federal government. Until 1903, the state controlled the militia units. The president had to call units into federal service through the governors of the states (see **Militia**). The National Defense Acts of 1920 and 1933 extended federal authority. Since that time, the president may order units to active duty for up to two years upon declaring a national emergency, or for up to six months without declaring a national emergency. State governors may order units to active duty during emergencies, such as storms, fires, earthquakes, or civil disturbances.

Joel Slackman

National historic site. See National Park System.
National Hockey League. See Hockey.
National Honor Society is an organization for high school students. Members are chosen on the basis of scholarship, leadership, service, and character. College scholarships are awarded each year to top-ranking senior members. The society is sponsored by the National Association of Secondary School Principals, which founded it in 1921. In 1929, the National Junior Honor Society was founded for students in middle-level schools. Both the senior society and the junior society have headquarters in Reston, Virginia.

Critically reviewed by the National Honor Society

National income is the total of all income earned in a nation during a specific period, usually a year. This figure shows whether a nation's economy is growing or declining. Economists use national income figures to compare the economies of various nations.

Determining national income. Economists calculate national income in either of two ways. One way is based on what individuals and businesses earn. The other is based on the production of goods and services. Each method provides the same national income figure because the amount that people earn equals the value of the goods and services produced.

United States national income

National income has soared since the Great Depression of the 1930's. This graph shows how much of the rise comes from the income of employees, the income of businesses, and interest and rent.

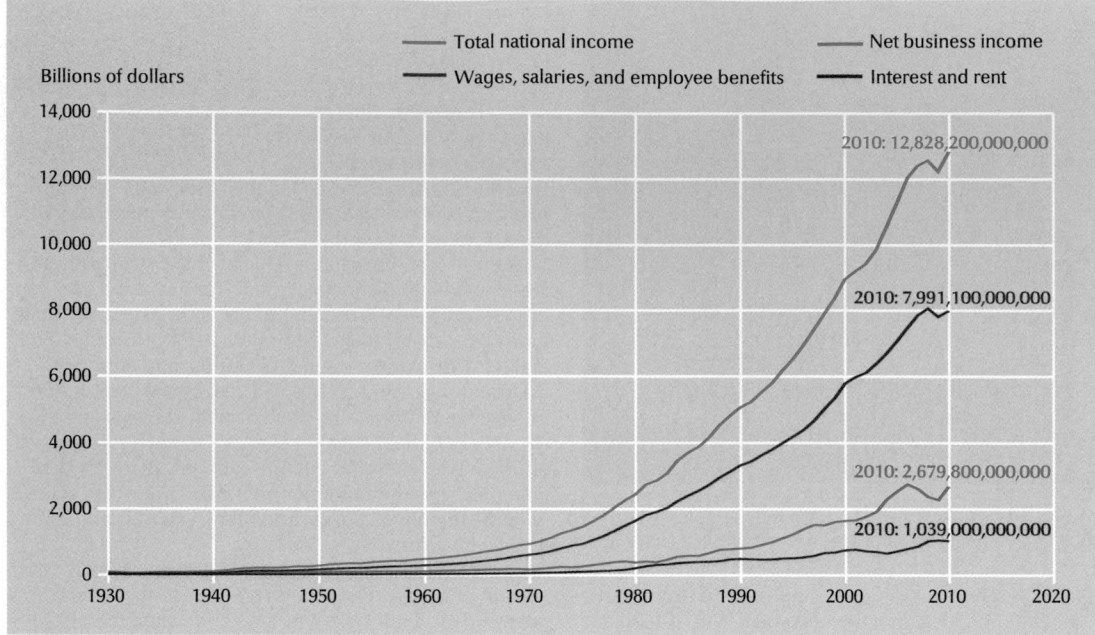

| ——— Total national income | ——— Net business income |
| ——— Wages, salaries, and employee benefits | ——— Interest and rent |

Billions of dollars

2010: 12,828,200,000,000

2010: 7,991,100,000,000

2010: 2,679,800,000,000

2010: 1,039,000,000,000

Source: U.S. Bureau of Economic Analysis.

National income based on earnings includes all the income a nation earns in a certain period. This income consists of wages, salaries, interest, profits, and rents.

To find national income based on production, economists first determine a nation's *gross national product.* This figure represents the total value of the goods and services produced by a nation during a specific period. Economists find the national income by subtracting *depreciation* and *indirect business taxes* from the gross national product. Depreciation includes the normal decline in the value of buildings and machinery as a result of doing business. Indirect business taxes are paid by buyers of goods and include sales and excise taxes. The difference between gross national product and depreciation is called the *net national product.*

National income may be affected by both *inflation* (rising prices) and *deflation* (falling prices). For example, if the amount people earn increases 10 percent in one year, the national income figure for that year will rise 10 percent. But if prices also rise 10 percent, people will not be able to buy any more goods or services than they did during the year before. Thus, the national income figure is 10 percent higher because of inflation, not because of economic growth.

In order to compare national income figures for two or more years, economists adjust the national income to include inflation or deflation. The adjusted figure is called *real national income.*

Importance of national income. National income figures show the rate at which a nation's economy changes. These figures also show the stability of the economy. For example, the economy may be unstable if national income varies greatly from year to year. National income figures also show how income is distributed in the forms of wages, interest, profits, and rent. In the United States, for instance, wages, salaries, and employee benefits account for about two-thirds of the national income. Interest, profits, and rents provide the rest of the national income.

Both government and industry adjust their budgets in terms of the level, distribution, and rate of change in national income. If national income falls, for example, the government might decrease taxes in order to allow people more after-tax income to spend. If people spent this additional income on goods and services, business activity would rise. As a result, more jobs would be created, and national income would increase.

National income figures include only payments and losses for which records are kept. As a result, these figures do not fully show the level of a nation's well-being. A homemaker receives no salary for doing housework, and so his or her work does not raise the national income. On the other hand, environmental pollution causes great economic loss. But no one knows the total cost of this loss, and so economists cannot subtract it from the national income.

Changes in national income. National income varies, depending on the efforts of workers, the level of employment, and the quality and quantity of *fixed capital.* Fixed capital includes the buildings and machinery that are used to provide goods and services. Improvements in fixed capital may create additional jobs and increase the national income. National income in the United States, Canada, and numerous other industrialized countries has generally risen. It has increased mainly because of additions to fixed capital, growth of the labor force, and improvements in the efficiency of both capital and labor.   Roberto Serrano

See also **Capital; Deflation; Gross domestic product; Income; Standard of living.**

National Industrial Recovery Act. See New Deal (Helping industry and labor).

National Institute for Occupational Safety and Health (NIOSH) is an agency of the United States Department of Health and Human Services. NIOSH is part of the department's Centers for Disease Control and Prevention. The institute's investigators study working conditions to determine the causes of employee illness and accidents. Employees or employers often request these investigations. NIOSH also recommends standards to control hazards on the job. It reports its findings to the Occupational Safety and Health Administration (OSHA), which establishes and enforces the standards.

NIOSH submits recommended standards determined by studies of worker exposure to dangerous chemicals or radiation, excessive noise, and other conditions on the job. The agency also examines existing health and safety policies in factories and businesses and develops methods to evaluate job hazards. Its duties also include approving respirators and other personal safety equipment and providing job safety and health training for employers and employees. NIOSH was created by the Occupational Safety and Health Act of 1970.   Critically reviewed by the National Institute for Occupational Safety and Health

See also **Centers for Disease Control and Prevention; Occupational Safety and Health Administration.**

National Institute of Standards and Technology is an agency of the United States Department of Commerce. The institute, often called NIST, develops measurement standards and techniques for American science and industry and for other government agencies. NIST also helps U.S. companies adopt new technologies to increase their international competitiveness.

The institute works to maintain, improve, and apply fundamental systems of measurement, including those of length, time, and mass. It compares and coordinates its measurement standards with those of other countries by working with international agencies. Although the institute has no regulatory authority, it helps private organizations promote the establishment of voluntary standards for commerce and industry.

NIST provides research and technical services in such areas as computer science and technology, materials science, building and fire safety, electronics, and automated manufacturing. Published information on NIST's research can be obtained from the National Technical Information Service of the Department of Commerce.

NIST was established as the National Bureau of Standards in 1901 and became part of the Department of Commerce in 1903. NIST got its present name in 1988.
Critically reviewed by the National Institute of Standards and Technology

National Institutes of Health (NIH) is an agency of the United States government. It is part of the Public Health Service of the Department of Health and Human Services. NIH conducts and supports a broad range of biomedical research and provides funds for the training of research scientists. It also classifies and distributes biological and medical information.

NIH conducts research at its laboratories in Bethesda, Maryland. There are 19 NIH institutes. They deal with (1) aging; (2) alcoholism; (3) allergy and infectious diseases; (4) arthritis and musculoskeletal and skin diseases; (5) biomedical imaging and bioengineering; (6) cancer; (7) child health and human development; (8) deafness and other communication disorders; (9) dental research; (10) diabetes and digestive and kidney disorder; (11) drug abuse; (12) environmental health sciences; (13) the eye; (14) general medical sciences; (15) the heart, lungs, and blood; (16) human genes; (17) mental health; (18) neurological disorders and stroke; and (19) nursing. The NIH Clinical Center, a research hospital, serves the institutes. NIH also includes the National Library of Medicine, the Fogarty International Center for Advanced Study in the Health Sciences, the National Center for Complementary and Alternative Medicine, the National Center on Minority Health and Health Disparities, and three support divisions that deal with information technology, research resources, and scientific review.

NIH traces its history to 1887, when the Hygienic Laboratory was set up at the U.S. Marine Hospital on Staten Island. The agency adopted its present name in 1948.
Critically reviewed by the National Institutes of Health

National Labor Relations Act, usually called the *Wagner Act,* is a law that guarantees the right of workers in the United States to form unions. It also ensures the right of employees to engage in *collective bargaining*—that is, to negotiate as a group with employers about wages, hours, and working conditions.

The rights of workers were originally protected by the National Industrial Recovery Act (NIRA) of 1933, which the Supreme Court declared unconstitutional in 1935. The Wagner Act was passed later that year to reaffirm those rights. Its main sponsor was Senator Robert F. Wagner, a New York Democrat.

The Wagner Act bans certain practices by employers. For example, it prohibits them from interfering with union efforts to bring workers into unions. The act also requires employers to negotiate with representatives elected by workers. The act established the National Labor Relations Board (NLRB) to enforce such provisions (see **National Labor Relations Board**).

The Wagner Act enables employees of individual companies to decide which union or person will negotiate for them. A worker or employer may request the NLRB to conduct an election among the workers to choose a representative. The employer must then bargain only with the elected representative.

Many employers believed the Wagner Act gave unions too much power. They complained that it allowed unions to force a business to hire only union members. Such a business is called a *closed shop.* The Taft-Hartley Act of 1947 amended the Wagner Act and outlawed some union activities.   James G. Scoville

See also **New Deal; Taft-Hartley Act.**

National Labor Relations Board (NLRB) was created as an independent agency by Congress in 1935 to administer the National Labor Relations Act, often called the Wagner Act. The NLRB works to correct or prevent unfair labor practices committed by either employers or unions. When a union represents 30 percent or more of a group of employees covered by the National Labor Relations Act, the NLRB conducts secret-ballot elections to determine whether employees wish to be represented in collective bargaining.

The president of the United States appoints the five board members and the general counsel, with the consent of the Senate. Each board member serves a five-year term. The general counsel has a four-year term. The NLRB's main offices are in Washington, D.C. Petitions for elections and charges of unfair labor practices are filed at regional offices.   James G. Scoville

See also **Industrial relations; National Labor Relations Act.**

National laboratory is any one of several major scientific laboratories owned and supervised by the United States Department of Energy. The laboratories do work for that department and for other federal agencies, such as the Department of Defense, National Research Council, and Environmental Protection Agency. Activities at the laboratories range from fundamental research intended to provide a better understanding of the universe to applied programs in national security, energy, and conservation. Research at the facilities has led to advances in such areas as nuclear power and nuclear medicine. Today, the laboratories are also studying human genetics, superconducting materials, fusion energy, global environmental change, and computers. In addition, the laboratories conduct programs for students and teachers to improve science education at all levels.

The national laboratories are operated by employees on contract from universities and private industries. Physicists, chemists, engineers, and environmental scientists often work as a team to pursue the solution to scientific problems. University faculty and students and industrial scientists also often work with the scientists at the laboratories.

Some of the laboratories developed as nuclear research centers during World War II (1939-1945). For example, a team of scientists created the first controlled, self-sustaining nuclear chain reaction at the University of Chicago in 1942. A few months later, the scientists moved the experiment to a site that was to become Argonne National Laboratory.   Toni Grayson Joseph

Related articles in *World Book* include:

Argonne National Laboratory	Lawrence Berkeley National
Brookhaven National	Laboratory
Laboratory	Lawrence Livermore National
Fermi National Accelerator	Laboratory
Laboratory	Los Alamos National
Idaho National Engineering	Laboratory
and Environmental	Oak Ridge National
Laboratory	Laboratory
	Sandia National Laboratories

National League. See Baseball (Major leagues; Professional baseball).

National League of Cities is an organization that represents United States cities. Membership is open to all cities and state federations of cities.

The league works to improve the quality of life for people who live in cities and to strengthen local government. Its officials discuss urban problems with members of Congress, officials in the executive branch, and other leaders to win support for a national urban policy. The organization sometimes takes legal action in federal courts on matters involving cities. It publishes a weekly newspaper called *Nation's Cities Weekly* and various reports on city policies and procedures. The league holds an annual convention called the Congress of Cities that is attended by mayors, city managers, council members, and other city officials. At this meeting, league members review, amend, and approve the organization's national municipal policy.

The history of the league dates back to 1924, when leaders of 10 state federations of cities formed the American Municipal Association. The organization changed its name to the National League of Cities in 1964. Its headquarters are in Washington, D.C.
Critically reviewed by the National League of Cities

National Library of Canada. See Library (Canadian government libraries).

National Library of Medicine. See Library (Government libraries).

National Mediation Board is a United States government agency that administers the Railway Labor Act. This law, enacted in 1926, governs labor-management relations in the railroad and airline industries. The board's two main functions are (1) to ensure the right of employees to organize into free and independent labor organizations, and (2) to help settle disputes over wages, rules, and working conditions.

In a dispute, either side may ask the board to *mediate* by suggesting solutions. The board may also enter the dispute without invitation. If mediation fails, the board asks the two sides to accept voluntary *arbitration.* If the parties agree, the board appoints a referee, whose decision is binding. If the parties refuse to arbitrate, the board formally notifies them that it has not been able to settle the dispute. A 30-day *cooling-off period* then follows while the board tries to settle the dispute. If an agreement is not reached by the end of this period, the parties are free to act on their own. As a last resort, the president of the United States may establish an emergency board to help end the dispute.

Congress created the board in 1934. It has three members, who are appointed by the president subject to the approval of the Senate.
Critically reviewed by the National Mediation Board

National Medical Association (NMA) is a professional organization that represents the interests of African American physicians. It was founded in 1895. The NMA is dedicated to ensuring that all career paths in the field of health care are open to African American physicians; that African Americans are well represented in the medical and health professions; and that quality health care is available and accessible to all patients, regardless of their ability to pay. The NMA publishes periodic reports and the *Journal of the National Medical Association,* a monthly scientific journal. The association also holds an annual convention. It has national headquarters in Washington, D.C.
Critically reviewed by the National Medical Association

National memorial. See National Park System.

National Meteorological Center. See Weather Service, National.

National monument. See National Park System.

National Motto, United States, is *In God We Trust.* Congress made this phrase the official motto of the United States in 1956. It has appeared on coins since 1864 and probably originated from verse 4 of "The Star-Spangled Banner": "And this be our motto: 'In God is our trust.'" See also E Pluribus Unum.

National Museum of African Art, a bureau of the Smithsonian Institution in Washington, D.C., features the

The National Museum of Natural History, in Washington, D.C., is a world center for the study of the natural sciences. Visitors entering the museum from the National Mall are greeted by a huge African bull elephant. It is thought to be the largest ever recorded, standing 13 feet (4 meters) tall at the shoulder.

Smithsonian Institution

traditional art of Africa south of the Sahara. It is the oldest museum in the United States devoted solely to the collection, exhibition, and study of African art. Works from central and west Africa make up a large part of the museum's collection. Also, the museum exhibits both ancient and contemporary art from the entire continent. The collection includes traditional works, such as masks and figures for ceremonial purposes, as well as ceramics, musical instruments, textiles, and furniture. The collection also displays modern African paintings, prints, sculptures, and other kinds of fine arts.

The National Museum of African Art was established in 1964 as a private educational institution called the Museum of African Art. It became a bureau of the Smithsonian Institution in 1979 and took its present name in 1981. The museum opened in a new underground building on the National Mall in 1987.

Critically reviewed by the National Museum of African Art

National Museum of American History features exhibits on the social, cultural, scientific, and technological development of the United States. The museum, in Washington, D.C., houses a large collection of historically significant items. It also conducts educational and research work. It is a bureau of the Smithsonian Institution.

The museum's collection includes displays of the cultural, military, and political development of the United States. Visitors can see George Washington's military uniform, the desk at which Thomas Jefferson wrote the first version of the Declaration of Independence, and the flag that inspired Francis Scott Key to write "The Star-Spangled Banner" (see **Star-Spangled Banner** [picture]).

The technology section features scientific and technological exhibits. These displays include Alexander Graham Bell's first telephone, Elias Howe's first sewing machine, and Samuel F. B. Morse's first telegraph.

The National Museum of American History originally formed part of the U.S. National Museum. In 1964, the history and technology items were put on display in a new building called the National Museum of History and Technology. The museum was renamed the National Museum of American History in 1980. It is supported by annual grants from Congress.

Critically reviewed by the National Museum of American History

National Museum of Natural History ranks as one of the world's major centers for the study of the natural sciences. The museum consists of the United States

government's collections of items relating to human beings, Earth and its environment, and outer space. In addition, the museum carries on educational and research work. It is in Washington, D.C.

Research conducted at the museum contributes to the advancement of medical knowledge, agricultural and mineral production, and environmental conservation. The museum houses exhibits on such subjects as the cultures of the Americas, the Pacific, Africa, and Asia; the evolution of human beings; dinosaurs and other fossils; and the ice age. The museum also has displays of gems and minerals, moon rocks, meteorites, mammals, birds, and marine life. Special features at the museum include a live insect zoo, a living coral reef, a naturalist center, and a "discovery room" where people of all ages can handle natural history specimens.

The museum is a branch of the Smithsonian Institution, which was founded in 1846. The American naturalist Spencer F. Baird began to develop the natural history collections during the 1850's. The museum is supported largely by annual grants from Congress.

Critically reviewed by the National Museum of Natural History

National Museum of the American Indian is a United States museum devoted to the histories and cultures of the native peoples of North, Central, and South America. The museum, also called the NMAI, works in cooperation with Native American communities to present objects, exhibits, and artworks of historical significance. Its collections also showcase modern Native American arts and cultures. The NMAI has three facilities: the George Gustav Heye Center in New York City; the Cultural Resources Center in Suitland, Maryland; and the museum on the National Mall in Washington, D.C. The NMAI is part of the Smithsonian Institution.

George Gustav Heye, an American art collector, established the Museum of the American Indian in New York City in 1916. In 1989, the U.S. Congress created the National Museum of the American Indian and moved Heye's collection to the Smithsonian Institution. The NMAI's museum in Washington, D.C., opened in 2004.

Critically reviewed by the National Museum of the American Indian

National Naval Medical Center. See Walter Reed National Military Medical Center Bethesda.

National Oceanic and Atmospheric Administration (NOAA) is an agency of the United States Department of Commerce that works to improve knowledge and use of the environment. It is responsible for forecasting the weather, for managing ocean resources, for providing various oceanic and atmospheric services, and for undertaking research relating to oceans and the atmosphere.

NOAA's major organizations include the National Environmental Satellite, Data and Information Service; the National Marine Fisheries Service; the National Ocean Service; the National Weather Service; and the Office of Oceanic and Atmospheric Research.

The agency was created in 1970. Its headquarters are in Washington, D.C.

Critically reviewed by the National Oceanic and Atmospheric Administration

See also **Weather Service, National.**

National Optical Astronomy Observatories (NOAO) are a group of astronomy research centers funded by the United States government. The NOAO includes Kitt Peak National Observatory near Tucson, Arizona; Cerro-Tololo Inter-American Observatory in northern Chile; and the National Solar Observatory in Arizona and New Mexico.

The NOAO was established in 1982 to combine the nation's major centers for *optical astronomy* into a single organization. Optical astronomy involves the use of *optical telescopes,* which capture visible light and *infrared* (heat) radiation to form images of the sun, planets, stars, galaxies, and other celestial objects.

The NOAO provides major research facilities to astronomers. Any astronomer can apply for time on NOAO telescopes to carry out research. In addition, the NOAO maintains a staff of astronomers who improve and develop the observatories' instruments, as well as conduct research.

Kitt Peak National Observatory is on Kitt Peak, about 60 miles (95 kilometers) southwest of Tucson. The observatory has a large collection of optical telescopes. Its biggest telescope is the 4-meter Mayall telescope, which contains a mirror 158 inches (4 meters) in diameter. Hundreds of astronomers from throughout the United States and other countries use Kitt Peak facilities each year.

Cerro Tololo Inter-American Observatory is on Cerro Tololo, a mountain about 50 miles (80 kilometers) east of La Serena, Chile. The observatory's 158-inch (4-meter) telescope is one of the largest optical telescopes south of the equator. Astronomers at the observatory study celestial objects that cannot be seen from the Northern Hemisphere.

The National Solar Observatory, based in Tucson, conducts studies of the sun. It operates the Dunn Solar telescope and other telescopes on Sacramento Peak, New Mexico, and the Robert R. McMath solar telescope at Kitt Peak. The McMath telescope has a mirror 60 inches (1.5 meters) in diameter. The telescope produces an image of the sun approximately 30 inches (75 centimeters) in diameter.

In addition, the NOAO conducts special programs in astronomy. One such program, called the Global Oscillation Network Group Project (GONG), uses a worldwide network of automated observatories to continuously study vibrations on the surface of the sun. Another such program, called the United States Gemini Program, participates in an international partnership that operates two 319-inch (8.1-meter) telescopes. The Gemini North telescope is on Mauna Kea in Hawaii, and the Gemini South telescope is on Cerro Pachón, near Cerro Tololo in central Chile.

The NOAO is operated by the Association of Universities for Research in Astronomy, Incorporated (AURA), a consortium of U.S. institutions and international affiliates. AURA is under contract to the National Science Foundation, a federal agency.

Critically reviewed by the National Optical Astronomy Observatories

See also **Sun** (History of modern solar study); **Telescope.**

National Organization for Women (NOW) is the largest women's rights organization in the United States. It is devoted to achieving full equality between women and men. NOW pushes for equality through public education, elections, and legislation as well as through rallies, demonstrations, and marches. The organization has hundreds of thousands of members—both men and women—in chapters throughout the nation. NOW is a nonprofit organization whose operating funds come from private donations and membership dues.

NOW seeks to eliminate discrimination against women in many settings, including employment, education, the legal system, and the family. The organization supports legalized abortion and access to birth control. Over the years, it has expanded its goals by backing racial equality and economic justice as well as calling for an end to discrimination on the basis of sexual orientation and disability.

NOW calls for the passage of an Equal Rights Amendment to the Constitution of the United States. The amendment would require that men and women be treated equally by law. The organization's first attempt to win approval of the amendment failed because only 35 of the necessary 38 states had approved it by a 1982 deadline. Since then, the amendment has been reintroduced in Congress a number of times but has not been passed.

Many people, including a large number of women, oppose the National Organization for Women's goals, its methods, or both. Some of these people object to the organization's support for abortion. Many of NOW's opponents believe that the welfare of society and of the family depends on preserving the traditional roles of men and women. These people criticize NOW for working to change women's roles. Some people dislike NOW's use of rallies, marches, and demonstrations to achieve its goals.

NOW disagrees that its activities weaken society or the family. The organization also points out that it supports the rights of all women, including homemakers, and that it acknowledges homemakers' vital contributions to society and the family.

NOW was established in 1966. The American writer Betty Friedan, one of NOW's founders, was the organization's first president. She served as president from 1966 to 1970. Friedan was the author of *The Feminine Mystique* (1963), which examined the effects of societies that encourage women to be homemakers and discourage them from seeking careers outside the home. NOW headquarters are in Washington, D.C.

Susan Gluck Mezey

See also **Equal Rights Amendment; Friedan, Betty.**

A national park is an area set aside to protect wildlife and preserve natural beauty. The magnificent scenery of Banff National Park in Canada, shown in this photograph, includes snow-covered mountains and sparkling lakes. Banff is one of the most popular national parks in North America.

National park

National park is an area set aside by a nation's government to protect natural beauty, wildlife, or other remarkable features. National parks also preserve places of cultural, historical, or scientific interest. Also, some parks protect entire environments, such as coral reefs, deserts, grasslands, mountain ranges, or rain forests. Governments create national parks to protect their natural treasures from the harmful effects of farming, hunting, logging, mining, and other economic development.

National parks and other protected areas serve important purposes. Many parks allow us to enjoy and appreciate majestic peaks, sparkling lakes, spectacular waterfalls, and other scenic wonders. Others let us see fascinating wild animals in their natural settings. Many national parks foster education by preserving important buildings, battlegrounds, and other features of a nation's cultural and historical heritage. Still others provide opportunities for boating, camping, hiking, and other recreation. As a means of attracting tourism, national parks are vital to the economies of many nations.

Parks help save endangered animals and plants. They provide natural laboratories for scientists seeking to understand relationships of animals and plants to their environment. Another goal of many parks is to protect the area's *biodiversity* (variety of plant and animal species). In this way, parks help maintain a healthy balance among species. They preserve the natural processes that support life on Earth.

National parks face a number of challenges. Many park managers must deal with pressures to develop park resources. They also are concerned about *poaching* (illegal hunting), the collection of rare plants, pollution, and overcrowding. Other concerns include the rights of the people who were the parks' original inhabitants and the wise management of natural forces such as fire and wildlife.

Outline

I. **Notable national park systems**
   A. Argentina
   B. Australia
   C. Canada
   D. Costa Rica
   E. Japan
   F. Kenya
   G. New Zealand
   H. South Africa
   I. The United States

II. **Other interesting national parks**

III. **Challenges for the parks**
   A. Development of park resources
   B. Changes in the environment
   C. Overcrowding
   D. The rights of original inhabitants
   E. Management of fire and wildlife

IV. **History**

The world's first national park, Yellowstone National Park, was established in the United States in 1872. National parks gradually spread throughout the world. Today, tens of thousands of national parks and other protected areas safeguard vast areas of land throughout the world. Many countries use the term *nature reserves* for areas similar to national parks. Together, the world's national parks and nature reserves cover an area about twice the size of Canada, China, or the United States.

Notable national park systems

A number of countries have developed important national park systems. These countries include Argentina, Australia, Canada, Costa Rica, Japan, Kenya, New Zealand, South Africa, and the United States.

Argentina has dozens of national parks. Its first national park, the National Park of the South, was established in 1922 to preserve an area of scenic mountains.

Argentina's national parks protect a huge range of geographical features, plants, and animals. The most notable parks include Nahuel Huapi, Los Glaciares, and Iguazú. Nahuel Huapi was originally called National Park of the South. It is Argentina's largest national park, covering about 2,700 square miles (7,000 square kilometers).

Only slightly smaller is Los Glaciares, which has more than 200 glaciers.

Together, Iguazú National Park in Argentina and Iguaçu National Park in Brazil protect the magnificent Iguaçu Falls and about 975 square miles (2,500 square kilometers) of tropical rain forest. This rain forest is home to more than 80 kinds of mammals and about 450 kinds of birds. The waterfall actually consists of 150 to 300 separate falls, depending on water flow. The combined falls measure about 2 miles (3 kilometers) wide and drop 237 feet (72 meters).

Australia has hundreds of national parks. Royal National Park was the first to be established, in 1879.

Australia's natural history makes its parks especially important to scientists. Australia has been isolated from other continents for about 200 million years. As a result, Australia's wildlife developed differently from the wildlife on other continents. Kangaroos, koalas, wombats, and thousands of other animals are unique to Australia. Many native plants are found nowhere else.

Australia's Great Barrier Reef Marine Park and Kakadu National Park are of exceptional interest. The Great Barrier Reef, which stretches along Australia's northeast coast, is the largest system of coral reefs in the world.

The spectacular Iguaçu Falls lies on the border between Brazil and Argentina and forms a part of national parks in each country. The waterfall actually consists of hundreds of separate falls. The combined falls measure about 2 miles (3 kilometers) wide and drop 237 feet (72 meters).

© Debra James, Shutterstock

The Great Barrier Reef Marine Park is one of the world's largest marine reserves. Its hundreds of colorful coral species and other wildlife attract divers from around the world.

The Great Barrier Reef Marine Park encompasses most of the reef. At about 133,000 square miles (345,000 square kilometers), it is one of the largest marine reserves in the world. The park is home to hundreds of species of coral and thousands of different species of fish and shellfish.

Kakadu National Park preserves Aboriginal culture and history, as well as a beautiful landscape. People have lived in the area for more than 50,000 years. The park includes one of the world's greatest collections of prehistoric cave paintings. Aboriginal peoples continue to live in the park and are recognized as its traditional owners. These traditional owners have leased their lands to the Australian government and cooperate in the management of the park.

Canada has dozens of national parks and park reserves. The Canadian system of national parks began in 1885, with land near Banff, Alberta. This area became part of what is now Banff National Park.

Canada has pioneered an *ecosystem* approach to park planning. An ecosystem consists of all the living and nonliving things in a given area and the relationships among them. An area's air, climate, soils, plants, and animals are all part of its ecosystem. Under the ecosystem approach, Canada's park service has divided the country into about 39 "natural regions," each with a different combination of land, water, plants, and animals. The government's goal is to have at least one national park in each region.

The Canadian park system is exceptionally diverse. Wood Buffalo National Park, in the Northwest Territories, is larger than Switzerland. It protects a large herd of bison and the nesting sites of whooping cranes. Banff, Jasper, Kootenay, and Yoho national parks protect almost 8,000 square miles (20,700 square kilometers) of mountain ecosystem. These four adjacent Rocky Mountain parks have rugged peaks, active glaciers, glistening

lakes, thundering waterfalls, and boiling hot springs. The parks are home to grizzly and black bears, bighorn sheep, deer, elk, moose, mountain goats, and dense forests of evergreen trees.

In addition, Canada has begun to develop a system of marine parks to protect underwater environments in the Atlantic, Pacific, and Arctic oceans and in the Great Lakes. Canada's first national marine park, Fathom Five, was established in 1987 in Lake Huron's Georgian Bay. The bay's cold, clear waters preserve several historic shipwrecks and provide opportunities for recreational divers. For a complete listing of Canada's national parks and historic sites, see **Canada** (National park system).

Costa Rica has many national parks and protected areas. More than 25 percent of Costa Rica's land area is protected, the most in the world. The national parks protect volcanoes, coral reefs, tropical rain forests, caves, and hot springs. These parks protect more than 75 percent of Costa Rica's plant and animal species, including more than 850 species of birds. That number is more bird species than live in Canada and the United States combined.

Poás Volcano National Park was created in 1971. It is the nation's oldest national park. Poás is 8,900 feet (2,700 meters) high, with a crater 950 feet (290 meters) deep. Visitors can walk to the rim and look down into an active volcano. The last major eruptions were in the 1950's. Braulio Carrillo National Park protects 170 square miles (440 square kilometers) of forests. The elevation of the park ranges from just above sea level to more than 9,500 feet (2,900 meters). An extraordinary diversity of life is found within the park, including more than 600 species of trees and 500 species of birds. Tortuguero National Park protects important sea-turtle nesting areas. Manuel Antonio National Park is popular for its beaches and

D. & J. Heaton, West Light

Mount Fuji, long considered a sacred place by the Japanese people, stands in Fuji-Hakone-Izu National Park. The beautifully shaped volcano attracts millions of visitors each year.

wildlife. Irazú National Park is a volcano from which visitors can sometimes see both the Caribbean Sea and the Pacific Ocean.

Japan has dozens of national parks. The national parks of Japan are rooted in both religion and recreation. Japan's major religions, Buddhism and Shintoism, stress harmony with nature and deep respect for living things. The Japanese people regard forests, islands, mountains, and other places of special beauty as sacred. For centuries, they treated such places as shrines and left them unspoiled. To protect the beauty of Japan's scenic mountains, the government created the country's first national park in 1934.

Japan is one of the most densely populated nations in the world. As a result, little unused land is available for the creation of national parks. Japan's solution has been to establish national parks that include private lands. The government then works with the landowners to preserve the natural beauty of each area. About a fourth of Japan's parkland is privately owned.

Japan's best-known scenic treasure is Mount Fuji, a beautiful volcano in Fuji-Hakone-Izu National Park. It attracts about 100 million visitors each year. About 200,000 of them climb to the summit.

Kenya has dozens of national parks and reserves. Its national park system protects the spectacular variety of wild animals native to East Africa. The national parks of Kenya date to the early 1900's, when colonial governments set aside wildlife reserves, mainly to provide sightseeing and hunting opportunities for Europeans. Today, money spent by tourists visiting the national parks is a major source of Kenya's national income.

Kenya's most famous protected areas include Tsavo and Amboseli national parks. Both lie in the grasslands of east Africa. Tsavo is Kenya's largest park. It covers about 8,800 square miles (22,800 square kilometers) and is known for its buffaloes, elephants, lions, rhinoceroses, and more than 500 species of birds. Amboseli is popular with tourists, who visit the park to view elephants and Mount Kilimanjaro, the highest mountain in Africa. The mountain's summit is about 30 miles (50 kilometers) to the south of Ambesoli, in Tanzania's Kilimanjaro National Park.

New Zealand has several national parks. The country's national park system was made possible by its native people, the Maori. Maori feared that Europeans settling in the country in the late 1800's would not respect their sacred volcanoes. In 1887, a Maori chief gave land to the government for a park. It was the first national park to be created by a gift from native peoples. The area became Tongariro National Park in 1894. The park has grown over time to cover about 300 square miles (775 square kilometers).

Preserving native wildlife has special importance in New Zealand, which has been isolated for about 80 million years. When Europeans began arriving in the 1800's, more than half of New Zealand's native plants and animals were unique to New Zealand. But European settlers introduced many species to New Zealand. These introduced species have devastated native plants and animals. New Zealand has made major efforts to preserve its native life.

Fiordland is New Zealand's largest national park. It covers about 4,800 square miles (12,500 square kilometers) on the South Island. The park is named for its *fiords,* narrow inlets of the sea between high cliffs.

The Great Limpopo Transfrontier Park, in Mozambique, South Africa, and Zimbabwe, is home to tens of thousands of large mammals, including elephants, giraffes, hippopotamuses, hyenas, lions, and Cape buffaloes, *shown here.* The park ranks as a leading center of wildlife research.

These fiords are up to 27 miles (43 kilometers) long and about 1,600 feet (500 meters) deep. This park also includes evergreen rain forests and Sutherland Falls, which drops 1,904 feet (580 meters). The national parks have helped make tourism and outdoor recreation major industries in New Zealand.

South Africa has a number of national parks. Nature observers have called South Africa's animal population "the greatest wildlife show on Earth." Not surprisingly, South Africa's national park system has focused on wildlife protection.

Kruger National Park began as the Sabi Game Reserve in 1898. In 1926, it became South Africa's first national park. It has become a world center for wildlife research. Kruger has thousands of buffaloes, elephants, impalas, and zebras, as well as hundreds of species of birds and plants. The park's grasslands are home to antelope, cheetahs, giraffes, hyenas, jackals, leopards, and lions. Crocodiles and hippopotamuses live in the rivers. In 2002, Kruger became part of the Great Limpopo Transfrontier Park, an international reserve that also includes parks in Mozambique and Zimbabwe. The establishment of the park is the first step in creating a larger transfrontier reserve that will eventually reach 39,000 square miles (100,000 square kilometers). That area is equivalent in size to Iceland.

Kalahari Gemsbok National Park was established in South Africa in 1931 to protect herds of migrating animals. In 2000, this park was merged with Gemsbok National Park in Botswana. The two parks formed the Kgalagadi Transfrontier Park. Kgalagadi covers about 15,000 square miles (38,000 square kilometers) of desert in the two countries. The park is famous for its variety of

(Continued on page 42h)

© Jon Arnold Images/Masterfile

The scenic Lake District National Park in England is one of Europe's natural treasures. About 15 lakes in the area, including Ullswater, *shown here,* attract writers, artists, and other visitors.

© Joakim Lloyd Raboff, Shutterstock

Tikal National Park in Guatemala protects ruins of pyramids and temples of the ancient Maya civilization. Tikal was an important city of the Maya. This civilization flourished between about A.D. 250 and 900.

Interesting national parks throughout the world

Examples of interesting national parks throughout the world are described below and on page 42g.

Name	Location	Outstanding features
AFRICA		
Amboseli	Kenya	Views of nearby Mount Kilimanjaro; elephants, leopards, and vervet monkeys
Bwindi Impenetrable	Uganda	Wide variety of animal and plant life, including mountain gorillas and a great diversity of trees
Chobe	Botswana	Elephants, giraffes, hippopotamuses, lions, and zebras
Comoe	Côte d'Ivoire	Elephants
Dzanga-Ndoki/ Nouabalé-Ndoki	Central African Republic/ Republic of the Congo	Chimpanzees, elephants, gorillas; rain forest
Etosha	Namibia	Savanna and woodland surrounding a shallow depression that fills with water in the rainy season; large elephant population, springboks, wildebeests, zebras, other wildlife
Garamba	Democratic Republic of the Congo	Habitat for buffaloes and white rhinoceroses
Great Limpopo	Mozambique/South Africa/ Zimbabwe	Savanna home to vast wildlife, including buffaloes, elephants, giraffes, and zebras
Hwange	Zimbabwe	Woodland and scrub savanna; buffaloes, elephants, giraffes, and zebras
Kabalega Falls (Murchison Falls)	Uganda	Murchison Falls, crocodiles, hippopotamuses, other wildlife
Kgalagadi	South Africa/Botswana	Desert area with migrating groups of springboks and gemsboks; cheetahs and lions
Kilimanjaro	Tanzania	Trails to the summit of Mount Kilimanjaro for mountaineers, elands and leopards
Lake Malawi	Malawi	Deep-water lake with hundreds of species of fish
Montagne d'Ambre	Madagascar	Volcanic area with crater lakes and waterfalls; tropical forests, lemurs, butterflies
Ngorongoro	Tanzania	Rim of ancient volcanic crater surrounds flat savanna; diverse wildlife
Niokolo-Koba	Senegal	River habitat, bordered by forest and savanna; buffaloes, crocodiles, and gazelles and other antelopes
Ranomafana	Madagascar	Rugged area of rain forest; endangered aye-ayes and ruffed lemurs
Ruwenzori (Queen Elizabeth)	Uganda	Two large lakes; chimpanzees and colobus monkeys, many antelopes
Selous	Tanzania	Buffaloes, elephants, other species
Serengeti/Maasai Mara	Tanzania/Kenya	Migrating wildebeests and zebras; diverse savanna wildlife
South Luangwa	Zambia	Woodland savanna for elephants, giraffes, leopards, other wildlife
Tsavo	Kenya	Largest park in Kenya; major elephant and rhinoceros populations
Victoria Falls/ Mosi-oa-Tunya	Zimbabwe/Zambia	Magnificent Victoria Falls
Virunga/Volcanoes	Democratic Republic of the Congo/Rwanda	Wide variety of habitats, including home of mountain gorillas
ASIA		
Angkor	Cambodia	Protected area for the ancient temples of Angkor
Bandipur/Mudumalai	India	In western Ghat mountains; one of the last strongholds for the Asian elephant
Corbett	India	Forest and grasslands provide habitat for Bengal tigers
Daisetsuzan	Japan (Hokkaido)	Mountainous habitat for brown bear and other wildlife; ski areas and hot springs
Fuji-Hakone-Izu	Japan	Scenic Mount Fuji; lakes; rocky coastline
Gunung Leuser	Indonesia (Sumatra)	Rain forest; orangutans, rhinoceroses, tigers, and the world's largest flower, the rafflesia
Kanha	India	Forests and bamboo thickets in central India; home to much wildlife, including swamp deer, tigers
Karatepe-Aslantas	Turkey	Archaeological site of former Hittite settlement; museum
Kaziranga	India	Elephants, rhinoceroses, wild buffaloes, birds
Keoladeo	India	Wetland for migrating waterfowl
Khao Yai	Thailand	Tropical, evergreen, and deciduous forests, as well as grassland; deer, elephants, and numerous bird species
Kinabalu	Malaysia (Borneo)	Jungle at the base of Mount Kinabalu; tree-level walkway through rain forest
Komodo	Indonesia	Habitat for the endangered Komodo dragon
Manas/ Royal Manas	India/ Bhutan	Foothills of Himalaya; varied forests, many bird species; golden langur monkeys, rhinoceroses, tigers
Mount Apo	Philippines (Mindanao)	Sanctuary for the great Philippine eagle
Nikko	Japan	Historic shrines and temples, mountainous scenery, rivers, and waterfalls
Royal Chitwan	Nepal	Grassland and forest; diverse animal and bird population, including rhinoceroses and tigers
Ruhuna (also called Yala)	Sri Lanka	Scrub woodland; elephants, spotted deer, and water buffaloes
Sagarmatha	Nepal	Includes Mount Everest, highest peak in the world
Sorak	South Korea	Peak of Mount Sorak; lush valleys and forests; Buddhist temples, waterfalls, and hiking trails
Stolby	Russia (Siberia)	Coniferous forests; granite hills; hiking and climbing
Taman Negara	Malaysia	Ancient tropical rain forest; buffaloes, hornbills, kingfishers, tapirs
Ujung Kulon	Indonesia (Java)	Wilderness for Javan gibbons, Javan rhinoceroses, leaf monkeys, and leopards
Wilpattu	Sri Lanka	Jungle habitat for leopards, sloth bears, spotted deer, other wildlife
Wolong	China	Rugged mountainous area of Sichuan province; forests, bamboo, rhododendrons; endangered giant pandas, golden monkeys, red pandas, takins
Yü Shan	Taiwan	Remote park, emperor pheasants, Formosan macaques, Taiwan black bears, and Taiwan serows
AUSTRALIA AND NEW ZEALAND		
Aoraki/Mount Cook	New Zealand	High mountains, Tasman Glaciers, native wildlife
Blue Mountains	Australia (New South Wales)	River-eroded gorges, waterfalls, eucalyptus forests
Cradle Mountain/Lake St. Clair	Australia (Tasmania)	Native plants, including pandanus; highlands, temperate rain forest, alpine moors, with glacial lakes
Daintree	Australia (Queensland)	Tropical rain forest, waterfalls, and diverse wildlife
Fiordland	New Zealand	New Zealand's largest park, has coastal fiords, rain forests, and Sutherland Falls
Great Barrier Reef	Australia (Queensland)	One of world's largest marine reserves; coral reefs and underwater species
Kakadu	Australia (Northern Territory)	Aboriginal cave paintings; includes tropical tidal flats, mangrove swamps, flood plains, woodlands, and sandstone escarpments
Tongariro	New Zealand	Active volcanoes; ancestral land of the Maori
Uluru-Kata Tjuta	Australia (Northern Territory)	Includes Uluru (also known as Ayers Rock) and the Olgas, rock domes in the desert; ancient cave paintings
EUROPE		
Askaniya Nova	Ukraine	Steppe wilderness and wetlands; summer home for migrating ducks and geese; spawning site for fish
Bayerischer Wald	Germany	Bavarian forest
Białowieza	Poland	Lowland forests, hundreds of species of flowering plants, virgin woods, European bison
Doñana	Spain	Wetland reserve for migrating waterfowl
Gran Paradiso/Vanoise	Italy/France (Alps)	Alpine landscape; chamois, ibex

Name	Location	Outstanding features
Lake District	United Kingdom	Mountains, valleys, and glacial lakes, picturesque scenery
North-East Greenland	Greenland	Arctic wildlife habitat, musk oxen, polar bears, walruses
Padjelanta/Sarek/ Stora Sjofallet	Sweden	Meadows, glacial peaks, and rugged valleys; grazing herds of reindeer, other wildlife
St. Kilda	United Kingdom	National scenic area; breeding ground for gannets, puffins, other marine birds
Swiss	Switzerland	Coniferous forests, alpine meadows, slopes, and outcrops
Tatransky/Tatra	Slovakia/Poland	Mountainous area with alpine plants and trees
Teberdinskiy	Russia (Caucasus)	Mountainous forests and meadows, glaciers and glacial lakes; home to deer, grouse, ibex, partridges, pheasants, and wild boars

NORTH AMERICA

Name	Location	Outstanding features
Banff/Jasper	Canada (Alberta)	Rocky Mountain scenery with glaciers and hot springs
Darien	Panama	Rain forest, mangrove swamps, white sand beaches
Denali	USA (Alaska)	Mount McKinley, highest mountain in North America; spectacular wildlife
Everglades	USA (Florida)	Subtropical wilderness with plentiful wildlife
Fundy	Canada (New Brunswick)	Rugged Bay of Fundy shoreline with coves and cliffs; some of the world's highest tides
Glacier	USA (Montana)	Glaciers and lakes among towering Rocky Mountain peaks
Grand Canyon	USA (Arizona)	Deep canyon with brightly colored walls and rock shapes
Great Smoky Mountains	USA (North Carolina/Tennessee)	High mountains; large hardwood and evergreen forests
Gros Morne	Canada (Newfoundland and Labrador)	Scenic Long Range Mountains; fiordlike lakes, waterfalls, and rugged seacoasts
Isle Royale	USA (Michigan)	Island wilderness with moose and wolves
Ixtacihuatl-Popocatepetl	Mexico	Mountain peaks, climbing and hiking trails
La Amistad	Costa Rica/Panama	Virgin forest; great biological diversity; dormant volcano
Mammoth Cave	USA (Kentucky)	Huge cave with several hundred miles of corridors
Mesa Verde	USA (Colorado)	Ancient Indian cliff dwellings
Olympic	USA (Washington)	Mountain wilderness, wild coastline, and rain forest; elk
Pacific Rim	Canada (British Columbia)	Beaches, rocky shore, islands, and forests; sea lions, whales
Redwood	USA (California)	World's tallest known tree in coastal redwood forest
Sian Ka'an	Mexico	Tropical forest, mangrove swamps, white sand beaches
Tikal	Guatemala	Ruins of the ancient Mayan civilization
Tortuguero	Costa Rica	Nesting area for the Atlantic green turtle; lowland rain forest
Wood Buffalo	Canada (Alberta/Northwest Territories)	Largest buffalo herd in North America and nesting grounds of rare whooping cranes
Yellowstone	USA (Wyoming/Montana/Idaho)	World's greatest geyser area; canyons and waterfalls; wide variety of wildlife
Yosemite	USA (California)	Mountain scenery with deep gorges and high waterfalls; sequoia forests

SOUTH AMERICA

Name	Location	Outstanding features
Amazonia	Brazil	Variety of ecosystems; anteaters, caimans, capybaras, monkeys, parrots, and toucans
Canaima	Venezuela	Angel Falls, the world's highest waterfall; grassland with flat-topped mountains, rain forests
Galapagos	Ecuador	Island ecosystems with unique wildlife
Iguaçu/Iguazú	Brazil/Argentina	Magnificent Iguaçu Falls; tropical rain forests; diverse bird and mammal species
Itatiaia	Brazil	Rugged area between Rio de Janeiro and São Paulo; diverse habitats ranging from rain forests to high plateaus with unique rock formations
Kaieteur	Guyana	Tropical rain forest, savannas; Kaieteur Falls; jaguars, ocelots, tapirs, and many species of birds
Los Glaciares	Argentina	Major glaciers from the southern Patagonian ice field
Manu	Peru	Undisturbed rain forest, with diverse plant and animal life; many species of birds and monkeys
Nahuel Huapi	Argentina	Mountains, glaciers, and glacial lakes and streams; hiking trails
Noel Kempff Mercado	Bolivia	Rain forest; jaguars, monkeys, tapirs, and the endangered giant otter
Pantanal	Brazil	Freshwater wetland near border with Bolivia; dense wildlife, including capybaras and hyacinth macaws
Raleighvallen-Voltzberg	Suriname	Rain forest along the Coppename River, Raleigh Falls; armadillos, macaws and toucans, pumas, and sloths
Rapa Nui	Chile (Easter Island)	Archaeological monuments and local cultural heritage
Torres del Paine	Chile	Dramatic peaks of southern Andes; Andean condors, eagles, rheas, and wild guanacos

© Pacific Stock/SuperStock

Indonesia's Komodo National Park protects the Komodo dragon. These rare lizards grow to more than 10 feet (3 meters) long and can weigh as much as 365 pounds (165 kilograms). Wildlife preservation is a key goal of national parks throughout the world.

© Steve Bloom Images/Alamy Images

The Wolong National Nature Reserve in China is one of several reserves that protect the rare giant panda, *shown here.*

antelope—including elands, gemsboks, springboks, steenboks, and wildebeests—as well as for cheetahs, hyenas, jackals, and lions.

The United States has dozens of national parks and hundreds of other protected areas. The U.S. government's work in establishing and managing parks has served as a model for countries around the world. The opening of Yellowstone National Park in 1872 was soon followed by the creation of many other important national parks. For more information on U.S. parks, see **National Park System**.

Other interesting national parks

Countries throughout the world have established national parks. A number of these parks are famous worldwide and attract millions of visitors annually. Tourists are often drawn by the variety of wildlife in a country's national parks. Many people are attracted by the outstanding features of individual parks as well. Some of these parks are considered world treasures. For example, Nepal's Sagarmatha National Park includes Mount Everest, which rises to 29,035 feet (8,850 meters) and is the highest peak in the world. Guatemala's Tikal National Park protects pyramids of the ancient Maya civilization.

Another famous protected area, Ecuador's Galapagos National Park, preserves the natural laboratory that influenced the British biologist Charles Darwin. Darwin's studies there contributed to his famous theory of evolution. The Lake District of England inspired the British poet William Wordsworth long before it became a national park in the 1950's. Victoria Falls National Park in Zimbabwe and Mosi-oa-Tunya National Park in Zambia share protection of the most famous waterfall in Africa. This landmark, the magnificent Victoria Falls, drops 355 feet (108 meters).

Many of the world's national parks are vital to wildlife preservation. Wolong National Nature Reserve in China shelters rare giant pandas. Indonesia's Komodo National Park provides habitat for the endangered Komodo dragon. India's national parks, such as Ranthambhore, have helped to save the tiger from extinction. The marshlands of Doñana National Park in Spain provide food and shelter to nearly half the bird species in Europe.

Challenges for the parks

People often think of the world's national parks as islands of unspoiled nature. We assume these parks are safely separated from a world rapidly becoming more urban, more industrial, and more artificial. The world's national parks, however, are part of the world in which we all live. What we do affects the parks and may threaten their existence.

Today, national parks face many challenges. Major threats come from pressures to develop park resources, from environmental change, and from overcrowding. Park managers also struggle to guarantee the rights of the land's original inhabitants and to ensure sound management of fire and wildlife.

Development of park resources. Many national parks were set aside in the belief that they had little or no commercial value. Later, people discovered that many of the parks contain valuable resources. For example, some parks contain valuable minerals. Also, resources inside parks become increasingly valuable as

© Masterfile

Poaching poses a major problem in a number of national parks that provide homes for threatened wildlife. The elephant tusks shown here were seized from ivory poachers in Africa.

resources outside the parks are exhausted. Parks contain trees that might be cut, grass that might be grazed, and land that might be farmed. The commercial development of park resources often will produce more jobs and economic growth in the short term than will preservation of the parks.

Pressures to develop park resources are limited in rich nations. People of wealthy nations do not need to use park resources for survival. In developing nations, however, the situation is different. Governments may feel great pressure to sacrifice parks in favor of economic development. Large corporations may acquire the right to use park resources by paying public officials for their cooperation. Many landless peasants seek park resources for survival. They may view the parks as the only lands available for collecting firewood, for building homes, for hunting food, or for raising crops.

Poachers also invade many parks. Many of these illegal hunters kill animals to sell the valuable body parts. For example, poachers slaughter leopards for their skins, elephants for their tusks, and rhinoceroses for their horns. Poachers also collect live animals for illegal sale as pets. Some people also take rare plants from the parks. Where these pressures on park resources are severe, the parks may not survive.

Changes in the environment also endanger the parks. Various forms of pollution—especially air and water pollution—present major threats because they easily cross park boundaries. For example, the scenic views of Grand Canyon National Park in the United States are often reduced due to air pollution from Los Angeles, which lies about 300 miles (480 kilometers) away. In addition, the park's environment has suffered from the construction of dams upstream on the Colorado River, which flows through the Grand Canyon. Changes in the flow of water have changed the ecosystem, harming water birds and other wildlife in the park.

Worldwide environmental problems also threaten national parks. These problems include *global warming,* the increase in Earth's average surface temperature. Scientists estimate that Earth's average surface temperature rose by about 1.4 Fahrenheit degrees (0.76 Celsius degree) from the mid-1800's to the early 2000's. Climate scientists believe that this increase was caused mostly by rising levels of carbon dioxide in the atmosphere. Carbon dioxide traps heat from the sun. The amount of carbon dioxide in the atmosphere has risen by about 40 percent since 1750. Most of the increase in carbon dioxide was caused by burning coal, gas, and oil for fuel.

Climate scientists predict that Earth's average surface temperature will rise an additional 2.0 to 11.5 Fahrenheit degrees (1.1 to 6.4 Celsius degrees) by 2100. Many scientists are concerned that such a large increase in temperature could have a devastating effect on human beings and the environment. They warn that global warming could cause many living things to become extinct.

Overcrowding. The world's national parks have experienced dramatic growth in tourism. Some popular parks are actually endangered by their visitors. Too many visitors can harm the natural environments that national parks are set aside to protect. In some popular national parks, for example, visitors' automobiles create traffic jams, kill wildlife, and pollute the air. In addition, overcrowded campgrounds increase the level of litter and destroy the unspoiled beauty of scenic areas.

Overcrowding creates a difficult choice for park managers. Tourist spending demonstrates that park preservation has economic as well as spiritual value. In fact, in many developing nations, income from tourists who visit national parks is vital to the economy. Nevertheless, managers have had to limit the number of visitors to protect park resources for future generations.

The rights of original inhabitants. The peoples who live in and near national parks are especially concerned about who benefits from tourism in the parks. In some countries, the benefits have gone to political officials who control the parks and to large foreign-based corporations. The original inhabitants may then see the parks as a foreign idea and one damaging to their lives. As a result, they may oppose the establishment and preservation of national parks.

Some park managers concerned for the rights of local peoples look to New Zealand and Australia for solutions. In those countries, the Maori and the Aborigines support the creation of national parks as a way to preserve their sacred places and traditional ways of life. The cooperative management of Kakadu National Park by Aboriginal groups and the Australian government may serve as a model for other countries.

Yellowstone National Park in the United States has more geysers and hot springs than any other area in the world. It is also home to a variety of animals, including American buffaloes. Yellowstone, the world's first national park, was established in 1872.

© Sascha Burkard, Shutterstock

Management of fire and wildlife. Fire and wildlife often cause problems for park managers. Both fire and wild animals must behave naturally to preserve a park's ecosystem. If allowed to burn freely, fire destroys old and diseased trees and shrubs and helps nourish the soil. These conditions promote new growth. Allowing animals to hunt and roam freely helps parks maintain a balanced and varied community of wildlife.

However, fire and wild animals may threaten neighboring crops, livestock, property, and people. Neither fire nor animals recognize park boundaries. As a result, the desire for a natural ecosystem inside the park may conflict with the interests of people who own property outside the park. Park officials may be required to build fences and put out fires to protect private property. But such actions can damage the ecosystem.

In Yellowstone National Park, wolves were killed off in the 1920's, partly to protect livestock outside the park. Without wolves to feed on elk, the number of elk increased. The park was overgrazed, damaging the ecosystem, and elk often starved to death. In the 1990's, wolves were brought back to the park. The wolves thrived in the park and helped to restore a more natural balance. However, wolves that move outside the park sometimes attack livestock.

History

Throughout history, people have preserved and protected places they considered special. But it was not until the 1800's that governments became active in establishing national parks.

The early national parks. The United States pioneered the development of national parks. Americans became interested in protecting the nation's wilderness as the country expanded westward during the 1800's. In 1832, the artist George Catlin became one of the first noted Americans to publicly call for the creation of a national park. In 1858, the writer Henry David Thoreau also promoted the idea. Catlin and Thoreau also saw national parks as places where American Indians could preserve their vanishing cultures. The dream of a great national park became a reality in 1872, when President Ulysses S. Grant signed a law creating Yellowstone National Park.

The national park idea spread to other countries. In 1885, the Canadian government established a park around the hot springs at Banff, Alberta. During the next 40 years, national parks opened in Australia, Germany, Italy, New Zealand, South Africa, Spain, Sweden, and Switzerland. Also during this period, Belgium and France established national parks in their colonial possessions in Africa.

International concern for national parks. The growth of national parks around the world led to the formation of international conservation organizations. The International Union for the Conservation of Nature and Natural Resources (IUCN) traces its history to 1948. The IUCN is a global federation of government and private conservation organizations. It works to conserve biodiversity and promote the sustainable use of natural resources. In 1960, the IUCN established an organization dedicated to national parks that is now called the World Commission on Protected Areas (WCPA). The WCPA works to encourage the creation and effective management of parks and protected areas around the world.

The First World Conference on National Parks was held in 1962. Since then, world meetings have taken place every 10 years. In 1972, the conference met at Yellowstone National Park in honor of the park's 100th anniversary. More recent world conferences have been held in Bali, Indonesia; Caracas, Venezuela; and Durban, South Africa.

The United Nations Educational, Scientific and Cultural Organization (UNESCO) established two other important conservation programs. It founded the Man and the Biosphere Programme in 1970 to preserve ecosystems throughout the world for scientific and educational purposes. In 1978, UNESCO released the first World Heritage List, which recognized areas of unique natural or cultural importance. Many national parks around the world have been designated under these programs as biosphere reserves or world heritage sites. This recognition is meant to reward and encourage protection by national governments.

The national park movement today. The idea of establishing national parks has proved popular and has spread to most of the world's countries. Increasingly, park planners work to create parks that will preserve the full range of a nation's plants, animals, and landscapes. Often, this requires establishing parks in areas of scientific and environmental importance even if those parks might not be particularly popular with tourists.

People are learning that national parks are not natural islands that can be maintained separately from the world around them. The survival of national parks depends on what we do both inside and outside the parks.

Craig W. Allin

Related articles in *World Book.* See the political maps in many country articles for locations of national parks. See also the following articles:
Audubon Society, National
Balance of nature
Biodiversity
Conservation
Ecology
Elephant (Protecting elephants)
Endangered species
Global warming
Great Limpopo Transfrontier Park
National Park System
National Trails System
National Wildlife Federation
National Wildlife Refuge System
Nature Conservancy
Park
Poaching
Rain forest
Sierra Club
Wildlife conservation

National Park Service is a bureau of the United States Department of the Interior. It manages the approximately 390 areas of the National Park System. The bureau preserves many natural landscapes and historic and archaeological sites and structures. The bureau was established in 1916, when the U.S. park system consisted of 37 areas. These areas included Yellowstone National Park, the world's first national park. The U.S. secretary of the interior appoints a director to head the bureau in its Washington, D.C., headquarters. The bureau has seven regional offices and a number of centers that provide support services.   Critically reviewed by the National Park Service

See also **National Cemetery; National Park System.**

© Reed Kaestner, Corbis

Yosemite National Park, in east-central California, was one of the first national parks created in the United States. The park is known for its spectacular scenery, including Lake Yosemite, *shown here.* Yosemite Falls, *background,* North America's highest waterfall, drops 2,425 feet (739 meters) from its hanging valley.

National Park System

National Park System consists of hundreds of areas in the United States that have been set aside for the benefit and enjoyment of the people. These areas, called *parklands,* are natural wonderlands, famous historic places, or sites for many kinds of outdoor recreation. They include national parks, monuments, battlefields, lakeshores, rivers, and historic buildings.

The nation's parklands range in size from millions of acres (or hectares) to a fraction of an acre (or hectare). The largest parkland in the United States is Wrangell-St. Elias National Park in Alaska. This park, which features many glaciers and high peaks, covers more than 8 million acres (3 million hectares). The smallest area in the National Park System is the Thaddeus Kosciuszko National Memorial in Philadelphia, a red brick building that occupies $\frac{1}{50}$ of an acre (.008 hectare). The building was briefly the home of Kosciuszko, a Polish patriot who fought in the Revolutionary War in America (1775-1783).

The United States government established the first national park in the world, Yellowstone National Park, in 1872. The National Park System developed with the creation of additional parklands. Today, the District of Columbia and every state except Delaware have at least one national parkland. The outlying U.S. regions American Samoa, Guam, Puerto Rico, and the Virgin Islands also have national parklands.

The National Park Service, a bureau of the U.S. Department of the Interior, manages nearly all the parklands.

The president of the United States appoints a director to head the National Park Service. The director names a superintendent to manage an individual area or a group of areas close together. Park rangers work to protect the parklands from damage and provide various services for visitors (see **National Park Service**). See also the articles on the various parklands listed in the tables with this article. For information on national parks throughout the world, see the *World Book* article **National park.**

Kinds of parklands

There are about 20 different types of areas in the National Park System, including national parks, national monuments, national memorials, and national historic sites. See the table of *Types of areas.*

The different types of areas in the National Park System are preserved for three basic reasons. Areas may have (1) beautiful or unusual natural features, (2) historical importance, or (3) attractive recreational features. Many areas are set aside for more than one reason.

Areas preserved for natural features. Most national parks are preserved chiefly for the outstanding beauty or scientific importance of their natural features. For example, Yellowstone National Park, which covers parts of Idaho, Montana, and Wyoming, is world famous for its natural wonders. They include hot geysers that erupt from the ground, thundering waterfalls that plunge into deep gorges, and sparkling lakes that lie high among snow-capped mountains. Death Valley National Park, partly in Nevada and partly in California, is preserved for

Continued on page 46

Parklands of the National Park System

These maps show the locations of the parklands in the National Park System. Because of space limitations on the large map, the parklands within the metropolitan areas of Boston, New York City, Philadelphia, and Washington, D.C., are listed on the right side of this map.

WORLD BOOK maps

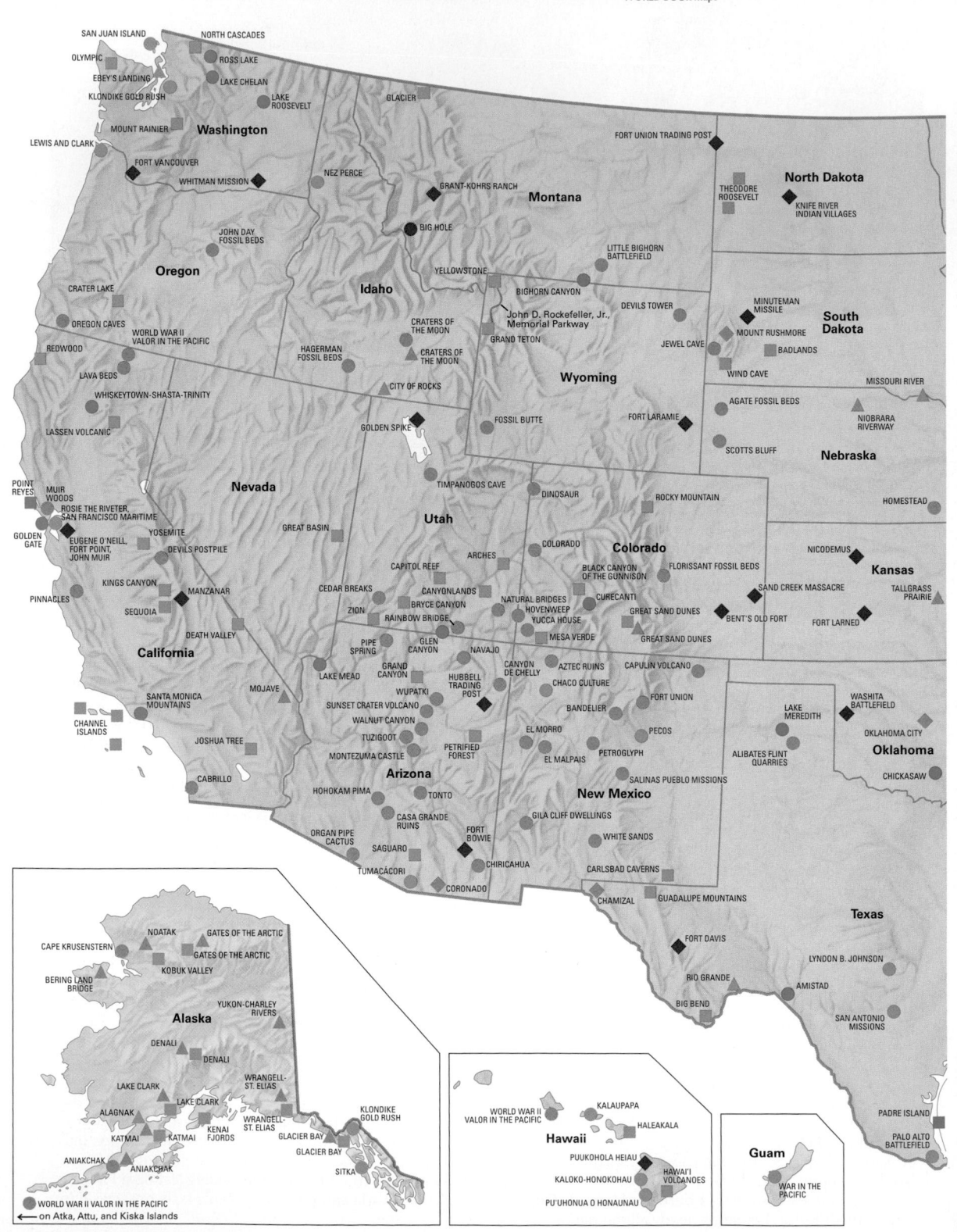

Legend:

- ■ National parks
- ● National recreation areas
- ● National monuments
- ◆ National historic sites
- ◆ National memorials
- ▲ National military parks

- ● National battlefields, national battlefield parks, and national battlefield sites
- ▲ National parkways and other national parklands
- ● National historical parks
- ■ National lakeshores and national seashores
- ▲ National preserves

Minnesota
- VOYAGEURS
- GRAND PORTAGE
- APOSTLE ISLANDS
- KEWEENAW
- ISLE ROYALE
- PICTURED ROCKS
- ST. CROIX RIVERWAY
- MISSISSIPPI RIVER
- PIPESTONE

Wisconsin
- SLEEPING BEAR DUNES

Michigan

Iowa
- EFFIGY MOUNDS
- HERBERT HOOVER

Illinois
- LINCOLN HOME

Indiana
- INDIANA DUNES
- DAYTON AVIATION HERITAGE
- WILLIAM HOWARD TAFT
- GEORGE ROGERS CLARK
- LINCOLN BOYHOOD

Missouri
- HARRY S. TRUMAN
- BROWN v. BOARD OF EDUCATION
- ULYSSES S. GRANT
- JEFFERSON NATIONAL EXPANSION MEMORIAL
- FORT SCOTT
- GEORGE WASHINGTON CARVER
- WILSON'S CREEK
- OZARK RIVERWAYS
- PEA RIDGE
- BUFFALO RIVER

Arkansas
- FORT SMITH
- LITTLE ROCK CENTRAL HIGH SCHOOL
- HOT SPRINGS
- ARKANSAS POST

Ohio
- PERRY'S VICTORY
- JAMES A. GARFIELD
- CUYAHOGA VALLEY
- FIRST LADIES
- HOPEWELL CULTURE

Kentucky
- ABRAHAM LINCOLN BIRTHPLACE
- MAMMOTH CAVE
- BIG SOUTH FORK
- CUMBERLAND GAP

Tennessee
- FORT DONELSON
- OBED RIVER
- ANDREW JOHNSON
- STONES RIVER
- GREAT SMOKY MOUNTAINS
- SHILOH
- RUSSELL CAVE
- BRICES CROSS ROADS
- LITTLE RIVER CANYON
- TUPELO

Alabama
- KENNESAW MOUNTAIN
- HORSESHOE BEND
- TUSKEGEE AIRMEN
- TUSKEGEE INSTITUTE

Mississippi
- NATCHEZ TRACE PARKWAY and SCENIC TRAIL
- VICKSBURG
- POVERTY POINT
- CANE RIVER CREOLE
- NATCHEZ

Louisiana
- BIG THICKET
- NEW ORLEANS JAZZ
- GULF ISLANDS
- JEAN LAFITTE

West Virginia
- FRIENDSHIP HILL
- HARPERS FERRY
- CEDAR CREEK AND BELLE GROVE
- GAULEY RIVER
- NEW RIVER GORGE
- BLUESTONE RIVER
- SHENANDOAH

Pennsylvania
- ALLEGHENY PORTAGE RAILROAD
- JOHNSTOWN FLOOD
- FLIGHT 93
- FORT NECESSITY
- HOPEWELL FURNACE
- GETTYSBURG
- EISENHOWER
- STEAMTOWN
- UPPER DELAWARE RIVER
- DELAWARE WATER GAP
- VALLEY FORGE
- Philadelphia

New York
- WOMEN'S RIGHTS
- MARTIN VAN BUREN
- T. ROOSEVELT INAUGURAL
- FORT STANWIX
- SARATOGA
- DELAWARE RIVER
- MORRISTOWN
- New York City

Maine
- ST. CROIX ISLAND
- ACADIA

Vermont
- MARSH-BILLINGS-ROCKEFELLER

New Hampshire
- SAINT-GAUDENS
- LOWELL
- Boston
- Mass.
- SPRINGFIELD ARMORY
- CAPE COD
- NEW BEDFORD WHALING
- Conn.
- R.I.
- ROGER WILLIAMS
- WEIR FARM
- ELEANOR ROOSEVELT, HOME OF F. D. ROOSEVELT, VANDERBILT MANSION
- New Jersey
- GREAT EGG HARBOR

Maryland / Delaware / Virginia
- HAMPTON
- FORT McHENRY
- Washington, D.C.
- PRINCE WILLIAM FOREST PARK
- THOMAS STONE
- GEORGE WASHINGTON BIRTHPLACE
- ANTIETAM, MONOCACY
- MANASSAS
- FREDERICKSBURG AND SPOTSYLVANIA
- MAGGIE L. WALKER
- Richmond
- COLONIAL
- APPOMATTOX COURT HOUSE
- PETERSBURG
- WRIGHT BROTHERS
- FORT RALEIGH
- BOOKER T. WASHINGTON
- CAPE HATTERAS
- ASSATEAGUE ISLAND

North Carolina
- GUILFORD COURTHOUSE
- BLUE RIDGE PARKWAY
- CARL SANDBURG HOME
- MOORES CREEK
- CAPE LOOKOUT

South Carolina
- COWPENS
- KINGS MOUNTAIN
- CHICKAMAUGA AND CHATTANOOGA
- CHATTAHOOCHEE RIVER
- NINETY SIX
- CONGAREE
- CHARLES PINCKNEY
- FORT SUMTER

Georgia
- MARTIN LUTHER KING, JR.
- OCMULGEE
- ANDERSONVILLE
- JIMMY CARTER
- FORT FREDERICA
- FORT PULASKI
- CUMBERLAND ISLAND
- TIMUCUAN
- FORT CAROLINE
- CASTILLO DE SAN MARCOS
- FORT MATANZAS

Florida
- CANAVERAL
- DE SOTO
- BIG CYPRESS
- BISCAYNE
- EVERGLADES
- DRY TORTUGAS

Appalachian Scenic Trail

Boston area
- ● BOSTON HARBOR ISLANDS
- ◆ BOSTON AFRICAN AMERICAN, FREDERICK LAW OLMSTED, JOHN FITZGERALD KENNEDY, LONGFELLOW, SALEM MARITIME, SAUGUS IRON WORKS
- ● ADAMS, BOSTON, MINUTE MAN

New York City area
- ● GATEWAY
- ● AFRICAN BURIAL GROUND, CASTLE CLINTON, GOVERNORS ISLAND, STATUE OF LIBERTY
- ◆ EDISON, SAGAMORE HILL, SAINT PAUL'S CHURCH, T. ROOSEVELT BIRTHPLACE
- ◆ FEDERAL HALL, GENERAL GRANT, HAMILTON GRANGE
- ■ FIRE ISLAND

Philadelphia area
- ◆ EDGAR ALLAN POE
- ◆ THADDEUS KOSCIUSZKO
- ● INDEPENDENCE

Washington, D.C. area
- ◆ CLARA BARTON, FORD'S THEATRE, FREDERICK DOUGLASS, MARY McLEOD BETHUNE COUNCIL HOUSE, PENNSYLVANIA AVENUE
- ◆ ARLINGTON HOUSE, FRANKLIN DELANO ROOSEVELT MEMORIAL, KOREAN WAR VETERANS, LINCOLN MEMORIAL, LYNDON B. JOHNSON GROVE, NATIONAL WORLD WAR II MEMORIAL, T. ROOSEVELT ISLAND, THOMAS JEFFERSON, VIETNAM VETERANS, WASHINGTON MONUMENT
- ▲ CONSTITUTION GARDENS, FORT WASHINGTON PARK, GEORGE WASHINGTON MEMORIAL PARKWAY, GREENBELT PARK, NATIONAL CAPITAL PARKS, NATIONAL MALL, PISCATAWAY PARK, POTOMAC HERITAGE SCENIC TRAIL, ROCK CREEK PARK, WHITE HOUSE, WOLF TRAP NATIONAL PARK FOR THE PERFORMING ARTS
- ● CHESAPEAKE AND OHIO CANAL

American Samoa
- AMERICAN SAMOA

Puerto Rico
- SAN JUAN

Virgin Islands
- VIRGIN ISLANDS CORAL REEF
- VIRGIN ISLANDS
- BUCK ISLAND REEF
- SALT RIVER BAY
- CHRISTIANSTED

Continued from page 43
its strange and beautiful rock formations. It has the lowest land surface in the Western Hemisphere—282 feet (86 meters) below sea level.

Many national monuments are preserved for unusual natural features. Among these national monuments are Agate Fossil Beds National Monument in Nebraska, which has deposits of ancient animal fossils, and Craters of the Moon National Monument in Idaho, which features lava fields with volcanic caves, cinder cones, craters, and tunnels.

Areas preserved for historical importance include ancient ruins, such as the remains at Georgia's Ocmulgee National Monument of American Indian mounds and towns, some dating from 8000 B.C. Other areas honor important people or events in the history of the United States. These areas include battlefields, forts, and other military sites, and historic bridges, buildings, dams, canals, and farms.

The homes of many United States presidents and other noted Americans are among the national historic sites. The most famous historical area is probably the White House, in Washington, D.C.

The historical areas look much as they did when they became important. Staff members sometimes restore buildings and natural features, raise animals on the farms, and wear clothing styles from the past.

Areas preserved for recreational use. National recreation areas, national seashores, and national lakeshores provide land and water resources for outdoor activities. For example, 68 miles (109 kilometers) of white

sand beaches and dunes line the Gulf of Mexico at Padre Island National Seashore in Texas. The area's fishing, horseback riding, sailing, and swimming attract visitors from all parts of the country.

In other areas of the National Park System, such features as roads, trails, and water reservoirs have been developed to provide recreational opportunities. For example, one of the world's largest artificially created lakes, 250-square-mile (650-square-kilometer) Lake Mead, is a popular playground for water sports. Formed by Hoover Dam, the lake is part of the Lake Mead National Recreation Area, which lies partly in Arizona and partly in Nevada.

The park system also has cultural areas that provide attractive settings for fine arts performances. One such area is the Wolf Trap National Park for the Performing Arts in northeastern Virginia, which presents concerts and other fine arts programs in its auditorium. Lawns around the auditorium provide seating space for thousands of additional people.

Visiting the parklands

Hundreds of millions of people visit the parklands in the National Park System each year. Many parklands offer free admission. Some areas allow camping or have lodgings for overnight stays.

Planning a visit. Learning about a parkland beforehand will increase the enjoyment of a visit. It is helpful to know what natural or historical features to look for and why they are important. For an overnight stay, visitors should find out whether the area has lodgings or campgrounds that will be open. It is also useful to know about available services and recreational activities, traveling routes, and various fees.

The tables with this article show which parklands have overnight lodgings, permit camping, are closed part of the year, or are not yet open to the public. The National Park Service provides additional information through its website at http://www.nps.gov to help plan a park visit.

Visitors should stop at a parkland's visitor center for pamphlets and maps that provide information about the area's features and activities. At many parklands, staff members offer campfire talks, guided trips, and amphitheater programs.

Visitors' costs. About two-thirds of the parklands are free to the public. The others charge a daily entrance fee. People younger than 16 and organized groups of high school age pay no entrance fee.

The United States government sells passes that may be used for a year at all parklands and certain other U.S. recreational lands that charge an entrance fee. People 62 or older may obtain an inexpensive lifetime pass. People with permanent disabilities may obtain a free lifetime pass. People who perform at least 500 hours of volunteer service for the National Park Service or for other agencies that maintain federal lands may obtain a free one-year pass.

Overnight lodgings vary in price, according to quality. They include cabins, cottages, lodges, motels, hotels, and trailer villages. These lodgings, available in dozens of areas, are operated privately under contract with the National Park Service. Visitors should make reservations early. The busiest periods, except in warm climates, are

Types of areas*

Classification	Number	Area In acres	In hectares
National parks	58	52,095,195	21,082,177
National recreation areas	18	3,700,833	1,497,674
National monuments	74	2,026,732	820,192
National historic sites	75	33,979	13,753
National memorials	28	10,642	4,306
National military parks	9	41,694	16,873
National battlefields	11	14,547	5,888
National battlefield parks	3	15,057	6,094
National battlefield site	1	1	0.4
National parkways and other parklands			
National parkways	4	178,159	72,098
International historic site	1	45	18
National reserves	2	33,740	13,654
National rivers	5	426,349	172,538
National scenic trails	3	247,710	100,245
National wild and scenic rivers and riverways	10	325,940	131,905
Other parklands	11	36,926	14,944
National historical parks	45	182,622	73,902
National seashores	10	596,561	241,421
National lakeshores	4	229,051	92,694
National preserves	18	24,184,651	9,787,180
Total	390	84,380,435	34,147,556

*Listed in the order that they appear in the following tables in this article.

from late May to mid-October, and weekends and holidays the rest of the year.

Camping is permitted in about 100 national parklands—in the wilderness or on campgrounds. A wilderness site may be a great distance from such conveniences as drinking water and food supplies. Wilderness campers must notify the superintendent or a park ranger of their plans. Back-country camping opportunities are available in more than 100 parks.

Inexperienced campers should camp on campgrounds. Some of these sites have few conveniences, and others have many, including play areas for children. Some campgrounds are designed for individuals or for families or other small groups. Other sites are intended for large, organized groups, such as school groups. Reservations can be made for group sites. Commercial reservation service is available for a few popular campgrounds. For camping tips, see the **Camping** article.

Visitors' responsibilities. Visitors share with park rangers the responsibility of protecting the parklands. Carelessness can start a forest fire that could destroy lives and valuable resources. Visitors are not allowed to remove or damage any natural feature—not even a flower. The National Park Service repeatedly warns the public not to feed, tease, or touch any animals of the parklands.

Preserving the parklands

Limits on activities. To keep the parklands in an unspoiled condition, the National Park Service strives to disturb the plant and animal life as little as possible. The Park Service allows fishing, but hunting, lumbering, and mining are prohibited in most areas. Livestock grazing is limited and is steadily being eliminated. In most areas, water resources may not be used for such purposes as irrigation or the production of hydroelectric power.

The National Park Service encourages recreational activities in the parklands if they do not disturb the surroundings. The service tries to teach people about the natural processes that have made the land of each area what it is. Park rangers and other staff members are trained to explain natural and scientific features to visitors. The service also encourages research and educational activities in all the nation's parklands.

Fires are an essential process in many natural areas, including forests and prairies. For this reason, the Park Service permits fires started by lightning to burn in certain parks, as long as the flames do not threaten human lives, buildings, or rare resources. But the Park Service fights any fire started by people, such as careless campers or smokers.

Crowds. The ever-increasing number of visitors puts pressure on the national parklands. Problems include demands for such basic services as food, water, lodging, and transportation. Only through careful planning and management can these problems be handled without spoiling the parklands. Otherwise, overcrowding could result in too much automobile traffic, air pollution from automobile fumes and campfire smoke, dirty streams, and jammed campgrounds.

The National Park Service has taken many steps to correct early mistakes in parkland development. It has tightened controls on air and water pollution, food supplies, and health care. In Yosemite National Park, for ex-

ample, public transportation was begun to reduce automobile traffic. The National Park Service also cut the number of campers permitted in overcrowded Yosemite Valley.

Establishing new parklands

National parks can be created only through acts of the U.S. Congress. Congress must also approve nearly all other new areas for the National Park System. The president may establish a national monument if the government owns the land. The secretary of the interior may approve a national historic site.

Congressional committees usually hold hearings about adding particular lands to the park system. The secretary of the interior makes recommendations based on a study of an area's significance conducted by Park Service personnel.

The National Park Service acquires new land through donations, exchanges, purchases, or reassignment of federal properties. Many parklands in the system include some land that the government does not own. The government is gradually acquiring these sections. Dozens of areas are owned by state, local, or private agencies. The National Park Service may contribute funds or provide technical advice and assistance to the agencies that manage these areas.

Continued on page 58

Redwood National Park is a redwood forest with some of the world's tallest trees. Visitors enjoy hiking in the forest.

National parks*

Name	Area In acres	In hectares	Location	Outstanding features
Acadia†‡	47,455	19,204	Maine	Highest land on Atlantic Coast of United States
American Samoa	9,000	3,642	American Samoa	Tropical rain forests with rare animal and plant life; white sand beaches and coral reefs
Arches†	76,679	31,031	Utah	Naturally formed rock arches, windows, and towers
Badlands†‡	242,756	98,240	South Dakota	Rugged ravines, ridges, and cliffs; prehistoric fossils
Big Bend†‡	801,163	324,219	Texas	Chisos Mountains and Desert in big bend of Rio Grande
Biscayne†	172,971	69,999	Florida	Living coral reef in Atlantic Ocean and Biscayne Bay
Black Canyon of the Gunnison†	30,750	12,444	Colorado	Steep-walled canyon with shadowed depths
Bryce Canyon†‡	35,835	14,502	Utah	Oddly shaped, beautifully colored rock formations
Canyonlands†	337,598	136,621	Utah	Canyons, mesas, and sandstone spires; 1,000-year-old Indian rock carvings
Capitol Reef†	241,904	97,895	Utah	Colorful ridge with white dome-shaped rock
Carlsbad Caverns	46,766	18,926	New Mexico	Huge underground caves with strange rock formations
Channel Islands†	249,561	100,994	California	Sea lion breeding place; nesting sea birds; animal fossils
Congaree†	26,546	10,743	South Carolina	Old-growth hardwood forest; wildlife sanctuary
Crater Lake†‡	183,224	74,148	Oregon	Lake in dead volcano; colorful lava walls almost 2,000 feet (610 meters) high
Cuyahoga Valley†‡	32,856	13,296	Ohio	About 20 miles (30 kilometers) of Cuyahoga River from Akron, Ohio, to Cleveland, Ohio
Death Valley†‡	3,373,042	1,365,021	California, Nevada	Great desert famous in Western history; lowest land surface in the Western Hemisphere
Denali†‡	4,740,911	1,918,579	Alaska	Mount McKinley, highest mountain in North America
Dry Tortugas†	64,701	26,184	Florida	Unusual bird and marine life; historic Fort Jefferson
Everglades†‡	1,509,152	610,732	Florida	Subtropical wilderness with plentiful wildlife
Gates of the Arctic	7,523,897	3,044,813	Alaska	Jagged peaks, Arctic valleys, wild rivers, and many lakes
Glacier†‡	1,013,322	410,076	Montana	Glaciers and lakes among towering Rocky Mountain peaks
Glacier Bay†‡	3,223,384	1,304,457	Alaska	Glaciers that move down mountainsides and into the sea
Grand Canyon†‡	1,217,403	492,666	Arizona	Canyon 1 mile (1.6 kilometers) deep with brightly colored walls and rock shapes
Grand Teton†‡	310,044	125,470	Wyoming	Rugged Teton peaks; winter feeding ground for elk
Great Basin†	77,180	31,234	Nevada	Jagged peaks, bristlecone pines, and limestone caves
Great Sand Dunes†	44,246	17,906	Colorado	Some of the largest and highest dunes in the United States
Great Smoky Mountains†‡	522,419	211,415	North Carolina, Tennessee	High mountains; large hardwood and evergreen forests
Guadalupe Mountains†	86,416	34,971	Texas	Fossil limestone reef; evergreen forest overlooking desert
Haleakala†‡	33,223	13,445	Hawaii	Inactive volcano with large, colorful crater
Hawaii Volcanoes†‡	323,431	130,888	Hawaii	Two active volcanoes; rare plants and animals
Hot Springs†	5,550	2,246	Arkansas	Mineral springs at base of Hot Springs Mountain
Isle Royale†‡§	571,790	231,395	Michigan	Island wilderness with large moose herd and wolves
Joshua Tree†	790,636	319,960	California	Joshua trees; desert plants and animals
Katmai†	3,674,378	1,486,968	Alaska	Valley of Ten Thousand Smokes, scene of 1912 volcanic eruption
Kenai Fjords	669,984	271,133	Alaska	The Harding Icefield, one of the major U.S. icecaps
Kings Canyon†‡	461,901	186,925	California	Mountain wilderness of giant sequoia trees
Kobuk Valley‡	1,750,716	708,490	Alaska	Rich in Arctic wildlife, including caribou, bears, and wolves; archaeological sites
Lake Clark‡	2,619,733	1,060,168	Alaska	Jagged peaks, granite spires, glaciers, and two volcanoes
Lassen Volcanic†‡	106,452	43,080	California	Active volcano; steep domes of lava
Mammoth Cave†‡	52,830	21,380	Kentucky	Huge cave with 212 miles (341 kilometers) of corridors
Mesa Verde†‡	52,485	21,240	Colorado	Ancient Indian cliff dwellings
Mount Rainier†‡	236,381	95,660	Washington	Greatest single-peak glacier system in United States
North Cascades†	504,781	204,278	Washington	Mountain wilderness with glaciers, lakes, and waterfalls
Olympic†‡	922,650	373,384	Washington	Oceanside mountain wilderness with rain forest and elk
Petrified Forest	221,621	89,687	Arizona	Ancient, rock-hard wood; Indian ruins; Painted Desert
Redwood†‡	112,618	45,575	California	World's tallest living tree in coastal redwood forest
Rocky Mountain†	265,758	107,548	Colorado	More than 100 peaks over 11,000 feet (3,350 meters) high
Saguaro	91,440	37,004	Arizona	Cactus forest, including giant saguaro cactuses
Sequoia†‡	404,063	163,518	California	Giant sequoia trees; Mount Whitney
Shenandoah†‡	199,100	80,573	Virginia	Blue Ridge Mountains; hardwood forest; Skyline Drive
Theodore Roosevelt†	70,447	28,509	North Dakota	Badlands along Little Missouri River and part of President Theodore Roosevelt's ranch
Virgin Islands†‡	14,737	5,964	Virgin Islands	White beaches; tropical plants and animals

See footnotes at end of table.

Continued on next page

National parks*

Name	Area In acres	In hectares	Location	Outstanding features
Voyageurs†‡	218,210	88,306	Minnesota	Beautiful northern forests of aspen, birch, pine, and spruce; more than 50 lakes
Wind Cave†	28,291	11,449	South Dakota	Limestone caverns; prairie wildlife
Wrangell-St. Elias†‡	8,323,147	3,368,258	Alaska	Country's largest collection of glaciers and of peaks more than 16,000 feet (4,877 meters)
Yellowstone†‡	2,219,791	898,318	Idaho, Montana, Wyoming	World's greatest geyser area; canyons and waterfalls; wide variety of wildlife
Yosemite†‡	761,268	308,074	California	Mountain scenery with deep gorges and high waterfalls
Zion†‡	146,597	59,326	Utah	Colorful canyons and mesas

*Each national park has a separate article in *World Book.*   †Camping permitted.   ‡Has overnight lodging.   §Closed part of the year.

National recreation areas

Name	Area In acres	In hectares	Location	Outstanding features
Amistad†	58,500	23,674	Texas	U.S. part of Amistad Reservoir on Rio Grande
Bighorn Canyon†	120,296	48,682	Montana, Wyoming	Reservoir created by Yellowtail Dam
Boston Harbor Islands	1,482	600	Massachusetts	Islands in Massachusetts Bay
Chattahoochee River	9,886	4,001	Georgia	48-mile (77-kilometer) stretch of the river
Chickasaw†	9,899	4,006	Oklahoma	Cold mineral springs; Lake of the Arbuckles
Curecanti†	41,972	16,986	Colorado	Blue Mesa and Morrow Point reservoirs
Delaware Water Gap	66,741	27,009	New Jersey, Pennsylvania	Scenery along Delaware River
Gateway	26,607	10,767	New Jersey, New York	Park in urban harbor area
Gauley River	11,560	4,678	West Virginia	White-water rapids; gorges and valleys
Glen Canyon†‡	1,254,117	507,523	Arizona, Utah	Lake Powell, formed by Glen Canyon Dam
Golden Gate	80,041	32,391	California	Urban recreational park
Lake Chelan†‡	61,949	25,070	Washington	Snow-fed Lake Chelan in forested valley
Lake Mead†‡	1,495,664	605,274	Arizona, Nevada	Lake Mead, formed by Hoover Dam; Lake Mohave, formed by Davis Dam
Lake Meredith†	44,978	18,202	Texas	Lake Meredith on Canadian River
Lake Roosevelt†	100,390	40,627	Washington	Franklin D. Roosevelt Lake; Grand Coulee Dam
Ross Lake†‡	117,575	47,581	Washington	Lakes and valleys among snow-capped peaks
Santa Monica Mountains†	156,673	63,403	California	Beaches, uplands and highlands
Whiskeytown-Shasta-Trinity†	42,503	17,200	California	Whiskeytown Reservoir, formed by Whiskeytown Dam

†Camping permitted.   ‡Has overnight lodging.

© Terry Donnelly/The Image Bank from Getty Images

Great Smoky Mountains National Park lies in the Great Smoky Mountains, on the boundary between North Carolina and Tennessee. The park contains about 150 kinds of trees, including the most extensive virgin hardwood and red spruce forests in the United States.

Wrangell-St. Elias National Park, in southeastern Alaska, is the largest national park in the United States. It covers more than 8 million acres (3 million hectares) and features many towering mountain peaks and glaciers.

National monuments

Name	Area In acres	Area In hectares	Location	Outstanding features
African Burial Ground	0.35	0.14	New York	Burial ground of about 15,000 free and enslaved Africans from the late 1600's to the mid-1790's
Agate Fossil Beds*	3,058	1,238	Nebraska	Deposits of animal fossils
Alibates Flint Quarries	1,371	555	Texas	Site of quarry used by prehistoric Indians in making tools and weapons
Aniakchak†	137,176	55,513	Alaska	30-square-mile (78-square-kilometer) crater in the Aleutian Mountains
Aztec Ruins*	318	129	New Mexico	Ruins of large Indian settlement of the 1100's
Bandelier†	33,677	13,629	New Mexico	Ruins of prehistoric Indian pueblos and cliff dwellings; canyons
Booker T. Washington*	239	97	Virginia	Birthplace and childhood home of famous African American leader and educator
Buck Island Reef*	19,015	7,695	Virgin Islands	Marine garden in Caribbean Sea
Cabrillo*	160	65	California	Memorial to Juan Rodríguez Cabrillo, the first European to reach the West Coast
Canyon de Chelly*†‡	83,840	33,929	Arizona	Ancient Indian ruins at base of cliffs and in caves
Cape Krusenstern‡	649,082	262,674	Alaska	Archaeological sites of Inuit (Eskimo) communities dating back 4,000 years
Capulin Volcano*	793	321	New Mexico	Cinder cone of dead volcano, with trails around rim and into crater
Casa Grande Ruins*	473	191	Arizona	Ruins of an adobe tower built by Indians 600 years ago
Castillo de San Marcos*	18	7	Florida	Fort begun by Spaniards in 1672 to defend St. Augustine
Castle Clinton*	1	0.4	New York	Landing depot for 8 ¼ million immigrants from 1855 to 1890
Cedar Breaks†	6,155	2,491	Utah	Natural amphitheater in colorful Pink Cliffs
Chiricahua†	11,985	4,850	Arizona	Strange, rocky landscape formed by nearly a billion years of erosion
Colorado*†	20,534	8,310	Colorado	Canyons and unusual sandstone formations
Craters of the Moon†	53,571	21,679	Idaho	Lava fields with volcanic caves, cinder cones, craters, and tunnels
Devils Postpile†§	798	323	California	Remains of lava flow forming rock columns up to 60 feet (18 meters) high
Devils Tower*†	1,347	545	Wyoming	Volcanic rock tower 865 feet (264 meters) high
Dinosaur†	210,278	85,096	Colorado, Utah	Fossil deposits of dinosaurs and other prehistoric animals; canyons cut by rivers
Effigy Mounds*	2,526	1,022	Iowa	Indian mounds in shapes of bears and birds
El Malpais	114,277	46,246	New Mexico	Unusual lava formations; historic Indian areas

See footnotes at end of table.

Continued on next page

National monuments

Name	Area In acres	In hectares	Location	Outstanding features
El Morro†	1,279	518	New Mexico	Soft sandstone with prehistoric rock carvings; inscriptions by early explorers and settlers
Florissant Fossil Beds*	5,998	2,427	Colorado	Fossil insects, leaves, seeds, and tree stumps
Fort Frederica*	284	115	Georgia	Built between 1736 and 1748 to protect British colonists from Spaniards
Fort Matanzas*	300	121	Florida	Spanish fort built in the 1740's to protect St. Augustine from French
Fort McHenry*	43	18	Maryland	Defended against British in War of 1812; battle inspired Francis Scott Key to write "The Star-Spangled Banner"
Fort Pulaski*	5,623	2,276	Georgia	Captured by Union forces during Civil War
Fort Stanwix*	16	6	New York	Site of treaty with Iroquois Indians in 1768 and American Revolution siege in 1777
Fort Sumter*	235	95	South Carolina	Site of beginning of American Civil War
Fort Union*	721	292	New Mexico	Ruins of fort built in 1851 to protect travelers on Santa Fe Trail
Fossil Butte*	8,198	3,318	Wyoming	Fish fossils from 40 million to 65 million years old
George Washington Birthplace*	662	268	Virginia	Plantation where Washington was born; memorial mansion and gardens
George Washington Carver*	210	85	Missouri	Birthplace and boyhood home of famous African American scientist
Gila Cliff Dwellings*	533	216	New Mexico	Prehistoric dwellings in overhanging cliff
Governors Island	23	9	New York	Historic outpost protecting New York harbor
Grand Portage*	710	287	Minnesota	Fur-trading post on portage of canoe route to Northwest
Hagerman Fossil Beds	4,351	1,761	Idaho	Fossil beds along banks of Snake River
Hohokam Pima#	1,690	684	Arizona	Remains of settlement of Hohokam Indians, ancestors of the Pima Indians
Homestead	211	85	Nebraska	One of the first land claims under Homestead Act of 1862
Hovenweep†	785	318	Colorado, Utah	Prehistoric Indian cliff dwellings, pueblos, and towers
Jewel Cave*	1,274	515	South Dakota	Underground limestone chambers connected by narrow corridors
John Day Fossil Beds*	13,944	5,643	Oregon	Plant and animal fossils from five consecutive epochs in Earth's history
Lava Beds*†	46,560	18,842	California	Unusual caves, cinder cones, and other results of volcanic action
Little Bighorn Battlefield*	765	310	Montana	Site of Battle of Little Bighorn in 1876
Montezuma Castle*	859	348	Arizona	Indian dwellings in limestone cliff
Muir Woods*	554	224	California	Grove of coast redwood trees
Natural Bridges†	7,636	3,090	Utah	Three gigantic natural bridges of sandstone
Navajo†	360	146	Arizona	Ruins of prehistoric Indian cliff dwellings
Ocmulgee*	702	284	Georgia	Remains of Indian mounds and towns, some dating from 8000 B.C.
Oregon Caves‡	488	197	Oregon	Limestone caverns with rock formations
Organ Pipe Cactus†	330,689	133,825	Arizona	Organ-pipe cactuses and other desert plants found nowhere else in United States
Petroglyph	7,272	2,943	New Mexico	Ancient Indian and Hispanic rock carvings
Pinnacles†	26,523	10,733	California	Spirelike rock formations from 500 to 1,200 feet (150 to 366 meters) high; many caves
Pipe Spring*	40	16	Arizona	Fort and other structures built by Mormon pioneers
Pipestone	282	114	Minnesota	Quarry where Indians took stone for making peace pipes
Poverty Point	911	369	Louisiana	Earth dwellings dating back 3,000 years
Rainbow Bridge*	160	65	Utah	Largest known natural bridge—290 feet (88 meters) high and 275 feet (84 meters) across
Russell Cave	310	126	Alabama	Tools and other evidence of human life from 7000 B.C. to A.D. 1650
Salinas Pueblo Missions	1,071	434	New Mexico	Ruins of Spanish missions and Indian pueblos
Scotts Bluff	3,005	1,216	Nebraska	Landmark on Oregon Trail
Statue of Liberty*	61	25	New Jersey, New York	Including pedestal, the world's tallest statue; gift of France
Sunset Crater Volcano†	3,040	1,230	Arizona	Volcanic cinder cone and crater formed about A.D. 1100
Timpanogos Cave*§	250	101	Utah	Limestone caverns known for coloring and twig-shaped wall formations
Tonto	1,120	453	Arizona	Indian cliff dwellings dating from 1300's

See footnotes at end of table.

Continued on next page

National Park Service

AP/Wide World

Saint-Gaudens National Historic Site, in Cornish, New Hampshire, was once the home of the famous American sculptor Augustus Saint-Gaudens. The site includes his studio, *shown here.*

Oklahoma City National Memorial has chairs that represent the 168 people killed on April 19, 1995, when a terrorist bomb destroyed the Murrah Federal Building that stood on this site.

National monuments

Name	Area In acres	In hectares	Location	Outstanding features
Tuzigoot	812	329	Arizona	Ruins of prehistoric Indian pueblos
Virgin Islands Coral Reef	12,708	5,143	Virgin Islands	Caribbean tropical marine ecosystem
Walnut Canyon	3,529	1,428	Arizona	Ancient cliff pueblos built in shallow caves under limestone ledges
White Sands*	143,733	58,167	New Mexico	Glistening white dunes of gypsum sand
World War II Valor in the Pacific	54	22	Alaska, California, Hawaii	Nine historic sites, including the USS *Arizona* Memorial, that commemorate the war in the Pacific
Wupatki*	35,422	14,335	Arizona	Red sandstone pueblos built by prehistoric Indians
Yucca House	34	14	Colorado	Ruins of large prehistoric Indian pueblo

*Has a separate article in *World Book.*   †Camping permitted.   ‡Has overnight lodging.   §Closed part of the year.   #Not open to the public.

National historic sites

Name	Area In acres	In hectares	Location	Outstanding features
Allegheny Portage Railroad	1,284	520	Pennsylvania	Honors Pennsylvania Canal and the railroad that carried canal boat passengers and cargoes over Allegheny Mountains
Andersonville	515	208	Georgia	Confederate prison camp during American Civil War
Andrew Johnson	17	7	Tennessee	Andrew Johnson's home, tailor shop, and grave
Bent's Old Fort	799	323	Colorado	Important fur-trading post of Old West
Boston African American	0.59	0.24	Massachusetts	Black community dwellings of the early 1800's
Brown v. Board of Education	1.9	0.8	Kansas	Honors U.S. Supreme Court decision ending racial segregation of schools at the site of Monroe School
Carl Sandburg Home	264	107	North Carolina	The poet's home and farm
Charles Pinckney	28	12	South Carolina	Estate of early American political leader
Christiansted	27	11	Virgin Islands	Honors Danish colonial development of Virgin Islands
Clara Barton	8.6	3.5	Maryland	Home of American Red Cross founder Clara Barton
Edgar Allan Poe	0.52	0.21	Pennsylvania	Home of American author Edgar Allan Poe
Eisenhower	690	279	Pennsylvania	Home and farm of Dwight D. Eisenhower during and after his presidency
Eleanor Roosevelt	181	73	New York	Val-Kill estate built for the first lady by her husband
Eugene O'Neill	13	5	California	Home of American playwright Eugene O'Neill
First Ladies	0.33	0.13	Ohio	Home of First Lady Ida Saxton McKinley
Ford's Theatre	0.30	0.12	District of Columbia	Ford's Theatre, where President Lincoln was shot, and the nearby house where he died; Lincoln Museum
Fort Bowie	999	404	Arizona	Military headquarters for operations against Geronimo and his Apache warriors
Fort Davis	474	192	Texas	Major fort in west Texas defense system against Apache and Comanche Indians
Fort Laramie	833	337	Wyoming	Major post that guarded covered wagons going west
Fort Larned	718	291	Kansas	Protection of Santa Fe Trail

See footnotes at end of table.

Continued on next page

National historic sites

Name	Area In acres	In hectares	Location	Outstanding features
Fort Point	29	12	California	Brick and granite fort of mid-1800's
Fort Raleigh	513	208	North Carolina	Site of first attempted English settlement in what is now United States, in 1585
Fort Scott	17	7	Kansas	Honors historic events of American Civil War period
Fort Smith	75	30	Arkansas, Oklahoma	One of first U.S. military posts in Louisiana Territory
Fort Union Trading Post	442	179	Montana, North Dakota	Major fur-trading post in upper Missouri River region
Fort Vancouver	194	79	Washington	Western headquarters of Hudson's Bay Company
Frederick Douglass	8.6	3.5	District of Columbia	Last home of Frederick Douglass, a leading black abolitionist and civil rights leader of the 1800's
Frederick Law Olmsted	7.2	2.9	Massachusetts	Home of 1800's park planner Frederick Law Olmsted
Friendship Hill	675	273	Pennsylvania	Home of Albert Gallatin, secretary of the treasury under Presidents Jefferson and Madison
Golden Spike	2,735	1,107	Utah	Honors completion in 1869 of first coast-to-coast railroad system in United States
Grant-Kohrs Ranch	1,618	655	Montana	One of the largest range ranches of the 1800's
Hampton	62	25	Maryland	Great mansion built in late 1700's
Harry S. Truman	10.5	4.2	Missouri	Home of Harry and Bess Truman in Independence
Herbert Hoover	187	76	Iowa	Birthplace, boyhood home, and burial place of President Herbert Hoover
Home of Franklin D. Roosevelt	792	321	New York	Birthplace, home, "Summer White House," and burial place of President Franklin D. Roosevelt
Hopewell Furnace	848	343	Pennsylvania	Rural ironmaking village of the 1800's
Hubbell Trading Post	160	65	Arizona	Shows role of Indian traders in settling West
James A. Garfield	7.8	3.2	Ohio	Former estate of President James A. Garfield
Jimmy Carter	72	29	Georgia	Past and present homes of President Jimmy Carter
John Fitzgerald Kennedy	0.09	0.04	Massachusetts	Birthplace of President John F. Kennedy
John Muir	345	140	California	Honors contributions to conservation and literature by explorer-naturalist
Knife River Indian Villages	1,758	712	North Dakota	Five Hidatsa Indian villages of 1845
Lincoln Home	12	5	Illinois	Only private home owned by Abraham Lincoln
Little Rock Central High School	27	11	Arkansas	Site of 1957 confrontation in the struggle to integrate public schools
Longfellow	2	0.8	Massachusetts	Home of American poet Henry Wadsworth Longfellow
Maggie L. Walker	1.3	0.5	Virginia	Home of Maggie L. Walker, a black leader and the first woman president of an American bank
Manzanar	814	329	California	Site of Japanese American internment camp
Martin Luther King, Jr.*	39	16	Georgia	Birthplace, church, and burial place of Martin Luther King, Jr.
Martin Van Buren§	285	115	New York	Home of President Martin Van Buren
Mary McLeod Bethune Council House	0.07	0.03	District of Columbia	Honors political and civil rights leader and educator
Minuteman Missile	15	6	South Dakota	Site of missile silo and launch facility of Cold War era
Nicodemus	4.6	1.9	Kansas	Pioneer town established by African Americans after the American Civil War
Ninety Six	1,022	414	South Carolina	Colonial trading post held briefly by the British during the American Revolution
Pennsylvania Avenue*	**	**	District of Columbia	Portion of Pennsylvania Avenue between the White House and U.S. Capitol
Puukohola Heiau	86	35	Hawaii	Ruins of a temple built by King Kamehameha I, first ruler of the kingdom of Hawaii
Sagamore Hill	83	34	New York	Last home of President Theodore Roosevelt
Saint-Gaudens§	148	60	New Hampshire	Home, studio, and gardens of sculptor Augustus Saint-Gaudens
Saint Paul's Church	6.1	2.5	New York	Site of events leading to the 1735 libel trial of newspaper editor John Peter Zenger
Salem Maritime	9	3.6	Massachusetts	Derby Wharf and other important structures in New England history
San Juan	75	30	Puerto Rico	Spanish fort begun in 1539 to protect Bay of San Juan
Sand Creek Massacre	12,583	5,092	Colorado	Site of the 1864 massacre of more than 160 Indian men, women, and children
Saugus Iron Works	8.5	3.4	Massachusetts	One of first ironworks in North America, built in 1640's
Springfield Armory	55	22	Massachusetts	Produced small arms for nearly 200 years
Steamtown	62	25	Pennsylvania	Steam locomotives of the early 1900's
Theodore Roosevelt Birthplace	0.11	0.04	New York	Birthplace of President Theodore Roosevelt
Theodore Roosevelt Inaugural	1	0.4	New York	House where Theodore Roosevelt was sworn in as president

See footnotes at end of table.

Continued on next page

National historic sites

Name	Area		Location	Outstanding features
	In acres	In hectares		
Thomas Stone	328	133	Maryland	Home of early American political leader Thomas Stone
Tuskegee Airmen	90	36	Alabama	Moton Field, the training base of the all-black Tuskegee Airmen air corps unit of World War II
Tuskegee Institute	58	23	Alabama	Student-made college buildings; home of Booker T. Washington; George Washington Carver Museum
Ulysses S. Grant	9.6	3.9	Missouri	Estate where Grant lived during the years immediately preceding the American Civil War
Vanderbilt Mansion	212	86	New York	Magnificent country home built in 1890's
Washita Battlefield	315	128	Oklahoma	Site of one of the largest battles between the Southern Great Plains tribes and the United States Army
Weir Farm	74	30	Connecticut	Home of Impressionist painter J. Alden Weir
Whitman Mission†	139	56	Washington	Site where American Indians killed missionaries Marcus Whitman and his wife
William Howard Taft	3.1	1.3	Ohio	President William H. Taft's birthplace

*Has a separate article in *World Book*.   §Closed part of the year.   **Acreage undetermined.

National memorials

Name	Area		Location	Outstanding features
	In acres	In hectares		
Arkansas Post	758	307	Arkansas	First permanent white settlement in lower Mississippi Valley, founded in 1686
Arlington House, The Robert E. Lee Memorial	28	11	Virginia	Home of General Robert E. Lee
Chamizal	55	22	Texas	Honors peaceful settlement in 1963 of 99-year-old border dispute with Mexico
Coronado	4,750	1,922	Arizona	Honors Francisco Coronado's exploration of Southwest
De Soto	30	12	Florida	Near site of 1539 landing of explorer Hernando de Soto
Federal Hall	0.45	0.18	New York	Site of first U.S. Capitol, 1789-1790
Flight 93 National Memorial	2,322	940	Pennsylvania	Memorial to passengers and crew of United Airlines Flight 93 who died resisting terrorist hijackers on Sept. 11, 2001. The memorial marks the crash site in Somerset County, Pennsylvania.
Fort Caroline	138	56	Florida	Stockade overlooking attempted French settlement in 1560's
Franklin Delano Roosevelt Memorial*	7.5	3	District of Columbia	Sculpture garden honoring Roosevelt
General Grant	0.76	0.31	New York	Tombs of Ulysses and Julia Grant
Hamilton Grange	1	0.4	New York	Home of Alexander Hamilton
Jefferson National Expansion Memorial	91	37	Illinois, Missouri	Museum and Gateway Arch 630 feet (192 meters) high honor U.S. expansion west of Mississippi River
Johnstown Flood	178	72	Pennsylvania	Memorial to more than 2,000 people killed in Johnstown Flood of 1889
Korean War Veterans*	2.2	0.9	District of Columbia	Statues of infantry soldiers; granite wall with etched figures of support personnel.
Lincoln Boyhood	200	81	Indiana	Farm site of most of Abraham Lincoln's boyhood home
Lincoln Memorial*	107	43	District of Columbia	Marble building with a statue of Lincoln
Lyndon Baines Johnson Memorial Grove on the Potomac	17	7	District of Columbia	Grove of 500 white pines
Mount Rushmore*	1,278	517	South Dakota	Heads of four presidents carved on granite cliff
National World War II Memorial*	2.5	1	District of Columbia	Honors those who served in the U.S. armed forces in World War II
Oklahoma City	3.3	1.3	Oklahoma	Commemorates those killed in 1995 bombing
Perry's Victory and International Peace Memorial	25	10	Ohio	Near site of U.S. naval victory in War of 1812; honors peace among United States, Canada, and the United Kingdom
Roger Williams	4.6	1.9	Rhode Island	Honors founder of Rhode Island colony, a pioneer leader for religious freedom
Thaddeus Kosciuszko	0.02	0.008	Pennsylvania	Honors Polish patriot of the Revolutionary War
Theodore Roosevelt Island	89	36	District of Columbia	Wooded island in Potomac River
Thomas Jefferson (Jefferson Memorial*)	18	7	District of Columbia	Circular marble building with a statue of Thomas Jefferson 19 feet (5.8 meters) high
Vietnam Veterans*	2	0.8	District of Columbia	Memorial to U.S. personnel who died serving in Vietnam War
Washington Monument*	106	43	District of Columbia	Four-sided pillar 555 feet (169 meters) high honoring George Washington
Wright Brothers	428	173	North Carolina	Site of Wright brothers' first airplane flight

*Has a separate article in *World Book*.

National military parks

Name	Area In acres	In hectares	Location	Outstanding features
Chickamauga and Chattanooga	9,036	3,657	Georgia, Tennessee	American Civil War battles of 1863— Chickamauga, Lookout Mountain, Missionary Ridge, and Orchard Knob
Fredericksburg and Spotsylvania County Battlefields Memorial	8,382	3,392	Virginia	American Civil War battles of Chancellorsville, Fredericksburg, Wilderness, and Spotsylvania Court House; 1862-1864
Gettysburg	5,989	2,423	Pennsylvania	American Civil War battle that stopped Confederate invasion, 1863
Guilford Courthouse	243	98	North Carolina	Battle of the American Revolution that led to British defeat at Yorktown, 1781
Horseshoe Bend	2,040	826	Alabama	Battle won by Andrew Jackson ending Creek Indian War, 1814
Kings Mountain	3,945	1,597	South Carolina	American Revolution victory of American patriots, 1780
Pea Ridge	4,300	1,740	Arkansas	Important Union victory of Civil War, 1862
Shiloh	5,964	2,414	Mississippi, Tennessee	Civil War battle, 1862; led to fall of Vicksburg
Vicksburg	1,795	726	Louisiana, Mississippi	Battle that gave Union control of Mississippi River, 1863

National battlefields, national battlefield parks, and national battlefield sites

Name	Area In acres	In hectares	Location	Outstanding features
Antietam (NB)	3,230	1,307	Maryland	American Civil War battle that stopped first Confederate invasion of North, 1862
Big Hole (NB)	1,011	409	Montana	Battle between U.S. soldiers and Chief Joseph's forces in Nez Perce Indian War, 1877
Brices Cross Roads (NBS)	1	0.4	Mississippi	Large Union force defeated by outnumbered Confederate cavalrymen, 1864
Cowpens (NB)	842	341	South Carolina	American victory during the American Revolution, 1781
Fort Donelson (NB)	1,007	408	Kentucky, Tennessee	First major Union victory of Civil War, 1862
Fort Necessity (NB)	903	365	Pennsylvania	Early battle in French and Indian War, 1754
Kennesaw Mountain (NBP)	2,853	1,155	Georgia	Civil War battle during General William T. Sherman's march to Atlanta, 1864
Manassas (NBP)	5,073	2,053	Virginia	Two battles of Manassas (Bull Run) in American Civil War, 1861 and 1862
Monocacy (NB)	1,647	667	Maryland	Union forces delayed General Jubal A. Early's march on Washington, 1864
Moores Creek (NB)	88	36	North Carolina	Patriots' victory over Loyalists in American Revolution, 1776
Petersburg (NB)	2,740	1,109	Virginia	Siege of Confederate railroad center, 1864-1865
Richmond (NBP)	7,131	2,886	Virginia	Several Union attempts to capture Richmond
Stones River (NB)	709	287	Tennessee	Beginning of Union drive to divide Confederacy into three parts, 1862-1863
Tupelo (NB)	1	0.4	Mississippi	Battle over General William T. Sherman's supply line during march to Atlanta, 1864
Wilson's Creek (NB)	2,369	959	Missouri	Confederate victory over Union, 1861

National parkways and other national parklands

Name	Area In acres	In hectares	Location	Outstanding features
Alagnak Wild River	30,665	12,410	Alaska	Abundant wildlife and sport fishing
Appalachian National Scenic Trail*†	236,715	95,795	From Maine to Georgia	Wilderness trail through Appalachian Mountains; about 2,000 miles (3,200 kilometers)
Big South Fork National River and Recreation Area	125,310	50,711	Kentucky, Tennessee	A scenic fork of the Cumberland River
Blue Ridge Parkway†‡	95,158	38,509	North Carolina, Virginia	Scenic mountain parkway 469 miles (755 kilometers) long
Bluestone Scenic River	4,310	1,744	West Virginia	Portion of river in Appalachian Plateau
Buffalo National River†‡	94,293	38,159	Arkansas	High bluffs and deep valleys along river
Catoctin Mountain Park†‡	5,874	2,377	Maryland	Mountain scenery
City of Rocks National Reserve	14,407	5,830	Idaho	Unusual rock formations

See footnotes at end of table.

Continued on next page

National parkways and other national parklands

Name	Area In acres	In hectares	Location	Outstanding features
Constitution Gardens	52	21	District of Columbia	Island gardens that honor the signers of Declaration of Independence
Delaware National Scenic River	1,973	799	New Jersey, Pennsylvania	Portion of river in Delaware Water Gap National Recreation Area
Ebey's Landing National Historical Reserve	19,333	7,824	Washington	Historic farms, Victorian seaport community, coastal beaches and cliffs
Fort Washington Park	341	138	Maryland	Site of Fort Washington, built in 1814
George Washington Memorial Parkway	6,922	2,801	Maryland, Virginia	Potomac River sites associated with Washington's life; 49-mile (79-kilometer) road
Great Egg Harbor Scenic and Recreational River	43,311	17,528	New Jersey	Longest canoeing river in the Pine Barrens
Greenbelt Park†	1,175	476	Maryland	Woodland; marked trails
John D. Rockefeller, Jr., Memorial Parkway†‡	23,777	9,622	Wyoming	82-mile (132-kilometer) parkway between Yellowstone and Grand Teton national parks
Mississippi National River and Recreation Area	53,775	21,762	Minnesota	69-mile (111-kilometer) segment of Mississippi River in eastern Minnesota
Missouri National Recreational River	34,159	13,824	Nebraska, South Dakota	One of the last free-flowing stretches of the Missouri River
Natchez Trace National Scenic Trail	10,995	4,450	Alabama, Mississippi, Tennessee	694-mile (1,117-kilometer) trail extending from Nashville, TN, to Natchez, MS
Natchez Trace Parkway†	52,302	21,166	Alabama, Mississippi, Tennessee	Scenic 450-mile (724-kilometer) road along Indian and frontier trail
National Capital Parks	6,726	2,722	District of Columbia, Maryland, Virginia	A 346-unit park system in and near Washington, D.C.
National Mall	146	59	District of Columbia	Between Capitol and Washington Monument
New River Gorge National River	72,186	29,213	West Virginia	Rugged, white water river that flows northward through deep canyons
Niobrara National Scenic Riverway	29,101	11,777	Nebraska, South Dakota	40-mile (64-kilometer) segment of the Missouri River
Obed Wild and Scenic River	5,073	2,053	Tennessee	Rugged scenery along the Obed River
Ozark National Scenic Riverways†‡	80,785	32,693	Missouri	Narrow river park along Current and Jacks Fork rivers; caves and springs
Piscataway Park	4,626	1,872	Maryland	View from Mount Vernon
Potomac Heritage National Scenic Trail	**	**	District of Columbia, Maryland, Virginia, West Virginia	704-mile (1,133-kilometer) trail along banks of Potomac River
Prince William Forest Park†‡	16,083	6,509	Virginia	Woodland with about 90 kinds of trees
Rio Grande Wild and Scenic River	9,600	3,885	Texas	Includes 191 miles (307 kilometers) of the Rio Grande
Rock Creek Park	1,755	710	District of Columbia	Large urban park
Saint Croix Island International Historic Site*	45	18	Maine	Site of an early French settlement in North America; on Maine-New Brunswick border
Saint Croix National Scenic Riverway†‡	92,748	37,534	Minnesota, Wisconsin	About 250 miles (400 kilometers) of Saint Croix and Namekagon rivers
Upper Delaware Scenic and Recreational River†‡	75,000	30,351	New York, Pennsylvania	Includes 100 miles (161 kilometers) of free-flowing stream
White House*	18	7	District of Columbia	President's home and office
Wolf Trap National Park for the Performing Arts	130	53	Virginia	Concerts and dance performances in Filene Center auditorium

*Has a separate article in *World Book*.   †Camping permitted.   ‡Has overnight lodging.   **Acreage undetermined.

National historical parks

Name	Area In acres	In hectares	Location	Outstanding features
Abraham Lincoln Birthplace	345	139	Kentucky	Log cabin inside memorial building on site of Lincoln's birthplace
Adams†	24	10	Massachusetts	Home of Adams family, including Presidents John Adams and John Quincy Adams
Appomattox Court House	1,774	718	Virginia	Site of Gen. Robert E. Lee's surrender to Gen. Ulysses S. Grant
Boston	43	17	Massachusetts	Includes Bunker Hill, Faneuil Hall, Old North Church, Paul Revere House
Cane River Creole	206	83	Louisiana	Landscapes, sites, and buildings associated with development of Creole culture
Cedar Creek and Belle Grove	3,712	1,502	Virginia	Site of Civil War battlefields and historic plantation
Chaco Culture	33,960	13,743	New Mexico	Ruins of pueblos built by prehistoric Indians
Chesapeake and Ohio Canal†	19,612	7,937	District of Columbia, Maryland, West Virginia	One of the nation's oldest and least-changed lock canals for mule-drawn boats

See footnotes at end of table.

Continued on next page

National historical parks

Name	Area In acres	In hectares	Location	Outstanding features
Colonial	8,677	3,511	Virginia	Major sites of colonial development—Jamestown, Williamsburg, and Yorktown
Cumberland Gap†	22,376	9,055	Kentucky, Tennessee, Virginia	Famous mountain pass explored by Daniel Boone and used by pioneers heading west
Dayton Aviation Heritage	86	35	Ohio	Wright brothers' flying field
George Rogers Clark	26	11	Indiana	Honors Clark's American Revolution victories
Harpers Ferry	3,661	1,482	Maryland, Virginia, West, Virginia	Scene of 1859 raid by John Brown, foe of slavery, and his capture
Hopewell Culture	1,170	473	Ohio	Burial mounds of prehistoric Indians
Independence	45	18	Pennsylvania	Independence Hall and other buildings and sites related to founding of United States
Jean Lafitte	22,983	9,301	Louisiana	Scene of Battle of New Orleans in War of 1812
Kalaupapa	10,779	4,362	Hawaii	Leper colony on island of Molokai
Kaloko-Honokohau	1,163	471	Hawaii	Site of early Hawaiian settlements
Keweenaw	1,870	757	Michigan	Site of first significant U.S. copper mining
Klondike Gold Rush	12,996	5,259	Alaska, Washington	Sites honoring the Alaska gold rush
Lewis and Clark National Historical Park	3,303	1,337	Oregon, Washington	Several sites, including Fort Clatsop, where Lewis and Clark spent the winter of 1805-1806
Lowell	141	57	Massachusetts	America's first planned industrial community
Lyndon B. Johnson	1,570	635	Texas	President Lyndon B. Johnson's birthplace
Marsh-Billings-Rockefeller	643	260	Vermont	Boyhood home of George Perkins Marsh
Minute Man	1,019	412	Massachusetts	Landmarks of American Revolution battles
Morristown	1,711	692	New Jersey	Campsites in American Revolution; Washington's headquarters in 1777 and 1779-1780
Natchez	108	44	Mississippi	Southern estates of the early 1800's
New Bedford Whaling	34	14	Massachusetts	Buildings and artifacts of the whaling industry
New Orleans Jazz	5.1	2.1	Louisiana	Preserves the history of jazz in New Orleans
Nez Perce	4,570	1,849	Idaho, Montana, Oregon, Washington	Honors history and life of Nez Perce Indian region, and Lewis and Clark expedition
Palo Alto Battlefield	3,442	1,393	Texas	Site of one of two Mexican War battles fought in United States
Pecos	6,669	2,699	New Mexico	Ruins of Spanish mission of 1600's and Indian pueblos of 1450's
Pu'uhonua o Honaunau	420	170	Hawaii	Prehistoric house sites and royal fishponds
Rosie the Riveter	145	59	California	Sites honoring World War II home front efforts
Salt River Bay	986	399	U.S. Virgin Islands	Only known site on U.S. territory where a party of Columbus expedition landed
San Antonio Missions	826	334	Texas	Four Catholic frontier missions; related historic dam and aqueduct system
San Francisco Maritime	50	20	California	Preserved ships of the 1800's docked at pier; National Maritime Museum
San Juan Island	2,072	839	Washington	Honors peaceful settlement of boundary dispute with Canada and Britain in 1872
Saratoga	3,394	1,374	New York	American victory in American Revolution
Sitka	112	45	Alaska	Site of Tlingit Indians' last stand against Russian settlers in 1804
Thomas Edison	21	8	New Jersey	Laboratories and home of inventor Thomas A. Edison
Tumacácori	360	146	Arizona	Spanish mission building constructed in 1700's
Valley Forge	3,468	1,403	Pennsylvania	Winter campsite of Washington's Continental Army in 1777-1778
War in the Pacific	2,037	824	Guam	Memorial to those participating in Pacific theater of World War II
Women's Rights	7.4	3	New York	Commemorates the birth of the women's rights movement in 1848

*Has a separate article in *World Book*.   †Camping permitted.

National seashores

Name	Area In acres	In hectares	Location	Outstanding features
Assateague Island†	41,320	16,722	Maryland, Virginia	Beaches and wild Chincoteague ponies
Canaveral	57,662	23,335	Florida	Beaches and birdlife
Cape Cod	43,607	17,647	Massachusetts	Beaches, birdlife, dunes, and marshes
Cape Hatteras†	30,351	12,283	North Carolina	Beaches, dunes, and birdlife; "Graveyard of the Atlantic," scene of many shipwrecks
Cape Lookout	28,243	11,430	North Carolina	Beaches, dunes, salt marshes, and lighthouse
Cumberland Island	36,347	14,709	Georgia	Beaches, dunes, marshes, lakes, and forests
Fire Island†	19,580	7,924	New York	Beaches, dunes, marshes, and wildlife
Gulf Islands†	137,989	55,842	Florida, Mississippi	Beaches, offshore islands, and historic forts
Padre Island†	130,434	52,785	Texas	Beaches, bird and marine life
Point Reyes†	71,028	28,744	California	Beaches, cliffs, lagoons, and wildlife

†Camping permitted.

National lakeshores

Name	Area		Location	Outstanding features
	In acres	In hectares		
Apostle Islands†	69,372	28,074	Wisconsin	Cliffs and rock formations on islands in Lake Superior; also on Bayfield Peninsula
Indiana Dunes	15,152	6,132	Indiana	Dunes along Lake Michigan; woodlands
Pictured Rocks†	73,236	29,638	Michigan	Beaches, dunes, woods, and cliffs
Sleeping Bear Dunes†	71,291	28,850	Michigan	Beaches, dunes, woods, and lakes

†Camping permitted.

National preserves

Name	Area		Location	Outstanding features
	In acres	In hectares		
Aniakchak†	464,118	187,822	Alaska	Adjacent to Aniakchak National Monument; crater contains a lake, a river, and a volcano that last erupted in 1931
Bering Land Bridge†	2,697,391	1,091,595	Alaska	Remains of land bridge that once connected Asia and North America
Big Cypress†‡	720,566	291,603	Florida	Everglades National Park freshwater supply; home of Seminole and Miccosukee Indians
Big Thicket†	105,806	42,818	Texas	Unusual combination of biomes, including desert, swamp, prairie, and woodland
Craters of the Moon†	410,733	166,218	Idaho	Adjacent to Craters of the Moon National Monument; lava fields, grasslands, and wildlife
Denali†	1,334,118	539,898	Alaska	Adjacent to Denali National Park; southern flanks of Mount McKinley; massive glaciers, Cathedral Spires, and wildlife
Gates of the Arctic†	948,608	383,888	Alaska	Adjacent to Gates of the Arctic National Park; habitat vital to the caribou, Dall's sheep, grizzly bear, moose, and wolf
Glacier Bay†‡	58,406	23,636	Alaska	Adjacent to Glacier Bay National Park; glaciers and migration routes
Great Sand Dunes†	41,686	16,870	Colorado	Adjacent to Great Sand Dunes National Park; alpine tundra and lakes and Rocky Mountain peaks
Katmai†‡	418,699	169,441	Alaska	Adjacent to Katmai National Park; habitat to protect brown bears and watersheds necessary for red salmon fisheries
Lake Clark†‡	1,410,292	570,725	Alaska	Adjacent to Lake Clark National Park; rugged mountains and valleys; much wildlife
Little River Canyon†	15,289	6,187	Alabama	Rock expanses and bluffs; endangered species of wildlife
Mojave†	1,535,509	621,398	California	Includes Mojave Desert; rugged mountains; wildlife
Noatak†‡	6,587,071	2,665,693	Alaska	Hundreds of archaeological sites and rich wildlife
Tallgrass Prairie	10,894	4,409	Kansas	Tallgrass ecosystem in the Flint Hills
Timucuan Ecological and Historic†	46,301	18,737	Florida	Timucuan Indian sites; coastal wetlands
Wrangell-St. Elias†	4,852,652	1,963,799	Alaska	Adjacent to Wrangell-St. Elias National Park; large area of wilderness; much wildlife
Yukon-Charley Rivers†	2,526,512	1,022,443	Alaska	Peregrine falcons; historic resources from gold rush era

†Camping permitted.   ‡Has overnight lodging.

Continued from page 47

History

During the 1800's, hunters and trappers returned from the Yellowstone region with reports of strange natural wonders. These stories—of hot springs, spurting geysers, and a mountain of black glass—seemed unbelievable. In 1870, an expedition led by General Henry D. Washburn, surveyor general of the Montana Territory, visited the region to check the reports.

After exploring by horseback, the men camped near the Madison River. They talked about the sights they had seen and discussed developing the land for resorts, or for lumbering and mining. Then, Cornelius Hedges, a Montana judge, proposed that the region be preserved as a national park to benefit all people for all time. The other men agreed enthusiastically.

Members of the expedition promoted the national park idea by writing articles in newspapers and magazines, giving lectures, and meeting with high government officials. Their efforts succeeded in 1872, when Congress established Yellowstone National Park, the world's first national park. During the 1890's, four more national parks were established—General Grant (now Kings Canyon), Sequoia, and Yosemite in California, and Mount Rainier in Washington.

In 1906, Congress passed the Antiquities Act to stop looting and destruction at prehistoric American Indian sites in the Southwest. This law gave the president the power to establish national monuments on land owned or controlled by the government. Later in 1906, Devils Tower National Monument in Wyoming became the first such area. More than 30 national monuments were established during the next 10 years.

In 1916, Congress set up the National Park Service as a bureau of the Department of the Interior. Stephen T. Mather, a Chicago businessman, became its first director. Mather did much to promote and expand the National Park System. In 1916, there were 16 national parks and 21 national monuments, with a total area of nearly 5 million acres (2 million hectares). When Mather retired in 1929, the system consisted of 25 national parks, 32 national monuments, and a national memorial. It had a total area of about 10 million acres (4 million hectares).

In 1933, Congress transferred more than 50 areas from other government agencies to the Department of the Interior. These areas, most of them historical, were added to the National Park System. In 1935, the Historic Sites Act gave the secretary of the interior the power to approve national historic sites.

The Park, Parkway, and Recreation Area Study Act of

1936 led to establishment of recreational areas in the National Park System. The first such area, the Blue Ridge Parkway, was established later that year. An act of 1946 allowed the Park Service to manage recreational areas under cooperative agreements with other government agencies that controlled the areas.

In the last half of the 1900's, much land was added to the National Park System. By the early 2000's, the system had grown to include about 390 areas and totaled more than 84 million acres (34 million hectares).

Critically reviewed by the National Park Service

Related articles. See the *World Book* articles on the national parklands as listed in the tables with this article. See also **Animal** (How human beings protect animals); **National park; National Park Service.**

Outline

I. Kinds of parklands
   A. Areas preserved for natural features
   B. Areas preserved for historical importance
   C. Areas preserved for recreational use
II. Visiting the parklands
   A. Planning a visit   C. Camping
   B. Visitors' costs   D. Visitors' responsibilities
III. Preserving the parklands
   A. Limits on activities
   B. Fires
   C. Crowds
IV. Establishing new parklands
V. History

Questions

Where is the largest national park in the United States?
What is done to preserve plant and animal life in the parklands?
What was the first national monument?
Who was the first director of the National Park Service?
How does the National Park Service acquire land?
What area became the first national park in the world in 1872?
What are the three basic reasons for including land in the National Park System?
What government agency must establish a new national park?
What national park has the lowest land surface in the Western Hemisphere?

National Primitive Baptist Convention is a religious organization that has hundreds of independent churches. Each church is independent in controlling its own membership. These Baptists follow three *ordinances* (established religious ceremonies)—baptism, Holy Communion, and foot washing rites. They believe that a definite number of the human race were chosen for redemption before the world was created, and these persons will be saved before the final judgment. The convention was formed in 1907. It consists of state conventions and associations. The organization's headquarters are in Tallahassee, Florida. See also **Baptists.**

Critically reviewed by the National Primitive Baptist Convention

National PTA. See **National Congress of Parents and Teachers.**

National Public Radio (NPR) is a public radio system in the United States. It acquires or produces news, cultural, and information programming and distributes it to hundreds of member stations in the United States, Puerto Rico, and Guam.

Member radio stations produce many of the cultural programs presented nationally by NPR. The cultural programming includes live performances of classical and jazz music. Reporters from member stations regularly file stories heard on NPR's newsmagazines.

The Corporation for Public Broadcasting, a private organization funded mainly by the federal government, created NPR to provide news programming and to link noncommercial radio stations across the United States. NPR was incorporated in 1970. Its first program transmission was live coverage of U.S. Senate hearings on the Vietnam War on April 19, 1971.

In 1977, NPR merged with the Association of Public Radio Stations and took on that organization's former responsibilities. For example, it began providing member stations with training and program promotion, and representing the interests of public radio before Congress and the Federal Communications Commission. In 1979, it established the first nationwide, satellite-delivered radio distribution network. NPR's headquarters are in Washington, D.C.   Critically reviewed by National Public Radio

See also **Corporation for Public Broadcasting.**

National Radio Astronomy Observatory (NRAO) is an organization that operates radio telescopes at Socorro, New Mexico; and at Green Bank, West Virginia. Scientists from the United States and other countries use these telescopes. The NRAO is financed by the U.S. National Science Foundation and has scientific offices in Charlottesville, Virginia.

The NRAO operates one of the world's most powerful radio telescopes, the Expanded Very Large Array, near Socorro. This instrument consists of 27 large, dish-shaped metal mirrors called *reflectors* that collect radio signals from space. Each reflector measures 82 feet (25 meters) in diameter. The reflectors operate as a single instrument. Another NRAO instrument, the Very Long Baseline Array telescope, consists of 10 reflectors at sites across U.S. territory, from Hawaii to the Virgin Islands. They are controlled from Socorro by radio signals sent by a computer, and they act as a single telescope.

At Green Bank, the NRAO operates the Robert C. Byrd Green Bank Telescope. The telescope's reflector has an unusual shape. Its rim is a flattened circle with a short-

NRAO/AUI

The National Radio Astronomy Observatory operates the Very Long Baseline Array (VLBA), a system of radio antennas across North America that act as a single giant telescope. This photograph shows a VLBA antenna in Owens Valley, California.

est diameter of 328 feet (100 meters) and a longest diameter of 361 feet (110 meters). Also at Green Bank, the NRAO operates a radio telescope that is 140 feet (43 meters) in diameter.

The NRAO was founded in 1956 by the National Science Foundation. Associated Universities, Inc., a not-for-profit science management corporation, operates it. Scientists using NRAO telescopes have detected radio waves given off by nearly all types of objects in space, ranging from nearby planets to distant quasars.

Critically reviewed by the National Radio Astronomy Observatory

See also **Telescope** (Radio and microwave telescopes).

National Railroad Passenger Corporation. See Amtrak.

National Recovery Administration (NRA) was a United States government agency in the early 1930's. It was established in 1933 under the National Industrial Recovery Act as part of the New Deal program (see **New Deal**). The NRA prepared and oversaw codes of fair competition for businesses and industries. Hugh S. Johnson was the first head of the agency. President Franklin D. Roosevelt abolished the NRA in 1935, after the Supreme Court of the United States ruled the National Industrial Recovery Act unconstitutional.

James T. Patterson

See also **Schechter v. United States.**

National recreation area. See National Park System.

National Republican Party was a political party that arose when the Democratic-Republican Party split during the administration of President John Quincy Adams (1825-1829). The National Republican Party supported Adams's administration. The split pitted the party against Andrew Jackson's followers. Groups including the National Republicans formed the Whig Party during Jackson's presidency (1829-1837) (see **Whig Party**).

William W. Freehling

National Research Council is a private, nonprofit organization in the United States that carries out much of the research of the National Academies. The National Academies include the council and the National Academy of Sciences, the National Academy of Engineering, and the Institute of Medicine. The council aids the other academies in promoting the development of science and technology and in advising the U.S. government and other groups. Thousands of scientists, scholars, and researchers serve as volunteers on its study committees.

The National Research Council was created by the National Academy of Sciences in 1916. It undertakes most of its activities at the request of the U.S. government. The council also initiates its own studies and carries out research at the request of private foundations and other organizations. Its headquarters are in Washington, D.C.

Critically reviewed by the National Research Council

See also **National Academies; National Academy of Sciences.**

National Rifle Association of America is an organization that encourages sharpshooting and the use of firearms for hunting and other shooting sports. It opposes what it considers unnecessary restrictions on the right to own guns. Such restrictions include laws that impose cost or inconvenience on law-abiding gun owners. The association, also known as the NRA, supports laws that provide longer prison terms for people who commit crimes with firearms.

The NRA has based its opposition to gun control laws on the Second Amendment to the Constitution of the United States. This amendment reads: "A well-regulated militia, being necessary to the security of a free state, the right of the people to keep and bear arms shall not be infringed." In 1939, the Supreme Court of the United States ruled that the amendment does not prohibit most gun control laws. However, in 2008, the court struck down a ban on handguns in the District of Columbia, ruling that Americans have a right to own guns for self-defense and hunting.

Many people, including many law enforcement professionals, believe that stricter laws against owning and using guns would reduce the crime rate. The NRA feels that such laws would not help fight crime but would restrict the legal use of guns. The NRA has been effective at persuading Congress to block the passage of gun control bills. The NRA was founded in 1871. Its headquarters are in Fairfax, Virginia.   Franklin E. Zimring

See also **Gun control; Second Amendment.**

National Right to Life Committee is a leading organization in the movement against legalized abortion in the United States. Members try to influence Congress and the state legislatures to pass laws restricting access to abortion. The committee also attempts to defeat legislation that would extend abortion rights. The committee has supported legislation to ban certain late-term abortion procedures and to prohibit the use of federal funds for abortions. In addition, the committee works to end *infanticide* (the killing of infants) and *euthanasia* (helping or allowing people to die).

The committee collects contributions from its members and gives the funds to political candidates it favors. It also conducts educational and outreach programs.

The committee was founded in 1973. That year, the Supreme Court of the United States made a landmark ruling in *Roe v. Wade* that states may not forbid abortions during the first three months of pregnancy. The committee has headquarters in Washington, D.C., and chapters in all 50 states.   David M. O'Brien

National Road. In the early 1800's, many pioneers began moving into the territory west of the Ohio River. These settlers wanted their section to grow rapidly and began demanding a better route from the East to the West. In 1811, work began on a road that, when completed, led from Cumberland, Maryland, to Vandalia, Illinois. It was known at first as the Great National Pike but later came to be called the National Road or the Cumberland Road. For many years, it was the chief road west. As railroads developed, the road became less important. See also **United States, History of the** (picture: The National Road).   Robert C. Post

National Safety Council is a not-for-profit public service organization that works to increase safety and occupational health in the United States. The council promotes safe practices on and off the job and supports accident prevention laws and standards. The council produces films, pamphlets, and other materials on preventing accidents and illness.

The council was founded in 1913 and chartered by the U.S. Congress in 1953. Its headquarters are in Itasca, Illinois.   Critically reviewed by the National Safety Council

National Science Foundation is an independent agency of the United States government. It promotes science and engineering research in the United States by (1) providing *fellowships* (monetary awards) to individuals for research and graduate study; (2) funding research institutions; and (3) supporting national research facilities, including the National Center for Atmospheric Research in Colorado and various supercomputing centers. The National Science Foundation (NSF) also funds and coordinates U.S. research in the Arctic and Antarctica, and it supports international research programs.

The NSF seeks to improve education in mathematics, science, and engineering. It supports programs that enhance teachers' skills and improve *curriculums* (courses of study) at the elementary through high school levels.

Congress established the NSF in 1950. A director, deputy director, and a 24-member National Science Board head the foundation. They are appointed by the president, subject to Senate approval. The agency's headquarters are in Arlington, Virginia.

Critically reviewed by the National Science Foundation

National Security Agency/Central Security Service is a high-technology agency within the United States Department of Defense. The agency, sometimes called the NSA/CSS, has two primary missions: (1) *information assurance* and (2) *signals intelligence.* Information assurance seeks to ensure the security of classified and sensitive information and systems within the U.S. government. Signals intelligence involves the gathering, analysis, and handling of secret information transmitted by foreign countries. The responsibilities of the NSA/CSS include both military and nonmilitary matters.

The NSA/CSS coordinates the work of analysts, computer experts, engineers, linguists, mathematicians, physicists, and other specialists. It is a *cryptologic* organization—that is, it is responsible for the research, analysis, and use of secret communication systems, such as codes and ciphers. The NSA/CSS is also an important center for foreign language analysis and research.

The National Security Agency was established in 1952. It became the National Security Agency/Central Security Service in 1972. The organization is based mainly in Fort Meade, Maryland.   Robert W. Taylor

See also **Codes and ciphers; Intelligence service.**

National Security Council (NSC) is a part of the Executive Office of the President of the United States. The council serves as an interdepartmental cabinet on defense, foreign policy, and intelligence matters. Members include the president, the vice president, and the secretaries of state and defense.

The NSC advises the president on many security problems. It brings together the departments and agencies most concerned with foreign policy and military matters. The council supervises the Central Intelligence Agency (see **Central Intelligence Agency**). The president calls meetings of the NSC. If a crisis develops, the president may call the group into immediate session.

The NSC is assisted by a staff headed by the assistant to the president for national security affairs. The staff works with the member departments and agencies to prepare studies and policy papers for the council's action. Congress created the council in 1947.

In 1986, the NSC was criticized for exceeding its authority as an advisory agency. This criticism arose when it was revealed that the NSC staff carried out secret arms sales to Iran and provided the profits to U.S.-supported rebels in Nicaragua. Some legal experts argued that both activities violated federal government policies at the time. In 1987, President Ronald Reagan responded to the criticism by adding a special legal adviser to the staff of the NSC.   Harvey Glickman

National Society of Professional Engineers (NSPE) is a professional society of engineers of all types in the United States. It promotes a positive image of engineering professionals and encourages competency, ethical practice, and professionalism among engineers through sound licensing practices. It also provides education, career development, and other resources to engineering professionals and students.

Membership in the NSPE, and in its state and territorial societies, includes licensed engineers, engineer interns, graduates of accredited engineering programs, and engineering students.

Critically reviewed by the National Society of Professional Engineers

National Trails System is a network of pathways and historic routes throughout the United States preserved for public enjoyment and in commemoration of significant periods or events in U.S. history. The system includes national scenic, historic, and recreation trails, and connecting or side trails that provide access to these paths. The trails wind through rural, wilderness, and urban areas. Three federal agencies—the National Park Service, the Forest Service, and the Bureau of Land Management—administer and coordinate the system.

National scenic trails provide opportunities for the enjoyment of natural beauty and of outdoor activities. National historic trails mark significant periods or events in U.S. history. National recreation trails are shorter trails that can be used for such activities as bicycling, cross-country skiing, hiking, horseback riding, and snowmobiling. The U.S. Congress established the National Trails System in 1968.   Critically reviewed by the National Park Service

See also **National Park System.**

National Weather Service. See **Weather Service, National.**

National Wildlife Federation is an organization founded to create interest and promote public education in the conservation of wildlife and wildlife habitats in the United States. The federation issues several free or inexpensive publications. It also publishes several magazines, including *National Wildlife* for its adult members, *Ranger Rick* for younger members, and *Your Big Backyard* for preschoolers.

State wildlife federations and conservation leagues, made up of local clubs, are affiliated with the national organization. The federation began in 1936.

Critically reviewed by the National Wildlife Federation

National Wildlife Refuge System consists of over 550 refuges established by the United States government to protect and increase wildlife and their habitats. The smallest refuge is Mille Lacs National Wildlife Refuge, two islands in Minnesota with a total area of about ⅖ acre (0.2 hectare). The largest, Yukon Delta National Wildlife Refuge, has nearly 20 million acres (8 million hectares) in Alaska. National refuges are run by the U.S. Fish and Wildlife Service.

Most refuges were created to protect migratory birds. Some protect threatened species of wildlife, including

U.S. Fish & Wildlife Service

The National Wildlife Refuge System in the United States protects many migratory birds. These American avocets are landing at the Bear River Migratory Bird Refuge in Utah.

bald eagles, brown pelicans, whooping cranes, sea turtles, and manatees. Refuges have helped rebuild populations of buffaloes, trumpeter swans, and pronghorns.

People also benefit from refuges. Refuges protect marshes, swamps, and other wetlands, which help control flooding, filter pollutants, and refill the supply of underground water. Most refuges are open to the public. Many offer educational programs on protecting the environment. Hunting and fishing are permitted on some refuges, but these activities are strictly regulated.

The first U.S. wildlife refuge was set up in 1903 on Pelican Island, off the east coast of Florida. President Theodore Roosevelt created it to help protect brown pelicans and other birds that nest on the island. More refuges were set up over time. In 1966, the U.S. Congress made these refuge areas the National Wildlife Refuge System.

Critically reviewed by the U.S. Fish and Wildlife Service

See also **Fish and Wildlife Service; Wildlife conservation.**

National World War II Memorial is a monument in Washington, D.C., that honors the millions of men and women who served in the United States armed forces during World War II (1939-1945) as well as the millions more who helped on the homefront. The memorial

© Tim Sloan, Getty Images

The National World War II Memorial stands on the Mall in Washington, D.C. The memorial includes 56 pillars that represent the District of Columbia and the states and territories of the war period. These pillars surround a pool and plaza.

stands on the National Mall at the east end of the Reflecting Pool, between the Lincoln Memorial and the Washington Monument.

At the memorial's center is a sunken pool surrounded by a granite plaza. Arches at the north and south ends of the plaza symbolize the two theaters of the war—Europe and northern Africa, and Asia and the Pacific. Fifty-six granite pillars, decorated with bronze wreaths, extend in semicircles from the arches. The pillars represent the U.S. states and territories of the war period. A curved wall on the plaza's west side is decorated with 4,000 gold stars. Each star honors 100 of the over 400,000 members of the U.S. armed forces who died in the war.

The Austrian-born American architect Friedrich St. Florian designed the memorial. It was dedicated in 2004.   Critically reviewed by the National World War II Memorial

See also **Washington, D.C.** (picture: War memorials).

National Zoological Park is a 163-acre (71-hectare) zoo maintained by the Smithsonian Institution along Rock Creek in Washington, D.C. The zoo exhibits hundreds of different *species* (kinds) of animals. Where possible, animals, plants, and other living things are presented together in natural settings. Millions of people visit the zoo every year. The zoo provides educational services to the public and conducts scientific research in animal behavior, ecology, zoo biology, animal reproduction, and exotic animal medicine. Conservation of endangered animal species is a major research focus at the zoo.

Critically reviewed by the National Zoological Park

Nationalism refers to a people's sense of common belonging and loyalty to a nation. Nationalism may arise from a long history of people who share such common traits as culture, language, origin, and tradition. It may develop as people join together to form a unified government. Nationalism may also originate as people fight to establish a unique ethnic or religious identity or struggle to prevent their identity from being changed or erased by a more powerful group. In each situation, nationalism creates a sense of connection and commitment to a group with a distinct set of beliefs, ideals, and traditions.

Although nationalism is widespread today, it once did not exist. Early people felt that they belonged to cities or tribes. As a result, people's loyalty and attachment were much more local. As people expanded their view of the world, they began to spread their loyalties among several groups. For example, during the Middle Ages, the period in European history from about the 400's through the 1400's, a French citizen might have vowed loyalty to the duke of Burgundy, the king of France, the Holy Roman emperor, and the pope.

The rise of nationalism can be traced to the development of a political unit known as the *nation-state.* A nation-state has three characteristics—(1) its people share some or all of such common traits as culture, history, language, and religion; (2) its people experience a feeling of unity; and (3) its people inhabit a specific area of land with its own independent government.

Nationalism is important in maintaining nation-states. The principles of nationalism, often referred to as the *doctrine of national self-determination,* argue that the nation is the only rightful basis for forming a political state. In this sense, nationalism frames all human activity as national in character. Those living in a nation are expected to adopt the national language, embrace the nation's symbols, learn and pass on the national music and folklore, and defend the nation's principles.

Nation-states began to develop at the end of the Middle Ages. In this period, people's sense of place changed. Travel and communication improved, and people became increasingly aware of the parts of a country that lay beyond their immediate community. As a result, loyalty to local and religious leaders weakened, and allegiance to a monarch grew stronger. By the 1700's, these factors enabled such European countries as England, France, and Spain to become nation-states. In the 1800's, additional nation-states, such as Germany and Italy, formed as the result of unification movements. In such cases, several provinces or states combined into a single political unit.

In the 1800's and 1900's, many nation-states also formed as a result of independence movements. Nationalist groups sought to break away from large empires and create smaller states. Argentina won independence from the Spanish Empire in 1816, Greece from the Ottoman Empire in 1829, and India from the British Empire in 1947. In the early 1990's, nationalism contributed to the breakup of several states in Eastern Europe, including Czechoslovakia, the Soviet Union, and Yugoslavia.

Smaller nationalist groups continue to struggle for the establishment of their own independent nation-state. These movements often are based on a desire for ethnic or religious separatism. In 1980, for example, people in the Basque provinces and the Catalonia region of Spain elected regional parliaments. Although both regions have limited self-government, both are striving for full independence. In the Middle East, Palestinians in the Gaza Strip and West Bank actively pursue the establishment of an independent state.

The effects of nationalism can be both good and bad. Nationalism gives people a sense of belonging and pride. It provides a cultural heritage and a common cultural ground. Nationalism also creates a willingness in people to make sacrifices for their country.

But nationalism also produces rivalry and tension between nations. When nationalist groups within a region desire independence from the nation, or when nation-states seek to extend their influence beyond their physical borders, military conflict often occurs. Historians commonly cite national independence movements as a primary cause of World War I (1914-1918). Feelings of nationalistic superiority have at times led nations to commit *genocide,* the deliberate and systematic mistreatment or extermination of an entire people. For example, Nazi Germany murdered millions of Jews during World War II (1939-1945) because of the Nazi belief that Germans were superior to Jews.

Nationalism also can be improperly used for the political gain of a person or party. In the early 1950's, United States Senator Joseph McCarthy used nationalism as a cover for falsely accusing U.S. government officials of cooperating with Communists. Such dictators as Adolf Hitler of Germany, Benito Mussolini of Italy, and Augusto Pinochet Ugarte of Chile used nationalism in demanding extreme loyalty from their people.   Karen A. Cerulo

See also **Nation; Patriotism.**

Nationalist China. See Taiwan.
Nationality, in law, is a person's status as a member of a certain country. Usually, a person's citizenship is the same as his or her nationality. But the terms do not mean exactly the same thing. For example, before the Philippine Islands became independent in 1946, their people were nationals of the United States. They owed allegiance to the United States but were not U.S. citizens.

Nationality is acquired at birth according to either of two principles. The first is the *jus sanguinis,* or *right of blood,* which gives to a child the nationality of one of the parents, usually the father. The second, called *jus soli,* or *right of the place of one's birth,* makes a person a national of the country in which he or she is born. Most countries use both principles. Every country has the right to determine who its nationals shall be.

In the Commonwealth of Nations, the difference between nationality and citizenship was once important. The Commonwealth is an association of mainly independent countries formerly under British rule. All people living in the Commonwealth were considered to be both British subjects and citizens of their own countries. Today, however, citizens of Commonwealth nations are not considered British subjects. A British subject also may be a citizen of a Commonwealth nation if he or she meets that nation's citizenship requirements.

Nationality groups. Nationality also refers to the fact that many people continue the habits, the customs, and even the language of their native land when they go to live elsewhere. Many groups of people in cities of the United States try to keep alive the customs and traditions of other countries. Some of these people were born outside the country. But in some cases, every member of the group was born in the United States.
Thomas M. DeFrank

See also **Citizenship; Naturalization.**
Nationalization is the control and ownership of an industry on a national scale by the government of a country. Industries that are most commonly nationalized include airlines, electric and gas utilities, mines, postal services, railroads, and telephone companies.

In some countries, nationalization plays a vital role in a set of economic, political, and social beliefs called *socialism.* These countries nationalize certain industries in order to provide better products or services for their citizens. Socialists say that nationalization ensures democratic control of these industries. In the past, the United Kingdom and France nationalized many industries for these purposes. However, since the 1980's, political changes have resulted in the sale of many of the British and French industries to private investors. The selling of nationalized industries to private investors is called *divestiture* or *privatization.*

Other countries, especially some developing nations, have nationalized certain industries to remove them from foreign ownership. In the 1960's and 1970's, for example, some countries in the Middle East and elsewhere began to take over oil companies that had been owned chiefly by Americans or Europeans. These countries gained higher profits for themselves by removing the oil industry from foreign ownership.

Forms of nationalization. There are several forms of nationalization, based on how the nationalized industry is managed. In the most common form, a *public corpo-*

ration is set up as an independent body by law. The government appoints a board of directors that manages the industry. In another form, a government department has control of the industry. Such action gives the government close control of the industry. In a third form, the government buys part of the stock in an ordinary corporation, and private investors own the rest.

Advantages and disadvantages. Nationalized industries have some advantages over private industries. A nationalized industry can provide vital products or services to the public that would not be profitable for private industry to provide. The government can encourage a nationalized industry to invest and expand during an economic *recession* (slowdown). Nationalized industries can also develop weak parts of the economy and help hold down prices during periods of inflation.

Supporters of nationalization say that—in certain industries—a nationalized corporation can provide more efficient service than private industries. Such industries include electric and gas utilities and telephone companies. Supporters also say that government is too weak unless it has some control over vital industries.

Nationalization has some disadvantages. Many nationalized industries do not make a profit. As a result, the government uses tax money to *subsidize* (help pay for) them. Critics of nationalization charge that a lack of competition causes nationalized industries to become inefficient. They say government subsidies keep unprofitable industries alive even if the industries are no longer useful. Critics additionally fear that a government has too much power if it controls vital industries.

Dennis L. Thompson

See also **Privatization; Socialism.**

Native Americans. See Indian, American.
Native cat. See Quoll.
Nativity. See Christmas; Jesus Christ (The Nativity).
NATO. See North Atlantic Treaty Organization.
Natsume Soseki, *NAHT soo* MEH *SOH seh* KEE (1867-1916), was Japan's first great modern novelist. Soseki was a member of the first generation of Japanese youth exposed to Western books and ideas. His writing reflects his response to the problems of living in the modern world. He wrote about doubt and faith; self assertion and self questioning; alienation from industrial, mechanized society; and personal identity.

Soseki wrote 10 novels and several short stories. His first works were satires of the Japanese society of his time. He gained immediate fame with his first novel, *I Am a Cat* (1905). This episodic story is narrated by a cat who sardonically observes his master and neighbors. *Little Master* (1906) also indicts modern society. The story is narrated by a country teacher whose old-fashioned virtues are of little use in his changing world. The best known of Soseki's later, and more somber, works is *Kokoro* (1914). The novel tells the story of a young man's relationships with an older man and his father, told partly through letters. His other novels include *The Three-Cornered World* (1906) and *Grass on the Wayside* (1915).

Soseki was born on Feb. 9, 1867, in Tokyo. His real name was Natsume Kinnosuke. He trained as a scholar of English literature, studying in England from 1900 to 1902. In 1907, he joined the staff of the *Asahi* newspaper, which published many of his novels in serial form. Soseki died on Dec. 9, 1916.   Laurel Rasplica Rodd

Natural gas. See Gas (fuel).
Natural gas liquids are certain chemical compounds that can be obtained in liquid form from natural gas. These compounds rank among the world's most valuable energy resources. Natural gas liquids, also called *NGL,* are widely used as fuel, and in manufacturing petrochemicals and other products.

The chief NGL compounds, in order of increasing *mass* of their molecules, are ethane, propane, butane, pentane, hexane, and heptane. A molecule's mass is the amount of matter it has. Chemical manufacturers use ethane to make *ethylene,* an important petrochemical. Butane and propane, and mixtures of the two, are classified as *LPG* (liquefied petroleum gas). LPG is used chiefly as a heating fuel in industry and homes. Pentane, hexane, and heptane are called *natural gasoline* or *condensate.* Refiners blend natural gasoline with other gasoline.

Natural gas liquids are classified as *light hydrocarbons.* Hydrocarbons are a group of compounds containing only hydrogen and carbon. Natural gas is made up chiefly of hydrocarbons. All hydrocarbons become liquid under certain combinations of temperature and pressure, depending on the mass of their individual molecules. Light hydrocarbons liquefy at lower temperatures and higher pressures than heavy hydrocarbons.

There are two main methods of producing NGL, *condensation* and *absorption.* In condensation, natural gas is chilled until it becomes a liquid from which the NGL are extracted. In absorption, processors mix gas with an oil that absorbs light hydrocarbons. NGL are then distilled from the oil. Natural gas processing plants produce most NGL.   Michael A. Adewumi

See also **Butane and propane; Ethane; Gas** (fuel).
Natural history. See Nature study.
Natural number. See Number theory.
Natural resources are those products and features of Earth that permit it to support life and satisfy people's needs. Minerals, land, and water are natural resources, as are such biological resources as flowers, trees, birds, wild animals, and fish. Mineral resources include oil, coal, metals, stone, and sand. Other natural resources are air, sunshine, and climate. Natural resources are used to make (1) food; (2) fuel; and (3) raw materials for the production of finished goods.

This article discusses natural resources in general. For information on the natural resources of specific areas, see the *Natural resources* section in each state and province article, and in various country articles.

Uses and importance. Biological resources are the most important natural resources. All the food we eat comes from plants or animals. Since early days, people have used wood from trees for fuel and shelter. Biological resources, in turn, are dependent on other natural resources. Most plants and animals could not live without air, sunshine, soil, and water.

Mineral resources are also extremely important to modern living. Mineral fuels—including coal, oil, and natural gas—provide heat, light, and power. Minerals serve as raw materials for making finished goods, such as cars, plastics, and refrigerators.

Natural resources contribute—but are not essential—to a nation's wealth. Such wealthy nations as Canada and the United States are rich in natural resources. But some well-to-do nations, such as Denmark and Japan, have few of them. Some poor, or *less developed,* countries have few natural resources, though some, like Peru and Congo (Kinshasa), have many.

Conservation and development. Because modern civilization—even life itself—depends on natural resources, many people have been concerned about whether there will always be enough.

Scientists and economists believe that people can never use up all the mineral raw materials like iron, aluminum, sand, and fertilizer. There are sufficient quantities in the land and the sea, and most of the materials can be reused. For example, scrap iron can be melted down and used again in steelmaking. But people may have to explore farther and dig deeper to get what they need. Or they may have to substitute one material for another that has become too scarce. For example, aluminum may be used in place of copper for many purposes. While copper is scarce, deposits of bauxite and clay contain more aluminum than people can ever use.

Mineral fuels are different and can all be used up. Earth contains enough mineral fuels to last only one or two centuries at current rates of use. When these supplies run out, people may depend more on solar energy to power autos and factories and on nuclear energy to heat homes. Even today, uranium and other nuclear fuels generate electric power. Such fuels will last for many centuries. Sunlight is already used to run the instruments in space satellites and may someday be widely used to provide energy. Scientists are now trying to generate power by combining the *nuclei* (cores) of hydrogen atoms. This process, called *nuclear fusion,* is a potentially limitless source of energy. See **Nuclear energy; Solar energy.**

Preserving the delicate balance of nature in biological resources appears to be the most difficult and important part of saving our natural resources. People have often upset this balance. For example, poor farming methods have ruined much farmland and left it barren. Each year, millions of tons of fertile topsoil that could produce good crops are washed away by rains. Chemicals sprayed on crops and washed off by rain sometimes end up in rivers and streams. Some of these chemicals kill the fish in the streams. Some entire species of birds and animals have been killed off by hunters.

Fumes from automobiles and trucks and smoke from factories poison the air. This *air pollution* in many cities kills trees and endangers human health. As more cars and factories are built, the problem tends to get worse. To correct these conditions, people have to reduce the amount of pollution produced by factories and automobiles. In the United States, the quality of both air and water has improved significantly since the 1970's because of government regulations. See **Air pollution.**

Even if natural resources are conserved and developed, Earth could not provide enough food if the population increases too much. With much effort, the amount of land under cultivation could be doubled, and farms in many developing countries could produce three or four times as much as they now do. Improved crop varieties can greatly increase yields. All this might increase the food supply 5 to 10 times what it now is. But eventually the growth of world population must slow if everyone is to have enough food.

Henry J. Aaron

Related articles in *World Book* include:
Air
Conservation
Developing country
Forest
Forestry
Game
Industry (Natural resources)
Mineral
National park (Development of park resources)
Soil
United Nations University
Water
Wildlife conservation

Natural selection is a process in nature by which the organisms best suited to their environment are the ones most likely to leave offspring. This process has been called *survival of the fittest,* though a more accurate term would be *reproduction of the fittest.* The theory of natural selection was first explained in detail in the 1850's by the British naturalist Charles R. Darwin. He believed all plants and animals had *evolved*—that is, developed by changing over many generations—from a few common ancestors by means of natural selection. Plants and animals produce many offspring, but some of the young die before they can become parents. According to Darwin's theory, natural selection determines which members of a species die prematurely and which ones survive and reproduce.

The theory of natural selection is based on the great variation among even closely related individuals. In most cases, no two members of a species are exactly alike. Each has a unique combination of such traits as size, color, and ability to withstand cold or other harsh conditions. Most of these traits are inherited.

Only a limited supply of food, water, and other necessities of life exists for all the organisms that are produced. Therefore, the organisms must constantly compete for these necessities. They also struggle against such dangers as being destroyed by animals that prey on them or by unfavorable weather. In any environment, some members of a species have combinations of traits that help them in the struggle for life. Other members have traits that are less suitable for that environment. The organisms with the favorable traits are most likely to survive, reproduce, and pass on those traits to their young. Organisms that are less able to compete are likely to die prematurely or to produce few or inferior offspring. As a result, the favorable traits replace the unfavorable ones in the species.

If the environment changes, different traits or combinations of traits may become favorable to survival, and the overall character of a species might change. In this way, a species adapts to its environment and avoids extinction. If two populations of a species live in different environments, they will probably develop differently. Eventually, they may differ so much that they become two separate species.

In 1858, Darwin and another British naturalist, Alfred R. Wallace, presented similar theories of natural selection. Many biologists rejected the idea at first. They incorrectly thought that natural selection and evolution would eventually stop because a species would have used up all its possible variations. Since then, scientists have learned that the cells of every living thing have tiny structures called *genes,* which determine the organism's hereditary traits. An organism inherits a set of genes from each parent. Variations occur in part because genes for new traits are constantly being introduced into a species and shuffled among individuals by reproduction. See **Gene; Heredity** (Heredity and natural selection).

Virtually all biologists believe that natural selection is an important process in evolution. But some religious groups reject the theory because it conflicts with their beliefs about the creation of life.   Jerry A. Coyne

See also **Darwin, Charles; Evolution; Races, Human** (Natural selection); **Wallace, Alfred R.**

Naturalism, in literature, is the attempt to apply scientific theory and methods to imaginative writing. Naturalists concentrate on the physical world to the exclusion of the supernatural. Naturalism thrived in the late 1800's and early 1900's and has been most important in the novel and in drama.

Theory of Naturalism. Naturalists have been the most uncompromising Realists. They believe that knowledge is acquired through the senses, and that the function of the writer is to report accurately what he or she observes. The Naturalist tries to be as objective as a laboratory scientist. In their theory of life, Naturalists are more pessimistic than Realists. The Realist believes people can make moral choices, but the Naturalist doubts that they can. Naturalists believe everything people do is determined by their heredity, or environment, or both. Naturalists believe people are trapped by forces such as money, sex, or power.

In picturing people as trapped, the Naturalist usually deals with the more sordid aspects of life. Characters in Naturalistic literature are driven by their most basic urges. They are often brutal and usually failures. They use coarse language, and their view of life is often bleak and without hope. Yet in the best Naturalistic works, there is a tone of compassion and even admiration for those characters who struggle against overwhelming odds.

Naturalism in fiction. The principles of Naturalistic fiction were first stated by the French author Émile Zola in *The Experimental Novel* (1880). Zola argued that novelists should treat their material as scientists treat theirs. Before 1880, psychological and physiological studies such as Zola recommended had appeared in works by Honoré de Balzac, Jules and Edmond de Goncourt, Gustave Flaubert, and other French writers. Zola's books shocked English and American readers, but his theories and novels established Naturalism as an important literary movement.

Naturalism never became popular in England, but it has been a major influence in the United States since the 1890's. Stephen Crane, Hamlin Garland, and Frank Norris were the first Americans consciously to adopt the Naturalistic style. Jack London and Edith Wharton developed it further. Most critics, however, consider Theodore Dreiser the best American Naturalist. Dreiser's novel *An American Tragedy* (1925) is a moving account of a young man trapped by circumstance. Later American Naturalistic novelists include Nelson Algren, John Dos Passos, James T. Farrell, Norman Mailer, and Richard Wright.

Naturalism in drama has the same goals as Naturalism in fiction. A highly realistic setting provides a sense of environment overwhelming the characters. The staging, acting, and plots try to resemble life, not art. Everything focuses upon the hopeless, but often admirable, struggle of the characters against fate.

Zola also led the movement in drama with his adaptation of his novel *Thérèse Raquin* into a play in 1873. August Strindberg of Sweden and Gerhart Hauptmann of Germany rank among the best European Naturalistic playwrights. Strindberg's *The Father* (1887) and *Miss Julie* (1889) are two violent studies of sex. *The Weavers* (1893) by Hauptmann, a grim portrait of a workers' revolt, set the style for German Naturalism. Naturalism also appears in plays by Henrik Ibsen of Norway and Leo Tolstoy and Maxim Gorki of Russia. In the United States, Naturalism became most popular and important in the plays of Eugene O'Neill. Many of O'Neill's plays, especially the trilogy *Mourning Becomes Electra* (1931), have pathetic characters and depressing atmosphere. Other American playwrights whose works contain Naturalistic elements include Arthur Miller, Clifford Odets, and David Mamet.

Naturalism today has declined in influence, but its methods and its view of life are responsible for much of the imaginative power in today's fiction and drama. Excessive though Naturalism may have been in its hopelessness and brutality, modern literature reveals life more honestly because of it.   Lawrence Lipking

See also **German literature** (Naturalism).

Additional resources

Innes, Christopher D., ed. *A Sourcebook on Naturalist Theatre.* Routledge, 2000.
Link, Eric C. *The Vast and Terrible Drama: American Literary Naturalism in the Late Nineteenth Century.* Univ. of Ala. Pr., 2004.

Naturalist. See **Nature study** and its list of *Related articles.*

Naturalization is a legal process by which a person becomes a citizen of an adopted country. Some nations,

AP/Wide World

Naturalization is the process by which a person becomes a citizen of an adopted country. Applicants for naturalization in the United States take an oath of allegiance to their new country at a special ceremony, *shown here.*

including Canada and France, give naturalized citizens the rights and duties of citizens by birth. Naturalized citizens of the United States cannot become president or vice president, but they have all the other rights and duties of people born as U.S. citizens.

A nation's naturalized citizens have the right to the protection of their adopted government when they travel abroad. However, some nations do not grant the right to give up citizenship. Such a nation could claim as a citizen any person who returned after being naturalized by another country. The adopted government might not be able to protect the individual in this situation.

Naturalization laws differ from nation to nation. For example, foreigners cannot be naturalized in the United States or Canada unless they have lived in their new country for a certain number of years. Israel, however, allows Jews from another country, with a few minor exceptions, to be naturalized on the day they arrive. Many nations naturalize only people who understand the rights and obligations of citizenship and can use the national language. In many countries, foreigners who meet the requirements for citizenship take part in a naturalization ceremony. This ceremony includes an oath of loyalty or allegiance to the adopted nation. In the United States and some other countries, such an oath includes giving up citizenship in any other nation.

A special act by a government may naturalize groups of people without requiring them to follow the usual naturalization procedure. For example, an act by the U.S. Congress naturalized the people of Puerto Rico in 1917. The United States had gained Puerto Rico following the Spanish-American War (1898). Treaties also may include naturalization provisions.

United States Citizenship and Immigration Services (USCIS), an agency of the Department of Homeland Security, administers naturalization in the United States. Similar departments and agencies in other countries include Citizenship and Immigration Canada, the UK Border Agency in the United Kingdom, Australia's Department of Immigration and Citizenship, Immigration New Zealand, the National Immigration Branch of the South African Department of Home Affairs, and the Bureau of Immigration in India.

Thomas M. DeFrank

See also **Alien; Citizenship; Citizenship and Immigration Services, United States; Immigration; Immigration and Naturalization Service.**

Nature Conservancy is an international conservation organization that saves rare plants and animals from extinction by protecting the places where they live. One of the many ways that the organization accomplishes this goal is to acquire land, which it purchases or receives as a gift.

With hundreds of preserves, the Nature Conservancy owns and manages the largest private system of nature sanctuaries in the world. Its Pine Butte Swamp Preserve in western Montana contains the site of the world's first discovery of baby dinosaurs in nests.

The Nature Conservancy was founded in 1951. Since then, it has protected millions of acres or hectares of critical habitats in the United States. The Nature Conservancy has also helped preserve several million acres in Latin America, including tropical rain forests. The organization publishes *Nature Conservancy Magazine,* a journal issued four times a year. The organization's headquarters are in Arlington, Virginia.

Critically reviewed by The Nature Conservancy

Nature study means watching and learning about things in nature. People who are students of nature may go on hikes in the countryside to observe the birds or to look for wildflowers. In the city, nature lovers may visit gardens, museums, parks, and zoos to learn about the natural world. Many youth organizations have nature study programs. Such organizations may sponsor outings or carry out special projects for the protection of the natural environment.

Careful observation is necessary in nature study. Many *naturalists* (students of nature) keep detailed records of their observations in the form of notes, sketches, or photographs. Some students of nature collect such things as flowers, insects, leaves, rocks, or shells. Naturalists have made many important contributions to our understanding of nature.

Related articles in *World Book* include:

American naturalists

Agassiz, Louis
Andrews, Roy C.
Audubon, John J.
Beard, Daniel C.
Beebe, William
Muir, John
Peterson, Roger Tory
Seton, Ernest Thompson

British naturalists

Bewick, Thomas	Hudson, William
Darwin, Charles R.	Wallace, Alfred R.
Durrell, Gerald	

Other naturalists

Adamson, Joy	Fabre, Jean H. C.
Asbjørnsen, Peter C.	Lamarck, Chevalier de
Cuvier, Baron	Linnaeus, Carolus
De Vries, Hugo	

Some nature study subjects

Animal	Insect
Astronomy	Lake
Balance of nature	Leaf
Bird	Mountain
Botany	Ocean
Butterfly	Plant
Conservation	River
Constellation	Rock
Desert	Season
Earth	Seed
Fish	Star
Flower	Tree
Forest	Vegetable
Forestry	Volcano
Fruit	Water
Gardening	Waterfall
Geology	Weather
Hobby	Zoology

Nature study organizations

Audubon Society, National
Boy Scouts
Camp Fire USA
Girl Scouts
Izaak Walton League of America
Scouts Canada

Other related articles

Aquarium, Public	Arbor Day

Botanical garden	Park
Museum	Planetarium
National forest	Telescope
National Park System	Terrarium
Observatory	Zoo

Nature worship is a religious practice followed by various cultures throughout history. It is based on the belief that nature is a god, goddess, divine power, or group of gods that can grant people favors and protect them from evil. Some peoples have worshiped specific natural forces, such as the sun, water, or the winds. In most cases, a community has worshiped the parts of nature most important to its survival. For example, early American Indians in agricultural areas asked the rain god for rain to make their crops grow.   Sarah M. Pike

See also **Animism; May Day; Pantheism; Religion** (Religion today).

Nauru, *NAH roo,* is a small island country in the central Pacific Ocean. It is part of Micronesia, one of the three groups of the Pacific Islands. Nauru consists of a single island, which has an area of only 8 square miles (21 square kilometers). It is the third smallest country in the world. Only Vatican City and Monaco are smaller. For many years, the mining of *phosphates,* valuable chemical compounds used in making fertilizers, earned the majority of the Nauruan government's revenue. However, phosphate reserves on the tiny island are now largely depleted.

Nauru has no capital city. The main government offices are in the southwestern part of the country. The Australian dollar is Nauru's basic unit of currency. For a picture of the flag of Nauru, see **Flag** (picture: Flags of Asia and the Pacific).

Government. Nauru is a republic and a member of the Commonwealth of Nations. An 18-member Parliament makes the country's laws. Parliament members are elected by the people to three-year terms. All Nauruans who are 20 years old or older are required to vote. The Parliament elects a president to a three-year term. The president selects a Cabinet. The president and the Cabinet carry out the executive functions of the government.

Land. Nauru, an oval-shaped coral island, lies about 40 miles (65 kilometers) south of the equator. Most of the island is a plateau, 200 feet (61 meters) high, which contains deposits of phosphates. Near the center of the plateau is a lagoon surrounded by a small area of fertile land. Another belt of fertile land lies along Nauru's coast. Most of the people live along the 12-mile (19-kilometer) coastline.

In the past, the people raised their own food. Now, they import most of their food and other products. Nauru has a tropical climate that is cooled by trade winds. Temperatures range from 76 to 93 °F (24 to 34 °C). About 80 inches (200 centimeters) of rain falls yearly.

People. About half of Nauru's population of 10,000 are Nauruans—people of mixed Polynesian, Micronesian, and Melanesian ancestry. They are Christians. Most of them speak both the Nauruan language and English. The rest of Nauru's people are mainly from Australia, China, Kiribati, and Tuvalu. They come for limited periods to help mine the phosphates.

The government provides Nauruans with modern homes at low rents, and government hospitals and clinics give them free medical care. Nauruan children from

Nauru

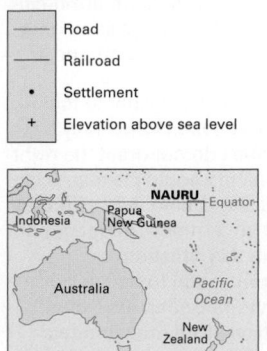

—	Road
—	Railroad
•	Settlement
+	Elevation above sea level

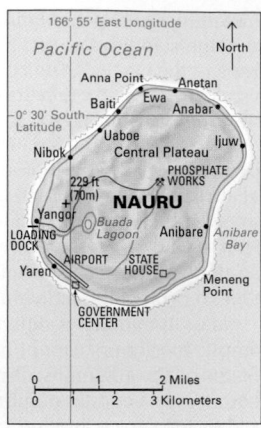

WORLD BOOK maps

the ages of 6 through 16 receive free education and must attend school. Some older Nauruan students attend the University of the South Pacific in Fiji, an island country to the south.

Economy. For many years, Nauru's economy has been dependent on phosphate mining. The government established a trust fund with revenue from phosphate sales. This trust fund was to help Nauru's economy after its phosphate reserves were exhausted. However, the phosphate reserves are now largely depleted and the trust fund is mostly spent. Because of these reasons, the island is nearly bankrupt and is heavily dependent on foreign aid. Nauru has little agricultural or industrial production and must import most of its food.

History. Nauru was first settled by Polynesian and Micronesian seafarers several thousand years ago. Captain John Fearn, an English explorer, was the first European to visit Nauru. He came in 1798. In 1888, Germany took over the island and administered it until 1914 when Australia took control. After World War I (1914-1918), Australia began to administer the island under a League of Nations mandate held also by the United Kingdom, Australia, and New Zealand.

Japan seized Nauru during World War II (1939-1945). In 1945, Australian forces retook the island. In 1947, the United Nations (UN) provided for Australian control of the island under a trusteeship held also by the United Kingdom and New Zealand. In 1964, Nauru began to work for independence and control of the phosphate industry. Nauru became independent in 1968 after a UN-supervised *plebiscite* (popular vote). In 1970, the Nauruan government gained control of the phosphate industry. It used revenue from phosphate exports to build homes, schools, and hospitals. Nauruans had a high standard of living through the 1980's. Since then, diminishing phosphate reserves, failed investments by the government, and problems in Nauru's banking industry have caused economic hardship.   Michael R. Ogden

Nausea, *NAW shuh* or *NAW shee uh,* is a disagreeable sensation in the area of the stomach. It is often followed by vomiting. In nausea, the muscles of the stomach wall slow or stop their movement. In turn, digestion of the contents of the stomach slows or stops. This action can help prevent the body from absorbing a poisonous substance that has been swallowed. If vomiting takes place, most of the substance will be expelled.

Nausea also may result from many other causes, both mental and physical. Mental causes include unpleasant sights, disgusting odors, and severe anxiety. Physical causes include severe pain, obstruction or irritation of the digestive tract, excessive physical exercise, and unnatural stimulation of the *vestibular system,* the organs of balance of the inner ear. Nausea from disturbances of the vestibular system is called *motion sickness* (see **Motion sickness**). Nausea often accompanies pregnancy, especially in the mornings of the first three months.

Some poisonous substances cause nausea by stimulating nerve endings in the lining of the stomach or intestine. Other poisons cause nausea after being absorbed into the blood. The blood carries the poison to special cells in the *medulla,* the lower part of the brain stem. These cells create nausea by sending impulses to higher parts of the brain, where sensations are received. Various drugs, including chlorpromazine and Dramamine, are used to control certain types of nausea (see **Chlorpromazine; Dramamine**).   K. E. Money

See also **Vomiting**.

Nautilus. See **Submarine** (History).

Nautilus, *NAW tuh luhs,* is a group of ocean animals that have a soft body partly covered with a coiled shell. A nautilus is a mollusk, a large group of animals that have no bones. Nautiluses live at depths of 20 to 1,000 feet (6 to 300 meters) along the coral reefs of the South Pacific and Indian oceans. They eat mainly marine worms and small *crustaceans,* a type of animal with a shell and jointed legs. They also feed on crustacean shells and animal remains. There are several *species* (kinds) of nautiluses. The most familiar is called the *chambered nautilus,* though this name is also used for other nautiluses. Scientists have found at least 2,000 fossil forms of nautiluses.

The body of an adult nautilus is about the size of a person's fist. Its cone-shaped head is surrounded by about 90 short *tentacles* (feelers) that can be pulled into the shell. These tentacles sense taste and touch. A nautilus shell is made up of many chambers. These chambers are lined with a rainbow-colored substance called *mother-of-pearl* or *nacre.* As a nautilus grows, it adds new chambers to its shell. Each new chamber is closed at the rear, so the animal always lives in the outermost chamber. The shell of an adult has about 30 chambers. The *siphuncle,* a coiled, blood-filled tube, extends through all the chambers of the shell.   Jennifer A. Basil

    Scientific classification. Nautiluses make up the genus *Nautilus.* The chambered nautilus is *Nautilus pompilius.*

See also **Shell** (Octopuses and squids).

Nauvoo, *naw VOO* or *NAW voo* (pop. 1,149), is a small community along the Mississippi River in western Illinois. Joseph Smith, the founder of the Mormon Church, founded it as a Mormon sanctuary in 1839. The site had previously been a failed settlement called Commerce. The Mormons fled to Nauvoo to escape persecution in Missouri. The name *Nauvoo* is a word of Hebrew origin meaning *the beautiful place.*

Soon after its founding, Nauvoo became a thriving city. In the mid-1840's, its population grew to about 12,000 people. For a time, it was the largest city in Illinois. The Illinois government granted Nauvoo *home rule* (local self-government), and the town had its own militia. The community developed considerable political

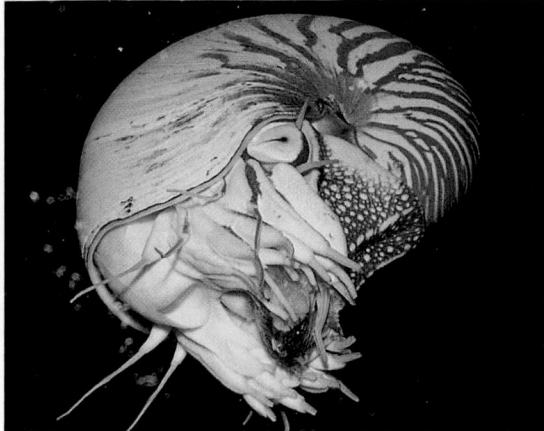

A nautilus has a spiral shell. The animal adds a new, larger chamber to its shell each time it outgrows its old one. Its cone-shaped head is surrounded by short tentacles.

and economic power, and nearby non-Mormons became hostile to it. In 1844, Smith and his brother Hyrum were assassinated. In 1846, mobs forced the Mormons out of Illinois. Most of them moved to what is now Utah.

In 1849, a French socialist named Étienne Cabet led a group of followers to Nauvoo and founded a *utopian community*—that is, a community based on a vision of political and social harmony. The settlers called their town Icaria. They practiced communal ownership of property and equality of work and profit. Icarians split into factions in 1856, and Cabet left with his own following. The Icarian community in Nauvoo ended in 1860.

In 2002, the Church of Jesus Christ of Latter-day Saints completed the rebuilding of the Nauvoo Temple, a historic place of worship built by the Mormons. The original temple had been destroyed about 1850. Today, visitors to Nauvoo may see the homes of Smith and of the Mormon leader Brigham Young, as well as other restored buildings.   Greg Hall

Navajo Indians, *NAV uh hoh,* also spelled *Navaho,* are the second largest Indian tribe in the United States. According to the 2000 U.S. census, there are about 269,000 Navajo. Only the Cherokee tribe has more members. The Navajo reservation, which covers 16 million acres (6.5 million hectares), is the nation's biggest reservation. It includes parts of Arizona, New Mexico, and Utah. The growth of industry on the reservation promises to make the Navajo one of the wealthiest tribes in America. The Navajo call themselves *Diné* (pronounced *dihn EH),* meaning *the people.*

About 143,000 Navajo live on the Navajo reservation. Some of them live in traditional tribal houses called *hogans,* which are made of earth and logs (see **Hogan**). Many Navajo practice the tribal religion. Large numbers of the tribe are farmers or sheep ranchers, but others are engineers, miners, teachers, or technicians. Skilled Navajo craftworkers weave wool blankets and rugs and make turquoise jewelry. The Navajo earn millions of dollars yearly, mainly from the mining of their vast coal deposits. The tribe also has a lumber mill and a manufacturing plant leased by an electronics firm. Diné College, the first community college to be owned and operated by Indians, is in Tsaile, Arizona, near Lukachukai, on the reservation.

About A.D. 1000, the ancestors of the Navajo migrated to the southwestern United States from what is now Alaska and Canada. Their Pueblo neighbors taught them to raise crops. During religious rituals, Navajo medicine men and medicine women created symbolic sand paintings to help heal the sick (see **Sand painting**).

During the 1600's, the Navajo began to raise sheep. An increasing number of white settlers established ranches on the Navajo lands, and the Indians fought to drive the ranchers away. In 1863 and 1864, U.S. Army troops led by Kit Carson destroyed the farms and homes of the Navajo. In 1864, the soldiers forced about 8,000 Indians to march more than 300 miles (480 kilometers) to Fort Sumner, New Mexico. The Navajo call this march the "Long Walk." Thousands of Indians died during the march and their imprisonment at the fort. In 1868, the Navajo agreed to settle on the reservation.

The Navajo reservation surrounds the Hopi Indian Reservation. The two tribes have disagreed over land ownership and use for many years, and the U.S. government has tried to solve some of these disputes. In 1974, Congress gave each tribe half of a 1,800,000-acre (730,000-hectare) land area in Arizona that the tribes had used jointly since 1962. However, many members of the Navajo tribe refused to move off the Hopi land. In the early 1990's, the Navajo and Hopi tribes reached an agreement, allowing Navajo families to remain on Hopi land for 75 years, living under Hopi law. Congress ratified this agreement in 1996. By the early 2000's, most Navajo families either had moved off Hopi land or had signed an agreement with the Hopi tribe.

Delilah Orr

See also **Code talkers; Indian, American** (pictures); **Manuelito.**

Additional resources

Iverson, Peter. *Diné: A History of the Navajos.* Univ. of N. Mex. Pr., 2002.
McIntosh, Kenneth. *Navajo.* Mason Crest, 2004.
Santella, Andrew. *Navajo Code Talkers.* Compass Point, 2004. Younger readers.

Naval Academy, United States. See United States Naval Academy.

Naval Observatory, United States, is the country's oldest national observatory. It was founded in 1830 and is operated by the U.S. Navy. It is headquartered in Washington, D.C.

The United States Naval Observatory is responsible for measuring the positions and motions of the sun, moon, planets, and stars, and for monitoring the position of Earth. The observatory also maintains the U.S. reference for precise time and distributes its data through such means as almanacs and related publications, electronic data links, and satellites. United States and international civilian and scientific agencies use information from the observatory primarily for navigation and scientific research.

In 1978, the observatory's largest telescope was used to discover Pluto's satellite Charon. The instrument, a reflecting telescope with a diameter of 61 inches (155 centimeters), is in Flagstaff, Arizona. Astronomers used another observatory instrument, a 26-inch (66-centimeter) refracting telescope, now in Washington, D.C., to dis-

cover the two moons of Mars, Phobos and Deimos, in 1877.   Critically reviewed by the United States Naval Observatory

Naval War College, in Newport, Rhode Island, is the postgraduate educational institution of the United States Navy. The college improves the professional decision-making abilities of senior officers in both command and management positions in the United States Navy. It also conducts research aimed at developing strategies and tactics for use in future naval warfare.

The Naval War College consists of four resident colleges, the Center for Naval Warfare Studies, and the Center for Irregular Warfare and Armed Groups. Some programs train U.S. officers from other branches of the armed forces. The Center for Naval Warfare Studies coordinates research and computerized war games that simulate actual combat conditions. The Center for Irregular Warfare and Armed Groups studies warfare with groups not part of national militaries. Commodore Stephen B. Luce founded the Naval War College in 1884. The website at http://www.usnwc.edu offers additional information.   Critically reviewed by the United States Navy

Nave. See Basilica; Cathedral.

Navel. See Umbilical cord.

Navigation is the process of finding an object's position and directing its movement. The word *navigate* comes from two Latin words meaning *ship* and *to drive.*

Navigation has long been used to guide ships. Today, navigation techniques can help guide almost anything— from cars, trains, airplanes, and spacecraft to packages and people. Modern navigation systems make it easy for almost everyone to find their way. Such systems have been developed using advanced mathematics, physics, engineering, and computer science.

Today, radio transmitters, computers, and satellites automatically perform much of the work of navigation. But early navigators had to rely on more basic tools and techniques. Some traditional techniques are still in use.

Traditional navigation

Among the most basic navigation aids are charts, maps, and compasses. Charts and maps show the physical characteristics of an area. They may give such information as the location of ports, the height of mountains, or the depth of water. Compasses determine direction. The simplest is a magnetic compass with a magnetized needle that points to the North Pole. Magnetic compasses, however, become wildly inaccurate near the North and South poles. In these regions, navigators may use electronic compasses called *gyrocompasses* that do not depend on Earth's magnetism. There are three chief methods of traditional navigation: (1) dead reckoning, (2) piloting, and (3) celestial navigation. Navigators may use one or more of the methods, depending on the means of travel, weather, and other factors.

Dead reckoning (DR), sometimes called *deduced reckoning,* involves estimating how far and in what direction an object has moved. This method is not particularly accurate. It does not consider such factors as water currents, wind, or steering errors. Any of these factors can make it difficult for navigators to accurately keep track of a vehicle's motion and direction, particularly in the case of ships and aircraft. Thus, navigators typically use other methods along with dead reckoning.

Piloting involves finding a vehicle's position in rela-

Air traffic controllers use navigation systems to safely guide airplanes to and from airports. Modern navigation systems use radio signals broadcast from stations on the ground and from satellites in orbit.

tion to one or more landmarks. Landmarks include such natural objects as mountains and islands. They also include artificial structures, such as buildings, buoys, and lighthouses. Successful piloting requires an up-to-date chart showing the positions of such landmarks.

In piloting, the navigator finds the *bearing* (direction) from the vehicle to a landmark in view. A magnetic compass can tell a landmark's bearing relative to the North Pole. Alternatively, a device called a *pelorus* can measure a landmark's bearing relative to a second landmark.

The navigator matches the landmark in view to its position on the chart. Then the navigator draws a line from the landmark on the chart in the same direction as the bearing. This line is called the *line of position*. The navigator can then figure out the vehicle's rough position on the chart, because it is on the line of position. However, to pinpoint a vehicle's position, two landmarks must be used. The two landmarks create two lines of position. The vehicle's position is at the point where the two lines cross each other.

Navigators may also pilot with the aid of a *depth finder*, a device that measures the depth of the water. A navigator compares the depths indicated by this device with the depths on the chart.

Piloting can be used to navigate most types of vehicles. Ships use this method when entering or leaving ports, or when sailing close to land. Sailors pilot many small boats with only a chart and compass.

Celestial navigation involves determining a vehicle's location by observing the sun, moon, planets, and stars. The navigator measures the angle between the horizon and such astronomical objects, also called *celestial* (heavenly) bodies. This angle is then used in complex mathematical calculations to determine the vehicle's position. Because the horizon is typically easy to view at sea, ships can make good use of celestial navigation.

Measuring angles. A device called a *sextant* enables navigators to easily measure the angle between a celestial body and the horizon. The sextant has a sighting tube, a fixed mirror called a *horizon glass* in which the horizon appears, and an adjustable mirror called an *index glass* that moves to give the navigator a view of the sun or a star. The sextant enables a navigator to take accurate measurements, even if the device is unsteady or jerks around, as on a moving ship.

On land, the navigator may not be able to see the horizon. The horizon also may not be perfectly flat, as it is at sea. To use celestial navigation on land, a navigator must thus use special techniques to approximate a flat horizon, from which to measure angles. One such technique involves using a carpenter's *level*, a device that forms a perfectly horizontal surface.

Keeping time. The moon, the stars, and other objects in the sky are in constant motion. Measuring their angles against the horizon thus yields different results at different times. For this reason, a navigator must know the time to use celestial navigation effectively. An English clockmaker named John Harrison invented the first accurate timekeeping device in the mid-1700's. The device, called a *chronometer*, made accurate celestial navigation possible.

Publications called *almanacs* list the positions of celestial bodies at all times during the year. Navigators could use almanacs along with accurate angle measurements and exact time measurements to determine position reliably.

One star never changes its position in the sky—the North Star, also called Polaris. In the Northern Hemisphere, stars seem to revolve around a point in the heavens called the *celestial north pole,* which lies above the North Pole. The North Star is so close to the celestial north pole that it appears stationary. Navigators in the

WORLD BOOK photo by Ralph Brunke

A sextant is an instrument used in celestial navigation. It measures the angle between the horizon and a star or other heavenly body. The sextant's location can be derived from this angle.

Northern Hemisphere can derive *latitude* (position north or south on Earth's surface relative to the equator) from the North Star's position, without regard to time. However, people in the Southern Hemisphere cannot see the North Star, so this technique does not work there.

Modern use. From Earth's surface, celestial navigation is possible only when the sky is clear. But airplanes and spacecraft fly over clouds and so can always use it. On spacecraft, celestial navigation is used to control the craft's *orientation* (direction in which it is pointed), rather than to find its position. A camera system called a *star tracker* does the work of a sextant, making celestial observations and measurements automatically.

Electronic navigation

The development of radio technology, computers,

and artificial satellites has revolutionized navigation. Such technology can automatically make measurements and calculations that navigators once had to do by hand.

Radio navigation. Most modern navigation systems use radio waves. Radio waves are invisible and can travel through air or space. Radio signals are useful for navigation because they can be used to measure distance and direction.

All radio navigation systems involve the use of one or more devices called *transmitters*. The transmitter sends out radio waves, which are eventually picked up by one or more devices called *receivers*.

In some radio navigation technologies, the transmitter sends radio waves to bounce off a moving object. Electronic equipment then measures how long the waves take to return to a receiver at their source. The returning waves reveal the distance and direction of the moving object, giving its position.

In other technologies, a receiver on a vehicle picks up radio waves from a transmitter. These waves may carry encoded information, such as the transmitter's position or the time the signal was sent. This information can be used to calculate the receiver's position and movement. Similarly, other systems use receivers on the ground to locate a moving transmitter.

Radio waves have various *frequencies*—that is, rates at which the wave *oscillates* (vibrates). Very high frequency (VHF) radio waves, such as those used in FM broadcasts, can more accurately pinpoint an object's position. But they can only travel in a straight line from the transmitter, called a *line of sight*. Thus, they cannot be transmitted over the curve of Earth's horizon. Airplanes and spacecraft avoid this problem because they fly high enough to have direct lines of sight to many places on the ground.

Low-frequency waves, such as those used in AM broadcasts, are less accurate. But they can travel beyond Earth's horizon by bouncing off an electrically charged part of the atmosphere called the *ionosphere*.

Radar uses radio waves with extremely high frequencies. It bounces the waves off moving objects to determine their direction and distance. *Radar* stands for *ra*dio

WORLD BOOK photo by Ralph Brunke

Celestial navigation—that is, navigation by the stars or other heavenly bodies—requires complex calculations to derive one's position. The navigator must know the angle from the horizon to a star, as well as the time at which the angle was measured.

detection and ranging. Air traffic controllers use radar to pinpoint the positions of aircraft in the sky. The controllers can share this information with the pilots through voice radio or text messaging. See **Radar**.

Radio direction finding involves determining the bearing of a transmitter called a *radio beacon.* A device called a *radio direction finder* (RDF) receives the beacon's signal. The navigator turns the RDF's antenna, and the device shows when it is pointed toward the beacon.

Omnirange is a short-range navigation system for aircraft flying over land. It makes use of ground stations shown on an aeronautical chart. They are called VOR's, for *V*ery High Frequency *O*mnidirectional *R*ange. The stations and the aircraft transmit radio waves to each other. These radio waves help determine the aircraft's range and bearing to each station.

The military uses a similar navigation system called TACAN, standing for *Tac*tical *A*ir *N*avigation. When VOR and TACAN equipment are on the same ground station, the station is called a *VORTAC* station. Almost all commercial airports have such stations.

Satellite navigation makes use of radio signals broadcast from artificial satellites orbiting Earth. There are several satellite-based navigation systems. Perhaps the best known is the Global Positioning System (GPS). The GPS includes at least 24 Navstar satellites, which are controlled by the United States Air Force. The word *Navstar* stands for *Nav*igation *S*atellite *T*racking *a*nd *R*anging.

The satellites circle Earth in six different orbits, with four or more satellites spread along each orbit. Each satellite broadcasts its exact position and time. A receiver picks up signals from at least three different satellites, analyzing how long each signal takes to reach it. The receiver then determines its location by calculating its distance from these satellites.

GPS makes accurate navigation possible in any weather condition. Many drivers, boaters, and hikers use a portable GPS receiver that displays their position on an electronic map. Many cell phones are also equipped with GPS receivers.

In addition, GPS signals serve as accurate timekeepers. Each satellite holds an extremely accurate atomic clock. The satellites broadcast their times to receivers. These signals are used around the world to *synchronize* communication systems—that is, to make them agree on what time it is.

Russia controls another satellite navigation system, GLONASS. The European Commission and the European Space Agency are building a satellite system called Galileo. China is also building a system called Compass, a version of their BeiDou satellite system. BeiDou is the Chinese name for the Big Dipper constellation.

Other radio navigation systems include *loran* and *omega.* They have been replaced by satellite navigation systems.

Loran stands for *lo*ng *ra*nge *n*avigation. It was used to guide ships and airplanes as they approached coastal waters from the sea. Multiple loran stations sent out low- or medium-frequency radio waves, which vehicles could detect over long distances. The vehicle's position could be determined accurately by comparing the signals from different stations.

Omega broadcast even lower frequency radio waves than loran did. The system used just eight transmitters throughout the world and required international cooperation to operate.

Inertial guidance involves the use of a computer and a type of gyroscope called an *inertial measurement unit* (IMU). The IMU constantly monitors changes in the vehicle's motion and sends this information to the computer. Specifically, IMU's measure the force produced when a vehicle accelerates. The computer uses these measurements to calculate the distance and direction traveled, and to continuously update the vehicle's velocity and ac-

U.S. Navy

Radar is an electronic navigation system that locates objects by bouncing radio signals off them. This operator on a military airplane is using radar to track other air traffic.

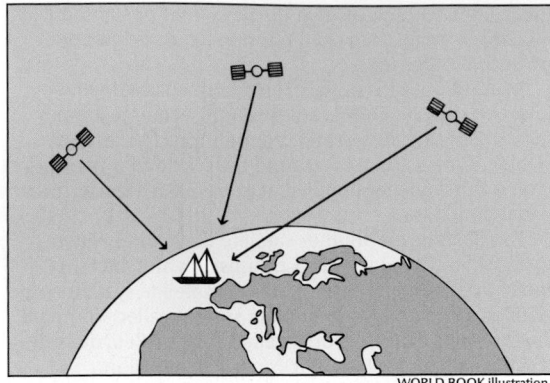

WORLD BOOK illustration

The Global Positioning System includes satellites that circle Earth and broadcast their positions. A receiver can find its location by computing its distance from at least three satellites.

celeration. Inertial navigation is used to guide satellites, aircraft, ships, and submarines. See **Inertial guidance.**

History

In ancient times, sailors navigated by observing heavenly bodies and constellations. They also studied the seasonal patterns in wind direction. During the Middle Ages (about the A.D. 400's through the 1400's), navigators drew simple charts. These charts included wind directions for different seasons, in addition to compass directions.

Early instruments. Many of today's navigation instruments developed from crude equipment used hundreds of years ago. For example, the first compass consisted of a magnetized piece of metal on a straw. The straw floated in a container of water.

For many centuries, the primary navigation tool was the sextant. Navigators used it to calculate a ship's latitude by measuring the angle of the sun or of a star above the horizon. The sextant developed from the *astrolabe* and the *quadrant,* two early instruments for measuring the angle between a celestial body and the hori-

zon. An astrolabe consisted of a disk, along with a sight that turned on a pivot. A quadrant had the same arrangement of two mirrors, one fixed and one adjustable, as a sextant had. A quadrant could measure larger angles than a sextant could. It could measure up to 90 degrees, or one-fourth of a circle, compared with the sextant's 60 degrees, or one-sixth of a circle. But navigators eventually preferred the sextant because it was more portable, and modern sextants can move up to 120 degrees.

Explorers. In the 1700's, the British navigator James Cook became the first person to use highly developed celestial navigation methods. Cook used these techniques in his three voyages to the Pacific Ocean.

The Lewis and Clark expedition, led by U.S. Army officers Meriwether Lewis and William Clark, used a quadrant and a sextant on their expedition up the Missouri River in 1803. The mountainous terrain often made it impossible to see the horizon. Instead, Lewis and Clark used a mirror and a level to create an "artificial horizon" from which to measure the relative angles to the sun and moon.

Electronic navigation. The development of radio, followed by its use on ships and airplanes in the early 1900's, marked the start of electronic navigation. During World War II (1939-1945), German scientists developed navigation systems to guide V-1 and V-2 rockets. Among the Allies, British and American scientists made important advances in radar technology that aided navigation.

Satellite navigation began with the launch of Sputnik in 1957. Scientists realized that a "constellation" of such satellites could be used for worldwide navigation. In 1960, the U.S. Navy launched a navigation satellite called TRANSIT 1B. The TRANSIT satellite navigation system operated from 1964 to 1996. It consisted of six operating satellites in widely spaced orbits, in addition to several spares. Several TRANSIT satellites are still in orbit and are used in scientific research.

In 1979, Canada, France, the United States, and the Soviet Union developed the COSPAS-SARSAT search and rescue satellite system. In this system, a transmitter on the ground sends a signal to a satellite. When an aircraft

Important dates in navigation

1100?-1200? Chinese and Mediterranean navigators used magnetic compasses to guide ships.

1519-1522 Ferdinand Magellan, a Portuguese navigator, led the first expedition to sail around the world.

1569 Gerardus Mercator, a Flemish geographer, invented the Mercator map, with which a navigator can accurately determine direction.

1730 John Hadley, an English mathematician, and Thomas Godfrey, an American astronomer and mathematician, independently invented the *sextant.* This device measures the angle between a celestial body and the horizon.

1735 John Harrison, an English clockmaker, made the first accurate *chronometer*—a device for measuring time.

1767 Nevil Maskelyne, an English astronomer, compiled the first *nautical almanac.* A nautical almanac is used to guide a ship by determining the positions of celestial bodies.

1802 Nathaniel Bowditch, an American mathematician and astronomer, wrote *The New American Practical Navigator.*

1842 Lieutenant Matthew F. Maury of the U.S. Navy charted the direction of winds and ocean currents. This information is used in *piloting,* a method of navigation.

1896 Guglielmo Marconi, an Italian inventor and electrical engineer, sent the first ship-to-shore radio signal.

1908 Hermann Anschütz-Kämpfe, a German engineer, invented the gyroscopic compass.

1910 J. A. D. McCurdy, a Canadian aviator, sent the first airplane-to-ground messages.

1933 P. V. H. Weems, an American navigator, compiled the first *air almanac,* used in guiding a plane by the positions of celestial bodies.

1939-1945 During World War II, British and American scientists made significant contributions to the development of radar.

1945-1950 American scientists developed a highly accurate *inertial guidance system,* which guides a vehicle without using outside signals.

1964-1996 The U.S. Navy operated its satellite navigation system TRANSIT.

1995 The U.S. Air Force's Navstar Global Positioning System became fully operational.

2005 Most cell phones in the United States were required to include GPS tracking ability for use in emergencies.

Granger Collection

A compass rose, like this one on a 1612 map of Virginia, indicates direction. Lines radiate from it in 32 points of direction.

or ship is in distress, its SARSAT transmitter is activated automatically. This transmitter is known as an Emergency Position Indicating Beacon, or EPIRB. One or more satellites receive the signal and locate the EPIRB. The system broadcasts this information to ground stations throughout the world, beginning search and rescue operations. The COSPAS-SARSAT system has helped save thousands of lives. Many countries share the responsibilities for its operation.

In the 1970's, the United States began to launch the first several satellites of the Navstar GPS. The GPS system became fully operational in 1995.   Daniel G. Jablonski

Related articles in *World Book* include:

Navigation aids and instruments

Airplane (Air navigation)	Lighthouse
Almanac	Log
Astrolabe	Map
Beacon	Radar
Buoy	Radio (Navigation)
Chronometer	Satellite, Artificial (Navigation
Compass	satellites)
Fathometer	Sextant
Global Positioning System	Ship (Navigating a ship)
Gyrocompass	Shoran
Gyroscope	Sonar
Inclinometer	

Famous navigators

Bowditch, Nathaniel
Cabral, Pedro Álvares
Columbus, Christopher
Cook, James
Da Gama, Vasco
Dias, Bartolomeu
Drake, Sir Francis
Henry the Navigator
Magellan, Ferdinand
Maury, Matthew Fontaine

Other related articles

Degree
Exploration
Great-circle route
Greenwich Observatory, Royal
Knot

Latitude
Longitude
Mercator, Gerardus
North Star
Time

Navigation Acts were several laws passed in the 1600's by the English Parliament. The purpose of the laws was to protect English trade. In 1645, Parliament passed a law that forbade the importation of whale oil into England in non-English vessels, or in ships that were not operated by English sailors.

The act known as the First Navigation Act was passed in 1651. It was aimed against the American Colonies and the Dutch, who were profiting from most of the overseas trade between the West Indies and Europe. The act provided that no products from any foreign country might be shipped into England in any but English-built ships operated by crews that were at least 75 percent English. But the act was not strictly enforced.

Parliament passed other trade laws in 1660, 1663, and 1672. The act of 1660 required that all the tobacco from the colonies must be brought to England. The act of 1663 (Second Navigation Act) declared that almost all goods imported into the colonies must be landed in England first. In 1672, an act was passed requiring that goods had to be shipped to England before they could pass from one of the American Colonies to another.

Before 1761, 29 acts limiting colonial trade had been passed. America suffered little from these laws because of smuggling by the colonists. Several parts of the acts favored American industry because they encouraged American shipping. But the Americans vigorously opposed the restrictions on commerce. This opposition was a main cause of the American Revolution (1775-1783). The British Parliament, in 1849, *repealed* (canceled) all the Navigation Acts.   Charles Carlton

See also **Colonial life in America** (Trade).

Navratilova, NAV *ruh tuh LOH vuh,* **Martina** (1956-   ), ranks among the greatest female tennis players in the history of the sport. Navratilova became noted for her aggressive, athletic style of play; her strong serve; and her skill at volleying. She won 59 grand slam titles—18 singles, 31 women's doubles, and 10 mixed doubles. The grand slam consists of the Australian Open, the French Open, the U.S. Open, and Wimbledon in England. In 1984, Navratilova and her partner Pam Shriver became the only women's doubles team to win all four grand slam championships in the same year.

Navratilova won a record 167 singles titles. She held the number-one ranking in women's tennis for 331 weeks. In 2003, at the age of 46, she became the oldest Wimbledon champion by winning the mixed doubles title with her partner Leander Paes of India. She also matched the American tennis star Billie Jean King's record of 20 Wimbledon titles.

Navratilova was born on Oct. 18, 1956, in Prague, then in Czechoslovakia and now in the Czech Republic. She defected to the United States in 1975 and became a U.S. citizen in 1981. Navratilova retired as an active player in 2006.   Tony Lance

See also **Tennis** (picture: Modern women tennis stars).

Navstar Global Positioning System. See Global Positioning System.

A naval task force consists of a temporary unit of ships formed to carry out an operation. In this British task force, a V/STOL aircraft carrier leads a group of smaller Royal Navy warships.

Navy

Navy is the branch of a nation's armed forces that consists of warships and support ships, their crews, and land bases and their personnel. Many navies also have an air force. Some navies include combat forces called *marines,* who are trained to fight in the air and on land.

Most nations that have a coastline have a navy. But the world's navies differ greatly in size, in fighting strength,

Norman Polmar, the contributor of this article, is the author of the reference book The Ships and Aircraft of the U.S. Fleet *and the former editor of the U.S. sections of* Jane's Fighting Ships.

and in the types of ships and aircraft that they have. Smaller navies consist mainly of warships called *small combatants,* such as patrol boats, missile boats, and minesweepers. The main task of a small navy is to defend its nation's coastline. Larger navies also have major warships, such as aircraft carriers, submarines, and frigates. These warships can operate far out at sea without returning to port for weeks or months. Nations use large navies to control the sea and, during times of war, to attack enemy shores.

The United States, China, and Russia have the largest navies in the world. For centuries, the most powerful nations were frequently those with the strongest navies. The development of aircraft and missiles in the 1900's reduced the importance of seagoing forces. Nevertheless, navies still have tremendous military and political value. Warships are flexible in operation, and they can travel the seas freely. International law allows ships to sail within 12 nautical miles (22.2 kilometers) of any country's coast without permission. Thus, a group of warships can serve as a temporary military base. More importantly, ships can carry out their mission independent of foreign land bases.

The role of navies

Nations use their navies in many different roles. A navy's role depends on its size and composition, and whether the nation is at war or at peace.

Peacetime roles. When a nation is at peace, it may show political support by sending its ships to an ally's port or by training with an ally's navy. Navies may also help deliver food, medicine, and other humanitarian aid to war-torn countries or to areas struck by a natural disaster. In addition, nations may use their navies to collect *intelligence* (information about potential enemies).

Sometimes, navies perform limited military operations during peacetime. For example, in the late 1980's, U.S. warships escorted oil tankers in the Persian Gulf to protect them from attack during the war between Iran and Iraq. This was a military action, even though the United States was not directly involved in the war.

Wartime roles. During a war, the primary role of a small navy is to defend its nation's coastline against enemies. Large navies have two principal wartime roles: (1) controlling the sea and (2) providing a base from which to launch attacks against the shore.

Controlling the sea means that a navy takes over specific areas of the ocean to ensure the safe passage of its own ships and to deny passage to enemy ships. Control of the sea involves defending ships against attack. It also may involve blockading enemy land bases so that enemy ships and aircraft cannot use them. A navy may control some areas of the sea by laying *naval mines* (explosive devices in the water). Naval mines can damage or destroy ships that try to pass over them.

A nation with a large navy also has the power to attack targets on land from the sea. Modern warships can launch attacks from positions far out at sea using missiles and aircraft. Navies may also launch *amphibious assaults*—invasions of enemy coastal areas by the combined action of land, sea, and air forces.

The organization of navies

Every navy has a shore-based branch and a seagoing branch. The shore-based branch includes headquarters, communications stations, airfields, shipyards, maintenance facilities, supply stations, naval schools, and their personnel. The seagoing branch, usually called the *fleet,* consists of a navy's ships, submarines, ship-based aircraft, and their crews. The organization of a fleet varies with the size, mission, and location of the navy. The U.S. Navy, for example, has separate fleets in the Atlantic and Pacific oceans. France has Atlantic and Mediterranean fleets. India's navy operates one fleet on India's western coast and a second fleet on its eastern coast.

Because ships are flexible in their operation, they can be organized in many combinations for different purposes. In most fleets, each ship is assigned to a permanent administrative unit called a *group, squadron,* or *division.* Large fleets may also organize their ships into

Detmar Modes, Bundesministerium Verteidigung

Navy personnel may be assigned to ships or bases on shore. This German naval officer serves aboard a small ship. From the *bridge* (navigational center), he watches a nearby auxiliary ship.

task forces. These are temporary groupings of ships formed to carry out a particular task. A task force may consist of one or more than a dozen ships, depending on the task. In the U.S. Navy, task forces are called *battle groups* when they contain one or more aircraft carriers.

Ships and aircraft

The world's navies operate many types of ships, ranging from huge aircraft carriers to small patrol boats. Navies also use many kinds of aircraft.

Mou Jianwei, Xinhua News Agency

Chinese sailors on the deck of a destroyer prepare a guided missile for launching. The large Chinese Navy operates mostly in coastal waters.

Aircraft carriers are the largest warships ever built. Carriers serve as mobile bases for many kinds of aircraft. Some carriers are designed for *conventional aircraft,* which would normally require a long runway. Conventional aircraft are launched from a carrier deck with the aid of a *catapult.* When the aircraft land, a device called a *tail hook* lowered from the rear of the plane catches one of the steel cables stretched across the deck. The Brazilian, French, Russian, and U.S. navies have conventional aircraft carriers. Other carriers can serve as a base only for *V/STOL aircraft,* which take off vertically or from a short runway. V/STOL stands for Vertical/Short Take-Off and Landing. India, Italy, Spain, Thailand, and the United Kingdom have V/STOL carriers. Helicopters fly from both types of carriers.

Most carriers are armed with guns and missiles for short-range defense, but they depend on their aircraft and other warships for protection. Russian carriers are more heavily armed than carriers in other fleets.

Cruisers are the next largest warships. Navies use cruisers primarily to defend aircraft carriers against air and submarine attacks. Cruisers are armed with missiles, rockets, and torpedoes. Some cruisers also carry powerful long-range missiles for attacking targets on land. Peru, Russia, and the United States use cruisers.

Destroyers are similar to cruisers, but they are smaller and less costly to build. They are armed with guns, rockets, torpedoes, and missiles. A destroyer's main role is to escort and defend other ships, but destroyers also perform independent missions. Several of the world's navies have destroyers.

Frigates are the most common large warships in the world's navies. Navies use them chiefly to defend other warships and cargo ships against enemy submarines. Frigates are armed with torpedoes and other antisubmarine weapons. Most frigates also have guns, and some have missiles for defense against air and surface attacks.

Amphibious ships—often called *amphibs*—carry marines to enemy shores for operations on land. Amphibs use helicopters and landing craft to carry troops and their equipment ashore.

Submarines are warships that travel underwater. They can remain at sea, fully submerged, for long periods. They are extremely difficult for enemies to attack. Navies have two principal kinds of submarines: *attack submarines* and *ballistic missile submarines.* Attack submarines carry torpedoes and missiles. They primarily at-

tack enemy surface ships and submarines. About 40 navies have attack submarines. Ballistic missile submarines carry long-range ballistic missiles with nuclear warheads for attacking targets on shore. The navies of China, France, Russia, the United Kingdom, and the United States have ballistic missile submarines.

Auxiliary ships are noncombatant ships, most of which support warships. *Underway replenishment* (UNREP) ships carry fuel, food, weapons, ammunition, and other supplies for warships at sea. Other auxiliary ships include supply and repair ships called *tenders,* hospital ships, tankers, salvage ships, and tugs.

Small combatants include missile and torpedo boats, minesweepers, and patrol boats. Small combatants operate mostly in coastal waters. Missile and torpedo boats have limited seagoing ability, but they carry powerful weapons for attacking larger ships. Minesweepers locate and destroy enemy mines. Patrol boats guard coastal waters.

Aircraft play a major role in modern naval operations. Navies use many types of aircraft, including fighter, attack, antisubmarine, cargo, and *reconnaissance* (observation) planes; and helicopters.

Major navies of the world

A powerful navy is modern, well trained, and can fight effectively. The world's largest navies, in terms of both number of major warships and number of personnel, belong to the United States, China, and Russia. Other countries with large navies include France, India, Italy, Japan, North Korea, South Korea, Taiwan, Turkey, and the United Kingdom. The size of a navy does not necessarily reflect its fighting strength, however. For example, one aircraft carrier can provide as much striking power as can several destroyers or submarines. Also, advanced weapons can give a small navy major striking power.

The United States has about 115 major surface warships, including 11 conventional aircraft carriers. The carriers, 10 of which are nuclear powered, are the backbone of the U.S. fleet. In addition to surface ships, the U.S. Navy operates about 70 nuclear-powered submarines. Approximately 340,000 men and women serve in the U.S. Navy. Another 204,000 belong to the Marine Corps, a separate branch of the Department of the Navy.

China has a large navy, but many of its ships are old, and its sailors have spent little time training at sea. Thus, the effectiveness of the Chinese Navy has been limited. China's fleet operates mostly in coastal waters. The Chinese Navy has about 70 major surface warships. It also has about 60 submarines, of which about 10 are nuclear powered. About 255,000 people, including marines, serve in the Chinese Navy.

Russia took control of most of the massive Soviet Navy after the Soviet Union broke apart in late 1991. Since then, Russia has taken many ships and submarines out of service because they cost too much to operate. Despite these reductions, the Russian Navy is still large, and most of its ships are modern.

The submarine is the most important ship in the Russian fleet. The Russian Navy has about 65 submarines, about 45 of which are nuclear powered. Russia also has about 30 major surface warships, including 1 aircraft carrier. The Russian Navy has about 161,000 men and women, including marines.

Zha Chunming, Xinhua News Agency

A destroyer from the Chinese fleet tests a guided missile for use against enemy ships, aircraft, and shore targets. Many types of warships may be armed with missiles.

India enlarged its navy during the 1980's as part of an arms build-up. It now has about 25 major surface warships, including 1 aircraft carrier. India also has about 15 submarines, mostly diesel-powered. About 58,000 people, including marines, serve in the Indian Navy.

France has a relatively small navy, but it is modern and well trained. It has about 25 major surface warships, including 1 conventional aircraft carrier. France also has about 10 submarines, all nuclear powered. About 40,000 people, including marines, serve in the French Navy.

The United Kingdom has a relatively small but effective navy. The navy of the United Kingdom, called the Royal Navy, operates about 25 major surface warships, including 1 aircraft carrier. It also has about 10 submarines, all nuclear powered. About 35,000 people, including marines, serve in the Royal Navy.

The history of navies

Ancient navies. By about 3000 B.C., the Egyptians were using small seagoing ships for military purposes. Between 2000 and 1000 B.C., the Greeks began building long, wooden ships called *galleys*. Galleys were propelled chiefly by oars, but most also had sails. Ancient Mediterranean civilizations used galleys to guard their coastlines and trading ships. Ancient galleys had pointed bows to ram other ships. Later, crews used *catapults* (weapons that resembled giant slingshots) to throw stones, hot coals, and pitch onto enemy ships.

In 483 B.C., the Greek *city-state* of Athens, which consisted of Athens and the surrounding villages and farmland, began to build a large fleet of galleys to defend itself against invaders from Persia. As a result, Athens soon became the dominant naval power in the Mediterranean Sea. Athens defeated the Persian fleet near the island of Salamis in 480 B.C. in the first naval battle for which an extensive record exists.

In 31 B.C., the fleets of two rival Roman leaders, Mark Antony and Gaius Octavian, fought a battle off Actium in western Greece. Antony was allied with Cleopatra, the queen of Egypt, and commanded their joint fleets. Octavian's fleet won the battle. He later became Emperor Augustus of Rome. Rome reigned as the supreme naval power in the Mediterranean for the next 250 years.

Navies in the Middle Ages. From the A.D. 700's to about 1100, bold Scandinavian sailors, now known as Vikings, raided coastal and river settlements throughout western Europe. In the late 800's, the English king Alfred the Great built a large fleet of galley warships to defend his country against Viking raiders.

During the 1200's, Europeans began to build ships with large, deep *hulls* (main bodies). Deep-hulled ships were faster and could travel more easily on the high seas than long, low galleys. Sails rather than oars became the principal means of propulsion, though some ships still used oars when there was no wind.

Most navies of the Middle Ages followed a standard battle plan. Attacking warships sailed alongside enemy ships and hurled rocks and flaming chemicals at them. Attackers then tried to ram or board enemy ships. After boarding, the crews fought hand-to-hand using swords, hatchets, and, later, guns. Some historians believe navies first used cannons during the 1300's. But naval guns did not come into wide use until the 1500's.

Between 1405 and 1433, a Chinese fleet led by Admiral Zheng He (also spelled Cheng Ho) made a series of seven expeditions to the Indian Ocean, the Middle East, and the eastern coast of Africa. These voyages established China as the unchallenged naval power in Asia for the first half of the 1400's. China's naval supremacy ended after leaders who disapproved of contact with foreigners took control.

The beginning of modern navies. The Italian city of Venice was the major sea power in the Mediterranean during the late Middle Ages. By 1400, Venice had a fleet of about 3,000 galleys. The Ottoman Empire, based in what is now Turkey, ranked as Venice's chief naval rival. In 1571, Venice, Spain, and their allies destroyed most of the Ottoman fleet in a battle off Lepanto in Greece. This was the last major battle between oar-driven galleys.

During the 1500's, Spain and England competed for control of the Atlantic Ocean. Both countries built *galleons,* which were large, sailing ships with three masts. In the late 1500's, English galleons began harassing Spanish galleons carrying gold and silver from the Americas. In response, Spain built a fleet called the Armada. In 1588, it tried to invade England. But England's galleons were smaller and easier to maneuver than Spain's, and English crews were better trained. The English defeated the Armada. England (later part of the United Kingdom) dominated the Atlantic for the next 300 years.

The Netherlands competed with England for control of the seas during the mid-1600's. The two countries fought several naval battles that brought important changes in military tactics at sea. By this time, fleets had become large and difficult to command. Naval commanders began issuing instructions before a battle to coordinate the movements of their ships during the fighting. Large groups of ships were divided into squadrons. Commanders used flags to signal to other ships.

The largest warships were called *battleships* or *ships of the line* because they were positioned in the main line of battle. Opposing lines of battleships sailed on parallel courses and bombarded each other with cannon fire. In the Battle of Trafalgar, off the coast of Spain in 1805, British Admiral Horatio Nelson won a major victory by breaking through and disrupting the battle line of the opposing French and Spanish navies.

Engineering advances. In 1814, the American inventor Robert Fulton built the first steam-powered warship. Steamships could cruise faster than sailing ships, and they could move against or without wind. But steamships faced a new problem. They needed fuel and had to depend on land bases to supply coal for refueling. Navies had to establish fueling stations overseas.

Improvements in the range, reliability, and accuracy of shipboard guns had a tremendous impact on naval warfare. During the 1820's, inventors developed naval guns that fired explosive shells rather than solid balls. In 1853, Russian ships fired the first explosive shells used in naval battle, destroying the wooden ships of the opposing Ottoman fleet during the Crimean War. In this war, Russia fought the allied forces of the United Kingdom, France, Sardinia, and the Ottoman Empire.

In the mid-1800's, shipbuilders began covering wooden hulls with heavy iron armor plates. Inventors developed rotating turrets so that naval guns could be fired in almost any direction without turning the ship. As the range and accuracy of guns increased, ships fought at

© North Wind Picture Archives, Alamy

In the Battle of Lepanto, near Greece, in 1571, the navies of Venice and Spain and their allies defeated the Ottoman fleet. It was the last major battle between fleets of oar-driven galleys.

greater distances. Crews no longer boarded enemy ships and fought hand-to-hand, as in the sailing era.

In 1862, during the American Civil War, the Union's *Monitor* fought the South's *Merrimack* (then named the *Virginia*) in the channel of Hampton Roads in Chesapeake Bay. Neither ship was sunk. But this battle is famous because it was the first battle between two iron-armored ships. It was also one of the first battles between ships powered entirely by steam.

In 1906, the British completed the battleship *Dreadnought.* The *Dreadnought* carried more large guns and was faster than any previous battleship. It made all other battleships out of date, and it pushed Germany and Britain into a race of modern shipbuilding.

World War I began in 1914. In the war, the Allies, who included France, Italy, Russia, the United Kingdom, and the United States, fought Germany, Austria-Hungary, and other Central Powers. The war featured two new weapons that revolutionized naval war: submarines and airplanes. Submarines armed with torpedoes sank many surface ships. Airplanes, flown from airfields ashore, attacked ships, submarines, and targets on land.

Most naval battles during World War I involved only a few ships. The war's largest naval battle occurred in 1916, when the United Kingdom and Germany fought the Battle of Jutland, off Denmark. Although the United Kingdom lost more ships, it forced the German fleet to withdraw and remain in port for the rest of the war.

When World War I ended in 1918, Japan, the United Kingdom, and the United States were engaged in costly shipbuilding programs. After extensive negotiations, these and other nations agreed to limit warship construction. The Treaty of Versailles, which ended military action against Germany, barred Germany from building a large navy. But Germany violated the treaty by secretly building submarines for other countries. When German dictator Adolf Hitler rose to power in the early 1930's, he ordered the construction of a large navy. Japan and the Soviet Union also began building major fleets.

World War II began in Europe in 1939. In that war, Germany, Italy, Japan, and smaller Axis nations fought the Allies, including Canada, China, the Soviet Union, the United Kingdom, and the United States. Naval combat broke out in the Atlantic in 1939, when German warships began attacking British ships. Germany's goal was to cut off the United Kingdom's supply of food and war materials. The United Kingdom sank most of Germany's surface ships, forcing Germany to resort to submarine warfare. The Allies fought German submarines with airplanes, antisubmarine ships, radar, sonar, and underwater bombs called *depth charges.* The Allies also intercepted and decoded German radio messages, which helped them predict enemy submarine movements.

Naval combat began in the Pacific Ocean on Dec. 7, 1941. That day, Japanese bombers flying from six aircraft carriers made a surprise attack on the U.S. Pacific Fleet at anchor in Pearl Harbor in Hawaii. The Japanese sank or heavily damaged five U.S. battleships. But all of the U.S. Navy's aircraft carriers survived because none were then in Pearl Harbor. After the attack, aircraft carriers became the principal warship of the U.S. Navy.

The Battle of the Coral Sea, in May 1942, was the first naval battle in which the opposing warships never sighted or fired on each other. The Japanese and U.S. navies attacked each other with warplanes launched from their aircraft carriers. The Battle of Midway in June 1942 was the turning point for naval war in the Pacific. In this battle, the U.S. Navy sank four Japanese aircraft carriers and one cruiser. The Battle for Leyte Gulf in the Philippines, in October 1944, was one of the largest naval battles in history. The battle involved about 280 Japanese and U.S. warships. It eliminated Japan as a major naval power.

When Japan surrendered in 1945 and World War II ended, only the United Kingdom and the United States still had major navies. The U.S. fleet was much larger than the rest of the world's seagoing forces combined.

Navies during the Cold War. The Cold War was a period of intense rivalry that developed after World War II between Communist and non-Communist countries. During this period, many countries carried out naval building programs. Many small navies were modernized with the addition of submarines, missiles, and other advanced weapons. The Soviet Union began a drive to enlarge and modernize its fleet in the late 1940's.

After World War II, aviation experts predicted that aircraft carrying nuclear bombs would be the principal weapon in future military conflicts. As a result, the U.S. Navy concentrated on building aircraft that could fly from large carriers and carry nuclear bombs.

The Korean War (1950-1953) proved, however, that conventional naval forces were still vital to modern conflicts. In this war, the United States and other members of the United Nations aided South Korea against North Korea, which was backed by China and the Soviet Union. Airpower was not the deciding factor in ending the war, and neither side used nuclear weapons. During the war, the U.S. Navy launched carrier-based air attacks, made amphibious landings, and used shipboard guns to bombard enemy coastal targets.

In 1954, the U.S. Navy launched the world's first nuclear-powered ship, the submarine *Nautilus.* The first Soviet nuclear submarine was completed about five years later. The first nuclear-powered surface warships were the U.S. aircraft carrier *Enterprise* and the cruiser *Long Beach,* both commissioned (put into active service) in 1961. By the mid-1960's, both the Soviet Union and the United States had submarines with ballistic missiles carrying nuclear warheads.

The world's navies were involved in numerous conflicts during the Cold War period. For example, in 1962, the U.S. Navy blockaded Cuba to force the Soviets to remove missiles and aircraft they had brought to the island. The U.S. Navy saw combat in the Vietnam War after the United States became heavily involved in the war in 1965. In 1982, the United Kingdom's Royal Navy battled Argentina for control of the Falkland Islands in the South Atlantic Ocean. The Royal Navy was victorious, proving that it could fight against modern weapons at great distances from the United Kingdom.

Navies after the Cold War. The Cold War ended in the early 1990's, after the Soviet Union broke apart and democratic reforms took place in Eastern Europe. Tensions eased between countries that had considered each other enemies.

Many countries, including the United Kingdom, Russia, and the United States, began reducing their navies. Older ships were cut up for scrap metal, newer ships were placed in reserve, and fewer new ships were built. Both Russia and the United States began reducing their fleets of ballistic missile submarines. However, some smaller navies, including those of France, India, and Israel, continued to build and modernize their fleets. Several of the former Soviet republics, especially Ukraine, began to build their own navies in the 1990's. Ukraine also took over a number of small ships that had belonged to the Soviet Navy. The U.S. Navy played a major role in the Persian Gulf War of 1991 and in the Iraq War (2003-2010).　　　　Norman Polmar

Related articles in *World Book* include:

Famous battles

Actium, Battle of	Salamis
Jutland, Battle of	Spanish Armada
Monitor and Merrimack	Trafalgar, Battle of

Kinds of ships

Aircraft carrier	Destroyer	Missile boat
Amphibious ship	Frigate	Submarine
Battleship	Galleon	Warship
Cruiser	Galley	

Other related articles

Aircraft, Military	Mine warfare
Amphibious warfare	Navy, United States
Canadian Armed Forces	Ship (History)
Depth charge	Torpedo
Guided missile	V/STOL
Marine	Zheng He
Marine Corps, United States	

Outline

I. **The role of navies**
　A. Peacetime roles　　　B. Wartime roles
II. **The organization of navies**
III. **Ships and aircraft**
　A. Aircraft carriers　　　F. Submarines
　B. Cruisers　　　　　　G. Auxiliary ships
　C. Destroyers　　　　　H. Small combatants
　D. Frigates　　　　　　I. Aircraft
　E. Amphibious ships
IV. **Major navies of the world**
　A. The United States　　B. Russia

C. China　　　　　　E. The United Kingdom
D. France　　　　　F. India
V. **The history of navies**

Questions

What is the primary task of a destroyer?
Why is a navy's size not necessarily an indication of its strength?
What is the principal warship of the Russian Navy?
What was the first battle between two iron-armored ships?
What do navies do during times of peace?
How were galleys and galleons powered?
What is the main task of a small navy during wartime?
Why did the *Dreadnought* make other warships out of date?
What was the first nuclear-powered warship?
What is a task force?

Additional resources

Friedman, Norman. *Seapower as Strategy: Navies and National Interests.* Naval Inst. Pr., 2001.
Lawrence, Richard R., ed. *The Mammoth Book of Eyewitness Naval Battles.* Carroll & Graf, 2003.
The Naval Institute Guide to Combat Fleets of the World. Naval Inst. Pr., published biennially.
Tucker, Spencer C., ed. *Naval Warfare: An International Encyclopedia.* 3 vols. ABC-CLIO, 2002.

Navy, Department of the, is a military department within the Department of Defense of the United States government. The department is responsible for having naval and marine forces trained and ready to carry out military missions ordered by the president or the secretary of defense.

The Department of the Navy has three parts: (1) the Navy Department, (2) the Operating Forces, and (3) the Shore Establishment. The Navy Department is the central executive authority of the U.S. Navy. It consists of the headquarters of the Navy and the U.S. Marine Corps in Washington, D.C. The Operating Forces consists of the fleets, including the Fleet Marine Forces, and other major sea commands. The U.S. Coast Guard functions as part of the Operating Forces in wartime or as directed by the president. The Shore Establishment operates within the United States. It performs various technical activities supporting the department's Operating Forces.

The *secretary of the Navy* heads the Department of the Navy, under the direction of the secretary of defense. The secretary of the Navy ranks equally with secretaries of the Army and the Air Force. The position carries general responsibility for all naval affairs. The principal civilian aides of the Navy secretary are an undersecretary, a deputy undersecretary, and four assistant secretaries.

The *chief of naval operations,* an admiral, is the Navy's highest-ranking military officer and a member of the Joint Chiefs of Staff. The chief is the principal naval adviser to the president and the Navy secretary on matters of war and the secretary's principal adviser and assistant.

The *commandant of the Marine Corps* is responsible for Marine Corps activities and is also a member of the Joint Chiefs of Staff. The commandant reports directly to the secretary of the Navy.

The United States Congress authorized the establishment of the Navy Department in 1798. As a result of the National Security Act of 1947, the Navy Department was renamed the Department of the Navy in 1949 and placed under the direction of the Department of Defense.

Critically reviewed by the Department of Defense

See also **Coast Guard, United States** (National defense); **Defense, Department of; Marine Corps, United States; Navy, United States.**

A nuclear-powered aircraft carrier, the USS *Abraham Lincoln,* joined the United States Navy's surface fleet in 1989. Carriers provide the fleet's main striking power.

U.S. Navy

Navy, United States, is the branch of the armed forces of the United States that acts to maintain command of the sea. In time of peace, the Navy often serves as an instrument of international relations. Navy ships also assist in humanitarian missions, such as carrying food and medical supplies to disaster areas. Merchant vessels and passenger ships often call on the Navy for aid in emergencies.

In time of war, the Navy seeks out and destroys the enemy on, under, or above the sea. It can also strike the enemy ashore. Naval amphibious forces can support troop landings on enemy-controlled shores. Nuclear-powered submarines can carry missiles and travel around the world underwater. Any enemy that might attack the United States must expect counterblows from these submarines, whose exact locations at sea cannot be pinpointed.

The Navy has just under 300 ships. They include aircraft carriers, cruisers, frigates, destroyers, submarines, and amphibious ships. These fighting ships depend on the services of ammunition ships, minesweepers, oilers, repair ships, supply ships, military sea-lift ships, maritime pre-positioning ships, and tugs. Both fighting ships and service ships rely on a shore organization, including naval bases, shipyards, docks, naval air stations, and

The U.S. Navy seal

training stations, for supplies, repairs, training, and other services.

The Navy operates under the Department of the Navy. The Navy has an active strength of about 336,000 men and women. Naval reserve forces total about 103,000. The Navy also maintains a Marine Corps, which has an active strength of about 204,000 men and women, and reserve forces numbering about 107,000. In wartime, or by decision of the president, the Coast Guard also operates under the Department of the Navy.

The Navy seal was adopted in 1957. "Anchors Aweigh" (1906) is the Navy's service song. Blue and gold are the official colors of the Navy.

Life in the Navy

Training a sailor. The enlisted ranks consist of three grades of seaman or airman and six grades of petty officer, from seaman recruit to master chief petty officer. Navy recruits first learn discipline and seamanship at *boot camp.* Boot camp takes place at the training center of Naval Station Great Lakes in Illinois. After successful completion of the training course, the sailors may attend a trade school, such as those for enginemen, cooks, and electricians. Or they may be assigned directly to a ship or a naval base where they learn their duties and practice their trades. Sailors take competitive examinations for advancement through the *ratings* (ranks). Some qualify to attend advanced schools. Qualified enlisted men and women can take examinations for admission to the U.S. Naval Academy at Annapolis, Maryland, or to other officer training programs.

Training an officer. Navy officers are trained at the U.S. Naval Academy or in the following naval programs: (1) the Naval Reserve Officers Training Corps (NROTC) for college and university students; (2) Officer Candidate School (OCS) for enlisted personnel and college graduates; and (3) programs to appoint warrant officers and limited-duty officers from within the enlisted ranks.

Doctors, dentists, lawyers, and ministers may be commissioned with little military training. Officer candidates train at the Officer Development School of Naval Station Newport in Rhode Island.

Naval officers are assigned to one of four divisions: (1) line, (2) staff, (3) limited duty, or (4) warrant. Unrestricted line officers command at sea or manage shore activities. Restricted line officers have specialized jobs, such as engineering or public affairs. Staff officers include doctors, dentists, nurses, supply officers, lawyers, and chaplains. Limited-duty or warrant officers are usually appointed from the enlisted ranks as administrative or technical specialists.

During officer training, officer candidates may apply for surface, submarine, aviation, or special warfare duty. After about four years of active duty, they become eligible for many technical postgraduate programs. Senior-ranking officers may take command and strategy courses at the Naval War College in Newport, Rhode Island, or at one of the joint service colleges, such as the National War College in Washington, D.C.

A typical day. Life at sea for *bluejackets* (sailors) varies with the type of ship on which they serve. Naval ships range from tugboats with a crew of five to giant aircraft carriers with a crew of thousands. Cargo ships spend long periods at sea. Repair ships usually stay in port, but they sometimes sail overseas to support operating forces. A sailor on a submarine gets to know every member of its crew. However, on an aircraft carrier, each crew member does a specialized job and may not be well acquainted with all areas of the ship or all of the members of the crew.

In peacetime aboard a naval ship, a typical day begins about 6 a.m. Meals are generally served at 7 a.m., noon, and 5 p.m. These hours may vary to meet operating requirements. The crew *musters* (assembles) at 7:30 a.m., after breakfast. Practically every crew member on a ship *stands watch,* or is at a post of duty, during four-hour periods. Each member has a battle station and a post for emergencies.

The Navy tries to make life aboard ship as comfortable and pleasant as possible for sailors who may have

Inspection in the ranks may be held ashore or aboard a ship. These Navy enlisted men are undergoing inspection with weapons. The officer marches in front.

to live in limited space for weeks or months at a time without seeing land. Some ships have a library for the crew, and many have recreation rooms and hobby shops. Sailors aboard most ships may participate in distance-learning programs, taking courses for college credit under the Navy College Program for Afloat College Education (NCPACE). Most ships have on-board television and radio stations. Tailor and shoe-repair shops, laundries, and stores on the ship provide for the crew's everyday needs. On large ships, doctors and dentists care for the sailors' health. When a ship is in port, crew members who are not on duty may be granted *liberty* (time off ashore).

Careers in the Navy. A first enlistment may prepare a person for a civilian job or a naval career. An applicant must be a U.S. citizen or a citizen of another country who resides legally in the United States. Applicants must be between the ages of 17 and 34, and they must meet the Navy's physical standards. They may enlist for four to six years.

Qualified enlisted personnel may advance to chief petty officer in 12 to 14 years. They receive a pay increase with each promotion, and extra pay for length of service. The Navy also pays money for *quarters* (housing) and *subsistence* (food). It gives additional pay for hazardous duty, such as submarine and aviation duty, or for sea duty and duty in some foreign countries. All Navy personnel are eligible for 30 days' *leave* (vacation) a year. They are entitled to free medical and dental care, and free hospital and medical care is available to their families. Sailors may retire with pay after 20 years' service.

Ships and weapons of the Navy

Combat ships of the U.S. Navy include warships, amphibious ships, and mine warfare ships. Smaller vessels—such as Mark V special operations craft or rigid-hulled inflatable boats (RIB's)—patrol coastlines, land troops, and operate on rivers and other shallow waterways. This section discusses the U.S. Navy's warships. For information on amphibious ships and mine warfare ships, see **Amphibious ship; Mine warfare.**

The U.S. Navy's *aircraft carriers* are its largest warships. Special helicopters and *amphibious assault ships* take part in helicopter amphibious assaults. *Guided missile cruisers* escort aircraft carriers and support amphibious forces. *Destroyers* defend aircraft carriers and amphibious ships. Some destroyers carry helicopters that can attack submarines. *Frigates* escort other warships and amphibious ships. *Submarines* operate against surface ships, other submarines, and shore positions. *Amphibious command ships* carry communications equipment and serve as command headquarters.

The Navy used to maintain large warships called *battleships* that bombarded enemy shore positions and attacked enemy ships. But no battleships serve in the Navy today.

Auxiliary ships provide maintenance, fuel, supplies, towing, and other services to warships. There are four main kinds of auxiliary ships: (1) underway replenishment ships, (2) fleet support ships, (3) sealift ships, and (4) special mission ships. *Service craft* usually are smaller and provide services similar to those of auxiliary ships.

Underway replenishment (UNREP) ships provide fuel, ammunition, food, spare parts, and other materials to warships at sea. UNREP ships transfer cargo to moving ships using lines rigged between the ships. Supplies can also be transferred using helicopters in a vertical replenishment (VERTREP).

Fleet support ships provide maintenance and other services to warships. Rescue and salvage ships offer towing, salvage, diving, firefighting, and heavy lifting capabilities. Submarine tenders provide maintenance for, and deliver supplies to, nuclear attack submarines. Other fleet support ships include tugs and hospital ships.

Sealift ships carry cargo from port to port but cannot land their cargo on beaches. Unlike UNREP ships, they cannot transfer cargo to moving ships. Maritime pre-positioning ships put supplies and equipment into position in preparation for the arrival of Marine Corps expeditionary forces. Special mission ships support warship development and operations. They include such vessels as surveillance ships, test support ships, ocean surveying ships, high-speed vessels, and ships that lay and repair communication cables.

Naval aviation enhances the defense of the fleet, joins amphibious attacks, and conducts strikes on ships and shore targets. Navy pilots fly attack, fighter, and special mission planes and helicopters from carriers. They also fly shore-based patrol aircraft. Carrier-based aircraft are built to withstand the great stress of take-off and landing. While they are on the flight deck, their wings can be folded to reduce the area needed for storage.

Navy attack aircraft include the F/A-18 Hornet and the F/A-18E/F Super Hornet. Navy aircraft can carry a variety of *ordnance* (weapons).

Special mission aircraft that operate from carriers include the S-3B Viking, a versatile jet aircraft used for surveillance as well as for battling enemy surface ships. The EA-6B Prowler, an electronic warfare plane, interferes with enemy electronic equipment. The P-3 Orion is a land-based antisubmarine warfare plane. The SH-60 Seahawk is a ship-based antisubmarine helicopter.

Naval aircraft are classified by letters and numbers. For example, the S-3B Viking is the third antisubmarine *(S)* aircraft in the Department of Defense system. The letter *B* indicates that it is the second model of the S-3 Viking. Other letters are *A,* attack; *C,* cargo/transport; *E,* electronic warfare; *F,* fighter; *H,* helicopter; *K,* tanker; *O,* observation; *P,* patrol; *T,* trainer; *U,* utility; *V,* vertical or short take-off and landing; and *X,* research.

Ordnance includes bombs, guns, mines, missiles, and torpedoes. Cruisers and destroyers carry Mk-45 5-inch guns that can shell targets more than 10 miles (16 kilometers) away. Some surface warships also carry Mk-75 76-millimeter and Mk-38 25-millimeter rapid-fire guns for defense.

Naval mines may be moored or mobile. The ASROC rocket-propelled missile is used against submarines. The Navy has air-launched, surface-launched, and subsurface-launched torpedoes. These torpedoes can be used against surface ships or submarines.

Surface-to-air missiles include the Rolling Airframe Missile (RAM), with a range of about 5 miles (8 kilometers), and the Standard Missile (SM-2), with a range of 45 to 100 miles (75 to 165 kilometers). Air-to-air missiles include the Advanced Medium-Range Air-to-Air Missile (AMRAAM), the Sidewinder, and the Sparrow. Such air-to-surface missiles as the High Speed Anti-Radiation

Missile (HARM) and the Maverick can support ground troops or hit targets at sea. The Harpoon and the Stand-Off Land Attack Missile-Expanded Response (SLAM-ER) are air/surface-to-surface missiles that can be launched from both planes and ships. Trident missiles have a range of about 4,600 miles (7,400 kilometers). Both surface ships and submarines can launch Tomahawk cruise missiles to destroy surface targets. See **Guided missile.**

Organization of the Navy

The U.S. Navy operates under the Department of the Navy in the Department of Defense. The Department of the Navy consists of the (1) Navy Department, (2) Operating Forces, and (3) Shore Establishment. The secretary of the Navy, a civilian, heads the Department of the Navy under the direction of the secretary of defense. The secretary of the Navy directs the affairs of the Department of the Navy, which include recruiting, organizing, supplying, equipping, training, and mobilizing naval forces.

The Navy Department, in Washington, D.C., is the central executive authority of the Department of the Navy. The Navy Department sets policy and directs and controls the Operating Forces and Shore Establishment. The Navy Department consists of the Office of the Secretary of the Navy; the Office of the Chief of Naval Operations; and Headquarters, Marine Corps.

The Operating Forces of the Navy and the Marine Corps consist of several fleets, other seagoing forces, Fleet Marine Forces (expeditionary troops), and other forces as directed by the president or the secretary of the Navy. These forces perform naval operations to carry out U.S. policies and advance U.S. interests.

The U.S. Fleet Forces Command, headquartered in Norfolk, Virginia, organizes, trains, and equips naval forces for the unified combatant commands of the U.S. military. It is at the top of the administrative chain of command for most naval units. The Fleet Forces Command is directly responsible for the Second Fleet in the western Atlantic Ocean and the Fourth Fleet in the Caribbean and Central and South America. The Fleet Forces Command oversees several subordinate commands, including the Naval Forces Southern Command, the Naval Network Warfare Command, Naval Submarine Forces, Naval Air Forces, Naval Surface Forces, the Naval Mine and Anti-Submarine Warfare Command, the First Naval Construction Division, the Navy Warfare Development Command, the Navy Expeditionary Combat Command, and the Navy Reserve Force.

Naval Forces Europe and Naval Forces Africa, headquartered in Naples, Italy, directs the operations of the Sixth Fleet in the Mediterranean and the Atlantic. The Naval Forces Central Command, headquartered in Manama, Bahrain, directs the Fifth Fleet in the Persian Gulf and the Indian Ocean. The U.S. Pacific Fleet, headquartered in Pearl Harbor, Hawaii, directs the Third Fleet and the Seventh Fleet in the Pacific Ocean.

The Naval Special Warfare Command, headquartered in San Diego, prepares SEAL (Sea, Air, and Land) teams and other special forces to carry out unconventional missions. The Operational Test and Evaluation Force, headquartered in Norfolk, Virginia, tests and evaluates ships, submarines, aircraft, and other equipment and systems. The Military Sealift Command, headquartered in Washington, D.C., transports equipment and supplies by sea to United States forces worldwide.

The Shore Establishment provides support to the Operating Forces. It includes naval bases managed by the Navy Installations Command. A naval base may include a shipyard, a naval station, or a naval air station.

A key part of the Shore Establishment are the systems commands, which design and develop equipment and systems for future use by the Operating Forces. These commands are the Naval Air Systems Command, the Naval Facilities Engineering Command, the Naval Sea Systems Command, the Naval Supply Systems Command, and the Space and Naval Warfare Systems Command. Other Shore Establishment units include the Bureau of Medicine and Surgery, the Naval Education and Training Command, the Naval Legal Service Command, the Office of Naval Intelligence, the Strategic Systems Programs, and the United States Naval Academy.

The active-duty Navy and reserves. The active-duty Navy consists of sailors who serve full-time. The Navy Reserve consists of the Ready Reserve, the Standby Reserve, and the Retired Reserve.

The Navy Reserve provides trained units and qualified individuals for active duty in time of war, military operations, or national emergency. The Ready Reserve is the core of the Navy Reserve. Its members are ready to be immediately mobilized. Ready reservists may be on active duty or in inactive duty status. *Selected reservists* are ready reservists who train for at least two days a month and perform two weeks of active duty a year. Standby Reserve and Retired Reserve members are subject to recall in a war or national emergency. But they do not get the amount or regularity of training that selected reservists do. In most cases, they would be mobilized only after selected reservists were called up. They might also be mobilized if their unique skill sets were needed.

The Marine Corps is a separate military service within the Department of the Navy. The commandant of the Marine Corps is responsible directly to the secretary of the Navy. The Marine Corps assigns forces to the Navy's fleets. The Marines have the primary jobs of amphibious warfare and land operations performed in connection with naval campaigns. They also provide security forces that guard naval stations and ships and U.S. embassies in other countries. See **Marine Corps, United States.**

The Coast Guard operates under the Department of the Navy in wartime or by decision of the president. In peacetime, the Coast Guard operates within the Department of Homeland Security. The Coast Guard provides air-sea rescue services, carries out antisubmarine patrols, and controls and guards shipping in U.S. ports. It also helps to prevent waterfront disasters, to enforce U.S. laws at sea, and to ensure safety at sea. See **Coast Guard, United States.**

History

The earliest colonial warships were privately owned vessels called *privateers.* These vessels usually operated on independent missions (see **Privateer**).

The Continental Congress established the Continental Navy in 1775. The Congress set up a Naval Committee and later a Marine Committee to administer naval affairs and to build and equip warships. Several merchant ships were converted into combat vessels. In 1776, Esek Hopkins, the Navy's first commodore and its first com-

U.S. Navy

U.S. Navy

U.S. Navy

U.S. Navy

Uniforms of the U.S. Navy include, *from left to right,* (1) the working uniform, (2) the service dress white uniform, (3) the service dress khaki uniform, and (4) the physical training uniform.

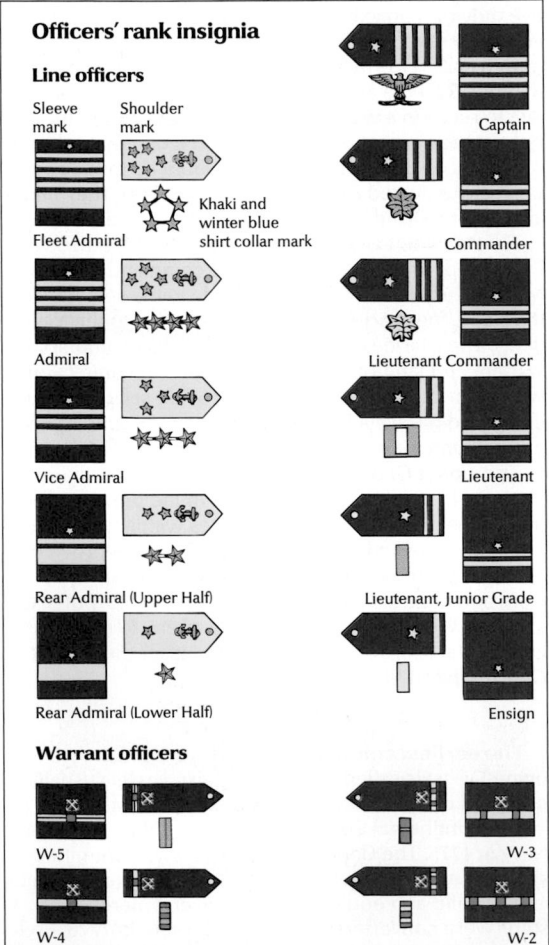

Officers' rank insignia

Line officers

Sleeve mark | Shoulder mark

Khaki and winter blue shirt collar mark

Fleet Admiral

Admiral

Vice Admiral

Rear Admiral (Upper Half)

Rear Admiral (Lower Half)

Captain

Commander

Lieutenant Commander

Lieutenant

Lieutenant, Junior Grade

Ensign

Warrant officers

W-5

W-4

W-3

W-2

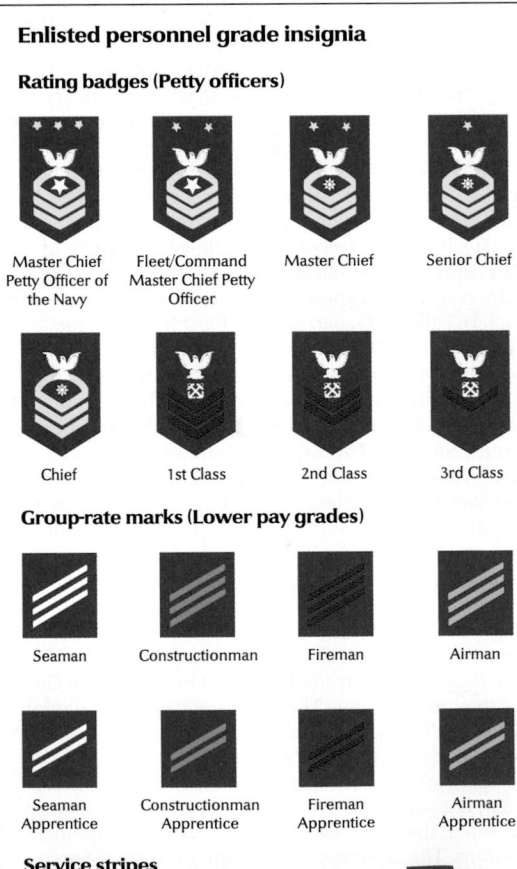

Enlisted personnel grade insignia

Rating badges (Petty officers)

Master Chief Petty Officer of the Navy | Fleet/Command Master Chief Petty Officer | Master Chief | Senior Chief

Chief | 1st Class | 2nd Class | 3rd Class

Group-rate marks (Lower pay grades)

Seaman | Constructionman | Fireman | Airman

Seaman Apprentice | Constructionman Apprentice | Fireman Apprentice | Airman Apprentice

Service stripes

Service stripes are worn near the bottom of the sleeve. Each stripe stands for four years of service.

Some officers' devices

The emblems are embroidered on the sleeves of blue uniforms to indicate specialties. They also are worn on shoulder boards, and on the collars of khaki and winter blue shirts of staff officers.

Officer (Staff corps)

Medical Corps · Supply Corps · (Christian) (Jewish) (Muslim) Chaplain Corps · Civil Engineer · Medical Service Corps · Judge Advocate General Corps · Dental Corps · Nurse Corps

Warrant officer (Line)

Boatswain · Cryptologic Technician · Security Technician · Repair Technician · Engineering Technician · Ship's Clerk · Ordnance Technician · Diving Officer

Some breast insignia

The emblems are worn by officers and enlisted personnel on the left breast of their uniform to indicate specialization. Emblems marked with an asterisk may be worn only by an officer.

Astronaut* · Naval Aviator · Surface Warfare* · Aircrew

Flight Surgeon* · Basic Parachutist · SSBN Deterrent Patrol · Submarine*

Submarine Medical · Submarine Engineering Duty · Submarine Combat Patrol · Special Warfare (SEAL)

Some specialty marks for general ratings

Specialty marks show the duties of enlisted personnel. Petty officers wear the marks on the rating badge, between the eagle's talons and the upper chevrons. Sailors in the lower pay grades wear them above the group-rate marks.

Aviation Electronics Technician · Aviation Machinist's Mate · Aviation Ordnanceman · Aerographer's Mate · Air Traffic Controller · Aircrew Survival Equipmentman

Machinist's Mate · Engineman · Electrician's Mate · Builder · Construction Mechanic · Construction Electrician · Gunner's Mate · Fire Control Technician

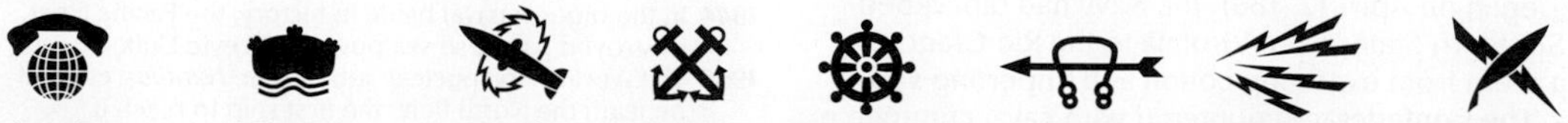

Interior Communications Electrician · Mineman · Missile Technician · Boatswain's Mate · Quartermaster · Sonar Technician · Information Systems Technician · Cryptologic Technician

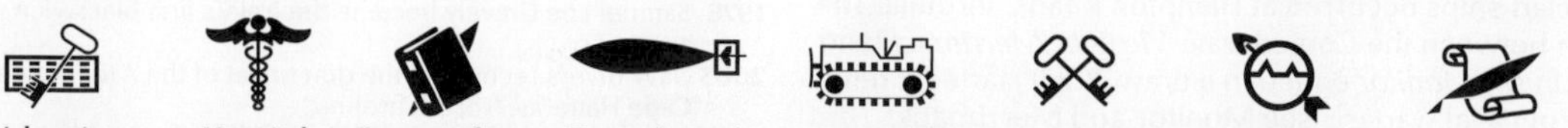

Disbursing Clerk · Hospital Corpsman · Personnelman · Torpedoman's Mate · Equipment Operator · Storekeeper · Operations Specialist · Journalist

mander in chief, raided Nassau in the Bahama Islands with a fleet of six ships. During the American Revolution, about 60 vessels served in the Continental Navy. Captain John Paul Jones's badly damaged *Bonhomme Richard* forced the British vessel *Serapis* to surrender in one of the war's most exciting battles. Jones uttered the Navy's famous watchword: "I have not yet begun to fight!" See **Revolution, American.**

The Navy ceased operations after the war. In 1785, the last warship was sold. But the need for a fleet soon arose again. Barbary *corsairs* (sea raiders) off North Africa preyed on American merchant ships and killed or captured American sailors. In 1794, Congress voted to build several *frigates*—at that time, fast three-masted warships—to fight the corsairs. This force operated under the secretary of war. The launching of the *United States* in 1797 marked the rebirth of the U.S. Navy.

Undeclared war with France. In the summer of 1796, the United States and France had reached a state of undeclared war. France and Britain (later also called the United Kingdom) were at war with each other at this time. The French treated U.S. merchant sailors like British subjects and, by 1798, had seized more than 300 U.S. merchant ships. That year, Congress created a Navy Department under a secretary of the Navy. The 44-gun frigates *Constitution* and *United States* and the 36-gun *Constellation* formed the basis of a new fleet that had grown to about 50 ships by 1801. Many battles raged between U.S. and French ships. The undeclared war with the United States ended after Napoleon Bonaparte seized power in France in 1799.

The War of 1812 (1812-1815). The United Kingdom declared a blockade of France when war broke out in 1803. It seized American ships that violated the blockade, and imprisoned their seamen. The U.S. Navy had only about 16 warships when the War of 1812 began.

In early victories, the *Constitution* captured and destroyed the British ships *Guerrière* and *Java,* and the *United States* captured the *Macedonian.* The British *Shannon* captured the American *Chesapeake.* Captain James Lawrence of the *Chesapeake* issued as his dying command: "Don't give up the ship!" The British clamped a tight blockade on American ports, but American privateers continued to operate. They captured more than 1,300 enemy vessels and damaged British overseas trade. American ships won decisive victories on Lake Erie and Lake Champlain. See **War of 1812.**

In the Mexican War (1846-1848), the Navy conducted amphibious operations and blockaded ports along Mexico's Gulf and Pacific coasts.

The American Civil War (1861-1865) found the Union Navy with only 42 ships. Within a month after the war began on April 12, 1861, the Navy had blockaded the Southern States from Virginia to the Rio Grande to keep them from exporting cotton and importing supplies. The Confederacy countered with naval commerce raiders and blockade runners, which were operated independently. In March 1862, the first battle between ironclad ships occurred at Hampton Roads, Virginia. The clash between the Confederate *Virginia (Merrimack)* and the Union *Monitor* ended in a draw. But it started a new kind of naval warfare (see **Monitor and Merrimack**).

Navy gunboats helped Union forces control the Tennessee, Cumberland, and Mississippi rivers, which led to the siege and capture of Vicksburg, Mississippi, in 1863. See **Civil War, American** (Siege of Vicksburg).

In August 1864, Rear Admiral David G. Farragut ran his fleet past defending forts at Mobile Bay, Alabama, and forced a Confederate fleet in the harbor to surrender. As Farragut entered the bay, he reportedly shouted, "Damn the torpedoes! Full speed ahead!"

In the Civil War, the Union Navy was essential to the success of the land armies and showed the powerful effect of control of the seas. It became the largest and most powerful naval force in the world. It had more than 670 ships and 57,000 men. See **Civil War, American.**

The Spanish-American War (1898) saw two major naval battles. On May 1, Commodore George Dewey's squadron steamed through the entrance to Manila Bay in the Philippines. As his flagship *Olympia* approached the Spanish fleet off Cavite, he gave the historic command: "You may fire when you are ready, Gridley." The battle ended with the 10-ship enemy fleet destroyed or burning. On July 3, Commodore Winfield S. Schley's warships defeated a Spanish fleet outside Santiago harbor in Cuba. See **Maine** (ship); **Spanish-American War.**

"The Great White Fleet." A force of 16 battleships and 4 destroyers of the Atlantic Fleet began a 14-month world cruise in 1907. It was called "the Great White Fleet" because the ships had been painted white. The 46,000-mile (74,000-kilometer) cruise proved that the Navy could easily shift from the Atlantic to the Pacific.

The Navy took other major steps in the early 1900's. In 1915, it established the office of chief of naval operations. Admiral William S. Benson was the first to fill this position. Naval aviation was born during this same period. In 1911, the Navy purchased its first airplane. Shortly before, on Nov. 14, 1910, Eugene Ely had made the first

Important dates in Navy history

1779 John Paul Jones's *Bonhomme Richard* outfought the *Serapis* and gave the Navy its famous watchword: "I have not yet begun to fight."

1794 The United States Navy was formally established in a law providing for ship construction.

1812 The *Constitution* under Isaac Hull overwhelmed the British ship *Guerrière* in the War of 1812.

1813 James Lawrence and the *Chesapeake* fell before the cannons of British warship *Shannon.* The dying Lawrence commanded: "Don't give up the ship!"

1862 The first battle between ironclad warships was fought between the *Monitor* and the *Merrimack (Virginia).*

1864 A Union fleet stormed into Mobile Bay as its commander, David Farragut, reportedly bellowed: "Damn the torpedoes! Full speed ahead!"

1898 The United States fleet under George Dewey crushed the Spanish fleet in Manila Bay.

1942 The Pacific Fleet repulsed a Japanese fleet that threatened Midway Island and Hawaii.

1944 In the biggest naval battle in history, the Pacific Fleet destroyed Japanese sea power off Leyte Gulf.

1958 The world's first nuclear submarine, *Nautilus,* cruised beneath the North Pole, the first ship to reach it.

1964 A nuclear-powered task force cruised around the world.

1972 Alene B. Duerk became the first woman in the Navy to be promoted to the rank of rear admiral.

1976 Samuel Lee Gravely became the Navy's first black vice admiral.

2003 Navy divers recovered the gun turret of the *Monitor* near Cape Hatteras, North Carolina.

2011 A team of Navy SEALs in Pakistan killed Osama bin Laden, the leader of the al-Qa'ida terrorist network.

shipboard take-off from a warship, the cruiser *Birmingham.* By 1914, the Navy had created its first permanent air station at Pensacola, Florida. In 1922, it *commissioned* (put into service) its first aircraft carrier, the *Langley.*

World War I (1914-1918) began for U.S. combat forces on May 4, 1917, when a destroyer division docked in Ireland for duty with the United Kingdom's Royal Navy. In April, Rear Admiral William S. Sims had arrived in London to command U.S. Naval Forces in European waters. The British predicted an Allied defeat in six months unless the German submarine attacks could be stopped. The Allied navies began convoys and assigned destroyers and submarine chasers to the Atlantic.

The Navy developed new types of mines and laid a mine *barrage* (field) in the North Sea. It planted about 56,000 mines in the largest mining operation in history. The Navy transported more than 2 million American soldiers across the Atlantic Ocean without a single loss of life. Naval aviation expanded rapidly with the establishment of bases in Europe. Navy pilots flew *reconnaissance* (observation), antisubmarine, and bombing missions. The Navy mounted five 14-inch (36-centimeter) guns on railroad cars for strategic shelling of German railways and supply depots in 1918. See **World War I.**

Women first served in the Navy during World War I. They performed *yeoman* (clerical and secretarial) duties to release enlisted men for active duty at sea.

The Navy declined after World War I. It scrapped, sank, or demilitarized about 2 million tons of ships, including 31 major warships, according to a treaty signed at the Washington Conference of 1921 and 1922 (see **Arms control**). By the 1930's, the United States had again started building ships. It planned a two-ocean Navy.

World War II (1939-1945). The Japanese attack against the Pacific Fleet at Pearl Harbor, Hawaii, on Dec. 7, 1941, brought the United States into World War II. Nearly four years later, the war ended with surrender ceremonies held aboard the battleship *Missouri* in Tokyo Bay, Japan.

The Navy had begun defense activities as early as 1939. The destroyer *Reuben James* became the Navy's first casualty of the undeclared war in the Atlantic when it was sunk by a German submarine on Oct. 31, 1941.

The Navy recovered quickly from its losses at Pearl Harbor. It salvaged and repaired many of the damaged or sunken ships. Admiral Ernest J. King became commander in chief of the United States Fleet. He later served as chief of naval operations. Admiral Chester W. Nimitz took command of the Pacific Fleet, and Admiral Royal E. Ingersoll commanded the Atlantic Fleet. By June 1942, the Navy's decisive victory in the Battle of Midway marked the end of Japanese expansion in World War II. When the war ended, the Navy had the most powerful fleet ever. It had 3,400,000 men and women and 2,500 ships, including 24 battleships, 35 aircraft carriers, 77 escort carriers, 92 cruisers, 501 destroyers, 406 destroyer escorts, and 262 submarines. See **World War II.**

In 1942, during World War II, Congress authorized the establishment of the Women's Reserve, a branch of the U.S. Navy Reserve. Navy women became known as WAVES (Women Accepted for Volunteer Emergency Service). Mildred H. McAfee, a distinguished educator, was the first director of the WAVES (see **McAfee, Mildred H.**). In 1948, women officially became a permanent part of the Regular Navy and the Navy Reserve.

The Korean War (1950-1953) involved naval forces almost immediately after the conflict began. Aircraft carriers and troop transports played roles in holding the Pusan perimeter during the first three months of the war. On Sept. 15, 1950, an amphibious landing at Inchon helped reverse the course of the war. A feature of the ground battles was the success of naval and Marine close air support, with aircraft and infantry operations closely coordinated. See **Korean War.**

The Vietnam War (1957-1975). The U.S. Navy entered combat in South Vietnam in 1964. The Seventh Fleet launched air strikes from aircraft carriers and bombarded enemy forces and positions ashore from cruisers, destroyers, and the battleship *New Jersey.* The Navy's Coastal Surveillance Force, River Patrol Force, and Riverine Assault Force operated along the coast and on rivers of South Vietnam. By March 29, 1973, the Navy had turned its responsibilities in Vietnam over to the South Vietnamese armed forces. See **Vietnam War.**

The Persian Gulf War of 1991. In August 1990, the United States sent naval forces to the Persian Gulf after Iraq invaded Kuwait. In January 1991, war broke out between Iraq and a U.S.-led multinational force. United States Navy planes made strikes against Iraqi troops and military installations. The battleships *Wisconsin* and *Missouri* bombarded Iraqi targets ashore. During the brief ground war, the threat of an amphibious landing of U.S. Marines in Kuwait kept as many as six Iraqi divisions pinned down. See **Persian Gulf War of 1991.**

Wars in Iraq and Afghanistan. Fighters and helicopters based on Navy carriers flew hundreds of missions in the Iraq War (2003-2010), which ended the dictatorship of Saddam Hussein. Navy ships also launched missiles at Iraqi targets. Navy SEALs fought in both Iraq and Afghanistan, often searching for enemy fighters and conducting small unit attacks and reconnaissance missions. In addition, Navy construction battalions built U.S. military facilities and helped with civilian reconstruction. In 2011, a team of Navy SEALs in Pakistan killed Osama bin Laden, the leader of the al-Qa'ida network responsible for the terrorist attacks of Sept. 11, 2001.

The nuclear age Navy. In 1948, the U.S. Navy and the Atomic Energy Commission established a joint program to develop nuclear-powered submarines. Unlike conventional submarines, which burn fuel oil, nuclear sub-

Names of naval ships

Since the 1970's, the United States Navy has generally named various types of ships after people, places, or things, as follows:

Aircraft carriers—Public officials *(Dwight D. Eisenhower, Carl Vinson, Theodore Roosevelt, Abraham Lincoln).*
Amphibious assault ships—Famous Navy ships *(Wasp).*
Battleships—States *(New Jersey).*
Cruisers—Battles *(Ticonderoga, Yorktown)* or states *(California, Virginia).*
Destroyers—Officers and enlisted personnel of the Navy and Marine Corps, Navy secretaries, members of Congress, or inventors who influenced naval matters *(Kidd, Coontz, Adams, David R. Ray, Fife).*
Frigates—Deceased Navy, Marine Corps, or Coast Guard personnel *(Lewis B. Puller, Jack Williams).*
Minesweepers—Descriptive qualities *(Avenger)* or birds *(Cardinal).*
Submarines—Trident ballistic missile submarines are named for states *(Ohio, Alaska).* Attack submarines are named for cities *(Los Angeles, Chicago).*

marines do not require air for combustion. They can thus travel long distances underwater. In 1954, the Navy commissioned the world's first nuclear-powered submarine, the *Nautilus.* In 1981, the Navy commissioned the *Ohio,* the first nuclear submarine armed with powerful Trident missiles. Today, the Navy has about 75 nuclear submarines, all of which carry missiles.

The Navy also developed nuclear-powered surface ships, which can steam at high speed for long distances without refueling. Its first nuclear surface ships, the cruiser *Long Beach* and the aircraft carrier *Enterprise,* were commissioned in 1961. Today, more than 40 per-

cent of the Navy's fighting vessels are nuclear powered.

In 1976, the lead ship of the *Tarawa* class of amphibious warfare ships was commissioned. This class of vessel transports landing craft and provides a flight deck for helicopters and vertical/short take-off and landing (V/STOL) aircraft. In 1991, the Navy commissioned the lead ship of the *Arleigh Burke* class of destroyers with weapons for fighting surface ships, submarines, and aircraft. The Navy decommissioned the last of its battleships in 1992. In 1997, the *Seawolf* class of nuclear-powered attack submarines entered service.

Robert Hodierne

Historic ships of the United States Navy

WORLD BOOK illustrations by Tak Murakami

Officer

The ***Bonhomme Richard,*** commanded by John Paul Jones, outfought the British ship *Serapis* in the American Revolution.

The ***Constitution,*** under the command of Isaac Hull, destroyed the British frigate *Guerrière* during the War of 1812.

Seaman

Officer

Officer

A **Civil War clash** in 1862 between the Union *Monitor* and the Confederate *Merrimack,* also called the *Virginia,* was the world's first battle between ironclad ships. The flat-topped *Monitor* was built of iron, but the *Merrimack* was a wooden frigate covered with iron plates.

Seaman

The ***Olympia,*** under the command of George Dewey, helped rout the Spanish fleet in the Battle of Manila Bay in 1898.

Officer

The ***Enterprise*** and other fast aircraft carriers formed the backbone of the U.S. Navy during World War II.

Seaman

The ***Missouri*** was the scene of the surrender ceremonies with Japan that marked the end of World War II.

Officer

The ***Nautilus*** was the first nuclear submarine. It made the first undersea cruise beneath the North Pole in 1958.

Related articles in *World Book.* See Navy with its list of *Related articles.* See also the following articles:

Navy SEALs, United States, are highly trained special forces troops in the U.S. Navy. Special forces troops work in small groups, usually in secret. The name *SEAL* stands for *SE*a, *A*ir, and *L*and. Navy SEALs are trained to fight in all three areas. SEAL missions include scouting and *intelligence* (information) gathering, hostage rescue, and counterterrorism activities. SEALs also fight in direct combat missions. There are about 2,500 SEALs. They are organized into nine active duty SEAL teams that are publicly acknowledged by the Navy. There are also two reserve teams and several support teams.

Training. Men must train for a year and a half to become SEALs. Women are not accepted for SEAL training. According to the Navy, only about 20 percent of men who attempt the training complete it. The training includes extreme physical exercise, such as swimming in cold surf, with limited food and sleep.

History. The SEAL teams developed from underwater demolition teams created during World War II (1939-1945). They were officially organized in 1962. SEALs have taken part in every war the United States has fought since then, as well as secret missions outside of wars.

The most famous SEAL operation was the nighttime helicopter raid on Osama bin Laden's secret compound in Abbottabad, Pakistan, in 2011. Bin Laden, who was shot and killed, was the leader of al-Qa'ida, the terrorist

organization responsible for the September 11 terrorist attacks.   Robert Hodierne

See also **Navy, United States** (The operating forces; Wars in Iraq and Afghanistan).

Naylor, Phyllis Reynolds (1933-), an American author, became known for her children's books dealing with the problems young people face growing up. Her books deal with such sensitive subjects as death, mental illness, and religious faith. Naylor has also written lighter books for children. In addition, she has written nonfiction books about family and peer relationships and about the craft of writing.

Naylor's novel *Shiloh* (1991) won the 1992 Newbery Medal, an annual award given to the best children's book written by an American. The novel tells about a young West Virginia boy who adopts a dog named Shiloh after the animal had run away from its abusive master. Naylor wrote two sequels, *Shiloh Season* (1996) and *Saving Shiloh* (1997). Naylor's "Alice" series portrays a high-spirited girl who must cope with the death of her mother as she matures through her teenage years. The series begins with *The Agony of Alice* (1985).

Phyllis Reynolds was born on Jan. 4, 1933, in Anderson, Indiana. She married Rex Naylor, a speech pathologist, in 1960, her second marriage.   Ann D. Carlson

Naypyidaw, *nay pyee DAW,* is the capital of Myanmar. Its name means royal capital city. The city lies in the center of the country (see **Myanmar** [map]). It replaced Yangon as the capital. Yangon had been the capital during colonial times and after Myanmar (then called Burma) gained independence from the United Kingdom in 1948.

In the beginning of the 2000's, construction started on what was widely believed to be a fortified military headquarters. In late 2005, the Myanmar government named the new city Naypyidaw and declared it the capital. Civilian government departments were ordered to move there from Yangon. Foreign embassies and many government offices stayed in Yangon, which remained the country's commercial center.   James F. Guyot

Nazareth, *NAZ uhr uhth* (pop. 62,700), is a town in northern Israel. For location, see **Israel** (political map). It was the home of Jesus Christ during his early youth. The town was in the Roman province of Galilee (see **Galilee**).

The Old Testament does not mention Nazareth. Nathanael in the New Testament expressed the attitude of the times about the village when he said, "Can anything good come out of Nazareth?" (John 1:46).

Nazareth remained insignificant for many years after the time of Christ. But pilgrims visited the town about A.D. 600, and a large basilica was built. The Arabs captured the city in the 600's. The crusaders built several churches there, but the Ottomans, who were Muslims, forced Christians to leave in 1517.

A new town of Nazareth stands on the site of the old town. The Latin Church of the Annunciation, completed in 1730, now rises where some people think the home of Mary, the mother of Jesus, stood. Since the 1700's, several religious denominations have built churches and monasteries in Nazareth. People there still take water from an ancient well, called Mary's Well.   Bernard Reich

Nazca, *NAHS kuh,* was an American Indian culture that thrived in the coastal desert of what is now southern Peru from as early as 100 B.C. to A.D. 800. The Nazca people are known for the huge etchings they made in the surface of the desert and for their colorful pottery. The name of the culture is also spelled Nasca.

The desert etchings, called the *Nazca lines,* include sets of parallel lines and the outlines of animals and geometric shapes. Some of the lines are several miles long, and some of the animal figures measure more than 400 feet (120 meters) in length. The Nazca made the markings by removing dark surface rocks to expose light-colored sand underneath. The Nazca may have used the markings to follow the positions of stars in the night sky and thus to keep track of the seasons.

Nazca pottery includes bowls and other vessels and such musical instruments as pipes, drums, and rattles. The Nazca decorated much of the pottery with plant and animal designs. Some vessels are shaped like animals or people. The Nazca also wove cotton and wool textiles.

The Nazca lived in villages. They built homes of canes tied together and covered with mud. Larger structures were made of adobe. They used irrigation to grow corn and other crops. About A.D. 800, Nazca culture became mixed with the Huari Indian culture, possibly after an invasion of the Nazca region.   Alexandra M. Ulana Klymyshyn

See also **Peru** (picture).

Nazism, *NAHT sihz uhm* or *NAT sihz uhm,* was a fascist political movement—and later a form of government—that developed in Germany during the 1920's. The Nazis (pronounced *NAHT seez),* led by Adolf Hitler, controlled Germany from 1933 to 1945. *Nazism,* sometimes spelled *Naziism,* also describes any governmental system or political beliefs like those of Hitler's Germany.

The Nazis called for aggressive nationalism, militarism, and the expansion of Germany's borders. Nazism placed great restrictions on personal freedom but permitted private ownership of property that did not conflict with the interests of the state. The Nazis glorified the Germans and other northern European peoples, whom they called Aryans. They claimed that Jews, Slavs, and other minority groups were inferior. Nazism opposed democracy, Communism, socialism, feminism, and other political systems and movements that claimed to favor equality. It promised to build a harmonious, orderly, and prosperous society for Germans. Instead, it brought terrorism, war, and mass murder.

The birth of Nazism. Germany experienced crippling political and economic crises after its defeat in World War I (1914-1918). Although a democratic government replaced the monarchy that had ruled the country for decades, Germany suffered from severe inflation and unemployment during the postwar years. Many Germans lacked faith in the new government and began to turn to political groups that called for extreme changes. One of these organizations was the German Workers' Party, which held its meetings in Munich. Hitler joined this group in 1919 and quickly gained control. He changed its name to the National Socialist German Workers' Party in 1920. *Nazi* stands for the first word in the German name of the party.

Nazism responded to deep problems in German history. Germany had not become a united nation until 1871, and many Germans felt that Germany was inferior to other countries. This feeling encouraged aggressive nationalism and a desire for expansion. Industry grew rapidly in the late 1800's and early 1900's and brought great wealth to the industrialists. But workers resented what they considered an unequal distribution of profits. Also, many middle-class and upper-class Germans had lived comfortably under the monarchy, and they feared and disliked the newly formed democratic government. Finally, many Germans blamed their problems on Jews.

Hitler's aims were primarily nationalistic, but he also promised social revolution to win support from the masses. The Nazi Party grew rapidly in the postwar crisis. The military supported Hitler's ideas of discipline, order, and military conquest. The middle classes and farmers were attracted by the promise of social reform. Wealthy industrialists joined to fight Communism. Powerless people responded to ideas of racial superiority, *anti-Semitism* (prejudice against Jews), and German strength. By 1923, the Nazi Party had 17,000 members.

The rise to power. Nazism did not gain wide support until the Great Depression, a worldwide business slump, began in 1929. Discontented Germans then turned to Nazism in increasing numbers. Nazism promised economic help, political power, and national glory. Hitler's fiery personality and talents as an orator also had a strong influence. The Nazi Party grew into a huge political organization with special divisions for children, youth, women, and professional people. It even had soldiers called *storm troopers,* who terrorized opponents.

In the elections of 1932, the Nazis emerged as the strongest party in Germany. On Jan. 30, 1933, Hitler became *chancellor* (prime minister). He quickly moved toward dictatorship, outlawing civil liberties and all political parties except the Nazi Party. The Nazis took over the press, the radio, and the school system. In time, they established a *totalitarian state* (a government that permits no opposition). They organized a powerful secret police force called the Gestapo and set up concentration camps for anyone suspected of opposing Nazism. Jews and members of other minority groups were also imprisoned in these camps, where the Germans either killed them or used them for forced labor.

Expansion, war, and collapse. Hitler and his followers hoped to make the Nazi state a world empire. In 1938, Germany annexed Austria. German forces occupied Czechoslovakia the following year. The Nazis attacked Poland later in 1939, and World War II began. The Nazis started a campaign to murder all European Jews. Hitler called this the "final solution." About 6 million Jews died by firing squad, in gas chambers, or by other methods. About 5 million others, including Roma (sometimes called Gypsies), political opponents of the Nazis, and Poles and other Slavs were also killed. These mass murders later became known as the Holocaust (see **Holocaust**). The United States, the United Kingdom, the Soviet Union, and other nations defeated Germany in 1945, and the Nazi government collapsed.

Neo-Nazism. Despite an official ban, a number of small *neo-Nazi* (new-Nazi) parties have emerged in Germany since World War II. They have sought to reestablish Nazi principles and to regain the lands Germany lost in the war. They also worked to reunify East Germany and West Germany, the two political units into which Germany was divided from 1949 to 1990. Some have denied that the Holocaust occurred. Neo-Nazi parties have gained support from former Nazis and from discontented or unemployed youth. After Germany's reunification in 1990, neo-Nazis began to make attacks on foreigners.

Neo-Nazi movements have grown in other countries since 1980. In the United States, Ku Klux Klan members, the Nazi Party, and Aryan Nation and other white-supremacist groups support neo-Nazi ideas. These people and organizations promote racism and anti-Semitism and use violence against minorities. Germany today is a strong democracy, and neo-Nazis have been largely left on the fringes of society.   Richard E. Rupp

Related articles in *World Book* include:

Auschwitz	Goebbels, Joseph	Kristallnacht
Bergen-Belsen	Göring, Hermann	Mein Kampf
Bonhoeffer,	Wilhelm	Mengele, Josef
Dietrich	Heydrich,	Nuremberg Trials
Bormann, Martin	Reinhard	Olympic Games
Buchenwald	Himmler, Heinrich	(Between the
Concentration	Hitler, Adolf	wars)
camp	Hitler Youth	Speer, Albert
Dachau	Jews (Beginnings	Swastika
Eichmann, Adolf	of Nazi persecu-	Treblinka
Germany (History)	tion; The	Wiesenthal, Simon
Gestapo	Holocaust)	World War II

NBC is the oldest broadcasting network in the United States. It was founded in 1926 as the National Broadcasting Company, the first permanent U.S. radio network. NBC is owned by NBC Universal, Inc.

The NBC television network was established by the Radio Corporation of America (RCA), a manufacturer of radio equipment. On April 30, 1939, NBC became the first network to introduce regular TV broadcasts when it demonstrated television at the opening day ceremonies at the New York World's Fair.

Among the most popular early NBC programs were the variety shows "The Texaco Star Theater" (1948-1956), which made the comedian Milton Berle the first big star of television, and "Your Show of Shows" (1950-1954), starring comedian Sid Caesar. NBC's dramatic program "Kraft Television Theatre" (1947-1958) featured Broadway actors in live telecasts. In 1956, NBC became the first network to televise national political conventions. NBC developed new styles of programming with the morning news show "Today," which began in 1952, and the late evening variety show "Tonight!" (later called "The Tonight Show"), which began in 1954. During the 1980's and 1990's, NBC dominated prime time with such highly acclaimed shows as "Hill Street Blues," "ER," "The Cosby Show," "Seinfeld," and "Friends."

In 1989, NBC News expanded into cable television, establishing a business channel, CNBC. In 1996, it teamed with Microsoft Corporation to establish MSNBC, a general cable news channel, and msnbc.com, an online news site. NBC is now the biggest television news organization in the United States.   Michael Curtin

See also **Sarnoff, David.**

NCAA. See National Collegiate Athletic Association.

N'Djamena, *ehn JAHM uh nuh,* is the capital and largest city of Chad. The city has a population of about 800,000. It lies on the southwest border of Chad where the Chari and Logone rivers meet (see **Chad** [map]).

N'Djamena is Chad's government center and a transportation hub. It is also a major regional market for grains, livestock, and other products. Meat processing is a major industry. The city has several hotels, a busy central market, a university, and an international airport. N'Djamena also has a spectacular *mosque* (Islamic house of worship) that was built in the 1970's. Most of the city's people live in adobe houses. There are also

© Victor Englebert

N'Djamena is the capital and largest city of Chad. The city is Chad's government center and a transportation hub. People in N'Djamena wear both traditional and Western-style clothing.

neighborhoods with more modern residences.

French troops founded the city in 1900 on the site of a fishing village. They had just defeated Rabah Zubayr Fadl-Allah, a Sudanese warlord who ruled the area in the 1890's. The French named the city Fort-Lamy, after the military leader who had led the conquest. In World War II (1939-1945), the Allies used Fort-Lamy as a military base. The French ruled Fort-Lamy and the rest of Chad until 1960, when Chad became independent. In 1973, Fort-Lamy was renamed N'Djamena.   Dennis D. Cordell

NEA. See National Education Association.

Neagh, Lough. See Lough Neagh.

Neandertals, *nee AN duhr tahlz,* were prehistoric human beings who lived in Europe and central Asia from about 150,000 to 35,000 years ago. Many scientists classify Neandertals (also spelled Neanderthals) as an early subspecies of *Homo sapiens.* However, others think they belong in a separate species, *Homo neanderthalensis.*

Neandertal adults stood about 5 feet 4 inches (165 centimeters) tall. They had strongly built bones and muscular bodies. Neandertal skulls were large and differed from those of modern people by having a large, projecting face; a low, sloping forehead; and a *browridge,* a raised strip of bone across the lower forehead. The Neandertal jaw also lacked a chin.

Neandertals lived in Europe during the Ice Age. They survived in that severe climate using skillfully made stone tools to hunt animals and gather plant foods. They used fire and built tentlike shelters from skins, often in the entrances to caves. At least some Neandertals buried their dead with care. Some isolated populations may have survived until about 28,000 years ago.

Anthropologists do not agree about the fate of the Neandertals. Most scientists think they became extinct about 35,000 years ago, when modern human beings migrated into Europe. In 2010, scientists announced that they had *sequenced* (determined the order of) the entire Neandertal *genome* (complete set of genes in a cell). The scientists found evidence that Neandertals interbred with ancient populations who settled Europe, Asia, and the Pacific Islands. This finding suggests that, though Neandertals are extinct, they are part of the ancestry of some modern peoples.   Alan E. Mann

See also **Prehistoric people** (The origin of *Homo sapiens;* How the Neandertals lived).

Nearsightedness. See Myopia.

Grant Heilman

Rolling farmland covers much of Nebraska, which ranks among the leading states in agricultural production. Nebraska devotes a greater percentage of land to farming than any other state.

Nebraska *The Cornhusker State*

Nebraska is one of the leading farming states in the United States. Yet it was once considered part of the "Great American Desert." The people of Nebraska, with their determined pioneer spirit, made the Nebraska "desert" a land of ranches and farms. They built irrigation systems and practiced scientific farming. Where crops could not be grown, Nebraskans grazed cattle.

Today, farms and ranches make up more than 90 percent of the state's area—a greater percentage than in any other state. In the west, fields of wheat stretch as far as the eye can see. In north-central and western Nebraska, huge herds of beef cattle graze on enormous ranches. On the fertile farms of the east, farmers grow corn, soybeans, sorghum grain, and other crops. The farmers there also raise hogs and fatten cattle for market.

But Nebraska is more than a farming state. Such service industries as finance and insurance play a major role in Nebraska's economy. Many of the state's service industries are in the Omaha and Lincoln metropolitan areas. Omaha is the largest city in the state. Lincoln is Nebraska's capital and its second largest city.

Manufacturing, especially food processing, is also im-

portant to the state's economy. Omaha is a leading food-processing center. A number of other cities in the state have large meat-packing plants.

Much of the history of Nebraska is the story of the tough, strong-willed Nebraska farmer. Many of the first farm settlers were called "sodbusters." They cut sod into blocks and used the blocks to build their homes because they found few trees on this grassy land. In the 1860's, the first great wave of homesteaders poured into Nebraska to claim free land granted by the federal government. However, hard times, insect pests, and droughts discouraged many farmers, and they returned to the East or moved to the mining areas of Colorado and California. But another wave of farmers poured into the state in the 1880's.

The independent, pioneer spirit of the people of Nebraska led them to adopt a *unicameral* (one-house) state legislature. This Legislature met for the first time in 1937. Nebraska is the only state in the nation with a unicameral legislature.

The name *Nebraska* comes from the Oto Indian word *nebrathka.* The word means *flat water* and was the Indian name for Nebraska's chief river, the Platte. Nebraska's official nickname is the *Cornhusker State.* This nickname comes from corn, the state's leading crop, and from the cornhusking contests that were once held each fall in many rural communities.

The contributors of this article are Donald R. Hickey, Professor of History at Wayne State College; and David Wishart, Professor of Geography at the University of Nebraska.

James Blank, FPG

Omaha's Gene Leahy Mall is a pleasant gathering place for people in the city. The Old Market rises in the background.

Interesting facts about Nebraska

WORLD BOOK illustration by Kevin Chadwick

Cowboy Horse Race

The Cowboy Horse Race began in Chadron on June 13, 1893. John Berry won the nine-man race to Buffalo Bill's Wild West show in Chicago, almost 1,000 miles (1,600 kilometers) away, in 13 days 16 hours. Berry won a prize of $1,000.

Nebraska has the largest planted forest in the United States. It covers about 22,000 acres (8,900 hectares) and is part of the Nebraska National Forest.

The National Museum of Roller Skating is located in Lincoln. It is the only museum in the world dedicated solely to roller skating, with exhibits on the sport and industry from 1819 to the present.

WORLD BOOK illustration by Stephen Brayfield

The largest mammoth fossil ever found was unearthed in 1922 near Wellfleet. Scientists have determined that the mammoth was 13 feet 4 ¼ inches (4.07 meters) tall. The fossil is on display at the University of Nebraska State Museum in Lincoln.

Largest mammoth fossil

Grant Heilman

Beef cattle provide Nebraska's largest single source of agricultural income. These ranchers are driving Hereford cattle to winter pasture.

Nebraska in brief

Symbols of Nebraska

The state flag, adopted in 1925, bears the state seal. The seal, adopted in 1867, includes a blacksmith with a hammer and anvil, a settler's cabin, sheaves of wheat, a steamboat on the Missouri River, and a train. The Rocky Mountains rise in the background. Above the landscape is a banner with the state motto, *Equality Before the Law.* At the bottom of the seal is the date of Nebraska's statehood, March 1, 1867.

State flag

Flag and seal from Secretary of State's Office, State of Nebraska

State seal

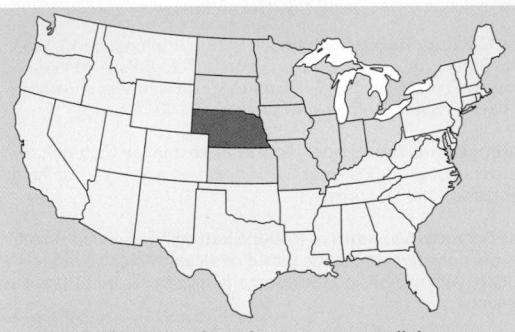

Nebraska (brown) ranks 15th in size among all the states and 3rd in size among the Midwestern States (yellow).

General information

Statehood: March 1, 1867, the 37th state.
State abbreviations: Nebr. or Neb. (traditional); NE (postal).
State motto: *Equality Before the Law.*
State song: "Beautiful Nebraska." Words by Jim Fras and Guy G. Miller; music by Jim Fras.

The State Capitol is in Lincoln, chosen as Nebraska's capital in 1867. The government moved there from Omaha a year later. Omaha was the capital from 1855 to 1868.

Land and climate

Area: 77,353 mi² (200,346 km²), including 481 mi² (1,247 km²) of inland water.
Elevation: *Highest*—5,426 ft (1,654 m) above sea level in southwestern Kimball County. *Lowest*—840 ft (256 m) above sea level in Richardson County.
Record high temperature: 118 °F (48 °C) at Geneva on July 15, 1934, at Hartington on July 17, 1936, and at Minden on July 24, 1936.
Record low temperature: –47 °F (–44 °C) at Camp Clarke, near Northport, on Feb. 12, 1899, and at Oshkosh on Dec. 22, 1989.
Average July temperature: 76 °F (24 °C).
Average January temperature: 23 °F (–5 °C).
Average yearly precipitation: 22 in (56 cm).

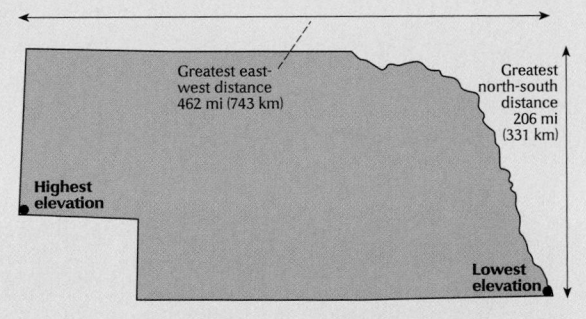

Greatest east-west distance 462 mi (743 km)

Greatest north-south distance 206 mi (331 km)

Highest elevation

Lowest elevation

Important dates

The United States bought the Louisiana territory, including Nebraska, from France.

One of the first free homesteads was claimed by Daniel Freeman near Beatrice.

| 1714 | 1803 | 1819 | 1863 |

Étienne Veniard de Bourgmont traveled up the Missouri River to the mouth of the Platte River.

The U.S. Army established Fort Atkinson.

State bird
Western meadowlark

State flower
Giant goldenrod

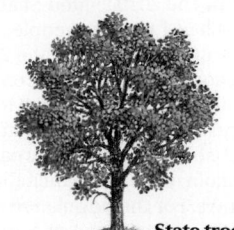

State tree
Eastern cottonwood

People

Population: 1,826,341
Rank among the states: 38th
Density: 24 per mi² (9 per km²), U.S. average 85 per mi² (33 per km²)
Distribution: 70 percent urban, 30 percent rural
Largest cities in Nebraska

Omaha	408,958
Lincoln	258,379
Bellevue	50,137
Grand Island	48,520
Kearney	30,787
Fremont	26,397

Source: 2010 census, except for distribution, which is for 2000.

Population trend

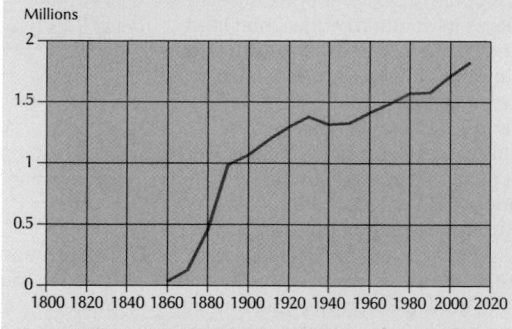

Millions

Year	Population
2010	1,826,341
2000	1,711,263
1990	1,578,385
1980	1,569,825
1970	1,483,493
1960	1,411,330
1950	1,325,510
1940	1,315,834
1930	1,377,963
1920	1,296,372
1910	1,192,214
1900	1,066,300
1890	984,120
1880	452,402
1870	122,993
1860	28,841

Sources: U.S. Census Bureau; Nebraska Historical Society.

Economy

Chief products

Agriculture: beef cattle, corn, hogs, milk, soybeans, wheat.
Manufacturing: chemicals, fabricated metal products, food products, machinery, medical equipment, transportation equipment.
Mining: limestone, natural gas, petroleum, portland cement, sand and gravel.

Gross domestic product

Value of goods and services produced in 2008: $86,099,000,000. *Services* include community, business, and personal services; finance; government; trade; and transportation and communication. *Industry* includes construction, manufacturing, mining, and utilities. *Agriculture* includes agriculture, fishing, and forestry.

Source: U.S. Bureau of Economic Analysis.

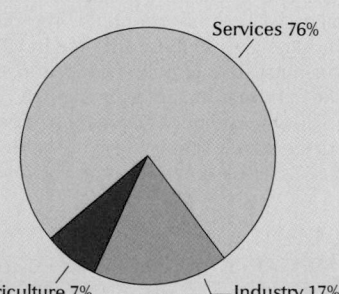

Services 76%

Agriculture 7%   Industry 17%

Government

State government

Governor: 4-year term
State senators: 49; 4-year terms
(Nebraska has a one-house legislature)
Counties: 93

Federal government

United States senators: 2
United States representatives: 3
Electoral votes: 5

Sources of information

Nebraska's official website at http://www.nebraska.gov provides a gateway to much information on the state's government, history, and economy.

In addition, the website at http://www.visitnebraska.gov provides information about tourism.

Nebraskans voted to adopt a one-house legislature.

Nebraska adopted Initiative 300, which prohibits corporations from buying farms or ranches in the state.

| 1867 | 1934 | 1967 | 1982 | 1997 |

Nebraska became the 37th state on March 1.

Nebraska adopted both a sales and an income tax.

A new school-financing law caused many small school districts to reorganize.

Population. The 2010 United States census reported that Nebraska had 1,826,341 people. The population had increased about 7 percent over the 2000 figure, 1,711,263. According to the 2010 census, Nebraska ranks 38th in population among the 50 states. About 55 percent of Nebraska's population live in the state's metropolitan areas (see **Metropolitan area**). The metropolitan areas are Lincoln; Omaha-Council Bluffs (Iowa); and Sioux City, Iowa. For the populations of these areas, see the *Index* to the political map of Nebraska.

Omaha, the state's largest city, is a chief food processing center. Omaha is a trade center. It is also an insurance, telemarketing, and health care center. Lincoln, the state's second largest city, is an educational, governmental, and retail shopping center. Bellevue, the state's third largest city, shares its southern edge with Offutt Air Force Base. Grand Island is Nebraska's fourth largest city. It serves as an important manufacturing, food processing, and distribution center. Only 12 other Nebraska cities have more than 10,000 people.

During the early history of Nebraska, Germans were the main immigrant group. They made up about 15 percent of the state's population in 1900. Today, Nebraska's largest population groups include people of German, Irish, English, Swedish, Czech, and Mexican descent.

Schools. In the 1820's, the U.S. Army established Nebraska's first school, at Fort Atkinson (near present-day Fort Calhoun). During the 1830's and 1840's, missionaries of various religious faiths founded schools in eastern Nebraska to teach the Indians. The first legislature of the Nebraska Territory adopted a free-school law in 1855. The state Constitution, adopted in 1875, provides for the present system of public education. Children must attend school from age 6 through 17.

The Department of Education supervises and administers the state's school system. The department consists of a State Board of Education and a state commissioner

Population density

About 60 percent of the people of Nebraska live in metropolitan areas. Eastern Nebraska includes the state's largest cities—Omaha and Lincoln—and is much more heavily populated than the west.

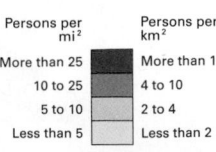

Persons per mi²	Persons per km²
More than 25	More than 10
10 to 25	4 to 10
5 to 10	2 to 4
Less than 5	Less than 2

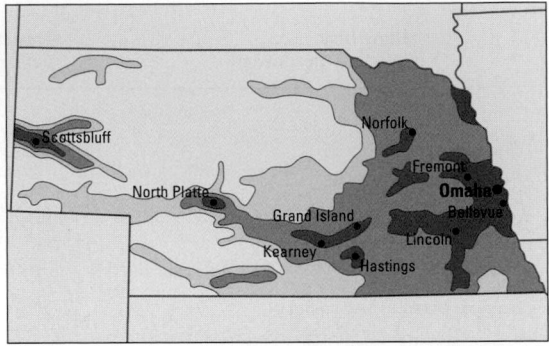

WORLD BOOK map; based on U.S. Census Bureau data.

of education. The people elect the eight members of the board to four-year terms. The members of the board appoint the commissioner. For the number of students and teachers in Nebraska, see **Education** (table).

Libraries. Nebraska's first library was established in 1820 at the Fort Atkinson military post. The Kansas-Nebraska Act of 1854 provided for a territorial library in Nebraska. This library later became the state law library.

In 1871, Omaha established the state's first public library. The Legislature passed a law in 1877 providing state funds to support public libraries. The Nebraska Library Commission was set up in 1901. It promotes, develops, and coordinates library services in the state. Nebraska has public libraries throughout the state.

The library system at the University of Nebraska-Lincoln houses special collections on American folklore and the author Willa Cather. The Nebraska State Historical Society Library in Lincoln collects books and documents on the history of the region. Some other significant libraries include the Lincoln City Libraries in Lincoln, and the Creighton University and University of Nebraska libraries in Omaha.

Museums. The Joslyn Art Museum in Omaha has collections ranging from ancient to modern art. Among its displays are objects crafted by American Indians and examples of art from Western frontier days. The University of Nebraska's Sheldon Museum of Art in Lincoln displays modern American paintings and sculptures.

The University of Nebraska State Museum in Lincoln has one of the largest collections of mammal fossils in the United States. Its exhibits include a mammoth skeleton and elephant skeletons from different periods. The Nebraska State Historical Society maintains a Museum of Nebraska History in Lincoln. The Historical Society also operates various other museums and sites. These include the Fort Robinson Museum in Crawford, the Senator George Norris State Historic Site in McCook, and the Willa Cather State Historic Site in Red Cloud. The Strategic Air and Space Museum near Ashland contains galleries of preserved aircraft.

Universities and colleges

This table lists the nonprofit universities and colleges in Nebraska that grant bachelor's or advanced degrees and are accredited by the North Central Association of Colleges and Schools.

Name	Mailing address
Bellevue University	Bellevue
Chadron State College	Chadron
Clarkson College	Omaha
Concordia University	Seward
Creighton University	Omaha
Doane College	Crete
Grace University	Omaha
Hastings College	Hastings
Midland Lutheran College	Fremont
Nebraska, University of	*
Nebraska Methodist College	Omaha
Nebraska Wesleyan University	Lincoln
Peru State College	Peru
St. Mary, College of	Omaha
Union College	Lincoln
Wayne State College	Wayne
York College	York

*For campuses, see Nebraska, University of.

Nebraska map index

Metropolitan areas

†Census designated place—unincorporated, but recognized as a significant settled community by the U.S. Census Bureau.
°County seat.
Places without population figures are unincorporated areas.
Source: 2010 census.

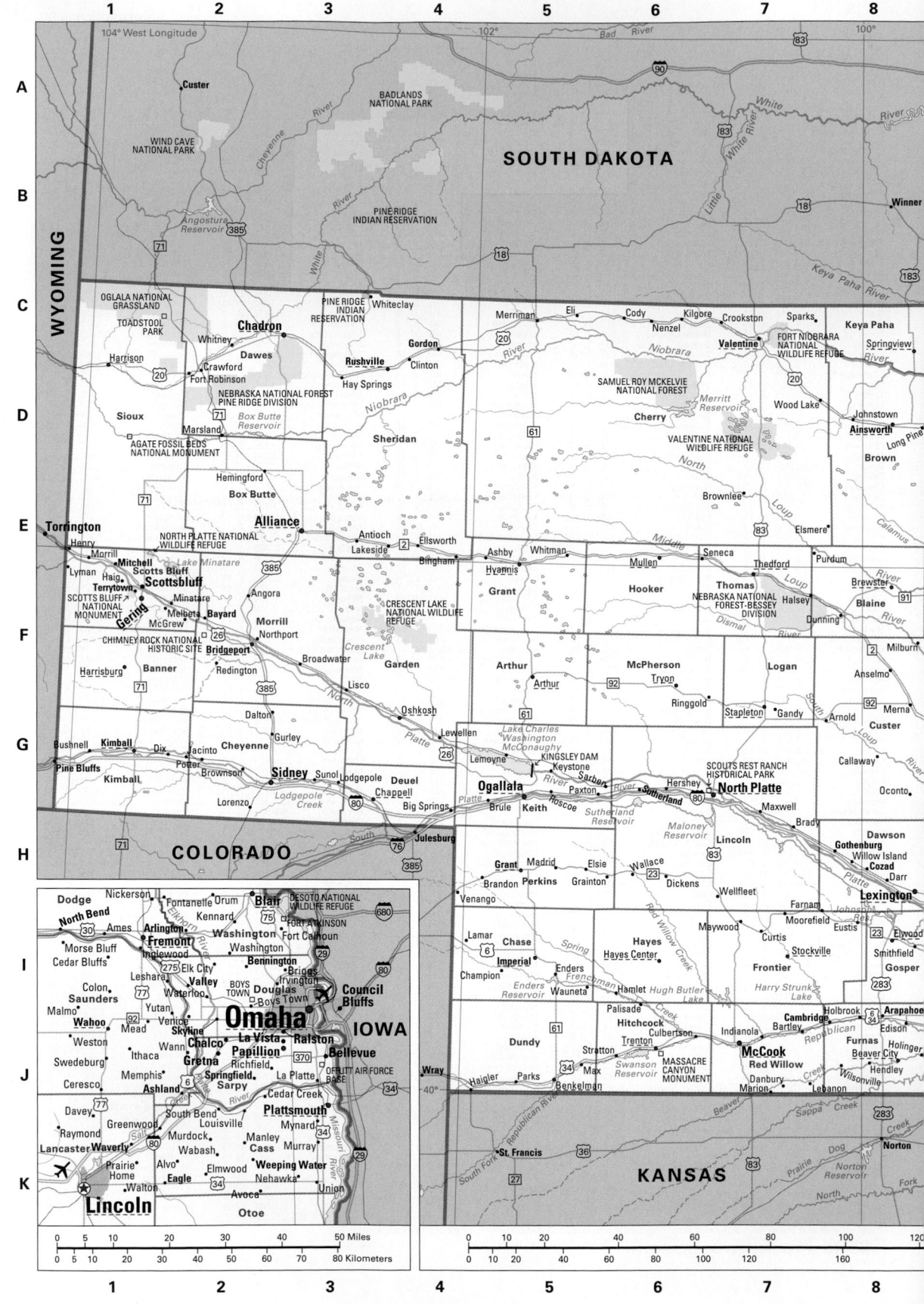

Nebraska political map

Legend:

Urban area	Hall — County name	Railroad
Park or other recreation area	State capital	Expressway
Forest or other conservation area	County seat	Other road
Indian reservation	City or town	80 Interstate highway
State boundary	Point of interest	20 U.S. highway
County boundary	Major airport	2 Other road

Lambert conformal conic projection
WORLD BOOK map

Every year, thousands of tourists drive along Nebraska highways that follow the historic Oregon and Mormon trails. Ruts left by the pioneers' covered wagons can still be seen along the roadsides. In northwestern Nebraska, the forests and rugged rocks of the Pine Ridge are a paradise for campers, bicyclists, and hikers. Other scenic spots include the valleys of the Platte, Niobrara, Big Blue, Loup, and Republican rivers and the bluffs along the Missouri River. The lakes and streams of the Sand Hills area teem with fish. On the prairies, hunters bag pheasants, quail, and other birds as well as deer.

The Nebraska State Fair and Nebraskaland Days are the state's most important annual events. The fair is held in Lincoln from late August to early September. It features exhibits of crops, farm machinery, household equipment, and livestock. Nebraskaland Days takes place in North Platte in June. It includes parades, a carnival, and the Buffalo Bill Rodeo. Almost every county has a fair during the summer, and many communities hold annual fall festivals.

Geraldine Rystrom

Children dressed in traditional clothes at the Swedish Festival in Stromsburg

Places to visit

Following are brief descriptions of some of Nebraska's many interesting places to visit:

Arbor Lodge, in Nebraska City, was the 52-room mansion of Julius Sterling Morton, a Nebraska journalist and the founder of Arbor Day. The site has about 270 *species* (kinds) of trees and shrubs.

Bellevue is the oldest town in Nebraska. It was established about 1823 as a fur-trading center. Some of the town's buildings are more than 100 years old.

Buffalo Bill State Historical Park, also known as Scout's Rest Ranch, near North Platte, is where Buffalo Bill, the famous scout and showman, lived when he was between tours with his popular Wild West show.

Great Platte River Road Archway Monument, a museum near Kearney, spans Interstate 80 and features exhibits on the road's history and the development of the West.

Henry Doorly Zoo, in Omaha, houses an indoor rain forest and an indoor desert.

Museum of the Fur Trade, near Chadron, has a large collection of Indian artifacts, early guns, and other fur trade relics.

Old Market, in Omaha, is a shopping and entertainment complex with restaurants, specialty shops, art galleries, and hotels.

Pioneer Village in Minden has an extensive collection of memorabilia from pioneer days.

Stuhr Museum of the Prairie Pioneer, near Grand Island, features a restored railroad town of the 1800's. A bank, general store, and post office are among 60 frontier buildings there.

National forests and parklands. Nebraska has two national forests, Nebraska in Blaine, Dawes, Sioux, and Thomas counties and McKelvie in Cherry County. The division of Nebraska National Forest that lies in Blaine and Thomas counties is the largest hand-planted forest in the United States. The Agate Fossil Beds National Monument in northwestern Nebraska contains deposits of animal fossils. The Homestead National Monument of America, near Beatrice, occupies the site of one of the first pieces of land claimed under the Homestead Act of 1862. The Scotts Bluff National Monument marks a landmark 800 feet (244 meters) above the North Platte River on the Oregon Trail. The spire at Chimney Rock National Historic Site rises about 500 feet (150 meters) above the North Platte.

State parks. Nebraska has several state parks and many historical parks and recreation areas. For more information about its parklands, visit the official website of the Nebraska Game and Parks Commission at http://outdoornebraska.ne.gov/.

Toadstool Geologic Park near Crawford

Gary Withey, Bruce Coleman Inc.

Chimney Rock National Historic Site near Bayard

© David Rees

Nebraska Department of Economic Development

Buffalo Bill's home at Scout's Rest Ranch near North Platte

Jim Holm, Nebraska Department of Economic Development

Nebraska's Big Rodeo in Burwell

The Sand Hills of west-central Nebraska are hills and ridges consisting of fine sand piled up by the wind. Grasses that cover the Sand Hills keep most of the sand in place.

© David Rees

Land regions. Nebraska rises in a series of rolling plateaus from the southeast to the extreme southwest. The land rises from about 800 feet (240 meters) above sea level to over 5,400 feet (1,650 meters). Nebraska has two major land regions. These are, from east to west: (1) the Dissected Till Plains and (2) the Great Plains.

The Dissected Till Plains cover about the eastern fifth of Nebraska and extend into South Dakota, Iowa, Missouri, and Kansas. Glaciers once covered the Till Plains. The last glacier melted several hundred thousand years ago. It left a thick cover of rich, soil-forming material called *till*. A deep deposit of windblown dust called *loess* then settled on the till. Streams have *dissected* (cut up) the region, giving it a rolling surface. In the southeastern section of Nebraska's Till Plains, the action of the streams has exposed glacial materials on the sides of the valleys. The northern section is known as the Loess Hills. Most of the Dissected Till Plains region is very well suited to farming with modern machinery.

The Great Plains region of Nebraska stretches westward from the Dissected Till Plains and extends into Wyoming and Colorado. A series of sand hills rises north of the Platte River in the central part of the region. The soil of the Sand Hills section consists of fine sand piled up by the wind. The sand was formed into hills and ridges. The section covers about 20,000 square miles (51,800 square kilometers), making it the largest area of sand dunes in North America. Grasses that now cover the Sand Hills hold most of the sand in place. Sometimes, however, overgrazing by cattle and extension of irrigated cropland kill the grass cover. The wind then cuts great holes called *blowouts* into the hillsides. Most ranchers take care not to overgraze the land. The Sand Hills make fine cattle country because of the area's

flowing streams, abundant well water, and excellent grasses. Some of the grass is cut as *wild hay*.

The soil of the Sand Hills acts like a giant sponge. It absorbs and holds most of the area's limited rainfall. The rainfall seeps down and creates vast underground reservoirs of *ground water*. Movement of the ground water makes it possible to pump irrigation water to the surface in areas around the Sand Hills.

A deep deposit of loess covers the central and south-central parts of the Great Plains. Some of this loess country is rough and hilly. But in the southeast, a relatively flat loess area, called the Loess Plain, covers about 7,000 square miles (18,000 square kilometers). It is farmed even more intensively than the Till Plains.

North and west of the Sand Hills are the High Plains, which cover about 12,000 square miles (31,100 square kilometers). The High Plains in the west rise to more than 1 mile (1.6 kilometers) above sea level along part of the Wyoming border. The High Plains receive less than 20 inches (51 centimeters) of rainfall. Farmers there must use irrigation or practice *dryland farming,* methods that

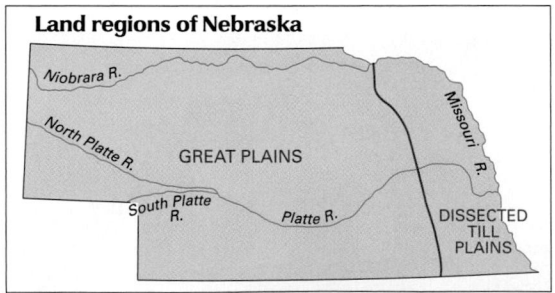

Land regions of Nebraska

WORLD BOOK map

Map index

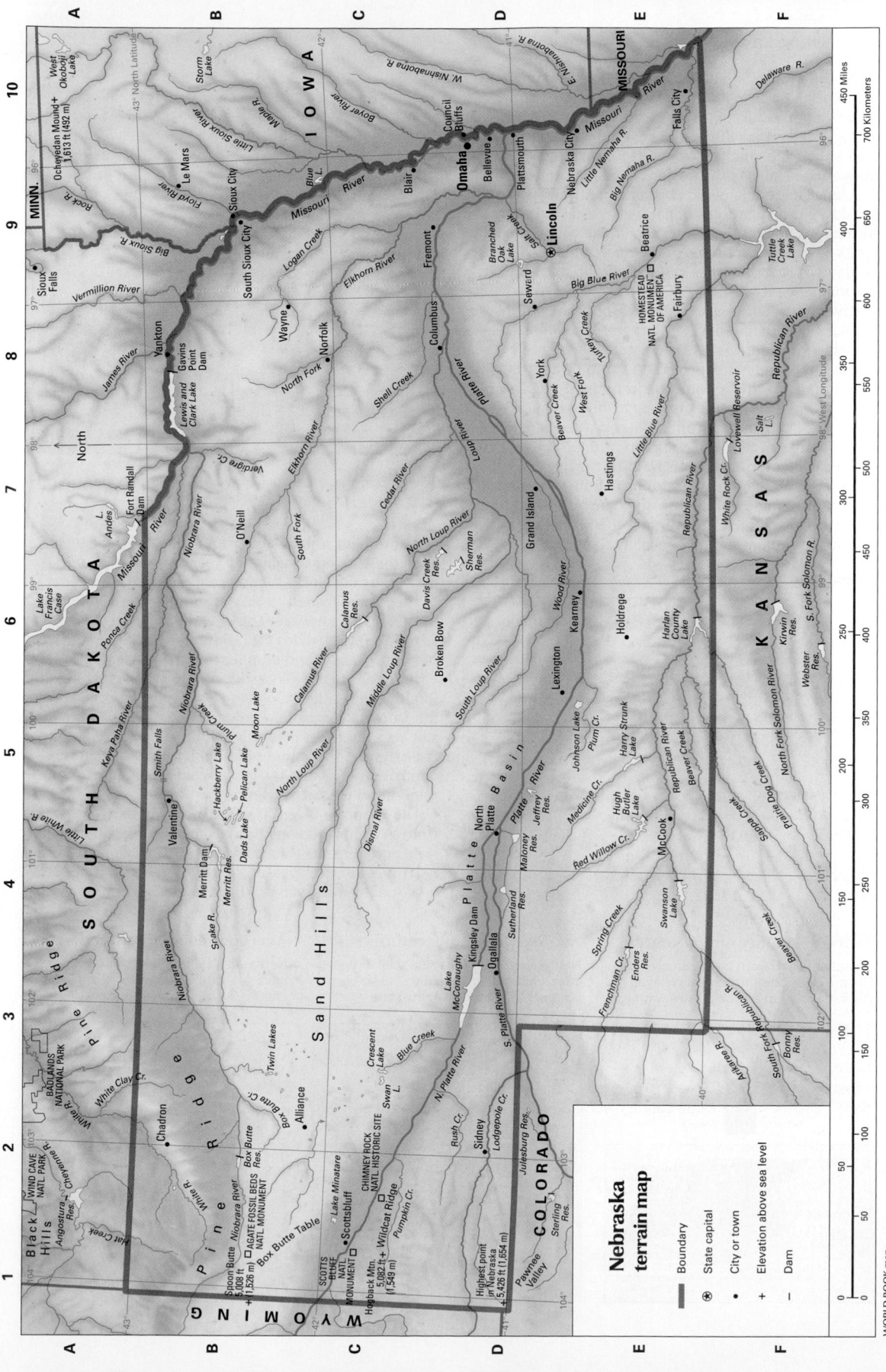

Nebraska
terrain map

Boundary

⊛ State capital

• City or town

+ Elevation above sea level

— Dam

WORLD BOOK map

A	B	C	D	E	F	

IOWA

MINN.

MISSOURI

SOUTH DAKOTA

WYOMING

COLORADO

KANSAS

Sand Hills

Pine Ridge

Black Hills

Badlands National Park

Wind Cave Natl. Park

West Okoboji Lake

Ocheyedan Mound+ 1,613 ft (492 m)

Storm Lake

Spirit Lake

Little Sioux River

Maple River

Boyer River

Rock R.

Floyd River

Le Mars

Sioux City

South Sioux City

Sioux Falls

Vermillion River

Big Sioux R.

Missouri River

Blue L.

Blair

Council Bluffs

Omaha

Bellevue

Plattsmouth

Nebraska City

Missouri River

Falls City

Delaware R.

W. Nishnabotna R.

E. Nishnabotna R.

Little Nemaha R.

Big Nemaha R.

Logan Creek

Elkhorn River

Fremont

Lincoln

Branched Oak Lake

Salt Creek

Seward

York

Big Blue River

Beatrice

Homestead Natl. Monument of America

Fairbury

Tuttle Creek Lake

Wayne

Norfolk

North Fork

Shell Creek

Columbus

Platte River

Turkey Creek

West Fork

Little Blue River

Republican River

Lovewell Reservoir

Salt L.

Republican River

James River

North

Yankton

Gavins Point Dam

Lewis and Clark Lake

Verdigre Cr.

Elkhorn River

South Fork

Cedar River

North Loup River

Sherman Res.

Davis Creek Res.

Grand Island

Hastings

Beaver Creek

White Rock Cr.

Fort Randall Dam

L. Andes

Niobrara River

O'Neill

Calamus Res.

Calamus River

Middle Loup River

Broken Bow

South Loup River

Wood River

Kearney

Lexington

Holdrege

Harlan County Lake

Republican River

Beaver Creek

Webster Res.

Kirwin Res.

Lake Francis Case

Ponce Creek

Keya Paha River

Smith Falls

Valentine

Hackberry Lake

Dads Lake

Pelican Lake

Moon Lake

Plum Creek

North Loup River

Dismal River

Johnson Lake

Plum Cr.

Medicine Cr.

Harry Strunk Lake

Hugh Butler Lake

McCook

Republican River

Swanson Lake

Red Willow Cr.

S. Fork Solomon R.

North Fork Solomon River

Prairie Dog Creek

Sappa Creek

Missouri River

Snake R.

Merritt Dam

Merritt Res.

Niobrara River

Plum Creek

Twin Lakes

Crescent Lake

Swan L.

Blue Creek

North Platte

Platte River

Jeffrey River

Jeffrey Res.

Maloney Res.

Sutherland Res.

Spring Creek

Frenchman Cr.

Enders Res.

Arikaree R.

South Fork Republican River

Bonny Res.

Sterling Res.

Pawnee Valley

Chadron

Box Butte Res.

White Clay Cr.

Box Butte Cr.

Alliance

Lake Minatare

Scottsbluff

Fox Butte Cr.

Chimney Rock Natl. Historic Site

Agate Fossil Beds Natl. Monument

Scotts Bluff Natl. Monument

Wildcat Ridge

Box Butte Table

Hogback Mtn. 5,082 ft (1,549 m)

Highest point in Nebraska +5,425 ft (1,654 m)

Spoon Butte 5,008 ft (1,526 m)

Niobrara River

White R.

Sidney

Lodgepole Cr.

Rush Cr.

N. Platte River

S. Platte River

Ogallala

Lake McConaughy

Kingsley Dam

Julesburg Res.

Platte Basin

White River

Cheyenne R.

Little White R.

Angostura Res.

Hat Creek

Pumpkin Cr.

make the most of the limited rainfall (see **Dryland farming**). Rough parts of the High Plains are used mainly to graze cattle. Some rough areas, including the Wildcat Ridge and the Pine Ridge, are covered with evergreen trees. The state's highest point is 5,426 feet (1,654 meters) above sea level in southwestern Kimball County.

A small area of Badlands is found in northwestern Nebraska. There, the forces of nature have carved weird formations in the sandstone and claylike rocks. The Badlands have little economic importance, but ranchers use some of the area to graze cattle, and tourists marvel at the magnificent scenery.

Rivers and lakes. The great Missouri River forms Nebraska's eastern and northeastern border. Nebraska's principal river, the Platte, flows into the Missouri at Plattsmouth. The North Platte and South Platte rivers join near the city of North Platte and form the Platte. The North Platte River enters the state from Wyoming, and the South Platte enters from Colorado. The Platte River winds across central and southern Nebraska. The Platte is too shallow for navigation. Nebraskans use the waters of the river and its branches for irrigation, recreation, and the production of hydroelectric power.

The Loup and Elkhorn rivers are the Platte's most important branches. Both rise in the Sand Hills.

Nebraska Department of Economic Development

The Pine Ridge is a beautiful, rugged area that forms part of the High Plains in northwestern Nebraska.

The abundant supplies of ground water in the Sand Hills keep these rivers flowing the year around. The Loup is formed by the North, Middle, and South Loup rivers.

The Republican River enters southwestern Nebraska from Kansas. It flows near the southern edge of Nebraska for about 200 miles (320 kilometers) and then turns back into Kansas and empties into the Kansas River. Other branches of the Kansas River in Nebraska include the Big Blue and Little Blue rivers. These three branches of the Kansas River usually flow gently. But heavy rainstorms sometimes cause them to overflow and flood the countryside. This danger has been reduced by flood-control projects and by dams built for irrigation and generating electric power.

The Niobrara River flows into northwestern Nebraska from Wyoming. It winds across the northern part of the state and joins the Missouri River in Knox County. This narrow, swift river passes through many scenic spots. It is part of the National Wild and Scenic Rivers System.

Average monthly weather

	Omaha					Scottsbluff				
	Temperatures °F		Temperatures °C		Days of rain or snow		Temperatures °F		Temperatures °C		Days of rain or snow
	High	Low	High	Low			High	Low	High	Low	
Jan.	32	12	0	–11	6	**Jan.**	38	11	3	–12	5
Feb.	38	18	3	–8	7	**Feb.**	44	16	7	–9	5
Mar.	50	28	10	–2	9	**Mar.**	52	23	11	–5	7
Apr.	63	40	17	4	10	**Apr.**	61	31	16	–1	9
May	74	51	23	11	12	**May**	71	42	22	6	11
June	84	61	29	16	11	**June**	82	52	28	11	11
July	87	66	31	19	10	**July**	89	57	32	14	8
Aug.	85	64	29	18	9	**Aug.**	87	55	31	13	7
Sept.	77	54	25	12	8	**Sept.**	77	44	25	7	7
Oct.	65	41	18	5	6	**Oct.**	64	31	18	–1	5
Nov.	48	28	9	–2	6	**Nov.**	48	20	9	–7	5
Dec.	35	16	2	–9	6	**Dec.**	40	12	4	–11	5

Average January temperatures

Nebraska winters can be extremely cold. The northeast has the coldest weather. The west and extreme south are warmest.

Degrees Fahrenheit	Degrees Celsius
Above 22	Above -6
20 to 22	-7 to -6
18 to 20	-8 to -7
Below 18	Below -8

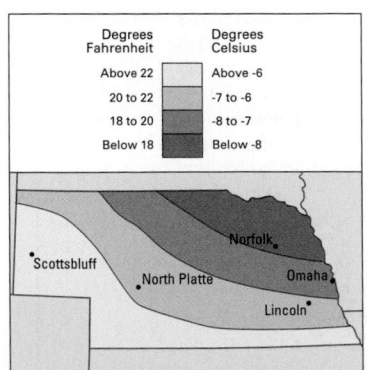

Average July temperatures

Nebraska has hot summers with temperatures varying only slightly. The far west is cooler than the rest of the state.

Degrees Fahrenheit	Degrees Celsius
Above 76	Above 25
75 to 76	24 to 25
74 to 75	23 to 24
Below 74	Below 23

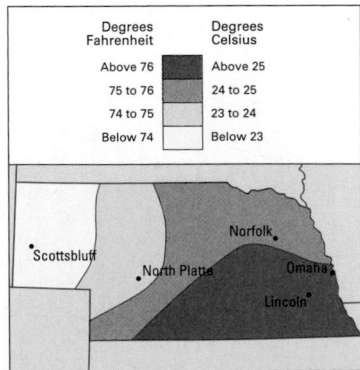

Average yearly precipitation

Nebraska may have wide ranges of precipitation from year to year. Rainfall decreases steadily from east to west.

WORLD BOOK maps

Inches	Centimeters
More than 28	More than 71
24 to 28	61 to 71
20 to 24	51 to 61
Less than 20	Less than 51

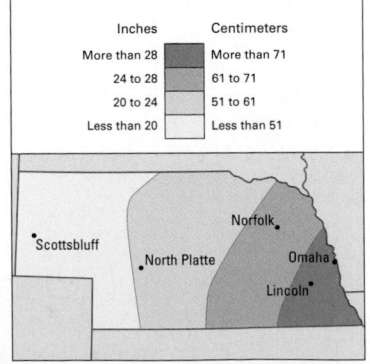

Nebraska has more than 2,000 lakes. None of the natural lakes are large. Hundreds of small, shallow lakes dot the Sand Hills. Lake McConaughy, Nebraska's largest lake, was artificially created. It covers about 55 square miles (142 square kilometers) and has a shoreline of 105 miles (169 kilometers). Lake McConaughy was formed on the North Platte River by Kingsley Dam.

Other important artificially created lakes on the Platte River irrigation and power system include Jeffrey and Sutherland reservoirs and Johnson Lake. Additional large artificially created lakes in Nebraska are Lewis and Clark Lake on the Missouri River, Swanson Lake and Harlan County Lake on the Republican River, and Enders Reservoir and Harry Strunk Lake on branches of the Republican River.

Plant and animal life. Forests cover only about 2 percent of Nebraska. Common trees in eastern and central Nebraska include ashes, basswoods, boxelders, cottonwoods, elms, hackberries, locusts, oaks, walnuts, and willows. Pines and cedars are among the trees that grow in the western part of the state.

Tall prairie grasses, especially bluestem, grow in uncultivated parts of eastern Nebraska. Short grasses, such as grama and buffalo grass, cover drier western regions. Eastern shrubs include wild plums and chokecherries. Evening primroses, phloxes, and violets bloom in the eastern regions in spring. During summer, blue flags, columbines, larkspurs, poppies, spiderworts, and wild roses thrive throughout the state. Goldenrod and sunflowers brighten roadsides and fields in late summer.

Nebraska's animal life consists chiefly of mule deer and such small animals as badgers, coyotes, muskrats, opossums, prairie dogs, rabbits, raccoons, skunks, and squirrels. Mountain lions, absent from the state since the end of the 1800's, began to be seen again in the 1990's. Game birds are plentiful. They include ducks, geese, pheasants, and quail. Common fish include bass, carp, catfish, crappies, perch, pike, and trout.

Climate. Nebraska's climate ranges from extremely hot in summer to extremely cold in winter. The weather changes suddenly—and sometimes violently. Hot, moist breezes from the Gulf of Mexico occasionally make summer nights uncomfortably warm in eastern areas. Nebraska sometimes has violent thunderstorms, tornadoes, blizzards, and hailstorms.

Temperatures vary only moderately from one area to another. Temperatures average about 76 °F (24 °C) in July and about 23 °F (–5 °C) in January. The state's record high temperature of 118 °F (48 °C) was set at Geneva on July 15, 1934; at Hartington on July 17, 1936; and at Minden on July 24, 1936. The lowest temperature, –47 °F (–44 °C), was reported at Camp Clarke, near Northport, on Feb. 12, 1899, and at Oshkosh on Dec. 22, 1989.

Rainfall decreases steadily from east to west. The east receives about 27 inches (69 centimeters) of rain yearly. Less than 20 inches (51 centimeters) fall in the west. The state has droughts in some years, floods in others. Most rain falls from April to September. The growing season ranges from about 165 days in the southeast to 120 days in the northwest. Snowfall averages almost 30 inches (76 centimeters) yearly in the east. The west generally has less snow.

Economy

Nebraska is one of the leading agricultural states. Farms and ranches take up more than 90 percent. That percentage is higher than in any other state. However, service industries, taken together, make up the largest part of Nebraska's *gross domestic product.* Gross domestic product is the total value of goods and services produced within the state in a year. Service industries and manufacturing benefit from the state's strong agricultural base. For example, processed foods are the state's leading manufactured product.

Natural resources. Soil and water are Nebraska's most precious natural resources. They are carefully conserved. Farmers rotate their crops. Some practice terracing and other soil-saving methods to keep the soil from wearing out or washing away. Nebraska has built many dams to provide water for livestock and irrigation. The dams also help control the flow of rivers and produce electric power. Nebraska may have more underground water than any other state. It lies above the High Plains Aquifer, a layer of porous rock and other material filled with water. This huge underground "lake" spreads from Texas to South Dakota. About two-thirds of it lies beneath Nebraska.

Soil. A fertile silt loam covers eastern Nebraska. The soil of the Sand Hills, in central Nebraska, consists of loose sand. It drifts badly if plowed, but left untouched, it supports grasses on which cattle can graze. The High Plains in the west have a loamy soil.

Minerals. Nebraska has few minerals. Fields of petroleum and natural gas lie chiefly in western and south-central Nebraska. Sand and gravel can be found along the Platte and Republican rivers and their branches. Limestone and clay are mined in the southeastern part of the state.

Service industries account for the largest portion of both the employment and the gross domestic product of Nebraska. Many of the state's service industries are in the Omaha and Lincoln metropolitan areas.

Omaha is a Midwestern financial center. Mutual of Omaha is headquartered in the city. The company ranks as one of the largest insurance companies in the United States. Omaha is also the home of Berkshire Hathaway, a large holding company of insurance companies and other businesses. ConAgra Foods, a major food processing and distributing company, is based in Omaha. So is Union Pacific, the nation's largest railroad company. Many hotels, restaurants, and retail trade establishments operate in the Omaha and Lincoln areas.

Lincoln, the state capital, is the center of government activities. Government services also include the operation of electric utilities and military bases. Nebraska is the only state in which publicly owned utilities provide all electric service. The headquarters of the U.S. Strategic Command (USSTRATCOM) is at Offutt Air Force Base near Bellevue. USSTRATCOM is the control center for U.S. nuclear offensive forces and military space operations. It also controls defense against nuclear and long-range conventional missile attacks on the United States.

Nebraska economy

General economy

Gross domestic product (GDP)* (2008) $86,099,000,000
  Rank among U.S. states   36th
Unemployment rate (2010)   4.7% (U.S. avg: 9.6%)

*Gross domestic product is the total value of goods and services produced in a year.
Sources: U.S. Bureau of Economic Analysis and U.S. Bureau of Labor Statistics.

Agriculture

Cash receipts $15,309,098,000
  Rank among U.S. states   4th
Distribution   52% livestock, 48% crops
Farms   47,200
Farm acres (hectares)   45,600,000 (18,450,000)
  Rank among U.S. states   4th
Farmland   92% of Nebraska

Leading products

1. Cattle and calves   (ranks 2nd in U.S.)
2. Corn   (ranks 3rd in U.S.)
3. Soybeans   (ranks 5th in U.S.)
4. Hogs
5. Wheat
Other products: beans, dairy products, eggs, hay, potatoes.

Manufacturing

Value added by manufacture* $15,969,148,000
  Rank among U.S. states   35th

Leading products

1. Food products
2. Chemicals
3. Medical equipment
4. Machinery
Other products: fabricated metal products, transportation
equipment.

*Value added by manufacture is the increase in value of raw materials after they
become finished products.

Electric power

Coal   66.3%
Nuclear   29.3%
Hydroelectric   2.3%
Other   2.1%

Production and workers by economic activities

Economic activities	Percent of GDP produced	Employed workers	
		Number of people	Percent of total
Finance, insurance, & real estate	21	133,600	11
Community, business, & personal services	18	363,000	29
Trade, restaurants, & hotels	14	256,500	20
Government	13	173,300	14
Manufacturing	11	105,000	8
Transportation & communication	10	86,000	7
Agriculture	7	57,800	5
Construction	4	73,800	6
Utilities	2	2,100	*
Mining	*	2,400	*
Total	100	1,253,500	100

*Less than one-half of 1 percent.
Figures are for 2008; employment figures include full- and part-time workers.
Source: *World Book* estimates based on data from U.S. Bureau of Economic Analysis.

Mining

Nonfuel mineral production* $152,000,000
  Rank among U.S. states   45th
Coal (tons)   †
Crude oil (barrels‡)   2,394,000
  Rank among U.S. states   21st
Natural gas (cubic feet§)   3,082,000,000
  Rank among U.S. states   25th

*Partial total, excludes values that must be concealed to not disclose company data.
†No significant mining of this product in Nebraska.
‡One barrel equals 42 gallons (159 liters).
§One cubic foot equals 0.0283 cubic meter.

Leading products

Petroleum and portland cement
Other products: lime, limestone, sand and gravel.

Figures are for 2008, except for the agricultural figures, which are for 2009.
Sources: U.S. Census Bureau, U.S. Department of Agriculture, U.S. Energy Information
    Administration, U.S. Geological Survey.

Economy of Nebraska

This map shows the economic uses of land in Nebraska and where the state's leading farm and mineral products are pro- duced. Major manufacturing centers are shown in red.

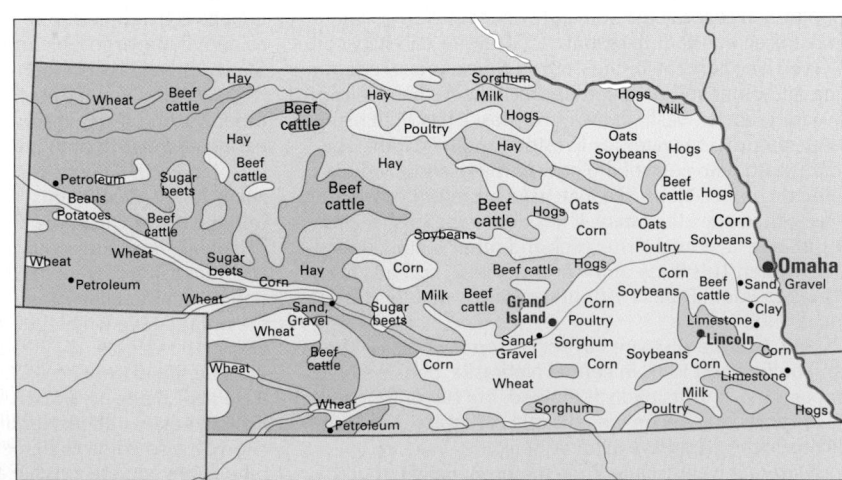

- Mostly cropland
- Woodland mixed with cropland
- Grazing land mixed with cropland
- Mostly grazing land
- ● Manufacturing center
- • Mineral deposit

WORLD BOOK map

ConAgra Foods

The headquarters of ConAgra Foods, a leading food process-ing and distribution company, are in Omaha. The city is a center for the processing of grain and meat products.

Manufacturing. Food processing is by far the lead-ing manufacturing activity in Nebraska. Meat products and grain products provide most of the income from food processing in Nebraska. Large meat-packing plants operate in the eastern and south-central areas. The state is one of the country's major centers of meat packing. The Omaha area is the state's chief center for the proc-essing of grain products. Breakfast cereal and livestock feed are important grain products.

Chemicals and machinery are also important manu-factured products. *Pharmaceuticals* (medicinal drugs) are Nebraska's leading chemical products. They are chiefly produced in Lincoln and Omaha. Plants in the Omaha area manufacture farm equipment. Farm equipment is the state's most important kind of machinery. Fabricated metal products, medical equipment, and transportation equipment are primarily produced in the south-central part of the state and in the Lincoln-Omaha area.

Agriculture. Farms and ranches cover more than 90 percent of Nebraska's land area. Nebraska's leading farm products are beef cattle, corn, hogs, soybeans, and wheat. Nebraska ranks among the leading producers of all these products. The state has many irrigated farms, especially in the central region.

Livestock and livestock products provide about half of Nebraska's farm income. Beef cattle are the most impor-tant farm product in the state. The rich grasses on the Sand Hills and in the western part of the state provide fine feed for range beef cattle. Some farmers raise dairy

cattle. Milk is another important source of farm income.

Hogs are the second most important livestock prod-uct in Nebraska. Eastern Nebraska is one of the country's leading hog-producing areas. Poultry farms are also found in this region.

Crops provide just under half of Nebraska's farm in-come. Corn is the state's chief crop. Corn grows in the central and eastern areas. The state's other leading crops are hay, soybeans, and wheat. Most of the hay is grown in the Great Plains region, especially the northern sec-tion. Most of the soybean farms lie in the Till Plains re-gion. Most of Nebraska's wheat farms lie in the west. Other crops raised in Nebraska include beans, grain sorghum, oats, potatoes, rye, and sugar beets.

Mining. Petroleum and portland cement are Nebras-ka's two leading mined products. Most of the state's crude oil is produced in Cheyenne, Dundy, Hitchcock, Kimball, and Red Willow counties. Portland cement is produced in Cass County. Construction companies use sand and gravel from the Platte Valley. Manufacturers use clay from southeastern Nebraska for bricks, tiles, and pottery. The state's limestone is used in construc-tion, in making cement, and in treating soil. Chase, Cheyenne, and Deuel counties are the state's leading producers of natural gas.

Electric power and utilities. Coal-burning power plants provide about two-thirds of the electric power generated in Nebraska. Nuclear plants at Brownville and Fort Calhoun supply more than a fourth of the state's power. Much of the remaining power comes from hy-droelectric plants and plants that burn natural gas.

Transportation. Thousands of pioneers crossed the Nebraska region on their way to the West. The Oregon, California, and Mormon trails followed Nebraska's Platte River. In 1865, the Union Pacific Railroad began laying track westward from Omaha. The track became part of the first transcontinental rail system in the United States. Today, the Union Pacific and the Burlington Northern Santa Fe railroads provide most of the freight service in the state. Nebraska has an extensive system of roads and highways. Interstate 80 is the most important highway. It runs east and west between Omaha and the Wyoming border. Nebraska's busiest airport is at Omaha. Lincoln also has a large airport. Ports in Nebraska City, Omaha, and South Sioux City send and receive freight by water.

Communication. D. E. Reed began Nebraska's first newspaper in 1854. It was called the *Nebraska Palladium and Platte Valley Advocate.* Today, Nebraska's leading daily newspaper is the *Omaha World-Herald.* Other Ne-braska newspapers with large circulations include *The Grand Island Independent,* the *Lincoln Journal Star,* and the *Norfolk Daily News.*

Government

Constitution of Nebraska was adopted in 1875. Ne-braska had one earlier constitution, adopted in 1866. Amendments may be proposed by the Legislature, by a constitutional convention, or by the people. A constitu-tional amendment proposed in the Legislature becomes law after approval by three-fifths of the Legislature and by a majority of voters casting ballots on the amend-ment, provided that these approving votes are no less

than 35 percent of the total votes cast in the election.

A proposal to call a constitutional convention also must be approved by three-fifths of the Legislature and by a majority of voters casting ballots on the proposal, provided that these approving votes are no less than 35 percent of the total votes cast in the election. Conven-tion proposals become law after they have been ap-proved by a majority of people voting on them. The

© David Rees

The Nebraska Legislature meets in the State Capitol in Lincoln. Nebraska is the only state with a *unicameral* (one-house) legislature. Its 49 members are called *senators.*

people of Nebraska may sign a *petition* (formal request) proposing a constitutional amendment. The number of signatures on a petition must equal at least 10 percent of the number of registered voters on the date the signatures are to be turned in to the secretary of state. The proposed amendment becomes law after approval by a majority of voters casting ballots on the amendment, providing that these votes are no less than 35 percent of the total votes cast in the election. The people also have the power of referendum, which may be invoked, by petition, to repeal acts of the Legislature.

Executive. Voters elect the governor, lieutenant governor, secretary of state, attorney general, treasurer, and auditor to four-year terms. The governor and treasurer may serve no more than two terms in succession. The other four officials have no term limits.

Legislature. Nebraska is the only state with a *unicameral* (one-house) legislature. The 49 members of the Legislature are called *senators.* Voters in each of the state's 49 legislative districts elect one senator. The people elect the senators on a *nonpartisan* ballot—that is, the ballot has no political party labels. Nebraska is the only state that chooses state legislators in nonpartisan elections. Senators are elected to four-year terms.

The Legislature meets every year. Regular sessions begin on the Wednesday after the first Monday in January. They are limited to 60 days in even-numbered years and 90 days in odd-numbered years. The governor may call special sessions.

Courts in Nebraska are headed by the state Supreme Court. It consists of a chief justice and one judge from each of the six judicial districts. The Court of Appeals has six judges, each representing one of the six judicial districts. Nebraska also has 12 district courts, with a total of 55 judges.

The state follows a merit plan for the selection of Supreme Court, appellate court, and district court judges. Under the plan, the governor appoints a judge to fill a vacancy in these courts from a list submitted by a nominating committee. Each judge appointed must be approved by the voters at the next general election after holding office for three years. If approved, he or she serves in the office for six more years. Thereafter, the

voters must approve the judge every six years.

There are 12 districts in Nebraska's county court system and 59 county judges. The state's three most populated counties—Douglas, Lancaster, and Sarpy—have separate juvenile courts. There are 10 juvenile court judges, who are selected and retained in the same manner as are judges of the state's Supreme Court and district courts. No political party labels are allowed on the ballot used for approving judges.

Local government. Nebraska has 93 counties. About two-thirds of the counties have the commissioner-precinct form of government, and the remainder have the supervisor-township form. Counties that have the commissioner-precinct form are governed by a board of commissioners of three or five members. The commissioners are elected to four-year terms. Counties with the supervisor-township form are governed by a seven-member board of supervisors. The supervisors are also elected to four-year terms. Other officials in both kinds of Nebraska counties include the county clerk, treasurer, sheriff, and attorney. Commissioners, supervisors, and all other elected county officials may serve any number of terms.

The governors of Nebraska

	Party	Term
David Butler	Republican	1867-1871
William H. James	Republican	1871-1873
Robert W. Furnas	Republican	1873-1875
Silas Garber	Republican	1875-1879
Albinus Nance	Republican	1879-1883
James W. Dawes	Republican	1883-1887
John M. Thayer	Republican	1887-1892
James E. Boyd	Democratic	1892-1893
Lorenzo Crounse	Republican	1893-1895
Silas A. Holcomb	Fusion	1895-1899
William A. Poynter	Fusion	1899-1901
Charles H. Dietrich	Republican	1901
Ezra P. Savage	Republican	1901-1903
John H. Mickey	Republican	1903-1907
George L. Sheldon	Republican	1907-1909
Ashton C. Shallenberger	Democratic	1909-1911
Chester H. Aldrich	Republican	1911-1913
John H. Morehead	Democratic	1913-1917
Keith Neville	Democratic	1917-1919
Samuel R. McKelvie	Republican	1919-1923
Charles W. Bryan	Democratic	1923-1925
Adam McMullen	Republican	1925-1929
Arthur J. Weaver	Republican	1929-1931
Charles W. Bryan	Democratic	1931-1935
Robert Leroy Cochran	Democratic	1935-1941
Dwight Griswold	Republican	1941-1947
Val Peterson	Republican	1947-1953
Robert B. Crosby	Republican	1953-1955
Victor E. Anderson	Republican	1955-1959
Ralph G. Brooks	Democratic	1959-1960
Dwight W. Burney	Republican	1960-1961
Frank B. Morrison	Democratic	1961-1967
Norbert T. Tiemann	Republican	1967-1971
J. James Exon	Democratic	1971-1979
Charles Thone	Republican	1979-1983
Robert Kerrey	Democratic	1983-1987
Kay A. Orr	Republican	1987-1991
E. Benjamin Nelson	Democratic	1991-1999
Mike Johanns	Republican	1999-2005
Dave Heineman	Republican	2005-

Nebraska has over 500 cities and villages. Most cities have the mayor-council form of government. Nebraska City uses the commission form, and a few cities use the council-manager plan. Most villages are governed by a five-member board of trustees. The Constitution gives *home rule* to cities with over 5,000 people. Such cities may operate under their own charters. Only Lincoln and Omaha have chosen to adopt their own charters.

Revenue. Taxes provide about half of the state government's *general revenue* (income). Most of the rest comes from federal grants and other U.S. government programs. The largest sources of state tax revenue are a general sales tax and a personal income tax. Other important tax revenue sources include taxes on corporate income, motor fuels, motor vehicle licenses, and tobacco products.

Politics. All members of the Legislature, all judges and school officials, and many local officials are elected or approved on nonpartisan ballots. This system has weakened party politics in the state. However, in most of the elections for governor, the winner has been a Republican. In most presidential elections, the state's electoral votes have gone to the Republican candidate. For Nebraska's electoral votes and voting record in presidential elections, see **Electoral College** (table).

Two of Nebraska's most famous citizens were political reformers. William Jennings Bryan ran for president unsuccessfully three times and served as secretary of state under President Woodrow Wilson. George W. Norris won fame as an independent politician during his 40 years in the United States House of Representatives and the United States Senate.

History

Early days. A prehistoric people probably lived in the Nebraska region between 10,000 and 25,000 years ago. Scientists base this belief on the discovery of tips of stone tools and weapons, which were found buried in the Nebraska earth.

During the 1700's, European explorers came in contact with several Indian tribes in the Nebraska region. The Missouri, Omaha, Oto, and Ponca Indians lived by farming, hunting, and fishing along the rivers. The Pawnee hunted buffalo and grew beans, corn, and squash. They fought fiercely with other tribes, especially with the Lakota Sioux who lived to the north and the Comanche to the south. But the Pawnee were friendly with white settlers, and Pawnee scouts helped the U.S. Army in wars against the Sioux and Cheyenne. The Arapaho, Cheyenne, Comanche, and Sioux hunted in western Nebraska. They moved from place to place in search of game. To keep their hunting grounds, some Arapaho, Cheyenne, and Sioux resisted the white settlers.

Other Indian tribes moved into the Nebraska region as whites drove them from their homes in the East. Among the last Indians to settle in Nebraska were the Winnebago, who originally lived in Wisconsin, and the Santee Sioux, who lived in Minnesota. White people drove the Winnebago first to Iowa and then to Minnesota and South Dakota. In 1863 and 1864, the Winnebago fled into what later became Thurston County. The Santee Sioux were forced from Minnesota in 1863. Some were moved to South Dakota and, in 1866, from there to northern Nebraska. The Omaha, Santee Sioux, and Winnebago now live on reservations in the state.

The Missouri, Oto, and Pawnee Indians were forced from Nebraska in the 1870's and 1880's and migrated to what is now Oklahoma. In 1876, the Ponca also were ordered to leave Nebraska. But Ponca leader Standing Bear led some of them back to the state in 1879.

Exploration. In 1541, Francisco Vásquez de Coronado, a Spanish explorer, led an expedition across the American Southwest and into present-day Kansas. Spain claimed all this territory, including Nebraska, though the Spaniards established no settlements.

In 1682, the French explorer René-Robert Cavelier, Sieur de La Salle, traveled down the Mississippi River to its mouth. He claimed for France all the land drained by the Mississippi and its branches. La Salle named this vast territory, which included Nebraska, *Louisiana,* after the French king, Louis XIV. French traders and trappers moved into the Louisiana region during the 1690's and early 1700's. In 1714, a French explorer and adventurer, Étienne Veniard de Bourgmont, traveled up the Missouri River to the mouth of the Platte River.

Spain objected to French explorers in regions that it claimed and decided to remove the French. In 1720, a Spanish expedition under Pedro de Villasur marched from Santa Fe into the Nebraska region. But the expedition met a group of Pawnee Indians along the Platte River and withdrew after being badly defeated.

Two French explorers, the brothers Pierre and Paul Mallet, traveled from French forts in Illinois to Santa Fe in 1739. They were probably the first Europeans to cross what is now the state of Nebraska.

The Louisiana Purchase. In 1762, France gave Louisiana to Spain. But French fur traders and trappers continued to operate in the Nebraska region, and the Spaniards never set up an effective government. In 1800, Napoleon Bonaparte, the ruler of France, forced Spain to return Louisiana to France. In 1803, he sold the Louisiana Territory to the United States. Nebraska, as part of the Louisiana Purchase, became part of the United States.

American exploration and settlement. In 1804, President Thomas Jefferson sent an expedition under Meriwether Lewis and William Clark to explore the Louisiana Territory. Lewis and Clark traveled up the Missouri River and explored the eastern edge of Nebraska. Another American explorer, Zebulon M. Pike, visited the south-central part of Nebraska in 1806. Manuel Lisa, a Spanish-American trader, established fur-trading posts along the Missouri River between 1807 and 1820. One of these posts was Fort Lisa, about 10 miles (16 kilometers) north of present-day Omaha.

In 1812, Robert Stuart, a fur agent, set out for New York City from the Astoria fur-trading post in Oregon. Stuart and his party spent the winter in Wyoming and entered Nebraska early in 1813. They traveled along the North Platte and Platte rivers and reached the Missouri River in April. Settlers moving to Oregon during the next 50 years followed the route explored by Stuart. This route became known as the Oregon Trail.

The U.S. Army established Fort Atkinson in 1819 on the Missouri River, about 16 miles (26 kilometers) north of present-day Omaha. The fort became the site of Nebraska's first school, library, sawmill, grist mill, and brickyard. The fort was abandoned in 1827.

In 1820, Major Stephen H. Long led an Army expedition across Nebraska through the Platte and North Platte river valleys. Long described the region of western Nebraska as "almost wholly unfit for farming." He called it the "Great American Desert."

During the 1820's, the American Fur Company and other fur companies set up trading posts at Bellevue and other points along the Missouri River. But until 1854, when Nebraska was made a territory, the federal government maintained Nebraska as Indian country. Except for Indian agents, missionaries, and licensed traders, no white families were allowed to settle there. In 1843, hundreds of pioneers began the "Great Migration" to the rich farmlands of Oregon. They followed the Oregon Trail through Nebraska to the West.

Territorial days. In 1854, the U.S. Congress passed the Kansas-Nebraska Act, which created the territories of Kansas and Nebraska and opened the region to white settlement. Earlier bills to create the territories had been defeated because Congress could not agree on the slavery question. Southerners in Congress did not want to open the northern plains for settlement because the Missouri Compromise of 1820 prohibited slavery there. The Kansas-Nebraska Act repealed the Missouri Compromise. It allowed the people living in the two territories to decide for themselves whether to permit slavery. Most Nebraskans opposed slavery.

The Nebraska Territory included what is now Nebraska and parts of Montana, North Dakota, South Dakota, Wyoming, and Colorado. President Franklin Pierce appointed Francis Burt of South Carolina as the first territorial governor. Burt died shortly after he took office, and the territorial secretary, Thomas B. Cuming, became acting governor. Cuming organized the territorial government and took a census so that elections could be held for the legislature. Nebraska had a population of 2,732 in 1854. By 1863, Congress had created several new territories from the region, and the Nebraska Territory was reduced to about the state's present area.

Many early settlers in the Nebraska Territory built their homes of sod because so few trees grew on the plains. This sod was known as "Nebraska marble." Pioneers cut out blocks of sod with spades and piled the blocks on top of one another to form walls. Most roofs consisted of sod blocks supported by a mat of branches, brush, and long grasses.

Statehood. By 1860, Nebraska's population had grown to 28,841. In 1862, Congress passed the first Homestead Act. This act granted 160 acres (65 hectares) of free land in the West to settlers. A great rush for land followed. One of the first homesteads was claimed by Daniel Freeman in 1863 near the present city of Beatrice. The 1862 Homestead Act and similar acts brought many thousands of homesteaders to Nebraska.

In 1865, the Union Pacific Railroad began building its line west from Omaha. The Union Pacific and the Burlington railroads also started campaigns to bring more settlers to Nebraska. The railroads sent pamphlets to people throughout the East, and even to Europe, describing Nebraska as a "Garden of Eden." These advertisements helped the population increase to 122,993 by 1870.

Early in 1867, Congress passed an act admitting Nebraska into the Union. In doing so, Congress overrode President Andrew Johnson's veto. Congress had required Nebraska to make certain changes in its Constitution. Johnson believed this action violated the U.S. Constitution. Johnson, a Democrat, also did not want Nebraska admitted into the Union because the territory had a Republican majority. The Republicans in Congress were trying to impeach Johnson, and the president believed that two additional Republican senators might have been enough to convict him. Nebraska became the 37th state on March 1, 1867. The people elected David Butler, a Republican, as the first governor.

In 1872, Nebraska became the first state to celebrate Arbor Day. Arbor Day is a special day set aside each year for planting trees. J. Sterling Morton, a newspaper publisher and political leader from Nebraska City, originated the idea of Arbor Day.

Pioneer settlers, such as these shown on a farm near Ansley, were often called "sodbusters." They cut sod into blocks and used the blocks to build their houses because so few trees grew on the plains.

Historic Nebraska

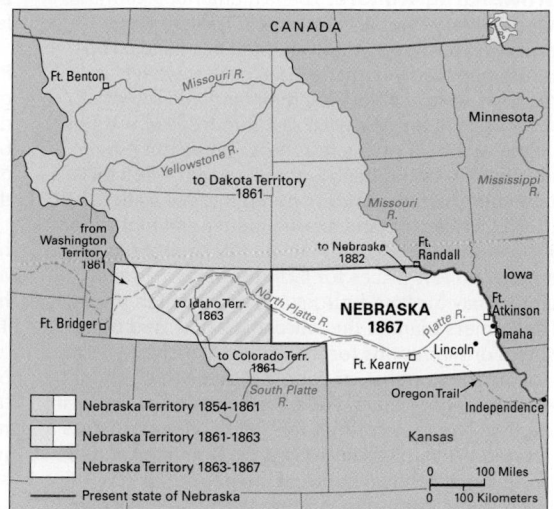

WORLD BOOK map

The Union Pacific Railroad began building west from Omaha in 1865 to complete its part of the first U.S. transcontinental line.

Nebraska became a part of the United States with the Louisiana Purchase of 1803. Earlier, France or Spain had claimed this area. Nebraska became a U.S. territory in 1854 and a U.S. state in 1867.

Buffalo Bill, whose real name was William Frederick Cody, was a noteworthy figure of the American West. He organized his famous Wild West Show in 1883 at his ranch near North Platte.

WORLD BOOK illustrations by Richard Bonson, The Art Agency

Important dates in Nebraska

1682 René-Robert Cavelier, Sieur de La Salle, claimed the region drained by the Mississippi River, including present-day Nebraska, for France.

1714 Étienne Veniard de Bourgmont traveled up the Missouri River to the mouth of the Platte River.

1720 The Pawnee Indians defeated Spanish forces under Pedro de Villasur along the Platte River.

1739 Pierre and Paul Mallet were probably the first Europeans to cross Nebraska.

1762 France gave the Louisiana Territory to Spain.

1800 Spain returned Louisiana to France.

1803 The United States bought the Louisiana Territory, including Nebraska, from France.

1804 Meriwether Lewis and William Clark traveled up the Missouri River and explored eastern Nebraska.

1806 Zebulon M. Pike explored south-central Nebraska.

1813 Robert Stuart and his party followed the North Platte and Platte rivers across Nebraska.

1819 The U.S. Army established Fort Atkinson.

1843 The "Great Migration" began through Nebraska along the Oregon Trail to the West.

1854 Congress passed the Kansas-Nebraska Act, creating the Nebraska Territory.

1863 One of the first free homesteads was claimed by Daniel Freeman near Beatrice.

1865 The Union Pacific Railroad began building its line west from Omaha.

1867 Nebraska became the 37th state on March 1.

1874-1877 Vast swarms of grasshoppers invaded the Nebraska farmlands and severely damaged crops.

1905 The North Platte River Project was begun to irrigate 165,000 acres (66,770 hectares) in western Nebraska.

1937 The unicameral legislature held its first session.

1939 Petroleum was discovered in southeastern Nebraska.

1944 Congress authorized the Missouri River Basin Project (now the Pick-Sloan Missouri Basin Program).

1960-1964 Nebraskans approved constitutional amendments that raised salaries and lengthened terms of government officials.

1982 Nebraska adopted Initiative 300, which prohibits corporations from owning farms or ranches in the state.

1997 The Legislature passed a measure giving aid to public schools based on an average cost per pupil, forcing many small school districts to reorganize.

2005 Governor Mike Johanns resigned from office after being appointed U.S. secretary of agriculture.

2006 A federal appeals court ruled that Nebraska's Initiative 300, which prohibited corporations from buying farms or ranches in the state, was unconstitutional.

Growth of agriculture. The settlement of Nebraska slowed down between 1874 and 1877, when vast swarms of grasshoppers invaded the farmlands. The grasshoppers badly damaged oat, barley, wheat, and corn crops. Many settlers left their land and returned East. Farmers in the Midwest saw hundreds of wagons traveling east bearing such signs as "Eaten out by grasshoppers. Going back East to live with wife's folks." But another rush of farmers poured into the state during the 1880's. Prices for land soared higher and higher. In 1890, land prices collapsed because of drought, overuse of credit, and low prices for farm products. Farmers could not pay for land bought on credit at high prices.

The farmers blamed the railroads, banks, and other business organizations for their difficulties. Many farmers joined the Populist, or People's Party, which sought reforms to help farmers. The party achieved its greatest strength in Nebraska during the 1890's. Many Populists supported William Jennings Bryan, a Democrat and the state's leading political figure of the period.

In the 1890's, Nebraska farmers started to use irrigation and dry-farming methods. Congress passed the Reclamation Act in 1902, authorizing federal aid for irrigation development. Three years later, construction started on the North Platte Project to irrigate 165,000 acres (66,770 hectares) in western Nebraska. The Kinkaid Act passed in 1904 and provided for 640-acre (259-hectare) homesteads in western Nebraska. But many settlers found much of the land unsuitable for farming. Cattle ranchers bought out most of the homesteaders and returned the land to grass.

Economic depression. A boom in farm prices ended during the early 1920's. During the Great Depression of the 1930's, farm prices fell still further. In addition, drought again hit the state. Many farmers faced bankruptcy and the loss of their land. Banks and insurance companies took over farmers' property because the farmers could not meet their mortgage payments. But so many families were affected that sheriffs often refused to carry out court orders for public sale of the land. As part of the New Deal, President Franklin D. Roosevelt's program to pull the nation out of the Great Depression, the federal government provided long-term, low-interest loans and other aid to farmers.

In 1915, a committee of the Nebraska legislature had recommended a unicameral legislature. The committee believed that a one-house legislature would increase the members' accountability and eliminate the delays that occur in two-house legislatures. The unicameral legislature would be more economical because there would be fewer members. The committee's recommendation formed the basis of discussions that lasted almost 20 years. In 1934, U.S. Senator George W. Norris of Nebraska sponsored an amendment to the state Constitution for the adoption of a unicameral legislature. The voters approved the amendment in November 1934. The new unicameral legislature held its first meeting in 1937.

The mid-1900's. Geologists discovered oil in southeastern Nebraska in 1939. Oil companies drilled many wells in the area during the early 1940's, and oil became the state's most important mineral.

During World War II (1939-1945), Nebraska farmers produced millions of tons of corn, oats, potatoes, and wheat to help meet wartime food shortages. The raising

of beef cattle also expanded greatly. By 1947, Nebraska's farm income reached more than $1 billion yearly.

In 1944, Congress approved the Missouri River Basin Project (now called the Pick-Sloan Missouri Basin Program). This huge project calls for construction of flood control dams, hydroelectric plants, and reservoirs in Nebraska and other states drained by the Missouri River. Nebraska has already benefited from the project, though it is far from completion.

In 1948, Offutt Air Force Base near Omaha became headquarters for the U.S. Strategic Air Command. When that command was eliminated in 1992, the base became home to the U.S. Strategic Command (USSTRATCOM). The base has been important to the economy of Omaha.

In 1949, geologists discovered oil fields in western Nebraska. During the 1950's, Nebraska farms became larger in size but fewer in number. The increased use of machinery lessened the need for farmworkers, and many of these workers moved to towns and cities in search of jobs. By 1970, over 60 percent of Nebraska's people lived in urban areas.

The shift in population made Nebraska aware of the need to expand its industries and to attract new ones. In 1960, the voters approved an amendment to the state Constitution allowing cities and counties to acquire and develop property for lease to private businesses. Many new firms moved to Nebraska in the 1960's, partly as a result of the state's campaigns to attract industry. Employment in manufacturing rose 44 percent in the 1960's.

During the 1960's, the Legislature passed much important legislation. It strengthened state government by raising salaries and lengthening terms of government officials. In 1963, it passed the Nebraska Education Television Act, and Nebraska became one of the first states

U.S. Strategic Command

The control center of the United States Strategic Command is near Omaha. The center would coordinate defense and warning systems and direct U.S. offensive nuclear forces in a nuclear war.

to cover its entire area with educational television (ETV) broadcasts. In 1967, it adopted sales and income taxes to make up for the revenue that was lost when the people voted out the state property tax in 1966.

The late 1900's. In 1982, Nebraskans adopted Initiative 300. The initiative was an amendment to the state Constitution that banned corporations from owning farm or ranch land in the state. Initiative 300 was designed to preserve family farms. But it was criticized for keeping land prices down and slowing the development of corporation-owned feedlots. In 2006, a federal appeals court ruled the initiative unconstitutional.

In 1986, State Treasurer Kay Orr, a Republican, defeated former Lincoln Mayor Helen Boosalis, a Democrat, in the election for governor. It was the first governor's election in U.S. history in which both major candidates were women. Orr became the first woman governor of Nebraska and the first Republican woman governor of a U.S. state.

In 1990, Nebraska's government passed a large tax increase to help finance public education. In a referendum, the voters approved the tax increase. At the same time, they rejected a proposal to limit government spending increases to 2 percent a year.

In 1996, the Legislature limited local property-tax-rate increases. As a result, schools faced a reduction in their chief source of income. In 1997, to offset that loss, the Legislature passed a measure providing increased state aid to public schools. The law based financial aid on a statewide average of spending per pupil. Although the formula benefited most schools, many small rural schools with higher than average per-pupil costs received little or no funding. Lawmakers expected the law to force the smallest school districts to reorganize.

The early 2000's. In 2005, Governor Mike Johanns resigned from office to become U.S. secretary of agriculture under President George W. Bush. Johanns had served as Nebraska's governor since 1999. In 2008, Johanns won election to the U.S. Senate. Also in 2008, Nebraska split its electoral votes in a presidential election for the first time. Nebraska and Maine are the only states in which all the electoral votes do not automatically go to the state's overall winner. Illinois U.S. Senator Barack Obama claimed an electoral vote in Nebraska's second congressional district—the Omaha area—and Arizona U.S. Senator John McCain secured the state's four remaining electoral votes. Obama won the general election.   Donald R. Hickey and David Wishart

Related articles in *World Book* include:

Biographies

Bryan, Charles W.	Flanagan, Edward	Norris, George W.
Bryan, William J.	Joseph	Pound, Roscoe
Cather, Willa	Ford, Gerald R.	Red Cloud
Cudahy, Michael	Morton, Julius S.	

Cities

Lincoln	Omaha

History

Homestead Act (Effects of the law)	Populism
Kansas-Nebraska Act	Railroad (The first transcontinental rail lines)
Louisiana Purchase	Western frontier life in America
Omaha Indians	
Oregon Trail	

Other related articles

Agate Fossil Beds National Monument	Great Plains
	Missouri River
Arbor Day	Offutt Air Force Base
Girls and Boys Town	Platte River

Outline

Questions

What is unusual about Nebraska's state Legislature?
Why did many early settlers in Nebraska build houses of sod?
Why are the Sand Hills important to Nebraska?
How did the railroads help attract settlers to Nebraska?
What famous pioneer trails crossed Nebraska?

Additional resources

Level I
Bjorklund, Ruth, and Richards, Marlee. *Nebraska.* 2nd ed. Marshall Cavendish Benchmark, 2010.
Heinrichs, Ann. *Nebraska.* Children's Pr., 2008.
Weatherly, Myra S. *Nebraska.* Children's Pr., 2009.

Level II
Hickey, Donald R., and others. *Nebraska Moments.* 2nd ed. Univ. of Neb. Pr., 2007.
Johnsgard, Paul A. *The Nature of Nebraska: Ecology and Biodiversity.* 2001. Reprint. Univ. of Neb. Pr., 2005.
Luebke, Frederick C. *Nebraska.* 2nd ed. Univ. of Neb. Pr., 2005.
Maher, Harmon D., Jr., and others. *Roadside Geology of Nebraska.* Mountain Pr. Pub. Co., 2003.
Olson, James C., and Naugle, R. C. *History of Nebraska.* 3rd ed. Univ. of Neb. Pr., 1997.
Wishart, David J. *An Unspeakable Sadness: The Dispossession of the Nebraska Indians.* Univ. of Neb. Pr., 1994.

Nebraska, University of, is a public university. Its main campus is the University of Nebraska-Lincoln (UNL). Other campuses include the University of Nebraska at Kearney (UNK), the University of Nebraska at Omaha (UNO), and the Omaha-based University of Nebraska Medical Center (UNMC). The Nebraska College of Technical Agriculture in Curtis is also part of the university.

UNL has colleges of agricultural sciences and natural resources, architecture, arts and sciences, business administration, education and human sciences, engineering, fine and performing arts, journalism and mass communications, and law. UNK has colleges of business and technology, fine arts and humanities, natural and social sciences, and education. UNO has colleges of arts and sciences; business administration; communication, fine arts, and media; education; information science and technology; and public affairs and community service. UNMC has a school of allied health professions as well as colleges of dentistry, medicine, nursing, pharmacy, and public health. It also has a hospital, a rehabilitation institute, and a laboratory cancer research center.

The University of Nebraska was chartered as a *land-grant college* in 1869. Land-grant colleges and universities receive federal aid to support education. The college held its first classes in 1871, in Lincoln. The current university system was established in 1968 by merging the University of Nebraska and the municipal University of Omaha and by creating a separate medical center. Kearney State College became the University of Nebraska at Kearney in 1991. The University of Nebraska is known as a strong research institution. It maintains agricultural research centers across the state. The university offers bachelor's, master's and doctor's degrees.

The university's athletic teams are called the Cornhuskers or Huskers. The school's website at http://www.nebraska.edu offers additional information.

Critically reviewed by the University of Nebraska

Nebuchadnezzar II, *nehb uh kuhd NEHZ uhr* (630?-562 B.C.), reigned as king of Babylon and ruler of the New Babylonian Empire from 605 to 562 B.C. The New Babylonian Empire included much of the Middle East. Babylon, a city near present-day Al Hillah, Iraq, was the empire's capital. Nebuchadnezzar was one of the most famous kings of the ancient world. He is best remembered for conquering the city of Jerusalem and for his great building projects. His name is also spelled *Nebuchadrezzar* and *Nabu-kudurri-usur.*

In 597 B.C., Nebuchadnezzar captured Jerusalem, the capital of a Jewish kingdom called Judah (now part of Israel). He deposed the king of Judah and appointed another king. He also took payment and hostages. About 10 years later, Judah rebelled against Babylonian control. In 587 or 586 B.C., Nebuchadnezzar took the city of Jerusalem again. His army destroyed the city's Temple and palace, and sent many Jews to Babylonia as prisoners. This period of Jewish history is called the *Babylonian Exile.*

Nebuchadnezzar launched many important building and renovation programs in Babylon. He built or improved a major palace, several temples, a monumental gate known as the Ishtar Gate, a paved avenue called the Processional Street, and a pyramid-shaped tower called a *ziggurat.*   Norman Yoffee

See also **Babylon; Seven Wonders of the Ancient World** (with picture).

Nebula, *NEHB yuh luh,* is a cloud of dust particles and gases in space. The term *nebula* comes from the Latin word for *cloud.* Early astronomers also used the term for distant galaxies outside Earth's galaxy, the Milky Way. Such galaxies, called *extragalactic nebulae,* looked like hazy patches of light among the stars. But modern telescopes showed that extragalactic nebulae are actually systems of stars similar to the Milky Way.

Today, most astronomers use the term *nebulae* only for the clouds of dust and gases in the Milky Way and other galaxies. They classify these masses into two general types: *diffuse nebulae* and *planetary nebulae.* Both types are also called *gaseous nebulae.*

Diffuse nebulae are the larger of the two types. Some diffuse nebulae contain enough dust and gases to form as many as 100,000 stars the size of the sun.

A diffuse nebula may occur near an extremely hot, bright star. The intense ultraviolet light from the star en-

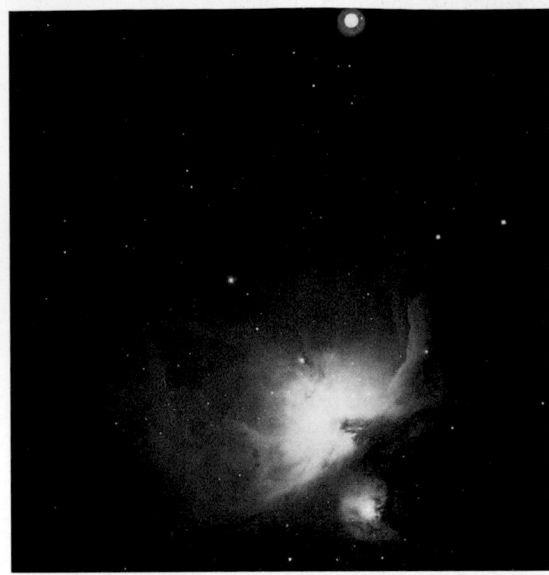

National Optical Astronomy Observatories

The Great Nebula in the constellation Orion is a huge cloud of dust and gas that appears as a misty spot in Orion's sword. The nebula's bright central area is shown in this photograph.

ergizes the gas atoms of the nebula and enables the mass to emit light. A diffuse nebula of this kind is called an *emission nebula.*

Astronomers believe some emission nebulae are places where new stars are forming. Gravity causes a portion of a nebula's dust and gases to contract into a much smaller, denser mass. Pressure and temperature build up within the mass of dust and gases as contraction continues for millions of years. In time, the mass becomes hot enough to shine—and forms a new star.

A diffuse nebula also may occur near a cool star. In this case, the ultraviolet light from the star is too weak to make the nebula's gas atoms give off light. But the dust particles in the diffuse nebula reflect the starlight. Astronomers refer to this kind of diffuse nebula as a *reflection nebula.* If a diffuse nebula occurs in an area that has no nearby stars, it neither emits nor reflects enough light to be visible. In fact, its dust particles blot out the light from the stars behind them. Astronomers call such a diffuse nebula a *dark nebula.*

Planetary nebulae are ball-like clouds of dust and gases that surround certain stars. They form when a star begins to collapse and throw off the outer layers of its atmosphere. When viewed through a small telescope, this type of nebula appears to have a flat, rounded surface like that of a planet.   C. R. O'Dell

See also **Astronomy** (Discovering other galaxies); **Galaxy; Milky Way.**

Nebular hypothesis, *NEHB yuh luhr hy PAHTH uh sihs,* is a theory about the origin of the solar system. Pierre Simon Laplace, a French astronomer and mathematician, formulated the theory in the late 1700's. According to Laplace, the solar system developed from a huge, extremely hot, rotating *nebula,* a cloud of dust particles and gases. The nebula cooled and contracted, leaving behind successive rings of matter as it became smaller. These rings, in turn, cooled and condensed, forming the planets. The remaining central core of the nebula became the sun.

Many of Laplace's ideas have been greatly modified by new discoveries. But most astronomers believe the solar system did develop from a nebula.   C. R. O'Dell

See also **Earth** (Formation of Earth); **Laplace, Marquis de; Nebula.**

Neck. See **Skeleton; Giraffe** (diagram); **Throat.**

Necktie is a band of material or a bow that is worn around the neck. The tie is the most visible item of men's clothing, and it reflects the wearer's personal tastes. The *four-in-hand* and *bow* ties worn today have been about the same style since they were first worn in the 1870's.

Neckties originated in the neckcloths that men folded and wrapped around their necks, with ribbon tied over them to hold the ends in place. In the 1700's, men wore a whalebone *stock.* They fastened it in back with a strap or buckle, and tied it in front with a bow or knot. The *cravats* of the 1600's and 1700's were often frilly and lace-trimmed. By the mid-1800's, narrow string ties, knotted bow ties, and ascots had replaced the more elaborate cravat. By about 1870, most men began to prefer wearing the wider four-in-hand necktie during the day. They wore white bow ties in the evening. Black bow ties appeared in the early 1900's. Today, necktie widths vary slightly in accordance with the styling of suit lapels.

Richard Martin

Necrology, *neh KRAHL uh jee,* is a record of deaths, especially one kept by a church. Usually it shows the day, month, and year of the death. A necrology may be a list of persons who have died within a certain time. It also may be an obituary notice.

Necropolis, *neh KRAHP uh lihs,* is a Greek word which means *city of the dead*—that is, a cemetery. Archaeologists and historians usually call the cemetery of an ancient city a *necropolis.*

Archaeologists have found large and well-known necropolises in Egypt, near such ancient cities as Memphis and Thebes. The tomb of Tutankhamun in the Valley of the Kings, near Luxor, is one of hundreds of tombs in the huge necropolis there (see **Tutankhamun; Valley of the Kings**). A necropolis also surrounds the pyramids at Giza. Another necropolis, dating from the Bronze Age, is at Hallstatt, Austria. Many necropolises have also been found in America. One at Paracas, an archaeological site in Peru, dates back to the days before the Inca ruled.

Ancient peoples often buried tools, weapons, and personal belongings with the dead. Sometimes they also carved or painted religious texts, information about the dead, and scenes from everyday life. Archaeologists and historians have learned much about ancient civilizations from necropolises.   Leonard H. Lesko

Nectar is a sugary liquid that is produced by flowering plants. Nectar is secreted from tissues called *nectaries* that are frequently in the flowers or other parts of flowering plants. Honey bees collect nectar to produce honey. While gathering nectar, bees usually spread pollen from one plant to another. Hummingbirds and many kinds of moths and butterflies also feed on nectar.

Richard C. Keating

See also **Bee** (Making honey).

Nectarine, *NEHK tuh REEN* or *NEHK tuh reen,* is a fruit much like the peach. The only important difference be-

WORLD BOOK illustration by Kate Lloyd-Jones, Linden Artists Ltd.

The nectarine is a fruit that resembles a peach, except that it has a smooth skin. The fruit encloses a single, large seed.

tween the two is that nectarines have smooth skins and peaches are fuzzy. They come from identical trees. Nectarines often originate from peach seeds, and peaches may come from nectarine seeds. Botanists do not know which originated first, nectarines or peaches.

James E. Pollard

Scientific classification. The nectarine is in the rose family, Rosaceae. It is *Prunus persica.*

See also **Peach.**

Needle is a simple-looking tool, with a fine point at one end and a tiny eye at the other. But needles are not easy to make. Each needle undergoes at least 20 production processes.

Sewing needles are made from coils of steel wire. These coils of wire are cut into pieces long enough for two needles by a wire straightening and cutting machine. The straightened wires are then ground to a point on each end on a grindstone. While the wires are being ground, they are held by a device which makes them turn all the time they are touching the grindstone. This turning makes the needle points fine and even.

After each end of the wire is ground to a point, the center section of the wire pieces is stamped by a machine. The machine stamps a flat place for the eyes. Next, the two eyes are punched in the middle of each piece of wire by another machine. A piece of wire is then run through the eyes. At this time, the needles are cut apart, leaving the needles hanging on the wire. Next, the heads, or eye ends, are rounded and smoothed. Finally, the needles are *tempered* (toughened), and polished, sorted, and packed.

Special needles are made for special uses. Sewing-machine needles are made with the eye near the point. In addition, they have a groove on one side, which acts as a guide for the thread that goes through the needle's eye.

A sewing needle for people with poor vision has the eye split so that the needle can be threaded through the top. A *crochet hook* is a type of needle with a hook at the end. The thread is caught in the hook instead of going through an eye. Upholstery sewing needles and

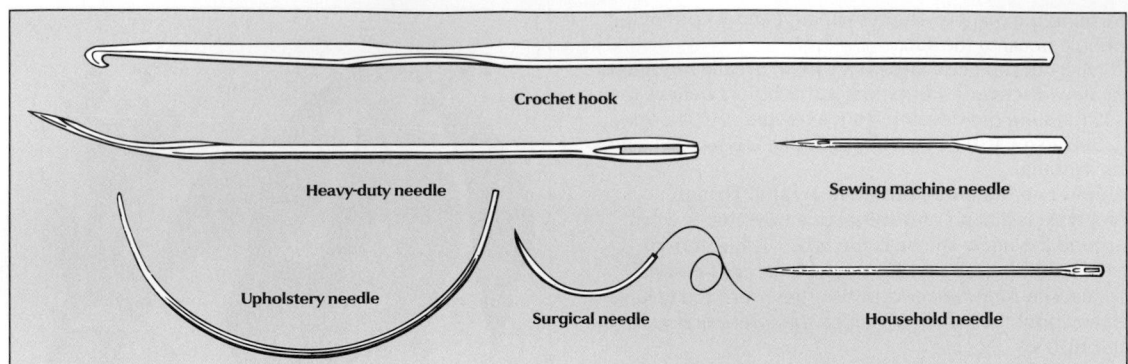

Different kinds of needles are made for special purposes. For example, a crochet hook has a hook to catch the thread. A heavy-duty needle is used to sew thick canvas or cloth for sails. Surgical needles are manufactured with thread attached to them for easy use in an operating room.

surgical needles are curved.   David A. Bagshaw

See also **Sewing**.

Needlepoint is a form of embroidery in which stitches are sewed through spaces or squares of an open-mesh fabric called the *canvas*. It is used to make clothing, pictures, purses, upholstery, and many other items. Needlepoint was once known as *tapestry*.

The pattern may be painted or printed on the canvas. The sewer uses a blunt-ended tapestry needle and soft threads. The threads may be cotton embroidery, crewel, knitting or Persian yarns, and sometimes leather strips or ribbon. Needlepoint stitches create a flat design.

The basic needlepoint stitch is the *cross stitch*. It oc-

cupies a square area over an intersection of the canvas mesh. Other stitches create various patterns and designs. These stitches include the slanting *basketweave* and *knotted* styles, and the *bargello*, a long vertical stitch. Needlepoint may be worked in fine thread and small stitches called *petit point,* or in large stitches known as *gros point*.   Dona Z. Meilach

See also **Embroidery; Lace; Petit point**.

Additional resources

Christensen, Jo I. *The Needlepoint Book.* Rev. ed. Fireside Paperbacks, 1999.
Pendray, Shay. *Piecework Magazine Presents the Needleworker's Companion.* Interweave, 2002.

Needletrades, Industrial and Textile Employees, Union of. See UNITE HERE.

Needlework. See Crochet; Embroidery; Knitting; Lace; Needlepoint; Petit point; Quilt; Sampler; Sewing.

Neem tree is an Asian tree that has many important uses for people. Manufacturers use parts of the neem tree to make *pesticides* (chemicals used to kill pests). In addition, people have treated diseases with the tree's leaves, seeds, bark, and roots for centuries.

The neem tree is native to south Asia, but it also grows in other parts of Asia and in Africa, the Caribbean, and Central America. The tree may grow up

There are dozens of needlepoint stitches, ranging from simple techniques to complicated ones. This photograph shows four popular stitches.

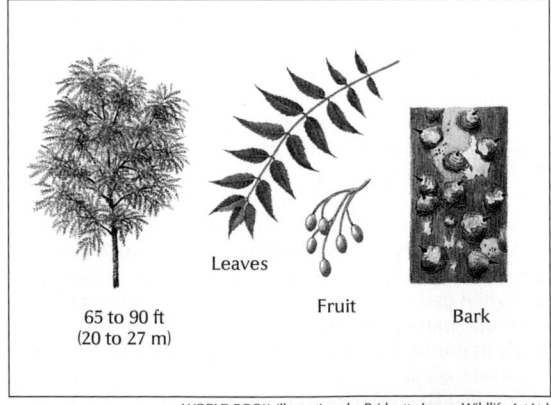

The neem tree produces olivelike fruits. Manufacturers use chemical compounds from the tree's seeds to make pesticides.

to 90 feet (27 meters) tall. It produces white, honey-scented flowers and olivelike fruits.

Seeds from the neem tree contain a compound called *azadirachtin.* People use azadirachtin along with other neem compounds to make pesticides. Such pesticides are environmentally safe and can help control hundreds of pests, including aphids, locusts, and mites. Manufacturers also use neem tree parts in such products as soap, toothpaste, and acne ointment.

People from south Asia have traditionally made a number of natural remedies from the neem tree. For example, they have produced antiseptic paste from the leaves to treat skin diseases and sores.   Michael J. Tanabe

Scientific classification. The scientific name of the neem tree is *Azadirachta indica.*

Nefertiti, *NEHF uhr TEE tee,* an ancient Egyptian queen, was the wife of Akhenaten, a *pharaoh* (king) who ruled from 1353 to 1336 B.C. Akhenaten was the first pharaoh to preach a form of *monotheism* (belief in one god). Nefertiti was a firm supporter of her husband's teachings and assisted him in the new religious ceremonies. He founded a new capital, Akhetaten (present-day Amarna). The reign of Akhenaten and Nefertiti is known as the Amarna Revolution because of the many changes they made in art, religion, and social practices.

Nefertiti and Akhenaten had six daughters. One of them, Ankhesenamun, married King Tutankhamun.   Salima Ikram

Painted limestone sculpture (about 1355 B.C.) by an unknown Egyptian artist; Egyptian Section, Staatliche Museen, Berlin

Nefertiti

See also **Egypt, Ancient** (The New Kingdom).

Negative number. See Algebra (Positive and negative numbers).

Negev, *NEH gehv,* is the triangular southern half of Israel. It extends from Beersheba south to the port of Elat on the Gulf of Aqaba (see **Israel** [terrain map]). The Negev is a semidesert tableland from 1,000 to 2,000 feet (300 to 610 meters) above sea level. It includes both flatlands and limestone mountains. Much of the Negev is covered by a layer of fertile loam, but rainfall needed for growing crops is insufficient. The Israelis have farmed part of the Negev by irrigation. They have irrigated the land with water brought from the Sea of Galilee through the National Water Carrier, a system of pipelines, canals, and tunnels. The Israelis have also mined phosphates and copper in the Negev.   Bernard Reich

Negligence is the legal term for carelessness. The law uses negligence as a test to determine whether a person involved in an accident is responsible for any loss or injury that occurs. The law considers negligence the failure to act the way a reasonably careful person would act under the same or similar circumstances. But the law does not say what specific conduct is negligent. The decision is made by a judge or a jury after consideration of the circumstances of each case. In general, a person whose negligence harms or kills another person or

damages that person's property must pay compensation. Such compensation is known as *damages.*

If the injured person was partly responsible for the occurrence, that person's carelessness is considered *contributory negligence.* In some cases, the contributory negligence prevents the injured person from being awarded compensation. In other cases, the judge or jury may compare the injured person's contributory negligence to the fault of the others involved. The injured person's compensation may then be reduced in proportion to his or her share of the blame.

English and American law do not regard negligence as a crime. But in cases where carelessness displays an extreme or willful disregard of the safety of others and results in a death, the negligent person may be charged with a crime called *manslaughter* or *negligent homicide.*
Steven R. Probst

See also **Damages; Malpractice suit; Product liability suit; Tort.**

Negotiable instrument, *nih GOH shuh buhl,* refers to a type of legal exchange or document that is either a promise or an order to pay money. Negotiable instruments can be used as evidence of indebtedness or as a substitute for money. A person holding a negotiable instrument is usually in a good legal position to collect from the person who signed it. The signer is called a *maker* or *drawer.* The use of negotiable instruments is regulated by the Uniform Commercial Code, which has been adopted in whole or in part by all 50 states in the United States. The rules for these instruments are similar in Australia, Canada, and the United Kingdom.

A negotiable instrument has six characteristics: (1) it must be in writing; (2) it must be signed by a maker or drawer, who promises to pay money; (3) it must contain an unconditional promise or order to pay; (4) payment must be a fixed amount of money; (5) it must be payable on demand or at a specific date; (6) it must be payable to the bearer or to the order of a person.

Forms. Common forms of negotiable instruments include *promissory notes* (signed promises to pay a debt in the future), *drafts* (orders to pay money from a specific bank), and *checks* (a type of draft).

Many instruments are not strictly negotiable but have some features of negotiable instruments. For example, instruments calling for the delivery of goods or property instead of money may possess many of the legal qualities of negotiability. A *bill of lading* (receipt given by a carrier, such as a railroad, showing a list of goods delivered to it for transportation) is an example.

Endorsement. Negotiable instruments are usually transferred or handed over to another person by *endorsement.* An endorsement is a signature or other writing on the back of the instrument that indicates or proves the instrument has been transferred.

An endorsement may be written in different ways. If the holder of the instrument simply signs it, the endorsement is called *in blank.* Anyone holding that instrument may receive payment. A *special endorsement* or an *endorsement in full* names the person to whom payment is to be made. A *restrictive endorsement* forbids further transfer. A check signed "Pay to First National Bank only" is a restrictive endorsement.

Every endorser of a negotiable instrument is usually liable for its face value, if the maker does not or cannot pay it. The endorser may add the words "without recourse" if he or she wishes to avoid liability. Such an endorsement does not affect the value of the instrument or prevent further endorsement.   Steven R. Probst

Related articles in *World Book* include:
Bond
Check
Commercial paper
Draft
Money order
Note

Negritos, *nih GREE tohz,* is a term used to refer to several ethnic groups that live in small, isolated populations in Southeast Asia. They are an *aboriginal people*—that is, their ancestors were the first people to live in the area. They spread from the Andaman Islands of the Indian Ocean to the Malay Peninsula, Indonesia, and the Philippines. Spanish explorers called them *negritos,* referring to their dark skin and short stature. Negritos traditionally lived by hunting and by gathering plants and fruits. Today, many have adopted the way of life of other agricultural peoples in their homeland.   Russell Zanca

Negro. See African Americans.

Negro History Week. See Black History Month.

Negroes. See African Americans.

Negroid race. See Races, Human (The three-race theory).

Nehemiah, *NEE uh MY uh,* **Book of,** is a book of the Hebrew Bible (also called the Old Testament). It is named for an important figure from the ancient country of Judea in southern Palestine. Appointed governor of Judea by the ruling Persians, Nehemiah served in that office from 445 to 433 B.C. and for several years after 432 B.C. Nehemiah's vigorous programs of political and religious reforms, recorded in the Book of Nehemiah, renewed and restored the faltering Jewish community in Palestine during the 400's B.C. See also **Ezra, Book of; Bible** (The Writings).   Carol L. Meyers

Nehru, *NAY roo* or *NEH roo,* is the family name of a father and his son, daughter, and granddaughter who became distinguished in Indian public affairs. The father and the son prefixed their names with their caste name, *pandit. Pandit* also means *scholar.* The daughter, the first woman president of the United Nations General Assembly, used Pandit as her last name (see **Pandit, Vijaya L.**). The granddaughter, Indira Gandhi, became the first woman prime minister of India (see **Gandhi, Indira**). Her son Rajiv Gandhi also served as prime minister (see **Gandhi, Rajiv**).

Motilal Nehru, *MOH tih lahl* (1861-1931), came from a distinguished family in the province of Kashmir. He was born in Agra on May 6, 1861. Nehru studied law at Muir College in Allahabad and built up a prosperous legal practice. He was at first a close friend of the English in India, a member of wealthy social groups, and a follower of Western ways. But in the 1920's, he was converted to the cause of Indian independence and became a follower of Mohandas Gandhi (see **Gandhi, Mohandas K.**). Nehru gave up his law practice and began to live in a simple manner.

Nehru wrote the *Nehru Report* in 1928. The report outlined a new constitution for India. In 1930, Nehru became active in Gandhi's civil disobedience movement. Nehru's energetic efforts on behalf of freedom and several terms in prison weakened his strength. Motilal

T. S. Satyan, Black Star
Jawaharlal Nehru was the first prime minister of India. He served from 1947 until his death in 1964.

Nehru died the next year, on Feb. 6, 1931.

Jawaharlal Nehru, *juh WAH hur lahl* (1889-1964), the son of Motilal Nehru, was India's first prime minister. He served as prime minister from 1947 until his death on May 27, 1964. He dominated Indian affairs. He worked to establish a democracy and to improve living standards. He favored a state-controlled economy.

Nehru gained international recognition for opposing alliances with the great powers and for promoting *neutralism* (nonalignment). He advocated nonaggression and ending atomic bomb tests. But he was criticized when Indian forces seized Goa and other Portuguese territories in India in 1961. Nehru acted as a spokesman for nonaligned nations in Asia and Africa. He favored admitting Communist China to the United Nations until Chinese forces attacked the Indian border in 1962.

Nehru and his father were fond and proud of each other, but occasionally disagreed. At one time, the father favored only dominion status for India, while the son demanded complete independence.

Nehru was born in Allahabad on Nov. 14, 1889. He went to school in England and graduated from Harrow School and Cambridge University. He returned to India after his schooling and became active in politics. He supported Mohandas Gandhi's civil disobedience movement in 1920. Nehru served as general secretary of the All India Congress Committee in 1929. That same year, he was elected president of the Indian National Congress. He held that post again in 1936, 1937, and 1946. The British often imprisoned him for his nationalistic activities during this period. Nehru was a master of English, and his writings are widely read. He died on May 27, 1964.   Robert LaPorte , Jr.

See also **India** (History); **Indian National Congress**.

Neihardt, *NY hahrt,* **John** (1881-1973), was an American author who was known for his poetry and fiction about American Indians. Neihardt's major work is a five-part epic poem called *The Cycle of the West.* The poem describes how white settlers conquered the Indians of the Great Plains in the 1800's. The epic consists of *The Song of Hugh Glass* (1915), *The Song of Three Friends* (1919), *The Song of the Indian Wars* (1925), *The Song of the Messiah* (1935), and *The Song of Jed Smith* (1941). Neihardt's *Black Elk Speaks* (1932), a biography of a Sioux medicine man, became his most widely read book.

John Gneisenau Neihardt was born on Jan. 8, 1881, near Sharpsburg, Illinois. He lived with the Omaha Indians in Nebraska from 1901 to 1907. Many of the themes in his works reflect his experiences among the Omaha and other tribes of the Great Plains. In 1921, Neihardt was named poet laureate of Nebraska. From 1926 to 1938, he was literary editor of the *St. Louis Post-Dispatch.* Neihardt served as poet-in-residence at the University of Missouri from 1949 to 1966. He died on Nov. 3, 1973.

Elmer W. Borklund

Nelson, Horatio (1758-1805), was the greatest British admiral and naval hero. In 1805, he defeated the combined French and Spanish fleets at Trafalgar in the greatest naval victory in British history. His victory broke France's naval power and established the United Kingdom's rule of the seas for the rest of the 1800's.

Early life. Nelson was born at Burnham-Thorpe in the English county of Norfolk on Sept. 29, 1758. His father was rector of the local church, and his mother was a member of the famous Walpole family. Nelson was a small, frail child. But he fell in love with the sea early in life and made up his mind to be a sailor. He spent much time piloting small boats on the river near his home. When Nelson was 12 years old, his uncle, Captain Maurice Suckling, planned a voyage to the Falkland Islands.

Nelson begged his family for permission to go along, and he was finally allowed to do so. Nelson owed much of his early training to Captain Suckling, who had him transferred from time to time to ships engaged in different types of service. Suckling also encouraged him to study navigation and to practice boat sailing.

Joins the navy. At the age of 15, Nelson went aboard the *Carcass* as a *coxswain* (steerer). He served there in an expedition to the Arctic seas. On his return, Nelson was sent to the East Indies on the *Seahorse.* On that voyage, he caught a fever that seriously damaged his health. But he became a lieutenant in the Royal Navy at 18.

In 1779, when not yet 21, Nelson was given command of the frigate *Hinchinbrook.* He was known as a capable officer. Nelson's professional ability and his talent for getting along with his men helped him to rise rapidly in the service. A cruise to Central America brought on a second tropical illness and Nelson was sent home in feeble health.

Nelson was given duty on the North Sea as soon as he recovered from the fever. He was then assigned to service in Canadian waters and developed a great fondness for Canada, where the climate strengthened his health. Nelson was given command of the frigate *Boreas,* stationed in the West Indies in 1784. He spent three years there.

Nelson married the widow of Josiah Nisbet, an English doctor, in the West Indies in 1787. Prince William, who later became King William IV of the United Kingdom, gave the bride away at the wedding. Nelson was recalled from active service soon afterward. He remained on the retired list until soon after the outbreak of war with France in 1793.

Wounded at Calvi. In 1793, Nelson was placed in command of the *Agamemnon* and sailed to join the British fleet in the Mediterranean Sea. This voyage began

Detail of *Nelson Falling* (1825), an oil painting on canvas by Denis Deighton;
National Maritime Museum, Greenwich, England

Horatio Nelson led the British to victory over the French and Spanish fleets at Trafalgar in 1805. Nelson, Britain's greatest naval hero, was fatally wounded in this battle, *above right.*

seven years of almost continual warfare at sea. Nelson was one of the British commanders who blockaded Toulon, France, and captured Corsica. He was wounded at Calvi, on the Corsican coast, and lost the sight of his right eye.

Brown Bros.
Horatio Nelson

Nelson next distinguished himself at the Battle of Cape St. Vincent in 1797. He served under Admiral Sir John Jervis, who defeated the combined French and Spanish fleets. Nelson was made a Knight of the Bath for his part in this victory. He had become a rear admiral a week before the battle. A few months later, Nelson led a small landing party in an attack on the strongly fortified port of Santa Cruz de Tenerife in the Canary Islands. The attack was a bold gamble, but unlike others, it failed. The British were driven off with heavy losses, and Nelson's right arm was badly mangled up to the elbow. The arm had to be cut off in a crude amputation in a pitching boat, and Nelson was invalided home to England in great pain. But he soon returned to duty.

Battle of the Nile. Napoleon, victorious in Europe, began to gather a French fleet for an expedition to conquer Egypt. Nelson was sent to watch the French ships at Toulon. A storm came up, and under its cover the French fleet escaped. Nelson followed it in a long and tiresome pursuit. He finally cornered the French ships in Abu Qir Bay. There, he attacked and almost destroyed the fleet on Aug. 1, 1798. This engagement is known to history as the Battle of the Nile. It cut off Napoleon's army in Egypt and ruined his Egyptian campaign. A year later, Napoleon deserted his army in Egypt and sneaked across the Mediterranean in a tiny ship. The victory in the Battle of the Nile made Nelson famous. He was made Baron of the Nile and given a large sum of money.

Nelson was wounded again in this battle, and he went to Naples to recover. Emma Lady Hamilton, wife of Sir William Hamilton, the British ambassador to Naples, fell in love with the battered naval hero and became his mistress. Her influence over Nelson became so great that he disobeyed his orders to leave Naples and join a squadron in the Mediterranean. It was Nelson's good fortune that no British defeat resulted from his refusal to leave Naples. Nelson was condemned for his conduct, however, when he returned to England.

Battle of Copenhagen. Nelson became a vice admiral in 1801 and sailed for Copenhagen, Denmark, in the squadron of Admiral Hyde Parker. The British had claimed the right to search neutral ships for contraband of war. However, Denmark refused to allow its ships to be searched. A council of war chose Nelson to attack the Danish fleet. Parker later became doubtful of the attack's outcome. He signaled Nelson to retire. But Nelson clapped his telescope to his blind eye and studied the signal. "I really do not see the signal," he said to an aide. He ignored Parker's order and turned what might have been a defeat into a great victory. After the Battle of Copenhagen, Nelson was given the title of viscount.

Victory at Trafalgar. Nelson was made commander in chief of the fleet in May 1803. Sailing on the flagship *Victory,* he once more went in search of the French. He found the French fleet at Toulon, but it slipped away from him. Nelson chased the French to the West Indies and back. It was more than two years before Nelson was able to bring the French fleet to battle off Cape Trafalgar on the coast of Spain, on Oct. 21, 1805 (see **Trafalgar, Battle of**). Nelson hoisted his famous signal, "England expects that every man will do his duty." With only 27 vessels, Nelson attacked the combined French and Spanish fleets. One of the great naval battles of all time followed. Napoleon's fleet, which had 33 warships, was destroyed.

Nelson was wounded at the height of the battle. He was carried below with a sharpshooter's bullet in his spine. Nelson died during the battle, but he lived long enough to know that the British fleet had defeated the French and Spanish fleets. Nelson's last words were, "Thank God I have done my duty."

One of Nelson's great characteristics as a commander was his willingness to give full credit to his officers and men. After the Battle of Copenhagen, he refused an honor given him by the City of London because he alone was to be honored. Nelson replied, "Never till the City of London thinks justly of the merits of my brave companions of the second of April can I, their commander, receive any attention from the City of London." The poet Robert Southey wrote of Nelson, "England has had many heroes. But never one who so entirely possessed the love of his fellow countrymen. All men knew that his heart was as humane as it was fearless … that with perfect and entire devotion he served his country with all his heart, and with all his soul, and with all his strength. And therefore they loved him as truly and fervently as he loved England."

Nelson monument. After Nelson's death, he became such a hero in the United Kingdom that the government erected a large column topped with a statue of him in Trafalgar Square, which was named for Nelson's last battle. The monument, called Nelson's Column, is one of the most famous landmarks in London. See **London** (picture: Trafalgar Square).   Philip Dwight Jones

Nelson, Thomas, Jr. (1738-1789), an American soldier and statesman, served as a Virginia delegate to the Continental Congress from 1775 to 1777 and again in 1779. He was one of the Virginia signers of the Declaration of Independence in 1776. During the American Revolution (1775-1783), Nelson commanded the Virginia militia and fought in the Battle of Yorktown in 1781. He also served as governor of Virginia that year. He was born on Dec. 26, 1738, in Yorktown, Virginia. He died on Jan. 4, 1789.

James H. Hutson

Nelson, William Rockhill (1841-1915), founded and built the *Kansas City* (Missouri) *Star,* a crusading newspaper, in 1880. The *Star* campaigned against municipal corruption, and for civic reform and a rehabilitation program. This program gave Kansas City broad boulevards, parks, and an art gallery. Nelson was born on March 7, 1841, in Fort Wayne, Indiana. He died on April 13, 1915.

Joseph P. McKerns

Nelson, Willie (1933-   ), is a popular country music composer and singer. Nelson began his music career composing songs for country singers. He launched his own singing career in the late 1960's and soon became one of the most popular performers in country music.

William Hugh Nelson was born on April 30, 1933, in Abbott, Texas. His parents abandoned him when he was 6 years old, and he was raised by grandparents. He moved to Nashville in 1960 and began his songwriting career, composing "Crazy" (1961), a hit for singer Patsy Cline. By the early 1970's, he helped launch the "outlaw" style in country music that attempted to return to a more authentic country sound.

In 1978, Nelson recorded the album *Stardust,* which included versions of pop standards, such as "Georgia on My Mind" and "Blue Skies." In 1980, Nelson composed one of his best-known songs, "On the Road Again." In 1982, he had a hit with the song "Always on My Mind." In 1984, Nelson and Julio Iglesias recorded the duet "To All the Girls I've Loved Before." It became a hit with pop music audiences as well as country music fans. Nelson attracted praise for organizing the first Farm Aid concert in 1985 to raise money for impoverished farmers. Also in 1985, Nelson joined Waylon Jennings, Johnny Cash, and Kris Kristofferson in forming the Highwaymen. They periodically toured and released popular albums in 1985, 1990, and 1995.

Nelson also appeared in motion pictures, including *The Electric Horseman* (1979), *Honeysuckle Rose* (1980), *Barbarosa* (1982), *Wag the Dog* (1997), and *Swing Vote* (2008). He has written an autobiography, a memoir, a novel, and other books. Nelson was elected to the Country Music Hall of Fame in 1993. William McKeen

Nelson River is the longest river in Manitoba. From its outlet at the northern end of Lake Winnipeg, it flows about 400 miles (640 kilometers) northeast to empty into Hudson Bay. It is the outlet of Lakes Winnipeg, Winnipegosis, and Manitoba, and the Winnipeg, Red, and Saskatchewan river systems. The watercourse to the head of the Saskatchewan's farthest tributary is 1,600 miles (2,580 kilometers) long. Once a transportation link for the Hudson's Bay Company, the river is now a source of hydroelectric power. Manitoba Hydro operates power stations at a number of locations along the river, including Kelsey Rapids, Jenpeg, Kettle Rapids, Limestone Rapids, and Long Spruce. John S. Brierley

Neman River is a waterway in eastern Europe. The Neman rises southwest of the city of Minsk in Belarus. It flows generally westward through Belarus and Lithuania and empties into the Baltic Sea (see **Europe** [terrain map]). The Neman flows 582 miles (937 kilometers) through a landscape of lakes and forests. Its chief branches are the Neris (Viliya), Shchara, Šešupė, and Merkys rivers. The Neman is called the Nyoman in Belarus and the Nemunas in Lithuania. Its historical names include the Memel and the Niemen.

The Neman is frozen from late November until March. Barges can sail up the river for about 400 miles (644 kilometers) from its source. A dam on the Neman near the city of Kaunas, Lithuania, has a hydroelectric power plant. The Nemunas River Delta Regional Park at the mouth of the river serves as a breeding ground for endangered birds. Guntis Smidchens

Nematode. See Roundworm.

Nene, *NAY nay,* also known as the Hawaiian goose, is a rare bird of Hawaii. It also is the official bird of Hawaii. Nenes measure 22 to 27 inches (56 to 69 centimeters) long and are brown with long, buff-colored neck feathers. They live in open country and feed chiefly on grass.

The female lays three to six creamy-white eggs. In 1950, only about 50 nenes existed. Since then, the number has greatly increased due to breeding and protection programs. See also **Bird** (picture: Birds of the Pacific Islands); **Hawaii** (picture: The state bird). Charles Walcott

Scientific classification. The nene's scientific name is *Branta sandvicensis.*

Neoclassicism. See Classicism.

Neocolonialism. See Colonialism.

Neodymium, *NEE uh DIHM ee uhm* (chemical symbol, Nd), is a metallic element belonging to the lanthanide group. Its *atomic number* (number of protons in its nucleus) is 60. Its *relative atomic mass* is 144.24. An element's relative atomic mass equals its *mass* (amount of matter) divided by $\frac{1}{12}$ of the mass of carbon 12, the most abundant form of carbon.

C. F. Auer von Welsbach of Austria discovered neodymium in 1885. He separated the so-called element didymium into neodymium and praseodymium.

Neodymium melts at 1021 °C and boils at 3074 °C. It has a density of 7.003 grams per cubic centimeter at 25 °C. It can be prepared by electrolysis of its halide salts, or by the reduction of these salts by alkaline earth metals in the presence of heat. The ceramic industry uses salts of neodymium to color glass and in glazes. The metal is present in *misch metal,* an alloy with many uses, and in the important Nd-YAG laser. Larry C. Thompson

See also **Element, Chemical** (tables); **Lanthanide.**

Neolithic Period. See Stone Age.

Neon is a chemical element that makes up about 1 part per 65,000 of Earth's atmosphere. The British chemists Sir William Ramsay and Morris W. Travers discovered the element in the atmosphere while they were studying liquid air in 1898. Ramsay had predicted the existence of this gas in 1897. Ramsay and Travers named the gas *neon,* for the Greek word that means *new.*

Neon is used chiefly for filling lamps and luminous sign tubes. Its usual color in lamps is bright reddish-orange. The addition of a few drops of mercury makes the light a brilliant blue.

Many airplane beacons use neon light because it can penetrate fog. Pilots have reported that neon beacons were visible for 20 miles (32 kilometers) when it was impossible for them to see other kinds of lights.

Neon lamps are made by removing the air from glass tubes and then filling them with neon gas. When about 15,000 volts of electrical energy are applied to the tube, an electric discharge occurs, and the tube glows fiery reddish-orange. Instead of a filament, a neon tube has two electrodes sealed within it. The neon forms a luminous band between these electrodes.

Commercially, neon is obtained as a by-product of liquid air manufacture. Neon liquefies under normal pressure at −246.048 °C, and it freezes at −248.67 °C. When air is liquefied at about −200 °C, neon is left behind as a gas. Neon is expensive, but little is needed for lamps. Signs use 1 quart per 200 to 300 feet (1 liter per 64 to 97 meters) of tubing. Liquid neon is often used as a low-temperature *refrigerant* (cooling agent).

Neon is a colorless, odorless gas. It does not react readily with other substances, though it may form a compound with fluorine. Neon is classed as a *noble gas.* Its symbol is Ne. It has an *atomic number* (number of protons in its nucleus) of 10. Its *relative atomic mass* is

David R. Frazier

Neon signs brighten entertainment and shopping areas. This hotel in Las Vegas, Nevada, has glowing signs to attract visitors. Stores often use neon signs to advertise products.

20.1797. An element's relative atomic mass equals its *mass* (amount of matter) divided by $\frac{1}{12}$ of the mass of carbon 12, the most abundant form of carbon.

Frank C. Andrews

See also **Electric light** (Neon lamps); **Noble gas**.

Neonatology, *NEE oh nay TAHL uh jee,* is the branch of medicine concerned with the care of infants during the first 28 days of life. The highest death rate in life occurs during this period, which is known as the *neonatal period.* A doctor who specializes in the care of newborn infants is called a *neonatologist.*

The major cause of neonatal death is premature birth—that is birth before the pregnancy reaches *term.* Birth occurs at term if it happens from the 38th through the 41st week of pregnancy. The more prematurely the baby is born, the less it weighs and the higher its risk of death. Most neonatal deaths occur among infants who weigh less than $5\frac{1}{2}$ pounds (2.5 kilograms) at birth. The average weight of a baby born at term is $7\frac{1}{2}$ pounds (3.4 kilograms). Many neonatal deaths also result from birth defects in the infant or medical problems of the mother, such as infectious diseases.

Many major medical centers have a neonatal intensive care unit. There, sick infants are usually cared for by a team of neonatologists, neonatal nurses, respiratory therapists, pediatric and surgical consultants, and other supporting staff. Advancements in neonatal intensive care have made it possible for infants born as much as 12 to 18 weeks prematurely to survive.   Kwang-sun Lee

Neoplasm. See Tumor.

Neoplatonism, *nee oh PLAY tuh nihz uhm,* was a dominant school of philosophy from the A.D. 200's to the 500's. Neoplatonism, which means *New Platonism,* developed from the philosophy of Plato. It also absorbed elements of Pythagorean, Aristotelian, and Stoic thought. Plotinus founded Neoplatonism. Other neoplatonists included his followers Porphyry and Proclus.

The Neoplatonists developed their philosophy from Plato's theory of *forms.* According to Plato, all things that can be perceived are only imperfect copies of forms, which are their perfect essence. Knowledge comes from grasping with the mind the essential form of a thing, rather than from perceiving with the senses its many incidental qualities. Plotinus went beyond this theory to divide Plato's realm of forms into various levels of reality. Each level depends for its reality on those above it.

Transcending all reality is *The One,* which is in itself unknowable. One cannot even say that The One *is,* because The One is beyond being. But The One expands or "overflows" into the levels beneath it, as light shines through darkness, becoming dimmer as it goes.

The highest level of reality is that of *Intellect,* in which forms exist as ideas beyond time and space. The next level, which is dimmer and less real, is that of *Soul.* Next is the level of *Nature,* which is the dark realm of material bodies. Beneath these levels is *Matter,* which Plotinus describes as "not-being" and as the principle of evil. We inhabit the lower levels but yearn to turn upward and return to the higher ones. Our souls can leave our bodies and "travel" to the realm of Intellect, where forms reside as ideas in the divine mind.

The Neoplatonists believed the purpose of philosophy is to escape from the attachment we feel to our bodies and physical environment. Thus, we achieve immortality by finding our true place in the world of forms.

Neoplatonism was an important philosophical movement. Plotinus influenced Saint Augustine in developing his principles of Christian theology. Proclus's views helped shape Christian *negative theology,* which points out the limits of human ability to comprehend a supreme being. Neoplatonist thought influenced Near Eastern philosophy as early as the A.D. 400's. The Neoplatonic emphasis on spiritual, as opposed to physical, beauty was important to the idea of *platonic love* during the Renaissance.   S. Marc Cohen

See also **Hypatia; Plato; Plotinus; Philosophy** (Plato; Neoplatonism).

Nepal, *nuh PAWL,* is a country in south-central Asia. The world's highest mountain range—the Himalaya—and a region of hills and valleys cover most of Nepal. The Tarai (or Terai)—a flat, fertile river plain along Nepal's border with India—covers the rest of the country.

Kathmandu is the capital of Nepal and its largest city. Mount Everest, the highest mountain in the world, rises 29,035 feet (8,850 meters) above sea level in the Himalaya on Nepal's border with Tibet, a region in China.

About 45 percent of Nepal's people live in the Tarai. The rest of the people live in the hills and valleys region or in the mountains. Patches of farmland lie among the mountains of Nepal. These cultivated areas account for only about 10 percent of the country's mountainous area, but almost all of the mountain people live there. Nepal is poor and undeveloped. The country also has a high rate of disease and illiteracy.

Facts in brief

Capital: Kathmandu.

Official language: Nepali.

Area: 56,827 mi² (147,181 km²). *Greatest distances*—east-west, 500 mi (805 km); north-south, 150 mi (241 km).

Elevation: *Highest*—Mount Everest, 29,035 ft (8,850 m) above sea level. *Lowest*—230 ft (70 m) above sea level.

Population: *Estimated 2012 population*—29,986,000; density, 528 per mi² (204 per km²); distribution, 83 percent rural, 17 percent urban. *2001 census*—23,151,423.

Chief products: Cattle, corn, potatoes, rice, water buffaloes, wheat.

National anthem: "Sayaun Thunga Phool Ka Haml" ("Hundreds of Flowers").

Flag: The flag has two red triangles trimmed in blue, one above the other. The top triangle shows the moon and the lower the sun, symbols of Nepal's long life. It is the only nonrectangular country flag. See **Flag** (picture: Flags of Asia and the Pacific).

Money: *Basic unit*—Nepalese rupee. One hundred paise equal one rupee.

Government. Nepal's 1990 Constitution made the country a constitutional monarchy with a king, a prime minister, and a two-house parliament. But in the early 2000's, King Gyanendra took full executive control of the government twice. In 2006 and 2007, Nepal's parliament stripped the king of most of his powers, and an *interim* (temporary) constitution was adopted. In April 2008, a Constituent Assembly was elected. The Constituent Assembly is responsible for writing a permanent constitution. In May 2008, the Assembly abolished the monarchy and declared Nepal a republic. Under Nepal's interim government, a prime minister serves as head of government, and a president serves as head of state.

The Supreme Court is Nepal's highest court. It consists of a chief justice and 14 judges.

Nepal is divided into 75 districts for purposes of local government. Each district is divided into cities and villages. The people elect a committee and a committee head to administer each district, city, and village.

People. Most Nepalese are closely related to the peoples of northern India. Other Nepalese are of Tibetan descent. Still others are of mixed Indian-Tibetan descent.

Most people live in small villages that consist of two-story houses made of stone or mud-brick.

About 75 percent of Nepal's people earn their living through farming. Most farms produce barely enough to support one family. Nepalese farmers trade any surplus crops they raise for such important items as kerosene and salt. Other Nepalese make their living as carpet weavers, clothing manufacturers, or craftworkers. Still others work as merchants, for the government, or in the tourist industry.

The Sherpas and the Gurkhas, two Nepalese groups, are known for their special skills. The Sherpas, a Himalayan people, have won fame as guides and porters for mountain-climbing expeditions. Sherpa men and women carry heavy loads up to high altitudes. Many Gurkhas serve as soldiers in the British or Indian army.

Most people in Nepal practice Hinduism. However, the Nepalese have combined the beliefs and practices of Hinduism with those of Buddhism. Buddha, the founder of Buddhism, was born in Nepal about 563 B.C. The Nepalese celebrate the festivals of both Buddhism and Hinduism, and Buddhist shrines and Hindu temples are considered equally sacred. Many Nepalese also worship local gods and spirits and consult *shamans* (magical healers) in times of illness. Nepal has few physicians, and such diseases as cholera, leprosy, and tuberculosis occur frequently. Since the early 1950's, the government has greatly reduced malaria. This has enabled many Nepalese from the mountains to settle in the Tarai, where malaria used to be widespread.

Some Hindus in Nepal practice *polygyny,* a form of marriage in which a husband has more than one wife. *Polyandry,* the practice of a wife having more than one husband, occurs among some of the Tibetan groups in northern Nepal. In most such cases, the woman marries two or more brothers. The children who are born of such marriages regard the oldest husband as their father and his brothers as uncles.

Illiteracy is one of Nepal's most serious problems. Tribhuvan University is Nepal's largest university. It has a main campus in Kathmandu and many other campuses.

Nepal

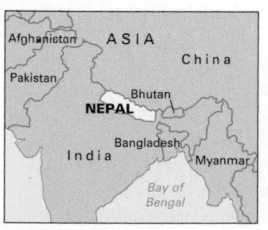

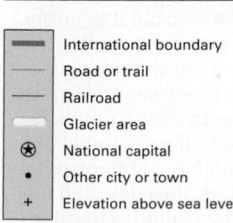

- ▬ International boundary
- ── Road or trail
- ── Railroad
- ▭ Glacier area
- ⊛ National capital
- • Other city or town
- + Elevation above sea level

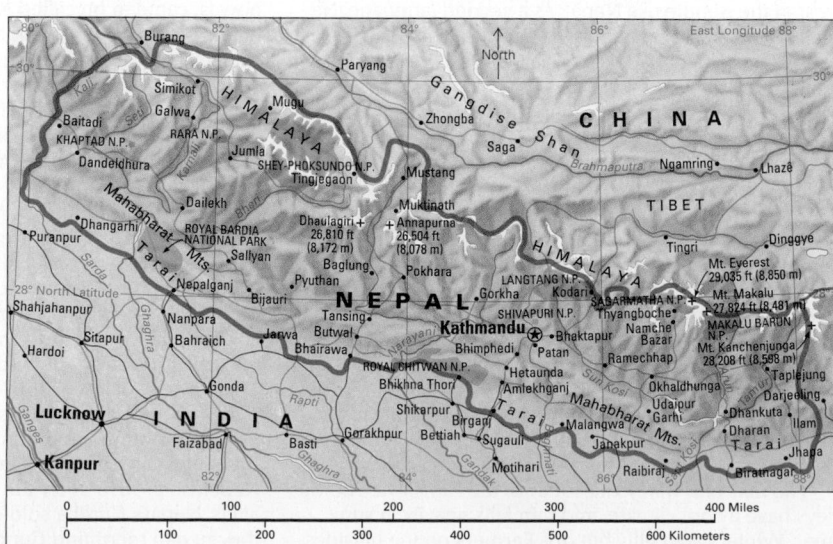

M. Philip Kahl, Jr., Bruce Coleman Inc.

Kathmandu, Nepal's capital and largest city, lies at the foot of the Himalaya. Many-storied temples called *pagodas,* such as the ones shown here, line many of Kathmandu's streets.

About half of the people speak Nepali—the country's official language—as their native tongue. Most of the rest of the people use Nepali as a second language. Nepali is related to the languages of northern India. More than 50 other languages and dialects are spoken in the country.

Land and climate. Nepal has three principal regions: (1) the Himalaya, (2) the hills and valleys, and (3) the Tarai. Altitude differences give each region a different climate. Each region also has its own kinds of plants and animals.

The Himalaya, in the north, covers much of Nepal. The mountains have long, harsh winters and short, cool summers. Steep rivers cut deep valleys through the snow-clad mountains of the Himalaya. Forests cover the mountains up to the altitude of about 12,000 feet (3,660 meters) above sea level. Only grasses, lichens, and moss can grow in the cold, dry air above this altitude.

Mountaineers in the Himalaya herd sheep. They also herd long-haired oxen called *yaks.* Some people claim that a mysterious creature called the Yeti, or Abominable Snowman, lives in the mountains.

The hills and valleys lie south of the Himalaya. The valleys have a cool climate, and rain falls heavily in summer. Winters are chilly but dry. Farmers on the hillsides and in the valleys raise many crops, including corn, millet, rice, and wheat. The farmers of the hills and valleys tend herds of cattle, goats, and sheep. A variety of trees and bamboo grasses grow in thick forests in this region.

The Tarai lies in southern Nepal. It has fertile farmland. Farmers grow corn, jute, millet, mustard, rice, sugar cane, tobacco, and other crops. Livestock raised in the region include cattle and water buffalo. The Tarai has a tropical climate. Its jungles and swamps provide a habitat for many wild animals, including crocodiles, deer, elephants, leopards, rhinoceroses, and tigers.

Economy. Nepal is one of the poorest countries in the world. Since the 1950's, large amounts of foreign aid have helped develop Nepal's economy. Several nations—including China, India, and Japan—have contributed money to Nepal. These funds have helped construct roads, maintain health centers, and start small industries. Hundreds of thousands of tourists visit Nepal annually. Money spent by visitors from other countries has helped improve economic conditions in Nepal.

Nepal's economy depends largely on agriculture. Nepal's farmers raise cattle, sheep, and water buffaloes. Leading crops include corn, potatoes, rice, sugar cane, and wheat.

Manufacturing and mining play a relatively small role in Nepal's economy. The country manufactures carpets, cement, clothing, and food products. Nepal has deposits of such minerals as coal, copper, gold, iron, lead, and zinc. However, the country has few mines. Nepal's greatest natural resources are its forests and rivers. Some of its swift mountain currents have been harnessed to produce hydroelectric power.

Nepal imports much more than it exports. The country's imports include electrical equipment, machinery, petroleum products, *pharmaceuticals* (medicinal products), and transportation equipment. Nepal exports carpets, clothing, food products, textiles, and yarn. India is, by far, Nepal's leading trade partner. Nepal also trades with China, Indonesia, Singapore, and the United States.

History. Until the late 1700's, Nepal consisted of a number of small, independent kingdoms. About A.D. 400, the Kathmandu Valley, where the Nepalese capital now is, came to be called Nepal. Through the centuries, bands of conquerors, nomads, and refugees moved into Nepal. They came from Central Asia, India, and Tibet and were the ancestors of the Nepalese.

In the mid-1700's, Prithwi Narayan Shah, a king from a small Nepalese kingdom called Gorkha, began a military campaign to unify the country. By the time of his death in 1775, he had conquered most of what is now Nepal. He took the title of king of Nepal, and his descendants have served as monarchs ever since.

In the early 1800's, Nepal fought a war against the United Kingdom. Nepal had tried to expand into northern India. The British East India Company, a trading firm, controlled much of India then, and British troops guarded India's borders. The British declared war on Nepal in 1814 after Nepalese troops attacked a British outpost. The British expected an easy victory, but the Nepalese were accustomed to mountain fighting. Although the British initially suffered heavy losses, they defeated the Nepalese in 1816. After the war, the countries became allies. Nepal's Gurkha soldiers impressed the British, and they began recruiting Gurkhas for their armies.

Malcolm Kirk from Peter Arnold

Porters on a mountain-climbing expedition carry heavy loads up a steep trail in Nepal. The country's rugged mountains attract thousands of climbers and hikers yearly.

A leader named Jung Bahadur seized control of Nepal in 1846. He took the title of *Rana* and declared that his family would lead the country from then on. The Rana family controlled Nepal until 1951. The Ranas dominated the army and imprisoned and killed their rivals. In the 1930's and 1940's, opposition to Rana rule grew. A revolution began in 1950. The revolution restored the monarchy to power under King Tribhuvan Shah in 1951.

In the early 1950's, the government tried to create a democracy. King Tribhuvan died in 1955. His son Mahendra succeeded him. Mahendra criticized the rivalry among political parties in democratic systems. In 1960, he dissolved the elected government, took power, and banned political parties. In 1962, Mahendra put into effect a constitution that established the panchayat system, in which the monarch holds most of the power. Under his rule, the government stressed economic development, tourism, road construction, and hydroelectric power. Mahendra died in 1972. His son Birendra succeeded him.

Many Nepalese staged violent protests in 1979, in part to demand a more democratic government. In response, Birendra allowed a national vote on the government system. By a narrow margin, the voters chose to continue Nepal's system. In 1990, violent protests calling for more democracy broke out again. The king lifted the ban on political parties, and an interim government was formed. In November 1990, a constitution was approved that made Nepal a constitutional monarchy. In May 1991, democratic parliamentary elections were held.

In 1996, rebels called Maoists began fighting to replace Nepal's constitutional monarchy with a Communist government. By the early 2000's, the Maoists controlled several districts and were active throughout much of Nepal. Both the Maoists and the national security forces used ruthless violence and intimidation against the people of Nepal. In 2001, the Maoists and the gov-

ernment began peace talks, though violence continued.

Additionally in 2001, King Birendra's son Dipendra killed the king and most of the royal family and then killed himself. Gyanendra, the brother of the king, took the throne. From 2002 to 2004 and from 2005 to 2006, Gyanendra took full executive control of the country after dismissing Nepal's prime minister and his cabinet. The king said that the prime minister had failed to deal effectively with the Maoists. In 2005, tens of thousands of people began pro-democracy protests. In April 2006, after weeks of renewed protests, the king reinstated Nepal's parliament, which had been dissolved in 2002. Political party leaders chose Girija Prasad Koirala as prime minister. In May 2006, parliament took away most of the king's powers.

In May 2006, the government began peace talks with the Maoists. In November, the two sides signed a peace deal. The deal brought an end to about 10 years of fighting, during which more than 13,000 people died. In early 2007, the Maoists joined the interim government.

In parliamentary elections held in April 2008, the Maoists won the most seats. In May, the government officially abolished the monarchy and declared Nepal a republic.   Graham P. Chapman

Related articles in *World Book* include:

Buddha
Colombo Plan
Gurkhas
Himalaya
Hinduism

Kathmandu
Mount Everest
Sherpas
Tenzing Norgay
Yeti

Nephrite. See Jade.

Nephritis, *nih FRY tihs,* formerly called Bright's disease, is a general term for several inflammatory diseases of the kidneys. *Glomerulonephritis* is the disease most often called nephritis. It involves an inflammation of the *glomeruli* (filtering units) of the kidneys. The inflammation often reduces the amount of urine produced by the kidneys, causing waste products normally eliminated in the urine to accumulate in the body. Severe or persistent glomerulonephritis can cause serious, permanent damage to the kidneys.

Most cases of glomerulonephritis follow an infection of the throat or skin caused by certain types of the bacteria called *streptococci.* In some people, such infections apparently cause the body to become allergic to the tissues of the glomeruli. The glomeruli may suffer serious damage as a result. If this damage occurs rapidly, the condition is called *acute glomerulonephritis.* If the damage continues over a period of years, the condition is called *chronic glomerulonephritis.*

Acute glomerulonephritis occurs mostly in children. Symptoms include facial swelling, fever, headache, high blood pressure, vomiting, and blood and proteins in the urine. There is no specific treatment. Nearly all patients recover from their first attack of acute glomerulonephritis, but many have later attacks of the disease.

Chronic glomerulonephritis develops mostly in adults. In most cases, the specific cause is unknown. Many cases involve only mild symptoms so that a person may not even know that he or she has the disease. For some patients, treatment with medications can stop or even reverse the damage. But for many others, chronic glomerulonephritis causes progressive, incurable kidney damage. Advanced stages may lead to kidney failure and a potentially fatal condition known as *uremia* (see **Uremia**). To prevent advanced uremia, physicians may connect the patient to a *dialysis machine,* which removes wastes from the patient's blood. Physicians may also treat chronic glomerulonephritis with *ambulatory dialysis,* in which the patient manually drains and replaces abdominal fluids. In certain severe cases of the disease, physicians may perform a kidney transplant to replace the damaged kidneys.   Laurence H. Beck

See also **Bright, Richard; Kidney; Transplant.**

Nepotism, *NEHP uh tihz uhm,* is the practice of giving important political or business positions to members of one's family. The word *nepotism* comes from the Latin word for *nephew.*

Neptune was the god of the sea in Roman mythology. He had power over the sea and seafaring. For example, he could cause—or prevent—storms at sea. Neptune resembled the Greek god Poseidon. Like Poseidon, he was also the god of earthquakes and horses.

The ancient Romans were a seafaring people and imported much of their food and other necessities by ship. As ruler of the sea, Neptune thus had an important role in their daily life. Sea travel was dangerous in ancient times, and Roman sailors prayed to Neptune for safe voyages. After the sailors returned, they often showed their gratitude by dedicating a valuable object to the god of the sea.

Neptune was the son of Saturn and Ops (called Cronus and Rhea by the Greeks). He married the sea nymph Amphitrite, and they had a son, Triton, who was half man and half fish. Triton played an important role in many ancient legends about the sea.

Neptune appears in a famous episode at the beginning of the *Aeneid,* an epic by the Roman poet Virgil. In this epic, Neptune calms a storm that had threatened to destroy the fleet of the Trojan hero Aeneas.

Many ancient and modern seascapes feature Neptune, Amphitrite, and Triton. Artists portray Neptune as a man carrying a *trident* (three-pronged spear). Some show him riding in a chariot pulled by seahorses and accompanied by dolphins. Many fountains, notably the Trevi Fountain in Rome, include a statue of Neptune. One of the planets is named for him.   Daniel P. Harmon

See also **Poseidon.**

Neptune is the most distant planet from the sun. It is the only planet that cannot be seen without a telescope. Neptune is about 30 times as far from the sun as Earth is. Neptune's average distance from the sun is about 2,793,100,000 miles (4,495,060,000 kilometers). Light can travel that distance in about 4 hours and 10 minutes.

Neptune's diameter at the equator is 30,775 miles (49,528 kilometers), or almost 4 times that of Earth. Neptune has 17 times as much *mass* (total matter) as does Earth. But Neptune is not as dense as Earth. Neptune has at least 13 *satellites* (moons) and several rings around it.

Neptune's orbit is *elliptical* (oval-shaped). But Earth's orbit, by comparison, is more than twice as *eccentric* (elongated) as Neptune's. Neptune orbits the sun once every 165 years. On its path around the sun, Neptune spins on its *axis.* The axis is an imaginary line through the planet's center. Neptune's day—the time it takes to rotate once—lasts about 16 hours and 3 minutes.

Neptune's axis is not *perpendicular* (at a right angle) to the planet's path around the sun. The axis tilts about 28°

Fountain of Neptune (1563-1567) by Giambologna in the Neptune Plaza in Bologna, Italy (Bridgeman Art Library)

Neptune was the Roman god of the sea. He was often portrayed holding a three-pronged spear called a *trident,* which he used to start and stop storms, smash rocks, and create earthquakes.

from the perpendicular position. Neptune's tilt causes the planet to have seasons. Each season on Neptune lasts about 40 years. Like Earth, Neptune has a magnetic field. Neptune's magnetic field is tilted about 47° from its axis of rotation. This fact makes magnetic north and geographic north relatively far apart on Neptune.

Structure and composition. Scientists believe that Neptune has three layers. The *core* (innermost layer) probably consists of mostly iron, nickel, and *silicates.* Silicates are minerals that also make up much of Earth's rocky *crust* (outer layer). Unlike Earth, Neptune has no solid surface. The layer above the core is a slushy *mantle* (middle layer) made of mostly ammonia, methane, and water ices. The large amount of ice within Neptune— and also Uranus—leads astronomers to label both plan-

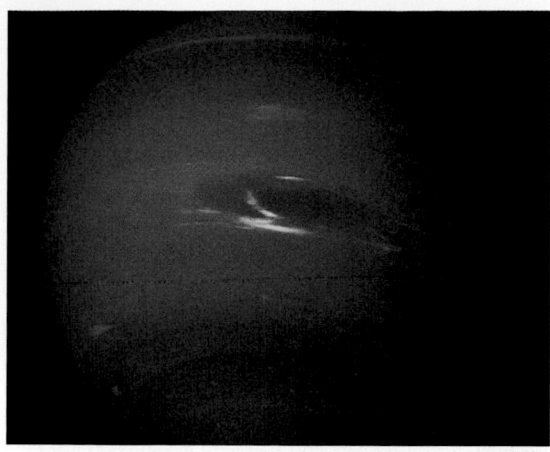

NASA/JPL

The planet Neptune is shrouded in bright blue clouds. They consist mainly of frozen methane. Winds that carry them may reach speeds up to about 900 miles (1,450 kilometers) per hour.

ets *ice giants.* Neptune's slushy mantle blends smoothly into its uppermost layer, a gaseous atmosphere of mostly hydrogen and helium. A small amount of methane gives the atmosphere a blue color.

High in Neptune's atmosphere, thick layers of clouds are in rapid motion. Winds blow these clouds at speeds up to about 900 miles (1,450 kilometers) per hour. Unlike the winds of Jupiter, Saturn, and Uranus, Neptune's winds tend to blow in the opposite direction of the planet's rotation. The highest clouds in Neptune's atmosphere consist mainly of frozen methane. Many scientists think that Neptune's darker, deeper clouds are composed of hydrogen sulfide. In 1989, the Voyager 2 spacecraft found that Neptune had a dark area of violently swirling gas that resembled a hurricane. This area, called the Great Dark Spot, was similar to the Great Red Spot on Jupiter. In 1994, the Hubble Space Telescope found that the Great Dark Spot had vanished.

Satellites and rings. Astronomers have identified 13 satellites of Neptune. But the planet probably has more that have yet to be discovered. Triton, Neptune's largest satellite, is about 1,700 miles (2,700 kilometers) in diameter. It lies about 220,440 miles (354,760 kilometers) from Neptune. It orbits in the opposite direction to that of Neptune's rotation. It is the only major satellite in the solar system that orbits a planet in this way. Triton has a circular orbit. It travels once around Neptune every six

Satellites of Neptune

Name	Mean distance from Neptune		Diameter of satellite		Year of discovery
	In mi	In km	In mi	In km	
Naiad	29,967	48,227	36	58	1989
Thalassa	31,115	50,075	50	80	1989
Despina	32,638	52,526	92	148	1989
Galatea	38,496	61,953	98	158	1989
Larissa	45,701	73,548	120	193	1989
Proteus	73,102	117,647	258	416	1989
Triton	220,440	354,760	1,681	2,705	1846
Nereid	3,425,900	5,513,400	211	340	1949
Halimede	10,321,597	16,611,000	39	62	2002
Sao	13,811,839	22,228,000	27	44	2002
Laomedeia	14,643,855	23,567,000	26	42	2002
Psamathe	29,885,469	48,096,000	24	40	2003
Neso	30,624,279	49,285,000	37	60	2002

days. The British brewer and amateur astronomer William Lassell discovered Triton in 1846. He found it just 17 days after Neptune was discovered.

Triton may once have been a large comet that traveled around the sun. At some point, Neptune's gravity probably captured the comet, and it became a satellite of Neptune. Triton has an orbit that is slowly dropping the satellite closer and closer to Neptune. In a few billion years, Triton will move so close that Neptune's gravity will break it apart, possibly forming an icy ring.

Voyager 2 also observed geyserlike eruptions of nitrogen gas and dust that rose up to 5 miles (8 kilometers) above Triton's surface. Triton's surface is about −390 °F (−223 °C), but many scientists believe the sun provides enough heat energy to drive the nitrogen plumes.

Triton has relatively few impact craters. Many scientists believe that the lack of craters on the moon's surface is the result of *cryovolcanism* (ice volcanoes). Neptune's gravitational pull compresses and heats Triton's interior. This additional heat may fuel the cryovolcanism, which, in turn, smooths over the moon's surface.

In 1949, the Dutch astronomer Gerard Kuiper discovered a second moon orbiting Neptune. The moon was named Nereid after the Nereids, sea nymphs in Greek mythology. In 1989, Voyager 2 provided the first close-up views of Neptune. It also discovered Neptune's rings and six of its moons—Despina, Galatea, Larissa, Naiad, Proteus, and Thalassa. Earth-based telescopes found the remaining five known moons in 2002 and 2003.

Neptune's six rings are much fainter and darker than those of Saturn. The rings consist of orbiting particles of dust. Neptune's outer ring is unlike any other planetary ring in the solar system. It is called the Adams ring in honor of John C. Adams, an English astronomer who studied Neptune. The Adams ring has five curved segments, called *arcs,* that are brighter and denser than the rest of the ring. Scientists believe small moons cause the dust to spread unevenly in the ring.

Discovery. Neptune was discovered by studying another planet, Uranus, and by means of mathematics. Astronomers observing Uranus noticed a subtle difference in the planet's observed orbit and its predicted orbit. They concluded that the gravitational force of some unknown planet was pulling on Uranus.

In 1843, John C. Adams, a young astronomer and mathematician, began working to find the planet. Adams calculated that the planet would be about 1 billion miles (1.6 billion kilometers) farther from the sun than Uranus. He completed his work in September 1845 and sent his computed orbit to Sir George B. Airy, the astronomer royal of England. The astronomer royal is a distinguished scientist who advises the king or queen on astronomical matters. However, Adams did not provide Airy with all the information needed to find Neptune.

Meanwhile, the French mathematician Urbain J. J. Le Verrier also became interested in the unseen planet. By mid-1846, Le Verrier had also calculated Neptune's orbit. However, Le Verrier in addition used his calculations to predict Neptune's position in the sky. He sent his predictions to the Urania Observatory in Berlin, Germany. Johann G. Galle, the director of the observatory, had just charted the stars in the area where the planet was believed to be. On Sept. 23, 1846, Galle and his assistant, Heinrich L. d'Arrest, found Neptune. The planet was in

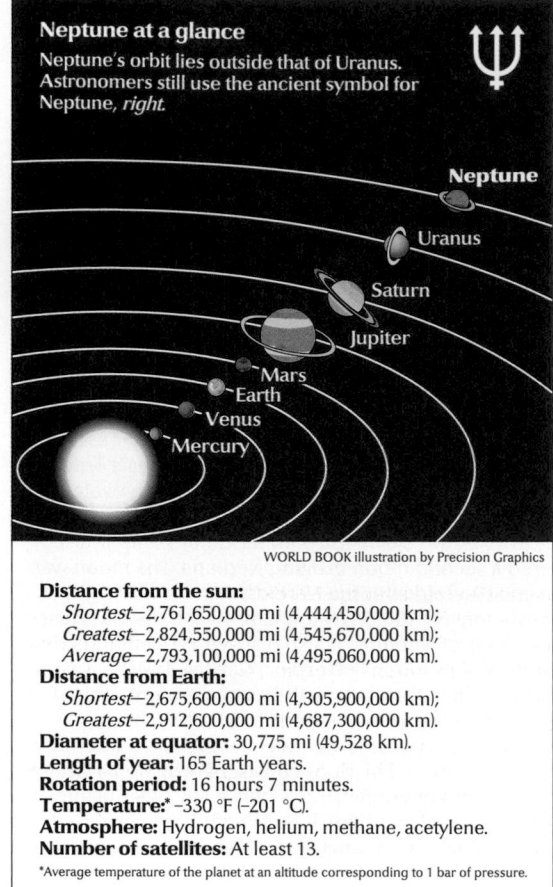

Neptune at a glance

Neptune's orbit lies outside that of Uranus. Astronomers still use the ancient symbol for Neptune, *right.*

Neptune
Uranus
Saturn
Jupiter
Mars
Earth
Venus
Mercury

WORLD BOOK illustration by Precision Graphics

Distance from the sun:
Shortest—2,761,650,000 mi (4,444,450,000 km);
Greatest—2,824,550,000 mi (4,545,670,000 km);
Average—2,793,100,000 mi (4,495,060,000 km).
Distance from Earth:
Shortest—2,675,600,000 mi (4,305,900,000 km);
Greatest—2,912,600,000 mi (4,687,300,000 km).
Diameter at equator: 30,775 mi (49,528 km).
Length of year: 165 Earth years.
Rotation period: 16 hours 7 minutes.
Temperature:* –330 °F (–201 °C).
Atmosphere: Hydrogen, helium, methane, acetylene.
Number of satellites: At least 13.
*Average temperature of the planet at an altitude corresponding to 1 bar of pressure.

almost exactly the position predicted by Le Verrier.

Traditionally, Adams and Le Verrier have been jointly credited with the discovery. However, after Adams's papers were rediscovered in 1998, some historians began to grant sole credit to Le Verrier. Adams's papers revealed that he had not fully explained where in the sky Neptune could be found and that his calculations lacked the accuracy of Le Verrier's. By contrast, Le Verrier's calculations of position led Galle and d'Arrest to find Neptune after only a 30-minute search.   Sally Dodson-Robinson

See also **Planet; Satellite** (Satellites of the gas giants); **Solar system; Triton.**

Neptunium, *nehp TOO nee uhm* (chemical symbol, Np), is a radioactive chemical element. Its *atomic number* (the number of protons in its nucleus) is 93. Almost all neptunium is created in nuclear reactors. Traces of the element exist in uranium ores. Neptunium was named for the planet Neptune. It follows uranium in the periodic table of the elements, just as Neptune follows Uranus in the solar system. See **Element, Chemical.**

There are 17 known forms or *isotopes* of neptunium. Different isotopes of an element have the same number of protons but different numbers of neutrons. Neptunium-237, the most stable isotope of neptunium, has 144 neutrons and an *atomic mass number* (total number of protons and neutrons) of 237. Isotopes of neptunium undergo radioactive decay—that is, their nuclei break

apart. As a result, their atoms turn into atoms of another isotope. The time that it takes half of a sample of an isotope to decay into another isotope is called its *half-life.* Neptunium-237 has a half-life of 2.14 million years.

Neptunium was discovered by the American physicists Edwin M. McMillan and P. H. Abelson at the University of California in 1940. They bombarded the isotope uranium-238 with neutrons to create the isotope neptunium-239. Neptunium-239 has a half-life of 2.4 days and decays to form the isotope plutonium-239, which can be used in nuclear reactors and nuclear weapons. Neptunium metal has a density of 20.25 grams per cubic centimeter at 20 °C. It melts at 639 °C.   Richard L. Hahn

Nereids, *NIHR ee ihdz,* were 50 beautiful sea nymphs who attended the sea divinities Poseidon and Amphitrite. They were the daughters of the sea goddess Doris and of Nereus, called the Old Man of the Sea. The Nereids lived under the sea and surfaced to dance in the waves. Their leader was Thetis, mother of the hero Achilles. Other famous Nereids included Psamathe and Galatea. See also **Andromeda; Nereus.**   Nancy Felson

Nereus, *NIHR oos,* was a kindly old sea god in Greek mythology. The poets Homer and Hesiod called him the Old Man of the Sea. Like other sea deities, Nereus had the gift of prophecy and the ability to change shapes. He foretold the fall of Troy in the Trojan War. The Greek hero Heracles (Hercules in Latin) captured him while he slept and held him fast as he rapidly changed forms. After Nereus finally resumed his original shape, he told Heracles where to find the garden of the Hesperides. The hero then let him go. With the sea goddess Doris, Nereus fathered 50 lovely sea nymphs called the Nereids. See also **Hesperides; Nereids.**   Nancy Felson

Neri, *NAIR ee,* **Saint Philip** (1515-1595), founded the Oratorians. He was also a reformer of Rome during the Counter Reformation. Pope Gregory XIII recognized his group of priests as the Congregation of the Oratory in 1575. Neri, a popular leader, also won over cardinals and popes to his unusual reform methods. He was born on July 21, 1515, in Florence, Italy. He died on May 26, 1595.   Marvin R. O'Connell

Nero, *NEER oh* (A.D. 37-68), was a Roman emperor who reigned from A.D. 54 until his death 14 years later. His rule is best known for a fire that destroyed much of Rome in A.D. 64. Nero built the Golden House, a colossal palace, in the center of the burned-out area. Rumors circulated that Nero had started the fire so he could build the palace. However, Nero blamed the Christians, then an unpopular group in Rome, and persecuted them.

Nero was born on Dec. 15, A.D. 37, in Antium. His given and family names were Lucius Domitius Ahenobarbus. His father, Gnaeus Domitius Ahenobarbus, was a nobleman. His mother was Agrippina the Younger, the great-granddaughter of Emperor Augustus. Nero's father died when Nero was still a child, and Agrippina married Emperor Claudius in A.D. 49. Claudius adopted Nero as his eldest son, naming him Nero Claudius Caesar Drusus Germanicus. In A.D. 53, Nero married Octavia, Claudius's daughter by a previous marriage. The next year, Claudius died. Many historians believe Agrippina poisoned him so that Nero could become emperor.

At first, Nero permitted two respected advisers to direct state affairs. These advisers were Seneca, a philosopher and writer, and Burrus, a military officer. However,

Bronze portrait bust of Nero, about A.D. 150; Uffizi Gallery, Florence, Italy (SCALA/Art Resource)

Emperor Nero, who ruled Rome from A.D. 54 to 68, ordered the death of many Christians and several of his own relatives.

Nero began to assume his own power in A.D. 59. That year, he had Agrippina murdered. In A.D. 62, Burrus died, and Seneca retired from political life. Soon afterward, Nero divorced Octavia and then had her killed so he could marry Poppaea Sabina. Poppaea was the former wife of a Roman military officer. Nero killed her a few years later. He also executed many Roman senators because they questioned his actions. These executions and Nero's scandalous life made him increasingly unpopular with the upper classes. A plan to overthrow Nero failed. As a result, more aristocrats were killed in A.D. 65.

Nevertheless, most of Rome's provinces were well governed and peaceful. Nero's military commanders put down rebellions in Britain and Judea and reasserted Rome's right to choose the king of Armenia.

Nero appreciated Greek civilization. He was a poet and actor and took an interest in architecture. In A.D. 66 and 67, Nero toured Greece and participated in games and festivals there. By then, military commanders in the provinces had begun to fear Nero's cruelty and wild suspicions. In A.D. 68, they revolted. Nero took his own life soon afterward. His last words were said to have been, "Alas, what an artist is dying in me." William G. Sinnigen

See also **Agrippina the Younger; Petronius; Seneca, Lucius Annaeus.**

Neruda, *nay ROOD uh,* **Pablo,** *PAH bloh* (1904-1973), a Chilean poet, won the 1971 Nobel Prize for literature. Because he continually changed his approach to poetry, Neruda's work cannot be easily characterized. He was one of the great adapters of surrealism in Spanish-language verse, producing obscure, violent imagery and conveying a sense of universal chaos (see **Surrealism**). Neruda also experimented with making poetic expression as direct and simple as possible.

Neruda was born in Perral, Chile. His real name was Neftalí Reyes. He first gained recognition with the lyrical and romantic *Twenty Poems of Love and One Desperate Song* (1924). The two parts of *Residence on Earth* contain his poetry from 1925 to 1935. They show the poet at his most surrealistic. Although not all their symbols are comprehensible, their vision of disintegration and despair are unmistakable. Neruda showed a new desire to make art speak for oppressed members of society in *Third Residence* (1947) and *General Song* (1950). His most playful and eloquent poems appear in *Elemental Odes* (1954). Naomi Lindstrom

Nerval, *nehr VAL,* **Gérard de,** *zhay RAR duh* (1808-1855), was a French poet. His charm, odd behavior, periodic mental disorders, and mysterious suicide made him a hero typical of the romantic movement. Critics consider him a major visionary poet.

Nerval believed in *metempsychosis,* the passing of a soul at death from one body to another. In *Les Chimères* (1854), a collection of sonnets, this belief underlies many obscure references to the legendary past which contribute to the haunting beauty of the poems. His search for the eternal feminine ideal is reflected in the short stories of *Les Filles du Feu* (1854), notably in "Sylvie," a tale set in the Valois countryside. *Aurélia* (1855), a prose confession, begins with the phrase "Our dreams are a second life." It describes this "life," including the hallucinations Nerval suffered during his periods of insanity. He was born in Paris. Jean-Pierre Cauvin

Nerve. See **Nervous system.**

Nerve gas. See **Chemical-biological-radiological warfare.**

Nervi, *NEHR vee,* **Pier Luigi,** *pyehr loo EE jee* (1891-1979), was an Italian architect and engineer. His designs reflect his belief that practical industrial structures should be beautiful and elegant through simplicity of design. Nervi was trained as an engineer, and he felt that architectural beauty could be derived from mathematical calculations rather than from aesthetic considerations. Nervi became especially noted for his free and graceful use of reinforced concrete. He developed a number of new structural techniques that utilized concrete.

Nervi was born in Sondrio. His first major work was a stadium completed in Florence in 1932. It has stairways that dramatically curve out over open space. Nervi designed two concrete exhibition halls (1948-1950) in Turin. Both were largely prefabricated. Nervi's other buildings include two Sports Palaces designed for the 1960 Summer Olympic Games in Rome, and the Palace of Labor (1961) in Turin. For pictures of Nervi's designs, see **Rome** (picture: The Sports Palace) and the introduction to **Architecture.** Nicholas Adams

Nervous breakdown is a term often used to refer to anything from fatigue caused by overwork to a severe mental illness. The term has no precise medical meaning. Psychiatrists and others who study and treat mentally ill patients do not use the term. It is used by those who believe it is an accepted medical term, or who want to avoid using the term "mental illness." The original idea behind the term was that mental symptoms of a person were caused by a failure of the nerves to function properly. Paula J. Clayton

See also **Mental illness.**

Nervous system is an internal communications network that enables an animal to adjust to changes in its environment. Almost all animals, except the simplest kinds, have some type of nervous system.

Animals without a backbone have a nervous system that ranges from a simple net of nerves to a highly organized system of nerve cords and a primitive brain. In human beings and other animals with backbones, the nervous system consists of the brain, the spinal cord, and the nerves. This article deals mainly with the human nervous system.

The human nervous system—especially the highly developed brain—makes people different from all other animals. The human brain functions much like a complicated computer that enables people to speak, solve difficult problems, and produce creative ideas.

The nervous system provides pathways by which information travels from a person's surroundings to the brain. The brain then sends instructions to various muscles via other pathways so that the body can respond to the information. The nervous system also regulates internal functions, such as breathing, digestion, and heartbeat. All of a person's movements, sensations, thoughts, and emotions are products of his or her nervous system.

How the nervous system works

The nervous system is made up of billions of special cells called *neurons* or *nerve cells.* Cordlike bundles of neuron fibers are called *nerves.* The nerves form a network of pathways that conduct information rapidly throughout the body.

A person's reaction to a situation may take only an instant, but it involves many complicated processes within the nervous system. For example, what happens in the nervous system of a person who sees a wild tiger and, an instant later, turns and runs away?

Specialized neurons called *receptors* are located in the ears and eyes and the other sense organs of the body. The receptors translate events in a person's surroundings—such as the sight of a tiger—into nerve messages, which are known as *impulses.* Nerve impulses travel along nerve fibers at speeds of 3 to 300 feet (0.9 to 90 meters) per second.

The receptor cells in the eyes respond to light rays that reflect off the tiger and translate the rays into a pattern of nerve impulses. These impulses then travel through neurons called *sensory neurons* and *association neurons.* The sensory neurons carry information from receptors in the sense organs to the association neurons, which are located in the brain and the spinal cord.

The neurons in the brain receive the impulses, analyze and interpret the message, and decide what action should be taken. A message consisting of the sight of a wild tiger is, of course, interpreted as danger. The person's brain immediately sends out a message—"Run!" — in the form of nerve impulses.

Next, the impulses travel through *motor neurons.* These nerve cells carry messages from the brain to the muscles and glands, which are called *effectors.* The effectors carry out the brain's instructions. Thus, the leg muscles respond and the person runs away. At the same time, the brain sends messages to various other parts of the body. For example, it sends messages to the heart to beat faster and send more blood to the leg muscles.

Divisions of the nervous system

The nervous system has three main parts, the *central nervous system,* the *peripheral nervous system,* and the *autonomic nervous system.* Each of these parts has special functions.

The central nervous system functions as a "main switchboard" that controls and coordinates the activities of the entire nervous system. The central nervous system consists of the *brain* and the *spinal cord.*

The brain is an extremely complicated organ. It consists of three principal parts, the *cerebrum,* the *cerebellum,* and the *brain stem.* This article provides basic information about the brain. For more detailed information on the brain and how it works, see the *World Book* article on **Brain.**

The cerebrum makes up about 85 percent of the brain and is the most complex part. It is above the cerebellum and the brain stem and almost surrounds them. Human beings have a highly developed cerebrum that directs their hearing, sight, and touch and their ability

How the nervous system works   The nervous system enables us to adjust to changes in our surroundings. Such *neurons* (nerve cells) as the *receptors* in the eyes translate information from the environment into nerve impulses. *Sensory neurons* carry the impulses to *association neurons* in the brain and spinal cord. *Motor neurons* then carry instructions from the brain to muscles, internal organs, and other body parts.

WORLD BOOK diagrams by Lou Bory Associates

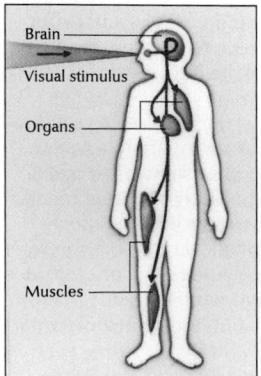

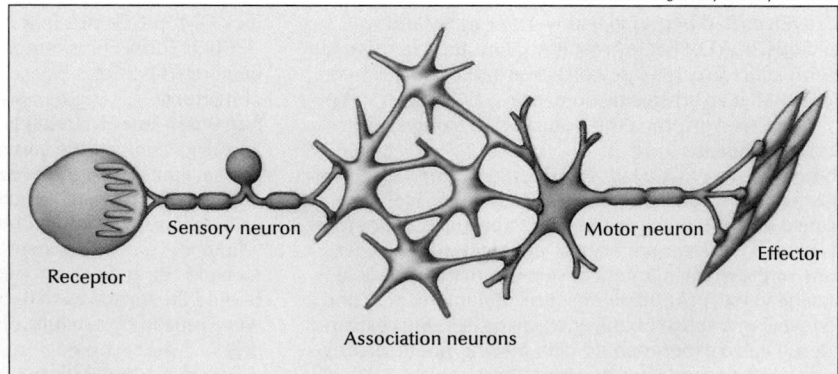

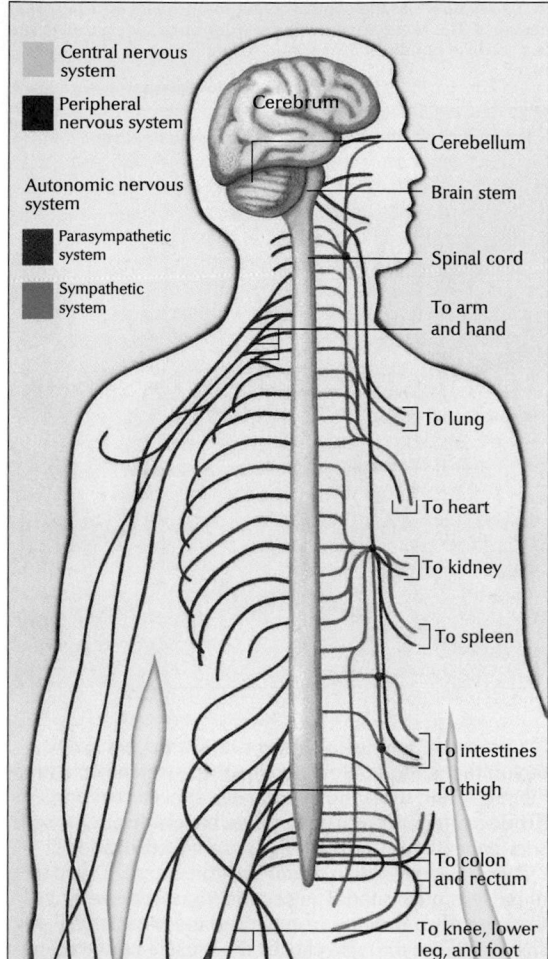

Central nervous system

Peripheral nervous system

Autonomic nervous system

Parasympathetic system

Sympathetic system

Cerebrum

Cerebellum

Brain stem

Spinal cord

To arm and hand

To lung

To heart

To kidney

To spleen

To intestines

To thigh

To colon and rectum

To knee, lower leg, and foot

WORLD BOOK diagram by Lou Bory Associates

The human nervous system has three main parts: (1) the *central nervous system,* (2) the *peripheral nervous system,* and (3) the *autonomic nervous system,* which consists of *sympathetic* and *parasympathetic* divisions. This simplified diagram shows only major nerves. It illustrates peripheral nerves only on the left side of the figure and autonomic nerves only on the right.

to think, use language, and feel emotions. The cerebrum is also the center of learning.

The cerebellum, which is about the size of an orange, is slightly above the brain stem. It helps maintain the body's sense of balance and coordinates muscular movements with sensory information.

The brain stem is a stalklike structure that is connected to the spinal cord at the base of the skull. The brain stem contains neurons that relay information from the sense organs. Many neurons that regulate automatic functions, such as balance, blood pressure, breathing, and heartbeat, are also in the brain stem.

The spinal cord is a cable of neurons that extends from the neck about two-thirds of the way down the backbone. The backbone surrounds and protects the spinal cord. The spinal cord contains pathways that carry sensory information to the brain. It also has pathways

that relay commands from the brain to the motor neurons.

The peripheral nervous system carries all the messages sent between the central nervous system and the rest of the body. The peripheral nervous system consists of 12 pairs of nerves that originate in the brain, plus 31 pairs of nerves of the spinal cord. These cranial and spinal nerves serve as "telephone wires" that carry messages to and from every receptor and effector in the body.

The autonomic nervous system is a special part of the peripheral nervous system. The autonomic nervous system regulates such automatic bodily processes as breathing and digestion without conscious control by the brain. This constant regulation enables the body to maintain a stable internal environment.

The autonomic nervous system has two parts, the *sympathetic system* and the *parasympathetic system.* The sympathetic system responds to the body's needs during increased activity and in emergencies. The actions of the sympathetic system include speeding up the heartbeat, sending additional blood to the muscles, and enlarging the pupils of the eyes to use all available light.

The parasympathetic system, in general, opposes the actions of the sympathetic system. The parasympathetic system's functions include slowing down the heartbeat, diverting blood from the muscles to the stomach and intestines, and contracting the pupils of the eyes. The balance of activity between the two systems is controlled by the central nervous system.

Parts of a neuron

A neuron has three basic parts, the *cell body,* the *axon,* and the *dendrites.* A thin *nerve membrane* surrounds the entire cell.

The cell body of a neuron is a ball-shaped structure about $\frac{1}{1000}$ of an inch (.025 millimeter) wide. Each neuron cell body is a center for receiving and sending nerve impulses. The cell body is also responsible for making proteins and using energy for the maintenance and growth of the nerve cell.

The vast majority of neuron cell bodies are within the central nervous system, where incoming messages are combined and outgoing messages are produced. The few neuron cell bodies outside the central nervous system are grouped into clusters called *ganglia.* The best-known ganglia are in the autonomic nervous system.

The axon, also called the *nerve fiber,* is a tubelike extension of a neuron cell body. The axon is specialized to carry messages. An axon of one neuron may have enough branches to make contact with as many as 1,000 other neurons.

Most axons in the central nervous system are less than $\frac{1}{25}$ of an inch (1 millimeter) long. However, many axons in the peripheral nervous system are longer, and some are much longer. For example, the axons that extend from the spinal cord to the muscles in the feet may be 30 to 40 inches (76 to 100 centimeters) long.

The structures commonly called *nerves* are actually bundles of axons lying next to one another in a cordlike formation. Nerves can be made up of the axons of motor neurons or sensory neurons, or of both.

Some axons are covered by a sheath of a white, fatty substance called *myelin.* The myelin increases the speed

Neurons and nerves   A neuron, *left,* has three basic parts. The *cell body* serves as the control center for the cell's activities. The *axon* is a tubelike extension that carries messages. The *dendrites* are shorter extensions specialized to receive messages. A nerve, *right,* consists of a cordlike bundle of axons from several neurons. The nerve shown runs from the spinal cord to a muscle.

WORLD BOOK diagrams by Lou Bory Associates

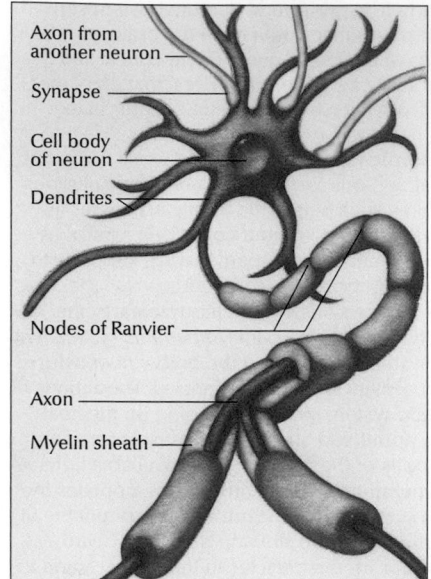

Axon from another neuron
Synapse
Cell body of neuron
Dendrites
Nodes of Ranvier
Axon
Myelin sheath

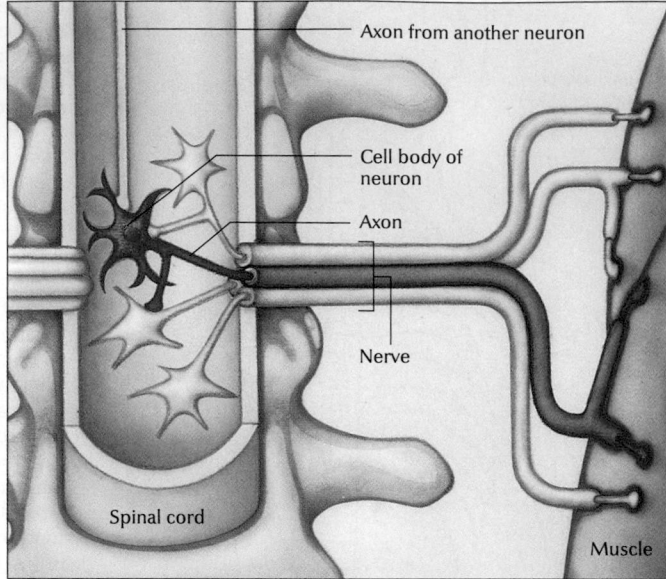

Axon from another neuron
Cell body of neuron
Axon
Nerve
Spinal cord
Muscle

of impulses along the axons. Myelin also causes the distinction between the *gray matter* and *white matter* in the nervous system. Gray matter consists largely of *unmyelinated axons* (axons without myelin sheaths) and neuron cell bodies. White matter consists mostly of axons with white myelin sheaths. Myelin is formed by special supporting cells called *glia* that surround the neuron cell bodies and axons. In the central nervous system, glial cells called *oligodendrocytes* produce myelin. In the peripheral nervous system, the myelin that surrounds the axons is produced by glia called *Schwann cells.*

The **dendrites** of a neuron are branching, tubelike extensions of the cell body that form a pattern resembling the limbs of a tree. Most neuron cell bodies have about six main dendrites, each of which is two or three times as thick as the axon of the cell. The distance between the cell body and the tips of the dendrites is about ⅟₅₀ of an inch (0.5 millimeter).

Dendrites are specialized structures for receiving impulses, mostly from the axon of another neuron. Dendrites and axons do not quite touch each other. In almost all cases, they are separated by an extremely narrow space called the *synaptic cleft,* over which nerve impulses are transmitted. These places where one neuron communicates with another are called *synapses.*

How messages are routed

Simple pathways. Much of the work of the nervous system depends upon established pathways between neurons. These pathways are called *neural circuits.* The simplest kind of neural circuit is a *reflex.* A reflex is an automatic and involuntary response to a stimulus. Simple reflexes do not involve the brain. Impulses in a reflex action follow a simple pathway that goes through the spinal cord and links a receptor and an effector.

One of the simplest reflexes is the *knee jerk reflex.* A tap on the tendon below the kneecap stretches the muscle there, and this action stimulates special receptors to produce an impulse. The impulse travels through a sensory neuron, over an axon to the spinal cord, and through a synapse to a motor neuron. There, a second impulse is generated. The second impulse travels over the axon of a motor neuron back to the muscle that was stretched. The impulse causes the muscle cells to contract and the leg to jerk.

Complex pathways. Many reflexes are more complicated and involve at least one association neuron between the sensory and motor neurons. The association neuron may be connected with many complex neural pathways, some of which may lead to the brain. A common but complex reflex is involved in withdrawing from a painful stimulus. For example, if a person steps on a sharp object, the immediate response is to lift the foot. In addition, association neurons stimulate the muscles of the other leg to adjust and maintain balance. Interconnecting neural pathways to the brain also may be stimulated so that the person is aware of what has happened.

Reflexes alone cannot account for the vast number and variety of actions performed by human beings. People, as well as some other kinds of animals, can learn new behavior patterns. Voluntary muscular movements necessary for learning new skills travel along complex nerve pathways that extend from the brain throughout the body. Complicated actions, such as riding a bicycle or walking, eventually can be performed without constant, conscious control after they have been learned.

How neurons carry impulses

During the 1800's, scientists discovered that nerve impulses involve electrical charges. They assumed a nerve impulse was simply an electric current flowing through nerves. By the 1900's, researchers had learned that different concentrations of certain ions in neurons and in their surrounding fluids create a potential electrical charge. It was also learned that nerve cell membranes have pores that allow only certain substances to pass through. Scientists then theorized that a nerve impulse was an electrochemical process controlled by the nerve cell membrane.

In the 1930's, researchers developed techniques to test the *membrane theory of nerve conduction,* which is the theory discussed in this section. This theory is the accepted explanation of how neurons carry impulses.

The beginning of an impulse. A nerve cell membrane has special protein molecules that control the opening and closing of its pores. When at rest, the membrane keeps the concentration of sodium ions in the neuron very low. The membrane also keeps the concentration of potassium ions and negative organic ions much higher in the cell than in the surrounding fluids. These differences in ion concentration make the inside of the neuron more negative than the outside, and so the membrane is said to be *polarized.* The resulting voltage difference across the membrane is called the *resting potential.*

A chemical, electrical, or mechanical stimulus applied to a neuron can affect the membrane's porosity and change the resting potential. The stimulus can cause the membrane's pores to open and allow more sodium ions into the cell. The increase in sodium ions makes the inside of the cell positively charged, and this voltage change is called a *depolarization.*

When a stimulus causes a neuron to depolarize, the neuron is said to *fire.* The firing is the start of a nerve impulse. A stimulus must be of a certain intensity, called the *threshold voltage,* for a neuron to fire.

All impulses from a particular neuron have the same size and duration, no matter how large the stimulus that caused the neuron to fire. The fact that neurons fire at maximum strength or not at all is called the *all-or-nothing phenomenon.* The brain probably detects the intensity of a stimulus by the frequency of impulses generated and the number of nerve fibers stimulated.

Conduction along the axon. The inside of an axon is filled with a solution that can conduct an electric charge. Depolarizations in one area of an axon spread through the solution to neighboring areas along the axon. This wave of depolarizations is called an *action potential.*

If the axon of a neuron has no myelin sheath, the nerve impulse sweeps continuously along the axon, like fire along a firecracker fuse. But in a myelinated axon, nerve impulses can occur only at the *nodes of Ranvier.* The nodes of Ranvier are areas along an axon where the myelin sheath is interrupted at regular intervals. The impulse hops from node to node.

Transmission across synapses. Certain chemicals, called *neurotransmitters,* transmit nerve impulses across synapses. When an impulse reaches the end of an axon, a neurotransmitter is released into the synaptic cleft. The neurotransmitter moves to the dendrites of the next nerve cell and causes certain pores of the nerve membrane to open. Ions move through these pores, and a voltage change, called a *postsynaptic potential,* results.

The postsynaptic potential is either *excitatory* or *inhibitory.* An excitatory postsynaptic potential spreads to the axon of a nerve cell and tends to produce another action potential. An inhibitory postsynaptic potential tends to prevent the axon from producing another ac–

Transmission of a nerve impulse

The transmission of a nerve impulse is an electrochemical process. Most experts believe the neuron membrane controls this process by selectively allowing ions to enter and leave the cell. These diagrams show how a motor neuron carries a message from an association neuron to an effector.

WORLD BOOK diagrams by Lou Bory Associates

A resting neuron is *polarized*—that is, its inside is more negative than its outside. The membrane maintains the polarity by restricting the flow of ions in and out of the cell.

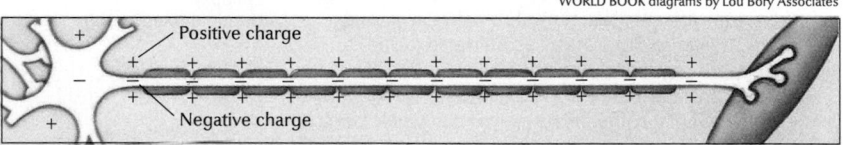

The impulse begins when neurotransmitters from the association neuron change the porosity of the motor neuron's membrane. This change results in depolarization.

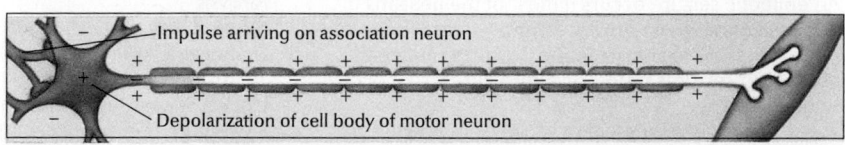

The impulse spreads down a myelinated axon as the depolarization hops from one node of Ranvier to the next. The impulse shown has gone nearly halfway down the axon.

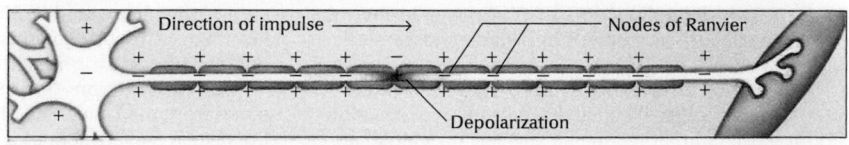

Chemical transmitters are released by specialized structures when the impulse gets to the neuron's end. These chemicals stimulate the effector, in this case a muscle.

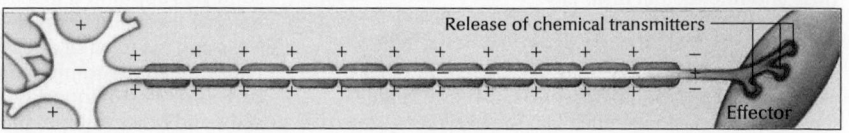

tion potential. Not every impulse that reaches a synapse is transmitted to the next neuron. The synapses thus help regulate and route the constant flow of nerve impulses throughout the nervous system.

Disorders of the nervous system

The nervous system can be damaged by injury and disease. Axons in the central nervous system cannot regrow after being damaged, but nerves in the peripheral nervous system may recover. Severely damaged nerve cells that die cannot be replaced.

Most neurons that perform a specific job are grouped together in the brain. Because of this grouping arrangement, called *localization of function,* damage to one area of the brain may affect only certain abilities and leave others intact. In some cases, undamaged areas of the brain gradually assume control of functions lost when another area of the brain was damaged. This action is called *recovery of function.*

The most common serious disorder of the nervous system is *stroke.* A stroke occurs if the blood supply to a certain area of the brain is cut off, resulting in the death of nerve cells. Stroke victims may lose the ability to perform functions controlled by the damaged area of the brain, such as speaking or moving a limb. Stroke victims may eventually recover some lost functions. But if respiration or some other vital function is affected, a stroke can be fatal.

The most common infectious diseases that affect the nervous system are mild virus infections that last only a few days and may produce headaches. More serious infectious diseases, such as *encephalitis* and *meningitis,* are caused by certain bacteria, viruses, or other microbes. Encephalitis is an inflammation of the brain, and meningitis is an inflammation of the membranes covering the brain and the spinal cord. See **Encephalitis; Meningitis.**

The cause of *multiple sclerosis,* a disease of the nervous system, is not known. Multiple sclerosis causes axons in various areas of the central nervous system to lose their myelin sheaths. As a result, these axons cannot conduct nerve impulses properly.

Another disorder of the nervous system is *epilepsy.* Victims of epilepsy suffer seizures that can cause muscle convulsions and a change in, or loss of, consciousness. An epileptic seizure occurs if most of the neurons in one area of the brain produce bursts of impulses at the same time. Physicians prescribe drugs to reduce the number of seizures or to prevent seizures from occurring at all.

Before the development of vaccines to prevent *poliomyelitis,* this virus disease of the nervous system was widespread. The polio virus can destroy motor neurons in the spinal cord and brain stem, leading to paralysis in some cases.

Some disorders of the nervous system can lead to mental illness or intellectual disability. For information about these conditions, see the articles on **Mental illness** and **Intellectual disability.**

The nervous system in other animals

In vertebrates. All vertebrates, including other mammals, as well as amphibians, birds, fish, and reptiles, have nervous systems much like the nervous system of a human being. The bodies of the nerve cells that make up the nervous systems of these animals are approximately the same size and shape as the bodies of human nerve cells.

The size of a specific area of the brain may indicate the importance of the function of that area for the animal. For example, dogs have a larger and better developed area for smell than do human beings. In contrast, human beings have a larger and more highly developed *cerebral cortex* than other animals. The cerebral cortex is the outer surface of the cerebrum, where such complicated skills as delicate motor control and the use of language are coordinated.

In invertebrates. Most species of invertebrates that consist of more than one cell have some sort of nervous system. Many of the neurons of these animals are larger than human neurons. In hydras and some other simple invertebrates, the nervous system may be a *nerve net,* in which nerve cells are spread throughout the organism. There is no distinction between axons and dendrites in nerve net systems, and impulses travel in all directions from the point of stimulation.

Other invertebrates, including worms and insects, have more complicated, centralized nervous systems. These systems consist largely of concentrations of neurons that form a nerve cord. Ganglia along the cord serve as centers for organizing and integrating various activities of the animals. Clusters of ganglia in the front end of the body act as a primitive "brain." Many insects also have such ganglia in the thorax region. These ganglia coordinate motor activities. The mechanisms of nerve impulses and synaptic potentials in higher invertebrates are the same as those in the human nervous system.   Charles F. Stevens

Related articles in *World Book* include:

Amyotrophic lateral sclerosis	Parkinson disease
Bell's palsy	Plexus
Brain	Poliomyelitis
Cerebrospinal fluid	Prion
Epilepsy	Reflex action
Huntington's disease	Sciatica
Migraine	Senses
Multiple sclerosis	Shingles
Myelin	Sleeping sickness
Neuritis	Spine
Neurofibromatosis	Stroke
Neurology	Tay-Sachs disease
Paralysis	Tourette syndrome

Ness, Eliot (1903-1957), was an American crime fighter. He became known during the late 1920's and early 1930's as a special agent in the Prohibition Bureau of the United States Department of Justice. Ness led a group of law enforcement officers against Chicago gangster Al Capone and his bootlegging activities. Ness's group earned the nickname "the Untouchables" because, unlike many other public officials of the time, they could not be bribed or frightened by mobsters.

Ness was born on April 19, 1903, in Chicago. He graduated from the University of Chicago in 1925. He joined the Justice Department as a special agent in 1928 and soon was appointed to lead an elite squad created to enforce the prohibition law. For more than two years, Ness and his team of about 10 Untouchables raided Capone's bootlegging operations. Ness's squad seized barrels of illegal liquor as well as beer delivery trucks, stills, and other equipment.

From 1935 to 1942, Ness acted as director of public safety in Cleveland, where he cleaned up corruption in the city's police force. From 1942 to 1945, he was director of the federal Social Protection Program, which was set up to handle certain public health issues on military bases. In 1945, Ness became a business executive. In 1947, Ness ran for mayor of Cleveland, but he was defeated. He died on May 7, 1957.

AP/Wide World

Eliot Ness

George T. Felkenes

Ness, Loch. See Loch Ness monster.

Nest is a place that an animal prepares for raising its young. See **Animal** (Animal homes and communities); **Ant** (Nests); **Bee** (The honey bee colony); **Bird** (Building a nest); **Hornet; Squirrel** (Obtaining shelter); **Wasp.**

Nestor. See Messenia.

Net is an open fabric. It is produced by knotting or looping together yarns, cords, wires, or other materials so that there are spaces left between the points where the material intersects. Most nets are made of cotton, nylon, or polyester, but some nets are made of silk.

There are many kinds of nets. Such household items as curtains, hammocks, tablecloths, and bedspreads are made of net. Many sports, including basketball, hockey, soccer, and tennis, feature nets. A type of light, fine net called *tulle* is used in ballet costumes and in veils.

Cargo is often loaded onto ships by means of heavy nets. Heavy nets also play an important role in the fishing industry. Some fishing nets weigh 10,000 pounds (4,500 kilograms) and are 2,000 feet (600 meters) long.

Nets were first made about 13,000 years ago. In the mid-1700's, nets were produced on warp-knitting machines. Today, most nets are made on bobbinet machines or raschel knitting machines.   Christine W. Cole

See also **Fishing industry** (How fish are caught); **Lace.**

Netanyahu, *neh tahn YAH hoo,* **Benjamin** (1949-   ), a Likud Party politician, began his second term as prime minister of Israel in 2009. After inconclusive elections that year, President Shimon Peres asked Netanyahu to form Israel's next government. Netanyahu was previously prime minister from 1996 to 1999.

Netanyahu has criticized the peace agreements between Israel and the Palestine Liberation Organization (PLO). These agreements, reached in the early and middle 1990's, provide for Palestinian self-rule in the Gaza Strip and West Bank, territories Israel had occupied since 1967. Netanyahu has claimed that the agreements did not include enough provisions for Israel, such as guaranteed security and allowance for its population growth.

During Netanyahu's first term as prime minister, Israel's peace negotiations with the PLO stalled. Netanyahu especially angered Palestinians with his decision to expand Israeli West Bank settlements and to build new Israeli housing in East Jerusalem.

Reuters/Archive Photos

Benjamin Netanyahu

Netanyahu was born on Oct. 21, 1949, in Tel Aviv. He served in the Israel Defense Forces from 1967 to 1972. He earned a master's degree in management from the Massachusetts Institute of Technology in 1976. From 1984 to 1988, he was the Israeli ambassador to the United Nations. He was elected to the Knesset (Israeli parliament) in 1988 and served as deputy minister of foreign affairs from 1988 to 1991. Netanyahu was elected leader of Likud in 1993. He resigned as Likud leader in 1999 after losing his bid for re-election as prime minister. From 2002 to 2003, Netanyahu served as Israel's foreign minister. From 2003 to 2005, he served as Israel's finance minister. In 2005, he was again elected leader of Likud.   Bernard Reich

B. A. Argentine, Shostal

Cargo net

Artstreet

Fishing net

© Bas Van Beek, Leo de Wys

Amsterdam, the capital of the Netherlands, is crisscrossed by canals. Canals serve as waterways throughout the Netherlands and help drain the country's low-lying land.

Netherlands

Netherlands is a small country on the North Sea in northwestern Europe. It is bordered by Belgium and Germany. The Netherlands is often called Holland, but this name officially refers only to the western part of the country. The people of the Netherlands call themselves Nederlanders. They are also known as the Dutch.

"God created the world, but the Dutch created Holland," according to an old Dutch saying. More than two-fifths of the country's land was once covered by the sea, or by lakes or swamps. The Dutch "created" this land by pumping out the water. These drained areas, called *polders,* became some of the richest farmlands of the Netherlands.

To make a polder, the Dutch build a dike around the area to be drained of water. The water is then pumped into a series of drainage canals. Windmills were once used to run the pumps, but electric motors have replaced most of them. Most polders are below sea level, and they collect excess water through seepage. As a result, pumping must continue after the polders are built.

The Zuider Zee (pronounced *ZY duhr ZAY),* once a large inlet of the North Sea, was cut off from the sea in 1932 by a dike 20 miles (32 kilometers) long. This changed the Zuider Zee into a freshwater lake called the IJsselmeer *(EYE suhl MEHR).* Much of the lake was then drained to make several large polders. This project added 637 square miles (1,650 square kilometers) of land for new farms and cities. The Netherlands gained an entire new province, Flevoland *(FLEE voh lahnt).*

The people of the Netherlands have great pride in their long battle against the sea. Because their country is one of the most densely populated countries in the world, they take extreme care to protect their hard-won land and to plan wisely the use of every acre. Several times during their history, however, the Dutch have opened the dikes and flooded the land to save their country from invaders.

Most of the Netherlands is flat, though it has some uplands. Many canals cut through the country. They not only drain the land but also serve as waterways.

Dairy farming is the most important form of agriculture in the Netherlands. The processing of dairy products is a major branch of Dutch manufacturing.

The country's rulers have included the Romans, a Germanic people called the Franks, the Spanish, and the French. The Dutch declared independence from Spain in 1581, and Spain recognized their independence in 1648. In 1815, the Netherlands became an independent kingdom united with Belgium. The two countries separated in 1830, when Belgium declared its independence.

The Dutch experienced a period of great prosperity and power—a Golden Age—during the 1600's. At that time, the country was the world's leading sea power, and it ruled a great colonial empire. Amsterdam was an important trading center, and Dutch businesses thrived. The Golden Age was also a time of cultural achievement, especially in painting.

Government

The Netherlands is a constitutional monarchy. It has a democratic government that is based on a constitution. Citizens aged 18 and older may vote.

National government. A king or queen is the country's head of state, but the monarch's duties are mostly ceremonial. The monarch signs all bills that are passed by the parliament and appoints government officials upon the advice of various government bodies.

Dutch monarchs, unlike those of other countries, are not crowned. Instead, they go through a ceremony called *investiture,* in which power is given to them by the people. This practice is based on a medieval tradition. In the Middle Ages—the period from about the A.D. 400's through the 1400's—new leaders traveled from town to town in their realm. They asked for oaths of allegiance from local authorities and, in return, promised to respect the rights of the townspeople. The investiture takes place in Amsterdam, the official capital. Another city, The Hague *(hayg),* is the seat of government.

A prime minister, appointed by the monarch, heads the government. The prime minister selects members of a Cabinet to run the government departments. If the Cabinet and the parliament cannot agree, either the Cabinet resigns, or the parliament is dissolved and a new election is held. The parliament of the Netherlands, the States-General, consists of two houses. The First Chamber has 75 members, who are elected to four-year terms by the legislatures of the country's provinces. The Second Chamber proposes new laws. It has 150 members, who are elected to four-year terms by the people. The members are chosen under a system called *proportional representation.* This system gives each political party a share of seats in the Second Chamber according to its share of the total votes cast.

Local government. The Netherlands is divided into 12 provinces, each governed by a commissioner and a council. The monarch appoints the commissioner. Council members are elected by the people to four-year terms. The number of council members varies according to population. The provinces are made up of *municipalities.* Each municipality has an elected council and an executive called a *burgomaster,* who is appointed by the monarch.

Politics. The largest political parties include the left-wing Dutch Labor and Socialist parties, a centrist party called the Christian Democratic Appeal, and the right-wing People's Party for Freedom and Democracy (also called the Liberal Party). There are also many small parties. No party has held a majority of seats in the Second Chamber since 1945, when World War II ended. Therefore, all governments are formed by party *coalitions* (partnerships).

Courts. The court system in the Netherlands consists of subdistrict courts, district courts, courts of appeal, and the Supreme Court. The monarch appoints all judges.

Armed forces. The Netherlands has an army, a navy, and an air force. All the men and women in the armed forces serve on a voluntary basis.

The Kingdom of the Netherlands. The Netherlands is part of a larger political unit called the Kingdom of the Netherlands. The kingdom also includes several islands in the Caribbean Sea. The islands of Aruba, Curaçao, and St. Martin (St. Maarten) are self-governing territories. All three have an appointed governor and a Council of Ministers headed by a prime minister. Three smaller Caribbean islands—Bonaire, Saba, and St. Eustatius—are overseas municipalities, with a status similar to that of towns in the Netherlands. Each Council of Ministers is responsible to a one-house legislature, whose members are elected by the islanders.

People

About 35 percent of the people of the Netherlands live in two coastal provinces—North Holland and South Holland. In these provinces are the three largest cities—Amsterdam, Rotterdam, and The Hague.

Ancestry. Most of the people in the Netherlands are of Dutch ancestry. The largest non-Dutch groups in the country include people from Indonesia, Morocco, Suriname, and Turkey.

Language. Dutch is the official language of the Netherlands. The Dutch language belongs to the Germanic language group. The people of the northern province of Friesland *(FREEZ lahnt)* speak Frisian *(FRIHZH uhn),* another Germanic language. Most people of the Netherlands also speak English, and many speak French or German as well.

Way of life

The Netherlands is one of the most densely populated countries in the world. Nearly half this small country lies below sea level, so the Dutch must carry on a continuous battle against the sea. Life in this environment has given the Dutch a practical, matter-of-fact outlook. To make the best use of their limited land and avoid overcrowding, the Dutch have developed a highly organized society. Neatness and self-control are prized. The Dutch tend to frown on extravagance and displays of wealth.

Although public life in the Netherlands is highly organized, there is a great deal of freedom in private life. The Dutch value personal privacy. They are also known for their good fellowship, called *gezelligheid (guh ZEHL ihk hyt).* This cozy friendliness among close friends and relatives is most frequently found when celebrating such occasions as birthdays and anniversaries. The Dutch are also interested in foreign countries, and many of them travel and work outside the Netherlands.

City life. For centuries, the Netherlands has been one of Europe's most urbanized regions. Nearly all Dutch cities were founded in the Middle Ages. The historic centers of these cities still have many shops and business and government offices. Public transportation includes subways and streetcars in the large cities.

Most city dwellers live in modern apartments and row houses. Because of high land prices, the cities have few single-family houses. Older residential sections of

Netherlands in brief

General information

Capital: Amsterdam.
Seat of government: The Hague.
Official language: Dutch.
Official name: Koninkrijk der Nederlanden (Kingdom of the Netherlands).
National anthem: "Wilhelmus van Nassouwe" ("William of Nassau").

Largest population centers: (2004 official estimates)

Cities	Metropolitan areas
Amsterdam (739,104)	Amsterdam (1,017,049)
Rotterdam (598,923)	Rotterdam (1,001,447)
The Hague (469,059)	The Hague (616,090)
Utrecht (270,244)	Utrecht (405,467)

The Dutch flag dates from about 1630. Until then, an orange stripe was at the top instead of a red one.

The coat of arms has old symbols of the Dutch royal family. The sword and arrows represent strength in unity.

Land and climate

Land: Netherlands is on the North Sea in northwestern Europe. It is bordered by Belgium and Germany. Most of the Netherlands is flat, though it has some uplands. Part of the country is made up of *polders,* land below sea level that was once covered by water. The Dutch built dikes around these areas and drained the water.

Area: 16,034 mi² (41,528 km²), including 2,929 mi² (7,587 km²) of inland water. *Greatest distances*—north-south, 196 mi (315 km); east-west, 167 mi (269 km). *Coastline*—228 mi (367 km).
Elevation: *Highest*—Vaalserberg, 1,053 ft (321 m) above sea level. *Lowest*—Prins Alexander Polder, 22 ft (6.7 m) below sea level.

Climate: The Netherlands has a mild, damp climate, with moderately warm summers and gentle winters. Temperatures average from 60 to 65 °F (16 to 18 °C) in summer, and a little above 30 °F (–1 °C) in winter. Extremely hot or cold temperatures are rare. Summer is the wettest season, though precipitation is fairly evenly distributed throughout the year. Most regions of the country receive about 25 to 30 inches (63 to 76 centimeters) of precipitation a year.

Government

Form of government: Constitutional monarchy.
Ceremonial head of state: Monarch (king or queen).
Head of government: Prime minister.
Legislature: States-General of two houses: 75-member First Chamber and 150-member Second Chamber.
Executive: Prime minister and Cabinet.
Political subdivisions: 12 provinces.

People

Population: *Estimated 2012 population*—6,726,000. *2008 official estimate*—16,404,282.
Population density: 1,043 per mi² (403 per km²).
Distribution: 82 percent urban, 18 percent rural.
Major ethnic/national groups: Almost entirely Dutch. Largest non-Dutch groups include people from Indonesia, Morocco, Suriname, and Turkey.
Major religions: About 30 percent Roman Catholic, about 20 percent Protestant (mostly Protestant Church in the Netherlands), about 5 percent Muslim. About two-fifths of the Dutch are not members of any church.

Population trend

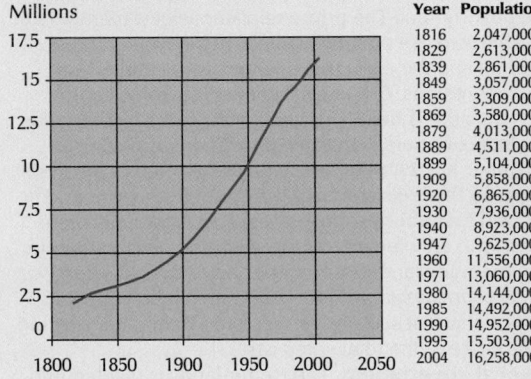

Year	Population
1816	2,047,000
1829	2,613,000
1839	2,861,000
1849	3,057,000
1859	3,309,000
1869	3,580,000
1879	4,013,000
1889	4,511,000
1899	5,104,000
1909	5,858,000
1920	6,865,000
1930	7,936,000
1940	8,923,000
1947	9,625,000
1960	11,556,000
1971	13,060,000
1980	14,144,000
1985	14,492,000
1990	14,952,000
1995	15,503,000
2004	16,258,000

Economy

Chief products: *Agriculture*—beef and dairy cattle, flowers and flower bulbs, hogs, potatoes, poultry, sheep, sugar beets, vegetables, wheat. *Fishing*—eels, herring, mackerel, mussels, plaice, shrimp, sole, whiting. *Manufacturing*—chemicals, dairy products, electronic equipment, machinery, processed meats, transportation equipment. *Mining*—natural gas, petroleum, salt.
Money: *Basic unit*—euro. One hundred cents equal one euro. The Dutch guilder was taken out of circulation in 2002.
Foreign trade: *Major exported goods*—automobiles, chemicals, dairy products, electronics equipment, flowers, meat, petroleum, vegetables. *Major imported goods*—automobiles, chemicals, clothing, electronics equipment, food products, iron and steel, machinery, paper and paper products, petroleum, plastics. *Main trading partners*—Belgium, China, France, Germany, Italy, Japan, Spain, United Kingdom, United States.

the major cities house many immigrants as well as university students and young adults.

Rural life. Because every region of the Netherlands has several cities, few rural areas are truly remote. Farms are commercial businesses, and rural life is not too different from life in the towns. Most villages are accessible by water and are well provided with services and public transportation.

People in farm areas and fishing villages sometimes wear the famous Dutch wooden shoes, called *klompen (KLAHMP uhn)*. These shoes are noisy, but they protect the feet from damp earth better than leather shoes do. The Dutch do not wear wooden shoes in their homes. They leave them outside and change to leather shoes.

In a few rural areas, the people still wear the traditional Dutch costume, which includes full trousers for men and full skirts and lace caps for women. These areas include the islands of the province of Zeeland *(ZAY lahnt)*, coastal fishing communities, and the towns of Staphorst *(STAHP hawrst)* and Spakenburg *(SPAH kuhn burk)*.

Food and drink. The Dutch diet is similar to that of other northern European countries. Breakfasts often consist of bread, cheese, and cold meat. Most people

© Arthur M. Greene, Bruce Coleman, Inc.

Bicycle riders cross an intersection in Gouda, *above*. Bicycling is popular among Dutch people of all ages, both as a recreational activity and as an important means of transportation.

eat a light lunch of a sandwich or salad. Most dinners include meat or fish, potatoes, and vegetables. Indonesian food is also popular. Traditional dishes include *hutspot* (a stew of meat, vegetables, and potatoes, pronounced *HUTS paht)*; raw herring sprinkled with onions; and large, thin pancakes covered with toppings. Beer and *jenever* (a juniper-flavored gin, pronounced *yuh NAY fur)* are popular alcoholic drinks.

Holidays and recreation. Most people in the Netherlands own a bicycle, and bicycle riding is a popular recreational activity. The Dutch also enjoy boating, sailing, and windsurfing on their many lakes, rivers, and canals. Miles of sandy beaches along the North Sea coast provide many places to swim.

Ice skating is extremely popular. But the Netherlands has mild winters, and the ice often does not get thick enough for skating. When the ice is hard enough, schools sometimes close to let the children skate. In exceptionally cold winters, an ice-skating race called the Elfstedentocht *(ehlf STEHD uhn tahkt)* takes place on the waterways of Friesland. The 124-mile (200-kilometer) course connects 11 cities of the northern province.

Every community has sport clubs that organize team sports for youths and adults. The most popular sports include field hockey, soccer, and tennis.

The Netherlands is the world's largest flower exporter, and Nederlanders are famous for raising tulips and other flowers. They hold many spectacular flower festivals each spring. Long parades of floats covered with blue, pink, red, and yellow blossoms wind through the towns near the bulb fields. Homes along the way are also decorated with beautiful floral designs.

The Dutch celebrate Queen's Day, the birthday of former Queen Juliana, on April 30 with local parades, games, and flea markets. Most towns hold a fair called a *kermis (KEHR mihs)* with carnival attractions and other entertainment.

The Dutch exchange gifts on St. Nicholas's Eve, December 5, instead of on Christmas. The children believe that Saint Nicholas visits their homes with presents for

© Glen Allison, Tony Stone Images

A Queen's Day celebration, held annually on April 30, includes a variety of entertainment. *Above,* people gather for festivities at a World War II monument in Amsterdam's Dam Square.

good boys and girls. A man dressed like a bishop represents Saint Nicholas and rides through the streets on a white horse. In Amsterdam, he arrives by steamship and is greeted by ringing bells and cheering crowds.

During the 1600's, the Dutch brought the custom of Saint Nicholas's visit with them to America. There, the English settlers changed his Dutch nickname, *Sinterklaas,* to *Santa Claus.*

Religion. Roman Catholics make up about 30 percent of the population. About 20 percent of the people are Protestants, most belonging to the Protestant Church in the Netherlands. The royal family traditionally belongs to this church, but it is not an official state church. Muslims make up about 5 percent of the population. About 40 percent of the people do not practice any religion.

Education. Dutch law requires children from ages 5 through 16 to go to school. All schools that meet national educational standards, including religious schools, receive government funds. The standards, set by law, include courses of study and hiring of teachers. Almost all adults can read and write. The Netherlands has no general high school program. Instead, it has several kinds of high schools. Each kind trains students for a special purpose, such as university work, advanced study in various institutes, or jobs in business or industry.

The Netherlands has several universities and many specialized institutions of higher education. Leiden University, founded in 1575, is the country's oldest university. The University of Amsterdam, the University of Groningen, and Utrecht University—all founded in the 1600's—are among the largest universities. The Open University, based in Heerlen, also has a large number of students. Founded in 1984, it carries out most of its instruction over the Internet.

Arts. The Netherlands has produced some of the world's greatest painters. During the 1600's, the country's Golden Age, the northern Netherlands was a republic. Without a royal court to order works of art, Dutch artists had to sell their creations to the country's prosperous bankers, merchants, and traders. Dutch buyers looked for small paintings suitable for private homes, rather than large-scale religious works, so Dutch artists often painted ordinary people and things. Frans Hals became a master painter of portraits. Pieter de Hooch *(PEE tuhr duh HOHK)* and Jan Vermeer *(yahn vuhr MEER)* often painted indoor scenes. Jacob van Ruisdael *(YAH kawp vahn ROYS dahl)* specialized in landscapes. Rembrandt painted masterpieces on many subjects.

Later Dutch painters include Vincent van Gogh and Piet Mondrian. Van Gogh, who painted in the late 1800's, is one of the most famous painters in modern art. Mondrian, who developed his extremely simplified geometric style of painting in the early 1900's, influenced modern architecture and commercial design as well as painting. Many museums in the Netherlands exhibit the works of the great Dutch artists. Among them are the Rijksmuseum and Stedelijk Museum in Amsterdam and the Gemeentemuseum in The Hague.

The Dutch enjoy reading and support many writers. But Dutch literature is little known outside the Netherlands, and few works have been translated. One of the most important Dutch writers is Joost van den Vondel *(YOHST vahn dehn VAHN duhl),* a celebrated poet and playwright of the Golden Age. Constantijn Huygens

Netherlands map index

*Does not appear on map; key shows general location.
†Populations are for municipalities, which may include rural areas as well as the urban center.
‡Population of metropolitan area, including suburbs.
Source: 2004 official estimates.

Netherlands
political map

International boundary
Expressway
Other road
Railroad
Canal
⊛ National capital
★ Provincial capital
• Other city

WORLD BOOK map

North

North Sea

East Frisian Islands

Norderney
Juist
Borkum
Borkum
Norden
Rottumeroog
Schiermonnikoog
Rottumeroog
Lauwerszee
Emden
Zoutkamp
Uithuizen
Appingedam
Delfzijl
Dollard Bay

West Frisian Islands

Terschelling
West Terschelling
Oost Vlieland
Vlieland
De Koog
Texel
Den Helder
Den Oever

Waddenzee

Ameland
Hollum
Schiermonnikoog
Holwerd
Dokkum
Buitenpost
Leeuwarden
Franeker
Harlingen
Bolsward
Sneek
Workum
Staveren

GRONINGEN
Groningen
Hoogezand-Sappemeer
Veendam
Winschoten
Oude Pekela
Aschendorf
Stadskanaal
Musselkanaal
Ter Apel
Emmen
Meppen

FRIESLAND

Bergum
Drachten
Roden
Makkinga
Heerenveen
Wolvega
★ Assen
Beilen
DRENTHE
Hoogeveen
Coevorden

BARRIER DAM
53°

North Holland Canal

Wieringermeer Polder
Schagen
Medemblik
Enkhuizen
Lemmer
Northeast Polder
Emmeloord
Urk
Staphorst
Steenwijk

IJsselmeer

Bergen aan Zee
Bergen
Heerhugowaard
Alkmaar
Egmond aan Zee
Heiloo
Hoorn
FLEVOLAND
Kampen
Staphorst
Hardenberg
Ommen
Nordhorn
Neuenhaus
Lingen

Markermeer

Heemskerk
Beverwijk
Velsen
Edam
Purmerend
Lelystad
Dronten
Elburg
Zwolle
Raalte
Den Ham
Ootmarsum
NORTH HOLLAND
Zaandam
Marken
Flevoland Polder
OVERIJSSEL
Hellendoorn
Almelo
Oldenzaal

North Sea Canal

Haarlem
Zandvoort
Heemstede
⊛ Amsterdam
Almere
Harderwijk
Nunspeet
Epe
Olst
Nijverdal
Borne
Hengelo
Losser
Ochtrup

Noordwijk
Lisse
Amstelveen
Weesp
Huizen
Ermelo
Deventer
Goor
Enschede
Grönau

NETHERLANDS

Katwijk aan Zee
Aalsmeer
Bussum
Spakenburg
Nijkerk
Apeldoorn
Lochem
Haaksbergen
Wassenaar
Hilversum
Baarn
Leiden
Alphen aan den Rijn
UTRECHT
Soest
Amersfoort
Voorst
Zutphen
Ahaus

The Hague
SOUTH HOLLAND
Woerden
Maarssen
De Bilt
Barneveld
Brummen
Groenlo

Monster
Rijswijk
Delft
Zoetermeer
Zeist
Ede
GELDERLAND
Rheden
Doetinchem
Winterswijk
Coesfeld
52° North Latitude
52°

Hoek van Holland
Naaldwijk
Maassluis
Gouda
Veenendaal
Renkum
★ Arnhem
Aalten
EUROPOORT
Rotterdam
Schoonhoven
Rhenen
Wageningen
Zevenaar
Bocholt
Borken

Haringvliet
Vlaardingen
Ridderkerk
Culemborg
Tiel
Waal
Nijmegen
Emmerich

Ouddorp
Spijkenisse
Sliedrecht
Gorinchem
Leerdam
Kleve
Haltern

Zwijndrecht
Dordrecht
Zaltbommel
Oss
Wijchen
Goch

Middelharnis
Willemstad
Waalwijk
Grave
Cuijk
Wesel
Dorsten

Zierikzee
Oosterhout
Vught
's Hertogenbosch
Uden
Boxmeer
Kevelaer
Dinslaken
Gelsenkirchen
Herne

Oosterschelde
Domburg
Stavenisse
Steenbergen
Etten
Dongen
NORTH BRABANT
Veghel
Venray
Geldern
Oberhausen
Bochum

Middelburg
Goes
Roosendaal
Breda
Gilze
Tilburg
Boxtel
Gemert
Deurne
GERMANY
Duisburg
Essen

ZEELAND
Zundert
Oirschot
Boxtel
Helmond
Krefeld

Vlissingen
Borssele
Bergen op Zoom
Eindhoven
Venlo

Oostburg
Terneuzen
Hulst
Veldhoven
Geldrop
Asten
Tegelen
Krefeld
Wuppertal
Remscheid
Solingen

Maldegem
Sas van Gent
Antwerp
Turnhout
Valkenswaard
LIMBURG
Roermond
Neuss
Mönchengladbach

Eeklo
Zelzate
Brasschaat
Herentals
Lommel
Weert
Echt
Düsseldorf

Ghent
Lokeren
Sint-Niklaas
Lier
Mol
Bree
Leverkusen

Dendermonde
Mechelen
Geel
Beringen
Julianakanaal
Sittard
51°

Aalst
Aarschot
Diest
Genk
Geleen
Brunssum
Jülich
Cologne

BELGIUM
Hasselt
Meerssen
Heerlen
Kerkrade
Düren
Troisdorf

Waregem
Louvain
Tienen
Maastricht ★
Vaals
Aachen
Eschweiler
Bonn

Ninove
⊛ Brussels
Sint-Truiden
Tongeren
Esther

Geraardsbergen
Halle
Wavre
Euskirchen

Ronse
Enghien
Braine-l'Alleud
Nivelles
Waremme
Liège
Verviers
Gembloux

Tournai
Ath
Soignies

0   25   50   75   100   125   150 Miles
0 25 50 75 100 125 150 175 200 225 Kilometers

In the Rijksmuseum in Amsterdam, visitors admire Rembrandt's famous painting *The Night Watch*. The Netherlands has many museums that exhibit masterpieces of Dutch art. The country has produced some of the world's greatest painters.

© Bas Van Beek, Leo de Wys

(KAHN stuhn TYN HY guhnz), another figure of the Golden Age, produced witty, elegant verse.

Other important writers include Willem Bilderdijk *(VIHL uhm BIHL duhr DYK)*, Multatuli *(MUL tuh TOO lee)*, and Louis Couperus *(loo EE koo PAY ruhs)*. Bilderdijk, a poet of the late 1700's and early 1800's, foreshadowed the Romantic era. Multatuli, the pen name of Eduard Douwes Dekker, was the author of *Max Havelaar* (1860), a novel about life in the Dutch East Indies that exposed the corruption and misrule there. Couperus, who wrote in the late 1800's and early 1900's, was acclaimed for his psychological novels. Famous Dutch novelists of the 1900's include Willem Frederik Hermans, Harry Mulisch, and Gerard Reve.

Among the better-known Dutch composers are organist Jan Pieterszoon Sweelinck *(yahn PEE tuhr SOHN SVAY lihngk)*, who achieved renown at the beginning of the 1600's for his organ compositions, and Willem Pijper *(VIHL uhm PY puhr)*, a leading composer in the first half of the 1900's. Several Dutch cities have fine symphony orchestras. The Royal Concertgebouw *(kahn SAIRT guh bow)* Orchestra of Amsterdam is world famous.

The land

The Netherlands has four main land regions: (1) the Dunes, (2) the Polders, (3) the Sand Plains, and (4) the Southern Uplands.

The Dunes are high, sandy ridges where tall grasses often grow. This region curves in a line along the country's entire North Sea coast. In the north, the line consists of the West Frisian Islands. The line is unbroken in the center, but it is broken in the south by wide river outlets.

The Polders lie mostly below sea level and are protected from the sea by sand dunes or by dikes. The Prins Alexander Polder, the lowest point in the Netherlands, is near Rotterdam. It lies 22 feet (6.7 meters) below sea level. The Polders region forms more than two-fifths of the country. It consists of flat, fertile areas of clay soils once covered by seas, swamps, or lakes. It has some of the country's most productive farmlands and largest cities.

Much of the southern part of the Polders consists of marshy islands and peninsulas that make up a delta. The delta is formed by the Maas *(mahs)* and Schelde *(SKEHL duh)* rivers and branches of the Rhine River. Massive dams prevent the sea from flooding the region. One of the dams has huge floodgates that allow salt water and natural tides to enter the protected area. This preserves the natural environment and the fishing economy of the region. During storms, the floodgates can be closed.

The Sand Plains lie less than 100 feet (30 meters) above sea level in most places. In the southwest, the region rises higher. Low, sandy ridges cross the plains

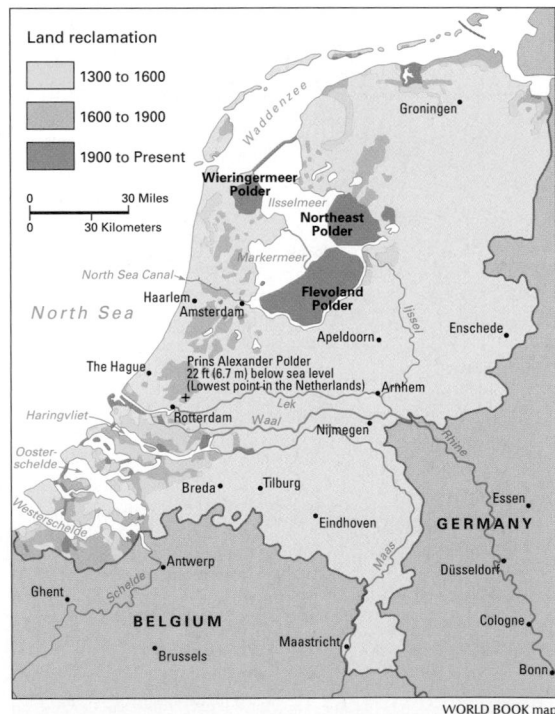

WORLD BOOK map

The Dutch have "created" land for centuries by pumping out the water that covered it. The drained areas are called *polders*. This map shows the development of polders since 1300.

and create a rolling landscape. Orchards are in the east. Forests cover much of the region. A broad valley of clay soils lies along the banks of the Maas, called the Meuse in French, and along the branches of the Rhine. These rivers and the canals that connect them with other rivers form an important transportation network.

The Southern Uplands form the highest land region. The highest point, Vaalserberg *(VAHL suhr behrk)*, rises 1,053 feet (321 meters) above sea level near Maastricht *(MAHS trihkt)*. The region has naturally fertile soils.

Climate

The Netherlands has a mild, damp climate. It has gentle winters and moderately warm summers. The sky is frequently overcast in winter, and fog often covers the land. Temperatures average from 60 to 65 °F (16 to 18 °C) in summer and a little above 30 °F (–1 °C) in winter. Extremely hot or cold temperatures are rare.

The Netherlands is small in area, and there are no great differences of climate from region to region. Most areas of the country receive about 25 to 30 inches (63 to 76 centimeters) of *precipitation* (rain, melted snow, and other forms of moisture) in a year. Summer is the wettest season, but precipitation is fairly evenly distributed throughout the year. The Dutch weather is changeable, and showers may fall unexpectedly.

Floods threaten the Netherlands from two directions. North Sea storms pound against the coastal dunes and sea dikes. Rain-swollen rivers, especially the Maas and the Rhine, press against the river dikes. Dike breaks in the past have resulted in many floods, sometimes with

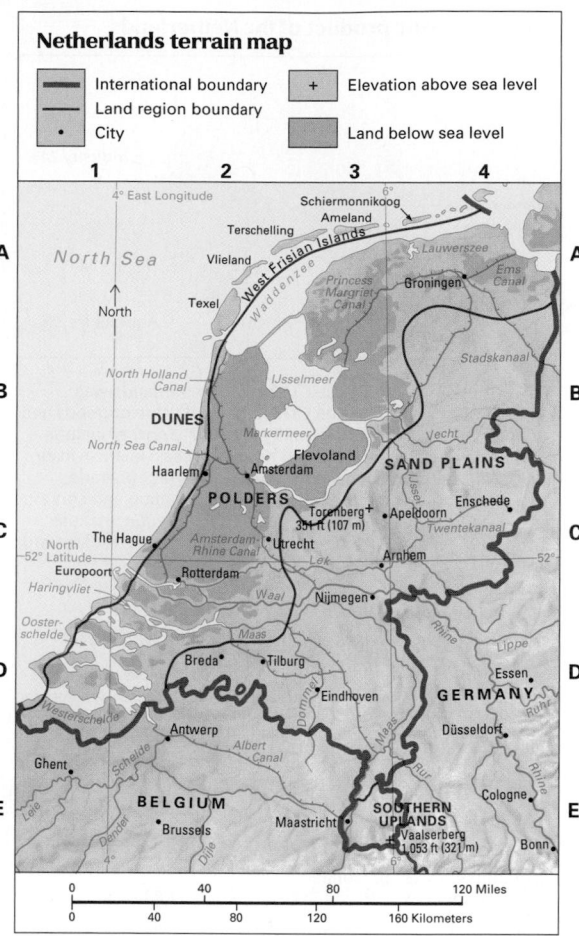

Netherlands terrain map

International boundary	+ Elevation above sea level
Land region boundary	Land below sea level
• City	

WORLD BOOK map

Physical features

Amsterdam-Rhine Canal	C	2	North Sea Canal	B	2
Dunes (region)	B	2	Oosterschelde	D	1
Ems Canal	A	4	Polders (region)	C	2
Europoort	C	1	Princess Margriet Canal	A	3
Flevoland (polder)	B	3	Rhine River	D	4
Haringvliet	C	1	Sand Plains (region)	C	4
IJsselmeer	B	3	Schelde River	E	1
IJssel River	C	3	Southern Uplands (region)	E	3
Lauwerszee	A	4	Vaalserberg (mountain)	E	3
Lek River	C	3	Vecht River	B	4
Maas River	D	3	Waal River	D	2
Markermeer	B	2	Waddenzee	A	2
North Holland Canal	B	2	Westerschelde	D	1
North Sea	A	1	West Frisian Islands	A	2

great loss of life. For example, a massive flood along the North Sea coast in 1953 caused about 1,800 deaths. The country is so low-lying that it would be flooded if global warming melted polar ice and raised the sea level.

Economy

The economy of the Netherlands is technically advanced and highly industrialized. Because the country has few natural resources, it depends heavily on foreign trade. Industries import most raw materials and export finished products. Modern farming techniques have made the small amount of farmland highly productive.

Service industries, taken together, account for about three-fourths of both the country's employment and its *gross domestic product* (GDP)—the total value of goods and services produced within the country in a year. Fi-

© Henk van der Leeden, The Picture Box

A polder is an area that was once covered by water. The Dutch built dikes around these areas and drained the water. This fertile land is an example of the many polders in the Netherlands.

Gross domestic product of the Netherlands

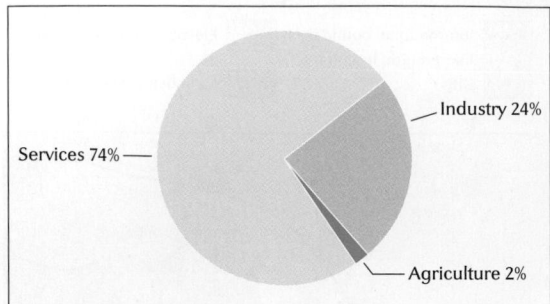

The gross domestic product (GDP) of the Netherlands was $776,211,000,000 in 2007. The GDP is the total value of goods and services produced within a country in a year. *Services* include community, social, personal, and health services; finance, insurance, real estate, and business services; government; trade, restaurants, hotels, and repair shops; transportation and communication; and utilities. *Industry* includes construction, manufacturing, and mining. *Agriculture* includes agriculture, fishing, and forestry.

Production and workers by economic activities

Economic activities	Percent of GDP produced	Employed workers Number of persons	Percent of total
Finance, insurance, real estate, & business services	28	1,897,000	22
Trade, restaurants, hotels, & repair shops	15	1,749,000	20
Manufacturing	14	923,000	11
Community, social, personal & health services	12	1,880,000	22
Government	11	898,000	10
Transportation & communication	7	474,000	6
Construction	6	495,000	6
Mining	3	8,000	*
Agriculture, forestry, & fishing	2	259,000	3
Utilities	2	30,000	*
Total	**100**	**8,613,000**	**100**

*Less than one-half of 1 percent.
Figures are for 2007.
Sources: Netherlands Central Bureau of Statistics, International Monetary Fund.

nance, insurance, real estate, and business services make up the leading service industry group. These services provide more than a fourth of the country's GDP—much more than any other industry group. Trade, restaurants, hotels, and repair shops combine to form the second most important service industry group.

Manufacturing accounts for about a seventh of the GDP. Several large international manufacturers have headquarters in the Netherlands. For example, Royal Philips Electronics, one of the world's largest electronics firms, has its headquarters in Amsterdam. The company produces medical equipment, lighting, household appliances, and consumer electronics. Other manufacturers produce automobiles and trucks, small commercial airplanes, and industrial machinery.

Food processing is a major manufacturing industry.

Dairy products are the chief food products. The Netherlands is one of the world's major cheese manufacturers. Other Dutch food products include beer, chocolate, processed meats, and sugar.

The chemical and petroleum industries are also important to the nation's economy. Rotterdam is the site of a huge complex of chemical plants and oil refineries. Amsterdam has long been a famous center of diamond cutting and polishing. Delft is known for producing earthenware pottery called *delftware*.

Agriculture. Because land is scarce, Dutch farmers work to make their soil as productive as possible. Most farms are under 75 acres (30 hectares). But by fertilizing the soil heavily and using modern equipment, Dutch farmers have become specialized producers of products sold throughout the world. The value of agricultural exports is larger than the value of agricultural imports.

More than half of the country's total land area is farmland. Dairy farming is the most important branch of agriculture. Most dairy farmers also raise crops, mainly to feed their livestock. The grazing land supports millions of cattle, chiefly dairy cows. Dutch farmers also raise beef cattle, hogs, poultry, and sheep.

Economy of the Netherlands

This map shows the economic uses of land in the Netherlands. It also indicates the country's main farm products, its chief mineral deposits, and its most important fishing products. Major manufacturing centers are shown in red.

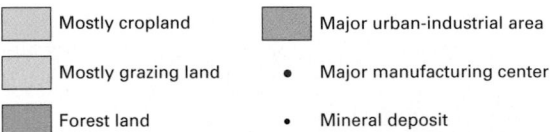

WORLD BOOK map

© Jose Fusta Raga

Modern windmills stand among dairy cows in the picture shown here. Dairy farming is the country's most important branch of agriculture.

© Zefa from The Stock Market

Tulip fields add splashes of color to the flat land of the Netherlands. Flowers and flower bulbs are important products of Dutch agriculture. Fresh flowers are flown to places all over the world.

The country's principal crops include potatoes, sugar beets, tomatoes, and wheat. An important specialty of Dutch agriculture is horticulture. Flowers and vegetables are grown in enormous greenhouses. They are trucked to neighboring countries, and fresh flowers are flown to most parts of the world. Flower bulbs, especially tulip bulbs, are also important.

Mining. The Netherlands has large deposits of natural gas and salt, and some petroleum. One of the world's largest natural gas fields lies near Slochteren *(SLAHK tuh ruhn)*, in the northeastern province of Groningen *(GROH nihng uhn)*. Oil wells operate offshore in the North Sea.

Fishing. The fish catch comes mainly from coastal waters and inlets, and from the North Sea. The major catches include eels, herring, mackerel, mussels, plaice, shrimp, sole, and whiting.

Energy sources. The Netherlands is a major producer of natural gas. But its oil wells supply only a small part of its petroleum needs. Natural gas provides most of the country's energy, and hydroelectric power, nuclear power, and petroleum provide most of the rest.

International trade. The Netherlands relies heavily on foreign trade because it has few natural resources. Its chief trading partner is Germany. Other important trading partners are Belgium, China, France, Italy, Japan, Spain, the United Kingdom, and the United States. The Netherlands exports more goods to other European Union countries than it imports. It imports more from the United States and Asian countries than it exports.

The main imports of the Netherlands include automobiles, chemicals, clothing, electronics equipment, food, iron and steel, machinery, paper and paper products, petroleum, and plastics. Among the exports are automobiles, chemicals, dairy products, electronics equipment, flowers, meat, petroleum, and vegetables.

Transportation. The Netherlands has an extensive network of navigable rivers and canals. The main rivers and many canals are important waterways. Barges on these waterways carry much of the country's freight. The country's railroads provide fast and frequent service.

© B&U International Picture Service

An oil refinery in Rotterdam processes petroleum. Rotterdam has a large complex of chemical plants and oil refineries. Oil wells operate off the shores of the Netherlands in the North Sea.

The Netherlands has an excellent network of paved roads. Almost all Dutch families own an automobile, and most people have a bicycle. The bicycle remains important for transportation as well as recreation. Bike paths are found throughout the country. Motor-driven bicycles called *bromfietsen* (pronounced *BRAHM feet suhn*), which literally means *roar bikes*, are common.

Rotterdam is Europe's busiest seaport. It serves as a gateway to and from much of Europe by way of the Rhine River, one of Europe's busiest inland waterways. Amsterdam, the second largest port in the Netherlands, is linked to the North Sea by the North Sea Canal, one of the world's deepest and widest artificial waterways. The canal is about 50 feet (15 meters) deep and 525 feet (160 meters) wide.

The country's most important airport, Schiphol *(SKIHP hohl),* near Amsterdam, is one of the busiest airports in Europe. KLM Royal Dutch Airlines has headquarters there. Established in 1919, KLM (now part of Air France-KLM) is the oldest airline in the world still in operation.

Communication. The Netherlands has many national and regional daily newspapers. The largest paper is *De Telegraaf,* published in Amsterdam and sold throughout the country.

Traditionally, private broadcasting companies have prepared most programs for the radio and television networks. Most of these companies represent political, religious, or cultural groups. In the late 1900's, commercial broadcasting emerged to supplement the traditional programming. Cable television also opened the country to a variety of foreign and commercial programs. Private firms provide postal and telecommunications services.

History

Early days. In the 50's B.C., Roman soldiers under Julius Caesar invaded what are now the Netherlands, Belgium, and Luxembourg. The Romans conquered much of the region, now called the Low Countries. The word *Netherlands* means *Low Countries,* but the Low Countries also include Belgium and Luxembourg.

In the A.D. 400's, a Germanic people called the Franks drove the Romans out of the Low Countries. The Frankish kingdom broke apart during the 800's. In 870, the Low Countries were divided between the East and West Frankish kingdoms (later Germany and France). The area that is now the Netherlands became part of the East Frankish kingdom.

The rise of commerce. Local dukes, counts, and bishops became increasingly powerful as the region developed. During the 1100's, trade and industry began to expand rapidly in the Low Countries. Fishing, shipbuilding, shipping, and textile manufacturing became especially important. Towns began to develop and grow.

Spanish control. Beginning in the 1300's, the French dukes of Burgundy won control of most of the Low Countries through inheritance, marriage, purchase, and war. The marriage of Mary of Burgundy to Maximilian of the House of Habsburg in 1477 joined the Low Countries with the Habsburg empire. In 1516, Mary and Maximilian's grandson Charles inherited the kingdom of Spain, putting the Low Countries under Spanish control. In 1519, Charles also became Archduke of Austria and Holy Roman Emperor Charles V.

Eighty Years' War. During the early 1500's, a Protestant movement called the Reformation spread through the Low Countries. Charles tried to stop this threat to Roman Catholicism by persecuting Protestants. Charles gave up rule of the Low Countries and of Spain, in 1555 and 1556, to his son, Philip II. Philip stepped up the struggle against Protestants and tried to take complete power over the Low Countries. In 1566, the people began to rebel. In 1568, William I (called the Silent), prince of Orange, led the nobles in revolt.

The Spanish troops were generally successful in land battles, but the rebels' ships controlled the sea. The Spaniards attacked Leiden in 1573, but the city held out bravely. In 1574, the people opened dikes that held back the sea, and a Dutch fleet sailed over the floodwaters to rescue Leiden from the Spaniards.

By 1579, the revolt had started to break apart. The southern provinces of the Low Countries (now Belgium) returned to Spanish control. Protestantism became stronger in the northern provinces (now the Netherlands). In 1579, most northern provinces formed the Union of Utrecht and pledged to continue the revolt.

On July 26, 1581, the northern provinces declared their independence from Spain, beginning what later became known as the Dutch Republic or the Netherlands. The Dutch fought for their freedom until 1648, except for a temporary peace from 1609 to 1621. Spain finally recognized Dutch independence in 1648.

Prosperity and power. The 1600's were the Golden Age of the Netherlands. The country became the leading sea power. Its merchant fleet tripled in size between 1600 and 1650, and the Dutch accounted for about half of Europe's shipping. Dutch explorers, including Willem Barents *(VIHL uhm BAHR uhnts)* and Abel Janszoon Tasman *(AH buhl YAHN sohn TAZ muhn),* found new sea routes and fisheries. Amsterdam became a great trading center of Europe. Dutch banks and businesses thrived. The Golden Age also brought major cultural achievements, especially in painting.

During the Golden Age, the Dutch Republic developed a great colonial empire. In 1602, Dutch firms trading with the East Indies combined to form the Dutch East India Company. The company founded Batavia (now Jakarta, Indonesia) as its headquarters. Company forces

Important dates in the Netherlands

50's B.C. Julius Caesar conquered much of the Low Countries, including what is now the Netherlands.

A.D. 400's-800's The Franks controlled the region.

870 The Netherlands became part of the East Frankish kingdom (now Germany).

1300's-1400's The French dukes of Burgundy united most of the Low Countries.

1516 Charles, ruler of the Low Countries, became King Charles I of Spain. In 1519, Charles became Holy Roman Emperor Charles V.

1581 The Dutch declared their independence from Spain.

1648 Spain recognized Dutch independence.

1600's The Netherlands became the world's major sea power and developed a great colonial empire.

1795-1813 France controlled the Netherlands.

1815 The Netherlands became an independent kingdom united with Belgium.

1830 Belgium revolted and became independent.

1940-1945 Germany occupied the Netherlands in World War II.

1949 The Netherlands granted independence to the Netherlands Indies (now Indonesia).

1954 The colonies of Suriname and Netherlands Antilles became equal partners in the Dutch kingdom.

1957 The Netherlands helped form the European Economic Community, a forerunner of the European Union (EU).

1962 The Netherlands gave up its last colony, West New Guinea (now the Papua region of Indonesia).

1975 Suriname became a fully independent nation.

1992 The Netherlands and 11 other European nations signed the Treaty on European Union, an agreement establishing the EU, in the Dutch city of Maastricht.

2010 The Netherlands Antilles broke apart into separate political units.

The Golden Age of the Netherlands was the 1600's. During this period, the country became a leading sea power, and it developed an extensive colonial empire. Ships bringing goods to and from Amsterdam, *above,* made the city one of the greatest trading centers of Europe.

largely drove the British and Portuguese out of what later became the Netherlands Indies (now Indonesia). The company also took control of Ceylon (now Sri Lanka) and colonized the southern tip of Africa. From the mid-1600's to the mid-1800's, the Dutch were the only Westerners allowed to trade with Japan.

The Dutch West India Company was founded in 1621 to trade in the New World and western Africa. In 1624, the company colonized New Netherland, which consisted of parts of present-day New York, New Jersey, Connecticut, and Delaware. In 1626, the colony's governor, Peter Minuit, bought Manhattan Island from the Indians for goods worth about $24. Dutch colonists had established New Amsterdam (now New York City) there the year before. From 1630 to 1654, the Dutch controlled Brazil. During that time, the Dutch also acquired a number of islands in the West Indies, including Aruba, Curaçao, and Saint Martin (spelled Sint Maarten in Dutch).

Wars with England and France. The Netherlands fought three naval wars with England from 1652 to 1674. The English hoped to seize the shipping and trading leadership from the Dutch, but they failed. During this period, the Dutch won what is now Suriname from the English, and the English gained New Netherland.

France and England formed a secret alliance against the Dutch Republic in 1670 and attacked it in 1672. The Dutch fleet prevented the English from landing by sea, but French troops seized a number of Dutch towns. William III, prince of Orange, was then elected *stadholder* (governor). He stopped the French by opening some dikes and flooding the land. Spanish and German troops also helped the Dutch. The English suffered major defeats at sea, and they made peace with the Dutch in 1674. The French were driven out, and they signed a peace treaty in 1678.

William's wife, Mary, was a member of the English royal family. In 1688, in what is called the Glorious Revolution, English leaders asked William to lead an invasion to overthrow the English King James II. In 1689, William and Mary became joint monarchs of England as William III and Mary II. The Netherlands, England, and other European countries battled France in two more wars, fought from 1689 to 1697 and from 1701 to 1714.

The 1700's. The long wars against France exhausted the Netherlands. Dutch industry and trade faltered, and the Netherlands entered a period of economic decline.

During the American Revolution (1775-1783), the Dutch aided the Americans against the British. Britain started a naval war against the Dutch in 1780. The Dutch were severely defeated by 1784. In 1795, the weakened Netherlands fell to invading French troops. The Dutch supporters of the French renamed the country the Batavian Republic and set up a new government. Britain seized most of the Dutch overseas possessions.

Independence. In 1806, Napoleon I of France forced the Dutch to accept his brother Louis as their king. The Batavian Republic became the Kingdom of Holland. Napoleon wanted tighter control over the country and made it part of France in 1810. The Dutch drove out the French in 1813.

In 1814 and 1815, Europe's political leaders remapped much of the continent at a series of meetings called the Congress of Vienna. They united Belgium, Holland, and Luxembourg into the Kingdom of the Netherlands to limit the power of France. William VI, prince of Orange, became King William I of the Netherlands and Grand Duke of Luxembourg.

The customs, economies, languages, and religions of the Dutch and the Belgians differed greatly. The majority of Belgians were Roman Catholics, and the upper classes spoke French. In 1830, Belgium declared its independence from the Kingdom of the Netherlands.

Luxembourg ended its political ties with the Dutch royal family in 1890. That year, 10-year-old Wilhelmina had become queen after the death of her father, William III. But Luxembourg's laws did not permit a female ruler.

The Netherlands stayed neutral during World War I (1914-1918). But the naval operations of the warring countries interfered with Dutch shipping and trading.

World War II. On May 10, 1940, during World War II, German troops invaded the Netherlands. Four days later, German bombers destroyed much of Rotterdam. The

After World War II, much of the Netherlands lay in ruins. For example, central Rotterdam, *shown here,* was destroyed, and its great port was crippled. The Dutch quickly rebuilt their country.

Dutch army surrendered. Most of the Dutch navy escaped capture and supported the Allies, the countries opposing Germany and its partners.

During the German occupation, from 1940 to 1945, the Dutch suffered greatly. The Germans killed about 75 percent of the nation's Jews—about 104,000 people—mostly in death camps. They also forced thousands of other Netherlanders to work in German factories. The Dutch resistance movement secretly published newspapers, hid Jews from capture, and committed acts of sabotage against the Germans. By the time Germany surrendered to the Allies in May 1945, about 250,000 Netherlanders had been killed or had starved to death.

The Netherlands was also involved in the war in the Pacific Ocean. In March 1942, the Netherlands Indies (now Indonesia) fell to Germany's ally Japan after the defeat of the Dutch fleet. The tens of thousands of Dutch then residing in the Indies became prisoners in Japanese camps.

Economic recovery. World War II left much of the Netherlands in ruins. Many of the nation's factories, bridges, and railroad lines had been destroyed. The great harbor at Rotterdam was crippled. Much of the land was flooded as a result of damage to the dikes.

After the war, the Dutch dedicated themselves to rebuilding their country, and the government supported close international cooperation to achieve this goal. In 1945, the Netherlands became a charter member of the United Nations (UN). In 1948, the Netherlands joined with Belgium and Luxembourg to eliminate all tariffs on trade among themselves, forming an organization called Benelux. In 1949, the Netherlands became part of the North Atlantic Treaty Organization (NATO), a defense alliance of European and North American nations.

In the 1950's, the Netherlands helped form the European Coal and Steel Community, the European Atomic Energy Community (Euratom), and the European Economic Community. These agencies later became the basis for the European Union, which works for economic and political cooperation among its members.

By 1955, Dutch industrial production had increased

about 60 percent over the pre-World War II level. Farm output was almost 20 percent greater.

Political changes. In 1948, the aging Queen Wilhelmina gave up the throne to her daughter, Juliana. At that time, a revolt was underway in the Netherlands Indies. The fighting, which had started in 1945, continued until 1949, when the Netherlands recognized Indonesia's independence. In 1954, Suriname and the Netherlands Antilles, which included six Caribbean islands, were made self-governing and equal members of the Dutch kingdom. In 1962, the Dutch gave up their last colony, West New Guinea (now the Papua region of Indonesia), to UN control. The UN turned the region over to Indonesia in 1963. In 1980, Juliana gave up the throne at the age of 71. Her oldest daughter, Beatrix, became queen.

Economic development. By the late 1900's, the Netherlands had achieved a high standard of living. Economic cooperation, both with other countries and at home, helped the Dutch to reestablish much of their prosperity after World War II. During the late 1940's and the 1950's, Dutch industry, labor, and government worked together to avoid strikes and expand industry. The discovery of a natural gas field in the northern part of the country in 1959 also provided a great economic boost. And Rotterdam, heavily damaged during the war, was rebuilt.

Immigration. In the late 1900's, hundreds of thousands of people from former Dutch colonies and from Mediterranean countries moved to the Netherlands. Many immigrants came from Indonesia. In the 1970's, people from the Molucca Islands demanded that the Dutch free their homeland from Indonesian control. In 1975, Suriname left the Kingdom of the Netherlands and became independent. Many people from Suriname moved to the Netherlands shortly before independence.

Liberal Dutch laws attracted refugees and immigrants from around the world. By the 1990's, many Dutch people wanted to reduce immigration. As a result, the government tightened the country's immigration laws, and some politicians adopted anti-immigrant platforms.

Recent developments. In 1992, the Netherlands signed the Treaty on European Union, also called the Maastricht Treaty for the Dutch city where it was signed. This treaty established the European Union (EU) and called for a single European currency, the *euro.* In 1999, the Netherlands and most other EU countries officially adopted the euro. Euro notes and coins replaced the notes and coins of the traditional Dutch currency, the guilder, in 2002. However, in 2005, Dutch voters rejected a proposed constitution for the EU.

After parliamentary elections in 2002, Jan Peter Balkenende of the Christian Democratic Appeal (CDA) party became prime minister at the head of a coalition government. He headed three more coalition governments, formed in 2003, 2006, and 2007. His fourth government collapsed in February 2010. In elections in June 2010, the CDA lost nearly half its seats. Balkenende resigned as CDA leader. He remained prime minister until a new coalition government formed in October. Mark Rutte of the People's Party for Freedom and Democracy became prime minister. In 2010, the Netherlands Antilles broke apart into separate political units, including the self-governing territories of Curaçao and St. Maarten.

Inez Hollander

Related articles in *World Book* include:

Political and military leaders

Beatrix
Grotius, Hugo
Juliana
Minuit, Peter
Stuyvesant, Peter

Tinbergen, Jan
Van Rensselaer,
  Kiliaen
Wilhelmina

William I
William I, Prince of
  Orange
William III

Cities

Amsterdam
Breda
Delft

Hague, The
Leiden

Rotterdam
Utrecht

History

Belgium (History)
Dutch East India Company
Dutch West India Company
Indonesia (History)
Luxembourg (History)
New Guinea

New Netherland
Operation Market Garden
Suriname
Vienna, Congress of
World War II (The invasion of
  the Low Countries)

Physical features

Meuse River
North Sea

Rhine River

Treaties and agreements

Benelux
Europe, Council of
European Union

North Atlantic Treaty
  Organization
Western European Union

Other related articles

Aruba
Christmas (In the Netherlands,
  Belgium, and Luxembourg)
Clothing (picture: Traditional
  costumes)
Delft (pottery)
Dollhouse
Europe (picture)
Flower (picture: A flower
  auction)
Furniture (The 1900's to the
  present; De Stijl)

Hyacinth
Keeshond
Mata Hari
Netherlands Antilles
Nicholas, Saint
Painting (The Dutch masters;
  De Stijl)
Royal Dutch/Shell Group
Santa Claus
Tulip
Windmill

Outline

I. **Government**
  A. National government
  B. Local government
  C. Politics
  D. Courts
  E. Armed forces
  F. The Kingdom of the
    Netherlands
II. **People**
  A. Ancestry
  B. Language
III. **Way of Life**
  A. City life
  B. Rural life
  C. Food and drink
  D. Holidays and recreation
  E. Religion
  F. Education
  G. Arts
IV. **The land**
  A. The Dunes
  B. The Polders
  C. The Sand Plains
  D. The Southern Uplands
V. **Climate**
VI. **Economy**
  A. Service industries
  B. Manufacturing
  C. Agriculture
  D. Mining
  E. Fishing
  F. Energy sources
  G. International trade
  H. Transportation
  I. Communication
VII. **History**

Additional resources

Andeweg, Rudy B., and Irwin, G. A. *Governance and Politics of the Netherlands*. 3rd ed. Palgrave, 2009.
Koopmans, Joop W., and Huussen, A. H., Jr. *Historical Dictionary of the Netherlands*. 2nd ed. Scarecrow, 2007.
State, Paul F. *A Brief History of the Netherlands*. Facts on File, 2007.
Wiarda, Howard J. *The Dutch Diaspora*. Lexington Bks., 2007.

Netherlands Antilles, *an TIHL eez,* was a part of the Kingdom of the Netherlands that consisted of islands in the Caribbean Sea. The Netherlands Antilles existed as a political unit from 1954 until 2010. It consisted of two groups of islands. One group included Aruba, Bonaire, and Curaçao, about 50 miles (80 kilometers) north of Venezuela. The other group included Saba, Saint Eustatius, and the southern part of Saint Martin. These islands are part of the Leeward Islands, about 160 miles (257 kilometers) east of Puerto Rico. Willemstad, on Curaçao, served as the capital of the entire Netherlands Antilles.

The Spanish first occupied Curaçao in 1527. The Dutch captured the Antilles area between 1630 and 1654. They used the area primarily for the slave trade. In 1845, the islands were united to form a colonial territory. The territory had a governor appointed by the Dutch monarchy. By the 1920's, large oil refineries were operating on Curaçao and Aruba. After World War II (1939-1945), these islands sought greater *autonomy* (self-government). In 1954, the Netherlands Antilles became a largely self-governing territory of the Kingdom of the Netherlands.

Due to a dispute with Curaçao, Aruba separated from the Netherlands Antilles in 1986. It became largely autonomous. *Referendums* (direct votes by the people) held from 2000 to 2005 determined the future of the remaining islands. The people of Curaçao and southern Saint Martin voted for more autonomy. The people of Bonaire, Saba, and Saint Eustatius voted for less.

The Netherlands Antilles dissolved in 2010. Curaçao and southern Saint Martin became autonomous countries within the Kingdom of the Netherlands, like Aruba. Bonaire, Saba, and Saint Eustatius became *overseas municipalities* of the Kingdom of the Netherlands. The overseas municipalities have a status similar to that of towns in the Netherlands.   Jeroen Dewulf

See also **Aruba; Curaçao; Willemstad.**

Nettle is the common name of a group of plants with stinging bristles. Nettles are coarse herbs that grow as weeds in Asia, Europe, and North America. They have tiny flower clusters and leaves that grow opposite each other on the stem. Nettle bristles contain a watery juice that produces an intense itch when it enters a person's skin. This itch does not last long. The bristles usually have no effect in places where the skin is thick.

Young shoots of nettles can be cooked and eaten as a vegetable. They are a good source of vitamins and protein. People have used nettles for medicinal purposes since ancient times. The stinging nettle of Europe and the United States has been cultivated for its fiber and used to make strong, coarse cloth.   Ronald L. Jones

Scientific classification. Nettles make up the genus *Urtica*. The stinging nettle is *Urtica dioica*.

See also **Ramie.**

Netzahualcóyotl, *NAY tsah wahl KOH yoht uhl* (pop. 1,104,585), is one of the largest cities of Mexico. An eastern suburb of Mexico city, it is in the state of México. Netzahualcóyotl is built on the dry lakebed of Lake Texcoco. (see **Mexico** [political map]).

Netzahualcóyotl was founded in 1900 but was not incorporated as a city until 1963. Since 1970, Netzahualcóyotl's population has more than doubled, making it a prime example of Mexico's booming urbanization. This rapid growth has produced such problems as a shortage of good housing, a lack of basic city services, and pollution. The city's population is largely working-class. A number of manufacturing plants operate there.

Samuel Brunk

Neumann, Saint John Nepomucene (1811-1860), was the first male United States citizen to be recognized as a saint by the Roman Catholic Church. He was *canonized* (declared a saint) in 1977.

Neumann was the bishop of Philadelphia from 1852 until his death on Jan. 5, 1860. As bishop, he increased the number of Catholic elementary schools in the city from 2 to almost 100. He helped bring several *sisterhoods* (groups of nuns) from Europe to run the schools.

Neumann was born on March 28, 1811, in Prachatitz, Bohemia (now in the Czech Republic). He came to the United States in 1836 and was ordained later that same year. In 1840, he joined the Redemptorist Fathers, a society of missionary priests. Neumann became a U.S. citizen in 1848. His feast day is January 5.   Robert P. Imbelli

Neuralgia, *nu RAL juh,* is a severe pain that occurs along a nerve. Its cause is not known. The pain may be limited to one part of the nerve, or it may extend along the nerve's branches. It may occur as repeated stabs of pain in the teeth, sinuses, eyes, face, tongue, or throat.

Neuralgia occurs most frequently in two cranial nerves. One nerve, the *trigeminal,* has three branches that enter the eyes, face, sinuses, and teeth. The other, the *glossopharyngeal,* leads to the back of the tongue and throat. Neuralgia is sometimes confused with other conditions called *neuritis* and *radiculopathy.* But these occur in many different parts of the body. True neuritis is an inflammation that can permanently damage a nerve. Neuralgia does not harm the nerve.

Tic douloureux is a type of neuralgia that is common among older people. The name is French for *painful twitching.* Tic douloureux affects the trigeminal nerve and causes facial pain. The face muscles may contract each time a stab of pain occurs. The pain occurs very suddenly and then shoots along one side of the face. It usually begins at a specific part of the nerve called the *trigger zone.* It may then spread along branches of the nerve, but it never involves other nerves. The pain may last a few hours or several weeks. It may then disappear for a few months or years, but it usually returns.

Glossopharyngeal neuralgia is a rare condition. It affects the throat and the back of the tongue.

Temporary relief for neuralgia may be obtained by using drugs, or by numbing the nerve with an injection of alcohol. If the pain does not disappear, the only cure is surgery to remove part of the nerve.   Daniel S. Barth

See also **Neuritis.**

Neuritis, *nu RY tihs,* is an inflammation of a nerve that is caused by disease or injury. It is a painful condition that may affect one or many nerves. Neuritis is sometimes confused with a disorder called neuralgia (see **Neuralgia**).

Bacteria, viruses, and diet and vitamin deficiencies can cause neuritis. Infections, such as tuberculosis, syphilis, and *herpes zoster* (shingles), can invade a nerve, resulting in neuritis. Neuritis can also develop when a disease, such as diabetes, changes the activities of the body's cells. Neuritis caused by physical injury to a nerve involves only the injured nerve.

If neuritis continues for a long time, a nerve may become so badly damaged that it can no longer function properly. As a result, a person may lose the ability to sense heat, pressure, and touch. The body also may lose control over such automatic activities as sweating. If a nerve no longer can stimulate a muscle, the muscle wastes away and eventually becomes paralyzed. Neuritis requires a doctor's care.   Daniel S. Barth

Neurofibromatosis, often abbreviated as NF, is an incurable hereditary disorder that affects the nervous system and the skin. NF is sometimes called *elephant man's disease* after the Englishman Joseph Merrick, whose disfigurement was mistakenly thought to have been caused by NF. In the 1980's, experts concluded that Merrick actually had a rarer disease called *Proteus syndrome.* NF may range in severity from a mild disorder to a severely disfiguring one. There are two forms of the disorder, called NF-1 and NF-2.

NF-1, also called *Von Recklinghausen's disease,* is more common and less severe. It occurs in about 1 out of every 4,000 births. The major signs are flat, light brown spots on the skin called *café-au-lait spots* and *benign* (noncancerous) tumors of the nerves. The tumors, called *neurofibromas,* often develop just beneath the surface of the skin, producing small to large skin growths. Tumors may affect many other parts of the body, including the bones. Many people with NF-1 have *scoliosis* (curvature of the spine). In some cases, tumors affect vital organs, and NF-1 may be life-threatening. Café-au-lait spots are usually present at birth. Neurofibromas usually appear at puberty.

NF-2, also called *bilateral acoustic neurofibromatosis,* is much rarer than NF-1, occurring in about 1 out of every 50,000 births. NF-2 is characterized by tumors in the brain, on the spinal cord, and on the nerves that control hearing. The tumors may lead to deafness, chronic headache, vision problems, partial paralysis, and, eventually, death. The first signs of NF-2 usually appear in the teens or early twenties.

The child of a person with NF has a 50 percent chance of inheriting NF. But about half of all NF victims have no family history of the disorder. There is no treatment other than surgical removal of the tumors. However, hopes for finding a treatment rose in 1990, when researchers identified the gene responsible for NF-1. This gene produces a protein, called *neurofibromin,* that researchers believe causes the disorder.   Allan E. Rubenstein

Neurology, *nu RAHL uh jee,* is the field of medicine concerned with the diagnosis and treatment of diseases of the nervous system and muscles. The nervous system consists of the brain, spinal cord, and nerves (see **Nervous system**). *Neurologists* are physicians who receive special training in neurology after completing medical school. Neurologists evaluate and treat patients who have experienced such symptoms as headaches, seizures, or paralysis, or who have such disorders as Alzheimer's disease, Huntington's disease, meningitis, multiple sclerosis, and Parkinson disease.

A neurologist begins an examination by asking the patient to fully describe the problem. The neurologist then evaluates the patient's mental functioning, emotional state, vision, hearing, speech, strength and reflexes, coordination, and perception of touch, pain, and temperature. Specialized imaging techniques may be used to view affected tissues and organs. These techniques include angiography, computed tomography, and magnetic resonance imaging (MRI). The neurologist interprets all this information to make a diagnosis and to determine treatment, which may include medications, physical therapy, or surgery.   William J. Weiner

Neuron. See Nervous system.

Neuropathology, NUR oh puh THAHL uh jee, is the science that studies alterations produced by diseases of the central nervous system, nerves, or muscles. It is also concerned with changes that result from normal activity in the nervous system. These may be changes in appearance that can be seen with the unaided eye or with an optical or electron microscope. See also **Nervous system; Pathology.**   Marianne Schuelein

Neurosis, nu ROH sihs, is a general term for a relatively mild type of mental illness. Symptoms of neurosis—which include anxiety, depression, and unreasonable fears—are usually distressing but not totally disabling. Conditions formerly categorized as neuroses are now known by more specific terms. The revolutionary psychological theories of the Austrian physician Sigmund Freud included the concept of neurosis as a disorder caused by conflict between conscious and unconscious impulses.   Nancy C. Andreasen

See also **Freud, Sigmund; Mental illness.**

Neutra, NOY trah, **Richard Joseph** (1892-1970), was an Austrian-born architect who worked in California. His best designs demonstrate his goal of creating buildings that meet biological and psychological needs, as well as artistic and technical considerations. In his book *Survival Through Design* (1954), Neutra stated that people can survive only by controlling their environment through design, architecture, and city planning.

Neutra was born on April 8, 1892, in Vienna, Austria. He moved to the United States in 1923 and settled in Los Angeles in 1925. His most famous work is the Lovell "Health" House (1927-1929) in Los Angeles, an early example of modern European architecture in the United States. A number of Neutra's later buildings, including the Tremaine House (1948) in Santa Barbara, California, suggest a continuous flow of space by the use of vast sheets of glass and thin supports. Neutra died on April 16, 1970.   Dennis Domer

© G. Brich, Shooting Star

Neutra's Lovell House in Los Angeles was one of the first homes in America with a light steel frame and an open plan.

Neutrality is the official status of a government that does not take part in a war. The nations that do not take part, either directly or indirectly, are called *neutrals.* The warring countries are called *belligerents.* Belligerents want to prevent their enemies from trading with neutrals. Neutrals want to stay out of the war and expect belligerents to respect neutral territory, freedom of the seas, and the right to trade. *Neutralization* describes the position of a nation that has been recognized as permanently neutral, such as Switzerland.

Since the late 1700's, the rights and duties of neutrals and belligerents have become part of international law. But warring nations have frequently ignored these rights and duties, and in most cases it has been difficult or impossible to enforce them. The rules of neutrality have been developed through both custom and treaty. In 1907, a group of nations at the second Hague Peace Conference set down in two treaties the traditional rules of neutrality on land and sea. These rules were an attempt to balance the differing, and often conflicting, interests of neutrals and belligerents. Individual governments also pass their own laws on neutrality.

Rights and duties. Traditionally, a neutral must not provide military assistance to either of the belligerents. In return, belligerents must respect the rights of neutrals. They must not fight on neutral territory, or move troops across neutral countries. If belligerent troops enter neutral territory, the neutral has the right to disarm them and *intern* (hold) them until the war is over.

A neutral must not build or arm warships for a belligerent. During the American Civil War (1861-1865), the United Kingdom failed to prevent the building and departure of the *Alabama* and other British warships for the Confederacy. These ships sank many Union ships. After the war, an international court ruled that the United Kingdom had violated its neutrality.

Belligerent warships may enter a neutral port in an emergency. But if they stay more than 24 hours, they can be interned. Belligerents may not use neutral ports for naval operations.

Neutrals have the right to trade with other neutrals. But belligerents may search neutral ships. If these ships are carrying war materials to the enemy, the belligerent has the right to seize the goods. Belligerents often decide for themselves what to consider as war materials. They may blockade enemy ports and seize neutral vessels that try to *run* (slip through) the blockade.

World War I (1914-1918). In 1914, Germany violated the rules of neutrality by invading Belgium, whose permanent neutrality had been guaranteed by treaty in 1831. The United States remained neutral in World War I from 1914 to 1917. During this time, the United States tried to defend its neutral rights at sea against violation by the United Kingdom, France, and Germany. The United Kingdom and France seized cargoes bound for neutral countries, such as Denmark and Norway. They argued that such cargoes might eventually reach Germany.

In 1917, the United States declared war against Germany, partly because Germany had violated U.S. neutrality. German submarines had sunk U.S. ships without warning. Under international law, Germany could capture ships carrying war materials to the enemy. But German submarines were unable to take captured ships into port, so they sank them. The loss of lives and property helped turn U.S. public opinion against Germany.

Between wars. Conflicts over neutral rights had twice been major causes for the United States to go to war, in 1917 and in 1812 (see **War of 1812** [Causes of the war]). In the 1930's, Congress passed several acts designed to keep the United States out of another war. These acts placed limits on U.S. neutral rights beyond those required by international law. They forbade the export of war materials and the extension of loans or credits to belligerents. They also provided that other goods could be exported only on a *cash-and-carry* basis. This meant that the belligerent had to pay cash and use its own ships to carry the goods. If the ships were sunk, the United States would not suffer any losses.

World War II (1939-1945). Early in World War II, Germany violated the neutrality of Belgium, Denmark, the Netherlands, Norway, and Yugoslavia. The United States soon shifted from a policy of impartial neutrality to one of aid to the Western allies. The laws of the mid-1930's were modified in November 1939 to permit the export of all materials to belligerents on a cash-and-carry basis.

When German victories threatened the United Kingdom, the United States violated its neutral obligations by sending 50 destroyers and other war materials to the British. In March 1941, Congress passed the Lend-Lease Act to aid countries fighting Nazi Germany. After Japan attacked Pearl Harbor in December 1941, the United States declared war on Japan. Germany, a Japanese ally, then declared war on the United States.

After World War II, many countries refused to support either the Communist or non-Communist blocs in the Cold War (see **Cold War**). They sought security through policies of nonalignment and noninvolvement. They were called *neutralist, nonaligned,* or *uncommitted* nations. However, the idea of opposing blocs lost meaning in 1991, when the Soviet Union—the leading Communist country during the Cold War—was dissolved.

Neutrality today. Total warfare and the growth of organizations like the United Nations (UN) have made neutrality more difficult to define. Total warfare has erased many distinctions between civilian and military activities and materials. This undercuts arguments neutrals previously used to support their rights of neutral trade. Collective action, such as use of a UN police force against an aggressor, is in many ways in disagreement with earlier practices of neutrality.   Robert J. Pranger

See also **High seas; International law; Third World.**

Neutralization, *NOO truh luh ZAY shuhn,* is a chemical reaction in which an acid and a base form a salt. If the reaction is complete—and the acid and base are both strong—the final salt is usually *neutral* (neither acidic nor basic).

Strong acids and bases in water solution *ionize* (break down) completely into positive and negative particles called *ions.* This reaction is shown below for hydrochloric acid (HCl) and sodium hydroxide (NaOH).

$$HCl \rightarrow H^+ + Cl^- \text{ and } NaOH \rightarrow Na^+ + OH^-$$

Weak acids and bases also break down in water. But they do not ionize completely.

When the acid and base react together, the hydroxide (OH⁻) ion from the base combines with the hydrogen (H⁺) ion from the acid to form water (H_2O).

$$H^+ + Cl^- + Na^+ + OH^- \rightarrow Na^+ + Cl^- + H_2O$$

The two remaining ions form a salt that may either *precipitate* (drop out of the solution as a solid) or stay in solution as ions. If the water is evaporated, the salt can be recovered in crystal form.   Marianna A. Busch

Related articles in *World Book* include:

Acid	Litmus	Phenolphthalein
Base	pH	Salt, Chemical
Ion		

Neutrino is any of three types of subatomic particles that have no electric charge. Experiments have shown that neutrinos have some *mass* (amount of matter). However, the masses of neutrinos are so small that scientists have not yet been able to measure them directly. A neutrino has no more than 1 millionth the mass of an *electron,* the lightest particle that has an electric charge.

Neutrinos travel at or near the speed of light. They are produced in reactions that occur in the *decay* (breaking apart) of unstable subatomic particles or nuclei. They are also created in reactions that produce energy in the sun and other stars. In addition, machines known as *particle accelerators* can produce neutrinos.

Neutrinos belong to the *lepton* family of particles. The other leptons carry an electric charge and have mass. They are, from lightest to heaviest, the electron, the *muon,* and the *tau.* A neutrino can change into a charged lepton by interacting with an atomic nucleus. Each type of neutrino can change into only one kind of charged lepton. The names of the neutrinos come from the names of the corresponding charged leptons. Thus, an *electron-neutrino* can change into an electron, a *muon-neutrino* into a muon, and a *tau-neutrino* into a tau.

The neutrinos also have *antimatter* counterparts called *antineutrinos* that differ from neutrinos in the direction of their *spin.* Spin is a measure of the internal rotation of a particle. There are *electron-antineutrinos, muon-antineutrinos,* and *tau-antineutrinos.*

The American physicists Frederick Reines and Clyde Cowan announced the discovery of the first neutrinos, electron-neutrinos, in 1956. In 1962, the American physicists Leon M. Lederman, Melvin Schwartz, and Jack Steinberger discovered the muon-neutrino. In 2000, an international team of scientists at Fermi National Accelerator Laboratory (Fermilab) in Batavia, Illinois, announced the first direct evidence for the tau-neutrino.

Neutrinos interact with other particles through a force called the *weak interaction.* This force is so feeble that neutrinos can pass through a large amount of matter with only a tiny chance of interacting with a particle in the matter. So, to detect enough neutrino interactions for study, researchers must build enormous detectors.

A detector senses a neutrino indirectly, after the neutrino interacts with a nucleus or collides with an electron. The interaction or collision releases charged particles that electronic devices can detect. But the devices can also detect other charged particles at Earth's surface. Therefore, to shield detectors from the other particles, scientists build them deep underground.

The most sensitive neutrino detector is the Sudbury Neutrino Observatory (SNO), which began operating in 1999 in a nickel mine in Ontario. The SNO detects several neutrino interactions per day. The Super-Kamiokande (Super-K) detector, in a zinc mine northwest of Tokyo,

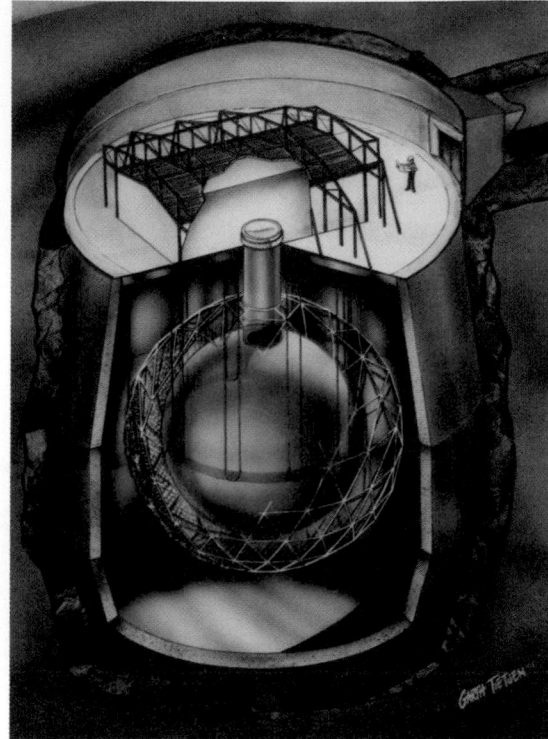

The Sudbury Neutrino Observatory consists of a large spherical water tank surrounded by sensors. The sensors detect flashes of light that occur when neutrinos interact with the water.

began operating in 1996 and has produced much valuable data. In 2005, the IceCube Neutrino Detector near the South Pole began collecting data. It was completed in 2010. IceCube is 1 cubic kilometer (0.24 cubic mile) in size and 1.4 kilometers (0.9 mile) below the ice.

Neutrino detectors have consistently observed fewer neutrinos from the sun than expected. Data from the SNO show that the shortage occurs because electron-neutrinos created in the sun turn into other varieties as they travel through space. The changes can occur only if neutrinos have mass.   Robert H. March

See also **Astronomy** (Neutrino astronomy); **Lepton; Observatory** (Neutrino observatories); **Subatomic particle.**

Neutron is a subatomic particle. Neutrons, together with subatomic particles called *protons,* form the nuclei of all atoms except that of ordinary hydrogen, whose nucleus consists of a single proton (see **Proton**). Neutrons and protons make up 99.9 percent of an atom's mass. A cloud of *electrons* around the nucleus accounts for the rest of the mass (see **Electron**). In the nucleus, a force called the *strong interaction* or the *strong nuclear force* holds neutrons and protons together.

The number of neutrons in an atom of any chemical element is equal to the difference between the element's *mass number* (total number of protons and neutrons) and its *atomic number* (number of protons). The atoms of lighter elements contain about an equal number of neutrons and protons. Heavier elements contain more neutrons than protons.

Neutrons consist of fundamental particles called *quarks* (see **Quark**). A neutron has no electric charge. Its diameter is approximately one-millionth of a nanometer. One nanometer equals one-millionth of a millimeter, or $\frac{1}{25,400,000}$ inch. The mass of a neutron is slightly greater than that of a proton. A free neutron decays into a proton, an electron, and an antineutrino. Free neutrons have an average life span of about 15 minutes.

Sir James Chadwick, a British physicist, discovered the neutron in 1932. Today, scientists use neutrons to make various elements radioactive. They bombard nuclei with neutrons in a nuclear reactor. After the nuclei absorb neutrons, they decay by giving off radiation. When a nucleus of the uranium isotope U-235 is struck by a neutron, it becomes unstable and splits into two parts. This process, called *fission,* releases a huge amount of energy and frees additional neutrons that cause more uranium nuclei to fission. A continuous series of such fissions, called a *nuclear chain reaction,* produces the energy in nuclear weapons and reactors.   Edward S. Fry

See also **Atom; Baryon; Chadwick, Sir James; Nuclear energy; Radiation; Subatomic particle.**

Neutron star is the smallest and densest type of star known. Neutron stars measure only about 12 miles (20 kilometers) across, but they have a mass between 1.4 times and 3 times that of the sun.

A neutron star can form when a fairly large star—roughly 8 to 11 times as massive as the sun or larger—runs out of fuel to burn. The star's intense gravitational force causes it to collapse. Gravity squeezes together the protons and electrons in the core of the star. These protons and electrons combine to form neutrons. The neutrons may, in turn, break down into elementary particles called *quarks.* The star then explodes as a *supernova,* leaving behind its spinning core—a neutron star.

Scientists believe the surface of a neutron star consists of a solid crust of atomic nuclei and electrons. Beneath the crust, the neutron star's core contains mainly neutrons. Its center may contain quarks. An extremely thin atmosphere of *plasma* (charged particles) may surround the crust. A neutron star has a magnetic field billions of times stronger than the most powerful magnets on Earth. This magnetic field creates an electric field that rips electrons and protons from the star's surface. In some cases, these particles produce a beam of radio waves, X rays, or other radiation that flows from the star.

Physicists predicted the existence of neutron stars in 1938. The prediction remained a theory until 1967. In that year, radio telescopes in the United Kingdom picked up regular bursts of radio waves from an object in space. Scientists later concluded that such objects, called *pulsars,* are actually neutron stars. In 1979, scientists first observed high-energy radiation from a type of neutron star similar to a typical pulsar, but with a magnetic field 100 to 1000 times as strong. These rare neutron stars were later called *magnetars.*

Some neutron stars orbit with a companion star. The neutron star's intense gravitational field pulls material from its companion, a process called *accretion.* The material falls into the neutron star, releasing a great deal of energy in the form of X rays. Accretion can make a neutron star spin at nearly 600 rotations per second. When accretion stops, the star becomes a special type of pulsar called a *millisecond radio pulsar.*   Jeremy S. Heyl

See also **Pulsar; Supernova.**

© James Blank, Stock, Boston

Red Rock Canyon, near Las Vegas, typifies the rugged desert landscape that covers most of the state of Nevada. Nevada receives less rainfall than any other state. More than 150 mountain ranges rise throughout Nevada.

Nevada *The Silver State*

Nevada, *nuh VAD uh* or *nuh VAH duh,* is a state in the western United States. It is a popular center of tourism. Nevada was the first state to allow widespread casino gambling. Large, luxurious gambling casinos attract visitors from all parts of the world to Lake Tahoe, Las Vegas, and Reno. Las Vegas is the largest city in Nevada, the state's chief tourist attraction, and one of the leading tourist destinations in the world.

Nevada is a land of rugged snow-capped mountains, grassy valleys, and sandy deserts. Pine forests cover many mountain slopes, and crystal-clear streams flow through steep, rocky canyons. Large trout swim in sparkling valley lakes. In many places, geysers erupt and hot springs gush amid the rocks.

In the south, bighorn sheep graze on jagged plateaus

that glow red in the brilliant sunshine. Glistening white patches called alkali flats stretch across the deserts. The flowers of cactus, yucca, and sagebrush plants add splashes of color to the landscape. The gray-green sagebrush gave Nevada one of its nicknames, the *Sagebrush State.*

Nevada's most common nickname is the *Silver State.* The name refers to the vast amounts of silver that were once taken from Nevada's numerous mines. Colorful ghost towns and historic mining towns, such as Virginia City, attract thousands of tourists to the state every year.

Mining remains important to Nevada's economy. Nevada ranks among the leading states in mining income. The state's most important mined product is gold, and Nevada leads the country in gold production. Other important mined products include copper, lime, sand and gravel, and silver.

Less rain falls in Nevada than in any other state. As a result, farming depends on irrigation. The Newlands Irrigation Project, near Reno, was the first system of its kind built by the federal government. Hoover Dam, on the Colorado River, created Lake Mead, one of the

The contributors of this article are Christopher H. Exline, former Professor and Chairman of the Department of Geography at the University of Nevada, Reno; and Hal Rothman, former Professor of History at the University of Nevada, Las Vegas.

Interesting facts about Nevada

The city of Aurora once took part in elections in two states. When the city was first settled, its inhabitants were not sure whether it was part of Nevada or California. Elections were held in 1863, and the citizens of Aurora selected candidates for offices in both states. A survey later determined that Aurora was in Nevada.

Reuel C. Gridley, an Austin grocer, collected $275,000 in 1864 by auctioning a single sack of flour over and over again. He gave all the money to the Sanitary Fund of the U.S. Sanitary Commission, the forerunner of the American Red Cross.

Gridley sack of flour

Several rare species of fish live in Nevada, the driest of the 50 states. These species include the cui-ui, a large sucker found only in Pyramid Lake, and the Devils Hole pupfish, which is found only in Devils Hole. These fish evolved separately from more common fish as a result of becoming isolated as prehistoric lakes dried up.

The only United States coins with a double mint mark were those produced by the U.S. Mint at Carson City from 1870 to 1893. They bore the mark *CC.* Gold coins, such as double eagles (face value $20), eagles ($10), and half eagles ($5), carried the distinctive mark. Silver coins, such as dollars, trade dollars, and half dollars, also had the double mint mark.

The federal government owns about three-fourths of Nevada's land. This proportion is the largest of any of the 50 states. Agencies that control the land include the Bureau of Land Management, the Fish and Wildlife Service, the Forest Service, the National Park Service, the United States Navy, and the United States Air Force.

WORLD BOOK illustration by Kevin Chadwick

© Caesars Palace

Las Vegas is Nevada's largest city and chief tourist attraction. Caesars Palace, *shown here,* is one of the city's many large, luxurious hotels and gambling casinos. Las Vegas's colorful entertainment and night life draw visitors from many parts of the world.

largest artificially created lakes in the world. The dam's power plant supplies electric power for Arizona, California, and Nevada.

Nevada is one of the most urbanized states in the nation. More than 90 percent of the state's people live in cities and towns. The vast majority of the population lives in the Las Vegas and Reno areas. The state has limited areas suitable for farming and ranching. Farming is less important in Nevada than it is in most other states.

Nevada lies mainly on a broad, rugged highland between the Rocky Mountains and the Sierra Nevada mountain range. In the 1820's and 1830's, the trappers Peter S. Ogden, Jedediah S. Smith, and Joseph Walker explored parts of the region in search of new fur sources. John C. Frémont began the first thorough exploration in 1843. By the 1860's, discoveries of gold and silver had brought thousands of miners to the area.

The name *Nevada* comes from a Spanish word meaning *snow-clad.* Miners and other settlers chose the name Nevada when the region became a territory in 1861. Nevada became a state in 1864 during the American Civil War and was nicknamed the *Battle Born State.*

© James Blank, West Stock

Lake Tahoe is a beautiful lake that lies in a valley of the Sierra Nevada mountains west of Carson City. Many people visit the lake to enjoy swimming, boating, and water-skiing.

Nevada in brief

Symbols of Nevada

The state flag, adopted in 1929, bears a silver star. The words *Battle Born* signify Nevada's admission to the Union during the Civil War. On the state seal, adopted in 1866, a railroad and a telegraph line symbolize Nevada's importance as a corridor between the Midwest and the West Coast. A tunnel, an ore cart, and an ore-crushing mill stand for the state's mineral wealth. A plow, a sickle, and a sheaf of wheat represent agriculture.

State flag

State seal

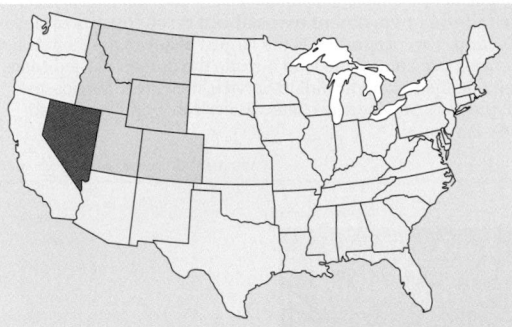

Nevada (brown) ranks seventh in size among all the states and second among the Rocky Mountain States (yellow).

General information

Statehood: Oct. 31, 1864, the 36th state.
State abbreviations: Nev. (traditional); NV (postal).
State motto: *All for Our Country.*
State song: "Home Means Nevada." Words and music by Bertha Raffetto.

The State Capitol is in Carson City, Nevada's capital since the Nevada Territory was created in 1861.

Land and climate

Area: 110,561 mi² (286,351 km²), including 735 mi² (1,903 km²) of inland water.
Elevation: *Highest*—Boundary Peak, 13,140 ft (4,005 m) above sea level. *Lowest*—470 ft (143 m) above sea level along the Colorado River in Clark County.
Record high temperature: 125 °F (52 °C) at Laughlin on June 29, 1994.
Record low temperature: –50 °F (–46 °C) at San Jacinto on Jan. 8, 1937.
Average July temperature: 73 °F (23 °C).
Average January temperature: 30 °F (–1 °C).
Average yearly precipitation: 9 in (23 cm).

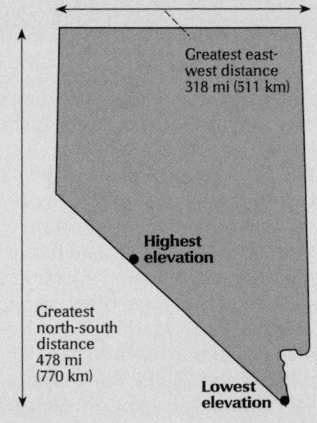

Greatest east-west distance 318 mi (511 km)

Highest elevation

Greatest north-south distance 478 mi (770 km)

Lowest elevation

Important dates

The U.S. received Nevada and other southwestern lands from Mexico under the Treaty of Guadalupe Hidalgo.

Nevada became the 36th state on October 31.

| 1825-1830 | 1848 | 1859 | 1864 |

Peter S. Ogden reached the Humboldt River. Jedediah S. Smith crossed southern Nevada.

The discovery of silver near Virginia City brought a rush of prospectors to western Nevada.

State bird
Mountain bluebird

State flower
Sagebrush

State trees
Nevada has two state trees—the Great Basin bristlecone pine, *left,* and the single-leaf piñon, *right.*

People

Population: 2,700,551
Rank among the states: 35th
Density: 24 per mi² (9 per km²), U.S. average 85 per mi² (33 per km²)
Distribution: 92 percent urban, 8 percent rural
Largest cities in Nevada

Las Vegas	583,756
Henderson	257,729
Reno	225,221
Paradise†	223,167
North Las Vegas	216,961
Sunrise Manor†	189,372

†Unincorporated place.
Source: 2010 census, except for distribution, which is for 2000.

Population trend

Millions

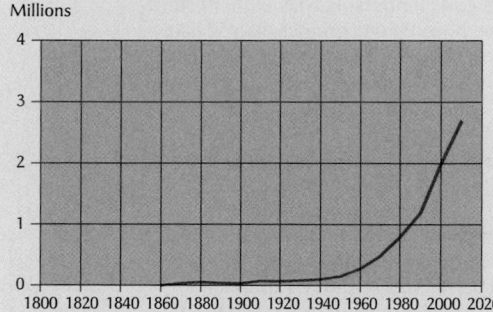

Year	Population
2010	2,700,551
2000	1,998,257
1990	1,201,833
1980	800,493
1970	488,738
1960	285,278
1950	160,083
1940	110,247
1930	91,058
1920	77,407
1910	81,875
1900	42,335
1890	47,355
1880	62,266
1870	42,491
1860	6,857

Source: U.S. Census Bureau.

Economy

Chief products

Agriculture: beef cattle, greenhouse and nursery products, hay, milk, onions, potatoes, sheep, wheat.
Manufacturing: computer and electronic products, concrete, fabricated metal products, food products, plastic products.
Mining: barite, copper, gold, lime, sand and gravel, silver.

Gross domestic product

Value of goods and services produced in 2008: $132,120,000,000. *Services* include community, business, and personal services; finance; government; trade; and transportation and communication. *Industry* includes construction, manufacturing, mining, and utilities. *Agriculture* includes agriculture, fishing, and forestry.

Source: U.S. Bureau of Economic Analysis.

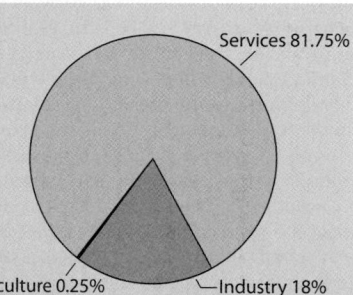

Services 81.75%
Agriculture 0.25%
Industry 18%

Government

State government

Governor: 4-year term
State senators: 21; 4-year terms
Assembly members: 42; 2-year terms
Counties: 17

Federal government

United States senators: 2
United States representatives: 3*
Electoral votes: 5†

*In 2013, Nevada will have 4 representatives.
†In 2012, Nevada will have 6 electoral votes.

Sources of information

Nevada's official website at http://nv.gov provides a gateway to much information on the state's government, history, and economy.

In addition, the website at http://travelnevada.com provides information about tourism.

Boulder Dam (now Hoover Dam) was completed.

The Nevada Legislature passed conservation laws to protect Lake Tahoe from pollution.

| 1931 | 1936 | 1963 | 1980 | 1990's |

The Nevada Legislature made gambling legal in the state.

The U.S. Supreme Court specified how much water Nevada could draw from the Colorado River.

Nevada's population grew by 66 percent, the fastest of any U.S. state during the decade.

Population. The 2010 United States census reported that Nevada had 2,700,551 people. The population had increased 35 percent over the 2000 figure, 1,998,257— the largest percentage increase among the U.S. states for that period. According to the 2010 census, Nevada ranks 35th in population among the 50 states.

About 90 percent of Nevada's people live in three metropolitan areas (see **Metropolitan area**). The metropolitan areas are Carson City, Las Vegas-Paradise, and Reno-Sparks. About 70 percent of Nevada's population lives in the Las Vegas-Paradise metropolitan area. The Reno-Sparks metropolitan area contains about 15 percent of the population. Las Vegas is Nevada's largest city, and Reno is the second largest city in the state.

Besides Las Vegas and Henderson, only eight of Nevada's urban areas have populations greater than 50,000. These areas are Enterprise, North Las Vegas, Paradise, Spring Valley, and Sunrise Manor, all near Las Vegas; Reno; Sparks; and Carson City, the state capital.

Hispanics account for over 25 percent of Nevada's population. African Americans make up about 8 percent.

People in the Las Vegas area have long depended on the tourism and gambling industries for employment. Since the 1980's, however, retirees and other newcomers to the area have helped create jobs in such fields as health care and real estate. Reno, another tourist favorite, is the center of banking, commerce, and transportation in northern Nevada.

Schools. The people of Nevada made plans for a tax-supported school system as early as 1861, when Nevada became a territory. In 1865, the year after Nevada became a state, the Legislature established the first school districts. Nevada had to overcome unusual problems in developing its public school system. Rural areas were thinly populated. In some places, taxpayers supported schools for as few as three or four school-age children living in a vast area. Some early schools were open only six months of the year because of a lack of funds. Until 1900, the state had only a few high schools.

A state Department of Education supervises Nevada schools. The department includes the State Board of Education and the superintendent of public instruction. The board has 10 voting members, who are elected by the people to four-year terms, and one nonvoting student representative. The board selects the superintendent of public instruction, who heads the Department of Education.

Population density

Nevada has a population of over 2 ½ million people. About 90 percent of the state's people live in or near Nevada's largest cities, Las Vegas and Reno.

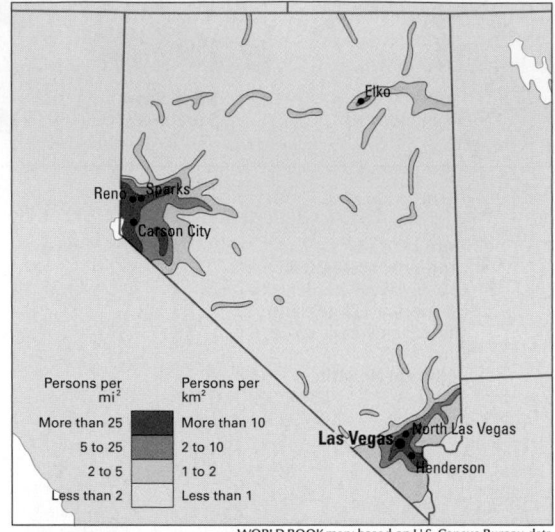

WORLD BOOK map; based on U.S. Census Bureau data.

© Richard Cummins, SuperStock

The University of Nevada, Las Vegas, was founded in 1957. It includes the Bigelow Health Sciences Building, *shown here.*

Each Nevada county makes up a school district. Each district has its own elected Board of Trustees. Children must attend school between the ages of 7 and 17. For

© Tom McHugh, Photo Researchers

The Reno skyline rises against the dramatic backdrop of the Virginia and Pah Rah mountain ranges. Reno is Nevada's second largest city.

statistics on Nevada schools, see **Education** (table).

Libraries. The University of Nevada has two of the largest libraries in the state on its campuses in Las Vegas and Reno. The Nevada State Library and Archives in Carson City serves as the official library for the state government and also as the reference and research center for other libraries throughout the state. Nevada has public libraries throughout the state.

Museums. The Nevada Historical Society in Reno and the Nevada State Museum in Las Vegas have exhibits on the region's history. The Nevada State Museum in Carson City houses such exhibits as an underground mine, a ghost town, a reconstructed mammoth, and a historic coin press. The Lost City Museum in Overton has items found at the Pueblo Grande de Nevada, an ancient Indian settlement. Lake Mead now covers part of the site of the ancient city.

The Old Las Vegas Mormon State Historic Park includes part of a fort built by Mormon pioneers. The University of Nevada, Las Vegas, operates the Marjorie Barrick Museum, devoted to the cultures of the American Southwest. The Northeastern Nevada Museum in Elko includes an extensive history gallery, photography exhibits, and historical reproductions of a ranch kitchen, a general store, and a printing shop. The National Automobile Museum in Reno has antique, classic, vintage, and special interest vehicles.

The Nevada Museum of Art in Reno houses a collection based on the theme of land and the environment. The W. M. Keck Museum at the University of Nevada in Reno focuses on mining and the history of mining.

Universities and colleges

This table lists the nonprofit universities and colleges in Nevada that grant bachelor's or advanced degrees and are accredited by the Northwest Commission on Colleges and Universities.

Name	Mailing address
Great Basin College	Elko
Nevada, University of	*
Roseman University of Health Sciences	Henderson
Sierra Nevada College	Incline Village
Southern Nevada, College of	North Las Vegas
Western Nevada College	Carson City

*Campuses at Las Vegas and Reno. See **Nevada System of Higher Education.**

Nevada map index

Metropolitan areas

Carson City	55,274
Las Vegas-Paradise	1,951,269
Reno-Sparks	425,417

Counties

Carson City‡	55,274	G 2
Churchill	24,877	F 4
Clark	1,951,269	M 10
Douglas	46,997	G 2
Elko	48,818	C 9
Esmeralda	783	J 5
Eureka	1,987	E 8
Humboldt	16,528	B 5
Lander	5,775	E 6
Lincoln	5,345	J 10
Lyon	51,980	G 3
Mineral	4,772	H 4
Nye	43,946	I 7
Pershing	6,753	D 4
Storey	4,010	F 2
Washoe	421,407	C 2
White Pine	10,030	F 10

Cities, towns and other populated places

Acoma		J 11
Adaven		J 9
Alamo†	1,080	K 9
Amargosa Valley		L 7
Ash Springs		J 9
Aurora		I 3
Austin†	192	F 6
Baker†	68	G 11
Barclay		J 11
Basalt		I 4
Battle Mountain†°	3,635	D 7
Beatty†	1,010	L 7
Beowawe		D 7
Berlin		F 6
Black Springs		F 2
Blue Diamond†	290	M 9
Boaz		C 9
Boulder City	15,023	N 10
Bunkerville†	1,303	L 11
Cactus Springs		L 8
Cal Nev Ari†	244	O 10
Caliente	1,130	J 11
Carlin	2,368	D 8
Carp		K 11
Carson City‡°	55,274	G 2
Caselton		J 11
Centerville		G 2
Charleston		A 9
Charleston Park		M 9
Cherry Creek		E 10
Cholona		C 3
Clark		F 2

Coaldale		I 5
Cobre		C 11
Cold Springs†	8,544	F 5
Contact		A 10
Copperfield		F 2
Cottonwood Cove		O 10
Crescent Valley†	392	D 7
Crestline		J 11
Crystal Bay†	305	G 2
Currant		H 9
Currie		D 10
Dayton†	8,964	G 2
Deeth		C 9
Denio†	47	A 4
Dixie Valley		F 5
Dresslerville		G 2
Dry Lake		L 10
Duck Valley Indian Reservation	953	A 8
Duckwater		G 9
Duckwater Indian Reservation	156	G 9
Dunphy		D 7
Dyer†	259	J 5
Eastgate		G 5
Echo Bay		M 11
Elburz		C 9
Elgin		K 11
Elko°	18,297	C 8
Ely°	4,255	G 10
Empire†	217	D 3
Enterprise*†	108,481	M 9
Etna		J 10
Eureka†°	610	F 8
Fallon°	8,606	F 3
Fallon Indian Reservation	581	F 4
Fallon Station*†	705	F 3
Fernley	19,368	F 3
Flanigan		E 2
Fort McDermitt Indian Reservation		A 6
Frenchman		G 4
Gabbs	269	G 5
Gardnerville†	5,656	G 2
Gardnerville Ranchos*†	11,312	G 2
Genoa†	939	G 2
Gerlach†	206	D 3
Glenbrook†	215	G 2
Glendale		L 11
Golconda†	214	C 6
Gold Acres		E 7
Gold Hill		F 2
Gold Point		K 6
Goldfield†°	268	J 6
Goodsprings†	229	N 9
Goshute Indian Reservation	15	E 11
Granite Point		E 4
Halleck		C 9
Harney		D 8
Hawthorne†°	3,269	H 4

Hazen		F 3
Henderson	257,729	M 10
Hiko†	119	J 9
Hogan		C 10
Holborn		C 10
Holbrook Junction		H 2
Humboldt		D 4
Imlay†	171	D 5
Incline Village†	8,777	G 2
Indian Hills*†	5,627	G 2
Indian Springs†	991	L 9
Islen		J 11
Jackpot†	1,195	A 10
Jarbidge		A 9
Jean		N 9
Jiggs		D 9
Johnson Lane*†	6,490	G 2
Jungo		C 4
Kampos		D 7
Kimberly		G 10
Kingsbury*†	2,152	G 2
Kingston†	113	G 6
Lages		E 10
Lamoille†	105	D 9
Lane		G 10
Las Vegas°	583,756	M 10
Laughlin†	7,323	O 11
Lawton		F 2
Lee		D 9
Lemmon Valley*†	5,040	F 2
Lida		J 6
Locks		H 9
Logandale		L 11
Lovelock°	1,894	E 4
Lundt		282 G 10
Luning		H 5
Majors Place		G 10
Mason		G 3
Massie		F 3
McDermitt†	172	A 5
McGill†	1,148	F 10
Mercury		L 8
Mesquite	15,276	L 11
Metropolis		B 9
Middlegate		G 5
Mill City		D 5
Mina†	155	H 5
Minden†°	3,001	G 2
Minerva		G 11
Moapa†	1,025	L 10
Moapa River Indian Reservation		L 10
Moapa Valley*†	6,924	L 11
Mogul†	1,290	F 2
Moleen		D 8
Montello†	84	B 11
Mosel		D 7
Mount Charleston*†	357	M 9
Mountain City		A 8

Mountain Springs		M 9
Nellis AFB†	3,187	M 10
Nelson†	37	N 10
New Empire		G 2
Nixon†	374	E 3
North Battle Mountain		D 7
North Las Vegas	216,961	M 10
Oasis†	29	C 11
Ocala		E 4
Oreana		D 4
Orovada†	155	B 5
Osino†	709	C 9
Overton		L 11
Overton Beach		M 11
Owyhee†	953	A 8
Pahrump†	36,441	M 8
Palisade		D 8
Panaca†	963	J 11
Paradise*†	223,167	M 9
Paradise Valley†	109	B 6
Parran		F 3
Patrick		F 2
Pequop		C 10
Pioche†°	1,002	J 11
Preston†	78	G 10
Proctor		C 11
Pronto		C 5
Pyramid		E 2
Pyramid Lake Indian Reservation	1,660	E 2
Rachel†	54	J 8
Rennox		D 7
Reno°	225,221	F 2
Rhyolite		L 7
Riverside		L 11
Rixies		D 7
Round Mountain		H 6
Rowland		A 8
Ruby Valley		D 9
Ruth†	440	G 10
Ryndon		C 9
Salt Wells		F 4
San Jacinto		A 10
Sand Pass		D 2
Sandy Valley†	2,051	N 9
Sano		D 2
Schurz†	658	G 3
Scotty's Junction		K 6
Searchlight†	539	O 10
Shafter		C 10
Shantytown		E 9
Silver City		G 2
Silver Peak†	107	J 5
Silver Springs†	5,296	F 3
Silver Zone		C 11
Sloan		N 9
Smith		H 2
Smith Valley*†	1,603	H 2
Spanish Springs*†	15,064	F 2

Sparks	90,264	F 2
Spring Creek†	12,361	C 9
Spring Valley†	178,395	M 10
Stagecoach†	1,874	F 2
Stateline†	842	G 2
Steamboat		F 2
Steptoe		F 10
Stewart		G 2
Stillwater		F 4
Sulphur		C 4
Summerlin South*†	24,085	M 10
Summit Lake Indian Reservation	1	B 3
Sun Valley*†	19,299	F 2
Sunnyside		H 10
Sunrise Manor*†	189,372	M 10
Sutcliffe†	253	E 2
Sweetwater		H 3
Te-Moak Indian Reservation		D 9
Thorne		H 4
Tobar		C 10
Tonopah†°	2,478	I 6
Toy		E 4
Trego		C 3
Tuscarora		B 8
Ursine†	91	J 11
Valmy†	37	C 6
Verdi†	1,415	F 2
Virginia City†°	855	F 2
Vya		B 2
Wabuska		G 3
Wadsworth†	834	F 3
Walker Lake†	275	H 3
Walker River Indian Reservation	746	J 4
Warm Springs		I 7
Washoe City		F 2
Washoe Indian Reservation		H 2
Weed Heights		G 3
Wellington		H 3
Wells	1,292	C 10
Weso		C 5
West Wendover	4,410	C 11
White Rock		A 7
Whitney	38,585	M 10
Wilkins		B 10
Winchester*†	27,978	M 9
Winnemucca°	7,396	C 5
Winnemucca Indian Reservation		C 5
Woolsey		D 4
Yerington°	3,048	G 3
Yerington Indian Reservation	151	G 3
Yomba Indian Reservation	95	G 6
Zephyr Cove†	565	G 2

*Does not appear on map; key shows general location.
†Census designated place—unincorporated, but recognized as a significant settled community by the U.S. Census Bureau.
‡Carson City is both a city and a county.

°County seat.
Places without population figures are unincorporated areas.
Source: 2010 census.

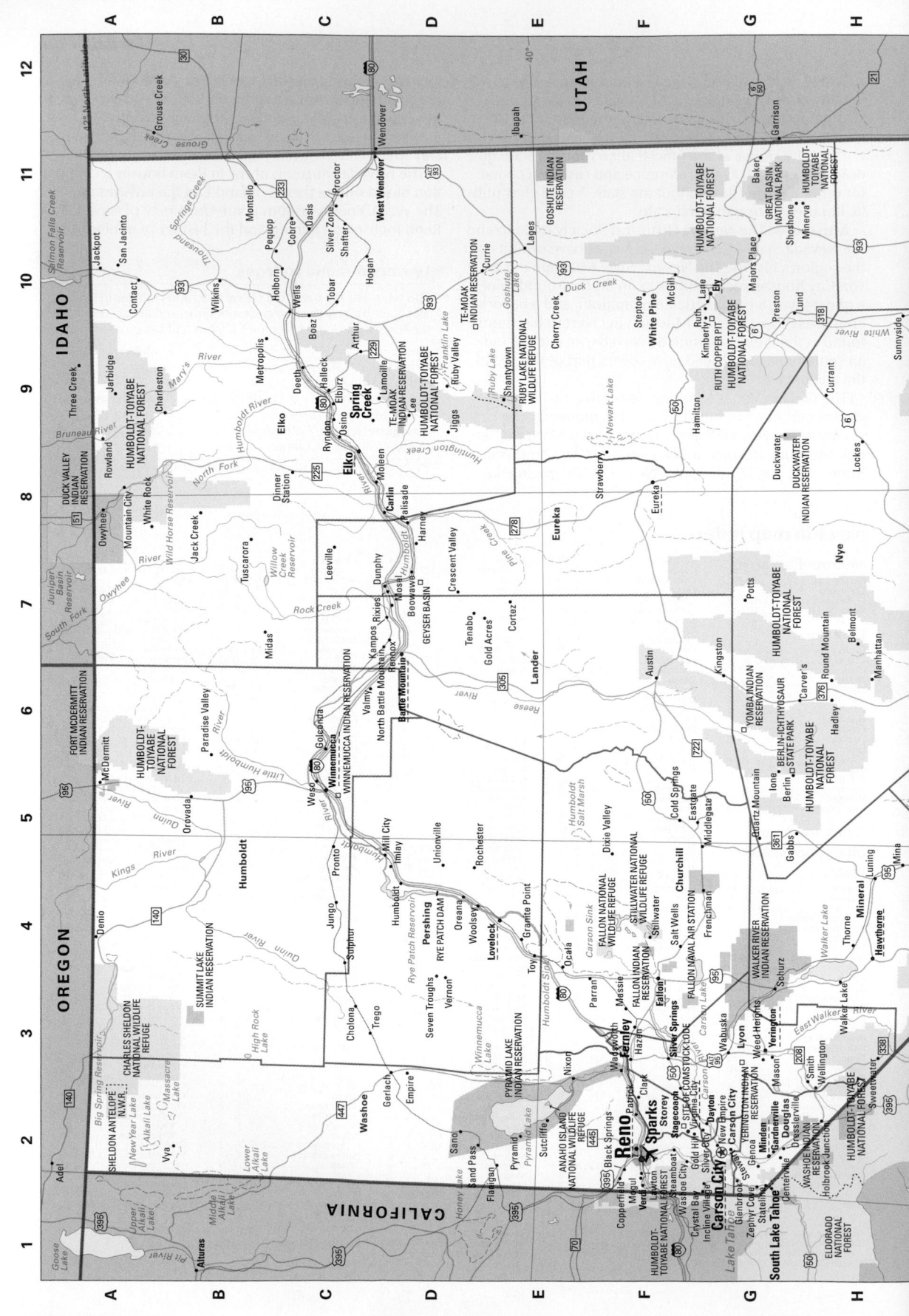

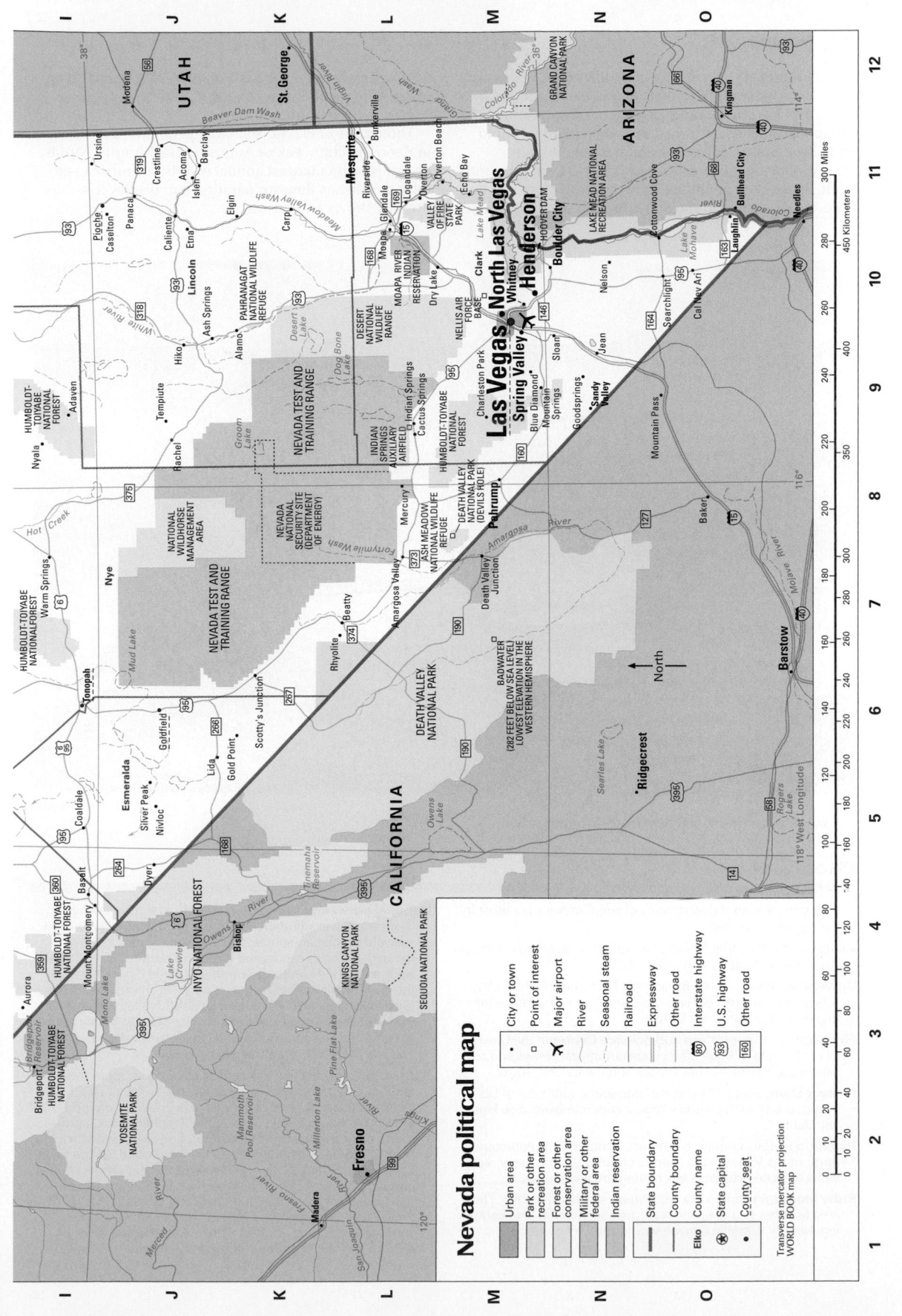

Nevada political map

	Urban area
	Park or other recreation area
	Forest or other conservation area
	Military or other federal area
	Indian reservation

	State boundary
	County boundary
Elko	County name
✪	State capital
•	County seat

•	City or town
□	Point of interest
✈	Major airport
	River
	Seasonal steam
	Railroad
	Expressway
	Other road
⑧⓿	Interstate highway
⑨③	U.S. highway
⑯⓿	Other road

Transverse mercator projection
WORLD BOOK map

Gambling and the colorful night life in Las Vegas and Reno draw millions of tourists every year. Virginia City and other historic Nevada towns remind travelers of the prospectors who came west seeking fortunes in gold and silver. Sports enthusiasts hunt mule deer and chukar partridge, and fish for catfish, bass, salmon, and trout. Skiers race down the snow-covered slopes of the Lake Tahoe basin and the Sierra Nevada near Reno, and

Mount Charleston near Las Vegas. Vacationers also enjoy swimming and water skiing at Lake Mead, Lake Tahoe, and Pyramid Lake.

Thousands of classic and vintage automobiles arrive in Reno the first week of August for Hot August Nights, one of Nevada's largest annual events. Visitors can admire the cars as they are paraded and displayed at numerous shows and events.

Bob and Ira Spring

Virginia City, a famous Western historic mining town

Places to visit

Following are brief descriptions of some of Nevada's most interesting places to visit:

Austin, a city in central Nevada, has authentic buildings from its days as a bustling mining settlement.

Bowers Mansion, a large Italian-style home near Carson City, was built by "Sandy" Bowers, a silver miner who made a fortune from the Comstock Lode.

Fleischmann Planetarium and Science Center at the University of Nevada in Reno offers planetarium star shows and realistic motion pictures about space and the natural world.

Hoover Dam, about 25 miles (40 kilometers) southeast of Las Vegas, is one of the world's largest concrete dams. See **Hoover Dam.**

Pioche, a famous county seat about 130 miles (210 kilometers) north of Las Vegas, has a historic courthouse and many remnants of its colorful past as a mining town in the 1800's.

Ruby Mountains are in a scenic region southeast of Elko. The area features skiing, hiking trails, fishing, hunting, and camping. Nearby Lamoille Canyon was formed by glaciers.

National parks and forests. Great Basin National Park lies in east-central Nevada. It includes rugged Wheeler Peak, 3,000-year-old bristlecone pines, and limestone caves. Wildlife in the park includes eagles and bighorn sheep (see **Great Basin National Park**). Humboldt-Toiyabe National Forest surrounds the park. Inyo National Forests is partly in Nevada and partly in California. The northeast corner of Death Valley National Park extends into Nevada from California (see **Death Valley National Park**). The National Park Service maintains Lake Mead as a national recreation area (see **Lake Mead**).

State parks. Nevada has a total of 24 state parks, monuments, and recreational areas. The largest is the Valley of Fire, near Overton. The rocks in this park have been worn into odd shapes by the weather. For example, Elephant Rock has the shape of an elephant's head. Berlin-Ichthyosaur State Park, near Gabbs, features the ruins of an abandoned mining town. Lake Tahoe State Park lies on the edge of Lake Tahoe, which is about 6,200 feet (1,900 meters) above sea level. For information about Nevada's state parks, write to Nevada Division of State Parks, Department of Conservation and Natural Resources, 901 S. Stewart Street, Suite 5005, Carson City, NV 89701-5248. The Web site is http://parks.nv.gov.

Hoover Dam near Las Vegas

U.S. Department of Transportation

NASCAR race in Las Vegas

© Thomas E. Donoghue

© Reno News Bureau

National Championship Air Races in Reno

Rene Pauli, Shostal

Rock formations in Valley of Fire State Park

Land and climate

Land regions. Nevada lies almost entirely within the Great Basin, a huge desert area that extends into Oregon, Idaho, Wyoming, California, and Utah (see **Great Basin**). The state has three main land regions: (1) the Columbia Plateau, (2) the Sierra Nevada, and (3) the Basin and Range Region.

The Columbia Plateau covers a small part of the northeastern corner of Nevada. Deep lava bedrock lies under the entire region. Streams and rivers have cut deep canyons, leaving steep ridges. The land flattens into open prairies near the Idaho border.

The Sierra Nevada, a rugged mountain range, cuts across a corner of the state west and south of Carson City. Lake Tahoe and other mountain lakes in this part of Nevada attract many vacationers each year. See **Sierra Nevada.**

The Basin and Range Region covers the remainder of the state. It consists mainly of an upland area broken by more than 150 north-south mountain ranges. The towering Sierra Nevada marks part of the western edge of the region. The Toiyabe and Toquima ranges rise in the center of the state. In the east are the Snake and Toana ranges. Between the mountains lie *buttes* (lone hills) and *mesas* (tablelike mountains), as well as flat valleys with lakes or alkali flats (see **Butte; Mesa**).

The elevation of the Basin and Range Region varies from less than 500 feet (150 meters) above sea level near the Colorado River to more than 13,000 feet (3,960 meters) in the southwest. Boundary Peak, the highest point in Nevada, rises 13,140 feet (4,005 meters) in Esmeralda County near the California border. Hot springs and geysers in many places show that Nevada is an area of dying volcanoes.

The southeastern tip of the Basin and Range Region is not part of the Great Basin. But the land here closely resembles that of the Great Basin.

Rivers and lakes. Most of Nevada's rivers are small and flow only during the wet season, from December to June. Only a few of the state's rivers have outlets to the sea. The Virgin and Muddy rivers join the Colorado in the southeastern tip of Nevada. The Owyhee (pronounced *oh WY hee* or *oh WY ee*), Bruneau, and Salmon rivers flow northward across the Columbia Plateau to Idaho's Snake River.

All of Nevada's other rivers empty into the Great Basin. They flow into lakes without outlets or into wide, shallow *sinks* (low spots in the earth). During summer, the water evaporates from the sinks and leaves salty mud flats and dry lakes. The snow-fed Humboldt River is the state's longest river. It flows westward from the mountains of Elko County for about 300 miles (480 kilometers) and empties into Humboldt Sink. The Carson River winds northeastward from California and empties into Carson Sink. The Walker River also rises in California

Jeff Gnass, West Stock

Lake Mohave is an artificial lake that forms part of the border between Nevada and Arizona. Engineers created the lake by building Davis Dam across the Colorado River.

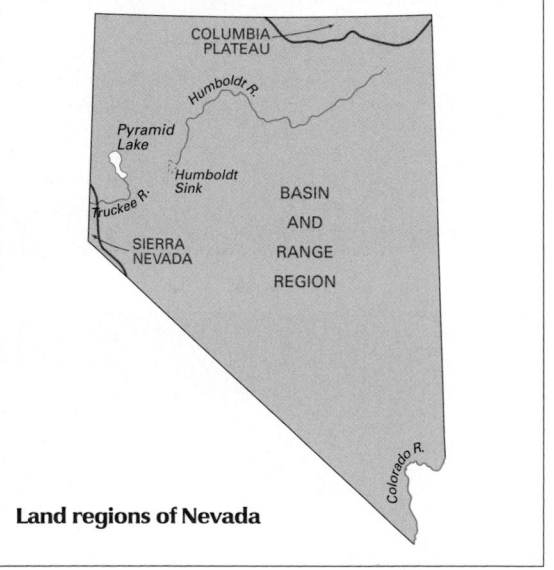

Land regions of Nevada

WORLD BOOK map

Map index

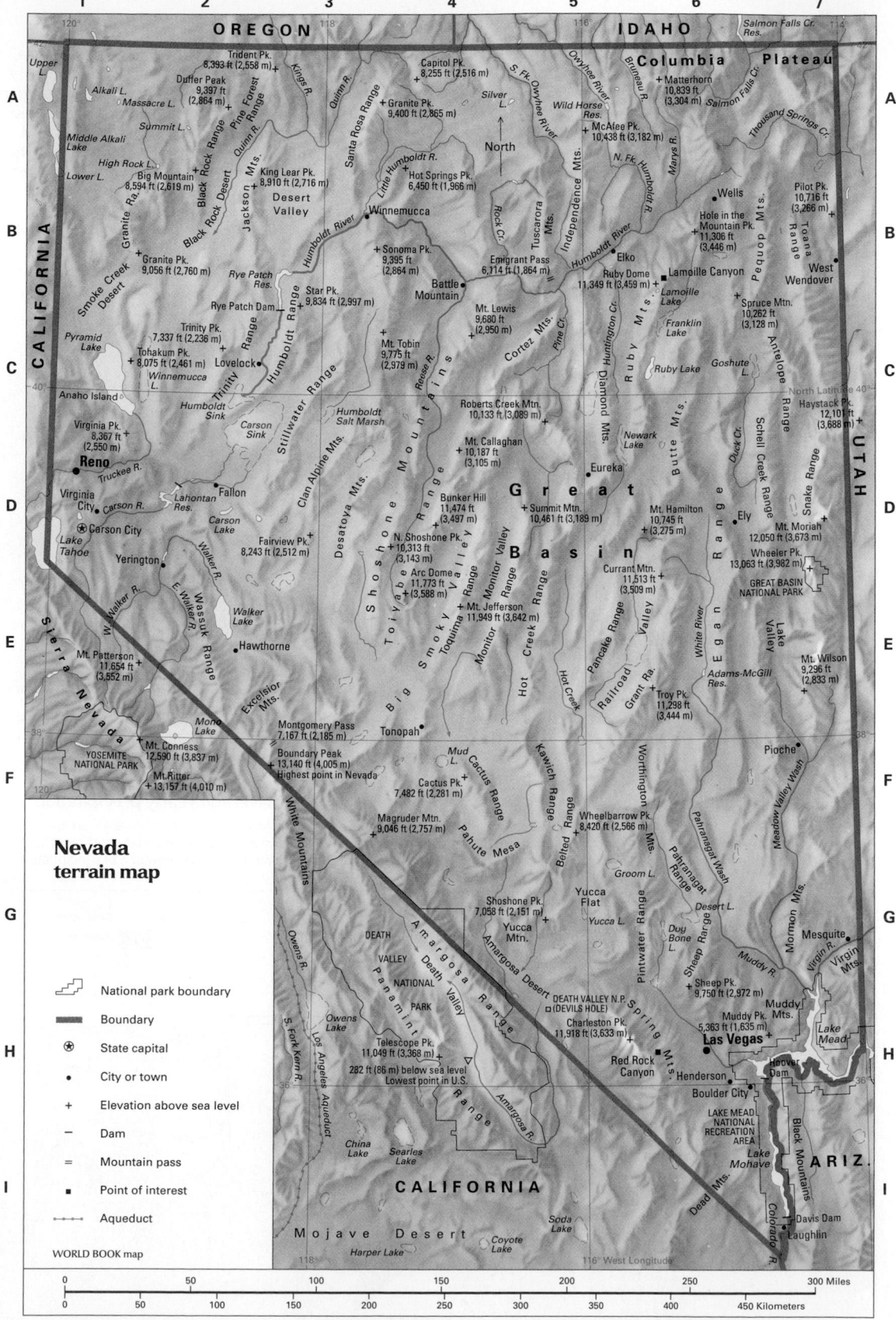

Nevada terrain map

Legend:
- ⌐┘ National park boundary
- ▬ Boundary
- ✦ State capital
- • City or town
- + Elevation above sea level
- − Dam
- = Mountain pass
- ■ Point of interest
- +·+·+ Aqueduct

WORLD BOOK map

| 0 | 50 | 100 | 150 | 200 | 250 | 300 Miles |

| 0 | 50 | 100 | 150 | 200 | 250 | 300 | 350 | 400 | 450 Kilometers |

Column headers: 1 2 3 4 5 6 7
Row labels: A B C D E F G H I

OREGON   IDAHO   Columbia Plateau

Salmon Falls Cr. Res.

Upper L.
Alkali L.
Massacre L.
Trident Pk. 8,393 ft (2,558 m)
Duffer Peak 9,397 ft (2,864 m)
Pine Forest Range
Capitol Pk. 8,255 ft (2,516 m)
Silver L.
Matterhorn 10,839 ft (3,304 m)
Salmon Falls Cr.
Thousand Springs Cr.

Middle Alkali Lake
Summit L.
High Rock L.
Lower L.
Big Mountain 8,594 ft (2,619 m)
King Lear Pk. 8,910 ft (2,716 m)
Granite Pk. 9,400 ft (2,865 m)
North
McAfee Pk. 10,438 ft (3,182 m)
Wild Horse Res.
Wells
Pilot Pk. 10,716 ft (3,266 m)

CALIFORNIA
Smoke Creek Desert
Granite Ra.
Granite Pk. 9,056 ft (2,760 m)
Black Rock Range
Black Rock Desert
Jackson Mts.
Desert Valley
Santa Rosa Range
Quinn R.
Kings R.
Little Humboldt R.
Hot Springs Pk. 6,450 ft (1,966 m)
Humboldt River
Winnemucca
Tuscarora Mts.
Independence Mts.
Rock Cr.
N. Fk. Humboldt R.
Marys R.
Hole in the Mountain Pk. 11,306 ft (3,446 m)
Toana Range
Pequop Mts.
West Wendover

Pyramid Lake
Rye Patch Res.
Sonoma Pk. 9,395 ft (2,864 m)
Battle Mountain
Emigrant Pass 6,114 ft (1,864 m)
Elko
Ruby Dome 11,349 ft (3,459 m)
Lamoille Canyon
Lamoille Lake
Spruce Mtn. 10,262 ft (3,128 m)

Rye Patch Dam
Star Pk. 9,834 ft (2,997 m)
Mt. Lewis 9,680 ft (2,950 m)
Franklin Lake

Anaho Island
Humboldt Sink
Trinity Pk. 7,337 ft (2,236 m)
Trinity Range
Lovelock
Humboldt Range
Tohakum Pk. 8,075 ft (2,461 m)
Winnemucca L.
Mt. Tobin 9,775 ft (2,979 m)
Reese R.
Cortez Mts.
Pine Cr.
Ruby Lake
Goshute L.
Haystack Pk. 12,101 ft (3,688 m)
UTAH
North Latitude 40°

Virginia Pk. 8,367 ft (2,550 m)
Carson Sink
Stillwater Range
Humboldt Salt Marsh
Roberts Creek Mtn. 10,133 ft (3,089 m)
Diamond Mts.
Newark Lake
Schell Creek Range
Duck Cr.
Snake Range

Reno
Virginia City
Truckee R.
Fallon
Carson R.
Lahontan Res.
Clan Alpine Mts.
Mt. Callaghan 10,187 ft (3,105 m)
Eureka
Butte Mts.
Antelope Range
Wheeler Pk. 13,063 ft (3,982 m)
GREAT BASIN NATIONAL PARK

Carson City
Lake Tahoe
Yerington
Carson Lake
Fairview Pk. 8,243 ft (2,512 m)
Desatoya Mts.
N. Shoshone Pk. 10,313 ft (3,143 m)
Bunker Hill 11,474 ft (3,497 m)
Great Basin
Summit Mtn. 10,461 ft (3,189 m)
Mt. Hamilton 10,745 ft (3,275 m)
Ely
Mt. Moriah 12,050 ft (3,673 m)

Sierra Nevada
Mt. Patterson 11,654 ft (3,552 m)
Walker R.
E. Walker R.
Walker Lake
Wassuk Range
Hawthorne
Shoshone Range
Toiyabe Range
Arc Dome 11,773 ft (3,588 m)
Big Smoky Valley
Monitor Valley
Mt. Jefferson 11,949 ft (3,642 m)
Toquima Range
Monitor Range
Hot Creek Range
Currant Mtn. 11,513 ft (3,509 m)
Pancake Range
White River Valley
Egan Range
Grant Ra.
Adams-McGill Res.
Lake Valley
Mt. Wilson 9,296 ft (2,833 m)

Mono Lake
Montgomery Pass 7,167 ft (2,185 m)
Tonopah
Mud Cactus Range
Kawich Range
Railroad Valley
Worthington Mts.
Troy Pk. 11,298 ft (3,444 m)
Pioche

YOSEMITE NATIONAL PARK
Mt. Conness 12,590 ft (3,837 m)
Mt. Ritter 13,157 ft (4,010 m)
Boundary Peak 13,140 ft (4,005 m) Highest point in Nevada
White Mountains
Cactus Pk. 7,482 ft (2,281 m)
Belted Range
Wheelbarrow Pk. 8,420 ft (2,566 m)
Pahranagat Range
Pahranagat Wash
Desert L.
Meadow Valley Wash

Magruder Mtn. 9,046 ft (2,757 m)
Pahute Mesa
Groom L.
Dug Bone L.
Sheep Range
Mormon Mts.
Mesquite
Virgin R.
Virgin Mts.

DEATH VALLEY NATIONAL PARK
Owens R.
Amargosa Range
Amargosa River
Amargosa Desert
Shoshone Pk. 7,058 ft (2,151 m)
Yucca Mtn.
Yucca Flat
Yucca L.
Pintwater Range
Sheep Pk. 9,750 ft (2,972 m)
Muddy R.
Muddy Pk. 5,363 ft (1,635 m)
Muddy Mts.

Owens Lake
Panamint Range
Spring Mts.
DEATH VALLEY N.P. (DEVILS HOLE)
Charleston Pk. 11,918 ft (3,633 m)
Las Vegas
Lake Mead

S. Fork Kern R.
Los Angeles Aqueduct
Telescope Pk. 11,049 ft (3,368 m)
282 ft (86 m) below sea level Lowest point in U.S.
Red Rock Canyon
Henderson
Boulder City
Hoover Dam
Black Mountains

China Lake
Searles Lake
Amargosa Range
LAKE MEAD NATIONAL RECREATION AREA
Lake Mohave
Dead Mts.
Colorado R.
ARIZ.

CALIFORNIA
Mojave Desert
Harper Lake
Coyote Lake
Soda Lake
Davis Dam
Laughlin

and empties into Walker Lake. The scenic Truckee River flows northeastward from Lake Tahoe and empties into Pyramid Lake.

Lake Tahoe, on the Nevada-California border, is one of the nation's loveliest lakes. Lamoille, Liberty, and other beautiful lakes lie among the peaks of the Ruby Range in Elko County. Ruby and Franklin lakes are at the eastern foot of the Ruby Range. Pyramid Lake and Walker Lake are the remains of Lake Lahontan, an ancient lake that gradually dried up. Thousands of years ago, Lake Lahontan covered about a tenth of the present state of Nevada.

Lake Mead, an artificially created lake, is the only Nevada lake with an outlet to the sea. Engineers formed this vast reservoir by building Hoover Dam across a canyon of the Colorado River.

Plant and animal life. Broad stretches of forests cover Nevada's mountainsides. Common trees include alders, aspens, cottonwoods, firs, hemlocks, junipers, pines, spruces, and willows.

Nevada's deserts are dotted with cactus, yucca, and a variety of low brush plants. The most common desert plants include the bitter brush, mesquite, rabbit brush, sagebrush, and shadscale. Grasses grow in mountain and valley meadows. Nevada's meadows bloom in spring with Indian paintbrush, larkspur, shooting stars, and violets. In early spring, blood-red blossoms of the snow plant push through the snow in the pine forests. Wild peach blossoms and desert lilies brighten Nevada's foothills in spring and summer.

Nevada has few large animals, but hundreds of small animals live in the state. Mule deer roam the mountain forests. Pronghorns live mainly in the Charles Sheldon Antelope Refuge in Washoe County. Bighorn sheep climb the steep, rocky slopes of the Sheep Range in Clark County. Nevada's small animals include badgers, coyotes, foxes, marmots, minks, muskrats, porcupines, rabbits, and raccoons. Several kinds of lizards and snakes live in the desert. Game birds include chukar partridges, ducks, geese, pheasants, quail, and sage hens. Hundreds of white pelicans nest in the Anahoe Island Refuge in Pyramid Lake. Several kinds of trout make the state a favorite fishing spot. The *cui-ui* is a large sucker found only in Pyramid Lake. It was once an important food fish among the local Indians. Other fishes that swim in Nevada waters include bass, carp, catfish, and crappies.

Leonard Lee Rue III, Shostal

Bighorn sheep in Nevada live on the steep, rocky slopes of the Sheep Range north of Las Vegas. Bighorn sheep, mule deer, and pronghorns are the state's largest wild animals.

Average January temperatures

The northeast has long, cool winters. Milder temperatures are found in the south and in the Reno-Carson City area.

Average July temperatures

Nevada has wide variations in summertime temperatures. Mountainous areas are much cooler than the rest of the state.

Average yearly precipitation

Nevada receives less rain than any other state. Much of the state gets less than 8 inches (20 centimeters) of precipitation.

WORLD BOOK maps

Degrees Fahrenheit	Degrees Celsius
Above 32	Above 0
30 to 32	-1 to 0
26 to 30	-3 to -1
Below 26	Below -3

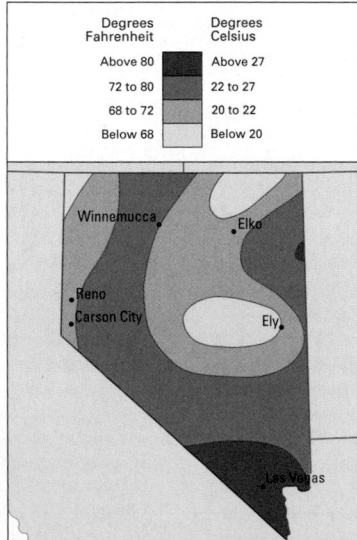

Degrees Fahrenheit	Degrees Celsius
Above 80	Above 27
72 to 80	22 to 27
68 to 72	20 to 22
Below 68	Below 20

Inches	Centimeters
More than 16	More than 41
12 to 16	30 to 41
8 to 12	20 to 30
Less than 8	Less than 20

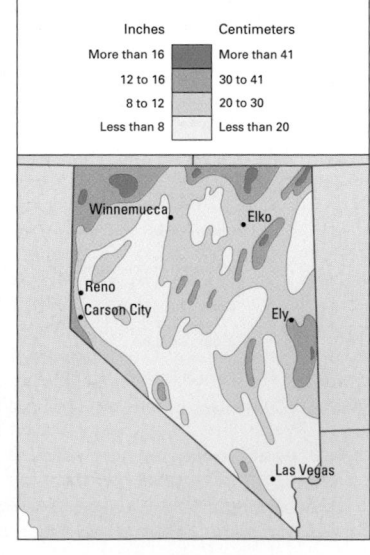

Average monthly weather

	Las Vegas						Elko				
	Temperatures				Days of rain or snow		Temperatures				Days of rain or snow
	°F		°C				°F		°C		
	High	Low	High	Low			High	Low	High	Low	
Jan.	57	37	14	3	3	Jan.	37	14	3	–10	9
Feb.	63	41	17	5	3	Feb.	43	20	6	–7	9
Mar.	70	47	21	8	3	Mar.	51	26	11	–3	9
Apr.	78	54	26	12	2	Apr.	59	30	15	–1	8
May	88	63	31	17	1	May	69	37	21	3	8
June	99	72	37	22	1	June	80	44	27	7	5
July	104	78	40	26	3	July	90	49	32	9	3
Aug.	102	77	39	25	3	Aug.	88	47	31	8	4
Sept.	94	69	34	21	2	Sept.	78	38	26	3	4
Oct.	81	57	27	14	2	Oct.	65	28	18	–2	5
Nov.	66	44	19	7	2	Nov.	48	21	9	–6	7
Dec.	57	37	14	3	3	Dec.	38	14	3	–10	9

Climate. Nevada has less precipitation than any other state. An average of only 9 inches (23 centimeters) of precipitation falls in Nevada annually. The driest regions of the state include the southeastern tip and the land near Carson Sink.

The rainiest parts of Nevada are in the Sierra Nevada and the eastern foothills of these mountains. As much as 25 inches (64 centimeters) of rain falls annually in the Lake Tahoe region of the Sierras. Most of it falls during winter. Clouds moving eastward from the Pacific Ocean bring the rain. But the clouds lose most of their moisture in California as they rise over the high Sierra Nevada.

Snowfall varies widely in the state. It ranges from about 300 inches (750 centimeters) a year in the highest sections of the Sierras to about 1 inch (2.5 centimeters) a year in the southeastern part of the state.

Nevada has a wide range of temperatures. The north and the mountains in all sections have cold, long winters and short, hot summers. The west has short, hot summers, but winters there are only mildly cold. In southern Nevada, summers are long and hot, and winters are mild.

July temperatures average about 70 °F (21 °C) in the north and in the mountains, and 86 °F (30 °C) in the extreme south. January temperatures average 24 °F (–4 °C) in the north and 43 °F (6 °C) in the south. The temperature often changes greatly during the day. In Reno, for example, the temperature may change more than 45 degrees Fahrenheit (25 degrees Celsius) on a summer day. The highest temperature ever recorded in Nevada was 125 °F (52 °C) at Laughlin on June 29, 1994. The temperature reached a record low of –50 °F (–46 °C) at San Jacinto on Jan. 8, 1937.

Economy

Service industries employ a large majority of Nevada's fast-growing work force. Heavy tourist spending benefits such service establishments as casino hotels, restaurants, and ski resorts. Agriculture and manufacturing are less dominant in Nevada than they are in most other states. Gold is Nevada's most important mined product.

Natural resources. Nevada's chief natural resources are its vast mineral deposits, wildlife, and beautiful scenery. In some areas of Nevada, poor soil and lack of water make it difficult or impossible to raise field crops. Thick grasses in some valleys provide grazing for cattle.

Soil. Most of Nevada is covered with a grayish-brown soil. Many areas have sparse coverings of grasses and brush. With irrigation, Nevada's soil can grow grain, hay, and other crops. In some valleys, thick layers of sodium carbonate form gleaming white alkali flats, where nothing grows. These flats are sometimes called *playas* or *dry lakes* because they may be covered with water after a storm. Much of southern Nevada is covered by light gray soil high in lime or gypsum. Much of the northern section has dark soil formed from volcanic rock.

Water. Nevada has a limited water supply because of its light rainfall. Water must be carefully conserved when used for personal needs and irrigation. Despite agriculture's limited impact on Nevada's economy, farming and ranching activities consume about three-fourths of the state's water. Farmers and ranchers pump underground water for their crops and livestock in the Carson, Diamond, Fish Lake, Mason, Smith, Spring, and White River valleys. The largest irrigation systems operate along the rivers. The Newlands Project includes the Lahontan Reservoir, which stores water from the Carson and Truckee rivers. It provides irrigation water for west-central Nevada. Other large irrigation projects include Rye Patch Dam on the Humboldt River, Topaz Reservoir on the Walker River, and Wild Horse Dam in the Owyhee River Valley. The Robert B. Griffith Water Project provides Lake Mead water to the Las Vegas area.

Minerals. Huge deposits of copper lie in Lander, Lyon, and White Pine counties. Central and northwestern Nevada have large tungsten deposits. Gold and silver are found in many areas. Other mined resources include barite, clays, diatomite, gemstones, lithium, magnesite, perlite, and salt. Nevada also has valuable deposits of gypsum, limestone, and sand and gravel. Petroleum is found in some eastern areas of the state.

Service industries account for over 80 percent of both Nevada's employment and its *gross domestic product*—the total value of goods and services produced in the state in a year. These industries are more important to Nevada's economy than they are to the economies of most other states. Most of Nevada's service industries are concentrated in the Las Vegas-Paradise and Reno-Sparks metropolitan areas.

Every year, tens of millions of visitors enjoy Nevada's night life, lovely scenery, and recreational activities. Nevada is one of the leading states in attracting visitors from other countries. Tourist activities contribute billions of dollars to the state annually. Although gambling is legal throughout the state, the vast majority of Nevada's large casinos are in Las Vegas, Reno, and the Lake Tahoe area. Well-known entertainers from the United States and Europe appear in floor shows at casinos and nightclubs. Dude ranches, fishing resorts, and hunting lodges operate in many areas of the state.

Hotels, restaurants, and retail trade establishments operate primarily in the Las Vegas area. Many of the hotels are casino hotels. Nevada's main financial centers

Nevada economy

General economy

Gross domestic product (GDP)* (2008) $132,120,000,000
   Rank among U.S. states   31st
Unemployment rate (2010)   14.0% (U.S. avg: 9.6%)

*Gross domestic product is the total value of goods and services produced in a year.
Sources: U.S. Bureau of Economic Analysis and U.S. Bureau of Labor Statistics.

Agriculture

Cash receipts $533,370,000
   Rank among U.S. states   44th
Distribution   52% livestock, 48% crops
Farms   3,100
Farm acres (hectares)   5,900,000 (2,390,000)
   Rank among U.S. states   37th
Farmland   8% of Nevada

Leading products

1. Cattle and calves
2. Hay
3. Dairy products
4. Onions
5. Greenhouse and nursery products
6. Potatoes
Other products: alfalfa, garlic, hogs, sheep and lambs, wheat

Manufacturing

Value added by manufacture* $8,950,077,000
   Rank among U.S. states   39th

Leading products
Computer and electronic products, fabricated metal products, food products, nonmetallic mineral products, plastic products.

*Value added by manufacture is the increase in value of raw materials after they become finished products.

Mining

Nonfuel mineral production $6,300,000,000
   Rank among U.S. states   2nd
Coal   *
Crude oil (barrels†)   436,000
   Rank among U.S. states   26th
Natural gas (cubic feet‡)   4,000,000
   Rank among U.S. states   32nd

*No significant mining of this product in Nevada.
†One barrel equals 42 gallons (159 liters).
‡One cubic foot equals 0.0283 cubic meter.

Leading products

1. Gold   (ranks 1st in U.S.)
2. Copper   (ranks 4th in U.S.)
3. Sand and gravel
4. Silver   (ranks 2nd in U.S.)
Other products: barite, diatomite, granite, gypsum, lime, limestone, lithium carbonate, magnesite.

Electric power

Natural gas   68.3%
Coal   22.3%
Hydroelectric   5.0%
Other   4.4%

Figures are for 2008, except for the agricultural figures, which are for 2009.
Sources: U.S. Census Bureau, U.S. Department of Agriculture, U.S. Energy Information Administration, U.S. Geological Survey.

Production and workers by economic activities

Economic activities	Percent of GDP produced	Employed workers Number of people	Percent of total
Finance, insurance, & real estate	25	210,400	13
Trade, restaurants, & hotels	24	523,700	32
Community, business, & personal services	17	432,800	26
Government	10	173,200	11
Construction	9	138,600	8
Transportation & communication	5	78,900	5
Manufacturing	4	52,600	3
Mining	3	16,600	1
Utilities	2	4,800	*
Agriculture	*	6,500	*
Total†	100	1,638,100	100

*Less than one-half of 1 percent.
†Figures do not add up to 100 percent due to rounding.
Figures are for 2008; employment figures include full- and part-time workers.
Source: World Book estimates based on data from U.S. Bureau of Economic Analysis.

Economy of Nevada

This map shows the economic uses of land in Nevada and where the leading farm and mineral products are produced. Major manufacturing centers are shown in red.

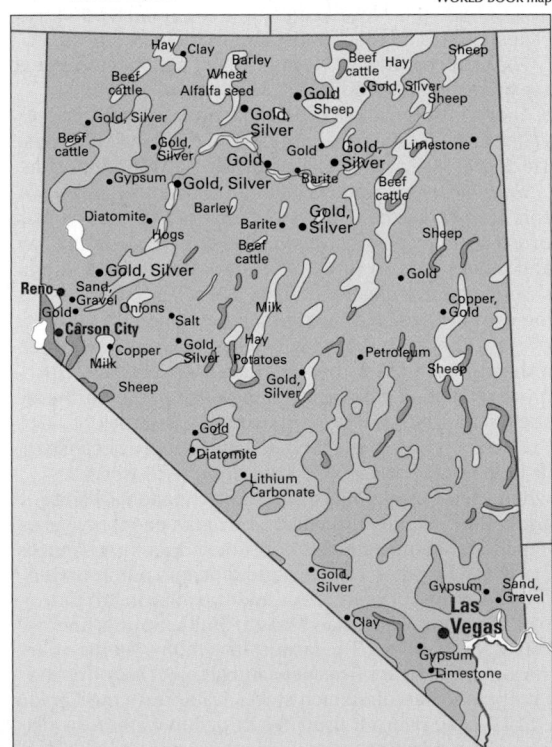

Gambling casinos, such as this one in Reno, attract tens of millions of tourists to Nevada each year. The tourist industry provides the state's single greatest source of income.

Tim Heneghan, West Stock

are Las Vegas and Reno. Real estate has become important as more people move to the state. Since 1980, Nevada has grown faster than any other state.

Government services are also important to Nevada's economy. Carson City, the state capital, is the center of state government activities. The federal government plays a major role in Nevada's economy because it owns most of the state's land. Two federal government facilities, the Nevada National Security Site and Nellis Air Force Base, employ thousands of people. The Nevada National Security Site's main function is to conduct experiments to maintain the safety of the country's nuclear stockpile.

Mining. Nevada ranks as one of the leading states in

David R. Frazier

Gold mining ranks as Nevada's most valuable mining activity. Nevada leads the nation in gold production. This engineer is laying out a surface mine near Elko.

mining income. Gold is Nevada's most valuable mined product, accounting for about four-fifths of the total mining income. Nevada mines about three-fourths of all the gold produced in the United States. The largest gold mines are in Elko, Eureka, Humboldt, Lander, and Nye counties. Several other Nevada counties produce significant amounts of gold. Nevada is also a leading producer of silver in the United States. The northern part of the state is the leading silver-producing region.

Nevada is a leading state in the production of diatomite, a chalky substance used to make filters. Most of the diatomite is obtained from areas that were once lakes in western Nevada. Nevada is also a leading producer of barite, copper, and gypsum, and the only state to produce lithium carbonate and magnesite.

Manufacturing. Manufacturing plays less of a role in Nevada's economy than it does in the economies of most other states. The Carson City, Las Vegas, and Reno areas are the chief manufacturing centers in the state.

Leading manufactured products include computer and electronic equipment, concrete, fabricated metal products, food products, and plastic products. Communication equipment, computers, and semiconductors are primarily produced in the Las Vegas and Reno areas. Concrete is mainly manufactured in the Las Vegas area. Machine shop products, sheet metal products, and structural metal products are the leading fabricated metal products. Baked goods and dairy products are mainly produced in the Las Vegas area. Minden processes coffee beans. Plastic products are primarily manufactured in the Las Vegas and Reno areas. The Las Vegas area also produces neon signs, and the Reno area also produces slot machines and other gaming equipment.

Agriculture. Livestock ranching accounts for about half of the state's agricultural activity. Most of Nevada's large cattle and sheep ranches are in the northern half of the state. Many ranchers graze their animals for part of the year on public lands that they rent from the federal government. Much of the milk production comes from Churchill, Lyon, and Nye counties.

Irrigated farms operate chiefly near the river valleys of northern and western Nevada. However, irrigated farming projects have been developed throughout the state. Hay is Nevada's most valuable field crop. The state's northwestern basins are the leading region for growing hay. Farmers also raise alfalfa seed, barley, garlic, mint, onions, potatoes, and wheat.

Electric power and utilities. Coal-burning plants and plants that burn natural gas provide most of Nevada's electric power. Hydroelectric plants at the Davis, Hoover, and Parker dams on the Colorado River provide much of the power for the southern portion of the state. Nevada is a leading producer of geothermal power. Geothermal power is mainly produced in the northern portion of the state.

Transportation. McCarran International Airport, in Las Vegas, is one of the nation's busiest airports. Reno/ Tahoe International Airport serves the Reno area. Rail lines provide freight service in the state, and passenger trains serve several Nevada cities.

Communication. Nevada's first printed newspaper, the *Territorial Enterprise,* was established at Genoa in 1858. The American author Mark Twain worked as a reporter on this paper from 1862 to 1864, after it moved to Virginia City. Today, daily newspapers with the largest circulations include the *Las Vegas Review-Journal* and the *Reno Gazette-Journal.*

Government

Constitution of Nevada was adopted in 1864, the year the state entered the Union. Nevada's Constitution may be *amended* (changed) only by a majority of the voters. An amendment proposed by the Legislature must be approved by a majority of both houses in two successive regular sessions. Then the voters must approve it in the next general election.

The people may amend the Constitution directly by using the *initiative.* In this procedure, voters who support the amendment first sign a petition. The number of signatures must equal at least 10 percent of the voters in the last general election in each of Nevada's three congressional districts. The petition states the proposed amendment and calls for a general election to vote on it. If the amendment is approved by a majority of the voters in two successive general elections, it becomes part of the Constitution.

The Nevada Constitution may also be revised by a constitutional convention. To call such a convention, two-thirds of each legislative house must vote for it. Then a majority of voters must approve the convention in the next general election.

Executive. The governor of Nevada is elected to a four-year term. The governor may serve no more than two elected terms.

Key Nevada state officials also are elected to four-year terms. Elected officials include the lieutenant governor, secretary of state, treasurer, controller, and attorney general. These officials may serve no more than two terms. The governor appoints the members of many bureaus, commissions, and administrative boards.

Legislature consists of a 21-member Senate and a 42-member Assembly. Nevada has 21 senatorial districts and 42 Assembly districts. Each senatorial district elects one senator. Each Assembly district elects one member to the Assembly. Members of the Senate serve four-year terms and may serve no more than three terms. Members of the Assembly serve two-year terms and may serve no more than six terms.

The Nevada Legislature meets on the first Monday of February in odd-numbered years. Legislators receive their salaries for 60 days, and legislative sessions are limited to 120 days. The governor can call special legislative sessions.

Courts. The Supreme Court of Nevada has a chief justice and six associate justices, all of whom are elected to six-year terms. One or two justices are elected every two years. A justice in the final two years of his or her term normally serves as chief justice.

Nevada has nine judicial districts, with 64 district judges who serve six-year terms. Court districts with large populations have divisions called *departments*. Each department is headed by a district judge. Municipal judges serve in Nevada's city courts, and justices of the peace serve in the state's townships.

Local government. Nevada has 17 counties. Three-member boards of county commissioners govern in Churchill, Esmeralda, Eureka, Lander, Mineral, Pershing, and Storey counties. Voters in Douglas, Elko, Humboldt, Lincoln, Lyon, Nye, Washoe, and White Pine counties

AP/Wide World

The Nevada Legislature meets in the State Capitol in Carson City. The Legislature consists of two chambers, the Senate and the Assembly. In this picture, Assembly members are sworn in on the first day of a legislative session.

elect five-member boards. Voters in Clark County elect a seven-member board. A five-member board of supervisors governs Carson City, which is both a city and a county. County commissioners serve four-year terms. Other elected county officials include the assessor, auditor and recorder, clerk, district attorney, public administrator, and sheriff. The state's local government officials may serve for no more than 12 years. Most of Nevada's cities have a mayor-council form of government.

Revenue. Taxes account for about two-thirds of Nevada's *general revenue* (income). Most of the rest comes from federal grants and other United States government programs. A sales tax is the state's most important source of revenue. Taxes on gambling are also important to the state. Nevada allows many forms of gambling that are not legal in most other states. Other important sources of state revenue include taxes on alcoholic beverages, insurance, mining, motor fuel, and tobacco; and license fees for automobiles and the transportation of passengers and freight. State and local governments share revenue from a property tax. Nevada has no personal or corporate income taxes.

To attract industry, Nevada enacted a "free port" tax law in 1949. This law applies to goods being held in Nevada for shipment outside the state. It allows manufacturers to process and store such goods in Nevada without paying property taxes on them. In most states, manufacturers must pay taxes on such goods. The free port law became part of the state Constitution in 1960.

Politics. The Republican Party is strong in much of Nevada. The Democratic Party's strength lies mainly in Las Vegas and the other communities of Clark County, where two-thirds of the state's voters live.

In elections for governor, Republicans have won

more often than Democrats. In presidential elections, voters have supported more Republican candidates than Democrats. For Nevada's votes and voting record in presidential elections, see **Electoral College** (table).

The governors of Nevada		
	Party	**Term**
Henry G. Blasdel	Republican	1864-1871
Lewis R. Bradley	Democratic	1871-1879
John H. Kinkead	Republican	1879-1883
Jewett W. Adams	Democratic	1883-1887
Charles C. Stevenson	Republican	1887-1890
Frank Bell	Republican	1890-1891
Roswell K. Colcord	Republican	1891-1895
John E. Jones	Silver	1895-1896
Reinhold Sadler	Silver	1896-1903
John Sparks	Silver-Dem.*	1903-1908
Denver S. Dickerson	Silver-Dem.	1908-1911
Tasker L. Oddie	Republican	1911-1915
Emmet D. Boyle	Democratic	1915-1923
James G. Scrugham	Democratic	1923-1927
Fred B. Balzar	Republican	1927-1934
Morley Griswold	Republican	1934-1935
Richard Kirman, Sr.	Democratic	1935-1939
Edward P. Carville	Democratic	1939-1945
Vail M. Pittman	Democratic	1945-1951
Charles H. Russell	Republican	1951-1959
Grant Sawyer	Democratic	1959-1967
Paul Laxalt	Republican	1967-1971
Mike O'Callaghan	Democratic	1971-1979
Robert List	Republican	1979-1983
Richard H. Bryan	Democratic	1983-1989
Bob Miller	Democratic	1989-1999
Kenny Guinn	Republican	1999-2007
Jim Gibbons	Republican	2007-2011
Brian Sandoval	Republican	2011-

*Silver-Democratic.

History

Indian days. Bones, ashes, and other remains discovered near Las Vegas indicate that Indians lived there thousands of years ago. Cave-dwelling Indians left picture writings on rocks in southern Nevada. Basket Makers once lived at Lovelock Cave, and Pueblo Indians lived around Las Vegas. Explorers of the early 1800's found Mohave, Paiute, Shoshone, and Washoe Indians in parts of the region.

Exploration. Francisco Garcés, a Spanish missionary, possibly was the first white man to enter the Nevada region. He may have traveled through southern Nevada while journeying from New Mexico to California in 1776. Fur traders and trappers began to explore the region between 1825 and 1830. Peter S. Ogden, a Canadian fur trader, explored the Humboldt River Valley with a group of trappers of the Hudson's Bay Company (see **Hudson's Bay Company**). Jedediah S. Smith, an American trader, led some trappers across the Las Vegas Valley region into California and then back across the Great Basin.

In 1830, the American frontiersman William Wolfskill blazed a route, called the Old Spanish Trail, from Santa Fe to Los Angeles. This trail opened Nevada to trade from the southeast. Joseph R. Walker, an American hunter and trapper, blazed a trail along the Humboldt River on his way to California in 1833. Hundreds of wagons rolled westward over this same trail after gold was

David Muench

Picture writings were made on rocks by cave-dwelling Indians thousands of years ago in Valley of Fire State Park.

discovered in California in 1848. Between 1843 and 1845, Lieutenant John C. Frémont explored the Great Basin and Sierra Nevada. Frémont provided the first accurate knowledge of the Nevada region.

Early settlement. At the end of the Mexican War in 1848, the United States acquired the Nevada region from Mexico. Nevada was then part of a territory that also included California, Utah, and parts of four other states (see **Mexican War** [The peace treaty]).

In 1849, the Mormon leader Brigham Young organized Utah, most of present-day Nevada, and parts of other present-day states as the State of Deseret. He asked Congress to admit his state to the Union. However, in 1850, Congress established the Utah Territory, which included Utah and most of present-day Nevada. President Millard Fillmore appointed Young governor of the territory.

In 1851, Mormons from the Great Salt Lake area in Utah built a trading post at Mormon Station (now Genoa) in the Carson Valley. The post supplied provisions for gold seekers heading for California. During the next few years, a few Mormon families came to farm and raise livestock in the Carson Valley and the surrounding region. This section of Utah Territory was organized into Carson County.

Many non-Mormons in Carson County did not want to be governed by Brigham Young. They pleaded unsuccessfully with Congress to make Carson County part of California. The Mormons themselves were troubled by a dispute with the federal government. In 1857, Young recalled the Mormon settlers to Great Salt Lake because he feared that federal troops would attack them. Two years later, the non-Mormons set up a provisional government in an attempt to establish Carson County as a separate territory. But Congress did not authorize the provisional government because only a few hundred persons lived in the Carson County area.

The Comstock Lode, a rich deposit of silver ore, was discovered in 1859 at the present site of Virginia City.

Henry Comstock, a prospector, took credit for the discovery, though other miners actually had found the ore. News of the Comstock Lode quickly spread to fortune hunters in California and the Eastern United States. Hundreds of prospectors rushed to Carson County to "strike it rich," settling in tents, rough stone huts, and hillside caves. Almost overnight, Virginia City became a thriving mining center.

The settlers of the area led a difficult and dangerous life. They paid unbelievably high prices for provisions that had to be hauled from California over the Sierra Nevada. Some miners became millionaires. However, many other miners found little or no wealth. Many mining camps were lawless, and many miners were rowdies or gunmen.

Nevada becomes a territory. By 1860, the booming mining camps of Carson County held more than 6,700 people. In March 1861, President James Buchanan signed an act creating the Nevada Territory. President Abraham Lincoln, who took office two days later, appointed James W. Nye, a New York City politician, governor of the territory.

The Civil War (1861-1865) began before Nevada's territorial government could be set up in Carson City. Most Nevadans favored the North. Lincoln needed another "northern" state to support his proposed antislavery amendments. He knew that most Nevadans favored his administration and would be likely to elect Republican senators who would support his policies. At the time, the Nevada Territory had far less than the 127,381 residents required by law to become a state. But Nevadans held a convention anyway and drew up a state constitution.

Statehood. The convention met in November 1863, but ended in failure. The voters rejected the proposed constitution because of its provisions for the taxing of mines. Congress then passed an act authorizing a second Nevada convention. In July 1864, this convention met and completed its work. In September, the revised

Genoa in 1859 prospered by supplying provisions for prospectors on their way to Virginia City to mine silver. Genoa is Nevada's oldest permanent white settlement. It was established in 1851 as a trading post called Mormon Station.

Historic Nevada

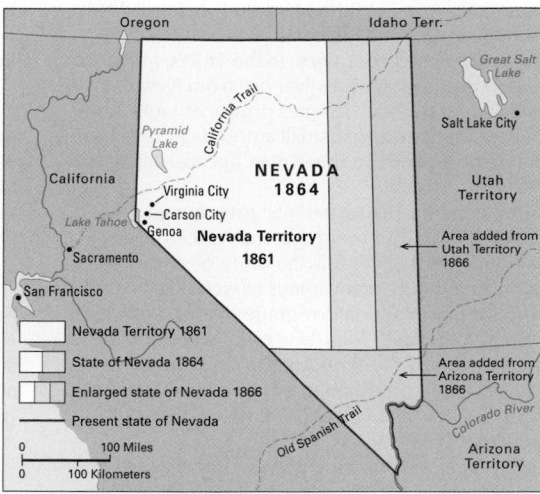

WORLD BOOK map

The Comstock Lode, a rich deposit of silver and gold ore, was discovered in 1859. Prospectors flocked to the area, and Virginia City quickly rose nearby.

Nevada was formed as the Nevada Territory in 1861. Land was added in 1864, the year Nevada became a state. In 1866, another addition of land gave the state its current boundaries.

Nuclear weapons testing began in 1951 at an Atomic Energy Commission center about 60 miles (97 kilometers) northwest of Las Vegas. Hundreds of tests were conducted at the site before the U.S. government halted testing in 1992.

Important dates in Nevada

WORLD BOOK illustrations by Richard Bonson, The Art Agency

1776 Francisco Garces, a friar, may have become the first European to enter the Nevada region.

1825-1830 Peter S. Ogden explored the Humboldt River. Jedediah S. Smith crossed southern Nevada.

1843-1845 John C. Frémont and Kit Carson explored the Great Basin and Sierra Nevada.

1848 The United States received Nevada and other lands in the Southwest from Mexico under the Treaty of Guadalupe Hidalgo.

1859 The discovery of silver near Virginia City brought a rush of prospectors to western Nevada.

1861 Congress created the Nevada Territory.

1864 Nevada became the 36th state on October 31.

1877-1881 The price of silver fell and caused many Nevada mines to close.

1880-1890 Unemployed people left Nevada, and the population dropped by almost 15,000.

1909 The Nevada Legislature passed laws that made gambling illegal. The laws went into effect in 1910.

1931 The Legislature reduced the divorce residence requirement to six weeks and also made gambling legal in the state.

1936 Boulder (now Hoover) Dam was completed.

1951 The Atomic Energy Commission began testing nuclear weapons in southern Nevada.

1963 The Supreme Court of the United States settled a 40-year dispute by specifying how much water the states of Arizona, California, and Nevada could draw from the Colorado River.

1967 The Nevada Legislature changed state gambling laws to allow corporations that sell stock to the public to buy casinos and to hold gambling licenses.

1971 The Water Project (now called the Robert B. Griffith Water Project) was completed.

1980 The Nevada Legislature passed conservation laws to protect Lake Tahoe from pollution.

1992 The U.S. government halted the testing of nuclear weapons, ending such tests in Nevada.

1990's Nevada's population grew by 66 percent, reaching a total of nearly 2 million by 2000. The growth rate was the highest of any U.S. state during the decade.

2000's Government officials and environmentalists debated a proposal to bury nuclear waste at Yucca Mountain.

constitution won the approval of the voters. The people elected Republican Henry G. Blasdel, a mining engineer, their first governor. President Lincoln proclaimed Nevada a state on Oct. 31, 1864.

Mine failure and recovery. In the 1870's, mining companies dug the richest silver ore from Nevada's mines. Some of the state's mines produced only "low-grade" ores that contained small amounts of silver. Mine owners made a profit on these ores because silver had a high value.

During the early 1870's, the U.S. government limited the use of silver in its money system. As the government's demand for silver fell, the value of silver also dropped. As a result, many mines closed because they could no longer produce low-grade ores at a profit, and many people lost their jobs. Unemployed people began to leave Nevada by the thousands to find work elsewhere. The state's population dropped from 62,266 in 1880 to 47,355 in 1890. Many thriving communities became ghost towns.

As mining failed, ranching grew in importance. However, the ranchers also faced difficult problems. They had to pay the railroad extremely high rates to ship their stock. In addition, severe winters during the late 1880's killed thousands of cattle. Many owners of small herds became bankrupt and had to sell out to operators of large ranches.

Nevada's economic recovery began with new mineral discoveries in 1900. Prospectors found huge deposits of silver at Tonopah. They could be mined profitably, though silver still had a low value. Prospectors uncovered copper ores at Ruth and Kimberly, near Ely. In 1902, gold was discovered at Goldfield. Rich deposits discovered the next year brought thousands of miners back to Nevada.

As the mining industry came to life again, the railroads built branch lines to the mining areas. Trains brought equipment to the mines and hauled ore away to processing plants. Cattle owners also used the new branch lines for speedy beef shipments.

Nevada's Newlands Irrigation Project, the country's first federal irrigation project, was completed in 1907. In this project, dams along the Carson and Truckee rivers create irrigation reservoirs and generate electricity. Water from this system supplies an agricultural region that developed near Fallon, which is in the west-central part of Nevada.

The richest of Nevada's gold and silver deposits were running out when the United States entered World War I in 1917. Industries then began to demand copper, tungsten, zinc, and other metals for weapons and wartime supplies. Many new mines opened in Nevada, and mine owners collected top prices for the metals. But prices fell after the war ended in 1918, and many mines closed.

In 1928, Congress authorized the construction of Hoover Dam on the Colorado River. Work on the dam began in 1930. The huge project was completed in 1935. Hoover Dam provides power and stores up irrigation water for parts of Nevada, Arizona, and California.

Legal gambling and easy divorce. As early as 1869, Nevada's legislature had permitted gamblers to operate games of chance in the state. By 1910, various groups of citizens had succeeded in having laws passed against gambling. However, Nevada's individualist culture and the limits of law enforcement made the laws largely ineffective. In 1931, Nevada made gambling legal. Numerous gambling casinos began to operate in the state during the 1930's.

In the early 1900's, Nevada had passed laws that made it easy to get a divorce. A person had to live in Nevada for only six months to get a divorce there. In 1927, the Nevada legislature passed a law allowing persons to obtain a divorce if they lived in the state for only three months. In 1931, the period was reduced to six weeks. During the mid-1900's, thousands of people went to Nevada each year to get divorces quickly and easily.

The mid-1900's. World War II (1939-1945) created new business for Nevada's mining industry. Manufacturers of military supplies purchased large amounts of the state's copper, lead, magnesite, manganese, tungsten, and zinc. After the war, mining decreased. The industry gradually switched to the production of gypsum, lime, and other nonmetallic minerals.

In the late 1940's, Nevada began a widespread campaign to attract new industry. Although the campaign brought a number of factories into the state, Nevada's economy during the 1950's and 1960's depended chiefly on nuclear research and tourism.

In 1950, the Atomic Energy Commission (AEC) set up a testing center about 60 miles (97 kilometers) northwest of Las Vegas. The next year, the AEC began testing nuclear weapons. Between 1951 and 1963, 127 aboveground atomic and nuclear tests took place in Nevada. Underground testing continued for 30 more years. In 1992, the federal government halted all nuclear weapons testing.

Tourism remained Nevada's largest and fastest-growing industry during the 1950's and 1960's. By the late 1960's, the Las Vegas area alone attracted annually about 15 million tourists, who spent about $400 million. Tourists also flocked to the state's two other main resort centers, Reno and the Lake Tahoe area.

In the late 1950's, the Nevada legislature set up strict gambling regulations to prevent cheating and to stop criminals from entering or influencing the gambling industry. The regulations require every gambling house to have a state license. A license is issued only after investigation by the Gaming Control Board and final approval by the Gaming Commission. In 1967, the legislature passed a law allowing corporations that sell stock to the public to hold gambling licenses. The new law was a further attempt to keep the underworld out of the gambling industry.

In 1963, the Supreme Court of the United States settled a 40-year dispute between Arizona, California, and Nevada over water supplies from the Colorado River. The court ruled on how much water each state could draw from the river every year.

Howard Hughes, an American businessman and one of the world's richest people, moved to Las Vegas in 1966. He then bought airports, casinos and hotels, large tracts of land, and a television station in the area.

In 1967, the Water Project (now called the Robert B. Griffith Water Project) was created to provide increased water supplies for the expected growth in the Las Vegas area. The final stage of the project, which brings water from Lake Mead, was completed in 1983.

The late 1900's. In the late 1970's, Las Vegas and Reno began projects to improve their airport facilities to accommodate a continuing increase in the number of tourists. Reno's project was completed in 1981. Expansion of the McCarran International Airport in Las Vegas was completed in 1998.

Air and water pollution became serious problems in Nevada in the late 1900's. In one program to control water pollution, Nevada joined with California in the Tahoe Regional Planning Compact in 1980 to fight pollution of Lake Tahoe. By the 1990's, the compact had resulted in environmental improvements in the area.

The early 2000's. Tourism remains Nevada's largest industry, but the manufacturing and construction industries are growing rapidly. The increase in tourism and the relocation of manufacturing facilities to the Las Vegas and Reno metropolitan areas have contributed to the growth of those areas. About 90 percent of Nevada's people now live in the Las Vegas and Reno areas. Growth also has made the state's population more ethnically and racially diverse.

Nevada cities face major problems as their populations continue to increase. Many of these problems require help from the state government. City dwellers are demanding better police and fire protection, improvements in education, better recreational facilities, and other services.

In 2002, President George W. Bush approved controversial legislation to bury nuclear waste in Nevada. The waste would have been buried at Yucca Mountain, on the federal lands in Nye County that include Nellis Air Force Base and the Nevada Test Site. Nevada officials and environmentalists opposed the legislation and filed several lawsuits to block it. They argued that the site would not be a safe place to store radioactive waste. In 2004, a federal appeals court ruled that the government could proceed with plans for the site if it devised stronger safeguards for protecting the surrounding environment from radiation. However, the plan continued to face political and public opposition. In 2009, U.S. Secretary of Energy Steven Chu said that the administration of President Barack Obama no longer considered Yucca Mountain an option for storing nuclear waste.

Christopher H. Exline and Hal Rothman

Related articles in *World Book* include:

Biographies

Carson, Kit
Frémont, John C.
Mackay, John William
McCarran, Patrick Anthony
Reid, Harry
Smith, Jedediah S.
Wovoka
Young, Brigham

Cities and towns

Carson City
Goldfield
Las Vegas
Reno
Virginia City

History

Comstock Lode
Guadalupe Hidalgo, Treaty of
Mexican War
Mormons
Western frontier life in America

Physical features

Colorado River
Desert
Great Basin
Lake Mead
Lake Tahoe
Sierra Nevada

Other related articles

Area 51
Death Valley National Park
Great Basin National Park
Hoover Dam
Irrigation
Nevada System of Higher Education
Ranching

Outline

I. **People**
   A. Population
   B. Schools
   C. Libraries
   D. Museums
II. **Visitor's guide**
III. **Land and climate**
   A. Land regions
   B. Rivers and lakes
   C. Plant and animal life
   D. Climate
IV. **Economy**
   A. Natural resources
   B. Service industries
   C. Mining
   D. Manufacturing
   E. Agriculture
   F. Electric power and utilities
   G. Transportation
   H. Communication
V. **Government**
   A. Constitution
   B. Executive
   C. Legislature
   D. Courts
   E. Local government
   F. Revenue
   G. Politics
VI. **History**

Questions

What are Nevada's main economic activities? Why is agriculture less important in Nevada than it is in most other states?

Why did many Nevada mining communities become ghost towns during the 1880's?

How does Nevada's "free port" law attract industry to the state?

From what country did the United States acquire the land that includes the present state of Nevada?

What ranks as the most valuable mined product produced in Nevada?

Why did President Abraham Lincoln support statehood for Nevada?

What is the longest river in Nevada? Where does this river stop flowing and disappear?

Why does the Nevada legislature enforce strict regulations on gambling?

Additional resources

Level I

Du l emple, Lesley A. *The Hoover Dam*. Lerner, 2003.
Heinrichs, Ann. *Nevada*. Children's Pr., 2008.
Stefoff, Rebecca. *Nevada*. 2nd ed. Marshall Cavendish Benchmark, 2010.
Williams, Suzanne M. *Nevada*. Children's Pr., 2009.

Level II

Bowers, Michael W. *The Sagebrush State: Nevada's History, Government, and Politics*. 3rd ed. Univ. of Nev. Pr., 2006.
Castor, Stephen B., and Ferdock, G. C. *Minerals of Nevada*. Univ. of Nev. Pr., 2004.
Drabelle, Dennis. *Mile-High Fever: Silver Mines, Boom Towns, and High Living on the Comstock Lode*. St. Martin's, 2009.
Dunar, Andrew J., and McBride, Dennis. *Building Hoover Dam*. 1993. Reprint. Univ. of Nev. Pr., 2001.
Grayson, Donald K. *The Desert's Past: A Natural Prehistory of the Great Basin*. 1993. Reprint. Smithsonian Institution, 1999.
Hulse, James W. *The Silver State*. 3rd ed. Univ. of Nev. Pr., 2004.
Moehring, Eugene P., and Green, M. S. *Las Vegas: A Centennial History*. Univ. of Nev. Pr., 2005.
Nicoletta, Julie. *Buildings of Nevada*. Oxford, 2000.
Orndorff, Richard L., and others. *Geology Underfoot in Central Nevada*. Mountain Pr. Pub. Co., 2001.

Nevada System of Higher Education is the public system of higher education for Nevada. The system operates universities at Reno and Las Vegas, a state college, three regional colleges, a community college, and an environmental research institute.

The University of Nevada, Reno, and the University of Nevada, Las Vegas, grant bachelor's, master's, and doctor's degrees. Nevada State College is in Henderson. The College of Southern Nevada, Great Basin College, and Western Nevada College offer degrees at a number of campuses and satellite centers. These three colleges are based in the Las Vegas area, in Elko, and in Carson City, respectively. Truckee Meadows Community College is in Reno. The Desert Research Institute studies atmospheric and water resources as well as other environmental concerns. It has facilities in Reno, Las Vegas, and Boulder City. The institute also operates the Storm Peak Laboratory in Steamboat Springs, Colorado.

The Nevada Board of Regents, which operates the system, was formed in 1865. However, the Nevada System of Higher Education was not created until 1968.

The system's website at http://system.nevada.edu/ provides additional information.

Critically reviewed by the Nevada System of Higher Education

Nevelson, *NEHV uhl suhn,* **Louise** (1899 or 1900-1988), was an American sculptor. She became best known for her *assemblages,* often grouped within boxlike frames. Many of the large black walls of her compartments express a feeling of quiet and majesty.

Most of Nevelson's assemblages are made out of wood that is painted either black or gold or left in the natural color. She was a pioneer in the creation of "total environments" of everyday "found" objects and utensils, strips of molding, woodwork decorations, or Victorian debris that form powerful unified wholes.

Nevelson was born on September 23 in 1899 or 1900 in Kiev, Ukraine (then part of the Russian Empire). She came to the United States with her family in 1905. She studied painting at the Art Students League in New York

A wooden sculpture painted black (1958); collection of the Norton Gallery of Art, West Palm Beach, FL. Gift of Mr. and Mrs. Joseph Rosenberg (Pace Gallery)

Louise Nevelson's *Sky Cathedral* is typical of the complex and mysterious wooden constructions that made her famous.

City. Nevelson died on April 17, 1988.   George Gurney

Nevins, *NEHV ihnz,* **Allan** (1890-1971), an American historian and educator, twice was awarded the Pulitzer Prize for biography. *Grover Cleveland: A Study in Courage* won the prize in 1933, and *Hamilton Fish: The Inner History of the Grant Administration* received the award in 1937. Nevins won the Bancroft Prize and the Scribner Centenary Prize for *The Ordeal of the Union* (1947). His works are noted for balance and thoroughness.

Nevins's 1940 biography *John D. Rockefeller* became popular. It was revised and republished in 1953 as *Study in Power: John D. Rockefeller, Industrialist and Philanthropist.* Nevins and the American writer Frank Ernest Hill completed *Ford: The Times, the Man, the Company,* a study of the automobile pioneer Henry Ford, in 1954.

Nevins also edited collections of the letters of noted historical people. He completed his first book, *Life of Robert Rogers,* in 1914, and followed it with more than 50 other volumes. His other books include *The American States During and After the Revolution* (1924), *Frémont: The West's Greatest Adventurer* (1927), *A Brief History of the United States* (1942), *The Emergence of Lincoln* (1950), and *Herbert H. Lehman and His Era* (1963).

Nevins was born on May 20, 1890, in Camp Point, Illinois. He graduated from the University of Illinois. He wrote editorials for the *New York Evening Post* from 1913 to 1923 and wrote for the magazine *The Nation* from 1913 to 1918. Nevins joined the staff of the *New York Sun* in 1924 and *The* (New York) *World* in 1925. He was a professor of history at Cornell University in 1927 and 1928 and at Columbia University from 1931 to 1958. In 1958, he became a senior fellow of research at the Henry E. Huntington Library in San Marino, California. Nevins lectured on American history at several universities in other nations. He served as a special representative for the Office of War Information in Australia and New Zealand in 1943 and 1944, during World War II. Nevins died on March 5, 1971.   Robert C. Sims

Nevis. See **Saint Kitts and Nevis.**

Nevis, Ben. See **Ben Nevis.**

New Age movement is a popular cultural movement that began in the early 1970's. The movement calls for keeping the body, mind, and spirit in harmony. Its followers believe in *intuition* (immediate understanding) and direct experience rather than science and rational thought. The New Age movement takes a strong interest in personal development. Followers often rely on spiritual means to achieve self-help. Such Asian religions as Zen Buddhism and the yoga school of Hinduism play a major role in the movement's spiritual life. New Age also emphasizes the *occult* (magic) and caring for the environment. Many followers believe in the coming of an age of peace and love.

Healing both the body and mind is central to the movement. New Age supports a *holistic* approach to health that is based on the interrelationship of many factors, including family relationships and working conditions. Many New Agers seek alternative health care, such as acupuncture and remedies made from herbs, rather than traditional Western medical treatments.

New Age music attempts to encourage spiritual well-being and inner peace through relaxation and meditation. New Age music typically is instrumental music that features such soothing instruments as the bamboo flute, wind chimes, and tuned quartz crystals.   Richard Kyle

See also **Acupuncture; Alternative medicine; Astrology; Holistic medicine; Yoga.**

New Amsterdam. See New York City (History).

New Bedford (pop. 95,072) is one of the leading commercial fishing ports of the United States. It is in southeastern Massachusetts. The city lies where the Acushnet River empties into Buzzards Bay, about 50 miles (80 kilometers) south of Boston. For location, see **Massachusetts** (political map). New Bedford; Providence, Rhode Island; and Fall River are part of a metropolitan area with 1,600,852 people.

New Bedford's chief industry is the production of seafood. The city's annual fish catch has a higher value than that of any other city in the United States. The city's fishing fleet is one of the leaders in the world in catching flounders and sea scallops. Other major industries produce electric equipment, rubber goods, and textiles. The city also is a trade and distribution center of southeastern Massachusetts. It has a growing tourist industry.

Through the years, large numbers of Portuguese immigrants have settled in New Bedford. The Feast of the Blessed Sacrament, a four-day midsummer Portuguese festival, attracts tens of thousands of visitors.

Wampanoag Indians lived in what is now the New Bedford area before white settlers arrived there. In 1652, a group of Pilgrims bought land from Massasoit, the Wampanoag chief, and founded a settlement. The settlement later was named for the Duke of Bedford.

New Bedford developed slowly until the 1760's, when the colonists established a whaling industry. By the mid-1800's, New Bedford had become the whaling capital of the world. The Wamsutta Mills, the city's first major textile plant, opened in 1846. New Bedford received a city charter in 1847.

New Bedford's whaling industry declined rapidly during the late 1800's, chiefly because petroleum products replaced whale oil for many purposes. A textile boom during the 1880's made the city a leading producer of cotton fabrics.

In 1966, New Bedford completed a dike that protects the city's harbor from hurricanes. In 1996, New Bedford Whaling National Historical Park was created to commemorate the port's whaling industry of the 1800's. The park spreads over 13 city blocks and includes the New Bedford Whaling Museum, a whaling schooner, and several historical structures. New Bedford has a mayor-council form of government.   Laurence A. Lewis

New Bern (pop. 29,524) is North Carolina's second oldest town, after Bath. It lies at the junction of the Trent and Neuse rivers, about 35 miles (56 kilometers) from the Atlantic Ocean (see **North Carolina** [political map]). In 1766, New Bern became the capital of the North Carolina colony and a major port. It remained the capital until 1778. The coming of the railroads in the mid-1800's contributed to the lessening of its importance as a port.

New Bern was founded in 1710 by Baron Christoph von Graffenried of Switzerland and German Palatines, who were seeking religious freedom. A colonial capitol and governor's residence called Tryon Palace was completed in 1770. The building was restored in the 1950's and is now a tourist attraction. New Bern, named for Bern, Switzerland, is the seat of Craven County. It has a council-manager government.   Jerry L. Surratt

New Britain is the largest of the more than 200 islands in the Bismarck Archipelago, which forms part of the nation of Papua New Guinea. New Britain lies off the northeast coast of New Guinea. It covers 14,093 square miles (36,500 square kilometers). Mountain ranges run the length of the island.

About 405,000 people live on New Britain. Almost all are Melanesians. The people fish and farm for a living. Most of the farming is done along the coasts. The island's north end is the most fertile area in Papua New Guinea. Rabaul is the island's largest urban community and port. It lies along the coast and has several active volcanoes around it. Rabaul suffered much damage in 1937 and 1994 when volcanoes erupted.

In 1700, the English navigator William Dampier reached New Britain. In 1884, it became a part of a German empire. Australian forces took the island from Germany in 1914, during World War I (1914-1918). The League of Nations gave Australia a *mandate* (order to rule) over New Britain in 1920. Japan captured Rabaul in 1942, during World War II (1939-1945), and held the area until 1945. During the war, bombing raids destroyed most of Rabaul, but the city was rebuilt. Australia regained control of the area after the war. In 1975, New Britain became part of the newly independent nation of Papua New Guinea.   David A. M. Lea

See also **Bismarck Archipelago; Papua New Guinea** (map).

New Britain, Connecticut (pop. 73,206), often called the *Hardware City,* has long been a producer of builders' hardware and carpenters' tools. New Britain lies in central Connecticut, about 10 miles (16 kilometers) southwest of Hartford (see **Connecticut** [political map]). Today, many factories in New Britain still produce small hardware items. Some factories make technological goods, such as computer components.

The New Britain Museum of American Art has a large collection of American paintings. Central Connecticut State University, founded in 1849, is in the city. It includes the Copernican Observatory and Planetarium. New Britain was settled in 1687 and became a city in 1870. It has a mayor-council government.   Bart Fisher

New Brunswick, New Jersey (pop. 55,181), is an educational and industrial center. It lies on the Raritan River in the north-central part of the state (see **New Jersey** [political map]). The city produces clothing, machinery, medical supplies, and pharmaceuticals. New Brunswick is in the New York (New York)-Northern New Jersey-Long Island (New York) metropolitan area. In World War II (1939-1945), nearby Camp Kilmer processed thousands of soldiers sent to Europe.

New Brunswick is the home of Rutgers, the State University of New Jersey; the New Brunswick Theological Seminary; and the New Jersey Agricultural Experiment Station. The town became a transportation center early in its history. The Raritan River was part of the land-water route from New York City to Philadelphia. New Brunswick was chartered in 1730. In the late 1900's, the city completed several projects downtown. The new construction included office buildings, a hotel and conference center, a cultural center, shopping facilities, and an automobile bridge over the Raritan River. New Brunswick has a mayor-council form of government. It is the seat of Middlesex County.   Robert M. Hordon

The Little Falls of the St. Croix River on the border with Maine

New Brunswick

New Brunswick is one of the four Atlantic Provinces of Canada. Clear, swift rivers rush down the many hills and sweep through the steep valleys of New Brunswick. Forests cover about 85 percent of the land and add to its natural beauty. Saint John is New Brunswick's largest city and chief industrial and shipping center. Fredericton is the capital. Moncton is a distribution center.

Every year, loggers cut millions of trees from New Brunswick's thick forests. Many trees are sawed into lumber. Even more go to pulp and paper mills, where they are processed into a soft mass called *pulp* and made into paper. Newsprint, the paper used in printing newspapers, is a leading manufactured product.

The province has rich mineral and energy resources that give it great potential for industrial growth. Huge deposits of copper, lead, silver, and zinc lie in northeast-

Greg Marquis, the contributor of this article, is Professor of History and Politics at the University of New Brunswick Saint John.

ern New Brunswick. During the 1950's, geologists mapped the area, and in the 1960's, new facilities were built to develop the area's resources. In the 1980's, large potash mines opened in southern New Brunswick. A nuclear power plant began operating in 1982. In addition, the province has the largest oil refinery in Canada, in Saint John.

New Brunswick has some moderately rich farmland in the Saint John River Valley and other regions. Potatoes rank as New Brunswick's leading field crop. The province has one of the world's largest frozen food industries. Dairy farming is extensive. Lobsters and crabs are the most important seafood catches. Fishing fleets on the Bay of Fundy and the Gulf of St. Lawrence make large hauls of herring and shrimp. The rivers and rolling woodlands of New Brunswick are among the best fishing and hunting grounds in North America.

In 1922, Andrew Bonar Law of New Brunswick became the only person born outside the United Kingdom or Ireland to serve as the British prime minister. Richard B. Bennett, another New Brunswicker, became prime

Interesting facts about New Brunswick

Middle Island and Chatham Lake, located about 1 mile (1.6 kilometers) from each other near Chatham, are exactly the same size and shape. The Mi'kmaq Indians of eastern Canada had many legends about an Indian folk hero called Glooscap, who supposedly shaped much of their landscape. According to a Mi'kmaq legend, Glooscap once became so enraged that he scooped out a handful of earth, forming Chatham Lake, and flung it into the Miramichi River, forming Middle Island.

Middle Island and Chatham Lake

The *Marco Polo,* a clipper ship built in 1851 in Saint John, earned the reputation as the fastest ship in the world. The ship sailed at record speed from England to Australia and back in 1852. The *Marco Polo* made the round trip in just under six months.

The Bay of Fundy has the world's highest tides. They sometimes are more than 50 feet (15 meters) high in the northern part of the bay, far surpassing the world average of 2 ½ feet (0.8 meter).

WORLD BOOK illustrations by Kevin Chadwick

The *Marco Polo*

Julia Catherine Beckwith Hart wrote *St. Ursula's Convent: Or, The Nun of Canada,* the first novel published in what later became Canada. The book was published in 1824.

© Jon Arnold Images Ltd./Alamy Images

Saint John, New Brunswick's largest city

minister of Canada in 1930. Other well-known New Brunswickers include Bliss Carman, one of Canada's most famous poets; novelist David Adams Richards; and playwright and novelist Antonine Maillet.

New Brunswick was named for the British royal family of Brunswick-Lüneburg (the House of Hanover). Most of its early settlers were American colonists who had remained loyal to England during the American Revolution (1775-1783). About 14,000 of these Loyalists, as they were called, arrived during and after the war, most of them in 1783. They settled among a few thousand French-speaking Acadians and several hundred Mi'kmaq and Maliseet (also known as Wolastoqiyik) Indians. As a result of these Loyalist settlers, New Brunswick received the nickname of the *Loyalist Province.* It is also called the *Picture Province* because of its natural beauty.

New Brunswick, along with Nova Scotia, Ontario, and Quebec, was one of the original provinces of Canada. For the relationship of New Brunswick to the other provinces, see **Canada; Canada, Government of; Canada, History of.**

Bill Brooks, Masterfile

Rolling hills around Millville in western New Brunswick

New Brunswick in brief

Symbols of New Brunswick

The provincial flag, adopted in 1965, is based on the provincial coat of arms. The coat of arms, adopted in 1868, has a shield with a British lion symbolizing New Brunswick's ties to the United Kingdom. The galley represents shipbuilding and seafaring, both important in the province's history. A crest and supporters were added in 1984. The crest is a salmon bearing St. Edward's crown. Two white-tailed deer support the shield.

Provincial flag

Provincial coat of arms

New Brunswick (brown) is eighth in size among the provinces and second among the Atlantic Provinces (yellow).

General information

Entered the Dominion: July 1, 1867; one of the original four provinces.
Provincial abbreviation: NB (postal).
Provincial motto: *Spem Reduxit* (Hope Restored).

The Legislative Building is in Fredericton, New Brunswick's capital since 1785. Some legislative sessions before 1788 were held in Saint John (then called Parrtown).

Land and climate

Area: 28,355 mi² (73,440 km²), including 520 mi² (1,350 km²) of inland water.
Elevation: *Highest*—Mount Carleton, 2,690 ft (820 m) above sea level. *Lowest*—sea level along the Atlantic coast.
Coastline: 1,410 mi (2,269 km).
Record high temperature: 103 °F (39 °C) at Nepisiguit Falls and at Woodstock on Aug. 18, 1935, and at Rexton on Aug. 19, 1935.
Record low temperature: −53 °F (−47 °C) at Sisson Dam on Feb. 1, 1955.
Average July temperature: 64 °F (18 °C).
Average January temperature: 14 °F (−10 °C).
Average yearly precipitation: 45 in (115 cm).

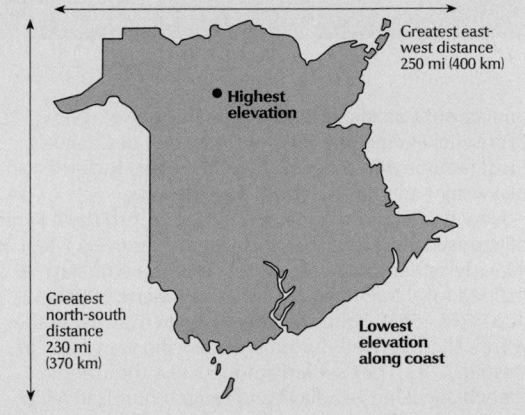

Greatest east-west distance 250 mi (400 km)

Highest elevation

Greatest north-south distance 230 mi (370 km)

Lowest elevation along coast

Important dates

Samuel de Champlain and Sieur de Monts spent the winter on St. Croix Island.

The New Brunswick-Maine boundary dispute was settled.

| 1534 | 1604 | 1784 | 1842 |

Jacques Cartier, a French explorer, arrived in Chaleur Bay.

New Brunswick became a separate province.

Bird
Black-capped chickadee

Tree
Balsam fir

Floral emblem
Early blue violet

People

Population: 729,997 (2006 census)
Rank among the provinces: 8th
Density: 26 persons per mi² (10 per km²), provinces average 13 per mi² (5 per km²)
Distribution: 51 percent urban, 49 percent rural
Largest cities and towns*

Saint John	68,043
Moncton	64,128
Fredericton	50,535
Dieppe	18,565
Miramichi	18,129
Riverview	17,832

*2006 census.
Source: Statistics Canada.

Population trend

Thousands

Year	Population
2006	729,997
2001	729,498
1996	738,133
1991	723,900
1986	710,422
1981	696,403
1976	677,250
1971	634,557
1966	616,788
1961	597,936
1951	515,697
1941	457,401
1931	408,219
1921	387,876
1911	351,889
1901	331,120
1891	321,263
1881	321,233
1871	285,594

Source: Statistics Canada.

Economy

Chief products

Agriculture: beef cattle, blueberries, floriculture and nursery, hogs, milk, potatoes, poultry.
Fishing industry: crab, herring, lobster, shrimp.
Forestry: fir, spruce.
Manufacturing: food products, paper products, wood products.
Mining: copper, lead, peat, potash, silver, zinc.

Gross domestic product

Value of goods and services produced in 2008: $27,288,000,000.*
Services include community, business, and personal services; finance; government; trade; and transportation and communication. *Industry* includes construction, manufacturing, mining, and utilities. *Agriculture* includes agriculture, fishing, and forestry.

*Canadian dollars.
Source: Statistics Canada.

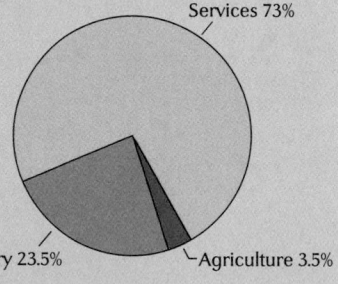

Services 73%
Industry 23.5%
Agriculture 3.5%

Government

Provincial government

Premier: term of up to 5 years
Members of the Legislative Assembly: 55; terms of up to 5 years

Federal government

Members of the House of Commons: 10
Members of the Senate: 10

Sources of information

New Brunswick's official website at http://www.new-brunswick.net provides a gateway to much information on the province's economy and history.

In addition, the website at http://www.tourismnewbrunswick.ca provides information about tourism.

Two national railway systems linked New Brunswick cities with Montreal.

Confederation Bridge, which connects New Brunswick and Prince Edward Island, opened.

1867 — **1890** — **1952-1953** — **1997**

New Brunswick became one of the original four provinces of the Dominion of Canada.

Large deposits of copper, lead, silver, and zinc were mapped in the Bathurst-Newcastle region.

Population. The 2006 Canadian census reported that New Brunswick had 729,997 people. The province's population had increased by less than 1 percent since the 2001 census, which reported a population of 729,498.

About half the people of New Brunswick live in urban areas. About a third of the people live in the metropolitan areas of Moncton and Saint John. Moncton and Saint John have the province's only Census Metropolitan Areas as defined by Statistics Canada.

Fredericton is the only other city in New Brunswick that has a population of more than 20,000. The province has only a few other cities and towns with populations of more than 10,000.

About 96 of every 100 New Brunswickers were born in Canada. About half of the others came from the United States or the United Kingdom.

New Brunswick has two official languages, English and French. It is the only legally bilingual province in Canada. About two-thirds of the people speak English as their native language. They include descendants of the Loyalists who left the American Colonies in the 1700's. Other English speakers include descendants of English, Irish, and Scottish immigrants who arrived in the 1800's. About one-third of New Brunswick's people, called Acadians, speak French as their native language. The south and west of the province are mostly English-speaking.

Population density

Most of New Brunswick's people live near the coast and in the southern part of the province. Large areas are thinly settled. Saint John is the largest city.

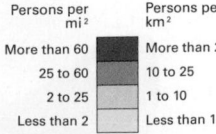

Persons per mi²		Persons per km²
More than 60		More than 25
25 to 60		10 to 25
2 to 25		1 to 10
Less than 2		Less than 1

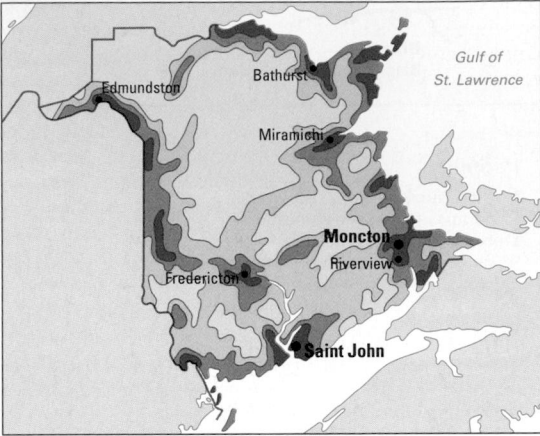

WORLD BOOK map; based on the *National Atlas of Canada*

The Acadians are concentrated in the north and east. About one-third of New Brunswickers speak both languages. About 18,000 people in New Brunswick have some *indigenous* (native, or American Indian) ancestry.

Schools. During the late 1700's, most schooling in the New Brunswick region took place in the home or in

© John Sylvester, Alamy Images

Acadians celebrate their heritage at the annual Tintamarre festival in Caraquet in northeastern New Brunswick. Acadians are the descendants of early French settlers in southeastern Canada.

© Claude Bouchard, First Light/Getty Images

Bouctouche, in eastern New Brunswick, includes Le Pays de la Sagouine, a historic reproduction of an Acadian village. Visitors reach the village by way of the curving footbridge shown here.

privately run schools. Most early schools were open only a few months of the year. Traveling teachers often taught the classes. An act of 1802 provided a small amount of money to help each *parish* (district within a county) pay for a school for younger children. However, not all parishes had schools. In 1805, an act established a *grammar* (high) school at Saint John. This act, along with others passed in 1816, helped to create a system of public schools by granting funds for education to each county. Parents and church groups also supported many schools in the 1800's. Since 1967, the provincial government has provided free public education for all children. New Brunswick also has privately funded Roman Catholic and other denominational schools.

District education councils consist of publicly and locally elected members. The members are responsible for establishing the direction and priorities for the school district. They are also responsible for deciding how to operate the districts and schools. Children are required to attend school from age 5 to age 18 or until they graduate. Students have the opportunity to learn in both English and French.

Libraries. The New Brunswick Public Library System provides library services throughout the province. The Legislative Library of New Brunswick is in Fredericton. Other libraries include the Harriet Irving Library of the University of New Brunswick in Fredericton, the Ralph Pickard Bell Library of Mount Allison University in Sackville, and the Champlain Library of the University of Moncton.

Museums. The New Brunswick Museum in Saint John is Canada's oldest museum. It was founded as the Museum of Natural History in 1842. Today, the museum has fine cultural, historical, and scientific exhibits. The Central New Brunswick Woodmen's Museum in Boiestown has exhibits of pioneer life in the province. The Acadian Museum at the Université de Moncton (University of Moncton) features material on Acadia, a region settled by the French in the 1600's that included what is now New Brunswick. The Atlantic Salmon Museum in

Universities

New Brunswick has four degree-granting universities that are members of the Association of Universities and Colleges of Canada.

Name	Mailing address
Moncton, Université de (University of Moncton)	Moncton
Mount Allison University	Sackville
New Brunswick, University of	*
St. Thomas University	Fredericton

*Campuses at Fredericton and Saint John.

Dennis Mills, Masterfile

The New Brunswick Museum, in Saint John, is the oldest museum in Canada. The institution was founded in 1842.

Doaktown has exhibits dealing with the Atlantic salmon and salmon fishing. The York Sunbury Museum in Fredericton depicts the history of central New Brunswick.

University of New Brunswick

The University of New Brunswick, in Fredericton, includes the Old Arts Building. Completed in 1828, this building is the oldest university building in Canada.

New Brunswick political map

Urban area

Park or other recreation area

Indian reserve

International boundary

Provincial boundary

County boundary

York County name

✪ Provincial capital

• County seat

• City or town

□ Point of interest

✈ Major airport

Railroad

Expressway

Other road

Trans-Canada highway

95 Interstate highway

1 U.S. highway

6 Other road

Lambert conformal conic projection
WORLD BOOK map

66° West Longitude

64°
Anticosti Island

North

Saint Lawrence River

Gaspé Passage

132

Cap-Chat

FORILLON NATIONAL PARK

Gaspé

132

Gaspé Peninsula

299

Cap d'Espoir

Chandler

132

QUEBEC

Grande Rivière

Rivière Bonaventure

Cascapédia River

132

Point La Nim

Campbellton

Atholville

Flatlands

Dalhousie

Charlo

Balmoral

Chaleur Bay

Petite-Rivière-de-l'Île

Miscou Island

Miscou Centre

Pigeon Hill

Ste-Marie-St. Raphaël

Île Lamèque

Shippagan

48° North Latitude

132

Rimouski River

Patapedia

Matapedia River

68°

Kedgwick River

Restigouche River

Robinsonville

17

Dawsonville

St. Arthur

Maltais

New Mills

Lorne

Jacquet River

11

Pointe-Verte

Petit-Rocher

Nicholas Denys

Robertville

Anse-Bleue

St. Léolin

Bertrand

Caraquet

Bas-Caraquet

113

St. Simon

Inkerman

St. Jean-Baptiste-de-Restigouche

Whites Brook

Kedgwick

St-Quentin

St. Martin-de-Restigouche

Restigouche

Nepisiguit Bay

Janeville

Tracadie-Sheila

Val-Comeau

Cabano

185

Temiscouata Lake

Madawaska

St. Joseph-de-Madawaska

St. Jacques

Edmundston

Madawaska

St. Basile

Bathurst

Gloucester

Salmon Beach

Notre Dame des Érables

Paquetville

St. Sauveur

St.-Isidore

St. Léonard

Rivière-du-Portage

Brantville

289

Lac-Baker

Baker Brook

Ste.-Anne-de-Madawaska

Siegas

St-Hilaire

Allardville

Lavillette

Lagacéville

Barryville

TABUSINTAC INDIAN RESERVE

11

Neguac

BURNT CHURCH INDIAN RESERVE

Portage Island

Conners

Clair

Green River

Saint John River

St. André

Riley Brook

Nepisiguit River

Bellefond

Loggieville

Escuminac

Point Escuminac

Pointe-Sapin

St. Léonard

Fish River

11

Square Lake

Grand Falls Grand-Sault

Grand River

2

Drummond

Victoria

New Denmark

Long Lake

MOUNT CARLETON PROVINCIAL PARK

Sisson Branch Res.

BIG HOLE TRACT INDIAN RESERVE

Curventon

Wayerton

Silikers

Whitney

Miramichi

Chatham

Derby

Barnaby River

Newcastle

Miramichi Bay

KOUCHIBOUGUAC NATIONAL PARK

Kouchibouguac Bay

Fontaine

PRINCE EDWARD ISLAND

TOBIQUE INDIAN RESERVE

Aroostook

Plaster Rock

Three Brooks

Arthurette

Northumberland

108

Renous

Trappist MONASTERY

Collette

Acadieville

St. Louis-de-Kent

St. Ignace

Summerside

Presque Isle

1

Aroostook River

Perth-Andover

Kilburn

Carleton

Upper Kent

Juniper

107

Bloomfield Ridge

Upper Blackville

Blissfield

Doaktown

Howard

Acadie Siding

8

Rogersville

St. Paul

126

Richibucto

Cap-Lumière

Rexton

St. Édouard-de-Kent

Bouctouche

St-Antoine

Cormierville

Cormier

Shediac Bridge

DORCHESTER CROSSING

Robichaud

CONFEDERATION BRIDGE

Cap-Pelé

MAINE

Houlton

95

WORLD'S LONGEST COVERED BRIDGE

Bath

Centreville

Knowlesville

Napadogan

Astle

McGivney

Nashwaak Bridge

Gasperaux Forks

BONAR LAW CAIRN

Bass River

Kent Junction

St. Lazare

Adamsville

Kent

Coal Branch

116

Shediac

15

Cocagne

Cap-des-Caissie

Shediac Cape

Johnville

Stickney

Hartland

Williamsburg

Boiestown

Southwest Miramichi River

Harcourt

Cape Tormentine

Melrose

Port Elgin

16

Aboujagane

Jacksontown

Jacksonville

Cloverdale

Stanley

Tay Creek

Hardwood Ridge

Sunbury

Chipman

Lutes Mountain

Moncton

Westmorland

112

Dieppe

Riverview

Memramcook

Point de Bute

Debec

Benton

Kirkland

Nackawic

Keswick Ridge

Ripples

New Canaan

Cumberland Bay

Minto

10

Youngs Cove

2

Havelock

Salisbury

Turtle Creek

Petitcodiac

Magagnetic

St. Joseph

Dorchester

Sackville

Amherst

104

Woodstock

Millville

Temperance Vale

Zealand

Durham Bridge

York

Taymouth

Marysville

Burton

Oromocto

8

Fredericton

Maugerville

Sheffield

Geary

Queenstown

Gagetown

102

Newtown

Berwick

Waterborough

Cambridge-Narrows

Kings

Penobsquis

Smiths Creek

Waterford

Sussex

Norton

Sussex Corner

Albert

114

Riverside-Albert

FUNDY NATIONAL PARK

Alma

Millinocket

Pemadumcook Lake

Harvey

Nasonworth

Tracy

Fredericton Junction

Central Blissville

Tweedside

Magaguadavic

Prince William

Kingsclear

Canterbury

Fosterville

4

Oromocto Lake

Grand Lake

Hoyt

Welsford

Wirral

Browns Flat

Welsford

Gondola Point

Renforth

Rothesay

Quispamsis

Hatfield Point

Shannon

Wickham

Queens

Cody's

Bloomfield

Hampton

Upham

Saint John

St. Martins

West Quaco

Ile Haute

Minas Channel

Cape Split

2

Annapolis Basin

Bangor

95

McAdam

St. Croix

Honeydale

Charlotte

Rollingdam

Oak Bay

Scotch Ridge

Old Town

6

Penobscot River

East Branch

Bonny River

St. Stephen

Calais

St. Andrews

ST. ANDREWS BLOCKHOUSE NATIONAL HISTORIC SITE

Back Bay

St. George

Blacks Harbour

Chance Harbour

Maces Bay

Prince of Wales

Lorneville

Black River

West Quaco

Grand Bay

Westfield

1

Musquash

Kennebecasis River

Graha Lake

1

Deer Island

Fairhaven

Wilsons Beach

ROOSEVELT CAMPOBELLO INTERNATIONAL PARK

North Head

Castalia

Grand Manan

Grand Harbour

Seal Cove

White Head Island

Grand Manan Island

Bay of Fundy

Sherbrooke Lake

12

NOVA SCOTIA

Fisher Lake

215

Kentville

Gaspereau Lake

River

101

8

Annapolis River

103

UNITED STATES

CANADA

Gulf of Saint Lawrence

Miscou Island

0 10 20   40   60   80   100 120 140 160 180 200 210 220 Miles

0 10 20   40   60   80   100   120   140   160 180   200 220   240   260   280   300   320   340   360 Kilometers

New Brunswick map index

Metropolitan areas

Counties

Cities, towns, and other populated places

*Does not appear on map; key shows general location.
†Parish.
°County seat.
Source: 2006 census. Places without populations are unincorporated.

© canadabrian/Alamy Images

Fredericton, in southern New Brunswick, is the provincial capital. Its City Hall, *shown here,* was built in 1876. The building was expanded in the 1970's.

Over a million people visit New Brunswick every year. These visitors enjoy boating and swimming off the beaches of the Northumberland Strait. In addition, the thick forests of New Brunswick offer excellent camping facilities.

New Brunswick offers some of the best fishing in North America. Fishing enthusiasts cast for fighting Atlantic salmon—the prize catch—and fish for bass, perch, smelt, and trout.

Many of New Brunswick's most popular attractions lie along the Bay of Fundy coastline. These attractions include Fundy National Park, Reversing Falls, and Hopewell Rocks. The Bay of Fundy's tides are among the highest in the world.

Malak

Kings Landing Historical Settlement in Prince William, near Fredericton

Places to visit

Following are brief descriptions of some of New Brunswick's many interesting places to visit:

Atlantic Salmon Museum, in Doaktown, shows the life cycle of the salmon with live samples.

Covered bridge, over the Saint John River in Hartland, is 1,282 feet (391 meters) long. It is believed to be the longest covered bridge in the world. The province also has a number of other covered bridges.

Hopewell Rocks, at Hopewell Cape in Albert County, rise in fantastic forms. These rocks are carved by tides from the Bay of Fundy.

Huntsman Marine Science Centre is in St. Andrews. It features laboratories and specimens of local marine life, including lobsters, salmon, and seals.

Islands in the Bay of Fundy. Campobello, Deer, and Grand Manan islands have fine harbors for yachting and colorful fishing villages. President Franklin D. Roosevelt of the United States kept a summer home on Campobello Island. See **Roosevelt Campobello International Park.**

Kings Landing Historical Settlement, a re-created village in Prince William, shows how the Loyalists and later settlers in the region lived in the period from 1783 through 1910. The settlement includes a church, houses, an inn, other businesses and shops, and a reception center. It is composed mainly of original buildings from a flooded area in the province.

Loyalist House, in Saint John, was built between 1811 and 1817 by David Merritt, a Loyalist from the United States. It was restored and opened in 1960.

Mactaquac Provincial Park is a 1,200-acre (500-hectare) park overlooking Mactaquac Dam near Fredericton. It has beaches, a marina, a camping area, and a golf course.

Magnetic Hill Complex is near Moncton. At this site, an optical illusion makes it seem as though automobiles can coast uphill. The complex also includes a zoo and a water park.

New Brunswick Aquarium and Marine Centre, in Shippagan, displays more than 100 forms of marine life from the Gulf of St. Lawrence.

Reversing Falls are at the mouth of the Saint John River in Saint John. Here, high tides from the Bay of Fundy force the river backwards through the falls two times a day.

Village Historique Acadien, near Caraquet, is a reconstructed Acadian settlement from 1770 to the early 1900's.

National parks and sites. New Brunswick has two national parks—Fundy National Park and Kouchibouguac National Park. National historic parks and sites include Carleton Martello Tower, Fort Beauséjour, and St. Andrews Blockhouse. For the areas and chief features of these parks and sites, see **Canada** (National Park System).

Provincial parks. For information on New Brunswick parks, visit the website at http//www.tourismnewbrunswick.ca.

© Sherman Hines, Masterfile

Carleton Martello Tower in Saint John

© Daniel Dempster Photography/Alamy Images

Roosevelt Cottage on Campobello Island

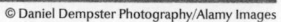

© Bill Brooks, Masterfile

Covered bridge over Saint John River in Hartland

Land regions. New Brunswick is in the northeastern extension of the Appalachian mountain system of the eastern United States. This area is called the Appalachian Region. Most of it consists of wooded highlands with clear, swift rivers in steep valleys. The Coastal Lowlands, also part of the Appalachian Region, make up the rest of the province.

The highlands areas of the Appalachian Region consist of the Central Highlands, the Northern Upland, and the Southern Highlands. The Central Highlands are the highest section of New Brunswick. These rugged hills increase in height from the southwest to the northeast. Many rise more than 2,000 feet (610 meters) above sea level. The hills include Mount Carleton, which stands 2,690 feet (820 meters) high. It is the highest point in New Brunswick. Northwest of the highlands is the flatter Northern Upland, with an elevation of about 1,000 feet (300 meters). The Southern Highlands, along the Bay of Fundy, have long ridges and valleys. Most of the hills are less than 1,000 feet (300 meters) high.

The Coastal Lowlands of the Appalachian Region are sometimes called the Eastern Plains. They slope gently down toward the east from the Central Highlands to the shores of the Gulf of St. Lawrence.

Coastline. New Brunswick has 1,410 miles (2,269 kilometers) of coastline. Deep bays and sharp inlets break

Flat, marshy land forms part of the Coastal Lowlands region of New Brunswick. The lowlands slope gently eastward from the Central Highlands of the Appalachian Region to the Gulf of St. Lawrence.

John de Visser, Masterfile

Bill Brooks, Masterfile

Mount Carleton is the highest point in New Brunswick. It rises 2,690 feet (820 meters) above sea level in the rugged Central Highlands of the Appalachian Region of the province.

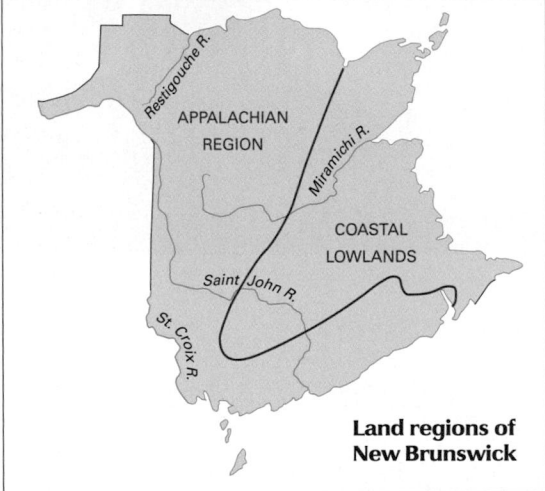

Land regions of New Brunswick

WORLD BOOK map

Map index

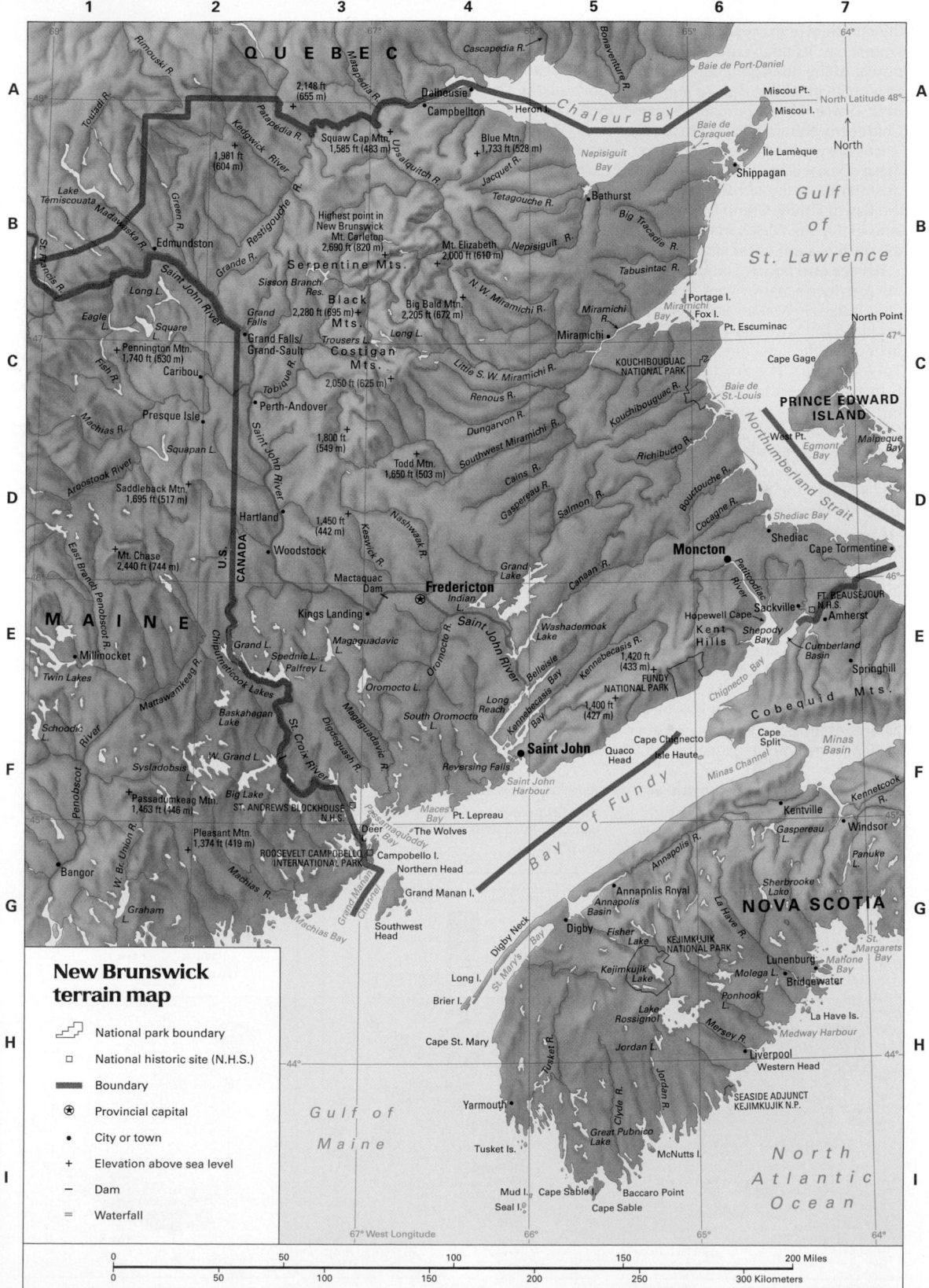

New Brunswick terrain map

- ⌐⌐ National park boundary
- □ National historic site (N.H.S.)
- ▬ Boundary
- ✪ Provincial capital
- • City or town
- + Elevation above sea level
- — Dam
- = Waterfall

WORLD BOOK map

QUEBEC

Rimouski R.
Cascapedia R.
Bonaventure R.
Baie de Port-Daniel
Miscou Pt.
Miscou I.
North Latitude 48°

2,148 ft (655 m)
Dalhousie
Campbellton
Heron I.
Chaleur Bay
Baie de Caraquet
Île Lamèque
North

Touladi R.
Kedgwick River
Matapédia R.
Patapédia R.
Squaw Cap Mtn. 1,585 ft (483 m)
Blue Mtn. 1,733 ft (528 m)
Upsalquitch R.
Jacquet R.
Nepisiguit Bay
Shippagan

Lake Témiscouata
Madawaska R.
Green R.
Restigouche R.
1,981 ft (604 m)
Highest point in New Brunswick Mt. Carleton 2,690 ft (820 m)
Mt. Elizabeth 2,000 ft (610 m)
Tetagouche R.
Bathurst
Big Tracadie R.
Tabusintac R.
Gulf of St. Lawrence

St. Francis R.
Edmundston
Grande R.
Saint John River
Serpentine Mts.
Sisson Branch Res.
Black Mts. 2,280 ft (695 m)
Big Bald Mtn. 2,205 ft (672 m)
Nepisiguit R.
N. W. Miramichi R.
Portage I.
Fox I.

Long L.
Eagle L.
Square L.
Grand Falls
Grand Falls/ Grand-Sault
Trousers L.
Costigan Mts.
Long L.
Little S. W. Miramichi R.
Miramichi R.
Miramichi
Miramichi Bay
Pt. Escuminac
North Point

Pennington Mtn. 1,740 ft (530 m)
Caribou
2,050 ft (625 m)
Renous R.
KOUCHIBOUGUAC NATIONAL PARK
Cape Gage

Machias R.
Presque Isle
Perth-Andover
Tobique R.
1,800 ft (549 m)
Dungarvon R.
Southwest Miramichi R.
Kouchibouguac R.
Baie de St-Louis
PRINCE EDWARD ISLAND
West Pt.
Egmont Bay
Malpeque Bay

Squapan L.
Saddleback Mtn. 1,695 ft (517 m)
Todd Mtn. 1,650 ft (503 m)
Cains R.
Richibucto R.
Bouctouche R.
Northumberland Strait

Aroostook River
Hartland
1,450 ft (442 m)
Keswick R.
Nashwaak R.
Gaspereau R.
Salmon R.
Cocagne R.
Shediac Bay

Mt. Chase 2,440 ft (744 m)
Woodstock
Mactaquac Dam
Fredericton
Indian
Grand Lake
Canaan R.
Moncton
Petitcodiac River
Shediac
Cape Tormentine

East Branch Penobscot R.
MAINE
Kings Landing
Magaguadavic R.
Oromocto R.
Saint John River
Washademoak Lake
Kennebecasis R.
Hopewell Cape
Kent Hills
FT. BEAUSÉJOUR N.H.S.
Sackville
Amherst

Millinocket
Grand L.
Spednic L.
Palfrey L.
Oromocto L.
Belleisle Bay
Kennebecasis Bay
1,420 ft (433 m)
FUNDY NATIONAL PARK
Shepody Bay
Cumberland Basin
Springhill

Twin Lakes
Baskahegan Lake
South Oromocto L.
Long Reach
1,400 ft (427 m)
Chignecto Bay
Cobequid Mts.

Schoodic L.
Penobscot River
Mattawamkeag R.
W. Grand L.
Digdeguash R.
Magaguadavic R.
Reversing Falls
Saint John
Quaco Head
Cape Chignecto
Isle Haute
Minas Channel
Minas Basin

Sysladobsis L.
Chiputneticook Lakes
St. Croix River
Saint John Harbour
Bay of Fundy
Cape Split
Kennetcook R.
Kentville
Windsor

Passadumkeag Mtn. 1,463 ft (446 m)
Big Lake
ST. ANDREWS BLOCKHOUSE N.H.S.
Passamaquoddy Bay
Maces Bay
Pt. Lepreau
Gasperau L.
Panuke L.

Pleasant Mtn. 1,374 ft (419 m)
Deer I.
The Wolves
ROOSEVELT CAMPOBELLO INTERNATIONAL PARK
Campobello I.
Northern Head
Annapolis R.
Sherbrooke Lake
NOVA SCOTIA
St. Margarets Bay

Bangor
Graham L.
Grand Manan Channel
Grand Manan I.
Southwest Head
Annapolis Basin
Annapolis Royal
La Have R.
Lunenburg
Mahone Bay
Molega L.
Bridgewater

Machias R.
Long I.
Brier I.
St. Marys Bay
Digby
Fisher Lake
KEJIMKUJIK NATIONAL PARK
Kejimkujik Lake
Ponhook L.
La Have Is.
Medway Harbour

Machias Bay
Cape St. Mary
Lake Rossignol
Mersey R.
Jordan L.
Liverpool
Western Head

Gulf of Maine
Yarmouth
Tusket R.
Jordan R.
Clyde R.
SEASIDE ADJUNCT KEJIMKUJIK N.P.
McNutts I.
North Atlantic Ocean

Tusket Is.
Mud I.
Seal I.
Cape Sable I.
Great Pubnico Lake
Baccaro Point
Cape Sable

67° West Longitude
66°
65°
64°

0	50	100	150	200 Miles

0	50	100	150	200	250	300 Kilometers

the coastline in many places. The Bay of Fundy is the largest bay. Its tides are among the world's highest. The power of the tides generally keeps the bay's harbors free of ice in winter. But ice floes close ports on the Gulf of St. Lawrence. Other major bays include Chaleur, Chignecto, Miramichi, and Passamaquoddy.

Heavily wooded islands lie off the coast. Many of these coastal islands are summer resort areas. Numerous islands, many of which are only jagged rocks, lie in the Bay of Fundy. Grand Manan Island is the largest island in the bay. Miscou Island and Île Lamèque lie off the northeastern coast of the province.

Rivers and lakes. The Saint John River, the longest of the province's many rivers, flows 418 miles (673 kilometers). It rises in Maine, and drains western New Brunswick and the lower part of the Coastal Lowlands. Its many branches include the Nashwaak, Oromocto, and Tobique rivers. The St. Croix River forms part of New Brunswick's border with Maine. The Restigouche River forms part of the border between New Brunswick and Quebec. Other major rivers include the Nepisiguit, Petitcodiac, and Southwest Miramichi.

The great tides of the Bay of Fundy rush into the Petitcodiac River and other rivers in a wall of water called a *bore.* This bore flows as far inland as Moncton, 20 miles (32 kilometers) away. The Moncton bore rises to about 24 inches (61 centimeters). The Bay of Fundy's tides also produce the Reversing Falls at the mouth of the Saint John River. At low tide, the river forms a falls as it rushes to the sea through a gap between high, rocky walls. When the tide comes in, however, it overpowers the river water and creates a falls in the opposite direction. At the town of Grand Falls, the Saint John River plunges 75 feet (23 meters) over a cliff.

Grand Lake, the largest lake in New Brunswick, forms an arm of the Saint John River. Other large lakes in the province include Magaguadavic, Oromocto, Washade-

Janet Foster, Masterfile

The rocks at Hopewell Cape on the Bay of Fundy are odd formations that have been carved out of the coast by strong tides.

moak, and the Chiputneticook chain of lakes.

Plant and animal life. Forests cover about 85 percent of the land area of New Brunswick—a higher percentage than in any other province. Almost unbroken forest covers the central and northern areas. Most of the trees are evergreens. The main varieties of trees in New Brunswick include balsam fir, birch, maple, pine, and spruce.

Purple violets and pink and white mayflowers carpet the forests late in spring. In summer, blackberries, blueberries, raspberries, and strawberries are plentiful. Fiddlehead ferns flourish along riverbanks.

New Brunswick offers outstanding hunting and fish-

Average January temperatures

The coastal regions of New Brunswick are milder during wintertime than the inland sections to the northwest.

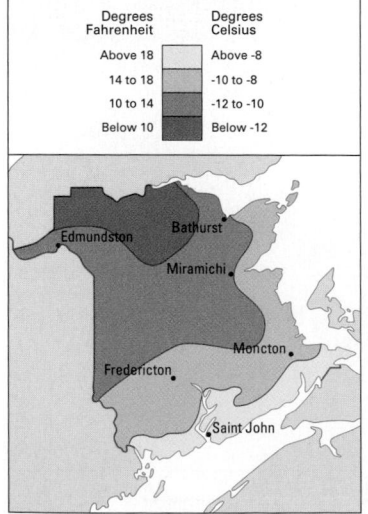

Degrees Fahrenheit	Degrees Celsius
Above 18	Above -8
14 to 18	-10 to -8
10 to 14	-12 to -10
Below 10	Below -12

Average July temperatures

New Brunswick has mild summers with generally even temperatures throughout the province.

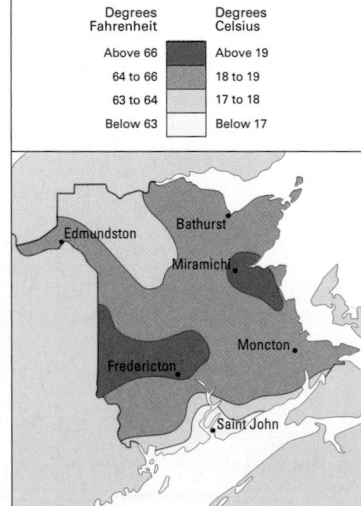

Degrees Fahrenheit	Degrees Celsius
Above 66	Above 19
64 to 66	18 to 19
63 to 64	17 to 18
Below 63	Below 17

Average yearly precipitation

Precipitation in New Brunswick is heaviest along the southern coastal region and the lightest in the northeastern area.

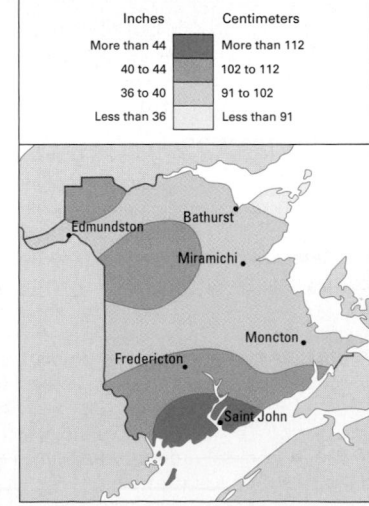

Inches	Centimeters
More than 44	More than 112
40 to 44	102 to 112
36 to 40	91 to 102
Less than 36	Less than 91

WORLD BOOK maps; based on the *National Atlas of Canada.*

ing. Forest animals include beavers, black bears, deer, moose, rabbits, skunks, and squirrels. Game birds include ducks, geese, partridges, pheasants, and woodcocks. Atlantic salmon, smallmouth bass, *landlocked salmon* (salmon in freshwater lakes), and trout are some of the province's game fish. Salmon stocks had become dangerously low in the Bay of Fundy by the late 1990's.

Climate. New Brunswick's coastal regions have quick changes in temperature, but the seasonal differences are not so great as those inland. Saint John, on the coast, averages 18 °F (-8 °C) in January and 62 °F (17 °C) in July. Inland, Fredericton averages 14 °F (-10 °C) in January and 67 °F (19 °C) in July. The record low, -53 °F (-47 °C), was set at Sisson Dam on Feb. 1, 1955. The record high was 103 °F (39 °C) in Nepisiguit Falls and Woodstock on Aug. 18, 1935, and in Rexton on Aug. 19, 1935.

Northern New Brunswick's *precipitation* (rain, melted snow, and other forms of moisture) averages 43 inches (108 centimeters) a year. The southern part of the province receives 48 inches (122 centimeters) a year.

Average monthly weather

	Saint John						Miramachi				
	Temperatures				Days of rain or snow		Temperatures				Days of rain or snow
	°F		°C				°F		°C		
	High	Low	High	Low			High	Low	High	Low	
Jan.	27	7	-3	-14	16	Jan.	23	3	-5	-16	14
Feb.	28	9	-2	-13	13	Feb.	27	5	-3	-15	11
Mar.	36	18	2	-8	15	Mar.	36	16	2	-9	14
Apr.	46	30	8	-1	14	Apr.	46	28	8	-2	14
May	59	39	15	4	14	May	61	39	16	4	15
June	68	46	20	8	13	June	72	50	22	10	13
July	72	54	22	12	12	July	77	55	25	13	15
Aug.	72	54	22	12	11	Aug.	75	54	24	12	13
Sept.	64	46	18	8	11	Sept.	66	45	19	7	12
Oct.	54	37	12	3	12	Oct.	54	34	12	1	14
Nov.	43	28	6	-2	14	Nov.	41	25	5	-4	14
Dec.	32	14	0	-10	17	Dec.	28	10	-2	-12	14/

Snowfall in New Brunswick averages about 124 inches (314 centimeters) a year.

Economy

In the early days, the economy of the New Brunswick region was based chiefly on the timber trade and fishing. Agriculture and shipbuilding became important during the 1800's. Today, service industries make up the largest part of New Brunswick's *gross domestic product* (GDP)—the total value of all goods and services produced in a province in a year.

Natural resources. The forests and wildlife of New Brunswick are important natural resources. Wilderness covers much of the land, and rugged terrain interfered with the early development of the province's minerals and other resources.

Minerals. The northeastern part of New Brunswick has large reserves of metallic minerals. These deposits include copper, lead, silver, and zinc. The southeastern part of the province has a major potash deposit. Bituminous coal deposits lie just north of Grand Lake. New Brunswick also has reserves of clay, gold, limestone, peat, and sand and gravel.

Soil is not fertile in most of New Brunswick. Farmers must use lime and fertilizers to make this soil productive. The flood plains of some rivers have a varying depth of extremely fertile black soil. Marshes and peat bogs cover parts of the east coast.

Service industries provide the largest portion of New Brunswick's gross domestic product and employment. Saint John and Moncton are the centers of trade and finance in New Brunswick. Fredericton, the provincial capital, is the center of government activities.

Manufacturing. Much of New Brunswick's manufacturing is dedicated to processing its agricultural and forest products. Leading food products include baked goods and dairy and fish products. McCain Foods, the world's largest French-fry producer, is headquartered in Florenceville. Paper products and wood products are also important. Pulp and paper mills and sawmills operate throughout the province. Saint John has a large oil refinery, and refined petroleum is an important export.

Mining. Metals provide the largest portion of New Brunswick's mining income. Zinc is the leading metal.

Copper, lead, and silver also rank high. Most metal mining occurs in the Bathurst area. Peat, used chiefly as fertilizer, is harvested in the northeast. Coal is mined in the Minto-Chipman field near Grand Lake. Potash, which is used to make fertilizer, is mined in the Sussex area.

Forestry. Most of the trees cut down in New Brunswick are balsam firs and spruces. Other commercially important trees include aspens, beeches, birches, cedars, maples, and pines. The forestry industry has planted more than 1 billion new trees since the 1970's.

Fishing industry. Lobster and crab are New Brunswick's most important catches. The province has a growing fish-farming industry, which produces salmon, trout, and several other types of fish.

© John de Visser, Masterfile

A huge paper mill operates in Saint John. The production of paper products is an important manufacturing activity in New Brunswick.

New Brunswick economy

General economy

Gross domestic product (GDP)* (2008) $27,288,000,000
  Rank among Canadian provinces   9th
Unemployment rate (2009)   8.9% (Canada avg: 8.3%)

*Gross domestic product is the total value of goods and services produced in a year and is
  in Canadian dollars.
Source: Statistics Canada.

Production and workers by economic activities

Economic activities	Percent of GDP produced	Employed workers	
		Number of people	Percent of total
Community, business, & personal services	22	129,200*	35*
Finance, insurance, & real estate	18*	15,800	4
Trade, restaurants, & hotels	15	81,600	22
Manufacturing	12	35,200	10
Government	10	25,500	7
Transportation & communication	9	32,200	9
Construction	7	23,900	7
Agriculture	3†	6,000	2
Utilities	3	4,900	1
Mining	1	11,700†	3†
Total	100	366,000	100

*Includes figures from establishments that manage other companies.
†Includes figures from forestry and fishing.
Figures are for 2008.
Source: Statistics Canada.

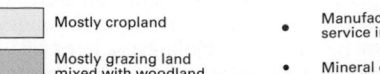

WORLD BOOK map

Agriculture

Cash receipts $471,373,000
  Rank among Canadian provinces   8th
Distribution   51% livestock, 49% crops
Farms (2006)   2,800
Farm acres (hectares)   967,800 (391,700)
  Rank among Canadian provinces   8th
Farmland   5% of New Brunswick

Leading products

1. Potatoes
2. Dairy
3. Hens and chickens
4. Floriculture and nursery
Other products: blueberries, cattle, eggs, hogs.

Fishing

Commercial catch $161,072,000
  Rank among Canadian provinces   4th

Leading catches

1. Lobster   (ranks 3rd in Canada)
2. Crab
3. Herring   (ranks 3rd in Canada)
Other products: alewives, scallops, sea urchins, shrimp.

Manufacturing

Value added by manufacture* $3,361,990,000
  Rank among Canadian provinces   7th

Leading products

Foods and beverages, paper products, wood products

*Value added by manufacture is the increase in value of raw materials after they
  become finished products.

Mining

Mineral production $1,540,180,000
  Rank among Canadian provinces   9th
Minerals and coal $1,540,180,000
Crude oil and crude oil equivalents   *
Natural gas   *

*No significant mining of this product in New Brunswick.

Leading product

Zinc   (ranks 1st in Canada)
Other products: copper, lead, peat, potash, sand and
  gravel, silver, stone.

Electric power

Nuclear   23.4%
Coal   21.9%
Petroleum   21.8%
Hydroelectric   15.9%
Natural gas   13.8%
Other   3.2%

Figures are for 2007, except for the agriculture and fishing figures, which are for 2008.
Dollar amounts are in Canadian dollars.
Source: Statistics Canada.

Economy of New Brunswick

This map shows the economic uses of land in New Brunswick
and where the province's leading farm, mineral, and forest products are produced. Manufacturing centers are shown in red.

- ☐ Mostly cropland
- ☐ Mostly grazing land mixed with woodland
- ☐ Forest land
- • Manufacturing and service industry center
- • Mineral deposit

Agriculture. Potatoes are the leading crop product in New Brunswick. Most of the potato crop comes from Carleton and Victoria counties. New Brunswick has also become an important producer of nursery products and ornamental flowers. Farmers also produce a number of fruit and vegetable crops. Dairy products rank as the leading livestock product. Much of the dairy production occurs in the southeast part of the province. Livestock farmers also raise beef cattle, hogs, and poultry.

Electric power and utilities. A nuclear power plant at Point Lepreau, near Saint John, provides much of the electric power generated in New Brunswick. Hydroelectric plants and plants that burn petroleum or coal produce most of the rest of the electric power.

Transportation. New Brunswick's busiest airports are in Fredericton, Moncton, and Saint John. Several national and regional airlines link these cities with cities in Canada and the United States. Railroads connect the province to the major cities of Quebec and Ontario.

New Brunswick's major highways run along the coastal areas and extend inward to Fredericton. The Trans-Canada Highway travels along the Saint John River and through Moncton.

Saint John is one of the few seaports of eastern Canada that is free of ice all year. Transatlantic liners can dock at Saint John during the winter, even when ice shuts the ports on the Gulf of St. Lawrence.

Communication. The first newspaper in New Brunswick, *The Royal Gazette and the New Brunswick Advertiser,* was founded in 1785. New Brunswick's daily papers include the *Telegraph-Journal* of Saint John, *The Daily Gleaner* of Fredericton, and the *Times & Transcript* of Moncton. *L'Acadie Nouvelle* of Caraquet is a French-language daily.

Government

Lieutenant governor of New Brunswick represents the British monarch, Queen Elizabeth II, in her role as the queen of Canada. The lieutenant governor is appointed by the *governor general in council*—that is, the governor general of Canada acting with the advice and consent of the Cabinet. The position of lieutenant governor is largely honorary.

Premier of New Brunswick is the actual head of the provincial government. The province, like the other provinces and Canada itself, has a *parliamentary* form of government. The premier is an elected member of the Legislative Assembly. The premier is usually the leader of the majority party in the Legislative Assembly. The premier presides over the Executive Council (cabinet). The premier chooses the council from among the members of the majority party in the Legislative Assembly. Each council member, called a minister, usually directs one or more departments of the provincial government. The council, like the premier, must resign if it loses the support of a majority of the Legislative Assembly.

Legislative Assembly of New Brunswick is a one-house legislature that makes the provincial laws. The Legislative Assembly is made up of 55 members who are elected from throughout the province. Terms served by the members of the Assembly may last up to five years. However, the lieutenant governor, on the advice of the premier, may call for an election before the end of the five-year period.

Courts. The highest court in New Brunswick is the Court of Appeal. It has a chief justice and five other justices. A panel of three judges hears most appeals, but some cases are argued before all six judges.

The Court of Queen's Bench has a chief justice and 20 other judges. The court has two divisions: the Trial Division and the Family Division. The Trial Division hears civil and criminal cases. The Family Division hears cases related to family matters, including divorce.

The governor general in council appoints the judges of the Court of Appeal and the Court of Queen's Bench. These judges may retire at age 65 or serve until age 75.

The Provincial Court has a chief judge and 25 other judges, all appointed by the provincial government. The court hears criminal matters, including cases involving juveniles. Lawyers may appeal Provincial Court verdicts

The premiers of New Brunswick

	Party	Term		Party	Term
Andrew R. Wetmore	Confederation	1867-1870	John B. M. Baxter	Conservative	1925-1931
George E. King	Conservative	1870-1871	Charles D. Richards	Conservative	1931-1933
George L. Hatheway	Conservative	1871-1872	Leonard P. de W. Tilley	Conservative	1933-1935
George E. King	Conservative	1872-1878	A. Allison Dysart	Liberal	1935-1940
John J. Fraser	Conservative	1878-1882	John B. McNair	Liberal	1940-1952
Daniel L. Hanington	Conservative	1882-1883	Hugh John Flemming	Progressive	1952-1960
Andrew G. Blair	Liberal	1883-1896		Conservative	
James Mitchell	Liberal	1896-1897	Louis J. Robichaud	Liberal	1960-1970
Henry R. Emmerson	Liberal	1897-1900	Richard Hatfield	Progressive	1970-1987
Lemuel J. Tweedie	Liberal	1900-1907		Conservative	
William Pugsley	Liberal	1907	Frank McKenna	Liberal	1987-1997
Clifford W. Robinson	Liberal	1907-1908	J. Raymond Frenette	Liberal	1997-1998
John D. Hazen	Conservative	1908-1911	Camille H. Thériault	Liberal	1998-1999
James K. Flemming	Conservative	1911-1914	Bernard Lord	Progressive	1999-2006
George J. Clarke	Conservative	1914-1917		Conservative	
James A. Murray	Conservative	1917	Shawn Graham	Liberal	2006-2010
Walter E. Foster	Liberal	1917-1923	David Alward	Progressive	2010-
Peter J. Veniot	Liberal	1923-1925		Conservative	

to the Court of Queen's Bench or, in some cases, directly to the Court of Appeal.

Local government. The provincial government assesses and collects local taxes and administers all matters relating to education, health, welfare, and justice. City, town, and village councils handle such things as fire and police protection and maintenance of streets, sewers, and water service.

All of the cities, towns, and villages in New Brunswick have mayors and councils. Some of the cities and towns in New Brunswick also have managers.

Revenue. New Brunswick gets about half of its *general revenue* (income) from taxes levied by the provincial government. Most of this revenue comes from taxes on personal income, retail sales, property, and gasoline sales. The province also receives revenue from national and provincial tax-sharing arrangements and federal assistance. Much of the other revenue comes from lottery sales and from license and permit fees.

Politics. The major political parties in New Brunswick are the provincial Liberal and Progressive Conservative parties. The Progressive Conservative Party was formerly named the Conservative Party, and today its members are usually called Conservatives. The third largest party is the New Democratic Party, commonly called the NDP or the New Democrats. The Conservatives have controlled the provincial government since a general election in 2010.

History

First Nations. The first European settlers in what is now New Brunswick found Mi'kmaq and Maliseet (Wolastoqiyik) First Nations people (American Indians) living in the region. Both of these peoples belonged to the Algonquian Indian family. The Mi'kmaq roamed the eastern part of the region. The Maliseet lived in the Saint John River Valley. Their name for themselves, Wolastoqiyik, comes from their name for the river, Wolastoq, meaning *beautiful river*. The First Nations people liked to camp downstream from waterfalls or near the farthest reaches of tidewater in rivers. These locations provided the best fishing for salmon and trout. The First Nations people also gathered clams and oysters along the coast.

Exploration and settlement. In 1534, the French explorer Jacques Cartier arrived in Chaleur Bay. He wrote of the region: "The land along the south side of it is as fine and as good land, as arable and as full of beautiful fields and meadows, as any we have ever seen."

© All Canada Photos/Alamy Images

First Nations peoples of the Algonquian Indian family lived in the New Brunswick region when Europeans arrived in the 1500's. They constructed birch bark tipis, like the one shown here.

No further exploration took place until 1604. That year, the French explorers Samuel de Champlain and Pierre du Gua (or du Guast), Sieur de Monts, sailed into the Bay of Fundy. They explored the coast and spent the winter on St. Croix Island, near the mouth of the St. Croix River. In 1605, they moved across the Bay of Fundy to Port-Royal, in what is now Nova Scotia. Later in the 1600's, French settlers established farms and fishing stations in the area. They called the region Acadia (see **Acadia**).

French rivals. The French, some of whom hoped to establish a fur trade, began to fight among themselves for control of the territory. The most famous struggle took place between Charles de la Tour and D'Aulnay de Charnisay. La Tour had a trading post and fort on the site of present-day Saint John. De Charnisay was a fur trader in Port-Royal. In 1645, after many years of rivalry, De Charnisay attacked La Tour's fort while La Tour was absent. Marie de la Tour, the trader's wife, led the defense of the fort but finally surrendered.

Competition among the French gradually gave way to rivalry between the French and the English. To the south, the English colonies grew rapidly. Many English fishing crews and other people were attracted to the New Brunswick region. The English conquered Acadia in 1654 but returned it to the French in the Treaty of Breda in 1667. The English invaded Acadia again in 1690. After Queen Anne's War (1702-1713), France gave the mainland Nova Scotia area of Acadia to Britain in the Treaty of Utrecht (1713). But France and Britain disputed the ownership of most of New Brunswick. Many Acadians remained in the New Brunswick region. In the last of the French and Indian wars, the British captured the region. They drove out many Acadians. The Treaty of Paris (1763) confirmed British ownership of the New Brunswick part of Acadia. See **French and Indian wars.**

British settlement. Traders from New England arrived in Saint John in 1762. In 1763, other New Englanders founded the settlement of Maugerville, near what is now Fredericton. That same year, the New Brunswick region became part of the British province of Nova Scotia. Many Acadians were allowed to return to the region. They received grants of lands in the north and east.

During and after the American Revolution (1775-1783), about 14,000 people loyal to Britain arrived from the United States, most in 1783. These Loyalists, as they were called, landed in Saint John. Most of them settled

Historic New Brunswick

WORLD BOOK map

Samuel de Champlain arrived at St. Croix Island, in the Bay of Fundy, in 1604. He and his party spent the winter on the island, near the mouth of the St. Croix River.

New Brunswick was once part of the British colony of Nova Scotia. In 1784, New Brunswick became a separate British province, and in 1867, it became one of Canada's first provinces.

The first nuclear power plant in the Atlantic Provinces, Point Lepreau Generating Station, began operating in New Brunswick in 1983.

Important dates in New Brunswick

WORLD BOOK illustrations by Richard Bonson, The Art Agency

1534 The French explorer Jacques Cartier arrived in Chaleur Bay.

1604 Samuel de Champlain and Sieur de Monts of France spent the winter on St. Croix Island.

1762 Traders from New England arrived in Saint John.

1763 France, in the Treaty of Paris, confirmed British ownership of the New Brunswick region.

1770's-1780's Thousands of Loyalists came from the United States to settle in New Brunswick.

1784 New Brunswick became a separate province.

1825 A great fire swept the Miramichi River region.

1842 The New Brunswick-Maine boundary dispute was settled.

1848 New Brunswick was granted self-government.

1867 New Brunswick became one of the original four provinces of the Dominion of Canada.

1890 Two national railway systems linked New Brunswick cities with Montreal.

1952-1953 Vast deposits of copper, lead, silver, and zinc were mapped in the Bathurst-Newcastle region.

1968 An industrial development program was completed in the Bathurst-Newcastle region, and a hydroelectric plant opened at Mactaquac Dam on the Saint John River near Fredericton.

1997 Confederation Bridge, which connects Prince Edward Island and New Brunswick, opened.

in the lower Saint John River Valley. They founded Fredericton. Others settled near Passamaquoddy Bay on the border with the United States. In 1784, Britain established New Brunswick as a separate province. In 1785, Saint John became the first incorporated city in what is now Canada. The following year, the Colonial Legislature was created, and the farmers and landowners elected the province's first Legislative Assembly.

Shipbuilding and the timber trade with the British grew during the 1800's. After 1815, thousands of English, Irish, and Scottish settlers came to New Brunswick because they could not find jobs in the United Kingdom. Some of these Irish immigrants were fleeing the Great Irish Famine of 1845-1850.

In 1825, a great forest fire blazed through about 6,000 square miles (16,000 square kilometers) in the Miramichi River region. The fire, fanned by its own hurricanelike winds, wiped out entire settlements and killed about 150 people. The homeless settlers received clothing, money, and supplies from the other provinces, the United Kingdom, and the United States.

By the 1830's, about four-fifths of New Brunswick was still *crown lands* (lands held in the name of the British government). Timber traders had to pay fees to operate in the forests. In 1833, the provincial legislature began a movement to acquire the crown lands. The British government gave the lands to New Brunswick in 1837.

The Aroostook War. Settlers from New Brunswick and Maine lived in the valley of the Aroostook River. The United Kingdom and the United States had never agreed on a boundary in this region, and disputes developed between New Brunswick and Maine loggers. The climax came in 1839 when militias from New Brunswick and Maine assembled to fight. No fighting took place, however. President Martin Van Buren of the United States sent U.S. Army General Winfield Scott to settle the dispute, which was called the Aroostook War. Scott arranged a truce. In 1842, British and American authorities established the New Brunswick-Maine boundary.

As the population of New Brunswick grew, so did demands for local autonomy. Political power shifted gradually from the British colonial office in London to the provincial legislature in Fredericton. In 1848, the United Kingdom granted New Brunswick almost complete control over its own affairs.

Confederation and progress. In 1864, delegates

from New Brunswick, Nova Scotia, and Prince Edward Island met in Charlottetown, Prince Edward Island, to discuss forming a united colony. Delegates from Upper Canada and Lower Canada, the southern parts of what are now Ontario and Quebec, joined them and proposed a confederation of all the British provinces of eastern North America. The delegates met again later in 1864 in Quebec. They drew up a plan for Canadian confederation that led to the creation of the Dominion of Canada.

Many New Brunswickers feared they would lose their political powers in the proposed union. Samuel L. Tilley, a provincial political leader, played a major part in convincing the people that the larger provinces would not control them. On July 1, 1867, New Brunswick became one of the four original provinces of the Dominion of Canada. The others were Nova Scotia, Ontario, and Quebec. Andrew R. Wetmore, of the Confederation Party, became the first premier of New Brunswick after confederation. The most prominent premier in the years following confederation was George E. King, who passed the act establishing free public schools in 1871.

The province's fishing, lumbering, and mining industries expanded gradually. But the increasing use of iron steamships led to the end of New Brunswick's sailing-ship industry. It was replaced by important textile and iron industries. During the 1870's and 1880's, many New Brunswickers moved to western Canada and the United States. These regions offered better job opportunities.

By 1890, two national railway systems linked cities in New Brunswick with Montreal. Saint John ranked with Halifax, Nova Scotia, as a chief winter port on Canada's east coast. However, Ontario and Quebec controlled manufacturing and trade in Canada. After 1900, the pulp industry became increasingly important in New Brunswick. Public works programs improved communication and transportation in the province during the early 1900's. But New Brunswick's industries suffered serious decline between 1919 and 1925. Recovery came slowly. The major growth during the 1920's and 1930's occurred in the paper industry.

The middle and late 1900's. After World War II (1939-1945), the province's pulp and paper industries expanded greatly, and shipbuilding became important in the Saint John area. Huge deposits of copper, lead, silver, and zinc were mapped in the Bathurst-Newcastle re-

The New Brunswick Museum

A fire in Saint John in 1837 destroyed a large part of the commercial district of the city. The lithograph at the left was made from a sketch by Thomas H. Wentworth, an eyewitness to the blaze.

gion in 1952 and 1953. In 1953 and 1957, the province completed hydroelectric plants that provided additional power for mining and manufacturing. The largest oil refinery in Canada was constructed in Saint John in 1960.

A construction program related to the Bathurst-Newcastle metal ore deposits began in 1962 and was completed by 1968. Projects in the program included chemical and fertilizer plants, docking and shipping facilities, milling and manufacturing firms, mines, and pipelines. Mining of the metal ores began to boom in 1964, when the region's largest mine started operations. Despite the economic stimulation provided by the construction program, New Brunswick's standard of living remained below the national average. Migration out of the province rose.

In 1968, a hydroelectric plant opened at Mactaquac Dam on the Saint John River near Fredericton. More than half the power from this plant goes to industries in the Bathurst-Newcastle region.

During the late 1960's, Premier Louis J. Robichaud, a Liberal, led the province in what he called a Program of Equal Opportunity. In this program, the provincial government took over the operation of all courts, schools, and health and welfare institutions. The action was taken to equalize the quality of services provided by such facilities throughout the province. The Robichaud era also was associated with a more active cultural, economic, and political role for New Brunswick's French-speaking Acadian minority.

In 1969, the New Brunswick Legislative Assembly passed a law that made French an official language of equal status with English in the legislature itself and in courts, government offices, and schools. Later that year, the Canadian Parliament passed the Official Languages Act. This law requires federal facilities to provide service in both languages in districts where at least 10 percent of the people speak French. Under this law, the whole province of New Brunswick is considered a bilingual district for federal services.

Economic developments. New Brunswick's shipping facilities were expanded in the 1970's. In 1970, North America's first deepwater terminal for oil tankers opened near Saint John. The next year, a terminal for container ships opened at Saint John.

In the mid-1970's, the Saint John area experienced major industrial expansion. The chief projects included the enlargement of shipbuilding and oil refining complexes. Food processing, mining, and forestry industries also expanded throughout New Brunswick.

In 1983, the first nuclear power plant in Atlantic Canada began operation at Point Lepreau. In 1983 and 1985, two large potash mines began operating in the Sussex region of southern New Brunswick. But in 1997, continued flooding caused the larger of the mines to close. Also in 1997, Confederation Bridge opened, providing a "fixed link" between New Brunswick and Prince Edward Island. Previously, travelers relied on ferry service to cross the Northumberland Strait. In the 1990's, the provincial government promoted investment in information technology businesses, such as telephone call centers.

An ongoing concern of provincial leaders has been how to provide jobs for the labor force, especially in the north, and to stop the emigration of young people to other parts of Canada. In 1996, the Royal Canadian Air Force base at Chatham closed. During the early 2000's, mills that produced pulp and other wood products closed at Bathurst, Dalhousie, Miramichi, and other locations. Other mills cut production. Hundreds of people lost their jobs. The Saint John dry dock and shipyard, which had produced state-of-the-art patrol frigates for the Royal Canadian Navy, also closed. In 2009, however, operations began at a liquefied natural gas receiving and regasification terminal in Saint John.   Greg Marquis

Related articles in *World Book* include:

Biographies

Beaverbrook, Lord	Foster, Sir George E.
Bennett, Richard Bedford	Law, Andrew B.
Carman, Bliss	LeBlanc, Roméo
Edmonds, Sarah Emma Evelyn	Roberts, Charles G. D.

Cities and towns

Fredericton	Saint John
Moncton	

Physical features

Bay of Fundy	Passamaquoddy Bay
Gulf of Saint Lawrence	Reversing Falls of Saint John
Miramichi River	Saint John River

Other related articles

Acadia	United Empire Loyalists
Canada	

Outline

I. **People**
  A. Population
  B. Schools
  C. Libraries
  D. Museums
II. **Visitor's guide**
III. **Land and climate**
  A. Land regions
  B. Coastline
  C. Rivers and lakes
  D. Plant and animal life
  E. Climate
IV. **Economy**
  A. Natural resources
  B. Service industries
  C. Manufacturing
  D. Mining
  E. Forestry
  F. Fishing industry
  G. Agriculture
  H. Electric power and utilities
  I. Transportation
  J. Communication
V. **Government**
  A. Lieutenant governor
  B. Premier
  C. Legislative Assembly
  D. Courts
  E. Local government
  F. Revenue
  G. Politics
VI. **History**

Additional resources

Acheson, T. W. *Saint John: The Making of a Colonial Urban Community.* 1985. Reprint. Univ. of Toronto Pr., 1993.
Campbell, Kumari. *Destination Saint John.* Fitzhenry & Whiteside, 1998. *New Brunswick.* Rev. ed. 2002. Younger readers.
Conrad, Margaret R., and Hiller, J. K. *Atlantic Canada: A History.* 2nd ed. Oxford, 2010.
Leroux, John. *Building New Brunswick: An Architectural History.* Goose Lane, 2008.
Marquis, Greg. *In Armageddon's Shadow: The Civil War and Canada's Maritime Provinces.* McGill-Queen's Univ. Pr., 1998.
Zimmerman, Karla, and Brash, Celeste. *Nova Scotia, New Brunswick, and Prince Edward Island.* Lonely Planet Pubns., 2007. A travel guidebook.

New Brunswick, *BRUHNZ wihk,* **University of,** is a public university with campuses in Fredericton and Saint John, New Brunswick. It was formed in Fredericton in 1785 as the Provincial Academy of Arts and Sciences. The school took its present name in 1859. The Saint John campus was established in 1964. The university offers bachelor's and graduate degrees. The Fredericton campus's athletic teams are called the Varsity Reds, and the Saint John campus's athletic teams are the Seawolves. The university's website at http://www.unb.ca offers additional information.

Critically reviewed by the University of New Brunswick

New Caledonia is an overseas possession of France. It lies in the South Pacific Ocean, about 1,200 miles (1,930 kilometers) northeast of Sydney, Australia. For location, see **Pacific Islands** (map). New Caledonia consists of one main island, also called New Caledonia, or Grand Terre; the Loyalty Islands; the Bélep Islands; the Isle of Pines; and a few uninhabited islands. The mountainous main island covers 6,321 square miles (16,372 square kilometers). The rest of the islands have a total area of only 851 square miles (2,203 square kilometers).

New Caledonia has a population of about 260,000. Nouméa, on the main island, is the capital and only city. Melanesians, also called Kanaks, are the largest group of people and make up about two-fifths of the population. Europeans are the second largest group. Others include Indonesians, Polynesians, and Vietnamese.

New Caledonia is one of the world's leading producers of nickel. Nickel mining and smelting are the leading industries. Other minerals produced in New Caledonia include chromite and cobalt. Farmers raise their own food and small amounts of coffee and copra for export. Tourism is another important industry.

New Caledonia's governmental responsibilities are shared by a locally elected congress and a French official appointed by the French government. The congress appoints a president and up to 10 other officials to carry out executive functions.

Melanesians, probably from New Guinea, reached New Caledonia at least 4,000 years ago. In 1774, James Cook, a British navigator, became the first European to land on the main island. He called it New Caledonia because it resembled Scotland *(Caledonia* in Latin). France took possession of New Caledonia in 1853. The United States had a large military base on the main island from 1942 to 1945. In the 1980's, many Kanaks demanded independence for New Caledonia. In a referendum held in

1987, New Caledonians voted to continue French control. But the Melanesians continued to demand independence. In 1988, violence erupted between some Kanaks and French officials. Later that year, voters approved a peace agreement. In a referendum held in 1998, New Caledonians voted in favor of greater self-government.   Nancy Davis Lewis

New Deal was President Franklin D. Roosevelt's program to pull the United States out of the Great Depression in the 1930's. The New Deal did not end the Depression. However, it relieved much economic hardship and gave Americans faith in the democratic system at a time when other nations hit by the Depression turned to dictators. Roosevelt first used the term *new deal* when he accepted the Democratic presidential nomination in 1932. "I pledge you, I pledge myself, to a new deal for the American people," he said.

When Roosevelt became president on March 4, 1933, business was at a standstill, the banking system was near collapse, and a feeling of panic had gripped the nation. The stock market crash in October 1929 had shattered the prosperity most Americans enjoyed during the 1920's. The Depression grew worse during the early 1930's, as banks, businesses, and factories closed. Workers lost their homes and farmers lost their farms because they could not meet mortgage payments. By 1933, an estimated 12 million to 15 million Americans—1 out of 4 workers—had no job. The Depression struck minority groups especially hard. In the African American community, unemployment rates hovered near 50 percent.

In his inaugural address, Roosevelt expressed confidence that the nation could solve its problems. "The only thing we have to fear is fear itself," he said.

The Hundred Days

Roosevelt called Congress into special session on March 5, 1933. From March 9 to June 16, Congress passed a series of laws aimed at speeding economic recovery, providing relief for victims of the Depression, and reforming financial, business, agricultural, and industrial practices. Most laws passed swiftly and with little opposition. Never before had Congress approved so many important laws so quickly. The session became known as the Hundred Days. Many historians would later refer to this period as the First New Deal.

The programs and policies that made up the New Deal did not come from one person. Roosevelt, his presidential advisers (also known as the "Brain Trust"), and congressional leaders all proposed ideas. Some programs conflicted with each other. For example, the Economy Act cut the salaries of federal employees while the Public Works Administration increased government spending. But Roosevelt was willing to experiment and tried the ideas of one group and then another.

Helping savers and investors. Roosevelt's first goal was to end the banking crisis. A wave of bank failures in February had frightened the public. Depositors rushed to withdraw their money before their banks failed. Roosevelt declared a "bank holiday," closing all banks on March 6. On March 9, Congress passed the Emergency Banking Act. The new law allowed government inspectors to check each bank's records and to reopen only those banks that were in strong financial condition. Within a few days, half the nation's banks reopened.

Shostal

Nouméa, the capital of New Caledonia, is the only city on the main island, called New Caledonia or Grand Terre.

These banks held 90 percent of the country's total deposits. This action did much to end the nation's panic.

The Glass-Steagall Banking Act of June 1933 provided further protection for investors. It gave the Federal Reserve Board more power to regulate loans made by banks and created the Federal Deposit Insurance Corporation (FDIC), which first insured bank deposits up to $2,500 and later, in July 1934, up to $5,000.

Congress passed the Securities Act of 1933, also called the Truth-in-Securities Act, in May 1933. This law required firms issuing new stocks to give investors full and accurate financial information. Congress created the Securities and Exchange Commission (SEC) in 1934 to regulate the stock market.

Helping the farmers. The Agricultural Adjustment Administration (AAA), created in May 1933, was a centerpiece of the Hundred Days. It sought to raise farm prices by limiting production. The AAA gave farmers "benefit payments" if they agreed not to produce as much as they had before. The plan increased farm income, but critics argued that farmers should not cut food and cotton production at a time when people were hungry and needed clothing. In addition, tenants and sharecroppers, many of whom were African American, rarely received any portion of the benefit payment given to the landowner. In fact, the measure encouraged landowners to evict tenants and sharecroppers because landowners had fewer acres to cultivate.

In *United States v. Butler* (1936), the Supreme Court of the United States declared the AAA unconstitutional. The government then paid farmers to leave some land vacant as part of new soil conservation programs.

Helping industry and labor. The National Industrial Recovery Act of June 1933 was another centerpiece of the Hundred Days. This act created the National Recovery Administration (NRA) to enforce codes of fair prac-

tices for business and industry. Representatives of firms within each industry wrote the codes, which allowed the firms to set quality standards and minimum prices. The codes primarily aided business.

The industrial codes set minimum wages and maximum hours, and supported the right of workers to join unions. However, some unions refused to admit African Americans. Many industries also refused to include black workers in the NRA protections and paid them less than whites. Some African Americans referred to the NRA as "Negro Run Around" or "Negroes Ruined Again." The Supreme Court declared the National Industrial Recovery Act unconstitutional in 1935, and the NRA was abolished (see **Schechter v. United States**).

Helping the needy. The Civilian Conservation Corps (CCC) launched the New Deal relief program. The CCC put young men from needy families to work at useful conservation projects, such as planting trees and building dams. The Federal Emergency Relief Administration provided the states with money for the needy. The Public Works Administration (PWA) created jobs for large numbers of people. It built thousands of schools, courthouses, bridges, dams, and other projects. The Tennessee Valley Authority (TVA) built dams to control floods and to provide electricity for residents of the Tennessee River Valley.

The Second Hundred Days

Congress approved several important relief and reform measures in 1935. These laws, which tended to emphasize economic security, became the heart of the lasting achievements of the New Deal. Most of these new laws were passed during the summer, and some historians call this period the *Second Hundred Days,* or the *Second New Deal.* The most important new measures included the Works Progress Administration

Leading New Deal agencies

AAA — Agricultural Adjustment Administration. Founded in 1933 to assist farmers and regulate farm production.

CCC —* Civilian Conservation Corps. Founded in 1933 to provide jobs for the unemployed.

CCC —* Commodity Credit Corporation. Founded in 1933 to support the Department of Agriculture.

FCA — Farm Credit Administration. Founded in 1933 to provide a credit system for farmers by making long-term and short-term credit available.

FCC —* Federal Communications Commission. Founded in 1934 to regulate radio, telephone, and telegraph systems.

FCIC — Federal Crop Insurance Corporation. Founded in 1938 to provide protection against crop losses.

FDIC —* Federal Deposit Insurance Corporation. Founded in 1933 to insure bank deposits.

FERA — Federal Emergency Relief Administration. Founded in 1933 to cooperate with the states in relieving hardships caused by unemployment and drought.

FHA —* Federal Housing Administration. Founded in 1934 to insure private lending companies against loss on home-mortgage loans and on loans for improving small properties.

FSA — Farm Security Administration. Founded in 1937 to help farmers buy needed equipment.

HOLC — Home Owners Loan Corporation. Founded in 1933 to grant long-term mortgage loans at low cost to homeowners in financial difficulties.

NLRB —* National Labor Relations Board. Founded in 1935 to administer the National Labor Relations Act.

NRA —* National Recovery Administration. Founded in 1933 to carry out plans made by the National Industrial Recovery Act to fight the Depression.

NYA — National Youth Administration. Founded in 1935 to provide job training for unemployed youths and part-time work for needy students.

PWA — Public Works Administration. Founded in 1933 to increase employment and purchasing power through the construction of useful public works, such as bridges, in the various states.

REA —* Rural Electrification Administration. Founded in 1935 to aid farmers in the electrification of their homes.

SEC —* Securities and Exchange Commission. Founded in 1934 to protect the public from investing in unsafe securities and to regulate stock market practices.

SSB — Social Security Board. Founded in 1935 to secure a sound social security system.

TVA —* Tennessee Valley Authority. Founded in 1933 to help develop the resources of the Tennessee Valley.

USHA — United States Housing Authority. Founded in 1937 to aid in the development of adequate housing throughout the nation.

WPA —* Works Progress Administration. Founded in 1935 to provide work for needy persons on public works projects. Renamed Work Projects Administration in 1939.

*Has a separate article in *World Book.*

Bettmann Archive

New Deal projects, such as this road construction project in New York City, put many Americans back to work. The New Deal helped the United States recover from the Great Depression.

(WPA), the National Labor Relations Act, and the Social Security Act.

Works Progress Administration provided jobs building highways, streets, bridges, parks, and other projects intended to have long-range value. It also created work for artists, writers, and performers. The WPA provided some work for about 8 ½ million people. It was renamed the Work Projects Administration in 1939.

The National Labor Relations Act guaranteed workers the right to organize unions. During the next few years, the American Federation of Labor (AFL) and the new Congress of Industrial Organizations (CIO) enrolled millions of workers in labor unions.

The Social Security Act provided pensions for the aged and insurance for the jobless. The law also provided payments for people with disabilities and for needy children (see **Social security**). However, by exempting farm and domestic workers, the law excluded two-thirds of the African American labor force from benefits.

The final measures

In its final and least successful phase, the New Deal aimed to expand the government's capacity to provide services to the people. Some historians call this period the *Third New Deal.*

In 1937, Roosevelt proposed a plan to add justices to the Supreme Court. Critics charged that he was trying to "pack" the court with judges who favored the New Deal. Roosevelt's plan divided the Democrats and cost him his solid support in Congress (see **Roosevelt, Franklin D.** [The Supreme Court]). Congress passed only two other important reform measures after 1936. The first was the United States Housing Act of 1937, which provided money for more public housing projects. The second was the Fair Labor Standards Act (FLSA) of 1938, which set a minimum wage of 25 cents an hour and a maximum workweek of 44 hours, with extra pay for extra

hours. The act also banned child labor. However, the FLSA excluded farm and domestic workers.

The economy faltered late in 1937. Farm prices dropped, and the number of jobless people rose from about 5 million in September 1937 to almost 11 million in May 1938. The Democrats retained majorities in both houses of Congress in the 1938 elections, but Republicans gained back seats for the first time since 1928. Strong opposition in Congress forced Roosevelt to avoid further reforms, and he soon became occupied primarily with the growing threat of Nazi Germany.

Results of the New Deal

Most scholars agree that the New Deal relieved much economic distress and brought about a measure of recovery. But about 8 million Americans still had no jobs in 1940. Military spending for World War II (1939-1945), rather than the New Deal, brought back prosperity.

The New Deal caused major political changes. The Democratic Party, generally a minority party since the American Civil War (1861-1865), became the largest political party. Its main strength shifted from the rural South to the urban North. Minorities, immigrants, union members, urban intellectuals, and reformers became more prominent in the party.

Most scholars agree that the New Deal preserved the essentials of the U.S. free enterprise system. Profits and competition continued to play a leading part in the system. But the program added new features. The federal government became responsible for the economic security of the people and the economic growth of the nation. After the New Deal, the government's role in public welfare and banking grew steadily, and organized labor became a key force in national affairs.   Margaret C. Rung

Related articles in *World Book.* See the separate articles listed in the table in this article. See also:

Fair Labor Standards Act	Roosevelt, Franklin D.
Hopkins, Harry Lloyd	Securities Exchange Act
Liberty League	Truman, Harry S. (Domestic program)

Additional resources

Edsforth, Ronald. *The New Deal.* Blackwell, 2000.
McElvaine, Robert. *The Depression and the New Deal: A History in Documents.* 2000. Reprint. Oxford, 2003.

New Delhi, *DEHL ee* (pop. 294,783), is the capital of India. It lies on the west bank of the Yamuna River in northern India, near the Thar, or Great Indian, Desert. New Delhi is about 3 miles (5 kilometers) south of Delhi, the former capital (see **India** [political map]).

New Delhi is an attractive, spacious city. It contrasts sharply with the crowded, older city of Delhi. The design of New Delhi and some of its buildings reflects the influence of the British, who ruled India from 1858 to 1947. New Delhi was built in the early 1900's to replace Delhi as India's capital. It became the capital in 1931.

The city. New Delhi is a carefully planned city. It has wide, treelined avenues, and many gardens and open areas. Huge government buildings, including Parliament House and a government office building called the Secretariat, dominate the center of the city. Large houses, originally built for government officials, and smaller houses for servants are nearby.

Rashtrapati Bhavan (Presidential House), the official residence of the president of India, stands west of the

WORLD BOOK photo by David R. Frazier

New Delhi, the capital of India, is a carefully planned city. Its wide, treelined avenues provide plenty of space for traffic and pedestrians. Tall, modern buildings dominate the skyline.

Secretariat. This majestic, copper-domed palace has 340 rooms. Several blocks east are white palaces that once were winter homes of Indian princes. The government turned most of the palaces into offices or museums after India became independent in 1947. The Dhyan Chand National Stadium, for field hockey, is east of the palaces.

The southern part of the city includes the Diplomatic Enclave, an area set aside for foreign embassies and fine residences. High government officials of other countries have offices on a street called *Shanti Path* (Peace Boulevard). A temple of the Bahá'í Faith is south of the capital. The temple, built in the shape of a lotus blossom, was completed in 1986.

New Delhi has many small neighborhoods and suburbs with distinctive bazaars. Many of these neighborhoods were settled by refugees from the section of India that became part of Pakistan in 1947. New Delhi also has several beautiful gardens, of which the Mughal Gardens at Rashtrapati Bhavan are the best known.

Connaught Place, the business center of New Delhi, lies north of the Secretariat and Parliament House. It is surrounded by a fashionable shopping area. A subway and elevated rail system serves the Delhi metropolitan area, which includes New Delhi.

Economy. The government of India is the main employer in New Delhi. The city has no factories. Craftworkers sell products in the Central Cottage Industries Emporium, a building near Connaught Place.

History. In 1912, the capital of India was moved from Calcutta (now Kolkata) to Delhi. Plans were also made to build a new capital just outside Delhi, away from that crowded city. The English architects Sir Herbert Baker and Sir Edwin L. Lutyens planned the layout and designed buildings for the new city. Construction began in 1912 but was delayed during World War I (1914-1918). In 1931, New Delhi was completed and became the capital

of India. The city remained the capital after India gained independence from the United Kingdom in 1947.

India's Constitution went into effect on Jan. 26, 1950. Since then, January 26 has been a national holiday called Republic Day. New Delhi has an annual Republic Day celebration, which features a huge parade.

Robert LaPorte, Jr.

See also **Delhi; India** (picture: New Delhi).

New Democratic Party (NDP) is a social-democratic political party in Canada. It is formally linked with the Canadian labor movement. The NDP supports strong social welfare policies, greater social rights, a more equal distribution of wealth, publicly funded universal health care, and limits on foreign ownership in Canada. It has never formed a national government, but it has often played a key role in minority governments. The NDP has had greater success at the provincial level. At times, it has controlled the governments of about half of Canada's provinces and territories.

The NDP traces its beginnings to the birth of another political party, the Co-operative Commonwealth Federation (CCF). The CCF was founded in 1932, during the Great Depression. It favored a greater role for government in economic planning, public health services, and public ownership of key industries.

In 1961, the CCF formed an alliance with unions in the Canadian Labour Congress and established the NDP. Saskatchewan Premier T. C. (Tommy) Douglas became the NDP's first leader. Under Douglas, the New Democrats did not achieve the national success they had expected, and they often placed third in federal elections. Until the early 2000's, the party never gained much support in Quebec or easternmost Canada.

The NDP at times has had significant influence in federal politics. From 1972 to 1974, the Liberal Party under Prime Minister Pierre Trudeau lacked a majority in Parliament. The Liberals relied on the support of the NDP, then led by labor lawyer David Lewis. The NDP's influence on the balance of power resulted in improvements in social programs. It also led to major reforms and the democratization of election financing, as well as the creation of the Foreign Investment Review Agency (FIRA, later Investment Canada) to oversee foreign investment in Canada. In the 1980's, under Ed Broadbent, the NDP made its greatest electoral gains up to that time. The party suffered major losses under Audrey McLaughlin in the 1993 federal election. Alexa McDonough led the NDP to a partial recovery in 1997 and 2000.

The NDP has steadily increased its votes and seats in Parliament since 2004, under the leadership of Jack Layton. In 2011, the NDP won the second most seats in the House of Commons and became the Official Opposition. Its dramatic increase in seats came largely from Quebec, where the separatist Bloc Québécois lost ground.

Alan Whitehorn

See also **McLaughlin, Audrey Marlene.**

New England is a region that consists of six states: Connecticut, Maine, Massachusetts, New Hampshire, Rhode Island, and Vermont. For information on this region, see **United States** (Regions). See also the articles on the states that make up the region.

New England, Dominion of, was a group of English colonies in America united in 1686 by King James II of England. The colonies in the dominion were Connecticut, Massachusetts, New Hampshire, East Jersey, West Jersey, New York, Plymouth, and Rhode Island. King James believed that if the colonies united under a single government, they would function better and could more easily defend themselves against England's major military rival, France. But the colonists had no voice in the government, and most of them opposed the dominion. James was overthrown in England in 1688. The dominion broke up the next year. Donna J. Spindel

New England Confederation was created in 1643. Four colonies—Massachusetts, Plymouth, Connecticut, and New Haven—formed the United Colonies of New England, as it was called. They worked to solve boundary and commercial disputes and to meet the increased danger of attacks by the Dutch, French, and Indians. Maine, New Hampshire, and Rhode Island were excluded from membership for political and religious reasons.

The four colonies agreed to "enter into a firm and perpetual league of friendship and amity, for offence and defence, mutual advice and succor upon all just occasions, both for preserving and propagating the truth and

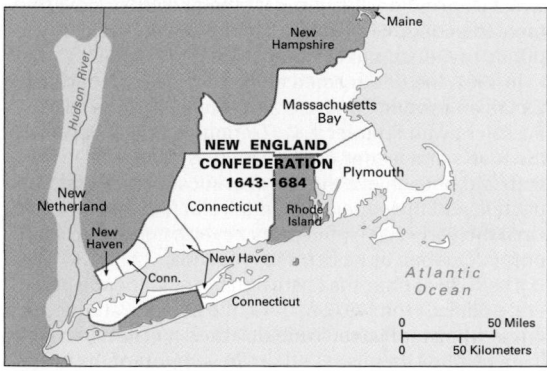

WORLD BOOK map

The New England Confederation was formed in 1643 by four New England colonies. The confederation hoped to discourage attacks by New Netherland, other nearby colonies, and Indians.

liberties of the gospel, and for their own mutual safety and welfare."

Two commissioners from each colony met each year to consider problems of mutual interest. Commissioners selected a president to preside over meetings. Under confederation regulations, three colonies comprised a decisive majority. The confederation had great power in theory, but, in practice, it could only advise. A test of the confederation's power came in 1653, when Plymouth, Connecticut, and New Haven favored a war against the Dutch of New Netherland. The fourth colony, Massachusetts, did not agree and absolutely refused to yield. This action lessened the prestige of the organization. After 1664, the commissioners met only every three years, and in 1684 the confederation came to an end. Despite serious weaknesses, the confederation provided valuable experience in cooperation among the colonies as well as America's first experiment in federalism. It also helped prevent the smaller colonies from being totally dominated by Massachusetts. Larry Gragg

New France was the French colonial empire in North America. The empire began during the early 1600's and lasted about 150 years. At its height in the early 1700's,

New France included three colonies—Canada, Acadia, and Louisiana. Canada and Acadia covered much of what is now eastern Canada. Louisiana lay in the Mississippi River Valley of the present-day United States.

The term *New France* often refers only to the colony of Canada, where about 75 percent of the empire's settlers lived. France lost this territory to Britain in the Seven Years' War (1756-1763). But the French influence on Canadian culture still remains strong. About 6 million Canadians, chiefly in the provinces of Quebec, Ontario, and New Brunswick, speak French. French, along with English, is an official language of Canada.

Exploration and settlement. The first official French expedition to North America occurred in 1524. That year, the Italian navigator Giovanni da Verrazzano explored the Atlantic Coast for King Francis I of France. The French explorer Jacques Cartier sailed to Canada in 1534, 1535, and 1541. He became the first European to reach the Gulf of St. Lawrence. Cartier claimed the area surrounding the Gulf of St. Lawrence for France.

During the 1500's, French fishing crews began to drop their nets off the coast of what is now the Canadian province of Newfoundland and Labrador. They also started to trade kettles, knives, and other European goods to local Indians for furs. Canadian furs, especially beaver pelts, became increasingly valuable because of the growing popularity of fur hats in Europe.

In 1604, the French explorers Pierre du Gua (or du Guast), Sieur de Monts, and Samuel de Champlain established Acadia along the Atlantic coast. Champlain founded the settlement of Quebec along the St. Lawrence River in 1608. Soon afterward, French fur traders established other settlements on the St. Lawrence River. Roman Catholic missionaries founded Montreal, at first named Ville-Marie, in 1642.

New France grew slowly. It had only a few thousand settlers by 1660. In 1663, King Louis XIV made New France a *royal province,* or colony, of France. Between 1665 and 1672, he sent over about 2,500 settlers. Among them were many women intended as brides for the soldiers and settlers already in the colony.

In 1672, Louis de Buade, Comte de Frontenac, became the governor general of New France. He encouraged fur traders and explorers to help expand the colony. Traders then began to establish a number of posts along the Great Lakes and Hudson Bay. Also, in 1672, the French-Canadian explorer Louis Jolliet and Jacques Marquette, a French missionary, became the first white people to find the upper part of the Mississippi River. The French explorer René-Robert Cavelier, Sieur de La Salle, followed the Mississippi to the Gulf of Mexico in 1682. He claimed the river valley for France and named it Louisiana to honor Louis XIV. In 1699, Pierre Le Moyne, Sieur d'Iberville, established the colony of Louisiana. The French built a chain of forts to link Louisiana with the rest of New France. The population of New France rose from almost 25,000 in 1720 to about 65,000 in 1760.

Colonial life. The chief governing officials of the royal province were the *governor general* and the *intendant.* The governor general supervised the army and relations with the Indians. The intendant controlled finance, law enforcement, and other local matters.

The fur trade was the chief economic activity in New France. Many young colonists were frontiersmen who

The **city of Quebec** served as the capital of New France. Quebec was also a religious and commercial center. This engraving from the 1700's shows a view of the city from the St. Lawrence River.

Granger Collection

made their living trading for furs. They were called *coureurs de bois* (vagabonds of the forest). Most coureurs de bois became farmers after they married, and agriculture grew in importance as an economic activity. Farmers raised livestock and grew mostly wheat and oats. Fishing and lumbering also developed into important industries. In addition, the colony had a brewery, an ironworks, and a shipyard.

By law, all colonists were Roman Catholics, and the Catholic church played a major role in New France. Female religious orders provided hospitals in the towns. They also ran schools.

The towns of Quebec, Montreal, and Trois-Rivières were the centers of trade and culture. Church and government officials and wealthy landowners lived in splendid stone homes in the towns. Merchants and craftworkers had smaller stone houses. Farmers lived on sections of land called *seigneuries*. The king of France granted the seigneuries to nobles, religious groups, military officers, and merchants, who rented the land to farmers. The landowners provided their tenants with a flour mill and a church. Most farmers lived in one- or two-room log cabins.

Both farmers and townspeople in New France often enjoyed dances and other merry social gatherings. Members of the upper class attended grand balls at the residence of the governor general. In winter, the colonists had sleighing parties and held horse races on the frozen rivers.

The British conquest. French and English settlers began fighting for control of the fur trade in the St. Lawrence River Valley in the early 1600's. The English colonies developed along the eastern coast of North America. French expansion during the 1600's angered the English colonists, who also wanted to expand westward.

Members of the two groups and their Indian allies fought each other in a series of wars from 1689 to 1763. Great Britain gained Newfoundland, the mainland Nova Scotia region of Acadia, and the French territory around Hudson Bay under the Treaty of Utrecht in 1713. During the next 30 years, the French built forts in the Ohio Valley and across the southern parts of what are now the Canadian provinces of Manitoba, Ontario, and Saskatchewan. Fighting began again in 1744. British colonists captured the French fort at Louisbourg on Cape Breton Island in 1745, but the French regained it in 1748.

The final struggle began in 1754. It is known as the French and Indian War in the United States. The conflict spread to Europe in 1756 and is called the Seven Years' War in Canada and Europe. The French were winning until 1758, when British forces captured Louisbourg and several key inland forts. In 1759, the British captured Quebec. The fighting ended when the British took Montreal in September 1760. France gave up Canada and part of Louisiana to Britain in the Treaty of Paris in 1763. France had given the rest of Louisiana to Spain in 1762. France reacquired Louisiana from Spain during the early 1800's and sold it to the United States in 1803.

John A. Dickinson

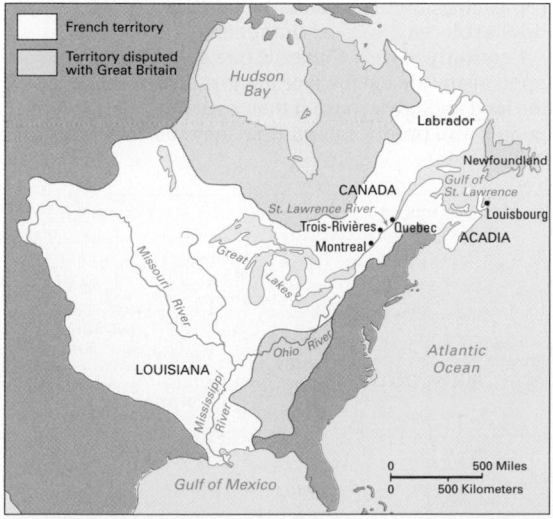

| | French territory |
| | Territory disputed with Great Britain |

New France in the early 1700's extended from Labrador to the Gulf of Mexico and included the Mississippi River Valley. The ownership of some areas, such as the region around Hudson Bay, was disputed between France and Great Britain.

WORLD BOOK map

Related articles in *World Book* include:
Acadia
Cartier, Jacques
Champlain, Samuel de
Coureurs de bois

French and Indian wars
Frontenac, Comte de
Jolliet, Louis
La Salle, Renê-Robert
Cavelier, Sieur de
Laval de Montmorency,
François Xavier de

Louisbourg
Louisiana Purchase
Marquette, Jacques
Quebec, Battle of
Seigneurial system
Talon, Jean Baptiste

Additional resources

Brandao, Jose A. *Your Fyre Shall Burn No More: Iroquois Policy Toward New France and Its Native Allies to 1701.* Univ. of Neb. Pr., 1997.
Greer, Allan. *The People of New France.* Univ. of Toronto Pr., 1997.

New Guinea is a large tropical island in the Pacific Ocean, north of Australia. It is the second largest island in the world. Greenland is the only island larger than New Guinea.

New Guinea has an area of about 309,000 square miles (800,000 square kilometers) and a population of about 9 million. Rugged mountains cover much of the interior of the island. Most of this area has a cool climate. In contrast, the lowlands along the northern and southern coasts are hot and humid.

Most New Guineans live in villages in rural areas. Almost half of the island's people dwell in isolated mountain valleys. Until the 1930's, these New Guineans had little contact with the outside world.

Political units. The island of New Guinea contains part of one nation and almost all of another. Papua is part of Indonesia, and Papua New Guinea is an independent country. Papua, formerly known as Irian Jaya, covers the western half of New Guinea and some small nearby islands to the north and west. See **Indonesia** (table: The chief islands; Papua).

Papua New Guinea occupies the eastern half of New Guinea and some islands to the east, including those of the Bismarck Archipelago. Formerly a territory of Australia, Papua New Guinea became an independent nation in 1975. Port Moresby, a city on the southeast coast of New Guinea, serves as the nation's capital. See **Papua New Guinea.**

People. Most New Guineans are Melanesians, a people who are native to the Pacific islands. Thousands of Asians, Australians, and Europeans also live on the island of New Guinea, most of them in coastal towns.

Large numbers of people from other Indonesian islands have settled in Papua.

In the highlands, most of the villagers live in round thatched houses and grow sweet potatoes as their main food. Pigs provide most of their meat. Many lowland villagers build their houses on stilts to keep them cool and dry. Their chief food crops are bananas, taro roots, and yams. People who live in the swamps of the coastal lowlands eat mostly sago, a starch that is taken from various kinds of palm trees.

New Guineans speak more than 700 languages. Because of the number of languages, many people cannot communicate with neighbors who live only a short distance away. A growing number of eastern New Guineans speak Pidgin English, or Tok Pisin, as a second language. This *lingua franca* (common language) enables speakers of different tongues to communicate with one another. In the west, many people speak Malay as a second language.

Land and climate. A great mountain system crosses New Guinea from east to west. It includes the Owen Stanley Range in the east and 16,503-foot (5,030-meter) Puncak Jaya, the highest point on the island, in the west. Mountain ridges, grassy plateaus, and deep, forested valleys cover much of the interior. Grasslands and jungles lie along the northern and southern edges of the island. Swamps with mangrove thickets border New Guinea in some areas.

Many streams and rivers flow down the mountain slopes and cross the lowlands. New Guinea's largest rivers, the Fly and Sepik, have large, swampy areas around them in the lowlands.

New Guinea's coastal lowlands have a hot, humid climate. The temperature and humidity drop as the altitude increases toward the center of the island. The annual rainfall in parts of New Guinea averages more than 200 inches (510 centimeters).

Native animals of New Guinea include crocodiles, tree kangaroos, and such snakes as the death adder, the Papuan black, and the taipan. The island also has many bright-colored birds and butterflies.

Economy of New Guinea is one of the least developed of any area in the world. Most of the people farm the land and grow most of their own food. Many farm people also produce goods that they sell, including co-

New Guinea

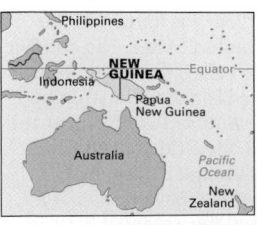

⊛ National capital
★ Provincial capital
• City or settlement
+ Elevation above sea level
— Road

WORLD BOOK maps

conuts, coffee, and cocoa. A few large plantations also
produce cocoa, coconuts, and coffee.

New Guinea has some large copper mines, including
one near Nabire in Papua. Another is in Papua New
Guinea, in mountains just east of the Indonesian border.
These mines also yield small amounts of gold. New
Guinea also has oil and natural gas deposits.

History. The earliest settlers in New Guinea probably
migrated thousands of years ago from the Asian mainland by way of the Malay Peninsula and Indonesia. In
1526, Jorge de Meneses, the Portuguese governor of the
Molucca Islands, became the first European to visit New
Guinea. Dutch, English, French, and Spanish explorers
stopped there during the next 300 years. The Netherlands claimed western New Guinea in 1828. In 1884, Germany gained the northeastern part of the island, and the
United Kingdom took the southeastern part. The United
Kingdom gave its territory to Australia in the early 1900's.
After Germany's defeat in World War I (1914-1918), the
League of Nations made northeastern New Guinea a
mandated territory under Australian rule (see **Mandated
territory**). Mandated territories were areas taken from
defeated nations and placed under the administration of
victorious nations.

Japan seized northern New Guinea in 1942, during
World War II (1939-1945). By 1944, the Allies had reconquered the area. After the war ended in 1945, the northeastern part became the United Nations (UN) Trust Territory of New Guinea under Australian administration.
Australia put the northeastern and southeastern units
(now part of Papua New Guinea) under one government.

Indonesia gained independence from the Netherlands in 1949 and claimed western New Guinea. In 1962,
the Netherlands agreed to turn over western New
Guinea to the UN. The UN placed the area under Indonesian administration in 1963, and Indonesia renamed the area Irian Barat (West Irian). In 1969, the people of the region voted to remain part of Indonesia.

During the 1960's, some New Guineans in both Irian
Barat and Papua New Guinea began demanding inde-
pendence. Irian Barat was renamed Irian Jaya in 1973.
That same year, Australia granted Papua New Guinea to-
tal control over its internal affairs. In 1975, Papua New
Guinea gained complete independence from Australia.

People of Irian Jaya continued to demand independence. In 2002, Indonesia increased the region's control
over local affairs and renamed it Papua, the name preferred by people native to the area.   David A. M. Lea

Related articles in *World Book* include:

Bird-of-paradise	Port Moresby
Bismarck Archipelago	Sculpture (Pacific Islands
Bougainville	sculpture)
Echidna	Wallaby
Indonesia	World War II (The South
Papua New Guinea	Pacific)
Pitohui	

Additional resources

Guile, Melanie. *Culture in Papua New Guinea.* Raintree, 2004.
   Younger readers.
Moore, Clive. *New Guinea: Crossing Boundaries and History.*
   Univ. of Hawaii Pr., 2003.
Smith, Michael F. *Village on the Edge: Changing Times in Papua
   New Guinea.* Univ. of Hawaii Pr., 2002.
Turner, Ann W. *Historical Dictionary of Papua New Guinea.* 2nd
   ed. Scarecrow, 2001.

Giorgio Ricatto, Shostal

Port Moresby, the capital of Papua New Guinea, lies on the
southeastern coast of the island of New Guinea. A deep, sheltered harbor helps make the city a commercial center.

Joe Viesti

A communications technician repairs office equipment in a
village in New Guinea. This woman is a Melanesian, the largest
population group in New Guinea.

Eric Carle, Shostal

The New Hampshire countryside is ablaze with orange, red, and yellow leaves during the fall season. Beautiful autumn colors surround a picturesque pond in Grafton County, *shown here.*

New Hampshire *The Granite State*

New Hampshire is one of the New England States of the United States. It is noted for its natural beauty and year-round outdoor activities. In summer, for example, vacationers flock to the state's rugged mountains, blue lakes, sandy beaches, and quiet villages. In the fall, visitors tour the countryside ablaze with red, orange, and yellow leaves. In winter, skiers race down snow-covered slopes. The scenic beauty and other attractions bring in millions of tourists from many parts of the world.

New Hampshire's large granite deposits give it the nickname *The Granite State.* Concord is the capital of New Hampshire, and Manchester is the largest city.

New Hampshire was first settled in 1623. Early settlers traded in fish, lumber, and furs. They soon carved farms out of a wilderness and worked the land for food. Later, the people turned their skills and their state's resources to industrial development. They cut down trees for the giant lumber and papermaking industries. They took minerals from the mountains and hills to start a mining industry. They used the rivers and lakes as sources of power for mills and factories. And they built ships along the state's short Atlantic coastline. In all, the people of New Hampshire changed a wilderness into a farming society and then into a thriving industrial state.

Today, service industries play a major role in New Hampshire's economy. Such activities as education, health care, real estate, retail trade, and tourism are important sources of income. The state's low taxes have attracted many new businesses and residents.

New Hampshire and its people have played important roles in United States history. On Jan. 5, 1776, New

The contributors of this article are Mark J. Okrant, Professor of Tourism Management and Director of the Institute for New Hampshire Studies at Plymouth State University, and Ann Page Stecker, Professor of Humanities at Colby-Sawyer College and coauthor of New Hampshire: Crosscurrents in Its Development.

Interesting facts about New Hampshire

WORLD BOOK illustrations by Kevin Chadwick

The first state general library law was enacted by New Hampshire on July 7, 1849. The law permitted cities, towns, and school districts to raise taxes for the support of libraries. It also required that every public library established under the law be open for use by all citizens.

The Brattle organ, in historic St. John's Episcopal Church in Portsmouth, is said to be the oldest pipe organ in the United States. Built in England and shipped to the colonies, it dates back to at least 1708. The organ is still in good condition and is played on special occasions.

Brattle organ

The treaty ending the Russo-Japanese War was signed in 1905 in Portsmouth. President Theodore Roosevelt arranged the peace conference between the Russians and Japanese. He was awarded the 1906 Nobel Peace Prize in recognition of his work in ending the war.

Artificial rain was first used to fight a forest fire on Oct. 29, 1947, near Concord. Scientists flew over the fire in airplanes and seeded clouds with dry ice to cause the rain. The experiment was part of Project Cirrus, a weather research program conducted by the General Electric Company, the U.S. Army Signal Corps, and the Office of Naval Research.

Fire fighting with artificial rain

Joan M. Eaton

A skier races down a slope during World Cup competition at Waterville Valley in New Hampshire's White Mountains.

Hampshire became the first of the 13 original colonies to adopt its own constitution. On June 21, 1788, it became the ninth state to ratify the United States Constitution. This act of ratification put the Constitution into effect. Since 1920, New Hampshire has held the nation's earliest presidential primary elections.

The U.S. Navy's first shipbuilding yard opened at Portsmouth in 1800. One of the country's first tax-supported public libraries was established at Peterborough in 1833. In 1853, Franklin Pierce of New Hampshire became the 14th president of the United States. Daniel Webster, a leading statesman and orator of the 1800's, was born in New Hampshire. So was Alan B. Shepard, Jr., who, in 1961, became the first American astronaut to travel in space. Christa McAuliffe, a New Hampshire schoolteacher, was chosen to be the first "ordinary citizen" in space. In 1986, McAuliffe was among the seven crew members killed when the space shuttle Challenger broke apart shortly after takeoff.

John Gauvin, Studio One

A downtown Manchester plaza is a pleasant gathering place for local residents. Manchester is the largest city and one of the chief manufacturing centers of New Hampshire.

New Hampshire in brief

Symbols of New Hampshire

The state flag, adopted in 1909, bears the state seal. A laurel wreath with nine stars shows that New Hampshire was the ninth state to approve the U.S. Constitution. The seal, adopted in 1931, displays the Revolutionary War frigate *Raleigh*, which was built in Portsmouth. The American flag of 1777 flies at the ship's stern. A granite boulder in the foreground symbolizes the state's rugged terrain and the character of its people.

State flag

State seal

New Hampshire (brown) ranks 44th in size among the states and is the 3rd largest of the New England States (yellow).

General information

Statehood: June 21, 1788, the ninth state.
State abbreviations: N.H. (traditional); NH (postal).
State motto: *Live Free or Die.*
State song: "Old New Hampshire." Words by John F. Holmes; music by Maurice Hoffmann.

The State Capitol is in Concord, the capital since 1808. Other capitals were Portsmouth (1679-1774), Exeter (1775-1781), and several different towns between 1781 and 1808.

Land and climate

Area: 9,282 mi² (24,041 km²), including 314 mi² (814 km²) of inland water.
Elevation: *Highest*—Mount Washington, 6,288 ft (1,917 m) above sea level. *Lowest*—sea level along the Atlantic coast.
Coastline: 18 mi (29 km).
Record high temperature: 106 °F (41 °C) at Nashua on July 4, 1911.
Record low temperature: –47 °F (–44 °C) at Mount Washington on Jan. 29, 1934.
Average July temperature: 68 °F (20 °C).
Average January temperature: 19 °F (–7 °C).
Average yearly precipitation: 42 in (107 cm).

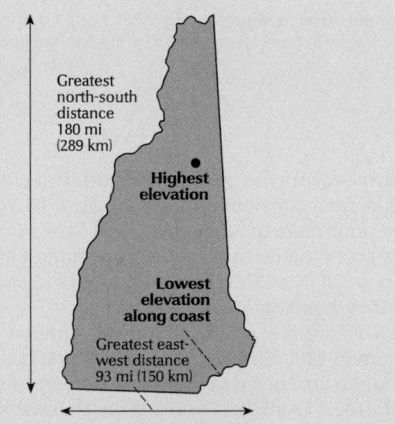

Greatest north-south distance 180 mi (289 km)

Highest elevation

Lowest elevation along coast

Greatest east-west distance 93 mi (150 km)

Important dates

David Thomson and Edward Hilton founded New Hampshire's first European settlements.

The state adopted its present constitution.

| 1603 | 1620's | 1776 | 1784 | 1788 |

Martin Pring of England sailed up the Piscataqua River.

New Hampshire broke away from Britain and adopted a temporary constitution.

New Hampshire became the ninth state on June 21.

State bird
Purple finch

State flower
Common lilac

State tree
White birch

People

Population: 1,316,470
Rank among the states: 42nd
Population density: 142 per mi²
(55 per km²), U.S. average 85 per mi²
(33 per km²)
Distribution: 59 percent urban,
41 percent rural
Largest cities in New Hampshire

Manchester	109,565
Nashua	86,494
Concord	42,695
Derry†	33,109
Dover	29,987
Rochester	29,752

†Unincorporated place.
Source: 2010 census, except for distribution, which is for 2000.

Population trend

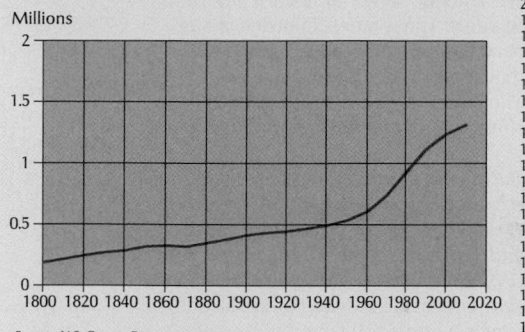

Millions

Source: U.S. Census Bureau.

Year	Population
2010	1,316,470
2000	1,235,786
1990	1,109,252
1980	920,610
1970	737,681
1960	606,921
1950	533,242
1940	491,524
1930	465,293
1920	443,083
1910	430,572
1900	411,588
1890	376,530
1880	346,991
1870	318,300
1860	326,073
1850	317,976
1840	284,574
1830	269,328
1820	244,161
1810	214,460
1800	183,858
1790	141,885

Economy

Chief products

Agriculture: apples, beef cattle, hay,
maple products, milk, nursery and
greenhouse products, sweet corn.
Manufacturing: computer and electronic products, fabricated metal
products, machinery.
Mining: gemstones, granite, sand
and gravel, traprock.

Gross domestic product

Value of goods and services produced in 2008: $59,131,000,000.
Services include community, business, and personal services; finance; government; trade; and
transportation and communication. *Industry* includes construction, manufacturing, mining, and
utilities. *Agriculture* includes agriculture, fishing, and forestry.

Source: U.S. Bureau of Economic Analysis.

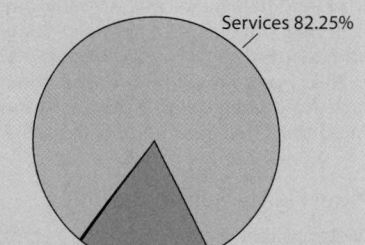

Services 82.25%

Agriculture 0.5%

Industry 17.25%

Government

State government

Governor: 2-year term
State senators: 24; 2-year terms
State representatives: 400; 2-year terms
Counties: 10

Federal government

United States senators: 2
United States representatives: 2
Electoral votes: 4

Sources of information

New Hampshire's official website at http://www.nh.gov provides a
gateway to much information on the state's government, history, and
economy.

In addition, the website at http://www.visitnh.gov provides information about tourism.

The first railroad in New
Hampshire was completed.

1838

The New Hampshire sweepstakes lottery began.
It was the first legal U.S. lottery since the 1890's.

1944 **1964** **1988** **1997-2003**

Jeanne Shaheen served as the first
woman governor of the state.

The International Monetary Conference
was held in Bretton Woods.

New Hampshire celebrated its
statehood bicentennial.

Population. The 2010 United States census reported that New Hampshire had 1,316,470 people. The state's population had increased about 6 ½ percent over the 2000 census figure of 1,235,786. According to the 2010 census, New Hampshire ranks 42nd in population among the 50 states.

About three-fifths of the state's people live in metropolitan areas. New Hampshire has two metropolitan areas. These areas are Boston (Massachusetts)-Cambridge (Massachusetts)-Quincy (Massachusetts) and Manchester-Nashua (see **Metropolitan area**). Manchester is the state's largest city. For the populations of these metropolitan areas, see the *Index* of the political map of New Hampshire.

In addition to Manchester, New Hampshire has 12 other incorporated cities. These cities, in order of size, are: Nashua, Concord (the capital), Dover, Rochester, Keene, Portsmouth, Laconia, Claremont, Lebanon, Somersworth, Berlin, and Franklin. See the articles on New Hampshire cities listed in the *Related articles* at the end of this article.

Many of New Hampshire's people are descendants of settlers who came from Canada and many European countries. The early settlers of New Hampshire came chiefly from England, Ireland, Scotland, and Wales. After the American Civil War, thousands of French Canadians and European immigrants came to New Hampshire to work in the state's mills, shops, and factories. Today, New Hampshire's largest population groups include people of English, French, French-Canadian, German, Irish, and Italian descent. African Americans, Asians, American Indians, and Hispanics together account for about 6 percent of New Hampshire's population.

New Hampshire's people, like other New Englanders, have long been called *Yankees.* This nickname calls to mind traits that are traditionally associated with the peo-

ple of New England. These traits include business ability, thrift, conservatism, and inventiveness. See **Yankee.**

Schools. The New Hampshire educational system dates from colonial days, when children of the settlers attended one-room schoolhouses. Some early schoolhouses still stand. Today's public schools operate under laws passed in 1789 and substantially revised in 1919. A seven-member State Board of Education and a commissioner of education administer state laws and regula-

Population density

The most thickly populated areas of New Hampshire are in the southeastern part of the state. The rugged White Mountain Region of northern New Hampshire has relatively few people.

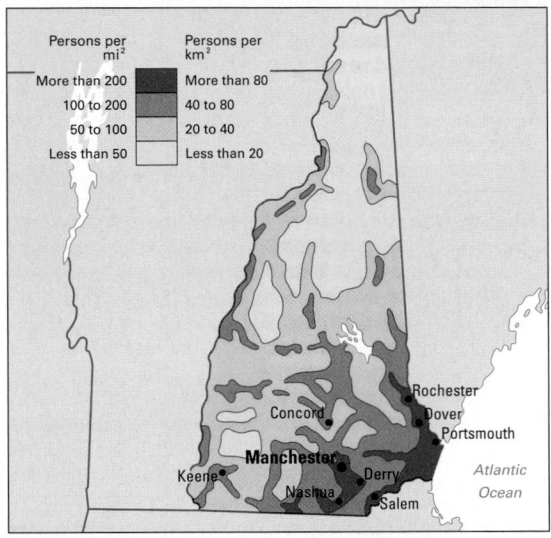

WORLD BOOK map; based on U.S. Census Bureau data.

New Hampshire map index

Metropolitan areas

Boston (MA)-
  Cambridge (MA)-
  Quincy (MA) 4,552,402
  (4,134,036 in MA,
  418,366 in NH)
Manchester-
  Nashua 400,721

Metropolitan division

Rockingham County-
  Strafford County ...418,366

Counties

Belknap ....60,088 ..K 7
Carroll ....47,818 ..I   7
Cheshire ....77,117 ..O 3
Coos ....33,055 ..D 7
Grafton ....89,118 ..J   4
Hillsborough ...400,721 ..N 5
Merrimack ......146,445 ..L   6
Rockingham .....295,223 ..N 8
Strafford ......123,143 ..L   8
Sullivan ....43,742 ..L   3

Cities and towns

Acworth▲ ....891 ..M 3
Albany▲ ....735 ..H   8
Alexandria▲ .....1,613 ..J   5
Allenstown▲ .....4,322 ..M 7
Alstead▲ ....1,937 ..M 3
Alton▲ ....5,250 ..K   8
Amherst▲ ....11,201 ..O 6
Andover▲ ....2,371 ..K   5
Antrim† 1,397
      ▲2,637 ..N 5
Ashland† 1,244
      ▲2,076 ..J   5
Ashuelot ....O 2
Atkinson▲ ....6,751 ..O 8
Auburn▲ ....4,953 ..N 7

Barnstead▲ ......4,593 ..L   7
Barrington▲ .....8,576 ..M 8
Bartlett▲ ....2,788 ..H   7
Bath▲ ....1,077 ..G   5
Bedford▲ ....21,203 ..N 6
Beebe River I   6
Belmont† 1,301
      ▲7,356 ..K   7
Bennington▲ .....1,476 ..N 5
Benton▲ ....364 ..H   5
Berlin ....10,051 ..E   8
Bethlehem▲ ......2,526 ..G   6
Boscawen▲ ....3,965 ..L   6
Bow*▲ ....7,519 ..M 6
Bow Center ....M 6
Bradford▲ ....1,650 ..L   5
Brentwood▲ ......4,486 ..N 8
Bretton Woods ....G   7
Bridgewater▲ ....1,083 ..J   5
Bristol† 1,688
      ▲3,054 ..K   6
Brookfield▲ ......712 ..K   8
Brookline▲ ......4,991 ..O 6
Campton▲ ....3,333 ..I   6
Canaan▲ ....3,909 ..J   4
Candia▲ ....3,909 ..N 7
Canobie Lake ....O 8
Canterbury▲ .....2,352 ..L   6
Carroll▲ ....763 ..F   6
Center Harbor▲ ..1,096 ..J   7
Charlestown† 1,152
      ▲5,114 ..M 3
Chatham▲ ....337 ..G   9
Chesham ....N 4
Chester▲ ....4,768 ..N 8
Chesterfield▲ ...3,604 ..O 2
Chichester▲ .....2,523 ..M 7
Chocorua I   8
Claremont ....13,355 ..L   3
Clarksville▲ .....265 ..B   7
Colebrook° 1,394
      ▲2,301 ..C   6
Columbia▲ ....757 ..C   6
Concord° ....42,695 ..M 6
Contoocook† .....1,444 ..M 6
Conway† 1,823
      ▲10,115 ..H   8

Coos Junction ....E   6
Cornish*▲ ....1,640 ..K   3
Cornish Center ....K   3
Crawford Notch ....G   7
Croydon▲ ....764 ..K   4
Dalton▲ ....979 ..F   6
Danbury▲ ....1,164 ..K   5
Danville▲ ....4,387 ..N 8
Deerfield▲ ......4,280 ..M 8
Deering▲ ....1,912 ..N 5
Derry† 22,015
      ▲33,109 ..O 7
Dorchester▲ ......355 ..J   5
Dover° ....29,987 ..M 9
Dublin▲ ....1,597 ..O 4
Dummer▲ ....304 ..E   8
Dunbarton*▲ .....2,758 ..M 6
Dunbarton
  Center ....M 6
Durham† 10,345
      ▲14,638 ..N 9
East Andover ....K   5
East Derry ....O 7
East Hampstead ....O 8
East Haverhill ....H   5
East Kingston▲ ..2,357 ..N 9
East Lempster ....M 4
East
  Merrimack*† ..4,197 ..O 7
East Swanzey ....O 3
East Wolfeboro ....J   8
Easton▲ ....254 ..G   5
Eaton▲ ....393 ..I   8
Effingham▲ ......1,465 ..J   9
Effingham Falls I   8
Elkins L   5
Ellsworth▲ ....83 ..I   5
Enfield† 1,540
      ▲4,582 ..J   4
Epping† 1,681
      ▲6,411 ..N 8
Epsom▲ ....4,566 ..M 7
Errol▲ ....291 ..D 8
Etna ....J   3
Exeter†° 9,242
      ▲14,306 ..N 9
Fabyan ....G   7

Farmington† 3,885
      ▲6,786 ..L   8
Fitzwilliam▲ ....2,396 ..O 4
Fitzwilliam Depot .....O 4
Francestown▲ ....1,562 ..N 5
Franconia▲ ......1,104 ..G   5
Franklin ....8,477 ..K   6
Freedom▲ ....1,489 ..I   8
Fremont▲ ....4,283 ..N 8
Georges Mills ....K   4
Gilford▲ ....7,126 ..K   7
Gilmanton▲ ......3,777 ..L   7
Gilmanton
  Iron Works L   7
Gilsum▲ ....813 ..N 3
Glen ....H   8
Goffstown† 3,196
      ▲17,651 ..N 6
Gonic L   9
Gorham† 1,600
      ▲2,848 ..F   8
Goshen▲ ....810 ..L   4
Gossville ....M 7
Grafton▲ ....1,340 ..K   5
Granite ....J   8
Grantham▲ ....2,985 ..K   4
Grasmere ....N 6
Greenfield▲ .....1,749 ..N 5
Greenland▲ ......3,549 ..N 9
Greenville† 1,108
      ▲2,105 ..O 5
Groton▲ ....593 ..J   5
Groveton† ....1,118 ..E   6
Guild L   4
Hampstead▲ ......8,523 ..O 8
Hampton† 9,656
      ▲14,976 ..N 9
Hampton
  Beach† ....2,275 ..O 9
Hampton Falls▲ ..2,236 ..N 9
Hancock▲ ....1,654 ..N 4
Hanover† 8,636
      ▲11,260 ..J   3
Harrisville▲ .....961 ..N 4
Hart's Location ...41 ..G   7
Haverhill▲ ......4,697 ..H   4
Hebron▲ ....602 ..J   5

Henniker† 1,747
      ▲4,836 ..M 5
Hill▲ ....1,089 ..K   6
Hillsborough† ...1,976
      ▲6,011 ..M 5
Hinsdale† 1,548
      ▲4,046 ..O 2
Holderness▲ .....2,108 ..J   6
Hollis▲ ....7,684 ..O 6
Hooksett† 4,147
      ▲13,451 ..M 7
Hopkinton▲ ......5,589 ..M 6
Hudson† 7,336
      ▲24,647 ..O 7
Intervale ....H   8
Jackson▲ ....816 ..G   8
Jaffrey† 2,757
      ▲5,457 ..O 4
Jefferson▲ ......1,107 ..F   7
Kearsarge ....H   8
Keene° ....23,409 ..N 3
Kensington▲ .....2,124 ..N 9
Kidderville C   7
Kingston▲ ....6,025 ..N 8
Laconia° ....15,951 ..K   7
Lakeport ....K   7
Lancaster†° 1,725
      ▲3,507 ..E   6
Landaff▲ ....415 ..G   5
Landaff Center ....G   3
Langdon▲ ....688 ..M 3
Lebanon ....13,151 ..J   3
Lee▲ ....4,330 ..M 9
Lempster▲ ....1,154 ..M 3
Lincoln† 993
      ▲1,662 ..H   6
Lisbon▲ ....1,595 ..G   5
Litchfield▲ .....8,271 ..O 7
Little Boars Head .....N 10
Littleton† 4,412
      ▲5,928 ..F   5
Livermore Falls ....J   6
Lochmere ....K   6
Lockehaven ....J   6
Londonderry† ...11,037
      ▲24,129 ..O 7
Loudon▲ ....5,317 ..L   7

tions. The governor and the Executive Council appoint the Board of Education members. The Executive Council approves the commissioner. School districts are governed by local school boards. Children from ages 6 to 18 must attend school in New Hampshire. For the number of students and teachers, see **Education** (table).

Dartmouth, New Hampshire's oldest college, ranks among the 10 oldest U.S. universities and colleges. It was chartered in 1769.

Libraries. In 1833, Peterborough founded a free, tax-supported public library. Many historians believe that this was the first library of its kind in the United States. But other historians claim that a library founded in Salisbury, Connecticut, was the first of this kind in the nation.

Most New Hampshire towns have at least one public library. The State Library's rural libraries project serves residents of rural areas in northern New Hampshire. The largest libraries outside of a university are the State Library in Concord and the Manchester City Library.

Museums. The Currier Museum of Art in Manchester has a fine collection of American and European art. It includes the Zimmerman House, designed by American architect Frank Lloyd Wright. The Museum of New Hampshire History in Concord houses historical furniture, landscape paintings, and memorabilia relating to famous residents of the state. The Canterbury Shaker Village is a restored religious community near Concord. Strawbery Banke, in Portsmouth, is a historic seaside community operated as a museum.

Craig Aurness, West Light

Dartmouth is the oldest college in New Hampshire and one of the 10 oldest universities and colleges in the United States. The college was founded in 1769 in Hanover.

Universities and colleges

This table lists the nonprofit universities and colleges in New Hampshire that grant bachelor's or advanced degrees and are accredited by the New England Association of Schools and Colleges.

Name	Mailing address
Chester College of New England	Chester
Colby-Sawyer College	New London
Daniel Webster College	Nashua
Dartmouth College	Hanover
Franklin Pierce University	Rindge
Granite State College	Concord
Keene State College	Keene
New England College	Henniker
New Hampshire, University of	*
New Hampshire, University of, School of Law	Concord
Plymouth State University	Plymouth
Rivier College	Nashua
St. Anselm College	Manchester
Southern New Hampshire University	Manchester
Thomas More College of Liberal Arts	Merrimack

*Campuses at Durham and Manchester.

Lower Gilmanton ....L 7	New Rye ....M 7	Peterborough† 3,103	Silver Lake ....I 8	Wallis Sands ....N 10

Lower Gilmanton ....L 7
Lower Bartlett ....H 8
Lyman▲ ....533 ..G 5
Lyme▲ ....1,716 ..I 4
Lyndeborough▲ ...1,683 ..O 5
Madbury▲ ....1,771 ..M 9
Madison▲ ....2,502 ..I 8
Manchester ...109,565 ..N 7
Maplewood ....G 6
Marlborough† 1,094
　　　　　　　▲2,063 ..O 3
Marlow▲ ....742 ..M 3
Mason▲ ....1,382 ..O 5
Meadows ....F 7
Melvin Mills ....L 5
Melvin Village† .....241 ..J 7
Meredith† 1,718
　　　　　　　▲6,241 ..J 7
Meriden ....K 3
Merrimack▲ ....25,494 ..O 7
Middleton▲ ....1,783 ..K 8
Milan▲ ....1,337 ..E 8
Milford† 8,835
　　　　　　　▲15,115 ..O 6
Milton▲ ....4,598 ..L 9
Milton Mills† ......299 ..K 9
Mirror Lake ....J 7
Monroe▲ ....788 ..G 4
Mont Vernon▲ ...2,409 ..O 6
Moulton-
　borough▲ ......4,044 ..J 7
Moultonborough
　Falls ....J 7
Moultonville ....J 8
Mount Sunapee ....L 4
Munsonville ....N 4
Nashua○ .....86,494 ..O 7
Nelson▲ ....729 ..N 4
New Boston▲ ...5,321 ..N 6
New Castle▲ ....968 ..N 10
New Durham▲ ...2,638 ..K 8
New Hampton▲ ...2,165 ..J 6
New Ipswich▲ ...5,099 ..O 5
New London† 1,415
　　　　　　　▲4,397 ..L 4

New Rye ....M 7
Newbury▲ ....2,072 ..L 4
Newfields▲ ....1,680 ..N 9
Newington▲ ....753 ..M 9
Newmarket† 5,297
Newport†○ 4,769
　　　　　　　▲6,507 ..L 4
Newton▲ ....4,603 ..O 9
Newton Junction ....O 8
Noone ....O 5
North Branch ....N 4
North Chatham ....G 8
North Chichester ....L 7
North Conway† ...2,349 ..H 8
North
　Hampton▲ ....4,301 ..N 9
North Haverhill ....H 4
North Richmond ....O 3
North Rochester ....L 9
North Salem ....O 8
North Sanbornton ....K 6
North Sandwich ....I 7
North Stratford ....D 6
North Village ....O 5
North Walpole† ...828 ..M 2
North
　Woodstock† ....528 ..H 6
Northfield▲ ......4,829 ..K 6
Northumber-
　land▲ ....2,288 ..E 6
Northwood▲ ....4,241 ..M 8
Northwood Ridge ....M 8
Nottingham▲ ...4,785 ..M 8
Orange▲ ....331 ..J 5
Orford▲ ....1,237 ..I 4
Orfordville ....I 4
Ossipee▲ ....4,345 ..J 8
Pages Corner ....M 6
Park Hill ....N 2
Pearls Corner ....L 7
Pelham▲ ....12,897 ..O 7
Pembroke▲ .....7,115 ..M 7
Penacook ....L 6
Percy ....E 7

Peterborough† 3,103
　　　　　　　▲6,284 ..O 5
Piermont▲ ....790 ..H 4
Pike ....H 4
Pinardville† .....4,780 ..N 6
Pittsburg▲ ....869 ..B 7
Pittsfield† 1,576
　　　　　　　▲4,106 ..L 7
Plainfield▲ ......2,364 ..K 3
Plaistow▲ ....7,609 ..O 8
Plymouth† 4,456
　　　　　　　▲6,990 ..J 6
Ponemah ....O 6
Portsmouth ...21,233 ..N 10
Potter Place ....K 5
Quaker City ....L 3
Quincy ....L 3
Randolph▲ ....310 ..F 7
Raymond† 2,855
　　　　　　　▲10,138 ..N 8
Redstone ....H 8
Reeds Ferry ....O 7
Richmond▲ .....1,155 ..O 3
Rindge▲ ....6,014 ..O 4
Riverton ....F 6
Rochester ......29,752 ..L 9
Rollinsford▲ ....2,527 ..M 9
Roxbury▲ ....229 ..N 3
Rumney▲ ....1,480 ..I 5
Rye▲ ....5,298 ..N 10
Rye Beach ....N 10
Salem▲ ....28,776 ..O 8
Salem Depot ....O 8
Salisbury▲ ....1,382 ..L 6
Salisbury
　Heights ....L 5
Sanbornton▲ ...2,966 ..K 6
Sanbornville† ...1,056 ..K 9
Sandown▲ ....5,986 ..N 8
Sandwich▲ ......1,326 ..I 7
Seabrook▲ ......8,693 ..O 9
Sharon▲ ....352 ..O 5
Shelburne▲ ....372 ..F 8
Shirley Hill ....N 6
Short Falls ....M 7

Silver Lake ....I 8
Smithtown ....O 9
Smithville ....O 5
Snowville ....I 8
Somersworth ...11,766 ..L 9
South Danbury ....K 5
South Danville ....O 8
South Hampton▲ ...814 ..O 9
South Hooksett† ..5,418 ..N 7
South Lyndeboro ....O 5
South Merrimack ....O 6
South Newbury ....L 4
South Weare ....N 6
South Wolfeboro ....K 8
Spofford ....N 3
Springfield▲ .....1,311 ..K 4
Stark ....556 ..E 7
Stewartstown▲ ...1,004 ..B 6
Stinson Lake ....I 5
Stoddard▲ ....1,232 ..N 4
Strafford▲ ....3,991 ..M 8
Stratford▲ ....746 ..D 6
Stratham▲ ......7,255 ..N 9
Sugar Hill▲ ....563 ..G 5
Sullivan▲ ....677 ..N 3
Sunapee▲ ......3,365 ..L 4
Suncook† ....5,379 ..M 7
Surry▲ ....732 ..N 3
Sutton▲ ....1,837 ..L 5
Swanzey▲ ......7,230 ..O 3
Tamworth▲ .....2,856 ..I 8
Temple▲ ....1,366 ..O 5
Thornton▲ ......2,490 ..I 6
Tilton▲ ....3,567 ..K 6
Tilton-
　Northfield*† ...3,075 ..K 6
Tinkerville ....G 5
Troy† 1,221
　　　　　　　▲2,145 ..O 4
Tuftonboro▲ ....2,387 ..J 8
Twin Mountain ....G 6
Union† ....204 ..K 9
Unity▲ ....1,671 ..L 3
Wadley Falls ....M 9
Wakefield▲ .....5,078 ..K 9

Wallis Sands ....N 10
Walpole▲ ....3,734 ..N 3
Warner▲ ....2,833 ..L 5
Warren▲ ....904 ..I 5
Washington▲ ....1,123 ..M 4
Waterloo ....L 5
Waterville
　Valley▲ ....247 ..H 6
Weare▲ ....8,785 ..M 6
Webster▲ ....1,872 ..L 6
Weirs Beach ....J 7
Wendell ....L 4
Wentworth▲ ......911 ..I 5
Wentworth
　Location▲ ......33 ..C 8
West Chesterfield ......O 2
West Epping ....J 8
West Lebanon ....J 3
West Milan ....E 7
West Ossipee ....I 8
West Peterborough ....O 4
West Rumney ....I 5
West Swanzey† ...1,308 ..O 3
Westmoreland▲ ..1,874 ..N 2
Westport ....O 3
Westville ....O 8
Whiteface ....I 7
Whitefield† 1,142
　　　　　　　▲2,306 ..F 6
Whittier ....I 7
Willey House ....J 6
Wilmot▲ ....1,358 ..K 5
Wilton† 1,163
　　　　　　　▲3,677 ..O 6
Winchester† 1,733
　　　　　　　▲4,341 ..O 3
Windham▲ ....13,592 ..O 7
Windsor▲ ....224 ..M 4
Winnisquam ....J 6
Wolfeboro† 2,838
　　　　　　　▲6,269 ..K 8
Wolfeboro Center ....J 8
Woodmere ....O 4
Woodstock▲ ....1,374 ..H 6
Woodsville†○ ....1,126 ..G 4

*Does not appear on map; key shows general location.
†Census designated place—unincorporated, but recognized as a significant settled community by the U.S. Census Bureau.

▲Entire town (township), including rural area.
Places without population figures are unincorporated areas.
Source: 2010 census.

○County seat.

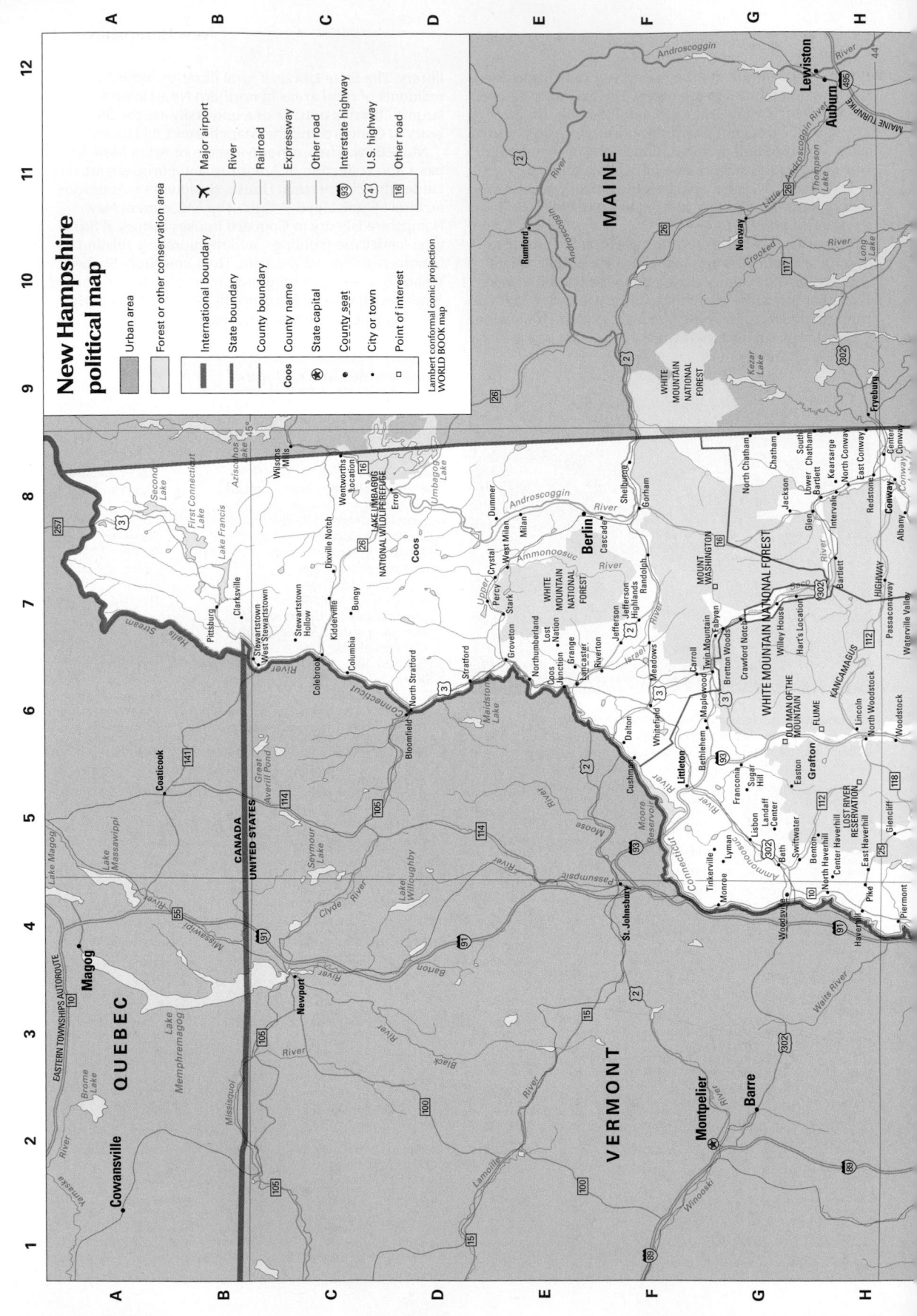

New Hampshire
political map

Lambert conformal conic projection
WORLD BOOK map

| | Urban area |
| | Forest or other conservation area |

	International boundary
	State boundary
	County boundary
Coos	County name
✳	State capital
●	County seat
•	City or town
□	Point of interest

✈	Major airport
	River
	Railroad
	Expressway
	Other road
93	Interstate highway
4	U.S. highway
16	Other road

QUEBEC

VERMONT

MAINE

CANADA
UNITED STATES

Coos

WHITE MOUNTAIN NATIONAL FOREST

Cowansville

Magog

Coaticook

Newport

St. Johnsbury

Montpelier

Barre

Rumford

Norway

Lewiston

Auburn

Fryeburg

Berlin

Littleton

Conway

Haverhill

Pittsburg

Clarksville

Stewartstown
West Stewartstown

Colebrook

Columbia

Kidderville

Bungy

Stewartstown
Hollow

Dixville Notch

Errol

Wilsons
Mills

Wentworths
Location

Bloomfield

North Stratford

Stratford

Groveton

Northumberland

Coos
Junction

Lost
Nation

Grange

Lancaster

Riverton

Jefferson

Meadows

Dalton

Whitefield

Custman

Dummer

West Milan

Milan

Upper
Percy

Stark

Crystal

Cascade

Gorham

Shelburne

Randolph

Jefferson
Highlands

Carroll

Twin Mountain

Fabyan

Bretton Woods

Maplewood

Bethlehem

Franconia

Sugar
Hill

Easton

Landaff
Center

Lisbon

Lyman

Monroe

Tinkerville

Woodsville

Benton

North Haverhill

Center Haverhill

East Haverhill

Pike

Piermont

Swiftwater

Bath

Glencliff

Grafton

North Woodstock

Lincoln

Woodstock

Waterville Valley

Passaconaway

Albany

Center
Conway

East Conway

Redstone

Intervale

North Conway

Kearsarge

Lower
Bartlett

Glen

Jackson

Chatham

South
Chatham

North Chatham

Bartlett

Willey House

Hart's Location

Crawford Notch

MOUNT
WASHINGTON

OLD MAN OF THE
MOUNTAIN

FLUME

LOST RIVER
RESERVATION

KANCAMAGUS
HIGHWAY

LAKE UMBAGOG
NATIONAL WILDLIFE REFUGE

WHITE
MOUNTAIN
NATIONAL
FOREST

WHITE
MOUNTAIN
NATIONAL
FOREST

EASTERN TOWNSHIPS AUTOROUTE

MAINE TURNPIKE

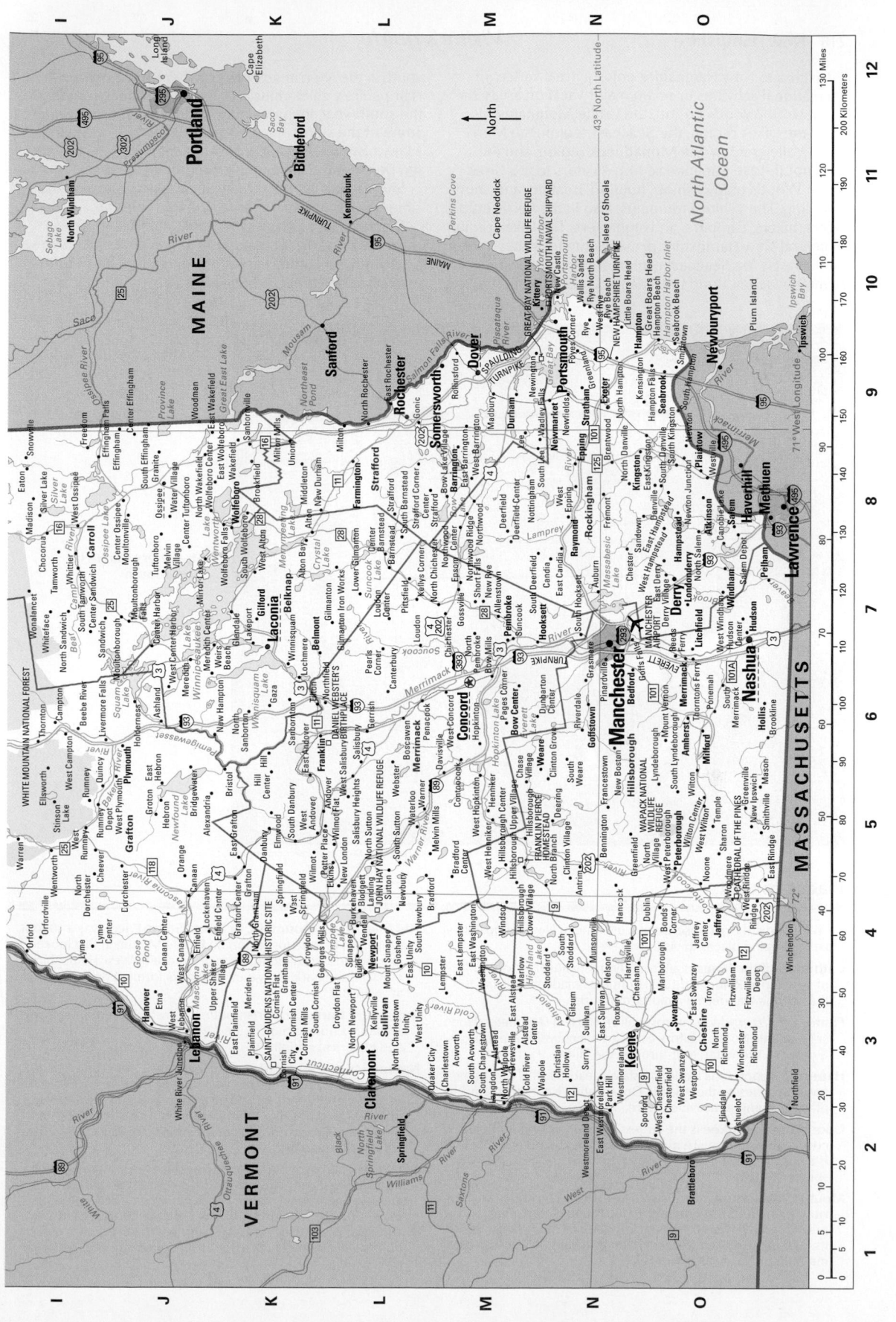

Visitors to New Hampshire enjoy a great variety of recreational activities in seven major vacation areas: the Great North Woods region, the White Mountains region, the Lakes region, the Seacoast region, the Merrimack Valley region, the Monadnock region, and the Dartmouth-Lake Sunapee region. Visitors to the Great North Woods enjoy fishing, hunting, boating, and snowmobiling. The White Mountains, also in the north, attract skiers, hikers, campers, and sightseers. The Lakes region of central New Hampshire provides fun for water-sports enthusiasts. The Seacoast region of the southeast has several beaches along the Atlantic Coast. Also in the south is the Merrimack Valley, where most of New Hampshire's chief cities are. The Monadnock region, in the southwest, includes many natural beauty spots and some of the state's most interesting towns and villages. Many historic sites and educational institutions are in the Dartmouth-Lake Sunapee region in the west.

Shopping is a popular activity among visitors to the state. New Hampshire has no general sales tax.

Many of New Hampshire's most popular annual events are sports contests. One of the state's best-known annual events is the League of New Hampshire Craftsmen's Fair at Mount Sunapee Resort.

Strawbery Banke in Portsmouth

New Hampshire Division of Travel and Tourism

Places to visit

Following are brief descriptions of some of New Hampshire's most interesting places to visit:

Cathedral of the Pines is an interdenominational outdoor place of worship at Rindge. In 1957, Congress made this shrine to the nation's war dead a national memorial.

Flume is a *chasm* (deep, narrow valley) 800 feet (240 meters) long at Franconia Notch. Visitors can view scenic wilderness on a ½-mile (0.8-kilometer) tour through the Flume.

Hampton Beach runs along the state's seacoast. It is one of the finest beaches on the Atlantic Ocean, and visitors enjoy many pleasant summer activities there.

Lake Winnipesaukee is the largest body of water in the state. It covers about 70 square miles (180 square kilometers). The lake is a popular place for sightseeing, boating, fishing, and water sports.

Mount Washington, near Fabyan, features a cog railway that runs 3 ½ miles (5.6 kilometers) to the mountaintop. The cog railway, which was completed in 1869, was the first railway of its kind in the United States. Mount Washington also has hiking trails and a scenic roadway.

Old Man of the Mountain, or Great Stone Face, was a 40-foot (12-meter) granite formation on Profile Mountain that looked like the side of an old man's face. It became New Hampshire's official trademark. However, the rocks forming the profile fell away in 2003.

Strawbery Banke, in Portsmouth, is a restored colonial seaport. It features homes built in the 1700's and 1800's, craft shops, and historical exhibits.

National forest and national historic site. The White Mountain National Forest lies in north-central New Hampshire. Part of the forest extends into Maine. Saint-Gaudens National Historic Site is in Cornish, near Claremont. The site includes the home, studio, and gardens of the American sculptor Augustus Saint-Gaudens.

State parks and forests. New Hampshire has many state parks, historic sites, and state forests. Many of the parks have lakes and groves of stately trees, especially white birch. For information on the state parks, historic sites, and forests, write to Director, Division of Parks, Department of Resources and Economic Development, P.O. Box 1856, Concord, NH 03302.

William Johnson, New Hampshire Dept. of Travel and Tourism

Lake Winnipesaukee

© James F. Harrington, New England Stock Photos/Digital Railroad

Hampton Beach

AP/Wide World

Sled Dog Derby in Laconia

Craig Aurness, Woodfin Camp, Inc.

Flume at Franconia Notch

Robert Frerck, Woodfin Camp, Inc.

Mount Washington Cog Railway

Land and climate

Land regions. New Hampshire has three main land regions. They are (1) the Coastal Lowlands, (2) the Eastern New England Upland, and (3) the White Mountains Region.

The Coastal Lowlands covers the extreme southeastern corner of the state. It is part of a larger land region of the same name that covers the entire New England coast. In New Hampshire, the region extends from 15 to 20 miles (24 to 32 kilometers) inland from the Atlantic Ocean. Along the coast, beaches provide popular recreational areas. Rivers winding through the Coastal Lowlands have long supplied water power for the region's industrial development. Great Bay is part of the Coastal Lowlands. Thousands of ducks and geese stop at the bay during their annual migrations.

The Eastern New England Upland covers most of southern New Hampshire. The entire Eastern New England Upland stretches from northern Maine to eastern Connecticut. In New Hampshire, the region consists of three areas: (1) the Merrimack Valley, (2) the Hills and Lakes region, and (3) the New Hampshire part of the Connecticut River Valley.

The Merrimack Valley extends northward from the Massachusetts border to central New Hampshire. It is named for the Merrimack River, which winds through the hilly, uneven valley. Large crops of hay and fruits grow in the rich soil between the hills. Many of the state's chief mill and factory towns are in the valley.

The Hills and Lakes region surrounds the Merrimack Valley on the east, north, and west. It extends in a broad half-circle from Maine almost to the Vermont border. Most of New Hampshire's large lakes nestle among forested hills in the region.

The Connecticut River Valley stretches in a long narrow strip down New Hampshire's western border. The Connecticut River flows through the area for 211 miles (340 kilometers). Rich farmland lies in the lowlands. Hardwood forests cover the hills. Hydroelectric plants supply power for public utilities. Their dams form long lakes in the valley.

The White Mountains Region lies north of the Eastern New England Upland. It has rugged mountains separated by narrow river valleys. Spruce, fir, and yellow birch provide wood for New Hampshire's paper mills

Manuel Dos Passos, Bruce Coleman Inc.

The Mount Washington Observatory stands on top of New Hampshire's highest peak. The observatory keeps daily records of weather conditions in the White Mountains.

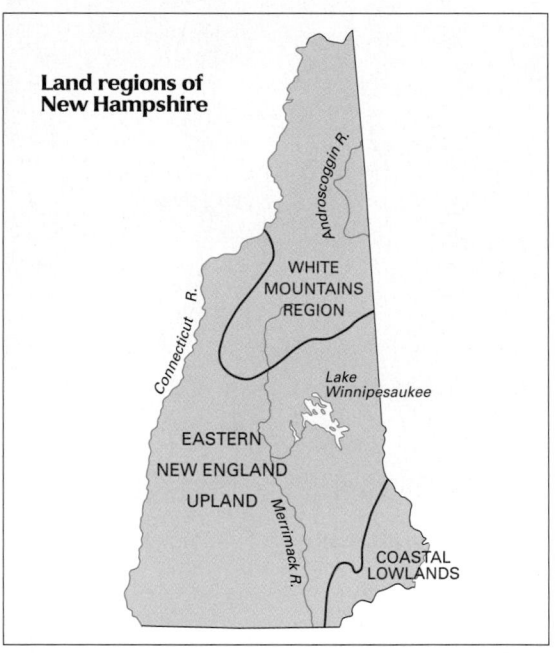

Land regions of New Hampshire

WHITE MOUNTAINS REGION

EASTERN NEW ENGLAND UPLAND

COASTAL LOWLANDS

Lake Winnipesaukee

WORLD BOOK map

Map index

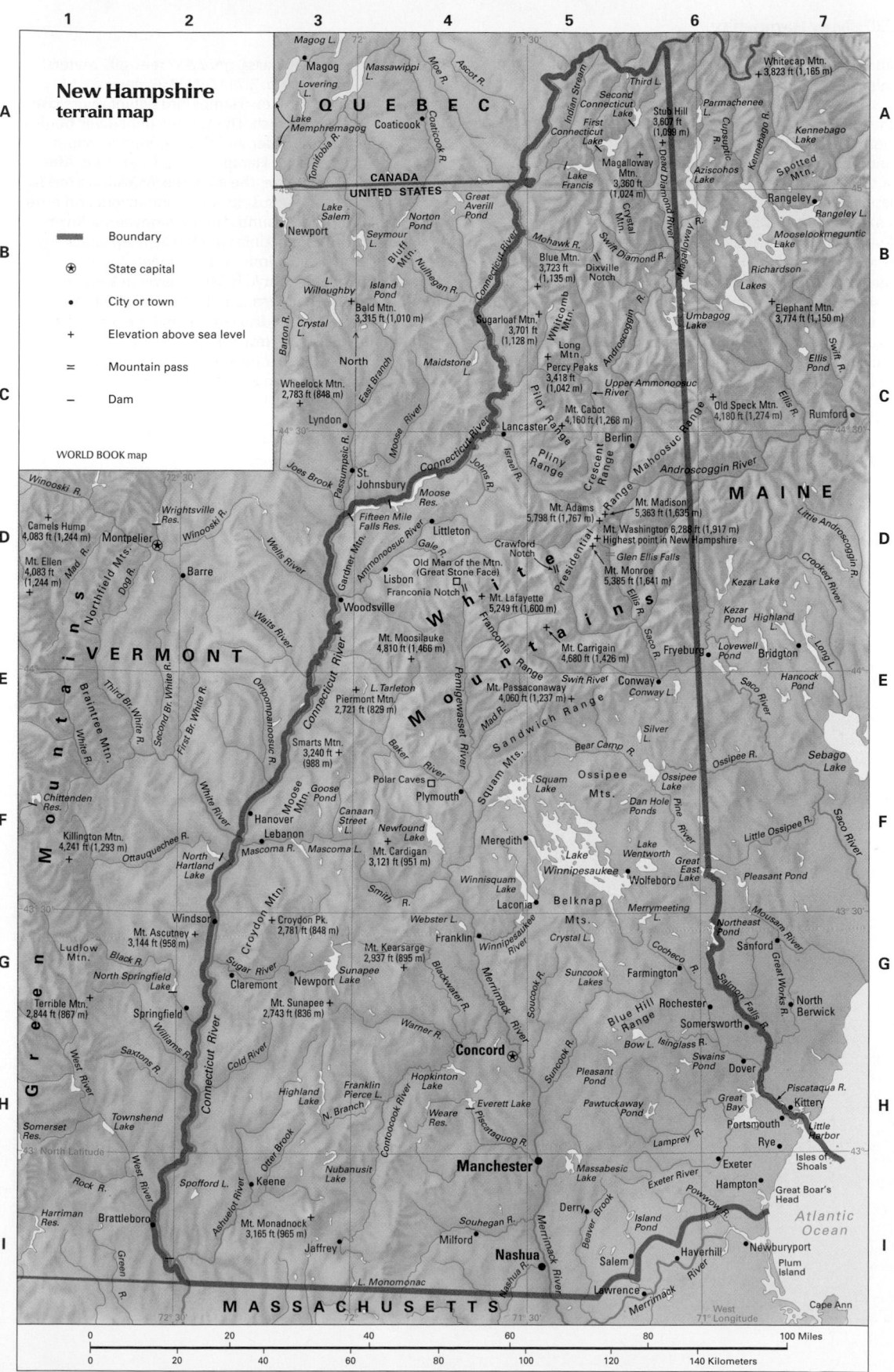

New Hampshire
terrain map

▬▬▬	Boundary
✪	State capital
•	City or town
+	Elevation above sea level
=	Mountain pass
−	Dam

WORLD BOOK map

and other wood products industries. The White Mountains attract summer and winter tourists.

An area of forest-covered hills in Coos County forms the northernmost part of the region. Lumbering and paper manufacturing are this area's chief industries. Dairy and potato farms thrive in the west.

Coastline. New Hampshire has a coast along the Atlantic of 18 miles (29 kilometers). This is the shortest coastline of any state bordering an ocean. Hampton, Rye, and other beaches lie along the shore. A group of islands called the Isles of Shoals lies 9 miles (14 kilometers) offshore. Four—Lunging, Seavey, Star, and White—belong to New Hampshire. The others are part of Maine.

Mountains. The Presidential Range of the White Mountains has the highest peaks in New England. Mount Washington is the highest mountain in this 86-peak range and reaches 6,288 feet (1,917 meters). Several other peaks in the Presidential Range are more than 1 mile (1.6 kilometers) high. These include Mount Adams, 5,798 feet (1,767 meters); Mount Jefferson, 5,715 feet (1,742 meters); Mount Clay, 5,532 feet (1,686 meters); Mount Monroe, 5,385 feet (1,641 meters); and Mount Madison, 5,363 feet (1,635 meters). The Franconia Range, also in the White Mountains, includes the famous Profile Mountain, a shoulder of Cannon Mountain. Profile Mountain was the site of a beloved New Hampshire landmark, a rock formation near the mountaintop that resembled a man's profile. It was called the Old Man of the Mountain (or Great Stone Face). But the rocks fell away in 2003.

New Hampshire's mountains include five *monadnocks.* A monadnock is made up of rock that did not wear down when all the land around it was leveled by erosion. The monadnocks and their heights are Mount Moosilauke, 4,810 feet (1,466 meters); Mount Monadnock, 3,165 feet (965 meters); Mount Cardigan, 3,121 feet

(951 meters); Mount Kearsarge, 2,937 feet (895 meters); and Sunapee Mountain, 2,743 feet (836 meters).

Rivers and lakes. New Hampshire's chief rivers rise in the mountainous north. The Connecticut River begins near the Canadian border and flows generally southward. It separates New Hampshire and Vermont. After leaving New Hampshire, the 407-mile (655-kilometer) river cuts across Massachusetts and Connecticut and empties into Long Island Sound. The Pemigewasset River flows south from Franconia Notch. The Merrimack River is formed where the Pemigewasset meets the Winnipesaukee River at Franklin. The Merrimack flows south into Massachusetts and then empties into the Atlantic Ocean. The Androscoggin and Saco rivers flow through northeastern New Hampshire and then cross into Maine. The Piscataqua and Salmon Falls rivers, in the southeast, form part of the New Hampshire-Maine border and empty into Portsmouth Harbor.

Average monthly weather

	Concord						Mt. Washington Observatory				
	Temperatures				Days of rain or snow		Temperatures				Days of rain or snow
	°F		°C				°F		°C		
	High	Low	High	Low			High	Low	High	Low	
Jan.	31	10	−1	−12	11	Jan.	14	−4	−10	−20	19
Feb.	34	13	1	−11	9	Feb.	15	−2	−9	−19	18
Mar.	44	23	7	−5	11	Mar.	21	6	−6	−14	19
Apr.	57	32	14	0	12	Apr.	29	16	−2	−9	18
May	70	42	21	6	12	May	42	30	6	−1	17
June	78	52	26	11	11	June	50	39	10	4	16
July	83	57	28	14	10	July	54	43	12	6	17
Aug.	81	56	27	13	10	Aug.	53	42	12	6	15
Sept.	72	47	22	8	9	Sept.	46	35	8	2	15
Oct.	61	35	16	2	9	Oct.	36	24	2	−4	15
Nov.	48	28	9	−2	11	Nov.	28	14	−2	−10	19
Dec.	36	16	2	−9	11	Dec.	19	2	−7	−17	20

Average January temperatures

New Hampshire winters are cold with heavy snowfalls. Southeastern New Hampshire has the mildest temperatures.

Average July temperatures

New Hampshire has cool summers with low humidity. The temperatures are warmer in the southern part of the state.

Average yearly precipitation

Much of the state's precipitation comes as snow. The heaviest precipitation is in the south and far north of the state.

WORLD BOOK maps

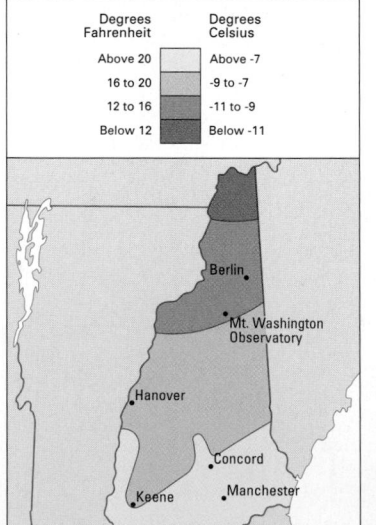

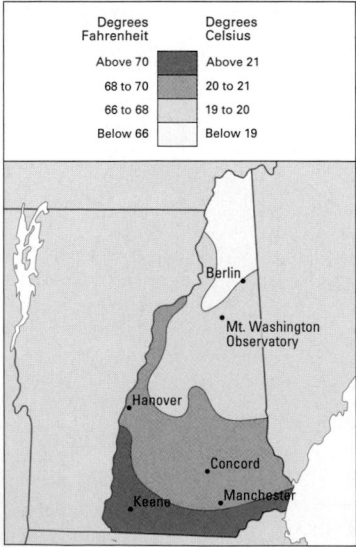

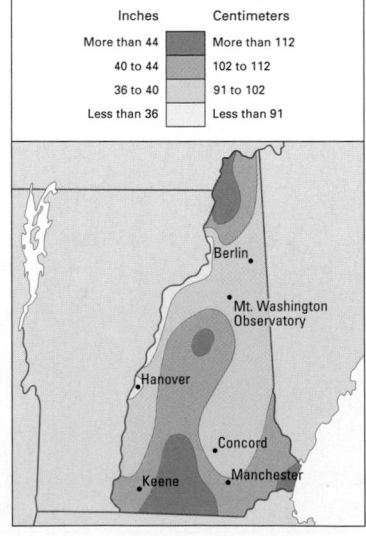

About 1,300 lakes lie scattered throughout the state's hills and mountains. The largest, Lake Winnipesaukee, is about 70 square miles (180 square kilometers) and has many islands. Other lakes include Ossipee, Squam, Sunapee, Umbagog (partly in Maine), and Winnisquam.

Plant and animal life. Forests cover about 85 percent of New Hampshire. Valuable trees include ashes, basswoods, beeches, birches, cedars, elms, firs, hemlocks, maples, oaks, pines, spruces, and tamaracks. Shrubs and flowering plants thrive in the state's forests. Shrubs include American elders, blueberries, mountain laurel, and sumacs. Wildflowers, which grow throughout the state, include black-eyed Susans, daisies, fireweed, gentians, goldenrod, purple trillium, violets, and wild asters.

Beavers, chipmunks, deer, foxes, mink, rabbits, raccoons, and squirrels are common throughout New Hampshire. Black bears and moose live in the northern forests. Game birds include ducks, geese, pheasants, ruffed grouse, and woodcocks. Among the many birds that nest in the state are bluebirds, purple finches, robins, sparrows, and warblers.

New Hampshire's freshwater fish include brook, brown, lake, and rainbow trout; largemouth and smallmouth bass; and landlocked salmon, pickerel, perch, whitefish, and bullheads. Saltwater fish include bluefish, cunner, cusk, flounder, haddock, hake, mackerel, pollock, striped bass, and tuna. The state's coastal waters have clams, lobsters, oysters, and shrimp.

Climate. New Hampshire has cool summers with low humidity. In winter, heavy snow falls in much of the state. January temperatures average about 16 °F (−9 °C) in the north and about 22 °F (−6 °C) in the south. The state's lowest temperature, −47 °F (−44 °C), was recorded at Mount Washington on Jan. 29, 1934. July temperatures average about 66 °F (19 °C) in the north and 70 °F (21 °C) in the south. The state's highest temperature, 106 °F (41 °C), was recorded at Nashua on July 4, 1911.

New Hampshire gets about 42 inches (107 centimeters) of precipitation a year. The state's average yearly snowfall ranges from about 50 inches (130 centimeters) near the Atlantic Ocean to more than 100 inches (250 centimeters) in the north and west.

Economy

Service industries provide the largest portion of New Hampshire's *gross domestic product*—the total value of goods and services produced in the state in a year. Manufacturing also ranks high among the economic activities. The beautiful seacoast, lakes, mountains, and unspoiled wilderness attract many visitors.

The low tax rates in New Hampshire have attracted many new businesses and residents. The state has no general sales tax. Residents pay a personal income tax only on their dividend or interest income, not on ordinary income. Thousands of people who work in Massachusetts live in New Hampshire to take advantage of the low taxes.

Natural resources. New Hampshire's climate and soils support dense forests. Minerals are found in many areas of the state, but the mining output is small.

Soil. Rock and a thin layer of soil cover most of New Hampshire's hills and mountains. The soil in New Hampshire's valleys is chiefly clay and loam, and coarse gravel and sand. The clay and loam support farm crops. The gravel and sand supply low-cost roadbuilding material.

Forests. Forests cover about 85 percent of New Hampshire. Commercially valuable softwood trees include balsam firs, cedars, hemlocks, spruces, tamaracks, and white pines. Valuable hardwoods include ashes, basswoods, beeches, birches, maples, and oaks.

Minerals. New Hampshire's chief mined resources include its deposits of granite, sand and gravel, and traprock. Large quantities of gray, pink, and other kinds of granite give New Hampshire the nickname of the Granite State.

Service industries account for about four-fifths of the state's employment and gross domestic product. These industries operate in towns and cities throughout the state, especially in southern New Hampshire.

Concord, the state capital, is the center of government activities. Manchester is the major insurance and banking center. Many hotels, restaurants, and retail trade establishments are also in the Manchester area. The White

Mountains and the lake and coastal areas of New Hampshire have many resorts. The Portsmouth area is the home of Portsmouth Naval Shipyard.

Manufacturing. Computer and electronic products are the state's leading products. Electronics, such as microchips and networking equipment, are made in the Manchester area. Plants in Nashua make military communication systems.

Fabricated metal products, including ball bearings and machine shop products, are made in the Manchester area. Southern New Hampshire produces printing and metalworking machinery, equipment for making lenses and other optical instruments, and other machinery products. New Hampshire also produces chocolates, concrete products, glass products, lighting equipment, and medical equipment.

Agriculture. Farmland covers only 8 percent of New Hampshire. Greenhouse and nursery products are the state's leading source of farm income. Hay is New Hampshire's leading field crop, apples are the leading fruit crop, and sweet corn is the leading vegetable. Maple syrup is also a major farm product.

Dairy farming is New Hampshire's most important livestock activity. Dairy farms operate throughout the state, but they are especially numerous in the west along the Connecticut River. Other livestock products in New Hampshire include beef cattle, eggs, and hogs.

Mining. Sand and gravel are the state's chief mined products. They are found in all of the state's counties, but production is heaviest in the south-central part of the state.

Granite is also important. Several parts of the state have granite quarries. The Concord quarries, in Merrimack County, have supplied granite for many famous buildings in the United States.

Electric power and utilities. The Seabrook Nuclear Power plant supplies about 40 percent of the state's power needs. Plants that burn coal, natural gas, or oil and plants that use renewable energy provide most of

New Hampshire economy

General economy

Gross domestic product (GDP)* (2008) $59,131,000,000
  Rank among U.S. states   41st
Unemployment rate (2010)   6.1% (U.S. avg: 9.6%)
*Gross domestic product is the total value of goods and services produced in a year.
Sources: U.S. Bureau of Economic Analysis and U.S. Bureau of Labor Statistics.

Agriculture

Cash receipts $178,903,000
  Rank among U.S. states   48th
Distribution   58% crops, 42% livestock
Farms   4,200
Farm acres (hectares)   470,000 (190,000)
  Rank among U.S. states   48th
Farmland   8% of New Hampshire

Leading products

1. Greenhouse and nursery products
2. Dairy products
Other products: apples, cattle and calves, chicken eggs,
  hay, hogs, honey, maple products, sweet corn.

Fishing

Commercial catch $20,789,000
  Rank among U.S. states   19th

Leading catches
Cod, crab, finfish, flatfish, goosefish, haddock, lobster,
  shark, shrimp, tuna.

Manufacturing

Value added by manufacture* $9,731,689,000
  Rank among U.S. states   37th

Leading products

1. Computer and electronic products
2. Machinery
Other products: electrical equipment, fabricated metal
  products, food products, medical equipment.
*Value added by manufacture is the increase in value of raw materials after they
  become finished products.

Mining

Nonfuel mineral production* $101,000,000
  Rank among U.S. states   47th
Coal   †
Crude oil   †
Natural gas   †
*Partial total, excludes values that must be concealed to not disclose company data.
†No significant mining of this product in New Hampshire.

Leading product

Sand and gravel
Other products: gemstones, granite, traprock.

Electric power

Nuclear   40.9%
Natural gas   30.9%
Coal   15.1%
Other   13.1%
Figures are for 2008, except for the agricultural figures, which are for 2009.
Sources: U.S. Census Bureau, U.S. Department of Agriculture, U.S. Energy Information
  Administration, U.S. Geological Survey, U.S. National Marine Fisheries Service.

Production and workers by economic activities

Economic activities	Percent of GDP produced	Employed workers Number of people	Percent of total
Community, business, & personal services	25	284,000	33
Finance, insurance, & real estate	25	85,900	10
Trade, restaurants, & hotels	17	205,600	24
Manufacturing	12	80,900	9
Government	10	95,600	11
Transportation & communication	5	32,800	4
Construction	4	59,900	7
Utilities	2	2,600	*
Agriculture	*	8,400	1
Mining	*	1,400	*
Total†	100	857,100	100

*Less than one-half of 1 percent.
†Figures may not add up to 100 percent due to rounding.
Figures are for 2008; employment figures include full- and part-time workers.
Source: *World Book* estimates based on data from U.S. Bureau of Economic Analysis.

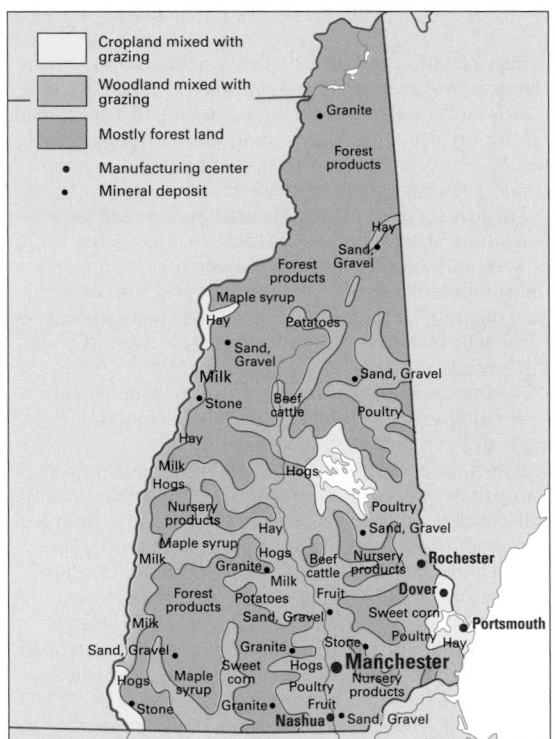

WORLD BOOK map

Economy of New Hampshire

This map shows the economic uses of land in New Hampshire
and where the state's leading farm, mineral, and forest products
are produced. Major manufacturing centers are shown in red.

the rest of the state's electric power. Hydroelectric
plants operate on the Connecticut and Merrimack rivers.
  Transportation. New Hampshire's first railroad began operating in 1838. Many rail lines provide freight
service in the state today. Amtrak passenger trains serve
a number of the state's cities and towns. New Hampshire's largest airport is in Manchester.
  The state has an extensive system of roads and highways. The New Hampshire Turnpike parallels the seacoast. The Spaulding Turnpike extends the seacoast

turnpike from Portsmouth to the Union area. The Everett Turnpike links Concord and Massachusetts. Interstate 89 connects Concord to Vermont.

Communication. New Hampshire's first newspaper, the *New Hampshire Gazette,* began publication in 1756

at Portsmouth. Today, the state's leading newspapers include *The Citizen of Laconia,* the *Concord Monitor, Foster's Daily Democrat* of Dover, *The Keene Sentinel,* the *New Hampshire Union Leader* of Manchester, the *Portsmouth Herald,* and *The Telegraph* of Nashua.

Government

Constitution of New Hampshire took effect in 1784. It replaced a temporary constitution that had been adopted in 1776. Constitutional amendments may be proposed by a three-fifths vote of each house of the New Hampshire state legislature or by a constitutional convention. To become law, a proposed constitutional amendment needs the approval of two-thirds of the people voting on the issue in an election. A majority of the members of both houses of the New Hampshire legislature may propose a constitutional convention. The proposal must be approved by two-thirds of the citizens voting on it. If no constitutional amendment is proposed, the question of holding a convention must be voted on by New Hampshire residents every 10 years.

Executive. The governor of New Hampshire holds office for a two-year term. A governor may be reelected any number of times.

The executive branch of the New Hampshire government is somewhat unusual. The state has no lieutenant governor. However, it does have an Executive Council, which is made up of five members. Members of the Executive Council are elected by the people to two-year terms. Most major executive officials appointed by the governor must be approved by the Executive Council.

The state governors of New Hampshire

	Party	Term		Party	Term
Meshech Weare	None	1776-1785	Natt Head	Republican	1879-1881
John Langdon	None	1785-1786	Charles H. Bell	Republican	1881-1883
John Sullivan	Federalist	1786-1788	Samuel W. Hale	Republican	1883-1885
John Langdon	*Dem.-Rep.	1788-1789	Moody Currier	Republican	1885-1887
John Sullivan	Federalist	1789-1790	Charles H. Sawyer	Republican	1887-1889
Josiah Bartlett	*Dem.-Rep.	1790-1794	David H. Goodell	Republican	1889-1891
John T. Gilman	Federalist	1794-1805	Hiram A. Tuttle	Republican	1891-1893
John Langdon	*Dem.-Rep.	1805-1809	John B. Smith	Republican	1893-1895
Jeremiah Smith	Federalist	1809-1810	Charles A. Busiel	Republican	1895-1897
John Langdon	*Dem.-Rep.	1810-1812	George A. Ramsdell	Republican	1897-1899
William Plumer	*Dem.-Rep.	1812-1813	Frank W. Rollins	Republican	1899-1901
John T. Gilman	Federalist	1813-1816	Chester B. Jordan	Republican	1901-1903
William Plumer	*Dem.-Rep.	1816-1819	Nahum J. Batchelder	Republican	1903-1905
Samuel Bell	*Dem.-Rep.	1819-1823	John McLane	Republican	1905-1907
Levi Woodbury	*Dem.-Rep.	1823-1824	Charles M. Floyd	Republican	1907-1909
David L Morrill	*Dem.-Rep.	1824-1827	Henry B. Quinby	Republican	1909-1911
Benjamin Pierce	*Dem.-Rep.	1827-1828	Robert P. Bass	Republican	1911-1913
John Bell	National Republican	1828-1829	Samuel D. Felker	Democratic	1913-1915
			Rolland H. Spaulding	Republican	1915-1917
Benjamin Pierce	Democratic	1829-1830	Henry W. Keyes	Republican	1917-1919
Matthew Harvey	Democratic	1830-1831	John H. Bartlett	Republican	1919-1921
Samuel Dinsmoor	Democratic	1831-1834	Albert O. Brown	Republican	1921-1923
William Badger	Democratic	1834-1836	Fred H. Brown	Democratic	1923-1925
Isaac Hill	Democratic	1836-1839	John G. Winant	Republican	1925-1927
John Page	Democratic	1839-1842	Huntley N. Spaulding	Republican	1927-1929
Henry Hubbard	Democratic	1842-1844	Charles W. Tobey	Republican	1929-1931
John H. Steele	Democratic	1844-1846	John G. Winant	Republican	1931-1935
Anthony Colby	Whig	1846-1847	Styles Bridges	Republican	1935-1937
Jared W. Williams	Democratic	1847-1849	Francis P. Murphy	Republican	1937-1941
Samuel Dinsmoor, Jr.	Democratic	1849-1852	Robert O. Blood	Republican	1941-1945
Noah Martin	Democratic	1852-1854	Charles M. Dale	Republican	1945-1949
Nathaniel B. Baker	Democratic	1854-1855	Sherman Adams	Republican	1949-1953
Ralph Metcalf	†American	1855-1857	Hugh Gregg	Republican	1953-1955
William Haile	Republican	1857-1859	Lane Dwinell	Republican	1955-1959
Ichabod Goodwin	Republican	1859-1861	Wesley Powell	Republican	1959-1963
Nathaniel S. Berry	Republican	1861-1863	John W. King	Democratic	1963-1969
Joseph A. Gilmore	Republican	1863-1865	Walter R. Peterson, Jr.	Republican	1969-1973
Frederick Smyth	Republican	1865-1867	Meldrim Thomson, Jr.	Republican	1973-1979
Walter Harriman	Republican	1867-1869	Hugh J. Gallen	Democratic	1979-1982
Onslow Stearns	Republican	1869-1871	John H. Sununu	Republican	1983-1989
James A. Weston	Democratic	1871-1872	Judd Gregg	Republican	1989-1993
Ezekiel A. Straw	Republican	1872-1874	Steve Merrill	Republican	1993-1997
James A. Weston	Democratic	1874-1875	Jeanne Shaheen	Democratic	1997-2003
Person C. Cheney	Republican	1875-1877	Craig Benson	Republican	2003-2005
Benjamin F. Prescott	Republican	1877-1879	John Lynch	Democratic	2005-

*Democratic-Republican.　　†Also called the Know-Nothing Party.

These officials include the attorney general and the heads of many departments and commissions. The New Hampshire legislature elects the secretary of state and state treasurer to two-year terms.

Legislature is called the General Court. By law, it consists of a 24-member Senate and a 400-member House of Representatives. The U.S. House of Representatives is the only legislative body in the country with more members than the New Hampshire House. The state's House districts are drawn so that each of the 400 representatives represents a roughly equal number of state residents. Voters in each of the 24 senatorial districts elect one senator. These districts are also based on population. Representatives and senators serve two-year terms.

Legislative sessions begin the Wednesday after the first Tuesday of January. The state legislators receive a fixed salary of $200 for their two-year term. Their allowance for travel expenses covers 45 session days. Legislators are paid for 15 business days during special sessions of the General Court. The governor or the General Court can call special sessions of the legislature.

Courts. The Supreme Court of New Hampshire has a chief justice and four associate justices. It is the state's only appellate court. The next lower court, the Superior Court, operates in 11 sites in the state—two in Hillsborough County and one in each other county. It is the only New Hampshire court that allows for trials by jury. A probate judge presides over each of the 10 probate courts, 1 in each county. The state also has municipal and district courts. The governor, with approval of the Executive Council, appoints all state and local judges.

Local government in New Hampshire operates as one of the purest forms of democracy in the world. The state's 221 towns are nicknamed "little republics." They are so named because they have almost complete self-government. Each year, the voters assemble for a town meeting at which they can participate directly in governmental decisions. Voters elect town officials, approve budgets, and make decisions on other local business. The chief administrative officials at the town level are the *selectmen*. Most of the towns have three selectmen. Selectmen serve three-year terms. A few towns have abandoned or modified the traditional form of government by giving greater power to an elected council and, in some cases, to an appointed executive.

New Hampshire's 13 incorporated cities use either the mayor-council or city-manager form of government. The cities have *home rule*. That is, they are free to write and amend their own charters. Each of the state's 10 counties also has its own government. County officials include the sheriff, attorney, treasurer, register of deeds, register of probate, and county commissioners. These officials are elected to two-year terms.

Revenue. Taxes account for about one-third of the state government's *general revenue* (income). About a fourth comes from federal government grants and programs. Charges for government services are another important source of income. The state collects no general sales tax. Residents pay a personal income tax only on dividend and interest income, not on ordinary income. Taxes on corporate income, motor fuels, and tobacco sales are the largest sources of tax revenue. A lottery helps finance public schools. But the state's contribution to schools is low, and towns and cities rely heavily on local property taxes to fund public schools.

Politics. New Hampshire became a Republican state shortly before the American Civil War (1861-1865). Until 1850, the state had usually voted Democratic. But most of New Hampshire's people opposed slavery and then became Republicans. Since 1856, Republicans have won most of the major elective offices in New Hampshire. But Democratic strength has increased since the 1960's.

Republicans have won the state's electoral votes in about three-fourths of the presidential elections since 1856. For the state's electoral votes and its voting record in presidential elections, see **Electoral College** (table).

History

Early days. About 5,000 American Indians probably lived in what is now New Hampshire before Europeans came. Most belonged to two branches of the Algonquian Indian family—the Abenaki and the Pennacook. The Abenaki branch included the Ossipee and the Pequawket tribes. The Pennacook included the Amoskeag, Nashua, Piscataqua, Souhegan, and Squamscot tribes. New Hampshire Indians built wigwams of bark and skins. They hunted and fished, and farmed small fields of corn. The tribes lived together in peace but often warred against their common enemy, the Iroquois.

Exploration. Historians do not know who were the first Europeans to reach New Hampshire. But wide-scale exploration of the area began in the early 1600's. In 1603, Martin Pring of England sailed a trading ship up the Piscataqua River. Pring and his crew may have landed in Portsmouth. The French explorer Samuel de Champlain landed on the New Hampshire coast in 1605. In 1614, the English captain John Smith reached the Isles of Shoals. He named them *Smith's Isles*.

Settlement. In 1619, England's King James I founded the Council for New England to encourage American settlement. The council granted David Thomson land in present-day New Hampshire. In 1623, Thomson and his followers settled at Odiorne's Point (now a part of Rye). Edward Hilton settled Hilton's Point (now Dover) in the 1620's. Some historians believe these settlements began at the same time. Others think Hilton's began later. Other early settlements include Strawbery Banke (now Portsmouth), established in 1630; and Exeter and Hampton, founded in 1638.

In 1622, the Council for New England gave John Mason and Sir Ferdinando Gorges a large tract of land in present-day New Hampshire and Maine. In 1629, the land was divided between the two men. In 1634, Mason and Gorges gained more land in the area. Mason called his land *New Hampshire,* after his native county, Hampshire, England. New Hampshire was made part of Massachusetts in 1641. But in 1680, King Charles II of England made New Hampshire a separate province. The king appointed John Cutt as New Hampshire's first provincial governor (then called president).

French and Indian wars were fought in New Hampshire and the rest of New England off and on from 1689

Historic New Hampshire

The Portsmouth Naval Shipyard was established in 1800. The shipyard built warships during World War I (1914-1918) and specialized in constructing submarines during World War II (1939-1945).

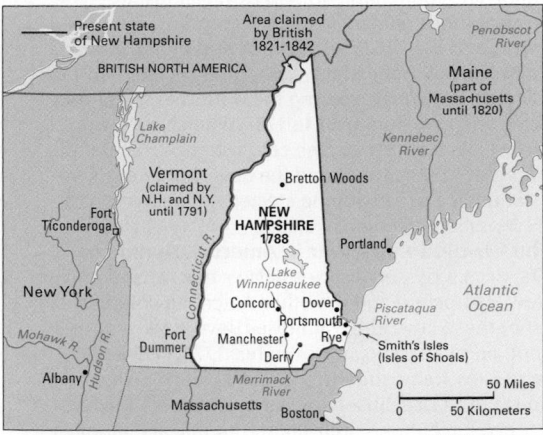

WORLD BOOK map

New Hampshire's first English settlements were established in the 1620's. New Hampshire was part of Massachusetts from 1641 to 1680, when England's King Charles II made New Hampshire a separate province. New Hampshire became a U.S. state in 1788.

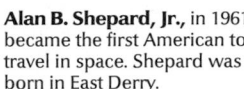

Alan B. Shepard, Jr., in 1961 became the first American to travel in space. Shepard was born in East Derry.

Important dates in New Hampshire

WORLD BOOK illustrations by Richard Bonson, The Art Agency

1603	Martin Pring of England explored the mouth of the Piscataqua River.
1614	Captain John Smith of England landed on the Isles of Shoals.
1620's	David Thomson and Edward Hilton established the first permanent settlements in New Hampshire.
1641	The Massachusetts Colony gained control of New Hampshire.
1680	New Hampshire became a separate royal colony.
1776	New Hampshire broke away from Britain and adopted a temporary constitution.
1784	New Hampshire adopted its present constitution.
1788	New Hampshire became the ninth state when it ratified the U.S. Constitution on June 21.

1853	Franklin Pierce of Hillsboro became the 14th president of the United States.
1944	The International Monetary Conference was held at Bretton Woods.
1961	Alan B. Shepard, Jr., of East Derry became the first American to travel in space.
1964	The New Hampshire sweepstakes lottery began. It was the first legal U.S. lottery since the 1890's.
1986	Christa McAuliffe, a Concord teacher, was among the seven crew members killed when the space shuttle *Challenger* broke apart shortly after take-off.
1997-2003	Jeanne Shaheen served three terms as governor of New Hampshire. Shaheen was the first woman to be elected to the office.

to 1763. The French and their Indian allies battled to gain control of the area from the British. Guided by Indians, French forces pushed down from Canada. Robert Rogers, the leader of a group of soldiers called Rogers's Rangers, and John Stark, both of New Hampshire, won fame as colonial military leaders during the French and Indian War (1754-1763). See **French and Indian wars**.

Colonial New Hampshire was a rural society. Most of the people kept busy clearing the wilderness, building houses, and growing food. In 1767, when New Hampshire took its first census, the colony had 52,700 people. The king of Britain appointed the governor and governor's council. But the people elected assemblymen to represent them in colonial affairs.

The Revolutionary War in America. During the 1760's, Britain passed a series of laws that caused unrest in New Hampshire and the other American colonies. Most of these laws either imposed severe taxes or restricted colonial trade. In December 1774, Paul Revere rode to New Hampshire to warn of a British military build-up in Massachusetts. A band of New Hampshire residents, led by John Sullivan, seized military supplies from a British fort in New Castle. This was one of the first armed actions by colonists against the British.

After the Revolutionary War in America broke out in Massachusetts in 1775, hundreds of New Hampshire "minutemen" hurried to Boston to fight the British. New Hampshire was the only one of the 13 original colonies in which no actual fighting occurred.

New Hampshire became the first colony to form a government wholly independent of Britain. It did so on Jan. 5, 1776, when it adopted a temporary constitution. On July 9, 1778, New Hampshire ratified the Articles of Confederation (the forerunner of the United States Constitution). On June 21, 1788, New Hampshire became the ninth state to ratify the U.S. Constitution. New Hampshire's ratification put the Constitution into effect.

The 1800's. New Hampshire remained an agricultural state from 1800 until the outbreak of the American Civil War in 1861. Then it began an industrial growth that has continued to the present day. In the 1830's, the Amoskeag Manufacturing Company built 30 textile mills in Manchester, along both sides of the Merrimack River. Manchester became New Hampshire's largest industrial center and, in 1846, the state's first incorporated city. Portsmouth developed as a leading clipper-ship port in the early 1800's, and the first railroad opened in 1838. During the 1850's, business leaders built hosiery plants, woolen mills, and factories that made boots and shoes, machine tools, and wood products.

Several people from New Hampshire gained national fame during this period. They included Franklin Pierce, the 14th president of the United States, and Daniel Webster, a leading orator and U.S. senator.

New Hampshire was a leading opponent of slavery. About 34,000 state residents served with the Union forces during the American Civil War, and the Portsmouth Naval Shipyard built ships that blockaded Southern ports.

Industrial development increased greatly after the Civil War ended in 1865. The textile, woodworking, and leather industries were among those that grew at record rates. Thousands of French-Canadian and European immigrants came to New Hampshire to fill the labor needs caused by expansion of mills and factories. At the same time, many farmers left the state to claim free land in the West. Farming activity decreased in New Hampshire as industry grew.

The early 1900's. During World War I (1914-1918), the Portsmouth Naval Shipyard built warships. New Hampshire's cotton and woolen textile industries declined in the 1920's and 1930's. Leather and shoe manufacturing became the state's leading industry. New Hampshire improved its highway system during the 1920's, and private utility companies built hydroelectric plants in the state. The Great Depression of the 1930's slowed the growth of the state's economy. Conditions improved after the Depression eased in the late 1930's.

The mid-1900's. During World War II (1939-1945), Portsmouth built submarines and repaired warships,

© SuperStock

AP/Wide World

The Old Man of the Mountain, before and after, is shown in these two photographs of Profile Mountain, in New Hampshire's Franconia Range. A rock formation on the mountain was called the Old Man of the Mountain or the Great Stone Face because people thought it resembled the profile of a man. It became the state's best-known symbol and drew many sightseers every year. In 2003, the rocks forming the famous profile were so weakened by erosion that they fell away.

and New Hampshire's textile mills supplied materials for military uniforms. These economic activities helped end depression conditions.

In 1944, representatives of 44 nations held the historic International Monetary Conference at Bretton Woods in the White Mountains. The representatives at Bretton Woods planned postwar world trade and simplified the transfer of money among nations. In addition, they drew up plans for two United Nations agencies—the International Monetary Fund and the World Bank. See **Bretton Woods.**

New Hampshire became increasingly urban and industrial during the mid-1900's. In the 1950's, the state approved the formation of a Business Development Corporation and established an Industrial Park Authority. These two agencies worked to aid new businesses in the state. They also tried to attract industry to New Hampshire.

New Hampshire's once important shoe industry declined sharply because of increased competition from other states as well as other countries, especially Italy. However, the rapid growth of New Hampshire's electronics industry more than made up for losses in the shoe industry.

In 1961, Alan B. Shepard, Jr., of New Hampshire became the first American to travel in space. Shepard was born in East Derry.

In 1963, New Hampshire adopted the first legal lottery in the United States since the 1890's. The first lottery was held in September 1964. The state uses the profits from the lottery to help pay for public education.

The late 1900's. Christa McAuliffe, a Concord high school teacher, was chosen to be the first "ordinary citizen" in space. She was among the seven crew members killed when the space shuttle Challenger broke apart shortly after take-off on Jan. 28, 1986.

During most of the 1980's, New Hampshire experienced economic prosperity and rapid population growth, especially in the southern part of the state. In the late 1980's and early 1990's, however, a national recession resulted in the loss of many jobs, particularly in the areas of real estate, banking, and the defense industry. New Hampshire's economy improved in the mid-1990's.

In 1996, voters elected New Hampshire's first woman governor, Jeanne Shaheen. Shaheen was reelected twice and held office until 2003.

The early 2000's. New Hampshire has remained one of the few states that does not collect a general individual income tax or a general sales tax. Residents pay a personal income tax only on dividend and interest income, not on ordinary income. This low-tax policy helps attract new industries and other businesses. But low taxes result in less money to pay for state-funded programs and services and less money for school funding and other aid to local communities.

In 2003, New Hampshire suffered the loss of its best-known symbol, the Old Man of the Mountain. The Old Man, also called the Great Stone Face, was a natural stone profile of a man's face that erosion had carved in Profile Mountain. The rocks forming the profile fell away in May 2003. In 2009, the New Hampshire legislature legalized same-sex marriage.

Mark J. Okrant and Ann Page Stecker

Related articles in *World Book* include:

Biographies

Adams, Sherman	Langdon, John	Souter, David H.
Bartlett, Josiah	McAuliffe, Christa	Stark, John
Dearborn, Henry	Pierce, Franklin	Thornton,
Frost, Robert	Porter, Fitz-John	Matthew
Gilman, Nicholas	Shepard, Alan B.,	Webster, Daniel
Hale, John P.	Jr.	Whipple, William

Cities and towns

Concord	Manchester	Nashua

Other related articles

Colonial life in America	Merrimack River
Connecticut River	Portsmouth Naval Shipyard
Dartmouth College case	White Mountains
French and Indian wars	

Outline

I. **People**
  A. Population
  B. Schools
  C. Libraries
  D. Museums
II. **Visitor's guide**
III. **Land and climate**

  A. Land regions ..... D. Rivers and lakes
  B. Coastline ..... E. Plant and animal life
  C. Mountains ..... F. Climate
IV. **Economy**

  A. Natural resources ..... E. Mining
  B. Service industries ..... F. Electric power and utilities
  C. Manufacturing ..... G. Transportation
  D. Agriculture ..... H. Communication
V. **Government**

  A. Constitution ..... E. Local government
  B. Executive ..... F. Revenue
  C. Legislature ..... G. Politics
  D. Courts
VI. **History**

Questions

Why was New Hampshire's ratification of the U.S. Constitution especially important?
What is the Executive Council of New Hampshire?
Where is New Hampshire's highest mountain?
What president of the United States was born in the state?
What are New Hampshire's leading manufactured products?
Why are New Hampshire's towns called "little republics"?
What important international conference was held in New Hampshire in 1944?
What are New Hampshire's three main land regions?
Why is New Hampshire's coastline unique?
What is New Hampshire's oldest college?

Additional resources

Level I
Hicks, Terry A. *New Hampshire.* Benchmark Bks., 2005.
Mattern, Joanne. *New Hampshire.* World Almanac Lib., 2003.
Shannon, Terry M. *New Hampshire.* Children's Pr., 2002.
Teitelbaum, Michael. *New Hampshire.* Children's Pr., 2004.

Level II
Heffernan, Nancy C., and Stecker, Ann Page. *New Hampshire.* 3rd ed. Univ. Pr. of New England, 2004.
Marshall, Susan E. *The New Hampshire State Constitution.* Praeger, 2004.
Piotrowski, Thaddeus, ed. *The Indian Heritage of New Hampshire and Northern New England.* McFarland, 2002.
Reid, John P. *Controlling the Law: Legal Politics in Early National New Hampshire.* Northern Ill. Univ. Pr., 2004.
Scala, Dante J. *Stormy Weather: The New Hampshire Primary and Presidential Politics.* Palgrave, 2003.
Wilderson, Paul W. *Governor John Wentworth and the American Revolution.* 1994. Reprint. Univ. Pr. of N. H., 2004.

University of New Hampshire

The University of New Hampshire in Durham is part of a public system of higher education. Thompson Hall, *shown here,* serves as the university's administration building.

New Hampshire, University of, is a public system of higher education. The official name of the system is the University System of New Hampshire. The system includes the main campus of the University of New Hampshire in Durham, another campus in Manchester, Keene

State College, Plymouth State University, and Granite State College, which offers degrees at centers throughout New Hampshire. The University of New Hampshire's athletic teams are called the Wildcats.

The university was founded in 1866 as the New Hampshire College of Agriculture and the Mechanic Arts. It became the University of New Hampshire in 1923. The university's website at http://www.usnh.edu offers additional information.

Critically reviewed by the University System of New Hampshire

New Harmony, Indiana (pop. 789), became famous as an educational and cultural center during the 1820's. Today, this quiet town in Posey County is a trading center for a farming region in the lower Wabash River Valley (see **Indiana** [map]).

George Rapp (1757-1847), the leader of a religious group called Harmonists, founded the village of Harmonie in 1814. Rapp brought the Harmonists from the kingdom of Württemberg in Germany to escape religious persecution. They spent 10 years in Butler County, Pennsylvania, before migrating to Indiana. The Harmonists were celibate and could not own property. In 1824, Rapp led his followers back to Pennsylvania and founded the village of Economy, which is now called Ambridge. The society died out there near the end of the 1800's.

Robert Owen, a wealthy social reformer and industrialist from Scotland, purchased the Harmonists' Indiana town in 1825. He renamed it New Harmony and attracted new residents with the promise of an earthly *utopia* (perfect society). Owen established a social order based on community ownership and equality of work and profit. His partner was William Maclure, a wealthy scientist from Philadelphia who is sometimes called the "Father of American Geology." In the 1820's, Maclure sent the first seed for the Chinese *golden-rain* trees to Thomas Say, a geologist in New Harmony. These gold-

Granger Collection; Jo Ann Holbrook

New Harmony, *below,* was a communal society. The restored hedge labyrinth, *left,* was first designed by George Rapp as entertainment.

en-rain, or *gate,* trees now line the streets of the town.

The experiment in community living made New Harmony famous. Scientists and scholars flocked to the town. But few of the 1,000 or more Owenites understood the principles of the experiment, and they split into several factions. By 1827, Owen's plan had failed. New Harmony remained an educational, scientific, and cultural center until the American Civil War (1861-1865). The Minerva Club, the first woman's club to have a constitution and bylaws, was organized at New Harmony in 1859. Some of the buildings constructed by the Harmonists and Owenites have been restored.

David L. Anderson

See also **Indiana** (Schools; Places to visit); **Owen, Robert; Owen, Robert Dale.**

New Haven (pop. 129,779) is the home of Yale University and the second largest city in Connecticut. Only Bridgeport has a larger population. New Haven and Milford form a metropolitan area with 862,477 people.

The city. A mayor and board of aldermen govern New Haven. The city lies on the northern shore of Long Island Sound. For location, see **Connecticut** (political map). Its bay is 4 miles (6.4 kilometers) long and 2 miles (3.2 kilometers) wide. Three small rivers, the Mill, Quinnipiac, and West, flow into the bay. At the northern border of the city stand two impressive rock hills—West Rock, rising 670 feet (204 meters), and East Rock, 359 feet (109 meters).

The historic downtown Green lies at the center of New Haven. Three churches built in the 1810's stand

F. Byrne Stoddard, Jr.

Center Church, a New Haven landmark dating from the early 1800's, stands on one side of the downtown Green. The tall building in the background is Yale University's Harkness Tower.

along one side of the Green. The Yale campus lies to the north and west of the Green. Offices and City Hall and other government buildings line the other sides of the Green.

A memorial in front of City Hall marks the site of the jail where the black slaves who rebelled on the ship *La Amistad* were held during their trial (see **Amistad Rebellion**). New Haven is now the home port for a life-sized replica of *La Amistad.*

Economy. Yale University and AT&T Connecticut (formerly Southern New England Telephone Company) are the city's largest employers. The Knights of Columbus, a Roman Catholic organization that is a major insurance provider, has its national headquarters in New Haven. The area's factories produce communications equipment, firearms, locks, medical instruments, packaging, razors, and a variety of other products.

Cultural life and recreation. Yale University, founded in 1701, is one of the oldest institutions of higher learning in the United States (see **Yale University**). Other New Haven colleges include Albertus Magnus College and Southern Connecticut State University.

Cultural attractions include the Peabody Museum of Natural History, the Eli Whitney Museum, the Yale Center for British Art, the Yale University Art Gallery, and the Beinecke Rare Book and Manuscript Library. New Haven is the home of the New Haven Symphony Orchestra, one of the oldest symphony orchestras in the United States. The city's theaters include the Long Wharf Theatre, the Yale Repertory Theatre, and the Shubert Theater. Yale's football team plays in the Yale Bowl.

History. The Quinnipiac Indians originally inhabited the area. Adriaen Block, a Dutch explorer, visited the harbor in 1614. A group of English Puritans led by Theophilus Eaton and John Davenport founded a town there in 1638. At first, they called it *Quinnipiac (Long River Place),* after the original Indian village. In 1640, they changed the town's name to New Haven, after the English city of Newhaven.

In 1784, New Haven became a city. Its first mayor was political leader and judge Roger Sherman (see **Sherman, Roger**). New Haven and Hartford were twin capitals of Connecticut from 1701 until 1875, when Hartford became the sole capital.

During the 1700's and the early 1800's, New Haven's business centered on its port. During the 1800's, the city became an industrial center. In addition, the growth of Yale University aided the development of the area. Renewal projects in the late 1900's included the Audubon Arts Center complex and Wooster Square. Once a run-down area, Wooster Square now includes a historic district and commercial and industrial buildings.

Stephen Fagin

New Hebrides Islands. See Vanuatu.

New Ireland is the second largest of the more than 200 islands of the Bismarck Archipelago, which forms part of the nation of Papua New Guinea. Only New Britain is larger than New Ireland in the island group. New Ireland is about 230 miles (370 kilometers) long and covers about 3,340 square miles (8,651 square kilometers) in the southwest Pacific Ocean (see **Papua New Guinea** [map]). It has about 90,000 people. Mountains cover much of the island, and coral reefs surround it.

David A. M. Lea

Atlantic City is a world-famous New Jersey resort. Hotels, gambling casinos, restaurants, shops, and beaches line the Atlantic City Boardwalk. New Jersey has many beautiful vacation areas along the Atlantic seaboard that attract millions of visitors to the state each year.

New Jersey *The Garden State*

New Jersey is a state of industrial cities and towns, glistening beaches, and popular summer resorts. It is the fifth smallest state of the United States. Only Hawaii, Connecticut, Delaware, and Rhode Island have a smaller area. But New Jersey ranks 11th in population among the states.

New Jersey is the most densely populated state. All of New Jersey's people live in one of the state's metropolitan areas. The state's cities include such communities as Camden, Elizabeth, Jersey City, Newark, Paterson, and Trenton. However, New Jersey also has many small, quiet towns. A large number of these towns are the homes of people who work in New York City or Philadelphia. Both of these giant cities are neighbors of New Jersey.

The thousands of New Jerseyites who work in New York City and in Philadelphia commute daily by train, automobile, or bus. The Holland and Lincoln tunnels, as well as the George Washington Bridge, link New Jersey with New York City. Four bridges connect New Jersey with Philadelphia.

The contributors of this article are Paul G. E. Clemens, Professor of History at Rutgers, the State University of New Jersey, and Grant Saff, Associate Professor of Global Studies and Geography at Hofstra University.

New Jersey's location gives it great economic importance. The state lies between the Hudson and Delaware rivers. It also lies between New York City and Philadelphia. Miles of wharves stretch along the New Jersey side of the Hudson. Ocean liners, container ships, freighters, and other ships from all parts of the world dock there and along the Delaware.

New Jersey remains a leading manufacturing state. New Jersey products find huge nearby markets in New York City and Philadelphia. New Jersey is one of the leading states in the production of chemical and *pharmaceutical* (medicinal drug) products. The state's other leading manufactures include electronics and food products.

Service industries are the leading part of the New Jersey economy. Many of the state's workers are employed in such activities as education, health care, and retail trade, especially in northeastern New Jersey.

New Jersey's vacation areas along the Atlantic Coast contrast sharply with the state's industrial cities. Dozens of resort cities and towns line the New Jersey coast. They include Atlantic City, Ocean City, and Cape May. The resort communities provide a wide variety of recreational activities for vacationers. Atlantic City's gambling casinos attract many visitors.

New Jersey and its people have played important roles in U.S. history. The state earned the nickname

WORLD BOOK illustrations by Kevin Chadwick

Interesting facts about New Jersey

The first drive-in motion-picture theater opened on June 6, 1933, on Crescent Boulevard outside Camden. The theater presented two shows each night on a 40 by 50 foot (12 by 15 meter) screen. Inclined rows at the theater accommodated 500 cars. Richard Hollingshead, Jr., the owner of the theater, originated the idea for the drive-in.

First drive-in theater

A huge clock in a riverfront park in Jersey City can be read from across the Hudson River in New York City. The clock, which came from the old Colgate-Palmolive building, is 50 feet (15 meters) across. The minute hand, about 26 feet (8 meters) long, moves 1 mile (1.6 kilometers) every 34 hours 4 minutes.

The first electric sewing machine was made in 1889 by the Singer Manufacturing Company at its factory in Elizabethport (now Elizabeth).

Colgate-Palmolive clock

G. Ahrens, H. Armstrong Roberts

A scenic mill stands in Clinton, a rural town in northwestern New Jersey. Despite its small size and large population, the state has many small, quiet towns.

Cockpit of the Revolution because of the many battles fought on its soil during the American Revolution (1775-1783). American patriots and British redcoats clashed nearly a hundred times in New Jersey. People compared these actions with cockfights. General George Washington turned the tide of the war at Trenton in 1776 when he led his tattered army across the Delaware River and surprised the enemy. Trenton and Princeton each served as the nation's capital during the 1780's.

In 1884, Grover Cleveland of New Jersey was elected the 22nd president of the United States. He was elected president again in 1892. Woodrow Wilson served as president of Princeton University and governor of New Jersey before he was elected the 28th president in 1912. Wilson was reelected in 1916 and led the nation through World War I (1914-1918).

Three of the world's greatest scientists and inventors worked in New Jersey for many years. Thomas Edison invented the electric light and the phonograph in his laboratory in Menlo Park. Samuel F. B. Morse developed the first successful U.S. electric telegraph near Morristown. Albert Einstein worked many years at the Institute for Advanced Study in Princeton.

New Jersey's many truck farms, orchards, and flower gardens give it the nickname of the *Garden State.* Trenton is the capital of New Jersey, and Newark is the largest city in the state.

© Graig Hammell, The Stock Market

Newark, New Jersey's largest city, is the center of a large industrial area in the northeastern part of the state. Newark ranks as one of the nation's leading manufacturing centers.

New Jersey in brief

Symbols of New Jersey

The state flag, adopted in 1896, bears a version of the state seal. On the seal, adopted in 1928, three plows on a shield represent agriculture. A helmet symbolizing sovereignty and a crest with a horse's head appear above the shield. Supporting the shield are Liberty, left, and Ceres, right, the Roman goddess of grain and a symbol of abundance.

State flag

State seal

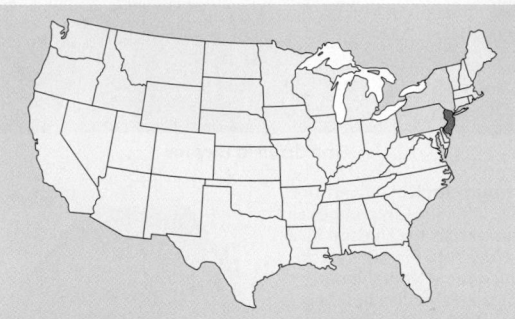

New Jersey (brown) ranks 46th in size among all the states and is the smallest of the Middle Atlantic States (yellow).

General information

Statehood: Dec. 18, 1787, the third state.
State abbreviations: N.J. (traditional); NJ (postal).
State motto: *Liberty and Prosperity.*
State song: none.

The State Capitol is in Trenton, the capital since 1790. Perth Amboy and Burlington served as twin capitals from 1703 to 1775. There was no definite capital from 1775 to 1790.

Land and climate

Area: 7,813 mi² (20,236 km²), including 396 mi² (1,025 km²) of inland water but excluding 401 mi² (1,040 km²) of coastal water.
Elevation: *Highest*—High Point, 1,803 ft (550 m) above sea level. *Lowest*—sea level along the Atlantic Ocean.
Coastline: 130 mi (209 km).
Record high temperature: 110 °F (43 °C) at Runyon on July 10, 1936.
Record low temperature: –34 °F (–37 °C) at River Vale on Jan. 5, 1904.
Average July temperature: 75 °F (24 °C).
Average January temperature: 31 °F (–1 °C).
Average yearly precipitation: 45 in (114 cm).

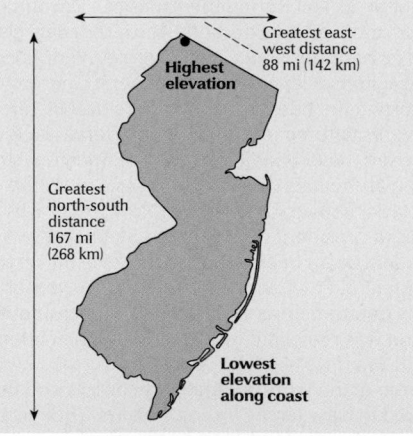

Greatest east-west distance 88 mi (142 km)

Highest elevation

Greatest north-south distance 167 mi (268 km)

Lowest elevation along coast

Important dates

The Dutch established a permanent settlement at Bergen (now part of Jersey City).

New Jersey became the 3rd state when it ratified the U.S. Constitution on December 18.

| 1524 | 1660 | 1776 | 1787 |

Giovanni da Verrazzano explored the New Jersey coast.

New Jersey adopted its first constitution.

State bird
American goldfinch

State flower
Common blue violet

State tree
Northern red oak

People

Population: 8,791,894
Rank among the states: 11th
Population density: 1,125 per mi² (434 per km²), U.S. average 85 per mi² (33 per km²)
Distribution: 94 percent urban, 6 percent rural

Largest cities in New Jersey

Newark	277,140
Jersey City	247,597
Paterson	146,199
Elizabeth	124,969
Edison†	99,967
Woodbridge†	99,585

†Township.
Source: 2010 census, except for distribution, which is for 2000.

Population trend

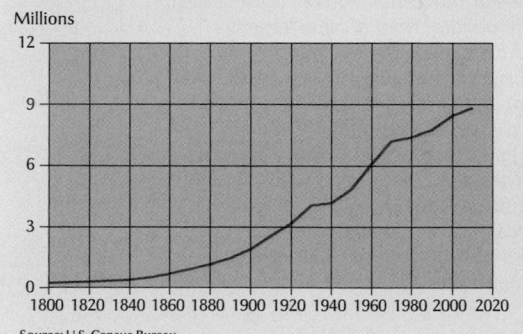

Millions

Source: U.S. Census Bureau.

Year	Population
2010	8,791,894
2000	8,414,350
1990	7,730,188
1980	7,364,823
1970	7,168,164
1960	6,066,782
1950	4,835,329
1940	4,160,165
1930	4,041,334
1920	3,155,900
1910	2,537,167
1900	1,883,669
1890	1,444,933
1880	1,131,116
1870	906,096
1860	672,035
1850	489,555
1840	373,306
1830	320,823
1820	277,575
1810	245,562
1800	211,149
1790	184,139

Economy

Chief products

Agriculture: blueberries, greenhouse and nursery products, horses, milk, peaches, vegetables.
Manufacturing: chemicals, computer and electronic products, fabricated metal products, food products, medical equipment, petroleum products.
Mining: granite, greensand marl, sand and gravel, traprock.

Gross domestic product

Value of goods and services produced in 2008: $486,556,000,000. *Services* include community, business, and personal services; finance; government; trade; and transportation and communication. *Industry* includes construction, manufacturing, mining, and utilities. *Agriculture* includes agriculture, fishing, and forestry.

Source: U.S. Bureau of Economic Analysis.

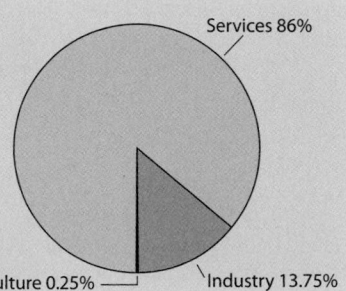

Services 86%
Agriculture 0.25%
Industry 13.75%

Government

State government

Governor: 4-year term
State senators: 40; 2- or 4-year terms
Members of the General Assembly: 80; 2-year terms
Counties: 21

Federal government

United States senators: 2
United States representatives: 13 (12 in 2013)
Electoral votes: 15 (14 in 2012)

Sources of information

New Jersey's official website at http://www.state.nj.us provides a gateway to much information on the state's government, history, and economy.

In addition, the website at http://www.visitnj.org/ provides information about tourism.

The first dinosaur skeleton discovered in North America was found buried in Haddonfield.

The New Jersey Turnpike opened.

Christine Todd Whitman served as New Jersey's first woman governor.

| 1858 | 1879 | 1952 | 1987 | 1994-2001 |

Thomas A. Edison invented the electric light in Menlo Park.

New Jersey celebrated the bicentennial of its statehood.

Population. The 2010 United States census reported that New Jersey had 8,791,894 people. The population of New Jersey had increased 4 ½ percent over the 2000 census figure, which was 8,414,350. According to the 2010 census, New Jersey ranks 11th in population among the 50 states.

All of the people in New Jersey live in metropolitan areas (see **Metropolitan area**). Seven metropolitan areas lie either partly or entirely in New Jersey. The areas are Allentown (Pennsylvania)-Bethlehem (Pennsylvania)-Easton (Pennsylvania), Atlantic City-Hammonton, New York (New York)-Northern New Jersey-Long Island (New York), Ocean City, Philadelphia (Pennsylvania)-Camden-Wilmington (Delaware), Trenton-Ewing, and Vineland-Millville-Bridgeton. For the populations of these areas, see the *Index* to the political map of New Jersey.

About three-fourths of New Jersey's people live in the New York (New York)-Northern New Jersey-Long Island (New York) metropolitan area. In terms of population, this metropolitan area is the largest in the United States.

Newark is New Jersey's largest city, with a population of about 277,000. The state's other cities with more than 75,000 people include Jersey City; Paterson; Elizabeth; Trenton, the state capital; Clifton; and Camden.

New Jersey ranks among the most ethnically and racially diverse states in the nation. New Jersey's largest

Population density

New Jersey is the most densely populated state. A majority of its people live in the northeast. The most thinly populated areas are in the northwest and the south.

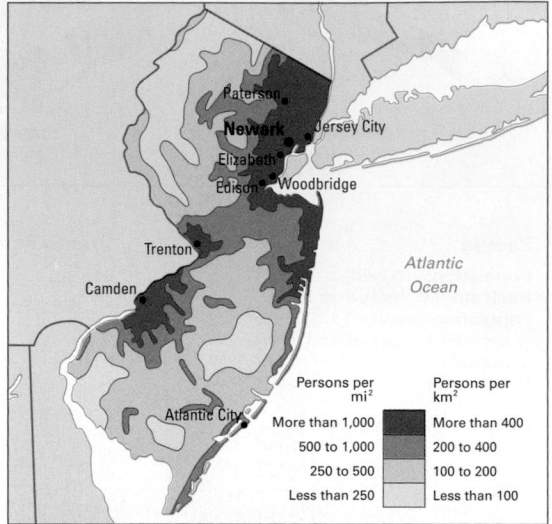

	Persons per mi²	Persons per km²
	More than 1,000	More than 400
	500 to 1,000	200 to 400
	250 to 500	100 to 200
	Less than 250	Less than 100

WORLD BOOK map; based on U.S. Census Bureau data.

David Overcash, Bruce Coleman, Inc.

Workers harvest cranberries from a bog near Chatsworth. New Jersey ranks as a leading cranberry-growing state. Farmers there also grow blueberries and peaches.

© J. T. Miller, The Stock Market

A roadside farmstand in Belle Mead sells flowers and produce. New Jersey's many truck farms, flower gardens, and orchards earn it the nickname the *Garden State*.

R. Krubner, H. Armstrong Roberts

The Cape May Mall has many quaint shops and restaurants. Cape May, one of New Jersey's most popular seaside resorts, is at the southern tip of the state.

Princeton University, founded in 1746, is one of the oldest institutions of higher learning in the United States. The Firestone Library in the background is one of the many beautiful buildings on the campus.

Michael J. Beanan, Princeton University

population groups include people of Italian, Irish, German, Polish, and English descent. Hispanic Americans account for over 15 percent of the population. Nearly 15 percent of New Jersey's people are African Americans. Asian Americans make up about 8 percent.

Schools. Colonial New Jersey had no public schools. Children attended school only if their parents could pay tuition. A public school system began in 1817, when the Legislature established a permanent school fund.

A state commissioner of education and a State Board of Education direct New Jersey public schools. The governor, with the Senate's approval, appoints the board members to six-year terms. The governor appoints the commissioner to a term that coincides with his or her own. The state government is responsible for education but delegates administrative responsibilities to local school boards. The Commission on Higher Education directs the state's higher education system.

New Jersey law requires children from age 6 to 16 to attend school. For the number of students and teachers in New Jersey, see **Education** (table).

Two of the oldest U.S. universities and colleges are in New Jersey. They are Princeton University (1746) and Rutgers, the State University of New Jersey (1766).

Libraries. Thomas Cadwalader founded New Jersey's first public library at Trenton in 1750. The State Library in Trenton has large law and general reference collections. The New Jersey Library Network includes many member libraries, organized by region. Member libraries can call on major libraries in each region for reference and interlibrary loan services. Princeton and Rutgers universities have the state's largest college libraries. The Harvey S. Firestone Memorial Library of Princeton University is the state's largest research library.

Museums. The New Jersey State Museum in Trenton features archaeology and ethnology, fine art, and cultural and natural history exhibits. It has an auditorium and a planetarium. The Newark Museum houses art and natural science exhibits, a small zoo, and a Buddhist altar. It also includes a planetarium and Ballantine House, a restored 1885 mansion. The Liberty Science Center in Jersey City features exhibits on the environment, inventions, and health. The Montclair Art Museum focuses on American and Native American art. The Princeton University Art Museum displays artwork from many periods and locations.

Universities and colleges

This table lists the nonprofit universities and colleges in New Jersey that grant bachelor's or advanced degrees and are accredited by the Middle States Association of Colleges and Schools.

Name	Mailing address	Name	Mailing address	Name	Mailing address
Bloomfield College	Bloomfield	Montclair State		Rutgers, the State	
Caldwell College	Caldwell	University	Montclair	University of	
Centenary College	Hackettstown	New Jersey, College of	Ewing	New Jersey	†
Drew University	Madison	New Jersey City University	Jersey City	St. Elizabeth,	
Fairleigh Dickinson		New Jersey Institute of		College of	Morristown
University	Teaneck	Technology	Newark	St. Peter's College	Jersey City
Felician College	Lodi	Princeton Theological		Seton Hall University	‡
Georgian Court		Seminary	Princeton	Somerset Christian	
University	Lakewood	Princeton University	Princeton	College	Zarephath
Kean University	Union	Ramapo College of		Stevens Institute of	
Medicine and	*	New Jersey	Mahwah	Technology	Hoboken
Dentistry of New		Richard Stockton College		Thomas Edison State	
Jersey, University of		of New Jersey	Pomona	College	Trenton
Monmouth University	West Long	Rider University	Lawrence-	William Paterson	
	Branch		ville	University of	
		Rowan University	Glassboro	New Jersey	Wayne

*Campuses at Newark, Piscataway, and Stratford. †For campuses, see **Rutgers, the State University of New Jersey.**
‡Campuses at Newark and South Orange.

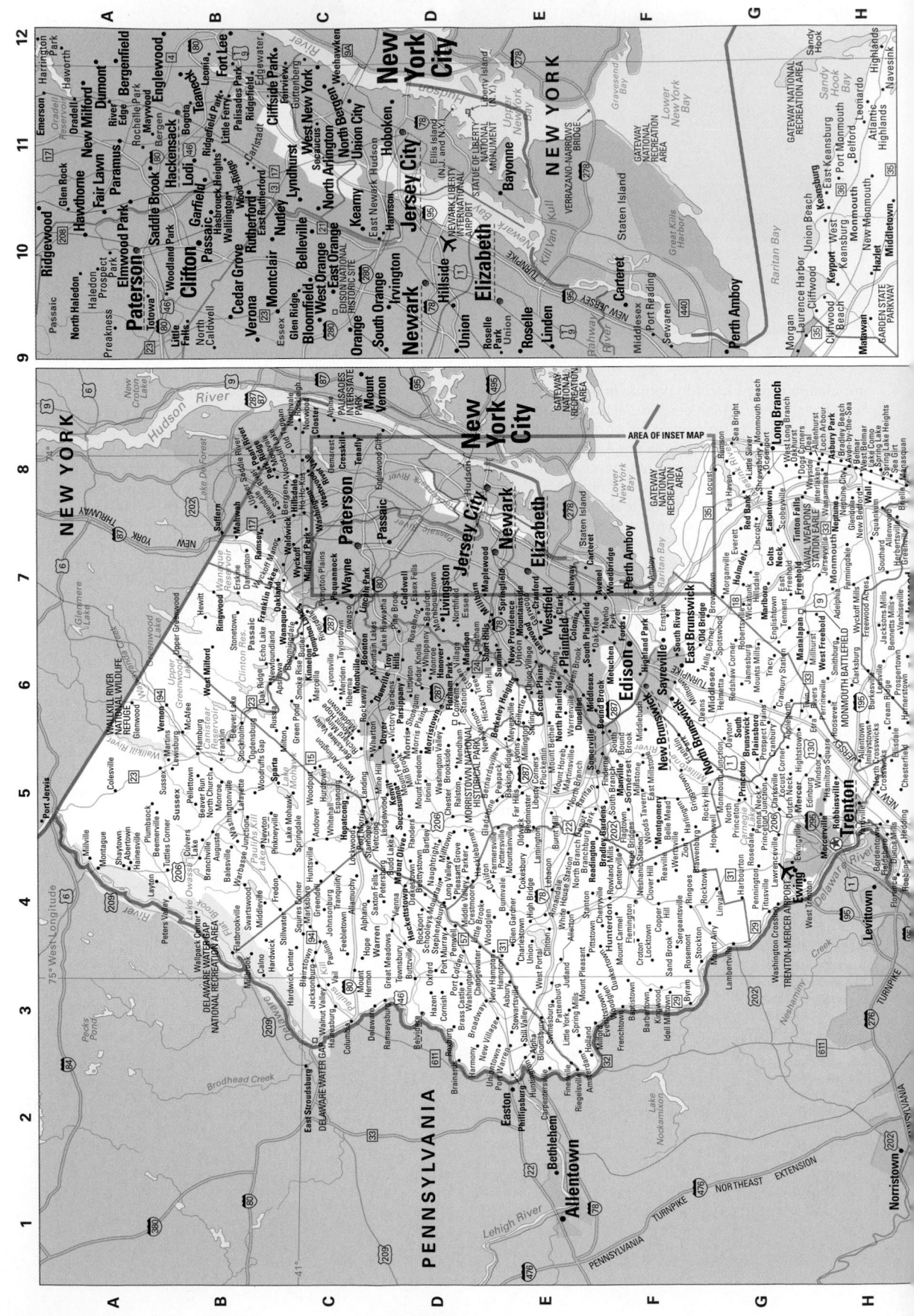

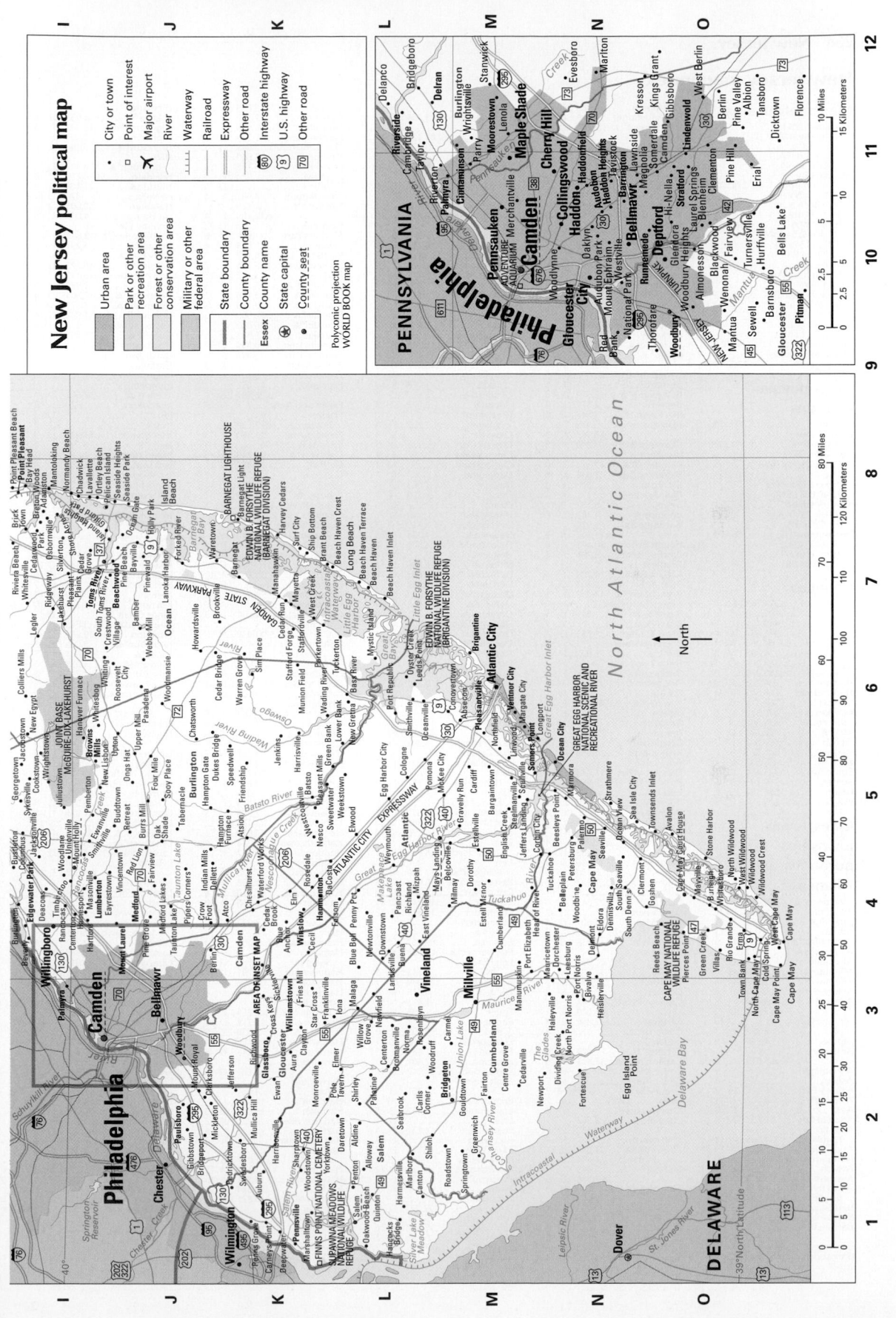

New Jersey map index

Metropolitan areas

Allentown (PA)-Bethlehem (PA)-Easton (PA) ... 821,173 (712,481 in PA, 108,692 in NJ)
Atlantic City-Hammonton ... 274,549
New York (NY)-Northern New Jersey-Long Island (NY) ... 18,897,109 (12,368,525 in NY, 6,471,215 in NJ, 57,369 in PA)
Ocean City ... 97,265
Philadelphia (PA)-Camden-Wilmington (DE) ... 5,965,343 (4,008,994 in PA, 1,316,762 in NJ, 538,479 in DE, 101,108 in MD)
Trenton-Ewing ... 366,513
Vineland-Millville-Bridgeton ... 156,898

Metropolitan divisions

Camden ... 1,250,679
Edison-New Brunswick ... 2,340,249
New York (NY)-White Plains (NY)-Wayne ... 11,576,251 (9,535,643 in NY, 2,040,608 in NJ)
Newark-Union ... 2,147,727 (2,090,358 in NJ, 57,369 in PA)
Wilmington (DE) ... 705,670 (538,479 in DE, 101,108 in MD, 66,083 in NJ)

Counties

Atlantic ... 274,549 .. L 5
Bergen ... 905,116 .. C 8
Burlington ... 448,734 .. J 5
Camden ... 513,657 .. K 4
Cape May ... 97,265 .. N 4
Cumberland ... 156,898 .. M 3
Essex ... 783,969 .. D 7
Gloucester ... 288,288 .. K 3
Hudson ... 634,266 .. D 8
Hunterdon ... 128,349 .. F 4
Mercer ... 366,513 .. G 5
Middlesex ... 809,858 .. G 6
Monmouth ... 630,380 .. H 7
Morris ... 492,276 .. D 5
Ocean ... 576,567 .. J 7
Passaic ... 501,226 .. B 6
Salem ... 66,083 .. L 1
Somerset ... 323,444 .. F 5
Sussex ... 149,265 .. B 5
Union ... 536,499 .. E 6
Warren ... 108,692 .. D 3

Cities, towns, townships, boroughs, and villages

Aberdeen*▲ ... 18,210 .. F 7
Absecon ... 8,411 .. M 6
Adelphia ... H 7
Albion ... O 11
Alexandria*▲ ... 4,938 .. E 3
Allamuchy▲ ... 4,323 .. C 4
Allendale ... 6,505 .. C 7
Allenhurst ... 496 .. H 8
Allentown ... 1,828 .. H 5
Allenwood† ... 925 .. H 8
Alloway† ... 1,402 ▲3,467 .. L 2
Almonesson ... O 10
Alpha ... 2,369 .. E 3
Alpine ... 1,849 .. C 8
Andover ... 606 ▲6,319 .. C 5
Annandale† ... 1,695 .. E 4
Asbury ... E 3
Asbury Park ... 16,116 .. H 8
Ashland*† ... 8,302 .. N 11
Atco ... K 4
Atlantic City ... 39,558 .. M 6
Atlantic Highlands ... 4,385 .. H 11
Audubon ... 8,819 .. N 10
Audubon Park ... 1,023 .. N 10
Avalon ... 1,334 .. O 5
Avenel† ... 17,011 .. F 7
Avon-by-the-Sea ... 1,901 .. H 8
Baptistown ... F 3
Bargaintown ... M 5
Barnegat† ... 2,817 ▲20,936 .. K 7
Barnegat Light ... 574 .. K 8
Barnsboro ... O 9
Barrington ... 6,983 .. N 11
Basking Ridge ... E 5
Bass River▲ ... 1,443 .. L 6
Bay Head ... 968 .. I 8
Bayonne ... 63,024 .. E 10
Bayville ... J 7
Beach Haven ... 1,170 .. L 7
Beach Haven West*† ... 3,896 .. K 7
Beachwood ... 11,045 .. J 7
Beattystown† ... 4,554 .. D 4
Bedminster▲ ... 8,165 .. E 5
Belford† ... 1,768 .. H 11
Belle Mead† ... 216 .. F 5
Belleplain† ... 597 .. N 4
Belleville▲ ... 35,926 .. C 10
Bellmawr ... 11,583 .. J 3
Belmar ... 5,794 .. H 8
Belvidere° ... 2,681 .. D 3
Bergenfield ... 26,764 .. A 12
Berkeley*▲ ... 41,255 .. I 7
Berkeley, see Holiday City [-Berkeley]
Berkeley Heights▲ ... 13,183 .. E 6
Berlin ... 7,588 ▲5,357 .. J 4
Bernards*▲ ... 26,652 .. E 5
Bernardsville ... 7,707 .. E 5
Bethlehem*▲ ... 3,979 .. E 3
Beverly ... 2,577 .. I 4
Blackwood† ... 4,545 .. O 10
Blairstown† ... 515 ▲5,967 .. C 3
Blawenburg† ... 280 .. F 5
Blenheim ... O 10
Bloomfield▲ ... 47,315 .. C 10
Bloomingdale ... 7,656 .. C 6
Bloomsbury ... 870 .. E 3
Blue Anchor ... K 4
Bogota ... 8,187 .. B 11
Boonton▲ ... 4,263 .. C 6
Bordentown*† ... 3,924 ▲11,367 .. H 5
Bound Brook ... 10,402 .. F 6
Bradley Beach ... 4,298 .. H 8
Bradley Gardens† ... 14,206 .. F 5
Brainards† ... 202 .. D 3
Branchburg*▲ ... 14,459 .. F 5
Branchburg Park ... F 5
Branchville ... 841 .. B 5
Brant Beach ... K 7
Brass Castle† ... 1,555 .. D 3
Breton Woods ... I 7
Brick*▲ ... 75,072 .. I 8
Brick Town ... I 7
Bridgeport ... J 2
Bridgeton° ... 25,349 .. M 2
Bridgewater*▲ ... 44,464 .. E 5
Brielle ... 4,774 .. H 8
Brigantine ... 9,450 .. M 6
Broadway ... E 3
Brookdale*† ... 9,239 .. B 10
Brooklawn* ... 1,955 .. J 3
Brookside ... D 5
Browns Mills† ... 11,223 .. I 5
Budd Lake† ... 8,968 .. D 5
Buena ... 4,603 .. L 4
Buena Vista*▲ ... 7,570 .. L 4
Bunnvale ... E 4
Burleigh† ... 725 .. O 4
Burlington ... 9,920 ▲22,594 .. I 4
Butler ... 7,539 .. C 6
Buttzville† ... 146 .. D 3
Byram*▲ ... 8,350 .. C 5
Caldwell† ... 7,822 .. D 7
Califon ... 1,076 .. E 4
Camden° ... 77,344 .. I 3
Candlewood* ... H 7
Cape May ... 3,607 .. O 4
Cape May Court House†° ... 5,338 .. O 4
Cape May Point ... 291 .. O 3
Cardiff ... M 5
Carlstadt ... 6,127 .. B 11
Carmel ... M 3
Carneys Point† ... 7,382 ▲8,049 .. K 1
Carteret ... 22,844 .. E 7
Cedar Brook ... K 4
Cedar Glen Lakes*† ... 1,421 .. I 6
Cedar Grove▲ ... 12,411 .. B 9
Cedar Knolls ... D 6
Cedar Run ... K 7
Cedarville† ... 776 .. M 2
Cedarwood Park ... I 7
Changewater ... E 4
Chatham ... 8,962 ▲10,452 .. E 6
Chatsworth ... J 5
Cherry Hill▲ ... 71,045 .. N 11
Chesilhurst ... 1,634 .. K 4
Chester† ... 1,649 ▲7,838 .. D 5
Chesterfield▲ ... 7,699 .. H 5
Cinnaminson▲ ... 15,569 .. M 11
Clark▲ ... 14,756 .. E 7
Clarksboro ... J 2
Clarksburg ... H 6
Clayton ... 8,179 .. K 3
Clementon ... 5,000 .. O 11
Clermont ... N 4
Cliffside Park ... 23,594 .. C 12
Cliffwood ... G 10
Clifton ... 84,136 .. B 10
Clinton*▲ ... 13,478 .. E 4
Clinton ... 2,719 .. E 4
Closter ... 8,373 .. C 8
Clover Hill* ... G 7
Cold Spring ... O 4
Collings Lakes*† ... 1,706 .. L 4
Collingswood ... 13,926 .. N 10
Cologne ... L 5
Colonia† ... 17,795 .. E 7
Colts Neck▲ ... 10,142 .. G 7
Columbia† ... 229 .. C 3
Columbus ... I 5
Commercial*▲ ... 5,178 .. N 3
Concordia*† ... 3,092 .. G 6
Conovertown ... M 6
Convent Station ... D 6
Cookstown ... I 5
Corbin City ... 492 .. M 4
Country Lake Estates*† ... 3,943 .. J 6
Cranbury† ... 2,181 ▲3,857 .. G 6
Crandon Lakes*† ... 1,178 .. B 4
Cranford▲ ... 22,625 .. E 7
Cresskill ... 8,573 .. C 8
Crestwood Village† ... 7,907 .. I 6
Cross Keys ... K 3
Crosswicks ... H 5
Culvers Lake ... B 4
Cumberland ... M 4
Darlington ... B 7
Dayton† ... 7,063 .. G 6
Deal ... 750 .. H 8
Deans ... G 6
Deepwater ... K 1
Deerfield*▲ ... 3,119 .. M 3
Delanco▲ ... 4,283 .. L 12
Delaware*▲ ... 4,563 .. G 4
Delmont ... N 4
Delran▲ ... 16,896 .. L 12
Demarest ... 4,881 .. C 8
Dennis*▲ ... 6,467 .. N 4
Dennisville ... N 4
Denville▲ ... 16,635 .. D 6
Deptford▲ ... 30,561 .. O 10
Dividing Creek ... N 3
Dorchester ... N 3
Dorothy ... M 4
Dover ... 18,157 .. D 5
Downe*▲ ... 1,585 .. N 3
Dumont ... 17,479 .. A 12
Dunellen ... 7,227 .. E 6
Dutch Neck ... G 5
Eagleswood*▲ ... 1,603 .. K 7
East Amwell*▲ ... 4,013 .. G 4
East Brunswick▲ ... 47,512 .. F 6
East Freehold† ... 4,894 .. G 7
East Greenwich*▲ ... 9,555 .. J 2
East Hanover*▲ ... 11,157 .. D 6
East Keansburg ... H 11
East Millstone† ... 579 .. F 5
East Newark ... 2,406 .. D 10
East Orange ... 64,270 .. C 10
East Rutherford ... 8,913 .. B 11
East Windsor*▲ ... 27,190 .. G 5
Eastampton*▲ ... 6,069 .. I 5
Eatontown ... 12,709 .. G 8
Echelon*† ... 10,743 .. O 11
Edgewater ... 11,513 .. B 12
Edgewater Park▲ ... 8,881 .. I 4
Edison▲ ... 99,967 .. F 6
Egg Harbor*▲ ... 43,323 .. M 5
Egg Harbor City ... 4,243 .. L 5
Elizabeth° ... 124,969 .. E 7
Elk*▲ ... 4,216 .. K 3
Ellisburg*† ... 4,413 .. N 11
Elmer ... 1,395 .. L 2
Elmwood Park ... 19,403 .. A 10
Elsinboro*▲ ... 1,036 .. L 1
Elwood ... 1,437 .. L 5
Emerson ... 7,401 .. A 11
Englewood ... 27,147 .. B 12
Englewood Cliffs ... 5,281 .. D 8
English Creek ... M 5
Englishtown ... 1,847 .. G 6
Erial ... O 11
Erma† ... 2,134 .. O 4
Espanong ... C 5
Essex Fells ... 2,113 .. D 7
Estell Manor ... 1,735 .. M 4
Evesboro ... N 12
Evesham*▲ ... 45,538 .. J 4
Ewan ... K 2
Ewanville ... I 5
Ewing▲ ... 35,790 .. G 4
Fair Haven ... 6,121 .. G 8
Fair Lawn ... 32,457 .. A 10
Fairfield*▲ ... 6,295 .. M 2
Fairfield*▲ ... 7,466 .. C 7
Fairton† ... 1,264 .. M 2
Fairview ... 13,835 .. C 12
Fanwood ... 7,318 .. E 6
Far Hills ... 919 .. E 5
Farmingdale ... 1,329 .. H 7
Fieldsboro ... 540 .. H 5
Finderne† ... 5,600 .. F 5
Finesville† ... 175 .. E 3
Flagtown ... F 5
Flanders ... D 5
Flemington° ... 4,581 .. F 4
Florence*† ... 4,426 ▲12,109 .. I 4
Florence ... O 12
Florham Park ... 11,696 .. D 6
Folsom ... 1,885 .. L 4
Fords† ... 15,187 .. F 7
Forked River† ... 5,244 .. J 7
Fort Lee ... 35,345 .. B 12
Frankford*▲ ... 5,565 .. B 5
Franklin*▲ ... 3,176 .. E 3
Franklin*▲ ... 3,195 .. F 3
Franklin*▲ ... 62,300 .. F 5
Franklin*▲ ... 16,820 .. L 3
Franklin ... 5,045 .. B 5
Franklin Lakes ... 10,590 .. C 7
Franklin Park† ... 13,295 .. F 5
Franklinville ... K 3
Fredon▲ ... 3,437 .. C 4
Freehold° ... 12,052 ▲36,184 .. G 7
Freewood Acres ... H 7
Frelinghuysen*▲ ... 2,230 .. C 4
Frenchtown ... 1,373 .. F 3
Fries Mill ... K 3
Galloway*▲ ... 37,349 .. M 6
Garfield ... 30,487 .. B 11
Garwood ... 4,266 .. E 7
Gibbsboro ... 2,274 .. O 11
Gibbstown† ... 3,739 .. J 2
Gilford Park ... I 7
Gillette ... E 6
Gladstone, see Peapack [and Gladstone]
Glassboro ... 18,579 .. K 3
Glen Gardner ... 1,704 .. E 4
Glen Ridge† ... 7,527 .. C 10
Glen Rock ... 11,601 .. A 10
Glendola ... H 8
Glendora† ... 4,750 .. O 10
Glenwood ... A 6
Gloucester*▲ ... 64,634 .. J 3
Gloucester City ... 11,456 .. N 10
Golden Triangle*† ... 4,145 .. N 11
Goshen ... N 4
Gouldtown ... M 2
Great Meadows† ... 303 .. D 4
Green*▲ ... 3,601 .. C 4
Green Bank ... K 5
Green Brook▲ ... 7,203 .. E 6
Green Creek ... O 4
Green Pond ... C 6
Green Village ... D 6
Greentree*† ... 11,367 .. N 7
Greenwich*† ... 2,755 ▲5,712 .. E 3
Greenwich*▲ ... 4,899 .. J 2
Greenwich▲ ... 804 .. M 2
Griggstown† ... 819 .. F 5
Groveville*† ... 2,945 .. H 5
Guttenberg ... 11,176 .. C 12
Hackensack° ... 43,010 .. B 11
Hackettstown ... 9,724 .. D 4
Haddon▲ ... 14,707 .. N 11
Haddon Heights ... 7,473 .. N 11
Haddonfield ... 11,593 .. N 11
Hainesport▲ ... 6,110 .. I 4
Haledon ... 8,318 .. A 10
Haleyville ... M 3
Hamburg ... 3,277 .. B 5
Hamilton*▲ ... 88,464 .. H 5
Hamilton*▲ ... 26,503 .. L 4
Hamilton Square† ... 12,784 .. H 5
Hammonton ... 14,791 .. K 4
Hampton*▲ ... 5,196 .. B 4
Hampton ... 1,401 .. E 3
Hancocks Bridge† ... 254 .. L 1
Hanover▲ ... 13,712 .. D 6
Harding*▲ ... 3,838 .. E 6
Hardwick▲ ... 1,696 .. C 4
Hardyston*▲ ... 8,213 .. B 5
Harmony† ... 441 ▲2,667 .. D 3
Harrington Park ... 4,664 .. A 12
Harrison*▲ ... 12,417 .. K 2
Harrison ... 13,620 .. D 10
Harrisonville ... K 2
Hartford ... I 4
Harvey Cedars ... 337 .. K 7
Hasbrouck Heights ... 11,842 .. B 11
Haworth ... 3,382 .. A 12
Hawthorne ... 18,791 .. A 10
Hazlet▲ ... 20,334 .. H 10
Heathcote*† ... 5,821 .. G 5
Hedding ... H 4
Heislerville ... N 3
Helmetta ... 2,178 .. G 6
Hewitt ... B 7
Hibernia ... C 6
High Bridge ... 3,648 .. E 4
Highland Lake*† ... 4,933 .. B 6
Highland Park ... 13,982 .. F 6
Highlands ... 5,005 .. H 12
Hightstown ... 5,494 .. G 6
Hillsborough*▲ ... 38,303 .. F 5
Hillsdale ... 10,219 .. C 8
Hillside▲ ... 21,404 .. D 9
Hi-Nella ... 870 .. O 11
Hoboken ... 50,005 .. D 11
Ho-Ho-Kus ... 4,078 .. C 8
Holiday City [-Berkeley]*† ... 12,831 .. J 7
Holland▲ ... 5,291 .. E 3
Holly Park ... J 7
Holmdel▲ ... 16,773 .. G 7
Hopatcong ... 15,147 .. C 5
Hope▲ ... 1,952 .. C 3
Hopewell*▲ ... 17,304 .. G 4
Hopewell*▲ ... 4,571 .. M 2
Hopewell ... 1,922 .. G 4
Hornerstown ... H 6
Howell*▲ ... 51,075 .. H 7
Huntington ... E 3
Hurdtown ... C 5
Hurffville ... O 10
Imlaystown ... H 6
Independence*▲ ... 5,662 .. D 4
Interlaken ... 820 .. H 8
Iona ... L 3
Ironia ... D 5
Irvington▲ ... 53,926 .. D 9
Iselin*† ... 18,695 .. E 7
Island Heights ... 1,673 .. I 7
Jackson*▲ ... 54,856 .. I 6
Jacobstown ... I 5
Jamesburg ... 5,915 .. G 6
Jefferson*▲ ... 21,314 .. C 5
Jersey City° ... 247,597 .. E 8
Johnsonburg† ... 101 .. C 4
Joint Base McGuire-Dix-Lakehurst ... I 6
Juliustown† ... 429 .. I 5
Keansburg ... 10,105 .. G 10
Kearny ... 40,684 .. C 10
Kendall Park*† ... 9,339 .. G 5
Kenilworth* ... 7,914 .. E 7
Kenvil† ... 3,009 .. D 5
Keyport ... 7,240 .. H 10
Kings Grant ... O 12
Kingwood▲ ... 3,845 .. F 3
Kinnelon ... 10,248 .. C 6
Knowlton*▲ ... 3,055 .. C 3
Lacey*▲ ... 27,644 .. J 7
Lafayette▲ ... 2,538 .. B 5
Lake Como ... 1,759 .. H 8
Lake Hiawatha ... D 6
Lake Mohawk† ... 9,916 .. C 5
Lake Telemark*† ... 1,255 .. C 6
Lakehurst ... 2,654 .. I 7
Lakewood† ... 53,805 ▲92,843 .. H 7
Lambertville ... 3,906 .. G 4
Landing ... D 5
Lanoka Harbor ... J 7
Laurel Springs ... 1,908 .. O 11
Laurence Harbor† ... 6,536 .. G 9
Lavallette ... 1,875 .. I 8
Lawnside ... 2,945 .. N 11
Lawrence*▲ ... 33,472 .. G 5
Lawrence*▲ ... 3,290 .. M 2
Lawrenceville† ... 3,887 .. G 5
Lebanon*† ... 1,358 ▲6,588 .. E 4
Ledgewood ... D 5
Leeds Point ... L 6
Leesburg ... N 3
Leisuretowne*† ... 3,582 .. K 5
Lenola, see Moorestown [-Lenola]
Leonardo† ... 2,757 .. H 11
Leonia ... 8,937 .. B 12
Liberty*▲ ... 2,942 .. D 4
Lincoln Park ... 10,521 .. C 7
Lincroft† ... 6,135 .. G 7
Linden ... 40,499 .. E 9
Lindenwold ... 17,613 .. O 11
Linwood ... 7,092 .. M 5
Little Egg Harbor*▲ ... 20,065 .. K 6
Little Falls▲ ... 14,432 .. B 9
Little Ferry ... 10,626 .. B 11
Little Silver ... 5,950 .. G 8
Livingston▲ ... 29,366 .. D 7
Loch Arbour ... 194 .. H 8
Locust ... G 8
Lodi ... 24,136 .. B 11
Logan*▲ ... 6,042 .. J 2
Long Beach*▲ ... 3,051 .. K 7
Long Branch ... 30,719 .. G 8
Long Hill*▲ ... 8,702 .. E 6
Long Valley† ... 1,879 .. D 4
Longport ... 895 .. M 6
Lopatcong*▲ ... 8,014 .. E 2
Lower*▲ ... 22,866 .. O 4
Lower Alloways Creek*▲ ... 1,770 .. L 1
Lower Bank ... L 5
Lumberton▲ ... 12,559 .. I 4
Lyndhurst▲ ... 20,554 .. C 10
Lyons ... E 5
Madison ... G 6
Madison ... 15,845 .. D 6

Madison Park*† ....7,144 ..F 6
Magnolia ....4,341 ..N 11
Mahwah▲ ....25,890 ..B 7
Malaga ....L 3
Manahawkin† ....2,303 ..K 7
Manalapan▲ ....38,872 ..G 6
Manasquan ....5,897 ..H 8
Manchester*▲ ..43,070 ..I 7
Mannington*▲ ..1,806 ..K 1
Mansfield*▲ ....7,725 ..D 4
Mansfield▲ ....8,544 ..H 5
Mantoloking ....296 ..I 8
Mantua▲ ....15,217 ..O 9
Manville ....10,344 ..F 5
Maple Shade▲ ....19,131 ..M 11
Maplewood▲ ..23,867 ..E 7
Marcella ....C 6
Margate City ....6,354 ..M 6
Marksboro† ....82 ..C 4
Marlboro▲ ....40,191 ..G 7
Marlton† ....10,133 ..N 12
Marmora ....N 5
Martinsville† ....11,980 ..E 5
Masonville ....I 4
Matawan ....8,810 ..H 9
Maurice River*▲ ....7,976 ..N 3
Mauricetown ....N 3
Mays Landing†○ ....2,135 ..M 5
Mayville ....O 4
Maywood ....9,555 ..A 11
McAfee ....B 6
McKee City ....M 5
Medford▲ ....23,033 ..J 4
Medford Lakes ....4,146 ..J 4
Mendham*† ....4,981 ▲5,869 ..D 5
Mercerville† ....13,230 ..H 5
Merchantville ....3,821 ..M 11
Metuchen ....13,574 ..F 6
Meyersville ....E 6
Mickleton ....J 2
Middle*▲ ....18,911 ..N 4
Middlebush† ....2,326 ..F 6
Middlesex ....13,635 ..F 6
Middletown▲ ..66,522 ..H 10
Midland Park ....7,128 ..C 7
Milford ....1,233 ..F 3
Millburn▲ ....20,149 ..E 7
Millhurst ....H 6
Millington ....E 6
Millstone*▲ ....10,566 ..H 6
Millstone ....418 ..F 5
Milltown ....6,893 ..F 6
Millville ....28,400 ..M 3
Milmay ....M 4
Mine Hill▲ ....3,651 ..D 5
Mizpah ....L 4
Monmouth Beach ....3,279 ..G 8
Monmouth Junction† ....2,887 ..G 5
Monroe*▲ ....39,132 ..G 6
Monroe*▲ ....36,129 ..K 3
Monroe ....B 5
Monroeville ....K 2
Montague▲ ....3,847 ..A 4
Montclair▲ ....37,669 ..C 9
Montgomery▲ ....22,254 ..F 4
Montvale ....7,844 ..C 8
Montville▲ ....21,528 ..C 6
Moonachie* ....2,708 ..D 7
Moorestown▲ ....20,726 ..M 11
Moorestown [-Lenola]† ....14,217 ..M 12
Morganville† ....5,040 ..G 7
Morris*▲ ....22,306 ..D 6
Morris Plains ....5,532 ..D 6
Morristown○ ....18,411 ..D 6
Mount Arlington ....5,050 ..C 5
Mount Bethel ....E 6
Mount Ephraim ....4,676 ..N 10
Mount Fern ....D 5
Mount Freedom ....D 5
Mount Hermon† ....141 ..C 3
Mount Holly○▲ ....9,536 ..I 4
Mount Hope ....C 5
Mount Laurel▲ ....41,864 ..J 4
Mount Olive▲ ....28,117 ..D 5
Mount Royal ....J 2
Mountain Lakes ....4,160 ..D 6
Mountainside ....6,685 ..E 6
Mullica*▲ ....6,147 ..L 5
Mullica Hill† ....3,982 ..K 2
Mystic Island† ....8,493 ..L 6
National Park ....3,036 ..N 9
Navesink† ....2,020 ..H 11
Neptune▲ ....27,935 ..H 8
Neptune City ....4,869 ..H 8
Nesco ....K 5
Neshanic Station ....F 5
Netcong ....3,232 ..D 5
New Bedford ....H 8
New Brunswick○ ..55,181 ..F 6
New Egypt† ....2,512 ..I 6
New Gretna ....L 6
New Hanover*▲ ....7,385 ..I 5
New Lisbon ....I 5
New Milford ....16,341 ..A 11
New Monmouth ....H 11
New Providence ..12,171 ..E 6
New Vernon ....D 6
New Village† ....421 ..E 3
Newark○ ....277,140 ..E 7
Newfield ....1,553 ..L 3
Newfoundland ....C 6
Newton○ ....7,997 ..C 4
Newtonville ....L 4
Norma ....L 3
North Arlington ....15,392 ..C 10
North Beach Haven*† ....2,235 ..L 7
North Bergen▲ ....60,773 ..C 12
North Branch ....E 5
North Brunswick▲ ....40,742 ..F 6
North Caldwell ....6,183 ..B 9
North Cape May† ....3,226 ..O 4
North Haledon ..8,417 ..A 10
North Hanover*▲ ....7,678 ..I 5
North Plainfield ....21,936 ..E 6
North Princeton ....G 5
North Wildwood ....4,041 ..O 4
Northfield ....8,624 ..M 5
Northvale ....4,640 ..C 8
Norwood ....5,711 ..C 8
Nutley▲ ....28,370 ..C 10
Oak Ridge ....C 6
Oak Valley*† ....3,483 ..O 9
Oakhurst† ....3,995 ..G 8
Oakland ....12,754 ..C 7
Oaklyn ....4,038 ..N 10
Oakwood Beach ....L 1
Ocean*▲ ....27,291 ..G 8
Ocean*▲ ....8,332 ..J 7
Ocean Acres*† ....16,142 ..J 6
Ocean Beach* ....I 8
Ocean City ....11,701 ..N 5
Ocean Gate ....2,011 ..J 7
Ocean Grove*† ..3,342 ..H 8
Ocean View ....N 5
Oceanport ....5,832 ..G 8
Oceanville ....L 6
Ogdensburg ....2,410 ..B 5
Old Bridge† ....23,753 ▲65,375 ..G 6
Old Tappan ....5,750 ..C 8
Oldmans*▲ ....1,773 ..K 1
Oldwick ....E 4
Oradell ....7,978 ..A 11
Orange▲ ....30,134 ..C 9
Oxford▲ ....2,514 ..D 3
Palisades Park ..19,622 ..B 12
Palmyra ....7,398 ..I 3
Paramus ....26,342 ..A 11
Park Ridge ....8,645 ..C 8
Parkertown ....K 7
Parsippany ....D 6
Parsippany-Troy Hills*▲ ....53,238 ..D 6
Passaic ....69,781 ..D 7
Paterson○ ....146,199 ..A 10
Pattenburg ....E 3
Paulsboro ....6,097 ..J 2
Peapack [and Gladstone] ....2,582 ..E 5
Pedricktown ....K 1
Pemberton ....1,409 ▲27,912 ..I 5
Pemberton Heights*† ....2,423 ..J 5
Pennington ....2,585 ..G 4
Penns Grove ....5,147 ..K 1
Penns Neck ....G 5
Pennsauken▲ ....35,885 ..M 10
Pennsville† ....11,888 ▲13,409 ..K 1
Penton ....L 1
Pequannock▲ ....15,540 ..C 7
Perrineville ....H 6
Perth Amboy ....50,814 ..F 7
Petersburg ....N 5
Phillipsburg ....14,950 ..E 2
Pilesgrove*▲ ....4,016 ..K 3
Pine Beach ....2,127 ..J 7
Pine Brook ....D 6
Pine Grove ....J 4
Pine Hill ....10,233 ..O 11
Pine Valley ....12 ..O 11
Pinewald ....J 7
Piscataway*▲ ....56,044 ..F 6
Pitman ....9,011 ..O 10
Pittsgrove*▲ ....9,393 ..L 3
Plainfield ....49,808 ..E 6
Plainsboro▲ ....22,999 ..G 5
Pleasantville ....20,249 ..M 6
Pluckemin ....E 5
Plumsted*▲ ....8,421 ..I 6
Pohatcong*▲ ....3,339 ..E 3
Point Pleasant ..18,392 ..I 8
Point Pleasant Beach ....4,665 ..I 8
Pomona† ....7,124 ..L 5
Pompton Lakes ....11,097 ..C 7
Pompton Plains ....C 7
Port Colden† ....122 ..D 4
Port Elizabeth ....M 3
Port Monmouth† ..3,818 ..H 11
Port Morris ....C 5
Port Murray† ....129 ..D 4
Port Norris† ....1,377 ..N 3
Port Reading† ..3,728 ..F 9
Port Republic ....1,115 ..L 6
Pottersville ....E 5
Presidential Lakes Estates*† ....2,365 ..J 6
Princeton ....12,307 ▲16,265 ..G 5
Princeton Junction† ....2,465 ..G 5
Princeton Meadows*† ..13,834 ..G 5
Prospect Park ....5,865 ..A 10
Quakertown ....F 4
Quinton† ....588 ▲2,666 ..L 1
Rahway ....27,346 ..E 7
Ramblewood*† ....5,907 ..J 4
Ramsey ....14,473 ..C 7
Ramtown*† ....6,242 ..H 7
Rancocas ....I 4
Randolph*▲ ....25,734 ..D 5
Raritan*▲ ....22,185 ..F 4
Raritan ....6,881 ..F 5
Readington▲ ..16,126 ..F 5
Reaville ....F 4
Red Bank ....12,206 ..G 8
Red Bank ....N 9
Richland ....L 4
Richwood† ....3,459 ..K 3
Ridgefield ....11,032 ..B 12
Ridgefield Park ....12,729 ..B 11
Ridgeway ....I 7
Ridgewood ....24,958 ..A 10
Riegelsville ....E 2
Ringoes ....F 4
Ringwood ....12,228 ..B 7
Rio Grande† ....2,670 ..O 4
River Edge ....11,340 ..A 11
River Vale▲ ....9,659 ..C 8
Riverdale ....3,559 ..C 7
Riverside▲ ....8,079 ..L 11
Riverton ....2,779 ..M 11
Riviera Beach ....I 7
Robbinsville▲ ..13,642 ..H 5
Robertsville† ....11,297 ..G 7
Rochelle Park▲ ....5,530 ..A 11
Rockaway*† ....6,438 ▲24,156 ..C 6
Rockleigh ....531 ..C 8
Rocky Hill ....682 ..G 5
Roebling† ....3,715 ..H 4
Roosevelt ....882 ..H 6
Roseland ....5,819 ..D 7
Roselle ....21,085 ..E 9
Roselle Park ....13,297 ..E 9
Rosenhayn† ....1,098 ..L 3
Rossmoor*† ....2,666 ..G 6
Roxbury*▲ ....23,324 ..D 5
Rumson ....7,122 ..G 8
Runnemede ....8,468 ..N 10
Rutherford ....18,061 ..B 10
Saddle Brook▲ ....13,659 ..A 11
Saddle River ....3,152 ..C 8
Salem○ ....5,146 ..L 1
Sandyston*▲ ....1,998 ..B 4
Sayreville ....42,704 ..F 6
Schooleys Mountain ....D 4
Scotch Plains▲ ....23,510 ..E 6
Scullville ....M 5
Sea Bright ....1,412 ..G 8
Sea Girt ....1,828 ..H 8
Sea Isle City ....2,114 ..N 5
Seabrook ....L 2
Seabrook Farms*† ....1,484 ..L 2
Seaside Heights ....2,887 ..J 8
Seaside Park ....1,579 ..J 8
Secaucus ....16,264 ..C 11
Sergeantsville ....F 4
Sewaren† ....2,756 ..F 9
Sewell ....O 10
Shamong*▲ ....6,490 ..J 4
Shiloh ....516 ..L 2
Ship Bottom ....1,156 ..K 7
Shore Acres ....I 8
Short Hills† ....13,165 ..E 7
Shrewsbury▲ ....1,141 ..G 8
Sicklerville ....K 3
Singac*† ....3,618 ..B 9
Smithville† ....7,242 ..L 6
Somerdale ....5,151 ..O 11
Somers Point ....10,795 ..M 4
Somerset*† ....22,083 ..F 6
Somerville○ ....12,098 ..F 5
South Amboy ....8,631 ..F 7
South Bound Brook ....4,563 ..F 6
South Branch ....F 5
South Brunswick▲ ....43,417 ..G 6
South Dennis ....N 4
South Hackensack*▲ ....2,378 ..D 7
South Harrison*▲ ....3,162 ..K 2
South Orange▲ ....16,198 ..D 9
South Plainfield ....23,385 ..E 6
South River ....16,008 ..F 6
South Seaville ....N 4
South Toms River ....3,684 ..I 7
Southampton*▲ ....10,464 ..J 4
Southard ....H 7
Sparta▲ ....19,722 ..C 5
Spotswood ....8,257 ..G 6
Spring Lake ....2,993 ..H 8
Spring Lake Heights ....4,713 ..H 8
Springdale*† ....14,518 ..N 11
Springfield*▲ ....3,414 ..I 5
Springfield▲ ....15,817 ..E 7
Stafford*▲ ....26,535 ..K 7
Stanhope ....3,610 ..C 5
Stanton ....F 4
Steelmanville ....M 5
Stevens ....H 4
Stewartsville† ....349 ..E 3
Stillwater▲ ....4,099 ..C 4
Stirling ....E 6
Stockholm ....B 6
Stockton ....538 ..F 3
Stone Harbor ....866 ..O 4
Stow Creek*▲ ....1,431 ..M 1
Stratford ....7,040 ..O 11
Strathmore*† ....7,258 ..F 7
Succasunna† ....9,152 ..D 5
Summit ....21,457 ..E 6
Surf City ....1,205 ..K 7
Sussex ....2,130 ..B 5
Swedesboro ....2,584 ..K 2
Tabernacle▲ ....6,949 ..J 5
Tansboro ....O 12
Tavistock ....5 ..N 11
Taylortown ....C 6
Teaneck▲ ....39,776 ..B 12
Tenafly ....14,488 ..C 8
Teterboro* ....67 ..D 8
Tewksbury*▲ ....5,993 ..E 4
Thorofare ....O 9
Three Bridges ....F 4
Tinton Falls ....17,892 ..G 8
Titusville ....G 4
Toms River†○ ....88,791 ▲91,239 ..I 7
Totowa ....10,804 ..A 10
Towaco ....C 6
Town Bank ....O 3
Trenton○ ....84,913 ..H 5
Troy Hills ....D 6
Tuckahoe ....N 4
Tuckerton ....3,347 ..L 6
Turnersville† ....3,742 ..O 10
Twin Rivers† ....7,443 ..G 6
Union▲ ....5,908 ..E 4
Union▲ ....56,642 ..D 9
Union Beach ....6,245 ..G 10
Union City ....66,455 ..C 11
Uniontown ....E 3
Upper*▲ ....12,373 ..N 5
Upper Deerfield*▲ ..7,660 ..L 2
Upper Freehold*▲ ..6,902 ..H 6
Upper Montclair*† ..11,565 ..B 11
Upper Pittsgrove*▲ ..3,505 ..K 2
Upper Saddle River ....8,208 ..B 8
Ventnor City ....10,650 ..M 6
Vernon▲ ....23,943 ..B 6
Vernon Valley*† ....1,626 ..A 6
Verona▲ ....13,332 ..B 9
Victory Gardens ....1,520 ..D 5
Vienna† ....981 ..D 4
Villas† ....9,483 ..O 4
Vincentown ....J 4
Vineland ....60,724 ..L 3
Vista Center*† ....2,095 ..H 7
Voorhees*▲ ....29,131 ..J 4
Waldwick ....9,625 ..C 7
Wall▲ ....26,164 ..H 8
Wallington ....11,335 ..B 10
Walpack*▲ ....16 ..B 4
Wanamassa† ....4,532 ..H 8
Wanaque ....11,116 ..C 7
Wantage*▲ ....11,358 ..B 5
Waretown† ....1,569 ..J 7
Warren*▲ ....15,311 ..E 6
Washington▲ ....9,102 ..C 8
Washington† ....6,461 ▲6,651 ..D 3
Washington*▲ ..18,533 ..D 4
Washington*▲ ..9,102 ..H 5
Washington*▲ ..48,559 ..K 3
Washington*▲ ....687 ..L 6
Washington Crossing ....G 4
Washington Valley ....D 6
Watchung ....5,801 ..E 6
Waterford*▲ ..10,649 ..K 4
Waterford Works ....K 4
Wayne▲ ....54,717 ..C 7
Weehawken▲ ....12,554 ..C 11
Wenonah ....2,278 ..O 10
West Amwell*▲ ....3,840 ..G 4
West Belmar† ....2,493 ..H 8
West Caldwell*▲ ..10,759 ..D 7
West Cape May ....1,024 ..O 4
West Creek ....K 7
West Deptford*▲ ..21,677 ..J 3
West Freehold† ....13,613 ..H 6
West Keansburg ....G 10
West Long Branch ....8,097 ..G 8
West Milford▲ ....25,850 ..B 6
West New York ....49,708 ..C 12
West Orange▲ ....46,207 ..C 9
West Wildwood ....603 ..O 4
West Windsor*▲ ..27,165 ..G 5
Westampton*▲ ....8,813 ..I 4
Westfield ....30,316 ..E 6
Westville ....4,288 ..N 10
Westwood ....10,908 ..C 8
Weymouth▲ ....2,715 ..L 4
Wharton ....6,522 ..D 5
Whippany ....D 6
White*▲ ....4,882 ..D 3
White Horse† ....9,494 ..H 5
White House Station† ....2,089 ..E 4
White Meadow Lake*† ....8,836 ..C 6
Whitesboro† ....2,205 ..O 4
Whiting ....I 6
Whittingham*† ..2,476 ..G 6
Wickatunk ....G 7
Wildwood ....5,325 ..O 4
Wildwood Crest ....3,270 ..O 4
Williamstown† ..15,567 ..K 3
Willingboro▲ ..31,629 ..I 4
Windsor ....H 5
Winfield*▲ ....1,471 ..E 7
Winslow▲ ....39,499 ..K 4
Wood-Ridge ....7,626 ..B 11
Woodbine ....2,472 ..N 4
Woodbridge† ....19,265 ▲99,585 ..F 7
Woodbury○ ....10,174 ..O 9
Woodbury Heights ....3,055 ..O 10
Woodcliff Lake ....5,730 ..C 8
Woodland*▲ ....1,788 ..J 6
Woodland Park ....11,819 ..B 10
Woodlynne ....2,978 ..N 10
Woodport ....C 5
Woods Tavern ....E 5
Woodstown ....3,505 ..K 2
Woolwich*▲ ....10,200 ..K 2
Wrightstown ....802 ..I 5
Wyckoff▲ ....16,696 ..C 7
Yardville† ....7,186 ..H 5
Yorketown*† ....6,535 ..G 6

*Does not appear on map; key shows general location.
†Census designated place—unincorporated, but recognized as a significant settled community by the U.S. Census Bureau.
▲Entire township, including rural area.

○County seat.
Places without population figures are unincorporated areas.
Source: 2010 census.

New Jersey is one of the great coastal playgrounds of the United States. Every year, millions of vacationers flock to the state's seaside resorts. They swim in the Atlantic Ocean, sunbathe on sandy beaches, and stroll along boardwalks lined with shops and museums.

Outdoors enthusiasts enjoy many options in New Jersey. They can catch game fish in the ocean or cast for trout in stocked streams. Hunters shoot ducks in coastal areas, and deer, pheasants, and rabbits on inland shooting grounds. Many areas are popular for camping, hiking, and bird watching. Sailing is popular in the coastal bays. The state also has fine ski areas and golf courses.

Many cultural festivals and historical celebrations are held in the state each year. One popular event is the reenactment of George Washington's crossing of the Delaware River, held every Christmas Day at Titusville.

Vincent Abbatiello, Rutgers University

Barnegat Lighthouse near Barnegat Light on Long Beach

Places to visit

Following are brief descriptions of some of New Jersey's many interesting places to visit:

Adventure Aquarium, in Camden, has exhibits featuring penguins, sharks, tropical fish, and many other marine animals.

Barnegat Lighthouse, near Barnegat Light, is a favorite subject of painters and photographers. The lighthouse is part of a state park that also includes a museum and a sandy beach.

Delaware Water Gap is a deep narrow gorge formed where the Delaware River cuts through the Kittatinny Mountains. This scenic gap separates New Jersey and Pennsylvania north of Columbia, New Jersey, and forms part of the Delaware Water Gap National Recreation Area.

Princeton is the home of Princeton University and Princeton Battlefield, the site of an important colonial victory in the American Revolution. The university's Nassau Hall served as the U.S. Capitol in 1783.

Seaside resorts include Cape May, Ocean City, Seaside Heights, and the Wildwoods. Atlantic City's boardwalk was the first built in the United States. In addition, the resort has a convention center for major events. Many visitors are attracted by Atlantic City's gambling casinos. Cape May, the oldest resort in the United States, has hundreds of Victorian buildings.

Trenton has many points of interest, including the New Jersey State Museum, the State Capitol, and the Old Barracks, used by British soldiers during the French and Indian wars (1689-1763) and by the Hessians at the Battle of Trenton (1776).

Waterloo Village, in Stanhope, is a restored village of the 1700's. The village includes a grist mill, blacksmith shops, and many furnished homes.

National park and historic site. Morristown National Historical Park, established in 1933, lies in and near Morristown. It includes Ford Mansion, George Washington's headquarters during the winter of 1779-1780; Fort Nonsense, a restoration of a fort built in 1777; and several camps used by American soldiers during the American Revolution. See **National Park System** (table: National historical parks). The Edison National Historic Site in West Orange includes Thomas A. Edison's home, laboratories, library, and models of his inventions.

State parks and forests. New Jersey has dozens of state forests, parks, marinas, and recreation areas. Liberty State Park, near the Statue of Liberty and Ellis Island, offers an excellent view of New York City's skyline. The park also has a science museum with interactive exhibits. For information on state parks, visit the New Jersey Department of Environmental Protection website at http://www.state.nj.us/dep/parksandforests.

Grass-covered dunes at
Island Beach State Park

G. Ahrens, H. Armstrong Roberts

Old Barracks Association

The Old Barracks in Trenton

© Pat Conklin

Blacksmith at Waterloo Village

G. Ahrens, H. Armstrong Roberts

Ford Mansion at Morristown National Historical Park

Land and climate

Land regions. New Jersey has four main land regions. They are, from northwest to southeast: (1) the Appalachian Ridge and Valley Region, (2) the New England Upland, (3) the Piedmont, and (4) the Atlantic Coastal Plain.

The Appalachian Ridge and Valley Region is a mountainous area in the northwestern corner of the state. It is part of a large region of the same name that runs from New York to Alabama. In New Jersey, it includes the Kittatinny Mountains and several valleys. The Kittatinny Mountains run parallel to New Jersey's northwestern border. The Delaware Water Gap, which is formed where the Delaware River cuts through the mountains, is one of the most scenic areas in the East. The Appalachian Valley lies southeast of the Kittatinny Mountains. This wide valley is part of the larger Great Valley. Shale and limestone formations lie in various parts of the Appalachian Valley. Herds of dairy cattle graze on grassy slopes in the valley, and farmers there raise apples and vegetables.

The New England Upland, usually called the *Highlands,* lies southeast of the Appalachian Ridge and Valley Region. The region extends into New York and Pennsylvania. Flat-topped ridges of hard rock, called *gneiss,* cover much of the New England Upland in New Jersey. Many lakes nestle among the ridges of the New England Upland in New Jersey. These lakes are among the state's most important tourist attractions.

The Piedmont crosses northern New Jersey in a belt 20 miles (32 kilometers) wide southeast of the New England Upland. The Piedmont covers an area from New York to Alabama. It covers only about a fifth of New Jersey, but about three-fifths of the state's people live there. The region includes such large industrial cities as Elizabeth, Jersey City, Newark, and Paterson. The cities of the Piedmont region owe much of their industrial importance to the many large rivers in the area. These rivers include the Hudson, the Passaic, the Ramapo, and the Raritan.

The Atlantic Coastal Plain is a gently-rolling lowland that covers the southern three-fifths of New Jersey. It is part of a plain with the same name that stretches from New York to Florida. In New Jersey, more than half the plain lies less than 100 feet (30 meters) above sea level. In the west and southwest, fertile soil supports many truck farms. Camden, Trenton, and other cities lie along the wide Delaware River in the western part of the plain. To the east, pine forests and salt marshes cover much of the Atlantic Coastal Plain. For this reason, large areas of the region are thinly populated. Salt marshes, shallow lagoons, and meadows lie near New Jersey's Atlantic coast. Over 50 resort cities and towns, including Atlantic City, Ocean City, and Cape May, lie on the eastern edge of the Atlantic Coastal Plain.

E. R. Degginger

A herd of dairy cattle grazes on a pasture in the Appalachian Ridge and Valley Region of northwestern New Jersey. This area includes the Kittatinny Mountains and several valleys.

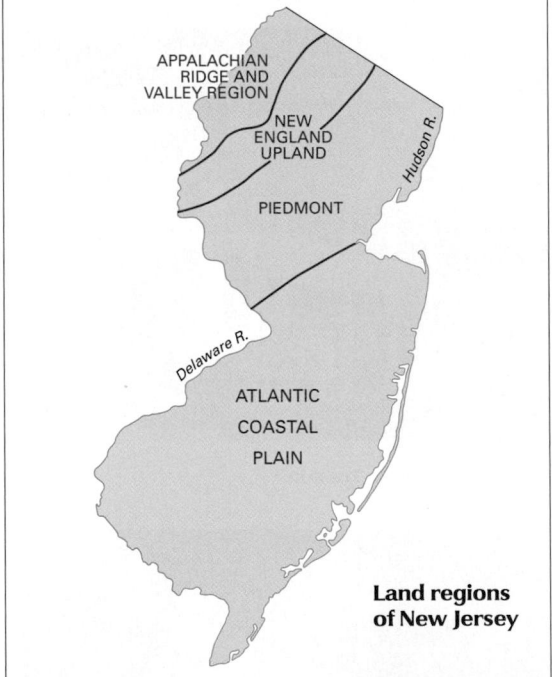

Land regions of New Jersey

WORLD BOOK map

Map index

New Jersey terrain map

Symbol	Description
National parkland boundary
Boundary
State capital
City or town
Elevation above sea level
Dam
Aqueduct

WORLD BOOK map

NEW YORK

High Point
1,803 ft (550 m)
Highest Point
in N.J.

DELAWARE WATER GAP
NATL. RECREATION AREA

Lake Wallenpaupack

Lehigh River

Pocono Mts.

Brodhead Cr.

Bush Kill

Tobyhanna Creek

Stroudsburg

Delaware Water Gap
280 ft (85 m)

Beltzville Lake

Lehigh River

Blue Mountain

Appalachian

Kittatinny Mountain

Delaware River

Culvers L.

Swartswood L.

Newton

Lake Mohawk

Paulins Kill

Jenny Jump Mtn.

Pequest R.

Pohatcong Cr.

Scotts Mtn.

Pohatcong Mtn.

Allamuchy Mtn.

Budd L.

Dover

Musconetcong Mtn.

Schooleys Mtn.

Sparta Mts.

Lake Hopatcong

Green Pond Mtn.

Green Pond

Bearfort Mtn.

Greenwood Lake

Monksville Res.

Wanaque Res.

Pompton Lakes

Ramapo Mts.

Ramapo R.

Lake Tappan

De Forest Lake

New Croton Res.

Kensico Res.

White Plains

The Palisades

Hudson River

Yonkers

Long Island Sound

Oradell Res.

Hackensack R.

Paterson

Clifton

Passaic

Union City

New York City

Harlem R.

Jersey City

Bayonne

Staten Island

Long Island

Lower New York Bay

Sandy Hook Bay

Sandy Hook

Keyport

Raritan Bay

Navesink

Shrewsbury R.

Red Bank

Eatontown

Long Branch

Asbury Park

Manasquan R.

Manasquan Inlet

Point Pleasant

Easton

Phillipsburg

Allentown

Bethlehem

Lehigh Valley

Musconetcong Mtn.

Spruce Run Reservoir

Round Valley Res.

Lamington R.

Morristown

Watchung Mts.

Passaic River

Elizabeth

Newark

Newark Bay

Rahway R.

Plainfield

Somerville

Woodbridge

Edison

Perth Amboy

PENNSYLVANIA

Lake Nockamixon

S. Branch

Raritan R.

New Brunswick

Raritan River

South R.

Piedmont

Green Lane Reservoir

Perkiomen Creek

Pottstown

Schuylkill R.

French Creek

West Chester

Doylestown

Neshaminy Creek

Norristown

Wissahickon Cr.

Sourland Mts.

Princeton

Carnegie Lake

Millstone R.

Delaware River

Trenton

Doctors Creek

Crosswick Cr.

Levittown

Pennypack Cr.

Burlington

Assiscunk Creek

Schuylkill R.

Philadelphia

Camden

Pennsauken

Cherry Hill

Bellmawr

Woodbury

Medford

Mt. Holly

Rancocas Cr.

Browns Mills

Metedeconk R.

Lakewood

Ridgeway Branch

Toms R.

Toms River

Cedar Creek

Silver Bay

Seaside Heights

Barnegat Bay

Barnegat Inlet

Atlantic Ocean

Chester

Darby Cr.

Chester Cr.

Brandywine Creek

Wilmington

Penns Grove

Mantua Cr.

Racoon Creek

Oldmans Cr.

Glassboro

Salem River

Pennsville

Salem

Chesapeake and Delaware Canal

Alloway Cr.

Cohansey Cr.

Smyrna

Leipsic R.

DELAWARE

Dover

St. Jones R.

Ben Davis Pt.

Egg Island Point

Deepwater Point

Christina R.

Vineland

Union Lake

Maurice R.

Bridgeton

Millville

Manantico Cr.

Mantico Cr.

Maumuskin Cr.

The Glades

East Pt.

Delaware Bay

Delaware River

Cape May

Hammonton

Makepeace Lake

Mullica River

Batsto R.

Wading R.

Mullica

Oswego R.

Great Egg Harbor R.

Pine Barrens

Coastal Plain

Barnegat

Forked R.

Little Egg Harbor

Beach Haven Inlet

Tucker I.

Little Egg Inlet

Great Bay

Little Bay

Reeds Bay

Absecon Bay

Pleasantville

Absecon Inlet

Atlantic City

Tuckahoe R.

Woodbine

Great Egg Inlet

Ocean City

Great Egg Bay

Corson Inlet

Ludlam Bay

Great Sound

Townsend Inlet

Hereford Inlet

Wildwood

Cape May

Cape May

North Latitude 39°30'

North

West Longitude

Coastline. A long, narrow sandbar makes up most of New Jersey's 130-mile (209-kilometer) coastline. Many inlets break the coast and lead to bays between the sandbar and the mainland. New Jersey's coastal bays include, from south to north, Great Egg Bay, Great Bay, Little Egg Harbor, Barnegat Bay, Sandy Hook Bay, Raritan Bay, and Newark Bay.

Mountains. New Jersey's most mountainous area is in the northwest. High Point, the state's highest peak, has an elevation of 1,803 feet (550 meters). It is in the Kittatinny Mountains in the Appalachian Ridge and Valley Region. The New Jersey Highlands, in the New England Upland Region, has mountains averaging more than 1,000 feet (305 meters). Other ranges in New Jersey include the Sourland and Watchung mountains, which generally rise about 450 feet (137 meters) in the Piedmont Region.

Rivers and lakes. New Jersey's most important rivers are the Delaware and the Hudson. The Delaware forms the state's western border and empties into Delaware Bay. The Hudson separates New Jersey and New York in the northeast and flows into the Atlantic Ocean. The Raritan is the longest river entirely within New Jersey. It flows about 75 miles (121 kilometers) through the north. Other important rivers in the north include the Hackensack, Millstone, Musconetcong, and Passaic. Southern New Jersey rivers include the Great Egg Harbor, Maurice, Mullica, and Toms.

New Jersey has more than 800 lakes and ponds, mostly in the north. Lake Hopatcong is the state's largest lake. Other large lakes include Budd Lake, Culvers Lake, Green Pond, Greenwood Lake (partly in New York), Lake Mohawk, and Swartswood Lake.

Plant and animal life. Forests cover about two-fifths of New Jersey. Beech, birch, maple, oak, sweet gums, yellow-poplar, and other hardwoods are the most valuable trees in the northern part of the state. Important trees of southern New Jersey include cedar, pitch pine, and short-leaf pine. The purple violet, the state flower, grows in wooded areas throughout the state. Honeysuckle, goldenrod, and Queen Anne's lace grow in many areas. Other flowers found in New Jersey include azaleas, buttercups, mountain laurels, rhododendrons, and Virginia cowslips.

The state's animals include deer, foxes, minks, muskrats, opossums, otters, rabbits, raccoons, and skunks. Wild ducks and geese are found along the marshy

Average monthly weather

	Newark						Atlantic City				
	Temperatures				Days of rain or snow		Temperatures				Days of rain or snow
	°F		°C				°F		°C		
	High	Low	High	Low			High	Low	High	Low	
Jan.	38	24	3	–4	11	Jan.	41	23	5	–5	11
Feb.	41	27	5	–3	10	Feb.	44	25	7	–4	10
Mar.	50	34	10	1	11	Mar.	52	32	11	0	11
Apr.	61	44	16	7	11	Apr.	61	40	16	4	11
May	71	54	23	12	12	May	71	50	22	10	10
June	80	64	27	18	10	June	80	59	27	15	9
July	85	69	29	21	10	July	85	65	29	18	9
Aug.	83	68	28	20	10	Aug.	83	64	28	18	9
Sept.	76	60	24	16	9	Sept.	77	56	22	13	8
Oct.	65	48	18	9	8	Oct.	66	44	19	7	7
Nov.	54	39	13	2	10	Nov.	56	36	13	2	9
Dec.	43	30	6	–1	11	Dec.	46	27	8	–3	10

Average January temperatures

New Jersey has cold winters. Temperatures are coldest in the north and mildest in the southern tip of the state.

Average July temperatures

Breezes from the Atlantic Ocean cool the coast in summer. The southwestern part of the state has the hottest temperatures.

Average yearly precipitation

New Jersey has a fairly even amount of precipitation, but the north gets much more annual snowfall than the south.

WORLD BOOK maps

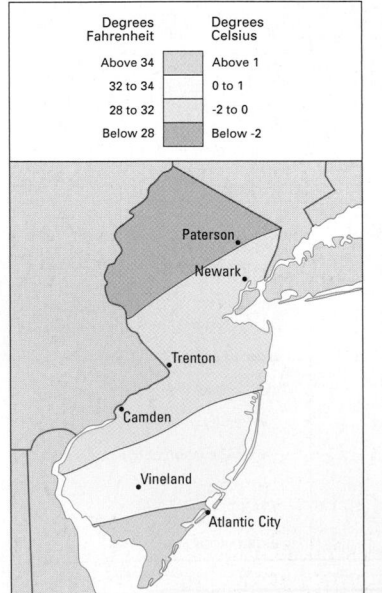

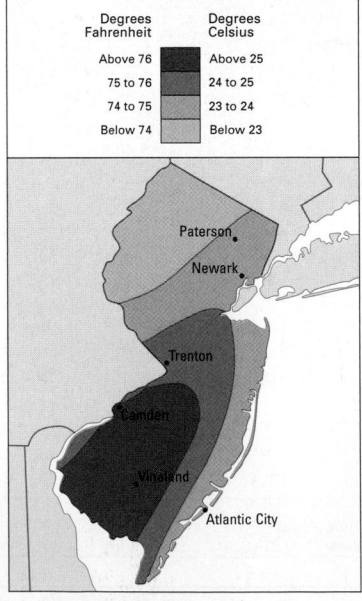

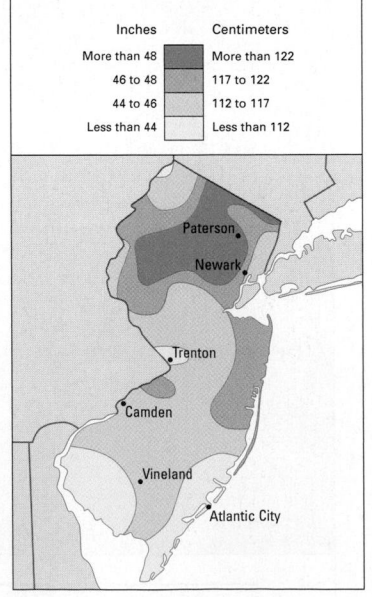

shores of the Atlantic Ocean. Game birds of the meadows and woodlands include partridges, pheasants, quail, ruffed grouse, and wild turkeys.

Clams, crabs, lobsters, menhaden, and oysters live in New Jersey's coastal waters. The state's bays and streams abound with bass, bluefish, crappies, pickerel, pike, salmon, shad, sturgeon, trout, and weakfish.

Climate. New Jersey has warm to hot summers and cold winters. Ocean breezes reduce summer temperatures and increase winter temperatures in a narrow strip along the eastern coast. Average July temperatures range from 76 °F (24 °C) in the southwest to 70 °F (21 °C) in the north. On July 10, 1936, Runyon had the state's highest temperature, 110 °F (43 °C). Average January temperatures range from 34 °F (1 °C) at Cape May to 26 °F (–3 °C) in the Appalachian Ridge and Valley Region. On Jan. 5, 1904, River Vale had the state's lowest temperature, –34 °F (–37 °C).

Snowfall averages about 13 inches (33 centimeters) a year in the south and 50 inches (127 centimeters) in the north. New Jersey averages about 45 inches (114 centimeters) of *precipitation* (rain, melted snow, and other forms of moisture) a year. Precipitation is fairly evenly distributed throughout the state.

E. R. Degginger

A salt marsh near Brigantine forms part of the Atlantic Coastal Plain region of New Jersey. This gently rolling lowland covers the southern three-fifths of the state.

Economy

Despite its small size, New Jersey ranks among the leading industrial states. Many of New Jersey's factories are in the northeastern part of the state. Service industries have become the pillar of the state's economy.

The 127-mile (204-kilometer) long, beach-lined Atlantic seaboard is the center of New Jersey's tourist trade. Tourist activities in the state account for tens of billions of dollars a year. New Jersey's proximity to New York City and Philadelphia helps the state's economy. These cities provide large markets for goods and services produced within New Jersey.

Natural resources of New Jersey include fertile soils and small deposits of minerals. Unlike many other states, New Jersey does not rely on its own resources for the raw materials of its industries.

Soil. Three types of soil are most common in New Jersey. In the north, the soil has a high limestone and glacial mineral content. Farmers in this region raise field crops and operate dairy farms. A subsoil of greensand marl, rich in phosphorus and potash, lies under loam in central New Jersey. This mixture yields good vegetable crops. When mixed with fertilizer, the sandy soil of the south supports fruit orchards and vegetable farms.

Minerals. Stone—especially granite and traprock—is New Jersey's most abundant mined resource. Northern and central New Jersey produce almost all the stone in the state. Sand and gravel are found throughout New Jersey. Counties in southern New Jersey produce sand and gravel for construction. Cumberland County produces a large amount of industrial sand for glassmaking and foundry work. Other mined resources include clay, greensand marl, and peat.

Service industries account for over five-sixths of both New Jersey's *gross domestic product*—the total value of all goods and services produced in the state in a year—and its employment. Most of New Jersey's service

industries are in the northeastern part of the state, near New York City.

Northern New Jersey is one of the nation's leading centers of commercial real estate. Prudential, one of the nation's largest life insurance companies, is headquartered in Newark. Northern New Jersey is also one of the country's leading centers for the wholesale trade of chemicals and machinery. The Port Newark/Elizabeth Marine Terminal is the leading container ship facility in the New York metropolitan area. The facility is run by the Port Authority of New York and New Jersey, and is among the busiest in the world. Most of New Jersey's hotels, restaurants, and retail trade establishments are in the northeastern part of the state.

Trenton, the state capital, is the center of government activities. Atlantic City has many casinos. One of the world's most famous private research complexes, Bell Laboratories, is in Murray Hill, near New Providence. Now part of Alcatel-Lucent, Bell Laboratories was formerly operated by AT&T Corp.

Manufacturing in New Jersey has declined since its heyday in the mid-1900's. But New Jersey still ranks among the leading states in manufacturing and processing. Many foreign manufacturers operate factories in New Jersey. Most of New Jersey's manufacturing is in the northeastern part of the state.

New Jersey is one of the leading states in chemical production, and chemicals rank as New Jersey's top manufactured product. *Pharmaceuticals* (medicinal drugs) are the most valuable types of chemicals made in the state. Such major pharmaceutical companies as Johnson & Johnson and Merck have their world headquarters in New Jersey. Sanofi-aventis, a major pharmaceutical manufacturer based in France, has its U.S. headquarters in Bridgewater. Shampoo, lotion, perfume, and other personal care products also make up an important

New Jersey economy

General economy

Gross domestic product (GDP)* (2008) $486,556,000,000
  Rank among U.S. states   7th
Unemployment rate (2010)   9.5% (U.S. avg: 9.6%)

*Gross domestic product is the total value of goods and services produced in a year.
Sources: U.S. Bureau of Economic Analysis and U.S. Bureau of Labor Statistics.

Production and workers by economic activities

Economic activities	Percent of GDP produced	Employed workers Number of people	Employed workers Percent of total
Finance, insurance, & real estate	29	687,600	13
Community, business, & personal services	23	1,801,700	35
Trade, restaurants, & hotels	16	1,103,300	21
Government	11	656,700	13
Manufacturing	8	313,600	6
Transportation & communication	7	316,500	6
Construction	4	258,600	5
Utilities	2	12,600	*
Agriculture	*	21,900	*
Mining	*	3,800	*
Total†	100	5,176,300	100

*Less than one-half of 1 percent.
†Figures may not add up to 100 percent due to rounding.
Figures are for 2008; employment figures include full- and part-time workers.
Source: *World Book* estimates based on data from U.S. Bureau of Economic Analysis.

Agriculture

Cash receipts $1,000,459,000
  Rank among U.S. states   39th
Distribution   87% crops, 13% livestock
Farms   10,300
Farm acres (hectares)   730,000 (300,000)
  Rank among U.S. states   45th
Farmland   15% of New Jersey

Leading products

1. Greenhouse and nursery products
2. Horses and mules   (ranks 2nd in the U.S.)
3. Blueberries   (ranks 3rd in the U.S.)
4. Tomatoes
5. Peaches   (ranks 3rd in the U.S.)
6. Green peppers
Other products: corn, cranberries, dairy products, eggs, soybeans, sweet corn.

Mining

Nonfuel mineral production* $345,000,000
  Rank among U.S. states   37th
Coal   †
Crude oil   †
Natural gas   †

*Partial total, excludes values that must be concealed to not disclose company data.
†No significant mining of this product in New Jersey.

Leading products

1. Sand and gravel
2. Traprock   (ranks 5th in the U.S.)
Other products: clays, granite, greensand marl, peat.

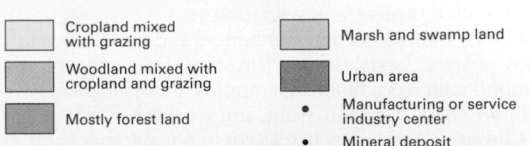

Cropland mixed with grazing	Marsh and swamp land
Woodland mixed with cropland and grazing	Urban area
Mostly forest land	• Manufacturing or service industry center
	• Mineral deposit

WORLD BOOK map

Economy of New Jersey

This map shows the economic uses of land in New Jersey and where the state's leading farm and mineral products are produced. Major manufacturing centers are shown in red.

Manufacturing

Value added by manufacture* $54,076,146,000
  Rank among U.S. states   13th

Leading products

1. Chemicals
2. Food and beverages
3. Petroleum and coal products
4. Computer and electronic products
5. Medical equipment
6. Fabricated metal products
Other products: machinery, nonmetallic minerals, plastics and rubber products, printed materials.

*Value added by manufacture is the increase in value of raw materials after they become finished products.

Figures are for 2008, except for the agricultural figures, which are for 2009.
Sources: U.S. Census Bureau, U.S. Department of Agriculture, U.S. Geological Survey.

continued on page 247

Fishing

Commercial catch	$168,653,000
Rank among U.S. states	8th

Leading catches

1. Scallops (ranks 2nd in U.S.)
2. Clams (ranks 2nd in U.S.)
3. Crabs

Other catches: finfish, flounder, goosefish, lobster, oyster, sea bass, squid, tuna.

Electric power

Nuclear	50.3%
Natural gas	32.5%
Coal	14.1%
Other	3.1%

Figures are for 2008.
Sources: U.S. Energy Information Administration and U.S. National Marine Fisheries Service.

part of the chemical industry of New Jersey.

Factories in northeastern New Jersey process a wide variety of foods, including bakery products, beverages, dairy products, meats, roasted coffee, and sugar and confectionery products. Food-processing plants in southwestern New Jersey process and can fruits and vegetables brought in from nearby orchards and *truck farms,* small farms that raise produce for market. Southwestern New Jersey also produces baked goods and sugar and confectionary products.

The state's main electronic manufacture is surveillance and navigation equipment. Large petroleum refineries operate in Linden and Paulsboro. Fabricated metal products and surgical supplies are manufactured in the northeastern part of the state, near New York City.

Agriculture. Farmland covers about one-sixth of New Jersey's land area. Greenhouse and nursery products are the most valuable source of agricultural income. New Jersey is an important state in the production of greenhouse and nursery products. These products are raised throughout New Jersey. Greenhouses raise chrysanthemums, geraniums, lilies, and poinsettias.

Milk is a valuable source of farm income in New Jersey. Dairy farms flourish in the northwestern part of the state, especially in Sussex and Warren counties. Burlington, Gloucester, and Salem counties in southern New Jersey also rank high in milk production. New Jersey ranks second to Kentucky in the raising of horses. Beef cattle and eggs are also leading livestock products.

New Jersey is also an important vegetable-growing state. The state is one of the nation's leading producers of bell peppers and spinach. Farmers also raise asparagus, cabbage, cucumbers, eggplant, lettuce, snap beans, squash, sweet corn, and tomatoes. The largest vegetable farms are in the southern half of the state.

Blueberries and peaches are the most valuable fruit crops grown in the state. New Jersey ranks among the leading states in the production of these fruits and of cranberries. Most of New Jersey's fruit orchards are in the southern half of the state.

Corn, hay, soybeans, and wheat New Jersey's chief field crops. Corn and hay are grown mainly in New Jersey's northwestern and southwestern counties. Soybeans and wheat are grown primarily in the southern third of the state.

Mining. The most important products mined in New Jersey are crushed stone and sand and gravel. The most valuable types of crushed stone quarried in New Jersey are granite and traprock, which come from the northern half of the state. Sand and gravel are mined throughout the state. The state's other mined products include clays, greensand marl, and peat. New Jersey is the only state to mine greensand marl.

Fishing industry. Scallops and clams are New Jersey's leading fish catches. New Jersey is a leading state in the catching of both scallops and clams. Huge clam beds extend from Barnegat Bay to Cape May. The fish catch also includes crab, finfish, flounder, goosefish, lobster, oysters, sea bass, squid, and tuna.

Cameramann International, Ltd., from Marilyn Gartman

Chemical plants, such as this one in Bayonne, operate throughout New Jersey. The production of chemicals is the state's leading manufacturing activity.

Nabisco Brands, Inc.

Cookies are inspected at a factory in Fair Lawn. Food processing ranks as one of New Jersey's leading manufacturing activities. New Jersey is an important food-processing state.

Cameramann International, Ltd. from Marilyn Gartman

The George Washington Bridge spans the Hudson River from Fort Lee to New York City. Thousands of commuters who live in New Jersey and work in New York City use it daily.

Electric power and utilities. Nuclear power plants provide about 50 percent of New Jersey's electric power. Plants that burn natural gas and coal-burning plants provide most of the remaining electric power.

Transportation. New Jersey lies between New York City and the western and southern states. This location makes its highways and railroads important links in the nation's transportation system. New Jersey is a leader in *containerization* (transporting goods by containers along a network of airplanes, ships, trains, and trucks).

Passenger trains connect many New Jersey cities with New York City and Philadelphia. These trains include swift commuter lines that carry thousands of New Jerseyites to jobs in these two large cities. A number of rail lines provide freight service in New Jersey.

In 1891, New Jersey became the first state to help local communities build roads. New Jersey now has an extensive system of roads and highways. The New Jersey Turnpike is 148 miles (238 kilometers) long. It runs between Deepwater in the southwest part of the state and Ridgefield Park in the northeast. The turnpike was opened in 1952 and was extended in 1956. It is 14 lanes wide in some areas, making it one of the widest highways in the United States. Hundreds of millions of vehicles travel the turnpike each year. The 173-mile (278-kilometer) Garden State Parkway crosses New Jersey between the New York state line near Montvale and Cape

May, at New Jersey's southern tip. The Garden State Parkway was completed in 1957.

Bridges and tunnels link New Jersey and neighboring states. The George Washington Bridge, one of the world's longest suspension bridges, spans the Hudson River between Fort Lee and New York City. The Bayonne Bridge, one of the longest steel arch bridges, crosses Kill Van Kull, a channel between Bayonne and Staten Island. Bridges across the Delaware River include the Benjamin Franklin Bridge between Camden and Philadelphia and the Delaware Memorial Bridge Twin Span between Deepwater and the New Castle, Delaware, area. The Holland and Lincoln auto tunnels and the PATH tubes—four rapid transit tunnels—link New Jersey and New York City, running beneath the Hudson River.

Newark Liberty International Airport is one of the country's busiest airports. It serves many passengers going to or from New York City as well as those headed to or from northeastern New Jersey. The first regular air passenger service in the United States began operating in 1919 between Atlantic City and New York City.

New Jersey has many important ports along the Hudson and Delaware rivers, in Newark and Raritan Bay, and along Kill Van Kull and Arthur Kill. New Jersey's part of the Atlantic Intracoastal Waterway extends for 118 miles (190 kilometers) from Manasquan Inlet to Cape May. This waterway is protected from the ocean by barrier beaches, and thus offers safe passage for small boats.

Communication. Numerous newspapers, many of them dailies, are published in New Jersey. The leading papers include the *Asbury Park Press* of Neptune, the *Courier-Post* of Cherry Hill, *The Press of Atlantic City, The Record* of Hackensack, *The Star-Ledger* of Newark, and *The Times* of Trenton. New York City and Philadelphia papers have wide circulation in New Jersey. The state's first weekly paper, the *New Jersey Gazette,* began publishing in Burlington in 1777. The first daily paper, the *Newark Daily Advertiser,* was founded in 1832.

New Jersey boasts many other "firsts" in communication. The first interstate long-distance telephone call was made from New Brunswick, New Jersey, to New York City in 1877. The first coast-to-coast direct dialing system was established in Englewood in 1951. Telstar 1, the first communications satellite to transmit live television across the Atlantic, was designed at New Jersey's Bell Laboratories. The satellite was launched in 1962.

Government

Constitution of New Jersey was adopted in 1947. New Jersey had two earlier constitutions, adopted in 1776 and 1844. Either house of the state Legislature may propose constitutional amendments. Amendments must be approved by three-fifths of the members of both houses, or by a majority vote of both houses in two successive years. To become law, amendments must also be approved by a majority of the voters in a general election. The Constitution does not provide for a constitutional convention that can amend the Constitution.

Executive. Historically, the governor was the only New Jersey executive official elected by the people. But in 2005 voters approved a constitutional amendment creating an office of lieutenant governor. The lieutenant

governor serves as governor if the governor dies, resigns, or is removed from office. Candidates for governor and lieutenant governor campaign as a team. The governor and lieutenant governor may serve any number of terms, but not more than two in succession. The state's first lieutenant governor took office in 2010.

The governor is responsible for appointing most of the high-level executive officials of New Jersey's government. These officials include the attorney general; secretary of state; state treasurer; and the commissioners of banking and insurance, personnel, community affairs, education, environmental protection, health and senior services, and labor. The state Board of Agriculture appoints the secretary of agriculture. Board members are recommended by an agricultural convention and appointed by the governor. All the governor's appointments must be approved by the state Senate. Most executive officials serve four-year terms.

Legislature of New Jersey consists of a 40-member Senate and an 80-member General Assembly. Voters in each of the state's 40 legislative districts elect one senator and two members of the Assembly. Senate terms are on 10-year cycles of two, four, and four years. Senators are elected to a two-year term in the election after each U.S. population census. The next two terms are each for four years. Members of the Assembly are elected to two-year terms. The New Jersey Legislature meets annually, beginning on the second Tuesday of January. Legislative sessions have no time limit.

Courts. New Jersey's highest court, the state Supreme Court, hears cases involving constitutional problems, capital punishment, and other major matters. The Supreme Court has a chief justice and six associate justices. The state Superior Court is New Jersey's chief trial court. It has three divisions—Appellate, Law, and Chancery. The governor, with the Senate's approval, appoints both the members of the Supreme and Superior courts to seven-year terms. If the governor reappoints them once, the judges may serve until they are 70 years old.

Lower courts include municipal courts, surrogate courts, and tax courts. The governor of New Jersey, with the Senate's approval, appoints all lower court judges except those of the single-municipal courts. Judges of single-municipal courts are appointed by local governments. New Jersey voters elect surrogate judges.

Local government. New Jersey is the only state in which county governments are called *boards of chosen freeholders.* This name comes from colonial days, when only *freeholders* (property owners) could hold public office. All 21 New Jersey counties have boards of from three to nine members. All freeholders in New Jersey's 21 counties are elected to three-year terms.

New Jersey has hundreds of cities, towns, townships, boroughs, and villages. Most have the mayor-council, commission, or council-manager form of government. Most of the large cities have the mayor-council form. Municipalities get their charters from the state. They choose from among a variety of charters. There are two ways a municipality can adopt a new charter or revise an existing one—either through direct petition, or by creating a charter study commission. Local voters must approve the new or revised charter.

Revenue. Taxes account for more than half of the state's *general revenue* (income). Most of the rest comes from federal grants, charges for government services, rents on leased property, casino fees, and a state lottery.

The state governors of New Jersey

	Party	Term		Party	Term
William Livingston	Federalist	1776-1790	David O. Watkins	Republican	1898-1899
William Paterson	Federalist	1790-1792	Foster M. Voorhees	Republican	1899-1902
Richard Howell	Federalist	1792-1801	Franklin Murphy	Republican	1902-1905
Joseph Bloomfield	Dem.-Rep.	1801-1802	Edward C. Stokes	Republican	1905-1908
John Lambert	Dem.-Rep.	1802-1803	John Franklin Fort	Republican	1908-1911
Joseph Bloomfield	Dem.-Rep.	1803-1812	Woodrow Wilson	Democratic	1911-1913
Aaron Ogden	Federalist	1812-1813	James E. Fielder	Democratic	1913
William S. Pennington	Dem.-Rep.	1813-1815	Leon R. Taylor	Democratic	1913-1914
Mahlon Dickerson	Dem.-Rep.	1815-1817	James E. Fielder	Democratic	1914-1917
Isaac H. Williamson	Dem.-Rep.	1817-1829	Walter E. Edge	Republican	1917-1919
Garret D. Wall	Democratic	1829 (declined)	William N. Runyon	Republican	1919-1920
			Clarence E. Case	Republican	1920
Peter D. Vroom	Democratic	1829-1832	Edward I. Edwards	Democratic	1920-1923
Samuel L. Southard	Whig	1832-1833	George S. Silzer	Democratic	1923-1926
Elias P. Seeley	Whig	1833	A. Harry Moore	Democratic	1926-1929
Peter D. Vroom	Democratic	1833-1836	Morgan F. Larson	Republican	1929-1932
Philemon Dickerson	Democratic	1836-1837	A. Harry Moore	Democratic	1932-1935
William Pennington	Whig	1837-1843	Clifford R. Powell	Republican	1935
Daniel Haines	Democratic	1843-1845	Horace G. Prall	Republican	1935
Charles C. Stratton	Whig	1845-1848	Harold G. Hoffman	Republican	1935-1938
Daniel Haines	Democratic	1848-1851	A. Harry Moore	Democratic	1938-1941
George F. Fort	Democratic	1851-1854	Charles Edison	Democratic	1941-1944
Rodman M. Price	Democratic	1854-1857	Walter E. Edge	Republican	1944-1947
William A. Newell	Republican	1857-1860	Alfred E. Driscoll	Republican	1947-1954
Charles S. Olden	Republican	1860-1863	Robert B. Meyner	Democratic	1954-1962
Joel Parker	Democratic	1863-1866	Richard J. Hughes	Democratic	1962-1970
Marcus L. Ward	Republican	1866-1869	William T. Cahill	Republican	1970-1974
Theodore F. Randolph	Democratic	1869-1872	Brendan T. Byrne	Democratic	1974-1982
Joel Parker	Democratic	1872-1875	Thomas H. Kean	Republican	1982-1990
Joseph D. Bedle	Democratic	1875-1878	James J. Florio	Democratic	1990-1994
George B. McClellan	Democratic	1878-1881	Christine Todd Whitman	Republican	1994-2001
George C. Ludlow	Democratic	1881-1884	Donald T. DiFrancesco	Republican	2001-2002
Leon Abbett	Democratic	1884-1887	John O. Bennett	Republican	2002
Robert S. Green	Democratic	1887-1890	Richard J. Codey	Democratic	2002
Leon Abbett	Democratic	1890-1893	James E. McGreevey	Democratic	2002-2004
George T. Werts	Democratic	1893-1896	Richard J. Codey	Democratic	2004-2006
John W. Griggs	Republican	1896-1898	Jon S. Corzine	Democratic	2006-2010
Foster M. Voorhees	Republican	1898	Christopher J. Christie	Republican	2010-

The chief sources of tax revenue are a personal income tax and a general sales tax. Other major sources are taxes on alcoholic beverages, corporate income, inheritance, insurance premiums, motor fuels, and tobacco products.

Politics. In the late 1800's, most New Jersey governors were Democrats. Since 1900, the office has been about equally divided between Democrats and Republicans. The Republicans had a majority in the state Senate and General Assembly during most of the early 1900's. But Democrats won increased support in state elections during the late 1950's and early 1960's. Since then, control of the houses of the legislature has passed between the Democrats and the Republicans several times.

Since 1856, New Jersey's electoral votes have been almost evenly split between Republican and Democratic presidential candidates. For New Jersey's electoral votes and voting record, see **Electoral College** (table).

History

Before European settlement, the Delaware Indians occupied the New Jersey area. They spoke an Algonquian dialect and called themselves Lenape, which means *the people* or *genuine people.* They inhabited small, scattered villages, where they lived by hunting, gathering, and farming. Trade began with the arrival of Europeans, and the Lenape traded furs for such items as beads and metal goods. See **Delaware Indians.**

Exploration. Giovanni da Verrazzano, an Italian navigator in the service of France, was probably the first European to explore the New Jersey coast. He reached the coast in 1524. Henry Hudson, an English sea captain employed by the Dutch East India Company, explored the Sandy Hook Bay area in 1609. He also sailed up the river that now bears his name.

Settlement. The Dutch and the Swedes were the first white settlers in New Jersey. The Dutch founded an outpost in Pavonia (now part of Jersey City) about 1630. Indian uprisings prevented permanent settlement until 1660. That year, the Dutch built the fortified town of Bergen (now part of Jersey City). Bergen was New Jersey's first permanent European settlement.

Sweden established Fort Christina in Delaware in 1638. Soon, traders and settlers crossed the Delaware River into neighboring New Jersey. The Dutch feared Swedish competition in the fur trade. The Dutch forced the Swedes out of the New Jersey area in 1655.

English control. English armies won control of New Jersey and other Dutch North American possessions in 1664. King Charles II of England gave the New Jersey area to his brother James, Duke of York. James, in turn, gave it to two of his friends, Lord John Berkeley and Sir George Carteret. James named the area *New Jersey* after Carteret's home island of Jersey, in the English Channel. Berkeley and Carteret offered to sell the land to colonists at low prices and allowed settlers to have political and religious freedom. These policies attracted settlers, who established such towns as Elizabeth, Middletown, Newark, Piscataway, Shrewsbury, and Woodbridge.

In 1674, a group of Quakers headed by Edward Byllynge bought Berkeley's share of New Jersey. Two years later, the colony was divided into two sections— West Jersey and East Jersey. Byllynge and his associates made West Jersey the first Quaker colony in America. Carteret owned East Jersey until his death in 1680. Another group of Quakers, called the Twenty-Four Proprietors, bought East Jersey in 1682.

New Jersey's political and religious freedom attracted a variety of groups. Puritans, Baptists, and Scotch-Irish arrived during the late 1600's. White settlers imported people from Africa to work as slaves. Increasing European settlement and disease wiped out much of the Lenape population, and the Indians were forced to sell their lands and move west. They moved first to western Pennsylvania, and eventually to the lands that are now Wisconsin and Oklahoma.

Rapid growth in the white population led to conflict among settlers over land ownership. The colonists also objected to paying rent to the owners. Many colonists rioted during the 1690's, and the owners gave up East and West Jersey in 1702. England then united the two colonies as a single royal colony.

Colonial days. New Jersey had twin capitals from 1703 to 1775. They were Perth Amboy, the former capital of East Jersey, and Burlington, the former capital of West Jersey. At first, the governor of New York also ruled New Jersey. But strong protests from the colonists forced England to give New Jersey its own governor in 1738. Lewis Morris, the first colonial governor, served from 1738 to 1746.

Colonial New Jersey was a rural society. By the 1760's, the colony had about 100,000 people. The English king appointed the colonial governor and a 12-member council. The people elected the colonial assembly, but only property owners could vote. In 1746, the Presbyterian Church founded the College of New Jersey (later Princeton University). Dutch Reformed clergy founded Queen's College (later Rutgers University) in 1766.

The American Revolution. During the 1760's, Britain passed a series of laws that caused unrest in New Jersey and the other American Colonies. Most of these laws either set up severe taxes or restricted colonial trade. Some New Jerseyites urged the colonists to remain loyal to Britain in spite of the laws. But many colonists believed that political and religious freedom could be retained only through independence from Britain.

In 1774, a group of New Jerseyites dressed as Indians burned a supply of British tea stored in a ship at Greenwich, near Salem. This event, called the Greenwich Tea Burning, was similar to the more famous Boston Tea Party of 1773. Like the Boston Tea Party, the action symbolized colonial opposition to British taxation policies. See **Boston Tea Party.**

The American Revolution began in Massachusetts in 1775. Large numbers of New Jerseyites joined the patriots in their fight for independence, and many other New Jerseyites fought on the British side. New Jersey's location between New York City and Philadelphia made it a major battleground during the war. The two sides fought nearly a hundred engagements in New Jersey. The most important ones included the battles of Trenton in 1776, Princeton in 1777, and Monmouth in 1778.

Detail of *Washington at Monmouth* (1857), an oil painting on canvas by Emanuel Leutze; Monmouth County Historical Association

George Washington led colonial forces in the Battle of Monmouth in 1778. The many important battles of the American Revolution fought in New Jersey gave it the nickname *Cockpit of the Revolution.*

Before the Battle of Trenton, George Washington made his famous surprise crossing of the Delaware River on Christmas night. During the war, Washington's army camped two winters at Morristown and a third at Bound Brook. See **Revolution, American** (The war in the North).

During the Revolutionary period, two New Jersey cities served as the temporary national capital. They were Princeton, from June 30 to Nov. 4, 1783, and Trenton, from Nov. 1 to Dec. 24, 1784.

New Jersey declared its independence from Britain and adopted its first constitution on July 2, 1776. On Nov. 26, 1778, it ratified the Articles of Confederation, the forerunner of the United States Constitution.

The New Jersey delegates to the Constitutional Convention of 1787 proposed a plan to protect the interests of small states. This New Jersey Plan suggested that all states have equal representation in Congress. But the convention adopted the Great Compromise instead. The compromise created the present two-house Congress. The states have equal representation in the Senate, but their representation in the House of Representatives is based on population. New Jersey became a state on Dec. 18, 1787, when it ratified the U.S. Constitution. It was the third state to do so. William Livingston became New Jersey's first state governor.

The 1800's. One of the most famous duels of all time was fought at Weehawken in 1804. Aaron Burr, the vice president of the United States, shot and killed his political rival, Alexander Hamilton. Also in 1804, New Jersey passed legislation to begin the gradual freeing of slaves held in the state. The act freed all children born into

slavery when the men reached the age of 25 and the women reached 21. Under this law, however, some people would still be held in bondage as the American Civil War (1861-1865) approached.

Public demand for a more democratic state government led to the adoption of a new state constitution in 1844. The new Constitution provided for the separation of powers among the legislative, judicial, and executive branches of the state government. The Constitution also provided for a bill of rights and for the election of the governor by the people. In 1845, Charles C. Stratton became the first New Jersey governor so elected.

About 88,000 New Jersey men served in the Union army during the American Civil War. But there was much pro-Southern sympathy in the state. In 1864, New Jersey was one of only three states that voted against the reelection of President Abraham Lincoln.

New Jersey was one of the first great industrial states. As early as 1792, Paterson had become a textile center. Later, the city became known for the manufacture of locomotives and for silk production. Other New Jersey cities grew because of industry. Trenton specialized in clay products, iron, and steel. John Roebling, who built the Brooklyn Bridge, had his firm in Trenton. Camden, Elizabeth, Jersey City, Newark, and Passaic all became major manufacturing centers in the 1800's.

Improvements in transportation during the first half of the 1800's helped New Jersey to grow industrially. New canals connected New Jersey cities to Philadelphia and New York City. New railroads expanded the transportation system. As industry grew, thousands of Europeans came to New Jersey cities to work in factories. At first,

Historic New Jersey

New Sweden 1638-1655

Present state of New Jersey

New York

Delaware R.

Quintipartite Deed 1676

Hudson R.

Connecticut

East Jersey 1676-1702

Morristown

Pavonia (Bergen)

New York City

Bound Brook

Perth Amboy

Pennsylvania

Sandy Hook Bay

Sandy Hook

Princeton

Battle of Princeton

Battle of Monmouth

Battle of Trenton

Trenton

NEW JERSEY 1787

Valley Forge

Delaware R.

Burlington

Philadelphia

Haddonfield

New Sweden 1638-1655

Maryland

Salem

West Jersey 1676-1702

Atlantic Ocean

Chesapeake Bay

Delaware

Somers Point

Delaware Bay

Cape May

0   20 Miles
0   20 Kilometers

WORLD BOOK map

Bergen, New Jersey's first permanent European settlement, was built by the Dutch in 1660. It is now part of Jersey City.

New Jersey was under Dutch control until the English won the area in 1664. The colony was divided into two sections in 1676 and united again in 1702. New Jersey became a U.S. state in 1787.

Washington crossed the Delaware at the head of the colonial army on Christmas night, 1776. The next day, his forces defeated a Hessian army—made up of German soldiers hired by the British—at Trenton.

Important dates in New Jersey

WORLD BOOK illustrations by Richard Bonson, The Art Agency

1524 Giovanni da Verrazzano explored the New Jersey coast.

1609 Henry Hudson explored Sandy Hook Bay and sailed up the Hudson River.

c. 1630 The Dutch established an outpost in Pavonia.

1660 The Dutch established a permanent settlement in Bergen (now part of Jersey City).

1664 The Dutch surrendered New Jersey to England.

1676-1702 The colony was divided into two sections—West Jersey and East Jersey.

1776 New Jersey adopted its first constitution.

1783-1784 Princeton and Trenton each served briefly as the national capital.

1787 New Jersey became the third state when it ratified the U.S. Constitution on December 18.

1844 New Jersey adopted its second constitution.

1858 The first dinosaur skeleton discovered in North America was found buried in Haddonfield.

1869 Rutgers defeated the College of New Jersey (now Princeton), by a score of 6 to 4, in New Brunswick in the world's first intercollegiate football game.

1879 Thomas A. Edison developed the first practical incandescent lamp in Menlo Park.

1911 Many reforms were enacted under Governor Woodrow Wilson.

1947 New Jersey adopted its third constitution.

1952 The New Jersey Turnpike opened.

1969 New Jersey voters approved a state lottery to raise money for the state government and for the schools.

1976 New Jersey adopted an individual income tax.

1978 Casino gambling began in Atlantic City.

1994-2001 Christine Todd Whitman served as New Jersey's first woman governor.

2001 More than 650 New Jerseyites died in a terrorist attack in neighboring New York City on September 11.

most came from Ireland and Germany. Later, large numbers came from Italy and eastern Europe. By 1910, more than half the state's people had been born outside the United States or had parents who were born in other countries. With the growth of industry, city populations increased and farm populations decreased. By 1900, more New Jerseyites were living in cities and towns than in rural areas.

During the late 1800's, New Jersey became the home of many of the nation's *trusts* (industrial monopolies). Trusts were illegal in many other states, but New Jersey law allowed them. During this period, New Jersey also attracted many *holding companies*—that is, companies that control the stock and policies of one or more other companies. By 1900, hundreds of large corporations obtained charters under New Jersey laws and set up headquarters in the state.

The early 1900's. Concern about the practices of big businesses led to a reform movement in New Jersey. In 1910, the people elected Woodrow Wilson, the president of Princeton University, as governor. Under Wilson, the state passed laws providing for direct primary elections, workers' compensation, and a public utilities commission. The legislature also passed laws restricting business monopolies. Wilson's achievements as governor helped lead to his election as president of the United States in 1912. He was reelected in 1916.

Thomas A. Edison helped develop the motion picture while working in New Jersey. Fort Lee became the motion-picture capital of the world in the early 1900's. There, Fatty Arbuckle, Mary Pickford, Pearl White, and other stars made movies that introduced a new era in entertainment.

After the United States entered World War I in 1917, Hoboken, on the Hudson River, became a major port for shipping troops overseas. Thousands of American soldiers sailed for France from the port. During the war, Camp Dix and Camp Merrit served as military training centers. New Jersey factories contributed chemicals, munitions, and ships to the war effort.

Between 1900 and 1930, New Jersey's population more than doubled. During the same period, the state's annual value of manufacturing rose from about $500 million to almost $4 billion. New Jersey, like other states, suffered widespread unemployment during the Great Depression of the 1930's.

The mid-1900's. New Jersey's electronics and chemical industries began large-scale operations about 1940. These industries grew during World War II (1939-1945), when the state produced communications equipment, ships, and weapons and ammunition.

In 1947, New Jersey voters approved a new state constitution. The Constitution extended the governor's term from three to four years and increased the powers of the office. The Constitution also reorganized the state's court system.

In the mid-1900's, the state's population expanded steadily into many rural areas. The expansion included construction of homes and of commercial and industrial plants. Commercial and industrial growth occurred most rapidly among chemical, electronics, food-processing, pharmaceutical, and research firms.

The New Jersey Turnpike opened in 1952 and soon became one of the nation's busiest highways. The turnpike links the Philadelphia and New York City metropolitan areas. The Garden State Parkway, completed in 1955, runs along the New Jersey coast.

During the 1960's, older New Jersey cities faced the problem of spreading slums, especially in African American neighborhoods. In July 1967, riots broke out in African American neighborhoods of several cities. The worst riot occurred in Newark, where 26 people were killed and more than 1,000 were injured. Property damage totaled between $10 million and $15 million.

In the late 1960's, the state adopted a sales tax and several bond issues to help pay for major government programs. One bond issue supplied money for new state colleges, highways, institutions, and commuter train facilities. Another paid for water conservation projects and for a program to fight water pollution. In 1969, voters approved a state lottery to raise money for the state government and for the schools.

The late 1900's. The state continued to seek new sources of revenue. In 1976, the Legislature adopted an individual income tax for the first time. Also in 1976, voters passed a referendum permitting gambling casinos in Atlantic City to help raise money for the elderly and people with disabilities. The first casino opened in 1978.

Large urban renewal projects of the late 1900's upgraded parts of several New Jersey cities. The program in Trenton included construction of a group of state government office buildings and a cultural center. In Newark, the state expanded college and university facilities, and a new performing arts center opened. In the 1990's, a minor league baseball stadium opened along the Passaic River.

Passenger railroad travel declined nationwide in the latter half of the 1900's, but New Jersey kept its position as a major rail center. Newark Airport began a major construction program in 1963 to expand passenger and cargo service. In the 1980's, it became one of the world's busiest airports.

In 1993, Christine Todd Whitman won election to the office of governor. She became the first woman to serve

Museum of Modern Art

Early motion pictures were made in studios at Fort Lee. Silent film star Mary Pickford, shown with director Maurice Tourneur, *left,* made *Poor Little Rich Girl* at Fort Lee in 1917.

as New Jersey's governor. Whitman took office in 1994.

The early 2000's. Whitman resigned as governor in 2001, when President George W. Bush named her to head the U.S. Environmental Protection Agency. Whitman headed the agency until 2003.

On Sept. 11, 2001, terrorists crashed two hijacked commercial jetliners into the twin towers of the World Trade Center in New York City. The approximately 3,000 people killed in the attacks included more than 650 New Jersey residents. In 2002, President Bush named former New Jersey Governor Thomas H. Kean to head a commission to investigate the attacks.

In 2004, Governor James E. McGreevey resigned. McGreevey, a married man, said that he was a homosexual and that he had had an extramarital affair with a man. He said he made the decision to resign because he believed that the circumstances surrounding the affair would be an obstacle to his governing effectively. The president of the state Senate served as governor until the next elected governor took office in 2006.

In 2005, New Jersey voters approved a state constitutional amendment creating the post of lieutenant governor. In the 2009 election, Kim Guadagno, a Republican and former sheriff of Monmouth County, was chosen as New Jersey's first lieutenant governor. In 2007, the New Jersey Legislature abolished the death penalty, replacing it with life in prison without parole.

Today, New Jersey faces problems related to overcrowding. Its high population density strains the environment and puts huge demands on the government to provide social services.   Paul G. E. Clemens and Grant Saff

Related articles in *World Book* include:

Biographies

Addams, Charles	Lawrence, James
Bradley, Bill	Livingston, William
Brearley, David	McClellan, George B.
Burr, Aaron	Paterson, William
Clark, Abraham	Pitcher, Molly
Cleveland, Grover	Roth, Philip
Crane, Stephen	Saint Denis, Ruth
Dayton, Jonathan	Schirra, Walter M., Jr.
Dayton, William L.	Schwarzkopf, H. Norman
Edison, Thomas Alva	Springsteen, Bruce
Einstein, Albert	Stockton, Richard
Halsey, William F., Jr.	Verrazzano, Giovanni da
Hart, John	Waksman, Selman A.
Hobart, Garret A.	Williams, William Carlos
Hudson, Henry	Wilson, Woodrow
Kilmer, Joyce	Witherspoon, John

Cities

Atlantic City
Camden
Elizabeth
Irvington
Jersey City
Newark
Paterson
Trenton

Physical features

Delaware Bay
Delaware River
Delaware Water Gap
Hudson River
Piedmont Region

Other related articles

Atlantic Intracoastal Waterway
Fort Monmouth
George Washington Bridge
Hudson River tunnels
New Netherland
New York City (Metropolitan area; Trade)
Port Authority of New York and New Jersey
Trenton, Battle of

Outline

Additional resources

Level I

Doak, Robin S. *New Jersey: 1609-1776.* National Geographic Children's Bks., 2005.
Kent, Deborah. *New Jersey.* Children's Pr., 2008.
Landau, Elaine. *George Washington Crosses the Delaware.* Enslow, 2009.
Moragne, Wendy, and Orr, T. B. *New Jersey.* 2nd ed. Benchmark Bks., 2009.
Weatherly, Myra. *The New Jersey Colony.* Child's World, 2004.

Level II

Coyne, Kevin. *Marching Home: To War and Back with the Men of One American Town.* Viking, 2003. Describes the experiences of six New Jersey men during and after World War II.
Fischer, David H. *Washington's Crossing.* Oxford, 2004. A history of George Washington's crossing of the Delaware River in December 1776 and the following campaign in New Jersey.
Fleming, Thomas J. *New Jersey.* Rev. ed. Norton, 1984.
Gale, Dennis E. *Greater New Jersey: Living in the Shadow of Gotham.* Univ. of Penn. Pr., 2006.
Gallagher, William B. *When Dinosaurs Roamed New Jersey.* Rutgers, 1997. Natural history and geology of New Jersey.
Hodges, Graham R. *Slavery and Freedom in the Rural North: African Americans in Monmouth County, New Jersey, 1665-1865.* Madison Hse., 1997.
Lurie, Maxine N., and Mappan, Marc, eds. *Encyclopedia of New Jersey.* Rutgers, 2004.
Salmore, Barbara G. and Stephen A. *New Jersey Politics and Government.* 3rd ed. Rivergate, 2008.
Siegel, Alan A. *Beneath the Starry Flag: New Jersey's Civil War Experience.* Rutgers, 2001.
Veit, Richard F. *Digging New Jersey's Past: Historical Archaeology in the Garden State.* Rutgers, 2002.

New Jersey Plan. See Constitution of the United States (The compromises); **New Jersey** (The Revolutionary War).

New Kingdom of Granada. See Colombia (History).

New Left was a radical political and social movement of the 1960's and early 1970's in the United States. The New Left included many college students and other young people. The movement was considered "new" in relation to the "old left" of the 1930's. The "old left" generally was guided by Marxist ideas and supported Soviet policies.

Members of the New Left demanded sweeping and fundamental changes in American society. They attacked most major institutions for claiming to support democratic principles but failing to end such injustices as poverty, racial discrimination, and class distinctions. Many New Leftists opposed capitalism and believed the desire for profits leads to *imperialism,* a policy that favors extending influence over another country.

People who identified themselves with the New Left were not all members of a single organization, and they frequently disagreed among themselves. Members of the New Left ranged from pacifists to violent revolutionaries. Many New Leftists favored such tactics as nonviolent civil disobedience. But their actions often led to bloody clashes with the police and other law enforcement officials. The most important elements of the New Left included the militant wings of the peace movement during the Vietnam War (1957-1975), the movement for racial equality, and the students' rights movement.

The peace and civil rights movements appealed especially to young people. Their experiences in civil rights and peace demonstrations convinced many of them that war and discrimination could be ended only by a general reformation of American society. Several radical student organizations appeared in the early 1960's, including the Students for a Democratic Society (SDS) and the Free Speech Movement. Radical students began to consider the university as an accomplice of war and racism. They used disruptive tactics in an effort to reform their universities or to use them as a base for revolutionary activities.

Most members of the New Left showed little interest in conventional politics and did little to get sympathetic candidates elected to public office. However, many people believe that the antiwar movement helped persuade President Lyndon B. Johnson not to run for reelection in 1968.

After 1968, the New Left split into several factions. For example, the revolutionaries split over tactics for defeating imperialism. Some urged an alliance with American workers, but others favored organizing the world's poor and nonwhite peoples.

The New Left failed to bring about radical changes in American society. But it formed the basis for several movements that remain active today, such as the women's and environmentalist movements.   Christopher Lasch

See also **Black Panther Party; Radicalism** (In the United States); **Riot** (During the 1900's); **Students for a Democratic Society.**

New London, Connecticut (pop. 27,620), is the home of the United States Coast Guard Academy. It is also the trading, banking, transportation, and distribution center for southeastern Connecticut. The city's position at the mouth of the Thames River, near the eastern entrance of Long Island Sound, makes it an important seaport (see **Connecticut** [political map]). New London and Norwich form a metropolitan area with 274,055 people. During the mid-1800's, New London's whaling fleet was second in size only to that of New Bedford, Massachusetts. Today, copper, paper products, and steel coils are the principal cargoes shipped to New London's Admiral Harold E. Shear State Pier.

Across the Thames River in Groton are Naval Submarine Base New London, the chief training center of the U.S. Navy's submarine force; and a submarine design and manufacturing facility. Their presence has attracted a number of defense-related consulting and engineering firms to New London. The city is the home of Connecticut College and Mitchell College.

New London was settled in 1646 and incorporated in 1784. In 1781, during the American Revolution, the city was burned by a British raiding party led by the American traitor Benedict Arnold. New London has a council-manager form of government.   Stephen Fagin

New mathematics was an educational movement during the late 1950's and the 1960's that attempted to change the teaching of mathematics in the United States. The growth of space exploration, computer technology, and other scientific fields had created a need for better training in mathematics. To meet this need, several independent groups of mathematicians and educators in the United States tried to design better math curriculums. The general goals of the groups were to modernize course content, give students a deeper understanding of mathematical principles, and encourage creative problem solving.

Traditional math programs stressed the development of basic computational skills—such as how to add, subtract, multiply, and divide—through repetitious drills and memorization. New math programs urged students to understand concepts rather than learn rules. To provide a better understanding of numbers, for example, many programs taught students to work problems in numeration systems with bases other than 10.

The educators who developed the new programs agreed on general goals but disagreed on specific goals and methods. As a result, many different curriculums were created. All became known as the *new mathematics* or *new math.*

Because of several obstacles, however, few schools established effective new math programs. For example, many institutions did not give teachers an adequate opportunity to learn the new material. Textbooks continued to present old methods and goals. Sections on new math topics—such as bases other than 10 and *sets* (collections of objects or ideas)—were merely added to the old lessons (see **Set theory**).

New math topics were often taught with the old focus on computational skills rather than on the learning of concepts. For example, teachers asked students to translate numbers from base 10 to another base rather than work math problems entirely within the non-10 base.

During the 1970's, students' achievement scores declined, and many people blamed new math. New math fell out of favor and was replaced by an even stronger focus on basic skills. Thus, new math was never widely implemented.   Karen Connors Fuson

© James Blank, West Stock

Scattered pines grow in a canyon near Los Alamos. Hundreds of thousands of people visit New Mexico each year to enjoy its warm climate, beautiful scenery, and rich Spanish and Indian cultures.

New Mexico *The Land of Enchantment*

New Mexico, a Southwestern state of the United States, is called the *Land of Enchantment* because of its scenic beauty and rich history. Every year, hundreds of thousands of tourists go to this state for hunting, fishing, skiing, or sightseeing. New Mexico is the fifth largest state in area. Only Alaska, Texas, California, and Montana have a greater area. But the state is thinly populated. Mountain ranges, rugged canyons, and rocky deserts cover much of New Mexico.

A person vacationing in New Mexico might see the state as a land of beautiful scenery, Spanish fiestas, and American Indian ceremonies. But a scientist would think of New Mexico as a center of research into rockets and nuclear energy. An oil company executive might regard the state as a rich source of gasoline for automobiles or of natural gas for cooking and heating. A retired couple

might choose to make their home in the southern part of New Mexico because its location and high altitude provide warm, sunny days and cool nights. A rancher might be impressed by New Mexico's vast stretches of grazing land.

Much of New Mexico's growing industry springs from the science of the nuclear age. The first atomic bomb was built and exploded in New Mexico in 1945. Today, scientists in New Mexico search for a way to make space rockets travel on nuclear power. Other scientists develop ways to use nuclear power for generating electricity, or work on improving nuclear weapons for defense.

New Mexico ranks among the leading states in mining. Natural gas and petroleum are New Mexico's most important mineral products by far. Large deposits of gas and petroleum lie in both the northwestern and southeastern parts of the state. In addition, New Mexico's resources include major deposits of coal, copper, potash, and uranium.

Cattle ranching is the most important type of farming in the state. More than a million cattle graze on the vast

The contributors of this article are Daniel P. Dugas, Assistant Professor of Geography at New Mexico State University, and Dulcinea M. Lara, Assistant Professor of History at New Mexico State University.

Interesting facts about New Mexico

El Camino Real (the Royal Highway) stretched from Santa Fe to Mexico City. It was the first road established by Europeans in what is now the United States. It was traveled about 1581 and was later used primarily as a trade route. Portions of it still exist and can be explored.

The Smokey Bear Historical State Park was established in Capitan in 1979. The symbol of Smokey was first used by the United States Forest Service in 1944. In 1950, a real "Smokey Bear" was found clinging to a burned tree after a fire swept through Lincoln National Forest. The orphaned bear cub became the living Smokey Bear. The bear died in 1976 and was buried in what is now Smokey Bear Historical State Park.

Smokey Bear

WORLD BOOK illustrations by Kevin Chadwick

The Palace of the Governors

The Palace of the Governors in Santa Fe is the oldest government building in the United States. The Spanish built it as part of a fortress during the winter of 1609-1610. In 1909, it was converted to the Palace of the Governors History Museum. The building now houses exhibits on Spanish, Mexican, and American colonization dating back to the late 1500's.

© Edna Douthat

Taos Pueblo is a Pueblo Indian village in north-central New Mexico. The Pueblo Indians have traditionally lived in stone or adobe structures that resemble modern apartment buildings.

plains and in the mountain valleys of New Mexico.

New Mexico's colorful past gives the state important tourist attractions. Still standing are the ruins of an apartment house with about 800 rooms built by the Indians hundreds of years before Christopher Columbus arrived in America. Spain ruled the land for more than 220 years. The Spanish influence may be seen today in the names of places, in the churches of early missionaries, in foods, and in customs and holidays. Colorful people such as Kit Carson, Geronimo, and Billy the Kid played major parts in the history of the New Mexico area in territorial days.

Many other historical features capture the interest of visitors to New Mexico. Within the state remain portions of the oldest road established by Europeans in the United States. This route, called El Camino Real (the Royal Highway), was first traveled about 1581. Santa Fe, the capital of New Mexico, ranks as the oldest seat of government in the United States. It was founded as the capital of a Spanish province as early as 1609 or 1610. The largest city in New Mexico is Albuquerque, which the Spaniards founded in 1706.

© Danita Delimont/Alamy Images

Albuquerque is New Mexico's largest city. It serves as an industrial, trade, and transportation center of the Southwest.

New Mexico in brief

Symbols of New Mexico

On the state flag, adopted in 1925, the ancient sun symbol of the Zia Pueblo Indians appears in red on a yellow field. These were the colors of Queen Isabella of Castile that the Spanish Conquistadors brought to the New World. On the state seal, adopted in 1913, a large eagle shielding a smaller eagle represents the annexation of New Mexico by the United States.

State flag

State of New Mexico
State seal

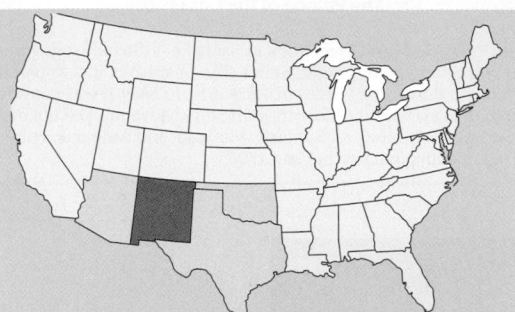

New Mexico (brown) ranks 5th in size among all the states and 2nd in size among the Southwestern States (yellow).

General information

Statehood: Jan. 6, 1912, the 47th state.
State abbreviations: N. Mex. or N.M. (traditional); NM (postal).
State motto: *Crescit Eundo* (It Grows as It Goes).
State song: "O, Fair New Mexico." Words and music by Elizabeth Garrett.

The State Capitol is in Santa Fe, which was founded as the capital of the Spanish province of New Mexico in 1609 or 1610.

Land and climate

Area: 121,590 mi² (314,915 km²), including 234 mi² (606 km²) of inland water.
Elevation: *Highest*—Wheeler Peak, 13,161 ft (4,011 m) above sea level. *Lowest*—2,817 ft (859 m) above sea level at Red Bluff Reservoir in Eddy County.
Record high temperature: 122 °F (50 °C) at Waste Isolation Pilot Plant near Carlsbad on June 27, 1994.
Record low temperature: –50 °F (–46 °C) at Gavilan, near Lindrith, on Feb. 1, 1951.
Average July temperature: 74 °F (23 °C).
Average January temperature: 34 °F (1 °C).
Average yearly precipitation: 13 in (33 cm).

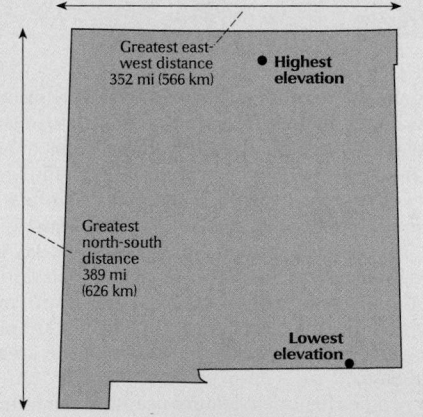

Greatest east-west distance 352 mi (566 km)

● **Highest elevation**

Greatest north-south distance 389 mi (626 km)

Lowest elevation ●

Important dates

—— Juan de Oñate founded New Mexico's first permanent Spanish settlement at San Juan.

—— Mexico ceded New Mexico to the United States.

| 1540-1542 | 1598 | 1821 | 1848 |

—— Francisco Vásquez de Coronado of Spain explored the New Mexico region.

—— New Mexico became a province of Mexico. William Becknell opened the Santa Fe Trail.

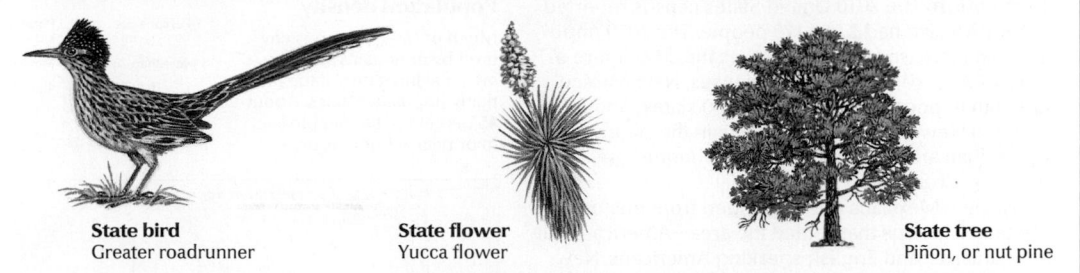

State bird
Greater roadrunner

State flower
Yucca flower

State tree
Piñon, or nut pine

People

Population: 2,059,179
Rank among the states: 36th
Density: 17 per mi² (7 per km²), U.S. average 85 per mi² (33 per km²)
Distribution: 75 percent urban, 25 percent rural

Largest cities in New Mexico

Albuquerque	545,852
Las Cruces	97,618
Rio Rancho	87,521
Santa Fe	67,947
Roswell	48,366
Farmington	45,877

†Unincorporated place.
Source: 2010 census, except for distribution, which is for 2000.

Population trend

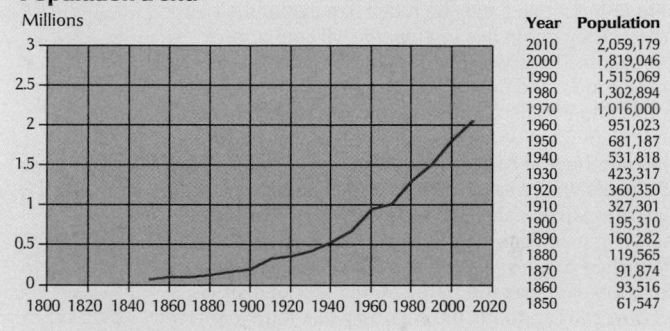

Millions

Year	Population
2010	2,059,179
2000	1,819,046
1990	1,515,069
1980	1,302,894
1970	1,016,000
1960	951,023
1950	681,187
1940	531,818
1930	423,317
1920	360,350
1910	327,301
1900	195,310
1890	160,282
1880	119,565
1870	91,874
1860	93,516
1850	61,547

Source: U.S. Census Bureau.

Economy

Chief products

Agriculture: beef cattle, hay, milk.
Manufacturing: chemicals, computer and electronic equipment, concrete, food products, transportation equipment.
Mining: coal, copper, natural gas, petroleum, potash.

Gross domestic product

Value of goods and services produced in 2008: $77,858,000,000. *Services* include community, business, and personal services; finance; government; trade; and transportation and communication. *Industry* includes construction, manufacturing, mining, and utilities. *Agriculture* includes agriculture, fishing, and forestry.

Source: U.S. Bureau of Economic Analysis.

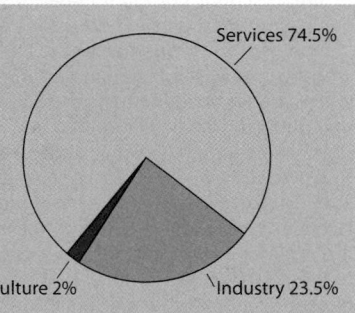

Services 74.5%

Agriculture 2%

Industry 23.5%

Government

State government

Governor: 4-year term
State senators: 42; 4-year terms
State representatives: 70; 2-year terms
Counties: 33

Federal government

United States senators: 2
United States representatives: 3
Electoral votes: 5

Sources of information

New Mexico's official website at http://www.newmexico.gov provides a gateway to much information on the state's government, history, and economy.

In addition, the website at http://www.newmexico.org provides information about tourism.

Geologists discovered oil in southeastern and northwestern New Mexico.

Completion of the San Juan-Chama project brought water through the Rocky Mountains to north-central New Mexico.

| 1912 | 1922 | 1945 | 1970's | 1998 |

New Mexico became the 47th state on January 6.

The world's first atomic bomb was exploded near Alamogordo.

New Mexico celebrated the 400th anniversary of the settlement of San Juan.

Population. The 2010 United States census reported that New Mexico had 2,059,179 people. The 2010 population had increased 13 percent over the 2000 figure of 1,819,046. According to the 2010 census, New Mexico ranks 36th in population among the 50 states. About 65 percent of New Mexico's people live in the state's four metropolitan areas. These areas are Albuquerque, Farmington, Las Cruces, and Santa Fe.

Most New Mexicans are descended from one of the three major groups that settled the area—American Indians, Spaniards, and English-speaking Americans. New Mexico has a higher percentage of Indians and Hispanics than any other state. About 45 percent of the people are Hispanic, and nearly 10 percent are Indian. The way of life of the Indians may be much like that of their ancestors. They might live in a *pueblo* (village) or on a reservation. The Spanish influence shows in place names, foods, and customs. Many people speak both English and Spanish. Non-Hispanic whites account for about 40 percent of the population. New Mexico has small numbers of African Americans and Asians.

Schools. In the early 1600's, Spanish Roman Catholic priests began establishing schools in New Mexico to teach Christianity to the Indians. Public education was established in the state in the late 1800's. A secretary of education oversees the state's public school districts. The governor appoints the secretary to a four-year term. A 10-member Public Education Commission advises the secretary. State law requires children from ages 5 to 18 to attend school. For the number of students and teachers in New Mexico, see **Education** (table).

Libraries and museums. The New Mexico Territorial Library was established in Santa Fe in 1851. Part of this collection was used to form the State Library. The state's first public library was founded in Cimarron in 1871.

The Museum of New Mexico in Santa Fe includes the New Mexico Museum of Art, Museum of Indian Arts and Culture, Museum of International Folk Art, and Palace of the Governors. The Wheelwright Museum of the American Indian also is in Santa Fe. The New Mexico Museum of Natural History and Science is in Albuquerque. The Bradbury Science Museum in Los Alamos has exhibits on the history and research of Los Alamos National Laboratory. The Albuquerque Museum of Art and History features art of the Southwest. Other museums include the New Mexico Farm and Ranch Heritage Museum in Las Cruces, the National Museum of Nuclear Science & History in Albuquerque, and the Roswell Museum and Art Center in Roswell.

Population density

Much of New Mexico is covered by mountains and deserts, making it one of the most thinly populated states. About 45 percent of the people live in or near Albuquerque.

	Persons per mi²	Persons per km²
	More than 25	More than 10
	10 to 25	4 to 10
	5 to 10	2 to 4
	Less than 5	Less than 2

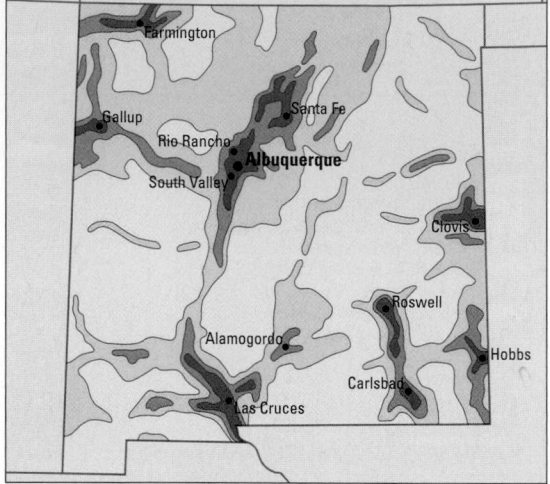

WORLD BOOK map based on U.S. Census Bureau data.

Universities and colleges

This table lists the nonprofit universities and colleges in New Mexico that grant bachelor's or advanced degrees and are accredited by the North Central Association of Colleges and Schools.

Name	Mailing address
Eastern New Mexico University	Portales
Institute of American Indian and Alaska Native Culture and Arts Development	Santa Fe
New Mexico, University of	Albuquerque
New Mexico Highlands University	Las Vegas
New Mexico Institute of Mining and Technology	Socorro
New Mexico State University	Las Cruces
Northern New Mexico College	Española
St. John's College	Santa Fe
Southwest, University of the	Hobbs
Southwestern College	Santa Fe
Western New Mexico University	Silver City

The University of New Mexico, in Albuquerque, is the state's largest university. Dane Smith Hall, *shown here,* has a number of classrooms and other spaces for students. It stands on the university's central campus.

New Mexico map index

Metropolitan areas

Albuquerque 887,077
Farmington 130,044
Las Cruces 209,233
Santa Fe 144,170

Counties

Bernalillo ....662,564 ..F 5
Catron ....3,725 ..I 3
Chaves ....65,645 ..I 10
Cibola ....27,213 ..G 3
Colfax ....13,750 ..C 9
Curry ....48,376 ..G 11
De Baca ....2,022 ..H 9
Doña Ana ....209,233 ..K 5
Eddy ....53,829 ..K 10
Grant ....29,514 ..K 2
Guadalupe ....4,687 ..G 9
Harding ....695 ..D 10
Hidalgo ....4,894 ..M 2
Lea ....64,727 ..J 11
Lincoln ....20,497 ..H 8
Los Alamos ....17,950 ..D 6
Luna ....25,095 ..L 4
McKinley ....71,492 ..E 3
Mora ....4,881 ..D 8
Otero ....63,797 ..K 7
Quay ....9,041 ..F 11
Rio Arriba ....40,246 ..C 5
Roosevelt ....19,846 ..H 11
San Juan ....130,044 ..C 3
San Miguel ....29,393 ..E 9
Sandoval ....131,561 ..E 5
Santa Fe ....144,170 ..E 7
Sierra ....11,988 ..J 4
Socorro ....17,866 ..H 5
Taos ....32,937 ..C 7
Torrance ....16,383 ..G 7
Union ....4,549 ..C 11
Valencia ....76,569 ..G 5

Cities, towns, and villages

Abeytas† ....56 ..G 5
Abiquiu† ....231 ..D 6
Acoma ....F 4
Acoma Indian
Reservation ....3,005 ..F 4
Acomita† ....416 ..F 4
Adelino*† ....823 ..G 5
Agua Fria† ....2,800 ..E 7
Alameda ....F 6
Alamillo† ....102 ..H 5
Alamo† ....1,085 ..G 4
Alamo Band
Navajo Indian
Reservation ....G 4
Alamogordo° ....30,403 ..J 7
Albert ....D 10
Albu-
querque° ....545,852 ..F 6
Alcalde† ....285 ..D 7
Algodones† ....814 ..E 6
Allison ....E 2
Alto ....I 7
Amalia ....B 7
Ambrosia Lake ....E 4
Amistad ....D 11
Anaconda ....F 3
Ancho ....H 7
Angel Fire ....1,216 ..C 8
Animas† ....237 ..L 2
Anthony† ....9,360 ..L 6
Anton Chico† ....188 ..F 8
Apache Creek† ....67 ..H 2
Aragon† ....94 ..H 2
Arenas Valley† ....1,522 ..K 3
Armijo ....F 5
Arrey† ....232 ..K 4
Arroyo Hondo† ....474 ..C 7
Arroyo Seco† ....1,785 ..C 7
Artesia ....11,301 ..J 9
Atoka† ....1,077 ..K 9
Aztec° ....6,763 ..B 3
Bard ....F 11
Barranca ....D 6
Bayard ....2,328 ..K 3
Belen ....7,269 ..G 5
Bell Ranch ....E 10
Bellview ....F 12
Bennett ....L 11
Bent† ....119 ..J 7
Berino† ....1,441 ..L 6
Bernalillo° ....8,320 ..F 6
Bingham ....H 6
Black Rock† ....1,323 ..F 2
Blanco† ....388 ..C 4
Bloomfield ....8,112 ..C 3
Bluewater ....F 3
Boles ....K 7
Bosque ....G 5
Bosque Farms ....3,904 ..F 6
Brazos† ....44 ..C 6
Brimhall ....E 2
Broadview ....F 11
Broadview Acres ....F 4
Buckeye ....K 11
Buckhorn† ....200 ..J 2
Buena Vista ....D 8
Bueyeros ....D 10
Burnham ....C 3
Caballo† ....112 ..J 4
Canjilon† ....256 ..C 6
Cannon AFB† ....2,245 ..G 11
Cañon Plaza ....C 6
Canoncito Indian
Reservation ....F 5
Capitan ....1,489 ..I 7
Caprock ....I 11
Capulin† ....66 ..C 10
Carlsbad° ....26,138 ..K 10
Carnuel*† ....1,232 ..F 6
Carrizozo° ....996 ..I 7
Casa Blanca ....F 4
Causey ....104 ..H 12
Cebolla ....C 6
Cedar Crest† ....958 ..F 6
Cedar Hill† ....847 ..B 4
Cedarvale ....G 7
Cerrillos ....E 6
Cerro ....C 7
Chacon ....D 8
Chama ....1,022 ..B 6
Chamberino† ....919 ..L 5
Chamisal† ....310 ..D 7
Chaparral† ....14,631 ..L 6
Chi Chil Tah ....F 2
Chilili† ....137 ..F 6
Chimayo† ....3,177 ..D 7
Chloride ....J 4
Church Rock† ....1,128 ..E 2
Cimarron ....1,021 ..C 8
Claunch ....H 7
Clayton° ....2,980 ..C 11
Cleveland ....D 8
Cliff† ....293 ..J 2
Clines Corners ....F 7
Cloudcroft ....674 ..J 7
Clovis° ....37,775 ..G 11
Cochiti† ....528 ..E 6
Cochiti Indian
Reservation ....E 6
Colonias ....F 9
Columbus ....1,664 ..M 4
Conchas Dam† ....186 ..E 10
Continental
Divide ....E 3
Contreras ....G 5
Corona ....172 ..H 7
Corrales ....8,329 ..F 6
Costilla† ....205 ..B 7
Cotton City† ....388 ..L 1
Cowles ....D 7
Coyote† ....128 ..D 6
Crossroads ....I 11
Crownpoint† ....2,278 ..E 3
Cruzville† ....72 ..H 2
Crystal† ....311 ..D 2
Cuba ....731 ..D 5
Cubero† ....289 ..F 4
Cuchillo ....J 4
Cuervo ....F 9
Cuyamungue*† ....479 ..D 7
Datil† ....54 ..H 4
Deming° ....14,855 ..L 4
Derry ....K 4
Des Moines ....143 ..B 10
Dexter ....1,266 ..J 9
Dixon† ....926 ..D 7
Domingo ....E 6
Doña Ana† ....1,211 ..K 5
Dora ....133 ..H 11
Dulce† ....2,743 ..B 5
Duran† ....35 ..G 8
Dusty ....I 4
Dwyer ....K 3
Eagle Nest ....290 ..C 8
Edgewood* ....3,735 ..F 6
Elephant Butte ....1,431 ..J 5
Elida ....197 ..H 11
Elkins ....I 10
El Prado ....C 7
El Rito† ....808 ..C 6
El Vado ....C 5
Encinal† ....210 ..F 4
Encino ....82 ..G 8
Ensenada† ....107 ..C 6
Escondida† ....47 ..H 5
Española ....10,224 ..D 6
Estancia° ....1,655 ..G 7
Eunice ....2,922 ..K 11
Fairacres† ....824 ..L 5
Farley ....C 10
Farmington ....45,877 ..C 3
Faywood† ....33 ..K 3
Fence Lake† ....42 ..G 2
Fierro ....J 3
Five Points ....F 5
Flora Vista† ....2,191 ..B 3
Florida ....H 5
Floyd ....133 ..H 11
Flying H ....J 8
Folsom ....56 ..B 10
Forrest ....G 11
Fort Stanton ....I 7
Fort Sumner° ....1,031 ..G 10
Fort Wingate ....E 2
Fruitland ....C 3
Gabaldon ....E 8
Gage ....L 3
Galisteo† ....253 ..E 7
Gallina† ....286 ..D 5
Gallup° ....21,678 ..E 2
Gamerco ....E 2
Garfield† ....137 ..K 4
Gavilan ....C 5
Gila† ....314 ..J 2
Gladstone ....C 10
Glencoe ....I 7
Glenrio ....F 12
Glenwood† ....143 ..J 2
Glorieta† ....430 ..E 7
Gonzales Ranch ....F 8
Grady ....107 ..F 11
Grants° ....9,182 ..F 3
Greenfield ....J 10
Grenville ....38 ..C 11
Guadalupita ....D 8
Hachita† ....49 ..L 3
Hagerman ....1,257 ..J 10
Hanover† ....167 ..J 3
Hatch ....1,648 ..K 5
Hayden ....D 11
High Rolls† ....834 ..J 7
Hillsboro† ....124 ..J 4
Hobbs ....34,122 ..K 12
Holloman AFB† ....3,054 ..J 6
Holman ....D 8
Hondo ....I 8
Hope ....105 ..K 9
House ....68 ..G 10
Humble City ....J 11
Hurley ....1,297 ..K 3
Isleta Indian
Reservation ....3,400 ..F 6
Isleta Pueblo ....F 5
Jal ....2,047 ..L 11
Jarales† ....2,475 ..G 5
Jemez Indian
Reservation ....1,815 ..E 5
Jemez Pueblo† ....1,788 ..E 5
Jemez Springs ....250 ..E 5
Jicarilla Apache
Indian
Reservation ....3,250 ..C 4
Kenna ....H 10
Kingston† ....32 ..J 4
Kirtland† ....7,875 ..C 3
La Cienega† ....3,819 ..E 6
Laguna† ....1,241 ..F 4
Laguna Indian
Reservation ....4,043 ..F 4
La Jara† ....207 ..D 5
Lajoya ....G 5
Lake Arthur ....436 ..J 9
Lakewood ....K 9
La Loma ....F 8
La Luz† ....1,697 ..J 7
La Madera† ....154 ..C 7
La Mesa† ....728 ..L 5
La Mesilla*† ....1,772 ..D 6
La Plata† ....612 ..B 3
La Puente ....C 6
Las Cruces° ....97,618 ..L 5
Las Nutrias† ....149 ..G 5
Las Tablas ....C 7
Las Tusas ....E 8
Las Vegas° ....13,753 ..E 8
La Union† ....1,106 ..L 5
Ledoux ....D 8
Lemitar† ....330 ..H 5
Leyba ....F 7
Lincoln ....I 8
Lindrith ....C 5
Lingo ....I 11
Llano ....D 7
Llaves ....C 5
Loco Hills† ....126 ..K 10
Logan ....1,042 ..E 11
Lordsburg° ....2,797 ..K 2
Los Alamos†° ....12,019 ..D 6
Los Chavez† ....5,446 ..G 5
Los Lunas° ....14,835 ..G 5
Los Montoyas ....E 8
Los Ojos† ....125 ..C 6
Los Padillas ....F 5
Los Pinos ....B 6
Los Ranchos de
Albuquerque ....6,024 ..F 5
Los Vigiles ....E 8
Loving ....1,413 ..L 10
Lovington° ....11,009 ..J 11
Lower Nutria ....F 2
Luis Lopez† ....107 ..H 5
Lumberton† ....73 ..B 5
Luna† ....158 ..H 2
Madrid† ....204 ..E 6
Magdalena ....938 ..H 4
Malaga† ....147 ..L 10
Maljamar ....J 11
Manuelito ....E 2
Manzano† ....29 ..G 6
Maxwell ....254 ..C 9
Mayhill† ....75 ..J 8
McAlister ....G 10
McCartys† ....48 ..F 4
McDonald ....J 11
McGaffey ....E 2
McIntosh† ....1,484 ..F 7
Meadow Vista,
see Sunland Park
Melrose ....651 ..G 11
Mentmore ....E 2
Mescalero† ....1,338 ..J 7
Mescalero
Apache Indian
Reservation ....3,613 ..J 7
Mesilla ....2,196 ..L 5
Mesita† ....804 ..F 4
Mesquite† ....1,112 ..L 5
Mexican
Springs ....D 2
Miami ....C 9
Milan ....3,245 ..F 3
Mills ....D 10
Milnesand ....I 11
Mimbres† ....667 ..J 3
Mogollon ....I 2
Monero ....B 5
Montezuma ....E 8
Monticello ....I 4
Montoya ....F 10
Monument† ....206 ..K 11
Mora†° ....656 ..D 8
Moriarty ....1,910 ..F 7
Mosquero° ....93 ..D 10
Mount Dora ....C 11
Mountain View ....F 6
Mountainair ....928 ..G 6
Mule Creek ....J 2
Nambe† ....1,818 ..D 7
Nara Visa† ....95 ..E 11
Naschitti† ....301 ..D 2
Navajo† ....1,645 ..D 2
Navajo Indian
Reservation ....42,127 ..C 2
New Laguna ....F 4
Newcomb† ....339 ..C 2
Newkirk† ....7 ..F 9
Nogal† ....96 ..I 7
North
Valley*† ....11,333 ..F 6
Ocate ....D 8
Oil Center ....K 11
Ojo Caliente ....C 7
Ojo Feliz ....D 8
Old Horse
Springs ....H 3
Organ† ....323 ..K 6
Orogrande† ....52 ..K 6
Otis ....K 10
Paguate† ....421 ..F 4
Pajarito ....F 5
Paradise Hills* ....4,256 ..F 5
Pastura† ....23 ..G 8
Pecos ....1,392 ..E 7
Peña Blanca† ....709 ..E 6
Peñasco† ....589 ..D 7
Pep ....H 11
Peralta ....3,660 ..F 5
Petaca ....C 7
Picacho ....I 8
Picuris Indian
Reservation ....1,886 ..D 7
Pie Town† ....186 ..H 3
Pilar ....D 7
Pinedale ....E 3
Piñon† ....25 ..K 8
Pinos Altos† ....198 ..J 3
Placitas† ....4,977 ..E 6
Pojoaque† ....1,907 ..D 7
Polvadera† ....269 ..H 5
Ponderosa† ....387 ..E 5
Portales° ....12,280 ..H 11
Prewitt ....E 3
Puerto de Luna ....F 9
Punta de Agua ....G 6
Quay ....F 10
Quemado† ....228 ..G 2
Questa ....1,770 ..C 7
Radium
Springs ....1,699 ..K 5
Rainsville ....D 8
Ramah ....370 ..F 2
Ranchito ....C 7
Ranchos
de Taos† ....2,518 ..C 7
Raton° ....6,885 ..B 9
Red River ....477 ..C 8
Redrock ....K 2
Regina† ....105 ..D 5
Rehoboth ....E 2
Rencona ....F 7
Reserve° ....289 ..I 2
Ribera† ....416 ..E 8
Rincon† ....271 ..K 5
Rio Commu-
nities*† ....4,723 ..G 5
Rio Rancho ....87,521 ..F 5
Rociada ....D 8
Rodeo† ....101 ..M 1
Rodey† ....388 ..K 5
Rogers ....H 11
Romeroville ....E 8
Roswell° ....48,366 ..I 9
Rowe† ....415 ..E 7
Roy ....234 ..D 10
Ruidoso ....8,029 ..J 7
Ruidoso
Downs ....2,815 ..I 7
Rutherton ....C 6
Sabinoso ....E 9
Sacramento† ....58 ..K 7
Saint Vrain ....G 11
Salem† ....942 ..K 5
San Acacia† ....44 ..H 5
San Antonio† ....94 ..H 5
San Cristobal† ....273 ..C 7
San Felipe
Pueblo† ....2,404 ..E 6
San Fidel† ....138 ..F 4
San Geronimo ....E 8
San Ildefonso† ....524 ..D 6
San Jon ....216 ..F 11
San Jose ....E 7
San Juan† ....137 ..D 6
San Lorenzo† ....97 ..K 3
San Mateo† ....161 ..E 4
San Miguel ....E 8
San Miguel† ....1,153 ..L 5
San Patricio ....I 8
San Rafael† ....933 ..F 3
San Ysidro ....193 ..E 5
Sandia Park† ....237 ..F 6
Sandia Indian
Reservation ....3,563 ..F 6
Sanostee† ....371 ..C 2
Santa Ana
Pueblo† ....610 ..E 6
Santa Clara ....1,686 ..K 3
Santa Clara
Indian Res-
ervation* ....11,021 ..D 6
Santa Cruz† ....368 ..D 7
Santa Fe° ....67,947 ..E 7
Santa Rosa° ....2,848 ..F 9
Santa Teresa† ....4,258 ..M 5
Santo Domingo
Pueblo† ....2,456 ..E 6
Santo Tomas ....L 5
Seboyeta† ....179 ..F 4
Sedan ....D 11
Sena† ....129 ..F 8
Seneca ....C 11
Serafina ....E 8
Seven Rivers ....K 9
Shiprock† ....8,295 ..B 2
Sile ....E 6
Silver City° ....10,315 ..K 3
Socorro° ....9,051 ..H 5
Solano ....D 10
South Carmen ....D 8
South
Valley*† ....40,976 ..F 6
Springer ....1,047 ..C 9
Standing Rock ....D 3
Stanley ....F 7
Stead ....D 11
Sunland Park
[-Meadow
Vista] ....14,106 ..M 6
Sunshine† ....420 ..L 3
Sunspot ....K 7
Taiban ....G 10
Tajique† ....130 ..G 6
Talpa† ....778 ..C 7
Taos° ....5,716 ..C 7
Taos Indian
Reservation ....4,329 ..C 8
Taos Pueblo† ....1,135 ..C 7
Tatum ....798 ..J 11
Tecolotito† ....232 ..F 8
Tererro ....E 7
Tesuque† ....925 ..E 7
Texico ....1,130 ..G 12
Thoreau† ....1,865 ..E 3
Three Rivers ....J 6
Tierra
Amarilla†° ....382 ..C 6
Tijeras* ....541 ..F 6
Tinnie ....I 8
Toadlena ....D 2
Tocito ....C 2
Tohatchi† ....808 ..D 2
Tome† ....1,867 ..G 5
Torreon† ....237 ..G 6
Trampas ....D 7
Trementina ....E 9
Tres Piedras ....C 7
Trujillo ....E 9
Truth or Conse-
quences° ....6,475 ..J 4
Tucumcari° ....5,363 ..F 10
Tularosa ....2,842 ..J 7
Turley ....C 4
Turquillo ....D 8
Tyrone† ....637 ..K 3
University
Park† ....4,192 ..L 5
Ute Park† ....71 ..C 8
Vado† ....3,194 ..L 6
Valdez ....C 7
Vallecitos ....C 6
Valencia† ....2,192 ..G 6
Valmont ....K 7
Valmora ....D 8
Vanadium ....K 3
Vaughn ....446 ..G 8
Veguita† ....232 ..G 5
Velarde† ....502 ..D 7
Villanueva† ....468 ..F 8
Virden ....152 ..K 1
Wagon
Mound ....314 ..D 9
Waterflow† ....1,670 ..B 3
Watrous† ....135 ..E 8
Weed† ....63 ..K 7
White Rock*† ....5,725 ..D 6
White Sands† ....1,651 ..K 6
Whites City† ....7 ..L 9
Willard ....253 ..G 7
Williamsburg ....449 ..J 4
Winston† ....61 ..I 4
Yeso ....G 9
Zuni Pueblo† ....6,302 ..F 2
Zuni Indian
Reservation ....7,891 ..F 2

*Does not appear on map; key shows general location.
†Census designated place—unincorporated, but recognized as a significant settled community by the U.S. Census Bureau.

°County seat.
Places without population figures are unincorporated areas.
Source: 2010 census.

UTAH
COLORADO
OKLAHOMA
TEXAS
ARIZONA

A B C D E F G H

12 11 10 9 8 7 6 5 4 3 2 1

ONLY POINT IN THE UNITED STATES COMMON TO FOUR STATE CORNERS

Muddy Creek Reservoir
Two Buttes
Boise City
Seneca
KIOWA NATIONAL GRASSLAND
Clayton
Des Moines
Grenville
Mount Dora
Union
Sedan
Stead
Hayden
Amistad
Bueyeros
Harding
Gallegos
Nara Visa
Logan
Bellview
Glenrio
Farwell
Clovis
Texico
Portales
Bovina
Causey
Rogers
Pep
Dora
Elida
Kenna

San Juan River
Animas River
Durango
Cortez
MESA VERDE NATIONAL PARK
UTE MOUNTAIN INDIAN RESERVATION
AZTEC RUINS NATIONAL MONUMENT
Aztec
Bloomfield
Flora Vista
Cedar Hill
Turley
Blanco
La Plata
San Juan
SALMON RUINS
Kirtland
Waterflow
Fruitland
Shiprock
Bikiahbito
Little Water
Farmington
Burnham
Blanco Trading Post
Nageezi
CHACO CULTURE NATIONAL HISTORICAL PARK
PUEBLO BONITO
Star Lake
Torreon
White Horse
Hospah
Pueblo Pintado
Seven Lakes
Crownpoint
Standing Rock
Smith Lake
Prewitt
Continental Divide
Thoreau
McKinley
Mariano Lake
Pinedale
Church Rock
Fort Wingate
Gamerco
Gallup
Rehoboth
Mentmore
Defiance
Manuelito
Yah-Ta-Hey
McGaffey
CIBOLA NATIONAL FOREST
Ramah
RAMAH NAVAJO INDIAN RESERVATION
EL MORRO NATIONAL MONUMENT
Fence Lake
NAVAJO INDIAN RESERVATION
Navajo
Mexican Springs
Tohatchi
Naschitti
Sheep Springs
Newcomb
Sanostee
Tocito
Toadlena
Crystal
Twin Lakes
Chi Chi Tah
Brimhall
Black Rock
Pescado
Zuni Pueblo
ZUNI INDIAN RESERVATION
Vanderwagen
Allison
St. Johns
Eagar
Red Hill
Luna
Cruzville
Apache Creek
Aragon
Old Horse Springs
Quemado
Pie Town
Omega
Datil
Mangas
Magdalena
APACHE NATIONAL FOREST
NATIONAL RADIO ASTRONOMY OBSERVATORY VLA TELESCOPE
CIBOLA NATIONAL FOREST
Alamo
San Antonio
Bingham
Lincoln
Ancho
Corona
Gran Quivira
Claunch
Cedarvale
Duran
Encino
Torrance
Willard
Mountainair
SALINAS PUEBLO MISSIONS NATIONAL MONUMENT
Punta de Agua
Abo
Manzano
Torreon
Tajique
Chilili
Estancia
McIntosh
Moriarty
Stanley
Galisteo
Lamy
Cerrillos
Madrid
Golden
San Pedro
Cedar Crest
Tijeras
Sandia Park
Placitas
SANDIA MILITARY RESERVATION
Bernalillo
Corrales
Rio Rancho
Alameda
Albuquerque
Mountain View
Bosque Farms
Peralta
Los Lunas
Valencia
Tome
Los Chavez
Belen
Jarales
Las Nutrias
Veguita
La Joya
Contreras
Abeytas
San Acacia
Lemitar
Polvadera
Escondida
Socorro
Luis Lopez
San Antonio
Bernardo
Sabinal
SEVILLETA NATIONAL WILDLIFE REFUGE
BOSQUE DEL APACHE NATIONAL WILDLIFE REFUGE
Florida
Alamillo

Durango
Waisenburg
Monte Vista
Alamosa
Trinidad
Raton
Colfax
Cimarron
CAPULIN VOLCANO NATIONAL MONUMENT
Capulin
Folsom
French
Maxwell
MAXWELL NATIONAL WILDLIFE REFUGE
Springer
Miami
Rayado
PHILMONT SCOUT RANCH
Eagle Nest
Angel Fire
TAOS INDIAN RESERVATION
Taos
Questa
Red River
Cerro
Costilla
Amalia
San Cristobal
Arroyo Hondo
Arroyo Seco
El Prado
Ranchos de Taos
Talpa
Pilar
Tres Piedras
Los Pinos
Antonito
Chama
Brazos
Tierra Amarilla
Los Ojos
Ensenada
Monero
Lumberton
Dulce
JICARILLA APACHE INDIAN RESERVATION
CARSON NATIONAL FOREST
El Vado Reservoir
El Vado
Cebolla
La Puente
Rutheron
Los Tablas
Vallecitos
La Madera
El Rito
Ojo Caliente
Abiquiu
Medanales
Velarde
Dixon
Chamisal
Peñasco
Vadito
Llano
Chacon
Holman
Mora
Ledoux
Cleveland
Rainsville
Ocate
Wagon Mound
Levy
Roy
Mills
KIOWA NATIONAL GRASSLAND
Solano
Albert
Mosquero
Bell Ranch
Variadero
Trementina
Sabinoso
Conchas
Conchas Dam
Newkirk
Cuervo
Santa Rosa
Puerto de Luna
Fort Sumner
Yeso
Taiban
Tolar
Melrose
McAlister
House
Montoya
Pastura
Vaughn
Duran
Ramon
Mesa
Yeso
De Baca
Pecos River
Guadalupe

Ghost Ranch
Coyote
Gallina
Regina
Cuba
Youngsville
Canones
Abiquiu
Cañon Plaza
Gavilan
Lindrith
Ojito
La Jara
Counselors
JEMEZ INDIAN RES.
JICARILLA APACHE INDIAN RESERVATION
SANTA FE NATIONAL FOREST
Jemez Springs
Ponderosa
Jemez Pueblo
San Ysidro
ZIA INDIAN RES.
BANDELIER NATIONAL MONUMENT
Los Alamos
White Rock
SANTA CLARA INDIAN RES.
Española
Santa Clara
Pojoaque
Nambe
Tesuque
Chimayo
Santa Cruz
San Ildefonso
San Juan
Alcalde
SANTA FE
La Cienega
Agua Fria
Cochiti
Peña Blanca
SANTO DOMINGO PUEBLO
Domingo
SAN FELIPE PUEBLO
Algodones
SANTA ANA PUEBLO
ISLETA INDIAN RES.
Isleta Pueblo
Los Padillas
Pajarito
LAGUNA INDIAN RESERVATION
Laguna
Paguate
Seboyeta
Paraje
Mesita
Los Lunas
New Laguna
Casa Blanca
Acomita
ACOMA INDIAN RESERVATION
Acoma
San Fidel
McCartys
Grants
San Rafael
Milan
Bluewater
Cubero
EL MALPAIS NATIONAL MONUMENT
Cibola
Broadview Acres
Correo
Armijo
Cibola
Correo

COCHITI INDIAN RES.

PECOS NATIONAL HISTORICAL PARK
Pecos
Glorieta
Rowe
Ribera
Villanueva
San Miguel
Serafina
Romeroville
San Jose
Bernal
Gabaldon
San Ignacio
Las Vegas
LAS VEGAS NATIONAL WILDLIFE REFUGE
Tecolotito
Sena
Gonzales Ranch
Aurora
Dahlia
Chaperito
Trujillo
Valmora
Watrous
FORT UNION NATIONAL MONUMENT
Sapello
Las Tusas
Los Vigiles
Montezuma
El Porvenir
Gascon
Rociada
San Miguel
Las Montoyas
Los Montoyas
San Geronimo
GERONIMO WILDLIFE REFUGE
Colonias
Esteros
Cibola
Corners
Newkirk
La Loma
Salado Creek
Salado River

Platoro Reservoir
Rio Grande
Huérfano River
Conejos River
Navajo River

Conchas Lake
Conchas River
Canadian River
Ute Creek
Ute Reservoir
Revuelto Creek
Pajarito
Caprock Hill
Broadview
Curry
Roosevelt
CANNON AIR FORCE BASE
GRULLA NATIONAL WILDLIFE REFUGE
Pleasant Hill
Bard
Cameron
Grady
St. Vrain
Field
Grier
Ranchvale
Floyd
Forrest
Tucumcari
Quay
San Jon
Logan
Garrison

Buena Vista
Guadalupita
Ojo Feliz
Shadybrook
PICURIS INDIAN RESERVATION
Picuris Pueblo
Truchas
Cordova
Cundiyo
Rociada
Las Vegas

CARSON NATIONAL FOREST
SANTA FE NATIONAL FOREST

Canjilon
Llaves
Nutrias
Cañones
Barranca

Rio Arriba
Sandoval

RIO GRANDE
Zuni River
Rio San Jose
Rio Puerco
Rio Salado
Canyon Largo
Chaco River
Mancos River
Dolores River
San Juan River
Las Animas River

WILD RIVERS NATIONAL RECREATION AREA
WHEELER PEAK
PECOS WILDERNESS
GLORIETA BATTLE SITE

Salado Creek del Perro
Laguna del Perro

Sofia
Gladstone
Abbott
Farley
Maxwell

Zuni Pueblo
Pescado
Thoreau

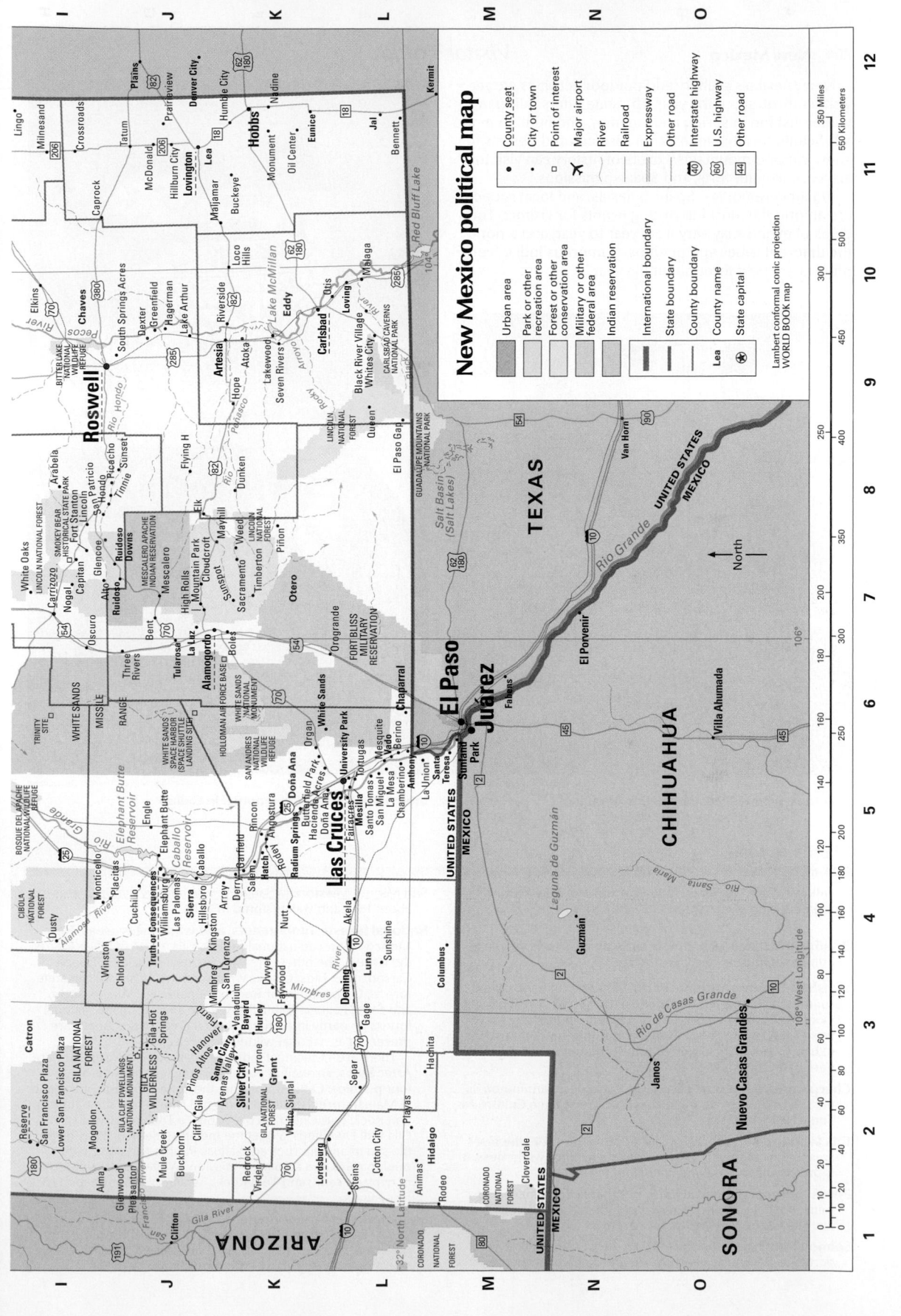

New Mexico political map

Legend:

Symbol	Description
●	County seat
·	City or town
□	Point of interest
✈	Major airport
	River
	Railroad
	Expressway
	Other road
40	Interstate highway
80	U.S. highway
44	Other road

Area shading	
	Urban area
	Park or other recreation area
	Forest or other conservation area
	Military or other federal area
	Indian reservation

Boundaries	
	International boundary
	State boundary
	County boundary
Lea	County name
⊛	State capital

Lambert conformal conic projection
WORLD BOOK map

0 50 100 150 200 250 300 350 Miles
0 50 100 150 200 250 300 350 450 500 550 Kilometers

New Mexico's scenery and outdoor activities attract visitors throughout the year. The state offers skiing in winter, fishing in spring and summer, and hunting in the fall. Scenic beauty ranges from rose-colored deserts to snow-capped mountains. Lovers of history can visit Indian ruins, frontier forts, and Spanish missions.

Indian ceremonies, Spanish fiestas, and local rodeos are among the most interesting events for visitors. The dates of events may vary from year to year, and among the different tribes and pueblos. Numerous Indian ceremonies are held throughout the year.

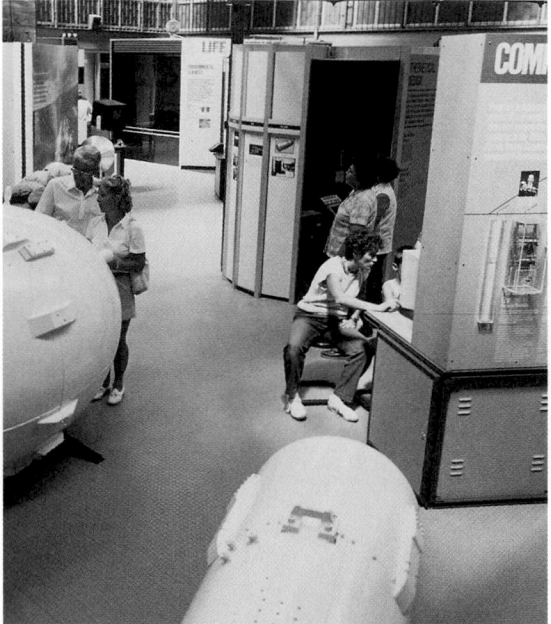

Los Alamos National Laboratory

Bradbury Science Museum in Los Alamos

Mark Nohl, New Mexico Tourism Department

Inter-Tribal Indian Ceremonial in Gallup

Places to visit

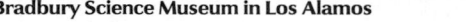

Following are brief descriptions of some of New Mexico's most interesting places to visit:

Bradbury Science Museum, in Los Alamos, shows the development of nuclear energy.

Carlsbad Caverns National Park. This series of huge caves in southeastern New Mexico is one of the world's great natural wonders. Lighted trails offer an excellent opportunity for visitors to see fantastic rock formations. Hundreds of thousands of bats fly out of the caverns at dusk and return at dawn. See **Carlsbad Caverns National Park.**

Chaco Culture National Historical Park, near Farmington, is the site of ruins of early Indian culture. See **Chaco Culture National Historical Park.**

Gila Wilderness, near Silver City, became—in 1924—the first area in the country to be set aside as a national wilderness. It is preserved in its natural condition.

Pecos National Historical Park, near Santa Fe, contains the ruins of what was once the largest Indian pueblo in New Mexico. See **Pecos National Historical Park.**

Salmon Ruins, near Bloomfield, is a site of archaeological importance. It features pueblo ruins and a nearby museum.

San Miguel Mission, in Santa Fe, was built by the Spaniards in about 1610 and was restored in 1710.

National forests, monuments, and wilderness areas. New Mexico has seven national forests. Gila, north of Silver City, is the largest. The others are Apache, near Luna and Reserve; Carson, near Taos; Cíbola, which consists of several separate forests; Coronado, near Rodeo; Lincoln, near Alamogordo; and Santa Fe, near Santa Fe. Apache and Coronado national forests lie partly in Arizona. Several areas of the forests are preserved as national wilderness areas.

There are 11 national monuments in New Mexico. They are Aztec Ruins, an ancient pueblo; Bandelier, the ruins of four pueblos; Capulin Volcano, the cone of an extinct volcano; El Malpais, prehistoric lava flows; El Morro, the site of Inscription Rock; Fort Union, an old Santa Fe Trail military post; the Gila Cliff Dwellings, a onetime Indian settlement; Petroglyph, the site of ancient rock art; Salinas Pueblo Missions, with pueblo ruins and a Spanish mission; White Sands, a deposit of gypsum sand; and Tent Rocks, which are cone-shaped rock formations.

State parks and monuments. New Mexico has 34 state parks and 6 state monuments. For detailed information about the parks and monuments, visit the New Mexico State Parks Division Web site at http://www.emnrd.state.nm.us/PRD.

AP/Wide World

International Balloon Fiesta in Albuquerque

Gail Russell

San Miguel Mission in Santa Fe

David Muench

Stalactites and stalagmites in Carlsbad Caverns

Land and climate

Land regions. New Mexico has four main land regions: (1) the Great Plains, (2) the Rocky Mountains, (3) the Basin and Range Region, and (4) the Colorado Plateau.

The Great Plains of New Mexico are part of the vast Interior Plain that sweeps across North America from Canada to Mexico. In New Mexico, the Great Plains cover roughly the eastern third of the state. They extend from a high plateau in the north to the Pecos River Valley in the south. Streams have cut deep canyons in the plateau as it slopes away from the Rocky Mountains. Cattle and sheep graze there. To the south are dry farming and irrigated agriculture. The eastern edge of the state, south of the Canadian River, is called the *High Plains* or *Llano Estacado* (Staked Plain). The Llano Estacado also covers much of northwestern Texas (see **Texas** [Land regions]).

The Rocky Mountains extend into north-central New Mexico from Colorado south to a point near Santa Fe. In winter, deep snow piles up on the mountains. In spring, the snow melts and provides water for irrigated crops in the fertile Rio Grande Valley. The Rio Grande, which rises in Colorado, cuts between ranges of mountains. To the east are the Sangre de Cristo (Blood of Christ) Mountains. Wheeler Peak, 13,161 feet (4,011 meters) high, is the highest point in the state. The Nacimiento and Jemez ranges are west of the river.

The Basin and Range Region covers about a third of the state. It extends south and west from the Rockies to the borders with Arizona and Mexico. This region includes scattered ranges of rugged mountains—the Guadalupe, Mogollon, Organ, Sacramento, and San Andres ranges. Broad desert *basins* (low places where the streams have no outlet) lie between the mountains. The largest basins are the Jornada del Muerto (Journey of the Dead) and the Tularosa. The Rio Grande flows through the Basin and Range Region.

The Colorado Plateau, in northwestern New Mexico, is a broken country of wide valleys and plains, deep canyons, sharp cliffs, and rugged, lonely, flat-topped hills called *mesas.* The best-known mesa in the state is Acoma. The Indians built a city on top of Acoma. To the west of Acoma is a 40-mile (64-kilometer) strip of *malpais,* an area of extinct volcanoes and lava plains. Ship Rock, a steep hill that resembles a ship under full sail, has been a famous landmark in San Juan County for hundreds of years. Ship Rock rises 1,678 feet (511 meters) above the flat land around it. The San Juan Basin lies in the northwest section of the Colorado Plateau. The *Continental Divide* passes through both the Colorado Plateau and the Basin and Range Region. Streams west of the divide run into the Pacific Ocean. Water east of it runs to the Gulf of Mexico.

Rivers and lakes. The Rio Grande runs like a backbone down the length of New Mexico. At the state's southern boundary it turns east and forms the border

Ken Gallard, Click/Chicago

Sheep graze on a New Mexico ranch. Farmers in the state raise sheep and cattle where low rainfall or rough land prevents crop farming. Ranching is the state's leading agricultural activity.

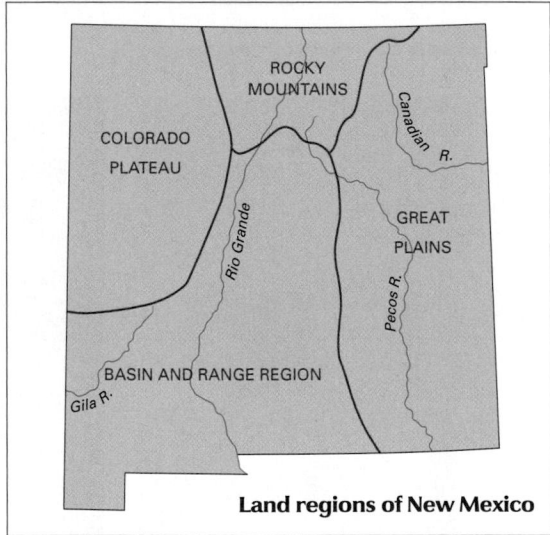

Land regions of New Mexico

WORLD BOOK map

Map index

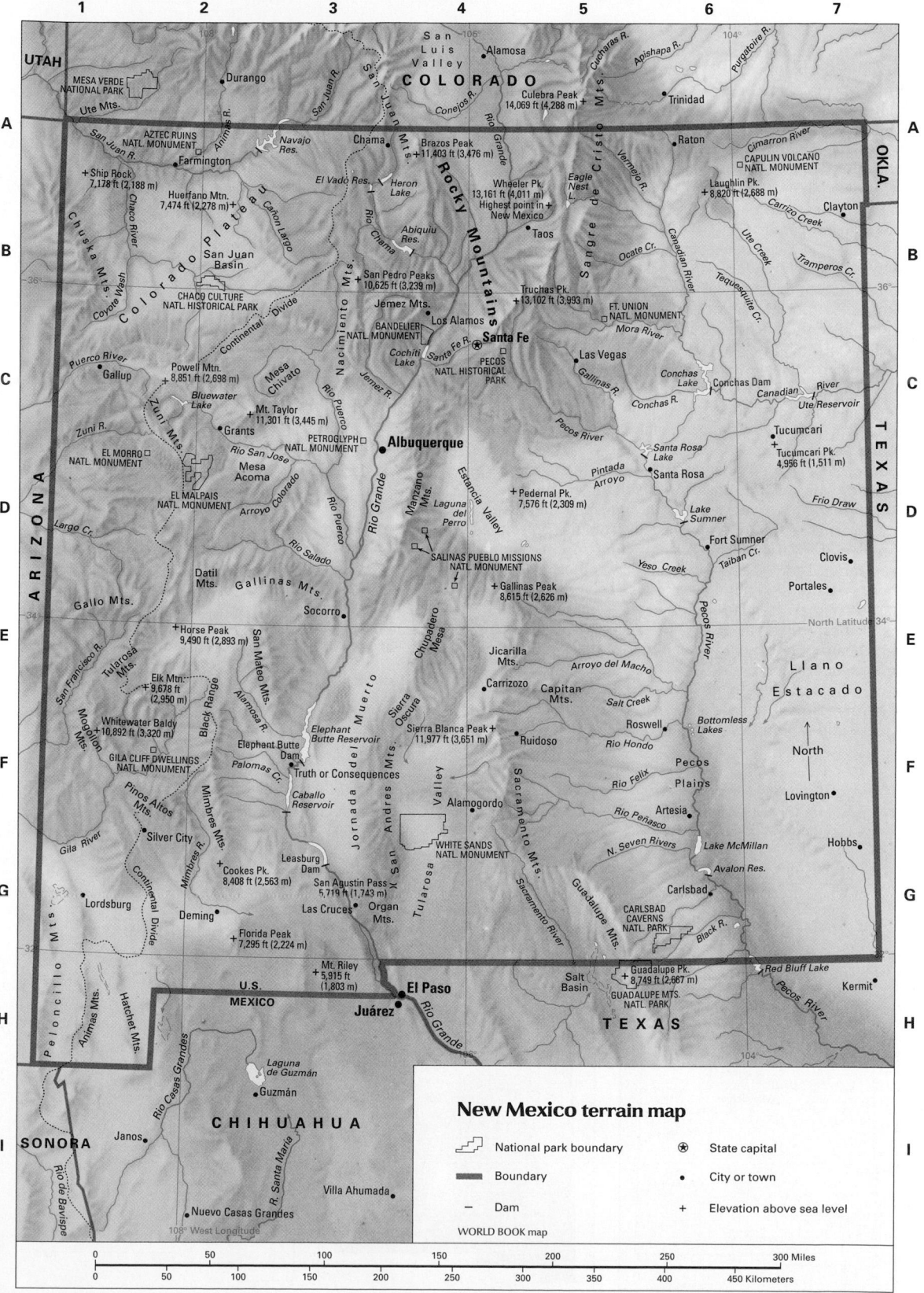

New Mexico terrain map

Legend			
⌐⌐	National park boundary	⊛	State capital
▬	Boundary	•	City or town
–	Dam	+	Elevation above sea level

WORLD BOOK map

Columns: 1 2 3 4 5 6 7

Rows: A B C D E F G H I

UTAH
COLORADO
ARIZONA
TEXAS
OKLA.
U.S.
MEXICO
SONORA
CHIHUAHUA

MESA VERDE NATIONAL PARK
• Durango
San Luis Valley
• Alamosa
Culebra Peak 14,069 ft (4,288 m) +
Cucharas R.
Apishapa R.
Purgatoire R.
• Trinidad

AZTEC RUINS NATL. MONUMENT
Navajo Res.
• Chama
Brazos Peak 11,403 ft (3,476 m) +
Wheeler Pk. 13,161 ft (4,011 m) Highest point in New Mexico +
Eagle Nest
Vermejo R.
• Raton
Cimarron River
CAPULIN VOLCANO NATL. MONUMENT
Laughlin Pk. + 8,820 ft (2,688 m)
Carrizo Creek
• Clayton

+ Ship Rock 7,178 ft (2,188 m)
• Farmington
Animas R.
San Juan R.
El Vado Res.
Heron Lake
Rio Grande
• Taos
Ocate Cr.
Canadian River
Ute Creek
Tramperos Cr.
Tequesquite Cr.

Huerfano Mtn. 7,474 ft (2,278 m) +
Cañon Largo
Abiquiu Res.
Rio Chama

San Juan Basin
• San Pedro Peaks + 10,625 ft (3,239 m)
Truchas Pk. + 13,102 ft (3,993 m)
FT. UNION NATL. MONUMENT
Mora River

CHACO CULTURE NATL. HISTORICAL PARK
Continental Divide
Jemez Mts.
Los Alamos
BANDELIER NATL. MONUMENT
Santa Fe
Las Vegas
Gallinas R.
Conchas Lake
Conchas Dam
Canadian River
Ute Reservoir

• Gallup
Puerco River
Powell Mtn. + 8,851 ft (2,698 m)
Mesa Chivato
Cochiti Lake
Santa Fe R.
PECOS NATL. HISTORICAL PARK
Conchas R.

Bluewater Lake
+ Mt. Taylor 11,301 ft (3,445 m)
• Grants
Zuni Mts.
PETROGLYPH NATL. MONUMENT
Albuquerque
Santa Rosa Lake
• Tucumcari
+ Tucumcari Pk. 4,956 ft (1,511 m)

Zuni R.
EL MORRO NATL. MONUMENT
Rio San Jose
Mesa Acoma
EL MALPAIS NATL. MONUMENT
Arroyo Colorado
Rio Puerco
Rio Grande
Manzano Mts.
Estancia Valley
Laguna del Perro
+ Pedernal Pk. 7,576 ft (2,309 m)
Pintada Arroyo
• Santa Rosa
Lake Sumner
• Clovis
Frio Draw

Largo Cr.
Rio Salado
SALINAS PUEBLO MISSIONS NATL. MONUMENT
+ Gallinas Peak 8,615 ft (2,626 m)
Yeso Creek
• Fort Sumner
Taiban Cr.
• Portales

Gallo Mts.
Datil Mts.
Gallinas Mts.
• Socorro
North Latitude 34°
Pecos River
Llano Estacado

+ Horse Peak 9,490 ft (2,893 m)
San Mateo Mts.
Chupadero Mesa
Jicarilla Mts.
Arroyo del Macho
North

San Francisco Mts.
Tularosa Mts.
Elk Mtn. + 9,678 ft (2,950 m)
Black Range
Alamosa R.
Sierra del Muerto
Sierra Oscura
• Carrizozo
Capitan Mts.
Salt Creek
• Roswell
Bottomless Lakes
• Lovington

Mogollon Mts.
+ Whitewater Baldy 10,892 ft (3,320 m)
GILA CLIFF DWELLINGS NATL. MONUMENT
Elephant Butte Reservoir
Sierra Blanca Peak + 11,977 ft (3,651 m)
• Ruidoso
Rio Hondo
Pecos Plains
Rio Felix
• Artesia
• Hobbs

Pinos Altos Mts.
Mimbres Mts.
Elephant Butte Dam
Palomas Cr.
Truth or Consequences
Jornada del Muerto
San Andres Mts.
Tularosa Valley
• Alamogordo
Sacramento Mts.
Rio Peñasco
N. Seven Rivers
Lake McMillan
Avalon Res.

Gila River
• Silver City
Continental Divide
Caballo Reservoir
+ Cookes Pk. 8,408 ft (2,563 m)
Leasburg Dam
WHITE SANDS NATL. MONUMENT
Sacramento River
• Carlsbad
CARLSBAD CAVERNS NATL. PARK

• Lordsburg
• Deming
San Agustin Pass 5,719 ft (1,743 m)
Las Cruces
Organ Mts.
Guadalupe Mts.
Black R.
Red Bluff Lake

Peloncillo Mts.
Animas Mts.
Hatchet Mts.
Florida Peak + 7,295 ft (2,224 m)
Mt. Riley + 5,915 ft (1,803 m)
El Paso
Salt Basin
Guadalupe Pk. + 8,749 ft (2,667 m)
GUADALUPE MTS. NATL. PARK
Pecos River
• Kermit

Juárez
Rio Grande
TEXAS

Rio Casas Grandes
R. Santa Maria
Laguna de Guzmán
• Guzmán
• Janos
Rio de Bavispe

• Villa Ahumada

• Nuevo Casas Grandes

108° West Longitude

106°
104°
36°
34°
32°

0		50		100		150		200	250	300 Miles
0	50	100	150	200	250	300	350	400	450 Kilometers	

between Texas and Mexico. A series of dams stores water for irrigation. Elephant Butte Dam, near Truth or Consequences, blocks the Rio Grande and forms Elephant Butte Reservoir, New Mexico's largest lake. Its water irrigates land in New Mexico, Texas, and Mexico. Another important river is the Pecos. It rises in the Sangre de Cristo Mountains and flows south. Pecos water irrigates the land around Carlsbad and Roswell. The San Juan River drains the northwest corner of the state. The Canadian River rises in the northeast part. Its waters are stored for irrigation at the Conchas Dam, near Tucumcari. The Gila River, in the southwest, flows west into Arizona.

New Mexico has few natural lakes. Most famous are the deep Bottomless Lakes, a group of pools near Roswell. Artificially created lakes other than Elephant Butte Reservoir include Abiquiu, Avalon, Bluewater, Caballo, Cochiti, Conchas, Eagle Nest, El Vado, Heron, McMillan, Navajo, Sumner, and Ute.

Plant and animal life. Forests cover about a fourth of New Mexico. Common trees include aspens, cottonwoods, Douglas-firs, junipers, piñons (nut pines), ponderosa pines, scrub oaks, spruces, and white firs. The yucca, New Mexico's state flower, grows in most areas. Desert plants include cactus, creosote bush, gramma grass, mesquite, white and purple sage, and soapweed. Cattle ranchers guard their livestock from the poisonous locoweed. Wild mountain plants include forget-me-nots, saxifrages, sedges, alpine larkspur, and other flowers.

Animal life is plentiful in New Mexico. Among the larger animals are black bears, coyotes, mountain lions, pronghorns, deer, and elk. Other animals include badgers, beavers, bobcats, chipmunks, foxes, jack rabbits, minks, otters, and prairie dogs.

Among the state's game birds are ducks, grouse, pheasants, quail, and wild turkeys. Many varieties of geese and sandhill cranes migrate to New Mexico for the winter. Common fishes include black bass, catfish, crappies, perch, suckers, and trout. Two kinds of poisonous snakes, the rattlesnake and the coral snake, live in New Mexico. The southwestern desert is the home of many spiders, including various kinds of tarantulas and the western black widow.

Climate. New Mexico has a dry, warm climate. A person may hang out clothes in the rain knowing the rain will stop soon and the air will dry the clothes quickly. The state averages less than 20 inches (51 centimeters) of *precipitation* (rain, melted snow, and other forms of moisture) a year. It varies from over 20 inches in the northern mountains to less than 10 inches (25 centimeters) in the south and central areas. Snow falls throughout the state. The south receives only about 2 inches (5 centimeters) a year. The high mountains may get as much as 300 inches (760 centimeters) of snow each year.

Average monthly weather

	Albuquerque						Roswell				
	Temperatures				Days of rain or snow		Temperatures				Days of rain or snow
	°F		°C				°F		°C		
	High	Low	High	Low			High	Low	High	Low	
Jan.	48	24	9	–4	4	Jan.	56	24	13	–4	4
Feb.	55	28	13	–2	4	Feb.	62	29	17	–2	3
Mar.	62	34	17	1	5	Mar.	70	36	21	2	3
Apr.	71	41	22	5	3	Apr.	78	43	26	6	3
May	80	50	27	10	4	May	86	53	30	12	4
June	90	60	32	16	4	June	94	62	34	17	5
July	92	65	33	18	9	July	95	67	35	19	6
Aug.	89	63	32	17	9	Aug.	92	66	33	19	8
Sept.	82	56	28	13	6	Sept.	86	58	30	14	6
Oct.	71	44	22	7	5	Oct.	77	46	25	8	5
Nov.	57	32	14	0	4	Nov.	65	33	18	1	3
Dec.	48	24	9	–4	4	Dec.	56	25	13	–4	4

Average January temperatures

Temperatures vary widely throughout the state during wintertime. The far southern section has the mildest winters.

Average July temperatures

The state has warm summers. The mildest temperatures occur in the mountainous areas of northern New Mexico.

Average yearly precipitation

New Mexico has a dry climate. Much of the west receives less than 12 inches (30 centimeters) of rain a year.

WORLD BOOK maps

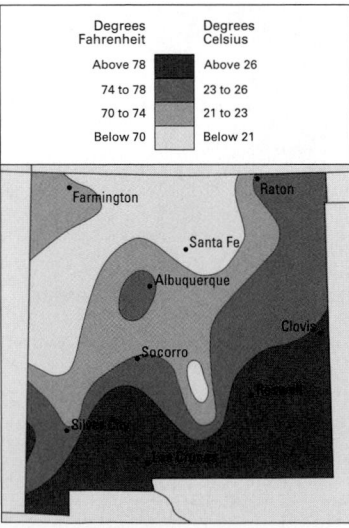

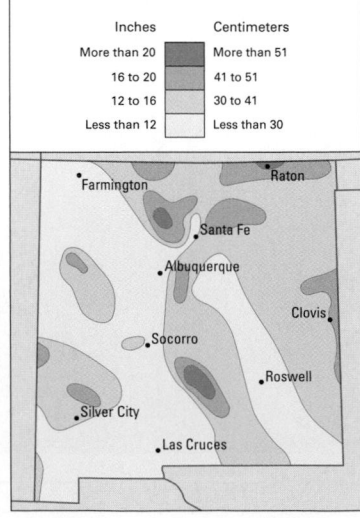

The average July temperature is about 74 °F (23 °C). January temperatures are generally warmer in the south than in the north. The state's average January temperature is 34 °F (1 °C). Day and night temperatures vary widely on the same day. The thin, dry air does not stay warm after sundown because of the high altitude. The lowest temperature recorded in New Mexico was –50 °F (–46 °C) at Gavilan, near Lindrith, on Feb. 1, 1951. The highest temperature was 122 °F (50 °C) near Carlsbad on June 27, 1994.

Economy

Although New Mexico has limited water resources and large tracts of desert, the state's natural resources play a major role in its economy. Tourism, mining, and agriculture provide valuable jobs for the state's workers.

The state's scenic beauty and reputation as an arts and cultural center attract tourists all year. The state's hand-crafted Indian pottery and jewelry are world famous. Tourists flock to New Mexico's many ski resorts in the winter. Large crude oil and natural gas reserves make New Mexico an important mining state. Cattle ranching and dairy farming provide the most farm income.

Large federal government research laboratories are among New Mexico's leading employers. Electronic products are the state's major type of manufacture.

Natural resources include large mineral deposits and rich, renewable resources based on the soil. These resources include forests, grasses, plants, and animals.

Minerals. New Mexico is rich in mined products that supply energy. It has large reserves of coal, crude oil, natural gas, and uranium. The state is the nation's leading producer of potash, a vital fertilizer material, and of perlite, a lightweight rock used in insulation and in potting mix. New Mexico has one of the largest copper reserves in the nation. Large reserves of carbon dioxide gas are found in a deposit called the Bravo Dome in the northeast part of the state. The state also ranks high in the production of molybdenum, pumice, and zeolites.

Soil. More than half of New Mexico's soil is stony and shallow, and not good for farming. Most of the crop and dairy farming occurs in the eastern part of the state, which has sandy soil. Important agricultural soils also occur along the Rio Grande valley.

Water is precious in New Mexico, and water resources are extremely important. New Mexico and other western states have joined with Mexico to share the use of water in various streams. Each area gets a share. For example, Colorado users must allow a certain amount of Rio Grande water to flow into New Mexico. New Mexico's resources include underground water.

New Mexico has a number of major storage projects that help make good use of water. These projects regulate the flow of the Canadian, Pecos, Rio Grande, and San Juan rivers, and that of some of their tributaries.

Forests cover about one-fourth of the state. There are commercially valuable timberlands in several mountain areas. The most common trees include the aspen, cottonwood, Douglas-fir, juniper, piñon, ponderosa pine, scrub oak, spruce, and white fir.

Service industries provide the greatest part of both New Mexico's employment and its *gross domestic product*—the total value of all goods and services produced in the state in a year. Many of the service industries are concentrated in the Albuquerque-Santa Fe area.

Government activities are important to New Mexico's economy. Santa Fe, the state capital, is the center of state government activities. Federal government research laboratories and military bases also play a major role in the state's economy. Los Alamos National Laboratory is a world leader in research of military and nonmilitary uses of nuclear energy. Sandia National Laboratories in Albuquerque is a center of nuclear weapons research. Military bases in New Mexico include Cannon Air Force Base in Clovis, Holloman Air Force Base near Alamogordo, Kirtland Air Force Base near Albuquerque, and White Sands Missile Range in the south-central part of the state. The Bureau of Indian Affairs, a federal government agency, assists the state's Indian population. Jobs at casinos on New Mexico's Indian reservations contribute to local government employment in the state.

Albuquerque is the chief banking and insurance cen-

Computer and electronic equipment is New Mexico's leading manufactured product. These technicians produce microprocessors at an Intel Corporation facility in Rio Rancho. They wear special clothing that prevents dust or hair from getting into the tiny circuits.

Intel Corporation

New Mexico economy

General economy

Gross domestic product (GDP)* (2008) $77,858,000,000
  Rank among U.S. states   37th
Unemployment rate (2010)   8.4% (U.S. avg: 9.6%)

*Gross domestic product is the total value of goods and services produced in a year.
Sources: U.S. Bureau of Economic Analysis and U.S. Bureau of Labor Statistics.

Production and workers by economic activities

Economic activities	Percent of GDP* produced	Employed workers Number of people	Percent of total
Community, business, & personal services	22	355,600	32
Government	19	212,700	19
Finance, insurance, & real estate	16	85,900	8
Trade, restaurants, & hotels	13	233,400	21
Mining	11	27,600	2
Construction	6	79,600	7
Transportation & communication	5	46,600	4
Manufacturing	5	41,600	4
Agriculture	2	29,900	3
Utilities	2	4,500	*
Total†	100	1,117,400	100

*Less than one-half of 1 percent.
†Figures may not add up to 100 percent due to rounding.
Figures are for 2008; employment figures include full- and part-time workers.
Source: World Book estimates based on data from U.S. Bureau of Economic Analysis.

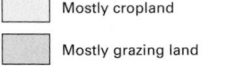

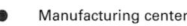

Mostly cropland — Forest land
Mostly grazing land — ● Manufacturing center
Desert shrubland — ∙ Mineral deposit

WORLD BOOK map

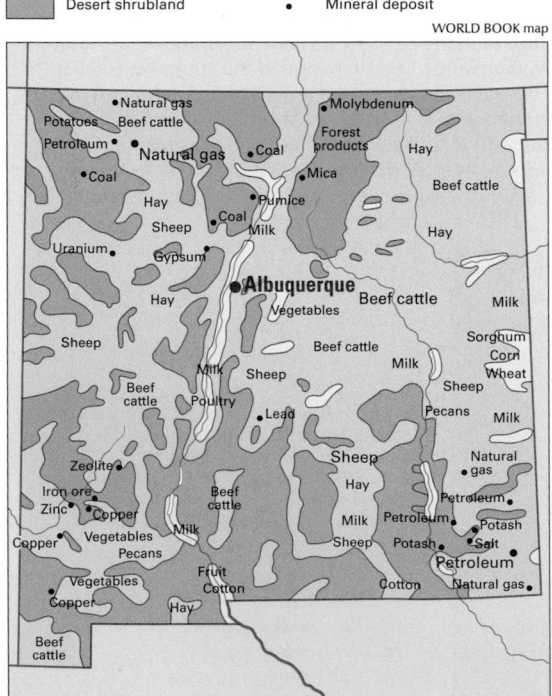

Agriculture

Cash receipts $2,698,524,000
  Rank among U.S. states   31st
Distribution   74% livestock, 26% crops
Farms   20,500
Farm acres (hectares)   43,000,000 (17,400,000)
  Rank among U.S. states   6th
Farmland   55% of New Mexico

Leading products

1. Cattle and calves
2. Dairy products
3. Hay
4. Pecans   (ranks 1st in U.S.)
5. Greenhouse and nursery products
6. Onions
Other products: chili peppers, corn, cotton, peanuts, potatoes, sorghum, wheat.

Manufacturing

Value added by manufacture* $7,115,060,000
  Rank among U.S. states   42nd

Leading product

Computer and electronic products
Other products: chemicals, fabricated metal products, food products, machinery, nonmetallic mineral products, transportation equipment.

*Value added by manufacture is the increase in value of raw materials after they become finished products.

Mining

Nonfuel mineral production $1,620,000,000
  Rank among U.S. states   15th
Coal (tons*)   25,645,000
  Rank among U.S. states   12th
Crude oil (barrels†)   59,403,000
  Rank among U.S. states   7th
Natural gas (cubic feet‡)   1,446,204,000,000
  Rank among U.S. states   4th

*One ton equals 0.9072 metric ton.
†One barrel equals 42 gallons (159 liters).
‡One cubic foot equals 0.0283 cubic meter.

Leading products

1. Natural gas   (ranks 4th in U.S.)
2. Petroleum
3. Coal
4. Copper   (ranks 3rd in U.S.)
5. Potash   (ranks 1st in U.S.)
Other products: molybdenum, perlite, portland cement, sand and gravel.

Electric power

Coal   73.0%
Natural gas   21.5%
Wind   4.4%
Other   1.1%

Figures are for 2008, except for the agricultural figures, which are for 2009.
Sources: U.S. Census Bureau, U.S. Department of Agriculture, U.S. Energy Information Administration, U.S. Geological Survey.

Economy of New Mexico

This map shows the economic uses of land in New Mexico and where the leading farm, mineral, and forest products are produced. Major manufacturing centers are shown in red.

ter. Many hotels, restaurants, and retail trade establishments are in the Albuquerque and Santa Fe areas. New Mexico's restaurants, hotels, and ski resorts benefit from the billions of dollars tourists spend in the state each year. Real estate is also important to New Mexico's economy. New Mexico's population growth has led to the development of many new homes and office buildings.

Manufacturing. Computer and electronic equipment is the leading manufactured product category by far. Intel, a major electronics company in the Albuquerque area, produces silicon chips for computers.

Other products manufactured in New Mexico include aircraft and aircraft parts, chemicals, concrete, food products, and petroleum products. Large oil refineries operate near Artesia, Bloomfield, and Gallup. The Albuquerque area is the state's chief manufacturing center.

Mining. New Mexico is a leading state in the annual value of mined products. Natural gas and petroleum together account for more than 85 percent of the state's total income from mined products. Both natural gas and petroleum are produced in northwestern and southeastern New Mexico. Coal, found mainly in surface mines in the northwest, is also a significant source of mining income. Carbon dioxide from Harding, Quay, and Union counties is used to help extract oil from fields in the Permian Basin of Texas and southeast New Mexico.

Copper and potash account for most of New Mexico's income from nonfuel mined products, and New Mexico is a leading producer of both minerals. Copper is mined primarily in Grant County. Potash comes mainly from deep underground mines in southeastern New Mexico. The state is also a leading producer of molybdenum, used in making steel alloys. A mine in Taos County produces nearly all of the state's molybdenum. Gold and silver are also mined.

Agriculture. Farmland covers over half of the state's land area. Cattle ranching is the leading agricultural activity. Ranchers raise beef cattle in almost every part of the state. Most of the beef cattle are shipped to other states for fattening and slaughtering. Dairy cattle are raised mainly in southern and eastern New Mexico.

Most of New Mexico's cropland is irrigated. Its leading crop is hay, used to feed cattle. The state is a leading producer of chili peppers and pecans. Other crops include corn, cotton, onions, potatoes, and wheat.

Electric power and utilities. Power plants that burn coal or natural gas supply the vast majority of the electric power generated in New Mexico. Electric power produced by wind, solar, water, and geothermal sources is of increasing importance in the state.

Transportation. New Mexico has an extensive system of roads and highways. The first road established by Europeans in what is now the United States—El Camino Real (the Royal Highway)—ran from Santa Fe to Mexico City, Mexico. Spaniards first traveled this route in about 1581. The Santa Fe Trail was opened in 1821 between Missouri and New Mexico. Today, Interstate 25 east of Santa Fe follows this old trail. Albuquerque International Sunport is the chief airport in New Mexico.

Communication. The first Spanish-language newspaper in New Mexico, *El Crepúsculo de la Libertad (The Dawn of Liberty),* began in 1834 at Santa Fe. The *Santa Fe Republican,* the first English-language paper, was founded in 1847. Today, the state's most widely read newspapers are the *Albuquerque Journal,* the *Las Cruces Sun-News,* and *The Santa Fe New Mexican.*

Government

Constitution. New Mexico is governed under its original state constitution. The Constitution was adopted in 1911, a year before New Mexico became a state.

Amendments may be proposed by either house of the state Legislature. They must be approved by a majority of the voters in a regular or special election. Some sections of the Constitution require special majority votes to be amended. These sections guarantee the voting rights and education of Spanish-speaking people. Amendments to these sections must be approved by three-fourths of the voters in the state and by two-thirds of the voters in each county. A constitutional convention may be called by a two-thirds vote of the Legislature, if a majority of the voters approve. The voters must approve amendments proposed by a constitutional convention.

Executive. New Mexico's governor serves a four-year term. Other executive officers elected to four-year terms are the lieutenant governor, secretary of state, auditor, treasurer, attorney general, and commissioner of public lands. Executive officers may hold office for any number of terms but not for more than two terms in a row.

Much of the governor's authority lies in the power of appointment. For example, the governor appoints four of the seven members of the State Board of Finance and is a member of the board as well. The governor also appoints most of the directors or board members who run state agencies and institutions. The governor may veto legislation passed by the state Legislature.

Legislature of New Mexico consists of a 42-member Senate and a 70-member House of Representatives. There are 42 senatorial districts and 70 representative districts. Voters in each senatorial district elect one senator. Voters in each representative district elect one representative. Senators serve four-year terms. Members of the House of Representatives serve two-year terms.

The Legislature meets every year beginning on the third Tuesday in January. Legislative sessions are limited to 60 days in odd-numbered years and to 30 days in even-numbered years. The governor or the Legislature itself may call a special session. The Constitution provides for the power of *referendum,* in which a proposed law is submitted to the voters for their approval, but not for *initiative,* in which voters may propose a law.

Courts. The state Supreme Court is the highest court. It has five justices elected to eight-year terms. Terms are staggered so an entirely new court is not elected in any one election. Every two years, the justices select a member of the court to be chief justice.

The Court of Appeals has 10 judges, who are elected to eight-year staggered terms. Panels made up of three judges hear appellate cases. Most cases that this court hears may be taken to the Supreme Court.

District courts are the state's principal trial courts. New Mexico has district judges elected from 13 judi-

WORLD BOOK photo by Michael Heller

The New Mexico House of Representatives meets in the House chambers in the State Capitol in Santa Fe. Each of the 70 representatives is elected to a two-year term.

The governors of New Mexico

	Party	Term
William C. McDonald	Democratic	1912-1916
Ezequiel C. de Baca	Democratic	1917
Washington E. Lindsey	Republican	1917-1918
Octaviano A. Larrazolo	Republican	1919-1920
Merritt C. Mechem	Republican	1921-1922
James F. Hinkle	Democratic	1923-1924
Arthur T. Hannett	Democratic	1925-1926
Richard C. Dillon	Republican	1927-1930
Arthur Seligman	Democratic	1931-1933
Andrew W. Hockenhull	Republican	1933-1934
Clyde Tingley	Democratic	1935-1938
John E. Miles	Democratic	1939-1942
John J. Dempsey	Democratic	1943-1946
Thomas J. Mabry	Democratic	1947-1950
Edwin L. Mechem	Republican	1951-1954
John F. Simms	Democratic	1955-1956
Edwin L. Mechem	Republican	1957-1958
John Burroughs	Democratic	1959-1960
Edwin L. Mechem	Republican	1961-1962
Tom Bolack	Republican	1962
Jack M. Campbell	Democratic	1963-1966
David F. Cargo	Republican	1967-1970
Bruce King	Democratic	1971-1974
Jerry Apodaca	Democratic	1975-1978
Bruce King	Democratic	1979-1982
Toney Anaya	Democratic	1983-1986
Garrey Carruthers	Republican	1987-1990
Bruce King	Democratic	1991-1994
Gary E. Johnson	Republican	1995-2003
Bill Richardson	Democratic	2003-2011
Susana Martinez	Republican	2011-

cial districts. They hold district court sessions in each of the state's 33 counties. District judges are elected for six-year terms. They also serve as juvenile judges if the defendant is younger than 18. Other New Mexico courts include magistrate, municipal, and probate courts.

Local government. New Mexico has 33 counties. A city-county council administers Los Alamos County. Each of the other counties is run by a board of commissioners. All commissioners are elected to four-year terms. They may serve two terms in a row but must then wait two years before they can be elected again to any public office.

State law gives *municipalities* (towns, villages, or cities) a wide choice of form of government. Most common are the mayor-council, commission, and city manager-commission forms. Cities can adopt their own charters. Alamogordo, Albuquerque, Clovis, Gallup, Las Vegas, Los Alamos, and Silver City have their own. Municipal elections occur every two years.

Revenue. Taxes account for about 40 percent of the state government's *general revenue* (income). Federal grants and other United States government programs and charges for state government services make up most of the rest. A general sales tax provides the greatest portion of New Mexico's tax revenue. Other sources of tax revenue include taxes on corporate and personal income, mining, and motor fuels.

Politics. In voter registration, Democrats usually outnumber Republicans. Democrats generally enjoy support in the state's larger cities, among newcomers to the state, and among Hispanic Americans. In the north-central counties, the Spanish American population has been largely Democratic since the early 1930's. The center of Republican strength lies in the southeast portion of the state. Voters there tend to be conservative and vote much like the residents of west Texas. For New Mexico's electoral votes and voting record in presidential elections, see **Electoral College** (table).

History

Indian peoples. American Indians have lived in what is now New Mexico for thousands of years. Stone spearheads found at Folsom and other places indicate that Indians hunted in northeastern New Mexico at least 10,000 years ago. The spearheads are known as *Folsom points.* See **Folsom point.**

From about 500 B.C. to A.D. 1200, the Mogollon Indians lived in the valleys in the area of the New Mexico-Arizona border. At first the Mogollon Indians lived in houses dug partly into the ground. Later, they built villages that stood above the ground. See **Mogollon.**

Another group of ancient Indians lived in the region where New Mexico, Arizona, Utah, and Colorado meet. These Indians were the Anasazi, who had one of the most highly developed civilizations in North America. The Anasazi raised corn and cotton and tamed wild turkeys. The large birds provided food and clothing. During the winter, the Indians wore robes made of turkey feathers and rabbit fur. Some Anasazi were cliff dwellers and built many-storied apartment houses of closely fitted stones. Many other Anasazi built apartment houses on flat surfaces. One such building, the Pueblo Bonito (pretty village), probably had about 600 or 700 rooms. Sometimes the Anasazi built towns on top of

The ruins of Indian cliff dwellings have been preserved at Bandelier National Monument near Santa Fe. The Anasazi people built homes on protected ledges, *lower right,* or lived in caves in cliff walls. Most cliff dwellings were built between A.D. 1000 and 1300.

Rubinsteen, West Stock

steep mesas. Today's Pueblo Indians are the descendants of these people. See **Anasazi.**

The Navajo and Apache tribes came from the north about A.D. 1500. The Ute and Comanche came a few years later.

Exploration, conquest, and settlement. The first Spanish explorers reached the New Mexico area almost by accident. Álvar Núñez Cabeza de Vaca was a member of a group seeking gold in Florida in 1528. He and others became separated from the expedition's ships. In an attempt to reach New Spain (now Mexico), they sailed on barges to the Texas coast. In 1536, after wandering for eight years, Cabeza de Vaca and three companions—two Europeans and an African—reached a settlement near the Pacific coast of New Spain. They told stories of seven cities of great wealth, called the Seven Cities of Cíbola, to the north. See **Cíbola, Seven Cities of.**

The Spaniards were determined to find the seven rich cities. Guided by Cabeza de Vaca's African companion, Estevanico, also called Estéban, a priest named Marcos de Niza made a search in 1539. He claimed the area as a province of Spain. Marcos de Niza also reported that he had seen one of the cities from a distance.

Francisco Vásquez de Coronado, also in search of the seven cities, explored present-day New Mexico and Arizona from 1540 to 1542. But he found only Indian pueblos. Fray Augustín Rodríguez and Captain Francisco Sánchez Chamuscado traveled up the Rio Grande from New Spain in 1581. The report of a later explorer, Antonio de Espejo, led to colonization of the region.

The first Spanish colony in New Mexico was established in 1598 at the Pueblo of San Juan de los Caballeros, near the Chama River. The colony was financed and established by Juan de Oñate. He became governor of

the province of New Mexico. Oñate was succeeded as governor by Pedro de Peralta, who moved the capital to Santa Fe in 1609 or 1610. Santa Fe is the oldest seat of government in the United States.

The colony had little wealth and grew very slowly. It was kept alive mainly by the efforts of missionaries. Roman Catholic priests from Spain established schools to teach Christianity to the Indians. But repeated quarrels occurred between the church and civil authorities, and between the Spaniards and the Indians.

The Spaniards set up a system of forced labor for the Indians that was much like slavery. The Spaniards also charged the Indians an annual tax of corn and blankets. In addition, they kept the Indians from worshiping their ancient gods. Popé, an Indian from the San Juan Pueblo, led a revolt in 1680. The Indians killed more than 400 Spaniards and drove the rest to what is now Ysleta del Sur Pueblo, near El Paso, Texas. The Indians destroyed almost every trace of the Roman Catholic Church. Historians have called the 1680 Pueblo revolt the most successful act of resistance by a native group against a European colonizer in North America.

In 1692, the Spanish governor Diego de Vargas took back the province. Four years of scattered fighting broke the power of the Pueblo Indians. The colonists and priests returned to build homes and missions in and near Santa Fe. For 125 years, the Spaniards and Pueblo Indians lived together in this lonely outpost of the Spanish Empire.

Mexican rule. During the early 1800's, trappers and traders came from the United States to the region that would later become New Mexico. Spanish officials feared the newcomers and expelled them or put them in prison. But the Spanish officials were replaced in 1821,

Historic New Mexico

Pueblo Bonito, built by Anasazi Indians about A.D. 900, had hundreds of rooms. The Anasazi, ancestors of the Pueblo Indians, lived in northwestern New Mexico.

WORLD BOOK map

New Mexico was ruled by Spain and Mexico before the United States gained control of the area in 1848. The area became part of the New Mexico Territory in 1850 and a U.S. state in 1912.

WORLD BOOK illustrations by Richard Bonson, The Art Agency

The Santa Fe Trail opened a new trade route to New Mexico. Trader William Becknell opened the trail in 1821 when he brought the first goods to Santa Fe from Missouri. Stagecoach service started from Independence, Missouri, in 1849. By the late 1860's, more than 5,000 wagons used the trail each year.

Important dates in New Mexico

c. 500 B.C.-A.D. 1200 The Mogollon Indians lived in the valleys in the area of the New Mexico-Arizona border.

c. 750-1150 The Anasazi, ancestors of the modern-day Pueblo Indians, thrived in northwestern New Mexico.

1540-1542 Francisco Vásquez de Coronado explored New Mexico.

1598 Juan de Oñate founded the first permanent Spanish colony, at San Juan.

c. 1610 The Spanish established Santa Fe.

1680 The Pueblo Indians revolted and drove the Spaniards out of northern New Mexico.

1692 Diego de Vargas reconquered New Mexico for Spain.

1706 Francisco Cuervo y Valdés founded Albuquerque.

1821 Mexico won its independence from Spain, and New Mexico became a province of Mexico. William Becknell opened the Santa Fe Trail.

1846 General Stephen W. Kearny took control of New Mexico during the Mexican War.

1848 Mexico ceded New Mexico to the United States.

1850 Congress created the Territory of New Mexico.

1853 New Mexico acquired part of the Gila Valley.

1862-1864 Colonel Kit Carson defeated the Mescalero Apache and Navajo Indians.

1881 The outlaw Billy the Kid was killed in Lincoln County.

1886 The surrender of Geronimo ended the Apache Wars.

1912 New Mexico became the 47th state on January 6.

1916 Mexican bandits, probably led by Pancho Villa, raided Columbus, killing 16 Americans.

1922 Geologists discovered oil in the southeastern and northwestern regions of New Mexico.

1945 The first atomic bomb was exploded at Trinity Site near Alamogordo.

1970's Completion of the San Juan-Chama project brought water to north-central New Mexico.

1998 New Mexico celebrated the 400th anniversary of the founding of the colony at San Juan.

2011 Susana Martinez became the first woman governor of New Mexico.

after Mexico won its freedom from Spain. New Mexico became a province of Mexico. That same year, William Becknell, an American trader, opened the Santa Fe Trail to bring goods to New Mexico from Missouri.

Mexico ruled the area for the next 25 years, a period filled with unrest. In 1837, Mexicans and Indians in New Mexico rebelled against the Mexican government. They executed the governor and seized the Palace of Governors in Santa Fe. A Taos Indian, José Gonzales, was installed as their chief executive. But a month later, Mexico's General Manuel Armijo crushed the rebellion and became governor.

In 1841, an expedition from Texas (then an independent country) invaded New Mexico. The Texans claimed the land east of the Rio Grande. However, Mexican troops defeated the invaders and sent them as captives to Mexico City. They were later freed.

The Mexican War. As colonists from the United States pushed west, trouble developed between the United States and Mexico. In 1846, war broke out, and U.S. forces under General Stephen W. Kearny took control of New Mexico with little resistance. The Treaty of Guadalupe Hidalgo ended the war in 1848, and the U.S. took possession of the region. See **Mexican War.**

Territorial days. In 1850, Congress organized New Mexico as a territory. The territory also included what is now Arizona and parts of present-day Colorado and Nevada. In 1853, the Gadsden Purchase enlarged the territory (see **Gadsden Purchase**). Mexico sold the United States land south of the Gila River, between the Rio Grande and the Colorado River. New Mexico got its present boundaries in 1863, after Congress organized the territories of Colorado and Arizona.

Early in the Civil War (1861-1865), Confederate forces from Texas captured much of the region, including Albuquerque and Santa Fe. Union forces recaptured the territory in March 1862, after two battles southeast of Santa Fe. The first clash was fought in Apache Canyon, and the second in Glorieta Pass. Between 1862 and 1864, Colonel Kit Carson, a famous frontier scout, led the New Mexicans in forcing both the Mescalero Apache and the Navajo Indian tribes to live on a reservation.

During the late 1870's, cattlemen and other groups fought for political control of Lincoln County. The bitterness burst into open violence with the murder of rancher John G. Tunstall. Billy the Kid and other outlaws took a leading part in the fighting, which became known as the Lincoln County War. General Lew Wallace was appointed territorial governor in 1878. He pardoned the fighters to end the bloodshed. Pat Garrett, the sheriff of Lincoln County, killed Billy the Kid in 1881. Sheriffs, including Garrett, and territorial governors helped establish order during the 1880's.

The Apache Chief Victorio led frequent attacks on settlers from 1879 until his death in 1880. Geronimo, an Apache warrior, continued to fight U.S. troops and settlers in the area until he surrendered on Sept. 4, 1886. During the late 1800's, after railroads linked the territory to the rest of the nation, New Mexico experienced a cattle and mining boom.

Early statehood. New Mexico became the 47th state on Jan. 6, 1912. The people elected William C. McDonald as the first state governor.

Mexican rebels, probably led by Pancho Villa, raided the town of Columbus in 1916, killing 16 Americans. The U.S. Army sent an expedition into Mexico to catch Villa, but it failed. During World War I (1914-1918), New Mexico sent more than 17,000 men into the armed forces.

In the early 1920's, a long drought made life difficult for farmers and ranchers. Livestock prices dropped, and the stock owners' financial troubles spread. Banks closed, and many people lost their savings. But new businesses developed. Oil was discovered in the 1920's, and huge potash deposits at Carlsbad were opened. In 1930, the famous caverns near Carlsbad became a national park, and the tourist industry grew.

World War II. When the United States entered World War II in 1941, the 200th Coast Artillery, composed of New Mexico soldiers, was in the Philippine Islands. The Japanese overwhelmed the regiment, along with the rest of the U.S. forces on Bataan Peninsula. Many of the soldiers were killed, and others spent years in Japanese prison camps. The war ended after U.S. planes dropped two atomic bombs on Japan in August 1945. The bombs had been produced at Los Alamos, a town and laboratory built secretly in the New Mexico mountains. The world's first atomic bomb was exploded at Trinity Site, near Alamogordo, on July 16, 1945.

The mid-1900's. After World War II ended in 1945, the government continued to spend large amounts of money in New Mexico for research. The state's economy and population both grew rapidly as the government provided funds for work on nuclear power develop-

© Jack Asby, Shostal

The world's first atomic bomb was exploded at Trinity Site, near Alamogordo, on July 16, 1945. Scientists produced the bomb at the weapons research laboratory in Los Alamos.

ment and experiments with rockets. The economy also was aided by the discovery of uranium in northwestern New Mexico in 1950.

The state's coal industry grew in the mid-1960's. A large coal mine was opened near Raton, and coal-burning electric generating plants were built near Farmington. But production of potash decreased in the Carlsbad area due to competition from Canadian potash mines.

During the 1960's, construction and improvement of winter sports resorts helped to increase tourism. Income from tourists almost doubled in the state.

Lack of water has always created problems in New Mexico. Some of these problems were solved with completion of the San Juan-Chama project in the 1970's. This project brings water to north-central New Mexico through tunnels from branches of the San Juan River in the Rocky Mountain area. Reservoirs built near Chama and Abiquiu as part of the project provide recreational facilities and water for irrigation.

Recent developments. Today, New Mexico ranks as a leading center for space and nuclear research. A leading private employer in the state is Sandia National Laboratories of Albuquerque, which conducts research and does engineering work on the uses of nuclear energy. At Los Alamos, government scientists work on many projects involving military and nonmilitary uses of nuclear energy. Military bases and manufacturing for military projects also contribute to the economy. Substantial reductions in military spending took place in the early 1990's after the Cold War ended. But the growth of non-government industries helped compensate for the military reductions. Manufacturing and construction industries in New Mexico experienced growth in the 1990's. In 1998, New Mexico celebrated the 400th anniversary of the founding of the colony at San Juan.

Tourism continued to play a strong role in the state's economy into the 2000's. Some academics and leaders of native groups, however, have charged that the state has promoted "cultural tourism" while neglecting the deep-seated poverty that remains in many native communities. In 2009, New Mexico abolished the death penalty. Also in 2009, construction began on Spaceport America, a project intended to aid in the commercial development of space. The project, at Upham, about 40 miles northeast of Las Cruces, was funded largely by the state government and by local tax increases. In 2011, Susana Martinez became the first woman governor of New Mexico and the first Hispanic woman governor in the United States.   Daniel P. Dugas and Dulcinea M. Lara

H. L Personius, Bureau of Reclamation

The San Juan-Chama project, completed in the 1970's, brings water to north-central New Mexico through tunnels from branches of the San Juan River in the Rocky Mountains.

Study aids

Related articles in *World Book* include:

Biographies

Baca, Elfego
Billy the Kid
Carson, Kit
Chavez, Dennis
Coronado, Francisco Vásquez de
Garrett, Pat
Geronimo

Hilton, Conrad Nicholson
Kearny, Stephen Watts
Larrazolo, Octaviano Ambrosio
Oñate, Juan de
Richardson, Bill
Ross, Edmund Gibson
Villa, Pancho

Cities

Albuquerque
Gallup

Las Cruces
Roswell

Santa Fe
Taos

History

Anasazi
Apache Indians
Cibola, Seven Cities of
Gadsden Purchase
Guadalupe Hidalgo, Treaty of
Indian, American
Indian wars

Jefferson Territory
Mexican War
Mission life in America
Mogollon
Navajo Indians
Pueblo Indians
Santa Fe Trail
Western frontier life in America
Zuni Indians

Physical features

Mesa
Pecos River

Rio Grande
Rocky Mountains

National parks and monuments

Aztec Ruins National Monument
Carlsbad Caverns National Park
Fort Union National Monument
Pecos National Historical Park

Other related articles

El Camino Real
Los Alamos National Laboratory
Sandia National Laboratories
White Sands Missile Range

Questions

What contribution did missionaries make to the development of New Mexico?
When and why did the Pueblo Indians revolt against the Spaniards in New Mexico?
How is Spanish influence evident in New Mexico?
Where is the oldest road established by Europeans in the United States? What is its name?
Why is New Mexico called the *Land of Enchantment?*
What states were formed or partly formed from the New Mexico Territory?
Where is the oldest seat of government in the United States?
What historic weapons were built in New Mexico during World War II?
What are some of the chief minerals in New Mexico?
What is the leading agricultural activity of New Mexico?

Additional resources

Level I
Bjorklund, Ruth. *New Mexico.* Benchmark Bks., 2003.
Burgan, Michael. *New Mexico.* World Almanac Lib., 2003.
Early, Theresa S. *New Mexico.* Rev. ed. Lerner, 2003.
Kent, Deborah. *New Mexico.* Children's Pr., 1999.
Lourie, Peter. *The Lost World of the Anasazi.* Boyds Mills, 2003.
McDaniel, Melissa. *New Mexico.* Benchmark Bks., 1999.

Level II
Bix, Cynthia O. *New Mexico.* Abrams, 1998. Emphasizes art in New Mexico.
Chavez, Thomas E. *An Illustrated History of New Mexico.* 1992. Reprint. Univ. of N. Mex. Pr., 2002.
Etulain, Richard W., ed. *New Mexican Lives.* Univ. of N. Mex. Pr., 2002.
Fagan, Brian M. *Chaco Canyon: Archaeologists Explore the Lives of an Ancient Society.* Oxford, 2005.
Kessell, John L. *Spain in the Southwest: A Narrative History of Colonial New Mexico, Arizona, Texas, and California.* Univ. of Okla. Pr., 2002.
Lynes, Barbara, and others. *Georgia O'Keeffe and New Mexico.* Princeton, 2004.
Reséndez, Andrés. *Changing National Identities at the Frontier: Texas and New Mexico, 1800-1850.* Cambridge, 2004.
Roberts, Calvin A. and Susan A. *New Mexico.* Rev. ed. Univ. of N. Mex. Pr., 2006.
Roberts, David. *The Pueblo Revolt.* Simon & Schuster, 2004.
Smith, Chuck. *The New Mexico State Constitution.* Greenwood, 1996.
Thompson, Jerry D., ed. *Civil War in the Southwest: Recollections of the Sibley Brigade.* Tex. A&M Univ. Pr., 2001.

New Mexico, University of, is a public school of higher education. The university's flagship campus is in Albuquerque, New Mexico. An additional campus near Albuquerque, in Rio Rancho, is called UNM West. Branch campuses of the University of New Mexico are in Gallup, Los Alamos, Taos, and Valencia County. The university's athletic teams are called the Lobos.

The university's Maxwell Museum of Anthropology contains a major collection of objects made by the Anasazi Indians, who were ancestors of the Pueblo Indians. In addition, the Albuquerque campus has museums of biology, geology, and meteoritics; art galleries; and a large concert hall, Popejoy Hall. The University of New Mexico was founded in 1889. The university's website at http://www.unm.edu offers additional information.

Critically reviewed by the University of New Mexico

New Mexico State University is a *land-grant university* in Las Cruces, New Mexico. A land-grant university is partly endowed by the United States government under the Morrill, or Land-Grant, Act of 1862. New Mexico State University offers a wide range of undergraduate and graduate programs. It was founded in 1888 as Las Cruces College. It became the New Mexico College of Agriculture and Mechanic Arts in 1889. The university received its present name in 1960.

The university's athletic teams are called the Aggies. The university's website at http://www.nmsu.edu offers additional information.

Critically reviewed by New Mexico State University

New Netherland was a region in America claimed by the Dutch in the early 1600's. It included parts of what are now Connecticut, Delaware, New Jersey, and New York.

In 1621, merchants in the Netherlands formed the Dutch West India Company to compete with the Spanish Empire, colonize New Netherland, and develop the region's fur trade. Thirty families, sponsored by the trading company, began a Dutch colony at the mouth of the Hudson River in 1624. In 1625, the Dutch settlers founded New Amsterdam (now New York City) there. Peter Minuit, the governor (or director-general) of New Netherland, bought Manhattan Island from the local American Indians in 1626. The Dutch set up trading posts at what are now Albany, New York; Hartford, Connecticut; and Trenton, New Jersey.

The Dutch West India Company attracted settlers from many European countries. About 20 languages were spoken in the colony, and many religions were represented. The Dutch colonists became allies of the Iroquois Indians, and they fought other tribes and neighboring French colonists. By the 1650's, a fierce trading rivalry had built up between the Dutch and the English. In 1664, the English sent a fleet of warships to capture New Netherland for the Duke of York. Many of the Dutch colonists refused to fight, and Governor Peter Stuyvesant was forced to surrender to the English. New Netherland became the English colony of New York.

Joan R. Gundersen

See also **Dutch West India Company; New York** (History); **Stuyvesant, Peter.**

© age fotostock/SuperStock

The historic French Quarter is one of the most famous attractions in New Orleans. Tourists on Bourbon Street, *shown here,* pass by some of the district's many restaurants and nightclubs.

New Orleans

New Orleans, *nyoo AWR lee uhnz* or *AWR luhnz,* (pop. 343,829; met. area pop. 1,167,764) is one of the world's busiest ports and the largest city in Louisiana. It is also a business, cultural, and industrial center of the southern United States. New Orleans lies along the Mississippi River about 100 miles (160 kilometers) north of where the river flows into the Gulf of Mexico. This location has helped make the city a great shipping center.

New Orleans has long been a popular city with tourists. The largest crowds come for the annual Mardi Gras celebration, with its parades and other festivities. Tourists are also attracted by the city's historic French Quarter, much of which has the charm of an old European town. In addition, a large number of visitors come to New Orleans to hear top jazz musicians perform in the city that helped give birth to jazz during the early 1900's.

New Orleans is the South's oldest major city. It was founded in 1718 by Jean Baptiste le Moyne, Sieur de Bienville. Bienville was governor of the French colony of Louisiana. He named the city after Philippe, Duke of Orleans, who ruled France for King Louis XV, then a youth. The flags of France, Spain, the Confederate States, and the United States have flown over New Orleans.

In August 2005, Hurricane Katrina struck the Gulf Coast, causing widespread destruction. For weeks, floodwaters covered much of New Orleans. Of the approximately 1,500 Louisianians who died because of the hurricane, most were from New Orleans. Hundreds of thousands of people left the city in the days before and after the storm.

By 2007, many restaurants and other businesses had reopened, and city officials and others had devised a plan to improve the city's infrastructure. However, much rebuilding work remained. Officials faced the prospect that many Orleanians who left the city might never return. The city's 2010 census population of 342,829 was about two-thirds of the total before the storm.

The city

New Orleans occupies all of Orleans Parish and has the same boundaries as the parish. In Louisiana, counties are called *parishes.*

New Orleans is often called the *Crescent City* because its original section—the French Quarter—lay along a giant curve in the Mississippi River. Today, the main part of the city lies between the river on the south and Lake Pontchartrain on the north.

Downtown New Orleans borders the east bank of the Mississippi. Most of the city's residential districts lie west, north, and east of the downtown area. The rest occupy a finger-shaped area on the river's west bank. This area, known as Algiers, is the only part of New Orleans on the west bank.

In the late 1800's, the federal government built about 130 miles (209 kilometers) of earthen barriers, called *levees,* around the city to protect it from flooding. The longest levees lie along the Mississippi River and Lake Pontchartrain. Following the construction of these earthworks, the city installed a massive pumping system to provide drainage during rainstorms. The pumps helped dry out the soils, and much of New Orleans sank below sea level. The combination of levees and pumps transformed the local landscape and led to suburban development in low areas.

Downtown New Orleans includes the French Quarter and the main business district. This area lies on higher ground than much of the city and suffered little damage from Hurricane Katrina in 2005. The French Quarter was named for the French colonists who settled there. It is also called the Vieux Carré (pronounced *vee yoo cair RAY),* meaning *Old Square.* Most buildings in the French Quarter, however, look more Spanish than French.

Fires swept through the downtown area in 1788 and 1794. At that time, Spain ruled Louisiana, and so the rebuilding favored the Spanish style of architecture. This style can be seen in many homes and other buildings, with their landscaped patios and graceful balconies of lacy iron grillwork.

Several of New Orleans's most historic structures border Jackson Square in the heart of the French Quarter. One landmark, the St. Louis Cathedral, was completed in 1851. It stands between the Presbytere and the Cabildo. The Presbytere, built from 1794 to 1813, was used as a courthouse. The Cabildo, begun in 1795 and completed in 1799, was the seat of the Spanish government in the Louisiana Territory. The United States acquired the territory from France in the Louisiana Purchase of 1803. The official transfer of the land took place in the Cabildo. The Presbytere and the Cabildo are now museums. Fire damaged much of the Cabildo in 1988. However, the museum has been fully restored.

The Pontalba Buildings, two block-long apartment buildings, face each other across Jackson Square. They were built as luxury town houses in 1849 and are among the city's most fashionable residences. The French Quarter is also known for its nightclubs on Bourbon Street and antique shops on Royal Street. It also has a number of restaurants famous for the local cuisine, which incorporates elements of African, French, Native American, and Spanish cooking.

New Orleans's main business district lies west of the French Quarter. Large hotels, some of them converted from department stores, stand along Canal Street, the district's main thoroughfare. This broad boulevard is 171 feet (52 meters) wide. The 33-story World Trade Center of New Orleans rises at the south end of Canal Street. The building includes a hotel and office space.

Many modern high-rise office buildings and hotels line Poydras Street between the riverfront and the gigantic Louisiana Superdome. The Superdome, one of the world's largest indoor stadiums, is used for sports events, conventions, and trade shows. City Hall stands in the nearby Civic Center.

Residential districts. West of downtown New Orleans is a large residential area known as Uptown. It includes some of the city's oldest neighborhoods. The most famous is the Garden District, with its majestic old mansions and beautiful gardens. Americans who came to New Orleans after the Louisiana Purchase in 1803 developed the Garden District.

Between the Garden District and the river lies the Irish Channel. This working-class neighborhood is filled with traditional New Orleans houses known as *shotguns* (narrow, one-room-wide houses), *shotgun doubles* (two attached shotgun houses), and *camelbacks* (shotguns with an upper level added at the rear). Also in Uptown are Tulane University, Loyola University New Orleans, and Audubon Park.

City Park and a number of attractive communities along the Lake Pontchartrain shore cover much of northern New Orleans. City Park occupies 1,300 acres (525 hectares) and is one of the nation's largest urban parks. The New Orleans Museum of Art is in the park. Lakeview and Pontchartrain Park are among the older lakefront communities. They were built in the mid-1900's, after the former marshlands were protected by levees and pumped dry. They both suffered serious flooding when Hurricane Katrina caused floodwalls to collapse in 2005. New Orleans Lakefront Airport and the University of New Orleans also lie on the lakefront.

Most of New Orleans's newest neighborhoods have been built in the northeastern part of the city, commonly called New Orleans East. Large-scale development began there during the 1960's. New Orleans East *subsided,* or sank, after its development, and the area experienced serious flooding due to Hurricane Katrina.

The metropolitan area of New Orleans-Metairie-Kenner extends over seven parishes—Jefferson, Orleans, Plaquemines, St. Bernard, St. Charles, St. John the Baptist, and St. Tammany. More than a million people, approximately 25 percent of Louisiana's people, lived in this area at the 2010 census. Fast-growing suburbs have sprung up along the Mississippi between New Orleans and Baton Rouge with the development of large industries. Suburbs north of Lake Pontchartrain have grown rapidly. Hurricane Katrina spurred suburban growth because many city residents moved to the suburbs.

People

African Americans make up about three-fifths of New Orleans's population. Whites make up about one-third

of the city's people. A small number of Hispanics and Asians account for most of the rest of the population.

Many white Orleanians are descendants of European immigrants who came to the city to find opportunity and freedom during the 1800's and early 1900's. Many other

Facts in brief

Population: *City*—343,829. *Metropolitan statistical area*—1,167,764.

Area: *City*—364 mi² (943 km²). *Metropolitan statistical area*—3,155 mi² (8,171 km²), excluding inland water.

Climate: *Average temperature*—January, 53 °F (12 °C); July, 83 °F (28 °C). *Average annual precipitation* (rainfall, melted snow, and other forms of moisture)—64 in (163 cm). For the monthly weather, see **Louisiana** (Climate).

Government: Mayor-council. *Terms*—4 years for the mayor and the seven council members.

Founded: 1718. Incorporated as a city in 1805.

Largest communities in the New Orleans area

Name	Population	Name	Population
New Orleans	343,829	Slidell	27,068
Metairie*	138,481	Terrytown*	23,319
Kenner	66,702	Harvey*	20,348
Marrero*	33,141	Gretna	17,736
Laplace*	29,872	Chalmette*	16,751

Source: 2010 census. *Unincorporated.

New Orleans's flag was adopted in 1918. The three stripes symbolize democracy. The fleurs-de-lis stand for the city's French heritage.

The city seal dates from 1852. The Indians honor the first inhabitants of the New Orleans area. The alligator represents the city's swamps.

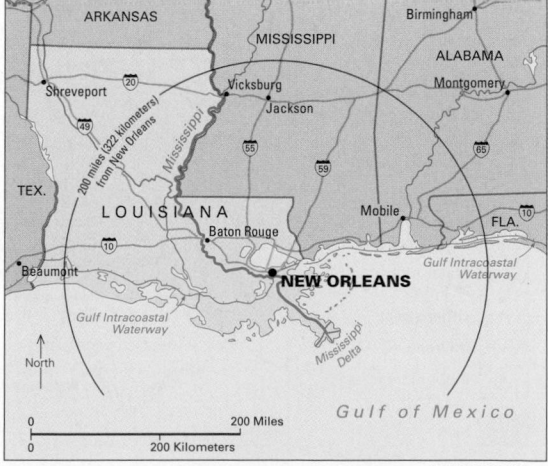

WORLD BOOK map

New Orleans lies in southwestern Louisiana.

Orleanians arrived from Latin American countries during the 1900's. Large numbers of blacks have lived in the city since the first slaves were brought to the area in the early 1700's. In addition, many free blacks immigrated from the West Indies, especially the Dominican Republic, from the late 1700's to the mid-1800's.

During the last half of the 1900's, the New Orleans metropolitan area experienced a shift in population common to other major urban centers in the United States. A large number of middle-class white families moved from the city to the suburbs. As a result of this population shift, wealthy whites and poor blacks formed the largest groups in New Orleans.

Ethnic groups. Nearly all the early African American residents of New Orleans came from Africa as slaves. They worked on farms and plantations near the city or in the city itself. In the early 1900's, African American musicians made New Orleans a world-famous center of jazz. Black jazz bands still follow a New Orleans custom and play as they march in funeral processions to and from cemeteries. See **Jazz** (Early jazz).

More than 325,000 African Americans lived in New Orleans before Hurricane Katrina struck in 2005. Many of them were poor and lived in mainly black communities near the downtown area. However, a sizable African American middle class lived mainly in eastern New Or-

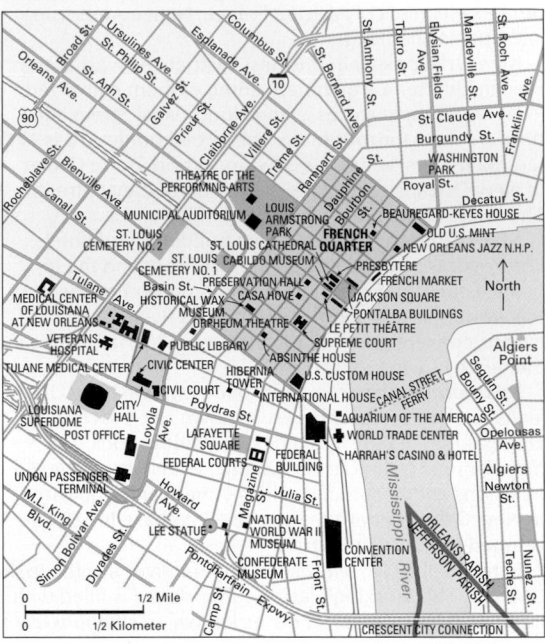

Downtown New Orleans

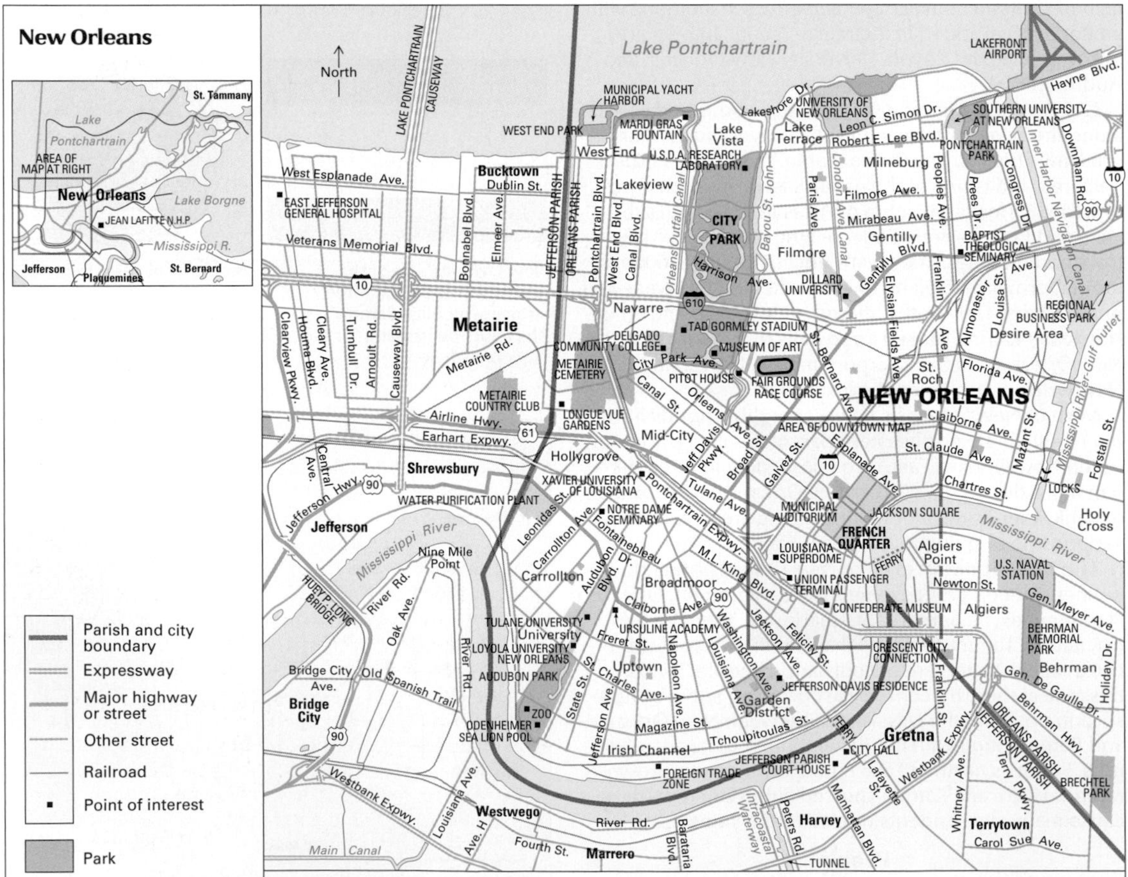

© Jon Arnold Images/SuperStock

A streetcar runs along St. Charles Avenue in the Garden District of New Orleans. The area, developed in the 1800's, is known for its charming old homes.

Richard Nowitz © New Orleans Metropolitan Convention and Visitors Bureau

Jazz musicians serenade passers-by outside a restaurant in the Garden District. New Orleans is known for its traditional brand of jazz. Musicians in the city helped give birth to jazz music in the early 1900's.

leans. Many neighborhoods damaged the most by the 2005 storm were largely black and poor. After the storm, about 100,000 African Americans left New Orleans and settled in other cities.

Other groups of Orleanians include those of Cuban, French, German, Irish, Italian, Honduran, Mexican, Polish, or Vietnamese ancestry. Many residents who came from Latin America live southeast of the downtown area.

The descendants of New Orleans's early African, French, Native American, and Spanish residents are known as Creoles. The term *Creole* comes from a Spanish word meaning *native to the place*. The Creole influence is still strong in New Orleans. For example, on All Saints' Day (November 1), a citywide holiday that honors the dead, many Orleanians follow the Creole tradition of going to the cemetery in family groups. Creole cooking, a spicy blend of African, French, Native American, and Spanish dishes, remains popular in restaurants throughout New Orleans.

Housing. At the time of the 2000 census, nearly half of New Orleans's families owned their homes. Most of the rest rented apartments. New high-rise apartment buildings stand in various parts of New Orleans. But about half the city's housing was built before 1950. In fact, much of the housing dates from the 1800's. Many of the older homes, especially those in the French Quarter and the Garden District, have been beautifully restored. But much other housing, greatly in need of repair, is neglected because the owners cannot afford the high cost of repairs. Yet, the traditional shotguns and doubles represent a local architectural tradition and contribute to the city's unique look.

Education. The Orleans Parish School Board, which consists of seven elected members, supervises the public school system in New Orleans. The New Orleans metropolitan area also has many Roman Catholic schools and a number of other church-supported and private schools.

Five years after the hurricane, nearly three-fourths of the city's schools had reopened. Many public schools that had closed reopened as charter schools run by public-private partnerships. A state organization called the Recovery School District took over some other public schools.

The University of New Orleans, the city's largest university, is part of the Louisiana State University system. Tulane University is New Orleans's oldest institution of higher learning. It was founded in 1834. Other universities and colleges in New Orleans include Dillard University; Loyola University New Orleans; New Orleans Baptist Theological Seminary; Notre Dame Seminary; Our Lady of Holy Cross College; Southern University at New Orleans; and Xavier University of Louisiana.

The arts. New Orleans is a leading cultural center of the South. The New Orleans Opera Association, the New Orleans Ballet Association, and the Louisiana Philharmonic Orchestra perform at various locations in the city. The Louisiana Philharmonic is completely owned by its musicians. Le Petit Théâtre du Vieux Carré is one of the city's best-known professional theater companies.

New Orleans has been known for its jazz ever since the city helped give birth to the music in the early 1900's. Black musicians and a number of white musicians helped to develop jazz in the bars and nightclubs on Basin, Rampart, and other streets both inside and outside the French Quarter. Today, old New Orleans-style jazz is still played in many places in the city. One of the most famous places is Preservation Hall, a small building where fans sit on wooden benches or stand to hear jazz.

Libraries and museums. The New Orleans Public Library operates a main library and several branches. Tulane University has an outstanding collection of books on Louisiana history. Tulane is also the home of the Amistad Research Center, which preserves books and other materials about African American life and culture. The Historic New Orleans Collection is one of the finest

Colorful Mardi Gras parades are a highlight of the carnival season in New Orleans. Mardi Gras festivities last for about two weeks and end the day before the religious season of Lent begins. Costumed riders on a parade float, *shown here,* toss beads and other trinkets to crowds along Canal Street.

repositories of material about the development of Louisiana and the South.

The New Orleans Museum of Art has fine collections of art from France and the Americas. The Louisiana State Museum operates eight historic buildings in New Orleans, including the Cabildo; the Presbytere; Madame John's Legacy, a beautifully restored house dating from the late 1700's; and the Old U.S. Mint, which features jazz memorabilia and other exhibits. Other New Orleans museums include the Pitot House, a former plantation; Louisiana's Civil War Museum at Confederate Memorial Hall; and the National World War II Museum.

Jean Lafitte National Historical Park and Preserve includes a large area of wetlands and the site of the Battle of New Orleans. A visitor center features displays about the battle, which was the last clash of the War of 1812 (1812-1815).

Recreation. New Orleans has dozens of parks. The two largest, City Park and Audubon Park, were plantations during the 1800's. City Park includes a botanical garden and two stadiums. Audubon Park's attractions include a large zoo. The Aquarium of the Americas, a large aquarium, stands in the French Quarter along the Mississippi River. Lake Pontchartrain and other nearby lakes are popular for boating, fishing, and sailing. The Bayou Sauvage National Wildlife Refuge in eastern New Orleans is an appealing outdoor attraction.

The city has two major league professional teams. It is the home of the New Orleans Saints of the National Football League and the New Orleans Hornets of the National Basketball Association.

Annual events. Every year, large numbers of visitors attend New Orleans's Mardi Gras festival in February or March. The celebration climaxes the city's carnival season, which begins in January. Mardi Gras activities last about two weeks and end on Shrove Tuesday, the day before the Christian observance of Lent starts. Mardi Gras features parades and elaborate costume balls sponsored by private carnival organizations known as *krewes.* On Shrove Tuesday, also called Mardi Gras Day, the king of the Rex krewe leads a parade of several hundred floats. Brightly costumed riders on the floats toss beads, toys, and imitation gold coins called *doubloons* to the crowds.

Another popular annual event in New Orleans is the Spring Fiesta, held in March, April, or May. It includes guided tours through charming old houses in the French Quarter and the Garden District. The Jazz and Heritage Festival is another popular spring event. New Orleans hosts the annual Sugar Bowl football game on or near New Year's Day. The game, held in the Superdome, features two of the nation's top college teams.

Social problems. The U.S. Census Bureau reported that, in the early 2000's, more than one-fourth of the city's families were poor. Most of the city's poor had little education and worked at low-paying jobs or were unemployed. Deteriorating housing in low-income areas was also a serious problem.

Economy

For months after Hurricane Katrina, many New Orleans businesses remained closed. But by 2007, the area's economy had improved, led by the tourism industry, which includes hotels, restaurants, and entertainment. The French Quarter suffered little damage, and most of its cultural and retail establishments soon reopened to accommodate visitors and city residents. Many workers came from across the country to help rebuild a city that suffered such great damage.

Trade and finance. The Port of New Orleans handles millions of tons of cargo a year. Hundreds of ships from around the world dock at the busy port annually. The chief exports include petroleum products and grain and other foods from the midwestern United States. The leading imports include aluminum, coffee, forest products, rubber, petroleum, and steel. The port's heaviest trading is with Latin America.

New Orleans has been a busy port for barges. The barges use the nation's two main inland waterways, the Mississippi River and the Gulf Intracoastal Waterway, which meet at New Orleans.

The New Orleans metropolitan area has been one of the South's chief centers for hotels, restaurants, and retail and wholesale trade. In addition, the New Orleans area has been a financial center. Many commercial banks and savings and loan associations have operated in the area. Their loans have helped finance business expansion projects and other civic developments. The Sixth Federal Reserve District Bank operates a branch bank in New Orleans.

Industry. The New Orleans metropolitan area has hundreds of manufacturing plants. At the Michoud Assembly Facility, several companies have produced equipment for the United States space program. Michoud made the Saturn 5 rocket that launched the Apollo 11 astronauts to the moon in 1969. In the 1980's, a huge new industrial center, the Almonaster-Michoud Industrial District (now called the New Orleans Regional Business Park), was begun. It was built around the Michoud Assembly Facility. The Avondale Shipyard, in Jefferson Parish, has been one of the largest shipbuilding centers in the United States. Other leading industries in the New Orleans area have included the making of food products, petrochemicals, petroleum products, and primary metals.

Transportation. Barges and oceangoing ships dock at wharves on the Mississippi River and the Inner Harbor Navigation Canal. The Navigation Canal links the Mississippi and Lake Pontchartrain. From 1968 to 2009, the 76-mile (122-kilometer) Mississippi River-Gulf Outlet (MRGO) gave shippers a 44-mile (71-kilometer) short cut between New Orleans and the Gulf of Mexico.

During the 2005 hurricane, *storm surges* (rapid rises in sea level produced when winds drive ocean waters ashore) moved rapidly up these artificial waterways, knocking down levees and flooding low-lying neighborhoods. In the storm's aftermath, some government proposals called for the closure of the MRGO. In 2009, the U.S. Army Corps of Engineers constructed a barrier to close the shipping channel.

Louis Armstrong New Orleans International Airport, in the nearby city of Kenner, serves many commercial airlines. Private aircraft use New Orleans Lakefront Airport. In addition, a large number of trucking companies and several passenger and freight rail lines serve the city. The Lake Pontchartrain Causeway, the longest bridge in the world, extends about 29 miles (47 kilometers). It spans the lake and links New Orleans and its northern suburbs.

Communication. New Orleans has one daily newspaper, *The Times-Picayune.* It has the largest circulation of Louisiana's daily newspapers. Several television stations and a number of radio stations serve the city.

Shipbuilding has been one of the leading industries in the New Orleans metropolitan area. The Avondale Shipyard of Jefferson Parish, *shown here,* has been a major U.S. shipbuilding center.

Government

The city has a mayor-council form of government. Voters elect the mayor and the seven members of the City Council to four-year terms. The mayor may serve any number of terms but not more than two in a row.

The mayor appoints a chief administrative officer to help direct the city government. The mayor also plans civic improvements. The council makes the city's laws. The mayor may veto bills passed by the council. However, any bill the mayor vetoes may still become law if at least five council members vote to repass it.

A sales tax is the city government's largest source of local revenue. But New Orleans, like other big cities, does not raise enough money from local taxes to pay for the increasing costs of services and improvements. As a result, the city has depended on the state and federal governments for about one-third of its revenue.

History

Chickasaw, Choctaw, and Natchez Indians lived in what is now the New Orleans area before Europeans arrived. In 1682, the French explorer René-Robert Cavelier, Sieur de La Salle, sailed down the Mississippi River from the Great Lakes region. He claimed the entire Mississippi Valley for France.

French and Spanish rule. Jean Baptiste Le Moyne, Sieur de Bienville, founded New Orleans in 1718. In 1722, he made it the capital of the French colony of Louisiana, which covered the central third of the present-day United States. In 1762, King Louis XV of France gave Louisiana to his cousin, King Charles III of Spain. The French Orleanians disliked the first Spanish governor of Louisiana, Antonio de Ulloa, and drove him from the city in 1768. But in 1769, soldiers arrived from Spain and restored Spanish rule in New Orleans.

The worst urban fire in what is now Louisiana broke out in New Orleans on March 21, 1788. It started in a house on Chartres Street and destroyed over 850 buildings. Rebuilding was underway when a fire swept through 200 more structures in 1794.

In 1800, France secretly regained the Louisiana region from Spain but did not reveal the fact until March 1803. The next month, France sold Louisiana to the United States. On November 30, in preparation for the region's official transfer, the French took down the Spanish flag that still waved over New Orleans and raised the French flag. On December 20, the American flag became the third flag to fly over the city in less than a month.

The early 1800's. In 1805, New Orleans was incorporated as a city. Louisiana joined the Union in 1812, and New Orleans became the state capital. Also in 1812, the steamboat *New Orleans* arrived at New Orleans after sailing down the Ohio and Mississippi rivers from Pittsburgh. It was the first steamer to navigate the Mississippi. River trade soon boomed at New Orleans.

During the War of 1812, British troops tried to capture New Orleans. The British sought the aid of Jean Laffite, leader of a pirate band based near the city. But Laffite joined the American forces that were defending New Orleans. General Andrew Jackson commanded the U.S. troops. His army and Laffite's pirates defeated the British in the Battle of New Orleans on Jan. 8, 1815. See **New Orleans, Battle of; War of 1812** ("The needless battle").

After the war, river trade brought increasing wealth to New Orleans. The city thrived as a cotton port and slave-trading center. The state capital was moved to Donaldsonville in 1830. But New Orleans again served as the capital from 1831 until 1849, when Baton Rouge became the capital. New Orleans held its first Mardi Gras celebration in 1838.

The Paris of America. By 1840, New Orleans had a population of 102,193 and was the nation's fourth largest city. In the mid-1800's, it attracted thousands of immigrants from Germany and Ireland. Professional opera and theater companies thrived in New Orleans during this period, and the lively and glamorous city became known as the *Paris of America.*

During the mid-1800's, New Orleans also gained a reputation as an unhealthy place. In 1832, a yellow fever epidemic swept through the city, taking about 7,700 lives. Doctors did not know that mosquitoes, which thrived in the swampy New Orleans area, were the chief carriers of the disease. The worst yellow fever epidemic in United States history hit New Orleans in 1853. It killed more than 11,000 people.

The American Civil War and Reconstruction. In 1861, Louisiana withdrew from the Union and joined the Confederate States against the North in the American Civil War (1861-1865). New Orleans's importance as a port made it a chief target of the Union forces. In April 1862, a Union fleet commanded by Captain David Farragut sailed up the Mississippi from the Gulf of Mexico. After bombarding several forts, the fleet reached New Orleans and forced it to surrender on May 1. General Benjamin F. Butler took charge of the city and made it the Union capital of Louisiana.

Union troops remained in New Orleans during the Reconstruction period after the war. African Americans and Northerners gained control of the city government. In 1866, a riot broke out between whites and blacks in New Orleans over a voting dispute. The riot resulted in the deaths of about 50 people—most of them blacks—and increased racial tension in the city. Widespread corruption in government and rising city debts also troubled New Orleans during Reconstruction. In 1877, the U.S. government withdrew its troops from the city.

During the late 1800's, New Orleans struggled to rebuild its economy. Trade at the port had slumped sharply after the Civil War, when the coming of the railroads to the Mississippi Valley caused steamboat traffic to decline. In 1878, another yellow fever epidemic killed more than 3,800 Orleanians.

Civic improvements. Port activity increased rapidly after 1879. That year, U.S. Army engineers directed by James B. Eads deepened the mouth of the Mississippi River. This project enabled oceangoing ships to reach New Orleans.

By 1900, New Orleans's population had reached about 287,000. It continued to climb steadily during the early 1900's, when thousands of Italian immigrants arrived. In 1905, New Orleans officials adopted a program to combat mosquitoes by destroying their breeding areas. This program ended the threat of yellow fever in the city.

By 1920, African American musicians had helped New Orleans win fame as a jazz center. They included Louis Armstrong, Jelly Roll Morton, and King Oliver.

During the 1920's, the development of tugboats powerful enough to push long lines of barges on the Mississippi River greatly increased trade at New Orleans's port. An annual threat of floods from the Mississippi was reduced with the completion of the Bonnet Carré Spillway in 1932. This channel connects the river to Lake Pontchartrain west of New Orleans. When floods threaten, water from the river is forced through the spillway and the lake to the Mississippi Sound.

In 1946, deLesseps S. Morrison, a Democratic reformer, was elected mayor of New Orleans. He served as mayor until 1961 and began a series of long overdue civic projects. In his first major accomplishment, Morrison combined five railroad stations into one, the Union Passenger Terminal. It opened in 1954. Other projects included the opening of the Greater New Orleans Bridge (now part of the Crescent City Connection) in 1958 and completion of the Civic Center in 1959.

Social changes. During the 1960's, far-reaching social changes occurred in New Orleans. In 1960, black students entered all-white public elementary schools in New Orleans for the first time since the Reconstruction period. The city's libraries, restaurants, and other public

Lithograph (1851) by T. H. Muller; Mariners' Museum, Newport News, Virginia (Katherine Young)

New Orleans's riverfront served as a chief port for steamboats that traveled on the Mississippi River in the mid-1800's. The booming river trade of this period brought great wealth to New Orleans, which thrived as a cotton port.

AP/Wide World

Floodwaters from Hurricane Katrina remained in low-lying New Orleans neighborhoods for weeks after the storm in 2005. The hurricane caused hundreds of deaths and great destruction.

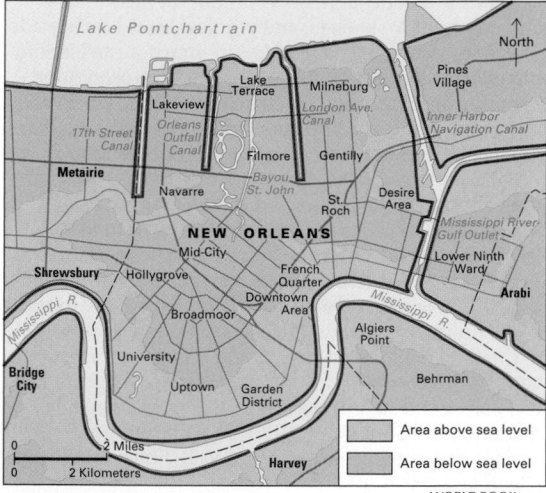

WORLD BOOK map

Much of New Orleans lies below sea level and is protected by a system of flood barriers called *levees*. The red lines on this map show the city's major levees. Areas below sea level suffered the greatest damage from Hurricane Katrina in 2005.

facilities also became integrated during the decade.

Large residential developments began in New Orleans East during the 1960's. In the mid-1960's, the production of rockets at the Michoud Assembly Facility made New Orleans a space age industrial center.

The late 1900's. The Louisiana Superdome opened in 1975. It led to the building of several hotels and motels in downtown New Orleans. A World's Fair was held in New Orleans in 1984.

Development of a 7,000-acre (2,800-hectare) business and industrial park in eastern New Orleans took place in the 1980's and 1990's. The park, reserved for business construction only, created jobs in the area.

In 1977, New Orleans voters elected Ernest N. (Dutch) Morial mayor. He was the city's first African American mayor. He was reelected in 1982 and remained in office

until 1986. Marc H. Morial, Ernest's son, served as mayor from 1994 to 2002.

The early 2000's. In August 2005, New Orleans suffered one of the worst disasters in American history when Hurricane Katrina struck the Gulf Coast. The hurricane caused hundreds of deaths and widespread destruction. After the levees failed, floodwaters covered about 80 percent of New Orleans and ruined thousands of homes. Hundreds of thousands of residents evacuated the city, and a majority were left homeless. Some suburbs and older neighborhoods that occupy higher ground survived the storm unharmed and largely returned to normal. However, many of the city's lakefront areas remained damaged. Repairs to the levees, homes, and businesses were expected to take years.

In September 2006, the Louisiana Superdome reopened for the first time since it was damaged by Hurricane Katrina in 2005. The damaged stadium served as a temporary shelter in the days after the storm. While it underwent repairs, New Orleans teams played in other facilities. Many people viewed the Superdome's reopening as a symbol of the city's recovery.

In 2007, officials unveiled a detailed plan for rebuilding the city. The plan included steps to improve the city's schools, roads, and hospitals. In 2008, the U.S. Army Corps of Engineers began construction on a 2-mile (3.2-kilometer) floodwall on the eastern edge of the city. The flood barrier was meant to protect such vulnerable neighborhoods as the Lower Ninth Ward from storm surges brought on by hurricanes. Also in 2008, city officials ordered an evacuation of the city as Hurricane Gustav approached the Gulf Coast. The hurricane caused major damage throughout Louisiana, but New Orleans was spared from widespread flooding. In 2010, voters elected Louisiana Lieutenant Governor Mitch Landrieu mayor. His father, Moon Landrieu, had served as the city's mayor from 1970 to 1978.   Craig E. Colten

Related articles in *World Book* include:

Outline

New Orleans, Battle of, was the last battle of the War of 1812 (1812-1815). The battle took place in southeastern Louisiana on Jan. 8, 1815. American troops led by Major General Andrew Jackson kept British troops led by Lieutenant General Sir Edward Pakenham from capturing the city of New Orleans. The battle has been called the "needless battle" because it was fought after the United States and the United Kingdom had signed a peace treaty.

In 1814, the British sought to capture New Orleans. On December 23, British soldiers captured a small force of American militia about 8 miles (13 kilometers) south of the city. That night, Jackson's U.S. troops attacked the British, but the British stopped their advance. Jackson withdrew his troops behind a canal about 4 miles (6.5 kilometers) south of New Orleans. Along the canal, Jackson's troops built a strong defensive position.

On December 24, the United States and the United Kingdom signed the Treaty of Ghent in Belgium. The treaty ended the war. But because of the slowness in carrying messages across the Atlantic Ocean, neither army knew of the peace treaty until February 1815.

On Jan. 8, 1815, General Pakenham's troops marched against Jackson's line and were badly defeated. Pakenham was killed while trying to rally his troops. During the battle, the British suffered about 300 soldiers killed, 1,250 wounded, and 500 captured. American losses totaled only 13 killed, 39 wounded, and 19 captured.

Because the battle took place after a peace treaty had been signed, it had no effect on the outcome of the war. However, the battle helped make Jackson a national hero. In 1828, Jackson was elected as the seventh president of the United States.   Gregory J. W. Urwin

See also **Jackson, Andrew; War of 1812** ("The needless battle").

New South Wales is the largest Australian state in terms of population. The state is on the east coast of the Australian continent. Sydney is the capital and largest city of New South Wales (see **Australia** [political map]).

Land and climate. The coast of New South Wales consists of many rugged cliffs. Some of these cliffs form rocky headlands that enclose good harbors. Sandy beaches line much of the coast. To the west, a narrow expanse of fertile land leads to the mountains of the Great Dividing Range. The highest peak in Australia, 7,310-foot (2,228-meter) Mount Kosciuszko, is part of this range. Grassy plains lie west of the mountains.

The state has a mild climate. Temperatures average about 50 °F (10 °C) in July and 75 °F (24 °C) in January. Average annual rainfall ranges from 80 inches (200 centimeters) in the eastern highlands to less than 10 inches (25 centimeters) on the western plains.

People. The 2006 Australian census reported that New South Wales had 6,549,177 people. Most of the state's population are of British or Irish descent. But many people from other parts of Europe have migrated to New South Wales since World War II (1939-1945), and many Asian immigrants have arrived since the 1970's. About 140,000 people in the state have Aboriginal or Torres Strait Islander ancestry. About two-thirds of the state's population lives in or near Sydney.

Children from 6 through 15 years of age

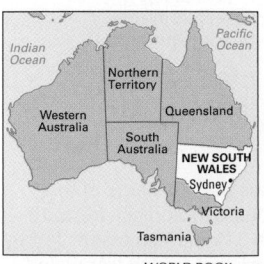

WORLD BOOK map
New South Wales

© Wayne Lawler, Corbis

Farmers raise about a third of Australia's sheep on the rich farmland of New South Wales. Other important crops include grains, bananas and citrus fruits, and sugar cane.

must attend school. New South Wales has 11 universities. They include the University of Sydney, Macquarie University, the University of Newcastle, the University of New England, and the University of New South Wales.

Economy. New South Wales has the most diverse economy in Australia. Service industries make up the largest sector. Sydney is a major center for finance and insurance in the Asia-Pacific region. Other service industries include education, government services, health and community services, and wholesale and retail trade.

Sydney, Newcastle, and Wollongong are the leading manufacturing centers. The chief manufactured goods include computers and electronic products, fabricated metal products, iron and steel, machinery, paper, *pharmaceuticals* (medicinal drugs), and processed foods.

Farmland lies on the coastal plain, in the foothills of the Great Dividing Range, and on the plains west of the mountains. Irrigation systems supply water to many inland areas. About a third of Australia's sheep are raised in New South Wales. The state also accounts for about a third of Australia's wheat production. Farmers also grow other grains, bananas and citrus fruits, and sugar cane.

Coal ranks as the state's leading mineral product. Huge deposits of black coal are mined in the northeastern part of the state. Australia's first gold discovery was made in New South Wales in 1851. Other important minerals in the state include copper, lead, limestone, opals, silver, and zinc.

Government. A governor with mostly ceremonial powers represents the British monarch in New South Wales. The actual head of state is the premier. The premier is assisted by a Cabinet of ministers. The state Parliament has a 42-member Legislative Council and a 93-member Legislative Assembly.

History. In 1770, the British navigator James Cook and his crew aboard the *Endeavour* became the first Europeans to reach the area. In 1788, Captain Arthur Phillip landed at Port Jackson in New South Wales with a group of convicts and soldiers to guard them. They founded the first white settlement in Australia. At that time, New South Wales was the name used for the eastern part of Australia and included land that is now the states of Queensland, Victoria, and part of South Australia. Free settlers began to arrive in the early 1800's. Convict immigration to New South Wales ended in 1840, though it was revived briefly in 1848 and 1849.

In 1851, the British gave Australian colonies the right to govern themselves in most matters. The colony of New South Wales became completely self-governing in

1856. In 1901, New South Wales became one of the six states of the Commonwealth of Australia. In 1911, the state began a transfer of land to the federal government to form the Australian Capital Territory, which covers 911 square miles (2,359 square kilometers). Canberra, the national capital, is in the territory.   Anthony W. Dennis

Related articles in *World Book* include:

Australia (History)	Canberra	Murray River
Australian Capital	Macquarie,	Newcastle
Territory	Lachlan	Sydney
Botany Bay	Mount Kosciuszko	Wollongong

New Sweden was the only Swedish colony in America. It extended along the Delaware River from the mouth of Delaware Bay to about what is now Trenton, New Jersey. Swedish settlers founded the colony in 1638 and built Fort Christina at what is now Wilmington, Delaware. New Sweden was a mildly successful fur-trading colony. The Dutch protested the existence of New Sweden because the land lay within the Dutch territory of New Netherland. In 1655, Peter Stuyvesant, governor of New Netherland, led a military expedition against New Sweden and forced its surrender. See also **Delaware** (History).   Oliver A. Rink

New Testament is the second part of the Christian Bible. *Testament* means *covenant* or *agreement.* The first part of the Christian Bible includes the *books* (individual writings) that became the Jewish Bible, also known as the Hebrew Bible. Christians call these writings the Old Testament. The Old and New Testaments together make up the Christian Bible.

Contents. The New Testament consists of 27 books. These books are called the *canon* of the New Testament—that is, the books that Christians officially accept as scripture. The books of the New Testament were written from about A.D. 50 to about 125. All were composed in the Greek language widely used at that time. Jesus Christ himself spoke Aramaic. At first, the books circulated separately. Later, they were gathered together.

Gospels. The first four books of the New Testament are the Gospels of Matthew, Mark, Luke, and John. The word *gospel* comes from an Old English word meaning *good news.* It refers to a kind of literature that contains stories about Jesus's words and deeds. The four Gospels tell the story of Jesus in different ways. Scholars do not know who actually wrote them. Mark probably was written in the A.D. 60's. Matthew, Luke, and John were written sometime between about A.D. 70 and 100.

The Acts of the Apostles follows the Gospels. This book is a continuation of the Gospel of Luke. It also is called simply Acts. It tells of the expansion of the early Christian church. Because Acts begins where Luke ends and was composed by the same author, scholars often refer to the two books together as Luke-Acts.

Letters. The next 21 books are called Epistles, meaning *letters.* The first 13 Letters claim to be written by the early Christian leader Paul. But many scholars doubt that Paul wrote all of them. They believe some of them are *pseudonymous.* Pseudonymous Letters are ones credited to one person but written by another. The Letters written by Paul were composed in the A.D. 50's and early 60's. They are the oldest books of the New Testament.

A Letter called Hebrews follows the Letters credited to Paul. It is called an *anonymous* Letter because its author is not named. After Hebrews come three Letters

that claim to be from the early church leaders James and Peter but probably were written by other people. The three Johannine Letters, 1-3 John, come next. They were written by the same community that composed the Gospel of John. The final Letter claims to be written by Jude, but some scholars believe it is pseudonymous.

Revelation, also called the Apocalypse, is the last book of the New Testament. It provides visions of God's judgment of the world and of the creation of a new heaven and earth.

Other early Christian writings. Besides the 27 books that make up the canon of the New Testament, early Christians produced many other writings. These include additional gospels, as well as letters and accounts of acts credited to the apostles. Such writings are called *apocryphal* or *noncanonical* writings. One of the most

Detail of *The Conversion of Saint Paul* (1542-1545), a fresco by Michelangelo in the Pauline Chapel in the Vatican (SCALA/Art Resource)

An account in the New Testament describes Saint Paul's conversion to Christianity while he was on the road to Damascus.

important noncanonical writings is the Gospel of Thomas, which preserves early sayings of Jesus.

Early church leaders wrote letters, defenses of the Christian faith, and works that sought to disprove beliefs that were not officially accepted by the church. By A.D. 400, the books that now comprise the New Testament had been widely accepted as scripture. Church councils later *ratified* (formally approved) the canon.

Critical studies. Scholarly study of the New Testament sometimes is called *criticism* of the New Testament. Used this way, the word *criticism* does not have an unfavorable meaning. Instead, it means the use of academic disciplines, such as history and literary studies, that are not directed by Christian teachings.

Redaction criticism looks at how authors of Biblical books used and *redacted* (edited) various sources to compose certain books. Some redaction critics study and compare the four Gospels.

The Gospels of Matthew, Mark, and Luke are called the Synoptic Gospels. The word *synoptic* comes from two Greek words meaning *seen together*. These three Gospels tell many of the same stories about Jesus, often in the same order and with nearly identical words. The similarity is so striking that most scholars think the authors of Matthew and Luke used Mark as a source.

Matthew and Luke also share certain similarities that do not extend to Mark. Scholars think the authors of Matthew and Luke might have used another common written source called Q, which is short for the German word *Quelle* (source). The writers of Matthew and Luke also added stories that are not in the other Gospels.

Historical Jesus research. The Gospels' writers told the story of Jesus in different ways, adding and leaving out certain teachings to meet their communities' needs. Some scholars compare and contrast the different Gospels. They also look to gospels and other sources that are not in the New Testament to reconstruct what the historical Jesus did and taught. This kind of research is called historical Jesus research.

Jesus and his early followers were Jews. Jesus was born during the time of King Herod the Great, who ruled Palestine from 37 B.C. to 4 B.C. Jesus grew up in a town in Galilee called Nazareth. The Gospels of Matthew and Luke claim that Jesus was born in Bethlehem, the hometown of King David. The Hebrew Bible says that the king of Israel should come from David's family.

According to Luke, Jesus was about 30 years old when he began his public ministry of healing and teaching. The Gospels suggest that his ministry lasted about one to three years. Jesus's followers believed that Jesus was the Christ or the Messiah. *Christ* and *Messiah* come from Greek and Hebrew words that mean *anointed* (rubbed with oil). In the Hebrew Bible and early Judaism, people who acted on behalf of God were actually anointed or considered to be anointed. They included the king, priests, and prophets.

The Roman authorities who ruled Judea crucified Jesus just outside Jerusalem. Death by crucifixion was the Roman punishment for revolutionaries. Christians commemorate Jesus's Crucifixion on Good Friday. Jesus's followers claimed that Jesus rose from the dead three days after the Crucifixion. Christians commemorate Jesus's Resurrection on Easter Sunday.

Christianity began as a movement within Judaism. But as Christianity spread beyond Palestine and throughout the Roman Empire, many Gentiles (non-Jews) began to join the Christian movement. Several New Testament documents address the problem of what requirements Gentiles had to meet to become Christians.

Authorship is another issue that Biblical critics study. For example, questions about the authorship of the 13 Letters credited to Paul existed as early as the A.D. 100's.

The Letters that all scholars agree Paul wrote are called the "undisputed" Pauline letters. They are Romans, Galatians, 1-2 Corinthians, Philippians, 1 Thessalonians, and Philemon. The other Letters credited to Paul differ in language, style, and theology from the undisputed Pauline letters. These "disputed" Pauline letters are Ephesians, Colossians, 2 Thessalonians, 1-2 Timothy, and Titus. Scholars who think that Paul did not write these letters call them Deutero-Pauline, meaning that Paul's followers wrote them. Most scholars consider 1-2 Timothy and Titus, also called the Pastoral Epistles, to be Deutero-Pauline letters. There is more debate about who wrote Ephesians, Colossians, and 2 Thessalonians.

Textual criticism. The original manuscripts written by the authors of the New Testament all have been lost. Only copies of them remain. Scholars called *textual critics* try to reconstruct the original form of the books of the New Testament. The earliest copies of these books date from the A.D. 100's. Thousands of later copies exist. Many variations of wording occur in the different copies. The people who made copies of the manuscripts are known as *scribes.* Some scribes accidentally made errors while copying the original manuscripts. Others intentionally changed the texts to address issues in the church at the time the scribes were making the copies.

The books of the New Testament were translated from Greek into other ancient languages. Some of the most important early translations were in the Latin, Syriac, and Coptic languages. Textual critics study variations between such early translations, as well as quotations from New Testament books used by early church leaders. With much research and comparison, scholars have combined the various wordings from different copies of the Greek New Testament to form the basis for most English translations of the Bible.   Henry W. Morisada Rietz

Related articles. See **Jesus Christ** and **Bible** and their lists of *Related articles* and *Additional resources.* See also the following articles on books of the New Testament:

Acts of the Apostles	Peter, Epistles of
Colossians, Epistle to the	Philemon, Epistle to
Corinthians, Epistles to the	Philippians, Epistle to the
Ephesians, Epistle to the	Revelation, Book of
Galatians, Epistle to the	Romans, Epistle to the
Gospels	Thessalonians, Epistles to the
Hebrews, Epistle to the	Timothy
James, Epistle of	Titus
John, Epistles of	

New Westminster (pop. 58,549) is a city in southwestern British Columbia. It lies on the Fraser River, 12 miles (19 kilometers) southeast of downtown Vancouver. For the location, see **British Columbia** (political map).

The Royal Columbian Hospital and Douglas College are the city's largest employers. Mills that once produced softwood lumber, pulp and paper, and shingles mostly have left the city. Many of its people work in nearby Vancouver, British Columbia's largest city.

The British Army's Royal Engineers began laying out

the city in 1858. The city was founded in 1859 and named Queensborough, for Queen Victoria of the United Kingdom. Later in 1859, the queen renamed it New Westminster, after the English town of Westminster (now part of Greater London). New Westminster served as the capital of the colony of British Columbia from 1859 to 1868. In 1860, it became British Columbia's first incorporated city. Fire destroyed the city's main business district in 1898, but it was soon rebuilt. New Westminster has a mayor-council form of government.   Robert A. J. McDonald

New World is another name for the Western Hemisphere, which includes the continents of North America and South America. See **Old World; Hemisphere.**

New Year's Day is the first day of the calendar year. People in almost every country celebrate this day as a holiday. The celebrations are both festive and serious. Many people make New Year's resolutions to break bad habits or to start good ones. Some think about how they have lived during the past year and look forward to the next 12 months.

Early customs. Many ancient peoples started the year at harvesttime. They performed rituals to do away with the past and purify themselves for the new year. For example, some people put out the fires they were using and started new ones.

In early times, the ancient Romans gave each other New Year's gifts of branches from sacred trees. In later years, they gave gold-covered nuts or coins imprinted with pictures of Janus, the god of gates, doors, and beginnings. January was named after Janus, who had two faces—one looking forward and the other looking backward. In addition to giving gifts to each other, the Romans also brought gifts to the emperor. The emperors eventually began to demand such gifts. But the Christian church outlawed this custom and certain other pagan New Year's practices in A.D. 567.

The ancient Persians gave New Year's gifts of eggs, which symbolized productiveness. The Celtic priests of what is now England gave the people branches of mistletoe, which was considered sacred.

The Celts took over many New Year's customs from the Romans, who invaded Britain in A.D. 43. By the 1200's, English rulers had revived the Roman custom of asking their subjects for New Year's presents. Common presents included jewelry and gold. Queen Elizabeth I acquired a large collection of richly embroidered and jeweled gloves through this custom. English husbands gave their wives money on New Year's Day to buy pins and other articles. This custom disappeared in the 1800's. However, the term *pin money* still means small amounts of spending money.

Many American colonists in New England celebrated the new year by firing guns into the air and shouting. They also visited taverns and houses to ask for drinks. Other colonists attended church. Some people held open house, welcoming visitors and feeding them.

Another old custom involved using the Bible to predict what would happen in the new year. People chose a passage of the Bible at random. They then applied the passage to the coming months of the new year.

Modern customs on New Year's Day include visiting friends and relatives; giving gifts; attending religious services; and making noise with guns, horns, bells, and other devices. Children in Belgium write their parents

New Year's messages on decorated paper. The children read the messages to their families on New Year's Day. The Chinese New Year begins between January 21 and February 20. The celebration lasts four days. On the last

San Francisco Visitors Bureau

A Chinese New Year celebration in San Francisco features a colorful dragon costume. The Chinese New Year begins between January 21 and February 20. The holiday lasts four days.

night, people dress as dragons to frighten and delight the children. In Japan, many people worship on New Year's Day.

In the United States, many people go to New Year's Eve parties. Crowds gather in Times Square in New York City, on State Street in Chicago, and in other public places. At midnight, bells ring, sirens sound, firecrackers explode, and everyone shouts, "Happy New Year!" People also drink a toast to the new year and sing "Auld Lang Syne" (see **Auld Lang Syne**).

On New Year's Day, many people in the United States visit relatives, attend religious services, or watch football games on television. Some attend parades, such as the Rose Parade at the Tournament of Roses in Pasadena, California, and the Mummers Parade in Philadelphia.

The date of New Year's. The early Roman calendar used March 1 as New Year's Day. Later, the ancient Romans made January 1 the beginning of the year.

During the Middle Ages (about A.D. 400 through the 1400's), most European countries used March 25, a Christian holiday called Annunciation Day, to start the year. By 1600, many Western nations had adopted a revised calendar called the Gregorian calendar. This calendar, used today, restored January 1 as New Year's Day. Britain and its colonies in America adopted it in 1752.

Many people celebrate the new year on dates established by their religion. For example, the Jewish New Year, a solemn occasion called Rosh Ha-Shanah, is observed during September or early October (see **Rosh Ha-Shanah**). Hindus in different parts of India celebrate the new year on various dates. Muslims use a calendar that has 354 days in most years. As a result, the Muslim New Year falls on different dates from year to year on the Gregorian calendar.   Robert J. Myers

See also **Chinese New Year.**

W. D. Murphy, Shostal

The Hudson River Valley at Bear Mountain Bridge in eastern New York is one of the state's many scenic areas. Much of the state is covered by wooded, rolling hills and sparkling lakes.

New York *The Empire State*

New York is a state that is a leading center of banking, communication, and finance in the United States. It is also a leader in manufacturing and in trade, restaurants, and hotels. According to the 2010 census, New York ranked as the nation's third largest state in population. Only California and Texas had more people. The capital of New York is Albany.

Much of the state's greatness lies in huge, exciting New York City. New York City is the largest city in the United States, and it ranks as one of the largest cities in the world. It is one of the world's leading centers of business. Its large number of theaters, museums, and musical organizations make it an important cultural center. New York City is a busy seaport. In its harbor stands the Statue of Liberty, long a symbol of freedom to people in all parts of the world. As the headquarters of the United Nations, New York City can be called the "capital of the world."

The contributors of this article are Adam W. Burnett, William R. Kenan Jr. Professor of Geography at Colgate University, and Milton M. Klein, Editor of The Empire State: A History of New York.

The state's factories turn out an incredible variety of products, from industrial machinery to fine jewelry. New York state is a leading producer in the United States of canned fruits and vegetables, chemicals, clothing, computer and electronics products, dairy products, jewelry, printed materials, and turbines. New York City ranks as the largest center of printing and publishing in the United States.

In addition to New York City, several other cities in the state are important centers of industry and trade. These cities include Albany, Buffalo, and Rochester. However, New York is not just a state of business and industry. It is also a land of fertile river valleys, forested hills, tall mountains, and sparkling lakes. New York's many scenic attractions draw tens of millions of tourists each year. Niagara Falls, the state's most magnificent natural wonder, is a chief attraction. New York City is also a major tourist center.

New York was one of the original 13 states. Henry Hudson, an English explorer sailing under the Dutch flag, claimed the New York region for the Netherlands in 1609. The Dutch named the region New Netherland. On Manhattan Island, the Dutch established New Amster-

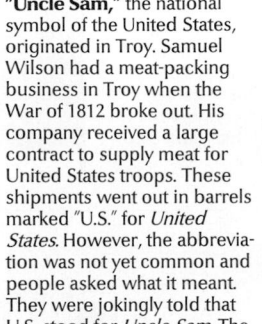

AP Photo

The Avenue of the Americas runs through the center of Manhattan in New York City, the largest city in the United States.

Interesting facts about New York

WORLD BOOK illustrations by Kevin Chadwick

"Uncle Sam," the national symbol of the United States, originated in Troy. Samuel Wilson had a meat-packing business in Troy when the War of 1812 broke out. His company received a large contract to supply meat for United States troops. These shipments went out in barrels marked "U.S." for *United States.* However, the abbreviation was not yet common and people asked what it meant. They were jokingly told that U.S. stood for *Uncle Sam.* The nickname eventually came to personify the nation. In 1961, Congress adopted a resolution recognizing Samuel Wilson as the person who inspired the Uncle Sam symbol.

Uncle Sam

Radio City Music Hall in New York City, the home of the famous Rockettes dance company, has a seating capacity of 5,900.

The first escalator was manufactured by the Otis Elevator Company of New York City in 1899. It was exhibited at the Paris Exposition in 1900. In 1901, the escalator was returned to the United States and installed in a building in Philadelphia.

License plates on automobiles began to be used in New York in 1901. New York was the first U.S. state to require automobile registration. Owners had to supply their own "plates," which were often made of leather with metal characters.

Radio City Music Hall

dam, which later became New York City. The English took control of New Netherland in 1664. They renamed it New York in honor of the Duke of York, a brother of England's king, Charles II.

About a third of all the battles of the American Revolution (1775-1783) were fought in New York. New York City served as the capital of the United States from 1785 to 1790. George Washington took the oath of office there as the first president of the United States. In the early 1800's, New York began its great era of canal and railroad building. By 1850, New York ranked as the leading manufacturing state.

By 1810, New York had become the most populous state in the United States. New York held that position until the 1960's, when California overtook it in population. During the 1990's, Texas also passed New York in population.

New York's nickname is the *Empire State,* which may have originated in a remark made by George Washington. Washington once called New York the "seat of the empire." New York is also known as the *Excelsior State. Excelsior,* a Latin word meaning *ever upward,* is the state motto.

Augusts Upitis, Shostal

The Empire State Plaza in Albany includes the State Capitol, *center,* and other government buildings.

New York in brief

Symbols of New York

The New York coat of arms appears on both the state flag and the state seal. On the arms, a shield displays a New York landscape with ships on a river, mountains, and a rising sun. A bald eagle perches on a globe above the shield. A figure representing Liberty stands to the left. The figure on the right symbolizes Justice. The flag was adopted in 1909, and the seal was adopted in 1882.

State flag

State seal

New York (brown) ranks 30th in size among all the states and is the largest of the Middle Atlantic States (yellow).

General information

Statehood: July 26, 1788, the 11th state.
State abbreviations: N.Y. (traditional); NY (postal).
State motto: *Excelsior* (Ever Upward).
State song: "I Love New York." Words and music by Steve Karmen.

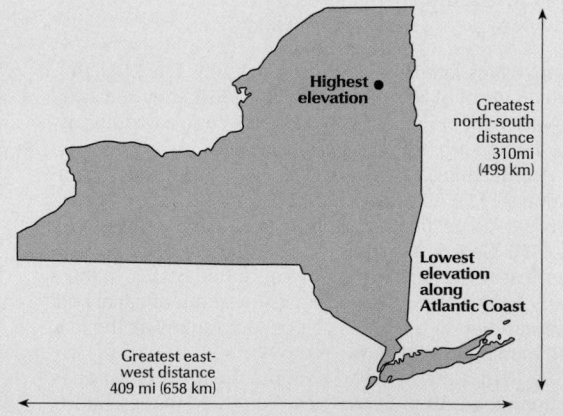

The State Capitol is in Albany, New York's capital since 1797. Kingston, Poughkeepsie, and New York City served as temporary capitals between 1777 and 1797.

Land and climate

Area: 49,109 mi² (127,191 km²), including 1,895 mi² (4,908 km²) of inland water but excluding 4,969 mi² (12,869 km²) of Great Lakes and coastal water.
Elevation: *Highest*—Mount Marcy, 5,344 ft (1,629 m) above sea level. *Lowest*—sea level along the Atlantic Ocean.
Coastline: 127 mi (204 km).
Record high temperature: 108 °F (42 °C) at Troy on July 22, 1926.
Record low temperature: –52 °F (–47 °C) at Old Forge on Feb. 18, 1979.
Average July temperature: 69 °F (21 °C).
Average January temperature: 21 °F (–6 °C).
Average yearly precipitation: 36 in (99 cm).

Highest elevation

Greatest north-south distance 310mi (499 km)

Lowest elevation along Atlantic Coast

Greatest east-west distance 409 mi (658 km)

Important dates

Dutch settlers began building New Amsterdam (New York City).

The Erie Canal was opened, linking the Hudson River and the Great Lakes.

| 1609 | 1625 | 1788 | 1825 |

Henry Hudson explored the Hudson River.

New York became the 11th state on July 26.

State bird
Eastern bluebird

State flower
Rose

State tree
Sugar maple

People

Population: 19,378,102
Rank among the states: 3rd
Density: 395 per mi² (152 per km²), U.S. average 85 per mi² (33 per km²)
Distribution: 87 percent urban, 13 percent rural
Largest cities in New York

New York City	8,175,133
Buffalo	261,310
Rochester	210,565
Yonkers	195,976
Syracuse	145,170
Albany	97,756

Source: 2010 census, except for distribution, which is for 2000.

Population trend

Millions

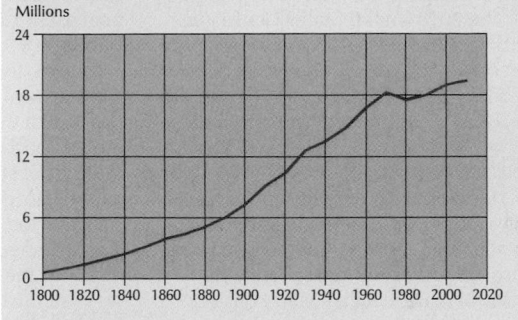

Source: U.S. Census Bureau.

Year	Population
2010	19,378,102
2000	18,976,457
1990	17,990,455
1980	17,558,072
1970	18,236,967
1960	16,782,304
1950	14,830,192
1940	13,479,142
1930	12,588,066
1920	10,385,227
1910	9,113,614
1900	7,268,894
1890	6,003,174
1880	5,082,871
1870	4,382,759
1860	3,880,735
1850	3,097,394
1840	2,428,921
1830	1,918,608
1820	1,372,812
1810	959,049
1800	589,051
1790	340,120

Economy

Chief products

Agriculture: apples, beef cattle, corn, greenhouse and nursery products, milk.
Manufacturing: chemicals, clothing, computer and electronic products, fabricated metals, food products, machinery, transportation equipment.
Mining: cement, limestone, natural gas, salt, sand and gravel.

Gross domestic product

Value of goods and services produced in 2008: $1,119,472,000,000. *Services* include community, business, and personal services; finance; government; trade; and transportation and communication. *Industry* includes construction, manufacturing, mining, and utilities. *Agriculture* includes agriculture, fishing, and forestry.

Source: U.S. Bureau of Economic Analysis.

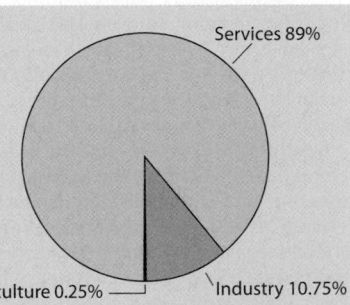

Services 89%
Agriculture 0.25%
Industry 10.75%

Government

State government

Governor: 4-year term
State senators: 62; 2-year terms
State representatives: 150; 2-year terms
Counties: 62

Federal government

United States senators: 2
United States representatives: 29 (27 in 2013)
Electoral votes: 31 (29 in 2012)

Sources of information

New York's official website at http://www.ny.gov provides a gateway to much information on the state's government, history, and economy.

In addition, the website at http://www.iloveny.com provides information about tourism.

The New York State Thruway (now the Governor Thomas E. Dewey Thruway) was completed.

1952

Construction of United Nations Headquarters in New York City was completed.

1960

New York voters approved a bond act to finance environmental projects, especially the cleaning up of hazardous waste sites.

1986

2001

The twin towers of the World Trade Center in New York City were destroyed in the worst terrorist attack in U.S. history.

Population. The 2010 United States census reported that New York had 19,378,102 people. The population of the state had increased about 2 percent over the 2000 figure of 18,976,457.

About 92 percent of New York's people live within the state's metropolitan areas (see **Metropolitan area**). Three of the state's 12 metropolitan areas have populations of 1 million or more. These areas are Buffalo-Niagara Falls, New York-Northern New Jersey-Long Island, and Rochester. For a complete list and populations of these areas, see the *Index* to the political map of New York.

New York City is the largest United States city in population. Its metropolitan area is also the largest in the United States in terms of population. New York City and its metropolitan area are among the world's largest cities in population. The 2010 United States Census reported that New York City had 8,175,133 people, and that its metropolitan area had 18,897,109 people. Four other cities in New York with more than 100,000 people are, in order of size, Buffalo, Rochester, Yonkers, and Syracuse.

New York, especially New York City, has long had a diverse population. Here, peoples of many countries and various ethnic groups have settled and adopted a common culture, while retaining many of their own customs. New York's largest population groups include people of English, German, Irish, Italian, and Polish descent. About 20 of every 100 people were born in another country. The largest groups born in other lands include people from China, Colombia, the Dominican Republic, Ecuador, Guyana, Haiti, India, Jamaica, and Mexico. Many Puerto Ricans have arrived since the end of World War II in 1945. About 800,000 Puerto Ricans live in New York City. Over 3 million African Americans live in New York—more than in any other state.

Schools. In 1784, the New York Legislature established the University of the State of New York. This agency is not a university in the usual sense of the word. It oversees all of the state's educational institutions— prekindergarten through graduate-level, both public and private—as well as a number of licensed professions. It also oversees many libraries and museums, the State Archives, public broadcasting facilities, and vocational rehabilitation services. A 17-member Board of Regents governs the agency. The New York State Legislature elects the regents to five-year terms. The regents serve without pay. The board's powers include setting educational standards, distributing public funds, issuing licenses and certificates, and incorporating colleges and universities.

The State Education Department administers the powers and duties of the regents. The regents appoint a commissioner of education to head the department for an indefinite term. The commissioner also serves as president of the University of the State of New York. The State Education Department supervises New York's local public school districts. Each district has its own school board. Districts have the authority to require children from age 6 to 17 to attend school.

In 1948, the State Legislature established the State University of New York. This statewide university system has one of the largest enrollments of any university in the United States. Its headquarters are in Albany. For the number of students and teachers in New York, see **Education** (table).

Libraries. The first libraries in New York were privately owned. In 1698, 1713, and 1730, clergymen gave books to the city for a public library. However, no library was established, and the books were destroyed during the American Revolution (1775-1783). The first circulating library was the New York Society Library, founded in New York City in 1754 and still in existence.

Today, the state has hundreds of public libraries. The New York Public Library in New York City includes research libraries and many branch libraries. This library system is one of the largest in the United States.

Columbia University in New York City has one of the largest collections of materials among the state's college and university libraries. Other large college and university libraries include those at Cornell University in Ithaca; the four centers of the State University of New York, in Albany, Binghamton, Buffalo, and Stony Brook; and Syracuse University. The Sibley Music Library of the University of Rochester has one of the few library build-

Population density

The New York City area is New York's most thickly populated region by far. The area between Albany and Buffalo is also heavily populated. Northern New York has relatively few people.

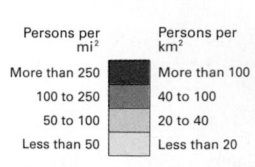

Persons per mi²	Persons per km²
More than 250	More than 100
100 to 250	40 to 100
50 to 100	20 to 40
Less than 50	Less than 20

WORLD BOOK map; based on U.S. Census Bureau data.

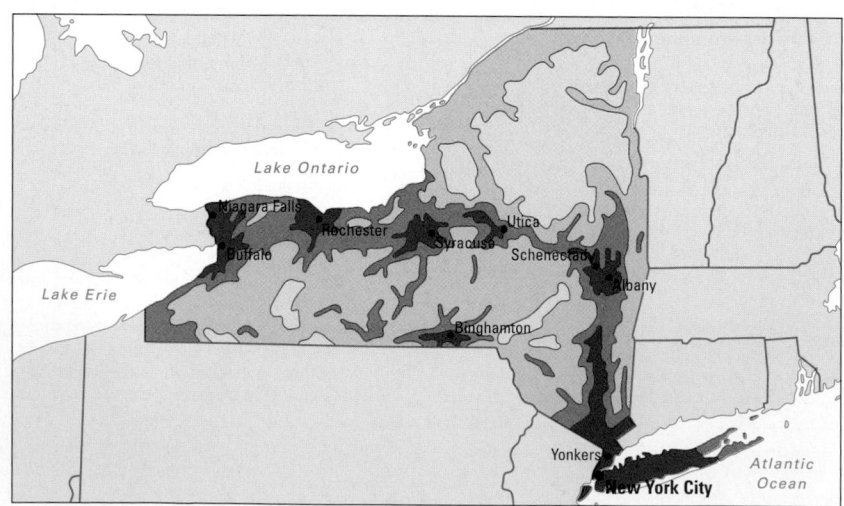

Cornell University's main campus is in Ithaca. The Uris Library and McGraw Tower, *center,* stand on the main quadrangle of the College of Arts and Sciences.

Cameramann International, Ltd. from Marilyn Gartman

Universities and colleges

This table lists the nonprofit universities and colleges in New York that grant bachelor's or advanced degrees and are accredited by the Middle States Association of Colleges and Schools.

Name	Mailing address	Name	Mailing address	Name	Mailing address
Adelphi University	Garden City	Jewish Theological		Roberts Wesleyan College	Rochester
Albany College of Phar-		Seminary of America	New York City	Rochester, University of	Rochester
macy and Health Sciences	Albany	Juilliard School	New York City	Rochester Institute of	
Albany Medical College	Albany	Keuka College	Keuka Park	Technology	Rochester
Alfred University	Alfred	King's College	New York City	Russell Sage College	Troy
Bank Street College		Le Moyne College	Syracuse	Sage College of Albany	Albany
of Education	New York City	Long Island University	†	Sage Graduate School	Troy
Bard College	Annandale-	Manhattan College	Bronx	St. Bonaventure University	St. Bona-
	on-Hudson	Manhattan School of Music	New York City		venture
Barnard College	New York City	Manhattanville College	Purchase	St. Francis College	Brooklyn
Boricua College	New York City	Marist College	Poughkeepsie	St. John Fisher College	Rochester
Briarcliffe College	Bethpage	Marymount Manhattan		St. John's University	Queens
Canisius College	Buffalo	College	New York City	St. Joseph's College,	
Cazenovia College	Cazenovia	Medaille College	Buffalo	New York	**
Christ the King Seminary	East Aurora	Mercy College	Dobbs Ferry	St. Joseph's Seminary	Yonkers
Clarkson University	Potsdam	Metropolitan College of		St. Lawrence University	Canton
Colgate University	Hamilton	New York	New York City	St. Rose, College of	Albany
Columbia University in		Molloy College	Rockville	St. Thomas Aquinas	
the City of New York	New York City		Centre	College	Sparkill
Concordia College	Bronxville	Mount St. Mary College	Newburgh	Sarah Lawrence College	Bronxville
Cooper Union	New York City	Mount St. Vincent,		Siena College	Loudonville
Cornell University	*	College of	Riverdale	Skidmore College	Saratoga
Culinary Institute of		Mount Sinai School of			Springs
America	Hyde Park	Medicine	New York City	Syracuse University	Syracuse
Daemen College	Amherst	Nazareth College of		Teachers College,	
Davis College	Johnson City	Rochester	Rochester	Columbia University	New York City
Dominican College		New Rochelle, College of	New Rochelle	Touro College	New York City
of Blauvelt	Orangeburg	New School	New York City	Unification Theological	
Dowling College	Oakdale	New York, City University of	‡	Seminary	Barrytown
D'Youville College	Buffalo	New York, State		Union College	Schenectady
Elmira College	Elmira	University of	§	Union Graduate College	Schenectady
Excelsior College	Albany	New York Chiropractic		Union Theological	
Fashion Institute of		College	Seneca Falls	Seminary	New York City
Technology	New York City	New York Institute of		United States Merchant	
Fordham University	Bronx	Technology	#	Marine Academy	Kings Point
Hamilton College	Clinton	New York Medical College	Valhalla	United States Military	
Hartwick College	Oneonta	New York University	New York City	Academy	West Point
Hebrew Union College—		Niagara University	Niagara	Utica College	Utica
Jewish Institute of		Northeastern Seminary	University	Vassar College	Poughkeepsie
Religion	New York City		Rochester	Vaughn College of Aero-	
Hilbert College	Hamburg	Nyack College	Nyack	nautics and Technology	Flushing
Hobart and William Smith		Pace University	New York City	Villa Maria College	
Colleges	Geneva	Paul Smith's College of		of Buffalo	Buffalo
Hofstra University	Hempstead	Arts and Sciences	Paul Smiths	Wagner College	Staten Island
Houghton College	Houghton	Polytechnic Institute of		Webb Institute	Glen Cove
Immaculate Conception,		New York University	Brooklyn	Wells College	Aurora
Seminary of the	Huntington	Pratt Institute	Brooklyn	Yeshiva University	New York City
Iona College	New Rochelle	Rensselaer Polytechnic			
Ithaca College	Ithaca	Institute	Troy		

*Main campus at Ithaca. Medical campus in New York City.
†Campuses at Brentwood, Brooklyn, Brookville, Orangeburg, Purchase, and Riverhead.
‡For campuses, see **New York, City University of.**

§For campuses, see **New York, State University of.**
#Campuses at New York City and Old Westbury.
**Campuses at Brooklyn and Patchogue.

ings in the United States devoted entirely to music.

The New York State Library was founded in Albany in 1818. The state library houses a comprehensive collection on New York history, including records of the early Dutch colonists. It also holds a number of important national documents. These holdings include autographs of all the signers of the Declaration of Independence, the preliminary Emancipation Proclamation, and George Washington's farewell address.

The New York State Library sponsors a statewide virtual library called the New York Online Virtual Electronic Library (NOVEL). NOVEL provides New Yorkers with access, through their local library, to thousands of national and international newspapers and magazines, health and medical resources, business collections, and age-appropriate materials for children.

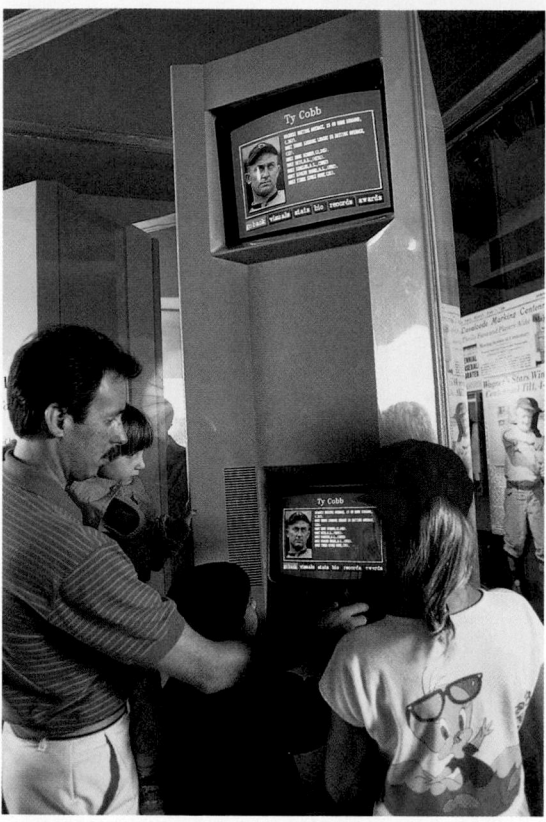

National Baseball Hall of Fame and Museum

New York State Museum

The New York State Museum in Albany includes exhibits on New York's history. This exhibit re-creates a scene from a New York City tenement neighborhood in the early 1900's.

The National Baseball Hall of Fame and Museum is in Cooperstown. The institution pays tribute to great players and features exhibits on the history of the game.

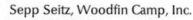

Sepp Seitz, Woodfin Camp, Inc.

The Juilliard School in New York City is a leading school for the performing arts. Courses of study include music, dance, and drama.

Museums. The New York State Museum, founded in Albany in 1836, is one of the oldest state museums in the nation. The regents of the University of the State of New York supervise this museum. The museum's collections deal with natural history, science, and the art and history of the state.

The Metropolitan Museum of Art in New York City is one of the finest and largest art museums in the world.

The state's other outstanding museums include the Museum of Modern Art, the American Museum of Natural History, and the Guggenheim Museum, all in New York City; and the National Baseball Hall of Fame and Museum and the Farmers' Museum, both in Cooperstown. The George Eastman House International Museum of Photography and Film in Rochester contains an outstanding collection of photographs.

The Guggenheim Museum in New York City displays works of art in an unusual circular building designed by Frank Lloyd Wright. Solomon R. Guggenheim founded the museum in 1937 to promote modern art and education in art.

Claus Dyrlund

Bill Foley, Black Star

Cadets celebrate graduation from the United States Military Academy in West Point. The academy's four-year program prepares young men and women for careers as Army officers.

Colour Library International from the Photo Source

The New York Public Library in New York City has more volumes and more branches than any other city public library in the United States.

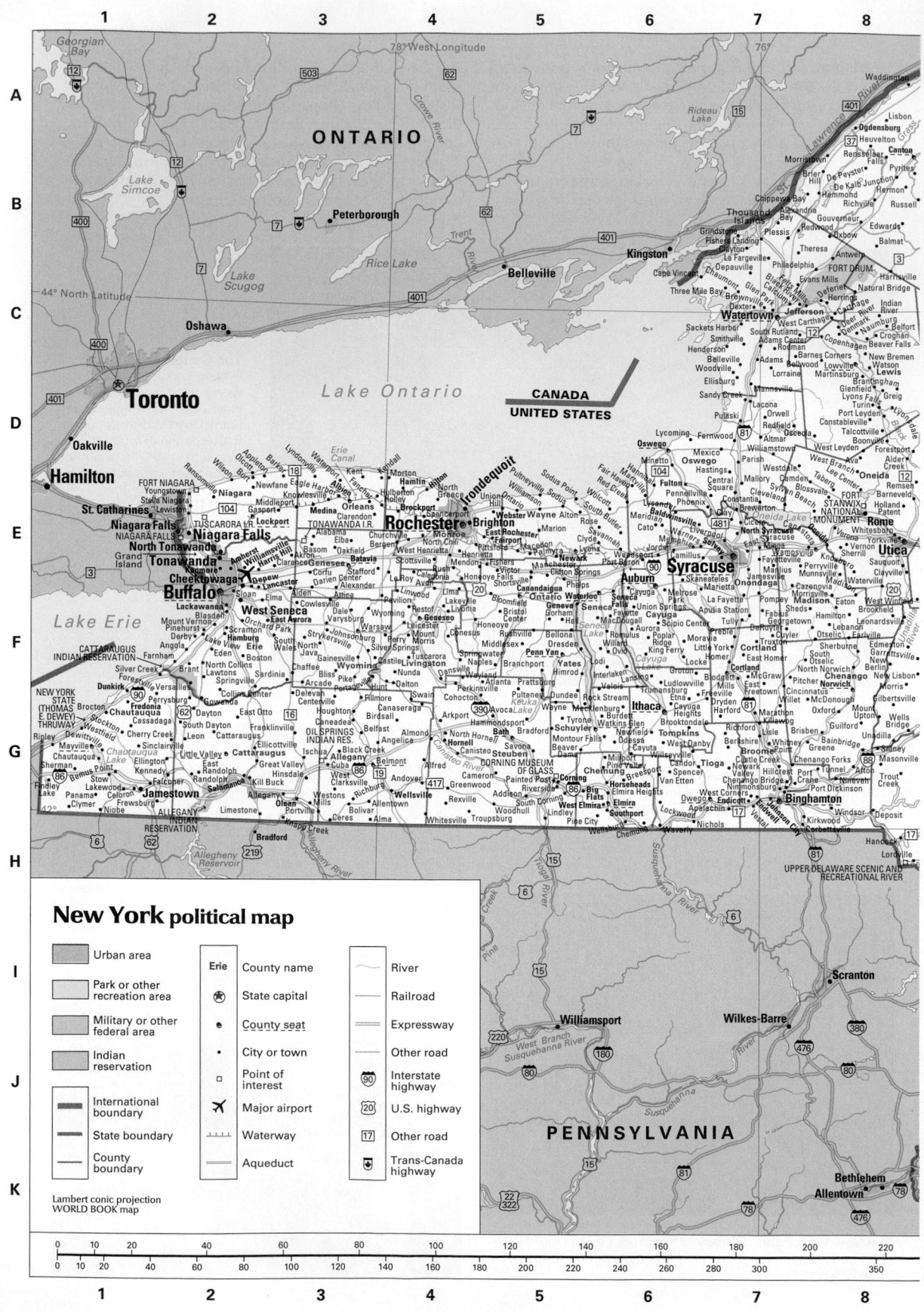

New York political map

Legend:

- Urban area
- Park or other recreation area
- Military or other federal area
- Indian reservation
- International boundary
- State boundary
- County boundary

- **Erie** County name
- ⊛ State capital
- ● County seat
- • City or town
- □ Point of interest
- ✈ Major airport
- Waterway
- Aqueduct

- River
- Railroad
- Expressway
- Other road
- 🄼 Interstate highway
- 🄴 U.S. highway
- 🄷 Other road
- Trans-Canada highway

Lambert conic projection
WORLD BOOK map

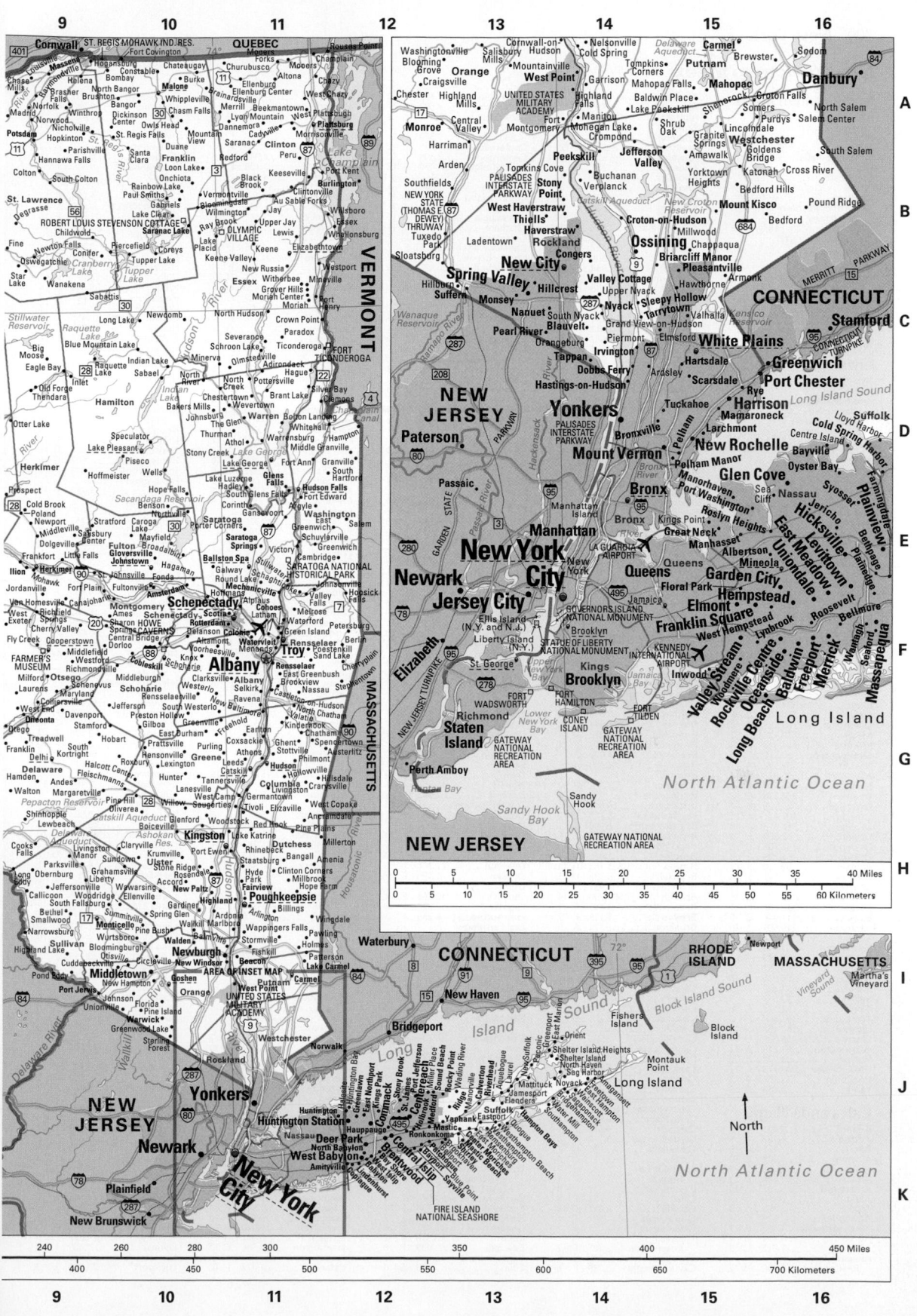

New York map index

*Does not appear on map; key shows general location.
†Census designated place—unincorporated, but recognized as a significant settled community by the U.S. Census Bureau.
‡Bronx, Brooklyn, Manhattan, Queens, and Staten Island are the five boroughs that make up New York City.
°County seat.
Places without population figures are unincorporated areas.
Source: 2010 census.

New York is one of the chief vacationlands in the United States. Its forested mountains, shimmering lakes, sandy beaches, and vast areas of unspoiled wilderness attract millions of summer vacationers yearly. Long Island's beaches and the Thousand Islands area are especially popular for fishing and water sports. Winter sports fans enjoy New York's excellent facilities for skiing, snowmobiling, tobogganing, iceboating, ice fishing, and ice-skating. Visitors also come to see New York's many historic forts and houses, and such magnificent wonders of nature as Niagara Falls. Every major urban center has places of historical and cultural interest. New York City's attractions draw millions of visitors a year. See **New York City**.

Many cultural festivals, historical celebrations, and sports competitions are held in New York every year. The New York State Fair is held annually in Syracuse in late August and early September. Buffalo, Niagara Falls, and Ogdensburg hold international festivals with the Canadian towns they border.

The Metropolitan Opera House at Lincoln Center in New York City

Thomas A. Moore, FPG

Places to visit

Following are brief descriptions of some of New York's many interesting places to visit.

Corning Museum of Glass, in Corning, features a factory that makes Steuben glass, a type of art glass. The museum also includes a teaching studio, a research library, and shops.

Farmers' Museum, near Cooperstown, has early agricultural tools and appliances. Nearby is the 19th Century Village. It includes a country school, law office, village store, blacksmith shop, print shop, doctor's office, church, tavern, and farmhouse and barn. All were built in the late 1700's or early 1800's.

Fort Niagara, near Youngstown, served as a base in the French and Indian War (1754-1763) and the War of 1812 (1812-1815).

Fort Ticonderoga, on Lake Champlain, is a reconstruction of the colonial fort where Ethan Allen and his Green Mountain Boys defied the British and forced them to surrender in 1775.

Home of Franklin D. Roosevelt National Historic Site, in Hyde Park, includes the president's grave and Val Kill, Eleanor Roosevelt's cottage. Nearby, the Franklin D. Roosevelt Library and Museum has many of Roosevelt's books, ship models, and other personal belongings.

Lake Placid, a village in the Adirondack Mountains, is a world-famous resort. It is noted for its glacial lake and its excellent facilities for winter and summer sports. The 1932 and 1980 Winter Olympics took place there.

Literary shrines may be seen throughout New York. They include John Burroughs's birthplace in Roxbury, Thomas Paine's home in New Rochelle, and Walt Whitman's birthplace near Huntington. Mark Twain's study and grave are in Elmira. The cottage in which Robert Louis Stevenson wrote several of his books is in Saranac Lake. The cottage in which Edgar Allan Poe wrote many poems is in the Bronx, in New York City.

National Baseball Hall of Fame and Museum, in Coopers-town, honors great baseball players and displays historic equipment of the game. The museum includes a theater that is modeled after the original Comiskey Park.

Niagara Falls, in the city of Niagara Falls, is the most famous, most accessible waterfall in the world. Water plunges into a steep-walled gorge at the rate of about 100,000 cubic feet (2,832 cubic meters) a second.

Saratoga Springs is a health resort noted for its mineral springs. The Saratoga Performing Arts Center is the summer home of the New York City Ballet, the New York City Opera, and the Philadelphia Orchestra. Saratoga Springs also has harness and thoroughbred race tracks. Museums include the National Museum of Racing and the National Museum of Dance.

West Point, on the Hudson River north of New York City, is the home of the United States Military Academy.

National parklands. New York's national parklands include many sites of historical importance and a number of areas preserved for their attractive recreational features. For example, Saratoga National Historical Park, near Stillwater, includes the battlefield on which the Americans defeated a British army in 1777 during the American Revolution. Castle Clinton National Monument, in New York City, originally a fort, was once a landing station for immigrants. Statue of Liberty National Monument stands in Upper New York Bay at the entrance to New York Harbor. Fire Island National Seashore features the beaches, dunes, marshes, and wildlife of Fire Island, a barrier island off Long Island.

State parks and forests. New York has more than 150 state parks and about 60 forest areas. Adirondack Park, covering 6 million acres (2.4 million hectares) in the Adirondacks, is the largest park in the nation. The state owns about 40 percent of the park. Watkins Glen State Park, with 18 waterfalls, is one of the scenic wonders of North America. Letchworth State Park, on the Genesee River, is famous for its scenic canyon, the Genesee Gorge. For information, write to the Office of Parks, Recreation, and Historic Preservation, Albany, NY 12238.

World-famous Niagara Falls

Anthony Morganti, FPG

Thanksgiving Day Parade in New York City

Jeffrey D. Smith, Woodfin Camp, Inc.

© Vespasian/Alamy Images

Reenactment of the French and Indian War at Fort Ticonderoga

© Brucepix/Shutterstock

The home of Franklin D. Roosevelt in Hyde Park

Land and climate

Land regions. In the Pleistocene Epoch, which ended about 11,500 years ago, a sheet of ice up to 2 miles (3.2 kilometers) thick in places spread across almost all the area in what is now New York. It formed many of the state's most striking natural features by deepening valleys, rounding off mountains, and depositing sand, stones, and pebbles. Most of New York's soils have been formed from materials deposited by the ice.

New York has eight land regions: (1) the Atlantic Coastal Plain, (2) the New England Upland, (3) the Hudson-Mohawk Lowland, (4) the Adirondack Upland, (5) the Tug Hill Plateau, (6) the St. Lawrence Lowland, (7) the Erie-Ontario Lowland, and (8) the Appalachian Plateau.

The Atlantic Coastal Plain covers Long Island and Staten Island. It forms part of the almost level coastal plain stretching along the Atlantic Ocean from Massachusetts to the southern tip of Florida. Staten Island and the western end of Long Island lie within New York City. Both islands are important residential districts.

Fishing is an important source of income on the Atlantic Coastal Plain. In addition, farmers raise vegetables, fruits, flowers, and poultry there. Long, offshore barrier islands and broad, sandy beaches contribute to Long Island's popularity as a summer resort area.

The New England Upland, a region of hills and low mountains, extends along the lower half of New York's eastern border. It includes the Taconic Mountains and the southern part of the Hudson River Valley. Also in the region is Manhattan Island, the heart of New York City.

In the Hudson Highlands near West Point, the Hudson River has cut a gorge 1,000-feet (300-meters) deep.

The Hudson-Mohawk Lowland covers most of the Hudson River Valley and the Mohawk River Valley. The lowland is about 10 to 30 miles (16 to 48 kilometers) wide and provides the nation's only natural navigable passage through the Appalachian Mountains. Since pioneer days, the Hudson and Mohawk river valleys have served as the most important transportation routes between the Atlantic Ocean and the Great Lakes. The fertile plains support fruit and dairy farms.

The Adirondack Upland is a roughly circular hill and mountain region about 100 miles (160 kilometers) in diameter in northeastern New York. The Adirondack Mountains are formed from hard, ancient rocks, perhaps the oldest in North America. More than 40 peaks rise over 4,000 feet (1,200 meters), with Mount Marcy, at 5,344 feet (1,629 meters), the highest point in the state. The region is a famous recreation area with hundreds of scenic lakes, streams, waterfalls, and peaks. Its thin soils are poor for farming, and the frost-free growing season is short. There is some lumbering and some lead, garnet, titanium, and zinc mining in the region.

The Tug Hill Plateau, an isolated part of the Appalachian Plateau, is a relatively flat rocky area. It is separated from the Adirondack Upland by the Black River Valley. The plateau stands in the path of cold winter air masses that cross unfrozen Lake Ontario and pick up heat and moisture.

Land regions of New York

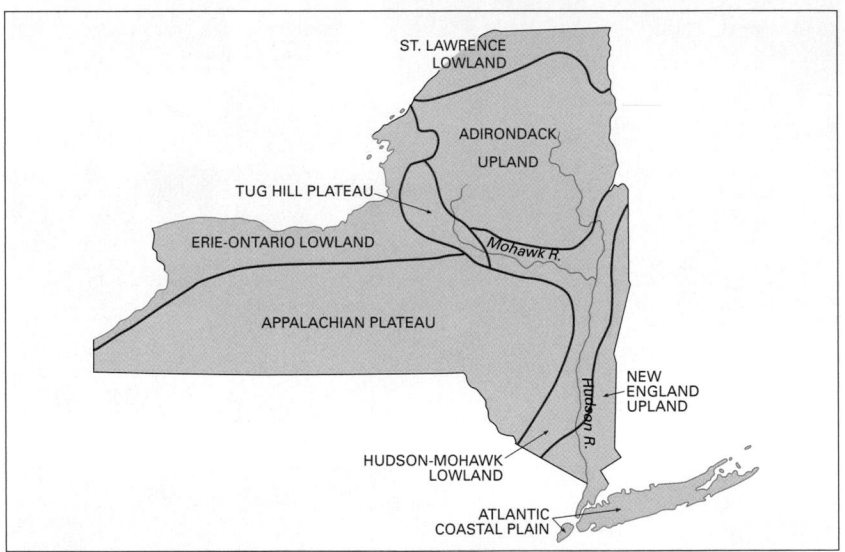

WORLD BOOK map

Map index

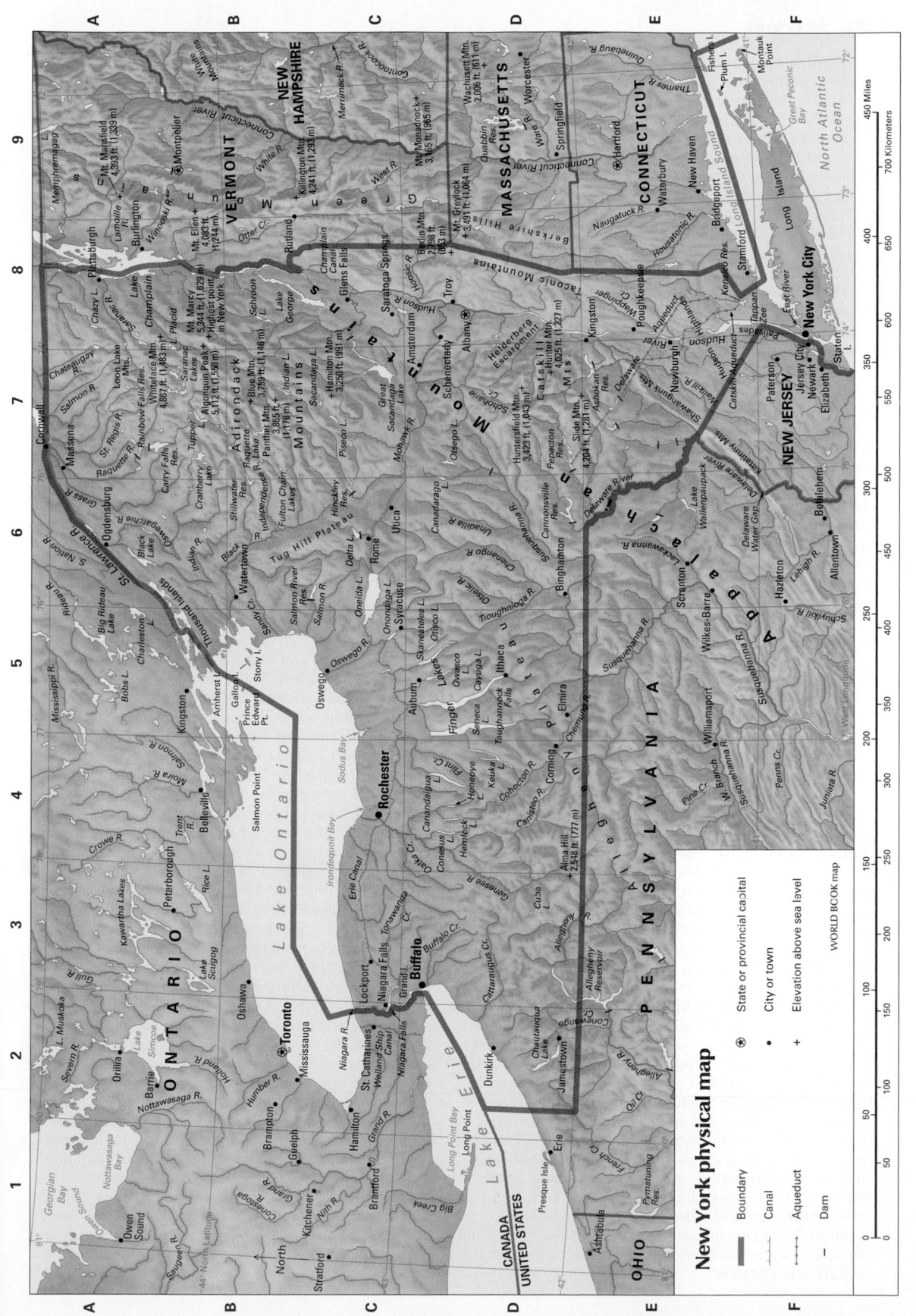

New York physical map

Boundary	
Canal	
Aqueduct	
Dam	

⊛ State or provincial capital

• City or town

+ Elevation above sea level

WORLD BOOK map

| 0 | 50 | 100 | 150 | 200 | 250 | 450 Miles |
| 0 | 50 | 100 | 150 | 200 | 250 | 300 | 350 | 400 | 450 | 550 | 650 | 700 Kilometers |

As a result, the plateau receives more snow—over 225 inches (572 centimeters) a year—than anyplace in the nation east of the Rocky Mountains. The harsh climate and thin soils restrict farming and settlement.

The St. Lawrence Lowland lies along the south bank of the St. Lawrence River and north of the Adirondack Upland. The region averages 18 miles (29 kilometers) in width. The land is level to rolling, with soils of widely varying fertility. The region has many dairy farms. Fruit orchards are common near Lake Champlain. Summer homes line the banks of the St. Lawrence River, particularly near the river's beautiful Thousand Islands.

The Erie-Ontario Lowland is a low plain south and east of Lake Erie and Lake Ontario. The plain is 5 miles (8 kilometers) wide along Lake Erie and broadens to 35 miles (56 kilometers) wide north of Syracuse. It has many swamps. Oval-shaped hills called *drumlins* rise from 50 to 200 feet (15 to 60 meters). They were formed from pebbles and other deposits of the ice sheet. A limestone and dolomite ridge stretching east-west between Lake Erie and Lake Ontario forms the ledge over which the Niagara River drops in its famous waterfall.

Fruit farming is a speciality in the lowland's unusually fertile soils. The region also has prosperous vegetable farms, greenhouses, plant nurseries, and dairy farms. The ease of reaching the Mohawk-Hudson transportation route to the east and an abundant supply of water power from falls on the Niagara and Genesee rivers spurred development in the region. These factors led to the growth of industrial, shipping, and service centers such as Buffalo, Rochester, and Syracuse.

The Appalachian Plateau, also known as the *Allegheny Plateau,* covers half of the state and is New York's largest land region. In the western and central portions of the plateau, broad uplands 800 to 2,000 feet (240 to 610 meters) above sea level are separated by ice-deepened valleys. At the Finger Lakes, the deepest valleys are now occupied by long, deep lakes.

In the south and east, the plateau rises. The Catskill Mountains, at 2,000 to 4,000 feet (610 to 1,200 meters) high, are a year-round recreation area. Reservoirs in the Catskills help supply New York City with water.

The rugged Appalachian Plateau supports only smaller cities, villages, and population centers except for Binghamton. Most Appalachian Plateau farms specialize in dairying. The most fertile and level lands lie to the north between the Finger Lakes, and along river valleys emptying out of the Catskills. Vineyards, nurseries, and vegetable farms can be found there.

Coastline and shoreline. New York's coastline stretches 127 miles (204 kilometers) along the Atlantic Ocean. This figure does not include the coastline along Long Island Sound. Including the shoreline of every bay and inlet on Long Island, the state's coastline is almost 1,850 miles (2,977 kilometers) long. New York City has one of the world's great natural harbors. The harbor is deep and almost completely protected by land. Excluding bays and inlets, the state has 275 miles (443 kilometers) of shoreline along Lakes Erie and Ontario, 192 miles (309 kilometers) along the Niagara and St. Lawrence rivers, and 212 miles (341 kilometers) along islands and Long Island Sound. Buffalo is New York's chief Great Lakes port. Oceangoing ships reach it through the St. Lawrence Seaway.

Mountains. The Adirondacks in northern New York are the state's highest range. Two peaks rise over 5,000 feet (1,500 meters). They are 5,344-foot (1,629-meter) Mount Marcy, and 5,112-foot (1,558-meter) Algonquin Peak (also known as Mount MacIntyre). At 4,204 feet (1,281 meters), Slide Mountain is the tallest peak in the Catskills. South of the Catskills, and extending into New Jersey, a 1,000- to 2,000-foot (300- to 600-meter) ridge known as the Shawangunk Mountains is famed among rock climbers. The Helderberg Escarpment presents a steep 1,000-foot (300-meter) cliff facing Albany to the northeast. The Taconic Mountains, which rise to 2,000 feet (610 meters) east of the Hudson, are a western extension of the Berkshire Mountains in Massachusetts.

Rivers. New York's most important rivers, the Hudson and the Mohawk, form one of the nation's great trade routes. The Hudson originates from a lake called Tear-of-the-Clouds high on Mount Marcy. It tumbles south through narrow gorges with many rapids and waterfalls. Oceangoing ships can sail from New York City 150 miles (241 kilometers) up the Hudson as far north as Albany. At Cohoes, about midway on the Hudson's 306-mile (492-kilometer) trip to the sea, the Mohawk enters.

The Mohawk River, the chief branch of the Hudson River, connects the Hudson with the Erie-Ontario Lowland. The Mohawk rises in Oneida County and flows southeastward for about 145 miles (233 kilometers). It drains central New York. The Mohawk was important in the development of the interior because the river and its tributaries provided water for the eastern half of the Erie Canal.

The Genesee River starts in Pennsylvania, flows north through western New York, and empties into Lake Ontario north of Rochester. At Letchworth State Park, it passes through a spectacular gorge 600 feet (180 meters) deep nicknamed "The Grand Canyon of the East." The Oswego River and its branch, the Seneca, also empty into Lake Ontario. The Delaware, an important sports fishing and canoeing river, tumbles out of the Catskills to form the eastern boundary between New York and Pennsylvania. The Susquehanna River originates from Otsego Lake and flows southwest past Binghamton before entering Pennsylvania.

Other rivers include the short but powerful Niagara, flowing 34 miles (55 kilometers) from Lake Erie to Lake Ontario, and the St. Lawrence. Both carry huge quantities of water and form part of the international boundary with Canada. The East River is actually a strait that connects Long Island Sound with New York Bay and separates Manhattan Island from Long Island.

Waterfalls. The state's most famous waterfall, Niagara Falls, is also New York's most important source of hydroelectric power. The American Falls, at 176 feet (54 meters), lie in New York. The St. Lawrence rapids near Massena have also been developed as a major source of power. The thin, delicate Taughannock Falls is the highest waterfall in the northeastern part of the nation. It drops 215 feet (66 meters) into a spectacular glen before entering Lake Cayuga in the Finger Lakes region.

Lakes. Most of New York's several thousand lakes lie in the Adirondack region. About 2,000 lakes and ponds are nestled among the hills and mountains there. Many of the larger Adirondack lakes support year-round resorts. Lake George, on the eastern edge of the Adirondacks, is a popular vacation spot. It empties into Lake Champlain. Lake Champlain lies on the New York-Vermont border and extends into the Canadian province of Quebec.

New York's largest lakes, by far, are Lake Erie and Lake Ontario. They form part of the boundary between the United States and Canada.

The long and narrow Finger Lakes lie parallel to one another in the Appalachian Plateau. Lakes Cayuga and Seneca are the largest and deepest of the 11 Finger Lakes. Lake Oneida, northeast of Syracuse, has the largest surface area lying entirely within the state. Covering 80 square miles (210 square kilometers), the lake is noted for its excellent boating and fishing. Chautauqua Lake in southwestern New York is a favorite summer resort. A famous arts and education center, the Chautauqua Institute, lies on its bank.

Plant and animal life. New York has many kinds of trees and plants. Forests cover about half the state, with the greatest ones in the Adirondacks. Smaller forests thrive throughout the Appalachian regions, where large areas of abandoned farmland have again become wood-

land. About 150 types of trees, of which about 135 are native, grow in New York. Trees of commercial importance include balsam fir, beech, black cherry, oak, pine, spruce, sugar maple, and yellow birch. Apple orchards are common in the Lake Ontario Lowland, along Lake Champlain, and in the Hudson River Valley.

Many wildflowers bloom along river valleys throughout New York. They include black-eyed Susans, devil's paintbrush, and Queen Anne's lace. Buttercups, goldenrod, violets, and wild roses grow along the borders of forests and in clearings. White and yellow water lilies thrive in many Adirondack lakes. Other wildflowers common in New York include bunchberry, enchanter's nightshade, goldenthread, Indian pipe, starflower, and trillium.

Some animals that once were common in New York are now endangered or extinct. These include such fur-bearing animals as marten, mink, and otters, and such

Average monthly weather

	Buffalo					New York City				
	Temperatures				Days of rain or snow		Temperatures			Days of rain or snow
	°F		°C				°F		°C	
	High	Low	High	Low			High	Low	High	Low	
Jan.	31	18	−1	−8	20	Jan.	39	27	4	−3	11
Feb.	33	19	1	−7	17	Feb.	41	28	5	−2	10
Mar.	43	26	6	−3	16	Mar.	50	35	10	2	11
Apr.	54	36	12	2	14	Apr.	60	44	16	7	11
May	66	48	19	9	13	May	71	54	22	12	11
June	75	57	24	14	11	June	79	64	26	18	10
July	80	62	27	17	10	July	85	70	29	21	9
Aug.	78	61	26	16	10	Aug.	83	69	28	21	9
Sept.	70	53	21	12	11	Sept.	76	62	24	17	8
Oct.	59	43	15	6	12	Oct.	65	51	18	10	8
Nov.	47	34	8	1	16	Nov.	54	42	12	6	10
Dec.	36	24	2	−4	19	Dec.	44	32	7	0	11

Average yearly precipitation

Precipitation in the state varies considerably. The wettest areas generally are in the mountains and in the southeast.

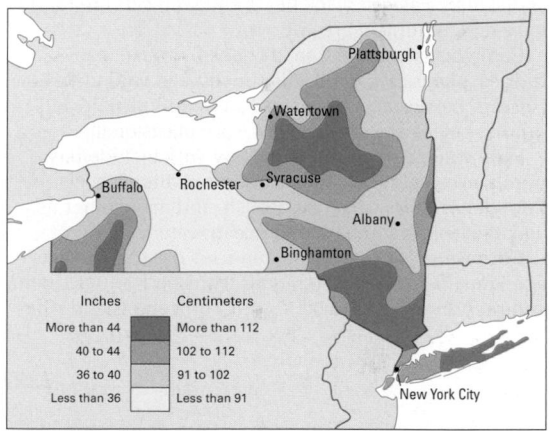

Average January temperatures

The northeastern part of New York has the lowest temperatures. The west and southeast have the mildest winters.

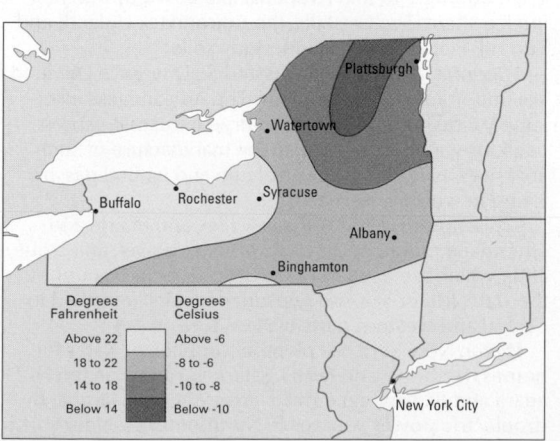

Average July temperatures

The state has fairly even summertime temperatures. The southeast and northwest are generally the warmest sections.

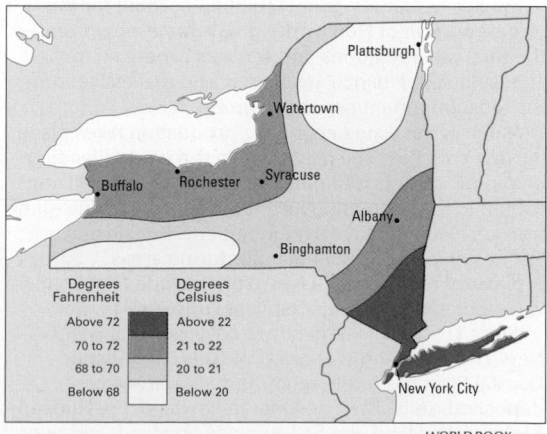

WORLD BOOK maps

Lake Placid, a beautiful glacial lake, lies in the Adirondack Mountains of northeastern New York. The village of Lake Placid is a popular summer and winter resort.

Don Mason, West Stock

important predators as the mountain lion, timber wolf, and wolverine. However, other native animals have adapted to human settlement. Porcupines, rabbits, red fox, squirrels, and woodchucks abound in some areas. Many deer roam the forests. The state's fur-bearing animals include beavers, muskrats, opossums, raccoons, and skunks. Eastern black bears and wild cats are found in remote mountain areas.

Game birds include Canada geese, grouse, partridges, pheasants, quail, wild ducks, and wild turkeys. Falcons, hawks, and owls can also be found. Bald and golden eagles are seen in New York occasionally.

Freshwater fish common in New York include bass, perch, pike, salmon, sunfish, and trout. Bluefish, clams, flounder, oysters, shad, swordfish, and many other fish and shellfish live in bays and ocean waters.

Climate. New York's climate varies greatly. The average January temperature ranges from 14 °F (–10 °C) in the central Adirondacks to 30 °F (–1 °C) on Long Island. The average July temperature is 66 °F (19 °C) in the central Adirondacks and 74 °F (23 °C) on Long Island. New York's record high temperature, 108 °F (42 °C), was recorded at Troy in east-central New York on July 22, 1926. Old Forge, in the Fulton Chain Lakes area, recorded a record low of –52 °F (–47 °C) on Feb. 18, 1979.

The frost-free growing season in New York ranges from an average high of 200 days on Long Island to less than 100 days in the central Adirondacks. New York's average annual *precipitation* (rain, melted snow, and other forms of moisture) ranges from 32 to 58 inches (81 to 147 centimeters). The most precipitation occurs on Tug Hill, the southwestern slopes of the Adirondacks, the central Catskills, and Long Island. In central, northern, and western New York, the Great Lakes, with their broad expanse of open water, supply moisture for many cloudy days and abundant winter snowfall. Syracuse, Rochester, and Buffalo routinely receive a greater annual snowfall than any other large city in the nation.

Economy

New York has a varied economy. Its excellent location, large population, and outstanding transportation facilities have helped make it a leader in business and industry. New York is a leading state in many economic areas, including accounting, banking, corporation management, insurance, manufacturing, publishing, and trade.

Service industries, taken together, account for the largest portion of New York's *gross domestic product*— the total value of goods and services produced in the state annually. Finance, insurance, and real estate form the most important economic group in New York.

Much of the state's economic production takes place in New York City. The city is one of the world's leading economic centers. But other parts of the state also contribute to the economy. Northern New York is one of the nation's leading dairy-farming regions. Buffalo and Rochester are important manufacturing areas.

Natural resources in New York include fertile soils, a variety of minerals, and abundant supplies of water.

Soils. The ice sheet that once covered what is now New York left behind a variety of soils. The Atlantic Coastal Plain has fertile sandy and *alluvial* (water-deposited) soils. The Erie-Ontario Lowland, the Hudson-Mohawk Lowland, the St. Lawrence Lowland, and river valleys throughout the Appalachian Plateau have fertile, well-drained soils. The soils of the rest of the Appalachian Plateau and the New England Upland tend to be poor, gray-brown, silty soils. These soils developed from glacial *drift.* Drift is material ranging in size from great boulders to fine rock dust laid down by the melting ice sheet. The Catskills, the Adirondack Upland, and Tug Hill Plateau have rough, stony soils.

Minerals. The Adirondacks and St. Lawrence Lowland are important suppliers of talc. The Adirondacks also supply a major part of the country's industrial garnets, used for watch jewels and in the manufacture of such abrasives as sandpaper. Petroleum and natural gas are found in western New York.

Clay is found in the Hudson Valley and in Erie and Onondaga counties. Deposits of sand, gravel, and stone, all of which are used in construction, occur throughout the state. Major salt and gypsum deposits are found in central and western parts of New York.

Water. New York has plentiful supplies of water for homes, factories, and farms. Falls and rapids on the Niagara and St. Lawrence rivers are among the largest hydroelectric power sources in North America. New York's rivers are also used for recreation and transportation.

New York economy

General economy

Gross domestic product (GDP)* (2008) $1,119,472,000,000
  Rank among U.S. states   3rd
Unemployment rate (2010)   8.4% (U.S. avg: 9.6%)

*Gross domestic product is the total value of goods and services produced in a year.
Sources: U.S. Bureau of Economic Analysis and U.S. Bureau of Labor Statistics.

Agriculture

Cash receipts $3,675,505,000
  Rank among U.S. states   28th
Distribution   54% livestock, 46% crops
Farms   36,600
Farm acres (hectares)   7,100,000 (2,870,000)
  Rank among U.S. states   36th
Farmland   23% of New York

Leading products

1. Dairy products   (ranks 3rd in U.S.)
2. Greenhouse and nursery products
3. Corn
4. Apples   (ranks 2nd in U.S.)
5. Cattle and calves
6. Soybeans
Other products: beans, cabbage, cucumbers, ducks, eggs, grapes, hay, maple products, onions, potatoes, tomatoes, turkeys, wheat.

Electric power

Natural gas   31.1%
Nuclear   30.6%
Hydroelectric   19.0%
Coal   13.6%
Petroleum   2.7%
Other   3.0%

Production and workers by economic activities

Economic activities	Percent of GDP produced	Employed workers	
		Number of people	Percent of total
Finance, insurance, & real estate	34	1,493,500	13
Community, business, & personal services	24	4,313,500	38
Trade, restaurants, & hotels	12	2,085,200	18
Government	11	1,528,400	14
Transportation & communication	8	648,700	6
Manufacturing	6	565,000	5
Construction	3	533,900	5
Utilities	2	40,400	*
Agriculture	*	66,100	1
Mining	*	14,300	*
Total	100	11,289,000	100

*Less than one-half of 1 percent.
Figures are for 2008; employment figures include full- and part-time workers.
Source: *World Book* estimates based on data from U.S. Bureau of Economic Analysis.

Fishing

Commercial catch $57,253,000
  Rank among U.S. states   16th

Leading catches

1. Clams   (ranks 4th in U.S.)
2. Lobsters
3. Squid
Other catches: bass, flounder, oysters, scallops, tilefish.

Figures are for 2008, except for the agricultural figures, which are for 2009.
Sources: U.S. Department of Agriculture, U.S. Energy Information Administration, U.S. National Marine Fisheries Service.

continued on page 310

Economy of New York

This map shows the economic uses of land in New York and where the state's leading farm and mineral products are produced. Major manufacturing centers are shown in red.

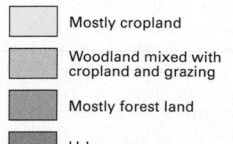

Mostly cropland
Woodland mixed with cropland and grazing
Mostly forest land
Urban area
• Manufacturing or service industry center
• Mineral deposit

WORLD BOOK map

Mining

Nonfuel mineral production	$1,480,000,000
Rank among U.S. states	16th
Coal (tons)	*
Crude oil (barrels†)	386,000
Rank among U.S. states	27th
Natural gas (cubic feet‡)	50,320,000,000
Rank among U.S. states	22nd

*No significant mining of this product in New York.
†One barrel equals 42 gallons (159 liters).
‡One cubic foot equals 0.0283 cubic meter.

Leading products

1. Natural gas
2. Salt   (ranks 3rd in U.S.)
3. Portland cement
4. Sand and gravel
Other products: clays, dolomite, garnet, gypsum, limestone, wollastonite, zinc.

Manufacturing

Value added by manufacture*	$87,126,225,000
Rank among U.S. states	8th

Leading products

1. Chemicals
2. Food and beverages
3. Computer and electronic products
4. Machinery
5. Fabricated metal products
6. Transportation equipment
Other products: clothing, jewelry, nonmetallic minerals, plastics and rubber products, printed materials.

*Value added by manufacture is the increase in value of raw materials after they become finished products.

Figures are for 2008.
Sources: U.S. Census Bureau, U.S. Energy Information Administration.

Service industries account for about 90 percent of New York's gross domestic product. Most of the service industries are concentrated in the state's metropolitan areas, but especially in the New York City area.

New York City, the nation's leading financial center, is the home of most of the largest U.S. financial companies. Large financial companies headquartered in the city include American Express, Citigroup, JPMorgan Chase & Co., and Morgan Stanley. The New York Stock Exchange is the largest securities exchange in the nation. The real estate business is also a major economic activity in New York City. A high demand for prime office space in Manhattan has resulted in some of the world's highest property values. Other important financial centers include Albany, Buffalo, and Rochester.

Hotels, restaurants, and retail trade establishments operate primarily in the New York City area, and also in Albany, Buffalo, and Rochester. New York's restaurants and hotels benefit from the tens of millions of tourists who visit each year. Many wholesale companies are based in New York City. The city's port handles much foreign trade. A large number of wholesale companies are also based in Albany and Buffalo and on Long Island.

State government offices are based in Albany. New

York City has many federal, state, and local government workers. Several of the world's largest law firms and advertising agencies are based in Manhattan. Verizon Communications, one of the largest U.S. communication companies, is headquartered in New York City.

Manufacturing. New York ranks among the leading manufacturing states. The state makes a wide variety of products—from huge machines to tiny computer chips.

Chemicals rank first among New York's manufactured products, and the state ranks as a leading chemical manufacturer in the United States. *Pharmaceuticals* (medicinal drugs) are the state's leading chemical products. Two major pharmaceutical producers, Bristol-Myers Squibb and Pfizer, are headquartered in New York City. Eastman Kodak, a leading maker of photographic chemicals and other products, is based in Rochester.

Computer and electronic products are also important. Leading products include computer components and microchips, and surveillance and navigation equipment. The chief centers of the electronic products industry are Binghamton, the Nassau-Suffolk area, New York City, and Rochester. International Business Machines Corporation (IBM), a major computer technology firm, has its headquarters just north of New York City.

© Andrew Gombert, EPA/Landov

The New York Stock Exchange ranks as the nation's largest stock exchange. The business, financial, and trading organizations in New York City play a major role in the economy of the United States and of the world.

New York's important food products include baked goods, canned fruits and vegetables, and dairy products. The state's major centers of food production include the Buffalo-Niagara Falls area, Nassau and Suffolk counties on Long Island, New York City, and Rochester.

The leading types of machinery include engines and turbines and industrial equipment. The major centers of machinery production in the state include Buffalo, the Nassau-Suffolk area, New York City, and Rochester.

Other manufacturing industries produce clothing, fabricated metal products, and printed materials. New York ranks as a leading producer of clothing, especially women's clothing. Important fabricated metal products include machine shop products and sheet metal. New York is a leading state in printing and publishing. New York City is the center of the publishing industry in the United States. Other important products manufactured in the state of New York include electrical equipment, jewelry, plastics and rubber products, and transportation equipment.

Agriculture. Farmland covers about a fourth of New York's land area. Livestock and livestock products provide slightly over half of New York's agricultural income. Milk is the state's leading agricultural product. New York ranks among the leading states in milk production. Milk is produced in the northern and western portions of the state.

Beef cattle and poultry products are also important sources of livestock income in New York. Leading poultry products include *broilers* (young, tender chickens), ducks, eggs, and turkeys.

Crops provide slightly less then half of New York's agricultural income. The state's leading field crops include hay and corn, which are used primarily as feed for the state's dairy cattle. Soybeans and wheat are also grown in New York.

Greenhouse and nursery products are another important source of agricultural income in New York. Suffolk County on Long Island is the leading county for greenhouse and nursery products.

New York is a leading center of fruit and vegetable production in the eastern United States. Orange and Suffolk counties, both near New York City, have many small vegetable farms, also called *truck farms.* Western New York also produces large amounts of vegetables. The most important vegetables grown in the state include cabbages, cucumbers, onions, potatoes, squash, sweet corn, and tomatoes.

Apples are the leading fruit crop in New York, and grapes rank second. New York ranks among the leading states in the production of both apples and grapes. The state's largest apple orchards lie near Lake Ontario and the Hudson River. Chautauqua County in far west New York leads in grape production.

Mining. New York's leading mined products include crushed stone, natural gas, salt, and sand and gravel. Limestone is the most important type of crushed stone quarried in the state. Natural gas is mined in western New York. Most salt-mining operations are in the Appalachian Plateau region of western New York. Sand and gravel are mined throughout the state. New York is the only state that produces wollastonite, used in ceramics. New York also ranks among the leading states in the production of garnet and talc.

Fishing industry. Commercial fishing takes place in Long Island waters and in Lake Erie and Lake Ontario. Clams, flounder, lobsters, scallops, and squid are taken from Long Island Sound. Bullheads, walleye, and yellow perch are caught in Lake Erie and Lake Ontario.

Electric power and utilities. Plants that burn natural gas and nuclear power plants each provide about 30 percent of New York's electric power. Coal-burning plants and hydroelectric plants supply most of the rest. New York's two largest hydroelectric power projects are the St. Lawrence-Franklin D. Roosevelt Power Project and the Niagara Power Project. They were developed jointly with Canada.

Transportation. New York lies in the heart of the most thickly populated part of the United States. It is the chief gateway to the United States from other countries. It has one of the finest natural harbors in the world and an excellent system of inland waterways. All these factors have helped New York become one of the nation's leaders in transportation.

Railroads. Rail lines provide freight service on thousands of miles of track in New York. The state's first railroad, the Mohawk and Hudson, began running between Albany and Schenectady in 1831. New York City's subway, the busiest in the nation, covers approximately 660 miles (1,060 kilometers). About 5 million riders jam these trains every working day.

Aviation. John F. Kennedy International Airport and La Guardia Airport are both in the Queens borough of New York City. Kennedy Airport ranks as one of the world's busiest airports. La Guardia Airport handles mostly domestic flights. People traveling to and from New York City also use the airport in nearby Newark, New Jersey. Albany, Buffalo, Islip, Rochester, and Syracuse also have busy airports.

Roads and highways. New York has an extensive system of roads and highways. The Governor Thomas E. Dewey Thruway is the longest toll superhighway in the United States. This 496-mile (798-kilometer) expressway runs across the state between New York City and the border with Pennsylvania at the western end of the state. It links Albany, Utica, Syracuse, Rochester, and Buffalo. Interstate 88 links Binghamton and Albany. Interstate 81 runs between the New York-Pennsylvania border south of Binghamton and the Canadian border, and Interstate 87 links Albany with the Canadian border.

New York has many great bridges. The Bear Mountain, George Washington, Mid-Hudson, Newburgh-Beacon, Rip Van Winkle, and Tappan Zee bridges span the Hudson River. The Brooklyn and Robert F. Kennedy bridges cross the East River. The Peace Bridge links Buffalo with Fort Erie in Canada. The 4,260-foot (1,298-meter) Verrazano-Narrows Bridge across the Narrows channel connects Brooklyn and Staten Island. The Verrazano-Narrows Bridge is the nation's longest suspension bridge. The Thousand Islands International Bridge connects the state with Canada.

Waterways. New York has one of the nation's largest internal waterway systems—the New York State Canal System. The system was completed in 1918 and includes parts of the old Erie Canal and several other waterways. The Erie Canal, which was opened in 1825, connected the Hudson River with Lake Erie. It played an important part in the economic growth of New York and the entire

United States. The New York State Canal System and its connecting waterways cover hundreds of miles. They extend from Lake Champlain and the Hudson River to Lake Erie and Lake Ontario. The St. Lawrence Seaway, which was opened in 1959, turned New York's Great Lakes ports into seaports.

Shipping. New York City's port, officially called the Port of New York and New Jersey, is one of the world's busiest seaports. Huge ocean liners and freighters from all parts of the world dock at this great port. Other major New York ports include Albany, Buffalo, Hempstead Harbor, and Port Jefferson. There is more limited shipping from Chester and Tarrytown. Albany is a major shipping center, though it lies about 150 miles (240 kilometers) from the Atlantic Ocean. The Hudson River has been deepened so that ocean ships can reach Albany.

Communication. New York leads the nation in producing books, magazines, and newspapers. William Bradford established New York's first newspaper, the *New-York Gazette,* in New York City in 1725. Today, one of the world's most influential newspapers, *The New York Times,* is published in New York City. Other well-known New York City newspapers are the *New York Post*—one of the nation's oldest papers—and the *Daily News. The Wall Street Journal,* a leading business newspaper, is published in New York City. *Good Housekeeping, Newsweek, Reader's Digest,* and many other magazines all have headquarters in or near New York City.

New York City is the headquarters of the major media companies CBS Corporation; News Corporation; NBC Universal, Inc.; Time Warner Inc.; and Viacom Inc. The Associated Press also is based there.

WNBT, the nation's first commercial television station, began operating in New York City in 1941. New York City is the corporate headquarters of three of the nation's four major broadcasting networks. The three networks are ABC, Inc.; CBS Broadcasting Inc.; and the NBC Television Network. The fourth major network, Fox Broadcasting Company, originates many of its programs from New York City.

Government

Constitution. New York adopted its first constitution in 1777. The present Constitution was adopted in 1894 and has been *amended* (changed) many times. An amendment may be proposed in the State Legislature. To pass, the proposal must be approved by a majority in both legislative houses of two successive, separately elected legislatures. It must then be approved by a majority of the people who vote on the proposal.

The Constitution may also be amended by a constitutional convention. A proposal to call a convention must be approved by a majority of the Legislature and by a majority of the voters. Constitutional amendments that are suggested by the convention become law after they have been approved by a majority of the citizens voting on them.

Executive. The governor of New York is elected to a four-year term and may serve an unlimited number of terms. The lieutenant governor, attorney general, and comptroller are also elected to four-year terms. The secretary of state is appointed by the governor with the approval of the state Senate. The governor heads the Executive Department. The governor, with the approval of the Senate, appoints most other department heads.

Legislature of New York consists of a Senate of 62 members and an Assembly of 150 members. Voters in senatorial and Assembly districts elect the members of both houses of the Legislature to two-year terms. The Legislature meets every year starting on the first Wednesday after the first Monday in January. Special sessions can be called by the governor or by petition of two-thirds of the Legislature. Regular and special sessions have no time limit.

Courts. New York is divided into 13 judicial districts. The voters in each district elect a varying number of Supreme Court judges to 14-year terms. Supreme Court justices have a mandatory retirement age of 70. However, they may be certified to serve for two-year periods up to the age of 76.

New York is also divided into four judicial departments. Each department has an appellate division of the Supreme Court. The appellate divisions hear appeals from the Supreme Court and other trial courts within their jurisdictions. The governor selects the appellate division justices from among the Supreme Court justices.

The highest court in New York is the Court of Appeals. It has a chief judge and six associate judges. Each of these judges is appointed to a 14-year term. This court hears cases only from the appellate divisions of the Supreme Court.

Each New York county, except those that make up New York City, has a county court. County courts hear civil and criminal cases. A surrogate court in each county deals with wills and estates. All counties have family courts that handle domestic matters. New York City has a civil court and a criminal court. In addition, there are

AP Photo

The New York State Legislature consists of an Assembly of 150 members and a Senate of 62 members. The Assembly meets in chambers in the State Capitol in Albany, *shown here.*

The state governors of New York

	Party	Term		Party	Term
George Clinton	None	1777-1795	Grover Cleveland	Democratic	1883-1885
John Jay	Federalist	1795-1801	David Bennett Hill	Democratic	1885-1891
George Clinton	*Dem.-Rep.	1801-1804	Roswell Pettibone Flower	Democratic	1892-1894
Morgan Lewis	*Dem.-Rep.	1804-1807	Levi Parsons Morton	Republican	1895-1896
Daniel D. Tompkins	*Dem.-Rep.	1807-1817	Frank Sweet Black	Republican	1897-1898
John Tayler	*Dem.-Rep.	1817	Theodore Roosevelt	Republican	1899-1900
De Witt Clinton	*Dem.-Rep.	1817-1822	Benjamin B. Odell, Jr.	Republican	1901-1904
Joseph C. Yates	*Dem.-Rep.	1823-1824	Frank Wayland Higgins	Republican	1905-1906
De Witt Clinton	*Dem.-Rep.	1825-1828	Charles Evans Hughes	Republican	1907-1910
Nathaniel Pitcher	Independent	1828	Horace White	Republican	1910
Martin Van Buren	*Dem.-Rep.	1829	John Alden Dix	Democratic	1911-1912
Enos T. Throop	Democratic	1829-1832	William Sulzer	Democratic	1913
William L. Marcy	Democratic	1833-1838	Martin Henry Glynn	Democratic	1913-1914
William H. Seward	Whig	1839-1842	Charles S. Whitman	Republican	1915-1918
William C. Bouck	Democratic	1843-1844	Alfred E. Smith	Democratic	1919-1920
Silas Wright	Democratic	1845-1846	Nathan L. Miller	Republican	1921-1922
John Young	Whig	1847-1848	Alfred E. Smith	Democratic	1923-1928
Hamilton Fish	Whig	1849-1850	Franklin D. Roosevelt	Democratic	1929-1932
Washington Hunt	Whig	1851-1852	Herbert H. Lehman	Democratic	1933-1942
Horatio Seymour	Democratic	1853-1854	Charles Poletti	Democratic	1942
Myron Holley Clark	Whig	1855-1856	Thomas E. Dewey	Republican	1943-1954
John Alsop King	Republican	1857-1858	W. Averell Harriman	Democratic	1955-1958
Edwin Denison Morgan	Republican	1859-1862	Nelson A. Rockefeller	Republican	1959-1973
Horatio Seymour	Democratic	1863-1864	Malcolm Wilson	Republican	1973-1974
Reuben Eaton Fenton	Republican	1865-1868	Hugh L. Carey	Democratic	1975-1982
John Thompson Hoffman	Democratic	1869-1872	Mario M. Cuomo	Democratic	1983-1994
John Adams Dix	Republican	1873-1874	George E. Pataki	Republican	1995-2007
Samuel Jones Tilden	Democratic	1875-1876	Eliot Spitzer	Democratic	2007-2008
Lucius Robinson	Democratic	1877-1879	David A. Paterson	Democratic	2008-2011
Alonzo B. Cornell	Republican	1880-1882	Andrew Cuomo	Democratic	2011-

*Democratic-Republican

many town justices, city court judges, and village courts in the state.

Local government. New York has 62 counties, including the 5 that make up the boroughs of New York City. A board of supervisors or a county legislature governs each county except the New York City boroughs. The officials of these boards and legislatures are elected either from the towns and cities of the county, or from county legislative districts. The major responsibilities of most counties in New York include the administration of courts, highways, and welfare. In addition to these responsibilities, counties deal with the administration of community colleges, libraries, garbage disposal, and parks and recreation.

Within New York's counties are villages, towns, and cities. An elected mayor and board of trustees governs each village. Each town is governed by an elected supervisor and town board.

Most New York cities have the mayor-council form of government. Some cities have the city manager form of government. The State Legislature has the authority to draw up city charters. Cities, in turn, may adopt and amend local laws and revise their charters, thus determining their own form of government. But New York City, because of its large population and area, has a different government from that of the other cities (see **New York City** [Government]).

Revenue. Taxes account for about half of the state government's *general revenue* (income). Federal grants and other U.S. government programs make up most of the rest. A personal income tax provides the greatest portion of the tax revenue. Other tax revenue sources include a general sales tax and taxes on alcoholic beverages, corporate income, motor fuels, motor vehicle licenses, public utilities, and tobacco products. A state lottery and charges for government services, such as toll-road collections, also contribute to the state's general revenue.

Politics. Enrolled Democratic voters in New York City usually significantly outnumber Republicans. But in the rest of the state, there are slightly more enrolled Republicans than Democrats. Albany and Erie Counties are often the only upstate counties to vote Democratic. Therefore, the two parties are fairly evenly matched, because New York City has about 40 percent of the state's total population. Republicans have generally controlled the Senate in New York, while Democrats have controlled the Assembly.

For most of the 1900's, New York had over 40 electoral votes, more than any other state. For this reason, New York played a key role in United States presidential elections. New York's governors were often considered possible presidential candidates. New York governors frequently introduced national issues into state politics. Four men served as governor of New York before becoming president—Martin Van Buren, Grover Cleveland, Theodore Roosevelt, and Franklin D. Roosevelt. Five other governors—Horatio Seymour, Samuel J. Tilden, Charles Evans Hughes, Alfred E. Smith, and Thomas E. Dewey—won their party's nomination for the presidency of the United States but failed to win the presidential election.

New Yorkers have voted for the winning candidate in most United States presidential elections. For New York's electoral votes and voting record, see **Electoral College** (table).

Early days. Two of the largest and most powerful Indian groups in North America lived in the New York region before European settlers came. One Indian group consisted of the Delaware, Mahican, Montauk, Munsee, and Wappinger tribes. These tribes made up the Algonquian family of Indians. The other Indian group was the Iroquois, or Five Nations. The Cayuga, Mohawk, Oneida, Onondaga, and Seneca tribes made up the Five Nations of the Iroquois Confederacy (see **Iroquois Indians**). Both Indian groups farmed, hunted, and fished. The Iroquois were especially advanced in political and social organization.

Exploration and settlement. Giovanni da Verrazzano, an Italian navigator and explorer, was probably the first European to visit the New York region. Verrazzano supposedly was hired by King Francis I of France to explore the northern part of America. Historians believe Verrazzano may have sailed into New York Bay and reached the Hudson River about 1524.

In 1609, Henry Hudson, an Englishman employed by the Dutch, sailed up the river that now bears his name. He was looking for a Northwest Passage to the Orient. Hudson's voyage gave the Netherlands a claim to the territory covering much of present-day New York, New Jersey, Delaware, and part of Connecticut. The territory was later named *New Netherland.*

Also in 1609, the French explorer Samuel de Champlain entered the northern part of New York from Quebec. His visit gave France a claim to the land.

The Dutch established several trading posts and prosperous settlements in the Hudson River Valley soon after Hudson's visit. There, they built up a profitable fur trade with the Indians. In 1621, a group of Dutch merchants formed the Dutch West India Company. The government of the Netherlands gave the company all rights to trade in New Netherland for the next 24 years. In 1624, the company sent about 30 families to settle in the region. Some of these families founded Fort Orange (now Albany), the first permanent white settlement in the colony. The rest of them established settlements in other parts of New Netherland.

In 1625, a group of Dutch colonists began building a fort and laying out a town on Manhattan Island. They named their settlement *New Amsterdam.* In 1626, Peter Minuit, the Dutch governor (or director-general), bought Manhattan from the Indians for goods worth 60 Dutch guilders, or about $24. During the next few years, Wiltwyck (now Kingston), Rensselaerswyck (now Rensselaer), Breuckelen (now Brooklyn), Schenectady, and other settlements were established in New Netherland by Dutch colonists.

In 1629, the Dutch West India Company set up the *patroon* (landowner) system to speed the settlement of New Netherland. Members of the company were given huge tracts of land, which they could keep if they colonized the land with settlers. Only one patroonship lasted into the 1700's, that of Kiliaen Van Rensselaer, an Amsterdam diamond merchant. His land covered much of present-day Albany, Columbia, and Rensselaer counties. Van Rensselaer began the practice of leasing his land to tenant farmers. The tenant system in New York lasted until the 1840's. A series of tenant revolts forced it to end. See **Patroon system.**

Under English rule. Many English colonists from Connecticut and Massachusetts settled on Long Island. For a long time, they cooperated with the Dutch. But gradually the English began to oppose the Dutch. In addition, King Charles II of England decided to take over New Netherland. He gave his brother James, the Duke of York, a charter for the territory. In 1664, the English sent a fleet to seize New Netherland. The warships dropped anchor in the harbor of New Amsterdam. Peter Stuyvesant, the Dutch governor, surrendered the settlement without a fight.

Copy (1670) of a drawing (1660) by Jacques Cortelyou; Museum of the City of New York

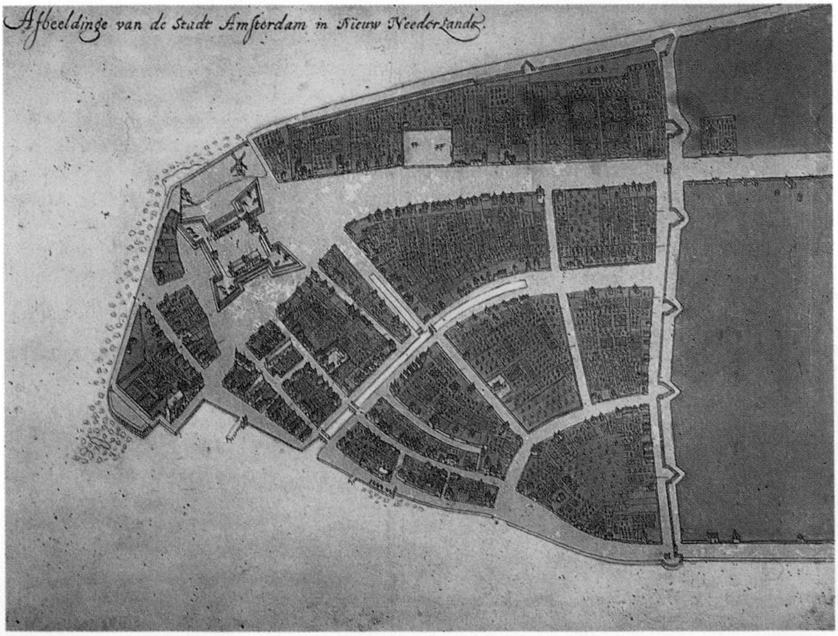

Afbeeldinge van de Stadt Amsterdam in Nieuw Neederlandt.

New Amsterdam was founded by Dutch settlers on Manhattan Island in 1625. This picture shows the layout of the settlement in 1660. The English later captured the colony and renamed it New York.

Fighting near Saratoga in 1777 resulted in a major victory for the American Army during the Revolutionary War. The patriots drove back about 1,500 British troops in the Second Battle of Freeman's Farm, *left.*

Oil painting on canvas; Fort Ticonderoga Museum

The English renamed the territory *New York,* after the Duke of York, who later became King James II of England. Under the Treaty of Breda, signed in 1667, the Dutch formally gave up all New Netherland to England.

Soon after the English won control of southern New York, the French began to take great interest in the northern part. In 1669, the French explorer René-Robert Cavelier, Sieur de La Salle, entered the Niagara region. In 1731, the French built a fortress at Crown Point on Lake Champlain. They prepared to take permanent possession of northern New York. Meanwhile, in 1689, war had broken out in Europe between England and France. New York soon became a battleground in the struggle between the two countries.

From 1689 until 1763, the region suffered severely through four wars, known in America as the French and Indian wars. Battles were fought at Crown Point, Fort Niagara, Fort Ticonderoga, and many other places. The French received aid from the Algonquian Indians in the wars, but the Iroquois Indians provided assistance to the British.

The French and Indian wars delayed settlement of the frontier regions and slowed the growth of sections that had already been settled. Britain and France signed a peace treaty—the Treaty of Paris—in 1763. However, the wars cost France almost all its possessions in North America. See **French and Indian wars.**

In 1735, John Peter Zenger, publisher of the *New-York Weekly Journal,* won a great victory for freedom of the press. Zenger had criticized the British governor, and was charged with seditious libel—that is, with making statements aimed at stirring up discontent or rebellion against the government. In a historic trial, the jury found Zenger innocent.

The Revolutionary War. British policies angered many people of New York. They did not like the presence of British troops, the authority of royal judges, or the taxes passed by the British Parliament. Other New Yorkers, called Loyalists or Tories, did not oppose the British. Nobody knows how many New Yorkers were

Loyalists. But during and after the Revolutionary War (1775-1783), perhaps as many as 30,000 people left the state.

During the Revolutionary War, New York was the scene of many battles. The British occupied New York City during the entire war. The Loyalists helped the British and persuaded the Iroquois Indians to fight the patriots. American patriots won the First and Second Battles of Freeman's Farm in New York in 1777. These victories led to a British surrender at Saratoga and marked a turning point in the war.

Statehood. On July 9, 1776, the provincial congress of New York met in White Plains. It approved the Declaration of Independence, which the Continental Congress had adopted on July 4. The congress also organized an independent government. The next year, New York adopted its first constitution. George Clinton was elected governor. Clinton later served as vice president under two U.S. presidents, Thomas Jefferson and James Madison.

On Feb. 6, 1778, New York approved the Articles of Confederation. It did not want a strong federal government. But it finally ratified the United States Constitution on July 26, 1788. New York was the 11th state to enter the Union. New York City served as the U.S. capital from 1785 to 1790. In 1789, George Washington was inaugurated as the nation's first president. The inauguration took place in Federal Hall in New York City.

Settlement of the interior progressed rapidly. In 1779, during the Revolutionary War, General Washington sent an expedition to crush the mighty Iroquois. Troops commanded by General James Clinton raided Indian villages up through the Mohawk Valley. The soldiers then moved down the Susquehanna River to Tioga, Pennsylvania. There, they joined troops commanded by General John Sullivan. The combined force of about 3,500 men marched through the Finger Lakes region to the Genesee Valley. The soldiers destroyed Indian villages, killed the Indians' livestock, and burned their fields. The heart of the Iroquois territory was left in ruin. The military

The Erie Canal opened in 1825 with a huge celebration. The canal provided an all-water route between the Hudson River and Buffalo. It greatly lowered the cost of transporting goods.

power of the Iroquois lay broken forever, leaving the area open to white settlement. After the Revolutionary War, soldiers who had fought in the area told of its level, fertile land. Many veterans settled on grants of land they received there. By 1810, New York had a population of 959,049, more people than any other state.

War broke out between the United States and Britain in 1812 (see **War of 1812**). Much of the fighting took place in frontier regions near the New York-Canada border. After the war, pioneers began to settle in the northern and western sections of the state. Many of these settlers came from other parts of New York, but many also came from Canada, New Jersey, Delaware, Pennsylvania, and especially New England. By 1820, about 500,000 people lived in frontier settlements, and the state had a population of over 1,370,000.

Growing prosperity. As the frontier was opened, the people of New York realized that better transportation would be needed between the coast and the interior.

Governor De Witt Clinton had long urged the construction of a canal to link the Atlantic Ocean and the Great Lakes. In 1825, the famous Erie Canal was completed. It crossed New York from Buffalo on Lake Erie to Troy and Albany on the Hudson River. The canal provided an important link in an all-water route between New York City and Buffalo. It greatly lowered the cost of transporting goods. Farmers in the West shipped their produce to the East by way of the Great Lakes and the Erie Canal. Products from New York's growing factories were, in turn, shipped on the canal to western markets.

The development of railroads across the state soon followed the opening of the Erie Canal. The canal and railroads greatly encouraged the state's growing prosperity. They also provided jobs for many of the thousands of European immigrants who were pouring into the state. By 1850, New York was firmly established as the *Empire State*. It led the nation in population, in manufacturing, and in commerce.

European immigrants came to the United States in great numbers during the 1840's and 1850's. Many of those immigrants landed at New York Harbor, *shown here.*

Historic New York

Manhattan was purchased in 1626 by Peter Minuit, the director-general of New Netherland. He paid the Manhattan Indians about $24 in goods for the island.

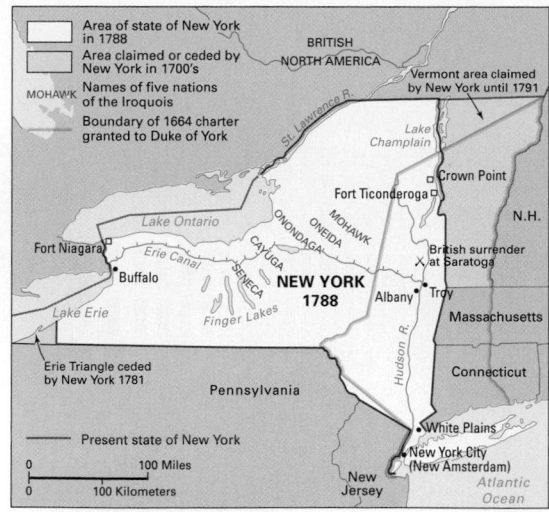

WORLD BOOK map

New York was home to several Indian groups before Dutch settlers arrived in the early 1600's. The English took over the territory during the 1660's. New York became a U.S. state in 1788.

The United Nations selected New York City as its permanent home in 1946. Construction of UN Headquarters was completed in 1952. This image shows a meeting of the UN General Assembly.

WORLD BOOK illustrations by Richard Bonson, The Art Agency

Important dates in New York

1609 Henry Hudson explored the Hudson River. Samuel de Champlain visited the New York region.

1624 The Dutch established Fort Orange (Albany), the first permanent white settlement in the New York region.

1625 Dutch settlers began building New Amsterdam (New York City).

1664 The Dutch surrendered New Amsterdam to England.

1735 Publisher John Peter Zenger was found innocent of libel, an important victory for freedom of the press.

1776 New York approved the Declaration of Independence.

1777 New York adopted its first constitution.

1779 Military expeditions under Generals James Clinton and John Sullivan opened Iroquois land to white settlement.

1788 New York *ratified* (approved) the Constitution of the United States and became the 11th state on July 26.

1789 George Washington was inaugurated in New York City as the first president of the United States.

1825 The Erie Canal opened.

1831 New York's first railroad, the Mohawk and Hudson, began running between Albany and Schenectady.

1863 Mobs rioted in New York City in opposition to drafting men into the Union Army.

1901 President William McKinley was assassinated at the Pan American Exposition in Buffalo.

1939-1940 New York held a World's Fair.

1941 The nation's first commercial television station began operating in New York City.

1948 New York established its first state university—the State University of New York.

1952 United Nations Headquarters was completed in New York City.

1959 The St. Lawrence Seaway opening made "ocean" ports of New York's ports on Lake Erie and Lake Ontario.

1960 The New York State Thruway (now the Governor Thomas E. Dewey Thruway) was completed.

1964-1965 New York held another World's Fair.

1967 The state legislature established a lottery with profits going to education.

1986 The voters approved a bond act to finance environmental projects, especially the cleaning up of hazardous waste sites.

2001 The twin 110-story towers of the World Trade Center in New York City were destroyed in the worst terrorist attack in U.S. history.

Civil War draft riots took place in New York City for four days in July 1863. Many people were opposed to the drafting of men into the Union Army. Mobs set fire to buildings and took over parts of the city. Troops called from the battlefield finally ended the riots, *shown here.*

Wealthy merchants and great landowners had controlled New York since colonial days. During the early 1800's, the state adopted more and more democratic practices. In the 1820's, white men no longer had to own property to be able to vote. A new constitution adopted in 1846 required that all major state officials be elected by the voters.

In 1839, the *antirent movement* began when tenant farmers refused to pay rent to wealthy landowners. The antirenters, disguised as Indians, ranged the Hudson and Mohawk river valleys and fought attempts by the landlords to evict them from their farms. The antirent movement grew rapidly and became a powerful political force in New York. During the 1840's, the great landlords began the process of breaking up their estates into small independent farms. See **Antirenters.**

Long before the Civil War began in 1861, many of New York's people strongly opposed slavery. But some did not. In July 1863, mobs rioted for four days in New York City. They objected to drafting men into the Union Army. The mobs burned, robbed, and murdered recklessly. They killed or wounded about 500 people and destroyed more than $1 \frac{1}{2}$ million worth of property. Troops called from the battlefield finally ended the riots. Despite the draft riots, New York provided more soldiers, supplies, and money to the Union war effort than any other state.

After the Civil War ended in 1865, new manufacturing centers grew up in various parts of New York. More and more products of the Middle West flowed through Buffalo, the state's western gateway. Increased commerce between the United States and other countries passed through New York City, the state's eastern gateway. New York City, already the nation's industrial and financial capital, also became a leading cultural center. As manufacturing continued to increase, new waves of immigrants poured in, drawn by employment opportunities.

They came from Italy, Poland, Russia, and other southern and eastern European countries. By 1900, the state had more than 7 million people.

The early 1900's. In 1901, a Pan American Exposition was held in Buffalo. The exhibition sought to promote unity and understanding between North and South America.

Theodore Roosevelt, a Republican, served as governor of New York in 1899 and 1900. He supported a number of reform bills, especially in the field of labor. In 1901, Roosevelt became vice president of the United States under President William McKinley. On Sept. 6, 1901, six months after the inauguration, an assassin shot McKinley while the president was attending the Pan American Exposition. McKinley died eight days later, and Roosevelt became president.

The United States entered World War I in 1917. New York City served as the great port from which thousands of American soldiers sailed for and returned from the battlefields of Europe.

The Great Depression of the late 1920's and the 1930's hit New York hard. Unemployment was severe. Men and women sold apples on street corners. Hungry people lined up at soup kitchens, or stood in bread lines that stretched for blocks.

Alfred E. Smith, a Democrat, served as governor of New York from 1919 to 1920 and from 1923 to 1928. He lost to Republican Herbert Hoover in the 1928 presidential election. Franklin D. Roosevelt was governor from 1929 to 1932. He served as president of the United States from 1933 until his death in 1945. Herbert H. Lehman succeeded Roosevelt as governor and served until 1942. Much of the social legislation supported by Governors Roosevelt and Lehman attacked the depression. This legislation later served as a model for federal laws urged by Roosevelt when he was president.

The mid-1900's. New York became a center of the

country's defense industry in the mid-1900's. Factories produced large amounts of war materials during World War II (1939-1945), the Korean War (1950-1953), and the Vietnam War (1957-1975). These materials came from the state's industrial centers—Buffalo, New York City, Rochester, Schenectady, and Syracuse—and hundreds of smaller communities. Growth occurred in several fields, including agriculture, banking, insurance, and manufacturing.

In 1946, the United Nations selected New York City as the site of its permanent home. Construction of UN Headquarters was completed in 1952. Two world's fairs were held in New York City during the mid-1900's—in 1939 and 1940 and in 1964 and 1965.

In 1948, New York established the State University of New York (SUNY), its first state university. SUNY has grown into a system of more than 60 campuses.

During the late 1950's, New York and the Canadian province of Ontario developed large hydroelectric projects on the St. Lawrence and Niagara rivers. In 1961, the Niagara Power Plant opened. It is one of the largest hydroelectric facilities in the world.

New York also greatly improved its transportation system. The St. Lawrence Seaway opened in 1959, allowing oceangoing ships to sail to ports on the Great Lakes. In 1960, New York completed the nation's longest toll superhighway, the New York State Thruway. This 496-mile (798-kilometer) expressway was renamed the Governor Thomas E. Dewey Thruway in 1964. Also in the 1960's, the federal government completed the New York portion of Interstate 81, stretching 180 miles (290 kilometers) from Pennsylvania to Canada. The 176-mile (283-kilometer) Adirondack Northway was also completed during this time. The scenic northway extends from Albany to Quebec. In 1964, the Verrazano-Narrows Bridge opened in New York City. It has one of the world's longest center spans.

During the 1960's, the Lincoln Center for the Performing Arts was built in New York City. The center serves as a home for some of the outstanding cultural institutions in the United States. These world-famous institutions include the Metropolitan Opera, the New York Philharmonic, the Juilliard School, the New York City Ballet, the New York City Opera, the Film Society of Lincoln Center, the Chamber Music Society of Lincoln Center, the Lincoln Center Theater, and the School of American Ballet. In addition, two branches of the New York Public Library are in the center.

The late 1900's. During the early 1970's, many manufacturing plants in New York closed, resulting in the loss of about 600,000 jobs. Many people moved away from the state as a result. However, this outflow of people leveled off during the 1980's, and the population showed an increase during the 1990's. The state's economy experienced a healthy recovery, due mainly to the tremendous growth in service industries and electronics manufacturing.

During the late 1900's, the state continued to maintain its great attractiveness for immigrants, especially Asians and Hispanics. New York ranks second only to California in the number of new immigrants it receives every year.

Like other states, New York began to deal with the

The City of New York (1884), a lithograph by Currier & Ives; Library of Congress

New York City served as the gateway for growing trade between the United States and other countries during the late 1800's. New York became the nation's financial and cultural center.

long-neglected problem of toxic industrial wastes. The state has hundreds of hazardous waste sites. One of the most critical sites was the Love Canal neighborhood of Niagara Falls. In the 1970's and early 1980's, chemical wastes that had leaked from a former disposal site threatened the health of the area's residents. Both the New York state government and the federal government provided financial aid to help move the families from Love Canal to other areas.

In addition to dealing with hazardous wastes, New York faced many other challenges in the late 1900's. These challenges, which continued into the 2000's, included improving social services and housing for the poor and mentally disabled and maintaining the state's extensive highway network. New York leaders also faced the need to provide better education for minority students, to curb drug abuse, and to improve the handling of the state's growing prison population.

The early 2000's. On Sept. 11, 2001, terrorists in hijacked commercial airplanes crashed the planes into the twin 110-story towers of the World Trade Center in New York City. Another hijacked plane crashed into the Pentagon Building, just outside Washington, D.C., and a fourth hijacked plane crashed in a field in Somerset County, Pennsylvania. The two Trade Center towers collapsed to the ground, and part of the Pentagon was destroyed. About 3,000 people were killed. The incidents were the worst terrorist attack in United States history.

In March 2008, Governor Eliot Spitzer resigned after it was revealed he had used a high-priced prostitution ring under investigation by the federal government. Lieutenant Governor David Paterson succeeded him. In 2011, Governor Andrew Cuomo signed a bill legalizing same-sex marriage in New York.

Adam W. Burnett and Milton M. Klein

Study aids

Related articles in *World Book.* See **New York City** with its list of *Related articles.* See also the following articles:

Biographies

Abzug, Bella
Arthur, Chester Alan
Astor, John Jacob
Auchincloss, Louis
Baldwin, James
Bryant, William Cullen
Buckley, William F., Jr.
Burr, Aaron
Cabrini, Saint Frances
Champlain, Samuel de
Chisholm, Shirley
Clark, Mark Wayne
Cleveland, Grover
Clinton, De Witt
Clinton, George
Clinton, Hillary Rodham
Cooper, James Fenimore
Cooper, Peter
Cornell, Ezra
Cuomo, Mario Matthew.
Curtiss, Glenn Hammond
Dewey, Thomas Edmund
Eastman, George
Fargo, William George
Farley, James Aloysius
Ferraro, Geraldine Anne
Fillmore, Millard
Fish, Hamilton
Floyd, William
Forrestal, James Vincent
Fulton, Robert
Gates, Horatio
Ginsburg, Ruth Bader
Goodrich, Benjamin Franklin
Gould, Jay
Greeley, Horace
Hale, Nathan
Hamilton, Alexander
Harriman, W. Averell
Hearst, William Randolph
Hudson, Henry
Hughes, Charles Evans
Irving, Washington
Jay, John

Kemp, Jack French
La Guardia, Fiorello Henry
Lewis, Francis
Lindsay, John Vliet
Livingston, Philip
Livingston, Robert R.
Mahan, Alfred Thayer
Miller, William Edward
Minuit, Peter
Morris, Gouverneur
Morris, Lewis
Moses, Grandma
Moynihan, Daniel Patrick
Ochs, Adolph Simon
Paine, Thomas
Powell, Adam Clayton, Jr.
Pulitzer, Joseph
Rangel, Charles Bernard
Rockefeller, Nelson Aldrich
Roosevelt, Eleanor
Roosevelt, Franklin Delano
Roosevelt, Theodore
Roosevelt, Theodore, Jr.
Root, Elihu
Rubin, Robert Edward
Runyon, Damon
Schuyler, Philip John
Seward, William Henry
Seymour, Horatio
Smith, Alfred Emanuel
Spellman, Francis Joseph
Stuyvesant, Peter
Sulzberger, Arthur Hays
Tilden, Samuel Jones
Tompkins, Daniel D.
Van Buren, Martin
Vanderbilt, Cornelius
Van Rensselaer, Kiliaen
Wagner, Robert Ferdinand
Walker, James John
Wharton, Edith
Wheeler, William Almon
Whitman, Walt
Zenger, John Peter

Cities and other communities

Albany
Buffalo
Cooperstown
Levittown

Mount Vernon
Oswego
Rochester
Schenectady

Syracuse
Utica
Yonkers

History

Albany Congress
Antirenters
Barnburners
Bucktails
Cayuga Indians
Colonial life in America
Dutch West India Company
Federal Hall
Fort Niagara
Fort Ticonderoga

Free Soil Party
French and Indian wars
Iroquois Indians
Locofocos
Mahican Indians
New Netherland
Patroon System
Revolution, American
Tammany, Society of
War of 1812

Physical features

Adirondack Mountains
Allegheny River
Catskill Mountains
Delaware River
Finger Lakes
Hudson River

Lake Champlain
Lake Erie
Lake Ontario
Lake Placid
Long Island
Mohawk River
Niagara Falls

Niagara River
Saint Lawrence Seaway
Susquehanna River
Thousand Islands

Other related articles

Castle Clinton National Monument
Chautauqua
Erie Canal
Fort Stanwix National Monument
Hall of fame

New York State Canal System
Oneida Community
Peace Bridge
Port Authority of New York and New Jersey
Sing Sing

Outline

I. People
  A. Population
  B. Schools
  C. Libraries
  D. Museums
II. Visitor's guide
III. Land and climate
  A. Land regions
  B. Coastline and shoreline
  C. Mountains
  D. Rivers
  E. Waterfalls
  F. Lakes
  G. Plant and animal life
  H. Climate
IV. Economy
  A. Natural resources
  B. Service industries
  C. Manufacturing
  D. Agriculture

E. Mining
F. Fishing industry
G. Electric power and utilities
H. Transportation
I. Communication
V. Government
A. Constitution
B. Executive
C. Legislature
D. Courts
E. Local government
F. Revenue
G. Politics
VI. History

Questions

Why have New York's governors often been considered possible presidential candidates?
What is New York's most magnificent natural wonder? In what part of the state is it?
Why was the Erie Canal so important in New York's history?
Where did George Washington take the oath of office as the first president of the United States?
What are some of the reasons that New York is a leader in business and industry?
Who established New York's first newspaper?
What was the *antirent movement?*
Why has the Hudson-Mohawk Lowland been so important in the development of New York?
What is the role of the University of the State of New York? When was it established?
Why do Rochester, Syracuse, and Buffalo get so much snow?

Additional resources

Level I
Doherty, Craig A. and Katherine M. *New York.* Facts on File, 2005.
Mis, Melody S. *The Colony of New York: A Primary Source History.* PowerKids Pr., 2007.
Schomp, Virginia. *New York.* 2nd ed. Benchmark Bks., 2006.
Somervill, Barbara A. *New York.* Children's Pr., 2008.

Level II
Berlin, Ira, and Harris, L. M., eds. *Slavery in New York.* New Pr., 2005.
Brumley, Charles, and Heilman, Carl. *Wild New York: A Celebration of Our State's Natural Beauty.* Voyageur Pr., 2005.
Eisenstadt, Peter R., ed. *The Encyclopedia of New York State.* Syracuse Univ. Pr., 2005.
Gage, Beverly. *The Day Wall Street Exploded: A Story of America in Its First Age of Terror.* Oxford, 2009.
Galie, Peter J. *Ordered Liberty: A Constitutional History of New York.* Fordham Univ. Pr., 1996.
Gilfoyle, Timothy J. *A Pickpocket's Tale: The Underworld of Nineteenth-Century New York.* Norton, 2006.
Holzer, Harold, ed. *State of the Union: New York and the Civil War.* Fordham Univ. Pr., 2002.
Jackson, Kenneth T., and Kameny, Fred, eds. *The Almanac of New York City.* Columbia Univ. Pr., 2008.
Klein, Milton M., ed. *The Empire State: A History of New York.* Cornell Univ. Pr., 2001.
Marshall, Bruce. *Building New York: The Rise and Rise of the Greatest City on Earth.* Universe, 2005.
Schneier, Edward V., and Murtaugh, Brian. *New York Politics.* M. E. Sharpe, 2000.

New York, City University of, is the largest urban public university system in the United States. It is often referred to as CUNY. The CUNY system consists of several senior colleges, community colleges, and graduate and professional schools throughout the five *boroughs* (districts) of New York City. These institutions offer a wide variety of academic programs leading to associate, bachelor's, master's, and doctor's degrees.

CUNY institutions in the borough of Manhattan include Baruch College, the City College of New York, the Graduate Center, the Graduate School of Journalism, Hunter College, the John Jay College of Criminal Justice, and the Sophie Davis School of Biomedical Education. CUNY institutions in the other four boroughs of New York City include Lehman College in the Bronx; Brooklyn College, Medgar Evers College, and the New York City College of Technology in Brooklyn; Queens College, York College, and the School of Law in Queens; and the College of Staten Island on Staten Island. Students in CUNY's Macaulay Honors College are spread throughout a number of CUNY campuses. In addition, the university has dozens of nationally recognized research centers and institutes.

The City University of New York traces its beginnings to the founding of the Free Academy in 1847. The Free Academy later became the City College. The New York State Legislature established CUNY in 1961 to join together the public municipal colleges throughout New York City.

Well-known CUNY graduates include U.S. Secretary of State Colin L. Powell and research scientist Jonas E. Salk. The university's website at http://www.cuny.edu offers additional information.

Critically reviewed by the City University of New York

New York, State University of, is the largest statewide public system of higher education in the United States. The university system, commonly called SUNY, has more than 60 campuses throughout the state of New York. These campuses include university centers and other institutions that grant doctor's degrees; university colleges; technology colleges; and community colleges. The State University of New York system was established in 1948. Its headquarters are in Albany.

SUNY's university centers are in Albany, Binghamton, Buffalo, and Stony Brook. They are large, broad-based research universities that offer bachelor's, master's, and doctor's degrees. SUNY also includes several specialized schools that offer degrees up to the doctor's level. These schools include the New York State College of Ceramics at Alfred University in Alfred; the College of Environmental Science and Forestry in Syracuse; the College of Optometry in the Manhattan borough of New York City; the Downstate Medical Center in the Brooklyn borough of New York City; the Upstate Medical University in Syracuse; and four colleges at Cornell University in Ithaca.

In addition, SUNY has a number of university colleges, which are arts and sciences colleges that offer degrees up to the master's level. The colleges at Brockport, Buffalo, Cortland, Fredonia, Geneseo, New Paltz, Old Westbury, Oneonta, Oswego, Plattsburgh, Potsdam, and Purchase are traditional residential colleges. Empire State College is a nonresidential, nontraditional college with multiple sites.

SUNY's technology colleges include the Maritime College in the Bronx borough of New York City and the SUNY Institute of Technology (SUNYIT) in Utica. SUNY also has technology colleges in Alfred, Canton, Cobleskill, Delhi, Farmingdale, and Morrisville. SUNY has numerous community colleges throughout the state. The university's website at http://www.suny.edu offers additional information.

Critically reviewed by the State University of New York

© Richard Berenholtz, Corbis Stock Market

New York City, the largest city in the United States, is a world center of business, culture, and trade. This photo shows Manhattan Island from the East River. The wide building in the foreground is United Nations Headquarters. Behind it, topped with arches and a spire, is the Chrysler Building.

New York City

New York City is the largest city in the United States and one of the largest in the world. It ranks as one of the world's most important centers of business, culture, and trade. It is also the home of the United Nations (UN). Much of what happens in New York City affects what happens throughout the United States and in other parts of the world.

New York City has a population of about 8 million. It has more than twice as many people as any other city in the United States. In fact, only 10 states—not including New York state—have more people than New York City. Ever since Dutch colonists settled the area at the southern tip of Manhattan Island in 1625, New York has been the destination of immigrants from throughout the world.

During the 1800's and the early 1900's, millions of Europeans seeking a better life in a free land poured into New York City. The Statue of Liberty, which was erected in New York Harbor in 1886, became the symbol of this new life.

Since the mid-1900's, many blacks from the Southern States and Spanish-speaking Americans from Puerto Rico have moved into the city. In the 1980's and 1990's, a new wave of immigrants flowed into New York City. These immigrants included many people from China, Central America, and Caribbean lands.

The business, financial, and trading organizations in New York City play a major role in the economy of the nation and of the world. The banks, stock exchanges, and other financial institutions in the city's famous Wall Street area help provide the money used by most large U.S. corporations. The skyscrapers that form the spectacular New York skyline house the home offices of many national and international business firms. The docks, the warehouses, and the shipping companies that line New York's huge natural harbor handle much of the nation's imports and exports. Three major airports serve numerous domestic and international airlines.

As a cultural center, New York City has no equal in the United States. Most of the publishing houses that select and produce the nation's books have their headquarters in New York. The city's world-famous Broadway area is the center of professional theater in the United States. New York is also the home of some of the nation's largest museums and art galleries. The city displays beautiful churches in the Gothic Revival style, gleaming modern skyscrapers, and other interesting styles of architecture. A great number of outstanding orchestras and opera and dance companies give performances at the Lincoln Center for the Performing Arts. Because of its prominence as a cultural and entertainment center, New York City is sometimes called the "Big Apple."

But along with all its greatness, the city has many serious problems. Thousands of immigrants have not found the opportunities they had hoped for in New York. Hundreds of thousands of New Yorkers receive welfare aid, and thousands live in slums. Other problems include air pollution, traffic jams, crime, drug abuse, racial conflicts, and increases in the cost of living in the city. All these problems are driving many families—especially middle-class families—to the suburbs.

New York City remains one of the most interesting and exciting cities in the United States. In fact, many people consider it the most fascinating city in the world.

The city

New York City lies in the southeast corner of New York state at the mouth of the Hudson River. It covers about 322 square miles (834 square kilometers). The city is divided into five areas called *boroughs*—Manhattan, the Bronx, Queens, Brooklyn, and Staten Island. The Bronx and Queens are also counties of the state of New York. Manhattan covers all of New York County. Brooklyn makes up Kings County, and Staten Island makes up Richmond County.

Manhattan, the smallest borough in area, covers 24 square miles (62 square kilometers). It occupies a long, narrow island bordered by the Hudson River on the west, the East River on the east, the Harlem River on the north and northeast, and Upper New York Bay (the mouth of the Hudson) on the south.

The Bronx lies across the Harlem River from Manhattan and covers 42 square miles (109 square kilometers). It extends north along the Hudson River and east along the East River. It is the only borough not separated from upstate New York by water.

Queens, the largest borough in area, occupies 112 square miles (290 square kilometers) on the northwest corner of Long Island. The East River separates it from the Bronx to the north and from Manhattan to the west.

Brooklyn covers 82 square miles (212 square kilometers) on the southwest tip of Long Island. It lies south and southwest of Queens and southeast of Manhattan across the East River.

Staten Island, formerly called the borough of Richmond, occupies a 60-square-mile (155-square-kilometer) island in Upper and Lower New York bays. It lies west of Brooklyn and southwest of Manhattan.

The state of New Jersey is directly west of New York City. It lies across two waterways, Arthur Kill and Kill Van Kull, from Staten Island; across Upper New York Bay from Brooklyn; and across the Hudson River from Manhattan and the Bronx.

Each of New York City's boroughs has a large population, important businesses and industries, and many fine educational and cultural institutions. Within the five boroughs are more than 100 neighborhoods, such as Manhattan's Chinatown, Greenwich Village, and Harlem. These neighborhoods are not official government units. They have similar types of housing or people with similar backgrounds or lifestyles.

The New York City metropolitan area spreads into northeastern New Jersey and southern New York. Some people who work in New York City live in suburban residential communities in the city's metropolitan area. Many industrial cities also lie in the metropolitan area.

Manhattan is the oldest and most important borough of New York City. It is about 13½ miles (21.7 kilometers) long and 2⅓ miles (3.8 kilometers) wide at its widest point. But about 1½ million people live there.

Manhattan has New York City's tallest buildings, some of the nation's largest schools and colleges, and the world's most famous financial and theatrical districts.

Facts in brief

Population: *City*—8,175,133. *Metropolitan division*—11,576,251 (9,535,643 in NY and 2,040,608 in NJ). *Metropolitan statistical area*—18,897,109 (12,368,525 in NY, 6,471,215 in NJ, and 57,369 in PA).

Area: *City*—322 mi² (834 km²). *Metropolitan division* (excluding inland water)—1,607 mi² (4,162 km²), consisting of 1,141 mi² (2,955 km²) in NY and 466 mi² (1,207 km²) in NJ. *Metropolitan statistical area* (excluding inland water)—6,725 mi² (17,418 km²), consisting of 2,340 mi² (6,061 km²) in NY, 3,838 mi² (9,940 km²) in NJ, and 547 mi² (1,417 km²) in PA.

Climate: *Average temperature*—January, 33 °F (1 °C); July, 77 °F (25 °C). *Average annual precipitation* (rainfall, melted snow, and other forms of moisture)— 46 in (117 cm). For information on the monthly weather in New York City, see **New York** (Climate).

Government: Mayor-council. *Terms*—4 years for the mayor, the public advocate, the comptroller, the 51 members of the City Council, and the five borough presidents.

Founded: 1625. Incorporated as a city in 1653.

The metropolitan divisions		The five boroughs	
Name	Population	Name	Population
New York-White Plains-Wayne, NY/NJ	11,576,251	Bronx	1,385,108
Nassau-Suffolk, NY	2,832,882	Brooklyn	2,504,700
Edison, NJ	2,340,249	Manhattan	1,585,873
Newark-Union, NJ/PA	2,147,727	Queens	2,230,722
		Staten Island	468,730

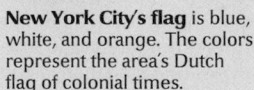

New York City's flag is blue, white, and orange. The colors represent the area's Dutch flag of colonial times.

The seal of New York City features an American eagle, an English sailor, and a Manhattan Indian.

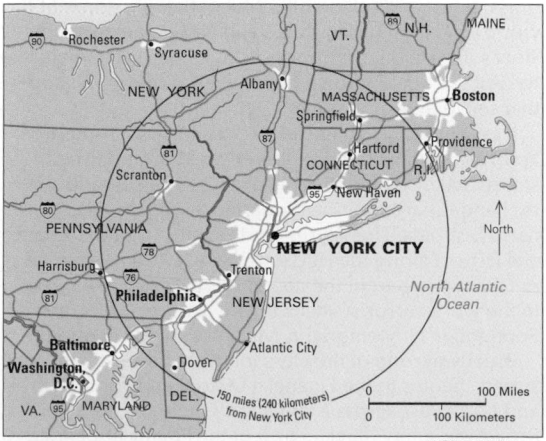

WORLD BOOK map

New York City lies at the center of a *megalopolis,* a group of metropolitan areas. These urban areas extend from Boston to Washington, D.C.

New York City metropolitan area

The metropolitan area of New York City includes parts of northeastern New Jersey and southwestern Connecticut. Hundreds of thousands of people who work in New York City do not live there. They commute daily from nearby areas, chiefly by train. The map shows major expressways and railroad lines.

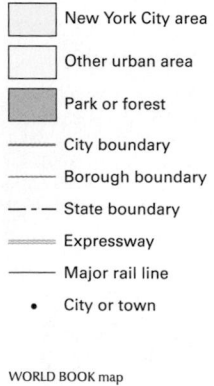

New York City area

Other urban area

Park or forest

——— City boundary

——— Borough boundary

— - — State boundary

═══ Expressway

——— Major rail line

• City or town

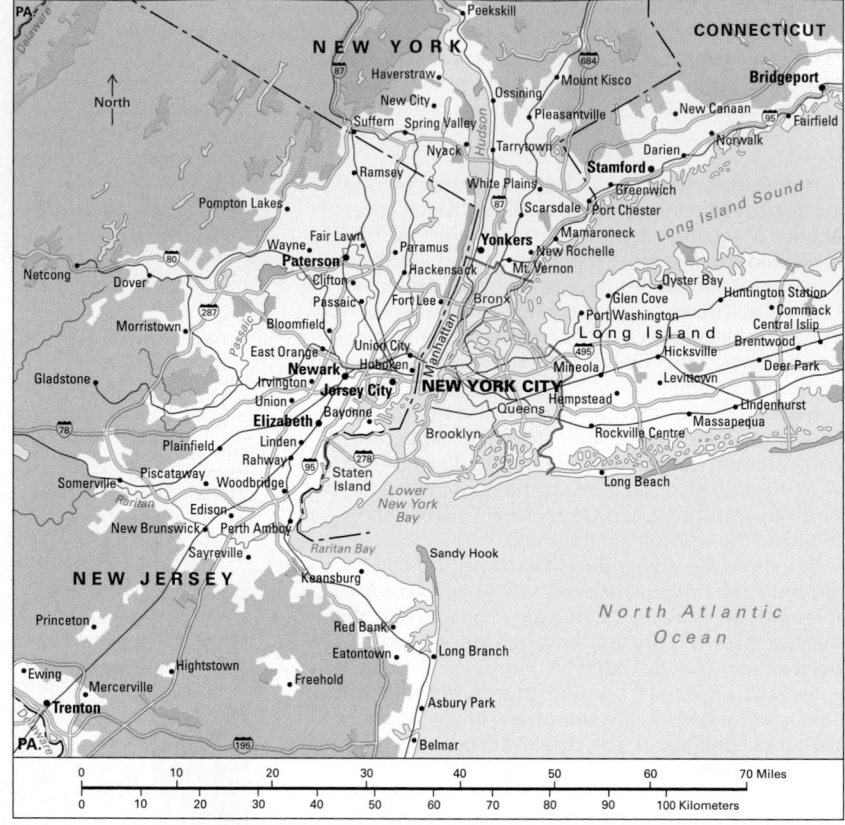

WORLD BOOK map

Manhattan is an area of many sharp contrasts. Some of the richest people in the United States live in its beautiful town houses and luxurious high-rise apartment buildings. But some of the nation's poorest people occupy its *tenements* (shabby apartment buildings) and low-rent public housing projects. Most of Manhattan is covered with concrete and asphalt, and skyscrapers make many of its streets look like deep canyons. But the borough's Central Park provides 840 acres (340 hectares) of grass, trees, and rolling hills. Manhattan has some of the world's most exclusive shops and largest department stores. They attract shoppers from all parts of the country. But the borough also has tiny neighborhood shops that sell to nearby residents.

New York City's Financial District lies at the southern tip of Manhattan and is centered on Wall and Broad streets. Many large banks, brokerage houses, and stock exchanges have their headquarters along the district's narrow streets. The World Trade Center is in the Financial District along the Hudson River. Twin 110-story towers that were part of the center were destroyed in 2001 in the worst terrorist attack in U.S. history. The National September 11 Memorial & Museum stands on the site.

Broadway, one of the city's longest and best-known streets, begins in the Financial District and runs north and northwest across Manhattan. On the east side of Broadway, a few blocks north of the Financial District, stands the Civic Center. The center includes City Hall, courthouses, and other government buildings.

Residential and commercial neighborhoods lie to the north and northeast of the Civic Center. These neighborhoods include Chinatown, Little Italy, and the Lower East Side. Both Chinatown and Little Italy have some of the city's oldest tenements. They also have many restaurants that specialize in Chinese or Italian food. For many years, most immigrants to New York City have first settled on the Lower East Side because of its many low-rent tenements. Jews once made up the largest group in the area. Today, Puerto Ricans are the largest single group there. Other groups, especially students and artists, have also been attracted to the Lower East Side by the low rents.

Greenwich Village lies west of Broadway and the Lower East Side. It attracts artists, writers, musicians, actors, and other people in the arts. The Village has a variety of housing, many interesting shops and art galleries, and several small theaters. Many people in the arts also live in the SoHo area, south of the Village.

North of Greenwich Village, Manhattan is laid out in a regular pattern of cross streets. Avenues run north and south, and numbered streets run east and west. Broadway cuts diagonally across this pattern.

Some of New York City's largest department stores are in the Herald Square and Greeley Square areas, where Broadway crosses the Avenue of the Americas (formerly Sixth Avenue). East of the department stores, on 34th Street, is the famous, 102-story Empire State Building, for many years the world's tallest building. The Garment District, center of the city's large clothing industry, lies north of Herald and Greeley squares.

The intersection of Broadway and Seventh Avenue,

between 42nd and 47th streets, forms world-famous Times Square, the heart of the New York Theater District. Since the late 1960's, the Times Square area has been undergoing redevelopment. A number of large office buildings have been constructed there. But the area remains the Theater District because many of the new buildings house theaters. Plans for further redevelopment also seek to maintain the area's theatrical activities.

United Nations Headquarters occupy 18 acres (7.3 hectares) along the East River between 42nd and 48th streets. The UN's beautiful modern buildings have become New York City landmarks.

Rockefeller Center is another of the city's landmarks. The center is a complex of buildings between Fifth and Seventh avenues and between 48th and 51st streets. It is the world's largest privately owned business and entertainment facility. Rockefeller Center's buildings include the GE Building, which is 850 feet (259 meters) high, and the 5,900-seat Radio City Music Hall, the home of the famous Rockettes dance company. Many of New York City's finest stores line Fifth Avenue both north and south of Rockefeller Center.

Central Park, which runs from 59th to 110th streets between Fifth Avenue and Central Park West, separates Manhattan's Upper East Side and Upper West Side. The Upper East Side has long been the most fashionable neighborhood in Manhattan. At one time, the area had many town houses that were owned by the city's richest residents. Today, cultural organizations and United Nations delegations occupy many of these buildings, and

New York City

This map shows the five boroughs of New York City—the Bronx, Brooklyn, Manhattan, Queens, and Staten Island. These boroughs are also counties of the state of New York. County names appear in parentheses under each borough name.

© Allyn Baum, Photo Researchers

Outdoor food markets and other small shops serve customers in many New York City neighborhoods. This fruit and vegetable market is in the Little Italy section of Manhattan.

most of the people in the area live in luxurious apartment buildings. The Upper West Side has been chiefly a middle-class neighborhood. It includes many apartment houses, hotels, tenements, and long blocks of brick and brownstone row houses. In the late 1900's, however, housing prices rose sharply in the area. Many of the Upper West Side's best buildings now rival the Upper East Side in price.

Harlem, the best-known black community in the United States, lies north of Central Park. It has long been a center of African American business and cultural activi-

ties. A series of model housing projects extends along the Harlem River at the northern edge of Harlem. But much of the area consists of tenements.

Morningside Heights—the site of Columbia University and several other educational, cultural, and religious institutions—lies west of Harlem along the Hudson River. City College of the City University of New York lies north of Morningside Heights, in an area that was once the country estate of the American statesman Alexander Hamilton.

Washington Heights and Inwood are at the northern tip of Manhattan. Both areas have aging tenements, as well as modern housing projects. Washington Heights was formerly inhabited by many Jewish immigrants who fled Europe to escape Nazi leader Adolf Hitler's brutal persecution of Jews in the 1930's and 1940's. Today the area is largely populated by immigrants from the Dominican Republic. Columbia University Medical Center; Yeshiva University; and the Cloisters, a museum featuring European art of the Middle Ages (from about the 400's through the 1400's), are in Washington Heights.

Brooklyn has more people than any other borough of New York City. If Brooklyn were an independent city, its population of about 2 ½ million would make it the nation's fourth largest city.

Brooklyn is an important port and industrial center. Hundreds of ships carry freight to and from Brooklyn's docks each year. The borough's factories, most of which are along the waterfront, make a wide variety of goods.

Housing in Brooklyn ranges from large houses and towering apartment buildings to small cottages and run-down rooming houses. But most Brooklynites live in row houses and small apartment buildings that line the streets throughout the borough.

Downtown Brooklyn, the borough's main business and shopping district, lies near the approaches to the Brooklyn and Manhattan bridges. These two bridges are the main links between Brooklyn and Manhattan. A third

WORLD BOOK photo by Donyale McRae

Harlem, a section of Manhattan, has long been a center of African American business and cultural activities. Shoppers on 125th Street, *shown here,* pass by a theater that dates from the early 1900's.

Manhattan

This map shows the central and lower parts of Manhattan.

Park

City boundary

Expressway

Other street

Road tunnel

■ Point of interest

WORLD BOOK map

North

NEW JERSEY

Union City

Weehawken

West New York

Hoboken

Jersey City

Liberty State Park

North Hudson Park

Palisade Ave.

Park Ave.

Boulevard E.

River Rd.

Bergenline Ave.

River Rd.

Palisade Ave.

Willow Ave.

Hudson St.

Park Ave.

Reservoir

Lincoln Tunnel

Holland Tunnel

Hudson River

RIVERSIDE CHURCH

COLUMBIA UNIVERSITY

Morningside Heights

MORNINGSIDE PARK

CATHEDRAL CHURCH OF ST. JOHN THE DIVINE

Harlem

Harlem Meer

Upper West Side

Henry Hudson Parkway

Riverside Drive

West End Ave.

Broadway

Amsterdam Ave.

Columbus Ave.

Central Park West

96th St.

86th St.

7th Ave.

116th St.

110th St.

120th St.

126th St.

MUSEUM OF THE CITY OF NEW YORK

MT. SINAI MEDICAL CENTER

JEWISH MUSEUM

COOPER-HEWITT MUSEUM

GUGGENHEIM MUSEUM

Madison Ave.

Lexington Ave.

3rd Ave.

2nd Ave.

1st Ave.

F.D. Roosevelt Drive

APOLLO THEATER

5th Ave.

MARCUS GARVEY PARK

JEFFERSON PARK

Bronx

East Harlem

Randalls Island

Wards Island

Hell Gate

ASTORIA PARK

Old Astoria

West Side

RIVERSIDE PARK

ROSE CENTER FOR EARTH AND SPACE

AMERICAN MUSEUM OF NATURAL HISTORY

NEW-YORK HISTORICAL SOCIETY

Reservoir

CENTRAL PARK

CLEOPATRA'S NEEDLE

The Lake

METROPOLITAN MUSEUM OF ART

WHITNEY MUSEUM OF AMERICAN ART

FRICK COLLECTION

82nd St.

86th St.

Yorkville

GRACIE MANSION

CARL SCHURZ PARK

COLER-GOLDWATER HOSPITAL

Robert F. Kennedy Bridge

Queens

Broadway

VIVIAN BEAUMONT THEATER

JUILLIARD SCHOOL

AVERY FISHER HALL

METROPOLITAN OPERA HOUSE

LINCOLN CENTER

NEW YORK STATE THEATER

FORDHAM UNIVERSITY

PASSENGER SHIP TERMINAL

DE WITT CLINTON PARK

INTREPID SEA, AIR & SPACE MUSEUM

JAVITS CENTER

Upper East Side

HUNTER COLLEGE

CHILDREN'S ZOO

ZOO

The Pond

TEMPLE EMANU-EL

SHERMAN STATUE

Columbus Circle

CARNEGIE HALL

AMERICAN FOLK ART MUSEUM

RADIO CITY MUSIC HALL

MUSEUM OF MODERN ART

TIFFANY & CO.

ROCKEFELLER UNIVERSITY

NEW YORK-PRESBYTERIAN HOSPITAL/ WEILL CORNELL MEDICAL CENTER

72nd St.

57th St.

48th St.

42nd St.

11th Ave.

12th Ave.

10th Ave.

9th Ave.

8th Ave.

7th Ave.

6th Ave.

5th Ave.

Madison Ave.

Park Ave.

Lexington Ave.

3rd Ave.

2nd Ave.

1st Ave.

TRAMWAY

Roosevelt Island

West Channel

East Channel

Ravenswood

QUEENSBRIDGE PARK

Queensbridge

Long Island City

Vernon Blvd.

37th Ave.

21st St.

31st St.

Theater District

TIMES SQUARE

ROCKEFELLER CENTER

ST. PATRICK'S CATHEDRAL

CITIGROUP CENTER

ST. BARTHOLOMEW'S CHURCH

WALDORF-ASTORIA HOTEL

BRYANT PARK

METLIFE BUILDING

PUBLIC LIBRARY

GRAND CENTRAL TERMINAL

34th St.

30th St.

Garment District

MADISON SQUARE GARDEN

CHELSEA PARK

MACY'S

HERALD SQUARE

CHRYSLER BUILDING

PENNSYLVANIA STATION

EMPIRE STATE BUILDING

FASHION INSTITUTE OF TECHNOLOGY

UNITED NATIONS HEADQUARTERS

23rd St.

Chelsea

111 EIGHTH AVENUE

NEW YORK LIFE BUILDINGS

MADISON SQUARE PARK

FLATIRON BUILDING

THEODORE ROOSEVELT BIRTHPLACE NATL. HISTORIC SITE

GRAMERCY PARK

NEW YORK UNIVERSITY MEDICAL CENTER

BELLEVUE HOSPITAL

VETERANS AFFAIRS HOSPITAL

Queens Midtown Tunnel

Hunters Point

COLER-GOLDWATER HOSPITAL

11th St.

Jackson Ave.

Thomson Ave.

Sunnyside

Long Island Expressway

Newtown Creek

Van Dam St.

Skillman Ave.

Queens Blvd.

UNION SQUARE

Greenwich Ave.

Bleecker Ave.

Avenue of the Americas

Broadway

Park Ave. S.

32nd St.

18th St.

14th St.

STUYVESANT SQUARE

Stuyvesant

WASHINGTON MEMORIAL ARCH

WASHINGTON SQUARE

NEW YORK UNIVERSITY

Greenwich Village

COOPER UNION

TOMPKINS SQUARE

Christopher St.

West St.

Varick St.

Hudson St.

12th St.

10th St.

4th St.

2nd St.

Ave. A

Ave. B

Ave. C

Ave. D

EAST RIVER PARK

Franklin D. Roosevelt Drive

East River

Greenpoint

GREENPOINT AVE.

Greenpoint Ave.

Kingsland Ave.

Manhattan Ave.

Humboldt St.

McGOLRICK PARK

SoHo **Manhattan**

Tribeca

Canal St.

Broadway

W. Broadway

Church St.

Lafayette St.

Bowery

Little Italy

Delancey St.

Houston St.

Bowery

Grand St.

Chinatown

AFRICAN BURIAL GROUND NATL. MONUMENT

E. Broadway

Lower East Side

CORLEARS HOOK PARK

Williamsburg Bridge

MCCARREN PARK

Bedford Ave.

Kent Ave.

Williamsburg

Grand St.

Brooklyn

Metropolitan Ave.

COOPER PARK

Bushwick Ave.

Montrose Ave.

Broadway

English Kills

WORLD FINANCIAL CENTER

WOOLWORTH BUILDING

WORLD TRADE CENTER SITE

Civic Center

CITY HALL

AMERICAN STOCK EXCHANGE

FEDERAL HALL NATL. MEMORIAL

TRINITY CHURCH

NEW YORK STOCK EXCHANGE

Wall St.

Financial District

BOWLING GREEN

CUSTOM HOUSE

CASTLE CLINTON NATIONAL MONUMENT

BATTERY PARK

Brooklyn-Battery Tunnel

STATEN ISLAND FERRY TERMINAL

SOUTH STREET SEAPORT MUSEUM

Brooklyn Bridge

Manhattan Bridge

WASHINGTON PLAZA

Brooklyn-Queens Expressway

Flushing Ave.

Penn. St.

Marcy Ave.

Broadway

Flatbush Ave.

CADMAN PLAZA

Brooklyn Heights

COMMODORE JOHN BARRY PARK

Beaver St.

Tompkins Park

© Geri Engberg, The Stock Market

Brooklyn includes hundreds of streets lined with long blocks of row houses and small apartment buildings. Brooklyn has the largest population of any of the five boroughs of New York City.

© Van Bucher, Photo Researchers

The Bronx extends along the Hudson River north of Manhattan. Most people in the Bronx live in large apartment buildings. But the borough also has many old private homes.

bridge, Williamsburg Bridge, also connects the two boroughs. Brooklyn's downtown area has large department stores, tall office buildings, and several schools and colleges. Flatbush Avenue, one of the main downtown streets, begins at the Manhattan Bridge and runs through the heart of the borough.

Two of Brooklyn's oldest neighborhoods, Brooklyn Heights and Cobble Hill, lie along the East River west of the downtown area. These neighborhoods have more than 1,000 houses over 100 years old. Many of the houses stand on handsome, treelined streets and are carefully preserved.

The site of the former U.S. Naval Shipyard, which had been one of Brooklyn's chief industries, lies northeast of downtown. The Navy gave up the yard in 1968, and the area became an industrial park for factories, shipbuilding, and warehouses.

Bedford-Stuyvesant, east of the downtown area, is the largest African American neighborhood in New York City. Blocks of well-kept row houses and many fine churches are found throughout the neighborhood. In contrast, Brownsville, a black and Puerto Rican neighborhood which lies southeast of Bedford-Stuyvesant, is one of the city's worst slum areas. It has few well-maintained areas, and many of its buildings are abandoned and decaying.

Prospect Park, in the center of Brooklyn, is one of the finest landscaped parks in the nation. The park is designed so that its lakes, meadows, woods, and other features look larger than they are. Flatbush, once a fashionable suburb of Brooklyn, begins on the southeast edge of the park. Large homes built during the 1890's and early 1900's line many of its shaded streets.

Coney Island lies at the southern tip of Brooklyn. The area once was an island, but land has been filled in to make it a peninsula. In summer, many New Yorkers ride subways to Coney Island's beaches. At one time, Coney Island also had great amusement parks, but they have been replaced by housing developments. In the late 1900's, large numbers of immigrants from Russia settled in Coney Island.

The Bronx has a population of about 1 ⅓ million and is chiefly a residential borough. The western part of the Bronx consists of a series of hills and valleys crossed by boulevards. A major boulevard in the Bronx, the Grand Concourse, runs north and south through the area. It is lined with apartment houses, commercial buildings, and stores. The eastern section of the borough is a broad plain, with peninsulas extending into the East River and Long Island Sound.

Bronx Park lies in the center of the Bronx. It includes the Bronx Zoo, one of the best-known zoos in the United States, and the New York Botanical Garden, an important scientific institution.

Fordham University and Lehman College have handsome campuses to the west of Bronx Park. The campus of Bronx Community College of the City University of New York includes the Hall of Fame for Great Americans, which honors the memory of outstanding Americans (see **Hall of fame**).

One of the most fashionable neighborhoods in the Bronx is Riverdale, in the northwest corner of the borough along the Hudson River. It has tall apartment buildings, estates and other large homes, and exclusive pri-

© Stan Ries

Queens is the largest borough in area. It has many unattached single-family homes, large apartment buildings, housing projects, and busy expressways. Much of the borough's development has occurred since the 1940's.

© Kay Honkanen from Carl Östman

Staten Island has several sections that look more like small towns than like parts of a major city. Staten Island is the only borough not connected to Manhattan by a bridge or a tunnel. The famous Staten Island ferries link the two boroughs.

vate schools. One of the poorest neighborhoods in the Bronx is Morrisania, which lies south of Bronx Park and east of Grand Concourse Boulevard. The area has many run-down and abandoned buildings.

Two huge housing developments lie in the eastern part of the Bronx. Parkchester, built from 1938 to 1942, is a rental and condominium development southwest of Bronx Park. Co-op City, built from 1968 to 1970, is in the northeast corner of the borough and is owned by its residents. Co-op City has more than 15,000 apartments, a large shopping area, and landscaped areas.

City Island lies east of the Bronx in Long Island Sound. It has several boat clubs and resembles a New England village. Edgewater Park and Silver Beach are at the southeastern tip of the Bronx. They were once summer resort communities. But the cottages in these areas have been winterized for year-round use.

Queens, with about 2 ¼ million residents, ranks second in population among New York City's boroughs. Queens grew rapidly from 1910 to 1930, when subways were built to connect it with Manhattan. A second period of fast growth began in the late 1940's, when the sub-

ways were extended, new highways were built, and two major airports were developed in the borough. Today, huge housing developments and busy expressways are the major features of Queens.

Much of the borough's industry is concentrated near the East River in an area called Long Island City. The area lies just south of the Ed Koch Queensboro Bridge, which connects Queens and Manhattan. It has giant rail yards and many industrial plants and warehouses. Maspeth, southeast of Long Island City, also has large industrial plants, as well as pleasant residential areas.

Forest Hills lies near the center of Queens. Within this neighborhood is Forest Hills Gardens, an attractive housing and shopping area built in 1910. Forest Hills Gardens was intended for families with middle incomes. But it immediately became—and has remained—a community for the wealthy.

Northeast of Forest Hills is Flushing Meadows Corona Park, site of the New York World's Fairs of 1939-1940 and 1964-1965. The park has several features left from the fairs, including a botanical garden, an indoor ice-skating rink, and a science museum.

La Guardia Airport is northwest of Flushing Meadows Corona Park, across Flushing Bay. The neighborhood of Flushing, northeast of the park, has a busy shopping area and many large apartment houses.

Jamaica, in southeastern Queens, is one of the borough's commercial hubs. It has large shopping and business areas and both rich and poor residential sections.

John F. Kennedy International Airport, the city's largest airport, lies immediately south of Jamaica. It has been expanding since 1942 and has become the borough's largest single source of employment.

Rockaway is a long peninsula that forms the southern border of Jamaica Bay. It has a sandy beachfront, attractive private homes, and modern apartment buildings. It also has many summer cottages, some of which are occupied the year around.

Staten Island has about 470,000 residents, making it the smallest borough in population. It is the only borough not connected to Manhattan by a bridge or a tunnel. Until the completion of the Verrazano-Narrows Bridge in 1964, much of the island consisted of small farms and undeveloped areas. The bridge, which connects Staten Island with Brooklyn, has led to the construction of new housing and to industrial growth. But many communities on Staten Island still look more like suburban towns than like sections of a major city.

St. George, on the northeast tip of Staten Island, serves as the downtown section of the borough and is the site of the Staten Island Ferry Terminal. The famous ferries carry automobiles and passengers between Staten Island and Manhattan and provide the only direct link between the two boroughs. A former U.S. Coast Guard station, government and private office buildings, and a variety of stores are also in St. George.

The eastern shore of Staten Island contains some decaying industrial areas. But handsome homes and several colleges lie on the wooded hills just inland. Parks and beaches line the southeastern and southern coasts of the island. Many of the historic buildings in Richmond Town, in the center of Staten Island, have been restored. Exhibits show how the community developed during the 1600's, 1700's, and 1800's.

The industrial communities of Mariners Harbor and Port Richmond lie on the north coast of Staten Island. One of the three bridges that connect Staten Island and New Jersey is near Mariners Harbor. The others are on the northwest coast and near the island's southern tip.

Small islands. Several small islands dot the waters surrounding New York City. The most famous is Liberty Island, site of the city's greatest landmark—the Statue of Liberty. Ellis Island lies near Liberty Island. The U.S. Immigration Service used Ellis Island until 1954 as a port of entry and a detention and deportation center. Liberty and Ellis islands now form the Statue of Liberty National Monument. Governors Island, at the mouth of the East River, was the site of a military installation from the late 1700's until 1997. The Governors Island National Monument, in the northern part of the island, includes two forts from the early 1800's. Roosevelt, Wards, Randalls, and Rikers islands are in the East River. Hospitals, prisons, and other institutions have been erected on these islands. An aerial cable car system connects Roosevelt Island and Manhattan. See **Ellis Island; Liberty Island.**

Metropolitan area. The New York-Northern New Jersey-Long Island metropolitan area spreads over 10 counties in New York, 12 counties in New Jersey, and 1 county in Pennsylvania. Nearly 19 million people live in this metropolitan area. In terms of population, this metropolitan area is the largest in the United States.

The New York-White Plains-Wayne metropolitan division consists of the five boroughs; Putnam, Rockland, and Westchester counties in southern New York; and Bergen, Hudson, and Passaic counties in New Jersey. About 11 ½ million people live in this division.

Many communities in the New York area are commuter suburbs. Their residents work in New York City and commute by automobiles, buses, ferries, railroads, and subways. Some of these suburbs, such as White

New York's Fifth Avenue is one of the city's famous shopping centers. It includes a number of stores known for their expensive merchandise. Fifth Avenue is also the site of such famous landmarks as Rockefeller Center, St. Patrick's Cathedral, and Trump Tower.

© Karl Kummels, Superstock

Manhattan's Central Park attracts many people on warm summer days. The huge park has athletic fields, fountains, gardens, a lake, playgrounds, wooded areas, and a zoo.

Plains in Westchester County, have become important centers of business and shopping outside the central city. Other communities in the New York area are industrial cities. They provide enough jobs so that most of their residents work in the communities themselves. Some of these industrial communities, such as Newark and Jersey City in New Jersey, are also experiencing the problems of pollution, poverty, and urban decay that affect New York City.

People

The people of New York City represent nearly all nationalities. During the 1650's, only about 1,000 people lived in the Dutch colony of New Amsterdam on Manhattan Island. But even then, 18 languages were spoken in the colony. Since that time, people from throughout the world have brought their skills, traditions, and ways of life to New York City.

People move to New York City for many reasons. Many are attracted by the city's job opportunities. Other people come to attend the city's schools and colleges or to enjoy its many cultural activities. Still others come simply because they want to be a part of a large, exciting city.

Ethnic groups. Five ethnic groups—black, Irish, Italian, Jewish, and Puerto Rican—make up about three-fifths of New York City's population. Neighborhoods consisting largely of people from these and many smaller groups are scattered throughout the city. Originally, most of the people in ethnic groups shared direct ties to a country, a language, or a common past with other members of their group. Today, such ties are less common. But the people still have some unity through such

things as common religious beliefs and common economic interests.

Blacks are the largest ethnic group in New York City and make up about 25 percent of the city's population. New York has about 2,100,000 blacks, more than any other city in the United States. Most of the blacks are migrants—or the children of migrants—from the rural South. But many have also come from the Caribbean. A large number of New York City's blacks live in poor neighborhoods. Many of them have been prevented from leaving the ghetto areas by discrimination in jobs and housing and by a lack of education. But more and more black New Yorkers are becoming part of the city's middle class. Thousands of blacks live in racially integrated areas, and thousands more live in middle-class black neighborhoods.

Jews make up about 12 percent of the population of New York City. New York's nearly 1 million Jews come from many countries. They are considered to be an ethnic group, however, because most of them live in Jewish neighborhoods and have similar religious and social beliefs. Many Jews own businesses. Many others work in garment factories, in offices, and in the legal, medical, and teaching professions.

Puerto Ricans make up about 10 percent of New York City's population. They are the largest of several Spanish-speaking ethnic groups in the city. Large numbers of Puerto Ricans began to come to New York in the 1950's. Many of them found jobs as unskilled workers, especially in hospitals, hotels, and restaurants. At first, nearly all Puerto Ricans lived in East Harlem in Manhattan. But today, Puerto Rican neighborhoods are found in all the boroughs. Neighborhood associations, large church organizations, and the public school system have all developed programs to help newly arrived Puerto Rican people learn English and adjust to life in the city.

About 8 percent of New York City's people are of Italian ancestry. New York Italians are known for their well-kept homes and for their close neighborhood ties. They are one of the largest single groups in the city's construction industry, and they play a key role in the restaurant and the wholesale and retail food-marketing industries. Many Italians have civil service jobs in the city's park, public works, sanitation, police, and fire departments. Most of New York City's Italians belong to the Roman Catholic Church.

The Irish have traditionally been active in New York City's political life. In the late 1800's and early 1900's, they controlled the city government. However, the percentage of Irish people in the city has dropped from 30 percent in 1870 to about 5 percent today. As a result, the Irish have lost much of their political power. But they are still one of the largest single groups employed by the city's police and fire departments. The Irish are also among the leaders of the Roman Catholic Church in the city.

New York City has a number of other ethnic groups besides the five major ones. Other large ethnic groups in the city include people of Chinese, Dominican, English, German, Asian Indian, Jamaican, Mexican, and Russian descent.

Housing in New York City differs in several ways from that in most other cities of the United States. About 70 percent of New York's families live in buildings with three or more units. In other cities, most people live in one- or two-family houses. About 65 percent of the families in New York rent their homes. In other U.S. cities, most families own their homes. About 40 percent of the housing in New York City was built before 1940. Most other cities in the United States have a far larger percentage of newer housing.

New York City has long been a leader in housing reform. In 1867, New York state, at the request of the city, passed the nation's first tenement house law. The law set minimum standards for room sizes and for ventilation and sanitation facilities. In 1943, the city passed a rent control law to protect tenants in privately owned buildings from unfair rent increases. Rent control laws passed in the 1970's were intended to help landlords make a reasonable profit. But many landlords complain that the higher rents they may charge do not cover rising costs. New York City has also built many public housing projects. Today, about 180,000 low-income families live in city-owned public housing.

But housing remains one of New York City's most serious and difficult problems. Many old buildings are becoming unusable, and the demand for new housing, especially among poor people, is rapidly increasing. Yet steadily rising construction costs and a lack of large areas of open land make the development of new housing difficult.

Education. New York City has the largest public school system of any city in the United States. The public school system includes more than 1,400 schools. In addition, there are hundreds of privately operated schools in the city.

© Allyn Baum, Photo Researchers

Jews form a large ethnic group in New York City. The people above are Hasidic Jews, who dress in a style that developed in Eastern Europe in the 1800's. Many Hasidic Jews live in Brooklyn.

The mayor controls the city's public school system. The mayor appoints a chancellor to head the Department of Education, the branch of city government that manages the public schools.

New York City has neighborhood high schools like those found in most other cities. But it also has a wide variety of specialized high schools that prepare students for a specific occupation or for further training at the college level. These institutions include schools of automobile mechanics, aviation, the performing arts, printing, and science. Grade schools in poor neighborhoods have special programs to aid underprivileged children and children who do not speak English.

Many of New York City's colleges, universities, and other institutions of higher learning are world famous. One of the largest universities in the world, the City University of New York, is operated by the city with state and federal assistance. The university consists of 11 senior colleges, 6 community colleges, an honors college, a graduate center, and schools of biomedical education, journalism, law, and professional studies.

Columbia University, founded in 1754, is the city's oldest private university. The city's largest private university is New York University. Fordham and St. John's universities are important Roman Catholic schools.

New York City also has many smaller and more specialized institutions of higher education. The New School deals mainly with adult education. Rockefeller University specializes in advanced research in biology and medicine. Pratt Institute and Cooper Union are largely devoted to architecture, engineering, and the fine arts. Other schools specialize in law, medicine, and social work.

Social problems. New York City has many of the same problems other cities have. But it is so much larger than other cities that the problems are greatly magnified. New York's major social problems include poverty, crime and drug addiction, and racial conflict.

Poverty is one of New York City's most expensive problems. The city budgets billions of dollars per year on welfare programs to provide food, clothing, housing, medical care, and other benefits for hundreds of thousands of people. Yet unskilled immigrants continue to move into the city, while the demand for unskilled labor continues to decline. As a result, the problem of poverty is difficult to solve.

Because of its large population, New York City has more crime than any other U.S. city. But the crime rate is actually lower in New York than in many other cities. New York's crime and drug addiction problems are closely related. A large number of drug addicts live in New York City. They commit many of the city's burglaries and attacks on individuals to get money for drugs.

Racial conflicts in New York City have had a number of causes. A major cause has been discrimination against blacks, Puerto Ricans, and other minority groups in jobs and housing. Many minority group members have had trouble obtaining well-paying jobs. Many also have had difficulty moving out of segregated neighborhoods and into neighborhoods where most of the people are white and of European ancestry. When members of a minority group have begun moving into such a neighborhood, the white residents often have begun moving out. In this way, segregated housing patterns have continued, and the chances for conflicts between the groups have increased.

Economy

New York City is one of the world's most important centers of industry, trade, and finance. Businesses, industries, and government agencies in the metropolitan area provide millions of jobs.

The economies of both New York City and its suburbs are growing. But since the 1940's, the economy of the suburban area has grown much faster than that of the city. The construction of new highways, a growing labor force, and the availability of land in the suburbs have led many businesses and industries to move from the crowded central city to the suburbs.

The types of jobs available in New York City have also been changing since the 1940's. The number of jobs for unskilled workers has decreased greatly because many industries have moved to the suburbs. This decrease has created a serious economic problem because most immigrants to the city are unskilled. At the same time, the number of jobs for skilled workers, especially office workers, has increased. But many of these jobs are being filled by people who live in the suburbs and commute to the city.

Industry. New York City, along with Chicago and Los Angeles, ranks among the leading manufacturing centers in the United States. New York City has thousands of industrial plants. The most important industries in the city are (1) printing and publishing and (2) clothing production.

New York City is one of the nation's chief printing and publishing centers. It has more printing plants than any other U.S. city. New York publishes a large percentage of the books published in the United States.

New York City's clothing industry is centered in Man-

hattan's famous Garment District, southwest of Times Square. But the garment industry has been declining in New York City. Many factories have closed. Other factories have left the Garment District because of the rising costs of doing business in the heart of Manhattan.

Other leading manufacturing industries include those that produce chemicals, food products, furniture, machinery, metal products, paper products, and textiles. The construction industry is also important.

Trade. New York City's port, officially called the Port of New York and New Jersey, is one of the world's largest and busiest seaports. The port ranks second to the Port of Los Angeles in total value of cargo handled annually. The port's cargo includes foreign imports and exports, and goods going to and coming from other U.S. ports.

New York City's port activity declined in the last half of the 1900's. One reason for the decline in port activity was the growth of other international seaports in the United States, especially along the Great Lakes. The opening of the St. Lawrence Seaway in 1959 allowed ships that previously docked in New York to reach Great Lakes ports.

Large amounts of cargo are also handled at airports in the New York City area. Foreign air freight goes through Kennedy Airport and nearby Newark Liberty International Airport in New Jersey. Domestic cargo is handled at Kennedy, La Guardia, and Newark airports.

The Port Authority of New York and New Jersey, a self-supporting agency of the states of New York and New Jersey, operates New York City's major airports and docking facilities, as well as several other transportation facilities. See **Port Authority of New York and New Jersey**.

Wholesale trade plays an important part in New York City's economy. The city has thousands of wholesale firms. Its wholesale grocery and dry-goods businesses are the largest in the United States.

© Ray Block

The Garment District in Manhattan is the center of New York City's important clothing industry. The district's streets are crowded with workers moving racks of clothing.

© Driendl Group/Getty Images

The New York Stock Exchange, *left,* stands at the corner of Wall and Broad streets in the heart of New York's Financial District. The cloaked statue of George Washington, *right,* marks the site where he was inaugurated as the first president of the United States in 1789.

The largest retail center in the United States is in midtown Manhattan. The department stores and specialty shops in midtown Manhattan are known throughout the world.

Finance. More of the nation's largest and most important financial institutions have their headquarters in New York City than in any other city. Banks, brokerage houses, insurance companies, real estate firms, stock exchanges, and other financial organizations in New York employ many people. Unlike most industries in the city, the financial organizations offer a steadily increasing number of jobs.

The most famous financial institution in New York City is the New York Stock Exchange, at the corner of Broad and Wall streets in the heart of the Financial District. It is the largest stock exchange in the United States. The American Stock Exchange, one of the nation's largest exchanges, is also in the Financial District. A number of

large brokerage houses have their headquarters near the exchanges.

New York City's banks are among the biggest in the world. These banks help finance business ventures throughout the United States and in many parts of the world. The largest of the city's banks are in the Financial District.

Transportation. New York City has a huge, complicated transportation system. Much of the system is centered in the area of Manhattan that is south of Central Park. Millions of people travel to and from that area each working day. Nearly all forms of air, land, and water transportation serve the city.

An extensive highway system has been developed to carry automobiles, buses, and trucks into, out of, and through New York City. The city's major expressways include the Major Deegan Expressway in the Bronx, the Shore Parkway and Gowanus Expressway in Brooklyn, and Grand Central Parkway and the Long Island Expressway in Queens. Franklin D. Roosevelt Drive carries traffic along the eastern edge of Manhattan.

New York City includes 65 square miles (168 square kilometers) of inland water, so many bridges and tunnels are needed to link the city's boroughs. The famous Brooklyn Bridge crosses the East River and connects Brooklyn and the southern tip of Manhattan. It was completed in 1883 and declared a national historic landmark in 1964. In addition to the Brooklyn Bridge, six other bridges cross the East River. They are, from south to north, the Manhattan, Williamsburg, Ed Koch Queensboro, Robert F. Kennedy, Bronx-Whitestone, and Throgs Neck bridges. The Y-shaped Robert F. Kennedy Bridge links Manhattan, the Bronx, and Queens.

The Harlem River is spanned by a number of bridges, including High Bridge, Henry Hudson Bridge, and Alexander Hamilton Bridge. High Bridge, which was opened in 1848, is one of the oldest bridges in New York City.

One bridge, the George Washington Bridge, crosses the Hudson River and connects Manhattan and New Jersey. The Bayonne Bridge stretches 1,675 feet (511 meters) over Kill Van Kull channel between Staten Island and New Jersey. It has one of the longest arch spans in the world. Goethals Bridge and Outerbridge Crossing, which cross Arthur Kill channel, also connect Staten Island and New Jersey.

The Verrazano-Narrows Bridge, which links Staten Island and Brooklyn, opened in 1964. Its 4,260-foot (1,298-meter) suspension span is one of the longest in the world.

The Queens Midtown Tunnel runs under the East River and connects Manhattan and Queens. The 9,117-foot (2,779-meter) Hugh L. Carey Tunnel links the southern tip of Manhattan with Brooklyn. The Lincoln and Holland tunnels run under the Hudson River between Manhattan and New Jersey. In addition to these tunnels for motor vehicles, several tunnels carry subway trains under the East River. Four rapid transit tunnels called the PATH (Port Authority Trans-Hudson) tunnels run under the Hudson River between Manhattan and New Jersey. See **Hudson River tunnels.**

The Metropolitan Transit Authority (MTA), a public corporation owned by the state of New York, operates New York City's subway and bus systems. New York

City's subway system, one of the largest in the world, provides passenger service on approximately 660 miles (1,060 kilometers) of track. The MTA also operates commuter rail and bus systems on Long Island and in the city's northern suburbs. New Jersey Transit operates commuter rail and bus systems in the city's western suburbs. Crowded Manhattan is famous for its huge fleet of taxicabs.

Two major railroad stations serve New York City—Grand Central Terminal (sometimes called Grand Central Station) at 42nd Street and Park Avenue and Pennsylvania Station on 31st Street at Seventh Avenue. In the mid-1960's, the upper level of Penn Station was torn down and replaced by Madison Square Garden, but trains continue to operate beneath street level. Before the rapid growth of air travel in the 1950's, hundreds of thousands of railroad passengers from all parts of the country passed through Grand Central and Penn stations each day. Today, hundreds of thousands of people still use the stations. Most of them, however, are commuters.

La Guardia, Kennedy, and Newark airports handle most of New York City's commercial air traffic. La Guardia serves domestic and Canadian airlines, and Kennedy and Newark serve domestic and international airlines. The New York City area also has numerous smaller airports.

Communications. New York City is the nation's most important center for mass communications. More publishing and broadcasting companies have their headquarters in New York than in any other city in the United States.

The *Daily News,* the *New York Post,* and *The New York Times* are general newspapers published daily in New York City. The *Times* is one of the world's best-known papers and is commonly used as a reference source. The city has a number of community, foreign-language, and trade and union papers. Daily papers printed in Spanish, Russian, Polish, Greek, and Chinese have large circulations. *The Wall Street Journal* is the major business paper. An international newspaper, its circulation is one of the largest of any paper in the United States.

Most major national magazines and many specialized magazines have their editorial offices in New York City. New York also has more book publishers and advertising agencies than any other city.

New York City has dozens of radio and television stations. It serves as the headquarters of three of the nation's four major broadcasting networks. The three networks are ABC, Inc.; CBS Broadcasting Inc.; and the NBC Television Network. They provide both television and radio programming to stations throughout the United States. The fourth network—Fox Broadcasting Company—originates many of its television programs from a studio in New York City.

Cultural life and recreation

New York City ranks as one of the world's greatest cultural centers. It has a number of art galleries, drama and

© Dennis Hallinan, FPG

The Theater District is near Times Square. Its many playhouses are called Broadway theaters, although few actually stand on Broadway. Some theaters feature musicals, and others specialize in comedies and serious dramas. Theatergoers line up in front of the Eugene O'Neill Theatre in this picture.

dance groups, musical and literary societies, and other cultural organizations. It also has some of the world's finest concert halls, museums, and theaters. Many of the nation's greatest actors, artists, musicians, poets, and writers live in New York.

There are several reasons for New York City's leading position as a cultural center. Many of the city's wealthy residents have long given financial support to cultural activities. Traditionally, the city has also offered people in the arts an atmosphere that encourages freedom of expression. In addition, New York's many advertising agencies, broadcasting and film studios, recording companies, and publishing houses have provided jobs that attract creative people.

The arts. Nearly all the arts thrive in New York City. Many new styles in American drama, literature, music, and painting have developed in New York and then spread to the rest of the country.

One of the city's most famous, popular forms of art is the theater. Most important American plays and musical comedies have their premieres in the city's famous Theater District. The theaters in this district are called *Broadway* theaters, though few are actually on that street. Most are on side streets near Times Square. Many plays and musicals are also presented in *off-Broadway* and *off-off-Broadway* theaters in Manhattan and Brooklyn.

Musical organizations in New York City include the New York Philharmonic, one of the world's great symphony orchestras, and the Metropolitan Opera Association, an outstanding opera company. Both the orchestra and the opera company perform at the Lincoln Center for the Performing Arts. Lincoln Center also houses the New York City Ballet and the Juilliard School. The New York City Center on West 55th Street offers a variety of

fine arts programs. Many concerts are held at Carnegie Hall, near Central Park.

Thousands of artists live and work in New York City. They display and sell their paintings, sculptures, and other works of art in the city's dozens of galleries. Many artists have made roomy studios in abandoned warehouses and factories in Manhattan. Most of the buildings were abandoned by industries that moved to suburban areas.

Architecture. New York's best-known style of architecture is the towering skyscraper. The giant buildings that form Manhattan's dramatic skyline are famous throughout the world.

One of the oldest and most famous skyscrapers in New York is the Flatiron Building, on 23rd Street where Broadway crosses Fifth Avenue. The 21-story building was completed in 1903. It has a triangular shape like that of an old-fashioned flatiron.

During the 1930's, several famous skyscrapers were built in New York City. The most famous, the 102-story Empire State Building, was completed in 1931. The Empire State Building ranked as the tallest building in the world for many years. The 77-story Chrysler Building at Lexington Avenue and 42nd Street and the 70-story RCA (now GE) Building in Rockefeller Center were also completed in the 1930's.

Many glass-walled skyscrapers have been built in New York since the 1950's. These buildings include the United Nations Secretariat Building along the East River at 44th Street, Lever House on Park Avenue between 53rd and 54th streets, and the Seagram Building on Park Avenue between 52nd and 53rd streets.

Several New York City churches are famous for their Gothic Revival style of architecture. They include the

© Toyohiro Yamada, FPG

Lincoln Center for the Performing Arts houses the New York Philharmonic, the Metropolitan Opera, the New York City Ballet, and several other cultural organizations.

The Metropolitan Museum of Art, which occupies four city blocks in New York, ranks as the largest art museum in the United States. Patrons enjoy viewing a vast array of paintings, sculptures, and other artworks in the "Met," as the museum is often called.

© Mike Yamashita, Woodfin Camp, Inc.

© Katrina Thomas, Photo Researchers

Neighborhood festivals allow New York City residents to enjoy cultural activities near their homes. The festivals are free and feature various types of music and other entertainment.

Episcopal Cathedral Church of St. John the Divine between 110th and 113th streets near Broadway, the Roman Catholic St. Patrick's Cathedral on Fifth Avenue between 50th and 51st streets, and the interdenominational Riverside Church on Riverside Drive and 122nd Street.

Other buildings of architectural interest in New York City include the many narrow brownstone houses that line side streets in Manhattan and Brooklyn. Most of these houses were built in the late 1800's as single-family homes. Today, many of them have been divided into apartments.

Libraries. New York City has three public library systems. The New York Public Library system serves Manhattan, the Bronx, and Staten Island. The Brooklyn Public Library serves Brooklyn, and the Queens Borough Public Library serves Queens. Altogether, the three systems have more than 200 branch libraries.

The New York Public Library system has about 85 of the branches—more than any other city public library in the United States. The system's Humanities and Social Sciences Library on Fifth Avenue at 42nd Street is a Manhattan landmark.

New York City also has over 1,000 libraries run by colleges, schools, and private organizations. Many of these libraries are highly specialized. For example, the Morgan Library & Museum has rare books and manuscripts, and the Dag Hammarskjöld Library at the United Nations specializes in books dealing with international affairs and world peace.

Nearly all museums in New York have associated libraries. The most important of these libraries include the Thomas J. Watson Library of the Metropolitan Museum of Art, the Frick Art Reference Library, and the American Museum of Natural History Research Library.

Museums. New York City has many kinds of museums. The Metropolitan Museum of Art on Fifth Avenue at 82nd Street is the largest art museum in the United States. It has more than 2 million works of art. These works represent nearly every culture of the last 5,000 years. The museum occupies four city blocks, yet it has space to display only part of its huge collection at one time. The Cloisters, a branch of the Metropolitan Museum, is devoted to European art and architecture of the Middle Ages (A.D. 400 through the 1400's). The building is designed like a medieval monastery. The Cloisters is in Fort Tryon Park at the northern tip of Manhattan.

Several New York City museums specialize in modern art, such as the Museum of Modern Art on West 53rd Street, the Whitney Museum of American Art on Madison Avenue and 75th Street, and the Guggenheim Museum on Fifth Avenue at 89th Street. The Guggenheim is in an unusual circular building designed by the famous American architect Frank Lloyd Wright. The Frick Collection on 70th Street at Fifth Avenue has a notable collection of art that dates from the 1300's through the 1800's. The museum occupies one of Manhattan's few remaining mansions.

The American Museum of Natural History stands at 79th Street and Central Park West. It has the largest exhibition space of any natural history museum in the world. The American Museum's exhibits include lifelike models of animals shown in reproductions of their natural surroundings.

New York City also has several historical museums. These museums include the Museum of the City of New York on Fifth Avenue at 103rd Street.

Parks. New York has more parks, playgrounds, beaches, and other recreational areas than any other U.S. city. Many parts of New York are so crowded, however, that children must still play in the city streets.

Central Park, in the middle of Manhattan, is the best known of the city's parks. This vast recreational site is 2 ½ miles (4 kilometers) long and ½ mile (0.8 kilometer) wide and has athletic fields, gardens, a lake, playgrounds, and wooded areas. Central Park includes the Mall, where outdoor concerts and other events are held, and the Ramble, a bird sanctuary.

The Gateway National Recreation Area forms a 26,607-acre (10,767-hectare) park. It covers shorelines and islands of Queens and Brooklyn, as well as part of the Staten Island shore and most of the Sandy Hook peninsula of New Jersey.

Other large parks in New York City include Bronx and Van Cortlandt parks in the Bronx, Prospect Park in Brooklyn, and Flushing Meadows Corona Park in Queens. In many parts of the city, small parks and playgrounds have been developed on any open land that was available, including single empty lots.

New York City has several zoos and botanical gardens. Central Park in Manhattan contains a zoo. The Bronx Zoo in Bronx Park has one of the largest collections of animals of any zoo in the United States. Bronx Park also includes the New York Botanical Garden, which features plants from most parts of the world. In addition, Brooklyn and Queens have outstanding botanical gardens.

Sports. The city has two major league baseball teams—the New York Yankees of the American League and the New York Mets of the National League. The Yankees play in Yankee Stadium in the Bronx. The Mets play in Citi Field in Queens.

In addition, the city has two National Football League teams. The New York Jets of the American Conference and the New York Giants of the National Conference both play in New Meadowlands Stadium in nearby East Rutherford, New Jersey.

New York City also has two professional hockey teams—the New York Islanders and New York Rangers of the National Hockey League—and a professional basketball team—the New York Knickerbockers of the National Basketball Association. The Islanders play in the Nassau Veterans Memorial Coliseum in Uniondale, New York. The Knickerbockers and Rangers play in New York City's Madison Square Garden.

A visitor's guide

Each year, many millions of tourists and delegates to conventions and trade shows visit New York City. To accommodate all these visitors, New York has hundreds of hotels, motels, and rooming houses, and thousands of restaurants. Some of the city's hotels rank among the world's most luxurious. Many restaurants specialize in a certain type of cooking, such as Chinese, French, German, or Italian. In fact, no other city in the world has so many kinds of restaurants as New York.

Following are descriptions of some of New York City's many interesting places to visit. Other places of interest in the city are discussed and pictured earlier in this article.

Empire State Building on Fifth Avenue between 33rd Street and 34th Street is a 102-story New York City landmark. Public observation decks on the 86th and 102nd floors of the Empire State Building offer visitors spectacular views of the city.

Financial District is centered on Wall and Broad streets near the southern tip of Manhattan. Many banks, brokerage houses, and stock exchanges are in the district. Tours are given of the New York Stock Exchange, at the corner of Wall and Broad streets.

Greenwich Village lies south of 14th Street and west of Broadway. Many actors, artists, musicians, and other people in the arts live in the area and in the SoHo area to the south. The Village and SoHo have several small theaters and many interesting shops and art galleries.

Museum of Modern Art on West 53rd Street between Fifth Avenue and the Avenue of the Americas displays modern paintings, sculptures, films, photographs, and other works of art.

Rockefeller Center lies between Fifth and Seventh avenues and between 48th and 51st streets. It includes the sunken Plaza, used for outdoor dining in summer and ice skating in winter; the 70-story GE Building, which has a public observation roof; Radio City Music Hall, a 5,900-seat theater featuring films and stage shows; and the studios of the NBC Television Network. Tours are given of Radio City Music Hall, of the NBC studios, and of the entire center.

Statue of Liberty

© John Lewis Stage, Photo Researchers

St. Patrick's Cathedral

© Kay Honkanen from Carl Östman

Rockefeller Center Plaza

© Superstock

St. Patrick's Cathedral is located at Fifth Avenue and 50th Street, across from Rockefeller Center. It is the seat of the Roman Catholic Archdiocese of New York. St. Patrick's Cathedral is one of the finest examples of Gothic Revival architecture in the United States. See **Saint Patrick's Cathedral.**

Statue of Liberty on Liberty Island in New York Harbor is the world-famous symbol of American freedom. Boats carry visitors to the island from Battery Park at the southern tip of Manhattan. See **Statue of Liberty.**

United Nations Headquarters lie along the East River between 42nd and 48th streets. Visitors may take tours of the Secretariat, General Assembly, and Confer-

ence buildings. A limited number of free tickets are available for meetings of the General Assembly and other United Nations organizations. See **United Nations.**

Government

New York City's government is presently organized under a charter that was adopted in 1961 and that became effective in 1963. The government of New York is more centralized than that of most other cities in the United States. In New York, the central government is responsible for public education, correctional institutions, libraries, public safety, recreational facilities, sanitation, water supply, and welfare services. In most of the

City Hall, completed in 1811, is one of New York City's architectural landmarks. The building is part of the Civic Center and is surrounded by City Hall Park and by other city government buildings. The mayor and the mayor's staff have their offices in City Hall.

© Lizabeth Corlett, Uniphoto

other cities in the United States, however, at least some of these services are provided by separate government units.

Until mid-1990, the New York City legislature consisted of a City Council and the Board of Estimate. In 1989, however, the Supreme Court of the United States declared that the composition of the Board of Estimate was unconstitutional because smaller boroughs had as many votes as larger boroughs. In November 1989, residents of New York City approved a plan to revise their city charter, which included abolishing the Board of Estimate. This revision was approved by the United States Department of Justice in December 1989. A number of changes went into effect immediately. The Board of Estimate was eliminated in September 1990.

New York City's government is headed by a mayor and a City Council. The mayor is the chief executive of New York City. The mayor is elected to a four-year term and is responsible for the administration of city government. The heads of about 50 city departments are appointed by the mayor. The mayor also may appoint one or more deputy mayors as assistants.

The City Council consists of representatives from each of the city's 51 districts, along with an official called the *public advocate.* Council members and the public advocate are elected in citywide elections and serve four-year terms. The public advocate presides over council meetings but does not have a vote. The council also elects one of its members to the position of council speaker. The council may pass laws and must approve the city's budget. It also has jurisdiction over most land use issues. The public advocate's main role is to investigate and answer complaints that New Yorkers make about ineffective city programs and services.

New York City has five boroughs. Each borough elects a borough president to a four-year term. The presidents advise the mayor on issues of interest to their boroughs. They also may serve on special city committees.

The city gets part of its income from about 20 different taxes, including an income tax, real estate tax, and sales tax. The real estate tax provides the most tax income. But the total tax income is far from enough to meet the city's expenses. The city gets additional money from the state and federal governments.

The Democratic Party has long been the most powerful political party in New York City. It has more than three times as many members as the Republican Party and usually controls between 75 and 85 percent of the city's elective offices. Neither the Democratic nor the Republican party in New York City has a strong citywide organization. Both political parties have separate organizations in each of the five boroughs.

Two minor political parties, the Liberal and the Conservative parties, also influence the city's politics. Both of these parties have affected city elections chiefly by supporting candidates from one of the two major parties.

History

The earliest people known to have lived in the New York City area were American Indians. Several tribes of the Algonquian family of Indians lived peacefully on the shores of New York Harbor and along the banks of the Hudson and East rivers. The Indians lived in small villages of bark houses. They fished, hunted, raised crops, and trapped animals. They traveled the area's waterways in sturdy canoes.

Exploration. The first European to enter New York Harbor was probably Giovanni da Verrazzano, an Italian explorer employed by the king of France. Verrazzano and his crew landed on Staten Island in 1524, while exploring the North American coast.

Other explorers visited the New York City region after Verrazzano. But none of these explorers reported seeing the island the Indians called *Man-a-hat-ta* (Island of the Hills). Finally, in 1609, Henry Hudson reached Manhattan and then sailed up the river that now bears his name.

Hudson was a citizen of England who was exploring for the Dutch, and so the Netherlands claimed the territory he had found. The region was later named New Netherland.

Settlement. In 1613, the Dutch trader and explorer Adriaen Block and his crew became the first Europeans to live on Manhattan Island. They built several huts and spent the winter near the southern tip of the island after their ship was destroyed by fire. Adriaen and his crew built a new ship and left Manhattan Island in the spring of 1614.

In 1624, the Dutch West India Company, a trading and colonizing firm, sent settlers to Manhattan. In 1625, the settlers laid out a town and built a fort called Fort Amsterdam at the island's southern tip. The next year, the governor (or director-general) of New Netherland, Peter Minuit, bought the island from the Indians for goods worth 60 Dutch guilders, the equivalent of about $24.

Soon after Fort Amsterdam was built, the entire settlement was named New Amsterdam. The colony grew slowly at first because the governors sent by the Dutch were poor administrators. But in 1647, Peter Stuyvesant became governor, and under his administration the town began to prosper rapidly.

About 1,000 people lived in New Amsterdam during the 1650's. Their houses stood along narrow dirt lanes. In 1653, the colonists built a wall along the northern edge of town because they feared attacks by Indians or by white enemies. But the wall fell down within a few years. Later, the colonists laid out a road in its place. The road became known as Wall Street.

While New Amsterdam was being established on Manhattan Island, colonists were also arriving in what is now the Bronx, Brooklyn, and Queens. Jonas Bronck, a Dutch citizen from Scandinavia, after whom the Bronx is named, became the first European settler in that area. Bronck set up a 500-acre (200-hectare) farm in 1641 and was soon followed by other settlers. Dutch and English colonists established small villages in Brooklyn and Queens. Staten Island developed more slowly than the other areas partly because settlers there often had trouble with Indians.

English rule. The Netherlands and England fought three naval wars between 1652 and 1674. In 1664, English warships sailed into New York Harbor and forced Peter Stuyvesant to surrender New Amsterdam. The

Dutch regained the colony a few years later but then gave it to England under the terms of a peace treaty. The English renamed the colony New York.

New York grew quickly under English rule. By 1700, its population reached about 7,000, and buildings filled lower Manhattan. The town's first newspaper, the *New-York Gazette,* appeared in 1725. King's College, now Columbia University, was founded in 1754.

New York City played an important role in the American Colonies' fight for freedom from Britain. In 1765, the Stamp Act Congress met in New York to protest unfair taxes. In 1770, New Yorkers clashed with British soldiers, and one man was killed in the fighting. Soon after the Revolutionary War in America began in 1775, American forces took possession of the city. But the British regained New York City after the Battle of Long Island in 1776. They held the city until the Revolutionary War ended in 1783.

In January 1785, New York City became the temporary capital of the United States. The Congress of the United States met in the city until August 1790. George Washington was inaugurated in New York City as the nation's first president in April 1789.

The growing city. During the early years of the United States, Philadelphia and Boston were larger and more prosperous than New York. But New York's economy and population expanded rapidly. The city took advantage of its excellent natural harbor to increase its trade with other East Coast ports and with foreign countries. European immigrants began to pour into the city. By 1800, New York had about 60,000 people, more than any other city in the country.

New York's growth continued during the early 1800's. In 1811, city officials, planning for further expansion, decided that all newly built Manhattan streets should run in straight lines. That decision resulted in the regular pattern of cross streets north of what is now Greenwich Village.

The Erie Canal opened in upstate New York in 1825. The canal provided an important link in an all-water route between New York City and the rapidly developing Midwestern States (see **Erie Canal**). An increasing number of banks, insurance companies, and investment firms added to the city's economic growth.

New York's neighboring communities also grew quickly during the early 1800's. Brooklyn, the most im-

New Amsterdam, 1650-63, The Prototype View; Museum of the City of New York

New Amsterdam was a Dutch settlement that became New York City. The settlers laid out the town on Manhattan Island in 1625. By the 1650's, New Amsterdam had about 1,000 residents.

portant of these communities, was incorporated as a village in 1816 with 3,300 residents. By the time it became a city in 1834, it had about 24,000 people.

During the 1800's, thousands of European immigrants arrived in New York City every year. Until about 1890, most of them came from Germany, Ireland, and other countries of northern and western Europe. After about 1890, most immigrants came from southern and eastern European countries. Many immigrants had difficulty adjusting to the city. They lived in crowded slums and had trouble finding jobs.

Politicians, especially members of the Democratic Party organization in Manhattan called Tammany Hall, offered jobs, gifts, and advice to immigrants. In return, the immigrants voted to keep Tammany Hall in power. But the politicians actually did little to solve the immigrants' most important problems, such as the need for better housing, education, and medical care. In 1871, Tammany boss William M. Tweed and some of his followers were arrested and charged with cheating the city out of several million dollars. The Tweed Ring, as his group was called, was driven from public life. But the Tammany organization soon regained power. See **Tammany, Society of.**

Formation of Greater New York. In 1883, engineers completed the Brooklyn Bridge, which provided the first direct link between Manhattan and Brooklyn. In 1898, Brooklyn and several other communities were united with Manhattan to form what was called Greater New York. The other communities were what became the Bronx, Queens, and Staten Island. The sprawling new city had more than 3 million residents.

Nearly 2 million of the people lived in Manhattan. However, during the early 1900's, subways and bridges were constructed to provide convenient transportation between Manhattan and the other boroughs. The city's

people then began to spread out. As the populations of the other boroughs grew, the population of Manhattan decreased.

But Manhattan remained the largest and most powerful borough of Greater New York, and so its Tammany Hall organization continued to control city politics. Occasionally, voters became angered enough by the illegal activities of Tammany leaders to elect mayors who promised reform. But none of these reform mayors lasted more than one term—until Fiorello La Guardia became mayor in 1934. La Guardia, an honest and outspoken reformer, served from 1934 to 1945. Since his administration, no political organization has been able to control New York politics.

Problems. Since the 1940's, New York City, like other communities, has been troubled by many problems. The severity of the problems began increasing during the early 1960's. Air and water pollution harmed New York City's environment. Highways and mass transportation systems became overcrowded and outdated. Housing shortages increased. Racial conflict worsened.

New York City has also faced a series of damaging strikes by public employees. In 1966, transit workers struck for 12 days, halting all subway and bus service. In 1968, striking sanitation workers let garbage pile up on city streets for 9 days. In 1971, police officers refused to go on patrols for 6 days. These and other strikes involved disputes over such matters as wages, benefits, and working conditions.

New York City experienced a financial crisis in 1975, when the city's government lacked enough money to pay all its bills for the year. The New York State Legislature helped ease the situation by establishing the Municipal Assistance Corporation, which lent the city some money. The federal government also provided funds for the city. To help pay its expenses during the late 1970's,

Harper's Weekly, The Newberry Library, Chicago

Tammany Hall, a powerful Manhattan political organization, was often attacked by cartoonist Thomas Nast. This cartoon appeared in 1871, after its leaders were caught cheating the city out of money.

Museum of the City of New York

Thousands of immigrants arrived in New York City every year during the 1800's. Before entering the city, many immigrants had to pass through the immigration station on Ellis Island. The island is now part of the Statue of Liberty National Monument.

Brown Brothers

Times Square in the 1930's was as much the heart of New York City's Theater District as it is today. Much of the area has been redeveloped, but it remains the center of the Theater District.

Russell Reif, Pictorial Parade

A financial crisis hit New York City in 1975 and caused great concern for the city's future. A rally in Times Square, *shown here,* supported the use of federal aid to help the city.

New York City increased city taxes, eliminated thousands of city government jobs, and reduced city services. In the 1980's, the city's economic situation improved.

In 1989, the Supreme Court of the United States declared the Board of Estimate of New York City unconstitutional. See the *Government* section of this article for details.

In February 1993, a powerful bomb exploded in a parking garage of the World Trade Center. The blast killed 6 people and injured more than 1,000. It caused more than $300 million in damage to the Trade Center. Four men, including Sheik Omar Abdel Rahman, an Egyptian Muslim cleric, were convicted of the bombing and sent to prison.

A time of change. Democrat Edward I. Koch was elected mayor of New York City in 1977. In 1981, he became the first person ever nominated mayor by both the Democratic and Republican parties. David N. Dinkins, a Democrat and an African American, served as mayor of New York City from 1990 to 1994. He was the city's first African American mayor. Republican Rudolph W. Giuliani was elected mayor in 1993. He was the first Republican to be chosen mayor since 1965. He served until the end of 2001.

A rise in the city's spirit took place about the same time Giuliani became mayor. About a million new immigrants and a booming New York-based stock market helped to invigorate the city's economy. New York City's crime rate dropped, and real estate prices soared. Neighborhood environmental efforts helped clean the city's air and the Hudson River.

On Sept. 11, 2001, terrorists in hijacked commercial airplanes crashed the planes into the twin 110-story towers of the World Trade Center. In related incidents that day, a hijacked plane crashed into the Pentagon Building, just outside Washington, D.C., and another hijacked

AP/Wide World

The collapse of a World Trade Center tower on Sept. 11, 2001, sent people fleeing. Terrorists sent two hijacked jetliners crashing into the center's twin towers, destroying both buildings.

plane crashed in Pennsylvania. The Trade Center towers collapsed to the ground. Part of the Pentagon was destroyed. About 3,000 people were killed. The terrorist attack was the worst in U.S. history.

In 2002, the New York State Legislature reorganized New York City's troubled public school system. The system, at one time under the control of the mayor, had been decentralized in 1969. The lawmakers returned power to the mayor and abolished the 32 local school boards.

In 2006, developers began constructing a skyscraper called One World Trade Center at the site where the World Trade Center once stood. Plans called for the tower to rise 1,776 feet (541 meters). The National September 11 Memorial opened on Sept. 11, 2011, at ground zero, the site of the World Trade Center attacks. The memorial includes twin reflecting pools that occupy the land where the twin towers once stood.

Michael Oreskes

Related articles in *World Book* include:

Business leaders

Baruch, Bernard M.	Rockefeller, John D.
Birdseye, Clarence	Sarnoff, David
Morgan, J. P.	Tiffany, Charles
Morgan, J. P., Jr.	Tiffany, Louis C.

Political leaders

Abzug, Bella S.	Morgenthau, Henry, Jr.
Arthur, Chester A.	Roosevelt, Franklin D.
Chisholm, Shirley	Roosevelt, Theodore
Dinkins, David N.	Smith, Alfred E.
Fish, Hamilton	Tilden, Samuel J.
Giuliani, Rudolph William	Tompkins, Daniel D.
La Guardia, Fiorello	Tweed, William M.
Lindsay, John V.	Wagner, Robert F.
Luce, Clare Boothe	Walker, James J.

Publishers and writers

Bennett, James G.	Melville, Herman
Bennett, James G., Jr.	Miller, Arthur
Bourke-White, Margaret	O'Neill, Eugene
Brisbane, Arthur	Pulitzer, Joseph
Dana, Charles A.	Ross, Harold W.
Greeley, Horace	Spingarn, Joel E.
Irving, Washington	Sturgeon, Theodore
Lippmann, Walter	Sulzberger, Arthur H.
Luce, Henry R.	

Other biographies

Berlin, Irving	Livingston, Robert R.
Burr, Aaron	Minuit, Peter
Copland, Aaron	Riis, Jacob A.
Gershwin, George	Rodgers, Richard
Gershwin, Ira	Streisand, Barbra
Goethals, George W.	Stuyvesant, Peter
Hammerstein, Oscar, II	Truth, Sojourner
Jay, John	Wald, Lillian D.
Kern, Jerome	Zenger, John P.
Lichtenstein, Roy	

Bridges and tunnels

Brooklyn Bridge	Hell Gate
George Washington Bridge	Hudson River tunnels

History

Federal Hall
Revolution, American (The war in the North)
September 11 terrorist attacks
Tammany, Society of
Triangle Shirtwaist Factory Fire

Institutions and buildings

American Museum of Natural History	Museum of Modern Art
	New York, City University of
American Stock Exchange	New York Stock Exchange
Columbia University	New York University
Empire State Building	Pierpont Morgan Library
Fordham University	Port Authority of New York
Frick Collection	and New Jersey
Guggenheim Museum	Saint Patrick's Cathedral
Hall of fame	Whitney Museum of American Art
Lincoln Center for the Performing Arts	can Art
	World Trade Center
Metropolitan Museum of Art	

Sections

Broadway	Liberty Island	Staten Island
Brooklyn	Manhattan Island	Wall Street
Ellis Island		

Other related articles

Cleopatra's Needles	New York (pictures)	Stock exchange Subway
Hudson River	Skyscraper	United Nations
	Statue of Liberty	(pictures)

Outline

I. The city
  A. Manhattan   E. Staten Island
  B. Brooklyn   F. Small islands
  C. The Bronx   G. Metropolitan area
  D. Queens
II. People
  A. Ethnic groups   C. Education
  B. Housing   D. Social problems
III. Economy
  A. Industry   D. Transportation
  B. Trade   E. Communications
  C. Finance
IV. Cultural life and recreation
  A. The arts   D. Museums
  B. Architecture   E. Parks
  C. Libraries   F. Sports
V. A visitor's guide
VI. Government
VII. History

Additional resources

Fodor's New York City. Fodor's Travel, published annually.
Homberger, Eric. *The Historical Atlas of New York City.* Rev. ed. Owl Bks., 2005.
McCully, Betsy. *City at the Water's Edge: A Natural History of New York.* Rivergate Bks., 2007.
Walsh, Frank. *New York City.* World Almanac Lib., 2004. Younger readers.
Walsh, Kevin. *Forgotten New York: Views of a Lost Metropolis.* HarperCollins, 2006.

New York Public Library is one of the most extensive library systems in the United States. It was founded in 1895. It operates four research libraries that depend heavily on private donations: the Stephen A. Schwarzman Building, which houses the library's humanities and social sciences collections; the Schomburg Center for Research in Black Culture; the New York Public Library for the Performing Arts; and the Science, Industry and Business Library. Public funds from New York City support branch libraries in the boroughs of Manhattan, the Bronx, and Staten Island. The research libraries have collections of books, manuscripts, films, and other materials for scholars. The branch libraries provide a variety of resources and services for local communities. The landmark main building of the library at Fifth Avenue and 42nd Street, now the Stephen A. Schwarzman Building, was designed by the American architects Thomas Hastings and John M. Carrère. Construction began in 1902, and the building was formally opened in 1911. The city has two other public library systems, the Brooklyn Public Library and the Queens Borough Public Library.

Critically reviewed by New York Public Library

New York State. See New York.

New York State Canal System connects the state's principal natural waterways. The state canal system was formally opened in 1918 as the New York State Barge Canal system. It updated and integrated four canals built between 1813 and 1828. The 524-mile (843-kilometer) system links two of the Great Lakes (Erie and Ontario), two of the Finger Lakes (Cayuga and Seneca), Lake Champlain, and navigable portions of the Mohawk and Hudson rivers. The Hudson River connects the system to New York City.

The New York State Legislature authorized construction of the canal system in 1903. It did so under strong pressure from business people anxious to create an enhanced alternative to the railroads. The project widened, deepened, and sometimes rerouted existing canals. The canal system has 57 locks, each 300 feet (91 meters) long and 43 ½ feet (13.3 meters) wide. It has a minimum overall channel depth of 12 feet (3.7 meters).

The system consists of four canals—the Erie, the Champlain, the Oswego, and the Cayuga and Seneca. The 348-mile (560-kilometer) Erie Canal connects Tonawanda on the Niagara River with Waterford on the Hudson River (see **Erie Canal**). The 60-mile (97-kilometer) Champlain Canal links Waterford with Whitehall on Lake Champlain. The 24-mile (39-kilometer) Oswego Canal links Oswego on Lake Ontario with Three Rivers on the Erie Canal. The 92-mile (148-kilometer) Cayuga and Seneca Canal extends from the Erie Canal at Montezuma to reach Ithaca at the southern end of Cayuga Lake and Watkins Glen at the southern end of Seneca Lake.

Since the 1950's, the use of the system for shipping cargo has declined, and its use for pleasure boating has increased. In 1992, the State Legislature transferred responsibility for the system from the Department of Transportation to the New York State Thruway Authority. It also took *Barge* out of the system's name to emphasize the recreational potential of the canals. Ray Bromley

New York Stock Exchange is the oldest stock exchange in the United States. Brokers and specialists on the exchange buy and sell stock in most of the largest U.S. corporations. They trade stock in many companies headquartered outside the United States.

The New York Stock Exchange, often called the NYSE or the Big Board, sets standards for those who want to trade there. All members must pass a written examination. They also must register with the Securities and Exchange Commission (SEC). The SEC is a United States government agency that administers and enforces federal laws governing the purchase and sale of stocks and bonds.

The New York Stock Exchange traces its roots to 1792, when a group of brokers and merchants gathered on Wall Street, in New York City, and agreed to trade securities on a commission basis. They called their agreement the Buttonwood Agreement after the buttonwood tree under which they met. The arrangement developed into a formal organization, the New York Stock and Exchange Board, in 1817. In 1863, the group changed its name to the New York Stock Exchange.

In 2006, the New York Stock Exchange merged with an electronic stock-trading company. The stock trades actually executed on the exchange had declined for years, and the NYSE wanted to gain a foothold in the fast-growing electronic-trading market. The two companies combined to form a new firm, the NYSE Group, Inc. The exchange became a for-profit, publicly traded company for the first time. In 2007, the holding company NYSE Euronext was created from the merger of the NYSE Group and Euronext N.V. The company NYSE Euronext now operates the New York Stock Exchange and the Euronext exchange, a European stock market. In 2008, NYSE Euronext acquired the American Stock Exchange. Critically reviewed by the New York Stock Exchange

See also **Stock exchange.**

New York University, often referred to as NYU, is a private institution of higher education in New York City. The university is not associated with any religion. NYU is one of the largest privately supported universities in the United States. The university was founded in 1831.

New York University is made up of a number of schools and colleges that operate at various centers in the borough of Manhattan. NYU is also formally affiliated with the Polytechnic Institute of NYU in Brooklyn.

The main NYU campus is around Washington Square Park in Greenwich Village. The Institute of Fine Arts is near the Metropolitan Museum of Art on the Upper East Side. The university operates a medical complex on the east side of Manhattan. The university's sports teams are called the Violets. The New York University website at http://www.nyu.edu offers additional information.

Critically reviewed by New York University

WORLD BOOK map

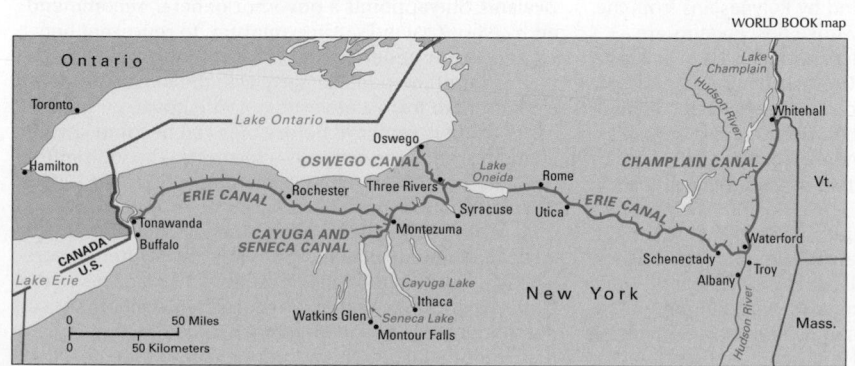

The New York State Canal System consists of the Erie Canal and three other canals. The system connects the principal natural waterways of New York and provides the shortest all-water route between the Atlantic Ocean and the Great Lakes.

Downtown Auckland lies on the North Island on a strip of land between two harbors. Auckland is New Zealand's largest city. Its tallest landmark is the 1,076-foot (328-meter) Sky Tower, *center.*

New Zealand

New Zealand is an island country in the southwest Pacific Ocean. It lies about 1,000 miles (1,600 kilometers) southeast of Australia. New Zealand consists of two main islands, called the North Island and the South Island, plus a number of smaller islands. The country belongs to a large island group called Polynesia. Wellington is the capital of New Zealand, and Auckland is the largest city.

New Zealand was first settled by Polynesians from the middle South Pacific region whose descendants are called the Maori. Many scholars think these Polynesians arrived by about the A.D. 1200's. British immigrants began settling in New Zealand during the early 1800's, and the country became part of the British Empire in 1840. Today, it is an independent member of the Commonwealth of Nations, an association of countries that replaced the empire.

New Zealand's current population represents many cultures. They include the Maori and other Polynesian groups; descendants of English, Irish, and other western European colonial settlers; and more recent immigrants from Asia, Africa, and eastern Europe.

New Zealand is a beautiful country of snow-capped mountains, green lowlands, beaches, and many lakes and waterfalls. No place is more than 80 miles (130 kilometers) from the coast, and most places have striking views of mountains or hills.

Government

New Zealand is a constitutional monarchy. Queen Elizabeth II of the United Kingdom is also Queen of New Zealand. She appoints a governor general, recommended by New Zealand's prime minister, to represent her. The governor general's main function is to arrange for the leader of the political party with the most support in Parliament to form a government. The governor general's consent is required before bills can become law, but this requirement is normally a formality. The legislature, prime minister, and Cabinet run the government.

The constitution. New Zealand has no formal written constitution. The country's unwritten constitution is a combination of *precedent* (tradition) and written material closely modeled on the constitutional practices of the United Kingdom. Written parts of New Zealand's constitution include Magna Carta, a 1215 document that put the king of England under the rule of law, and the

Facts in brief

Capital: Wellington.
Official languages: English, Maori, and New Zealand Sign Language.
Area: 104,454 mi² (270,534 km²). *North Island*—44,701 mi² (115,777 km²); *South Island*—58,385 mi² (151,215 km²); *Stewart Island*—674 mi² (1,746 km²); *Chatham Islands*—372 mi² (963 km²); other islands—322 mi² (837 km²). *Coastline*—9,404 mi (15,134 km).
Elevation: *Highest*—Mount Cook, 12,316 ft (3,754 m) above sea level. *Lowest*—sea level along the coast.
Population: *Estimated 2012 population*—4,455,000; density, 43 per mi² (16 per km²); distribution, 86 percent urban, 14 percent rural. 2006 census—4,027,947.
Chief products: *Agriculture*—apples, barley, beef, dairy products, eggs, grapes, kiwi fruit, lamb, mutton, onions, potatoes, wool. *Fishing industry*—blue grenadier (hoki). *Forestry*—Monterey pine. *Manufacturing*—food products, machinery, paper, textiles, transportation equipment, wood products. *Mining*—coal, gold, ironsand, limestone.
Anthems: "God Defend New Zealand" (national); "God Save the Queen" (royal).
Money: *Basic unit*—New Zealand dollar. One hundred cents equal one dollar.

New Zealand's flag, officially adopted in 1902, features the British Union Flag and four stars of the constellation Southern Cross against a royal blue background.

Coat of arms. Symbols on the shield represent the value of farming, mining, and trade to New Zealand. The crown represents the British monarch, who is also the monarch of New Zealand.

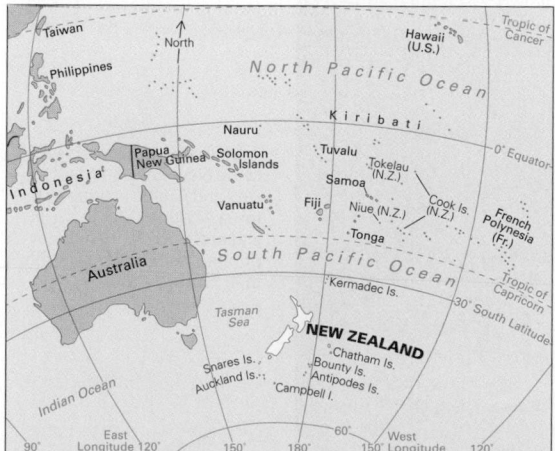

WORLD BOOK map
New Zealand, a country in the Pacific Ocean, lies about 1,000 miles (1,600 kilometers) southeast of Australia. New Zealand consists of the North Island, the South Island, and smaller islands.

Habeas Corpus Act of 1679, which protects people from being imprisoned unjustly.

The legislature. New Zealand's Parliament consists of the monarch, represented by the governor general, and an elected House of Representatives, also called the Parliament. The House usually has 120 members. The size of the House may change slightly depending on the votes cast in a general election. Voters directly elect 69 House members. Several of the directly elected seats are reserved for Maori. The rest of the House is chosen on the basis of *proportional representation.* Under this method, each political party that receives at least 5 percent of the popular vote gets a number of seats based on the percentage of the vote it receives. A parliamentary election must be held every three years or sooner. All citizens and permanent residents at least 18 years old may vote in general elections.

The prime minister and Cabinet. The leader of the political party that wins the most seats in a parliamentary election becomes prime minister. The leading party may also form a coalition government with other parties if it does not gain a majority in Parliament.

On the advice of the prime minister, the governor general appoints the Cabinet to run the various government departments. The Cabinet members, called *ministers,* are members of Parliament. The prime minister and the Cabinet are called the Government. The Government proposes most new legislation in Parliament. If Parliament votes in favor of the bill, it becomes law.

Political parties. The largest political parties in New Zealand are the National Party and the Labour Party. Traditionally, the Labour Party has favored government control and public regulation of industry, whereas the National Party has favored free enterprise. Since 1984, however, both parties have adopted similar economic policies.

Local government. New Zealand has a *unitary* system of government. In this system, Parliament has the power to create and authorize local governments. The country's local government structure provides for 11 elected regional councils and 67 territorial authorities. Agencies created by the central government provide community services, including land-use planning, water supply and waste disposal, recreation, and cultural facilities. Private companies deliver some of these community services.

Ombudsman is an official selected by Parliament to investigate complaints by citizens against government departments and related organizations. If an ombudsman believes a complaint is justified, he or she reports it to the department concerned along with any recommendation for action.

Courts. The Supreme Court of New Zealand is the country's highest court. The Supreme Court consists of a chief justice and four other judges. The Court of Appeal hears mainly cases that have been appealed from a lower court.

Below the Court of Appeal in New Zealand are the High Court and district courts. The High Court deals with major crimes, important civil claims, and appeals from lower courts. It also reviews administrative actions. District courts serve specific regions. Justices of the peace and community magistrates hear traffic and minor criminal charges. A number of courts also have special functions, such as the Coroners Court, Environment Court, Family Court, Maori Land Court, and Youth Court.

Armed forces of New Zealand are called the New Zealand Defence Force (NZDF). The NZDF consists of a navy, army, and air force, together with civilian employees. Military service is voluntary.

Overseas territories. New Zealand governs two overseas territories. They are Ross Dependency, a part of Antarctica; and Tokelau, an island group northeast of New Zealand. New Zealand formerly governed the Cook Islands and the island of Niue. The Cook Islands became self-governing in 1965 and Niue in 1974. But the people of these islands are still considered citizens of New Zealand, and the country still has some responsibility for the islands' defense and foreign affairs.

People

New Zealand has two main ethnic groups, Maori and whites of European ancestry. Maori make up about 15 percent of the population and form the country's largest minority group. About 70 percent of the people are of European ancestry. The number of people of other Pacific Island or Asian ancestry is growing. People of non-Maori ancestry are called *Pakeha (PAH keh hah)*. Many Pakeha are descended from British colonists who came to the country during the 1800's, and so many New Zealand customs resemble British customs. However, New Zealand has developed its own sense of identity as a country of both British and Polynesian heritage.

New Zealand has three official languages: English, Maori, and New Zealand Sign Language. English is the most widely used. Other languages spoken include Cook Island Maori, Dutch, Greek, Italian, Niuean, Samoan, and Tongan.

Way of life

City life. New Zealand's cities offer a wide range of economic and social opportunities. City dwellers can work in New Zealand's business, communication, manufacturing, and shipping industries. Urban New Zealanders enjoy easy access to the fine arts, education, entertainment, and night life. New Zealand's cities are fairly uncrowded. Some city dwellers live in high-rise apartment buildings, but most own their own homes.

Rural life in New Zealand centers mainly around agricultural activities such as raising sheep and cattle and growing fruits, vegetables, and grain. Many people in the northern part of New Zealand's North Island raise dairy cattle. In other parts of North Island and on South Island, beef cattle and sheep are more common. Farmers produce large amounts of apples, kiwi fruit, and other fruits. Vineyards mainly in the southern regions of North Island, the northern regions of South Island, and the eastern regions of both islands grow grapes and produce New Zealand wine.

Food and drink. New Zealand's cooking combines British traditions with foods grown in the country. Traditionally, New Zealanders have favored beef, mutton, and venison served as steaks, as sausages, or in meat pies. But vegetarianism is increasing in popularity. New Zealand's coastal waters offer an abundance of seafood. Dairy products such as milk, cheese, and ice cream are important foods. A favorite dish is a sweet meringue dessert called *pavlova*. Tea, coffee, beer, and wine are popular beverages.

Recreation. Sports and outdoor activities are important forms of recreation in New Zealand. New Zealanders enjoy Rugby Union, a form of rugby football generally regarded as the national sport. New Zealand's national Rugby Union football team is called the All Blacks. Cricket is another popular spectator sport. In the summer, New Zealand's mountainous terrain offers mountaineering, hiking, and climbing. In the winter, skiing and other snow sports are popular. New Zealand's

A Maori woodcarver works at the New Zealand Maori Arts and Crafts Institute in Rotorua. Modern Maori artists and craftspeople have incorporated traditional styles into their work.

Rugby Union football is widely popular in New Zealand and is regarded as the national sport. The country's national Rugby Union team is the All Blacks, shown here in black uniforms.

AP/Wide World

coastal waters attract many boaters and surfers. Horse racing has always been a favored leisure activity.

Fishing and hunting are popular pastimes. Rainbow trout and brown trout abound in New Zealand's lakes and rivers. The North Island's warm coastal waters provide excellent line fishing and spear fishing. Boating offers the additional attraction of deep-sea fishing for marlin, shark, or tuna. The chief game birds for hunters are duck, swan, pheasant, quail, and geese.

Religion. The Anglican Church is the largest religious group in New Zealand. Approximately 14 percent of the people are Anglicans. About 13 percent are Roman Catholics, and 10 percent are Presbyterians. New Zealand society has become more *secular* (nonreligious). At the 2006 census, 35 in 100 people reported no religious affiliation.

Education. New Zealand has public schools funded by the state and private schools, a majority of which are church sponsored. All children from the ages of 6 to 16 must attend school, though most children begin at the age of 5. Students who live in isolated areas or who have special physical or psychological needs may receive instruction from the Correspondence School in Wellington. In addition, the school serves adults and pupils who wish to study courses not offered at their local schools. Almost all of the adults in New Zealand can read and write.

The country has eight universities. They are Massey University in Palmerstown North; Victoria University of Wellington; Lincoln University, near Christchurch; the University of Auckland; Auckland University of Technology; the University of Canterbury in Christchurch; the University of Otago in Dunedin; and the University of Waikato in Hamilton. A number of technical and professional institutions also offer degrees. Institutions known as *wananga* provide technical and university-level programs for Maori students, with an emphasis on Maori culture and language.

The arts. New Zealand literature first gained widespread attention in the early and middle 1900's. Katherine Mansfield wrote sensitive short stories about her childhood in New Zealand. Sylvia Ashton-Warner is known for her fiction and autobiographical books that draw upon her experiences as a teacher in rural New Zealand. Keri Hulme won fame for her fiction and poetry that deal with the language and culture of the Maori. Other important New Zealand writers include James K. Baxter, Janet Frame, Ngaio Marsh, and Frank Sargeson.

Important New Zealand painters include Colin McCahon, Rita Angus, and Toss Woollaston. All three were leaders in introducing modern styles to New Zealand art in the 1900's. McCahon painted intense landscapes and religious scenes. Angus created vivid portraits and landscapes in both oil and water color. Woollaston painted landscapes as well as portraits of family and friends. Maori have maintained a long tradition of folk art, especially carefully detailed woodcarvings and intricate, swirling tattoos. Modern Maori artists have incorporated traditional Maori styles into painting and sculpture.

In music, opera singer Kiri Te Kanawa won international acclaim as one of the finest sopranos of the later 1900's. The New Zealand Symphony Orchestra is internationally recognized. The Royal New Zealand Ballet, established in 1953, is the oldest professional dance company in the country. The New Zealand School of Dance and Te Kura Toi Whakaari o Aotearoa: New Zealand Drama School offer courses in the performing arts. There are many local theater and music groups.

New Zealand has many public museums and art galleries. New Zealand's national museum—Te Papa Tongarewa, Museum of New Zealand—opened in Wellington in 1998. The New Zealand Film Archive collects and preserves a national collection of New Zealand's motion-picture history. The New Zealand Historic Places Trust preserves archaeological sites, historic areas and buildings, and sites of special significance to Maori.

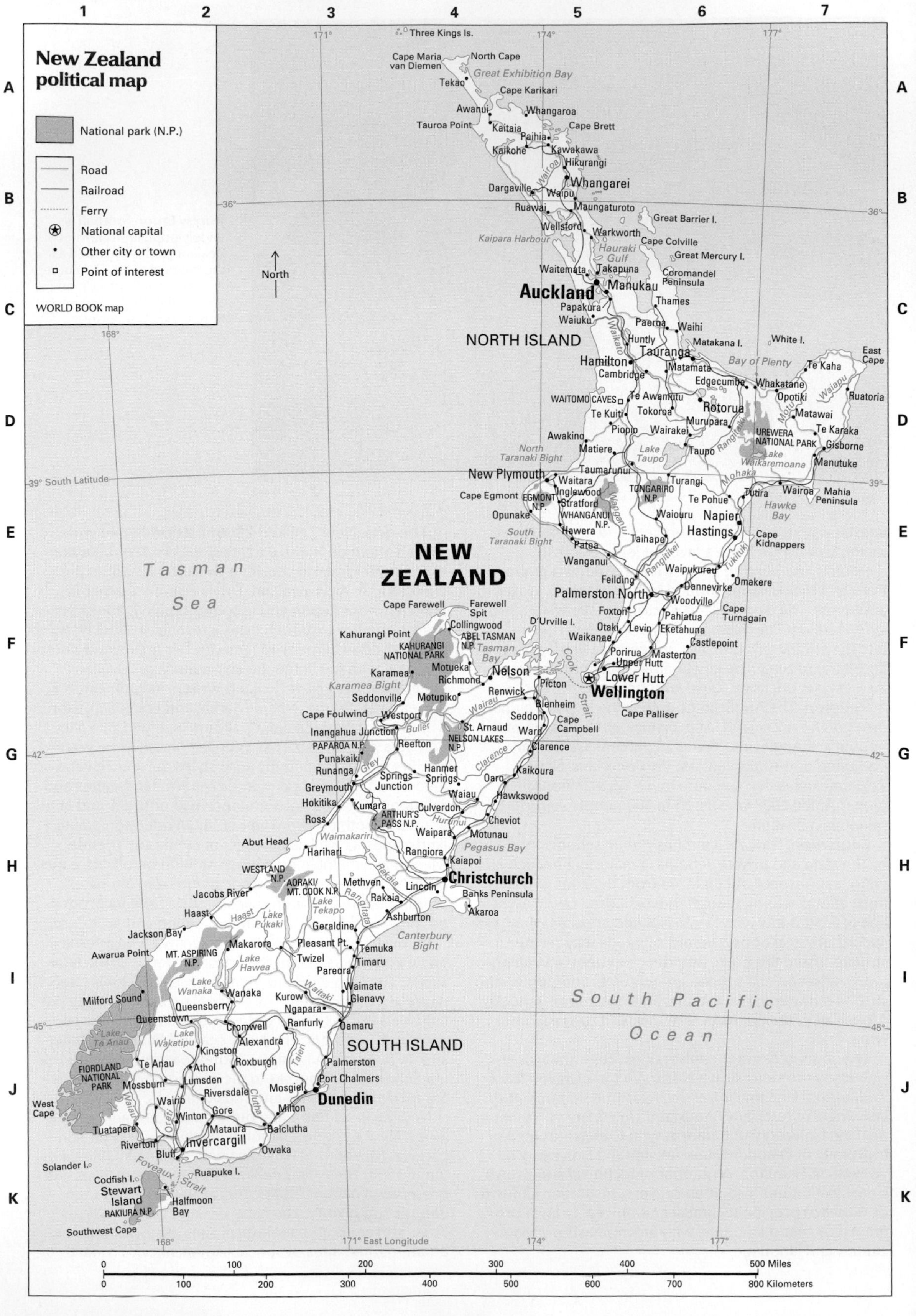

New Zealand political map

National park (N.P.)

Road
Railroad
Ferry
National capital
Other city or town
Point of interest

WORLD BOOK map

North

1 2 3 4 5 6 7

Three Kings Is.

Cape Maria van Diemen
North Cape
Great Exhibition Bay
Tekao
Cape Karikari
Awanui
Whangaroa
Tauroa Point
Kaitaia
Paihia
Cape Brett
Kaikohe
Kawekawa
Hikurangi
Dargaville
Whangarei
Waipu
Ruawai
Maungaturoto
Great Barrier I.
Wellsford
Warkworth
Cape Colville
Kaipara Harbour
Waitemata
Hauraki Gulf
Takapuna
Great Mercury I.
Coromandel Peninsula
Auckland
Manukau
Papakura
Thames
Waiuku
Paeroa
Waihi
Matakana I.
White I.
NORTH ISLAND
Huntly
Tauranga
East Cape
Hamilton
Matamata
Bay of Plenty
Cambridge
Edgecumbe
Whakatane
Te Kaha
WAITOMO CAVES
Te Awamutu
Opotiki
Ruatoria
Te Kuiti
Tokoroa
Rotorua
Matawai
Piopio
Wairakei
Murupara
Te Karaka
Awakino
Matiere
Lake Taupo
Taupo
UREWERA NATIONAL PARK
Gisborne
North Taranaki Bight
Taumarunui
Lake Waikaremoana
Manutuke
New Plymouth
Waitara
Turangi
Mohaka
Cape Egmont
Inglewood
TONGARIRO N.P.
Te Pohue
Tutira
Wairoa
Mahia Peninsula
EGMONT N.P.
Stratford
Napier
Opunake
WHANGANUI N.P.
Waiouru
Hastings
Hawera
Cape Kidnappers
NEW ZEALAND
Patea
Taihape
Wanganui
Waipukurau
Feilding
Dannevirke
Omakere
Palmerston North
Woodville
Cape Turnagain
Foxton
Pahiatua
Cape Farewell
Farewell Spit
Otaki
Levin
Ekatahuna
Castlepoint
Collingwood
D'Urville I.
Waikanae
Kahurangi Point
ABEL TASMAN N.P.
Tasman Bay
Porirua
Masterton
KAHURANGI NATIONAL PARK
Motueka
Upper Hutt
Karamea
Motupiko
Richmond
Nelson
Picton
Lower Hutt
Cook Strait
Wellington
Karamea Bight
Renwick
Cape Palliser
Seddonville
Motupiko
Blenheim
Cape Foulwind
Westport
Seddon
Cape Campbell
Inangahua Junction
St. Arnaud
Ward
PAPAROA N.P.
Reefton
NELSON LAKES N.P.
Punakaiki
Clarence
Runanga
Hanmer Springs
Clarence
Greymouth
Springs Junction
Kaikoura
Hokitika
Kumara
Waiau
Oaro
Hawkswood
Ross
ARTHUR'S PASS N.P.
Culverden
Cheviot
Abut Head
Waimakariri
Waipara
Motunau
Harihari
Rangiora
Pegasus Bay
WESTLAND N.P.
Kaiapoi
Methven
Lincoln
Christchurch
Jacobs River
AORAKI/ MT. COOK N.P.
Rakaia
Banks Peninsula
Haast
Lake Tekapo
Ashburton
Akaroa
Jackson Bay
Lake Pukaki
Geraldine
Canterbury Bight
Makarora
Pleasant Pt.
MT. ASPIRING N.P.
Temuka
Awarua Point
Lake Hawea
Twizel
Timaru
Pareora
Milford Sound
Lake Wanaka
Wanaka
Kurow
Waimate
Queensberry
Ngapara
Glenavy
Queenstown
Ranfurly
Oamaru
Lake Wakatipu
Cromwell
SOUTH ISLAND
South Pacific Ocean
FIORDLAND NATIONAL PARK
Alexandra
Palmerston
Lake Te Anau
Kingston
Roxburgh
Port Chalmers
Te Anau
Athol
Mosgiel
West Cape
Mossburn
Lumsden
Milton
Dunedin
Wairio
Riversdale
Winton
Gore
Tuatapere
Mataura
Balclutha
Riverton
Invercargill
Owaka
Bluff
Solander I.
Ruapuke I.
Codfish I.
Stewart Island
Halfmoon Bay
RAKIURA N.P.
Southwest Cape

Tasman Sea

171° 174° 177°
36°
168°
39° South Latitude
42°
45°
171° East Longitude

0 100 200 300 400 500 Miles
0 100 200 300 400 500 600 700 800 Kilometers

New Zealand map index

Main islands

Map key	Island	Population	Area In mi²	In km²
C 5	**North Island**	3,059,418	44,701	115,777
J 3	**South Island**	967,908	58,385	151,215
K 1	**Stewart Island**	402	674	1,746

Cities and towns

Alexandra ....J   2
Ashburton* .....27,372 ..H   4
Ashhurst† ....F   5
Auckland 404,658
..........†1,208,094 ..C   5
Balclutha ....J   3
Birkenhead† C   5
Blenheim§ .....28,527 ..G   5
Bluff ....K   2
Cambridge ....D   5
Carterton*† ....7,098 ..F   6
Christchurch ..348,435 ..H   4
Cromwell I   2
Dannevirke ....F   6
Dargaville ....B   5
Devonport† C   5
Dunedin ....118,683 ..J   3
East Coast Bays† C   5
Eastbourne† ....F   5
Ellerslie† C   5
Feilding§ .....13,887 ..E   5
Gisborne* ......44,460 ..D   7
Glen Eden† C   5
Gore* ....12,108 ..J   2
Green Island† ....J   3
Greymouth§ ....9,672 ..G   3
Hamilton .....129,249 ..C   5
Hastings* ....70,839 ..E   6
Havelock North† ....E   6
Henderson† C   5
Heretaunga-
Pinehaven† ....F   5
Hokitika ....G   3
Hornby† ....H   4
Howick† C   5
Huntly C   5
Invercargill ....50,328 ..K   2
Kaiapoi ....H   4
Kaikohe ....B   4
Kaitaia ....A   4
Kapiti Coast*† ..46,200 ..F   5
Kawerau*† ......6,921 ..D   6
Levin§ ....19,134 ..F   5
Lower Hutt ....97,701 ..F   5
Lyttelton† ....H   4
Manukau .....328,968 ..C   5
Marton* ......22,623 ..F   6
Masterton* ....22,623 ..F   6
Matamata ....D   6
Morrinsville† C   6
Mosgiel ....J   3
Motueka ....F   4
Mount Albert† C   5
Mount Eden† C   5
Mount Maun-
ganui† C   6
Mount Roskill† C   5
Mount Wel-
lington† C   5
Napier ....55,359 ..E   6

Nelson ....42,891 ..F   4
New
Plymouth* ....68,901 ..E   5
Ngaruawahia† C   5
North
Shore† ......205,608 ..C   5
Northcote† C   5
Oamaru§ ....12,681 ..I   3
One Tree Hill† C   5
Onehunga† C   5
Opotiki* ....8,973 ..D   7
Otahuhu† C   5
Otaki ....F   5
Paeroa C   6
Palmerston
North ....75,543 ..F   5
Papakura† ....45,183 ..C   5
Papatoetoe† C   5
Petone† ....F   5
Picton ....F   5
Porirua ......48,546 ..F   5
Port Chalmers ....J   3
Pukekohe†§ ...22,518 ..C   5
Putaruru† ....D   6
Queenstown I   2
Rangiora ....H   4
Riccarton† ....H   4
Richmond ....F   4
Rotorua* ....65,901 ..D   6
St. Kilda† ....J   3
Sockburn† ....H   4
Southland*† ....28,440 ..K   1
Stratford* ....8,892 ..E   5
Takapuna C   5
Taumarunui ....D   5
Taupo* ....32,418 ..D   6
Tauranga ....103,635 ..C   6
Tawa† ....F   5
Te Awamutu ....D   6
Te Kuiti ....D   5
Te Puke† ....D   6
Temuka I   3
Thames C   6
Timaru* ....42,867 ..I   3
Tokoroa§ ......13,527 ..D   6
Turangi ....E   6
Upper Hutt ......38,415 ..F   5
Waihi ....F   5
Waikanae ....F   5
Wainuiomata† ....F   5
Waipukurau ....E   6
Wairoa* ....8,484 ..E   7
Waitakere† ....186,444 ..C   5
Waitara ....E   5
Waitemata C   5
Waiuku C   5
Wanganui* .....42,636 ..E   5
Wellington 179,466
...............‡360,624 ..F   5
Westport ....G   3
Whakatane† .....33,300 ..D   7
Whangarei* .....74,463 ..B   5

*Population of district, which may include rural areas as well as the city or town.
†Does not appear on the map; key shows general location.
‡Metropolitan area, including suburbs.
§Population of *urban areas*—population centers with no administrative or legal basis.
Source: 2006 census, data are unavailable for places without populations.

The land

New Zealand lies in the southwest Pacific Ocean. The North Island and the South Island are New Zealand's largest islands. They extend in a curve more than 1,000 miles (1,600 kilometers) long and cover about 99 percent of the country's total area. Cook Strait, which is about 16 miles (26 kilometers) wide at its narrowest point, separates the islands.

The North Island can be divided into three main land regions: (1) the Northern Peninsulas and Waikato Basin, (2) the Volcanic Region and Western Hill Country, and (3) the Eastern Hills.

The Northern Peninsulas and Waikato Basin occupy most of the northern part of the island. This region has forests, rich lowlands, and undeveloped hill country. In the lower lands, many farmers grow citrus or kiwi fruits or raise dairy cattle. Beef cattle and sheep are raised in the hill country. Long, sandy beaches line the west coast, and many inlets mark the east coast.

The Volcanic Region and Western Hill Country cover the western half of the island south of the Northern Peninsulas and Waikato Basin. Much of the region consists of volcanic rock. A large plateau covered with soft, yellow-brown soil made up of crushed *pumice*—the porous stone thrown off by volcanoes—rises along the eastern part of the region in the center of the island.

This region has several active volcanoes, including Mount Tongariro, and the highest peak on the island, 9,175-foot (2,797-meter) Mount Ruapehu. This region also has many hot springs and geysers.

The Eastern Hills occupy the eastern and southern parts of North Island. A mountain system runs through the region from East Cape to Cook Strait. The eastern slopes consist mainly of rugged hills. Ranchers use this land for grazing sheep and beef cattle. Lowlands along the east coast are used for growing vegetables and fruits. To the west of the mountains are lowlands and plains. Farmers raise dairy cattle, other livestock, and crops in this region.

The South Island has three main regions: (1) the Southern Alps and High Country, (2) the Canterbury Plains, and (3) the Otago Plateaus and Basins.

The Southern Alps and High Country cover most of the island. The highest peak in New Zealand, 12,316-foot (3,754-meter) Aoraki/Mount Cook, rises in the Southern Alps. *Aoraki,* also spelled *Aorangi,* is the Maori name for the mountain. It is usually translated as *cloud piercer.*

© Gerald Cubitt

Majestic Aoraki/Mount Cook, New Zealand's highest mountain, soars 12,316 feet (3,754 meters) on the South Island. Aoraki/Mount Cook and other peaks attract many climbers.

Physical features

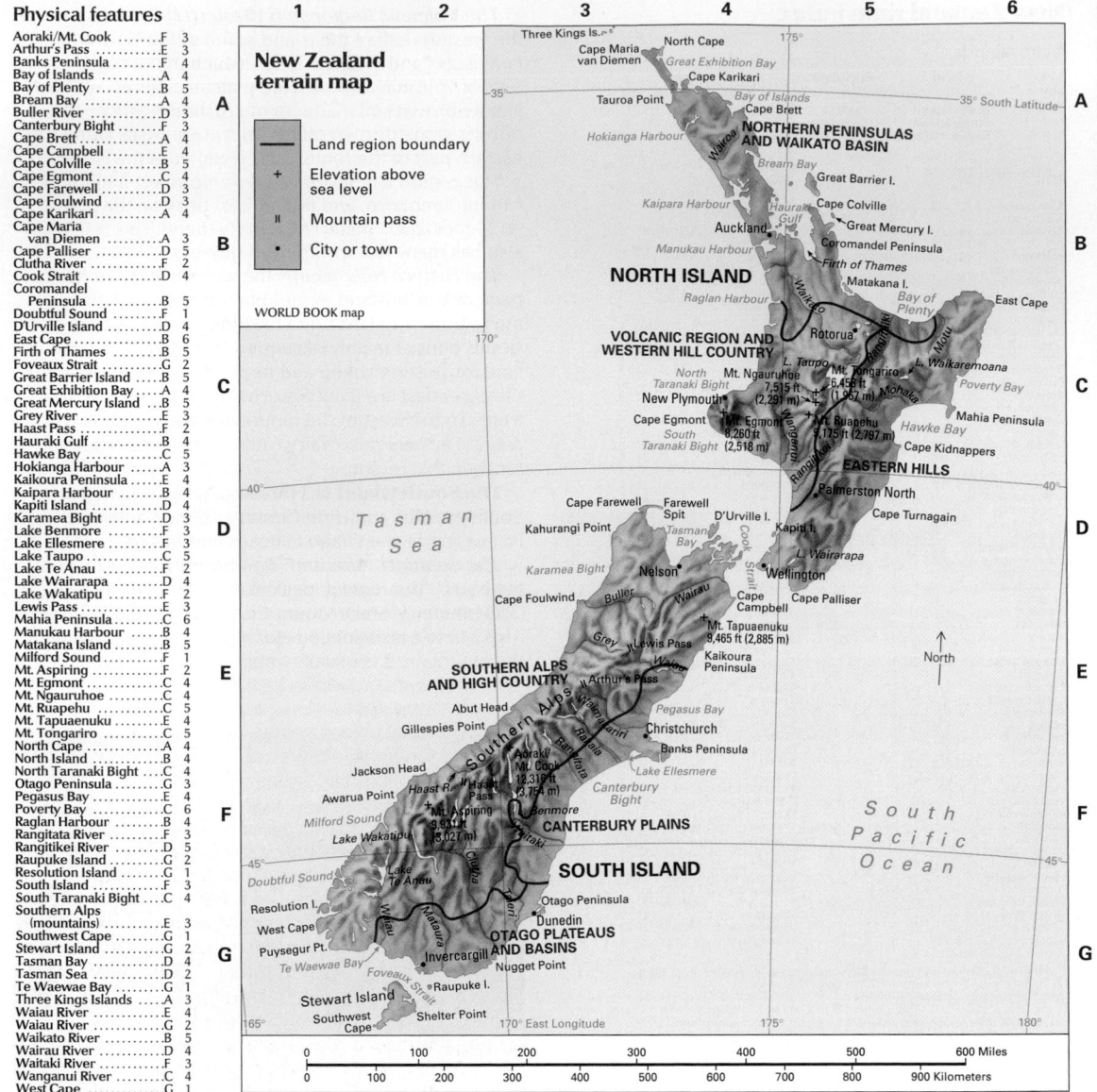

The Aoraki/Mount Cook region has some of New Zealand's most spectacular scenery. Glaciers lie on mountain slopes high above thick, green forests. Sparkling lakes nestle in valleys throughout the regions.

The western slopes of the Southern Alps and High Country region are forested, rainy, and rugged. The eastern slopes are lower and much less rainy. Along the southwest coast, long inlets of the sea called *fiords* cut into the land, creating a jagged coastline. Forested mountains border many of the fiords.

The Canterbury Plains lie along the east-central coast of the South Island. They form New Zealand's largest area of flat or nearly flat land and make up the chief grain-growing region. The plains are laid out in a patch-work of fields on which farmers grow barley, fodder crops, oats, and wheat. The plains are also an important region for raising sheep.

The Otago Plateaus and Basins lie in the southeast corner of the South Island. The region has plains and rolling hills, where crops and livestock are raised.

Other islands. Stewart Island lies about 20 miles (32 kilometers) south of the South Island. Scrubby bushes cover most of the island. Most of the people earn their living by fishing and oyster gathering. The Chatham Islands lie about 530 miles (850 kilometers) east of the South Island. Most Chatham Islanders are Maori. Fishing and sheep farming are their main occupations.

Other islands and island groups are the Antipodes Islands, the Auckland Islands, the Bounty Islands, Campbell Island, the Kermadec Islands, the Snares Islands, Solander Island, and the Three Kings Islands. Of these, only Campbell Island has a permanent population.

Lakes, rivers, and waterfalls. New Zealand has many rivers, lakes, and waterfalls. In the alpine regions of the South Island, mountain snows and glaciers feed many rivers. The North Island has New Zealand's longest river, the Waikato, flowing 264 miles (425 kilometers). The island also has the largest lake, Lake Taupo, which covers 234 square miles (606 square kilometers) and is a vacation area famous for trout fishing.

On both islands, the rivers rise in the mountains and flow down to the sea. Most of the rivers flow swiftly and are difficult to navigate. The Clutha River on the South Island carries the largest volume of water. The rapid flow of the rivers makes them important sources of hydroelectric power.

New Zealand has many waterfalls. Sutherland Falls tumbles 1,904 feet (580 meters) down a mountain near Milford Sound on the South Island.

Animal life. The islands of New Zealand were isolated for about 80 million years. As a result, the animal life is unique but limited in variety. There are many species of beetles, flies, and moths. The islands have several types of frogs, geckos, and skinks, and an ancient reptile called the tuatara. The only native land mammals are bats, but dolphins, seals, and whales live in the surrounding ocean. There are also many species of coastal and wetland birds. The flightless kiwi lives only in New Zealand. *Kiwi* has become a nickname for a New Zealander. The kea is a parrot noted for its playfulness.

Settlers introduced many animal species from other lands. Maori ancestors introduced the dog and one type of rat to the islands. Europeans brought many other animals, including deer and rabbits, as well as cattle, pigs, and sheep. Wallabies and brush-tailed possums came from Australia. The new species have depleted the native species to the extent that many are now severely endangered.

Plant life. About 7,000 years ago, rain forests covered most of what is now New Zealand. In the relatively dry Otago Plains in the south of the South Island, grasses and shrubs flourished. As the climate cooled, plant species sensitive to frost diminished, while more cold-tolerant species thrived, especially in upland areas. Low forests developed on the South Island. On the North Island, broadleaf and cone-bearing trees, such as the kauri, became more widespread. Beech forests grow on the cooler uplands of both islands. Since 1900, people have introduced many foreign trees into New Zealand.

Earthquakes. New Zealand has about 100 earthquakes every year that are strong enough to be felt. The country's most disastrous earthquake occurred near Hawke Bay in 1931. It killed 256 people and badly damaged the cities of Hastings and Napier.

Climate

The country has a mild, moist climate. New Zealand lies south of the equator, so its seasons are opposite those of the Northern Hemisphere. July is New Zealand's coldest month, and January and February are the warmest months. The country's mild climate results from ocean breezes that bring warmth in winter and cool temperatures in summer. Average summer temperatures range from about 59 °F (15 °C) to about 69 °F (20 °C), but summer temperatures occasionally rise above 90 °F (32 °C). Average winter temperatures range from about 35 °F (2 °C) to about 53 °F (12 °C).

Climate regions. On the North Island, the northern tip of the Northland Peninsula is warm and humid all year. The island's central plateau has hot, sunny weather in summer and sharp frosts with occasional snow in winter. Wellington lies exposed to the frequent gales of Cook Strait. On the South Island, the rainy west contrasts with the drier east. Southern New Zealand is cooler than northern New Zealand.

Rainfall. The mountains chiefly control the distribution of rainfall in New Zealand. Winds from the west carry moisture from the ocean. This moisture falls as rain on the western slopes of the mountain ranges. Almost the entire west coast of the South Island averages more than 80 inches (200 centimeters) of rain a year. Milford Sound, on the South Island, averages about 260 inches (660 centimeters) of rain each year. East of the mountains, the winds lose most of their moisture. Some eastern regions in the country average less than 20 inches (51 centimeters) of rain a year. Snow seldom falls in lowland areas, though some mountain peaks remain snow-capped all year.

Economy

For many years, New Zealand's economy depended on agriculture. Agriculture remains important, but changing domestic and international conditions have caused a shift in economic activity. Today, the main economic sector is service industries. Service industries account for over two-thirds of both New Zealand's employment and its *gross domestic product*—the total value of all goods and services produced within the country in a year. Tourism is important to New Zealand's economy. Millions of people visit from Australia, the United Kingdom, the United States, and other countries.

Manufacturing. Much of New Zealand's manufacturing is dedicated to making dairy products, meat, paper, wood, and other agricultural and forest products. Factories also manufacture machinery, textiles, and transportation equipment. These industries tend to be based in the larger commercial centers, especially Auckland. Since the mid-1900's, manufactured products have become an important export.

Agriculture. New Zealand's agriculture centers on raising cattle and sheep for dairy products, meat, and wool. These products are among the country's leading exports. New Zealand is one of the world's leading producers of both milk and wool. Cattle are raised throughout the North Island, and many sheep are raised in the Eastern Hills. On the South Island, cattle and sheep are both primarily raised in the Canterbury Plains and at the southern end of the island. Chickens provide eggs and meat. The major crops include apples, barley, grapes, kiwi fruit, onions, potatoes, and wheat.

Mining. New Zealand contains a wide variety of minerals. The country is probably best known for its gold, but the mining industry also produces *ironsand* (sand containing iron ore), clay, coal, dimension stone, lime, limestone, marble, natural gas, oil, salt, silver, and other mineral products.

Forestry. Much of New Zealand's *indigenous* (native) forests grow in the mountain regions on the west coast of the South Island. A small percentage of the country's total forest production is harvested from indigenous forests. The vast majority of the timber comes from planted forests, mostly the fast-growing Monterey pine. The logs are manufactured into plywood, wood pulp, veneer, and other wood products.

Fishing industry. New Zealand's exclusive economic fishing zone is one of the largest in the world, an area about 15 times larger than the country's land mass. Valuable commercial fish include blue grenadier (also called hoki), jack mackerels, orange roughy, snoek (also called barracouta), southern blue whiting, squid, and tuna. Mussels, oysters, and salmon are important aquaculture products.

Energy. Water power provides over half of New Zealand's electric power. Underground steam in the North Island's volcanic area has become an increasingly important source of power. Most of the remaining power comes from coal, natural gas, and oil. Wind power supplies a small, but growing, amount of energy.

International trade. New Zealand's leading trade partners are Australia, China, Japan, and the United States. The country also conducts trade with Germany, Malaysia, Singapore, South Korea, and the United Kingdom. New Zealand's leading exports include aluminum, dairy products, fish, fruits, machinery, meat, wood and wood products, and wool. The country imports aircraft, machinery, petroleum and petroleum products, and plastics.

Transportation. New Zealand has tens of thousands of miles of roads and millions of motor vehicles. The country also has an extensive rail system to carry both passengers and freight.

Air transportation is important to New Zealand. Air New Zealand is the major domestic airline. The country's largest international airports are in Auckland, Christchurch, and Wellington. Though international air links have helped overcome the country's geographical isolation, New Zealand still relies heavily on sea transport for overseas trade. Auckland is the nation's chief seaport.

Communication is one of the most rapidly growing sectors of the New Zealand economy. Television New Zealand operates two television channels, and Radio New Zealand Limited operates a radio network. The country also has privately owned radio and television stations. Maori language radio and television stations promote Maori culture.

New Zealand has many daily newspapers, most of which are published in the evening. *The New Zealand Herald,* based in Auckland, has the largest circulation.

History

New Zealand's first settlers, the people who became known as Maori, migrated from the islands of eastern Polynesia. These people probably had established settlements along the coast by the A.D. 1200's. They survived by fishing, hunting, and raising crops. Maori did not see themselves as one nation. Instead, they considered themselves members of their *hapu* (sub-tribe) and *iwi* (tribe). These groups jealously defended their territories. Wars among them were common.

Early European contact. In 1642, the Dutch explorer Abel Janszoon Tasman became the first European to sight New Zealand. Maori attacked his boats, and Tasman left without going ashore. In 1769, the British explorer James Cook landed on New Zealand and claimed it for Britain (now also called the United Kingdom). Although Cook was cautious, he and his crew also had several violent clashes with Maori groups.

In the 1790's and early 1800's, the seals and whales in New Zealand's coastal waters attracted many American, Australian, and European hunters. Traders also came to buy New Zealand flax and kauri timber from Maori. Christian missionary groups targeted Maori as possible converts. By the 1830's, these groups had begun to settle New Zealand. The settlers heavily relied on Maori tribes.

Before 1840, no legal government had authority over the settlers and traders who came to New Zealand. Warfare between Maori groups and disputes between missionary and trading settlements were common. In 1835, a group of Maori leaders called the Confederation of Chiefs of the United Tribes of New Zealand signed a declaration proclaiming the country's independence. The

© Superstock

Sheep are raised in many parts of New Zealand. These animals provide mutton, lamb, and wool. Many sheep are sold at auctions. New Zealand ranks as one of the world's most important sheep-producing countries.

declaration requested the British monarch to act as the country's protector.

European colonization. Reports of lawless conditions and fear of competition from French and American settlers led the United Kingdom to declare New Zealand a colony. In 1840, the British negotiated the Treaty of Waitangi with the Maori. About 500 Maori chiefs eventually signed the treaty.

The Treaty of Waitangi was written in English and then translated into Maori. Problems with the translation of some important words have led to disputes over which rights the Maori kept and which they signed away. For example, in English the treaty proposed that the Maori hand over their sovereignty—that is, their right to rule themselves—in exchange for recognition of their ownership of the land and the right to be protected as British subjects. But in the Maori translation, the words used for *sovereignty* and *ownership* could be understood as giving the British limited powers to govern, rather than full sovereignty.

In the United Kingdom, the British colonial organizer Edward Gibbon Wakefield created the New Zealand Company. The company established settlements at Wellington and Wanganui in 1840, New Plymouth in 1841, and Nelson in 1842. Other groups founded settlements at Dunedin in 1848 and Christchurch in 1850.

The South Island began to prosper soon after the British claimed New Zealand as a colony. The island's rich grasslands provided good grazing for sheep imported from Australia, and soon the settlers began exporting wool. In 1861, prospectors discovered gold in Otago. Immigrants poured into the country, hoping to strike it rich. Few miners were successful, but many stayed to become farmers.

The New Zealand Wars. As the colonists' demand for Maori land grew, disputes over land ownership became more common and more violent. War broke out in 1860 when a group of Maori disputed the government's purchase of tribal land in the Taranaki region. Government forces seized a Maori fortification built on the disputed land near Waitara. The initial fighting in the Waitara region lasted about a year.

In July 1863, the British governor Sir George Grey or dered the invasion of the Waikato district, a Maori-occupied region on the North Island's western side. Grey had heard rumors that the Waikato Maori forces intended to attack Auckland. He was supported by the settlers who wanted to open up the Waikato's fertile grazing lands to British settlement. The wars continued until 1872.

In 1865, the colonial government created an agency called the Native Land Court to establish individual titles to land. The court defied the traditional Maori belief that land belonged to the entire tribe, not to individuals. By the end of the 1800's, settlers had taken most Maori land. The Maori were forced to withdraw into the harshest and most isolated regions of the country.

Depression and social reform. The expense of fighting the Maori, along with shrinking profits from South Island gold mines, took a severe toll on New Zealand's economy. Heavy government borrowing to support colonization and development projects also weakened the economy. In the late 1870's, the country entered an economic depression that lasted until the 1890's. In 1890, the Liberal Party won control of the government and remained in power for 21 years.

The Liberal Party represented the first stable nationwide political party in New Zealand's history. The party, under the leadership of Richard John Seddon from 1893 to 1906, carried out an extensive program of social reform. In 1893, New Zealand became the first country to give women full voting rights.

Dominion status. In the early 1900's, New Zealanders began to develop a sense of national identity. In 1907, the United Kingdom granted New Zealand's request to become a *dominion*, a self-governing country within the British Empire. New refrigeration methods developed in the late 1800's contributed to New Zealand's growing prosperity. These methods made it possible to export large quantities of butter, cheese, and meat.

During World War I (1914-1918), New Zealand sent about 100,000 troops to Europe to fight with the Allies against Germany. These soldiers suffered heavy casualties, with about 1 in 7 killed.

The Great Depression. New Zealand was hard-hit by the worldwide Great Depression that began in the late 1920's. Unemployment and desperate living conditions led to rioting against the government in the major cities. In 1935, the people elected a Labour Party government. The party increased public works projects, such as railway and road construction and forest planting, to put men to work. In 1938, the government set up a social security program that included health care for all citizens and special benefits for the aged, children, and widows.

World War II. In 1939, New Zealand followed the United Kingdom in declaring war on Germany. New Zealand troops fought beside British troops in Europe and the Middle East. When Japan entered the war in 1941, New Zealand began to fear a Japanese invasion. As British power declined in the Pacific, New Zealand increasingly relied on the United States. New Zealand fought beside the United States in the Pacific Islands.

During the war, New Zealand's domestic economy boomed. Manufacturing and farm production rose, and wages and prices stabilized. By the war's end in 1945, the country had climbed out of the Great Depression. The mid-1900's brought many years of prosperity.

International tensions developed between New

Important dates in New Zealand

A.D. 1200	Polynesian settlers arrived in New Zealand.
1642	Abel Janszoon Tasman became the first European to sight New Zealand.
1769	James Cook landed on New Zealand and claimed it for Britain (now the United Kingdom).
1840	The British and Maori signed the Treaty of Waitangi, giving the British the right to govern New Zealand.
1860-1872	Settlers on the North Island fought the Maori in the New Zealand Wars.
1861	The New Zealand gold rush began.
1893	New Zealand became the first country to grant women the right to vote.
1907	New Zealand became a dominion within the British Empire.
1938	New Zealand set up a social security program that included health care for all citizens.
1984	New Zealand adopted a policy that banned nuclear weapons and nuclear-powered ships from its ports.
1997	Jenny Shipley became the first woman prime minister of New Zealand.

A drawing (1642) by Isaac Gilsemans from Abel Janszoon Tasman's Journal;
Alexander Turnbull Library, Wellington, New Zealand

Maori in canoes attacked vessels of Dutch explorer Abel Janszoon Tasman along the New Zealand coast in 1642. Tasman and
his crew had become the first Europeans to sight New Zealand.

Zealand and some of its overseas allies in the 1980's. In
1981, a tour by a South African rugby team caused controversy as many New Zealanders protested South Africa's policy of *apartheid* (racial segregation).

In 1984, Labour Party Prime Minister David Lange announced that New Zealand would ban ships carrying
nuclear weapons or powered by nuclear reactors from
entering its ports. This ban brought New Zealand into
disagreement with the United States, a military ally. In
1986, the United States suspended its military duties to
New Zealand under the ANZUS mutual defense treaty.
The ANZUS treaty had been signed by Australia, New
Zealand, and the United States in 1951. This suspension
was partially lifted in 1999 to allow U.S. and New Zealand troops to participate in joint United Nations (UN)
peacekeeping operations.

New Zealand also strongly opposed France's testing
of nuclear weapons in the South Pacific. In 1985, the environmental organization Greenpeace planned to use its
ship *Rainbow Warrior* to protest French nuclear tests in
the Pacific. But French agents bombed and sank the ship
in Auckland Harbour. France apologized for sinking the
ship in New Zealand's waters but prevented the agents
from serving out their prison terms in New Zealand. In
1996, New Zealand cosponsored a UN resolution to ban
nuclear weapons from the Southern Hemisphere.

Maori-Pakeha relations. Since the 1840's, the Maori
had protested abuses of the Treaty of Waitangi. In 1975,
the Maori showed their discontent with a march to Wellington. In 1975, the New Zealand government set up a
panel called the Waitangi Tribunal to investigate tribal
land claims and suggest possible settlements. The panel
consists of half Maori and half Pakeha members appointed by the governor general.

In 1995, the government reached a historic settlement
with a group of Maori known as the Tainui. The settlement included the return of land, money, and a formal
apology. Since then, the government has made settlements with several other Maori groups.

Political changes. In 1993, New Zealand adopted a
mixed member proportional system of electing members of Parliament. In this system, some chairs are re-

served for elected legislators, while others are divided
among the parties that receive 5 percent or more of the
popular vote according to their share of the total votes
cast. In the 1996 election, the first held under the new
system, no party won an outright majority. The number
of seats held by third parties and Maori increased dramatically. To obtain a majority, the National Party formed
a coalition with the New Zealand First Party.

In 1997, Jenny Shipley became National Party leader
and New Zealand's first woman prime minister. In 1999
elections, a coalition of the Labour and Alliance parties
won a majority of seats in Parliament. Helen Clark,
Labour's leader, became prime minister. In elections in
2002, a coalition of the Labour and Progressive Coalition
parties won the most seats in Parliament. Clark remained
as prime minister. In a September 2005 election, Labour
won the most votes. Labour then entered into formal
and working alliances with three other parties, and Clark
began a third term as prime minister. The National Party
defeated Labour in parliamentary elections in late 2008,
and National Party leader John Key replaced Clark as
prime minister.   Giselle M. Byrnes

Related articles in *World Book* include:

Biographies

Cities

Other related articles

Outline

E. Fishing industry
F. Energy
G. International trade
H. Transportation
I. Communication

VII. History

Additional resources

Jackson, William K., and McRobie, Alan. *Historical Dictionary of New Zealand.* 2nd ed. Scarecrow, 2005.
New Zealand. Lonely Planet, frequently updated.
Nile, Richard, and Clerk, Christian. *Cultural Atlas of Australia, New Zealand, and the South Pacific.* Facts on File, 1996.
Sinclair, Keith, ed. *The Oxford Illustrated History of New Zealand.* 2nd ed. Oxford, 1996.

Newark, Delaware (pop. 31,454), is the home of the University of Delaware and a manufacturing and research center. It lies in northern Delaware, about halfway between New York City and Washington, D.C. For the location of Newark, see **Delaware** (political map).

Newark's products include cleaning supplies and *pharmaceuticals* (medicinal drugs). Engineers develop electronic components in the city's research facilities. Newark was chartered in 1758. It has a council-manager form of government.   Peter W. Rees

Newark, New Jersey (pop. 277,140), is the largest city in New Jersey and one of the leading centers of transportation in the United States. Newark lies on Newark Bay at the mouth of the Passaic River, about 10 miles (16 kilometers) west of New York City. For location, see **New Jersey** (political map). Newark is in the New York (New York)-Northern New Jersey-Long Island (New York) metropolitan area.

In 1666, 30 Puritan families from the Connecticut Colony settled in what is now eastern New Jersey. Developers of the area had offered them religious freedom and inexpensive farmland. The settlers founded a village on the Passaic because the site included a harbor and level, unforested land. They named the village Newark—probably for Newark-on-Trent, the English town where their pastor had entered the ministry. The name may also have originated in the phrase *new ark,* a reference to the Ark of the Covenant mentioned in the Bible (see **Ark of the Covenant**).

The city. Newark, the county seat of Essex County, covers about 24 square miles (62 square kilometers). Downtown Newark has the city's tallest building, the 34-story National Newark Building. Nearby is the First Presbyterian Church, Newark's oldest house of worship, completed in 1791. The Gateway Center, a group of office buildings and a hotel, rises in the eastern part of the downtown area.

African Americans make up more than half of Newark's population. The city also has many people of Italian, Portuguese, or Puerto Rican descent.

Economy. The production of drugs and chemicals ranks as the leading industrial activity in the city. Newark also manufactures electric equipment, processed food, metal products, and nonelectrical machinery.

Newark Liberty International Airport, a major passenger and cargo center, lies at the south end of town. Port Newark, a leading port, handles the ships of more than 100 ship companies. It is one of the largest ports in the United States for container ships, which carry cargo in large, separate containers. Passenger and freight railroads and numerous trucking firms serve the city.

Newark ranks as the nation's third largest insurance

New Jersey Newsphotos

Newark, New Jersey, lies on the west bank of the Passaic River, *rear,* where the river flows into Newark Bay. The city forms the center of a large industrial area in northeastern New Jersey.

center. Only companies in Hartford, Connecticut, and in New York City sell more insurance. Newark is the home of Prudential Insurance Company of America, one of the country's largest life insurance firms. The city also serves as New Jersey's leading center of finance and trade. Newark has one daily newspaper, *The Star-Ledger.*

Education and cultural life. The Newark School District is one of the oldest public school systems in New Jersey. The city's Barringer High School, established in 1838, was the first high school in the state. The city also has a number of parochial and private schools. Institutions of higher learning include the University of Medicine and Dentistry of New Jersey; the New Jersey Institute of Technology; the Newark campus of Rutgers, the State University of New Jersey; and the Seton Hall University School of Law.

The New Jersey Symphony Orchestra and the New Jersey State Opera perform in the New Jersey Performing Arts Center. The Newark Museum features art collections, exhibits of science and industry, and a planetarium. The New Jersey Historical Society has a library and a museum of historic items.

Newark's largest park is Branch Brook Park. It covers 360 acres (145 hectares) and includes more than 2,000 cherry trees.

Government. Newark has a mayor-council form of government. The voters elect a mayor and nine council members to serve four-year terms. Property taxes are the city's leading source of revenue.

History. Delaware Indians lived in what is now the Newark area before white settlers first arrived in 1666. During the late 1700's, a number of tanners settled in Newark. The area had many hemlock trees, which furnished the bark used in making leather. By the early 1800's, about a third of the labor force worked in shoe-making and other leather products industries.

The work of Seth Boyden, a Newark inventor, helped the city grow industrially during the early 1800's. Boyden developed such products as patent leather and an improved kind of cast iron. Advances in transportation also contributed to Newark's industrial growth. For example, the Morris Canal, completed in 1831, linked Newark with coal-mining areas in the Lehigh Valley of Pennsylvania. By 1834, a railroad connected Newark and the Hudson River, which separates New Jersey and New York City. Newark had a population of 19,732 when it was incorporated in 1836.

From 1840 to 1860, many German and Irish immigrants settled in Newark to fill the growing number of industrial jobs. By 1860, the city had 71,941 people. A wave of immigration that began in the late 1880's brought thousands of people from eastern and southern Europe to Newark. In 1910, the city had 347,469 people.

Port Newark opened in 1915, during World War I (1914-1918). Newark's chemical industry, which began in the 1870's, expanded greatly during the war and the 1920's. In 1930, the population reached a peak of 442,337.

During the Great Depression of the 1930's, more than 600 Newark factories closed and many neighborhoods became shabby. During World War II (1939-1945), jobs in defense plants drew thousands of African Americans from the South to Newark. They crowded into the city's run-down areas. Beginning in the 1950's, many middle-income families moved from Newark to the suburbs. By 1960, the city's population had fallen to 405,220.

By the mid-1960's, Newark had a large proportion of poor people. The city lacked money to provide adequate services. Almost half the voters were African Americans, but they had little political power. As a result, racial tensions mounted. In July 1967, five days of rioting shook the African American sections of Newark, causing 26 deaths and more than $10 million in property damage. Blacks had charged that widespread dishonesty existed in the city government. A series of investigations following the riots led to the conviction of Mayor Hugh Addonizio and other politicians for sharing illegal refunds on city contracts.

In 1970, the voters elected Newark's first African American mayor, Kenneth A. Gibson. Gibson had been city engineer. He won reelection three times and served as mayor until 1986.

In 1971, a dispute over working conditions developed between white Newark teachers and the city's board of education. As a result of appointments made by Gibson, the board had a majority of black and Puerto Rican members. The dispute led to an 11-week strike by the teachers, the longest in the history of a major U.S. city. This strike increased racial tension in Newark. The school board has since become an elective body.

During the late 1900's, Newark leaders worked to increase the city's job opportunities and improve its housing. The federal and state governments contributed large sums of money to help with such problems. Much new construction took place. A series of urban renewal projects begun in the 1960's resulted in the construction of some factories and office buildings. Newark (now Newark Liberty International) Airport started a major expansion program in 1963. Several new university campuses and seaport expansion projects were completed in the 1970's. Construction of new office buildings continued into the early 2000's.   Robert M. Hordon

For the monthly weather, see **New Jersey** (Climate).

Newbery, John (1713-1767), was an English publisher and bookseller. He is famous in the history of children's literature as the first person to print and sell books for children. He published *A Little Pretty Pocket-Book* (1744) and *The History of Little Goody-Two-Shoes* (1765) and many other little volumes bound in "flowery gilt," a colorful paper from the Netherlands. Many of his books were reprinted in America between 1749 and 1831.

Newbery's bookshop, The Bible and Sun, was in St. Paul's Churchyard, London. He was the friend and patron of Oliver Goldsmith, Samuel Johnson, and other literary people. Goldsmith portrayed Newbery in his novel *The Vicar of Wakefield* (1766). It is believed that Goldsmith wrote some of the quaint penny books published by Newbery. These little books are now highly prized.

Newbery was born in Berkshire in July 1713. The Newbery Medal, which has been awarded each year since 1922 for the finest children's book written by an American, was named for him (see **Newbery Medal**). He died on Dec. 22, 1767.   Jill P. May

See also **Literature for children** (The 1700's); **Mother Goose.**

Newbery Medal is an annual award given to the author of the most distinguished contribution to American children's literature published in the preceding year. The award was established and endowed in 1921 by Frederic G. Melcher, chairman of the board of R. R. Bowker Co., publishers of the *Library Journal* and *Publishers' Weekly.* He named it for John Newbery, an English publisher and bookseller. Melcher also founded the Caldecott Medal. This award is presented annually to the illustrator of the outstanding children's picture book of the preceding year.

American Library Association

The Newbery Medal is awarded to a children's author.

The American sculptor René Chambellan designed the Newbery Medal. The Association for Library Service to Children of the American Library Association awards it.   Critically reviewed by the Association for Library Service to Children

See also **Caldecott Medal; Melcher, Frederic Gershom; Newbery, John.**

Newcastle (pop. 493,466) is one of the largest cities in the Australian state of New South Wales. Newcastle lies along the southeast coast of Australia (see **Australia** [political map]). Newcastle is an important industrial and shipping center. The city's major industries include the production of steel and base metals. Many buildings date from the 1800's, including Fort Scratchley, the Customs House, Public School, and Railway Station. The

Newbery Medal winners

Year	Author	Winning book	Year	Author	Winning book
1922	Hendrik van Loon	The Story of Mankind	1969	Lloyd Alexander	The High King
1923	Hugh Lofting	The Voyages of Dr. Dolittle	1970	William H. Armstrong	Sounder
1924	Charles Hawes	The Dark Frigate	1971	Betsy Byars	The Summer of the Swans
1925	Charles Finger	Tales from Silver Lands	1972	Robert C. O'Brien	Mrs. Frisby and the Rats of NIMH
1926	Arthur Chrisman	Shen of the Sea	1973	Jean Craighead George	Julie of the Wolves
1927	Will James	Smoky	1974	Paula Fox	The Slave Dancer
1928	Dhan Gopal Mukerji	Gay-Neck: The Story of a Pigeon	1975	Virginia Hamilton	M.C. Higgins, the Great
1929	Eric Philbrook Kelly	The Trumpeter of Krakow	1976	Susan Cooper	The Grey King
1930	Rachel Field	Hitty, Her First Hundred Years	1977	Mildred Taylor	Roll of Thunder, Hear My Cry
1931	Elizabeth Coatsworth	The Cat Who Went to Heaven	1978	Katherine Paterson	Bridge to Terabithia
1932	Laura Armer	Waterless Mountain	1979	Ellen Raskin	The Westing Game
1933	Elizabeth Lewis	Young Fu of the Upper Yangtze	1980	Joan W. Blos	A Gathering of Days: A New England Girl's Journal
1934	Cornelia Meigs	Invincible Louisa			
1935	Monica Shannon	Dobry	1981	Katherine Paterson	Jacob Have I Loved
1936	Carol Ryrie Brink	Caddie Woodlawn	1982	Nancy Willard	A Visit to William Blake's Inn
1937	Ruth Sawyer	Roller Skates	1983	Cynthia Voigt	Dicey's Song
1938	Kate Seredy	The White Stag	1984	Beverly Cleary	Dear Mr. Henshaw
1939	Elizabeth Enright	Thimble Summer	1985	Robin McKinley	The Hero and the Crown
1940	James Daugherty	Daniel Boone	1986	Patricia MacLachlan	Sarah, Plain and Tall
1941	Armstrong Sperry	Call It Courage	1987	Sid Fleischman	The Whipping Boy
1942	Walter D. Edmonds	The Matchlock Gun	1988	Russell Freedman	Lincoln: A Photobiography
1943	Elizabeth Janet Gray	Adam of the Road	1989	Paul Fleischman	Joyful Noise: Poems for Two Voices
1944	Esther Forbes	Johnny Tremain			
1945	Robert Lawson	Rabbit Hill	1990	Lois Lowry	Number the Stars
1946	Lois Lenski	Strawberry Girl	1991	Jerry Spinelli	Maniac Magee
1947	Carolyn S. Bailey	Miss Hickory	1992	Phyllis R. Naylor	Shiloh
1948	William Pène du Bois	The Twenty-One Balloons	1993	Cynthia Rylant	Missing May
1949	Marguerite Henry	King of the Wind	1994	Lois Lowry	The Giver
1950	Marguerite de Angeli	The Door in the Wall	1995	Sharon Creech	Walk Two Moons
1951	Elizabeth Yates	Amos Fortune, Free Man	1996	Karen Cushman	The Midwife's Apprentice
1952	Eleanor Estes	Ginger Pye	1997	Elaine Konigsburg	The View from Saturday
1953	Ann Nolan Clark	Secret of the Andes	1998	Karen Hesse	Out of the Dust
1954	Joseph Krumgold	. . . And Now Miguel	1999	Louis Sachar	Holes
1955	Meindert DeJong	The Wheel on the School	2000	Christopher Paul Curtis	Bud, Not Buddy
1956	Jean Lee Latham	Carry On, Mr. Bowditch	2001	Richard Peck	A Year Down Yonder
1957	Virginia Sorenson	Miracles on Maple Hill	2002	Linda Sue Park	A Single Shard
1958	Harold Keith	Rifles for Watie	2003	Avi	Crispin: The Cross of Lead
1959	Elizabeth G. Speare	The Witch of Blackbird Pond	2004	Kate DiCamillo	The Tale of Despereaux
1960	Joseph Krumgold	Onion John	2005	Cynthia Kadohata	Kira-Kira
1961	Scott O'Dell	Island of the Blue Dolphins	2006	Lynne Rae Perkins	Criss Cross
1962	Elizabeth G. Speare	The Bronze Bow	2007	Susan Patron	The Higher Power of Lucky
1963	Madeleine L'Engle	A Wrinkle in Time	2008	Laura Amy Schlitz	Good Masters! Sweet Ladies! Voices from a Medieval Village
1964	Emily C. Neville	It's Like This, Cat			
1965	Maia Wojciechowska	Shadow of a Bull	2009	Neil Gaiman	The Graveyard Book
1966	Elizabeth Borton de Treviño	I, Juan de Pareja	2010	Rebecca Stead	When You Reach Me
1967	Irene Hunt	Up a Road Slowly	2011	Clare Vanderpool	Moon over Manifest
1968	Elaine Konigsburg	From the Mixed-Up Files of Mrs. Basil E. Frankweiler			

city is the home of the University of Newcastle.

Permanent European settlement of Newcastle began in 1804, when convicts were sent there from Sydney. Newcastle was a place of punishment for prisoners until 1824. It received city status in 1885. Alan Fitzgerald

Newcastle upon Tyne (pop. 259,573; met. area pop. 1,075,979) is a commercial and manufacturing center of northern England. The city, usually called Newcastle, anchors the Tyne and Wear metropolitan area. Newcastle lies on the River Tyne, near the North Sea (see **England** [political map]). It is named after a castle built about 1080 by a son of William the Conqueror, a king of England.

Coal mining and shipbuilding were the city's chief industries from the 1700's until the 1930's. The expression "carrying coals to Newcastle" means taking something to a place that has more than it needs. Coal mining and shipbuilding have been largely replaced by food processing and the manufacture of chemical products and heavy engineering equipment. The city is the home of Newcastle University. M. Trevor Wild

Newcomen, *noo KUHM uhn,* **Thomas** (1663-1729), an English inventor, built the first commercially successful steam engine in 1712. His steam engine was used widely for more than 60 years in Europe and throughout the coal-mining regions of Britain (later also called the United Kingdom) to remove water from mines.

While selling tools, Newcomen learned of the difficulty of pumping water from tin mines. He developed an engine driven by air pressure. Water was injected into a cylinder filled with steam, condensing the steam and creating a vacuum. The weight of the atmosphere then pushed a piston to the bottom of the cylinder, pulling up the pumps linked to the piston and raising water. To sell his engines, Newcomen formed a partnership with inventor Thomas Savery, who had a patent on a different device that raised water from mines. Newcomen engines could pump over 3 ½ million gallons (13.2 million liters) of water a day. Newcomen was born in Dartmouth and died in London on Aug. 5, 1729. Bruce E. Seely

See also **Steam engine** (History; picture).

Fishing boats docked at St. John's, Newfoundland and Labrador's capital and largest city

Newfoundland and Labrador

Newfoundland and Labrador, *NOO fuhnd LAND,* is Canada's newest province. It became a province in 1949. It includes the island of Newfoundland and the coast of Labrador, a part of the Canadian mainland. St. John's, the capital and largest city of Newfoundland and Labrador, ranks among the oldest communities in North America.

For many years, the province's official name was simply Newfoundland. Canada's Parliament changed the official name to Newfoundland and Labrador in 2001.

Fewer people live in Newfoundland and Labrador than in any other province except Prince Edward Island. Most of the land in Newfoundland and Labrador is rugged, especially along the rocky coast. Thick forests grow along tumbling rivers and around sparkling blue lakes. Barren, rocky ridges rise above the green valleys and surround many brown *peat bogs* (swamps of decayed plants). Arctic winds and ocean currents chill the land and keep the climate cool. Storms occur frequently. Fog often covers the coast.

Almost all of the province's people live near the sea. Hundreds of villages and fishing settlements nestle in small, sheltered bays along the coast. Some places, too small to appear on maps, have such unusual names as Crow Head, Dragon's Bay, and Juniper Stump.

Most people in Newfoundland and Labrador belong to families that originally came from the United Kingdom and Ireland. The people of the many small fishing settlements, known as *outports,* have kept much of the language and customs of their ancestors. But the decline of the fishing industry and the rapid extension of modern transportation and communication systems threaten this traditional way of life. At the same time, works by urban artists in the province celebrate outport life.

Newfoundland and Labrador's coastal waters historically were one of the world's richest fishing areas. For more than 300 years, fishing fleets from various nations have shared in the bounty of the shallow Grand Banks, southeast of Newfoundland. However, bigger trawlers and more efficient ways of finding and catching fish have led to a drop in the numbers of cod and other fishes. As a result, Canada's government has established restrictions on fishing off Newfoundland.

Mining is an important industry in Newfoundland and Labrador. Offshore oil production became a valuable mining activity in the late 1990's. Iron ore mining on the Labrador Peninsula is also extremely important. Seafood

Interesting facts about Newfoundland and Labrador

WORLD BOOK illustrations by Kevin Chadwick

The first successful transatlantic telegraph cable was completed when the *Great Eastern,* the steamship laying the cable, landed at Heart's Content on July 27, 1866. The *Great Eastern,* the largest ship in the world at the time, laid the cable on the ocean floor from Valentia, Ireland, to Newfoundland.

First transatlantic cable

Guglielmo Marconi received the first transatlantic wireless message at St. John's on Dec. 12, 1901. The Morse Code signal he received was a letter *s* sent from Cornwall, England. The signal was picked up by an aerial attached to a kite.

Sir Humphrey Gilbert, an English explorer, arrived in Newfoundland in August 1583. It is sometimes considered England's oldest possession in North America. However, the United Kingdom did not formally recognize Newfoundland as a colony until 1824.

Guglielmo Marconi

Bill Brooks, Masterfile

Beach at Middle Cove, near Torbay

products are the leading manufactured products in the province. Refined petroleum and wood pulp and paper are also important products of the province's manufacturing industry.

Newfoundland and Labrador is the oldest English-speaking region of North America. Norse (Scandinavian) adventurers established a settlement at L'Anse aux Meadows about A.D. 1000. Sailors from the English port of Bristol likely reached the island of Newfoundland in the late 1400's. In 1497, John Cabot, an Italian explorer in England's service, sailed through the rich fishing waters near Newfoundland. He brought news of the fishing back to Europe. The fisheries attracted many fishing crews, and some of those people settled on the island. In the 1500's, Basque people of southwestern France and northern Spain established semipermanent whaling and fishing settlements along the Labrador coast. Though its ships used Newfoundland as a fishing area for many years, the United Kingdom did not recognize it as a colony until 1824.

For the relationship of Newfoundland and Labrador to the other provinces, see **Canada; Canada, Government of; Canada, History of.**

George Hunter, National Film Board of Canada

Open-pit iron mine on the Labrador Peninsula

Newfoundland and Labrador in brief

Symbols of Newfoundland and Labrador

The provincial flag was adopted in 1980. The blue section represents Newfoundland and Labrador's ties to the United Kingdom. The red and gold symbolize hope for the future, with the arrow pointing the way. The coat of arms was granted by King Charles I of England in 1637 and officially adopted as a provincial symbol in 1928. The shield has two lions and two unicorns representing the United Kingdom. The Indians symbolize Newfoundland and Labrador's first inhabitants.

Provincial flag

Provincial coat of arms

Province of Newfoundland and Labrador

Newfoundland and Labrador (brown) is the seventh largest province and the largest of the Atlantic Provinces (yellow).

General information

Entered the Dominion: March 31, 1949, the 10th province.
Provincial abbreviation: NL (postal).
Provincial motto: *Quaerite Prime Regnum Dei* (Seek Ye First the Kingdom of God).
Provincial song: "The Ode to Newfoundland." Words by Sir Cavendish Boyle; music by Sir Hubert Parry.

The Confederation Building, headquarters of the Newfoundland and Labrador provincial government, is in St. John's, the capital since 1729.

Land and climate

Area: 156,649 mi² (405,720 km²); the island of Newfoundland, 43,008 mi² (111,390 km²); Labrador, 113,641 mi² (294,330 km²).
Elevation: *Highest*—Mount Caubvick (called Mont d' Iberville in Quebec), 5,420 ft (1,652 m) above sea level. *Lowest*—sea level.
Coastline: The island of Newfoundland, 7,176 mi. (11,548 km). Labrador, 5,078 mi (8,172 km).
Record high temperature: 100 °F (38 °C) at Happy Valley-Goose Bay on July 4, 1944.
Record low temperature: −55 °F (−48 °C) at Ashuanipi on Feb. 7, 1950.
Average July temperature: 59 °F (14 °C).
Average January temperature: 19 °F (−7 °C).
Average yearly precipitation: 44 in (111 cm).

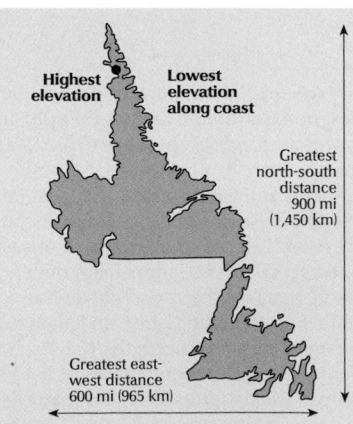

Highest elevation

Lowest elevation along coast

Greatest north-south distance 900 mi (1,450 km)

Greatest east-west distance 600 mi (965 km)

Important dates

The Treaty of Utrecht gave Newfoundland to Britain.

Britain obtained Labrador from France in the Treaty of Paris.

| 1583 | 1713 | 1763 | 1832 |

Sir Humphrey Gilbert landed in Newfoundland and claimed the region for England.

The United Kingdom granted Newfoundland the right to elect a general assembly.

Bird
Puffin

Tree
Black spruce

Floral emblem
Purple pitcher plant

People

Population: 505,469 (2006 census)
Rank among the provinces: 9th
Density: 3 persons per mi² (1 per km²), provinces average 13 per mi² (5 per km²)
Distribution: 58 percent urban, 42 percent rural
Largest cities and towns*

St. John's	100,646
Mount Pearl	24,671
Conception Bay South	21,966
Corner Brook	20,083
Grand Falls-Windsor	13,558
Paradise	12,584

*2006 census.
Source: Statistics Canada.

Population trend

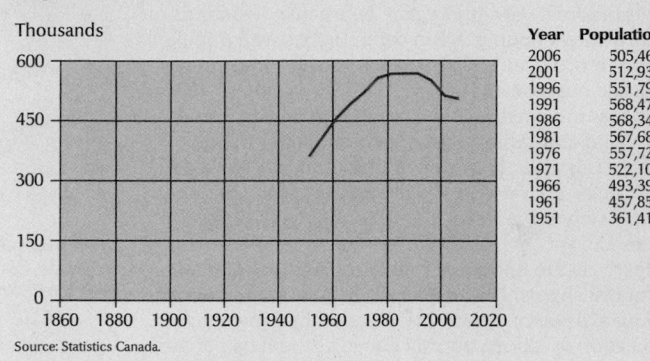

Thousands

Year	Population
2006	505,469
2001	512,930
1996	551,792
1991	568,474
1986	568,349
1981	567,681
1976	557,725
1971	522,104
1966	493,396
1961	457,853
1951	361,416

Source: Statistics Canada.

Economy

Chief products

Agriculture: chickens, eggs, milk, nursery products.
Forestry: fir, spruce.
Manufacturing: paper products, seafood products, wood products.
Mining: iron ore, nickel, petroleum.

Gross domestic product

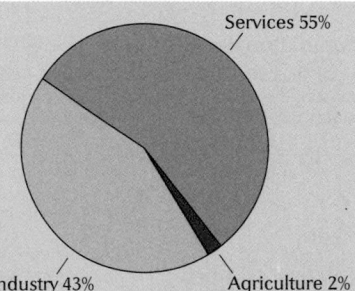

Services 55%
Industry 43%
Agriculture 2%

Value of goods and services produced in 2008: $31,458,000,000.*
Services include community, business, and personal services; finance; government; trade; and transportation and communication. *Industry* includes construction, manufacturing, mining, and utilities. *Agriculture* includes agriculture, fishing, and forestry.

*Canadian dollars.
Source: Statistics Canada.

Government

Provincial government

Premier: term of up to 4 years
Members of the House of Assembly: 48; terms of up to 4 years

Federal government

Members of the House of Commons: 7
Senators: 6

Sources of information

Newfoundland and Labrador's official website at http://www.gov.nf.ca provides a gateway to much information on the province's economy, government, and history.

In addition, the website at http://www.newfoundlandlabrador.com provides information on tourism in the province.

Newfoundland appealed to the United Kingdom for financial assistance and became a British dependency.

Construction began on a $950-million hydroelectric plant in Churchill Falls in Labrador.

1934   **1949**   **1967**   **2001**

Newfoundland became the 10th province on March 31.

Newfoundland's name was officially changed to Newfoundland and Labrador.

Population. The 2006 Canadian census reported that Newfoundland and Labrador had 505,469 people. The province's population had decreased by about 1 ½ percent since the 2001 census, which reported a total of 512,930 people.

St. John's, on the Avalon Peninsula, is Newfoundland and Labrador's capital and largest city. St. John's is the center of the province's only Census Metropolitan Area as defined by Statistics Canada. For the population of the metropolitan area, see the *Index* to the political map of Newfoundland and Labrador. About one-third of Newfoundland and Labrador's people live in the St. John's metropolitan area.

Corner Brook and Mount Pearl are Newfoundland and Labrador's only other cities. More than two-thirds of the province's people live in communities with populations of more than 1,000 people. Almost all these settlements lie near the coast.

Only approximately 3 of every 100 people in Newfoundland and Labrador live in communities on the coast of Labrador. For more information, see the separate articles on Newfoundland and Labrador cities and towns listed in the *Related articles* at the end of this article.

Nearly all the people of Newfoundland and Labrador are of British, Irish, French, or Aboriginal (Innu, Inuit, or Mi'kmaq) descent. About 2 percent of the province's population was born outside Canada. About half of the people who were born outside Canada came from the

Wayne Sproul, Hot Shots

The small village of Salvage lies on the rugged coast of Bonavista Bay. Less than a third of Newfoundland and Labrador's people live in communities that have fewer than 1,000 people.

United Kingdom or from the United States.

Schools in Newfoundland and Labrador operate under the authority of the province's Minister of Education. Several elected school boards manage the daily operations of the schools. One of the school boards manages the *francophone* (French-speaking) school district, which covers the entire province. Provincial law requires children in Newfoundland and Labrador to attend school from age 6 to age 16.

The province's one university—Memorial University of Newfoundland—was founded in 1925. Its main campus is in St. John's.

In addition to the publicly funded education system, the province regulates a number of private elementary and secondary schools and vocational and technical training schools. These institutions operate either as businesses, as not-for-profit organizations, or as specially funded schools.

Libraries and museums. In 1934, Newfoundland established its first public library, the Gosling Memorial Library in St. John's. The Arts and Culture Centre in St. John's houses the Newfoundland & Labrador Collection of the Provincial Resource Library.

The Rooms, which is in St. John's, features art, cultural, and historical exhibits. The Rooms unites the Provincial Museum, the Provincial Art Gallery, and the Provincial Archives into one location.

The Provincial Seamen's Museum in Grand Bank is a branch of The Rooms. It has exhibits on the maritime history of the southern coast of Newfoundland. The North Atlantic Aviation Museum, in Gander, features vintage aircraft and exhibits on the aviation history of that community.

Community museums highlight local heritage collections throughout the Newfoundland and Labrador province.

Population density

More than 90 percent of the province's people live near the coast of the island of Newfoundland. St. John's is the capital and largest city. The Labrador area has relatively few people.

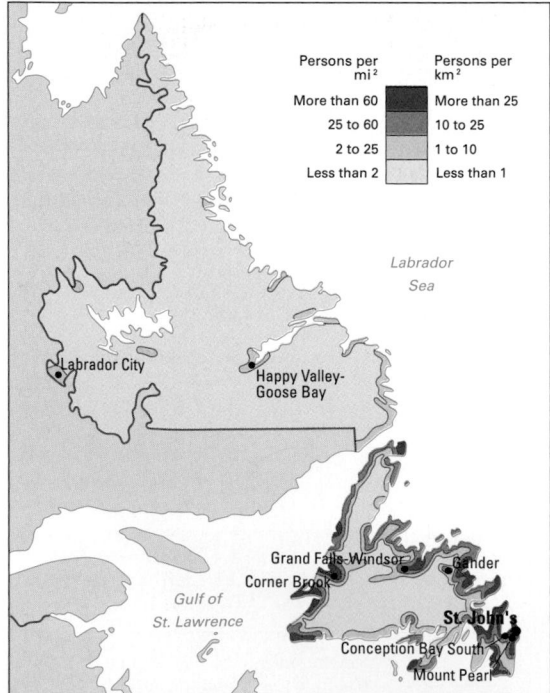

Persons per mi²	Persons per km²
More than 60	More than 25
25 to 60	10 to 25
2 to 25	1 to 10
Less than 2	Less than 1

Labrador Sea

Labrador City

Happy Valley-Goose Bay

Grand Falls-Windsor
Corner Brook
Gander

Gulf of
St. Lawrence

St. John's

Conception Bay South
Mount Pearl

WORLD BOOK map; based on the *National Atlas of Canada*

Memorial University of Newfoundland, in St. John's, is Newfoundland and Labrador's only university. The school was founded in 1925 as Memorial University College and began granting degrees in 1950.

E. Otto, Miller Services

Newfoundland and Labrador map index

*Does not appear on map; key shows general location.
Places without populations are unincorporated.
Source: 2006 census.

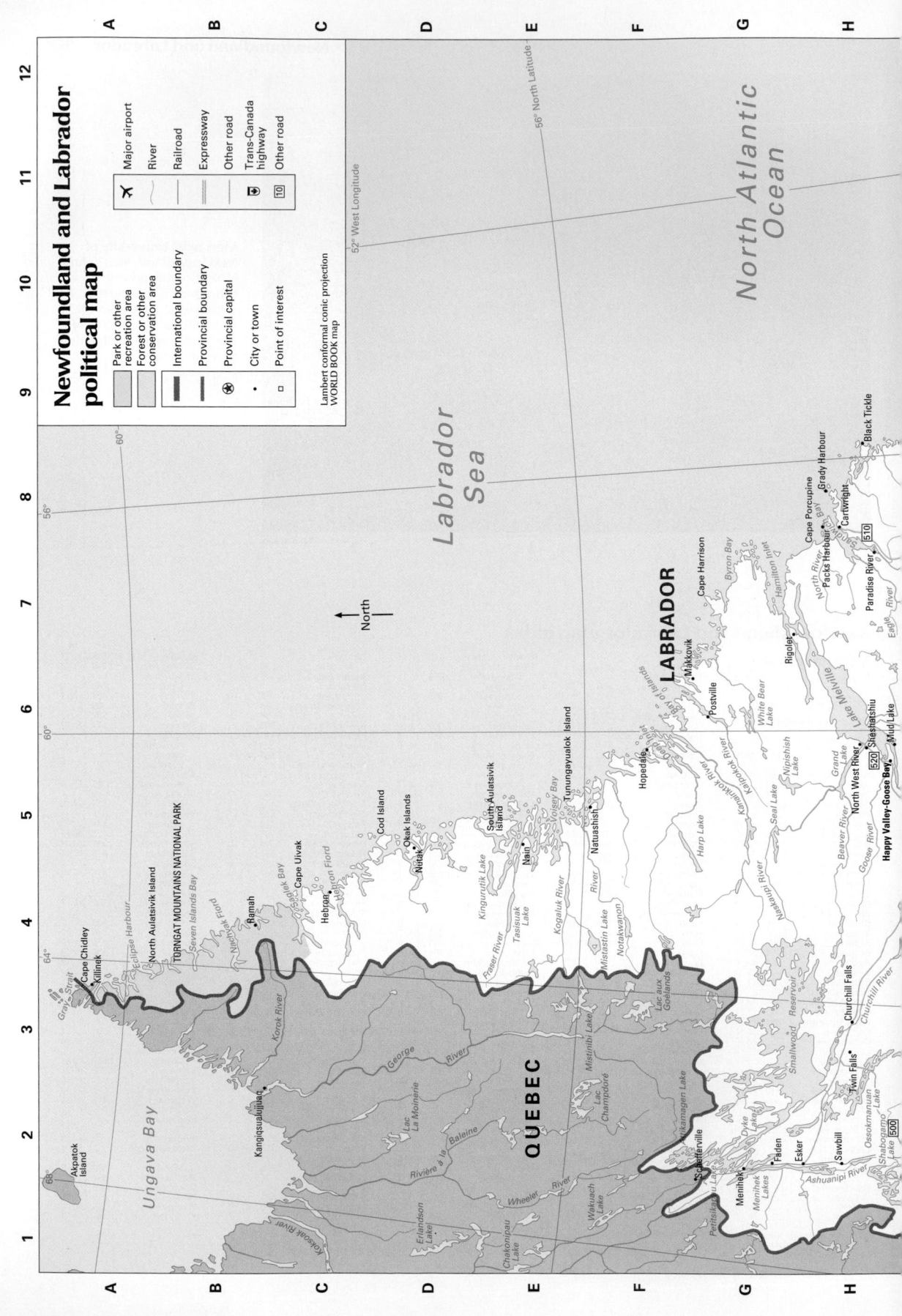

Newfoundland and Labrador political map

	Park or other recreation area
	Forest or other conservation area
	International boundary
	Provincial boundary
⊛	Provincial capital
•	City or town
□	Point of interest

✈	Major airport
	River
	Railroad
	Expressway
	Other road
⊞	Trans-Canada highway
10	Other road

Lambert conformal conic projection
WORLD BOOK map

North

North Atlantic Ocean

Labrador Sea

Ungava Bay

QUEBEC

LABRADOR

Akpatok Island

Cape Chidley
Killinek
Grays Strait
Eclipse Harbour
North Aulatsivik Island
TORNGAT MOUNTAINS NATIONAL PARK
Seven Islands Bay
Nachvak Fiord
Ramah
Saglek Bay
Cape Uivak
Hebron
Bryan Fiord
Cod Island
Okak Islands
Nutak
Kangiqsualujjuaq
Korok River
Fraser River
Tasisuak Lake
Kinguratik Lake
South Aulatsivik Island
Nain
Kogaluk River
Tununayualok Island
Voisey Bay
Bay of Islands
Natuashish
Hopedale
Postville
Makkovik
Cape Harrison
Byron Bay
Hamilton Inlet
Rigolet
North River
Cape Porcupine
Packs Harbour
Grady Harbour
Cartwright
Paradise River
Eagle River
Black Tickle
510

George River
Lac La Moinerie
Rivière à la Baleine
Erlandson Lake
Chakonipau Lake
Kossak River
Wheeler River
Petitsikapau Lake
Menihek
Menihek Lakes
Fermont
Esker
Schefferville
Mistinibi Lake
Lac Champdoré
Notakwanon
Mistastin Lake
Lac aux Goélands
Kamagen Lake
Dyke Lakes
Wabush
Labrador City
500
Ossokmanuan Lake
Shabogamo Lake
Ashuanipi River
Twin Falls
Churchill Falls
Churchill River
Smallwood Reservoir
Naskaupi River
Beaver River
Goose River
Grand Lake
North West River
Happy Valley-Goose Bay
Sheshatshiu
Mud Lake
520
Lake Melville
Nipishish Lake
Seal Lake
Harp Lake
White Bear Lake
Kanairiktok River

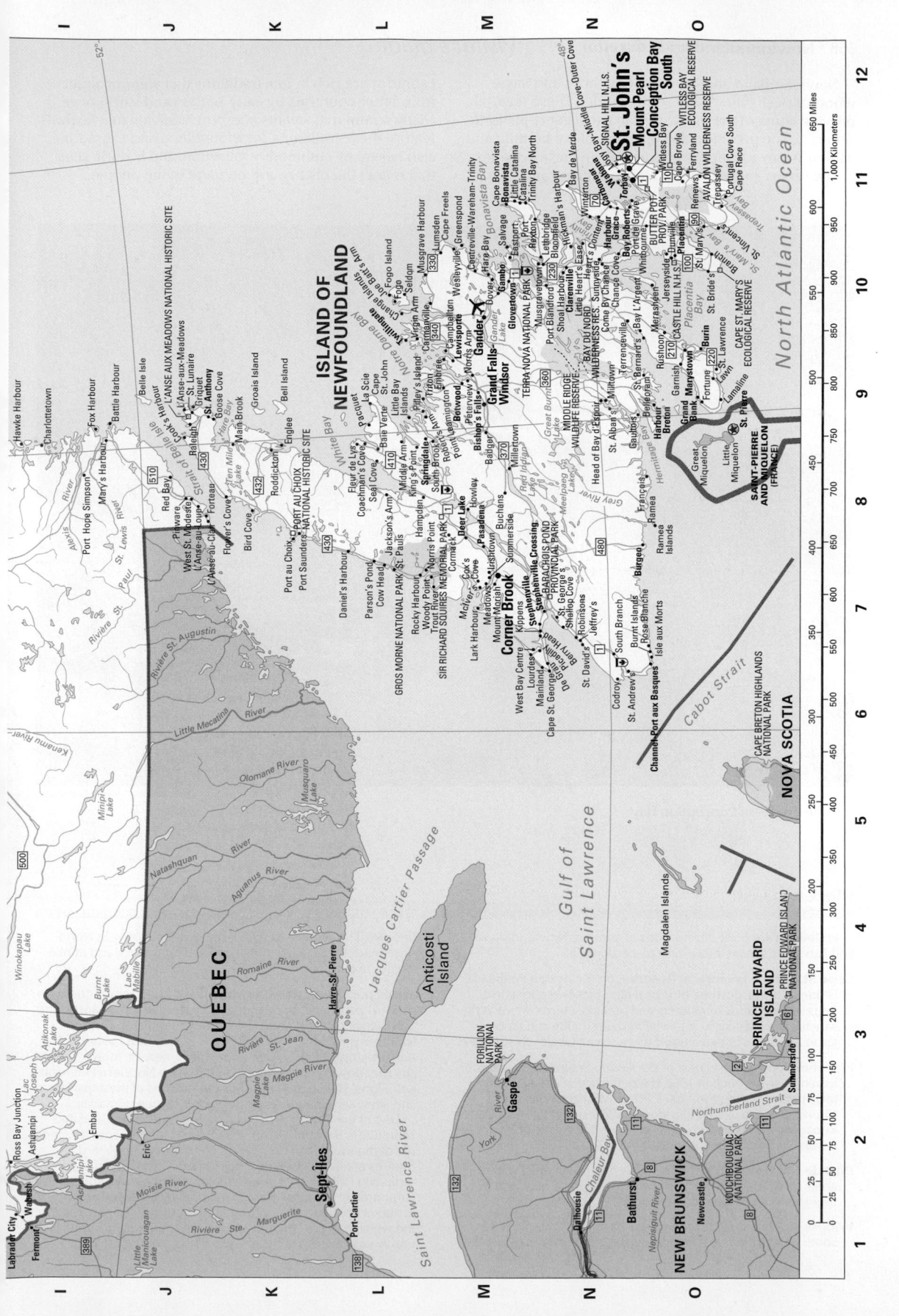

Newfoundland and Labrador has capes and bays, wooded river valleys, and Arctic tundra. These features provide some of the most spectacular scenery in North America. The province also offers excellent hunting and fishing. Many vacationers participate in these activities.

The towns and villages of Newfoundland and Labrador are rich in folk traditions that were brought from other countries by early settlers and still survive. Many community events and provincewide folk festivals feature these traditions. Newfoundland and Labrador also has many community museums and historic sites that reflect the history and heritage of the people.

Bruce Paton, Canadian Tourism Commission

Port de Grave on Conception Bay

Places to visit

Following are brief descriptions of some of Newfoundland and Labrador's most interesting places to visit:

Cape St. Mary's Ecological Reserve, on the Avalon Peninsula, is one of the largest sea bird breeding places in the world. Tens of thousands of gannets and other sea birds arrive at the sanctuary each year to raise their young on the cliff faces. Cape St. Mary's is also a good place to see whales in summer.

Placentia, on the west coast of the Avalon Peninsula, was established by the French in 1662. It was the scene of several historic battles during the 1700's. Prime Minister Winston Churchill of the United Kingdom and President Franklin D. Roosevelt of the United States drew up the Atlantic Charter on a warship near Placentia in 1941.

Port de Grave, on Conception Bay, is one of the most scenic areas in Newfoundland. It attracts sightseers, artists, and photographers from all over the world.

Witless Bay is a small fishing village 20 miles (32 kilometers) south of St. John's. Just offshore is the Witless Bay Ecological Reserve. The reserve has the largest puffin colony in North America. It is also a good place to see humpback and minke whales in summer.

National parks and sites. Newfoundland and Labrador has two national parks and one national park reserve. Gros Morne and Terra Nova national parks are on Newfoundland. Torngat Mountains National Park Reserve is in northern Labrador. National historic sites include Cape Spear, near St. John's; L'Anse aux Meadows; Port au Choix, on the Great Northern Peninsula; and Signal Hill, in St. John's. For the features of these parks and sites, see **Canada** (National Park System of Canada).

One of the largest provincial parks in Newfoundland and Labrador is Barachois Pond Park near St. George's, in the middle of the towering Long Range Mountains. Sir Richard Squires Memorial Park, on the Humber River, includes the famous Big Falls. Every spring, Atlantic salmon make spectacular jumps up the falls to reach their *spawning* (egg-laying) grounds upstream. For information on provincial parks, visit the website of the Newfoundland and Labrador Parks and Natural Areas Division at http://www.env.gov.nl.ca/parks .

St. John's Day parade

Atlantic puffins at Witless Bay

Cape St. Mary's Ecological Reserve

Viking settlement at L'Anse aux Meadows

Land regions. Newfoundland and Labrador includes parts of two land regions: (1) the Canadian Shield, and (2) the Appalachian Region.

The Canadian Shield covers about half of Canada, including all of Labrador. It is a rough plateau made up of ancient rocks. In Labrador, the edge of this plateau is cut by valleys and by swift rivers that drain into the Atlantic Ocean. Forests cover more than half of Labrador. Southwestern Labrador has many lakes. It also has rich deposits of iron ore. See **Canadian Shield.**

The Appalachian Region extends through the eastern part of North America from the island of Newfoundland to Alabama. Lowlands form the eastern edge of the island. To the west, the land gradually rises to a plateau with parts more than 2,000 feet (610 meters) above sea level. In the central part of the island, rocky ridges rise from forested valleys. Lakes, ponds, and bogs dot the area. Three peninsulas—the Great Northern, the Avalon, and the Burin—stick out from the island. The mountainous Great Northern Peninsula points northeast toward Labrador. Forests cover most of it. The Avalon Peninsula, in the southeast, is the most heavily populated part of the province. About 40 percent of the people live there. To the west, across Placentia Bay, lies the hilly Burin Peninsula.

Coastline of Newfoundland and Labrador is broken by *fiords* (long inlets) and many bays. The island of Newfoundland has 7,176 miles (11,548 kilometers) of coastline. Labrador's coastline is 5,078 miles (8,172 kilometers) long. Thousands of small islands with a total coastline of 5,739 miles (9,236 kilometers) dot the coastal waters.

Mountains. The highest point in Newfoundland and Labrador is Mount Caubvick. This peak in the Torngat Mountains is part of the boundary between Quebec and Newfoundland and Labrador. In Quebec, it is known as Mont d'Iberville. It rises 5,420 feet (1,652 meters) above sea level. The Mealy Mountains, in southern Labrador, are over 4,000 feet (1,200 meters) high. On the island of Newfoundland, the chief mountains are the Long Range Mountains. The Lewis Hills have the island's highest elevation—2,672 feet (814 meters) above sea level.

Rivers and lakes. The Churchill River in Labrador is Newfoundland and Labrador's longest river. It rises near the Quebec border and flows 600 miles (966 kilometers) to the Atlantic Ocean. On the island of Newfoundland, the Exploits River flows 153 miles (246 kilometers) northeast from Red Indian Lake into Notre Dame Bay.

Labrador's largest lake is Lake Melville. It covers 1,133 square miles (2,934 square kilometers). The next largest Labrador lakes are Michikamau, Lobstick, and Dyke

Hans Blohm, Masterfile

Rocky ridges rise from forested valleys in the Appalachian Region of the province. This region covers the entire island of Newfoundland and includes many lakes, ponds, and bogs.

Land regions of Newfoundland and Labrador

CANADIAN SHIELD

LABRADOR

Naskaupi R.

Churchill R.

APPALACHIAN REGION

NEWFOUNDLAND ISLAND

Exploits R.

WORLD BOOK map

Map index

Newfoundland and Labrador terrain map

National park boundary

□ National historic site (N.H.S.)

Boundary

⊛ Provincial capital

• City or town

+ Elevation above sea level

= Waterfall

WORLD BOOK map

QUEBEC

Akpatok Island
Killiniq I.
Cape Chidley
Ungava Bay
North Aulatsivik I.
Four Peaks 4,415 ft (1,346 m)
Abloviak Fiord
Stony Point
Mt. Eliot 4,553 ft (1,388 m)
Seven Islands Bay
Innuit Mtn. 4,950 ft (1,509 m)
Nachvak Fiord
TORNGAT MOUNTAINS NATIONAL PARK
Mount Caubvick (Mont d'Iberville) 5,420 ft (1,652 m) Highest point in Newfoundland and Labrador
Saglek Bay
Cape Uivak
Labrador Sea
Hebron Fiord
North
Koksoak R.
Kuujjuaq
L. LeMoyne
Riviere-à-la-Baleine
George River
Kaumajet Mts.
Cod Island
Okak Islands
Wheeler River
Fraser R.
Labrador Highland
South Aulatsivik I.
Lac Champdore
Nain
Dog I.
North Latitude 56°
Wakuach L.
+ 2,873 ft (876 m)
Lac aux Goelands
Kogaluk R.
Voisey Bay
Tunungayualok I.
Mistastin L.
Hopedale
North Atlantic Ocean
Schefferville
Petitsikapau L.
Attikamagen L.
Riviere de Pas
Harp Lake
Ugjoktok Bay
Deep Inlet
Bay of Islands
Cape Makkovik
Dyke L.
Kanairiktok R.
Adlavik Is.
Cape Harrison
Menihek Lakes
Smallwood Reservoir
Sandgirt L.
Lobstick L.
Michikamau L.
Seal L.
White Bear L.
Kaipokok R.
Byron Bay
Naskaupi River
Nipishish L.
Hamilton Inlet
Ashuanipi L.
Churchill Falls 245 ft (75 m)
Churchill Falls
Ossokmanuan L.
Grand L.
Goose R.
Lake Melville
+ 4,300 ft (1,311 m)
Cape Porcupine
Sandwich Bay
Table Bay
Labrador City
Shabogamo L.
Lac Joseph
Happy Valley-Goose Bay
Mealy Mts.
Cartwright
Island of Ponds
Wabush
Winokapau L.
Kenamu R.
Eagle River
Hawke I.
Opocopa L.
Churchill River
3,245 ft (989 m)
St. Michaels Bay
Atikonak L.
Ashuanipi L.
Minipi L.
Little Mecatina
Paradise R.
Alexis R.
Port Hope Simpson
St. Lewis R.
Belle Isle
Moisie River
Natashquan River
St. Augustin River
St. Paul R.
Bradore Hills
Cape Bauld
Strait of Belle Isle
L'ANSE AUX MEADOWS N.H.S.
Hare Bay

QUEBEC

3,440 ft (1,049 m)
Riviere Ste. Marguerite
R. St. Jean
Romaine River
Aguanus River
Olomane River
L. Musquaro
Groais I.
Grey Islands
Bell I.
Magpie River
Havre-St-Pierre
Sept Îles
Mingan Archipelago
Pte. de Natashquan
Cape Whittle
PORT AU CHOIX N.H.S.
Great Northern Peninsula
Long Range Mts.
White Bay
Horse I.
Cape St. John
Island of Newfoundland
West Point
Jacques Cartier Passage
Anticosti Island
Gros Morne 2,644 ft (806 m)
GROS MORNE NATIONAL PARK
Notre Dame Bay
New World I.
Fogo I.
St. Lawrence River
Mt. Jacques Cartier 4,160 ft (1,268 m)
FORILLON NATIONAL PARK
Heath Point
Bay of Islands
Sandy L.
Gander R.
Cape Freels
Gaspé Peninsula
Cape Gaspé
Corner Brook 2,672 ft (814 m)
Grand Lake
Exploits R.
Gander L.
Gander
Bonavista Bay
Cape Bonavista

QUEBEC

Red Indian L.
Grand Falls-Windsor
Lewis Hills
Port au Port Peninsula
Cape St. George
Meelpaeg Lake
TERRA NOVA NATIONAL PARK
Gulf of St. Lawrence
St. George's Bay
Long Range Mts.
Victoria L.
King George IV L.
Grey R.
Jeddore L.
Mt. Sylvester 1,250 ft (381 m)
Trinity Bay
Campbellton
Chaleur Bay
Cape Anguille
Cape Ray
Channel-Port aux Basques
Hermitage Bay
Fortune Bay
Placentia Bay
St. John's
Cape Spear
Avalon Peninsula
Placentia
Mt. Carleton 2,690 ft (820 m)
Nepisiguit R.
Île Lamèque
Magdalen Island
Cabot Strait
Great Miquelon
ST.-PIERRE AND MIQUELON (France)
Burin Peninsula
Placentia Bay
Concepcion Bay
NEW BRUNSWICK
KOUCHIBOUGUAC NATIONAL PARK
Miramichi Bay
Cape North
CAPE BRETON HIGHLANDS NATIONAL PARK
St.-Pierre
Cape St. Mary's
Cape Pine
Cape Race
Trepassey Bay
Grand Banks
PRINCE EDWARD ISLAND
NOVA SCOTIA
60° West Longitude

QUEBEC

Labrador

Labrador Sea

0   100   200   300   400   500   600 Miles

0   100   200   300   400   500   600   700   800   900 Kilometers

lakes, and Lac Joseph. On the island of Newfoundland, Grand Lake is the largest, followed by Red Indian and Gander lakes. Grand Lake covers 205 square miles (531 square kilometers).

Plant and animal life. Forests cover about 87,000 square miles (225,000 square kilometers) of the province. Balsam fir and spruce are the most common trees. They supply wood for Newfoundland and Labrador's pulp and paper industry. Other trees include the aspen, birch, larch, pine, and white spruce. Shrubs, lichens, and mosses grow at high elevations. Wildflowers, such as butterworts, Canada mayflowers, goldthreads, Indian pipes, pink lady's-slippers, starflowers, and twinflowers, also grow in the province. The purple pitcher plant, Newfoundland and Labrador's provincial flower, grows in bog areas.

Many species of fish have flourished in the shallow waters surrounding the island of Newfoundland and extending along the Labrador coast. The main species there include capelin, cod, crab, flounder, herring, lobster, plaice, redfish, and scallops.

About 30 kinds of animals live in the province. They include Arctic hares, bears, beavers, caribou, foxes, lynxes, moose, otters, rabbits, seals, and weasels. Two famous breeds of dogs, the Labrador retriever and the Newfoundland, originated in the province (see **Labrador retriever; Newfoundland dog**).

Some birds live in Newfoundland and Labrador all year, but many kinds visit the province. Ptarmigans and ruffed grouse live in the province. Ducks, geese, and snipes visit every summer. Gulls, loons, murres, puffins, terns, and other sea birds feed in the coastal waters.

Climate. The cold Labrador Current and Arctic winds keep the province cool (see **Labrador Current**). But the climate varies greatly between Labrador and Newfound-

land. On the island, January temperatures in St. John's average 23 °F (−5 °C). Along the Labrador coast, average January temperatures range from 4 to −2 °F (−16 to −19 °C). July temperatures average about 59 °F (15 °C) in St. John's and about 50 °F (10 °C) in coastal Labrador. The province's highest and lowest temperatures occurred in central Labrador. Happy Valley-Goose Bay had the highest temperature, 100 °F (38 °C), on July 4, 1944. The record low, −55 °F (−48 °C), occurred at Sandgirt Lake on Jan. 17, 1946, and at Ashuanipi on Feb. 7, 1950.

Newfoundland and Labrador's annual *precipitation* (rain, melted snow, and other forms of moisture) ranges from about 20 inches (51 centimeters) in Northern Labrador to 60 inches (150 centimeters) at St. John's. Average yearly snowfall ranges from 77 inches (196 centimeters) on the island to about 170 inches (430 centimeters) in Labrador.

Average monthly weather

	Nain					St. John's				
	Temperatures				Days of rain or snow		Temperatures				Days of rain or snow
	°F		°C				°F		°C		
	High	Low	High	Low			High	Low	High	Low	
Jan.	7	−9	−14	−23	12	Jan.	30	16	−1	−9	22
Feb.	7	−9	−14	−23	10	Feb.	28	16	−2	−9	19
Mar.	19	0	−7	−18	13	Mar.	34	21	1	−6	20
Apr.	32	14	0	−10	13	Apr.	41	28	5	−2	18
May	41	27	5	−3	13	May	52	36	11	2	16
June	52	34	11	1	14	June	61	43	16	6	15
July	59	41	15	5	14	July	68	52	20	11	13
Aug.	61	43	16	6	13	Aug.	68	52	20	11	14
Sept.	52	37	11	3	14	Sept.	61	46	16	8	16
Oct.	39	28	4	−2	13	Oct.	52	37	11	3	19
Nov.	28	18	−2	−8	13	Nov.	43	30	6	−1	20
Dec.	16	1	−9	−17	14	Dec.	34	21	1	−6	22

Average January temperatures

The province's winters are much colder on the Labrador mainland than they are on the island of Newfoundland.

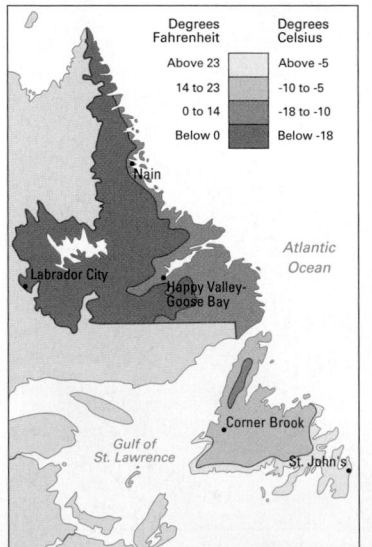

Degrees Fahrenheit	Degrees Celsius
Above 23	Above -5
14 to 23	-10 to -5
0 to 14	-18 to -10
Below 0	Below -18

Average July temperatures

The province generally is cool during summertime. The warmest temperatures are found on the island of Newfoundland.

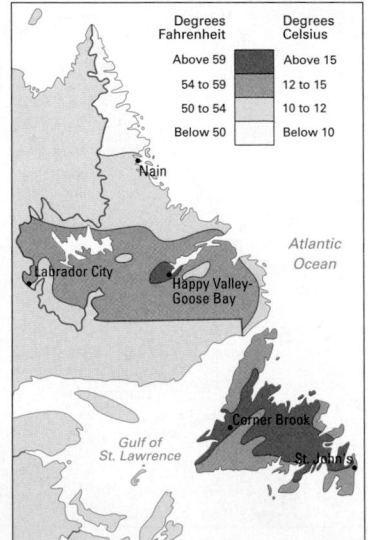

Degrees Fahrenheit	Degrees Celsius
Above 59	Above 15
54 to 59	12 to 15
50 to 54	10 to 12
Below 50	Below 10

Average yearly precipitation

The island of Newfoundland and the southern mainland receive the most precipitation. The north is the driest section.

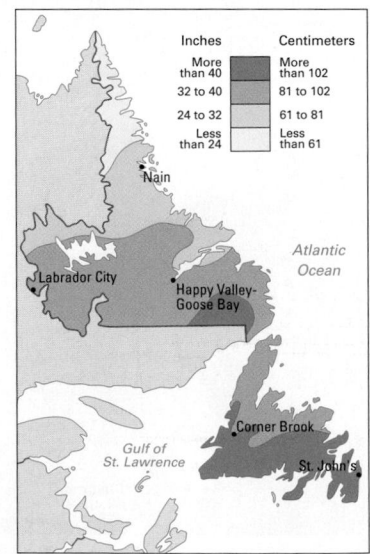

Inches	Centimeters
More than 40	More than 102
32 to 40	81 to 102
24 to 32	61 to 81
Less than 24	Less than 61

WORLD BOOK maps; based on the *National Atlas of Canada.*

Newfoundland and Labrador economy

General economy

Gross domestic product (GDP)* (2008)	$31,458,000,000
Rank among Canadian provinces	9th
Unemployment rate (2009)	15.5% (Canada avg: 8.3%)

*Gross domestic product is the total value of goods and services produced in a year and is in Canadian dollars.
Source: Statistics Canada.

Production and workers by economic activities

Economic activities	Percent of GDP* produced	Employed workers Number of people	Employed workers Percent of total
Mining	30	15,900*	7*
Community, business, & personal services	19	77,400†	35†
Finance, insurance, & real estate	12†	7,500	3
Trade, restaurants, & hotels	10	48,800	22
Government	7	18,600	8
Transportation & communication	6	18,900	9
Manufacturing	5	14,100	6
Construction	4	16,700	8
Utilities	3	1,600	1
Agriculture	2*	900	‡
Total**	100	220,400	100

*Includes figures from forestry and fishing.
†Includes figures from establishments that manage other companies.
‡Less than one-half of 1 percent
**Figures do not add up to 100 percent due to rounding.
Figures are for 2008. Source: Statistics Canada.

WORLD BOOK map

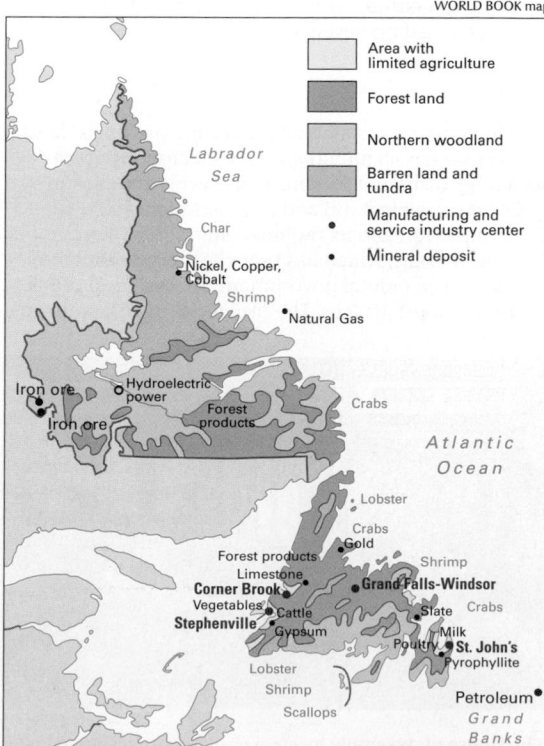

	Area with limited agriculture
	Forest land
	Northern woodland
	Barren land and tundra
●	Manufacturing and service industry center
●	Mineral deposit

Labrador Sea

Char
Nickel, Copper, Cobalt
Shrimp
Natural Gas
Iron ore
Hydroelectric power
Iron ore
Forest products
Crabs
Atlantic Ocean
Lobster
Crabs
Forest products
Gold
Limestone
Shrimp
Corner Brook
Grand Falls-Windsor
Vegetables
Cattle
Crabs
Stephenville
Gypsum
Slate
Milk
Poultry
St. John's
Pyrophyllite
Lobster
Shrimp
Scallops
Petroleum
Grand Banks

Agriculture

Cash receipts	$110,095,000
Rank among Canadian provinces	10th
Distribution	86% livestock, 14% crops
Farms (2006)	600
Farm acres (hectares)	91,900 (37,200)
Rank among Canadian provinces	10th
Farmland	Less than ⅒ of 1% of the province

Leading product

Dairy
Other products: cattle and calves, eggs, floriculture and nursery products, hens and chickens, hogs, vegetables.

Fishing

Commercial catch	$527,487,000
Rank among Canadian provinces	2nd

Leading catches

1. Shrimp (ranks 1st in Canada)
2. Crab (ranks 1st in Canada)
3. Cod (ranks 1st in Canada)
4. Lobster
Other catches: clams, flatfishes, Greenland turbot, herring, mackerel.

Manufacturing

Value added by manufacture*	$1,175,657,000
Rank among Canadian provinces	9th

Leading product

Food and beverage products
Other products: computer and electronic products, fabricated metal products, paper products, printed materials, refined petroleum, transportation equipment, wood products.

*Value added by manufacture is the increase in value of raw materials after they become finished products.

Mining

Mineral production	$15,181,281,000
Rank among Canadian provinces	2nd
Minerals	$4,949,381,000
Coal	*
Crude oil and crude oil equivalents	15,181,281,000
Natural gas	*

*No significant mining of this product in Newfoundland and Labrador.

Leading products

1. Petroleum (ranks 2nd in Canada)
2. Nickel (ranks 2nd in Canada)
3. Iron (ranks 1st in Canada)
4. Copper (ranks 3rd in Canada)
Other products: cobalt, stone, zinc.

Electric power

Hydroelectric	96.3%
Petroleum	3.2%
Other	0.5%

Figures are for 2007, except for agriculture and fishing statistics, which are for 2008.
Dollar amounts are in Canadian dollars.
Source: Statistics Canada.

Economic map of Newfoundland and Labrador

This map shows the economic uses of land in Newfoundland and Labrador and where the leading farm, mineral, and forest products are produced. Industrial centers are shown in red.

Natural resources have provided the foundation of the Newfoundland and Labrador economy for centuries. These resources include iron ore from Labrador, pulpwood from the island of Newfoundland, fish from the Atlantic Ocean, and since the 1990's, oil extracted off the province's coast. However, service industries are the economy's leading sector. They account for the largest part of the province's *gross domestic product* (GDP)—the total value of goods and services produced in a year.

Natural resources. Newfoundland and Labrador has some of the world's largest known iron-ore deposits. It also has significant deposits of cobalt, copper, nickel, and oil. Natural gas deposits exist in the area but have not yet been developed. The province's large forests are valuable natural resources.

Because of a depletion of fish stocks in the Atlantic Ocean off the province's coast, a series of fishing restrictions went into effect beginning in the early 1990's. In 2003, the Canadian government banned cod fishing in the Atlantic Ocean northeast of the province.

Service industries account for most of the province's GDP and employment. Many of these industries are in St. John's, the provincial capital. St. John's is the center of government activities and the province's banking industry. Memorial University of Newfoundland in St. John's is one of the world's leading centers of ocean research.

Mining. Oil production is the province's newest mining activity. Production started from the large offshore Hibernia field in late 1997. Within a few years, oil had become the province's most valuable mined product.

Iron ore also ranks among the province's leading mined products. All of the iron ore comes from two mines in Labrador. One mine is at Labrador City, and the other is at Wabush. Voisey Bay in Labrador produces nickel, copper, and cobalt.

Manufacturing plays a lesser role in Newfoundland and Labrador than it does in any other province. Much of the province's manufacturing involves processing its natural resources. Seafood products are the leading food product. Large paper mills and sawmills operate in the province. Come by Chance has an oil refinery.

Fishing has traditionally been important to the economy. Before fishing restrictions were imposed in the early 1990's, cod was the leading fish catch. Today, such shellfish as crab and shrimp are the leading catches.

Forestry. Fir and spruce provide much of the timber harvest. The province's timber is used to make firewood, lumber, and newsprint.

Agriculture. Because of the lack of fertile soil, agriculture provides less income in Newfoundland and Labrador than in any other province. The leading farm products include dairy products, chickens, eggs, and floriculture and nursery products.

Electric power and utilities. Hydroelectric plants supply almost all of the electric power produced in the province. The largest hydroelectric plant lies on the Churchill River in Labrador.

Transportation. Newfoundland and Labrador lies nearer Europe than any other part of North America except Greenland. This location made the province an important stopping point for airplanes and ships traveling across the Atlantic. But increases in the range of planes and ships have reduced the need for refueling stops.

Gander and St. John's have international airports. Part of the Trans-Canada Highway runs on the island of Newfoundland from St. John's to Channel-Port aux Basques (see **Trans-Canada Highway**). Ferry services also operate in the province.

Communication. The *Telegram* of St. John's is the province's leading newspaper.

Government

Lieutenant governor of Newfoundland and Labrador represents the British monarch, Queen Elizabeth II, in her role as queen of Canada. The *governor general in council* appoints the lieutenant governor. The governor general in council is the governor general of Canada acting with the advice and consent of the Executive Council (also called the Cabinet). The lieutenant governor is considered the head of state, but the position is largely ceremonial.

Premier of Newfoundland and Labrador is the actual head of the provincial government. The province has a *parliamentary* form of government. The premier is an elected member of the House of Assembly. The person who serves as premier is usually the leader of the majority party in the Assembly. The premier must have the support of a majority of the Assembly.

The premier presides over the Cabinet. The Cabinet includes ministers appointed by the lieutenant governor on the advice of the premier. Most of them belong to the premier's party in the Assembly. Most ministers direct one or more branches of the government. The Cabinet, like the premier, must have the support of the majority of the Assembly. Otherwise, the Cabinet must resign, or its supporters must win a majority of seats in the Assembly in a new general election.

House of Assembly of Newfoundland and Labrador

is a one-house legislature. It passes the provincial laws. The House has 48 members, each elected from 1 of 48 Assembly districts. Elections occur every four years.

Courts in Newfoundland and Labrador include the Supreme Court and its regional judicial centers, and the Provincial Court, which has branches throughout the province. The federal government of Canada appoints Supreme Court justices. The provincial government ap-

Office of the Speaker

The House of Assembly meets in chambers in the Confederation Building in St. John's. The Assembly has 48 members.

The premiers of Newfoundland and Labrador

	Party	Term
Joseph R. Smallwood	Liberal	1949-1972
Frank D. Moores*	Progressive Cons.	1972-1979
A. Brian Peckford*	Progressive Cons.	1979-1989
Thomas Rideout*	Progressive Cons.	1989
Clyde Kirby Wells	Liberal	1989-1996
Brian Tobin	Liberal	1996-2000
Beaton Tulk	Liberal	2000-2001
Roger D. Grimes	Liberal	2001-2003
Danny Williams*	Progressive Cons.	2003-2010
Kathy Dunderdale	Progressive Cons.	2010-

*Progressive Conservative.

points judges to Newfoundland and Labrador's Provincial Court.

Local government. St. John's, Corner Brook, and Mount Pearl, Newfoundland and Labrador's three cities, operate under city acts passed by the provincial legislature. An elected council governs each incorporated town and incorporated community in the province.

Revenue. Taxes account for over half of Newfoundland and Labrador's *general revenue* (income). Most of this is generated from personal income taxes, retail sales taxes, and royalties from offshore oil production. Much of the rest comes from the federal government.

Politics. The main provincial parties in Newfoundland and Labrador are the Liberal, New Democratic, and Progressive Conservative (PC) parties. Of these, the New Democratic Party is the least conservative. The PC Party is the most conservative. Other parties include the Labrador Party and the Green Party.

Aboriginal government. Through an agreement with the governments of Newfoundland and Labrador and Canada, the Inuit of Labrador established the regional Nunatsiavut Government in 2005. This government has several departments that are responsible for such matters as land and natural resources; health and social development; culture, recreation, and tourism; finance and human resources; and education and economic development. Several Inuit *community governments* exist under the Nunatsiavut Government. An Inuit Angajukkak (mayor and chief executive officer) heads each community government.

History

Early European exploration. Norse explorers probably were the first white people to live in Newfoundland. In 1961, archaeologists discovered the ruins of a Norse settlement on the northern tip of the island. This settlement was established about A.D. 1000.

English fishing crews from Bristol probably reached Newfoundland in the late 1400's. John Cabot, an Italian explorer in the service of England, may have landed on Newfoundland or Nova Scotia in 1497. Cabot brought news of Newfoundland's rich fishing to Europe.

Following Cabot's voyage, hundreds of French, Portuguese, and Spanish fishing fleets visited Newfoundland. Among them were Basque whalers from France and Spain. Some Basques established a base at Red Bay, on the southeast coast of Labrador. At that time, Beothuk Indians lived in Newfoundland. In the 1700's, Mi'kmaq Indians settled chiefly along the southern coast of Newfoundland. The Beothuk depended on access to coastal and marine resources. The growing presence of European fishing enterprises and coastal settlements led the Beothuk to retreat inland. Inland, the Beothuk found too few resources to support them, and European diseases weakened them. By 1829, the Beothuk had disappeared.

The Innu, formerly called the Naskapi and Montagnais, and the Inuit, formerly called Eskimos, have lived in Labrador for centuries. The Innu lived in southern and central Labrador and the Inuit along the northern coast.

Colonization. By the late 1500's, English fishing fleets worked and settled mainly along the southeastern coast of Newfoundland. French fishing fleets controlled the north and south coasts. But English, French, Spanish, and Portuguese ships often anchored in the same harbor. A "fishing admiral" ruled each harbor. This official was the master of the first ship to arrive at the beginning of the fishing season. In 1634, King Charles I officially gave authority to the English fishing admirals.

In 1583, the English explorer Sir Humphrey Gilbert arrived in St. John's. He claimed Newfoundland as part of his new colony. But Gilbert and his crew were lost at sea on their journey home without having established a settlement in Newfoundland. John Guy, a merchant, arrived in 1610 with settlers sent by an English company. Guy formed a colony at Cupids, on Conception Bay. Cupids failed as a commercial venture, but people continued to live there. In 1621, Sir George Calvert (later Lord Baltimore) founded a major colony at Ferryland. In 1629, after an unusually cold winter, Calvert requested a royal grant of land farther south. He went on to establish the colony of Maryland in what is now the United States.

In 1637, King Charles I granted Newfoundland to Sir David Kirke and other nobles. Kirke set up headquarters at Ferryland but had no authority over English fishing fleets who visited the island. The Ferryland colony developed successfully under Kirke and, later, under his wife, Lady Sara Kirke. The English government recalled Kirke to England in 1651 and discouraged further attempts at colonization in Newfoundland. But the descendants of the early English colonists served as the core of a growing permanent population of European ancestry there.

War with France. French settlers founded Placentia in 1662. Placentia quickly grew into a fortified colony that threatened the English in Newfoundland. William III became king of England in 1689. William declared war on France, and the French and English colonies in North America, including Newfoundland, became part of the battleground. In 1696 and 1697, the French destroyed all English settlements in Newfoundland. However, the war in Europe went against the French and, in 1713, the Treaty of Utrecht gave all of the island of Newfoundland to the British. France kept only the privilege of using part of the northeastern and western shore for drying fish. That area became known as the French Shore. The 1783 Treaty of Versailles signed by Britain (now also called the United Kingdom) and France shifted the boundaries of the French Shore to the north and west.

In 1729, the British government began to appoint naval officers as royal governors to rule Newfoundland during the fishing season each summer. Captain Henry

ℋistoric 𝒩ewfoundland and ℒabrador

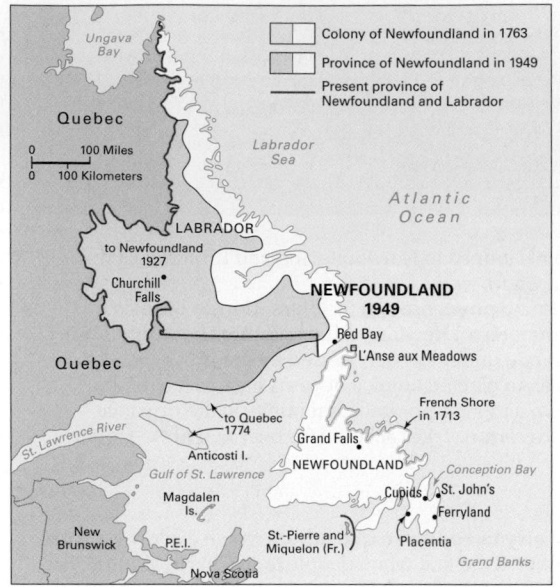

WORLD BOOK map

Norse explorers were probably the first Europeans to live on the island of Newfoundland. A Norse settlement on the island dates back to about A.D. 1000.

Newfoundland, a British colony in 1763, included the island of Newfoundland and a strip of land along the Labrador coast. The British Privy Council established the current western boundary of Labrador in 1927. Newfoundland became a province in 1949.

The British and French battled for control of what is now Newfoundland and Labrador during the Seven Years' War. In 1762, a French fleet, *shown here,* seized St. John's. But the war ended as a great British victory in 1763.

WORLD BOOK illustrations by Richard Bonson, The Art Agency

Important dates in Newfoundland and Labrador

1497 John Cabot raised the banner of King Henry VII on a "new found land" which may have been the island of Newfoundland or Nova Scotia.

1583 Sir Humphrey Gilbert landed in Newfoundland and claimed the region as part of his new colony.

1637 King Charles I granted Newfoundland to Sir David Kirke and his partners.

1662 The French established a garrison at Placentia.

1713 The Treaty of Utrecht gave Newfoundland to Britain (now also called the United Kingdom).

1729 Captain Henry Osborne became Newfoundland's first naval governor.

1763 In the Treaty of Paris, France surrendered Labrador to Britain.

1832 The United Kingdom granted Newfoundland the right to elect a general assembly.

1855 Newfoundland gained a "responsible government" that was controlled by an elected assembly.

1927 The British Privy Council established the present boundary between Quebec and what is now the province of Newfoundland and Labrador.

1934 The United Kingdom suspended Newfoundland's government, established a Commission of Government, and assumed Newfoundland's debts.

1949 Newfoundland became Canada's 10th province on March 31.

1958 Newfoundland introduced free hospitalization and programs for educational improvements.

1967 Construction began on a $950-million hydroelectric plant in Churchill Falls in Labrador. The plant's first two generators began operating in 1971.

2001 Canada's Parliament officially changed Newfoundland's name to Newfoundland and Labrador.

Osborne became the first such "naval governor."

Britain obtained nearly all the rest of France's possessions in Canada by the Treaty of Paris, which ended the Seven Years' War in 1763. France received St.-Pierre and Miquelon islands from Britain and regained its right to use the French Shore. France gave up this right in 1904.

After the Treaty of Paris, the British government placed the Labrador coast under the authority of Newfoundland's naval governor. The Labrador coast was placed under Quebec-British rule in 1774 and returned to Newfoundland's control in 1809.

Representation and independence. By 1815, about 40,000 people lived in Newfoundland. In 1817, Sir Francis Pickmore became the first governor to remain on the island after the close of the fishing season. Many people wanted a strong local government. Led by William Carson, a Scottish surgeon, the people repeatedly asked Parliament for authority to make their own laws. In 1832, the British government established a legislature for Newfoundland. It consisted of a governor, a council, and a general assembly elected by the people.

Newfoundland's government was a "representative government" because its legislature could make laws. But the British Parliament had to approve the laws, and a British governor enforced them. The general assembly soon asked for a "responsible government" in which the assembly rather than the governor controlled the cabinet. The British had granted their other Canadian colonies responsible government in the 1840's. They allowed Newfoundland to set up such a government in 1855.

Economic developments. Until the mid-1800's, Newfoundland's economy was based chiefly on fishing and sealing. Dried cod and seal products were major exports of Newfoundland. In the 1860's, mineral exploration began, and by 1888, copper mining had become an important industry in Newfoundland. In the 1890's, an iron ore mine opened on Bell Island. A railway was built across Newfoundland from 1882 to 1896. The colony's first paper mill began operating in Grand Falls in 1909. But Newfoundland's new mining and forestry industries depended on external markets, and railway construction burdened the colony with a large public debt.

In 1927, the British Privy Council established the present boundary between the coast of Labrador and Quebec. This decision gave Newfoundland the vast mineral resources of the Knob Lake and Wabush Lake regions.

Ruin and recovery. After World War I ended in 1918, Newfoundland's prosperity began to fade, chiefly because of a depression in international trade. The cost of the war also increased Newfoundland's public debt. In the 1920's, Newfoundland tried to revive its lagging industries and develop new ones. But by 1930, the Great Depression had struck most of the world. Newfoundland's fish, iron ore, and newsprint markets collapsed. The colony's finances began to fail.

Under Prime Minister Frederick C. Alderdice, Newfoundland appealed to the United Kingdom for financial assistance under a new form of government. In 1934, the United Kingdom suspended Newfoundland's government and established a Commission of Government. It consisted of a British governor and six other men, three of them Newfoundlanders. Newfoundland became a dependency, and the United Kingdom took over its debts.

Economic recovery came slowly. The government re-

organized the civil service, improved education and health facilities, and sponsored research to improve agriculture. Newfoundland's fishing and logging industries got much-needed financial aid. World War II (1939-1945) gave new life to Newfoundland's economy. The factories, fisheries, and mines increased production to fill wartime demands. Canada and the United States built military bases in Newfoundland. People at these bases created new demand for local products.

Confederation with Canada. In 1948, Newfoundland voters chose to unite with Canada rather than keep the Commission of Government or return to independent self-government. On March 31, 1949, Newfoundland became the 10th province of Canada. Joseph R. Smallwood, leader of the Liberal Party, was the first premier of the new province. Newfoundland was in sound financial condition at the time of confederation. But a wide gap existed between the standard of living in Newfoundland and many of the other nine provinces. Through confederation, Newfoundland began to share in federal social security benefits. The province also participated in such federal programs as the development of trade schools and the construction of more than 500 miles (800 kilometers) of the Trans-Canada Highway.

The late 1900's. In the 1960's, Newfoundland expanded its industrial and educational facilities and its production and distribution of electric power. After a boom in mineral production, mining began to rival fishing as a major industry. New mines opened, mostly in Labrador.

By the late 1960's, Newfoundland's rural electrification program had brought electric service to over 100 isolated communities in the province. The main project in the electrification program was a huge hydroelectric plant in Churchill Falls in Labrador. The plant began producing power in 1971, and all of its 11 generators were operating by 1974. The plant is one of the largest hydroelectric projects in the Western Hemisphere.

From the time it became a province to the mid-1970's, Newfoundland's population grew rapidly, and many people had to leave the province to find work. In 1979, a major oil field was discovered off the eastern coast. But low oil prices contributed to a delay in the development of the field, and oil production did not begin until 1997.

In the early 1990's, the federal government restricted fishing for cod in waters in and around Newfoundland because of a sharp drop in their numbers. It also placed restrictions on other species. In 1994, the Northwest Atlantic Fisheries Organization (NAFO) agreed to observe the restrictions. NAFO is an intergovernmental fisheries science and management organization.

Recent developments. In 2001, Canada's Parliament changed the official name of the province to Newfoundland and Labrador. Newfoundland and Labrador experienced economic difficulties during the first few years of the 2000's. In 2003, the government banned cod fishing in the Atlantic Ocean northeast of Newfoundland and Labrador. Thousands of Newfoundlanders lost jobs in the fishing industry. Weakened international markets for newsprint also caused two of the province's major pulp and paper mills to shut down in 2005 and 2009.

In 2008, oil-related revenue transformed Newfoundland and Labrador from a "have-not" into a "have" province under the system by which Canada's government transfers money from wealthier to poorer provinces. By

2010, revenue from offshore oil production was largely responsible for the province's relative prosperity during a global economic recession.   Sean Cadigan

Related articles in *World Book* include:

Biographies

Bartlett, Robert A.	Grenfell, Sir Wilfred T.
Gilbert, Sir Humphrey	Prendergast, Maurice B.

Cities and towns

Corner Brook	Placentia	St. John's

Physical features

Churchill River	Gulf Stream
Grand Banks	Labrador Current
Gulf of Saint Lawrence	Labrador Peninsula

Other related articles

Atlantic Provinces	Terra Nova National Park
Beothuk Indians	

Outline

I. People
   A. Population   C. Libraries and museums
   B. Schools
II. Visitor's guide
III. Land and climate
   A. Land regions   D. Rivers and lakes
   B. Coastline   E. Plant and animal life
   C. Mountains   F. Climate
IV. Economy
   A. Natural resources   F. Forestry
   B. Service industries   G. Agriculture
   C. Mining   H. Electric power and utilities
   D. Manufacturing   I. Transportation
   E. Fishing   J. Communication
V. Government
   A. Lieutenant governor   E. Local government
   B. Premier   F. Revenue
   C. House of Assembly   G. Politics
   D. Courts   H. Aboriginal government
VI. History

Additional resources

Beckett, Harry. *Newfoundland and Labrador.* Weigl, 2008. Younger readers.

Blake, Raymond B. *Canadians at Last: Canada Integrates Newfoundland As a Province.* 1994. Reprint. Univ. of Toronto Pr., 2004.

Cadigan, Sean T. *Newfoundland and Labrador: A History.* Univ. of Toronto Pr., 2009.

Hubbard, Mina B., and others. *The Woman Who Mapped Labrador.* McGill-Queen's Univ. Pr., 2005. Includes Hubbard's edited expedition diary and a biography of Hubbard by Ann Hart.

O'Flaherty, Patrick. *Lost Country: The Rise and Fall of Newfoundland, 1843-1933.* Long Beach Pr., 2005. *Old Newfoundland: A History to 1843.* 1999.

Rompkey, Bill. *The Story of Labrador.* McGill-Queen's Univ. Pr., 2003.

Stortini, Helen. *Newfoundland and Labrador.* Whitecap Bks., 2006. Younger readers.

Newfoundland dog, *NOO fuhnd* LAND, is one of the largest and strongest breeds of dog. Male Newfoundlands weigh about 140 pounds (64 kilograms) and stand about 28 inches (71 centimeters) high at the shoulder. Females are slightly smaller. Newfoundlands have a thick coat that protects against all types of weather. The most common color is black, often with a patch of white on the chest, chin, or toes. These dogs also may be gray, brown, or white with black markings.

No one knows exactly when the Newfoundland was developed. The breed was used for heavy work, both on land and in water. Early steamships and sailing vessels frequently included a Newfoundland as a crew member. These dogs are still known for their work in the water and their tendency to help swimmers in distress.

Newfoundlands are even-tempered, intelligent, and confident. Their patience, playfulness, and protectiveness make them excellent companions for children.

Critically reviewed by the Newfoundland Club of America

See also **Dog** (picture: Working dogs).

Newgate Prison was England's main criminal jail for over 700 years. It was built in London in 1188 and was enlarged and redesigned many times. It was torn down in 1902 after years of protests about its harsh conditions. The site then became incorporated into London's Central Criminal Court, also known as the Old Bailey.

Beginning in 1783, Newgate housed the London gallows. Executions were at first held in public but were moved inside the prison in 1868. In addition to its history of brutality, Newgate played a key role in prison reform. In 1813, Elizabeth Fry, a British social reformer, began working to improve the conditions of the prison and the treatment of the inmates, especially the women and their children. Until Fry's policies were established, women, children, debtors, and convicted criminals were held together in open cells. In 1858, the interior was rebuilt with single cells.   Mary Bosworth

Newman, Barnett (1905-1970), an American painter, was a leading member of the Abstract Expressionist movement. Newman developed a simple style. Most of his works consist of a large vertical stripe on a background of one intense color. Newman used large surfaces to induce viewers to scan his paintings broadly and thereby sense their vast scale and spacious, uncluttered vision. He believed the abstract nature of his paintings gave them philosophical and spiritual meaning.

Newman began to paint in his simplified style in 1949. His works became highly controversial and were often attacked during the 1950's. However, his style had a strong impact on many painters of the 1960's and 1970's.

Newman helped establish the principles of Minimalism, an American style that rejected emotion and subject matter in painting and emphasized color and form. His use of large areas of color also influenced a movement called Color-Field Painting.

Newman was born on Jan. 29, 1905, in New York City. He died on July 4, 1970.   Dore Ashton

See also **Abstract Expressionism.**

Newman, John Henry (1801-1890), became a cardinal of the Roman Catholic Church in 1879, after converting to the Catholic faith in 1845. Before his conversion, Newman distinguished himself as a scholar and a preacher of the Church of England at Oxford University. In 1833, he joined the Oxford Movement, a movement to rid the Church of England of political domination and to ground it more firmly in traditional beliefs (see **Oxford Movement**). Newman shocked his fellow reformers by joining the Catholic Church in 1845. In 1846, he became a priest. For most of his life as a Catholic, he lived in Birmingham, England, as *rector* (head priest) of an *oratory*—that is, a group of men devoted to prayer and study.

Newman was born in London on Feb. 21, 1801. He was one of the great thinkers of the 1800's. Newman's writings include his autobiography, the *Apologia pro Vita Sua* (1864); a lecture titled "The Idea of a University"

(1852); the book *The Grammar of Assent* (1870); and the hymn "Lead, Kindly Light" (1833). Newman died on Aug. 11, 1890. In 2010, Pope Benedict XVI *beatified* Cardinal Newman. Beatification is an important step toward declaring an individual a saint in the Roman Catholic Church.   Peter W. Williams

Newman, Paul (1925-2008), an American actor, won fame for his action roles and convincing character studies in motion pictures. He portrayed outsiders or rebels in many films. He won the Academy Award as best actor for his performance in *The Color of Money* (1986). In 1986, Newman received an honorary Academy Award "for his personal integrity and dedication to his craft."

Paul Leonard Newman was born on Jan. 26, 1925, in Cleveland. He studied acting at Kenyon College, Yale University, and the Actors Studio. His first movie was *The Silver Chalice* (1954). He gained stardom in *Somebody Up There Likes Me* (1957). His other films include *Cat on a Hot Tin Roof* (1958), *Exodus* (1960), *The Hustler* (1961), *Hud* (1963), *Harper* (1966), *Hombre* (1967), *Cool Hand Luke* (1967), *Butch Cassidy and the Sundance Kid* (1969), *The Sting* (1973), *The Towering Inferno* (1974), *Slap Shot* (1977), *The Verdict* (1982), *Mr. and Mrs. Bridge* (1990), and *Road to Perdition* (2002). He also starred on Broadway in *Sweet Bird of Youth* (1959). Newman directed *Rachel,*

AP/Wide World

Paul Newman

Rachel (1968), *The Effect of Gamma Rays on Man-in-the-Moon Marigolds* (1972), and *The Glass Menagerie* (1987). All three starred his wife, Joanne Woodward.

Newman was a professional race car driver and co-owned an automobile racing team. In 1982, he cofounded Newman's Own, a food company, from which all proceeds go to charity. For his charitable work, Newman received the Jean Hersholt Humanitarian Award during Academy Award ceremonies in 1994. Newman died on Sept. 26, 2008.   Louis Giannetti

Newport, Rhode Island (pop. 24,672), is best known as a summer resort. The city lies on Narragansett Bay (see **Rhode Island** [political map]). Today, Newport is also a tourist and convention center. Its attractions include more than 300 buildings from colonial days. One of them, the Colony House, was built in 1739 and served as one of Rhode Island's capitols until 1900. Another historic landmark is the Touro Synagogue. Built in 1763, it is the oldest Jewish house of worship in the United States. The city hosts the annual Newport Music Festival.

Newport was founded in 1639 by nine families from the Massachusetts Bay Colony who sought religious freedom. Before the American Revolution (1775-1783), Newport rivaled Boston and New York City as a shipping center. The city won fame in the late 1800's as the summer home of wealthy railroad and banking families. Newport is the home of the Naval War College and Salve Regina University. It has a council-manager government.   Stanford E. Demars

See also **Rhode Island** (Places to visit; pictures).

Newport, Christopher (1560?-1617), was an English sea captain who commanded the fleet that first brought settlers to present-day Virginia in 1607. Newport helped establish the Jamestown colony, the first permanent English settlement in North America.

Newport was born in England in 1560 or 1561. He went to sea as a young man and served aboard privateering vessels that raided Spanish treasure ships and colonies in the Caribbean Sea. Newport gained his first independent command in 1590. That same year, Newport lost his right arm fighting the Spanish off the coast of Cuba. Two years later, he captured the Spanish vessel *Madre de Dios,* which held a valuable cargo of spices and gems. It was one of the largest seizures of Spanish treasure in the 1500's.

Because of Newport's navigational skills and reputation as a mariner, the Virginia Company of London hired him to transport colonists to the New World (see **London Company**). In December 1606, Newport, his crew, and more than 100 settlers left London aboard three ships, the *Susan Constant, Godspeed,* and *Discovery.* During the voyage, Newport suspected the headstrong soldier John Smith of plotting a mutiny. Newport imprisoned and threatened to hang Smith, who later would serve as the leader of the Jamestown colony. Newport's ships reached the southern entrance to Chesapeake Bay in April 1607. Newport helped select the colony's location along the James River in May. In June, he returned to England to obtain additional supplies and men.

Newport sailed back to Virginia four times from 1608 to 1611. During his third voyage to Virginia, in 1609, he commanded the *Sea Venture* (also called *Sea Adventure),* which wrecked on the island of Bermuda. In the winter of 1609 and 1610, Newport and other survivors constructed two new vessels from the wreckage and then sailed on to Virginia. Many historians and literature experts believe these events inspired the play *The Tempest* (1611) by the English dramatist William Shakespeare. In 1612, Newport went to work for the East India Company (see **East India Company**). He died in what is now Indonesia in August 1617.   Phillip Hamilton

Newport News (pop. 180,719) is a shipbuilding center in eastern Virginia. It lies on the north shore of the harbor called Hampton Roads. See **Hampton Roads; Virginia** (political map). Newport News is part of a metropolitan area that includes Norfolk and Virginia Beach. The area has a population of 1,671,683.

Northrop Grumman Shipbuilding in Newport News is Virginia's largest private employer. The city is a large coal-exporting center. Other industries include seafood processing and the manufacture of automotive parts, electronic parts, escalators, printers, and photocopiers. Newport News is the home of the Mariners' Museum.

Newport News was named for Christopher Newport, who led a group of colonists to Jamestown, Virginia, in 1607. He reportedly brought news that more colonists were on the way. Although settlement began about 1620, the area did not develop as a city until the railroad arrived in 1881. Newport News merged with Warwick and took over Warwick County in 1958. It has a council-manager form of government.   Susan L Woodward

News media. See Journalism.

News service. See Associated Press; Thomson Reuters; United Press International.

The newsroom of a major newspaper is alive with activity as the editorial staff hurries to prepare stories on events and issues. Reporters and editors work on computers joined in a network, enabling them to pass stories along in electronic form so that all may complete their tasks.

Newspaper

Newspaper is a publication devoted chiefly to presenting and commenting on the news. Newspapers provide a good means of keeping informed on current events. They also play a role in shaping public opinion.

A large daily newspaper provides a great variety of information. News stories cover the latest developments in such fields as government, politics, sports, science, business, and the arts. Other news stories report crimes, disasters, and special events of human interest. Editorials and opinion columns comment on controversial issues. Informative feature articles examine a wide range of subjects, including psychology, fashion, health, and child care. Most newspapers have both print and online editions. An online edition might have features not found in the print version, such as videotaped interviews and *blogs* (online journals) by journalists. Other items, such as comic strips and puzzles, might be available only in the print paper.

Producing a daily newspaper requires great speed and efficiency. Reporters, editors, and photographers work under the constant pressure of deadlines. A large daily also employs many other workers, including advertising salespeople, artists, librarians, printing-press operators, truckdrivers, and Web site designers.

This article describes the kinds, organization, production, and business operations of newspapers in the United States. It then discusses newspapers in other countries and traces the history of newspapers. For information on major issues in U.S. journalism, see **Journalism**.

Kinds of newspapers

Newspapers are printed on coarse paper called *newsprint*. There are two major sizes of newspapers—*standard* and *tabloid*. A standard-sized newspaper in the United States is usually printed on paper known as *broadsheet*. Broadsheets are around 30 inches (76 centimeters) wide by 24 inches (61 centimeters) deep. When this paper is folded in half, it makes a page of a normal size for a standard newspaper—that is, about 15 inches (38 centimeters) wide by 24 inches deep. Tabloids are smaller and are sold flat instead of folded in half. They are not usually organized into separate sections as are broadsheet newspapers.

The standard and tabloid sizes are both used in publishing printed newspapers. The three main kinds of printed papers are (1) daily newspapers, (2) weekly newspapers, and (3) special-interest newspapers.

Daily newspapers print world, national, state, and local news. They also carry editorials, opinion columns, feature articles, and entertainment items. Big-city dailies print many stories on social and political issues, such as the quality of schools and the efficiency of government. Many metropolitan papers include one or more sections of suburban news several times a week. Some dailies are distributed in the evening, and others are morning papers. Only a few large cities have more than one daily newspaper. The United States has about 1,400 daily newspapers. The total circulation of U.S. dailies is about 50 million copies. The largest dailies sell more than a million copies.

Additional features and more advertising make Sunday newspapers much larger than weekday editions. Numerous Sunday papers have special sections on such topics as entertainment, finance, and travel. Many also include a Sunday magazine and comics in color.

In the United States, most daily newspapers chiefly serve a particular metropolitan area or local region. Many other countries, however, have newspapers with a national circulation. In these countries, most governmental decisions are made on the national level. However, in the United States, many governmental decisions are made locally. Largely for that reason, there are few national newspapers in the United States. Instead, many small U.S. newspapers report local happenings.

In the United States, *The New York Times, USA Today,* and *The Wall Street Journal* circulate nationally, but mostly in urban areas. Other notable dailies in the United States include the *Chicago Tribune, The Dallas Morning News, The Detroit News,* the *Los Angeles Times, The Miami Herald,* the *Daily News* of New York City, *The Philadelphia Inquirer,* the *St. Louis Post-Dispatch,* and *The Washington Post.*

Weekly newspapers, in general, serve much smaller areas than daily papers and publish news of a more personal nature. In small communities, many people know one another and take great interest in the activities of their friends and neighbors. Weddings, births, and deaths are major news items. A fire or traffic accident gets front-page coverage in a weekly newspaper. Weeklies also report news of local business and politics. Most weekly newspapers do not carry state, national, or world news.

Special-interest newspapers print news of concern to particular groups. Many business associations and labor unions publish newspapers for their members. Newspapers printed in foreign languages serve foreign-born residents in big cities. Some newspapers specialize in news about African Americans, Asian Americans, Hispanics, and other ethnic groups. Special-interest papers may also focus on specific topics, such as sports or the arts. Many high schools and most colleges also have a newspaper of their own.

Online newspapers are not distributed in printed form. Instead, they are produced as collections of information found at Web sites on the Internet. Many newspapers, especially dailies, produce an online version in addition to a printed version. Some online newspapers include many of the same news stories and features that appear in the printed version. Others include expanded articles, additional commentary on news stories, features that do not appear in their printed version, and content that can only be published online, such as audio or video recordings called *podcasts.* The online versions of some major papers have certain information that is available only by subscription, for which a computer user pays a fee.

The staff of a newspaper

The number of people needed to produce a newspaper varies widely. The smallest weekly papers may have only 1 to 3 workers, who do everything from writing the news, to selling ads, to running the press. Some larger weeklies employ 10 to 30 people. The largest metropolitan dailies have 2,000 or more employees.

The staff of most dailies is headed by the publisher, who directs all the departments. The staff of such a paper is divided into three main departments: (1) editorial, (2) business, and (3) mechanical.

The editorial department is responsible for the news and features that the paper prints. The head of the department is called the editor in chief, executive editor, or simply editor. This individual must have a thorough knowledge of all phases of newspaper work and know how to deal well with people.

Staff members of a small weekly newspaper generally perform a greater variety of tasks than their counterparts at a large daily newspaper. A staff of only a few people must do all the work, from gathering and writing the news to printing the paper. These editors are checking the facts in a story.

A managing editor helps the editor in chief direct the members of the editorial staff. Under the managing editor are assistant managing editors and news editors. Other editors have charge of news in certain areas. For example, most large dailies have a city editor, a suburban editor, a national editor, a feature editor, and an international editor. Each of the various sections and departments of the paper, such as the sports, arts, and financial sections, also has its own editor. Each editor supervises a staff of reporters, writers, and other workers. Some editors, such as the sports and financial editors, may write a daily column in addition to their supervisory duties. An art director works with the editors in planning the illustrations and photographs to accompany stories. The art director oversees a staff of artists and photographers.

The editor in chief directs the news staff and editorial writers. In many cases, the publisher helps guide these writers. For that reason, a newspaper's editorials often express the views of the publisher. Metropolitan dailies also employ special columnists to write columns of humor, advice, or general information.

Many newspapers provide special facilities to assist the editorial staff. For example, a library keeps copies of past stories and pictures plus such resources as almanacs and encyclopedias. The library also has computers for searching national and international databases. In addition, artists need special facilities to do their work. Some newspapers have a lab where photographic film can be developed quickly.

The business department tries to ensure that the paper makes a profit. A business manager heads the department with the help of an advertising manager, a circulation manager, and a promotion manager. The advertising manager directs a staff that sells advertising space to stores, manufacturers, and other businesses as well as classified ads to individuals and firms. The circulation manager supervises the distribution of the newspaper. The promotion manager develops ways of drawing attention to the paper to attract new readers and advertisers. The business department also has accountants and bookkeepers to handle the financial records.

The mechanical department prints the newspaper. A production manager directs the department's operations. Some workers create layouts of pages, and others set the type. Still other workers produce the printing plates from which the newspaper is printed. The printing-press operators lock the plates on the presses and print the papers. Mailroom personnel assemble the papers and turn them over to the circulation department.

How newspapers are produced

Gathering information is the first step in the production of the news in a newspaper. A paper gets the news it prints from two main sources: (1) its own reporters and (2) news services.

Reporters use interviews, research, and investigative techniques to gather information for their stories. They must have well-developed news judgment to sort out important stories from those with little public interest.

A newspaper employs several kinds of reporters. Many reporters cover a specialty called a *beat.* Some beat reporters are assigned to particular locations, including city hall, police headquarters, and the criminal courts. Other beat reporters cover a particular subject, such as science, religion, education, or consumer affairs. Certain other reporters, called *general assignment reporters,* cover any story to which they are assigned or which they find on their own.

The news staff of a big-city newspaper also includes *investigative reporters* and *stringers.* Investigative reporters search out and expose political corruption or other wrongdoing. They may work weeks or months to get a story or a series of stories. Stringers do not work full time for the newspaper, but they occasionally write a story for it. Many stringers for big-city newspapers have a regular job with a suburban newspaper, a regional magazine, or a small radio station.

Many metropolitan papers have a staff of reporters in the state capital and in Washington, D.C. The largest pa-

© Gannett Company Inc.

Interviews help newspaper reporters gather information for their stories. A reporter carefully prepares interview questions to gain the information that is of most interest to the readers.

AP/Wide World

News services supply newspapers with stories and pictures electronically. This photo researcher is looking for particular types of images in a news service's archive of photographs.

pers also have foreign correspondents in such cities as London, Paris, Moscow, and Tokyo.

News services. Not even the largest newspapers can afford to have reporters in all the major cities of the United States and the world. As a result, newspapers depend on news services for at least part of their national and international news. The chief U.S. news service is the Associated Press (AP). The Associated Press has reporters throughout the United States and the world. Major news services in other countries include Agence France-Presse in France, Thomson Reuters in Canada and the United Kingdom, and ITAR in Russia (referred to as ITAR-TASS in its bureaus outside Russia). News services were formerly known as *wire services* because they sent their stories by wire to printing devices called teletypewriters. Today, stories and photographs are sent electronically.

Many papers also get news from *news syndicates.* A news syndicate is owned by a newspaper or chain of newspapers with a large staff of reporters worldwide.

Newspapers also receive many press releases from private companies and government departments. An organization's press release sometimes leads to major news coverage of the event it describes.

Writing and editing stories. In writing a news story, reporters begin by giving the important facts in the first paragraph, which is called the *lead*. They then present details in the rest of the space given to the story by the city editor or news editor. The completed story goes to a copy editor, or copyreader, who checks it for accuracy and writes a headline for it. The copy editor may change the wording to make the story more readable. The copy editor must also cut material if the story is too long. A proofreader checks the story for spelling and punctuation errors.

Most reporters and editors prepare their stories on computers that have word processing software. The computers are linked in a network so that several individuals can use their own computers to perform successive writing and editing operations on a single story.

Many stories are accompanied by photographs, charts, or illustrations. Some photos, especially those of major news events, come from news services. They may be received over telephone lines or by satellite. Most newspapers also have a staff of photographers who take pictures of local events. Graphic artists usually design charts and illustrations on computers.

Writing editorials and features. A newspaper's editorial writers hold meetings to select topics for editorials. They also decide what viewpoint to take in the editorials. Unlike a news story, an editorial expresses an opinion and tries to sway readers to that way of thinking.

Feature writers prepare stories on subjects they think would interest the newspaper's readers. Common types of feature articles include interviews with famous entertainers, stories on unusual organizations, and descriptions of places to visit. Newspapers also get feature material from *feature syndicates,* which resemble news syndicates. Feature syndicates provide such items as political cartoons, comic strips, crossword puzzles, and columns on chess, gardening, and financial matters.

Preparing advertisements. Newspapers carry two forms of advertising—*display ads* and *classified ads.* Most display ads include illustrations and may be as

Newspaper terms

Banner is the top headline on page 1.

Beat is a news field to which a reporter is regularly assigned, such as city hall or consumer affairs.

By-line is the name of the writer of a news story, feature article, or special column. In most cases, it appears just beneath the headline.

Copy means the manuscript of any news matter prepared for typesetting.

Dateline refers to the line at the beginning of a news story that tells where and, in some cases, when the story originated.

Edition means any issue of the newspaper. Large newspapers issue several editions during the day or night.

Lead is the opening paragraph of a news story. In most cases, it summarizes the important information in the story.

Masthead includes the title of the newspaper and the names of the publisher and principal editors. In most cases, it appears on the editorial page.

Subhead is a short heading used to break up the paragraphs of a long news story.

large as two pages. Some metropolitan newspapers add booklets of display ads, called *inserts,* to the newspaper. Many newspapers have a staff of graphic artists to help prepare display ads. Classified ads, also called *want ads,* usually appear in a separate section of the newspaper. Most consist of a few lines of print and advertise such things as used cars or apartments for rent.

Making up the pages. Artists prepare a *layout,* or sketch, of each newspaper page. A layout shows where the stories, pictures, and advertisements should appear on the page. Most newspapers use computers to create layouts. Computer layouts enable artists to make precise measurements and to rearrange page contents quickly.

Many newspapers also assemble the pages by computer. Workers merge two kinds of files, following the layouts: (1) text files, and (2) graphics files. Text files consist of the words in stories, advertising copy, and other material. Graphics files are digital representations of photographs and other illustrations. Some graphics are photographed with digital cameras or are received as computer data from outside sources. Photographs shot on film and illustrations drawn on paper are converted to digital form using an electronic device called a *scanner.* Workers using a computer to assemble a page can see exactly where the text and the illustrations, which are represented by boxes called *windows,* will appear on the page.

An older method of making up pages uses images of illustrations and individual columns of type on paper. A special machine coats the back of the paper with wax, which makes the paper stick to plastic. Using the layouts as a guide, workers prepare a *paste-up* by attaching the pieces of paper for one or two pages to a large plastic sheet.

When pages are produced and assembled on a computer, any of several methods may be used to produce printing plates. In one method, called *computer-to-plate* or *direct-to-plate,* the digital files representing the pages are transmitted electronically to an imagesetting or platesetting device, which produces the printing plates. In another method, the page is printed out on a computer printer. The text and graphics appear where the worker positioned the windows. The printed page may then be photographed to produce a negative. Or the page

How a newspaper is produced

The pictures on this page show some of the steps commonly used in producing newspapers and preparing them for shipment. Some publishers use different methods for laying out pages.

© Gannett Company Inc.

Writing a story. A reporter gathers information by doing research and performing interviews. The writer then uses a computer with word-processing software to prepare the story.

Walter P. Calahan Photography for *USA Today*

Assembling a page. With the aid of a computer, a worker lays out the stories and the other elements of the page. The layout can be transmitted electronically to a laser platesetter.

© Pam Roberts, *Ely Echo*

Mounting the printing plate. A worker wraps the printing plate around a cylinder on the printing press. The plate is made so that ink will adhere only to the image areas.

Uniphoto

Printing a newspaper. A newspaper is printed by *offset lithography.* Ink transfers from the printing plates to *rubber blanket cylinders* and then to a long roll of paper.

Walter P. Calahan Photography for *USA Today*

Producing individual newspapers. Special equipment cuts sections from the printed roll and folds them to make individual newspapers. The papers are ready to be bundled for shipment.

Walter P. Calahan Photography for *USA Today*

Shipping the newspapers. Most of the papers are bundled and sent to a loading dock. Workers put the papers on trucks, which deliver them to newsstands and distribution centers.

image can be transferred onto light-sensitive paper or film that will then be transferred to a printing plate.

For certain applications, a negative is produced with the graphics windows taking the place of the illustrations. A worker then cuts away the paper or plastic from the image areas and inserts negatives of the graphics. When pages are assembled via the paste-up method, workers photograph the sheets to make negatives of the pages.

Printing the newspaper. The majority of newspapers use a printing method called *offset lithography.* In *offset,* as it is usually called, the image to be printed is on the same level of the printing plate as the areas that do not print. Offset is done on *rotary presses,* which have cylinders that hold curved printing plates. The plate does not come into contact with the paper. Instead, the printed images are transferred—that is, offset—to a rubber "blanket" cylinder that then prints them on the paper.

In one common method of producing a plate, the negative of a page is placed on a thin metal or plastic plate with a light-sensitive coating. It is then exposed to bright light. The light passes through the transparent (image) parts of the negative and hardens the coating under these parts. The other parts of the negative block the light, and the coating under them remains soft. Workers treat the plate with a solution of developer and lacquer. The lacquer adheres only to the hardened image areas. The plate is washed, and a gum is applied to thoroughly cleanse the nonimage areas so they will repel any ink. During printing, only the lacquered areas accept ink.

Printers mount the plates on the rotary press. After all the plates have been made and are mounted on the press, the press goes into action. In the most commonly used kind of press, a large *web* (roll) of paper is drawn between the blanket cylinders, receiving the print images of all of the plates. The printed pages are then transferred to a machine that cuts the sheets and folds them into pages. Other machines place the different sections of the paper together and stack the newspapers into piles.

Some newspapers are printed by methods other than offset. For more information on printing, see **Printing** (Methods of printing).

Business operations

Newspapers in the United States earn a large part of their income from the sale of advertising. Most newspapers get the rest of their income from sales of the paper. The syndication of news stories or features provides additional revenue for some large papers. A newspaper's advertising department handles the sale of ads, and the circulation department manages the distribution and sales of the newspaper. Some special-interest newspapers are circulated without charge and earn all their income from advertising.

Advertising fills much of the space in U.S. newspapers. Papers sell most of this space to local businesses and individuals. National firms buy the rest.

The advertising manager of a large newspaper directs division supervisors. The division supervisors have charge of various kinds of advertising, such as advertising for automobile dealers, department stores, and su-

Janet Heintz, *Chicago Tribune*
A newspaper display advertisement is inserted on a page electronically. An advertising agency prepared the ad and handled the purchase of the newspaper space for it.

permarkets. Each division supervisor has a staff of sales representatives who sell ads to businesses. Workers in the classified-ad department sell ads over the telephone. They also help people write their want ads. People may also purchase ads through a newspaper's Web site. In addition to the local advertising staff, many newspapers have sales representatives in other cities.

Circulation. Newspaper distribution is a complex operation. After the papers are printed and assembled, conveyor belts carry them to the mailroom. Most of the papers are grouped into bundles with plastic strapping. The rest are addressed for mailing. The bundles travel on chutes to a loading dock, where trucks wait to haul them to newsstands and distribution centers.

National newspapers are printed simultaneously throughout the country. Communications satellites relay images of the newspaper pages to printing plants in major cities. Some large metropolitan papers have a central plant as well as plants in outlying areas that print the paper from satellite images.

The circulation manager oversees the distribution of papers and works with the promotion manager to try to increase the number of readers. Supervisors of city sales, suburban sales, and home delivery work under the circulation manager. District circulation supervisors look after sales in various areas of the city or suburbs. Independent newspaper carriers also make up an important part of the distribution system. They pick up papers at distribution centers and deliver them to homes in the city and suburbs.

Newspapers in other countries

Newspapers in most countries have far fewer pages than do those in the United States. Many papers in other countries have no more than 8 or 10 pages. They devote more of their stories to political and governmental affairs, and they have fewer ads and features.

Countries with exceptionally high newspaper readership include Finland, Japan, Norway, and Sweden. Daily circulation for both China and India have grown dramatically since 2000. In general, circulations are larger in industrialized nations, but readership in developing nations is growing rapidly.

In most nations, the government controls to some extent what newspapers may publish. Governmental control of the news media is strongest in Communist nations. In these nations, the government owns and operates the media. Many countries in Africa, Asia, and Latin America severely restrict press freedom. In these countries, the government controls the press through censorship or through laws that make it dangerous to criticize the government. Only a small minority of nations allow newspapers to print any news they wish. Freedom of the press exists mainly in English-speaking nations, in most of the countries of Western Europe, and in Israel and Japan. See **Freedom of the press.**

In Canada, newspapers are similar to U.S. papers in size and content. The leading English-language dailies in Canada include *The Gazette* of Montreal and two Toronto papers—the *Toronto Star* and *The Globe and Mail. Le Journal de Montréal* is the largest French-language daily in Canada.

In Europe, newspapers in the United Kingdom most closely resemble those of the United States and Canada. All the largest British newspapers have their main offices in London and are distributed nationally. They include the country's most influential papers, *The Times, The Guardian, The Independent, The Daily Telegraph,* and the *Financial Times.* The British papers with the highest circulations include the *Daily Mail,* the *Daily Mirror,* and *The Sun.*

Before World War II (1939-1945), most newspapers in France were associated with some political party or special-interest group. Each of these papers wrote its news from a particular political viewpoint. Today, *L'Humanité,* which maintains an affiliation with the Communist Party, is the only such paper with a wide circulation in France. Other French papers have political leanings, but they report news from a basically neutral point of view. Some French newspapers, such as the Paris papers *Le Figaro* and *Le Monde,* provide excellent coverage of the arts. Other French newspapers that are widely circulated include *La Croix, France-Soir,* and *Le Parisien.* All of these newspapers are published in Paris.

Newspaper circulation is generally smaller in Russia than in most European countries. Russia's leading dailies are *Komsomolskaya Pravda* and *Trud.* Other large dailies include *Moskovsky Komsomolets* and *Izvestia.*

In Germany, the daily with the highest circulation is *Bild.* Outstanding German newspapers include the *Frankfurter Allgemeine Zeitung* of Frankfurt (am Main), *Süddeutsche Zeitung* of Munich, and *Die Welt* and *Berliner Zeitung* of Berlin. Italy's leading papers include *La Stampa* of Turin, *La Repubblica* of Rome, and *Il Giorno* and *Corriere della Sera* of Milan.

In Africa and the Middle East, the governments of most nations maintain tight control over what appears in the press. Israel and South Africa have a free press. But the governments of both countries exercise control over certain types of information, such as military news. Most Arab countries have laws that allow government officials to censor news before publication. In Egypt, the government owns all the newspapers, including the respected *Al Ahram* of Cairo. Some daily papers are read throughout the Middle East, including *Al-Sharq Al-Awsat* and *Al-Hayat,* both of which are published out of London.

In Latin America, government control of the press is common. Some Latin American nations officially restrict what newspapers may print. Certain others practice indirect forms of censorship. For example, the government may own the nation's paper supplies. In that case, a newspaper that criticizes government leaders may find it difficult to buy newsprint. Major Latin American newspapers include *La Prensa* and *La Nación* of Buenos Aires, Argentina; *O Estado de São Paulo* of São Paulo, Brazil; and *Excélsior* of Mexico City, Mexico.

In Asia, Japan and China have the most highly developed press systems. Japan's leading dailies—*Asahi Shimbun, Mainichi Shimbun,* and *Yomiuri Shimbun*—circulate nationally. Each paper publishes a Tokyo edition and several regional editions. *Yomiuri Shimbun* has the largest circulation of any paper in the world—more than 14 million copies per day. One of China's largest newspapers is *Renmin Ribao (People's Daily)* of Beijing, the official paper of the Chinese Communist Party.

In Australia and New Zealand, newspapers resemble those of the United States and Canada. Major dailies in Australia include *The Daily Telegraph* and *The Sydney Morning Herald* of Sydney and the *Herald Sun* and *The Age* of Melbourne. New Zealand's leading daily is *The New Zealand Herald,* published in Auckland.

History

Handwritten newssheets posted in public places probably were the first newspapers. The earliest known daily newssheet was *Acta Diurna (Daily Events),* which started in Rome in 59 B.C. The world's first printed newspaper was a Chinese circular called *Dibao,* also spelled *Ti-pao.* The Chinese began printing *Dibao* from carved wooden blocks around A.D. 700. The first regularly published newspaper in Europe, *Avisa Relation oder Zeitung,* started in Germany in 1609.

Development of U.S. newspapers. In 1690, Benjamin Harris of Boston founded *Publick Occurrences Both Forreign and Domestick,* the first newspaper in the American Colonies. However, the colonial government ordered it stopped after one issue. In 1704, John Campbell established *The Boston News-Letter,* the colonies' first regularly published newspaper. By 1765, the colonies had more than 20 newspapers.

Newspapers in the United States developed rapidly in the 1800's. By 1830, the country had about 1,000 papers. But they were available only by subscription, and they cost about 6 cents a copy, which was more than working-class people could afford. Then in 1833, Benjamin H. Day started the *New York Sun,* the first of many successful penny newspapers. In the late 1800's, papers tried to outdo one another with sensational reports of crimes, disasters, and scandals. The most sensational newspapers included two New York City dailies—William Randolph Hearst's *Journal* and Joseph Pulitzer's *World.* Edward Wyllis Scripps established the first newspaper chain during the late 1800's. The number of U.S. newspapers peaked in 1909, when the country had about 2,600 dailies and about 14,000 weeklies. For more on the early history of U.S. newspapers, see **Journalism** (History).

Newspapers in the 1900's. Since the 1960's, newspaper chains in the United States have bought up papers at an especially rapid rate. The 10 largest chains account for more than half of the total daily circulation in the United States. The nation's largest chain is Gannett Co., Inc., which owns more than 80 papers. Other major chains include Advance Publications, Inc.; the McClatchy Company; and the New York Times Company.

In the last decades of the 1900's, newspapers in the United States, western Europe, Latin America, Australia, and New Zealand struggled to remain profitable. Initially, high operating expenses, especially the rising cost of labor and newsprint, drove many papers out of business. Many cities lost competing dailies and were left with only one newspaper. In some cities that kept their competing dailies, the rival publishers printed their papers on the same presses to reduce costs. Financial problems hit hardest at major metropolitan papers, which faced special distribution problems.

Recent trends. The economic problems of the newspaper business grew worse in the early 2000's. Newspaper circulation, in decline since the 1950's, suddenly showed a more marked decrease. Increasing competition from suburban papers and TV newscasts was part of the problem. But by the 1990's, the Internet played a large part in the drop in print newspaper readership.

The first electronic newspaper was published before the introduction of the Internet. In 1980, *The Columbus Dispatch* of Ohio became the first electronic newspaper in the United States. Besides a print edition, the *Dispatch* began transmitting some of its editorial content to computers in the homes, businesses, and libraries of a small number of subscribers via the CompuServe network. The growing popularity of the Internet in the 1990's allowed many more people to access news online.

Today, most papers offer online versions. The Internet has allowed papers to quickly and easily make corrections and to update or add stories at any point in a day. But newspapers have lost much of the more profitable parts of their business—especially classified ads—to online sites. In addition, advertisers do not pay as much for spots on a website as they would spots in a print newspaper. These shifts have led to declining profits and closures for hundreds of newspapers.   Robert K. Stewart

Related articles. See the *Communication* section of the various country, state, and province articles. See also:

American newspaper journalists

Bennett, James G.	Grady, Henry W.
Bennett, James G., Jr.	Hecht, Ben
Bierce, Ambrose	Landers, Ann
Bly, Nellie	Lardner, Ring
Bonfils, Frederick Gilmer	Lippmann, Walter
Bourke-White, Margaret	Lovejoy, Elijah P.
Bradford, William	Marquis, Don
Bradford, William, III	Mencken, H. L.
Brisbane, Arthur	Pyle, Ernie
Bryant, William Cullen	Reid, Whitelaw
Buchwald, Art	Rice, Grantland
Cary, Mary Ann Shadd	Riis, Jacob A.
Dana, Charles A.	Rowan, Carl T.
Dunne, Finley P.	Royall, Anne Newport
Ephron, Nora	Runyon, Damon
Field, Eugene	Schurz, Carl
Garrison, William Lloyd	Van Buren, Abigail
Godkin, Edward L.	Wells-Barnett, Ida Bell

White, William A.	Zenger, John Peter
Winchell, Walter	

American newspaper publishers

Abbott, Robert S.	Graham, Katharine	Ochs, Adolph S.
Bradford, William, III	Greeley, Horace	Pulitzer, Joseph
	Hearst, William	Raymond, Henry J.
Cox, James M.	Randolph	Scripps, Edward
Curtis, Cyrus H. K.	Knox, Frank	W.
Field, Marshall, I (His family)	McCormick, Robert R.	Sulzberger, Arthur Hays
Franklin, Benjamin	Medill, Joseph	Thomas, Isaiah
Goddard, Mary K.	Nelson, William R.	Weed, Thurlow
Goddard, William		

Other newspaper journalists and publishers

Beaverbrook, Lord	Herzen, Alexander	Northcliffe,
Bourassa, Henri	Ivanovich	Viscount
Brown, George	Hunt, Leigh	Reuter, Baron de
Davies, Robertson	Murdoch, Rupert	Steele, Sir Richard
Harris, Benjamin		

Editorial cartoonists

Block, Herbert L.	Mauldin, Bill	Outcault,
Darling, Ding	Nast, Thomas	Richard F.
Daumier, Honoré	Oliphant, Patrick B.	Tenniel, Sir John

Other related articles

Advertising (Newspapers)	Fourth estate	Stars and Stripes
	Freedom of the	Stereotyping
Associated Press	press	Thomson Reuters
Cartoon	Journalism	United Press
Comics	Linotype	International
Editorial	Printing	War
Fax machine	Publishing	correspondent
Foreign correspondent	Pulitzer Prizes	

Outline

I. Kinds of newspapers
  A. Daily newspapers
  B. Weekly newspapers
  C. Special-interest newspapers
  D. Online newspapers

II. The staff of a newspaper
  A. The editorial department
  B. The business department
  C. The mechanical department

III. How newspapers are produced
  A. Gathering information
  B. Writing and editing stories
  C. Writing editorials and features
  D. Preparing advertisements
  E. Making up the pages
  F. Printing the newspaper

IV. Business operations
  A. Advertising
  B. Circulation

V. Newspapers in other countries
  A. In Canada
  B. In Europe
  C. In Africa and the Middle East
  D. In Latin America
  E. In Asia
  F. In Australia and New Zealand

VI. History

Questions

How much of their income do newspapers in the United States earn from the sale of advertising space?

Where do newspapers obtain such items as political cartoons, crossword puzzles, and comic strips?

Why does the United States have few national newspapers?

What jobs are performed by the staff of a newspaper's business department?

What are online newspapers?
Which newspaper has the largest circulation in the world?
How do newspapers in most other countries differ from those in
the United States?
What is a *beat?* A *lead?* A *by-line?*

Additional resources

Barnhurst, Kevin G., and Nerone, John C. *The Form of News: A History.* Guilford, 2001.
Granfield, Linda. *Extra! Extra! The Who, What, Where, When and Why of Newspapers.* Orchard Bks., 1994. Younger readers.
Mogel, Leonard. *The Newspaper: Everything You Need to Know to Make It in the Newspaper Business.* GATFPress, 2000.

Newsprint. See **Paper** (Special kinds of paper).

Newt, *noot,* is a small animal with a slender body, thin skin, and four weak legs. It is a type of salamander and is classified as an amphibian, along with frogs and caecilians (see **Amphibian**).

Newts and other salamanders are *tailed amphibians.* The tail of the adult newt is flatter than that of most other salamanders. Newts hatch from eggs that are laid singly in the spring on the leaves of plants underwater. The young hatch after three to five weeks. They live in the water and breathe by means of gills. After a few months,

WORLD BOOK illustration by Richard Lewington, The Garden Studio

The red-spotted newt, the most common type of newt in the United States, is a small amphibian with a long tail.

they develop lungs and may take to the land. People then call them *efts.* Efts are bright orange and are easily seen on the forest floor. Other animals seldom bother them because their skin is poisonous. Efts may stay on land up to seven years before they return to water, where they live and breed as adult newts. Both efts and adult newts shed their skins and often eat them. If an eft or adult loses a body part, such as a leg, it can grow the part back. The kind of newt best known in the United States is the *red-spotted newt.* It measures about 4 inches (10 centimeters) long. Newts eat insects, mollusks, and worms.   Don C. Forester

Scientific classification. Newts are in the salamander family, Salamandridae. The red-spotted newt is *Notophthalmus viridescens viridescens.*

Newton, is the unit of force in the International System of Units, commonly referred to as the metric system. Its symbol is *N.* The newton was named for the English scientist Sir Isaac Newton. One newton is the force required to increase or decrease the velocity of a 1-kilo-

gram object by 1 meter per second every second. The number of newtons needed to accelerate an object can be calculated by using Newton's Second Law of Motion. That law can be expressed by the formula: $F = ma$. The mass *(m)* of the object in kilograms is multiplied by the acceleration *(a)* in meters per second squared to determine the force *(F)*.

Force is measured in pounds in the inch-pound system of measurement customarily used in the United States. One newton equals about 0.225 pound of force. See also **Pascal.**   Robert B. Prigo

Newton, Sir Isaac (1642-1727), an English scientist, astronomer, and mathematician, invented a new kind of mathematics, discovered the secrets of light and color, and showed how the universe is held together. He is sometimes described as "one of the greatest names in the history of human thought" because of his great contributions to mathematics, physics, and astronomy.

Newton discovered how the universe is held together through his theory of gravitation. He discovered the secrets of light and color. He invented a branch of mathematics, *calculus,* also invented independently by Gottfried Leibniz, a German mathematician (see **Calculus**). Newton made these three discoveries within 18 months from 1665 to 1667.

The theories of motion and gravitation. Newton said the concept of a universal force came to him while he was alone in the country. He had been forced to flee there because of the outbreak of plague in the city of Cambridge. During this time, Newton realized that one and the same force pulls an object to Earth and keeps the moon in its orbit. He found that the force of universal gravitation makes every pair of bodies in the universe attract each other. The force depends on (1) the amount of matter in the bodies being attracted and (2) the distance between the bodies. For instance, the force by which Earth attracts or pulls a large rock is greater than its pull on a small pebble because the rock contains more matter. Earth's pull is called the *weight* of the body. With this theory, Newton explained why a rock weighs more than a pebble.

Newton also proved that many types of motion are due to one kind of force. He showed that the gravitational force of the sun keeps the planets in their orbits, just as the gravitational force of Earth attracts the moon and keeps it in its orbit. The falling of objects on Earth seems different from the motion of the moon because the objects fall straight down to Earth, while the moon moves approximately in a circle around Earth. Newton showed that the moon falls just like an object on Earth. If the moon did not fall constantly toward Earth, it would move in a straight line and fly off at a tangent to its orbit. Newton calculated how much the moon falls in each second and found the distance is $\frac{1}{3,600}$ of the distance an object on Earth falls in a second. The moon is 60 times as far from Earth's center as such an object. Consequently, the force of Earth acting on an object 60 times as far away is $\frac{1}{3,600}$ of the force of Earth acting on an object on Earth's surface.

The *Principia.* Newton concluded his first investigations on gravity and motion in 1665 and 1666. Nothing was heard of the investigations for nearly 20 years. His original theory had been based on an inaccurate measurement of Earth's radius, and Newton realized differences between the theory and the facts. Although he later learned the true value of Earth's size, he was not led to complete his investigation or to produce a book for publication.

At a meeting of the Royal Society in January 1684, Edmond Halley, an English astronomer; Robert Hooke, an English scientist; and Christopher Wren, an English architect, were discussing what law of force produced the visible motion of the planets around the sun. They were unable to solve this problem. Halley went to Cambridge in the summer of 1684 to ask Newton about it. He found Newton in possession of a nearly completed proof of the law of gravity. Halley persuaded Newton to publish his findings. Halley paid all the expenses, corrected the proofs, and laid aside his own work to publish Newton's discoveries.

Newton's discoveries on the laws of motion and theories of gravitation were published in 1687 in *Philosophiae naturalis principia mathematica (Mathematical Principles of Natural Philosophy)*. This work, usually called *Principia* or *Principia mathematica*, is considered one of the greatest single contributions in the history of science. Prior to Newton's theory of universal gravitation, it was widely believed that the laws of planetary motion were different from the laws of motion for bodies on Earth. The *Principia* was the first book to contain a unified system of scientific principles that explained what happens in both the heavens and on Earth.

Light and color. Newton's discoveries in optics were equally spectacular. He published the results of his experiments and studies in *Opticks* (1704).

Newton's discoveries explained why bodies appear to be colored. The discoveries also laid the foundation for the science of spectrum analysis. This science allows us to determine the chemical composition, temperature, and even the speed of such hot, glowing bodies as a distant star or an object heated in a laboratory.

By passing a beam of sunlight through a glass prism and studying the colors that were produced, Newton discovered that sunlight is a mixture of light of all colors. According to this model of light, a green sweater looks green in sunlight because it largely reflects the green light in the sun and absorbs most of the other colors. If the green sweater were lighted by a red light or any color light not containing green, it would not appear green.

The study of light led Newton to consider constructing a new type of telescope in which a reflecting mirror was used instead of a combination of lenses. Newton's first reflecting telescope was 6 inches (15 centimeters) long, and, through it, he saw the satellites of Jupiter.

Early life. Newton was born at Woolsthorpe, Lincolnshire, on Dec. 25, 1642. He attended Grantham grammar school. As a boy, he was more interested in making mechanical devices than in studying. His youthful inventions included a small windmill that could grind wheat and corn, a water clock run by the force of dropping water, and a sundial. He left school when he was 14 to help his widowed mother manage her farm. But he spent so much time reading, he was sent back to school.

He entered Trinity College, Cambridge University, in 1661. He showed no exceptional ability during his college career and graduated in 1665 without any particular distinction. He returned to Cambridge as a fellow of Trinity College in 1667.

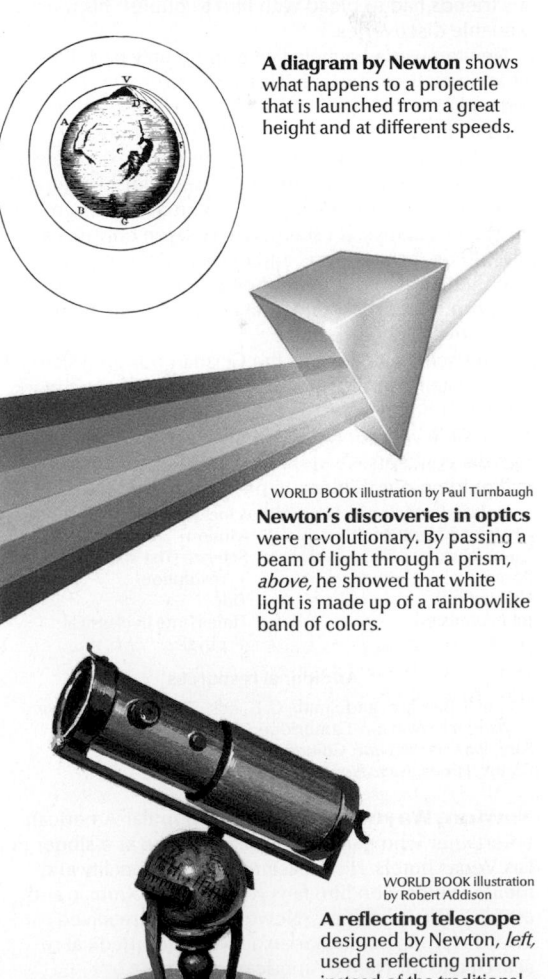

Oil painting on canvas (about 1726) by an unknown artist; National Portrait Gallery, London
Sir Isaac Newton was a famous English scientist.

A diagram by Newton shows what happens to a projectile that is launched from a great height and at different speeds.

WORLD BOOK illustration by Paul Turnbaugh
Newton's discoveries in optics were revolutionary. By passing a beam of light through a prism, *above,* he showed that white light is made up of a rainbowlike band of colors.

WORLD BOOK illustration by Robert Addison
A reflecting telescope designed by Newton, *left,* used a reflecting mirror instead of the traditional combination of lenses.

Newton became professor of mathematics at Cambridge in 1669. He lectured once a week on arithmetic, astronomy, geometry, optics, or other mathematical subjects. He was elected to the Royal Society in 1672.

Public life. Newton became active in public life after the publication of *Principia*. He became the Cambridge University member of Parliament in 1689 and held his seat until Parliament dissolved the next year. He became warden of the mint in 1696. He was appointed master of the mint in 1699, a position he held until his death.

In 1699, Newton also became a member of the Royal Society council and an associate of the French Academy. He was elected to Parliament again from the university in 1701. He left Cambridge and settled in London in that same year. He became president of the Royal Society in 1703 and was reelected annually until his death. Queen Anne knighted Newton in 1705. He died on March 20, 1727, and was buried in Westminster Abbey.

Personal characteristics. Newton did not enjoy the scientific arguments that arose from his discoveries. Many new scientific theories are opposed violently when they are first announced, and Newton's did not escape criticism. He was so sensitive to such criticism that his friends had to plead with him to publish his most valuable discoveries.

Newton was a bachelor who spent only part of his time on mathematics, physics, and astronomy. He studied and experimented with alchemy. He also spent time on questions of theology and Biblical chronology.

Although Newton's achievements were extremely important, he spoke modestly of himself shortly before his death, saying, "I do not know what I may appear to the world, but to myself I seem to have been only like a boy playing on the seashore, and diverting myself in now and then finding a smoother pebble or a prettier shell than ordinary, whilst the great ocean of truth lay all undiscovered before me."

Later scientists, such as the German-born physicist Albert Einstein, modified and challenged Newton's work. Einstein admitted that his own work would have been impossible without Newton's discoveries. He also said that the concepts Newton developed "are even today still guiding our thinking in physics."   Mary Domski

Related articles in *World Book* include:

Additional resources

Cohen, I. Bernard, and Smith, G. E., eds. *The Cambridge Companion to Newton.* Cambridge, 2002.
Fara, Patricia. *Newton.* Columbia Univ. Pr., 2002.
Gleick, James. *Isaac Newton.* Pantheon, 2003.

Newton, Wayne (1942-   ), is a popular American entertainer who gained his greatest fame as a singer in Las Vegas hotels. His pleasing stage personality and mellow voice won him fans with both pop music and country music listeners. Newton has also received awards for his humanitarian activities for medical research and for Native American causes.

Carson Wayne Newton was born on April 3, 1942, in Norfolk, Virginia. He dropped out of high school in 1959

and performed at the Fremont Hotel in Las Vegas from that year to 1963. The American singer Bobby Darin discovered Newton singing in a New York City hotel in 1963 and produced Newton's first hit record, "Danke Schoen" (1963). His other hit recordings include "Red Roses for a Blue Lady" (1965) and "Daddy Don't You Walk So Fast" (1972). Newton began singing in major Las Vegas hotels in the late 1960's and soon became one of the city's biggest stars. Newton performed in Branson, Missouri, during much of the 1990's but returned to performing mainly in Las Vegas in 2000. He wrote an autobiography, *Once Before I Go* (1989).   Dan Zeff

Newton's rings are a series of alternating bright and dark concentric circles produced by the interference of light (see **Interference**). They occur when two microscope slides are pressed tightly together at one point,

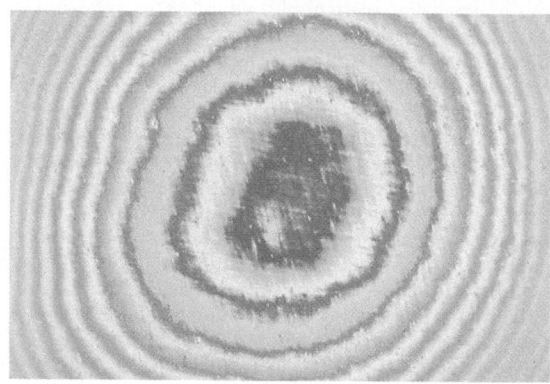

David M. Roessler, General Motors Research Laboratories

Newton's rings, *shown here*, were created by pressing two microscope slides tightly together at one point.

or when a slightly convex piece of glass is placed on top of a flat piece of glass. Light reflected off the flat surface travels slightly farther than—and interferes with—light reflected off the curved surface. If viewed in strong white light, such as sunlight, the rings show the colors of the spectrum. If the viewing light is a single color, the rings have only that color. The rings were named for the English scientist Sir Isaac Newton, who first studied them in detail.   David M. Roessler

Next of kin is a legal phrase for the closest blood relatives of a person who has died without making a valid will. These next of kin share in the personal property of the dead person. Each state's laws determine which relatives get the personal property left by a resident of that state who did not leave a will. Usually, such laws provide for the distribution of both real and personal property to the same people, thus treating next of kin the same as heirs (see **Heir**). The relatives sharing the property are called *next* of kin because they are generally the closest surviving relatives of the dead person. Thus, a dead person's children are favored over cousins in the distribution of property.   William M. McGovern

Ney, *nay,* **Michel,** *mee SHEHL* (1769-1815), a French general, was one of Napoleon I's great soldiers. Ney was brave, but he was not effective as a commander.

Ney served with great distinction in the campaign of 1792, when the French Army of the North defeated the Prussians and Austrians. He soon distinguished himself by his cool courage and military skill. Napoleon made him a marshal of France in 1804. Ney received the title Duke of Elchingen for defeating the Austrians at Elchingen in 1805. He fought at Jena and Eylau and commanded an army at Friedland, where the French defeated the Russians in 1807. Ney's conduct at Friedland won him Napoleon's praise. He took charge of Napoleon's army for the march into Russia in 1812 and became Prince of Moscow. Napoleon left the army after its defeat and hastened back to France. But Ney remained with the Grand Army during the terrible retreat from Russia.

When Napoleon was forced from power in 1814, Ney abandoned him and became a supporter of King Louis XVIII, who succeeded Napoleon. But Napoleon escaped from Elba in 1815 and landed on the coast of France. Ney told King Louis that he would "bring Napoleon back in an iron cage" and started out with an army. He met Napoleon, who was marching toward Paris with a new army. But emotion swayed Ney. He embraced Napoleon and joined him in the march on Paris. The king fled as the army approached, and Ney and Napoleon entered the capital together.

The period of Napoleon's return to power, called the Hundred Days, ended in his defeat. Ney led the last French charge at Waterloo in 1815. But he was seized, tried for treason and rebellion, and condemned to death. He was shot on Dec. 7, 1815. Ney was born on Jan. 10, 1769, in Saarlouis, in the Saar Basin in what is now Germany.　Eric A. Arnold, Jr.

See also **Napoleon I.**

Nez Perce Indians, *nehz PURS,* are a tribe that lives in north-central Idaho. According to the 2000 United States census, there are about 2,300 Nez Perce. The rich farmlands and forests in the area form the basis for the tribe's chief industries—agriculture and lumber. Many Nez Perce also make a living by fishing, by hunting, and by gathering wild plants.

The name *Nez Perce* means *pierced nose,* but few of the Indians ever pierced their noses. In 1805, a French interpreter gave the name to the tribe after seeing some members wearing shells in their noses as decorations. The Indians kept the name, but they do not use the French form of the name, *Nez Percé* (pronounced *nay pehr SAY).*

The Nez Perce originally lived in the region where the borders of Idaho, Oregon, and Washington meet. Prospectors overran the Nez Perce reservation after discovering gold there in the 1860's.

Part of the tribe resisted the efforts of the government to move them to a smaller reservation. In 1877, fighting broke out between the Nez Perce and U.S. troops. Joseph, a Nez Perce chief, tried to lead a band of the Indians into Canada. But he surrendered near the United States-Canadian border.　Deward E. Walker, Jr.

See also **Joseph, Chief; Indian wars** (The Nez Perce War).

NFO. See **National Farmers Organization.**

NGL. See **Natural gas liquids.**

Ngo Dinh Diem, *uhng oh dihn zih ehm* (1901-1963), was the first president of South Vietnam. He served from 1955 until a group of army officers seized control of the government and killed him in 1963.

Diem was born in central Vietnam on Jan. 3, 1901, the son of a government official. In the late 1940's, he worked for Vietnam's independence from France and opposed Communist control of Vietnam. In 1954, Communist-led rebels defeated the French forces in Vietnam. The country was then divided into two parts, South Vietnam and North Vietnam. Bao Dai, emperor of South Vietnam, appointed Diem as his prime minister. Diem was elected president when South Vietnam became a republic in 1955.

At first, Diem restored some order to his war-torn country. However, he soon began ruling like a dictator, and he became increasingly unpopular. Special police units brutally crushed Diem's opponents. In addition, Diem was unable to stop Viet Cong (Communist-led guerrilla) attacks on villages in South Vietnam. Many of his harsh actions were attributed to advice from his brother Ngo Dinh Nhu and his sister-in-law, Madame Nhu. Nhu and Diem were killed together on Nov. 2, 1963.　David P. Chandler

See also **Vietnam** (History); **Vietnam War.**

Niacin. See **Vitamin** (Water-soluble vitamins).

Niagara Falls is one of the most spectacular natural wonders of North America. Niagara Falls is on the Niagara River, about halfway between Lake Erie and Lake Ontario. The river forms part of the United States-Canadian border.

Niagara Falls actually consists of two waterfalls, the Horseshoe Falls and the American Falls. The Horseshoe Falls is on the Canadian side of the border in the province of Ontario. The American Falls is on the United States side in the state of New York. At night, wide beams of colored lights illuminate the falls. Millions of people visit Niagara Falls annually.

Description. At the falls, the Niagara River plunges

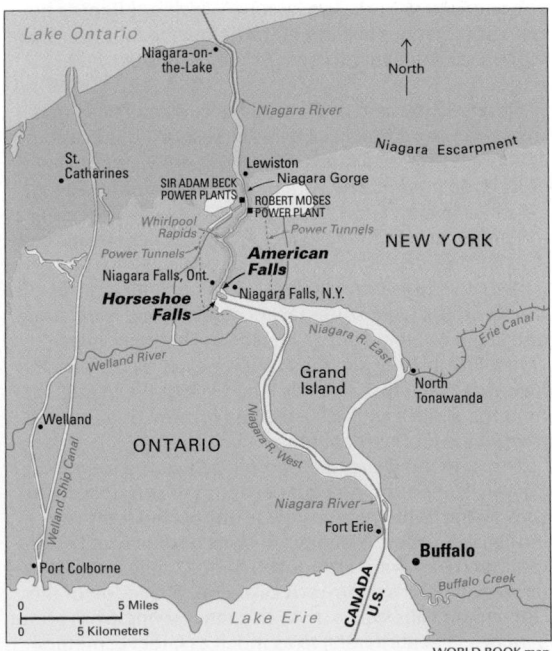

WORLD BOOK map

Niagara Falls lies on the United States-Canadian border. It consists of the American Falls and the Horseshoe Falls on the Niagara River, about halfway between Lakes Erie and Ontario.

Frederick Lewis, Inc.

The spectacular waterfalls of the Niagara River attract millions of tourists annually. Parks with observation areas line both sides of the river where it splits and plunges into a steep gorge. Goat Island lies between the American Falls, *left,* and the Horseshoe Falls, *right.*

into a steep, canyonlike gorge. The gorge extends beyond Niagara Falls for about 7 miles (11 kilometers), to Lewiston, New York. The famous Whirlpool Rapids begin about 3 miles (5 kilometers) below the falls. Here, the violent current has carved a round basin out of the rocks.

About 85 percent of the water at Niagara Falls flows over the Horseshoe Falls. The Horseshoe Falls is about 167 feet (51 meters) high and 2,600 feet (792 meters) wide at its widest point. The American Falls is about 176 feet (54 meters) high and 1,000 feet (305 meters) wide.

The gorge is about 200 feet (61 meters) deep and consists of layers of different kinds of stone. A hard rock called *dolomite* about 80 feet (24 meters) thick forms the top layer. It covers softer layers of limestone, sandstone, and shale. Water erodes soft stone faster than hard stone. For this reason, the top layer extends beyond the lower layers in many places. The Cave of the Winds, behind the American Falls, has been formed under an extended shelf of harder stone.

Through the years, the gorge has become longer and longer. The pounding water erodes the soft underlying rock layers, which causes the unsupported hard rock ledge to collapse. Niagara Falls was originally at Lewiston, but it has gradually moved about 7 miles (11 kilometers) back upstream toward Lake Erie. The ledge of the Horseshoe Falls wears away at a rate varying from about 3 inches (8 centimeters) to as much as 6 feet (2 meters) per year. The ledge of the American Falls erodes more slowly because less water flows over it. Each year, about 1 inch (2.5 centimeters) wears away.

Tourism. Niagara Falls attracts visitors throughout the year. However, most visitors come during the tourist season, from April 1 to October 31. Several steamers called *The Maid of the Mist* take sightseers close to the churning waters at the base of the falls. Parks line both sides of the river near Niagara Falls. Excellent views of the falls may be seen from such sites as Prospect Point, Table Rock, and Terrapin Point. Four observation towers, ranging from 282 to 500 feet (86 to 150 meters) high, also provide fine views of the falls.

Water flow. United States and Canadian hydroelectric plants divert some of the water through tunnels from the Niagara River before it reaches Niagara Falls (see **Niagara River** [Water power]). For scenic reasons, however, the amount of water that may be diverted is regulated by a treaty between the United States and Canada. The treaty states that at least 100,000 cubic feet (2,800 cubic meters) of water a second must pass over the falls during daylight hours of the tourist season. At other times, the flow may be decreased to 50,000 cubic feet (1,400 cubic meters) a second.

History. Niagara Falls was probably formed about 12,000 years ago, after the last great ice sheet melted from the region. The melting ice caused Lake Erie to overflow. The overflow formed the Niagara River. The river ran northward over a high cliff called the *Niagara Escarpment.* The Niagara River cut through the escarpment and, over the centuries, formed Niagara Falls.

Indian tribes lived in the area long before the first Europeans arrived. The name *Niagara* comes from the Iroquois word *Onguiaahra,* meaning *the strait.*

Louis Hennepin, a Roman Catholic priest who traveled with the French explorer Robert Cavelier, Sieur de La Salle, left a written account of his visit to Niagara Falls. In a book published in 1683, Hennepin wrote: "These waters foam and boil in a fearful manner. They thunder continually."

Large numbers of tourists began visiting Niagara Falls during the 1800's. Many hotels and taverns were built on the American and Canadian sides of the falls. In addition, numerous industries began to operate along the Niagara River.

Some people believed that the rapid development of tourism and industry ruined the scenic beauty of the area around Niagara Falls. In 1885, the government of New York took control of the land bordering the American Falls. It then established Niagara Falls Park, covering about 430 acres (174 hectares), on the land. In 1886, Canada established Queen Victoria Park on 196 acres (79 hectares) of land near the Horseshoe Falls. Since the 1880's, much more land in the Niagara Falls area has been set aside for parks, especially on the Canadian side.

Rock slides have gradually changed the appearance of Niagara Falls through the years. In 1931, about 80,000 tons (73,000 metric tons) of rock fell from the American Falls. Several years later, approximately 30,000 tons (27,000 metric tons) of rock broke off the upper edge of the Horseshoe Falls. In 1954, about 185,000 tons (167,800 metric tons) of rock tumbled from the American Falls and nearby Prospect Point.

In 1969, U.S. Army engineers built a dam to stop the flow of water temporarily over the American Falls. A board of experts from the United States and Canada then studied the rock ledge to determine how to prevent further erosion. However, the board decided that

Robert H. Glaze, Artstreet

A sightseeing boat, one of several steamers called *The Maid of the Mist,* gives visitors a close-up view of the foaming water and fallen rocks at the base of the American Falls.

Power Authority, State of New York

Power plants harness the water power of the Niagara River to generate electricity for a wide area. The Robert Moses plant and reservoir, *shown here,* lie on the American side of the river below Niagara Falls. Two Canadian power plants are just across the river. Both hydroelectric projects remove water from the river by tunnel before it reaches the falls.

Niagara Falls erosion

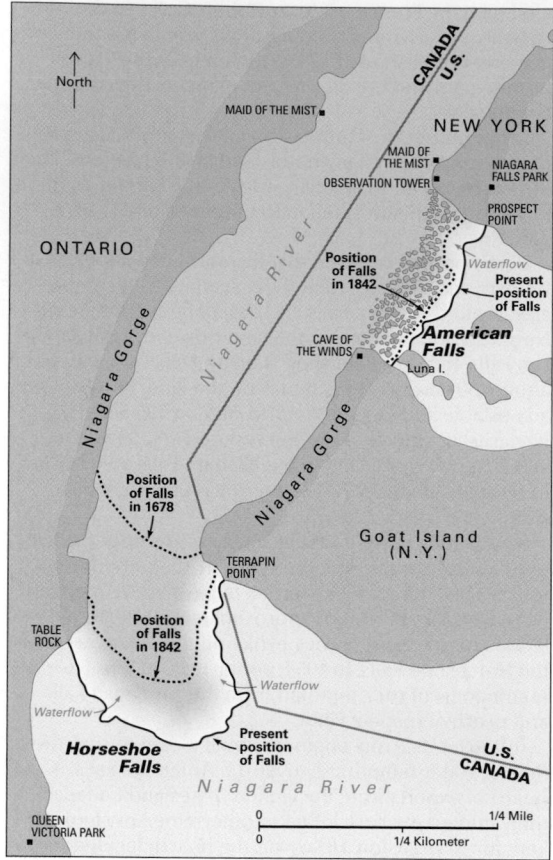

WORLD BOOK map

The falls change constantly through erosion. The swirling currents of the Niagara River slowly wear away the walls of the gorge and sometimes cause major rock slides. In this map, the dotted lines indicate earlier positions of the falls, which are gradually moving upstream.

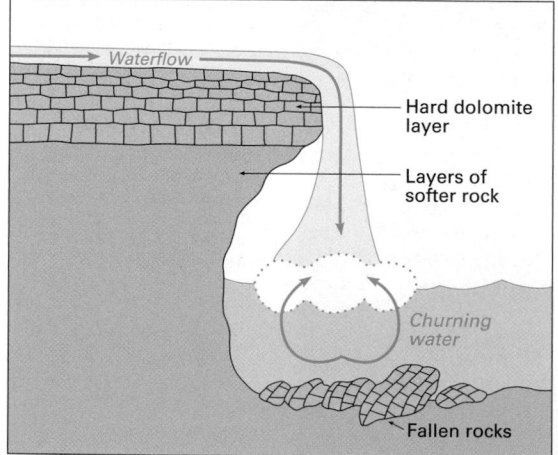

WORLD BOOK diagram

The churning water at the base of the falls eats away the soft underlying rock layers of the gorge, as shown in this diagram. The unsupported hard top rock then breaks off.

the cost of halting erosion would be too high. It recommended that nothing be done except small measures to improve public safety.   Adam W. Burnett

See also **New York** (picture: World-famous Niagara Falls); **Ontario** (picture: Horseshoe Falls).

Additional resources

Berton, Pierre. *Niagara: A History of the Falls.* McClelland, 1992.
Pierre Berton's Picture Book of Niagara Falls. 1993.
Fisher, Leonard E. *Niagara Falls.* Holiday Hse., 1996. Younger readers.
Whitcraft, Melissa. *The Niagara River.* Watts, 2001. Younger readers.

Niagara Movement was an organization founded by African Americans to fight racial discrimination in the United States. It existed from 1905 to 1910. At its height, the Niagara Movement had 30 branches in American cities. It failed to win the support of most blacks, but many of the movement's ideas were adopted in 1909 by a new interracial organization—the National Association for the Advancement of Colored People (NAACP).

The Niagara Movement was founded in Niagara Falls, Canada. W. E. B. Du Bois, an African American professor at Atlanta University, led the organization (see **Du Bois, W. E. B.**). The movement placed the responsibility for racial problems in the United States on whites. The Niagara Movement thus opposed the view of the famous African American educator Booker T. Washington, who urged blacks to stop demanding equal rights (see **Washington, Booker T.**). Various branches of the movement demanded voting rights for African Americans, opposed school segregation, and worked to elect candidates who promised to fight race prejudice.

Otey M. Scruggs

Niagara River is a short river that connects Lake Erie and Lake Ontario. The river forms part of the border between the state of New York and the Canadian province of Ontario. Water from all the Great Lakes except Lake Ontario drains into the Niagara River. Most of this water drops over Niagara Falls, which is about halfway along the Niagara River's course.

The Niagara River is 35 miles (56 kilometers) long. It drops 326 feet (99 meters) during its course, an unusually sharp descent for so short a river. The dramatic drop in elevation creates a swift current and some of the roughest rapids in the world. Hydroelectric power plants along the river produce much electric power.

Description. The Niagara River starts at Lake Erie as a quiet stream approximately 600 yards (550 meters) wide. The river flows north, broadens, and then divides as it passes both sides of Grand Island. Beyond the island, the river becomes about 2 miles (3 kilometers) wide. It then turns sharply west and narrows before plunging over Niagara Falls.

Beyond the falls, the Niagara River turns north again and flows swiftly through a narrow gorge about 7 miles (11 kilometers) long. The Whirlpool Rapids begin in the gorge about 3 miles (5 kilometers) below the falls. The water in the rapids twists violently and circles at a speed of about 27 miles (43 kilometers) per hour. The river forms another series of rapids below the Whirlpool Rapids and then flows quietly on before emptying into Lake Ontario.

Water power. Several hydroelectric power plants stand on both sides of the Niagara River below Niagara

Falls. The major power plants are the Robert Moses power plant on the American side of the river and the two Sir Adam Beck power plants on the Canadian side. The Robert Moses power plant and a nearby pumping-generating station together have a capacity of about 2,400,000 kilowatts. The Robert Moses plant is the largest hydroelectric plant in the eastern United States and one of the largest hydroelectric plants in the world. The two Sir Adam Beck plants and a small pumping-generating station have a combined capacity of more than 1,800,000 kilowatts.

Water for the Robert Moses and Sir Adam Beck power plants is taken from the Niagara River before the river reaches Niagara Falls. The water plunges down tunnels dug along the American and Canadian sides of the river. The tunnels carry the water into canals. The water then flows into the power plants. Each of the power projects has a large reservoir. When the demand for electric power is low, water from the tunnels is pumped into the reservoirs. When the demand increases, the reservoir water is used by the pumping-generating stations to produce additional electric power.

Commerce and industry. Ships cannot sail the full length of the Niagara River because of the falls and rapids. However, the nearby Welland Ship Canal, built by the Canadian government, provides a route for ships traveling between lakes Erie and Ontario (see **Welland Ship Canal**).

The hydroelectric power plants along the Niagara River have attracted to the region many industries that use large amounts of electric power. Most of the industries are centered in Niagara Falls, Ontario, and in the area between Niagara Falls, New York, and Buffalo, New York. During the 1970's, many people in the area became concerned about water pollution caused by some of the industries.   George Macinko

See also **Niagara Falls**.

Niamey, *nyah MAY* (pop. 400,000), is the capital and largest city of Niger. The city lies on the Niger River in the southwestern part of the country (see **Niger** (map).

Niamey is the chief trade and exporting center for farm products raised in Niger. It has two marketplaces, where people buy and sell farm products. Niamey has some small food-processing plants, but few other industries. The city's main buildings include government office buildings and a *mosque* (Muslim house of worship). Most of the people live in crowded areas along the Niger River. Niamey has a small international airport.

In the early 1900's, France took control of Niger from black Africans who had long lived there. In 1926, the French founded Niamey as the capital of their colony of Niger. Niger gained independence from France in 1960. At the time, Niamey's population was about 30,000.

Robert I. Rotberg

Nibelungenlied, *NEE buh lung uhn LEET,* is a German epic poem written about A.D. 1200. The title means *Song of the Nibelungs.* The author is unknown but undoubtedly came from the Danube area of southeastern Germany or Austria. Several versions of the author's story exist today.

The poem tells of Siegfried, who owns the fabulous Nibelung treasure and a cloak of invisibility. He has also killed a dragon and bathed in its blood. The blood hardened Siegfried's flesh, protecting it from wounds. But a linden leaf had fallen between his shoulders while he bathed, leaving an unprotected spot on his back.

Siegfried wants to marry Kriemhild, the sister of King Gunther of Burgundy. To gain Kriemhild, Siegfried helps Gunther win the maiden Brunhild, Queen of Iceland. Brunhild will marry only the man who can overcome her in combat. So Siegfried disguises himself as Gunther and beats Brunhild, winning her for Gunther. Years later, Kriemhild tells Brunhild that Siegfried, not Gunther, had beaten her, adding some insulting lies to the revelation. In revenge, Brunhild orders Hagen, one of Gunther's servants, to murder Siegfried. Hagen kills Siegfried by thrusting a spear into the unprotected spot on his back.

Several years later, Kriemhild marries Etzel, mighty king of the Huns. But she never forgets Siegfried. Kriemhild invites the Burgundians to visit her and has them slaughtered. Only Hagen survives. Kriemhild asks him to reveal where he has hidden the Nibelung treasure. When he refuses, she kills him. Hildebrand, a warrior at the court of Etzel, horrified by Kriemhild's treachery, kills her.

The background. Two actual events form the basis for parts of the *Nibelungenlied.* In A.D. 437, the Huns destroyed the Burgundians, an east Germanic tribe. The Burgundian king and members of his royal household died in the battle. The king of the Huns, Attila (called Etzel in the poem), was not connected with this event. Attila died on his wedding night in 453. Some historians said that he was murdered by his Germanic bride.

The Nibelungen-poet clearly was not the first to deal with this story material. The Icelandic *Edda,* composed before the *Nibelungenlied,* contains *lays* (short poems) on the same themes. The early Germanic peoples composed lays to celebrate the great heroes and events of their past. The lays were revised, and in the course of centuries the original historical events were greatly altered. Unknown poets combined the events of 437 and 453 into a single historic lay. In this lay, a Burgundian bride kills Attila to gain revenge for the death of her relatives, who had been killed by Attila's Huns.

Many of the themes and much of the plot of the older Germanic lays can still be found in the *Nibelungenlied,* but the poet changed the material. Scholars have not been able to trace the *Nibelungenlied* story of Siegfried's death to particular historical personalities and events. In fact, Siegfried's supernatural powers give his story the quality of a fairy tale.

The style. The *Nibelungenlied* is written in stanzas. Each stanza consists of four long lines of two pairs of rhymed couplets. The author shows a keen understanding of human psychology in developing the motives that cause the proud figures in the poem to act as they do. The great climaxes lie in the tense dialogues in which the rivals confront each other.

Scholars cannot say precisely what the Nibelungen-poet retained and what he or she inserted. The courtly aspects were probably added around 1200, when courtly culture flourished in Germany. The love between Siegfried and Kriemhild, the festivals of knights and ladies, and the many heroes reflect courtly virtues. These softer accents contrast with and heighten the effect of the tragic ending.   James F. Poag

See also **Fafnir**.

Nicaea, Councils of. See Nicene councils.

David Mangurian

The Nicaraguan countryside includes sharply rising mountains and grazing land for cattle and other livestock. This scene is in western Nicaragua, near the city of León.

Nicaragua

Nicaragua, *NIHK uh RAH gwuh,* is the largest country of Central America in area. It extends from the Pacific Ocean to the Caribbean Sea. About three-fifths of the country's people live in a fertile region on the Pacific side. In this region is Managua, the capital and largest city of Nicaragua.

Most Nicaraguans have both American Indian and Spanish ancestors. In the early 1500's, Spaniards began arriving in what is now Nicaragua. They named the land for an Indian chief and his tribe—both called Nicarao— who lived there. The Nicarao way of life, like that of most other Indians of Nicaragua, has blended with Spanish customs and traditions. Today, Nicaragua has only a few Indian groups that follow traditional ways of life.

Coffee is one of Nicaragua's leading sources of income. It is grown in the Pacific Region of western Nicaragua and in the Central Highlands. Few people live in the thickly forested Caribbean Region in the eastern part of the country.

Government

A president heads the national government of Nicaragua. The people elect the president and a vice president to five-year terms. The president appoints a Cabinet to help carry out the day-to-day operations of the government. The National Assembly makes the country's laws. The people elect 90 members of the Assembly to five-year terms. All Nicaraguans 16 years of age and older may vote in elections.

Nicaragua is divided into 15 *departments* and 2 *autonomous* (self-governing) regions on the Caribbean coast. The country is further divided into municipalities for purposes of local government. The people elect a mayor and a council to administer each municipality.

Nicaragua has a number of political parties, which of-

ten form alliances. Two major parties are the Sandinista National Liberation Front (FSLN), commonly called the Sandinistas, and the Liberal Constitutionalist Party (PLC).

The Supreme Court of Justice is Nicaragua's highest court. It hears appeals from lower courts. It has 16 judges. The judges are elected by the National Assembly to five-year terms.

The armed forces of Nicaragua consist of an air force, army, and navy. Service is voluntary.

People

The majority of Nicaraguans are *mestizos* (people with Spanish and Indian ancestors). The mestizos' way of life is similar to that of Spanish Americans in other Central American countries. About half of the Nicaraguan people belong to the Roman Catholic Church.

A majority of Nicaraguans speak Spanish. The only Indian groups in Nicaragua that still speak their own languages and follow their traditional ways of life live in the thinly populated Caribbean Region. The Caribbean Re-

Facts in brief

Capital: Managua.
Official language: Spanish.
Area: 50,337 mi² (130,373 km²). *Greatest distances*—north-south, 293 mi (472 km); east-west, 297 mi (478 km). *Coastlines*—Pacific, 215 mi (346 km); Caribbean, 297 mi (478 km).
Elevation: *Highest*—Pico Mogotón, 6,913 ft (2,107 m) above sea level. *Lowest*—sea level along the coasts.
Population: *Estimated 2012 population*—6,039,000; density, 120 per mi² (46 per km²); distribution, 57 percent urban, 43 percent rural. *2005 census*—5,142,098.
Chief products: *Agriculture*—beans, beef and dairy products, coffee, corn, peanuts, rice, sugar cane, tobacco. *Manufacturing*—food and beverage products, clothing, textiles.
National holiday: Independence Day, September 15.
Money: *Basic unit*—gold córdoba. One hundred centavos equal one gold córdoba.

gion also has several black and mixed Indian-black communities that largely follow Indian customs and traditions.

About two-fifths of Nicaraguans are poor people who farm for a living. Many of those in the Pacific Region are peasants who work on their own farms, on cooperatives or state farms, or on large private farms. In warmer areas, agricultural workers live in palm- or metal-roofed houses. In the colder areas of the Central Highlands, farmers live in adobe houses with tile roofs. The Indians and blacks of the Caribbean Region live chiefly by farming small plots or by fishing, lumbering, or mining.

Nicaraguan law requires children to go to school from ages 6 through 12. Before 1980, only about half of Nicaraguan children did so, and most of these children lived in cities or towns. Nicaragua had too few schools, and many rural areas had no schools at all. But since then, the government has built hundreds of rural schools. The government also conducted a successful literacy campaign headed mainly by young volunteer teachers.

Nicaragua has several universities. The National University of Nicaragua, in León and Managua, is the oldest and largest university. It was founded in 1812 and has more than 22,000 students.

The land and climate

Nicaragua has three main land regions: (1) the Pacific Region, (2) the Central Highlands, and (3) the Caribbean Region. The climate is chiefly tropical, with some differences among these regions.

The Pacific Region is largely a low area extending from Honduras to Costa Rica. Several volcanoes, some of them active, are in this low area. Lake Managua and Lake Nicaragua lie in the central and southern sections. Mountains up to 3,000 feet (910 meters) high rise along the Pacific coast. Nicaragua's largest cities and many large farms are in the Pacific Region.

The region receives about 60 inches (150 centimeters) of rain a year. The rainy season lasts from May to November. Temperatures average about 80 °F (27 °C) throughout the year.

The Central Highlands make up Nicaragua's highest and coolest region. They include the country's highest point, Pico Mogotón, a peak on the border with Honduras, north of Ocotal, that rises 6,913 ft (2,107 m) above sea level. Forests cover most of the region's slopes. Deep valleys lie between the mountains.

Some areas receive over 100 inches (250 centimeters) of rain a year. Most people live on farms in drier areas. Like the Pacific Region, the Central Highlands have a rainy season from May to November. Temperatures average 60 to 70 °F (16 to 21 °C).

The Caribbean Region is mostly a flat plain, with some highlands sloping upward toward the west. Many rivers that rise in the Central Highlands flow through the plain. The region's only good farmland lies along the riverbanks. Rain forests cover most of the region. There are grasslands with palm and pine forests in the north. A number of small islands lie off the coast.

Easterly trade winds drench the Caribbean Region with an annual average of 165 inches (419 centimeters) of rain, which falls throughout most of the year. Temper-

Nicaragua's flag was adopted in 1908 from that of the United Provinces of Central America. This union of the early 1800's consisted of Nicaragua and four other nations.

The coat of arms appears on the flag. The volcanoes stand for the Central American union, the triangle for equality, the rainbow for peace, and the cap for liberty.

© Shepard Sherbell, SABA
Managua is the capital, largest city, and chief commercial center of Nicaragua. The city is located in western Nicaragua.

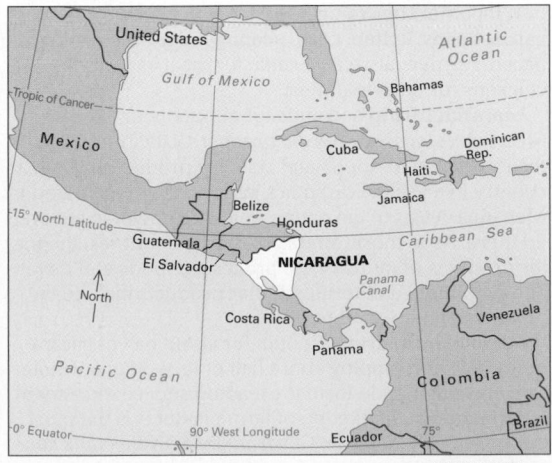
WORLD BOOK map
Nicaragua is bordered by Honduras, the Caribbean Sea, Costa Rica, and the Pacific Ocean.

Land regions of Nicaragua

Distance scale
0   100 Miles
0   100 Kilometers

WORLD BOOK map

atures in the Caribbean Region average approximately 80 °F (27 °C).

Economy

Nicaragua is one of the poorest countries in Latin America. *Remittances* (money sent home) from Nicaraguans living abroad are important to the economy. Nicaragua's economy also relies on foreign aid.

Nicaragua's major natural resource is the rich soil of the Pacific Region. Ash from volcanoes makes this soil fertile. Farming is a leading economic activity. Nicaragua has some deposits of copper, gold, and silver. However, mining provides only a small part of the nation's income. Nicaragua has no oil or gas reserves. The country must import these products to meet its needs. Thick forests cover much of the land.

Agriculture is one of the leading economic activities in Nicaragua. About one-third of the country's workers are involved in raising crops and livestock. Farming activities center in the Central Highlands and the Pacific Region. Farm products provide much of Nicaragua's export income. The country's leading crops include bananas, beans, coffee, corn, peanuts, sugar cane, and tobacco. Farmers also raise cattle for meat and milk and chickens for eggs and meat.

Manufacturing accounts for about one-fifth of Nicaragua's *gross domestic product* (GDP). The GDP is the total value of goods and services produced within a country in a year. Nicaragua's industry is concentrated in Managua. Most of the nation's electric power is generated there. As in most Central American countries, the major products of industry are processed foods and beverages, clothing, and textiles. Other products include cement, machinery, and petroleum.

Service industries account for about half of Nicaragua's GDP and employ about half of its workers. Wholesale and retail trade form the leading service industry in Nicaragua. The marketing of farm products is the most important type of trade. Government activities rank second in importance.

Foreign trade. Nicaragua imports more than it exports. The country imports electronics, machinery, mo-

tor vehicles, petroleum and petroleum products, and *pharmaceuticals* (medicinal drugs). Leading exports include beef, coffee, gold, lobster, shrimp, and sugar. The United States is Nicaragua's chief trading partner. Important Latin American trading partners include Costa Rica, El Salvador, Guatemala, Honduras, Mexico, and Venezuela. Nicaragua belongs to the Central American Common Market, an economic union of nations.

Transportation. Nicaragua's road system is in poor condition. Most of the roads are unpaved. The Pan American Highway is the country's major highway (see **Pan American Highway**). This highway runs through the western part of Nicaragua. Many populated areas cannot be reached by automobile. The people in these areas use mules or oxcarts. Few Nicaraguans own an automobile. Bluefields, Corinto, and Puerto Sandino have major seaports. Managua has an international airport.

Communication. Nicaragua has few newspapers. The largest are *La Prensa* and *El Nuevo Diario,* both of Managua. Radio and TV stations are the leading sources of information.

History

The Indian period. Little is known of what is now Nicaragua before the Spaniards arrived in the early 1500's. A series of Indian states occupied the Pacific Region and the Central Highlands. They built fortified towns. They had highly developed markets and a system of social classes that included slaves. Less developed Indian societies lived in the Caribbean Region.

The colonial period. In 1502, Christopher Columbus, an Italian navigator in the service of Spain, arrived at what is now Nicaragua. He claimed the land for Spain. A Spanish expedition from Panama explored the Pacific Region in 1522. Many of the Nicarao Indians who lived there were baptized as Roman Catholics.

Another expedition from Panama arrived in 1524. The leader was Francisco Fernández de Córdoba. He founded Granada and León near the main sources of Indian labor. The Indians worked on the Spaniards' farms and in their mines. In 1570, Nicaragua came under the control of the Audiencia of Guatemala. The Audiencia was a high court of Spanish judges and administrators that ruled most of Central America. Nicaragua was part of the colony of New Spain. But the court had great power because Nicaragua was so far from Mexico City, the colonial capital.

The Spaniards explored the Caribbean coast of Nicaragua but did not settle there. In the 1600's and 1700's, other Europeans—chiefly the English—occupied that region from time to time. English, Dutch, and French pirates had hideouts there. They attacked Spanish shipping in the Caribbean Sea. The pirates also raided Spanish towns to the west. In the 1700's, the English gained control over the Miskito (also called Mosquito) Indians of the Caribbean coast. The United Kingdom gave up its hold on the region to Nicaragua in the mid-1800's.

Independence. On Sept. 15, 1821, Nicaragua and other Central American states declared their independence. These states later became part of the Mexican Empire. They broke away from the empire in 1823 and established the United Provinces of Central America. In general, this union followed liberal economic and political policies. For example, the members established civil

Nicaragua
map index

Departments

Boaco ....150,636 ..D 3
Carazo ....166,073 ..E 2
Chinandega ...378,970 ..D 1
Chontales ....153,932 ..D 3
Esteli ....201,548 ..C 2
Granada ......168,186 ..E 2
Jinotega ......331,335 ..C 2
León ....355,779 ..D 1
Madriz ....132,459 ..C 2
Managua ....1,262,978 ..D 2
Masaya ......289,988 ..E 2
Matagalpa ....469,172 ..C 2
Nueva
 Segovia ....208,523 ..B 2
R.A.A.N.* ......314,130 ..B 5
R.A.A.S.† ....306,510 ..E 5
Río San Juan ...95,596 ..F 4
Rivas ....156,283 ..E 2

Cities and towns‡

Acoyapa ....16,946 ..E 3
Altagracia ....19,955 ..E 3
Belén ....16,428 ..E 2
Bluefields ....45,547 ..E 5
Boaco ....49,839 ..D 3
Bonanza ....18,633 ..B 4
Camoapa ....34,962 ..D 3
Chichigalpa .....44,769 ..D 1
Chinandega ...121,793 ..D 1
Ciudad Darío ....41,014 ..D 2
Ciudad
 Sandino§ ....75,083 ..D 2
Condega ....28,481 ..C 2
Corinto ....16,624 ..D 1
Corn Island§ ....6,626 ..D 5
Diriamba ....57,542 ..E 2
Diriomo§ ......22,352 ..E 2
El Castillo ......19,864 ..F 4
El Jícaro§ ......25,901 ..B 2
El Rama ....52,482 ..D 4
El Sauce ....27,900 ..D 2
El Viejo ....76,775 ..D 1
Esquipulas .....15,877 ..D 2
Esteli ....112,084 ..C 2
Granada ......105,171 ..E 2
Jalapa ....54,491 ..B 2
Jinotega ....99,382 ..C 2
Jinotepe ....42,109 ..E 2
Juigalpa ....51,838 ..D 3
La Concep-
 ción§ ....31,950 ..E 2
La Libertad .....11,429 ..D 3
La Paz
 Centro ....28,118 ..D 1
La Trinidad .....20,041 ..C 2
Larreynaga .....27,898 ..D 2
León ....174,051 ..D 1
Managua ......937,489 ..D 2
Masatepe ....31,583 ..E 2
Masaya ....139,582 ..E 2
Matagalpa .....133,416 ..C 2
Mateare ....28,775 ..D 2
Matiguás ....41,127 ..C 3
Muelle de los
 Bueyes ....22,082 ..D 4
Muy Muy ......14,721 ..D 3
Nagarote ....32,303 ..D 2
Nandaime ......34,288 ..E 2
Nindirí ....38,355 ..E 2
Niquino-
 homo§ ....14,847 ..E 2
Nueva Guinea ...66,936 ..E 4
Ocotal ....34,580 ..B 2
Paiwas§ ....31,762 ..D 3
Palacagüina ....12,825 ..C 2
Prinzapolka .....16,105 ..C 5
Pueblo
 Nuevo ....20,620 ..C 2
Puerto
 Cabezas ......66,169 ..B 5
Río Blanco .....30,785 ..C 3
Rivas ....41,080 ..E 2
San Carlos .....37,461 ..F 4
San Isidro ......17,412 ..C 2
San Jorge ....8,024 ..E 3
San Juan de
 Limay ....13,455 ..C 1
San Juan
 del Sur ......14,741 ..F 2
San Lorenzo§ ...23,666 ..D 3
San Marcos§ ...29,019 ..E 2
San Rafael
 del Norte .....17,789 ..C 2
San Rafael
 del Sur ....42,417 ..E 2
San Sebastián
 de Yalí ....26,979 ..C 2
Santo
 Domingo ....12,182 ..D 4
Santo Tomás ...16,404 ..D 3
Sébaco ....32,221 ..C 2
Siuna ....64,092 ..B 4
Somotillo ......29,030 ..E 1
Somoto ....33,788 ..C 2
Telica ....23,266 ..D 1

Tipitapa ....101,685 ..D 2
Villa Sandino ...13,152 ..D 4
Waspam ....47,231 ..A 5
Wiwilí [de
 Jinotega] .....57,485 ..B 3

Physical features

Amaka (river) ....B 3
Archipiélago
 Solentiname
 (islands) ....F 3
Bambana (river) ....D 4
Bay of Bluefields ....E 5
Bay of Punta Gorda ....F 5
Bocay (river) ....B 3
Cabo Gracias
 a Dios (cape) ....A 5
Coco (river) ....B 3

Cordillera
 Chontaleña
 (mountains) ....E 4
Cordillera Darienes
 (mountains) ....C 3
Cordillera de
 los Marrabios
 (mountains) ....D 1
Cordillera
 Isabelia
 (mountains) ....B 3
Escondido (river) ....D 4
Estero Real (river) ......C 1
Gulf of Fonseca ....C 1
Indio (river) ....F 5
Isla de Ometepe
 (island) ....E 3
Isla del Venado
 (island) ....E 5

Kukalaya (river) ....B 5
Laguna Bismuna
 (lagoon) ....A 5
Laguna de Perlas
 (lagoon) ....D 5
Laguna de Wounta
 (lagoon) ....B 5
Laguna Páhara
 (lagoon) ....A 5
Lake Managua ....D 2
Lake Nicaragua ....E 3
Mico (river) ....D 4
Mosquito Coast ....D 5
Pearl Cays ....D 5
Prinzapolka (river) ......C 5
Punta Gorda (point) .....A 5
Punta Gorda (river) .....E 4
Punta Grindstone
 Bay (point) ....E 5

Punta Mono (point) .....E 5
Punta Perlas
 (point) ....D 5
Río Grande de
 Matagalpa (river) .....C 4
San Juan (river) ....F 4
Serranías de
 Yolaina
 (mountains) ....E 4
Serranías Huapí
 (mountains) ....D 4
Siquia (river) ....D 4
Tuma (river) ....C 3
Tyra Cays ....C 5
Viejo (river) ....D 2
Volcán Concepción
 (volcano) ....E 3
Waspuk (river) ....B 4
Wawa (river) ....B 5

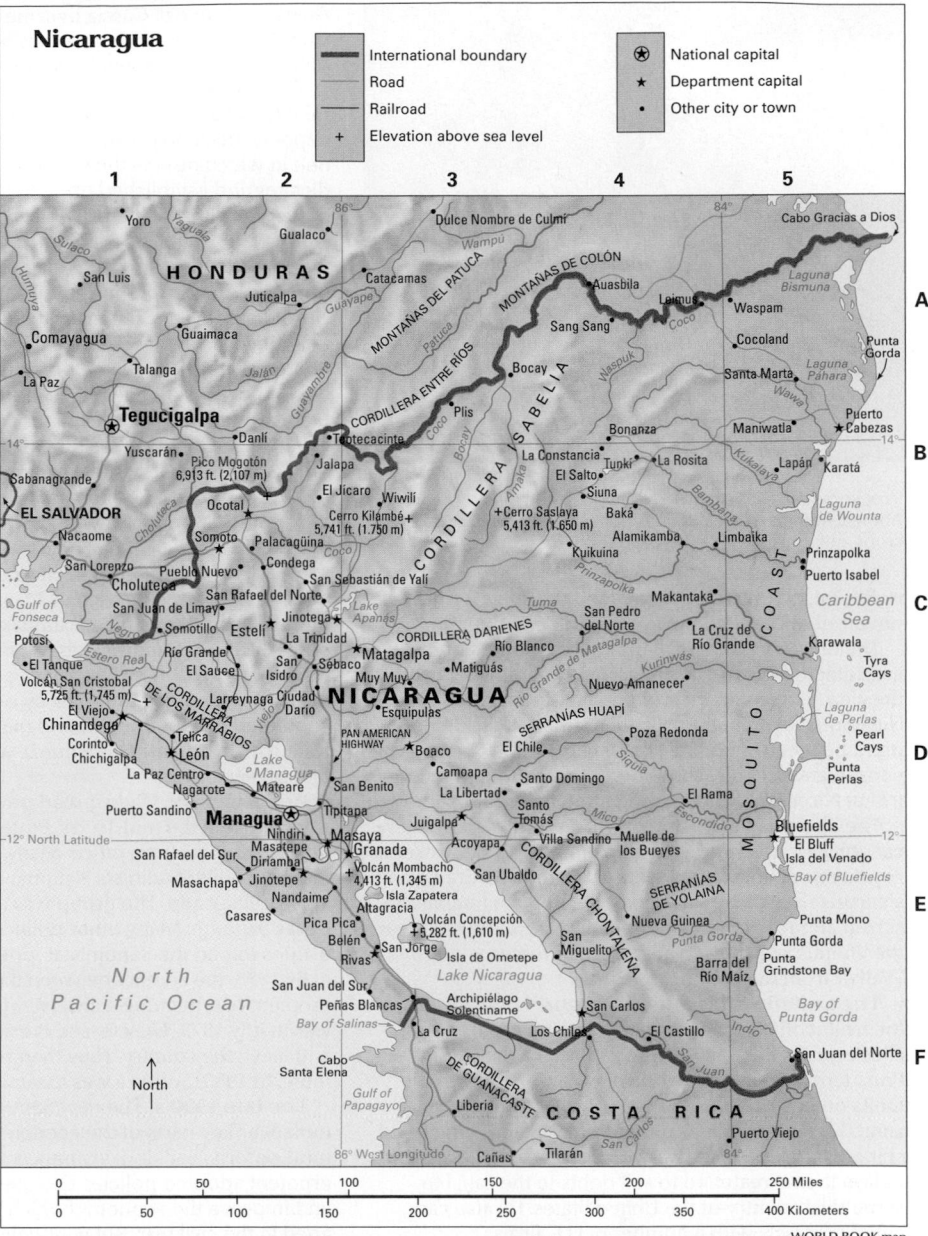

WORLD BOOK map

*Región Autónoma Atlántico Norte.
†Región Autónoma Atlántico Sur.
‡Population of municipalities, which may include rural areas as well as the urban center.
§Does not appear on the map; key shows general location.
Source: 2005 census.

© Bill Gentile, Sipa

Workers load bananas at a Nicaraguan port, *shown here.* About two-fifths of Nicaragua's people make a living by raising crops and livestock for export and for domestic use.

rights. In addition, they also ended the special rights of powerful nobles and the Roman Catholic Church.

The union began to collapse under various pressures, including efforts by the conservative landowners and the clergy to regain their old privileges. In 1838, Nicaragua left the union. By then, a dispute had developed between León, the liberal center, and Granada, the conservative center. These two cities struggled for control of Nicaragua, and fighting often broke out.

The liberals of León asked William Walker, an American military adventurer, to help them. In 1855, Walker arrived with a band of followers and captured Granada in a surprise attack. But instead of helping the liberals, he seized control of the government in 1856. The next year, the liberals and conservatives joined forces and drove Walker from the country.

The United States and Nicaragua. For many years, the United States had wanted to build a canal across Nicaragua to link the Atlantic and Pacific oceans. In 1901, President José Santos Zelaya of Nicaragua set certain limits on U.S. rights in the proposed Nicaragua Canal zone. The United States did not accept these limits, and shifted its attention to Panama as the site of the canal. Zelaya then threatened to sell rights to the canal to some rival country of the United States. He also canceled contracts with a number of U.S. firms.

In 1909, a revolt broke out against Zelaya, a harsh ruler. He was driven from office after the United States sided with the rebels. In 1911, U.S. banks began to lend money to Nicaragua under agreements that gave them control over its finances until the debts were paid in 1925. At the request of the banks and President Adolfo Díaz, U.S. marines landed in Nicaragua in 1912 to put down forces opposed to American control. The marines remained in Nicaragua almost continuously until 1933 to protect United States interests and supervise elections.

Rebels led by General Augusto César Sandino tried to make the U.S. forces leave Nicaragua. From 1927 to 1933, the rebels raided the U.S. marines from hideouts in the mountains. The United States trained a new Nicaraguan army, called the National Guard, to help the marines.

Anastasio Somoza García became head of the National Guard. In 1934, after the marines had left, Somoza had members of the National Guard murder Sandino.

The Somoza period. In 1936, Somoza forced President Juan Sacasa to resign. Somoza, who was Sacasa's nephew, became president the next year after an election in which he was the only candidate. He ruled as a dictator and established great political and economic power for himself and his family.

From 1937 until 1979, a Somoza ruled Nicaragua either as president or as the real power behind the government. Anastasio Somoza was assassinated in 1956. His older son, Luis, then replaced him as president. Luis held the presidency until 1963. His brother, Anastasio Somoza Debayle, became president in 1967. In general, the Somozas were eager to cooperate with the United States and had support from the U.S. government.

Political stability under the Somoza family rule attracted U.S. investments, and Nicaragua's economy expanded. The 160-mile (257-kilometer) Rama Road was built between 1968 and 1980 with U.S. aid. It helped connect the Pacific and Caribbean coasts of Nicaragua.

In 1972, an earthquake in Nicaragua killed about 5,000 people. It destroyed much of Managua. The city was rebuilt near the site of the earthquake. Also in 1972, President Anastasio Somoza Debayle turned over formal power to a civilian *junta*—that is, a small group that takes over a government and rules by decree. However, he continued to rule from behind the scenes as head of the National Guard. In 1974, Somoza was elected president for six years.

Rebel victory. Widespread protests against Somoza's rule began in the mid-1970's. Protesters demanded Somoza's removal from office. Many of the opponents belonged to the Sandinista National Liberation Front, then a guerrilla group. The group was named after Augusto César Sandino. Many other political and economic groups joined the Sandinistas' protests.

By 1978, the conflict between the rebels and the government had become a civil war. The rebels won the war in July 1979. They forced President Somoza to resign and leave the country. They then set up a new government. In 1980, Somoza was assassinated in Paraguay.

The late 1900's. The new Sandinista government took over key parts of the economy, including agricultural exports, banking, insurance, and mining. The government adopted policies designed to help the poor and improve the economy, which had been badly damaged in the civil war. But economic recovery from the war was slow, and hardships remained for many people.

In the early 1980's, internal opposition to the Sandinistas developed concerning economic policy and the type of government to be established. In 1981, the United States charged that Nicaragua was providing weapons to rebels in other Central American countries, and it cut off aid to Nicaragua. In that year, former members of Somoza's National Guard and others stepped up attacks from bases over the border in Honduras. In response, the Nicaraguan government declared a state of emergency and launched a campaign to build up its military forces. In 1983, several thousand anti-Sandinistas invaded northeastern Nicaragua. Fighting between the invaders—called *contras*—and the government forces resulted in a large number of deaths from 1983 to 1990.

The United States gave financial aid to the contras. The government was aided by the Soviet Union, Cuba, Western European nations, and other countries.

Daniel Ortega became head of the Sandinista government. He was elected president of Nicaragua in 1984. United States President Ronald Reagan charged that the Sandinistas had set up a Communist dictatorship and were providing aid to rebels in other Central American countries. In late 1983 and early 1984, the United States helped the contras place mines in Nicaraguan harbors. In 1985, Reagan ordered an embargo on U.S. trade with Nicaragua. Before the embargo, the United States had been Nicaragua's chief trading partner.

Some people in the United States opposed U.S. financial aid to the contras. In the 1980's, the U.S. Congress voted sometimes for and sometimes against further aid to the rebels. In 1986, the International Court of Justice concluded that the United States had acted illegally in helping the contras. United States officials rejected the conclusion.

In March 1988, the Sandinistas and the contras negotiated a cease-fire. They held talks to try to resolve their differences. Although no peace agreement was reached, the level of fighting declined following the talks. But fighting resumed after the government refused to extend the cease-fire past Oct. 31, 1989.

In elections in February 1990, Violeta Barrios de Chamorro of the anti-Sandinista National Opposition Union (UNO) was elected president. The government and the contras signed a cease-fire agreement in April 1990. By June 1990, the contra troops had been disbanded.

After the election of Chamorro, the United States ended its trade embargo with Nicaragua. During the 1990's, the government began to privatize some areas of the economy, such as banking and mining, that had been nationalized by the Sandinistas. But Nicaragua still faced severe economic problems, including high inflation and poor industrial performance.

In a presidential election held in 1996, José Arnoldo Alemán Lacayo of the rightist Liberal Alliance defeated Daniel Ortega of the Sandinistas and several other candidates. The main party in the Liberal Alliance was the Liberal Constitutionalist Party (PLC).

In 1998, Hurricane Mitch struck Nicaragua, producing floods and landslides. The storm killed about 3,000 people and caused more than $1 billion in damage.

Recent developments. In a 2001 presidential election, Enrique Bolaños Geyer of the PLC defeated Ortega, who again ran as the Sandinista candidate. In 2003, former President Alemán was convicted of corruption and sentenced to 20 years of house arrest. Nicaraguan voters reelected Daniel Ortega president in 2006. Ortega took office in early 2007. Dario A. Euraque

Related articles in *World Book* include:

Central America	León
Chamorro, Violeta	Managua
Barrios de	Mosquito Coast
Darío, Rubén	Ortega, Daniel
Granada	Sandino, Augusto César
Iran-contra affair	Somoza García, Anastasio
Lake Nicaragua	

Outline

I. **Government**
II. **People**

© Bill Gentile, Sipa Press

Sandinista soldiers, *shown here,* fought rebels called *contras* in Nicaragua during the 1980's. The war ended in 1990.

III. **The land and climate**
   A. The Pacific Region
   B. The Central Highlands
   C. The Caribbean Region
IV. **Economy**
   A. Agriculture
   B. Manufacturing
   C. Service industries
   D. Foreign trade
   E. Transportation
   F. Communication
V. **History**

Questions

How did Nicaragua get its name?
What is the main source of Nicaragua's income?
What family controlled Nicaragua from 1937 to 1979?
What is the most heavily populated part of Nicaragua?
What led to the landing of U.S. Marines in Nicaragua in 1912?
Which two cities struggled for power in the 1800's?
Why is the Pacific Region's soil especially fertile?
What was the Audiencia of Guatemala?

Additional resources

Gutierrez, Catalina, and others. *Making Work Pay in Nicaragua.* World Bank, 2008.
Hendrix, Steven E. *The New Nicaragua.* Praeger, 2009.
Volz, Eric. *Gringo Nightmare.* St. Martin's, 2010.
White, Steven F., and Calderon, Esthela. *Culture and Customs of Nicaragua.* Greenwood, 2008.

Nice, *nees* (pop. 347,060; met. area pop. 940,017), is a resort city on the French Riviera and a Mediterranean port. It lies at the foot of the Alps near Italy (see **France** [political map]). The city has wide avenues, luxurious hotels, and villas surrounded by gardens. The Paillon River divides it into the Old Town to the east and the modern, western part. The Alps protect Nice from cold northern winds and give it a mild winter climate.

Most of the people depend for their living on the tourist trade. Most tourists come during the winter vacation season between January and April, or else from July to September. The Mardi Gras, the height of the Riviera Carnival, is one of Nice's many winter festivals (see **Mardi Gras**). The industries of Nice produce olive oil, perfumes, processed fruit, soap, cement, and other products. Railroad lines to Marseille and to the Italian cities of Genoa and Turin pass through Nice. Greek settlers founded Nice about 400 B.C. William M. Reddy

Nicene Councils, *ny SEEN,* were two councils of the early Christian church held in Nicaea (now Iznik in northwest Turkey). The Roman Emperor Constantine called the first council in 325 to settle the dispute caused by the Arian views of the Trinity. Arius was a priest of Alexandria, Egypt, who believed that Jesus Christ was not of the same *essence* (substance) as God. The council adopted the so-called Nicene Creed, which declared that God and Jesus Christ as God were of the same essence. The council also fixed the time for observing Easter. In some regions, the Christian Easter had been observed on the same day as the Jewish Passover. In others, Easter had been observed on the following Sunday.

The Nicene Creed summarized the chief articles of the Christian faith. It was adopted originally in the following form, but has been expanded since then:

> We believe in one God, the Father Almighty, maker of all things, both visible and invisible; and in one Lord, Jesus Christ, the Son of God, Only begotten of the Father, that is to say, of the substance of the Father, God of God and Light of Light, very God of very God, begotten, not made, being of one substance with the Father, by whom all things were made, both things in heaven and things on earth; who, for us men and for our salvation, came down and was made flesh, was made man, suffered, and rose again on the third day, went up into the heavens, and is to come again to judge both the quick and the dead; and in the Holy Ghost.

Empress Irene of the Byzantine Empire and her son Constantine called the second council in 787. The Emperor Leo, Irene's deceased husband, had forbidden the use of images for any religious purpose. Irene and Constantine called the council because of opposition to Leo's decree. Irene canceled the decree after the council had established principles governing the *veneration* (honoring) of images.   Eugene TeSelle

See also **Arianism; Easter; Trinity.**

Nicholas I (1796-1855) was czar of Russia from 1825 to 1855 and a member of the Romanov line of rulers. He was a hard-working leader whose conservatism kept him from moving Russia into the modern world.

Nicholas was born on July 6, 1796, in Tsarkoye Selo, an estate near St. Petersburg, Russia. He succeeded his brother Alexander I after Alexander's death in December 1825. At that time, a group of liberal army officers, later known as Decembrists, tried to take power. Nicholas had five of the leaders executed and the others exiled to Siberia. He fought liberalism in Russia and revolution in Europe. In 1830-1831, he put down a Polish uprising aimed at freeing Poland from the Russian Empire. In 1849, he sent Russian armies into Hungary to crush a revolt for Hungarian independence from Austria.

Within the Russian Empire, Nicholas demanded loyalty to himself and to the Russian Orthodox Church. Censorship was severe during his reign. But Russian literature, art, and music thrived. Some reforms did occur. With his approval, Russia's first modern law code was issued in the 1830's. Nicholas also authorized improvements in the living conditions of certain peasants.

In 1828-1829, Nicholas won territory for Russia and helped win independence for Greece in a war with the Muslim Ottoman Empire. The Ottoman Empire was centered in what is now Turkey. He again went to war with the Ottomans in what became the Crimean War (1853-1856). Fearful of Russian expansion, the United Kingdom

and France helped the Ottomans defeat the Russians. Nicholas died on March 2, 1855.   Joseph T. Fuhrmann

See also **Alexander II; Crimean War; Romanov; Russia** (History).

Nicholas II (1010?-1061) became pope in 1059. His reign is best known for the Lateran *synod* (assembly) of 1059, which reformed the procedures for electing a new pope. *Lateran* refers to the Basilica of St. John Lateran in Rome. The synod issued a decree stating that the *cardinal bishops* (high-ranking cardinals) in effect would propose a candidate for pope. Then all the cardinals would "elect" the candidate, which actually meant they would accept him. The pope-elect would be presented to the people of Rome for approval. A notice then would be sent to the Holy Roman emperor for his approval. The decree's purpose was to prevent Roman nobles from interfering with papal elections. Later, the decree also was used to limit the emperor's influence on papal elections.

The synod also issued laws enforcing *celibacy* (unmarried life) of the clergy and prohibiting *simony* (selling church offices) and *lay investiture,* by which nonreligious rulers presented clergymen with the symbols of their offices. Lay investiture enabled rulers to control who received church offices. To secure his electoral decree, Nicholas allied the papacy with the Normans, a group of Scandinavians in southern Italy. At times, this alliance effectively protected the popes from troubled Roman politics and German interference. At other times, the Normans themselves interfered in Rome.

Nicholas was born in Burgundy, or possibly Lorraine, France. His given name was Gerhard. He died on Oct. 27, 1061.   Thomas F. X. Noble

See also **Pope** (The early Middle Ages).

Nicholas II (1868-1918), the last czar of Russia, ruled from 1894 to 1917. A member of the Romanov line of rulers, he succeeded his father, Alexander III. Nicholas believed a czar must have absolute power and opposed parliamentary government.

Nicholas was born on May 18, 1868, in St. Petersburg, Russia. During his reign, industry developed rapidly in Russia. Literature, science, and other branches of learning also made impressive gains. But the middle class increasingly felt the monarchy was out of touch with the needs of the new industrial society. Workers in the cities became dissatisfied with living and working conditions.

Meanwhile, Nicholas tried to expand Russian territory in Asia. This effort led to the Russo-Japanese War (1904-1905), which Russia lost. The war sharpened dissatisfaction with the government, and the people revolted in 1905. Workers, peasants, and intellectuals joined to force Nicholas to make reforms. He agreed to establish an elected legislature and granted the people civil liberties. Beginning in 1906, Nicholas's government expanded public education, gave workers some insurance against illness and injury, and allowed peasant families to assume ownership of the village land they were farming. But these reforms were interrupted by the outbreak of World War I in 1914. Nicholas's approval of a buildup of Russian troops along the country's borders with Germany and Austria-Hungary helped trigger the war.

Russia suffered severe losses in World War I. In 1915, Nicholas assumed direct command of the army. As a result, the people blamed him for Russia's military failures. Many Russians also unjustly accused Alexandra, his

Brown Bros.

Nicholas II, the last czar of Russia, and his family posed for this photograph shortly before the Russian Revolution of 1917. The czar's family included, *clockwise from lower left,* his son, Grand Duke Alexis; his wife, Empress Alexandra; and his daughters, the Grand Duchesses Maria, Tatiana, Olga, and Anastasia.

German-born wife, of treason. These problems and shortages of food and fuel led the people to revolt in March 1917. Nicholas lost all political support, and he gave up his throne on March 15.

In November 1917, revolutionaries called Bolsheviks (later known as Communists) seized power. They imprisoned Nicholas and his wife and children in Yekaterinburg in the Ural Mountains and killed them there on July 17, 1918.　　Joseph T. Fuhrmann

See also **Duma; Rasputin, Grigori E.; Russia** (History); **Russo-Japanese War; World War I** (Causes of the war; Beginning of the war).

Additional resources

King, Greg. *The Court of the Last Tsar: Pomp, Power, and Pageantry in the Reign of Nicholas II.* Wiley, 2006.
King, Greg, and Wilson, Penny. *The Fate of the Romanovs.* Wiley, 2003.

Nicholas V (1397-1455) was elected pope in 1447. Nicholas was the first true Renaissance pope. He drew inspiration from intellectual developments in Florence, the leading humanist center in Italy (see **Renaissance** [Humanism]). Nicholas spent vast sums on an important collection of ancient Greek, Roman, and early church manuscripts. These writings became the core of the Vatican Library. Nicholas sponsored many humanists in Rome as translators of Greek works into Latin, seeing the papal role not only as head of the church but also as head of Western civilization.

Nicholas aimed to once again make Rome the capital of the Christian world. He proclaimed 1450 a jubilee year, which attracted many pilgrims to Rome. He also rebuilt many structures in the city and made ambitious plans to rebuild the Vatican. Nicholas was born on Nov.

15, 1397, in Sarzana, Italy, near La Spezia. His given and family name was Tommaso Parentucelli. He died in Rome on March 24 or 25, 1455.　　Charles L. Stinger

Nicholas, Saint (A.D. 300's), is one of the most popular saints of the Christian church. He is the patron saint of sailors, travelers, bakers, merchants, and especially children. Little is known about his life except that he was Bishop of Myra in Lycia, on the coast of Asia Minor. According to tradition, he was born in Lycia. Some legends say he made a pilgrimage as a boy to Egypt and Palestine, that he was imprisoned during Diocletian's persecution, and released under Constantine the Great. In addition, legends say Nicholas attended the Council of Nicaea in 325. Numerous miracles were credited to him.

Much of Europe still observes December 6, Saint Nicholas's feast day and the supposed day of his death, as special holidays. For example, in Germany, Switzerland, the Netherlands, and Belgium, men in bishops' robes pose as Saint Nicholas. They visit children, examine them on their prayers, urge them to be good, and give them gifts. This custom probably originated in the legend that Saint Nicholas gave gold to three girls who did not have dowries and so could not get married.

Nicholas evolved into Father Christmas in Germany and Protestant northern Europe. Dutch immigrants brought the tradition of "the visit of Saint Nicholas" to America. The Dutch settlers and their English neighbors transformed Nicholas into the kind and jolly patron of American Christmas. The name *Santa Claus* comes from *Sinterklaas,* Dutch for *Saint Nicholas.*　　Stanley K. Stowers

See also **Christmas** (Gift giving); **Netherlands** (Holidays and recreation); **Saint Nicholas, Feast of; Santa Claus.**

Nicholas of Cusa, *KOO suh* (1401-1464), was a German theologian, scholar, and statesman. Nicholas wrote extensively on philosophy, theology, mathematics, and astronomy. In his most famous work, *On Learned Ignorance* (1440), Nicholas argued that reason is inadequate to determine truth. In his writings on astronomy, Nicholas suggested that Earth is in motion and is not the center of the universe. Thus, he was a forerunner of the theories developed in the 1500's by the Polish astronomer Nicolaus Copernicus.

Nicholas was born at Kues, Germany, near Trier. The Latin form of *Kues* is *Cusa.* In 1437, with the approval of Pope Eugene IV, Nicholas traveled to Constantinople to arrange a meeting between Eastern and Western church officials to discuss reunification. In 1438, Nicholas went to Germany to help regain for the papacy the allegiance of the Holy Roman Empire. This mission succeeded in 1448 with the signing of the Concordat of Vienna. Pope Nicholas V made Nicholas a cardinal in 1449. He became bishop of Brixen (now Bressanone), Italy, in 1450. He died on Aug. 11, 1464.　　Timothy B. Noone

Nichols, Mike (1931-　　), is a famous German-born director known for his work in motion pictures and on the stage. Nichols won an Academy Award for directing *The Graduate* (1967), his second movie. His other films include *Who's Afraid of Virginia Woolf?* (1966), *Catch-22* (1970), *Carnal Knowledge* (1971), *Silkwood* (1983), *Working Girl* (1988), *Postcards from the Edge* (1990), *The Birdcage* (1996), *Primary Colors* (1998), *Closer* (2004), and *Charlie Wilson's War* (2007).

Nichols began his directing career with *Barefoot in*

the Park (1963), a Broadway comedy. Nichols later directed such plays as *The Knack* (1964), *The Odd Couple* (1965), *Luv* (1966), *Streamers* (1976), *The Real Thing* (1984), *Biloxi Blues* (1988), and *Monty Python's Spamalot* (2004).

Nichols was born Michael Igor Peschkowsky in Berlin, Germany, on Nov. 6, 1931. He came to the United States in 1939 and became a U.S. citizen in 1944. He joined a Chicago theater group in 1955. Later, he and another member of the group, Elaine May, formed a team that put on satirical comedy skits.   Gene D. Phillips

Nicholson, Ben (1894-1982), was an English artist noted for his abstract paintings. Nicholson's most valued artistic contribution is the *relief,* a three-dimensional abstract picture created by cutting, carving, and painting flat boards. His early reliefs are painted white. His later reliefs incorporate subtle color and texture.

Benjamin Lauder Nicholson was born on April 10, 1894, in Denham, near London. His father was Sir William Nicholson, also an artist. Ben Nicholson's early works were charming and realistic decorative paintings. He also painted still lifes that demonstrate the influence of the French artist Paul Cezanne and the Cubism movement. Nicholson died on Feb. 6, 1982..   Pamela A. Ivinski

Nicholson, Jack (1937-   ), is an American motion-picture actor who often plays a cocky, rude outsider or free-spirited individualist. Nicholson has won three Academy Awards. He won the 1975 best actor award for *One Flew Over the Cuckoo's Nest* and the 1997 award for *As Good As It Gets.* He won the 1983 award as best supporting actor for *Terms of Endearment.*

Nicholson was born in Neptune, New Jersey, on April 22, 1937. He made his film debut in *The Cry Baby Killer* (1958) and first gained recognition in *Easy Rider* (1969). His other major films include *Five Easy Pieces* (1970), *Carnal Knowledge* (1971), *The Last Detail* (1973), *Chinatown* (1974), *The Shining* (1980), *Prizzi's Honor* (1985), *The Witches of Eastwick* (1987), *Batman* (1989), *Wolf* (1994), *About Schmidt* (2002), *Something's Gotta Give* (2003), *The Departed* (2006), *The Bucket List* (2007), and *How Do You Know* (2010). Nicholson has also directed films, beginning with *Drive, He Said* (1971).   Rachel Gallagher

M. Ginies, Sipa Press

Jack Nicholson

Nickel is a white metallic chemical element used in alloys. Nickel is magnetic, takes a high polish, and does not tarnish easily or rust. It can be hammered into thin sheets or drawn into wires. One pound (0.4 kilogram) of pure nickel could be drawn into a wire 80 miles (130 kilometers) long. The Chinese used an alloy of nickel more than 2,000 years ago. Pure nickel was first isolated in 1751 by the Swedish scientist Axel Cronstedt.

Nickel's *atomic number* (number of protons in its nucleus) is 28. The *relative atomic mass* of nickel is 58.6934. An element's relative atomic mass equals its *mass* (amount of matter) divided by $\frac{1}{12}$ of the mass of carbon 12, the most abundant form of carbon. Nickel melts at 1455 °C, and it has a density of 8.908 grams per cubic

Leading nickel-producing areas

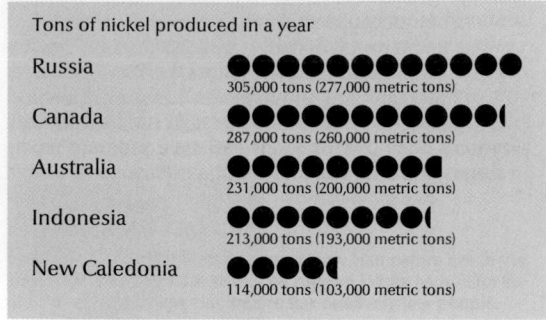

Tons of nickel produced in a year	
Russia	305,000 tons (277,000 metric tons)
Canada	287,000 tons (260,000 metric tons)
Australia	231,000 tons (200,000 metric tons)
Indonesia	213,000 tons (193,000 metric tons)
New Caledonia	114,000 tons (103,000 metric tons)

Figures are for 2008.
Source: U.S. Geological Survey.

centimeter at room temperature (see **Density**).

Industrial uses. Nickel is used in structural work and in electroplating because it resists corrosion. Printing plates electroplated with nickel withstand hard use (see **Electroplating**). *Nickel peroxide,* a nickel compound, forms the active material of the positive electrode in the Edison storage battery. Nickel is also used in the nickel-cadmium storage battery (see **Battery**). An important use for nickel is to promote certain chemical reactions by *catalysis* (see **Catalysis**). The nickel itself is not changed in the process and can be used repeatedly. It is used as a catalyst in a process called *hydrogenation* to produce solid vegetable oils for cooking. See **Hydrogenation**.

Nickel-iron alloys. Perhaps the largest use for nickel is as an additive to cast iron and steel. It makes iron more *ductile* (easily formed) and increases its resistance to corrosion. Nickel also makes steel more resistant to impact. Manufacturers often use steel alloyed with nickel to make armor plate and machine parts.

Invar is an alloy of nickel, iron, and other metals. It is valued for meter scales and for pendulum rods. Invar expands or contracts little as its temperature changes.

Monel metal is an alloy of nickel and copper used in sheet-metal work. It has an especially high resistance to corrosion. See **Monel metal**.

Nickel silver, also called *German silver,* is a nickel alloy used in tableware.

Mining nickel. The chief mineral ore of nickel is *pentlandite,* a mixture of sulfur, iron, and nickel. Other nickel ores include *millerite* and *niccolite.*

Canada and Russia are the leading nickel producers. They combine to produce about one-third of the world total. Australia, Indonesia, and New Caledonia are also important nickel-producing areas.   Marianna A. Busch

Nickel is the common name for a United States copper-nickel coin worth five cents. Its official name is the five-cent piece. The current nickel has a picture of Thomas Jefferson on the *obverse* (front) and Monticello, Jefferson's home, on the *reverse* (back). Jefferson and Monticello first appeared on the nickel in 1938. Redesigned nickels, with a new picture of Jefferson and an updated image of Monticello, began circulating in 2006.

The earliest U.S. five-cent pieces had a shield on the obverse and a *5* on the reverse. They were minted between 1866 and 1883. Nickels made from 1883 through 1912 had a head of Liberty on the obverse and a *V* (Roman numeral five) on the reverse. A nickel with an Indi-

The U.S. nickel shows Thomas Jefferson and Monticello.

an head on the obverse and a buffalo on the reverse was minted from 1913 through 1938. In 2004 and 2005, the U.S. government issued special nickels to commemorate the Louisiana Purchase of 1803 and the Lewis and Clark expedition of 1804 to 1806.   Burton H. Hobson

Nickelodeon. See Motion picture (The history of motion pictures; picture).

Nicklaus, *NIHK luhs,* **Jack** (1940-   ), an American, ranks among the greatest players in the history of golf. Nicklaus was the first player to win all four major golf titles at least twice. He won the British Open in 1966, 1970, and 1978; the United States Open in 1962, 1967, 1972, and 1980; the Masters Tournament in 1963, 1965, 1966, 1972, 1975, and 1986; and the United States PGA (Professional Golfers' Association) Championship in 1963, 1971, 1973, 1975, and 1980. He won the U.S. Amateur tournament in 1959 and 1961 before turning professional.

Jack William Nicklaus was born in Columbus, Ohio, on Jan. 21, 1940. He defeated Arnold Palmer in a playoff for the 1962 U.S. Open championship for his first professional victory. He joined the Senior PGA Tour in 1990. Nicklaus retired from competitive golf in 2005. He ended his career with 73 PGA tournament victories, second only to Sam Snead's 82. He has also designed several golf courses.   Marino A. Parascenzo

See also **Golf** (picture).

Nickname. See Name (Nicknames).

Nicolet, *nee kaw LEH* or *nihk uh LAY,* **Jean,** *zhahn* (1598-1642), also spelled Nicollet, was a French explorer, fur trader, and interpreter. He was the first European to enter Lake Michigan and travel in what is now Wisconsin, adding to French knowledge of North America.

Nicolet was born Jean Nicolet de Belleborne in Cherbourg, France. He traveled to North America in 1618 with Samuel de Champlain, a French explorer. For two years, Nicolet lived among Algonquin Indians of Allumette Island on the Ottawa River, in present-day Quebec. In 1620, Champlain sent Nicolet to Lake Nipissing, in what is now Ontario. Nicolet traded there until 1629.

In 1634, Nicolet traveled north on Lake Huron and then west to Lake Michigan. He established friendly relations with Winnebago Indians who lived along Lake Michigan's Green Bay. He then traveled along the Fox River and explored southward, near the Wisconsin River. But he failed to achieve one of the goals of his voyage—to find a route to Asia. Nicolet returned to Quebec in 1635 and settled in Trois-Rivières in 1637, where he lived until his death on Nov. 1, 1642.   D. Peter MacLeod

Nicosia, *NIHK uh SEE uh,* is the capital and largest city of Cyprus, an island republic in the Mediterranean Sea (see **Cyprus** [map]). The municipality of Nicosia has a

population of about 250,000. A municipality may include rural areas as well as the urban center. Nicosia serves as the island's business center and as a trade center in the Mesaoria Plain. Goods produced there include almonds, fruit, olive oil, wheat, and wine.

In 1974, Turkish troops invaded Cyprus. Nicosia was divided into a Turkish Cypriot section and a Greek Cypriot section. The island's main government offices are in the southern section.   Theofanis G. Stavrou

Nicotine is a substance largely responsible for both the pleasurable and the addictive effects of tobacco use. It and other ingredients in tobacco and cigarette smoke are responsible for a wide variety of health problems. Nicotine is found in small amounts in the leaves, roots, and seeds of the tobacco plant. In nature, it acts as a poison that protects the plant from being eaten by certain insects. Nicotine can also be made synthetically. Chemists classify nicotine as an *alkaloid* (see **Alkaloid**).

A smoker takes in about 0.05 milligram to 2 milligrams of nicotine per cigarette. Nicotine is quickly absorbed into the bloodstream from the lungs and rapidly distributed throughout the body. Blood saturated with nicotine reaches the brain within seconds and accounts for the feeling of euphoria or "rush" felt from smoking. In pregnant women, nicotine can harm the developing fetus. The chemical easily crosses the *placenta,* the organ that supplies the fetus with food and oxygen. Smokers have nicotine in all their bodily fluids, including breast milk.

Nicotine stimulates certain receptors in the brain, increasing levels of the chemical *dopamine.* Dopamine plays a key role in motivation, pleasure, and addiction. Nicotine improves memory and relaxes the muscles of the body. It also increases heart rate, blood pressure, and the force of heart muscle contractions, putting added stress on the heart.

The liver breaks down most nicotine in the body, and the kidneys excrete the remainder through urine. Frequent smokers suffer withdrawal symptoms when they have low levels of nicotine in their blood. They may feel irritable and anxious and crave cigarettes. Many smokers smoke throughout the day to maintain the accustomed nicotine levels in their blood.   Diane Burgermeister

See also **Smoking; Tobacco.**

Nictitating membrane. See Cat (Head); Eye (Eyes of animals); Frog (Senses).

Niebuhr, *NEE boor,* **H. Richard** (1894-1962), was an influential Protestant theologian. He was an authority on Christian ethics and religion in the United States.

In *The Social Sources of Denominationalism* (1929), Niebuhr argued that race and social class were important in determining most Americans' religious affiliation. In *The Kingdom of God in America* (1937) and *Christ and Culture* (1951), he showed how Christian principles have helped shape American culture and warned Christians not to allow society to overly influence their values. Other writings focused on the need for religious people to integrate their beliefs with their daily lives.

Helmut Richard Niebuhr was born on Sept. 3, 1894, in Wright City, Missouri. He died on July 5, 1962. His brother, Reinhold, was also a theologian.   Charles H. Lippy

Niebuhr, *NEE boor,* **Reinhold** (1892-1971), was a prominent American theologian known for his writings on ethics. Karl Paul Reinhold Niebuhr was born on June 21, 1892, in Wright City, Missouri. After graduating from

Yale Divinity School in 1915, he was a pastor at an Evangelical church in Detroit for 13 years. Niebuhr believed that Christian ethical teaching and socialism could offer solutions to social conflicts. He also was a pacifist.

In 1928, Niebuhr became a professor of the philosophy of religion at Union Theological Seminary in New York City. About this time, he began to abandon his earlier views in favor of a new approach called Christian Realism. According to this philosophy, an ideal society will always be beyond humanity's grasp, but moral individuals should still work for social justice. In doing so, Christians should apply moral principles in a way that is flexible enough to account for certain situations. For example, the Christian Realist approach led Niebuhr to abandon pacifism when the Nazis came to power in Germany. Niebuhr believed the Nazis were a symbol of an evil greater than the evil of war.

Niebuhr wrote several books on ethics. His most influential work is the two-volume *Nature and Destiny of Man* (1941, 1943). Niebuhr's brother, H. Richard Niebuhr, was also a prominent theologian. Reinhold Niebuhr died on June 1, 1971. Charles H. Lippy

Nielsen, *NEEL suhn,* **Carl August** (1865-1931), was one of Denmark's greatest composers. His music was little performed during his lifetime, but it has become internationally known since his death on Oct. 3, 1931.

Nielsen wrote in the traditional forms of the 1800's. His early works reflect the influence of the composers Johannes Brahms of Germany and Franz Liszt of Hungary. But Nielsen's own style grew steadily. He eventually developed a more modern musical language, especially in his use of dissonant harmonies. Nielsen's compositions include six symphonies, symphonic poems for orchestra, and concertos for clarinet, flute, and violin. He also wrote chamber music, 10 cantatas, and works for both piano and organ. One of his last major compositions is *Piano Music for Young and Old* (1930), a set of 24 pieces in all keys. Nielsen was born on June 9, 1865, near Odense, Denmark. Daniel T. Politoske

Niemeyer, *NEE my uhr,* **Oscar** (1907-   ), is a Brazilian architect. He is best known as the designer of the principal buildings of Brasília, the Brazilian capital (see **Brasília**). Niemeyer often uses primary forms for entire buildings, and in repetitious architectural elements. He has said that his designs are inspired by Brazilian climatic and social conditions, and the nation's colonial baroque art heritage.

Niemeyer was born Dec. 15, 1907, in Rio de Janeiro. His early work was influenced by brief contact with the architect Le Corbusier. An example of this work is the Gustavo Capanema Palace (1937-1943) in Rio de Janeiro. It is shaped like a slab, with windows set deeply into the concrete building to provide sun shades. In the early 1940's, he was chief architect for Pampulha, a residential area near Belo Horizonte. Among his other works are the French Communist Party headquarters (1968-1975) in Paris; the Oscar Niemeyer Museum (1967-2003) in Curitiba, Brazil; and the Oscar Niemeyer International Cultural Center (2011) in Avilés, Spain. Dennis Domer

See also **Brasília** (picture); **Brazil** (picture: Modern Brazilian architecture).

Niépce, *nyehps,* **Joseph Nicéphore,** *zhoh ZEHF nee say FAWR* (1765-1833), a French scientist, invented the first photographic technique, *heliography*. He started ex-

perimenting in 1816. He succeeded in making a crude photograph of a courtyard in 1826. Niépce sensitized a metal plate with *bitumen* (a dark tarlike substance) and exposed it for eight hours. This plate, the world's first photograph, can be viewed in the Gernsheim Collection at the University of Texas at Austin (see **Photography** [History; picture]).

In 1829, Niépce became the partner of L. J. M. Daguerre, a French stage designer and painter who introduced the first popular form of photography. Daguerre based his research for the *daguerreotype* process for making photographs on Niépce's technique of heliography (see **Daguerre, Louis J. M.**). Niépce was born on March 7, 1765, in Chalon-sur-Saône, France. He died on July 5, 1833. Richard Rudisill

Nietzsche, *NEE chuh,* **Friedrich,** *FREE drihkh* (1844-1900), was a German philosopher and classical scholar. He deeply influenced many philosophers, artists, and psychologists of the 1900's.

Classical scholarship. Nietzsche's first book was *The Birth of Tragedy* (1872). It presented a new theory of the origins of classical Greek culture. He believed that Greek culture could best be understood as resulting from a conflict between two basic human drives, the Apollonian and the Dionysian. The Apollonian was represented by Apollo, the god of the sun. The Dionysian was represented by Dionysus, the god of wine and intoxication.

The Apollonian is a drive to create clarity and order. It is a desire for a world in which everything possesses a clear identity and can be distinguished from other things. The Apollonian tendency finds expression in the visual arts, where each form stands out clearly from other forms. Nietzsche argued that, in reality, the world lacks any clear distinctions, that it is confused, chaotic, and cruel. The Apollonian drive tries to redeem the horrors of the real world by giving it the illusion of order and beauty, thus making it tolerable.

The Dionysian is a drive that tries to rip apart Apollonian illusions and reveal the reality that lies behind them. This revelation takes place only in special states of ecstasy or religious frenzy induced by drinking, wild music, and sexual license.

Nietzsche and religion. Nietzsche was a severe critic of religion, especially Christianity. In *Thus Spake Zarathustra* (1883 to 1885), he proclaimed that "God is dead." This was his dramatic way of saying that most

Messerschmidt, FPG

The Presidential Offices was one of many buildings designed by Oscar Niemeyer in the 1950's for Brazil's capital, Brasília.

people no longer believed in God. Thus, religion could no longer serve as the foundation for moral values.

Nietzsche believed that the time had come to examine traditional values critically. In *Beyond Good and Evil* (1886) and *The Genealogy of Morals* (1887), he examined the origins of our moral systems. He argued that the warriors who dominated earlier societies had defined their own strength as "good" and the weakness of the common people they dominated as "bad." Nietzsche called this "master morality" because it represented the values of the masters.

Later, the priests and common people, who wanted to take power, defined their own weakness and humility as "good." They called the aggressive strength of the warriors "evil." Nietzsche identified these values, which he called "slave morality," with the values of the Judeo-Christian tradition that dominates Western culture. He criticized these values as being expressions of the fear and resentment of the weak against the strong.

Psychological ideas. Nietzsche's major psychological theory states that all human behavior is inspired by a "will to power." He wanted to disprove and replace a common prevalent psychological theory that was known as *hedonism*. Hedonism holds that human behavior is inspired by a desire to experience pleasure and avoid pain. Nietzsche argued that people are frequently willing to increase their pain, strain, or tension to accomplish tasks that allow them to feel power, competence, or strength.

Nietzsche did not mean that people wanted only to dominate each other, nor that they were only interested in physical or political power. He wrote that we also want to gain power over our unruly drives and instincts. He thought that the self-control exhibited by artists and people who practice self-denial for religious reasons was actually a higher form of power than the physical bullying of the weak by the strong.

Nietzsche's ideal was the *overman* (or *superman*), a passionate individual who learns to control his or her passions and use them in a creative manner. This superior human being channels the energy of instinctual drives into higher, more creative, and less objectionable forms. Nietzsche believed that such "sublimation" of energy is far more valuable than the suppression of the instincts urged by Christianity and other religions.

His life. Nietzsche was born on Oct. 15, 1844, in Röcken, Saxony, near present-day Leipzig, Germany. He was a professor of classics at the University of Basel in Switzerland from 1868 to 1878, when he retired because of poor health. He then devoted himself to writing. In 1889, Nietzsche suffered a mental breakdown from which he never recovered. He died on Aug. 25, 1900. Nietzsche is often wrongly considered a racist, anti-Semite, and forerunner of Nazism. These charges are largely the result of distortions of his ideas by his sister Elisabeth and by Nazi propagandists after his death.

Ivan Soll

See also **Ethics** (Nietzsche).

Additional resources

Andreas-Salome, Lou. *Nietzsche.* 1988. Reprint. Univ. of Ill. Pr., 2001.
Safranski, Rudiger. *Nietzsche.* Norton, 2001.
Solomon, Robert C., and Higgins, Kathleen M. *What Nietzsche Really Said.* Schocken, 2000.

Niger, *NY juhr,* is a large, landlocked country in west Africa. Barren desert and mountains cover most of northern Niger. A grassy, thinly wooded plain extends along the southern border. The country, officially called the Republic of Niger, takes its name from the Niger River, which flows through its southwest corner. Niamey is Niger's capital and largest city.

The people of Niger belong to many different ethnic groups, each with its own language and customs. A large majority of the people are Muslims. Most people work as farmers and live in the south, where water and land are available.

Niger became an independent nation in 1960. France had ruled it for about 60 years before independence.

Government. The president is the most powerful official in the government. The president appoints a prime minister and other members of the cabinet, determines their responsibilities, and may end their appointments at any time. The president is elected by the people to a five-year term.

The National Assembly is responsible for making Niger's laws. The members of the National Assembly are elected to five-year terms. The Constitutional Court is Niger's highest court in constitutional matters, and the Supreme Court is the highest court in other matters.

People. The people of Niger are called Nigeriens *(nee ZHEH ree ehnz)*. The major ethnic groups in Niger include the Hausa, Djerma-Songhai, Tuareg, Fulani, and Kanuri.

Niger

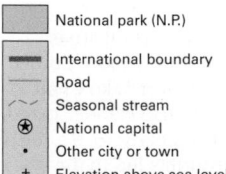

National park (N.P.)

International boundary
Road
Seasonal stream
National capital
Other city or town
Elevation above sea level

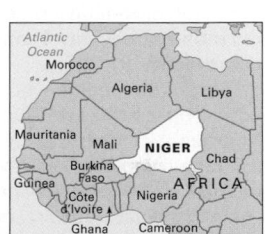

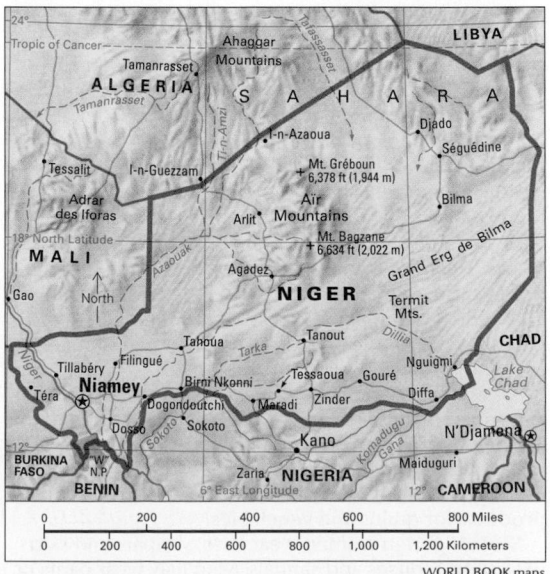

WORLD BOOK maps

Facts in brief

Capital: Niamey.
Official language: French.
Area: 489,191 mi² (1,267,000 km²). *Greatest distances*—east-west, 1,100 mi (1,770 km); north-south, 825 mi (1,328 km).
Elevation: *Highest*—Mount Bagzane, 6,634 ft (2,022 m) above sea level.
Population: *Estimated 2012 population*—17,031,000; density, 35 per mi² (13 per km²); distribution, 83 percent rural, 17 percent urban. *2001 census*—11,060,291.
Chief products: *Agriculture*—cattle, cotton, cowpeas, millet, peanuts, rice, sorghum. *Mining*—coal, gold, iron ore, phosphate, tin, uranium.
Flag: Horizontal stripes of orange, white, and green; an orange circle on the white stripe. See **Flag** (picture: Flags of Africa).
Money: *Basic unit*—CFA franc. CFA stands for Communauté Financière Africaine (African Financial Community).

The Hausa make up more than half of the population of Niger. They live mainly in the south and work as farmers. About one-fourth of the people are members of the Djerma-Songhai ethnic group. The Djerma-Songhai are farmers and live in the southwestern corner of the country, along the Niger River. The Kanuri make up about 5 percent of the population. They farm the rich land in southeast Niger.

Many of the Tuareg and the Fulani are *nomadic* (traveling) people who raise livestock for food. The Tuareg and the Fulani each make up about 10 percent of the country's population. During the rainy season, which lasts from July through September, these two groups live in the barren desert country of northern Niger. In dry months, they travel south in search of water and pastureland.

Most of the people who live in Niger's rural areas raise crops and livestock for food and for export. Some Nigeriens who live near the Niger River or Lake Chad fish for a living. The nomadic groups raise camels, cattle, goats, and sheep. In the late 1960's and early 1970's, and again in the early 1980's, severe droughts led to the deaths of many of the nomads' animals. As a result, many nomads were forced to become farmers or move to urban areas.

Niamey, Niger's capital, is its largest city by far. Other large cities include Agadez (Agades), Maradi, Tahoua, and Zinder. A majority of urban workers in Niger are employed in the government and other services, or in business.

Houses in rural Niger are built according to the traditions of the ethnic groups. The Hausa live in crowded villages and towns, in houses built of sun-dried mud bricks. The nomadic Tuareg live in tents made of skins or mats. The nomadic Fulani build houses out of straw and branches, and must construct new homes every time they move. The Nigerien government has built low-cost single-family houses in Niamey.

Nigeriens eat mainly grains and dairy products. Several popular dishes are made with millet and sorghum. The grains are often cooked into a porridge and served with a sauce. The nomadic Fulani and Tuareg live mainly on milk products from their herds. They also trade these products for grains and vegetables.

Most Nigerien women wear long, wraparound skirts with short blouses and sandals. Men may wear pants or knee-length shorts with loose shirts or robes. Tuareg men wear turbans with veils. The Fulani and Tuareg, who travel in desert areas, wear long, loose robes for protection from the sun.

Education in Niger is free, but many areas do not have schools. The government operates the public schools. Many places have Qur'ānic schools, which teach Muslim religious knowledge. A system of "tent schools" serves the nomadic groups in the north. When a group moves, the school moves with it. Most of Niger's adults cannot read or write.

French is the official language of Niger and is widely used in the schools. However, most Nigeriens commonly speak the language of their ethnic group, instead of French. More than 85 percent of the population understand the Hausa language, which serves as the language of trade. The language of the Djerma-Songhai is the second most widely spoken language. Some Nigeriens speak Arabic.

Most Nigeriens are Muslims. A small percentage of urban dwellers are Christians. Some rural Nigeriens practice traditional African religions.

The ethnic groups in Niger have produced many kinds of crafts, music, dance, and art. Craftworkers make gold and silver jewelry, pottery, leatherwork, cloth, and wood carvings. People in both urban and rural areas enjoy traditional African styles of music. Popular forms of recreation include cycling, basketball, and soccer.

Land and climate. Sandy plateaus and desert cover the northern two-thirds of Niger. In the center of this region, a large area of mountain ranges called the Aïr Mountains rises above the flat landscape. These mountains include the highest peak in Niger, Mount Bagzane, which stands 6,634 feet (2,022 meters) above sea level. Less than 7 inches (17.5 centimeters) of rain falls each year in the mountains. The surrounding desert receives

Naud, AAA Photo

Hausa women in Niger work in the grain fields near their village. The Hausa people make up the country's largest ethnic group. Most Hausa make their living by farming.

even less rain. Temperatures in the area can reach as high as 122 °F (50 °C).

Niger's most productive zone for herding animals and growing crops is the *savanna,* a grassy, thinly wooded plain in the south. The savanna extends from the Niger River in the west to Lake Chad in the east. It is one of the world's hottest places, with average daily temperatures in Niamey reaching 95 to 100 °F (35 to 38 °C). Most of Niger's rain falls in the savanna area. The city of Zinder receives about 22 inches (55 centimeters) annually.

Niger is a landlocked nation, with no outlet to the sea. The Niger River flows for about 350 miles (563 kilometers) across the southwest corner of Niger. The river floods each January and February and provides irrigation water for growing crops along its banks. Part of Lake Chad lies in southeastern Niger.

Niger's plant and animal life vary from north to south. Few plants grow in the desert, except near oases, where the date palm tree is common. Such wild animals as barbary sheep, foxes, gazelles and other antelope, and ostriches live in the north. Acacia, baobab, kapok, mahogany, and palm trees grow in the south. Wild animals in the south include baboons, crocodiles, elephants, giraffes, and wart hogs.

Economy. Niger is one of the world's poorest countries. Only a small part of its land is used to grow crops, and it has few natural resources. At times, droughts have caused sharp reductions in crop and livestock production, devastating the economy. Most of Niger's people live by farming and herding. Agricultural products include cattle, cotton, cowpeas, millet, peanuts, rice, and sorghum. Niger is a major producer of uranium. Coal, gold, iron ore, phosphate, and tin are also mined.

Niger exports livestock and uranium, and it imports machinery and petroleum products. France, Nigeria, and the United States are Niger's chief trading partners.

Poor transportation has hampered economic development in Niger. The country has no railroads, and most of its roads are not paved. Few Nigeriens own an automobile. Trucks carry freight, and people get around by buses or on foot. Niamey has an international airport.

Niger has one daily newspaper. The government controls much of the communications media in the country.

History. About A.D. 1000, Tuareg people began moving south from the middle of the Sahara into what is now Niger. They eventually controlled the trade routes across the desert and south to the coast. In the 1400's, a Tuareg empire grew up around the city of Agadez. The Songhai Empire became powerful in the 1400's. Its capital was Gao, in what is now Mali. During the 1500's, the empire conquered the Tuareg at Agadez and controlled much of central and western Niger. In 1591, an army from Morocco captured Gao, and the empire collapsed. See **Africa** (The empires of west Africa).

European explorers first arrived in Niger during the early 1800's. The French occupied parts of west Africa under agreements reached in 1885 and 1890 between the various European groups. France gained control of most of Niger by 1900. It put down a strong Tuareg resistance in 1906. Niger became part of the large French territory called French West Africa in 1922. Niger gained independence from France on Aug. 3, 1960.

Hamani Diori, leader of the Niger Progressive Party (Parti Progressiste Nigérien, or PPN), was elected Niger's first president. In the late 1960's and early 1970's, a severe drought struck Niger, causing widespread food shortages. In 1974, army officers headed by Seyni Kountché overthrew Diori. Kountché became president of the Supreme Council (formerly called the Supreme Military Council), which held all governing power. He died in 1987, and the council chose Colonel Ali Saïbou to succeed him. Niger's economy suffered during the 1980's because worldwide prices of uranium declined.

In 1992, Niger adopted a multiparty political system. Mahamane Ousmane was elected president in 1993. In 1995, the government signed peace accords with Tuareg and Toubou groups who had been in rebellion since 1990. A military coup led by General Ibrahim Baré Maïnassara overthrew the government in January 1996. Maïnassara won a presidential election in July, but opposition leaders claimed it was fraudulent. He was assassinated in April 1999, and military leaders created a new constitution, which was approved in July 1999. Mamadou Tandja, head of the National Movement for Society Development (Mouvement National pour la Société du Développement, or MNSD), was elected president in late 1999 and reelected in 2004. In February 2010, Tandja was overthrown in a military coup. The coup leaders set up a junta called the Supreme Council for the Restoration of Democracy. Since 2007, renewed Tuareg unrest in the north has resulted in some violence and the displacement of thousands of people.   Ronald Bruce St John

Related articles in *World Book* include:

French West Africa	Fulani	Niamey	Tuareg
	Hausa	Sahara	

Niger River, *NY juhr,* is the third longest river in Africa. Only the Nile and Congo rivers are longer. The Niger flows about 2,600 miles (4,180 kilometers) in western Africa. It carries more water than any other African river except the Congo. The Niger drains about 580,000 square miles (1,500,000 square kilometers) of land in the countries of Benin, Guinea, Mali, Niger, and Nigeria. Niger and Nigeria take their names from the river.

The Niger begins in the highlands of southern Guinea, about 150 miles (240 kilometers) from the Atlantic Ocean, near Guinea's border with Sierra Leone. It flows northeast into Mali, where it turns southeastward. After leaving Mali, the river cuts through the southwestern part of Niger and the northern tip of Benin. It then flows through western Nigeria, where it is joined by its main tributary, the Benue River. Near southern Nigeria's coast, it flows through a large delta region and empties into the Gulf of Guinea, an arm of the Atlantic Ocean.

Fishing and transportation are important activities on the Niger. Boats can navigate the river for about 1,000 miles (1,600 kilometers) in Mali and about 400 miles (640 kilometers) in Nigeria the year around. Rapids, waterfalls, and other obstacles prevent navigation on other parts of the Niger. The delta region of the Niger has major deposits of petroleum. The Kainji Dam in Nigeria is one of the largest power projects on the river. The dam, which holds back the Niger to form Kainji Lake, produces much of Nigeria's electric power. The Niger's name probably came from a Tuareg phrase meaning *river of rivers.* The Scottish explorer Mungo Park was the first European to explore its course, leading expeditions in 1796 and 1797 and in 1805 and 1806.   Vernon Domingo

See also **Africa** (political map); **Park, Mungo.**

Women harvest peanuts, one of Nigeria's leading crops, at a farm in the northern part of the country. Nigeria has more people than any other country in Africa. About half of Nigerians live in rural areas and earn their livelihood by farming, fishing, or herding.

© Joe B. Blossom, Photo Researchers

Nigeria

Nigeria, *ny JIHR ee ah,* a nation on the west coast of Africa, has more people than any other country in Africa. Nigeria ranks as one of the most populous countries in the world.

Nigeria is a land of great variety. It has hot, rainy swamplands; dry, sandy areas; grassy plains; and tropical forests. High plateaus and rocky mountains rise in various parts of the country. The population of Nigeria consists of more than 250 *ethnic* (cultural) groups. Approximately half of the country's people live in rural areas. Nigeria also has several large, crowded cities. Lagos is the chief commercial center. Abuja is the capital of the country.

Most Nigerians earn their livelihood by farming, fishing, or herding. The country is a leading producer of cacao, peanuts, and other crops. In addition, Nigeria has mineral resources, including large deposits of petroleum. Since the late 1960's, profits from Nigeria's oil industry have brought new wealth to the nation. Nigeria has used this wealth to develop new industry, improve its educational system, and modernize its agriculture.

A number of ancient kingdoms developed in the area that is now Nigeria hundreds of years ago. Some of the kingdoms became important cultural and trade centers. The United Kingdom gained control of Nigeria in the late 1800's and the early 1900's. Nigeria was a British colony and protectorate until 1960, when it gained independence.

Government

Military leaders controlled Nigeria's government from 1966 to 1979 and from 1983 to 1999. Civilian rule was restored in 1999, and a new constitution was adopted.

National government. A president heads the government of Nigeria. The president is elected by the people to a four-year term and cannot serve more than two terms. A vice president and Cabinet assist the president in handling the day-to-day operations of the government. The people elect the vice president. The president appoints members of the Cabinet with the approval of the Senate.

The National Assembly is Nigeria's legislature. The National Assembly consists of the House of Representatives and the Senate. The Nigerian people elect their representatives and senators to four-year terms. All Ni-

Facts in brief

Capital: Abuja.
Official language: English.
Official name: Federal Republic of Nigeria.
Area: 356,669 mi² (923,768 km²). *Greatest distances*—east-west, 800 mi (1,287 km); north-south, 650 mi (1,046 km). *Coastline*— 478 mi (769 km).
Elevation: *Highest*—Dimlang Peak, 6,699 ft (2,042 m) above sea level. *Lowest*—sea level.
Population: *Estimated 2012 population*—164,055,000; density, 460 per mi² (178 per km²); distribution, 52 percent rural, 48 percent urban. *2006 census*—140,431,790.
Chief products: *Agriculture*—cacao, cashews, cassava, cattle, chickens, corn, millet, palm oil and palm kernels, peanuts, rice, rubber, yams. *Mining*—coal, columbite, limestone, natural gas, petroleum, tin. *Manufacturing*—cement, chemicals, food products, footwear, textiles.
National anthem: "Arise, O Compatriots."
Money: *Basic unit*—naira. One hundred kobo equal one naira.

gerian citizens who are 18 years of age or older may vote.

Local government. Nigeria is divided into 36 states and the Federal Capital Territory of Abuja. Each state is governed by a House of Assembly and a governor. Assembly members and the governor are elected by the people to four-year terms. Nigeria's 36 states are divided into over 770 local government areas. Elected local government councils administer these areas.

Courts. The Supreme Court is the highest court in Nigeria. The country's judicial system also includes federal courts of appeal, the Federal High Court, and state high courts.

Nigeria has a number of religious courts. These courts have traditionally ruled only on questions of Islamic personal law for people who are practicing Muslims. The highest such court is the Sharī`ah Court of Appeal in Abuja. In the early 2000's, a number of largely Muslim northern states adopted Sharī`ah (also spelled Sharī`a), which is the body of Islamic law, as the basis of their legal codes. As a result, Sharī`ah is now applied to both civil and criminal cases in those states.

Armed forces. Nigeria has an army, a small navy and air force, and a federal police force. All military service is voluntary.

People

Ancestry. Almost all Nigerians are black Africans. The country has more than 250 ethnic groups. These groups differ from one another in language and in some of their customs and traditions. Nigeria's three largest ethnic groups are, in order of size, the Hausa, the Yoruba, and the Igbo (also spelled Ibo). These three ethnic groups account for about three-fifths of the total population of Nigeria.

The Hausa people live primarily in northern Nigeria and in the neighboring countries of Niger and Chad. Most of them are farmers, and many Hausa also are craftworkers and traders. The Hausa have lived in the area for more than a thousand years. During the 1200's, the Fulani, a people who originally came from what are now Senegal and Gambia, began to settle in the Hausa territory. The Fulani took control of the region during the early 1800's. The two peoples intermixed so much that the group is sometimes called the Hausa-Fulani.

The Yoruba live mainly in the southwestern part of the country and in Benin and Togo, two nations that lie to the west of Nigeria. Many of the Yoruba live in cities and farm the land in the surrounding countryside. Several Yoruba cities, including Lagos, were founded hundreds of years ago.

The Igbo form a majority of the population in southeastern Nigeria. In addition, a large number of Igbo live in other areas of the country. During the period of British rule in the 1900's, many Igbo accepted Western education and ways of life more quickly than the other Nigerian ethnic groups. The Igbo were also more willing to travel. As a result, the Igbo held many important positions in business and government during the period of colonial rule.

Other leading ethnic groups in the country include the Nupe and Tiv of central Nigeria; the Edo, Urhobo, and Itsekiri of the Edo and Delta states; the Ijaw of the

© Marcus Rose, Panos Pictures

Abuja, officially the capital of Nigeria since 1991, lies in a hilly region in the central part of the country. Aso Rock, *background,* and other huge rock formations stand in or near the city.

Nigeria's flag was adopted in 1960. The green represents agriculture, and the white symbolizes unity and peace.

Coat of arms. The design on the shield stands for Nigeria's fertile soil and main rivers, the Niger and the Benue.

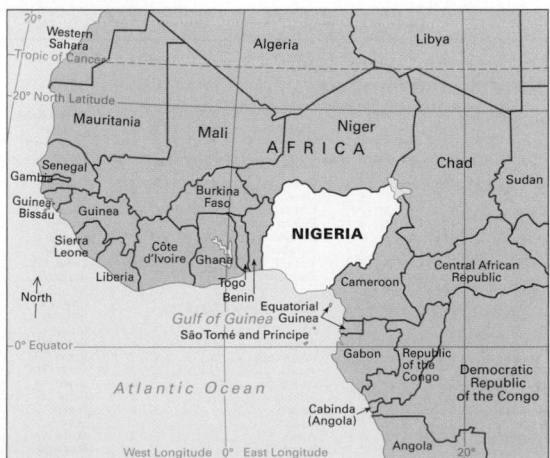

WORLD BOOK map

Nigeria, a large country in West Africa, lies on the Gulf of Guinea, just north of the equator.

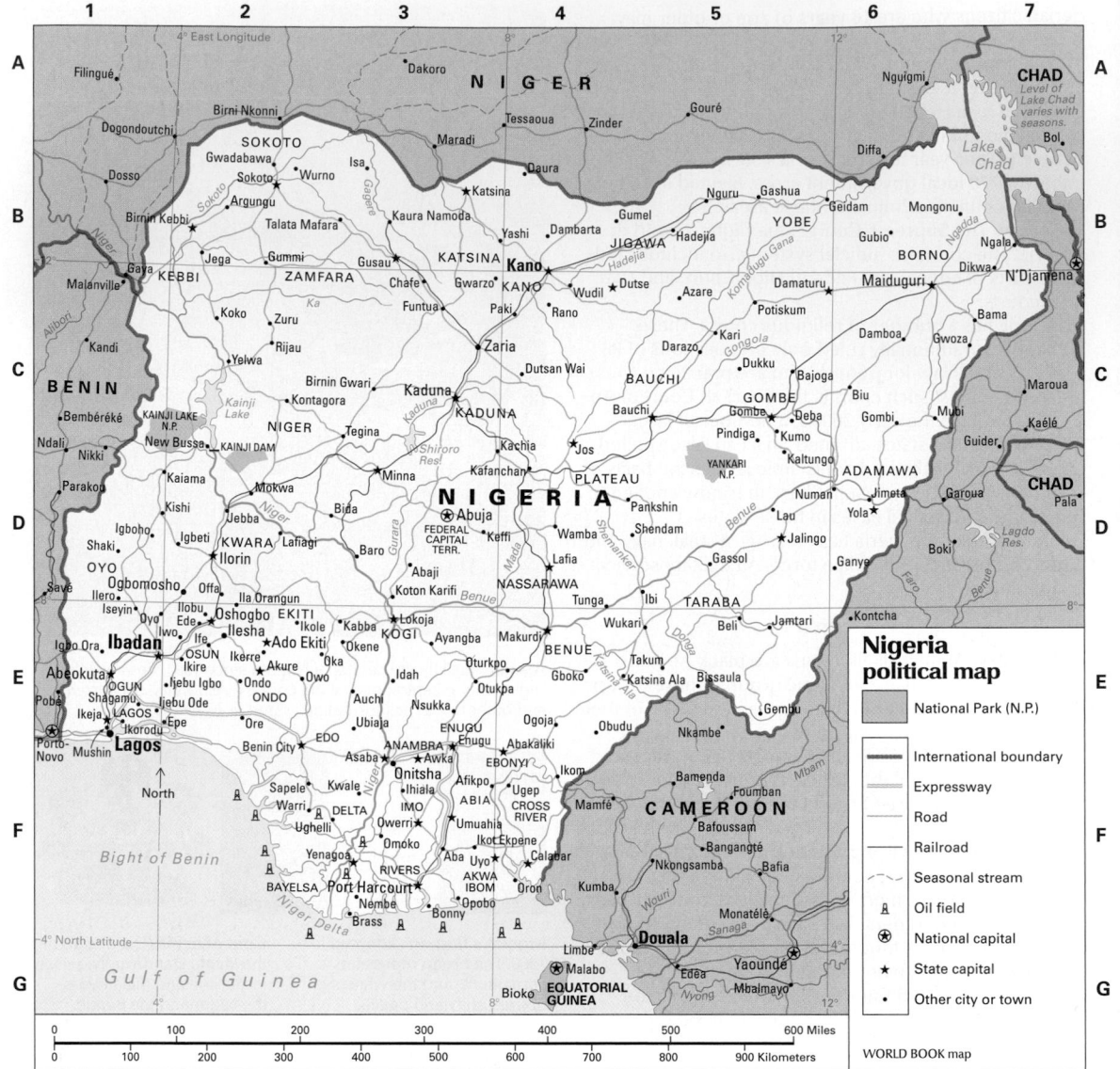

Nigeria political map

WORLD BOOK map

	National Park (N.P.)
	International boundary
	Expressway
	Road
	Railroad
	Seasonal stream
	Oil field
	National capital
	State capital
	Other city or town

Nigeria map index

*Not shown on map; key indicates general location.
Source: 2006 census.

Rivers state; the Efik and Ibibio of the Cross River State; and the Kanuri of northeastern Nigeria. The Kanuri trace their ancestry back to the ancient Kanem empire, which began during the A.D. 700's.

Languages. English is the official language of Nigeria and is taught in schools throughout the country. However, English is not the country's most commonly used language. Each of the more than 250 ethnic groups that live in Nigeria has its own distinct language. The three most widely used languages are those of the three largest ethnic groups—Hausa, Yoruba, and Igbo.

A majority of the people of Nigeria speak more than one language. They may use the language of their ethnic group on most occasions and speak English or another language at other times. In addition, Nigerians who are Muslims use Arabic while taking part in various religious activities.

Way of life. About half of Nigeria's people live in rural areas. Most homes in rural Nigeria are made of grass, dried mud, or wood and have roofs of asbestos cement sheets, corrugated metal, or thatch. A typical village consists of several *compounds* (clusters of houses). A group of related families lives in each compound. Well-to-do city dwellers in Nigeria live in modern houses or apartment buildings. The cities also have slums, where people live in mud huts that line unpaved streets. Overcrowding has become a serious problem in many Nigerian cities since the 1960's, when increasing numbers of people began moving from rural to urban areas in search of jobs.

In the cities, many Nigerians wear clothing similar to that worn by North Americans and Europeans. But other city dwellers and most people in rural areas wear traditional clothing. Traditional garments for men and women in Nigeria include long, loose robes made of white or brightly colored fabrics. The men may also wear short, full jackets with shorts or trousers. Small round caps are popular head coverings for men, and Nigerian women often wear scarves tied like turbans.

The chief foods of Nigeria include yams, corn, rice, and beans. The people also eat *plantains* (a kind of banana) and the roots of the cassava plant. Nigerian food is often cooked in palm oil or peanut oil, and it may be highly seasoned with red peppers. Some Nigerian meals feature beef, chicken, fish, or lamb. But in general, most Nigerians eat little meat. Popular beverages in Nigeria include beer and a wine that is made from the sap of palm trees. Some city dwellers also drink coffee and tea. Nigerian Muslims who obey the laws of Islam may not drink alcoholic beverages.

Religion. About half the people of Nigeria are Muslims. They make up the majority of the population in the north. Nearly 40 percent of the people are Christians. They live mainly in southern and central parts of Nigeria. Many Nigerians, especially in the rural areas, practice traditional religions based on the worship of many gods and spirits. People throughout the country may combine Christian or Muslim religious practices with traditional beliefs.

Education. About half of Nigeria's adults can read and write. For the country's literacy rate, see **Literacy** (table: Literacy rates). Nigeria does not have enough schools or teachers to provide an education for all school-age children, and laws do not require school at-

© John Cole, Impact Photos

Lagos, which served as Nigeria's capital from 1914 to 1991, is the nation's chief port and commercial and manufacturing center. Downtown Lagos has a number of tall, modern buildings.

© James Morris, Panos Pictures

A typical village house in Nigeria is made of grass, dried mud, or wood and has a roof of asbestos cement sheets, corrugated metal, or thatch. Most villages consist of clusters of houses.

© Giles Moberly, Impact Photos

Nigerian Muslims dressed in traditional costumes take part in a *durbar* (parade) at a festival in Katsina in northern Nigeria. About half the people of Nigeria are Muslims.

© Jason Lauré

Music and dance are popular forms of entertainment in Nigeria. These Hausa musicians and dancers from Kano in northern Nigeria are performing in Lagos.

tendance. Nigeria has many universities. The largest include Ahmadu Bello University, in Zaria; the University of Lagos; Lagos State University; and Olabisi Onabanjo University, in Ogun state.

Recreation. People in urban and rural areas of Nigeria enjoy performances of traditional songs and dances. Motion pictures attract many people in the large cities, where radio and television are also popular. Soccer is the favorite sport in Nigeria. Art festivals and special sports contests are held in many parts of the country.

The arts. Nigeria is famous for the variety and quality of its art. The art of Nigeria and other African countries has influenced art movements in many other parts of the world. For example, traditional African sculpture influenced Pablo Picasso and other modern Western artists.

The oldest known African sculptures are *terra-cotta* (clay) figures created by the Nok civilization in central Nigeria as early as 500 B.C. Other famous traditional sculptures include the brass figures of Benin and Ife, and the woodcarvings of the Yoruba people. Various peoples who live in the forest areas of Nigeria are known for their elaborately carved wooden masks. Most of the traditional Nigerian painting is done on sculp-

tures and textiles, or as body decoration.

Nigerian music often features drums, xylophones, and various string and wind instruments. Dance and dramatic performances are popular forms of entertainment in Nigeria. Many of these performances portray themes from folk stories or topics related to the everyday life of the people.

Most of Nigeria's traditional literature is oral, rather than written. Popular forms of such literature include chants, folk stories, proverbs, and riddles. During the mid-1900's, many Nigerian authors began to write novels, stories, and poetry. These works were written in English and in local languages. In 1986, the Nigerian playwright, poet, and novelist Wole Soyinka became the first African writer to win the Nobel Prize in literature.

The land and climate

Land regions. Nigeria can be divided into 10 land regions. They are (1) the Sokoto Plains, (2) the Chad Basin, (3) the Northern High Plains, (4) the Jos Plateau, (5) the Niger-Benue River Valley, (6) the Western Uplands, (7) the Eastern Highlands, (8) the Southwestern Plains, (9) the Southeastern Lowlands, and (10) the Niger Delta.

The Sokoto Plains occupy the northwestern corner of Nigeria. Several rivers flow across the flat, low-lying plains and flood the area during the rainy season. The floodwaters deposit fertile soil that allows farmers to grow various crops in the area. But the floods also occasionally destroy homes and farms.

The Chad Basin extends across northeastern Nigeria, south and west of Lake Chad. Sandy ridges cut across parts of the low-lying basin. During the rainy season, parts of the region become swampy. However, long dry spells occasionally cause serious droughts in the region. Short grasses and thinly scattered trees grow in the Chad Basin.

The Northern High Plains cover almost a fifth of Nigeria's total area. They consist largely of flat grasslands, with a few hills and granite ridges. Most of the plains area has an elevation of about 2,500 feet (762 meters) above sea level.

Several branches of the Niger River have their source in the Northern High Plains. These branches include the Gongola, Sokoto, and Kaduna rivers. They flow gently across the plains and form beautiful waterfalls as they tumble into deep gorges in parts of the region.

© James Morris, Panos Pictures

The Niger River serves as a major transportation route in Nigeria. The river flows southward through west-central Nigeria and cuts through grassland, tropical forests, and swampy plains. It empties into the Gulf of Guinea, an arm of the Atlantic Ocean.

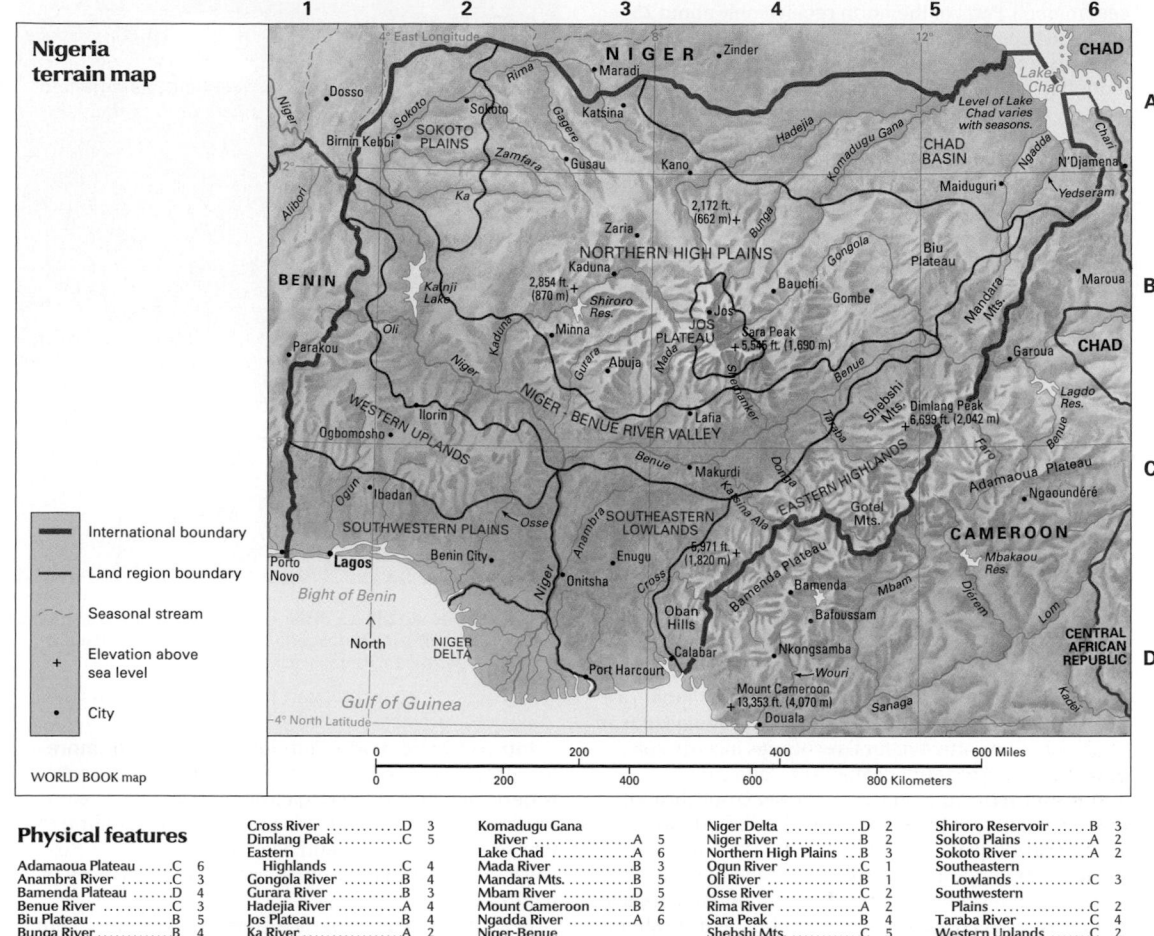

Nigeria terrain map

1	2	3	4	5	6

Legend:
- International boundary
- Land region boundary
- Seasonal stream
- + Elevation above sea level
- • City

WORLD BOOK map

0   200   400   600 Miles
0   200   400   600   800 Kilometers

Physical features

Adamaoua Plateau	C 6	Cross River	D 3	Komadugu Gana		Niger Delta	D 2
Anambra River	C 3	Dimlang Peak	C 5	River	A 5	Niger River	B 2
Bamenda Plateau	D 4	Eastern		Lake Chad	A 6	Northern High Plains	B 3
Benue River	C 3	Highlands	C 4	Mada River	B 3	Ogun River	C 1
Biu Plateau	B 5	Gongola River	B 4	Mandara Mts.	B 5	Oli River	B 1
Bunga River	B 4	Gurara River	B 3	Mbam River	D 5	Osse River	C 2
Chad Basin	A 5	Hadejia River	A 4	Mount Cameroon	B 2	Rima River	A 2
		Jos Plateau	B 4	Ngadda River	A 6	Sara Peak	B 4
		Ka River	A 2	Niger-Benue		Shebshi Mts.	C 5
		Kainji Lake	B 2	River Valley	C 3	Shemanker River	C 4

Shiroro Reservoir	B 3
Sokoto Plains	A 2
Sokoto River	A 2
Southeastern	
Lowlands	C 3
Southwestern	
Plains	C 2
Taraba River	C 4
Western Uplands	C 2
Zamfara River	A 2

The Jos Plateau lies near the center of Nigeria. It rises sharply from the surrounding plains. Parts of the region lie more than 5,000 feet (1,500 meters) above sea level. Dairy cattle graze on the plateau's grasslands, and the area also has important tin mines.

The Niger-Benue River Valley forms an arc across central Nigeria, from east to west. The Niger River flows southeastward from Benin through west-central Nigeria. The Benue River cuts across east-central Nigeria. The two rivers meet near the center of the country and flow southward to the Niger Delta. Grasslands, palm forests, and swampy plains cover parts of the valley. Other areas are marked by rugged, rocky hills.

The Western Uplands, also known as the Plateau of Yorubaland, lie about 1,000 to 2,000 feet (300 to 610 meters) above sea level in west-central Nigeria. Dome-shaped granite hills dot the grassy plains of the uplands.

The Eastern Highlands stretch along the eastern border of Nigeria. They consist of plateaus and low, rocky mountains and hills. Much of the region is more than 4,000 feet (1,200 meters) above sea level. Dimlang Peak, the highest point in Nigeria, rises 6,699 feet (2,042 meters) above sea level in the Shebshi Mountains.

The Southwestern Plains consist of a heavily forested area that slopes gently northward from the Gulf of

Guinea, an arm of the Atlantic Ocean. Swamps and lagoons cover much of the coastal region. Lagos, the largest city of Nigeria, occupies several islands in the Lagos Lagoon.

The Southeastern Lowlands resemble other parts of southern Nigeria, with swamps and forested plains covering much of the region. In the northwestern part of this region, however, steep-sided plateaus rise to about 1,000 feet (300 meters) above sea level.

The Niger Delta forms the southernmost region of Nigeria, along the Gulf of Guinea. It consists of deposits of clay, mud, and sand at the mouth of the Niger River. Lagoons and mangrove swamps cover much of the region. This area is also the site of Nigeria's important petroleum deposits.

Climate. Most of Nigeria has a tropical climate, with warm temperatures throughout the year. The north is generally hotter and drier than the south. The average annual temperature in the north is about 85 °F (29 °C), but daily temperatures may rise above 100 °F (38 °C). The average annual temperature in the south is about 80 °F (27 °C).

Southern Nigeria receives far more rainfall than the northern part of the country. The coastal areas of Nigeria have an average annual rainfall of about 150 inches (381 centimeters). Parts of the north receive only about 25 inches (64 centimeters) of rainfall annually. The rainy season lasts from April to October in most parts of Nigeria, though it usually extends for a longer time in the south.

Economy

Nigeria has a developing economy based on agriculture and mining. Agriculture employs about three-fifths of all Nigerian workers, and it accounts for about one-third of the country's *gross domestic product* (GDP). The GDP is the total value of goods and services produced within a country in a year. Since the late 1960's, the development of the oil industry has made mining the fastest-growing part of the economy. Today, mining accounts for about one-third of the country's GDP. Revenue from oil exports provides the government with its chief source of income. Despite the increase in oil income, Nigeria has a high poverty rate.

Natural resources. Nigeria has a variety of natural resources. Much of Nigeria's land is suitable for farming and grazing. However, only a small percentage of the country's total area is used for growing crops. Forests also cover much of Nigeria. Lakes, rivers, and streams provide an abundance of fish.

Petroleum ranks as Nigeria's most valuable natural resource. Large oil fields lie in southwestern Nigeria and offshore in the Gulf of Guinea. The Jos Plateau of central Nigeria has important deposits of tin and columbite, a mineral that is used in the production of certain kinds of steel. Other important natural resources include coal, iron ore, lead, limestone, natural gas, and zinc.

Agriculture. Nigerian farmers grow crops throughout the country. Nigeria is the world's leading producer of cassava and yams. The country ranks among the world's leading producers of cacao, palm oil and palm kernels, and peanuts. Nigeria's other important crops include cashews, corn, millet, rice, rubber, and sorghum. Farmers raise cattle, chickens, goats, and sheep. Nigerian fishing crews catch catfish, shrimp, tilapia, and a variety of other seafoods.

Nigeria does not grow enough food for its own population, and the country must import much of its food. Most of the country's farmers use old-fashioned tools and methods. The government sponsors programs to distribute fertilizer, insecticides, and new varieties of seeds to farmers.

Mining. Nigeria ranks as one of the world's leading producers and exporters of petroleum. Foreign oil companies operate most of the petroleum wells, but they pay the Nigerian government much of their profits. In addition to petroleum, Nigeria produces coal, columbite, gold, iron ore, lead, limestone, natural gas, tin, and zinc.

Manufacturing. Nigeria's factories produce a wide variety of goods. However, manufacturing employs only about 2 percent of the country's work force. Manufacturing also only accounts for about 2 percent of Nigeria's GDP. Most businesses and industries in Nigeria are privately owned, but the federal government shares in the ownership of some. Leading industries in Nigeria produce cement, chemicals, fertilizers, food products, footwear, textiles, and tires. The country also has motor vehicle assembly plants, petroleum refineries, and steel mills.

© Eric Miller, Lauré Communications

An oil worker steadies a drilling pipe at an oil platform off the coast of southern Nigeria. Nigeria is a world leader in the production of petroleum, its most valuable natural resource.

International trade. Petroleum accounts for more than 90 percent of the total value of Nigeria's exports. Nigeria belongs to the Organization of the Petroleum Exporting Countries (OPEC), an association of countries whose economies depend heavily on oil exports. Because of the large oil exports, Nigeria exports more than it imports.

In addition to oil, Nigeria exports cacao beans, natural gas, and rubber. Chief imports include chemical products, electronics, food products, machinery, petroleum products, and transportation equipment. Nigeria's most important trade partners are Brazil, China, France, Germany, India, South Korea, the United Kingdom, and the United States.

Transportation and communication. Railroads and paved roads link Nigeria's major cities. But many of the country's roads are unpaved and rutted. Few Nigerians own an automobile. Buses and taxis—often jammed with passengers—operate along the main roads.

Nigeria's chief ports are Lagos and Port Harcourt. Bonny has Nigeria's main port for petroleum shipments. Abuja, Kano, Lagos, and Port Harcourt have international airports.

A number of daily newspapers, representing a variety of political opinions, are published in Nigeria. These newspapers are both privately and government owned. The national and state governments operate radio and television systems that broadcast in more than a dozen languages. The country also has several private radio and television stations.

History

People lived in what is now Nigeria thousands of years ago. In parts of Nigeria, archaeologists have found stone tools that are 40,000 years old. Human skeletons, rock paintings, and other remains of prehistoric settlements have also been found.

The Nok civilization flourished in what is now central Nigeria from about 500 B.C. to A.D. 200. The clay figures of animals and people produced by this civilization are among the oldest known examples of African sculpture.

Early kingdoms. The kingdom of Kanem developed in about the A.D. 700's in what is now Chad. Beginning in the 1000's, Kanem adopted Islam as its religion and gradually expanded its territory. By the 1300's, Bornu (now called Borno), in what is now northeastern Nigeria, had become the political center of the kingdom. The Kanem-Bornu kingdom traded with countries in Africa, Asia, and Europe.

After about A.D. 1000, a number of Hausa states grew up in the region west of Bornu. Some of these states, such as Kano and Katsina, traded with other countries in North Africa and the Middle East. Kano, Kebbi, and some other Hausa states became part of the Songhai Empire, a west African state that flourished during the 1400's and 1500's. During the early 1800's, Usman dan Fodio (also called Uthman ibn Fudi), a Fulani who was a Muslim religious leader, declared war on the Hausa states. His forces gained control of almost all northern Nigeria except Bornu. He turned the area into a Muslim empire called the Sokoto Caliphate.

In the south, the Yoruba people had established an important cultural center at Ife as early as the mid-900's. Yoruba rulers from Ife later founded states in various parts of the surrounding territory. The most important of these was the kingdom of Oyo, which extended into what is now the country of Benin during the 1700's.

The kingdom of Benin flourished from the early 1400's to the 1800's. It developed between Lagos and the Niger Delta and grew into a prosperous trade center. The kingdom also became famous for its sculptures of brass, bronze, and ivory.

The coming of the Europeans. The Portuguese were the first Europeans to reach Nigeria. They established a trade center near Benin in the late 1400's and developed a trade in slaves with the African leaders. British, Dutch, and other European traders later competed for control of the trade. By the 1700's, the British were the leading slave traders on the Nigerian coast.

In 1807, the British government outlawed the slave trade. The United Kingdom signed treaties with other European countries and with local African rulers in an attempt to end the trade. British ships sailed along the Nigerian coast and captured ships that carried slaves. The British then set the slaves free at Freetown in Sierra Leone. British missionaries converted many of the freed slaves to Christianity. Some of the freed slaves later returned to Nigeria and helped spread Christianity along the coastal areas and in the southwest.

British rule. After 1807, British traders began to deal in palm oil and other agricultural products of the Nigerian coastal region. They explored the Niger River and other waterways in search of valuable natural resources. In 1851, the United Kingdom seized the port of Lagos to increase its influence over the area. Lagos served as a base from which the British continued their war against the slave trade. Lagos became a British colony in 1861.

During the late 1800's, the United Kingdom established protectorates in parts of southern Nigeria. A British trading firm called the Royal Niger Company ruled most of northern Nigeria until 1900. That year, the British government made the region the Protectorate of Northern Nigeria. In 1906, all of southern Nigeria, including Lagos, became the Colony and Protectorate of Southern Nigeria. Nigerians in many areas, especially in the north, fought unsuccessfully against the establishment of British rule. In 1914, the United Kingdom joined the northern and southern regions into one unit—the Colony and Protectorate of Nigeria.

Independence. During the 1920's, Nigerians began to demand representation in the British colonial government. In the 1940's, their demands began to be met.

In 1946, the United Kingdom divided Nigeria into three regions—north, west, and east. Each region had an assembly composed of Nigerian and British members. The assemblies acted as advisory bodies to the central government in Lagos. A Constitution adopted in 1954 gave the assemblies increased powers and established Nigeria as a federation. Abubakar Tafawa Balewa, a northern leader, became the federation's first prime minister in 1957. On Oct. 1, 1960, the United Kingdom granted Nigeria independence. Balewa remained prime minister. Nnamdi Azikiwe, a political leader from the eastern part, became the first person to hold the ceremonial office of president of Nigeria.

In 1961, the United Nations (UN) organized a referendum in western Cameroon, a UN trust territory that bordered Nigeria on the east. As a result of the referendum, the northern part of the territory joined Nigeria, and the southern part joined Cameroon.

During the early 1960's, various ethnic groups competed for political power within Nigeria's three regions. In 1963, a Mid-Western Region was created out of the Western Region. Some people in the Northern and Eastern regions also demanded separate political units.

At the same time, the different groups competed for control of the central government. The people of southern Nigeria, especially the Igbo, resented the power of the Hausa people of the north. The northerners controlled the central government because the north had more people than the other regions. Censuses conducted in 1962 and 1963 showed that the north had an even

Important dates in Nigeria

c. 500 B.C.-A.D. 200 The Nok civilization thrived in what is now central Nigeria.

c. A.D. 1000-1400's Various kingdoms, including Benin, Kanem-Bornu, Ife, and the Hausa states, began to develop in different parts of Nigeria.

Late 1400's The Portuguese became the first Europeans to reach Nigeria.

1851 The British seized control of Lagos.

1914 The British formed the Colony and Protectorate of Nigeria.

1960 Nigeria became independent.

1966 In January, military leaders overthrew Nigeria's government. In July, a second revolt established a new military government in Nigeria.

1967-1970 Nigeria's Eastern Region declared itself an independent republic called Biafra. Biafra and the rest of Nigeria fought each other in a civil war until Biafra surrendered in 1970.

1979 Civilian rule was restored in Nigeria.

1983 Military leaders took control of Nigeria's government.

1999 Nigeria returned to civilian rule.

An independence ceremony attended by representatives of the United Kingdom marked the opening of Nigeria's parliament. Nigeria gained independence from the United Kingdom in 1960.

larger population than had been expected. Many southerners protested against the census figures. Charges of dishonesty in a 1964 federal election and a 1965 regional election led to violent riots and added to the turmoil.

Civil war. In January 1966, a group of Army officers, mainly Igbo, overthrew the central and regional governments. They killed Prime Minister Balewa and the prime ministers of the Northern and Western regions. General Johnson Aguiyi-Ironsi, commander of the Army and an Igbo, took control of the government. In May, he abolished the federal system of government. He set up a strong central government and appointed many Igbo as advisers. Many northerners feared that these actions would give the Igbo control over the nation. Riots broke out in the north, and thousands of Igbo were killed.

In July 1966, a group of northern Army officers revolted against the government and killed Aguiyi-Ironsi. Yakubu Gowon, the Army chief of staff, became head of a new military government. But Colonel Odumegwu Ojukwu, the military governor of the Eastern Region, refused to accept Gowon as head of state.

In 1967, Gowon replaced the country's 4 political regions with 12 states to give some of the smaller ethnic groups more political power. Ojukwu refused to accept the division of the Eastern Region into 3 states. On May 30, 1967, he declared the Eastern Region an independent republic called Biafra. Civil war between Biafra and the rest of Nigeria broke out in June 1967. Biafra surrendered in January 1970. The civil war caused widespread death and destruction in southeastern Nigeria. Beginning in 1970, the government sponsored reconstruction and relief programs to overcome the effects of the war. Many Igbo, including some who had fought with rebel forces, were given government positions.

Oil wealth. During the early 1970's, Nigeria's growing oil industry provided the country with an important source of wealth. Oil profits enabled the government to plan development programs to improve the standard of living of Nigerians. Major goals included the establishment of manufacturing industries, new schools, and improved transportation facilities. But political problems continued in Nigeria. In 1975, military leaders overthrew General Gowon. General Murtala Ramat Muhammad became head of state and commander in chief of Nigeria's armed forces. In 1976, a group of military officers tried to overthrow the government. They failed, but they killed General Muhammad. Lieutenant General Oluse-

gun Obasanjo succeeded him. Also in 1976, Nigeria increased its number of states from 12 to 19. Military rule ended in 1979. The people elected a new civilian government to replace the military government. Shehu Shagari became president. He was reelected in 1983.

The wealth that Nigeria gained from its oil exports in the 1970's attracted many people from neighboring lands. These people came to Nigeria to find work. But in the early 1980's, declining oil prices began to hurt Nigeria's economy. In 1983 and again in 1985, the government ordered foreigners who were living in Nigeria illegally to leave the country. Many people from Ghana and other countries were required to leave Nigeria.

In 1980, Nigeria's government began building a new city, Abuja, near the country's center to replace Lagos as the capital. Abuja became the official capital in 1991.

Changes in government. In December 1983, the military overthrew the civilian government. Major General Muhammadu Buhari became head of a new military government. In 1985, he was overthrown by other military leaders. Major General Ibrahim Badamosi Babangida became government head. He announced that Nigeria would return to civilian rule. The government formed two political parties in 1989. Elections for a new National Assembly occurred in 1992. Elections for a civilian president were held in June 1993. But Babangida canceled the presidential election results, charging that the voting had been dishonest. Many Nigerians rioted in protest.

In November 1993, General Sani Abacha overthrew the Interim National Government that Babangida had set up in the summer. That government was headed by a civilian, Earnest Shonekan. Abacha made himself head of state and commander in chief of the armed forces. He dissolved the National Assembly, outlawed political parties, and dismissed all elected local government officials. In 1995, he ended the ban on political parties. In 1996, Nigeria increased the number of its states to 36.

Abacha died in June 1998. General Abdulsalami Abubakar became president. In 1999, Nigeria held elections for the National Assembly and for the presidency and adopted a new constitution. Olusegun Obasanjo, who as a military ruler had handed over power to a democratically elected government in 1979, was elected president as a civilian. He was reelected in 2003.

Internal conflict. Since 1999, ethnic, religious, and political tensions in Nigeria have sparked outbreaks of violence, leaving tens of thousands of people dead. Many conflicts have been over access to land or other scarce resources. The adoption of Shari`ah (Islamic law) in several northern Nigerian states has led to clashes between Muslims and Christians.

In 2007, Umaru Yar'Adua, governor of the northern state of Katsina, was elected president. He died in 2010 after a long illness. Vice President Goodluck Jonathan succeeded him and then won the 2011 presidential election. Northern Muslims protested the results, leading to riots that killed more than 200 people. Despite the violence, observers called the election free and fair.

Oil pollution. Decades of oil spills have severely damaged parts of the Niger Delta, contaminating land and water. In 2011, the Dutch oil company Shell accepted blame for much of the damage. Shell stopped operating in the area in 1993, but its remaining pipelines and other facilities continue to cause pollution. A UN report estimated it would take 25 to 30 years to restore the environment. Ebere Onwudiwe

Related articles in *World Book* include:

Abuja	Hausa	Lagos
Achebe, Chinua	Ibadan	Nok
Africa (picture)	Ife	Songhai Empire
Benin	Igbo	Soyinka, Wole
Fulani	Kanem	Yoruba

Additional resources

Anderson, Martha G., and Peek, P. M., eds. *Ways of the Rivers: Arts and Environment of the Niger Delta.* Univ. of Calif. Pr., 2002.
Falola, Toyin. *Culture and Customs of Nigeria.* Greenwood, 2001. *The History of Nigeria.* 1999.
Levy, Patricia. *Nigeria.* 2nd ed. Benchmark Bks., 2004. Younger readers.
Oyewole, Anthony, and Lucas, John. *Historical Dictionary of Nigeria.* 2nd ed. Scarecrow, 2000.

Night. See Day and night.

Night vision systems are electronic devices used by military forces to detect and track targets at night. Police officers and hunters also use these devices.

The most advanced night vision system is the Forward-Looking Infrared (FLIR) system, developed in the late 1960's. The FLIR uses a technique called *thermal imaging,* which detects and records minute temperature variations. The FLIR converts the temperature readings

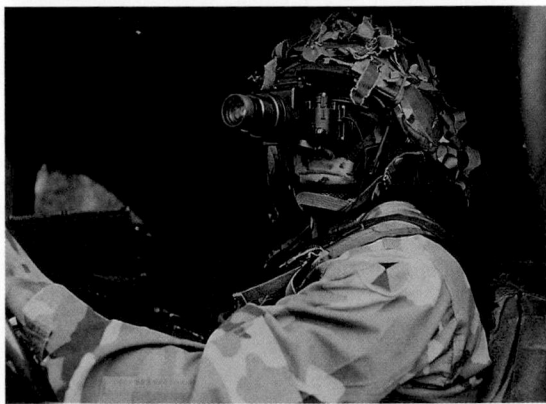

Night vision goggles help a soldier see at night. The goggles magnify starlight and moonlight reflected by objects to produce an image of the objects. Lon Harding, Litton Industries, Inc.

into electrical signals that generate a clear, black-and-white video image in which hot areas appear bright and cold areas appear dull. FLIR systems cannot be easily detected. Combined with powerful lenses, these systems have a long range. They perform well even in bad weather or smoky conditions.

The first night vision systems sent out infrared rays to illuminate an area. The infrared rays were invisible except when viewed through a special filter. Infrared systems were easily detected. They had a limited range, and they did not work well in bad weather or smoky conditions. In the early 1960's, *image intensifying systems* (sometimes called *starlight scopes)* were introduced. These systems magnify the starlight and moonlight reflected by objects. They focus the light on a viewing screen to produce an image. Kenneth S. Brower

WORLD BOOK illustration by John Rignall, Linden Artists Ltd.
The common nighthawk often flies in urban areas during the evening, hunting for insects that are attracted by the city lights.

Nighthawk, also called the *bullbat* and the *mosquito hawk,* is a bird that catches insects on the wing. There are several *species* (kinds). Nighthawks are not hawks. The common nighthawk measures about 10 inches (25 centimeters) long. It has brown, black, and white feathers; a white throat patch; and a white bar on each wing. Soon after sunset, the common nighthawk flies to look for insects. It breeds in North America. In winter, it lives in South America. The female lays two speckled eggs on the ground or on gravel rooftops. Bertin W. Anderson

Scientific classification. Nighthawks are in the nightjar family, Caprimulgidae. The common nighthawk is *Chordeiles minor.*

Nightingale is a small, dull-colored bird famed for its beautiful, sad song. The bird lives in central and western Europe for most of the year, but it spends winters in Africa. The name *nightingale* also refers to a number of other, less common birds.

The nightingale grows about 6 to 7 inches (15 to 18 centimeters) long. The upper parts of its body are russet-brown, and the underparts are predominantly grayish-white. The bird has a rounded tail. Its relatively long legs are well suited to traveling on land.

Nightingales usually live in dense woodland undergrowth and along streams in swampy thickets or hedges. They normally feed on insects and worms. When searching for food, the birds hop rapidly along

Jose Luis G. Grande, Photo Researchers
The nightingale is a small bird known for its melancholy song. Nightingales nest in thickets or hedges near the ground.

the ground for a few moments and then stand motionless to listen for prey. Their songs are heard most often during spring or summer, usually in the early morning or late evening. Sometimes the songs last well into the night. The songs vary in their notes and may include imitations of other bird calls.

Nightingales usually have one brood of young each year. They build a nest near the ground in dense thickets or hedges. The female lays four to six olive-brown eggs. Both parents care for the young.   Donald F. Bruning

Scientific classification. The nightingale's scientific name is *Luscinia megarhynchos.*

Nightingale, Florence (1820-1910), was the founder of the nursing profession as we know it today. British soldiers who were wounded in the Crimean War (1853-1856) called her "The Lady with the Lamp" when she walked the halls of their hospital at night. The light that Nightingale carried has come to mean care for the sick, concern for the welfare of the ordinary soldier, and freedom for women to choose their own work.

Early years. Florence Nightingale was named for Florence, Italy, where she was born on May 12, 1820, while her wealthy British parents were living abroad. Her childhood was spent on the family estates in England with her mother, father, and sister Parthenope. The girls' mother, Frances, taught her daughters the social graces and how to run a large household. Their father, William, tutored them in languages, history, and philosophy.

At the age of 16, Florence thought she heard the voice of God telling her she had a special mission in life. She suspected this mission had something to do with helping other people. Florence had always enjoyed caring for the babies of her parents' visitors and for sick farmers on her father's estates.

She followed her own sense of purpose by turning down suitors, declining many parties, and spending much time studying health and reforms for the poor. Her mother could not accept such behavior, which was not considered proper for a wealthy young woman.

Her family's opposition initially prevented Nightingale from working in a hospital. She took a step toward independence when she entered the Institution of Deaconesses, a Protestant school for training nurses, in Kaiserswerth, a town near Düsseldorf, Germany. She later studied in Paris. At 33, she became superintendent of a women's hospital in London.

Service in Crimea. The United Kingdom and France went to war with Russia in the Crimea, now part of Ukraine, in 1854. The British people were angry when they heard that their troops had been sent to battle without enough supplies, to die under terrible conditions. The secretary of war asked Florence Nightingale to take charge of nursing. She sailed for the Crimea with 38 nurses.

Nightingale and the other nurses stepped ashore in the mud of Scutari, across from

Brown Bros.

Florence Nightingale

Constantinople (now Istanbul, Turkey), in late 1854. They faced a job that seemed impossible. Wounded troops had just arrived from the Battle of Balaklava, where the charge of the "Light Brigade" had taken place. About 250 of the British cavalry had been killed or wounded in the battle in 20 minutes.

The hospital was an old Turkish barracks, rat-infested, dirty, and poorly furnished. Many of the wounded lay on floors, bleeding and neglected. There were not enough cots, mattresses, or bandages, and no washbasins, soap, or towels. Nightingale found a few men well enough to clean the place, and she put them to work at once. She set up a nursing schedule for patient care and work. At night, her lamp burned as she walked the miles of corridors or wrote countless reports and letters demanding supplies from British military officials. When the hospital was running smoothly, she started classes to teach convalescent soldiers to read and write.

At first, doctors and officials resented the "dictatorship of a woman." But they eventually came to respect her tireless efforts and professional skills.

While on a visit to the front lines, Nightingale became seriously ill and nearly died. By that time, she had become famous, and even Queen Victoria kept an anxious watch on her recovery.

After she returned to the Scutari hospital, Nightingale was urged to go to England to get her strength back. She replied firmly that she was "ready to stand out the war with any man." Nightingale's success at Scutari became so widely recognized that she was given charge of all the British Army hospitals in the Crimea. By the end of the war, Nightingale had saved many lives and had brought about worldwide reforms in hospital administration and in nursing.

Return to England. England greeted her arrival in 1856 with big celebrations. Instead of attending them, Nightingale went quietly home to her family, and then moved to London. The strain of overwork and her Crimean illness had injured her health. Nightingale became a semi-invalid and seldom left her rooms. Instead, the world came to her. Ministers, heads of government, authors, reformers, and politicians came to ask her advice. Nightingale's report of over 1,000 pages to the British War Department brought about the formation of the Royal Commission on the Health of the Army in 1857. By correspondence and constant reading, she made studies of health conditions in India. Another Royal Commission was appointed in 1859, resulting in the establishment of a Sanitary Department in India in 1868.

In 1860, Nightingale used donations of about $222,000 to found the Nightingale Training School for Nurses at St. Thomas's Hospital in London. She became a world authority on scientific care of the sick. The United States asked Nightingale's advice for setting up military hospitals during the American Civil War (1861-1865). Nightingale received many honors and was the first woman to be given the British Order of Merit. She died on Aug. 13, 1910.   Kenneth R. Manning

Nightjar. See Goatsucker.

Nightmare is a frightening dream or dreamlike experience that often awakens a sleeper. People who have nightmares can frequently report details of the experience. Nightmares may occur in times of severe tension. They may also follow a hurtful or shocking experience.

Many people experience nightmares after watching films or television shows with themes involving horror, suspense, or the bizarre. Nightmares can also be triggered by eating before bedtime or by an illness—especially when accompanied by fever. Withdrawal from alcohol and certain drugs can also cause nightmares.

Most nightmares occur during a stage of sleep called REM (rapid eye movement) sleep, as do most dreams. REM sleep is typically concentrated during the second half of the night. Frequent nightmares among older children and adults may indicate a physical or emotional problem. In severe cases, nightmares can be treated with antidepressant or antianxiety medications, hypnosis, or psychotherapy.   Lawrence J. Wichlinski

See also **Dream.**

Nightshade is the common name for the family of plants that have the scientific name Solanaceae. Thousands of *species* (kinds) of plants belong to this family. They grow throughout the world, especially in South America and Central America.

Various species in the nightshade family are grown for food. These include the potato, tomato, eggplant, capsicum (red, chili, and bell peppers), and such tropical species as naranjilla and tree tomatoes. The family also

Some members of the nightshade family

E. R. Degginger
Belladonna

E. R. Degginger
Jimson weed

© Giuseppe Mazza
Potatoes

© Bruce Coleman Ltd.
Tomatoes

includes some poisonous plants used to make medicines, such as henbane, jimson weed, belladonna (also called deadly nightshade), and the mandrakes. Other species yield an important source of food for many wild animals. The petunia, a garden flower, and the tobacco plant also belong to the family.

Superstitions and folklore surround many plants in the family. Europeans once associated some species with witchcraft. In the 1500's, many people believed tomatoes and potatoes were poisonous.   John E. Averett

Related articles in *World Book* include:

Belladonna	Henbane	Petunia	Tobacco
Bittersweet	Jimson weed	Potato	Tomato
Eggplant	Mandrake		

Nihilism, *NY uh lihz uhm,* is the name used for a variety of extreme, pessimistic philosophical and political views. The term *nihilism* comes from a Latin word meaning *nothing.* The most radical nihilist would deny that anything exists. A slightly less radical view, usually called *skepticism,* denies that anything can be known.

Nihilism is most commonly understood as the view that no absolute values exist. The Russian author Fyodor Dostoevsky challenged this view in his novel *The Brothers Karamazov* (1879-1880). He wrote that if no God existed, then everything would be permitted. He argued that belief in God was necessary for believing in any absolute values.

The term *nihilist* first came into popular use in the mid-1800's in Russia. It applied to radical opponents of the czar, some of whom committed terrorist acts against the government. Used more broadly, *nihilism* referred to any extreme challenge to authority. The Russian author Ivan Turgenev portrayed a nihilist in his novel *Fathers and Sons* (1862). This character believes in reason and a scientific view of the world but rejects traditional religious beliefs and moral values.   Stephen Nathanson

Nijinsky, *nih ZHIHN skee* or *nih JIHN skee,* **Vaslav,** *vahts LAHF* (1889?-1950), was the most famous male

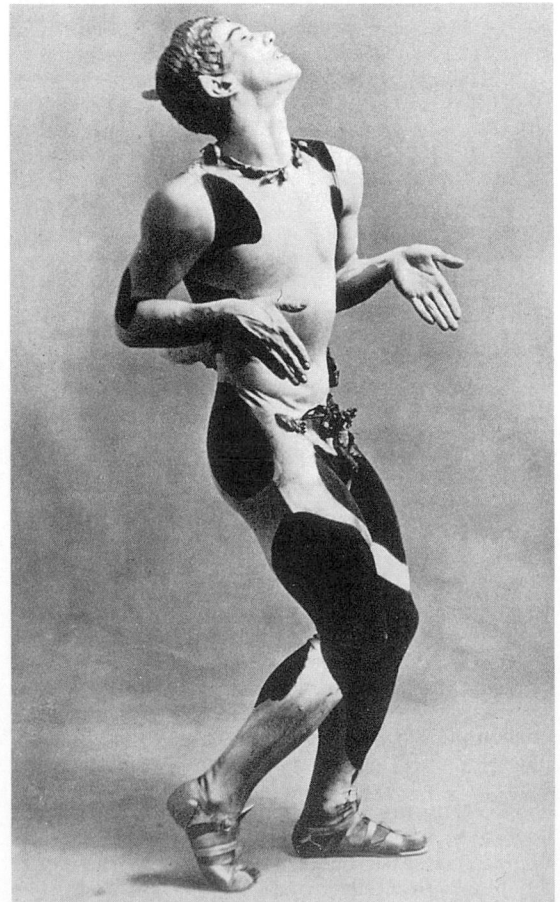
Bettmann Archive
Vaslav Nijinsky created the choreography and also danced the part of the faun in *The Afternoon of a Faun* in 1912.

dancer of his time. He was short, with thick thighs and sloping shoulders. Yet he acted out his roles so completely that his appearance seemed to change from one role to another.

Nijinsky had such amazing body control that his dancing looked spontaneous and effortless. One legend tells of a dramatic leap Nijinsky made through an open window as his exit in *Le Spectre de la Rose.* He rose slowly, soared across the window ledge, appeared to stop in midair, and was still at the height of his jump as he disappeared.

Nijinsky was born in Kiev, Ukraine, on March 12 (February 28 according to the calendar then in use), probably in 1889. At that time, Kiev was a part of the Russian Empire. He first studied dancing at the St. Petersburg Imperial School of Ballet in 1898. Nijinsky traveled with Sergei Diaghilev's ballet company to Paris in 1909 and had great international success until 1913. He married a ballet student with the company in that year, and Diaghilev dismissed him. Nijinsky rejoined the company in the United States in 1916, dancing as brilliantly as ever. But in 1917, mental illness ended his career. Nijinsky died on April 8, 1950.   Katy Matheson

See also **Ballet** (Ballet in Russia; picture: Vaslav Nijinsky and Anna Pavlova).

Nike, Temple of. See Acropolis.

Nike of Samothrace. See Winged Victory.

Nile River is the longest river in the world. It flows for 4,160 miles (6,695 kilometers) through northeast Africa. The Nile rises near the equator and flows into the Mediterranean Sea. It irrigates about 6 million acres (2.4 million hectares) of land in Egypt and about 2 ¾ million acres (1.1 million hectares) in Sudan. For much of Egypt and Sudan, the Nile is the sole source of water.

The Nile Valley and the Nile Delta rank among the most fertile farming areas in the world. Until 1968, water from the Nile deposited fertile *silt* (particles of soil) in the valley and on the delta where the Nile flows into the Mediterranean. The Nile also flooded certain areas every summer.

In 1968, the Aswan High Dam in southeastern Egypt began operating. This dam ended the annual floods and trapped the Nile's silt behind the dam in Lake Nasser. Without regular deposits of silt, Egyptian farmers must

Nancy Palmer Photo Agency Inc.

The Nile River irrigates large strips of farmland. The Egyptian farm village shown here lies north of the Aswan High Dam.

Nile River

――――	International boundary
•	City
□	Historical site
::::	Swamp

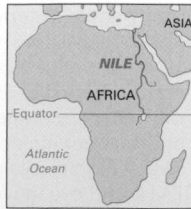

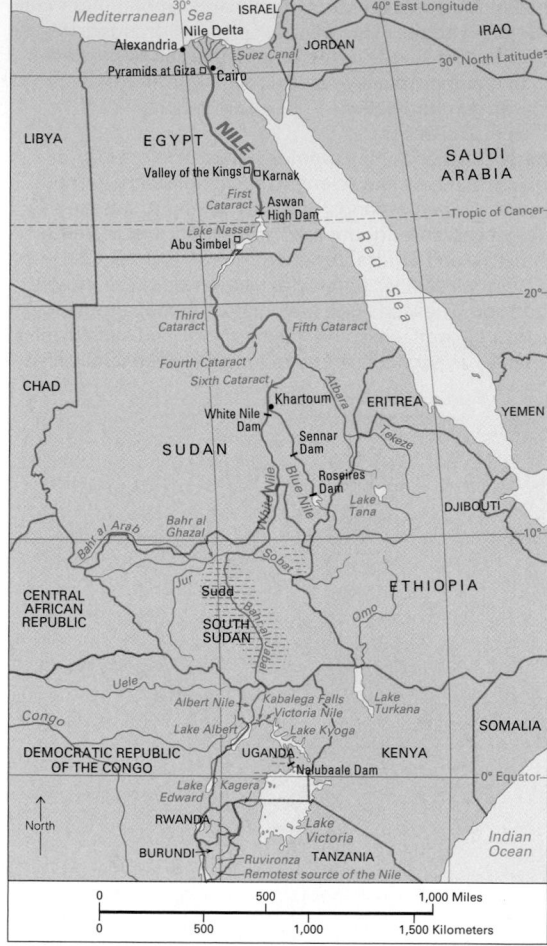

WORLD BOOK maps

use more artificial fertilizers on their soil. But the high dam and other dams generate electric power and provide a steady flow of water for irrigation.

The course of the Nile. The Nile flows generally northward. Its southernmost source is the Ruvironza River in Burundi. Its largest source is Lake Victoria. The Nile flows through the enormous swamps of the Sudd region in South Sudan, where high temperatures cause about half of the water to evaporate. North of Cairo, Egypt, the Nile divides into the Rosetta and Damietta branches and enters the Nile Delta. The delta has highly fertile soil, as well as swamps and salt lakes.

The White Nile from Burundi joins the Blue Nile from Ethiopia at Khartoum, Sudan. The Atbara River, another source of the Nile, drains into it in Sudan north of Khar-

C. Pierre, De Wys, Inc.

The Blue Nile, one of the two main branches of the Nile, has carved out a deep valley in Ethiopia, *shown here.*

Marc & Evelyne Bernheim, Woodfin Camp, Inc.

Kabalega Falls is on the Victoria Nile, part of the White Nile in Uganda, about 20 miles (32 kilometers) east of Lake Albert.

toum. The White Nile is longer than the Blue Nile, but about 70 percent of the Nile's water comes from the Blue Nile.

The Nile Valley and Nile Delta make up about 3 percent of Egypt's total area. Almost all Egyptian farms lie in this densely populated region. Water from the Nile enables farmers in the valley and delta to raise various crops the year around. These crops include clover, wheat, and beans in the winter, and cotton, corn, rice, and millet in the summer. Cotton is Egypt's most important financial crop.   Ronald Bruce St John

See also **Africa** (picture); **Aswan High Dam; Delta; Egypt** (The land; picture); **Lake Nasser.**

Nimitz, *NIHM ihts,* **Chester William** (1885-1966), served as commander in chief of the United States Pacific Fleet during World War II (1939-1945). He took command on Dec. 31, 1941, about three weeks after the fleet had been almost completely disabled in the Japanese at-

tack on Pearl Harbor. Admiral Nimitz painstakingly rebuilt U.S. strength in the Pacific. As commander of the Pacific Fleet and the Pacific Ocean Areas, he directed the Navy and the Marine Corps forces. His calm assurance of final victory helped restore the faith of the Navy in its own power and ability.

In early 1942, Nimitz refused to attack before United States forces were fully ready, in spite of angry questions from Congress and the press. He waited until he had enough ships, supplies, and troops to assure victory. He developed much of the strategy of seizing key islands from which attacks on other key islands could be launched. Nimitz gave the orders that led to the Battle of Midway, in which U.S. forces destroyed four Japanese aircraft carriers. He led the Pacific Fleet to many victories until it drove the Japanese back to Japan. He became a fleet admiral in 1944. Nimitz signed for the United States during the Japanese surrender ceremonies in Tokyo Bay in 1945. See **World War II** (The war in Asia and the Pacific).

After the war, Nimitz became chief of naval operations. He left active duty in December 1947 and then became special assistant to the secretary of the Navy. Nimitz headed the United Nations commission that mediated the dispute over Kashmir in 1949. Nimitz was born on Feb. 24, 1885, in Fredericksburg, Texas, and graduated from the U.S. Naval Academy in 1905. He died on Feb. 20, 1966.   Adrian R. Lewis

Nineteenth Amendment. See **Constitution of the United States** (Amendment 19); **Woman suffrage.**

9/11, the terrorist attacks. See **September 11 terrorist attacks.**

Nineveh, *NIHN uh vuh,* became the last capital of the ancient Assyrian Empire in 704 B.C. It stood near present-day Mosul, Iraq. The site had a sizable settlement from as early as the 6000's B.C., but it is best known for the palaces built there in the 700's and 600's B.C. A coalition of Babylonians, Medes, and Scythians destroyed the city in 612 B.C. Archaeologists have recovered much of the royal library of King Ashurbanipal, who reigned from 668 to 627 B.C. It includes some 5,000 administrative, literary, religious, and scientific texts. See also **Assyria.**   Seth F. C. Richardson

Nintendo is one of the oldest, most successful producers of electronic games and electronic game machines. Nintendo characters, such as the gorilla Donkey Kong and the adventuring plumber Mario, rank among the most recognizable figures in the history of popular culture. Nintendo has its main headquarters in Kyoto, Japan.

Nintendo was founded in 1889 to manufacture traditional Japanese playing cards called *hanafuda.* In the 1960's, the company expanded to include video games and electronic toys. In 1977, Nintendo hired Shigeru Miyamoto, a Japanese artist. Miyamoto became one of Nintendo's most important video game designers.

In 1974, Nintendo developed an image-projection system used in early *arcade machines.* Arcade machines are coin-operated games at commercial facilities. The 1981 arcade machine *Donkey Kong* became Nintendo's first major success in the United States. Donkey Kong introduced the character Jumpman, later renamed Mario.

In 1985, Nintendo released a home *console* (gaming

machine) internationally known as the Nintendo Entertainment System (NES). Early games for this machine established many of Nintendo's best-known characters, stories, and game designs. Such games included *Super Mario Bros.* (1985), *The Legend of Zelda* (1986), and *Metroid* (1987).

Nintendo's next major success was the Game Boy. It was a battery-powered, handheld system released in 1989. Game Boy used a primitive *liquid crystal display* (LCD). Liquid crystals are molecules that respond to electric signals by either blocking or not blocking a beam of light. Game Boy sold well with a variety of games.

Throughout the 1990's and early 2000's, Nintendo released more advanced home and handheld consoles. These machines included the Super Nintendo Entertainment System (SNES), Nintendo 64, the Nintendo GameCube, and the Game Boy Advance. Nintendo later released consoles with innovative game controls. The handheld Nintendo DS, for example, features a stylus-controlled touchscreen. The Wii home console introduced a wandlike motion-sensitive controller.

Ivan A. Games and Kurt Squire

See also **Electronic game.**

Niobe, *NY oh bee,* was a queen in Greek mythology who was famous for mourning her dead children. Niobe was the daughter of King Tantalus and Queen Dione, and married Amphion, king of Thebes. She boasted that because of her six (or seven) fine sons and six (or seven) beautiful daughters, she deserved worship more than the goddess Leto, who had only two children, Apollo and Artemis. In anger, Leto ordered Apollo and Artemis to kill Niobe's children with their arrows. As Niobe wept unceasingly for her loss, the gods in pity changed her into a rock that spouted water like tears. According to tradition, this rock with a waterfall below stands on Mount Sipylon in what is now Turkey.

Jon D. Mikalson

Niobium, *ny OH bee uhm,* also called *columbium,* is a soft, silver-white or gray metallic element. In nature, it occurs chiefly combined with *tantalum,* another rare metal. Manufacturers alloy much niobium with nickel and steel to make strong structural materials that resist high temperatures. Niobium is also used in the cores of certain nuclear reactors because it allows neutrons to penetrate easily and can withstand high-temperature reactor coolants. At extremely low temperatures, it becomes a *superconductor,* and so it is used in making superconducting magnets (see **Superconductivity**).

Niobium has the chemical symbol Nb. Its *atomic number* (number of protons in its nucleus) is 41. Its *relative atomic mass* is 92.90638. An element's relative atomic mass equals its *mass* (amount of matter) divided by $\frac{1}{12}$ of the mass of carbon 12, the most abundant form of carbon. Niobium melts at 2468 ± 10 °C and boils at 4742 °C. Niobium has a density of 8.57 grams per cubic centimeter at 20 °C (see **Density**). Charles Hatchett, a British chemist, discovered niobium in 1801.   Marianna A. Busch

See also **Element, Chemical** (Periodic table).

NIOSH. See **National Institute for Occupational Safety and Health.**

Nippon. See **Japan.**

Nirvana, *nihr VAH nuh,* according to Buddhist belief, is perfect peace and *blessedness* (happiness or contentment). The attainment of nirvana enables a person to escape from a painful, continuous cycle of death and rebirth. This cycle is caused by worldly desires, such as a craving for fame, immortality, and wealth. People attain nirvana when such desires are completely eliminated. When they die, their cycle of death and rebirth ends.

The Buddha, the founder of Buddhism, preached that nirvana could be attained by following a Middle Way between self-indulgence and self-denial, and by practicing the Noble Eightfold Path. The path consists of eight aspects of correct living, including proper behavior, meditation, and insight into truth.   Frank E. Reynolds

See also **Buddhism** (The dharma).

Nirvana, *nihr VAH nuh,* was an American group that changed rock music in the 1990's. Nirvana played a forceful style of music called *grunge.* Grunge had a raw, fiery sound and an angry, rebellious attitude. Nirvana was the first grunge group to reach a wide audience.

Nirvana was formed in Aberdeen, Washington, in 1987 by singer and guitarist Kurt Cobain (1967-1994) and bassist Krist Novoselic (1965-   ). Drummer Chad Channing (1967-   ) joined the band in 1988. The group's first single, "Love Buzz," was released in 1988. In 1989, guitarist Jason Everman (1967-   ) joined the group. Nirvana released its first album, *Bleach,* in 1989. That

© Frank Micelotta, Getty Images

Kurt Cobain led Nirvana, a popular American rock band. In 1993, Cobain and Nirvana appeared on the TV show "MTV Unplugged," *shown.* Nirvana broke up after Cobain's death in 1994.

year, Dave Grohl (1969-   ) joined the group as drummer. In 1990, Channing and Everman left Nirvana.

Nirvana's second album, *Nevermind,* was released in 1991 and became a best seller. A hit video for the album's single "Smells Like Teen Spirit" helped Nirvana gain a huge following. Many rock fans and critics consider the song and album to be among rock's greatest. In 1992, the band issued *Incesticide,* a collection of previously recorded material. That album was followed by another hit album, *In Utero,* in 1993.

Nirvana broke up in 1994 after Cobain committed suicide. Two popular albums of live Nirvana performances were issued after Cobain's death, *MTV Unplugged in New York* (1994) and *From the Muddy Banks of the Wishkah* (1996). Later in 1994, Grohl formed the rock band the Foo Fighters.   Shawn Brennan

See also **Rock music** (Alternative rock).

Nitrate is any kind of compound that contains the inorganic nitrate ion (NO_3^-). Nitric acid (HNO_3) is a nitrate. Most metals form nitrate salts when combined with nitric acid. In nature, there are relatively few nitrate minerals. Two important nitrates, potassium nitrate (KNO_3) and ammonium nitrate (NH_4NO_3), are used as fertilizers to replenish nitrogen in the soil. Bacteria in the soil form nitrates from organic compounds containing nitrogen. Plants use these nitrates to make proteins. Nitrates can also form in the atmosphere. There, nitrogen oxide may combine with water to produce nitric acid, a part of the pollutant acid rain. Nitrates are also used in explosives, fireworks, and heart medicines. People take in nitrates daily, primarily from vegetables. But consuming large amounts of nitrates can help produce toxic substances in the body. See also **Nitric acid; Nitrogen cycle.**

Emily Jane Rose

Nitrate of silver. See Silver nitrate.

Nitric acid is a strong inorganic acid that has many industrial uses. Its principal use is for the production of fertilizers and explosives. Large quantities of nitric acid are produced during thunderstorms and fall to the earth in rain. The rain falls as a very weak solution of nitric acid. The production of nitric acid during thunderstorms allows nitrogen from the air to become part of the soil in a form that plants can use (see **Nitrogen cycle**). Nitric acid was one of the first acids known. Many alchemists of the Middle Ages used it in their experiments.

Nitric acid is such a powerful oxidizing agent that it dissolves many metals. But it does not attack gold and platinum. A drop of nitric acid on a piece of jewelry tells whether it is made of genuine gold or platinum. These two metals can be dissolved by *aqua regia,* a mixture of nitric acid and hydrochloric acid.

Nitric acid is used to manufacture ammonium nitrate, NH_4NO_3, an ingredient of many fertilizers, and to make explosives, flares, and rocket propellants. The chemical industry uses nitric acid to prepare nylon and many organic compounds that are used as dyes and drugs. Nitric acid reacts with toluene in the presence of sulfuric acid to form trinitrotoluene, better known as TNT.

Commercially, most nitric acid is produced by oxidizing ammonia using a platinum catalyst. Ammonia and air are passed through heated platinum gauze. The gases react to form water, nitric oxide (NO), and nitrogen dioxide (NO_2). Upon cooling, this gaseous mixture forms nitric acid. This method is called the *Ostwald process,* after Wilhelm Ostwald, the German chemist who developed it. Nitric acid is also produced by heating saltpeter with sulfuric acid. In this process, nitric acid is recovered by distillation.

Nitric acid is a colorless liquid with a suffocating odor. It develops a yellow color if kept in bottles that are not tightly stoppered. This is due to nitrogen dioxide gas that results from decomposition of the acid. Nitric acid stains the skin yellow and can cause burns. Its chemical formula is HNO_3. The metal salts of nitric acid, called *nitrates,* are soluble in water.   Marianna A. Busch

Nitrite is a compound of the nitrite *anion* (NO_2^-) and some other element. An anion is a negatively charged ion. Inorganic nitrites are stable and soluble in water. Most organic nitrites are made from alcohols. They are unstable when in the presence of acid, but they are preserved satisfactorily in neutral or mildly alkaline solutions. Nitrites are used in medicine for heart ailments. Sodium nitrite is important in making dyes. It is also used to cure meats, such as bacon, to prevent botulism and to give the meat a pinkish color. Under certain conditions, sodium nitrite may combine with chemicals called amines to form nitrosamines, which can cause cancer. The U.S. Department of Agriculture limits the amount of sodium nitrite allowed in cured meats. Nitrites are also used in photography and in the manufacture of organic materials.   Patrice C. Bélanger

Nitrogen is a nonmetallic chemical element. It occurs in nature as a colorless, odorless, and tasteless gas. This gas makes up about 78 percent of Earth's atmosphere by volume. Daniel Rutherford, a Scottish physician, discovered nitrogen in 1772.

The chemical symbol for nitrogen is N. Nitrogen gas consists of two nitrogen atoms bonded together to form a molecule with the chemical formula N_2. The gas may be condensed to a liquid that boils at –195.8 °C and freezes at –209.9 °C. Nitrogen gas does not combine easily with other elements. But nitrogen atoms are part of many chemical compounds. Nitrogen's *atomic number* (number of protons in its nucleus) is 7. Its *relative atomic mass* is 14.0067. An element's relative atomic mass equals its *mass* (amount of matter) divided by $\frac{1}{12}$ of the mass of an atom of carbon 12, the most abundant form of carbon.

Nitrogen and life

All organisms must have nitrogen to live. Nitrogen is part of all *amino acids,* the building blocks of proteins. Plants make all the amino acids they need. Animals produce only some of these compounds and must get the rest by eating other animals and plants.

Nitrogen is constantly being removed from the air and returned to it in a series of chemical reactions known as the *nitrogen cycle.* In the first part of this process, called *nitrogen fixation,* nitrogen gas is converted to nitrogen compounds that plants can use. Nitrogen in the air reacts with water to form nitric acid, which is deposited in the soil by rain. Certain bacteria and yeasts also change nitrogen from the air into compounds plants can use. Bacteria in swellings on the roots of *legumes,* such as peas and beans, can also do this.

In the next stage of the nitrogen cycle, plants use nitrogen compounds in the soil to make protein. Fertilizers increase the usable nitrogen in the soil. Plant proteins are then eaten by animals. In the final stage, the decay of animal wastes and of dead plants and animals returns nitrogen compounds to the soil and nitrogen gas to the atmosphere. See **Nitrogen cycle.**

Uses of nitrogen

Manufacturers obtain pure nitrogen by making liquid air. They then separate the nitrogen from the oxygen and other gases in air by the process of distillation (see **Liquid air**). During the process of distillation, the nitrogen is collected and stored under pressure in specially designed metal containers. Small amounts of nitrogen can be prepared by gently heating a water solution of ammonium nitrate.

Pure nitrogen gas is used as a "blanket" by certain industries to keep oxygen away from specific areas. For example, the food industry uses nitrogen to prevent oxygen from reaching such foods as fresh fruits and spoiling them. The food industry also uses liquid nitrogen to quick-freeze food and to refrigerate food during transport. Scientists use liquid nitrogen to produce the low temperatures needed in some experiments.

Production of nitrogen compounds. The principal use of nitrogen is in the production of ammonia (NH_3), a gas that consists of nitrogen and hydrogen. Manufacturers produce ammonia chiefly by the Haber process. In this process, nitrogen and hydrogen are combined at high temperatures and pressures (see **Haber process**). Ammonia is used as a fertilizer, as a refrigerant, and in the production of nitric acid and other chemicals. Household ammonia, which is a cleaning agent, consists of a dilute solution of ammonia gas in water. See **Ammonia**.

Nitric acid is a second major nitrogen compound produced by industry. It is made from ammonia in a series of reactions called the Ostwald process. Nitric acid is used mainly to make fertilizer (see **Nitric acid**). Nitrogen compounds are also important in drugs, dyes, explosives, poisons, and synthetic fibers.

Nitrogen in agriculture. Almost all fertilizers contain nitrogen, which is necessary for the healthy growth of plants. Farmers may inject ammonia gas directly into the soil. Liquefied ammonia and such compounds as ammonium sulfate and ammonium nitrate also are used as nitrogen fertilizers. Other sources of nitrogen include nitrate compounds, manure, and *guano,* the waste material of sea birds. See **Fertilizer**.

Farmers can also supply nitrogen to their fields by rotating crops. In crop rotation, a farmer plants a field one year with corn, wheat, or some other crop that removes nitrogen from the soil. The next year, the farmer plants the field with legumes that restore nitrogen to the soil.

Nitrogen and pollution

People influence the nitrogen cycle. The use of nitrogen fertilizers adds nitrogen to the soil. Rain water carries unused fertilizer and other nitrogen compounds into streams and lakes, where the compounds cause water plants and algae to multiply. As the plants and algae die and decay, they use up oxygen, endangering animal life in the body of water.

Nitrogen oxides pollute the air. Pollutants are released by burning fossil fuels, such as coal and gasoline. Sunlight causes nitrogen oxides in the lower atmosphere to react with oxygen to form ozone, an irritating substance in *smog.* Nitrogen oxides can also return to earth as nitric acid, a major ingredient of *acid rain.*

Jet engines produce nitrogen oxides in the upper atmosphere, where the compound may harm the environment in a different way. Nitrogen oxides can promote the decomposition of ozone in the upper atmosphere. Here, ozone benefits animals and plants by shielding them from harmful ultraviolet light. Emily Jane Rose

Related articles in *World Book* include:

Borazon	Nitrate	Nitroglycerin
Environmental pollution	Nitric acid	Nitrous oxide
	Nitrite	Saltpeter

Nitrogen cycle is the circulation of nitrogen among the atmosphere, the soil and water, and the plants and animals of the earth. All living things require nitrogen, but most organisms cannot use the nitrogen gas (N_2) that

makes up about 78 percent of the atmosphere. They need nitrogen that has combined with certain other elements to form organic compounds. But the supply of this *fixed nitrogen* is limited, so complex methods of recycling nitrogen have developed in nature.

One part of the nitrogen cycle involves circulation of nitrogen between the soil and living things. After plants and animals die, they undergo decomposition by certain bacteria and fungi. These microorganisms produce ammonia (NH_3) from nitrogen compounds in dead organic matter and in body wastes excreted by animals. Plants absorb some of the ammonia and use it to make proteins and other substances essential to life. The rest of the ammonia is changed into nitrates (NO_3^- compounds) by *nitrifying bacteria.* First, nitrifying bacteria called *nitrite bacteria* convert ammonia into nitrites (NO_2^- compounds). Then *nitrate bacteria* change nitrites into nitrates. Plants absorb most of the nitrates and use them in the same way as ammonia. Animals get nitrogen by eating plants or by feeding on animals that eat plants.

In another part of the cycle, a process called *nitrogen fixation* constantly puts additional nitrogen into biological circulation. In this process, *nitrogen-fixing* bacteria in the soil or water, or living within plants such as legumes, convert nitrogen from the atmosphere into nitrogen-containing organic substances.

While nitrogen fixation converts nitrogen from the atmosphere into organic compounds, a series of processes called *denitrification* returns an approximately equal amount of nitrogen to the atmosphere. *Denitrifying bacteria* convert nitrates and nitrites in soil into nitrogen gas or into gaseous compounds such as nitrous oxide (N_2O) or nitric oxide (NO). However, fixed nitrogen may circulate many times between organisms and the soil before denitrification returns it to the atmosphere.

Some human activities influence the nitrogen cycle. Industry fixes vast quantities of nitrogen to produce fertilizer, much of which is washed off farmland and into waterways, polluting the water. The combustion of certain fuels produces nitrogen compounds that pollute the air. These compounds may also play a part in the warming of the earth's climate (see **Greenhouse effect**).

William A. Reiners

See also **Nitrogen; Legume; Nitrate; Nitrite.**

Nitroglycerin, *NY truh GLIHS uhr ihn,* also called *nitroglycerol,* is a powerful explosive. Its chemical formula is $C_3H_5(ONO_2)_3$. It is the principal explosive ingredient in dynamite. Nitroglycerin also is used by doctors as a heart medication.

As an explosive. Nitroglycerin is a heavy, clear or straw-colored liquid with a sweet, burning taste. The liquid freezes at slightly below room temperature to form needlelike crystals that explode when heated or broken. An explosion of nitroglycerin is about three times as powerful as that of an equal amount of gunpowder.

Chemists once made nitroglycerin by slowly adding glycerol, also known as glycerin, to concentrated nitric and sulfuric acids. After the mixture was stirred, the nitroglycerin formed a layer on top of the two acids. This layer was drawn off and washed, first with water, and then with a solution of sodium carbonate. Today, chemists make nitroglycerin in smaller, safer batches in a type of tank called a *Biazzi nitrator.*

Ascanio Sobrero, an Italian chemist, discovered

The nitrogen cycle   Nitrogen makes up about 78 percent of Earth's atmosphere, but most organisms cannot use nitrogen in its gaseous form. *Nitrogen-fixing bacteria* convert atmospheric nitrogen into a form that
other living things can use. After nitrogen has been fixed by the bacteria, it circulates repeatedly
between organisms and the soil. *Denitrifying bacteria* help regulate the amount of nitrogen in biological circulation by changing some fixed nitrogen back into a gas.

WORLD BOOK diagram

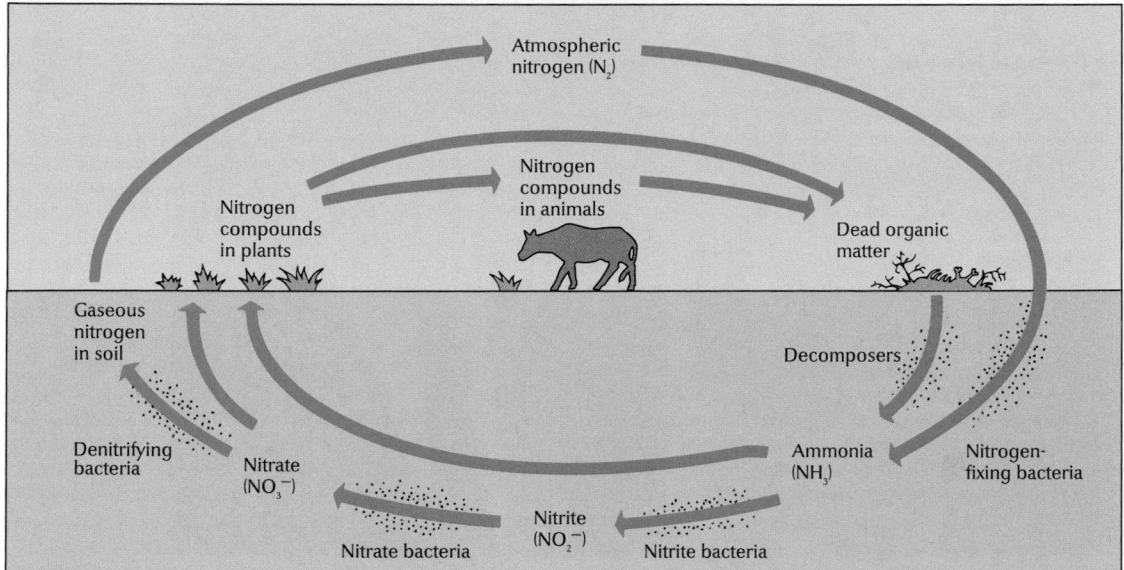

nitroglycerin in 1846. For years, nitroglycerin was not used widely because it did not *detonate* (explode) reli-ably when ignited. Alfred Nobel, a Swedish chemist, de-veloped a detonating cap that proved ideal for explod-ing nitroglycerin. In 1867, Nobel patented dynamite, a safe and convenient means for transporting and using nitroglycerin. Nitroglycerin became the most widely used explosive and remained so until about the 1950's.

As a medication. Sobrero noted that tasting a tiny drop of nitroglycerin gave him a violent headache. Doc-tors knew that amyl nitrite, a substance discovered a few years before nitroglycerin, relieved chest pain and low-ered blood pressure. The fact that amyl nitrite also caused severe headaches led doctors to study the effect of nitroglycerin on the heart and on blood circulation.

Today, nitroglycerin is used to treat *angina,* severe chest pain that occurs when the heart does not receive enough oxygen through the blood. Nitroglycerin works by causing the blood vessels to widen, reducing the heart's workload and permitting more blood and oxygen to reach the heart.

To relieve an angina attack, most patients take nitro-glycerin in the form of a tablet that is placed under the tongue or against the cheek, where it slowly dissolves. An oral spray is also used to treat attacks. Swallowing the medication delays its effectiveness because the liver rapidly converts nitroglycerin to slower-acting forms. To prevent angina, a nitroglycerin patch containing a sup-ply of the medication is attached to the skin like an adhe-sive bandage. The patch slowly and continuously releas-es nitroglycerin, which seeps through the skin to the bloodstream. Nitroglycerin also may be taken in capsule form or applied as an ointment.   Robert J. Linhardt

See also **Dynamite; Explosive; Glycerol; Heart** (Coro-nary artery disease).

Nitrous oxide, *NY truhs AHK syd,* is a colorless, odor-less gas that physicians and dentists use to make pa-tients insensitive to pain. Such drugs are called *anesthet-ics.* Nitrous oxide is commonly called *laughing gas* because people sometimes become excited and silly af-ter they inhale it. Nitrous oxide causes unconsciousness if enough of it is inhaled.

Nitrous oxide is pleasant to inhale, and it takes effect quickly. It also wears off rapidly and is nonflammable. Doctors always give oxygen with nitrous oxide because the body needs a certain amount of oxygen that the anesthetic gas does not supply.

Nitrous oxide only works as an anesthetic at high con-centrations. However, at lower concentrations, nitrous oxide can relieve pain without producing true anesthe-sia and loss of consciousness. Doctors sometimes ad-minister such *subanesthetic* doses to women during childbirth and to patients undergoing dental treatment. However, the greatest use of nitrous oxide is as a sup-plement to more powerful anesthetics during major surgery.

Nitrous oxide was first prepared in 1772 by Joseph Priestley, a British chemist. In 1844, Horace Wells, a Hart-ford, Connecticut, dentist, was the first person to actual-ly use nitrous oxide. He inhaled the gas himself before having a tooth extracted, and the tooth was pulled pain-lessly. Nitrous oxide anesthesia became widely used in dentistry during the 1860's. The introduction of anesthe-sia marked the beginning of modern dentistry.

Nitrous oxide is also called *nitrogen monoxide* or *dini-trogen monoxide.* Its chemical formula is N_2O. It is used in industry as a propellant in aerosol products and as a "tracer gas" to locate leaks in vacuum and pressure lines.
J. Lance Lichtor

See also **Aerosol; Priestley, Joseph.**

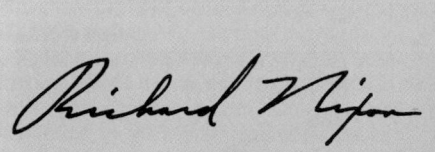

**37th president of
the United States 1969-1974**

L. Johnson
36th president
1963-1969
Democrat

Nixon
37th president
1969-1974
Republican

Ford
38th president
1974-1977
Republican

**Spiro T.
Agnew**
Vice president
1969-1973

Gerald R. Ford
Vice president
1973-1974

The White House

Nixon, Richard Milhous (1913-1994), was the only president of the United States ever to resign from office. He left the presidency on Aug. 9, 1974, while facing certain impeachment for his involvement in the Watergate scandal. This scandal included a break-in at the Democratic national headquarters and other illegal activities by employees of Nixon's 1972 reelection committee and members of his executive staff. Nixon's attempts to cover up these crimes became a major part of the scandal.

Nixon was succeeded as president by Vice President Gerald R. Ford. One month after Nixon resigned, Ford pardoned him for all federal crimes he may have committed during his presidency.

Although Nixon left office in disgrace, he won respect for his conduct of foreign policy. As president, he ended U.S. military participation in the Vietnam War in 1973 and eased the tension that had existed for years between the United States and both China and the Soviet Union. He became the first president to visit China while in office. He also visited the Soviet Union. He won congressional approval of U.S.-Soviet trade agreements and agreements to limit the production of nuclear weapons.

At home, Nixon was challenged by sharply rising prices. He placed government controls on wages and prices to halt inflation, but the controls had little effect. Nixon ended the military draft and created an all-volunteer system for the U.S. armed services. He signed into law a wide variety of economic, social, and environmental legislation that made him seem almost a liberal.

When Nixon was elected president in 1968, he cli-

maxed one of the most extraordinary political comebacks in U.S. history. In 1960, while serving as vice president under President Dwight D. Eisenhower, Nixon ran for the presidency and lost to John F. Kennedy. In 1962, Nixon was defeated when he ran for governor of California, his home state. After this loss, Nixon held what he called his "last press conference." Reporters wrote his political obituary.

But in 1968, Nixon showed that he was politically very much alive. He won several primary elections and again became the Republican candidate for president. This time, Nixon defeated Vice President Hubert H. Humphrey, his Democratic opponent, and former Governor George C. Wallace of Alabama, the candidate of the American Independent Party. In 1972, Nixon won a second term in a landslide victory over Democratic Senator George S. McGovern of South Dakota.

Important dates in Nixon's life

1913	(January 9) Born in Yorba Linda, California.
1934	Graduated from Whittier College.
1940	(June 21) Married Thelma Catherine (Pat) Ryan.
1942-1946	Served in the U.S. Navy during World War II.
1946	Elected to the U.S. House of Representatives.
1948	Reelected to the House.
1950	Elected to the U.S. Senate.
1952	Elected vice president of the United States.
1956	Reelected vice president.
1960	Defeated for president by John F. Kennedy.
1962	Defeated for governor of California by Governor Edmund G. (Pat) Brown.
1968	Elected president of the United States.
1972	Reelected president.
1974	(August 9) Resigned as president.
1994	(April 22) Died in New York City.

Melvin Small, the contributor of this article, is Professor of History at Wayne State University and author of The Presidency of Richard Nixon.

Tragedy and triumph both left an imprint on the Nixon presidency. The Vietnam War, *above,* continued through the early 1970's, though Nixon began a withdrawal of U.S. troops in 1969. A new era of space exploration began that same year, when Neil A. Armstrong and Buzz Aldrin became the first people to set foot on the moon. Armstrong photographed Aldrin on the moon, *left.*

The world of President Nixon

Antiwar protests on college campuses and elsewhere disrupted the nation during the late 1960's and early 1970's.
The women's liberation movement gained strength. In 1973, in *Roe v. Wade,* the Supreme Court ruled that the U.S. Constitution allows a woman to decide for herself if she will have an abortion in the first three months of pregnancy.
Concern for the environment developed as air and water pollution became increasingly serious problems.
Golda Meir, a former Milwaukee schoolteacher, became prime minister of Israel in 1969. She served until 1974.
School desegregation rulings by federal courts in the early 1970's resulted in the busing of students from one neighborhood to another in a number of U.S. cities.
China joined the United Nations in 1971.
The minimum voting age in all U.S. elections was lowered from 21 to 18 by the 26th Amendment to the Constitution, ratified in 1971.
Civil war in Pakistan in 1971 resulted in the creation of Bangladesh from the territory that had been East Pakistan.
Revolution in Chile in 1973 led to the death of President Salvador Allende. Allende had been the first Marxist elected democratically to head a nation in the Western Hemisphere.
The fourth Arab-Israeli war erupted in October 1973, when Egypt and Syria attacked Israel.
An Arab oil embargo reduced supplies of petroleum to the United States and other nations in 1973 and 1974.
Watergate stunned the nation as it developed into the biggest political scandal in U.S. history. It led to the resignations of top White House aides and, eventually, Nixon himself.

Robert Ellison, Black Star; NASA

Among the group of vice presidents who became president, Nixon was the first who did not succeed the president under whom he had served. Nixon became vice president under Eisenhower at the age of 40. He was the second youngest man to hold that office. John C. Breckinridge was 36 when he became vice president under James Buchanan in 1857. Before Nixon was elected vice president, he was elected twice to the U.S. House of Representatives and once to the U.S. Senate.

Friends knew Nixon as a painfully sensitive man. Nixon felt especially hurt by what he considered unfair criticism. But in politics, he won fame as a tough, forceful campaigner. He liked a good fight and had a fierce determination to succeed.

Early life

Boyhood. Richard Milhous Nixon was born on Jan. 9, 1913, in Yorba Linda, California, a village 30 miles (48 kilometers) southeast of Los Angeles. He was the second of the five sons of Francis Anthony (Frank) Nixon and Hannah Milhous Nixon. Nixon's father had moved from Ohio to southern California. There he met and married Hannah Milhous, who had come from Indiana with her parents and a group of other Quakers. Frank Nixon later gave up his Methodist faith and became a Quaker. At one time or another, he worked as a streetcar conductor, a carpenter, a laborer, and a farmer.

In 1922, the Nixon family moved to East Whittier (now Whittier). There Frank Nixon opened a combination grocery store and gasoline station. Richard had four brothers, Harold (1909-1932), Donald (1914-1987), Arthur (1918-1925), and Edward (1930-   ).

At the age of about 10, Richard began working part-time as a bean picker. During his teens, he worked as a handyman in a packing house, janitor at a swimming pool, and barker at an amusement park. While in college, he served as bookkeeper and as manager of the vegetable department of his father's store.

Education. Nixon attended elementary schools in Yorba Linda, Whittier, and nearby Fullerton. At Whittier High School, history and civics were his favorite subjects. An excellent student, he also played football and starred in debating. At the age of 17, Nixon entered Whittier College, a Quaker institution. He won several debating awards, and he became president of the student body.

© Chad Slattery, After Image

Richard Nixon's birthplace was this small frame house in Yorba Linda, California. He was the second of the five sons of Francis Anthony (Frank) Nixon and Hannah Milhous Nixon.

Nixon graduated from Whittier in 1934 and won a scholarship from the Duke University School of Law in Durham, North Carolina. Walter F. Dexter, then president of Whittier College, wrote in a letter of recommendation for Nixon: "I believe he will become one of America's important, if not great, leaders." At Duke, Nixon was elected president of the student law association. He also won election to the Order of the Coif, the national law fraternity for honor students. Nixon ranked third in the 1937 graduating class of 44 students.

Lawyer. The Great Depression still gripped the United States when Nixon left Duke. There were few jobs. Nixon tried unsuccessfully to join the Federal Bureau of Investigation and then a law firm in New York City. He finally returned home and joined a Whittier law firm, in which he became a partner. Nixon and several investors later formed a company to make and market frozen orange juice, but it went bankrupt in 18 months. At the age of 26, Nixon became the youngest member of the Whittier College Board of Trustees.

Nixon's family. Shortly after returning to Whittier, Nixon met Thelma Catherine Ryan (1912-1993). She had been born in a mining camp at Ely, Nevada. Her father nicknamed her Pat because she was born on the eve of St. Patrick's Day. When Pat was a baby, her parents moved to a farm in California. They died before Pat finished high school. Pat put herself through the University of Southern California, occasionally working as an extra in Hollywood films.

When Nixon met Pat, she was teaching commercial subjects at Whittier High School. They met during tryouts for a community theater play. They were married on June 21, 1940. The Nixons had two daughters, Patricia (Tricia), born in 1946, and Julie, born in 1948. Julie married David Eisenhower, grandson of former President Eisenhower, in 1968. Tricia married Edward Cox in 1971.

Naval officer. In January 1942, during World War II, Nixon left Whittier to take a job in the tire rationing section of the Office of Price Administration in Washington, D.C. Eight months later, he joined the Navy as an ensign. Nixon served in a naval air transport unit in the Pacific and was promoted to lieutenant commander before the war ended in 1945.

Career in Congress

Since 1936, the voters of Nixon's home congressional district had elected a Democrat, Jerry Voorhis, to the U.S. House of Representatives. Republican leaders searched for a "new face" to oppose Voorhis in the 1946 election. Nixon, then awaiting discharge from the Navy, convinced a number of leading Republicans that he was the best candidate.

Professional politicians gave Nixon little chance of defeating Voorhis, a veteran campaigner. But Nixon campaigned aggressively, implying that Voorhis was supported by Communists, though there was little evidence to prove that he was. Nixon won the election.

U.S. representative. In the House of Representatives, Nixon was proudest of his work on a committee that laid the groundwork for the Marshall Plan and other foreign aid programs (see **Foreign aid**). Nixon helped write the Taft-Hartley Act, which established controls over labor unions. In addition, he became a member of the House Committee on Un-American Activities.

In 1948, Nixon was reelected to the House. The Alger Hiss case, which began that same year, brought Nixon into national prominence. Hiss, a former State Department official, was accused of having passed classified State Department documents to a Soviet spy ring during the 1930's. The matter rested with Hiss's word against that of his accusers. Many members of the Un-American Activities Committee wanted to drop the case, but Nixon insisted that Hiss was a traitor. The question of Communists in government was a fierce political issue at the time. In 1950, a federal District Court jury convicted Hiss of perjury in that he had ever given secret documents to Soviet agents. See **Hiss, Alger.**

U.S. senator. In 1950, at the peak of his prominence in the Hiss case, Nixon ran for the U.S. Senate. He opposed Representative Helen Gahagan Douglas, a New Deal Democrat. During the campaign, Nixon emphasized charges, made originally by Douglas's foes in the Democratic primary election, that she was "soft" on Communism. He called her the "Pink Lady." Douglas took revenge by labeling Nixon "Tricky Dick." In one of California's most savage political contests, Nixon defeated Douglas by nearly 700,000 votes.

In the Senate, Nixon served on the Labor and Public Welfare Committee. He also became a popular speaker at Republican Party affairs and at civic meetings in all parts of the United States.

The 1952 campaign. In 1952, the Republican National Convention nominated Nixon for vice president to run with General Dwight D. Eisenhower. A highlight of the campaign was a dispute over an $18,000 fund set up by Nixon's supporters in California. They had organized the fund in 1950 to enable Nixon to campaign for Republican programs and candidates in both election and non-election years. Nixon and his friends showed that they had used the money only for political expenses, but members of the media labeled it a "secret slush fund." Many Republicans, fearing that Nixon might hurt Eisenhower's chances of victory, demanded that Nixon withdraw from the ticket.

UPI/Bettmann Newsphotos

Representative Nixon won national attention during the Alger Hiss case. He worked with Whittaker Chambers, *left,* who accused Hiss of spying, and investigator Robert Stripling, *right.*

Nixon's cause seemed hopeless. Then, on Sept. 23, 1952, Nixon stated his case in an emotional address over television and radio. He discussed his personal finances in detail, showing that he had not profited personally from the fund. He said that "Pat doesn't have a mink coat. But she does have a respectable Republican cloth coat." And he vowed to keep Checkers, a cocker spaniel that had been a gift to his daughters. After the program, Republicans hailed Nixon as a hero. Eisenhower put his arm around Nixon when they next met and declared, "You're my boy."

During the campaign, Nixon accused his Democratic opponents of not recognizing the Communist threat to the United States and the world. He charged that a vote for the Democrats was a vote for socialism at home and surrender abroad. Eisenhower and Nixon went on to defeat their Democratic opponents, Governor Adlai E. Stevenson of Illinois and Senator John J. Sparkman of Alabama.

Vice president (1953-1961)

Eisenhower succeeded Democratic President Harry S. Truman in 1953. He gave Nixon the job of working with members of Congress to smooth out possible quarrels with the new administration. Eisenhower also assigned Nixon to preside over Cabinet meetings and the National Security Council in the president's absence. Nixon took a greater role in the executive branch of the government than any previous vice president.

Eisenhower's illnesses. Nixon's biggest test as vice president began Sept. 24, 1955, when Eisenhower suffered a heart attack. Nixon calmly went about his normal duties, presided at Cabinet meetings, and kept the wheels of government moving smoothly. He also stepped in when the president suffered another illness in June 1956 and a stroke in November 1957. The arrangement Nixon worked out with Eisenhower later served as a basis for the 25th Amendment to the Constitution of the United States. The amendment, ratified in 1967, provides for the vice president acting for the president when the president is unable to perform the duties of the office.

The 1956 election. Many people wondered whether Eisenhower would ask Nixon to run with him again in 1956. For a while, the president seemed to be considering the idea of dropping his controversial running mate. Finally, however, the president declared: "Anyone who attempts to drive a wedge of any kind between Dick Nixon and me has just as much chance as if he tried to drive it between my brother and me." Eisenhower and Nixon defeated the Democratic nominees, Adlai E. Stevenson and Senator Estes Kefauver of Tennessee.

Overseas missions. Nixon frequently acted as spokesperson for the government on trips to other nations. As vice president, he toured nearly 60 countries, visiting every continent except Antarctica. During a tour of Latin America in the spring of 1958, Nixon faced violence and danger. In Peru, Communist agents led groups that booed and stoned him and even spit at him. In Venezuela, mobs smashed the windows of Nixon's car. However, he was not hurt.

Nixon traveled to the Soviet Union in July 1959 to open an American exhibit in Moscow. As he and Premier Nikita S. Khrushchev walked through a model

UPI/Bettmann Newsphotos

Nixon and Dwight D. Eisenhower were a winning team during the presidential campaigns of 1952 and 1956.

home, they argued over which economic system was better, capitalism or Communism. At one point in the "kitchen debate," Nixon startled his hosts by pointing his finger at Khrushchev and saying bluntly: "You don't know everything."

Defeat by Kennedy. Few people doubted that Nixon would be the Republican presidential candidate in 1960. Some party leaders thought Governor Nelson Rockefeller of New York might make an all-out fight for the nomination. But Rockefeller withdrew, and the Republican National Convention nominated Nixon on the first ballot. Nixon chose Henry Cabot Lodge, Jr., U.S. ambassador to the United Nations, as his vice presidential running mate. The Democrats nominated Senator John F. Kennedy of Massachusetts for president and Senator Lyndon B. Johnson of Texas for vice president.

The presidential campaign was close and hard-fought from start to finish. Kennedy argued that Republican

AP/Wide World

The "kitchen debate" occurred in 1959, when Nixon and Soviet Premier Nikita Khrushchev toured a U.S. exhibit in Moscow and argued about differences in Soviet and American lifestyles.

UPI/Bettmann Newsphotos

Presidential candidates John F. Kennedy and Richard M. Nixon took part in four televised debates in 1960. It was the first time presidential candidates had met in face-to-face debates.

methods had slowed U.S. economic growth, contributing to what he called a loss of American prestige abroad. Nixon cited figures to show that the economy was growing at a satisfactory rate. Kennedy also charged that the Republicans had allowed the Soviet Union to overtake the United States in missile production.

Nixon and Kennedy took part in a unique series of four televised debates. The television and radio audiences included most of the nation's voters. These "great debates" marked the first time in U.S. history that presidential candidates argued campaign issues face-to-face. Kennedy's calm manner and appearance in the first debate, contrasted with Nixon's apparent nervousness, helped Kennedy win over many voters who had been undecided about their choice.

Nixon lost to Kennedy in one of the closest presidential elections in U.S. history. Kennedy won by 114,673 popular votes out of nearly 69 million total votes. Nixon carried 26 states to 22 for Kennedy, but Kennedy received 303 electoral votes compared to Nixon's 219. Senator Harry F. Byrd of Virginia got 15 electoral votes. Widespread charges of fraudulent vote counting in Illinois and Texas cast some doubt on Kennedy's victory.

Political comeback

Defeat in California. In 1961, Nixon began to practice law in Los Angeles. In 1962, he decided to run for governor of California. Nixon won the Republican nomination for governor by defeating Joseph C. Shell in the state primary election. But the victory was costly. Conservative Republicans had supported Shell, and Nixon's triumph split the party. In the election, California's governor, Democrat Edmund G. (Pat) Brown, beat Nixon by about 300,000 votes.

New York City lawyer. Nixon moved to New York City in 1963 and began a new law practice. He became a partner in a Wall Street law firm, and his associates placed his name first in the list of partners.

Some of Nixon's supporters wanted him to run for president in 1964, but Nixon felt that most Republicans

favored Senator Barry M. Goldwater of Arizona. Goldwater won the Republican presidential nomination, and Nixon campaigned for him and other party candidates. President Lyndon B. Johnson, seeking his first full term, defeated Goldwater by a huge margin.

Goldwater's overwhelming defeat put Nixon back into the political limelight. Liberal and conservative Republicans were quarreling bitterly, and Nixon was the only nationally prominent man whom both groups could accept. In 1966, Nixon campaigned vigorously for Republican candidates in congressional elections. Republicans won 47 House seats and 3 Senate seats that had been held by Democrats. Nixon received much credit for the Republican victories.

In 1967, Nixon traveled around the world. His trip included visits to the Soviet Union and South Vietnam.

The 1968 election. In February 1968, Nixon announced that he would be a candidate for the Republican presidential nomination. Many Republicans wondered whether he could regain his voter appeal. They feared that his defeats by Kennedy and Brown had given him the image of a loser. But Nixon won primary elections by large margins in New Hampshire, Wisconsin, Indiana, Nebraska, Oregon, and South Dakota.

Nixon's chief opponents for the presidential nomination were Governors Nelson Rockefeller of New York and Ronald Reagan of California. But Nixon easily won nomination on the first ballot at the Republican National Convention in Miami Beach. The convention nominated Nixon's choice as running mate, Governor Spiro T. Agnew of Maryland.

The Democrats chose Vice President Hubert H. Humphrey and Senator Edmund S. Muskie of Maine. Former Governor George C. Wallace of Alabama and retired General Curtis E. LeMay ran as the candidates of the American Independent Party.

Both Nixon and Humphrey promised to make peace in Vietnam their main goal as president. The Vietnam War had begun in 1957 as a battle for control of South Vietnam between South Vietnam's non-Communist government and the Communist-led National Liberation Front, the Viet Cong. By the mid-1960's, the United States was deeply involved in the war as an ally of the South Vietnamese government.

Nixon called for a program of what he termed "new internationalism." Under this program, other nations would take over from the United States more of the responsibility for preserving world peace and helping developing countries. This plan later became known as the Nixon Doctrine. Nixon also pledged to strengthen law enforcement in the United States.

In the election, Nixon defeated Humphrey by only about 511,000 popular votes, 31,785,148 to 31,274,503. Wallace received 9,901,151 popular votes. Nixon won a clear majority of electoral votes, with 301. Humphrey received 191 electoral votes, and Wallace got 46. For the electoral vote by states, see **Electoral College** (table).

Nixon's first administration (1969-1973)

Foreign policy. Nixon's major goal was settlement of the Vietnam War. In his first inaugural address, Nixon said: "The greatest honor history can bestow is the title of peacemaker. This honor now beckons America."

The Vietnam War. The Vietnam peace talks, begun in

Nixon's first election

Place of nominating convention	Miami Beach, Florida
Ballot on which nominated	1st
Democratic opponent	Hubert H. Humphrey
American Independent opponent	George C. Wallace
Electoral vote*	301 (Nixon) to 191 (Humphrey) and 46 (Wallace)
Popular vote	31,785,148 (Nixon) to 31,274,503 (Humphrey) and 9,901,151 (Wallace)
Age at inauguration	56

*For votes by states, see Electoral College (table).

1968, continued in Paris. But the negotiators made little progress. In March 1969, Nixon ordered a stepped-up training program for South Vietnamese forces so they could gradually take over the major burden of fighting. He also ordered secret bombings of supply routes in Cambodia. In July, he began a gradual withdrawal of U.S. combat troops from Vietnam, a policy known as *Vietnamization.* Many Americans favored it, but many others wanted U.S. involvement to end immediately. Protests and demonstrations swept the nation.

In 1970, United States troops invaded Cambodia to attack North Vietnamese supply depots there. Nixon said the action would shorten the war, but many people felt it was expanding it. Protests broke out on hundreds of college campuses. At Kent State University in Ohio, National Guardsmen fired into a crowd of demonstrators, killing four students and wounding nine others. The shocked reaction of the nation and student strikes at other colleges, many of which closed until fall, forced Nixon to cut short the Cambodian campaign.

In May 1972, in response to a Communist offensive, Nixon ordered a blockade of North Vietnam to cut off its war supplies from the Soviet Union and China. The blockade included the mining of North Vietnam's ports and the bombing of its rail and highway links to China. In December 1972, after peace negotiations broke down, Nixon ordered extensive bombing of Hanoi, the North Vietnamese capital.

AP/Wide World

In his inaugural address in 1969, President Nixon pledged that the United States would seek "the title of peacemaker." Vice President Spiro T. Agnew is at Nixon's left.

Relations with China. In 1969, Nixon approved the removal of some restrictions on travel by Americans to China. He also encouraged the reopening of trade between China and the United States. The two nations had stopped trading with each other during the Korean War (1950-1953). In 1971, Nixon approved the export of certain goods to China. In February 1972, the president visited China for seven days, and he began the process that led to formal recognition of China by the United States in 1979.

Relations with the Soviet Union. In May 1972, Nixon visited the Soviet Union for nine days. During this visit, Nixon and Leonid I. Brezhnev, leader of the Soviet Communist Party, signed agreements to limit the production of nuclear weapons. Later that year, the Soviet Union became a major buyer of U.S. wheat.

The national scene. In August 1969, Nixon proposed a series of major domestic reforms, which he termed the *New Federalism.* One of the reforms called for a minimum federal payment to every needy family with children. Nixon also called for a form of national health insurance and suggested a *revenue sharing* plan in which the federal government would share its tax revenues with state and local governments. But action on the reforms was stalled as key Democrats and Republicans in Congress asked for major changes.

Major legislation. In spite of the legislative slowdown, Congress did enact several far-reaching laws. In 1969, it passed Nixon's proposal to establish a lottery system for

Vice presidents and Cabinet

Vice president	* Spiro T. Agnew†
	* Gerald R. Ford (1973)
Secretary of state	William P. Rogers
	* Henry A. Kissinger (1973)
Secretary of the treasury	David M. Kennedy
	* John B. Connally (1971)
	* George P. Shultz (1972)
	William E. Simon (1974)
Secretary of defense	* Melvin R. Laird
	* Elliot L. Richardson (1973)
	James R. Schlesinger (1973)
Attorney general	* John N. Mitchell
	Richard G. Kleindienst (1972)
	* Elliot L. Richardson (1973)
	William B. Saxbe (1974)
Postmaster general**	Winton M. Blount
Secretary of the interior	Walter J. Hickel
	Rogers C. B. Morton (1971)
Secretary of agriculture	Clifford M. Hardin
	Earl L. Butz (1971)
Secretary of commerce	Maurice H. Stans
	Peter G. Peterson (1972)
	Frederick B. Dent (1973)
Secretary of labor	* George P. Shultz
	James D. Hodgson (1970)
	Peter J. Brennan (1973)
Secretary of health, education, and welfare	Robert H. Finch
	* Elliot L. Richardson (1970)
	* Caspar Weinberger (1973)
Secretary of housing and urban development	George W. Romney
	James T. Lynn (1973)
Secretary of transportation	John A. Volpe
	Claude S. Brinegar (1973)

*Has a biography in World Book.
**Reduced to non-Cabinet rank, 1971.
†Resigned on Oct. 10, 1973.

National Archives

Nixon toured the Great Wall of China during his historic visit to that country in 1972. Relations between the United States and China improved dramatically during Nixon's presidency.

the military draft. Also in 1969, Congress approved extensive reforms in federal tax laws. These reforms included increases in personal income tax deductions and cuts in tax benefits for foundations and oil companies. In 1970, Congress established independent agencies to replace the Post Office Department and to operate the passenger trains that linked the nation's major cities. Also in 1970, Congress approved the lowering of the minimum voting age in federal elections to 18. It began the process that led to the ratification in 1971 of the 26th Amendment to the U.S. Constitution, which set the voting age at 18 for elections. In 1972, Congress approved Nixon's revenue sharing program. The legislation provided billions of dollars in federal tax money to state and local governments.

Inflation was one of Nixon's chief domestic concerns. Many Americans found that although they were earning more money than ever before, rising prices sharply cut their gains. In 1971, Nixon, concerned about how the economy might affect his reelection, set up a Pay Board to stop inflationary wage and salary increases and a Price Commission to regulate price and rent increases. The economy improved in 1972. In addition, the inflation rate slowed.

The ABM system. In March 1969, Nixon proposed a plan to build an antiballistic missile (ABM) system called *Safeguard.* Nixon said the new missiles were needed to protect U.S. underground missiles and bomber bases from enemy missile attack and to match comparable systems in the Soviet Union. The plan became one of the

most heavily debated issues of Nixon's administration. Critics charged that the system would step up the arms race between the United States and the Soviet Union. They also claimed the new missiles would cost too much money and fail to destroy enemy missiles. In August, the Senate narrowly approved construction of the two ABM bases Nixon had requested.

Civil rights. Nixon developed a successful "Southern strategy" that resulted in virtually all the Southern States switching from Democratic to Republican during his time in office. The Democrats were perceived to be the party of civil rights and desegregation, while Nixon's Republicans appeared to be more supportive of the interests of Southerners not in favor of desegregation. For example, Republicans fiercely opposed the Supreme Court's 1971 ruling that children could be bused to integrate public schools. However, it was during Nixon's administration that legal segregation in Southern schools was finally ended. In addition, Nixon introduced the Philadelphia Plan, an affirmative action program for hiring in companies with large government contracts.

Supreme Court nominations. In 1969, Nixon's appointment of Warren E. Burger as chief justice of the United States was approved. However, in that same year and again in 1970, Nixon suffered a stinging defeat when he tried to appoint a conservative Southerner to the Supreme Court. In May 1969, Associate Justice Abe Fortas resigned from the court under charges of personal misconduct (see **Fortas, Abe**). Nixon nominated Judge Clement F. Haynsworth, Jr., of South Carolina to succeed Fortas. Some critics claimed that Haynsworth was anti-black. Others charged he was unethical for ruling in a case in which he had a financial interest. In November, the Senate rejected the nomination by a 55 to 45 vote.

In January 1970, Nixon nominated Judge G. Harrold Carswell of Florida for the seat. Opposition to Carswell grew quickly after several judges and law school deans rated him unqualified for the Supreme Court. In April, the Senate defeated the nomination by a 51 to 45 vote. It was the first time that two Supreme Court nominees of a president had been rejected since 1894, when Grover Cleveland was president.

After Carswell's defeat, Nixon charged that the Senate would not confirm a Southerner to the court. In May, the Senate unanimously approved Nixon's third choice, Judge Harry A. Blackmun of Minnesota. In 1971, the Senate approved Nixon's selection of Lewis F. Powell, Jr., and William H. Rehnquist for the court.

The U.S. space program opened a new era of exploration and discovery in 1969. On July 20, Apollo 11 astronauts Neil A. Armstrong and Buzz Aldrin became the first people to set foot on the moon. Through a special telephone connection while they were on the moon Nixon told them, "Because of what you have done, the heavens have become part of man's world."

Environmental problems attracted more and more attention during Nixon's administration. Many Americans began to realize that pollution of the air, land, and water endangered not only the quality of life but also life itself. In 1970, Nixon set up the Environmental Protection Agency to deal with pollution problems.

In addition, although Nixon was not known to be an environmentalist, he approved of the Clean Air Act Amendments, the Coastal Zone Management Act, the

Marine Mammal Protection Act, the Endangered Species Act, and the Safe Drinking Water Act. He also transferred land to the states for 642 new parks.

The 1972 election. Nixon and Agnew easily won renomination at the 1972 Republican National Convention in Miami Beach, Florida. The Democrats nominated Senator George S. McGovern of South Dakota for president. Sargent Shriver, former director of the Peace Corps, became McGovern's running mate.

In the election, Nixon won a landslide victory. He received almost 18 million more popular votes than McGovern—the widest margin of any U.S. presidential election. Nixon got 520 electoral votes, and McGovern received 17. John Hospers of the Libertarian Party won 1 electoral vote. See **Electoral College** (table).

Life in the White House. The Nixons brought a calm and reserved way of life to the White House. They preferred formal dress, including white ties and coats with tails for men and long gowns for women. They also favored fox trots and waltzes for dancing.

The Nixons' taste in art also was conservative. They replaced a number of the op art paintings on White House walls with traditional landscapes and portraits. Nixon was the first president to play the piano since Harry Truman. He occasionally played for guests. Nixon followed sports closely and impressed many visitors with his knowledge of baseball and football.

Pat Nixon worked hard to encourage Americans to volunteer to help deal with the country's social problems. She frequently traveled across the nation to support volunteer organizations.

A private man, Nixon did much of his work in a remote office in the Executive Office Building across from the White House. Shortly after taking office, he bought an estate in San Clemente, a beach resort in southern California. It became known as the Western White House because Nixon spent working vacations there. He also maintained a home in Key Biscayne, Florida.

Nixon's second administration (1973-1974)

Foreign affairs. On Jan. 27, 1973, the United States

Nixon's second election

Place of nominating convention	Miami Beach, Florida
Ballot on which nominated	1st
Democratic opponent	George S. McGovern
Electoral vote*	520 (Nixon) to 17 (McGovern) and 1 (Hospers)
Popular vote	47,170,179 (Nixon) to 29,171,791 (McGovern)
Age at inauguration	60

*For votes by states, see **Electoral College** (table).

and the other participants in the Vietnam War signed agreements to stop fighting immediately and begin exchanging prisoners. The agreements climaxed several weeks of bargaining between North Vietnamese officials and Henry A. Kissinger, Nixon's national security adviser, who had begun secret talks with the Communists in 1969. The United States completed its troop withdrawal from South Vietnam in March. Nixon privately assured South Vietnam that the United States would use "full force" to aid the South Vietnamese if the Communists violated the agreements. Fighting did continue in 1973, but no U.S. troops reentered the war. Later that year, Kissinger became secretary of state.

Nixon continued his efforts to improve relations between the United States and China. In 1973, the two nations sent representatives to serve in each other's capital and exchanged visits by cultural groups.

Events at home. Nixon carried out a key campaign pledge in January 1973 when he ended the military draft. The military then became an all-volunteer force.

Disputes with Congress. Nixon's relations with the Democratic-controlled Congress grew increasingly strained during 1973. Nixon angered many members of Congress by *impounding* (not spending) several billion dollars in federal aid on projects that Congress had approved. Nixon called the projects wasteful.

The president suffered a major defeat when Congress forced him to end U.S. bombing in Cambodia. Nixon had argued that the bombing was needed to prevent a Com-

National Archives, Nixon Project

The Nixon family gathered in the White House for this portrait. Standing are, *left to right,* son-in-law David Eisenhower, President Nixon, Mrs. Nixon, and son-in-law Edward Cox. Seated are the Nixon daughters, Julie Nixon Eisenhower, *left,* and Patricia Nixon Cox.

munist take-over of that nation. But Congress refused to provide money for bombing beyond Aug. 15, 1973.

Nixon received another major setback in 1973 when Congress overrode his veto of a resolution that limited presidential war powers. The War Powers Resolution gives Congress the power to halt after 60 days the use of any U.S. armed forces that the president has ordered into combat abroad. Passage of the resolution was the strongest action ever taken by Congress to spell out the warmaking powers of Congress and the president.

Economic problems continued to challenge Nixon in 1973. In January, he ended most of the government-required limits that had been placed on wage and price increases in 1971. But prices soared, and another brief use of controls resulted in a shortage of beef and other foods. By the end of 1973, inflation had risen 8.8 percent, the largest increase in any year since 1947.

Also in 1973, a fuel shortage led to reduced supplies of oil for home heating and industry and to gasoline rationing in a number of states. In 1974, Congress approved Nixon's proposal to set up a Federal Energy Administration to deal with the energy shortage.

The Watergate scandal hit the Nixon administration during 1973. It arose from a break-in at the Democratic Party headquarters in the Watergate building complex in Washington, D.C., on June 17, 1972. Employees of Nixon's 1972 reelection committee were arrested in the break-in and convicted of burglary. Early in 1973, evidence was uncovered that linked several top White House aides with either the break-in or later attempts to hide information related to it.

Nixon insisted that he did not participate in the Watergate break-in or the cover-up. In addition, he promised a full investigation of the case. In May, Archibald Cox, a Harvard Law School professor, was named to head the investigation as the special prosecutor.

In July, a Senate investigating committee learned that

Nixon had secretly made tape recordings of conversations in his White House offices since 1971. The president said that he taped the conversations to preserve an accurate record of his administration. Cox and the Senate committee asked Nixon to give them certain tapes that they believed could aid their investigations. Nixon refused. He argued that the Constitution gives a president the implied right to maintain the confidentiality of private presidential conversations. Nixon said the loss of that right would endanger the presidency.

In August, Cox and the committee filed petitions in court to obtain the tapes. U.S. District Court Judge John J. Sirica decided to review the tapes himself and ordered Nixon to give them to him. Nixon appealed the order, but a U.S. court of appeals supported Sirica.

On October 19, Nixon offered to supply summaries of the tapes to the Senate committee and to Cox. Cox refused, arguing that summaries would not be regarded as proper evidence in court. Nixon ordered Attorney General Elliot L. Richardson to fire Cox, but Richardson refused and resigned, as did Deputy Attorney General William G. Ruckelshaus. Nixon named Robert H. Bork acting attorney general, and Bork fired Cox. Leon Jaworski, a noted Texas attorney, later succeeded Cox. But Nixon's actions resulted in a move for his impeachment.

The resignation of Agnew on Oct. 10, 1973, further stunned the nation. Earlier that year, federal officials had begun to investigate Agnew in connection with charges of graft in Maryland. They uncovered evidence he had accepted illegal payments as an officeholder in Maryland and as vice president. After he resigned, Agnew pleaded *nolo contendere* (no contest) to a charge that he had cheated on his federal income tax payment for 1967.

National Archives

During the Watergate scandal, Nixon appeared on TV with transcripts of tape recordings of White House conversations. He refused to give the actual tapes to investigators.

Quotations from Nixon

The following quotations come from some of Richard Nixon's speeches and writings.

Crises can indeed be agony. But it is the exquisite agony which a man might not want to experience again—yet would not for the world have missed.

Introduction to *Six Crises,* published in 1962

We have found ourselves rich in goods, but ragged in spirit; reaching with magnificent precision for the moon, but falling into raucous discord on earth. We are caught in war, wanting peace. We are torn by divisions, wanting unity.

First Inaugural Address, Jan. 20, 1969

If when the chips are down, the world's most powerful nation ... acts like a pitiful, helpless giant, the forces of totalitarianism and anarchy will threaten free nations ...throughout the world.

Speech announcing invasion of Cambodia, April 30, 1970

Let us reject the narrow visions of those who would tell us that we are evil because we are not yet perfect ... that all the sweat and toil and sacrifice that have gone into the building of America were for naught because the building is not yet done. Let us see that the path we are traveling is wide, with room in it for all of us, and that its direction is toward a better nation in a more peaceful world.

State of the Union Address to Congress, Jan. 20, 1972

Always give your best, never get discouraged, never be petty; always remember, others may hate you. Those who hate you don't win unless you hate them. And then you destroy yourself.

Final speech before leaving office, Aug. 9, 1974

Years later, in 1981, a Maryland court ordered Agnew to pay the state the amount of the bribes it declared he had accepted, plus interest. In 1983, Agnew paid $268,482.

Nixon became the first president to appoint a vice president under procedures established by the 25th Amendment to the Constitution. He named House Minority Leader Gerald R. Ford as Agnew's successor, and Ford became vice president on Dec. 6, 1973.

The impeachment hearings began before the House Judiciary Committee in October 1973. The committee had obtained from the president several tapes and edited transcripts of many tapes of White House conversations. The committee issued *subpoenas* (legal demands) for additional tapes, but the president resisted and took his case to the Supreme Court.

In July 1974, before the court made its decision, a majority of the committee members voted to recommend three articles of impeachment against Nixon. The first article charged that the president obstructed justice by withholding evidence, counseling his aides to give false testimony, and otherwise interfering with the Watergate investigation. The second impeachment article charged that Nixon abused presidential powers, and the third accused him of refusing to obey subpoenas.

In late July, the Supreme Court ruled that Nixon had to turn over the tapes. Nixon made the tapes public on August 5. One tape revealed that he had spoken of a cover-up as early as June 23, 1972, six days after the burglary. Republican congressional leaders warned Nixon that he faced almost certain impeachment by the House of Representatives and removal from office by the Senate.

Resignation and pardon. Nixon told his family on August 7 that he planned to resign. He announced his decision to the American people in a nationwide television address the next evening. On August 9, with about 2 ½ years remaining in his second term, Nixon submitted his resignation as president. At noon that day, Vice President Gerald R. Ford was sworn in as the 38th president.

Nixon's resignation ended the prospect of a struggle over impeachment. But many Americans continued to debate whether he should be prosecuted for his role in the cover-up. On September 8, Ford granted Nixon a pardon for all federal crimes Nixon may have committed while president. Ford said he made the decision to "reconcile divisions in our country and heal the wounds that had festered too long."

Later years

After leaving office, Nixon returned to San Clemente. He avoided active participation in politics and spent much of his time playing golf and writing. Nixon maintained a strong interest in international affairs, and his opinions on U.S. foreign policy were highly regarded by many people, including both Democratic and Republican presidents who served after him.

In 1978, Nixon wrote *RN: The Memoirs of Richard Nixon.* In 1980, he moved to New York City and wrote *The Real War,* a book on U.S. foreign policy. Nixon moved to Saddle River, New Jersey, in 1981 and to Park Ridge, New Jersey, in 1991. He also wrote *Leaders* (1982), *Real Peace: A Strategy for the West* (1983), *No More Vietnams* (1985), *1999: Victory Without War* (1988), *In the Arena* (1990), *Seize the Moment* (1992), and *Beyond Peace* (1994).

Alex Webb, Magnum

Nixon left the White House on Aug. 9, 1974, and became the first president to resign. With him were Mrs. Nixon and Vice President and Mrs. Ford. Ford succeeded Nixon as president.

In 1990, the Richard Nixon Library and Birthplace opened in Yorba Linda, California. It includes a museum. Nixon's wife, Pat, died of lung cancer on June 22, 1993, at their home in Park Ridge. On April 18, 1994, Nixon suffered a stroke at home just before dinner and was taken by ambulance to a hospital in New York City. Three days later, he lapsed into a coma. He died the following day, April 22. Nixon and his wife are buried on the grounds of the Richard Nixon Library and Birthplace, near the house in which he was born.   Melvin Small

Related articles in *World Book* include:

Agnew, Spiro T.	Kennedy,	President of the
Cold War	John F.	United States
Eisenhower,	Kissinger,	Republican Party
Dwight D.	Henry A.	Vice president of
Ford, Gerald R.	Lodge,	the United
Hiss, Alger	Henry C., Jr.	States
Humphrey,	Moynihan,	Vietnam War
Hubert H.	Daniel P.	Watergate

Outline

I. **Early life**
  A. Boyhood   D. Nixon's family
  B. Education   E. Naval officer
  C. Lawyer
II. **Career in Congress**
  A. U.S. representative
  B. U.S. senator
  C. The 1952 campaign
III. **Vice president (1953-1961)**
  A. Eisenhower's illnesses C. Overseas missions
  B. The 1956 election   D. Defeat by Kennedy
IV. **Political comeback**
  A. Defeat in California
  B. New York City lawyer
  C. The 1968 election
V. **Nixon's first administration (1969-1973)**
  A. Foreign policy   C. The 1972 election
  B. The national scene D. Life in the White House
VI. **Nixon's second administration (1973-1974)**
  A. Foreign affairs
  B. Events at home
VII. **Later years**

Questions

When did Nixon win election to his first national political office?
What was the "kitchen debate"?
Why was Nixon's election as president in 1968 one of the greatest political comebacks in U.S. history?
How was Nixon's career almost ruined in 1952?
Why was the 1960 presidential campaign unique?
What was Vietnamization? The New Federalism?
Why did Nixon resign from the presidency?

Additional resources

Black, Conrad. *Richard M. Nixon: A Life in Full.* PublicAffairs, 2007.
Frick, Daniel. *Reinventing Richard Nixon: A Cultural History of an American Obsession.* Univ. Pr. of Kans., 2008.
Frost, David. *Frost/Nixon: Behind the Scenes of the Nixon Interviews.* HarperPerennial, 2007.
Perlstein, Rick. *Nixonland: The Rise of a President and the Fracturing of America.* Simon & Schuster, 2008.

Nizhniy Novgorod, *NIHZH nee NAHV guh RAHD,* (pop. 1,311,252), is an industrial center in Russia. It lies at the fork of the Volga and Oka rivers (see **Russia** [political map]). Nizhniy Novgorod is one of the oldest cities in Russia and is known as the *Cradle of the Russian Empire.* The city's upper part contains a fortress and historic cathedrals. The lower town is the industrial section. One of Russia's largest automobile factories is in Nizhniy Novgorod. Other products include locomotives, airplanes, machine tools, and chemicals.

Nizhniy Novgorod was an important commercial center in the Middle Ages, a period in history that lasted from about the 400's through the 1400's. During this period, west-east travel along the Oka River and through a low pass in the Ural Mountains met north-south travel on the Volga River. In 1932, when Russia was a republic of the Soviet Union, the city was renamed Gorki in honor of the Russian writer Maxim Gorki. The city was renamed Nizhniy Novgorod in 1990, about a year before the Soviet republics became independent.

Roman Szporluk

Nkrumah, *ehn KROO muh,* **Kwame,** *KWAH mee* (1909-1972), was president of Ghana from 1960 to 1966. Army leaders ousted him in 1966, and Nkrumah went into exile in nearby Guinea. President Sékou Touré of Guinea made Nkrumah Guinea's honorary president.

As president of Ghana, Nkrumah worked to develop the economy and improve living conditions. He promoted industrialization, introduced health and welfare programs, and expanded the educational system. But Nkrumah made enemies with the methods he used to achieve these goals. He imprisoned his opponents. Ghana's economy began to weaken, and corruption became widespread. Army leaders took over the government while Nkrumah was visiting China.

Nkrumah was born in September 1909 in Nkroful, the Gold Coast. He led his country's drive for independence from the British in the 1950's. He was prime minister of the Gold Coast and kept that office when the colony became Ghana, an independent country, in 1957. Nkrumah died on April 27, 1972. Immanuel Wallerstein

NLRB. See National Labor Relations Board.

No Child Left Behind Act is a United States law that regulates public education in elementary and secondary schools. The law, sometimes called the NCLB, seeks to improve student performance, hold schools accountable for student progress, and provide assistance and options for students in failing schools. A central feature of the law is a student-testing program designed to identify schools that fail to meet basic educational standards. The act significantly expanded the role of the federal government in public education. Congress passed the law in 2001, and President George W. Bush signed it into law on Jan. 8, 2002.

The No Child Left Behind Act calls for annual student testing in mathematics, reading, and science. If test scores for a particular school fail to show an adequate improvement over several years, the school may be closed or its staff replaced. The law requires schools to report their *annual yearly progress* (AYP) toward meeting educational goals. Under the law, the parents of students in failing schools have the option to transfer their children to other schools in the same school district. In addition, the law seeks to improve the quality of instruction by establishing strict federal requirements for teacher training.

The No Child Left Behind Act has stirred controversy. Most educators and teachers organizations support the goals of the act. But many say that the federal government has failed to provide adequate funding to carry out testing, provide extra tutoring, and meet other requirements of the law. Some critics have charged that the complexity of the act has caused confusion over how to implement testing programs and meet various federal requirements. Critics of the act also charge that too many schools will unfairly face punishments.

The No Child Left Behind Act reauthorized and amended the Elementary and Secondary Education Act (ESEA). Initially passed in 1965, ESEA is a federal program that supports elementary and secondary education in the United States. Lawrence O. Picus

See also **Elementary and Secondary Education Act.**

No-fault divorce. See Divorce.

No-fault insurance is a type of automobile accident insurance that was first proposed in the 1960's. It provides that if a driver, passenger, or pedestrian is injured, an insurance company—usually the driver's company—must pay, no matter who caused the accident. Injured people receive payment for medical costs and loss of income. Many no-fault plans restrict a victim's right to sue for pain and suffering or other nonfinancial damage. Such restrictions forbid a suit for nonfinancial damage unless the medical expenses exceed a certain amount or the victim was disfigured, disabled, or killed. Many other types of insurance, including fire, health, and life insurance, have always been no-fault.

Supporters of no-fault automobile insurance believe it corrects flaws in the older system. They argue that it brings quicker legal settlements and fairer distribution of damages. Under the traditional system, fault must first be determined before claims are settled. Determining fault often involves costly legal battles. As a result, many victims of automobile accidents must wait for years before receiving payment. Insurance companies fight large claims more vigorously than small ones. As a result, many seriously injured victims receive either nothing or little in damages after lengthy delays.

Opponents of no-fault insurance argue that it is unfair to free careless drivers of their responsibility for injuries they cause. These opponents believe that no-fault plans do not provide appropriate *incentives* (motives) for people to drive safely. They also argue that such plans give a financial reward to irresponsible drivers, because some accident costs are paid by drivers who are not at fault.

Kevin C. Ahlgrim

Noah, *NOH uh,* according to the Bible, was the only righteous, God-fearing man of his time. Genesis 6-9 tells that he was chosen by God to keep some people and animals alive during the Deluge, or great Flood. Noah warned people for 120 years that the Flood was coming. During that time, he built a ship, called the ark, which was 450 feet (137 meters) long. He took into the ark his family and enough birds and animals to repopulate Earth. The rain poured down for 40 days and 40 nights (Genesis 7:12, 24).

The waters dropped enough 150 days after the Flood started that the ark was able to rest on the mountains of Ararat, in what is now Turkey (see **Ararat**). Noah let loose a raven that only flew back and forth because the waters had not yet dried up. Then he sent out a dove, and it returned because it could find no place to perch. He sent out the dove two more times. On the second flight, it returned with an olive branch in its mouth.

Noah and the animals left the ark later to begin a new life. Noah offered sacrifice to God for deliverance, and God promised that he would never send another flood to destroy Earth. God made the rainbow a sign of that promise. He commanded Noah and his descendants to respect human life and to punish murder with the death penalty.

Noah's sons were Shem, Ham, and Japheth. Shem became father of the Semitic peoples, including the Jews and the Arabs. Ham was the father of the Hamitic peoples. Japheth was the father of peoples of Asia Minor and Europe. In traditions originally unrelated to the Flood, Noah is portrayed as a gardener and credited with the discovery of wine (Genesis 9:18-27).

Carole R. Fontaine

Nobel, *noh BEHL,* **Alfred Bernhard** (1833-1896), a Swedish chemist and industrialist, invented dynamite. He established the Nobel Prizes, using profits from the manufacture of chemical explosives to provide funds for the prizes (see **Nobel Prizes**).

Nobel began experimenting with nitroglycerin in his father's factory. Liquid nitroglycerin is a powerful explosive that is dangerous because of its tendency to explode when handled roughly. Nobel tried many ways of making nitroglycerin safe to use. The best way, he discovered, was to mix it with a fine, porous powder called *kieselguhr.* Nobel named the resulting powdery mixture dynamite (see **Dynamite**).

He received a patent for it in 1867. Construction and mining companies and the military ordered large quantities of dynamite because of its relative safety and explosive power. Nobel set up factories around the world, and sales of dynamite and other explosives brought him great wealth. His other chemical research provided valuable information

Amer. Swedish News Exch., Inc.
Alfred Nobel

on the preparation of artificial forms of rubber, leather, silk, and precious stones.

Nobel was born on Oct. 21, 1833, in Stockholm, Sweden, and was educated in St. Petersburg, Russia, where his family had moved in 1842. He traveled widely as a young man and became fluent in five languages. Nobel was greatly interested in literature and wrote poetry, novels, and plays in his spare time. In his will, Nobel set up a fund of about $9 million. The interest from the money was to be used to award annual prizes to people whose work most benefited humanity. Nobel wanted the profits from explosives to be used to reward human ingenuity. The Nobel Prizes, first awarded in 1901, remain the most honored prizes in the world. Nobel died on Dec. 10, 1896. Julia Brazas

Additional resources

Binns, Tristan B. *Alfred Nobel.* Watts, 2004. Younger readers.
Fant, Kenne. *Alfred Nobel.* Arcade Pub., 1993.
Feldman, Burton. *The Nobel Prize.* Arcade Pub., 2000.
Larsson, Ulf, ed. *Cultures of Creativity: The Centennial Exhibition of the Nobel Prize.* Science History Pubs., 2001.

Nobel Prizes, *noh BEHL,* are awarded each year to people, regardless of nationality, who have made valuable contributions to the "good of humanity." In his will, the Swedish inventor Alfred Nobel directed that the income from his $9-million estate be used to fund five annual prizes. The awards are given for the most important discoveries or inventions in physics, chemistry, and physiology or medicine; the most distinguished literary work of an idealistic nature; and the most effective work in the interest of international peace. The prizes were first presented in 1901. A sixth prize—the Bank of Sweden Prize in Economic Sciences in Memory of Alfred Nobel—was first awarded in 1969. This prize was established by the Bank of Sweden and is funded by the bank. The value of each of the six prizes is approximately $1 ⅓ million.

The Royal Swedish Academy of Sciences in Stockholm, Sweden, chooses the physics, chemistry, and economics winners. The Nobel Assembly at the Karolinska Institute in Stockholm awards the prize in physiology or medicine. The Swedish Academy in Stockholm awards the prize in literature. The Norwegian Nobel Committee elected by the Norwegian *Storting* (parliament) awards the prize for peace.

A candidate may not apply directly for a prize. A qualified person must submit each name in writing. For the literary prize, the Swedish Academy considers only works that have appeared in print. The academy usually selects an author for his or her complete work rather than for one book.

The organizations that award the prizes appoint 15 deputies who elect a board of directors. The board holds office for two years and administers the funds. Prizewinners receive their awards on December 10, the anniversary of the death of Alfred Nobel. The peace prize is awarded in Oslo, Norway. The other prizes are presented in Stockholm. Two or three people may share a prize. Sometimes, prizes are not awarded or are awarded in a later year.

Critically reviewed by the Nobel Foundation

There is a biography in *World Book* of each prizewinner whose name is marked with an asterisk in the tables on the following pages.

(Front)
Alfred Nobel

(Back)
Physics and chemistry

(Back)
Physiology or medicine

(Back)
Literature

Nobel Prizes consist of a medal and a cash award. Prizes are awarded for achievement in chemistry, physics, physiology or medicine, literature, world peace, and economics. The front side of each medal has a bust of Alfred Nobel, a Swedish chemist who established most of the prizes in the late 1800's. The bust is the same on the physics and chemistry, physiology or medicine, and literature medals, *shown here*. The physics and chemistry medals have identical back sides. The front and back sides of the peace and economics medals are shown at the far right.

Nobel Prizes in physics

1901 *Wilhelm C. Roentgen (German) for discovering X rays.

1902 *Hendrik Antoon Lorentz and *Pieter Zeeman (Dutch) for discovering the Zeeman effect of magnetism on light.

1903 *Antoine Henri Becquerel (French) for discovering natural radioactivity and *Pierre and Marie Curie (French) for their research on radiation.

1904 Baron Rayleigh (British) for studying the density of gases and discovering argon.

1905 Philipp Lenard (German) for studying the properties of cathode rays.

1906 *Sir Joseph John Thomson (British) for studying electrical discharge through gases.

1907 *Albert A. Michelson (American) for his design of precise optical instruments and for the accurate measurements he obtained with them.

1908 Gabriel Lippmann (French) for his method of color photography.

1909 *Guglielmo Marconi (Italian) and Karl Ferdinand Braun (German) for developing the wireless telegraph.

1910 Johannes D. van der Waals (Dutch) for studying the relationships of liquids and gases.

1911 Wilhelm Wien (German) for his discoveries on the heat radiated by black objects.

1912 Nils Dalén (Swedish) for inventing automatic gas regulators for lighthouses.

1913 Heike Kamerlingh Onnes (Dutch) for experimenting with low temperatures and liquefying helium.

1914 Max T. F. von Laue (German) for using crystals to measure X rays.

1915 *Sir William Henry Bragg and Sir William L. Bragg (British) for using X rays to study crystal structure.

1916 No award

1917 Charles Barkla (British) for studying the diffusion of light and the radiation of X rays from elements.

1918 *Max Planck (German) for stating the quantum theory of light.

1919 Johannes Stark (German) for discovering the Stark effect of spectra in electric fields.

1920 Charles E. Guillaume (French) for discovering nickel-steel alloys with slight expansion, and the alloy invar.

1921 *Albert Einstein (German) for contributing to mathematical physics and stating the law of the photoelectric effect.

1922 *Niels Bohr (Danish) for studying the structure of atoms and their radiations.

1923 *Robert A. Millikan (American) for measuring the charge on electrons and working on the photoelectric effect.

1924 *Karl M. G. Siegbahn (Swedish) for working with the X-ray spectroscope.

1925 James Franck and *Gustav Hertz (German) for stating laws on the collision of an electron with an atom.

1926 Jean Baptiste Perrin (French) for studying the discontinuous structure of matter and measuring the sizes of atoms.

1927 Arthur H. Compton (American) for discovering the Compton effect on X rays reflected from atoms, and Charles T. R. Wilson (British) for discovering a method for tracing the paths of ions.

1928 Owen W. Richardson (British) for studying thermionic effect and electrons sent off by hot metals.

1929 *Louis Victor de Broglie (French) for discovering the wave character of electrons.

1930 *Sir Chandrasekhara Venkata Raman (Indian) for discovering a new effect in radiation from elements.

1931 No award

1932 *Werner Heisenberg (German) for founding quantum mechanics, which led to discoveries in hydrogen.

1933 Paul Dirac (British) and *Erwin Schrödinger (Austrian) for discovering new forms of atomic theory.

1934 No award

1935 *Sir James Chadwick (British) for discovering the neutron.

1936 *Carl David Anderson (American) for discovering the positron, and Victor F. Hess (Austrian) for discovering cosmic rays.

1937 Clinton Davisson (American) and George Thomson (British) for discovering the diffraction of electrons by crystals.

1938 *Enrico Fermi (Italian) for discovering new radioactive elements beyond uranium.

1939 *Ernest O. Lawrence (American) for inventing the cyclotron and working on artificial radioactivity.

1940-1942 No award

1943 Otto Stern (American) for discovering the molecular beam method of studying the atom.

1944 Isidor Isaac Rabi (American) for recording the magnetic properties of atomic nuclei.

1945 *Wolfgang Pauli (Austrian) for discovering the exclusion principle (Pauli principle) of electrons.

1946 *Percy Williams Bridgman (American) for his work in the field of very high pressures.

*Has a biography in *World Book*.

(Front)   (Back)   (Front)   (Back)

Peace   **Economics**

© The Nobel Foundation

Nobel Prizes in physics (continued)

1947 Sir Edward V. Appleton (British) for exploring the ionosphere.

1948 Patrick M. S. Blackett (British) for his discoveries in cosmic radiation.

1949 *Hideki Yukawa (Japanese) for his prediction of the existence of mesons.

1950 Cecil Frank Powell (British) for his photographic method of studying atomic nuclei and his discoveries concerning mesons.

1951 *Sir John D. Cockcroft (British) and *Ernest T. S. Walton (Irish) for work on the transmutation of atomic nuclei by artificially accelerated atomic particles.

1952 Felix Bloch and Edward Mills Purcell (American) for developing magnetic measurement methods for atomic nuclei.

1953 Frits Zernike (Dutch) for inventing the phase contrast microscope for cancer research.

1954 *Max Born (German) for research in quantum mechanics, and Walther Bothe (German) for discoveries he made with his coincidence method.

1955 *Willis E. Lamb, Jr. (American), for discoveries on the structure of the hydrogen spectrum, and Polykarp Kusch (American) for determining the magnetic moment of the electron.

1956 *John Bardeen, *Walter H. Brattain, and *William Shockley (American) for inventing the transistor.

1957 *Tsung Dao Lee and *Chen Ning Yang (American) for work disproving the law of conservation of parity.

1958 Pavel A. Cherenkov, Ilya M. Frank, and Igor Y. Tamm (Soviet) for discovering and interpreting the Cherenkov effect in studying high-energy particles.

1959 Emilio Segrè and Owen Chamberlain (American) for their work in demonstrating the existence of the antiproton.

1960 Donald A. Glaser (American) for inventing the bubble chamber to study subatomic particles.

1961 Robert Hofstadter (American) for his studies of nucleons, and *Rudolf L. Mössbauer (German) for his research on gamma rays.

1962 Lev Davidovich Landau (Soviet) for his research on liquid helium.

1963 *Eugene Paul Wigner (American) for his contributions to the understanding of atomic nuclei and the elementary particles, and *Maria Goeppert Mayer (American) and *J. Hans Jensen (German) for their work on the structure of atomic nuclei.

1964 Charles H. Townes (American) and Nikolai G. Basov and *Alexander M. Prokhorov (Soviet) for developing *masers* and *lasers.*

1965 Sin-Itiro Tomonaga (Japanese) and Julian S. Schwinger and *Richard P. Feynman (American) for basic work in quantum electrodynamics.

1966 Alfred Kastler (French) for his work on the energy levels of atoms.

1967 Hans Albrecht Bethe (American) for his contributions to the theory of nuclear reactions, especially his discoveries on the energy production in stars.

1968 Luis W. Alvarez (American) for his contributions to the knowledge of subatomic particles.

1969 *Murray Gell-Mann (American) for his discoveries concerning the classification of nuclear particles and their interactions.

1970 Hannes Olof Gösta Alfvén (Swedish) for his work in *magnetohydrodynamics*, the study of electrical and magnetic effects in fluids that conduct electricity, and Louis Eugène Félix Néel (French) for his discoveries of magnetic properties that applied to computer memories.

1971 *Dennis Gabor (British) for his work in *holography*, a method of making a three-dimensional photograph with coherent light produced by a laser.

1972 *John Bardeen, Leon N. Cooper, and John Robert Schrieffer (American) for their work on *superconductivity*, the disappearance of electrical resistance.

1973 Ivar Giaever (American), Leo Esaki (Japanese), and Brian Josephson (British) for their work on the phenomena of electron "tunneling" through semiconductor and superconductor materials.

1974 Antony Hewish (British) for his decisive role in the discovery of pulsars, and Sir Martin Ryle (British) for his use of small radio telescopes to "see" into space with great accuracy.

1975 L. James Rainwater (American) and Aage N. Bohr and Ben R. Mottelson (Danish) for their work on the structure of the atomic nucleus.

1976 Burton Richter and Samuel Chao Chung Ting (American) for their discovery of an elementary nuclear particle called the *psi,* or *J, particle.*

1977 Philip W. Anderson and John H. Van Vleck (American) and Sir Nevill F. Mott (British) for helping develop semiconductor devices.

1978 Pyotr Kapitsa (Soviet) for his research in low-temperature physics, and Arno Penzias and Robert Wilson (American) for their discovery and study of cosmic microwave background radiation.

1979 Sheldon L. Glashow and Steven Weinberg (American) and Abdus Salam (Pakistani) for developing a principle that unifies the weak nuclear force and the force of electromagnetism.

1980 James W. Cronin and Val L. Fitch (American) for their research on subatomic particles revealing that the fundamental laws of symmetry in nature could be violated.

1981 Nicolaas Bloembergen and Arthur L. Schawlow (American) for their contribution to the development of laser spectroscopy, and Kai Siegbahn (Swedish) for his contribution to the development of high-resolution electron spectroscopy.

*Has a biography in *World Book.*

Nobel Prizes in physics (continued)

1982 Kenneth G. Wilson (American) for his method of analyzing the behavior of matter when it changes form—for example, from water to steam.

1983 *Subrahmanyan Chandrasekhar and William A. Fowler (American) for work on the evolution and death of stars.

1984 Carlo Rubbia (Italian) and Simon van der Meer (Dutch) for contributions to the discovery of two subatomic particles—the *W particle* and the *Z particle.*

1985 Klaus von Klitzing (West German) for developing a precise way of measuring electrical resistance.

1986 Ernst Ruska (West German) for his invention of the electron microscope and Gerd Binning (West German) and Heinrich Rohrer (Swiss) for their invention of the scanning tunneling microscope.

1987 J. Georg Bednorz (West German) and K. Alex Müller (Swiss) for their discovery of superconductivity in a ceramic material.

1988 Leon M. Lederman, Melvin Schwartz, and Jack Steinberger (American) for their work on subatomic particles called *neutrinos.*

1989 Hans G. Dehmelt (American) and Wolfgang Paul (German) for isolating and measuring single atoms, and Norman F. Ramsey (American) for work that led to the atomic clock.

1990 Jerome Friedman and *Henry Kendall (American) and Richard Taylor (Canadian) for experiments that proved the existence of subatomic particles called *quarks.*

1991 Pierre-Gilles de Gennes (French) for his analyses of alignments and other orderly arrangements of molecules in certain substances.

1992 Georges Charpak (French) for the invention of devices that detect subatomic particles in particle accelerators.

1993 Russell A. Hulse and Joseph H. Taylor, Jr. (American) for discovering dense pairs of stars called *binary pulsars.*

1994 Clifford G. Shull (American) and Bertram N. Brockhouse (Canadian) for using neutrons to probe the atomic structure of solids.

1995 Martin Perl (American) for research on a subatomic particle called the *tau,* and Frederick Reines (American) for his discovery of a subatomic particle called the *neutrino.*

1996 David M. Lee, Robert C. Richardson, and Douglas D. Osheroff (American) for discovering that a type of helium called *helium 3* becomes a *superfluid,* a rare form of matter, at an extremely low temperature.

1997 Steven Chu and William D. Phillips (American) and Claude Cohen-Tannoudji (French) for developing a way to trap atoms with laser light.

1998 Robert B. Laughlin (American), Horst L. Störmer (German-born American), and Daniel C. Tsui (Chinese-born American) for discovering the *fractional quantum Hall effect.*

1999 Gerardus 't Hooft and Martinus J. G. Veltman (Dutch) for creating calculation methods used with the *electroweak theory,* which deals with subatomic particle behavior.

2000 Zhores I. Alferov (Russian) and Herbert Kroemer (German-born American) for developing certain layered structures that are used in electronic devices, and *Jack Kilby (American) for his part in the invention of the integrated circuit.

2001 Eric A. Cornell (American), Wolfgang Ketterle (German), and Carl E. Wieman (American) for the discovery and study of a *Bose-Einstein condensate,* a state of matter.

2002 Raymond Davis, Jr. (American) and Masatoshi Koshiba (Japanese) for their development of equipment used to detect subatomic particles known as *neutrinos* that come from outer space, and Riccardo Giacconi (Italian-born American) for work that led to the discovery of X-ray sources in outer space.

2003 Alexei A. Abrikosov (Russian-born American), Vitaly L. Ginzburg (Russian), and Anthony J. Leggett (British and American) for contributions to the theory of superconductors and superfluids.

2004 David J. Gross, H. David Politzer, and Frank A. Wilczek (American) for developing a theory to explain the force that binds quarks together.

2005 Roy J. Glauber (American) for his contribution to the study of optics in quantum theory, and John L. Hall (American) and Theodor W. Hänsch (German) for developing more precise techniques for laser spectroscopy.

2006 John C. Mather and George F. Smoot III (American) for their discoveries confirming the *big bang* theory of the early universe.

2007 Albert Fert (French) and Peter A. Grünberg (German) for discovering a phenomenon called *giant magnetoresistance,* which enabled the development of small, high-capacity computer hard drives.

2008 Yoichiro Nambu (Japanese-born American) for his explanation of broken symmetry, an important property of subatomic particles; and Makoto Kobayashi and Toshihide Maskawa (Japanese) for identifying the particles that must exist for Nambu's explanation to work.

2009 Charles K. Kao (Chinese-born British-American) for groundbreaking achievements concerning the transmission of light in fibers for optical communication, and Willard S. Boyle (Canadian-born American) and George E. Smith (American) for the invention of the charge-coupled device (CCD) sensor, an imaging semiconductor circuit.

2010 Andre Geim (Russian-born Dutch) and Konstantin Novoselov (British and Russian) for pioneering experiments regarding the two-dimensional material *graphene,* a single sheet of graphite. Graphene is an ultra-thin, extremely strong material.

Nobel Prizes in chemistry

1901 Jacobus Henricus Van't Hoff (Dutch) for discovering laws of chemical dynamics and osmotic pressure.

1902 Emil Fischer (German) for synthesizing sugars, purine derivatives, and peptides.

1903 Svante August Arrhenius (Swedish) for his dissociation theory of ionization in electrolytes.

1904 *Sir William Ramsay (British) for discovering helium, neon, xenon, and krypton, and determining their place in the periodic system.

1905 Adolf von Baeyer (German) for his work on dyes and organic compounds, and for synthesizing indigo and arsenicals.

1906 Henri Moissan (French) for preparing pure fluorine and developing the electric furnace.

1907 Eduard Buchner (German) for his biochemical researches

and for discovering cell-less fermentation.

1908 *Ernest Rutherford (New Zealand-born) for discovering that radioactive elements change into other elements.

1909 *Wilhelm Ostwald (German) for his work on catalysis, chemical equilibrium, and the rate of chemical reactions.

1910 Otto Wallach (German) for work on alicyclic substances.

1911 *Marie Curie (French) for discovering radium and polonium, isolating radium, and studying radium's compounds.

1912 François A. V. Grignard (French) for discovering the Grignard reagent to synthesize organic compounds, and Paul Sabatier (French) for his method of using nickel as a hydrogenation catalyst.

1913 Alfred Werner (Swiss) for his coordination theory on the arrangement of atoms.

*Has a biography in *World Book.*

Nobel Prizes in chemistry (continued)

1914 Theodore W. Richards (American) for determining the atomic weights of many elements.

1915 Richard Willstätter (German) for his research on chlorophyll and other coloring matter in plants.

1916-1917 No award

1918 Fritz Haber (German) for the Haber-Bosch process of synthesizing ammonia from nitrogen and hydrogen.

1919 No award

1920 Walther Nernst (German) for his discoveries concerning heat changes in chemical reactions.

1921 *Frederick Soddy (British) for studying radioactive substances and isotopes.

1922 Francis W. Aston (British) for finding many isotopes by means of the mass spectrograph and for discovering the whole number rule on the structure and weight of atoms.

1923 Fritz Pregl (Austrian) for inventing a method of microanalyzing organic substances.

1924 No award

1925 Richard Zsigmondy (Austrian) for his method of studying colloids.

1926 Theodor Svedberg (Swedish) for his work on dispersions and on colloid chemistry.

1927 Heinrich O. Wieland (German) for studying gall acids and related substances.

1928 Adolf Windaus (German) for studying sterols and their connection with vitamins.

1929 Sir Arthur Harden (British) and Hans August Simon von Euler-Chelpin (German) for their research on sugar fermentation and enzymes.

1930 Hans Fischer (German) for studying the coloring matter of blood and leaves and synthesizing hemin.

1931 Carl Bosch and Friedrich Bergius (German) for inventing high-pressure methods of manufacturing ammonia and liquefying coal.

1932 Irving Langmuir (American) for his discoveries about molecular films absorbed on surfaces.

1933 No award

1934 *Harold Clayton Urey (American) for discovering deuterium (heavy hydrogen).

1935 Frédéric and *Irène Joliot-Curie (French) for synthesizing new radioactive elements.

1936 Peter J. W. Debye (Dutch) for his studies on dipole moments, the diffraction of electrons, and X rays in gases.

1937 Sir Walter N. Haworth (British) for his research on carbohydrates and vitamin C, and Paul Karrer (Swiss) for studying carotenoids, flavins, and vitamins A and B_2.

1938 Richard Kuhn (German) for his work on carotenoids and vitamins (declined).

1939 Adolph Butenandt (German) for studying sex hormones (declined), and Leopold Ružička (Swiss) for his work on polymethylenes.

1940-1942 No award

1943 Georg von Hevesy (Hungarian) for using isotopes as indicators in chemistry.

1944 *Otto Hahn (German) for his discoveries in fission.

1945 Artturi Virtanen (Finnish) for inventing new methods of agricultural biochemistry.

1946 James B. Sumner (American) for discovering that enzymes can be crystallized, and Wendell M. Stanley and *John H. Northrop (American) for preparing pure enzymes and virus proteins.

1947 Sir Robert Robinson (British) for his research on biologically significant plant substances.

1948 Arne Tiselius (Swedish) for his discoveries on the nature of the serum proteins.

1949 William Francis Giauque (American) for studying reactions to extreme cold.

1950 Otto Diels and Kurt Alder (German) for developing a method of synthesizing organic compounds of the diene group.

1951 Edwin M. McMillan and *Glenn T. Seaborg (American) for their work in discovering plutonium and other elements.

1952 Archer J. P. Martin and Richard Synge (British) for developing the partition chromatography process, a method of separating compounds.

1953 Hermann Staudinger (German) for discovering a way to synthesize fiber.

1954 *Linus Pauling (American) for his work on the forces that hold matter together.

1955 Vincent Du Vigneaud (American) for discovering a process for making synthetic hormones.

1956 Sir Cyril Hinshelwood (British) and Nikolai N. Semenov (Soviet) for their work on chemical chain reactions.

1957 Lord Todd (British) for his work on the protein composition of cells.

1958 *Frederick Sanger (British) for discovering the structure of the insulin molecule.

1959 Jaroslav Heyrovský (Czech) for developing the polarographic method of analysis.

1960 *Willard F. Libby (American) for developing a method of radiocarbon dating.

1961 Melvin Calvin (American) for his research on photosynthesis.

1962 *Sir John Cowdery Kendrew and Max Ferdinand Perutz (British) for their studies on globular proteins.

1963 Giulio Natta (Italian) for his contributions to the understanding of polymers, and Karl Ziegler (German) for his production of *organometallic compounds,* which consist of organic compounds and metal atoms. Their work resulted in improved plastics.

1964 *Dorothy C. Hodgkin (British) for X-ray studies of such compounds as vitamin B_{12} and penicillin.

1965 Robert Burns Woodward (American) for his contributions to organic synthesis.

1966 *Robert S. Mulliken (American) for developing the molecular-orbital theory of chemical structure.

1967 Manfred Eigen (German) and Ronald G. W. Norrish and George Porter (British) for developing techniques to measure rapid chemical reactions.

1968 Lars Onsager (American) for developing the theory of reciprocal relations of various thermodynamic activities.

1969 Derek H. R. Barton (British) and Odd Hassel (Norwegian) for studies relating chemical reactions with the three-dimensional shape of molecules.

1970 Luis Federico Leloir (Argentine) for his discovery of chemical compounds that affect the storage of chemical energy in living things.

1971 Gerhard Herzberg (Canadian) for his research in the structure of molecules, particularly for his work on molecular fragments called *free radicals.*

1972 Christian B. Anfinsen, Stanford Moore, and William H. Stein (American) for fundamental contributions to the chemistry of *enzymes,* basic substances of living things.

1973 Geoffrey Wilkinson (British) and Ernst Fischer (German) for their work on organometallic compounds.

1974 Paul John Flory (American) for work in polymer chemistry.

1975 John Warcup Cornforth (Australian-born) and Vladimir Prelog (Swiss) for their work on the chemical synthesis of important organic compounds.

1976 William N. Lipscomb, Jr. (American), for his studies on the structure and bonding mechanisms of *boranes,* complex compounds of boron and hydrogen.

*Has a biography in *World Book.*

Nobel Prizes in chemistry (continued)

1977 Ilya Prigogine (Belgian) for his contributions to non-equilibrium thermodynamics.

1978 Peter Mitchell (British) for his studies of cellular energy transfer.

1979 Herbert C. Brown (American) and Georg Wittig (German) for developing compounds capable of producing chemical bonds useful in the manufacture of drugs and in other industrial processes.

1980 Paul Berg and Walter Gilbert (American) and *Frederick Sanger (British) for their studies of the chemical structure of nucleic acids.

1981 Kenichi Fukui (Japanese) and Roald Hoffmann (American) for applying the theories of quantum mechanics to predict the course of chemical reactions.

1982 Aaron Klug (British) for his work with the electron microscope and for his research into the structure of nucleic acid-protein complexes.

1983 Henry Taube (American) for his research on the transfer of electrons between molecules in chemical reactions.

1984 R. Bruce Merrifield (American) for developing a rapid, automated method for making *peptides,* the building blocks of proteins.

1985 Herbert A. Hauptman and Jerome Karle (American) for developing techniques for quickly determining the chemical structure of molecules vital to life.

1986 Dudley R. Herschbach and Yuan T. Lee (American) and John C. Polanyi (Canadian) for their pioneering research on basic chemical reactions.

1987 Jean-Marie Lehn (French) and Donald J. Cram and Charles J. Pedersen (American) for their development of, and work with, artificial molecules that function like natural organic molecules.

1988 Johann Deisenhofer, Robert Huber, and Hartmut Michel (West German) for revealing the structure of proteins that are essential to photosynthesis.

1989 Sidney Altman and Thomas R. Cech (American) for their discovery that ribonucleic acid (RNA) is able to assist chemical reactions in cells.

1990 Elias James Corey (American) for developing techniques for artificially duplicating such natural substances as compounds that can be used as drugs.

1991 Richard R. Ernst (Swiss) for improvements in the use of nuclear magnetic resonance (NMR) to analyze chemicals.

1992 Rudolph A. Marcus (American) for analyzing the transfer of electrons between molecules.

1993 Kary B. Mullis (American) for his method of copying genetic material, and Michael Smith (Canadian) for his method of altering DNA molecules.

1994 George A. Olah (Hungarian-born) for discovering ways to break up hydrocarbon molecules and stabilize the resulting parts.

1995 Mario Molina and F. Sherwood Rowland (American) and Paul Crutzen (Dutch) for work leading to the discovery of a "hole" in Earth's protective layer of ozone.

1996 Richard E. Smalley and Robert F. Curl, Jr. (American), and Sir Harold W. Kroto (British) for discovering carbon molecules called *fullerenes.*

1997 Paul D. Boyer (American), Jens C. Skou (Danish), and John E. Walker (British) for discoveries about adenosine triphosphate (ATP), a molecule living things use to store energy.

1998 Walter Kohn (Austrian-born American) for his mathematical analysis of chemical bonds, and John A. Pople (British) for new techniques for determining molecular structure.

1999 Ahmed H. Zewail (Egyptian-born American) for his work in detecting the individual steps of chemical reactions.

2000 Alan J. Heeger (American), Alan G. MacDiarmid (New Zealand-born American), and Hideki Shirakawa (Japanese) for the discovery and development of polymers that can conduct electric current.

2001 William S. Knowles (American), Ryoji Noyori (Japanese), and K. Barry Sharpless (American) for their development of molecules that are used to produce a number of drugs.

2002 John B. Fenn (American), Koichi Tanaka (Japanese), and Kurt Wüthrich (Swiss) for the development of methods used to identify and analyze the structure of proteins and other large molecules that are parts of living things.

2003 Peter Agre and Roderick MacKinnon (American) for discoveries concerning channels in cell membranes.

2004 Aaron Ciechanover and Avram Hershko (Israeli) and Irwin Rose (American) for discovering a process living cells use to destroy unwanted proteins.

2005 Yves Chauvin (French), Robert H. Grubbs (American), and Richard R. Schrock (American) for their development of the *metathesis method,* a technique used in the manufacture of organic chemicals.

2006 Roger D. Kornberg (American) for his description of how cells use information from genes to make proteins.

2007 Gerhard Ertl (German) for his studies of chemical processes on solid surfaces.

2008 Osamu Shimomura (Japanese-born American) and Martin Chalfie and Roger Y. Tsien (American) for the discovery and development of the green fluorescent protein, an important tool used in bioscience, first observed in jellyfish.

2009 Venkatraman Ramakrishnan (Indian-born American), Thomas A. Steitz (American), and Ada E. Yonath (Israeli) for studies of the structure and function of the *ribosome,* a protein-making cell structure.

2010 Richard F. Heck (American), Ei-ichi Negishi (Japanese), and Akira Suzuki (Japanese) for developing techniques to synthesize complex carbon molecules, including medicines.

Nobel Prizes in physiology or medicine

1901 Emil von Behring (German) for discovering the diphtheria antitoxin.

1902 Sir Ronald Ross (British) for working on malaria and discovering how malaria is transmitted.

1903 Niels Ryberg Finsen (Danish) for treating diseases, especially *lupus vulgaris,* with concentrated light rays.

1904 *Ivan Petrovich Pavlov (Russian) for his work on the physiology of digestion.

1905 *Robert Koch (German) for working on tuberculosis and discovering the tubercule bacillus and tuberculin.

1906 *Camillo Golgi (Italian) and Santiago Ramon y Cajal (Spanish) for their studies of nerve tissue.

1907 *Charles Louis Alphonse Laveran (French) for studying diseases caused by protozoans.

1908 *Paul Ehrlich (German) and *Élie Metchnikoff (Russian) for their work on immunity.

1909 Emil Theodor Kocher (Swiss) for his work on the physiology, pathology, and surgery of the thyroid gland.

1910 Albrecht Kossel (German) for studying cell chemistry, proteins, and nucleic substances.

1911 Allvar Gullstrand (Swedish) for his work on dioptrics, the refraction of light through the eye.

1912 Alexis Carrel (French) for suturing blood vessels and grafting vessels and organs.

1913 Charles Robert Richet (French) for studying allergies caused by foreign substances, as in hay fever.

1914 Robert Bárány (Austrian) for work on function and diseases of equilibrium organs in the inner ear.

*Has a biography in *World Book.*

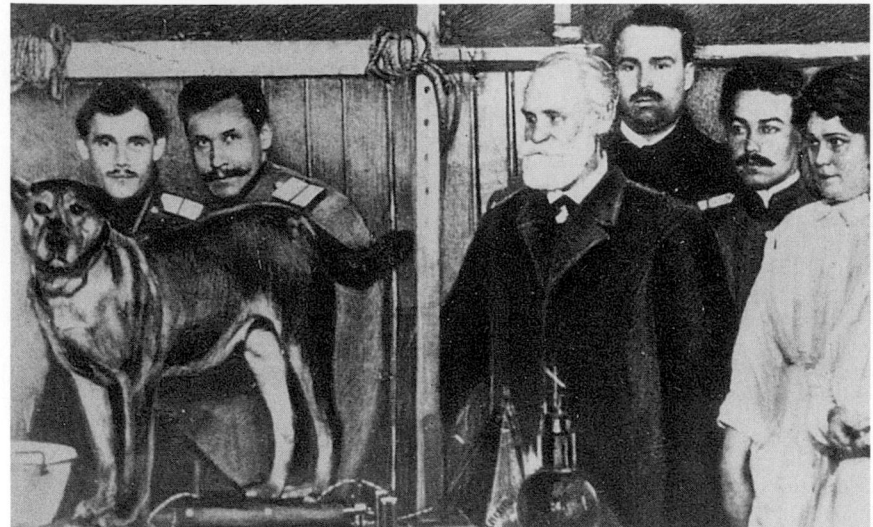

Ivan Petrovich Pavlov,
a Russian physiologist,
won the 1904 prize in
physiology or medicine.
Pavlov and his staff experimented with dogs to learn
how nerves affect the
process of digestion.

Bettmann Archive

Nobel Prizes in physiology or medicine (continued)

1915-1918 No award

1919 Jules Bordet (Belgian) for discoveries on immunity.

1920 August Krogh (Danish) for discovering the system of action of blood capillaries.

1921 No award

1922 Archibald V. Hill (British) for his discovery on heat production in the muscles, and Otto Meyerhof (German) for his theory on the production of lactic acid in the muscles.

1923 *Sir Frederick G. Banting (Canadian) and John J. R. Macleod (Scottish) for discovering insulin.

1924 *Willem Einthoven (Dutch) for his discovery of the way in which electrocardiography works.

1925 No award

1926 Johannes Fibiger (Danish) for discovering a parasite that causes cancer.

1927 Julius Wagner von Jauregg (Austrian) for discovering the fever treatment for paralysis.

1928 Charles Nicolle (French) for his work on typhus.

1929 Christiaan Eijkman (Dutch) for discovering vitamins that prevent beriberi, and Sir Frederick Hopkins (British) for finding vitamins that aid growth.

1930 *Karl Landsteiner (American) for discovering the four main human blood types.

1931 Otto H. Warburg (German) for discovering that enzymes aid in respiration by tissues.

1932 Edgar D. Adrian and Sir Charles S. Sherrington (British) for their discoveries on the function of neurons.

1933 *Thomas H. Morgan (American) for studying the function of chromosomes in heredity.

1934 George R. Minot, William P. Murphy, and George H. Whipple (American) for their discoveries on liver treatment for anemia.

1935 Hans Spemann (German) for discovering the organizer effect in the growth of an embryo.

1936 Sir Henry H. Dale (British) and Otto Loewi (German-born) for their discoveries on the chemical transmission of nerve impulses.

1937 *Albert Szent-Györgyi (Hungarian) for his discoveries in connection with oxidation in tissues, vitamin C, and fumaric acid.

1938 Corneille Heymans (Belgian) for his discoveries concerning the regulation of respiration.

1939 *Gerhard Domagk (German) for discovering Prontosil, the first sulfa drug (declined).

1940-1942 No award

1943 Henrik Dam (Danish) for discovering vitamin K, and Edward Doisy (American) for synthesizing it.

1944 Joseph Erlanger and Herbert Gasser (American) for their work on single nerve fibers.

1945 *Alexander Fleming (British) for discovering penicillin, and *Howard W. Florey and *Ernst B. Chain (British) for developing its use as an antibiotic.

1946 Hermann Joseph Muller (American) for discovering that X rays can produce mutations.

1947 Carl F. and Gerty Cori (American) for their work on insulin, and Bernardo Houssay (Argentine) for studying the pancreas and the pituitary gland.

1948 Paul H. Müller (Swiss) for discovering the insect-killing properties of DDT.

1949 Walter R. Hess (Swiss) for discovering how certain parts of the brain control organs of the body, and António Egas Moniz (Portuguese) for originating prefrontal lobotomy.

1950 Philip S. Hench and Edward C. Kendall (American) and Tadeus Reichstein (Swiss) for discoveries on cortisone and ACTH.

1951 Max Theiler (South African who worked in the United States) for developing the yellow fever vaccine 17-D.

1952 *Selman A. Waksman (American) for his work in the discovery of streptomycin.

1953 *Fritz Albert Lipmann (American) and *Hans Adolf Krebs (British) for discoveries in biosynthesis and metabolism.

1954 *John F. Enders, Thomas H. Weller, and Frederick C. Robbins (American) for discovering a simple method of growing polio virus in test tubes.

1955 Hugo Theorell (Swedish) for his discoveries on the nature and action of oxidation enzymes.

1956 André F. Cournand, Dickinson W. Richards (American), and Werner Forssmann (German) for using a catheter to chart the interior of the heart.

1957 Daniel Bovet (Italian) for discovering antihistamines.

1958 *George Wells Beadle and Edward Lawrie Tatum (American) for their work in biochemical genetics, and *Joshua Lederberg (American) for his studies of genetics in bacteria.

*Has a biography in *World Book*.

Nobel Prizes in physiology or medicine (continued)

1959 Severo Ochoa and Arthur Kornberg (American) for producing nucleic acid by artificial means.

1960 *Sir Macfarlane Burnet (Australian) and Peter B. Medawar (British) for research in transplanting human organs.

1961 Georg von Békésy (American) for demonstrating how the ear distinguishes among various sounds.

1962 *James D. Watson (American) and *Francis H. C. Crick and *Maurice H. F. Wilkins (British) for work on nucleic acid.

1963 Sir John Carew Eccles (Australian) for his research on the transmission of nerve impulses, and Alan Lloyd Hodgkin (British) and Andrew Fielding Huxley (British) for their description of the behavior of nerve impulses.

1964 *Konrad E. Bloch (American) and *Feodor Lynen (German) for their work on cholesterol and fatty acid metabolism.

1965 François Jacob, André Lwoff, and Jacques Monod (French) for their discoveries concerning genetic control of enzyme and virus synthesis.

1966 *Francis Peyton Rous (American) for discovering a cancer-producing virus, and Charles B. Huggins (American) for discovering uses of hormones in treating cancer.

1967 Ragnar Granit (Swedish) and H. Keffer Hartline and *George Wald (American) for their findings about chemical and physiological processes that take place in the eye.

1968 Robert W. Holley, H. Gobind Khorana, and Marshall W. Nirenberg (American) for explaining how genes determine the function of cells.

1969 Max Delbrück, Alfred Hershey, and Salvador Luria (American) for their work with *bacteriophages* (viruses that attack bacteria).

1970 Julius Axelrod (American), Bernard Katz (British), and Ulf Svante von Euler (Swedish) for their discoveries of the role played by certain chemicals in the transmission of nerve impulses.

1971 Earl W. Sutherland, Jr. (American) for his discovery of the ways hormones act, including the discovery of cyclic AMP, a chemical that influences the actions of hormones on body processes.

1972 Gerald M. Edelman (American) and Rodney R. Porter (British) for their discovery of the chemical structure of antibodies.

1973 *Nikolaas Tinbergen (Dutch-born) and *Konrad Z. Lorenz and *Karl von Frisch (Austrian) for their studies on animal behavior.

1974 Christian de Duve (Belgian) and Albert Claude and George E. Palade (American) for their pioneer work in cell biology.

1975 David Baltimore, Renato Dulbecco, and Howard M. Temin (American) for their research on how certain viruses affect the genes of cancer cells.

1976 Baruch S. Blumberg and D. Carleton Gajdusek (American) for their discoveries concerning the origin and spread of infectious diseases.

1977 Roger Guillemin, Andrew Schally, and Rosalyn Yalow (American) for their research concerning the role of hormones in the chemistry of the body.

1978 Werner Arber (Swiss) and Daniel Nathans and Hamilton O. Smith (American) for discoveries in molecular genetics.

1979 Allan MacLeod Cormack (American) and Godfrey N. Hounsfield (British) for their contributions to development of the computerized tomographic (CT) scanner.

1980 Baruj Benacerraf and George D. Snell (American) and Jean Dausset (French) for their discoveries concerning the genetic regulation of the body's immune system.

1981 Roger W. Sperry and David H. Hubel (American) and Torsten N. Wiesel (Swedish) for their research on the organization and functioning of the brain.

1982 Sune K. Bergstrom and Bengt I. Samuelsson (Swedish) and John R. Vane (British) for their discoveries regarding prostaglandins and related substances.

1983 *Barbara McClintock (American) for her discovery that genes sometimes behave unexpectedly inside cells.

1984 Niels K. Jerne (British-born), Georges J. F. Köhler (German), and Cesar Milstein (Argentine) for their discoveries in immunology.

1985 Michael S. Brown and Joseph L. Goldstein (American) for explaining how high cholesterol causes heart disease.

1986 Stanley Cohen (American) and Rita Levi-Montalcini (Italian-born) for their research on cell and organ growth.

1987 Susumu Tonegawa (Japanese) for his discoveries on how genes change to produce antibodies against specific disease agents.

1988 *Gertrude B. Elion and George H. Hitchings (American) and Sir James Black (British) for their discoveries of important principles for drug treatment.

1989 J. Michael Bishop and Harold E. Varmus (American) for their research on cancer-causing genes called *oncogenes*.

1990 Joseph E. Murray and E. Donnall Thomas (American) for their work in transplanting human organs and bone marrow.

1991 Erwin Neher and Bert Sakmann (German) for discovering how cells communicate with one another.

1992 Edmond Fischer and Edwin Krebs (American) for discovering a chemical process in cells that is linked to cancer and to rejection of transplanted organs.

1993 Richard J. Roberts (British-born) and Phillip A. Sharp (American) for their discoveries regarding the structure and function of genes.

1994 Alfred G. Gilman and Martin Rodbell (American) for their research into signaling mechanisms in cells.

1995 Edward B. Lewis and Eric Wieschaus (American) and Christiane Nüsslein-Volhard (German) for their studies of how genes control early embryo development.

1996 Peter C. Doherty (Australian) and Rolf M. Zinkernagel (Swiss) for discovering the signals that alert white blood cells to kill virus-infected cells.

1997 Stanley B. Prusiner (American) for his discovery of prions, a new type of infectious particle that appears to consist only of protein.

1998 Robert F. Furchgott, Louis J. Ignarro, and Ferid Murad (American) for their discovery that the gas nitric oxide acts as an important signal molecule in the heart and blood vessels.

1999 Günter Blobel (German-born) for his discoveries on the movement of proteins within the cells of living organisms.

2000 Arvid Carlsson (Swedish) and Paul Greengard and Eric Kandel (American) for their research on the transmission of impulses between nerve cells.

2001 Leland H. Hartwell (American) and Timothy Hunt and Sir Paul Nurse (British) for their discoveries regarding genetic control of cell division in living organisms.

2002 Sydney Brenner and John E. Sulston (British) and H. Robert Horvitz (American) for their discoveries on the development, growth, and death of cells in organisms.

2003 Paul Christian Lauterbur (American) and Sir Peter Mansfield (British) for their contributions to the development of magnetic resonance imaging (MRI).

2004 Richard Axel and Linda B. Buck (American) for discovering odor receptors and the organization of smell in animals.

2005 Barry J. Marshall and J. Robin Warren (Australian) for their discovery of the bacterium *Helicobacter pylori* and its role in gastritis and peptic ulcer disease.

*Has a biography in *World Book.*

Nobel Prizes in physiology or medicine (continued)

2006 Andrew Z. Fire and Craig C. Mello (American) for their discovery of RNA interference, a mechanism for controlling the action of genes.

2007 Mario R. Capecchi and Oliver Smithies (American) and Sir Martin John Evans (British) for discoveries that led to a technique used to modify genes in mice.

2008 Françoise Barré-Sinoussi and Luc Montagnier (French) and Harald zur Hausen (German) for their discoveries of the viruses that cause AIDS and cervical cancer.

2009 Elizabeth H. Blackburn (Australian-born American), Carol W. Greider (American), and Jack W. Szostak (American) for their discovery of how chromosomes are protected by *telomeres,* structures that form the ends of chromosomes, and *telomerase,* the enzyme that replenishes the telomere.

2010 Robert G. Edwards (British) for the development of *in vitro fertilization,* the combining of an egg cell with a sperm cell in a laboratory to produce an embryo.

Nobel Prizes in literature

1901 Sully Prudhomme (French) for his poems.

1902 Theodor Mommsen (German) for his historical narratives, particularly his history of Rome.

1903 Bjørnstjerne Bjørnson (Norwegian) for his novels, poems, and dramas.

1904 *Frédéric Mistral (French) for his poems, and José Echegaray y Eizaguirre (Spanish) for his dramas.

1905 *Henryk Sienkiewicz (Polish) for his novels.

1906 *Giosuè Carducci (Italian) for his poems.

1907 *Rudyard Kipling (British) for his stories, novels, and poems.

1908 Rudolf Eucken (German) for his philosophic writings.

1909 *Selma Lagerlöf (Swedish) for her novels and poems.

1910 Paul von Heyse (German) for his poems, novels, and dramas.

1911 *Maurice Maeterlinck (Belgian) for his dramas.

1912 *Gerhart Hauptmann (German) for his dramas.

1913 *Rabindranath Tagore (Indian) for his poems.

1914 No award

1915 *Romain Rolland (French) for his novels.

1916 Verner von Heidenstam (Swedish) for his poems.

1917 Karl Gjellerup (Danish) for his poems and novels, and Henrik Pontoppidan (Danish) for his novels and short stories.

1918 No award

1919 Carl Spitteler (Swiss) for his epics, stories, and essays.

1920 *Knut Hamsun (Norwegian) for his novels.

1921 *Anatole France (French) for his novels, short stories, and essays.

1922 Jacinto Benavente (Spanish) for his dramas.

1923 *William Butler Yeats (Irish) for his poems.

1924 Władysław S. Reymont (Polish) for his novels.

1925 *George Bernard Shaw (Irish-born) for his plays.

1926 Grazia Deledda (Italian) for her novels.

1927 *Henri Bergson (French) for his philosophic writings.

1928 *Sigrid Undset (Norwegian) for her novels.

1929 *Thomas Mann (German) principally for his novel *Buddenbrooks.*

1930 *Sinclair Lewis (American) for his novels.

1931 Erik Axel Karlfeldt (Swedish) for his lyric poetry.

1932 *John Galsworthy (British) for his novels, plays, and short stories.

1933 *Ivan Bunin (Soviet) for his novels, short stories, and poems.

1934 *Luigi Pirandello (Italian) for his dramas.

1935 No award

1936 *Eugene O'Neill (American) for his dramas.

1937 Roger Martin du Gard (French) for his novels.

1938 *Pearl S. Buck (American) for her novels.

1939 Frans Eemil Sillanpää (Finnish) for his novels.

1940-1943 No award

1944 Johannes V. Jensen (Danish) for his poems and novels.

1945 *Gabriela Mistral (Chilean) for her poems.

1946 *Hermann Hesse (German) for his novels, poems, and essays.

1947 *André Gide (French) for his novels.

1948 *T. S. Eliot (British) for his poems, essays, and plays.

1949 *William Faulkner (American) for his novels. (Award delayed until 1950.)

1950 *Bertrand Russell (British) for his philosophic writings.

1951 *Pär Fabian Lagerkvist (Swedish) for his novels, particularly *Barabbas.*

1952 *François Mauriac (French) for his novels, essays, and poems.

1953 *Sir Winston Churchill (British) for his essays, speeches, and historical writings.

1954 *Ernest Hemingway (American) for his novels and short stories.

1955 Halldór K. Laxness (Icelandic) for his novels.

1956 *Juan Ramón Jiménez (Spanish) for his poems.

1957 *Albert Camus (French) for his novels.

1958 *Boris Pasternak (Soviet) for his novels, especially *Dr. Zhivago* (declined).

1959 Salvatore Quasimodo (Italian) for his lyric poems.

1960 *Saint-John Perse (French) for his poems.

1961 Ivo Andrić (Yugoslav) for his novels, especially *The Bridge on the Drina.*

1962 *John Steinbeck (American) for his novels, especially *The Winter of Our Discontent.*

1963 George Seferis (Greek) for his lyric poetry.

1964 *Jean-Paul Sartre (French) for his philosophical works (declined).

1965 *Mikhail Sholokhov (Soviet) for his novels.

1966 *Shmuel Yosef Agnon (Israeli) for his stories of Eastern European Jewish life, and *Nelly Sachs (German-born) for her poetry and plays about the Jewish people.

1967 *Miguel Angel Asturias (Guatemalan) for his writings rooted in national individuality and Indian traditions.

1968 Yasunari Kawabata (Japanese) for his novels.

1969 *Samuel B. Beckett (Irish-born) for his novels and plays.

1970 *Alexander Solzhenitsyn (Soviet) for his novels.

1971 *Pablo Neruda (Chilean) for his poems.

1972 *Heinrich Böll (German) for his novels, short stories, and plays.

1973 *Patrick White (Australian) for his novels.

1974 Eyvind Johnson (Swedish) for his novels and short stories, and Harry Edmund Martinson (Swedish) for his essays, plays, novels, and poems.

1975 *Eugenio Montale (Italian) for his poems.

1976 *Saul Bellow (American) for his novels.

1977 *Vicente Aleixandre (Spanish) for his poems.

*Has a biography in *World Book.*

Nobel Prizes in literature (continued)

1978 *Isaac Bashevis Singer (Polish-born) for his novels and short stories.

1979 Odysseus Elytis (Greek) for his poems.

1980 Czesław Miłosz (Polish-born) for his poems.

1981 Elias Canetti (Bulgarian-born) for his fiction and nonfiction.

1982 *Gabriel García Márquez (Colombian) for his novels and short stories.

1983 *William Golding (British) for his novels.

1984 Jaroslav Seifert (Czech) for his poems.

1985 Claude Simon (French) for his novels.

1986 *Wole Soyinka (Nigerian) for his plays, poems, and novels.

1987 *Joseph Brodsky (Soviet-born) for his poems.

1988 *Naguib Mahfouz (Egyptian) for his novels and short stories.

1989 Camilo José Cela (Spanish) for his novels.

1990 *Octavio Paz (Mexican) for his poems and essays.

1991 *Nadine Gordimer (South African) for her novels and short stories.

1992 *Derek Walcott (St. Lucian-born) for his poetry.

1993 *Toni Morrison (American) for her novels.

1994 *Kenzaburo Oe (Japanese) for his novels.

1995 *Seamus Heaney (Irish) for his poetry.

1996 *Wisława Szymborska (Poland) for her poetry.

1997 Dario Fo (Italian) for his plays.

1998 José Saramago (Portugal) for his novels.

1999 *Günter Grass (German) for his novels.

2000 Gao Xingjian (Chinese) for his plays, novels, and essays.

2001 *V. S. Naipaul (West Indian-born) for his novels.

2002 Imre Kertész (Hungarian) for his novels.

2003 *J. M. Coetzee (South African) for his novels.

2004 Elfriede Jelinek (Austrian) for her novels and plays.

2005 *Harold Pinter (British) for his plays.

2006 Orhan Pamuk (Turkish) for his novels.

2007 *Doris Lessing (British) for her novels.

2008 J.-M. G. Le Clézio (French) for his novels, essays, and stories.

2009 Herta Müller (Romanian-born German) for her novels, essays, and poetry.

2010 *Mario Vargas Llosa (Peruvian) for his novels.

Nobel Peace Prizes

1901 *Jean Henri Dunant (Swiss) for founding the Red Cross and originating the Geneva Convention, and Frédéric Passy (French) for founding a French peace society.

1902 Élie Ducommun (Swiss) for his work as honorary secretary of the International Peace Bureau, and Charles Albert Gobat (Swiss) for his work as administrator of the Inter-Parliamentary Union.

1903 Sir William Cremer (British) for his activities as founder and secretary of the International Arbitration League.

1904 The Institute of International Law for its studies on the laws of neutrality and other phases of international law.

1905 Baroness Bertha von Suttner (Austrian) for promoting pacifism and founding an Austrian peace society.

1906 *Theodore Roosevelt (American) for negotiating peace in the Russo-Japanese War.

1907 Ernesto T. Moneta (Italian) for his work as president of the Lombard League for Peace, and Louis Renault (French) for organizing international conferences and representing France at two peace conferences.

1908 Klas Pontus Arnoldson (Swedish) for founding the Swedish Society for Arbitration and Peace, and Fredrik Bajer (Danish) for his work on the International Peace Bureau.

1909 Auguste M. F. Beernaert (Belgian) for his work on the Permanent Court of Arbitration, and Paul d'Estournelles (French) for founding and directing the French Parliamentary Arbitration Committee and League of International Conciliation.

1910 The International Peace Bureau for promoting international arbitration and organizing peace conferences.

1911 Tobias M. C. Asser (Dutch) for organizing conferences on international law, and Alfred H. Fried (Austrian) for his writings on peace as editor of *Die Friedenswarte*.

1912 *Elihu Root (American) for settling the problem of Japanese immigration to California and organizing the Central American Peace Conference.

1913 Henri Lafontaine (Belgian) for his work as president of the International Peace Bureau.

1914-1916 No award

1917 The International Committee of the Red Cross for doing relief work during World War I.

1918 No award

1919 *Woodrow Wilson (American) for attempting a just settlement of World War I and advocating the League of Nations. (Award delayed until 1920.)

1920 Léon Bourgeois (French) for his contribution as president of the Council of the League of Nations.

1921 Karl Hjalmar Branting (Swedish) for promoting social reforms in Sweden and serving as the Swedish delegate to the League of Nations, and Christian Lous Lange (Norwegian) for his contribution as secretary-general of the Inter-Parliamentary Union.

1922 *Fridtjof Nansen (Norwegian) for doing relief work among Russian prisoners of war and in famine areas in Russia.

Hull House Association

Jane Addams, an American social worker, shared the 1931 peace prize for her work with an international peace group.

*Has a biography in *World Book*.

Nobel Peace Prizes (continued)

1923-1924 No award

1925 Sir Austen Chamberlain (British) for helping work out the Locarno Peace Pact, and *Charles G. Dawes (American) for originating a plan for payment of German reparations.

1926 *Aristide Briand (French) for his part in forming the Locarno Peace Pact, and Gustav Stresemann (German) for persuading Germany to accept plans for reparations.

1927 Ferdinand Buisson (French) for his contribution as president of the League of Human Rights, and Ludwig Quidde (German) for his writings on peace and his work in international peace congresses.

1928 No award

1929 Frank Billings Kellogg (American) for negotiating the Kellogg-Briand Peace Pact.

1930 Nathan Söderblom (Swedish) for writing on and working for peace.

1931 *Jane Addams (American) for her work with the Women's International League for Peace and Freedom, and Nicholas M. Butler (American) for his work with the Carnegie Endowment for International Peace.

1932 No award

1933 Sir Norman Angell (British) for his work with the Royal Institute of International Affairs, the League of Nations, and the National Peace Council.

1934 Arthur Henderson (British) for his contribution as president of the World Disarmament Conference.

1935 Carl von Ossietzky (German) for promoting world disarmament. (Award delayed until 1936.)

1936 Carlos Saavedra Lamas (Argentine) for negotiating a peace settlement between Bolivia and Paraguay in the Chaco War.

1937 Edgar Algernon Robert Gascoyne Cecil (British) for promoting the League of Nations and working with peace movements.

1938 The Nansen International Office for Refugees for directing relief work among refugees.

1939-1943 No award

1944 The International Committee of the Red Cross for doing relief work during World War II.

1945 *Cordell Hull (American) for his peace efforts as secretary of state.

1946 John R. Mott (American) for his YMCA work and for aiding displaced persons, and Emily Greene Balch (American) for her work with the Women's International League for Peace and Freedom.

1947 The Friends Service Council and the American Friends Service Committee for humanitarian work.

1948 No award

1949 John Boyd Orr (British) for directing the United Nations Food and Agriculture Organization.

1950 *Ralph J. Bunche (American) for his work as UN mediator in Palestine in 1948 and 1949.

1951 Léon Jouhaux (French) for his work helping to organize national and international labor unions.

1952 *Albert Schweitzer (German-born) for his humanitarian work in Africa. (Award delayed until 1953.)

1953 *George C. Marshall (American) for promoting peace through the European Recovery Program.

1954 Office of the United Nations High Commissioner for Refugees for providing protection for millions of refugees and seeking permanent solutions to their problems.

1955-1956 No award

1957 *Lester B. Pearson (Canadian) for organizing a United Nations force in Egypt.

1958 Dominique Georges Pire (Belgian) for his work in resettling displaced persons.

*Has a biography in *World Book*.

United Press Int.

Albert Schweitzer won the 1952 Nobel Peace Prize. He devoted most of his life to humanitarian work in Africa.

1959 Philip Noel-Baker (British) for his work in promoting peace and disarmament.

1960 *Albert John Luthuli (South African) for his peaceful campaign against racial restrictions in South Africa.

1961 *Dag Hammarskjöld (Swedish) for his efforts to bring peace to the Congo (awarded posthumously).

1962 *Linus Pauling (American) for efforts to ban nuclear weapons and nuclear testing.

1963 International Committee of the Red Cross and League of Red Cross Societies for humanitarian work.

Karsh, Ottawa, from Pix

Lester B. Pearson was the first Canadian to win the peace prize. He won the 1957 award for his work in the United Nations.

Nobel Peace Prizes (continued)

Wide World

Martin Luther King, Jr., won the 1964 peace prize for leading nonviolent civil rights demonstrations in the United States.

1964 *Martin Luther King, Jr. (American) for leading the black struggle for equality in the United States through nonviolent means.

1965 United Nations Children's Fund for its aid to children.

1966-1967 No award

1968 René Cassin (French) for promoting human rights.

1969 International Labour Organization (ILO) for its efforts to improve working conditions.

1970 *Norman E. Borlaug (American) for his role in developing high-yield grains that increased food production in developing countries.

1971 *Willy Brandt (German) for his efforts to improve relations between Communist and non-Communist nations.

1972 No award

1973 *Henry A. Kissinger (American) and Le Duc Tho (North Vietnamese) for their work in negotiating the Vietnam War cease-fire agreement (Le Duc Tho declined).

1974 Sean MacBride (Irish) for working to guarantee human rights through international law, and Eisaku Sato (Japanese) for his efforts to improve international relations and stop the spread of nuclear weapons.

1975 *Andrei D. Sakharov (Soviet) for his work in promoting peace and opposing violence and brutality.

1976 Mairead Corrigan and Betty Williams (Irish) for organizing a movement to end Protestant-Catholic fighting in Northern Ireland. (Award delayed until 1977.)

1977 Amnesty International for helping political prisoners.

1978 *Menachem Begin (Israeli) and *Anwar el-Sadat (Egyptian) for their efforts to bring about a settlement of the Arab-Israeli conflict.

1979 *Mother Teresa (Indian) for aiding India's poor.

1980 Adolfo Pérez Esquivel (Argentine) for his role in Service for Peace and Justice in Latin America, a group promoting the cause of human rights.

1981 Office of the United Nations High Commissioner for Refugees for protection of millions of Vietnamese and other refugees.

1982 *Alva R. Myrdal (Swedish) and Alfonso García Robles (Mexican) for contributions to UN disarmament negotiations.

1983 *Lech Wałęsa (Polish) for his efforts to prevent violence while trying to gain workers' rights.

1984 *Desmond Tutu (South African) for leading a nonviolent campaign against racial segregation in his country.

1985 International Physicians for the Prevention of Nuclear War for educating the public on the effects of nuclear war.

1986 *Elie Wiesel (American) for his vigorous efforts to help victims of oppression and racial discrimination.

1987 *Oscar Arias Sánchez (Costa Rican) for authoring a plan to end civil wars in Central America.

1988 The United Nations peacekeeping forces for helping control military conflict in the Middle East and other areas.

1989 *The Dalai Lama (Tibetan) for his nonviolent struggle to end China's rule of Tibet.

1990 *Mikhail S. Gorbachev (Soviet) for his efforts to promote world peace.

1991 *Aung San Suu Kyi (Burmese) for her nonviolent struggle for democracy and human rights in Myanmar.

1992 *Rigoberta Menchú (Guatemalan) for her work to gain respect for the rights of Guatemala's Indian peoples.

1993 *Nelson Mandela and *Frederik W. de Klerk (South African) for working to end apartheid in South Africa and to enable its nonwhites to fully participate in government.

1994 *Yasir Arafat (Palestinian), *Shimon Peres (Israeli), and *Yitzhak Rabin (Israeli) for promoting peace in the Middle East.

1995 The organization known as the Pugwash Conferences on Science and World Affairs and its president, Joseph Rotblat (British), for efforts to eliminate nuclear weapons.

1996 Carlos Ximenes Belo and José Ramos-Horta (Timorese) for work on behalf of the people of East Timor.

1997 International Campaign to Ban Landmines and its coordinator, Jody Williams (American), for their work to end the use of land mines worldwide.

*Has a biography in *World Book.*

Nobel Peace Prizes (continued)

1998 John Hume and David Trimble (British) for working to end Protestant-Catholic fighting in Northern Ireland.

1999 †Doctors Without Borders (French) for its pioneering work in providing medical care and humanitarian aid to victims of disasters on several continents.

2000 Kim Dae Jung (South Korean) for his efforts to end hostility between North Korea and South Korea.

2001 *Kofi Annan (Ghanaian) and the United Nations for their efforts to build peace and security throughout the world.

2002 *Jimmy Carter (American) for his efforts to seek peaceful solutions to international conflicts and to promote democracy and human rights.

2003 Shirin Ebadi (Iranian) for her work to promote democracy and human rights in Iran and other countries.

2004 Wangari Muta Maathai (Kenyan) for her efforts to promote environmental conservation, economic development, democracy, human rights, and women's rights in Kenya and the rest of Africa.

2005 Mohamed ElBaradei (Egyptian) and the International Atomic Energy Agency for their efforts to prevent the use of nuclear weapons.

2006 Grameen Bank and its founder, Muhammad Yunus (Bangladeshi), for pioneering work in microcredit as a means of relieving poverty.

2007 *Al Gore (American) and the United Nations Intergovernmental Panel on Climate Change for their work in spreading awareness of global warming.

2008 Martti Ahtisaari (Finnish) for his efforts to resolve international conflicts on several continents.

2009 *Barack Obama (American) for his "extraordinary efforts to strengthen international diplomacy and cooperation between peoples."

2010 Liu Xiaobo (Chinese) for his "long and non-violent struggle for fundamental human rights in China."

Bank of Sweden Prizes in Economic Sciences in Memory of Alfred Nobel

1969 *Ragnar Frisch (Norwegian) and *Jan Tinbergen (Dutch) for their work in econometrics, a method of analyzing economic activity.

1970 *Paul A. Samuelson (American) for raising the level of scientific analysis in economic theory.

1971 *Simon Kuznets (American) for his interpretation of economic growth.

1972 *Kenneth J. Arrow (American) and Sir John Hicks (British) for their pioneering contribution to general equilibrium theory and to welfare theory.

1973 Wassily Leontief (American) for his development of the input-output method of economic analysis.

1974 Friedrich von Hayek (Austrian) and *Gunnar Myrdal (Swedish) for their work in the theory of money and economic change and in the relationship between economic and social factors.

1975 Leonid V. Kantorovich (Soviet) and Tjalling C. Koopmans (American) for their work on how economic resources should be distributed and used.

1976 *Milton Friedman (American) for his work in the fields of economic consumption, monetary history and theory, and price stabilization policy.

1977 James Meade (British) and Bertil Ohlin (Swedish) for their studies of international trade and finance.

1978 *Herbert A. Simon (American) for his research on the decision-making process in business.

1979 *Sir Arthur Lewis (St. Lucian-born) and Theodore W. Schultz (American) for their research into the economic problems of developing countries.

1980 *Lawrence R. Klein (American) for using econometric models to analyze economic policies and the rise and fall in business activity.

1981 James Tobin (American) for his analyses of financial markets and their effect on how businesses and families spend and save money.

1982 George Stigler (American) for his research on industrial organization, markets, and regulation.

1983 Gerard Debreu (American) for developing a mathematical model that proved the theory of supply and demand.

1984 Sir Richard Stone (British) for developing methods of measuring the performance of national economies.

1985 Franco Modigliani (American) for his theories on personal savings and financial markets.

1986 James M. Buchanan (American) for developing methods of analyzing the decision-making process in government.

1987 Robert Solow (American) for his development of a mathematical model that identified technology as the dominant factor in long-term economic growth.

1988 Maurice Allais (French) for his theories on economic markets and the efficient use of resources.

1989 Trygve Haavelmo (Norwegian) for his development of statistical techniques that led to the creation of mathematical models used in making economic predictions.

1990 Harry M. Markowitz, Merton H. Miller, and William F. Sharpe (American) for their theories in corporate finance.

1991 Ronald H. Coase (British-born) for his theories on the economic importance of property rights and of the costs of carrying out business transactions.

1992 Gary S. Becker (American) for extending economic theory to aspects of behavior that previously had been dealt with only by such fields as sociology and criminology.

1993 Robert W. Fogel and Douglass C. North (American) for their work in economic history.

1994 *John F. Nash (American), John C. Harsanyi (American), and Reinhard Selten (German) for their work in game theory.

1995 Robert E. Lucas, Jr. (American) for his analysis of the impact of government economic policies on the economic decisions of individuals.

1996 William S. Vickrey (American) and James A. Mirrlees (British) for contributing to the economic theory of incentives.

1997 Robert C. Merton and Myron S. Scholes (American) for work in determining proper prices for financial options.

1998 Amartya Sen (Indian) for his studies of such problems as famine and poverty from an ethical point of view.

1999 Robert A. Mundell (Canadian-born) for his theories on how international factors affect governments' efforts to stabilize their economies.

2000 James Heckman and Daniel McFadden (American) for their work in the statistical analysis of the economic behavior of individuals and households.

2001 George A. Akerlof, A. Michael Spence, and Joseph E. Stiglitz (American) for showing how buyers and sellers with different amounts of information affect market systems.

2002 Daniel Kahneman (Israeli-born) and Vernon L. Smith (American) for their use of psychological research and experimental methods in the study of economics.

2003 Robert F. Engle (American) and Clive W. J. Granger (British) for their development of statistical methods for the study of sets of economic observations recorded over time.

2004 Finn E. Kydland (Norwegian) and Edward C. Prescott (American) for their research on economic policymaking and the factors that influence business cycles.

*Has a biography in *World Book*.   †Has a separate article in *World Book*.

2005 Robert J. Aumann (Israeli and American) and Thomas C. Schelling (American) for their use of game theory to examine conflict and cooperation in society.

2006 Edmund Phelps (American) for advancing understanding about the trade-offs between such economic objectives as saving and consuming or unemployment and inflation.

2007 Leonid Hurwicz (Russian-born), Eric S. Maskin (American), and Roger B. Myerson (American) for their work on the development of *mechanism design theory,* which helps economists understand why markets work well in certain situations but not in others.

2008 Paul Krugman (American) for his analysis of trade patterns and location of economic activity.

2009 Elinor Ostrom (American) for her analysis of *economic governance* (the use of authority to manage public resources and economic problems), especially the *commons* (resources, goods, services, and assets that must be produced and used by people as a group), and Oliver E. Williamson (American) for his analysis of economic governance, especially the boundaries of the firm.

2010 Peter A. Diamond (American), Dale T. Mortensen (American), and Christopher A. Pissarides (Cypriot-British) for their analysis of how the job market is affected by regulation and economic policy.

Nobelium is an artificially produced radioactive element. It has an *atomic number* (number of protons) of 102. Its chemical symbol is No. Scientists have discovered 12 *isotopes* of nobelium, forms of the element with the same number of protons but different numbers of neutrons. These isotopes have *atomic mass numbers* (total numbers of protons and neutrons) from 250 to 260. The most stable isotope has a mass number of 259 and a *half-life* of 58 minutes—that is, due to radioactive decay, only half the atoms in a sample of isotope 259 would still be atoms of that isotope after 58 minutes.

In 1957, scientists at the Nobel Institute for Physics in Stockholm, Sweden, claimed that they had produced an element whose atomic number was 102. They proposed to name the element *nobelium,* after the Swedish inventor Alfred Nobel. But their claim could not be confirmed.

In 1958, scientists at Lawrence Radiation Laboratory (now Lawrence Berkeley National Laboratory) in Berkeley, California, published the first in a series of claims that they had created element 102. The Berkeley scientists also proposed the name *nobelium.* The International Union of Pure and Applied Chemistry (IUPAC) accepted this name. The IUPAC is the recognized authority in crediting the discovery of elements and naming them.

In the 1950's and 1960's, the Joint Institute for Nuclear Research (JINR) in Dubna, Russia, near Moscow, claimed that its scientists had discovered element 102. In 1986, the IUPAC and the International Union of Pure and Applied Physics formed a working group to review the histories of the elements with atomic numbers from 101 to 109. In 1993, the IUPAC accepted the working group's conclusion that the discovery of element 102 was first proved in 1966 at the JINR. The JINR scientists had bombarded americium, whose atomic number is 95, with nitrogen, whose atomic number is 7.   Richard L. Hahn

Nobility is a class of people who are considered to stand at the top of their society. They have special political and social status. Nobility is inherited, and it carries titles such as *duke* or *earl.* Some nobles are the descendants of lords of the Middle Ages (about A.D. 400 through the 1400's) and have inherited their property as well as their titles. Others trace their ancestry to a person who was awarded a title for service to a monarch.

In the United Kingdom

The British nobility is called the *peerage,* and noblemen are known as *peers.* There are five grades of peers. From highest to lowest, they are duke; marquess, or marquis; earl; viscount; and baron. The wives of noblemen, and women who hold titles in their own right, are called *peeresses.* The five grades are duchess, marchioness, countess, viscountess, and baroness.

The title of earl is the oldest grade of peer. It dates back to the Danish nobles who ruled much of England from the 800's to the 1000's. The rank of baron was introduced by the Normans when they conquered England in 1066. King Edward III of England created the rank of duke in 1337, when he named his oldest son as Duke of Cornwall. The title of marquess was created in 1385, and the first viscount was introduced in 1440.

The creation of peerages. The British monarch now grants peerages on the recommendation of the prime minister. The monarch issues documents called *letters patent,* which create the peerage and specify how it will be inherited. In most cases, a peer's title passes to his oldest son. If he has no son, it usually goes to his closest male relative. The other children are commoners. The title becomes extinct if there is no male heir. Some medieval peerages were created by royal orders called *writs of summons.* These types of peerages may pass to a daughter if the holder leaves no male descendant. If the daughter then has a son, he usually inherits the title.

Today, the British monarch rarely grants hereditary peerages. Each year, however, the monarch may grant titles called *life peerages* to distinguished persons. A life peerage involves the same privileges as a hereditary peerage, but it does not descend to the holder's children. Life peerages may be awarded to both men and women, and the title given is baron or baroness. Today, there are about 1,300 peers, including about 750 hereditary peers and about 600 life peers.

Privileges of the peerage. Until 1999, all peers who were at least 21 years old—except peers of Ireland and individuals who had been declared bankrupt or insane—were summoned to the House of Lords. The House of Lords is the upper house of the British Parliament. In 1999, reforms began that limited the number of hereditary peers sitting in the House of Lords to 92. Life peers continued to serve as members of the Lords.

Peers are summoned because of the feudal agreement that lords and vassals should consult on important business. Women who are peeresses in their own right may also serve in the House of Lords. Peers who are in the House of Lords may not also serve in the lower house of Parliament—the House of Commons—and they cannot vote in parliamentary elections. Until 1948, peers accused of a felony or of treason had the right to be tried in the House of Lords by their fellow peers.

Dukes, marquesses, and earls have lesser titles besides the one by which they are known. Traditionally, the oldest son of one of these peers uses the highest of his father's lesser titles as a *courtesy title.* For example, the oldest son of the Duke of St. Albans uses the courtesy title Earl of Burford, but he is not a peer. A younger son of a duke adds *Lord* to his name, as in Lord Peter Grey. His sister would be Lady Helen Grey.

In other countries

Most other countries have officially abolished titles of nobility. A person who inherits a title may use it as part of his or her name. But the individual has none of the privileges of nobility. Titles of nobility ended in France in 1871, in Russia in 1917, in Germany in 1918, and in Japan—except those of the imperial family—in 1946. The titles were often eliminated as part of a revolution or a major social and political effort to modernize the country. The Constitution of the United States forbids the government to give anyone a title of nobility. The Constitution also prohibits federal officials from accepting any title from a foreign country without the special consent of Congress.   Joel T. Rosenthal

Related articles in *World Book* include:

Baron	Duke	Lady
Burke's Peerage	Heraldry	Lord
Count	House of Lords	Viscount

Noble gas refers to any of a group of six chemical elements. These elements are argon (Ar), helium (He), krypton (Kr), neon (Ne), radon (Rn), and xenon (Xe). They occur naturally and can be found in the atmosphere. The British scientists Lord Rayleigh and William Ramsay discovered the noble gases during the late 1890's.

Unlike most gaseous elements, the noble gases are *monatomic*—that is, they occur as single atoms instead of as molecules of two or more atoms. The atoms have stable *configurations* (arrangements) of electrons. Therefore, the atoms do not, under normal conditions, gain or lose electrons or share electrons with other elements. The six gases are called "noble gases" or *inert gases* because they do not readily react with other elements. But most of the noble gases will form certain compounds under specialized conditions.

The noble gases have various uses. Except for radon, which is highly radioactive, all of them are used as light sources in incandescent and gaseous-discharge lamps (see **Electric light**). Some also are used in devices called *gas lasers* (see **Laser** [Kinds of lasers]).

Argon and helium are used in a welding process called *arc welding*. They provide a chemically inactive atmosphere in which certain metals, such as aluminum, can be heated to their melting points without reacting chemically. Helium also is used in balloons that carry scientific instruments high into the atmosphere, and in low-temperature research. Each noble gas has a separate article in *World Book*.   Frank C. Andrews

Noël. See Christmas.

Noguchi, Isamu (1904-1988), was an American sculptor whose work represents a wide variety of styles. Noguchi said that he was "suspicious of the whole business of style." He called style "a form of inhibition."

Noguchi worked in nearly every sculptural material. He sought to preserve the nature of the material. Almost all his work has no recognizable subject matter. He was intrigued by problems of weight, mass, and tension.

Noguchi was born on Nov. 17, 1904, in Los Angeles. His mother was an American, and his father was a well-known Japanese poet and scholar. Noguchi lived in Japan from age 2 to age 13. He gave up medical studies at Columbia University to return to sculpture, his earlier ambition. In the late 1920's, he studied in Paris with the Romanian-born sculptor Constantin Brancusi, who

The Seed (1946), *left, Strange Bird* (1945), *center,* and *Metamorphosis* (1946), *right,* in white marble and slate (Michio Noguchi, Isamu Noguchi Garden Museum)

Isamu Noguchi's sculptures typically portray abstract forms in arrangements of smooth, highly polished stone.

strongly influenced his work. Noguchi designed furniture and settings for ballets. He also collaborated with architects in planning gardens, playgrounds, and bridges. He died on Dec. 30, 1988.   George Gurney

Noh. See Drama (Asian drama); Japanese literature (Early medieval period).

Noise is random or unwanted sound. Unwanted signals, such as static that interferes with radio transmission, are also referred to as noise. The sound we hear is caused by vibrations of air molecules. A tuning fork produces a *pure tone,* with only one *frequency,* or rate of vibration (see **Tone**). Musical instruments produce *harmonic sound.* Such sound contains many frequencies that are harmonically related (see **Harmonics**). *Random sound* has many frequencies that are not harmonically related. *Unwanted sound* can be caused by any kind of sound—tones, harmonic sound, or random sound. Techniques to reduce unwanted sound include *filtering* and *averaging.* Filtering can eliminate certain unwanted frequencies. Averaging causes unwanted sound waves to cancel each other out through *interference* (see **Interference**).   Edward J. Tucholski

See also **Acoustics; Decibel; Muffler; Sound.**

Nok, *nahk,* was a West African civilization that flourished from about 500 B.C. until around A.D. 200. Archaeologists became aware of Nok in the 1940's, when small clay statues were discovered along the Jos Plateau in central Nigeria. These statues are the oldest sculptures ever found in Africa south of the Sahara. Bernard Fagg, a British archaeologist, studied these sculptures and other objects to learn about Nok's people and culture. Fagg determined that Nok was spread along an area between the Niger and Benue rivers, southwest of the Jos Plateau.

He named the culture Nok after the modern-day Nigerian village of Nok, where the statues were discovered.

The Nok sculptures are human and animal figures made of *terra cotta* (baked clay). Most stand no more than a foot (30 centimeters) high, but some are nearly life-sized. Distinctive features of Nok sculpture include a semicircular or triangular shape of the eyes. Most figures are hollow, with holes in the pupils, ears, noses, and mouths. Scholars are unsure what function the sculptures served. The figures may have been placed above the front doors of houses or displayed on altars.

Nok's people were among the earliest ironworkers in Africa. They used low, circular iron-smelting furnaces. They also worked with some stone tools, particularly polished stone axes.

Little is known about the details of Nok society. Archaeologists' efforts to learn more about Nok have been hindered by looting of the Jos region. Thieves have taken many of the terra-cotta sculptures and sold them on the international art market.   Kevin C. MacDonald

Nomad is a person who moves from place to place as a way of obtaining food, finding pasture for livestock, or otherwise making a living. The word *nomad* comes from a Greek word that means *one who wanders for pasture.* Most nomadic groups follow a fixed annual or seasonal pattern of movements and settlements.

Nomads keep moving for different reasons. *Nomadic foragers* move in search of game, edible plants, and water. The Australian Aborigines, Negritos of Southeast Asia, and San of Africa, for example, traditionally move from camp to camp to hunt and to gather wild plants. Some American Indians followed this way of life. *Pastoral nomads* make their living raising livestock, such as camels, cattle, goats, horses, sheep, or yaks. These nomads travel to find water and pastures for their herds. Bedouin herders, for example, move camels, goats, and sheep through the deserts of Arabia and northern Africa. The Fulani and their cattle travel through the grasslands of Niger in western Africa. Some nomadic peoples, especially herders, may also move to raid settled communities or avoid enemies. Nomadic craftworkers and merchants travel to find and serve customers. They include the Lohar blacksmiths of India, the Romani (Gypsy) traders, and the Irish Travellers.

Most nomads travel in groups of families called *bands* or *tribes.* These groups are based on kinship and marriage ties or on formal agreements of cooperation. A council of adult males makes most of the decisions, though some tribes have chiefs.

The nomadic way of life has become increasingly rare. Many governments dislike nomads because it is difficult to control their movement and to obtain taxes from them. Many countries have converted pastures into cropland and forced nomadic peoples into permanent settlements.   Russell Zanca

Related articles in *World Book* include:

Aborigines, Australian	Negritos
Africa (Rural life)	Roma
Agriculture (Pastoralism)	Sahara (People)
Asia (Country life)	San
Bedouins	Tuareg
Fulani	

Nome (pop. 3,598) is the transportation and commercial hub for northwestern Alaska. It lies 140 miles (225 kilo-

meters) south of the Arctic Circle on the southern coast of the Seward Peninsula. It faces Norton Sound of the Bering Sea (see **Alaska** [political map]). Nome can be reached only by water or air, as no roads link it to any other cities.

An Inuit group known as the Iñupiat make up about half of Nome's people. Many hunt and fish for much of their food. Nome is the finish for the annual Iditarod Trail Sled Dog Race. The race honors a heroic dog sled run through blizzards and extremely low temperatures to deliver diphtheria serum during a 1925 epidemic.

Major industries in Nome include mining for gold and other minerals, local and state government, oil and gas development, tourism, commercial reindeer herding, and native arts and crafts. *The Nome Nugget,* first published in 1900, is Alaska's oldest newspaper.

Gold was discovered near Nome in 1898. In 1900, Nome's population reached 12,500, making it the Alaska region's largest city at the time. Nome was incorporated in 1901. The city is named for Cape Nome, which supposedly got its name when a mapmaker misread the term *? name* on a chart and recorded it as *C. Nome,* or *Cape Nome.*   Cary W. de Wit

Nominative case. See Case.

Nonaggression pact is a treaty by which two or more nations agree to settle mutual disputes peacefully and not to attack each other. Between World War I (1914-1918) and World War II (1939-1945), many nations signed nonaggression pacts because there was no international force strong enough to prevent aggression.

Nonaggression pacts sometimes were not effective because they lacked enforcement procedures and also because participating nations violated their agreements. For example, during the 1920's and 1930's, the Soviet Union signed pacts with many of its neighbors. But the Soviet Union violated its agreements with Estonia, Latvia, and Lithuania when it occupied them in 1939 and 1940. Germany signed a nonaggression pact with the Soviet Union in 1939 but attacked the Soviets in 1941.

Since the end of World War II, there have been fewer attempts to establish nonaggression pacts. Many nations believe that the United Nations Charter contains adequate provisions for the peaceful settlement of disputes.

A major problem with nonaggression pacts is to decide an acceptable definition of *aggression.* The United Nations has debated this question but reached no agreement. Some nations believe aggression includes only direct military attacks. Others believe when one country aids revolution in another country through propaganda, through subversion, or by taking over government posts, it is indirect aggression.   Robert J. Pranger

See also **League of Nations; United Nations.**

Nonaligned nation. See Third World.

Nonfiction. See Literature (Nonfiction); Literature for children (Biography; Information books; Children's nonfiction); Writing (Nonfiction).

Nonmetal. See Metal.

Non-Proliferation of Nuclear Weapons, Treaty on the. See Nuclear Nonproliferation Treaty.

Nonverbal behavior. See Body language; Kinesics.

Nonviolent resistance. See African Americans (The growing movement); Chavez, Cesar Estrada; Gandhi, Mohandas Karamchand; King, Martin Luther, Jr.

Noon. See Day and night; Time.

Detail of *Habitations at Nootka Sound* (1784), an engraving after a drawing by John Weber; Royal British Columbia Museum, Victoria

The Nootka Indians fished and hunted whales off the Northwest Coast of North America. They built houses of cedar planks.

Nootka Indians, *NOOT kuh,* live along the west coast of Vancouver Island in the province of British Columbia and at the tip of the Olympic Peninsula in the state of Washington. The Nootka on Vancouver Island call themselves the Nuu-chah-nulth or West Coast natives. The Nootka in Washington call themselves the Makah. There are more than 8,000 Nootka. They make their living mainly by fishing and lumbering in their traditional lands or by working in nearby cities. Many still speak dialects of the Nootkan language.

The Nootka were once noted for their skill in hunting whales from graceful dugout canoes. They lived in wooden plank houses on sheltered beaches and coves. Nootka artists carved and painted masks, large puppets, totem poles, and other objects used in religious ceremonies and in feasts called *potlatches.* The Nootka were first described in detail by the British navigator Captain James Cook in 1778. In the late 1700's and the 1800's, they were devastated by diseases introduced by Europeans, Americans, and Canadians.   Robert S. Grumet

See also **Indian, American** (Indians of the Northwest Coast).

Nopal. See **Prickly pear.**

NORAD is a military alliance responsible for defending the United States and Canada against air attack. NORAD stands for *Nor*th *A*merican *A*erospace *D*efense Command. It oversees a large network of radars and other sensing devices that monitor air traffic, such as passenger airplanes. The network can also detect and track enemy bombers and missiles.

NORAD was established in 1957. It has headquarters at Peterson Air Force Base in Colorado Springs, Colorado. The commander of NORAD is traditionally a general in the U.S. military, and the second in command is a Canadian general. NORAD works with many government agencies to ensure that it is prepared to respond quickly to potential threats or attacks. The U.S. Air Force, Army, Navy, and National Guard support NORAD operations. Fighter aircraft stationed around the United States are ready to intercept suspicious aircraft at a moment's notice.   Critically reviewed by NORAD

See also **North Warning System.**

Nordenskjöld, *NOOR duhn SHOOLD,* **Nils Adolf Erik,** *nihls AH dawlf AY rihk* (1832-1901), Baron Nordenskjöld, was a Swedish polar explorer, mineralogist, and map authority. In 1878 and 1879, he became the first person to sail through the Northeast Passage between the Atlantic and Pacific oceans. He sailed along the northern coast of Europe and Asia. He tells of this journey in his book *Voyage of the Vega* (1881).

Nordenskjöld was born on Nov. 18, 1832, in Helsinki, Finland. He moved to Sweden in 1857 and became a Swedish citizen. He led two expeditions in an attempt to reach the North Pole. On the first one, in 1868, he took his ship, the *Sofia,* to within about 575 miles (925 kilometers) of the Pole. Nordenskjöld studied the geology of Greenland in 1870. He returned there in 1883 and penetrated the ice barrier off the east coast. He determined that ice covered the island's interior. Nordenskjöld died on Aug. 12, 1901.   William Barr

Nordhoff and Hall were a team of American authors. Charles Bernard Nordhoff (1887-1947) and James Norman Hall (1887-1951) became famous for their three novels about an actual mutiny in the British Navy in 1789. These novels are *Mutiny on the Bounty* (1932), *Men Against the Sea* (1934), and *Pitcairn's Island* (1934). The first novel describes how the crew of the *Bounty* mutinied against their cruel captain, William Bligh. The second novel tells about the hardships of Bligh and his followers after they were set adrift in a small boat. The final novel follows the lives of the crew and their descendants after they settled on Pitcairn Island and Norfolk Island in the South Pacific Ocean.

Nordhoff was born on Feb. 1, 1887, in London, and Hall was born on April 22, 1887, in Colfax, Iowa. They met while serving as pilots during World War I (1914-1918). In 1920, they sailed for Tahiti, where they lived for many years. Nordhoff and Hall wrote several novels together as well as works individually. Nordhoff died on April 11, 1947, and Hall died on July 6, 1951.

Samuel Chase Coale

See also **Bligh, William; Pitcairn Island.**

Norfolk, *NAWR fuhk,* Virginia (pop. 242,803), is a leading United States port. It lies in southeastern Virginia (see **Virginia** [political map]). Norfolk is the state's second largest city. Only Virginia Beach has more people. Norfolk, Virginia Beach, and Newport News form a metropolitan area with 1,671,683 people.

Hampton Roads, one of the world's finest natural deepwater harbors, forms Norfolk's northwestern boundary. Naval Station Norfolk employs more people and harbors more ships than any other naval base in the United States. It serves as headquarters of the United States Joint Forces Command, the U.S. Navy's Fleet Forces Command, and the U.S. Marine Corps Forces Command.

In 1680, the Virginia General Assembly founded a port in Norfolk County to serve ships sailing to and from England and the West Indies. The port was later named Norfolk for the county. It became an independent borough in 1736 and an independent city in 1845.

Description. Norfolk covers 66 square miles (171 square kilometers). The Elizabeth River borders the city on the west. Chesapeake Bay is on the north.

Features of downtown Norfolk include a cultural and convention center called Scope. This complex includes

Chrysler Hall, where the Virginia Symphony Orchestra performs. Norfolk's Chrysler Museum of Art houses a large collection. A science museum called Nauticus celebrates the region's seafaring heritage. Next to Nauticus on the downtown waterfront, the World War II battleship U.S.S. *Wisconsin* is open for tours.

The city's colleges and universities include Norfolk State University, Old Dominion University, and Virginia Wesleyan College. Norfolk is also home to Eastern Virginia Medical School. Every year, many visitors come to Norfolk for the Norfolk NATO Festival (formerly called the International Azalea Festival) and for a festival called Harborfest. Many tourists also visit St. Paul's Church, which dates from 1739. This church was one of only a few buildings that survived a British bombardment during the American Revolution (1775-1783).

Economy of Norfolk depends heavily on its port. Naval Station Norfolk is the city's largest employer. The Norfolk International Terminals (NIT) is a huge center on the waterfront for loading and unloading cargo from container ships from all over the world. The cargo is loaded onto trucks and trains for distribution across North America. NIT and terminals in the neighboring cities of Portsmouth and Newport News are part of the Virginia International Terminals, which handle millions of tons of cargo a year. Norfolk International Airport handles domestic and international flights.

The Norfolk metropolitan area has hundreds of manufacturing companies. Their chief products include processed foods, ships, and trucks.

Government and history. Norfolk has a council-manager form of government. The voters elect a mayor and seven other council members to four-year terms. The council hires a city manager to carry out its policies.

Powhatan Indians lived in what is now the Norfolk area when European explorers first arrived there in the early 1600's. Early Norfolk served as a tobacco and naval supply port. In 1776, during the American Revolution, a British fleet bombarded and destroyed much of the town. Norfolk was incorporated as a city in 1845.

The city grew slowly until the Navy began to build the Norfolk naval station in 1917, shortly after the nation entered World War I. During World War II (1939-1945), thousands of civilians moved to the city to work in the navy yards and on the base. The population of Norfolk rose from 144,332 in 1940 to 213,513 in 1950.

The city launched an urban renewal program in 1951 that included slum clearance and the construction of public housing. In the 1970's, the city constructed several high-rise buildings and a waterfront hotel. In 1983, the Waterside, a festival marketplace, was completed on the downtown waterfront. Downtown revitalization continued through the late 1900's and into the 2000's. MacArthur Center mall opened in 1999.   Elizabeth Thiel

For Norfolk's monthly weather, see **Virginia** (Climate).

Norfolk Island, *NAWR fuhk,* lies in the South Pacific Ocean, about 1,000 miles (1,600 kilometers) northeast of Sydney, Australia. For location, see **Pacific Islands** (map). Norfolk Island covers 14 square miles (35 square kilometers). About 2,000 people live on the island. Tourism is the main source of income. The island has fertile volcanic soil, and people there grow bananas, citrus fruits, and vegetables. Many of the island's inhabitants are descendants of crew members of the British naval ship

Bounty. In 1789, those sailors *mutinied* (rebelled) against the way they were treated by their captain, William Bligh. They settled on Pitcairn Island in 1790. In 1856, 194 of their descendants moved to Norfolk Island.

In 1774, the British explorer James Cook became the first European to reach Norfolk Island. From 1788 to 1814, the island was used as a penal settlement by the British colony of New South Wales in Australia. It again served as a penal settlement from 1825 until 1856, when the settlement was abolished. In 1914, the island was separated from New South Wales and became a territory of Australia. The Norfolk Island Act 1979 set up a local government on the island. The act preserved Australia's overall responsibility for the island.   Kate Darian-Smith

Norfolk terrier, *NAWR fuhk,* is a breed of dog that originated in the United Kingdom. Norfolk terriers and Norwich terriers were exhibited at dog shows as one breed until 1964. That year, the Kennel Club in England registered them as separate breeds. The main difference between the two breeds is the way they carry their ears. Norfolks have ears that drop forward, and Norwich terriers have ears that stand erect. The American Kennel Club recognized the dogs as separate breeds in 1979.

The Norfolk terrier is hardy and active and instinctively hunts small animals. It was originally bred as a com-

WORLD BOOK photo by Tom Weigand

The Norfolk terrier is an affectionate pet.

panion dog and makes a fine pet. It may be black and tan, or any shade of red. It has a straight, wiry outer coat and a harsh undercoat. The dog has short, sturdy legs. The tail is sometimes *docked* (cut) to 3 or 4 inches (8 to 10 centimeters) in length. A full-grown Norfolk weighs from 10 to 12 pounds (4.5 to 5.4 kilograms) and stands about 10 inches (25 centimeters) tall at the shoulder.

Critically reviewed by the Norwich and Norfolk Terrier Club

See also **Norwich terrier.**

Norgay, Tenzing. See Tenzing Norgay.

Noriega, *nawr YAY gah,* **Manuel Antonio,** *mah NWEHL* (1934-   ), was a military leader who controlled Panama from 1983 to 1989. In December 1989, United States President George H. W. Bush ordered troops into Panama. Bush said the troops were a response to the killing of a U.S. marine lieutenant by Panamanian soldiers and charges of drug trafficking and racketeering against Noriega. In January 1990, Noriega surrendered to U.S. officials and was taken to the United States to stand trial. In 1992, he was convicted of drug trafficking, money laundering, and racketeering and was sent to prison. In 1993 and 1994, Panamanian courts convicted Noriega of involvement in the murders of two of his political opponents, and in 1999, a French court convicted him of money laundering. Noriega completed his United States prison term in 2007. He remained in a U.S. prison while his lawyers fought a request from France to hand him over to serve a prison term there. In 2010, the United States sent Noriega to France to face a new trial for money laundering. He was convicted and sentenced to seven years in jail.

Noriega was born on Feb. 11, 1934, in Panama City. He graduated from a military academy in Peru in 1962. That year, Noriega enlisted in Panama's military. He soon became a lieutenant. Following a military take-over of the government in 1968, he quickly rose through the ranks. Noriega became commander of Panama's military intelligence agency in 1970 and expanded his power. He took charge of the military in 1983 and became increasingly involved in the drug trade. Beginning in 1987, the United States tried to force him to resign.   Steve C. Ropp

Norman, Marsha (1947-   ), an American playwright, won the 1983 Pulitzer Prize for drama for *'night, Mother* (1982). The emotional and somber play describes the last night in the life of an unhappy woman who tells her mother she plans to commit suicide. Norman had previously gained praise for another grim and realistic drama, *Getting Out* (1977). It portrays the struggle of a woman on parole from prison as she seeks a new life. Norman won a 1991 Tony Award for her book for the musical *The Secret Garden*. She also wrote the lyrics for the show's songs. Norman wrote the book for the musical *The Color Purple* (2005).

Marsha Williams was born on Sept. 21, 1947, in Louisville, Kentucky. She was married to Michael Norman, a teacher, from 1969 to 1974. Marsha Norman established herself as a playwright with *Getting Out*, her first produced work. Her other plays include *Circus Valentine* (1979), *Traveler in the Dark* (1984), *Sarah and Abraham* (1988), *D. Boone* (1992), and *Last Dance* (2003). She also wrote the screenplay for *'night, Mother* (1986) and a novel, *The Fortune Teller* (1987).   Dan Zeff

Norman architecture is a regional adaptation of Romanesque architecture. It originated in Normandy in northwest France. The style reached its highest development in England during the late 1000's, after the Norman Conquest of 1066, and in the 1100's. Norman architecture is noted for its massive character, development of the six-part vault ceiling, and the use of Celtic and Carolingian patterns of carved ornamentation. Examples of the style include the churches of St. Étienne and La Trinité in Caen, France, and Ely and Durham cathedrals in England. See also **Architecture** (picture: Romanesque architecture).   J. William Rudd

Norman Conquest was the conquest of England in 1066 by William, Duke of Normandy. The duke, also known as William the Conqueror, led a Norman army across the English Channel into England (see **Normans**).

William was a proud and ruthless ruler and a vassal of the king of France. He hoped to follow his distant cousin, King Edward the Confessor, as king of England. William claimed that Edward had named him as his successor. The chief English contender for the throne was Harold, Earl of Wessex. But William also claimed that Harold, who had visited Normandy in 1064, had sworn a solemn oath to support William's claim to the throne. In 1066, King Edward died. The Anglo-Saxon *witenagemot* (great council) chose Harold as king (see **Harold II**).

William at once declared his right to the throne. He claimed to have the support of the pope and gathered an army from northern France. William landed in England without opposition at Pevensey, between Eastbourne and Hastings.

The Normans were aided in their successful landing by a chance happening. While Harold was waiting for the Normans to arrive, he got news that a Norwegian force had landed in the north of England. He hastened north and defeated the Norwegians. Meanwhile, William's forces landed on the unprotected coast. Harold then marched back across England. But as he neared Hastings, he was attacked by William on Oct. 14, 1066. This was the historic Battle of Hastings, which established the Norman rule of England. Harold was defeated and slain. William entered London and was crowned king of England on Christmas Day, 1066. At first, he tried to win over the English nobles. But they opposed him stubbornly, and he spent several years subduing them.

William established Norman rule in England on a strong foundation. He hesitated at no act that he thought would increase the power of the crown. William took almost all the land of the English nobility, keeping some of it for himself and dividing most of the rest among his Norman followers. William forced all landholders to swear loyalty to himself. In this way, he put all the lords of England under his direct control. To know the conditions in England, William directed the preparation of the famous Domesday Book, a survey of all the regions in his kingdom (see **Domesday Book**).

The descendants of the Normans became the ruling

Norman architecture flourished in England in the 1000's and 1100's. Ely Cathedral, *shown here,* is a masterpiece of the style.

Detail of the Bayeux Tapestry (late 1000's), embroidery on linen by unknown artists; William the Conqueror Center, Bayeux, France (SCALA/Art Resource)

The Norman Conquest of England began in 1066 when William the Conqueror sailed his army across the Channel.

class in England. For a time, they kept themselves aloof from the Anglo-Saxons and treated them as a conquered people. As the years went by, however, the Normans and the Anglo-Saxons intermarried. The two peoples, which even in the beginning were similar, blended into one. Today, a large number of English families claim—though few can prove—descent from the Norman conquerors.

The Normans contributed much to the English language and to English literature and architecture. At first, the Normans spoke French. Later, the Norman French blended with the Germanic tongue of the Anglo-Saxons and became English.   John Gillingham

See also **England** (The Norman Conquest); **Hastings, Battle of; Ireland** (The Norman invaders); **William I, the Conqueror.**

Normandy is a region in northwestern France. It was named after the Norse people who conquered the area in the 800's. It lies along the English Channel coast between the regions of Picardy and Brittany (see **France** [political map]). Famous towns include Rouen, the capital of the old province; Le Havre, a leading port; Honfleur; Caen; Bayeux; and Cherbourg. The inhabitants are well known as sailors and farmers. The farmers specialize in dairying and raising fruits, especially apples for cider and brandy. Iron ore is mined near Caen. Tourism is an important industry along the coast.

In A.D. 911, the Carolingian king, Charles the Simple, granted much of what is now Normandy to the Norman chieftain Rollo, or Hrolf. One of Rollo's most famous descendants was William the Conqueror, who won the English crown after the Battle of Hastings in 1066. Events of the battle are pictured on the famous Bayeux Tapestry, a medieval wallhanging housed in the William the Conqueror Center in Bayeux, France. Normandy was united with England during the reign of the English king Henry I (1100-1135). England and France struggled for control of Normandy during the Hundred Years' War. The English recovered the region twice, but finally lost it in 1449 to Charles VII, king of France. Joan of Arc became famous as the leader of French troops in the fight for Normandy.

On June 6, 1944, during World War II, Normandy attracted worldwide attention when Allied troops landed on its beaches. From Normandy, the Allies drove the Germans out of France. Many of the towns in Normandy were damaged in the fighting.   Hugh D. Clout

See also **Bayeux Tapestry; France** (picture); **Normans; World War II** (D-Day).

Normandy, Duke of. See William I, the Conqueror.

Normans were a group of Vikings, or *Norsemen* (Scandinavians), who first settled in northern France, then advanced into England, southern Italy, and Sicily. In the 800's, Norman warriors began their conquests by raiding French coasts and river valleys. By the early 900's, they had settled in the French territory near the mouth of the Seine River now known as Normandy. In 911, the Carolingian king, Charles the Simple, granted much of the region to the Norman chief, Rollo, or Hrolf, and Rollo became the king's vassal. The Normans became Christians and adopted French customs. A large number of Normans became famous administrators, clergymen, and crusaders.

Norman power grew after 950. The Normans invaded the Rhineland, an area in present-day Germany. In 1066, under the leadership of William, Duke of Normandy, they conquered England. After the conquest, Norman influence spread steadily throughout what are now the United Kingdom and Ireland. (see **William I, the Conqueror**). In the same period, Normans won great victories in other lands. Robert Guiscard (1015?-1085), son of Tancred of Hauteville, conquered southern Italy. Roger, another of Tancred's sons, took the island of Sicily from the Muslims. These two territories were later united in the famous Kingdom of the Two Sicilies by Roger's son, Roger II. Major advances in architecture and sculpture occurred in the period of Norman domination in western Europe. An architectural style called *Romanesque* owed much to the Normans.   Malcolm Todd

See also **Norman Conquest; Normandy; Vikings.**

Norns were the three Fates of Scandinavian mythology. They were three sisters: Urd (Past), Verdandi (Present), and Skuld (Future). Urd was old and looked toward the past. Verdandi faced straight ahead into the present.

Skuld looked in a direction opposite from that of Urd. The fate of people and gods was decided by the Norns. The early Scandinavians believed that there were many lesser Norns, and one for each person.   C. Scott Littleton

Norodom Sihanouk (1922-   ), *NAWR uh dum SEE uh nuk,* is a former king of Cambodia. He was an important figure in Cambodian politics from 1941 to 2004.

Sihanouk was born in Phnom Penh on Oct. 31, 1922. He became king in 1941. Cambodia was part of French Indochina at that time. He became a supporter of Cambodian independence. In 1953, Cambodia became independent. In 1955, he gave up the throne and was elected prime minister. He was elected head of state in 1960.

In 1970, during the Vietnam War, the prime minister, Lieutenant General Lon Nol, and Prince Sisowath Sirik Matak ousted Sihanouk and forced him into exile. Sihanouk had publicly proclaimed Cambodian neutrality in the war. But he secretly allowed North Vietnamese Communists—the enemies of the United States and South Vietnam—to establish bases in Cambodia.

In 1975, a Communist group called the Khmer Rouge gained control of Cambodia and set up a harsh political regime. Sihanouk was allowed to return to Cambodia as head of state, but he had no real political power.

In 1978, Vietnamese forces invaded Cambodia, and Sihanouk fled to China. A civil war broke out among the Khmer Rouge, the Vietnamese, and other Communist and non-Communist groups. The opposing groups signed a peace agreement in 1991 and elections were held. In 1993, a new National Assembly made Sihanouk king again. In 2004, he gave up the throne because of poor health. He was replaced by his son Norodom Sihamoni.   Nguyen Thi Dieu

Norris, Frank (1870-1902), was an American novelist and journalist and a leader of the naturalism movement. Norris believed that a novel should serve a moral purpose. "The novel with a purpose," he explained, "brings the tragedies and griefs of others to notice" and "prove(s) that injustice, crime, and inequality do exist."

Benjamin Franklin Norris, Jr., was born in Chicago on March 5, 1870. He moved to San Francisco with his family. While attending the University of California, he was influenced by French naturalist writer Émile Zola. He began to write *McTeague* (1899), one of his finest novels. It tells how alcoholism, heredity, economic circumstances, and chance compel a man to become a murderer.

Norris planned a three-novel series called *Epic of the Wheat* to tell about the production, distribution, and consumption of wheat in the United States. *The Octopus* (1901) dramatizes how a railroad controlled a group of wheat farmers. The book emphasizes the control of "forces," such as wheat and railroads, over people and groups. It ranks with *McTeague* as Norris's finest work. Both novels show the author's weakness for melodrama but illustrate his genius for revealing character and writing exciting action scenes. The second book of the series, *The Pit,* was published in 1903, after Norris died on Oct. 25, 1902, following an operation for appendicitis.

Alan Gribben

Norris, George William (1861-1944), was one of the great independent politicians of American public life. During his 40 years in Congress, he ignored party politics to fight for whatever he believed to be right.

Norris was elected to the United States House of Representatives as a Republican from Nebraska in 1902. He served for 10 years. In 1910, he led the fight to reduce the power of the speaker of the House. Norris was elected a U.S. senator from Nebraska in 1912. His main interest lay in developing public ownership of utilities. He wanted the United States government to develop the electric power of the Tennessee River Valley, despite the policies of the Republican Party. In 1933, Congress passed his bill to create the Tennessee Valley Authority (TVA).

Norris realized how the rise of Nazism and Fascism in Europe endangered the United States. He supported aid to Britain in the early years of World War II. Norris was defeated for reelection in 1942. He was born on July 11, 1861, in Sandusky County, Ohio. Norris died on Sept. 2, 1944.   Robert W. Cherny

Norris-La Guardia Act of 1932 was one of the first laws that encouraged labor union activity in the United States. It restricted federal courts from issuing *injunctions* (orders) to stop union activities, including strikes, that involved no violence. The law made it impossible to enforce *yellow-dog contracts.* Many employers had forced their workers to sign such agreements, in which employees promised not to join or aid a union. The Norris-La Guardia Act prohibited employers from suing employees for breaking yellow-dog contracts. As a result, employers eventually stopped using them. The act was sponsored by Senator George W. Norris of Nebraska and Representative Fiorello H. La Guardia of New York.

Before Congress passed the Norris-La Guardia Act, an employer could obtain an injunction to stop any union activity that hurt the employer's business in any way. The act banned such injunctions unless the employer had made every possible effort to settle the dispute through negotiations with the union. It also required an employer to prove that denial of an injunction would hurt the employer more than an injunction would hurt the union. The Taft-Hartley Act of 1947 allowed injunctions in certain other cases (see **Taft-Hartley Act**).   James G. Scoville

Norse mythology. See Mythology (Teutonic mythology).

Norsemen. See Vikings.

North, Andrew. See Norton, Andre.

North, Lord (1732-1792), Frederick, Earl of Guilford, was British prime minister from 1770 to 1782. His shortsighted treatment of the American Colonies helped bring on the Revolutionary War (1775-1783).

North managed the House of Commons in the interests of the king, George III (see **George III**). Even when he disagreed with the king's policy, he did not oppose it. He supported the tea tax that became one of the causes of the Revolutionary War (see **Boston Tea Party**). As the war went on, North's administration became increasingly disorganized and demoralized. In 1782, he persuaded the king to accept his resignation. In 1783, he became joint secretary of state with Charles Fox but resigned after only nine months (see **Fox, Charles J.**).

North was born on April 13, 1732, in London and attended Eton College and Oxford University. In 1754, his father had him elected to Parliament from a family-owned "pocket borough." He later served in the Treasury and the Privy Council. He became chancellor of the exchequer and leader of the House of Commons in 1767. North died on Aug. 5, 1792.   John L. Bullion

© Eric Carle, Bruce Coleman Inc.

The Canadian Rockies

© Lee Balterman from Marilyn Gartman

Downtown Chicago

© Brian Vikander, West Light

Rural Mexico

North America

North America, the third largest continent in area, extends from the Arctic Ocean in the north to South America in the south. Only Asia and Africa cover larger areas. North America ranks fourth among the continents in population, after Asia, Africa, and Europe.

North America includes Canada, Greenland, the United States, Mexico, Central America, and the islands of the Caribbean Sea. Canada and the United States make up what is sometimes called Anglo-America (English-America) because many of their settlers came from England. English is the dominant language in Anglo-America. Mexico, Central America, and the Caribbean Islands are sometimes called Middle America because they lie between Anglo-America and South America. Spanish is the dominant language in Middle America, though English is spoken on many Caribbean Islands.

Anglo-America has valuable supplies of coal, natural gas, petroleum, and other underground resources. It has thick forests and vast farmlands. Anglo-America produces about a fourth of the world's manufactured goods. It also exports more food than any other region in the world. Some Middle American countries, on the other hand, rank among the world's poor countries. Limited natural resources, inefficiently managed economies, and political problems have hampered their economic development.

North America offers other contrasts. Its climate is the most varied of any continent. Northern ice-covered plains differ widely in temperature from sunny Caribbean beaches. The landscape ranges from magnificent mountain peaks to flat grasslands. Luxuriant redwood forests along the Pacific coast contrast sharply with the parched sands of the southwestern deserts. North America has the world's largest island, Greenland, and the world's largest freshwater lake, Lake Superior.

People

The earliest North Americans were Indians who came to the continent from Asia. Most scientists think they ar-

Facts in brief

Area: 9,352,000 mi² (24,221,000 km²). *Greatest distances* (mainland)—north-south, 4,500 mi (7,200 km); east-west, 4,000 mi (6,400 km); (including islands)—north-south, 5,400 mi (8,900 km); east-west, 5,400 mi (8,900 km). *Coastline*—about 190,000 mi (300,000 km).

Population: *Estimated 2012 population*—549,433,000; density, 59 per mi² (23 per km²).

Elevation: *Highest*—Mount McKinley in Alaska, 20,320 ft (6,194 m) above sea level. *Lowest*—near Badwater, Death Valley, California, 282 ft (86 m) below sea level.

Physical features: *Chief mountain ranges*—Alaska, Appalachian, Cascade, Coast, Rocky, Sierra Madre Occidental, Sierra Madre Oriental, Sierra Nevada. *Chief rivers*—Arkansas, Colorado, Columbia, Fraser, Hudson, Mackenzie, Mississippi, Missouri, Nelson, Ohio, Platte, Rio Grande, St. Lawrence, Saskatchewan, Snake, Tennessee, Yukon. *Chief lakes*—Athabasca, Erie, Great Bear, Great Salt, Great Slave, Huron, Michigan, Nicaragua, Ontario, Superior, Winnipeg. *Chief deserts*—Chihuahuan, Colorado, Great Basin, Mojave, Painted, Sonoran, Vizcaíno, Yuma. *Chief waterfalls*—Niagara, Ribbon, Silver Strand, Takakkaw, Yosemite. *Chief islands*—Baffin, Banks, Cuba, Ellesmere, Greenland, Hispaniola, Jamaica, Newfoundland, Prince Edward, Puerto Rico, Vancouver, Victoria.

Number of independent countries: 23.

rived about 15,000 years ago. But some people believe they came as early as 35,000 years ago. The Indians crossed the Bering Strait—dry land then—while following the large mammals they hunted. They eventually settled throughout the continent, but especially in Middle America. The ancestors of today's Inuit migrated from Asia to North America several thousand years ago.

The first Europeans to discover North America were the Norse, or Viking, explorers from Scandinavia. They visited Greenland and the Labrador coast of Canada in the late 900's. Europeans began settling the continent in the late 1400's and early 1500's. Explorers from Spain were the first to sail across the Atlantic Ocean to Middle America. About 100 years later, British and French people settled in what are now the United States and Canada. People from Africa were originally brought to North America by the Spanish to work as slaves on sugar plantations in the Caribbean. African slaves later were brought to the North American mainland.

Population. About 549 million people live in North America, or about 8 percent of the world's population. Few people live in the cold northern part of the continent or in its western deserts. Many large cities lie along the eastern Great Lakes, the St. Lawrence River, and the Atlantic coast from Massachusetts to Virginia. Since the 1950's, a number of people have moved from the northeastern and midwestern United States to California and states in the Southwest and along the Gulf Coast. In Middle America, most people live in the cool highlands where the Indians originally settled. Mexico City, in these highlands, is one of the world's largest metropolitan areas. Since 1900, many Mexicans, Puerto Ricans, and Cubans have moved to the United States.

Ancestry. Most North Americans are descendants of Europeans. Immigrants from every European country have settled in North America. More than a fourth of the

Independent countries of North America*

Map key	Name	Area In mi²	In km²	Population	Capital	Official language	Date of independence
L 12	**Antigua and Barbuda**	171	442	90,000	St. John's	English	1981
L 9	**Bahamas**	5,382	13,939	354,000	Nassau	English	1973
M12	**Barbados**	166	430	278,000	Bridgetown	English	1966
M 8	**Belize**	8,867	22,966	327,000	Belmopan	English	1981
G 7	**Canada**	3,855,103	9,984,670	34,967,000	Ottawa	English; French	1931
N 9	**Costa Rica**	19,730	51,100	4,763,000	San José	Spanish	1821
L 9	**Cuba**	42,427	109,886	11,268,000	Havana	Spanish	1898
M12	**Dominica**	290	751	73,000	Roseau	English	1978
L 10	**Dominican Republic**	18,792	48,671	10,464,000	Santo Domingo	Spanish	1844
N 8	**El Salvador**	8,124	21,041	6,275,000	San Salvador	Spanish	1821
M12	**Grenada**	133	344	106,000	Saint George's	English	1974
M 8	**Guatemala**	42,042	108,889	15,065,000	Guatemala City	Spanish	1821
M10	**Haiti**	10,714	27,750	10,411,000	Port-au-Prince	French	1804
M 8	**Honduras**	43,433	112,492	7,907,000	Tegucigalpa	Spanish	1821
M 9	**Jamaica**	4,244	10,991	2,760,000	Kingston	English	1962
L 6	**Mexico**	758,450	1,964,375	112,965,000	Mexico City	Spanish	1821
N 8	**Nicaragua**	50,337	130,373	6,039,000	Managua	Spanish	1821
N 9	**Panama**	29,157	75,517	3,608,000	Panama City	Spanish	1903
L 11	**St. Kitts and Nevis**	101	261	51,000	Basseterre	English	1983
M12	**St. Lucia**	238	616	177,000	Castries	English	1979
M12	**St. Vincent and the Grenadines**	150	389	109,000	Kingstown	English	1979
M12	**Trinidad and Tobago**	1,981	5,130	1,351,000	Port-of-Spain	English	1962
J 7	**United States†**	3,609,778	9,349,280	314,431,000	Washington, D.C.	None	1776

Dependencies in North America*

Map key	Name	Area In mi²	In km²	Population	Status
L 11	**Anguilla**	37	96	16,000	British overseas territory; some self-government
M10	**Aruba**	69	180	108,000	Self-governing part of the Netherlands
J 11	**Bermuda**	20	53	65,000	British overseas territory; some self-government
M11	**Bonaire**	111	288	15,000	Overseas municipality of the Netherlands
M 9	**Cayman Islands**	101	262	56,000	British overseas territory
M11	**Curaçao**	171	444	144,000	Self-governing part of the Netherlands
D 9	**Greenland**	836,331	2,166,086	57,000	Province of Denmark
L 12	**Guadeloupe**	658	1,705	470,000	Overseas region and department of France
M12	**Martinique**	436	1,128	408,000	Overseas region and department of France
L 11	**Montserrat**	39	102	6,000	British overseas territory
L 11	**Puerto Rico**	3,425	8,870	4,001,000	United States commonwealth
M11	**Saba‡**	5	13	2,000	Overseas municipality of the Netherlands
L 11	**St-Barthélemy‡**	8	21	7,000	Overseas collectivity of France
M11	**St. Eustatius‡**	8	21	3,000	Overseas municipality of the Netherlands
M11	**St. Martin (St. Maarten)‡**	17	43	37,000	Self-governing part of the Netherlands
L 11	**St-Martin‡**	20	53	31,000	Overseas collectivity of France
H 11	**St-Pierre and Miquelon**	93	242	6,000	Overseas collectivity of France
L 10	**Turks and Caicos Islands**	366	948	27,000	British overseas territory
L 11	**Virgin Islands (U.S.)**	134	347	110,000	U.S. organized unincorporated territory
L 11	**Virgin Islands, British**	58	151	25,000	British overseas territory; some self-government

*Each country and dependency in North America, except for Bonaire, Saba, St-Barthélemy, St. Eustatius, St. Martin, and St-Martin, has a separate article in *World Book*.
†Excludes 6,461 square miles (16,734 square kilometers) and 1,315,000 people for Hawaii.
‡Not on map; key shows general location.

Populations are 2012 estimates for independent countries and dependencies based on the latest figures from official government and United Nations sources.

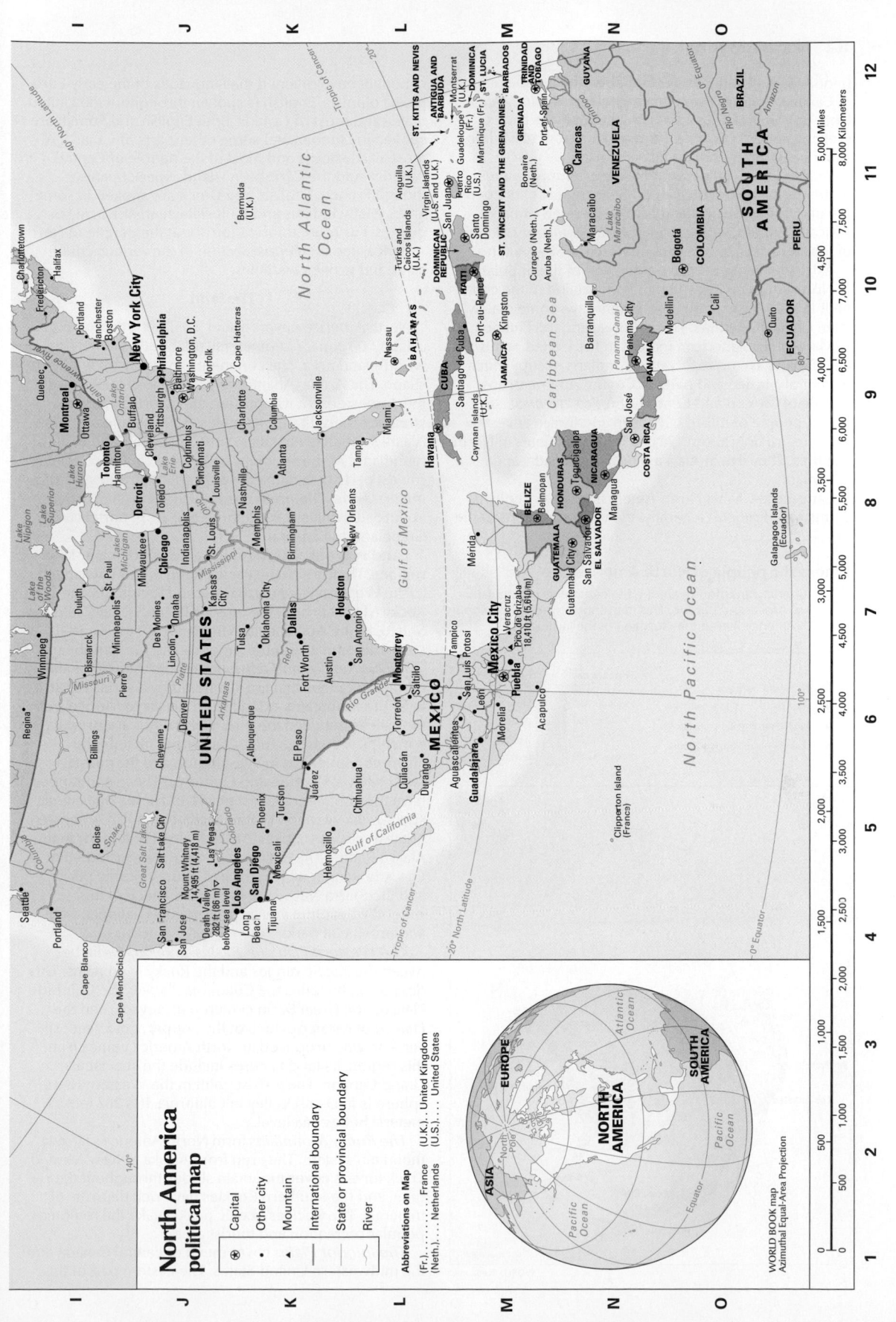

North America political map

Abbreviations on Map

(Fr.) . . . . France
(Neth.) . . . . Netherlands

(U.K.) . . . . United Kingdom
(U.S.) . . . . United States

⊛ Capital
• Other city
▲ Mountain
— International boundary
— State or provincial boundary
〜 River

WORLD BOOK map
Azimuthal Equal-Area Projection

people of the United States and about half of the people of Canada have ancestors from England, Ireland, Scotland, or Wales. About a sixth of all Canadians have French ancestors. Most European ancestors of Middle Americans came from Spain.

People of African descent make up about 13 percent of the population of the United States. Most of the people of the Caribbean Islands are descended from Africans. Other Caribbean people are *mulattoes,* people of mixed African and European descent. See **Mulatto.**

Asians make up a small percentage of the population of North America. They began immigrating to the continent in the 1800's. Asian immigrants have come mainly from China, Indochina, Japan, Korea, and the Philippines.

Many of the American Indians in the United States and Canada live on reservations. Indians occupy much of central Mexico and parts of Central America. Most people of Mexico and Central America are *mestizos*—that is, people of mixed European and Indian ancestry.

There are only about 175,000 Inuit and Aleuts in North America. They live in Alaska, northern Canada, and Greenland.

Languages. Most North Americans speak English, Spanish, or French. Generally, the various regions of the

Where the people of North America live

North America ranks fourth among the continents in population, after Asia, Africa, and Europe. This map shows where the people of North America live and the location of the largest cities.

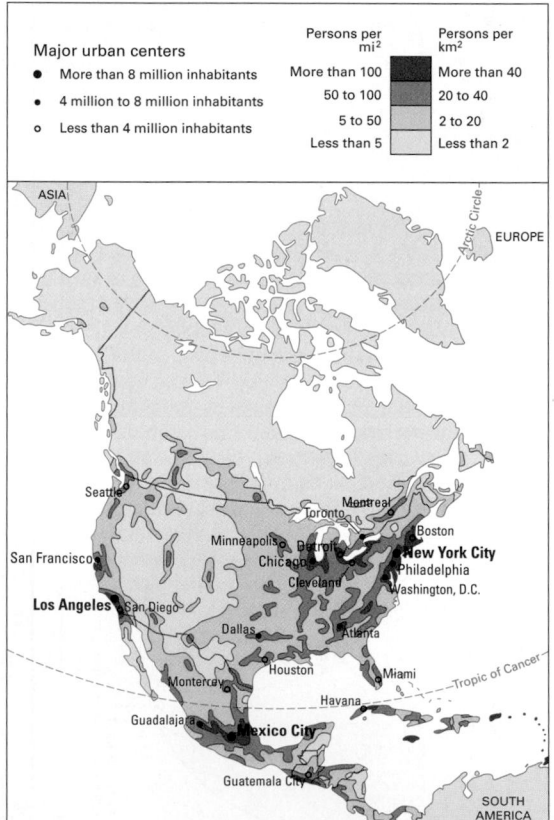

Major urban centers		Persons per mi²	Persons per km²
●	More than 8 million inhabitants	More than 100	More than 40
●	4 million to 8 million inhabitants	50 to 100	20 to 40
○	Less than 4 million inhabitants	5 to 50	2 to 20
		Less than 5	Less than 2

ASIA
EUROPE
Arctic Circle
Seattle
Montreal
Toronto
Boston
Minneapolis   Detroit
New York City
San Francisco   Chicago
Philadelphia
Cleveland
Washington, D.C.
Los Angeles   San Diego
Dallas
Atlanta
Houston
Miami
Tropic of Cancer
Monterrey
Havana
Guadalajara
Mexico City
Guatemala City
SOUTH AMERICA

WORLD BOOK map

continent have retained the languages of the early European colonists. English is spoken throughout the United States and most of Canada. Both English and French are spoken in Quebec and some other parts of Canada. Almost all Mexicans and most of the people of Central America and the Caribbean Islands speak Spanish, though French, English, and Dutch are spoken in some areas. Many Indians and Inuit still use their native languages. For more information about the people of North America, see the *People* section of the various country, state, and province articles.

The land

North America covers about 9,352,000 square miles (24,221,000 square kilometers), or about a sixth of the world's land area. The continent is roughly triangular in shape. The Arctic, Atlantic, and Pacific oceans border the three sides. At its northern end, North America stretches more than 5,400 miles (8,900 kilometers) from Alaska's Aleutian Islands to the Canadian island of Newfoundland. At the southern end of the continent, the narrowest parts of Panama are only about 30 miles (50 kilometers) wide. The greatest north-south distance spans about 5,400 miles (8,900 kilometers), from northern Greenland to Panama.

Land regions. North America has eight major land regions. They are (1) the Pacific Ranges and Lowlands, (2) the Western Plateaus, Basins, and Ranges, (3) the Rocky Mountains, (4) the Interior Plains, (5) the Canadian Shield, (6) the Appalachian Highlands, (7) the Coastal Lowlands, and (8) Central America and the Caribbean.

Pacific Ranges and Lowlands consist of two parallel mountain ranges that are separated by a series of valleys. The mountains extend from Alaska to Mexico. Fertile valleys between the mountain ranges are productive agricultural centers. The outer ranges include the Olympic Mountains in Washington and the coastal mountains of Oregon and California. The inland ranges have the continent's tallest peaks and some of its most spectacular scenery. Mount McKinley, North America's highest mountain, rises 20,320 feet (6,194 meters) in the Alaska Range. The inland mountains also include the Cascade Range, which features many volcanic peaks, and the Sierra Nevada of California. Much of this ruggedly beautiful area is preserved as national, state, and provincial parks.

The Western Plateaus, Basins, and Ranges lie between the Pacific ranges and the Rocky Mountains. This dry region includes the Columbia Plateau, the Colorado Plateau, the Great Basin centered in Nevada, and the Plateau of Mexico. Much of the copper, gold, lead, silver, and zinc produced in North America comes from this region. Its land features include the spectacular Grand Canyon. The lowest point in the Western Hemisphere is in Death Valley in California. It is 282 feet (86 meters) below sea level.

The Rocky Mountains form North America's largest mountain system. They run from Alaska to New Mexico. Thick forests cover mountain slopes throughout the region, and the southern Rockies have rich deposits of minerals. The Rockies' scenic peaks make the region a popular recreation and tourist area.

The Interior Plains cover much of central Canada and the midwestern United States. The eastern part of this

North America
terrain map

Land region boundary
International boundary
• City
+ Elevation above sea level
▽ Depression

WORLD BOOK map

| 0 | 500 | 1,000 | 1,500 | 2,000 | 2,500 | 3,000 Miles |

| 0 | 500 | 1,000 | 1,500 | 2,000 | 2,500 | 3,000 | 3,500 | 4,000 | 4,500 Kilometers |

Physical features

Tropical islands, including Aruba, *shown here,* dot the Caribbean Sea. Their beaches attract large numbers of tourists.

© Roy Morsch, Bruce Coleman Inc.

Dry, rugged land, like California's Death Valley, *shown,* covers much of the southwestern United States and northern Mexico.

flat, low-lying region is North America's most productive agricultural area. Corn, hogs, and soybeans rank among the leading products. The drier western part—the Great Plains—supplies most of the continent's wheat and much of its cattle, coal, petroleum, and natural gas.

The Canadian Shield is a huge area of ancient rock that covers most of Canada east of the Great Plains and north of the Great Lakes. Few people live in this region because of the poor soil and cold climate. Many valuable minerals lie beneath its surface. A vast *boreal* forest—consisting mainly of evergreens—extends across the southern part of the region.

The Appalachian Highlands extend from the island of Newfoundland to Alabama. The region includes low, rounded mountains; plateaus; and valleys. One of the world's most productive coal fields lies in the Allegheny Plateau, in the central part of the region. Hardwood forests grow in the northern and southern sections.

The Coastal Lowlands stretch along the Atlantic Ocean and the Gulf of Mexico, from New York City to Mexico's Yucatán Peninsula. The rich soil in much of this region creates good farmland. Many of North America's best harbors and great port cities are along the Atlantic and Gulf coasts. The region's broad, sandy beaches and warm waters attract millions of tourists each year.

Central America and the Caribbean consist of the narrow bridge of land at the southern tip of North America and the islands in the Caribbean Sea. A chain of volcanoes forms a mountainous spine along the Pacific coast of Central America. Most of the Caribbean islands were created by volcanic eruptions. Others are coral and other limestone formations.

Rivers. West of the Rocky Mountains, the rivers of North America drain into the Pacific Ocean or the Gulf of California, an arm of the Pacific. East of the Rockies, rivers flow into the Arctic Ocean, Hudson Bay, the Atlantic Ocean, or the Gulf of Mexico. The high ridge of the Rockies that separates the waters is called the Great Divide, or the Continental Divide. The divide continues through Mexico and Central America and also separates the flow of rivers in those areas.

West of the Rockies, such rivers as the Yukon, Fraser, and Columbia rush to the Pacific through gaps in the coastal ranges. The Colorado River cuts through the Grand Canyon as it flows toward the Gulf of California.

The Mackenzie River, which forms part of Canada's longest river system, flows from Great Slave Lake into the Arctic Ocean. Many Canadian streams and rivers empty into Hudson Bay. East of the Appalachian Mountains, several short rivers, such as the Connecticut and the Hudson, drain into the Atlantic. Many of the main rivers in Mexico, such as the Lerma and Balsas, are not as long as those in the north. However, they provide water that is vital to irrigation, hydroelectric power, and wildlife habitats.

The continent's longest river system, the Mississippi-Missouri-Ohio, flows into the Gulf of Mexico. This system, which is about 4,700 miles (7,600 kilometers) long, drains almost all of the United States between the Rockies and the Appalachian Mountains. The Rio Grande, which forms most of the border between the United States and Mexico, also empties into the gulf.

Lakes. Lake Superior is the largest freshwater lake in the world. It is one of the five Great Lakes, which make up part of North America's most important inland waterway. Four of the Great Lakes—Superior, Huron, Erie, and Ontario—lie on the border between Canada and the United States. The fifth, Lake Michigan, lies entirely within the United States. A chain of big lakes extends northwest from the Great Lakes to Great Bear Lake, Canada's largest lake. Utah's Great Salt Lake, one of the natural wonders of North America, is saltier than the ocean.

Many of the rivers in the United States and Canada have been dammed to form large but narrow artificial lakes, or reservoirs. Lake Mead and Lake Powell on the Colorado River are among the largest such lakes in the United States. Smallwood Reservoir on the Churchill River in Newfoundland is Canada's largest artificial lake.

Waterfalls. North America's most famous waterfall is Niagara Falls, on the U.S.-Canadian border between Lake Erie and Lake Ontario. Niagara Falls consists of two waterfalls, the Horseshoe Falls and the American Falls. The Horseshoe Falls is only 167 feet (51 meters) high, but more water passes over it than over any other waterfall in North America. A number of higher falls—several more than 1,000 feet (300 meters) high—plunge through the Cascade Range and the Sierra Nevada. North America's highest waterfall, Yosemite Falls, is a main attraction at Yosemite National Park in the Sierra Nevada. Yosemite Falls drops 2,425 feet (739 meters).

Deserts. Most North American deserts lie in the southwestern United States and northern Mexico. One vast dry area reaches from southern Idaho and Oregon into Mexico. It includes the Great Basin, the Mojave Desert and Death Valley, and the Sonoran Desert. Another area, the Chihuahuan Desert, extends from southern New Mexico through western Texas into Mexico.

Coastline and islands. North America has a longer total coastline than any other continent. Including the continent's many islands, the coastline is about 190,000 miles (300,000 kilometers) long.

Mountains line the Pacific and north Atlantic coasts, and many bays cut into the rocky land. Plains slope gently to the coasts along the Gulf of Mexico, the Caribbean Sea, and the Atlantic south of New York City. There, the coastline is relatively smooth and even.

A number of islands lie off the coasts of North America. Greenland is in the North Atlantic Ocean. Newfoundland and other islands lie off the Canadian coast in the Atlantic Ocean. In the Pacific Ocean, Vancouver and many other islands lie off Canada, the Aleutian Islands extend westward from the tip of the Alaska Peninsula, and the Channel Islands are off California's southern coast. The islands in the Caribbean Sea are called the West Indies. They include the Bahamas, the Greater Antilles, and the Lesser Antilles. Cuba, one of the Greater Antilles, is the largest Caribbean island.

Climate

North America is the only continent that has every kind of climate, from the dry, bitter cold of the Arctic to the steamy heat of the tropics. An ice sheet permanently covers the interior of Greenland, where the temperature almost never rises above freezing. In the North American *tundra,* the vast treeless plain of the far north, the temperature rises above freezing for only a short period each summer. In the low-lying areas of the far south, it is hot and rainy all the time.

Most of the rest of North America is cold in the winter and warm in the summer, with moderate precipitation. Some areas have mild winters and long, hot summers. Other areas have harsh winters and short summers. The highest temperature ever recorded in North America was 134 °F (57 °C) at Death Valley in 1913. The lowest was –87 °F (–66 °C) at Northice in Greenland in 1954.

Animal life

North America has abundant animal life, which varies with the climate and plant life of each region. Caribou, musk oxen, polar bears, seals, snowy owls, whales, and

What North America's climate is like

Icecap–Always cold, average monthly temperature never above freezing. Precipitation almost always snow.

Tundra–Always cold, with a brief, chilly summer. Little precipitation in all seasons.

Subarctic–Short, cool summers and long, cold winters. Light to moderate precipitation, mostly in summer.

Humid continental–Mild summers and cold winters. Moderate precipitation in all seasons.

Humid oceanic–Moderately warm summers and generally cool winters. Moderate precipitation in all seasons.

Humid subtropical–Warm to hot summers and cool winters. Moderate precipitation in all seasons.

Subtropical dry summer–Hot, dry summers and mild, rainy winters. Moderate precipitation in winter.

Semiarid–Hot to cold. Great changes in temperature from day to night except in coastal areas. Light precipitation.

Desert–Hot to cool. Great changes in temperature from day to night except in coastal areas. Very little precipitation.

Highland–Climate depends on altitude. Climates at various altitudes are like those found in flat terrain.

Tropical wet and dry–Always hot, with alternate wet and dry seasons. Heavy precipitation in wet season.

Tropical wet–Always hot and wet. Heavy precipitation well distributed throughout year.

WORLD BOOK map

wolverines live in the cold north. Jaguars, monkeys, and colorful birds are found in tropical Central America. Rocky Mountain sheep and goats graze on the slopes of the Rockies. The southwestern deserts have a wide variety of lizards and rattlesnakes. Coyotes and pronghorns—animals that are found only in North America—roam the Great Plains. The forests of Canada and the eastern United States have beavers, black bears, deer, ermines, minks, moose, muskrats, and porcupines. Canada geese, ducks, egrets, pelicans, and spoonbills are among the birds that winter in the marshes of the Coastal Lowlands, and alligators live in the coastal wa-

ters of the far south. Raccoons, skunks, and squirrels are common throughout the continent.

The oceans supply commercial fishing crews with valuable catches of flounder, salmon, and many other kinds of fish and shellfish. Crabs are plentiful in the northern Pacific, lobsters in the northern Atlantic, and menhaden all along the Atlantic coast. Shrimp and oysters are abundant in the Gulf of Mexico.

Some kinds of wildlife have decreased sharply over the years. These include the bison (buffalo), whooping crane, and bald eagle. Game laws and the establishment of protected areas help such animals survive today.

Animals of North America

This map shows some of the many kinds of mammals, birds, and reptiles of North America. The continent's abundant animal life varies with each region's climate and plant life.

WORLD BOOK map

Plant life

The plant life of North America is related to the continent's various climates. Nothing grows on Greenland's ice sheet. Only grasses, mosses, and lichens survive in the vast cold plains that border the Arctic Ocean. A kind of moss called *sphagnum* or *peat* fills the marshes of the Canadian Shield and is an important export from this region. Huge saguaro cactuses and other cactus plants grow in the southwestern deserts. Short grasses and small bushlike plants, such as tumbleweed, cover the dry Great Plains.

Most of the rest of the continent has forests and level or rolling grasslands called *prairies*. The prairies stretch across the center of the continent. The forests cover the continent's western mountain regions, most of Canada, and the eastern half of the United States. A tropical rain forest grows along the Caribbean coast.

The finest North American forests are those along the Pacific coast. The towering redwoods stand there, as well as forests of cedar, fir, hemlock, and spruce.

The Canadian forests include spruce, larch, pine, and fir trees. Hardwood trees, such as maple and beech, grow in the northeastern United States. Many trees that

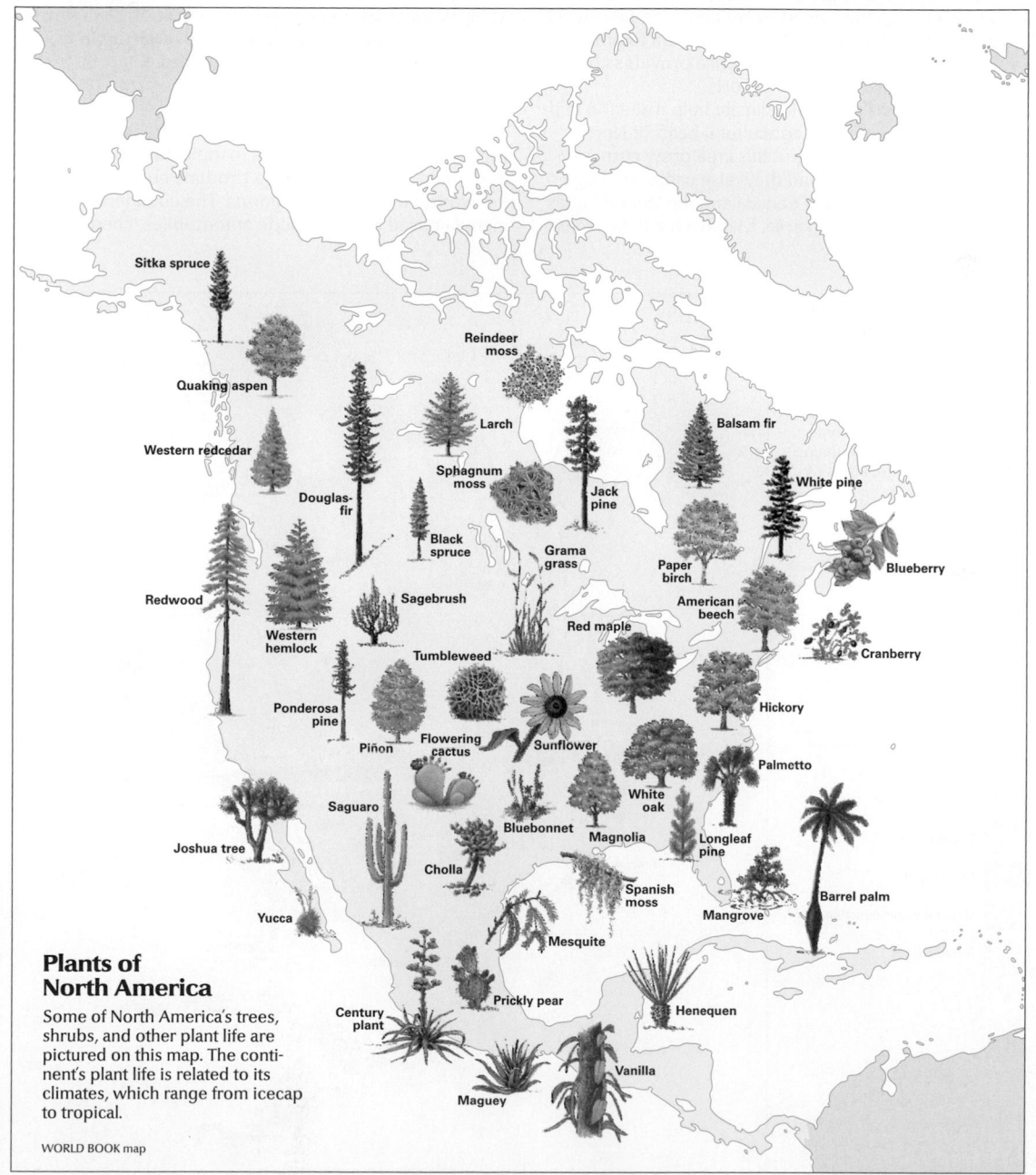

Plants of North America

Some of North America's trees, shrubs, and other plant life are pictured on this map. The continent's plant life is related to its climates, which range from icecap to tropical.

WORLD BOOK map

grow in Canada and the northeastern United States are processed into wood pulp for newsprint. Hickory, oak, and pine trees fill the forests of the southern United States. Central America's tropical forests include mahogany and rosewood trees, used to make furniture.

Agriculture

North America ranks third among the continents, after Asia and Europe, in agricultural production. Its farms grow about two-fifths of the world's corn and soybeans and about half the world's flaxseed. North American farms produce about a fourth of the world's sorghum; a fifth of its citrus fruits, cotton, and oats; and a sixth of its wheat. Farmers in the United States and Canada grow so much food that large quantities may be sent to other countries. For example, North America provides about two-fifths of the world's grain exports.

Fertile soil and a favorable climate help make the midwestern United States the agricultural heart of North America. Farmers throughout this area grow corn, soybeans, and other crops, and they raise cattle and hogs. The Great Plains region of Canada and the United States is a major wheat-growing area. Massive feedlots, where

cattle are fattened before going to market, are also in this region. Large cattle and sheep ranches cover the Western basins and plateaus. Irrigation enables farmers in these areas to produce many varieties of fruits, nuts, and vegetables. Other crops, such as cotton and alfalfa, are grown in abundance. Corn, dry beans, and rice are important food crops in Middle America. Large plantations in the region produce such crops as bananas, coffee, cotton, and sugar cane.

Only about 2 percent of United States and Canadian workers farm. Most of the farmers own all or at least part of their land. In Middle America, about 20 percent of the people farm, and few of them own their own land. Many work as laborers on large plantations. Some own or rent small plots of land on which they struggle to grow enough food to feed their families.

Industry

Manufacturing. North America ranks second to Europe among the continents in manufacturing. Together, the United States and Canada produce about a fourth of the world's manufactured goods. The continent's chief manufactured goods include automobiles, chemicals,

Agriculture and fishing in North America

This map shows the major uses of land in North America. It locates the chief agricultural products and shows the most important crops in large type. The map also shows the major fishing areas and the kinds of fish caught.

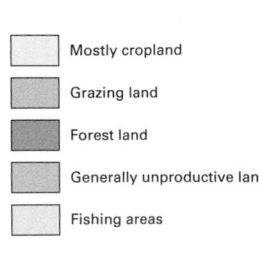

- Mostly cropland
- Grazing land
- Forest land
- Generally unproductive land
- Fishing areas

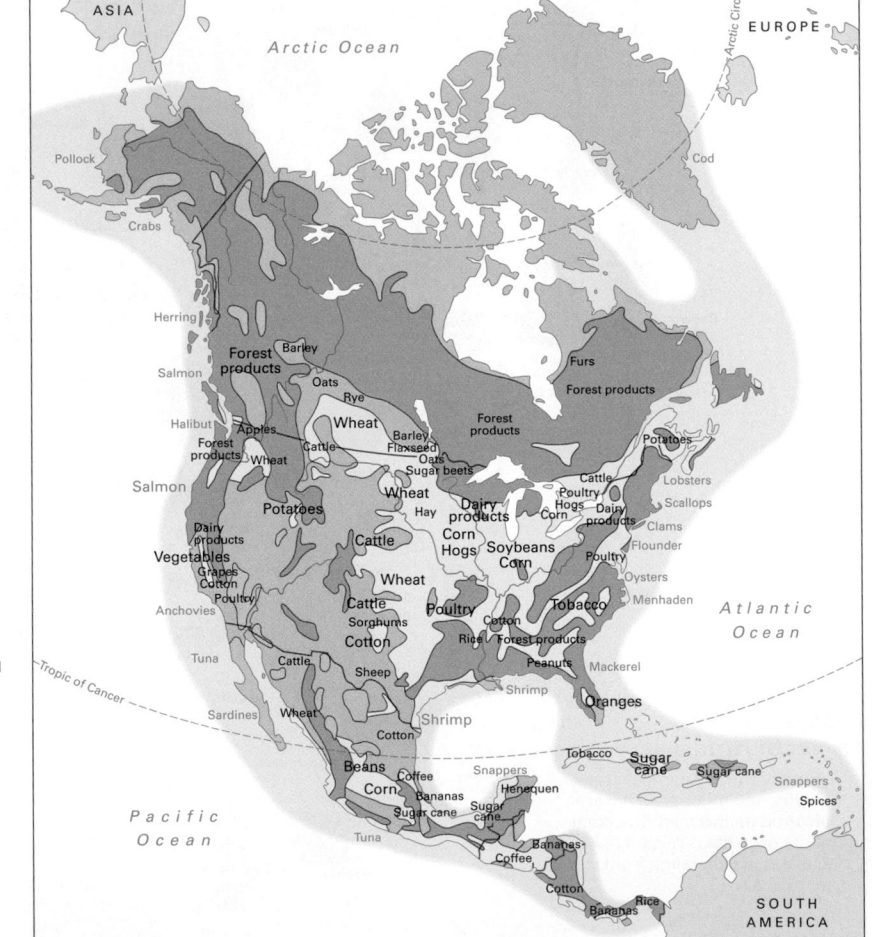

WORLD BOOK map

and food products. Manufacturing employs about one-eighth of all North American workers.

The midwestern and northeastern United States and the Canadian provinces of Ontario and Quebec have long been North America's major manufacturing centers. Since the mid-1900's, however, industry has expanded rapidly in the southern United States and along its Pacific coast. The chief products from factories in these newer industrial areas include aircraft and missiles, computers and electronic components, and petroleum and *petrochemicals* (chemicals made from petroleum or natural gas). Manufacturing also has grown in Middle America, particularly Mexico. Modern factories in Mexico now supply the world with automobiles, automobile parts, and electronics. Other countries in Middle America produce chemicals, clothing and textiles, food products, and medicines.

Mining. North America has large supplies of a broad range of minerals. The continent produces about one-third of the world's supply of potash and uranium. About a fourth of the world's natural gas and silver come from North America, as does a fifth of its coal, lead, nickel, and phosphate rock. North America also produces about a sixth of the world's copper, crude oil, and gold. Fewer than 1 percent of all North American workers have jobs in mining.

Most of North America's petroleum and natural gas comes from the Great Plains region, Alaska, and offshore deposits in the Gulf of Mexico. Major coal fields lie in the Appalachian Plateau, the central United States, and the Rocky Mountain region. Metallic minerals come mainly from the Canadian Shield, the Rockies and other western mountains, and the Appalachian Highlands.

Transportation and communication

North America lies between the Atlantic and Pacific oceans in the middle of the world's major trade routes. The Panama Canal at the southern tip of the continent connects the two oceans. Large ports line North America's east and west coasts. New York City, New Orleans, and Houston handle the most cargo of ports that serve the Atlantic coast. The leading ports on the Pacific Coast are Valdez Harbor, Alaska; Vancouver, British Columbia; and Long Beach, California.

The United States and southern Canada have one of the world's most highly developed transportation systems, including inland waterways, highways, and railroads. The Mississippi River system, the Great Lakes, and the St. Lawrence Seaway form North America's most important inland waterways. Highways and railroad tracks crisscross the United States and southern Canada. Few roads lead into northern Canada. In Mexico, paved roads and railroad lines link major cities. In Central America and the Caribbean, most local roads are unpaved, and most railroad companies are small, private lines that connect sugar or banana plantations with processing plants and ports.

North America has the world's best regional airline network. Most flights serve the large cities of the United States and southern Canada. Many of the world's busiest airports are in the United States.

North America also has the best communications system of any continent. Radios and televisions are common in U.S. and Canadian households. Many people in

Mining and manufacturing in North America

This map shows the location of North America's chief mineral resources and manufacturing centers. Major mineral-producing areas are shown in large type, and lesser ones in small type.

WORLD BOOK map

Middle American countries own radios, but televisions are less widespread. Most North American newspapers and radio and television broadcasting stations are privately owned, except in Cuba, where the government controls most communications. Since the mid-1990's, Internet usage has grown tremendously, especially in Anglo-America. Today, most Americans and Canadians have Internet access. A smaller proportion of people in Middle America have Internet access, with usage rates on Caribbean islands higher than those elsewhere in Middle America.   Jefferson S. Rogers

Related articles in *World Book* include:

Countries, colonies, and territories

Anguilla	Guadeloupe	Saint-Pierre and
Antigua and Bar-	Guatemala	Miquelon
buda	Haiti	Saint Vincent and
Bahamas	Honduras	the Grenadines
Barbados	Jamaica	Trinidad and
Belize	Martinique	Tobago
Bermuda	Mexico	Turks and Caicos
Canada	Montserrat	Islands
Cayman Islands	Netherlands	United States
Costa Rica	Antilles	Virgin Islands,
Cuba	Nicaragua	British
Dominica	Panama	Virgin Islands, U.S.
Dominican	Puerto Rico	
Republic	Saint Kitts and	
El Salvador	Nevis	
Greenland	Saint Lucia	
Grenada		

Large cities

Baltimore
Calgary
Chicago
Dallas
Detroit
Guadalajara
Havana
Houston

Indianapolis
Los Angeles
Memphis
Mexico City
Monterrey
Montreal
New York City
Philadelphia

Phoenix
San Antonio
San Diego
San Francisco
Toronto
Washington, D.C.

Natural features

See the list of *Related articles* with the articles on **Desert; Island; Lake; Mountain; River; Waterfall.** See also the following articles on important North American physical features:

Appalachian
 Mountains
Arkansas River
Badlands
Blue Ridge Mountains
Bridalveil Fall
Canadian Shield
Coast Ranges
Colorado River
Columbia River
Death Valley
Everglades
Grand Canyon
Great Basin
Great Bear Lake
Great Divide
Great Lakes
Great Plains

Great Salt Lake
Great Slave Lake
Greenland
Klondike
Labrador
 Peninsula
Lake Nicaragua
Lake Winnipeg
Mackenzie River
Mississippi River
Missouri River
Nelson River
Newfoundland
 and Labrador
Niagara Falls
Niagara River
Orizaba, Pico de
Painted Desert
Paricutín

Piedmont Region
Popocatépetl
Ribbon Falls
Rio Grande
Rocky Mountains
Saint Lawrence
 River
Shenandoah
 Valley
Sierra Madre
Sierra Nevada
Takakkaw Falls
West Indies
Yellowstone National Park
Yosemite Falls
Yosemite National
 Park
Yukon River

Coastal waters

Arctic Ocean
Atlantic Ocean
Bay of Fundy
Bering Sea
Caribbean Sea
Chesapeake Bay
Delaware Bay
Gulf of California

Gulf of Mexico
Gulf of Saint Lawrence
Hudson Bay
James Bay
Long Island Sound
Pacific Ocean
Puget Sound

People

African Americans
Asian Americans
City
Clothing
Food
Hispanic Americans

Indian, American
Inuit
Literacy (table)
Metropolitan area
Population
World

History

See the *History* section of the articles on the countries, states, and provinces of North America. See also the following articles:

Canada, History of
Central America
Exploration

Latin America (History)
United States, History of

Outline

I. **People**
  A. Population
  B. Ancestry
  C. Languages
II. **The land**
  A. Land regions
  B. Rivers
  C. Lakes
  D. Waterfalls
  E. Deserts
  F. Coastline and islands
III. **Climate**
IV. **Animal life**
V. **Plant life**
VI. **Agriculture**
VII. **Industry**
  A. Manufacturing
  B. Mining
VIII. **Transportation and communication**

Additional resources

Level I

Lacey, Theresa, J. *The Blackfeet.* Chelsea Hse., 2006.
McIntosh, Marsha. *Teen Life on Reservations and in First Nation Communities.* Mason Crest, 2008.
Woods, Michael and Mary B. *Seven Natural Wonders of North America.* 21st Century Bks., 2009.

Level II

Dailey, Donna. *North America: A Guide to the Places You Must See in Your Lifetime.* Barron's, 2009.
Hayes, Derek. *America Discovered: A Historical Atlas of North Amerian Exploration.* D & M Pubs., Inc., 2004.
Wesson, Cameron B. *The A to Z of Early North America.* Scarecrow, 2009.

North American Aerospace Defense Command. See NORAD.

North American Free Trade Agreement (NAFTA) is a pact that unites Canada, Mexico, and the United States in one of the world's largest free-trade zones. It builds on a free-trade agreement between the United States and Canada that became effective in 1989. NAFTA took effect in January 1994.

Under NAFTA, tariffs on most goods produced and sold in North America were gradually eliminated over 10 years. Trade of a few additional products was restricted for another 5 years. The first reductions took place in 1994, and almost all tariffs were eliminated by 2008.

NAFTA also establishes rights and obligations regarding trade in services, intellectual property, and international investment. These provisions could serve as models for future global and regional trade agreements.

NAFTA generated extensive opposition in the United States because of concerns that it would result in a loss of U.S. jobs. Opponents feared the job losses would result from increased Mexican imports and from a shift in U.S. production to Mexican plants. Environmental groups feared NAFTA would increase air and water pollution. In response to this opposition, the three countries established commissions to monitor developments related to environmental and labor issues and to help solve problems that may arise.   Jeffrey J. Schott

North Atlantic Treaty Organization (NATO) is a military alliance consisting of the United States, the United Kingdom, Canada, and more than 20 other member countries. NATO seeks to protect the freedom and security of its member countries through political and military efforts. The organization also participates in a variety of international peacekeeping and crisis management efforts.

NATO was established in 1949, after the start of the Cold War. The Cold War was a period of intense rivalry between Communist countries, led by the Soviet Union, and non-Communist countries, led by the United States. Originally, the central purpose of NATO was to discourage an attack by the Soviet Union on the non-Communist nations of Western Europe. By joining NATO, each member country agreed to treat an attack on any other member as an attack on itself. NATO's collective defense policy was known as *deterrence* because it was designed to *deter* (discourage) a Soviet attack. In 1955, the Soviet Union and its allies formed their own military alliance, called the Warsaw Pact, to oppose NATO.

The Cold War ended in the early 1990's. Since then, the main focus of NATO has shifted toward general crisis management and peacekeeping. Today, the organization's central aims include resolving international conflicts and crises, developing and enforcing international security policies, fighting terrorism, and working to maintain peace and stability. NATO's website at http://www.nato.int presents information on its activities.

Organization. NATO has a civilian branch and a military branch. The civilian branch includes the North Atlantic Council, the highest authority in NATO. The council consists of the heads of government or other representatives for every NATO country. Decisions of the council must be unanimous.

NATO's military branch includes two commands: (1) Allied Command Operations, which is responsible for NATO's military operations; and (2) Allied Command Transformation, which is responsible for improving NATO's military capabilities.

History. NATO was created by the North Atlantic Treaty, signed by 12 countries in 1949. The countries were Belgium, Canada, Denmark, France, Iceland, Italy, Luxembourg, the Netherlands, Norway, Portugal, the United Kingdom, and the United States. NATO established its central office in London, but it was moved to Paris in 1952.

During the Cold War, NATO helped maintain peace in Europe through its policy of deterrence. However, it also experienced disagreements among its members. In particular, the United States often favored more aggressive policies toward the Soviet Union than other members wanted. For instance, U.S. officials generally insisted that NATO rely on nuclear weapons to deter a Soviet attack. But some NATO countries opposed the use of these weapons.

Greece and Turkey joined the NATO alliance in 1952. West Germany joined in 1955. France withdrew from NATO in 1966. Because of this, NATO moved its headquarters from Paris to Brussels, Belgium, in 1967. Spain joined NATO in 1982. Germany replaced West Germany as a member in 1990, when West and East Germany were united.

In 1991, the Warsaw Pact was dissolved, and the Soviet Union broke apart into a number of independent states. Most of these states rejected Communism. Some people felt that, without its traditional Communist enemies, NATO had lost its purpose and should disband. However, the alliance shifted its focus and launched the Partnership for Peace program in 1994. More than 20 countries—including Russia and many Eastern European nations—joined the program, which provides for joint military planning and exercises with NATO members.

During the 1990's, NATO became involved in efforts to stop civil wars in Bosnia-Herzegovina and Yugoslavia (then made up of Serbia and Montenegro). In Yugoslavia in 1999, NATO launched extensive air strikes against military targets. The targets included Serbian troops from the Yugoslav army who were fighting ethnic Albanian rebels in Kosovo. The action by NATO became the closest thing to a conventional war ever fought by the organization. The bombing ended in June 1999 after Yugoslavia began withdrawing its troops. NATO troops then entered Kosovo as peacekeepers.

In 1997, Russia had announced that it would not oppose the eastward expansion of NATO. In 1999, the Czech Republic, Hungary, and Poland became NATO members. Bulgaria, Estonia, Latvia, Lithuania, Romania, Slovakia, and Slovenia joined in 2004.

In 2001, NATO sent troops to Macedonia to help maintain a cease-fire agreement between Albanian rebels and the Macedonian government. NATO troops were given the task of collecting and destroying the rebels' weapons.

Later that year, following the September 11 terrorist attacks in the United States, NATO announced that it considered the attacks against the United States as attacks against all NATO members. In the following months, many NATO nations provided assistance in a U.S.-led military campaign against terrorist targets in Afghanistan. The campaign led to the fall of Afghanistan's ruling party, the Taliban. In 2003, NATO took command of an international peacekeeping force in Kabul, the capital of Afghanistan. In 2005, NATO sent additional troops into southern Afghanistan, and in 2006, NATO assumed command from the coalition forces of peacekeeping efforts there. In 2011, U.S. president Barack Obama announced a plan to withdraw NATO-led American forces from Afghanistan by 2014.

In 2002, NATO and Russia established the NATO-Russia Council. This body allows Russia and NATO to work together on a range of projects and policies, including counterterrorism, arms control, and crisis management. The creation of the council marked Russia's entry into NATO as a limited partner.

The Iraq War (2003–2010) created significant disagreements among NATO countries. Several European nations—including France and Germany—opposed the U.S.-led invasion of Iraq, which led to the fall of the Iraqi government of Saddam Hussein. Following the invasion, NATO helped the new government of Iraq train its security forces.

France, which had withdrawn from NATO in 1966, rejoined the organization as a member state in 2009. Albania and Croatia also became member nations of NATO in 2009. That same year, NATO began military operations in the Indian Ocean and Gulf of Aden, aimed at fighting piracy in the region.

In 2011, conflict erupted in Libya between the Libyan military and protesters opposed to the rule of Mu'ammar al-Qadhafi. NATO-led military operations aimed at protecting civilians in this conflict.   Bruce Cronin

See also **Cold War; Flag** (picture: Flags of world organizations); **Warsaw Pact.**

Members of NATO

Original members of NATO do not have dates after their names. Other nations are listed with the years they became members.

Albania (2009)	Germany (1955)*	Poland (1999)
Belgium	Greece (1952)	Portugal
Bulgaria (2004)	Hungary (1999)	Romania (2004)
Canada	Iceland	Slovakia (2004)
Croatia (2009)	Italy	Slovenia (2004)
Czech Republic	Latvia (2004)	Spain (1982)
(1999)	Lithuania (2004)	Turkey (1952)
Denmark	Luxembourg	United Kingdom
Estonia (2004)	Netherlands	United States
France	Norway	

*West Germany became a member in 1955. Germany replaced West Germany in 1990, when West and East Germany were united.

Ed Blair, Shostal

A smoky mist rises over the Blue Ridge Mountains near Asheville. This forest-covered range, which cuts across western North Carolina, is famous for its beautiful scenery.

North Carolina *The Tar Heel State*

North Carolina leads all the states of the United States in tobacco farming and in the manufacture of tobacco products. It ranks among the nation's leaders in the production of textiles and wooden furniture.

Raleigh is North Carolina's capital. Charlotte is the state's largest city.

North Carolina is a Southern state with a long coastline on the Atlantic Ocean. Islands, reefs, and sand bars make its shores some of the most treacherous in the world. Many ships have been wrecked at Cape Hatteras by the rough seas and difficult currents. Cape Hatteras is called the *Graveyard of the Atlantic.*

The state stretches westward from the coast across swamps and fertile farms. The land rises through lovely

hills into industrial cities and towns. Rugged mountains cover much of the far western part of North Carolina. Mount Mitchell, which rises more than 1 ¼ miles (2 kilometers) above sea level, is the highest peak in the eastern United States.

Service industries are the major part of North Carolina's economy. The leading services include finance, health care, private research, real estate, and retail trade. Research Triangle Park, a large research complex in the Raleigh-Durham area, is an important center of research for the electronics, medical, and other industries. Manufacturing is also an important economic activity. North Carolina is a leading state in raising *broilers* (young, tender chickens), hogs, and turkeys. One of the state's main crops is tobacco. Tobacco fields, with neat rows of tobacco plants, are scattered throughout North Carolina.

In 1584, English explorers looked for a suitable site for a settlement along the North Carolina coast. As a result, the first groups of English settlers in America built colonies on Roanoke Island off the coast in 1585 and 1587. The earlier group returned to England. The later group vanished from the island, leaving behind only a mystery

The contributors of this article are Stephen S. Birdsall, Professor of Geography at the University of North Carolina at Chapel Hill and coauthor of Regional Landscapes of the United States and Canada; *and Harry L. Watson, Professor of History at the University of North Carolina at Chapel Hill and author of* An Independent People: The Way We Lived in North Carolina, 1770-1820.

Charlotte is the largest city in North Carolina. It serves as a major financial, transportation, and wholesaling center.

that has puzzled the ages. This group has been named the Lost Colony. Virginia Dare, the first child born to English parents in America, was a member of the Lost Colony.

During colonial days, groups of patriots in North Carolina, such as the Sons of Liberty, defied English taxes and English rule. After the Revolutionary War began in 1775, North Carolina was the first colony to instruct its delegates at the Continental Congress to vote for independence.

Before the outbreak of the Civil War (1861-1865), North Carolina tried to preserve the Union even after most other Southern states had withdrawn. But after North Carolina left the Union, it did its best to help the Confederate cause. More than 10 Civil War battles were fought on North Carolina soil. About a fourth of all Confederate soldiers killed came from North Carolina.

North Carolina's nickname, the *Tar Heel State,* refers to one of the state's earliest products—tar. According to legend, some Confederate troops retreated during a fierce Civil War battle. They left the North Carolina soldiers to fight the Union soldiers alone. The North Carolinians supposedly threatened to put tar on the heels of the other Confederate soldiers so that they would "stick better in the next fight."

Interesting facts about North Carolina

Virginia Dare, the first English child to be born in America, was born on Roanoke Island on Aug. 18, 1587. Nothing else is known about her, because the colony into which she was born mysteriously disappeared.

Virginia Dare

The first state governor to be impeached was William Woods Holden of North Carolina. He had gained a reputation for waste and corruption after two years in office. On March 22, 1871, he was removed from office by vote of the state legislature.

The first operating silver mine in the United States opened in 1838 near Lexington. The mine was later named the Silver Hill Mine. It no longer operates.

The first interstate railroad opened in 1833 between Blakely, in Northampton County, and Petersburg, Va. The 75-mile (120-kilometer) Petersburg Railroad helped to increase tobacco trade

First interstate railroad

from the Roanoke Valley into Virginia. The town of Blakely no longer exists, but the railroad still operates as part of the Seaboard System Railroad.

The Cape Hatteras lighthouse overlooks a part of North Carolina's Atlantic coast known for rough seas and difficult currents.

North Carolina in brief

Symbols of North Carolina

The state flag, adopted in 1885, displays two dates. May 20, 1775, is the supposed date of the Mecklenburg Declaration of Independence proclaiming Mecklenburg County's independence from Britain. On April 12, 1776, North Carolina authorized its delegates to the Continental Congress to vote for independence. The state seal, adopted in 1984, also has these dates. The standing figure represents Liberty; the seated figure, Plenty.

State flag

Secretary of State, North Carolina
State seal

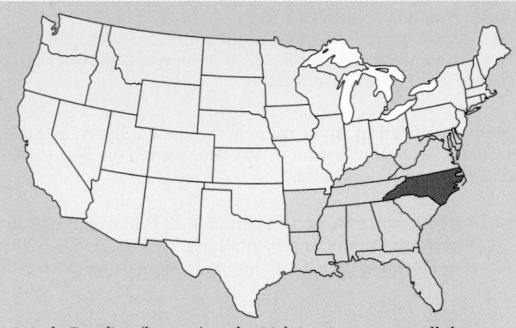

North Carolina (brown) ranks 28th in size among all the states and 4th in size among the Southern States (yellow).

General information

Statehood: Nov. 21, 1789, the 12th state.
State abbreviations: N.C. (traditional); NC (postal).
State motto: *Esse Quam Videri* (To Be, Rather Than to Seem).
State song: "The Old North State." Words by William Gaston; musical arrangement by Ora Huffman Randolph.

The State Capitol is in Raleigh, North Carolina's capital since 1792. New Bern was the capital from 1766 to 1778. There was no fixed capital from 1778 to 1792.

Land and climate

Area: 52,671 mi² (136,416 km²), including 3,960 mi² (10,255 km²) of inland water.
Elevation: *Highest*—Mount Mitchell, 6,684 ft (2,037 m) above sea level. *Lowest*—sea level along the Atlantic Ocean.
Coastline: 301 mi (484 km).
Record high temperature: 110 °F (43 °C) at Fayetteville on Aug. 21, 1983.
Record low temperature: −34 °F (−37 °C) at Mount Mitchell near Asheville on Jan. 21, 1985.
Average July temperature: 70 °F (21 °C).
Average January temperature: 41 °F (5 °C).
Average yearly precipitation: 50 in (127 cm).

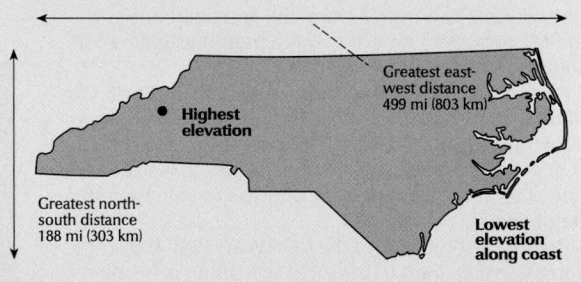

Greatest east-west distance 499 mi (803 km)

Highest elevation

Greatest north-south distance 188 mi (303 km)

Lowest elevation along coast

Important dates

The English established their first American colony at Roanoke Island.

Colonists in North Carolina began to resist enforcement of the British Stamp Act and other tax laws.

| 1524 | 1585 | c.1650 | 1765 |

Giovanni da Verrazzano explored the North Carolina coast.

North Carolina's first permanent white settlers came to the Albemarle region from Virginia.

State bird
Northern cardinal

State flower
Flowering dogwood

State tree
Pine

People

Population: 9,535,483
Rank among the states: 10th
Density: 181 per mi² (70 per km²), U.S.
average 85 per mi² (33 per km²)
Distribution: 60 percent urban, 40 percent rural
Largest cities in North Carolina

Charlotte	731,424
Raleigh	403,892
Greensboro	269,666
Winston-Salem	229,617
Durham	228,330
Fayetteville	200,564

Source: 2010 census, except for distribution, which is for 2000.

Population trend

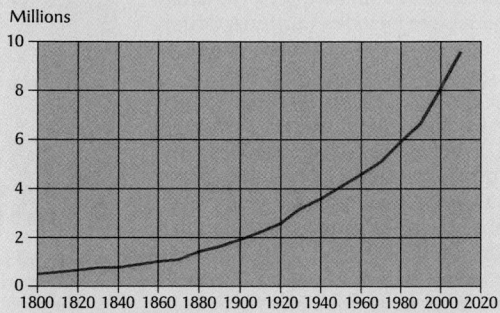

Millions

Source: U.S. Census Bureau.

Year	Population
2010	9,535,483
2000	8,049,313
1990	6,628,637
1980	5,881,766
1970	5,082,059
1960	4,556,155
1950	4,061,929
1940	3,571,623
1930	3,170,276
1920	2,559,123
1910	2,206,287
1900	1,893,810
1890	1,617,949
1880	1,399,750
1870	1,071,361
1860	992,622
1850	869,039
1840	753,419
1830	737,987
1820	638,829
1810	555,500
1800	478,103
1790	393,751

Economy

Chief products

Agriculture: broilers, cotton, hogs, greenhouse and nursery products, tobacco, turkeys.
Manufacturing: chemicals, computer and electronic products, fabricated metal products, food products, machinery, textiles, tobacco products.
Mining: granite, limestone, phosphate rock, sand and gravel.

Gross domestic product

Value of goods and services produced in 2008: $404,567,000,000. *Services* include community, business, and personal services; finance; government; trade; and transportation and communication. *Industry* includes construction, manufacturing, mining, and utilities. *Agriculture* includes agriculture, fishing, and forestry.

Source: U.S. Bureau of Economic Analysis.

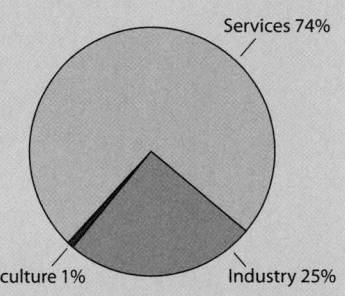

Services 74%
Agriculture 1%
Industry 25%

Government

State government

Governor: 4-year term
State senators: 50; 2-year terms
State representatives: 120; 2-year terms
Counties: 100

Federal government

United States senators: 2
United States representatives: 13
Electoral votes: 15

Sources of information

North Carolina's official website at http://www.ncgov.com provides a gateway to much information on the state's government, history, and economy.

In addition, the website at http://www.visitnc.com provides information about tourism.

Constitutional changes gave greater representation to the counties of western North Carolina.

A new state constitution went into effect.

| 1789 | 1835 | 1959 | 1971 | 1989 |

North Carolina became the 12th state on November 21.

The Research Triangle Park, which serves industry, opened near Durham.

North Carolina marked the bicentennial of its statehood.

Population. The 2010 United States census reported that North Carolina had 9,535,483 people. The state's population had increased 19 percent over the 2000 figure, which was 8,049,313. According to the 2010 census, North Carolina ranks 10th in population among the 50 states.

About 70 percent of North Carolina's people live in metropolitan areas (see **Metropolitan area**). Thirteen metropolitan areas lie entirely in North Carolina. These areas are Asheville, Burlington, Durham-Chapel Hill, Fayetteville, Goldsboro, Greensboro-High Point, Greenville, Hickory-Lenoir-Morganton, Jacksonville, Raleigh-Cary, Rocky Mount, Wilmington, and Winston-Salem. The Charlotte-Gastonia-Rock Hill area extends into South Carolina. The Virginia Beach (Virginia)-Norfolk (Virginia)-Newport News (Virginia) area includes Currituck County in North Carolina. For the populations of these areas, see the *Index* to the political map of North Carolina.

Charlotte is the state's largest city, with a population of about 730,000. North Carolina's other cities with more than 200,000 people, in order of population, include Raleigh, the state capital; Greensboro; Winston-Salem; Durham; and Fayetteville. All these cities lie inland. The state's largest coastal city is Wilmington, with a population of about 106,000.

About 21 of every 100 North Carolinians are African Americans. The state's other large population groups include people whose ancestors came from England, Germany, Ireland, Northern Ireland, and Scotland. A number of North Carolinians are of American Indian descent.

Schools. Churches and religious leaders controlled most of the early education in North Carolina. In 1705,

Murray and Associates, Inc.

A furniture factory in Thomasville produces wooden furniture. Furniture manufacturing is a major industry in North Carolina, which leads the states in household furniture production.

Food and beverage production provides employment for a large number of North Carolinians. The workers shown here are packaging doughnuts from a conveyor belt at a bakery goods store in Raleigh.

© Jeff Greenberg, Alamy Images

Population density

About half of North Carolina's people live in a stretch of land that extends from Charlotte to the Atlantic Coast. This area includes most of the state's largest cities.

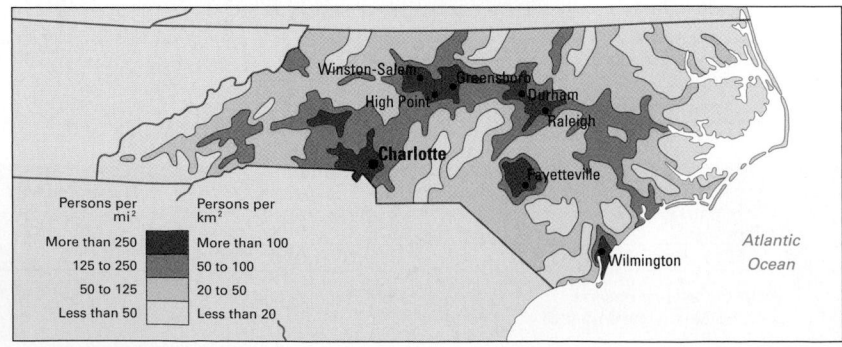

Persons per mi²	Persons per km²
More than 250	More than 100
125 to 250	50 to 100
50 to 125	20 to 50
Less than 50	Less than 20

WORLD BOOK map;
based on U.S. Census Bureau data.

Charles Griffin, a schoolteacher and Anglican Church member, set up what was probably North Carolina's first school. It was at Symons Creek near Elizabeth City.

The Constitution of 1776 provided for the establishment of a public school system and for chartering the University of North Carolina. In 1795, this university became the first state university in the United States to hold classes. But North Carolina did not build its first public school until 1840. In 1901, Governor Charles B. Aycock began to improve the state's system of public education.

The State Board of Education supervises North Carolina's public school system and makes its policies. The board consists of the lieutenant governor, the state treasurer, and 11 other members who are appointed by the governor to eight-year terms. The state superintendent of public instruction, who is elected to a four-year term, serves as the chief administrator and secretary of the State Board. Children between the ages of 7 and 16 must attend school. For the number of students and teachers in the state, see **Education** (table).

Libraries. The state's first public library was founded in Bath about 1700 by Thomas Bray, an English missionary. Bray established the first free lending libraries in the American Colonies. Bath was incorporated as a town in 1705, and it became the first town in North Carolina.

In 1897, the state passed its first public-library law, and the state's first tax-supported library opened in Durham. Today, in addition to its public libraries, North Carolina has several cooperative library organizations that provide for the sharing of services and resources.

Libraries at Duke University and at the University of North Carolina at Chapel Hill own the largest collections of books in the state. Both universities have excellent collections of documents on Southern history and social sciences. The State Library of North Carolina in Raleigh

Murray and Associates, Inc.

Duke University, in Durham, is named for James B. Duke, a tobacco millionaire who gave a large endowment to the school.

houses materials on the history of the state. The archives and history division retains state records.

Museums. One of the outstanding art museums in the South, the North Carolina Museum of Art, opened in Raleigh in 1956. The University of North Carolina's art museums include the Ackland Art Museum in Chapel Hill and the Weatherspoon Art Museum in Greensboro.

Highlights at the North Carolina Museum of Natural Sciences in Raleigh include dinosaur and whale skeletons, as well as re-created North Carolina habitats. The North Carolina Museum of History in Raleigh and the Greensboro Historical Museum portray the history of the state. The International Civil Rights Center & Museum in Greensboro has exhibits depicting the civil rights movement, including a re-creation of the Greensboro lunch counter where African American students began a sit-in after they were refused service in 1960.

Universities and colleges

This table lists the nonprofit universities and colleges in North Carolina that grant bachelor's or advanced degrees and are accredited by the Southern Association of Colleges and Schools.

Name	Mailing address	Name	Mailing address	Name	Mailing address
Appalachian State University	Boone	Greensboro College	Greensboro	University of North Carolina State	Winston-Salem
Barton College	Wilson	Guilford College	Greensboro	University	Raleigh
Belmont Abbey College	Belmont	High Point University	High Point	North Carolina	
		Johnson C. Smith University	Charlotte	Wesleyan College	Rocky Mount
Bennett College for Women	Greensboro	Lees-McRae College	Banner Elk	Peace College	Raleigh
Brevard College	Brevard	Lenoir-Rhyne University	Hickory	Pfeiffer University	Misenheimer
Cabarrus College of Health Sciences	Concord	Livingstone College	Salisbury	Queens University of Charlotte	Charlotte
Campbell University	Buies Creek	Mars Hill College	Mars Hill	St. Andrews	
Catawba College	Salisbury	Meredith College	Raleigh	Presbyterian College	Laurinburg
Chowan University	Murfreesboro	Methodist University	Fayetteville	St. Augustine's College	Raleigh
Davidson College	Davidson	Mid-Atlantic Christian University	Elizabeth City	Salem College	Winston-Salem
Duke University	Durham	Montreat College	Montreat	Shaw University	Raleigh
East Carolina University	Greenville	Mount Olive College	Mount Olive	Southeastern Baptist Theological Seminary	Wake Forest
Elizabeth City State University	Elizabeth City	North Carolina, University of	*	Wake Forest University	Winston-Salem
Elon University	Elon	North Carolina Agricultural and Technical State University	Greensboro	Warren Wilson College	Asheville
Fayetteville State University	Fayetteville	North Carolina Central University	Durham	Western Carolina University	Cullowhee
Gardner-Webb University	Boiling Springs	North Carolina School of the Arts,		Wingate University	Wingate
				Winston-Salem State University	Winston-Salem

*For campuses, see North Carolina, University of.

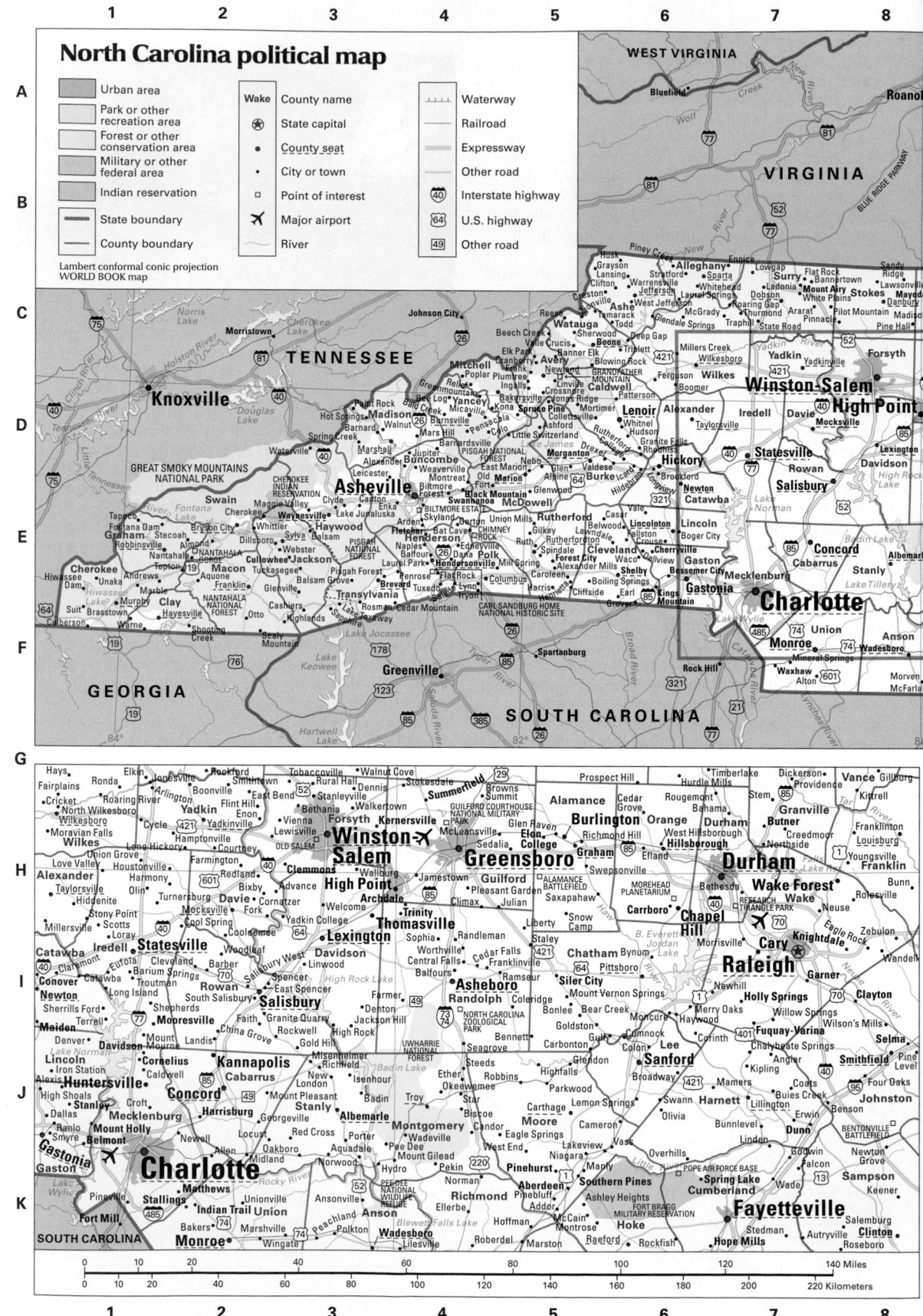

North Carolina political map

Urban area
Park or other recreation area
Forest or other conservation area
Military or other federal area
Indian reservation

State boundary
County boundary

Wake — County name
State capital
County seat
City or town
Point of interest
Major airport
River

Waterway
Railroad
Expressway
Other road
Interstate highway
U.S. highway
Other road

Lambert conformal conic projection
WORLD BOOK map

WEST VIRGINIA
VIRGINIA
TENNESSEE
GEORGIA
SOUTH CAROLINA

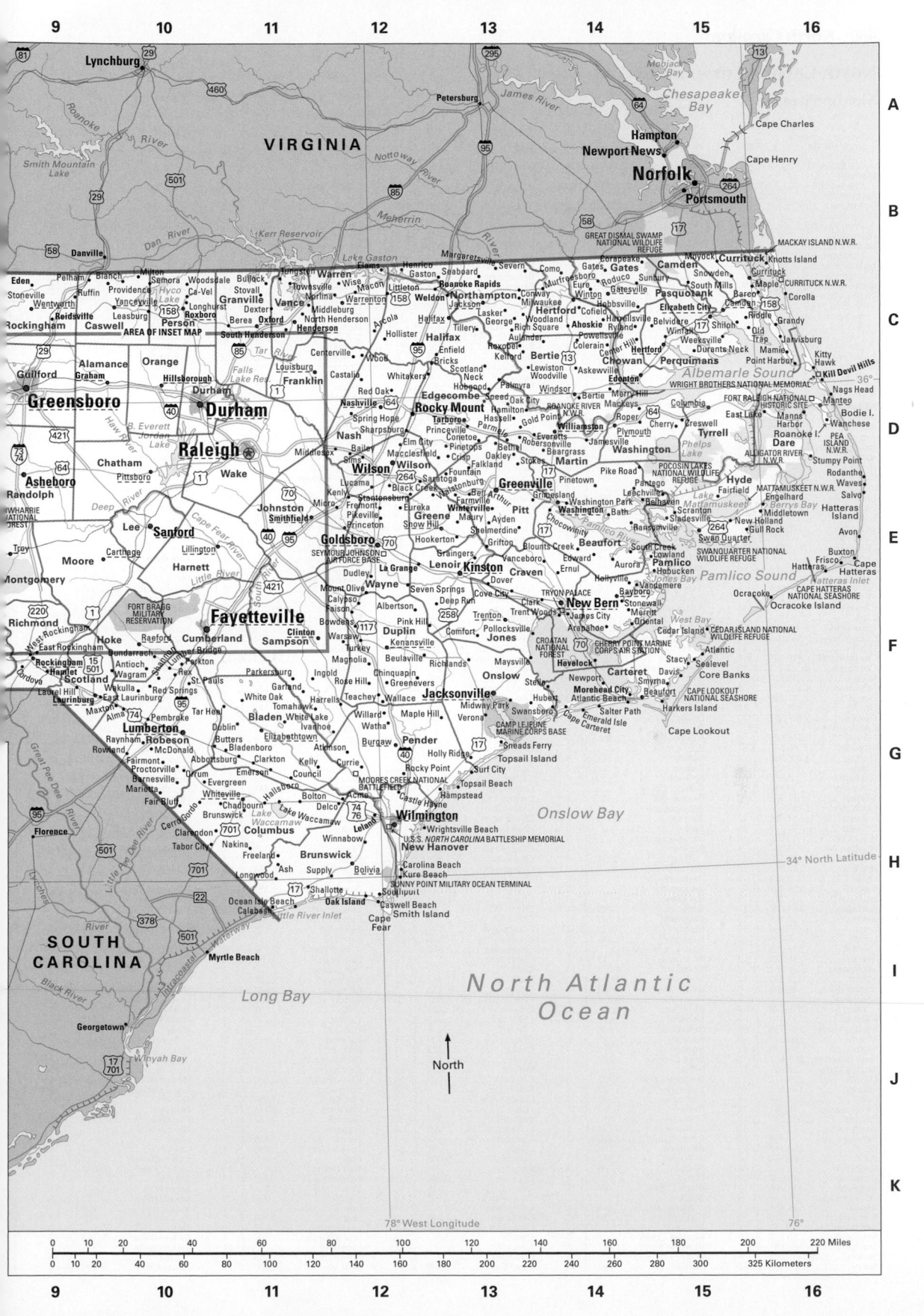

North Carolina map index

Many Northerners come to North Carolina's Sandhills area for relief from the cold winter weather. Blossoming mountain laurels, azaleas, and rhododendrons in spring and summer, and the beautiful colors of autumn, lure visitors to the mountains. Hunters track quail and deer through the mountains. Swimmers, sunbathers, and people who like fishing enjoy North Carolina's lakes, rivers, and coastlines. Historic sites, battlefields, old

mansions, and beautiful gardens attract sightseers and students of American history.

One of the most popular annual events in North Carolina is the performance of *The Lost Colony.* This historical drama is staged at Fort Raleigh in Manteo during June, July, and August. The play portrays some of the hardships faced by the early English colonists who disappeared mysteriously from Roanoke Island.

The North Carolina Zoological Park in Asheboro

Chip Henderson

Places to visit

Following are brief descriptions of some of North Carolina's many interesting places to visit:

Alamance Battlefield, near Burlington, was the scene of a historic battle shortly before the American Revolution (1775-1783). About 2,000 frontiersmen, called the Regulators, rebelled against the eastern planters. The Regulators were defeated on May 16, 1771.

Battleship *North Carolina* Memorial is on the Cape Fear River at Wilmington. Visitors may tour the U.S.S. *North Carolina,* a famous battleship that took part in every major offensive in the Pacific during World War II (1939-1945).

Bentonville Battlefield, near Smithfield, was the scene of one of the last important American Civil War battles. There, in March 1865, General William T. Sherman's Union forces defeated the Confederate troops of General Joseph E. Johnston.

Biltmore Estate covers about 8,000 acres (3,200 hectares) of forests and farmlands in Asheville. The Biltmore House, a masterpiece of early French Renaissance architecture, is the chief feature of the estate.

Cherokee Indian Reservation, at Cherokee, includes a replica of an American Indian village as it looked in the 1700's. Visitors can see demonstrations of Cherokee handicraft.

Chimney Rock is a unique rock formation that towers high above the mountains in Rutherford County. Chimney Rock offers an excellent view of the Blue Ridge Mountains.

Grandfather Mountain, near Linville, looks like the huge sleeping face of an old man. Tourists may walk across a swinging bridge 1 mile (1.6 kilometers) high.

Morehead Planetarium and Science Center, at the University of North Carolina in Chapel Hill, is a widely known planetarium. Spectators can watch the movements of stars and planets across a 68-foot (21-meter) dome.

Nantahala Gorge, in Swain County, plunges deep into the mountains. American Indians in the region believed the gorge was haunted.

NASCAR Hall of Fame, in Charlotte, has exhibits honoring the history of NASCAR, the organization that governs the nation's most popular form of stock car automobile racing.

North Carolina Zoological Park, in Asheboro, ranks as one of the largest zoos in the world. It has more than 1,100 animals and more than 30,000 plants. People may visit more than 500 acres (200 hectares) of exhibit area.

Ocracoke Island, a hideout of Blackbeard, the pirate, lies about 25 miles (40 kilometers) offshore, southeast of Pamlico Sound. The island was the site of many shipwrecks.

Old Salem is a restored colonial village in Winston-Salem. Moravians founded the village of Salem in 1766.

Tryon Palace, in New Bern, is the restored governor's mansion originally built by William Tryon, a royal governor. American patriots defied British authority by meeting in the palace in 1774.

National parks, forests, and memorials. North Carolina has four national forests: Croatan, Nantahala, Pisgah, and Uwharrie. North Carolina shares the Blue Ridge Parkway with Virginia, and the Great Smoky Mountains National Park with Tennessee (see **Great Smoky Mountains National Park**). The state has 12 national wilderness areas. The Wright Brothers National Memorial at Kill Devil Hills near Kitty Hawk honors the first powered airplane flight. For other areas, see the tables in **National Park System.**

State parks. North Carolina has a number of state parks and recreation areas. For more information, visit the official website of the North Carolina Division of Parks and Recreation at http://www.ncparks.gov/Visit/main.php.

Biltmore Estate in Asheville

Photri from Marilyn Gartman

North Carolina Division of Travel and Tourism

The Lost Colony drama at **Manteo**

H. Morton, Shostal

Grandfather Mountain near Linville

Land and climate

Land regions. North Carolina has three main land regions. These are, from east to west: (1) the Atlantic Coastal Plain, (2) the Piedmont, and (3) the Mountain Region.

The Atlantic Coastal Plain extends from New Jersey to southern Florida. North Carolina's coastal plain extends inland through an area of low, level marshland, covered by trees and water. Many swamps, shallow lakes, and rivers reflect moss-hung baldcypress trees. The Dismal Swamp in the northeast is one of the country's largest swamps. Treeless, grassy prairies cover parts of the eastern coastal plain. The western coastal plain has rich farmland. Sand hills rise along the southern part of the coastal plain.

The Piedmont is a hilly region that extends from Delaware to Alabama. In North Carolina, the Piedmont rises from about 300 feet (90 meters) at the edge of the coastal plain to about 1,500 feet (460 meters) at the mountains. The boundary between the Piedmont and the coastal plain is called the Fall Line. Along the Fall Line, rivers fall from the rocky Piedmont onto the softer, flat coastal plain. Most of the state's manufacturing industries are in the Piedmont. The area has more people than the coastal and mountain regions together.

The Mountain Region stretches from southern Pennsylvania to northern Georgia. The Blue Ridge Mountains are North Carolina's chief range. But the region also includes a number of other ranges. They include the Bald, Black, Brushy, Great Smoky, South, Stone, and Unaka ranges. All these mountains form part of the Appalachian Mountains. The Mountain Region rises from the Piedmont to heights of more than 1 mile (1.6 kilometers) above sea level. Mount Mitchell rises 6,684 feet (2,037 meters) and is the highest peak east of the Mississippi River. Forests cover much of the mountains, and the valley bottoms have good farmland. Great Smoky Mountains National Park and the Blue Ridge Parkway are in this region.

Coastline. The general coastline of the North Carolina mainland stretches 301 miles (484 kilometers). The tidal shoreline, which includes sand bars, islands, bays, and the mouths of rivers, measures 3,375 miles (5,432 kilometers). Sand bars, called the *Outer Banks,* form an almost continuous barrier along the coast. The Outer Banks jut into the Atlantic Ocean, forming Cape Fear, Cape Lookout, and Cape Hatteras. Their shifting sands have caused many shipwrecks. Cape Hatteras is called the *Graveyard of the Atlantic.*

Rivers, waterfalls, and lakes. Most of North Carolina's rivers start in the Mountain Region or in the Piedmont. They flow southeastward down the slopes of the western mountains and hills until they reach the edge of the Piedmont region. The rivers move through narrow channels above the Fall Line. Some flow through rapids where there is a noticeable drop at the Fall Line. Below the Fall Line, the rivers widen and flow slowly and then end in wide *estuaries* (river mouths). Boats can sail inland from the coast on several of the larger rivers as far west as the Fall Line.

One of the state's largest rivers, the Roanoke, flows into northeastern North Carolina, and empties into Albemarle Sound. The Neuse and Tar rivers drain the central part of North Carolina and flow into Pamlico Sound. The Cape Fear River crosses the southeastern portion of the Atlantic Coastal Plain. Several swift streams west of the Blue Ridge Mountains drain into Tennessee. North Carolina's largest dams are in this western area on the Hiwassee, Little Tennessee, and Nantahala rivers. Large dams also span the Catawba River, east of the Blue Ridge Mountains near Marion, and the Roanoke River near Roanoke Rapids.

Many lovely waterfalls add to the beauty of southwestern North Carolina. Whitewater Falls, near Brevard, plunges 411 feet (125 meters) and is one of the highest falls in the Eastern United States. North Carolina's only natural lakes are on the Atlantic Coastal Plain. Lake Mattamuskeet, the largest, is about 15 miles (24 kilometers) long and 6 miles (10 kilometers) wide.

Plant and animal life. Forests cover about half of North Carolina. Common trees include baldcypresses, hickories, maples, oaks, pines, sweet gums, tupelos, white-cedars, and yellow-poplars. In January, camellias bloom along the coastline. By April, redbud and dogwood blossoms have spread across the state. In May and June, azaleas and rhododendrons color the moun-

Land regions of North Carolina

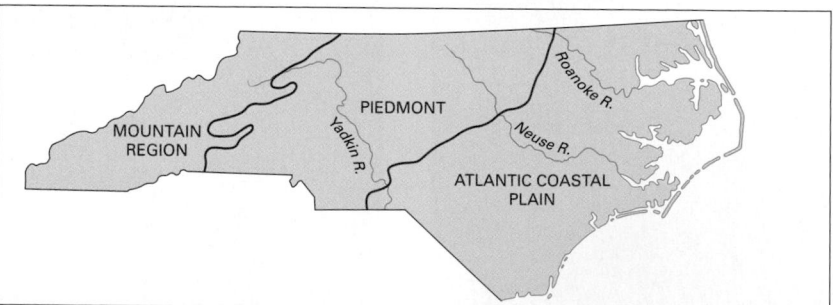

WORLD BOOK map

Map index

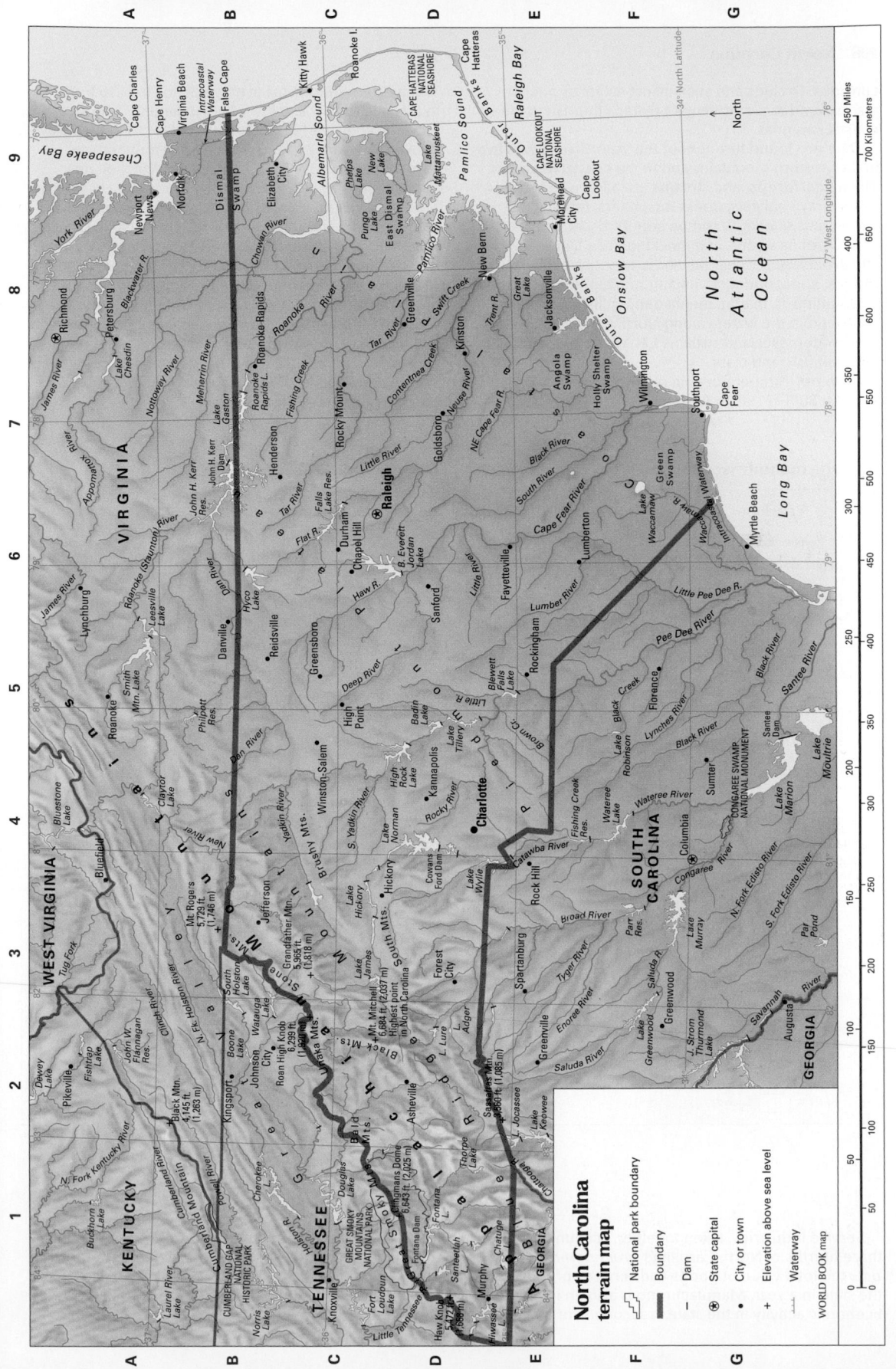

North Carolina
terrain map

National park boundary
Boundary
Dam
State capital
City or town
Elevation above sea level
Waterway

WORLD BOOK map

tainsides. Orchids and such insect-eaters as pitcher plants, sundews, and Venus's-flytraps flourish in the coastal savannas.

Deer are found throughout the state. Black bears live in the western mountains and in the coastal lowlands. The fields, forests, and streams are filled with beavers, foxes, gray squirrels, opossums, otters, rabbits, raccoons, and skunks. Common songbirds include cardinals, Carolina wrens, and mockingbirds. Ducks, geese, and swans winter near the coast. Mourning doves, partridges, and woodcocks inhabit much of the state.

Dolphinfish, marlin, menhaden, sailfish, and sturgeon are found in the waters along North Carolina's coast. Freshwater lakes and streams have bass, bluegills, crappies, sunfish, and trout.

Climate. Temperatures in southeast North Carolina average 80 °F (27 °C) in July and 48 °F (9 °C) in January.

The western mountains average 60 to 70 °F (16 to 21 °C) in July and as low as 28 °F (-2 °C) in January. The state's highest recorded temperature was 110 °F (43 °C) at Fayetteville on Aug. 21, 1983. The lowest temperature recorded was -34 °F (-51 °C) at Mount Mitchell near Asheville on Jan. 21, 1985.

Rain makes up most of the state's *precipitation* (rain, melted snow, and other moisture). The Atlantic Coastal Plain averages about 50 inches (125 centimeters) a year, the Piedmont about 47 inches (120 centimeters), and the Mountain Region about 60 inches (150 centimeters). Snowfall ranges from 40 inches (100 centimeters) a year in some mountains to only a trace in some coastal areas.

Because of the way its coastline juts into the Atlantic Ocean, North Carolina has often been the target of destructive hurricanes. The state experiences an average of one hurricane every four years.

Average monthly weather

	Charlotte							Asheville					
	Temperatures °F High Low		Temperatures °C High Low		Days of rain or snow			Temperatures °F High Low		Temperatures °C High Low		Days of rain or snow	
Jan.	51	32	11	0	10		Jan.	46	26	8	-3	10	
Feb.	56	34	13	1	10		Feb.	50	28	10	-2	10	
Mar.	64	42	18	6	11		Mar.	58	35	14	2	12	
Apr.	73	49	23	9	9		Apr.	67	42	19	6	10	
May	80	58	27	14	10		May	74	51	23	11	12	
June	87	67	31	19	10		June	80	58	27	14	12	
July	90	71	32	22	11		July	83	63	28	17	12	
Aug.	88	69	31	21	10		Aug.	82	62	28	17	13	
Sept.	82	63	28	17	7		Sept.	76	55	24	13	10	
Oct.	73	51	23	11	7		Oct.	67	43	19	6	8	
Nov.	63	42	17	6	8		Nov.	57	35	14	2	9	
Dec.	54	35	12	2	10		Dec.	49	29	9	-2	10	

Average yearly precipitation

North Carolina has a wet climate. The far west and the area along the Atlantic Ocean receive the most precipitation. Snow is usually concentrated in the mountains of the Mountain Region.

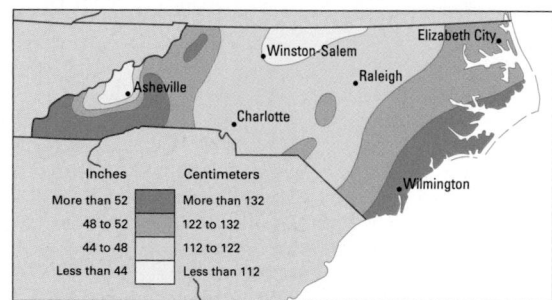

Inches	Centimeters
More than 52	More than 132
48 to 52	122 to 132
44 to 48	112 to 122
Less than 44	Less than 112

Average January temperatures

North Carolina has short, mild winters. The southeastern part of the state has the warmest wintertime temperatures. The coolest temperatures are found in the mountainous western area.

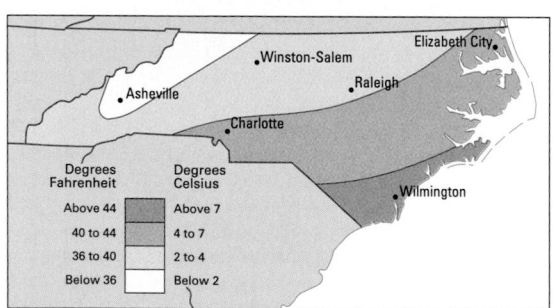

Degrees Fahrenheit	Degrees Celsius
Above 44	Above 7
40 to 44	4 to 7
36 to 40	2 to 4
Below 36	Below 2

Average July temperatures

The state has hot summers with little variation in temperature. Generally the southeastern section of North Carolina is somewhat warmer than the area to the northwest.

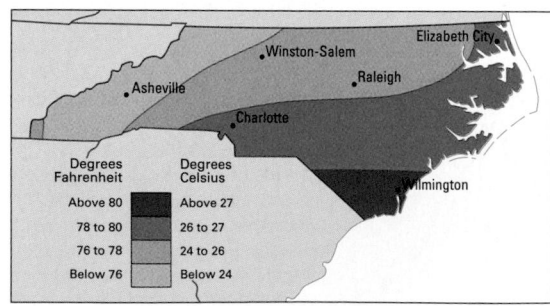

Degrees Fahrenheit	Degrees Celsius
Above 80	Above 27
78 to 80	26 to 27
76 to 78	24 to 26
Below 76	Below 24

WORLD BOOK maps

Economy

Service industries, taken together, account for nearly three-fourths of North Carolina's *gross domestic product*—the total value of goods and services produced in the state in a year. Manufacturing is also an important economic activity in the state. It accounts for a fifth of

North Carolina's gross domestic product. The leading manufactured goods are chemicals and tobacco products. Community, business, and personal services is the leading employer among North Carolina's service industry groups.

North Carolina economy

General economy

Gross domestic product (GDP)* (2008) $404,567,000,000
   Rank among U.S. states   9th
Unemployment rate (2010)   10.2% (U.S. avg: 9.6%)

*Gross domestic product is the total value of goods and services produced in a year.
Sources: U.S. Bureau of Economic Analysis and U.S. Bureau of Labor Statistics.

Agriculture

Cash receipts $9,187,821,000
   Rank among U.S. states   8th
Distribution   62% livestock, 38% crops
Farms   52,400
Farm acres (hectares)   8,600,000 (3,480,000)
   Rank among U.S. states   32nd
Farmland   26% of North Carolina

Leading products

1. Broilers   (ranks 4th in U.S.)
2. Hogs   (ranks 2nd in U.S.)
3. Greenhouse and nursery products   (ranks 5th in U.S.)
4. Tobacco   (ranks 1st in U.S.)
5. Soybeans
Other products: cattle and calves, corn, cotton, dairy products, eggs, sweet potatoes, turkeys.

Manufacturing

Value added by manufacture* $101,342,064,000
   Rank among U.S. states   6th

Leading products

1. Chemicals
2. Tobacco products
3. Food and beverage products
4. Computer and electronic products
5. Fabricated metal products
Other products: furniture, machinery, textiles and textile products, transportation equipment.

*Value added by manufacture is the increase in value of raw materials after they become finished products.

Production and workers by economic activities

Economic activities	Percent of GDP produced	Employed workers Number of people	Percent of total
Finance, insurance, & real estate	23	542,500	10
Manufacturing	19	537,000	10
Community, business, & personal services	18	1,688,400	31
Government	14	851,200	15
Trade, restaurants, & hotels	13	1,136,500	21
Construction	5	392,800	7
Transportation & communication	5	239,700	4
Agriculture	1	88,600	2
Utilities	1	13,700	*
Mining	*	7,500	*
Total†	100	5,497,900	100

*Less than one-half of 1 percent.
†Figures may not add up to 100 percent due to rounding.
Figures are for 2008; employment figures include full- and part-time workers.
Source: *World Book* estimates based on data from U.S. Bureau of Economic Analysis.

Mining

Nonfuel mineral production $1,090,000,000
   Rank among U.S. states   23rd
Coal   *
Crude oil   *
Natural gas   *

*No significant mining of this product in North Carolina.

Leading product

Granite   (ranks 1st in U.S.)
Other products: clay, feldspar, limestone, phosphate rock, sand and gravel, traprock.

Figures are for 2008, except for the agricultural figures, which are for 2009.
Sources: U.S. Census Bureau, U.S. Department of Agriculture, U.S. Geological Survey.

Continued on page 488

Economy of North Carolina

This map shows the economic uses of land in North Carolina and where the state's leading farm, mineral, and forest products are produced. Major manufacturing centers are shown in red.

WORLD BOOK map

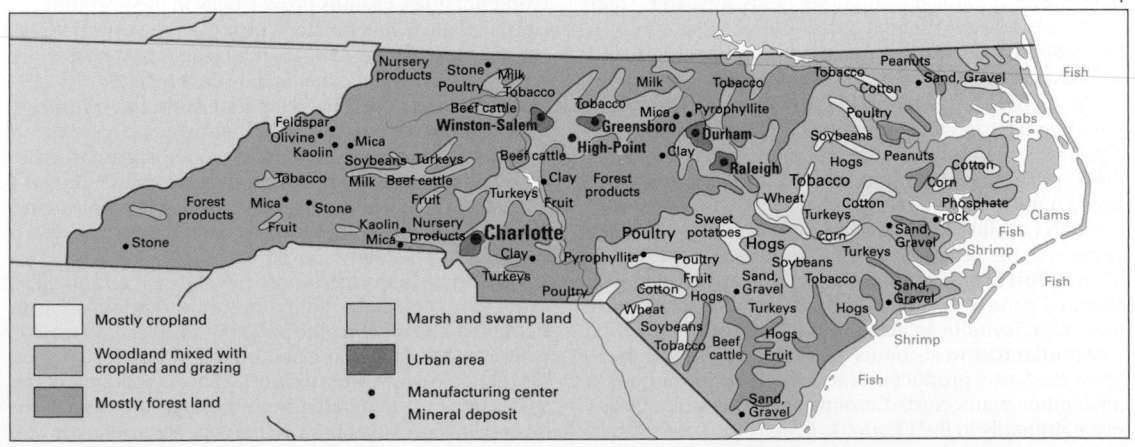

Fishing

Commercial catch	$86,716,000
Rank among U.S. states	12th

Leading catches

1. Crab	
2. Shrimp	(ranks 5th in U.S.)
3. Flounder	(ranks 2nd in U.S.)
4. Tuna	(ranks 5th in U.S.)

Other catches: bass, clams, croakers, mackerels, oysters.

Electric power

Coal	60.5%
Nuclear	31.8%
Natural gas	3.3%
Hydroelectric	2.4%
Other	2.0%

Figures are for 2008.
Sources: U.S. Energy Information Administration, U.S. National Marine Fisheries
Service.

Natural resources of North Carolina include rich soils and mineral deposits, and thick forests.

Soil. Red and yellow soils cover most of the state, except along the coast and in the mountains. Light and level sandy loam soils make the central and western coastal plain the richest farmland in the state. Some coastal land has marshy soils formed by dark peat or muck. Drained properly, these soils provide good farmland. Deep sandy soils cover the sand hills along the southern part of the Fall Line. The Piedmont has sandy, clay, and silt loams, mostly red in color. Strips of dark *alluvial* (water-deposited) soils lie along most of the streams. Grayish-brown loams cover most of the mountain area.

Minerals. North Carolina, sometimes called "Nature's Sample Case," has deposits of more than 300 different minerals and rocks. The mountains contain rich stores of feldspar and kaolin. The Mountain and Piedmont regions have large deposits of gneiss. Limestone and sand and gravel are found throughout the state. The Piedmont region has clays, granite, and shale.

Forests cover about half of the state. Oaks and pines are the most common trees. Oaks grow along with such other hardwoods as hickories, maples, and yellow-poplars over the entire state. Tupelo and sweet gum forests spread along the coastal plain rivers and streams. Loblolly pine, the state's most common softwood, grows over the entire coastal plain. Pond pine, black tupelo, baldcypress, and white-cedar are found in the swamps.

Service industries account for about three-fourths of North Carolina's gross domestic product and about four-fifths of its employment. Most services are concentrated in the state's metropolitan areas.

Raleigh, the state's capital, is the center of government activities. Duke University in Durham is a leading center of research in medicine and other fields. Research Triangle Park is a large research complex in the Raleigh-Durham area. Charlotte is one of the country's major financial centers. Bank of America Corporation, a large banking company, is based in the city. Lowe's Companies, Inc., a large wholesale distributor of building materials, is headquartered in Mooresville. Hotels, restaurants, and retail establishments are primarily in the state's metropolitan areas.

North Carolina has one of the largest public university systems in the United States. Military bases in the state include Fort Bragg, Marine Corps Base Camp Lejeune, Marine Corps Air Station Cherry Point, Pope Air Force Base, and Seymour Johnson Air Force Base.

Manufacturing accounts for a larger portion of the gross domestic product in North Carolina than it does in most other states. North Carolina's manufacturing takes place primarily in the Charlotte, Greensboro, Raleigh-

Durham, and Winston-Salem areas.

Chemicals and tobacco products are the leading manufactured products. *Pharmaceuticals* (medicinal drugs) are the leading chemical product. Factories in the Raleigh area make pharmaceuticals. North Carolina makes more tobacco products than any other state. Factories in Greensboro, Winston-Salem, and other cities produce cigarettes. North Carolina produces about half of the cigarettes made in the United States.

Computer and electronic products, machinery, and transportation equipment are primarily manufactured in the metropolitan areas. North Carolina ranks as a leader in poultry processing and textile production. It leads the states in the production of household furniture.

Agriculture. Farmland covers about a fourth of North Carolina. Livestock products provide over half of the agricultural income. North Carolina ranks among the leading states in the production of both *broilers* (young, tender chickens) and hogs. Broilers and hogs together account for about three-fourths of the state's income from livestock. Most hogs are raised in the eastern part of the state. The largest numbers of broilers come from southern and central Piedmont and from Wilkes County.

North Carolina is also a leading turkey-raising state. and Sampson counties raise the most turkeys. Dairy farming is mainly in the western part of the state. Other livestock products include beef cattle and eggs.

North Carolina is the leading tobacco-growing state. Fire-cured tobacco is grown in many parts of the state. Burley tobacco is grown in mountainous areas near Asheville and also north of Winston-Salem. Corn, cotton, and soybeans also rank as important crops. They grow in the eastern part of the state.

North Carolina is a leading producer of peanuts and sweet potatoes. Peanuts grow chiefly in the northern coastal plain. Sweet potatoes grow in the western coastal plain. Blueberries are the leading fruit crop.

Mining. Crushed stone, mainly granite, is North Carolina's leading mined product. Limestone and traprock are also mined from the state's quarries.

Other leading mined products are phosphate rock and sand and gravel. Phosphate rock is mined in Beaufort County. Sand and gravel are produced mainly in the coastal plain. North Carolina is a leading producer of feldspar, mica, and pyrophyllite.

Fishing industry. The most valuable fish and shellfish caught are blue crabs, flounder, shrimp, and tuna. North Carolina's *aquaculture* industry raises catfish and trout in natural and artificially created bodies of water.

Electric power and utilities. About 60 percent of the state's power is generated from coal-burning plants. Nuclear plants provide about 30 percent. Hydroelectric and natural gas burning plants also provide power.

Transportation. Rivers served as the first highways in North Carolina. Roads began to appear in the 1700's, but most remained poor until well into the 1900's. The state began a major campaign to improve its roads in the 1920's. The first two major railroads—the Wilmington and Raleigh, and the Raleigh and Gaston—began service in 1840. At that time, the 161-mile (259-kilometer) Wilmington line was the longest in the world.

Today, the state has an extensive system of roads and highways. Seven interstate highways link North Carolina's cities. Many bridges span inlets and rivers along the state's coast. Numerous rail lines provide freight service in North Carolina. The busiest airport is at Charlotte. The Raleigh-Durham area and Greensboro also have major airports. Harbors at Morehead City, Southport, and Wilmington are part of the Atlantic Intracoastal Waterway (see **Atlantic Intracoastal Waterway**).

Communication. James Davis, a printer and editor, established North Carolina's first newspaper, the *North Carolina Gazette,* at New Bern in 1751. The weekly *Raleigh Register* was founded in 1799. Today, *The Charlotte Observer* and *The News and Observer* of Raleigh are the state's largest dailies.

Government

Constitution of North Carolina became effective in 1971. The state had two earlier constitutions, adopted in 1776 and 1868. Amendments to the Constitution can be proposed in the state legislature or by a constitutional convention. An amendment proposed in the legislature must be approved by three-fifths of both houses. Then it must be approved by a majority of the voters in a general election. A constitutional convention must be approved by two-thirds of both houses, and by the voters, before it can meet to propose and adopt amendments to the Constitution.

Executive. North Carolina's governor and lieutenant governor serve a four-year term. They may serve any number of terms but not more than two in a row. The governor can appoint a number of important state officials, including the heads of nine executive departments. The voters elect eight other top administrative officers to four-year terms. They are the attorney general, auditor, secretary of state, superintendent of public instruction, treasurer, and commissioners of agriculture, labor, and insurance. These officials and the lieutenant governor make up the Council of State, an advisory council to the governor.

Legislature of North Carolina is called the General Assembly. It consists of a 50-member Senate and a 120-member House of Representatives. North Carolina has 50 senatorial districts and 120 representative districts. Members of both houses serve two-year terms. The lieutenant governor is president of the Senate. The House of Representatives elects a speaker to preside over it.

The legislature meets every year. In odd-numbered years, it has a regular session that begins on the Wednesday after the second Monday in January. In even-numbered years, a short session is held, usually in June, to review financial matters and conclude any business from the previous year.

Courts. North Carolina's court system has three divisions: an Appellate Division, a Superior Court Division, and a District Court Division. The Appellate Division consists of the Supreme Court, the state's highest court; and the Court of Appeals, an intermediate appellate court. The appellate courts hear cases appealed from lower courts. The Supreme Court consists of a chief justice and 6 associate justices, and the Court of Appeals has 15 judges.

The Superior Court Division is divided among eight divisions and 46 judicial districts across the state. Superior Court judges hear civil and criminal trials. District Court judges handle minor civil and criminal cases.

Supreme Court justices, Court of Appeals judges, and Superior Court judges are elected to eight-year terms. District Court judges are elected to four-year terms. If any leaves office, the governor appoints a successor.

Local government. North Carolina has 100 counties. Each county is governed by a board of county commissioners. The boards consist of three to seven members, elected to two- or four-year terms, depending on the county. The board members meet at least monthly to supervise county affairs and to perform such duties as appropriating funds and levying taxes. County officials include the sheriff, register of deeds, superior court clerk, county manager, finance officer, attorney, and tax officials.

State laws grant cities and towns *home rule* (self-government) to the extent that they may make certain amendments to their charters. But supervision and control remain in the hands of the General Assembly.

North Carolina has more than 500 incorporated municipalities. An area may incorporate by petitioning the General Assembly. Most of the larger cities in the state have the council-manager form of government. Other forms of municipal government are mayor-council and commission.

Revenue. Taxes account for about half of the state government's *general revenue* (income). Federal grants and other U.S. government programs make up most of the rest. A personal income tax provides the greatest portion of the tax revenue. Other important tax revenue sources in North Carolina include a general sales tax and taxes on corporate income, motor fuels, and motor vehicle licenses.

Politics. The Democratic Party traditionally has dominated the state's politics. But Republicans have gained strength since the mid-1960's. From the Reconstruction period (1865-1877) through 1964, the Democratic candidate won the state's electoral votes in almost every presidential election. But since 1968, the Republican has won in almost all of the presidential elections. For North Carolina's voting record in presidential elections, see **Electoral College** (table).

In 1972, James E. Holshouser, Jr., became the first Republican to be elected governor of North Carolina since 1896. Also in 1972, Jesse A. Helms became the first Republican elected to the United States Senate from the state since 1895.

The state governors of North Carolina

	Party	Term		Party	Term
Richard Caswell	None	1776-1780	†W. W. Holden	Republican	-1865
Abner Nash	None	1780-1781	Jonathan Worth	Democratic	1865-1868
Thomas Burke	None	1781-1782	W. W. Holden	Republican	1868-1871
Alexander Martin	None	1782-1784	T. R. Caldwell	Republican	1871-1874
Richard Caswell	None	1784-1787	C. H. Brogden	Republican	1874-1877
Samuel Johnston	Federalist	1787-1789	Z. B. Vance	Democratic	1877-1879
Alexander Martin	Unknown	1789-1792	T. J. Jarvis	Democratic	1879-1885
R. D. Spaight, Sr.	*Dem.-Rep.	1792-1795	A. M. Scales	Democratic	1885-1889
Samuel Ashe	*Dem.-Rep.	1795-1798	D. G. Fowle	Democratic	1889-1891
W. R. Davie	Federalist	1798-1799	Thomas M. Holt	Democratic	1891-1893
Benjamin Williams	*Dem.-Rep.	1799-1802	Elias Carr	Democratic	1893-1897
James Turner	*Dem.-Rep.	1802-1805	D. L. Russell	Republican	1897-1901
Nathaniel Alexander	*Dem.-Rep.	1805-1807	Charles B. Aycock	Democratic	1901-1905
Benjamin Williams	*Dem.-Rep.	1807-1808	R. B. Glenn	Democratic	1905-1909
David Stone	*Dem.-Rep.	1808-1810	W. W. Kitchin	Democratic	1909-1913
Benjamin Smith	*Dem.-Rep.	1810-1811	Locke Craig	Democratic	1913-1917
William Hawkins	*Dem.-Rep.	1811-1814	Thomas W. Bickett	Democratic	1917-1921
William Miller	*Dem.-Rep.	1814-1817	Cameron Morrison	Democratic	1921-1925
John Branch	*Dem.-Rep.	1817-1820	Angus Wilton McLean	Democratic	1925-1929
Jesse Franklin	*Dem.-Rep.	1820-1821	O. Max Gardner	Democratic	1929-1933
Gabriel Holmes	Unknown	1821-1824	J. C. B. Ehringhaus	Democratic	1933-1937
H. G. Burton	Unknown	1824-1827	Clyde R. Hoey	Democratic	1937-1941
James Iredell, Jr.	*Dem.-Rep.	1827-1828	J. Melville Broughton	Democratic	1941-1945
John Owen	Democratic	1828-1830	R. Gregg Cherry	Democratic	1945-1949
Montfort Stokes	Democratic	1830-1832	W. Kerr Scott	Democratic	1949-1953
D. L. Swain	Whig	1832-1835	William B. Umstead	Democratic	1953-1954
R. D. Spaight, Jr.	Democratic	1835-1836	Luther H. Hodges	Democratic	1954-1961
E. B. Dudley	Whig	1836-1841	Terry Sanford	Democratic	1961-1965
J. M. Morehead	Whig	1841-1845	Daniel K. Moore	Democratic	1965-1969
W. A. Graham	Whig	1845-1849	Robert W. Scott	Democratic	1969-1973
Charles Manly	Whig	1849-1851	James E. Holshouser, Jr.	Republican	1973-1977
D. S. Reid	Democratic	1851-1854	James B. Hunt, Jr.	Democratic	1977-1985
Warren Winslow	Democratic	1854-1855	James G. Martin	Republican	1985-1993
Thomas Bragg	Democratic	1855-1859	James B. Hunt, Jr.	Democratic	1993-2001
John W. Ellis	Democratic	1859-1861	Mike Easley	Democratic	2001-2009
Henry T. Clark	Democratic	1861-1862	Beverly Perdue	Democratic	2009-
Z. B. Vance	Democratic	1862-1865			

*Democratic-Republican   † Provisional governor

History

Indian days. About 35,000 Indians, belonging to about 30 tribes, lived in the North Carolina region when Europeans first arrived. The most important tribes were the Cherokee in the western mountains; the Hatteras along the coast; and the Catawba, Chowanoc, and Tuscarora of the coastal plain and the Piedmont.

Exploration and settlement. Giovanni da Verrazzano, sailing in the service of France, was the first known European to explore the North Carolina coast. He visited the Cape Fear area in 1524. Verrazzano sent glowing reports of what he saw to King Francis I of France. But the king was not interested in colonizing the region. Two years later, an expedition led by Lucas Vásquez de Ayllón of Spain may have stopped near Cape Fear to scout for a place to settle. Vásquez and his followers decided the area was unsuitable, and the expedition moved farther south to settle on the coast of South Carolina or Georgia. In 1540, Hernando de Soto of Spain led an expedition over the mountains at the southwestern tip of the North Carolina region. He hoped to find gold. Instead, he became the first European to reach the Mississippi River. He arrived at the river in 1541. Neither Spain nor France established any permanent settlements.

In 1584, Sir Walter Raleigh of England sent explorers to the North Carolina coast to find a suitable site for a settlement. The next year, the first English colony in America was established on Roanoke Island. But misfortunes forced the settlers to return to England in 1586. Raleigh sent a later expedition to Roanoke Island in 1587, with John White as governor. White established a colony and sailed back to England for supplies that same year. When Queen Elizabeth allowed White to return to Roanoke Island in 1590, his colony had disappeared. No one knows what happened to the more than a hundred men, women, and children of what has come to be called the Lost Colony (see **Lost Colony**).

In 1629, King Charles I of England granted his attorney general, Sir Robert Heath, the southern part of the English claim in America. This included a strip of land containing what is now both North Carolina and South Carolina. The land was named the Province of *Carolana* (land of Charles). Heath's attempts at settlement failed.

The first permanent European settlers in Carolina came from Virginia. They settled in the Albemarle Sound region around 1650. In 1663, Charles II of England regranted Carolina to eight of his favorite nobles. He made them *lords proprietors* (ruling landlords). These men divided Carolina into three counties: (1)

Historic North Carolina

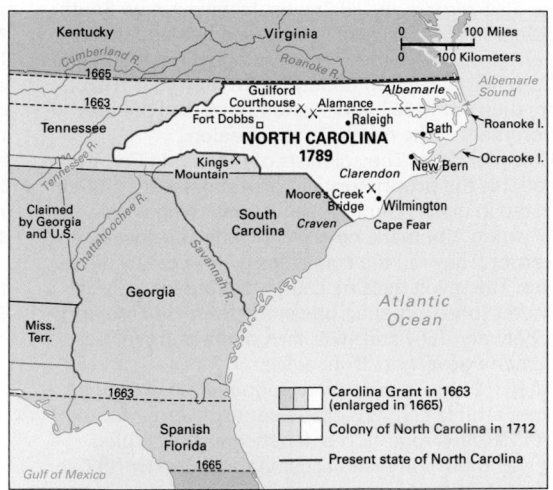

WORLD BOOK map

The Lost Colony was a group of more than 100 English colonists who settled on Roanoke Island in 1587. Three years later, a supply ship found the colony had disappeared. One of its only traces was the word *Croatoan* carved on a tree.

North Carolina was part of a charter England's King Charles II granted to several nobles in 1663. The area became a separate colony in 1712. North Carolina became a U.S. state in 1789.

The Wright brothers made the world's first successful power-driven airplane flight near Kitty Hawk on Dec. 17, 1903.

WORLD BOOK illustrations by Richard Bonson, The Art Agency

Important dates in North Carolina

1524   Giovanni da Verrazzano, a Florentine explorer sailing for France, visited the North Carolina coast.

1585   The English established at Roanoke Island their first colony in what is now the United States.

1629   King Charles I of England granted *Carolana* to Sir Robert Heath.

c. 1650   The first permanent settlers came to the Albemarle region from Virginia.

1663   King Charles II granted the Carolina colony to eight lords proprietors.

1664   North Carolina's first permanent government was established in Albemarle County.

1711   The Tuscarora Indians attacked settlements between the Neuse and Pamlico rivers. The colonists defeated the Indians in 1713.

1712   The North Carolina region became a separate colony.

1729   North Carolina came under direct royal rule.

1765   Colonists in North Carolina began to resist enforcement of the British Stamp Act and other tax laws.

1774   North Carolina sent delegates to the First Continental Congress in Philadelphia.

1776   The Whigs defeated the Tories at Moore's Creek Bridge. North Carolina adopted its first constitution.

1781   British forces withdrew from North Carolina and surrendered in Virginia.

1789   North Carolina *ratified* (approved) the U.S. Constitution and became the 12th state on November 21.

1835   Constitutional changes gave greater representation to the counties of western North Carolina.

1861   North Carolina seceded from the Union.

1865   General Joseph E. Johnston surrendered to General William T. Sherman near Durham.

1868   North Carolina was readmitted to the Union.

1903   The Wright brothers made the first successful powered airplane flight near Kitty Hawk.

1915   The state legislature set up a highway commission.

1933   The state took over the support of public schools.

1949   North Carolina voters approved a large bond issue for road and public-school construction.

1950   Great industrial expansion began.

1959   Research Triangle Park, operated by three North Carolina universities to serve industry, opened.

1960   Four African American students launched a sit-in movement at a lunch counter in Greensboro.

1971   A new state constitution went into effect.

1972   James E. Holshouser, Jr., became the first Republican to be elected governor of North Carolina since 1896.

1989   North Carolina marked the bicentennial of its statehood.

2009   Beverly Perdue became North Carolina's first woman governor.

Albemarle, in the northern part; (2) Clarendon, in the Cape Fear region; and (3) Craven, in what is now South Carolina. In 1664, William Drummond was appointed governor of Albemarle County, and government began in Carolina. Clarendon County lasted only until 1667. From then until 1689, Albemarle County had the only government in the North Carolina region.

Colonial days. The colonists of Albemarle County believed that the proprietors and governors were more interested in making money than in governing wisely. In 1677, some Albemarle colonists revolted against their governor. They ran the county for over a year by themselves. The revolt became known as Culpeper's Rebellion after John Culpeper, one of the leaders of the uprising. Between 1664 and 1689, the colonists drove five Albemarle governors from office.

After 1691, governors were appointed to govern the entire Carolina colony, with a deputy governor for the North Carolina region. The deputy governors ruled wisely and the colonists accepted them. The North Carolina region became a separate colony in 1712.

During the late 1600's and early 1700's, increasing numbers of settlers came to North Carolina. In 1705, North Carolina's first town, Bath, was incorporated near the mouth of the Pamlico River. By 1710, settlements had spread down the coast and along the riverbanks as far south as the Neuse River. In 1710, Swiss and Germans founded New Bern, a community several miles inland on the Neuse, in Tuscarora Indian territory. At dawn on Sept. 22, 1711, enraged Tuscarora Indians, whose land had been seized by European settlers, attacked New Bern and other settlements. Within two hours, most of the settlements between the Neuse and Pamlico rivers lay in ruins. The Indians had massacred hundreds of settlers, burned their homes, stolen their valuables, and destroyed their crops. The massacre marked the beginning of the Tuscarora War, the worst Indian war in North Carolina's history. The colonists defeated the Indians on March 25, 1713.

While settlers battled the wilderness and the Indians during the late 1600's and early 1700's, pirates terrorized North Carolina's coastline. Most piracy along the Atlantic Coast ended with the death of the pirate Blackbeard in a battle near Ocracoke Island in 1718.

In 1729, the lords proprietors sold their land back to the king of the United Kingdom. North Carolina became a royal colony, ruled by royal governors named by the king. The governors ruled wisely and helped the colony grow. In 1729, only about 36,000 people lived in North Carolina, mostly along the coast. By 1775, the population had grown to nearly 350,000, and settlement had spread westward across the Piedmont and into the mountains.

North Carolina contributed money and troops to help the United Kingdom fight several colonial wars. Those wars included Queen Anne's War (1702-1713), King George's War (1744-1748), and the French and Indian War (1754-1763). In 1760, Hugh Waddell of Wilmington led North Carolina troops to an important victory over the Cherokee Indians at Fort Dobbs, near present-day Statesville. In 1761, the Cherokee signed a peace treaty that opened a vast area of western Virginia and the Carolinas to settlement. See **French and Indian wars**.

Revolution and independence. The United Kingdom placed additional taxes on the American Colonies to help pay for the colonial wars. But the colonists objected to taxes levied without their consent. Protestors in North Carolina and other colonies called the Sons of Liberty led demonstrations and even armed rebellions against these taxes. Meanwhile, some farmers in western North Carolina rose up against the high taxes and dishonest officials forced upon them by the wealthy eastern planters. The western rebels were called the Regulators. William Tryon, the royal governor, needed more than a thousand troops to defeat the Regulators at the Battle of Alamance on May 16, 1771.

North Carolina sent delegates to Philadelphia to attend the First Continental Congress in 1774. After the Revolutionary War began in April 1775, North Carolinians quickly took sides. Those who opposed the British were called Whigs. Those who remained loyal to the king were called Tories. On Feb. 27, 1776, Whig forces, under Colonels Richard Caswell and Alexander Lillington, crushed the Tories in the Battle of Moore's Creek Bridge. This was the first battle of the Revolutionary War in North Carolina. The Whig victory prevented a planned British invasion of North Carolina. On April 12, 1776, North Carolina became the first colony to instruct its delegates to the Continental Congress to vote for independence. Later that year, North Carolina adopted its first constitution and chose Caswell as governor. On July 21, 1778, North Carolina *ratified* (approved) the Articles of Confederation.

Much of the Revolutionary War was fought outside North Carolina's borders. But North Carolinians joined the fight against the British in Virginia, Georgia, and South Carolina. Inside the state, warfare between Whigs and Tories produced much bloodshed and bitterness. In 1780, British forces led by Lord Charles Cornwallis marched toward North Carolina from the south. Part of Cornwallis's army was slaughtered in the Battle of Kings Mountain, just south of North Carolina. But after a retreat, Cornwallis moved northward again, this time into North Carolina. On March 15, 1781, Cornwallis's troops outlasted the American General Nathanael Greene's forces in the Battle of Guilford Courthouse. But the severely weakened British abandoned North Carolina soon afterward.

Statehood. North Carolinians delayed approving the United States Constitution because they opposed a strong federal government. At the Hillsborough Convention of 1788, they rejected the Constitution and suggested many amendments to it. The Bill of Rights to the Constitution, proposed by Congress in 1789, included some of these suggestions. North Carolina finally ratified the Constitution on Nov. 21, 1789.

During the early 1800's, North Carolina was a backward state. It had little commerce or industry. It lacked seaports and transportation facilities. North Carolina planters relied heavily on slave labor, and black slaves made up about a third of the population. Many people left North Carolina, including three men who later became president—Andrew Jackson, James K. Polk, and Andrew Johnson.

North Carolina began to progress in 1835, after revising its Constitution. The new Constitution gave greater representation to the people of the western region and encouraged the development of that area. Public schools, railroads, and roads were built. Agriculture increased, and manufacturing started to grow. North Carolina led the nation in gold production until the California Gold Rush of 1849.

The Civil War and Reconstruction. Although North Carolina was part of the South, it tried to preserve the Union even after most other Southern states had *seceded* (withdrawn). The Civil War began on April 12, 1861. When President Abraham Lincoln asked for troops to fight the Confederate States, North Carolina refused. The state seceded from the Union on May 20, 1861.

Union forces captured much of North Carolina's coastline early in the war. But the port at Wilmington remained open to Confederate supply ships until January 1865. More than 10 battles took place in North Carolina. The bloodiest of these was fought at Bentonville from March 19 to 21, 1865. There, Union forces under General William T. Sherman defeated the Confederate troops of General Joseph E. Johnston. Johnston surrendered to Sherman near Durham on April 26. North Carolina supplied 125,000 men to the Confederate cause. About a fourth of all the Confederate soldiers killed came from North Carolina. However, many North Carolinians sympathized with the Union and resisted the Confederacy.

During the Reconstruction period, federal troops supervised the state's government until 1868. That year, a new state Constitution abolished slavery and gave blacks the right to vote. The Republican Party then gained control of North Carolina. Its members included blacks, white Union sympathizers, and a few Northerners called *carpetbaggers* (see **Carpetbaggers**). The state rejoined the Union on June 25, 1868.

During the Reconstruction years, bitter struggles took place between Republicans and Democrats, and between blacks and whites. The Ku Klux Klan and other secret groups supported white supremacy and tried to keep blacks from voting. Democrats gained control of the state legislature in 1870. They impeached Republican Governor William W. Holden in 1871, and removed him from office. In 1875, the Democratic legislature added 30 amendments to the Constitution, thus ensuring white, Democratic control of county government.

Economic progress. The Civil War had brought death and destruction to North Carolina. But it also freed about 350,000 of the state's black slaves. After slavery was abolished, North Carolina planters divided their land into small farms. They rented these farms to tenants in return for a share of the crop. Under this system of *sharecropping,* the number of farms in the state grew from about 75,000 in 1860 to 150,000 in 1880.

The people of North Carolina rebuilt their state quickly. By the 1880's, farm production equaled what it had been before the war. Tobacco and cotton crops led the growth. Industry also grew rapidly. Many new cotton mills opened. Tobacco-manufacturing and furniture-making also became large-scale industries. Industrialist James Buchanan Duke built up the American Tobacco Company until it had eliminated most competition. Farmers left the farms for industrial jobs in the cities.

In 1898, the Democrats won control of the state legislature in a campaign based on racial hatred. They amended the state Constitution to deprive most blacks of voting rights. New laws required the racial segregation of schools, restaurants, railroad trains, streetcars, and other public facilities.

The early 1900's. In 1901, Governor Charles B. Aycock started a far-reaching program to improve North Carolina's public education system. In 1915, the legislature created the State Highway Commission, which began the largest roadbuilding program in the state's history. That program earned North Carolina the nickname of the "Good Roads State" during the 1920's.

The state's industries developed at a tremendous rate during the early 1900's. By the late 1920's, North Carolina led the nation in the production of cotton textiles, tobacco products, and wooden furniture.

The Great Depression of the 1930's brought sudden drops in prices and wages. Businesses failed and banks closed. Workers lost their jobs and farmers lost their farms. The federal and state governments tried to fight the effects of the depression. The North Carolina government reduced local taxes and took control of all highways and public schools. Federal control of agricultural production raised farm prices and income. The state passed welfare measures, raised teachers' salaries, and reduced working hours to help North Carolina out of the depression by the late 1930's.

The mid-1900's. During World War II (1939-1945), North Carolina mills supplied the armed forces with more textiles than any other state. Its mines supplied more than half the mica used in U.S. war production.

In the late 1940's, North Carolina built new hospitals and mental health facilities, and it paved many roads in rural areas. Two dams increased the state's power output. Fontana Dam, at the edge of the Great Smoky Mountains, started operating in 1945, and Kerr Dam, near Henderson, went into operation in 1954.

North Carolina blacks began to gain greater rights during the mid-1900's. A key event occurred in 1954, when the Supreme Court of the United States ruled that compulsory school segregation was illegal. In 1960, four black students remained seated at a restricted lunch counter in Greensboro after they were refused service. Their action sparked a wave of sit-in demonstrations throughout the South. Such protests contributed to the passage of the Civil Rights Act of 1964, which banned the segregation of public facilities.

During the 1950's, North Carolina continued to shift from a rural, agricultural economy to an urban, industrial economy. The state worked to attract new industries by providing businesses with technical and engineering assistance and by reducing taxes on corporations. In 1956, three universities—Duke University at Durham, North Carolina State University at Raleigh, and the University of North Carolina at Chapel Hill—combined their research resources. They helped form the North Carolina Research Triangle Park, a research center that serves industry. The center opened in 1959.

In 1963, the legislature set up a system of community colleges and technical institutes. Also in 1963, the state adopted a single university plan for the University of North Carolina, beginning with campuses at Chapel Hill, Greensboro, and Raleigh. By 1972, the University of North Carolina had 16 campuses. These included the North Carolina School of the Arts, which had become the nation's first state-supported school for the arts when it opened in Winston-Salem in 1965.

The late 1900's. In 1971, in a case involving a Charlotte school district, the Supreme Court of the United

States ruled that children could be bused to achieve racial integration. Most North Carolina school districts were integrated soon afterward. The Charlotte busing program became a model for the rest of the country.

The Republican Party increased its strength in the state in the late 1900's. In 1972, James E. Holshouser, Jr., became the first Republican to be elected governor of North Carolina since 1896. Also in 1972, Jesse A. Helms became the first Republican candidate to be elected to the United States Senate from North Carolina since 1895.

The development of Research Triangle Park brought prosperity to Durham, Raleigh, Chapel Hill, and the surrounding area. In the late 1980's and the 1990's, many of North Carolina's urban areas experienced growth in the finance and technology industries. However, employment in many traditional industries, including tobacco and textiles, declined. During the 1980's and the 1990's, North Carolina experienced growth in agricultural-related businesses, such as hog, poultry, and sweet

potato production. The filmmaking industry also flourished. Population growth in the state's urban areas increased demand for better schools, highways, health care facilities, and other government services.

Recent developments. In 1999, school busing was discontinued in the Charlotte school district. A federal judge ruled that forced integration was no longer necessary because all traces of intentional discrimination had disappeared.

North Carolina suffered one of the worst natural disasters in its history in September 1999. Hurricane Floyd's floodwaters left drowned livestock and flooded farms and towns across the eastern part of the state. Officials estimated the damage costs to be billions of dollars.

In 2005, the General Assembly approved a state lottery as a means to fund education. Lottery ticket sales began in 2006. In 2009, Beverly Perdue became North Carolina's first woman governor.

Stephen S. Birdsall and Harry L. Watson

Study aids

Related articles in *World Book* include:

Biographies

Aycock, Charles B.
Blackbeard
Blount, William
Bragg, Braxton
Dare, Virginia
Dole, Elizabeth H.
Edwards, John
Helms, Jesse A.
Hewes, Joseph
Hooper, William
Johnson, Andrew
King, William R. D.
Penn, John
Polk, James Knox
Spaight, Richard D.
Vance, Zebulon B.
Williamson, Hugh

Cities

Asheville
Charlotte
Durham
Greensboro
Raleigh
Winston-Salem

History

Civil War, American
Colonial life in America
Franklin, State of
Lost Colony
Reconstruction
Revolution, American
Watauga Association

Physical features

Blue Ridge Mountains
Cape Hatteras
Dismal Swamp
Fall line
Great Smoky Mountains
Piedmont Region

Other related articles

Camp Lejeune
Fort Bragg
Lumbee Indians
North Carolina, University of
Tennessee Valley Authority

Outline

I. **People**
   A. Population
   B. Schools
   C. Libraries
   D. Museums
II. **Visitor's guide**
III. **Land and climate**
   A. Land regions
   B. Coastline
   C. Rivers, waterfalls, and lakes
   D. Plant and animal life
   E. Climate
IV. **Economy**
   A. Natural resources

B. Service industries
C. Manufacturing
D. Agriculture
E. Mining
F. Fishing industry
G. Electric power and utilities
H. Transportation
I. Communication
V. **Government**
   A. Constitution
   B. Executive
   C. Legislature
   D. Courts
   E. Local government
   F. Revenue
   G. Politics
VI. **History**

Additional resources

Level I
Cannavale, Matthew C. *North Carolina, 1524-1776.* National Geographic Children's Bks., 2007.
Heinrichs, Ann. *North Carolina.* Children's Pr., 2009.
Niz, Xavier. *The Mystery of the Roanoke Colony.* Capstone Pr., 2007.
Wiener, Roberta, and Arnold, J. R. *North Carolina.* Raintree, 2005.

Level II
Alexander, John R., and Lazell, James D. *Ribbon of Sand: The Amazing Convergence of the Ocean and the Outer Banks.* 1992. Reprint. Univ. of N.C. Pr., 2000.
Barnes, Jay. *North Carolina's Hurricane History.* 3rd ed. Univ. of N.C. Pr., 2001.
Barney, William L. *The Making of a Confederate: Walter Lenoir's Civil War.* Oxford, 2008.
Bennett, D. Gordon, and Patton, J. C. *A Geography of the Carolinas.* Parkway Pubs., 2008.
Culp, Ronald K. *The First Black United States Marines: The Men of Montford Point, 1942-1946.* McFarland, 2007.
Powell, William S. *North Carolina Through Four Centuries.* Univ. of N.C. Pr., 1989.
Powell, William S., ed. *Dictionary of North Carolina Biography.* 6 vols. Univ. of N.C. Pr., 1979-1996.
Powell, William S., and Mazzocchi, Jay, eds. *Encyclopedia of North Carolina.* Univ. of N.C. Pr., 2006.
Reid, Richard M. *Freedom for Themselves: North Carolina's Black Soldiers in the Civil War Era.* Univ. of N.C. Pr., 2008.

University of North Carolina

The University of North Carolina at Chapel Hill is the oldest institution in the university system. It includes the Louis Round Wilson Special Collections Library, *shown here.*

North Carolina, University of, is a state-supported system of higher education. The statewide system includes 16 institutions that grant bachelor's degrees. Most of them also award master's and doctor's degrees. In addition, the system includes the North Carolina School of Science and Mathematics (NCSSM), a public residential high school in Durham for gifted students. Each of these 17 schools has its own chancellor. A president heads the entire system. The University of North Carolina's website at http://www.northcarolina.edu offers additional information.

Six of the postsecondary schools are called the University of North Carolina (UNC). They are in Asheville, Chapel Hill, Charlotte, Greensboro, Pembroke, and Wilmington. The other 10 postsecondary institutions are Appalachian State University (in Boone), East Carolina University (in Greenville), Elizabeth City State University, Fayetteville State University, North Carolina Agricultural and Technical State University (in Greensboro), North Carolina Central University (in Durham), North Carolina State University (in Raleigh), the University of North Carolina School of the Arts (in Winston-Salem), Western Carolina University (in Cullowhee), and Winston-Salem State University.

UNC-Chapel Hill is the oldest institution in the UNC system. Its athletic teams are called the Tar Heels. North Carolina State University is the largest UNC school. Its athletic teams are called the Wolfpack.

The University of North Carolina was chartered in 1789. In 1795, it became the first public institution of higher education in the United States to begin enrolling students. The university's first campus, at Chapel Hill, was the only campus throughout the 1800's and early 1900's. From 1931 to 1972, the North Carolina General Assembly gradually brought all of the state's public four-year colleges and universities into the University of North Carolina system. The NCSSM opened in 1980 and became affiliated with the UNC system in 1985.

Critically reviewed by the University of North Carolina

North Cascades National Park is in northwestern Washington. The park's magnificent scenery includes mountain ridges, forested valleys, alpine lakes and meadows, waterfalls, and glaciers. Among the animals that live in the park are bears, cougars, deer, moose, mountain goats, and wolverines. The park also has magnificent cedar and fir forests.

The park was established in 1968, along with the adjacent Lake Chelan National Recreation Area and Ross Lake National Recreation Area. For the area of North Cascades National Park, see **National Park System** (table: National parks). For the location of the park, see **Washington** (political map).

Critically reviewed by the National Park Service

Robert McKenzie, Tom Stack & Assoc.

North Cascades National Park provides visitors with many scenic attractions, including snow-capped mountains, forested valleys, alpine lakes, and numerous forms of wildlife.

North Central States are the 12 states in the north-central part of the United States. They include Illinois, Indiana, Iowa, Kansas, Michigan, Minnesota, Missouri, Nebraska, North Dakota, Ohio, South Dakota, and Wisconsin. These states are also known as the Midwestern States.

The western North Central States, which are sometimes called the Great Plains States, contain some of the richest farming land in the world. Corn and wheat fields cover the plains. The states on the eastern edge of the region are sometimes called the Lake States. These states are known for their great industrial centers, in addition to their farms.

Steep buttes rise beyond a farm near Medora, in southwestern North Dakota. Farms and ranches cover much of the state. North Dakota's economy depends heavily on agriculture.

North Dakota   *The Flickertail State*

North Dakota is a Midwestern state of the United States. It borders Canada and lies at the center of the North American continent. The geographic center of North America is near the town of Rugby. Bismarck is the capital of North Dakota, and Fargo is the largest city.

North Dakota is mainly a farm state. Its economy is based more heavily on farming than most other states. Many North Dakota factories process farm products or manufacture farm equipment. Many of the state's merchants also rely on agriculture. North Dakota has a larger percentage of agricultural workers than most other states, but increased mechanization has led to declines in the total number of farmworkers.

Farms and ranches cover nearly all North Dakota. They stretch from the flat Red River Valley in the east, across rolling plains, to the rugged Badlands in the west. The chief crop, wheat, is grown in nearly every county. North Dakota harvests more than 90 percent of the nation's canola and flaxseed. It is also the country's top producer of barley and sunflower seeds and a leader in the production of beans, honey, lentils, oats, peas, and sugar beets.

The contributors of this article are Douglas C. Munski, Professor of Geography, University of North Dakota, and Chairperson, North Dakota Geographic Alliance; and Kimberly Porter, Professor of History, University of North Dakota.

Soil is North Dakota's most precious resource. It is the base of the state's great agricultural wealth. But North Dakota also has enormous mineral resources. These resources include billions of tons of *lignite,* a low-quality coal. In addition, North Dakota has large oil reserves. Petroleum was discovered in the state in 1951 and quickly became one of North Dakota's most valuable mineral resources.

Few white settlers came to the North Dakota region before the 1870's because railroads had not yet entered the area. In the early 1870's, the Northern Pacific Railroad began to push across the Dakota Territory. Large-scale farming also began during the 1870's. Eastern corporations and some families established huge wheat farms in the Red River Valley. The farms made such enormous profits that they were called *bonanza* farms. White settlers, attracted by the success of the bonanza farms, flocked to North Dakota. In 1870, North Dakota had 2,405 people. By 1890, the population had grown to 190,983.

North Dakota was named for the Sioux Indians who once lived in the territory. The Sioux called themselves *Dakota* or *Lakota,* meaning *allies* or *friends.* One of North Dakota's nicknames is the *Peace Garden State.* This nickname honors the International Peace Garden, which lies on the state's border with Manitoba, Canada. North Dakota is also called the *Flickertail State* because of the many flickertail ground squirrels that live in the central part of the state.

Interesting facts about North Dakota

North Dakota is one of the leading producers of lignite coal in the United States. The low-quality coal can be found throughout the western portion of the state. The deposit, which contains billions of tons of lignite coal, is considered one of the largest single concentrations of solid fuel in the world.

North and South Dakota were admitted to the Union simultaneously. On Nov. 2, 1889, President Benjamin Harrison signed the proclamation that made North and South Dakota states. He shuffled the states' admission papers so that one state could not claim to have been admitted before the other. Today, the two are listed alphabetically, making North Dakota the 39th and South Dakota the 40th.

Lignite coal

WORLD BOOK illustrations by Kevin Chadwick

International golf course

An international golf course is based in Portal. Part of the course lies in the United States and part is in Canada. An international hole-in-one can be scored on the ninth hole. The tee for the ninth hole is in Canada, and the cup is in the United States. George Wegener scored the first international hole-in-one there in 1934.

The geographic center of North America is near the town of Rugby in Pierce County.

Sheldon Green

Petroleum is the most profitable mineral in North Dakota. Most of the petroleum is recovered from the thousands of wells in the western part of the state.

Sheldon Green

Ranchers round up cattle on a North Dakota farm. Beef cattle rank as the state's most valuable livestock animals. Farmers in North Dakota also raise hogs and dairy cattle.

Sheldon Green

Fargo is the largest city in North Dakota. It is one of only five cities in the state with a population of more than 25,000. The other four cities are Bismarck, Grand Forks, Minot, and West Fargo.

North Dakota in brief

Symbols of North Dakota

The state flag, adopted in 1911, bears a modified version of the coat of arms of the United States. On the state seal, adopted in 1889, a tree in an open field is surrounded by bundles of wheat, which represent agriculture. A plow, anvil, and sledge also symbolize farming. The bow and arrows and the Indian on horseback chasing a buffalo represent the Indian nations that thrived in the North Dakota region for hundreds of years.

State flag

North Dakota Secretary of State's Office
State seal

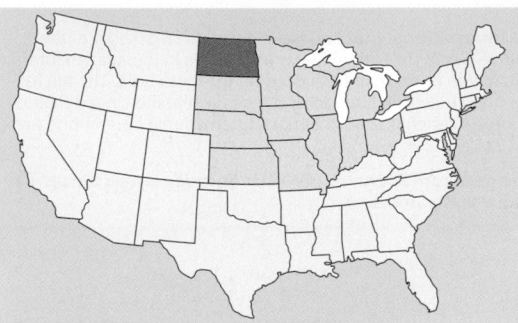

North Dakota (brown) ranks 17th in size among all the states and 5th in size among the Midwestern States (yellow).

General information

Statehood: Nov. 2, 1889, the 39th state.
Abbreviations: N. Dak. or N.D. (traditional); ND (postal).
State motto: *Liberty and Union, Now and Forever, One and Inseparable.*
State song: "North Dakota Hymn." Words by James W. Foley; music by C. S. Putnam.

The State Capitol is in Bismarck, the capital since North Dakota became a state in 1889.

Land and climate

Area: 70,700 mi² (183,112 km²), including 1,724 mi² (4,465 km²) of inland water.
Elevation: *Highest*—White Butte, 3,506 ft (1,069 m) above sea level. *Lowest*—750 ft (229 m) above sea level in Pembina County.
Record high temperature: 121 °F (49 °C) at Steele on July 6, 1936.
Record low temperature: −60 °F (−51 °C) at Parshall on Feb. 15, 1936.
Average July temperature: 70 °F (21 °C).
Average January temperature: 7 °F (−14 °C).
Average yearly precipitation: 17 in (43 cm).

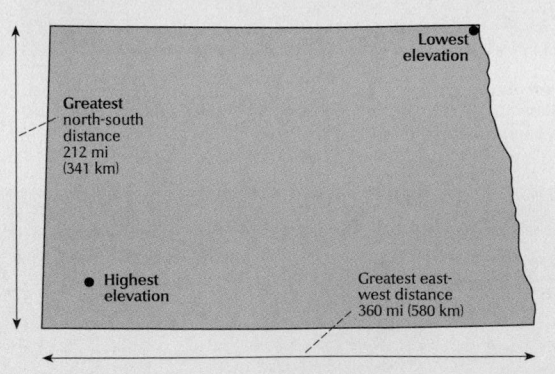

Lowest elevation

Greatest north-south distance 212 mi (341 km)

Highest elevation

Greatest east-west distance 360 mi (580 km)

Important dates

The United States acquired southwestern North Dakota through the Louisiana Purchase.

The Dakota Territory was opened for homesteading.

| 1738 | 1803 | 1818 | 1863 |

Pierre Gaultier de Varennes, Sieur de La Vérendrye, made the first explorations in North Dakota.

The United States acquired northeastern North Dakota in a treaty with the United Kingdom.

State bird
Western meadowlark

State flower
Wild rose

State tree
American elm

People

Population: 672,591
Rank among the states: 48th
Density: 10 per mi² (4 per km²), U.S. average 85 per mi² (33 per km²)
Distribution: 56 percent urban, 44 percent rural
Largest cities in North Dakota

Fargo	105,549
Bismarck	61,272
Grand Forks	52,838
Minot	40,888
West Fargo	25,830
Mandan	18,331

Source: 2010 census, except for distribution, which is for 2000.

Population trend

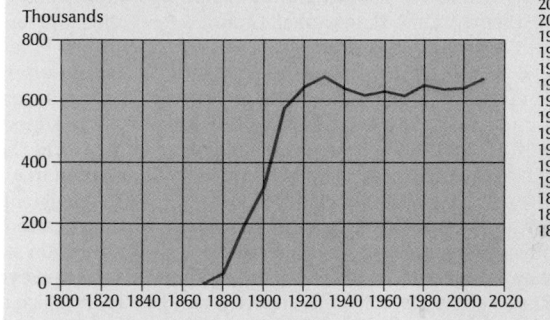

Thousands

Source: U.S. Census Bureau.

Year	Population
2010	672,591
2000	642,200
1990	638,800
1980	652,717
1970	617,761
1960	632,446
1950	619,636
1940	641,935
1930	680,845
1920	646,872
1910	577,056
1900	319,146
1890	190,983
1880	36,909
1870	2,405

Economy

Chief products

Agriculture: barley, beans, beef cattle, canola, corn, hay, milk, peas, potatoes, soybeans, sugar beets, sunflowers, wheat.
Manufacturing: computer and electronic products, fabricated metals, food products, machinery.
Mining: coal, natural gas, petroleum.

Gross domestic product

Value of goods and services produced in 2008: $31,246,000,000. *Services* include community, business, and personal services; finance; government; trade; and transportation and communication. *Industry* includes construction, manufacturing, mining, and utilities. *Agriculture* includes agriculture, fishing, and forestry.

Source: U.S. Bureau of Economic Analysis.

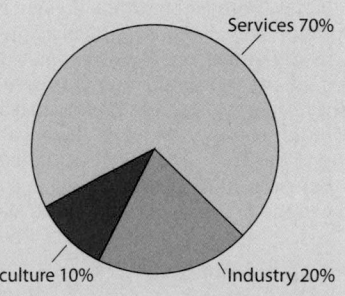

Services 70%

Agriculture 10%

Industry 20%

Government

State government

Governor: 4-year term
State senators: 47; 4-year terms
State representatives: 94; 4-year terms
Counties: 53

Federal government

United States senators: 2
United States representatives: 1
Electoral votes: 3

Sources of information

North Dakota's official website at http://www.nd.gov provides a gateway to much information on the state's government, history, and economy.

In addition, the website at http://www.ndtourism.com provides information about tourism.

Oil was discovered near Tioga.

Construction began on the Garrison Diversion Project to increase the state's water supply.

1889   **1951**   **1956**   **1968**   **1997**

North Dakota became the 39th state on November 2.

The first generator at Garrison Dam began to produce electric power.

Flooding along the Red River of the North caused severe damage, especially in Grand Forks.

Population. The 2010 United States census reported that North Dakota had 672,591 people. The population had increased by about 5 percent over the 2000 figure, 642,200. According to the 2010 census, North Dakota ranks 48th in population among the 50 states.

Nearly half of the people of North Dakota live within one of the state's three metropolitan areas (see **Metropolitan area**). The Bismarck metropolitan area is entirely in North Dakota, and the Fargo and Grand Forks areas extend into Minnesota. For the populations of these metropolitan areas, see the *Index* to the political map of North Dakota.

North Dakota has few large manufacturing industries to encourage the growth of big cities. Only five cities in the state have more than 25,000 people. They are, in order of size, Fargo; Bismarck, the state capital; Grand Forks; Minot; and West Fargo. The larger cities still serve their original function as centers of shipping, supply, and trade for the surrounding agricultural regions.

White settlers began to pour into North Dakota by the thousands in the 1870's and 1880's. They were attracted by reports of the large profits made in wheat farming and the availability of free government land.

Settlers came from states to the east and south and from Europe. The largest number from other nations came from Norway. They settled throughout the region. Germans from Russia settled in the south-central area, and Canadians moved into the northern Red River Valley. Today, the largest population groups in the state are made up of people of German and Norwegian descent.

Today, population trends present North Dakota with a number of challenges, particularly in the areas of health care and education. The state's metropolitan areas have grown, but many rural counties have lost population. North Dakota also has a higher than average proportion of elderly people, and it has had problems keeping its young people from migrating to other states.

Schools. In 1818, Roman Catholic missionaries established the first school in the North Dakota region. This school was at Pembina, in the northeast. The missionaries taught Métis (people of mixed white and Indian ancestry) of the region and the children of Scottish and Irish settlers who came from Canada. The school closed in 1823, when Pembina was abandoned. In 1848, George Belcourt, a Catholic priest, reopened the school as an Indian mission.

In the early days, teachers traveled from village to village, teaching groups of children in homes. As the settlements grew, the colonists built schools and hired teachers. Railroad companies, anxious to attract settlers, helped by supplying building materials.

In 1862, the first legislature of the Dakota Territory passed "An Act for the Regulation and Support of Common (public) Schools." Between 1862 and statehood in 1889, the territory reorganized its educational system several times. The first state legislature created a fund for the support of all schools teaching the English language. Taxes now support the state's public schools.

The superintendent of public instruction administers the North Dakota public school system. He or she is elected to a four-year term. This official and a special staff make up the state Department of Public Instruction. Children must attend school from ages 7 through 15. For education statistics in the state, see **Education** (table).

Libraries and museums. Women's clubs did much to organize and improve North Dakota's early libraries. In 1897, a women's club opened the state's first public library at Grafton. Today, North Dakota has numerous public libraries around the state. North Dakota's statewide library catalog—which includes academic, public, school, and special libraries—is available on the Internet.

North Dakota State University in Fargo and the University of North Dakota in Grand Forks have the largest libraries in the state. Both house large collections on North Dakota's history. The State Historical Society in Bismarck also operates a library with large collections relating to the state's history.

The North Dakota Heritage Center, in Bismarck, is the largest museum in the state. The museum also serves as the headquarters of the State Historical Society. The center features exhibits on the life of early North Dakota Indians, pioneer days, and natural history. The Pembina State Museum, in Pembina, focuses on regional history.

Population density

Only about half the residents of North Dakota live in urban areas. About two-fifths live in the state's four largest cities— Bismarck, Fargo, Grand Forks, and Minot.

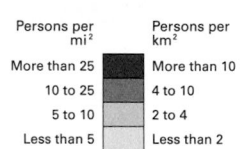

Persons per mi²		Persons per km²
More than 25		More than 10
10 to 25		4 to 10
5 to 10		2 to 4
Less than 5		Less than 2

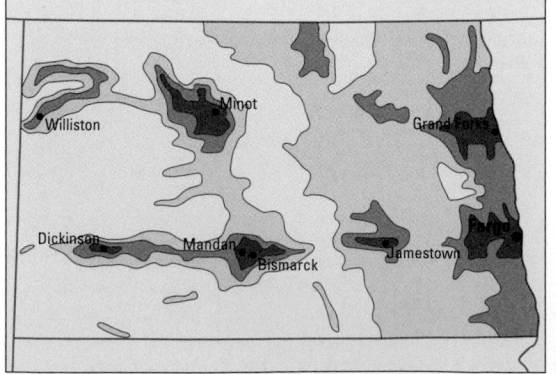

WORLD BOOK map, based on U.S. Census Bureau data.

Universities and colleges

This table lists the nonprofit universities and colleges in North Dakota that grant bachelor's or advanced degrees and are accredited by the North Central Association of Colleges and Schools.

Name	Mailing address
Dakota College at Bottineau	Bottineau
Dickinson State University	Dickinson
Jamestown College	Jamestown
Mary, University of	Bismarck
Mayville State University	Mayville
Medcenter One College of Nursing	Bismarck
Minot State University	Minot
North Dakota, University of	Grand Forks
North Dakota State University	Fargo
Sitting Bull College	Fort Yates
Trinity Bible College	Ellendale
Turtle Mountain Community College	Belcourt
Valley City State University	Valley City
Williston State College	Williston

North Dakota map index

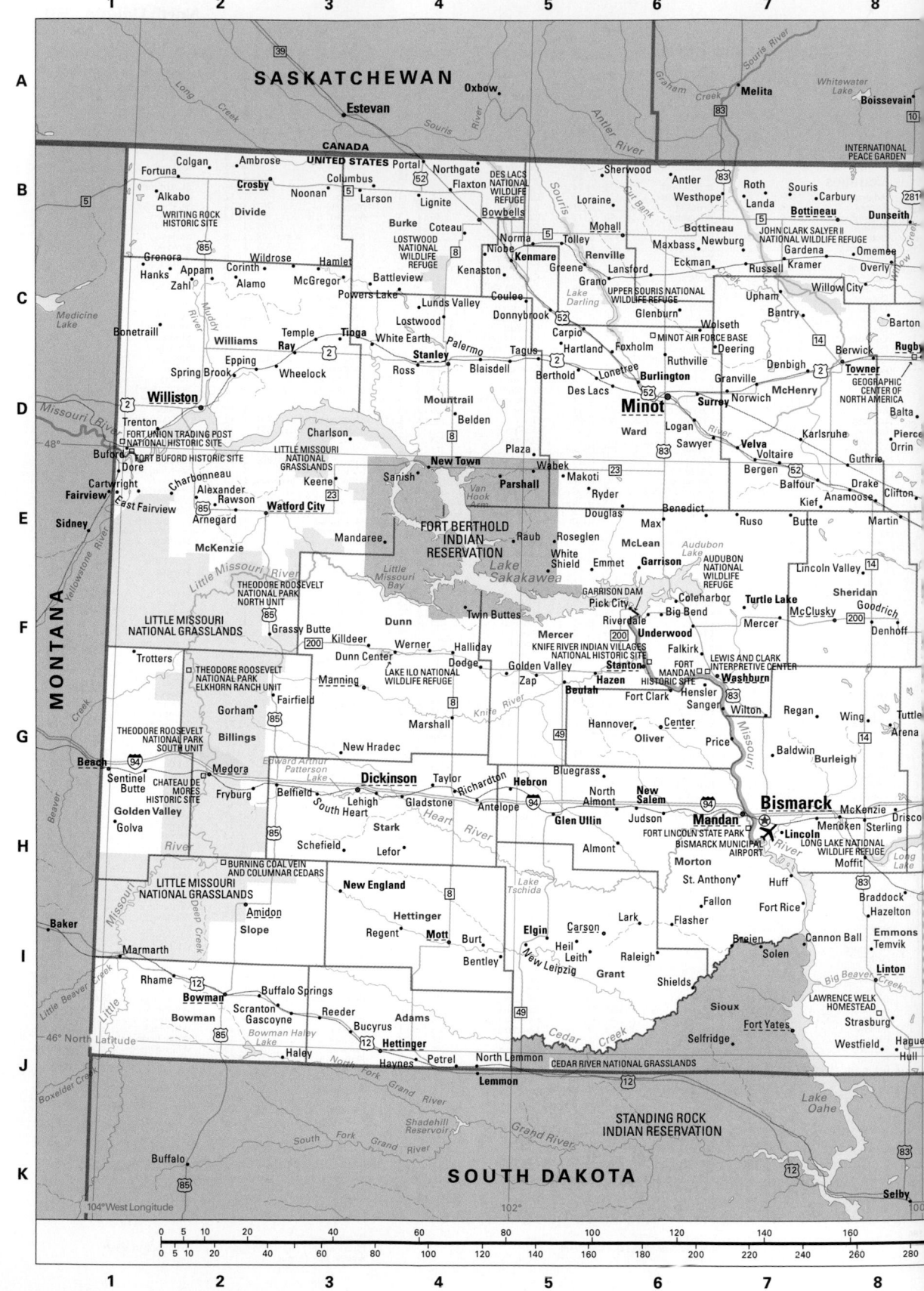

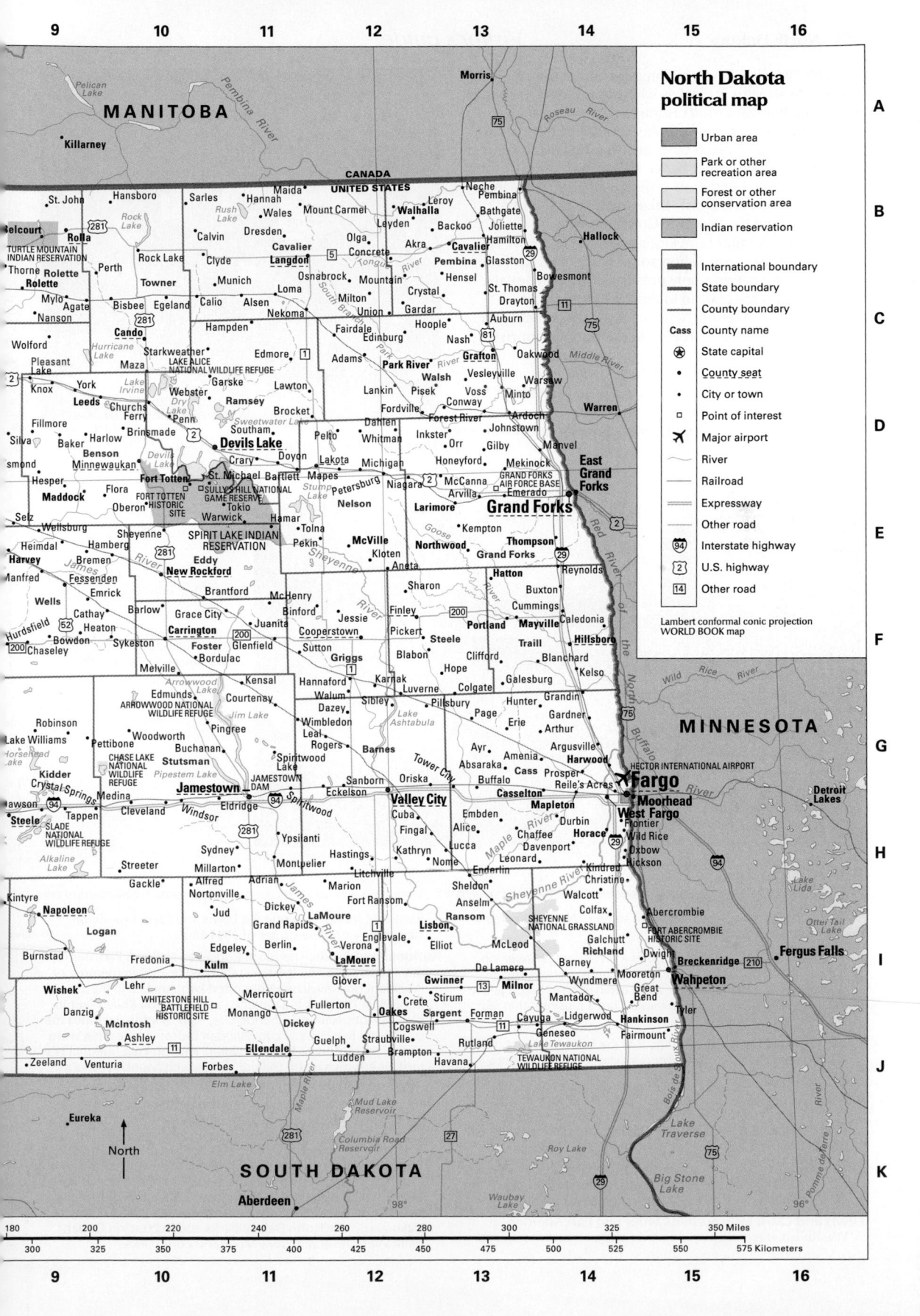

North Dakota
political map

- Urban area
- Park or other recreation area
- Forest or other conservation area
- Indian reservation

International boundary
State boundary
County boundary
Cass County name
✪ State capital
• County seat
• City or town
▫ Point of interest
✈ Major airport
River
Railroad
Expressway
Other road
94 Interstate highway
2 U.S. highway
14 Other road

Lambert conformal conic projection
WORLD BOOK map

9 10 11 12 13 14 15 16

A
Morris
75

MANITOBA
• Killarney
Pelican Lake
Pembina River
Roseau River
75

CANADA
UNITED STATES

B
St. John • Hansboro Sarles • Hannah Maida Leroy • Neche Pembina
Belcourt Wales Mount Carmel Bathgate Hallock
Rolla Dresden Leyden Backoo Joliette
TURTLE MOUNTAIN INDIAN RESERVATION 281 Calvin Olga Akra **Cavalier** Hamilton 29
Thorne Perth Rock Lake Clyde Concrete Pembina Glasston Bowesmont
Rolette Rolette Cavalier Osnabrock Hensel St. Thomas Drayton
Rock Lake 5 Langdon Mountain Crystal Auburn 11
Mylo • Agate Bisbee Egeland Loma Milton Gardar Oakwood 75

C
Nanson Cando Munich Alsen Union Hoople Nash
Wolford Hampden Fairdale Edinburg Grafton
Pleasant Lake Starkweather Edmore 1 Adams **Park River** Vesleyville Warsaw
Knox York Leeds Garske Lawton **Walsh** Minto
Fillmore Webster Brocket Lankin Pisek Voss Warren
Silva Baker Harlow Brinsmade Penn Dahlen Fordville Conway Ardoch
Benson Devils Lake Crary Doyon Whitman Inkster Orr Johnstown Manvel East Grand Forks

D
Minnewaukan Fort Totten Bartlett Mapes Michigan Honeyford Mekinock GRAND FORKS AIR FORCE BASE
Maddock Flora SULLY'S HILL NATIONAL GAME RESERVE Petersburg Niagara McCanna Arvilla Emerado **Grand Forks**
Oberon FORT TOTTEN HISTORIC SITE Warwick Tokio Hamar Larimore
Selz Wellsburg Sheyenne SPIRIT LAKE INDIAN RESERVATION Tolna **Nelson** Goose River

E
Heimdal Hamberg Eddy Pekin McVille Kempton Thompson
Harvey Bremen New Rockford Kloten Northwood Grand Forks Reynolds 29
Manfred Fessenden Brantford Aneta Hatton
Wells Emrick McHenry Sharon Buxton
Barlow Grace City Finley Cummings
Hurdsfield Cathay Heaton Binford Jessie Pickert Steele **Portland** Mayville Caledonia

F
52 Bowdon Sykeston Juanita Cooperstown Blaben **Traill** Hillsboro
Chaseley Melville Carrington Glenfield Sutton Hope Clifford Blanchard Kelso
200 Foster Bordulac Griggs Hannaford Karnak Luverne Colgate Galesburg

G
Robinson Edmunds Kensal Walum Dazey Sibley Pillsbury Grandin
Lake Williams ARROWWOOD NATIONAL WILDLIFE REFUGE Courtenay Jim Lake Wimbledon Page Hunter Gardner
Pettibone Woodworth Pingree Leal Rogers Erie Arthur MINNESOTA
Kidder CHASE LAKE NATIONAL WILDLIFE REFUGE Buchanan Spiritwood Lake **Barnes** Ayr Amenia Argusville
Crystal Springs Stutsman JAMESTOWN DAM Sanborn Oriska Tower City **Cass** Prosper Reile's Acres HECTOR INTERNATIONAL AIRPORT

H
Dawson Medina Jamestown Eckelson **Valley City** Casselton **Fargo** Detroit Lakes
Steele Cleveland Windsor Eldridge Cuba Embden Mapleton Moorhead
SLADE NATIONAL WILDLIFE REFUGE Tappen 281 Ypsilanti Fingal Alice Durbin West Fargo
Napoleon Sydney Hastings Kathryn Chaffee Davenport Horace Frontier Wild Rice 29 Oxbow
Streeter Millarton Montpelier Litchville Nome Leonard Kindred Dickson 94

I
Kintyre Gackle Alfred Adrian Marion Sheldon Walcott Christine
Logan Nortonville Fort Ransom Anselm Colfax
Burnstad Jud Dickey LaMoure Ransom McLeod Abercrombie
Fredonia Grand Rapids Berlin Verona Elliot Galchutt FORT ABERCROMBIE HISTORIC SITE
Wishek Lehr Edgeley **LaMoure** Englevale Barney Richland Dwight Fergus Falls
WHITESTONE HILL BATTLEFIELD HISTORIC SITE Kulm 1 De Lamere SHEYENNE NATIONAL GRASSLAND Wyndmere Mooreton Breckenridge 210
Danzig Merricourt Glover **Gwinner** Crete Stirum **Milnor** Mantador Great Bend **Wahpeton**

J
McIntosh Monango Fullerton Cayuba Lidgerwood Tyler
Ashley Dickey **Oakes** Sargent Forman Hankinson
Zeeland Venturia 11 Guelph Cogswell Geneseo Fairmount
Ellendale Straubville Rutland Lake Tewaukon Bois de Sioux River
Forbes Ludden Brampton Havana TEWAUKON NATIONAL WILDLIFE REFUGE

K
Elm Lake SOUTH DAKOTA Mud Lake Reservoir Lake Traverse
Eureka North 281 Columbia Road Reservoir 27 Roy Lake Big Stone Lake 75 96°
Aberdeen 98° Waubay Lake 29

180 200 220 240 260 280 300 325 350 Miles
300 325 350 375 400 425 450 475 500 525 550 575 Kilometers

9 10 11 12 13 14 15 16

North Dakota's crisp autumn days attract thousands of hunters to streams and lakes where migrating waterfowl pause on their way south. Hunters also shoot ducks, geese, grouse, ring-necked pheasants, and other game birds. Vacationers catch bass, catfish, northern pike, walleye, trout, and other fishes. Favorite summer-resort areas include the Badlands region, with Theodore Roosevelt National Park; Devils Lake; Killdeer and Turtle mountains; and the Pembina Gorge.

During the summer, musicals are offered at Fort Totten, on an Indian reservation south of Devils Lake. Fort Totten has the nation's only preserved "cavalry square." Variety shows are offered in the Burning Hills Amphitheatre near Medora, a picturesque old West town that has been restored. The town is a popular tourist attraction.

Summer visitors to North Dakota also enjoy colorful Indian powwows conducted on various reservations in the state. Many tourists attend the exciting rodeos that are held in numerous communities throughout North Dakota.

Clayton Wolt, C. J. Photos

The General Store at Bonanzaville, USA

International Peace Garden near Dunseith

Clayton Wolt, C. J. Photos

Places to visit

Following are brief descriptions of some of North Dakota's many interesting places to visit:

Bonanzaville, USA, in West Fargo, is a preserved pioneer village. It has 40 buildings, including a church, a one-room schoolhouse, a general store, a log cabin, a town hall, a jail, a drugstore, a hotel and bar, a market, and a museum that features American Indian items.

Chateau de Mores, near Medora, was the home of a Frenchman, the Marquis de Mores, who founded Medora in 1883.

International Peace Garden is a park that lies partly in North Dakota and partly in Manitoba. It symbolizes the long friendship between the United States and Canada. See **International Peace Garden.**

Lake Sakakawea, the reservoir for Garrison Dam, is about 60 miles (97 kilometers) north of Bismarck. The site is popular for swimming, boating, fishing, camping, and picnicking.

Lewis and Clark Interpretive Center and Fort Mandan, at Washburn, offers displays, exhibits, and a reconstructed and furnished fort like the one the Lewis and Clark Expedition stayed in during the winter of 1804-1805.

National parklands. Theodore Roosevelt National Park lies in the scenic Badlands. It was established in 1947 in memory of President Roosevelt, who operated two ranches in the area in the 1880's. The park is a wildlife sanctuary. The Knife River Indian Villages National Historic Site, near Stanton, includes the remains of five Hidatsa and Mandan Indian villages that were occupied until 1845. The Fort Union Trading Post National Historic Site, which North Dakota shares with Montana, was a major fur-trading post in the mid-1800's.

State parks. North Dakota has about 20 state parks and campgrounds and many historic and military sites. Fort Abraham Lincoln State Park, near Mandan, is an important historic site. In 1876, Lieutenant Colonel George A. Custer set out from Fort Abraham Lincoln on the expedition that ended in the Battle of the Little Bighorn. Fort Totten, a state historic site on the Fort Totten Indian Reservation, includes a U.S. military post that dates from 1867. For information on the state parks of North Dakota, visit the North Dakota Parks and Recreation Department Web site at http://www.ndparks.com/parks.

United Tribes Powwow
in Bismarck

Clayton Wolt, C. J. Photos

Combine demolition derby
at State Fair in Minot

Sheldon Green

Jeff Gnass, West Stock

A log cabin at Theodore
Roosevelt National Park

The Red River Valley is one of the most fertile farming areas in the world. It lies along the Red River of the North, which forms the North Dakota-Minnesota border.

Sheldon Green

Land regions. North Dakota has three major land regions: (1) the Red River Valley, (2) the Drift Prairie, and (3) the Great Plains. These regions rise in three broad steps from east to west.

The Red River Valley lies along the Minnesota border. This region is extremely flat. The valley is part of the bed of an ancient glacial lake, Lake Agassiz (see **Lake Agassiz**). The *silt* (soil particles) of the former lake bottom makes this valley one of the most fertile farming areas in the world. Livestock farms and fields of wheat and other crops cover most of the region. The valley is the most heavily populated part of North Dakota.

The Drift Prairie rises on the western border of the Red River Valley. An *escarpment* (steep slope) separates the two regions. The escarpment is steepest in the north in the Pembina Hills (sometimes called the Pembina Mountains), which tower several hundred feet or meters above the Red River Valley. Generally, the Drift Prairie rises gradually toward the west and southwest. Near the region's western border, the land is from 300 to 2,000 feet (91 to 610 meters) above the Red River Valley. The glaciers that crossed the Drift Prairie during the Pleistocene Epoch, which ended about 11,500 years ago, left rich deposits of earth materials called *drift*. The passage of glaciers also earned the area the name *Glaciated Plains*. Most of the region has rolling hills and is cut by stream valleys. In the north, the Turtle Mountains rise about 550 feet (168 meters) above the surrounding plains. The Drift Prairie has many small lakes where thousands of wild ducks nest every year.

The Great Plains cover the southwestern half of North Dakota. This region is part of the immense highland that extends from northern Canada to southern Texas (see **Great Plains**). North Dakotans call the region the *Mis-*

souri Plateau. The region begins at the Couteau Slope. The slope rises 300 to 400 feet (91 to 120 meters) above the Drift Prairie just east of the Missouri River. It crosses the state from northwest to southeast. The area is hilly, and is used for grazing cattle. It is also rich in mineral deposits.

A narrow band of lowlands called the *Missouri Breaks* follows the sweep of the Missouri River. The area south and west of the river is called the *Slope*. There, rough valleys and *buttes* (steep hills that stand alone) break up the flatness of the plains. Many small streams wind around the hills as they flow toward the larger rivers.

The Badlands of the Little Missouri River lie in the southwest. This strip of rough, beautiful land is 6 to 20 miles (10 to 32 kilometers) wide and about 190 miles (306 kilometers) long. The Badlands are a sandstone, shale, and clay valley in which wind and water have carved weird formations. Buttes, domes, pyramids, and cones—colored with bands of browns, reds, grays, and yellows

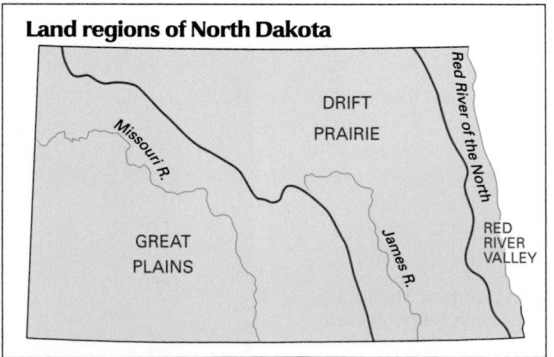

Land regions of North Dakota

WORLD BOOK map

Map index

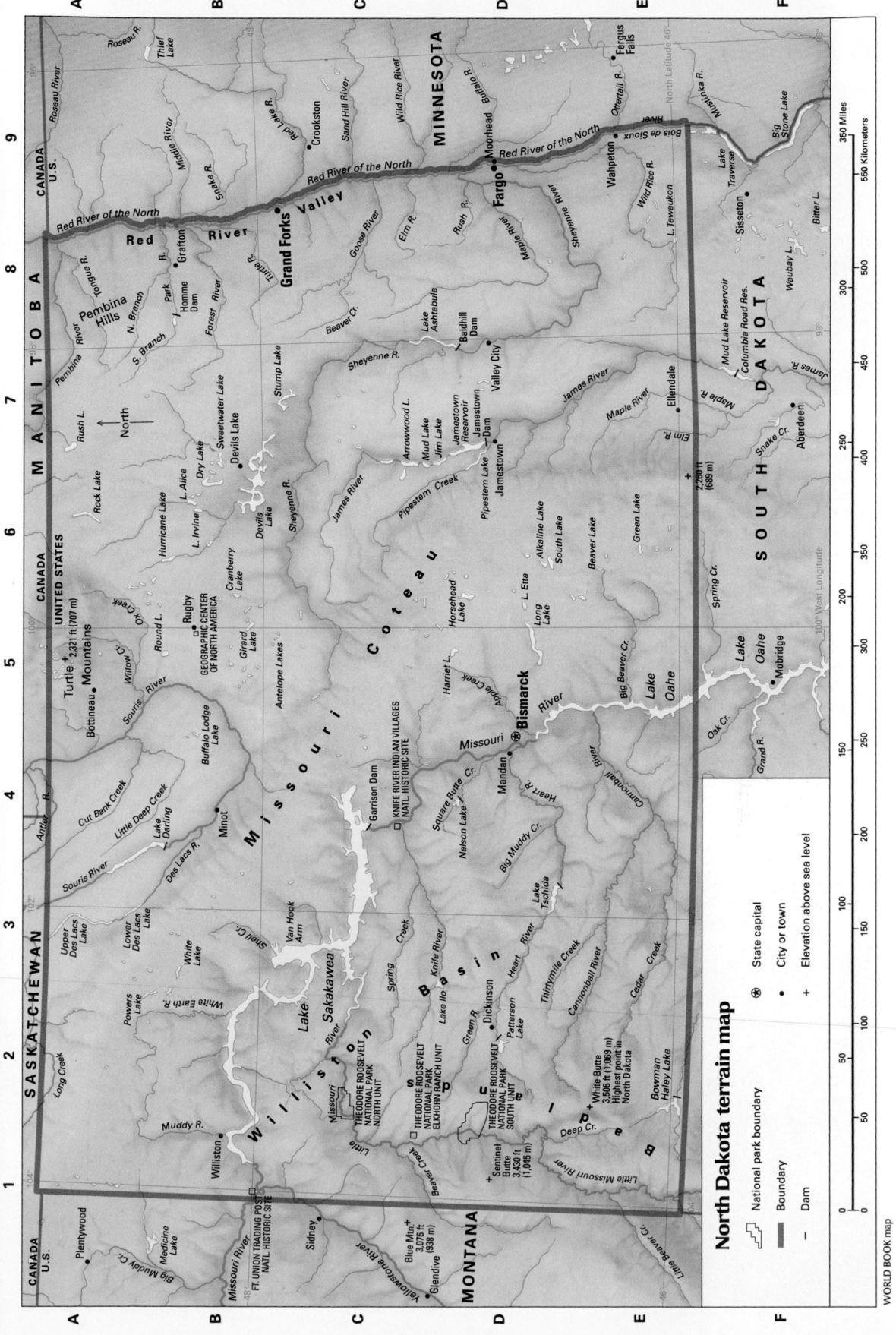

North Dakota terrain map

National park boundary

Boundary

Dam

⊛ State capital

• City or town

+ Elevation above sea level

WORLD BOOK map

0   50   100   150   200   250   300   350 Miles
0   50 100 150 200 250 300 350 400 450 500 550 Kilometers

The Badlands of North Dakota lie in the southwestern part of the state along the Little Missouri River. Wind and water have carved unusual formations out of sandstone, shale, and clay in this rugged area.

Sheldon Green

—rise from the floor of the valley. One of the buttes, White Butte, is 3,506 feet (1,069 meters) above sea level, the highest point in North Dakota. In parts of the Badlands, the rocks contain lignite coal. Some coal beds have been burning for many years, turning the clay above them bright red and pink. This burned material, called *scoria,* is used for surfacing roads.

Rivers and lakes. The Missouri River drains about 60 percent of North Dakota, and the Red River of the North drains most of the rest of North Dakota. The great Missouri winds through the western part of the state. Its branches include the Cannonball, Heart, Knife, and Little Missouri rivers. The James River begins in central North Dakota and flows southward into South Dakota. Garrison Dam, 12,000 feet (3,658 meters) long, spans the Missouri near Riverdale. The waters above the dam form Lake Sakakawea. This narrow lake is 178 miles (286 kilometers) long. The dam helps control floods and provides water for irrigation and hydroelectric power.

The Red River of the North and its branches flow northward through eastern North Dakota and empty into Lake Winnipeg in Canada. The largest branches include the Goose, Park, Pembina, and Sheyenne rivers. The Souris River drains a flat, fertile area in the north-central section. It flows southward from Saskatchewan and then circles back north into Manitoba. The Bois de Sioux River forms part of the border between North Dakota and Minnesota.

Small lakes dot the Drift Prairie. Many lie in beds scooped out by the glaciers. Devils Lake, in the north-central part of the region, is the largest natural lake in North Dakota. The lake, which is prone to flooding, has an artificial outlet on the Sheyenne River. Its water, however, is salty and high in minerals, and can harm wildlife and soil fertility in the area.

Plant and animal life. Forests cover only about 1 percent of North Dakota. Trees that grow in the east include the ash, aspen, basswood, boxelder, elm, oak, and poplar. The largest stands of timber are in the Turtle Mountains and Pembina Hills and in the hills surround-

Sheldon Green

Lake Sakakawea was formed when engineers built Garrison Dam across the Missouri River. The lake is 178 miles (286 kilometers) long and an average of 3 ½ miles (5.6 kilometers) wide.

Average January temperatures
Winters can be bitterly cold. Temperatures are coldest in the northeast and warmest in the southwest.

Average July temperatures
North Dakota has pleasant, sunny summers with low humidity. Temperatures are generally even throughout the state.

Average yearly precipitation
North Dakota is one of the driest of the states. The southeastern corner of the state receives the most precipitation.

WORLD BOOK maps

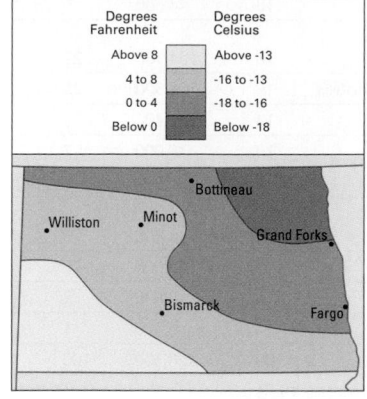

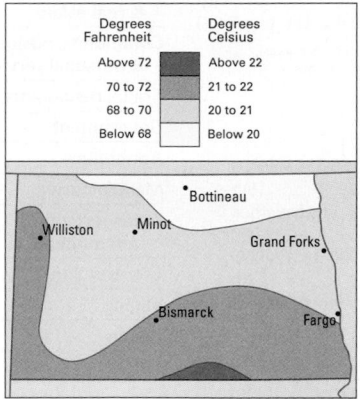

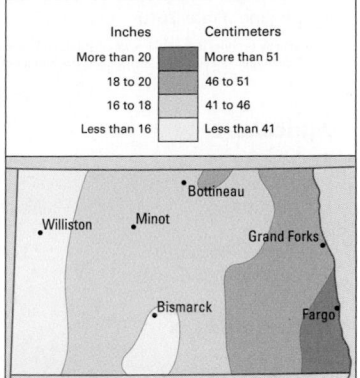

ing Devils Lake. Ash, cottonwood, elm, and willow trees grow along the Missouri River and its branches.

In spring and summer, brilliantly colored flowers bloom. They include beardtongues, black-eyed Susans, gaillardias, pasqueflowers, prairie mallows, red lilies, and wild prairie roses. Chokecherries, highbush cranberries, and wild plums grow in many parts of North Dakota. Bluegrass thrives in the northeast, and buffalo and grama grasses grow in the southwest.

White-tailed deer graze throughout North Dakota. Mule deer and pronghorns range the western plains. In the Badlands, prairie dogs live in scattered colonies called *dog towns.* Fur-bearing animals found in the state include badgers, beavers, bobcats, coyotes, foxes, lynxes, minks, muskrats, rabbits, raccoons, skunks, and weasels. Flickertail ground squirrels are common.

Every summer, ducks migrate to North Dakota to breed in the lakes, marshes, and grainfields. More waterfowl hatch in North Dakota than in any other state. Game birds include grouse, Hungarian partridges, and pheasants. Fish in the state's waters include bass, carp, catfish, perch, trout, and walleye pike.

Climate. Summers in North Dakota are generally clear and pleasant. The sun shines more than 15 hours on each clear day from mid-May through July. Even the hottest days are seldom uncomfortable because the humidity is low. Winters can be severe. Winds that sweep across the plains make the cold bitter.

July temperatures average 67 °F (19 °C) in northern North Dakota and 73 °F (23 °C) in the south. The state's

Average monthly weather

	Williston					Fargo			
	Temperatures				Days of rain or snow		**Temperatures**				Days of rain or snow
	°F High	°F Low	°C High	°C Low			°F High	°F Low	°C High	°C Low	
Jan.	19	–3	–7	–19	8	Jan.	16	–2	–9	–19	9
Feb.	28	6	–2	–14	6	Feb.	23	5	–5	–15	7
Mar.	40	17	4	–8	8	Mar.	35	19	2	–7	8
Apr.	56	29	13	–2	8	Apr.	55	32	13	0	8
May	68	41	20	5	10	May	70	45	23	7	10
June	77	50	25	10	11	June	77	55	25	13	11
July	83	55	28	13	9	July	82	59	28	15	10
Aug.	83	54	28	12	7	Aug.	81	57	27	14	9
Sept.	70	42	21	6	7	Sept.	70	46	21	8	8
Oct.	57	30	14	–1	6	Oct.	56	34	13	1	7
Nov.	36	15	2	–9	6	Nov.	35	18	2	–8	6
Dec.	24	2	–4	–17	8	Dec.	21	4	–6	–16	8

record high temperature was 121 °F (49 °C), at Steele on July 6, 1936. January temperatures average 3 °F (–16 °C) in the northeast part of the state and 14 °F (–10 °C) in the extreme southwest. The state's lowest temperature, –60 °F (–51 °C), was recorded at Parshall on Feb. 15, 1936.

The southeast has the most precipitation—about 20 inches (51 centimeters) a year. Some western areas of the state receive only about 13 inches (33 centimeters). Most of the rain in North Dakota falls between April and September. Snowfall averages about 32 inches (81 centimeters) yearly.

Economy

The large output of such commodities as grain, beef cattle, and petroleum help make agriculture and mining more important in North Dakota than they are in most other states. However, services and manufacturing continue to grow in economic importance in the state.

Service industries account for the majority of North Dakota's *gross domestic product*—the total value of

goods and services produced annually. The strong agricultural base greatly benefits the service industries. For example, trains carry wheat to wholesale distributors in the state's large cities. Trains are part of the transportation and communication industry; and wholesale distributors are part of the trade industry. Agriculture also benefits North Dakota's manufacturing industry. The state's

North Dakota economy

General economy

Gross domestic product (GDP)* (2008)	$31,246,000,000
Rank among U.S. states	49th
Unemployment rate (2010)	3.8% (U.S. avg: 9.6%)

*Gross domestic product is the total value of goods and services produced in a year.
Sources: U.S. Bureau of Economic Analysis and U.S. Bureau of Labor Statistics.

Agriculture

Cash receipts	$6,351,969,000
Rank among U.S. states	18th
Distribution	88% crops, 12% livestock
Farms	32,000
Farm acres (hectares)	39,600,000 (16,030,000)
Rank among U.S. states	7th
Farmland	88% of North Dakota

Leading products

1. Wheat   (ranks 1st in U.S.)
2. Soybeans
3. Corn
4. Cattle and calves
5. Barley   (ranks 1st in U.S.)
6. Sunflowers   (ranks 1st in U.S.)
7. Dry beans
8. Sugar beets   (ranks 2nd in U.S.)
Other products: canola, dairy products, flaxseed, hay,
   hogs, honey, lentils, peas, potatoes.

Manufacturing

Value added by manufacture*	$4,731,266,000
Rank among U.S. states	46th

Leading products

1. Machinery
2. Food products
Other products: computer and electronic products, fabricated metal products, transportation equipment, wood
products.

*Value added by manufacture is the increase in value of raw materials after they
become finished products.

Electric power

Coal	90.6%
Wind	5.2%
Other	4.2%

Production and workers by economic activities

Economic activities	Percent of GDP produced	Employed workers Number of people	Percent of total
Finance, insurance, & real estate	18	44,600	9
Community, business, & personal services	16	134,100	27
Trade, restaurants, & hotels	16	108,300	22
Government	13	81,400	16
Agriculture	10	36,000	7
Manufacturing	9	27,900	6
Transportation & communication	7	24,400	5
Construction	4	29,900	6
Mining	4	8,400	2
Utilities	3	3,500	1
Total*	100	498,500	100

*Figures may not add up to 100 percent due to rounding.
Figures are for 2008; employment figures include full- and part-time workers.
Source: *World Book* estimates based on data from U.S. Bureau of Economic Analysis.

Mining

Nonfuel mineral production*	$38,700,000
Rank among U.S. states	49th
Coal (tons†)	29,627,000
Rank among U.S. states	10th
Crude oil (barrels‡)	62,776,000
Rank among U.S. states	6th
Natural gas (cubic feet§)	61,437,000,000
Rank among U.S. states	21st

*Partial total, excludes values that must be concealed to not disclose company data.
†One ton equals 0.9072 metric ton.
‡One barrel equals 42 gallons (159 liters).
§One cubic foot equals 0.0283 cubic meter.

Leading products

1. Petroleum
2. Natural gas
3. Coal
4. Sand and gravel
Other products: clay, crushed stone, lime.

Figures are for 2008, except for the agricultural figures, which are for 2009.
Sources: U.S. Census Bureau, U.S. Department of Agriculture, U.S. Energy Information
   Administration, U.S. Geological Survey.

Economy of North Dakota

This map shows the economic uses of land in North Dakota and where the leading farm
and mineral products are produced. The state's major urban areas are shown in red.

☐	Mostly cropland
☐	Grazing land mixed with cropland
☐	Shrubland mixed with grassland
☐	Woodland
●	Manufacturing center
●	Mineral deposit

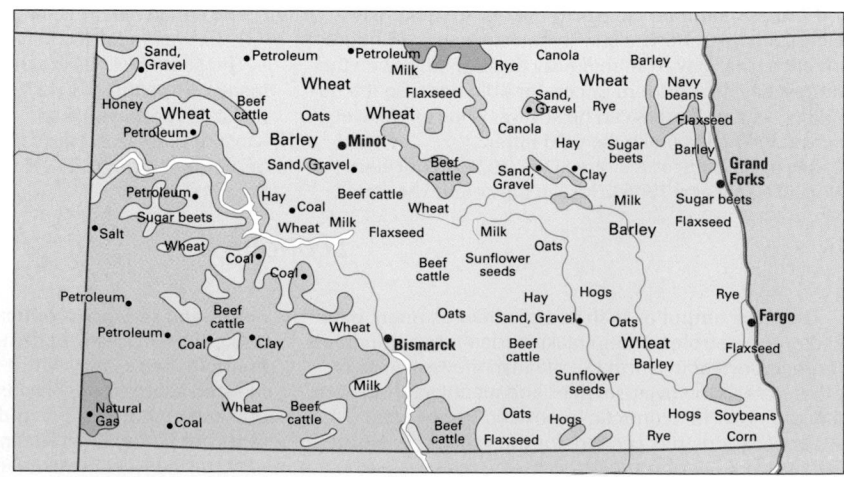

WORLD BOOK map

A combine harvests wheat on a North Dakota farm. Wheat is the state's leading farm product. North Dakota ranks among the leading states in wheat production.

Clayton Wolt, C. J. Photos

leading manufactured products include farm machinery and processed foods.

Natural resources. North Dakota's greatest natural resources are its outstandingly fertile soil and its enormous mineral deposits.

Soil is North Dakota's most valuable resource. It is the basis of one of the state's major industries—agriculture. North Dakota's richest soil lies in the Red River Valley. This fertile black soil is free of stones and contains much *organic matter* (decayed plant and animal remains). Loamy and sandy soils lie on the Drift Prairie west of the Red River Valley. Shale and limestone make up most of the soil of the Great Plains region.

Minerals. North Dakota has large deposits of petroleum in the west. These deposits lie in the Williston Basin, which extends from North Dakota into northern South Dakota, eastern Montana, and southern Canada. Bowman County in the southwest and other oil-producing counties in the west have natural-gas wells.

North Dakota has large deposits of *lignite,* also called *brown coal,* a low-grade coal. These deposits lie in the western North Dakota. Sand and gravel are found throughout the state. The southwest has great amounts of clay, ranging in quality from common brick to the finest pottery clay.

Service industries provide most of North Dakota's employment and its gross domestic product. Service industries are concentrated in the Bismarck and Fargo areas.

Fargo is North Dakota's center of banking and insurance. Bismarck, Fargo, and Grand Forks have large medical centers. Many hotels, restaurants, and retail trade establishments also operate in these areas. Such businesses benefit from the state's tourism industry, which has grown in importance since the late 1900's. The wholesale trade of farm machinery, food products, and mined products is also important in North Dakota.

Bismarck, the state capital, is the center of state government activities. Government services also include the operation of U.S. Air Force bases near Grand Forks and Minot and the operation of four Indian reservations either partially or completely in the state. The U.S. government administers many wildlife refuges in North Dakota.

Transportation and communication are more important in North Dakota than in most other states because North Dakota's small population is widely scattered.

Farm products and mined products often must travel great distances to reach market. Trucks and railroads transport much of the state's farm and coal output. Pipelines transport petroleum and natural gas.

Agriculture accounts for a larger portion of the gross domestic product in North Dakota than in most other states. Cropland and pastures cover nearly 90 percent of North Dakota's total land area.

Wheat brings in more income than any other farm product in North Dakota, and the state is a leading producer of this crop. Wheat is grown throughout the state. Much of the wheat grown in northwestern North Dakota is *durum* wheat—a hard form of wheat used to make spaghetti and other kinds of pasta. North Dakota farmers grow over half of the nation's durum wheat.

North Dakota is the leading producer of barley and sunflower seeds. Barley is grown throughout the state. Many sunflowers grow in the northern portion of the state. North Dakota farmers produce the majority of the nation's flaxseed. The state also ranks among the leading producers of beans, canola seed, oats, and sugar beets. Corn is primarily grown in the southeastern part of the state. The central and western parts of North Dakota produce the most hay. Soybeans are grown in the east.

Livestock and livestock products account for about a sixth of North Dakota's agricultural income. The raising of beef cattle is the leading type of livestock farming in the state. The central and western plains of North Dakota provide good pastureland and winter feed for beef cattle. Many dairy farms are in the south-central part of the state. North Dakota farmers raise hogs in the eastern part of the state, where corn is plentiful. North Dakota is among the leading states in honey production.

Manufacturing. Food processing and machinery production are North Dakota's leading manufacturing activities. Food processing benefits greatly from the state's strong agricultural base. North Dakota's major food products include bread and pasta, dairy products, meat, oils from oil seeds, and refined sugar. Most food-processing plants are in the eastern part of the state. The Bobcat Company, a leading manufacturer of construction machinery, is headquartered in West Fargo and has plants in Bismarck and Gwinner. Many cities manufacture farm machinery.

Other manufactured products include computer and electronics products, fabricated metal products, transportation equipment, and wood products. Circuit boards are the most important electronic manufacture. Fabricated metal products are primarily made in eastern North Dakota. Airplane parts, motor vehicle parts, and other kinds of transportation equipment are also produced in the eastern part of the state. Factories in southeastern North Dakota manufacture wood products.

Mining. Petroleum is the leading mined product in North Dakota. Oil fields lie in the Williston Basin, which is in the western part of North Dakota. Bowman, McKenzie, Mountrail, and Williams counties are the leading producers in the state.

Coal and natural gas are also important mined products in North Dakota. Beds of lignite coal lie under almost all of the western part of the state. McLean, Mercer, and Oliver counties in west-central North Dakota provide most of the coal. The only major natural gas field lies in the southwest corner of the state. Natural gas is obtained as a by-product of oil and coal processing.

Among North Dakota's other mined products, sand and gravel provide the most income. Several areas of the state produce sand and gravel. North Dakota's other mined products include clays, crushed stone, and lime.

Electric power and utilities. Steam plants that burn lignite coal generate about 90 percent of North Dakota's electric power. Major coal-burning plants are at Beulah, Center, Stanton, and Underwood. Wind and water power are also important. Wind turbines generate electric power in many parts of the state. A hydroelectric project is at Garrison Dam in Mercer County.

Transportation. North Dakota is a large state with a relatively small population. In addition, it is far from the nation's large population centers. Thus, the state's transportation system is extremely important. The first railroad in North Dakota, the Northern Pacific, reached Fargo in 1872 and Bismarck in 1873. By 1881, the railroad line ran to the Montana border.

Also by 1881, the Great Northern Railway had established a route between Fargo and Grand Forks. The railway built a line westward through Minot and Williston to the Montana border by 1887. Today, rail lines provide freight service for North Dakota. In addition, passenger trains serve several North Dakota cities.

North Dakota has an extensive system of roads and highways. Interstate highways 94 and 29 are the state's main trucking routes. Fargo is home to the state's busiest airport.

Communication. North Dakota's first newspaper, the *Frontier Scout,* was published in Fort Union in 1864. In 1873, Colonel Clement A. Lounsberry founded the *Bismarck Tribune,* the oldest newspaper still published in the state. In 1876, Lounsberry wrote the first story of the Battle of the Little Bighorn. In this battle, Indians killed Lieutenant Colonel George A. Custer and all the troops under his immediate command. To write the story, Lounsberry used notes found in the buckskin pouch of Mark Kellogg, a reporter who was killed in the battle. The largest daily newspapers in North Dakota include the *Bismarck Tribune, The Fargo Forum,* the *Grand Forks Herald,* and the *Minot Daily News.*

Government

Constitution. North Dakota is governed under its original constitution, adopted in 1889. An *amendment* (change) to the Constitution may be proposed in the state legislature. The proposed amendment must be approved by a majority of each house of the legislature. Then a majority of citizens voting on the proposal must approve it. The people may also sign a *petition* (formal request) proposing an amendment. After 4 percent of the people have signed the petition, the proposal is put on a statewide ballot. The proposal becomes law if a majority of voters approve it.

Executive. The governor of North Dakota is elected to a four-year term. The governor may serve an unlimited number of terms.

The lieutenant governor, attorney general, secretary of state, treasurer, auditor, and superintendent of public instruction are also elected to four-year terms. All of these state officials may serve an unlimited number of terms. The people of North Dakota also elect three public-service commissioners and one commissioner each of agriculture, of insurance, and of taxation.

The governor, attorney general, and commissioner of agriculture make up the state Industrial Commission. This commission regulates the state's oil industry. In addition, it oversees the operation of such state-owned enterprises as the Bank of North Dakota in Bismarck and the North Dakota Mill and Elevator in Grand Forks.

Legislature. The state's legislature, called the Legislative Assembly, has a 47-member Senate and a 94-member House of Representatives. Voters in each of the state's 47 legislative districts elect one senator and two representatives. Both senators and representatives serve four-year terms.

The state Assembly holds its regular session in odd-numbered years, beginning usually on the first Tuesday after the first Monday in January. Regular sessions of the Assembly are limited to 80 legislative, or working, days. The governor may also call special sessions.

Courts of North Dakota are headed by the state Supreme Court. The Supreme Court has five justices, all elected to 10-year terms. The people of North Dakota's seven judicial districts elect a total of 42 district court judges to six-year terms. The Supreme Court and district court judges elect a chief justice of the Supreme Court to a five-year term.

The state's municipal courts handle violations of local ordinances. Places of at least 5,000 people have municipal courts, and places of less than 5,000 people may decide whether to do so. Municipal court judges serve four-year terms. All judges in the state are elected on a "no party" ballot—the ballot has no political party labels.

Local government. North Dakota has 53 counties. Each county is governed by a board of commissioners of three to five members elected to four-year terms. North Dakota has about 360 incorporated cities. The 1967 legislature classed all cities and towns in North Dakota as cities. The cities are organized under mayor-council, city-manager, or commission government.

Revenue. Taxes bring in about 45 percent of the state government's *general revenue* (income). Most of the re-

Sheldon Green

The North Dakota House of Representatives meets in the house chambers in the State Capitol, in Bismarck. Each of the House's members is elected to serve a four-year term.

The governors of North Dakota

	Party	Term
John Miller	Republican	1889-1891
Andrew H. Burke	Republican	1891-1893
Eli C. D. Shortridge	Independent	1893-1895
Roger Allin	Republican	1895-1897
Frank A. Briggs	Republican	1897-1898
Joseph M. Devine	Republican	1898-1899
Frederick B. Fancher	Republican	1899-1901
Frank White	Republican	1901-1905
E. Y. Sarles	Republican	1905-1907
John Burke	Democratic	1907-1913
L. B. Hanna	Republican	1913-1917
Lynn J. Frazier	Republican	1917-1921
R. A. Nestos	Republican	1921-1925
A. G. Sorlie	Republican	1925-1928
Walter Maddock	Republican	1928-1929
George F. Shafer	Republican	1929-1933
William Langer	Republican	1933-1934
Ole H. Olson	Republican	1934-1935
Thomas H. Moodie	Democratic	1935
Walter Welford	Republican	1935-1937
William Langer	Republican	1937-1939
John Moses	Democratic	1939-1945
Fred G. Aandahl	Republican	1945-1951
C. Norman Brunsdale	Republican	1951-1957
John E. Davis	Republican	1957-1961
William L. Guy	Democratic	1961-1973
Arthur A. Link	Democratic	1973-1981
Allen I. Olson	Republican	1981-1984
George A. Sinner	Democratic	1985-1992
Edward T. Schafer	Republican	1992-2000
John Hoeven	Republican	2000-2010
Jack Dalrymple	Republican	2010-

maining revenue comes from federal grants and charges for government services. The largest sources of North Dakota's tax revenue are a general sales tax and a personal income tax. Other important tax revenue sources in the state include taxes on corporate profits, motor fuels, motor vehicle licenses, and oil and coal production.

Politics. Throughout most of its history, North Dakota has strongly favored the Republican Party. The Nonparti-san League, a political organization of farmers, was founded in North Dakota in 1915. During its early years, the league often controlled the Republican Party. In 1956, however, the league joined with the state Democratic Party and helped elect Democrats.

In 1889, the people elected a Republican as their first governor. Since then, most of North Dakota's governors have been Republicans. North Dakotans have voted for Republican candidates in most presidential elections.

History

Indian days. Seven groups of Indians lived in North Dakota when white explorers and fur traders first arrived there. The Mandan, Hidatsa, and Arikara Indians lived in permanent earthen lodges along the Missouri River. They were farmers but also hunted. The Chippewa resided and hunted in the northeast. Nomadic groups of Assiniboine lived along what would become the United States-Canada border. The Yankton Sioux lived in the James and Sheyenne river valleys, where they hunted. The largest and most powerful tribe, the Lakota or Teton Sioux, lived in the southwest and were hunters. Led by the great chiefs Sitting Bull and Gall, the Lakota Sioux fiercely resisted the United States Army.

Exploration and early settlement. In 1682, René-Robert Cavelier, Sieur de La Salle, claimed for France all the land drained by the Mississippi River system. The territory La Salle claimed included the southwestern half of North Dakota, because the Missouri River flows into the Mississippi. France also claimed the vast region south of Hudson Bay, which included the northeastern half of North Dakota. In 1713, France gave all of this territory to Britain (now also called the United Kingdom).

North Dakota was first explored by a French Canadian, Pierre Gaultier de Varennes, Sieur de La Vérendrye. He set out from Canada in 1738 and reached the Mandan Indian villages near present-day Bismarck.

In 1762, France gave its land west of the Mississippi to Spain. Spain returned it to France in 1800. In 1803, the United States bought this region, then called Louisiana, from France (see **Louisiana Purchase**).

In 1804, President Thomas Jefferson sent Meriwether Lewis and William Clark to explore the Louisiana Territory and to blaze a trail to the Pacific Ocean. They reached central North Dakota in October 1804 and built Fort Mandan on the east bank of the Missouri River, across from present-day Stanton. The explorers stayed at Fort

The Mandan Indians performed a buffalo dance to ensure success in hunting buffalo. Several Indian tribes lived in the North Dakota region before European explorers arrived there.

Water color (1832-1834) by Karl Bodmer; Joslyn Art Museum, Omaha, Nebraska

Mandan until April 1805. They passed through North Dakota again in 1806 on their return from the Pacific.

In 1812, Scottish and Irish families from Canada made a permanent settlement in North Dakota, in Pembina. In 1818, the United States obtained northeastern North Dakota by a treaty with the United Kingdom. All of present-day North Dakota then became U.S. territory. The 1818 treaty also set the United States-Canadian border at the 49th parallel. Some of the Pembina settlers moved north to be sure they were on British territory. The rest left in 1823, when a survey confirmed that Pembina was actually in the United States. A number of Métis (people of mixed white and Indian descent) remained in the region after the settlers left.

Territorial days. Congress created the Dakota Territory in 1861. President Abraham Lincoln appointed William Jayne as governor. The territory included the present states of North and South Dakota and much of Montana and Wyoming. The first legislature met in Yankton (now in South Dakota) in 1862.

In 1863, the territory opened for homesteading. Settlers were given free land if they lived on it and improved it. But the territory developed slowly. Transportation was poor, and the settlers feared the Indians. In 1862, Sioux Indians killed hundreds of settlers in an uprising in Minnesota. Some of the Indians then fled to the Dakota Territory. The United States government sent troops into the territory to punish the Indians who had taken part in the Minnesota uprising. Several battles were fought as the soldiers pursued the Indians across the territory.

The federal government signed several treaties with the Indians in the Dakota Territory, giving them land on reservations. But the whites often broke the treaties, causing more Indian uprisings. Peace came in 1881, when the great Sioux leader Sitting Bull voluntarily surrendered to U.S. troops. See **Sitting Bull.**

Large-scale farming began about 1875, when eastern corporations and some families established huge wheat farms. Most of the farms were in the Red River Valley and ranged from 3,000 to 65,000 acres (1,200 to 26,300 hectares). The farms earned such tremendous profits

that they became known as *bonanza* farms. The farmers used machinery and orderly methods of planting, harvesting, and marketing. This type of farming was possible because only one crop—wheat—was raised. In time, other crops were introduced on the bonanza farms. As the bonanza farms developed, cattle companies from the southern plains moved into the Badlands. The future President Theodore Roosevelt was among those who helped open up the land along the Little Missouri River. Most of the bonanza farms were divided into smaller lots and sold to newcomers because low wheat prices in the 1890's made them unprofitable.

Statehood. During the 1870's, the people began to ask Congress to divide the Dakota Territory into two parts. The population centers had developed in far corners of the territory—in the northeast and the southeast. North-south travel between these two centers was difficult because the railroads had laid their tracks in an east-west direction. The two groups of settlers had little in common and wanted their own governments.

In February 1889, Congress established the present boundary between North Dakota and South Dakota. It also passed an enabling act, allowing the two regions to set up the machinery to become states. On Nov. 2, 1889, North Dakota became the 39th state and South Dakota the 40th state. John Miller, a Republican, became North Dakota's first governor.

The early 1900's. North Dakota's population increased rapidly following statehood. The state had 190,983 people in 1890. In 1910, it had 577,056 people. Farming also grew rapidly. However, the farmers disliked having to deal with banks, grain companies, and railroad interests in Minnesota. In addition, they disliked the power that these out-of-state businesses held in North Dakota politics.

In 1915, the Nonpartisan League was founded in North Dakota. This organization supported the farmers and called for a state-owned grain elevator, flour mill, packing house, and cold-storage plant. It also wanted banks in farming areas that would grant loans at cost. Thousands of farmers joined the league.

In 1916, a league-supported candidate, Republican

Historic North Dakota

Pierre Gaultier de Varennes, Sieur de La Vérendrye, was the first European to explore the North Dakota region. In 1738, he reached the Mandan Indian villages near present-day Bismarck while searching for a route to the Pacific Ocean.

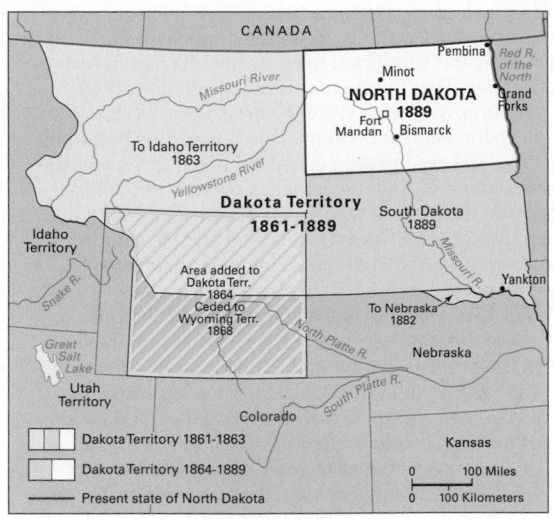

WORLD BOOK map

North Dakota was formed from the vast Dakota Territory, created by Congress in 1861. The border between North Dakota and South Dakota was set in 1889, the year both areas became states.

The Northern Pacific Railroad built a line to Fargo by 1872 and reached westward as far as Bismarck by 1873. Railroad building brought a rush of settlers to the region, and farming prospered in eastern North Dakota. By 1881, the railroad line ran to the Montana border.

Important dates in North Dakota

WORLD BOOK illustrations by Richard Bonson, The Art Agency

1682 René-Robert Cavelier, Sieur de La Salle, claimed for France all the land drained by the Mississippi River. This land included southwestern North Dakota.

1738 Pierre Gaultier de Varennes, Sieur de La Vérendrye, made the first European explorations in North Dakota.

1803 The United States acquired southwestern North Dakota through the Louisiana Purchase.

1804-1806 Meriwether Lewis and William Clark passed through North Dakota on their expedition to and from the Pacific Ocean.

1812 Scottish and Irish settlers made the first attempt at permanent European settlement in North Dakota, at Pembina.

1818 The United States acquired northeastern North Dakota by a treaty with the United Kingdom.

1861 Congress created the Dakota Territory.

1863 The Dakota Territory was opened to settlers for homesteading.

c. 1875 The era of bonanza farming began.

1889 North Dakota became the 39th state on November 2.

1915 The Nonpartisan League was founded.

1951 Oil was discovered near Tioga.

1956 The first generator at Garrison Dam began to produce electric power. The dam was completed in 1960.

1968 Construction began on the Garrison Diversion Project to increase the state's water supply.

1986 Congress approved a modified version of the Garrison Diversion Project.

1989 North Dakota celebrated its statehood centennial.

1997 Spring flooding produced enormous damage in the Red River Valley, especially in the city of Grand Forks.

Lynn J. Frazier, was elected governor of North Dakota. He was reelected in 1918 and 1920. During Frazier's first two terms, the Nonpartisan League dominated the state legislature and supported the passage of a number of progressive laws. Rural schools got more funds. Taxes on farm improvements were lowered. An Industrial Commission was set up to manage businesses begun by the state. The commission consisted of the governor, the attorney general, and the commissioner of agriculture.

In 1919, the Bank of North Dakota was founded in Bismarck. In 1922, the North Dakota Mill and Elevator in Grand Forks began operating. The Industrial Commission still oversees these state-owned businesses.

In the 1920 election, anti-league Republicans won control of the state's House of Representatives. They called for an investigation of the Industrial Commission, and the investigation provided evidence of mismanagement. Also, an economic downturn that included falling prices for farm products, decreasing land values, and bank failures contributed to voter dissatisfaction with Frazier's administration. In 1921, the state held a recall election. Frazier and the other two members of the Industrial Commission were removed from office. Frazier became the first governor of a U.S. state to be recalled. But he was elected to the U.S. Senate the following year and served as a senator from 1923 to 1940.

The Great Depression struck the entire nation during the 1930's. In addition, North Dakota suffered a severe drought. The state's farm production plunged sharply, and its population also began to decline. The state and federal governments took many steps to help North Dakota farmers. In 1937, the State Water Conservation Commission was created. Since then, state, federal, and private agencies have set up projects to provide irrigation and stop soil erosion.

The mid-1900's. North Dakota's economy recovered during World War II (1939-1945). Farmers broke all their production records in supplying food for the armed forces. But in the late 1940's, farm prices sagged as a result of farm surpluses throughout the country. The increased use of machines on farms left large numbers of farmworkers unemployed. Many found jobs in towns and cities, and North Dakota's urban population increased. But thousands could not find jobs in the state and left in search of opportunities elsewhere.

The great Garrison Dam near Riverdale was constructed between 1947 and 1960. This dam provides flood control, hydroelectric power, and water for irrigation.

Oil was discovered near Tioga in 1951. By 1970, oil wells were operating throughout western North Dakota.

In 1957, North Dakota established an Economic Development Commission to attract industry to the state. Dozens of North Dakota communities also had their own development commissions. Largely as a result of these commissions, the state's rate of industrial growth ranked among the highest in the country from 1958 to 1969. The U.S. Air Force helped the state's economy during the 1960's. It built bases near Grand Forks and Minot.

The Garrison Diversion Project was started in 1968. It included the construction of a canal system to bring water for irrigation from the Missouri River to large sections of North Dakota farmland. It also included plans to supply water to a number of cities and towns.

Late 1900's. During the early 1970's, growing concerns about the environmental effects of the Garrison Diversion Project slowed construction. For example, the Canadian government protested because the project, which called for the transfer of U.S. water into Canada, could have introduced pollutants into Canadian waters. In 1986, the U.S. Congress modified the project in response to some of these environmental concerns.

During the 1970's, North Dakota increased coal, oil, and natural gas production as a step toward broadening its economy. Farm production remained high in the 1980's and 1990's, but state leaders continued to seek new industry for North Dakota. The number of nonagricultural jobs increased, but not enough to keep up with the decline in farm jobs.

Recent developments. In 1993, after a prolonged wet period, Devils Lake in northeast North Dakota began to rise. The lake, which had no natural outlet, flooded large areas of farmland and hundreds of homes. The state developed a plan to construct an overflow outlet from the lake to the Sheyenne River. The Sheyenne empties into the Red River, which flows north into the Canadian province of Manitoba. Manitoba objected to the plan, however, in part because of the lake's poor water quality. North Dakota began building the outlet in 2002. It opened in 2005, after North Dakota, Minnesota, and Manitoba reached an agreement providing for improved filtration for water flowing through the outlet.

In 1997, heavy snowfalls produced damaging spring floods. Flooding of the Red River of the North forced almost 90 percent of the people of Grand Forks to evacuate. Over 70 percent of the buildings in Grand Forks experienced water damage. High river levels tested Fargo's flood defenses in 1997 and again in 2009.

In 2000, Congress replaced the Garrison Diversion Project with a new act called the Dakota Water Resources Act. The new law authorized over $600 million for water supply and recreation projects in the state.

Due in part to an oil boom in the Williston area, North Dakota's economy grew rapidly during the early 2000's. Features of the strong economy included low unemployment and state budget surpluses. Rural areas of North Dakota continued to deal with an exodus of residents, especially young adults, to the state's larger cities.

In 2010, John Hoeven was elected to the U.S. Senate and became the state's first governor to voluntarily resign. Lieutenant Governor Jack Dalrymple took Hoeven's place as governor.   Douglas C. Munski and Kimberly Porter

Study aids

Related articles in *World Book* include:

Biographies

Burke, John	L'Amour, Louis	Sitting Bull
Eielson, Carl Ben	Sacagawea	

Cities

Bismarck	Fargo

History

Lake Agassiz	Western frontier life
Lewis and Clark expedition	in America
Louisiana Purchase	

Physical features

Badlands	Missouri River
Great Plains	Red River of the North

Other related articles

Dryland farming
Garrison Dam
Geographic center of North America
Theodore Roosevelt National Park

Outline

I. **People**
 A. Population
 B. Schools
 C. Libraries and museums
II. **Visitor's guide**
III. **Land and climate**
 A. Land regions   C. Plant and animal life
 B. Rivers and lakes   D. Climate
IV. **Economy**
 A. Natural resources   E. Mining
 B. Service industries   F. Electric power and utilities
 C. Agriculture   G. Transportation
 D. Manufacturing   H. Communication
V. **Government**
 A. Constitution   E. Local government
 B. Executive   F. Revenue
 C. Legislature   G. Politics
 D. Courts
VI. **History**

Additional resources

Level I

McDaniel, Melissa, and Kras, S. L. *North Dakota.* 2nd ed. Marshall Cavendish Benchmark, 2010.
Sanders, Doug. *North Dakota.* Benchmark Bks., 2004.
Silverman, Robin L. *North Dakota.* Children's Pr., 2009.
Stille, Darlene R. *North Dakota.* Children's Pr., 2010.

Level II

Handy-Marchello, Barbara. *Women of the Northern Plains: Gender and Settlement on the Homestead Frontier, 1870-1930.* Minn. Hist. Soc., 2005.
Leahy, James E. *The North Dakota State Constitution: A Reference Guide.* Praeger, 2003.
Lysengen, Janet D., and Rathke, A. M., eds. *The Centennial Anthology of North Dakota History.* State Hist. Soc. of N. Dak., 1996.

North Dakota, University of, is a state-supported liberal arts institution in Grand Forks, North Dakota. It was founded in 1883. The university's athletic teams are called the Fighting Sioux. The university's website at http://www.und.nodak.edu offers additional information.
Critically reviewed by the University of North Dakota

North Dakota State University is a public school at Fargo, North Dakota. The university includes extension service and research experiment stations across North Dakota. North Dakota State University awards bachelor's, master's, and doctor's degrees. The school was founded in 1890 as the North Dakota Agricultural College. It took its present name in 1960. The university's athletic teams are called the Bison. The university's website at http://www.ndsu.edu offers additional information.
Critically reviewed by North Dakota State University

North Korea. See Korea, North.

North Platte (pop. 24,733) is the center of a farming and cattle-raising region in western Nebraska. For location, see **Nebraska** (political map). North Platte plays an important role in the United States rail network. Most transcontinental traffic on the Union Pacific Railroad passes through the city's Bailey Yard, a facility for sorting freight cars into trains. Besides railroading, major economic activities in the city include retail trade, tourism, and processing agricultural products.

The famous frontiersman Buffalo Bill built a home near North Platte in 1886. The home is now the site of the Buffalo Bill Ranch State Historical Park. The city also hosts a statewide celebration, Nebraskaland Days, in June each year. The celebration includes a rodeo.

The city was first settled in 1866. It began as a construction camp for workers who were building the Union Pacific Railroad.

North Platte is the seat of Lincoln County. The city has a mayor-council form of government.   Laura Johnston

North Pole is a term used for several invisible surface points in the Arctic region. The best known is the north geographic pole. But other important north poles include the instantaneous north pole, the north pole of balance, the north magnetic pole, and the geomagnetic north pole.

The north geographic pole lies near the center of the Arctic Ocean where all Earth's lines of longitude meet. The American explorer Robert E. Peary led the first expedition usually credited with reaching this pole. The expedition included Matthew Henson, who was Peary's assistant, and four Inuit (formerly called Eskimos). They made the trip by dog team in 1909. The American explorers Richard E. Byrd and Floyd Bennett are credited with reaching the pole by airplane in 1926, though evidence indicates they might not have succeeded. In 1958, the USS *Nautilus* became the first submarine to pass under the Arctic ice to the pole. In 1978, Naomi Uemura of Japan became the first person to reach the pole alone. He traveled by dog sled.

The instantaneous north pole lies at the point where Earth's *axis* (an imaginary line through Earth) meets the surface. Earth wobbles slowly as it turns around its axis, causing the instantaneous north pole to move. This pole takes about 14 months to move clockwise around an irregular path that is called the Chandler Circle. The diameter of this path varies from less than 1 foot (30 centimeters) to about 70 feet (21 meters).

The north pole of balance lies at the center of the Chandler Circle. Its position locates the north geographic pole. Each year since 1900, the north pole of balance has moved about 6 inches (15 centimeters) toward North America. This motion has caused tiny changes in the latitude and longitude of points around Earth.

The north magnetic pole is the farthest point on Earth in the direction of magnetic north. This pole can move many miles or kilometers in a few years. Today, the north magnetic pole is in the Arctic Ocean off northern Canada.

The geomagnetic north pole lies near Etah, Greenland, north of the town of Thule. In the upper atmosphere, Earth's magnetic field points down toward this point.   William C. Mahaney

Related articles in *World Book* include:

Arctic (Arctic exploration)   Exploration (Arctic exploration)
Arctic Ocean (maps)
Byrd, Richard E.   Henson, Matthew A.
Cook, Frederick A.   Peary, Robert E.
Earth (How Earth moves)   Submarine (Nuclear submarines)

North Sea is a wide arm of the Atlantic Ocean that lies between the island of Great Britain and the mainland of Europe. Seven nations—the United Kingdom, Norway, Denmark, Germany, the Netherlands, Belgium, and France—border the sea. The North Sea is a major trade and transportation route. It is also an important source of petroleum, natural gas, and fish.

The North Sea covers 218,178 square miles (565,078 square kilometers). It extends almost 600 miles (960 kilometers) from north to south and about 360 miles (580 kilometers) from west to east. It has an average depth of 100 feet (30 meters) in the south and 400 feet (120 meters) in the north. The Strait of Dover and the English Channel connect the North Sea with the Atlantic Ocean. Skagerrak, an arm of the sea, links it with the Strait of Kattegat and the Baltic Sea. The Kiel Canal also connects the North and the Baltic seas.

Weather conditions in the North Sea are unpredictable, especially in winter. Winds of up to 100 miles (160 kilometers) an hour and severe storms sometimes occur, making navigation extremely dangerous.

In the 1960's, vast amounts of petroleum and natural gas were found under the North Sea. Today, the United Kingdom and Norway get large quantities of petroleum from the area. Natural gas is piped ashore to the United Kingdom and Germany.

The North Sea's fishing grounds rank among the richest in the world. Fish caught in the area include cod, haddock, herring, mackerel, pilchard, plaice, sole, and whiting. The sea also provides many kinds of shellfish. But overfishing has depleted the stocks of many fish.

The North Sea is one of the world's most important waterways for commercial activity. Its many major ports include London, England; Hamburg, Germany; Amsterdam and Rotterdam, the Netherlands; Antwerp, Belgium; and Dunkerque, France. But increased air travel has dramatically reduced ferry travel across the sea.

The North Sea has been used for trade and transportation since ancient times. Its position made it important during World War I (1914-1918) and World War II (1939-1945). During World War I, the United Kingdom controlled the North Sea and largely prevented the German Navy from using it as a route to the Atlantic Ocean. During World War II, Germany controlled the part of the sea between Norway and France. But the United Kingdom controlled the English Channel and the northern

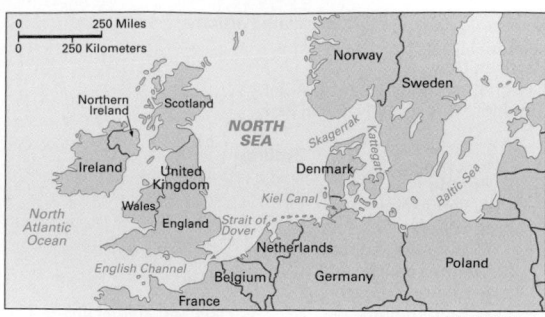
WORLD BOOK map
Location of the North Sea

approaches to the sea, allowing Allied ships to use the waterway.   Neil Kent

North-South Ministerial Council is a political body that addresses matters of concern to the entire island of Ireland. It brings together government representatives from the independent Republic of Ireland in the south and from Northern Ireland, which is part of the United Kingdom. The council deals with issues in such areas as agriculture, education, the environment, and health. Its decisions are subject to the approval of the Irish Parliament and the Northern Ireland Assembly, an elected body that has jurisdiction over most local affairs.

The North-South Ministerial Council was established by the 1998 Northern Ireland political settlement. This agreement aimed at ending the violence between Irish nationalists and unionists over control of Northern Ireland. Through the years, the nationalists have wanted Northern Ireland to become part of the Republic of Ireland, but the unionists have favored keeping Northern Ireland part of the United Kingdom. The council meets some goals of both groups. For example, it gives the nationalists an all-island institution. But it also provides the unionists with a way to cooperate with the Republic of Ireland without unification.   Brendan O'Leary

See also **Northern Ireland** (History).

North Star is a readily visible star that appears to be almost directly above the North Pole. The term *polestar* is sometimes used for North Star. The North Star is presently Polaris, the brightest star in the constellation Ursa Minor. Polaris is within one degree of the place where the northern extension of the earth's axis pierces the sky. Because of its position, Polaris appears stationary, while other stars seem to revolve around the earth's axis as the earth rotates. As a result, Polaris has served as a guide for navigators through the centuries. Polaris is a star of the second *magnitude*. The brighter a star is, the lower is its magnitude (see **Star** [Brightness of stars]).

Polaris will not always be the North Star because the earth's axis will not always point toward Polaris. The earth's rotational axis changes direction in a circular motion called *precession*. Each end of the axis traces out a fictitious circle in the sky. One complete trip around the circle takes about 26,000 years. Thus, the brighter stars on or near the precessional circle above the earth's North Pole each become the North Star for a certain period. For example, in about 12,000 years, the earth's axis will point north to a spot near Vega in the constellation Lyra. In about 22,000 years, Thuban in the constellation Draco will become the North Star. About 26,000 years

© Ed Pritchard, Getty Images
Tugboats on a frozen North Sea wait to bring cargo ships into the port of Bremerhaven, Germany. The North Sea's shipping lanes are among the busiest in the world.

from now, Polaris will return to its present location relative to Earth's axis and will be the North Star.

Sumner Starrfield

See also **Astronomy** (map: The stars and constellations of the Northern Hemisphere).

North Vietnam. See Vietnam.

North Warning System is a long-range radar network built to provide the United States and Canada with warning of an air attack from the north. It was completed in 1994. The system extends from northwest Alaska across northern Canada and down the coast of Labrador. It consists of 54 radar stations. NORAD, a U.S.-Canadian military alliance, controls the North Warning System (see **NORAD**).

In 1985, the United States and Canada agreed to improve surveillance by replacing the DEW (*D*istant *E*arly *Wa*rning) line's aging radars and building additional radars. The improved system was renamed the North Warning System. The North Warning System replaced the DEW line after that system was deactivated in 1993.

Critically reviewed by NORAD

North West Company was a Canadian fur-trading company based in Montreal in the late 1700's and early 1800's. It became the main competition of the powerful Hudson's Bay Company (see **Hudson's Bay Company**). North West Company traders explored and mapped little-known regions of northern and western Canada.

Britain took control of French Canada in 1763, and the organization of the fur trade in Montreal changed. During the 1770's, various groups of Montreal fur merchants began to combine their operations to compete more effectively with the Hudson's Bay Company. In 1784, following a period of joint ventures, these groups collectively adopted the name North West Company.

The North West Company also competed with other Montreal fur-trading companies, such as the XY Company and John Jacob Astor's Pacific Fur Company. It united with the XY Company in 1804 and bought Fort Astoria (now Astoria, Oregon) from Astor in 1813. Competition between the North West and Hudson's Bay companies then became especially strong. By 1821, both organizations faced financial difficulties, and the natural resources upon which they depended were diminishing. That year, they merged under the name Hudson's Bay Company.

Ann M. Carlos

See also **Fraser, Simon; Fur trade** (The early fur trade); **Mackenzie, Sir Alexander; McGillivray, William; McTavish, Simon.**

North-West Mounted Police. See Royal Canadian Mounted Police.

North West Rebellion was a conflict that arose in 1885 between the *Métis* (people of mixed white and Indian ancestry) and the Canadian government in what is now Saskatchewan. It came from Métis fears that government plans to encourage new farming settlements in the northwest would threaten their communities.

North Star
(Polaris)

Dubhe

Big Dipper

Merak

The North Star appears at the center of circular tracks made by other stars in a time-exposure photograph. Earth's rotation on its axis makes other stars seem to rotate around the North Star, which lies near the axis. The North Star may be located by using the group of stars called the Big Dipper, also shown here. Two of these stars, Dubhe and Merak, are almost in line with the North Star.

The Métis had opposed the government in the Red River Rebellion in 1869 and 1870, in what is now the Canadian province of Manitoba. That conflict also had involved Métis fears about the effects of white settlement on their lands. The Métis demanded, and obtained, guarantees that the Canadian government would protect their property, cultural, religious, and language rights. The guarantees, however, proved too weak. As a result, the Métis retreated west and established new communities in the valleys of the North and South Saskatchewan rivers. There, the Métis laid out their small farms in the traditional French river lot pattern, in long strips bordering the rivers.

By the early 1880's, the Métis became concerned about the effects of the nearly completed transcontinental railroad and the government's plans for white settlement in Saskatchewan. The government wanted the land divided into square lots, and it refused to approve Métis claims for new lots laid out in riverfront strips.

The Métis again called on Louis Riel, the leader of their earlier protest in Manitoba. In March 1885, Riel established a temporary Métis government to negotiate with the Canadian government. The Canadian government regarded this as an act of treason. All possibility of negotiation ended when the Métis and North-West Mounted Police fought near Duck Lake on March 26, 1885. People on both sides were killed. In addition, scattered fighting broke out between some Cree Indians and settlers.

Canada's government sent a military force to Saskatchewan. These troops, joined by the North-West Mounted Police and local volunteers, moved against the Métis at Batoche. The Métis, seriously outnumbered and poorly equipped, were defeated at Batoche in May 1885. Gabriel Dumont, their military leader, escaped to the United States. Riel was arrested, tried for treason, and hanged in Regina in November 1885.

After the rebellion, people in the northwest gained representation in the Canadian Parliament. Many French-speaking Canadians sympathized with the Métis, and the rebellion led to increased tension between French- and English-speaking Canadians. The rebellion accomplished little for the Métis.   T. D. Regehr

See also **Crowfoot; Dumont, Gabriel; Poundmaker; Riel, Louis.**

North Yemen. See Yemen.

Northcliffe, Viscount (1865-1922), a famous English journalist and publisher, pioneered in the use of comics, special features, religious news, and tabloid newspapers. He also played an important part in the formation in 1916 of the Coalition Cabinet led by David Lloyd George. Northcliffe owned the Amalgamated Press, a large magazine publishing house, and the London *Evening News,* the *Daily Mail,* the *Daily Mirror,* and *The Times.* He was born on July 15, 1865, in County Dublin, Ireland. His given and family name was Alfred Charles William Harmsworth. He died on Aug. 14, 1922.

Joseph P. McKerns

Northeast Passage. See Arctic Ocean.

Norther is a cold winter wind that sweeps over the southern United States, the Gulf of Mexico, and the east coast of Central America, destroying crops and wrecking ships. The northers occur most frequently between October and April. Northers often cause the temperature to rapidly drop as much as 30 to 50 °F (17 to 28 °C).

The wind usually blows over regions that border the western part of the Gulf of Mexico. Sometimes the wind reaches as far south as Panama. Occasionally, a norther starts as far north as Canada and extends over the entire Mississippi Valley. Scientists can predict a norther about 24 hours in advance. In Central America, this wind is called *el norte.*   Richard A. Dirks

Northern harrier, sometimes called *marsh hawk,* is the only *species* (kind) of harrier that lives in North America. It also lives in Europe, where it is called a *hen harrier,* and in northern and central Asia. A *harrier* is a type of hawk.

Northern harriers have long wings, tails, and legs. The birds measure 17 to 24 inches (43 to 61 centimeters) long with a wingspread of 40 to 54 inches (101 to 137 centimeters). The females grow slightly larger than the males. Adult male northern harriers are mostly light gray above and white below. Adult females have brown coloring above with dark streaking below. The young birds resemble the females but have less streaking below.

Like owls, northern harriers have a saucer-shaped ruff of feathers around the eyes. This ruff, called a *facial disk,* reflects sound to the harrier's ear openings. The northern harrier usually hunts small birds and mammals. Its

WORLD BOOK illustration by John Rignall, Linden Artists Ltd.

Northern harriers help farmers by eating harmful pests. The adult female, *left,* is brown. The adult male, *right,* is gray.

facial disk helps it detect prey by sound. The bird then swoops down and kills its victim.

Northern harriers nest on the ground. The males are the only North American birds of prey that typically mate with more than one female during the same period. Females usually lay from four to six eggs.

Richard D. Brown

Scientific classification. The scientific name of the northern harrier is *Circus cyaneus.*

See also **Harrier; Hawk.**

Northern Hemisphere. See Hemisphere.

Belfast is the capital and largest city of Northern Ireland. Donegall Place, in the heart of Belfast, *shown here,* features an outdoor mall lined with shops and offices.

The landscape of Northern Ireland has many fertile, rolling plains inland and low mountains near the coast. Shown here are mountains sloping down to a beach on the northern coast.

Northern Ireland is the smallest of the four political divisions that make up the United Kingdom of Great Britain and Northern Ireland. England, Scotland, and Wales are the other divisions of the United Kingdom, which is often called the U.K. or Britain. Belfast is Northern Ireland's capital and largest city.

Northern Ireland occupies the northeastern corner of the island of Ireland. It takes up about a sixth of the island. The independent Republic of Ireland occupies the rest. Northern Ireland is often called Ulster. Ulster was the name of a large province of Ireland until 1920, when Northern Ireland was separated from the rest of Ireland.

Religion has long divided Northern Ireland. About half of the people are Protestants, who have traditional ties to the rest of the United Kingdom. Nearly all the rest are Roman Catholics, as are most people in the Republic of Ireland. Most Protestants are Unionists, who want Northern Ireland to remain in the United Kingdom. Most Catholics are Nationalists, who want Northern Ireland to become part of the Irish Republic. The dispute sometimes led to riots, bombings, and other outbreaks of violence and terrorism, often called the Troubles. A political settlement in 1998 promised an end to the Troubles. But the agreement proved difficult to implement as the two sides struggled to overcome their mutual mistrust.

This article tells about the people, geography, economy, and history of Northern Ireland. For a discussion of the United Kingdom as a whole, see **United Kingdom.** For information on the Republic of Ireland, see **Ireland.**

Government

The United Kingdom is a constitutional monarchy. The monarch is the head of state, but a cabinet of officials called *ministers* actually governs. The prime minister, who chairs the cabinet, is the head of government.

Parliament. Laws for the United Kingdom are made by the British Parliament, which consists of the House of Commons and the House of Lords. Northern Ireland elects a small number of the 600 members of the House of Commons. The House of Lords consists mainly of honorary appointees. For more information on the British government, see **United Kingdom** (Government).

The Northern Ireland Office handles a variety of matters including human rights and law and order. The British prime minister appoints a secretary of state for Northern Ireland to head the office.

The 1998 political settlement created three new political bodies: the Northern Ireland Assembly, the North-South Ministerial Council, and the British-Irish Council. These groups began meeting in 1999.

The Northern Ireland Assembly assumes many of the responsibilities formerly handled by the Northern Ireland Office. It enacts local laws in such areas as agriculture, finance, and health and social services. Voters in Northern Ireland elect the Assembly's 108 members. Complex rules attempt to create a balance of power between unionists and nationalists.

The North-South Ministerial Council handles affairs of the entire island of Ireland. It includes representatives

Facts in brief

Capital: Belfast.

Official language: English.

Area: 5,242 mi² (13,576 km²). *Greatest distances*—east-west, 111 mi (179 km); north-south, 85 mi (137 km). *Coastline*—330 mi (531 km).

Elevation: *Highest*—Slieve Donard, 2,796 ft (852 m) above sea level. *Lowest*—The Marsh, near Downpatrick, 1.3 ft (0.4 m) below sea level.

Population: *Estimated 2012 population*—1,733,000; density, 331 per mi² (128 per km²); distribution, 70 percent urban, 30 percent rural. *2001 census*—1,685,267.

Chief products: *Agriculture*—cattle, chickens, eggs, hogs, sheep. *Manufacturing*—aircraft, Irish linen and other textiles, machinery, pottery and china, ships.

Northern Ireland's flag and coat of arms have a six-pointed star and the ancient Ulster symbol of a red hand. The star and hand appear over the St. George's cross of the English flag. Northern Ireland's flag and arms ceased to be official symbols after the United Kingdom took direct control of the country's government in 1972. The flag is often flown by private citizens, but the official flag is the British Union flag.

from the governments of both Northern Ireland and the Republic of Ireland. The council's decisions are subject to the approval of the Irish Parliament and the Northern Ireland Assembly.

The British-Irish Council, also called the Council of the Isles, addresses issues concerning all of Ireland and the United Kingdom. The council brings together representatives from the parliaments of Ireland and the United Kingdom; the assemblies of Northern Ireland, Scotland, and Wales; and the governments of the Channel Islands and the Isle of Man, two British dependencies.

Local government. Northern Ireland is divided into 26 districts, each governed by an elected council. Council members serve four-year terms. The councils handle such services as parks and environmental protection.

People

Ancestry. About half of the people are descended from English and Scottish settlers who have arrived in Ireland since the 1600's. Most of the rest trace their ancestry to the earlier Celtic, Viking, and Norman settlers of the island of Ireland.

Language. English is the official language of Northern Ireland, and all the people there speak it. The Irish language, a form of Gaelic once used throughout Ireland, is taught to children in Roman Catholic schools and in some Protestant schools.

Way of life

About two-thirds of the people of Northern Ireland live in urban areas. Many live in or near the cities of Belfast and Londonderry, which is also called Derry. About a third of the people live in rural areas, and most of them earn their living by farming.

Food and drink. The people of Northern Ireland enjoy meals of meat, potatoes, vegetables, and bread. They also eat large amounts of poultry, eggs, dairy products, and fish. Tea is the most popular drink. A favorite alcoholic beverage is beer.

Recreation. Many people in Northern Ireland relax in the evening by watching television. Motion pictures are also popular. As in the rest of the United Kingdom, *pubs* (public houses) are an important part of the social lives of many people in Northern Ireland. People gather in pubs to drink beer and other beverages, eat sandwiches, talk with friends, and listen to music.

The most popular organized sport is football, the game Americans call soccer. Other popular sports include *cricket,* which is played with bats and a ball; *Gaelic football,* which resembles soccer; handball; *hurling* and *camogie,* which are somewhat similar to field hockey; and *rugby,* a game played with an oval ball. Many people also enjoy boating, fishing, golf, and swimming.

Education. All children in Northern Ireland from age 4 through 16 are required to attend school. Nearly all of them go to schools supported by public funds. Children attend a primary school from age 4 to 11. Some then attend a secondary school, which provides general and vocational education, or a grammar school, which prepares students for higher education. Others attend a comprehensive school, which provides both secondary and grammar school courses.

Catholics operate their own schools, so education in Northern Ireland is largely segregated along religious lines. However, some integrated schools have been established by Catholic and Protestant parents who are concerned about the continued segregation.

Northern Ireland has two universities. Queen's University is in Belfast. The University of Ulster has branches in Belfast, Coleraine, Jordanstown, and Londonderry.

Religion. About half of the people are Protestants. Most of the rest are Roman Catholics. The Church of Ireland and the Presbyterian Church are the largest Protestant churches. The Church of Ireland belongs to the Anglican Communion, which also includes the Church of England and the Episcopal Church in the United States.

An organization of Protestant men called the Orange Order, also known as the *Orangemen,* holds parades every July 12. The parades celebrate the victory of King William III, a Protestant, over King James II, a Roman Catholic, in the Battle of the Boyne in 1690. The "Twelfth" is a public holiday in Northern Ireland. A similar association of Roman Catholics, the Ancient Order of Hibernians, holds parades on August 15 and sometimes on March 17. August 15 is the Roman Catholic Feast of the Assumption of the Virgin Mary. March 17 is St. Patrick's Day. Saint Patrick is the patron saint of Ireland.

The arts. The most famous cultural event in Northern Ireland is the international arts festival hosted each November by the Queen's University of Belfast. This festival features musical performances, dramatic productions, art exhibits, motion pictures, lectures, and other events.

The Ulster Orchestra and Opera Northern Ireland, both of which perform in Belfast, are well known. In addition, several musicians from Northern Ireland have established international reputations, including the flutist James Galway and the pianist Barry Douglas.

Northern Ireland is also known for talented writers. Poet Seamus Heaney won the 1995 Nobel Prize for literature. Other widely known writers include poet John Hewitt, novelist Brian Moore, and playwright Brian Friel.

The land

Northern Ireland lies on the northeast corner of the island of Ireland. On the south and west, it is bordered by the Republic of Ireland, which occupies the rest of the island. The North Channel separates Northern Ireland from Scotland to the northeast. The Irish Sea separates Northern Ireland from England to the southeast. For more information about the geography and climate of Northern Ireland, see *The land* and *Climate* sections in the **United Kingdom** article.

Northern Ireland

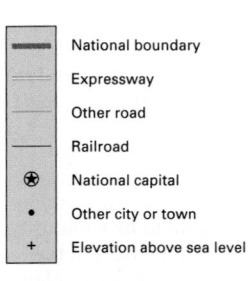

National boundary
Expressway
Other road
Railroad
National capital
Other city or town
Elevation above sea level

WORLD BOOK maps

Surface features. Northern Ireland is a land of rolling plains and low mountains. The plains, which cover the central part of the region, include fertile fields and pasturelands. The mountains, which are near the coast, have many deep, scenic valleys. In some areas, the plains reach to the coast.

The highest peak in Northern Ireland is Slieve Donard (pronounced *sleev DAHN uhrd*). It rises 2,796 feet (852 meters) in the Mourne Mountains near the southeast coast. Other mountain ranges include the Sperrin Mountains in the northwest and the Mountains of Antrim in the northeast.

Lakes, rivers, and bays. Northern Ireland has many smooth, clear lakes called *loughs* (pronounced *lahks*). Lough Neagh *(lahk NAY)*, near the center of the land, covers about 150 square miles (388 square kilometers). It is the largest lake in the United Kingdom and the largest body of water on the island of Ireland.

The longest river in Northern Ireland is the River Bann. The Bann is actually two rivers. The Upper Bann, which is 47$\frac{1}{2}$ miles (76.4 kilometers) long, begins in the Mourne Mountains and flows northwest into the southern end of Lough Neagh. The Lower Bann begins at the northern end of the lake and flows north 38 miles (61 kilometers) into the Atlantic Ocean.

Several large bays, which are also called loughs, cut into the coast. Lough Foyle and Belfast Lough provide excellent harbors for Londonderry and Belfast.

Economy

Service industries rank as leading employers. The major service industries include education, government services, health care, and wholesale trade.

Manufacturing. One of Northern Ireland's most famous manufactured products is Irish linen, which is known for its excellent quality. Most linen mills are near Belfast and Londonderry. Other mills produce woolen and cotton textiles and synthetic fibers.

Beautiful pottery and hand-cut crystal are also made in Northern Ireland. The village of Belleek in the district of Fermanagh is famous for its delicate china.

Shipyards in the Belfast area have built many warships, ocean liners, and tankers. Aircraft plants in the area make commercial and military planes. Other products manufactured in Northern Ireland include automobile parts, chemicals, computer chips, processed foods, and videocassette recorders.

Agriculture and fishing. Cattle, chickens, eggs, hogs, milk, potatoes, and sheep are among Northern Ireland's most important agricultural products. Much barley and hay are grown for animal feed. Other farm products include butter, cheese, mushrooms, and turnips. Orchards in the district of Armagh produce apples, pears, and plums.

The fishing fleet of Northern Ireland brings in large catches of cod, herring, mackerel, shrimp, and whiting, mainly from the Irish Sea. Salmon and trout are netted in the Rivers Foyle and Bann.

Transportation and communication. An excellent road system crisscrosses Northern Ireland. A government-operated railroad system links Belfast and Londonderry with each other, with Portadown and Bangor in

Karin Daher, Gamma/Liaison

A demonstration in Londonderry marks an anniversary of Sunday, Jan. 30, 1972. On that day, 14 Catholics were killed when British soldiers fired at a crowd of protesters. Violent incidents have been part of the long conflict between those who want Northern Ireland to remain in the United Kingdom and those who want it to become part of the Republic of Ireland.

northern Ireland, and with Dublin in Ireland. Large amounts of freight pass through the seaports of Belfast, Coleraine, Larne, Londonderry, and Warrenpoint. Regular passenger ferry service connects Belfast and Larne with cities in western Scotland. Belfast International Airport is the only airport in Northern Ireland that handles international flights.

Northern Ireland has several daily newspapers. The leading papers are *The Belfast Telegraph, The Irish News,* and *The News Letter*, all published in Belfast. Two British Broadcasting Corporation television channels and two independent channels serve Northern Ireland.

History

This section deals mainly with the history of Northern Ireland from the Protestant settlement in the 1600's to recent developments. For information on the early history of the island of Ireland, see **Ireland** (History).

Protestant settlement. In 1541, King Henry VIII of England became king of Ireland. The Reformation, during which Henry changed England from a Roman Catholic to a Protestant nation, had little effect on Ireland. English rule there was ineffective, and most Irish people remained Catholics.

In 1607, local Irish chieftains who opposed the English fled from Ulster, a large province in northern Ireland. King James I of England then gave the chieftains' land to English and Scottish Protestants. This action was partly responsible for the Protestant majority found in Northern Ireland today.

In the 1600's, two attempts were made to reestablish Catholic power in Ireland. The first was an uprising that began in 1641 and was not put down by English forces until 1653.

The second attempt was made under James II, a Catholic who became king of England in 1685. Many English people were unhappy with James's policies and feared that a Catholic succession to the throne would be established. In 1688, the English invited William of Orange, a

Protestant, to invade England with Dutch forces. James fled, and William of Orange was crowned as King William III in 1689. Meanwhile, James went to France and then to Ireland, where he organized an army to fight William. But James was defeated by William in the Battle of the Boyne in 1690. After the battle, Anglican Protestants owned most of the land in Ireland, controlled Ireland's Parliament, and restricted the rights of Catholics and Presbyterian Protestants alike.

Union with Britain. In 1801, the Act of Union took effect. This act abolished the Irish Parliament and created the United Kingdom of Great Britain and Ireland. During the 1800's, the standard of living in northern Ireland rose as manufacturing flourished. But southern Ireland, where most of the Catholics lived, had a low living standard due to unequal distribution of land and a growing population.

In 1886, the British Liberal Party proposed a plan for Ireland called *home rule*. Under this plan, Ireland would have remained part of the United Kingdom, but it would have had its own parliament for domestic affairs. Ulster Protestants, who feared that such a parliament would be Catholic, opposed the plan. The plan was defeated in the British Parliament.

The division of Ireland. By the early 1900's, most Irish Catholics favored complete independence from Britain. But most of the Protestants in Ulster opposed independence because they did not want to be a minority in a Catholic country. In 1919, 73 Irish members of the British Parliament met in Dublin and declared all Ireland an independent state. Guerrilla warfare then broke out between the Irish rebels and British forces.

In 1920, the British Parliament passed the Government of Ireland Act. This act divided Ireland into two separate political units and gave each some powers of self-government. Ulster Protestants accepted the act, and the state of Northern Ireland was formed from six counties in Ulster. But southern Catholics rejected the act and demanded complete independence for a single, united Irish republic. In 1921, southern leaders and the United Kingdom signed a treaty that created the Irish Free State from 23 southern counties and 3 counties of Ulster. In 1937, the Irish Free State adopted a new constitution and changed its name to Éire (in Gaelic) or Ireland (in English). In 1949, Ireland cut all ties with the United Kingdom and became an independent republic.

Under the 1920 act, Northern Ireland was given its own governor, parliament, prime minister, and cabinet. The governor served as the official head of state, but the prime minister and cabinet held most of the power. Northern Ireland's two-house Parliament handled such matters as administering the educational system and regulating commerce and agriculture. Certain other powers, such as levying income taxes and maintaining armed forces, were reserved for the British Parliament. Throughout Northern Ireland's period of self-rule, the Unionist Party—which favored continued union with the United Kingdom—controlled the government.

Problems of division. Many Roman Catholics in Northern Ireland refused to accept the 1920 division of Ireland, and the new government made little effort to win their loyalty. In some areas where Catholics formed a majority, election districts were set up to ensure that Unionist minorities won control of local councils.

The division of Ireland was also opposed by the Irish Free State and, later, by the Republic of Ireland. Beginning in 1921, armed groups crossed into Northern Ireland and attacked British installations. They hoped to force the British to give up control of Northern Ireland.

The Troubles. Catholics in Northern Ireland had long claimed that Protestants violated their civil rights and discriminated against them in jobs, housing, and other areas. In the late 1960's, the struggle for civil rights turned violent, and a period known as the Troubles began. When the government tried to stop a civil rights demonstration in Londonderry in 1968, bloody riots broke out. Serious riots occurred again in 1969 in Belfast and Londonderry. Troops were sent to Northern Ireland to restore order but failed to prevent further rioting. Meanwhile, the pro-Catholic Irish Republican Army (IRA) and other militant nationalist groups carried out bombings and other terrorist attacks. Loyalist paramilitary groups, such as the Ulster Defence Association and the Ulster Volunteer Force, also carried out attacks.

The conflict led the British to suspend Northern Ireland's government in 1972 and to rule the region directly. But the Troubles continued. In 1973 and 1982, the United Kingdom set up assemblies in Northern Ireland to restore control over local affairs to the region. But lack of cooperation between Protestants and Catholics led the British government to dissolve both assemblies.

In 1985, the United Kingdom and the Republic of Ireland signed the Anglo-Irish Agreement, which gave the government of the Irish Republic an advisory role in Northern Ireland's affairs. Both Unionists and the IRA strongly opposed the agreement, and protests against the British government took place.

In the late 1980's and early 1990's, terrorist bombings by the IRA and related groups intensified. The attacks led to violent responses by Protestant terrorist groups. In 1994, both the IRA and Protestant groups declared an end to violence, but bombings resumed in 1996.

Recent developments. The IRA announced another cease-fire in mid-1997. In September 1997, formal talks began that aimed to end the Northern Ireland violence. The talks were the first to include all parties involved in the conflict. In April 1998, the talks ended with the Good Friday Agreement. It was put to referendums in both Ireland and Northern Ireland. Voters approved the agreement, which included a commitment to using peaceful means to resolve political differences. The agreement called for the creation of a Northern Ireland legislative assembly with control over many local matters. It also called for a North-South Ministerial Council, which would include government representatives from Northern Ireland and Ireland, and a British-Irish Council, which would include representatives from the Irish parliament and the various British legislative assemblies.

The new governing bodies began meeting in December 1999. Early in 2000, the agreement was suspended when the Protestants threatened to withdraw from the government to protest a lack of disarmament by the IRA. After months of negotiations, the IRA proposed a new disarmament plan, and the power-sharing government resumed. However, civil unrest between Catholics and Protestants continued. In October 2002, the United Kingdom suspended the power-sharing government.

In 2005, the IRA announced it would stop using violence and destroy its weapons. In response, the United Kingdom began to reduce its troops stationed in Northern Ireland. In May 2006, the Northern Ireland Assembly met for the first time since it had been suspended in 2002. A new power-sharing government began in May 2007.   A. T. Q. Stewart and Brendan O'Leary

Related articles in *World Book* include:

Adams, Gerry	Irish Republican	Orange Order
Belfast	Army	Paisley, Ian
Bloody Sunday	Londonderry	Trimble, David
Boyne, Battle of the	Lough Neagh	Troubles
British-Irish Council	North-South Minis-	Ulster Unionist
Giant's Causeway	terial Council	Party

Additional resources

Edwards, Aaron, and Bloomer, Stephen, eds. *Transforming the Peace Process in Northern Ireland.* Irish Academic Pr., 2008.
Gillespie, Gordon. *Historical Dictionary of the Northern Ireland Conflict.* Scarecrow, 2008.
Schubotz, Dirk, and Devine, Paula, eds. *Young People in Post-Conflict Northern Ireland.* Russell Hse., 2008.
Van Til, Jon. *Breaching Derry's Walls.* Univ. Pr. of Am., 2008.

Northern lights. See Aurora.

Northern Mariana Islands, Commonwealth of the, is a chain of 16 islands in the Pacific Ocean. The islands are a United States commonwealth. They lie about 1,000 miles (1,600 kilometers) south of Japan and about 1,500 miles (2,400 kilometers) east of the Philippines.

The Northern Marianas extend about 337 miles (543 kilometers) from north to south and cover about 179 square miles (464 square kilometers) of land. They are part of a larger region in the Pacific Ocean called Micronesia. Together with Guam, the Northern Marianas make up the Mariana Islands.

About 91,000 people live in the Northern Marianas. About 90 percent of the population lives on Saipan, the capital and largest island. Most of the rest of the people

Northern Mariana Islands

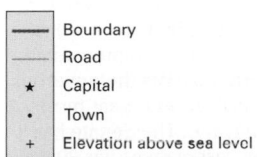

— Boundary
— Road
★ Capital
• Town
+ Elevation above sea level

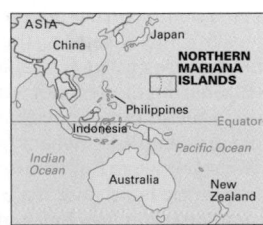

WORLD BOOK maps

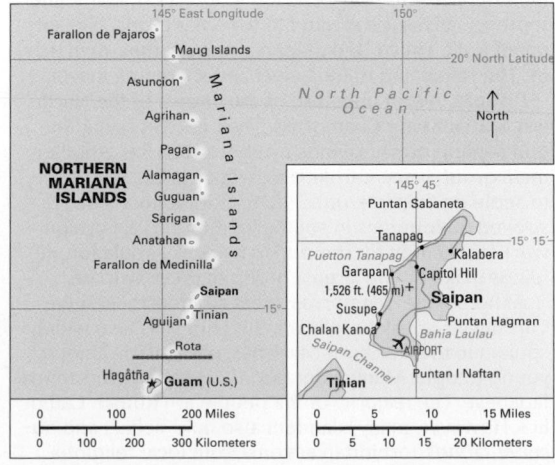

Frederick McDonald

The Commonwealth of the Northern Mariana Islands is in the Pacific Ocean. Chalan Kanoa, *shown here,* is one of the commonwealth's largest towns. It lies on the island of Saipan.

live on Tinian, the second largest island; and Rota, the third largest. The largest community is San Antonio, on Saipan. Government offices are in Susupe and Capitol Hill, which are also on Saipan.

In 1947, the United States began administering the Northern Marianas as part of the Trust Territory of the Pacific Islands. The Northern Marianas became a self-governing commonwealth of the United States in 1986. The commonwealth government handles the commonwealth's internal affairs. The United States is responsible for defense and foreign affairs. Island residents are U.S. citizens, but they cannot vote in presidential elections.

Government. A governor heads the commonwealth government. A lieutenant governor assists the governor. The voters elect both these officials to four-year terms. A two-house legislature makes the laws. The Senate has 9 members, and the House of Representatives has 20 members. Senators are elected to four-year terms, and representatives are elected to two-year terms. The voters of Rota, Tinian, and Saipan also elect their own mayor. The remaining islands elect and share one mayor.

People. About one-third of the people of the Northern Marianas are Chamorros. Their ancestors had begun settling on the islands by about 1500 B.C. Another main group is the Carolinians, whose ancestors began to settle on Saipan around 1815 after typhoons destroyed their homes in southern Micronesia. Foreign workers account for more than half the population. Filipinos make up the largest group of these workers.

At home, the Chamorros speak Chamorro, and the Carolinians speak Carolinian. But English is also widely spoken in the Northern Marianas, particularly among young people. Many older people speak conversational Japanese. The majority of the people are Roman Catholics. However, many islanders also hold beliefs and observe *taboos* (forbidden actions) from local religions.

The law requires children from 6 through 16 years of age to attend school. Postsecondary education is available from Northern Marianas College, which mostly grants degrees at the associate's level. The school does, however, grant a bachelor's degree in education.

Many houses on the islands are made of wood or concrete block with sheet metal roofs. Saipan has some modern apartment buildings and condominiums.

Land and climate. The Northern Marianas are the peaks of a huge undersea mountain range. The range rises more than 6 miles (9.5 kilometers) off the bottom of the Mariana Trench, the deepest known spot in the world's oceans. Volcanic rock covers the northern islands. Seven of them—Alamagan, Anatahan, Agrihan, Farallon de Pajaros, Guguan, Sarigan, and Pagan—still have active volcanoes. Limestone terraces cover volcanic rock on the southern islands. The Maug Islands, a cluster of three islands, are sometimes counted as one island. The Northern Marianas have an average year-round temperature of about 84 °F (29 °C) and an average annual rainfall of about 84 inches (213 centimeters).

Economy. The government is the major employer in the Northern Marianas. Tourism ranks as the most important economic activity. The garment industry is the only significant manufacturing activity. Imports in the Northern Marianas far outnumber exports. More than half of the work force in the Northern Marianas are foreigners. The majority of the garment workers are Chinese or Thai. Many islanders hold government jobs.

History. The ancestors of the present-day Chamorros had begun living on the Northern Marianas by about 1500 B.C. In A.D. 1521, Ferdinand Magellan, a Portuguese explorer in the service of Spain, discovered Rota and Guam. Spain claimed the islands in 1565. But Spain did not begin ruling them until 1668, after Spanish Jesuits established a missionary settlement on Guam.

At the end of the Spanish-American War in 1898, Spain turned Guam over to the United States. The next year, Spain sold the Northern Marianas to Germany. Germany ruled the Northern Marianas until the Japanese seized them at the beginning of World War I in 1914. After the war ended in 1918, a mandate from the League of Nations gave Japan control of the islands.

The United States gained control of the Northern Marianas in 1944, during World War II. In 1947, the United States began administering the islands as part of the United Nations Trust Territory of the Pacific Islands. In 1975, the United States agreed to make the Northern Marianas a self-governing U.S. commonwealth. The agreement took effect Nov. 3, 1986.   Michael R. Ogden

See also **Pacific Islands, Trust Territory of; Saipan.**

Northern pike. See Pike.

Northern Rhodesia. See Zambia.

Northern Territory is a vast area in north-central Australia that has large regions of only partly explored land. The Northern Territory covers 519,800 square miles (1,346,200 square kilometers). The 2006 Australian census reported that the Northern Territory had 192,898 people, including many Aborigines whose ancestors lived in Australia before white people arrived (see **Australia** [The Aborigines]). Most of the territory's Aborigines live in communities in remote areas. Darwin is the capital and largest city in the Northern Territory.

Land and climate. The territory's flat coastline of

© Manfred Gottschalk, Tom Stack & Associates

Darwin is the capital and largest city of the Northern Territory of Australia. It is also the chief port of the territory. The city lies along Australia's northern coast on the Beagle Gulf, an arm of the Timor Sea. It is named in honor of the British naturalist Charles Darwin.

1,040 miles (1,674 kilometers) has many bays. The interior is mostly flat. The northern area has excellent grazing regions. Rivers in the north include the Victoria, Daly, and Roper. The southern area has low rainfall and no permanent rivers. Average January temperatures in the Northern Territory range between 80 and 95 °F (27 and 35 °C), and July temperatures average 77 °F (25 °C). The annual rainfall varies throughout the Northern Territory. Darwin, on the northern coast, has an average of 58 inches (147 centimeters) a year. In the dry interior, rainfall seldom exceeds 11 inches (28 centimeters) a year.

Economy. Mining is the Northern Territory's chief industry. Bauxite, gold, lead, manganese, oil, uranium, and zinc are the chief minerals. Tourism and cattle breeding are also leading industries. Cattle graze on large *stations* (farms). Fruit and vegetable growing is also important. The fishing industry is largely based on the production of barramundi, prawns, and snapper.

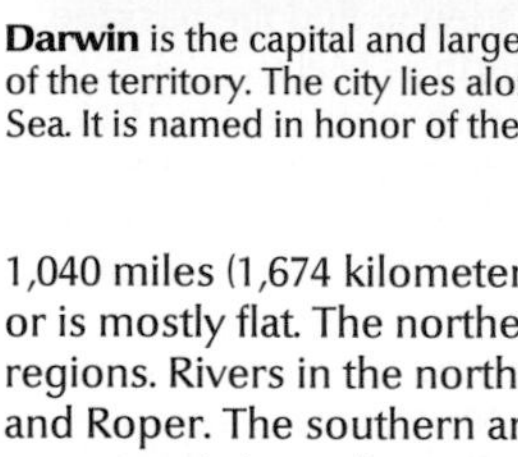

Government. An official appointed by the governor general of Australia on the advice of the federal government administers the government of the Northern Territory. A Legislative Assembly with 25 members is elected every four years. The territory elects two members to the federal House of Representatives and two members to the federal Senate.

WORLD BOOK map

The Northern Territory

© Manfred Gottschalk, Tom Stack & Associates

The Northern Territory covers a huge area in north-central Australia. The interior of the territory is dry and flat except for some low mountains and scattered rock formations.

The federal government provides medical services for the Northern Territory. A "Flying Doctor" operation uses radio and aircraft service to help the sick and injured at isolated mines and cattle stations.

History. The Scottish-born explorer John McDouall Stuart first entered the Northern Territory in 1860. His explorations opened up much of the territory. An overland telegraph line, completed in the 1870's, followed Stuart's trail from Adelaide to Darwin.

The Northern Territory was part of New South Wales until 1863, when South Australia took over the territory from the British government. The Australian federal government took over the administration of the territory in 1911. In 1978, the federal government granted the Northern Territory self-government.   John Brendan Loizou

See also **Darwin; Uluru.**

Northfield (pop. 20,007) is a city in southeastern Minnesota. It lies about 40 miles (64 kilometers) south of St. Paul. For the location of Northfield, see **Minnesota** (political map). The notorious Jesse James gang tried to rob a bank in Northfield in 1876, but the bank clerk refused to open the vault. James escaped, but several gang members were killed or captured. The bank is now a historical museum. The city is the home of Carleton and St. Olaf colleges. Northfield's industries include food processing and the production of electronic circuits. The city is named for John W. North, who founded it in 1855. Northfield has a mayor-council form of government.   Clifford E. Clark, Jr.

Northrop, John Howard (1891-1987), an American biochemist, shared the 1946 Nobel Prize in chemistry with James B. Sumner and W. M. Stanley. Northrop prepared in crystalline form several pure enzymes and one of the viruses that destroy bacteria (see **Enzyme**). Northrop's writings on enzymes include *Crystalline Enzymes* (1939).

Northrop was born on July 5, 1891, in Yonkers, New York. He received his doctor's degree from Columbia University in 1915 and was a member of the Rockefeller Institute (now Rockefeller University) in New York City from 1924 until his death on May 27, 1987.

Eric Howard Christianson

Northwest Ordinance was an important law passed by the United States Congress on July 13, 1787. The ordinance provided for the government of the region north of the Ohio River and west of Pennsylvania, then called the Northwest Territory. It became a model for all territories that later entered the Union as states. The ordinance was largely the work of General Nathan Dane and political leaders Rufus King and Manasseh Cutler.

Under the terms of the ordinance, the territories could achieve equality with the older states by passing through three steps leading to full self-government: (1) Congress, which governed the territory, appointed a governor, a secretary, and three judges. (2) When the territory, or any division of it, attained an adult male population of 5,000, it could choose a legislature and send to Congress a delegate who could speak there but not vote. (3) When the total population reached 60,000, the territory could apply for admission into the Union on terms of full equality with the older states. The ordinance removed the danger of colonial rebellion because it assured the territories of participation in the national government.

The Northwest Ordinance provided more than a plan of government. It laid the groundwork for social and political democracy in the West. It forbade slavery. All people were guaranteed trial by jury and freedom of religious worship. The ordinance guaranteed fair treatment for the Indians and declared that "means of education shall forever be encouraged."

The terms of the Northwest Ordinance were so attractive that pioneers poured into the new territory. In 1788, one of the first groups of settlers founded the town of Marietta, Ohio. Thousands of families followed the first settlers in the westward movement. The territory eventually became five states—Ohio, Indiana, Illinois, Michigan, and Wisconsin. The territory included what is now the part of Minnesota east of the Mississippi River.

William E. Foley

See also **Northwest Territory** (Early history); **Ohio Company.**

Northwest Passage is a water route, long sought by explorers, across or around North America. The explorers who followed Christopher Columbus soon found that North America was not a part of Asia, as they had believed at first. At that time, English, French, and Dutch adventurers were more interested in finding an easy route to Asia than they were in exploring and settling North America. So they began to look for a "Northwest Passage," or waterway, that would take them around or through the North American continent.

The search for the Northwest Passage is a tale of adventure and heroism. In 1524, Giovanni da Verrazzano, sailing under the French flag, tried to find the passage. He probably explored as far north as Maine.

Jacques Cartier, while exploring for France in 1535, found the St. Lawrence River. He was seeking a route to China. Henry Hudson was sent out many years later by the Dutch East India Company to find a shorter route to the South Seas. He thought he had found that route in 1609 when he sailed into New York Bay and some distance up the Hudson River. In 1610, Hudson explored the Hudson Strait and Hudson Bay while searching for the Northwest Passage.

No country tried harder than England to find the passage. Sir Martin Frobisher began a series of English expeditions in 1576. Other English navigators continued these explorations for 300 years. Frobisher made many important findings, including Frobisher Bay, an indentation in Baffin Island. John Davis followed Frobisher and sailed into the strait that now bears Davis's name. In 1616, William Baffin and Robert Bylot sailed up Davis Strait and around the great channel that has ever since been known as Baffin Bay. Russia, the Netherlands, and Denmark took an interest in the search.

By the late 1700's, the territory that had been explored included Hudson Strait, Hudson Bay, Davis Strait, Baffin Bay, and the icy seas from Greenland to Svalbard and from Svalbard to Novaya Zemlya. See **Exploration.**

Commander John Ross, a Scottish explorer, began the final series of expeditions in 1818. The most noted of the explorers to follow him was Sir John Franklin, a British explorer. Franklin found a passage to Asia during a voyage from 1845 to 1847. His ships reached King William Island, near waters that led directly to the Asian shore. But Franklin and his crew died after their ships became jammed in the ice, and their discovery was not known

The Northwest Passage

This map shows routes traveled by explorers in search of a northern sea passage between Europe and Asia.

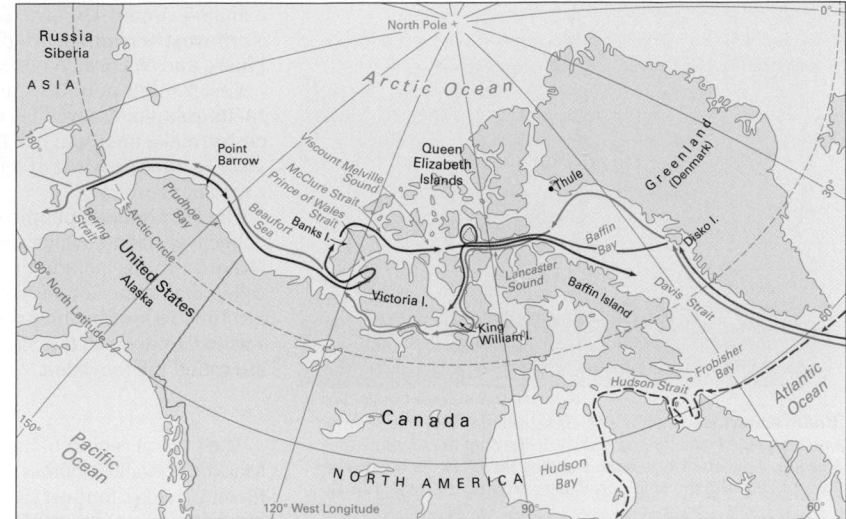

---- Henry Hudson 1610-1611

——— Sir John Franklin 1845-1847

━━━ Sir Robert McClure 1850-1854

——— Roald Amundsen 1903-1906

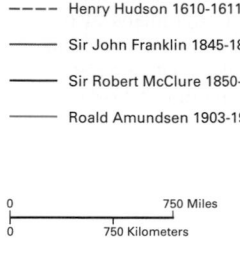

0   750 Miles

0   750 Kilometers

WORLD BOOK map

until later expeditions found relics of their trip. In 1850, Sir Robert McClure, a British explorer, sailed from the west to the northern shore of what is now Banks Island. Thick ice then halted his voyage. McClure and his crew continued by sled to Melville Island, where they transferred to another ship. On that ship, McClure and his crew completed the first journey across the Northwest Passage in 1854.

In 1906, Roald Amundsen's ship, the *Gjöa*, carried the first group to sail all the way through the passage. He traveled from east to west. The first west-to-east voyage through the passage was completed in 1942 by the Royal Canadian Mounted Police schooner *St. Roch*.

McClure Strait was conquered in 1954 by United States Navy and Coast Guard icebreakers. Three U.S. Coast Guard cutters, the *Spar,* the *Bramble,* and the *Storis*, aided by the Canadian Navy icebreaker the *Labrador,* made the west-to-east trip in 1957. The four cutters traveled through Bellot Strait. This channel permits cargo ships to unload supplies for the North Warning System radar line in northern Canada. The *Spar* was the first ship to sail completely around North America on a continuous voyage. The ship started in Bristol, Rhode Island, went south to the Panama Canal, then up the Pacific Coast, through the Northwest Passage, and back to Bristol.

In 1960, the U.S. atomic submarine *Seadragon* made the first underwater crossing of the Northwest Passage.

Colored lithograph (1854) by Lt. S. Gurney Cresswell; Peabody Essex Museum, Salem, Massachusetts

The *Investigator,* a ship captained by the British explorer Sir Robert McClure, sailed to the north shore of Banks Island in 1850. There, thick ice prevented further sailing. But McClure and his crew continued by sled and ship, completing the first expedition through the Northwest Passage in 1854.

Bancroft Library, University of California, Berkeley

Roald Amundsen's ship, the *Gjøa,* sailed through the Northwest Passage from 1903 to 1906, the first ship to complete the journey. A weary Amundsen, standing far left in the picture below, posed with the ship's crew after arriving in Nome, Alaska.

Bancroft Library, University of California, Berkeley

It traveled 850 miles (1,368 kilometers) from Lancaster Sound, through the Canadian Arctic islands, and into McClure Strait. In 1969, the U.S. icebreaker-tanker *Manhattan* became the first commercial ship to complete the passage. The *Manhattan* sailed to Alaska by way of the Prince of Wales Strait.   William Barr

Related articles in *World Book* include:

Amundsen, Roald	Franklin, Sir John	Hudson, Henry
Baffin, William	Frobisher, Sir	McClure, Sir Robert
Cabot, Sebastian	Martin	John Le Mesurier
Cartier, Jacques	Gilbert, Sir	Parry, Sir William
Davis, John	Humphrey	Edward

Northwest Territories is a vast region in northern Canada. It stretches from the northern boundaries of the provinces of British Columbia, Alberta, and Saskatchewan north to islands in the Arctic Ocean. The Northwest Territories is a cold, rugged region with relatively few people. Politically, it is one of three territories in northern Canada. It lies between the two other territories: Yukon, to the west, and Nunavut, to the east. The capital of the Northwest Territories is Yellowknife.

People

The Northwest Territories is sparsely populated. It has only about 35 scattered and mostly tiny communities. Yellowknife is the only city. It is the territorial capital and

a mining center. About 45 percent of the people of the Northwest Territories live there. Fort Smith, Hay River, Inuvik, and Norman Wells are incorporated towns.

First Nations people (American Indians), Inuit, and Métis (people of mixed European and First Nations ancestry) make up about half the population of the Northwest Territories. Most of the remaining people have European ancestry.

The First Nations people in the area call themselves collectively Dene, which means *people.* Individual First Nations groups include the Bear Lake Indians (also called the Sahtu Gotine), the Chipewyan (Denesuline), the Tlicho (Dogrib), the Gwich'in (Kutchin), the Hare (Kasho Gotine), and the Slavey. The Inuit of the region are called the Inuvialuit.

Land

The central region of the Northwest Territories is the Mackenzie Valley. Within this region is the Mackenzie River, Canada's longest river and one of the longest in North America. The Mackenzie Mountains extend along the Northwest Territories' western border. Most of the

Northwest Territories

National park (N.P.)

Boundary
Road
Railroad
★ Capital
• Other city or town
+ Elevation above sea level

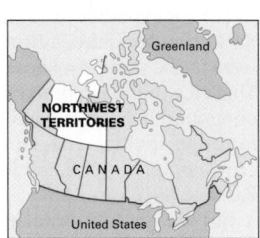

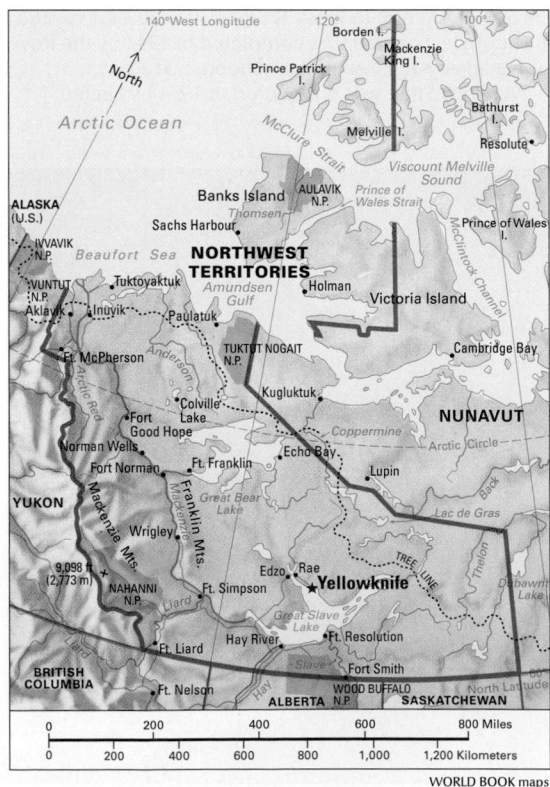

WORLD BOOK maps

The spectacular scenery of
the Northwest Territories
includes Alexandra Falls on
the Hay River south of Great
Slave Lake. The southern part
of the vast, rugged Territories
includes mountains, lakes,
and rivers. The northern part
is a cold, harsh area of islands
and icy waters.

Bob and Ira Spring

far eastern and northern parts of the Territories consist of treeless, rocky terrain.

The Mackenzie Mountains stretch from the Beaufort Sea, in the north, to British Columbia, in the south. The tallest mountain in the Northwest Territories is an unnamed peak that rises 9,098 feet (2,773 meters) in the southern part of the range. The highest named peak is Mount Sir James MacBrien, which is 9,062 feet (2,762 meters) high. Few people live in the Mackenzie Mountains. The region is difficult to travel through and has few marketable resources.

The Mackenzie Valley lies east of the Mackenzie Mountains and largely defines the Northwest Territories. The region is a northward extension of the Great Central Plain of North America. It is dominated by the Mackenzie River, which flows 1,100 miles (1,770 kilometers) from Great Slave Lake in the south to the Beaufort Sea in the north. A number of communities with roots in the 1800's fur trade lie along the river.

The Franklin Mountains stand about 5,000 feet (1,500 meters) tall to the east of the Mackenzie River. Two of the largest lakes in Canada, Great Bear Lake and Great Slave Lake, are east of the Franklin Mountains. Yellowknife lies on the shores of Yellowknife Bay, a projection at the northern end of Great Slave Lake.

Barren grounds. The rest of the Northwest Territo-ries typically is described as part of the *barren grounds,* a vast expanse of rolling, rocky terrain that is largely treeless and extends eastward far into Nunavut. Lakes dot the area, and many streams cut through it.

The Northwest Territories also includes a number of islands in the Arctic Ocean. Several of these are divided between the Northwest Territories and Nunavut. Like the Arctic portion of the mainland Territories, these islands support a small population and little vegetation. A number of small Inuit communities developed on the islands after World War II (1939-1945).

National parklands are spread throughout the Northwest Territories. In the southwest corner is Nahanni National Park Reserve, noted for its attractive rivers and majestic waterfalls. Wood Buffalo National Park straddles the border between the Northwest Territories and Alberta. It is home to Canada's largest remaining herd of buffalo and serves as the spring nesting ground of the endangered whooping crane. Tuktut National Park lies on the northern coast of the Northwest Territories' mainland, and Aulavik National Park occupies part of Banks Island in the Arctic Ocean.

Climate

The Northwest Territories is one of the coldest areas in North America. It has long, bitterly cold winters and short, cool summers. Summer in the Mackenzie Valley is warmer than in the area north of the *tree line,* the northern limit of forest growth. Inuvik, in the northern Mackenzie Valley, has average temperatures of about 57 °F (14 °C) in July and about −18 °F (−28 °C) in January. To the south, along the border with Alberta, average temperatures are about 61 °F (16 °C) in July and about −10 °F (−23 °C) in January. The highest temperature recorded in the Northwest Territories was 103 °F (39 °C) at Fort Smith on July 18, 1941. The lowest, −79 °F (−62 °C), was recorded at Fort Good Hope on Dec. 31, 1910.

During the longest days of summer, the Territories receives nearly 19 hours of sunlight near its southern border and 24 hours of sunlight in the far north. In midwinter, the far south gets about 9 hours of daylight, while areas north of the Arctic Circle have one or more days when the sun does not rise above the horizon.

The average annual precipitation in the Northwest

Facts in brief

Capital: Yellowknife.

Government: *Parliament*—members of the Senate, 1; members of the House of Commons, 1. *Territorial*—members of the territorial Legislative Assembly, 19.

Area: 501,570 mi² (1,299,070 km²), including 42,860 mi² (111,000 km²) of inland water. *Greatest distances*—north-south, 1,320 mi (2,125 km); east-west, 860 mi (1,385 km). *Coastline*—6,835 mi (11,000 km).

Elevation: *Highest*—An unnamed peak in the Mackenzie Mountains, 9,098 ft (2,773 m) above sea level. *Lowest*—sea level along the coast.

Population: *2006 census*—41,464; density, 8 per 100 mi² (3 per 100 km²).

Chief products: *Fishing industry*—lake trout, whitefish. *Manufacturing*—food products, printed materials. *Mining*—diamonds, natural gas, petroleum.

Yellowknife is the capital and largest city of the Northwest Territories of Canada. The city stands on Yellowknife Bay, a projection at the northern end of Great Slave Lake.

Territories is only 11 inches (27 centimeters). Most of it falls as snow. The mainland gets about 60 inches (150 centimeters) of snow each year, and less than 40 inches (100 centimeters) falls on most of the islands. Much of the Territories has nearly desertlike conditions.

Economy

The landscape and climate of the Northwest Territories limit its economic development. Mining dominates the economy. Government services also play an important role and employ much of the population. Many tourists come to the region for its natural beauty and outdoor activities.

Mining. Diamonds rank as the leading mined product of the Northwest Territories. Canada's first diamond mine opened in 1998 near Lac de Gras, about 185 miles (300 kilometers) north of Yellowknife. Additional mines followed in the early 2000's.

The petroleum industry has become increasingly important in the Northwest Territories. Oil drilling began at Norman Wells after World War I (1914-1918). Oil was discovered in the Beaufort Sea in the 1970's. The Northwest Territories also has substantial quantities of natural gas. However, it lacks the pipeline facilities needed to carry the gas to market. Debates over the construction of a gas pipeline have continued since the 1970's.

Government at several levels is the largest employer in the Northwest Territories. About one-fourth of all workers hold jobs with the federal, territorial, or *municipal* (town or city) governments.

Tourism, like the petroleum industry, has become increasingly important to the economy. People from Europe, Japan, the United States, and other parts of the world visit the Northwest Territories to enjoy its rugged beauty and participate in such activities as fishing, hunting, photography, and skiing. In winter, tourists are attracted by the magnificent natural display of light called the *aurora borealis* (northern lights).

Fishing and forestry employ relatively few people and produce few exports. Commercial fishing in the Northwest Territories centers on Great Slave Lake, which provides whitefish and lake trout. Forestry is limited by the area's distance from outside markets and by the slow growth rate and small size of many of the trees. However, loggers do harvest birch, pine, poplar, and spruce, especially in the south near Hay River.

Transportation. The large size, diverse terrain, extreme climate, and small population of the Northwest Territories make transportation difficult. Moving passengers and goods is costly and slow, and it presents technological challenges.

The Mackenzie Northern Railway operates between Alberta and the town of Hay River, on Great Slave Lake. The Northwest Territories has few permanent roads. The main one, the Mackenzie Highway, runs alongside the railway. Temporary ice roads are used to transport supplies to diamond mines and isolated communities. The main route for carrying goods is the Mackenzie River. However, the river is navigable only three or four months each year. A tug and barge system operates from Hay River and serves communities along the Mackenzie River, to the Beaufort Sea.

Air service is the chief method of passenger travel in the Northwest Territories. It also plays an important role in transporting fresh foods and other perishable goods. Most communities have regular air service. Planes that use floats, skis, and landing gear with wheels serve isolated mining and prospecting sites.

Communications. Newspapers are published in Yellowknife and in most towns in the Northwest Territories. A system of *terrestrial* (on land), microwave, and satellite technologies provides radio, telephone, television, and Internet access to all communities. The Canadian Broadcasting Corporation has radio stations in Yellowknife and Inuvik.

Education

Two district educational authorities—public and Roman Catholic—operate schools in Yellowknife. Regional education boards coordinate schools' activities in other parts of the Territories. First Nations authorities control many local schools, and schools throughout the education system incorporate *aboriginal* (native) curriculum.

Government

As a territory of Canada, the Northwest Territories does not have all the same political rights and freedoms as the provinces, and it relies heavily on the federal government for financial support. The people elect one member to the Canadian House of Commons. The Northwest Territories has one appointed representative in Canada's Senate.

Canada's federal government appoints a commissioner to serve as honorary head of government for the Northwest Territories. A premier actually leads the government. The Legislative Assembly of the Northwest Territories elects the premier and the council from among its own members.

The members of the Legislative Assembly are elected to four-year terms as independents rather than as members of political parties. The Assembly governs by *consensus* (general agreement). This method of government is more in keeping with aboriginal traditions.

The court system includes the Court of Appeal, the Supreme Court, and the Territorial Court. The Court of Appeal hears civil and criminal appeals from the Supreme Court, and criminal appeals from the Territorial Court. The Supreme Court hears civil and criminal cases. The federal government appoints the judges of the Court of Appeal and the Supreme Court.

The Territorial Court handles the majority of criminal cases that enter the court system. It also may hear some civil cases. Its justices, appointed by the territorial government, travel throughout the Territories to hear cases. Justices of the peace appointed by the territorial government also may conduct certain judicial proceedings.

The Northwest Territories has several *settlement areas* resulting from land-claim and self-government agreements with aboriginal peoples, including the Dene, Inuit, and Métis. The agreements generally recognize aboriginal control of a small percentage of land in the settlement areas. They also give the aboriginal people a one-time cash contribution; *royalties* (payments) from the development of natural resources; and administrative and political input in the management of the areas. The agreements require the establishment of *resource boards* with both aboriginal and nonaboriginal representatives. Resource boards manage land, water, and wildlife in the settlement areas.

A growing number of aboriginal groups have some form of *autonomy* (self-government). These communities exercise control over local education, health care, economic development, and cultural affairs.

History

Early inhabitants. People have lived in what is now the Northwest Territories for thousands of years. Before Europeans arrived there, groups of Inuit and First Nations people moved across the land to find natural resources and favorable weather. These people developed sophisticated cultural, economic, social, and spiritual systems.

European exploration. The first European to reach the area was Samuel Hearne, an employee of the Hudson's Bay Company, a British trading firm. King Charles II of England had granted the company trading rights in a region that included what is now the Northwest Territories. Hearne set out overland from Churchill, in what is now Manitoba, in 1770. He reached the mouth of the Coppermine River the next year. Hearne explored the Great Slave Lake region on his return journey.

In 1789, the Scottish-born Canadian explorer Alexander Mackenzie followed what is now known as the Mackenzie River in search of an overland route to the Pacific Ocean. His journey took him instead to the Arctic Ocean. As a result of Mackenzie's exploration, the fur trade expanded into the Northwest Territories region. The arrival of traders in the area spread European diseases to the aboriginal population. More than half the native people died by the early 1800's.

Political development. In the mid-1800's, the area that is now the Northwest Territories was under the authority of the Hudson's Bay Company. But the company and the British government did little to administer the area. In 1870, the recently created Dominion of Canada agreed to take over the company's landholdings and established the North-West Territories. The North-West Territories originally covered an area extending from the Rocky Mountains in the west to the Labrador Peninsula in the east, and from the United States border in the south to the northern coast of mainland North America. Because of a Métis uprising in the Red River Valley, Canada also made part of the company's lands into the province of Manitoba in 1870. In 1880, Canada took over the Arctic islands that now form part of the Territories.

In 1898, the federal government created Yukon by carving out part of the North-West Territories. A rapid increase in settlement on the Canadian prairies, along with demands for regional representation, resulted in the establishment of Alberta and Saskatchewan in 1905. Like Yukon, these new provinces had been part of the Territories. The North-West Territories was renamed the Northwest Territories in 1906. Manitoba, Ontario, and Quebec were expanded northward in 1912, further diminishing the Territories' area.

The early and middle 1900's. Development of the region through the early 1900's was linked strongly to the discovery of marketable resources there. These resources included baleen whales, hunted from the late 1880's to the early 1900's, and, later, mined products, such as crude oil, gold, and radium ore.

The Canadian government's presence in the Territories consisted of a small number of schools, post offices, and weather stations, and occasional geological surveys and medical services. The government relied upon small detachments of the North-West Mounted Police to provide oversight and services to the widely scattered population. Few nonaboriginal people ventured into the northeastern portion of the territory following the decline of the whaling industry in the early 1900's.

During World War II (1939-1945), the United States launched the Northwest Defense Projects as part of its strategy to defend North America from Japanese attack. In the Northwest Territories, these projects included the construction of airfields and the development of barge facilities along the Mackenzie River. The Territories' radium deposits also became important during World War II because they contained uranium, which was used to develop the first atomic bomb. In the middle of the war, the Canadian government assumed responsibility for mining the region's radium and uranium ore.

In the 1950's, the Canadian government moved aboriginal people off their land and onto government-built communities. The government enacted housing, employment, education, health care, and cultural programs to improve aboriginal people's social and economic conditions. However, threats to the aboriginal hunting-and-gathering culture, as well as the absence of meaningful wage employment in the new communities, made the transition from a mobile to a settled lifestyle painful and disruptive. It began an era of intense cultural dislocation and personal crisis for native peoples across the region.

In the 1950's and 1960's, private industry and the Canadian government began to develop the Northwest Territories' natural resources. Work expanded at the gold

Symbols of the Northwest Territories

Territorial flag

Territorial coat of arms

Territorial bird
Gyrfalcon

Floral emblem
White (eight-petaled) mountain avens

The territorial flag, which includes most of the coat of arms, was adopted in 1969. On the coat of arms, the wavy blue line represents the Northwest Passage. The gold bars symbolize mineral wealth. The white fox represents the fur industry. Two *narwhals* (Arctic whales) guard a compass rose, which symbolizes the north magnetic pole. The coat of arms was adopted in 1957. The gyrfalcon and the white mountain avens also symbolize the Northwest Territories.

new political unit controlled largely by the Inuit from the eastern Territories. The Canadian Parliament authorized the division of the Northwest Territories in 1993, and the territory of Nunavut came into existence in 1999. With the creation of Nunavut, the area of the Northwest Territories was reduced by more than half—from 1,322,910 square miles (3,426,320 square kilometers) to 501,570 square miles (1,299,070 square kilometers).

The economy of the Northwest Territories improved dramatically in the 1990's with the beginning of diamond mining in the region. The mines marketed Canadian diamonds as an alternative to *blood diamonds*—that is, diamonds mined by rebels in African countries to fund violent conflicts.

Recent developments. The Northwest Territories is a region in transition. Its economy remains vulnerable to changes in the market values of such resources as oil, natural gas, and diamonds. The resolution of aboriginal land claims has empowered most First Nations and Inuit communities in the Territories. Aboriginal people play an active role in regional government, and autonomous communities have gained greater control over education, health care, and economic development. Though social problems, such as alcohol abuse, persist, the First Nations, Inuit, and Métis communities have experienced significant improvements.   Ken S. Coates

Related articles in *World Book* include:

Arctic Ocean	Inuvik	Northwest
Baffin Island	Mackenzie, Sir	Passage
Ellesmere Island	Alexander	Nunavut
Great Bear Lake	Mackenzie River	Southampton
Great Slave Lake	Melville Island	Island
Inuit		Yellowknife

Northwest Territory was a vast tract of land lying north of the Ohio River, west of Pennsylvania, and east of the Mississippi River. It extended to the northern limits of the United States. The states of Ohio, Indiana, Illinois, Michigan, Wisconsin, and part of Minnesota east of the Mississippi were carved out of the territory.

Early history. The French first occupied the region and founded posts by the early 1700's. Competition between French traders operating from these posts and British trappers from Pennsylvania helped start the French and Indian War (1754-1763). The war ended with the area's cession to a victorious Britain (now also called the United Kingdom). See **French and Indian wars.**

During the American Revolution (1775-1783), violent fighting took place in the Northwest between the settlers and the British and their Indian allies. The campaign of George Rogers Clark against British-controlled settlements helped win the territory for the United States. The region was ceded after the war. Before the government could open the region to settlement, it had to deal with the claims of Massachusetts, Connecticut, Virginia, and New York. These states insisted that their colonial charters extended their boundaries into this area. The states ceded their claims to Congress between 1781 and 1785, because Maryland refused to approve the Articles of Confederation until it received assurance that the other states would yield their claims.

The land then became a territory of the United States. Congress, eager for revenue from the sale of lands there, adopted the Ordinance of 1785. This law provided for orderly rectangular surveys into mile-square units

fields at Yellowknife and at the Norman Wells oil field. A lead zinc mine opened at Pine Point. Petroleum exploration in the Beaufort Sea showed promise. The Canadian government supported resource development by building roads and funding the construction of a railway to Pine Point. But many mines closed after a short time. During the 1970's, aboriginal-led protests stalled plans for a natural gas pipeline from the Beaufort Sea.

Before 1967, the Northwest Territories' government had been based in Ottawa, thousands of miles away. A regional administrative center operated at Fort Smith. The decision to make Yellowknife the capital in 1967 brought about rapid growth of the city. The creation of the new capital was part of a process of *devolving* (shifting) government responsibilities from the federal government to the Territories. The Territories attained *responsible government*, a system in which the elected officials, rather than the appointed commissioner, were directly responsible for managing territorial affairs.

The late 1900's. The Inuit of the eastern Territories felt that the government in Yellowknife was out of touch with aboriginal needs, and they wanted more control over their own affairs. A 1992 *plebiscite* (direct vote by the people) resulted in formal approval to create a huge

Granger Collection

The Northwest Territory's first settlement and its first capital were established at Marietta, Ohio, in 1788. The engraving of the Marietta courthouse and jail shown here dates from 1842.

called *sections.* These were sold at auction at a minimum price of $1 an acre. Congress also struggled with the problem of a government for the territory. Thomas Jefferson in 1784 had drafted a plan that would have divided the territory into several units. These could become states when the population of any one unit equaled the population of the smallest state in the Union. The Eastern States rejected this proposal, because they feared that the many Western States would dominate Congress. Instead, Congress adopted the Northwest Ordinance, or Ordinance of 1787. This provided for the division of the region into from three to five states, and the establishment of a governmental system that would allow them eventual membership in the Union. See **Northwest Ordinance.**

Settlement began at once. The first arrivals were sent out by a New England speculating group called the Ohio Company (see **Ohio Company**). They founded the town of Marietta at the mouth of the Muskingum River in Ohio. Other interests soon established rival settlements at such villages as Gallipolis and Cincinnati. To the north, colonists clustered about Cleveland in the "Western Reserve" area retained by Connecticut when it ceded its lands to Congress (see **Western Reserve**). Arthur St. Clair, a Scottish-born political and military leader, became the first governor of the Northwest Territory in 1787. He inaugurated the first territorial government on July 15, 1788.

The population grew slowly at first because of continual Indian attacks. President George Washington sent three expeditions to fight the Indians, but the first two met with disaster. The territory became more peaceful after General Anthony Wayne defeated the Indians in the Battle of Fallen Timbers in 1794. In 1795, Wayne forced the Treaty of Greenville on the Indians. In the Treaty of Greenville, the Indians ceded most of the lands of southern Ohio and part of eastern Indiana to the United States. Other land cessions followed during the early 1800's. See **Indian wars** (Conflicts in the Midwest).

As more settlers moved into the region, the Northwest Territory was divided. In 1800, the western part of the region became the Territory of Indiana, with William Henry Harrison—later president of the United States—as governor. The Michigan Territory was created in 1805, and the Illinois Territory in 1809. Ohio became a state in

1803, Indiana in 1816, Illinois in 1818, Michigan in 1837, and Wisconsin in 1848.   Jerome O. Steffen

See also **Clark, George Rogers; Harrison, William Henry; Saint Clair, Arthur.**

Northwestern University is a private institution that has its main campuses in Evanston and Chicago, Illinois. Northwestern University was founded by Methodists in 1851, but the school has no religious affiliation today. Women first enrolled at Northwestern in 1869.

Most of Northwestern's undergraduate and graduate programs are on the Evanston campus. The school grants degrees in many fields, including arts and sciences and education. Northwestern is noted for its programs in music and theater as well as its efforts in the development of children's theater. The Technological Institute houses the school of engineering, another respected program. Northwestern is also known for its business school, the Kellogg School of Management, and its school of journalism and marketing communications, Medill.

Northwestern's Chicago campus, opened in 1926, serves as a center for professional studies. The university's Feinberg School of Medicine is based on the Chicago campus. Research hospitals in Chicago affiliated with the university and its medical school include Children's Memorial Hospital and Northwestern Memorial Hospital. The university's Law School is also on the Chicago campus.

Northwestern's Law School organized one of the first scientific crime detection laboratories. The university also established one of the first programs in African studies. Its Materials Research Science and Engineering Center and Transportation Center are nationally known. Northwestern also operates the National High School Institute, offering a summer program for high school students. The university's sports teams are called the Wildcats. Its website at http://www.northwestern.edu offers more information.

Critically reviewed by Northwestern University

Norton, Andre (1912-2005), was an American author of science fiction. She wrote more than 130 books, most of them for young people. Norton often drew on history and folklore for her action-packed plots, which include such elements as magic, time travel, and animals with powers of telepathy.

Norton's first books were spy stories and historical novels. Her first science-fiction book was *Star Man's Son, 2250 A.D.* (1952). Other books include *The Beast Master* (1959), *Operation Time Search* (1967), *Wraiths of Time* (1976), and *Dare to Go A-Hunting* (1990).

Norton wrote numerous books with other authors. For example, she collaborated with Sasha Miller on a fantasy series that includes *To the King a Daughter* (2000), *Knight or Knave* (2001), and *A Crown Disowned* (2002).

Norton was born on Feb. 17, 1912, in Cleveland. From 1932 to 1951, she worked as a children's librarian in Cleveland. Norton's given name was Mary Alice. She changed her name to Andre because of fears that her first novel, *The Prince Commands* (1934), would not be accepted if publishers knew its author was a woman. Norton also wrote science fiction under the pen name Andrew North. She died on March 17, 2005.

Kathryn Pierson Jennings

© N. Beeckman, Mittet Foto

Norway is known for the scenic beauty of its rugged mountains and its deeply indented coast. Many inlets of the sea called *fiords* extend far into the country. The village of Stryn on the Nord Fiord, *shown here,* lies about 60 miles (100 kilometers) from the coast.

Norway

Norway is a long, narrow country on the northwestern edge of the European continent. The northern third of Norway lies above the Arctic Circle and is called the *Land of the Midnight Sun.* Because this region is so far north, it has long periods every summer when the sun shines 24 hours a day. Oslo, Norway's capital and largest city, is in the southern part of the country.

Most of the Norwegian people live near or along the sea. Winds warmed by the sea give the coast much warmer winters than other regions so far north, and snow melts quickly there. Even north of the Arctic Circle, nearly all of Norway's harbors are free of ice the year around. Inland areas are colder, and snow covers the ground much of the year. For thousands of years, the people have used skis for travel over the snow. Today, skiing is Norway's national sport. Most Norwegians learn to ski before they even start school.

Norway, along with Denmark and Sweden, is one of the Scandinavian countries. Vikings lived in all three countries about 1,000 years ago. Vikings from Norway sailed west and established colonies in Iceland and Greenland. About A.D. 1000, Leif Eriksson (also spelled Ericson, Ericsson, or Eiriksson) sailed from Greenland and headed probably the first European expedition to the American mainland.

Since the time of the Vikings, the Norwegians have been a seafaring people. Norway's coast is famous for its many long, narrow inlets of the sea called *fiords,* which provide fine harbors. Rich fisheries lie off the west coast, and dried fish were an important export as early as the

1200's. Norway began developing its great shipping fleet during the 1600's. Today, Norway's fishing and shipping industries rank among the world's largest.

Norway is mostly a high, mountainous plateau covered by bare rock, and it has a relatively small amount of farmland. But the rivers that rush down from the moun-

Facts in brief

Capital: Oslo.
Official language: Norwegian (Bokmål and Nynorsk).
Official name: Kongeriket Norge (Kingdom of Norway).
Area: 148,718 mi² (385,179 km²), including Svalbard and Jan Mayen. *Greatest distances*—northeast-southwest, 1,089 mi (1,752 km); northwest-southeast, 267 mi (430 km). *Coastline*—1,647 mi (2,650 km).
Elevation: *Highest*—Galdhøppigen, 8,100 ft (2,469 m) above sea level. *Lowest*—sea level along the coast.
Population: *Estimated 2012 population*—4,960,000; density, 33 per mi² (13 per km²); distribution, 79 percent urban, 21 percent rural. *2001 census*—4,520,947.
Chief products: *Agriculture*—barley, eggs, fruits, milk, potatoes, wheat, wool. *Fishing*—blue whiting, cod, haddock, herring, mackerel. *Forestry*—pine, spruce. *Manufacturing*—aluminum, computers, processed foods, refined petroleum products, ships, wood pulp and paper. *Mining*—coal, iron ore, limestone, natural gas, nickel, petroleum, pyrites, zinc.
National anthem: "Ja, vi elsker dette landet" ("Yes, We Love This Land").
National holiday: Constitution Day, May 17.
Money: *Basic unit*—Norwegian krone. One hundred øre equal one krone.

© Superstock

© A. Thelin, Mittet Foto

The midnight sun is a famous symbol of Norway. It shines 24 hours a day for 10 weeks each year at North Cape, *shown here,* a rocky point of land on the shore of the Arctic Ocean.

Oslo, Norway's capital and largest city, is home to almost 1 of 8 Norwegians. Oslo is also the chief commercial, industrial, and shipping center of Norway.

tains provide cheap electric power. Norway generates more hydroelectric power per person than any other country. Norwegian manufacturing is based on this cheap power.

Government

Norway is a constitutional monarchy with a king or a queen, a Cabinet led by a prime minister, and a parliament. The government is based on the Norwegian Constitution of 1814, which divides the government into three branches—executive, legislative, and judicial. The prime minister is the actual head of the government. The monarch has little power.

The monarch usually appoints the leader of the strongest political party or *coalition* (group of parties) in the parliament to be prime minister. Other high government officials, including judges and county governors, are appointed by the monarch on the advice of the Cabinet. Like the other Scandinavian countries, Norway has a government official called an *ombudsman.* This official investigates complaints by citizens against government actions or decisions. See **Ombudsman.**

National government. Executive power in the Norwegian government is exercised by the Cabinet, also known as the Council of State. It consists of the prime minister and about 18 other officials, each of whom heads a department or ministry. The monarch officially appoints the Cabinet members, but they are actually selected by the party or coalition in power in the parliament. To keep the powers of the executive and legislative branches separate, Cabinet members cannot also

The Norwegian flag was adopted in 1898. The civil flag, *shown here,* is rectangular. The state flag has a *swallowtail* (forked tail).

Norway's coat of arms dates from the 1280's, when the ax and crown of Saint Olav were added to the lion.

WORLD BOOK map

Norway is a country in northern Europe. It borders Sweden, Finland, and Russia.

Norway map index

Cities and towns

Ålesund	39,373	.F	2	Egersund	13,324	.I	2	Hammerfest	9,020	.A	6	
Alta	17,159	.A	6	Eidsvoll	18,035	.H	3	Harstad	23,092	.B	5	
Arendal	39,554	.I	2	Farsund	9,497	.I	2	Haugesund	30,742	.H	1	
Askim	13,673	.H	3	Flekkefjord	8,839	.I	2	Kongsberg	22,657	.H	3	
Baerum*	101,497	.H	3	Flora	11,323	.G	2	Kongsvinger	17,366	.H	3	
Bergen	233,291	.G	1	Fredrikstad	68,505	.H	3	Kragerø	10,610	.H	3	
Bodø	41,760	.C	4	Gjøvik	27,093	.G	3	Kristiansand	73,977	.I	2	
Drammen	55,862	.H	3	Grimstad	18,307	.I	2	Kristiansund	17,009	.F	2	
				Halden	27,204	.H	3	Larvik	40,795	.H	3	
				Hamar	26,952	.G	3	Lillehammer	24,796	.G	3	

Mandal	13,417	.I	2	Sandefjord*	40,079	.H	3	
Molde	23,876	.F	2	Sandnes	54,929	.H	2	
Moss	27,338	.H	3	Sarpsborg*	48,555	.H	3	
Namsos	12,352	.E	3	Skien	49,936	.H	3	
Narvik	18,495	.C	5	Stavanger	109,710	.H	1	
Notodden	12,240	.H	3	Steinkjer	20,483	.E	3	
Odda	7,575	.H	2	Tønsberg*	35,326	.H	3	
Oslo	512,589	.H	3	Tromsø	60,524	.B	5	
Porsgrunn	33,122	.H	3	Trondheim	151,408	.F	3	
Ringerike*	27,912	.H	3	Voss	13,751	.G	2	

*Does not appear on map; key shows general location.
Source: 2002 official estimates.

be members of the parliament.

The Cabinet is responsible for forming government policies. A Cabinet remains in office as long as it has the support of a majority of the parliament. The Cabinet must resign if it loses a vote of confidence in the parliament. If a vote of no confidence or some other government crisis occurs, an alternate Cabinet—usually from a minority party—is appointed to govern during the rest of the parliament's term.

The parliament, Norway's lawmaking body, is called the Storting. It consists of 169 members elected to four-year terms. The people directly elect 150 of the members. The remaining 19 members are chosen from national electoral lists. The Storting consists of one house. But after each election, its members form two sections to discuss and vote on proposed laws. They elect about a fourth of their number to the Lagting. The remaining members make up the Odelsting.

To become law, most bills must first be approved by the Odelsting and then by the Lagting. If the two sections do not agree on a bill, it can be approved by two-thirds of the parliament as a whole. Certain matters, including bills that deal with taxation and spending, are voted on only by the entire parliament.

Courts. Norway's highest court is the Supreme Court of Justice. Five Superior Courts try the most serious cases and hear appeals of decisions made by the county and town courts. Each county and town also has a Conciliation Council, which tries to settle disputes before they go to court. This body consists of three people elected to four-year terms.

Local government. Norway has 19 counties, one of which is the city of Oslo. Each of the counties, except Oslo, has a governor. Norway's cities, towns, and village districts elect councils of varying size to four-year terms. These councils select a chairman, or mayor, who serves two years.

Politics. Norway has several major political parties. The largest is the socialist Labor Party. Members of the Labor Party favor social welfare programs, and they also favor government action to foster economic growth and full employment. The Conservative Party's members support lower taxes and less government control of the economy. The Christian People's Party is a center-right party whose members promote democracy based on a Christian outlook. Norway's other major political parties include the Center Party, the Liberal Party, the Progress Party, and the Socialist Left Party. All Norwegians who are at least 18 years old can vote.

Armed forces. Norway's army, navy, and air force have a total of about 27,000 troops. Norwegian men between the ages of 19 and 44 are required to serve from 12 to 15 months in the armed forces. About 85,000 men and women serve in the Home Guard.

People

Ancestry. The Norwegians are a Scandinavian people, closely related to the Danes and the Swedes. The people of Norway have strong ties with Americans. From the mid-1800's to the early 1900's, more than 750,000 Norwegians migrated to the United States in search of better job opportunities.

The Sami (formerly known as Lapps) are concentrated in far northern Norway (see **Sami**). Several thousand

people of Finnish ancestry also live in that region. In addition, Norway has a large number of immigrants. They include people from the Middle East, Africa, Pakistan, Turkey, the former Yugoslavia, and other European countries.

Language. The Norwegian language has two forms— Bokmål and Nynorsk. They are similar enough for someone who speaks either form to understand a person who speaks the other. Both Bokmål and Nynorsk belong to the Scandinavian group of Germanic languages. Local school boards may select either as the chief form of communication in a school, but all students learn to read both. The Sami also use their own language, which is similar to Finnish.

Bokmål, also called Riksmål, is the major form used in the cities and towns and in most Norwegian schools. Bokmål is a Norwegian form of Danish. It has almost the same vocabulary and spelling as Danish but is pronounced much differently. Bokmål developed during Norway's political union with Denmark, which lasted from 1380 to 1814. During that period, it replaced Old Norse, the early Norwegian language.

Nynorsk, originally called Landsmål, was created during the mid-1800's as a reaction against the Danish influence. Nynorsk was based on the many *dialects* (local forms of speech) that developed in rural areas during Norway's union with Denmark.

Way of life

City life. About 80 percent of Norway's people live in urban areas. But Norway is less urban than Denmark and Sweden, where about 85 percent of the people live in cities. Oslo, Norway's capital and largest city, has about half a million people. Other large cities include Bergen, Drammen, Kristiansand, Stavanger, Tromso, and Trondheim. See the articles on Norwegian cities listed in the *Related articles* at the end of this article.

Norwegian cities sprawl into surrounding suburbs, but they are smaller than most other European cities. They have fewer high-rise commercial buildings and lack the fast pace of life often found in cities of other industrial nations.

Norway's high standard of living and its social welfare system have kept the cities free of slums and substandard housing. Most Norwegians and immigrant workers live in modern apartment buildings in or near the principal urban areas. Wealthier Norwegians often own single-family homes built of wood. A number of Norwegians also own small cottages along the coast or in the mountains, which they visit on weekends or holidays.

Although Norway's cities have bus and train services, traffic congestion is a problem. Norway has little industrial pollution because of its extensive use of hydroelectric power and natural gas in industry. Unemployment is extremely low by international standards. Many of Norway's immigrants work in low-paying jobs in the cities. Their presence has caused discontent among some Norwegians because of the benefits the immigrants get through the social welfare system.

Rural life. About 20 percent of Norway's people live in rural areas. The rural population is concentrated in southeastern Norway, which has gently rolling hills suitable for farming; along the western coast; and in the northern regions. Many people who live in rural areas

Frogner Park in Oslo has about 150 works by Gustav Vigeland, one of Norway's greatest sculptors.

Norwegian fishermen process a catch of fish. The fishing industry provides a livelihood for many rural Norwegians.

fish for a living. Some spend weeks or even months away from home on fishing ships in the North Sea and the North Atlantic Ocean.

Many rural homes are old, wooden farmhouses that have been modernized. Almost all of them have electric stoves, refrigerators, and other appliances.

Norway's numerous fiords, rivers, and mountains prevent many rural Norwegians from traveling easily. However, roads and tunnels built since the late 1900's have helped connect parts of Norway that had been isolated. Snow and ice still make many roads impassable during much of the year. For these reasons, rural people rely heavily on boats and the country's electrified railway system for transportation.

Food and drink. Norwegians usually eat four meals a day, but many farm families have five. Breakfast generally includes cereal and open-faced sandwiches with cheese, jam, herring, marmalade, or sliced meat. Goat cheese is a favorite sandwich spread. Sandwiches are also eaten at lunch and at a late-evening supper. Dinner is usually the only hot meal of the day. It includes soup, meat or fish, potatoes, vegetables, and dessert. People

in the cities and towns eat dinner in the evening. Some people in farm areas have dinner at midday.

Norwegians drink coffee throughout the day and especially at mealtimes. Many Norwegians also enjoy beer, which is sometimes served with a strong, colorless liquor called *aquavit.* Tea, milk, and soft drinks also are popular in Norway.

Recreation. Outdoor sports are an important part of Norwegian life. Recreation areas lie within short distances of all homes. Skiing, Norway's national sport, may have started there thousands of years ago as a means of crossing the snow-covered land. Many Norwegians take cross-country ski trips to the country's mountains or wooded hills. Almost every town has a ski jump. The second most popular winter activity is ice-skating. Norwegians also have long enjoyed *bandy,* a form of hockey played by 11-player teams on large rinks. Soccer is the favorite summer sport.

Norway's forests and mountains provide many other recreational opportunities. On weekends, many Norwegians enjoy hiking through hills and forest areas. Some Norwegians travel to cabins in the mountains, where

Championship ski-jumping at Holmenkollen attracts thousands of spectators each year. Skiing is Norway's national sport.

Edvard Munch's painting *Evening on Karl Johans Gate* expresses a terrifying sense of isolation in the characters on a crowded street in Oslo. Munch was a strong influence on the Expressionist art style of the early 1900's.

they may spend several weeks during the summer vacation season. Many adults also enjoy hunting. Sailing is popular along the coast. In addition, Norway's numerous fiords, lakes, and rivers attract many fishing enthusiasts. Swimming is also a popular activity.

Social welfare. Norway's government provides the people with many welfare services. All people living in Norway who support children younger than 18 are entitled to a child benefit, or family allowance. The government guarantees paid vacation for all employed people. Large families with medium or low incomes pay little or no national taxes, and their local taxes are reduced.

The National Insurance Act, which went into effect in 1967, combined many existing welfare programs. All Norwegians are required to take part in this combined plan. It includes old-age pensions, job retraining, and aid for mothers, orphans, widows, widowers, and people with disabilities. Another insurance plan provides free medical and hospital care, plus cash payments to employees during illness. The costs of these plans are shared by the insured people, their employers, and the national and local governments.

Religion. The Norwegian Constitution establishes the Evangelical Lutheran Church as the nation's official church, but other religions have complete freedom of worship. More than 80 percent of the people are Evangelical Lutherans. The government largely controls the Evangelical Lutheran Church. It appoints the pastors and church officials and pays their salaries.

Other religious groups in Norway include Baptists, Free Lutherans, Methodists, Pentecostals, and Roman Catholics. The Oslo region is home to a large Muslim community.

Education. Almost all people in Norway can read and write. Norwegian law requires children from the age of 6 to 16 to go to school. The elementary school program lasts seven years. It is followed by three years of junior high school and three years of senior high school. Senior high school provides academic courses for those who wish to go on to college and also provides vocational courses.

Ås (near Oslo), Bergen, Oslo, Stavanger, Tromsø, and Trondheim each have a university. Another university has campuses in the counties of Vest-Agder and Aust-Agder in southern Norway. Schools of higher education also include a network of regional colleges, and several technical and other specialized institutions.

The University of Oslo Library is the largest library in Norway. Oslo also has the country's largest city library. All cities and towns are required by law to have free public libraries. These libraries are partly supported by government grants.

Arts. Norwegians have contributed much to the development of the arts. Henrik Ibsen's realistic plays of the late 1800's brought him worldwide fame as the father of modern drama. Three Norwegian writers—Bjørnstjerne Bjørnson, Knut Hamsun, and Sigrid Undset—have won the Nobel Prize in literature.

The painter Edvard Munch was a strong influence on the Expressionist art style of the early 1900's. Statues by Gustav Vigeland, perhaps Norway's greatest sculptor, stand in Oslo's Frogner Park. Edvard Grieg, Norway's best-known composer, used melodies from Norwegian folk songs and dances in his orchestral works. For more

information on Norwegian artists, see the biographies listed in the *Related articles* at the end of this article.

The land

Land regions. Most of Norway is a high, mountainous plateau. Its average height is more than 1,500 feet (457 meters) above sea level. Only about a fifth of Norway, including two major lowlands, lies lower than 500 feet (150 meters). Norway has three main land regions: (1) the Mountainous Plateau, (2) the Southeastern Lowlands, and (3) the Trondheim Lowlands.

The Mountainous Plateau is covered largely by bare rock that was smoothed and rounded by ancient glaciers. Glaciers also formed many lakes and deep valleys, especially in the 4,500-square-mile (11,700-square-kilometer) Hardanger Plateau, Europe's largest highland plain. In Norway's uplands above 6,500 feet (1,980 meters), permanent snow and ice cover about 1,200 square miles (3,110 square kilometers). The 188-square-mile (487-square-kilometer) Jostedalsbreen is the largest glacier in Europe outside Iceland.

In the narrow northern half of Norway, the Kjølen mountain range extends along the border with Sweden. Norway's highest mountains rise in the wider southern half of the country. The Dovre Mountains extend in an east-west direction, and the Long Mountains rise to the south. The Jotunheimen range of the Long Mountains includes Galdhøpiggen, northern Europe's tallest mountain, which rises 8,100 feet (2,469 meters).

The Southeastern Lowlands consist mostly of the middle and lower valleys of the Glåma River, which is 372 miles (598 kilometers) long, and several other rivers. The rivers are used to float timber to pulp mills and sawmills. Their many waterfalls provide hydroelectric energy. The region also has narrow lakes, including Lake Mjøsa. Slopes are gentler than in most of the country, and the region is more suitable for farming and

Ernst A. Weber, Photo Researchers

The Trondheim Lowlands include the lower ends of several wide, flat valleys that are suitable for farming. Crops include barley and potatoes. The region also has much dairy farming.

forestry. These lowlands are the most thickly settled part of Norway. They include Oslo, the capital and chief commercial, industrial, and shipping center.

The Trondheim Lowlands include the lower ends of several wide, flat valleys. In addition to providing good farmland, the valleys also serve as important railroad routes to other parts of Norway and to Sweden.

The lowlands have long been a major region of settlement. Trondheim, founded in A.D. 998, was an important religious center in Norway during the Middle Ages. Today, it is a leading center of industry and trade.

Coast and islands. Many long, narrow inlets of the sea indent the rocky coast of Norway. These inlets, called *fiords,* make the coastline one of the most jagged in the world. The longest, Sogne Fiord, extends inland for 127 miles (204 kilometers). Norway has a coastline of about 1,647 miles (2,650 kilometers). Including all the fiords and peninsulas, the full length of the coast is about 13,267 miles (21,351 kilometers), which is approximately half the distance around the world.

About 150,000 islands lie off the Norwegian coast. Some are only rocky reefs called *skerries,* which shield the coastal waters from stormy seas. The Lofoten and Vesterålen islands are the largest offshore island groups. The waters around them have rich cod fisheries.

The famous Maelstrom current sweeps between the two outermost Lofotens, sometimes forming dangerous whirlpools. Jan Mayen and Svalbard are island possessions of Norway in the Arctic Ocean.

Climate

The climate of Norway is much milder than that of most other regions as far north, especially along the country's west coast. Near the Lofoten Islands, for example, January temperatures average 45 °F (25 °C) higher than the world average for that latitude. Snow that falls along the coast melts almost immediately. The warm North Atlantic Current of the Gulf Stream keeps nearly all the seaports ice-free, even in the Arctic (see **Gulf Stream**).

During winter, Norway's inland regions are colder than the coast because mountains block the warm west winds from the sea. Snow covers the ground at least three months a year. During the summer months, when the sea is cooler than the land, the west winds cool the coast more than the inland. The warmest summers are in the inland valleys of the southeast. Less rain falls inland than along the coast.

The far north, known as the *Land of the Midnight Sun,* has continuous daylight from mid-May through July. The

Physical features

Alta River	A	5
Andøya (island)	B	4
Arnøy (island)	A	4
Barents Island	B	2
Bokna Fiord	F	2
Dovre Mountains	D	3
Edge Island	B	2
Folden Fiord	C	3
Galdhøpiggen (mountain)	E	3
Glåma River	E	3
Hardanger Fiord	E	2
Hardanger Plateau	E	2
Hinlopen Strait	A	1
Hinnøya (island)	B	4
Hitra (island)	D	3
Is Fiord	B	1
Jaekkevarri (mountain)	B	4
Jostedalsbreen (Jostedal Glacier)	E	2
Jotunheimen (mountains)	E	3
Kjølen Mountains	C	4
Kvaløy (island)	A	4
Lågen River	F	3
Lake Femund	E	3
Lake Mjøsa	E	3
Langøya (island)	B	4
Lapland	B	5
Lindesnes (cape)	F	2
Lofoten Islands	B	3
Long Mountains	E	2
Lopp Bay	A	5
Maelstrom (current)	B	3
Namsen River	D	3
Newtontoppen (mountain)	A	1
Nord Fiord	E	2
North Cape	A	5
North East Land	A	2
Olga Strait	B	2
Oslo Fiord	F	3
Otra River	F	2
Porsanger Fiord	A	5
Ringvassøy (island)	A	4
Rolvsøya (island)	A	5
Romsdals Fiord	D	2
Røs Lake	C	4
Senja (island)	B	4
Skagerrak (channel)	F	3
Smøla (island)	D	2
Sogne Fiord	E	2
Sørøya (island)	A	5
Spitsbergen (island)	A	1
Stor Fiord	B	2
Svalbard (islands)	B	2
Svartisen (mountain)	C	4
Trondheim Fiord	D	3
Varanger Fiord	A	6
Vega (island)	C	3
Vesterålen (islands)	B	4
Vest Fiord	B	4

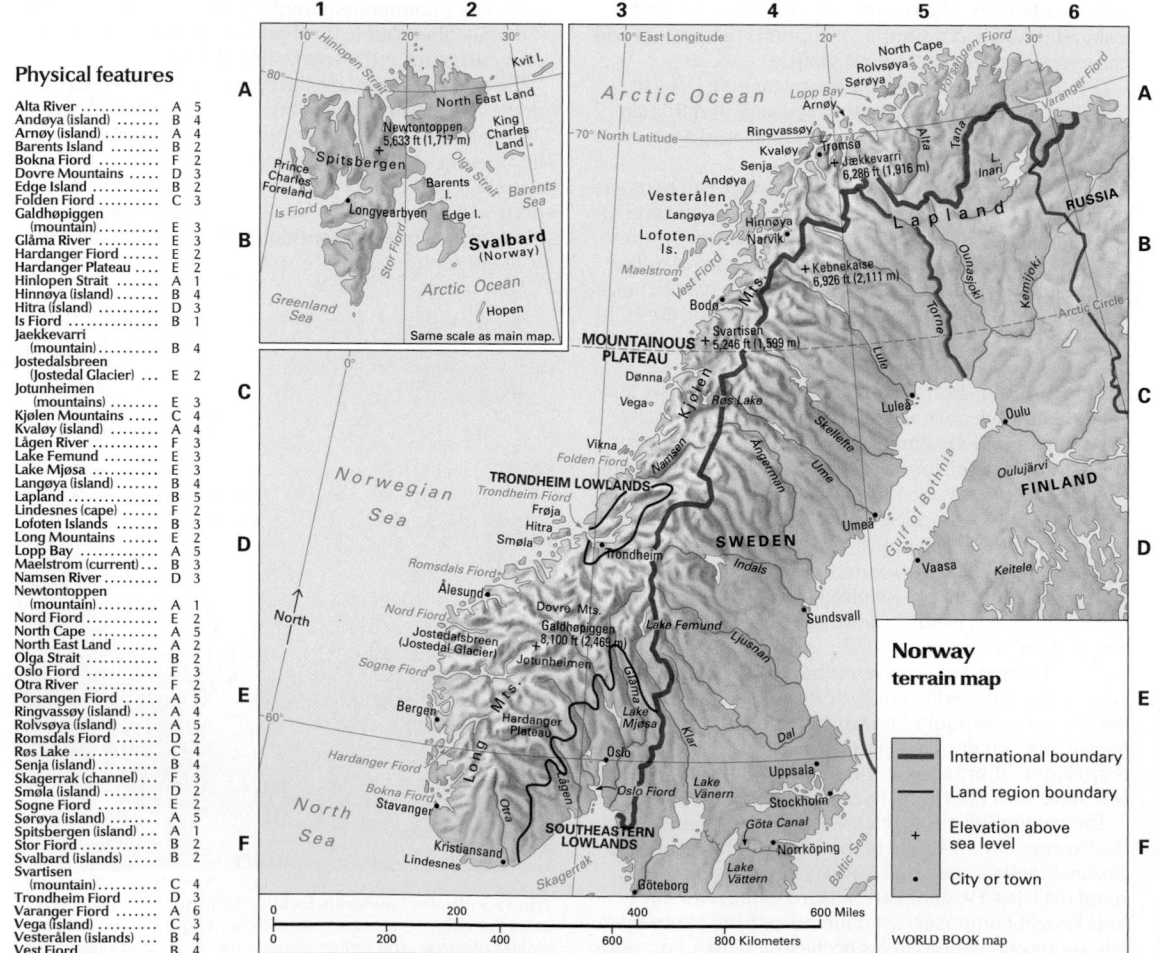

Norway terrain map

——	International boundary
—	Land region boundary
+	Elevation above sea level
•	City or town

0   200   400   600 Miles
0   200   400   600   800 Kilometers

WORLD BOOK map

period of midnight sun decreases southward, and there is no 24-hour sunshine south of the Arctic Circle. In winter, northern Norway has similar periods of continuous darkness. See **Midnight sun.**

Economy

Norway has a well-developed economy, with a low unemployment rate. Norway ranks as one of the leading countries in *gross domestic product* (GDP)—that is, the total value of all goods and services produced within the country in a year—per capita. The GDP per capita can be determined by dividing the total GDP by the nation's population.

Norway's economy is partially free market and partially government controlled. The government controls the petroleum industry and, each year, invests some of the petroleum revenue. Norway plans for these investments to continue to provide some income after the oil reserves are exhausted.

Natural resources. Norway's waters provide its most valuable resources. Important petroleum and natural gas fields lie offshore in the North Sea. The offshore areas and the country's rivers are rich in fish. Norway's many swift mountain rivers are used to produce hydroelectric power.

Norway's land is not rich in natural resources. About 60 percent of the country consists of mountains and plateaus that are covered mostly by bare rock. Only about 3 percent of Norway is farmland. Productive forests cover about 25 percent of the land.

Service industries are those economic activities that provide services instead of producing goods. Service industries account for over half of Norway's total GDP and about three-fourths of the country's employment. Community, government, and personal services is Norway's leading service industry group. This group includes such activities as education, government, and health care. Hotels, restaurants, and shops greatly benefit from the millions of tourists who visit Norway each year. Most of these tourists come from Denmark, Germany, the Netherlands, Spain, Sweden, the United Kingdom, and the United States.

Mining became a major Norwegian economic activity during the 1970's, when the country began producing petroleum and natural gas from North Sea fields. Today, petroleum and natural gas account for a large part of the country's income. Norway ranks as one of the world's leading countries in the production of natural gas. However, since about 2000, Norway's petroleum production has been diminishing.

Iron ore and pyrites, from which copper and sulfur are taken, are also mined in Norway. Other minerals include aluminum, limestone, nickel, titanium, and zinc. Coal is mined only in Svalbard, an island territory north of Norway.

Manufacturing developed much later in Norway than in the major industrial countries. Those countries had their own coal to provide power with which to run machines. In the 1800's, Norway had to import coal for its factories, which made manufacturing costly and held back the country's growth.

By 1900, Norway had started to develop its sources of cheap hydroelectric power. The country's factories turned to hydroelectric power to meet their needs. As a result, manufacturing in Norway expanded rapidly.

Today, manufacturing is one of Norway's most valuable industries. The most important products include petroleum products, such metals as aluminum and magnesium, processed foods, and ships. Norway is an important aluminum-producing country. This metal is processed from imported bauxite. The nation also produces computers and electrical equipment, machinery, and wood pulp and paper.

Agriculture. Farms in Norway lie on narrow strips of land in inland valleys and along the coast. Many Norwegian farmers have a second occupation so they can earn enough to support their families. Farmers own much of Norway's commercial forests, and many are also loggers. Some farmers also fish commercially.

Dairy farming and livestock production account for most of Norway's farm income. Farmers raise beef and

Norway's gross domestic product

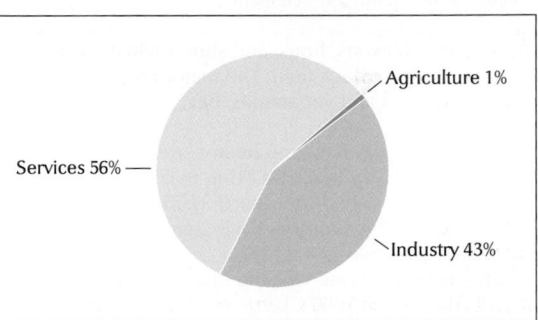

Agriculture 1%

Services 56%

Industry 43%

Norway's gross domestic product (GDP) was $388,232,000,000 in 2007. The GDP is the total value of goods and services produced within a country in a year. *Services* include community, government, and personal services; finance, insurance, real estate, and business services; trade, restaurants, and hotels; and transportation and communication. *Industry* includes construction, manufacturing, mining, and utilities. *Agriculture* includes agriculture, forestry, and fishing.

Production and workers by economic activities

Economic activities	Percent of GDP produced	Employed workers Number of people	Employed workers Percent of total
Mining	25	39,000	2
Community, government, & personal services	20	953,000	39
Finance, insurance, real estate, & business services	18	324,000	13
Trade, restaurants, & hotels	10	425,000	17
Manufacturing	10	277,000	11
Transportation & communication	8	158,000	6
Construction	5	180,000	7
Utilities	2	17,000	1
Agriculture, forestry, & fishing	1	69,000	3
Total*	100	2,442,000	100

Figures are for 2007.
*Figures do not add up to 100 percent due to rounding.
Sources: Statistics Norway; International Labour Organization, International Monetary Fund.

Mittet Foto

Norway possesses rich petroleum and natural gas deposits in the North Sea. Exports of petroleum and natural gas have greatly stimulated Norway's economy.

NTB Foto

Hydroelectric plants, such as the Alta River dam, *shown here,* harness the energy of Norway's many swiftly flowing rivers. The plants provide inexpensive power for homes and industry.

dairy cattle, chickens, hogs, and sheep. Most cropland is used to grow livestock feed. The major crops of Norway are barley, fruits and vegetables, hay, oats, potatoes, and wheat.

Fishing. Norway has long been a great fishing country. Norwegian fishing crews bring in large numbers of blue whiting, cod, haddock, herring, mackerel, and saithe. Most of the country's fishing catch comes from the Norwegian Sea.

Norway's once-great whaling industry declined sharply during the 1960's. Large catches by Norway and other major whaling nations made many kinds of whales increasingly scarce. In 1987, Norway joined an international *moratorium* (temporary halt) on commercial whaling (see **Whale** [The future of whales]). It continued to take some whales for research purposes. In 1993, Norway resumed limited commercial whaling of minke whales, claiming they were no longer in danger.

Forestry has been an important industry in Norway for hundreds of years. Lumber became a major export in the 1500's. Today, much timber is also used to make pulp and paper. The most important commercial trees are pine and spruce. Tens of thousands of miles of forest roads have been built to transport the logs. Timber is also moved by way of rivers. Much of the timber production comes from the southeastern portion of the country.

Energy sources. Since the early 1900's, hydroelectric stations have generated most of the power used in Norway's industry and homes. But since the mid-1970's, the extraction of Norway's rich oil and natural gas deposits in the North Sea has led to more extensive use of petroleum products in industry and transportation. A small amount of energy comes from such solid fuels as coal, peat, and wood.

Foreign trade. Norway depends heavily on foreign trade to help keep its standard of living high. The nation exports much more than it imports. Norway's trade is one of the largest in the world in relation to its population. Norway, with limited natural resources, imports a wide variety of foods and minerals as well as automobiles, chemicals, machinery, and petroleum products.

Petroleum and natural gas rank as Norway's chief exports, and Norway is one of the leading countries in the export of both products. Other exports include chemicals, fish, food products, machinery, metals, transportation equipment, and wood pulp and paper. Norway's large merchant fleet is also an important source of income for the country. The fleet provides shipping services for countries in all parts of the world.

Norway's leading trade partners are Denmark, France, Germany, Sweden, and the United Kingdom. Norway also trades with other European countries, China, Japan, and the United States.

Transportation. Norway's merchant fleet ranks as one of the world's largest. Several hundred vessels link the coastal cities and towns of Norway. Inland, ferries cross many fiords and rivers.

Norway has an extensive road system. Almost all Norwegian households own an automobile. The world's longest highway tunnel, the Lærdal Tunnel, opened in 2000. It extends 15.2 miles (24.5 kilometers) under the Jotunheimen mountain range in southern Norway.

The government owns and operates nearly all the railroads. It also owns part of the Scandinavian Airlines System, which flies throughout the world. Several airlines provide regular service to all parts of Norway. Oslo International Airport, which is about 30 miles (50 kilometers) north of Oslo in Gardermoen, is Norway's busiest airport. Bergen, Stavanger, and Trondheim also have large international airports.

Communication. Norway has dozens of daily newspapers. The most important dailies include the *Aftenposten, Dagbladet,* and *Verdens Gang* of Oslo; the *Bergens Tidende* of Bergen; and *Adresseavisen* of Trondheim. Many of the country's newspapers support the views of one of the major political parties.

The government-owned Norwegian Broadcasting Corporation operates the national radio and television systems. The corporation is mainly funded by license fees on all television sets in the country. In 1992, Norway's first nationally broadcast commercial television station, TV2, began operating. Now there are several commercial television and radio stations.

History

Early days. Almost 11,000 years ago, people lived along the northern and western coasts of what is now Norway. Most of the region was covered by thick ice sheets, which took thousands of years to melt. By 2000 B.C., people had started to settle there permanently. By the time of Christ, Germanic tribes had spread throughout the region, and they continued to arrive for hundreds of years. These tribes formed local and regional communities ruled by chiefs and kings.

The Viking period. Viking sea raiders from the Norwegian communities spread terror through much of western Europe for about 300 years. Beginning with Great Britain and Ireland in A.D. 793, they attacked coastal towns and sailed away with slaves and treasure. The Vikings also sailed to the west and established colonies in the Faroe Islands and other North Atlantic islands. About 870, they explored farther west and colonized Iceland. Erik the Red brought the first group of settlers to Greenland about 985. About 1000, his son Leif Eriksson led what is believed to have been the first voyage of Europeans to the mainland of America. See **Erik the Red; Leif Eriksson; Vikings** (The Norwegian Vikings).

About 900, much of present-day Norway was united under Norway's first king, Harald I (also called Harald Fairhair). He defeated many local chieftains and kings, and others recognized his leadership. King Olav I Tryggvason began the widespread conversion of Norway to Christianity in the 990's. In the early 1000's, Olav II achieved full Norwegian unity and firmly established Christianity. He became recognized as Norway's patron saint soon after his death in 1030.

The Viking period ended around 1100. The church grew in power, foreign trade expanded, and religious and trading centers became important cities. Political confusion and bitter struggles for royal power also developed. Beginning in 1130, many regional leaders claimed the throne. They were defeated in a series of civil wars that lasted until 1240. Peace was restored under Haakon IV. By 1300, Norway's economy was largely controlled by north German merchants. Norwegians had become dependent on them for grain imports. Norway was weakened further in 1349 and 1350, when about half of its people died in an epidemic of plague.

Union with Denmark. Margaret, the wife of King Haakon VI of Norway, was also the daughter of the king of Denmark. After her father died in 1375, she had her young son elected king and she ruled Denmark as regent. Haakon died in 1380, and Margaret became regent of Norway as well. In 1388, during political confusion in Sweden, Swedish noblemen elected her to rule that country, too. In 1397, in the Union of Kalmar, Margaret united Norway, Denmark, and Sweden, with power centered in Denmark. Sweden revolted against Danish rule several times, and broke away from the union in 1523.

Under the Danish-controlled union, Norway grew weaker and Denmark became stronger. In 1536, Denmark declared Norway a Danish province and made Lutheranism the official Norwegian religion. Although Danish law acknowledged Norway as a separate kingdom in 1665, the monarch of Denmark continued to rule Norway.

During the 1500's, Norway exported increasing

Important dates in Norway

c. 870 Norwegian Vikings colonized Iceland.
c. 900 Harald I united Norway.
c. 985 Erik the Red colonized Greenland.
c. 1000 Leif Eriksson sailed to North America.
1349-1350 An epidemic of plague killed about half the people of Norway.
1380 Norway was united with Denmark.
1536 Norway became a Danish province. Lutheranism was made Norway's official religion.
1814 Denmark gave up Norway to Sweden but kept Norway's island colonies.
1884 The cabinet of Norway became responsible to the parliament instead of the king.
1905 Norway became independent.
1940-1945 German troops occupied Norway in World War II.
1945 Norway joined the United Nations.
1949 Norway became a member of the North Atlantic Treaty Organization.
1957 King Haakon VII died and was succeeded by Olav V.
1960 Norway and six other nations formed the European Free Trade Association.
1967 Norway began its greatest welfare program, which combined many established social security plans under the National Insurance Act.
1970's Norway began producing petroleum and natural gas from North Sea fields, greatly stimulating the economy.
1991 King Olav V died and was succeeded by Harald V.

amounts of lumber to the countries of western Europe. As a result, Norway began to develop a great shipping industry during the late 1600's. The industry expanded rapidly throughout the 1700's.

Union with Sweden. In 1807, during the Napoleonic Wars, Denmark sided with France against the United Kingdom. The United Kingdom had been Norway's chief trading partner, but now the British ended the trade. British warships blockaded Norway's trade with other countries, and many Norwegians starved. Norway was cut off from Denmark by the British blockade and began to manage its own affairs. The Norwegians secretly began to trade with the British again.

Denmark was defeated in 1813 by Sweden, an ally of the United Kingdom against France. In 1814, in the Treaty of Kiel, Denmark gave Norway to Sweden. Denmark kept Norway's island colonies—Greenland, Iceland, and the Faroe Islands.

© J. Brun, Mittet Foto

Norwegian Vikings sailed long wooden ships—like this one preserved in an Oslo museum—in raids along the coast of western Europe. They also explored the North Atlantic Ocean.

The National Assembly, Eidsvoll 1814 by Oscar Wergeland.
Storting, Oslo (O. Vaering)

The Constitution of Norway was adopted in 1814 by an elected assembly at Eidsvoll, near Oslo. It has remained in effect since then with only minor changes. This painting of the assembly, presented to the parliament in 1885, hangs in the Storting's main chamber.

The Norwegians did not recognize the Treaty of Kiel. Later in 1814, they elected an assembly to draw up a constitution for an independent Norway. The constitution was adopted on May 17, but Sweden refused to grant Norway independence. Swedish forces attacked Norwegian troops and quickly defeated them. In November 1814, the Norwegian parliament accepted King Charles XIII of Sweden as Norway's ruler as well. Charles promised to respect the Norwegian constitution.

In 1884, after a long political struggle, the parliament won the right to force the cabinet to resign. Until that time the cabinet had been responsible only to the king.

Independence. During the 1890's, Norway's merchant fleet was one of the largest in the world. But the Swedish foreign service handled Norway's shipping affairs in overseas trading centers. Norway demanded its own foreign service, but Sweden refused. In May 1905, the Norwegian parliament passed a law creating a foreign service, but the Swedish king vetoed it. On June 7, the parliament ended the union with Sweden.

Sweden nearly went to war against Norway. However, Sweden recognized Norway's independence in September 1905, after all but 184 Norwegians voted for independence. In November, the people approved a Danish prince as their king. He became Haakon VII.

By the time of independence, Norway had started to develop its many mountain streams to produce hydroelectric power. Its industries expanded rapidly with this cheap power source. Norway's economy increased further during World War I (1914-1918). Norway remained neutral, but its merchant fleet carried much cargo for the Allies. About half its ships were sunk by German submarines and mines.

An economic depression hit Norway following the end of World War I. The nation's economy, dependent on trade and shipping, suffered further during the worldwide depression of the 1930's. Between a fourth and a third of Norway's workers were usually unemployed during this period.

World War II began in 1939, and Norway tried to remain neutral. But on April 9, 1940, Germany invaded Norway by attacking all its main seaports at once. The Norwegians fought bravely for two months, aided by some British, French, and Polish troops. On June 7 of that year, King Haakon VII and the Cabinet fled to London where they formed a government-in-exile. The Germans made Vidkun Quisling, a Norwegian who supported them, premier of Norway. His last name became an international word for *traitor.*

A secret Norwegian resistance army conducted sabotage against the German occupation force. These Norwegians were trained chiefly to join a hoped-for Allied invasion of Norway. Other Norwegians fled their country and trained in Sweden or the United Kingdom for the invasion. Some took part in British commando raids in Norway. After each raid, the Germans shot, tortured, or imprisoned many Norwegians.

Norwegian fighter pilots trained in Canada, and operated from bases in the United Kingdom and Iceland. Norway's merchant fleet carried war supplies for the Allies. The Norwegian navy helped protect Allied shipping, and took part in the invasion of France in 1944.

On May 8, 1945, after Germany fell, the 350,000 German troops in Norway surrendered. Haakon VII returned in triumph on June 7, the 40th anniversary of Norwegian independence. About 10,000 Norwegians died during the war, and about half the merchant fleet was sunk. The far northern counties of Finnmark and Troms lay largely in ruins. See **World War II.**

Postwar developments. After the war, loans from the United States helped Norway rebuild its merchant fleet and industries. By the late 1950's, the Norwegian economy was thriving.

Norway became a charter member of the United Nations in 1945. The next year, Trygve Lie of Norway became the first secretary-general of the UN. In 1949, Norway became a charter member of the North Atlantic Treaty Organization (NATO). But Norway refused to permit NATO bases or nuclear weapons on its territory for fear of angering the Soviet Union, its neighbor on the northeast. (The Soviet Union had been formed under Russia's leadership in 1922, and it existed until 1991.) In 1960, Norway and six other countries formed the European Free Trade Association, an economic union (see **European Free Trade Association**).

In 1957, Haakon VII died. His son became King Olav V of Norway.

Social and economic changes. In 1966, the parliament passed the National Insurance Act. The program combined such social security plans as old-age pensions, job retraining, and aid for mothers, orphans, widows, widowers, and people with disabilities. Norway based much of its expanded social welfare program on the Swedish system, which provided many benefits.

In 1972, Norway signed a preliminary treaty to join the European Community, an economic organization of European nations. In September 1972, Norway's voters rejected the membership treaty. The Norwegian government then reached a more limited agreement with the European Community to eliminate tariffs on most industrial goods.

Norway began producing petroleum and natural gas from North Sea fields during the early 1970's. The extraction and processing of petroleum and gas greatly stimulated economic growth. Norway's petroleum exports help to fund its generous social welfare program.

Political changes. Norway's Labor Party held a majority of seats in the Storting from 1935 to 1981, except for brief periods in the 1960's and 1970's. In 1981, Labor lost its majority, and Norway entered a period of rapidly shifting coalitions and governments.

In 1981, Gro Harlem Brundtland became the first woman to serve as Norway's prime minister. Although her first term lasted less than a year, she held the post again from 1986 to 1989 and from 1990 to 1996.

Until 1990, only a king could serve as monarch of Norway. That year, the Storting amended the Constitution to allow women to inherit the throne. Olav V died in 1991. His son, Prince Harald, succeeded him as King Harald V. In 1993, Norway fostered peace negotiations between Israel and the Palestine Liberation Organization, which led to the Oslo accords.

In the 1990's, the European Community grew into the European Union (EU), an organization that promotes political and economic cooperation among member states. In 1992, the Storting voted in favor of joining the European Economic Area. Membership provided greater access to the common European market, but it also required Norway to follow EU policies. Many Norwegians urged that the country take the next step and join the EU. But in November 1994, Norwegians voted against joining the EU.

Recent developments. In elections in 2005, the Labor Party won more seats than any other party. It joined with the Center and Socialist Left parties to form a government. For the first time since the mid-1980's, the governing coalition held a majority of seats in the Storting.

In 2011, 77 people died in Norway's worst terrorist violence since World War II. A domestic terrorist detonated a bomb in downtown Oslo, killing eight people. The bomber then traveled to nearby Utøya Island, where he shot and killed 69 people at a youth camp. The terrorist,

a right-wing extremist, claimed he wanted to reverse Norway's immigration policies and the spread of Islam.

Terje I. Leiren

Related articles in *World Book* include:

Biographies

Amundsen, Roald	Hamsun, Knut	Lie, Trygve
Asbjørnsen,	Harald I (of	Munch, Edvard
Peter C.	Norway)	Nansen, Fridtjof
Bjerknes, Vilhelm	Harald III (of	Quisling, Vidkun
Erik the Red	Norway)	Undset, Sigrid
Flagstad, Kirsten	Ibsen, Henrik	Wergeland,
Grieg, Edvard	Leif Eriksson	Henrik A.

Cities

Bergen	Trondheim
Oslo	

History

Canute	Vikings
Europe, Council of	World War II
European Union	

Physical features

Arctic	Lapland	Midnight sun
Barents Sea	Maelstrom	Svalbard
Fiord		

Other related articles

Christmas (In Denmark,	Sami
Norway, and Sweden)	Scandinavia
European Free Trade	Skiing
Association	Theater (Scandinavia)

Outline

I. **Government**
    A. National government   D. Politics
    B. Courts   E. Armed forces
    C. Local government
II. **People**
    A. Ancestry
    B. Language
III. **Way of life**
    A. City life   E. Social welfare
    B. Rural life   F. Religion
    C. Food and drink   G. Education
    D. Recreation   H. Arts
IV. **The land**
    A. Land regions
    B. Coast and islands
V. **Climate**
VI. **Economy**
    A. Natural resources   G. Forestry
    B. Service industries   H. Energy sources
    C. Mining   I. Foreign trade
    D. Manufacturing   J. Transportation
    E. Agriculture   K. Communication
    F. Fishing
VII. **History**

Questions

What families are covered by Norway's family allowance program?

Who led what was probably the first voyage of Europeans to the mainland of America?

What makes Norway's cities different from other European cities?

What country dominated Norway from 1380 to 1814?

Who chooses and who appoints the members of Norway's Cabinet?

What role does the Cabinet play in the government?

How did Norway's two official languages develop?

Why is Norway's large merchant fleet helpful to the country's economy?

What are Norway's chief sources of energy?

When and why did mining become an important economic activity in Norway?

What led to Norway's independence from Sweden?

Additional resources

Fodor's Norway. Fodor's Travel, frequently updated.
Heidar, Knut. *Norway.* Westview, 2001.
Kagda, Sakina, and Cooke, Barbara. *Norway.* 2nd ed. Benchmark Bks., 2006. Younger readers.
Morgan, Patti J. *Island Soul: A Memoir of Norway.* 2000. Reprint. Island Soul, 2004.
Norway. Lonely Planet Pubns., frequently updated. Travel guide.
Sjåvik, Jan. *Historical Dictionary of Norway.* Scarecrow, 2008.

Norwegian elkhound is a hunting dog that originated in Norway, probably between 5000 and 4000 B.C. Hunters claim the elkhound can scent an elk 3 miles (5 kilometers) away. The elkhound stalks its prey quietly and holds it at bay until the hunter arrives. It is also used in hunting bear and game birds. The elkhound's coat is thick and gray with black tips. The dog weighs about 50 pounds (23 kilograms).

Critically reviewed by the Norwegian Elkhound Association of America

See also **Dog** (picture: Hounds).

Norwich terrier is a breed of dog that developed in England about 1880. Norwich terriers are alert, quick, sturdy, and instinctively good at hunting mice, rats, and other small animal pests. They make good pets as long as they get plenty of exercise and attention.

Norwich terriers are similar to Norfolk terriers. But the

WORLD BOOK photo by Tom Weigand

The Norwich terrier originated in England.

ears of Norwich terriers stand erect, and those of Norfolk terriers drop forward. The Kennel Club in England recognized the dogs as separate breeds in 1964. The American Kennel Club recognized them as different breeds in 1979. See **Norfolk terrier.**

Norwich terriers may be any shade of red, or black and tan. They have a straight, wiry outer coat and a harsh undercoat. The dogs have short, sturdy legs, and sometimes their tail is *docked* (cut) to 3 to 4 inches (8 to 10 centimeters) in length. Full-grown Norwich terriers stand approximately 10 inches (25 centimeters) high at the shoulder and weigh from 10 to 12 pounds (4.5 to 5.4 kilograms).

Critically reviewed by the Norwich and Norfolk Terrier Club

Nose is the organ used for breathing and smelling. It forms part of the face, just above the mouth. Outwardly, it seems simple, but it is complicated inside.

When we breathe, air enters the nose through two openings called *nostrils.* The nostrils are separated by the *septum,* a thin wall of *cartilage* (tough tissue) and bones. Air passes from the nostrils into two tunnels called the *nasal passages,* which lead back to the upper part of the throat. From the nasal passages, air passes through the pharynx and trachea into the lungs.

Both nasal passages have a lining of soft, moist mucous membrane covered with microscopic, hairlike projections called *cilia.* The cilia move in coordination, passing dust, bacteria, and fluids from the nose to the throat for swallowing. Each nasal passage also has three large, shelflike bones that are called *conchae* or *turbinates.* The top two conchae on each side are actually *processes* (extensions) of the ethmoid bone. The lowest concha on each side is a separate bone. The conchae warm the air before it enters the lungs. These bones also stir up the air so that dust in the air sticks to the mucous membrane of the conchae and does not pass into the lungs.

The perception of smell occurs in the highest part of the nasal cavity, where *olfactory nerve receptors* lie in a

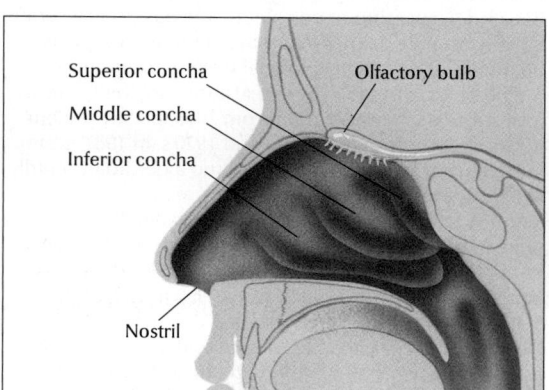

Superior concha
Middle concha
Inferior concha
Olfactory bulb
Nostril

The nose is outwardly simple but inwardly complex. Its interior, *above,* consists of two passages. Each passage contains three shelflike bones called *conchae,* which are covered by mucous membranes. These bones help warm inhaled air. Nerve fibers extending from an *olfactory bulb* at the top of each passage contain odor-detecting *olfactory nerve receptors.* The exterior of the nose, *below left,* consists largely of a connective tissue called *cartilage.* So also does the frontmost part of the *septum,* the wall that separates the nasal passages, *below right.*

WORLD BOOK illustrations by Charles Wellek

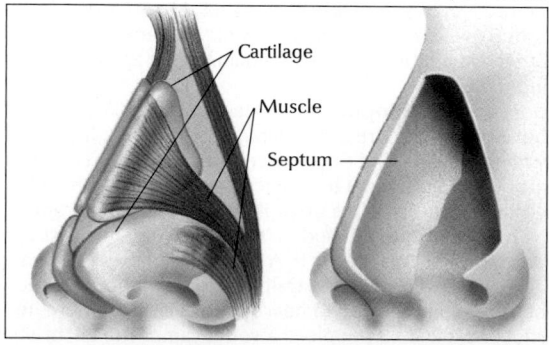

Cartilage
Muscle
Septum

small, flat piece of mucous membrane about the size of a thumbnail. These receptors generate nerve impulses in response to chemicals in the air. *Olfactory nerve fibers* then carry the impulses to a part of the brain called the *olfactory bulb.* One olfactory bulb lies just above each nasal passage. From there, the impulses are carried to other parts of the brain, where they are translated into sensations of odor.

The sense of smell is closely related to the sense of taste. Some experts believe that much of our taste sensations are sensations of odor that we have associated with certain tastes. For example, we really smell coffee, tobacco, wine, apples, and potatoes more than we taste them. If a person is blindfolded and the nose stopped up so that the person cannot smell, the person has great difficulty telling apples from potatoes by taste. Red wine and plain coffee taste almost alike to such a person when they are at the same temperature and consistency.

We cannot smell when we have a cold, because the infection inflames the mucous membrane of the nasal passages and blocks the passage of air to the center of smell. It is important to keep nasal passages clean and to treat any inflammation of the mucous membrane right away. When neglected, colds can lead to more serious ailments, such as bronchitis and pneumonia. Sinuses, which empty into the nose, may also become infected.

Anthony J. Weinhaus

Related articles in *World Book* include:

Adenoids	Mucus	Rhinitis
Cilia	Nosebleed	Sinus
Cold, Common	Respiration (with	Smell (with
Cold sore	diagram)	diagram)

Nosebleed is a discharge of blood from the nose. Most nosebleeds result from minor irritations of the tissue that lines the lower nasal passages. But nosebleeds may also occur as a symptom of a serious illness or as the result of a head or neck injury. The medical term for nosebleed is *epistaxis.*

The nasal passages are lined with a thin, moist tissue called *mucous membrane.* Many small vessels carry blood close to the membrane's surface. If the membrane becomes dry, even slight knocks or scratches can break the blood vessels. This type of nosebleed commonly occurs in the winter, when nasal tissues become irritated by dry, cool air and by colds and influenza.

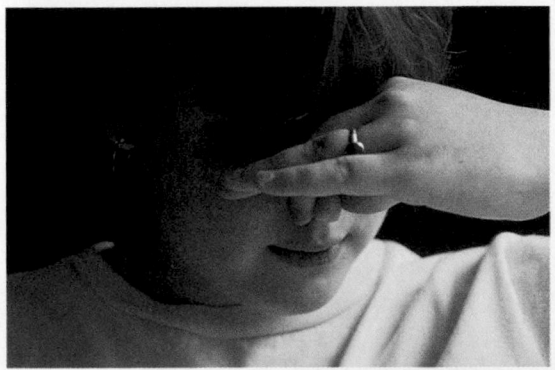

WORLD BOOK photos by Dan Miller

To stop minor nosebleeds, lean forward and pinch your nostrils together for about 10 minutes. If bleeding cannot be controlled, seek medical attention.

Minor nosebleeds frequently result from irritations of the mucous membrane that covers the *nasal septum,* the structure that separates the two nostrils. Some people have a *deviated septum,* which curves into one of the two nostril chambers. A deviated septum lies directly in the path of air entering the nose, and therefore is likely to become dried and to bleed if irritated.

To stop a minor nosebleed, sit down and lean forward with your chin toward your chest. Then, pinch your nostrils together for about 10 minutes, or until the bleeding stops. If the nosebleed does not stop after using these measures, seek medical attention.

Severe nosebleeds may be a symptom of a blood-clotting disorder, leukemia, or the rupture of a large blood vessel at the back of the nose. Heavy bleeding from the nose may be life-threatening and thus requires emergency medical care. If a head or neck injury is suspected, do not move the person. Prevent the head and neck from moving by stabilizing them with your hands. Have someone call for an ambulance immediately.

David D. Caldarelli Critically reviewed by the American Red Cross

Nostradamus, *NAHS truh DAY muhs* (1503-1566), was the Latin name of Michel de Notredame, a French astrologer and physician. His fame rests on his book *Centuries* (1555), a series of prophecies in verse. He won lasting fame in 1559, when King Henry II of France died in a manner predicted in the *Centuries.*

Nostradamus was born on Dec. 14, 1503, in St.-Rémy, in southern France. He earned a doctor's degree in 1532 and became a professor at the University of Montpellier. The success of *Centuries* gained him an appointment as court physician to King Charles IX of France. Nostradamus also became

Bettmann Archive

Nostradamus

an adviser to Catherine de Médicis, wife of King Henry II of France. Nostradamus died on July 2, 1566.

Nostradamus's prophecies are vague and open to interpretation. One prophecy seemed to predict World War II (1939-1945). During that war, the Nazis issued their own versions of Nostradamus's prophecies to convince the German people and their European enemies of the Nazis' ultimate victory.   John Bell Henneman

Nostril. See Nose.

Notary public, *NOH tuhr ee,* is an officer authorized by law to certify certain documents and to take oaths. Many documents, such as deeds, must be notarized before they become legally effective. The purpose of notarizing a document is to protect those who use it from forgeries. The notary signs the document to certify that the individual

The notary public seal is pressed into paper with a small hand stamp.

who signed it appeared in person and swore to the notary that the signature is genuine. The notary records that fact, then stamps a seal on the document.

In most states of the United States, any responsible person can get a commission as a notary public, on payment of a fee. Notaries are usually allowed to charge for their services. In the United Kingdom, notaries must be lawyers or must have had certain legal training.

Jack M. Kress

Notation, *noh TAY shuhn,* is any system of symbols and abbreviations that helps people work with a particular subject. Mathematics uses notation to simplify and consolidate ideas and problems. The Arabic numeral system is a notational device for writing numbers and doing arithmetic. Chemistry, music, physics, and other subjects also have notation systems.   Howard W. Eves

See also **Arabic numerals; Music** (Musical notation); **Scientific notation; Symbol.**

Note is an unconditional written promise to pay a specified sum of money on demand or at a given date to a designated person. The signer of the note is called the *maker.* The one to whom it is made payable is called the *payee.* This written promise is known as a *promissory note.* It is sometimes called a *note of hand.*

Suppose that Arlene Shaw, a retail merchant with a good business and a good financial standing, needs $500 worth of merchandise but does not have the cash to pay for it. She knows that she has accounts coming due within 60 days. She will be able to pay the $500 when she is paid by those who owe her. She goes to Henry Brown, a wholesale merchant, who sells her the goods and takes her note. The note is as follows:

$500   San Francisco
                                              March 1, 2011
Sixty days after date I promise to pay to the order of
Henry Brown $500, with interest at 10 percent. Value received.

                                              Arlene Shaw

Brown can endorse the note and cash it at the bank if he needs the money before 60 days. Shaw will then pay the bank when her note becomes due. Sometimes the maker specifies the actual date of payment in the note.

Liability of the maker. A note is *negotiable* when it is made payable to "bearer" or includes the word "order," like the one given above. When a note has been transferred by endorsement, the person in possession of the note is known as the *holder.* The holder can trans-

G. Marche, FPG

The Cathedral of Notre Dame is a masterpiece of Gothic architecture and one of the most famous buildings in Europe. It stands on a small island in the Seine River in the heart of Paris. The cathedral was built between 1163 and 1250. This picture shows the main entrance.

fer it to another by endorsing it, and so on indefinitely, just as a bank check can be transferred. When the note falls due, the holder looks to the maker for payment. The law protects the holder under almost all conditions, including some kinds of fraud or cheating by the payee.

An endorser is liable in case the maker fails to pay the note when it falls due. The endorser is served with a notice called a *protest.* It is signed by a notary public, and one copy is sent to each endorser if there is more than one (see **Notary public**).

Caution. No one should sign a document without fully understanding what is being signed. A lawyer should examine any document that the maker does not understand. The law holds the maker responsible for his or her signature, except when any part, or all, of the document is proved fraudulent in court, or is proved to have been altered without the maker's knowledge, after it was signed in good faith.   Joanna H. Frodin

See also **Commercial paper; Negotiable instrument.**

Notre Dame, *NOH truh DAHM,* **Cathedral of,** is a famous cathedral in Paris. It stands on the Île de la Cité, a small island in the Seine River, in the center of Paris. The cathedral is dedicated to *Notre Dame,* the French expression for *Our Lady,* the Virgin Mary. The cathedral is one of the finest examples of Gothic architecture.

The cathedral stands on the site of two earlier churches. Construction of the present building occurred between 1163 and 1250. During the French Revolution (1789-1799), Notre Dame was heavily damaged by mobs who regarded the church as a symbol of the hated monarchy. Beginning in 1845, the French architect Eugène Emmanuel Viollet-le-Duc directed extensive restorations of Notre Dame. He was responsible for much of the cathedral's present appearance.

Notre Dame was one of the first buildings to have *flying buttresses* (arched exterior supports). The buttresses strengthen the walls and permit the use of large stained-glass windows that allow light to enter the building. The cathedral's main entrances are elaborately decorated with stone sculptures. A number of other cathedrals are also named Notre Dame, including those in Amiens, Chartres, and Reims, France.   William J. Hennessey

Notre Dame, *NOH tuhr DAYM,* **University of,** is a private, Roman Catholic school in Notre Dame, near South Bend, Indiana. It is governed by two groups, the Fellows of the University and the Board of Trustees. Both groups include priests of the Congregation of Holy Cross—the order that founded the university—and lay people. Students of all faiths may attend the university. Notre Dame was founded in 1842.

The campus. Notre Dame has a large campus with twin lakes and wooded areas. The center of campus is dominated by two architectural landmarks, a church called the Basilica of the Sacred Heart and the golden-domed Main Building. Nearby are the Grotto of Our Lady of Lourdes, a replica of a shrine at Lourdes, France; and the Log Chapel, which is a replica of the first building erected at Notre Dame.

The Theodore M. Hesburgh Library was completed in 1963. Its important collections include the Dante Collection of books from the 1400's and 1500's, the Joyce Sports Research Collection of materials relating to American sports, and several collections of Spanish and Latin American literature and cultural documents.

The university's athletic teams are known as the Fighting Irish. The Fighting Irish football team plays at Notre Dame Stadium. Great football figures, such as Coach Knute Rockne, player George Gipp, and the Four Horsemen of Notre Dame (four players that formed the backfield of Notre Dame's 1924 team), brought the university much fame (see **Rockne, Knute**).

Programs. Notre Dame offers a wide variety of undergraduate, graduate, and professional programs. Its law school was the first law school at a Roman Catholic university in the United States.

The university has awarded the Laetare Medal nearly every year since 1883. The award honors a leading Roman Catholic of the United States for his or her contributions to society.

Notre Dame strongly emphasizes research. It receives millions of dollars in research grants annually. The university conducts research in radiation chemistry at a ra-

University of Notre Dame

The library at the University of Notre Dame is one of the largest university library buildings in the world. The 14-story building was built at a cost of $12 million. The exterior features a mural, 132 feet (40 meters) high, made of about 6,700 granite pieces. The mural depicts Jesus Christ, the apostles, and various scholars.

diation laboratory built by the United States Atomic Energy Commission. The Medieval Institute conducts research in the culture, life, and thought of the Middle Ages, the period from about A.D. 400 through the 1400's. The university also conducts research in a variety of other areas. Notre Dame's website at http://www.nd.edu presents information about the school.

Critically reviewed by the University of Notre Dame

See also Hesburgh, Theodore Martin.

Nottingham, *NAHT ihng uhm* or *NAHT ihng HAM,* is an industrial city in central England. It is the chief city and administrative center of the county of Nottinghamshire. Nottingham lies on the north bank of the River Trent (see **England** [political map]). The district of Nottingham, which includes the city and some surrounding areas, has a population of about 267,000.

An old castle towers above the center of Nottingham. Other landmarks include the University of Nottingham and St. Mary's Church, which is a good example of English church architecture of the 1400's. Sherwood Forest, near Nottingham, was supposedly the home of the legendary English outlaw Robin Hood (see **Robin Hood**).

Nottingham existed by the 800's and became a major center of the wool trade during the Middle Ages, which lasted through the 1400's. During the late 1700's and early 1800's, the city prospered and its population grew because of the hosiery, knitting, and lacemaking industries there. Factories built during the late 1800's and early 1900's manufacture such products as bicycles, cigarettes, and pharmaceutical goods.   G. Malcolm Lewis

Nouakchott, *nwahk SHAHT* (pop. 558,195), is the capital and largest city of Mauritania. It lies in western Mauritania, along the Atlantic Ocean. For location, see **Mauritania** (map).

Government buildings and foreign embassies dominate the center of the city. Nouakchott is overcrowded. Severe droughts during the 1970's and 1980's forced large numbers of rural people to move to the city to obtain food and work. Many of them live in shacks and tents. Nouakchott has some modern housing. Its products include hand-woven woolen carpets and other handicrafts, soft drinks, and chemical products.

Nouakchott was founded in 1957, when France ruled Mauritania. It was established to replace Saint-Louis, Senegal, as the seat of Mauritania's colonial administration. It became the capital when Mauritania gained independence from France in 1960.   Lansiné Kaba

Noun is a part of speech that identifies people, places, objects, actions, qualities, and ideas. The English language has a great variety of nouns. These nouns have been grouped into several classifications, some of which overlap.

Mass nouns and count nouns. Mass nouns identify things that cannot be divided into separate units, such as *fruit* and *soil.* Count nouns identify things that can be divided into units, such as *apple* and *rose.*

Mass nouns and count nouns do not differ completely. Some words may belong to either group. In the sentence *I bought cheese,* for example, *cheese* is a mass noun. But in the sentence *I bought the cheeses, cheese* is a count noun. Count nouns, but not mass nouns, occur in the plural and with articles *(a, an, the).* When what is ordinarily a mass noun is used as a count noun, it generally refers to a specific type, as in *types of cheese.*

Abstract and concrete nouns. Abstract nouns identify ideas and qualities that have no physical existence. *Bravery, effort,* and *knowledge* are abstract nouns. In contrast, concrete nouns identify objects that can be seen, heard, smelled, touched, or tasted. *Airplane, layer cake,* and *skyscraper* are concrete nouns. Some words can be used as either abstract or concrete nouns. *Red* as an abstract noun may specify the quality of redness. As a concrete noun, it may represent the color.

Abstract nouns usually function as mass nouns do. We do not say *She had two knowledges* or *She had the knowledge.* However, when a specific type of knowledge is discussed, it may be treated as a count noun, as in *She has a good knowledge of atomic physics* or *She has the knowledge not to act badly.*

Proper and common nouns. Proper nouns identify particular names or titles and are always capitalized. Examples include *Apollo 11, Beacon Street, Cherokee Park, New Year's Eve,* and *President Lincoln.* Proper nouns are generally used without articles, but there are exceptions, such as *the United States* or names of rivers, such as *the Mississippi River.*

All nouns that are not proper nouns are common nouns. They identify general categories of things, such as *experiment, helper, holiday,* and *river.*

Collective nouns identify groups of persons, animals, or things. Examples include *audience, class, crowd, family, flock, government,* and *team.* A collective noun may be considered singular if the word is used as a unit. In this instance, the noun takes a singular verb. For example, *The cast of the play* was *at its best.* A collective noun is considered plural if the word is used in terms of its parts. The noun then takes a plural verb— *The cast* were applauded *loudly for their performances.*

Nominals are words and phrases that function as nouns. Pronouns are the most common nominals, but other parts of speech may be used as nouns:

Adjective: *The* strongest *was not best.*
Gerund: *Clam* digging *is fun.*
Infinitive: To err *is human.*
Prepositions: *We knew the* ins *and* outs.
Pronoun: He *took a walk.*

Number and case. English nouns may have endings that show *number* and *case.*

Number is the form which indicates that the noun refers to one (singular) or to more than one (plural). Singular nouns indicate one, such as *pear, apple, man,* and *mouse.* Plural forms for these nouns are *pears, apples, men,* and *mice.* Abstract nouns, mass nouns, and proper nouns do not ordinarily have distinct plural forms. In special cases, these may be used as count nouns and take plurals, as in *There are three* Sams *in this room.*

Case is the form that helps show the relation of a noun to other words in a sentence. In some languages, words have many different endings to show relationships. In English, word order, rather than endings, shows relationships. Modern English nouns have only two cases, *common case* and *possessive case.* Boys, man, and Sam are common-case forms. Boys', man's, and Sam's are possessive-case forms.

Gender. In English, nouns are sometimes said to have gender, but this is not regularly shown by endings. An English noun has gender only in the sense that it is referred to by one of three sets of pronouns: *he* or *him,* *she* or *her,* or *it.* For example, *I found Jim and brought* him *home; I found Sally and brought* her *home;* and *I found a book and brought* it *home.*

Nouns for which the corresponding pronoun is *he* or *him* are *masculine* nouns. Nouns for which the corresponding pronoun is *she* or *her* are *feminine* nouns. Nouns for which the corresponding pronoun is *it* are *neuter* nouns. Usually, masculine nouns name males, feminine nouns name females, and neuter nouns name inanimate or sexless things. However, there are some exceptions. Some people refer to ships as *she,* though most authorities prefer *it.* Babies are often referred to as *it,* except where the sex is known. Even when the sex is known, *it* is more common for many animals. In many languages, the relationship between gender and natural sex is not as close as it is in English. For example, learners of German must memorize noun genders.

There is a tendency in modern English to stop using special words for women. Some pairs are still common, such as *actor* and *actress,* but words like *aviatrix* for a female aviator are virtually obsolete.   Susan M. Gass

Related articles in *World Book* include:

Case	Person
Declension	Sentence (Subject and
Inflection	predicate)
Number	

Nova is an explosion that causes a star to become from 10,000 to 100,000 times as bright as the sun. The star may shine this brightly for a week, a month, or longer before fading to its original brightness. A nova hurls huge masses of gas and dust into space. The word *nova* comes from the Latin word for *new.* People once mistook novae for new stars.

Stars that undergo *fast novae* reach maximum brightness several hours after the explosion. They begin to fade after a few days. Stars that undergo *slow novae* take much longer to reach maximum brightness. But they stay extremely bright for months or years before they fade to their original brightness. Fast novae propel gas and dust outward at speeds of several thousand kilometers per second. Slow novae do so about a tenth as fast.

Astronomers believe that novae occur in *close binaries.* A close binary is a double star system in which two stars revolve closely around each other (see **Binary star**). For a nova to occur, one of the stars must be medium-sized, and the other must be a small, extremely dense star called a *white dwarf.* The two stars are so close that the gravitational pull of the white dwarf draws material rich in hydrogen from the larger star. This material collects on the white dwarf and eventually triggers reactions of *nuclear fusion* there. In such reactions, hydrogen nuclei combine to form helium nuclei, and a large amount of energy is released. The reactions quickly become a runaway process, which results in a nova.

During the last 100 years, astronomers have observed some stars that have undergone more than one nova. Astronomers call such explosions *recurrent novae.* All novae may be recurrent, but for some of them the interval between explosions may be hundreds or even thousands of years. This much time may be required for a white dwarf to accumulate enough hydrogen for nuclear fusion to recur. On the other hand, the causes of recurrent and ordinary novae may differ, and ordinary novae may occur only once in a close binary.

Some close binaries undergo small explosions every month or so. These *dwarf novae* do not throw out material during an outburst, and they become only 10 to 100 times as bright as the sun. Their cause is unknown. Other stars undergo explosions called *supernovae,* which are thousands of times as bright as ordinary novae. Some supernovae occur in binaries, while others result from the collapse of extremely massive stars.

Karen Vanlandingham

See also **Supernova; White dwarf.**

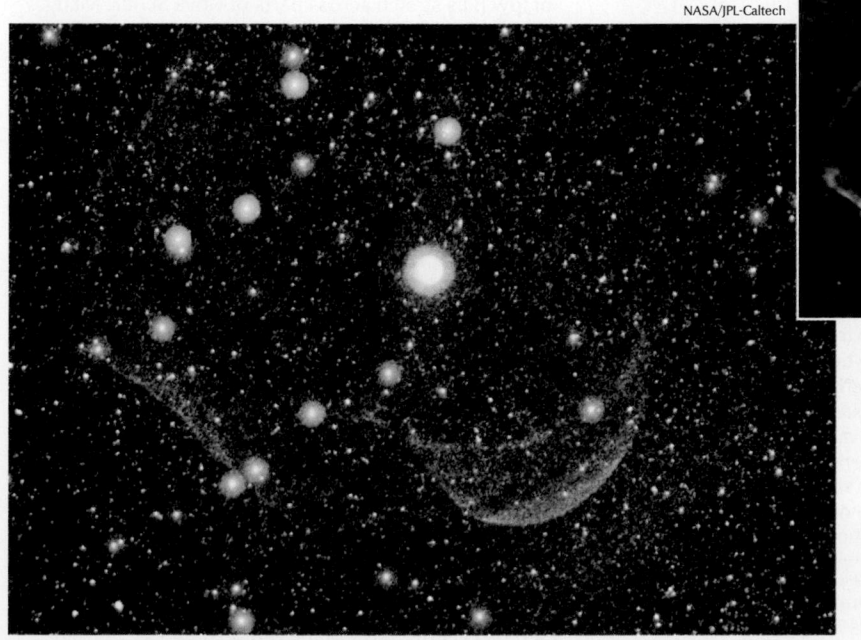

NASA/JPL-Caltech

Novae and dwarf novae, two types of star explosions, both occur in the binary star system Z Camelopardalis. The image at left, taken in ultraviolet light, shows the star system during a dwarf nova. The image above, which has been processed to reduce background clutter, shows a shell of gas expelled by an earlier, nondwarf nova.

Peggy's Cove, on the scenic rocky coast of Nova Scotia

Nova Scotia

Nova Scotia, *NOH vuh SKOH shuh,* is one of the four Atlantic Provinces of Canada. The province includes a peninsula that juts out of the Canadian mainland into the Atlantic Ocean and also Cape Breton Island. Each year, many visitors enjoy the beaches and resorts in Nova Scotia.

No part of Nova Scotia is more than 35 miles (56 kilometers) from the sea. The Atlantic Ocean, the Gulf of St. Lawrence, and the Bay of Fundy surround almost the entire province. Only a narrow strip of land—the Isthmus of Chignecto—joins the peninsula to the Canadian mainland. Ocean tides can rise extremely high in parts of Nova Scotia. Sometimes the tide rises more than 50 feet (15 meters) at the head of the Bay of Fundy. Sable Island, which is formed entirely of sand, lies about 100 miles (160 kilometers) offshore toward the southeast. Sailors call Sable Island the *Graveyard of the Atlantic* because it has been the scene of many shipwrecks.

The sea keeps the climate of Nova Scotia from becoming either extremely hot or extremely cold. Thick

The contributors of this article are A. J. B. Johnston, a historian with Parks Canada in Halifax, Nova Scotia, and Hugh Millward, Professor of Geography at St. Mary's University.

forests cover much of the province. In the north, ranges of low hills stretch across parts of Nova Scotia. Many rivers, some freshwater and some seawater, reach inland. The Annapolis Valley, famous for its apple orchards, produces a range of crops.

White-tailed deer roam the wilderness areas. Many kinds of sea birds nest along the shore and on offshore islands. Lobsters, scallops, and other seafood caught off Nova Scotia help make the province one of the leaders in the Canadian fishing industry.

Service industries are the leading economic activity in Nova Scotia. These industries include education, government, and hotels and restaurants. Manufacturing is also important to the economy. The leading manufactured products include food products, paper products, plastic and rubber products, and transportation equipment. Nova Scotia leads Canada in mining gypsum.

People have lived in the Nova Scotia region for about 10,000 years. *Aboriginal* (native) people inhabited the area when European explorers arrived in the late 1400's or early 1500's. The first French settlement in Nova Scotia was on Sable Island in 1598. Scottish settlers first came to Nova Scotia in 1629. In 1713, Britain (now also called the United Kingdom) gained control of mainland Nova Scotia through a treaty with France. The Latin words *Nova Scotia* mean *New Scotland,* the name a Scottish charter gave to the region.

Interesting facts about Nova Scotia

WORLD BOOK illustrations by Kevin Chadwick

First airplane flight

The first airplane flight in Canada was made on Feb. 23, 1909, over Bras d'Or Lake near Baddeck Bay. J. A. D. McCurdy flew the *Silver Dart,* which was designed and built by the Aerial Experiment Association under Alexander Graham Bell. It flew 10 to 30 feet (3 to 9 meters) off the ground at a speed of 40 miles (65 kilometers) per hour for a distance of half a mile (0.8 kilometer). The flight was the first by a British subject in the British Empire.

Steamship mail service

The first regular mail service by steamship between the United Kingdom, Canada, and the United States was established by Sir Samuel Cunard of Halifax. The paddle steamer *Britannia* began the mail service by crossing from Liverpool to Halifax to Boston in 14 days 8 hours in July 1840.

The first newspaper in Canada was the *Halifax Gazette.* John Bushnell published the first issue on March 23, 1752.

© age fotostock/SuperStock

Halifax, a busy seaport, is the capital of Nova Scotia. Its harbor, *shown here,* is one of the largest in the world. Most of Halifax lies on a peninsula between the harbor and an inlet of the Atlantic Ocean called the North West Arm.

The American poet Henry Wadsworth Longfellow made Nova Scotia famous in his poem *Evangeline* (1847). The poem describes how British troops drove French colonists, called Acadians, from their homes. The poem nicknamed the Annapolis Valley *Land of Evangeline.*

Beginning in 1749, settlers from Britain, Germany, and New England began coming to Nova Scotia in increasing numbers. During and after the American Revolution (1775-1783), many people who remained loyal to Britain fled from the United States to Nova Scotia. The settlers included many enslaved and free people of African descent. By the 1820's, Nova Scotians had acquired the nickname "bluenosers," which probably came from locally grown blue potatoes. Today, Nova Scotians still call themselves "Bluenosers."

Nova Scotia—along with New Brunswick, Ontario, and Quebec—was one of the four original Canadian provinces. These four formed the Dominion of Canada in 1867. For the relationship of Nova Scotia to other provinces, see **Atlantic Provinces; Canada; Canada, Government of; Canada, History of.**

Outline

I. **People**
   A. Population
   B. Schools
   C. Libraries
   D. Museums
II. **Visitor's guide**
III. **Land and climate**
   A. Land regions
   B. Coastline
   C. Rivers and lakes
   D. Plant and animal life
   E. Climate
IV. **Economy**
   A. Natural resources
   B. Service industries
   C. Manufacturing
   D. Fishing
   E. Mining
   F. Agriculture
   G. Forestry
   H. Electric power and utilities
   I. Transportation
   J. Communication
V. **Government**
   A. Lieutenant governor
   B. Premier
   C. House of Assembly
   D. Courts
   E. Local government
   F. Revenue
   G. Politics
VI. **History**

Nova Scotia in brief

Symbols of Nova Scotia

The provincial flag and coat of arms, adopted in their present form in 1929, bear a blue cross of St. Andrew on a white background and the arms of Scotland. The American Indian on the coat of arms represents Nova Scotia's original inhabitants, and a royal unicorn symbolizes Scotland. Under their feet, Scottish thistle is entwined with the mayflower, Nova Scotia's floral emblem.

Provincial flag

Provincial coat of arms

Nova Scotia (brown) ranks ninth in size among all the provinces and third among the Atlantic Provinces (yellow).

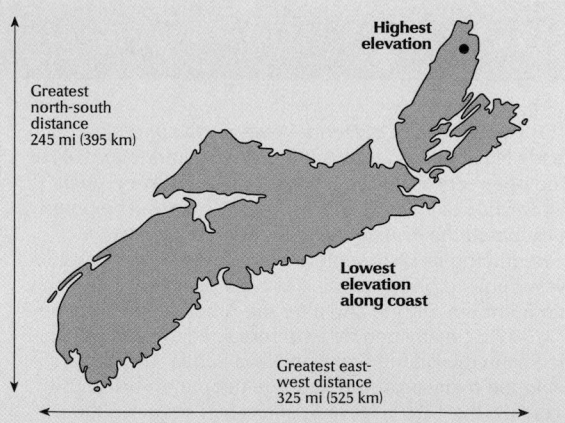

Province House is in Halifax, the capital of Nova Scotia since 1749. Annapolis Royal served as the region's capital from 1710 to 1749.

General information

Entered the Dominion: July 1, 1867; one of the original four provinces.
Provincial abbreviation: NS (postal).
Provincial motto: *Munit Haec et Altera Vincit* (One Defends and the Other Conquers).

Land and climate

Area: 21,423 mi² (55,490 km²), including 1,023 mi² (2,650 km²) of inland water.
Elevation: *Highest*—1,747 ft (532 m) above sea level in Cape Breton Highlands National Park. *Lowest*—sea level.
Coastline: 4,709 mi (7,579 km).
Record high temperature: 101 °F (38 °C) at Collegeville, near Antigonish, on Aug. 19, 1935.
Record low temperature: –42 °F (–41 °C) at Upper Stewiacke on Jan. 31, 1920.
Average July temperature: 64 °F (18 °C).
Average January temperature: 23 °F (–5 °C).
Average yearly precipitation: 53 in (134 cm).

Highest elevation

Greatest north-south distance 245 mi (395 km)

Lowest elevation along coast

Greatest east-west distance 325 mi (525 km)

Important dates

Pierre du Gua, Sieur de Monts, founded Port-Royal.

Troops from Britain and New England began removing Acadians from Nova Scotia, Île Saint-Jean, and Île Royale.

| 1497-1524 | 1605 | 1713 | 1755 |

European explorers reached Nova Scotia while seeking a sea route to Asia.

France gave Britain the mainland of Nova Scotia under the Peace of Utrecht.

Bird
Osprey

Tree
Red spruce

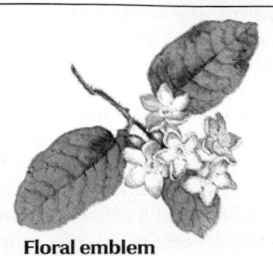

Floral emblem
Mayflower

People

Population: 913,462 (2006 census)
Rank among the provinces: 7th
Density: 43 persons per mi² (16 per km²), provinces average 13 per mi² (5 per km²)
Distribution: 55 percent urban, 45 percent rural
Largest cities and towns*

Halifax†	372,679
Cape Breton†	102,250
Truro	11,765
Queens†	11,177
Amherst	9,505
New Glasgow	9,455

*2006 census. †Regional municipality.
Source: Statistics Canada.

Population trend

Millions

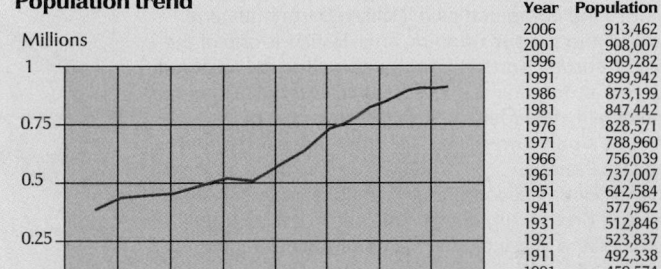

Year	Population
2006	913,462
2001	908,007
1996	909,282
1991	899,942
1986	873,199
1981	847,442
1976	828,571
1971	788,960
1966	756,039
1961	737,007
1951	642,584
1941	577,962
1931	512,846
1921	523,837
1911	492,338
1901	459,574
1891	450,396
1881	440,572
1871	387,800

Source: Statistics Canada.

Economy

Chief products

Agriculture: beef and dairy cattle, blueberries, chickens and eggs.
Fishing industry: cod, crab, haddock, herring, lobster, scallops, shrimp.
Manufacturing: paper products, plastic and rubber products, processed foods, transportation equipment, wood products.
Mining: gypsum, natural gas, petroleum, stone.

Gross domestic product

Value of goods and services produced in 2008: $34,209,000,000.*
Services include community, business, and personal services; finance; government; trade; and transportation and communication. *Industry* includes construction, manufacturing, mining, and utilities. *Agriculture* includes agriculture, fishing, and forestry.

*Canadian dollars.
Source: Statistics Canada.

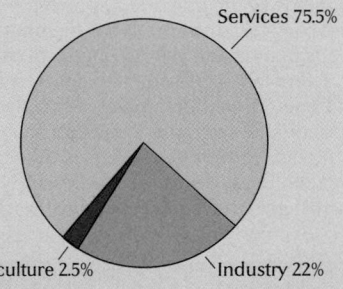

Services 75.5%
Agriculture 2.5%
Industry 22%

Government

Provincial government

Premier: term of up to 5 years
Members of the House of Assembly: 52; terms of up to 5 years

Federal government

Members of the House of Commons: 11
Members of the Senate: 10

Sources of information

Nova Scotia's official Web site at http://www.gov.ns.ca provides a gateway to much information on the province's government, history, and economy.

In addition, the Web site at http://novascotia.com provides information about tourism.

Nova Scotia joined with New Brunswick, Ontario, and Quebec in forming the Dominion of Canada.

The New Democratic Party won a provincial election for the first time in Nova Scotia's history.

1763   **1867**   **1955**   **2009**

Under the Peace of Paris, France officially gave Cape Breton Island and St. John's Island to Britain.

The Canso Causeway was opened, linking the Nova Scotia mainland with Cape Breton Island.

People

Population. The 2006 Canadian census reported that Nova Scotia had 913,462 people. The province's population had increased by less than 1 percent since the 2001 census, which reported a total of 908,007.

A majority of Nova Scotians have ancestors who originally came from the United Kingdom and Ireland. Significant numbers of others are of French, German, Dutch, African, and Mi'kmaq ancestry. A small number of people in Cape Breton still speak the Gaelic language of their Scottish ancestors. A larger number of Acadians and Mi'kmaq in Nova Scotia still speak French and the Mi'kmaq language, respectively.

Halifax is the capital of Nova Scotia and by far the largest of the province's three regional municipalities. It includes the communities of Halifax, Dartmouth, and Bedford and the surrounding area. Halifax is one of the most important ports in Canada, as well as the chief railway and air terminal in Nova Scotia. The Halifax Regional Municipality includes the population center of the province's only Census Metropolitan Area as defined by Statistics Canada.

Nova Scotia's second largest regional municipality is the Cape Breton Regional Municipality. It is on Cape Breton Island and includes the communities of Sydney and Glace Bay.

Schools. Public schools in Nova Scotia operate under the provincial Education Act. Nova Scotia's first Education Act was passed in 1766. The provincial Department of Education supervises the public school system. Locally elected school boards control local schools. Each board may include one appointed member of Mi'kmaq descent and one appointed member of African Nova Scotian descent. School boards do not have taxing powers. Provincial and municipal governments fund the schools. The federal government also provides funding for certain programs. Provincial law requires children to attend school from age 5 to 16. Alternatives to public education include private schools and home schooling, which are both subject to provincial standards.

Population density

Most of Nova Scotia's people live near the coast. Most of the interior is uninhabited or thinly settled. Halifax is the province's capital and largest regional municipality.

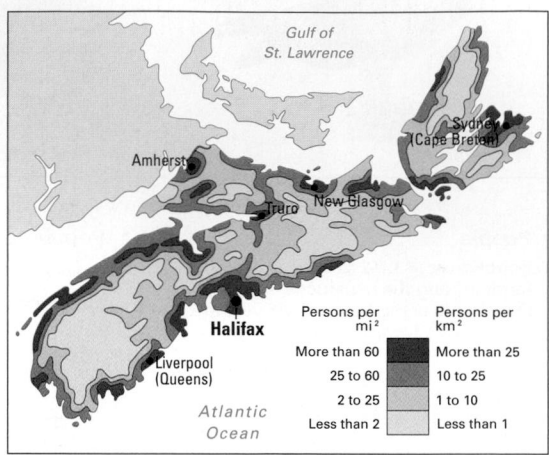

WORLD BOOK map; based on the *National Atlas of Canada.*

Libraries. Nova Scotia has nine regional library systems and a number of college and university libraries. The Nova Scotia Provincial Library is in Halifax.

Museums. The Nova Scotia Museum is a group of more than 25 museums and historic sites throughout the province. These museums and sites include the Maritime Museum of the Atlantic and the Museum of Natural History in Halifax; the Fisheries Museum of the Atlantic in Lunenburg; and Sherbrooke Village, a restored town of the 1800's, in Sherbrooke. Many of Nova Scotia's Mi'kmaq communities have museums or cultural centers. The Black Cultural Centre for Nova Scotia in Dartmouth deals with the history of African Nova Scotians. Other museums include the Army Museum at the Halifax Citadel National Historic Site, a military fort of the 1800's; and the Alexander Graham Bell National Historic Site in Baddeck.

© age fotostock/SuperStock

Dalhousie University, founded in 1818, is one of Canada's leading research and teaching universities. The Arts and Administration Building, *shown here,* stands in the center of the campus.

Universities and colleges

Nova Scotia has 10 degree-granting universities and colleges that are members of the Association of Universities and Colleges of Canada.

Name	Mailing address
Acadia University	Wolfville
Cape Breton University	Sydney
Dalhousie University	Halifax
King's College, University of	Halifax
Mount St. Vincent University	Halifax
Nova Scotia Agricultural College	Truro
NSCAD University	Halifax
St. Francis Xavier University	Antigonish
St. Mary's University	Halifax
Ste. Anne University	Church Point

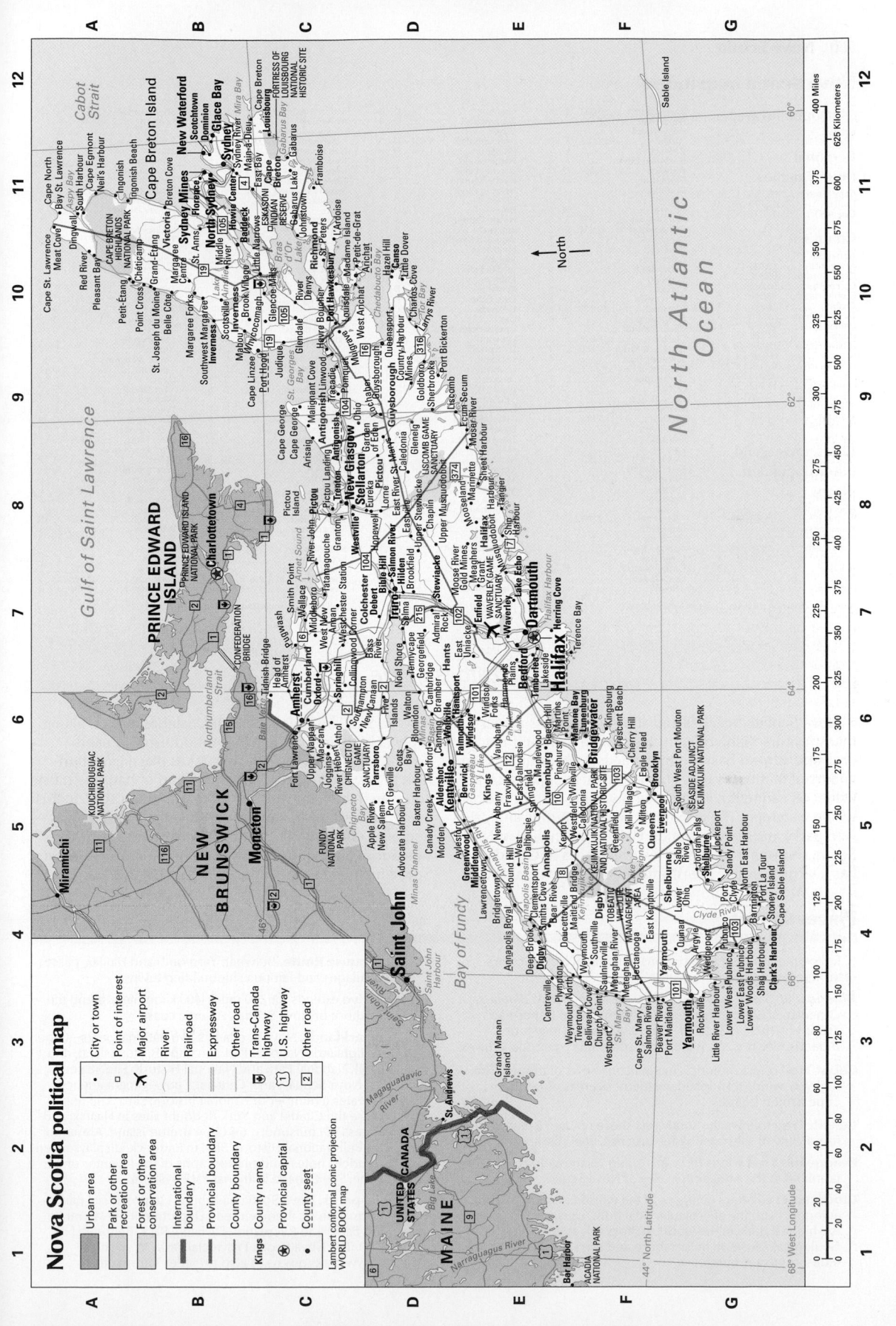

Nova Scotia political map

Urban area	
Park or other recreation area	
Forest or other conservation area	

•	City or town
▫	Point of interest
✈	Major airport
~	River
	Railroad
	Expressway
	Other road
	Trans-Canada highway
Kings	County name
⊛	Provincial capital
•	County seat

	International boundary
	Provincial boundary
	County boundary
◈	U.S. highway
⬭	Other road

Lambert conformal conic projection
WORLD BOOK map

Gulf of Saint Lawrence

Cabot Strait

PRINCE EDWARD ISLAND

Charlottetown

PRINCE EDWARD ISLAND NATIONAL PARK

CONFEDERATION BRIDGE

NEW BRUNSWICK

Miramichi

KOUCHIBOUGUAC NATIONAL PARK

Moncton

Saint John

Saint John Harbour

St. Andrews

Grand Manan Island

MAINE

UNITED STATES

CANADA

Bar Harbor

ACADIA NATIONAL PARK

Narraguagus River

Magaguadavic River

Bay Breze
Northumberland Strait

Turkish Bridge

Head of Amherst

Amherst

Fort Lawrence

Upper Nappan

Maccan

Joggins

River Hébert

Athol

CHIGNECTO GAME SANCTUARY

Parrsboro

Port Greville

Apple River

New Salem

Advocate Harbour

Baxter Harbour

FUNDY NATIONAL PARK

Cumberland

Oxford

Springhill

Collingwood Corner

Southampton

Five Islands

Bass River

Economy

West New Annan

Westchester Station

Wallace

Pugwash

Tatamagouche

River John

Smith Point

Pictou Island

Pictou

Pictou

Scotsburn

Granton

Trenton

New Glasgow

Stellarton

Eureka

Hopewell

East River St. Mary

Caledonia

Garden of Eden

Glenelg

Sherbrooke

Goldboro

Port Bickerton

Liscomb

LISCOMB GAME SANCTUARY

Ecum Secum

Moser River

Sheet Harbour

Tangier

Mooseland

Marinette

Upper Musquodoboit

Middle Musquodoboit

Upper Stewiacke

Chaplin

Ohio

Antigonish Landing

Antigonish

Tracadie

Linwood

Malignant Cove

Arisaig

Cape George

Cape George

Larrys River

Port Bickerton

Charlos Cove

Little Dover

Hazel Hill

Canso

Queensport

Country Harbour

Guysborough

Lochaber

PICTOU

COLCHESTER

Truro

Hilden

Bible Hill

Brookfield

Salmon River

Debert

Brentwood

Stewiacke

Maitland

Noel Shore

Kennetcook

Cambridge

Brooklyn

Hants Border

Windsor Forks

Windsor

Falmouth

Hantsport

Avonport

Grand Pré

Wolfville

Canning

Canard

Blomidon

Medford

Aldershot

Kentville

Berwick

KINGS

New Minas

Waterville

Kingston

Greenwood

Middleton

Lawrencetown

Round Hill

Annapolis Royal

Granville Ferry

Clementsport

Bear River

Deep Brook

Smiths Cove

Digby

Weymouth

Plympton

Centreville

Weymouth North

Tiverton

Bellivue Cove

Church Point

Westport

Salmon River

Port Maitland

Yarmouth

Argyle

Rockville

Wedgeport

Lower East Pubnico

Lower West Pubnico

Pubnico

Shag Harbour

Clark's Harbour

Barrington

North East Harbour

Lower Woods Harbour

Cape Sable Island

Stoney Island

Port La Tour

Sandy Point

Port Clyde

Clyde River

Ohio

Lower Sable River

Sable River

Jordan Falls

Lockeport

Shelburne

Sable River

Liverpool

Brooklyn

Eagle Head

Western Head

Mill Village

Port Mouton

South West Port Mouton

SEASIDE ADJUNCT KEJIMKUJIK NATIONAL PARK

KEJIMKUJIK NATIONAL PARK AND NATIONAL HISTORIC SITE

Greenfield

Caledonia

Maitland Bridge

Kempt

East Kemptville

TOBEATIC WILDLIFE MANAGEMENT AREA

Meteghan River

Meteghan

Saulnierville

Southville

Dalhousie

Doucetteville

QUEENS

SHELBURNE

Crescent Beach

Kingsburg

Lunenburg

LUNENBURG

Bridgewater

Mahone Bay

Martins River

Pinehurst

Maplewood

New Germany

New Albany

Springfield

Vaughan

Newport

Mount Uniacke

Enfield

WAVERLEY GAME SANCTUARY

Waverley

Dartmouth

Bedford

Timberlea

Lakeside

Halifax

Herring Cove

Terence Bay

Halifax Harbour

Prospect

Lake Echo

Ship Harbour

Musquodoboit Harbour

Meaghers Grant

Gold Mines

East Uniacke

Beech Hill

Chester

HALIFAX

East

Admiral Rock

Georgefield

Cherry Hill

Bay of Fundy

Minas Channel

Minas Basin

Chignecto Bay

Cobequid Bay

St. Marys Bay

Mira Bay

Aspy Bay

Bras d'Or Lake

St. Georges Bay

Chedabucto Bay

Northumberland Strait

Cape Breton Island

New Waterford

Scotchtown

Dominion

Glace Bay

Sydney Mines

North Sydney

Sydney

Florence

Howie Center

Louisbourg

FORTRESS OF LOUISBOURG NATIONAL HISTORIC SITE

Cape Breton

Gabarus

Framboise

Main-à-Dieu

Sydney River

St. Anns

Victoria

Inverness

Baddeck

Middle River

Little Narrows

ESKASONI INDIAN RESERVE

Grand Etang

Chéticamp

CAPE BRETON HIGHLANDS NATIONAL PARK

Belle Côte

St. Joseph du Moine

Point Cross

Petit-Étang

Margaree Forks

Southwest Margaree

Margaree Centre

Mabou

Glencoe Mills

Scotsville

Brook Village

Whycocomagh

West Bay

Orangedale

Iona

River Denys

Judique

Port Hood

Cape Linzee

L'Ardoise

St. Peters

Petit-de-Grat

Arichat

Madame Island

Richmond

Port Hawkesbury

Mulgrave

Havre Boucher

Auld's Cove

ANTIGONISH

GUYSBOROUGH

Cape North

Meat Cove

Bay St. Lawrence

Cape St. Lawrence

Dingwall

South Harbour

Pleasant Bay

Red River

Neil's Harbour

Ingonish

Ingonish Beach

North Atlantic Ocean

Sable Island

North

DIGBY

ANNAPOLIS

YARMOUTH

HANTS

Bridgetown

Middleton

Aylesford

Morden

Canady Creek

Margaretsville

Fraxville

West Dalhousie

Nova Scotia map index

Visitor's guide

Nova Scotia's beaches and shoreline resorts attract many visitors. Fishing enthusiasts catch haddock, mackerel, and striped bass along the coast, and salmon, shad, and trout in the streams. Visitors can also enjoy such activities as canoeing, sailing, sea kayaking, hiking, and whale watching. The province has many public and private parks and campgrounds. Halifax, the capital of Nova Scotia and one of the most historic places in Canada, has a large number of historic buildings. See **Halifax.**

Nova Scotians enjoy festivities celebrating the many aspects of their heritage. The Antigonish Highland Games is a Scottish festival that takes place in Antigonish in July. Visitors listen to the sound of bagpipe music and watch the Scottish sport of tossing the caber. In this event, contestants throw a *caber* (heavy wooden pole) end over end as far as they can. Halifax hosts many festivals during the summer and fall. Winter sports in Nova Scotia include curling, hockey, skating, and skiing.

Places to visit

Following are brief descriptions of some of Nova Scotia's many interesting places to visit:

Bluenose II, based in Halifax Harbour, is a replica of *Bluenose,* a Canadian schooner that won the International Fisherman's Trophy in 1921, 1922, 1931, and 1938. Visitors may tour *Bluenose II* when it is in port and sometimes may take cruises.

Cabot Trail offers motorists magnificent views of the sea. This highway winds through the wilderness areas of northern Cape Breton Island.

Ceilidh Trail follows the southwest shore of Cape Breton. It offers a view of saltwater bluffs, beaches, and hills and valleys.

Evangeline Trail winds through fishing villages and rolling farmland in the Annapolis Valley of Nova Scotia.

Glooscap Trail offers glimpses of the world-famous fossil cliffs at Joggins and the spectacular tidal bore, caused by some of the highest tides in the world. Visitors can stop at the Fundy Geological Museum in Parrsboro and see some of Canada's oldest dinosaur bones.

The Lighthouse Route, between Yarmouth and Halifax, passes fishing villages and famous shipbuilding towns.

Marine Drive extends for 250 miles (400 kilometers) along the eastern shore of Nova Scotia's Atlantic coast.

National parklands. Nova Scotia has two national parks—Cape Breton Highlands National Park, on Cape Breton Island, and Kejimkujik National Park and National Historic Site, in southwestern Nova Scotia. Parks Canada, a government agency, also operates a number of national historic sites. The best known are the Citadel and York Redoubt sites in Halifax, and the Fortress of Louisbourg on Cape Breton Island. Alexander Graham Bell National Historic Site, in Baddeck, displays inventions, models, notes, and photographs of the inventor of the telephone. See **Canada** (National Park System).

Provincial parks. Nova Scotia has about 120 provincial parks. For information on them, write to Department of Natural Resources, Parks and Recreation Division, RR 1, Belmont, NS B0M 1C0. The Nova Scotia Provincial Parks Web site at http://www.parks.gov.ns.ca also provides information.

© Peter Gridley, FPG

View from winding Cabot Trail on Cape Breton Island

© Parks Canada

Kejimkujik National Park and National Historic Site

© Radius Images/Alamy Images

Cape Split, in the Bay of Fundy

Nova Scotia Department of Tourism, Culture and Heritage

Old Town Lunenburg, established in 1753

Land regions. Nova Scotia has three main land regions. They are (1) the Atlantic Plateau, (2) the Northern Highlands, and (3) the Lowlands.

The Atlantic Plateau rises gradually from sea level on the Atlantic coast to about 700 feet (220 meters) inland. Hard rocks from 400 million to 500 million years old lie beneath the surface of the region. These rocks were worn down to sea level to form a plain. About 70 million years ago, the plain uplifted slightly and tilted so that it sloped to the southeast. In the last ice age, which ended about 11,500 years ago, glaciers removed most of the topsoil, exposing bedrock in many places. The action of glaciers also created many lakes and bogs. Today, forests cover the Atlantic Plateau, and the land is unsuitable for farming.

The Northern Highlands consist of masses of harder rocks that are generally over 400 million years old. These rocks form the rugged slopes of the Cobequid Mountains, the Pictou-Antigonish Highlands, and the Cape Breton Highlands. The highest point in Nova Scotia rises to 1,747 feet (532 meters) above sea level in Cape Breton Highlands National Park.

The Lowlands lie mainly in central and northern Nova Scotia. Soft rocks about 200 million to 350 million years old lie beneath the surface of the region. They have worn down more rapidly than the harder rocks in the hills and plateaus of Nova Scotia's other regions.

The Lowlands are gently rolling plains. They have Nova Scotia's finest soils and mineral deposits. The rich farmland of the Annapolis Valley is south of North Mountain, which rises along the Bay of Fundy. Fertile marshlands, protected by dikes, lie at the head of the Bay of Fundy, along the inlets called Chignecto Bay and Minas Basin. These marshlands also extend far inland along many rivers. Beneath the Lowlands are rich deposits of coal and gypsum. There are also deposits of limestone, quartz, rock salt, sandstone, and shale.

Coastline of Nova Scotia measures 4,709 miles (7,579 kilometers). This includes 2,517 miles (4,051 kilometers) of mainland, 1,170 miles (1,883 kilometers) of major islands, and 1,022 miles (1,645 kilometers) of minor islands. The rocky southern shore has many inlets. Fishing fleets use the large inlets as harbors. Hundreds of small islands lie off the southern coast.

Rivers and lakes. Nova Scotia's rivers are all narrow, and few are over 50 miles (80 kilometers) long. The Mersey and the St. Mary's rivers, both 72 miles (116 kilometers), are the longest in the province. The Mersey rises on South Mountain and flows through several lakes, including Lake Rossignol. Rich farmland lies along the Annapolis and Shubenacadie rivers, which flow into the Bay of Fundy. Other important rivers include the La Have and Musquodoboit, which flow into the Atlantic, and the Margaree on Cape Breton Island. Many of Nova Scotia's rivers rise and fall with the tides near their mouths and carry salt water inland. Dikes around the Bay of Fundy and the Minas Basin, and along nearby rivers, protect farmlands from flooding at high tide.

Nova Scotia has more than 400 lakes. Most of them are small. Bras d'Or Lake, the largest, covers 425 square miles (1,100 square kilometers) on Cape Breton Island. This saltwater lake nearly divides the island in two. The

Sherman Hines, Masterfile

The southern coastline of Nova Scotia has many inlets. Numerous small islands lie off the province's southern shore.

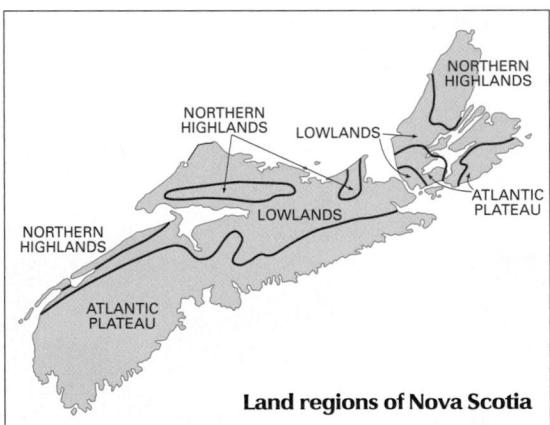

Land regions of Nova Scotia

WORLD BOOK map

Map index

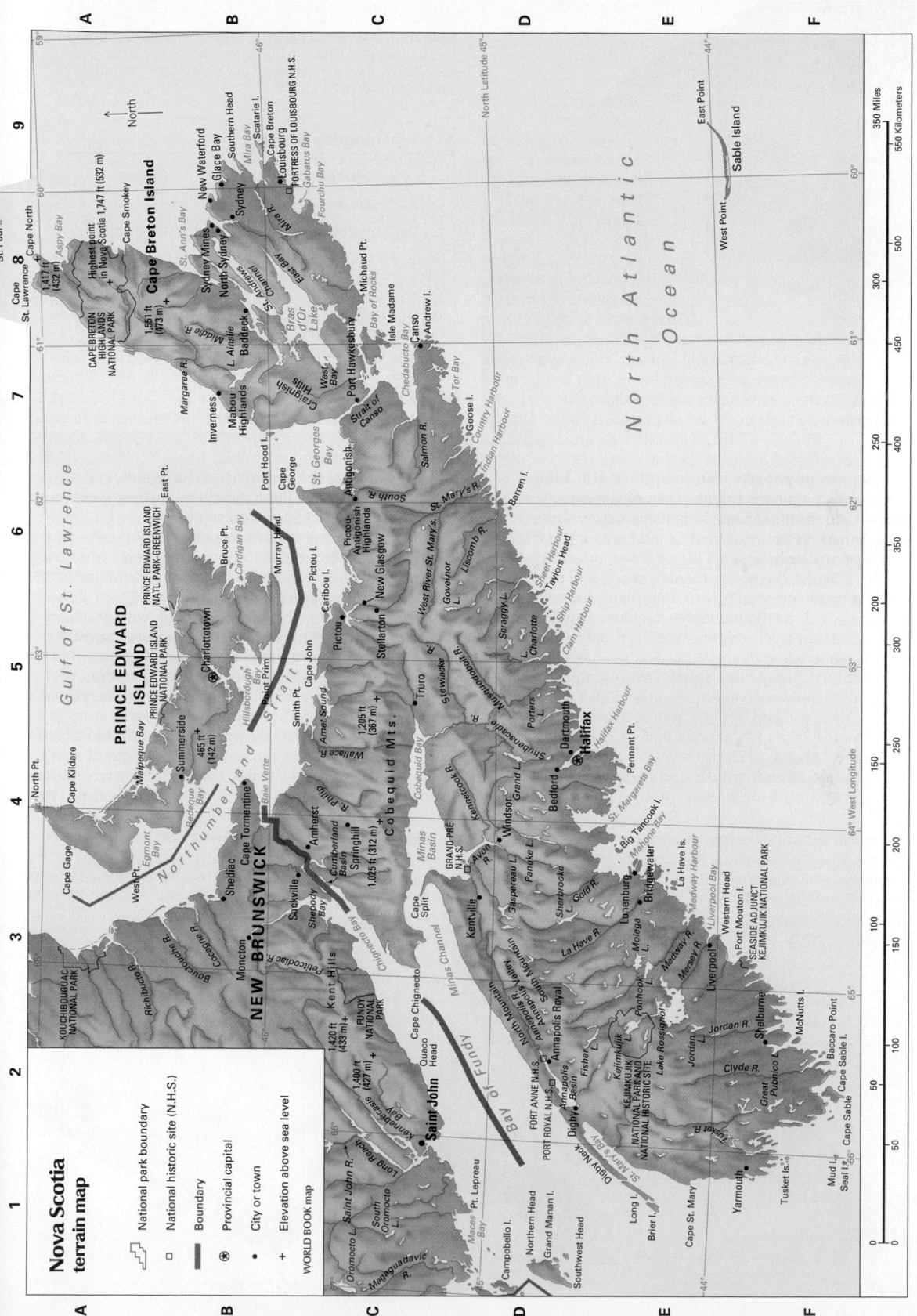

Nova Scotia
terrain map

- ⬚ National park boundary
- □ National historic site (N.H.S.)
- ▬ Boundary
- ⊛ Provincial capital
- • City or town
- + Elevation above sea level

WORLD BOOK map

North

PRINCE EDWARD ISLAND

PRINCE EDWARD ISLAND NATL. PARK-GREENWICH

PRINCE EDWARD ISLAND NATIONAL PARK

North Pt.
Cape Kildare
West Pt.
Cape Gage
Egmont Bay
Malpeque Bay
Summerside
465 ft (142 m) +
Bedeque Bay
Cardigan Bay
Bruce Pt.
East Pt.
Charlottetown ⊛
Hillsborough Bay
Northumberland Strait
Point Prim
Murray Head

Gulf of St. Lawrence

Cape St. Lawrence Cape North
1,417 ft (432 m) +
Aspy Bay
Cape North
1,551 ft (473 m) +
CAPE BRETON HIGHLANDS NATIONAL PARK
Highest point in Nova Scotia 1,747 ft (532 m) +
Cape Smokey
St. Ann's Bay
New Waterford
Glace Bay
Southern Head
Scatarie I.
Sydney Mines
North Sydney
Sydney
Louisbourg
FORTRESS OF LOUISBOURG N.H.S. □
Cape Breton
Gabarus Bay
Fourchu Bay
Mira Bay

Cape Breton Island

Margaree R.
Inverness
Mabou
Middle R.
L. Ainslie
Baddeck
Bras d'Or Lake
Carigush Hills
West Bay
East Bay
Mira R.
St. Andrews Channel
Great Bras d'Or Channel
Port Hawkesbury
Strait of Canso
Michaud Pt.
Bay of Rocks
Isle Madame
Andrew I.
Canso

Port Hood
Cape George
Port Hood I.
St. Georges Bay
Antigonish
Pictou-Antigonish Highlands
South R.
Salmon R.
Tor Bay
Goose I.
Country Harbour
Chedabucto Bay
Indian Harbour

Chaleur Bay
Richibucto R.
KOUCHIBOUGUAC NATIONAL PARK
Buctouche R.
Cocagne R.
Moncton
Shediac
Petitcodiac R.
Sackville
Amherst
Springhill
Cumberland Basin
1,025 ft (312 m) +
Shepody Bay
Cape Chignecto
Minas Channel
Chignecto Bay
Cape Tormentine
Baie Verte

NEW BRUNSWICK

Kent Hills
1,420 ft (433 m) +
1,400 ft (427 m) +
FUNDY NATIONAL PARK
Quaco Head

Saint John

FORT ANNE N.H.S.
PORT ROYAL N.H.S.
Kennebecasis R.
Long Reach
Saint John R.
Oromocto L.
South Oromocto L.
Magaguadavic R.
Maces Bay
Pt. Lepreau
Northern Head
Grand Manan I.
Southwest Head
Campobello I.

Bay of Fundy

North Mountain
Annapolis Valley
Annapolis Royal
South Mountain
Digby
Annapolis Basin
Digby Neck
Long I.
Brier I.
St. Mary's Bay

Cape Split
Cape Blomidon
Minas Basin
GRAND-PRÉ N.H.S.
Avon R.
Windsor
Kentville
Cape d'Or

Cobequid Mts.

1,205 ft (367 m) +
Amet Sound
Wallace R.
R. Philip
Cape John
Smith Pt.
Caribou I.
Pictou I.
Pictou
Truro
Stewiacke
Shubenacadie R.
Stellarton
New Glasgow
West River St. Mary's
Governor L.
Liscomb R.
Sheet Harbour
Taylors Head
Ship Harbour
Clam Harbour
Barren I.
St. Mary's R.
Straggly L.
Charlotte L.
Porters L.

Windsor
Bedford
Dartmouth
⊛ Halifax
Halifax Harbour
Pennant Pt.
Kennetcook R.
Grand L.
St. Margarets Bay
Panuke L.
Jasperau L.
Big Tancook I.
Mahone Bay
Sherbrooke
Gold R.
Sheet Harbour
La Have Is.
Lunenburg
Bridgewater
La Have R.
Mushamush R.
Medway Harbour
Western Bay
Port Mouton I.

Cape Chignecto
Jordan R.
Mersey R.
Jordan L.
Medway R.
Molega L.
Ponhook L.
Lake Rossignol
Liverpool
Liverpool Bay
Shelburne
Clyde R.
Great Pubnico
Cape Sable I.
McNutts
Baccaro Point
Cape Sable

KEJIMKUJIK NATIONAL PARK
KEJIMKUJIK L.
KEJIMKUJIK NATIONAL PARK AND NATIONAL HISTORIC SITE
SEASIDE ADJUNCT KEJIMKUJIK NATIONAL PARK
Fisher L.
Tusket R.
Yarmouth
Cape St. Mary
Mud I.
Seal I.
Tusket Is.

North Atlantic Ocean

East Point
West Point
Sable Island

North Latitude 45°

0   50   100   150   200   250   300   350 Miles
0   50   100 150 200 250 300 350 400 450 500 550 Kilometers

Blomidon Provincial Park, on Cape Blomidon, features forested seaside cliffs, such as those shown here. The cape lies along the western shore of the Minas Basin, an extension of the Bay of Fundy.

Average monthly weather

	Halifax							Sydney				
	Temperatures °F		Temperatures °C		Days of rain or snow			Temperatures °F		Temperatures °C		Days of rain or snow
	High	Low	High	Low				High	Low	High	Low	
Jan.	30	12	-1	-11	19		Jan.	30	14	-1	-10	20
Feb.	30	14	-1	-10	15		Feb.	28	12	-2	-11	16
Mar.	37	21	3	-6	16		Mar.	36	19	2	-7	17
Apr.	46	30	8	-1	15		Apr.	43	28	6	-2	16
May	59	41	15	5	14		May	55	37	13	3	14
June	68	50	20	10	13		June	66	46	19	8	13
July	75	57	24	14	12		July	73	54	23	12	12
Aug.	73	57	23	14	10		Aug.	73	55	23	13	13
Sept.	66	48	19	9	11		Sept.	64	48	18	9	14
Oct.	55	39	13	4	12		Oct.	54	39	12	4	16
Nov.	45	30	7	-1	15		Nov.	45	32	7	0	18
Dec.	34	19	1	-7	18		Dec.	36	21	2	-6	21

largest freshwater lakes are, in order of size, Lake Rossignol in Queens County, Lake Ainslie and Mira River on Cape Breton Island, Kejimkujik Lake in Queens and Annapolis counties, and Grand Lake near Halifax.

Plant and animal life. Forests cover about 75 percent of Nova Scotia. Birch, firs, maples, pines, and spruces are the most common trees. Other plants found in the province include the blueberry, bracken, lambkill, mayflower, raspberry, rhodora, sweet fern, and wintergreen.

The white-tailed deer is Nova Scotia's most common large animal. Some black bears, coyotes, moose, and wildcats also live in wilderness areas. Small animals of Nova Scotia include beavers, minks, muskrats, otters, porcupines, red foxes, skunks, and weasels. The province has several kinds of geese and ducks, as well as pheasants, ruffed grouse, and woodcocks. Salmon and trout swim in the streams of Nova Scotia. The

coastal waters of the province contain clams, crabs, flounder, haddock, halibut, herring, lobsters, mackerel, pollock, redfish, scallops, and swordfish.

Climate. The sea nearly surrounds Nova Scotia and keeps the climate from becoming extremely hot or cold. The province has an average January temperature of 23 °F (-5 °C). The average July temperature is 64 °F (18 °C). The Atlantic coast is the coolest area of Nova Scotia in summer, but it has the mildest temperatures in winter. The interior and north have hotter summers and colder winters. But even in these areas, winter temperatures seldom fall below 0 °F (-18 °C). In winter, winds crossing the ice-filled Gulf of St. Lawrence chill coastal areas of the northern mainland and western Cape Breton Island.

In spring and early summer, fogs are frequent along the Atlantic and Fundy coasts. Late summer and autumn bring sunny skies and pleasant southwesterly winds to

Average January temperatures

The North Atlantic coast from Sydney to Yarmouth is the mildest area of the province during the wintertime.

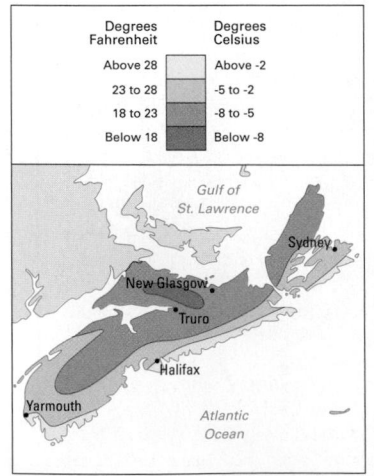

Degrees Fahrenheit	Degrees Celsius
Above 28	Above -2
23 to 28	-5 to -2
18 to 23	-8 to -5
Below 18	Below -8

Average July temperatures

Nova Scotia has cool summers along the foggy Atlantic coast. Inland and to the north, temperatures are warmer.

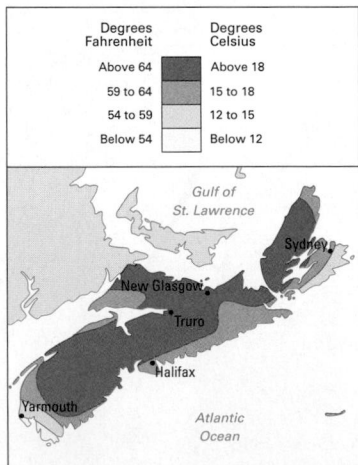

Degrees Fahrenheit	Degrees Celsius
Above 64	Above 18
59 to 64	15 to 18
54 to 59	12 to 15
Below 54	Below 12

Average yearly precipitation

The Atlantic coastal area is the wettest part of Nova Scotia. Precipitation declines toward the northwest.

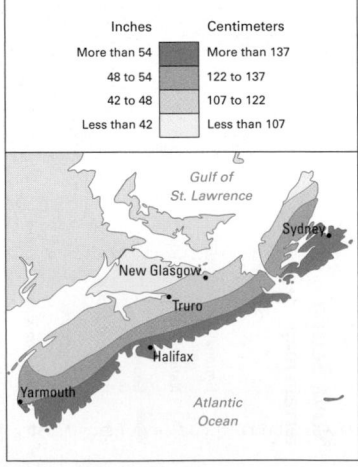

Inches	Centimeters
More than 54	More than 137
48 to 54	122 to 137
42 to 48	107 to 122
Less than 42	Less than 107

WORLD BOOK maps; based on the *National Atlas of Canada.*

the southern coast of the province.

The province's highest temperature, 101 °F (38 °C), occurred at Collegeville, near Antigonish, on Aug. 19, 1935. Upper Stewiacke recorded Nova Scotia's lowest temperature, −42 °F (−41 °C), on Jan. 31, 1920.

Nova Scotia's precipitation averages 53 inches (134 centimeters) a year. Rainfall is heaviest along the Atlantic coast. Annual snowfall is highest where onshore winds blow onto highlands and is greater than 110 inches (280 centimeters) in the Cape Breton Highlands.

Economy

The vast majority of Nova Scotia's workers find jobs in service industries, which include education, finance, health care, tourism, and trade. In addition, Nova Scotia has important manufacturing and fishing industries.

Natural resources. Nova Scotia's most valuable resources include its mineral deposits, forests, and fertile lowlands.

Soil. The Annapolis Valley has Nova Scotia's best farmland. Other good farming areas include reclaimed marshlands at the head of the Bay of Fundy, the central lowlands near Truro, and the coastal lowlands along the Northumberland Strait. The Northern Highlands and Atlantic Plateau regions have shallow, rocky soil.

Minerals in Nova Scotia include two of North America's largest deposits of gypsum, at Windsor and East Milford. Although the province's last underground coal mine closed in 2001, significant coal deposits still lie underground from Chignecto on the mainland to Glace Bay on Cape Breton Island. A few surface coal mines still operate in Nova Scotia. Natural gas and oil deposits lie beneath the shallow waters around Sable Island.

Service industries, taken together, produce the largest portion of Nova Scotia's *gross domestic product* (GDP)—the total value of all goods and services produced in the province in a year. Service industries employ a large number of Nova Scotians. Many of these industries are in the Halifax area.

Halifax, the provincial capital, is the center of federal and provincial government activities. The Halifax area is the largest financial center in the Atlantic Provinces. The city is also the center of trade and tourism in Nova Scotia. A large naval base operates at Halifax.

Manufacturing. Much of Nova Scotia's manufacturing industry is centered on processing the province's natural resources. Food and beverage processing is a leading activity. Food products include dairy products, fish products, meat and poultry products, and preserved fruits. The manufacturing of wood and paper products is also important to the province.

Establishments in Nova Scotia also manufacture aerospace products, aircraft parts, boats, and ships. Large Michelin tire plants operate near Bridgewater, Kentville, and New Glasgow. The Halifax area has an oil refinery.

Fishing. Nova Scotia ranks first among the provinces in the value of fish caught. Lobsters are Nova Scotia's most valuable catch. The once-important cod stocks in the waters around Nova Scotia have been greatly depleted. *Aquaculture* (fish farming) has become increasingly important in sheltered waters along the Atlantic coast and Bras d'Or Lake.

Mining. Nova Scotia's most valuable mineral products are gypsum, natural gas, and petroleum. Natural gas and petroleum are mined near Sable Island, which lies off Nova Scotia's southeastern coast. Gypsum comes from Hants, Inverness, and Victoria counties.

Agriculture. Livestock and livestock products provide most of the province's farm income. Milk is the leading farm product. The chief dairying regions are in Colchester County and the Annapolis Valley. Other important farm products in the province include beef cattle, chickens and eggs, and hogs.

Apples, blueberries, and strawberries are Nova Scotia's most valuable fruits. The raising of *floriculture* (ornamental plants) and nursery products is also important. Christmas tree nurseries are a leading part of this sector.

Forestry. Nova Scotia's forests supply wood for its pulp and paper mills, lumber mills, boatyards, and furniture factories. Maples and birches are the chief hardwoods of the province. The chief softwoods include balsam fir and spruces.

Electric power and utilities. Power plants fueled by coal, natural gas, and oil generate most of Nova Scotia's electric power. Hydroelectric plants supply most of the rest. The first tidal power plant in North America operates at the mouth of the Annapolis River.

Transportation. Major provincial highways connect locations throughout Nova Scotia. Older scenic roads run mainly along the coastal areas. Part of the Trans-Canada Highway stretches from Amherst to North Sydney. Motor vehicles and trains travel from the Nova Scotia mainland to Cape Breton Island over a *causeway* (elevated road), 1 ½ miles (2.4 kilometers) in length, across the Strait of Canso.

Halifax has the province's largest airport and seaport. It is a port of call for many cruise ships. Sydney and Yarmouth also have airports. Railways link Nova Scotia's largest cities to a national railroad network. Ferries connect Nova Scotia with other provinces and Maine.

© Ron Garnett, AirScapes

Manufacturing is an important industry in Nova Scotia. Pulp mills, such as this one in Port Hawkesbury on Cape Breton Island, produce a material called *pulp* that is used to make paper.

Nova Scotia economy

General economy

Gross domestic product (GDP)* (2008) $34,209,000,000
  Rank among Canadian provinces   7th
Unemployment rate (2009)   9.2% (Canada avg: 8.3%)

*Gross domestic product is the total value of goods and services produced in a year and is in Canadian dollars.
Source: Statistics Canada.

Agriculture

Cash receipts $474,644,000
  Rank among Canadian provinces   7th
Distribution   72% livestock, 28% crops
Farms (2006)   3,800
Farm acres (hectares)   998,000 (403,900)
  Rank among Canadian provinces   7th
Farmland   7% of Nova Scotia

Leading products
1. Dairy
2. Hens and chickens
3. Blueberries   (ranks 3rd in Canada)
Other products: apples, cattle, eggs, floriculture and nursery products, hogs, potatoes, strawberries.

Fishing

Commercial catch $661,405,000
  Rank among Canadian provinces   1st

Leading catches
1. Lobster   (ranks 1st in Canada)
2. Scallops   (ranks 1st in Canada)
3. Crabs   (ranks 2nd in Canada)
Other catches: cod, haddock, halibut, herring, shrimp.

Manufacturing

Value added by manufacture* $4,032,795,000
  Rank among Canadian provinces   6th

Leading products
Fabricated metals, food and beverage products, paper
products, plastic and rubber products, transportation
equipment, wood products

*Value added by manufacture is the increase in value of raw materials after they become finished products.

Production and workers by economic activities

Economic activities	Percent of GDP produced	Employed workers	
		Number of people	Percent of total
Community, business, & personal services	23	161,000*	36*
Finance, insurance, & real estate	21*	22,300	5
Trade, restaurants, & hotels	14	108,600	24
Manufacturing	11	39,100	9
Government	10	30,300	7
Transportation & communication	8	38,400	8
Construction	6	31,300	7
Mining	3	12,700†	3†
Agriculture	3†	6,400	1
Utilities	2	3,100	1
Total‡	100	453,200	100

*Includes figures from establishments that manage other companies.
†Includes figures from forestry and fishing.
‡Figures do not add up to 100 percent due to rounding.
Figures are for 2008.
Source: Statistics Canada.

Mining

Mineral production $1,647,136,000
  Rank among Canadian provinces   8th
Minerals and coal $327,705,000
Crude oil and crude oil equivalents $343,692,000
Natural gas $975,739,000

Leading products
1. Natural gas
2. Petroleum
3. Gypsum   (ranks 1st in Canada)
4. Stone
Other products: coal, sand and gravel, zinc.

Figures are for 2007, except for the agriculture and fishing figures, which are for 2008.
Dollar amounts are in Canadian dollars.
Sources: Statistics Canada, Government of Nova Scotia.

Economic map of Nova Scotia

This map shows the economic uses of land in Nova Scotia and where the province's leading farm, mineral, and forest products are produced. Major manufacturing centers are shown in red.

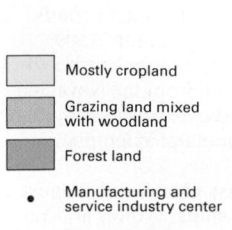

Mostly cropland

Grazing land mixed with woodland

Forest land

• Manufacturing and service industry center

• Mineral deposit

Communication. The *Halifax Gazette,* founded in 1752, was the first newspaper published in Canada. It is still published as the *Royal Gazette* by the provincial government. Daily newspapers with the largest circulations are *The Chronicle Herald* of Halifax and the *Cape Breton Post* of Sydney.

Government

Lieutenant governor of Nova Scotia represents the British monarch, Queen Elizabeth II, in her role as the queen of Canada. The *governor general in council*—that is, the governor general of Canada acting with the advice and consent of the Cabinet—appoints the lieutenant governor on the recommendation of the prime minister. The position of lieutenant governor is largely honorary.

Premier of Nova Scotia is the actual head of the provincial government. Nova Scotia, like Canada itself, has a parliamentary form of government. The premier is an elected member of the House of Assembly. The person who serves as premier is usually the leader of the majority party in the Assembly.

The premier presides over a cabinet called the Executive Council. The cabinet is made up of the premier and other ministers. All the ministers belong to the Assembly's majority party. They are chosen by the premier. Each cabinet member usually directs one or more governmental departments. The cabinet resigns if it loses the support of a majority of the Assembly.

House of Assembly makes the provincial laws. This one-house legislature has 52 members who are elected by the people. An election for the Assembly must be held at least every five years. But the lieutenant governor, on the advice of the premier, may call for an election at any time. A premier who loses the support of the majority of the House of Assembly must resign.

Courts. Nova Scotia's Supreme Court is the province's highest trial court. Other courts include provincial, small claims, family, bankruptcy, and probate courts. Judges of the Court of Appeal and the Supreme Court are appointed by the federal government and may serve until the age of 75. The provincial government of Nova Scotia appoints other provincial judges and justices of the peace, who may serve until the age of 70.

Local government. Nova Scotia has 18 counties and a number of towns. Nine of Nova Scotia's counties are single rural municipalities, six are divided into two rural municipalities apiece, and the other three are regional municipalities. Voters from each regional municipality and town elect a mayor and a council. An elected council governs each rural municipality. Council members elect a *warden* (chief councilor) from their group.

Revenue. Nova Scotia gets about half of its *general revenue* (income) from taxes levied by the provincial government. Most of this money comes from taxes on income and on goods and services. Sales of gasoline and tobacco products are also taxed. Other sources of revenue include national and provincial tax-sharing programs, license and permit fees, and royalties from offshore petroleum production.

Politics. Nova Scotia's leading political organizations are the provincial Progressive Conservative, New Democratic, and Liberal parties. Since July 1867, when Nova

The premiers of Nova Scotia

	Party	Term
Hiram Blanchard	Conservative	1867
William Annand	Liberal	1867-1875
Philip C. Hill	Liberal	1875-1878
Simon H. Holmes	Conservative	1878-1882
John S. D. Thompson	Conservative	1882
William T. Pipes	Liberal	1882-1884
William S. Fielding	Liberal	1884-1896
George H. Murray	Liberal	1896-1923
Ernest H. Armstrong	Liberal	1923-1925
Edgar N. Rhodes	Conservative	1925-1930
Gordon S. Harrington	Conservative	1930-1933
Angus L. Macdonald	Liberal	1933-1940
A. Stirling MacMillan	Liberal	1940-1945
Angus L. Macdonald	Liberal	1945-1954
Harold Connolly	Liberal	1954
Henry D. Hicks	Liberal	1954-1956
Robert L. Stanfield	*Prog. Cons.	1956-1967
George I. Smith	*Prog. Cons.	1967-1970
Gerald Regan	Liberal	1970-1978
John Buchanan	*Prog. Cons.	1978-1990
Roger S. Bacon	*Prog. Cons.	1990-1991
Donald W. Cameron	*Prog. Cons.	1991-1993
John Savage	Liberal	1993-1997
Russell MacLellan	Liberal	1997-1999
John F. Hamm	*Prog. Cons.	1999-2006
Rodney MacDonald	*Prog. Cons.	2006-2009
Darrell Dexter	New Democrat	2009-

*Progressive Conservative.

Scotia became a province, Liberals have held the office of premier about twice as long as have Conservatives and Progressive Conservatives combined. In 2009, Nova Scotia voters elected the first New Democratic government in the province's history.

History

Early inhabitants. Human beings have lived in Nova Scotia at least 10,000 years. The earliest people, whom archaeologists call Paleo-Indians, were hunters who lived mainly off herds of caribou. When Europeans first reached Nova Scotia, the Mi'kmaq people lived in the area. Today, the Mi'kmaq consider themselves descendants of the earliest people in Nova Scotia. The region's early inhabitants hunted and fished along the coast in the summer and in the forested interior during winter.

Exploration and settlement. In 1497, John Cabot, an Italian navigator in the service of England, landed on Cape Breton Island or Newfoundland. Cabot believed that he had landed in Asia. Between 1520 and 1524, several other explorers reached Nova Scotia while trying to find a westward sea route to Asia. They included the Italian navigator Giovanni da Verrazzano and two Portuguese sailors, João Alvares Fagundes and Esteban Gómez (also spelled Estêvão Gomes). Verrazzano explored in the service of France. Gómez sailed in the service of Spain. Some historians think that Fagundes founded a colony on Cape Breton Island. During the summers of the late 1500's, French and Basque fishing crews used Nova Scotia's harbors for drying codfish they had caught offshore. These crews returned to France every autumn.

In 1598, King Henry IV of France granted a fur-trading monopoly in a vast area of Atlantic Canada to a French nobleman, the Marquis de La Roche-Mesgouez. La Roche accompanied an expedition of about 50 men to Sable Island, which he named the Île de Bourbon. La Roche returned to France later that year, but the other men stayed on the island. Many of the men died. However, a few survivors made their way back to France in 1603.

In 1603, King Henry granted land and trading rights over an area that included Nova Scotia to the French nobleman Pierre du Gua (or du Guast), Sieur de Monts. De Monts and other explorers, including Samuel de Champlain, sailed together along the coast of what is now Nova Scotia, New Brunswick, and Maine in 1604. Champlain made the first accurate charts of the coast. The Nova Scotia region and the land around it became known as Acadie or Acadia. De Monts established a base at the mouth of the St. Croix River, which separates New Brunswick from Maine. In 1605, after a difficult winter, the base was moved to Port-Royal, near present-day Annapolis Royal. The new settlement served as an outpost for trading fur with the Mi'kmaq and as a base for French missionaries.

The struggle in Acadia. In 1613, an English expedition from Virginia burned down the French settlement at Port-Royal. Samuel Argall, a sea captain, led the attack. For the next 150 years, the English and the French battled, off and on, for control of Acadia.

In 1621, King James (who ruled as James I in England and James VI in Scotland) made a land grant to the Scotsman Sir William Alexander. The grant included what are now Nova Scotia (including Cape Breton Island), New Brunswick, Prince Edward Island, and parts of Quebec and Maine. The charter granted by the king called the region *Nova Scotia,* Latin for *New Scotland.* In 1629, Alexander's son, Sir William the younger, built Charles Fort near the site of the former French settlement at Port-Royal. The colony lasted until 1632, when a

© Parks Canada

Rock carvings called *petroglyphs* were created by the native Mi'kmaq people of Nova Scotia. The Mi'kmaq were living in the region when Europeans first arrived there during the 1500's.

peace treaty returned control of Acadia to France. Colonists sent by a French company took control of the Port-Royal area but settled primarily at La Have, on Nova Scotia's southern coast. Around 1636, many of these settlers relocated to the Port-Royal area, which had better potential for agriculture. Their main settlement, called Port-Royal, was about 10 miles (16 kilometers) from the original Port-Royal settlement. By building dikes, they reclaimed marshland from the sea for farming.

English troops under Sir William Phips captured Port-Royal in 1690. But England gave Port-Royal back to France under the Treaty of Ryswick in 1697. A combined force of British troops from England and New England took Port-Royal again in 1710. That year, the British changed the name of Port-Royal to Annapolis Royal, which became the capital of the colony in 1713.

France gave up mainland Nova Scotia under the Treaty of Utrecht in 1713. The treaty made British subjects of the Acadians who remained there. The treaty allowed France to keep Île Royale (now Cape Breton Island) and Île Saint-Jean (now Prince Edward Island). Both nations claimed authority over most of what is today New Brunswick. The French built a fortified town at Louisbourg on Île Royale to assert their power in the region. Troops from New England, an area controlled by Britain, captured the fortress in 1745 with the aid of Britain's Royal Navy. France regained it in 1748 under the Treaty of Aix-la-Chapelle, which settled a European war. But Louisbourg later fell to the British in 1758, during the Seven Years' War.

British settlers established Halifax in 1749, and it became the capital of Nova Scotia the same year. Many French, German, and Swiss Protestants moved to Nova Scotia during the early 1750's.

In 1755, the Nova Scotia Council ordered the deportation of all Acadians. At the time, Britain and France were fighting for control of North America, and the council doubted the Acadians' loyalty to Britain. In the following years, until 1763, troops from Britain and New England forcibly removed about 10,000 Acadians from Nova Scotia, Île Saint-Jean, and Île Royale. At first, they sent the Acadians to Britain's American Colonies. Later, they sent them to France. Diseases and shipwrecks killed many Acadians during this upheaval. After 1763, Acadians were allowed to return to Nova Scotia provided that they swore an oath of loyalty to Britain. Many Acadians migrated to Louisiana from about 1763 to 1785.

Also during the 1700's, the British agreed to a series of peace and friendship treaties with the native Mi'kmaq people. These treaties, created from 1725 to 1779, today form the basis for a land claim by the Mi'kmaq.

Progress as a province. In 1758, the British government allowed colonists in Nova Scotia to elect a representative assembly. The first assembly met in Halifax. It gave the people some voice in their government, but a governor and a council appointed by the king continued to rule the province. In 1763, the Peace of Paris officially gave Cape Breton Island (formerly Île Royale) and St. John's Island (formerly Île Saint-Jean) to Britain, and they became part of Nova Scotia. St. John's Island became a separate colony in 1769, and its name was changed to Prince Edward Island in 1799. Cape Breton Island existed as a separate colony from 1784 to 1820, when it once again became part of Nova Scotia.

Historic Nova Scotia

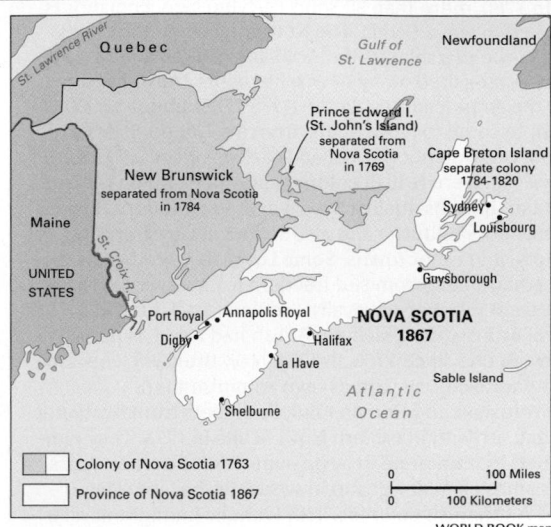

WORLD BOOK map

Halifax was founded in 1749 by Edward Cornwallis, a British soldier and colonial official. Cornwallis became governor of Nova Scotia and made Halifax its capital.

Nova Scotia once included Prince Edward Island and New Brunswick. Prince Edward Island became a separate colony in 1769, and New Brunswick separated from Nova Scotia in 1784.

Port-Royal, one of the oldest towns in North America, was first established by French settlers in 1605. The French reestablished Port-Royal around 1636 at the site of present-day Annapolis Royal. The British captured the settlement in 1710 and changed its name to Annapolis Royal.

Important dates in Nova Scotia

WORLD BOOK illustrations by Richard Bonson, The Art Agency

1497-1524 European explorers reached Nova Scotia while seeking a sea route to Asia.

1598 The Marquis de La Roche-Mesgouez established a settlement on Sable Island.

1603 King Henry IV of France granted Pierre du Gua, Sieur de Monts, land and trading rights in Nova Scotia.

1604 Samuel de Champlain charted the Nova Scotia coast.

1605 De Monts founded Port-Royal.

1710 The British captured Port-Royal and changed its name to Annapolis Royal.

1713 Under the Peace of Utrecht, France gave Britain the mainland of Nova Scotia.

1749 The British founded Halifax.

1755 The Nova Scotia Council ordered the deportation of all Acadians from Nova Scotia.

1758 Nova Scotia's first provincial parliament met in Halifax.

1763 Under the Peace of Paris, France officially gave Cape Breton Island and St. John's Island to Britain.

1776-1785 United Empire Loyalists settled in Nova Scotia.

1784 New Brunswick was separated from Nova Scotia and became another British colony.

1848 Nova Scotia became the first part of Canada to get local self-government.

1867 Nova Scotia became part of the Dominion of Canada.

1917 A French munitions ship exploded in Halifax Harbour and killed about 2,000 people.

1955 The Canso Causeway opened, linking mainland Nova Scotia with Cape Breton Island.

1996 Halifax, Dartmouth, Bedford, and the rest of Halifax County joined to form the Halifax Regional Municipality.

2009 The New Democratic Party won a provincial election for the first time.

In 1760, more than 20 ships carrying New Englanders arrived in Nova Scotia. The New Englanders took over the fertile marshlands the Acadians had reclaimed, and they established many new settlements. During and after the American Revolution (1775-1783), about 35,000 people came to Nova Scotia from the United States. Most of these people, called Loyalists or United Empire Loyalists, were British colonists in America who refused to take up arms against Britain in the revolution. They established Shelburne and also settled in Guysborough, Digby, and other towns. Some Loyalists were blacks who had been promised freedom from slavery in Nova Scotia. A number of Loyalists settled in what is today New Brunswick, which the British had ruled as part of Nova Scotia since 1763. In 1784, New Brunswick became a separate colony with its own administration.

Protestant and Roman Catholic settlers from Scotland began arriving in eastern Nova Scotia in 1773. They continued to immigrate in large numbers for over 50 years, becoming a major group in what later became Pictou and Antigonish counties. Irish Catholic immigrants also arrived in the early 1800's, settling chiefly in and around Halifax. More blacks came from the United States during the War of 1812 (1812-1815).

In 1848, the British government gave Nova Scotia's elected representative assembly authority over the colony's executive cabinet. Thus, Nova Scotia became the first self-governing colony within the British Empire. Joseph Howe, a forceful editor and statesman of Nova Scotia, had led the fight for self-government.

During the 1800's, Nova Scotia thrived with growing industries and increasing world trade. Shipbuilders used timber from the province's forests to build merchant ships. By 1860, Nova Scotia had one of the largest merchant fleets in the world.

In 1867, Nova Scotia joined with New Brunswick, Ontario, and Quebec in forming a confederation called the Dominion of Canada. But many Nova Scotians opposed the union and soon voted out the leaders who had supported confederation.

The next 25 years were a period of economic hardship for Nova Scotia. Investors abandoned shipping in an unsuccessful effort to industrialize the province. During the late 1890's, however, Nova Scotia's coal and steel industries began to thrive.

The early to middle 1900's. During World War I (1914-1918), Halifax served as the headquarters of Allied convoys sailing between North America and Europe. In 1917, a French ship carrying explosives collided with a Norwegian vessel in Halifax Harbour. The resulting blast, known as the Halifax explosion, killed about 2,000 people and damaged much of the city.

Following World War I, Nova Scotia experienced an economic crisis and political unrest. Many people left the province. After a brief period of prosperity during World War II (1939-1945), hard times returned.

In the mid-1950's, Canada's overall postwar prosperity began to trickle down to Nova Scotia, and the provincial economy grew. Schools, hospitals, and modern roads were constructed. The Nova Scotia section of the Trans-Canada Highway was built. In 1955, the Canso Causeway, linking the mainland and Cape Breton Island, was completed. It contributed to the province's economic growth and an expansion of the tourist industry. During this period, the rural population of Nova Scotia declined as people moved to the province's urban areas.

Beginning in the 1950's, Canada's federal government and Nova Scotia's provincial government worked to promote economic growth within Nova Scotia. A series of provincial and federal agencies sought to close outdated industries and attract new ones. These agencies included Industrial Estates Limited (established in 1957), the Cape Breton Development Corporation (1967), Sydney Steel Corporation (1969), and Nova Scotia Power Corporation (1973).

The expansion of industry and port facilities helped improve Nova Scotia's economy in the 1970's. For example, a container terminal opened in 1970 at the Port of Halifax to handle large container ships. During the early 1970's, an industrial park was built on the shores of the Strait of Canso.

The late 1900's and early 2000's. Several important economic developments occurred in Nova Scotia in the late 1900's and early 2000's. Expanded and upgraded facilities at the Port of Halifax enabled the province to handle increasing amounts of cargo, especially shipping containers. In 1995, the government legalized gambling casinos to provide a new source of income for the province. The production of natural gas, which had been discovered in the 1970's near Sable Island, began in 1999. In addition, cruise ships brought large numbers of tourists to the province, especially Halifax.

However, the province also faced economic challenges. During the 1990's, efforts to balance the federal budget led to reduced funding for Nova Scotia. As a result, government enterprises were cut back. Some municipal governments, hospital and school boards, and institutions of higher education were combined in an effort to save money. In 1992, the government sold Nova Scotia Power, the province's main provider of electric service, to private investors. In addition, Atlantic Canada's cod-fishing industry virtually collapsed because of overfishing.   A. J. B. Johnston and Hugh Millward

Related articles in *World Book* include:

Biographies

Borden, Sir Robert L.	Howe, Joseph
Champlain, Samuel de	MacLennan, Hugh
Cornwallis, Edward	Poutrincourt, Jean de
Dawson, George M.	Stanfield, Robert L.
Dawson, Sir John W.	Thompson, Sir John S. D.
Du Gua, Pierre, Sieur de Monts	Tupper, Sir Charles

Communities

Annapolis Royal
Dartmouth
Grand Pré
Halifax
Louisbourg

Physical features

Bay of Fundy
Cape Breton Island
Gulf of Saint Lawrence
Sable Island

Other related articles

Acadia
Bluenose
British North America Act
French and Indian wars

Halifax explosion
King's College, University of
United Empire Loyalists

Additional resources

Beckett, Harry. *Nova Scotia.* Weigl, 2010. Younger readers.
Boudreau, Hélène. *Life in a Fishing Community.* Crabtree Pub.
Co., 2009. Younger readers.
Bruce, Harry. *An Illustrated History of Nova Scotia.* Nimbus, 1997.
Faragher, John M. *A Great and Noble Scheme: The Tragic Story
of the Expulsion of the French Acadians from Their American
Homeland.* Norton, 2005.
Forbes, E. R., and Muise, D. A., eds. *The Atlantic Provinces in
Confederation.* 1993. Reprint. Univ. of Toronto Pr., 2001.
Johnston, A. J. B. *Control and Order in French Colonial Louis-
bourg, 1713-1758.* Mich. State Univ. Pr., 2001. *Endgame 1758:
The Promise, the Glory, and the Despair of Louisbourg's Last
Decade.* Univ. of Neb. Pr., 2007.
McDonald, Laura M. *Curse of the Narrows.* Walker, 2005. A his-
tory of the 1917 Halifax harbor explosion.
Reid, John G. *Nova Scotia.* Fernwood Pub., 2009.

Nova Scotia duck tolling retriever is a breed of dog developed in Nova Scotia for duck hunting. Hunters used this breed, often called simply the *toller,* to *toll* (lure) and retrieve birds. A male toller should grow 18 to 21 inches (46 to 53 centimeters) high at the shoulder and weigh 45 to 51 pounds (20 to 23 kilograms). A female may be slightly smaller.

The toller's muscular body has a waterproof double coat of moderately long, thick hair. This coat was originally developed to protect the dog from the icy waters it had to enter when hunting. Tollers also have a wedge-shaped head, triangular ears with rounded tips, and an elongated tail with long, feathered hair. Coloring can include any shade of red, with distinctive white markings on the feet, chest, face, and tail tip.

The Nova Scotia duck tolling retriever was originally developed in the early 1800's. This intelligent dog has a friendly, loyal personality and can make an excellent family pet.

Critically reviewed by the Nova Scotia Duck Tolling Retriever Club (USA)

Novalis, *noh VAH lihs* (1772-1801), was the pen name of Baron Friedrich von Hardenberg, a German romantic poet. Five poems by Novalis, called *Hymns to the Night* (1800), express his religious, mystical nature, and a longing for death. In the essay *Christianity or Europe* (1799), he tried to show that people lived more meaningfully in the spiritual unity of the Catholic Middle Ages (from about the 400's through the 1400's) than in his own time. This attitude became a theme of German Romanticism.

Novalis was born on May 2, 1772, in Saxony. The death of his fiancée in 1797 deepened his melancholy and his religious temperament. His work as a mining engineer brought him close to the land and intensified his love of nature and its mysteries. Novalis died on March 25, 1801.   Jeffrey L Sammons

Novaya Zemlya, *NOH vuh yuh ZEHM lee AH,* is a group of islands in the Arctic Ocean that separate the Barents Sea from the Kara Sea. The islands are part of Russia. The Russian name means *new land* and commonly refers to the two largest islands. The northern large island covers about 20,000 square miles (52,000 square kilometers). Glaciers blanket much of it. The southern large island has an area of about 15,000 square miles (38,800 square kilometers), most of which is a treeless plain. Both islands have large deposits of coal and some copper, lead, and zinc.

Early Russians first discovered Novaya Zemlya between the 1000's and 1100's. But the islands remained uninhabited until 1877, when an Arctic people called Nenets established the first permanent settlements.

A small colony of Russians and Nenets live on the southern island. Islanders raise reindeer, trap and hunt animals, and collect *eider down* (the feathers of eider ducks). The Soviet Union tested nuclear bombs on the northern island in the 1950's. Today, the island shows harmful levels of radiation.   Craig ZumBrunnen

Novel is a long fictional story written in prose. It is one of the most popular forms of literature.

The subject matter of novels covers the whole range of human experience and imagination. Some novels portray true-to-life characters and events. Writers of such *realistic novels* try to represent life as it is. In contrast to realistic novels, *romantic novels* portray idealized versions of life. Some novels explore purely imaginary worlds. For example, *science-fiction novels* may describe events that take place in the future or on other planets. Other popular kinds of novels include detective novels and mysteries, whose suspenseful plots fascinate readers.

Some novels point out evils that exist in society and challenge the reader to seek social or political reforms. Novels may also provide knowledge about unfamiliar subjects or give new insights into familiar ones.

The novel has four basic features that together distinguish it from other kinds of literature. First, a novel is a *narrative*—that is, a story presented by a teller. It thus differs from a drama, which presents a story through the speech and actions of characters on a stage.

Second, novels are longer than short stories, fairy tales, and most other types of narratives. Novels vary greatly in length, but most exceed 60,000 words. Because of their length, novels can cover a longer period and include more characters than can most other kinds of narratives.

Third, a novel is written in prose rather than verse. This feature distinguishes novels from narrative poems.

Fourth, novels are works of fiction. They differ from histories, biographies, and other long prose narratives that tell about real events and people. Novelists sometimes base their stories on actual events or the lives of real people. But these authors also make up incidents and characters. Therefore, all novels are partly, if not entirely, imaginary.

The basic features of the novel make it a uniquely flexible form of literature. Novelists can arrange incidents, describe places, and represent characters in an almost limitless variety of ways. They also may narrate their stories from different points of view. In some novels, for example, one of the characters may tell the story. In others, the events may be described from the viewpoint of a person outside of the story. Some novelists change the point of view from one section of a story to another. Novelists also vary their treatment of time. They may devote hundreds of pages to the description of the events of a single day, or they may cover many years within a few paragraphs.

Origins of the novel

This article discusses the development of the novel in Western literature. The history of the novel is marked by an almost continual development of variations on old narrative forms. No matter how up to date or localized novels may seem, their stories still employ many themes and issues from narrative forms dating back to the ancient Greeks and Romans.

Ancient Greek and Roman narratives. In ancient times, most long narratives were composed in verse. Histories were among the few kinds of long narratives written in prose. The earliest known histories were written by two Greek authors, Herodotus and Thucydides, during the 400's B.C.

The finest fictional narratives of ancient Greece were long poems called *epics*, which told about the deeds of legendary heroes and mythical gods. The *Iliad* and the *Odyssey*, the two most famous epics, were probably composed by Homer between 800 and 700 B.C.

The Greeks also wrote long fictional adventure stories. These tales described fantastic adventures in foreign countries or related the plights of young lovers. Some writers composed *pastoral* tales, which told of love between shepherds and maidens. One of the best-known Greek pastorals is *Daphnis and Chloe* (A.D. 100's or 200's) by Longus.

The most important Roman narratives in prose included *Satyricon* (about 60 A.D.) by Petronius and *Metamorphoses*, or *The Golden Ass* (mid-100's A.D.), by Lucius Apuleius. These earthy stories contrast sharply with the love stories of the Greeks. *Satyricon* vividly portrays the adventures of three Roman scamps. *Metamorphoses* tells of a man who is changed into a donkey and travels through various countries observing the weaknesses and failings of humans.

Medieval narratives. The word *novel* originally referred to prose stories that were topical. The word for *novel* in French and other languages deriving from classical Latin is *roman*. The word reflects the fictions called *romances* in which it had its roots. Love and adventure stories called *romances of chivalry* became widely popular during the late Middle Ages. Many of the romances dealt with the legendary British King Arthur and his Knights of the Round Table.

Early novels. During the 1500's and 1600's, many English romances were written in an extremely decorative style. After John Lyly of England wrote *Euphues: The Anatomy of Wit* (1578), this highly artificial style was called *euphuistic* and was widely imitated. In France, many romances and romance histories were written by important women writers. Madeleine de Scudéry wrote historical narratives, such as *Artamene, or The Great Cyrus* (1649-1653). Marie-Madeleine de La Fayette wrote the most psychologically powerful of these novels, *The Princess of Cleves* (1678).

In Spain, several narratives that were more realistic appeared during the 1500's. One of the most influential was *Lazarillo de Tormes* (1554), by an unknown Spanish author. Some critics consider it the first *picaresque novel*. These novels describe the adventures of a young *picaro* (rogue) who makes his way in the world through cunning and treachery. Picaresque novels are episodic like romances about knights, but in *Lazarillo de Tormes*, the rogue replaces the knight as the hero.

The first classic novel, according to some critics, was the Spanish masterpiece *Don Quixote* (part I 1605, part II 1615) by Miguel de Cervantes. Cervantes's story combines the chivalric romance and the picaresque adventure. The central character in *Don Quixote* is a middle-aged country landowner who imagines himself a knight, battling injustice. He differs significantly from the unbelievably heroic or clever characters in romances and picaresque narratives. Cervantes's characters resemble real people and often make foolish and costly mistakes.

The rise of the English novel

The novel form tends to emphasize realistic social themes. Sophisticated novels of this kind first appeared in England in the early 1700's. At that time, the urge to record the details of ordinary life began to replace the older narrative focus on wondrous, supernatural, remote, and heroic material.

The first English novelists. Some critics regard Daniel Defoe as the first novelist, though others credit Aphra Behn with combining the novel form and the romance in her fascinating slave narrative, *Oroonoko* (1688). Defoe's *Robinson Crusoe* (1719) and *Moll Flanders* (1722) consist of a series of episodes in the lives of clever and resourceful, but ordinary, characters.

Samuel Richardson wrote novels with well-developed plots rather than a sequence of episodes. His *Pamela; or Virtue Rewarded* (1740) tells of a virtuous female servant who resists her master's attempts to seduce her. The story is told in the form of letters, most of which are written by Pamela, the heroine, to her family. Through the letters, Richardson reveals key psychological aspects of the central character.

Henry Fielding wrote *The History of Tom Jones, a Foundling* (1749), which is especially noted for its elaborate, unified plot. This novel tells of the comical adventures of a young orphan, first as he grows up in rural England, and then as he travels toward London, meeting a variety of characters in English life.

Tobias Smollett wrote amusing, loosely constructed novels about eccentric characters. *The Expedition of Humphry Clinker* (1771) is a novel in letter form about a variety of English travelers and personality types.

Laurence Sterne was one of the greatest experimenters in the history of the novel. *The Life and Opinions of Tristram Shandy, Gentleman* (1760-1767). *Tristram Shandy* is an unconventional novel about an unconventional family. The story humorously portrays character types, philosophical ideas, and social customs.

Gothic novels became widely popular in England during the late 1700's through the 1800's. These horror stories tell of mysterious events that take place in gloomy, isolated castles. They have suspenseful, action-packed plots. Mary Shelley's *Frankenstein* (1818), about a scientist who creates a monster from parts of dead bodies, and Bram Stoker's *Dracula* (1897), about a nobleman who is secretly a vampire, became the most enduring examples of the type.

The 1800's

During the 1800's, English writers elaborated on the techniques of the early novelists and produced many great works. Authors in France, the United States, and Russia also wrote novels of major literary importance. The *romantic movement*, which stressed the need for full expression of human emotions and imagination, dominated the literature of the early 1800's. It was followed by the *realistic movement,* which demanded that literature accurately represent life as it is.

Britain. Sir Walter Scott, a Scottish writer, created and popularized *historical novels.* Such novels re-create the atmosphere of a past period and include actual characters and events from history. Scott wrote a long series of historical novels, including *Waverley* (1814), about a Scottish rebellion against England.

The *novel of manners* appeared in England during the late 1700's. Fanny Burney was one of the first writers in the tradition with *Evelina* (1778), a novel about a young woman's introduction to London life. Jane Austen perfected the novel of manners in the early 1800's. Her masterpiece, *Pride and Prejudice* (1813), centers on the social conventions surrounding courtship and marriage.

The English novel flourished during the 1800's, expanding to explore society's classes and institutions. Emily Bronte's *Wuthering Heights* (1847) added both Gothic and romance elements to the novel of manners. Charlotte Bronte's *Jane Eyre* (1847) merged Gothic romance and fictional biography. William Makepeace Thackeray wrote satirically on the hypocrisies of life in London and Paris in *Vanity Fair* (1847-1848). Charles Dickens wrote many great novels about English urban life. *Oliver Twist* (1837-1839) deals with the London underworld.

Anthony Trollope wrote long, detailed novels centering on politics, society, and religion as in the witty *Barchester Towers* (1857). George Eliot portrayed English rural and small-town life. Her greatest work, *Middlemarch* (1871-1872), deals with the profound moral crises in the lives of landowners and rural professionals. Robert Louis Stevenson wrote *Treasure Island* (1883) and other popular adventure novels. In the late 1800's, Thomas Hardy wrote novels such as *Jude the Obscure* (1895), in which tortured characters were fated to lead desperate lives.

France. French writers greatly influenced the development of the novel in the 1800's. Honoré de Balzac wrote a series of novels in the 1830's and 1840's under the collective title *The Human Comedy.* These were the first novels to fully explore the manners and morals of an entire society. Stendhal contributed to the development of the psychological novel in *The Red and the Black* (1830) and to the political novel in *The Charterhouse of Parma* (1839). Alexandre Dumas *père* and Victor Hugo wrote massive historical novels. The most famous include Dumas's *The Count of Monte Cristo* (1844-1845) and Hugo's *Les Misérables* (1862).

Gustave Flaubert wrote *Madame Bovary* (1856), which tells about a woman unhappy in her marriage to a village doctor. Flaubert's precise objective style influenced many other writers. Émile Zola helped establish *naturalism* as an important literary movement in the late 1800's. According to the theory of naturalism, a person's life is determined by heredity and environment. Naturalistic novels portray people who are trapped by circumstances beyond their control. Many of these novels deal with grim subjects. Zola's *Germinal* (1885), for example, describes the suffering of French miners.

The United States. The early American novel was less concerned with social and historical tradition than the European novel. From its beginnings, the American novel explored intense family themes, as in Charles Brockden Brown's *Wieland* (1798), about a man who

goes insane and murders his wife and children. American novels also dealt with the frontier landscape, as in James Fenimore Cooper's *The Last of the Mohicans* (1826). Cooper's novel includes one of America's great folk heroes, the frontiersman Natty Bumppo.

The mid-1800's produced classic American novels of moral dilemmas and obsession. Nathaniel Hawthorne's tale of sin, *The Scarlet Letter* (1850), and Herman Melville's symbolic whaling story, *Moby-Dick* (1851), are examples. Harriet Beecher Stowe's *Uncle Tom's Cabin* (1851-1852) was one of the first novels to raise the nation's consciousness about slavery.

In the late 1800's, Mark Twain captured American humor and colloquial speech in *The Adventures of Tom Sawyer* (1876) and *Adventures of Huckleberry Finn* (1884). The later book in particular has been praised for its attack on the social evils of the day and its vivid and realistic portrait of life on the Mississippi River.

William Dean Howells, in his novel *The Rise of Silas Lapham* (1885), became the first American writer to draw on the tradition of social realism coming out of European fiction in the 1800's. Henry James has been acclaimed for his psychological portrayals of sensitive, intelligent characters. James spent much time in England and followed the English tradition of writing about social manners in *The Portrait of a Lady* (1880-1881) and other novels.

During the late 1800's and early 1900's, the French naturalist movement influenced many American writers, notably Stephen Crane, Theodore Dreiser, Frank Norris, and Upton Sinclair. Crane's first novel, *Maggie: A Girl of the Streets* (1893), portrays the cruelty and vulgarity of slum life. Dreiser's *Sister Carrie* (1900) tells of a poor, lonely woman in Chicago. Norris's *The Octopus* (1901) depicts the expansion of the American railroad. Sinclair's *The Jungle* (1906) attacked the Chicago-based meatpacking industry so effectively that the novel led directly to government reforms.

Russia produced its two greatest novelists, Leo Tolstoy and Fyodor Dostoevsky, during the 1800's. Tolstoy and Dostoevsky rank as masters of the realistic novel.

Tolstoy's famous masterpiece, *War and Peace* (1869), centers on the 1812 invasion of Russia by the French emperor Napoleon I. The account of the war is interwoven with stories about the lives of several Russian families. Dostoevsky won fame for his probing psychological insight and his treatment of philosophical ideas. In his novel *Crime and Punishment* (1866), he explored the anguished mind of a student who commits two murders.

The modern novel

During the 1900's. Novelists experimented with various styles, techniques, and types of plots. World War I (1914-1918) had a major impact on many writers. The noble ideals and high hopes with which nations entered the war were shattered by the length and destruction of the conflict. After the war, many novelists dealt with the social changes and personal disillusionments of modern times. After World War II (1939-1945), novelists continued to explore the problems of modern life, especially the threat of nuclear war.

New directions in the novel. Older forms of the novel persisted in the early 1900's, notably in the works of Arnold Bennett and Rudyard Kipling in England. However, more experimental novelists began to gain prominence. In such novels as *Nostromo* (1904), the Polish-born English novelist Joseph Conrad changed the form of the adventure story. Conrad's stylistic experiments and probing psychological analysis helped shape the future of the novel in the 1900's.

In England, D. H. Lawrence broke many social taboos in writing about sexual passion in such novels as *Women in Love* (1920). Ford Madox Ford experimented with narration in *The Good Soldier* (1915), in which the narrator discovers that his wife and his best friend have been lovers for years. E. M. Forster raised issues of class and race in *A Passage to India* (1924).

Marcel Proust of France wrote the masterpiece *Remembrance of Things Past* (1913-1927). This seven-part novel deals with many subjects and portrays French society in the process of change during the early 1900's. The hero of French author Louis-Ferdinand Céline's *Journey to the End of the Night* (1932) wanders aimlessly through war-torn Europe.

The Irish writer James Joyce became one of the greatest novelists of the 1900's. In *Portrait of the Artist as a Young Man* (1916), a largely autobiographical novel about his youth, Joyce began to use techniques of narration in which the author presents the thoughts, sensations, and memories that flow through a character's mind. He perfected this technique, called *interior narration,* or *stream of consciousness,* in *Ulysses* (1922). This challenging novel compares one day in the life of a 1904 Dublin resident with events in Homer's *Odyssey.*

The English author Virginia Woolf also experimented with interior narration. Her best novels, such as *To the Lighthouse* (1927), are known for their brilliant structure and the emotional power of their style.

The greatest American novelists of the early 1900's included Edith Wharton, Sinclair Lewis, F. Scott Fitzgerald, Ernest Hemingway, William Faulkner, and John Steinbeck. Wharton followed Henry James in such novels of manners as *The Age of Innocence* (1920), about aristocratic New Yorkers of the 1870's. Lewis wrote about middle-class Americans in *Babbitt* (1922). In *The Great Gatsby* (1925), Fitzgerald pictured the false glamour and moral emptiness of wealthy, pleasure-seeking Americans of the 1920's, an era called the *Jazz Age.* Hemingway captured the personal letdown and sense of loss that many people felt after World War I in *The Sun Also Rises* (1926). In *The Sound and the Fury* (1929) and other novels, Faulkner dealt with the decline of Southern aristocratic families and the breakdown of traditional standards of behavior. Steinbeck wrote about the Great Depression in such powerful novels as *The Grapes of Wrath* (1939).

The American detective novel made a significant contribution to the modern novel with its realistic language and cynicism. The most important of these novels included *The Maltese Falcon* (1930) by Dashiell Hammett and *The Big Sleep* (1939) by Raymond Chandler.

Franz Kafka, a Czech author who wrote in German, produced puzzling novels that have an atmosphere of fantasy and nightmare. In *The Trial* (1925), Kafka portrayed the frustration and despair of an ordinary man entangled in the workings of a bureaucratic legal system. The German novelist Thomas Mann also wrote about the frustrations of modern life, but the main char-

acters in his novels are sensitive and intellectually gifted. Mann's major novels include *The Magic Mountain* (1924).

Existentialism, a philosophical movement, greatly influenced French literature during the late 1930's and the 1940's. Existentialists emphasized that individuals must choose their own way to live and act in an essentially meaningless world and then accept full responsibility for their actions. The rise of existentialism in France resulted in a number of existential novels, including *Nausea* (1938) by Jean-Paul Sartre and *The Stranger* (1942) by Albert Camus. Sartre and Camus focused on moral issues rather than on experimental techniques.

After World War II. During the 1950's, an experimental form called the *nouveau roman* (new novel) appeared in France. The nouveau roman writers rejected traditional features of novels, such as organized plots and clear-cut types of characters. Instead, they wrote novels that focused on exact descriptions of objects and events. The nouveau roman writers included Alain Robbe-Grillet, Marguerite Duras, and Michel Butor. *Jealousy* (1957) by Robbe-Grillet typifies the nouveau roman. Perhaps the most original novelist of the 1940's and 1950's was Samuel Beckett, an Irish-born author who wrote in both French and English. Beckett was influenced by James Joyce and used the interior narration technique in *Malone Dies* (1951). This novel centers on the repressed hysteria of a dying tramp named Malone.

In England, the leading postwar novelists included Evelyn Waugh, George Orwell, and Graham Greene. Waugh wrote light satirical novels before the war, but his tone later deepened in *Brideshead Revisited* (1945), a study of an aristocratic Roman Catholic family. Orwell's *1984* (1949) deals with life in a totalitarian state. Greene wrote about religious and moral problems in *The Heart of the Matter* (1948). Other postwar English novelists included Kingsley Amis, Anthony Burgess, Doris Lessing, Iris Murdoch, C. P. Snow, and Muriel Spark.

American writers produced fairly conventional novels during the 1950's. One of the most popular novels of this period was *The Catcher in the Rye* (1951) by J. D. Salinger. It tells about the problems of a prep school dropout in New York City. The novels of Saul Bellow, Philip Roth, and Bernard Malamud deal partly with Jewish life in the United States. Bellow followed the form of the picaresque narrative in *The Adventures of Augie March* (1953), about a Chicago youth who grows up during the Great Depression. In *The Assistant* (1957), Malamud portrayed the relationship between a poor Jewish shopkeeper and his helper. In *Goodbye, Columbus* (1959), Roth wrote of the strained love affair between a young middle-class Jewish man and a wealthy Jewish girl.

The American novelists Ralph Ellison and James Baldwin focused on the difficulties faced by African Americans. Ellison's *Invisible Man* (1952) describes a young black man's growing awareness of the turmoil over race in the United States. Baldwin's *Go Tell It on the Mountain* (1953) tells of a poor black family in the Harlem section of New York City. Other brilliant writers in the 1950's produced well-crafted and powerful novels. Flannery O'Connor explored religious fanaticism in the South in *Wise Blood* (1952). The Russian-born Vladimir Nabokov wrote *Lolita* (1955), a funny and controversial novel about an older man's obsession with a young girl.

The middle and late 1900's. The *black humor* style in fiction became popular during the 1960's. Black humorists treat serious subjects in a darkly comic manner. Their novels are both funny and tragic. For example, *Catch-22* (1961), by the American author Joseph Heller, deals humorously with the absurdities of warfare and military organizations, but also captures the terrifying confusion of war.

John Updike's *Rabbit, Run* (1960) is an ironic novel about suburban life in the eastern United States. Philip Roth's *Portnoy's Complaint* (1969) deals with the sexual neuroses of a young man from a Jewish family.

Science fiction played a prominent role in novels of the middle and late 1900's. Key works include *Fahrenheit 451* (1953) by Ray Bradbury, *Stranger in a Strange Land* (1961) by Robert A. Heinlein, *Dune* (1965) by Frank Herbert, *The Andromeda Strain* (1969) by Michael Crichton, *Neuromancer* (1984) by William Gibson, and *The Handmaid's Tale* (1985) by Margaret Atwood.

The novel today features international trends that appeared during the 1960's and 1970's. One of the trends was introduced by a group of authors who wrote *nonfiction novels.* These novelists combined a documentary style with fictional techniques to tell about actual events and people.

The American writer Truman Capote originated the term "nonfiction novel" to describe his *In Cold Blood* (1965). Capote based this work on an actual 1959 murder case in which two men killed a Kansas farm family. Many other American authors, including William Styron and Norman Mailer, followed Capote in writing nonfiction novels. In *The Confessions of Nat Turner* (1967), Styron told the story of an 1831 slave rebellion in Virginia led by Nat Turner, a black preacher. Mailer wrote *The Armies of the Night* (1968), which describes his experiences in a 1967 protest march in Washington, D.C.

One group of writers created highly imaginative and inventive novels. In some cases, they modernized myths, fairy tales, and other old stories, or they created fantasy worlds. Latin American fiction gained recognition with a kind of novel called *magic realism,* which blends dreams and magic with everyday reality. The originator of this style was the Argentine writer Jorge Luis Borges. The Colombian writer Gabriel García Márquez wrote a classic of magic realism, *One Hundred Years of Solitude* (1967), about generations of a strange Latin American family. Manuel Puig of Argentina wrote *Kiss of the Spider Woman* (1976), about the relationship between two men who share a prison cell. Several other Latin American novelists contributed to the tradition of magic realism, often writing in newer, more experimental forms. These authors included Carlos Fuentes of Mexico in *The Death of Artemio Cruz* (1962), Mario Vargas Llosa of Peru in *The Time of the Hero* (1962), and Luisa Valenzuela of Argentina in *The Lizard's Tail* (1983).

Postwar German novelists produced their own style of magic realism in the fiction of Günter Grass. In Grass's *The Tin Drum* (1959), the main character can stop time and drown out history. Grass wrote about postwar stress in Germany and Poland in *The Call of the Toad* (1992). Heinrich Böll dealt with postwar German memories in *Group Portrait with Lady* (1971).

The Italian writers Italo Calvino and Umberto Eco took the novel back to its roots in allegory, fable, and fairy tale. Calvino wrote *The Castle of Crossed Destinies* (1973), and Eco wrote *The Name of the Rose* (1980).

Eastern Europe produced its own style of experimental fiction, often with a political slant. Christa Wolf described the difficulty of living in East Germany before the 1990 reunification in *The Quest for Christa T.* (1968). Milan Kundera dealt with human relationships in Czechoslovakia near the time of a Russian invasion in 1968 in *The Unbearable Lightness of Being* (1984).

Another international trend in the novel was fiction that reflected the breakup of colonial empires in Africa, Asia, and the Caribbean. Some authors wrote about changes in Australia and Canada. Works reflecting these trends included the South African novels *In the Heart of the Country* (1977) by J. M. Coetzee and *Burger's Daughter* (1979) by Nadine Gordimer. Chinua Achebe used Nigerian themes in *Things Fall Apart* (1958). V. S. Naipaul wrote several highly praised novels set in the West Indies, notably *Guerrillas* (1975). Salman Rushdie wrote about Indian and Muslim traditions in *The Satanic Verses* (1988). Patrick White wrote sweeping novels about his homeland of Australia, such as *The Tree of Man* (1955). Robertson Davies wrote sophisticated novels about Canada, including *What's Bred in the Bone* (1985).

British novelists still write in a realistic style, but they have widened the range of their works. Graham Swift wrote about rural life in *Waterland* (1983). Kingsley Amis's son Martin Amis wrote about world finance in *Money: A Suicide Note* (1984). David Lodge used an academic setting in *Small World: An Academic Romance* (1984). Julian Barnes dealt with the world of ideas in *A History of the World in 10½ Chapters* (1989). Jeanette Winterson explored myth and sexuality in *Sexing the Cherry* (1989). Kazuo Ishiguro wrote about world politics in *The Remains of the Day* (1989). Ireland produced gritty novels about lower-class urban characters, such as *Paddy Clarke Ha Ha Ha* (1993) by Roddy Doyle.

Several African American and Asian American women writers created important novels that explored aspects of the modern black and Asian experience. These authors included Toni Cade Bambara in *The Salt Eaters* (1980), Bette Bao Lord in *Spring Moon* (1981), Al-ice Walker in *The Color Purple* (1982), Toni Morrison in *Beloved* (1987), and Amy Tan in *The Joy Luck Club* (1989).

The novel today continues to explore national themes. Examples include *American Pastoral* by Philip Roth, *Mason & Dixon* by Thomas Pynchon, and *Underworld* by Don DeLillo (all of the United States, all published in 1997), and *The God of Small Things* (1997) by Arundhati Roy of India.   Michael Seidel

Related articles. See the articles on the various national literatures, such as **American literature** and **French literature,** and their lists of *Related articles.* See also the following articles:

Black humor	Literature	Romanticism
Detective story	Naturalism	Science fiction
Epic	Prose	Short story
Existentialism	Realism	Westerns
Fiction	Romance	
Gothic novel		
Graphic novel		

Additional resources

Levasseur, Jennifer, and Rabalais, Kevin, eds. *Novel Voices.* Writer's Digest, 2003.
Schellinger, Paul, ed. *Encyclopedia of the Novel.* 2 vols. Fitzroy Dearborn, 1998.

November is the 11th month of the year according to the Gregorian calendar, which is used in almost all the world today. It takes its name from *novem,* the Latin word for *nine.* In the early Roman calendar, November was the ninth month. Because July was named for Julius Caesar and August for Augustus Caesar, the Roman Senate offered to name the 11th month for Tiberius Caesar. He refused modestly, saying, "What will you do if you have 13 emperors?" Originally there were 30 days in November, then 29, then 31. From the time of Augustus, the month has had 30 days.

November is a month of remembrance. On Día de los muertos, November 2, Mexicans honor the dead. This holiday is somber, yet has many playful characteristics as well. On November 11, Americans honor war veterans with a national holiday called Veterans Day. In Canada, the holiday is called Remembrance Day. This holiday, also known as Armistice Day in some countries, commemorates the signing of the *armistice* (temporary peace agreement) that ended World War I (1914-1918).

On the second Sunday of the month, Father's Day is celebrated in Sweden. Children's Book Week is observed in November in many places. November 14 is Children's Day in India. The Japanese festival Shichi-Go-San (Three-Five-Seven) is a special day set aside for children who are 3, 5, or 7 years old. It is held on November 15. Election Day in the United States falls on the first Tuesday after the first Monday of the month.

People in the United States celebrate Thanksgiving Day on the fourth Thursday of November. On Guy Fawkes Day, November 5, people in the United Kingdom recall the Gunpowder Plot of 1605, an unsuccess-

Important November events

1 All Saints' Day observed by Christians.
— Crawford W. Long, American physician who first used ether as an anesthetic in surgery, born 1815.
2 All Souls' Day observed by Christians.
— Daniel Boone, American frontiersman, born 1734.
— Marie Antoinette, French queen, born 1755.
— Spanish expedition led by Gaspar de Portolá reached San Francisco Bay, 1769.
— James K. Polk, 11th U.S. president, born 1795.
— Warren G. Harding, 29th U.S. president, born 1865.
— North Dakota became the 39th U.S. state, 1889.
— South Dakota became the 40th U.S. state, 1889.
3 Benvenuto Cellini, Italian goldsmith, born 1500.
— Stephen Austin, colonizer of Texas, born 1793.
— Vilhjalmur Stefansson, Canadian explorer, born 1879.
— Panama declared its independence from Colombia, 1903.
4 Erie Canal formally opened at New York, 1825.
— Will Rogers, American humorist, born 1879.
— Iranian revolutionaries took over U.S. Embassy in Tehran and seized some U.S. citizens as hostages, 1979.
— Yitzhak Rabin, prime minister of Israel, assassinated 1995.
5 Guy Fawkes Day in the United Kingdom marks failed Gunpowder Plot to blow up Houses of Parliament, 1605.
— Eugene V. Debs, American labor leader, born 1855.
— Will Durant, American historian, born 1885.
6 John Philip Sousa, American bandmaster, born 1854.
— First U.S. intercollegiate football game, Rutgers versus College of New Jersey (Princeton), at Rutgers, 1869.
7 General William Henry Harrison defeated Indians in Battle of Tippecanoe, 1811.
— Marie Curie, French physicist, born 1867.
— Albert Camus, French author, born 1913.
— Bolsheviks ousted provisional Russian government, 1917. (October 25 on the Russian calendar then in use.)

8 Edmond Halley, British astronomer, born 1656.
— Mount Holyoke Female Seminary (today Mount Holyoke College) opened, 1837.
— Montana became the 41st U.S. state, 1889.
9 Ivan Turgenev, Russian novelist, born 1818.
— Edward VII of the United Kingdom born 1841.
— Kaiser Wilhelm II abdicated German throne, 1918.
— *Kristallnacht,* when Jewish businesses and synagogues throughout Germany were attacked by the Nazis, 1938.
— Cambodia became independent in 1953.
— Opening of the Berlin Wall, Germany, 1989.
10 Martin Luther, German religious leader, born 1483.
— William Hogarth, English painter, born 1697.
— Friedrich Schiller, German playwright and poet, born 1759.
— Sir John S. D. Thompson, Canadian prime minister, born 1844.
— Donald MacMillan, American Arctic explorer, born 1874.
11 Remembrance Day, Canada.
— Fyodor M. Dostoevsky, Russian novelist, born 1821.
— Ned Kelly, Australian bushranger, hanged 1880.
— Washington became the 42nd U.S. state, 1889.
— Poland was proclaimed an independent republic in 1918.
— Armistice signed ending World War I, 1918.
— Veterans Day first celebrated in United States, 1954.
12 Joseph Hopkinson, American jurist, born 1770.
— Elizabeth Cady Stanton, American reformer, born 1815.
— Bahá'u'lláh, Baháí prophet, born 1817.
— Auguste Rodin, French sculptor, born 1840.
13 Robert Louis Stevenson, Scottish novelist, born 1850.
— Louis D. Brandeis, American jurist, born 1856.
— Holland Tunnel opened in New York City, 1927.
— Mariner 9, the first human-made object to orbit another planet, began orbiting Mars, 1971.
14 Robert Fulton, American inventor, born 1765.
— Claude Monet, French painter, born 1840.

Nov. birthstone—
topaz

Nov. flower—
chrysanthemum

Nov. 4—Will
Rogers born

Nov. 6—first inter-
collegiate football game

ful attempt to blow up the Houses of Parliament. The day is marked with fireworks and bonfires. In Thailand, Loy Krathong, a water festival, is held in mid-November.

Religious holidays in November include the Christian All Saints' Day on November 1. The Bahá'í observance of the birth of Bahá'u'lláh, who founded the faith, occurs on the 12th. Sikhs commemorate the birth of Nanak, the first Sikh *guru* (spiritual teacher), in November.

November's flower is the chrysanthemum. The topaz is November's birthstone.   Carole S. Angell

Quotations

November woods are bare and still;
November days are clear and bright;
Each noon burns up the morning's chill,
The morning's snow is gone by night.
                                    Helen Hunt Jackson

November's sky is chill and drear,
November's leaf is red and sear.
                                    Sir Walter Scott

Autumn wins you best by this, its mute
Appeal to sympathy for its decay.
                                    Robert Browning

The wild November comes at last
Beneath a veil of rain;
The night wind blows its folds aside,
Her face is full of pain.
                                    Richard Henry Stoddard

Related articles in **World Book** include:

Calendar	Thanksgiving Day
Chrysanthemum	Topaz
Fawkes, Guy	Veterans Day

Important November events

14 Jawaharlal Nehru, Indian statesman, born 1889.
— Frederick Grant Banting, Canadian physician who discovered insulin, born 1891.
— Aaron Copland, American composer, born 1900.
— Prince Charles, heir to British throne, born 1948.
15 Shichi-Go-San (Three-Five-Seven) festival, Japan.
— William Pitt the Elder, British statesman, born 1708.
— William Herschel, English astronomer, born 1738.
— Draft of Articles of Confederation approved by U.S. Congress, 1777.
— Felix Frankfurter, American jurist, born 1882.
— First meeting of League of Nations Assembly, 1920.
— Manuel Quezon inaugurated as first president of the Philippines, 1935.
16 Louis H. Fréchette, Canadian poet, born 1839.
— Paul Hindemith, German American composer, born 1895.
— Oklahoma became the 46th U.S. state, 1907.
17 U.S. Congress first met in Washington, D.C., 1800.
— Suez Canal opened, 1869.
18 Louis Jacques Daguerre, French painter and inventor of the daguerreotype, born 1787.
— Asa Gray, American botanist, born 1810.
— Sir William S. Gilbert, English dramatist who worked with composer Sir Arthur Sullivan, born 1836.
— Ignace Jan Paderewski, Polish pianist, composer, and statesman, born 1860 (November 6 on the Russian calendar then in use).
— Standard time began in the United States, 1883.
— Eugene Ormandy, American conductor, born 1899.
— United States and Panama signed treaty providing for Panama Canal, 1903.
19 George R. Clark, American frontiersman, born 1752.
— Ferdinand de Lesseps, French promoter of Suez Canal, born 1805.
— James A. Garfield, 20th U.S. president, born 1831.
— Abraham Lincoln delivered Gettysburg Address, 1863.

— Indira Gandhi, first woman prime minister of India, born 1917.
20 Sir Wilfrid Laurier, Canadian statesman, born 1841.
— Selma Lagerlöf, Swedish novelist, born 1858.
— Kenesaw Mountain Landis, first commissioner of professional baseball, born 1866.
— United States forces landed on Tarawa, World War II, 1943.
21 Sieur de La Salle, French explorer, born 1643.
— Voltaire, French author and philosopher, born 1694.
— North Carolina ratified the U.S. Constitution, 1789.
22 Independence Day, Lebanon.
— George Eliot, English novelist, born 1819.
— Charles de Gaulle, French statesman, born 1890.
— Benjamin Britten, British composer, born 1913.
— First transpacific air-mail flight began, 1935.
— U.S. President John F. Kennedy assassinated, 1963.
23 Franklin Pierce, 14th U.S. president, born 1804.
24 Baruch Spinoza, Dutch philosopher, born 1632.
— Father Junípero Serra, Franciscan missionary, born 1713.
— Laurence Sterne, British novelist, born 1713.
— Zachary Taylor, 12th U.S. president, born 1784.
— Henri de Toulouse-Lautrec, French painter, born 1864.
25 Lope de Vega, Spanish playwright, born 1562.
— Andrew Carnegie, American industrialist, born 1835.
— Pope John XXIII born 1881.
— Joe DiMaggio, American baseball star, born 1914.
26 First national Thanksgiving Day in United States proclaimed by President George Washington, 1789.
27 Charles A. Beard, American historian, born 1874.
28—William Blake, English poet and artist, born 1757.
— Stefan Zweig, Austrian biographer, born 1881.
— Mauritania became independent in 1960.
29 Louisa M. Alcott, American author, born 1832.
— American Commander Richard E. Byrd and crew of three became first to fly over South Pole, 1929.
30 Jonathan Swift, English author, born 1667.
— Mark Twain, American author, born 1835.
— Sir Winston Churchill, British statesman, born 1874.

WORLD BOOK illustrations by Mike Hagel

Nov. 19—Lincoln's Gettysburg Address

Nov. 19—Indira Gandhi born

Nov. 22—John F. Kennedy assassinated

Nov. 26—first national Thanksgiving Day in U.S.

Novgorod. See Velikiy Novgorod.
Novi Sad, *NAW vee SAHD,* is a center of manufacturing and transportation in Serbia and one of Serbia's largest cities. The municipality of Novi Sad has a population of 299,294. A municipality may include rural areas as well as the urban center. About 45 miles (72 kilometers) northwest of Belgrade, Novi Sad lies on the main highway and railroad between Belgrade and Budapest, Hungary (see **Serbia** [map]). The Danube River meets the Mali Bački Canal at Novi Sad. The canal is part of a system of waterways that link the Danube and Tisa rivers. The city produces electrochemical equipment and processed foods. It is home to the University of Novi Sad.

Novi Sad was founded in the early 1690's as the headquarters of the Serbian Orthodox Church. It grew as a trade center for the nearby farm area. A boom began in Novi Sad during the 1960's after petroleum and natural gas were found near the city.   Sabrina P. Ramet
Novosibirsk, *NAW vah sih BEERSK* (pop. 1,425,508), is an important center of manufacturing in Russia. The city lies on the Ob River, about 1,700 miles (2,740 kilometers) east of Moscow, in Siberia. Novosibirsk is the largest city in Siberia (see **Russia** [political map]).

Many factories in Novosibirsk manufacture heavy equipment, including farm and mining machinery and diesel trucks. The city also produces steel. Airlines, railroads, and riverboats serve Novosibirsk.

Novosibirsk was founded in 1893 as a settlement for workers building a railroad across Siberia. The city grew as a transportation center. Industry boomed during World War II (1939-1945), when many factories in combat areas in western areas of the country were moved to the safety of Novosibirsk. In 1958, the government built Akademgorodok (Academy City), a suburb of Novosibirsk, as a science research center.   Craig ZumBrunnen
NOW. See National Organization for Women.
Noyce, Robert (1927-1990), is one of the two inventors of the microchip, or *integrated circuit,* which contains all the components of an electronic circuit. Microchips are used in computers and other electronic equipment.

Noyce made his chip in 1959 while working at Fairchild Semiconductor Corporation, a company he helped found. Jack Kilby, an electrical engineer, developed a similar chip at about the same time, but working independently. Kilby's patent was filed first. But Noyce's design made the connections between components a part of the manufacturing process, while Kilby's did not.

In 1968, Noyce left Fairchild. He and Gordon Moore, a research scientist from Fairchild, founded Intel Corporation, now a leading maker of semiconductor chips.

Robert Norton Noyce was born on Dec. 12, 1927, in Burlington, Iowa. He graduated from Grinnell College in 1949 and earned a doctorate in physics from Massachusetts Institute of Technology in 1953. Noyce died on June 3, 1990.   Paul N. Edwards

See also **Computer chip; Kilby, Jack.**
Noyes, *noyz,* **Alfred** (1880-1958), was one of the most popular English poets of the early 1900's. He became famous for his ballads and lyric poems about English history. Many of Noyes's poems also show his love of the sea. His reputation has declined since the mid-1900's, but some of his poetry remains popular with children, especially the exciting ballad "The Highwayman" (1906).

Noyes was born on Sept. 16, 1880, in Wolverhampton.

He established himself as a leading poet with the epic *Drake* (1906-1908). *Drake* deals with the famous English sea captain Sir Francis Drake. In *The Golden Hynde* (1908), Noyes filled his poems with colorful images of the sea and sea voyages. *Tales of the Mermaid Tavern* (1913) describes the adventures of noted Englishmen who lived during the reign of Queen Elizabeth I.

Noyes's most ambitious work was perhaps *The Torchbearers,* a long three-part poem honoring great scientists. It consists of *The Watchers of the Sky* (1922), *The Book of Earth* (1925), and *The Last Voyage* (1930).

In 1927, Noyes converted to Roman Catholicism. His conversion influenced many of his later writings. In *The Unknown God* (1934), he wrote a prose account of his change from an unbeliever to a devout Christian.

In addition to verse, Noyes wrote biographies, literary criticism, novels, plays, and short stories. Noyes also wrote an autobiography, *Two Worlds from Memory* (1953). He died on June 28, 1958.   Garrett Stewart
NRA. See National Rifle Association of America.
NSPE. See National Society of Professional Engineers.
Nubia, *NOO bee uh,* was an ancient African region that covered part of what is now Sudan. Nubia extended along the Nile River from the southern boundary of ancient Egypt almost to present-day Khartoum, Sudan. Although Egypt periodically controlled Nubia, powerful independent states also emerged in the region. The earliest state was Kerma, which lasted from about 2400 to 1500 B.C. The kingdom of Kush developed in Nubia after

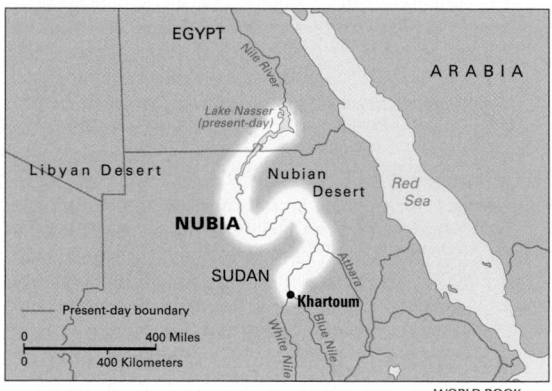

The ancient region of Nubia, *shown in yellow,* occupied an area along the Nile River in what is now Sudan.

1000 B.C. and became a center for agriculture and trade. From 750 to 660 B.C., Kushites conquered and ruled Egypt. Kush itself lasted until about A.D. 350. See **Kush.**

The Egyptians regarded Nubia as a source of gold, cattle, and soldiers, and as a trading center for goods from the African interior. Although Egyptian influence in Nubia increased over time, Nubians maintained their own cultures, worshiped their own gods, and had their own forms of architecture.

Most Nubians were converted to Christianity in the A.D. 500's. Many remained Christian until the 1300's, when Arab Muslim invaders conquered the area and made Islam the dominant religion.   Kevin C. MacDonald
Nuclear bomb. See Nuclear weapon.

Patrick Aventurier, Gamma/Liaison

A nuclear power plant uses the heat of a controlled nuclear reaction to produce steam, which then generates electric energy. The plant shown here, southeast of Paris on the Seine River, has tall structures called *cooling towers* to dispose of excess heat.

Nuclear energy

Nuclear energy, also called *atomic energy,* is the powerful energy released by changes in the *nucleus* (core) of atoms. The heat and light of the sun result from nuclear energy. Scientists and engineers have found many uses for this energy. They include the production of electric power, the explosion of nuclear weapons, and the diagnosis and treatment of medical conditions.

Scientists knew nothing about nuclear energy until the early 1900's, though they knew that all matter consists of atoms. Through further study, scientists learned that a nucleus makes up most of the *mass* (quantity of matter) of every atom. They also learned that this nucleus is held together by an extremely strong force. A huge amount of energy is concentrated in the nucleus because of this force. The next step was to make nuclei let go of much of that energy.

Scientists first released nuclear energy on a large scale at the University of Chicago in 1942, three years after the beginning of World War II. This achievement led to the development of the atomic bomb. The first atomic bomb exploded in the desert near Alamogordo, New Mexico, on July 16, 1945. In August of that year, United States airplanes dropped atomic bombs on the Japanese cities of Hiroshima and Nagasaki. The bombs largely destroyed both cities and helped end World War II.

Since 1945, scientists have developed peaceful uses of nuclear energy. The energy released by nuclei cre-

ates large amounts of heat. This heat can be used to make steam. The steam, in turn, can be used to drive machines that generate electric power. Engineers have built devices called *nuclear reactors* to produce and control nuclear energy.

A nuclear reactor operates somewhat like a furnace. However, instead of using such fossil fuels as coal or oil, almost all reactors use uranium. Fossil fuels are made from once-living material that has been dead for millions of years. Instead of burning in the reactor, the uranium *fissions*—that is, its nuclei split into two or more fragments. As a nucleus splits, it releases energy that is converted largely into heat. The fission of 1 pound of uranium releases more energy than the burning of 3 million pounds (1,500 tons) of coal. Stated in metric terms, the fission of 1 kilogram of uranium releases more energy than the burning of 3 million kilograms (3,000 metric tons) of coal.

One peaceful use of nuclear energy is the production of electric power. Nuclear energy also powers some submarines, surface ships, and spacecraft. Nuclear reactions produce particles and rays called *nuclear radiation* that have uses in medicine, industry, and science. However, large doses of nuclear radiation can be dangerous. Exposure to too much radiation can result in a condition called *radiation sickness* (see **Radiation sickness**).

This article deals mainly with nuclear energy as a

source of electric power. To learn about other uses of nuclear energy, see **Nuclear weapon; Ship** (Nuclear power and automation); **Submarine.**

The role of nuclear energy in power production

Almost all the world's electric power is produced by *hydroelectric* or *thermal* power plants. Hydroelectric plants use the force of rushing water from a dam or waterfall to generate electric power. Thermal plants use the force of steam from boiling water. Most thermal plants burn fossil fuels—coal, oil, and natural gas—to produce heat to boil water. The remaining thermal plants fission uranium.

Few countries have enough water power to generate large amounts of hydroelectric power. Many regions have already fully exploited their hydroelectric capacity. Thus, most countries depend mainly on fossil fuels. But fossil fuels are a nonrenewable resource, and burning them produces gases that can damage the environment. Therefore, many experts predict that nuclear power will become increasingly important.

Worldwide use of nuclear energy. Nuclear power reactors produce electric power in about 30 countries. There are about 440 reactors worldwide. These reactors produce about 15 percent of the world's electric power. The United States is the world's leading producer of nuclear energy. In addition to these reactors, there are more than 3,000 nuclear facilities worldwide that are used for applications in research, medicine, industry, and agriculture.

Advantages and disadvantages of nuclear energy. Nuclear power plants have two main advantages over fossil-fuel plants. (1) Once built, a nuclear plant can be less expensive to operate than a fossil-fuel plant, mainly because a nuclear plant uses a much smaller volume of fuel. (2) Uranium, unlike fossil fuels, releases no chemical or solid pollutants into the air during use.

However, nuclear power plants have three major disadvantages. These disadvantages have slowed the development of nuclear energy in some countries. (1) Nuclear power plants cost more to build than fossil-fuel plants. (2) Nuclear plants must meet stricter government regulations than fossil-fuel plants have to meet. The regulations are meant to prevent hazardous amounts of radioactive material from being released. For example, a nuclear plant must satisfy the government that it can quickly and automatically deal with any kind of emergency. (3) Used nuclear fuel produces radiation long after it has been removed from the reactor. Some of the solid fission fragments are unstable and release radiation as they decay into other elements. As a result, safe disposal of nuclear waste presents a challenge.

The full development of nuclear energy. Many experts believe that the benefits of nuclear energy outweigh any problems involved in its production. According to these experts, oil may be so scarce by the mid-2000's that it will be too expensive to drill. Canada, China, Germany, India, Russia, the United States, and some other countries have enough coal to meet their energy requirements for hundreds of years at present rates of use. However, coal releases large amounts of sulfur and other pollutants into the air when it is burned (see **Environmental pollution**). If nuclear energy were fully developed, it could completely replace oil and coal as a source of electric power.

But a number of problems must be solved before nuclear energy can be fully developed. For example, almost all today's power reactors use a scarce type of uranium known as U-235. If U-235 continues to be used at

Share of electric power from nuclear energy

This graph shows the percentage of total electric power derived from nuclear energy by selected countries.

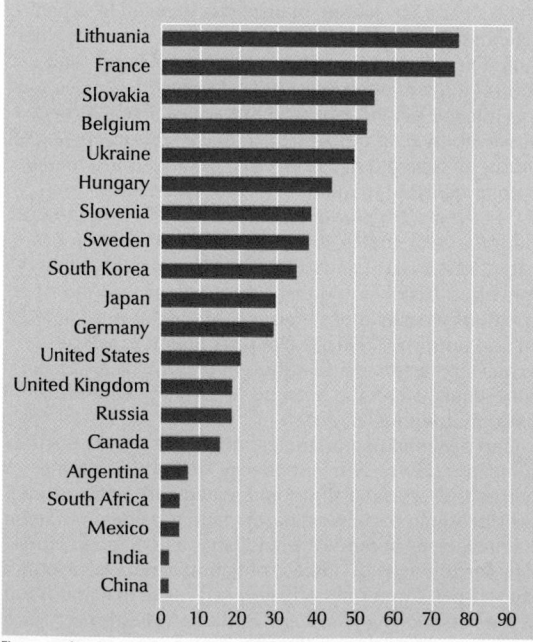

Figures are for 2009. Source: International Atomic Energy Agency.

Leading nuclear energy producing countries

Nuclear energy produced in a year

United States	●●●●●●●●●●●●
	796,900,000,000 kilowatt-hours
France	●●●●●●◖
	391,800,000,000 kilowatt-hours
Japan	●●●●◖
	263,100,000,000 kilowatt-hours
Russia	●●◖
	152,800,000,000 kilowatt-hours
South Korea	●●◖
	141,100,000,000 kilowatt-hours
Germany	●●
	127,700,000,000 kilowatt-hours
Canada	●◖
	85,100,000,000 kilowatt-hours
Ukraine	●◖
	78,000,000,000 kilowatt-hours
China	●
	65,700,000,000 kilowatt-hours
United Kingdom	●
	62,900,000,000 kilowatt-hours

Figures are for 2009.
Source: International Atomic Energy Agency.

its present rate, the world's supply of it will become so small that it will be too expensive to mine and process by 2100. Therefore, for nuclear energy to replace other energy sources in the future, it must be based on fuel that is much more plentiful than U-235.

The composition of matter

The process by which a nucleus releases energy is called a *nuclear reaction*. To understand the various types of nuclear reactions, a person must know something about the nature of matter.

All the matter that makes up all solids, liquids, and gases is composed of *chemical elements*. The chemical elements, in turn, are composed of atoms. A chemical element is a substance that cannot be broken down chemically into simpler substances. There are over 100 known chemical elements. Ninety-three of them are found on or in Earth, including tiny amounts of an element called plutonium. All the other elements are artificially created.

Scientists rank the elements according to *mass,* a measure of the quantity of matter in an object. An object's mass is proportional to its weight. Hydrogen is the lightest natural element, and plutonium is the heaviest. Most of the artificially created elements are heavier than plutonium.

Nuclear energy terms

Atom consists of a positively charged nucleus and one or more negatively charged electrons. The electrons revolve about the nucleus.

Atomic mass number is the total number of neutrons and protons in the nucleus of an atom.

Chain reaction is a continuous, self-sustaining series of fission reactions in a mass of uranium or plutonium.

Fission is the type of nuclear reaction that occurs when a nucleus of uranium or another heavy element is split into two nearly equal parts.

Fusion is a type of nuclear reaction that occurs when two lightweight nuclei *fuse* (combine) and form a heavier nucleus. Fusion produces the sun's energy.

Half-life is the time required for half the atoms of a radioactive substance to decay into another substance.

Isotopes are different forms of the same element. The atoms that make up each of the different forms have different mass numbers. The atoms are also called isotopes.

Neutron is an electrically *neutral* (uncharged) particle in the nucleus of an atom.

Nuclear radiation consists of high-energy particles and tiny packets of energy called *photons* that are given off during a nuclear reaction.

Nuclear reaction involves a change in the structure of a nucleus. Fission, fusion, and radioactive decay are the most important types of nuclear reactions.

Nuclear reactor is a device for producing nuclear energy by means of controlled chain reactions.

Nucleus is the core of an atom and carries a positive charge. The nuclei of all elements except hydrogen consist of neutrons and protons. An ordinary hydrogen nucleus has one proton and no neutrons.

Proton is a positively charged particle in a nucleus.

Radioactive decay, or radioactivity, is the process by which a nucleus *spontaneously* (naturally) changes into the nucleus of another isotope or element. The process releases energy mainly in the form of nuclear radiation.

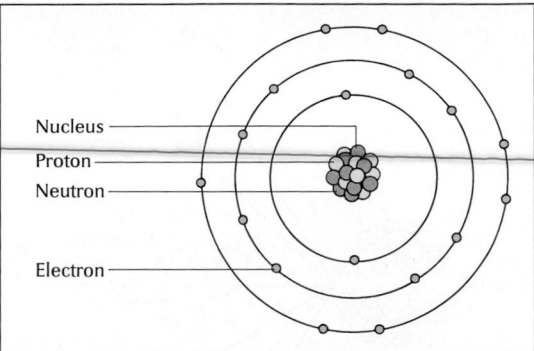

WORLD BOOK diagram by Arthur Grebetz

An atom consists of a nucleus and one or more electrons. The nucleus, which makes up almost all of an atom's mass, consists of tiny particles called *protons* and *neutrons*. They are held together by an extremely strong force.

Atoms and nuclei. An atom consists of a positively charged nucleus and one or more *electrons,* which are negatively charged particles. The nucleus makes up almost all of an atom's mass. The electrons, which have almost no mass, revolve around the nucleus. Electrons determine how an atom chemically reacts with other atoms (see **Chemistry** [Fundamental ideas of chemistry]). However, electrons do not play an active part in nuclear reactions.

The nuclei of chemical elements consist of particles called *protons* and *neutrons*. An ordinary nucleus of hydrogen, the lightest element, has one proton and no neutrons. Heavier elements, such as uranium and plutonium, have large numbers of protons and neutrons.

Protons carry a positive charge. Neutrons have no net charge. Extremely strong forces called *nuclear forces* hold the protons and neutrons together in the nucleus. These nuclear forces determine the amount of energy required to release neutrons and protons from the nucleus of an atom.

Isotopes. Most chemical elements have more than one form. These different forms are called the *isotopes* of an element. An element's isotopes have the same number of protons, but different numbers of neutrons.

Scientists identify an isotope by its *atomic mass number*—that is, the total number of protons and neutrons in each of its nuclei. All the isotopes of a given element have the same number of protons in every nucleus. Every hydrogen nucleus, for example, has just 1 proton. Every uranium nucleus has 92 protons.

However, each isotope of an element has a different number of neutrons in its nuclei and so has a different atomic mass number. For example, the most plentiful isotope of uranium has 146 neutrons. Its atomic mass number is therefore 238 (the sum of 92 and 146). Scientists call this isotope *uranium 238* or *U-238*. The uranium isotope that almost all nuclear reactors use as fuel has 143 neutrons, and so its atomic mass number is 235. This isotope is called *uranium 235* or *U-235*.

No two elements have the same number of protons in their atoms. If an atom gains or loses one or more protons, it becomes an atom of a different element. However, if an atom gains or loses one or more neutrons, it becomes another isotope of the same element.

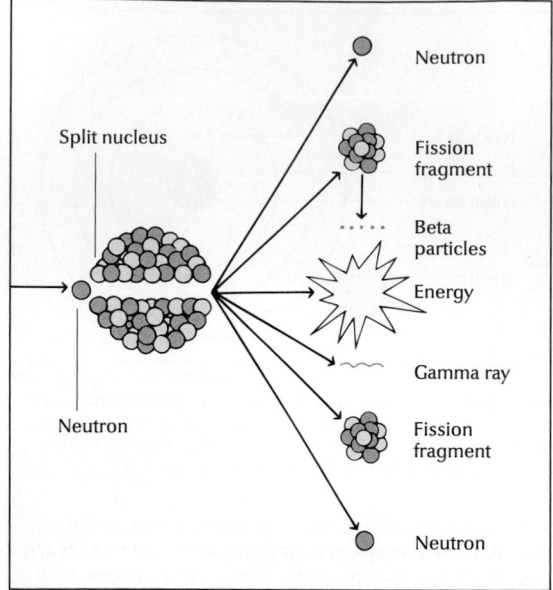

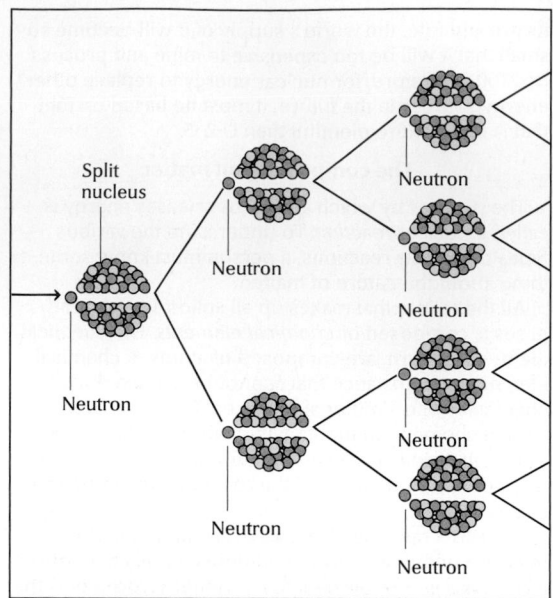

Nuclear fission is the chief method of producing nuclear energy. It involves using a neutron to split a nucleus of a heavy element, such as uranium, into two *fission fragments.* Besides heat energy, fission releases neutrons and such radiation as gamma rays. The fragments give off beta particles and gamma rays.

A chain reaction results in the continuous fissioning of nuclei and so produces a steady supply of energy. To produce a chain reaction, each fissioned nucleus must give off neutrons to fission at least two more nuclei, *shown here.* Uranium and plutonium are the materials used to produce a chain reaction.

Nuclear reactions

A nuclear reaction changes the structure of a nucleus. The nucleus gains or loses one or more neutrons or protons. It thus changes into the nucleus of a different isotope or a different element. If the nucleus changes into the nucleus of a different element, the change is called a *transmutation* (see **Transmutation of elements**).

Three types of nuclear reactions release useful amounts of energy. These reactions are (1) radioactive decay, (2) nuclear fission, and (3) nuclear fusion. During each reaction, the matter involved loses mass. The mass is lost because it changes into energy.

Radioactive decay, or radioactivity, is a process by which a nucleus changes into the nucleus of another isotope or element. The process releases energy chiefly in the form of particles and rays called *nuclear radiation.* Many elements have isotopes that are *stable,* meaning they cannot decay. But radioactive uranium, thorium, and several other elements are *unstable* and decay naturally. They contribute to the natural, or *background,* radiation that is always present on Earth. Nuclear reactors produce radioactive isotopes artificially. Nuclear radiation accounts for about 10 percent of the energy produced in a reactor.

Nuclear radiation consists largely of alpha particles, beta particles, and gamma rays. An *alpha particle,* which is made up of two protons and two neutrons, is identical to a helium nucleus. A *beta particle* is simply an electron. It results from the breakdown of a neutron in a radioactive nucleus. The breakdown also produces a proton, which remains in the nucleus. *Gamma rays* are electromagnetic waves similar to—but more powerful than—X rays (see **Electromagnetic waves**).

Scientists measure the rate of radioactive decay in units of time called *half-lives.* A half-life equals the time required for half the atoms of a particular radioactive element or isotope to decay. Half-lives range from a fraction of a second to billions of years. See **Isotope** (Radioactive isotopes).

Nuclear fission is the splitting of heavy nuclei to release energy. All commercial nuclear reactors produce energy in this way. The two atomic bombs dropped on Japan in World War II used nuclear fission.

To produce fission, a reactor requires a *bombarding particle,* such as a neutron, and a *target material,* such as U-235. Nuclear fission occurs when the bombarding particle splits a nucleus in the target material into two or more parts called *fission fragments.* Each fragment consists of a nucleus with about half the neutrons and protons of the original nucleus. The energy is released in many forms. But most of the energy released eventually takes the form of heat in the surrounding matter.

The bombarding particle must first be captured by a nucleus for fission to occur. Reactors use neutrons as bombarding particles. They are the only atomic particles that are both easily captured and able to cause fission. Neutrons can also pass through most kinds of matter, including uranium.

The target material. Commercial power reactors use uranium as their target material, or fuel. Uranium has one of the easiest nuclei to split because of its large number of protons. Protons naturally repel one another, and so a nucleus with many protons has a tendency to "fly apart." It can thus be split with little difficulty.

Uranium also makes a good nuclear reactor fuel because it can sustain a continuous series of fission reactions. As a result, uranium can produce a steady supply of energy. To create a series of reactions, each fissioned nucleus gives off neutrons. Each of these neutrons can split another uranium nucleus, thus releasing still more neutrons. As this process is repeated over and over, it becomes a self-sustaining *chain reaction*. Chain reactions can produce an enormous amount of energy. Only nuclei that have many more neutrons than protons, such as uranium nuclei, can produce a nuclear chain reaction.

Nuclear power plants rely on the scarce uranium isotope U-235. It is the only natural material that nuclear reactors can use to produce a chain reaction. Nuclei of the much more abundant U-238 isotope usually absorb neutrons without fissioning. An absorbed neutron simply becomes part of the U-238 nucleus.

Neutrons released in fission travel too rapidly to be absorbed by U-235 nuclei in numbers large enough to sustain a chain reaction. Reactors can use U-235 as a fuel because they utilize other materials called *moderators*. The moderators slow the neutrons down, making nuclear fission much more likely to occur. Some reactors use water as a moderator, and others use graphite or *heavy water*. Heavy water contains an isotope of hydrogen called *deuterium*. A normal hydrogen nucleus has no neutrons, but deuterium has one neutron. Deuterium is also known as *heavy hydrogen*.

The slowed neutrons travel at a velocity of about 2.2 kilometers per second and are known as *thermal neutrons*. Reactors that use moderators are called *thermal reactors*. The vast majority of today's reactors are thermal reactors.

Thermal neutrons are highly effective in causing fission in U-235. Therefore, the uranium in a thermal reactor can have a low percentage of U-235 content. Depending on their design, modern power reactors use a U-235 content ranging from 0.71 percent—the percentage in natural uranium—to almost 5 percent. Special-purpose reactors may use fuel with a higher percentage of U-235.

Scientists have also developed *fast reactors*, in which high-velocity neutrons cause fissions without the use of a moderator. These reactors use plutonium or uranium 233 fuel. *Fast breeder reactors* produce more fuel material than they consume. A fast breeder reactor that converts U-238 to plutonium can greatly extend the use of uranium as an energy resource. In addition, a fast reactor can be designed to consume certain radioactive elements that have long lives and are present in used fuel. Such a reactor would reduce the amount of certain radioactive wastes that must be disposed of. The section *Research on new types of reactors* in this article discusses fast reactors in more detail.

Nuclear fusion occurs when two lightweight nuclei *fuse* (combine) and form a nucleus of a heavier element. The products of the fusion reaction have less mass than the original nuclei had. The lost mass has therefore been changed into energy.

Fusion reactions that produce large amounts of energy require extremely intense heat. Such reactions are called *thermonuclear reactions*. The sun's energy comes from thermonuclear reactions. Thermonuclear weapons—also called *hydrogen bombs*—are typically much more powerful than fission weapons. But scientists have not yet succeeded in harnessing the energy of fusion to produce electric power.

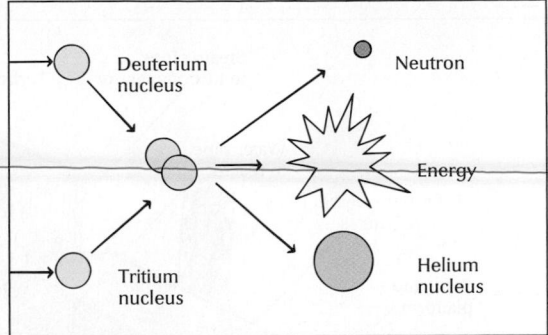

WORLD BOOK diagram by Arthur Grebetz

Nuclear fusion occurs when two lightweight nuclei unite and form a heavier nucleus. In the example shown here, nuclei of deuterium and tritium unite and form a helium nucleus. This process releases energy and a neutron. Repeated many times, fusion creates the energy of the sun and the hydrogen bomb. But scientists have yet to control fusion for energy production.

A thermonuclear reaction can only occur in a form of matter called *plasma*. Plasma is a gaslike substance made up of free electrons and *free nuclei* (nuclei that have no electrons revolving about them). Normally, nuclei repel one another because of the positive charges of their protons. However, if a plasma containing lightweight atomic nuclei is heated many millions of degrees, the nuclei begin moving so fast that they overcome the force of repulsion and fuse. See **Plasma** (in physics).

Problems of controlling fusion. In their fusion experiments, scientists generally work with plasmas that are made from the three isotopes of hydrogen—protium, deuterium, and tritium. The most common hydrogen isotope, protium, has a nucleus that consists of a single proton. Deuterium is the second most common isotope. It has a nucleus made up of one proton and one neutron. The nucleus of the rarest isotope, *tritium,* consists of one proton and two neutrons. Tritium is not found in nature. Scientists produce tritium artificially by bombarding lithium nuclei with neutrons. Of the three isotopes of hydrogen, only tritium is radioactive.

A mixture of deuterium and tritium is an excellent thermonuclear fuel because ordinary seawater contains plentiful stocks of deuterium and lithium. One barrel of seawater contains enough of these substances to produce as much energy as the burning of about one-fifth of a barrel of oil.

To produce a controlled thermonuclear reaction, a plasma of one or more hydrogen isotopes must be heated many millions of degrees. Thermonuclear weapons—unlike nuclear reactors—quickly explode and so do not need to hold the hot plasma for an extended time. Scientists have yet to develop a container that can hold plasma this hot. The plasma expands quickly. In addition, the walls of the container must be kept at low temperatures to prevent them from melting. But if the plasma touches the walls, it becomes too cool to produce fusion. The plasma must therefore be kept away from the walls of the container long enough for its nuclei to fuse and produce usable amounts of energy.

Fusion devices. Most experimental fusion reactors are designed to contain hot plasma in "magnetic bottles"

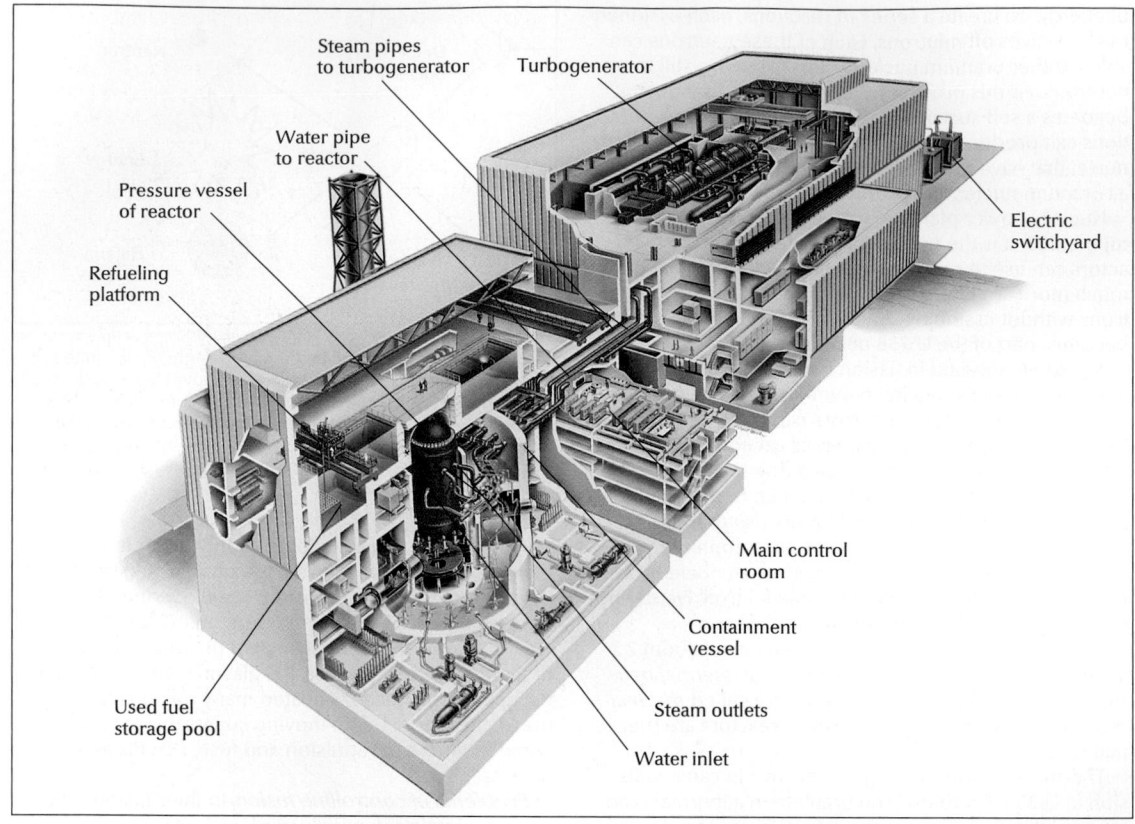

Steam pipes
to turbogenerator   Turbogenerator

Water pipe
to reactor

Pressure vessel
of reactor

Refueling
platform

Electric
switchyard

Main control
room

Containment
vessel

Used fuel
storage pool

Steam outlets

Water inlet

GE Nuclear Energy

A nuclear power plant uses a nuclear reactor to convert water to steam. The steam drives turbogenerators that produce electric energy. This energy flows through wires to a switchyard, where
other wires carry it from the plant. This plant uses a *boiling water reactor,* which produces steam
inside its pressure vessel. After the steam drives the turbogenerators, it is cooled so that it turns
back into water. This water is recirculated into the reactor. A steel and concrete containment vessel
guards against the escape of radioactive material from an accidental leak in the reactor.

twisted into various shapes. The walls of the bottles are
made of copper or some other metal and are surrounded by electromagnets. Plasma, unlike gas, responds
strongly to magnetic fields. The electromagnets can thus
push the plasma away from the walls. All the fusion devices thus far developed, however, use much more energy than they create. The section *Research on new
types of reactors* discusses experimental fusion reactors
in greater detail.

How nuclear energy is produced

All large commercial nuclear power plants produce
energy by fissioning U-235. But U-235 makes up only
about 0.71 percent of the uranium found in nature.
About 99.28 percent of all natural uranium is U-238. The
two types occur together in uranium ores, such as
carnotite and *pitchblende.* Separating the U-235 from the
U-238 in these ores is difficult and costly. For this reason,
the fuel used in reactors consists largely of U-238. But
the fuel has enough U-235 to produce a chain reaction.

Nuclear fuel requires special processing before and
after it is used. The processing begins with the mining
of uranium ore and ends with the disposal of fuel
wastes.

This section deals chiefly with the methods used in
the U.S. nuclear power industry. These methods resemble those used in other countries.

Power plant design. Most nuclear power plants cover an area of 200 to 300 acres (80 to 120 hectares). The
majority are built near a large river or lake because nuclear plants require enormous quantities of water for
cooling purposes.

A nuclear plant consists of several main buildings,
one of which houses the reactor and its related parts.
Another main building houses the plant's turbines and
electric generators. Every plant also has facilities for
storing unused and used fuel. Many plants are largely
automated. Each of these plants has a main control
room, which may be in a separate building or in one of
the main buildings.

The reactor building, or *containment building,* has a
thick concrete floor and walls of steel or of concrete
lined with steel. The concrete and steel guard against
the escape of radioactive material from an accidental
leak in the nuclear reactor.

Power reactors used in U.S. nuclear power plants
consist of three main parts: (1) a reactor vessel, also
called a pressure vessel; (2) a core; and (3) a set of con-

trol rods. In addition, reactor operations depend upon two substances—moderators and coolants.

The *reactor vessel* is a tanklike structure that encloses the other main parts of the reactor. The vessel has steel walls that are typically at least 6 inches (15 centimeters) thick and capable of containing the high pressure exerted in a reactor.

The *core* contains the nuclear fuel, in which the fission chain reaction occurs. The core sits in the lower half of the reactor vessel. A great many *fuel assemblies* stand upright in the core between an upper and lower support plate. Each fuel assembly contains a bundle of *fuel rods*. A fuel rod consists of pellets of fuel inside a metal tube. The pellet material is usually a dense powder made of *uranium dioxide*. The tubing material is typically *zircaloy*, a mixture of the metal zirconium and one or more other metals. Neutrons can pass from the fuel through the tube walls, but most other nuclear particles cannot.

The *control rods* are long metal rods that are used to regulate fission in the fuel. The control rods contain such neutron-absorbing materials as boron, cadmium, hafnium, or silver. A mechanism outside the reactor vessel is attached to the rods. This mechanism inserts the rods into the core and withdraws them when necessary. When inserted fully into the core, the control rods absorb many neutrons and so prevent a fission chain reaction. To begin operation of the reactor, the control rods are partially withdrawn until a chain reaction occurs at a constant rate. To increase power in the reactor, the rods are withdrawn slightly more. Thus, fewer neutrons are absorbed, and more are available to cause fission. To stop the chain reaction, the rods are inserted all the way into the core to absorb most of the neutrons.

The *moderator* slows down neutrons as they pass through it, making fission more likely. The moderator fills the space between the rods in the fuel assemblies.

The *coolant* is a liquid or gas that carries off the heat

Parts of a nuclear reactor

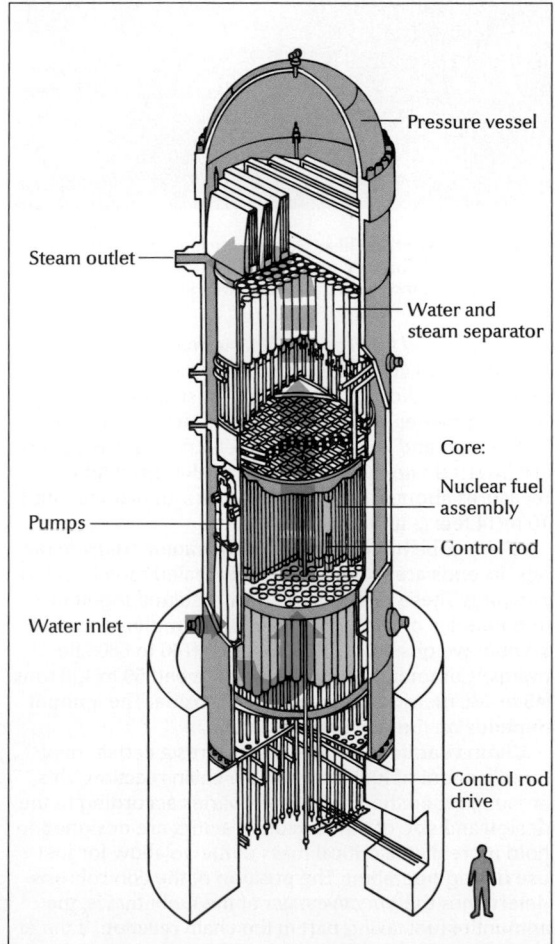

General Electric (WORLD BOOK diagrams)

The core is the heart of a nuclear reactor. Nuclear fuel in the core of this boiling water reactor produces heat that converts water to steam. The steam runs machinery outside the reactor. A pressure vessel encloses the core and various other equipment.

How a reactor works

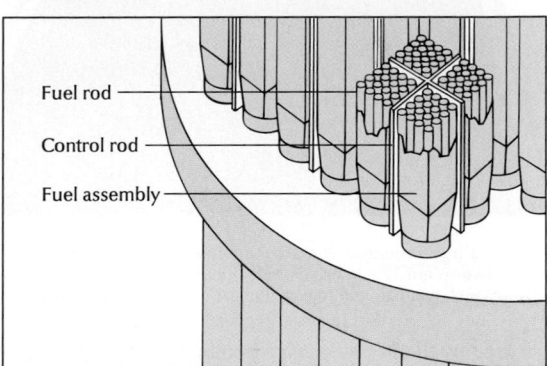

Fuel assemblies in the reactor's core hold individual fuel rods that contain atoms of nuclear fuel. As the fuel nuclei split, they produce energy and release neutrons. Other fuel nuclei split when struck by the neutrons, and thus the reaction continues.

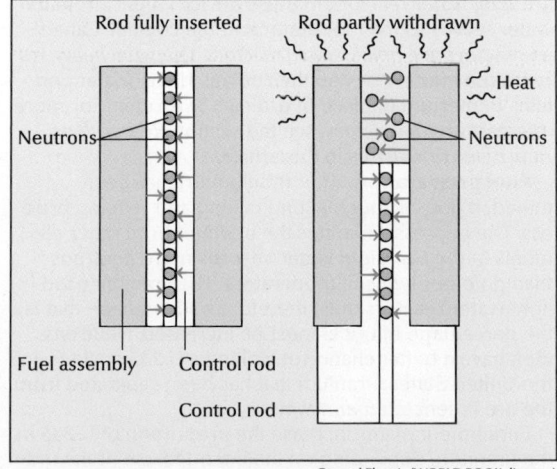

General Electric (WORLD BOOK diagram)

Control rods limit the number of fuel nuclei that can split. Materials in the rods absorb neutrons. When fully inserted in the core, the rods absorb so many neutrons that few nuclei can split. To start the reactor, some rods are partly withdrawn.

Assembling a reactor. A *reactor internal* is lowered into place at a power plant. The internal holds nuclear fuel and *control rods,* which regulate the rate of nuclear reactions in the fuel.

Refueling a reactor. These workers are loading a new *fuel assembly* into the core of a nuclear reactor. The assembly consists of a bundle of long metal tubes filled with uranium pellets.

created by the fission chain reaction. The coolant circulates throughout the core. It carries the heat from the reactor to an energy conversion system. Thus, the coolant keeps the fuel rods from getting too hot. It also transfers energy to where electric power can be generated.

All commercial power reactors in the United States are *light water reactors.* In these devices, *light* (ordinary) water serves as the moderator and the coolant. Canadian reactors are *heavy water reactors.* They use *heavy water* as the moderator and the coolant. Heavy water contains deuterium in place of ordinary hydrogen. For more information on reactors, see the section *Research on new types of reactors* in this article.

Fuel preparation. After uranium ore has been mined, it goes through a long milling and refining process. The process separates the uranium from other elements in the ore. Light water absorbs more neutrons than do other types of moderators. The uranium used in light water reactors must therefore be *enriched*—that is, the percentage of U-235 must be increased. Neutrons then have a better chance of striking a U-235 nucleus. In the United States, uranium that has been separated from the ore is sent to an *enrichment plant.*

Enrichment plants increase the proportion of U-235 in the uranium, depending on the intended use of the uranium. Most light water reactors use fuel with about 2 to 4 percent U-235. Much higher amounts of U-235 are needed in nuclear weapons and in the fuel for the reactors that power nuclear ships. The enriched uranium is

shipped to *fuel fabrication plants* to make fuel rods.

A fuel fabrication plant changes enriched uranium into uranium dioxide. The plant then shapes the uranium dioxide powder into pellets about ⅓ inch (8 millimeters) in diameter and ½ inch (13 millimeters) long. The pellets are inserted into tubes made of zircaloy. Each tube measures about ½ inch (13 millimeters) in diameter and 10 to 14 feet (3 to 5 meters) long.

After a tube has been filled with uranium dioxide pellets, its ends are welded shut. This sealed tube is called *cladding.* These fuel rods are then fastened together into bundles of 30 to 300 each. Each bundle, or *fuel assembly,* weighs 300 to 1,500 pounds (140 to 680 kilograms). Commercial power reactors need 50 to 150 tons (45 to 136 metric tons) of uranium dioxide. The amount depends on the size of the reactor.

Chain reactions. A reactor requires a certain minimum amount of fuel to keep up a chain reaction. This amount, called the *critical mass,* varies according to the design and size of the reactor. Reactors are designed to hold more than a critical mass of fuel to allow for fuel use during operation. The position of the control rods determines the *effective mass* of the fuel—that is, the amount of fuel taking part in the chain reaction. If the effective mass is decreased below the critical mass, the chain reaction will die out and reactor power will decrease. If the effective mass is increased above the critical mass, the chain reaction will become more rapid and reactor power will increase. In an emergency, if the chain reaction became too rapid, the reactor could over-heat. However, the control rods are available to slow down the chain reaction if it becomes too rapid.

To prepare a reactor for operation, the fuel assemblies are loaded into the core with the control rods completely inserted. In a light water reactor, the water used as a moderator fills the spaces between the fuel assemblies. The control rods are then slowly withdrawn, and a chain reaction begins. The farther the rods are withdrawn, the greater the rate of the reaction because fewer neutrons are absorbed. More neutrons thus are available to cause fission.

When the desired power is reached, the control rods are positioned so that the effective mass is equal to the critical mass. The water in the core carries off the heat created by the chain reaction. To stop the reaction, the rods are again inserted all the way into the core to absorb most neutrons.

Steam production. The light water reactors used by almost all U.S. nuclear plants are of two main types. One type, the *pressurized water reactor,* produces steam outside the reactor vessel. The other type, the *boiling water reactor,* makes steam inside the vessel.

Most nuclear plants in the United States use pressurized water reactors. These reactors heat the moderator water in the core under high pressure. The pressure allows the water to heat past its normal boiling point of 212 °F (100 °C) without actually boiling. The chain reaction heats the water to about 600 °F (315 °C). Pipes carry this extremely hot—though not boiling—water to *steam generators* outside the reactor. These generators transfer heat from the pressurized water to a separate supply of water that boils at a lower pressure and so produces steam.

In a boiling water reactor, the chain reaction boils the moderator water in the core. Steam is therefore produced inside the reactor vessel. Pipes carry the steam from the reactor to the plant's turbines.

In producing electric energy, a nuclear plant's steam turbines and electric generators work like those in a fossil-fuel plant. The steam produced by a reactor spins the blades of the plant's turbines, which drive the generators. Many plants have combination turbines and generators called *turbogenerators.*

After steam has passed through a plant's turbines, it is piped to a *condenser.* The condenser transfers heat to a separate water stream and changes the steam back into water. A reactor can thus use the same water over and over. But a condenser requires a constant supply of cool, fresh water to cool the steam. Most plants pump this water from a nearby river or lake. The water, which warms as it passes through the condenser, is then pumped back into the river or lake. This wastewater's heat must be kept within limits so that the water in the river or lake does not endanger plants and animals that live there. The discharge of the warmer wastewater is sometimes called *thermal pollution.*

To minimize thermal pollution, new nuclear plants have *cooling towers.* Hot water from the steam condensers is moved through the towers in such a way that the heat passes into the atmosphere. Some water also evaporates. The cooled water is returned to the steam condenser for reuse.

Hazards and safeguards. An ordinary power reactor cannot explode like an atomic bomb. Only a greatly *supercritical* mass of plutonium 239 or of highly enriched uranium 235 can explode in this way. A supercritical mass contains much more than the amount of plutonium or uranium required to sustain a chain reaction.

The chief hazards of nuclear power production result from the great quantities of radioactive material that a reactor produces, including fission products and transmuted materials in the reactor vessel. These materials give off radiation in the form of alpha and beta particles and gamma rays. The reactor vessel is surrounded by thick concrete blocks called a *shield.* Normally, the

WORLD BOOK diagram by Arthur Grebetz

A nuclear steam supply system

The system shown in this diagram uses a *pressurized water reactor,* which heats water under high pressure. The pressure allows the water to heat past its normal boiling point without actually boiling. Heat from this water boils water in a *steam generator,* which produces steam. The water from the reactor is pumped back to the reactor for reuse. After the steam has operated the plant's turbine, it is sent to a *steam condenser,* which changes it back to water for reuse in the steam generator.

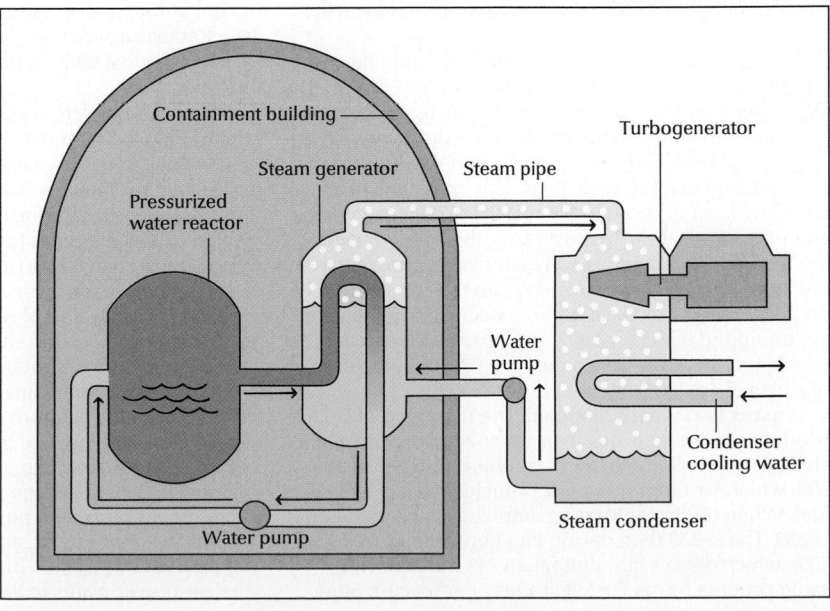

Containment building

Pressurized water reactor

Steam generator

Steam pipe

Turbogenerator

Water pump

Condenser cooling water

Steam condenser

Water pump

The main control room of a nuclear power plant contains a variety of computers, switches, recorders, and other devices. Some of these devices help regulate the production of nuclear energy. Others monitor the plant's safety systems.

David R. Frazier

shield prevents almost all radiation from escaping.

Federal regulations limit the amount of radiation allowed from U.S. nuclear plants. Every plant has instruments that continually measure the radioactivity in and around the plant. They automatically set off an alarm if the radioactivity rises above a predetermined level. If necessary, the reactor is shut down.

A plant's routine safety measures greatly reduce the possibility of a serious accident. Nevertheless, every plant has emergency safety systems that remove heat from radioactive products. Possible emergencies range from a break in a reactor water pipe to a leak of radiation from the reactor vessel. Any such emergency automatically activates a system that instantly shuts down the reactor, a process called *scramming*. The usual method of scramming is to insert the control rods rapidly in the core.

A leak or break in a reactor water pipe could have dangerous consequences if it results in a loss of coolant. Even after a reactor has been shut down, the radioactive materials remaining in the reactor core produce large amounts of heat. They can become so hot without sufficient coolant that the core melts. This condition, called a *meltdown,* could result in the release of dangerous amounts of radiation. In most cases, the large containment structure that houses a reactor would prevent radioactive material from escaping into the atmosphere. To prevent such an accident from occurring, all reactors are equipped with an *emergency core cooling system,* which automatically floods the core with water in case of a loss of coolant.

Wastes and waste disposal. The fissioning of U-235 produces more neutrons than are needed to continue a chain reaction. Some of them combine with U-238 nuclei, which far outnumber U-235 nuclei in the reactor fuel. When U-238 captures a neutron, it is changed into U-239. The U-239 then decays into neptunium 239 (Np-239), which decays into plutonium 239 (Pu-239). This same process forms Pu-239 in a breeder reactor. Slow

neutrons can fission Pu-239, as well as U-235. Some of the newly formed Pu-239 is thus fissioned during the fissioning of U-235. The rest of the Pu-239 remains in the fuel assemblies.

The fissioning of U-235 also produces many other radioactive isotopes, such as strontium 90, cesium 137, and barium 140. Fuel wastes can remain dangerously radioactive for hundreds of years because of the strontium and cesium isotopes. After that time, enough of the strontium and cesium will have decayed into stable isotopes so that they no longer present a severe problem. However, the plutonium and other artificially created elements from U-238 transmutation remain radioactive for thousands of years. Even in small amounts, plutonium can cause cancer or genetic damage in human beings. Larger amounts can cause radiation sickness and death (see **Radiation sickness**). Safe disposal of these wastes is one of the most difficult problems involved in nuclear power.

Most nuclear plants need to replace about a third of their fuel assemblies every year. The radioactive wastes generate heat, and so used fuel assemblies must be cooled after removal from a reactor. Nuclear plants cool the assemblies by storing them underwater in specially designed *storage pools* for several years. Later, the wastes are transferred to air-cooled concrete casks.

A storage site for nuclear waste must lie in a highly stable area that is free of earthquakes, faulting, and other geologic activity. The site must be dry so that the waste containers cannot be corroded and water supplies cannot be contaminated. The site also must be constructed so that future generations do not dig into it and release radioactivity. In 2002, the U.S. government selected Yucca Mountain, Nevada, as the country's single nuclear waste storage site. In 2009, however, the government said that it no longer considered Yucca Mountain an option for storing nuclear waste after facing political opposition. In the meantime, commercial nuclear power plants in the United States continue to store used fuel assemblies and other wastes in pools of water and in concrete cakes.

Other countries, including France, Japan, and Russia, are pursuing a *reprocessing* plan. Under this plan, nuclear plants would ship their used fuel assemblies to the reprocessing plants for removal of Pu-239 and unused U-235. These radioactive isotopes would then be recycled into fuel for nuclear reactors. However, this method would leave radioactive isotopes in the chemical solutions used for reprocessing. These solutions would have to be changed into a solid form that could be safely stored.

The nuclear energy industry

In every country that has a nuclear energy industry, the government plays a role. But this role varies greatly among countries. This section deals mainly with the U.S. and Canadian nuclear energy industries.

Organization of the industry. Private utility companies own most of the nuclear power plants in the United States. The rest are publicly owned. Private companies also manufacture reactors, mine uranium, and handle most other aspects of U.S. nuclear power production.

Canada's nuclear power plants are all publicly owned. Atomic Energy of Canada Limited (AECL), a government corporation, has overall responsibility for the country's nuclear research and development. AECL also designs the CANDU (CANada Deuterium oxide-Uranium) heavy water reactors used by all Canadian nuclear plants. Private companies make the various reactor parts and process the country's uranium. Canada has no enrichment plants because CANDU reactors operate with natural uranium as fuel.

The industry and the economy. The main economic advantage of nuclear power plants is that their fuel is less expensive than fossil fuels. But nuclear plants cost somewhat more to build than do fossil-fuel plants. Under normal economic conditions, a nuclear plant's savings in fuel eventually make up for its higher construction expenses. At first, these expenses add to the cost of producing electric power. But after some years, a plant will have paid off its construction costs. It can then produce electric power more cheaply than a fossil-fuel plant can.

The industry and the environment. Unlike fossil fuel plants, nuclear plants do not release solid or chemical pollutants into the atmosphere. For this reason, nuclear power is expected to play a major role in enabling several countries to meet the objectives of the Kyoto Protocol, a 1997 agreement calling for reduced emissions of various heat-trapping gases. However, a nuclear plant releases small amounts of radioactive gas into the air. In addition, the cooling water used in pressurized water plants picks up a small amount of radioactive tritium in the steam condenser. The tritium remains in this water when it is returned to a river or lake. But these small amounts of radiation released into the environment are not believed to be harmful, and are actually less than the radioactivity released by plants that burn fossil fuel. Thermal pollution remains a problem at some nuclear plants. But cooling towers help correct this problem.

In a small number of nuclear accidents, hazardous amounts of radiation have been released into the atmos-

phere. Accidental releases of radioactive substances have occurred in Japan, Russia, the United Kingdom, and the United States. An especially serious accident occurred in 1986 at the Chernobyl nuclear power plant in Ukraine (then part of the Soviet Union).

Critics of nuclear power also fear another danger to the environment. As power production grows, the problem of storing high-level radioactive wastes also grows.

Government regulation. The Nuclear Regulatory Commission (NRC), an agency of the federal government, regulates nonmilitary nuclear power production in the United States. The NRC works to ensure that nuclear power plants operate safely. Every nuclear reactor and power plant must be inspected and licensed by the NRC before it may begin operations. The NRC also supervises the manufacture and distribution of nuclear fuels, and it controls the disposal of radioactive wastes from commercial production.

The Canadian Nuclear Safety Commission, a Canadian government agency, regulates Canada's nuclear energy industry. The board's duties resemble those of the Nuclear Regulatory Commission.

Careers in nuclear energy cover a wide range of occupations and require widely varying amounts of training. A high percentage of the jobs require a college degree or extensive technical education. Many of these jobs are in large research laboratories, which work to improve nuclear processes and to lessen their hazards. Other careers requiring advanced training are in such areas as uranium mining and processing, reactor manufacturing and inspection, power plant operation, and government regulation.

Many colleges and universities offer undergraduate and graduate degrees in such highly specialized fields as nuclear engineering, nuclear physics, and nuclear technology. The industry also employs many workers with college degrees in various branches of engineering and in such fields as biology, chemistry, geology, and medicine. Many vocational and technical schools and some high schools prepare students for specialized jobs in the industry.

The development of nuclear energy

In 1972, scientists discovered that a natural chain reaction had released nuclear energy nearly 2 billion years ago in a uranium deposit in west-central Africa. Two billion years ago, there had been so little radioactive decay that the ore contained enough U-235 for a chain reaction. An accumulation of *ground water* (water beneath the surface) acted as a moderator to begin the chain reaction. As heat from the reaction changed the water into steam, less and less water was available to serve as a moderator and the reaction died out. Except for such rare natural occurrences, nuclear energy was not released on a large scale on Earth until 1942. That year, scientists produced the first artificially created chain reaction. Scientific discoveries that have taken place since the late 1800's have led to the large-scale release of nuclear energy.

Early developments. Before the late 1800's, scientists did not suspect that atoms could release nuclear energy. Then in 1896, the French physicist Antoine Henri Becquerel found that uranium constantly gives off energy in the form of invisible rays. Becquerel thus became the discoverer of radioactivity. Other scientists soon began experiments to learn more about this mysterious phenomenon.

The beginning of nuclear physics. In 1898, the great New Zealand-born physicist Ernest Rutherford identified two kinds of radioactive "rays," which he called *alpha rays* and *beta rays.* He and other researchers later showed that these rays are actually high-energy particles, which became known as *alpha* and *beta* particles. Experiments with these particles then led Rutherford to discover the atom's nucleus. This achievement, which Rutherford announced in 1911, marked the beginning of a new science—nuclear physics.

About 1914, scientists began doing experiments to see what happens when nuclear particles collide. The scientists used alpha particles from naturally radioactive materials to bombard the nuclei of light atoms. Light nuclei do not repel positively charged particles, such as alpha particles, as strongly as heavy nuclei do. Rutherford used this method to produce the first artificial transmutations in a series of experiments from 1917 to 1919. He bombarded nitrogen atoms with alpha particles. In rare collisions, a nitrogen 14 nucleus absorbed an alpha particle (a helium 4 nucleus). At the same time, the alpha particle pushed a proton out of the nitrogen nucleus. The nucleus thereby became an oxygen 17 nucleus.

Artificial fission. To produce nuclear reactions in heavy nuclei, scientists needed a particle that heavy nuclei would not repel. In 1932, the British physicist James Chadwick discovered such a particle—the neutron. In 1938, two German radiochemists, Otto Hahn and Fritz Strassmann, reported they had produced the element barium by bombarding uranium with neutrons.

At first, scientists could not explain how uranium had produced barium, which is much lighter than uranium. All previous transmutations had resulted in an element about as heavy as the original one. Then in 1939, the Austrian physicist Lise Meitner and her nephew Otto Frisch showed that Hahn and Strassmann had in fact produced the first known artificial fission reaction. A uranium nucleus had split into two nearly equal fragments, one of which consisted of a barium nucleus. Two neutrons were also emitted. The other fragment consisted of a nucleus of krypton, a somewhat lighter element than barium. These two nuclei, together with the emitted neutrons, are lighter than a uranium nucleus and a neutron. The reaction had therefore produced more energy than it consumed.

Scientists soon realized that if many uranium nuclei could be made to fission, a tremendous amount of energy would be released. The amount of energy could be calculated from a theory developed by the great German-born physicist Albert Einstein in 1905. The theory shows that matter can change into energy and that matter and energy are related by the equation $E = mc^2$. This equation states that the *energy (E)* into which a given amount of matter can change equals the *mass (m)* of that matter multiplied by the *speed of light squared (c^2).* The speed of light squared is obtained by multiplying the speed of light by itself. Using this equation, scientists determined that the fissioning of 1 pound (0.45 kilogram) of uranium would release as much energy as 8,000 tons (7,300 metric tons) of TNT. Uranium could therefore be used to make a powerful bomb.

The development of nuclear weapons. World War II broke out in Europe in September 1939. The month before, Einstein had written to United States President Franklin D. Roosevelt urging him to commit the United States to develop nuclear energy technology, including an atomic bomb. Einstein had fled to the United States from Germany to escape Nazi persecution. He warned Roosevelt that German scientists might already be working on a nuclear bomb. Roosevelt acted on Einstein's urging, and early in 1940 scientists received the first funds for uranium research in the United States. The United States entered World War II in 1941. The government then ordered an all-out effort to build an atomic bomb and in 1942 established the top-secret Manhattan

Detail of a 1957 painting by Gary Sheahan; Chicago Historical Society (University of Chicago)

The first nuclear reactor was built by scientists at the University of Chicago beneath the stands of the university's athletic field. The reactor, made of tons of uranium oxide and uranium embedded in graphite, produced the first artificial chain reaction in 1942.

Project to achieve this goal (see **Manhattan Project**).

A group of scientists at the University of Chicago had charge of producing plutonium for the Manhattan Project. The group included such noted physicists as Enrico Fermi, Leo Szilard, and Eugene Wigner, all of whom had been born in Europe and had settled in the United States. Fermi headed the group. Under the scientists' direction, workers built an atomic *pile,* or reactor, beneath the stands of the university athletic field. The pile consisted of 50 tons (45 metric tons) of natural uranium oxide and uranium embedded in 500 tons (450 metric tons) of graphite. The graphite served as a moderator. The pile was designed to demonstrate a controlled nuclear chain reaction in the uranium. Cadmium rods controlled the reaction. On Dec. 2, 1942, this reactor produced the first artificial chain reaction.

The success of the University of Chicago project led the U.S. government to build a plutonium-producing plant in Hanford, Washington. The government also built a uranium enrichment plant in Oak Ridge, Tennessee. Plutonium and greatly enriched uranium from these plants were used in the two atomic bombs that the United States dropped on Japan in August 1945.

After World War II, scientists began work on developing a hydrogen bomb. The United States exploded the first hydrogen bomb in 1952 and so achieved the world's first large-scale thermonuclear reaction. The Soviet Union tested its first atomic bomb in 1949 and its first full-scale hydrogen bomb in 1953. China, France, India, Pakistan, South Africa, and the United Kingdom have also exploded nuclear weapons. For more information on the development of nuclear weapons, see **Nuclear weapon.**

The first peaceful uses. While research on nuclear weapons continued, various countries also began experimenting with nuclear reactors. The United States and the Soviet Union had built uranium enrichment plants for nuclear weapons. Both countries therefore started to develop light water reactors, which require enriched uranium fuel. Canada, France, and the United Kingdom worked on reactors moderated by graphite or heavy water. These reactors cost more to build than light water reactors but use natural uranium.

The U.S. Congress set up the Atomic Energy Commission (AEC) in 1946 to direct and control all aspects of nuclear energy development in the United States. In 1954, Congress allowed private industry to take over most aspects of commercial nuclear power development. But the AEC became responsible for regulating the nuclear energy industry. It also kept control in such areas as uranium enrichment and waste disposal.

The United States made the world's first full-scale use of controlled nuclear energy in 1954. That year, the U.S. Navy launched the first nuclear-powered vessel, the submarine *Nautilus.* The world's first full-scale nuclear power plant began operations in 1956 at Calder Hall in northwestern England. In 1957, the first large-scale nuclear plant in the United States opened in Shippingport, Pennsylvania. It supplied electric power to the Pittsburgh area until 1982, when the plant was closed. Canada opened its first full-scale plant in 1962 at Rolphton, Ontario.

The successful start of the nuclear power industry convinced world leaders of the need for international cooperation in the field. In 1957, the United Nations (UN) established the International Atomic Energy Agency to promote the peaceful uses of nuclear energy (see **International Atomic Energy Agency; United Nations** [Peaceful uses of nuclear energy]). Also in 1957, Belgium, France, Italy, Luxembourg, the Netherlands, and West Germany formed the European Atomic Energy Community (Euratom). The organization encourages the development of nuclear power among its member countries. Today, the countries that make up the European Union are all members of Euratom (see **European Union**).

The spread of nuclear capability. During the 1960's and early 1970's, a number of countries acquired reactors and used them to start nuclear power development. Progress was also made during this period toward limiting nuclear weapons tests and stopping the spread of nuclear weapons. In 1970, for example, a nuclear *nonproliferation treaty* went into effect. The treaty prohibits the nuclear powers that have agreed to abide by the document from giving nuclear weapons to nations that do not already have them. The nonproliferation treaty also prohibits nations without nuclear weapons from acquiring them.

But the nonproliferation treaty does not prohibit nations from selling or buying nuclear reactors. A reactor can be used not only for peaceful purposes but also to produce plutonium for nuclear weapons. India used a research reactor for this purpose and in 1974 exploded its first atomic bomb. Canada had supplied the reactor to India with the understanding it would be used for peaceful purposes only. Canada has signed the nonproliferation treaty, but India has not. Critics of India's action questioned the wisdom of supplying reactors to countries that do not already have them.

Meanwhile, the United States had been greatly increasing its nuclear power capacity. But opposition to nuclear power development also increased in the United States during the late 1960's and early 1970's. Critics began to question nearly every aspect of nuclear power production, from the cost of uranium enrichment to the problems of waste disposal.

Many critics of the United States nuclear program charged that the government overlooked various safety risks at nuclear plants to promote nuclear power development. Partly as a result of such criticism, Congress disbanded the Atomic Energy Commission (AEC) in 1974 and divided its functions between two newly formed agencies. The Energy Research and Development Administration (ERDA) took over the AEC's development programs. The Nuclear Regulatory Commission (NRC) took over its regulatory duties. The NRC, it was believed, could better regulate the industry if it was not also responsible for the industry's growth and development. In 1977, Congress abolished ERDA and transferred its responsibilities to the newly created Department of Energy. See **Energy, Department of; Nuclear Regulatory Commission.**

In 1992, the U.S. Congress passed the Energy Policy Act, opening the way for deregulation of the electric power industry. Since then, many nuclear utilities have consolidated. In 2000, the NRC began approving extensions of operating life for existing nuclear plants.

Safety concerns. There have been a number of accidents at nuclear power plants. Most have not been seri-

The Chernobyl power plant, near Kiev in Ukraine, was the scene of the worst nuclear accident in history. In 1986, an explosion and fire ripped apart the reactor and released large amounts of radioactive substances into the atmosphere. This photo shows the Chernobyl plant after the accident.

Sovfoto

ous. However, in 1957, a fire at the Windscale plutonium production plant in northern England resulted in the release of a large quantity of radioactivity. The British government banned the sale of milk from cows in that part of England for more than a month after the fire.

In the United States, concerns about the safety of nuclear reactors increased after a serious accident in 1979 at the Three Mile Island nuclear power plant near Harrisburg, Pennsylvania. Mechanical and human failures resulted in a breakdown of the reactor's cooling system and serious damage to the reactor core. Scientists and technicians prevented a failure of the reactor vessel that might have released large amounts of radioactive isotopes into the reactor containment building. Cleanup of the plant was completed in the early 1990's.

The worst nuclear accident in history occurred in 1986 at the Chernobyl nuclear power plant near Kiev in Ukraine, which was then part of the Soviet Union. An explosion and fire ripped apart the reactor and released large amounts of radioactive isotopes into the atmosphere. Unlike most Western reactors, the Chernobyl reactors had a different type of enclosure that was unable to prevent radioactive isotopes from escaping. Soviet officials reported that 31 people died from radiation sickness or burns and more than 200 others were seriously injured. The radioactive substances spread over parts of what are now Ukraine, Russia, and Belarus, and were carried by wind into northern and central Europe. Experts expected a significant increase in the number of cancer deaths among those near the reactor. But they predicted that the health effects outside the area would be slight. The last working reactor at Chernobyl was shut down in 2000.

As a result of the accidents at Three Mile Island and Chernobyl, opposition to nuclear power increased in

many countries during the late 1980's. In the United States, the NRC tightened its control of nuclear plants.

Experts have expressed particular concern over the safety of older Soviet-designed reactors now operating in Russia, Ukraine, and several countries of the former Soviet bloc. Western scientists and engineers are helping to remedy some of the most urgent safety problems in these reactors. Most have been closed or redesigned to eliminate their original design flaws.

On March 11, 2011, a tremendous earthquake struck off the east coast of Japan, causing a nuclear crisis at the Fukushima Daiichi Nuclear Power Station. The earthquake created a massive *tsunami* (series of ocean waves) that flooded the power plant. The plant's reactors survived the quake and tsunami intact, and the plant's automatic systems successfully inserted the control rods. But the disaster crippled the plant's cooling system. Without cooling water, the plant's fuel rods overheated from radioactive decay heat, generating several explosions and widely spreading radioactivity. The Japanese government struggled to spray water on the reactors and evacuated citizens in a 20-mile (32-kilometer) radius.

Research on new types of reactors. New research on reactors was sparked by fears of a shortage of U-235 to fuel fission reactors. But in the 1970's, nuclear power production grew less rapidly than expected. Geologists also discovered that there was much more uranium on Earth than had originally been estimated. Therefore, the expected near-term shortage did not occur.

Today, scientists seek to develop safer and more efficient reactors. Researchers have concentrated their efforts on the development of a fusion reactor and advanced fission reactors.

Experimental fusion devices. Most experiments on controlled nuclear fusion have concentrated on the de-

A tokamak fusion reactor heats hydrogen nuclei so that they *fuse* (join), releasing energy. Researchers are trying to develop a fusion reactor that can produce commercially valuable amounts of energy.

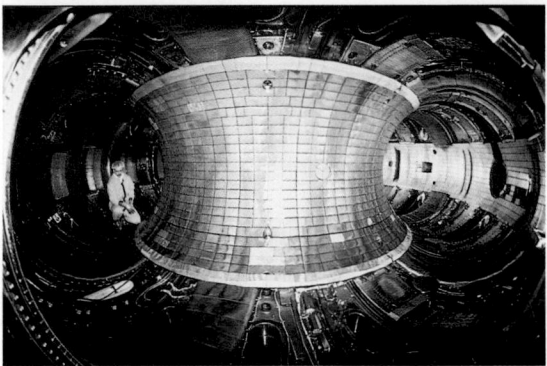

Inside a tokamak is a chamber, being examined here by a worker, in which hydrogen nuclei are forced to fuse. The tokamak produces fusion by heating a *plasma* (a mixture of nuclei and electrons) to at least 180,000,000 °F (100,000,000 °C).

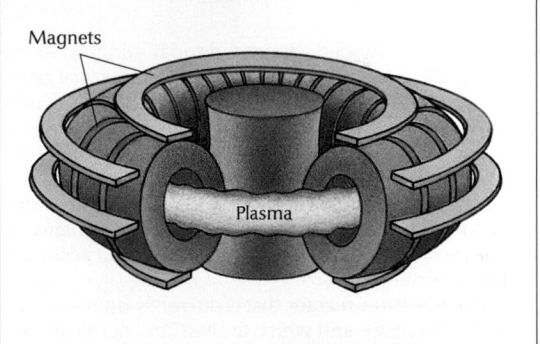

Plasma in a tokamak is held away from the chamber walls by a magnetic field produced by two sets of magnets. If the plasma were to touch the walls, its temperature would fall so sharply that nuclei in the plasma could not fuse.

velopment of reactors that would use deuterium and tritium plasma as the fuel. The most successful type of fusion reactor, called a *tokamak,* was originally designed by Soviet scientists. The term *tokamak* comes from Russian words meaning *toroidal* (doughnut-shaped) *chamber and magnetic coil.* Like many other experimental fusion reactors, a tokamak uses *magnetic confinement.* A magnetic field pushes plasma away from the tokamak's containing walls. The tokamak also passes a strong electric current through the plasma. The current interacts with the magnetic field to help confine the plasma.

One goal of fusion research is to reach the *breakeven level,* the level of energy production equal to the energy needed to create and heat the plasma. To reach this level, a tokamak of the design presently under development must heat the plasma to at least 180,000,000 °F (100,000,000 °C). Also, each cubic centimeter (0.061 cubic inch) of the plasma must contain about 100 trillion nuclei, and the magnetic field must confine the plasma for about 1 second.

Researchers working with tokamaks have reached these three goals, but never in the same experiment. By

the mid-1990's, individual experiments on plasmas made up of deuterium and tritium atoms had achieved about 30 percent of the breakeven level.

Another kind of fusion reactor uses *inertial confinement.* In this case, no container holds the fuel during fusion. Rather, the fuel's *inertia,* its natural tendency to remain in the same place, holds it long enough for fusion to occur. In one kind of inertial confinement fusion (ICF) reactor, extremely powerful laser beams strike a cylindrical case made of metal. Inside the case is a pea-sized sphere containing deuterium and tritium gas. The laser beams heat the case, causing it to turn to plasma. The plasma, in turn, bombards the sphere with X rays, rapidly heating the shell of the sphere. As a result, the shell both expands and pushes inward. The inward push compresses the fuel, causing fusion.

The most powerful laser-driven reactor is operated by the National Ignition Facility at Lawrence Livermore National Laboratory in Livermore, California. The facility uses 192 separate lasers to deliver a huge pulse of energy lasting a tiny fraction of a second.

Advanced fission reactors. Research, development, and design work on advanced fission reactors has con-

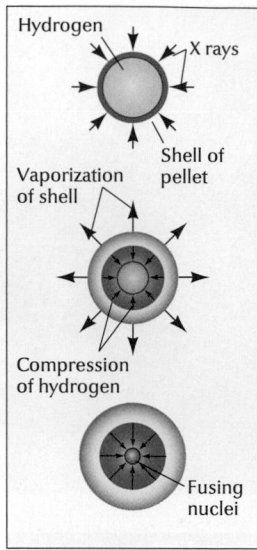

An inertial confinement fusion reactor heats a target so rapidly that nuclei fuse before the target can fly apart. Laser beams hit a target in a spherical chamber, *above,* producing X rays. The rays strike a hydrogen-filled pellet, *right,* vaporizing its shell and compressing the hydrogen. The hydrogen becomes so hot that nuclei fuse.

WORLD BOOK diagram by Mark Swindle

centrated on advanced versions of today's light-water reactors (LWR's), on other types of advanced thermal reactors, and on fast reactors. The goals of this work include improved operating efficiency, simplified design, lower cost, and increased use of *passive* safety systems. A passive safety system does not depend upon mechanical devices, such as pumps and valves operated by people or powered by electric energy, to prevent core damage and to remove heat from the reactor core if an accident occurs.

A type of fission reactor that is currently operating in Japan and France—and which the NRC has certified for use in the United States—is the *advanced light water reactor* (ALWR). ALWR's have many passive safety features. One ALWR design relies on pools of water positioned at various heights. Gravity, rather than pumps, circulates a supply of cooling water that would be needed in certain emergencies.

A *high-temperature gas-cooled reactor* (HTGR) is a smaller power plant that uses a pressurized gas, usually helium, as the coolant. The fuel consists of ceramic-coated pellets of uranium oxycarbide. The purpose of this design is to make it extremely unlikely for the fissions in a pellet to produce enough heat to rupture the casing, even if the reactor were to lose all its coolant. If the pellets remained intact, radioactive material would not be released.

A group of reactors known as *fast reactors* have long-term advantages. A fast breeder reactor can be designed to both consume plutonium as a fuel and convert U-238 to more plutonium. The plutonium, in turn, can be used as reactor fuel. The breeder thus creates more fissionable material than it consumes. Because uranium is plentiful, the use of breeders would extend its potential as an energy resource enormously. Several countries have built experimental breeders. A unit in France, called the Superphénix, produced 1.2 million kilowatts of electric power.

Fast reactors can also be developed to consume some of the long-lived radioactive materials, such as plutonium and americium, that are in spent nuclear

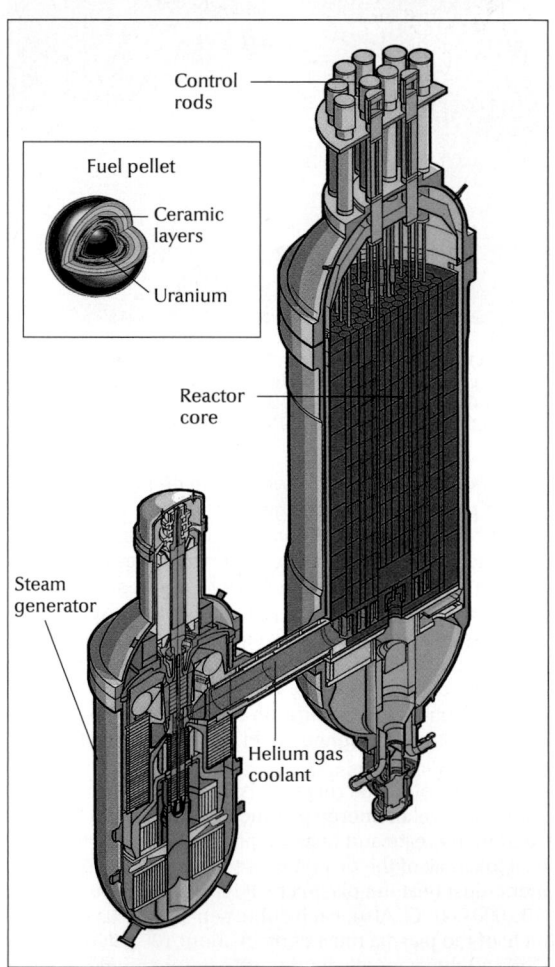

General Atomics

An experimental reactor uses pellets of uranium and a ceramic casing. The pellets are designed to prevent heat from rupturing the casings if the coolant were lost.

fuel from light water reactors. They thus avoided the need to contain these materials in a repository for thousands of years.   Michael L. Corradini

Related articles in *World Book.* See **National laboratory** and its list of *Related articles.* See also:

Biographies

Outline

Additional resources

Level I
Parker, Steve. *Nuclear Energy.* Gareth Stevens, 2004.
Saunders, Nigel, and Chapman, Steven. *Nuclear Energy.* Raintree, 2004.
Scarborough, Kate. *Nuclear Waste.* Bridgestone, 2003.

Level II
Garwin, Richard L., and Charpak, Georges. *Megawatts and Megatons: A Turning Point in the Nuclear Age?* Knopf, 2001.
Lüsted, Marcia and Greg. *A Nuclear Power Plant.* Lucent Bks., 2005.
Newton, David E. *Nuclear Power.* Facts on File, 2006.

Nuclear fission. See Fission; Nuclear energy.

Nuclear Nonproliferation Treaty is an international agreement that attempts to prevent the spread of nuclear weapons. Its official name is the Treaty on the Non-Proliferation of Nuclear Weapons. It was approved by the United Nations in 1968 and took effect in 1970. In 1995, the treaty's signers agreed to make it permanent.

Under the treaty, nations with nuclear weapons agree not to help countries without such weapons to acquire them; to help nonnuclear-armed countries benefit from the peaceful uses of nuclear energy; and to seek nuclear disarmament. Also, countries without nuclear weapons agree not to acquire nuclear weapons and to accept safeguards arranged by the International Atomic Energy Agency (IAEA). The safeguards allow the IAEA to inspect nuclear facilities and materials in each country.

A vast majority of all countries have ratified the treaty, including such nuclear-armed nations as China, France, Russia, the United Kingdom, and the United States. Some countries that have not agreed to the treaty either possess nuclear weapons or are able to produce them. These nations include India, Israel, and Pakistan. North Korea withdrew from the treaty in 2003 after revealing that it had a program to develop nuclear weapons. In 2006, the country tested a nuclear device, though experts believed the device was small. The test caused the United Nations to impose economic sanctions on North Korea. Another nation that has caused concern is Iran. Iran signed the treaty in 1968. In the early 2000's, however, IAEA inspectors began investigating Iran's uranium-enrichment program. The IAEA feared the uranium was intended for weapons instead of energy purposes.
   Robert E. Williams

Nuclear physics is the study of atomic nuclei and the application of nuclear processes to technology. Nuclear physics began in about 1900 as the study of radioactive materials, such as radium and uranium.

Three major nuclear processes are (1) *radioactivity,* involving the decay of a nucleus; (2) *fission,* the breakup of a nucleus to form two smaller nuclei; and (3) *fusion,* the joining of two nuclei to form a larger nucleus. Both fusion and fission create the energy of nuclear weapons.

Radioactivity is the *emission* (giving off) of particles and energy by a nucleus. An atomic nucleus lies at the center of an atom. The simplest nucleus is that of the lightest *isotope* (form) of hydrogen. It consists of a single particle, called a *proton,* which carries a positive electric charge. All other nuclei consist of at least one proton and one *neutron.* A neutron has internal charges that cancel one another out, making it electrically neutral.

The location of individual protons and neutrons in a nucleus depends on their energy and other factors. The protons and neutrons of certain isotopes, called *radioisotopes,* will change their locations by means of radioactive decay. In one kind of decay, two protons and two neutrons leave the nucleus together as a unit known as an *alpha particle.* Decay occurs *spontaneously*—that is, no input of particles or energy is needed to trigger it.

Physicians can use radioisotopes to diagnose disease. To detect heart ailments, for example, doctors inject a radioactive substance called a *tracer* into a patient's bloodstream. A camera equipped with a radiation detector then records the flow of the tracer through the heart. In another medical application, physicians treat cancer by bombarding tumors with radiation.

Other scientists make use of the fact that radioisotopes decay at an exact and uniform rate. One application, known as *radiocarbon dating,* uses the rate of decay of a carbon isotope to determine the age of ancient plants and animals.

Fission creates energy in a nuclear power plant. In this process, a heavy nucleus, such as a uranium nucleus, absorbs a subatomic particle, then splits into two smaller nuclei. In each fission, a tiny amount of nuclear matter changes into heat energy. Electric generators in the power plant convert the heat to electric energy.

Fusion powers the sun and other stars. In one kind of

fusion reaction, two protons come together. One of them emits a positively charged particle called a *positron* and a neutral particle known as a *neutrino*. The emissions then turn the proton into a neutron, so the resulting nucleus consists of a proton and a neutron. During fusion, some nuclear matter changes into heat energy. Scientists are experimenting with ways to produce electric energy from the energy of fusion.

William Karl Pitts

Related articles in *World Book* include:

Atom	Nuclear weapon
Fission	Radiation (Radiation and
Fusion	radioactivity)
Nuclear energy	Radiocarbon

Nuclear power. See Nuclear energy.

Nuclear reactor is a device in which controlled nuclear fission reactions take place. See **Isotope** (Artificial radioisotopes); **Nuclear energy** (Power reactors); **Rocket** (Nuclear rockets; picture); **Submarine** (The power plant; pictures).

Nuclear Regulatory Commission is an independent agency of the United States government. The commission, also called the NRC, was organized to ensure that the use of nuclear energy for civilian purposes does not endanger the health and safety of the public and the environment. It licenses and oversees the construction and operation of nuclear reactors that produce electric power. The NRC also regulates the use of radioactive materials in agriculture, industry, and medicine, and the packaging of such materials for transport.

The Energy Reorganization Act of 1974 abolished the Atomic Energy Commission (AEC) and replaced it with the NRC and the Energy Research and Development Administration (ERDA). The NRC began operations in 1975. In 1977, ERDA was abolished and its responsibilities were transferred to the Department of Energy.

Critically reviewed by the Nuclear Regulatory Commission

Nuclear waste. See Nuclear energy (Wastes and waste disposal).

Nuclear weapon is a weapon that gets its destructive power by turning matter into energy. All nuclear weapons are explosive devices. They are carried in missiles, bombs, artillery shells, mines, or torpedoes. The most powerful nuclear weapons are far more destructive than any *conventional* (nonnuclear) weapon. A nuclear weapon set off in a large city could kill millions of people. A large nuclear war could devastate Earth's climate and ability to support life.

Nuclear weapons work through reactions in the *nuclei* (cores) of atoms. They can be divided into two groups: *fission weapons* and *thermonuclear weapons*. Fission weapons are also called *atomic bombs*. Thermonuclear weapons are also called *hydrogen bombs* or *fusion weapons*. Thermonuclear weapons are generally far more powerful than fission weapons.

The first nuclear weapons were the only ones ever used. They were two fission bombs dropped by the United States on the Japanese cities of Hiroshima and Nagasaki in 1945, during World War II (1939-1945). The bombs killed from 110,000 to 140,000 people. They also destroyed large areas of both cities. The terrible destruction became a major factor in Japan's decision to surrender to the United States and its Allies. Japan's surrender ended the war.

After World War II, the United States and the Soviet Union entered a period of intense rivalry called the Cold War. But the deadly risk of nuclear war was so great that neither side actually attacked the other.

Today, eight countries in the world have nuclear *arsenals* (weapon supplies). The United States and Russia (formerly part of the Soviet Union) have most of the world's nuclear weapons. Other countries with nuclear arms include China, France, India, Israel, Pakistan, and the United Kingdom. North Korea tested nuclear devices in 2006 and 2009. But experts disagree about whether the tests succeeded. In addition, many experts believe that Iran is planning to build nuclear weapons. South Africa once possessed nuclear weapons. But the country voluntarily destroyed its arsenal in the early 1990's. Several other nations might have the ability to build nuclear weapons. Many experts believe the greatest threat to international peace and security is the possibility that a terrorist group could acquire and use a nuclear weapon.

How nuclear weapons work

Conventional bombs get energy from *chemical reactions*. Such reactions involve changes in the structure of *molecules* (groups of atoms). But they leave the nuclei of the atoms themselves unchanged. In contrast, nuclear weapons get energy through *nuclear reactions*. Such reactions change the structure of atomic nuclei. In the process, matter in the nuclei is converted into energy. The result is a huge explosion.

The particles that make up an atom's nucleus are called *protons* and *neutrons*. They have much more mass than the electrons that swirl around the nucleus. The number of protons in an atom's nucleus determines what kind of element an atom is. For example, the lightest element, hydrogen, has one proton. Helium has two protons. Uranium has 92 protons.

Nuclear reactions involve not only specific elements but also specific *isotopes* of those elements. An element's various isotopes have the same number of protons, but different numbers of neutrons.

Fission weapons generate their destructive power through the *fission* (splitting) of atomic nuclei. Only three materials are known to be *fissionable*—that is, ca-

Photri

U.S. Army

Photri

Nuclear weapons include missiles and artillery shells. The top photograph at the left shows the launching of two long-range nuclear missiles. Such missiles carry extremely powerful thermonuclear devices. The explosion of such a device creates a huge mushroom-shaped cloud like the one shown at the right. A self-propelled howitzer, *bottom left,* can fire nuclear artillery shells.

pable of fission—in weapons. They are two isotopes of uranium and one isotope of plutonium.

Nuclear fission occurs when a neutron strikes, and splits, the nucleus of a uranium or plutonium atom. Splitting the nucleus transforms a small amount of its matter into a large amount of energy. In addition, the fission releases two or three additional neutrons. These neutrons may then split other nuclei. If this process continues, a self-sustaining *chain reaction* begins. In a chain reaction, many nuclei split rapidly. Their combined energies produce a fission explosion. To generate a self-sustaining chain reaction, a nuclear weapon must have a certain amount of fissionable material. This amount is known as the *critical mass.* A mass too small to support a chain reaction is called a *subcritical mass.*

A fission weapon uses one of two methods to create a critical mass, the *gun-type method* or the *implosion method.* In the gun-type method, two subcritical pieces of material are placed in a device similar to a gun's barrel. One piece rests at one end of the barrel. The other is some distance from the first piece. This second piece has a powerful conventional explosive behind it. The barrel is sealed at both ends. When the weapon's fuse is triggered, the explosive propels the second subcritical mass at high speed into the first. The resulting combined mass immediately becomes *supercritical* (greater than critical). The result is a rapid, self-sustaining chain reaction, and thus a nuclear explosion. The United States used a gun-type fission bomb at Hiroshima.

In the implosion method, a subcritical mass is made supercritical by compressing it into a smaller volume. The subcritical mass is in the center of the weapon. It is surrounded by conventional explosives. When the fuse

is triggered, all the conventional explosives go off at the same time. The explosions squeeze the mass into a high-density supercritical mass. The result is a chain reaction and an explosion. The United States used an implosion-type fission bomb at Nagasaki.

Thermonuclear weapons get their power from the *fusion* (combining) of nuclei under intense heat. The nuclei are those of special isotopes of hydrogen. When the hydrogen nuclei fuse, they form a helium nucleus. The fusion also releases vast energy and extra neutrons.

Fusion reactions require temperatures equal to, or greater than, those found in the sun's core—about 27 million °F (15 million °C). The only practical way to achieve such temperatures on Earth is with a fission explosion. Thus, a thermonuclear weapon contains an implosion-type fission device that, in turn, triggers fusion.

When the fission device explodes, it releases neutrons. The neutrons bombard a compound inside the weapon called lithium 6 deuteride. It consists of lithium and deuterium, an isotope of hydrogen with an extra neutron. When struck with neutrons, the compound's lithium splits into helium and another hydrogen isotope, called tritium, with two extra neutrons. Pairs of the two hydrogen isotopes—two deuteriums, two tritiums, or one of each—fuse together. A small amount of matter from each nucleus converts to a large amount of energy. Thus, a thermonuclear explosion occurs.

The *yield* (explosive power) of a thermonuclear weapon can be increased by blanketing the lithium 6 deuteride with uranium. The uranium fissions from the extra neutrons released during the reactions. On the other hand, a *neutron bomb*—also called an e*nhanced radiation* (ER) *weapon,* has a low explosive yield. In a neutron bomb, most of the neutrons escape into the air. The neutrons kill living things while causing comparatively little damage to buildings and other structures.

Types of nuclear weapons

The explosive material in a nuclear weapon must be attached to a delivery system. Such a system may be a bomb or a guided missile. Nuclear weapons can thus also be classified by their delivery systems. In addition, they can be divided into two main types, depending on the role for which they are designed. These types are *strategic* nuclear weapons and *tactical* nuclear weapons.

Strategic nuclear weapons are designed primarily to attack targets in an enemy's homeland from great distances. Strategic nuclear weapons generally target cities, industrial centers, and the enemy's nuclear arsenal. These weapons can be delivered by long-range bombers or by missiles. The missiles with the longest range are called *intercontinental ballistic missiles* (ICBM's). They can deliver explosive devices to targets beyond 3,400 miles (5,500 kilometers) from the launch

site. Some missiles are based on land. Others are based underwater on submarines. They are called *submarine-launched ballistic missiles* (SLBM's). Some strategic missiles have several nuclear devices or *warheads.* Each warhead carries explosive material to a separate target.

Tactical nuclear weapons are designed for use on a military battlefield. They could be used, for example, to attack an invading enemy's troop formations. Tactical nuclear weapons are used in *military theaters* (combat areas). Thus, they are sometimes called *theater nuclear weapons.* Tactical nuclear weapons generally have smaller yields than strategic nuclear weapons. They are also delivered from shorter ranges. They include bombs delivered by fighter aircraft, short and medium-range ballistic missiles, and jet-powered *cruise missiles.* Tactical nuclear weapons also include nuclear artillery shells, surface-to-air missiles (SAM's), mines, and torpedoes.

Effects of nuclear weapons

Nuclear explosive devices have different yields. Most large thermonuclear weapons are about 8 to 40 times as

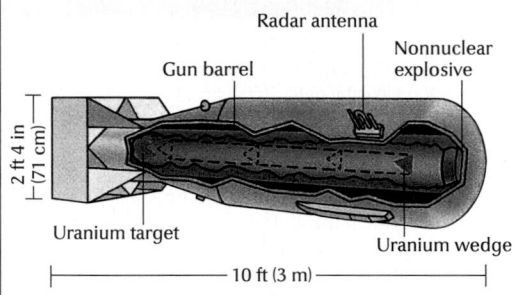

Gun-type fission bomb

Radar antenna

Gun barrel

Nonnuclear explosive

2 ft 4 in (71 cm)

Uranium target

Uranium wedge

10 ft (3 m)

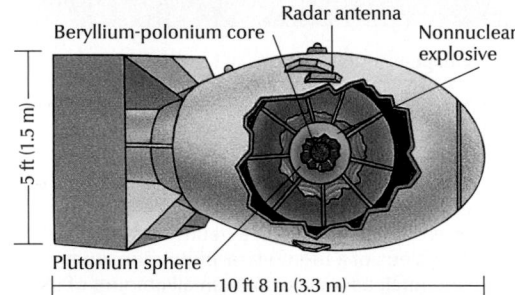

Implosion-type fission bomb

Radar antenna

Beryllium-polonium core

Nonnuclear explosive

5 ft (1.5 m)

Plutonium sphere

10 ft 8 in (3.3 m)

WORLD BOOK illustrations by J. Harlan Hunt (adapted from artwork by Van Dyke, Dec. 19, 1960, *Newsweek*)

UPI/Bettmann Newsphoto

Hiroshima, Japan, was largely destroyed by a gun-type fission bomb called the Little Boy bomb, *top,* on Aug. 6, 1945. The bomb was dropped from a B-29 bomber. When the bomb reached 1,850 feet (564 meters), a radar echo set off an explosive inside. This explosive drove a wedge of U-235 into a larger piece of U-235, setting off the nuclear blast. This photograph shows Hiroshima after the explosion.

Atomic Energy Commission

Nagasaki, Japan, was struck by an implosion-type fission bomb called the Fat Man bomb, *top,* on Aug. 9, 1945. In this bomb, an explosive crushed a hollow sphere of plutonium into a core made up of the chemical elements beryllium and polonium. This core then released neutrons, which triggered a fission chain reaction in the plutonium. This photograph shows Nagasaki after the nuclear blast.

powerful as the Hiroshima bomb. Some bombs made during the Cold War had yields of about 20 *megatons,* equivalent to the yield of about 1,540 Hiroshima bombs. A megaton is the amount of energy released by 1 million tons (907,000 metric tons) of TNT. Today, most nuclear devices have yields of less than 1 megaton.

The effects of a nuclear explosion can vary greatly, depending on a number of factors. These factors include the weapon's yield, the weather, the terrain, and the altitude of the explosion. This section describes the possible effects of a 1-megaton nuclear weapon. The weapon's explosion would produce four basic effects. They are a blast wave, thermal radiation, prompt nuclear radiation, and residual nuclear radiation.

Blast wave. The explosion begins with the formation of a *fireball.* The fireball is a cloud of dust and hot gases under high pressure. A fraction of a second after the explosion, the gases begin to expand. They form a *blast wave,* also called a *shock wave.* This wave is a wall of compressed air. It moves rapidly in all directions from the fireball. The blast wave created by a 1-megaton explosion could travel about 12 miles (19 kilometers) from *ground zero* in just 50 seconds. Ground zero is the point on the ground directly below the explosion.

The blast wave causes most of the damage. As the wave advances, it creates *overpressure,* atmospheric pressure above the normal level. A 1-megaton explosion can produce enough overpressure to destroy most buildings within 1 mile (1.6 kilometers) of ground zero. This overpressure can also cause moderate to severe damage within 6 miles (10 kilometers) of ground zero.

Strong winds accompany the blast wave. These winds may reach speeds of 400 miles (640 kilometers) per hour at 2 miles (3.2 kilometers) from ground zero. The blast wave and wind probably would kill most of the people within 3 miles (4.8 kilometers) of ground zero. The blast and wind probably would cause some deaths between 3 and 6 miles (4.8 and 9.7 kilometers) from ground zero. Many other people within 6 miles would be injured.

Thermal radiation consists of heat and light given off by the fireball. The explosion's blinding light can cause eye injuries. Heat from the explosion creates skin burns, called *flash burns.* Flash burns caused from 20 to 30 percent of the deaths at Hiroshima and Nagasaki.

Thermal radiation also can ignite flammable materials, such as newspapers and dry leaves, causing large fires. Some scientists theorize that, in a major nuclear war, the smoke from such fires would absorb enough sunlight to lower Earth's surface temperature for several months or years. The lowered temperatures would result in widespread crop failure and famine. This possible effect of nuclear war is called *nuclear winter.* However, the effects of thermal radiation can vary, depending on conditions at the time of the explosion. In a light atmospheric haze, for example, the effects could be only one-hundredth as strong as they would be in clear air.

Solid, nontransparent objects—such as walls, trees, and rocks—can shield people from the direct effects of thermal radiation. In addition, light-colored clothing reflects heat. It can thus help protect a person from some flash burn effects. However, thermal radiation from a 1-megaton explosion can produce *second-degree burns* (blistering) of exposed human skin up to 11 miles (18 kilometers) from ground zero. The thermal radiation

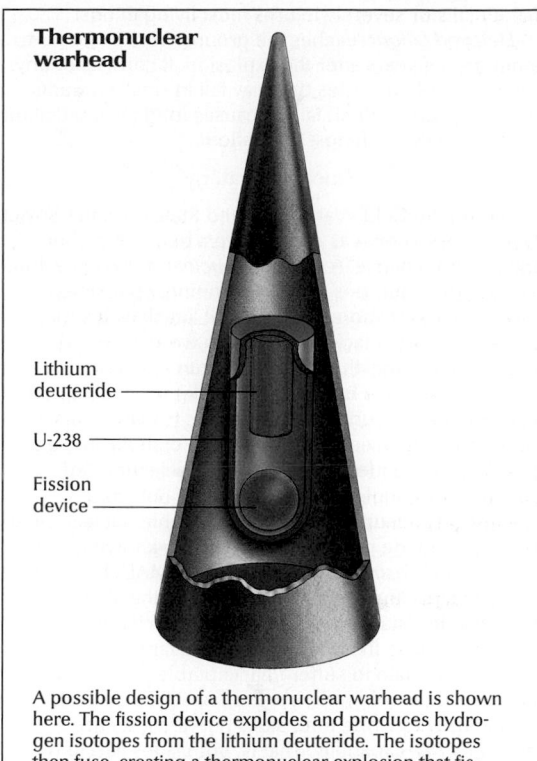

Thermonuclear warhead

Lithium deuteride

U-238

Fission device

A possible design of a thermonuclear warhead is shown here. The fission device explodes and produces hydrogen isotopes from the lithium deuteride. The isotopes then fuse, creating a thermonuclear explosion that fissions the U-238 and increases the warhead's power.

WORLD BOOK illustration by J. Harlan Hunt. Adapted from artwork in Howard Morland's *The Secret That Exploded,* Random House, 1981.

would last only about 10 seconds. Thus it would char, but not burn up, heavy fabrics and thick wood or plastic.

Prompt nuclear radiation begins at the instant of the explosion. It lasts about a minute. It consists of neutrons and *gamma rays.* Gamma rays are a form of radiation similar to—but more powerful than—X rays. The fireball emits neutrons and some of the gamma rays almost instantly. The rest of the gamma rays come from a huge mushroom-shaped cloud of radioactive material formed by the explosion. Nuclear radiation can destroy living cells and prevent normal cell replacement. Large doses of radiation can cause death. For more information about how radiation affects the body, see **Radiation** (Effects of radiation) and **Radiation sickness.**

Prompt radiation rapidly loses strength as it moves away from ground zero. Thus, people farther from ground zero suffer less harm from such radiation.

Residual nuclear radiation is given off later than one minute after the explosion. Residual radiation created by fission consists of gamma rays and electrons. Residual radiation from fusion is made up primarily of neutrons. The radiation strikes particles of debris in the mushroom-shaped cloud created by the explosion. As a result, these particles become radioactive. They fall to the ground as *fallout.* The closer an explosion occurs to Earth's surface, the more fallout it produces.

Early fallout reaches the ground within 24 hours of the explosion. Its heavier particles are highly radioactive. Most particles fall downwind from ground zero. Early fallout kills or severely injures most living things.

Delayed fallout reaches the ground from 24 hours to a number of years after the explosion. It consists of tiny, often invisible particles that may fall in small amounts over large areas. Such fallout causes long-term radiation damage to living things. See **Fallout.**

Nuclear strategy

During the Cold War, the United States and the Soviet Union were known as *superpowers* because of their military dominance. A policy of *nuclear deterrence* dominated both countries' military planning. Both sides threatened to respond to any initial attack with a major nuclear counterattack. Such threats were intended to *deter* (discourage) the other side from attacking first.

Many historians believe nuclear deterrence helped keep the peace during the Cold War. However, many experts think deterrence became more complicated after the Cold War ended. In the case of nuclear-armed terrorists, for example, deterrence might not work.

Mutually assured destruction. Stable nuclear deterrence was made possible by a situation known as *mutually assured destruction* (MAD). Under MAD, both the United States and the Soviet Union had the ability to launch a devastating nuclear attack, even if the opponent struck first. In the event of a nuclear war, both sides would be certain to suffer unacceptable damage. Thus, neither side would have a reason to start a conflict.

For MAD to work, both sides needed a secure *second-strike* capability. That is, both sides had to be able to absorb a massive nuclear attack and retain the ability to launch a devastating counterattack.

MAD would have been undermined if one side could launch a *splendid first strike*. This term refers to a nuclear attack that completely destroys the enemy's nuclear arsenal. A country that could launch a splendid first strike need not fear a nuclear counterattack. It might therefore be tempted to start a nuclear war. As a result, the superpowers went to great lengths during the Cold War to make sure that their nuclear weapons could survive an attack. For example, the United States placed nuclear weapons in submarines and in hardened missile silos. It also kept nuclear-armed bomber planes continuously in the air. Such measures made it more difficult for the Soviet Union to attack U.S. nuclear weapons.

Nuclear superiority. During the Cold War, strategists debated whether *nuclear superiority* contributed to nuclear deterrence. Nuclear superiority means having a larger and better arsenal of nuclear weapons than an opponent. Advocates of nuclear superiority argued that their opponent might not be deterred from launching a nuclear attack if it could inflict significantly more damage. Critics believed that a second-strike capability was itself enough to deter an opponent. Nevertheless, the United States and the Soviet Union both built tens of thousands of nuclear weapons. This massive build-up is called an *arms race*. It was motivated by each country's fear of its opponent achieving nuclear superiority.

Nuclear defense. The United States and the Soviet Union also tried to build defenses against nuclear weapons. *Missile defenses* use missiles to target and destroy an opponent's nuclear-armed missiles before they can reach their target. *Civil defenses* include underground bunkers and fallout shelters. These facilities are designed to help people survive during and after a nuclear war. Critics argued that such defenses were expensive and ineffective. They also claimed that defenses could undermine MAD. They reasoned that if one side felt protected from nuclear attack, it might not be deterred from starting a nuclear war.

Post-Cold War strategy. Many experts believe that nuclear deterrence has become more complicated since the end of the Cold War. Many more countries have nuclear weapons. Each nuclear-armed country today might have multiple nuclear-armed enemies. In addition, MAD might not hold for countries with smaller nuclear arsenals. New nuclear powers also have less experience managing nuclear weapons. Thus, they may be more likely to have a nuclear accident. Experts worry that regional nuclear powers—such as India and Pakistan—could someday fight a nuclear war.

Nuclear terrorism became a concern after the terrorist attacks of Sept. 11, 2001. Most experts believe that nuclear deterrence will not work against terrorists. Terrorists are often well hidden. They may be willing to carry out a suicide attack with nuclear weapons. Such factors make it difficult—or pointless—to threaten terrorists with a second strike. Experts believe that a terrorist group with nuclear weapons would likely use them. The key to stopping nuclear terrorism is thus to prevent terrorists from acquiring nuclear weapons at all.

Controlling nuclear weapons

Because of the great dangers associated with nuclear weapons, many nations have made attempts to control their spread. The chief approaches to control have been *arms control* and *nuclear nonproliferation.*

Arms control refers to agreements between nuclear-armed countries to limit the size and deadliness of their nuclear arsenals. Arms control agreements can contribute to stability by ensuring mutually assured destruction. The agreements also can stop expensive arms races. In addition, they can limit the amount of damage that would occur if a nuclear war broke out.

Some arms control treaties limit the size of nuclear arsenals. In 1972, for example, the United States and the Soviet Union signed the Strategic Arms Limitation Treaty (SALT I). It froze each country's number of missile launchers at the existing levels. In 2010, the United States and Russia signed the New Strategic Arms Reduction Treaty (New START). It limits each side's *deployed* (positioned for use) strategic warheads to 1,550.

Other arms control agreements place limits on testing. *Test bans* make it difficult for countries to design and build new nuclear weapons. The bans also protect people and the environment from harmful radiation produced by nuclear tests. The first major arms control treaty was the Limited Test Ban Treaty (LTBT) of 1963. The treaty banned nuclear weapons tests in the atmosphere, in outer space, and underwater. The Comprehensive Test Ban Treaty (CTBT) of 1996 calls for the end of all nuclear weapons tests. To go into effect, the treaty must be ratified by all countries that have *nuclear reactors* (devices for producing nuclear energy). About three-fourths of those countries have ratified the treaty, including Russia. The United States has not ratified it.

Nuclear nonproliferation refers to efforts to prevent additional countries or terrorist groups from acquiring nuclear weapons. Nonproliferation measures include international treaties, economic *sanctions* (penalties), military strikes, *inducements* (rewards), and nuclear security.

Treaties. The Nuclear Nonproliferation Regime is a set of international agreements designed to prevent the spread of nuclear weapons. The cornerstone of the regime is the Nuclear Nonproliferation Treaty (NPT), which came into force in 1970. The NPT recognizes China, France, Russia, the United Kingdom, and the United States as nuclear weapon states. Other countries signed the treaty as nonnuclear weapon states. These countries agreed never to acquire nuclear weapons. In exchange, the states without nuclear weapons receive a number of benefits. The benefits include assurances that their rivals will not acquire nuclear weapons. The benefits also include help with nuclear technology for peaceful purposes. In addition, nuclear weapon states promised to negotiate to give up nuclear weapons in the future.

Nearly every country in the world is a member of the NPT. India, Israel, and Pakistan—countries that later obtained nuclear weapons—did not sign the treaty. North Korea withdrew from the treaty in 2003 after revealing that it had a program to develop nuclear weapons.

Sanctions. Countries use economic sanctions to deter other countries from acquiring nuclear weapons. Sanctions limit trade and investment in target countries. They aim to force a country to choose between nuclear weapons and a healthy economy. From 2006 to 2010, for example, the United Nations (UN) passed four rounds of economic sanctions against Iran. The sanctions came in response to Iran's violations of its NPT commitments.

Military strikes have also been used to prevent—or at least delay—countries from acquiring nuclear weapons. Such a strike may destroy the facilities used to build nuclear weapons. For example, during World War II, the United States targeted Nazi Germany's nuclear research facilities. In 2007, Israel bombed a nuclear reactor in Syria, which was thought to be part of a weapons program.

Inducements. Countries also use inducements to encourage other countries not to develop nuclear weapons. The promises under the NPT to provide peaceful nuclear technology are one example of inducements. The United States also provides security guarantees to many of its allies. As part of these guarantees, the United States promises to retaliate if another country attacks the ally with nuclear weapons. These guarantees are sometimes called a *nuclear umbrella* or *extended deterrence.* They are designed to convince U.S. allies that they can be secure without nuclear weapons of their own.

Security. Since the September 11 terrorist attacks, nuclear security has become an important part of international nonproliferation efforts. Terrorists can most easily obtain nuclear weapons or materials by stealing them from a nuclear-armed state. A number of international agreements thus have triggered steps to increase the security of nuclear materials and facilities. These agreements include UN Security Council Resolution 1540 and the Global Initiative to Combat Nuclear Terrorism.

History

Scientists gained an understanding of the basic structure of the atom during the late 1800's and early 1900's. In 1938, researchers discovered that splitting the nucleus of a uranium atom released much energy. See **Atom**

(Development of the atomic theory); **Nuclear energy** (The development of nuclear energy).

World War II. By early 1939, only months before the start of World War II, physicists in the United States had become aware of the potential military applications of nuclear energy. They grew concerned that Nazi Germany might develop a nuclear weapon. In August 1939, the German-born physicist Albert Einstein helped alert U.S. President Franklin D. Roosevelt to the potential military applications of nuclear fission. World War II began on Sept. 1, 1939. The United States entered the war in December 1941. In 1942, the U.S. government set up the Manhattan Project to design a fission bomb.

On July 16, 1945, Manhattan Project scientists led by the American physicist J. Robert Oppenheimer exploded the first experimental nuclear device. The test, at the Trinity Site near Alamogordo, New Mexico, used an implosion-type design and yielded 22 kilotons.

The first nuclear weapon used against Japan was a gun-type fission bomb. Its yield was about 13 kilotons. An American B-29 aircraft dropped the bomb on Hiroshima on Aug. 6, 1945. Three days later, another B-29 dropped a 22-kiloton implosion-type fission bomb on Nagasaki. These bombs largely destroyed both cities. But the number of deaths differed greatly. The smaller bomb killed from 70,000 to 100,000 people in Hiroshima, which has a flat terrain. The larger bomb killed about 40,000 in Nagasaki, which is hilly. Other people in both cities died later of injuries and radiation. On Aug. 14, 1945, Japan agreed to surrender, ending World War II.

The Cold War. In 1949, the Soviet Union tested its first fission device amid rising tension between the superpowers. In 1952, during the Korean War (1950-1953), the United States exploded the first experimental thermonuclear device. The Soviet Union set off its first weapons-grade thermonuclear device in 1955. In the mid-1950's, the Soviets equipped submarines with nuclear missiles. In 1957, they test-launched the first land-based intercontinental ballistic missile (ICBM). The United States developed its first ICBM's and SLBM's in 1959.

In the 1960's, several crises almost led the United States and the Soviet Union to nuclear war. One was the Cuban missile crisis. In 1962, the United States learned that the Soviet Union had installed missiles in Cuba. The United States considered invading the Soviet-allied island country. The U.S. Navy also threw up a blockade around Cuba against Soviet ships. In the end, the Soviet Union removed the missiles (see **Cuban missile crisis**).

As time went on, the strategic nuclear balance stabilized. The frequency of nuclear crises between the superpowers diminished. By the 1970's, the superpowers reached a cooling of tensions known as *détente.* This situation allowed for the negotiation and conclusion of a number of nuclear arms control treaties.

The superpowers also cooperated on nuclear nonproliferation. They were the key actors behind the establishment of the Nuclear Nonproliferation Treaty. Both the United States and the Soviet Union were successful in preventing most of their allies from acquiring nuclear weapons. But during the Cold War, the United Kingdom (1952), France (1960), China (1964), and Israel (1967) succeeded in gaining nuclear weapons.

The end of the Cold War in the early 1990's reduced the political tensions between the superpowers. United

States and Soviet leaders began reducing their nuclear arsenals. The threat of a nuclear war between the superpowers had diminished. As a result, many experts shifted their attention to the threat of nuclear proliferation.

After the Soviet Union broke up in 1991, the Soviet military left nuclear weapons in the newly independent countries of Belarus, Kazakhstan, and Ukraine. These countries quickly returned the weapons to Russia.

In 1998, both India and Pakistan conducted nuclear tests. Like the superpowers before them, India and Pakistan soon experienced a series of crises. These crises threatened to draw them into a nuclear war. In 1999, fighting broke out between the two countries over control of a mountainous region called Kashmir.

After the terrorist attacks of Sept. 11, 2001, many experts assessed that nuclear terrorism posed the greatest threat to international peace and security. World leaders began focusing on countries that had nuclear programs and ties to terrorist organizations. The U.S.-led invasion of Iraq in 2003 was partially motivated by the belief that Iraq might transfer nuclear weapons and other *weapons of mass destruction* (WMD's) to terrorist groups. However, no WMD's were found in Iraq.

The international community also put pressure on nuclear programs in Iran, Libya, and North Korea. Libya gave up its nuclear program in 2003. But North Korea conducted nuclear tests in 2006 and 2009. Iran continued to develop its nuclear capabilities. But the country claimed that such development was only for peaceful energy purposes.   Matthew Kroenig

Related articles in *World Book* include:

Biographies

Einstein, Albert	Teller, Edward
Oppenheimer, J. Robert	Truman, Harry S.

Countries

Canada, History of (The return of the Liberals)
India (Recent developments)
Iran (Recent developments)
Korea, North (Nuclear tensions)
Pakistan (Struggle for democracy)
Russia (History)
United States, History of (The Cold War; The end of the Cold War)

Treaties and agreements

North Atlantic Treaty Organization
Nuclear Nonproliferation Treaty
Strategic Arms Reduction Treaty

Wars and other conflicts

Cold War	World War II (The atomic
Cuban missile crisis	bomb)
War (Limited war)	

Weapons and armed forces

Air force (Air forces in the nuclear age)
Air Force, United States (Defense and deterrence; Missiles)
Army (Armies in the nuclear age)
Army, United States (History)
Bomb (Nuclear bombs)
Guided missile
Submarine (Nuclear submarines)
Weapon (World War II)

Installations

Los Alamos National Laboratory
Sandia National Laboratories
White Sands Missile Range

Other related articles

Arms control	Manhattan Project	Plutonium
Civil defense	Nagasaki	United Nations
Hiroshima	Neutron	(Arms control)
Hydrogen (Isotopes)	Nuclear energy	Uranium
	Nuclear winter	

Additional resources

Bernstein, Jeremy. *Nuclear Weapons.* Cambridge, 2008.
DeGroot, Gerard J. *The Bomb.* Harvard Univ. Pr., 2005.
Diehl, Sarah J. and Moltz, J. C. *Nuclear Weapons and Nonproliferation.* 2nd ed. ABC-CLIO, 2008.
Reed, Thomas C., and Stillman, D. B. *The Nuclear Express: A Political History of the Bomb and Its Proliferation.* Zenith Pr., 2009.
Rhodes, Richard. *The Twilight of the Bombs.* Knopf, 2010.

Nuclear winter refers to the deadly worldwide climate change that would result from a major nuclear war. Even a relatively small nuclear war between neighboring countries would change climate dramatically.

Nuclear winter would develop from fires created by nuclear explosions in cities and industrial areas. Large amounts of smoke from these fires would spread to cover the entire planet. The smoke would prevent most sunlight from reaching the ground. Temperatures would drop substantially, and rainfall would be reduced. These conditions would last for several years or more. With greatly reduced sunlight, less rain, and lower temperatures, farming would stop, and worldwide famine would result. Nuclear winter also would reduce Earth's ozone layer, which protects people and other forms of life from the sun's dangerous ultraviolet light.

Scientists estimate that the nuclear explosions in a major nuclear war could kill 500 million people. But 4 billion more people could starve to death in the next year because of nuclear winter. Thus, nuclear winter could endanger every country.   Alan Robock

Nucleic acid. See DNA; RNA.

Nucleus. See Ameba; Atom; Cell; Comet; Nuclear energy; Radioactivity.

Nuer, *NOO uhr,* are a cattle-keeping people of northeast Africa. About 900,000 Nuer live in the grasslands and swamps along the Nile River in South Sudan and western Ethiopia. They speak a language called Nuer, which belongs to the Nilo-Saharan family of African languages that also includes Dinka and Maasai.

Cattle play a central role in the social and religious life of the Nuer. A Nuer bridegroom gives a large gift of cattle to his bride's family. The Nuer sacrifice cattle to their supreme god and to lesser spirits. Milk and milk products make up much of their diet, but the Nuer do not kill their cattle for meat.

The Nuer move to higher ground during the rainy season, from May to December, when the Nile River floods. There they raise peanuts, a grain called *millet,* and other vegetable crops. The Nuer build houses of sun-dried mud and make thatched roofs for them.

The Nuer are divided into clans whose members have a common ancestor. Until the 1900's, the Nuer were not organized under the control of leaders. A religious expert called the *kuuarmuon* or *leopard-skin chief* helped settle disputes and presided over religious ceremonies. The United Kingdom and Egypt made Sudan a protectorate in 1899 and brought many changes to the Nuer, including the creation of tribal chiefs and administrators.

Arabic-speaking Muslims from northern Sudan controlled Sudan's government after the nation gained independence in 1956. In the 1980's, the Nuer joined other black African groups, including the Dinka, to form an opposition group called the Sudan People's Liberation Army (SPLA). Southern Sudan suffered brutal fighting and numerous famines as the SPLA battled for independence from the Muslim north. In 2005, Sudan's National Assembly approved a new constitution and established a regional government in the south, ending the civil war. South Sudan became an independent nation in 2011. But conflicts between the Nuer and neighboring ethnic groups continue to occur.   Elliot Fratkin

See also **Africa** (picture: African artists sometimes use the human body); **Dinka; Maasai; Sudan** (Independence; Civil war).

Nuevo Laredo, *NWAY voh lah RAY doh* or *noo AY voh luh RAY doh* (pop. 373,725), is a city on Mexico's border with the United States. For location, see **Mexico** (political map). Three road bridges across the Rio Grande link the city with Laredo, Texas, just north of the border. Nuevo Laredo is a major point of entry into Mexico. It lies at the northern end of a stretch of the Pan American Highway, a major road to Mexico City.

© Bob Daemmerich, The Image Works

Nuevo Laredo lies on Mexico's border with the United States. This photograph shows a main business district of the city.

The city of Laredo was founded in 1755. It then included what are now Laredo and Nuevo Laredo. Laredo and Nuevo Laredo became separate cities in 1848, when the Treaty of Guadalupe Hidalgo established the boundary between Mexico and Texas. *Nuevo* in the name Nuevo Laredo means *new.* At one time, the city attracted millions of tourists annually. During the early 2000's, however, tourism declined because rivalries between drug cartels increased crime in the area.   Julian C. Bridges

Nullification, *NUHL uh fuh KAY shuhn,* is the action of setting aside a law by declaring it *null and void.* The Constitution of the United States does not provide any way for a law of Congress to be declared unconstitutional after the president has signed it. Some delegates

to the Constitutional Convention believed the courts would naturally assume this authority. Only in 1803, with the case of *Marbury v. Madison,* did the Supreme Court of the United States flatly assert the right of the courts to pass on the constitutionality of an act of Congress.

The theory that the states, rather than any branch of the federal government, should have the right to *nullify* (declare unconstitutional) a law of Congress, developed slowly. The Kentucky and Virginia Resolutions of 1798 protested the Alien and Sedition Acts passed by Congress. Many people believed that these acts violated the First Amendment. They wanted all the states to declare the acts unconstitutional. But no other state would join in the action. In 1799, the Kentucky legislature stated its belief in the legality of nullification, but merely entered a protest against the Alien and Sedition Acts.

Nullification was next seriously proposed in 1828, when John C. Calhoun prepared a document known as the South Carolina Exposition. Rising industrial interests of the Northeast had persuaded Congress to include in the tariff law of 1828 (the "tariff of abominations") protective duties that the cotton-growing South disliked. Sentiment against the tariff was strongest in South Carolina. People even talked of secession.

Calhoun's motive in recommending nullification was to provide an alternative to secession. He argued that the federal government had no right to judge the constitutionality of its acts. He also insisted that the states had given certain powers to Congress and were alone competent to say whether or not Congress had exceeded its powers. Calhoun's reasoning was set forth by Senator Robert Y. Hayne in his famous debate with Senator Daniel Webster in 1830. Webster said nullification would break up the Union and closed with the words: "Liberty *and* Union, now and forever, one and inseparable!"

In 1832, Congress again passed a protective tariff act. South Carolina passed an ordinance that declared the tariff laws of 1828 and 1832 null and void in that state. It threatened to leave the Union if the federal government tried to enforce the tariff laws anywhere in South Carolina. President Andrew Jackson warned the people that the laws would be enforced. He also took measures to make sure that the tariff would be collected at the important port of Charleston. After Congress passed a law called a *force bill* to uphold Jackson's position, it became clear that resistance was unwise. Besides, the Compromise Tariff of 1833, engineered through Congress by Henry Clay, greatly reduced the tariff duties.

Nullification was only one manifestation of the doctrine of states' rights. That doctrine, insofar as it meant the supremacy of the states over the nation, was ended by the American Civil War (1861-1865).   Robert M. Weir

See also **Calhoun, John C.; Force bill; Hayne, Robert Y.; States' rights; Webster, Daniel.**

Numbat is an Australian marsupial with distinctive striped coloring. It grows about 10 inches (25 centimeters) long and has a bushy tail. The numbat is rusty-red above and white below. The hind third of the back is crossed by about six white stripes. A black stripe runs through the eye from snout to ear. Unlike many female marsupials, female numbats do not have an enclosed pouch for carrying their young. Instead, females have an open pouch with long guard hairs. The young cling to the mother's hair and *teats* (nipples).

The numbat has distinctive white stripes on the hind end of its rusty-red back. This mammal also has a pointed snout, erect ears, and a bushy tail. Numbats inhabit woodland areas in the southwestern corner of Australia. They feed primarily on termites.

© Steven David Miller, Nature Picture Library

Numbats feed during the day on termites, which they catch by scratching open the insect's underground tunnels. The termites are caught on the numbat's long, sticky, cylindrical tongue. Numbats live in scrub woodland. They nest at night in hollow logs. The numbat was once common over much of the southern half of Australia but is now found only in the southwest corner. It is in danger of dying out completely.   Marissa L. Parrott

Scientific classification. The numbat's scientific name is *Myrmecobius fasciatus.*

Number, in grammar, is a feature of language that indicates how many persons or objects are referred to. In English, the form of a noun shows whether the reference is to one person, place, object, or idea, or to more than one. The form that indicates only one is called the *singular.* The form that indicates more than one is called the *plural.* Some other languages have a singular form, indicating one; a *dual* form, indicating two; and a plural form, indicating more than two. The plurals of English nouns are formed in *regular* and *irregular* ways.

Regular plurals are formed by adding *-s* or *-es* to the singular forms of the noun, as in *cap, caps* and *church, churches.* Compound nouns form plurals with the addition of *-s* or *-es,* but the placement varies. For example, the plural of *brother-in-law* is *brothers-in-law.* But the plural of *grown-up* is *grown-ups.* And in *manservant,* both parts take the plural form—*menservants.*

Irregular plurals are not formed according to any established rule, as are regular plurals. The plurals of some nouns of Old English origin are formed by a vowel change, as in *man, men* and *tooth, teeth.* A small number of nouns still have the Old English plural ending *-en*—for example, *ox, oxen* and *child, children.*

About a dozen nouns that end in *-f* or *-fe* are changed to *-ves* in the plural, among them *half, halves* and *wife, wives.* But not all nouns that end in *-f* or *-fe* follow this pattern. For example, *roof* and *chief* form regular plurals —*roofs* and *chiefs.*

Some nouns, such as *barracks, deer,* and *sheep,* have the same form in both the singular and the plural. A few expressions use a singular form even though a plural is actually called for. These include *two-inch nail, six-foot man,* and *two-gallon bucket.*

Some nouns, including *cowardice* and *brilliance,* have no plural. They differ from such nouns as *deer* and *sheep* because *two sheep* is correct, but *two cowardices* is not. The plural of *cowardice* would usually be expressed by saying something like *There are different kinds of cowardice.*

Foreign plurals. Words coming into English from foreign languages sometimes keep their foreign plurals. Such foreign plurals are mostly from Greek and Latin words. Some of these are *phenomenon, phenomena; criterion, criteria; alumnus, alumni; alumna, alumnae; fungus, fungi;* and *thesis, theses.* There is a strong tendency for such words to go into the regular English plural group. For example, at an earlier period the plural of *stadium* was the foreign form *stadia.* Now, however, *stadiums* is the plural form commonly used.

The spelling of plurals in English has many irregularities that are not reflected in speech. Singular nouns that end in *-y,* following a consonant, are changed to *-ies* in the plural—for example, *lady, ladies; flurry, flurries;* and *candy, candies.* For those ending in *-y,* preceded by a vowel, *-s* is added, as in *alley, alleys* and *day, days.* Some nouns that end in *-o* have *-s* added: *silos* and *pianos.* Others, for no special reason, have *-es* added: *tomatoes* and *heroes.* Several even have optional forms, such as *zeroes* or *zeros* and *ghettoes* or *ghettos.*

English pronouns also have plurals, but the relationship is not so consistent as in nouns. *We* can be called the plural of *I,* and *they* the plural of *he, she,* and *it. These* is the plural of *this,* and *those* the plural of *that.*

English verbs reflect number by agreeing with the subject. For example, the verb *play* occurs with a plural subject in the sentence *The boys play baseball every day.* The verb appears with a singular subject in *The boy plays baseball every day.*   Patricia A. Moody

See also **Declension; Inflection; Noun** (Number and case); **Pronoun; Verb.**

Number, in mathematics, represents a quantity or an amount. A number can tell how many objects there are in a certain set, as in *one* apple or *five* letters. Numbers can also describe the order of objects—for example, the *third* planet from the sun. In addition, numbers can measure *properties* (characteristics) of objects, such as an object's length, weight, or temperature.

By themselves, numbers are just ideas. But we can write or discuss numbers using symbols called *numerals*. For example, several different numerals can represent the number we think of as *twelve*. They include the decimal numeral *12,* the Roman numeral *XII*, and the binary numeral *1100*. These three numerals all represent the same idea—the number *twelve*. Decimal, Roman, and binary are three kinds of *numeral systems*. Numeral systems, also called *systems of numeration,* are ways of counting and naming numbers.

Numeral systems

Numeral systems differ in the symbols they use. They also differ in the way they group symbols to represent larger numbers.

The decimal system is the most commonly used numeral system. It uses 10 numerals, called *digits*. They are *0, 1, 2, 3, 4, 5, 6, 7, 8,* and *9*. The decimal system is also called the *base 10 system*. The word decimal comes from the Latin word *deca,* meaning *ten*.

The decimal system represents larger numbers using groups of 10. Suppose you want to count how many pennies you have saved. You could stack them in groups of 10 pennies each. If there are 10 or more such stacks, you can bunch the piles together to form an even larger group of 10 tens—or 100—pennies.

**2 groups of 10 stacks   4 stacks of   8 pennies
  of 10 pennies   10 pennies**

In this picture, there are eight (8) single pennies, four (4) stacks of 10 pennies, and two (2) groups of 100 pennies. Thus, we say there are 248 pennies. The decimal number *248* is organized the same way as the pennies. It is short for saying that there are 2 hundreds, 4 tens, and 8 single pennies.

The decimal system is an example of a *place-value system,* also called a *positional system*. That is, the value of each digit in a decimal number depends on its place. In the number *248,* the *2* is in the hundreds place. It actually means *200*. The *4* is in the tens place. It means *40*. The *8* is in the ones place. It simply means *8*.

The digit *0* has special importance in the decimal system. It lets us show that a certain place is empty. For example, the decimal number *205* means *2 hundreds, no tens, and 5 ones*. Ancient numeral systems lacked a symbol for zero. They thus found it difficult to represent numbers using place values.

In the decimal system, each place represents a *power* of 10. In mathematics, the word *power* means the result of multiplying a number by itself a certain number of times. For example, 10 to the third power—written *10³*—

means $10 \times 10 \times 10$. The following table shows several place values and their corresponding powers of 10:

Decimal number	Place value	Power of 10
1	1 one	$10^0 = 1$
10	1 ten	$10^1 = 10$
100	1 hundred	$10^2 = 10 \times 10$
1,000	1 thousand	$10^3 = 10 \times 10 \times 10$
10,000	1 ten-thousand	$10^4 = 10 \times 10 \times 10 \times 10$

The *2* in *10²,* the *3* in *10³,* and so on are called *exponents*. The number 10 is called the *base*. This is why the decimal system is also called the base 10 system.

There is no particular mathematical reason to base a numeral system on the number 10. Rather, the decimal system likely began simply because humans have 10 fingers for counting. In fact, the word *digit* means *finger*.

The binary system only uses two digits—generally *1* and *0*. It is also called the *base 2 system*. The word *binary* comes from a Latin word meaning *two at a time*. Computers use binary numbers for processing information and performing other basic functions.

The binary system, like the decimal system, uses places. But in the binary system, the places are powers of 2, not 10. For example, the binary number *10* means *1 two,* not *1 ten*. The binary number *11* means *1 two and 1 one*. This adds up to the decimal number *3*. The following table shows several place values in the binary system and the corresponding powers of two:

Binary number	Place value	Power of 2
1	1 one	$2^0 = 1$
10	1 two	$2^1 = 2$
100	1 four	$2^2 = 2 \times 2$
1000	1 eight	$2^3 = 2 \times 2 \times 2$
10000	1 sixteen	$2^4 = 2 \times 2 \times 2 \times 2$

In the decimal system, the number *1101* means *1 thousand, 1 hundred, 0 tens, and 1 one*. But in binary, the places are powers of 2, not of 10. So the binary number *1101* means *1 eight, 1 four, no twos, and 1 one*. The binary number *1101* is thus equal to the decimal number *13*.

Roman numerals express numbers using letters, such as *M* (1,000), *C* (100), *X* (10), *V* (5), and *I* (1). This system does not make use of place value. Instead, the individual values are often added together. For example, the Roman numeral *VII* is equal to the decimal number *7* (5 + 1 + 1). See **Roman numerals**.

Kinds of numbers

The numbers discussed so far are all members of the set of *natural numbers*. There are infinitely many natural numbers. Even so, math uses many more numbers.

Natural and whole numbers. Natural numbers are also called *counting numbers* or *positive integers*. They are the numbers 1, 2, 3, and so on. The set of *whole numbers* is often said to include the natural numbers, plus zero. Some mathematicians include zero with the natural numbers.

Integers. The set of integers includes zero and all the natural numbers along with their negatives. It can be written: {… –3, –2, –1, 0, 1, 2, 3, …}. The integers go on forever in both directions. Negative integers are not part of the set of natural numbers.

Rational numbers. Integers, along with natural and whole numbers, have one feature in common: Their members are separated by "gaps" of one whole unit, with nothing in between. But in daily life, we must often represent quantities between two integers—for example, *half* a loaf of bread or a distance of *two and a quarter* miles.

We can represent such quantities using the set of *rational numbers*. This set includes all the ratios of integers. *Half a loaf of bread* can be expressed using the rational number ½. Ratios written in this way are also called *fractions*. *Two and a quarter miles* can be expressed using the number 2 ¼, or ¾.

The integer –7 is also a rational number, because it can be written as ⁻⁷⁄₁. Thus, the set of rational numbers includes every integer. Any two integers, when divided, produce a rational number—with one exception. Division by zero is impossible.

Every rational number can be written as either a *terminating* decimal—one that ends—or a repeating decimal. For example, ¾ is equal to a decimal, 0.75, which *terminates* (ends). The number ⁴⁄₃₃ equals a repeating decimal, 0.121212…. The pattern of alternating *1*'s and *2*'s repeats forever.

Irrational numbers. The set of rational numbers seems large. But even it has many "gaps" between its members. Many numbers, called *irrational numbers,* cannot be written as ratios of integers. The most famous irrational number is the number *pi* (π). Pi is the ratio of a circle's circumference to its diameter. No fraction of integers describes this quantity.

Unlike a rational number, an irrational number can be represented by a nonterminating, nonrepeating decimal. No group of digits in such a number repeats itself in exactly the same order. For example, the first eight decimal digits of π are 3.1415927. But the digits go on forever after that, with no pattern.

Real numbers. If we combine all rational and irrational numbers, we get the larger set of the *real numbers*. This set is "complete" in the sense that there are no more gaps between its members.

Complex numbers. In advanced mathematics, there is a still larger set of numbers, the *complex numbers*. Complex numbers take the form $a + bi$. In this formula, a and b are real numbers. The quantity i equals the square root of –1. No real number, when multiplied by itself, results in a negative number. Thus, the quantity i is called the *imaginary unit*. The word "imaginary" does not mean the number is made-up or fictional. Nor does the word "real" mean that real numbers are more real than other numbers.

Examples of complex numbers include $3 + 2i$ and $-5 + i$. The real number 7 is also a complex number, because it can be written as $7 + 0i$. Likewise, $4i$ is a complex number. It can be written $0 + 4i$.

Thus, the real numbers are a subset of the complex numbers. Likewise, the rational numbers are a subset of the real numbers. The integers are a subset of the rational numbers. Each set is a subset of the next one.

History

Ancient people had several ways of recording the few numbers they needed. A shepherd, for example, could collect pebbles to represent the number of sheep in a flock. Each pebble meant one sheep. A bag of pebbles stood for the whole flock.

Later, people developed other ways to record the number of their possessions. They tied knots in a leather thong or scratched tally marks on the side of a rock. They then matched the knots or marks against each item. Later, people began to use words to represent numbers. These words described "how many" and helped people match items mentally. For example, people used the word for *wings* to mean two objects. For five items, they used the word that meant *hand*.

Finally, people began to count by arranging the names of numbers in a certain order. To count, they spoke or wrote the word that meant *one,* next the word for *two,* then the word for *three,* and so on. In time, people in many parts of the world developed various kinds of counting systems. Some were based on 5, others on 10, and still others on 12 or 60. People still use such measures as 12 inches in a foot and 60 minutes in an hour, descended from these ancient systems.

In most early numeral systems, people formed numerals simply by repeating basic symbols and adding the values to get the number they wanted. The Egyptians, Greeks, and Romans used systems of this kind. The Maya of Central America and the Hindus of India used systems that followed the principle of place value. These systems used a symbol that meant *not any,* a forerunner of our modern zero. The Hindu system ultimately developed into the decimal numeral system.

The Egyptians. About 3000 B.C., the ancient Egyptians used *hieroglyphics* (picture writing) to write numerals, as shown here.

1 **/** Stroke	1,000	Lotus flower
10 ∩ Arch	10,000	Finger
100 **⑨** Coiled rope	100,000	Tadpole

The Egyptian system was based on 10. But it did not include a zero symbol. Nor did it use the principle of place value. The Egyptians formed numerals by putting basic symbols together. For example, they wrote the numeral 1,326 like this:

The Babylonians used *cuneiform* (wedge-shaped) symbols to write numbers. An early system of about 2100 B.C. was based on 60. In this system, a numeral contained groups of symbols. One group stood for the number of 1's, the next group stood for 60's, the next for 3600's (60 × 60), and so on.

The Greeks. About 500 B.C., the Greeks developed a system based on 10. This system used a 27-letter Greek alphabet—the present-day 24-letter alphabet plus 3 letters no longer used. The first 9 letters stood for numbers, from 1 through 9. The next 9 letters stood for 10's, from 10 through 90. The last 9 letters were symbols for 100's, from 100 through 900.

The Greek philosopher Pythagoras, who lived about 550 B.C., explored beyond the representation of numbers to their very nature. Pythagoras believed that everything could be understood in terms of whole numbers or their ratios. About 400 B.C., however, the Greeks discovered irrational numbers. They recognized that Pythagoras's ideas were incomplete.

The Romans used letters as symbols for numbers. But the early Roman system of about 500 B.C. differed from the system we use today. For example, the ancient Romans wrote 4 as IIII and 9 as VIIII. Today, we usually use IV for 4 and IX for 9. A table of Roman numerals appears in the *World Book* article **Roman numerals.** People throughout Europe widely used Roman numerals until the A.D. 1500's. The numerals are still used on clock faces, in outlines, and for other purposes.

The Chinese, by the 100's B.C., had devised a decimal system of numbers. It included fractions, zero, and negative numbers.

The Maya used a numeral system based on 20. A dot represented the number one, and a bar represented five. The Maya system was a place-value system, and the Maya used a zero before A.D. 600. Their system was as advanced as the systems that gave rise to the modern decimal system.

The Hindu-Arabic numeral system. Hindu mathematicians of the 300's and 200's B.C. used a system based on 10. The Hindus had symbols for each number from one to nine. They had a name for each power of 10, and used these names when writing numerals. For example, Hindus wrote "1 sata, 3 dasan, 5" to represent the number we write as 135. They wrote "1 sata, 5" for the number we write as 105.

The Hindus gradually developed a way of eliminating place names. They invented the symbol *sunya* (meaning *empty*), which we call *zero.* With this symbol, they could write "105" instead of "1 sata, 5."

During the 700's, the Arabs learned Hindu arithmetic. In the 800's, a Persian mathematician named al-Khwārizmī wrote a book that used the Hindu numeral system. His book was translated into Latin about 300 years later. This translation brought the Hindu-Arabic numerals into Europe. Modern decimal numerals are sometimes called *Arabic numerals* for this reason.

Several centuries passed before the Hindu-Arabic system became widely used. After Europeans learned to print from movable type in the 1400's, they published many mathematics textbooks. Most of the books showed calculations using the Hindu-Arabic system. These books brought the system into widespread use.

Binary numbers. During the late 1600's, the German mathematician and philosopher Gottfried Wilhelm Leibniz developed and promoted the binary numeration system. However, the binary system only reached widespread importance with the invention of electronic computers, which began in the 1930's and 1940's. Computers and other electronic devices used the binary system because they could represent any number with circuits that were in one of two states, on or off.

Beyond real numbers. In the 1500's, mathematicians first encountered imaginary numbers. They gave the numbers the name *imaginary* because they were confused about the nature of the numbers. In the late 1700's, scholars gradually began to accept imaginary and complex numbers into mathematics. Such numbers have numerous practical applications in physics and engineering. For example, engineers use complex numbers in calculations dealing with mechanical vibrations and electric circuits.   Eli Maor

Related articles in *World Book* include:

Abacus	Addition	Algebra
Al-Khwārizmī	Fraction	Rational number
Arabic numerals	Infinity	Roman numerals
Arithmetic	Mathematics	Root
Binary number	Multiplication	Scientific notation
Decimal system	Notation	Set theory
Division	Number theory	Square root
Duodecimal	Power	Subtraction
system	Progression	Zero

Number theory is the branch of mathematics concerned with the properties of the natural numbers 1, 2, 3, 4, and so on. Number theory also deals with a type of natural numbers called *prime numbers.* A prime number, such as 2, 5, or 71, is a natural number that can be divided without a remainder only by itself and 1.

About 300 B.C., the Greek mathematician Euclid discussed prime numbers in his book *Elements.* He proved that there are infinitely many prime numbers. Euclid's *Elements* also stated a famous property of natural numbers called the *fundamental theorem of arithmetic.* This theorem states that every natural number can be written as a product of prime numbers in exactly one way.

The systematic study of number theory began with the work of the French mathematician Pierre de Fermat in the 1600's. A landmark book in number theory was *Disquisitiones Arithmeticae* (1801), by the German mathematician Carl Friedrich Gauss. It developed a comprehensive theory of natural numbers, including a proof of the fundamental theorem of arithmetic.   Thomas Butts

See also **Fermat, Pierre de; Gauss, Carl Friedrich.**

Numbers, Book of, is the fourth book of the Bible. Its title reflects parts of the book that describe the *numbering* (census) of the Twelve Tribes of Israel. The Hebrew title *In the Wilderness* is perhaps more accurate because the book tells about the Israelites during their traditional 40 years of wandering in the wilderness after their departure from Egypt.

The Book of Numbers begins at Mount Sinai with God ordering the Israelite leader Moses to take a census of the Israelites. The book ends with the Israelites camped on the plains of Moab, an area east of the Jordan River, just before entering Canaan. The book highlights the personal virtue of Moses as the leader of the difficult and rebellious Israelites. An assortment of religious material is interwoven with the main story. This material includes stories that describe the priestly role of the Levites, one of the Twelve Tribes of Israel. Other passages give procedures for such religious rituals as purification rites and sacrificial offerings to God.

Carol L. Meyers

See also **Pentateuch.**

Numeral. See Number.

Numerator. See Arithmetic (Common fractions); Fraction.

Numerology, *NOO muh RAHL uh jee,* is the practice of using numbers to analyze character and foretell the future. It is based on the belief that the universe is governed by numerical laws and that each number has special powers and qualities. Most scientists believe that numerology has no scientific basis, but many people throughout the world practice it.

Numerologists believe that a person's name is an important clue to that person's character. Each letter in the name is changed to a number using a system based on ancient Greek and Hebrew alphabets. The numbers are added together, and the separate figures in the total are combined to arrive at a number from one to nine. Suppose the numbers derived from a person's name total 75. The 75 is broken into a 7 and a 5, which add up to 12. The 12 is separated into a 1 and a 2, which total 3. This number supposedly reflects the person's character. For example, people with the number one are said to be ambitious and forceful. Those with the number two supposedly are quiet and shy.

Another number that numerologists believe reveals character is the *birth number,* which is determined by adding the figures in a person's birth date. Numerologists also combine the birth number with the figures in any year to find a *personal year number.* This number predicts what is going to happen to the person in that year.   Christopher McIntosh

See also **Fortunetelling.**

Numidia, *noo MIHD ee uh,* was an area in northern Africa during ancient times. It occupied the eastern part of what is now Algeria. Numidia was allied with nearby Carthage when the Second Punic War between Carthage and Rome began in 218 B.C. But Massinissa, a Numidian chieftain, sided with the Roman general Publius Cornelius Scipio. In return, as Scipio's ally, Massinissa was rewarded with territory and became king of all Numidia about 200 B.C. Soon afterward, the Numidians helped Scipio defeat the Carthaginians, who were led by Hannibal, at Zama in northern Africa.

Several times after the war, Massinissa seized land from Carthage. Finally, Carthage fought back, helping bring about the Third Punic War (149-146 B.C.). Rome destroyed Carthage in the war but also halted Numidian expansion. By 112 B.C., Jugurtha, adopted grandson of Massinissa, had seized all of Numidia in defiance of Rome. The Roman general Marius defeated him in 106 B.C. In 46 B.C., Numidian King Juba I fought Julius Caesar and was defeated. Caesar annexed Numidia and made most of it a Roman province. The Vandals, a Germanic tribe, conquered Numidia in A.D. 436.   David L. Stone

Numismatics. See **Coin collecting.**

Nummulite, *NUHM yuh lyt,* is an extinct, one-celled marine organism with a shell shaped like a flat disk. On the inside, the shell is coiled and divided into many little chambers. Nummulites range in diameter from less than ½ inch (1.3 centimeters) to more than 2 inches (5 centimeters). The ancient Egyptians used nummulite shells as coins. In fact, *nummulite* comes from a Latin word

© Colin Keates, Natural History Museum, London/Dorling Kindersley
Coinlike nummulite shells, the remains of an extinct marine organism, are scattered through this rock.

meaning *little coin.* Scientists classify nummulites in a group of living things called *protists.*

From about 65 million to 34 million years ago, nummulites lived in great numbers in the sea. Their shells form thick layers of rock, especially in southern Asia and in the Mediterranean. The pyramids of ancient Egypt were built with nummulitic limestone.

Many scientists believe that nummulites lived with tiny photosynthetic organisms called *algae.* The algae may have helped produce the shells, which consist of calcium carbonate.   Irwin Richard Isquith

Scientific classification. Nummulites make up the family Nummulitidae.

Nun is a woman who belongs to a religious community and dedicates her life to carrying out its goals. Various major religions, including Buddhism, Christianity, and Taoism, have orders of nuns. The Roman Catholic Church has more of these orders than any other Christian denomination.

Most Roman Catholic orders of nuns have different requirements for permanent membership, but they all require years of preparation. When a woman enters an order, she begins a period of spiritual training called a *novitiate.* During this period, which in many orders lasts several years, she becomes thoroughly acquainted with the obligations of religious life (see **Religious life**). After her novitiate, the woman takes her first vows, and after several more years, final vows. She promises to give up possession of worldly goods, obey her superiors in the order, and remain unmarried. These promises may be either *simple vows* or *solemn vows.* Solemn vows are more binding.

A woman who has taken simple vows is known as a *sister.* One who has taken solemn vows is properly called a nun. But the term *sister* is commonly used as a form of address for a nun.

The first convents for women were founded in the Egyptian desert during the early 300's by Saint Pachomius. During the Middle Ages, from about the 400's through the 1400's, nuns led strictly *cloistered* (secluded) lives in such convents. In 1633, Saint Vincent de Paul and Saint Louise de Marillac founded the Daughters of Charity (often called the Sisters of Charity), an order devoted to charity work outside the convent. The members cared for orphans and the sick and taught children and adults.

The nun's way of life was modernized by Vatican Council II, a worldwide council of the Roman Catholic Church held from 1962 to 1965. Many orders now permit their members to live in small informal groups rather than in a convent. Many nuns no longer must wear the traditional robe and veil. Nuns continue to work in charitable and educational fields. They now also counsel youths in juvenile courts and perform other services as well.   Anne E. Carr

Related articles in *World Book* include:

Carmelites	Dominicans
Cistercians	Franciscans
Convent	Monasticism

Nunavut, *NOO nuh voot,* is a Canadian territory in the northeastern part of the country. It was created from the eastern part of the Northwest Territories in 1999 to provide more self-government for the Inuit, who make up most of the population. *Nunavut* means *Our Land* in Inuktitut, an Inuit *dialect* (language variation). Iqaluit is

Iqaluit is Nunavut's capital and largest town. It stands on Baffin Island, on the shores of Frobisher Bay. The Inuit had long used Iqaluit as a seasonal fishing camp when Europeans arrived in the area in 1576. The town's name in Inuktitut, an Inuit language, means *place of fish.*

Nunavut's capital and largest town.

Nunavut is part of a vast Arctic region that has long, cold winters and short, cool summers. The territory is sparsely populated because of its harsh climate, but it has rich mineral deposits. It covers about 810,000 square miles (2.1 million square kilometers) and makes up about one-fifth of Canada's land area.

People

Most of Nunavut's people are Inuit, which means *the people* in Inuktitut. They live in dozens of small, government-built, mainly coastal communities. Iqaluit, with about 6,000 residents, is the largest populated place. Many of Nunavut's people play sports, and most hunt or fish for food and as a cultural activity. The territory has three official languages—English, French, and the Inuit language, which includes the Inuktitut and Inuinnaqtun dialects.

Nunavut has a number of social problems, such as high rates of unemployment, suicide, and drug abuse. Nunavut also has a housing shortage, and the people have serious concerns about losing their traditional language and culture.

Land and resources

Location and description. Much of Nunavut lies north of the Arctic Circle. The territory is bordered on the south by the province of Manitoba, on the west by the Northwest Territories, and on the north by the Arctic Ocean. To the east lies Greenland, a province of Denmark, separated from Nunavut by Baffin Bay and Davis Strait. Many of the islands north of the Canadian mainland are part of Nunavut. The territory's islands include Baffin, Ellesmere, and Southampton islands, all part of a

region known as the Arctic Archipelago. Cape Columbia on Ellesmere Island is Canada's northernmost point.

Nunavut consists mainly of rocky, rugged, treeless terrain. Much of the ground beneath the surface is *permafrost* (permanently frozen ground). Some permafrost in Nunavut is more than 2,000 feet (600 meters) thick. Only the top 6 to 60 inches (15 to 150 centimeters) of ground thaws in the summer.

Glaciers cover parts of Baffin and Ellesmere islands, which also have rugged mountains and deep *fiords* (long, narrow bays). Ellesmere Island has a high mountain range called the United States Range. The range's highest peak, Mount Barbeau, rises 8,584 feet (2,616 meters) above sea level.

Nunavut is home to a variety of wildlife, including caribou, musk oxen, polar bears, wolves, Arctic foxes, and Arctic hares. Caribou traditionally have been important to the Inuit, providing them with food and clothing. Narwhals and other whales swim in the icy waters of the Arctic Ocean, along with seals and walruses. Ravens,

Facts in brief

Capital: Iqaluit.

Government: *Parliament*—members of the Senate, 1; members of the House of Commons, 1. *Territorial*—members of the territorial Legislative Assembly, 19.

Area: 808,185 mi² (2,093,190 km²).

Elevation: *Highest*—Mount Barbeau in the United States Range, 8,584 ft (2,615 m) above sea level; *Lowest*—sea level along the coast.

Population: *2006 census*—29,474; density, 4 persons per 100 mi² (1 per 100 km²).

Chief products: *Fishing and hunting*—char, caribou, turbot. *Manufacturing*—fine arts and crafts.

Nunavut

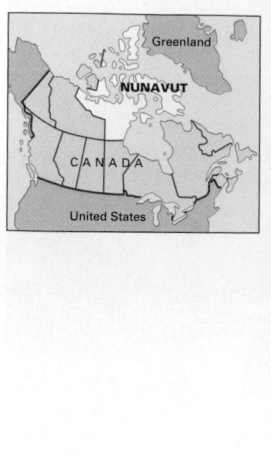

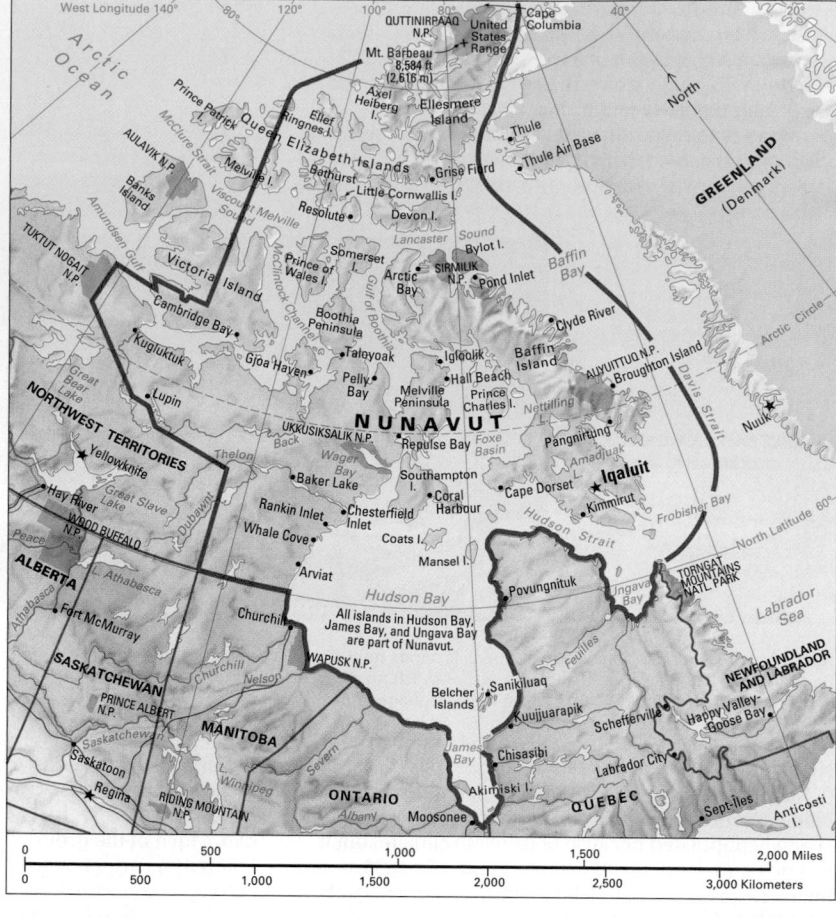

National park (N.P.)

Glacier or ice field

Boundary

Road

Railroad

★ Capital

• Other city or town

+ Elevation above sea level

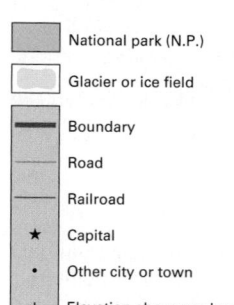

WORLD BOOK maps

gyrfalcons, and ptarmigan live in Nunavut the year around. Many other birds, such as eider ducks and snowy owls, migrate to the region in the spring. Snow geese nest on Baffin Island. *Polynas* (areas of open water surrounded by ice) provide for diverse and rich ecosystems in such areas as Lancaster Sound.

Nunavut is rich in mineral resources. It has large deposits of copper, diamonds, gold, iron, lead, nickel, silver, uranium, and zinc. However, many of these resources have not been developed because of the region's harsh climate and the difficulty of transportation there. As part of a global effort to develop Arctic resources, several companies are exploring for oil and natural gas in the region.

Climate. Nunavut has long, cold winters and short, cool summers. Average winter temperatures range from about –20 °F (–29 °C) in southern Baffin Island to below –35 °F (–37 °C) on Ellesmere Island. Summer temperatures range from above 50 °F (10 °C) in southern Nunavut to about 36 °F (2 °C) in the north.

Nunavut has a dry climate. Nearly all the territory receives less than 12 inches (300 millimeters) of precipitation a year. Northern Nunavut gets so little precipitation that it is often considered a polar desert.

Economy

Nunavut does not have a fully developed economy.

The harsh climate and terrain hinder access to areas rich in natural resources. The Inuit are making the transition from *subsistence hunting* (hunting for their own use) and dependence on the government to a wage-earning economy. Training skilled workers and providing secure jobs are a high priority of the government.

The Nunavut government is the largest employer in the territory. Mining is also important to Nunavut's economy. In 2010, the province began mining gold. The territory has a small, but growing, fishing industry. Char, shrimp, and turbot are the main fishing catches. Hunting and trapping also provide income for some Nunavut residents.

The spectacular scenery of the region and its rich array of wildlife attract tourists to Nunavut. Inuit organizations and communities offer tourist services. Visitors engage in such activities as exploring, fishing, hiking, hunting, and kayaking. Hearty travelers visit Nunavut's four national parks—Auyuittuq, Quttinirpaaq, Sirmilik, and Ukkusiksalik.

Arts and crafts have provided income for some Inuit since emerging as an economic sector in the 1950's and 1960's. Galleries worldwide sell Inuit soapstone carvings. Prints from Cape Dorset and Pangnirtung are famous. Inuit weavers produce tapestries at weaving centers in Pangnirtung.

Nunavut has few roads and no railroads. Airplanes are

the primary means of transportation between Nunavut's communities. Ships and barges deliver supplies to the communities annually. Many people use snowmobiles. However, traditional dog sled teams still are in common use. Modern telecommunications have helped to overcome problems created by the great distances between communities in Nunavut. All communities have radio and television, transmitted by a satellite relay system. All communities also have telephone service.

Education

All Nunavut communities offer schooling through grade 12. Many schools teach classes in Inuktitut in the lower grades and then switch to English instruction in the higher grades. Although Nunavut's literacy rate is lower than the national rate, an increasing number of students are attending and completing high school.

Nunavut Arctic College provides adult basic education, college and technical courses, and some university programs through partnerships with other institutions. In addition to its three campuses at Cambridge Bay, Iqaluit, and Rankin Inlet, the college has Community Learning Centres in many Nunavut communities.

The territorial government is working to improve education by reducing class sizes, training and hiring more Inuit teachers, and developing a curriculum focused more on Inuit culture, history, and language. The survival of Inuktitut is a major concern of Nunavut's government, which also wants the territory's youth to be able to work in Canada's largely English-language economy.

Government

Nunavut is one of Canada's three territories. The other two are the Northwest Territories and Yukon. The people of Nunavut elect one representative to the Canadian House of Commons. Nunavut also has one representative in the Canadian Senate. Canadian territories have fewer powers than the provinces and require substantial subsidies from the federal government.

A premier heads Nunavut's government with the assistance of an Executive Council. The Executive Council handles the administration of the government and its relations with the provinces and the federal government.

Fishing is an important source of food for some people of Nunavut. Most residents also hunt and fish for pleasure. These Inuit are fishing in the waters off the southern tip of Baffin Island.

© John de Visser, Masterfile

Symbols of Nunavut

The territorial flag

| The territorial coat of arms | Territorial bird Rock ptarmigan | The floral emblem Purple saxifrage |

The territorial flag and the coat of arms bear representations of an *inuksuk*—that is, a traditional Inuit stone monument—and the North Star. On the coat of arms, the Inuit stone lamp next to the inuksuk symbolizes the warmth of family and community. An igloo and crown appear at the top, and a caribou and narwhal support the shield. The motto, in Inuktitut, means *Nunavut Our Strength*. The rock ptarmigan is well adapted to Nunavut's harsh climate, and the hardy purple saxifrage can flourish in rocky ground.

Nunavut's Legislative Assembly makes Nunavut's laws and elects the premier and Executive Council from its membership. Voters elect Assembly members for terms of up to five years. Nunavut has no political parties. Members of the Assembly are elected as independents. This type of government is called *consensus government.* It is more in keeping with aboriginal tradition than party politics are. The territorial government is decentralized, with operations spread across dozens of communities. *Hamlet councils* carry out local government. However, many *hamlets* (small communities) lack the resources to attend to local issues.

History

Early history. Ancestors of the Inuit have inhabited the Arctic for thousands of years. The pre-Dorset culture, the first Canadian Arctic culture, spread eastward from Alaska some 4,000 years ago. About 3,000 years ago, a new culture called the Dorset spread rapidly across the Arctic. The Dorset people adapted well to life in the harsh Arctic climate. They made snow knives from bones and may have been the first people to use the snowhouses called *igloos.* Stone lamps fueled by animal fat heated their houses.

About 1,000 years ago, another new culture called the

Thule *(THOO lee)* culture spread across the region, and the Dorset culture disappeared. The Thule people lived in villages. Their houses had stone floors and walls made from whale ribs or boulders covered with turf. Whaling was the cornerstone of their culture. After whaling declined, these people hunted caribou and seals. The importance of villages then declined, and smaller groups lived in seasonal camps of snowhouses and tents. By about 1700, the Thule culture had become the modern Inuit culture.

Arrival of the Europeans. The Vikings were probably the first Europeans to visit Nunavut. They may have sighted the shores of Nunavut and Greenland about A.D. 1000. About the 1500's, the riches of China encouraged many explorers to look for a Northwest Passage, a sea route through North America to Asia. Martin Frobisher, an English seaman searching for the Northwest Passage, became the first known European to reach Nunavut. He arrived at Baffin Island in 1576. Frobisher claimed to have discovered gold, but further expeditions showed that he had found iron pyrite, a compound of iron and sulfur known as *fool's gold.*

In 1670, King Charles II of England granted part of what later became Nunavut to the Hudson's Bay Company, a British fur-trading company. The company paid little attention to the area. In 1870, the Dominion of Canada acquired Rupert's Land and the North-Western Territory, the company's massive landholdings that included most of what are now northern and western Canada. The Canadian government created Manitoba, Canada's fifth province, from a small part of the land and organized the remainder as the North-West Territories (later renamed the Northwest Territories).

The Canadian government made part of the North-West Territories into the territory of Yukon in 1898 and cut off additional land to form the provinces of Alberta and Saskatchewan in 1905. In 1912, Manitoba, Ontario, and Quebec acquired certain areas that had belonged to the Territories. The federal government in Ottawa governed the remaining territorial lands, called the Northwest Territories, until 1967.

Development of the modern Canadian North. The Inuit of the Northwest Territories adapted readily to new economic activity in their region. They participated actively in the whaling industry that operated around Baffin Island and in Hudson Bay in the 1800's and early 1900's. They adopted new technologies and proved themselves talented commercial hunters and traders.

Canada's government played a minimal role in the region until after World War II (1939-1945). It relied on widely scattered Royal Canadian Mounted Police (RCMP) posts, occasional RCMP patrols, and annual visits by supply ships to attend to local concerns.

Conditions changed rapidly during and after World War II. During the war, the United States built several military bases in the Canadian North, including a major airfield at Frobisher Bay (now Iqaluit). Security concerns during the Cold War resulted in the development in the 1950's of the Distant Early Warning (DEW) line, a series of radar stations across the Arctic. The Cold War was an intense rivalry that developed after World War II between Communist and non-Communist nations.

From the late 1940's to the 1960's, the Canadian government sent many Inuit suffering from tuberculosis to hospitals farther south, and many of them died there. The collapse of caribou harvesting and the fur trade economy caused widespread hardship in the mid-1900's. As a result, Canada's government relocated many Inuit to different parts of the Arctic from the mid-1950's through the early 1960's. The coming of government housing, modern medical care, *residential schools,* and welfare payments also brought sweeping change to the Inuit in the mid-1900's. Residential schools were boarding schools aimed at integrating indigenous children into mainstream society. Many Inuit who had lived off the land had to adjust to a more settled existence in government-built communities.

Establishment of Nunavut. For many years, the Inuit of the eastern Northwest Territories had called for their own political unit. They argued that their culture was distinct from other cultures of the Northwest Territories. They also said that Yellowknife, the capital, was too far away. Yellowknife is near Great Slave Lake, some 1,500 miles (2,400 kilometers) west of Frobisher Bay. Negotiations in the 1970's and 1980's between indigenous organizations and the Canadian government focused on Inuit demands for land, resources, revenues, and self-government. In 1982, the people of the Northwest Territories voted to divide the Territories between east and west.

In 1992, the people of the Northwest Territories approved a boundary to divide the Territories. The new eastern territory would be called Nunavut. In 1993, the Canadian Parliament passed the Nunavut Act, which approved the division of the Northwest Territories and the creation of Nunavut. In 1993, Parliament also passed the Nunavut Land Claims Agreement Act, which gave the Inuit exclusive ownership of nearly one-fifth of Nunavut's land area, about 135,000 square miles (350,000 square kilometers). Nunavut came into being on April 1, 1999. During its first decade, the government struggled with high expectations, great economic and social challenges, and the difficulties of addressing Inuit needs.

Global climate change focused attention on Nunavut in the early 2000's. Issues included defining the extent of the Arctic continental shelf, the prospects of gas and oil development in the Arctic, control over the Northwest Passage, and the environmental impact of warmer temperatures on Arctic communities.   Ken S. Coates

Related articles in *World Book* include:

Arctic Ocean	Ellesmere Island
Baffin Island	Inuit
Boothia Peninsula	Iqaluit
Canada (Arctic life; The Arctic Islands)	Melville Island
	Southampton Island

Nuremberg, *NOO ruhm BEHRG* (pop. 493,397), is an industrial city in southern Germany. For location, see **Germany** (political map). The city's name is sometimes spelled Nuremburg. Its German name is Nürnberg. The Pegnitz River divides the central part of Nuremberg in half. A wall completed in the 1400's encircles the city's center. Allied bombing attacks during World War II (1939-1945) destroyed or damaged many of Nuremberg's historic buildings. The city's remaining landmarks include the medieval churches of St. Lawrence and St. Sebaldus, and the restored house of the famous artist Albrecht Dürer. Nuremberg's many industries include the production of automobiles, beer, bicycles, electrical equipment, office machinery, and toys.

Nuremberg's founding date is unknown, but the city dates from at least the 1000's. During the late Middle Ages, Nuremberg became a prosperous trade and cultural city. Nuremberg was a center of Nazi activities in the 1930's. In 1935, the Nazi-controlled German national assembly approved the anti-Jewish Nuremberg Laws, which were drafted in the city. The laws deprived Jews of citizenship and forbade "Aryan" Germans to marry Jews. Nuremberg was the site of Allied trials of Nazi war criminals (see **Nuremberg Trials**). Melvin Croan

See also **Clock** (picture); **Germany** (pictures).

Nuremberg Trials, *NOO ruhm BEHRG,* were legal proceedings against Nazi Germany's former leaders for crimes committed before and during World War II (1939-1945). The trials took place from 1945 to 1949 in Nuremberg, Germany, where Adolf Hitler's Nazi Party had once held its political rallies. The trials were the first successful war crimes trials conducted against senior national officials. The four countries that had defeated and then occupied Germany—France, the Soviet Union, the United Kingdom, and the United States—organized the first trial.

The trials. The defendants were charged with four kinds of crimes—conspiracy, crimes against peace, war crimes, and crimes against humanity. Conspiracy is the act of planning crimes in advance. This legal concept allowed the prosecutors to try the Nazi government's prewar acts. Crimes against peace included launching a war in violation of international agreements. War crimes covered the mistreatment of prisoners of war, the plunder of occupied areas, and crimes on the *high seas* (areas of the oceans that lie outside the authority of any nation). Crimes against humanity involved the persecution and murder of people based on their political beliefs, race, or religion. A charter signed by the Allies before the trials established, for the first time, an international legal definition of crimes against humanity. This definition included acts committed before or during the war.

The first trial ran from November 1945 to October 1946. The International Military Tribunal, made up of British, French, Soviet, and U.S. judges and prosecutors, conducted the trial. The tribunal tried 22 high-ranking German leaders, including top Nazis Hermann Göring and Rudolf Hess; military leaders, such as Wilhelm Keitel and Karl Dönitz; foreign minister Joachim von Ribbentrop; minister of armaments Albert Speer; and Ernst Kaltenbrunner, second in command of the elite Nazi Party guard known as the SS (Schutzstaffel). Twelve defendants received death sentences, seven received prison sentences, and three were found not guilty.

Individual countries conducted later trials of Nazi officials. At Nuremberg, U.S. military tribunals held 12 trials from 1946 to 1949. Each trial examined a different set of crimes. For example, one trial focused on Nazi doctors who conducted experiments on concentration camp prisoners. Another involved the leaders of SS forces that had committed mass killings of Jews. Of the 185 defendants involved in the U.S. trials, 24 received death sentences, 107 received prison sentences, 35 were found not guilty, and 19 were released on other grounds.

Reaction. The Nuremberg Trials triggered some criticism. The sentences were harsh, and no procedure existed for appealing the judgments. In addition, the Soviets, who participated in the International Military Tribunal, had engaged in war crimes themselves. Such charges as crimes against peace and humanity were new. As a result, some critics argued that the German defendants had violated moral rules but had not committed legal violations. Despite these criticisms, the Nuremberg Trials had far-reaching effects. They carefully documented Nazi actions, from launching World War II to murdering millions of European Jews. They also set the legal example, later adopted by the United Nations, that leaders can stand trial for crimes committed against their own citizens. Norman J. W. Goda

See also **Holocaust; International law; War crime** (World War II); **World War II** (picture: The Nuremberg Trials).

Nureyev, *nu RAY yuhf,* **Rudolf** (1938-1993), was one of the great ballet dancers of the 1900's. He became known for his exciting stage personality and his strong, expressive dance technique. Nureyev danced more than 100 roles. In 1962, he began a partnership with the famous English ballerina Dame Margot Fonteyn. Nureyev and Fonteyn performed together in such ballets as *Giselle, Swan Lake,* and *Les Sylphides.* As a *choreographer* (creator of dances), Nureyev created versions of such ballets as *Don Quixote* and *The Nutcracker.*

Nureyev was born on March 17, 1938, near Irkutsk, in Russia. He joined the Kirov Ballet in 1958 and soon became its principal dancer. In 1961, Nureyev defected to the West while the Kirov Ballet was performing in Paris. He then danced with ballet and modern dance companies throughout the Western world and appeared in several dance films. He was director of the Paris Opera Ballet from 1983 until 1989. Nureyev died on Jan. 6, 1993. Katy Matheson

See also **Ballet** (Ballet in Russia); **Fonteyn, Margot** (picture).

Nurmi, *NUR mee,* **Paavo,** *PAH vaw* (1897-1973), a Finnish athlete, is considered the greatest distance runner in track and field history. His achievements from 1920 to 1932 made him a national hero of Finland. During that period, Nurmi set many world records in distances from 1,500 meters to 20,000 meters. He also won nine gold

© Martha Swope

Rudolf Nureyev became one of the most famous ballet dancers of the 1900's. He won praise for his exciting stage personality and powerful leaps in such ballets as *Swan Lake, shown here.*

medals in the Olympic Games of 1920, 1924, and 1928. At the 1924 Games, he won five gold medals, a record in track and field. Over his career, he won 12 Olympic medals in seven events, including gold medals in six events. Both achievements also represent Olympic records in track and field.

Paavo Johannes Nurmi was born on June 13, 1897, in Turku, Finland. He was the first distance runner to scientifically plan his races. For example, he used a stop watch to help run at a desired pace. His Olympic career was cut short just before the 1932 games. The International Amateur Athletic Federation (now the International Association of Athletics Federations) declared that he had accepted too much money for expenses during a European tour, making him a professional athlete and therefore ineligible for the Olympics. Nurmi died on Oct. 2, 1973.   Michael Takaha

Nurse. See Nursing.

Nurse shark is a bottom-dwelling shark that lives in shallow coastal waters. The nurse shark is tan to dark brown. It hunts at night for food on the sea floor.

The nurse shark has a broad head with a small mouth. It has *barbels* (fleshy whiskerlike growths) around the mouth. The shark uses these barbels to detect prey by touch in the dark. The shark's long tail fin makes up about a quarter of its overall length. The nurse shark typically reaches about 8 ½ feet (2.6 meters) long. It usually weighs about 250 pounds (110 kilograms).

The nurse shark lives in warm waters along the Atlantic and Pacific coasts of North and South America. It also is found around islands in the Caribbean Sea. The shark also lives along the Atlantic coast of Africa and a small part of Europe. It usually swims near coral reefs.

The nurse shark feeds on fish. In addition, it eats crabs, shrimp, and other *crustaceans* (animals with a shell and jointed legs). It also eats squid, octopuses, and other *mollusks* (boneless animals that often have an outer shell). The shark's mouth can produce powerful suction. It typically sucks in prey from holes in the reef.

Females give birth to live young that they carry for about six months. They give birth to about 30 pups over several weeks. Nurse sharks may live for more than 25 years in captivity.

Nurse sharks bite people only rarely, usually when ha-

rassed. The shark may hold onto a person so strongly that it cannot be removed without using tools. If given a clear path of escape, however, the shark will usually release its bite and swim away. People sometimes call the sand tiger shark the *gray nurse shark.* But it is not closely related to the true nurse shark.   Nicholas M. Whitney

Scientific classification. The scientific name of the nurse shark is *Ginglymostoma cirratum.*

See also **Shark** (picture: Some kinds of sharks).

Nursery produces and raises plants for transplanting into fields, gardens, orchards, and landscaped areas. Nurseries raise trees, shrubs, ground covers, and other plants, including flowers and vegetables. Some nurseries specialize in tropical plants. Most nurseries operate as businesses. Certain governmental agencies maintain nurseries to help reforest public and private lands.

Nurseries produce plants from seeds or cuttings or by *grafting,* attaching buds or stems from mature plants to the root systems of other plants. Nurseries also grow certain plants from bulbs or other plant parts. Workers care for the plants by fertilizing and irrigating the soil, and by protecting them from disease, insects, and weeds. Nurseries grow and sell many plants in containers. They sell some larger field-grown plants *balled and burlapped*—that is, with their roots and soil wrapped in burlap—or *bare-root,* with the roots packed in moist material to prevent drying.

Three kinds of commercial nurseries exist. *Wholesale nurseries* sell to other nurseries and handle large quantities of a small variety of plants. *Retail nurseries* sell directly to the public and handle relatively small quantities of many kinds of plants. Most retail nurseries operate in cities or along busy highways. Some provide planting and maintenance services and offer planting designs for home gardens and yards. *Mail-order nurseries* distribute catalogs and maintain Internet sites describing the plants they sell. Many grow only a small portion of their plants and buy the rest from wholesale nurseries.

Various nursery associations worldwide enable nurseries to exchange ideas on nursery practices and business management. The major United States association is the American Nursery and Landscape Association, headquartered in Washington, D.C.   Douglass F. Jacobs

Nursery rhyme is a rhythmical poem that amuses or soothes young children. Many nursery rhymes also pass along cultural information and values. These poems are a vital form of folk literature. They appeal to children because of their pleasing rhymes and sounds and compelling rhythms. Youngsters often keep time with the musical rhythm of the words by clapping their hands or rocking back and forth. Nursery rhymes help children appreciate the many sounds and rhythms of a language.

The great variety of stories and characters in the verses stimulates the imagination. Children delight in the humor and surprises in such rhymes as "Mary Had a Little Lamb" and "Hey Diddle Diddle." Other rhymes, including "Three Little Kittens" and "Old Mother Hubbard," introduce children to their first stories. A child's familiarity with nursery rhymes can lead to a lasting appreciation of poetry and prose.

Types

The most popular types of nursery rhymes include (1) lullabies, (2) singing game rhymes, (3) nonsense rhymes,

© Robert Paul van Beets, Shutterstock

Workers at a nursery in the Netherlands tend tulip plants being grown for sale.

(4) rhyming riddles, (5) counting-out rhymes, (6) tongue twisters, (7) verse stories, and (8) cumulative rhymes.

Lullabies are simple, soothing melodies sung to children to help them fall asleep. "Rock-a-bye Baby" is probably the best-known lullaby in the English language.

> Rock-a-bye, baby, on the tree top,
> When the wind blows the cradle will rock;
> When the bough breaks the cradle will fall,
> Down will come baby, cradle, and all.

Singing game rhymes accompany dances or certain games. For example, "Ring-a-Ring O'Roses" is sung by a group of children who join hands and dance in a circle.

> Ring-a-ring o'roses,
> A pocket full of posies,
> A-tishoo! A-tishoo!
> We all fall down.

Nonsense rhymes provide a verbal release from the "sensible" requirements of everyday life. This one has the humor and wit typical of such verses.

> I eat my peas with honey,
> I've done it all my life.
> It makes the peas taste funny,
> But it keeps them on the knife.

Rhyming riddles ask children to unravel a mystery or identify a certain object from clues in the verse.

> Runs all day and never walks,

Illustration (1916) by Blanche Fisher Wright from *The Real Mother Goose;* © 1916, 1944 Rand McNally

Nursery rhymes are short poems for children. This picture illustrates the nursery rhyme "Peter, Peter, Pumpkin-Eater," which tells about a man who keeps his wife in a pumpkin shell.

> Often murmurs, never talks;
> It has a bed and never sleeps;
> It has a mouth and never eats.

The answer is a *river*.

Counting-out rhymes provide formulas that help children choose sides for games. The verse "One, Two, Three, Four, Five" is an example.

> One, two, three, four, five!
> I caught a hare alive;
> Six, seven, eight, nine, ten!
> I let her go again.

Such rhymes may also help children learn the days of the week, the months of the year, and how to count.

Tongue twisters are difficult to say without making a mistake. The playful challenge of these rhymes comes from reciting them accurately as fast as possible, as in the famous tongue twister "Peter Piper."

> Peter Piper picked a peck of pickled peppers;
> A peck of pickled peppers Peter Piper picked;
> If Peter Piper picked a peck of pickled peppers,
> Where's the peck of pickled peppers Peter Piper picked?

Verse stories are short dramatic tales that often are longer than other types of nursery rhymes. "The Queen of Hearts" is a popular verse story.

> The Queen of Hearts,
> She made some tarts,
> All on a summer's day;
> The Knave of Hearts,
> He stole those tarts,
> And took them clean away.
> The King of Hearts
> Called for the tarts,
> And beat the knave full sore;
> The Knave of Hearts
> Brought back the tarts,
> And vowed he'd steal no more.

Cumulative rhymes, in each successive verse, repeat the information presented in the earlier verses. Thus, each verse is longer than the previous one. Here is the first verse of "The House That Jack Built."

> This is the house that Jack built.

The second verse has two lines.

> This is the malt
> That lay in the house that Jack built.

The third verse adds another line to the story.

> This is the rat
> That ate the malt
> That lay in the house that Jack built.

This cumulative rhyme then continues for many more verses.

History

For centuries, nursery rhymes have been passed orally from generation to generation. Every culture has its own nursery rhymes, plus additional ones that have been adopted from other societies. The verses have a wide variety of origins. Some nursery rhymes are fragments of ballads, prayers, proverbs, or tavern songs. Others came from ancient customs or rituals. Still others, such as "Old King Cole" and "Hey Diddle Diddle," may have been based on real people and events. Many nursery rhymes developed a number of versions as they passed orally from generation to generation.

Most nursery rhymes probably originated after 1600, but some rhymes may have been created earlier, such as "Little Tom Tucker." One of the earliest English collections of nursery rhymes, *Mother Goose's Melody,* was brought out in 1781 by an English publisher. This collection was reprinted in 1786 by an American publisher, Isaiah Thomas.

Many nursery rhymes that date from before 1800 were intended to entertain adults, not children. Rhymes written especially for youngsters included alphabet rhymes, lullabies, and verses that were used in games.

The term *nursery rhyme* first appeared in print in 1824 in *Blackwoods's Edinburgh Magazine,* a Scottish periodical. Before then, the rhymes were known as songs or ditties. James Halliwell, a British author, compiled the first large-scale collections of nursery rhymes. The collections were called *The Nursery Rhymes of England* (1842) and *Popular Rhymes and Nursery Tales* (1849). These books served as the basis of nursery rhyme collections in English until the publication in 1951 of *The Oxford Dictionary of Nursery Rhymes.* This work was edited by Iona and Peter Opie, a husband-and-wife team of British scholars.   John Cech

See also **Folklore; Literature for children** (Poetry; Books to read [Poetry]); **Mother Goose; Newbery, John.**

Nursery school. See Preschool.

Nurse's aide is a person who works in health care under the supervision of a registered nurse. A nurse's aide also may be called a *certified nursing assistant* or a *patient care assistant.*

Nurse's aides help by answering patients' calls; feeding, washing, and walking patients; and recording vital signs and other indications of a patient's care. If patients have to go to some other part of the hospital, nurse's aides may go along. They may help support patients during treatment or help move them onto or off beds and stretchers.

Nurse's aides give important social and emotional support to patients, as the registered nurses may not have enough time to spend with the patients. In larger hospitals, nurse's aides may act as diet assistants or as clerks.

The Red Cross and other schools train nurse's aides. Most certified nursing assistant training programs can be completed in 6 to 12 weeks. Most require only a high school diploma. Many young people work as nurse's aides in a hospital for a while to find out whether or not they want to become nurses.

Rossana Segovia-Bain

See also **Nursing.**

Nursing is a profession that provides care to the sick, the injured, and other people in need of medical assistance. Nurses perform a wide variety of duties in many settings. Many nurses work in hospitals, outpatient clinics, or other health care facilities. Other nurses work in health insurance companies, research institutions, and *pharmaceutical* (medicinal drug) companies. Nurses also work in schools, in factories, and in the armed forces. Nurses may run general health screening or immunization clinics and blood drives.

Patients often get most of their direct health care through nurses. Among their duties, nurses record patient medical histories and symptoms, help perform medical tests, administer treatment and medications, operate medical machinery, and help with follow-up care and rehabilitation. They also provide advice and emotional support to patients and their families.

Nurses educate patients about various medical conditions. They teach patients and their families how to manage illnesses or injuries. They explain home care needs, including diet, nutrition, and exercise programs; physical therapy; and how to take medication. Some nurses work to promote public knowledge about health and health care. They may give public lectures on health and medical topics.

More women serve in the field of nursing than in any other profession except teaching. However, this trend is changing. Until the 1960's, men made up only 1 percent of professional nurses. By the early 2000's, men made up more than 10 percent of students enrolled in undergraduate professional nursing programs. Men make up about 6 percent of professional nurses.

Nursing careers

Nurses participate in every kind of health care, so there are a wide variety of career paths within nursing. In the United States, Canada, Australia, and many other countries, most nurses are *registered nurses* (RN's). These nurses have graduated from an approved nursing education program. In the United States and some provinces of Canada, they have also passed a national licensing exam. Nurses with similar qualifications are called *level one nurses* in the United Kingdom.

Hospital nurses. Most registered nurses work in hospitals. RN's manage the daily care of patients, supervising nurse's aides or nursing assistants. RN's administer prescribed medicines to patients. They teach patients medication use and safety. A registered nurse also educates patients about their illness and any necessary medical procedures.

The well-being of patients is of first importance to nurses. RN's are taught to recognize and understand patients' needs. They provide emotional support as well as physical care, taking time to reassure worried patients and boost their morale.

Each type of patient has special needs, requiring nurses with specialized knowledge or training. As a result, hospital nurses typically choose an area of specialization, just as most doctors develop a specialty. Nursing specializations range from basic primary care to fields requiring highly developed technical skills. Such specializations include surgical nursing, *cardiovascular nursing* (care of the heart and blood vessels), *oncology nursing* (cancer care), *renal nursing* (kidney care), *orthopedic nursing* (bone and muscle care), and *neurological nursing* (care of the nervous system). Nurses also specialize in *radiology* (the use of X rays to diagnose diseases and injuries) and *anesthesiology* (the administration of drugs for the relief of pain). Many of these technical specialties require additional certification by professional boards or associations.

RN's in many other institutions perform in much the same way as hospital nurses. Such institutions include nursing homes and mental hospitals.

They can conduct physical examinations and diagnose and treat illness and injury. Nurse practitioners also advise and educate patients on health problems.

The role of nurse practitioner has grown to include working together with physicians. Depending on their specialties, nurse practitioners may work in hospitals. Many nurse practitioners operate private offices in partnership with a physician or independently.

Community health nursing. Community health nurses usually help take care of large groups of people in their homes and communities. Those who wish to enter this field must take college courses approved for community health work.

Visiting nurses are community health or public health nurses who go into homes to care for patients. They may visit patients who have just returned from hospitals. They often teach patients with chronic illnesses, such as cancer and diabetes, how to care for themselves. Visiting nurses also educate patients and their families about proper diet, cleanliness, and other ways of preventing illness.

Community health nurses may take part in many community projects, such as immunization programs. Some of them work in schools and summer camps. Some community health nurses work for the city or state. Others work for private hospitals that provide home health services to their patients.

Occupational and industrial health nursing. Nurses work in factories, stores, banks, and many business offices. These nurses give first aid to the injured. They give employees physical examinations and screen employees for illnesses. They treat workers for colds, bruises, and other minor ailments. They also promote programs to prevent accidents on the job.

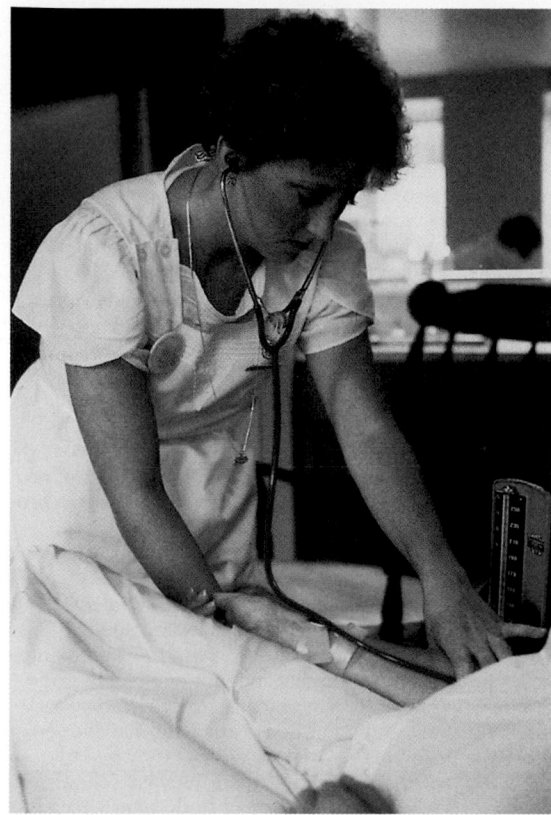

WORLD BOOK photo by Dan Miller

Most nurses work in hospitals, where they help comfort and care for people who are sick, injured, or recovering from surgery. This nurse is taking a patient's blood pressure.

Licensed practical nurses (LPN's) work under the direct supervision of RN's and doctors. In Texas and California, they are also called licensed vocational nurses (LVN's). They may work in hospitals, private homes, nursing homes, public health agencies, and doctors' offices. LPN's perform many patient care tasks. These include measuring a patient's temperature, blood pressure, pulse, weight, and other vital signs. LPN's often care for mothers and babies, the aged, and people with *chronic* (long-lasting) illnesses. Frequently, they are responsible for such tasks as making beds, giving baths, and feeding those who cannot feed themselves. However, LPN's cannot perform certain tasks that an RN can, such as administering prescription drugs or *intravenous* fluids, which are given into a vein.

Nurse managers supervise the nurses in a unit or section of a hospital. The position of nurse manager usually requires an advanced degree in business or adminstration in addition to the requirements of nursing. In Australia and the United Kingdom, nurse managers are sometimes called *nursing sisters.*

Nurse practitioners are nurses who have earned a master's degree and received special *advanced practice* education. Some nurse practitioners specialize in *geriatrics* (caring for the aged). Others specialize in *pediatrics* (caring for children). Nurse practitioners perform many functions that were once done only by physicians.

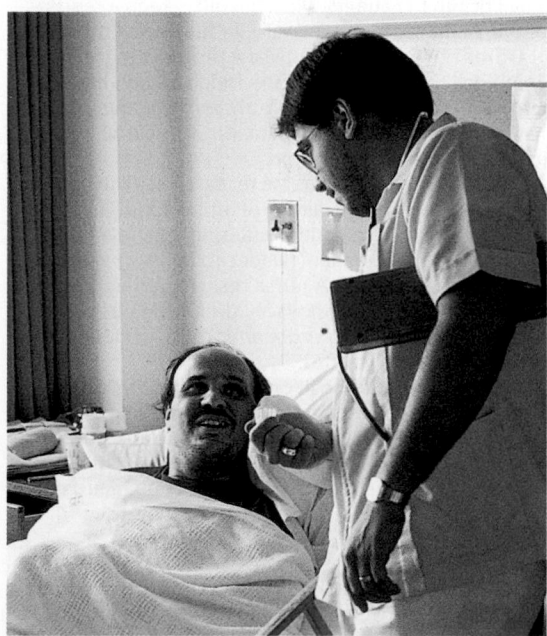

WORLD BOOK photo by Dan Miller

A male nurse gives medication to a patient. Although most nurses are women, more and more men are enrolling in nursing education programs or pursuing careers in practical nursing.

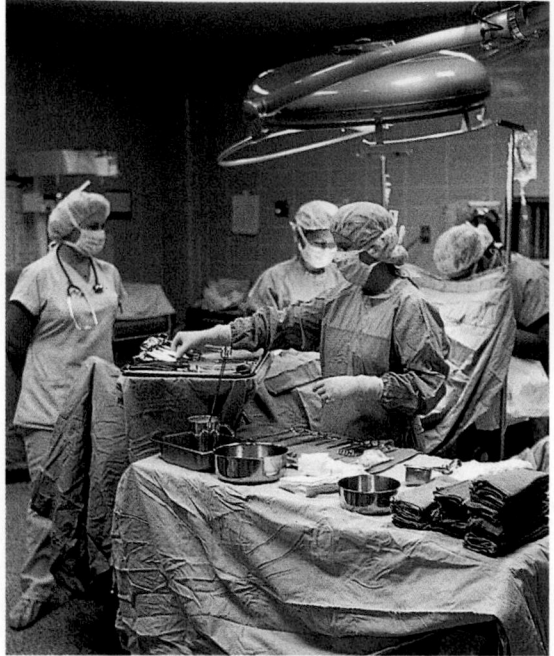

WORLD BOOK photo by Dan Miller

Operating room nurses assist surgeons during operations. These nurses must react instantly and accurately to the surgeons' requests for operating instruments.

Private duty nurses, unlike other nurses, are employed by the patient rather than by the hospital. Private duty nurses may devote all their time to only one patient who needs constant care. Sometimes, they care for a small group of patients. Most hospitals keep a registry, or file, of nurses who are available for private duty.

Other nursing careers. Many professional nurses combine the professions of teaching and nursing. To teach in a school of nursing, a professional nurse must have advanced college preparation. A doctoral degree in nursing is usually required.

Many nurses work as nurse researchers. They can conduct research on a variety of topics. Examples include how to relieve patient suffering and how to decrease vomiting in patients undergoing *chemotherapy* (treatment with drugs). A nurse researcher might also study injuries in the workplace, identifying possible causes and developing *ergonomic* tools, designed to reduce or eliminate injuries.

Some nurses hold positions in nursing organizations. Others write books and articles about nursing. Companies that manufacture drugs and medical equipment often employ nurses as consultants on their products. Nurses serve in the armed forces. Other branches of the government also have nurses on their staffs.

Planning a nursing career

Nursing offers satisfaction to those who desire to help others. It also provides a wide range of job opportunities. A capable nurse—especially one with an advanced degree—can generally feel sure of a job. Salaries for nurses are often high compared with those for other professions.

People considering a career in nursing should consider a number of additional factors. Hospital nurses must be active and remain on their feet a great deal. They may have to do strenuous work, such as lifting patients. Special body mechanics courses taught in nursing schools help the nurse prepare for such activities.

A nurse must like people and want to help them. A nurse must also have self-reliance and good judgment. Patience, tact, honesty, responsibility, and the ability to work easily with others are valuable traits. Good health is another requirement.

Most nursing schools accept only candidates who rank in the upper half or upper third of their high school graduating class. Entrance requirements for licensed practical nursing are less strict. High school graduates are preferred. However. many LPN training programs accept candidates who have passed high school equivalency exams if they have not completed high school.

Professional nursing education. Three types of programs provide the necessary training for a career in professional nursing. They are (1) associate degree programs, (2) diploma programs, and (3) baccalaureate programs.

Associate degree programs consist of a two-year course of study in nursing care and related subjects. These programs lead to an associate degree in nursing. Many junior and community colleges offer such programs. Students also gain practical experience by working in hospitals and other health agencies that cooperate in the programs.

Diploma programs are offered by hospital schools. They require two or three years of study, after which the student receives a diploma. Students take nursing courses in classrooms and laboratories. They work with patients in the hospital and at health agencies.

Baccalaureate programs offered by colleges and universities lead to a bachelor of science degree. The course work requires four to five years. It includes experience with patients in hospitals and health agencies as well as courses in nursing and in the humanities.

All nursing education programs provide both classroom training and practical experience. They prepare the student for obtaining a license to practice as a registered nurse.

Classroom work. Nursing students study such subjects as anatomy, chemistry, nutrition, *pharmacology* (the study of the effects of drugs on living things), *physiology* (the study of body functions), psychology, and *sociology* (the study of human society). They also learn the fundamentals of nursing care. They learn to care for the sick by working in the nursing laboratory. Frequently, the students practice on one another. For example, one student may take another's temperature, blood pressure, and pulse rate.

Clinical experience. All schools of nursing integrate classroom work or theory with practice. Clinical experience, or practice, means the time that the student spends in learning to care for patients. As part of their clinical experience, students also learn about hospital routine and the functions of various departments.

Nursing students have experience with all types of patients. A teacher who is an expert nurse supervises all their early activities. As students gain experience and knowledge, they work more independently.

Licensing. The requirements for a license to practice nursing vary from country to country. In most countries, including Australia and the United Kingdom, a nurse must have graduated from a university's nursing program or from an approved school of nursing. In some countries, including the United States, India, South Africa, and some Canadian provinces, nurses must also pass a written examination after graduation. The nurse then receives a license to practice in the state or province. She or he is now a registered nurse.

Nurses may advance their careers by additional study and experience. A master's degree is often the step to specialization, teaching, or administration. To advance further, a nurse may earn a doctoral degree as preparation for teaching and conducting research.

Practical nursing courses usually last one year. Like professional nursing education, practical nursing courses combine classroom study with actual experience.

There are two types of schools of practical nursing, public and private. Some public schools teach practical nursing as part of their vocational-training or adult-education programs. Hospitals, health agencies, and some junior colleges and universities operate private schools of practical nursing.

Credits for courses taken at vocational nursing schools often cannot be directly transferred to professional nursing schools. However, some nursing school programs allow vocational nurses to obtain a degree without repeating basic courses.

In all the states, and in some Canadian provinces, a practical nurse, like a professional nurse, must obtain a license to practice. He or she then becomes a licensed practical nurse or licensed vocational nurse. Nurses with similar qualifications are called *enrolled nurses* in Australia and New Zealand and *level two nurses* in the United Kingdom.

Career information. A high school student who wants to learn about a nursing career should talk with a vocational guidance counselor, school nurse, or other nurses. Many high schools have "future nurses" clubs whose members visit hospitals and schools of nursing and do volunteer work. Serving as a nurse's aide or as an orderly in a hospital is another way to learn more about nursing (see **Nurse's aide**).

History

Some form of nursing care has probably been practiced for thousands of years. For example, the early Israelites and Egyptians hired women, later called *midwives,* who assisted at births.

Modern nursing traces its roots to early Christian times. It was then that nurses first organized into groups. Noblewomen, including the wives of the emperors, helped care for the ill in ancient Rome. During the Crusades, a series of religious wars waged by Christians against Muslims from 1096 to the 1500's, military nursing orders of monks and knights tended the sick and wounded.

Many monasteries closed during the Reformation, a religious movement of the 1500's that led to Protestantism. There were only a few places where religious orders could nurse the sick. The years from 1600 to 1850 were the darkest period in the history of nursing. Hospitals often were built as charity hospitals. They were usu-

ally staffed by untrained, sometimes disreputable, women. Wealthy people never went to hospitals. The importance of sanitation and hygiene was unknown. People did not understand how diseases spread. Nurses who took care of patients with contagious diseases often contracted these diseases themselves.

Nursing as we know it began in the 1850's with the work of the English nurse Florence Nightingale. Nightingale was the founder of modern professional nursing. She established the first school of nursing, the Nightingale Training School for Nurses, in London in 1860. Graduates of this school traveled to all parts of the world to teach nursing.

The first nursing schools in the United States were established in 1873 at Massachusetts General Hospital in Boston, Bellevue Hospital in New York City, and the New Haven (Connecticut) Hospital. The American Nurses Association, Inc., an organization of registered nurses, was organized in 1896.

Many nurses have won world fame. They include Clara Barton, Edith Cavell, Elizabeth Kenny, and Lillian D. Wald. Rossana Segovia-Bain

Related articles in *World Book* include:
Barton, Clara
Cavell, Edith L.
Hospital
Kenny, Elizabeth
Medicine (with pictures)
Midwife
Nightingale, Florence
Nurse's aide
Nutting, Mary Adelaide
Physical therapy
Red Cross
Wald, Lillian D.

Nursing home is a residential institution that provides medical or nonmedical care, chiefly for people who are 65 years old or older. Nearly all homes also accept younger patients. In the United Kingdom, some private maternity hospitals are called nursing homes. The best nursing homes strive to provide a comfortable, homelike environment for their residents.

Most nursing homes are privately owned. Others are operated by federal, state, provincial, or local governments. Some private nursing homes are run by corporations, which try to earn a profit for the owners. Others are sponsored by religious or civic groups, which do not have a primary goal of making money.

Most countries have laws governing the operation of nursing homes and require the institutions to have a license. Inspectors visit the homes periodically to make sure they follow these laws.

Types of nursing homes

There are three types of nursing homes: (1) skilled nursing care homes, (2) intermediate care facilities, and (3) supervised assisted living facilities. They differ according to the types of patients they care for and the kinds of services they offer.

Skilled nursing care homes provide more extensive services than the other types of nursing homes. For example, they offer diagnostic, laboratory, and medication services; therapy programs; and dental care. Registered nurses supervise the care of patients according to the instructions of the institution's medical director. Physi-

At a nursing home, registered nurses supervise the care of patients according to the instructions of the institution's medical director.

© Andrew Gentry, Shutterstock

cians visit these homes frequently. Most skilled nursing care homes are run by licensed administrators.

Most of the patients in skilled nursing care homes require medical attention around the clock. Some have serious illnesses or disabilities. Others stay in these institutions after being hospitalized. They receive additional treatment before returning home.

Most skilled nursing care homes have transfer agreements with hospitals, intermediate care facilities, and other health-care institutions. Patients who become so ill that they need more medical care than a nursing home can provide are taken to a hospital. Those whose health improves, but who still require some nursing care, are transferred to an intermediate care facility or other health-care institution.

Intermediate care facilities, also called basic nursing care homes, provide basic nursing services. Registered nurses examine the residents periodically to determine what treatment is needed. Most patients in intermediate care facilities suffer from a long-term illness, such as Alzheimer's disease or Parkinson disease. However, they require only minor medical care. Doctors visit these nursing homes regularly.

Registered nurses direct the nursing programs in intermediate care facilities, but an administrator runs these institutions.

Supervised assisted living facilities provide nonmedical services. These services include preparing and serving the residents' meals and helping the men and women care for themselves. For example, members of the staff assist residents who have difficulty dressing themselves. The institutions also plan outings and other social activities for the residents.

Most residents of assisted living facilities need only routine medical examinations, and physicians visit these homes only when necessary. A supervisor of residential care directs the services provided.

Selecting a nursing home

Quality of care. In selecting a nursing home, it is important to match both the medical and psychological needs of a person with the resources of the caregiving institution. For example, not all older adults require the same amount of medical care. A study of nursing homes revealed that a number of relatively healthy people lived in institutions that had extensive medical facilities. The study also found that many people who needed medical treatment lived in nursing homes that did not have adequate medical services.

Nursing homes also should provide for the psychological needs of their residents. Most people in nursing homes can still lead productive lives. However, some low-quality institutions have few or no activities for residents. The best nursing homes encourage residents to stay active and to participate in a variety of community service and social activities.

Emotional effects. Many families feel guilty about placing an elderly relative in a nursing home. In most cases, they agree to this action only as a last resort. They do so when the person's health problems grow too severe and the family's social and financial resources become too strained to keep the relative at home.

Many elderly people suffer stress when they must adjust to the unfamiliar environment of a nursing home. Some older people regard it as the final step before death. The strain of the move can result in depression, increased health problems, and, in certain cases, even death.

There are several ways to lessen the strain on older people, including involving them in the decision to move to a nursing home and in the choice of a facility. The institution should allow patients to keep personal belongings in their new room. In addition, it is important to choose a nursing home where the staff is well trained and concerned about the patients.

Nancy P. Kropf

See also **Day care; Foster care; Hospital; Old age.**

Nut, Egyptian goddess. See **Mythology** (Egyptian mythology).

Nut is the popular name for many kinds of edible, dry seeds or fruits that grow in a woody shell. The word *nut* can refer to both the shell and the nutmeat, or kernel, in-

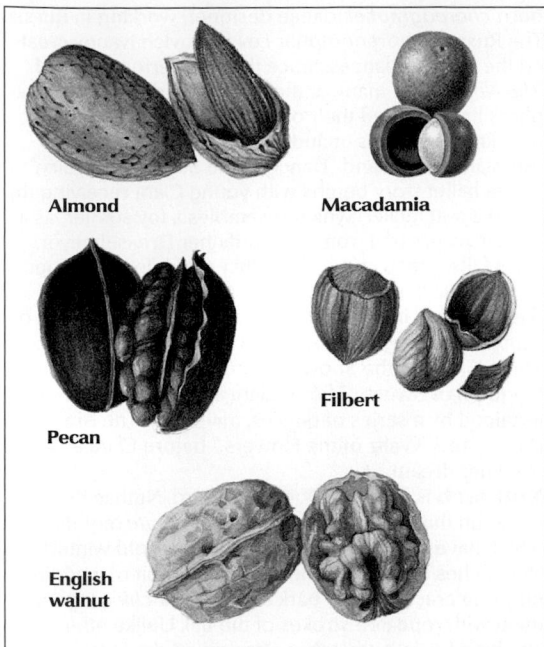

Almond

Macadamia

Pecan

Filbert

English
walnut

WORLD BOOK illustrations by Kate Lloyd-Jones, Linden Artists Ltd., and James Teason

Nuts grow nearly everywhere in the world. Some popular nuts produced in the United States are almonds, macadamia nuts, pecans, filberts or hazelnuts, and English walnuts.

side or to the kernel alone. Nut-bearing plants grow in almost every part of the world.

Botanists define a nut as a dry, one-seed fruit surrounded by a hard shell that does not open on its own. Some edible nuts, including chestnuts and filberts, fit this definition of a true nut. But people also eat other kinds of "nuts," including almonds, coconuts, and peanuts, that are not true nuts. In fact, peanuts are related to peas.

Uses of nuts. People commonly eat nuts as snacks or use them as flavoring in cooking. For example, food processors use peanuts in peanut butter, candies, and cookies. Most nuts provide large amounts of protein and fat, though chestnuts and a few others have more starch than protein. In Italy, bakers sometimes produce bread from flour made with chestnuts.

Prehistoric human beings probably ate nuts as a regular part of their diet, and many people today still rely on nuts for this purpose. Some scientists believe that nuts will become more widely used as a source of protein in parts of the world that have food shortages.

In addition to their value as food, certain nuts provide useful oil. For example, peanut oil and walnut oil are used in cooking. Walnut oil is also used to clean and polish wooden furniture. Jojoba nuts furnish a valuable lubricant for precision instruments. Tung oil is used in paints and varnishes.

Kinds of nuts. Hundreds of shrub and tree species produce nuts. However, growers raise only about 25 kinds of nuts as crops. Peanuts rank among the most important and widespread nut crops. Leading peanut-growing countries include China, India, Nigeria, and the United States.

Growers in California, Iran, and the Mediterranean region produce much of the world's almonds. Pecans, a type of hickory nut, are raised in the United States, Australia, Mexico, South Africa, and the Middle East.

Leading walnut-producing countries include China, Iran, Turkey, and the United States. Filberts grow on large shrubs or small trees and rank as a major crop in Italy, Turkey, and the northwestern United States. Pistachios are grown in Iran, the United States, and the Mediterranean region. These nuts have a delicate flavor and a distinctive green color. Processors often use them in ice cream.

Various species of chestnuts are produced throughout the world. Many people roast sweet chestnuts and eat them whole, and others turn them into sauces. During the early 1900's, a disease called *chestnut blight* almost wiped out the American chestnut trees of the eastern part of North America. Though some of these diseased trees still sprout from old stumps, they do not produce seeds.

A number of important nuts grow in tropical regions, including macadamia nuts, Brazil nuts, cashews, and coconuts. Macadamia nuts come from macadamia trees, which are native to Australian rain forests. Australia and the United States rank as the leading producers of these nuts. Most U.S. macadamia nut production occurs in Hawaii. Brazil nuts are native to the Amazon rain forest in South America. Harvesting of these nuts ranks as a major economic activity in the Amazon region. Cashew nuts originally came from Brazil, and people now cultivate them in Brazil, India, Vietnam, and sub-Saharan Africa. Cashews have a sweet flavor and are rich in protein. Coconuts grow primarily in Southeast Asia and Brazil. They contain a crisp, sweet-tasting *meat* and a sugary liquid called coconut *milk.*

Nut growing. Most kinds of nut trees produce nuts only if they have been *cross-pollinated*—that is, pollinated by flowers from another tree of the same species. Nut growers raise new trees by grafting certain parts of one tree to the roots of another (see **Grafting**).

Nut trees—and nuts themselves—may be damaged by a number of pests and diseases. For example, mice, squirrels, weevils, and some species of birds eat nuts and feed on nut crops. Nut trees can be harmed by certain insects and diseases that attack the leaves, stems, or nuts. Nut growers commonly protect their crops from insects and diseases by spraying the trees with pesticides. They use firearms, mechanical barriers, poisons, repellents, traps, and various other means to control birds and rodents. Breeding programs also help growers develop disease-resistant varieties of trees.

William A. DiMichele

Related articles in *World Book* include:

Nutcracker is a small bird that feeds mainly on the seeds of pine cones. The *species* (kind) known as Clark's nutcracker lives in ever-green forests in the mountains of western North America. It is gray with black and white wing and tail feathers and is 12 inches (30 centimeters) long. The Eurasian nutcracker is found in similar regions in Europe and Asia. This bird is reddish-brown with white markings, and it has black wings. Nutcrackers have a strong, direct flight.

WORLD BOOK illustration by John Rignall, Linden Artists Ltd.

Clark's nutcracker

Clark's nutcracker feeds chiefly on the seeds of pine cones. It holds the cones in its sharp, heavy, curved claws while opening them with its bill. The Eurasian nutcracker feeds on the seeds of pine cones and hazelnuts. Nutcrackers also eat insects, berries, and the eggs of other birds. They often store seeds and nuts for winter. Clark's nutcracker hides its nest at the top of a tall pine. During winter, the female lays from three to five speckled, grayish-green eggs. Both parents care for the eggs and the young.   Sandra L. Vehrencamp

Scientific classification. Nutcrackers make up the genus *Nucifraga.* Clark's nutcracker is *Nucifraga columbiana.* The Eurasian nutcracker is *N. caryocatactes.*

Nutcracker, The, is a popular classical ballet that has become a tradition during the Christmas season. *The Nutcracker* is known for its spectacle and its familiar music. *The Nutcracker* suite (1892), which consists of the most familiar melodies from the ballet, ranks among the standard works for symphony orchestras.

The Russian composer Peter Ilich Tchaikovsky wrote the music for *The Nutcracker,* which received its first performance in St. Petersburg, Russia, in 1892. The ballet is based on a story called "Nutcracker and the Mouse King" (1816) by the German writer E. T. A. Hoffmann. The ballet story was prepared by Marius Petipa, a French-born *choreographer* (dance designer) working in Russia. The Russian choreographer Lev Ivanovich Ivanov created the original dances. Since the first performance of *The Nutcracker,* many of the world's leading choreographers have created their own versions of the ballet. Its best-known dances include "Waltz of the Flowers," "Russian Dance," and "Dance of the Sugar-Plum Fairy."

The ballet story begins with young Clara receiving the gift of a nutcracker, which resembles a toy soldier, as a Christmas present from her godfather Drosselmeyer. Clara falls asleep and dreams that she defends the nutcracker against the King of the Mice. The nutcracker then changes into a handsome prince. He takes Clara on a journey through a snowstorm, where they meet the Snow King and the Snow Queen, and finally enter the Kingdom of Sweets. There, Clara and the prince are entertained by a series of dances, including "The Arabian Dance" and "Waltz of the Flowers," before Clara awakes from her dream.

Nuthatch is a tree-climbing songbird. Nuthatches are common throughout the world's *temperate* regions, which have warm summers and cool or cold winters. Nuthatches get their name from their habit of wedging nuts into cracks in tree bark and then *hatching* (opening) them with repeated strokes of the bill. Unlike other climbing birds, nuthatches often creep down tree trunks headfirst.

The best-known North American species is the *white-breasted nuthatch.* This bird lives the year around in the United States and southern Canada and can be found in woodlands, orchards, and yards. It measures about 5 to 6 inches (13 to 15 centimeters) in length. The top of its head and upper neck are black, its back is dark gray, and its underparts are white.

White-breasted nuthatches eat nuts and grain, as well as insects and insect *larvae* (young) that they find underneath the bark of trees. In winter, these birds are easily attracted to feeding stations, where they eat sunflower seeds and *suet* (animal fat). The white-breasted nuthatch builds its nest in holes in trees or stumps. The female lays from 5 to 10 white eggs that are speckled with reddish-brown or lavender markings.

Other North American nuthatches are the *red-breasted nuthatch,* which lives in southern Canada and in the northern and western parts of the United States; the

© Lindsay Hebberd, Digital Railroad

The Nutcracker is one of the most popular classical ballets. The story follows the adventures of a girl named Clara, who receives a nutcracker, which resembles a toy soldier, from her godfather as a Christmas present. Clara dreams that the nutcracker turns into a handsome prince who takes her on a journey through a snowstorm. The wintry landscape, *shown here,* forms the setting of one of the ballet's dances, led by the Snow Queen, *foreground.*

Red-breasted nuthatch

Wayne Lankinen, DRK Photo

brown-headed nuthatch, found in the Southern States; and the *pygmy nuthatch,* found in western North America and in Mexico. These species are smaller than the white-breasted nuthatch. Martha Hatch Balph

Scientific classification. Nuthatches belong to the nuthatch family, Sittidae. The scientific name for the white-breasted nuthatch is *Sitta carolinensis.*

See also **Bird** (pictures: Birds of forests and woodlands; Birds' eggs).

Nutmeg is a tropical tree that is grown commercially for the spice it provides. The spice, also called *nutmeg,* comes from the inner part of the tree's brown seeds. The seeds develop in small fruits that look like golden-yellow pears when ripe. Nutmeg trees are native to the Molucca (Spice) Islands. They are now raised in Indonesia, the West Indies, Brazil, India, and Sri Lanka.

The nutmeg tree grows up to 70 feet (21 meters) tall and is an evergreen. It has gray-green leaves that are

WORLD BOOK illustration by Kate Lloyd-Jones, Linden Artists Ltd.
Nutmeg is a tropical tree that bears small fruits. The spices mace and nutmeg are obtained from the seeds of the fruits.

long and pointed with well-marked veins. The small, pale-yellow flowers droop in clusters and develop into fruit. As the fruit ripens, the fleshy part becomes rather hard. It finally splits open showing a bright-scarlet membrane that partly covers the kernel of the seed. The spice called *mace* comes from this membrane (see **Mace**). Nutmeg is made by grating or grinding the kernels. It has a sweet, spicy flavor.

Nutmeg trees do not bear fruit until they are about 9 years old. Each tree produces from 1,500 to 2,000 seeds yearly. The fleshy part of the fruit is sometimes preserved and eaten like candy. A clear oil called *oil of nutmeg* is made from the kernels. David S. Seigler

Scientific classification. Nutmeg trees belong to the nutmeg family, Myristicaceae. Their scientific name is *Myristica fragrans.*

Nutmeg State. See **Connecticut** (Colonial life).

Nutria, *NOO tree uh,* or *coypu, KOY poo,* is a large rodent that lives near water. Nutrias are native to South America. They were introduced into many parts of Europe and North America to be raised for their fur. However, most attempts to raise nutrias commercially have not been profitable.

Bruce Coleman, Bruce Coleman Ltd.
Nutrias are large aquatic rodents that originated in South America. The animals are valued for their brown, beaverlike fur.

The nutria has brown fur with a whitish-tipped muzzle. It has small ears; webbed hind feet; and a long, scantily haired tail. The tail makes up nearly half the total body length, which measures up to 40 inches (100 centimeters). Wild nutrias may weigh up to 20 pounds (9 kilograms).

Nutrias live along the banks of lakes, marshes, ponds, and rivers. They are excellent swimmers. They feed chiefly on water plants. Female nutrias give birth to an average of four or five young at a time.

Nutrias are serious pests in some regions of the southeastern United States. They dig holes in earthen dams and dikes and disrupt the balance of nature by destroying water plants. They also damage rice and sugar cane crops.

Nutrias are trapped in Louisiana. The fur is made into coats and gloves. The meat is used for pet food.
Hugh H. Genoways

Scientific classification. The nutria belongs to the family Myocastoridae. Its scientific name is *Myocastor coypus.*

© Lawrence Migdale

A balanced diet is the key to good nutrition. It supplies all the food substances the body needs. The family shown here enjoys a breakfast that includes fruit, cereal, bread, and milk. The daily diet should include several servings of these foods.

Nutrition

Nutrition is the science that deals with food and how the body uses it. People, like all living things, need food to live. Food supplies the energy for every action we perform, from reading to running. Food also provides substances that the body needs to build and repair its tissues and to regulate its organs and systems.

What we eat directly affects our health. A proper diet helps prevent certain illnesses and aids in recovery from others. An improper or inadequate diet increases the risk of various diseases. Eating a balanced diet is the best way to ensure that the body receives all the food substances it needs. Nutrition experts recommend that the daily diet include a certain number of servings from each of the five major food groups: (1) breads, cereals, rice, and pasta; (2) vegetables; (3) fruits; (4) milk, yogurt, and cheese; and (5) meat, poultry, fish, dried beans and peas, eggs, and nuts. Fats are also essential, but, like sweets, should be eaten in small quantities.

Workers in the field of nutrition oversee school food services, plan menus for hospitalized patients, and provide nutrition counseling for individuals. They administer international food programs and investigate the relationship between diet and health. They seek improved ways of processing, packaging, and distributing foods, and they create new foods.

How the body uses food

Food provides certain chemical substances needed

Johanna T. Dwyer, the contributor of this article, is Professor in the Friedman School of Nutrition Science and Policy and in the School of Medicine at Tufts University and Director of the Frances Stern Nutrition Center at Tufts Medical Center.

for good health. These substances, called *nutrients,* perform one or more of three functions: (1) they provide materials for building, repairing, or maintaining body tissues; (2) they help regulate body processes; and (3) they serve as fuel to provide energy. The body needs energy to maintain all its functions.

The body breaks food down into its nutrients through the process of digestion. Digestion begins in the mouth. As food is being chewed, saliva moistens the particles. The saliva begins to break down such starchy foods as bread and cereals. After the food is swallowed, it passes through the *esophagus,* a tube that leads into the stomach. In the stomach, digestive juices speed up the breakdown of such foods as meat, eggs, and milk.

The partly digested food, called *chyme* (pronounced *kym),* passes from the stomach into the small intestine. In the small intestine, other juices break down the food into molecules that pass through the walls of the intestine and into the blood.

Blood distributes nutrients throughout the body. In the body's cells and tissues, the nutrients are broken down to produce energy, or are used to rebuild tissues or to regulate chemical processes. Some nutrients are stored in the body, and others are used over and over again. But most of the nutrients undergo chemical changes as they are used. These chemical changes produce waste products, which go into the bloodstream.

Some of these wastes are carried to the kidneys, which filter them from the blood. The body expels these wastes in the urine. The liver also filters out some wastes and concentrates them into a liquid called *bile.* In addition to concentrating certain wastes, bile helps digest fats.

Bile is stored in the gallbladder until it is needed to aid in digestion. Then the gallbladder empties bile into the small intestine. Bile then passes into the large intestine, along with parts of the food not digested in the small intestine. The large intestine absorbs water and small amounts of minerals from this waste material. This material, along with bacteria present in the large intestine, becomes the final solid waste product, the *feces,* and it is eliminated from the body.

Kinds of nutrients

The foods we eat contain thousands of different chemicals. However, only a few dozen of these chemicals are absolutely essential to keep us healthy. These few dozen are the *nutrients*—the substances we must obtain from the foods we consume.

Nutritionists classify nutrients into six main groups: (1) water, (2) carbohydrates, (3) fats, (4) proteins, (5) minerals, and (6) vitamins. The first four groups are called *macronutrients,* from a Greek prefix meaning *large,* because the body needs them in large amounts. The last two groups, which are required in small quantities, are known as *micronutrients,* from a Greek prefix meaning *very small.*

Water is needed in great amounts because the body consists largely of water. Usually, between 50 and 75 percent of a person's body weight is made up of water.

The body requires large quantities of carbohydrates, fats, and proteins because these nutrients provide energy. Food energy is measured in units called *kilocalories.* A kilocalorie is equal to 1,000 *calories.* A calorie is the energy required to raise the temperature of one gram of water one Celsius degree. However, kilocalories are often referred to as simply "calories." The "calories" mentioned in this article are actually kilocalories.

Although minerals and vitamins are needed in only small amounts, they are as vital to health as any other nutrients. Minerals and vitamins are needed for growth and to maintain tissues and regulate body functions.

Water is, perhaps, the most critical nutrient. We can live without other nutrients for several weeks, but we can go without water for only about one week. The body needs water to carry out all of its life processes. Watery solutions help dissolve other nutrients and carry them to all the tissues. The chemical reactions that turn food into energy or tissue-building materials can take place only in a watery solution. The body also needs water to carry away waste products and to cool itself. Adults should consume about $2 \frac{1}{2}$ quarts (2.4 liters) of water a day in the form of beverages or water in food.

Carbohydrates include all sugars and starches. They serve as the main source of energy for living things. Each gram (0.035 ounce) of carbohydrate provides about 4 calories.

There are two kinds of carbohydrates—*simple* and *complex.* Simple carbohydrates, all of which are sugars, have a simple molecular structure. Complex carbohydrates, which include starches, have a larger and more complicated molecular structure that consists of many simple carbohydrates linked together.

Most foods contain carbohydrates. The main sugar in food is *sucrose,* ordinary white or brown sugar. Another important sugar, *lactose,* is found in milk. *Fructose,* an extremely sweet sugar, comes from most fruits and many vegetables. Foods containing starches include beans, breads, cereals, corn, *pasta* (macaroni, spaghetti, and similar foods made of flour), peas, and potatoes.

Fats are a highly concentrated source of energy. Each gram of fat provides about 9 calories.

All fats are composed of an alcohol called *glycerol* and substances called *fatty acids.* A fatty acid consists of a long chain of carbon atoms, to which hydrogen atoms are attached. There are three types of fatty acids: *saturated, monounsaturated,* and *polyunsaturated.* A saturated fatty acid contains as many hydrogen atoms as its carbon chain can hold. A monounsaturated fatty acid is lacking one pair of hydrogen atoms. In a polyunsaturated fatty acid, the carbon chain contains at least four fewer hydrogen atoms than it could hold. A process called *hydrogenation* can attach additional hydrogen atoms to the carbon chains of unsaturated fatty acids. Hydrogenation may produce *trans fats,* in which newly added hydrogen atoms are connected in a slightly different position than the one in which they attach naturally.

Most saturated fatty acids occur in foods derived from animals, such as butter, lard, dairy products, and fatty red meats. But some come from vegetable sources, such as coconut oil or palm oil.

Polyunsaturated fatty acids are found in the oils of such plants as corn and soybeans and in such fish as salmon and mackerel. Certain polyunsaturated fatty acids called *essential fatty acids* must be included in the diet because the body cannot manufacture them. These essential fatty acids serve as building blocks for the membranes that surround every cell in the body. Common sources of monounsaturated fatty acids include olives and peanuts.

Proteins provide energy—4 calories per gram, as carbohydrates do—but more importantly, proteins serve as one of the main building materials of the body. Muscle, skin, cartilage, and hair, for example, are made up largely of proteins. In addition, every cell contains proteins called *enzymes,* which speed up chemical reactions. Cells could not function without these enzymes. Proteins also serve as *hormones* (chemical messengers) and as *antibodies* (disease-fighting chemicals).

Proteins are large, complex molecules made up of smaller units called *amino acids.* The body must have a sufficient supply of 20 amino acids. It can manufacture enough of 11 of them. Nine others, called *essential amino acids,* either cannot be made by the body or cannot be manufactured in sufficient amounts. They must come from the diet.

The best sources of proteins are cheese, eggs, fish, lean meat, and milk. Proteins in these foods are called *complete proteins* because they contain adequate amounts of all the essential amino acids. Cereal grains, *legumes* (peanuts and other plants of the pea family), nuts, and vegetables also supply proteins. These proteins are called *incomplete proteins* because they lack adequate amounts of one or more essential amino acids. However, a combination of two incomplete proteins can provide a complete amino acid mixture. For example, beans and rice are both incomplete proteins, but together they provide the correct balance of amino acids.

Minerals are needed for the growth and maintenance of body structures. They are also needed to maintain the composition of digestive juices and the fluids that are found in and around cells. People need only small amounts of minerals each day.

Unlike vitamins, carbohydrates, fats, and proteins,

minerals are *inorganic compounds*—that is, they are not created by living things. Plants obtain minerals from the water or soil, and animals get minerals by eating plants or plant-eating animals. Unlike other nutrients, minerals are not broken down by the body.

Required minerals include calcium, chlorine, magnesium, phosphorus, potassium, sodium, and sulfur. Calcium, magnesium, and phosphorus are essential for healthy bones and teeth. Calcium is also necessary for blood clotting. Milk and milk products are the richest sources of calcium. Cereals and meats provide phosphorus. Whole-grain cereals, nuts, legumes, and green leafy vegetables are good sources of magnesium.

Still other minerals are needed only in extremely tiny amounts. These minerals, called *trace elements,* include chromium, copper, fluorine, iodine, iron, manganese, molybdenum, selenium, and zinc. Iron is an important part of hemoglobin, the oxygen-carrying molecule in red blood cells. Copper helps the body make use of iron to build hemoglobin. Manganese and zinc are required for the normal action of various enzymes. Green leafy vegetables, whole-grain breads and cereals, seafood, and liver are good sources of trace elements.

Vitamins are essential for good health because they regulate chemical reactions in which the body converts food into energy and tissues. There are 13 vitamins: vitamin A; the vitamin B complex, which is a group of 8 vitamins; and vitamins C, D, E, and K. Scientists divide vitamins into two general groups, *fat-soluble vitamins* and *water-soluble vitamins.* The fat-soluble vitamins—vitamins A, D, E, and K—dissolve in fats. The vitamins of the B complex and vitamin C dissolve in water. Small amounts of these compounds are needed daily.

Vitamin A is necessary for healthy skin and development of strong bones. Sources of this vitamin include liver, green and yellow vegetables, and milk.

Vitamin B_1, also called *thiamine,* is necessary for changing starches and sugars into energy. It is found in meat and whole-grain cereals.

Vitamin B_2, also known as *riboflavin,* is essential for complicated chemical reactions that take place during the body's use of food. Milk, cheese, fish, liver, and green vegetables supply vitamin B_2.

Vitamin B_6, also called *pyridoxine,* and two other B vitamins known as *pantothenic acid* and *biotin* all play a role in chemical reactions essential for growth. Liver, yeast, and many other foods contain these vitamins.

Vitamin B_{12} and folic acid, also called *folate,* are both needed for forming red blood cells and for a healthy nervous system. Vitamin B_{12} is found in animal products, especially liver. Folic acid is present in green leafy vegetables. Doctors recommend that all pregnant women consume small amounts of folic acid each day to reduce the risk of *spina bifida,* a serious birth defect.

Niacin is also part of the B complex. Cells need niacin to release energy from carbohydrates. Liver, yeast, lean meat, fish, nuts, and legumes contain niacin.

Vitamin C, also called *ascorbic acid,* is needed for the maintenance of ligaments, tendons, and other supportive tissue. It is found in fruits and in potatoes.

Vitamin D is necessary for the body's use of calcium. It is present in fish-liver oil and vitamin D-fortified milk. Vitamin D also forms when skin is exposed to sunlight.

Vitamin E, also known as *tocopherol,* helps maintain cell membranes. Vegetable oils and whole-grain cereals are especially rich in this vitamin. It is also found in small amounts in most meats, fruits, and vegetables.

Vitamin K is necessary for proper clotting of blood. Green leafy vegetables contain vitamin K. It is also manufactured by bacteria in the intestine.

Nutrition guidelines

Eat a balanced diet. Nutritionists have devised various systems to aid in planning a balanced diet. The Food Guide Pyramid was one such system, developed by the United States Department of Agriculture (USDA). The USDA introduced the pyramid in 1992 and revised it in 2005. The pyramid's shape and colors called attention to the recommended amounts of each of the major food groups that make up a healthy diet. The department replaced the pyramid in 2011 with the MyPlate symbol. This symbol is combined with guidelines to help encourage people to eat healthfully and make better food choices. The MyPlate guidelines encourage people to eat more fruits, vegetables, whole grains, and fat-free or low-fat milk and milk products. The guidelines emphasize that a healthful diet should be low in saturated fats, trans fats, cholesterol, salt, and added sugars. They also recommend moderate to vigorous physical activity for at least 30 minutes each day.

In the United States, the Food and Nutrition Board of the National Academy of Sciences issues Recommended Dietary Allowances (RDA's). RDA's are estimated amounts of various nutrients needed daily to avoid deficiency and maintain good nutrition in healthy people. The board issues a standard called *adequate intake* (AI) in cases where the board's experts feel there is insufficient evidence to establish an RDA. RDA's and AI's for particular nutrients may vary, depending on a person's sex or age. This article includes a table of certain RDA's.

RDA's and AI's are part of a larger category of standards called *dietary reference intakes* (DRI's). DRI's also include guidelines called *tolerable upper intake levels* (UL's). UL's define the maximum daily intake that is unlikely to harm health. DRI's are being developed jointly by the U.S. Food and Nutrition Board and Health Canada.

The Nutrition Labeling and Education Act of 1990 requires that all packaged and processed food sold in the United States carry labels with nutritional information. These labels help people compare the nutritional content of the foods they eat with their daily dietary needs. Nutrition labels list the amounts of fats, carbohydrates, cholesterol, and other nutrients in one serving of the food. The nutrients listed are those considered most important to health, as determined by the U.S. Food and Drug Administration (FDA). The label also provides a *Daily Value* percentage for each nutrient to show how it fits into a healthful diet. The percentages are based on guidelines called *Daily Reference Values* (DRV's), which the FDA established as the amounts of these nutrients that a healthy person should consume each day.

In addition, health claims, such as "reduces risk of heart disease," and descriptive terms, such as "fresh" and "low fat," can appear on food packages only in accordance with FDA regulations. A list of some of these descriptive terms and an illustration of a standard nutrition label accompany this article.

People vary in their needs for energy. A person who

MyPlate nutrition guidelines

The United States Department of Agriculture (USDA) designed an interactive food guidance system called MyPlate to help people develop individual programs of diet for better health. The colored portions of the plate and cup represent the five food groups in proportions that reflect a healthful diet. MyPlate is designed to remind people to eat wisely. It also provides tips to help consumers make better food choices.

U.S. Department of Agriculture

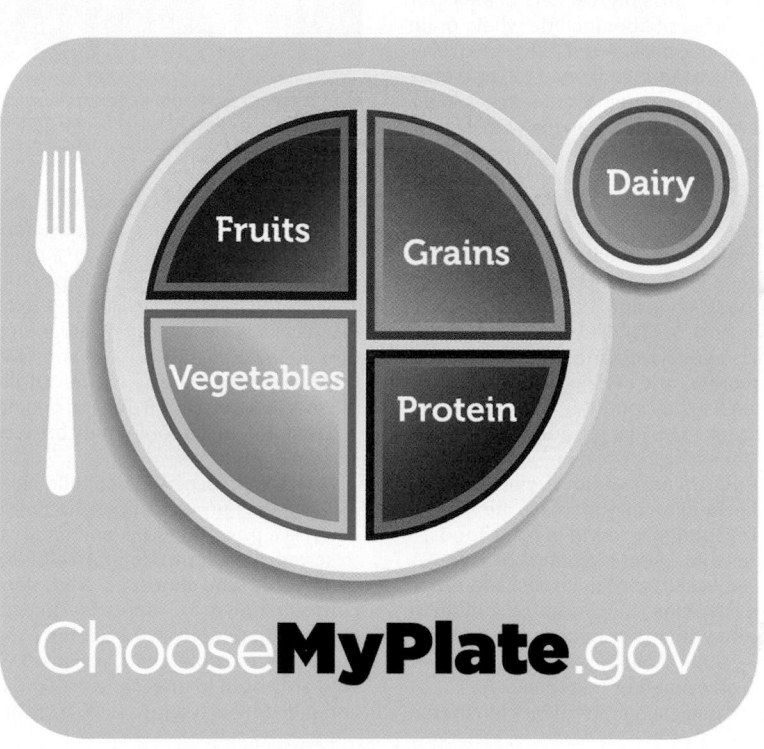

Some tips for a great plate of food

Balance calories

Find out how many calories you need for a day as a first step in managing your weight. Being physically active also helps you balance calories. Pay attention to hunger and fullness cues before, during, and after meals. Use them to recognize when to eat and when you have had enough.

Eat these foods more often

Eat more vegetables, fruits, whole grains, and fat-free or 1 percent milk and dairy products. These foods have the nutrients you need for health—including potassium, calcium, vitamin D, and fiber. Make these foods the basis for meals and snacks.

Make half your plate fruits and vegetables

Choose dark green, orange, and red vegetables, such as broccoli, sweet potatoes, and tomatoes, along with other vegetables for your meals. Add fruit to meals as part of main or side dishes or as dessert.

Make half your grains whole grains

To eat more whole grains, substitute a whole-grain product for a refined grain product. For example, eat whole-wheat bread instead of white bread or brown rice instead of white rice.

Eat these foods less often

Cut back on foods high in salt, solid fats, and added sugars. Such foods include cakes, candies, cookies, ice cream, pizza, sweetened drinks, and fatty meats, such as bacon, hot dogs, ribs, and sausages. Use these foods as occasional treats, rather than as everyday foods.

plays sports daily, for example, needs more calories than someone who does little physical work. Children need more calories than their size would indicate because they are growing. Pregnant women need extra calories to provide enough nutrients for a healthy baby.

Include fiber. Dietary fiber consists of complex carbohydrates that cannot be absorbed by the body. Fiber passes out of the body as waste. Fiber moves food along through the stomach and intestines, thus helping to prevent *constipation* (difficulty in emptying the bowels). Many experts believe that fiber also helps reduce the risk of such rectal and intestinal disorders as hemorrhoids, diverticulitis, and, possibly, cancers of the colon and rectum. Good sources of fiber include whole-grain breads and cereals, beans, peas, vegetables, and fruit.

Limit intake of saturated fats, trans fats, and cholesterol. Health experts recommend a diet that is low in saturated fats, trans fats, and *cholesterol,* a waxy substance found in many animal foods. Consumption of these substances raises the level of cholesterol in a person's blood, which increases the risk of heart disease. Animal products are the source of all dietary cholesterol and most saturated fats except coconut oil and other tropical oils. To reduce intake of saturated fats and cholesterol, experts suggest choosing lean meats, fish, poultry without skin, and low-fat dairy products. They also advise using fats and oils sparingly. Trans fats occur chiefly in solid margarines and certain processed foods. Nutrition labels often list the amount of trans fats. The words *partially hydrogenated* in a product's ingredients often indicate that trans fats are present.

Limit intake of sodium and sugar. A diet that includes a great deal of sodium may increase the risk of high blood pressure. Sodium is found in many foods, including canned vegetables, frozen dinners, pickles, processed cheese, table salt, and such snack foods as pretzels, chips, and nuts. One way to reduce sodium intake is to use herbs and other seasonings instead of salt in cooking and at the table. Another way is to select fresh foods rather than canned or frozen items.

Foods that contain much sugar are often high in calo-

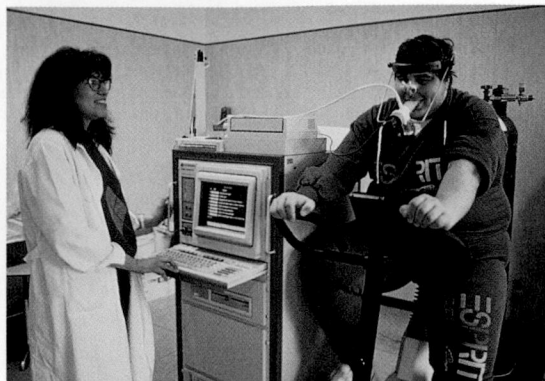

© R. Benzi, Custom Medical

Obesity may result from poor nutrition. Medical personnel should be consulted to develop and monitor a weight-loss program involving both diet and physical exercise.

ries and fat but low in minerals, proteins, and vitamins. Nutritionists sometimes call these foods "empty calorie" foods, because they may make a person feel full but provide few nutrients. In addition, sugar that remains in and around the teeth contributes to tooth decay. Foods that have a large amount of sugar include candies, pastries, many breakfast cereals, and sweetened canned fruits. In place of sugary foods, nutritionists advise people to snack on fresh fruits and vegetables. They also recommend that people drink unsweetened juices instead of soft drinks.

Beware of alcohol. Alcoholic beverages supply calories, but they provide almost no nutrients. In addition, alcohol is a powerful drug, and habitual drinking can lead to serious health problems. Health experts recommend that people who choose to drink alcoholic beverages consume only small amounts. They further recommend that certain people avoid alcohol altogether, including children and adolescents; pregnant women; people who are about to drive; anyone who is taking medicine; and individuals who are unable to limit their drinking.

Recommended daily dietary allowances of some chief nutrients

	Age	Calcium (mg)*	Iron (mg)	Vitamins								
				A (µg RE)	B₆ (mg)	B₁₂ (µg)	C (mg)	D (µg)*	E (mg TE)	Niacin (mg NE)	Riboflavin (mg)	Thiamine (mg)
Children	1-3	500	7	300	0.5	0.9	15	5	6	6	0.5	0.5
	4-8	800	10	400	0.6	1.2	25	5	7	8	0.6	0.6
	9-10	1,300	8	600	1.0	1.8	45	5	11	12	0.9	0.9
Males	11-13	1,300	8	600	1.0	1.8	45	5	11	12	0.9	0.9
	14-18	1,500	11	900	1.3	2.4	75	5	15	16	1.3	1.2
	19-30	1,000	8	900	1.3	2.4	90	5	15	16	1.3	1.2
	31-50	1,000	8	900	1.3	2.4	90	5	15	16	1.3	1.2
	51+	1,200	8	900	1.7	2.4	90	10-15	15	16	1.3	1.2
Females	11-13	1,300	8	600	1.0	1.8	45	5	11	12	0.9	0.9
	14-18	1,300	15	700	1.2	2.4	65	5	15	14	1.0	1.0
	19-30	1,000	18	700	1.3	2.4	75	5	15	14	1.1	1.1
	31-50	1,000	18	700	1.3	2.4	75	5	15	14	1.1	1.1
	51+	1,200	8	700	1.5	2.4	75	10-15	15	14	1.1	1.1

g = grams; mg = milligrams; µg = micrograms; RE = retinol equivalents; NE = niacin equivalents; TE = tocopherol equivalents.
Above recommendations designed for the maintenance of good nutrition of practically all healthy people in the United States.
*Adequate Intake (AI). The AI is a value based on experimentally derived intake levels or approximations of observed mean nutrient intakes by a group or groups of healthy people. Because there is less information on which to base allowances, these figures are not classified as RDA's.
Source: The National Academy of Sciences. Courtesy of the National Academy Press, 2000, 2001.

Food labels All packaged and processed foods sold in the United States must carry a label with the title *Nutrition Facts*. An example of a standard food label is illustrated below. Foods in small packages or foods that contain limited nutrients may carry a simplified version of this label. Fresh fruits and vegetables, single-ingredient raw meats, and a few other foods are not required to carry labels.

Food and Drug Administration (World Book *chart)*

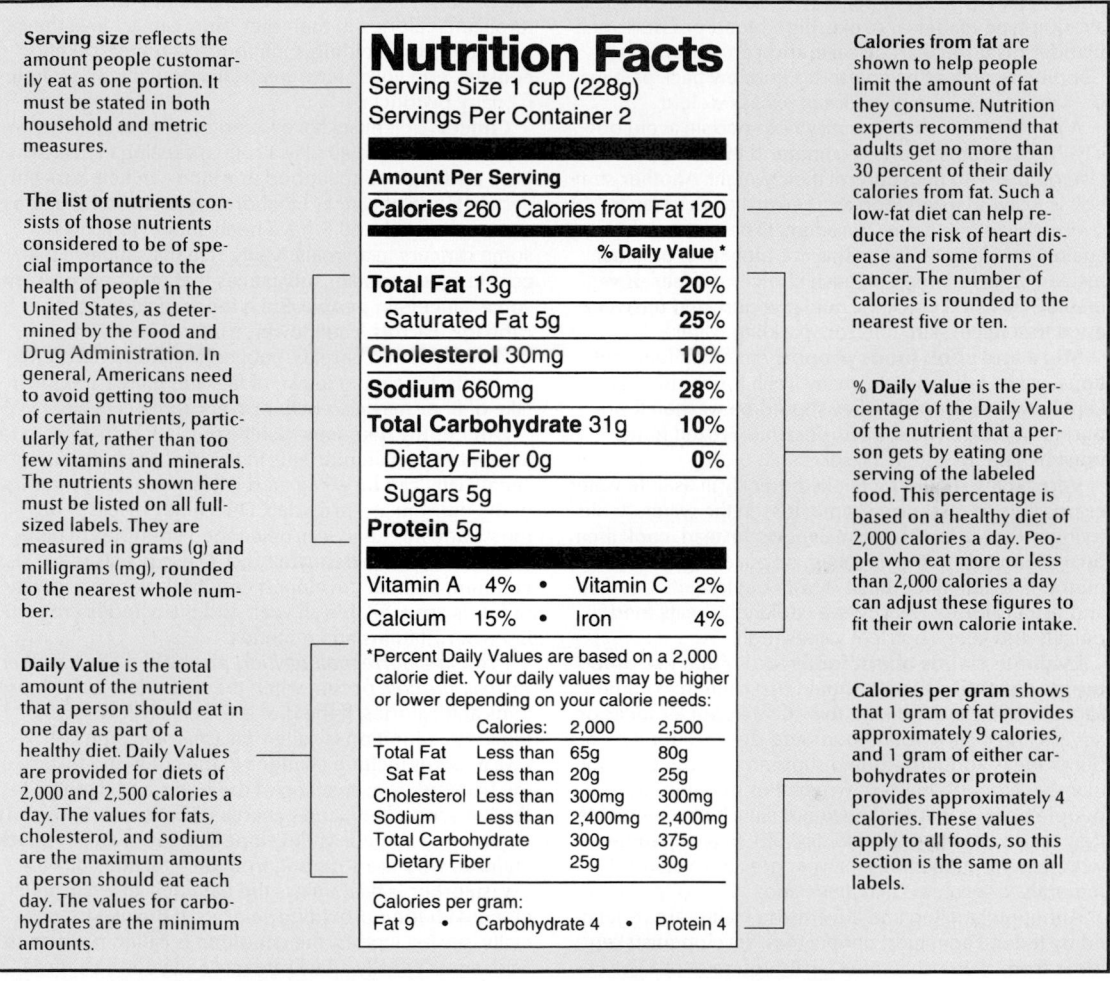

Serving size reflects the amount people customarily eat as one portion. It must be stated in both household and metric measures.

The list of nutrients consists of those nutrients considered to be of special importance to the health of people in the United States, as determined by the Food and Drug Administration. In general, Americans need to avoid getting too much of certain nutrients, particularly fat, rather than too few vitamins and minerals. The nutrients shown here must be listed on all full-sized labels. They are measured in grams (g) and milligrams (mg), rounded to the nearest whole number.

Daily Value is the total amount of the nutrient that a person should eat in one day as part of a healthy diet. Daily Values are provided for diets of 2,000 and 2,500 calories a day. The values for fats, cholesterol, and sodium are the maximum amounts a person should eat each day. The values for carbohydrates are the minimum amounts.

Calories from fat are shown to help people limit the amount of fat they consume. Nutrition experts recommend that adults get no more than 30 percent of their daily calories from fat. Such a low-fat diet can help reduce the risk of heart disease and some forms of cancer. The number of calories is rounded to the nearest five or ten.

% Daily Value is the percentage of the Daily Value of the nutrient that a person gets by eating one serving of the labeled food. This percentage is based on a healthy diet of 2,000 calories a day. People who eat more or less than 2,000 calories a day can adjust these figures to fit their own calorie intake.

Calories per gram shows that 1 gram of fat provides approximately 9 calories, and 1 gram of either carbohydrates or protein provides approximately 4 calories. These values apply to all foods, so this section is the same on all labels.

Nutrition Facts

Serving Size 1 cup (228g)
Servings Per Container 2

Amount Per Serving

Calories 260   Calories from Fat 120

	% Daily Value *
Total Fat 13g	**20%**
Saturated Fat 5g	**25%**
Cholesterol 30mg	**10%**
Sodium 660mg	**28%**
Total Carbohydrate 31g	**10%**
Dietary Fiber 0g	**0%**
Sugars 5g	
Protein 5g	

Vitamin A 4%	•	Vitamin C 2%
Calcium 15%	•	Iron 4%

*Percent Daily Values are based on a 2,000 calorie diet. Your daily values may be higher or lower depending on your calorie needs:

	Calories:	2,000	2,500
Total Fat	Less than	65g	80g
Sat Fat	Less than	20g	25g
Cholesterol	Less than	300mg	300mg
Sodium	Less than	2,400mg	2,400mg
Total Carbohydrate		300g	375g
Dietary Fiber		25g	30g

Calories per gram:
Fat 9   •   Carbohydrate 4   •   Protein 4

Some terms used in labeling food

Certain descriptive terms can appear on food packages only if the food meets requirements set by the Food and Drug Administration. A list of some of these terms follows.

Free means the food contains nutritionally insignificant amounts of the specified nutrient. For example, a can of chicken soup labeled "sodium-free" must contain no sodium or an insignificant amount of sodium.
Fresh, as in "fresh orange juice," means the food is raw, contains no preservatives, and has not been processed, heated, or frozen.
Healthy means the food is low in fat and saturated fat and contains no more than 480 milligrams of sodium and 60 milligrams of cholesterol per serving.
High, as in "high in fiber" or "high in protein," means the food provides 20 percent or more of the Daily Value of the specified nutrient per serving.
Lean applies to meats, poultry, and seafoods that contain fewer than 10 grams of fat, 4 grams of saturated fat, and 95 milligrams of cholesterol per serving.
Less means the food contains at least 25 percent less of the specified nutrient than does a similar, specified food. For example, a package of pretzels could be labeled "less fat than potato chips," provided that the pretzels have at least 25 percent less fat.
Light or **lite,** as in "lite sour cream," means the food has been altered during processing to contain one-third fewer calories or one-half less fat or sodium than the regular product.
Low, as in "low fat" or "low sodium," means the food can be eaten frequently without exceeding Daily Value guidelines for the specified nutrient.
More means the food contains at least 10 percent more of the Daily Value for the specified nutrient than does a similar, specified food. For example, grapefruit juice could be labeled "more vitamin C than orange juice," provided the grapefruit juice has at least 10 percent more vitamin C.
Source of or **Good source of,** as in "source of calcium" or "good source of fiber," means a serving has 10 to 19 percent of the Daily Value of a particular nutrient.

Do not overeat. When people consume more calories than they need, their bodies store most of the extra calories as fat. Accumulation of fat can result in *obesity,* a condition in which a person has too much body fat for good health. Obesity increases the risk of such diseases as adult-type diabetes, stroke, high blood pressure, gall bladder disease, heart disease, and certain cancers. Conditions such as osteoarthritis and low back pain may be worsened by the pressure of excess weight.

A number of techniques may help people avoid obesity. Most health experts recommend that people exercise regularly to help control their weight. Another strategy is to avoid using food as a reward or as a way to overcome loneliness or boredom. Experts also advise against snacking on foods that are high in fat or sugar. Instead, they recommend such choices as fruits or vegetables, unsalted crackers, nonfat yogurt, and unsweetened fruit juice, skim milk, or sparkling water.

Store and cook foods properly to retain their nutritional value. For example, many fresh foods should be kept in the refrigerator. They should be washed thoroughly and eaten as soon as possible. Frozen foods must be kept frozen in a freezer.

Vegetables should be cooked quickly in as little water as possible to minimize vitamin loss in the water. Avoid frying meats and other animal foods. Instead, cook them by broiling, stir-frying, braising, or poaching. These methods result in food that is tasty but free of added fat and extra calories. Microwave cooking reheats food quickly and keeps nutrient values high.

Evaluate claims about foods and dietary supplements carefully. People should use caution, common sense, and critical thinking to evaluate popular ideas or advertising claims about foods and dietary supplements. Some ideas about foods and supplements become popular even though they are wrong. For example, some people believe that they need not eat a balanced diet if they take a vitamin pill every day. But, in fact, people who rely on vitamin pills may not get all the calories, minerals, or proteins that they need.

Although labeling and advertising claims are regulated by federal agencies, people may develop mistaken ideas from claims that meet legal requirements. For example, some people think they can eat unlimited quantities of foods labeled "low fat." In fact, careful comparison of labels shows that many low-fat foods contain almost as many calories as do versions not labeled low-fat.

People should carefully consider the source of nutritional claims. Reliable sources of information include state, provincial, and national health and nutrition agencies; public departments of agriculture; and universities with expert knowledge in health and nutrition.

Nutrition and disease

An improper or inadequate diet can lead to a number of diseases. On the other hand, good nutritional habits can help prevent certain diseases.

Heart disease in its most common form is called *coronary artery disease* (CAD). CAD narrows coronary arteries and so reduces the blood supply to the heart. It can lead to crippling attacks of chest pain and, eventually, to life-threatening heart attacks. High blood pressure and high levels of blood cholesterol are two of the major risk factors for CAD. In many cases, people can low-

er these risk factors with good nutritional practices.

Many people can reduce mild high blood pressure by limiting their intake of salt and calories. Similarly, many people can lower their blood cholesterol level by reducing the amount of fat—particularly saturated fat—cholesterol, and calories in their diet. They can achieve these reductions by avoiding such foods as butter, cakes, cookies, egg yolks, fatty meats, tropical oils, and whole-fat dairy products.

Cancer. Scientists have found that heredity, environment, and lifestyle all play a role in causing cancer. They have also learned that good nutrition can help prevent certain kinds of cancer in laboratory animals. Large doses of vitamins A and C have been shown to prevent some cancers in animals. Many scientists believe that certain foods contain substances that may help prevent some cancers in people. Such foods include broccoli, cabbage, carrots, cauliflower, fruits, spinach, whole-grain breads and cereals, cooked tomatoes, and some seafoods. Lessening intake of fats and increasing the intake of fiber may also help prevent some cancers.

Deficiency diseases result from an insufficient amount of certain nutrients in the diet. Such diseases can usually can be eliminated when adequate amounts of the nutrient are provided. Deficiency diseases are most widespread in less developed countries, where people may lack adequate food. These diseases are less common in most developed countries, where a variety of foods are available all year, and many foods are fortified with vitamins and minerals.

Protein-calorie malnutrition, also called *protein-energy malnutrition,* occurs when the diet is low in both proteins and calories. If the diet is especially low in proteins, the condition is called *kwashiorkor.* Signs of kwashiorkor include changes in the color and texture of the hair and skin; swelling of the body; and damage to the intestines, liver, and pancreas. The disease, which is common in some less developed nations, usually attacks children who are suffering from an infectious disease. Kwashiorkor is fatal unless the patient is given protein along with food providing calories. If the diet is especially low in calories, the condition is called *marasmus.* Marasmus usually attacks infants and young children, and it causes extreme underweight and weakness.

Vitamin deficiencies. The signs and symptoms of

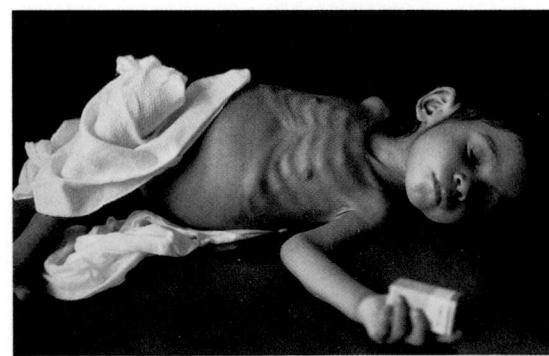

Fred Griffing, UNICEF

A diet especially low in proteins may cause *kwashiorkor,* a disease that generally strikes children. In severe cases, the muscles waste away and the skin swells with body fluids.

vitamin deficiencies vary according to the missing vitamin. Vitamin C deficiency, also called *scurvy,* causes sore and bleeding gums, slow repair of wounds, and painful joints. Vitamin D deficiency, also called *rickets,* causes abnormal development of bones. A deficiency of niacin and the amino acid tryptophan, found in protein, causes *pellagra.* The early symptoms of pellagra include weakness, lack of appetite, diarrhea, and indigestion.

Mineral deficiencies. The most common mineral deficiency disease is *iron-deficiency anemia.* In this disease, lack of iron prevents formation of enough oxygen-carrying red blood cells. As a result, the blood cannot supply the tissues with sufficient oxygen. Thus, the person feels weak or tired. Other symptoms include dizziness, headaches, rapid heartbeat, and shortness of breath. A lack of iodine can cause *goiter,* a disease in which the thyroid gland becomes enlarged.

Other diseases may result from poor nutritional habits. For example, excessive intake of alcohol causes some forms of liver disease. The risk of *osteoporosis* (loss of bone tissue) is higher for people—especially women— whose intake of calcium and level of physical activity are low. To prevent osteoporosis, physicians recommend a lifelong combination of regular exercise and a diet with adequate calcium.

Careers in nutrition

Nutrition offers a variety of careers in work settings that range from restaurants to research laboratories. Jobs in this field require at least a high school education. Some positions require a two-year associate's degree or a bachelor's degree. High school students interested in a career in the field of nutrition should take such science courses as biology and chemistry. College students preparing for a career in nutrition study physiology—the science that deals with how the body works—as well as biochemistry—the science of the chemical reactions that take place in living things. Other required courses include bacteriology and general chemistry. Students interested in careers in medical nutrition learn how diseases affect the body. Students pursuing careers in food service take such courses as food preparation, food purchasing, accounting, and personnel management.

Work as a *dietetic technician* requires an associate's degree. Dietetic technicians work as members of a food service staff or a health care team, under the supervision of a *registered dietitian.* These technicians supervise support staff, develop nutrition care plans, and provide nutrition counseling for individuals or small groups.

A bachelor's degree and a period of supervised practice are necessary to become a registered dietitian. Candidates must also pass a registration examination. Many registered dietitians manage food services in schools, nursing homes, and restaurants. Others work in hospitals or clinics, planning special diets for people who are ill. Some registered dietitians coordinate disease prevention programs for public health organizations or work with community food programs. Others work for corporations, helping to develop food products. A number of registered dietitians offer personal nutrition counseling directly to the public.

People with advanced degrees may teach; conduct research projects for government, business, industry, and health care institutions; or hold administrative positions

© Joseph Sterling, Tony Stone Worldwide from Click/Chicago

Food services in schools, nursing homes, and restaurants offer career opportunities in the field of nutrition. The nutritionist pictured here, *left,* directs the preparation of meals.

in international food or agricultural programs. These experts may investigate the effect of diet on health or develop improved methods for processing and packaging food. Some create new foods, such as artificial sweeteners or fat substitutes.   Johanna T. Dwyer

Related articles in *World Book* include:

Dietary diseases

Allergy	Goiter	Pellagra
Anemia	Kwashiorkor	Rickets
Beriberi	Malnutrition	Scurvy

Nutrients

Albumin	Gluten	Protein
Amino acid	Iron	Starch
Carbohydrate	Lipid	Sugar
Fat	Potassium	Vitamin

Other related articles

Antioxidant	Diet	Metabolism
Baby (Feeding procedures)	Digestive system	Rice (Food)
Biochemistry	Family and consumer sciences	Seafood
Calorie	Fat substitute	Starvation
Cancer (Nutrition)	Fiber, Dietary	Trace elements
Center for Science in the Public Interest	Food	Trans fats
Cholesterol	Food preservation	Vegetarianism
	Health food	Weight control
	Meat	Wheat (Food for people)

Outline

I. **How the body uses food**
II. **Kinds of nutrients**
    A. Water   D. Proteins
    B. Carbohydrates   E. Minerals
    C. Fats   F. Vitamins
III. **Nutrition guidelines**
    A. Eat a balanced diet
    B. Include fiber
    C. Limit intake of saturated fats, trans fats, and cholesterol
    D. Limit intake of sodium and sugar
    E. Beware of alcohol
    F. Do not overeat
    G. Store and cook foods properly
    H. Evaluate claims about foods and dietary supplements carefully
IV. **Nutrition and disease**
    A. Heart disease   C. Deficiency diseases
    B. Cancer   D. Other diseases
V. **Careers in nutrition**

Questions

Why is water an essential nutrient?
How do complete proteins differ from incomplete proteins?
   What are some foods that supply complete proteins?
What are some symptoms of iron-deficiency anemia?
Why must essential fatty acids be included in the diet?
What is *kwashiorkor? Marasmus?*
What are some dangers of obesity?
What are some ways to reduce sodium intake?
What three main functions do nutrients perform?
What are some roles of a registered dietitian?
Why is it important to include fiber in the diet?

Additional resources

Level I

Body Needs. 5 vols. Heinemann Lib., 2003. Each volume focuses on a basic nutrient, such as fats, proteins, and vitamins.
Gregson, Susan R. *Healthy Eating.* LifeMatters Bks., 2000.
Westcott, Patsy. *Diet and Nutrition.* Raintree Steck-Vaughn, 2000.

Level II

Bellenir, Karen, ed. *Diet Information for Teens.* Omnigraphics, 2001.
James, Delores C. S. *Nutrition and Well-Being A to Z.* Macmillan Reference, 2004.
Ronzio, Robert A. *The Encyclopedia of Nutrition and Good Health.* 2nd ed. Facts on File, 2003.

Nutting, Mary Adelaide (1858-1948), was a leader in the development of professional nursing in the United States. She helped establish professional standards in nursing education and the practice of nursing. She developed a model training program that supplemented practical experience in a hospital with practical instruction in nursing principles.

Nutting was born on Nov. 1, 1858, in Quebec, Canada. In 1889, she went to Baltimore to enter the first class of the Johns Hopkins Hospital Training School for Nurses. After graduating in 1891, she served as a head nurse at the school. In 1894, she became the school's principal. Nutting held this position until 1907. That year, she joined the faculty of Teachers College at Columbia University in New York City and became the world's first professor of nursing. Nutting headed the Department of Nursing and Health at the college from 1910 until she retired in 1925. She died on Oct. 3, 1948.

Kenneth R. Manning

Nuuk, *nook* (pop. 14,350), is the capital and largest town of Greenland. Called Godthåb in Danish, it lies on Davis Strait near the entrance of Nuuk Fiord (see **Greenland** [map]). With a harbor that remains free of ice all year, Nuuk serves as the island's leading seaport. The Greenland National Museum and the University of Greenland are in Nuuk.

In the 900's, Norse explorers settled the area near Nuuk, but they disappeared by 1350. A Norwegian missionary, Hans Egede, set up a mission on an island in the fiord in 1721. Godthåb was founded in 1728 when the mission moved onshore. The town became Greenland's administrative center during Danish colonial rule. In 1979, it took the Greenlandic name Nuuk.   Mark Nuttall

Nyasa, Lake. See Lake Nyasa.

Nye, Bill (1850-1896), was a popular American humorist. He became famous for his clever essays and *anecdotes* (brief stories) on a variety of subjects ranging from the American West to journalism. Nye was also a successful comic lecturer.

Nye was born on Aug. 25, 1850, in Shirley, Maine. His full name was Edgar Wilson Nye. In 1876, Nye moved to Wyoming. He first gained national fame as a columnist for the Laramie *Boomerang,* a newspaper he founded in 1881. In 1886, Nye moved to New York City and wrote humorous columns for *The* (New York) *World* newspaper. His books include *Bill Nye's History of the United States* (1894) and *Bill Nye's History of England* (1896). Both were widely popular for their satirical treatment of the past. Nye died on Feb. 22, 1896.   David B. Kesterson

Nyerere, *nih RAIR ee,* **Julius Kambarage,** *JOOL yuhs kahm BAH rah guh* (1922-1999), was president of Tanzania from 1964 until he retired in 1985. Tanzania consists of Tanganyika, a region on the African mainland; and Zanzibar, a nearby island group. Tanganyika and Zanzibar were formerly ruled by the United Kingdom. Nyerere led the movement that resulted in Tanganyika's independence from the United Kingdom in 1961. He became the president of Tanganyika in 1962. He also helped unite Tanganyika and Zanzibar to form Tanzania in 1964, and he became the new country's president. He was first elected president in 1965 and was reelected in 1970, 1975, and 1980. Nyerere retired as president in 1985 and as chairman of the only legal political party in 1990. But he remained a major influence in Tanzania until his death on Oct. 14, 1999.

As Tanzania's president, Nyerere became a leading spokesman for cooperation among black African nations, and he helped unite Tanzania's many ethnic groups. In 1979, Nyerere sent Tanzanian troops to Uganda, after Uganda had invaded Tanzania. The Tanzanian troops helped overthrow the dictatorship of Idi Amin Dada in Uganda.

Nyerere was born on April 13, 1922, near what is now Musoma, Tanzania. He was educated at various schools in what are now Tanzania and Uganda and at the University of Edinburgh in Scotland.   Robert I. Rotberg

See also **Tanzania** (History).

Nylon is the general term for a group of synthetic products. These products are made from chemicals derived from coal, water, air, petroleum, agricultural by-products, and natural gas. Nylon is one of the most important chemical discoveries. It is a tough elastic substance that can be formed into fibers, bristles, sheets, rods, and tubes. It also can be made in powdered form for use in molding operations.

Nylon fibers and fabrics are noted for their strength, ability to be dyed, low shrinkage, silklike appearance, and resistance to abrasion, mildew, and insects. They are not harmed by most kinds of oil and grease or by household cleaning fluids. Nylon fabrics dry rapidly because nylon absorbs little water.

Uses. Nylon is used primarily in fibers and fabrics. It was the first synthetic fabric thought to be superior to natural fabrics. Nylon hosiery came on the market in 1939. Since then, many uses have been found for nylon, including carpets, tires, upholstery, dresses, underwear, bathing suits, lace, and parachutes. Single threads of nylon are used for fishing line and for bristles in brushes. Surgeons use nylon thread to sew up wounds.

Nylon is also important in the plastics industry. Nylon plastics are noted for their electrical properties, toughness, and resistance to chemicals, fire, and wear. They are used in such products as electrical equipment, gears, tubing, and sporting equipment. Plastic nylon body panels have replaced steel on some automobiles.

How nylon is made. Most nylon produced in the United States is made from two chemical compounds— *hexamethylenediamine* and *adipic acid.* Both of these compounds contain carbon and hydrogen. Manufacturers combine the compounds to form *hexamethylene-di-ammonium-adipate,* commonly called *nylon salt.*

Most nylon factories make the substance by placing a solution of nylon salt in a machine called an *autoclave.* The autoclave heats the solution under pressure. The water is removed, and the molecules that make up each of the compounds combine to form large molecules. This process of making large molecules from smaller ones is called *polymerization.* In some factories, the newly formed nylon comes out of the machine as a plastic ribbon. The ribbon is cooled, hardened, and cut into chips that are used in making a variety of nylon products. See **Plastics** (How plastics are made).

Nylon fibers are made by forcing molten nylon through tiny holes in a device called a *spinneret.* In some factories, the molten nylon travels to the spinneret as soon as the polymerization process is completed. Other factories melt nylon chips and pump the melted nylon through the spinneret. The streams of nylon harden into filaments when they strike the air. Then they are wound onto bobbins. From 1 to as many as 2,520 filaments are united into a textile nylon yarn.

Nylon fibers are *drawn* (stretched) after they cool. Some factories draw nylon after it has been spun into yarn. Others spin and draw the yarn in one operation. Drawing involves unwinding the yarn or filaments from one spool and winding them onto another. The winding rate is four or more times as fast as the unwinding rate. The pull between the spools stretches the fibers. Drawing makes the molecules in each filament fall into parallel lines. This process gives the fiber strength and elasticity. After being drawn, the yarn may be twisted a few turns per yard or per meter as it is wound onto spools. It may also be treated to give it a special texture or bulk.

The size of nylon yarn is measured in *deniers.* A denier is the weight in grams of 9,000 meters (9,843 yards) of the yarn. For example, if 9,000 meters of a nylon yarn weigh 15 grams, the yarn is called *15-denier* yarn.

History. Wallace H. Carothers, a chemist of the DuPont Company, was a leader in the development of nylon. In the late 1920's, he began to experiment with polymerization. He used a machine called the "molecular still," which made it possible to make longer molecules than had been made before. Carothers found that many of the fibers made from compounds that he polymerized could be pulled out to several times their original length after they were cooled. This pulling process made the fibers much stronger and more elastic.

But most compounds that Carothers had made so far melted at a temperature too low to make them practical for textiles that must be ironed. Then, in 1935, he polymerized hexamethylenediamine and adipic acid. The product was called *polyhexamethylene adipamide.* This material had a melting point of 482 °F (250 °C), which is satisfactory for textiles. The new fiber was named nylon and was hailed as a great discovery. Later, chemists referred to this original kind of nylon as *nylon 66* because both chemicals used in making it had six carbon atoms.

Before nylon could be produced for the public, scientists had to find a way to make large amounts of hexam-

ethylenediamine and adipic acid. Researchers at DuPont eventually developed a method for making these chemicals from petroleum, natural gas, and agricultural by-products. Nylon production began in 1938, and the first products made from nylon were introduced in 1939.

Most manufacturers in the United States have continued to produce nylon 66. However, other types of nylon have also been developed. Nylon 6, made from a six-carbon chemical called *caprolactam,* is a major fiber produced in the United States and numerous other countries. A silklike nylon with the trademark *Qiana* is a popular fiber that is used for clothing.   Marvis E. Hartman

See also **Velcro.**

Nymph, in entomology. See **Larva.**

Nymph, *nihmf,* was a lovely maiden of Greek and Roman mythology who guarded the different realms of nature. *Oreads* watched over the hills and mountains, and *Nereids* kept watch over the Mediterranean Sea. The *naiads* were the nymphs of the rivers, brooks, and streams. The ocean was protected by the *Oceanids.* The *dryads* and *hamadryads* took care of the trees and forests.

A number of the naiads watched over springs that were believed to inspire those who drank their waters. The naiads were thought to have powers to prophesy and to inspire people. The oreads were also known by names that came from the hills or mountains where they lived.

Nymphs were sometimes shy. But at other times, they were passionate lovers. They were generally friendly and kind to mortals but occasionally punished people who offended them. Nymphs are represented with fauns and satyrs in the forest, or playing around the keels of ships. Nymphs lived for a long time, but they were not usually considered immortal.   Justin M. Glenn

Nystagmus, *nihs TAG muhs,* is an involuntary, rhythmical movement of the eyes. The eyes may move from side to side, up and down, in a circle, or in a combination of these movements. The motions may be rapid or slow, and jerky or smooth. Nystagmus occurs normally, as when a person watches scenery from a moving train. This condition may also be produced by diseases of the eye, the ear, or the brain. Some people are born with nystagmus.   Ronald Klein

Nzinga Nkuwu, *ehn ZIHNG ah ehn KOO woo* (?-1506), was the ruler of the Kongo kingdom in west-central Africa. His subjects believed he was God in human form.

After the first Portuguese trading ships came to Kongo in 1485, Nzinga Nkuwu welcomed trade with Portugal and established a friendly relationship with the Europeans. Portugal sent carpenters, farmers, traders, and other specialists to Kongo. But eventually the Europeans became more interested in developing the slave trade than in aiding the Kongolese.

After Christian missionaries came to Mbanza, Kongo's capital, Nzinga Nkuwu accepted Christianity as one of Kongo's religions. He was baptized in 1491 and took the name John I, or *João,* the name of Portugal's king. However, he gave up Christianity around 1495 because of disputes in his court between supporters and opponents of Christianity. Nzinga Mbemba, Nzinga Nkuwu's son, gained power shortly after Nzinga Nkuwu's death in 1506. A Christian supported by the Portuguese, Nzinga Mbemba took the name Afonso I.   Kevin C. MacDonald

See also **Kongo.**

Oo

O is the 15th letter of the alphabet used for the modern English language. The letter *O* is also used in a number of other languages, including French, German, and Spanish.

The letter *O* is the fourth of the English vowel letters (see **Vowel**). The letter has several sounds in English. The sound in *cot* is a short *O,* and the sound in *book* is a short *OO* (double *O*). The sound in *November* is a long *O* and the sound in *loose* is the long *OO* sound. In some English words in which the letter appears in pairs, each *O* is pronounced separately, as in the word *cooperate.* These words are sometimes spelled with a hyphen, as *co-operate,* for example.

Scholars believe the letter *O* evolved from an Egyptian *hieroglyph* (pictorial symbol) that represented an eye. Hieroglyphs were adapted to be used for a Semitic language by around 1500 B.C. The alphabet for this Semitic language—the earliest known alphabet—is called Proto-Sinaitic. By 1100 B.C., an alphabet for another Semitic language, Phoenician, had evolved from Proto-Sinaitic. See **Semitic languages.**

The Phoenician letter that can be traced to the Egyptian eye hieroglyph is the 16th letter of the Phoenician alphabet, `ayn, the Phoenician word for *eye.* The Phoenicians used the letter to represent a gargling sound that is not used as a speech sound in English. This sound was not used in ancient Greek. So, around 800 B.C., when the Greeks adapted the Phoenician alphabet, `ayn became *omicron.*

The Etruscans adopted the Greek alphabet about 700 B.C. Although they had no *O* sound in their language, the Etruscans kept letters for which they had no need. By around 650 B.C., the Romans adopted the alphabet from the Etruscans. The Romans used the letter evolved from *omicron* for their *O* sound.   Peter T. Daniels

See also **Alphabet.**

Development of the letter *O*

Seafarers and traders aided the transmission of letters along the coast of the Mediterranean Sea.

The Latin alphabet was adopted from the Etruscans by the Romans around 650 B.C. The Roman letter *O was* somewhat more oval in shape than earlier letters, such as *omicron.*

The Etruscan alphabet was adopted from the Greek about 700 B.C. The Etruscan letter for the *O* sound evolved from *omicron.*

Large and small *o* are not as different as are the versions of some of the other letters. Small letters evolved because curved, connected lines were faster to write than imitations of the *inscriptional* (carved) Roman letters. The inscriptional forms of the letters developed into capital letters. The curved forms developed into small letters. The letter *O* was already a curved letter and so did not change much.   A.D. 300   1500   Today

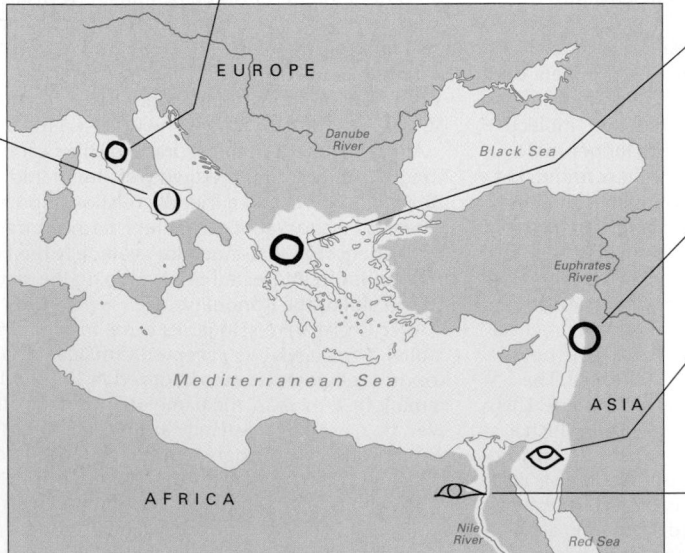

The Greek alphabet evolved from the Phoenician by around 800 B.C. The Greek letter *omicron,* which was adapted from `ayn, was one of two letters used for the *O* sound. The other letter, *omega* (Ω), was used in some dialects of Greek for a long *O* sound.

The Phoenician alphabet had evolved from the Proto-Sinaitic by around 1100 B.C. The Phoenician letter looked less eyelike, but the Phoenician word `ayn meant *eye.*

A Proto-Sinaitic alphabet for a Semitic language evolved from Egyptian hieroglyphs by around 1500 B.C. The Proto-Sinaitic letter that came from the eye hieroglyph was the letter `ayn.

The Egyptians, about 3000 B.C., drew a hieroglyph representing an eye.

EUROPE

Danube River

Black Sea

Euphrates River

ASIA

Mediterranean Sea

AFRICA

Nile River

Red Sea

O Canada is the national anthem of Canada. The Canadian Parliament adopted the song as the national anthem on June 27, 1980. Calixa Lavallée, a Canadian musician, composed the music in 1880. The song has both French and English lyrics. Sir Adolphe Basile Routhier, a Canadian judge, wrote the French lyrics in 1880. Another Canadian judge, Robert Stanley Weir, wrote the English words in 1908. In 1968, some of the wording in the English version was changed. The English lyrics are not a translation of the French lyrics.

The first stanza of the English lyrics is given below, followed by the first stanza of the French lyrics.

> O Canada! Our home and native land!
> True patriot love in all thy sons command.
> With glowing hearts we see thee rise,
> The True North strong and free!
> From far and wide, O Canada,
> We stand on guard for thee.
> God keep our land glorious and free!
> O Canada, we stand on guard for thee.
> O Canada, we stand on guard for thee.
>
> O Canada! Terre de nos aïeux,
> Ton front est ceint de fleurons glorieux!
> Car ton bras sait porter l'épée,
> Il sait porter la croix!
> Ton histoire est une épopée
> Des plus brillants exploits.
> Et ta valeur, de foi trempée,
> Protégera nos foyers et nos droits,
> Protégera nos foyers et nos droits.

Valerie Woodring Goertzen

Oahu. See **Hawaii** (The islands).

Oak is any of a large variety of trees or shrubs that bear acorns. There are several hundred *species* (kinds) of oaks. All of them grow naturally only in the Northern Hemisphere. Most species of oaks are found in tropical and warm regions. Only a few grow in Canada and other regions with short summers and long winters. Oaks thrive in forests throughout the continental United States except for Alaska. They also grow in forests of China, Japan, and central and southern Europe.

Oaks vary widely in size and in the way they grow. Some oaks never become taller than small shrubs. Others reach heights of more than 100 feet (30 meters). Many oaks that grow in warm climates do not lose their leaves in the autumn. They are called *evergreens.* But most oaks found in regions with cold winters are *deciduous*—that is, they shed their leaves each autumn. The leaves of many deciduous oaks turn beautiful colors, such as deep red or golden-brown, in early autumn.

In the spring, oaks produce small, yellowish-green flowers. The male flowers, which form in dangling clusters called *catkins,* produce large amounts of pollen. The wind carries the pollen to the female flowers and fertilizes them. Once fertilized, a female flower will become an acorn. The acorn is the fruit of the oak. Acorns vary in length from less than ½ inch (13 millimeters) to more than 2 inches (51 millimeters).

Oaks grow slowly and usually do not bear acorns until they are about 20 years old. But these trees live a long time. Most oaks live for 200 to 400 years.

Oaks are an important source of lumber. Oak wood is heavy, hard, and strong, and it has a beautiful grain. Manufacturers use it for furniture, barrels, and railroad ties. The wood and bark of some oaks contain *tannin,* a bitter substance used in the preparation of leather. Cork comes from the bark of certain oaks. Acorns are an important source of food for wildlife. In the past, many Indians of North America used acorns for food. Today, oaks are grown as ornamental trees worldwide.

North American oaks

Hundreds of species of oaks are native to North America. Only a few dozen of these grow north of Mexico. Botanists divide oaks into two groups: (1) white oaks and (2) red oaks, sometimes called *black oaks.* The trees in these two groups differ chiefly in the shape of their leaves and in how long it takes their acorns to mature.

White oaks have lobed leaves, and the tips of the lobes are rounded. Many red oaks also have lobed leaves, but these leaves have pointed tips that end in a hairline bristle. Some red oaks have unlobed, oval leaves with a sharp tip.

The acorns of white oaks form in the spring, mature during the summer, and are shed in the autumn. The acorns of red oaks need two growing seasons to mature. In general, white oak acorns taste less bitter than do red oak acorns.

White oaks thrive throughout deciduous forests of eastern North America. A species that is named the *white oak* is especially common. It is easily recognized by its grayish bark, which forms shinglelike plates about 20 to 30 feet (6 to 9 meters) up the trunk. Its leaves usually have seven or nine lobes. The wood of the white oak makes excellent furniture.

Several other white oaks are important members of eastern deciduous forests. The *post oak* grows in dry soils. It has gray bark and leaves with five lobes. The *overcup oak,* the *swamp chestnut oak,* and the *swamp white oak* are common in swampy areas. The leaves of these three species usually have more than seven lobes. The *bur oak* ranges from the eastern part of the Great Plains east to New Brunswick and Nova Scotia. This species produces large acorns.

Only a few species of white oaks grow in western North America. The *California white oak* is common along streams and in moist valleys of California, where it provides shade for livestock. This oak has leaves with 7, 9, or 11 lobes. It bears long, slender acorns. The *Oregon white oak* is found in river valleys and warm, dry areas from central California to southwestern British Columbia. The leaves of the Oregon white oak resemble those of the California white oak, but it has much plumper acorns. The Oregon white oak also grows as a low shrub along the Oregon coast and in mountainous regions. This oak may be found as high as 4,000 feet (1,200 meters) above sea level.

Red oaks are common in forests of eastern North America. The *northern red oak* grows from the southern Appalachian Mountains north to Ontario and Nova Scotia, and west into Arkansas and Missouri. It is often found along with two other red oak species, the *black oak* and the *scarlet oak.* These three species look similar and even experts sometimes confuse them. All three species usually have leaves with seven or nine lobes. But the leaves of black oaks have yellow hairs on the underside. Most scarlet oak leaves have sharply pointed tips and deep notches between the lobes. These oaks are an important source of timber and tannin.

Many red oaks grow only in certain soils or locations. For example, the *blackjack oak* grows in soils that contain much clay. This oak has pear-shaped leaves with golden hairs on the underside. The *turkey oak* is found in sandy soils of the Atlantic coastal plain. Its leaves have deeply notched edges.

Evergreens in the red oak group are often called *live oaks*. The live oak of the Southern States grows in the Gulf and Atlantic coastal plains. Its large, spreading branches are often draped with Spanish moss. In coastal dune areas, these trees grow as shrubs. Live oaks are also common in dry regions of Texas. The *California live oak* grows on hillsides along the southern California coast, where little rain falls during the summer.

A number of shrubby, evergreen oaks grow in dry areas of California and the Southwest. The *California scrub oak* is found in regions that have frequent wildfires. Some reach a height of only 3 to 4 feet (0.9 to 1.2 meters). The roots of this oak have many buds. Following a fire, these buds sprout and grow into new shrubs. The *shrub live oak* is one of several species of shrubby oaks found in the deserts of the southwestern United States and of Mexico. The shrub live oak is common on mountain slopes.

Other oaks

In the United Kingdom and northern Europe, two common deciduous trees are the *English oak* and the *sessile oak*, also called the *durmast oak*. These two species of oaks are easy to tell apart by how their acorns grow. The acorns of English oaks grow on long stalks. The acorns of sessile oaks attach directly to twigs. Both oaks may grow to a height of more than 110 feet (34 meters). Some have lived more than 800 years. The wood of these oaks is used for beams and shipbuilding.

Several deciduous species of oaks also grow in the mountain forests of southern Europe. These include the *Hungarian oak* and the *Pyrenean oak*. Both are used for ornament and shade in gardens worldwide.

Live oaks grow in regions of southern Europe that have mild winters. The *holm oak* looks much like the live oaks of the southwestern United States. It is an important timber tree and an excellent source of charcoal. The holm oak is grown in parks and along roads throughout the world. The *cork oak* is found chiefly in Spain and Portugal. Cork comes from the bark of this tree.

Many oak species grow in the forests of central and eastern Asia. The *Lebanon oak* is common in mountainous regions of the Middle East. The *Mongolian oak* is an important timber tree in eastern Asia, including Japan. Both of these species can be found in parks and gardens in the United States.   Norman L. Christensen, Jr.

Scientific classification. Oaks are in the beech family, Fagaceae, and make up the genus *Quercus*. The scientific name for the white oak is *Quercus alba*, the northern red oak is *Q. rubra*, the live oak of the Southern States is *Q. virginiana*, and the English oak is *Q. robur*.

See also **Acorn; Cork; Live oak; Tree** (Broadleaf and needleleaf trees [pictures]).

Oak, Silky. See Silky oak.

Oak Ridge National Laboratory, in Oak Ridge, Tennessee, is one of the largest and most diverse energy research and development centers in the United States. Work at the laboratory focuses primarily on basic energy research and nuclear energy technology.

Oak Ridge researchers conduct experiments with nuclear fission and nuclear fusion. The laboratory is also the major source in the United States for radioactive and stable isotopes used in medicine, industry, and research. Other fields of study at Oak Ridge include nuclear physics, metallurgical and solid-state physics, biology, and energy conservation. Scientists there also work

Some kinds of oaks   There are more than 600 species of oaks. All of them grow naturally only in the Northern Hemisphere. Botanists divide oaks into two general groups: *white oaks* and *red oaks*. Three species of oaks are illustrated below. The drawings include the leaf and the acorn of each species.

The white oak is common in eastern North America. It has grayish bark and leaves with seven or nine lobes.

The English oak is found in forests of Britain and northern Europe. Its acorns grow on long stalks.

The holm oak is an important timber tree of southern Europe. It is found in parks throughout the world.

to develop more efficient methods of using coal and other nonnuclear sources of energy. In addition, scientists study how the use of various forms of energy affects the environment and human health.

Oak Ridge National Laboratory was established in 1943 as part of the World War II Manhattan Project to build the atomic bomb. During the war, the laboratory's main objective was to develop a process for separating plutonium, an explosive material used in atomic bombs, from uranium. Today, the University of Tennessee and Battelle Memorial Institute, a research and development organization, operate the laboratory under contract with the U.S. Department of Energy.   Toni Grayson Joseph

Oakland (pop. 390,724) is one of the busiest shipping centers in California. The city lies on the eastern shore of San Francisco Bay, an inlet of the Pacific Ocean. Oakland is 3 miles (4.8 kilometers) across the bay from San Francisco (see **California** [political map]). Oakland was founded after the discovery of gold in California in 1848. The city was named for the oak trees that grew on its hills.

Description. Oakland is the seat of Alameda County. Oakland, San Francisco, and Fremont are part of a metropolitan area.

Lake Merritt lies in the heart of downtown Oakland. The oldest wildlife refuge in North America was established at Lake Merritt in 1870. Jack London Square includes the bay waterfront that was visited frequently by the author for whom it was named. Museums and other cultural institutions in the city include the Oakland Museum of California, the Chabot Space & Science Center, and the Oakland East Bay Symphony. The African American Museum and Library at Oakland includes letters, diaries, and photographs that share the experiences of blacks in California.

Institutions of higher education in Oakland include California College of the Arts, Holy Names University, Mills College, and Patten University. Oakland is home to the Oakland Athletics baseball team of the American League, the Oakland Raiders of the National Football League, and the Golden State Warriors of the National Basketball Association.

Economy. Oakland is a major transportation center. The Port of Oakland is one of the world's busiest ports

Facts in brief

Population: *City*—390,724. *Metropolitan division*—2,559,296. *Metropolitan statistical area*—4,335,391.
Area: *City*—54 mi² (140 km²). *Metropolitan division*—1,458 mi² (3,776 km²). *Metropolitan statistical area*—2,474 mi² (6,408 km²).
Climate: *Average temperature*—January, 51 °F (11 °C); July, 65 °F (18 °C). *Average annual precipitation* (rainfall, melted snow, and other forms of moisture)—23 inches (58 cm).
Government: Mayor-council. *Terms*—4 years for the mayor and the 8 council members. City administrator appointed by the mayor.
Founded: 1852. Incorporated as a town, 1852; as a city, 1854.

for container ships. The western terminals of several freight railroad systems are in Oakland. Passenger trains link Oakland with other cities in the United States. The Bay Area Rapid Transit system (BART), a regional rail system, has its headquarters in the city. Air travelers use Oakland International Airport.

A majority of Oakland's workers are employed in service industries. Important economic activities in the city include business and health care services, food processing, and transportation.

Government and history. Oakland has a mayor-council form of government. The voters elect a mayor and eight council members to four-year terms. The mayor appoints a city administrator to carry out city policies.

Ohlone, also called Costanoan, Indians lived in what is now Oakland before European settlers arrived. In the 1770's, Spanish explorers and missionaries became the first Europeans to reach the region. In 1820, Luís María Peralta, a Spanish soldier, received a land grant that included most of the area that is now Alameda County.

By 1849, merchants, loggers, and gold seekers had begun to settle the region. Oakland was incorporated as a town in 1852 and as a city in 1854.

Oakland's population grew rapidly after it was chosen as the western *terminus* (end) of the first transcontinental railroad in 1869. About 65,000 people settled in the city in 1906 after fleeing the San Francisco earthquake.

Industrial expansion took place in Oakland through the 1920's. Many automakers and food processing and steel companies were established in the city. Oakland

Oakland Convention Bureau

Oakland, California, lies on the eastern shore of San Francisco Bay, 3 miles (4.8 kilometers) across the bay from San Francisco. Lake Merritt, *shown here,* is a large saltwater lake in the heart of downtown Oakland.

became a major port and shipbuilding center during World War II (1939-1945).

In the 1970's, the city began several urban renewal projects in the downtown area. Construction on Oakland City Center, a complex of office buildings and retail stores, was completed in 1990. Preservation Park, a showplace of historic homes that were moved from other parts of the city, opened in 1991.

In October 1989, a strong earthquake struck Oakland and the surrounding area. As a result of the earthquake, a portion of the upper level of the city's double-decked Nimitz Freeway, or Interstate Highway 880, collapsed onto the lower level. The earthquake caused 43 deaths and extensive property damage in Alameda County. In October 1991, a brush fire in Oakland killed 25 people and caused much property damage.

Redevelopment continued into the 2000's. In the late 1990's, businesses and residents began relocating from overcrowded San Francisco to Oakland.   Betty Marvin

Oakley, Annie (1860-1926), was a famous American sharpshooter who starred in Buffalo Bill's Wild West show for more than 16 years. She was assisted by her husband, Frank Butler, and part of her act was to shoot a dime out of his hand or a cigarette out of his mouth. Oakley also could hit a playing card thrown into the air 90 feet (27 meters) away from her. She gained worldwide fame on European tours for such daring deeds as shooting a cigarette held in the mouth of the German Crown Prince Wilhelm.

Annie Oakley was born Phoebe Ann Moses on Aug. 13, 1860, in Darke County, Ohio. She took the name Oakley from a district in Cincinnati. She learned to shoot at age 8 and helped support her family by killing game for a Cincinnati hotel. At age 15, she defeated Butler, a professional marksman, in a shooting exhibition. In 1876, they married. She then adopted the stage name Annie Oakley and took part in shooting exhibitions.

Oakley was only 5 feet (150 centimeters) tall. The Sioux Indian chief Sitting Bull, who toured briefly with Buffalo Bill's Wild West show, called her "Little Sure Shot." Oakley joined the show in 1885, and Butler became her manager. In 1901, she was injured in a train accident and resigned from the show. She joined a theatrical group and starred in *The Western Girl* (1902). During World War I (1914-1918), she gave shooting exhibitions and instruction to American soldiers. She died on Nov. 3, 1926.

The popular musical comedy *Annie Get Your Gun* (1946), which has songs by composer Irving Berlin, is loosely based on Oakley's life. It portrays her as an outspoken tomboy. In reality, she was a quiet, simple person who did needlepoint in her free time.   Odie B. Faulk

Oar. See Rowing.

Oarfish is the longest bony fish. It normally measures 16 to 35 feet (5 to 11 meters) long. However, people have reported seeing oarfish more than 55 feet (17 meters) in length. The fish live in *temperate* (mild) and warm seas, normally at depths of 1,000 to 2,000 feet (300 to 610 meters). They have flat-sided, silvery bodies with bright red fins. On the underside of an adult's body, two long pelvic fins end in blade-shaped swellings. These fins resemble the oars of a rowboat, giving the fish its name.

Oarfish have no teeth and feed chiefly on tiny shrimplike creatures called *krill*. Scientists know little about oarfish because the fish live in deep water and have never been kept in aquariums.   John E. McCosker

Scientific classification. The oarfish is in the family Regalecidae. It is *Regalecus glesne*.

See also **Fish** (picture: Fish of the deep ocean).

OAS. See **Organization of American States; France** (France under de Gaulle).

Oasis is a fertile, vegetated area in a desert where underground water comes close enough to the surface for

Annie Oakley became famous as one of the world's most accurate shots with pistol, rifle, and shotgun.
Bettmann Archive

S. Fiore, Shostal

Irrigation ditches filled with water from deep wells or underground springs support date palms and other crops raised on oases, such as this one in western Africa.

wells and springs to exist. Water that occurs at an oasis originally fell as rain or snow in distant mountains or hills. After seeping into the ground, the water slowly filters through the underground rocks toward low places in the desert. It then reappears at the surface to form springs or is shallow enough to be found in wells. Fertile, vegetated areas along permanent streams in deserts are sometimes also called oases.

Soil in desert regions is generally fertile but lacks the moisture to encourage plant growth. Because oases have water, almost all of them are areas of farming and settlement. Some oases are small and can support only a few people, but others are large enough to support millions of people.   Paul R. Bierman

See also **Africa** (picture: Deserts); **Desert; Merv; Sahara** (picture: An oasis village).

Oates, *ohts,* **Joyce Carol** (1938-   ), is an American author. She gives most of her novels and short stories a nightmarish quality and emphasizes sex and violence. But her most significant subjects are society and the insanity it generates. At the core of her work is a moral vision. Oates has written more than 100 books of fiction, nonfiction, and poetry. Some critics argue she would profit from polishing her fiction, but most agree that her pictures of society are accurate.

Oates dramatizes the way that she believes American society treats the poor in *A Garden of Earthly Delights* (1967). *Them* (1969) portrays the violent lives of a poor family in Detroit. *Unholy Loves* (1979) is a comic novel set on a college campus in the United States. *A Bloodsmoor Romance* (1982) satirizes Romantic novels of the 1800's.

© Marco Secchi, Photoshot/Landov
Joyce Carol Oates

Oates's first novel was *With Shuddering Fall* (1964). Her other novels include *Expensive People* (1968), *Wonderland* (1971), *Do with Me What You Will* (1973), *Marya* (1986), *You Must Remember This* (1987), *Because It Is Bitter, and Because It Is My Heart* (1990), *Black Water* (1992), *Foxfire* (1993), *We Were the Mulvaneys* (1996), *Broke Heart Blues* (1999), *Blonde* (2000), *Rape* (2003), *The Falls* (2004), *Missing Mom* (2005), *Black Girl/White Girl* (2006), and *The Gravedigger's Daughter* (2007).

Oates's novels for young adults include *Big Mouth & Ugly Girl* (2002), *Freaky Green Eyes* (2003), *Sexy* (2005), and *After the Wreck, I Picked Myself Up, Spread My Wings, and Flew Away* (2006). *Naughty Chérie!* (2008) is a children's picture book about a misbehaving kitten.

Oates's stories have been collected in such volumes as *By the North Gate* (1963), *The Wheel of Love* (1970), *Last Days* (1984), *Heat* (1991), *Will You Always Love Me?* (1996), *Faithless* (2001), *I Am No One You Know* (2004), *The Female of the Species* (2006), *High Lonesome* (2006), *Dear Husband,* (2009), and *Sourland* (2010). Her *Twelve Plays* was published in 1991. Her nonfiction has been published in *The Profane Art* (1983), *Where I've Been, and Where I'm Going* (1999), *Uncensored: Views and (Re)views* (2005), and *In Rough Country* (2010).

Oates's poetry appears in *Love and Its Derangements* (1974) and *The Time Traveler* (1989). She discusses the craft of writing in *The Faith of a Writer* (2003). *The Journal of Joyce Carol Oates, 1973-1982* was published in 2007. She is also an editor and anthologist. She writes thrillers under the name Rosamond Smith. Oates was born on June 16, 1938, in Lockport, New York.   Arthur M. Saltzman

Oath is a pledge or promise. The *judicial oath* is probably the most common form. It is used in a court of law, at a deposition, or before a notary public or other judicial officer (see **Deposition; Notary public**). A witness taking this oath swears that all of his or her statements are true. Often the person must lay a hand on the Bible while taking the oath. This gesture means that the person is making a declaration through God. A person swearing to the truth of an affidavit may be given the following oath: "You do solemnly swear that the contents of this affidavit by you subscribed are true, so help you God." A person who takes an oath in court and then makes a dishonest statement while under oath is guilty of perjury, a crime punishable by a fine or jail sentence.

All of us are familiar with oaths in everyday life. For example, a person who promises to give up a bad habit is said to "take an oath." This kind of oath is called *extrajudicial* because it has no force in a court of law.

Affirmation. Some religious groups, such as Quakers, disapprove of swearing by an oath. They believe in the Bible's command "Swear not at all." When members of such groups testify in court, they take an *affirmation* instead of an oath. The affirmation binds them to the truth as strongly as an oath would. If a person violates an affirmation, he or she becomes guilty of perjury.

Oath of office. Many officials must take a pledge when they enter a public office. This *oath of office* is a promise to carry out the duties of the office honestly and faithfully. According to the Constitution of the United States, the nation's president must take the following oath at the inauguration: "I do solemnly swear (or affirm) that I will faithfully execute the Office of the President of the United States, and will to the best of my ability, preserve, protect and defend the Constitution of the United States." All U.S. government officers lower in rank than the president take oaths much like the one above. An officer taking over a state public office promises to protect the state constitution as well as the U.S. Constitution.

In Canada, many government officials take a pledge upon entering public office. Members of the federal Parliament and of provincial legislatures take the following oath: "I do swear that I will be faithful and bear true allegiance to His (or Her) Majesty ..."

Military oaths are taken by people who enter the armed forces. In the United States, a person must take the following oath: "I do solemnly swear (or affirm) that I will support and defend the Constitution of the United States against all enemies, foreign and domestic; that I will bear true faith and allegiance to the same; and that I will obey the orders of the President of the United States and the orders of the officers appointed over me, according to regulations and the Uniform Code of Military Justice. So help me God." Members of the armed forces of Canada, the United Kingdom, and other countries take a similar oath.   Sherman L. Cohn

See also **Citizenship; Hippocrates** (The Hippocratic oath); **Perjury.**

Oatmeal is a food product prepared from oats. It is commonly eaten as a cooked breakfast cereal. Oatmeal is made by removing the outer husk of the oat kernel. The *groats,* or inner portion of the kernel, is scoured to remove some of the outer skin. Then it is partially cooked by steaming and rolled to form flakes.

Oatmeal is a good source of B vitamins and iron. One cup (240 milliliters) of cooked oatmeal contains about 23 grams of carbohydrates, 5 grams of protein, and 2 grams of fat. One cup is made up of about 85 percent water and has 130 calories.   Jane Ann Raymond Bowers

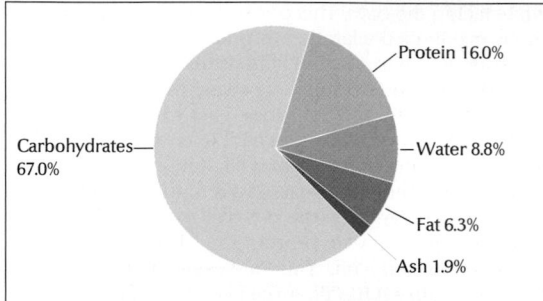

Protein 16.0%

Carbohydrates— 67.0%

Water 8.8%

Fat 6.3%

Ash 1.9%

Source: U.S. Department of Agriculture, Agricultural Research Service.

The food value of oatmeal makes it a nourishing breakfast cereal. One cup of oatmeal has about 130 calories.

Oats are an important grain crop. Farmers grow them mainly to feed livestock, but oats also provide nourishing food for many people. The seeds of oat plants are processed and used in such foods as oatmeal, oatcakes, cookies, and ready-to-eat breakfast cereals.

Oats are a cereal grain and belong to the same family of plants as wheat, rice, corn, and barley. Oats have a higher food value than any other cereal grain. They are rich in starch and high-quality protein, and they provide a good source of Vitamin B$_1$. Some nutritionists believe that the addition of *oat bran* (the seed covering of oats) to the diet helps reduce cholesterol.

Most of the oats grown in the United States are used as feed for livestock. Oats are the best grain to feed horses. Many farmers use the straw from oats as bedding for their livestock.

Russia is the leading oat-growing country. Other leading countries include Australia, Canada, Poland, and the United States. The world's annual production of oats totals about 27 million tons (24 million metric tons).

The oat plant has a stem that grows from 2 to 4 feet (60 to 120 centimeters) high. The stem ends in a head called a *panicle,* which consists of many small branches. Each branch ends in a single *spikelet* (flower cluster). The majority of oat plants have from 40 to 50 spikelets. Most spikelets contain two seeds, each enclosed by a husk called the *hull.* The hull must be removed before the seeds can be processed into oatmeal or other food products. The oat seed, called a *groat,* is usually the same color as the hull. Different varieties of oat seeds may be white, yellow, red, gray, or black.

The chief kinds of cultivated oats include common oats, red oats, side oats, and hull-less oats. Common oats are the type most widely grown in the United States. Red oats have reddish seeds. Side oats have all their branches on one side of the stalk. Hull-less oats, unlike the other types, have loose husks that separate from the seeds during harvesting.

Growing oats. Oats can be grown in a variety of climates and soils. But they grow especially well in areas that have a cool, moist climate and fertile soil. Farmers may add fertilizer to poor soil to increase the yield.

Farmers grow two types of oats, *spring oats* and *winter oats.* Spring oats are planted in early spring and harvested in summer. The date of planting and harvesting depends on the climate of the area. Winter oats are

Leonard Lee Rue III, Bruce Coleman Ltd.

Oat plants have heads called *panicles.* Each panicle has many flower clusters called *spikelets,* which contain the seeds. Each seed is enclosed by a hull.

TSW/Chicago Ltd.

Harvesting oats, a farmer may use a *combine.* This machine cuts down the stalks and separates the grain from them.

Leading oat-growing countries

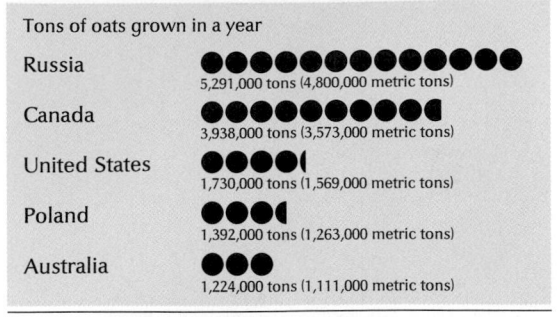

Tons of oats grown in a year

Russia — 5,291,000 tons (4,800,000 metric tons)

Canada — 3,938,000 tons (3,573,000 metric tons)

United States — 1,730,000 tons (1,569,000 metric tons)

Poland — 1,392,000 tons (1,263,000 metric tons)

Australia — 1,224,000 tons (1,111,000 metric tons)

Figures are for a three-year average, 2004-2006.
Source: Food and Agriculture Organization of the United Nations.

Leading oat-growing states and provinces

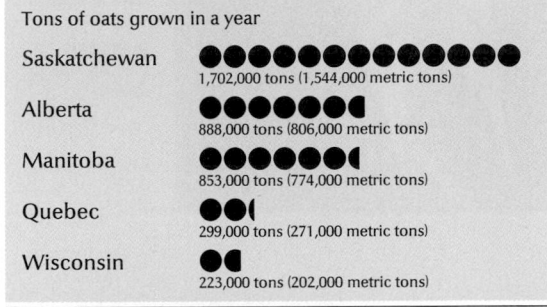

Tons of oats grown in a year

Saskatchewan — 1,702,000 tons (1,544,000 metric tons)

Alberta — 888,000 tons (806,000 metric tons)

Manitoba — 853,000 tons (774,000 metric tons)

Quebec — 299,000 tons (271,000 metric tons)

Wisconsin — 223,000 tons (202,000 metric tons)

Figures are for a three-year average, 2004-2006.
Sources: U.S. Department of Agriculture; Statistics Canada.

planted in fall and harvested the next summer. They start growing before the weather turns cold. Growth stops in the winter and begins again in spring. Winter oats are not as hardy as other winter grains, and so they are grown chiefly in areas with mild winters.

Oats are planted either by simply scattering the seeds over the field or by sowing the seeds with a *grain drill.* This machine drops the seeds into furrows and covers them with soil. The seeds are planted in rows about 6 to 7 inches (15 to 18 centimeters) apart and covered with about 2 inches (5 centimeters) of soil. Most farmers use sowing rates of 60 to 90 pounds per acre (65 to 100 kilograms per hectare) of land.

Harvesting oats. Oats are harvested after the plants become dry and yellow and the seeds harden. The grain should not contain more than 12 to 14 percent moisture when harvested. Farmers can take samples of the seed to a grain elevator for a moisture test.

Some oats are grown for hay or *silage.* Silage consists of chopped plant stalks, which are stored in a silo and used to feed livestock during the winter. Oats grown for hay or silage are harvested while the plants are still green and the seeds are soft.

Most farmers harvest oats with a machine called a *combine,* which cuts the stalks and separates the grain from the *chaff* (stiff, strawlike bits surrounding the grain). Before oat grain is made into human food products, the hulls are removed from the seeds at processing plants. Hulls are not removed from grain used as livestock feed. The average yield of oats in the world is about 1,900

pounds per acre (2,100 kilograms per hectare). The United States average is about 2,000 pounds per acre (2,200 kilograms per hectare).

Diseases and insect pests. Diseases can attack oats and sharply reduce the yield. They include smuts, rusts, septoria, and barley yellow dwarf. Oat crops can also be damaged by such insects as aphids, armyworms, cutworms, cereal leaf beetles, and grasshoppers. Aphids are especially troublesome because they spread the barley yellow dwarf disease. Some farmers use chemical sprays to control diseases and insects. But the best protection comes from planting resistant varieties of oats. Researchers continually develop new varieties that are more resistant to diseases and insects. The new varieties often also produce higher yields and better grain. See **Aphid; Armyworm; Cutworm; Rust; Smut.**

Robert D. Wych

Scientific classification. Oats make up the genus *Avena.* Common oats belong to the species *A. sativa.*

See also **Furfural; Grain; Oatmeal.**

Oaxaca, *wah HAH kah* (pop. 255,029), is the capital of Oaxaca, a poor state in southern Mexico. The state has a large American Indian population. The city's official name is Oaxaca de Juárez. Oaxaca has won fame for its handicrafts and its impressive colonial architecture. The city's economy relies largely on tourism and the sale of cattle, dairy products, and hardwoods. The ruins of several ancient Indian cities, including Mitla and Monte Albán, lie near Oaxaca. Some historians believe the Aztec founded Oaxaca in 1486. But the Zapotec and the Mixtec Indians had lived in the area for many centuries before that date. Samuel Brunk

See also **Mixtec Indians; Monte Albán; Zapotec Indians.**

Ob River, *ahb, awb,* or *ohb,* is a chief river of Russia in Asia. It rises in the Altai Mountains of Siberia and flows northwest for 2,268 miles (3,650 kilometers) before emptying into the Kara Sea through the Gulf of Ob (Obskaya Guba). The river drains about 1,130,000 square miles (2,930,000 square kilometers). For location, see **Russia** (terrain map).

The navigable waterways of the Ob and its tributaries total about 19,000 miles (30,600 kilometers). The lower Ob is 2 to 4 miles (3 to 6 kilometers) wide, and the Gulf of Ob averages about 35 miles (55 kilometers) in width. It is blocked with ice from October to June. In summer, the Ob is a major water route for shipping grain, dairy products, livestock, wool, and meat. Craig ZumBrunnen

Obadiah, *OH buh DY uh,* **Book of,** is a book of the Hebrew Bible, or Old Testament, named for an Israelite prophet. The book, which has 21 verses, is the shortest in the Bible. It was probably composed after the Babylonians destroyed Jerusalem in 587 or 586 B.C.

The Book of Obadiah has three sections. They deal with the destruction of Edom (verses 1-9), the misdeeds of Edom against Israel (verses 10-14), and the restoration of Israel at the expense of other nations (verses 15-21). Edom was an ancient kingdom in what is now Jordan. Obadiah (verses 1-9) closely parallels the Book of Jeremiah (49: 7-21), which also predicts the destruction of Edom. The familiarity of Obadiah's author with such prophetic themes as "The Day of the Lord" (verses 15-21) places him in the mainstream of late Biblical prophecy.

Eric M. Meyers

**44th president
of the United States 2009-**

G. W. Bush
43rd president
2001-2009
Republican

Obama
44th president
2009-
Democrat

Joe Biden
Vice president
2009-

The White House

Obama, *oh BAH muh,* **Barack,** *buh RAHK* (1961-   ), became in 2009 the first African American president of the United States. Obama, a Democrat, had represented Illinois in the United States Senate from 2005 to 2008. Before being elected to the U.S. Senate, Obama served for eight years in the Illinois Senate. In the 2008 presidential election, Obama defeated Senator John McCain, a Republican from Arizona.

Obama had served only two years in the U.S. Senate before announcing his run for the presidency. During the presidential campaign, Obama's opponents charged that he was too inexperienced to be president. Obama, however, pledged "a new kind of politics" and sought to represent a change from the administration of President George W. Bush. Bush, a Republican, faced low approval ratings, due in part to a struggling economy and the unpopular Iraq War, which had begun in 2003.

Obama, the child of a black Kenyan father and a white American mother, stressed that his mixed-race status gave him the perspective to understand issues related

to race and ethnicity. He spent his boyhood in Hawaii and Indonesia, and he said his experiences as an "outsider" helped him see the United States as others see it. He believed that such a viewpoint could help him repair the nation's international reputation, which many people believed was damaged by the Iraq War (2003-2010).

In 2009, Obama won the Nobel Peace Prize. The Nobel committee honored him for what it called his "extraordinary efforts to strengthen international diplomacy and cooperation between peoples." Obama became the third sitting U.S. president to win the award. Theodore Roosevelt won the award in 1906, and Woodrow Wilson won it 1919. Obama had also been only the third sitting U.S. senator to be elected president. Warren Harding, in 1920, and John F. Kennedy, in 1960, were the others.

Early life

Family background. Barack Hussein Obama, Jr., was born on Aug. 4, 1961, in Honolulu. His first name comes from the Swahili word *baraka*, which means *blessing*.

Obama's father, Barack Hussein Obama, Sr. (1936-1982), was born in the village of Nyang'oma Kogelo, near Kisumu, in western Kenya. His family were members of the Luo, one of the country's largest ethnic groups.

Obama's mother, Stanley Ann Dunham (1942-1995), was born in Kansas. She was named after her father, Stanley Dunham (1918-1992), a furniture salesman. Her mother, Madelyn (1922-2008), became a bank executive after the family moved to Hawaii during the late 1950's.

Obama's father met Stanley Ann, called Ann, while he was a student at the University of Hawai'i. The two married in 1960. Initially, both sets of parents disapproved of the union. It was uncommon at the time for people of different races to marry.

Important dates in Obama's life

1961	(Aug. 4) Born in Honolulu.
1967	Moved to Indonesia.
1971	Returned to Hawaii.
1983	Graduated from Columbia University.
1991	Graduated from Harvard Law School.
1992	(Oct. 3) Married Michelle Robinson.
1996	Elected to the Illinois Senate.
2004	Elected to the U.S. Senate.
2008	Elected president of the United States.
2009	Won Nobel Peace Prize.

When young Barack, called Barry, was 2 years old, his father left the family to study at Harvard University. Barry's parents divorced in 1964, and the elder Obama later returned to Kenya, where he worked in several government positions. The father saw his son only once more before dying in a 1982 automobile accident in Nairobi, Kenya.

Boyhood. Barry spent his earliest years in Honolulu with his mother in his grandparents' home. Friends described Barry as a happy child who loved spending time at the beach with his grandparents, whom he called "Toot" and "Gramps."

In 1967, when Barry was 6 years old, his mother remarried. Lolo Soetoro, an Indonesian student studying at the University of Hawai'i, became Barry's stepfather. The family soon moved to Jakarta, Indonesia. Barry attended two schools there. Ann worked as an English teacher and as an anthropologist.

Obama had eight siblings, including Maya, a teacher who was born in Indonesia to Barack's mother and stepfather. In Kenya, Barack's father had seven other children. They were Abongo, called Roy, an accountant; Auma, a social worker; Mark, a marketing consultant; David, who died in a motorcycle accident; Abo, a store manager; Bernard, a businessman; and George.

In 1971, Obama received a scholarship to attend the Punahou School, a well-known private school in Honolulu. He moved back to Hawaii to stay with his grandparents while attending school.

Obama excelled at his studies and made a diverse group of friends in the ethnic melting pot of Hawaii. But he sometimes struggled to define his racial identity as a black child being raised by his white mother and grandparents. "I was trying to raise myself to be a black man in

UPI/Landov

Obama's grandparents Stanley and Madelyn Dunham visited Barack while he was a student at Columbia University. Obama lived with the Dunhams for much of his childhood.

America," he wrote, "and beyond the given of my appearance, no one around me seemed to know exactly what that meant."

Obama was a reserve player on the Punahou School basketball team that won the state title in 1979. For his success at making long-range jump shots, his teammates gave him the nickname "Barry O'Bomber."

College. After graduation from high school, Obama enrolled at Occidental College in Los Angeles. He was popular among his classmates and became known as a serious student and an accomplished basketball player. While at Occidental, Obama participated in demonstrations to encourage the college to withdraw its investments from South Africa because of that country's policy of *apartheid* (rigid racial segregation). Obama credited the experience with getting him involved in public policy issues.

During his time at Occidental, Obama began to call himself Barack, his given name. Friends said Obama made the change to be taken more seriously and perhaps also to feel a stronger connection to his African

UPI/Landov

Obama as a toddler is held by his mother, Ann Dunham, in the early 1960's. Dunham met Obama's father, Barack Obama, Sr., a Kenyan, when both were students at the University of Hawaii.

AP/Wide World

Obama taught constitutional law at the University of Chicago Law School from 1992 to 2004. During his time as a university lecturer, Obama also worked as a lawyer and as a state senator.

heritage. In 1981, Obama transferred to Columbia University in New York City. Obama received a bachelor's degree in political science from the university in 1983.

Community organizer. In 1985, Obama moved to the South Side of Chicago to work for a community development organization in low-income African American neighborhoods. In this role, Obama worked to reform schools and public housing, and to help residents organize for job-training and health-related issues.

About this time, Obama met his half-sister Auma. He later traveled to Kenya to visit his father's country and to meet his extended family.

Law school. Obama entered Harvard Law School in 1988 and graduated *magna cum laude* (with great honor) in 1991. In law school, he became the first African American to serve as president of the *Harvard Law Review. Law Review* members are selected on the basis of their grades and writing ability, and membership is a prized honor. The members prepare articles for publication and elect a president to oversee their work. As president of the *Law Review,* Obama gained praise from fellow law students, both liberal and conservative, for his willingness to provide a forum for differing viewpoints.

Obama's family. In 1989, while working as a summer associate at a Chicago law firm, Obama met Michelle Robinson (1964-   ). Michelle was a lawyer who later became a hospital executive. The couple married on Oct. 3, 1992. They have two children: Malia (1998-   ) and Natasha, commonly called Sasha (2001-   ). Obama's mother died of ovarian cancer in 1995.

Early career

After graduating from Harvard, Obama practiced law in Chicago, specializing in civil rights issues. He also began teaching constitutional law at the University of Chicago.

While still in law school, Obama had begun writing what became the autobiography *Dreams from My Father: A Story of Race and Inheritance* (1995). In the book, Obama writes about his family. He describes the father from Kenya whom he barely knew; his strong-willed,

idealistic mother; and the grandparents who helped raise him. The book details his work as a community organizer in Chicago and how it helped him find a place in the African American community. The book had only modest sales after its initial publication. But after Obama gave a celebrated speech at the 2004 Democratic National Convention, the book became a best seller.

Entry into politics

State senator. In 1995, Obama began campaigning for a seat in the Illinois Senate. He won the November 1996 race and took office in 1997. In the state Senate, he focused on such issues as health care, poverty, crime, ethics, and education. For much of his early legislative career, Obama's Democrats were the minority party in the state Senate. Many of his early proposals failed, but he became known as a politician who would listen respectfully to opponents and their views.

Obama did have some successes in the Illinois Senate, notably in ethics reform and criminal justice issues. In 1998, he sponsored legislation that banned nearly all gifts from lobbyists. The law also required lawmakers to report all contributions and expenditures into an electronic database. In 2003, Obama cooperated with law enforcement officials and conservative legislators to reform police procedures. They enacted new rules requiring the police to videotape interrogations and confessions in death penalty cases. The new rules came after reports showed that many inmates on death row had been innocent of their crimes.

United States senator. In 2003, Obama decided to run for a U.S. Senate seat that was held by a retiring Republican. He easily won the Democratic nomination in 2004. In the November election, Obama faced Alan Keyes, a conservative commentator who before the campaign had been living in Maryland. Obama won the election with 70 percent of the vote. He took office in January 2005, becoming the only African American in the Senate.

Convention speech. The summer before the 2004 election, Senator John Kerry, the Democratic presidential nominee, asked Obama to give the keynote address at the Democratic National Convention in Boston. The speech solidified Obama's status as a rising star within the party. He discussed what he called the "politics of hope," saying, "It's the hope of slaves sitting around a fire singing freedom songs; the hope of immigrants setting out for distant shores; . . . the hope of a skinny kid with a funny name who believes that America has a place for him, too."

Legislative accomplishments. In the Senate, Obama voted with his party on a majority of bills. But he also cooperated with Republicans on several issues. In 2006 and 2007, Obama worked with Senator Richard Lugar, a Republican from Indiana, on the Lugar-Obama threat reduction initiative. The act, signed into law by President Bush in 2007, expanded the role of the United States in helping other nations destroy stockpiles of conventional weapons, including shoulder-fired missiles.

A second autobiography. Obama's second autobiographical book, *The Audacity of Hope: Thoughts on Reclaiming the American Dream* (2006), presented his views on the differences and similarities between Republicans and Democrats and on such topics as values, religion, race, and foreign policy. He wrote that politics

Obama's family includes, *from left,* his wife, Michelle, and daughters Sasha and Malia. In this picture, the family departs an airplane in Indianapolis. Obama campaigned in the city prior to Indiana's Democratic primary in May 2008.

© Jason Reed, Reuters/Landov

can reflect the common values and hopes that bind Americans together despite their different views.

The book took its name in part from a sermon titled "The Audacity to Hope" by Jeremiah A. Wright, Jr., the pastor of Trinity United Church of Christ in Chicago. Obama had attended the church since the 1980's.

Presidential nomination. In February 2007, Obama held a rally in Springfield, Illinois, to announce that he would seek the 2008 Democratic nomination for president. His rivals for the nomination included Governor Bill Richardson of New Mexico, former U.S. Senator John Edwards of North Carolina, U.S. Representative Dennis Kucinich of Ohio, and U.S. Senator Hillary Rodham Clinton of New York.

Late in 2007, Obama trailed Clinton by more than 20 percentage points in national polls. On Jan. 3, 2008, he scored a surprise victory in the Iowa caucuses, but Clinton won the New Hampshire primary about a week later.

A historic choice. By February, most of the Democratic hopefuls had dropped out of the race, and the nomination came down to a contest between Obama and Clinton. The match-up ensured that for the first time, a major party would nominate either an African American or a woman candidate for president.

Clinton and Obama took similar positions on many issues, including immigration reform and tax policy. Both candidates offered similar plans regarding the withdrawal of U.S. troops from Iraq. Obama stressed that he had strongly opposed the war even before it began. In 2002, when the administration of President Bush was proposing to invade Iraq, Obama gave a speech declaring: "I know that even a successful war against Iraq will require a U.S. occupation of undetermined length, at undetermined cost, with undetermined consequences . . . I am not opposed to all wars. I'm opposed to dumb wars." Clinton, who had voted in Congress for the measure to

AP/Wide World

The 2004 Democratic National Convention in Boston helped make Barack Obama a rising star in his party. Senator John Kerry of Massachusetts, the party's presidential nominee, asked Obama to deliver the convention's keynote address. In this image from the speech, Obama discusses "the politics of hope." He was a candidate for the U.S. Senate at the time.

The race for the 2008 Democratic nomination was one of the closest in history. Obama's main rival, Senator Hillary Rodham Clinton of New York, joined him onstage before a debate.

authorize the war, claimed she had the greater experience to handle international crises.

Controversies. Media coverage of the nominating campaign often centered on verbal blunders and other controversial remarks by the candidates or their associates. Sermons by Obama's pastor, Jeremiah A. Wright, Jr., drew heavy media attention. Wright had accused the U.S. government of creating HIV, the virus that causes AIDS, to harm African Americans. Wright also said that U.S. foreign policy was partly responsible for the terrorist attacks of Sept. 11, 2001. Obama distanced himself from his pastor's remarks, concerned that such accusations would undermine his message of racial unity. Obama left the church in May 2008.

Some of Obama's opponents tried to take advantage

of public fears regarding terrorism and Muslim extremist groups hostile to the United States. They spread rumors that Obama was a Muslim and often mentioned his Muslim-sounding middle name Hussein. Opponents also questioned Obama's patriotism, noting that he had been critical of some U.S. foreign policy.

Race in the United States. On March 18, in a Philadelphia speech, Obama responded to the issue of race in the campaign, in part inspired by the heated reaction to his pastor's remarks. Obama spoke of his unusual racial identity and discussed such issues as white resentment of affirmative action programs and the continued legacy of discrimination against blacks. He asked Americans for their help to put aside such resentments and to focus instead on shared goals, such as better health care and economic and educational opportunities.

Securing the nomination. The contest between Obama and Clinton intensified on February 5—a day known as "Super Tuesday" because almost half the states held nominating contests. Obama and Clinton ended the day nearly tied in the race for delegates to the national convention. In other February contests, however, Obama gained victories in a number of states. Some of the victories came in caucus states where Clinton had chosen not to seriously compete.

In early June, after the last primaries in South Dakota and Montana, Obama gained enough delegates to secure the Democratic nomination. He reached the necessary total with the help of so-called *superdelegates*—Democratic party leaders and officials who can vote for a candidate regardless of the results of their state's primary election or caucus. Political observers described the tight Clinton-Obama race as the longest and most expensive nominating contest in the history of the United States. Each candidate raised hundreds of millions of dollars, setting fund-raising records.

The 2008 election

In August, at the Democratic National Convention in Denver, Obama formally became the party's presidential nominee. At Obama's request, the delegates nominated Senator Joe Biden of Delaware as their candidate for vice president. Obama and Biden faced the Republican nominees McCain and Alaska Governor Sarah Palin.

During the general election campaign, Obama and

At the 2008 Democratic National Convention in Denver, Obama and U.S. Senator Joe Biden of Delaware thank the audience after accepting the Democratic nomination for president and vice president.

© Jim Bourg, AFP/Getty Images

Three televised debates between Obama and his Republican opponent, Senator John McCain of Arizona, *left,* were key events leading up to the 2008 election. This picture shows the first debate, at the University of Mississippi in Oxford.

McCain worked to rally their political bases while reaching out to independent voters. Obama and other Democrats attempted to link McCain with President Bush, whose approval ratings were at record lows. They highlighted McCain's similarities to Bush on such issues as taxes and the Iraq War. Meanwhile, Obama's opponents argued that his policies, especially with regard to taxation and government spending, were too liberal.

Following the conventions, public opinion polls indicated that McCain's choice of Palin had energized the Republicans' conservative base. However, in television interviews, she stumbled over a number of questions. Many Americans began to question Palin's qualifications to be "a heartbeat away" from the presidency.

Major issues during the campaign included energy policy, world affairs, and the economy. Both candidates pledged to reduce U.S. dependence on foreign oil, but they differed on how to achieve such a goal. The candidates contrasted in their views on the Iraq War and negotiating with hostile nations. Obama favored a timetable for withdrawing from Iraq and said the United States should not be afraid to negotiate with its enemies. McCain opposed a timetable and said that negotiations could hurt U.S. interests by legitimizing enemy regimes.

During the summer and fall, many U.S. financial firms suffered huge losses, largely related to risky mortgages called *subprime mortgages.* The economy slumped badly. In October, Congress passed legislation that provided up to $700 billion for the government to purchase bad debts from troubled lenders. Most political experts said the troubled economy helped Obama and the Democrats win the election.

One of the greatest contrasts between Obama and McCain was the 25-year age gap separating them. In polls, many voters expressed concerns about McCain's age. At 72 years old, he would have been the oldest president inaugurated for a first term. Obama, born during the "baby boom" generation from 1946 to 1964, presented himself as a more youthful candidate and an agent of change in national government. His campaign used the effective slogan "Change We Can Believe In."

In the November election, Obama defeated McCain. Obama became the nation's 44th president. Obama received about 53 percent of the vote, compared with about 46 percent for McCain.

Obama's administration

On Jan. 20, 2009, Obama was sworn in as president. In his inaugural address, Obama struck a sober tone in listing the challenges the nation faced, including a troubled economy, political gridlock, and overseas conflicts. "Our challenges may be new," he said. "The instruments with which we meet them may be new. But those values upon which our success depends—hard work and honesty, courage and fair play, tolerance and curiosity, loyalty and patriotism—these things are old."

Domestic issues. In February, Obama signed a $787-billion economic stimulus bill that was meant to shore up an economy reeling from high unemployment and slumping financial markets. The law, called the American Recovery and Reinvestment Act, included investments in education, energy, science, and transportation projects. The act also included tax cuts and extended unemployment benefits. Obama said he hoped the measures would create or save millions of jobs.

Later in February, in his first formal address to Congress, Obama discussed the state of the nation's economy. He spoke about his hopes for the economic stimulus package and laid out goals in the areas of education, energy, and health care. He said, "Now is the time to act boldly and wisely, to not only revive this economy, but to build a new foundation for lasting prosperity."

In April, political observers noted Obama's accomplishments after his first 100 days in office. The economic crisis remained his main challenge. In addition to the massive stimulus bill, Obama's response included measures to shore up the financial industry and to bail out troubled automakers. He promised a major push to overhaul the nation's education and health care systems. He lifted restrictions on the federal funding of stem-cell research, and signed legislation making it easier for women to sue their employers for job discrimination.

Obama's opponents, including Republicans in Congress and commentators on conservative radio and television programs, criticized his policies, often calling his expansion of government spending "socialist." On April 15, Tax Day in the United States, groups of conservatives held symbolic "Tea Parties" to express their discontent with the government bailouts of the finance industry and their opposition to Obama's programs in general.

Obama's election

Place of nominating convention	Denver
Ballot on which nominated	1st
Republican opponent	John McCain
Electoral vote	365 (Obama) to 173 (McCain)*
Popular vote	69,456,897 (Obama) 59,934,814 (McCain)
Age at inauguration	47

*For votes by states, see **Electoral College** (table).

In May, Obama nominated federal appeals judge Sonia Sotomayor to the Supreme Court of the United States. The Senate confirmed the nomination in August. Sotomayor became the first Hispanic American on the court. She replaced Justice David Souter, who retired.

During the summer of 2009, administration officials noted improvements in the housing and manufacturing sectors of the economy. They said such signs indicated the stimulus plan was working. But by October, the nation's unemployment rate had climbed to over 10 percent, the highest since 1983.

Health care bills in Congress caused heated debate in 2009. In September, Obama outlined his proposals on health care reform before a joint session of Congress. Obama's plan would make it mandatory for Americans to have health insurance and require employers to either provide coverage or help employees cover the costs of health care. He also supported a *public option*—that is, a nonprofit insurance plan set up by the government—saying it would force private insurance companies to lower costs. Republicans overwhelmingly opposed a public option, saying it would drive many private insurers out of business.

In his January 2010 State of the Union address, Obama asked lawmakers to put political differences aside and pursue goals shared by both parties. He said that common-sense reforms to the financial and health care industries were needed for the nation to create *sustain-*

Vice president and Cabinet

Vice president	*Joe Biden
Secretary of state	*Hillary Rodham Clinton
Secretary of the treasury	Timothy F. Geithner
Secretary of defense	Robert M. Gates (2006)
	Leon E. Panetta (2011)
Attorney general	*Eric H. Holder, Jr.
Secretary of the interior	Kenneth L. Salazar
Secretary of agriculture	Tom Vilsack
Secretary of commerce	Gary Locke
	John Bryson (2011)
Secretary of labor	Hilda Solis
Secretary of health and human services	Kathleen Sebelius
Secretary of housing and urban development	Shaun Donovan
Secretary of transportation	Ray LaHood
Secretary of energy	Steven Chu
Secretary of education	Arne Duncan
Secretary of veterans affairs	Eric K. Shinseki
Secretary of homeland security	Janet Napolitano

*Has a separate biography in *World Book*.

able (lasting) economic growth. He said that the 2009 stimulus bill had saved millions of jobs and called for Congress to pass a bill that gave tax credits to companies that create jobs in the United States. He also pledged to extend tax cuts for the middle class and end tax breaks for oil companies and people making more than $250,000 a year.

In March 2010, Obama signed a historic health insurance reform bill that extends coverage to about 30 million uninsured Americans. The Patient Protection and Affordable Care Act expands Medicaid coverage; provides a tax credit to help small businesses with health care costs; and prevents insurers from dropping coverage for patients with preexisting medical conditions. It creates a system of *health insurance exchanges* in which insurance providers offer a variety of plans for uninsured and self-employed people to purchase. The law also contains cost-cutting measures intended to decrease long-term expenditures on health care.

Provisions of the health insurance reform law were to take effect at various times between 2010 and 2020. The plan is funded by increased taxes on investment income and high-end medical insurance plans. No Republicans in Congress supported the bill.

In April 2010, an explosion on an offshore oil rig killed 11 people and caused about 200 million gallons (760 million liters) of oil from an underwater well to pour into the Gulf of Mexico, 50 miles (80 kilometers) off Louisiana. For nearly three months, the U.S. Coast Guard and BP, the well's principal operator, worked to stop the flow of oil. BP engineers capped the well in July and permanently sealed it in September. Officials called the spill one of the worst environmental disasters in U.S. history.

In May 2010, Obama nominated U.S. Solicitor General Elena Kagan to replace retiring Justice John Paul Stevens on the Supreme Court of the United States. Kagan was confirmed in August.

Obama signed a sweeping financial reform bill into law in July. The Dodd-Frank Wall Street Reform and Consumer Protection Act sought to bring openness to complex financial transactions and end taxpayer-funded bailouts of large financial institutions. It also created a new consumer protection agency to regulate financial services.

In the summer of 2010, administration officials pointed to reports that said earlier stimulus plans had saved or created millions of jobs. The nation's unemployment rate remained high, however, at about 9.5 percent. Economists worried that other economic indicators, such as declining home sales, showed that the economic recovery was a fragile one.

In November 2010, voter frustration with the slow pace of the economic recovery contributed to a Republican take-over of the House of Representatives. Obama, who called the Democrats' election experience a "shellacking," vowed to work with Republicans on economic issues. But he pledged to block any efforts to overturn the landmark health insurance reform law. Later in November, a children's book Obama wrote was published. *Of Thee I Sing: A Letter to My Daughters* (2010) tells about the inspiring lives of 13 important Americans.

In military matters, Obama promised to work with Congress and military leaders to end the "don't ask don't tell" policy. The policy barred openly gay soldiers from

President Obama's national security team met at the White House in May 2011 to monitor the raid that killed terrorist leader Osama bin Laden. The team included Vice President Joe Biden and Obama, *seated at left;* and Secretary of State Hillary Clinton, *seated at right.*

serving in the armed forces. In December, Congress passed, and Obama signed, a law ending "don't ask don't tell." Many observers called the law's passage a major civil rights achievement. A number of conservative lawmakers, however, expressed concern that the change could disrupt combat operations in Afghanistan.

Also in December, Obama signed a bill that represented a tax compromise with Republicans. The bill extended tax cuts—including those for the wealthiest Americans—passed during the administration of President George W. Bush. The bill also extended unemployment benefits and cut payroll taxes. Payroll taxes are the taxes workers contribute to the Social Security system.

In 2011, Obama and leaders of both parties in Congress battled over whether to increase the nation's debt limit. The debt limit is the amount the U.S. Department of the Treasury is allowed to borrow to meet government expenses. Republicans in Congress had insisted an increase in the debt limit be paired with deep cuts in government spending. Many Democrats had called for spending cuts to be offset by increasing tax revenues.

In August 2011, both houses of Congress passed, and Obama signed, a bill that largely followed the Republican plan. The bill also created a joint congressional committee to recommend measures to further reduce federal budget deficits. Economic experts had warned that a failure to extend the nation's borrowing authority would harm the already struggling economy. Jobless rates remained high—more than 9 percent—during 2011.

In September 2011, Obama proposed a $447-billion job creation plan to stimulate the economy. The plan included tax cuts, spending on roads and schools, and aid to states to preserve the jobs of teachers. Obama said he would fund the plan by increasing taxes on the wealthiest Americans and by eliminating tax loopholes for the oil and gas industry. The proposal faced significant opposition in Congress.

Foreign affairs. Soon after Obama took office in 2009, he addressed a number of diplomatic and military issues facing the United States. Obama eased restrictions on family travel to Cuba and *remittances* (money sent) to the island nation.

In a major speech in Cairo, Egypt, in June 2009, Oba-

ma sought to repair the troubled relationship that the United States had with the Muslim world. Obama also criticized North Korea for conducting nuclear weapons and missile tests during the spring of 2009.

Obama stated that all U.S. combat operations in Iraq would cease by Aug. 31, 2010. In accordance with a U.S.-Iraq security agreement, United States combat troops withdrew from the country's cities by June 30. United States and other coalition forces continued to provide air support and other assistance to Iraqi forces from bases outside of cities. By the end of August 2010, all U.S. combat troops had left Iraq. About 50,000 soldiers remained in the country to combat terrorism, provide security, and train Iraqi troops.

In Afghanistan, about 20,000 U.S. troops were sent during the spring and summer of 2009 in an effort to provide stability and push back the Taliban forces. The Taliban are a militant Islamic group allied with al-Qa'ida, the terrorist organization responsible for the attacks of Sept. 11, 2001 (see **September 11 terrorist attacks**).

By the summer of 2010, Obama had added nearly 100,000 U.S. troops to the number in Afghanistan. For the first time since 2003, more soldiers were stationed in Afghanistan than in Iraq. Also in 2010, Obama declared plans to send 1,200 additional National Guard troops to increase security along the border with Mexico.

In 2011, violent protests in Libya led to an open, armed rebellion against the regime of Mu'ammar al-Qadhafi. The protesters called for Qadhafi's resignation, but he refused to step down. In March, Libyan warplanes attacked rebel strongholds in several cities.

The United Nations (UN) Security Council voted to authorize a no-fly zone for Libyan warplanes over Libya. It also passed a resolution calling for "all necessary measures" to protect Libyan civilians. The United States joined an international force to help protect the Libyan people. Air strikes led by United States, French, and British warplanes then hit Libyan government positions. In a nationally televised speech, Obama said the military intervention was necessary to prevent a massacre in Libya. As fighting continued, the North Atlantic Treaty Organization (NATO) took over the military operations aimed at protecting civilians. By August, rebel forces controlled most of Libya, including Tripoli, the capital. Qadhāfī went into hiding. In October, Qadhāfī was killed in his hometown of Surt (also spelled Sirte).

On the night of May 1, 2011, President Obama had announced on national television that the terrorist leader Osama bin Laden had been killed. Bin Laden, the leader of the al-Qaʾida terrorist network, had evaded capture since the 1990's. In late April 2011, Obama approved an operation to kill bin Laden at the terrorist leader's compound in Abbottabad, in northern Pakistan. Early on the morning of May 2 (May 1 in the United States), a team of Navy SEALs shot and killed bin Laden in a nighttime helicopter raid on the compound. Obama called the death of bin Laden "the most significant achievement to date" in the effort to defeat al-Qaʾida.

In August 2011, Obama joined a number of European leaders in calling for Syrian President Bashar al-Assad to step down from power. Beginning in March, Bashar's regime had violently cracked down on antigovernment protesters. Hundreds were killed. Obama also issued an executive order tightening economic sanctions on Syria's state-owned energy industries.   Yanek Mieczkowski

See also **Democratic Party; McCain, John; Obama, Michelle Robinson; President of the United States.**

Obama, *oh BAH muh,* **Michelle Robinson** (1964–   ), an American lawyer, is the wife of Barack Obama, who was elected president of the United States in 2008. She became first lady of the United States after her husband's inauguration in January 2009. She is the first African American to become first lady.

Michelle Obama was born Michelle LaVaughn Robinson on Jan. 17, 1964, in Chicago. Her father, Fraser, worked at the city's water department. Her mother, Marian, was a stay-at-home mother to Michelle and Michelle's older brother, Craig. Craig starred in basketball at Princeton University and later coached the sport at the college level. Michelle followed him to Princeton, majoring in sociology and graduating in 1985. She received a law degree from Harvard Law School in 1988.

© Ethan Miller, Getty Images
Michelle Obama

After graduating from law school, Michelle worked at a private law firm in Chicago. In 1989, she was assigned to mentor Barack Obama, who was working as a summer associate at the firm. The couple married on Oct. 3, 1992. They have two children: Malia, born in 1998, and Natasha, commonly called Sasha, born in 2001.

In 1991, Michelle Obama began working for the city of Chicago. In 1993, she helped start a Chicago office for a nonprofit group that encouraged young people to consider public service. She later became a director of community outreach efforts for the University of Chicago Medical Center.

Michelle Obama said that one of her priorities as first lady would be to speak out on issues that affect military families. The first lady also worked to combat childhood obesity.   Yanek Mieczkowski

Obelisk, *AHB uh lihsk,* is a great, upright, four-sided stone pillar. The sides slope slightly so that the top is smaller than the base. The top is shaped like a pyramid and ends in a point. The Washington Monument in Washington, D.C., is a good example of an obelisk.

Ancient Egyptians erected huge obelisks that were cut from single blocks of granite. Most obelisks had inscriptions in *hieroglyphics* (picture writing). They were often erected in pairs at entrances to temples. Two obelisks, now known as Cleopatra's Needles, were originally at Heliopolis, Egypt. In the 1800's, one was taken to New York City and the other to London (see **Cleopatra's Needles**). An obelisk from Luxor, Egypt, is now in Paris.

Obelisks were cut right at the quarry. The ancient Egyptians first made a horizontal, three-sided form by cutting deep trenches all around it. Then they split away the fourth side either by inserting copper or wooden wedges, or by pounding through the underside with balls of diorite, a hard rock. Finally, they polished the obelisk. Still unexplained is how they raised the huge stone pillar to an upright position at its final site. Some scientists think the Egyptians might have begun by hauling the obelisk up a gravel and stone ramp to the edge of a pit filled with sand. The obelisk was lowered into the pit by slowly removing the sand while crews pulled on ropes to guide it into place.   Leonard H. Lesko

See also **Paris** (Gardens, squares, and parks; picture).

Obesity, *oh BEE suh tee,* is the condition of having an excessive amount of body fat. Obesity increases a person's risk for many conditions and diseases, including diabetes, heart disease, *hypertension* (high blood pressure), arthritis, and cancer. Physicians typically use a simple, inexpensively obtained measurement called the *body mass index* (BMI) to determine whether a person is overweight or obese. The body mass index represents the proportion between a person's weight and height.

You can calculate your BMI by dividing your weight in kilograms by the square of your height in meters. For example, a woman weighing 130 pounds (59 kilograms) who is 5 feet 4 inches (1.6 meters) tall has a BMI of about 23—that is, 59 divided by 2.56 (or 1.6^2). Another way to calculate your BMI is to multiply your weight in pounds by 703 and then divide that figure by the square of your height in inches. In adults, a BMI of 25 to 29.9 indicates that the individual is overweight, and a BMI of 30 and above indicates obesity.

In children, the normal range of BMI varies with age and differs between boys and girls. Physicians do not have a standard definition of obesity for children. Physicians often use the terms *obese* and *overweight* interchangeably. To determine if a child is overweight, physicians use growth charts that compare BMI with age, called *BMI-for-age* charts. They use separate BMI-for-age charts for boys and girls. A physician locates a child's BMI on the appropriate chart and then compares it to statistical rankings called *percentiles,* which are shown as curved lines. Physicians consider a child overweight if the BMI-for-age is equal to or greater than the 95th percentile. A ranking in the 95th percentile means that the child's BMI is higher than that of 95 percent of other boys or girls at the same age. A BMI in the 85th to 95th percentile indicates a risk of becoming overweight.

Rates of obesity vary widely throughout the world. People in industrialized countries tend to be heavier

Height (in)	Underweight	Normal weight	Overweight	Obese	Very obese																		
60	23	25	27	29	31	33	35	37	39	41	43	45	47	49	51	53	55	57	59	63	66	70	74	78
62	22	24	26	27	29	31	33	35	37	38	40	42	44	46	48	49	51	53	55	59	62	66	70	73
64	21	22	24	26	28	29	31	33	34	36	38	40	41	43	45	46	48	50	52	55	58	62	65	68
66	19	21	23	24	26	27	29	31	32	34	36	37	39	40	42	44	45	47	49	52	55	58	61	65
68	16	20	21	23	24	26	27	29	30	32	34	35	37	38	40	41	43	44	46	48	52	55	58	61
70	17	19	20	22	23	24	26	27	28	30	32	33	35	36	37	38	40	42	43	46	48	52	55	57
72	16	18	19	20	22	23	24	26	27	29	30	31	33	34	35	37	38	39	41	43	46	49	52	54
74	15	17	18	19	21	22	23	24	26	27	28	30	31	32	33	35	36	37	39	41	44	48	49	51
76	15	16	17	18	20	21	22	23	24	26	27	28	29	30	32	33	34	35	37	40	41	44	48	49
Weight (lb)	120	130	140	150	160	170	180	190	200	210	220	230	240	250	260	270	280	290	300	320	340	360	380	400

WORLD BOOK chart

Physicians use a measurement called body mass index (BMI) to determine whether a person is overweight or obese. The BMI represents the proportion between a person's weight and height. To find your BMI on this chart, locate your weight in pounds along the bottom and your height in inches along the left. The number where these two values intersect is your BMI.

than people who live in less developed countries. The rate of obesity is rising in many countries. In the early 2000's, the Centers for Disease Control and Prevention (CDC) estimated that about one-third of adults and about one-sixth of children and adolescents in the United States were obese.

Causes of obesity

Obesity results from an energy imbalance in which a person consumes more calories in food and drink than he or she *burns* (uses as energy) over time. Genetic and environmental factors influence how much a person eats and how many calories the person burns. In some cases, obesity may result from specific diseases, such as *Prader-Willi syndrome,* a condition that includes an uncontrollable urge to eat. Hormone imbalances or medications may also cause obesity. However, these causes account for relatively few cases of obesity and are not related to the increase in obesity occurring in the United States and many other countries. Medical experts link the overall rise in obesity to changing lifestyles.

A person's genetic makeup helps determine the person's body size, build, and *metabolism,* the ability of the body to convert food into energy and living tissue. But personal choices about food and beverage consumption and physical activity can affect a person's weight. Medical experts know that some behaviors and habits are associated with higher rates of overweight and obesity. These include eating fatty foods, not getting enough fruits and vegetables, skipping breakfast, frequently eating at fast-food restaurants, eating meals with large portion sizes, and maintaining a *sedentary* (inactive) lifestyle.

Physical inactivity has become an important cause of obesity. Much of this inactivity results from a modern lifestyle. Many people in industrialized countries work sedentary jobs, which involve sitting or standing still for long periods. People in these countries also tend to engage in social and leisure activities that burn few calories. Such activities include watching television, playing video games, using computers, and traveling by automobile instead of walking or bicycling.

Individual decisions concerning diet and exercise generally determine whether a person will become obese or not. However, societal and environmental factors can significantly influence a person's decisions and thus can contribute to obesity. In the United States and other developed areas, widespread fast-food restaurants and convenience stores typically offer high-calorie meals and snacks. Food portions of meals served at restaurants often exceed the nutritional amounts recommended for maintaining a healthy weight. Commercial advertisements for foods typically focus on convenient foods that are high in fat, sugar, and calories, influencing eating habits. Suburban communities in the United States frequently lack sidewalks, making trips by automobile more convenient and safer than walking or riding a bicycle. In addition, many inner-city areas lack parks, playgrounds, and other facilities for physical activity and exercise.

Consequences of obesity

Obesity *impairs* (weakens) the function of many organ systems in the body, such as the circulatory system. The risk of serious medical conditions increases with higher BMI values. Obesity-related health problems include Type 2 diabetes, heart disease, hypertension, high blood cholesterol, back and joint problems, *sleep apnea* (a condition in which breathing passages are repeatedly blocked during sleep), and certain cancers. In addition, obesity reduces quality of life, complicates recovery from surgery, and contributes to premature death from other causes.

Obesity and obesity-related health problems increase health care costs for individuals and communities. Medical costs associated with obesity include direct and indirect costs. Direct medical costs result from the diagnosis and treatment of obesity and related complications. Indirect costs include the value of income lost because of decreased productivity, restricted activity, and more frequent absences, all of which are associated with obesity. Indirect costs also include the value of future income lost by premature death. Medical experts have suggested that the health care costs related to obesity in the United States are comparable to those associated with smoking.

Social researchers have found that obese people often experience higher-than-normal rates of discrimination and social isolation. For children, the emotional and social consequences of obesity can include low self-esteem, negative body image, depression, exposure to teasing and discrimination, and social isolation.

Prevention of obesity

Scientists are discovering that tastes, eating habits, and attitudes about diet are established at a young age and often persist throughout a person's lifetime. In addition, scientists have found that children who are overweight have a much higher risk of being overweight as adults. Many scientists have therefore concluded that the most effective way to prevent obesity is to prevent unhealthy weight gain beginning in childhood.

Successful prevention programs involve promoting a balanced, nutritious diet and encouraging physical activity for all children, not just those perceived to be overweight. Health experts also emphasize the importance of helping children develop healthy attitudes toward food. They advise encouraging children to learn to recognize internal signals that indicate *satiety* (fullness) during meals. Parents and caregivers can help by setting a healthy example in their food choices and other eating behavior.

To assist in the development of a healthy lifestyle, the United States Department of Agriculture (USDA) issued a new food guide system in 2011 called MyPlate. The guide outlines dietary recommendations for each food group that can help prevent obesity. The program encourages people to eat more fruits, vegetables, whole grains, lean meats, and fat-free or low-fat milk and milk products. It also emphasizes that a healthful diet should be low in saturated fats, trans fats, cholesterol, salt, and added sugars.

The *Dietary Guidelines for Americans,* published by the United States Department of Health and Human Services (HHS) and the USDA, recommends that children and teenagers engage in at least 60 minutes of exercise or other physical activity each day. They also suggest that children be as active as possible. Adults should aim for at least 30 minutes of activity daily and should take part in moderate or vigorous activity, such as running or bicycling, three or more times a week.

Public health experts point out that communities can make changes to promote healthy lifestyles and help prevent obesity. For example, communities can encourage people to increase their physical activity by constructing parks, playgrounds, and bike paths. Schools can improve the availability of nutritious foods and beverages, promote nutrition education classes, and offer quality physical education.

Treatment of obesity

Treatments for obesity involve first losing the excess weight. Guidelines published by the United States National Institutes of Health (NIH) recommend weight loss for overweight individuals who have two or more risk factors associated with weight. These risk factors include hypertension, diabetes, and arthritis. Other health care organizations recommend weight loss for all overweight individuals.

Specific weight loss goals and methods differ for each individual. For obese adults, treatment should begin with a thorough clinical assessment by a physician. The physician can help develop a behavior modification plan tailored to the individual to promote weight loss. In some cases, drugs and surgery can help in the treatment of obesity. However, medical experts recommend discussing these methods with a physician to explore the risks and advantages.

An important challenge in treating obesity is to prevent excessive weight gain from occurring again in the future. Obesity is a chronic condition. Successful treatment often requires long-term, structured therapy. Support from physicians, caregivers, family, and friends and the appropriate use of medical treatments can increase a person's chances for lasting success in maintaining a healthy weight.

Changes in behavior. Medical experts often advise a person who aims to maintain or lose weight to review personal habits and behaviors to determine what improvements can be made. Physicians recommend that anyone beginning a weight-loss program start slowly and set reasonable goals. Initial changes can be as simple as switching from whole milk to low-fat milk or increasing the distance walked each day. A healthy and effective program aims for slow weight loss through a reduction in dietary fat and an increase in physical activity. Researchers have found that such a program can help ensure successful weight loss and long-term weight maintenance.

Surgery. Some severely obese people require a surgical operation to reduce the size of their stomach or the length of their small intestine. This surgery, called *bariatric surgery,* has become increasingly common for obese people who cannot lose weight by traditional means or for people who suffer from serious health problems related to obesity. The operation promotes weight loss by restricting food intake or by interrupting the digestive process so that the body cannot absorb many of the calories from food.

Several different types of bariatric surgery exist. Each type of surgery involves some risks and requires patients to make lifelong changes to their diet and lifestyle. A patient should only undergo bariatric surgery after consulting with a physician and carefully evaluating the long-term risks and benefits of the operation.

Treatment for children. Unless serious health concerns are involved, physicians typically recommend weight maintenance for overweight children rather than weight loss. Medical experts worry that restricting calories to promote weight loss might result in a child consuming inadequate nutrients to sustain healthy growth. Parents and children can work together to identify possible contributors to weight gain and then develop simple weight-maintenance goals. By keeping a steady weight, a child can often outgrow overweight.

Bariatric surgery is sometimes considered as a treatment option for adolescents who are severely overweight. However, physicians have many concerns about the long-term effects of the surgery on adolescents, who are still developing physically and mentally. Physicians recommend that bariatric surgery be considered only when adolescents are *severely obese* (a BMI of greater than or equal to 40), have reached their adult height, and have serious weight-related health problems. In addition, they advise that adolescent patients and their parents be evaluated to ensure they are emotionally prepared for the surgery and the lifestyle changes that it requires.

Effects of weight loss. Weight loss in obese people improves or eliminates obesity-related medical conditions and may also improve quality of life. Many of the results relate directly to the amount of weight lost. Obese people therefore do not have to become lean to benefit from weight loss. Beneficial health effects result from modest weight losses and increase with greater weight loss. Loss of as little as 10 percent of total body weight can produce significant health benefits in an obese person, even if the person remains obese.

Elena Serrano

See also **Bariatric surgery; Binge eating; Nutrition** (Nutrition guidelines); **Weight control.**

Oboe is the smallest and highest-pitched of the double-reed woodwinds. The name comes from two French words: *haut,* meaning *high,* and *bois,* meaning *wood.*

WORLD BOOK illustration by Oxford Illustrators Limited

Keys

Tone holes

Northwestern University (WORLD BOOK photo by Ted Nielsen)

Bell

The oboe is a high-pitched woodwind instrument. It is played by blowing gently through the mouthpiece and opening and closing the tone holes with the fingers.

The oboe is approximately 21 inches (53 centimeters) long. It was developed in the 1600's, probably by two French musicians, Jean Hotteterre and André Philidor. Its range is almost three octaves. The tone is produced by means of a small double reed. Predecessors of the oboe, called *shawms,* had a raucous, penetrating sound. However, today the oboe is known for its smooth and beautiful tone.

The oboe is important in symphony orchestras, concert bands, and small ensembles. Composers who wrote works for the oboe include Ludwig van Beethoven of Germany and Wolfgang Amadeus Mozart of Austria. The English horn is an alto oboe, a fifth lower in pitch than the oboe.   André P. Larson

See also **English horn; Music** (Wind instruments).

Obregón, *OH bray GAWN,* **Álvaro,** *AHL vah roh* (1880-1928), was president of Mexico from 1920 to 1924. He succeeded Venustiano Carranza as president, after Carranza was killed in a revolt led by Obregón. As president, Obregón distributed some land among the peasants, built many schools, and supported a strong labor union movement. He was reelected president in 1928 but was assassinated on July 17, 1928, before he could take office.

Obregón was born on Feb. 19, 1880, in the municipal district of Navojoa in Sonora. In 1912, he raised a force of Yaqui Indians and defended President Francisco Madero during a revolution against the government. In 1913, Victoriano Huerta seized the presidency, and Madero was murdered. That same year, Obregón joined Venustiano Carranza in a revolt against Huerta and, in 1914, fought Pancho Villa to help Carranza become acting chief of Mexico. Obregón later opposed Carranza after Carranza refused to support his efforts to become president.   W. Dirk Raat

See also **Carranza, Venustiano; Mexico** (Reforms of the early 1900's); **Villa, Pancho** (with picture).

O'Brien, Robert C. (1918-1973), was the pen name of Robert Leslie Conly, an American author of children's books. O'Brien won the 1972 Newbery Medal for *Mrs. Frisby and the Rats of NIMH* (1971). This novel tells about a widowed mouse who willingly faces many dangers to save her invalid son. She receives aid from superintelligent rats who have escaped from a laboratory at the National Institute of Mental Health (NIMH).

O'Brien was born on Jan. 11, 1918, in New York City. His first children's book was *The Silver Crown* (1968). His last book, *Z for Zachariah,* a mystery story for young readers, was published in 1974, after his death. O'Brien died on March 5, 1973.   Nancy Lyman Huse

Obscenity and pornography are terms used to designate written, recorded, or pictorial material—including motion pictures—that many people consider indecent and thus find offensive. The term *obscenity* can also refer to any language or behavior believed to corrupt public morals. The term *pornography* refers chiefly to written or sexually explicit pictorial material intended primarily to cause sexual stimulation. Some people use the term to refer to written or pictorial material that glorifies violence against women or degrades women. In many cases, however, the terms *obscenity* and *pornography* are used interchangeably.

In the United States, most states and cities have laws against publishing, distributing, or selling obscene materials. There are also federal laws against the interstate sale and distribution of such material and against the presentation of obscene material on radio or television. But these laws have been hard to enforce, in part because it is difficult to determine what is obscene according to the law.

The nature of obscenity and pornography and the laws governing them have been a continuing source of controversy. Some people believe that the distribution of pornographic material corrupts public morality. Others focus on the extent to which some printed or photographic material portrays violence against women—and the degradation of women—as appropriate behavior. From this perspective, the problem is not in the portrayal of sex, but in the portrayal of women as existing for the sexual satisfaction of men. Others believe existing antiobscenity laws and proposed antipornography laws violate the rights of free speech and press guaranteed by the First Amendment to the U.S. Constitution.

Congress passed the first federal law against obscenity as part of the Tariff Act of 1842. This law made it illegal to bring what it called "indecent and obscene" material into the country. The Comstock Law, passed in 1873, prohibited the mailing of indecent materials.

In 1957, in the case of *Roth v. the United States,* the Supreme Court ruled that freedom of speech and the press—as guaranteed by the First Amendment—restricted prosecution to only those materials that a court had determined to be legally obscene. But the Supreme Court provided only loose guidelines for the definition of legally obscene material.

In 1973, in the case of *Miller v. California,* the Supreme Court held that material could be considered legally obscene only if (1) the average person, applying contemporary community standards, would find that the material, taken as a whole, appeals to the *prurient* (sexually arousing) interest; (2) the material shows, in a clearly offensive way, sexual conduct specifically described in the applicable law; and (3) the material lacks serious literary, artistic, political, or scientific value, when evaluated in accordance with national standards. In 1974, in *Jenkins v. Georgia,* the Supreme Court unanimously determined that local standards play a very limited role in the determination of what is to be considered obscene. Today, as a result of *Jenkins v. Georgia, Miller v. California,* and other cases, obscenity prosecutions are rare.

A national Commission on Obscenity and Pornography reported in 1970 that it found no reliable evidence that pornography caused crime among adults or delinquency among young people. The commission recommended repeal of all laws prohibiting the sale of pornography to consenting adults. But it also recommended that each state adopt laws against the sale of obscene pictorial material to young people. In 1986, however, the Attorney General's Commission on Pornography determined that a relationship existed between sexually violent or degrading materials and the amount of sexual violence in society. It also recommended increased prosecution of cases dealing with *child pornography*—that is, pornographic materials that involve photographs of children.

In other countries. Many nations have antiobscenity laws. In some, including Ireland and Italy, such laws are strictly enforced. In Canada, antiobscenity groups have fought for years for stricter laws and stricter enforcement. Many members of these groups seek recognition of the harm resulting from materials that endorse sexual violence against women. But some nations have repealed their obscenity laws. In the late 1960's, for example, Denmark dropped all legal barriers against pornography for adults.   Frederick Schauer

See also **Censorship; Comstock Law.**

Additional resources

Cothran, Helen, ed. *Pornography: Opposing Viewpoints.* 2nd ed. Greenhaven, 2001.

Harrison, Maureen, and Gilbert, Steve, eds. *Obscenity and Pornography Decisions of the United States Supreme Court.* Excellent Bks., 2000.

Mackey, Thomas C. *Pornography on Trial: A Handbook with Cases, Laws, and Documents.* ABC-CLIO, 2002.

Slade, Joseph W. *Pornography in America.* ABC-CLIO, 2000.

Observatory is a research institution where astronomers study planets, stars, galaxies, and other celestial objects. An observatory has at least one telescope or other kind of observation device. Most such devices are housed in structures built on the ground, but observation equipment is also used underground, in airplanes, and in satellites. Certain satellites that house telescopes are also known as observatories.

The term *observatory* can also refer to certain ancient structures that people probably used to keep track of important days of the year. One such structure, Stonehenge, in Wiltshire, England, consists of large stone slabs set in the ground. People may have used Stonehenge to determine, for example, when summer began. At the beginning of summer, the sun would rise above an imaginary line between a certain pair of slabs.

Observatories with telescopes

Where observatories are built. Earth's atmosphere influences the selection of sites for telescopes. Telescopes work with visible light and other forms of *electromagnetic radiation* sent out by objects in space. The radiation travels in waves, and the forms differ in *wavelength,* distance between successive wave crests. The forms of electromagnetic radiation are—from the shortest to the longest wavelength—gamma rays, X rays, ultraviolet rays, visible light, infrared rays, and radio waves.

The atmosphere blocks gamma rays and X rays as well as certain wavelengths of infrared and ultraviolet rays. Telescopes built to work with such radiation must therefore operate aboard satellites. The atmosphere also partially blocks other infrared and ultraviolet wavelengths. But telescopes on high mountains can detect some infrared and ultraviolet rays. Telescopes in aircraft that fly at high altitudes can observe more infrared wavelengths. To "see" the remaining infrared and ultraviolet wavelengths, a telescope must operate in space.

Visible light and radio waves pass readily through the atmosphere. So *optical* telescopes—those that detect visible light—and radio telescopes can be on the ground.

Ground-based observatories. Optical telescopes are built on mountaintops or high plains to avoid air pollution, illumination from city lights, and the distorting effect of the atmosphere. The distorting effect, which also causes the stars to twinkle, blurs images of stars and

Mauna Kea, on the island of Hawaii, has some of the largest optical telescopes in the world. The two spherical structures in the left center of this photo are the W. M. Keck Observatory of the United States. In the cylindrical building beside them is the Subaru telescope of Japan.

© Richard Wainscoat

other heavenly objects. A high-altitude location will also more likely offer a large percentage of clear nights because it is above low-lying clouds.

Radio telescopes must be shielded from radio waves that are used for communications. So some radio observatories are built in valleys so that the surrounding hills shield them. Others are on mountaintops or high plains.

One of the chief mountain sites is Mauna Kea, a volcano that rises 13,796 feet (4,205 meters) above sea level on the island of Hawaii. Major optical telescopes on Mauna Kea include Keck I and Keck II, operated by a partnership of the University of California and the California Institute of Technology (Caltech); and Subaru, operated by Japan's National Astronomical Observatory.

A radio telescope known as the Robert C. Byrd Green Bank Telescope (GBT) is in a valley in Green Bank, West Virginia. A group of 27 radio telescopes called the Very Large Array (VLA) stands on a high plain near Socorro, New Mexico. The National Radio Astronomy Observatory of the United States operates the GBT and the VLA.

Airborne observatories. From 1975 to 1995, the Gerard P. Kuiper Airborne Observatory (KAO) made observations at infrared wavelengths. The KAO was a modified C-141 cargo plane equipped with a telescope whose light-gathering mirror was 36 inches (91 centimeters) across. The craft flew at altitudes as high as 45,000 feet (13.7 kilometers). The National Aeronautics and Space Administration (NASA) of the United States operated the KAO.

Satellite observatories. The best-known satellite observatory is the Hubble Space Telescope, launched in 1990 to observe infrared, visible, and ultraviolet radiation. It was the first of NASA's four "Great Observatories" to go into orbit. The second was the Compton Gamma Ray Observatory, which circled Earth from 1991 to 2000. The third is the Chandra X-ray Observatory, launched in 1999. The last of the four, an infrared observatory called the Spitzer Space Telescope, was launched in 2003.

How observatories are operated. The staff of a ground-based, telescopic observatory consists of astronomers, engineers, technicians, telescope operators,

computer programmers, optics experts, and administrators. But astronomers who are not on the staff do most of the research.

Teams of astronomers share time on the major telescopes. Teams wishing to use a telescope must submit research proposals to a special committee. The committee approves certain proposals and divides up the time available on the telescope. In general, a team will have limited access—often only a few nights of use a year.

Large ground-based telescopes are so complex that a telescope operator is usually present at the observatory. However, an astronomer does not necessarily have to go to the observatory to use one of its telescopes—the astronomer can work via computer links. Computer-controlled light detectors mounted on the telescope convert the results of the observations to electric signals, so the data can be transferred over the links. Orbiting observatories are operated by radio commands sent from a control center on the ground.

Other kinds of observatories

Neutrino observatories detect subatomic particles called *neutrinos* that come from space. Neutrinos rarely interact with other kinds of matter, so a neutrino observatory must use a huge quantity of matter as a neutrino target. Neutrino observatories are built beneath Earth's surface because large numbers of other particles would interact with a target on the surface.

The target at the Sudbury Neutrino Observatory (SNO) in Greater Sudbury, Ontario, is 1,100 tons (1,000 metric tons) of *heavy water* held in an underground tank. Heavy water is slightly heavier than ordinary water because it contains *deuterium,* a hydrogen atom that weighs more than the ordinary hydrogen atom. SNO is operated by Sudbury Neutrino Observatory Institute, an organization with representatives from Canada, the United Kingdom, and the United States.

Gravitational observatories. Astronomers are building ground-based observatories to detect *gravitational waves.* According to the general theory of relativity announced by the German-born American physicist

Albert Einstein in 1915, gravity can travel in waves. However, such waves have not yet been directly detected.

To detect gravitational waves directly, the observatories will use objects that are large enough to be measurably affected by them. An observatory known as the Laser Interferometer Gravitational-Wave Observatory (LIGO) has three detectors—two in Hanford, Washington, and one in Livingston, Louisiana. Each detector uses two metal tubes, each 2 ½ miles (4 kilometers) long. When a wave passes through the tubes, it changes their lengths. Each detector has a laser system designed to sense the changes. Caltech and the Massachusetts Institute of Technology operate LIGO.   Kevin Krisciunas

Related articles in *World Book* include:

Arecibo Observatory	Jodrell Bank Observatory	Naval Observatory, United States
Astronomy	Keck Observatory	Neutrino
Black hole	Lick Observatory	Palomar Observatory
Electromagnetic waves	Mauna Kea	Satellite, Artificial
Gravitation	Mount Wilson Observatory	Southern African Large Telescope
Green Bank Telescope	National Optical Astronomy Observatories	Space exploration
Greenwich Observatory, Royal	National Radio Astronomy Observatory	Stonehenge Telescope
Hubble Space Telescope		Yerkes Observatory

Obsessive-compulsive disorder (OCD) is a common mental illness in which people feel burdened by unwanted thoughts or forced to repeat troublesome actions. Unwanted thoughts, called *obsessions*, often include unreasonable fear of dirt or germs. Another common obsession involves fear of losing control and hurting oneself or others. Many patients also feel a need to perform repeated actions, called *compulsions*, to prevent harmful events. Some wash their hands excessively to avoid infection. Unreasonable repetition of everyday routines—for example, checking that faucets or stoves are turned off—is also common.

Most people have certain routines and habits that they find comforting. For example, a person may like to get dressed or prepare for bed in a certain way. But most people can change their routines when the need arises. People with obsessive-compulsive disorder feel trapped and unable to change, even though they know that their obsessions and compulsions are unrealistic.

Many experts believe that obsessive-compulsive disorder involves an imbalance in *serotonin,* one of the brain's most important messenger chemicals. Doctors may treat the disorder with medicines that correct serotonin levels. People may also be helped by behavior therapy, which teaches patients ways to resist their unreasonable thoughts and actions.   Donald W. Black

See also **Hoarding; Mental illness** (Anxiety disorders); **Serotonin.**

Obsidian, *ahb SIHD ee uhn,* is a natural glass formed from lava flows that cooled quickly. Most obsidian has the same chemical composition as granite. But it cooled too quickly for the minerals to form crystals. The result is a smooth glass instead of granite. Most obsidian is black, or black with red bands. It is brittle. Indians used it to make tools, arrowheads, and knives. See also **Granite; Igneous rock.**   Mark A. Helper

Obstetrics and gynecology, *ahb STEHT rihks,* GY *nuh KAHL uh jee,* are branches of medicine that deal with women's health. *Obstetrics* is concerned with pregnancy, childbirth, and the six-week period following delivery. Doctors who practice obstetrics are called *obstetricians. Gynecology* deals with diseases of the female reproductive organs. Doctors who practice gynecology are called *gynecologists.*

During a woman's pregnancy, an obstetrician is responsible for the health of both the mother and the *fetus* (unborn child). The obstetrician must take special care to avoid harming the fetus when treating diseases in the mother. During childbirth, the obstetrician helps deliver the baby. Thereafter, the obstetrician examines the mother periodically to make sure she recovers from the changes that occurred in her body during pregnancy.

A gynecologist deals with disorders involving the uterus, the ovaries, the fallopian tubes, and other organs of the female reproductive system. Such disorders may be present at birth, or they may result from infections, tumors, injuries, or improper balances of *hormones* (body chemicals). The gynecologist may prescribe drugs, use radiation, or perform surgery to treat the patient.   Gretajo Northrop

See also **Childbirth; Infertility; Pregnancy.**

Ocarina, *AHK uh REE nuh,* is a small wind instrument of the whistle type. It is made of molded clay or plastic, and is shaped like an elongated egg or a sweet potato, which it is often called in the United States. It has a mouthpiece through which air is blown and 8 to 10 holes that sound a simple scale. Its tone is pleasant and soft. An Italian named Giuseppe Donati developed the standard Western ocarina in the 1860's, but forms of the ocarina were known in ancient China. Varieties of the ocarina are often used to play folk music.   André P. Larson

Claire Rydell

Ocarina

O'Casey, Sean, *shawn* (1880-1964), was perhaps the greatest Irish playwright of his time. O'Casey was born in the Dublin slums on March 30, 1880, and was largely self-educated. He gained fame when Dublin's Abbey Theatre staged three of his plays—*The Shadow of a Gunman* (1923), *Juno and the Paycock* (1924), and *The Plough and the Stars* (1926). Each play deals with the violence in Ireland from 1916 to 1924, during and after its fight for independence from England. O'Casey showed egotism, slogans, and abstract ideals, such as patriotism, as the enemies of life and happiness. The plays are full of colorful characters and speech and are written in a vivid, realistic style.

O'Casey left Ireland for England in 1926, after *The Plough and the Stars* provoked rioting during its opening week. Some of the audience thought the play slandered Ireland's patriots and womanhood. O'Casey broke with the Abbey Theatre in 1928 after it refused to stage his play *The Silver Tassie.* Like his earlier work, this play was antiwar in tone, and shows war as the destroyer of individuality and heroism. The play also developed Expressionistic tendencies found in O'Casey's earlier work.

Symbolism and Expressionism became more important in O'Casey's later plays.

Most of O'Casey's plays in the 1930's and early 1940's have revolutionary heroes and call for a radical transformation of society. The plays include *Purple Dust* (published in 1940) and *Red Roses for Me* (published in 1942).

O'Casey returned to Irish themes late in his career. He presented an Ireland that had exchanged British domination for domination by the Roman Catholic Church of Ireland and the new commercial class. Plays of this period include *Cock-a-Doodle Dandy* (1949), *The Bishop's Bonfire* (1955), and *The Drums of Father Ned* (completed in 1958). O'Casey's most important nondramatic work is an autobiography in fictional form. He died on Sept. 18, 1964.   Edward Hirsch

Occam, William of. See William of Ockham.

Occultism, *uh KUHL tihz uhm,* is a term that refers to a wide range of beliefs and practices involving magical, secret, or unseen forces. Occultism includes astrology, fortunetelling, magic, and *spiritualism*—the belief that spirits of the dead communicate with the living. People who believe in occultism consider it to be based on hidden knowledge that ordinary people do not have.

Some scientists reject all occult practices. Others believe in telepathy, extrasensory perception (ESP), and certain other powers, which they call *paranormal* (outside normal awareness). Opinion regarding some practices has changed through the years. Until the late 1800's, for example, most scientists considered hypnotism an occult practice. However, many scientists accept hypnosis today and use it in medicine and psychology.

Since the mid-1900's, there has been a widespread revival of occultism in the Western world, including Europe, where occultism dates back hundreds of years. Today, it is also common in isolated, nonindustrial societies throughout the world.   Sarah M. Pike

Related articles in *World Book* include:

Alchemy	Graphology	Psychical research
Astrology	Hypnosis	Spiritualism
Clairvoyance	Magic	Superstition
Divination	Numerology	Telepathy
Extrasensory perception	Ouija board	Witchcraft (Witchcraft as a religion)
Fortunetelling	Palmistry	
	Parapsychology	

Occupancy, *AHK yuh puhn see,* is a legal method by which a person or nation acquires title to something that no one else owns. It usually refers to taking possession of *real property* (land and anything built on that land) through a process known as *adverse possession.*

To gain title to real property by occupancy, a person or nation must take possession of the property with the intention of keeping it. Typically, the property must be occupied continually, openly, and exclusively for a specified period. A primary purpose of the law in allowing occupancy and adverse possession is to reward those who use land productively. For example, British settlers claimed Bermuda for Britain (now also called the United Kingdom) by occupancy in 1609. At that time, the islands had no other inhabitants.   Steven R. Probst

Occupation. See Careers.

Occupational disease. See Disease (Environmental and occupational diseases).

Occupational medicine is the branch of medicine that deals with diseases caused by hazards that people encounter on the job or at their workplace. Health care providers in this specialty may work independently, or for a hospital or clinic. Others may have jobs with a large company, providing care for its employees. Most specialists in occupational medicine treat workplace-related injuries and illnesses. They also focus on prevention and education for employers and employees, working to reduce or eliminate problems by modifying the work environment.

Two important tools of occupational medicine are *epidemiology* and *toxicology.* Epidemiology is the science of investigating the causes, distribution, and control of disease by studying groups of affected people. Toxicology is the study of poisonous materials and their effects on living things.

Health care providers in occupational medicine are always on the alert to identify diseases caused by chemicals or industrial processes. For example, one physician noticed that several workers with a rare type of liver cancer worked with vinyl chloride, a gas used to make plastic. Using epidemiologic techniques, he showed that the workers' exposure to vinyl chloride caused this cancer. Companies worldwide took steps to prevent the disease by reducing workers' exposure to the gas.

By using knowledge of toxicology, occupational medicine specialists try to predict the diseases that chemicals could cause. Then they tell companies that use the chemicals how to protect their employees. These employees undergo periodic testing to ensure that they are not getting sick from their exposure at work. Because the physicians identify the hazards, companies can take steps to prevent disease by reducing exposure and monitoring workers' health.

This focus on the health of both the individual and the group is a special feature of preventive medicine, the branch of medicine concerned with prevention of disease. This combined approach distinguishes an occupational medicine specialist from the other medical specialists. Specialists in occupational medicine can save lives by identifying the cause of a disease and then sharing their discovery.

Occupational medicine is a recognized specialty in many countries, and the demand for specialists is great. A health care worker who decides to specialize in occupational medicine receives advanced training in toxicology, epidemiology, statistical methods, and public health. The health care worker can then become certified by meeting the requirements of national authorities.   Rossana Segovia-Bain

See also Ergonomics; Repetitive strain injury.

Occupational Safety and Health Administration (OSHA) is an agency of the United States Department of Labor that promotes safe and healthful working conditions. OSHA's chief responsibility is the development and enforcement of job safety and health regulations. The agency also works to educate employers and employees about industrial hazards.

OSHA regulations deal with fire prevention, protective garments and railings, and many other safety matters. The rules also establish maximum levels of exposure to asbestos, lead, and other substances that could endanger the health of workers. OSHA inspectors check factories and other sites for violations, and employers who fail to make required changes are fined.

The agency encourages the states to develop their

own health and safety programs to replace OSHA itself. Many states have programs approved by the agency. The federal government pays half the cost of such programs.

OSHA was established by the Williams-Steiger Occupational Safety and Health Act of 1970 and began operating in 1971. Many leaders of both business and labor have criticized the agency's performance. Executives complain that OSHA demands too much paperwork and too many costly changes that do not increase safety. Labor leaders charge that the agency lags in developing new regulations and fails to enforce existing ones. To improve the agency's performance, OSHA began additional training programs for inspectors and planned more efficient procedures.   Harvey Glickman

See also **National Institute for Occupational Safety and Health.**

Occupational therapy is a form of treatment that uses everyday activities to help people with illnesses or disabilities recover, develop, or maintain practical skills. Doctors often recommend occupational therapy for patients with health problems that interfere with their ability to perform daily tasks at home, school, or work. For example, a person who uses a wheelchair may need to learn how to get around in the kitchen and prepare a meal from a sitting position. A person who has lost sight or the use of an arm or leg may need to learn new ways to bathe or dress. Occupational therapy is often called *curing by doing* because patients improve their own physical and mental well-being by carrying out activities themselves.

Professionals called *occupational therapists* plan and supervise treatment activities for their patients. *Occupational therapy assistants* work under the supervision of an occupational therapist and do much of the hands-on work with patients, helping them learn and practice

American Occupational Therapy Association, Inc.
Occupational therapy may involve the use of games or other physical activities that help disabled children strengthen their muscles and improve coordination.

skills. Occupational therapists and assistants work in such settings as hospitals, rehabilitation centers, mental health centers, schools, facilities for older adults, and day care centers. Many occupational therapists also provide treatment in people's homes.

How occupational therapy helps patients

An occupational therapist first needs to evaluate a patient's health problems, background, and interests. The therapist uses this information to plan an individual program that will meet each patient's needs and make the most of each patient's abilities.

Helping people with physical disabilities. People who have a serious illness or injury may lose strength and coordination. For example, a person with multiple sclerosis (MS) may become weak and have difficulty balancing because the disease damages the nerves that control muscles. An occupational therapist will help an MS patient learn activities that preserve strength and maintain the greatest possible range of useful activities. In addition to teaching activities, the therapist may make a splint for the person's hand, arm, or leg to prevent weakened muscles from stretching or shrinking.

Occupational therapy plays a vital part in helping people with permanent disabilities, such as blindness or the loss of a limb. A blind person might learn to travel to a commercial district and shop alone. The therapist may help a patient find resources, such as special tools or equipment, to replace lost skills or functions. For example, someone whose arm or leg was amputated might learn to drive a specially equipped car.

Specially designed computers enable people with spinal cord injuries, blindness, hearing impairment, or cerebral palsy to communicate, operate household equipment, and find and hold a job. An occupational therapist may suggest rearranging furniture or equipment in a patient's home to make him or her more independent. The therapist may also recommend structural changes, such as widening doorways, lowering sinks and counters, and installing automatic door openers for people who use wheelchairs.

Occupational therapy helps people with chronic illnesses, such as emphysema or heart disease, redirect their interests into activities within their physical limits. For example, someone recovering from a heart attack might substitute walking for tennis.

Occupational therapy also aids people who become injured at work or develop health problems that affect their ability to do their jobs. Modifications to an employee's work environment or job responsibilities may enable the person to return to work and avoid reinjury.

Occupational therapy can also aid the growth and development of children. Many children receive treatment at school. Occupational therapists help these children interact with others, develop self-confidence, and take full advantage of opportunities in the classroom and playground. Therapists also work closely with the children's family members and teachers.

Occupational therapy for children often includes playing with toys or participating in games. A child with learning disabilities may have difficulty recognizing colors and shapes. He or she may play games that involve matching objects of different size, shape, texture, and color. A child with cerebral palsy may have difficulty

Occupational therapists work with patients to help them develop or maintain skills needed for living and working. Here, a therapist works with a patient in a simulation of a supermarket to help her learn how to shop from a wheelchair.

© Hank Morgan, Photo Researchers

dressing. An occupational therapist might provide the child with a toy that features zippers and buttons. Playing with the toy helps the child develop the skills needed to get dressed.

Helping people with mental illness. Occupational therapists also help people who have mental and emotional illnesses, such as anxiety, depression, and schizophrenia. These illnesses may interfere with a person's ability to cope with daily life. People with mental illness may need to learn how to plan their day, how to manage stress, or how to communicate effectively with family and co-workers. A therapist can help a patient identify the most significant problem areas in his or her life. Together, the therapist and patient can plan a program of strategies to help the patient gain a sense of accomplishment and satisfaction. For example, a person who is depressed might create a daily schedule of goals and activities and check off those that have been completed.

History

Occupational therapy as a profession dates back only to the early 1900's, but people have long known that work and other activities speed recovery from illness or injury. In A.D. 172, the Greek physician Galen said, "Employment is nature's best medicine and essential to human happiness."

During the late 1700's, physicians in several countries began to prescribe useful activities as treatment for patients with mental illnesses. These doctors included Philippe Pinel in France, Johann Christian Reil in Germany, and Benjamin Rush in the United States. As early as 1798, medical professionals at the Pennsylvania Hospital for the Insane in Philadelphia taught patients such skills as carpentry, needlework, and shoe repair.

Modern occupational therapy developed from a nursing course called Invalid Occupations. This course was first offered to student nurses in 1906 by Susan E. Tracy,

a Boston nurse. American architect George E. Barton originated the term *occupational therapy.* He himself received this form of treatment after one of his feet was amputated. The need to help disabled veterans of World Wars I (1914-1918) and II (1939-1945) stimulated the growth of occupational therapy. The World Federation of Occupational Therapists was established in Liverpool, England, in 1952.

Careers

Anyone who is interested in a career as a professional occupational therapist must first earn a bachelor's or master's degree in occupational therapy from an accredited college or university. Accredited programs include courses in biology, psychology, sociology, and occupational therapy theory and practice. All programs require students to complete a period of supervised clinical training. Most teaching, research, and administrative positions in occupational therapy require a master's or doctor's degree.

A person who wants to become an occupational therapy assistant must complete an associate degree program. Associate's programs also include academic coursework and supervised clinical training.

Upon completion of the program, graduates must pass a certification examination. Assistants must also take an exam. The American Occupational Therapy Association, Association of Occupational Therapists of Ireland, British Association/College of Occupational Therapists, Canadian Association of Occupational Therapists, Singapore Association of Occupational Therapists, and similar professional groups in other countries can provide information on training programs and careers.

Critically reviewed by the American Occupational Therapy Association, Inc.

See also **Disability; Physical therapy; Vocational rehabilitation.**

NASA/Goddard Space Flight Center & ORBIMAGE/SeaWiFS Project

Ocean waters cover most of Earth's surface. This satellite view shows the Indian Ocean, partly bordered by Africa, Asia, and Australia, and below it the Southern Ocean surrounding Antarctica.

Ocean

Ocean is the great body of water that covers nearly 71 percent of Earth's surface. People also call it the sea. The ocean serves as a source of food, energy, minerals, and recreation. Ships sail the ocean to carry cargo between continents. The sea also plays a major role in Earth's climate system by regulating the air temperature and by supplying the moisture for rainfall. If there were no

ocean, life as we know it could not exist on our planet.

The ocean contains about 97 percent of all the water on Earth. Most of the remaining water occurs frozen in ice sheets and other ice formations. The rest is underground, in the air, or in such bodies of water as lakes and rivers.

The bottom of the ocean has features as varied as those on land. Huge plains spread across the ocean floor, and long mountain chains rise toward the surface. Volcanoes erupt from the ocean bottom, and trenches and valleys plunge to great depths.

Scientists called *oceanographers* work to discover the

Philip L. Richardson, the contributor of this article, is Scientist Emeritus, Physical Oceanography Department, Woods Hole Oceanographic Institution.

ocean's secrets. They study how the ocean moves and how it affects the atmosphere. They investigate the chemical composition of seawater and monitor the forces that shape the sea floor. They also study how organisms live in the sea and how people affect the ocean.

The world ocean

The ocean forms one great connected body of water often called the *world ocean* or the *global ocean.* Geographers and oceanographers divide the world ocean into five major parts. They are the Pacific Ocean, the Atlantic Ocean, the Indian Ocean, the Southern Ocean, and the Arctic Ocean. Each ocean includes smaller bodies of water called *seas, gulfs,* or *bays,* which lie along the ocean margins. For example, the Caribbean Sea and the Mediterranean Sea are part of the Atlantic, and the Bering Sea and the South China Sea are part of the Pacific. The word *sea* also refers to the ocean in general.

Area. The world ocean covers about 71 percent of Earth's surface. Most of the ocean lies in the Southern Hemisphere—that is, south of the equator. The Southern Hemisphere consists of about 80 percent ocean, and the Northern Hemisphere about 60 percent.

The Pacific Ocean ranks as the largest ocean by far. It covers about 66 million square miles (171 million square kilometers)—about one-third of Earth's surface. Near the equator, the Pacific stretches about 11,000 miles (17,700 kilometers) from Panama to the Malay Peninsula. North and South America border the Pacific on the east, and Asia and Australia lie to the west. To the north, the Bering Strait links the Pacific with the Arctic Ocean. See **Pacific Ocean.**

The Atlantic Ocean covers about 34 million square miles (88 million square kilometers). Europe and Africa lie east of the Atlantic, and North and South America lie west. See **Atlantic Ocean.**

The Indian Ocean has an area of about 26.6 million square miles (69 million square kilometers). Africa lies to the west. Australia and Indonesia lie to the east. Asia borders this ocean on the north. See **Indian Ocean.**

The Southern Ocean covers about 8.5 million square miles (22 million square kilometers). It surrounds the continent of Antarctica. See **Southern Ocean.**

The Arctic Ocean covers about 3.7 million square miles (9.6 million square kilometers). It is bounded by Asia, Europe, and North America. See **Arctic Ocean.**

Depth. The world ocean has an average depth of 13,000 feet (4,000 meters), but parts of the ocean plunge

---

Interesting facts about the ocean

WORLD BOOK illustrations by John Eggert and Robin Bouttell, WildLife Art Limited

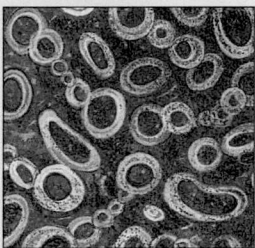

Life began in the ocean according to most scientists. Fossils of one sea creature, *pictured here,* which belongs to a group of soft-bodied animals called mollusks, show that the organism has remained unchanged for over 500 million years.

There is a bit of "ocean" inside us. The body of an adult male contains about 19 quarts (18 liters) of salt water. The composition of this fluid is similar to seawater.

The world ocean would rise about 200 feet (60 meters) if the Greenland and Antarctic ice sheets should suddenly melt. New York City would be submerged, with only the tops of the tallest buildings above water.

The Atlantic Ocean's floor spreads about 0.6 inch (1.5 centimeters) yearly, widening the ocean basin. The Pacific floor spreads about 5 inches (13 centimeters) yearly. The edges of this floor sink under continents, so the basin does not widen.

Tsunami **waves**—powerful waves usually caused by an earthquake or underwater landslide—can reach speeds of 600 miles (970 kilometers) per hour and travel across an entire ocean.

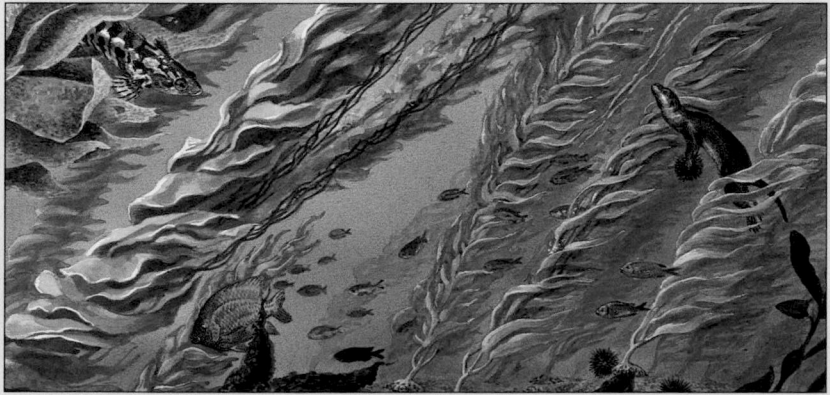

Giant kelp, a large seaweed, may grow up to 200 feet (60 meters) long. Great underwater forests of kelp exist in many parts of the ocean. These forests provide shelter for numerous animals, including fish. Other animals, such as sea otters, roam the kelp forests in search of food.

much deeper. The deepest areas occur in trenches—long, narrow valleys on the sea floor. The deepest known spot is in the Mariana Trench in the western Pacific Ocean, near the island of Guam. It lies 35,840 feet (10,924 meters) below sea level. If the world's highest mountain, 29,035-foot (8,850-meter) Mount Everest, were placed in that spot, more than 1.3 miles (2.1 kilometers) of water would cover the mountaintop.

The Java Trench is the lowest point in the Indian Ocean. It lies 23,812 feet (7,258 meters) deep. The deepest point of the Atlantic lies in the Puerto Rico Trench at 28,232 feet (8,605 meters) below the surface. In the Southern Ocean, the deepest point exists 23,737 feet (7,235 meters) below sea level at the southern end of the South Sandwich Trench. The Arctic's deepest point lies in a deep plain north of the islands of Svalbard and

The world ocean

This map shows the world ocean, which includes the Atlantic, Arctic, Indian, Pacific, and Southern oceans. It also shows the ocean's major surface currents.

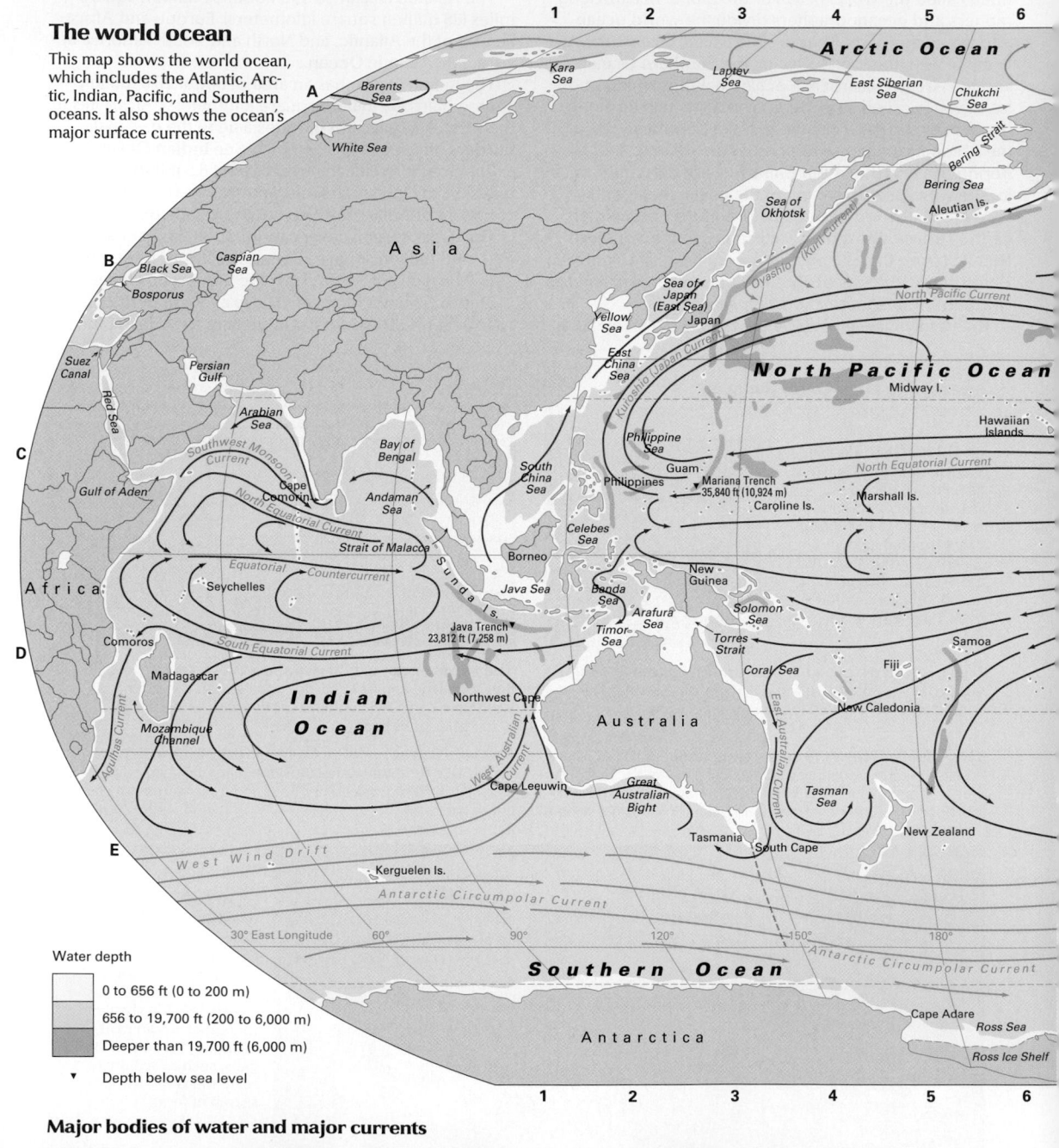

Water depth

☐	0 to 656 ft (0 to 200 m)
☐	656 to 19,700 ft (200 to 6,000 m)
☐	Deeper than 19,700 ft (6,000 m)
▾	Depth below sea level

Major bodies of water and major currents

Antarctic Circumpolar Current	E 2	Baltic Sea	B 12	Black Sea	B 1	Coral Sea	D 5	Gulf Stream	B 10
Arabian Sea	C 2	Barents Sea	A 1	Brazil Current	D 10	East China Sea	C 4	Indian Ocean	D 2
Arctic Ocean	A 5	Bay of Bengal	C 2	Canary Current	C 11	Greenland Sea	A 11	Irish Sea	B 11
Baffin Bay	A 9	Beaufort Sea	A 7	California Current	B 7	Gulf of Guinea	C 12	Java Sea	D 3
		Bering Sea	B 6	Caribbean Sea	C 9	Gulf of Mexico	C 8	Kara Sea	A 2

measures 15,305 feet (4,665 meters) below sea level.

Temperature. The surface temperature of the ocean varies from about 28 °F (−2 °C) near the North and South poles to about 86 °F (30 °C) near the equator. In polar regions, surface seawater freezes. The western tropical Pacific has the warmest surface water. Ocean currents affect surface temperature. Some currents carry warm tropical water toward the poles. Other currents bring cold surface waters from the poles toward the equator.

Ocean temperature also varies with depth. In general, the temperature falls as the depth increases. The warm surface waters extend to depths of about 500 to 1,000 feet (150 to 300 meters). Below the surface waters, the temperature decreases rapidly, forming a layer called the *thermocline*. The thermocline varies in thickness, from about 1,000 to 3,000 feet (300 to 900 meters). From

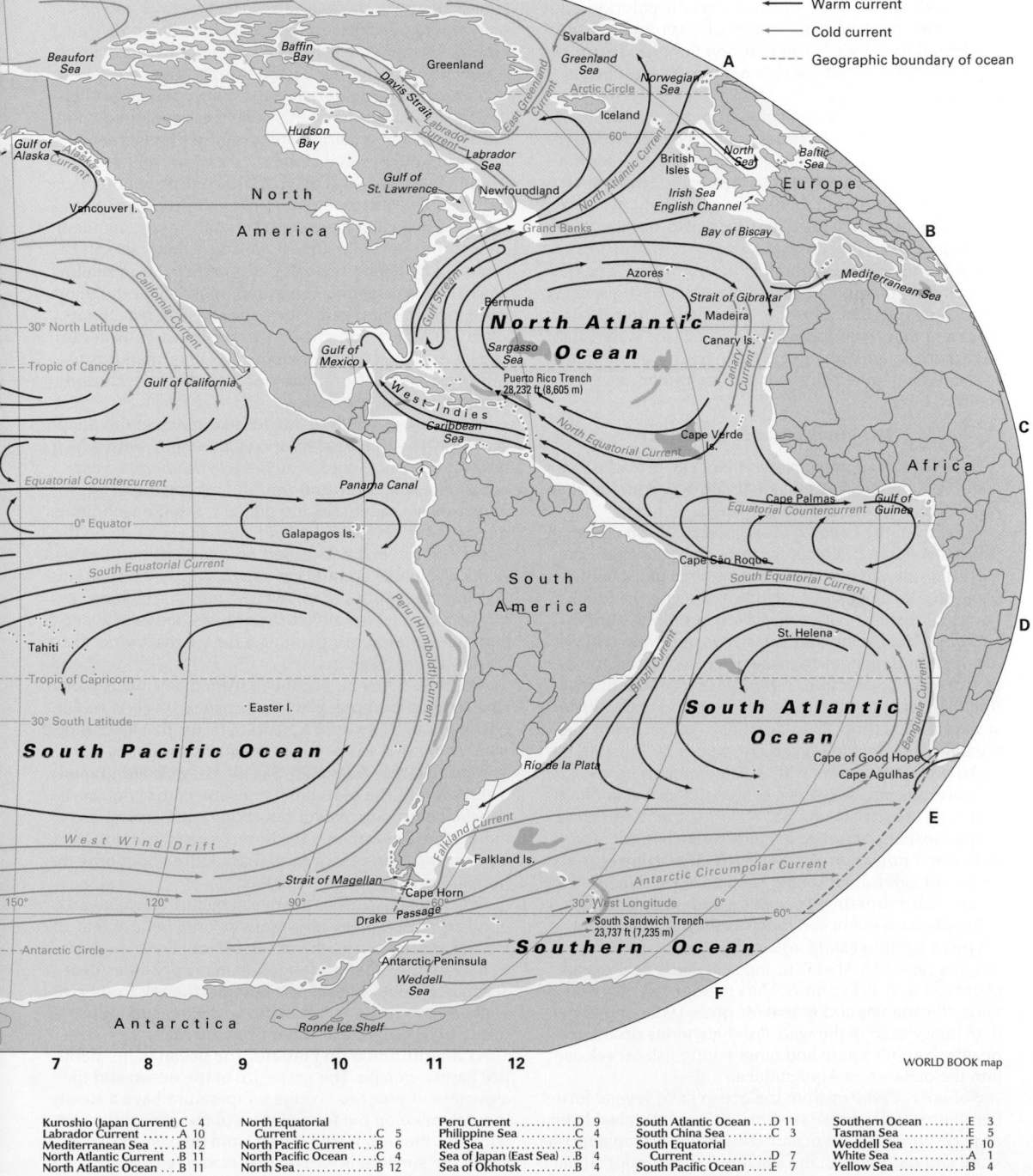

WORLD BOOK map

the thermocline to the sea floor, the temperature decreases more slowly. Ocean temperature ranges between 34 and 39 °F (1 and 4 °C) near the bottom. In some regions, colder and deeper water rises to the surface, lowering the surface water temperature.

Composition. The ocean likely contains every natural chemical element. However, the sea is best known for its salts. On average, the weight of seawater contains about 3.5 percent salts. Eleven *ions,* or molecules with electrical charges, account for the ocean's *salinity* (saltiness). They are, in order of concentration, chloride, sodium, sulfate, magnesium, calcium, potassium, bicarbonate, bromide, borate, strontium, and fluoride. The most abundant form of salt consists of the ions sodium and chloride.

Many ions in the ocean come from the dissolving of rocks on land. As rocks break down, rivers carry the resulting ions to the ocean. Volcanoes and undersea hot springs also contribute ions to the ocean. Evaporation and precipitation further affect ocean salinity. Evaporation removes fresh water from the ocean surface, leaving behind salts. Precipitation, however, returns fresh water to the ocean. Evaporation in subtropical areas is greater than precipitation, so these areas have especially salty surface waters. Closer to the equator, precipitation is greater than evaporation, making surface waters less salty there. In addition, rivers bring fresh water to the ocean, which lowers the salinity of seawater near river mouths.

The importance of the ocean

As a wealth of resources. The ocean provides many major resources. They include (1) food, (2) sources of energy, (3) sediments, and (4) medicines.

Food from the ocean consists mainly of fish and shellfish. Most of the catch comes from coastal waters. The world's fishing fleets harvest many kinds of fish and shellfish. The chief kinds include anchovies, haddock, herring, lobsters, mackerel, oysters, sardines, shrimp, and tuna. The fishing industry also is developing new products and markets to make use of less familiar types of seafood. For example, *surimi,* a fish product developed in Japan, can be made into imitation crab, lobster, scallop, and shrimp. Processors use many fish not traditionally eaten, including certain species of flounder, to make protein powders with which to enrich foods.

Seaweeds also serve as a source of food, in addition to having industrial uses. *Kelp,* a large seaweed, is one of the most important. Kelp contains such nutrients as iodine and potassium. However, its chief value is as a source of *algin,* a thickening substance used in ice cream, salad dressing, cosmetics, and other products.

People farm the ocean much as they farm the land. In a type of farming called *aquaculture* or *mariculture,* farmers raise fish, shellfish, and seaweeds near ocean shores as well as in ponds. They use special methods to make the animals and seaweeds grow faster and larger than they would in the wild. Fish hatcheries produce healthy young salmon and other young fish for release into the ocean. See **Aquaculture.**

Sources of energy from the ocean have several forms. Petroleum and natural gas rank as the most valuable energy resources of the ocean. Offshore wells tap deposits of oil and gas beneath the sea floor. Today, approximately 30 percent of worldwide oil and gas comes from offshore production. Scientists think that there are huge reserves of oil and gas still remaining beneath the ocean floor. As gas and oil reserves on land are used up or become too difficult and expensive to obtain, undersea deposits will become increasingly important. See **Gas** (Producing gas).

The ocean tides also provide energy. Tidal power facilities use the energy in the rise and fall of the tides to produce electric power. Unlike petroleum and gas, this source of energy is renewable. The first tidal power plant opened in 1966 on the Rance River near St.-Malo, France. Ocean waves also provide potential sources of renewable energy. See **Energy supply** (Tidal energy).

Sediments are materials deposited at the bottom of the ocean. Ocean sediments collect as sand, mud, minerals, and other materials. Important sediments recovered from the ocean include sand and gravel mined from the sea floor and used to make construction materials. People also use some sand to restore damaged beaches. Seawater itself contains such important minerals as bromide and magnesium. These minerals can be removed by letting seawater evaporate in large shallow basins under sunlight. The evaporation leaves the mineral deposits behind in the form of salts. The salts themselves and such elements as magnesium and bromide can be extracted from the deposits. Other methods to remove minerals from seawater include chemical and electrochemical processes.

The mineral wealth of the ocean extends to the deep-sea floor. The deep-sea floor contains vents from which hot water flows. Deposits at these *hydrothermal vents* contain copper, iron, and zinc. But mining the ores would prove expensive and difficult, and the techniques must still be developed. Manganese deposits lie on the ocean bottom in lumps called *nodules.* The nodules also contain valuable amounts of cobalt, copper, and nickel. Possible techniques to mine these nodules include using buckets that run on conveyor belts between a ship and the sea floor, or operating a device that works like a giant vacuum cleaner.

Medicines may be produced from many forms of marine life. For example, plantlike organisms called *red algae* could provide *anticoagulants,* drugs that keep blood from clotting. A family of marine snails produces substances that may treat pain. Sea life has also aided medical research. The blood of horseshoe crabs contains a substance used to test for infections and bacteria contamination. Researchers study nerve cells from lobsters, squids, and marine worms to learn more about how the human nervous system functions.

Other products from the ocean include coral, pearls, and shells used in jewelry. Many people believe that natural sponges from the ocean bottom are of higher quality than synthetic sponges. In many dry areas near seacoasts, people *desalinate* (remove the salt from) seawater to produce fresh water for drinking and industrial uses (see **Water** [Fresh water from the sea]).

As an influence on climate. The ocean helps stabilize Earth's climate. The great size of the ocean and the slowness of water to change temperature have a steadying influence on the temperature of the atmosphere. In summer, the ocean stores heat from the sun. In winter, when the sunlight is weaker, the ocean releases the stored heat into the air. Currents carry the heat of tropical waters toward the poles, thereby cooling the tropics and warming the polar regions.

The ocean is the source of most precipitation that falls on Earth. The sun's heat evaporates water from the ocean surface. The water rises as invisible vapor and forms clouds as it cools. It then falls back to Earth as rain, sleet, hail, or snow.

As a vast highway. The ocean has been a highway for trade since people built the first ships thousands of years ago. Shipping ranks as an important use of the ocean in international trade. See **Ship; Transportation.**

Life in the ocean

An incredible variety of living things resides in the ocean. Marine life ranges in size from microscopic one-celled organisms to the blue whale, which may measure up to 100 feet (30 meters) long. In a process called *photosynthesis,* ocean plants and plantlike animals use sunlight, carbon dioxide, water, and nutrients to produce their own food and materials for growth. Sea animals eat these organisms and one another. Marine plants and plantlike organisms can live only in the sunlit surface waters of the ocean, which is called the *photic zone.* The photic zone extends only about 330 feet (100 meters) below the surface. Beyond that point, the light is insufficient to support organisms that rely on photosynthesis. Animals, however, live throughout the ocean, from the surface waters to the greatest depths.

Three basic categories of marine organisms inhabit the oceans. They are (1) the plankton, (2) the nekton, and (3) the benthos.

The plankton includes plantlike organisms and animals that drift with ocean currents. They have little ability to move through water on their own. Most of them are so small that they cannot be seen without a microscope. Plantlike organisms of the plankton are called *phytoplankton,* and they include such simple creatures as diatoms and other algae. Animals of the plankton are among the organisms known as *zooplankton.*

Phytoplankton consist of several kinds of plantlike organisms. Most have only one cell and float in the photic zone, where they obtain sunlight and nutrients for photosynthesis. Although the organisms generally drift about, some kinds have long, whiplike parts called *flagella* that enable them to swim. Phytoplankton serve as food for zooplankton and some larger marine animals.

The most numerous phytoplankton are diatoms and dinoflagellates. A diatom consists of one cell enclosed in a hard, glasslike shell made of silica. Diatoms live mainly in colder regions of the ocean. Some even live within sea ice. Most dinoflagellates also are one-celled organisms. They generally live in more tropical regions. A dinoflagellate has two flagella it can use to move in a swirling motion. Sudden increases in certain dinoflagellate populations are called *red tides,* from the reddish discoloration that millions of these cells create in the water. Some dinoflagellates produce powerful poisons. When such species become plentiful, they may create a red tide that kills many sea animals (see **Red tide).** Other kinds of phytoplankton include coccolithophores, one-celled organisms with a hard shell made of calcite; and silicoflagellates, which have a skeleton of hollow silica rods.

Zooplankton consist of many kinds of creatures, such as single-celled organisms and small animals that are unable to swim. They live at all depths in the ocean. Some planktonic animals float about freely throughout their lives. The rest spend only the early part of their lives as plankton. As adults, some become strong swimmers and join the nekton. Others settle to the sea floor or attach themselves to it and become part of the benthos. Crustaceans, a large group of *invertebrates* (animals without backbones), make up about 70 percent of all zooplankton. Tiny swimmers called copepods are the most numerous crustaceans. Shrimplike krill, another group of crustaceans, provide food for fish, sea birds, seals, squids, and whales.

The nekton consists of animals that can swim freely in the sea. They are strong swimmers and include fish, squids, and marine mammals. Most nektonic species live near the sea surface, where food is plentiful. But many other animals of the nekton live in the deep ocean.

Fish rank among the most important animals of the nekton. About 14,500 kinds of fish live in the ocean. One of the world's smallest fishes, a goby with the scientific name *Trimmatom nanus,* lives in the Indian Ocean. It grows to about 0.4 inch (1 centimeter) long. The largest fish, the whale shark, measures as much as 40 feet (12 meters) long. Such fish as tuna and mackerel have streamlined bodies that enable them to swim rapidly. Many fish of the deeper parts of the ocean have light-producing organs that may help attract prey. Such fish include deep-sea anglerfish and lanternfish.

Squids are free-swimming mollusks, a group of soft-bodied invertebrates, and have eight arms and two tentacles. Related animals include octopuses and cuttlefish. Squids live in surface and deep waters. They measure from less than 1 foot (0.3 meter) to as much as 60 feet (18 meters) long, including the tentacles. A squid moves backward through the water in a jetlike action by forcing water through a tube beneath its head.

Nektonic mammals include dugongs, manatees, porpoises, and whales, all of which remain in the ocean for their entire lives. Other marine mammals, such as sea otters, seals, and walruses, also spend time on land.

The benthos is made up of marine organisms that live on or near the sea floor. Animals of the benthos may burrow in the ocean floor, attach themselves to the bottom, or crawl or swim about within the bottom waters. Where sunlight can reach the sea floor, the benthos supports plants and plantlike organisms, such as kelp and sea grass, which become anchored to the bottom. Common benthos animals include clams, crabs, lobsters, starfish, and various worms. Some fish have features specially suited for life on the sea floor. For example, halibut and sole, which lie sideways on the bottom, have both eyes on the side of the head facing up.

Most bottom-dwelling creatures are part of the plankton and drift with the currents during the early stages of their development. They then sink to the sea floor where, as adults, they become part of the benthos. Such animals include barnacles, clams, corals, oysters, and a variety of snails and worms.

The food cycle in many parts of the sea begins with the phytoplankton that produce food by photosynthesis. Certain zooplankton eat the phytoplankton. Those animals, in turn, become food for other zooplankton or for

Life in the ocean
The ocean contains a remarkable variety of life, from tiny microorganisms to gigantic whales. Different kinds of organisms inhabit different levels of depth in the ocean waters.

Plankton

WORLD BOOK illustrations by Alex Ebel

Plankton consists mostly of small marine organisms that drift with ocean currents. The plantlike organisms are called *phytoplankton*. Planktonic animals are among the organisms known as *zooplankton*.

Phytoplankton

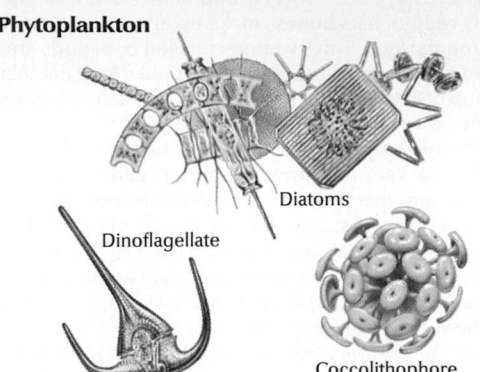

Diatoms

Dinoflagellate

Coccolithophore

Zooplankton

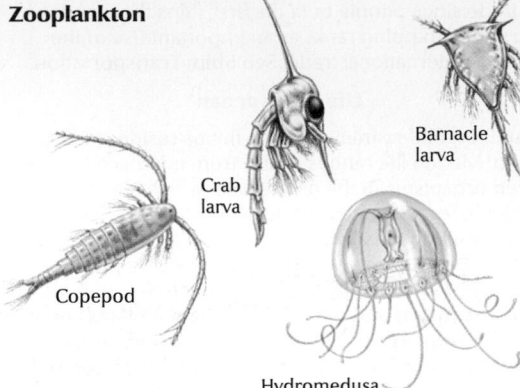

Barnacle larva

Crab larva

Copepod

Hydromedusa

Nekton
Nekton is made up of fish and other animals that have the ability to swim freely in water without the help of currents. Most nektonic creatures live in the upper layer of the ocean.

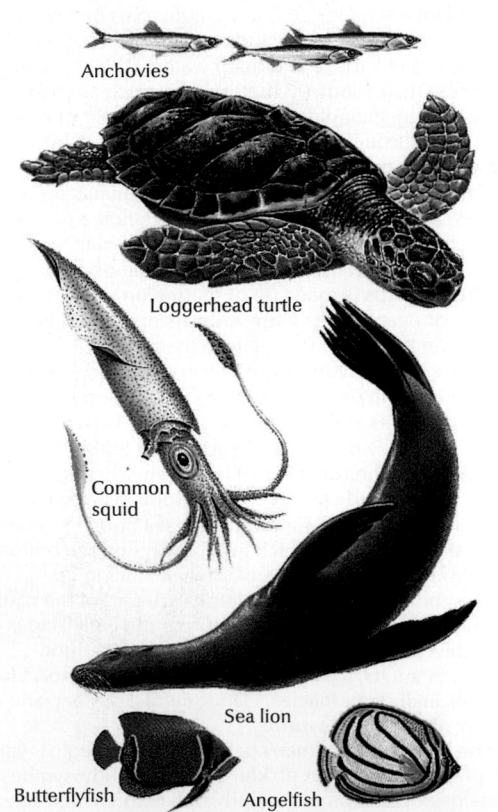

Anchovies

Loggerhead turtle

Common squid

Sea lion

Butterflyfish

Angelfish

Benthos
Benthos consists of marine organisms that live on the ocean bottom. Some members of the benthos are attached to the bottom in one position throughout their lives.

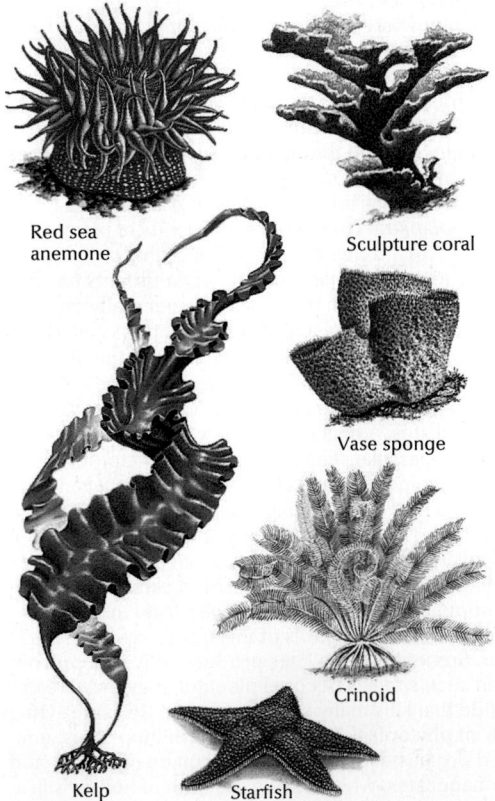

Red sea anemone

Sculpture coral

Vase sponge

Crinoid

Kelp

Starfish

The ocean's cycle of life

The creatures of the ocean make up a complex web of life. For most marine life, the food cycle begins with tiny organisms called *plankton*. Plantlike *phytoplankton* use sunlight, carbon dioxide, water, and nutrients in the water to make food. *Zooplankton,* which are animals, eat phytoplankton or other zooplankton. These organisms, in turn, serve as food for fish, whales, and other animals that swim, called the *nekton.* Many larger creatures of the nekton eat smaller nektonic animals. Animals of the *benthos* (sea floor), such as sponges and sea lilies, depend on organic debris falling from the upper ocean. Finally, *upwellings* (deep waters that rise to the surface) carry waste products and other organic debris back to the surface, where they serve as nutrients for the phytoplankton.

WORLD BOOK illustrations by George Fryer, Bernard Thornton Artists

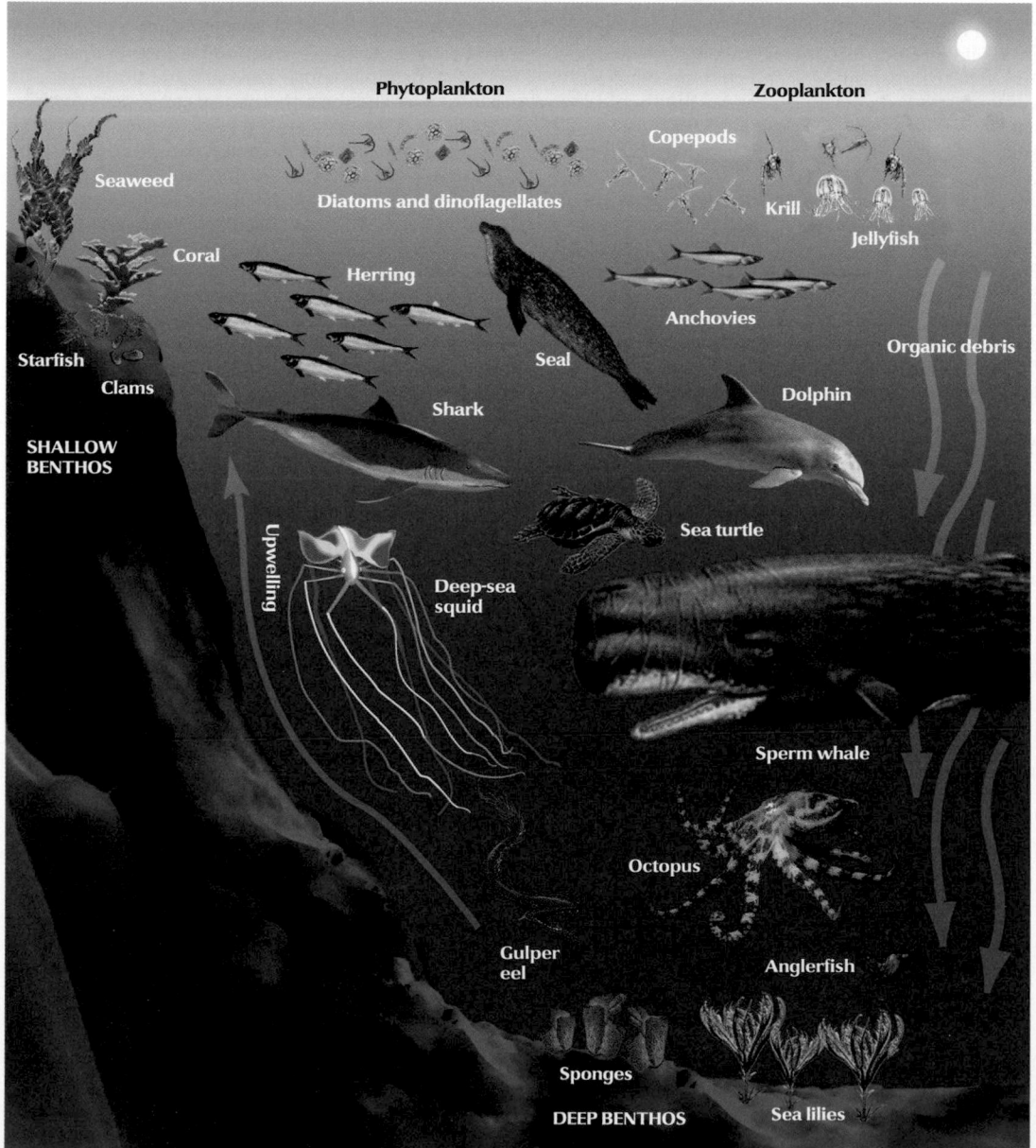

658   **Ocean**

fish and other animals of the ocean.

After ocean organisms die, they begin to sink. Before most dead organisms sink far, they are eaten by creatures dwelling at lower depths. Dead organisms that are not eaten immediately begin to decompose. Bacteria and fungi cause the organisms to decompose by breaking them down into *nutrients* (nourishing chemicals). In addition, bacteria and fungi break down waste products given off by marine life. Rising currents carry the nutrients to the surface, where phytoplankton use them for photosynthesis, completing the food cycle.

Hydrothermal vents support thriving marine life. However, the food cycle at hydrothermal vents is not based on phytoplankton. Instead, such microscopic organisms as bacteria and *archaea* serve as the food base. Archaea are single-celled organisms that rank among the oldest forms of life on Earth. In a process called *chemosynthesis,* these microorganisms use energy from chemicals in the water instead of sunlight to produce food and grow. Other living things rely on archaea for food.

How the ocean moves

Ocean currents move through the sea like giant meandering rivers. Winds and earthquakes create waves across the surface of the ocean. The gravitational pull of the moon and sun causes movement, producing the daily rise and fall of the tides.

Circulation. Two main types of circulation exist in the ocean. They are (1) *wind-driven currents* and (2) *thermohaline circulation.*

Wind-driven currents result from wind blowing on the ocean surface. The wind sets surface waters into motion as currents. Currents generally flow horizontal-ly—that is, parallel to Earth's surface. The wind mainly affects only the upper 330 to 660 feet (100 to 200 meters) of water. However, the flow of wind-driven currents may extend to depths of 3,300 feet (1,000 meters) or more.

Wind-driven currents move in enormous circular patterns called *gyres.* Gyres flow clockwise in the subtropics of the Northern Hemisphere and counterclockwise in the subtropics of the Southern Hemisphere. Several conditions influence the direction of wind-driven currents and make them form gyres. Earth's wind systems drive the currents in an easterly or westerly direction. Continents direct the flow toward the north or south. Earth's rotation further causes the currents' circular paths. Major wind-driven currents include the North and South Equatorial currents, the California Current, the Canary Current, the Gulf Stream, the Kuroshio (Japan Current), the Labrador Current, and the Peru Current. The Antarctic Circumpolar Current is the strongest ocean current and the only one that circles Earth without hitting continents. See *The world ocean* map in this article for the location of the major currents.

In some areas, *upwelling* occurs when winds cause surface waters near the coast to move offshore. Colder, deeper waters, which are rich in nutrients, then rise to the surface near the coast. The upwelling of deeper waters provides nutrients for the growth of phytoplankton, which fish and other sea animals eat. Upwelling areas have great numbers of fish and, in fact, yield half of the world's fish catch. Important upwelling regions include the coasts of Peru and northwestern Africa, as well as along the equator and around Antarctica.

Thermohaline circulation produces great vertical movements of water that flow from the surface to the

Ocean currents result from two forces: (1) the action of the wind on surface waters, and (2) the differences in temperature and salt content of surface and deeper waters. The earth's general wind circulation produces the major currents—great streams that carry the ocean's surface waters in roughly circular patterns. Wind also causes *upwelling,* which occurs when coastal waters are blown offshore and replaced by colder, deeper waters. *Thermohaline circulation* takes place because colder, saltier water sinks. This action produces great vertical currents in the ocean.

WORLD BOOK illustration by Sarah Woodward

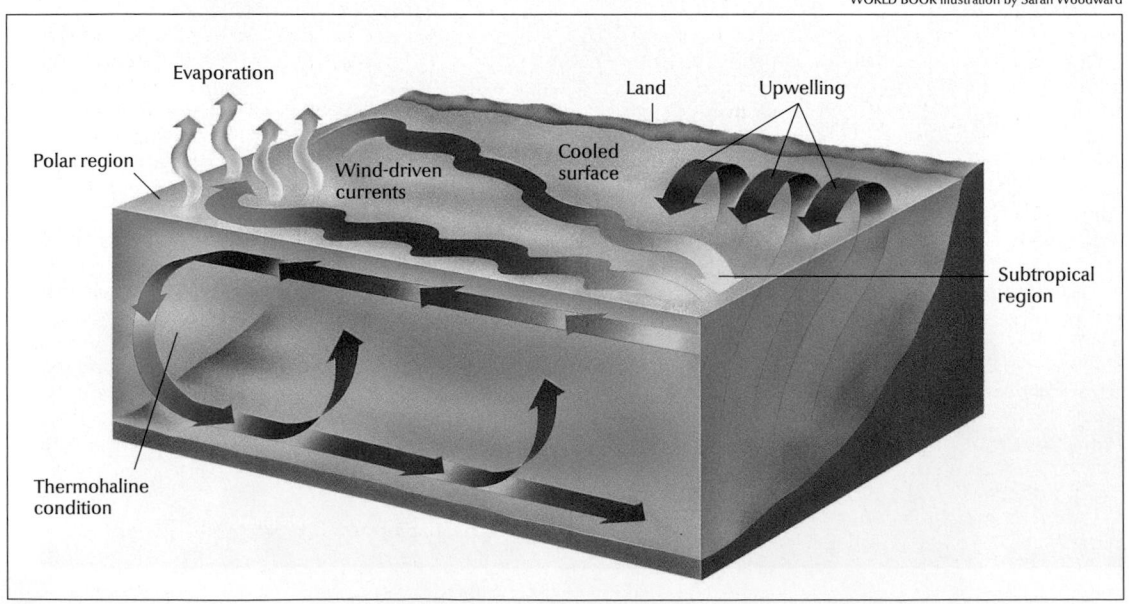

The ocean as a conveyor belt

Thermohaline circulation produces a worldwide current comparable to a conveyor belt. Cold, dense waters descend from the surface in the North Atlantic and spread first to the Southern Ocean, then around Antarctica, and then into the Indian and Pacific oceans. In the North Pacific, the waters migrate upward as they become warmer and less saline. They then travel back to the Indian Ocean and through the southern Atlantic. The waters eventually reach the North Atlantic, where the conveyor belt begins again.

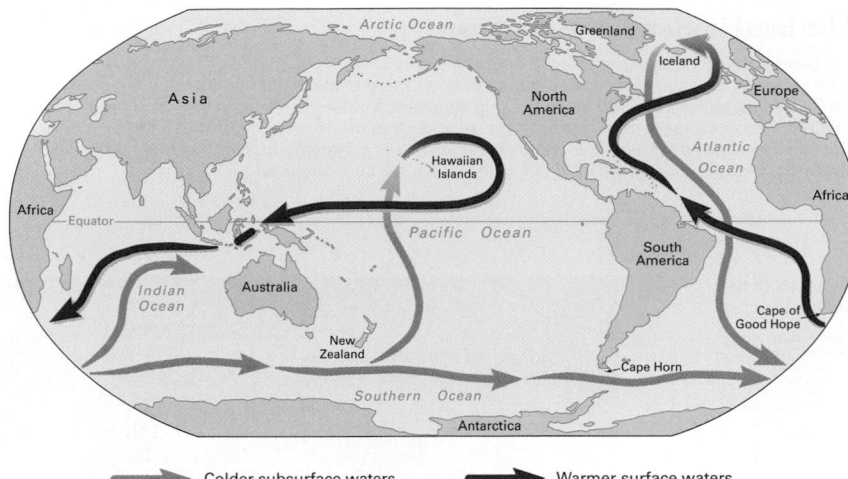

WORLD BOOK map

→ Colder subsurface waters   → Warmer surface waters

ocean depths. The circulation results from differences in water temperature and salinity. In the polar regions, surface waters are colder and saltier. Being colder and saltier makes these waters heavier, and they sink toward the ocean bottom. They then gradually flow back toward the surface and replace the surface waters that sink.

Thermohaline circulation produces a worldwide circuit comparable to a conveyor belt. Cold, dense waters descend from the surface in the North Atlantic and spread southward in deep areas of the ocean. Upon reaching the Southern Ocean, these waters sweep eastward around Antarctica and then spread northward into the Indian and Pacific oceans. In the North Pacific, the waters migrate upward as they become warmer and less saline. They then follow the surface circulation, returning southward into the Indian Ocean and through the southern Atlantic around the Cape of Good Hope. They eventually reach the North Atlantic, where the conveyor belt begins another global circuit. Such waters take about 1,000 years to make one complete circuit.

Waves. In addition to creating currents, wind produces the up and down movements of an ocean wave. Little or no forward motion of water occurs as a wave goes through the water. The action of an ocean wave resembles waves you can make in a rope that is tied to a tree. If you shake the rope's free end, waves run along it. But the rope itself does not move forward. But when an ocean wave reaches land, it starts to drag on the bottom. The wave becomes steeper and breaks, producing a rush of water against the shore called *surf.* See **Waves.**

Ocean waves vary in size from small ripples to giant hurricane waves more than 100 feet (30 meters) high. Wave size depends on wind speed, on how long the wind blows, and on how far it blows over the ocean. The waves continue to move over the ocean surface and can travel great distances from where they began. If the wind stops, the waves become smoother and longer. Waves created by strong winds in the open ocean may become so steep that they break in a manner similar to surf. These breaking waves are called *whitecaps.*

The action of ocean waves changes the shoreline. Waves cut away sloping land and leave steep cliffs. They break up exposed rocks and form beaches. The movement of the waves and currents shapes beaches and

builds up sand bars along the shore. Waves also carry beach sand away, particularly during storms.

Another type of wave results from a disturbance such as a submarine earthquake, landslide, or volcanic eruption. Such a disturbance can generate a series of waves called a *tsunami.* Some people call tsunami waves *tidal waves,* though the tide does not cause them. On the surface of the open ocean, the waves of a tsunami can barely be seen. The waves typically measure about 3 feet (1 meter) high or less. But they can travel as fast as 600 miles (970 kilometers) per hour. As they approach a coast, they slow down and may pile up to a tremendous height, causing great damage along the coast. Most tsunamis strike land areas in or bordering the Pacific Ocean. Sometimes, scientists can predict when a tsunami may form and warn people in its path. See **Tsunami.**

Tides are the rhythmic rise and fall of ocean waters. In many coastal areas, water slowly rises along the shoreline for about six hours every day. Then it slowly falls back for about six hours. Tides are caused chiefly by the gravitational pull of the moon on Earth. The moon's pull is strongest on the surface of Earth directly facing the moon. When ocean waters face the moon, the moon pulls the water up and forms a high tide in that area. The moon's pull is weakest on the side of Earth opposite from the moon, enabling water there to move away from Earth as it rotates. This action produces another high tide bulge. As Earth rotates each day, high tide bulges move around the planet.

The sun's gravitational pull also affects the ocean. But the sun causes tides only about half as high as those caused by the moon. The gravitational pull of the moon and sun combine during the full moon and new moon. At such times, the sun, moon, and Earth are in a straight line. The tides then rise higher and fall lower than usual. They are called *spring tides.* When the moon is in its first and third quarters, the sun and moon are at right angles to each other with respect to Earth. The resulting tides do not rise or fall as much as usual. They are called *neap tides.* See **Tide.**

The land at the bottom of the sea

The ocean floor is a region of spectacular contrasts. Broad plains cover huge distances, towering mountain

The land beneath the oceans

The geography of the land beneath the oceans features long mountain ridges, broad basins, and deep trenches. This computer-generated map shows many of the major landforms of the ocean floor. Oceanographers created the map using information gathered from a variety of sources, including radar equipment from satellites and sonar devices on ships and in the sea. Deeper elevations on the map appear in darker colors, while shallower elevations appear in lighter colors. The map index below indicates the locations of individual sea floor features.

WORLD BOOK map; image provided by National Oceanic and Atmospheric Administration, National Geophysical Data Center

Features of the ocean floor

Water depth

0
656 ft (200 m)
1,640 ft (500 m)
4,921 ft (1,500 m)
9,843 ft (3,000 m)
16,404 ft (5,000 m)
22,966 ft (7,000 m)
29,528 ft (9,000 m)
36,089 ft (11,000 m)

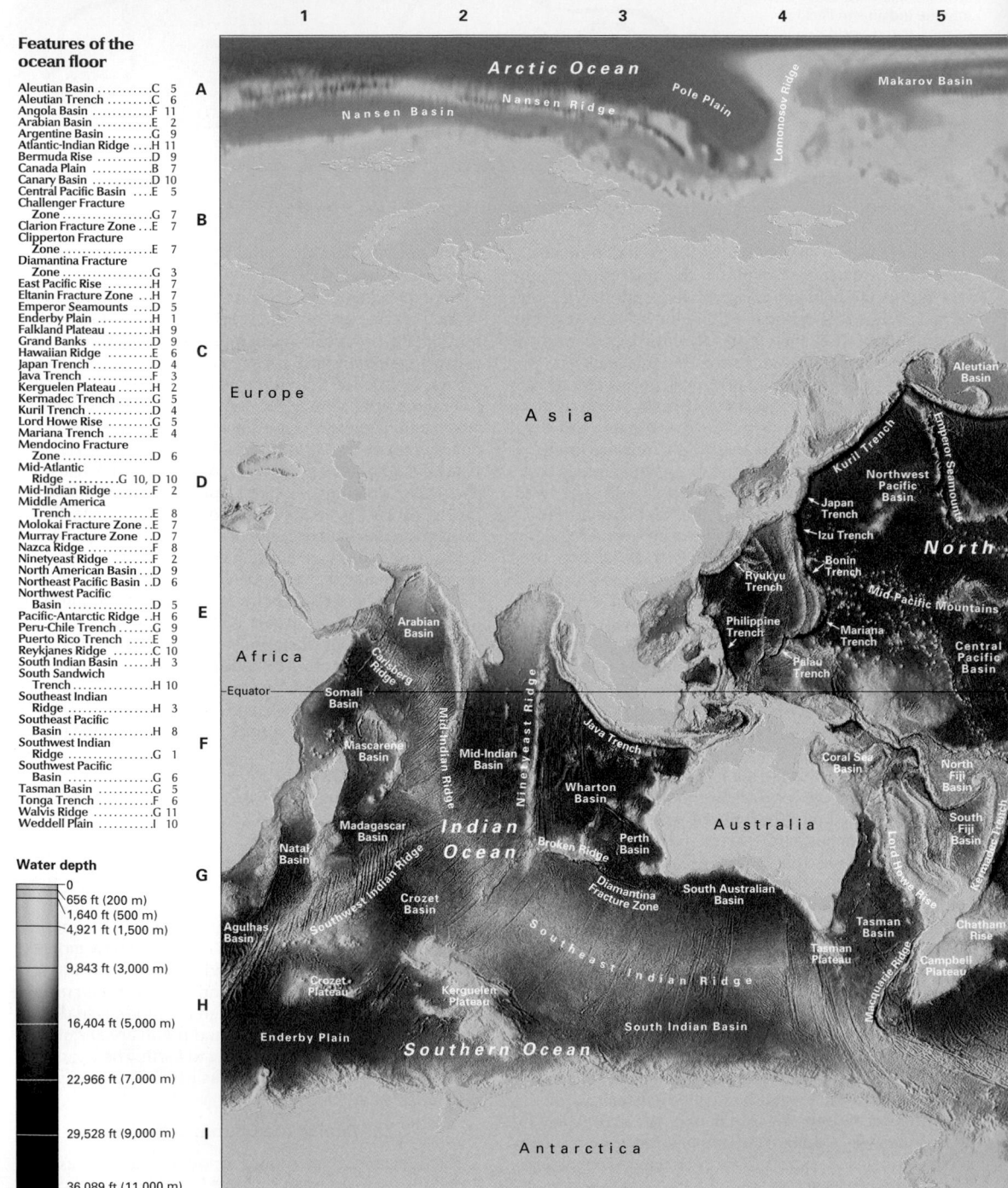

chains circle the planet, undersea volcanoes rise toward the surface, and trenches and valleys reach great depths.

The continental margin forms the part of the seabed that borders the continents. It consists of (1) the continental shelf, (2) the continental slope, and (3) the continental rise.

The continental shelf is the submerged land at the edge of the continents. It begins at the shoreline and

gently slopes underwater to a depth less than 660 feet (200 meters). The width of the continental shelf usually ranges between 19 and 190 miles (30 and 300 kilometers). In certain areas, such as parts of the Arctic Ocean, the shelf extends over 620 miles (1,000 kilometers). In other areas, particularly those bordering much of the Pacific, it measures only 1 mile (1.6 kilometers) or less. Valleys of varying depths cut through the shelf. Sediment carried into the ocean by rivers collects on the shelf.

The continental slope begins at the outer edge of the shelf. The slope is much steeper than the shelf and plunges to depths of 2.2 miles (3.6 kilometers). The slope forms the sides of continents. Its width ranges from 12 to 60 miles (20 to 100 kilometers). In many places, deep underwater canyons gash the slope. Some canyons rival the gigantic Grand Canyon of North America in size. Many underwater canyons lie offshore from large rivers, and sediment-laden waters may have carved them.

The continental rise consists of sediment from the continental shelf and slope that accumulates at the bottom of the slope. The thick sediment deposits of the continental rise extend up to about 600 miles (1,000 kilometers) from the slope.

Deep-sea peaks, valleys, and plains lie beyond the continental margin in the ocean basin. *Mid-ocean ridges* form a chief feature of the basin. The ridges consist of a chain of mountains that runs through the world ocean. Estimates of the chain's total length range from 30,000 to 50,000 miles (50,000 to 80,000 kilometers). Scientists discovered the mountain chain independently in each ocean basin and gave it different names, including Mid-Atlantic Ridge, East Pacific Rise, and Mid-Indian Ridge. Most mountains of the mid-ocean ridges stand about 5,000 feet (1,500 meters) above the sea floor. Some peaks rise above the surface and form islands, such as the Azores and Iceland in the Atlantic Ocean. Deep valleys often cut across the ridges, producing a rugged, fractured surface. Some mid-ocean ridges have valleys down through the center of them. Frequent volcanic eruptions and earthquakes occur along such valleys.

The sides of the mid-ocean ridges slope down to the *abyssal plains.* Accumulation of sediment buries most features of the ocean floor on the abyssal plains, which are flat as a result. The chief sources of deep-sea sediment are the land itself and marine life. The breaking down and wearing away of rock produces land sediment, which rivers carry to the ocean. Wind also carries dust from deserts and other regions to the ocean. In addition, volcanic eruptions spread large amounts of ash over the ocean. Marine life sediment consists mainly of tiny shells and the remains of dead planktonic organisms. When such biological matter makes up a major part of a sediment, scientists call it an *ooze*.

Other features of the deep-sea basin include long, narrow trenches and underwater mountains called *seamounts.* Trenches form the deepest parts of the ocean. Volcanic eruptions produce seamounts. These mountains have steep sides and may rise thousands of feet or meters above the sea floor.

How the sea floor was formed. Since the late 1800's, scientists have developed several theories to explain how the sea floor formed. The theory of *continental drift* first received wide attention in the early 1900's. According to this theory, the continents originally were a single great land mass surrounded by one ocean. The land mass broke up into continents, which slowly drifted apart. New oceans, including the Atlantic and Indian oceans, resulted from the drift of the continents.

At first, many scientists rejected the continental drift theory because no one could explain what forces might move continents. Then in the 1960's, a theory called *sea-floor spreading* provided some explanation. According to the theory, the sea floor itself moves, carrying the continents along. Circulating movements deep within Earth's *mantle*—that is, the partly molten layer of hot rock beneath the earth's crust—make the sea floor move. The circulating movements carry melted rock up to the mid-ocean ridges and force it into the central valleys of the ridges. As the melted rock cools and hardens, it forms new sea floor and pushes the old floor and the continents away from the ridges.

A theory called *plate tectonics* combines and expands on the ideas of sea-floor spreading and continental drift. According to plate tectonics, Earth's outer shell consists of huge rigid plates that move continuously. As the plates move, they carry the ocean floor and the continents with them. The relative movement of two neighboring plates is generally about 0.5 to 4 inches (1 to 10 centimeters) a year. Sea-floor spreading—and the formation of new sea floor—occurs where plates move apart. The mid-ocean ridges mark such areas.

As plates move away from one another in one place, they must move toward one another elsewhere. When two plates collide, one may pile up against the other, forming mountains. Or one plate may be drawn down into the mantle under the other plate. Such action produces trenches and volcanoes. Earthquakes occur at or near plate boundaries, where plates spread apart, collide, or slide past each other. The Atlantic Ocean is slowly growing wider, and the Pacific smaller, because of plate tectonics. See **Earth** (Earth's plates); **Plate tectonics.**

The oceanic crust forms the ocean floor. It consists of hard rock called *basalt.* The continents lie on the continental crust, which consists mainly of granite. Granite is lighter than basalt, and so the continental crust basically "floats" on the mantle, above the oceanic crust. Ocean basins, as sunken areas, thus collect water. Most scientists believe that the water now in the oceans came from a number of asteroids and comets that struck Earth as it formed nearly 4.6 billion years ago. Much of it was released from rocks within Earth by volcanic activity.

Exploring the ocean

By exploring and understanding the ocean, we can learn to manage its resources wisely.

Tools of exploration. The tools that oceanographers use in their efforts to explore the sea include (1) research ships, (2) research submarines called *submersibles,* (3) satellites, and (4) computers.

Research ships are typically about 100 to 300 feet (30 to 90 meters) long and include laboratory space where scientists can work while at sea. Oceanographers use research vessels to make measurements, perform experiments, and study marine processes. They may stay at sea for weeks or months at a time. They often work in rough seas and in distant locations around the world.

Oceanographers use several types of instruments on research ships. They operate underwater cameras to

Computer-generated images provide information about water temperatures in the ocean and about the ocean's geological history. In this view of coastal California, light gray, red, and orange colors represent the shallowest, warmest waters. Blue and purple indicate the deepest, coldest waters. The picture also shows how erosion has shaped the sea floor, creating canyons and other features.

© William Haxby, Lamont-Doherty Earth Observatory/Columbia University

photograph the sea floor. Electronic devices measure the depth of the sea by sending out sound waves and recording their echoes from the ocean floor. The most powerful of such instruments detect echoes from deep within Earth's crust. Scientists analyze the records to learn about the structure of the crust. Oceanographers also measure temperature, salinity, and a wide array of chemicals in the ocean. Nets towed behind research ships gather samples of marine life for study.

Oceanographers also use a number of floating devices. For example, a *mooring* consists of an anchor and a float connected by a cable. The float may be placed at the sea surface or at a specific depth. Scientists attach various instruments to the cable of a mooring. Some instruments measure the speed and direction of ocean currents at different depths. Other devices record the temperature and salinity of the water. A mooring may remain at sea several years before the research ship picks up the device and the data it has collected.

Other floating devices include *buoys,* which drift with the ocean's surface currents. Buoys chiefly provide information about ocean circulation. But they may also record air pressure or surface water temperature. Buoys relay data to scientists through orbiting satellites. Some buoys can drift with currents below the ocean surface.

Oceanographers use specialized equipment to collect samples from the ocean bottom. Scientists can gather rock samples from the mid-ocean ridge by towing a dredge along the sea floor. Other ships can drop long, heavy pipes into the sea floor to collect vertical samples of sediments called *cores.* Because sediments are deposited in layers over time, studies of cores can determine how old the sediments are. The age and composition of the sediments can reveal how oceans have changed over time. See **Ocean drilling programs.**

Submersibles can descend to the depths of the ocean. They enable scientists to observe features on the sea floor that may be missed by instruments lowered from research ships on the surface.

Piloted submersibles, such as the U.S. *Alvin,* carry a human crew. The crew members take photographs and use a mechanical arm outside the vessel to gather samples and set out instruments.

Other submersibles, called *remotely operated vehicles* (ROV's) or *autonomous underwater vehicles* (AUV's), carry no crew. ROV's usually are controlled from a ship by a cable. They have television cameras and sensors that can return information about the sea floor environment. In 1985, two remotely operated submersibles—the

U.S. *Argo* and the French *Sar*—found and explored the wreckage of the *Titanic,* a British passenger ship that sank in the Atlantic in 1912. AUV's are self-contained vehicles controlled by an onboard computer programmed with instructions. They can explore specific areas of the ocean, take measurements, and collect samples. AUV's return to the control ship or station to recharge batteries, return data and samples, and receive new instructions in their computers. See **Diving, Underwater.**

Satellites transmit data from buoys and other instruments at sea to oceanographers on shore. They also provide views of vast expanses of the sea from their position high above Earth. In general, satellites supply information more quickly over a larger area than do research ships.

Satellite images can show the distribution of sea ice, the extent of surface oil slicks, and the cloud formations over the ocean. Satellites can help map the temperature and color of the ocean surface. Some satellites can even detect the small differences in the elevation of the sea surface caused by ocean currents. Such data help oceanographers in many ways. For example, scientists can study variations in the routes and patterns of ocean currents and their effects on climate and weather. Researchers can also determine biological activity in the ocean's surface waters, as well as understand how the

Woods Hole Oceanographic Institution

The submersible *Alvin* can carry a crew of scientists to the ocean floor, where they take photographs and gather samples.

ocean affects weather and climate.

Computers enable oceanographers to collect and analyze the enormous amounts of data obtained every day from satellites, from instruments on research ships, and from buoys. Scientists also use computers to create *models* (mathematical representations) of the ocean's movement and structure. The models enable them to understand and predict the ocean's behavior and its effect on the environment.

Discoveries. Oceanographers constantly make new and interesting discoveries about the sea. One of the exciting discoveries occurred in 1977, when scientists first detected a hydrothermal vent on the sea floor near the Galapagos Islands in the eastern Pacific Ocean. Similar vents have been found elsewhere in the ocean, especially along mid-ocean ridges, volcanic regions where new sea floor forms as tectonic plates move apart. Hydrothermal vents occur at a range of depths, from the shallow water around volcanic islands to more than 12,000 feet (3,600 meters) beneath the ocean's surface.

Hot seawater containing such chemicals as copper, iron, manganese, zinc, and sulfate flows from the vents. As the hot water mixes with colder seawater containing oxygen, chemical reactions form dark-colored mineral particles. These particles produce deposits around the vents. The deposits take the shape of "chimneys" through which the water shoots out. The dark-colored minerals make the water look like black smoke, and so these hydrothermal vents are called *black smokers.*

Communities of strange marine life live at hydrothermal vents. Scientists discovered that some kinds of bacteria and archaea that live there use chemosynthesis to produce food. Such organisms serve as the base of the food chain for the vent communities. Scientists previously thought that all food chains throughout the ocean began with the energy from sunlight and the photosynthesis that takes place in shallow waters. Other forms of life found near hydrothermal vents include clams up to 1 foot (30 centimeters) long and giant tubeworms up to about 5 feet (1.5 meters) long. Scientists have also discovered various species of crabs, fish, shrimp, and other animals in the vent communities. Most of the animals were previously unknown species of marine life.

Oceanographers often make discoveries as they apply new instruments and techniques to study the ocean. The use of specialized research ships, satellites, and computers has increased their knowledge of oceanic processes. For example, such technology has enabled us to better understand the effects of El Niño in Earth's weather and climate systems. El Niño is an interaction between the atmosphere and the waters of the Pacific Ocean that occurs about every two to seven years. During an El Niño, a warm current flows southward along the west coast of South America, warming the normally cold coastal waters of Ecuador and Peru. The warming of the ocean waters kills many fish and the sea birds that rely on fish for food. A typical El Niño lasts about 18 months.

For years, El Niño was considered only a local phenomenon. In the 1960's, however, scientists observed a connection between El Niño and a change in the normal trade winds over the tropical Pacific Ocean. In the 1990's, oceanographers used a variety of ships, satellites, and electronic instruments to study the ways in which the tropical ocean and atmosphere interact to produce El

Niño events. They discovered that El Niño and an opposite pattern called La Niña that often follows are part of a larger atmospheric pattern known as the Southern Oscillation. El Niño studies have also enabled scientists to predict El Niño events—and their effects—from 6 to 18 months in advance. These effects include rainfall and drought conditions, as well as severe forest fires and floods. See **El Niño.**

International cooperation. Increasingly, many countries now cooperate with one another in conducting scientific studies of the ocean. Major international investigations have studied such issues as the circulation of ocean waters, the changes in the sea's chemical content, and the structure of marine ecosystems. In addition, efforts are underway to develop a global ocean observing system to better understand natural and human-induced changes in the marine environment.

Ocean problems

For thousands of years, people used the ocean and its vast resources with little concern for their conservation. But during the last two centuries, increases in human population, industrial development, and use of coastal regions has put the health of the sea at risk, forcing people to address ocean conservation problems. Many of the major problems involve marine pollution, depletion of fisheries, habitat modification, and climate change.

Marine pollution. *Pollutants* (substances that cause pollution) enter oceans through accidents, carelessness, and the deliberate disposal of wastes. The ocean can absorb some types of pollutants in certain quantities because of its great size and the natural chemical processes that occur within it. But the ocean's capacity to absorb and recycle pollutants can become overwhelmed.

People pollute the oceans in several ways. Major ocean pollutants include waste products, which people often dump deliberately into the ocean, and oil, which usually enters the sea by accident.

Waste products that enter the ocean include sewage, plastic litter, and industrial wastes. Sewage, such as human waste and ground-up garbage, often fouls coastal regions. This kind of waste contains organic matter that decomposes and reduces the levels of oxygen in the water. Low oxygen levels make the water unfit for animals. Sewage also contains nitrates, phosphates, and other nutrients that stimulate the growth of phytoplankton. An overabundance of certain phytoplankton produces a condition called *eutrophication,* which also reduces the water's oxygen levels. Rapid growth of some phytoplankton can create *red tides.* Red tide phytoplankton produce toxins that poison marine life.

Plastic litter can severely damage the ocean because it does not break down easily. Sea birds, turtles, seals, whales, and other marine animals can get tangled in plastic nets, bags, and packing material. They may also mistake plastic items for food and die of starvation if the plastic blocks their digestive system. Plastics and other litter also make the marine environment less attractive. Many countries ban the disposal of plastics into the ocean, but such litter remains a problem on shorelines.

The deliberate dumping of industrial waste into the sea from ships and barges has also polluted oceans. Such wastes have included ash from power plants, contaminated sediments dredged from harbors, and even radioactive wastes. Since the 1970's, many countries have begun banning ocean dumping of most wastes. But the disposal of some types of wastes, such as dredged sediments, may likely continue.

Oil pollution enters the ocean from oil spills on land or in rivers. Oil also seeps into the ocean naturally from cracks in the sea floor. Oil tanker and oil well accidents at sea account for only a small portion of ocean oil pollution, but their effects may be disastrous. One of the largest accidental oil spills in history occurred in 2010, when an explosion on an offshore oil rig caused about 206 million gallons (780 million liters) of oil to spill into the Gulf of Mexico. The world's largest oil spill occurred when Iraq deliberately released between 240 million and 465 million gallons (910 million and 1,760 million liters) of oil into the Persian Gulf during the Persian Gulf War of 1991. In water, much of the oil forms tarlike lumps. It fouls beaches and other coastal areas. Oil also coats fish, birds, and mammals and kills many of them.

Fisheries. Since the latter part of the 1900's, the world's fishing industry has harvested fish from many ocean fisheries faster than the fish stocks can renew themselves. Some fishing techniques have proved especially destructive. These techniques include the use of dynamite and cyanide to stun or kill fish on coral reefs. They also include the use of nets that capture, injure, or kill species other than the ones being sought. In some cases, the depletion of commercially valuable fish species can alter marine ecosystems by making less valuable species more abundant. Such problems have led many countries to enforce limits on catch and even temporarily close a number of valuable fisheries.

Habitat modification. People have harmed marine ecosystems in many coastal regions by destroying such vital habitats as marshes; mangrove swamps, where the spreading roots of mangrove trees catch and hold silt from the water; and tidal flats, which are covered and uncovered twice daily by the tides. These environments often play an essential role in maintaining a healthy marine ecosystem. As a result, conservationists are attempting to stop further damage to such habitats and, in some cases, to restore the habitats to their natural state.

Climate change. Natural processes cause most kinds of climate change. But increasing evidence indicates that human activities can also produce changes in climate. Over the past 150 years, the combustion of such *fossil fuels* as petroleum, coal, and natural gas has increased the amount of carbon dioxide gas in the atmosphere by about 30 percent. Carbon dioxide traps heat from the sun in a process called the *greenhouse effect.* Increases in atmospheric carbon dioxide may enhance the greenhouse effect and significantly raise temperatures on Earth. Such changes in climate could greatly affect all marine ecosystems. See **Greenhouse effect.**

Scientists are working to determine the role of the ocean in climate, as well as the effects of human activities on climate change. Scientists have studied the possibility of disposing of carbon dioxide into the depths of the ocean as a way to keep Earth from overheating.

Who owns the ocean? This question has become more important as countries have learned that fish and other ocean resources can be used up and that valuable minerals and sources of energy lie on and under the sea floor. The United Nations has worked to develop an

AP/Wide World

Oil spills harm marine wildlife. These volunteers gather penguins that have become soaked with oil from a spill in South Africa. Such animals must be cleaned if they are to survive.

agreement on ownership of the sea. Its efforts resulted in the Law of the Sea Convention, drafted in 1982. This treaty went into effect in 1994, after more than 60 nations ratified it. The treaty provides for a system to protect the economic and environmental interests of coastal nations, while allowing the free passage of other countries' ships.

Under the Law of the Sea Convention, the laws of a coastal nation apply throughout its territorial sea, which extends 12 nautical miles (22 kilometers) from the na-

© Donna Rona, Bruce Coleman Inc.

A marine biologist, *shown here,* studies life in the ocean. A net is used to gather tiny animals and plantlike organisms.

© Ocean Drilling Program, Texas A&M University

Marine geologists study features of the ocean bottom. These scientists are examining and describing vertical samples of sediment called *cores.* Cores are drilled from beneath the sea floor.

tion's shoreline. An *exclusive economic zone* (EEZ) lies beyond the nation's territorial sea and extends, in most cases, 200 nautical miles (370 kilometers) from the nation's shoreline. Each coastal nation, even if it is an island, has total control over resources and research within its EEZ. The remaining ocean area is defined as the *high seas,* where no nation may make a territorial claim. However, even on the high seas, various international agreements govern fishing methods and fishing catches, as well as disposal of wastes.

The United States has not joined the Law of the Sea Convention. At the time the treaty was drafted, the U.S. government supported most of its provisions but believed it did not adequately protect private industries involved in deep-sea mining. In 1994, the United States signed an agreement that addressed these deep-sea mining concerns. However, the U.S. Senate has not approved the 1994 agreement or the original convention.

Careers in oceanography

The ocean can be studied in many ways, and the science of oceanography includes several specialties. *Physical oceanographers* study waves, tides, currents, and the action of the ocean and the atmosphere on each other. *Chemical oceanographers* study the chemical reactions that occur in the ocean. *Marine geologists* and *marine geophysicists* analyze the form and composition of the sea floor, as well as the forces that shape the ocean floor. Marine geologists mainly study the sediments and surface features of the ocean bottom. Marine geophysicists deal with the deeper oceanic crust. *Biological oceanographers* and *marine biologists* study marine life, from microscopic bacteria to large marine mammals. *Ocean engineers* design instruments to study the ocean, develop methods for obtaining minerals and other resources from the sea, and design structures for use in the ocean and on the sea floor.

To become an oceanographer, one needs a background in science and mathematics. Solid knowledge of at least one basic science, such as biology, chemistry, or geology, is required. Most oceanographers acquire detailed knowledge of oceans through graduate training.

An oceanographer may choose from several types of careers after completing training. Research jobs are

available at colleges and universities, at oceanographic institutions, in government, and in industry laboratories. Colleges and universities also provide teaching jobs. Some oceanographers go on long research expeditions or make deep-sea dives. Others formulate theories or interpret scientific observations. Oceanographers may also work with computers in an attempt to re-create, analyze, and predict ocean behavior.   Philip L. Richardson

Related articles in *World Book* include:

Oceans

Arctic Ocean	Indian Ocean	Southern Ocean
Atlantic Ocean	Pacific Ocean	

Seas

Adriatic Sea	Caribbean Sea	Mediterranean
Aegean Sea	China Sea	Sea
Arabian Sea	Coral Sea	North Sea
Azov, Sea of	Ionian Sea	Red Sea
Baltic Sea	Irish Sea	Tasman Sea
Barents Sea	Japan, Sea of	Tyrrhenian Sea
Bering Sea	Kara Sea	White Sea
Black Sea	Marmara, Sea of	Yellow Sea

Currents

El Niño	Kuroshio	Peru Current
Gulf Stream	Labrador Current	

Life in the ocean

Animal (Animals of	Deep sea	Plankton
the oceans)	Diatom	Seaweed
Archaea	Dinoflagellate	Sponge
Coral	Fish	Whale
Crustacean		

Other related articles

Bay	Life (Modern	Seiche
Cable	explanations)	Seven seas
Calms, Regions of	Maelstrom	Ship
Climate	Marine biology	Skin diving
Conservation	Navigation	Sonar
(Ocean	Ocean drilling	Tide
conservation)	programs	Transportation
Coral reef	Oceanography	Tsunami
Deep	Oil spill	United Nations
Diving,	Pearl	(Peaceful uses
Underwater	Plate tectonics	of outer space
Estuary	Red tide	and the seabed)
Fathometer	Sargasso Sea	Water (Fresh wa-
Fishing industry	Scripps Institution	ter from the sea)
Geology	of Oceanogra-	Waves
Grand Banks	phy	Woods Hole
Hydrothermal vent	Sea level	Oceanographic
Ice formation	Seamount	Institution
Law of the Sea	Seashore	
Convention		

Outline

I. **The world ocean**
    A. Area
    B. Depth
    C. Temperature
    D. Composition

II. **The importance of the ocean**
    A. As a wealth of resources
    B. As an influence on climate
    C. As a vast highway

III. **Life in the ocean**
    A. The plankton
    B. The nekton
    C. The benthos
    D. The food cycle

IV. **How the ocean moves**
    A. Circulation
    B. Waves
    C. Tides

V. **The land at the bottom of the sea**
    A. The continental margin
    B. Deep-sea peaks, valleys, and plains

C. How the sea floor was formed

Additional resources

Level I
Ganeri, Anita. *Oceans.* Gareth Stevens, 2003.
Littlefield, Cindy A. *Awesome Ocean Science: Investigating the Secrets of the Underwater World.* Williamson, 2003.

Level II
Sverdrup, Keith A., and Duxbury, A. C. and A. B. *An Introduction to the World's Oceans.* 7th ed. McGraw, 2003.
World Atlas of the Oceans. Firefly Bks., 2001.

Ocean drilling programs are a series of scientific expeditions to study Earth beneath the ocean floor. They aim to help scientists understand the processes that have shaped Earth. Ocean drilling also provides information on the evolution of prehistoric marine life, the development of ice ages, and changes in Earth's climate during the past 200 million years. The Integrated Ocean Drilling Program (IODP), the latest such program, began in 2003. The IODP continues the work of the Ocean Drilling Program (ODP) and the Deep Sea Drilling Project.

Ocean drilling programs use special ships called *drillships.* A long strand of pipe called a *drill pipe* passes through a hole in the ship's hull. Machinery on the ship rotates the drill pipe, which bores deep into the ocean floor. Tools passed through the center of the pipe remove cylindrical samples of sediment and rock called *cores.* Many of the cores contain fossils and minerals that have accumulated over thousands or even millions of years. Scientists have recovered cores in water more than 27,000 feet (8,200 meters) deep. In laboratories aboard the drillships, scientists analyze and catalog the cores. The cores are later moved to special libraries called *core repositories.* Once a core has been taken, scientists can place devices called *sensors* inside the drilled hole to monitor temperature and pressure.

Teams of scientists from around the world participate in IODP cruises that last from several weeks to months. Many nations contribute funding to the program. The ODP operated the *JOIDES Resolution* from 1985 to 2003. *JOIDES* stands for *J*oint *O*ceanographic *I*nstitutions for *D*eep *E*arth *S*ampling. The program identified populations of primitive microbes living in hot water beneath the ocean crust and analyzed evidence of past climate change. It also studied *natural gas hydrates,* frozen deposits of methane gas and water that could someday be used for fuel. United States members of the IODP operated the *JOIDES Resolution* from 2003 to 2005. From 2006 to 2009, the U.S. partners rebuilt the *JOIDES Resolution.* The renovated ship resumed drilling in 2009.

Japanese members constructed a heavy drillship named the *Chikyu,* the Japanese word for *Earth.* The ship can drill up to 23,000 feet (7,000 meters) into the ocean floor, more than three times deeper than previous drillships. The *Chikyu* began drilling in 2007. European IODP partners have provided equipment for special missions, such as icebreakers for expeditions to the Arctic Ocean.

The Deep Sea Drilling Project operated the drillship

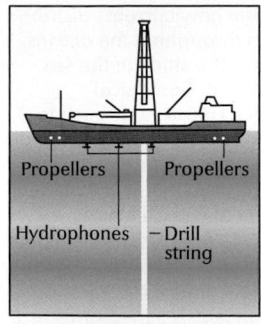

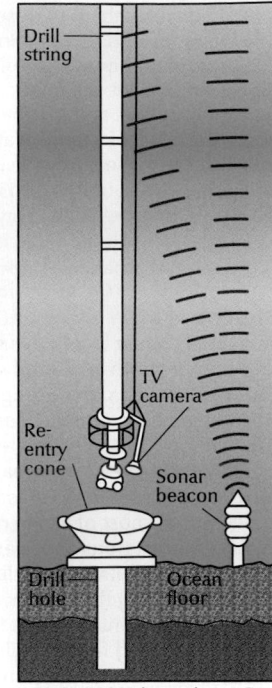

A deep-sea drilling ship uses propellers to stay in place despite wind and waves. Devices called *hydrophones* help maintain its position. They receive signals from a sonar beacon on the sea floor.

A drill string of pipe can be put back into a drill hole after removal for repairs. A remote television camera helps researchers guide the pipe to a reentry cone above the hole.

WORLD BOOK diagrams by Amie Zorn, Artisan-Chicago

Glomar Challenger from 1968 to 1983. Among its many achievements, the project provided data to support the theory of *plate tectonics.* The theory holds that Earth's surface is made up of rigid plates moving about on a layer of hot rock. The project produced evidence that newly created sea floor spreads from underwater ridges, a key element of tectonic theory (see **Plate tectonics**).   Frank R. Rack

See also **Ocean** (Tools of exploration).

Oceania. See **Pacific Islands.**

Oceanography is the scientific study of Earth's oceans. Oceanographers study the sea floor, seawater, and sea life. They may specialize in biology, chemistry, engineering, geology, or physics. Oceanographers gather information using research ships, submarines, robotic vehicles, and various collecting tools and measuring instruments. Several countries have ocean-observing systems. Such systems continuously monitor the ocean's properties, including temperature and currents. Oceanographers develop ways to store and analyze this data.

Biological oceanography is the study of ocean life and its interaction with the ocean's physical, chemical, and biological features, such as temperature, oxygen levels, and other organisms. This includes the study of the diversity, characteristics, and activities of ocean life.

Chemical oceanography studies the elements and compounds in seawater, sea-floor rocks, sea life, and the atmosphere. Many chemical oceanographers study *elemental cycles,* the processes and reactions that cause chemicals to cycle between these domains.

Physical oceanography involves the use of physics, mathematics, and computer models to understand the ocean's physical characteristics. Physical oceanographers study currents, evaporation, ice formation, light, rainfall, salt content, sound, and temperature. This information enables them to describe how currents distribute water, heat, or living things throughout the oceans.

Geological oceanography is the study of the sea floor and ancient sea floors on land. Geological oceanographers and marine geologists study such topics as Earth's crust, underwater volcanoes, and earthquakes. They also study the changing nature of coasts, including river outflow, erosion, and the record of Earth's history revealed in layers of coastal lands.

Critically reviewed by the Woods Hole Oceanographic Institution

Related information in *World Book.* For more information on the oceans, see **Ocean** and its list of related articles.

Ocelot, *AHS uh laht* or *OH suh laht,* is a medium-sized animal of the cat family. It is known as the *leopard cat* or *tiger cat* of North and South America. It is 3 ½ to 4 feet (107 to 120 centimeters) long including the tail, which is 15 inches (38 centimeters) long. The ocelot stands 16 to 18 inches (41 to 46 centimeters) high at the shoulder.

The ocelot lives in an area ranging from southeastern Arizona and southern Texas to Paraguay in South America. It spends most of its life on the ground, but it often hunts in forest trees and is an agile climber. It eats mice, wood rats, rabbits, snakes, lizards, birds, young deer, and monkeys. In the tropics, a favorite food is agoutis.

The ground tint of ocelot fur varies greatly in different animals, ranging from reddish-yellow to smoky-pearl. Black spots vary in size from dots on the legs and the feet to large shell-shaped spots on other body parts. The ocelot has a pink nose and large, translucent eyes.

Ocelots have been widely hunted for their fur, and their number has fallen sharply. Laws that ban hunting of ocelots have been hard to enforce.   Duane A. Schlitter

Scientific classification. The ocelot's scientific name is *Leopardus pardalis.*

See also **Animal** (picture: Animals of the tropical forests).

Ochs, *ahks,* **Adolph Simon** (1858-1935), rose from a job as a newsboy to become the publisher and guiding influence of *The New York Times.* He separated editorial comment from news in the *Times* and sought to present news free from prejudice. In 38 years, the daily circulation of the *Times* rose from 9,000 to 460,000. Ochs also founded *Current History* magazine and gave $500,000 toward publication of the *Dictionary of American Biography.* Ochs began his career at 11 as an errand boy at the *Knoxville* (Tennessee) *Chronicle.* Later, he bought a half-interest in the *Chattanooga Times* and made it one of the area's strongest papers. He became manager of *The New York Times* in 1896 and gained controlling interest in 1900. He was born on March 12, 1858, in Cincinnati. He died on April 8, 1935.   William McKeen

Ockham, William of. See William of Ockham.

Ocmulgee National Monument, *ohk MUHL gee,* is in central Georgia. It contains the most important prehistoric Indian mounds in the Southeast, including a restored council chamber. Ruins dating from 8000 B.C. were found there. The monument was established in 1934. For area, see **National Park System** (table: National monuments).   Critically reviewed by the National Park Service

O'Connell, Daniel (1775-1847), an Irish statesman, helped lead the struggle of Roman Catholics to gain political rights in the United Kingdom. This struggle resulted in the passing of the Catholic Emancipation Act of 1829. That act gave Catholic men the right to serve in the

British Parliament and to hold most other public offices. Previously, Catholics were denied these rights in the primarily Protestant United Kingdom. The new law had a major effect in Ireland, then a part of the United Kingdom where most of the people were Catholics. O'Connell, called "the Liberator," became the first Irish Catholic to win election to the British House of Commons. He served there from 1829 to 1847.

O'Connell was born on Aug. 6, 1775, in Cahirciveen, County Kerry. He became a lawyer in 1798. He formed the Catholic Association in 1823 to seek the political rights of Catholics. In Parliament, he played a key role in passing the Reform Act of 1832, which gave most middle class men the right to vote. He was arrested in 1843 for supporting Ireland's complete independence from the United Kingdom. In 1844, he was convicted of plotting against the government and spent 14 weeks in jail. He died on May 15, 1847.   Thomas E. Hachey

O'Connor, Flannery (1925-1964), was an American author whose novels and stories are filled with characters who are physically deformed or emotionally or spiritually disturbed. Some are obsessed with religion and the possibility of their own damnation or salvation. But O'Connor's books also contain humor, irony, and satire.

Mary Flannery O'Connor was born on March 25, 1925, in Savannah, Georgia. Her Southern heritage and Roman Catholicism strongly influenced her writing. O'Connor suffered from poor health most of her life and could complete only a few works. They include two novels, *Wise Blood* (1952) and *The Violent Bear It Away* (1960).

O'Connor died on Aug. 3, 1964. Her stories were collected in *A Good Man Is Hard to Find* (1955) and *Everything That Rises Must Converge,* published in 1965 after her death. The stories in these two collections are included in *Flannery O'Connor: The Complete Stories,* published in 1971. This collection won the 1972 National Book Award for fiction. *Mystery and Manners,* essays and lectures on literature and writing, was published in 1969. A collection of her letters called *The Habit of Being* was published in 1979.   Noel Polk

O'Connor, Sandra Day (1930-   ), became the first woman to serve on the Supreme Court of the United States when she became an associate justice of the court in 1981. President Ronald Reagan appointed her to replace Justice Potter Stewart, who retired. O'Connor retired from the court in January 2006 after the U.S. Senate confirmed Samuel A. Alito, Jr., as her successor.

As a Supreme Court justice, O'Connor often sided with conservative court members. But she was sympathetic to liberal views on some issues. She provided the deciding vote in many important cases, involving such issues as affirmative action, abortion, and states' rights.

O'Connor was born on March 26, 1930, in El Paso, Texas. She graduated from Stanford Law School in 1952. In 1965, she became an assistant attorney general of Arizona. In 1969, she was appointed to an

Dane Penland, Supreme Court of the United States

Sandra Day O'Connor

unexpired term in the Arizona Senate. She won election to that body in 1970, was reelected in 1972, and was named Senate majority leader in 1973. O'Connor was elected a judge of a Maricopa County trial court in 1974. In 1979, she was named to the Arizona Court of Appeals, the state's second highest court. Dennis J. Hutchinson

See also **Supreme Court of the United States** (picture).

Ocotillo, OH kuh TEEL yoh, is a shrub that grows in the deserts of Mexico and the southwestern United States. It is also called candlewood, coachwhip, and vine cactus.

The ocotillo plant stands 6 to 25 feet (1.8 to 7.6 meters) tall. It has many long, spiny stems growing from its base. After moderate to heavy rains, the stems bear leaves and bunches of scarlet flowers. But in the dry season, they stand bare as dry spiny sticks. Ocotillos make good hedges that are hard to pass through.

Philip W. Rundel
Scientific classification. Ocotillo's scientific name is *Fouquieria splendens.*

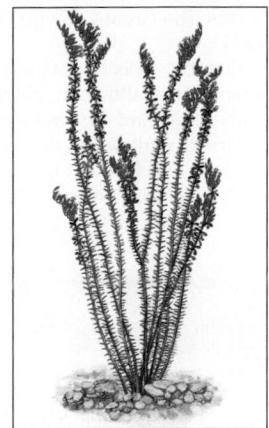

WORLD BOOK illustration by Lorraine Epstein

Ocotillo looks like a bunch of dry sticks thrust into the sand in dry periods. After a heavy rain, tiny green leaves cover the plant's stems, and brilliant red blossoms form at the tips.

Octagon is a plane figure with eight sides. It is a type of polygon. The sides of an octagon meet at points called *vertices* to form eight interior angles. The interior angles of an octagon always add up to 1080°. A type of octagon called a *regular octagon* has equal sides and equal angles. The area of a regular octagon equals one-half the product of the perimeter and the *apothem,* the distance from the center of a regular polygon to the midpoint of one of its sides. Blake E. Peterson

Octahedron is any solid, three-dimensional figure with eight faces. It is a type of *polyhedron* (solid figure with many faces). The faces of an octahedron need not have the same shape. Some may be triangles and others another kind of polygon. A variety of octahedron called a *regular octahedron* is a convex polyhedron in which all of the eight faces are congruent equilateral triangles. Blake E. Peterson

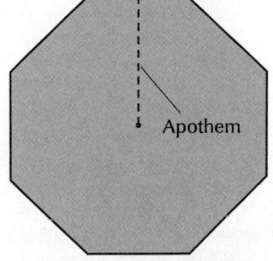

WORLD BOOK illustration
A regular octagon has eight equal sides.

WORLD BOOK illustration
A regular octahedron has eight faces, each of which is a congruent equilateral triangle.

Octane, AHK tayn, is any of 18 chemical compounds that consist of 8 carbon atoms and 18 hydrogen atoms. Octanes are among the main ingredients of gasolines. An octane called *isooctane* is used in a test mixture to determine how well a gasoline resists knocking (see **Octane number**). Gasolines with a high octane number can prevent engine knock better than those with lower octane number. Octanes belong to a group of chemicals called *hydrocarbons* (see **Hydrocarbon**). All octanes are colorless liquids, all are highly flammable, and all have the same molecular formula, C_8H_{18}. But they have different molecular structures and therefore different chemical and physical properties. For example, *normal octane,* also called *n-octane,* boils at 258.2 °F (125.7 °C), but isooctane boils at 210.6 °F (99.2 °C). Geoffrey E. Dolbear

Octane number, AHK tayn, is a number that tells how well a motor fuel resists "knocking." "Knocking" occurs when portions of the fuel in an engine cylinder ignite too soon, causing all of the fuel to burn too quickly.

Engineers determine a gasoline's octane number by comparing its resistance to knocking with the antiknock performance of reference fuels in a test engine. Each reference fuel is a blend of two *hydrocarbons,* organic compounds that contain only hydrogen and carbon. These two hydrocarbons are *normal heptane,* which is knock-prone, and *isooctane,* which is knock-resistant. Normal heptane has an octane number of 0, and isooctane a value of 100. A motor fuel has an octane number of 85 if it produces the same knock as a reference fuel made of 85 percent isooctane and 15 percent normal heptane. Octane numbers above 100 are measured with a reference fuel containing isooctane and chemical antiknock compounds.

Automotive engineers typically measure octane number in two ways. Thus, every gasoline has two octane numbers: a *research octane number* (RON) and a *motor octane number* (MON). The RON is determined in a special one-cylinder engine in a laboratory. The MON is determined in the same engine, but under conditions that simulate the normal operation of an ordinary engine. The MON is typically about 10 numbers lower than the RON. For example, a gasoline with a RON of 95 may have a MON of 87. The octane number displayed on the pump at a gas station is usually the average of the RON and the MON. Most commercially available gasolines have octane numbers from 87 to 93. Edward C. Mozdzen

See also **Gasoline.**

Octavia, ahk TAY vee uh (69?-11 B.C.), was the older half-sister of the Roman ruler Octavian, who became the emperor Augustus in 27 B.C. Octavia married Octavian's co-ruler Mark Antony in 40 B.C. The marriage sealed a peace pact that ended a civil war between Octavian and Antony. Octavia bore Antony two daughters, Antonia the Elder and Antonia the Younger.

Antony treated Octavia badly. He and Cleopatra, queen of Egypt, had been lovers before he married Octavia. In 37 B.C., he left Octavia to live with Cleopatra. He divorced Octavia in 32 B.C. Afterward, Octavia raised Antony's children by his first wife, Fulvia, and her own children by Antony and her first husband, Marcellus. Octavia also raised Antony's children by Cleopatra after Antony and Cleopatra died in 30 B.C. Judith P. Hallett

See also **Antony, Mark; Augustus; Cleopatra.**
Octavian. See Augustus.

October is the 10th month of the year, according to the Gregorian calendar, which is used in most parts of the world today. Its name comes from the Latin word for *eight.* October was the eighth month of the early Roman calendar. It later became the 10th month when the ancient Romans moved the beginning of the year from March 1 to January 1. October has had 31 days since the time of the Roman emperor Augustus.

Various kinds of holidays occur in this month. South Koreans celebrate National Foundation Day on October 3. This holiday marks the establishment of the kingdom of Choson in 2333 B.C. According to legend, Tangun, a son of a heavenly being, founded *Choson,* meaning *land of morning calm,* in present-day North Korea. Chulalongkorn Day falls on October 23 in Thailand. This national holiday honors King Chulalongkorn, also known

as Rama V, who abolished slavery and introduced many reforms. New Zealand observes Labour Day on the fourth Monday in October.

The second Monday in October is Thanksgiving Day in Canada. Columbus Day in the United States also occurs on this day. It marks the arrival of Christopher Columbus in America on Oct. 12, 1492. The week including October 9 is Fire Prevention Week in the United States. The Great Chicago Fire raged from October 8-10, 1871.

October 31 is Halloween in some countries. On the evening of Halloween, children disguise themselves with masks and costumes and go door to door asking for treats. Halloween developed from ancient new year festivals and festivals of the dead. The ancient Celts celebrated Samhain, a harvest festival, on November 1. On

Important October events

1 Free rural mail delivery began in the United States, 1896.
— First "Model T" Ford put on the market, 1908.
— Jimmy Carter, 39th U.S. president, born 1924.
— People's Republic of China was established in 1949.
— Nigeria became independent in 1960.
2 Mohandas Gandhi, Indian political leader, born 1869.
— Cordell Hull, American statesman, born 1871.
— Guinea became independent in 1958.
3 George Bancroft, American historian, born 1800.
— Eleonora Duse, Italian actress, born 1858.
4 Jean François Millet, French painter, born 1814.
— Rutherford B. Hayes, 19th U.S. president, born 1822.
— Frederic Remington, American artist, born 1861.
— U.S.S.R. launched Sputnik I, first artificial satellite, 1957.
— Lesotho became independent in 1966.
5 Gregorian calendar introduced, 1582.
— Denis Diderot, French author, born 1713.
— Chester A. Arthur, 21st U.S. president, born 1829.
— Joshua Logan, American playwright, born 1908.
— U.S. President Harry S. Truman made the first presidential telecast address from the White House, 1947.
6 Jenny Lind, Swedish singer, born 1820.
— George Westinghouse, American inventor, born 1846.
— Le Corbusier, Swiss-born architect, born 1887.
— Anwar el-Sadat, president of Egypt, assassinated 1981.
7 First double-decked steamboat, the *Washington,* arrived at New Orleans, 1816.
— James Whitcomb Riley, American poet, born 1849.
— Niels Bohr, Danish physicist, born 1885.
8 John M. Hay, American statesman, born 1838.
— Great Chicago Fire began, 1871.
— Eddie Rickenbacker, American air ace, born 1890.
9 Uganda became independent in 1962.
— Camille Saint-Saëns, French composer, born 1835.
10 Sports Day, Japan

— Henry Cavendish, English scientist, born 1731.
— U.S. Naval Academy opened at Annapolis, Maryland, 1845.
— Fridtjof Nansen, Norwegian explorer and statesman, born 1861.
— Helen Hayes, American actress, born 1900.
11 Arthur Phillip, first governor of New South Wales, Australia, born in London, 1738.
— Eleanor Roosevelt, wife of U.S. President Franklin D. Roosevelt, born 1884.
— François Mauriac, French novelist, born 1885.
12 Christopher Columbus landed in America, 1492.
— Ralph Vaughan Williams, British composer, born 1872.
13 U.S. White House cornerstone laid, 1792.
— Rudolf Virchow, German scientist, born 1821.
— Margaret Thatcher, British prime minister, born 1925.
14 William the Conqueror won the Battle of Hastings, 1066.
— William Penn, founder of Pennsylvania, born 1644.
— Eamon de Valera, president of the Irish Republic, born 1882.
— Dwight D. Eisenhower, 34th U.S. president, born 1890.
— E. E. Cummings, American poet, born 1894.
15 Virgil, Roman poet, born 70 B.C.
— J. F. Pilâtre de Rozier became first person to ascend in a captive balloon, 1783.
— Helen Hunt Jackson, American novelist, born 1830.
— Friedrich Nietzsche, German philosopher, born 1844.
— Clayton Antitrust Act became U.S. law, 1914.
16 Noah Webster, American dictionary editor, born 1758.
— Oscar Wilde, Irish-born dramatist, born 1854.
— David Ben-Gurion, Israeli prime minister and Zionist leader, born 1886.
— Eugene O'Neill, American playwright and Nobel Prize winner, born 1888.
17 British General John Burgoyne surrendered his army at Saratoga, New York, American Revolution, 1777.

Oct. birthstone—
opal

Oct. flower—
calendula

Oct. 1—first
Model T Ford

Oct. 8—Great Chicago
Fire

the night before the festival, they honored Saman, the Celtic lord of death. This celebration also marked summer's end. October 31 is All Hallows' Eve in Christian cultures. It is the eve of All Saints' Day, on which Christians honor all the known and unknown saints who have died.

The calendula and cosmos are October's flowers. October's birthstones are the opal and the tourmaline.

Carole S. Angell

Quotations

October turned my maple's leaves to gold;
The most are gone now; here and there one lingers;
Soon these will slip from out the twig's weak hold,
Like coins between a dying miser's fingers.

Thomas Bailey Aldrich

There is something in October sets the gipsy blood astir;
We must rise and follow her,
When from every hill of flame
She calls, and calls each vagabond by name.

Bliss Carman

October gave a party;
The leaves by hundreds came;
The ashes, oaks, and maples,
And those of every name.

George Cooper

Related articles in *World Book* include:

Autumn	Columbus Day	Indian summer
Calendar	Cosmos	Opal
Calendula	Halloween	Tourmaline

October Revolution. See Union of Soviet Socialist Republics (The October Revolution).

Important October events

17 Abolitionist John Brown and his men seized U.S. arsenal at Harpers Ferry, Virginia (now West Virginia), 1859.
18 Henri Bergson, French philosopher, born 1859.
— Pierre Elliott Trudeau, prime minister of Canada, born 1919.
19 First general court in New England held, Boston, 1630.
— British troops under Cornwallis surrendered at Yorktown, ending the American Revolution in 1781.
— Thomas Edison first demonstrated his electric light, 1879.
20 Sir Christopher Wren, English architect, born 1632.
— The Báb, first prophet in Age of Fulfillment in Baha'i faith, born 1819.
— John Dewey, American philosopher, born 1859.
21 Magellan entered strait that bears his name, 1520.
— Samuel Taylor Coleridge, English poet, born 1772.
— U.S.S. *Constitution,* better known as *Old Ironsides,* launched, 1797.
— British Admiral Nelson was killed at Trafalgar, 1805.
— Alfred Nobel, Swedish philanthropist and founder of the Nobel Prize, born 1833.
22 Franz Liszt, Hungarian composer, born 1811.
— Sam Houston inaugurated as first president of the Republic of Texas, 1836.
23 British began offensive at El Alamein in Egypt in World War II, 1942.
— Battle for Leyte Gulf in the Philippines began in World War II, 1944.
24 Anton van Leeuwenhoek, Dutch naturalist, born 1632.
— First transcontinental telegram sent, 1861.
— United Nations formally established, 1945.
— Northern Rhodesia became independent and was renamed Zambia in 1964.
25 Henry V of England defeated French at Agincourt in Hundred Years' War, 1415.
— Thomas B. Macaulay, British historian, born 1800.
— "Waltz King" Johann Strauss, Jr., born 1825.

— Georges Bizet, French composer, born 1838.
— Pablo Picasso, Spanish painter, born 1881.
— Richard E. Byrd, American polar explorer, born 1888.
26 International Red Cross Day.
— Helmuth von Moltke, Prussian general, born 1800.
— Erie Canal opened to traffic, 1825.
27 Captain James Cook, British explorer, born 1728.
— Niccolò Paganini, Italian violinist, born 1782.
— The *Federalist* papers began appearing in the New York newspaper *Independent Journal,* 1787.
— Theodore Roosevelt, 26th U.S. president, born 1858.
28 Harvard College founded, 1636.
— Statue of Liberty dedicated, 1886.
— Jonas Salk, American developer of a polio vaccine, born 1914.
29 Republic Day, Turkey.
— James Boswell, Scottish biographer of Samuel Johnson, born 1740.
— Bill Mauldin, American cartoonist, born 1921.
— Collapse of U.S. stock market (Black Tuesday), 1929.
30 John Adams, second U.S. president, born 1735.
— Benito Mussolini, founder of fascism, became prime minister of Italy, 1922.
31 Halloween in many countries.
— UNICEF Day in United States.
— According to tradition, the day Martin Luther nailed his 95 theses to the door of a church at Wittenberg, 1517.
— Jan Vermeer, Dutch painter, born 1632.
— King's College (now Columbia University) founded, 1754.
— John Keats, English poet, born 1795.
— Nevada became the 36th U.S. state, 1864.
— Sir Hubert Wilkins, Australian explorer, born 1888.
— Indira Gandhi, Indian prime minister, assassinated 1984.

WORLD BOOK illustrations by Mike Hagel

Oct. 12—Christopher Columbus's arrival in America

Oct. 17—John Brown's raid

Oct. 19—British surrender at Yorktown

Oct. 28—Statue of Liberty dedicated

© Neil McDaniel

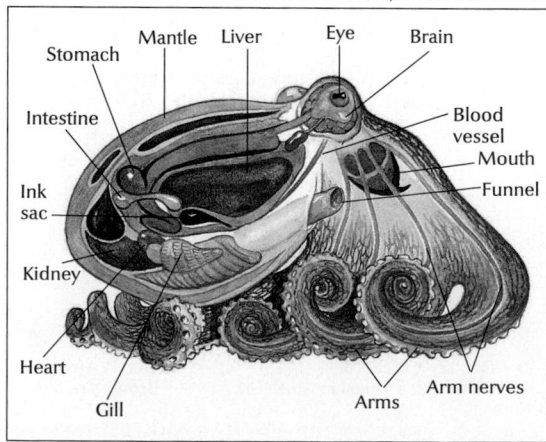

© Fred Bavendam from Peter Arnold

© Waina Cheng, Bruce Coleman Inc.

Octopuses are soft-bodied sea animals with eight arms. Suckers on the underside of each arm enable an octopus to cling to rocks or prey. The *North Pacific giant octopus, left,* lives in the Pacific Ocean. Octopuses lay transparent eggs, *top right,* from which the young hatch, *bottom right.*

Octopus is any of a group of sea animals with a rounded body, large eyes, and eight long arms. The best-known *species* (kinds) of octopuses inhabit rocky, sandy, or muddy bottoms in shallow parts of oceans worldwide. Many octopuses live in deep waters. Some kinds are *pelagic,* inhabiting the surface water of open oceans.

Octopuses vary greatly in size. The largest species, the *North Pacific giant octopus* of the Pacific Ocean, can weigh up to 150 pounds (68 kilograms). It measures more than 20 feet (6 meters) from the tip of one arm to the tip of another on the opposite side of the body. The smallest species, found in the Indian Ocean, weighs less than 1 ounce (28 grams) and measures about 1 inch (2.5 centimeters) from arm tip to arm tip.

Octopuses belong to a large group of animals called *mollusks.* This group also includes clams, oysters, and snails. Like squids and cuttlefish, octopuses are mollusks that have no external shell or skeleton.

The body of an octopus is soft and boneless. A fleshy, muscular covering called the *mantle* surrounds the main part of the body, forming a cavity that encloses the gills. An octopus breathes by drawing water into the mantle cavity. The circulation of water provides oxygen for the gills. The mantle then contracts and forces the water out through a tube called the *funnel* or *siphon.* Octopuses have a main *systemic heart* and two additional *branchial hearts.* The branchial hearts supply blood to the animal's gills.

Octopuses have good vision. The animal's two large

eyes lie on each side of the creature's head.

Eight arms extend from the head of an octopus. At their base, the arms are united by a membrane web. Round, muscular suckers line the underside of each arm. An octopus uses its arms and suckers to move along the ocean bottom and capture prey. The suckers can provide enormous suction, enabling the octopus to attach firmly to rocks and prey. If an octopus loses an

The body of an octopus

WORLD BOOK illustration by Oxford Illustrators Limited

Stomach · Mantle · Liver · Eye · Brain · Intestine · Blood vessel · Mouth · Ink sac · Funnel · Kidney · Heart · Gill · Arms · Arm nerves arm, a new one grows in its place. Octopuses have a beaklike mouth below the head at the base of the arms.

The life of an octopus. Octopuses feed chiefly on clams, crabs, and snails. Many species also eat fish and even other octopuses. Certain octopuses can make a hole in the shells of clams, crabs, or snails and then inject a poison that paralyzes the animals.

Many sea animals—especially seals, whales, and certain fish—prey on octopuses. An octopus has various means of avoiding predators. It can swim quickly backward by forcing a powerful jet of water through its funnel. The octopus may conceal itself by discharging a cloud of inky fluid. In some cases, the shape of the ink cloud resembles the octopus and thus acts as a decoy.

In addition, an octopus can escape danger by rapidly changing colors. Its skin contains cells called *chromatophores,* each of which contains a single-colored pigment. Sudden contractions of muscles surrounding the chromatophores can produce the animal's rapid color changes. These color changes may startle a predator or enable the octopus to blend with its surroundings. Octopuses also may use color changes to communicate with one another and as a courtship display.

Octopuses reproduce sexually. In some species, females can lay more than 100,000 eggs. A female octopus cares for the eggs until they hatch into tiny, immature octopuses. The young swim at or near the surface of the water for several weeks as part of *plankton* (see **Plankton**). Many of the young are eaten by fish and other marine animals. In most octopus species, the remaining young descend to the ocean bottom and develop into adults. In a few pelagic octopuses, the young never become bottom dwellers.

Octopuses have short lives. Many live one year or less. The largest species live about three years.

Octopuses and people. Most octopuses are not dangerous to human beings. However, octopuses sometimes bite, so use caution when handling them. The small *blue-ringed octopuses* of Australia have a venom that can kill people. In some countries, octopus is an important food. Octopus fisheries occur in many regions, most notably off Japan, in the Mediterranean, and off the northwest coast of Africa.   Robert S. Prezant

Scientific classification. Octopuses make up the order Octopoda in the class Cephalopoda. The scientific name for the North Pacific giant octopus is *Enteroctopus dofleini.* Blue-ringed octopuses belong to the genus *Hapalochlaena.*

See also **Argonaut; Cuttlefish; Mollusk; Nautilus; Squid.**

Ocular. See Microscope (How an optical microscope works); Telescope (Optical telescopes).

Odd Fellows, Independent Order of, is one of the major fraternal and benevolent orders in the United States. The order was founded in England. The date of its founding is not known, but Odd Fellows' groups probably existed in the early 1700's. The members founded a system of benefits and helped one another in time of misfortune. Branches called *lodges* grew up in the various English cities, but each branch refused to admit the superior rank of any other. Adjustments were finally made, and in 1814, the Manchester Unity of the Independent Order of Odd Fellows was organized. Today, this organization has branches in various countries, but it has no connection with the order in the United States.

The American order. In 1819, the Washington Lodge of Odd Fellows was organized in Baltimore. The next year, Washington Lodge became a subordinate lodge in the Manchester Unity. Other American lodges were established later and assumed a like position.

In 1843, the American lodges separated themselves from the parent order in England. The United States grand lodge became the head of the order in America and reserved for itself the right to found new lodges in Europe. The Canadian branch operated under a separate charter until 1852. During that year, the society in Canada was merged with the grand lodge of the United States.

Purpose and organization. The chief purpose of the Order of Odd Fellows is to give aid, assistance, and comfort to its members and their families. It also does local charitable and volunteer work. It has its own system of rites and passwords. The three links in its symbol represent friendship, love, and truth.

A local lodge can confer three degrees of membership upon an Odd Fellow. When a member has reached the highest of these three degrees, he is ready for membership in an encampment. The encampment also has three degrees of membership, the Patriarchal, the Golden Rule, and the Royal Purple. The Patriarchal is an English degree. Since 1884, there has also been a military or uniformed degree called the Patriarchs Militant.

The Rebekah lodges in Odd Fellows are chiefly for women, although some men belong. Rebekah assemblies were organized in 1851, and they continue to provide much volunteer work for the order. The headquarters of the order are in Winston-Salem, North Carolina.

Critically reviewed by the Independent Order of Odd Fellows

Ode, *ohd,* is a poem of moderate length that usually expresses exalted praise. Greek dramatists wrote *choral odes* that had three parts. Two parts, a *strophe* and an *antistrophe,* had identical meter. The third part, called an *epode,* had a contrasting meter. Pindar, of ancient Greece, wrote odes in praise of athletic heroes. He used the strophic form, which came to be called *Pindaric* (see **Pindar**). Horace, of ancient Rome, wrote odes made up of uniform stanzas, called *stanzaic* form.

English poetry, from the time of Ben Jonson, included a variety of Pindaric odes, stanzaic odes, and *irregular* odes, or those with no particular stanza structure. John Dryden wrote two irregular odes in praise of Saint Cecilia. "Ode to Evening," by William Collins, is a notable stanzaic ode. The great irregular and stanzaic odes of the 1800's include William Wordsworth's "Ode: Intimations of Immortality," Percy Bysshe Shelley's "Ode to the West Wind," John Keats's "Ode on a Grecian Urn," and Alfred, Lord Tennyson's "Ode on the Death of the Duke of Wellington."   Paul B. Diehl

See also **Greek literature** (Lyric poetry).

O'Dell, Scott (1898-1989), an American author, became known for his historical novels for children. Many of his works are set in Mexico and southern California. O'Dell's first children's book, *Island of the Blue Dolphins* (1960), won the 1961 Newbery Medal. His other children's books include *The King's Fifth* (1966), *The Black Pearl* (1967), *Sing Down the Moon* (1970), and *Streams to the River, River to the Sea* (1986). O'Dell wrote three related novels about a 16-year-old Spanish boy's experiences in the New World. The series consists of *The Captive*

(1979), *The Feathered Serpent* (1981), and *The Amethyst Ring* (1982). O'Dell was born on May 23, 1898, in Los Angeles. He died on Oct. 15, 1989.   Virginia L. Wolf

Oder River, *OH duhr,* is an important waterway in central Europe. It is about 530 miles (855 kilometers) long and drains about 46,000 square miles (119,000 square kilometers).

The Oder, also called Odra, rises in the Sudeten Mountains of the Czech Republic. It then flows northward across western Poland where it is joined by the Neisse (Nysa) River—officially Lausitzer Neisse (Nysa Łużycka). The joined rivers form most of the boundary between Poland and Germany. The Oder empties into the Baltic Sea by way of the Stettin Lagoon (see **Poland** [terrain map]). Oceangoing vessels use the Polish port of Szczecin south of the lagoon. Other major cities on the Oder include Frankfurt in Germany, the Polish cities of Wrocław and Opole, and Ostrava in the Czech Republic.

The Oder's tributaries include the Warta (Warthe) River. The Warta links the Oder with the Vistula River in Poland by the Noteć (Netze) River and a canal. Canals also link the Oder with the Polish industrial city of Gliwice and with the Havel and Spree rivers in Germany.

The Oder-Neisse boundary between Poland and East Germany was established after World War II ended in 1945. East Germany recognized this boundary in 1950. West Germany opposed the boundary until 1970, when it signed treaties with both Poland and the Soviet Union confirming the boundary. East Germany and West Germany unified in 1990.   Leszek A. Kosiński

Odessa, *oh DEHS uh* (pop. 1,029,000), is a seaport city in Ukraine. It lies on the southwestern coast, near the Romanian border. Odessa is on the Black Sea, 32 miles (51 kilometers) southwest of the mouth of the Dnieper River. For location, see **Ukraine** (political map).

Odessa is one of Ukraine's industrial centers. Its refineries produce large amounts of petroleum products. Factories make machinery, automobiles, airplanes, and motion-picture equipment. Odessa is an important transfer point for rail and ocean transportation. The city is also known for its health resorts.

Odessa is built in a circular shape and slopes down toward a harbor. A long stairway leads up from the harbor. The stairway is called the Potemkin Steps in memory of the crew of the ship *Potemkin,* who mutinied in Odessa during the Russian Revolution of 1905.

Historians are not sure when the first settlement was established on the site where Odessa now stands. The area was conquered by the Tatars in the 1200's, followed by the Lithuanians in the 1300's and the Ottomans in the 1500's. Russia gained control of the site in 1792 and built a port and a fortress there. In 1795, Russia named the city Odessa. In 1944, Odessa became part of the Ukrainian Soviet Socialist Republic of the Soviet Union. The Soviet Union had been formed under Russia's leadership in 1922. In 1991, following an upheaval in the Soviet Union, the Ukrainian republic declared itself an independent nation. In December of that year, the Soviet Union was dissolved.   Jaroslaw Bilocerkowycz

Odets, *oh DEHTS,* **Clifford** (1906-1963), an American dramatist, is best known for his plays of social conflict written during the 1930's. His most successful works were presented by the famous Group Theatre.

Odets's one-act play *Waiting for Lefty* (1935) is about a taxi drivers' strike. It ranks among the most important of the many plays written in the 1930's that deal with the struggle of the working class. Odets's *Awake and Sing!* (1935) is less propagandistic than *Waiting for Lefty.* It tells the story of a poor Jewish family in the Bronx during the Great Depression. Odets also wrote *Paradise Lost* (1935), *Golden Boy* (1937), *Night Music* (1940), *The Big Knife* (1948), and *The Country Girl* (1950).

Odets was born in Philadelphia on July 18, 1906. He helped form the Group Theatre in 1931. He was a film scriptwriter from 1936 until shortly before his death on Aug. 14, 1963.   Frank R. Cunningham

Odin, *oh DIHN,* was the chief god in Norse mythology. In German, he is called Wotan *(WOH tuhn).* Odin became the ruler of the universe after he and his two brothers, Ve and Vili, killed the frost giant Ymir, the first living being. From Ymir's body, they made Midgard, the earth; and began to build Asgard, the dwelling place of the gods. Valhalla was Odin's home in Asgard. There he feasted with the souls of heroes who had died in battle. Odin, a fearless fighter, carried a spear as his weapon, and rode an eight-legged horse called Sleipnir. He inspired ferocious human warriors called Berserkers who fought recklessly without armor and felt no wounds.

Odin was the wisest god. He gave up one eye for the right to drink from the spring of wisdom, guarded by Mimir, a supernaturally wise creature. Odin was also known for his magic powers. By wounding and hanging himself from a tree, he acquired the power of spells called *runes.* They let him predict the future, change his shape at will, and visit the underworld. Odin's sons included Thor, the god of thunder and lightning, and Balder, the god of goodness. According to Norse myths, Odin will lead the gods against the evil giants at Ragnarok, the battle that will destroy the world. He will be eaten by Fenrir, a ferocious wolf.

The Anglo-Saxons' name for Odin was Woden. It was the source of the word *Wednesday.*   Carl Lindahl

See also **Mythology** (Teutonic mythology); **Valhalla.**

Odoacer, *OH doh AY suhr* (A.D. 434?-493), was the Germanic leader who overthrew the last emperor of Rome in the West, ending the West Roman Empire.

Odoacer was probably born near the Danube River in what is now Germany. He joined the West Roman army and became a leader of *barbarian* (non-Roman) troops serving the Romans. In 476, when the Roman government refused to give his troops land for settlement, Odoacer led them in a revolt. Odoacer deposed the West Roman emperor, Romulus Augustulus, and became the first barbarian king of Italy. Historians consider this event the end of the West Roman Empire. But for years, barbarian generals had been its real rulers. The emperors were symbolic rulers.

Odoacer ruled independently, though he pretended to serve Zeno, the East Roman emperor. Zeno never recognized Odoacer as ruler of Italy. In 488, Zeno sent the Ostrogoth king Theodoric to attack Odoacer. Odoacer retreated to Ravenna, where he surrendered in 493. He was executed on March 15 of that year (see **Theodoric**).   William G. Sinnigen

Odometer. See **Speedometer.**

Odyssey, *AHD uh see,* an epic poem, is perhaps the most influential and most popular work in ancient Greek literature. The *Odyssey* ranks among the greatest adven-

Red-figure painting on a cup (about 490 B.C.) by Douris; Kunsthistorisches Museum, Vienna (Interfoto Pressebildagentur/Alamy Images)

Odysseus was an important character in the Greek epics the *Iliad* and the *Odyssey.* This ancient Greek painting portrays the bearded Odysseus giving the armor worn by the slain Greek hero Achilles to Achilles's warrior son Neoptolemus.

Red-figure painting (about 475 B.C.) on a terra cotta vase; Granger Collection

Odysseus encountered the Sirens during his voyage home. The Sirens, part bird and part woman, lured seamen to their death with beautiful singing. Odysseus had himself tied to the mast so he could safely enjoy the singing.

ture stories in literature. It became a model for many later adventure stories.

According to tradition, the *Odyssey* was composed by the Greek poet Homer, probably in the 700's B.C. The central character is Odysseus (Ulysses in Latin), the king of Ithaca. The poem describes Odysseus's journey home after fighting for Greece against the city of Troy in the Trojan War. The author told about this war in the *Iliad,* another great epic poem. See **Homer.**

The *Odyssey* consists of 24 *books* (sections). The story takes place over about 10 years. The tale begins after much of the action has already occurred. This device of starting a story in the middle and returning to the start is called *in medias res.* Many later writers used it.

The *Odyssey* begins on the island of Ogygia, where Odysseus has been the prisoner of the sea nymph Calypso for seven years. At a council of the gods on Mount Olympus, Zeus decides the time has come for Odysseus to return to his wife, Penelope, in Ithaca.

The scene then changes to Odysseus's palace in Ithaca, where a group of unruly young noblemen has settled. The noblemen want Penelope to assume that her husband is dead. They demand that she marry one of them and thus choose a new king of Ithaca. Odysseus's son, Telemachus, resents the noblemen. The goddess Athena suggests that he go on a journey to seek news of his father. Telemachus agrees and leaves Ithaca.

The tale next returns to Odysseus's adventures. The god Hermes makes Calypso release Odysseus. Odysseus sails away on a raft, but the sea god Poseidon causes a storm, and Odysseus is shipwrecked on the island of the Phaeacians. Nausicaa, the beautiful daughter of the Phaeacian king, discovers him.

Odysseus describes his wanderings since the Trojan War while being entertained by the Phaeacians. He

tells of his visit to the land of the lotus-eaters, whose magic food makes people forget their homeland. Some of his men who ate the food wanted to stay with the lotus-eaters, but Odysseus forced them to leave with him. Odysseus and his men then sailed to an island where they were captured by Polyphemus, a one-eyed giant called a Cyclops. They escaped after blinding the Cyclops with a heated stake. But the Cyclops prayed to his father, Poseidon, to avenge him by making Odysseus's homecoming as difficult as possible.

After more adventures, the ship carrying Odysseus and his men landed on the island of the enchantress Circe. Circe changed Odysseus's men into pigs and made Odysseus her lover. She told Odysseus that to get home, he must visit the underworld to consult the prophet Teiresias. In the underworld, Odysseus saw the ghosts of his mother and of Trojan War heroes. He also witnessed the punishment of sinners.

Teiresias warned Odysseus of the dangers awaiting him, and Circe told him how to sail past the sea monsters Scylla and Charybdis. Circe also warned him about the Sirens, sea nymphs who use their beautiful singing to lure sailors to death on a magic island. Odysseus's ship sailed past these dangers and seemed ready to reach Ithaca without further trouble. But some of Odysseus's men stole and ate the sacred cattle of the sun on the island of Thrinacia. As punishment, the ship was destroyed by a thunderbolt, and the men drowned. Odysseus washed up on Ogygia, where the story began.

Odysseus returns home. After Odysseus finishes his story, the Phaeacians take him to Ithaca. Athena tells him of the noblemen in his palace and advises him to return home in disguise. Odysseus goes to his palace disguised as a beggar. Penelope has agreed to marry the man who can string Odysseus's huge bow and shoot an arrow through 12 axes. Odysseus wins the contest, kills the noblemen, and is reunited with Penelope.

The *Odyssey* as literature. The *Odyssey* is a skillfully told adventure story. The story combines realistic accounts of life in ancient Greece and elements of historical events with fairy tales about imaginary lands.

The work also contains skillful characterization. Odysseus represents the model of a man of courage and determination. In spite of many setbacks, he never abandons his goal of returning home. However, Odysseus has other human traits that keep him from being only a symbol. He enjoys life, even while struggling to get home. He is restless, clever, and even tricky and is able to invent lies easily. In fact, some later Greek dramatists made Odysseus a symbol of deceit. Penelope stands for the faithful, loving wife. Telemachus symbolizes the youth who matures by facing a difficult challenge. The travels of Odysseus and Telemachus may represent the human journey through life and the search for self-fulfillment and self-knowledge.

Cynthia W. Shelmerdine

Related articles in *World Book* include:

Aeneid	Iliad
Aeolus	Lotus-eaters
Capri	Penelope
Circe	Scylla
Cyclops	Sirens
Homer	Ulysses

Oe, *oh ay,* **Kenzaburo,** *kehn zah bu roh* (1935-   ), a Japanese novelist, won the Nobel Prize in literature in 1994. Much of Oe's fiction is political in tone, emphasizing his country's search for its cultural roots. He also writes about the sense of betrayal and alienation many Japanese felt following Japan's defeat in World War II (1939-1945).

Oe was born on Jan. 31, 1935, in Shikoku, Japan. He graduated from the University of Tokyo in 1959 with a degree in French literature. Oe gained recognition with his earliest works, which explored violence and insanity and created controversy for their unconventional, rough literary style. Among Oe's early works are the story "Lavish Are the Dead" (1957), written while he was a student, and the novel *Nip the Buds, Shoot the Kids* (1958). The short novel *Prize Stock* (1958) describes the friendship between a Japanese boy and an African American prisoner of war.

Oe's later writings are dominated by his experiences as the father of a son who has brain damage. Many of these intense and painful works reflect the attitudes of postwar Japanese youth who feel themselves culturally adrift. The books include *A Personal Matter* (1964), *Hiroshima Notes* (1964, revised 1995), *The Silent Cry* (1967), and *Rouse Up O Young Men of the New Age* (1984). Some of Oe's short stories were collected in *The Crazy Iris and Other Stories of the Atomic Aftermath* (1984). Four of his short novels, including *Prize Stock*, are collected in *Teach Us to Outgrow Our Madness* (1969). Oe also wrote a study of Japanese mythology called *M/T* (1986).   Laurel Rasplica Rodd

OECD. See Organisation for Economic Co-operation and Development.

Oedipus, *EHD uh puhs,* was a king of Thebes in Greek mythology. Many ancient authors wrote different versions of the story of Oedipus. The following version is

Painting on a cup (about 465 B.C.) by an unknown Greek artist; Vatican Museums, Rome (SCALA/Art Resource)

Oedipus, a hero in Greek mythology, solved the riddle of the Sphinx. The Thebans rewarded him by making him king.

based largely on *Oedipus Rex,* a tragedy by the Greek playwright Sophocles.

The *oracle* (prophet) of Delphi told King Laius of Thebes that a son born to his wife, Queen Jocasta, would kill him (see **Delphi**). After Jocasta gave birth to a son, Laius ordered the baby taken to a mountain and left to die. However, a shepherd rescued the child and brought him to King Polybus of Corinth. Polybus adopted the boy and named him Oedipus.

Oedipus grew up in Corinth. As a young man, he learned from the oracle that he would kill his father and marry his mother. Believing that Polybus was his father, Oedipus tried to avoid the prophecy by fleeing Corinth. On the road to Thebes, he quarreled with a man and killed him. The stranger was King Laius.

Near Thebes, Oedipus encountered a monster called the Sphinx. She had a woman's head, a lion's body, and a bird's wings. The Sphinx killed everyone who could not solve this riddle: What has one voice and becomes four-footed, two-footed, and three-footed? The Sphinx asked Oedipus the riddle, which no one had solved. He answered: Man, who crawls on all fours as a baby, then walks on two legs, and finally needs a cane in old age. The Sphinx killed herself because Oedipus had solved the riddle. Oedipus was rewarded by being made king of Thebes. He married Jocasta, the widowed queen.

Several years later, a plague struck Thebes. The oracle said it would end when the murderer of Laius had been driven from Thebes. Oedipus investigated the murder and came to realize that Laius was the man he had killed on the road to Thebes. He then discovered that Laius was his father and Jocasta his mother. Oedipus blinded himself, and Jocasta hanged herself. Oedipus was banished from Thebes. He died at Colonus, near Athens.

John Hamilton

See also **Mythology** (Greek heroes).

Oedipus complex, *EHD uh puhs,* a concept used in psychoanalysis, is a child's unconscious desire for sexual attachment with the parent of the opposite sex. This desire includes jealousy toward the parent of the same sex and the unconscious wish for that parent's death.

The term *Oedipus complex* was first used by the Austrian physician Sigmund Freud. It comes from the myth of Oedipus, a Greek hero who unknowingly killed his father and married his mother (see **Oedipus**). Freud used the term to describe the unconscious feelings of children of both sexes toward their parents. However, later researchers used the term *Electra complex* for the complex in girls. According to Greek legend, a woman named Electra helped plan the murder of her mother.

Freud believed that the Oedipus complex is a normal part of human psychological growth. The Oedipal phase of development is commonly considered to last from the age of 2 ½ to 6. During this period, children experience intense feelings—love and hate, yearning and jealousy, fear and anger—that produce emotional conflicts. Most people outgrow the Oedipal phase, but some individuals with mental illness have a strong Oedipus complex as adults. According to Freud, the principal reason for the weakening of the complex in boys is the fear of punishment from the father.

Freud thought that all peoples experience the Oedipus complex. But many anthropologists and researchers in psychoanalysis doubt that the complex exists in certain non-Western societies. They believe it develops as a result of a person's social environment and does not occur in everyone.   Nancy C. Andreasen

Oersted, *UR stehd,* **Hans Christian** (1777-1851), a Danish physicist, laid the foundation for the science of electromagnetism (see **Electromagnetism**). In 1820, he noticed that the needle of a compass wavered every time he put it near a wire carrying a current. He had discovered that every conductor carrying an electric current is surrounded by a magnetic field. Oersted is also credited with producing the first aluminum, in 1825 (see **Aluminum** [The first aluminum]). He wrote *Spirit of Nature* (1850). Oersted was born on Aug. 14, 1777, in Rudkøbing, Denmark. He died on March 9, 1851. The *oersted,* a unit of measure of magnetic field intensity, is named for him.   Julia Borst Brazas

Offenbach, *AW fuhn bahk,* **Jacques,** *zhahk* (1819-1880), a French composer, created the French style of operetta. His operettas are humorous, witty, and satirical. He enjoyed poking fun at the politics and society of his day and quoting familiar themes from other compositions (especially operas). Offenbach's success internationally helped to establish operetta as an accepted musical form and led to the development of musicals in the United States in the 1900's.

Many of Offenbach's operettas are *opéras bouffes* (comic or light operas). He completed more than 90 works for the stage. His first success was *Orpheus in the Underworld* (1858). His most popular compositions appeared in the 1860's. They include *La Belle Hélène* (1864), *La Vie Parisienne* (1866), *La Grande-Duchesse de Gérolstein* (1867), and *La Périchole* (1868). In 1877, he began his most famous work, the opera *The Tales of Hoffmann,* which was unfinished at his death. See **Operetta.**

Offenbach was born on June 20, 1819, in Cologne, Germany. He moved to Paris in 1833 to study the cello. For many years, he had a successful career as a cellist. He became a conductor at the Théâtre-Français in 1850.

In 1855, he founded the Théâtre des Bouffes-Parisiens, a theatrical company that staged many of his operettas. Offenbach became a French citizen in 1860. He died on Oct. 5, 1880.   Katherine K. Preston

Office of . . . See articles on offices listed under their key word, as in **Management and Budget, Office of.**

Office work is the process of recording, storing, and distributing the information needed to operate a business. The managers of the business use this information to make administrative decisions.

Millions of people in industrialized countries are employed as office workers. They include secretaries, assistants, computer technicians, and accountants. Office workers do not include people involved in such activities as buying, selling, or management.

An office may receive information by telecommunications, by mail, or by computer. An office worker must have skill in language and arithmetic to handle business information properly. Almost all office jobs require at least a high school education. Many employers prefer to hire people who have taken courses beyond the high school level. A person can receive advanced training at a community college, junior college, or business or vocational school. This training may include instruction in operating computers, calculators, copying machines, and other office equipment.

An office requires a staff of managers to plan and direct work. As a business grows, so does the amount of information handled by its office workers. The managers coordinate the activities of these employees so that accurate records can be kept concerning correspondence, inventory, payroll, sales, and taxes.   Richard M. Hodgetts

Related articles in *World Book* include:

Office equipment

Calculator	Fax machine	Typewriter
Computer	Printer	Word processing
Copying machine		

Other related articles

Bookkeeping	Information retrieval
Careers (Administrative	Microfilm
support)	Secretarial work
E-mail	Shorthand

Officer. See Rank, Military; Reserve Officers Training Corps.

Offset is a printing process in which an image is first transferred from a printing plate to a rubber blanket covering a rotating cylinder. The impression is transferred to paper by the pressure of other cylinders. The term *offset* describes the transfer, or offsetting, of the ink from a printing plate to rubber and then to paper.

All ordinary offset printing is done from the metal surfaces of lithographic plates (see **Lithography**). The material to be printed is transferred onto the plates through a photographic process or directly from computer files. The plates are chemically treated so only the image areas of the print will take up the ink. Other types of plates can be used for offset printing. Some printing is done from ordinary type and cuts, some from thin plastic relief or letterpress plates, some from gelatin surfaces, and some from *intaglio* plates, metal sheets or cylinders that carry the ink in sunken lines.

Offset lithography is usually done on a press having three cylinders. A lithographic plate is wrapped around the first cylinder. This plate is a sheet of aluminum or zinc about as thick as heavy paper. The plate prints on the second cylinder, which is covered by the rubber blanket. The impression on the rubber is printed on the paper carried by the third cylinder. The third cylinder is equipped with steel fingers, called *grippers,* to hold the paper in position while it is squeezed against the rubber surface. Three-cylinder presses of this type can turn out 10,000 to 20,000 printed impressions an hour.

These cylinders are almost hidden while the press is in operation. They are covered by a great number of rollers which supply the lithographic plate with ink and water. The cylinders are also concealed by a mechanism for feeding and removing sheets or rolls of paper.

Offset has several advantages over other types of printing. The elastic rubber transfers the impression to a rough surface as easily as to a smooth one. This makes it possible to print on rough paper, as well as on tin, plastic, and other materials. Another advantage of offset is that the rubber on the cylinder fits easily to uneven surfaces. This reduces the time workers must spend preparing the presses for printing.

Offset was developed in the early 1900's in the United States. It has been applied to almost every class of printing, from the cheapest to the most expensive. Offset has replaced the older forms of lithography in which the impression was made directly on the paper from stone or metal plates. An offset press can turn out bank notes, letterheads, magazines, mail-order catalogs, newspapers, posters, and stock certificates. The offset press is used to print many daily newspapers. Offset can be combined with *rotogravure,* another printing process, to make colored illustrations that are clear and delicate. It is also used for facsimile reproduction of old books.

Offset continues to be improved and applied to new purposes. Offset presses have been designed to print on a *web* (roll) of paper. In a process called *perfecting,* paper on this *web press* is passed between two rollers covered with rubber blankets, printing on both sides at the same time.   Frank J. Romano

See also **Intaglio; Printing.**

Offutt Air Force Base, Nebraska, is headquarters of the United States Strategic Command (USSTRATCOM), an interservice command under the Department of Defense. The Strategic Command is the control center for U.S. nuclear offensive forces and military space operations, and for defense against nuclear and long-range conventional missile attacks on the United States. USSTRATCOM was created in 1992.

The base covers 4,063 acres (1,644 hectares) south of Omaha. On this site, the U.S. Army established Fort Crook in 1891. In 1921, the Army completed construction of an airfield there. In 1924, the airfield was named Offutt Field after First Lieutenant Jarvis J. Offutt, a pilot killed in World War I. In 1946, the Army Air Forces gave the name Offutt Field to all of Fort Crook. In 1948, the newly created U.S. Air Force acquired Offutt Field and named it Offutt Air Force Base. It served as Strategic Air Command headquarters from 1948 until 1992, when the Air Force eliminated the command.   Wayne Thompson

See also **Strategic Air Command.**

O'Flaherty, *oh FLA huhr tee,* **Liam,** *LEE uhm* (1896-1984), was an Irish writer of novels and short stories. He wrote many of his works in Gaelic and translated them into English. O'Flaherty was born on Aug. 28, 1896. Much of his fiction vividly depicts the barren, rocky landscape and remote villages of the Aran Islands, where he was born and raised. Other works, reflecting his later life, describe grinding poverty in impersonal cities.

O'Flaherty's best-known novel is the harshly realistic *The Informer* (1925). He also wrote *The Black Soul* (1924), *The Assassin* (1928), *Skerrett* (1932), and *Famine* (1937). In these novels, young, poor, and disadvantaged people struggle against overwhelming odds and lose.

O'Flaherty wrote many short stories in economic, lyrical prose. Many are collected in *Spring Sowing* (1924) and *The Stories of Liam O'Flaherty* (1956). These stories portray children, peasants, or animals with emotions, who are helpless in the face of passing time and the destructive force of nature. O'Flaherty died on Sept. 7, 1984.

Janet Egleson Dunleavy

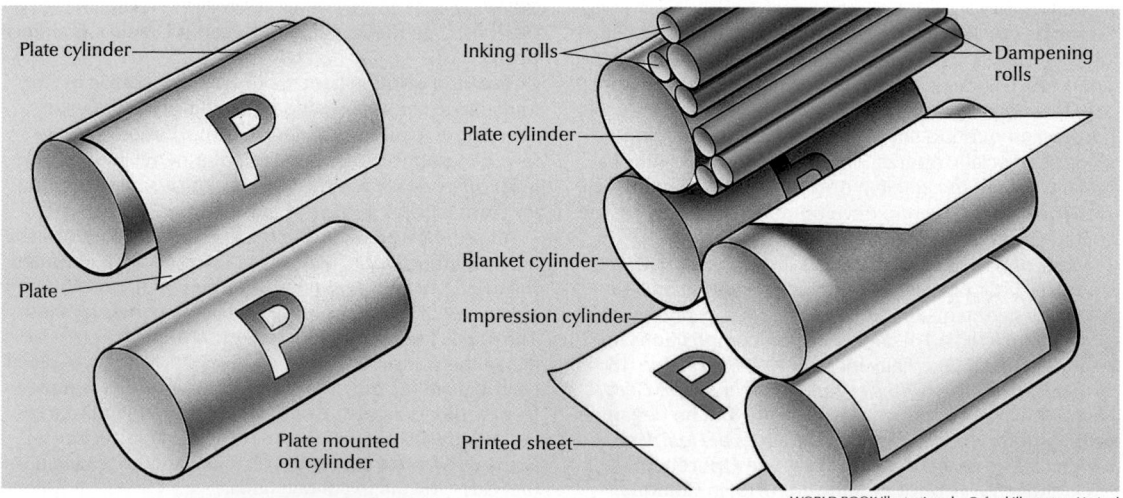

WORLD BOOK illustrations by Oxford Illustrators Limited

Offset lithography printing is not done directly from a printing plate or from type. Instead, the plate cylinder *offsets* (transfers) the inked images onto a rubber blanket cylinder. The rotating blanket cylinder offsets the images onto the paper carried by the impression cylinder.

Ogden, *AHG dehn* or *AWG dehn* (pop. 82,825), is one of the largest cities in Utah. It lies in the northern part of the state, 35 miles (56 kilometers) north of Salt Lake City. For location, see **Utah** (political map). Ogden and Clearfield form part of a metropolitan area of 547,184.

Ogden's industries process agricultural products, produce missiles and automobile air bags, and extract minerals from the Great Salt Lake. Regional headquarters of the Internal Revenue Service and the Forest Service are in the city. Ogden is the home of Weber State University and the Utah Schools for the Deaf and the Blind.

Mormons came to the Ogden region in 1848. Ogden was incorporated in 1851 and grew rapidly after becoming a link in the transcontinental railroad system in 1869. The Golden Spike, driven near Ogden in May 1869, completed the railroad. Ogden was named for Peter Skene Ogden, an early fur trader.

Ogden is the seat of Weber County. It has a mayor-council form of government. Pat Bean

Oglala Indians. See Red Cloud; Sioux Indians.

Oglethorpe, *OH guhl THAWRP,* **James Edward** (1696-1785), an Englishman, founded the colony of Georgia. He was born on Dec. 22, 1696, in London and attended Eton College and Oxford University. He joined the British Army at 14. He was elected to Parliament in 1722. There, he became interested in people sent to prison for not paying debts. He hoped to help them by establishing an American colony for debtors. In 1732, he and a group of associates received a charter from King George II for the colony. It was to be founded between the Savannah and Altamaha rivers. Parliament also granted him $50,000.

Oglethorpe and about 120 colonists arrived in America in January 1733. In February, he set up his first settlement where the city of Savannah now stands. But few debtors ever came to the new colony. Oglethorpe governed for nine years and drove invading Spanish troops back into Florida. He defeated the Spaniards badly in the Battle of Bloody Marsh on St. Simons Island, in 1742.

Oglethorpe was so much in debt from his loans to colonists that he had to return to England in 1743. His enemies called him a coward for not capturing St. Augustine, Florida, when he attacked the Spaniards there in 1743. A court-martial dismissed the charges. He and the other trustees returned the Georgia charter to George II in 1752, and Georgia became a royal province. Oglethorpe died on June 30, 1785. Dan T. Carter

See also **Georgia** (Colonial period).

Oh, Sadaharu (1940-), was a Japanese baseball star. Oh dominated baseball in Japan for almost 20 years with his power hitting, making him a national sports hero. During his career, Oh hit 868 home runs, more than any other player in professional baseball history.

Oh spent his entire playing career with the Tokyo-based Yomiuri Giants of the Central League. Oh led the league in home runs 15 times and in runs batted in 13 times, and he was named the league's Most Valuable Player 9 times. He was inducted into the Japanese Baseball Hall of Fame in 1994.

Oh was born on May 20, 1940, in Tokyo, of a Chinese father and a Japanese mother. In 1959, Oh signed to play with Yomiuri as a pitcher but quickly was moved to first base. He led the Giants to 11 league championships. Oh retired in 1980 but remained with Yomiuri as an assistant manager from 1981 to 1983 and as manager from 1984

to 1988. The Giants won the league pennant in 1987. After 1988, Oh left baseball. In 1995, however, he returned as manager of the Fukuoka Daiei Hawks (later the Fukuoka SoftBank Hawks) of the Pacific League, leading the team to league championships in 1999, 2000, and 2003 and the Japanese Series championships in 1999 and 2003. He retired as manager of the Hawks following the 2008 season. Neil Milbert

O'Hara, John (1905-1970), was an American novelist and short-story writer. He gained fame for his realistic observations on the manners and morals of the American middle class. O'Hara set a number of his novels and stories in the fictional town of Gibbsville, Pennsylvania.

John Henry O'Hara was born on Jan. 31, 1905, in Pottsville, Pennsylvania. He worked as a journalist until he turned to fiction after the success of his first novel, *Appointment in Samarra* (1934), an ironic picture of upper middle-class life in a Pennsylvania city. O'Hara's other important novels include *Butterfield 8* (1935), *Ten North Frederick* (1955), *From the Terrace* (1958), and *Elizabeth Appleton* (1963). Many of O'Hara's books were made into motion pictures, and two of his novels, *Hope of Heaven* (1938) and *The Big Laugh* (1962), are set in Hollywood.

O'Hara's short fiction received special praise. His story collections include *The Doctor's Son* (1935), *Sermons and Soda Water* (1960), *The Cape Cod Lighter* (1962), *The Hat on the Bed* (1963), and *Good Samaritan* (published in 1974, after his death on April 11, 1970). O'Hara collaborated with the American composer Richard Rodgers and the lyricist Lorenz Hart to turn his story sequence *Pal Joey* (1940) into a musical comedy. Barbara M. Perkins

O'Hara, Mary (1885-1980), was the pen name of Mary O'Hara Alsop, an American author. She wrote of people on the plains and their love for horses in her novels *My Friend Flicka* (1941) and *Thunderhead* (1943). She also wrote *The Son of Adam Wyngate* (1952), a novel of spiritual experiences. She was born on July 10, 1885, in Cape May Point, New Jersey, and died on Oct. 14, 1980.

O'Hare International Airport. See Airport; Chicago (Transportation).

O. Henry. See Henry, O.

O'Higgins, Bernardo (1778-1842), was the chief liberator of Chile and its first leader after independence. He headed the nation from 1817 to 1823.

In 1814, O'Higgins became commander in chief of Chilean rebel forces fighting to gain independence from Spain. In October, the Spaniards defeated the rebels at the Battle of Rancagua, and O'Higgins fled with his army to Argentina. There, he joined forces with the Argentine general José de San Martín. In 1817, the combined armies crossed the Andes Mountains and defeated the Spaniards at Chacabuco, near Santiago. O'Higgins was then named *supreme director* of Chile. O'Higgins and San Martín won a final victory over the Spanish forces in 1818 at the Maipo River.

O'Higgins backed a number of reforms for Chile but met with strong opposition from aristocrats, provincial chiefs, and the Roman Catholic Church. Lack of support for his policies caused him to resign in 1823.

Bernardo O'Higgins Riquelme was born on Aug. 20, 1778, in Chillán, Chile. His Irish-born father, Ambrosio O'Higgins, was a colonial official in the service of Spain. O'Higgins died in October 1842. Michael L. Conniff

See also **Chile** (History; picture).

David M. Dennis

A scenic meadow in central Ohio forms part of the Appalachian Plateau region. This region includes rolling hills and valleys and some of the state's largest forests.

Ohio　*The Buckeye State*

Ohio is one of the leading industrial states in the United States. Its industries produce chemicals, machine parts, metal products, motor vehicles, processed foods, steel, and many other products. Ohio ranks 7th among the states in population, though it is 35th in area. Columbus is Ohio's largest city and state capital. Cleveland, the state's chief industrial center, is Ohio's second largest city.

Ohio took its name from the Iroquois Indian word meaning *something great.* The Iroquois used the word for the Ohio River, which forms the state's southeastern and southern borders. Ohio is called the *Buckeye State* because of the buckeye trees that once grew plentifully on its hills and plains. Pioneers cut down many of the buckeyes to build log cabins.

In 1803, Ohio became the first state to be carved out of the Northwest Territory. Ohio later served as an important link to the West as canals, railways, and roads

crossed the state. It was called the *Gateway State.*

Several natural advantages helped Ohio become a great manufacturing state. Ohio has an abundant supply of water and large deposits of coal, salt, and other important minerals. Its central location, near raw materials and major markets, has helped attract many large industries. Ohio ranks high among the states in the manufacture of cars and trucks, chemicals, fabricated metal products, industrial machinery, motor vehicle parts, processed foods, and steel.

But manufacturing is only part of the Ohio economy. A majority of the state's workers are employed in service industries, which include such activities as education, finance, government, health care, insurance, and trade. Cleveland and Columbus are important financial centers of the United States. Cleveland is among the nation's leading health care centers. Cincinnati, Ohio's third-largest city, is an important center of manufacturing and trade.

Farmland covers about half of Ohio. Soil in the Till Plains area of western Ohio is especially fertile. Ohio is a major producer of corn and soybeans.

Ohio claims the title of the *Mother of Presidents.*

The contributors of this article are Andrew Cayton, Distinguished Professor of History at Miami University; and Thomas W. Schmidlin, Professor of Geography at Kent State University.

Ray F. Hillstrom, Jr.

Downtown Cleveland includes Public Square, with the 46-story BP Building, also known as 200 Public Square, rising in the background.

Interesting facts about Ohio

WORLD BOOK illustrations by Kevin Chadwick

The first electric traffic signal lights on record were invented by James Hoge of Cleveland. They were installed in Cleveland on Aug. 5, 1914, at Euclid Avenue and East 105th Street by the American Traffic Signal Company. Brackets on poles at each corner held red or green lights 15 feet (4.5 meters) above the street. When the lights were about to change, a bell rang to warn the motorists.

First traffic lights

The first public weather forecasting service in the United States was started in Cincinnati. Cleveland Abbe, the director of the Cincinnati Observatory, issued the first of his daily statements of "probabilities" on Sept. 1, 1869. He predicted prevailing easterly and southerly winds for September 2.

The first book matches were manufactured by the Diamond Match Company at its factory in Barberton in 1896. The company had obtained the patent of book matches from the man who invented them, Joshua Pusey, a Philadelphia attorney. The patent date, Sept. 27, 1892, appeared on Diamond matchbooks for years.

The oldest known watercraft in North America is a dugout canoe built about 1600 B.C. It was found in 1977 in a peat bog at the head of the Vermilion River in Ashland County. The canoe is now on display at the Cleveland Museum of Natural History.

Oldest watercraft

Seven presidents of the United States were born in Ohio, more than in any other state except Virginia. In historical order, the presidents born in Ohio were Ulysses S. Grant, Rutherford B. Hayes, James A. Garfield, Benjamin Harrison, William McKinley, William Howard Taft, and Warren G. Harding. William Henry Harrison was living in Ohio when he became president of the United States.

Two of the nation's most famous astronauts were born in Ohio. Neil A. Armstrong, the first person to set foot on the moon, was born in Auglaize County near Wapakoneta. John H. Glenn, Jr., the first American astronaut to orbit Earth, was born in Cambridge and grew up in New Concord. He was elected to the United States Senate from Ohio in 1974.

Many famous inventors also came from Ohio. Thomas A. Edison, the wizard of electricity, developed his scientific curiosity as a small boy in Milan. Orville and Wilbur Wright made test flights in their first power-driven airplane from a field near Dayton. Charles F. Kettering of Dayton developed a self-starter for automobiles. The aluminum-refining process was discovered by Charles M. Hall of Oberlin.

Honda

An aircraft manufacturing plant in Columbus produces bomber parts for the United States Air Force. Ohio ranks among the leading manufacturing states.

Ohio in brief

Symbols of Ohio

The state flag was adopted in 1902. The triangle represents Ohio's hills and valleys, and the stripes symbolize roads and waterways. The 17 stars stand for Ohio as the 17th state. The white circle with a red center represents Ohio's initial and the buckeye nut. The seal, adopted in 1967, bears a sheaf of wheat and a bundle of 17 arrows. A sun with 13 rays rising over mountains symbolizes the 13 original colonies.

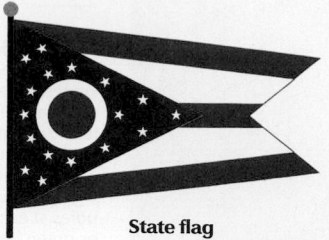

State flag

State seal

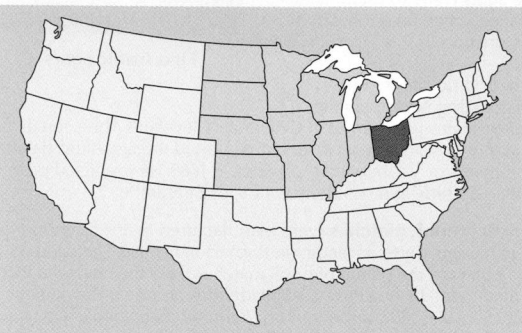

Ohio (brown) ranks 35th in size among all the states and 11th in size among the Midwestern States (yellow).

General information

Statehood: March 1, 1803, the 17th state.
State abbreviations: O. (traditional); OH (postal).
State motto: *With God, All Things Are Possible.*
State song: "Beautiful Ohio." Words by Ballard MacDonald, music by Mary Earl.

The State Capitol is in Columbus, the capital of Ohio since 1816. Earlier capitals were Chillicothe (1803-1810, 1812-1816) and Zanesville (1810-1812).

Land and climate

Area: 41,326 mi² (107,034 km²), including 378 mi² (978 km²) of inland water but excluding 3,499 mi² (9,062 km²) of Great Lakes water.
Elevation: *Highest*—Campbell Hill in Logan County, 1,550 ft. (472 m) above sea level. *Lowest*—433 ft. (132 m) above sea level along the Ohio River in Hamilton County.
Record high temperature: 113 °F (45 °C) near Gallipolis on July 21, 1934.
Record low temperature: –39 °F (–39 °C) at Milligan, near New Lexington, on Feb. 10, 1899.
Average July temperature: 73 °F (23 °C).
Average January temperature: 28 °F (–2 °C).
Average yearly precipitation: 38 in (97 cm).

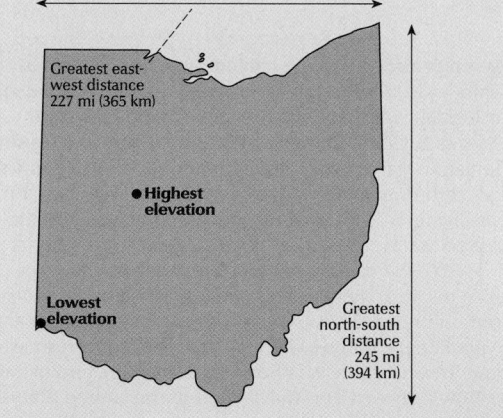

Greatest east-west distance 227 mi (365 km)

●Highest elevation

Lowest ●elevation

Greatest north-south distance 245 mi (394 km)

Important dates

The first permanent white settlement in Ohio was established at Marietta.

The Ohio and Erie Canal was completed.

c. 1670 — 1788 — 1803 — 1832

La Salle probably became the first white person to explore the Ohio region.

Ohio became the 17th state on March 1.

State bird
Northern cardinal

State flower
Scarlet carnation

State tree
Ohio buckeye

People

Population: 11,536,504
Rank among the states: 7th
Density: 279 per mi^2 (108 per km^2), U.S.
average 85 per mi^2 (33 per km^2)
Distribution: 77 percent urban, 23 percent rural

Largest cities in Ohio

Columbus	787,033
Cleveland	396,815
Cincinnati	296,943
Toledo	287,208
Akron	199,110
Dayton	141,527

Source: 2010 census, except for distribution, which is for 2000..

Population trend

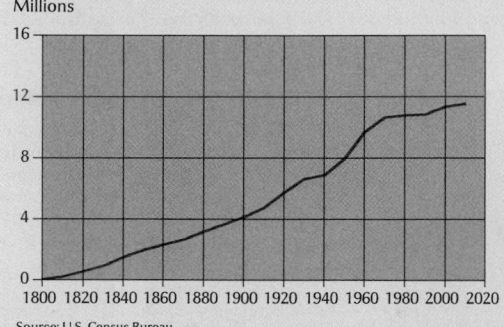

Millions

Source: U.S. Census Bureau.

Year	Population
2010	11,536,504
2000	11,353,140
1990	10,847,115
1980	10,797,630
1970	10,652,017
1960	9,706,397
1950	7,946,627
1940	6,907,612
1930	6,646,697
1920	5,759,394
1910	4,767,121
1900	4,157,545
1890	3,672,329
1880	3,198,062
1870	2,665,260
1860	2,339,511
1850	1,980,329
1840	1,519,467
1830	937,903
1820	581,434
1810	230,760
1800	45,365

Economy

Chief products

Agriculture: beef cattle, corn, greenhouse and nursery products, hogs, milk, poultry products, soybeans.
Manufacturing: chemicals, fabricated metal products, machinery, plastics and rubber products, primary metals, processed foods, transportation equipment.
Mining: coal, limestone, natural gas, petroleum, salt, sand and gravel.

Gross domestic product

Value of goods and services produced in 2008: $477,245,000,000. *Services* include community, business, and personal services; finance; government; trade; and transportation and communication. *Industry* includes construction, manufacturing, mining, and utilities. *Agriculture* includes agriculture, fishing, and forestry.

Source: U.S. Bureau of Economic Analysis.

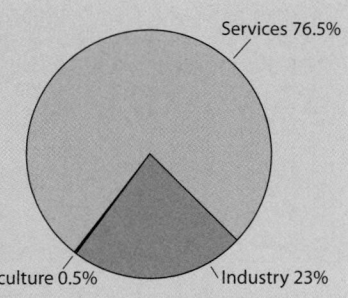

Services 76.5%
Agriculture 0.5%
Industry 23%

Government

State government

Governor: 4-year term
State senators: 33; 4-year terms
State representatives: 99; 2-year terms
Counties: 88

Federal government

United States senators: 2
United States representatives: 18 (16 in 2013)
Electoral votes: 20 (18 in 2012)

Sources of information

Ohio's official website at http://ohio.gov provides a gateway to much information on the state's government, history, and economy.

In addition, the website at http://consumer.discoverohio.com provides information about tourism.

	The Miami River Valley flood-control project was completed.		Ohio adopted a state income tax.	
1914	1922	1955	1971	1993
Ohio passed the Conservancy Act after floods in 1913.		The Ohio Turnpike was opened to traffic.		Voters approved a $200-million state park and recreation area improvement project.

Population. The 2010 United States census reported that Ohio had 11,536,504 people. The state's population had increased by about 1 ½ percent over the 2000 census figure, 11,353,140. According to the 2010 census, Ohio ranks 7th in population among the 50 states.

About 80 percent of Ohio's people live in the state's metropolitan areas. About half of the people live in the three largest metropolitan areas—Cincinnati-Middletown, Cleveland-Elyria-Mentor, and Columbus.

Ohio has 16 metropolitan areas. Ten of these lie entirely within Ohio. Six metropolitan areas are partly in Ohio and partly in one or more of the bordering states of Indiana, Kentucky, Pennsylvania, and West Virginia (see **Metropolitan area**). For the names and populations of these areas, see the *Index* to the political map of Ohio.

Columbus, with a population of 711,470, ranks as the largest city in Ohio. Five other cities in the state have populations of 100,000 or more. These cities are Cleveland, Cincinnati, Toledo, Akron, and Dayton.

The largest population groups in Ohio include people of German, Irish, and English descent. Other large groups include people of Polish, French, or Scottish descent. About 11 percent of the state's people are African Americans. People of Hispanic and Asian origin each account for less than 2 percent of Ohio's population.

Schools. The first school in Ohio opened in 1773 at Schoenbrunn, near present-day New Philadelphia. It was set up for Indian children by David Zeisberger, a Moravian missionary. Ohio's public-school system began in 1825, and public high schools were authorized in 1853. During the 1800's, several Ohio educators wrote school textbooks that were used in public schools throughout

Population density

About 80 percent of Ohio's people live in the state's metropolitan areas. About half of the state's people live in the metropolitan areas of Cincinnati, Cleveland, and Columbus.

Persons per mi²		Persons per km²
More than 500		More than 200
250 to 500		100 to 200
100 to 250		40 to 100
Less than 100		Less than 40

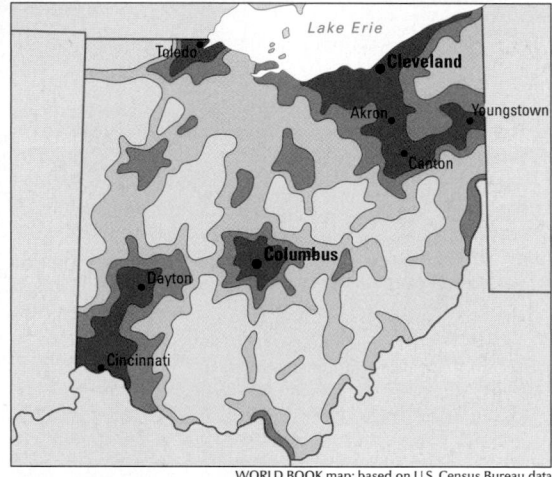

WORLD BOOK map; based on U.S. Census Bureau data

J. Kevin Fitzsimons, Ohio State University

Ohio State University at Columbus has one of the largest student populations of any campus in the United States. University Hall, *shown here,* is located in the center of the campus.

© Toledo Botanical Garden

The Toledo Botanical Garden is known for its elegant displays of plants and sculpture. Throughout the year, the garden hosts weddings, educational events, and art and music festivals.

the United States. The most famous of these educators was William H. McGuffey (see **McGuffey, William H.**).

Many colleges were founded in Ohio in the 1800's. Oberlin College, established in 1833, became the first college in the United States for both men and women.

The State Board of Education supervises all elementary schools and high schools in Ohio. This board consists of 11 members elected to four-year terms and 8 members appointed by the governor to four-year terms. The board members appoint the state superintendent of public instruction. Ohio law requires children between the ages of 6 and 18 to attend school. For the number of students and teachers in Ohio, see **Education** (table).

Libraries. A subscription library opened at Belpre in 1795. In 1804, the famous Coonskin Library was founded at Ames (now Amesville). Pioneers bought its first books with animal skins. Many of these books have been preserved by the Ohio Historical Society in Columbus. The State Library of Ohio in Columbus was established in 1817 as a reference library for state officials.

The Cleveland Public Library is one of the biggest in the United States. Other large Ohio libraries include the Public Library of Cincinnati and Hamilton County, the University of Cincinnati library system, and the Ohio State University library system in Columbus, which is Ohio's largest library center. The library of the Rutherford B. Hayes Presidential Center in Fremont honors the 19th U.S. president. In 1916, it became the nation's first presidential library. The Cincinnati Historical Society Library highlights early Ohio and metropolitan Cincinnati.

Museums. The Cleveland Museum of Art, the Cincinnati Art Museum, and the Toledo Museum of Art all own renowned collections of art from many different periods and cultures. The Taft Museum of Art in Cincinnati displays paintings and Chinese ceramics. The National Museum of the United States Air Force at Wright-Patterson Air Force Base near Dayton exhibits old and modern airplanes. The Rock and Roll Hall of Fame and Museum in Cleveland has displays and interactive exhibits about the history of rock music.

Universities and colleges

This table lists the nonprofit universities and colleges in Ohio that grant bachelor's or advanced degrees and are accredited by the North Central Association of Colleges and Schools.

Name	Mailing address	Name	Mailing address	Name	Mailing address
Air Force Institute of Technology	Wright-Patterson Air Force Base	God's Bible School and College	Cincinnati	Notre Dame College	South Euclid
		Hebrew Union College— Jewish Institute		Oberlin College	Oberlin
				Ohio Christian University	Circleville
Akron, University of	Akron	of Religion	Cincinnati	Ohio College of Podiatric Medicine	Cleveland
Antioch University	Yellow Springs	Heidelberg University	Tiffin		
Antioch University McGregor	Yellow Springs	Hiram College	Hiram	Ohio Dominican University	Columbus
		John Carroll University	Cleveland	Ohio Northern University	Ada
Art Academy of Cincinnati	Cincinnati	Kent State University	†	Ohio State University	§
Ashland University	Ashland	Kenyon College	Gambier	Ohio University	#
Athenaeum of Ohio	Cincinnati	Kettering College of Medical Arts	Kettering	Ohio Wesleyan University	Delaware
Baldwin-Wallace College	Berea			Otterbein College	Westerville
Bluffton University	Bluffton	Lake Erie College	Painesville	Pontifical College Josephinum	Columbus
Bowling Green State University	*	Laura and Alvin Siegal College of Judaic Studies	Beachwood	Rio Grande, University of	Rio Grande
Capital University	Columbus	Lourdes College	Sylvania	St. Mary Seminary and Graduate School of Theology	Wickliffe
Case Western Reserve University	Cleveland	Malone University	Canton		
Cedarville University	Cedarville	Marietta College	Marietta	Shawnee State University	Portsmouth
Central State University	Wilberforce	Mercy College of Northwest Ohio	Toledo	Tiffin University	Tiffin
Chancellor University	Cleveland			Toledo, University of	Toledo
Cincinnati, University of	Cincinnati	Methodist Theological School in Ohio	Delaware	Trinity Lutheran Seminary	Columbus
Cincinnati Christian University	Cincinnati	Miami University	‡	Union Institute & University	Cincinnati
Cincinnati College of Mortuary Science	Cincinnati	Mount Carmel College of Nursing	Columbus	United Theological Seminary	Dayton
Cleveland Institute of Art	Cleveland	Mount St. Joseph, College of	Cincinnati	Urbana University	Urbana
Cleveland Institute of Music	Cleveland	Mount Union, University of	Alliance	Ursuline College	Cleveland
				Walsh University	North Canton
Cleveland State University	Cleveland	Mount Vernon Nazarene University	Mount Vernon	Wilberforce University	Wilberforce
Columbus College of Art & Design	Columbus			Wilmington College	Wilmington
Dayton, University of	Dayton	Muskingum University	New Concord	Winebrenner Theological Seminary	Findlay
Defiance College	Defiance			Wittenberg University	Springfield
Denison University	Granville	Northeastern Ohio Universities Colleges of Medicine and Pharmacy	Rootstown	Wooster, College of	Wooster
Findlay, University of	Findlay			Wright State University	Dayton
Franciscan University of Steubenville	Steubenville			Xavier University	Cincinnati
Franklin University	Columbus	Northwestern Ohio, University of	Lima	Youngstown State University	Youngstown

*Campuses at Bowling Green and Huron.
†Campuses at Burton Township, Canton, Kent, New Philadelphia, and Salem.

‡Campuses at Hamilton, Middletown, and Oxford.
§For campuses, see **Ohio State University.**

#Campuses at Athens, Chillicothe, Lancaster, St. Clairsville, and Zanesville.

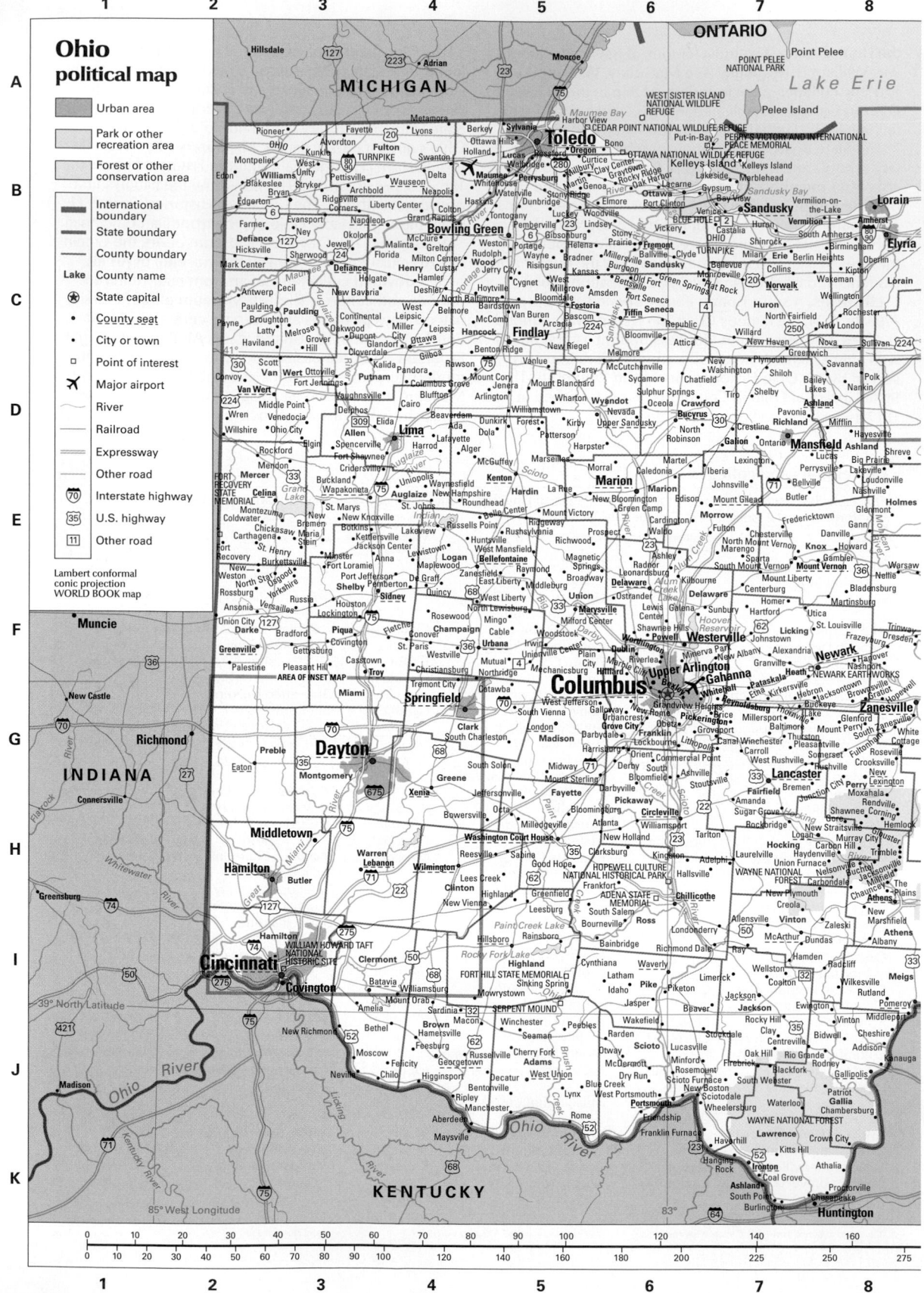

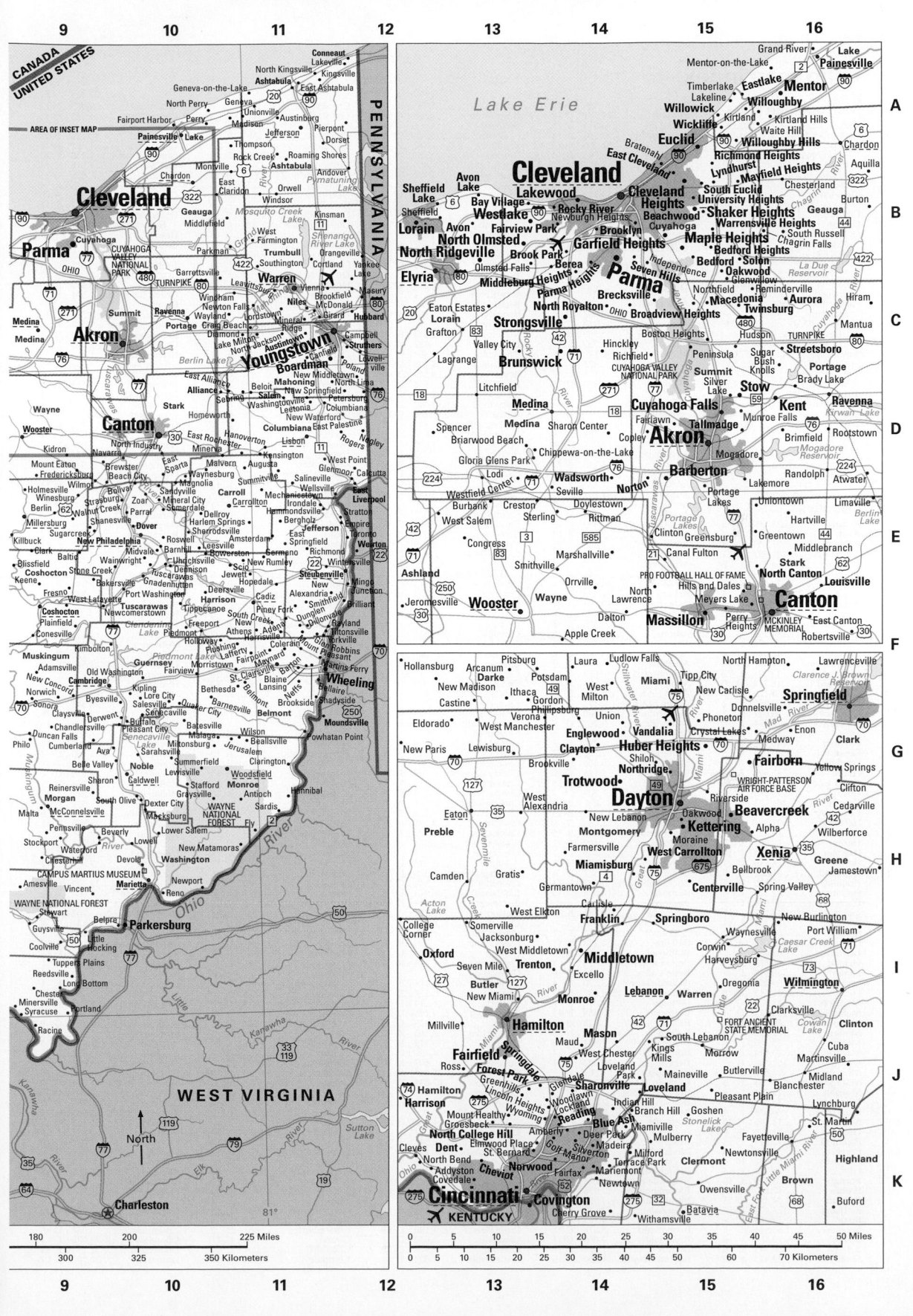

Ohio map index

Landen*† ... 6,782 .. H 4
La Rue ... 747 .. E 5
Laura ... 474 .. F 14
Laurelville ... 527 .. H 7
Leavittsburg† ... 1,973 .. C 11
Lebanon° ... 20,033 .. H 3
Leesburg ... 1,314 .. I 5
Leesville ... 158 .. E 10
Leetonia ... 1,959 .. D 11
Leipsic ... 2,093 .. C 4
Lewisburg ... 1,820 .. G 13
Lewisville ... 176 .. G 10
Lexington ... 4,822 .. D 7
Liberty Center ... 1,180 .. B 4
Lima° ... 38,771 .. D 4
Lincoln Heights .. 3,286 .. K 13
Lincoln Village*† ... 9,032 .. G 6
Lindsey ... 446 .. B 6
Lisbon° ... 2,821 .. D 11
Lithopolis ... 1,106 .. G 7
Lockbourne ... 237 .. G 6
Lockland ... 3,449 .. J 14
Lodi ... 2,746 .. D 13
Logan° ... 7,152 .. H 7
Logan Elm Village*† ... 1,118 .. H 6
London° ... 9,904 .. G 5
Lorain ... 64,097 .. B 8
Lordstown ... 3,417 .. C 11
Lore City ... 325 .. F 10
Loudonville ... 2,641 .. E 8
Louisville ... 9,186 .. E 16
Loveland ... 12,081 .. J 14
Loveland Park† .. 1,523 .. J 4
Lowell ... 549 .. H 10
Lowellville ... 1,155 .. C 12
Lucas ... 615 .. D 8
Lucasville† ... 2,757 .. J 6
Luckey ... 1,012 .. B 5
Ludlow Falls ... 208 .. F 14
Lynchburg ... 1,499 .. J 16
Lyndhurst ... 14,001 .. B 15
Lyons ... 562 .. A 4
Macedonia ... 11,188 .. C 15
Mack*† ... 11,585 .. K 13
Macksburg ... 186 .. H 10
Madeira ... 8,726 .. K 14
Madison ... 3,184 .. A 11
Magnetic Springs .. 268 .. E 5
Magnolia ... 978 .. E 10
Maineville ... 975 .. J 15
Malinta ... 265 .. B 4
Malta ... 671 .. G 9
Malvern ... 1,189 .. D 10
Manchester ... 2,023 .. J 5
Mansfield° ... 47,821 .. D 7
Mantua ... 1,043 .. C 16
Maple Heights ... 23,138 .. B 15
Maple Ridge*† ... 761 .. D 10
Marble Cliff ... 573 .. F 6
Marblehead ... 903 .. B 7
Marengo ... 342 .. E 7
Mariemont ... 3,403 .. K 14
Marietta° ... 14,085 .. H 10
Marion° ... 36,837 .. E 6
Marseilles ... 112 .. D 5
Marshallville ... 756 .. E 14
Martins Ferry ... 6,915 .. F 11
Martinsburg ... 237 .. F 8
Martinsville ... 463 .. J 16
Marysville° ... 22,094 .. F 5
Mason ... 30,712 .. J 14
Massillon ... 32,149 .. F 15
Masury† ... 2,064 .. C 12
Maumee ... 14,286 .. B 5
Mayfield* ... 3,460 .. B 15
Mayfield Heights ... 19,155 .. B 15
McArthur° ... 1,701 .. I 7
McClure ... 725 .. B 4
McComb ... 1,648 .. C 4
McConnelsville° ... 1,784 .. H 9
McDonald ... 3,263 .. C 11
McGuffey ... 501 .. D 4
Mechanicsburg ... 1,644 .. F 5
Medina° ... 26,678 .. C 9
Melrose ... 275 .. C 3
Mendon ... 662 .. D 3
Mentor ... 47,159 .. A 16
Mentor-on-the-Lake ... 7,443 .. A 16
Metamora ... 627 .. A 4
Meyers Lake ... 569 .. F 15
Miamisburg ... 20,181 .. H 14
Middleburg Heights ... 15,946 .. C 14
Middlefield ... 2,694 .. B 10
Middle Point ... 576 .. D 3
Middleport ... 2,530 .. I 8
Middletown ... 48,694 .. I 14
Midland ... 315 .. J 16
Midvale ... 754 .. E 10
Midway ... 322 .. G 5
Milan ... 1,367 .. C 7
Milford ... 6,709 .. K 14
Milford Center ... 792 .. F 5
Millbury ... 1,200 .. B 5
Millersburg° ... 3,025 .. E 9
Millersport ... 1,044 .. G 7
Millville ... 708 .. I 13
Mineral City ... 727 .. E 10
Mineral Ridge† ... 3,892 .. C 11
Minerva ... 3,720 .. D 10
Minerva Park ... 1,272 .. F 6
Minford† ... 693 .. J 6
Mingo Junction ... 3,454 .. E 12
Minster ... 2,805 .. E 3
Mogadore ... 3,853 .. D 15
Monfort Heights* ... 11,948 .. K 13
Monroe ... 12,422 .. I 14
Monroeville ... 1,400 .. C 7
Montgomery* ... 10,251 .. K 14
Montpelier ... 4,072 .. B 3
Montrose-Ghent*† ... 5,177 .. D 14
Moraine ... 6,307 .. H 15
Moreland Hills* .. 3,320 .. B 15
Morral ... 399 .. D 6
Morristown ... 303 .. F 10
Morrow ... 1,188 .. J 15
Moscow ... 185 .. J 3
Mount Blanchard ... 492 .. D 5
Mount Carmel*† ... 4,741 .. K 14
Mount Cory ... 204 .. D 4
Mount Eaton ... 241 .. E 9
Mount Gilead° ... 3,660 .. E 7
Mount Healthy ... 6,098 .. J 13
Mount Healthy Heights*† ... 3,264 .. K 13
Mount Orab ... 3,664 .. I 4
Mount Pleasant ... 478 .. F 11
Mount Repose*† ... 4,672 .. J 14
Mount Sterling ... 1,782 .. G 5
Mount Vernon° ... 16,990 .. E 7
Mount Victory ... 627 .. E 5
Mowrystown ... 360 .. I 4
Mulberry† ... 3,323 .. K 15
Munroe Falls ... 5,012 .. D 15
Murray City ... 449 .. H 8
Napoleon° ... 8,749 .. B 4
Navarre ... 1,957 .. D 10
Neffs† ... 993 .. F 11
Nelsonville ... 5,392 .. H 8
Nevada ... 760 .. D 6
New Albany ... 7,724 .. F 7
New Alexandria ... 272 .. E 11
New Athens ... 320 .. F 11
New Blomington ... 515 .. E 6
New Boston ... 2,272 .. J 6
New Bremen ... 2,978 .. E 3
New Carlisle ... 5,785 .. F 15
New Concord ... 2,491 .. F 9
New Franklin* ... 14,227 .. E 15
New Holland ... 801 .. H 5
New Knoxville ... 879 .. E 3
New Lebanon ... 3,995 .. H 14
New Lexington° ... 4,731 .. G 8
New London ... 2,461 .. C 8
New Madison ... 892 .. G 12
New Matamoras ... 896 .. H 11
New Miami ... 2,249 .. I 13
New Middletown ... 1,621 .. C 12
New Paris ... 1,629 .. G 12
New Philadelphia° ... 17,288 .. E 10
New Richmond ... 2,582 .. J 3
New Riegel ... 249 .. C 5
New Straitsville ... 722 .. H 8
New Vienna ... 1,224 .. H 4
New Washington ... 967 .. D 7
New Waterford ... 1,238 .. D 11
Newark° ... 47,573 .. F 8
Newburgh Heights ... 2,167 .. B 14
Newcomerstown ... 3,822 .. F 9
Newton Falls ... 4,795 .. C 11
Newtonsville ... 392 .. K 15
Newtown ... 2,672 .. K 14
Ney ... 354 .. B 3
Niles ... 19,266 .. C 11
North Baltimore ... 3,432 .. C 5
North Bend ... 857 .. K 12
North Canton ... 17,488 .. E 16
North College Hill ... 9,397 .. K 13
North Fairfield ... 560 .. C 7
North Hampton ... 478 .. F 16
North Kingsville ... 2,923 .. A 11
North Lewisburg ... 1,490 .. F 5
North Madison*† ... 8,547 .. B 11
North Olmsted .. 32,718 .. B 13
North Perry ... 893 .. A 10
North Randall* ... 1,027 .. B 15
North Ridgeville ... 29,465 .. B 13
North Robinson ... 205 .. D 6
North Royalton ... 30,444 .. C 14
North Star ... 236 .. F 2
North Zanesville*† ... 2,816 .. G 8
Northbrook*† ... 10,668 .. K 13
Northfield ... 3,677 .. C 15
Northgate*† ... 7,377 .. J 13
Northridge† ... 7,572 .. F 4
Northwood* ... 5,265 .. B 5
Norton ... 12,085 .. E 14
Norwalk° ... 17,012 .. C 7
Norwood ... 19,207 .. K 13
Oak Harbor ... 2,759 .. B 6
Oak Hill ... 1,551 .. J 7
Oakwood ... 9,202 .. H 15
Oakwood ... 608 .. C 3
Oakwood ... 3,667 .. B 15
Oberlin ... 8,286 .. C 8
Obetz ... 4,532 .. G 6
Ohio City ... 705 .. D 3
Old Washington ... 279 .. F 10
Olmsted Falls ... 9,024 .. B 13
Ontario ... 6,225 .. D 7
Orange* ... 3,323 .. B 15
Oregon ... 20,291 .. B 5
Orient ... 270 .. G 2
Orrville ... 8,380 .. E 14
Orwell ... 1,660 .. B 11
Osgood ... 302 .. F 3
Ostrander ... 643 .. F 6
Ottawa° ... 4,460 .. C 4
Ottawa Hills ... 4,517 .. A 5
Ottoville ... 976 .. D 3
Owensville ... 794 .. K 15
Oxford ... 21,371 .. J 12
Painesville° ... 19,563 .. A 10
Pandora ... 1,153 .. D 4
Park Layne*† ... 4,343 .. G 15
Parma ... 81,601 .. B 14
Parma Heights .. 20,718 .. C 14
Parral ... 218 .. E 9
Pataskala ... 14,962 .. F 7
Paulding° ... 3,605 .. C 3
Payne ... 1,194 .. C 2
Peebles ... 1,782 .. J 5
Pemberville ... 1,371 .. B 5
Peninsula ... 565 .. C 15
Pepper Pike* ... 5,979 .. B 15
Perry ... 1,663 .. A 10
Perry Heights† ... 8,441 .. D 10
Perrysburg ... 20,623 .. B 5
Perrysville ... 735 .. D 8
Phillipsburg ... 557 .. G 14
Philo ... 733 .. G 9
Pickerington ... 18,291 .. G 7
Pigeon Creek*† ... 882 .. D 14
Piketon ... 2,181 .. I 6
Pioneer ... 1,380 .. A 3
Piqua ... 20,522 .. F 3
Pitsburg ... 388 .. G 13
Plain City ... 4,225 .. F 5
Plains, The† ... 3,080 .. H 8
Pleasant City ... 447 .. G 10
Pleasant Grove*† ... 1,742 .. G 8
Pleasant Hill ... 1,200 .. F 3
Pleasant Run† ... 4,953 .. K 13
Pleasant Run Farms*† ... 4,654 .. J 13
Pleasantville ... 960 .. G 7
Plymouth ... 1,857 .. D 7
Poland ... 2,555 .. C 12
Polk ... 336 .. D 8
Pomeroy° ... 1,852 .. I 8
Port Clinton° ... 6,056 .. B 6
Port Jefferson ... 371 .. F 4
Port Washington ... 569 .. E 10
Portage ... 438 .. B 5
Portage Lakes† .. 6,968 .. E 15
Portsmouth° ... 20,226 .. J 6
Potsdam ... 288 .. F 14
Powell ... 11,500 .. F 6
Powhatan Point .. 1,592 .. G 11
Proctorville ... 574 .. K 8
Prospect ... 1,112 .. E 6
Quaker City ... 502 .. G 10
Quincy ... 706 .. F 4
Racine ... 675 .. J 9
Ravenna° ... 11,724 .. C 10
Rawson ... 570 .. D 4
Rayland ... 417 .. F 11
Reading ... 10,385 .. J 13
Reminderville ... 3,404 .. C 15
Republic ... 549 .. C 6
Reynoldsburg .. 35,893 .. G 7
Richfield ... 3,648 .. C 14
Richmond ... 481 .. E 11
Richmond Heights ... 10,546 .. B 15
Richwood ... 2,229 .. E 5
Ridgeway ... 338 .. E 5
Rio Grande ... 830 .. J 8
Ripley ... 1,750 .. J 4
Risingsun ... 606 .. C 5
Rittman ... 6,491 .. E 14
Riverlea ... 545 .. F 6
Riverside ... 25,201 .. G 15
Roaming Shores ... 1,508 .. A 11
Rock Creek ... 529 .. A 11
Rockford ... 1,120 .. D 2
Rocky Ridge ... 417 .. B 6
Rocky River ... 20,213 .. B 13
Rogers ... 237 .. D 11
Rosemount† ... 2,112 .. J 6
Roseville ... 1,852 .. G 8
Ross† ... 3,417 .. J 13
Rossford ... 6,293 .. B 5
Rushsylvania ... 516 .. E 5
Russells Point ... 1,391 .. E 4
Russellville ... 561 .. J 5
Russia ... 640 .. F 3
Rutland ... 393 .. I 8
Sabina ... 2,564 .. H 5
St. Bernard ... 4,368 .. K 13
St. Clairsville° ... 5,184 .. F 11
St. Henry ... 2,427 .. E 2
St. Louisville ... 373 .. F 8
St. Marys ... 8,332 .. E 3
St. Paris ... 2,089 .. F 4
Salem ... 12,303 .. D 11
Salineville ... 1,311 .. D 11
Sandusky° ... 25,793 .. B 7
Sardinia ... 980 .. I 4
Savannah ... 413 .. D 8
Scio ... 763 .. E 11
Sciotodale† ... 1,081 .. J 6
Scott ... 286 .. D 3
Seaman ... 944 .. J 5
Sebring ... 4,420 .. D 11
Senecaville ... 457 .. G 10
Seven Hills ... 11,804 .. B 14
Seven Mile ... 751 .. I 13
Seville ... 2,296 .. E 14
Shadyside ... 3,785 .. G 11
Shaker Heights ... 28,448 .. B 15
Sharonville ... 13,560 .. J 14
Shawnee ... 655 .. G 8
Shawnee Hills ... 681 .. F 6
Shawnee Hills*† ... 2,171 .. H 16
Sheffield ... 3,982 .. B 12
Sheffield Lake ... 9,137 .. B 12
Shelby ... 9,317 .. D 7
Sherrodsville ... 304 .. E 10
Sherwood ... 827 .. C 3
Sherwood*† ... 3,719 .. K 14
Shiloh ... 649 .. D 7
Shreve ... 1,514 .. D 8
Sidney° ... 21,229 .. F 4
Silver Lake ... 2,519 .. D 15
Silverton ... 4,788 .. K 14
Smithfield ... 869 .. E 11
Smithville ... 1,252 .. E 13
Solon ... 23,348 .. B 15
Somerset ... 1,481 .. G 8
Somerville ... 281 .. I 13
South Amherst ... 1,688 .. B 8
South Bloomfield ... 1,744 .. G 6
South Canal*† ... 1,100 .. C 11
South Charleston ... 1,693 .. G 5
South Euclid ... 22,295 .. B 15
South Lebanon ... 4,115 .. J 15
South Point ... 3,958 .. K 7
South Russell ... 3,810 .. B 16
South Salem ... 204 .. I 5
South Solon ... 355 .. G 5
South Vienna ... 384 .. G 5
South Webster ... 866 .. J 7
South Zanesville ... 1,989 .. G 8
Sparta ... 161 .. E 7
Spencer ... 753 .. D 12
Spencerville ... 2,223 .. D 3
Spring Valley ... 479 .. H 16
Springboro ... 17,409 .. I 15
Springdale ... 11,223 .. J 13
Springfield° ... 60,608 .. G 4
Steubenville° .. 18,659 .. E 12
Stockport ... 503 .. H 9
Stone Creek ... 177 .. E 9
Stony Prairie† ... 1,284 .. B 6
Stoutsville ... 560 .. G 7
Stow ... 34,837 .. D 15
Strasburg ... 2,608 .. E 9
Stratton ... 294 .. E 12
Streetsboro ... 16,028 .. C 16
Strongsville ... 44,750 .. C 14
Struthers ... 10,713 .. C 12
Stryker ... 1,335 .. B 3
Sugar Grove ... 426 .. H 7
Sugarcreek ... 2,220 .. E 8
Summerfield ... 254 .. G 10
Summerside*† ... 5,083 .. K 14
Sunbury ... 4,389 .. F 7
Swanton ... 3,690 .. B 4
Sycamore ... 861 .. D 6
Sylvania ... 18,965 .. A 5
Syracuse ... 826 .. I 9
Tallmadge ... 17,537 .. D 15
Tarlton ... 282 .. H 7
Terrace Park ... 2,251 .. K 14
Thornville ... 991 .. G 7
Thurston ... 604 .. G 7
Tiffin° ... 17,963 .. C 6
Tiltonsville ... 1,372 .. F 11
Timberlake ... 675 .. A 15
Tipp City ... 9,689 .. G 15
Tiro ... 280 .. D 7
Toledo° ... 287,208 .. A 5
Tontogany ... 367 .. B 5
Toronto ... 5,091 .. E 12
Tremont City ... 375 .. F 4
Trenton ... 11,869 .. I 13
Trimble ... 390 .. H 8
Trotwood ... 24,431 .. G 14
Troy° ... 25,058 .. F 3
Turnpike Interchange* ... C 11
Turpin Hills*† ... 5,099 .. K 14
Tuscarawas ... 1,056 .. E 10
Twinsburg ... 18,795 .. C 15
Uhrichsville ... 5,413 .. E 10
Union ... 6,419 .. G 14
Union City ... 1,666 .. F 2
Uniontown† ... 3,309 .. E 16
Uniopolis ... 222 .. E 4
University Heights ... 13,539 .. B 15
Upper Arlington ... 33,771 .. F 6
Upper Sandusky° ... 6,596 .. D 6
Urbana° ... 11,793 .. F 4
Urbancrest ... 960 .. G 6
Utica ... 2,132 .. F 7
Valley View* ... 2,034 .. B 14
Valleyview* ... 620 .. G 6
Van Buren ... 328 .. C 5
Van Wert° ... 10,846 .. D 3
Vandalia ... 15,246 .. G 15
Vanlue ... 359 .. D 5
Venedocia ... 124 .. D 3
Vermilion ... 10,594 .. B 8
Verona ... 494 .. G 13
Versailles ... 2,687 .. F 3
Vienna Center*† ... 650 .. C 11
Vinton ... 222 .. J 8
Wadsworth ... 21,567 .. D 14
Waite Hill ... 471 .. A 16
Wakeman ... 1,047 .. C 8
Walbridge ... 3,019 .. B 5
Waldo ... 338 .. E 6
Walton Hills* ... 2,281 .. B 14
Wapakoneta° ... 9,867 .. E 3
Warren° ... 41,557 .. C 11
Warrensville Heights ... 13,542 .. B 15
Warsaw ... 682 .. E 8
Washington Court House° ... 14,192 .. H 5
Washingtonville ... 801 .. D 11
Waterford† ... 450 .. H 10
Waterville ... 5,523 .. B 5
Wauseon° ... 7,332 .. B 4
Waverly° ... 4,408 .. I 6
Wayne ... 887 .. C 5
Wayne Lakes* ... 718 .. F 2
Waynesburg ... 923 .. D 10
Waynesfield ... 847 .. E 4
Waynesville ... 2,834 .. I 15
Wellington ... 4,802 .. C 8
Wellston ... 5,663 .. I 7
Wellsville ... 3,541 .. E 11
West Alexandria ... 1,340 .. H 13
West Carrollton ... 13,143 .. H 14
West Farmington ... 499 .. B 11
West Hill*† ... 2,273 .. C 12
West Jefferson ... 4,222 .. G 5
West Lafayette ... 2,321 .. F 9
West Leipsic ... 206 .. C 4
West Liberty ... 1,805 .. F 4
West Manchester ... 474 .. G 13
West Mansfield ... 682 .. E 5
West Milton ... 4,630 .. F 14
West Portsmouth† .. 3,149 .. J 6
West Salem ... 1,464 .. E 12
West Union° ... 3,241 .. J 5
West Unity ... 1,671 .. B 3
Westerville ... 36,120 .. F 6
Westfield Center ... 1,115 .. E 13
Westlake ... 32,729 .. B 13
Weston ... 1,590 .. B 4
Wharton ... 358 .. D 5
Wheelersburg† ... 6,437 .. J 7
White Oak*† ... 19,167 .. I 4
Whitehall ... 18,062 .. G 6
Whitehouse ... 4,149 .. B 4
Wickliffe ... 12,750 .. A 15
Wilberforce† ... 2,271 .. H 16
Willard ... 6,236 .. C 7
Williamsburg ... 2,490 .. I 4
Williamsport ... 1,023 .. H 6
Willoughby ... 22,268 .. A 15
Willoughby Hills ... 9,485 .. A 15
Willowick ... 14,171 .. A 15
Willshire ... 397 .. D 2
Wilmington° ... 12,520 .. H 4
Wilmot ... 304 .. E 9
Winchester ... 1,051 .. J 5
Windham ... 2,209 .. C 11
Wintersville ... 3,924 .. E 11
Withamsville† ... 7,021 .. K 14
Woodlawn ... 3,294 .. J 14
Woodmere* ... 884 .. B 10
Woodsfield° ... 2,384 .. G 11
Woodstock ... 305 .. F 5
Woodville ... 2,135 .. B 5
Wooster° ... 26,119 .. D 9
Worthington ... 13,575 .. F 6
Wright-Patterson AFB† ... 1,821 .. G 15
Wyoming ... 8,428 .. J 13
Xenia° ... 25,719 .. G 4
Yellow Springs ... 3,487 .. G 16
Yorkville ... 1,079 .. F 11
Youngstown° .. 66,982 .. C 11
Zaleski ... 278 .. I 8
Zanesfield ... 197 .. E 5
Zanesville° ... 25,487 .. G 8

*Does not appear on the map; key shows general location.
†Census designated place—unincorporated, but recognized as a significant settled community by the U.S. Census Bureau.

°County seat.
Places without population figures are unincorporated areas.
Source: 2010 census.

Ohio has hundreds of historical, recreational, and scenic attractions. Historical points of interest include huge Indian burial mounds and forts that date back to prehistoric times.

The 2,500 lakes and 44,000 miles (70,800 kilometers) of rivers and streams in Ohio provide many opportunities for boating, fishing, and swimming. Lake Erie is a major tourist and recreational attraction. Hunters shoot deer, ducks, and rabbits in the state's woods and on the rolling plains. Many vacationers enjoy hiking in the hilly eastern section of Ohio, which has some of the state's most beautiful scenery.

Two historical plays performed outdoors rank among Ohio's most popular annual events. *Tecumseh!* (1973), a drama about the Shawnee chief, is held near Chillicothe. *Trumpet in the Land* (1970), which concerns Ohio's first permanent white settlement, is performed near New Philadelphia. Both plays run from June to September.

**Great Serpent Mound
near Hillsboro**

Steve Bulkley, Foto/Find

Places to visit

Following are brief descriptions of some of Ohio's most interesting places to visit:

Adena State Memorial, in Chillicothe, is a restored stone house built in 1807 by Thomas Worthington, who later became governor of Ohio. It is furnished with rare American antiques of the 1700's and early 1800's.

Campus Martius Museum, in Marietta, stands on the site of the fortified stockade built by the first permanent white settlers in Ohio. The museum includes the home of Rufus Putnam, the founder of Marietta. The nearby Ohio River Museum exhibits models, pictures, and relics of riverboats.

Fort Recovery, in the village of Fort Recovery, is a reproduction of part of the fort that General Anthony Wayne ordered built in 1793. Wayne used the fort during the Indian wars in Ohio.

Historic Roscoe Village, in Coshocton, is a restored community that illustrates life on the Ohio and Erie Canal in the 1830's. It features homes, businesses, and a horse-drawn canal boat.

Indian Mounds and other earthworks may be seen throughout the state. Fort Ancient, near Lebanon, is the largest hilltop earth structure in the United States. Its earthen walls are more than 20 feet (6 meters) high and 3 miles (5 kilometers) long. Fort Hill, near Bainbridge, is a 1,200-acre (486-hectare) area with a great earthwork enclosure on a high hill. Great Serpent Mound, near Hillsboro, is one of the best-known prehistoric structures in the world and is shaped like a snake. It rises about 3 feet (0.9 meters) and extends over ¼ mile (0.4 kilometer). Newark Earthworks, at Newark, includes an octagonal earthen ridge that encloses about 50 acres (20 hectares), and circular earthen walls that enclose about 20 acres (8 hectares).

Kelleys Island, in Lake Erie near Sandusky, is a summer resort famous for its glacial markings and Inscription Rock. The markings—grooves cut into surface limestone by glaciers—are among the world's best examples of glacial action. Inscription Rock is a boulder with traces of ancient Indian carvings.

Pro Football Hall of Fame, in Canton, honors outstanding professional football players. It includes a museum of equipment worn by famous players and used in famous games.

Rock and Roll Hall of Fame and Museum, in Cleveland, celebrates the living legacy of rock and roll. Exhibits include stage costumes, sheet music, instruments, and other items that portray the historical progression of rock music.

Rutherford B. Hayes Presidential Center, in Fremont, includes a library and museum at the former president's Spiegel Grove estate. The presidential library has papers of Hayes and books on American life during the 1800's. The museum features exhibits on the life and times of Hayes and his family.

Schoenbrunn Village, near New Philadelphia, consists of reconstructed portions of the Moravian mission settlement founded there in 1772 for Indians. The site includes a replica of the first schoolhouse in what is now Ohio.

Wright-Patterson Air Force Base, near Dayton, is one of the nation's largest U.S. Air Force bases and home of the Air Force Research Laboratory. The base includes the field on which the Wright brothers conducted their airplane experiments. The base also includes the world's oldest and largest military aviation museum.

Zoar Village, near New Philadelphia, was founded in 1817 by a group of Germans seeking freedom from religious persecution. Visitors can see restored buildings once used by the community members and the Zoar garden.

National forests and parklands. Wayne National Forest, the only national forest in Ohio, lies in the southeastern part of the state. Perry's Victory and International Peace Memorial stands at Put-in-Bay on South Bass Island in Lake Erie. It honors the American victory in the Battle of Lake Erie during the War of 1812 (1812-1815), as well as the long-lasting peace between the United States, Canada, and the United Kingdom. The granite shaft, 352 feet (107 meters) high, is one of the nation's tallest memorials. It has an observation deck near the top. Hopewell Culture National Historical Park, near Chillicothe, has many prehistoric Indian mounds. The Cuyahoga Valley National Park stretches along the Cuyahoga River between Akron and Cleveland. The William Howard Taft National Historic Site, in Cincinnati, includes the birthplace of the 27th president.

State parks and forests. Ohio has dozens of state parks and state forests. The official website of the Ohio Department of Natural Resources at http://www.dnr.state.oh.us provides more information.

Horse-drawn canal boat at Roscoe Village

Roscoe Village

Ohio Outdoor Historical Drama Association, Inc.

Historical pageant near New Philadelphia

Pro Football Hall of Fame

Pro Football Hall of Fame in Canton

Artstreet

National Museum of the United States Air Force near Dayton

Land regions. Several glaciers moved down from the north during the Pleistocene Epoch, which ended about 11,500 years ago. They covered all of what is now Ohio except the southeastern part. These separate glacial movements helped create the state's four main land regions. These four regions are (1) the Great Lakes Plains, (2) the Till Plains, (3) the Appalachian Plateau, and (4) the Bluegrass Region.

The Great Lakes Plains of northern Ohio form part of the fertile lowland that lies along much of the Great Lakes. In Ohio, these plains make up a narrow strip of land that borders Lake Erie. The region is 5 to 10 miles (8 to 16 kilometers) wide in the east, and broadens to more than 50 miles (80 kilometers) in the Maumee Valley to the west. A few low, sandy ridges along the Lake Erie shore break the flatness of the plains. A wide variety of crops, especially fruits and vegetables, grows in the region's fertile soil. The region is one of the busiest manufacturing, shipping, trading, and recreational areas in the United States. It includes many lake ports and large industrial cities. The most heavily populated part of Ohio, the Cleveland metropolitan area, is in the Great Lakes Plains region.

The Till Plains are the easternmost part of the rich midwestern Corn Belt, which stretches westward from Ohio. This region ranks among the most fertile farming areas in the country.

Some hills dot the gently rolling plains, which lie in most of western Ohio. One of them, Campbell Hill in Logan County, rises 1,550 feet (472 meters) and is the highest point in Ohio. From there, the land gradually slopes downward to the southwestern corner of the state in Hamilton County. This area, 433 feet (132 meters) above sea level, is Ohio's lowest point. Farmers of the Till Plains produce grain, soybeans, and livestock. The area has many industrial cities where a wide variety of products is manufactured. It also includes Columbus, the state capital.

The Appalachian Plateau includes most of the eastern half of Ohio. This highland extends eastward into Pennsylvania and West Virginia. The southern two-thirds of the region was not covered by glaciers. As a result, this section is the most rugged part of the state, with steep hills and valleys. Most of the soil is thin and not fertile. The northern third of the plateau has rolling valleys and hills, and has less fertile soil than that of the Till Plains.

The rugged Appalachian Plateau has some of Ohio's most beautiful scenery, including the state's largest forests and some waterfalls. It also has Ohio's richest mineral deposits—clay, coal, natural gas, oil, and salt. A few of its cities are important manufacturing centers.

The Bluegrass Region, Ohio's smallest land region, is an extension of the Bluegrass Region of Kentucky. This triangular area in southern Ohio has both hilly and gently rolling land. The hills of the Bluegrass Region have thin, less fertile soil.

Shoreline of Ohio stretches for 312 miles (502 kilometers) along Lake Erie, from Conneaut in the east to Toledo in the west. It includes 53 miles (85 kilometers) along Sandusky Bay, and 66 miles (106 kilometers) along offshore islands. The eastern half of the shoreline consists of clay bluffs about 10 to 18 feet (3 to 5 meters) high. The western half has beaches of clay or sand. Many harbors indent the shoreline. Two of the busy lake ports lie on large bays—Toledo on Maumee Bay, and Sandusky on Sandusky Bay. North and northwest of Sandusky in Lake Erie are some small islands. The largest ones, Kelleys and North, Middle, and South Bass islands, are used chiefly as recreation areas.

Rivers and lakes. Ohio has more than 44,000 miles (70,800 kilometers) of rivers and streams. They flow either south into the Ohio River or north into Lake Erie. A series of low hills separates the two groups of rivers. This *divide* lies approximately along the southern boundary of the Great Lakes Plains and extends into Indiana. Except for the Maumee River, all the longer, wider rivers flow into the Ohio River. They drain about 70 percent of the state.

The Ohio River, one of the chief rivers of North America, flows more than 450 miles (724 kilometers) along Ohio's southern and southeastern borders. The northern bank of the river forms the state boundary. Many bluffs from 200 to 500 feet (61 to 150 meters) high rise along the river, which winds through a valley less than 2 miles (3 kilometers) wide.

The Ohio River's longest tributary in Ohio is the Scioto River, which is 237 miles (381 kilometers) long. Other rivers flowing into the Ohio include the Hocking,

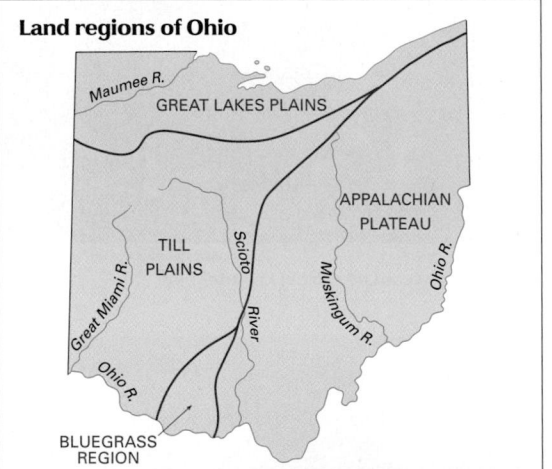

Land regions of Ohio

WORLD BOOK map

Map index

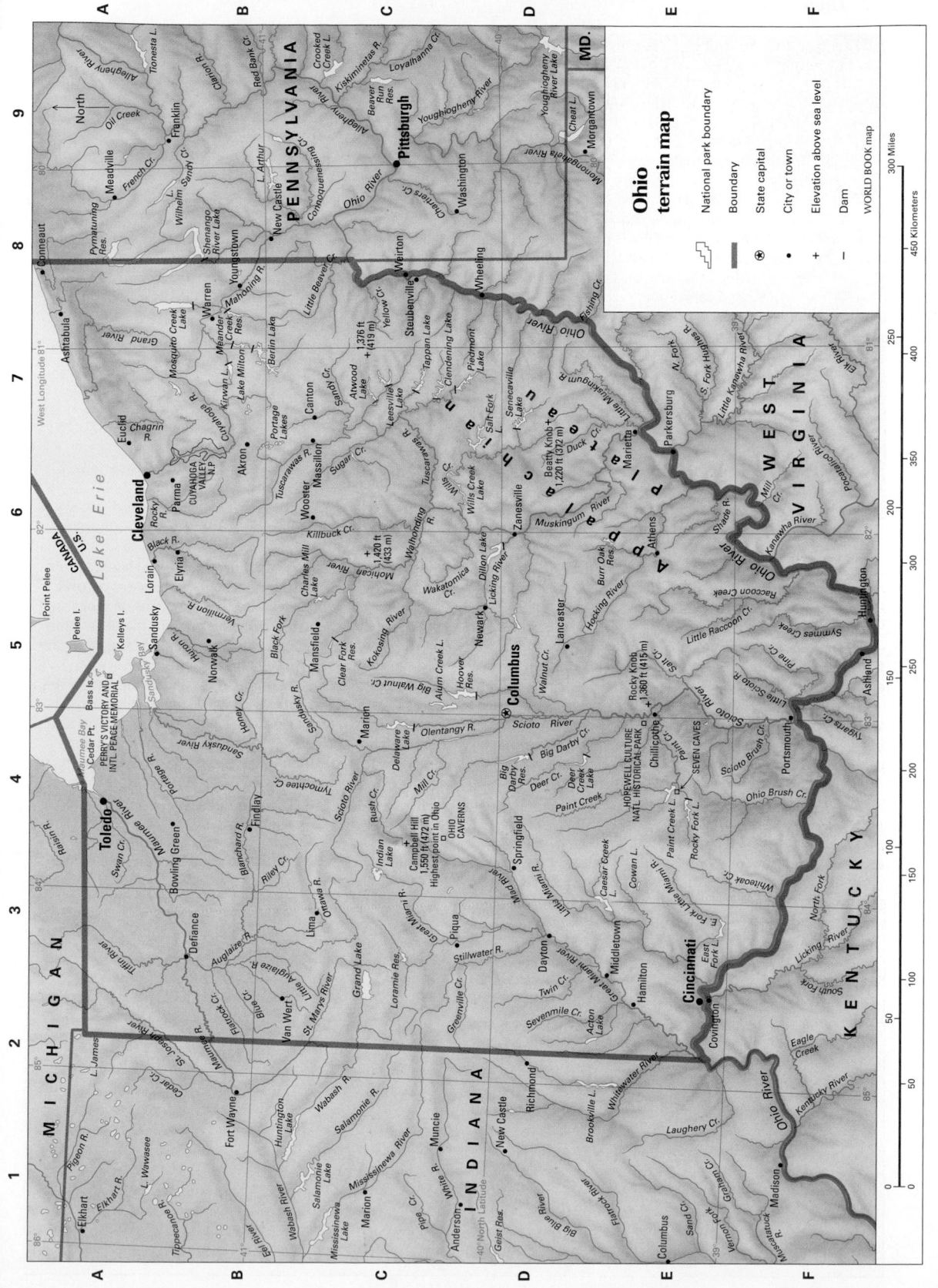

Ohio
terrain map

	National park boundary
▓	Boundary
⊛	State capital
•	City or town
+	Elevation above sea level
—	Dam

WORLD BOOK map

0   50   100   150   200   250   300 Miles
0   50 100 150 200 250 300 350 400 450 Kilometers

The Ohio River forms Ohio's southern border. Gallipolis, settled in the 1790's, overlooks West Virginia across the river.

Irvin L. Oakes, Foto/Find

Little Miami, Great Miami, and Muskingum. The largest rivers that flow into Lake Erie are the Cuyahoga, Grand, Huron, Maumee, Portage, Sandusky, and Vermilion. Some underground streams in Ohio have formed caverns, such as Seven Caves near Bainbridge and Ohio Caverns near West Liberty. Many swift streams in northeastern Ohio have rapids and waterfalls.

Ohio's lake waters include 3,499 square miles (9,062 square kilometers) of Lake Erie. The International Line between the United States and Canada runs through Lake Erie about 20 miles (32 kilometers) north of the

Ohio shore. The state has more than 2,500 lakes larger than 2 acres (0.8 hectare). Over 20 of them are natural lakes with an area of 40 acres (16 hectares) or more. These lakes were formed by the ancient glaciers. Ohio also has more than 180 artificially created lakes that cover at least 40 acres (16 hectares) each.

Several lakes were created in Ohio during the 1830's and 1840's to feed water into two canals. These canals were the Ohio and Erie Canal, between Cleveland and Portsmouth, and the Miami and Erie Canal, between Toledo and Cincinnati. They were Ohio's chief means of

Average January temperatures

Ohio has cold winters. Only the far southern section has temperatures that average above the freezing level.

Average July temperatures

The state has warm, humid summers. The south is the warmest and the areas along Lake Erie have the mildest summers.

Average yearly precipitation

The southern part of Ohio is the wettest, and the northwest is the driest. The northeast receives the heaviest snowfall.

WORLD BOOK maps

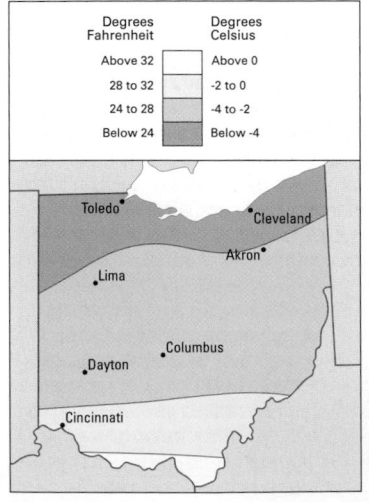

Degrees Fahrenheit	Degrees Celsius
Above 32	Above 0
28 to 32	-2 to 0
24 to 28	-4 to -2
Below 24	Below -4

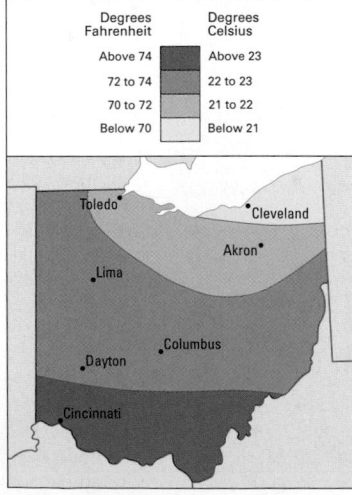

Degrees Fahrenheit	Degrees Celsius
Above 74	Above 23
72 to 74	22 to 23
70 to 72	21 to 22
Below 70	Below 21

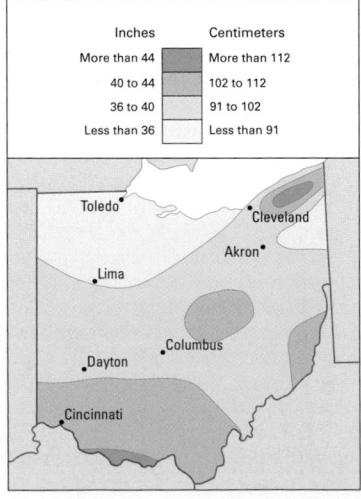

Inches	Centimeters
More than 44	More than 112
40 to 44	102 to 112
36 to 40	91 to 102
Less than 36	Less than 91

Average monthly weather

	Cleveland							Cincinnati					
	Temperatures				**Days of**			**Temperatures**				**Days of**
	°F		**°C**		**rain or**			**°F**		**°C**		**rain or**
	High	**Low**	**High**	**Low**	**snow**			**High**	**Low**	**High**	**Low**	**snow**
Jan.	33	19	1	–7	17		Jan.	38	21	3	–6	12
Feb.	36	21	2	–6	14		Feb.	43	25	6	–4	11
Mar.	46	29	8	–2	15		Mar.	54	34	12	1	13
Apr.	57	38	14	3	14		Apr.	65	43	18	6	13
May	69	48	21	9	13		May	74	53	23	12	12
June	77	58	25	14	11		June	82	62	28	17	11
July	81	62	27	17	10		July	86	66	30	19	10
Aug.	79	61	26	16	10		Aug.	85	64	29	18	9
Sept.	72	54	22	12	10		Sept.	78	57	26	14	8
Oct.	61	44	16	7	11		Oct.	66	45	19	7	8
Nov.	49	35	9	2	14		Nov.	54	36	12	2	11
Dec.	37	25	3	–4	16		Dec.	43	26	6	–3	12

transportation until the coming of the railroads in the 1840's. The largest lake in Ohio is 12,700-acre (5,140-hectare) Grand Lake in the west-central part of the state. It was created during the 1840's by damming two nearby creeks to provide water for the Miami and Erie Canal. Other large artificially created lakes include Berlin, Indian, Mosquito Creek, and Senecaville lakes.

Plant and animal life. Forests cover about a fourth of Ohio. Most of the state's trees are hardwoods. They include beeches, black walnuts, hickories, maples, red and white oaks, sycamores, white ashes, white elms, and yellow-poplars. Among the common shrubs found in Ohio are azalea, dogwood, hawthorn, sumac, and viburnum. The state's wildflowers include anemones, blazing stars, blue sages, Indian pipes, lilies, saxifrages, toothworts, and wild indigos.

Ohio has few large wild animals. Only white-tailed deer are plentiful. Smaller wild animals include minks, muskrats, opossums, rabbits, raccoons, red foxes, skunks, squirrels, and woodchucks. Among Ohio's songbirds are blackbirds, brown thrashers, cardinals, chickadees, and wrens. Bald eagles and various shore birds live along Lake Erie. Game birds include ducks, geese, pheasants, quail, ruffed grouse, and wild turkeys. Fish living in the state's waters include bass, bluegills, catfish, muskellunge, perch, pike, and walleye.

Climate. Ohio has cold winters and warm, humid summers, with an average annual temperature of 52 °F (11 °C). The average January temperature is 28 °F (–2 °C), and the July temperature averages 73 °F (23 °C). Ohio's lowest recorded temperature, –39 °F (–39 °C), occurred at Milligan, near New Lexington, on Feb. 10, 1899. The highest recorded temperature was 113 °F (45 °C) near Gallipolis on July 21, 1934.

Ohio's annual precipitation averages 38 inches (97 centimeters). The wettest area in the state is the southwest, where Wilmington's yearly precipitation averages 44 inches (112 centimeters). The driest part of Ohio lies along Lake Erie between Sandusky and Toledo. That region gets 32 inches (81 centimeters) of precipitation a year. Snowfall in Ohio averages 29 inches (74 centimeters) a year. It increases from west to east and from south to north. Northeastern Ohio receives about 100 inches (254 centimeters) of snow annually and has several ski areas.

Economy

In the heart of the industrial region of the northeastern United States, Ohio has long been known as an important manufacturing center. Ohio's manufacturing industry is characterized by the wide variety of goods produced. The manufacture of machinery, motor vehicles, plastics, processed foods, soap, steel, and tires are all important businesses in Ohio.

Service industries, taken together, account for the largest portion of Ohio's *gross domestic product*—the total value of goods and services produced annually. Finance, insurance, and real estate is the state's leading service industry group. Coal and natural gas are the leading mined products. Corn and soybeans rank as Ohio's most valuable agricultural products.

Natural resources. Fertile soils and valuable minerals are Ohio's most important natural resources.

Soil. Fertile soils deposited by ancient glaciers are found in all parts of Ohio except the southeast. Many layers of these soils are several feet deep. Materials in the various kinds of soils include limestone, sandstone, and shale. The soil is less fertile in the southeastern part of the state, which was not covered by glaciers during the most recent ice age, which ended about 11,500 years ago.

Minerals. Coal and natural gas are Ohio's most important mined products. Coal is primarily mined in eastern and southeastern Ohio. Oil and natural gas are found in eastern Ohio. The state also contains huge reserves of rock salt and saltwater. The state could supply the United States with all the salt it needs for thousands of years. Most of the salt lies in deep rock-salt beds in northeastern Ohio. Other mined products in the state include large deposits of cement, clays, limestone and dolomite, sand and gravel, and sandstone.

Service industries, as a group, account for the largest portion of Ohio's gross domestic product and employ more people than any other type of industry. Most of the service industries are concentrated in the state's metropolitan areas.

Finance, insurance, and real estate is important to Ohio's economy. Most of Ohio's largest banks are based in Cleveland and Columbus. Cleveland is the headquarters of the Fourth Federal Reserve District Bank, one of 12 federal banks established by Congress. Cincinnati is also the home of several large financial companies, including Fifth Third Bancorp. Several large insurance companies, including Nationwide Mutual Insurance Company & Affiliated Companies and Progressive Casualty Insurance Company, have headquarters in Ohio.

Columbus, the state capital, is the center of government activities. Cleveland is a leading center of health care in the United States. Many hotels, restaurants, and retail trade establishments operate in the Cincinnati, Cleveland, and Columbus areas. The ports of Cincinnati and Toledo handle much wholesale trade. Several large shipping companies lie along Lake Erie and the Ohio

Ohio economic statistics

General economy

Gross domestic product (GDP)* (2008) $477,245,000,000
  Rank among U.S. states   8th
Unemployment rate (2010)   10.3% (U.S. avg: 9.6%)

*Gross domestic product is the total value of goods and services produced in a year.
Sources: U.S. Bureau of Economic Analysis and U.S. Bureau of Labor Statistics.

Agriculture

Cash receipts $6,835,590,000
  Rank among U.S. states   16th
Distribution   67% crops, 33% livestock
Farms   74,900
Farm acres (hectares)   13,800,000 (5,580,000)
  Rank among U.S. states   22nd
Farmland   52% of Ohio

Leading products

1. Soybeans
2. Corn
3. Dairy products
4. Hogs
5. Chicken eggs   (ranks 3rd in U.S.)
6. Cattle and calves
7. Greenhouse and nursery products
Other products: apples, broilers, hay, peppers, sweet corn,
  tomatoes, turkeys, wheat.

Electric power

Coal   85.2%
Nuclear   11.4%
Natural gas   1.6%
Other   1.8%

Production and workers by economic activities

Economic activities	Percent of GDP produced	Employed workers	
		Number of people	Percent of total
Finance, insurance, & real estate	23	690,400	10
Community, business, & personal services	21	2,230,400	33
Manufacturing	17	765,900	11
Trade, restaurants, & hotels	15	1,436,000	21
Government	11	847,400	12
Transportation & communication	6	352,100	5
Construction	3	357,500	5
Utilities	2	22,600	*
Agriculture	1	91,600	1
Mining	*	25,100	*
Total†	100	6,819,000	100

*Less than one-half of 1 percent.
†Figures do not add up to 100 percent due to rounding.
Figures are for 2008; employment figures include full- and part-time workers.
Source: *World Book* estimates based on data from U.S. Bureau of Economic Analysis.

Fishing

Commercial catch $5,315,000
  Rank among U.S. states   25th

Leading catches

1. Perch   (ranks 1st in U.S.)
2. Bass
3. Catfish   (ranks 5th in U.S.)
Other catches: buffalofish, carp, drum, whiting.

Figures are for 2008, except for the agricultural figures, which are for 2009.
Sources: U.S. Department of Agriculture, U.S. Energy Information Administration,
    U.S. National Marine Fisheries Service.

continued on page 697

Economy of Ohio

This map shows the economic uses of land in Ohio and where the state's leading farm and mineral products are produced. Major manufacturing centers are shown in red.

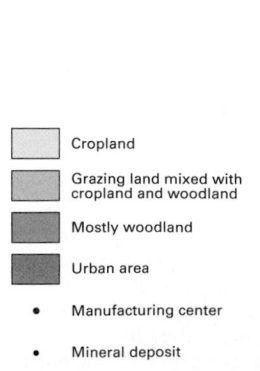

Cropland

Grazing land mixed with cropland and woodland

Mostly woodland

Urban area

●   Manufacturing center

●   Mineral deposit

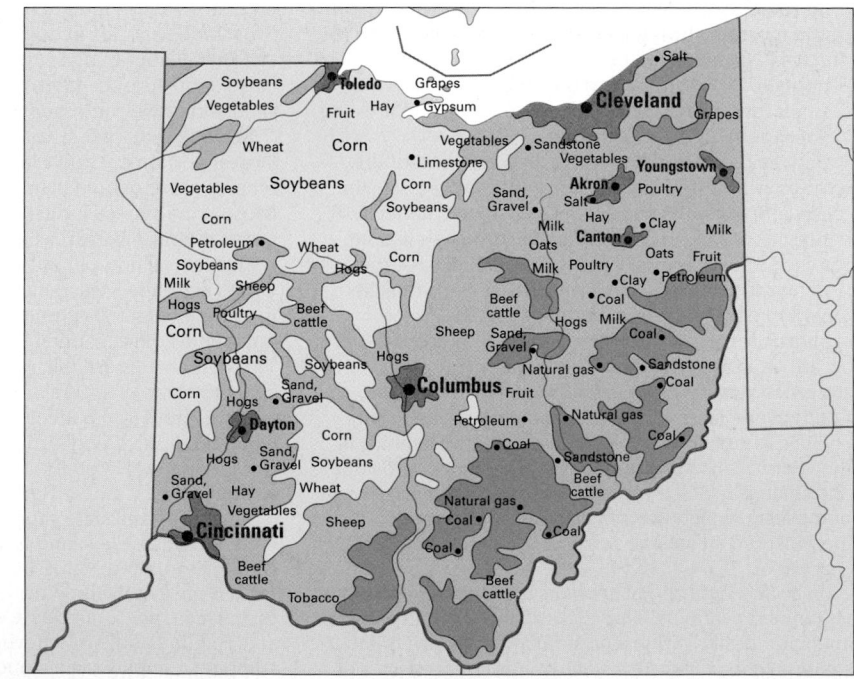

WORLD BOOK map

Mining

Mining	
Nonfuel mineral production	$1,270,000,000
Rank among U.S. states	19th
Coal (tons*)	26,251,000
Rank among U.S. states	11th
Crude oil (barrels†)	5,715,000
Rank among U.S. states	18th
Natural gas (cubic feet‡)	84,858,000,000
Rank among U.S. states	20th

*One ton equals 0.9072 metric ton.
†One barrel equals 42 gallons (159 liters).
‡One cubic foot equals 0.0283 cubic meter.

Leading products

1. Coal
2. Natural gas
3. Petroleum
Other products: clays, lime, limestone, salt, sand and gravel.

Manufacturing

Manufacturing	
Value added by manufacture*	$121,527,105,000
Rank among U.S. states	3rd

Leading products

1. Transportation equipment
2. Fabricated metal products
3. Chemicals
4. Food and beverages
5. Primary metal products
6. Machinery
Other products: computer and electronic products, glass products, plastics and rubber products.

*Value added by manufacture is the increase in value of raw materials after they become finished products.

Figures are for 2008.
Sources: U.S. Census Bureau, U.S. Geological Survey.

River. Wright-Patterson Air Force Base lies near Dayton.

Many large companies are headquartered in Ohio. The Cincinnati area is the home of several major retail companies, including Macy's, Inc. and the Kroger Co. Wendy's, a leading restaurant chain, is headquartered in Dublin. Columbus is the home of Battelle Memorial Institute, one of the world's largest private research organizations. Roadway Express, a major trucking company, is headquartered in Akron.

Manufacturing. Ohio ranks high among the states in total value added by manufacture. Akron, Cincinnati, Cleveland, Columbus, Dayton, and Toledo are among the leading manufacturing cities.

Transportation equipment is Ohio's leading manufactured product by far. The most important types of transportation equipment made in Ohio are motor vehicles and motor vehicle parts. Ohio is a leading producer of both cars and trucks. Motor vehicle parts come mainly from the Cleveland, Dayton, Toledo, and Warren areas. Ohio also manufactures airplanes and aircraft parts.

Food products are also important. The Cincinnati, Cleveland, and Columbus areas are Ohio's main food-processing centers. Mariemont has a plant that makes cookies and crackers. Solon makes frozen dinners. The world's largest yogurt manufacturing plant is in Minster. Napoleon has a large soup factory. A factory at Wellston is the world's leading producer of frozen pizzas.

Ohio is a leading U.S. producer of both fabricated metal and primary metal products. Machine shop products are the leading fabricated metal product. The Cleveland area leads Ohio in fabricated metal production. Ohio ranks second nationally in raw steel production. The largest steelmaking centers are in the Canton, Cleveland, Middletown, and Warren areas. Cincinnati, Cleveland, and other cities have aluminum foundries.

Chemicals, glass products, machinery, and plastics and rubber products are also produced in Ohio. Ohio's leading chemical products include industrial chemicals, paints and varnishes, and soaps and cleansers. The Procter & Gamble Company, a major manufacturer of soaps and cosmetics and many other products, is based in Cincinnati. Toledo and other cities in Ohio make glass. Plentiful deposits of sand and natural gas, which are used in glassmaking, helped establish the glassmaking industry in the state. Ohio's major machinery products

include heating and cooling equipment and machine tools and machine tool parts. Cincinnati, Cleveland, and Dayton are the chief centers of machinery production. Factories in Akron, Dayton, and Findlay make such rubber products as hoses and tires. Goodyear Tire & Rubber Company, an important manufacturer of tires and other rubber products, has its headquarters in Akron. Many cities in Ohio produce plastic products.

Agriculture. Farms cover about half of Ohio's land area. Crops account for about two-thirds of the state's agricultural income.

Field crops provide much of Ohio's farming income. Soybeans are the state's leading farm product. Corn ranks second. Ohio ranks among the leading producers of both soybeans and corn. Farmers grow these two crops in nearly all parts of the state, especially in the Till Plains region. Other field crops raised in the state include hay, tobacco, and wheat.

Ohio has been an important fruit-producing state since pioneer days, when Johnny Appleseed roamed the countryside planting apple seeds (see **Appleseed, Johnny**). In addition to apples, Ohio farmers produce grapes, peaches, and strawberries. Vineyards on the plains along Lake Erie and on the offshore islands grow grapes. Warm lake winds protect the grapes from frosts in late spring and early autumn.

Ohio growers produce large crops of cabbages, cucumbers, green peppers, potatoes, squash, sweet corn, and tomatoes. The rich soils of the Great Lakes Plains and the warmer lowlands along the Ohio River are especially good for growing vegetables. During the cold season, vegetables are grown in heated glass shelters called *hothouses.* The Great Lakes Plains and Till Plains also have tree nurseries and flower greenhouses.

Milk is the leading livestock product in Ohio. The state's leading dairy-farming areas include Columbiana, Holmes, Stark, Tuscarawas, and Wayne counties in the northeast, and Mercer County in the west. The state ranks as a leading producer of cheese and ice cream.

Many farmers in Ohio raise beef cattle. Ohio also ranks as a major hog-producing state. Farmers in the Miami River Valley developed the famous Poland China hog during the 1800's. A monument to the Poland China breed stands near Monroe. Farmers also raise sheep for both mutton and wool, chiefly in the central part of the state. Ohio produces more wool than any other state east of the Mississippi River.

Ohio is one of the leading states in egg production. Most of the egg-producing poultry farms are in the west-central part of the state. Ohio poultry farmers also raise turkeys and *broilers* (young, tender chickens).

Mining. Coal and natural gas are the greatest sources of Ohio's mining income. The state's great fields of *bituminous* (soft) coal lie mainly in the east and southeast. Belmont, Harrison, and Monroe counties produce the most coal. The fields there form part of the great Appalachian coal fields that include parts of Pennsylvania and West Virginia. The eastern part of the state is the leading area for natural gas production.

Ohio is a leader in the production of *dimension sandstone,* which is cut in blocks. Sandstone is taken chiefly from quarries in eastern and northern Ohio. The best-known variety of sandstone, Berea or *grit,* comes from Lorain County. Ohio is also a leading producer of both common and fire clays. These clays are used in such products as bricks and tile, cement, pottery, and stoneware. Ohio is an important producer of limestone and also a leader in the production of lime, made from limestone. Other uses of limestone include the manufacture of cement, chemicals, fertilizers, and steel.

Ohio's oldest mining industry is the production of salt, and the state is one of the nation's leading salt producers. The deepest salt mine in the United States is near Fairport Harbor, northeast of Cleveland. Petroleum is mined in several parts of eastern Ohio. Sand and gravel are produced throughout the state.

Electric power and utilities. Ohio's largest utility companies are American Electric Power of Columbus and FirstEnergy Corp. of Akron. Plants that burn coal provide most of the electric power generated in Ohio. Nuclear plants produce most of the remaining power.

Transportation. Ohio is a transportation link between the eastern and western United States. Cross-country railways and roads began going westward through the state during the 1800's.

The first east-west roads in Ohio were the natural trails that followed the sandy ridges along Lake Erie. Later roads, paved with logs, followed Indian trails. The historic Zane's Trace, built for the federal government by Ebenezer Zane, opened in 1797. It ran between what is now Wheeling, West Virginia, and Maysville, Kentucky, through the present-day Ohio cities of Zanesville, Lancaster, and Chillicothe. Maysville was then the northern end of the road to New Orleans. During the early 1800's, the National (Cumberland) Road became an important link between the East and the West (see **National Road**).

Today, Ohio has an extensive system of roads. Many multilane highways and expressways cross the state. The Ohio Turnpike runs across northern Ohio between the Pennsylvania and Indiana borders. Freight railroads operate on thousands of miles of rail line in the state.

Cleveland Hopkins International Airport is Ohio's busiest airport. Other major airports serve the Akron-Canton, Columbus, Dayton, and Toledo areas. The largest airport serving the Cincinnati area lies in nearby Boone County, Kentucky.

The Great Lakes and the St. Lawrence Seaway connect Ohio with the Atlantic Ocean. Ice closes this passage in January and February. The Great Lakes also link Ohio with the north-central states and Canada. Another major waterway, the Ohio River, connects the state with the Mississippi River and the Gulf of Mexico. The entire length of this waterway is navigable all year.

Communication. The first newspaper published north and west of the Ohio River, the *Centinel of the North-Western Territory,* was founded in Cincinnati in 1793. The nation's first antislavery newspaper, the *Philanthropist,* began publication in Mount Pleasant in 1817. Today, Ohio's largest daily newspapers include the *Akron Beacon Journal, The Blade* of Toledo, *The Cincinnati Enquirer, The Columbus Dispatch,* the *Dayton Daily News, The Plain Dealer* of Cleveland, and *The Repository* of Canton.

Government

Constitution of Ohio, the second in the state's history, was adopted in 1851. Ohioans adopted their first constitution in 1802. An amendment may be proposed by (1) the state legislature, (2) a petition signed by 10 percent of the voters, or (3) a constitutional convention. A convention may be called if it is approved by two-thirds of each house of the legislature and by a majority of the voters. Ohioans also vote every 20 years as to whether they wish to call a constitutional convention. Amendments to the Constitution must be approved by a majority of the people voting on them in an election.

Executive. The governor and lieutenant governor of Ohio are elected to four-year terms. They can serve an unlimited number of terms but not more than two terms in succession.

The governor has the power to appoint the heads of many of the state's administrative departments and agencies and the trustees of state-supported universities and institutions. Some appointments of the governor must be approved by the state Senate.

Voters also elect the secretary of state, attorney general, treasurer, and auditor in Ohio. These officials may not serve more than two terms in succession.

Legislature, called the General Assembly, consists of a 33-member Senate and a 99-member House of Representatives. Voters in each of Ohio's 33 senatorial districts elect one senator. Senators serve four-year terms and may not serve more than two terms in succession. Voters in the state's 99 representative districts elect one representative. Representatives serve two-year terms and may not serve more than four terms in succession. Regular legislative sessions begin on the first Monday of January in odd-numbered years and have no time limit.

A 1903 amendment to the state Constitution required that each county have at least one representative, regardless of its population. In 1964, the Supreme Court of the United States ruled this amendment unconstitutional. In 1965, Ohio's governor, the state auditor, and the secretary of state drew up a *reapportionment* (redivision) plan for the Senate and House of Representatives. They set up single-member legislative districts that were as equal in population as possible. A special three-judge

The governors of Ohio

	Party	Term		Party	Term
Edward Tiffin	* Dem.-Rep.	1803-1807	George Hoadly	Democratic	1884-1886
Thomas Kirker	Dem.-Rep.	1807-1808	Joseph B. Foraker	Republican	1886-1890
Samuel Huntington	Dem.-Rep.	1808-1810	James E. Campbell	Democratic	1890-1892
Return J. Meigs, Jr.	Dem.-Rep.	1810-1814	William McKinley	Republican	1892-1896
Othneil Looker	Dem.-Rep.	1814	Asa S. Bushnell	Republican	1896-1900
Thomas Worthington	Dem.-Rep.	1814-1818	George K. Nash	Republican	1900-1904
Ethan Allen Brown	Dem.-Rep.	1818-1822	Myron T. Herrick	Republican	1904-1906
Allen Trimble	Federalist	1822	John M. Pattison	Democratic	1906
Jeremiah Morrow	Dem.-Rep.	1822-1826	Andrew L. Harris	Republican	1906-1909
Allen Trimble	Federalist	1826-1830	Judson Harmon	Democratic	1909-1913
Duncan McArthur	Federalist	1830-1832	James M. Cox	Democratic	1913-1915
Robert Lucas	Democratic	1832-1836	Frank B. Willis	Republican	1915-1917
Joseph Vance	Whig	1836-1838	James M. Cox	Democratic	1917-1921
Wilson Shannon	Democratic	1838-1840	Harry L. Davis	Republican	1921-1923
Thomas Corwin	Whig	1840-1842	A. Victor Donahey	Democratic	1923-1929
Wilson Shannon	Democratic	1842-1844	Myers Y. Cooper	Republican	1929-1931
Thomas W. Bartley	Democratic	1844	George White	Democratic	1931-1935
Mordecai Bartley	Whig	1844-1846	Martin L. Davey	Democratic	1935-1939
William Bebb	Whig	1846-1849	John W. Bricker	Republican	1939-1945
Seabury Ford	Whig	1849-1850	Frank J. Lausche	Democratic	1945-1947
Reuben Wood	Democratic	1850-1853	Thomas J. Herbert	Republican	1947-1949
William Medill	Democratic	1853-1856	Frank J. Lausche	Democratic	1949-1957
Salmon P. Chase	Republican	1856-1860	John W. Brown	Republican	1957
William Dennison	Republican	1860-1862	C. William O'Neill	Republican	1957-1959
David Todd	Republican	1862-1864	Michael V. DiSalle	Democratic	1959-1963
John Brough	Republican	1864-1865	James A. Rhodes	Republican	1963-1971
Charles Anderson	Republican	1865-1866	John J. Gilligan	Democratic	1971-1975
Jacob Dolson Cox	Republican	1866-1868	James A. Rhodes	Republican	1975-1983
Rutherford B. Hayes	Republican	1868-1872	Richard F. Celeste	Democratic	1983-1991
Edward F. Noyes	Republican	1872-1874	George V. Voinovich	Republican	1991-1998
William Allen	Democratic	1874-1876	Meridian Hollister	Republican	1998-1999
Rutherford B. Hayes	Republican	1876-1877	Bob Taft	Republican	1999-2007
Thomas L. Young	Republican	1877-1878	Ted Strickland	Democratic	2007-2011
Richard M. Bishop	Democratic	1878-1880	John Kasich	Republican	2011-
Charles Foster	Republican	1880-1884			

*Democratic-Republican

federal district court approved the plan for use until a permanent plan could be drawn. The Supreme Court of the United States approved the federal district court's decision. In 1967, the Constitution was amended to provide for a permanent reapportionment plan.

Courts. The highest appeals court in Ohio is the Supreme Court. It has a chief justice and six other justices—all elected to six-year terms. Ohio also has 12 courts of appeals. The court of Cuyahoga County has 12 judges. The other districts in Ohio have from 3 to 8 judges each. The highest trial courts in Ohio are the courts of common pleas. Each of the state's 88 counties has one such court. These courts have varying numbers of judges, all of whom are elected to six-year terms. Other courts in Ohio include county, juvenile, municipal, mayor, and probate courts.

Local government. Ohio has 88 counties. All of the counties except Summit are governed by an elected three-member board of commissioners. Summit County is governed by an elected county executive and a seven-member council. By law, counties may have *home rule*—that is, a county may adopt its own charter. But only Summit County has done so.

Most Ohio cities have more than 5,000 people. Villages generally have populations of less than 5,000. Officially, Ohio has no towns. Ohio law allows cities and villages to adopt home rule, and about a fourth of them have done so. The home-rule cities and villages have mayor-council, council-manager, or commission gov-

ernments. In 1913, Dayton became the nation's first large city to adopt council-manager government. About three-fourths of Ohio's cities and villages have a mayor-council government.

Revenue. Taxes account for about half of the state government's *general revenue* (income). Most of the rest comes from federal grants and other U.S. government programs. A general sales tax and a personal income tax are the leading sources of tax revenue. Other state taxes include those on corporate income, motor fuels, motor vehicle licenses, and tobacco products. Other revenue comes from charges for government services and from a state lottery.

Politics. Both the Democratic and Republican parties have much strength in Ohio. The Democratic Party is strongest in Cleveland and other metropolitan areas in northeastern Ohio. The Republican Party is dominant in most rural areas and is also strong in the Cincinnati and Columbus metropolitan areas. Since the end of World War II in 1945, Democratic and Republican candidates have won elections for governor about an equal number of times.

Ohio is often called a *barometer state* in national politics. That is, the political views of Ohioans frequently indicate those of most Americans. For example, the winning presidential candidates have won Ohio's electoral votes in a great majority of presidential elections since 1804. For Ohio's electoral votes and its voting record in presidential elections, see **Electoral College** (table).

History

Indian days. Thousands of years ago, prehistoric Indians lived in what is now Ohio. These Indians were the ancestors of peoples called Mound Builders, some of whom had high forms of civilization. The Mound Builders left more than 6,000 burial mounds, forts, and other earthworks throughout the Ohio region. The Indians included the Adena and Hopewell peoples, who lived there from about 600 B.C. to about A.D. 500. See **Mound Builders**.

When the early white settlers arrived, several Indian tribes lived in the Ohio region. These tribes included the Delaware, Miami, Shawnee, and Wyandot, or Huron.

Exploration and settlement. The French explorer René-Robert Cavelier, Sieur de La Salle, was probably the first European to reach present-day Ohio. He is believed to have visited the region about 1670. The French based their claim to the entire Northwest on La Salle's explorations. But the British claimed all the territory extending inland from their Atlantic colonies. In 1750, the Ohio Company of Virginia sent Christopher Gist to explore the upper Ohio River Valley. This company, organized in 1747, was made up of English people and Virginians who planned to colonize the Ohio region. See **La Salle, René-Robert Cavelier, Sieur de; Ohio Company** (The first Ohio Company).

The dispute between Britain and France over territory in North America, including the Ohio region, led to the French and Indian War (1754-1763). In the peace treaty of 1763, France gave Britain most of its lands east of the Mississippi River. Pontiac, an Indian chief believed to have been born in Ohio, started an Indian rebellion against the British in 1763 after the peace treaty was signed. See **French and Indian wars; Pontiac**.

Fighting during the American Revolution (1775-1783) forced a Moravian mission settlement named Schoenbrunn, near present-day New Philadelphia, to close down. The settlement, founded in 1772 by David Zeisberger, was abandoned in 1776. In 1780, George Rogers Clark defeated Shawnee Indian allies of the British in the Battle of Piqua, near present-day Springfield. Clark's campaigns in the Northwest helped the United States claim the region in the 1783 treaty that ended the American Revolution.

The region, including Ohio, became the Northwest Territory in 1787. The Northwest Ordinance of 1787 provided for the eventual statehood of Ohio and other divisions of the territory. That year, the Ohio Company of Associates bought land northwest of the Ohio River in the Muskingum River Valley. Members of this company came from New England. On April 7, 1788, the company founded Marietta, the first permanent white settlement in Ohio. Rufus Putnam, a general who fought in the American Revolution, was superintendent of the colony. Marietta became the first capital of the Northwest Territory in July 1788. Soon other communities developed along the Ohio River. Many settlers were veterans of the American Revolution who received land in payment for their military service. See **Northwest Territory; Ohio Company** (The second Ohio Company); **Putnam, Rufus**.

For several years, Indians resisted the expansion of white settlements. Several raids were led by Little Turtle, a Miami chief. In 1794, General Anthony Wayne defeated the Indians near present-day Toledo in the Battle of Fallen Timbers. The next year, in the Treaty of Greenville, the Indians ceded the United States about two-thirds of what is now Ohio. The Indians accepted the treaty largely through the influence of Tarhe, or Crane, a Wyandot chief. With peace restored, more and more settlers poured into the region. Many settlements were founded in the valleys of rivers flowing into the Ohio. Pioneers also settled in northeastern Ohio in the area called the Western Reserve (see **Western Reserve**).

In 1800, Congress passed the Division Act. This legislation created the Indiana Territory out of the western part of the Northwest Territory. Chillicothe became the capital of the eastern part, which continued to be called the Northwest Territory.

Statehood. Preparation for Ohio statehood began in November 1802, when a convention in Chillicothe drew up the state's first constitution. Ohio became the 17th state on March 1, 1803, when the first state legislature met. Edward Tiffin, a Democratic-Republican, was the

Oil painting on canvas (1873) by William Henry Powell; Senate Wing of the Capitol (National Graphic Center)

Commodore Oliver H. Perry defeated the British in the Battle of Lake Erie during the War of 1812. While the battle raged, he rowed from a disabled ship, the *Lawrence,* to take command on the undamaged *Niagara.*

Historic Ohio

The Underground Railroad in Ohio helped slaves reach Canada. Many slaves escaped from the South across the Ohio River. Ohio abolitionists ran the informal network of escape routes and hiding places.

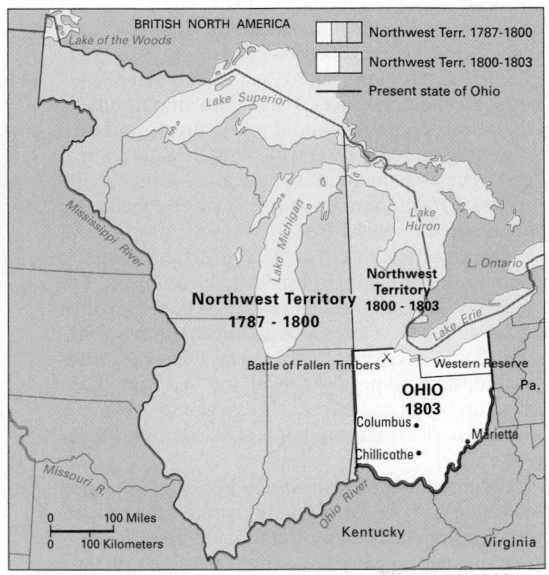

WORLD BOOK map

Ohio was originally part of the Northwest Territory. The territory was formed in 1787 and reduced in size in 1800. Ohio became a state in 1803.

The Cincinnati Red Stockings (now the Reds) became the first professional baseball team in 1869. The team was one of the original members of the National League, formed in 1876.

Important dates in Ohio

WORLD BOOK illustrations by Richard Bonson, The Art Agency

c. 1670	The French explorer René-Robert Cavelier, Sieur de La Salle, was probably the first European to reach the Ohio region.
1747	The Ohio Company of Virginia was organized to colonize the Ohio River Valley.
1763	France surrendered its claim to the Ohio region to Britain (now the United Kingdom).
1787	The Northwest Territory was established.
1788	The first permanent white settlement in Ohio was established in Marietta.
1795	Indian wars in the Ohio region ended with the Treaty of Greenville.
1800	The Division Act divided the Northwest Territory into two parts, and Chillicothe became the capital of the new Northwest Territory.
1803	Ohio became the 17th state on March 1.
1813	Commodore Oliver H. Perry's fleet defeated the British in the Battle of Lake Erie.
1832	The Ohio and Erie Canal was completed.
1833	Oberlin College became the first college in the United States to enroll both men and women.
1836	The Ohio-Michigan boundary dispute was settled.

1845	The Miami and Erie Canal was completed.
1870	Benjamin F. Goodrich began the manufacture of rubber goods in Akron.
1901	The Wright Brothers built North America's first wind tunnel in Dayton. They used it to conduct experiments that led to the first successful airplane flight.
1914	Ohio passed the Conservancy Act after floods in 1913.
1922	The Miami River Valley flood-control project was finished.
1938	The flood-control project in the Muskingum River Valley was completed.
1955	The Ohio Turnpike opened to traffic.
1959	Terms of the governor and other high state officials were increased from two years to four.
1967	Ohio voters approved a plan for reapportionment of the state legislature.
1971	Ohio adopted an income tax.
1993	Ohio voters approved the sale of $200 million worth of bonds to finance improvements and expansion in the state's parks and other recreation areas.
2003	Ohio celebrated its bicentennial.

first governor. Ohio's population was about 70,000. Chillicothe was the capital from 1803 to 1810, when Zanesville became the capital. Chillicothe again became the capital in 1812, and Columbus in 1816.

The Louisiana Purchase in 1803 gave Ohio settlers a river outlet for their products. They could ship goods down the Mississippi River and through the port of New Orleans. A thriving river trade with New Orleans soon developed. The first steamboat to travel the Ohio River was the *New Orleans,* a wood-burning side-wheeler. It first went down the river in 1811.

Ohio took an active part in the War of 1812 (1812-1815). Commodore Oliver H. Perry sailed from Put-in-Bay at South Bass Island off the Ohio shore to battle a British fleet on Sept. 10, 1813. Perry won an important naval victory in this Battle of Lake Erie (see **Perry, Oliver H.**). After the war, thousands of people moved to Ohio from the eastern states. Many came from New England, New York, and Pennsylvania. Immigrants arrived from Britain and Germany.

In 1818, the steamboat *Walk-in-the-Water* became the first steamboat on Lake Erie. It demonstrated the practical use of the Great Lakes as a waterway to the West. The Erie Canal across New York from Lake Erie opened in 1825. The Ohio and Erie Canal, joining Cleveland and Portsmouth, was completed in 1832. The Miami and Erie Canal, connecting Toledo and Cincinnati, was completed in 1845. These canals served as busy trade routes for more than 25 years. But the coming of the railroads reduced canal traffic. Ohio canals and railroads brought increased prosperity, and many mills and factories were built between 1830 and 1860.

An old border dispute between Ohio and the Territory of Michigan flared up in 1835 and led to the "Toledo War." Before any actual fighting broke out, President Andrew Jackson sent agents to Toledo to persuade the governors of Ohio and Michigan to accept a truce. In 1836, Congress awarded the disputed area, about 520 square miles (1,350 square kilometers) along Lake Erie, to Ohio. In 1841, William Henry Harrison of North Bend became the ninth President.

The Civil War. During the years before the Civil War (1861-1865), many Ohioans had strong feelings on the question of slavery. Many *abolitionists* (black and white people opposed to slavery) lived throughout Ohio. They helped slaves who had escaped across the Ohio River on their flight to Canada (see **Underground Railroad**). Most of Ohio's Southern sympathizers lived in southern and north-central parts of the state. In 1862, Clement L. Vallandigham of Dayton became leader of the Peace Democrats Party, which opposed President Abraham Lincoln's administration. Vallandigham and other Southern sympathizers were known as Copperheads.

Famous Civil War commanders born in Ohio included Ulysses S. Grant and William T. Sherman. Ohio supplied about 345,000 men to the Union Army. This was more than the total quotas requested by 10 presidential calls for soldiers from the state. In 1863, Confederate cavalrymen known as Morgan's Raiders crossed into Ohio and brought Civil War fighting to its northernmost point. Led by General John Hunt Morgan, they were captured in Columbiana County. Morgan later escaped and returned to the South. See **Morgan, John Hunt**.

Ohio's industrial centers grew rapidly after the Civil

Ohio Historical Society

Floodwaters caused enormous destruction in the Miami River Valley during the spring of 1913. Floods killed about 350 people.

War. Many workers from other countries settled in the state. The shipping of coal, iron ore, and other bulk goods on Lake Erie increased. Farming continued to be a leading industry, but Ohio also developed into a top manufacturing state. In 1869, the Cincinnati Red Stockings (now Reds) became the first all-professional baseball team. Benjamin F. Goodrich began manufacturing rubber products in Akron in 1870.

Five Ohio-born Presidents, all Republicans, were elected during the 1800's. They were Ulysses S. Grant, Rutherford B. Hayes, James A. Garfield, Benjamin Harrison, and William McKinley. President William Henry Harrison of Ohio was born in Virginia.

The early 1900's. Ohio's government was torn by scandal and corruption during the late 1800's. Marcus A. "Mark" Hanna, political boss of Cleveland, and George B. Cox, boss of Cincinnati, both Republicans, dominated state politics. Around 1900, Mayors Samuel Jones of Toledo and Tom Johnson of Cleveland led influential movements to reform city governments. William Howard Taft of Cincinnati became the 27th President of the United States in 1909.

Ohio suffered the worst floods in its history during the spring of 1913. About 350 people lost their lives after rivers overflowed their banks, and damage totaled about $100 million. Most of the destruction occurred in the Miami River Valley, especially at Dayton. In 1914, the state legislature passed the Conservancy Act, the first legislation of its kind in the United States. The chief purpose of the act was to permit the establishment of flood-control districts based on entire river systems. Many flood-control dams and reservoirs were built under the Conservancy Act, including those completed by 1922 in the Miami River Valley. The federal government also built about 20 flood-control dams in Ohio.

After the United States entered World War I in 1917, the state produced vast supplies of war materials. Newton D. Baker of Cleveland served as secretary of war in President Woodrow Wilson's wartime Cabinet.

Between world wars. In 1921, Warren G. Harding of Marion became the 29th president. His Democratic opponent was Governor James M. Cox of Dayton. The 1920's were prosperous years in Ohio, because of continued industrial development. Cincinnati, Cleveland, Dayton, Toledo, and other industrial cities expanded rapidly. Many nearby farms disappeared as the cities grew. The Great Depression that began in 1929 hit these cities hardest in Ohio. Thousands of workers lost their jobs as factories closed. Many farmers lost their land when farm prices dropped sharply.

Government funds and federal agencies such as the Works Progress Administration (WPA), later called Work Projects Administration, helped Ohio recover from the Depression during the 1930's. In 1934, work began on the Muskingum River Valley flood-control project. This project came to national attention in 1937, when most of the dams withstood heavy floodwaters of the Ohio River. It was completed in 1938. Robert A. Taft, who became one of the most powerful U.S. senators, began his first term as Republican senator from Ohio in 1939.

The mid-1900's. During World War II (1939-1945), Ohio produced aircraft, ships, and weapons. It also contributed steel, tires, and materials to the war effort. The armed services established a number of training centers in the state. During the 1950's, the Atomic Energy Commission (AEC) built several installations in Ohio. They included the Portsmouth Area Project in Pike County, which produces uranium-235 for use in nuclear reactors. In 1955, the 241-mile (388-kilometer) Ohio Turnpike across northern Ohio opened. Since 1958, the National Aeronautics and Space Administration (NASA) has operated the John H. Glenn Research Center at Lewis Field in Cleveland. Scientists there conduct research on space propulsion systems.

Ohio's industrial growth moved forward rapidly during the 1960's. In 1963, the state launched a giant economic development program to attract more industry. Industrial expansion included new aluminum plants and

Scientists check water quality from a research vessel in Lake Erie by measuring the quantity and types of microscopic animals called *zooplankton* in the water.

chemical factories in cities in a region along the Ohio River that offered cheap, coal-generated power.

Ohio also entered international trade. Eight Ohio cities on Lake Erie—Ashtabula, Cleveland, Conneaut, Fairport, Huron, Lorain, Sandusky, and Toledo—became ports of the St. Lawrence Seaway, which opened in 1959. By 1970, Ohio ranked fourth among the states in the value of goods exported annually.

Several significant changes occurred in state government. In 1959, Ohio voters increased the terms of the governor and other elected executive officials from two to four years. The Supreme Court of the United States ruled in 1964 that Ohio must *reapportion* (redivide) its House of Representatives to provide more equal representation based on population. The state legislature drew up a reapportionment plan for both the House and the Senate. The voters approved the plan in 1967.

Recent developments. The state legislature enacted an income tax in 1971 to help pay for the rising costs of state government. In 1972, voters approved an amendment to the state constitution permitting a state lottery to help fund public schools.

Ohio continues to struggle with the issue of funding public education. Between 1966 and the mid-1970's, several school districts closed schools because of a lack of funds. State income taxes were increased in the early 1980's to help provide funding for public schools and the state-supported university system, and to support other state public services. In the 1997 case *DeRolph v. State of Ohio,* the Ohio Supreme Court ruled that the school funding system was unconstitutional. The decision created controversy that continued into the 2000's.

Ohio has also had to deal with problems caused by decreasing energy resources. Fuel shortages during the mid-1970's caused an increase in fuel prices and a decrease in production. During a severe winter in 1977, a shortage of natural gas forced many of the state's factories, offices, and schools to close temporarily.

In the mid-1980's, however, abundant natural gas and cheaper petroleum gave a boost to many of Ohio's important manufacturing industries, including the production of automobiles and chemicals. In 1985, Ohio voters approved a $100 million bond issue to finance research on ways to develop technologies to reduce the high-sulfur content of the state's coal. The goal was to make the coal meet environmental standards, thus increasing its use. An electric power plant using low-sulfur coal that resulted from the research opened in 1993.

Another serious problem for Ohio has been the pollution of Lake Erie and the state's rivers. Federal and state antipollution laws and controls have now cleaned up state rivers and Lake Erie for both commercial fishing and recreation. In 1993, Ohio voters approved a $200 million bond issue to finance improvements and expansion in the state's parks and other recreation areas.

Nevertheless, Ohio continues to have serious problems. Ohio manufacturers—especially the steel industry—face increasing foreign competition. Some of Ohio's industries have moved to states with warmer climates and cheaper labor. Many Ohio farmers have also had difficulties. Periodic declines in prices for crops and livestock result in lower incomes for farmers. Many smaller farmers have been forced out of business by such slumps.   Andrew Cayton and Thomas W. Schmidlin

Study aids

Related articles in *World Book* include:

Biographies

Anderson, Sherwood	Logan
Appleseed, Johnny	McGuffey, William H.
Armstrong, Neil A.	McKinley, William
Boehner, John Andrew	Nicklaus, Jack
Brant, Joseph	Pendleton, George H.
Bricker, John W.	Perry, Oliver H.
Bromfield, Louis	Pontiac
Chase, Salmon P.	Putnam, Rufus
Cox, James M.	Rockefeller, John D.
Dunbar, Paul Laurence	Shawnee Prophet
Edison, Thomas A.	Sherman, John
Firestone, Harvey S.	Sherman, William T.
Garfield, James A.	Steinem, Gloria
Glenn, John H., Jr.	Stokes, Carl B.
Goodrich, Benjamin F.	Taft, Robert A.
Grant, Ulysses S.	Taft, William H.
Green, William	Tecumseh
Hanna, Mark	Thurman, Allen G.
Harding, Warren G.	Vallandigham, Clement L.
Harrison, Benjamin	Wayne, Anthony
Harrison, William Henry	Woodhull, Victoria C.
Hayes, Rutherford B.	Wright brothers
Kettering, Charles F.	

Cities

Akron	Cincinnati	Columbus	Toledo
Canton	Cleveland	Dayton	Youngstown

History

French and Indian wars	Pioneer life in America
Indian Wars	Underground Railroad
Mound builders	War of 1812
Northwest Ordinance	Western Reserve
Northwest Territory	Westward movement in
Ohio Company	America

Other related articles

Battelle Memorial Institute	Lake Erie
Cuyahoga Valley	National Road
National Park	Ohio River
Erie Canal	Rock and Roll Hall of Fame
Flood	and Museum

Outline

I. People
   A. Population
   B. Schools
   C. Libraries
   D. Museums
II. Visitor's guide
III. Land and climate
   A. Land regions
   B. Shoreline
   C. Rivers and lakes
   D. Plant and animal life
   E. Climate
IV. Economy
   A. Natural resources
   B. Service industries
   C. Manufacturing
   D. Agriculture
   E. Mining
   F. Electric power and utilities
   G. Transportation
   H. Communication
V. Government
   A. Constitution
   B. Executive
   C. Legislature
   D. Courts
   E. Local government
   F. Revenue
   G. Politics
VI. History

Additional resources

Level I

Barker, Charles F. *Under Ohio: The Story of Ohio's Rocks and Fossils.* Ohio Univ. Pr., 2007.
Heinrichs, Ann. *Ohio.* Child's World, 2006.
Sherrow, Victoria. *Ohio.* 2nd ed. Benchmark Bks., 2008.
Stille, Darlene R. *Ohio.* Children's Pr., 2009.

Level II

Cayton, Andrew R. L. *Ohio: The History of a People.* Ohio State Univ. Pr., 2002.
Cayton, Andrew R. L., and Hobbs, S. D., eds. *The Center of a Great Empire: The Ohio Country in the Early American Republic.* Ohio Univ. Pr., 2005.
Dee, Christine, ed. *Ohio's War: The Civil War in Documents.* Ohio Univ. Pr., 2006.
Jones, Robert H. *Guarding the Overland Trails: The Eleventh Ohio Cavalry in the Civil War.* Arthur H. Clark, 2005.
Mersman, Joseph J. *The Whiskey Merchant's Diary: An Urban Life in the Emerging Midwest.* Ed. by Linda A. Fisher. Ohio Univ. Pr., 2007.
Schieber, Randall L., and Smith, Robin. *Ohio Then & Now: Contemporary Rephotography.* Westcliffe, 2006.
Schiff, Thomas R. *Panoramic Ohio: Photographs.* Cincinnati Art Museum, 2002.
Steinglass, Steven H., and Scarselli, G. J. *The Ohio State Constitution: A Reference Guide.* Praeger, 2004.
Zaidan, Abe, and Green, J. C. *Portraits of Power: Ohio and National Politics, 1964-2004.* Univ. of Akron Pr., 2007.

Ohio Company. There were two Ohio Companies in American history. The purpose of each was to colonize the Ohio River Valley.

The first Ohio Company was formed in 1747. It is sometimes called the Ohio Company of Virginia. Its members included London merchants and wealthy Virginians. Among them were George Washington's brothers, Lawrence and Augustine Washington. In 1749, King George II granted the company 200,000 acres (81,000 hectares) west of the Allegheny Mountains in Maryland, Pennsylvania, and Virginia, and on both sides of the Ohio River. The company surveyed the Ohio River Valley. It traded with Indians, built storehouses and roads, and established the first fort at the forks of the Ohio. In 1753, a settlement called Gist's Plantation was founded near Mount Braddock, Pennsylvania. The French destroyed the company's strongholds in 1754. The French and Indian War (1754-1763) blocked efforts to settle in the West. The company went out of business in 1792.

The second Ohio Company was more important. Its official name was the Ohio Company of Associates. It was organized at the Bunch of Grapes Tavern in Boston on March 1, 1786. Eleven delegates, elected by people interested in the venture, set up the company. They planned to raise up to $1 million in Continental money by selling shares. Each share cost $1,000 in Continental money, which was almost worthless, plus $10 in gold or silver. The company appointed Manasseh Cutler, Samuel Parsons, and Rufus Putnam to petition the Congress of the Confederation to sell it a tract beyond the Ohio River. Congress approved and later passed the Northwest Ordinance of 1787 (see **Northwest Ordinance**).

At first the Ohio Company contracted to buy 1 ½ million acres (610,000 hectares) at 66 ⅔ cents an acre. But because of financial difficulties, these terms were never fully carried out. Congress finally granted title to 750,000 acres (304,000 hectares) in what is now southeastern Ohio. The agreement provided that 214,285 acres (86,718 hectares) could be bought with army warrants and that 100,000 acres (40,000 hectares) were to be offered free to settlers. One section of each township was reserved for schools, one for religion, and three sections for future disposal by Congress. This last term was designed to keep speculators from monopolizing the territory. Two townships of 46,080 acres (18,648 hectares) were set aside "for the support of an institution of higher learning." This institution was founded at Athens, Ohio, in 1804, and became Ohio University.

The Ohio Company appointed Rufus Putnam as its superintendent. He led an advance party of 47 surveyors, carpenters, boatbuilders, blacksmiths, and laborers to lay out a town where the Muskingum and Ohio rivers joined. The group arrived at the mouth of the Muskingum on April 7, 1788. It founded there the first settlement under the Northwest Ordinance and named it Marietta in honor of Queen Marie Antoinette of France. The settlers also built a fort called Campus Martius to protect their village. On July 15, Governor Arthur St. Clair established the first capital of the Northwest Territory at Marietta. By April 1789, three new settlements had been established. The Ohio Company completed its land operations by 1797. It divided its assets among the shareholders, but did not go out of business until about 1832.

Richard J. Hopkins

See also **Northwest Territory; Putnam, Rufus.**

Ohio River is the second most heavily used commercial river in the United States. Only the Mississippi River has more cargo shipped on it. The Ohio flows 981 miles (1,579 kilometers) through some of the nation's busiest industrial regions and richest farmlands. About 230 million tons (209 million metric tons) of freight are transported annually on the Ohio. The river serves some of the country's principal coal fields and several major steel-producing districts. It drains an area of about 204,000 square miles (528,400 square kilometers).

The Ohio River begins in Pittsburgh, Pennsylvania, where the Allegheny and Monongahela rivers meet. The Ohio flows mainly southwestward and forms the southern borders of Ohio, Indiana, and Illinois, and the northern boundaries of West Virginia and Kentucky. It empties into the Mississippi River at Cairo, Illinois. Major branches of the Ohio include the Muskingum, Kanawha, Big Sandy, Scioto, Licking, Great Miami, Kentucky, Green, Wabash, Cumberland, and Tennessee rivers.

Navigation. Almost all the cargo transported on the Ohio River moves on large barges. These barges are pushed by tugboats. Dams and canals provide a minimum water depth of 9 feet (2.7 meters). Locks in the canals raise and lower the water level in the river, enabling ships to travel the entire length of the Ohio River.

Coal makes up more than half the total freight shipped on the Ohio. Other major cargoes include agricultural products, chemicals, crushed rock, gravel, petroleum products, sand, and steel products. Among the chief ports along the Ohio are Pittsburgh and Aliquippa, Pennsylvania; Huntington, West Virginia; Cincinnati, Ohio; Louisville, Kentucky; and Mount Vernon, Indiana.

Animal and plant life. Forests of beech, hickory, oak, poplar, and sycamore trees cover the Ohio River Valley. Animals in these forests include chipmunks, muskrats, raccoons, red foxes, squirrels, white-tailed deer, and woodchucks. Among the fishes in the Ohio are bullheads, bass, catfish, and trout.

Community and industrial wastes and farming chemicals pollute the Ohio. Pollution threatens fish and other wildlife. The Ohio River Valley Water Sanitation Commission regulates the release of river pollutants.

History. In 1669, the French explorer René-Robert Cavelier, Sieur de La Salle, became the first European to see the Ohio River. At that time, Shawnee and other In-

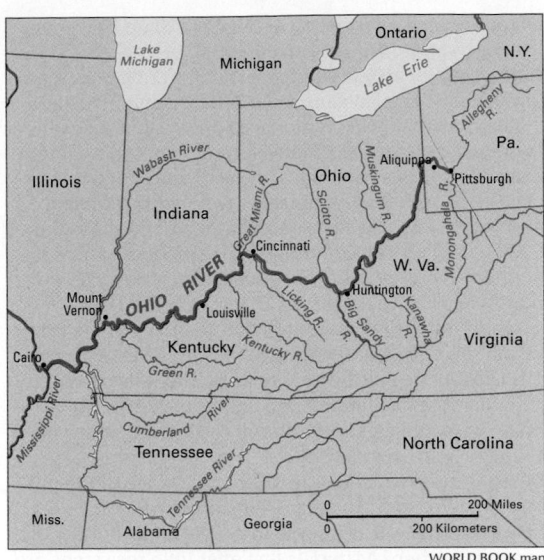

WORLD BOOK map

Location of the Ohio River

dians lived along its shores. Throughout the 1700's, traders used the river to explore the entire Ohio River Valley. Settlers traveled on the Ohio to the Northwest Territory after that region was established in 1787.

More than 60 steamboats were active on the Ohio by 1820. After the American Civil War ended in 1865, the river became a major corridor for the shipment of raw materials and industrial products. During the early 1900's, the steamboats were gradually replaced by powerful tugboats pushing heavy barges.

Flooding along the Ohio often causes heavy damage. Severe floods in 1937, 1945, and 1963 brought great losses of life and property. Since the 1950's, the federal government has worked with the states bordering the river to build or update about 20 dam and canal structures that control most flooding on the Ohio.

John Edwin Coffman

Related articles in *World Book* include:

Allegheny River	Kanawha River	Tennessee River
Cumberland River	Monongahela River	Wabash River

Ohio State University is a state-assisted coeducational institution with campuses in Columbus, Lima, Mansfield, Marion, and Newark, Ohio. The main campus is in Columbus. The university also operates two facilities in Wooster, Ohio—the Agricultural Technical Institute, a two-year college; and the Ohio Agricultural Research and Development Center.

Ohio State University was founded in 1870 as a *land-grant* college. Land-grant colleges and universities receive federal aid to support education. Originally called Ohio Agricultural and Mechanical College, the school opened in 1873. It took its present name in 1878. The other campuses were founded between 1957 and 1960. Athletic teams on the Columbus campus are called the Buckeyes.

Ohio State University operates its own radio and television stations and has an airport near the Columbus campus. The university's Franz Theodore Stone Laboratory, in Put-in-Bay, Ohio, studies the biology of the Great Lakes. The university's website at http://www.osu.edu offers additional information about Ohio State University.

Ohio University is a public institution of higher learning that has its main campus in Athens, Ohio. The university also maintains regional campuses in Chillicothe, Ironton, Lancaster, St. Clairsville, and Zanesville. Ohio University grants bachelor's, master's, and doctoral degrees. The university also has a school of osteopathic medicine. Students study journalism and media in the Scripps College of Communication. The university's Kennedy Museum of Art includes a large collection of Southwest Native American art.

Ohio University was founded in 1804. It was the first institution of higher learning in the vast Midwestern region called the Northwest Territory. The university's athletic teams are called the Bobcats. Its website at http://www.ohio.edu offers additional information.

Ohm is the unit used to measure resistance to the passage of an electric current. All materials resist the flow of electric current. But some materials offer more resistance than others. Materials that offer little resistance are called *conductors.* Materials that offer great resistance are called *insulators.* Electrical resistance, measured in ohms *(R),* is equal to the electromotive force producing an electric current, measured in *volts (E),* divided by the current, measured in *amperes (I):*

$$\text{ohms} = \frac{\text{volts}}{\text{amperes}} \text{ or } R = \frac{E}{I}$$

The resistance of a conductor depends on its dimensions and its temperature as well as on the material from which the conductor is made. For example, the resistance of a wire increases as its length increases or as its diameter decreases. Generally, the resistance of a metal increases as its temperature rises.

The international standard for the ohm was adopted in 1990. It was based on a sensitive measurement of the resistance of a conducting material in a magnetic field. When cooled to extremely low temperatures, the material's resistance can have only certain, precise values. Engineers have worked out the resistance of standard-sized wires for people who work with electric circuits. Resistance in an electric circuit can be measured with an *ohmmeter.* More accurate measurements can be obtained by using a device called a *Wheatstone bridge* (see **Wheatstone bridge**).   Michael Dine

Ohm, Georg Simon (1789-1854), a German physicist, in 1827 described the mathematical law of electric currents called Ohm's law (see **Ohm's law**). The *ohm,* a unit of electrical resistance, was named for him. His discovery was neglected until 1833, when he became a professor of physics at Nuremberg. He was appointed a physics professor at the University of Munich in 1849.

Ohm was born on March 16, 1789, in Erlangen, Germany. He graduated from the University of Erlangen. Ohm died on July 6, 1854.   Julia Borst Brazas

Ohm's law is a mathematical formula that expresses the relationship between the electromotive force, electric current, and resistance in a circuit. This relationship was discovered by the German physicist Georg Ohm and was published in 1827.

When applied to a direct-current circuit, Ohm's law states that the electromotive force *(E),* measured in volts, equals the current *(I)* in amperes multiplied by the resistance *(R)* in ohms:

$$E = IR$$

When the law is used for an alternating-current circuit, resistance is replaced by *impedance (Z),* also in ohms. The flow of alternating current produces a *counter-electromotive force,* which resists the current. The strength of such resistance depends on how rapidly the electric current alternates. Impedance consists of this resistance, called *reactance,* combined with the circuit's regular resistance.

Electricians use Ohm's law to determine the efficiency of circuits. For example, they can calculate how the flow of current will be affected by various arrangements of such circuit components as connecting wires, capacitors, and resistors.   Michael Dine

Oil is any greasy substance that does not dissolve in water but can be dissolved in a liquid called *ether.* Many different kinds of oil exist. Most oils are lighter than water and are liquid at room temperature. A few oils, such as lard and butterfat, are solid at room temperature.

People obtain oils from animal, mineral, or plant sources. Oil from minerals, also called *petroleum* or *crude oil,* consists of a mixture of compounds that can be separated into fuel oils, mineral oil, and other petroleum products. This article discusses animal and plant oils, which differ chemically from mineral oils. For more information on mineral oils, see **Petroleum.**

Animal and plant oils consist chiefly of carbon, hydrogen, and oxygen. They belong to a family of materials called *lipids.* People classify animal and plant oils as *fixed* or *volatile,* depending on whether the oil evaporates under normal conditions.

Fixed oils, which do not evaporate under ordinary conditions, are also called *fatty oils* or simply *fats.* They include all animal oils and many oils from plants. Butterfat, lard, and tallow rank as the chief animal oils. Margarine and salad oil consist mainly of fixed plant oils. Other products that are made from fixed oils include candles, linoleum, lubricants, paint, and soap.

Butter makers churn cream to produce butter. People *render* (heat) fatty animal tissues to obtain other kinds of animal oil. Lard is made from fatty tissues of hogs, and tallow from cattle, goats, or sheep. Oils from such sea animals as fish and whales are called *marine oils.*

Most fixed plant oils are extracted from such seeds as corn, cottonseed, and soybeans. Processors obtain olive and palm oils from the fruit pulp surrounding the seed. For information on the processing of such oils, see **Vegetable oil.**

Exposure to air causes fixed oils to thicken. Depending on the degree of thickening, they can be classified as (1) drying, (2) semidrying, or (3) nondrying.

Drying oils absorb oxygen from the air to form a tough film. They are widely used to make paints and varnishes. Important drying oils include hemp, linseed, oiticica, perilla, poppy seed, soybean, sunflower, tung or chinawood, and walnut. Linseed oil, one of the most important drying oils, comes from flaxseeds. It is used in making paints and varnishes. Tung oil is a valuable oil used in waterproof varnishes and quick-drying enamels.

Semidrying oils absorb oxygen from the air to become thick, but not hard. Cottonseed, corn, and sesame oils are of the semidrying type.

Nondrying oils absorb oxygen from the air with little increase in thickness, but they often become *rancid*—that is, they develop unpleasant odors and flavors. Grape-seed, olive, and peanut oils, butterfat, and lard are examples of nondrying types.

Volatile oils, also called *essential oils,* evaporate quickly, especially when heated. Some of these oils come from plants, and others are artificially created. People use volatile oils chiefly for their flavor or odor. The taste of such food flavorings as lemon, mint, and vanilla extracts results from the volatile oils they include. Volatile oils also flavor chewing gum, tobacco, and toothpaste. Most fine perfumes include fragrant oils obtained from roses and other flowers. Manufacturers use such volatile oils as lemon oil to give a scent to soaps and other cleaning products.

Natural volatile oils are extracted from various parts of plants, including bark, flowers, leaves, roots, seeds, and twigs. Methods of obtaining plant oils used for their scent are described in the **Perfume** article. Food-processing companies follow similar procedures in extracting natural volatile oils for flavoring.

Manufacturers use chemical processes to make artificial volatile oils from coal, petroleum, wood, and other substances. Some artificial oils duplicate natural oils. Others differ from any substance found in nature. Such products as artificial oil of rose and artificial vanilla extract cost much less than similar natural substances.

Martha H. Stipanuk

Related articles in *World Book* include:

Butter	Hydrogenation	Peanut
Canola oil	Lard	Peppermint
Castor oil	Linseed oil	Petitgrain oil
Copra	Lipid	Sesame
Corn oil	Margarine	Soybean
Cottonseed oil	Olive oil	Tung oil
Fat	Palm oil	Vegetable oil

Oil painting. See Painting.

Oil refinery. See Petroleum.

Oil shale is a soft, fine-grained sedimentary rock from which oil and natural gas are obtained. Oil shale consists of light brown layers of silt and darker layers of *kerogen,* a waxy organic substance that originated from the remains of *cyanobacteria* (blue-green algae) and other living matter. Vast deposits of oil shale occur in southern Brazil, northeastern China, Estonia, Sweden, and the United States.

Heating oil shale releases crude oil and natural gas from the kerogen in a process called *retorting.* However, it takes huge quantities of rock to obtain a useful amount of oil. As a result, the oil is expensive to produce. The high cost of production has limited the commercial use of the oil. Only a few countries now use oil shale.

Two methods are used to obtain oil from oil shale. In the first process, the mined rock is crushed, transported to a processing plant, and heated to temperatures higher than 900 °F (480 °C). The heat drives oil vapors from the rock, and they condense into liquid oil.

The second process for extracting oil from oil shale is called the *in situ* (in place) method. In this method, miners dig a hole into the bottom of a shale deposit. They then dynamite the deposit, which collapses and shatters. A mixture of air and gas is pumped into the deposit and ignited, heating the rock. Oil vapors then separate from

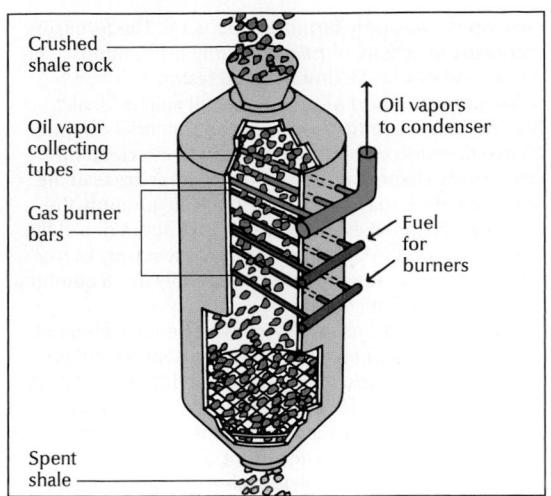

Labels: Crushed shale rock; Oil vapor collecting tubes; Gas burner bars; Spent shale; Oil vapors to condenser; Fuel for burners

WORLD BOOK diagram

Crude oil is obtained from oil shale by a process called *retorting,* shown here. Crushed shale rock is heated to more than 900 °F (480 °C) by gas burners. The heat releases oil vapors from the rock, and the vapors liquefy in a condenser.

the rock and condense, and oil is pumped out.

Bob Williams

Oil spill is the release of petroleum products into the environment. Oil can spill on land, in lakes and rivers, in the ocean, or around coastal areas. Once spilled, oil interacts with the environment in many ways. The oil can cause great damage to living things. Because oil spills are so destructive, people have devised a number of methods to clean them up.

Effects. Oil is a liquid form of petroleum, which forms deep underground. Most oil is less dense than water. Thus, spilled oil typically floats on water. But the floating oil soon begins to change through a process called *weathering.* Weathering refers to changes in the chemical and physical properties of the oil after it has been exposed to the environment. Some changes are caused by the activities of living things in the water. As the oil weathers, waves and currents can help break it up into smaller pieces. They may carry the pieces far away from the spill location. In addition, some oil may sink through the water and gather in sediments at the bottom. The oil can remain in sediments for decades.

Birds, fish, turtles, and many other animals can become heavily coated with spilled oil. The animals typically die as a result. Oil can also coat seagrass beds and marshlands. In doing so, it kills plants and poisons animals that live in such areas. In addition, oil contains toxic chemicals that harm living things over a long time. Such chemicals may cause *tumors* (abnormal growths) or prevent animals from reproducing.

Damaging effects from oil spills can persist in specific areas for decades. A small spill in a fragile environment can cause more damage than a larger spill elsewhere.

Responses. Workers can set up *booms* (floating barriers) to block the spread of oil. They can also spread *sorbent* materials. These materials act as oil-absorbing sponges. Skimmers and nets can also recover oil. *Dispersing agents,* also called *dispersants,* are chemicals that push the oil into deeper waters. In *bioremediation,* cleanup crews apply fertilizers to the oil. The fertilizers increase the activity of *microbes* (tiny living things). The microbes help break down the oil faster.

No single method of treating an oil spill is ideal. Booms, nets, skimmers, and sorbent materials are ineffective in rough waters and can do little to clean up large spills. Dispersants move oil to other areas in the ocean where it may still pose threats. In addition, the dispersants themselves can be toxic to some ocean life. Bioremediation depends on a sufficient supply of oxygen for the microbes. Workers generally use a combination of response techniques.

Petroleum consists chiefly of two chemical elements: carbon and hydrogen. These two elements combine, forming *compounds,* in thousands of different ways. A source of oil typically has a unique mixture of compounds. This mixture acts as a chemical "fingerprint." By examining an oil spill's fingerprint, scientists can often trace the oil to the party that spilled it. A government can then hold the party responsible for the environmental damage and cleanup efforts.

In the United States, the Environmental Protection Agency (EPA) coordinates the response to oil spills in inland waters or on land. The U.S. Coast Guard coordinates the response for oil spills on the seashore or in the open ocean. Each agency directs the cleanup using private, corporate, and government resources. Other developed countries coordinate responses to oil spills in similar ways. But poor countries often lack the resources or political stability to direct effective responses. Oil spills are common in the Niger Delta region of the African country Nigeria, for example. There, hundreds of millions of gallons (1 to 2 billion liters) of oil have probably been spilled since the 1950's, when oil was first discovered in the region. But the Nigerian government rarely cleans up the oil effectively, and safety features to prevent spills are poorly maintained.

Notable spills. One of the largest oil spills ever recorded on land began in 1910, in Kern County, Califor-nia. Over a period of 18 months, about 360 million gallons (1.36 billion liters) of oil spilled out from an uncontrolled blowout at an oil well.

In 1989, the *Exxon Valdez* oil tanker struck a reef off Alaska, spilling about 11 million gallons (42 million liters). The disaster brought attention to oil tanker safety.

During the 1991 Persian Gulf War, the Iraqi government purposely dumped well over 200 million gallons (760 million liters) of crude oil into the Persian Gulf. Troops also set fire to hundreds of oil wells on land, burning or spilling even greater amounts of oil.

The Gulf oil spill of 2010 was the largest spill ever recorded in U.S. waters. An explosion at the *Deepwater Horizon* oil rig spilled around 200 million gallons (760 million liters) of oil into the Gulf of Mexico off Louisiana.

Edward S. Van Vleet

Related articles in *World Book* include:
Exxon Valdez oil spill
Gulf oil spill of 2010
Ocean (Oil pollution)
Petroleum (Spills and seeps)
Tanker (Oil spills)

Oil well. See Petroleum.

Oilbird is a cave-dwelling bird found in the tropics of northern South America that somewhat resembles an owl. Oilbirds have cinnamon-brown feathers with white dots. Adults measure from 12 to 18 inches (30 to 46 centimeters) long. Young oilbirds are unusually plump and contain so much oily fat that they were once slaughtered by people who used the fat as lamp oil and cooking oil. Oilbirds are also called *guácharos.*

Oilbirds spend most of their time roosting or flying because their feet are poorly developed for walking. They are active at night and feed largely on the fruits of palm and laurel trees. They build nests of seeds and bird droppings on top of rocks or ledges deep in caves. An oilbird finds its way about caves and at night by means of *echolocation.* The bird makes sharp clicking sounds that echo off objects to tell it where to fly. Oilbirds also

An oil spill can cause great environmental damage. In this photograph, a shrimp boat uses floating barriers called *booms* to clean up spilled oil in the Gulf of Mexico, off the coast of Louisiana. About 200 million gallons (760 million liters) of oil spilled into the Gulf after an oil rig exploded in 2010.

Bertram G. Murray, Jr., Animals Animals

Oilbirds dwell in caves in tropical regions of northern South America. They have rich brown feathers and large eyes that reflect red in the dark. Oilbirds feed on palm and laurel fruits.

make loud, shrill calls at night.   Donald F. Bruning

Scientific classification. The oilbird's scientific name is *Steatornis caripensis*.

Ojibwa Indians. See Chippewa Indians.

Okapi, *oh KAH pee,* is a rare animal that lives in dense forests around the Congo River Basin in Africa. The okapi stands about 5 feet (1.5 meters) high at the shoulder. It is related to the giraffe, but its neck is much shorter. The okapi has a dark chestnut body, a white face, and white stripes on its rump and upper legs. The male has a pair of short, hairy horns.

The okapi eats leaves, fruit, and seeds. It travels alone or in pairs. The okapi has keen hearing and flees when disturbed.   Wendy C. Turner

Scientific classification. The okapi's scientific name is *Okapia johnstoni*.

Kenneth W. Fink, Ardea

The okapi is a relative of the giraffe. It has a reddish-brown body, a white face, and white stripes on its legs. Okapis live in rain forests of the Congo River Basin in Africa.

Oil painting on canvas (1936); © Georgia O'Keeffe, photo by Malcolm Varon

Georgia O'Keeffe gained fame for her paintings of the desert region of the American Southwest. *Summer Days, shown here,* is typical of O'Keeffe's works. Animal bones, flowers, and the desert landscape appear in many of her paintings.

Okeechobee, Lake. See Lake Okeechobee.

O'Keeffe, Georgia (1887-1986), was an American painter who found most of her inspiration in nature. O'Keeffe's flower paintings, which she created throughout her career, are her best-known works. She is additionally famous for her paintings of animal skulls and desert landscapes. O'Keeffe painted in a highly personalized style, using strong, vibrant colors. Her forms are sensually smoothed and simplified, often into highly abstract designs.

O'Keeffe was born on Nov. 15, 1887, in Sun Prairie, Wisconsin. She studied at several schools, including the Art Institute of Chicago, the Art Students League, and Columbia University. From 1912 to 1918, O'Keeffe taught in Texas, Virginia, and South Carolina. In Texas, she first became interested in the American Southwest. The region's desert landscape greatly influenced her work.

The American photographer Alfred Stieglitz first showed O'Keeffe's paintings in 1916 at "291," his experimental gallery in New York City. For years, he displayed her work at two other galleries he operated in New York City. Stieglitz and O'Keeffe married in 1924. In 1929, O'Keeffe began spending much time in New Mexico. Stieglitz died in 1946. O'Keeffe settled near Abiquiu in 1949.

Toward the end of her life, O'Keeffe's eyesight began to fail. She then began to work with ceramics, shaping beautifully rounded, sensuous forms and pottery. O'Keeffe died on March 6, 1986.   Deborah Leveton

See **Painting** (picture: *Black Iris).*

Okefenokee Swamp, *OH kuh fuh NOH kee,* lies mostly in southeastern Georgia. A small part of it ex-

Artstreet

Okefenokee Swamp covers about 700 square miles (1,800 square kilometers) of marshy wilderness, chiefly in southeastern Georgia. The United States government has set aside about two-thirds of the region as the Okefenokee National Wildlife Refuge. The preserve provides a recreation area for people, as well as a safe home for many unique varieties of mammals, birds, fish, and plants.

tends into northeastern Florida. Okefenokee Swamp is a marshy, subtropical wilderness.

The United States government has owned most of it since 1937. The government has set aside about 630 square miles (1,630 square kilometers) of the region as the Okefenokee National Wildlife Refuge.

The name *Okefenokee* comes from the Indian word *Owaquaphenoga,* which means *trembling earth.* It refers to the trembling of the small bushes and water weeds that float on the lakes of Okefenokee.

Okefenokee Swamp covers 700 square miles (1,800 square kilometers). Fine timberlands and freshwater lakes lie next to the marshy stretches. The St. Marys and the Suwannee rivers drain the region. Other bodies of water wind through the swamp. There are dozens of islands there.

Okefenokee Swamp was once a favorite hunting ground of the Creek and Seminole Indians. Today, as a government preserve, the swamp is the home of many animals, including alligators, bears, bobcats, deer, opossums, and otters. The swamp is also the winter refuge of hundreds of bird species. There are dozens of kinds of fish in its waters. Plants that grow there include baldcypress trees, white and golden lilies, and Spanish moss.

James O. Wheeler

See also **Georgia** (map; picture).

Okinawa, *OH kuh NOW wuh,* or in Japanese, *AW kee NAH wah,* is the largest and most important island of the Ryukyu Islands. The Ryukyus are a chain of islands in the North Pacific Ocean that are part of Japan.

Okinawa covers 465 square miles (1,204 square kilometers). It is the largest island in Japan's Okinawa *prefecture* (district), which has a population of 1,361,594. The Okinawa prefecture also includes the southern Ryukyu Islands. Almost all of the prefecture's population lives on the island of Okinawa. Naha, the capital of Okinawa prefecture and largest city of the Ryukyus, is on Okinawa.

Okinawa was under Japanese control before World War II (1939-1945). The United States occupied Okinawa after the war and administered it and the other Ryukyu islands until 1972. In that year, the United States returned the islands to Japanese control.

Okinawa has had great military importance for the

United States because it lies within easy flying distance of China, mainland Japan, the Philippines, Taiwan, and Vietnam. The United States built air bases and other installations on the island and continued to maintain them after returning control of the island to Japan. But in the mid-1990's, growing dissatisfaction among Okinawans with the U.S. military presence prompted the United States to agree to give up part of the land it administers.

Okinawa

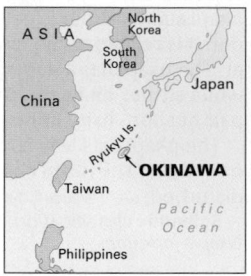

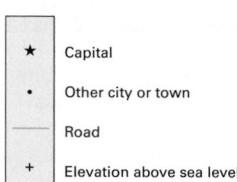

★ Capital

• Other city or town

— Road

+ Elevation above sea level

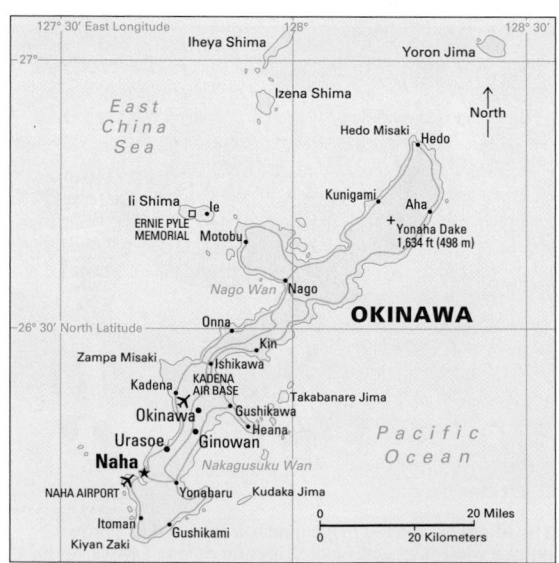

WORLD BOOK maps

Government. Voters elect a governor to head the prefecture of Okinawa. The prefecture's legislature is called the Prefectural Assembly. The prefecture's voters also elect representatives to the Diet (national parliament) in Tokyo.

People. The Okinawan language is related to Japanese. Okinawan is in decline, and most Okinawans speak only Japanese.

Most Okinawans live in urban areas. Naha and other cities in Okinawa have modern buildings and traffic-choked streets. A few Okinawans still live in small villages of red tile-roofed houses. Their main food is rice, but they also eat much pork. Most village people farm or fish for a living.

The University of the Ryukyus, in Naha, is Okinawa's major institution of higher education. The Okinawa Prefectural Board of Education oversees public elementary, junior high, and high schools.

Land and climate. Okinawa is 67 miles (108 kilometers) long and from 2 to 16 miles (3 to 26 kilometers) wide. Mountains and jungle cover the northern part of the island. The southern part has low, rocky hills. Most of the people live in the south.

Okinawa has a subtropical climate. The average daily temperature in Naha is 72 °F (22 °C) the year around. Rainfall averages about 83 inches (211 centimeters) yearly, most of it falling in the typhoon season, from April to October.

Economy. Before World War II, Okinawa was a poor agricultural island. Today, it has one of the highest *per capita* (per person) incomes in East Asia. Okinawa's chief crops include pineapples, rice, sugar cane, and sweet potatoes.

Tourism has become the island's main industry. Most of the tourists come from other parts of Japan to enjoy Okinawa's warm climate and natural beauty.

Okinawan craftworkers make ceramics, lacquerware, and woven and dyed cloth. A pottery kiln in Naha has been operating since the 1600's. Okinawan arts and crafts are prized by art collectors, especially in Japan.

History. Japan and China both claimed Okinawa and the rest of the Ryukyus until 1874, when China recognized Japan's rule. For the history of the island before that time, see the article on **Ryukyu Islands.**

One of the bloodiest campaigns of World War II was fought on Okinawa between U.S. and Japanese troops. The Americans landed on the island on April 1, 1945, and conquered it in late June. During the fighting, more than 90 percent of the island's buildings were destroyed. See **World War II** (Closing in on Japan).

The peace treaty that ended the war gave the United States control of the Ryukyu Islands. In 1950, the United States began to grant some self-rule to the Ryukyuans. It returned the northern Ryukyus to Japan in 1953 but kept Okinawa and the southern islands. The United States built military bases on Okinawa after the Chinese Communists gained control of China in 1949 and the Korean War broke out in 1950.

During the 1950's and 1960's, many Okinawans demanded that the island be returned to Japanese rule. The United States returned the island to Japan in 1972. Under an agreement between the two nations, U.S. military bases remain on Okinawa, but nuclear weapons may not be kept on the island without Japan's consent. In 1996, the United States announced that within the coming years it would return to Okinawa 20 percent of the land held by the U.S. military.

David L. Howell

David Moore, Black Star

An Okinawan farmworker cuts pineapples from their plants and drops them into a basket strapped to her back. Pineapples rank among the leading exports of Okinawa.

Pan-Asia Newspaper Alliance

Naha, Okinawa's largest city, is a major commercial center on the island. The busy International Avenue, *shown here,* is the main street of the city.

© David G. Fitzgerald

Granite mounds rise in Quartz Mountain State Park near Lugert. Oklahoma's varied landscape includes rugged hills and mountains, vast plains, green forests, and fertile farmlands.

Oklahoma *The Sooner State*

Oklahoma is a major fuel and food producing state in the southwestern part of the United States. Thousands of oil and natural gas wells dot the Oklahoma landscape. Millions of white-faced beef cattle graze on Oklahoma's flat plains and low hills. Fertile fields produce vast crops of wheat.

Service industries and manufacturing are also important in Oklahoma. The state's location midway between the east and west coasts makes it an important transportation, communication, and distribution center. Oklahoma's manufacturing plants turn out large amounts of aerospace equipment, food products, machinery, refined petroleum, and tires.

The development of Oklahoma's vast natural resources began with the American Indians. In the 1800's, the United States government made most of the region a huge Indian reservation called the Indian Territory. Most of the Indians had been forcibly moved there from ancestral homelands in the southeastern United States. The Indians established separate nations, with their own governments and their own schools. The name *Oklahoma* is a combination of two Choctaw Indian words—

okla, meaning *people,* and *homma,* meaning *red.*

The government first opened Oklahoma to white settlement during the late 1880's. Oklahoma became known as the *Sooner State* because some settlers were there "sooner" than the land was opened. The land was settled rapidly, and whites soon far outnumbered the Indians.

During the early 1900's, the farms and ranches of Oklahoma were fertile and productive. But in the 1920's, unsustainable farming practices led to severe soil erosion in many parts of the state. In the 1930's, a long dry period and low farm prices brought disaster to the farmers. Large numbers of farmers and other workers left the state, and the population of Oklahoma dropped.

Both these periods of Oklahoma history have become famous. The story of the state's farmers and cattlemen in territorial days is told in the musical play *Oklahoma!* (1943). The title song from the play became Oklahoma's state song. John Steinbeck's famous novel *The Grapes of Wrath* (1939) included a fictional, but widely accepted, description of the drought of the 1930's.

Today, farmers protect their land from drought with modern soil and water conservation methods. The state's oil and gas wells continue to yield their valuable products, and the state is working to attract new industries. Oklahoma City, the state capital and largest city in population, is one of the largest cities in area in the United States. It covers more than 600 square miles (1,550 square kilometers).

The contributors of this article are Brad A. Bays, Associate Professor of Geography at Oklahoma State University, and Deena K. Fisher, Associate Professor of History at Northwestern Oklahoma State University.

© David G. Fitzgerald

Beavers Bend State Park has scenic woodlands covering more than 3,500 acres (1,400 hectares) in the Ouachita Mountains.

Interesting facts about Oklahoma

Downtown Guthrie has dozens of buildings—a large portion of the downtown area—on the National Register of Historic Places. Guthrie was the first capital of Oklahoma. But in 1910, the capital was moved to Oklahoma City. The booming town suddenly became quiet. Buildings erected during the days of early statehood were preserved and older buildings were not torn down to make room for newer ones. Thus, the town became a treasure of historical architecture. A major architectural restoration project in the 1980's brought the town's historic character back to life.

Guthrie

The first automatic parking meter was installed in Oklahoma City on July 16, 1935.

Oklahoma City was barren prairie on the morning of April 22, 1889, but its population numbered more than 10,000 by nightfall. That day unassigned land was opened to settlement.

Oklahoma is a major center of American Indian culture. The state has a large and varied Indian population. More than 60 different Indian tribes live in Oklahoma.

The Oklahoma State Capitol is the nation's only statehouse with oil wells on its grounds. The wells were drilled after the capitol was built, and the state owns the mineral rights to its grounds.

Indian culture

WORLD BOOK illustrations by Kevin Chadwick

Randy Bennett, Oklahoma City Public Information Office

Oklahoma City is the capital and largest city of Oklahoma. Modern buildings stand close together in the downtown section of the city, *left.* Myriad Gardens, in the foreground, provides open space in the crowded downtown area.

Oklahoma in brief

Symbols of Oklahoma

The state flag, adopted in 1925, displays an Osage warrior's shield decorated with eagle feathers. Crossing the shield are two symbols of peace—an olive branch and a peace pipe. On the state seal, adopted in 1907, an Indian and a white frontiersman shake hands before the figure of Justice to show the cooperation of the people of Oklahoma. The large star displays symbols of the Five Civilized Tribes, which moved to the region in the 1800's.

State flag

State of Oklahoma
State seal

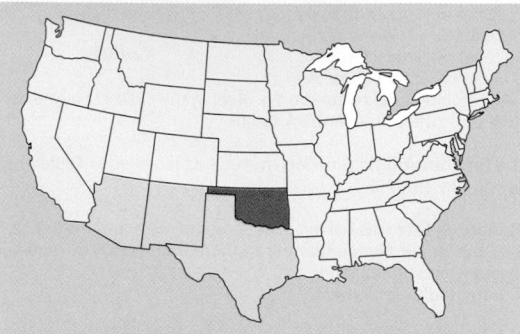

Oklahoma (brown) ranks 18th in size among all the states and is the smallest of the Southwestern States (yellow).

The State Capitol is in Oklahoma City, the capital of Oklahoma since 1910. Guthrie served as capital from 1890 to 1910.

General information

Statehood: Nov. 16, 1907, the 46th state.
State abbreviations: Okla. (traditional); OK (postal).
State motto: *Labor Omnia Vincit* (Labor Conquers All Things).
State song: "Oklahoma!" Words by Oscar Hammerstein II; music by Richard Rodgers.

Land and climate

Area: 69,898 mi² (181,036 km²), including 1,231 mi² (3,189 km²) of inland water.
Elevation: *Highest*—Black Mesa, 4,973 ft (1,516 m) above sea level. *Lowest*—287 ft (87 m) above sea level along the Little River in McCurtain County.
Record high temperature: 120 °F (49 °C) at Alva on July 18, 1936; at Altus on July 19 and Aug. 12, 1936; at Poteau on Aug. 10, 1936; at Tishomingo on July 26, 1943; and at Tipton on June 27, 1994.
Record low temperature: −27 °F (−33 °C) at Vinita on Feb. 13, 1905, and at Watts on Jan. 18, 1930.
Average July temperature: 82 °F (28 °C).
Average January temperature: 37 °F (3 °C).
Average yearly precipitation: 33 in (84 cm).

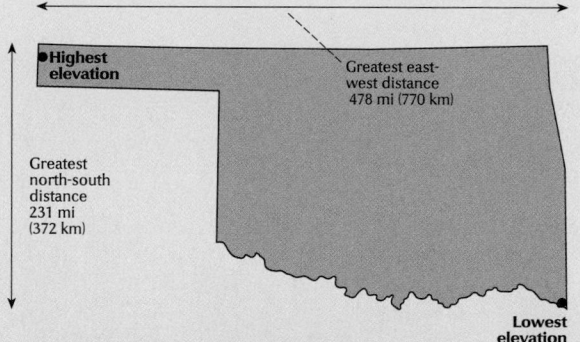

Highest elevation

Greatest east-west distance 478 mi (770 km)

Greatest north-south distance 231 mi (372 km)

Lowest elevation

Important dates

La Salle claimed Oklahoma as part of French Louisiana.

The U.S. government established Fort Gibson and Fort Towson, the region's first military posts.

| 1541 | 1682 | 1803 | 1824 |

Francisco Vásquez de Coronado crossed western Oklahoma in search of gold.

The United States bought the Oklahoma region, except the Panhandle, as part of the Louisiana Purchase.

State bird
Scissor-tailed flycatcher

State flower
Oklahoma rose

State tree
Eastern redbud

People

Population: 3,751,351
Rank among the states: 28th
Density: 54 per mi² (21 per km²), U.S. average 85 per mi² (33 per km²)
Distribution: 65 percent urban, 35 percent rural
Largest cities in Oklahoma

Oklahoma City	579,999
Tulsa	391,906
Norman	110,925
Broken Arrow	98,850
Lawton	96,867
Edmond	81,405

Source: 2010 census, except for distribution, which is for 2000.

Population trend

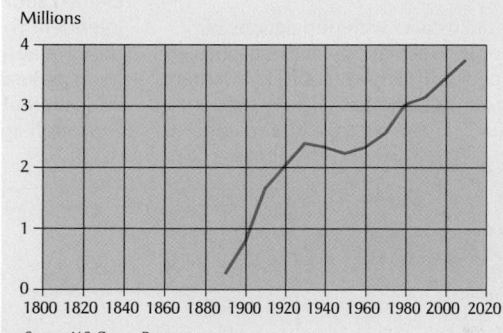

Millions

Source: U.S. Census Bureau.

Year	Population
2010	3,751,351
2000	3,450,654
1990	3,145,585
1980	3,025,290
1970	2,559,229
1960	2,328,284
1950	2,233,351
1940	2,336,434
1930	2,396,040
1920	2,028,283
1910	1,657,155
1900	790,391
1890	258,657

Economy

Chief products

Agriculture: beef cattle, broilers, dairy products, greenhouse and nursery products, hay, hogs, wheat.
Manufacturing: fabricated metal products, food products, machinery, petroleum products, transportation equipment.
Mining: natural gas, petroleum.

Gross domestic product

Value of goods and services produced in 2008: $151,406,000,000. *Services* include community, business, and personal services; finance; government; trade; and transportation and communication. *Industry* includes construction, manufacturing, mining, and utilities. *Agriculture* includes agriculture, fishing, and forestry.

Source: U.S. Bureau of Economic Analysis.

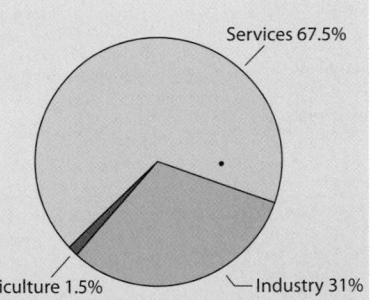

Services 67.5%

Agriculture 1.5%

Industry 31%

Government

State government

Governor: 4-year term
State senators: 48; 4-year terms
State representatives: 101; 2-year terms
Counties: 77

Federal government

United States senators: 2
United States representatives: 5
Electoral votes: 7

Sources of information

Oklahoma's official website at http://www.ok.gov provides a gateway to much information on the state's government, history, and economy.

In addition, the website at http://www.travelok.com provides information about tourism.

The Cherokee Outlet was opened to white settlement, creating Oklahoma's greatest land rush.

The Oklahoma City oil field opened.

1889   1893   1907   1928   1990

Parts of Oklahoma opened to white settlement on April 22.

Oklahoma became the 46th state on November 16.

Oklahoma became the first state to pass term limits on members of its state Legislature.

Population. The 2010 United States census reported that Oklahoma had 3,751,351 people. The state's population had increased about 9 percent over the 2000 census figure of 3,450,654. According to the 2010 census, Oklahoma ranks 28th in population among the 50 states.

Most of the state's population is concentrated in a corridor that runs from southwest to northeast Oklahoma. This corridor includes three of the state's four metropolitan areas (see **Metropolitan area**). These areas are Oklahoma City, Tulsa, and Lawton.

The fourth metropolitan area is based in Fort Smith, Arkansas, and extends into part of east-central Oklahoma. For the populations of the four metropolitan areas, see the *Index* to the political map of Oklahoma in this article.

Oklahoma has about 20 cities with populations of more than 20,000 people. The majority of these cities are near Oklahoma City or Tulsa. Oklahoma City is a center of industry and trade. Tulsa started as a Creek Indian village in the early 1800's. The city boomed after oil was discovered in nearby Red Fork in the early 1900's. Norman, the state's third-largest city, is the home of the University of Oklahoma. Lawton serves Fort Sill, a neighboring military center.

Oklahoma's largest population groups include people of European and American Indian descent. Other sizable groups include Hispanics and African Americans.

Schools. The first schools in Oklahoma were established for the Indians in the 1820's by missionaries. By the late 1840's, several tribes, including the Cherokee and the Choctaw, had established their own advanced educational systems. Schools for white children were first established in Oklahoma in 1890.

Oklahoma's present school system is headed by an elected superintendent of public instruction. The superintendent works with a Board of Education whose members are appointed by the governor. The U.S. government maintains two boarding schools to assist in the education of Indian children. By law, children from age 5 through age 17 must attend school. For the number of

Population density

About 60 percent of the people of Oklahoma live in the metropolitan areas of Oklahoma City and Tulsa. Western Oklahoma, including a narrow strip called the Panhandle, is more thinly populated.

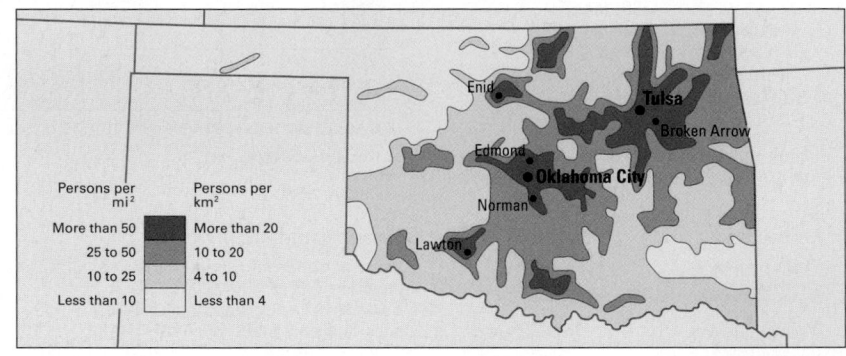

Persons per mi²	Persons per km²
More than 50	More than 20
25 to 50	10 to 20
10 to 25	4 to 10
Less than 10	Less than 4

WORLD BOOK map;
based on U.S. Census Bureau data.

© Monica Armstrong, Dreamstime

Tulsa's skyline rises along the Arkansas River in northeastern Oklahoma. Tulsa is the state's second largest city and a center for manufacturing and trade. Many administrative services for the U.S. petroleum industry are based in the city.

students and teachers in Oklahoma, see **Education** (table).

Libraries. Oklahoma has a system of public libraries and a number of college and university libraries. The state's first public library was founded in Guthrie in 1901.

The Oklahoma Department of Libraries and the library division of the Oklahoma Historical Society are both in Oklahoma City. The University of Oklahoma Library in Norman has the History of Science Collections, the Harry W. Bass Business History Collection, and a collection of materials on the history of the American West.

Museums. Oklahoma's museums own many fine collections on Indian history and art. The Gilcrease Museum, in Tulsa, is devoted largely to such collections. Lawton is the home of the Museum of the Great Plains. The Woolaroc Museum near Bartlesville owns one of the world's finest collections of Indian blankets. The Southern Plains Indian Museum and Crafts Center is in Anadarko.

The Oklahoma History Center is in Oklahoma City. The National Cowboy & Western Heritage Museum, also in Oklahoma City, features art of the American West. It also houses the Rodeo Hall of Fame, the Hall of Great Westerners, and the Hall of Great Western Performers.

The Philbrook Museum of Art in Tulsa displays paint-

ings from the Italian Renaissance and collections of African and Native American art. Science Museum Oklahoma, in Oklahoma City, includes exhibits that visitors are encouraged to touch and explore. The 45th Infantry Museum, also in Oklahoma City, features various exhibits related to the state's contributions to the nation's defense. Fort Sill, a military center near Lawton, has an artillery museum that displays unusual weapons.

Oklahoma State University

Oklahoma State University, in Stillwater, was founded in 1890. The university library, *shown in this photograph,* stands in the central part of the campus.

Universities and colleges

This table lists the nonprofit universities and colleges in Oklahoma that grant bachelor's or advanced degrees and are accredited by the North Central Association of Colleges and Schools.

Name	Mailing address
Bacone College	Muskogee
Cameron University	Lawton
Central Oklahoma, University of	Edmond
East Central University	Ada
Langston University	Langston
Mid-America Christian University	Oklahoma City
Northeastern State University	Tahlequah
Northwestern Oklahoma State University	Alva
Oklahoma, University of	*
Oklahoma Baptist University	Shawnee
Oklahoma Christian University	Oklahoma City
Oklahoma City University	Oklahoma City
Oklahoma Panhandle State University	Goodwell
Oklahoma State University	†
Oklahoma Wesleyan University	Bartlesville
Oral Roberts University	Tulsa
Phillips Theological Seminary	Tulsa
Rogers State University	Claremore
St. Gregory's University	Shawnee
Science and Arts of Oklahoma, University of	Chickasha
Southeastern Oklahoma State University	Durant
Southern Nazarene University	Bethany
Southwestern Christian University	Bethany
Southwestern Oklahoma State University	Weatherford
Tulsa, University of	Tulsa

*For campuses, see Oklahoma, University of.
†For campuses, see Oklahoma State University.

R. Krubner, H. Armstrong Roberts

The Philbrook Museum of Art in Tulsa is known for its beautiful gardens. The museum's collections include paintings from the Italian Renaissance as well as Native American art..

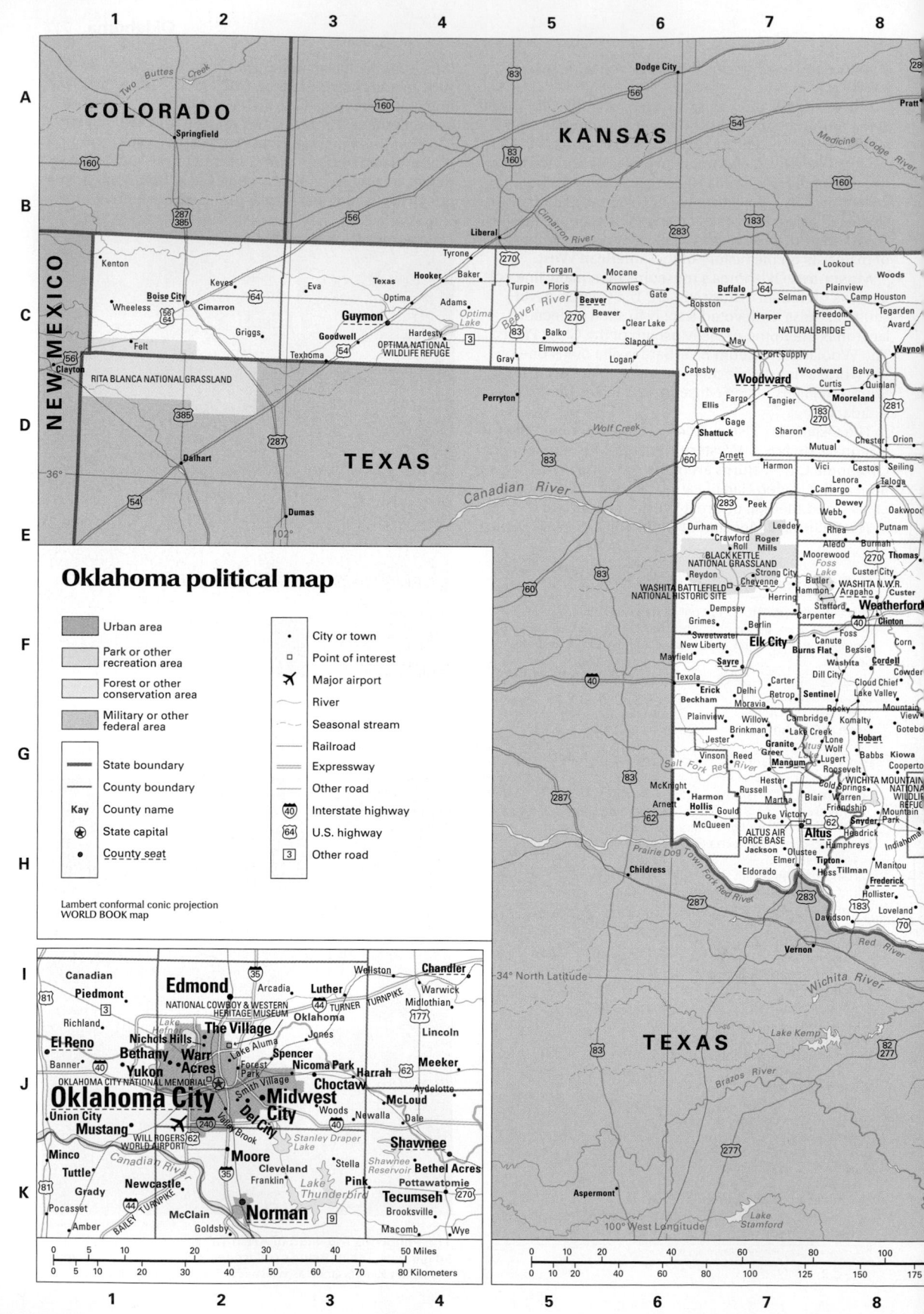

Oklahoma political map

Legend:

- Urban area
- Park or other recreation area
- Forest or other conservation area
- Military or other federal area
- State boundary
- County boundary
- Kay — County name
- State capital
- County seat

- City or town
- Point of interest
- Major airport
- River
- Seasonal stream
- Railroad
- Expressway
- Other road
- 40 — Interstate highway
- 64 — U.S. highway
- 3 — Other road

Lambert conformal conic projection
WORLD BOOK map

States and regions labeled: COLORADO, KANSAS, NEW MEXICO, TEXAS, OKLAHOMA

Selected places (main map):
Springfield, Dodge City, Pratt, Kenton, Keyes, Eva, Texas, Hooker, Baker, Tyrone, Forgan, Mocane, Knowles, Lookout, Woods, Boise City, Cimarron, Optima, Adams, Turpin, Floris, Beaver, Gate, Buffalo, Selman, Plainview, Camp Houston, Wheeless, Griggs, Goodwell, Hardesty, Balko, Beaver, Clear Lake, Rosston, Harper, Freedom, Tegarden, Avard, Felt, Texhoma, Gray, Elmwood, Slapout, Logan, May, Laverne, NATURAL BRIDGE, Waynoka, Clayton, Catesby, Port Supply, Woodward, Belva, Quinlan, RITA BLANCA NATIONAL GRASSLAND, Perryton, Ellis, Fargo, Tangier, Curtis, Mooreland, Dalhart, Shattuck, Gage, Sharon, Chester, Orion, Mutual, Arnett, Harmon, Vici, Cestos, Seiling, Dumas, Peek, Leedey, Dewey, Camargo, Webb, Oakwood, Putnam, Durham, Crawford, Roger Mills, Rhea, Aledo, Burmah, Thomas, Roll, Moorewood, Custer City, BLACK KETTLE NATIONAL GRASSLAND, Strong City, Cheyenne, Butler, Arapaho, Custer, WASHITA BATTLEFIELD NATIONAL HISTORIC SITE, Reydon, Hammon, Stafford, WASHITA N.W.R., Dempsey, Herring, Carpenter, Weatherford, Grimes, Berlin, Clinton, New Liberty, Sweetwater, Canute, Corn, Mayfield, Elk City, Burns Flat, Bessie, Cordell, Texola, Sayre, Washita, Cowder, Erick, Delhi, Carter, Dill City, Cloud Chief, Lake Valley, Beckham, Moravia, Retrop, Sentinel, Plainview, Willow, Rocky, Mountain View, Brinkman, Jester, Lake Creek, Cambridge, Komalty, Gotebo, Vinson, Lone Wolf, Granite, Greer, Lugert, Babbs, Kiowa, Cooperton, Reed, Mangum, Roosevelt, Hester, Russell, Blair, Cold Springs, Warren, WICHITA MOUNTAINS NATIONAL WILDLIFE REFUGE, McKnight, Harmon, Martha, Victory, Friendship, Mountain Park, Arnett, Hollis, Gould, Duke, Snyder, McQueen, Blair, Headrick, Indiahoma, ALTUS AIR FORCE BASE, Jackson, Olustee, Altus, Humphreys, Childress, Eldorado, Elmer, Tipton, Hess, Tillman, Manitou, Frederick, Davidson, Hollister, Loveland, Vernon, Aspermont

Inset map — Oklahoma City area:
Canadian, Edmond, Wellston, Chandler, Piedmont, Arcadia, Luther, Warwick, Richland, NATIONAL COWBOY & WESTERN HERITAGE MUSEUM, Oklahoma, TURNER TURNPIKE, Midlothian, El Reno, The Village, Jones, Lincoln, Nichols Hills, Banner, Bethany, Warr Acres, Spencer, Nicoma Park, Meeker, Yukon, Forest Park, Harrah, OKLAHOMA CITY NATIONAL MEMORIAL, Smith Village, Choctaw, Aydelotte, Oklahoma City, Midwest City, McLoud, Union City, Del City, Woods, Newalla, Dale, Mustang, WILL ROGERS WORLD AIRPORT, Stanley Draper Lake, Shawnee, Minco, Moore, Stella, Bethel Acres, Tuttle, Cleveland, Pink, Tecumseh, Newcastle, Franklin, Pottawatomie, Grady, Lake Thunderbird, Shawnee Reservoir, Brooksville, Pocasset, McClain, Macomb, Amber, Goldsby, Norman, Wye

Rivers: Two Buttes Creek, Medicine Lodge River, Cimarron River, Beaver River, Wolf Creek, Canadian River, Salt Fork Red River, Red River, Prairie Dog Town Fork Red River, North Canadian River, Wichita River, Brazos River, Lake Kemp, Lake Stamford

34° North Latitude
100° West Longitude
36°
102°

Scale bars:
0 5 10 20 30 40 50 Miles
0 5 10 20 30 40 50 60 70 80 Kilometers
0 10 20 40 60 80 100
0 10 20 40 60 80 100 125 150 175

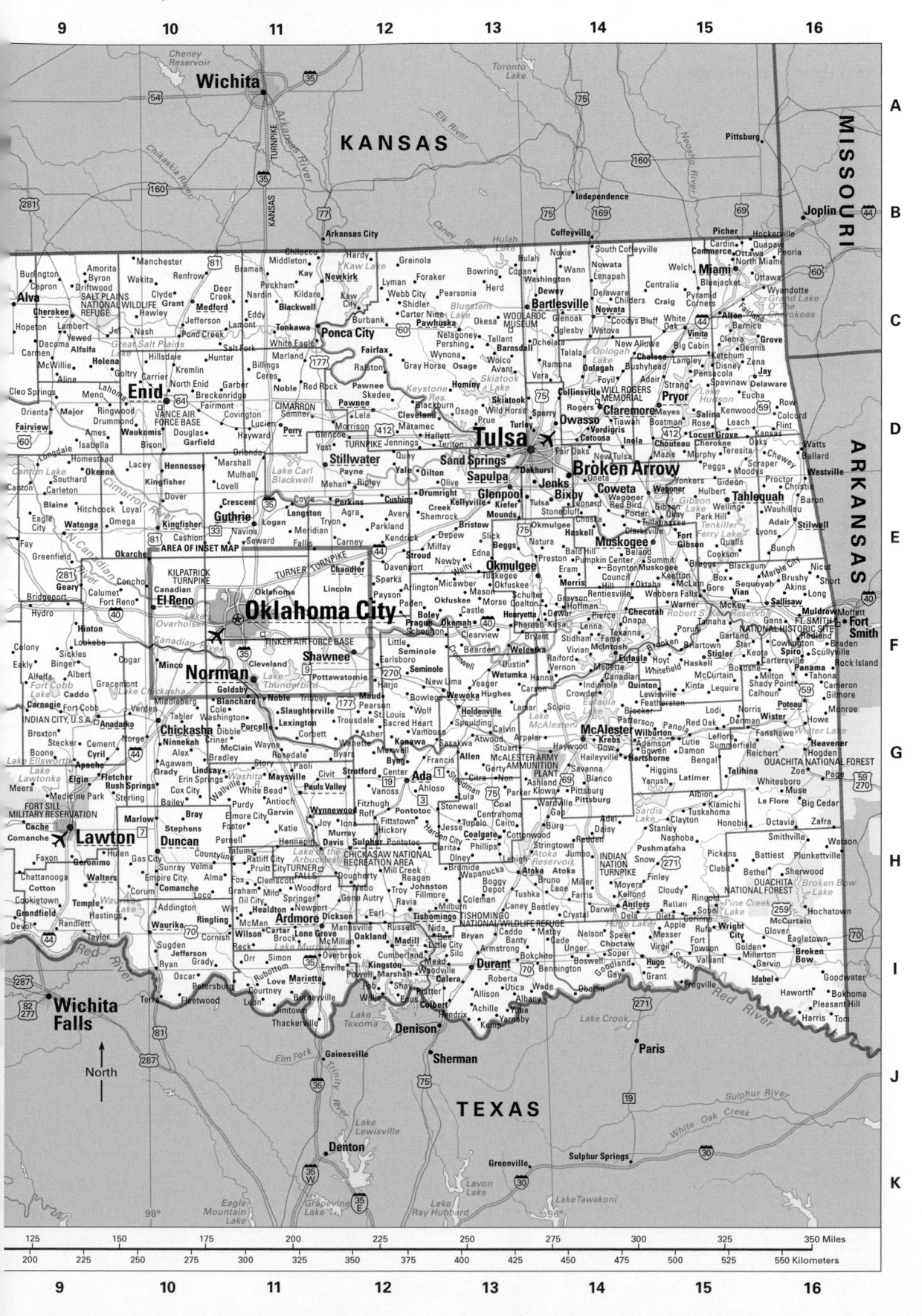

Oklahoma map index

Kingston ... 1,601 .. I 12
Kinta ... 297 .. F 15
Kiowa ... 731 .. G 14
Knowles ... 11 .. C 6
Komalty ... G 8
Konawa ... 1,298 .. G 12
Krebs ... 2,053 .. G 14
Kremlin ... 255 .. C 10
Kusa ... F 14
Lacey ... D 10
Lahoma ... 611 .. D 10
Lake Aluma ... 88 .. J 2
Lake Creek ... G 7
Lake Valley ... F 8
Lamar ... 158 .. F 13
Lambert ... 6 .. C 9
Lamont ... 417 .. C 11
Lane† ... 414 .. H 14
Langley ... 819 .. C 15
Langston ... 1,724 .. E 11
Laverne ... 1,344 .. C 6
Lawrence Creek* ... 149 .. D 12
Lawton○ ... 96,867 .. H 9
Leach† ... 237 .. D 15
Leedey ... 435 .. E 7
Leflore ... 190 .. G 15
Lehigh ... 356 .. H 13
Lela ... D 12
Lenapah ... 293 .. C 14
Lenna ... F 14
Lenora ... D 8
Leon ... 91 .. I 11
Leonard ... E 14
Lequire ... F 15
Lewisville ... F 15
Lexington ... 2,152 .. G 11
Liberty* ... 220 .. E 13
Lima* ... 53 .. F 13
Lindsay ... 2,840 .. G 11
Little ... F 12
Little City ... I 12
Loco ... 122 .. H 10
Locust Grove ... 1,423 .. D 15
Lodi ... G 15
Logan ... C 6
Lone Grove ... 5,054 .. I 11
Lone Wolf ... 438 .. G 8
Long† ... 370 .. E 16
Longdale ... 262 .. D 9
Lookeba ... 166 .. F 9
Lookout ... B 7
Lotsee* ... 2 .. D 13
Loveland ... 13 .. H 8
Lovell ... D 10
Loyal ... 79 .. E 10
Lucien† ... 88 .. D 11
Lugert ... G 7
Lula ... G 13
Luther ... 1,221 .. I 3
Lutie ... G 15
Lyman ... C 12
Lyons ... E 16
Macomb ... 32 .. K 4
Madill○ ... 3,770 .. I 12
Manchester ... 103 .. B 10
Mangum○ ... 3,010 .. G 7
Manitou ... 181 .. H 8
Mannford* ... 3,076 .. D 13
Mannsville ... 863 .. I 12
Maramec ... 91 .. D 12
Marble City ... 263 .. E 16
Marietta○ ... 2,626 .. I 11
Marland ... 225 .. C 11
Marlow ... 4,662 .. H 10
Marshall ... 272 .. D 10
Martha ... 162 .. G 7
Mason ... E 13
Matoy ... I 13
Maud ... 1,048 .. F 12
Maxwell ... G 12
May ... 39 .. C 7
Mayfield ... F 6
Maysville ... 1,232 .. G 11
Mazie ... D 15
McAlester○ ... 18,383 .. G 14
McBride* ... I 12
McCurtain ... 516 .. F 15
McKey† ... F 15
McKnight ... G 6
McLain ... E 15
McLoud ... 4,044 .. J 3
McMan ... H 11
McMillan ... I 12
McQueen ... H 7
McWillie ... C 9
Mead ... 122 .. I 13
Medford○ ... 996 .. C 10
Medicine Park ... 382 .. G 9
Meeker ... 1,144 .. J 4
Meers ... G 9
Mehan ... D 12
Mellette ... F 14
Meno ... 235 .. D 9
Meridian ... 38 .. E 11
Messer ... I 15
Miami○ ... 13,570 .. B 15
Micawber ... E 13
Middleberg ... G 10
Middleton ... B 11
Midlothian ... I 4
Midwest City ... 54,371 .. J 2
Milburn ... 317 .. H 13
Milfay ... E 12
Mill Creek ... 319 .. H 12
Miller ... H 14
Millerton ... 320 .. I 15
Milo ... H 11
Milton ... F 16
Minco ... 1,632 .. F 10
Mocane ... B 6
Moffett ... 128 .. F 16
Monroe ... G 16
Moodys ... D 15
Moore ... 55,081 .. K 2
Mooreland ... 1,190 .. D 8
Moorewood ... E 7
Moravia ... F 7
Morris ... 1,479 .. E 14
Morrison ... 733 .. D 12
Morse ... E 13
Mounds ... 1,168 .. E 13
Mountain Park ... 409 .. G 8
Mountain View ... 795 .. G 8
Moyers ... H 14
Muldrow ... 3,466 .. F 16
Mulhall ... 225 .. D 11
Murphy† ... 219 .. D 15
Muse ... G 16
Muskogee○ ... 39,223 .. E 15
Mustang ... 17,395 .. J 1
Mutual ... 61 .. D 8
Nardin† ... 52 .. C 11
Nash ... 204 .. C 10
Nashoba ... H 15
Natura ... E 14
Navina ... E 11
Nelagoney ... C 13
Nelson ... I 14
New Alluwe ... 90 .. C 14
New Cordell* ... 2,915 .. F 8
New Liberty ... F 7
New Lima ... F 12
New Tulsa ... D 14
New Woodville* ... 132 .. I 12
Newalla ... J 3
Newby ... E 13
Newcastle ... 7,685 .. K 2
Newkirk○ ... 2,317 .. C 11
Newport ... H 11
Nichols Hills ... 3,710 .. J 2
Nicoma Park ... 2,393 .. J 3
Nicut† ... 360 .. E 16
Nida ... I 13
Ninnekah ... 1,002 .. G 10
Noble ... 6,481 .. F 11
Non ... G 13
Norge ... 145 .. G 10
Norman○ ... 110,925 .. F 11
Norris ... G 15
North Enid ... 860 .. D 10
North Miami ... 374 .. B 15
Nowata○ ... 3,731 .. C 14
Oak Grove* ... 18 .. D 12
Oakhurst† ... 2,185 .. D 13
Oakland ... 1,057 .. I 12
Oaks ... 288 .. D 15
Oakwood ... 65 .. E 8
Oberlin ... I 14
Ochelata ... 424 .. C 13
Octavia ... H 16
Oglesby ... C 14
Oil City ... H 11
Oilton ... 1,013 .. D 12
Okarche ... 1,215 .. E 10
Okay ... 620 .. E 15
Okeene ... 1,204 .. D 9
Okemah○ ... 3,223 .. F 13
Okesa ... C 13
Okfuskee ... E 13
Oklahoma City○ ... 579,999 .. F 11
Okmulgee○ ... 12,321 .. E 13
Oktaha ... 390 .. E 14
Oleta ... H 15
Olive ... D 13
Olney ... H 13
Olustee ... 607 .. H 7
Omega ... E 9
Onapa ... F 14
Oneta ... D 14
Oolagah ... 1,146 .. C 14
Optima ... 356 .. C 4
Orienta ... D 9
Orion ... D 8
Orlando ... 148 .. D 11
Orr ... I 11
Osage ... 156 .. D 13
Oscar ... I 10
Ottawa ... B 15
Overbrook ... I 11
Owasso ... 28,915 .. D 14
Paden ... 461 .. F 12
Page ... G 16
Panama ... 1,413 .. F 16
Panola ... G 15
Paoli ... 610 .. G 11
Paradise Hill* ... 85 .. E 16
Park Hill† ... 3,909 .. E 15
Parker ... G 13
Parkland ... E 12
Patterson ... G 15
Pauls Valley○ ... 6,187 .. G 11
Pawhuska○ ... 3,584 .. C 13
Pawnee○ ... 2,196 .. D 12
Payson ... E 12
Pearson ... G 12
Pearsonia ... C 13
Peckham ... C 11
Peek ... E 7
Peggs† ... 813 .. D 15
Pensacola ... 125 .. C 15
Peoria ... 132 .. B 16
Perkins ... 2,831 .. E 12
Pernell ... H 11
Perry○ ... 5,126 .. D 11
Pershing ... C 13
Peterman Ridge* ... D 12
Petersburg ... I 11
Pharoah ... F 13
Phillips ... 135 .. H 13
Picher ... 20 .. B 15
Pickens ... H 15
Piedmont ... 5,720 .. I 1
Pierce ... F 14
Pink ... 2,058 .. K 3
Pittsburg ... 207 .. G 14
Plainview ... C 8
Plainview ... G 7
Platter ... I 13
Pleasant Hill ... I 16
Plunkettville ... H 16
Pocasset ... 156 .. K 1
Pocola* ... 4,056 .. F 16
Ponca City ... 25,387 .. C 11
Pond Creek ... 856 .. C 10
Pontotoc ... H 12
Porter ... 566 .. E 14
Porum ... 727 .. F 15
Poteau○ ... 8,520 .. F 16
Powell ... I 12
Prague ... 2,386 .. F 12
Preston ... E 13
Proctor† ... 231 .. D 16
Prue ... 465 .. D 13
Pruitt City ... H 11
Pryor○ ... D 15
Pryor Creek* ... 9,539 .. D 15
Pumpkin Center ... E 14
Purcell○ ... 5,884 .. G 11
Purdy ... G 11
Putnam ... 29 .. E 8
Pyramid Corners ... C 15
Qualls ... E 15
Quapaw ... 906 .. B 15
Quay ... D 12
Quinlan ... D 8
Quinton ... 1,051 .. F 15
Raiford ... F 14
Ralston ... 330 .. C 12
Ramona ... 535 .. C 13
Randlett ... 438 .. I 9
Ratliff City ... 120 .. H 11
Rattan ... 310 .. H 15
Ravia ... 528 .. H 12
Reagan ... H 12
Reck ... I 11
Red Bird ... 137 .. E 14
Red Oak ... 549 .. G 15
Red Rock ... 283 .. C 11
Redden ... H 14
Redland ... F 16
Reed ... G 7
Reichert ... G 16
Renfrow ... 12 .. B 10
Rentiesville ... 128 .. E 14
Retrop ... F 7
Reydon ... 210 .. E 6
Rhea ... E 8
Richland ... I 1
Rigsby* ... D 12
Ringling ... 1,037 .. I 11
Ringold ... H 15
Ringwood ... 497 .. D 9
Ripley ... 403 .. D 12
Roberta ... I 13
Rock Island ... 646 .. F 16
Rocky ... 162 .. F 8
Roff ... 725 .. H 12
Roland* ... 3,169 .. F 16
Roll ... E 7
Roosevelt ... 248 .. G 8
Rose† ... 285 .. D 15
Rosedale ... 68 .. G 11
Rosston ... 31 .. C 6
Row ... D 16
Rubottom ... I 11
Rufe ... I 15
Rush Springs ... 1,231 .. G 10
Russell ... G 7
Russett ... I 12
Ryan ... 816 .. I 10
Sacred Heart ... G 12
St. Louis ... 158 .. G 12
Salina ... 1,396 .. D 15
Sallisaw○ ... 8,880 .. F 16
Salt Fork ... C 10
Sand Point* ... I 13
Sand Springs ... 18,906 .. D 13
Sapulpa○ ... 20,544 .. D 13
Sasakwa ... 150 .. G 13
Savanna ... 686 .. G 14
Sawyer ... 321 .. I 15
Sayre○ ... 4,375 .. F 7
Schoolton ... F 13
Schulter ... 509 .. F 14
Scipio ... G 14
Scraper† ... 191 .. D 15
Scullyville ... F 16
Seiling ... 860 .. D 8
Selman ... C 7
Seminole ... 7,488 .. F 12
Sentinel ... 901 .. F 8
Seward ... E 11
Shady Point ... 1,026 .. F 16
Shamrock ... 101 .. E 12
Sharon ... 135 .. D 7
Shattuck ... 1,356 .. D 6
Shawnee○ ... 29,857 .. F 12
Shay ... I 12
Sherwood ... H 16
Shidler ... 441 .. C 12
Short† ... 293 .. E 16
Sickles ... F 9
Silo ... 331 .. I 13
Simon ... I 11
Skedee ... 51 .. D 12
Skiatook ... 7,397 .. D 13
Slapout ... C 6
Slaughterville ... 4,137 .. G 11
Slick ... 131 .. E 13
Smith Village ... 66 .. J 2
Smithville ... 113 .. H 16
Snow ... H 15
Snyder ... 1,394 .. H 8
Sobol ... H 15
Soper ... 261 .. I 14
South Coffeyville ... 785 .. B 14
Southard ... D 9
Sparks ... 169 .. E 12
Spaulding ... 178 .. G 13
Spavinaw ... 437 .. C 15
Speer ... I 14
Spencer ... 3,912 .. J 2
Sperry ... 1,206 .. D 13
Spiro ... 2,164 .. F 16
Sportsmen Acres* ... 322 .. D 15
Springer ... 700 .. H 11
Stafford ... F 8
Star ... F 15
Stecker ... G 9
Steedman ... G 12
Stella ... K 3
Sterling ... 793 .. G 9
Stidham ... 18 .. F 14
Stigler○ ... 2,685 .. F 15
Stillwater○ ... 45,688 .. D 11
Stilwell○ ... 3,949 .. E 16
Stonebluff ... E 14
Stonewall ... 470 .. G 13
Story ... G 11
Strang ... 89 .. C 15
Stratford ... 1,525 .. G 12
Stringtown ... 410 .. H 13
Strong City ... 47 .. E 7
Stroud ... 2,690 .. E 12
Stuart ... 180 .. G 13
Sugden ... 43 .. I 10
Sulphur○ ... 4,929 .. H 12
Summerfield ... G 15
Summit ... 139 .. E 14
Sumner ... D 11
Sunray ... H 10
Sweetwater ... 87 .. F 6
Tabler ... G 10
Taft* ... 250 .. E 14
Tahlequah○ ... 15,753 .. E 15
Tahona ... F 16
Talala ... 273 .. C 14
Talihina ... 1,114 .. G 15
Tallant ... C 13
Taloga○ ... 299 .. D 8
Tamaha ... 176 .. F 15
Tangier ... D 7
Tatums ... 151 .. H 11
Taylor ... H 10
Tecumseh ... 6,457 .. K 4
Tegarden ... C 8
Temple ... 1,002 .. H 9
Teresita† ... 159 .. D 15
Terlton ... 106 .. D 12
Terral ... 382 .. I 10
Texanna† ... 2,261 .. F 14
Texhoma ... 926 .. C 3
Texola ... 36 .. F 6
Thackerville ... 445 .. I 11
Thomas ... 1,181 .. E 8
Tiawah† ... 189 .. D 14
Timberlane* ... D 12
Tipton ... 847 .. H 8
Tishomingo○ ... 3,034 .. H 12
Tom ... I 16
Tonkawa ... 3,216 .. C 11
Tribbey ... 391 .. F 12
Trousdale ... G 12
Troy ... H 12
Tryon ... 491 .. E 12
Tullahassee ... 106 .. E 14
Tulsa○ ... 391,906 .. D 13
Tupelo ... 329 .. H 13
Turley† ... 2,756 .. D 13
Turpin† ... 467 .. C 5
Tushka ... 312 .. H 13
Tuskahoma† ... 151 .. G 15
Tuskegee ... E 13
Tuttle ... 6,019 .. K 1
Tyrone ... 762 .. B 4
Unger ... I 14
Union City ... 1,645 .. J 1
Utica ... I 13
Valley Brook ... 765 .. J 2
Valley Park* ... 77 .. D 14
Valliant ... 754 .. I 15
Vamoosa ... G 12
Vanoss ... G 12
Velma ... 620 .. H 10
Vera ... 241 .. C 14
Verden ... 530 .. G 10
Verdigris ... 3,993 .. D 14
Vernon ... F 14
Vian ... 1,466 .. E 15
Vici ... 699 .. D 7
Victory ... H 7
Village, The ... 8,929 .. I 2
Vinita○ ... 5,743 .. C 15
Vinson ... G 6
Vivian ... F 14
Wade ... I 13
Wagoner○ ... 8,323 .. D 15
Wainwright* ... 165 .. E 14
Wakita ... 344 .. C 10
Wallville ... G 11
Walters○ ... 2,551 .. H 9
Wanette ... 350 .. G 12
Wann ... 125 .. B 14
Wapanucka ... 438 .. H 13
Wardville ... G 13
Warner ... 1,641 .. F 15
Warr Acres ... 10,043 .. J 2
Warren ... G 8
Warwick ... 148 .. I 4
Washington ... 618 .. G 11
Watonga○ ... 5,111 .. E 9
Watova ... C 14
Watson ... H 16
Watts ... 324 .. D 16
Wauhillau† ... 345 .. E 16
Waukomis ... 1,286 .. D 10
Waurika○ ... 2,064 .. I 10
Wayne ... 688 .. G 11
Waynoka ... 927 .. C 8
Weatherford ... 10,833 .. F 8
Webb ... E 8
Webb City ... 62 .. C 12
Webbers Falls ... 616 .. E 15
Welch ... 619 .. B 15
Weleetka ... 998 .. F 13
Welling† ... 771 .. E 15
Wellston ... 788 .. I 4
Welty ... E 13
West Siloam Springs* ... 846 .. D 16
Westport* ... 298 .. D 13
Westville ... 1,639 .. D 16
Wetumka ... 1,282 .. F 13
Wewoka○ ... 3,430 .. F 13
Wheeless ... C 1
White Bead ... G 11
White Oak† ... 263 .. C 15
Whitefield ... 391 .. F 15
Whitesboro† ... 250 .. G 16
Wilburton○ ... 2,843 .. G 15
Wild Horse ... D 13
Willis ... I 12
Willow ... 149 .. G 7
Wilson ... 1,724 .. I 11
Winchester* ... 516 .. E 13
Wirt ... H 11
Wister ... 1,102 .. G 16
Wolco ... C 13
Wolf ... G 12
Woodford ... H 11
Woodlawn Park* ... 153 .. F 10
Woods ... J 3
Woodville ... I 12
Woodward○ ... 12,051 .. D 7
Wright City ... 762 .. I 15
Wyandotte ... 333 .. C 16
Wye ... K 4
Wynnewood ... 2,212 .. H 11
Wynona ... 437 .. C 13
Yale ... 1,227 .. D 12
Yanush ... G 15
Yarnaby ... I 13
Yeager ... 75 .. F 13
Yewed ... C 9
Yonkers ... D 15
Yost ... D 12
Yuba ... I 13
Yukon ... 22,709 .. J 1
Zafra ... H 16
Zena† ... 122 .. C 15
Zoe ... G 16

*Does not appear on the map; key shows general location.
†Census designated place—unincorporated, but recognized as a significant settled community by the U.S. Census Bureau.

○County seat.
Places without population figures are unincorporated areas.
Source: 2010 census.

Visitor's guide

Will Rogers, the famous Oklahoma cowboy humorist, once said: "There ought to be a law against anybody going to Europe until they have seen the things we have in this country." Rogers may have been thinking of some of the scenic spots in his home state. Oklahoma's attractions include beautiful lakes, rugged terrain, prairie vistas, and striking modern buildings. A statue at the Will

Rogers Memorial Museum, in Claremore, bears his famous statement: "I never met a man I didn't like."

Many Oklahoma towns and cities hold annual festivals that celebrate local history, food, and cultures. One of the most famous annual events in Oklahoma is the *Trail of Tears* (1969) outdoor drama. This play takes place in an amphitheater in Tahlequah.

Oklahoma Tourism

Will Rogers Memorial in Claremore

AP Photo

***Trail of Tears* outdoor drama in Tahlequah**

Places to visit

Following are brief descriptions of some of Oklahoma's many interesting places to visit:

Arbuckle Wilderness, in Davis, is an exotic animal park. Wild, exotic, and rare animals roam in habitats similar to their own.

Bricktown District, in Oklahoma City, is a popular entertainment and dining area. Visitors can enjoy numerous restaurants, nightclubs, and shops.

Cherokee Heritage Center, southeast of Tahlequah, includes the Tsa-La-Gi Ancient Village, a re-creation of an Indian village. Cherokee Indians give tours during the summer months.

Fort Sill, a military center near Lawton, includes three historical sites—Stone Corral, Old Guardhouse, and an artillery museum. The fort was established in 1869.

Gilcrease Museum, in Tulsa, is an art gallery and library. It houses a huge collection of art of the American West.

National Cowboy & Western Heritage Museum, in Oklahoma City, displays art, artifacts, and memorabilia of the American West. The center includes the Rodeo Hall of Fame and a re-creation of an old pioneer town.

National Wrestling Hall of Fame, in Stillwater, has a hall of fame, a collection of memorabilia highlighting the sport's history, and a library.

Oklahoma City Museum of Art, in Oklahoma City, displays

paintings, sculptures, photographs, and decorative arts from Asia, Europe, and the United States.

Oklahoma City National Memorial, in Oklahoma City, honors the victims, survivors, and rescuers of the bombing of the Murrah Federal Building in 1995.

Oklahoma History Center, at the Capitol Complex in Oklahoma City, has numerous exhibits on the state's history.

Will Rogers Memorial Museum, in Claremore, tells the life story of Will Rogers through paintings, manuscripts, and other personal belongings. Rogers is buried at the site.

Woolaroc Museum & Wildlife Preserve, southwest of Bartlesville, displays thousands of historical artifacts. Much of its collection deals with the history of the Southwest.

National Recreation Area and Forest. The Chickasaw National Recreation Area lies in south-central Oklahoma. The area has public campgrounds, and facilities for swimming and boating at the Lake of the Arbuckles. Two sections of the Ouachita National Forest are in southeastern Oklahoma.

State parks. Oklahoma has dozens of state parks and resorts that offer a wealth of water sports, hiking, camping, and other recreational activities. For more information, visit the official website of the Oklahoma Tourism & Recreation Department at http://www.TravelOK.com/state_parks.

The grave of Apache chief Geronimo at Fort Sill

Professional basketball's Oklahoma City Thunder

International Finals Rodeo in Oklahoma City

**National Cowboy & Western Heritage
Museum in Oklahoma City**

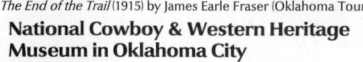

**Little Sahara State Park
near Waynoka**

Land regions. Oklahoma has 10 main land regions. These regions are (1) the Ozark Plateau, (2) the Prairie Plains, (3) the Ouachita Mountains, (4) the Sandstone Hills, (5) the Arbuckle Mountains, (6) the Wichita Mountains, (7) the Red River Region, (8) the Red Beds Plains, (9) the Gypsum Hills, and (10) the High Plains.

The Ozark Plateau extends into the northeastern part of Oklahoma from Missouri and Arkansas. This hilly region has swift streams and steep-sided river valleys. The areas between the river valleys are broad and flat. Bluffs have been formed where streams cut into the plateau.

The Prairie Plains include the land west and south of the Ozark Plateau. Farming and cattle ranching are the most important activities in this region. The Arkansas River Valley, east of Muskogee, produces such pasture crops as alfalfa and hay. Much of the area's cultivated land also produces corn, soybeans, and nursery products. Much of the state's coal comes from this region.

The Ouachita Mountains rise in the southeastern part of the state on the border between Oklahoma and Arkansas. These mountains are a series of high sandstone ridges that form the roughest land surface in Oklahoma. The ridges run in a general east-west direction. They include Blue Bouncer, Buffalo, Jackfork, Kiamichi, Rich, and Winding Stair. The timber industry and poultry farms are major contributors to the region's economy.

The Sandstone Hills region extends south from the border with Kansas to near the Red River in southern Oklahoma. It is a region of hills 250 to 400 feet (76 to 120 meters) high. Many areas are covered with blackjack and post oak forests. Much of the early Oklahoma oil development took place in these hills. The Sandstone Hills region still has important oil fields. Ranching is also important there.

The Arbuckle Mountains are wedged into an area of 1,000 square miles (2,600 square kilometers) in south-central Oklahoma. Millions of years ago, these were tall mountains. Erosion has worn them down until they now rise only 600 to 700 feet (180 to 210 meters) above the surrounding plains. The erosion uncovered unusual rock formations that are often studied by geology students. The principal formations of this region include conglomerates, granite, limestone, sandstone, and shale. Ranchers use the land to raise cattle.

The Wichita Mountains are rough granite peaks in southwestern Oklahoma. The region has a number of small artificial lakes. These lakes were created by damming the mountain streams to provide water for the irrigation of cotton fields. Such lakes remain important for recreational use. The Fort Sill military reservation and a federal wildlife refuge lie mostly within the Wichita Mountains region.

The Red River Region is a rolling prairie and forest

© David G. Fitzgerald

Rugged mesas rise in the Oklahoma Panhandle, which forms part of the High Plains region of northwestern Oklahoma. The rest of this region consists mainly of level grassland.

Land regions of Oklahoma

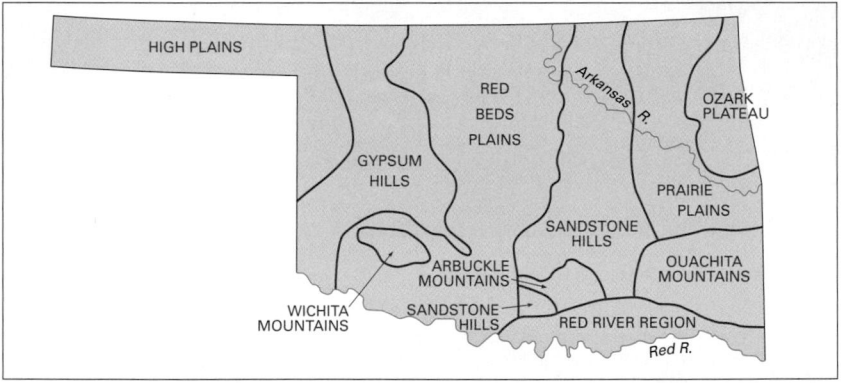

WORLD BOOK map

Map index

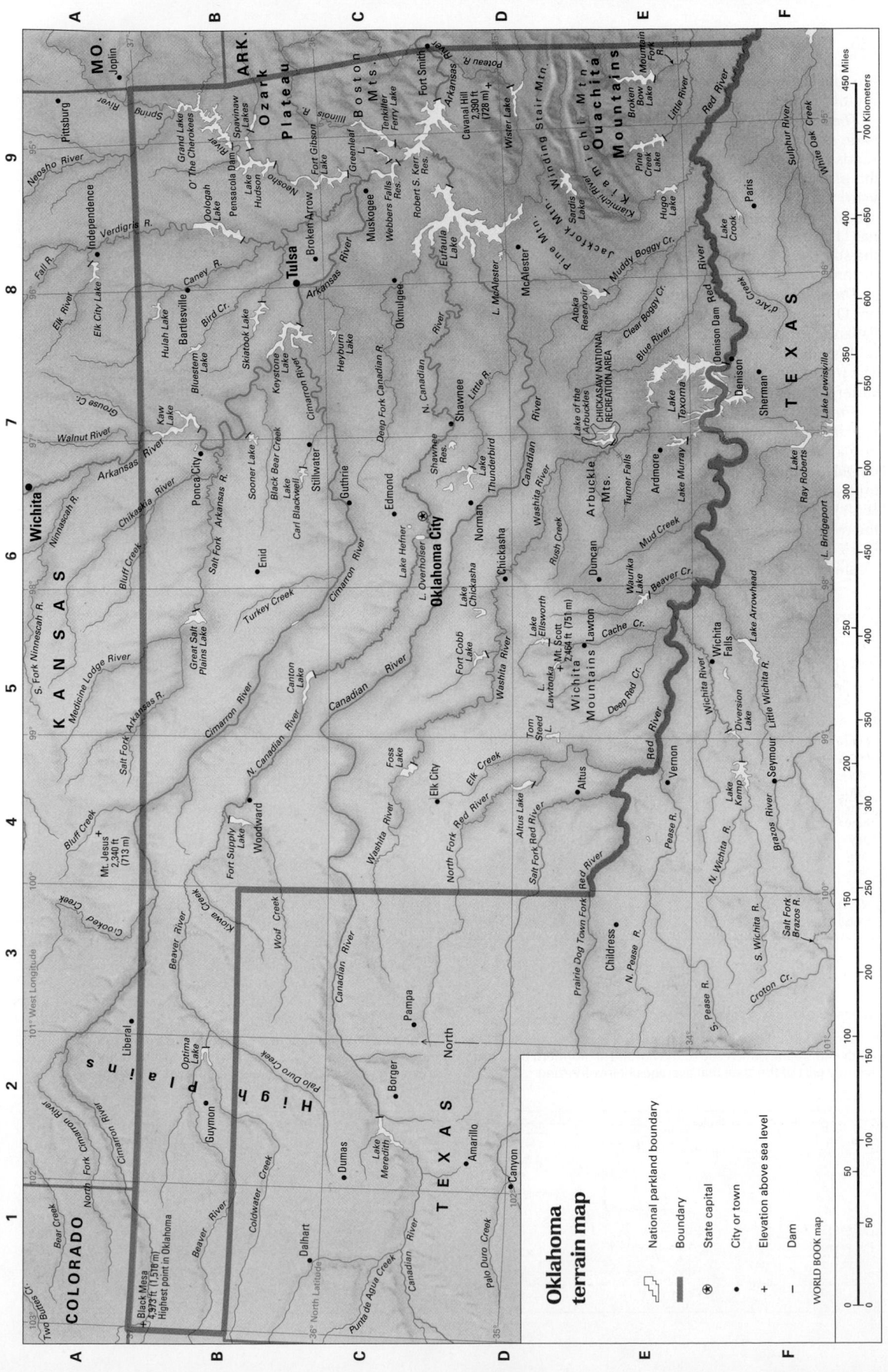

Oklahoma
terrain map

	National parkland boundary
▬	Boundary
⊛	State capital
•	City or town
+	Elevation above sea level
−	Dam

WORLD BOOK map

area. Much of the soil is sandy and fertile. Farmers in the region grow cotton, peanuts, and vegetables.

The Red Beds Plains extend from Kansas to Texas in a wide sweep through the middle of Oklahoma. Soft red sandstone and shale lie under the soil. This gently rolling plain, Oklahoma's largest land region, slopes downward from west to east. The eastern part has woodland areas, and the western part is mostly grassy. The region has fairly fertile soil. Farmers grow cotton and wheat in the southwestern part. Oil fields have been developed in some parts of the Red Beds Plains.

The Gypsum Hills is an area of varied terrain in western Oklahoma. The region includes rolling sand dunes, flatlands, and isolated tablelands of small mesas and buttes called the Glass (pronounced *glahs)* Mountains. The mountains are named for the crystals of *selenite*—a variety of the mineral gypsum—that cover their surface.

The High Plains, an area of level grassland, occupy the state's northwestern section, which includes Oklahoma's Panhandle. The Panhandle is the western portion of Oklahoma, a strip of land 166 miles (267 kilometers) long and 34 miles (55 kilometers) wide. The land of the High Plains rises from about 2,000 feet (610 meters) on the region's eastern edge to 4,973 feet (1,516 meters) at Black Mesa, the highest point in Oklahoma, in the northwestern corner of the state.

Oklahoma Tourism

Turner Falls tumbles 77 feet (23 meters) into Honey Creek in the Arbuckle Mountains region of south-central Oklahoma. Erosion has created unusual rock formations in this region.

Average monthly weather

Oklahoma City					Tulsa				
	Temperatures			Days of rain or snow		Temperatures			Days of rain or snow
	°F		°C			°F		°C	
	High	Low	High	Low		High	Low	High	Low	
Jan.	47	26	8	–3	5	Jan.	47	26	8	–3	6
Feb.	54	31	12	–1	6	Feb.	53	31	12	–1	7
Mar.	63	39	17	4	7	Mar.	62	40	17	4	8
Apr.	71	48	22	9	8	Apr.	72	50	22	10	9
May	79	58	26	14	10	May	80	59	27	15	11
June	87	66	31	19	9	June	88	68	31	20	9
July	93	71	34	22	6	July	94	73	34	23	6
Aug.	93	70	34	21	6	Aug.	93	71	34	22	7
Sept.	84	62	29	17	7	Sept.	84	63	29	17	7
Oct.	73	51	23	11	7	Oct.	74	51	23	11	7
Nov.	60	38	16	3	6	Nov.	60	39	16	4	7
Dec.	50	29	10	–2	6	Dec.	50	30	10	–1	7

Average yearly precipitation

Oklahoma has wide differences in precipitation. The amount of precipitation decreases from the eastern to the western part of the state. Most of the snow falls in northwestern Oklahoma.

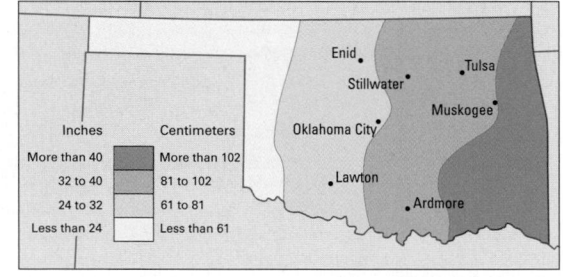

Inches	Centimeters
More than 40	More than 102
32 to 40	81 to 102
24 to 32	61 to 81
Less than 24	Less than 61

Average January temperatures

Oklahoma has mild winters. The temperatures are highest in the south and steadily decrease to the north. The northern border is the only part of the state that averages below freezing.

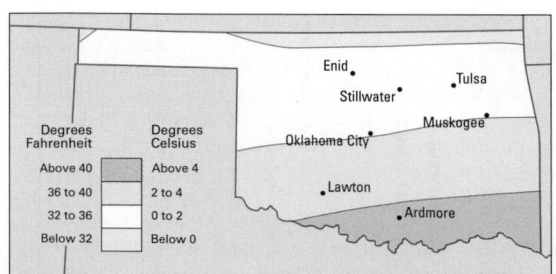

Degrees Fahrenheit	Degrees Celsius
Above 40	Above 4
36 to 40	2 to 4
32 to 36	0 to 2
Below 32	Below 0

Average July temperatures

Oklahoma has hot summers with little variation in temperatures throughout the state. The northeastern corner and the Panhandle area to the west have the coolest summer temperatures.

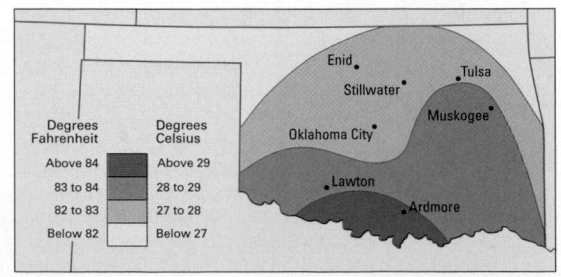

Degrees Fahrenheit	Degrees Celsius
Above 84	Above 29
83 to 84	28 to 29
82 to 83	27 to 28
Below 82	Below 27

WORLD BOOK maps

Rivers and lakes. Oklahoma is drained by two great river systems—the Red and the Arkansas. These systems carry water from the state's rivers and streams eastward to the Mississippi River, which empties into the Gulf of Mexico. The winding Red River forms Oklahoma's southern boundary with Texas. Its main tributaries drain southern Oklahoma. These streams include the Blue, Kiamichi, Little, Mountain Fork, and Washita rivers; Cache Creek; and the North Fork of the Red River.

The Arkansas River flows through northeastern Oklahoma. Its principal southern tributaries flow in a broad, irregular semicircle across the entire width of the state. These include the Canadian, North Canadian, and Cimarron rivers. The Chikaskia, Illinois, Neosho (or Grand), Poteau, Salt Fork, and Verdigris rivers, which drain northern and eastern Oklahoma, are also important branches.

Oklahoma has more than 200 artificially created lakes and about 100 small natural lakes. Lake Texoma, covering 91,200 acres (36,910 hectares), is the most popular resort center. Part of it lies in Texas. Grand Lake O' The Cherokees is in northeastern Oklahoma. It backs up the waters of the Neosho River for 65 miles (105 kilometers). Lake Eufaula, in the east-central portion, covers over 100,000 acres (40,000 hectares). Fort Gibson Lake, Greenleaf Lake, Lower Spavinaw Lake, Upper Spavinaw Lake, Tenkiller Ferry Lake, and Lake Wister are in eastern Oklahoma. They have resorts for fishing and boating. Other lakes and reservoirs in Oklahoma include Altus, Canton, Ellsworth, Fort Supply, Foss, Great Salt Plains, Heyburn, Keystone, Lawtonka, Murray, and Oologah.

Plant and animal life. Forests cover about a fifth of Oklahoma. Important trees include ashes, elms, hickories, oaks, pines, sweet gums, and walnut trees. The main commercial forests are in southeastern Oklahoma.

Prairie grasses in the state provide grazing for millions of cattle. Among these grasses are bluestems, Indian grass, sand grass, and the shorter buffalo grass, grama, and wire grass. Other common prairie plants are mesquite and sagebrush. Dogwoods and redbuds grow in the east, central, and southern areas. Anemones, goldenrods, wild indigos, petunias, phlox, primroses, spiderworts, sunflowers, black-eyed Susans, verbena, and violets grow in all regions of Oklahoma.

Armadillos, coyotes, prairie dogs, and rabbits are common on the plains of Oklahoma. Forest animals include deer, opossums, raccoons, foxes, and gray and fox squirrels. Common birds in the state include blue jays, cardinals, crows, doves, meadowlarks, mockingbirds, robins, scissor-tailed flycatchers, and house sparrows. Fishes in Oklahoma's waters include bass, buffalo fish, carp, catfish, crappie, drumfish, paddlefish, and sunfish.

The Oklahoma Department of Wildlife Conservation serves a large population of active hunters and fishing enthusiasts. Significant game species include whitetail deer, turkey, and quail. Catfish, hatchery-raised trout, and several kinds of bass are popular sportfishing species.

Climate. Most of Oklahoma has a warm, dry climate. Northwestern Oklahoma is cooler and drier than the southeastern part. Precipitation varies greatly throughout the state. Average precipitation ranges from 50 inches (130 centimeters) a year in the southeast to 15 inches (38 centimeters) in the western Panhandle. Snowfall ranges from about 2 inches (5 centimeters) a year in the southeast to 25 inches (64 centimeters) in the northwest. The Panhandle gets the most snow.

The average July temperature in Oklahoma is 82 °F (28 °C), and the average January temperature is 37 °F (3 °C). The state's highest temperature, 120 °F (49 °C), was recorded on four occasions during the summer of 1936—at Alva on July 18, at Altus on July 19 and August 12, and at Poteau on August 10. The same figure was reached at Tishomingo on July 26, 1943, and at Tipton on June 27, 1994. The record low temperature, −27 °F (−33 °C), was registered at two locations—at Vinita on Feb. 13, 1905, and at Watts on Jan. 18, 1930.

Economy

Service industries account for the largest part of Oklahoma's *gross domestic product*—the total value of goods and services produced in the state in a year. Manufacturing and mining are also important. Machinery is the leading manufactured product. Oklahoma ranks as a leading producer of natural gas and petroleum. Beef cattle are the leading farm product.

Natural resources. Oklahoma has vast reserves of minerals and large areas of fertile soils. Its mineral wealth includes petroleum and natural gas. Large supplies of water and a favorable climate combine with rich soils to make Oklahoma a major food producer.

Minerals. The state's oil reserves are among the largest in the nation. Natural gas is also present in most of the oil fields. Deposits of natural gas and petroleum have been found in nearly every county in Oklahoma.

Small beds of coal lie in the east-central and northeastern parts of the state. The eastern part also has clays and stone. Other mineral resources include gypsum, iodine, limestone, salt, and sand and gravel. The natural gas of the Panhandle contains helium.

Soil varies from the fertile deposits in the river valleys to the unproductive shale and granite of the mountains. Much of the plains and grasslands area has a rich, productive soil. Other areas have poor red clay soil.

Service industries account for the largest portion of both Oklahoma's employment and its gross domestic product. Most service industries are concentrated in the Oklahoma City and Tulsa metropolitan areas.

Oklahoma City and Tulsa are the state's chief financial and insurance centers. Most hotels, restaurants, and retail trade establishments are also in the Oklahoma City and Tulsa areas. Oklahoma City, the state capital, is the center of government activities. The University of Oklahoma Health Sciences Center in Oklahoma City is one of the nation's leading medical facilities. Tinker Air Force Base, near Oklahoma City, is a major employer in the state. Several rental car companies are headquartered in Tulsa. American Airlines also has a large facility there.

Some service industries are dedicated to Oklahoma's oil production. The wholesale trade of oil and gas is important in the state. Pipeline companies transport the state's huge oil and gas production. Companies that rent oil field equipment are also important to Oklahoma.

Oklahoma economy

General economy

Gross domestic product (GDP)* (2008) $151,406,000,000
  Rank among U.S. states   29th
Unemployment rate (2010)   6.8% (U.S. avg: 9.6%)

*Gross domestic product is the total value of goods and services produced in a year.
Sources: U.S. Bureau of Economic Analysis and U.S. Bureau of Labor Statistics.

Agriculture

Cash receipts $4,844,882,000
  Rank among U.S. states   23rd
Distribution   74% livestock, 26% crops
Farms   86,500
Farm acres (hectares)   35,100,000 (14,200,000)
  Rank among U.S. states   8th
Farmland   78% of Oklahoma

Leading products

1. Cattle and calves
2. Broilers
3. Hogs
4. Wheat
5. Greenhouse and nursery products
Other products: corn, cotton, dairy products, eggs, hay,
  sorghum grain, soybeans.

Manufacturing

Value added by manufacture* $26,933,513,000
  Rank among U.S. states   29th

Leading products

1. Machinery
2. Petroleum and coal products
3. Fabricated metal products
4. Food products
5. Transportation equipment
Other products: chemicals, plastics and rubber products.

*Value added by manufacture is the increase in value of raw materials after they
  become finished products.

Electric power

Coal   47.5%
Natural gas   44.2%
Other   8.3%

Production and workers by economic activities

Economic activities	Percent of GDP produced	Employed workers Number of people	Employed workers Percent of total
Community, business, & personal services	17	634,600	29
Government	17	363,800	16
Finance, insurance, & real estate	15	183,200	8
Trade, restaurants, & hotels	13	426,600	19
Mining	13	95,100	4
Manufacturing	12	159,000	7
Transportation & communication	6	98,400	4
Construction	4	133,700	6
Agriculture	2	100,600	5
Utilities	2	11,300	1
Total*	100	2,206,300	100

*Figures do not add up to 100 percent due to rounding.
Figures are for 2008; employment figures include full- and part-time workers.
Source: World Book estimates based on data from U.S. Bureau of Economic Analysis.

Mining

Nonfuel mineral production $810,000,000
  Rank among U.S. states   27th
Coal (tons*)   1,463,000
  Rank among U.S. states   22nd
Crude oil (barrels†)   64,065,000
  Rank among U.S. states   5th
Natural gas (cubic feet‡)   1,913,029,000,000
  Rank among U.S. states   3rd

*One ton equals 0.9072 metric ton.
†One barrel equals 42 gallons (159 liters).
‡One cubic foot equals 0.0283 cubic meter.

Leading products

1. Natural gas   (ranks 3rd in U.S.)
2. Petroleum   (ranks 5th in U.S.)
3. Limestone
4. Portland cement
Other products: gypsum, iodine, sand and gravel.

Figures are for 2008, except for the agricultural figures, which are for 2009.
Sources: U.S. Census Bureau, U.S. Department of Agriculture, U.S. Energy Information
  Administration, U.S. Geological Survey.

Economy of Oklahoma

This map shows the economic uses of land in Oklahoma and where the state's leading farm and mineral products are produced. Major manufacturing centers are shown in red.

Mostly cropland

Woodland mixed with cropland

Grazing land mixed with cropland

Grazing land mixed with shrubland

Mostly forest land

•   Manufacturing center
•   Mineral deposit

WORLD BOOK map

Karl Kummels, Shostal

An oil derrick rises from the Oklahoma plains, symbolizing the importance of petroleum to the state's economy. Oklahoma ranks among the leading oil-producing states.

© Louie Psihoyos, Corbis

The manufacture and repair of transportation equipment contribute significantly to Oklahoma's economy. This worker is retrieving parts at an airplane repair facility near Oklahoma City.

Manufacturing. Much of Oklahoma's manufacturing is dedicated to processing its agricultural and mining products. Dozens of meat-packing plants operate in the state. Bakery goods are also made in Oklahoma. Large oil refineries operate in Ardmore, Ponca City, Tulsa, and Wynnewood. Several cities make oil field machinery.

Fabricated metal products, machinery, and transportation equipment are primarily made in the Oklahoma City and Tulsa areas. Fabricated metal products include heat exchangers and machine shop products. Machinery products include construction machinery, engines and turbines, and refrigeration and heating equipment. Buses, motor vehicle parts, and trucks are important transportation products made in the state. Plants in Tulsa make aircraft and aerospace equipment. Factories in

Ardmore and Lawton produce tires.

Mining. Natural gas and petroleum are Oklahoma's leading mineral products by far. Oklahoma ranks among the leading states in both natural gas and petroleum production. The heaviest natural gas production occurs in the western part of the state. Central Oklahoma is the leading area for petroleum production.

Oklahoma is a leading producer of gypsum. Other mineral products include coal, crushed stone, iodine, and sand and gravel. Most coal is produced in eastern Oklahoma. Limestone quarries in northeast and south-central Oklahoma provide much of the crushed stone. Oklahoma is the only state that produces iodine. It is mainly produced in the northwest part of the state as a by-product of oil field brine. Sand and gravel come mainly from pits near Oklahoma City and Tulsa.

Agriculture. Farmland covers about three-fourths of Oklahoma. The production of beef cattle is the leading source of agricultural income, and Oklahoma is one of the country's most important sources of beef. Ranchers throughout Oklahoma raise beef cattle. Other important livestock income comes from *broilers* (young, tender chickens), hogs, and milk. Oklahoma's farmers raise broilers in the eastern portion of the state. Hogs are primarily raised in the Panhandle. Dairy farms are found in Grady County and in the northeastern and southwestern portions of the state.

Winter wheat is the state's most valuable field crop, and Oklahoma is a leading wheat-growing state. Most wheat is produced in the Panhandle and in the southwestern portion of the state. Hay ranks second in value among Oklahoma's field crops. Oklahoma is the leading producer of rye. The state's other important crops include corn, cotton, grain sorghum, oats, peaches, peanuts, pecans, and soybeans. Greenhouse and nursery products are an important source of income.

Tom McHugh, Photo Researchers

Beef cattle graze in a field of tall grass near Cleo Springs. The production of beef cattle is Oklahoma's leading source of agricultural income.

Electric power and utilities. Coal-burning plants and plants that burn natural gas supply the majority of Oklahoma's electric power. Hydroelectric plants in the eastern part of Oklahoma and wind power plants in the western part of the state provide much of the remaining power.

Transportation. Oklahoma has hundreds of thousands of miles of roads and highways. The state has an extensive system of toll highways, including the Turner Turnpike, which links Oklahoma City and Tulsa.

Freight railroads operate on thousands of miles of rail line in Oklahoma. The state's first railroad was the Missouri-Kansas-Texas Railroad, called the "Katy." It was built across Oklahoma to Denison, Texas, from 1870 to 1872. Passenger trains connect Oklahoma City with Fort Worth, Texas. Oklahoma City and Tulsa have the state's major commercial airports. Muskogee and the Tulsa Port of Catoosa are Oklahoma's chief ports. The McClellan-Kerr Arkansas River Navigation System links these two port cities with Mississippi River ports.

Pipelines carry Oklahoma's oil, natural gas, and refined products to other states. Most of the pipelines run through central Oklahoma from southwest to northeast.

Communication. Oklahoma's first newspaper, the *Cherokee Advocate,* was published in Tahlequah in 1844. It was printed in both English and Cherokee. Today, the largest newspapers are *The Oklahoman* of Oklahoma City and the *Tulsa World.*

Government

Constitution. The Oklahoma Constitution was adopted in 1907, the year Oklahoma became a state. It may be amended by a majority vote of the people. Amendments may be proposed by the Legislature or by petitions from the voters. A constitutional convention may be called by the Legislature, subject to voter approval. The Constitution contains initiative and referendum clauses that allow the voters to propose and pass laws directly (see Initiative and referendum).

Executive. The governor is elected to a four-year term. The governor may serve an unlimited number of terms, but not more than two terms in a row. The governor appoints the secretary of state and the heads of the chief revenue and budget departments. Some department heads are chosen by a board or by a commission. The lieutenant governor, attorney general, treasurer, auditor and inspector, superintendent of public instruction, insurance commissioner, labor commissioner, and corporation commissioners are all elected to serve four-year terms.

Legislature of Oklahoma consists of a Senate with 48 members and a House of Representatives with 101 members. Each senator and representative is elected from a separate district. Senators are elected to four-year terms and representatives to two-year terms. Each senator and representative is limited to no more than 12 total years of elected service as a state legislator. The Legislature meets in annual sessions that begin on the first Monday in February. In odd-numbered years, the Legislature also meets on the first Tuesday after the first Monday in January to verify election results.

Courts. The Oklahoma Supreme Court has nine justices. They select a chief justice from their group. The governor appoints the justices with the advice of a judicial nominating commission. At the first general election following the appointment, voters decide on nonpartisan ballots whether to retain or dismiss the justice. A vote of retention means the justice may then serve a six-year term. The state also has a Court of Civil Appeals with at least 12 judges and a Court of Criminal Appeals with 5 judges. All of these judges are chosen in the same way that Supreme Court justices are selected.

Local government in Oklahoma operates in 77

Oklahoma Capitol
The Oklahoma House of Representatives meets in the House chambers in the State Capitol in Oklahoma City.

The governors of Oklahoma

	Party	Term
Charles N. Haskell	Democratic	1907-1911
Lee Cruce	Democratic	1911-1915
R. L. Williams	Democratic	1915-1919
James B. A. Robertson	Democratic	1919-1923
John C. Walton	Democratic	1923
Martin E. Trapp	Democratic	1923-1927
Henry S. Johnston	Democratic	1927-1929
William J. Holloway	Democratic	1929-1931
William H. Murray	Democratic	1931-1935
Ernest W. Marland	Democratic	1935-1939
Leon C. Phillips	Democratic	1939-1943
Robert S. Kerr	Democratic	1943-1947
Roy J. Turner	Democratic	1947-1951
Johnston Murray	Democratic	1951-1955
Raymond D. Gary	Democratic	1955-1959
J. Howard Edmondson	Democratic	1959-1963
George Nigh	Democratic	1963
Henry Bellmon	Republican	1963-1967
Dewey F. Bartlett	Republican	1967-1971
David Hall	Democratic	1971-1975
David L. Boren	Democratic	1975-1979
George Nigh	Democratic	1979-1987
Henry Bellmon	Republican	1987-1991
David Walters	Democratic	1991-1995
Frank Keating	Republican	1995-2003
Brad Henry	Democratic	2003-2011
Mary Fallin	Republican	2011-

counties and about 600 cities and towns. The counties have three commissioners, each elected from a separate district. Most cities and towns use the mayor-council or council-manager form of government. Larger cities can adopt and amend their own charters and thus can take some control over their affairs.

Revenue. State taxes, including money from licenses, permits, and fees, provide about half of the state government's *general revenue* (income). Major sources of tax revenue include a personal income tax, a sales tax, and a severance tax on petroleum and natural gas production. Most of the rest of the revenue comes from bond sales and U.S. government programs.

Politics. Oklahoma was once almost solidly Democratic. The state began to develop a two-party system during the 1960's. Oklahoma voters elected the state's first Republican governor in 1962. Oklahomans have favored Republican candidates in most presidential elections held since 1948. For Oklahoma's voting record in presidential elections, see **Electoral College** (table).

History

Early days. Before white people came, bands of American Indians roamed the plains of the region that now includes Oklahoma. The Indians followed the huge herds of buffalo that grazed on the grasslands. The tribes included the Plains Apache, Caddo, Comanche, Kiowa, Osage, Pawnee, and Wichita.

Europeans first reached the Oklahoma region in 1541. That year, the Spanish explorer Francisco Vásquez de Coronado led an expedition from Tiguex, New Mexico. He reached what is now Oklahoma. Later the same year, Hernando de Soto, another Spaniard, probably entered the area. Both Coronado and De Soto were searching for gold, but they found none.

In 1682, the French explorer Robert Cavelier, Sieur de La Salle, traveled down the Mississippi River. He did not reach the Oklahoma area. However, he claimed for France all the land drained by the Mississippi, including the Oklahoma region. Soon afterward, other French explorers—notably Bernard de La Harpe—and traders entered the Oklahoma area.

American ownership. France claimed the Oklahoma region as part of Louisiana until 1762, when France ceded Louisiana to Spain. Napoleon I regained the province for France in 1800, but he needed money to fight wars in Europe. In 1803, he sold Louisiana to the United States (see **Louisiana Purchase**).

Congress reorganized the administration of Louisiana several times. The section that included present-day Oklahoma was first called the District of Louisiana. In 1805, it became the Louisiana Territory. Seven years later, in 1812, the Missouri Territory was organized from the Louisiana Territory. In 1819, the United States settled several boundary disputes with Spain. As a result, the present Oklahoma Panhandle, one of the disputed areas, was given to Spain. The rest of Oklahoma became part of the Arkansas Territory, which was created in 1819. Miller Court House (in present-day McCurtain County), Salina, and Three Forks were among the first white settlements established in Oklahoma.

The Indian nations. After 1819, the federal government began prodding the Indian tribes in the southeastern United States to move to the Oklahoma area. The tribes—the Cherokee, Chickasaw, Choctaw, Creek, and Seminole—had lived in close contact with white people for more than a hundred years. They adopted many of the habits and customs of the whites, and they became known as the Five Civilized Tribes.

In the early 1800's, Oklahoma was largely unoccupied. In 1824, to prepare the area for the Indian migration, the U.S. Army built Fort Towson and Fort Gibson. The government soon forced the five tribes to give up most of their eastern lands and begin the move west.

Between 1830 and 1842, sad processions of Indians moved into the hills and grasslands of eastern Oklahoma. Thousands died along the way. The Indians who moved included the Cherokee, who called their own trip the *Trail of Tears.* This term is sometimes used to refer to the removal of the other tribes as well.

The immigrant Indians were given the right to all of present-day Oklahoma except the Panhandle. Each of the five tribes formed a nation. By treaties, the United States promised to protect the Indian nations. The government guaranteed that the Indians would own their lands "as long as grass shall grow and rivers run." Each Indian nation established its own legislature, courts, and written laws, and each built its own capital. Most settlements were in the eastern part of the region.

After the first hard years, the Indians began to build schools and churches, clear land, and operate farms and ranches. They were protected from white settlement by their treaties, so the general westward movement of the pioneers passed them.

The American Civil War (1861-1865) destroyed the prosperity and protection the Indians enjoyed. The Five Civilized Tribes had come from the South, and many of the Indians owned slaves. Delegations from Texas and Arkansas urged the Indians to join the Confederacy. In 1861, a Confederate military leader, Albert Pike, made treaties of alliance with some of the tribes. These tribes included some Plains Indians who had moved into the area. At first the Cherokee leader, Chief John Ross, tried to avoid taking sides. But after the Confederates won a battle near the Cherokee border, at Wilson's Creek in Missouri, Ross pledged the Cherokee to the South. Pike then recruited and led a brigade of Indians to fight for the South. One Cherokee, Stand Watie, became a Confederate brigadier general. Other Indians, however, fought for the Union.

After the Civil War, Congress forced the Five Civilized Tribes to give up the western part of their land because they had supported the South. Some of this land was given or sold to other Indian tribes.

The land that bordered the Indian Territory filled rapidly with settlers. Soon there was no more free or cheap land available. The whites wanted to use the fertile Indian lands. During the late 1860's, many cattlemen drove their herds across Oklahoma on their way from Texas to the Kansas railroad centers. Some cattle ranchers paid the Indians for grazing rights, but others did not. From 1866 to 1885, over 6 million longhorn cattle crossed the

Indian lands. The East Shawnee, West Shawnee, Chisholm, and Western trails were the leading routes. In 1883, an association of cattle ranchers leased more than 6 million acres (2.4 million hectares) from the Indians for five years. But the U.S. government declared all the leases invalid. President Benjamin Harrison ordered the whites' cattle removed in 1890.

Great land rushes. "Boomers" urged the government to open the land for white settlement. The boomer leaders included C. C. Carpenter, William Couch, and David Payne. Finally the government yielded. It bought over 3 million acres (1.2 million hectares) from the Creek and Seminole tribes. Authorities declared almost 1,900,000 acres (769,000 hectares) in central Oklahoma open for settlement at noon, April 22, 1889. Thousands of settlers moved to the border to await the opening. The Army held them back until a pistol shot signaled the opening. Then a wild race began to claim the best farms and townsites. About 50,000 people had moved into Oklahoma by that evening. In a single day, Guthrie and Oklahoma City became cities of 10,000 people.

Some settlers, called Sooners, went into the area before the opening to claim the best land. To hide their early entry, many Sooners ran their horses hard on the day of the opening. Then the tired horses would be shown to the pioneers who had followed the rules, to "prove" that the owner had just arrived.

The Territory of Oklahoma was established by Congress in May 1890, with Guthrie as the capital. The same act added the Panhandle to the territory. The Panhandle had become U.S. territory when Texas joined the Union in 1845. President Harrison appointed George W. Steele as the first territorial governor.

Many African American settlers came to the Great Plains in the late 1800's. They fled the hostile environment they faced in the South after the Reconstruction period that followed the Civil War. Such all-black towns as Langston were established in Oklahoma.

During the 1890's, more and more Indian tribes accepted individual *allotment* of their lands. This meant that individual Indians, not the tribe, owned the land. Land not allotted to tribe members was opened for settlement. In some areas, settlers got their land by *run,* or land rush. Other land was distributed by a lottery.

The greatest opening occurred on Sept. 16, 1893. That day, the Cherokee Outlet, in north-central Oklahoma, and the Tonkawa and Pawnee reservations were opened. Over 50,000 people claimed land in the 6 ½-million-acre (2.6-million-hectare) area the first day.

Progress toward statehood. After 1890, maps showed the Oklahoma area as the Twin Territories—Indian Territory and Oklahoma Territory. Indian Territory was the remaining land of the Five Civilized Tribes, plus a small area owned and settled by other tribes. The rest of the region was Oklahoma Territory.

White settlers now wanted the remaining Indian lands. In 1893, Congress created the Dawes Commission to bargain for the land and to dissolve the Indian nations. Agents of the commission helped the tribes incorporate towns and prepare for citizenship. The commission divided the remaining land among members of the tribes. By 1905, commission leaders felt the Indian Territory was ready to become a state.

Leaders of the Five Civilized Tribes called a constitutional convention at Muskogee in 1905 and invited white citizens to take part. At the time, whites in the Indian Territory outnumbered the Indians 5 to 1. The convention adopted a constitution for the proposed state of Sequoyah, and the people approved it in an election. But Congress refused to accept the area as a state. Congress wanted one state to be created from the Twin Territories. In 1906, delegates from both territories met in Guthrie to draw up a constitution.

Early statehood. On Nov. 16, 1907, Oklahoma became the 46th state in the Union. Charles N. Haskell of Muskogee was elected the first governor. The new state had a population of 1,414,177. Guthrie was the first capital. In 1910, Oklahoma City became the capital.

Even before statehood, Oklahoma had become a center of oil production. A small well was drilled near Chelsea in 1889. The first important well was drilled at Bartlesville in 1897. Tulsa became an oil center after the Red Fork-Tulsa field opened in 1901.

There were problems, however, especially among farmers. The prices of farm products were low, and many settlers found they did not have enough land to farm profitably. After the United States entered World War I in 1917, these problems disappeared in the huge demand for Oklahoma's farm and fuel products.

The 1920's. During the 1920's, many of Oklahoma's problems returned. Farm prices dropped again, and economic distress led to unrest. Secret organizations, such as the Ku Klux Klan, stirred into action (see **Ku Klux Klan**). The Klan won many members all over the state, and controlled or elected many municipal and county officials. But Governor James B. A. Robertson, who served from 1919 to 1923, fought the Klan and refused to allow any state official to join the organization.

In 1923, John C. Walton became governor, but he was soon impeached for abusing his powers. The state Legislature removed him from office after only 9 months and 14 days. Among other things, Walton had used the National Guard to prevent a grand jury from meeting. Lieutenant Governor Martin E. Trapp became governor and served until 1927. Trapp was a "hard roads" governor who pushed the construction of all-weather highways. Trapp also backed a law that made it illegal to wear masks at public gatherings. This law helped control the Klan. Henry S. Johnston became governor in 1927, but he, too, was impeached. After two years in office, Johnston was found guilty of incompetence and removed by the Legislature. In March 1929, Lieutenant Governor William J. Holloway became governor.

Important discoveries of oil and gas helped Oklahoma during this period. The huge Oklahoma City field opened in 1928. It had more than 1,500 producing wells within 10 years. The Greater Seminole area led the nation in production from 1925 to 1929.

The 1930's. The campaign of 1930 was highlighted by the election as governor of one of Oklahoma's most colorful politicians, William H. "Alfalfa Bill" Murray. A former congressman, Murray appealed to the "common folks" to vote for him. After his election, Murray shut down over 3,000 flowing oil wells. The price of oil had been dropping, and Murray wanted to keep some oil off the market to force up the price. After three months, he permitted production to start again.

Oklahoma suffered many hardships during the Great

ℋistoric Oklahoma

WORLD BOOK map

A forced relocation of thousands of Indians to Oklahoma from the southeastern United States took place during the 1830's. Many Indians died during the difficult journeys, which became known as the Trail of Tears.

Oklahoma was part of several different U.S. territories before the U.S. government forced Indian groups to move to the region in the 1830's. Congress formed the Oklahoma Territory in 1890. Oklahoma became a state in 1907.

The Dust Bowl formed in the 1930's, forcing many Oklahoma farmers to move elsewhere. Unsustainable farming practices and drought led to soil erosion and huge dust storms.

Important dates in Oklahoma

WORLD BOOK illustrations by Richard Bonson, The Art Agency

1541   Francisco Vásquez de Coronado crossed western Oklahoma in a search for gold.

1682   Robert Cavelier, Sieur de La Salle, claimed Oklahoma as part of French Louisiana.

1762   France gave Louisiana, including the Oklahoma region, to Spain.

1800   France regained Louisiana.

1803   The United States bought the Oklahoma region, except for the Panhandle, as part of the Louisiana Purchase.

1819   The Oklahoma region, except the Panhandle, became part of the Territory of Arkansas.

1824   The government established Fort Gibson and Fort Towson, the region's first military posts.

1830-1842 The Five Civilized Tribes moved to Oklahoma.

1870-1872 The Missouri-Kansas-Texas railroad was built across the region.

1872   Oklahoma's first commercial coal was mined near McAlester.

1889   The United States opened part of Oklahoma to white settlement. The region's first producing oil well was drilled near Chelsea.

1890   Congress established the Territory of Oklahoma and added the Panhandle region to it.

1893   Congress established the Dawes Commission to manage the affairs of the Five Civilized Tribes. The Cherokee Outlet was opened to white settlement.

1898   Congress passed the Curtis Act, which gradually dissolved tribal laws and courts, and brought members of the Five Civilized Tribes under the laws and courts of the United States. White settlement boomed in the territory.

1907   On November 16, Oklahoma became the 46th state to join the Union.

1920   The Osage County oil fields began to produce.

1928   The Oklahoma City oil field opened.

1963   Henry Bellmon became the first Republican governor of Oklahoma.

1990   Oklahoma became the first state to pass term limits on members of its state legislature.

1995   A terrorist bomb blew up a federal government building in Oklahoma City, killing 168 people.

2007   Oklahoma celebrated the centennial of its statehood.

Tulsa Port of Catoosa

Tulsa's port and a large industrial area are at nearby Catoosa on the Verdigris River. Barges haul goods between this port, the busiest in Oklahoma, and Mississippi River ports.

Depression of the 1930's. Business was bad, and farm prices were extremely low. Many banks failed, and people lost their savings. The entire Great Plains region suffered a severe water shortage. Crops failed for lack of rain, and there were unusually hot summers. High winds stripped away large areas of fertile topsoil and whipped the dry dirt into massive dust storms that turned day into night. Much of the plains area became known as the Dust Bowl (see **Dust Bowl**). Many farmers, miners, and oil workers left the state to try their luck elsewhere. Oklahoma suffered a large loss of population. See **Great Depression** (Human suffering).

The mid-1900's. During World War II (1939-1945), Oklahoma's major products—food and fuels—again came into great demand. Increased use of soil conservation practices helped restore many farms that had been damaged during the drought of the 1930's.

From 1943 to 1947, Governor Robert S. Kerr brought about reforms in education, state finances, and pardon and parole procedures for convicts. After serving his term as governor, Kerr won election to the U.S. Senate.

During the 1950's, Oklahoma's economy began to shift from an agricultural to an industrial base. Both the size and number of farms declined. Johnston Murray, the son of Alfalfa Bill Murray, became governor in 1951 and started a campaign to develop new industry in the state.

New industries and construction projects highlighted the state's economic progress during the 1960's. Two large electronics plants were built in Oklahoma City, and Tulsa became the site of a space equipment factory. The Federal Aviation Administration built an aeronautics center in Oklahoma City. In 1963, Henry Bellmon became the state's first Republican governor.

Construction of a number of dams and creation of several lakes began in the mid-1900's. Some of these projects were completed in the 1960's, and others were finished in the 1970's. The lakes were created to increase the state's hydroelectric power and water storage capacities. The new dams and lakes helped the efforts of business and political leaders to broaden the state's industrial activity. The state government advertised Oklahoma's abundant supplies of fuel, water, and electric power. In addition, the Legislature revised the state's tax structure to attract manufacturers. As a result, Oklahoma gained new industries that did not depend on the products of its farms and mines.

The late 1900's. The McClellan-Kerr Arkansas River Navigation System, completed in 1970, made shipping an important activity in Oklahoma. The waterway enables barges on the Mississippi River to reach Oklahoma ports on the Arkansas River. Tulsa and Muskogee are important ports on the river system.

Between 1976 and 1980, a strong world demand for energy led to an economic boom in Oklahoma. The state's petroleum and natural gas industries thrived and brought much income to Oklahoma. In addition, rising tourism contributed to the state's economy.

During the early 1980's, however, the prices of oil and gas fell sharply, and the economic boom in the state ended. In addition, a deep decline in agricultural prices contributed to an economic crisis for thousands of Oklahoma residents. Hundreds of oil wells shut down, and many farmers lost their farms. Unemployment increased rapidly, and many people left the state in search of jobs. Once again, the state's leaders emphasized the need to attract new industries that would help lessen Oklahoma's dependence on its traditional mineral and agricultural industries.

In 1982, betting on horse races became legal in Oklahoma. In 1984, the state gave each county the right to decide whether to end restrictions on alcoholic beverage sales within its borders. In 1959, the state had repealed a 1907 law banning alcohol sales but left some restrictions in place. In 1990, Oklahomans voted to limit state legislators to no more than 12 total years of elective service. This was the first time any state's voters passed such term limits.

In 1995, a bomb set off by American terrorist Timothy J. McVeigh blew up Oklahoma City's Murrah Federal Building, killing 168 people. The incident was one of the worst terrorist acts in the United States. McVeigh was convicted of murder and conspiracy in 1997 and was executed in 2001. See **Oklahoma City bombing.**

The 2000's. The Oklahoma City National Memorial, established on the site of the Murrah Federal Building, was dedicated in 2000. A new federal building was completed near the site in 2003.

In 2002, a dome was completed atop the State Capitol Building in Oklahoma City. In 2007, Oklahoma celebrated its centennial with parades and other events in Oklahoma City and Guthrie.   Brad A. Bays and Deena K. Fisher

Study aids

Related articles in *World Book* include:

Biographies

Albert, Carl Bert   Chouteau, Jean P.

Harris, Roy	Tallchief, Maria
Rogers, Will	Thorpe, Jim
Ross, John	Watie, Stand
Sequoyah	Watts, J. C., Jr.

Cities

Oklahoma City	Tulsa

History

Caddo Indians
Cheyenne Indians
Comanche Indians
Five Civilized Tribes
Fort Sill
Indian, American
Indian Territory
Louisiana Purchase
Osage Indians
Trail of Tears
Westward movement in America

Physical features

Arkansas River
Dust Bowl
Lake Texoma
Ozark Mountains
Pensacola Dam
Red River

Outline

I. People
- A. Population
- B. Schools
- C. Libraries
- D. Museums

II. Visitor's guide

III. Land and climate
- A. Land regions
- B. Rivers and lakes
- C. Plant and animal life
- D. Climate

IV. Economy
- A. Natural resources
- B. Service industries
- C. Manufacturing
- D. Mining
- E. Agriculture
- F. Electric power and utilities
- G. Transportation
- H. Communication

V. Government
- A. Constitution
- B. Executive
- C. Legislature
- D. Courts
- E. Local government
- F. Revenue
- G. Politics

VI. History

Questions

Why did Congress take land away from the Indians in the Oklahoma area after the American Civil War?
How were Oklahoma's earliest schools established?
How may Oklahoma's Constitution be amended?
What term did the Cherokee and other Indians use to refer to their forced migration from their homelands east of the Mississippi River to the Oklahoma area in the 1830's?
What activity is the state's leading source of agricultural income?
Why is Oklahoma called the *Sooner State?*
What part of Oklahoma is called the Panhandle?
Which city was Oklahoma's first capital?
Why is the phrase "as long as grass shall grow and rivers run" important in Oklahoma history?
Why did Oklahoma suffer a decrease in its population during the 1930's?

Additional resources

Level I

Brown, Jonatha A. *Oklahoma.* Gareth Stevens, 2006.
Heinrichs, Ann. *Oklahoma.* Child's World, 2006.
Orr, Tamra B. *Oklahoma.* Children's Press, 2008.
Sanders, Doug. *Oklahoma.* Benchmark Bks., 2006.

Level II

Adkison, Danny M., and Palmer, L. M. *The Oklahoma State Constitution.* Greenwood, 2001.
Baird, W. David, and Goble, Danney. *Oklahoma, a History.* Univ. of Okla. Pr., 2008.
Baker, Terri M., and Henshaw, C. O., eds. *Women Who Pioneered Oklahoma: Stories From the WPA Narratives.* Univ. of Okla. Pr., 2007.
Faulk, Odie B., and Welge, W. D. *Oklahoma: A Rich Heritage.* Am. Hist. Pr., 2004.
Goins, Charles R., and Goble, Danney. *Historical Atlas of Oklahoma.* 4th ed. Univ. of Okla. Pr., 2006.
Stein, Howard F., and Hill, R. F., eds. *The Culture of Oklahoma.* Univ. of Okla. Pr., 1993.

Oklahoma, University of, is a public institution in Norman, Oklahoma. The university also has campuses at Oklahoma City and Tulsa. Research facilities on the Norman campus include the Center for Analysis and Prediction of Storms and the Carl Albert Congressional Research and Studies Center. The University of Oklahoma has a law school and a medical school. The university also has museums of art and of natural history. It was founded in 1890. Its athletic teams are called the Sooners. Its website at http://www.ou.edu offers additional information. Critically reviewed by the University of Oklahoma

Oklahoma City (pop. 579,999; met. area pop. 1,252,987) is the capital and largest city of Oklahoma. About a third of the state's people live in the Oklahoma City metropolitan area. The city ranks as one of the chief centers of oil production in the United States. It is a commercial and manufacturing center of Oklahoma and a distribution point for a large farming area.

Oklahoma City lies on the North Canadian River, near the geographic center of the state. For location, see **Oklahoma** (political map).

White settlers first came to what is now the Oklahoma City area in 1889. The United States government had originally set this land aside for Indians. But the government later opened central Oklahoma for white settlement. On the first day, about 10,000 settlers flocked to a site near the Atchison, Topeka and Santa Fe Railway (now part of the Burlington Northern Santa Fe Corporation) tracks and pitched their tents. This settlement became Oklahoma City. The city's name came from two Choctaw Indian words—*okla,* meaning *people,* and *homma,* meaning *red.*

The city covers 621 square miles (1,608 square kilometers), including 14 square miles (36 square kilometers) of inland water. The metropolitan area consists of seven counties—Canadian, Cleveland, Grady, Lincoln, Logan, McClain, and Oklahoma—and covers an area of about 5,518 square miles (14,292 square kilometers).

The State Capitol stands in a major oil field near the heart of the city. A statue called *Tribute to Range Riders* (1930), nicknamed "The Cowboy," by the American sculptor Constance Whitney Warren stands in front of the Capitol. An oil well on the Capitol grounds, long a tourist attraction, ended production in 1986. Other producing wells are scattered throughout the city.

The Cox Convention Center is one of the leading convention sites in the United States. The 36-story Chase Tower is the city's tallest building.

About 97 percent of the city's people were born in the United States. African Americans make up about 15 percent of the city's population. About 15 percent of the people are Hispanic Americans. American Indians and Asian Americans each make up about 4 percent of the population.

Economy. The leading industries of Oklahoma City produce construction equipment, electronic equipment, food products, and petroleum products. Other Oklahoma City products include building materials, cottonseed oil, iron and steel products, paper products, telephone equipment, and transportation equipment. The city has hundreds of manufacturing plants.

The federal and state governments provide jobs for many of Oklahoma City's workers. Tinker Air Force Base is the largest single employer. This important repair and supply station for the U.S. Air Force employs several thousand civilians. The Federal Aviation Administration has a regional office in the city.

Much of Oklahoma City's industrial importance results from its location in an area rich in natural resources for both oil production and farming. Oklahoma County has hundreds of oil and natural gas wells. The city processes and distributes such farm products as feed, flour, and meat. It is the leading cattle market in the United States.

Will Rogers World Airport lies in the southwestern part of the city. Buses, trucks, and freight and passenger trains also serve the city. Oklahoma City has one daily newspaper, *The Oklahoman.*

Education and cultural life. An eight-member elected Board of Education supervises Oklahoma City's public school system. The city also has church-supported and private schools. Colleges and universities in Oklahoma City include Mid-America Christian University, Oklahoma Christian University, Oklahoma City University, and the University of Oklahoma Health Sciences Center. The University of Oklahoma is in nearby Norman.

Randy Bennett, Oklahoma City Public Information Office

Oklahoma City is the capital and largest city of Oklahoma. Its downtown area, *shown here,* includes towering office buildings and hotels. Some of the buildings were constructed as part of a renewal program that began in the mid-1900's.

Southern Nazarene University is in nearby Bethany. The University of Central Oklahoma is just north of Oklahoma City, in Edmond. The Metropolitan Library System has a number of full-service public libraries and small extension libraries that serve Oklahoma County.

Oklahoma City has several community theaters. The Oklahoma City Philharmonic performs at the Civic Center Music Hall. The National Cowboy & Western Heritage Museum displays paintings and sculptures of the American West. The Oklahoma City Museum of Art features European and American paintings and sculptures, as well as drawings, prints, photography, and glass artworks.

The Oklahoma History Center has a collection of exhibits tracing the history of Oklahoma. Science Museum Oklahoma includes aviation and space exhibits, hands-on science exhibits, cultural galleries, gardens, a planetarium, and a theater. The science museum also houses the International Photography Hall of Fame and Museum and a museum of American Indian culture called the Red Earth Museum.

Oklahoma City has dozens of parks. Lincoln Park, the largest park, includes the Oklahoma City Zoo and Botanical Garden. The Oklahoma City Thunder plays in the National Basketball Association.

Government. Oklahoma City has a council-manager form of government. The voters elect a mayor and eight council members to four-year terms. The council appoints a city manager.

In 1971, the voters elected Patience S. Latting mayor. She became the first woman mayor of a United States city of more than 200,000 people. Sales taxes provide most of the city's revenue.

History. Creek and Seminole Indians lived in what is now the Oklahoma City area before white settlers first arrived. In 1889, the U.S. government bought the land there from the two tribes. On April 22 of that same year, the government opened the area for white settlement, and a great land rush began. By the evening of April 22, approximately 10,000 settlers had arrived there. Oklahoma City was incorporated in 1890. By 1910, it was the state's largest city. Its population rose from 10,037 in 1900 to 64,205 in 1910. During that period, four railroads began to serve the city, and two meat-packing plants opened. In 1910, Oklahoma City replaced Guthrie as the state capital.

The city's greatest problem during its early years was a lack of water sources. Shortly after 1900, Oklahoma City built its first municipal well. In 1919, it completed its first reservoir, Lake Overholser. Since then, the city has built several more reservoirs.

By 1920, Oklahoma City had 91,295 people. Oil was discovered in the city in 1928, and an oil boom began. Many oil companies built refineries, and the area became a center of the nation's petroleum industry.

Tinker Air Force Base was built in Oklahoma City during World War II (1939-1945). By 1950, the population of the city had risen to 243,504.

Industrial expansion occurred during the 1950's and 1960's. Iron and steel plants were built, and the city also became a center of the electronics industry. Development also took place in downtown Oklahoma City. During the 1960's, the city annexed many surrounding areas, and its area increased from about 310 square miles (803

A terrorist bomb destroyed Oklahoma City's Murrah Federal Building, *shown here,* on April 19, 1995. The bomb killed 168 people, including 19 children. After a long search for victims, the building was razed.

square kilometers) in 1960 to about 635 square miles (1,645 square kilometers) in 1970. Oklahoma City's population continued to grow. It reached 403,484 by 1980.

Since the late 1960's, Oklahoma City has undertaken several urban renewal projects to replace old buildings and wipe out slums. One of the projects, called the Medical Center Project, was completed in 1978. It includes a dental college, a hospital, a nursing school, and headquarters for the State Health Department.

The Central Business District Project, which included the construction of several office buildings and a convention center, was completed in 1985. The John F. Kennedy Project involved renovating or replacing 1,260 acres (510 hectares) of slum housing. It was completed in 1988. A race track opened in northeast Oklahoma City in 1988. In 1998, a 13,000-seat minor league baseball stadium was completed in Bricktown, a restored historic district near downtown.

In 1995, a terrorist bomb exploded in front of a United States government building in downtown Oklahoma City. The explosion killed 168 people. For more information on the attack, see **Oklahoma City bombing.**

In the early 2000's, the city completed further downtown redevelopment. Projects included the Civic Center Music Hall and a sports and entertainment arena, the Ford Center. The Ronald J. Norick Downtown Library, named for a former mayor, opened in 2004.   Ed Kelley

See also **National Park System** (picture); **Oklahoma** (Climate; pictures).

Oklahoma City bombing was one of the worst terrorist acts carried out in the United States. It occurred on April 19, 1995, in downtown Oklahoma City, Oklahoma. One or more terrorists set off a bomb in a truck in front of the Alfred P. Murrah Federal Building. The explosion destroyed the building and killed 168 people. The victims included 19 children, most of them at a day-care center in the building.

Timothy J. McVeigh and Terry L. Nichols, both U.S. citizens, were arrested and charged with the crime. The charges stated that they made the bomb and that McVeigh drove the truck to the building and set off the bomb. Earlier, McVeigh and Nichols had publicly expressed strong opposition to the federal government. A third U.S. citizen, Michael Fortier, was charged with aiding them.

Fortier pleaded guilty and agreed to testify in the trials of the two other men. In 1998, he was sentenced to 12 years in prison. He was released in 2006 after his sentence was reduced for good behavior in prison. McVeigh was convicted of murder and conspiracy in 1997 and sentenced to death. He was executed on June 11, 2001. Nichols was convicted of conspiracy and involuntary manslaughter. In 1998, he was sentenced to life in prison without parole.

In 2004, Nichols was tried a second time. His first conviction and sentencing had been in federal court for the deaths of eight federal employees killed in the explosion. However, the state of Oklahoma brought murder charges against him for the deaths of all the other victims. Prosecutors sought the death penalty. A jury found Nichols guilty but could not agree on a sentence. The trial judge then sentenced him to life in prison without parole.

The Oklahoma City National Memorial, established on the site of the destroyed building, was dedicated in 2000. A new federal building was completed near the site in 2003.   Ed Kelley

See also **National Park System** (picture: Oklahoma City National Memorial).

Oklahoma State University is a public university system with four campuses. The system's main campus is in Stillwater, Oklahoma. Oklahoma State University also has campuses in Oklahoma City, Okmulgee, and Tulsa. The university system maintains several agricultural experiment stations and a state extension service.

Oklahoma State University was established in 1890 and opened to students in 1891. The university's athletic men's teams are called the Cowboys, and the women's teams are known as the Cowgirls. Oklahoma State's website at http://system.okstate.edu provides additional information.

Critically reviewed by Oklahoma State University

Okra, *OH kruh,* also called *gumbo* or *okro,* is a plant cultivated for its immature pods. People eat the pods as a vegetable. Cooks typically fry okra or use it as an ingredient in stews or soups.

The okra plant is an *annual* and must be raised from seed each year. Gardeners plant the seeds in spring. The plant grows 2 to 8 feet (0.6 to 2.4 meters) high. It bears rounded, fine-lobed leaves, and greenish-yellow flow-

WORLD BOOK illustration by Kate Lloyd-Jones, Linden Artists Ltd.

Okra is a tall plant raised for its sticky green pods, which are used in cooking. The plant bears greenish-yellow flowers.

ers. The pods on the plant measure from 4 to 6 inches (10 to 15 centimeters) long. But they sometimes exceed 1 foot (30 centimeters) when fully grown. Okra pods are cooked and canned when they are young and tender.

Okra is a kind of hibiscus and is related to cotton. It is a native of Africa. Okra is raised in large quantities in the southern United States.   S. J. Locascio

Scientific classification. Okra is a member of the mallow family, Malvaceae. Okra is *Hibiscus esculentus.*

Oktoberfest is a lively annual beer festival held in Munich, Germany. It usually lasts 16 days, starting on a Saturday in the second half of September and normally ending on the first Sunday in October. Since it began in 1810, Oktoberfest has become one of the world's largest festivals. Each year, millions of people fill huge tents to enjoy food, beer, and music. German settlers carried the tradition to other places. Today, communities around the world hold their own local Oktoberfest celebrations.

Oktoberfest commemorates the marriage of Crown Prince Ludwig of Bavaria to Princess Therese of Saxony-Hildburghausen on Oct. 12, 1810. The prince invited Munich's people to celebrate with a great festival on the fields near the city gates. The festival lasted five days and concluded with a horse race. Other activities were added as it became an annual event. Oktoberfest continues to be held at the same location, now called Theresienwiese (Therese's Meadow) in honor of the princess. In the late 1800's, the start of the festival was moved to September, when Munich's weather is milder.

Heide A. Crawford

See also **Germany** (picture: Oktoberfest).

Olajuwon, *oh LY juh wahn,* **Hakeem,** *ah KEEM* (1963-   ), ranks among the greatest centers in the history of the National Basketball Association (NBA). Standing 7 feet (213 centimeters) tall, he became known on offense for his quick, graceful moves and accurate jump shot. Defensively, he was the leading shot-blocker in NBA history with 3,830 blocked shots. Olajuwon led the Houston Rockets to the NBA championship in 1993-1994

and again in 1994-1995. During the 1993-1994 season, he became the first ever to be named the league's Most Valuable Player, defensive player of the year, and Most Valuable Player in the play-off finals in the same season.

Hakeem Abdul Olajuwon was born on Jan. 21, 1963, in Lagos, Nigeria. He played soccer, handball, and basketball in Nigeria. From 1981 to 1984, he attended the University of Houston, where he was a star player. In the 1984 draft, the Houston Rockets selected him as the first player. Houston traded him to the Toronto Raptors after the 2000-2001 season. He retired in 2002 and was elected to the Basketball Hall of Fame in 2008. His name was spelled *Akeem* early in his career. He then changed it to *Hakeem.* He became a U.S. citizen in 1993.   Sam Smith

Old age cannot be defined exactly because it does not have the same meaning in all societies. In many parts of the world, people are considered old because of certain changes in their activities or social roles. For example, people may be considered old when they become grandparents or when they begin to do less or different work. In the United States, people are often considered old if they have lived a certain number of years. Many Americans think of 65 as the beginning of old age because U.S. workers traditionally became eligible to retire with full Social Security benefits at age 65. People in the 65-and-older age group are often called *senior citizens.* Starting in 2003, the age of eligibility for full Social Security benefits began to increase gradually. It will reach age 67 in 2027.

Worldwide, the number of people 65 or older is increasing faster than ever before. Most of this increase is occurring in less developed countries. In the United States, the percentage of people 65 or older grew from 4 percent in 1900 to about 12 percent in the early 2000's. In 1900, only about 3 million of the nation's people had reached 65. By 2008, the number of senior citizens had increased to nearly 39 million. Population experts estimate that about 72 million Americans—about 20 percent of the population—will be 65 or older in 2030. The number of elderly people is growing around the world chiefly because more children reach adulthood.

In most parts of the world, women live, on average, longer than men. In the United States in the early 2000's, life expectancy at birth was 80 years for women and 75 years for men. American women who were age 65 in the early 2000's could expect to live about 20 additional years. Men who were 65 could expect to live about 17 additional years.

The study of aging and old age is called *gerontology.* Many universities and colleges offer courses in gerontology for people who wish to provide services for the elderly. *Geriatrics* is the branch of medicine that deals with old age and its diseases. Most medical schools offer courses in geriatrics.

The rest of this article mainly discusses attitudes toward old age and tells about ways of life of the elderly in the United States. For information on the medical and physical aspects of old age, see the *World Book* articles on **Aging** and **Geriatrics.**

Attitudes toward old age

In all societies, old people are generally more respected if they control important resources, such as information, money, or land. In many countries, for example, the ability of the elderly to provide information based on their extensive experience gives them a respected position in society. This is particularly true in nonindustrial countries, which have few books or computers to store information. In modern industrial nations, however, many people do not regard the elderly as wiser or more knowledgeable. Also in industrial nations, where income from work is a major resource and where having a job earns a person respect, people may lose status when they retire.

Many beliefs about older people are untrue. Some employers, for example, think that younger workers are more efficient and reliable than older ones. But in many types of jobs, older people are better workers than younger people. The ideas that people become less intelligent as they age and that old people cannot learn new skills are also not true. Some researchers have called the many incorrect ideas about old people *ageism.*

Ways of life of the elderly

Older people in the United States follow many different ways of life. How a particular older person lives has much to do with how that person lived in earlier years. Important factors include the financial resources the person has accumulated, the interests the person has developed, and the relationships the person has established with other people.

Finances. The most important source of income for many retired workers is Social Security. Workers and their employers pay equal shares of a payroll tax into the Social Security fund. The fund is administered by the federal government. After the workers retire, they receive a monthly payment from the Social Security fund. The amount of their payment is determined by the salary they earned as well as the number of years that they worked. Widows and widowers continue to receive the pension after the death of their spouses. See **Social security.**

Some retired people also receive a pension from their employer or have their own savings. Most retired people receive less than half as much as they earned while working. But in many cases, their expenses are also lower.

Employment and other activities. The majority of Americans over 65 do not have a job. Only about 15 percent of the men above this age and 8 percent of the women are employed. Under United States law, workers in most jobs cannot be forced to retire because of their age. However, even when employers were still allowed to enforce a retirement age, most people stopped working for other reasons. Health and expected retirement income were, and still are, the chief factors in the decision to retire.

Some senior citizens join private groups for social and recreational activities. These groups include church organizations and senior citizens' clubs. Some elderly people join AARP (formerly the American Association of Retired Persons) or similar organizations. These groups offer a large number of services, including educational and travel programs, medical insurance, and newsletters. In addition, such organizations also tell politicians about older people's views on medical care, Social Security, and related issues. An organization called the Gray Panthers, whose members include both young and old, works to fight ageism in U.S. society.

The U.S. government provides several programs that enable senior citizens to help other people. For example, the Service Corps of Retired Executives (SCORE) attracts retired business people who enjoy advising community organizations and small businesses. The Foster Grandparent Program (FGP) uses seniors to help care for children. People over 60 may also join the Retired Senior Volunteer Program (RSVP) to work in hospitals, libraries, schools, and other institutions.

Older people seem to have a greater involvement in politics than do members of any other age group in the United States. A higher percentage of elderly people than other individuals vote in elections.

Housing. Most Americans over 65 are closely involved with their families. However, only about one-eighth of all elderly Americans live with a relative other than their husband or wife. A large number of elderly parents and their children prefer the independence and privacy of living in separate dwellings. In other countries, the percentage of elderly parents who live with their children is much higher. In Japan, for example, about two-thirds of all elderly parents live with one of their children.

In the United States, only about 5 percent of the elderly live in a nursing home or other institution. Some of the senior citizens in the United States live in special housing called *retirement communities.* These communities may consist of apartment buildings, individual houses, or groups of mobile homes. In retirement communities, residents are guaranteed medical care for as long as they live.

Health care. The federal government administers Medicare, a medical insurance program for senior citizens that pays part of their expenses for physicians and hospital care. Medicare also pays a portion of the cost of medical services at home or in a nursing home. However, medical expenses remain a serious problem for many older people and their families, especially if long-term care is needed because of a chronic illness. Finding ways for older people to receive high-quality, long-term care is a major problem facing American policymakers today. See **Medicare.**   Jennie Keith

Related articles in *World Book* include:
AARP
Day care (Day care for the elderly)
Gray Panthers
Library (Services for special groups)
Life expectancy
Nursing home
Retirement
Welfare

Additional resources

Disney, Richard. *Can We Afford to Grow Older?* MIT Pr., 1996.
Gould, John. *Tales from Rhapsody Home: Or, What They Don't Tell You About Senior Living.* Algonquin Bks., 2000.
Hebeler, Henry K. *Your Winning Retirement Plan.* Wiley, 2001.
Posner, Richard A. *Aging and Old Age.* 1995. Reprint. Univ. of Chicago Pr., 1997.

Old-Age, survivors, and disability insurance. See Social security.

Old Bailey is the common name for the Central Criminal Court in London. The Old Bailey has several courts, and each one holds sessions at least four times a year. It is on a street called Old Bailey. This street once formed part of a *bailey* (area between the inner and outer city walls) in medieval London.

The city government built the Sessions House in 1550. This building became known as the Old Bailey. People held at nearby Newgate Prison were tried in the Old Bailey (see **Newgate Prison**). Famous cases held there included the treason trial of judges responsible for the execution of King Charles I; the treason trial of William Joyce, who broadcast for Nazi Germany during World War II (1939-1945) as Lord Haw Haw; and the morals trial of the Irish author Oscar Wilde.   Robert E. Dowse

Old Catholic churches are a group of Christian churches that split away from the Roman Catholic Church. Most of them were formed by Catholics who opposed the teaching of *papal infallibility* proclaimed at the first Vatican Council in 1870. This teaching states that the pope is free from error when he speaks as head of the church on matters of faith and morals.

The Catholics who withdrew from the church at that time established an independent church. Most of these Catholics lived in Germany, the Netherlands, Switzerland, and the Austro-Hungarian Empire. In 1889, the independent church formed a loose relationship with other *dissenting* (disagreeing) Catholic churches under the terms of an agreement called the Union of Utrecht. Some of the dissenting churches had been established as early as 1724.

Old Catholic churches generally follow Roman Catholic teachings, though the clergy may marry. The churches encourage Bible study.   Marvin R. O'Connell

Old English. See **English language** (Old English); **English literature** (Old English literature).

Old English sheepdog is best known for its long hair, "bobbed" tail, and odd, shuffling walk. Its hair hangs down over its eyes. Much brushing is required to keep the dog's long coat neat. The coat serves as excellent insulation. It is gray or blue, often with white markings, or mostly white with gray or blue markings. The dog stands about 22 inches (56 centimeters) high and weighs from 50 to 65 pounds (23 to 29 kilograms).

Critically reviewed by the American Kennel Club

See also **Dog** (picture: Herding dogs); **Sheepdog**.

Old Faithful. See **Wyoming** (picture); **Yellowstone National Park**.

Old Glory. See **United States flag**.

Old Ironsides, locomotive. See **Baldwin, Matthias William**.

Old Ironsides, ship. See **Constitution** (ship).

Old North Church is the popular name for Christ Church, the oldest public building in Boston. The red-brick structure has a slender white steeple in the Christopher Wren style. Church *sexton* (caretaker) Robert Newman hung two lanterns there as a signal from Paul Revere that the British were coming to seize arms and gunpowder at Concord, Massachusetts, at the start of the American Revolution (1775-1783). The tower contains the first set of church bells in the American Colonies, cast in 1744. Storms in 1804 and 1954 toppled the spire. In 1955, it was rebuilt to its original height of 190 feet (58 meters). See also **Boston; Revere, Paul**.   William J. Reid

Old Spanish Trail. See **Santa Fe Trail**.

Old Testament is the Christian name for the writings that make up the first part of the Christian Bible. The in-

dividual writings collected in the Bible are known as *books*. The second part of the Christian Bible is the New Testament. The books that are officially accepted by any religious group as part of its Bible are called its *canon*.

Many of the books of the Old Testament come from the older Jewish Bible. The Jewish Bible is commonly called the Hebrew Bible because most of it was written in the Hebrew language. Roman Catholic and Orthodox Christian versions of the Old Testament also include some books that are not in the Hebrew Bible. See **Bible** (table: The books of the Bible).

Many scholars avoid using the term Old Testament because it is a Christian term and Jews also use the books to which it refers. Instead, these scholars use the more neutral terms Hebrew Bible and Tanak. Tanak incorporates the first letters of three Hebrew words that represent the three sections of the Jewish Bible—Torah (Law), Nebi'im (Prophets), and Ketubim (Writings).

Origins. The ancestors of the Jewish people composed the books collected in the Old Testament between about 1000 and 165 B.C. Much of the material existed in oral form before it was written down. Some books were rewritten several times by different people. These people composed new material and added other texts and teachings to the earlier writings.

The Old Testament begins with stories about the creation of the world and God's promises to Abraham and Abraham's wife Sarah, the ancestors of the Jews. It describes how Moses led Abraham and Sarah's descendants, the Israelites, out of slavery in Egypt to the Promised Land of Canaan (later called Palestine). Canaan consisted of an area that extended roughly from east of the Jordan River to the Mediterranean Sea. The Old Tes-

Vic Bider, The Stock Market

The graceful steeple of historic Old North Church pierces the skyline near the business district of Boston.

tament also tells stories about how the Israelites conquered and settled Canaan. Eventually, King David and his son Solomon established a line of rulers. Some of the earliest stories in the Old Testament may have been written down during the reigns of David and Solomon.

In 922 B.C., the kingdom of the Israelites split into two nations—Israel and Judah. The Jews composed and circulated many teachings included in the Old Testament in oral and written forms during the time of the divided kingdom, from 922 to 586 B.C.

Some of the most important prophets and poets of the Old Testament lived during a period called the Babylonian Exile. The exile began in 587 or 586 B.C., with the Babylonian conquest of Judah, and lasted until 538 B.C. During that period, the Babylonians held many Jews captive in Babylonia. The captives collected, expanded, and edited many of the teachings, laws, and historical records in the Old Testament.

Other books were written after the exile. Daniel was the last to be written, about 165 B.C.

Ancient translations. Most of the books in the Old Testament originally were composed in Hebrew. Some chapters in the Books of Daniel and Ezra were composed in Aramaic, a language similar to Hebrew.

In the 200's B.C., Jewish scholars in Alexandria, Egypt, translated the Hebrew Torah into Greek. Their translation is called the Septuagint. The Septuagint gradually expanded to include other books of the Hebrew Bible, plus some books not in the Hebrew Bible.

The Old Testament books were later translated into Syriac, Ethiopic, Coptic, Slavonic, and Latin. In A.D. 405, the Christian scholar Jerome (later Saint Jerome) completed a Latin translation of the Bible called the Vulgate. It included the Old and New Testaments and was the official Bible of the Roman Catholic Church for centuries.

Contents. The Old Testament has four parts. They are the Pentateuch, the historical books, the wisdom books, and the Prophets. The Pentateuch, from the Greek word for *five,* comprises the first five books of all Bibles—Genesis, Exodus, Leviticus, Numbers, and Deuteronomy. In Hebrew, the Pentateuch is called the Torah, meaning *the teaching.* When the Pentateuch was translated into Greek, the word *torah* was translated as *law.* People sometimes call the Pentateuch the Books of the Law. According to tradition, Moses wrote the Pentateuch. Consequently, the Pentateuch is also called the Books of Moses. But scholars recognize that different authors and editors composed the Pentateuch over many centuries.

The three parts of the Old Testament that follow the Pentateuch differ in Catholic, Orthodox, and Protestant Bibles. The historical books in Catholic Bibles are Joshua, Judges, Ruth, 1 and 2 Samuel, 1 and 2 Kings, 1 and 2 Chronicles, Ezra, Nehemiah, Tobit, Judith, Esther, and 1 and 2 Maccabees. The wisdom books are Job, Psalms, Proverbs, Ecclesiastes, Song of Songs, the Wisdom of Solomon, and Sirach (also called Ecclesiasticus and Ben Sirah). The Prophets includes Isaiah, Jeremiah, Lamentations, Baruch, Ezekiel, Daniel, Hosea, Joel, Amos, Obadiah, Jonah, Micah, Nahum, Habakkuk, Zephaniah, Haggai, Zechariah, and Malachi.

Several books in the Catholic version of the Old Testament are called *deuterocanonical,* meaning *canonized second.* They officially became part of the Catholic canon after other Old Testament books did. They are To-

bit, Judith, 1 and 2 Maccabees, the Wisdom of Solomon, Sirach, and Baruch. The deuterocanonical books also are found in the Septuagint and the Vulgate.

The Greek Orthodox Old Testament includes all the books in the Catholic Old Testament plus five more—1 and 2 Esdras, the Prayer of Manasseh, Psalm 151, and 3 Maccabees. An *appendix* (supplement) also contains 4 Maccabees. The Ethiopian Orthodox Old Testament has additional books, including Jubilees and 1 Enoch.

Today, the Protestant Old Testament includes most of the books in the Catholic Old Testament. However, the Books of Esther and Daniel are shorter in the Protestant Bible than in the Catholic Bible. The Protestant Old Testament also excludes the deuterocanonical books. In the A.D. 1500's, some Protestant scholars became concerned that the Old Testament included books not found in the Hebrew Bible. Protestants removed these books from the Old Testament and called them Apocrypha, meaning *hidden.* Some Protestant Bibles, however, have a separate section for Apocrypha.   Henry W. Morisada Rietz

See also **Bible** and its list of *Related articles.*

Old World is a general term applied to the Eastern Hemisphere. The Old World includes the continents of Europe, Asia, Africa, and Australia. But the term *Old World* is often used to refer just to Europe or to European civilization. See also **New World; Hemisphere.**

Oldenburg, Claes, *klaws* (1929-   ), an American sculptor, was a leader of the Pop Art movement in the early 1960's. He created exaggerated, oversized sculptures representing such familiar objects as ice cream cones, electric plugs, lipstick tubes, and Mickey Mouse.

Using everyday objects as the single subjects of his

Enameled burlap and plaster (1962); The Museum of Modern Art, New York City, Philip Johnson Fund

Oldenburg's *Two Cheeseburgers with Everything* illustrates his use of soft materials to depict familiar objects.

works, Oldenburg has created two principal types of sculpture. One of these types consists of sculptures that are made of soft material, thus contradicting the hardness of the actual objects. This soft material is frequently in a bright color that is related to its subject. The second type is made up of huge steel monuments of common objects designed to be placed in landscapes or among buildings (see **Des Moines** [picture]). By creating these caricatures of everyday objects, Oldenburg changes recognizable objects into abstract forms.

Oldenburg was born on Jan. 28, 1929, in Stockholm,

Sweden. He became a United States citizen in 1953. Oldenburg is also noted for excellent preparatory drawings for his sculptures and for prints of his sculpture subjects. Deborah Leveton

See also **Pop Art.**

Oldfield, Barney (1878-1946), was the first person to drive an automobile at a speed of 1 mile (1.6 kilometers) per minute. His name became synonymous with speed after he did this in a famous test at Indianapolis on June 15, 1903. Henry Ford built Oldfield's first racing car, the "999." In it, Oldfield won his first race at Detroit in 1902. In 1910, at Daytona Beach, Florida, he raced a mile at an average speed of 131 miles per hour (211 kilometers per hour), a record then. Berner Eli Oldfield was born on Jan. 29 or June 3, 1878, in Wauseon, Ohio. He died on Oct. 4, 1946. Sylvia Wilkinson

See also **Aviation** (picture: Airplanes raced against automobiles).

Olds, Ransom Eli (1864-1950), was a pioneering automobile inventor and manufacturer. Two automobiles were named for him: the Oldsmobile and the Reo (from his initials). Olds was one of only a few early auto manufacturers who made reliable, inexpensive cars for the common people.

Olds was born on June 3, 1864, in Geneva, Ohio. He dropped out of high school and went into his family's steam engine business. In 1887, Olds adapted a steam engine to a three-wheeled vehicle. He gradually improved the design. Olds became convinced that steam-powered cars had a limited future. He then experimented with internal combustion engines.

In 1897, Olds secured a patent for a carriage with a gasoline engine. In 1899, he moved to Detroit and established the Olds Motor Works. The company introduced the Curved Dash Oldsmobile in 1901. By 1904, Olds Motor Works assembled more than 5,000 cars, making it the world's largest motorcar manufacturer. Workers at Olds's factories assembled cars on moving platforms, similar to the assembly lines later made famous by the American automobile manufacturer Henry Ford.

In 1904, Olds left Olds Motor Works. That same year, he founded the Reo Motor Car Company. He served as its president and chairman before retiring in 1936. Olds died on Aug. 26, 1950. John A. Heitmann

See also **Automobile** (History).

Olduvai Gorge, on the Serengeti Plain in northern Tanzania, is an important source of fossilized bones of prehistoric human beings. The gorge is a Y-shaped canyon about 30 miles (50 kilometers) long and as much as 330 feet (100 meters) deep. Over the past 2 million years, geological processes have produced seven sediment layers, called *beds,* at the site—four major layers beneath three thinner ones. Prehistoric human beings and other animals were preserved as fossils as the layers accumulated. Over time, seasonal water runoff from the Olduvai River and wind erosion carved the gorge out of the sediments, exposing the fossil bones.

German scientists discovered and explored the gorge in the early 1900's, but World War I (1914-1918) interrupted their work. In the 1930's, the British anthropologists Louis and Mary Leakey began exploring the gorge. In the early 1960's, they found fossils of early human ancestors called *Homo habilis.* This species is considered by most anthropologists to be one of the earliest types of

human beings. The fossils, found in the lower beds, are nearly 2 million years old. Simple stone tools and fossil animal bones with butchery marks made by the sharp edges of stone tools were also found. Today, excavations at Olduvai Gorge continue to yield important fossils of prehistoric human beings. Alan E. Mann

See also **Homo habilis; Leakey, Louis Seymour Bazett; Leakey, Mary Douglas; Tanzania** (map).

Oleander, OH lee AN duhr, is a popular ornamental flowering shrub. The plant sometimes grows 15 feet (4.6 meters) tall. It has leathery, lance-shaped leaves and colorful roselike flowers. The two most common varieties have red and white blossoms. The oleander is native to the warm parts of Asia and to the Mediterranean region. Gardeners plant the oleander outdoors in warm climates. But they grow it indoors in pots and tubs in temperate regions, which have cool or cold winters. The oleander is a favorite porch plant in summer.

Gardeners raise oleander from cuttings. When the cuttings are placed in water, they form roots in a few weeks. After the cuttings root, they must be transplanted to moist, rich soil, where they grow well. All parts of the oleander are poisonous to eat. Walter S. Judd

Scientific classification. The oleander's scientific name is *Nerium oleander.*

O'Leary, Hazel Rollins (1937-   ), served as the United States secretary of energy under President Bill Clinton from 1993 to 1997. She was the first woman and the first African American to hold that post.

Before O'Leary became secretary, she worked for the U.S. Federal Energy Administration and the Department of Energy under Presidents Gerald Ford and Jimmy Carter. In these positions, she was responsible for federal government programs designed to conserve energy and protect the environment. From 1989 to 1993, O'Leary was an executive of the Northern States Power Company, a utility based in Minneapolis.

Hazel Reid was born on May 17, 1937, in Newport News, Virginia. She earned a bachelor's degree from Fisk University in 1959 and a law degree from Rutgers University in 1966. Her first marriage, to Carl Rollins, ended in divorce. In 1980, she married John F. O'Leary, a former deputy secretary of energy. Barbara A. Reynolds

Oleic acid. See Fat (Structure).

Oleomargarine. See Margarine.

Olericulture. See Horticulture.

Olfactory bulb. See Nose; Smell.

Oligarchy, AHL uh GAHR kee, is any type of government in which power is held by relatively few people. An oligarchy may take many different forms. For example, a republic may be an oligarchy if only a few people have the right to vote (see **Republic**). An aristocracy, in which rulers come from the "best" members of the community, is also a form of oligarchy (see **Aristocracy**). In most oligarchies, the ruling group has power because of its wealth or military authority.

Oligarchies have existed throughout history. Most ancient Greek city-states, such as Sparta, were good examples of oligarchy. In those city-states, political power was restricted to a small group of citizens. Modern oligarchies have included the South African government that operated until 1994 under *apartheid.* Apartheid was a system of racial segregation that also limited political power to a minority of white citizens. Thomas S. Vontz

Oligopoly. See Monopoly and competition.
Oliphant, *AHL ih fuhnt,* **Patrick Bruce** (1935-   ), is a well-known editorial cartoonist. The figures in his cartoons have exaggerated features, and his work is more biting than most other editorial cartoonists. Most Oliphant cartoons include Punk the Penguin, a character that usually comments on the action in the drawings. Oliphant won the Pulitzer Prize for cartooning in 1967.

Oliphant was born on July 24, 1935, in Adelaide, Australia. In 1955, he became the editorial cartoonist of *The (Adelaide) Advertiser.* He came to the United States in 1964 to join the *Denver Post* as editorial cartoonist. From 1975 to 1981, he worked on *The Washington Star.* Universal Press Syndicate distributes Oliphant's cartoons. Many collections of his work have been published, including *Oliphant's Presidents* (1990) and *Leadership* (2007).   Roy Paul Nelson

Olive is the fruit of a tree that is native to the Mediterranean region. Olives are cultivated both for their oil and for the fruit itself. People have grown olives since prehistoric times. Olive trees first grew in the eastern Mediterranean basin. Centuries ago, they began to grow wild around the Mediterranean Sea. The Spaniards brought olive trees to South America, and they were introduced into California in 1769. More recently, they have been introduced to Australia.

Appearance of the fruit and tree. The fruit may be oval or oblong. As it matures, it turns from green to yellow to red to purple-black. It has a smooth skin, and its flesh surrounds a hard pit. Both the flesh and the seed in the pit contain oil, which makes up 10 to 40 percent of the mature fresh fruit's weight. Fresh olives contain *oleuropein,* a bitter substance that makes them unpleasant to eat before processing. During processing, this substance is largely or entirely removed.

The olive tree's bark and leaves are a soft gray-green, and its trunk becomes gnarled as it ages. Olive trees live longer than most other fruit trees. There are olive trees in the Middle East that may be over 2,000 years old.

A mature olive tree may have as many as 500,000 small flowers. Most of the flowers are imperfect, and fruit cannot grow from them. They give off pollen, which is usually carried from flower to flower by the wind. Most varieties of olive trees bear a large crop one season and a small crop the next.

Cultivation. Parts cut off from an olive tree may take root and grow into new trees. The trees will grow in many types of soil but need good drainage. To produce large fruit, the grower must irrigate and prune the trees. Fertilizers that add nitrogen to the soil can increase yields. The olive tree grows best where the climate is hot and dry. But for bearing good fruit, the tree needs a moderate supply of water. The fruit matures from October to January and is injured if the temperature falls below 26 °F (–3 °C). The tree itself is not seriously injured until the temperature falls to 16 °F (–9 °C). The fruit needs much heat to have a good quality when mature. The air must be dry when the flowers blossom, and also when the fruit begins to grow.

Harvesting and preparation for market. Most olive-producing nations grow olives primarily for their oil. Until the early 2000's, nearly all olives grown in the United States were processed to be eaten. Now, more olives are processed for oil than for eating.

Harvesting olives requires careful handling. Olives grown for their oil may be mechanically harvested. Olives grown for eating have traditionally been picked by hand to reduce damage to the fruit.

Olives are harvested later than other fruit crops, in the fall and winter. Generally, olives that are harvested later accumulate more oil and have milder flavors.

Olives processed for eating are either green or black. One of three major processing methods may be used: (1) the Spanish, (2) the American, and (3) the Greek.

Most green olives are prepared by the Spanish process. In this process, unripe, yellowish-green olives are placed in a solution of sodium hydroxide (also called lye). The sodium hydroxide removes most of the bitter taste of the oleuropein. The olives are washed and then fermented in brine. They are kept submerged continuously to prevent darkening, which can result from exposure to the air. The fermented olives may be pitted and stuffed with such fillings as almonds and pimentos. The fruit is then packed in fresh brine and pasteurized.

In the United States, most black olives are prepared by the American process. This process ripens immature, yellow-to-red olives artificially. The fruit is alternately submerged in sodium hydroxide and exposed to the air until no bitterness remains and the olives have turned brown to black. The fruit is then washed and pickled. After canning, the olives are sterilized at 240 °F (116 °C).

In the Greek process, ripe, purple-black olives undergo a slow fermentation in brine. During fermentation, the fruit's bitterness decreases. This process traditionally does not use sodium hydroxide.

Production. Nations along the Mediterranean Sea grow most of the world's olives. Spain is the largest producer, followed by Italy, Greece, and Turkey. World olive production is about 19 million tons (17 million metric tons) yearly. The United States olive crop comes almost entirely from California. California is the only part of the country that has a Mediterranean climate. Olive trees also grow along the Gulf of Mexico but do not bear fruit there.   Vito S. Polito

Scientific classification. The olive tree's scientific name is *Olea europaea.*

See also **Olive oil; Spain** (picture: Olive orchards).

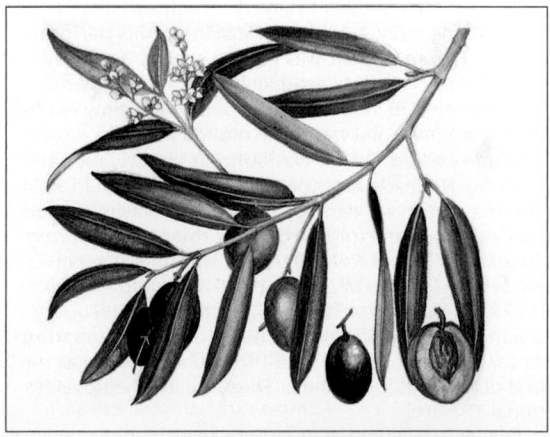

WORLD BOOK illustration by Kate Lloyd-Jones, Linden Artists Ltd.
Olives are a small, oval or oblong fruit. They are grown chiefly for their oil, which can make up about half the flesh of the fruit.

Olive oil is a fragrant, edible oil made from olives. It is used primarily as a salad dressing and as a cooking oil. It ranges in taste from sweet to bland and consists almost entirely of unsaturated fat (see **Fat**). Most olive oil has a light greenish-yellow color.

Olive oil is widely used in countries along the Mediterranean Sea. Spain is the world's leading producer. Greece and Italy also make large quantities of olive oil. In the United States, it is produced only in California.

Olive oil is made by crushing and pressing ripe olives. Whole olive fruit consists of 10 to 40 percent oil, and the fruit pulp is 60 to 80 percent oil. Producers use hydraulic presses to squeeze the oil out of the fruit under low pressure. This technique, called *cold-pressing,* generates little heat, and so the oil retains its flavor, color, and nutritional value. Thus, olive oil, unlike most other vegetable oils, needs no further processing before being packaged. In addition, olive oil can be stored for months without refrigeration or danger of spoilage.

Pressing commonly occurs in several stages, with only some of the oil being extracted at each stage. The process remains basically the same throughout, but the quality of the oil declines with each pressing. In most cases, olives are pressed at temperatures no higher than 80 °F (27 °C). Pressing the fruit produces a mixture of oil and water. The oil is separated from the water in a spinning machine called a *centrifuge,* or it is skimmed off the water's surface in a process called *decanting.*

The first pressing gives the highest quality oil, usually called *virgin* or *extra-virgin* olive oil. Virgin olive oil costs more than other vegetable oils. The lower-quality oils from later pressings are often blended in small amounts with such refined oils as soybean or cottonseed oil. Olive oil from the final pressing is inedible. This oil, called *olive residue* or *olive foots,* is used in cosmetics, detergents, medicines, soap, and textiles.   M. E. Parish

See also **Olive; Vegetable oil.**

Olives, Mount of. See Mount of Olives.

Olivier, *oh LIHV ee AY,* **Laurence** (1907-1989), became one of the leading English actors of the 1900's. Olivier was a versatile performer and was especially known for his acting in the plays of William Shakespeare. His film versions of Shakespeare's *Henry V* (1944), *Hamlet* (1948), and *Richard III* (1955) are considered classics. Olivier produced, directed, and starred in all three films. He won an Academy Award as best actor for his performance in *Hamlet.* Olivier also was given a special Academy Award for his work as producer, director, and star of *Henry V.* In 1979, he received a special Academy Award for his lifetime achievement in motion pictures.

Laurence Kerr Olivier was born on May 22, 1907, in Dorking. He made his professional stage debut in 1924. His first screen appearance was in 1930. Olivier gained international fame for his romantic roles in *Wuthering Heights* (1939) and *Rebecca* (1940). His other films include *The Divorce of Lady X* (1938), *Pride and Prejudice* (1940), *Lady Hamilton* (1941), *The Entertainer* (1960), *Sleuth* (1972), *Marathon Man* (1976), and *The Boys from Brazil* (1978). From 1963 until 1973, Olivier served as the first director of the National Theatre (now the Royal National Theatre).

Olivier was knighted in 1947. In 1970, he became Lord Olivier of Brighton, the first actor in English history to be named a baron. His autobiography, *Confessions of an*

Culver Pictures

Laurence Olivier gained international fame for his romantic performance in the 1940 film *Rebecca,* co-starring Joan Fontaine.

Actor, was published in 1982. *On Acting* (1986) is a series of essays about his professional life. He was married to the British actress Jill Esmond from 1930 to 1940, the British actress Vivien Leigh from 1940 to 1960, and the British actress Joan Plowright from 1961 until his death on July 11, 1989.   Daniel J. Watermeier

Olivine, *AHL uh veen,* is a rock-forming mineral that consists of silicon, oxygen, magnesium, and iron. Olivine occurs primarily in dark igneous rocks rich in iron and magnesium but poor in silicon. It usually appears as grainy masses or embedded crystals. It is generally one of the first minerals to crystallize from dark-colored *magma* (melted rock material).

Most types of olivine range in color from clear green to yellow-green, but iron-rich varieties may be brown. Olivine is relatively hard and cannot be scratched by a knife. The most common olivine is forsterite, which is rich in magnesium. Clear green olivine used as a gemstone is called *peridot* (see **Peridot**).   Mark A. Helper

Olmec Indians, *OHL mehk,* developed what may have been the earliest civilization in North America. The Olmec civilization flourished between about 1250 and 400 B.C. on the Mexican Gulf Coast, in what are now the states of Veracruz and Tabasco. Some scholars recognize Olmec influences in the artwork and religious practices of later American cultures. These cultures include the Maya and the Aztec.

The Olmec built their largest sites atop natural rises within seasonally flooded lowlands. Olmec workers leveled some of these hills. They built massive earthen mounds on others. The largest Olmec site, called San Lorenzo today, covered more than 2 square miles (5 square kilometers). It was the biggest American settlement of its time. The Olmec grew crops on lands made fertile by seasonal flooding. They also fished and collected wild plant foods. Rivers served as important routes for transportation, communication, and trade.

The Olmec are best known for their colossal carved stone sculptures. These include huge human heads, massive tabletop altars, and figures with both animal and human features. Some of the sculptures weigh up to 20 tons (18 metric tons). Olmec artisans carved the sculptures from gigantic stones that were transported from sites more than 50 miles (80 kilometers) away. Other objects found at Olmec sites include polished stone mirrors, blocks of a stone called *serpentine,* polished stone axes, and carved wooden human busts. Many of these materials came from hundreds of miles away. Some of these objects were placed in symbolic positions at Olmec sites. Others were stored in large *caches* (hidden storage places). Carl J. Wendt

See also **Maya** (History); **Sculpture** (American Indian sculpture).

Olmert, *OHL mehrt,* **Ehud,** *eh HOOD* (1945-   ), was prime minister of Israel from May 2006 to March 2009. He had served as acting prime minister after Prime Minister Ariel Sharon suffered a stroke earlier in 2006.

Olmert was elected to the Knesset (Israeli parliament) as a member of the conservative Likud party in 1973. He served under Prime Minister Yitzhak Shamir as minister without portfolio responsible for minority affairs from 1988 to 1990 and as health minister from 1990 to 1992. From 1993 to 2003, Olmert was mayor of Jerusalem. As mayor, he helped develop Jerusalem's road system.

In 2003, Sharon appointed Olmert deputy prime minister. Olmert also served as communications minister and as finance minister. He was one of the first Israeli ministers to suggest that Israel withdraw troops and settlers from the Gaza Strip, an area on the Mediterranean coast that Israel had occupied since 1967.

In 2005, Sharon quit Likud to form Kadima, a moderate party, after many Likud members opposed his plan for withdrawal from the Gaza Strip. Olmert was one of the first to join. The withdrawal was completed in 2005. Olmert became head of Kadima in 2006.

Starting in late 2006, Olmert faced multiple corruption investigations. He denied any wrongdoing. In July 2008, Olmert announced that he would resign as prime minister and head of Kadima. Tzipi Livni replaced him as Kadima leader in September. After elections in February 2009, Benjamin Netanyahu replaced Olmert as prime minister.

Olmert was born in what is now Binyamina, Israel, on Sept. 30, 1945. His father was also a Knesset member. Olmert served in the Israel Defense Forces and later became an army reporter. He holds a law degree from the Hebrew University of Jerusalem. Jonathan Mendilow

See also **Kadima.**

Olmsted, Frederick Law (1822-1903), was an American landscape architect, city planner, and writer on social issues. Olmsted's career was shaped by his idea of a civilized society. Through his landscape designs and writings, he tried to recast the form of cities and suburbs in the United States, and to promote the refinement and culture he thought the citizens of a republic could attain. Olmsted criticized the slaveholding South because he believed it lacked the social and cultural institutions that would raise the level of civilization there.

In 1858, Olmsted and the English architect Calvert Vaux submitted a plan for New York City's Central Park, the first great urban park in the United States. Olmsted then supervised construction of the park and modified its design to give the park its most distinctive features. These features include the separation of all forms of traffic and the sweeping natural scenery that would provide New Yorkers with an alternative to the sights and sounds of the city. After 1872, Olmsted and various part-

ners designed Belle Isle Park in Detroit, Mount Royal Park in Montreal, and Roger Williams Park in Providence, Rhode Island. Olmsted planned park systems for Seattle; Boston; Atlanta; New York City; and Louisville, Kentucky.

Olmsted planned suburban developments, colleges, and the grounds for many institutions and public buildings. His most notable designs include the grounds of the U.S. Capitol in Washington, D.C. (1874) and the layout for the World's Columbian Exposition in Chicago (1893). He also designed such communities as Riverside, Illinois; and Parkside, in Buffalo, New York.

Olmsted was born in Hartford, Connecticut, on April 26, 1822. He died on Aug. 28, 1903. His son Frederick Law Olmsted, Jr., was also a well-known landscape architect and city planner. David Schuyler

Olson, Charles (1910-1970), was one of the most influential American poets of his time. In 1948, Olson began teaching at Black Mountain College, an experimental school in Black Mountain, North Carolina. He served as the school's *rector* (head) from 1951 to 1956. At the college, Olson taught Robert Creeley, Robert Duncan, and other young writers who became leading poets.

Charles John Olson was born on Dec. 27, 1910, in Worcester, Massachusetts. His chief work was a long *cycle* (series of poems) called *The Maximus Poems.* Publication of this complex work began in 1953 and ended in 1975, after his death. In it, Olson used Gloucester, Massachusetts, symbolically to praise what he admired in human life and to attack the greed and commercialism he saw in American culture.

Olson first gained recognition with *Call Me Ishmael* (1947), a critical study of the American author Herman Melville. Olson's major poems and critical writings appear in *Selected Writings* (1966). This collection includes Olson's well-known essay "Projective Verse" (1950), in which he discussed his complicated style of poetry. Olson's *Collected Prose* was published in 1997, after his death. He died on Jan. 10, 1970. Elmer W. Borklund

Olympia, *oh LIHM pee uh,* is a valley about 11 miles (18 kilometers) from Pírgos, Greece. In ancient times, religion, politics, and athletics centered at Olympia. The Olympic Games, held there every four years, were so important in Greek life that they were used as the basis for the calendar. All the buildings in Olympia were for worship or for games. The religious buildings clustered in the *Altis* (sacred grove), which lies where the Cladeus River flows into the Alfios River. The buildings included the temples of Zeus and Hera, the Pelopion, the Philippeion, and the great altars.

The athletic buildings lay just outside the Altis. They included a gymnasium; the palaestra, a wrestling and boxing school; the stadium; and the hippodrome, where chariot and horse races were held.

The Olympic Games were banned in A.D. 393, and a fort was built in the Altis. Later, earthquakes and floods covered Olympia under 20 feet (6 meters) of earth.

In 1829, a French expedition began excavations at the temple of Zeus. The German government continued this work. Between 1875 and 1879, the entire Altis and many of the surrounding buildings were uncovered. Fragments of sculpture, coins, terra cottas, and bronzes have been found. The major discoveries were two statues, the *Victory of Paeonius* (423 B.C.) and the *Hermes of*

Praxiteles. The originals of all discoveries remained in the possession of Greece. The Germans reserved the right to take casts from sculptures, coins, or other discoveries. A museum with Olympian relics stands at the modern town of Olympia at the edge of the ruins. The modern town provides hotels and other services to the many tourists who visit the ruins.   John J. Baxevanis

See also **Olympic Games.**

Olympia, *oh LIHM pee uh* (pop. 46,478; met. area pop. 252,264), is the capital of the state of Washington. An important port city, it lies at the southern tip of Puget Sound. For location, see **Washington** (political map).

Pioneers first settled the area in 1845. Edmund Sylvester founded Olympia in 1850. It became the capital of the Washington Territory when the territory was created in 1853. The city was incorporated in 1859. Olympia was named the state capital when Washington became a state in 1889. The city is the seat of Thurston County and has a council-manager form of government.

For hundreds of years, the Squaxin, Nisqually, Chehalis, Suquamish, and Duwamish Indians shared access to abundant shellfish and salmon in the area. Today, the Olympia oyster is an important local export.

Olympia began as a shipping center for the area's products, including lumber, sandstone, coal, and grain. Over the years, lumber mills and fruit canneries developed, attracting new immigrants as workers.

Today, many Olympians work for the state government. The State Capitol sits on a bluff above Budd Inlet, south of downtown. Completed in 1927, the Capitol's 287-foot (87-meter) white dome towers over the area. Area schools include the Evergreen State College and St. Martin's University. Joint Base Lewis-McChord, a combined U.S. Air Force and Army base, lies between Olympia and Tacoma.   Edward L. Echtle, Jr.

Olympiad, *oh LIHM pee ad.* In the Greek system of telling time, an Olympiad was the period of four years that elapsed between two successive celebrations of the Olympian, or Olympic, Games. This way of figuring time became common about 300 B.C. All events were dated from 776 B.C., the start of the first known Olympiad.

This method of counting time ceased about A.D. 440, after the 304th Olympiad. The Olympiads were used as measures of time by later Greek historians and other writers to refer to preceding centuries, but they were never in everyday use, as were months and years.

The beginning of the year of the Olympiad was determined by the first full moon after the *summer solstice,* the moment when the sun reaches its northernmost position in the sky. The first full moon after the solstice occurs about July 1.   Bruce F. Field

Olympians. See **Mythology** (Greek mythology).

Olympias, *oh LIHM pih uhs* (375?-316 B.C.), was the wife of Philip II of Macedonia and the mother of Alexander the Great. She had much influence on Alexander. She told him that his real father was the god Zeus-Ammon, not Philip. She feared that Philip might choose another heir. Many people believe she had Philip killed to ensure that Alexander would become king. After Alexander's death in 323 B.C., Olympias tried to keep the empire for her grandson, Alexander IV. She failed, and in 316 B.C. was captured by Cassander, a Macedonian prince. Olympias was eventually killed. See also **Alexander the Great** (His youth); **Philip II.**   Judith P. Hallett

Olympic Games

Olympic Games are the most important international athletic competition in the world. The Olympics bring together thousands of the world's finest athletes to compete against one another in a variety of individual and team sports. Millions of people have attended the games, and more than 1 billion people throughout the world watch the Olympics on television.

The Olympic Games originated in ancient Greece and were held from 776 B.C. to A.D. 393. The modern games began in 1896. The organizers revived the games to encourage world peace and friendship and to promote healthy sporting competition for the youth of the world.

The Olympic Games consist of the Summer Games and the Winter Games. From 1896 to 1992, the Olympics were held every four years, except in 1916 during World War I, and in 1940 and 1944 during World War II. The Winter Games, which were established in 1924, took place the same year as the Summer Games. Beginning in 1994, the Winter and Summer Games were divided and scheduled on four-year cycles two years apart.

Olympic ceremonies and symbols

Colorful ceremonies combine with thrilling athletic competition to create the special feeling of excitement in the Olympics. The Opening Ceremony is particularly impressive. The Olympic athletes of Greece march into the stadium first, in honor of the original games held in ancient Greece. The other athletes follow in alphabetical order by country according to the spelling in the lan-

Sites of the Olympic Games

Year	Summer	Winter
1896	Athens, Greece	Not held
1900	Paris, France	Not held
1904	St. Louis, U.S.	Not held
1908	London, U.K.	Not held
1912	Stockholm, Sweden	Not held
1916	Not held	Not held
1920	Antwerp, Belgium	Not held
1924	Paris, France	Chamonix, France
1928	Amsterdam, the Netherlands	St. Moritz, Switzerland
1932	Los Angeles, United States	Lake Placid, U.S.
1936	Berlin, Germany	Garmisch-Partenkirchen, Germany
1940	Not held	Not held
1944	Not held	Not held
1948	London, United Kingdom	St. Moritz, Switzerland
1952	Helsinki, Finland	Oslo, Norway
1956	Melbourne, Australia	Cortina, Italy
1960	Rome, Italy	Squaw Valley, U.S.
1964	Tokyo, Japan	Innsbruck, Austria
1968	Mexico City, Mexico	Grenoble, France
1972	Munich, West Germany	Sapporo, Japan
1976	Montreal, Canada	Innsbruck, Austria
1980	Moscow, Soviet Union	Lake Placid, U.S.
1984	Los Angeles, U.S.	Sarajevo, Yugoslavia
1988	Seoul, South Korea	Calgary, Canada
1992	Barcelona, Spain	Albertville, France
1994		Lillehammer, Norway
1996	Atlanta, United States	
1998		Nagano, Japan
2000	Sydney, Australia	
2002		Salt Lake City, U.S.
2004	Athens, Greece	
2006		Turin, Italy
2008	Beijing, China	
2010		Vancouver, Canada
2012	London, United Kingdom	
2014		Sochi, Russia
2016	Rio de Janeiro, Brazil	

The **Opening Ceremony** of the Olympic Games features the entry of the athletes into the stadium. Athletes from Greece enter first, followed by teams from the other countries.

Paul J. Sutton, Duomo

The **Olympic symbol** consists of five interlocking rings that represent Africa, Asia, Australia, Europe, and the Americas.

guage of the host country. The athletes of the host country enter last. The president or other head of state of the host country opens the games. The Olympic flag is raised, trumpets play, and cannons boom in salute.

The most dramatic moment of the Opening Ceremony is the lighting of the Olympic flame. The flame symbolizes the light of spirit, knowledge, and life; and it is a messenger of peace. The fire is ignited in Olympia, Greece, by using a mirror to concentrate the rays of the sun. Runners transport the flame in a torch relay from Greece to the site of the games.

Most runners carry the Olympic flame on foot. But many other kinds of transportation, including airplanes, horses, and skis, have been used. The final runner lights a huge *caldron* (kettle). The flame burns throughout the games and then is extinguished during the Closing Ceremony.

The Olympic symbol, created in 1913, consists of five interlocking rings that represent the continents of Africa, Asia, Australia, Europe, and the Americas. The colors of the rings, from left to right, are blue, yellow, black, green, and red. The flag of every nation competing in the games has at least one of these colors. Under the rings is the Olympic motto, the Latin words *Citius, Altius, Fortius.* The words are translated as *Swifter, Higher, Stronger.*

The International Olympic Committee

The International Olympic Committee (IOC) is the governing body of the Olympic Games. The IOC has headquarters in Lausanne, Switzerland. The committee approves the sports and events to be included in the games. The IOC also selects the host cities for the Summer Games and Winter Games, seven years in advance. The cities bidding for the games must prove they can provide athletic facilities for the games and housing for the athletes, coaches, officials, and visiting spectators. Host cities provide a special housing compound called the Olympic Village for the athletes and coaches. The prospective hosts must also convince the IOC that they

The **Olympic flame** is lighted during the Opening Ceremony. The fire is ignited in Olympia, Greece, and transported by relay to the site of the games. The flame symbolizes the light of spirit, knowledge, and life, and it is a herald of peace.

Manny Millan, *Sports Illustrated*

The **medal ceremony** takes place after the finals of each event. The top three finishers receive a medal and a diploma. They stand at attention on a platform while the flags of their countries are raised and a band plays the national anthem of the country of the gold medal winner.

David Black

can furnish adequate transportation, food service, and cultural activities. Host cities are chosen by a majority vote of the IOC.

Originally, members of the IOC were elected for life. But according to a rule change in 1995, all members must retire before they reach the age of 81. Members elected in 1999 or later must retire the year they turn 70. IOC members are not allowed to accept instructions on voting from any government or other group or individual. New members of the IOC are elected by current members. There are no rules setting the size of the IOC or what countries should be represented.

Olympic competition

Every country or territory competing in the Olympic Games is represented by a national Olympic committee. In the early 2000's, more than 200 nations and territories had such groups. Each committee is responsible for selecting its national team, providing uniforms and equipment, and furnishing transportation to the Olympic site.

Most countries use government funds to pay their Olympic expenses. The IOC also provides financial aid. The United States is the only large nation whose government does not give its team financial support. The U.S.

The Closing Ceremony comes after the end of the athletic competition. The Ceremony is marked by spectacle and concludes with the extinguishing of the Olympic flame, which had burned throughout the competition.

AP/Wide World

team is largely financed by contributions from private corporations and individuals.

Selection of the athletes. In many countries, athletes qualify for the Olympics by winning or finishing high in competitions called *selection trials*. In most cases, athletes are invited to the trials based on their performance in national and international competitions.

An athlete representing a country must be a citizen of that country. For many years, only amateur athletes competed in the games. This gave an advantage to wealthy athletes who could devote all their time to training without worrying about earning money. Professional athletes are now eligible to compete in all Olympic sports except boxing.

Entries. Each sport has its own standards for eligibility for the Olympics. There are special "wild-card" entry provisions for countries that do not meet the standard. In addition, nations that fail to qualify in any sport are allowed to enter up to two men and two women, though only in track and field or swimming. If a nation receives a wild-card entry in another sport, that entry is subtracted from its quota of two men and two women.

Team sports are limited to 8 to 16 teams per sport. National teams must win or place high in qualifying tournaments to make the final competition. The host country is allowed to enter a team in every team event.

Medals. The top three finishers in each event receive a medal and a diploma. The next five finishers get only a diploma. Each first-place winner receives a gold medal, which is actually made of silver and coated with gold. The second-place medal is made of silver, and the third-place medal is bronze. All members of a winning relay team get a medal, including those who participated only in qualifying rounds. In team sports, all the members of a winning team who have played in at least one of the games during the competition receive a medal.

The top three finishers receive their medals in a ceremony after the event. The medal winners stand at attention on a platform, with the gold medalist in the middle. The silver medalist stands on the gold medalist's right and the bronze medalist on the left. The flags of their countries are raised, and a band plays the national anthem of the country of the gold medal winner.

Olympic competition is intended to test the skill of individuals and teams, not nations. No country "wins" the Olympics. However, medal totals are compiled by the press and by the IOC.

The Summer Games

The Summer Games are held during the summer season of the host city, usually between July and October, and last 17 days. Athletes compete in about 300 separate events during the Summer Games. A sport must be played in at least 75 countries on four continents before it can be considered for men's competition. To be eligible for women's competition, a sport must be played in 40 countries on three continents.

The Summer Games have grown enormously. In the first modern games in 1896, about 245 male athletes representing 14 nations competed. Today, more than 10,000 male and female athletes representing more than 200 countries and territories participate.

The Winter Games

The Winter Games are usually held in February and last 17 days. A sport must be played in at least 25 countries on three continents to be considered. The Winter Olympics include over 85 events. The games attract approximately 2,500 athletes from about 80 countries.

Text continued on page 750.

2010 Winter Olympic Games

Medal-winning nations

Nation	Gold	Silver	Bronze	Total
United States	9	15	13	37
Germany	10	13	7	30
Canada	14	7	5	26
Norway	9	8	6	23
Austria	4	6	6	16
Russia	3	5	7	15
South Korea	6	6	2	14
China	5	2	4	11
Sweden	5	2	4	11
France	2	3	6	11
Switzerland	6	0	3	9
Netherlands	4	1	3	8
Czech Republic	2	0	4	6
Poland	1	3	2	6
Italy	1	1	3	5
Japan	0	3	2	5
Finland	0	1	4	5
Australia	2	1	0	3
Belarus	1	1	1	3
Slovakia	1	1	1	3
Croatia	0	2	1	3
Slovenia	0	2	1	3
Latvia	0	2	0	2
United Kingdom	1	0	0	1
Estonia	0	1	0	1
Kazakhstan	0	1	0	1

Alpine skiing

Event	Winner	Nation	Time
Men			
Downhill	Didier Defago	Switzerland	1 min 54.31 s
Combined	Bode Miller	United States	2 min 44.92 s
Slalom	Giuliano Razzoli	Italy	1 min 39.32 s
Giant slalom	Carlo Janka	Switzerland	2 min 37.83 s
Super G	Aksel Lund Svindal	Norway	1 min 30.34 s
Women			
Downhill	Lindsey Vonn	United States	1 min 44.19 s
Combined	Maria Riesch	Germany	2 min 09.14 s
Slalom	Maria Riesch	Germany	1 min 42.89 s
Giant slalom	Viktoria Rebensburg	Germany	2 min 27.11 s
Super G	Andrea Fischbacher	Austria	1 min 20.14 s

Biathlon

Event	Winner	Nation
Men		
10-kilometer sprint	Vincent Jay	France
12.5-kilometer pursuit	Bjorn Ferry	Sweden
15-kilometer mass	Evgeny Ustyugov	Russia
20-kilometer individual	Emil Hegle Svendsen	Norway
30-kilometer relay	Hanevold, Svendsen, Bjoerndalen, Boe	Norway
Women		
7.5-kilometer sprint	Anastazia Kuzmina	Slovakia
10-kilometer pursuit	Magdalena Neuner	Germany
12.5-kilometer mass	Magdalena Neuner	Germany
15-kilometer individual	Tora Berger	Norway
24-kilometer relay	Bogaliy-Titovets, Medvedtseva, Zaitseva, Sleptsova	Russia

Bobsledding

Event	Winner	Nation	Time†
Two-man	Lange, Kuske	Germany	3 min 26.65 s
Four-man	Holcomb, Mesler, Tomasevicz, Olsen	United States	3 min 24.46 s
Two-woman	Humphries, Moyse	Canada	3 min 32.28 s

Kim Yu-Na of South Korea won the gold medal in women's figure skating at the 2010 Winter Olympic Games in Vancouver, Canada. The judges awarded her a record 228.56 points. Many observers described her performance as one of the greatest in Olympic figure-skating history.

© Kevork Djansezian, Getty Images

Cross-country skiing

Event	Winner	Nation	Time
Men			
1.3-kilometer sprint	Nikita Kriukov	Russia	3 min 36.3 s
15-kilometer free	Dario Cologna	Switzerland	33 min 36.3 s
30-kilometer pursuit	Marcus Hellner	Sweden	1 h 15 min 11.4 s
50-kilometer classic	Petter Northug	Norway	2 h 5 min 35.5 s
Team sprint	Pettersen, Northug	Norway	19 min 01.0 s
40-kilometer relay	Richardsson, Hellner, Soedergren, Olsson	Sweden	1 h 45 min 05.4 s
Women			
1.1-kilometer sprint	Marit Bjoergen	Norway	3 min 39.2 s
10-kilometer free	Charlotte Kalla	Sweden	24 min 58.4 s
15-kilometer pursuit	Marit Bjoergen	Norway	39 min 58.1 s
30-kilometer classic	Justyna Kowalczyk	Poland	1 h 30 min 33.7 s
Team sprint	Sachenbacher-Stehle, Nystad	Germany	18 min 03.7 s
20-kilometer relay	Skofterud, Steira, Bjoergen, Johaug	Norway	55 min 19.5 s

Curling

Winning nation

Canada (men)
Sweden (women)

Figure skating

Event	Winner	Nation
Men	Evan Lysacek	United States
Women	Yu-Na Kim	South Korea
Pairs	Shen, Zhao	China
Ice dancing	Virtue, Moir	Canada

Freestyle skiing

Event	Winner	Nation
Men		
Aerials	Alexei Grishin	Belarus
Moguls	Alexandre Bilodeau	Canada
Ski cross	Michael Schmid	Switzerland
Women		
Aerials	Lydia Lassila	Australia
Moguls	Hannah Kearney	United States
Ski cross	Ashleigh McIvor	Canada

Ice hockey

Winning nation

Canada (men)
Canada (women)

Luge

Event	Winner	Nation	Time
Men's singles	Felix Loch	Germany	3 min 13.085 s
Women's singles	Tatjana Huefner	Germany	2 min 46.524 s
Men's doubles	Linger, Linger	Austria	1 min 22.705 s

Nordic combined skiing

Event	Winner	Nation
Individual NH	Jason Lamy Chappuis	France
Individual LH	Bill Demong	United States
Team	Gruber, Gottwald, Stecher, Kreiner	Austria

Short-track speed skating

Event	Winner	Nation	Time
Men			
500 meters	Charles Hamelin	Canada	42.123 s
1,000 meters	Jung-Su Lee	South Korea	1 min 32.023 s
1,500 meters	Jung-Su Lee	South Korea	2 min 17.611 s
5,000-meter relay	Hamelin, Hamelin, Jean, Tremblay	Canada	6 min 43.610 s
Women			
500 meters	Meng Wang	China	44.725 s
1,000 meters	Meng Wang	China	1 min 31.932 s
1,500 meters	Yang Zhou	China	2 min 42.801 s
3,000-meter	Sun, Wang, Zhang, Zhou	China	4 min 06.610 s*

Skeleton

Event	Winner	Nation	Time†
Men's singles	Jon Montgomery	Canada	3 min 29.73 s
Women's singles	Amy Williams	United Kingdom	3 min 35.64 s

Ski jumping

Event	Winner	Nation
90 meters	Simon Ammann	Switzerland
120 meters	Simon Ammann	Switzerland
120-meter team	Loitzl, Morgenstern, Schlierenzauer, Kofler	Austria

Snowboarding

Event	Winner	Nation
Men		
Cross	Seth Wescott	United States
Parallel giant slalom	Jasey Jay Anderson	Canada
Halfpipe	Shaun White	United States
Women		
Cross	Maelle Ricker	Canada
Parallel giant slalom	Nicolien Sauerbreij	Netherlands
Halfpipe	Torah Bright	Australia

© Kevork Djansezian, Getty Images

Shaun White of the United States won the gold medal in the halfpipe event in snowboarding competition at the 2010 Winter Olympic Games in Vancouver, Canada.

Speed skating

Event	Winner	Nation	Time
Men			
500 meters	Tae-Bum Mo	South Korea	1 min 9.82 s
1,000 meters	Shani Davis	United States	1 min 8.94 s
1,500 meters	Mark Tuitert	Netherlands	1 min 45.57 s
5,000 meters	Sven Kramer	Netherlands	6 min 14.60 s*
10,000 meters	Seung-Hoon Lee	South Korea	12 min 58.55 s*
Team pursuit	Giroux, Makowsky, Morrison	Canada	3 min 41.37 s*
Women			
500 meters	Sang-Hwa Lee	South Korea	1 min 16.09 s
1,000 meters	Christine Nesbitt	Canada	1 min 16.56 s
1,500 meters	Ireen Wust	Netherlands	1 min 56.89 s
3,000 meters	Martina Sablikova	Czech Republic	4 min 02.53 s
5,000 meters	Martina Sablikova	Czech Republic	6 min 50.91 s
Team pursuit	Anschutz Thoms, Beckert, Mattscherodt, Friesinger-Postma	Germany	3 min 02.82 s

*Olympic record.   †Time is total of four races.

2008 Summer Olympic Games

Leading medal-winning nations

Nation	Gold	Silver	Bronze	Total
United States	36	38	36	110
China	51	21	28	100
Russia	23	21	28	72
United Kingdom	19	13	15	47
Australia	14	15	17	46
Germany	16	10	15	41
France	7	16	17	40
South Korea	13	10	8	31
Italy	8	10	10	28
Ukraine	7	5	15	27

Winners of team sports

Sport	Nation
Baseball (men)	South Korea
Basketball (men)	United States
Basketball (women)	United States
Field hockey (men)	Germany
Field hockey (women)	Netherlands
Handball (men)	France
Handball (women)	Norway
Soccer (men)	Argentina
Soccer (women)	United States
Softball (women)	Japan
Volleyball (men)	United States
Volleyball (women)	Brazil
Water polo (men)	Hungary
Water polo (women)	Netherlands

Archery

Event	Winner	Nation
Individual (men)	Viktor Ruban	Ukraine
Individual (women)	Zhang Juan Juan	China
Team (men)		South Korea
Team (women)		South Korea

Badminton

Event	Winner	Nation
Singles (men)	Lin Dan	China
Singles (women)	Zhang Ning	China
Doubles (men)	Markis Kido, Hendra Setiawan	Indonesia
Doubles (women)	Yu Yang, Du Jing	China
Mixed doubles	Lee Yongdae, Lee Hyojung	South Korea

Continued on next page.

Beach volleyball

Event	Winner	Nation
Men	Philip Dalhausser, Todd Rogers	United States
Women	Kerri Walsh, Misty May-Treanor	United States

Boxing

Class	Winner	Nation
48 kilograms (106 lbs)	Zou Shiming	China
51 kilograms (112 lbs)	Somjit Jongjohor	Thailand
54 kilograms (119 lbs)	Badar-Uugan Enkhbat	Mongolia
57 kilograms (126 lbs)	Vasyl Lomachenko	Ukraine
60 kilograms (132 lbs)	Alexey Tishchenko	Russia
64 kilograms (141 lbs)	Felix Diaz	Dominican Republic
69 kilograms (152 lbs)	Bakhyt Sarsekbayev	Kazakhstan
75 kilograms (165 lbs)	James Degale	United Kingdom
81 kilograms (179 lbs)	Zhang Xiaoping	China
91 kilograms (201 lbs)	Rakhim Chakhkiev	Russia
Over 91 kilograms	Roberto Cammarelle	Italy

Canoeing and kayaking

Event	Winner	Nation
Men		
Single kayak slalom	Alexander Grimm	Germany
Kayak 500-meter singles	Ken Wallace	Australia
Kayak 500-meter doubles	Saul Craviotto, Carlos Perez	Spain
Kayak 1,000-meter	Tim Brabants	United Kingdom
Kayak 1,000-meter doubles	Martin Hollstein, Andreas Ihle	Germany
Kayak 1,000-meter fours	R. Piatrushenka, A. Abalmasau, A. Litvinchuk, V. Makhneu	Belarus
Singles canoe slalom	Michal Martikan	Slovakia
Pairs canoe slalom	Pavol Hochschorner, Peter Hochschorner	Slovakia
Canoe 500-meter	Maxim Opalev	Russia
Canoe 500-meter doubles	Meng Guanliang, Yang Wenjun	China
Canoe 1,000-meter singles	Attila Sandor Vajda	Hungary
Canoe 1,000-meter doubles	Andrei Bahdanovich, Aliaksandr Bahdanovich	Belarus
Women		
Kayak slalom	Elena Kaliska	Slovakia
Kayak 500-meter singles	Inna Osypenko-Radomska	Ukraine
Kayak 500-meter doubles	Katalin Kovacs, Natasa Janics	Hungary
Kayak 500-meter fours	N. Reinhardt, F. Fischer, K. Wagner-Augustin, C. Wassmuth	Germany

Cycling

Event	Winner	Nation
Men		
BMX	Maris Strombergs	Latvia
Road race	Samuel Sanchez	Spain
Individual time trial	Fabian Cancellara	Switzerland
Madison sprint	Juan Esteban Curuchet, Walter Fernando Perez	Argentina
Keirin sprint	Chris Hoy	United Kingdom
Men's sprint	Chris Hoy	United Kingdom
Team sprint	C. Hoy, J. Kenny, J. Staff	United Kingdom
Individual pursuit	Bradley Wiggins	United Kingdom
Team pursuit	E. Clancy, P. Manning, G. Thomas, B. Wiggins	United Kingdom
Points race	Joan Llaneras	Spain
Mountain bike	Julien Absalon	France

Women

BMX	Anne-Caroline Chausson	France
Road race	Nicole Cooke	United Kingdom
Individual time trial	Kristin Armstrong	United States
Sprint	Victoria Pendleton	United Kingdom
Individual pursuit	Rebecca Romero	United Kingdom
Points race	Marianne Vos	Netherlands
Mountain bike	Sabine Spitz	Germany

Equestrian

Event	Winner	Nation
Eventing, individual	Hinrich Romeike	Germany
Eventing, team	P. Thomsen, F. Ostholt, H. Romeike, I. Klimke, A. Dibowski	Germany
Dressage, individual	Anky van Grunsven	Netherlands
Dressage, team	H. Kemmer, N. Capellmann, I. Werth	Germany
Jumping, individual	Eric Lamaze	Canada
Jumping, team	M. Ward, L. Kraut, W. Simpson, B. Madden	United States

Fencing

Event	Winner	Nation
Men		
Epee	Matteo Tagliariol	Italy
Epee, team	F. Jeannet, J. Jeannet, U. Robeiri	France
Foil	Benjamin Kleibrink	Germany
Sabre	Zhong Man	China
Sabre, team	J. Pillet, B. Sanson, N. Lopez	France
Women		
Epee	Britta Heidemann	Germany
Foil	Maria Vezzali	Italy
Foil, team	E. Lamonova, V. Nikichina, A. Shanaeva, S. Boyko	Russia
Sabre	Mariel Zagunis	United States
Sabre, team	O. Khomrova, H. Pundyk, O. Kharlan, O. Zhovnir	Ukraine

Gymnastics

Event	Winner	Nation
Men		
All-around	Yang Wei	China
Vault	Leszek Blanik	Poland
Pommel horse	Xiao Qin	China
Horizontal bar	Zhou Kai	China
Parallel bars	Li Xiaopeng	China
Rings	Cheng Yibing	China
Floor exercise	Zhou Kai	China
Team		China
Trampoline	Lu Chunlong	China
Women		
All-around	Nastia Liukin	United States
Balance beam	Shawn Johnson	United States
Uneven bars	He Kexin	China
Vault	Hong Un Jong	North Korea
Floor exercise	Sandra Izbasa	Romania
Team		China
Trampoline	He Wenna	China

Judo

Class	Winner	Nation
Men		
60 kg (132 lbs)	Choi Minho	Korea
66 kg (146 lbs)	Masato Uchishiba	Japan
73 kg (161 lbs)	Elnur Mammadli	Azerbaijan
81 kg (179 lbs)	Ole Bischof	Germany
90 kg (198 lbs)	Irakli Tsirekidze	Georgia
100 kg (220 lbs)	Tuvshinbayar Naidan	Mongolia
Over 100 kg	Satoshi Ishii	Japan

Women

48 kg (106 lbs)	Alina Alexandra Dumitru	Romania
52 kg (115 lbs)	Xian Dongmei	China
57 kg (126 lbs)	Giulia Quintavalle	Italy
63 kg (139 lbs)	Ayumi Tanimoto	Japan
70 kg (154 lbs)	Masae Ueno	Japan
78 kg (172 lbs)	Yang Xiuli	China
Over 78 kg	Tong Wen	China

Modern pentathlon

Event	Winner	Nation
Men	Andrey Moiseev	Russia
Women	Lena Schoneborn	Germany

Rhythmic gymnastics

Event	Winner	Nation
Individual	Evgeniya Kanaeva	Russia
Team	M. Aliychuk, A. Gavrilenko, T. Gorbunova, E. Posevina, D. Shkurikhina, N. Zueva	Russia

Rowing

Event	Winner	Nation
Men		
Single sculls	Olaf Tufte	Norway
Heavyweight double sculls	David Crawshay, Scott. Brennan	Australia
Lightweight double sculls	Zac Purchase and Mark Hunter	United Kingdom
Quadruple sculls	K. Wasielewski, M. Kolbowicz, M. Jelinski, A. Korol	Poland
Pairs	Drew Ginn, Duncan Free	Australia
Fours	T. James, S. Williams, P. Reed, and A. Triggs Hodge	United Kingdom
Lightweight fours	T. Ebert, M. Joergensen, M. Christian Kruse Andersen, E. Balschmidt Ebbesen	Denmark
Eights	K. Light, B. Rutledge, A. Byrnes, J. Wetzel, M. Howard, D. Seiterle, A. Kreek, K. Hamilton, B. Price	Canada
Women		
Single sculls	Rumyana Neykova	Bulgaria
Double sculls	Georgina Evers-Swindell, Caroline Evers-Swindell	New Zealand
Lightweight double sculls	Kirsten van der Kolk, Marit van Eupen	Netherlands
Quadruple sculls	T. Bin, J. Ziwei, X. Aihua, Z. Yangyang	China
Pairs	Georgeta Andrunache, Viorica Susanu	Romania
Eights	E. Cafaro, L. Shoop, A. Goodale, E. Logan, A. Cummins, S. Francia, C. Lind, C. Davies, M. Whipple	United States

Sailing

Class	Winner	Nation
Open		
49er dinghy sailing	Warrer Jonas, Martin Kirketerp Ibsen	Denmark
Laser	Paul Goodison	United Kingdom
Tornado	Fernando Echavarri, Anton Paz	Spain
Men		
Finn	Ben Ainslie	United Kingdom
470	Nathan Wilmot, Malcolm Page	Australia
Star	Iain Percy, Andrew Simpson	United Kingdom
RS:X	Tom Ashley	New Zealand

Women

Laser Radial	Anna Tunnicliffe	United States
470	Elise Rechichi Tessa Parkinson	Australia
Yngling	Sarah Ayton, Sarah Webb, Pippa Wilson	United Kingdom
RS:X	Yin Jian	China

Shooting

Event	Winner	Nation
Men		
Trap shotgun	David Kostelecky	Czech Republic
Double trap shotgun	Walton Eller	United States
Skeet shotgun	Vincent Hancock	United States
10-meter air rifle	Abhinav Bindra	India
50-meter prone rifle	Artur Ayvazian	Ukraine
50-meter 3 position rifle	Qiu Jian	China
10-meter air pistol	Pang Wei	China
50-meter pistol	Jin Jong Oh	South Korea
25-meter rapid-fire pistol	Oleksandr Petriv	Ukraine
Women		
Trap shotgun	Satu Makela-Nummela	Finland
Skeet shotgun	Chiara Cainero	Italy
10-meter air rifle	Katerina Emmons	Czech Republic
50-meter 3 position rifle	Du Li	China
10-meter air pistol	Guo Wenjun	China
25-meter pistol	Chen Ying	China

Swimming and diving

Event	Winner	Nation	Time
Men			
50-meter freestyle	Cesar Cielo Filho	Brazil	21.30 s †
100-meter freestyle	Alain Bernard	France	47.21 s
200-meter freestyle	Michael Phelps	United States	1 min 42.96 s*
400-meter freestyle	Park Taehwan	South Korea	3 min 41.86 s
1,500-meter freestyle	Oussama Mellouli	Tunisia	14 min 40.84 s
100-meter backstroke	Aaron Peirsol	United States	52.54 s*
200-meter backstroke	Ryan Lochte	United States	1 min 53.94 s*
100-meter breaststroke	Kosuke Kitajima	Japan	58.91 s*
200-meter breaststroke	Kosuke Kitajima	Japan	2 min 07.64 s †
100-meter butterfly	Michael Phelps	United States	50.58 s †
200-meter butterfly	Michael Phelps	United States	1 min 52.03 s*
200-meter medley	Michael Phelps	United States	1 min 54.23 s*
400-meter medley	Michael Phelps	United States	4 min 03.84 s*
4x100-meter medley relay	A. Peirsol, B. Hansen, M. Phelps, J. Lezak	United States	3 min 29.34 s*
4x100-meter freestyle relay	M. Phelps, C. Jones, G. Weber-Gale, J. Lezak	United States	3 min 08.24 s*
4x200-meter freestyle relay	M. Phelps, R. Lochte P. Vanderkaay, R. Berens	United States	6 min 58.56 s*
10-kilometer marathon	Maarten van der Weijden	Netherlands	1 h 51 m 51.6 s
Platform diving	Matthew Mitcham	Australia	
Springboard diving	He Chong	China	
Synchronized 3-meter platform	Wang Feng, Qin Kai	China	
Synchronized 10-meter platform	Lin Yue, Huo Liang	China	

*World record   †Olympic record.

Continued on next page

Women

50-meter freestyle	Britta Steffen	Germany	24.06 s †
100-meter freestyle	Britta Steffen	Germany	53.12 s †
200-meter freestyle	Federica Pellegrini	Italy	1 min 54.82 s*
400-meter freestyle	Rebecca Adlington	United Kingdom	4 min 03.22 s
800-meter freestyle	Rebecca Adlington	United Kingdom	8 min 14.10 s*
100-meter backstroke	Natalie Coughlin	United States	58.96 s
200-meter backstroke	Kirsty Coventry	Zimbabwe	2 min 05.24 s*
100-meter breaststroke	Leisel Jones	Australia	1 min 05.17 s †
200-meter breaststroke	Rebecca Soni	United States	2 min 20.22 s*
100-meter butterfly	Lisbeth Trickett	Australia	56.73 s
200-meter butterfly	Liu Zige	China	2 min 04.18 s*
200-meter medley	Stephanie Rice	Australia	2 min 08.45 s*
400-meter medley	Stephanie Rice	Australia	4 min 29.45 s*
4x100-meter freestyle relay	I. Dekker, M. Veldhuis R. Kromowidjojo, F. Heemskerk	Netherlands	3 min 33.76 s †
4x100-meter medley relay	E. Seebohm, L. Jones, J. Schipper, L. Trickett	Australia	3 min 52.69 s*
4x200-meter freestyle relay	S. Rice, B. Barratt, K. Palmer, L. Mackenzie	Australia	7 min 44.31s*
10-kilometer marathon	Larisa Ilchenko	Russia	1 h 59 m 27.7s
Synchronized swimming, duet	Anastasia Davydova, Anastasia Ermakova	Russia	
Synchronized swimming, team		Russia	
Platform diving	Chen Ruolin	China	
Springboard diving	Guo Jingjing	China	
Synchronized 3-meter springboard	Guo Jingjing, Wu Minxia	China	
Synchronized 10-meter platform	Wang Xin, Chen Ruolin	China	

Table tennis

Event	Winner	Nation
Singles (men)	Ma Lin	China
Singles (women)	Zhang Yining	China
Team (men)	Ma Lin, Wang Hao, Wang Liqin	China
Team (women)	Guo Yue, Zhang Yining, Wang Nan	China

Tae kwon do

Event	Winner	Nation
Men		
Under 58 kg (128 lbs.)	Guillermo Perez	Mexico
Under 68 kg (150 lbs.)	Son Taejin	South Korea
Under 80 kg (176 lbs.)	Hadi Saei	Iran
Over 80 kg	Cha Dongmin	South Korea
Women		
Under 49 kg	Wu Jingyu	China
Under 57 kg (126 lbs.)	Lim Sujeong	South Korea
Under 67 kg (148 lbs.)	Hwang Kyungseon	South Korea
Over 67 kg	Maria del Rosario Espinoza	Mexico

Tennis

Event	Winner	Nation
Singles (men)	Rafael Nadal	Spain
Singles (women)	Elena Dementieva	Russia
Doubles (men)	Roger Federer, Stanislas Wawrinka	Switzerland
Doubles (women)	Serena Williams, Venus Williams	United States

© Fei Machua, Xinhua /Landov

Stephanie Rice of Australia won the 200-meter individual medley, *shown here.* Rice also won the 400-meter individual medley. She set a world record in winning the gold in both races.

© Richard Dole, Bloomberg News/Landov

Yelena Isinbayeva of Russia won the women's pole vault event. Isinbayeva broke her own world record and won her second consecutive Olympic women's pole vault gold medal.

Track and field

Event	Winner	Nation	Time or distance
Men			
100 meters	Usain Bolt	Jamaica	9.69 s*
200 meters	Usain Bolt	Jamaica	19.30 s*
400 meters	LaShawn Merritt	United States	43.75 s
800 meters	Wilfred Bungei	Kenya	1 min 44.65 s
1,500 meters	Asbel Kipruto Kiprop	Kenya	3 min 33.11 s
5,000 meters	Kenenisa Bekele	Ethiopia	12 min 57.82 s †
10,000 meters	Kenenisa Bekele	Ethiopia	27 min 01.17 s †
110-meter hurdles	Dayron Robles	Cuba	12.93 s
400-meter hurdles	Angelo Taylor	United States	47.25 s
3,000-meter steeplechase	Brimin Kiprop Kipruto	Kenya	8 min 10.34 s
Marathon	Samuel Kamau Wansiru	Kenya	2 h 6 min 32 s †
4x100-meter relay	N. Carter, M. Frater, U. Bolt, A. Powell	Jamaica	37.10 s*
4x400-meter relay	L. Merritt, A. Taylor, D. Neville, J. Wariner	United States	2 min 55.39 s †
20-kilometer walk	Valeriy Borchin	Russia	1 h 19.01 s
50-kilometer walk	Alex Schwazert	Italy	3 h 37 min 9 s
High jump	Andrey Silnov	Russia	2.36 m (7 ft 9 in)
Long jump	Irving Jahir Saladino Aranda	Panama	8.34 m (27 ft 4 ½ in)
Triple jump	Nelson Evora	Portugal	17.67 m (57 ft 11 ⅔ in)
Pole vault	Steve Hooker	Australia	5.96 m (19 ft 6 ⅔ in) †
Discus	Gerd Kanter	Estonia	68.82 m (225 ft 9 ½ in)
Javelin	Andreas Thorkildsen	Norway	90.57 m (297 ft 1¾ in) †
Shot-put	Tomasz Majewski	Poland	21.51 m (70 ft 7 in)
Hammer	Primoz Kozmus	Slovenia	82.02 m (269 ft 1 in)
Decathlon	Bryan Clay	United States	8,791 points

Women

100 meters	Shelly-Ann Fraser	Jamaica	10.78 s
200 meters	Veronica Campbell-Brown	Jamaica	21.74 s
400 meters	Christine Ohuruogu	United Kingdom	49.62 s
800 meters	Pamela Jelimo	Kenya	1 min 54.87 s
1,500 meters	Nancy Jebet Langat	Kenya	4 min 00.23 s
5,000 meters	Tirunesh Dibaba	Ethiopia	15 min 41.40 s
10,000 meters	Tirunesh Dibaba	Ethiopia	29 min 54.66 s †
100-meter hurdles	Dawn Harper	United States	12.54 s*
400-meter hurdles	Melaine Walker	Jamaica	52.64 s †
3,000–meter steeplechase	Gulnara Samitova-Galkina	Russia	8 min 58.81 s*
4x100-meter relay	E. Polyakova, A. Fedoriva, Y. Gushchina, Y. Chermoshanskaya	Russia	42.31 s
4x400-meter relay	M. Wineberg, A. Felix, M. Henderson, S. Richards	United States	3 min 18.54 s
20-kilometer walk	Olga Kaniskina	Russia	1 h 26 min 31 s †
High jump	Tia Hellebaut	Belgium	2.05 m (6 ft 8 ¾ in)
Long jump	Maurren Higa Maggi	Brazil	7.04 m (23 ft 1 in)
Triple jump	Francoise Mbango Etone	Cameroon	15.39 m (50 ft 6 in) †
Pole vault	Yelena Isinbayeva	Russia	5.05 m (16 ft 6 ¾ in)*
Discus	Stephanie Brown Trafton	United States	64.74 m (212 ft 5 in)
Javelin	Barbora Spotakova	Czech Republic	71.42 m (234 ft 3 ¾ in)
Shot-put	Valerie Vili	New Zealand	20.56 m (67 ft 5 ¼ in)
Hammer	Aksana Miankova	Belarus	76.34 m (250 ft 5 ½ in) †
Marathon	Constantina Tomescu	Romania	2 h 26 min 44 s
Heptathlon	Nataliia Dobrynska	Ukraine	2 h 17 min 72 s

*World record   †Olympic record

Triathlon

Event	Winner	Nation
Men	Jan Frodeno	Germany
Women	Emma Snowsill	Australia

© Mike Theiler, UPI/Landov

Shawn Johnson of the United States won four medals in the women's gymnastics competition, including the gold medal in the balance beam event.

© Hou Deqiang, Xinhua/Landov

Anne-Caroline Chausson of France won the gold medal in the women's BMX cycling race. The race was held for the first time in the 2008 games.

© Kyodo/Landov

Usain Bolt of Jamaica won the 200-meter race in men's track and field competition, *shown here*. Bolt also won the 100-meter race. He set world records in winning both events. Bolt also ran on the Jamaica 4×100-meter relay team that won the gold medal.

Weightlifting

Class	Winner	Nation	Weight
Men			
56 kg (123 lbs)	Long Qingguan	China	292 kg (644 lbs)
62 kg (136 lbs)	Zhang Xiangxiang	China	319 kg (703 lbs)
69 kg (152 lbs)	Liao Hui	China	348 kg (767 lbs)
77 kg (169 lbs)	Sa Jaehyor	South Korea	366 kg (807 lbs)
85 kg (187 lbs)	Lu Yong	China	394 kg (869 lbs)
94 kg (207 lbs)	Ilya Ilin	Kazakhstan	406 kg (895 lbs)
105 kg (231 lbs)	Andrei Aramnau	Belarus	436 kg (961 lbs)*
Over 105 kg	Matthias Steiner	Germany	461 kg (1,016 lbs)
Women			
48 kg (106 lbs)	Chen Xiexia	China	212 kg (467 lbs) †
53 kg (117 lbs)	P. Jaroenrat-tanatarakoon	Thailand	221 kg (487 lbs)
58 kg (128 lbs)	Chen Yanqing	China	244 kg (538 lbs) †
63 kg (139 lbs)	Pak Hyon Suk	North Korea	241 kg (531 lbs)
69 kg (152 lbs)	Liu Chunhong	China	286 kg (631 lbs)*
75 kg (165 lbs)	Cao Lei	China	282 kg (622 lbs) †
Over 75 kg	Jang Miran	South Korea	326 kg (719 lbs)*

*World record   †Olympic record. Weight is total of two lifts: (1) snatch and (2) clean and jerk.

Wrestling

Class	Winner	Nation
Freestyle (Men)		
55 kg (121 lbs)	Henry Cejudo	United States
60 kg (132 lbs)	Mavlet Batirov	Russia
66 kg (146 lbs)	Ramazan Sahin	Turkey
74 kg (163 lbs)	Buvaysa Saytiev	Russia
84 kg (185 lbs)	Revazi Mindorashvili	Georgia
96 kg (212 lbs)	Shirvani Muradov	Russia
120 kg (265 lbs)	Artur Taymazov	Uzbekistan
Freestyle (Women)		
48 kg (106 lbs)	Carol Huynh	Canada
55 kg (121 lbs)	Saori Yoshida	Japan
63 kg (139 lbs)	Kaori Icho	Japan
72 kg (159 lbs)	Wang Jiao	China
Greco-Roman style		
55 kg (121 lbs)	Nazyr Mankiev	Russia
60 kg (132 lbs)	Islam-Beka Albiev	Russia
66 kg (146 lbs)	Steeve Guenot	France
74 kg (163 lbs)	Manuchar Kvirkelia	Georgia
84 kg (185 lbs)	Andrea Minguzzi	Italy
96 kg (212 lbs)	Aslanbek Khushtov	Russia
120 kg (265 lbs)	Mijain Lopez	Cuba

The ancient games

Athletics played an important role in the religious festivals of ancient Greece. Historians believe the ancient Greeks first organized athletic games as part of funeral ceremonies for important people. This practice probably existed by the 1200's B.C. Later, games became part of religious festivals honoring the gods. Many Greek cities held festivals every two or four years.

Over time, four great religious festivals developed that brought together people from throughout the Greek world. These festivals were the Isthmian, Nemean, Pythian, and Olympic games. The Olympic Games, which ranked as the most important, honored Zeus, the king of the gods.

The first recorded Olympic contest took place in 776 B.C. at Olympia in western Greece. The first winner was Koroibos (also spelled Coroebus), a cook from Elis. The Olympic Games were held every four years. They were so important to the ancient Greeks that time was measured in *Olympiads,* the four-year intervals between games. The only event in the first 13 games was the *stadion,* a running race of 192 meters (210 yards). Through the years, longer running races were added.

Other types of competition became part of the ancient Olympics. In 708 B.C., wrestling and the pentathlon were added. The pentathlon was a combination of jumping, running, the discus throw, the javelin throw, and wrestling. Boxing joined the program in 688 B.C., and the four-horse chariot race was added in 680 B.C. Horse racing was included in 648 B.C., as was the *pancratium* (also spelled *pankration),* a combination of boxing,

wrestling, and kicking. Some unusual events were included in the Olympics, such as a race in armor, a chariot race called the *apene* in which two mules pulled the chariot, and a competition for trumpeters.

The ancient Olympics produced several famous champions. Milo of Kroton won the wrestling competition five times between 532 and 516 B.C., and Leonidas of Rhodes won three running races in each of four Olympics from 164 to 152 B.C.

The Romans conquered Greece during the 140's B.C., and the games soon lost their religious meaning. In A.D. 393, Emperor Theodosius I banned the games.

The modern games

The modern games begin. In 1875, a group of German archaeologists began to excavate the ruins of the stadium and temples of Olympia, which had been destroyed by an earthquake and buried by a landslide and floods. Their discoveries inspired Baron Pierre de Coubertin, a French educator, to organize a modern international Olympics. He first proposed the idea publicly in 1892. In 1894, the first IOC was formed.

The first modern Olympic Games were held in Athens, Greece, in 1896. The athletes competed in nine sports: (1) cycling, (2) fencing, (3) gymnastics, (4) lawn tennis, (5) shooting, (6) swimming, (7) track and field, (8) weightlifting, and (9) wrestling. James B. Connolly of the United States became the first modern Olympic champion, winning the triple jump (then known as the *hop, step, and jump).*

The games of 1900 and 1904 attracted little attention. The 1900 Olympics were held as part of the Universal

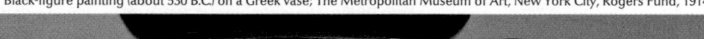

Black-figure painting (about 530 B.C.) on a Greek vase; The Metropolitan Museum of Art, New York City, Rogers Fund, 1914

The ancient Olympic Games were held every four years in Olympia in western Greece. The first recorded games took place in 776 B.C. For the first 13 competitions, the only event was a running race for male athletes, *shown here,* of 192 meters (210 yards). Other events were added over the years.

Exposition, a world's fair in Paris. Competition was spread out over five months. Attendance was poor, and some athletes did not even realize they had participated in the Olympics.

The 1900 Olympics included the first competitions involving women, in lawn tennis and golf. The first women gold medalists were British tennis player Charlotte Cooper and American golfer Margaret Abbott. Poor attendance and other problems also plagued the 1904 Olympics, held as part of the Louisiana Purchase Exposition in St. Louis.

In the early years of the Olympics, competitions were held in several sports that were later dropped. They included polo, croquet, tug of war, the high jump on horseback, and a swimming obstacle race.

The Olympic movement might have died except for the *Intercalated,* or *Interim,* Games held in Athens in 1906. The IOC does not consider these games official. However, they were popular and held the movement together until the next official games in London in 1908. The most dramatic moment of the 1908 games came in the marathon. Dorando Pietri of Italy entered the stadium in first place but collapsed before reaching the finish line. Officials dragged Pietri across the finish line and declared him the winner, but he was later disqualified because he did not finish under his own power.

The 1912 Olympics in Stockholm, Sweden, were the first well-organized Olympic Games. The hero of Stockholm was Jim Thorpe, a Native American who easily won the 10-event decathlon and the 5-event pentathlon. Thorpe's medals were taken away after it was discovered that he had played baseball for a small salary before the games, making him a professional athlete and therefore ineligible for the Olympics. In 1982, the IOC voted to return the medals to Thorpe's family and put his name back in the record books as an Olympic champion.

Between the wars. The 1916 games were canceled because of World War I (1914-1918). The 1920 Olympics in Antwerp, Belgium, marked the first appearance of the great Finnish distance runner Paavo Nurmi. He competed in all three Olympics of the 1920's, winning nine gold medals.

Figure skating was included in the 1908 games, and both figure skating and ice hockey were part of the 1920 games. The first separate Winter Games took place in Chamonix, France, in 1924, with 278 men and 13 women representing 16 countries.

The 1924 Summer Games were held in Paris. One of the stars was American swimmer Johnny Weissmuller, who later became famous portraying Tarzan in motion pictures. Other famous athletes included British sprinters Harold Abrahams and Eric Liddell, later portrayed in the film *Chariots of Fire* (1981).

The 1928 Summer Games, held in Amsterdam, the Netherlands, were the first in which women competed in track and field. In the Winter Games in St. Moritz, Switzerland, Sonja Henie of Norway won her first gold medal in women's figure skating. She repeated as champion in the 1932 and 1936 Winter Games before becoming a star of Hollywood musicals.

The 1932 Summer Games were held in Los Angeles. These games introduced automatic timing for races and the photo-finish camera. The first Olympic Village was

Hulton Deutsch from All Sport

Jim Thorpe of the United States won the decathlon and pentathlon at the 1912 Summer Games. His medals were taken away after he was declared ineligible, but they were restored in 1982.

also erected. The games produced the first U.S. female Olympic star, Babe Didrikson (later Babe Didrikson Zaharias). She qualified for five track and field events but was allowed to enter only three. She won the javelin throw and the hurdles race and finished second in the high jump.

In 1931, the IOC chose Berlin, Germany, as the site for the 1936 Summer Games and Garmisch-Partenkirchen, Germany, for the Winter Games. Two years later, Adolf Hitler and his Nazi Party rose to power in Germany. As Hitler's policies became known, there were pleas to move the Summer Games, but the IOC refused.

The Berlin games were the first to be preceded by a torch relay of the Olympic flame from Greece, and they were the first games to be shown on television. But the 1936 Summer Olympics are best remembered for Hitler's failed attempt to use them to prove his theory of racial superiority. The Nazis glorified the Germans and other northern European peoples, while claiming that Jews, blacks, and other groups were inferior. But the most successful athlete in the Summer Games was Jesse Owens, an African American who won four gold medals in track and field. The German spectators, ignoring Hitler's speeches against black people, treated Owens as their favorite hero of the games.

The postwar games. The Olympics scheduled for 1940 and 1944 were canceled because of World War II (1939-1945). The first postwar Summer Games were held in London in 1948 and the Winter Games again in St. Moritz. The most popular athlete in the Summer Games was Fanny Blankers-Koen of the Netherlands, a home-

AP/Wide World

All Sport

Early women Olympic stars included Babe Didrikson of the United States and Sonja Henie of Norway. Didrikson, *running far right,* won the hurdles in the 1932 Summer Games. She also won the javelin throw and finished second in the high jump. Henie, *shown here,* won the gold medal in figure skating in 1928, 1932, and 1936, the only woman to win the event three times.

maker who won four gold medals in track and field. A star of the Winter Games was Dick Button of the United States, who won the gold medal in figure skating, an achievement he repeated in the 1952 games. Barbara Ann Scott of Canada won the women's figure-skating title, becoming the first Canadian figure skater to win an Olympic gold medal.

Athletes from the Soviet Union made their first Olympic appearance in the 1952 Summer Games in Helsinki, Finland. By the 1956 games, Soviet athletes were winning more medals than the athletes of any other country. In Helsinki, Emil Zátopek of Czechoslovakia became the only runner to win the 5,000 meters, 10,000 meters, and marathon races in the same Olympics.

The 1956 Summer Games were held in Melbourne, Australia, the first to be held in the Southern Hemisphere. Because of Australian quarantine laws concerning horses, the equestrian events were staged separately in Stockholm. In the weeks preceding the Melbourne games, Israel invaded Egypt and Soviet troops invaded Hungary. These actions led to the first boycotts of the modern Olympics. Egypt, Iraq, and Lebanon withdrew to protest the Israeli take-over of the Suez Canal. The Netherlands and Spain boycotted to protest the Soviet invasion.

The 1960 Winter Games at Squaw Valley in California and the Summer Games in Rome were the first to be televised to the United States. The track and field stars of the Summer Games included American sprinter Wilma Rudolph and marathon winner Abebe Bikila of Ethiopia, the first black African to win a gold medal. American boxer Cassius Clay won the light heavyweight gold medal. He later gained international fame as professional boxer Muhammad Ali.

In 1964, the Summer Games were held in Tokyo, the first Asian city to serve as host. Ukrainian gymnast Laris-

sa Latynina won six medals. In her career, she won a record 18 Olympic medals. The Tokyo games were the last Summer Games for more than 20 years to be free of major controversy.

The 1968 games. The 1968 Summer Games were held in Mexico City during a period of political turmoil throughout the world. The most controversial episode took place during the medal ceremony for the men's 200-meter dash. The gold and bronze medals were won by African American sprinters Tommie Smith and John Carlos. To protest racism in the United States, both athletes bowed their heads and raised clenched fists during the playing of the U.S. national anthem. At the insistence of the IOC, the U.S. Olympic Committee suspended both men from the Olympic team and ordered them to leave the Olympic Village.

Mexico City's high altitude was disastrous for athletes in long-distance races and other endurance events, but it contributed to world records in many other contests. The most famous record was 29 feet 2 $\frac{1}{2}$ inches (8.90 meters) in the long jump, set by Bob Beamon of the United States. The jump became a world record that lasted for 23 years.

The 1968 Winter Games in Grenoble, France, produced one of the great Olympic heroes of the 1960's. French skier Jean-Claude Killy won three gold medals and became an international celebrity.

Terrorism in Munich. The 1972 Summer Games were held in Munich, in what was then West Germany. The Munich Olympics are remembered for the events of September 5. Eight Palestinian terrorists broke into the Olympic Village and entered the dormitory where the Israeli team was staying. They killed two Israelis and took nine hostages. They demanded that Israeli authorities release more than 200 Arab prisoners being held in Israel. During a battle with West German sharpshooters, all the Israeli hostages were killed, along with five terrorists and one policeman.

The highlight of the competition was swimmer Mark Spitz of the United States, who won seven gold medals. The Soviet Union also won a controversial victory over the U.S. men's basketball team in the championship game. The Americans led by 1 point when the buzzer sounded to end the game. But the officials twice ordered the game to continue, first for 1 second and then for 3 seconds more, enabling the Soviet team to score the winning basket.

Boycotts. The 1976 Summer Games, held in Montreal, Canada, were hit by a boycott led by Tanzania. More than 20 African nations and 2 other countries refused to compete. The boycotters demanded that New Zealand be banned from competition because a New Zealand rugby team had toured South Africa. At that time, South Africa had a white-controlled government that enforced a policy of rigid racial segregation called *apartheid.* South Africa was barred from the Olympics because of its racial policies, but the IOC said it had little control over the travel of rugby teams because rugby was not an Olympic sport.

In spite of the absence of hundreds of top athletes, the 1976 games were filled with outstanding performances. A 14-year-old gymnast from Romania named Nadia Comaneci caused a sensation by earning the first perfect score of 10 ever awarded in the Olympics. She eventually earned seven scores of 10 and won three gold medals.

The 1980 Summer Games in Moscow were disrupted by another boycott, this one led by U.S. President Jimmy Carter. The boycott protested the Soviet Union's 1979 invasion of Afghanistan. Carter urged other nations to join the boycott, and about 50 nations stayed away.

The 1980 Winter Games in Lake Placid, New York, were among the most exciting in history. Eric Heiden won all five speed-skating races, setting an Olympic or world record in each race. He became the first athlete to

Wide World

Jesse Owens of the United States was the hero of the 1936 Summer Games. Owens won four gold medals in track and field.

win five individual gold medals in one Olympics. Mark Spitz had won three of his seven gold medals as a member of a winning relay team.

Also at the 1980 Winter Games, the United States ice hockey team won an unexpected gold medal. The American team upset the Soviet Union team in an emotional semifinal match and then defeated Finland in the finals.

The games returned to Los Angeles in 1984. With the games being held in the United States, the Soviet Union launched a revenge boycott. Only 13 countries joined the boycott, but they included such sports powers as Bulgaria, East Germany, Cuba, and Hungary. Among the sports that lost most of their medal favorites were gymnastics, weightlifting, wrestling, women's swimming, and women's track and field. However, China competed in the Olympics for the first time in more than 30 years. China was led by the popular gymnast Li Ning, who won six medals. United States track and field star Carl Lewis matched Jesse Owens's 1936 feat of winning four gold medals.

Charges of steroid use. The 1988 Summer Games were held in Seoul, South Korea, and were boycotted by North Korea and Cuba. Instead of political controversy, disputes over the use of drugs called *anabolic steroids* marked the 1988 games. Anabolic steroids are artificial forms of male hormones used to increase strength and weight. Their use is banned in Olympic competition. Since 1968, the International Olympic Committee has tested athletes for steroids and other performance-enhancing drugs.

In the 1988 Olympics, Ben Johnson of Canada defeated Carl Lewis in the 100-meter dash and set a world record. Three days later, the IOC announced that Johnson had tested positive for steroids and was disqualified. Lewis was awarded the gold medal, thus becoming the first man to win the 100-meter dash twice. He also won the long jump for the second time. Other notable performers were swimmers Matt Biondi of the United States, who won five gold medals, and Steffi Graf of West Germany, who won the gold medal in women's singles as part of a season in which she won all four grand slam tennis titles.

In the 1988 Winter Games in Calgary, Canada, Katarina Witt of East Germany won the women's figure-skating title. Witt also had won the event in 1984. She was the first woman to repeat as champion since Sonja Henie.

The recent games. The 1992 Summer Games in Barcelona, Spain, reflected the breakup of the Soviet Union and the collapse of Communist governments in Eastern Europe. Germany entered a unified team representing the former countries of East and West Germany. The Baltic states of Estonia, Latvia, and Lithuania, previously part of the Soviet Union, competed as separate nations. Russia and other former Soviet republics competed as the Unified Team. However, when athletes from the Unified Team won a medal, they were honored by the raising of the flag of their own republic and by the playing of their own national anthem. South Africa, which had ended apartheid, rejoined the Olympics and competed for the first time since 1960.

The 1992 Olympics also marked the first time that professional basketball players were eligible for the competition. This rule change led to the creation of a U.S. "Dream Team" that included Magic Johnson, Larry Bird,

Michael Jordan, Charles Barkley, and other stars of the National Basketball Association. The American team easily won the gold medal.

Speed-skater Bonnie Blair was a star of the Winter Games of 1988, 1992, and 1994. She won five gold medals and a bronze medal in the three games.

The 1996 Summer Games were held in Atlanta. Stars included Russian gymnast Alexei Nemov, who won six medals; Birgit Schmidt of Germany, who won her fifth

AP/Wide World

Controversy erupted in 1968 when American sprinters Tommie Smith, *center,* and John Carlos raised clenched fists at a medal ceremony to protest racism in the United States.

career gold medal in canoeing; and Michael Johnson of the United States, the first male to win the 200-meter and 400-meter races in the same Olympics.

The 2000 Summer Games in Sydney, Australia, were the largest in Olympic history, with athletes competing for medals in 300 events. Drug problems continued to cast a cloud over the games. Several athletes were disqualified for taking illegal drugs. Some forfeited medals after failing drug tests. Stars of the games included sprinter Maurice Greene of the United States, Australian swimmer Ian Thorpe, Chinese diver Fu Mingxia, and cyclist Leontien Ziljaard of the Netherlands.

A controversy arose in the 2002 Winter Games over the judging of the figure skating pairs competition. Judges first awarded the gold medal to Elena Berezhnaya and Anton Sikharulidze of Russia and the silver medal to Jamie Sale and David Pelletier of Canada. After a protest and investigation, the Canadians were awarded a gold medal along with the Russians.

Drug problems remained a problem in the 2004 Summer Games in Athens, Greece. Numerous athletes were disqualified before or during the games for failing or refusing to take drug tests. The star of the games was American swimmer Michael Phelps, who won six gold medals and tied a record by winning eight medals during a single Olympics. German canoeist Birgit Fischer-Schmidt became the first athlete in any sport to win two medals in each of five Olympics. Other stars included Australian swimmer Ian Thorpe, Moroccan runner Hicham El Guerrouj, American swimmer Aaron Peirsol, British runner Kelly Holmes, and Chilean tennis player Nicolas Massu.

No single athlete dominated the 2006 Winter Olympics in Turin, Italy. The top medal winners were Canadian speed skater Cindy Klassen, who won five medals; South Korean short track speed skater Ahn Hyun-soo, who won four medals; and German biathlete Michael Greis, who won three gold medals.

Focus on Sports

Paul J. Sutton, Duomo

Great moments in Olympic competition occurred in the 1976 and 1980 games. In the 1976 Summer Games, Nadia Comaneci of Romania, *shown here,* became the first gymnast in Olympic history to score a perfect 10. In the 1980 Winter Games, the United States ice hockey team upset the Soviet team in the semifinals, *shown here,* and then defeated Finland to win the gold medal.

Andrew Bernstein, *Sports Illustrated*

The "Dream Team" was the name given to the American men's basketball team that won the gold medal at the 1992 Summer Games. The stars of the team came from the National Basketball Association. The 1992 Olympics marked the first time professional players could participate.

In 2007, the IOC announced the establishment of the Youth Olympics for athletes from 14 to 18 years old. The first Summer Youth Olympics is scheduled for 2010 and is expected to attract about 3,500 competitors. The first Winter Youth Olympics is scheduled for 2012 with about 1,000 athletes expected to enter.

The 2008 Summer Olympics in Beijing, China, were dominated by the American swimmer Michael Phelps and the Jamaican sprinter Usain Bolt. Phelps became the first athlete to win eight gold medals at a single Olympics, winning five individual races and competing on three winning relay teams. Phelps's eight victories included seven world records and an Olympic record. Bolt won the 100-meter and 200-meter sprints and ran on Jamaica's winning 400-meter relay team, setting world records in all three events. The United States won the most medals in the games with 110. China won the most gold medals with 51. At the 2010 Winter Olympics in Vancouver, Canada, the United States set a Winter Games record by winning 37 total medals. Canada won 14 gold medals, another Winter Games record. Two Norwegian cross-country skiers were the leading medal winners. Petter Northug won four medals in men's competition, and Margit Bjoergen won five medals in women's competition.   David Wallechinsky

Related articles. *World Book* has separate articles on many Olympic sports, including gymnastics, ice skating, swimming, and track and field. See also the following:

Blair, Bonnie	Olympia
Blood doping	Olympiad
Comaneci, Nadia	Owens, Jesse
Horse (Horse shows and	Phelps, Michael
sports)	Rudolph, Wilma
International Olympic	Scott, Barbara Ann
Committee	Thorpe, Jim
Joyner-Kersee, Jackie	Zaharias, Babe Didrikson
Lewis, Carl	

© Cameron Spencer, Getty Images

Michael Phelps is one of the greatest swimmers in the history of the sport. At the 2008 Summer Olympic Games in Beijing, he won gold medals for the United States in eight events—five individual events and three relay races. Phelps became the first athlete ever to win eight gold medals at a single Olympics.

Outline

I. **Olympic ceremonies and symbols**
II. **The International Olympic Committee**
III. **Olympic competition**
    A. Selection of the athletes
    B. Entries
    C. Medals
IV. **The Summer Games**
V. **The Winter Games**
VI. **The ancient games**
VII. **The modern games**

Additional resources

Guttmann, Allen. *The Olympics: A History of the Modern Games.* 2nd ed. Univ. of Ill. Pr., 2002.
Macy, Sue. *Freeze Frame: A Photographic History of the Winter Olympics.* National Geographic Soc., 2006. *Swifter, Higher, Stronger: A Photographic History of the Summer Olympics.* 2004. Younger readers.
Perrottet, Tony. *The Naked Olympics: The True Story of the Ancient Games.* Random Hse., 2004.

Olympic Mountains, *oh LIHM pihk,* are part of the Pacific Coast Ranges. The Olympics rise in northern Washington, south of Juan de Fuca Strait. They occupy an area of about 3,500 square miles (9,060 square kilometers), most of which lies in Olympic National Park.

Mount Olympus (7,965 feet, or 2,428 meters) is the highest peak. There are over 100 small glaciers in the mountains. Forests of spruce, fir, cedar, and hemlock cover the lower slopes. The southwestern slopes receive over 140 inches (356 centimeters) of rain a year, one of the highest averages in the United States.
Jois C. Child

Olympic National Park, *oh LIHM pihk,* lies in the Olympic Peninsula of Washington, not far from Seattle and Tacoma. The Olympic Range's jagged peaks cover much of the national park. For the park's area, see **National Park System** (table: National parks). The park has campgrounds and winter sports activities for tourists. Olympic National Park headquarters are at Port Angeles, Washington, a resort city on the Strait of Juan de Fuca.

Of special interest are the rain forests consisting mainly of Sitka spruce, western hemlock, western red-cedar, and Douglas-fir. These rain forests, resulting from good soil and exceptionally heavy rainfall, are almost tropical in luxuriance, with an undergrowth of vine maple, bigleaf maple, ferns, and other junglelike growth. Mosses drape the branches and tree trunks. The park is the home of the world's largest herd of Roosevelt elk, estimated at 5,000 animals. Other wildlife species include black bear, cougar, and black-tailed deer.

This wilderness of glacier-clad peaks, flower-strewn alpine meadows, turbulent streams, jewellike lakes, and deep valleys supporting a rich forest growth is often described as America's "last frontier." Highways penetrate only its outer fringes, but the park has several hundred miles of hiking and horseback riding trails. Nearly 1,000 varieties of flowers grow in the park's meadows and on its mountain slopes. Some varieties, such as the Piper bellflower, grow nowhere else.

Part of this region was set aside as Mount Olympus National Monument by President Theodore Roosevelt in 1909. In 1938, President Franklin D. Roosevelt signed the act establishing Olympic National Park. The park was formally dedicated in 1946. The Queets Corridor and Olympic Ocean Strip were added to the park by presidential proclamation in 1953.

Critically reviewed by the National Park Service

See also **Washington** (pictures).

Olympics. See Olympic Games.

Olympus. See Mount Olympus.

Omaha, *OH muh HAW* or *OH muh HAH* (pop. 409,958; met. area pop. 865,350), is the largest city in Nebraska and one of the world's leading food processing centers. The city is the trading center for eastern Nebraska and western Iowa. For location, see **Nebraska** (political map).

Omaha took its name from the Omaha Indians. In 1854, this tribe gave most of its hunting grounds in the eastern Nebraska area to the United States government. That same year, the Council Bluffs and Nebraska Ferry Company, a land development firm, founded the town of Omaha City. The name of the town was later shortened to Omaha. The company chose the site for settlement because of its location on a bluff at a ferry crossing at the start of the Mormon Trail.

The city covers 115 square miles (298 square kilometers) on the west bank of the Missouri River. The city of Council Bluffs, Iowa, lies across the river and makes up part of the Omaha metropolitan area. This area covers 4,363 square miles (11,300 square kilometers) and consists of Cass, Douglas, Sarpy, Saunders, and Washington counties in Nebraska and Harrison, Mills, and Pottawattamie counties in Iowa.

Omaha's main business district lies near the Missouri River. In the heart of the downtown area stands the city's tallest building, the 45-story First National Tower.

People of European descent make up nearly 75 percent of Omaha's population. About 15 percent of the people are African Americans. Hispanics, who may be of any race, make up nearly 15 percent. The city has a small number of Asian Americans and American Indians.

Economy. Omaha has hundreds of manufacturing plants. Food processing ranks as the city's most important industry. Omaha is one of the chief frozen food producers in the United States.

Other major Omaha industries include machinery manufacturing, metalworking, printing, publishing, and the manufacture of telephone and electric equipment. The city is a national center for telemarketing companies, which promote and sell products by telephone. Omaha is also an insurance center. A number of insurance firms have their home offices in the city, including Mutual of Omaha, one of the largest insurance companies in the United States.

Railroads provide freight and passenger service to Omaha. Airlines use Eppley Airfield. Bus lines and trucking firms also operate in Omaha. Barge lines help make the city an important Missouri River port. Omaha has one daily newspaper, the *Omaha World-Herald*.

Education. Boys Town, a famous community for homeless and underprivileged children, is just west of Omaha (see **Boys Town**). Colleges and universities in Omaha include the University of Nebraska at Omaha, Creighton University, the University of Nebraska Medical Center, Clarkson College, the College of St. Mary, Grace University, and Nebraska Methodist College. Bellevue University is in Bellevue, a suburb that lies south of Omaha.

Cultural life and recreation. The Joslyn Art Museum features works from ancient to modern times, with a special emphasis on European and American art of the 1800's and 1900's. The museum is noted for its collection of art of the American West. Other museums include the Omaha Children's Museum and the Durham Museum, a history museum in a restored railroad station. The city has a symphony orchestra. The Omaha Community Playhouse, which first opened in 1925, presents plays in two theaters.

Omaha has more than 200 parks. The Henry Doorly Zoo, in the southeastern part of the city, attracts many visitors. The zoo's Lied Jungle is an indoor re-creation of rain forests of Asia, Africa, and South America. Lauritzen Gardens, Omaha's Botanical Center, is just north of the zoo. Fontenelle Forest, the largest unbroken tract of forestland in Nebraska, lies south of Omaha.

Every June, top college baseball teams come to Omaha to compete in the National Collegiate Athletic Association College World Series. The Knights of Ak-Sar-Ben, a civic organization, sponsors a rodeo and livestock show every September. This organization, whose name is *Nebraska* spelled backwards, was founded in 1895.

Government. Omaha has a mayor-council form of government. The voters elect the mayor and the seven council members to four-year terms. Omaha gets most of its income from a property tax and a city sales tax.

History. Many American Indian tribes, including the Omaha and the Oto, once hunted buffalo in what is now the Omaha area. The famous expedition headed by Meriwether Lewis and William Clark passed through the area in 1804 on its way to the West.

In 1854, a treaty between the United States government and the Omaha Indians opened the newly created Nebraska Territory for settlement. The Council Bluffs and Nebraska Ferry Company surveyed and laid out the site of Omaha. The firm sold land for $25 per lot. In 1855, the first territorial legislature selected Omaha as the capital. Omaha was incorporated as a city in 1857.

In the late 1850's, Omaha became an outfitting point for wagon trains headed for the newly discovered gold

Greater Omaha Convention and Visitors Bureau

An outdoor concert in Omaha draws many people. The Joslyn Art Museum presents the free "Jazz on the Green" programs in the summer on its east lawn and grand staircase.

fields of Colorado. But the city grew slowly and, in 1860, had a population of only 1,183.

Many Nebraskans had opposed the selection of Omaha as the territorial capital. More than half the territory's people lived south of the Platte River. They felt that the capital should not be north of the Platte, as Omaha is. After Nebraska became a state in 1867, the city of Lincoln was chosen as the new capital. The state government moved to Lincoln, 50 miles (80 kilometers) southwest of Omaha, in 1868.

In 1863, President Abraham Lincoln had selected the Council Bluffs area as the starting point of the Union Pacific Railroad. In 1865, the first tracks were laid westward from Omaha. The Union Pacific thus became part of the first U.S. transcontinental rail system, which was completed in 1869. Omaha began to grow rapidly.

During the 1880's, Omaha developed into an important meat-processing center. The city's location in a great cattle-raising area and at the heart of a rail network helped this growth. The opening of the Union Stockyards in 1884 hastened the growth. Thousands of immigrants, many from southern and central Europe, worked in Omaha's meat-packing plants.

In 1898, the Knights of Ak-Sar-Ben organized the Trans-Mississippi and International Exposition, which attracted more than 2 ½ million visitors to Omaha. By 1900, the city had 102,555 people. The population reached 191,601 in 1920 and 223,844 in 1940. The number of factories grew from 150 in 1900 to 450 in 1950. In 1948, the U.S. Air Force established the headquarters of the Strategic Air Command (SAC) at Offutt Air Force Base, near Omaha. SAC was eliminated in 1992 during a reorganization of the Air Force. The base is now the headquarters of the U.S. Strategic Command.

Changes in the city during the last half of the 1900's included turning a wholesale fruit and vegetable market south of downtown into an attraction called Old Market. Old Market is a brick-paved district with shops, art galleries, and restaurants. Other projects included the construction of a hotel and several large office buildings downtown. The Gene Leahy Mall also was completed, linking the city's business district to the riverfront. A new convention center and arena on the northeast edge of downtown opened in 2003.

In 2006, Nebraska passed a law that would have divided Omaha's public school district into three divisions. Each division would have a majority or near-majority of one of three different ethnic groups—blacks, whites, and Hispanics. Opponents charged that the law amounted to state-sponsored segregation. In 2007, however, the Legislature passed a law intended to keep the district together and to help solve the schools' funding and academic performance problems.   Lawrence H. Larsen

For the monthly weather in Omaha, see **Nebraska** (Climate). See also **Nebraska** (pictures).

Omaha Indians live mainly in northeast Nebraska. Many make their homes on a reservation there. Many others live in Lincoln or Omaha or in Sioux City, Iowa. The city of Omaha was named after the Omaha Indians.

The Omaha once lived in the Ohio River Valley along with ancestors of the Kansa, Osage, Ponca, and Quapaw Indians. They all spoke similar Siouan languages. Eventually, the groups separated, and most of them moved west. The Omaha arrived in Nebraska about 1700. Many Omaha still speak their own language.

In Nebraska, the Omaha traditionally lived in *earth lodges* in villages near the Missouri River. An Omaha earth lodge consisted of a circular log frame covered with layers of branches, grass, and earth. The Omaha planted corn and other crops in the spring. In summer, they moved west to hunt buffalo and lived in tipis. In the fall, they returned to the village with supplies of dried buffalo meat and harvested their corn. They hunted deer in the winter.   John Ludwickson

Oman, *oh MAHN,* is a small country on the southeastern end of the Arabian Peninsula. Most of the land is desert, but it holds large deposits of petroleum. Muscat is Oman's capital and largest city.

Oman lies on the Gulf of Oman and the Arabian Sea. Yemen borders Oman on the southwest, and Saudi Arabia lies to the west. The United Arab Emirates separates the northern tip of Oman, the Musandam Peninsula, from the rest of Oman. The peninsula lies on the strategic Strait of Hormuz. This narrow waterway separates the Persian Gulf from the Indian Ocean, which opens to the east of the Gulf of Oman. All oil exported by ship from the Persian Gulf must pass through the strait.

Oman was extremely poor until oil was discovered there in 1964. The government has used oil revenues to finance economic improvements, and the standard of living of the population has risen. Nevertheless, most Omanis still struggle to earn a living.

Government. Oman is ruled by a monarch called the *sultan.* The sultan appoints cabinet members who oversee the government's operations. Two councils advise the sultan. The sultan appoints the Council of State. Omani men and women from throughout the country's 59 *wilayats* (districts) elect the members of the Consultative Council. Oman has a Chief Court and local courts. All judges are experts in Islamic law.

People. Most of the population is Arab, and these people belong to various tribal and religious groups.

Oman

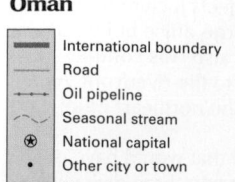

- ▬▬▬ International boundary
- —— Road
- ⊢—⊣ Oil pipeline
- ⌒⌒ Seasonal stream
- ⊛ National capital
- • Other city or town
- + Elevation above sea level

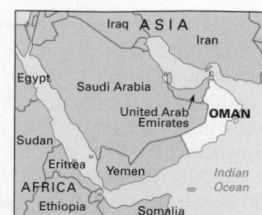

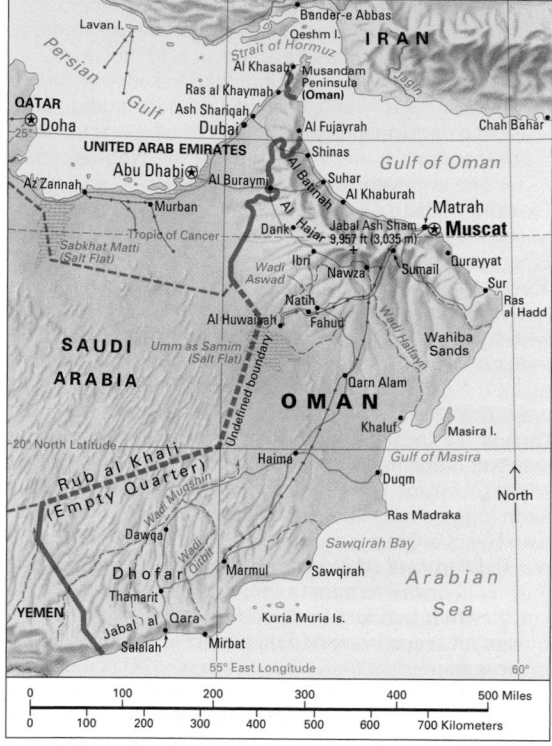

WORLD BOOK maps

Facts in brief

Capital: Muscat.
Official language: Arabic.
Official name: Saltanat Uman (Sultanate of Oman).
Area: 119,499 mi² (309,500 km²). *Greatest distances*—north-south, 500 mi (805 km); east-west, 400 mi (644 km). *Coastline*—about 1,060 mi (1,700 km).
Elevation: *Highest*—Jabal Ash Sham, 9,957 ft (3,035 m) above sea level. *Lowest*—sea level.
Population: *Estimated 2012 population*—3,088,000; density, 26 per mi² (10 per km²); distribution, 72 percent urban, 28 percent rural. *2003 census*—2,340,815.
Chief products: *Agriculture*—alfalfa, bananas, coconuts, dates, limes, onions, pomegranates, tobacco, tomatoes, wheat. *Fishing industry*—abalone, anchovies, cod, sardines, sharks, tuna. *Mining*—petroleum, natural gas, copper, chromite.
National anthem: "Nashid as-Salaam as-Sultani" ("Sultan's National Anthem").
Flag: The flag has a vertical red stripe and three horizontal stripes of white, red, and green. The national emblem, which features crossed swords and a dagger, appears at the top of the vertical stripe. See **Flag** (picture: Flags of Asia and the Pacific).
Money: *Basic unit*—Omani rial, or riyal. One thousand baizas equal one rial. See also **Rial**.

The largest of the many non-Arab minorities who live in Oman are Balochis—that is, people from the Arabian Sea coast of Iran and Pakistan—and Asian Indians. The country's official language is Arabic.

Most rural Omanis live in villages. Most people who live in coastal villages work on date palm plantations. Some fish for a living. Farmers in the interior villages grow dates, fruits, and grain. Some also raise animals.

Old Omani houses in coastal villages are made of palm leaves to allow the sea breezes to cool them. Old houses in villages in the interior are built of mud brick and stone. Newer housing is constructed from cement blocks. Some major towns have large stone fortresses that were built hundreds of years ago and beautifully decorated palaces where prominent families once lived.

Nomads make up about 5 percent of Oman's population. Nomads move from place to place as they search for water and grazing for their herds of goats, camels, and small cattle. They live in tents.

Omanis depend on wells for water for most or all of the year. Before the Arabs took over Oman, Persians lived there and built canals called *aflaj* (singular *falaj*) to carry water to the villages. Many aflaj carry water from underground wells tapped by tunnels called *qanat*.

Growing numbers of urban Omanis have jobs in industry, including the petroleum industry. Most city dwellers, however, are government workers, laborers, merchants, or sailors. Their houses are generally constructed of whitewashed mud brick. These houses are built around a central courtyard, and many have flat roofs surrounded by high walls. Some people sleep on these roofs during hot weather. The larger cities also have modern high-rise buildings.

Most Omanis are Muslims. Many belong to the moderate Ibadi (also spelled *Ibadhi*) branch of the Kharijite division of Islam. Ibadi Muslims have traditionally believed that the religious leader, the *imām*, should be elected based on merit. See **Islam** (Divisions of Islam).

The lives of most Omani women center on their homes and families. They follow Islamic religious rules about modest dress. When Omani women leave their houses, they wrap themselves in long black cloaks called *abayas*, and some also wear black masks called *burqas* to cover their faces. These garments also protect them from the sun. Many Omani men wear a long white robe called a *dishdashah*. They often carry decorative knives called *khanjars*, which they wear in brightly colored sashes. In rural areas, some men carry rifles.

Since 1970, the government has built many schools for children and has established literacy programs for adults. Because of these efforts, the number of Omani people 15 years old or older who can read and write is rising. Sultan Qaboos University, the first university in Oman, opened in the Muscat region in 1986.

Land and climate. Most of Oman is dry and rocky. The Musandam Peninsula in the north consists of barren mountains. Al Batinah, a narrow coastal plain, lies along the Gulf of Oman. Date palms thrive in this fertile region.

Steep, rugged mountains called Al Hajar separate the Batinah from the interior. The interior is a vast, flat wasteland. The Rub al Khali (Empty Quarter), a desert, extends into western Oman from Saudi Arabia. Most of Oman's coast along the Arabian Sea is barren and rocky. But tropical vegetation grows along the coast in Dhofar,

© Robert Azzi, Woodfin Camp, Inc.

An Omani craftsman uses a potter's wheel to make pottery. Like most Omani men, this potter wears loose, white garments and a turban for protection from Oman's strong sun.

© David Hume Kennerly, Gamma/Liaison

Barren wasteland covers much of Oman. In this wasteland, farmers struggle to earn a living by grazing cattle or other livestock. Life in rural Oman has changed little through the years.

a region in the south. Dhofar is famous for its frankincense trees, the best of which grow on a plateau north of the Jabal al Qara, a mountain range.

Temperatures in Oman may reach 130 °F (54.4 °C) in the summer. Most of Oman receives less than 6 inches (15 centimeters) of rain each year. Dhofar, however, receives up to 25 inches (63.5 centimeters) of rain annually.

Economy. Oman's economy is largely based on oil and natural gas production. But many Omanis work in traditional occupations, such as farming and fishing. Chief crops include bananas, dates, limes, and tomatoes. Nomads and some settled farmers raise camels, cattle, chickens, goats, and sheep. Oman's fishing fleet catches sardines, tuna, and other fish and shellfish. Oil and natural gas account for about three-fourths of Oman's exports. Its chief imports include automobiles, food, iron and steel, and machinery. Oman's main trading partners include China, Japan, and the United Arab Emirates.

History. Human beings have lived in Oman for more than 5,000 years. Beginning in ancient times, Oman's wooden sailing ships carried goods throughout the Persian Gulf and to coastal areas in south Asia and east Africa. In the 1500's, Portuguese military forces built forts in Muscat and other Omani seaports as well as elsewhere in the Persian Gulf to control this rich trade. The Omani navy and tribal fighters, under the leadership of Sultan bin Saif al-Yaribi, forced the Portuguese from Oman in 1650. The Omanis then attacked rival shipping on the high seas and established control over trading ports along much of the east coast of Africa.

For centuries after the arrival of Islam in Oman during the 600's, members of the Ibadi branch of the faith had come into repeated conflict with the dynasties and foreign powers ruling Oman. In the 1740's, Ahmad bin

Said, the first ruler of the Al Bu Said family, united the Omanis and took power. Ahmad died in 1783. Oman was then increasingly divided between the hereditary Al Bu Said rulers, whose power was based in coastal Muscat, and the more traditional Ibadi tribes of the country's interior, who looked to elected imams for leadership.

In 1798, the sultan signed the first of several treaties with the United Kingdom. The British competed against Oman for trade dominance in the Indian Ocean. Gradually, Oman's sea trade declined and its economy suffered. Oman also lost control of its outposts in the east.

Oman was reunited in 1955 by Sultan Said bin Taimur. With British help, the sultan defeated rebellious Ibadi tribesmen of interior Oman in 1959. In the early 1960's, another rebellion against Said began in Dhofar. In 1970, Said's son Qaboos bin Said overthrew him. Qaboos put down the Dhofar rebellion in the mid-1970's.

Said had been opposed to making Oman a modern state. But Qaboos immediately started to modernize Oman. He developed the oil industry. He also built new irrigation systems and made many other agricultural improvements. He built roads, schools, and hospitals. Before Qaboos became sultan, few Omani children—and hardly any girls—ever went to school. He encouraged Omanis to educate their daughters as well as their sons.

In 1981, Oman and five other Arab states bordering the Persian Gulf formed the Gulf Cooperation Council (GCC). GCC members work together on military defense and economic projects. Following Iraq's invasion of Kuwait in 1990, Omani military forces, as part of the GCC and the allied coalition, took part in the 1991 ground campaign that liberated Kuwait.

In 2011, antigovernment protests erupted in several Omani cities. Protesters called for democratic reform and improved living conditions. In response, Sultan Qaboos promised to create more jobs and help those seeking employment. The protests in Oman followed similar events in Tunisia, Egypt, and elsewhere in the region.   Mary Ann Tétreault

See also **Arabs** (picture: Traditional Arab architecture); **Muscat.**

Omar. See Muhammad (His religious life).

Omar Khayyam, *OH mahr ky YAHM* (1048-1131), was a Persian poet, astronomer, and mathematician. He was famous during his lifetime for his reform of the Islamic calendar. About 100 years after his death, collections of poems appeared bearing his name. These poems express religious skepticism and a rather world-weary *hedonism* (love of pleasure). The verses show a mind acutely conscious of human ignorance and of the brevity of life. A collection called the *Rubaiyat of Omar Khayyam, The Astronomer-Poet of Persia* first attracted attention in the West in 1859, when English writer Edward FitzGerald published his free translation of a number of the stanzas arranged as a continuous poem.

Omar Khayyam was born on May 18, 1048, in Nishapur, in what is now northwestern Iran. His name, which probably reflects an ancestor's trade, means *the tentmaker.* He died on Dec. 4, 1131.   Dick Davis

See also **FitzGerald, Edward; Rubaiyat.**

Ombudsman, *AHM buhdz MUHN,* is a nonpartisan public official who investigates people's complaints about government officials or agencies. Most of an ombudsman's work involves complaints of unjust or harsh treatment of people by police, prosecuting attorneys, or judges, and such matters as housing, taxation, voting, or welfare payments. After investigating a complaint, the ombudsman may dismiss it or may seek correction of the problem—by persuasion, by publicity, or, occasionally, by recommending prosecution.

The idea of the ombudsman originated in Sweden in 1809 and spread to other countries. Today in the United States, Hawaii has a comprehensive ombudsman plan, and other states and some cities have modified plans. The idea also has gained popularity in large organizations, including corporations and universities. Its growing popularity coincides with the increasing complexities of administration and the need for impartial and informal handling of complaints.   David R. Berman

Omdurman, *AHM dur MAHN* (pop. 1,849,659), is the largest city in Sudan. It lies on the west bank of the Nile River, across the river from Khartoum, Sudan's capital. For location, see **Sudan** (map).

Omdurman is a regional market. It is also a religious and cultural center for Sudanese Muslims. The tomb of Muhammad Ahmad, a Muslim leader called the *Mahdi* (divinely appointed guide), stands in the city center. Muhammad Ahmad founded the city in 1885. Near the tomb is a large market area called the *suq.* Many people who work in Khartoum live in Omdurman. Omdurman has modern apartment buildings and houses. It also has small houses made of sun-dried mud-brick. Tents and shacks on the outskirts of the city provide shelter for many refugees from western and southern Sudan and nearby countries.   Kenneth J. Perkins

Omen is a sign of future good or bad luck. A good omen foretells a desirable event, and a bad omen forecasts disaster. For example, a person may regard a dream about gold as an omen of success in business. Or the person may believe that the death of a relative will follow a dream about losing a tooth. Sometimes omens come from a deliberate attempt to look into the future, such as a fortuneteller's tarot cards.

Many ancient societies believed that lightning, thunder, or the behavior of animals foretold events. For example, the Mesopotamians thought fire would destroy the king's palace if a dog were seen lying on the throne. In Greece, the cry of a hawk warned of danger. Many

leaders, when trying to decide on a course of action, asked the gods for a sign. In folklore, many people die after disregarding such signs.   Sarah M. Pike

See also **Augur; Divination; Superstition.**

Omnibus bill, *AHM nuh buhs,* is a term which is sometimes used for a bill that includes several unrelated measures when it is put before a legislative assembly. An omnibus bill is used to pass several bills at once. It is named for an *omnibus* (bus), a vehicle that carries a number of people.

Omnibus bills are considered bad practice. When a number of unrelated items are crowded into one bill, it is hard to give each the study it deserves. In addition, an omnibus bill may include provisions that would be unlikely to pass on their own merits. Sometimes, legislators attach an amendment called a *rider* to an important bill. Opponents are forced to accept the rider if they want the rest of the bill to become law. The constitutions of most states and provinces provide that a single bill shall relate to one topic only.   Douglas Greenberg

Omsk, *awmsk* (pop. 1,134,016), is a major manufacturing center of Russia. It lies along the Irtysh River, about 1,360 miles (2,190 kilometers) east of Moscow, in Siberia (see **Russia** [political map]). Omsk is one of the largest cities in Siberia. Omsk factories manufacture farm machinery for the surrounding agricultural area. The city also has large aerospace, food-processing, oil-refining, and petrochemical industries.

Omsk was founded in 1716, during the Russian expansion into Siberia. The Trans-Siberian Railroad reached the city in 1894, and Omsk became a commercial center of western Siberia. During World War II (1939-1945), the government moved many factories from combat zones in the western part of Russia to safe areas in Siberia. Omsk developed rapidly as a result, and its industries have continued to expand.   Zvi Gitelman

Onager, *AHN uh juhr,* is the name of a fast-running relative of the donkey. It is the *wild ass* mentioned in the Bible. The onager travels in herds on the hot, dry plains of west-central Asia. Its color varies from cinnamon-brown in summer to yellow-brown in winter. A yellow patch covers each thigh and a broad black stripe runs along its back. The onager also has a mane and a tuft of

Onagers resemble donkeys but run as swiftly as horses. This onager stands with her foal.

hair at the end of its tail. It stands about 4 feet (1.2 meters) tall at the shoulder. Steven D. Price

Scientific classification. The onager's scientific name is *Equus hemionus.*

Onassis, Jacqueline Kennedy (1929-1994), the wife of President John F. Kennedy, was one of the most popular first ladies in United States history. President Kennedy was assassinated in 1963. Five years later, Jacqueline Kennedy married Aristotle Onassis, a Greek businessman.

Jacqueline Lee Bouvier was born on July 28, 1929, in Southampton, New York. She graduated from George Washington University in 1951. From 1951 to 1953, she worked for the *Washington Times-*

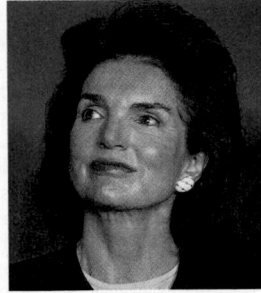

© Ira Wyman, Sygma
Jacqueline Kennedy Onassis

Herald, where she produced a daily column as an inquiring photographer. She asked people human-interest questions, such as whether they had done their Christmas shopping, and wrote up the replies. She took pictures of the people, which accompanied the column.

In 1953, Jacqueline Bouvier married Kennedy, who was then a U.S. senator. The couple had two children who survived infancy: Caroline, born in 1957; and John F., Jr., 1960. A daughter was stillborn in 1956, and a son born prematurely in 1963 lived only two days. Kennedy became president in 1961. As first lady, Jacqueline—often called "Jackie"—became known for her elegance in hairstyle, clothing, and other elements of fashion. She won admiration for her composure and dignity following the assassination of her husband on Nov. 22, 1963.

Jacqueline Kennedy married Onassis in 1968. He died in 1975. From 1975 until her death on May 19, 1994, Jacqueline Onassis worked as an editor for book publishers. Kathryn Kish Sklar

See also **Kennedy, John Fitzgerald.**

Oñate, *oh NYAH tay,* **Juan de** (1550?-1626?), was a Spanish explorer. He is remembered mainly for colonizing the territory now called New Mexico in 1598. His explorations extended from the Colorado River to the plains of Kansas. Oñate served as governor of the territory but quarreled with the settlers and was forced to resign in 1607. He was tried and found guilty of immorality and abuse of power. It was largely due to Oñate that the city of Santa Fe was founded in about 1610. Oñate was born near Zacatecas, Mexico. Helen Delpar

Oncology, *ahng KAHL uh jee,* is the study of the development, treatment, and prevention of cancer. It includes both research and clinical care. Doctors who specialize in oncology are called *oncologists.*

In the laboratory, oncologists compare human cancer cells with normal cells to try to understand the cellular mechanisms that control the growth of normal tissues. By understanding these mechanisms, oncologists hope to find ways to correct abnormal tissue growth.

Similarly, oncologists study cancers in animals to learn how the body itself often controls the growth of cancer cells. The scientists study how naturally occurring chemicals called *interleukins* stimulate an animal's

immune system to eliminate cancer cells. Through such research on animals, oncologists hope to develop methods of cancer prevention and treatment for people.

Clinical oncologists diagnose and treat cancer. A diagnosis is made by examining a bit of abnormal tissue under a microscope. This procedure, called a *biopsy,* determines if the tumor is cancerous. Treatment depends on whether tumors are limited to one site or organ or whether cancer cells have spread. Surgery, radiation, drug therapy, or combination treatments may be used (see **Cancer** [Cancer treatment]). Janice Phillips Dutcher

One-celled organism. See **Protist; Protozoan.**

O'Neal, Shaquille, *sha KEEL* (1972-), was a star center in the National Basketball Association (NBA). O'Neal stands 7 feet 1 inch (216 centimeters) tall and weighs about 315 pounds (142.9 kilograms). He became known for his strength and for his powerful slam dunks. He consistently ranked among the NBA leaders in scoring, shooting percentage, rebounds, and blocked shots. He led the NBA in scoring in the 1994-1995 season with a 29.3 point average per game. O'Neal led the NBA in scoring again in the 1999-2000 season with a 29.7 point average and was voted the league's Most Valuable Player. O'Neal announced his retirement following the 2010-2011 season. He ended his 19-season career in the NBA with 28,596 points, ranking fifth in career NBA scoring.

Shaquille Rashaun O'Neal was born on March 6, 1972, in Newark, New Jersey. O'Neal attended Louisiana State University, leaving in 1992 after his junior year to turn professional. The Orlando Magic selected him as the first player in the 1992 NBA draft. He was named the league's Rookie of the Year for 1992-1993. In 1996, he signed as a free agent with the Los Angeles Lakers and helped that team win three straight NBA championships in 2000, 2001, and 2002. O'Neal was traded to the Miami Heat in 2004, to the Phoenix Suns in 2008, and to the Cleveland Cavaliers in 2009. He signed to play with the Boston Celtics in 2010. O'Neal has also appeared in motion pictures, recorded as a rap artist, and done many commercials and product endorsements. Sam Smith

See also **Basketball** (picture).

O'Neale, Peggy (1799?-1879), was a central figure in one of the greatest disputes in the history of Washington, D.C., society. The dispute caused President Andrew Jackson to reorganize his Cabinet.

Margaret O'Neale was born in Washington, D.C., the daughter of an innkeeper. According to her own account, she was born on Dec. 3, 1799. Margaret, known by the nickname Peggy, married John B. Timberlake, a Navy purser. She lived at the O'Neale tavern while Timberlake was at sea. Senator John H. Eaton of Tennessee lived there in 1818 and became fond of Peggy. Andrew Jackson, who became a United States senator from Tennessee in 1823, met Peggy at the inn. Peggy's husband died in 1828, and she married Eaton on Jan. 1, 1829.

Eaton became secretary of war in 1829. Washington society refused to receive Peggy, because of her father's occupation and because of gossip about her conduct with Eaton. President Jackson stood by her. Several Cabinet members resigned, and Eaton resigned his post in 1831. Peggy died on Nov. 8, 1879. James C. Curtis

See also **Jackson, Andrew** (Split with Calhoun).

Onega, Lake. See **Lake Onega.**

Oneida Community, *oh NY duh,* a cooperative community in Oneida, New York, was founded by John Humphrey Noyes in 1848. Noyes hoped to make the community a *utopia* (perfect society). Noyes, a preacher, believed in a radical form of Christianity known as Perfectionism. Perfectionism taught that people could abolish sin from their lives and become perfect. Noyes began the community in Putney, but he and his followers were forced to leave because of their beliefs.

The members of the Oneida Community believed that the best way to achieve perfection was to live communally, sharing the burden of labor as well as all possessions. The community abolished the private family and, in its place, set up a system called *complex marriage*. In this system, every man was considered to be married to every woman. The community also planned the birth of its babies and raised its children. In 1869, the community began to choose combinations of parents that it believed would produce the best children.

The Oneida Community flourished financially. It became wealthy by manufacturing and selling a type of steel game trap invented by one of its members. The community also earned money by canning and by manufacturing steel chains and silk thread.

In 1879, outside opposition to complex marriage forced the community to give up the practice. In 1881, the community was reorganized as a joint-stock company called Oneida Community Ltd. In the 1890's, the manufacture of silverware became the company's main industry. Today, the company exists as Oneida Ltd. The Oneida Community Mansion House, the former home of the Oneida Community, is a national historic landmark and museum.   Benjamin Zablocki

Oneida Indians. See Iroquois Indians.

O'Neill, Eugene (1888-1953), is regarded as America's greatest playwright. In 1936, O'Neill received the Nobel Prize in literature. Four of his plays won Pulitzer Prizes— *Beyond the Horizon* in 1920; *Anna Christie* in 1922; *Strange Interlude* in 1928; and *Long Day's Journey into Night* in 1957, after his death.

O'Neill's plays show his fascination with philosophy and religion and his intense self-examination. By incorporating experimental techniques of European theater into his plays, O'Neill is credited with raising the previously narrow and insubstantial American drama into an art form that gained worldwide respect.

His life. Eugene Gladstone O'Neill was born on Oct. 16, 1888, in New York City. His father, James O'Neill, was one of America's most popular actors. Between national tours, the family spent the summers in New London, Connecticut. Their home was the setting for two of O'Neill's greatest plays—*Ah, Wilderness!* (1933) and *Long Day's Journey into Night* (written from 1939 to 1941 and first performed in 1956). In New London, he discovered his mother's addiction to morphine and rebelled against his father's theatrical conservatism. O'Neill was raised a Roman Catholic, but he rejected religion. He married in 1909 but was divorced within three years. By 1912, he had worked as a gold prospector in Honduras and as a seaman and had become a frequenter of cheap saloons and flophouses in New York City. That year, he returned to New London and became ill with tuberculosis.

O'Neill's reading while recovering at a sanitarium inspired him to become a playwright. In 1914, he studied drama with George Pierce Baker at Harvard University.

In 1916, O'Neill joined the Provincetown Players, an experimental theater group on Cape Cod in Massachusetts. In July, the group presented *Bound East for Cardiff,* the first staging of an O'Neill play.

O'Neill's second marriage, to writer Agnes Boulton, in 1918 ended in divorce in 1929. Later that year, he married actress Carlotta Monterey. He wrote until the mid-1940's, when a muscular disease resembling Parkinson disease prevented further work. O'Neill died largely forgotten on Nov. 27, 1953. But in 1956, a revival of *The Iceman Cometh* (written in 1939) and the premiere of *Long Day's Journey into Night* renewed interest in his plays.

His plays. O'Neill's career consisted of two periods of Realism divided by a middle period of experimentation. He first wrote one-act plays that utilized his youthful experiences, especially at sea. The best of these plays include four Realistic works that trace the changing relationships among seamen of the S.S. *Glencairn* amid the tensions of World War I (1914-1918).

In the early 1920's, O'Neill rejected Realism and determined to capture on stage the "force behind" human life. He was influenced by the ideas of the German philosopher Friedrich Nietzsche, the Austrian psychologist Sigmund Freud, the Swiss psychologist Carl Jung, and the Swedish playwright August Strindberg.

In *The Emperor Jones* (1920), an Expressionistic play, O'Neill traced the personal and racial past of a black porter who becomes a Caribbean dictator. *The Hairy Ape* (1922) blends Realistic and Expressionistic elements in the story of an alienated man's attempts to belong in modern society. *Desire Under the Elms* (1924) transplants the Greek myth of Phaedra and Hippolytus and elements of other myths to a New England farm.

In *The Great God Brown* (1926), the characters wear masks that express or hide their inner natures. In the nine-act *Strange Interlude* (1928), characters voice inner thoughts that frequently contradict their public utterances. *Mourning Becomes Electra* (1931) is a trilogy that shifts the Greek tragic trilogy the *Oresteia* to the United States immediately after the American Civil War (1861-1865). The gods and Furies of Greek mythology are replaced by the workings of the subconscious mind.

O'Neill's final period was his best as he returned to Realism and gave in to a lifelong impulse to write autobiographical plays. *The Iceman Cometh* immortalizes the unrealistic "pipe dreams" of the friends from the flophouses and Greenwich Village. The play's characters shield themselves from the bitter truth of failure through their mutually supportive illusions. *A Touch of the Poet,* written from 1935 to 1942 and first staged in 1957, is the only complete drama of a planned 11-play cycle. O'Neill intended the cycle to trace the life of an Irish American family and the spiritual decline of America from the early 1800's. In his greatest play, *Long Day's Journey into Night,* the Tyrone family is clearly based on O'Neill's own family in 1912. *A Moon for the Misbegotten* (written from 1941 to 1943 and first performed in 1957) is a sequel that portrays the last days of O'Neill's alcoholic brother, Jamie.   Frederick C. Wilkins

See also **American literature** (picture).

O'Neill, Thomas Philip (1912-1994), a Massachusetts Democrat, served as speaker of the United States House of Representatives from 1977 until 1987, when he retired. His retirement ended a 34-year career in the

House. O'Neill had served as majority *whip* (assistant leader) of the House from 1971 to 1973 and as majority leader from 1973 to 1977.

O'Neill was born on Dec. 9, 1912, in Cambridge, Massachusetts. He was given the nickname Tip as a boy, after baseball player James Edward (Tip) O'Neill. Thomas O'Neill graduated from Boston College in 1936 and was elected to the Massachusetts House of Representatives that same year. He became minority leader in 1947 and speaker of the Massachusetts House in 1948.

O'Neill won election to the U.S. House of Representatives in 1952. As a representative, he supported several changes in House rules. For example, he led a successful fight to record all votes in the House. Previously, representatives had voted on amendments to bills with no record of whether they favored or opposed the legislation. In 1967, O'Neill became one of the first House leaders to publicly oppose U.S. involvement in the Vietnam War. He died on Jan. 5, 1994.   Guy Halverson

Onion is a vegetable that has a strong odor and flavor. Onions rank as one of the world's most popular foods. They are used chiefly as a seasoning and are eaten raw, cooked, dehydrated, and pickled. When cut, raw onions give off a vapor that causes people's eyes to water.

The onion plant. Most onion plants are *biennials* (plants that require two years to complete their life cycle). When fully grown, they consist of leaves, a bulb, and roots. The long, slender leaves are hollow cylinders that grow upright. They thicken at the base to form a bulb, the part of the plant that people eat most frequently. Onion bulbs grow partially aboveground. They tend to be globe-shaped, but some are wide and flat. Others are slender and upright. A thin, papery covering made up of dried outer leaves encloses the bulb.

Onion bulbs may be red, white, or yellow. A cluster of short root fibers grows from the bottom of the bulb. During its second year of growth, an onion plant produces rounded clusters of small, greenish-white, seed-bearing flowers at the tips of its stalks. Most onions are harvested during the first year and thus do not flower.

Onions are classified as *short-day onions* or *long-day onions.* Short-day onions require 10 to 11 hours of daylight and grow best in the southern United States. Long-day onions need 14 to 15 hours and grow best in the northern part of the country. Varieties of short-day onions include Red Creole, Texas Grano 1015Y, White Grano, Yellow Bermuda, and Yellow Granex. Long-day varieties include Candy, Southport Yellow Globe, Super Star, Vaquero, Walla Walla, and Yellow Sweet Spanish. To form a bulb, all onion plants require an average temperature greater than 60 °F (16 °C).

Cultivation. Onion growers plant onion *sets* (small bulbs), seeds, or seedlings. Seedlings are grown in a greenhouse or in an area with warm winters. Seeds are planted about ½ inch (1.3 centimeters) deep. Sets are pressed into the ground but left uncovered.

Onions need rich soil and plenty of water, especially when they are young. When the bulb is ready to be harvested, the plant's leaves grow limp and fall over. Growers dry and store harvested bulbs in a cool place to avoid decay.

Onions differ in the strength of their flavor. People use such strong-tasting onions as the Southport White Globe in soups and stews. Mild onions, including the

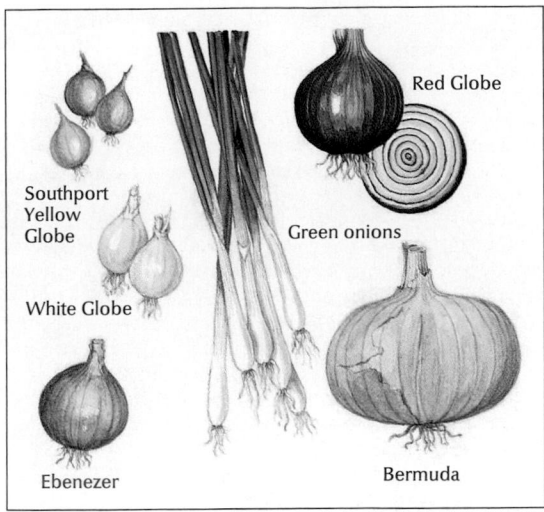

WORLD BOOK illustrations by Kate Lloyd-Jones, Linden Artists Ltd.

The onion is a vegetable with a bulb that can be eaten raw or used in cooking. Onions come in many shapes, sizes, and colors. This illustration shows some common kinds of onions.

Yellow Bermuda and Yellow Granex, are often eaten raw in salads or on sandwiches. Onions harvested when their bulbs are immature are called *green onions* or *salad onions* and are sold with leaves attached.

Onions probably first grew in central or southwestern Asia. Today, the leading onion-growing countries include China, India, and the United States. In the United States, leading onion-growing states include California, Oregon, and Washington.   Christopher S. Cramer

See also **Bulb; Chive; Garlic; Leek; Ramp.**

Scientific classification. The onion's scientific name is *Allium cepa.*

Onizuka, *ahn uh zoo kah,* **Ellison Shoji,** *EHL uh suhn SHOH jee* (1946-1986), in 1985 became the first Asian American in space. He was also one of the seven United States astronauts killed in the 1986 Challenger disaster.

On his first space flight in January 1985, Onizuka and his fellow astronauts on the space shuttle Discovery completed a secret three-day mission for the Department of Defense. As part of his second mission, Onizuka and the other astronauts aboard the space shuttle Challenger planned to release two satellites, a retrievable satellite to study Halley's Comet and a communications satellite. On Jan. 28, 1986, an accident destroyed the shuttle shortly after liftoff. Structural failures caused the shuttle to break apart. The accident killed Onizuka and the six other crew members (see **Space exploration** [The Challenger disaster]).

Onizuka was born on June 24, 1946, in Kealakekua, Hawaii. His family had moved to Hawaii when his grandparents left Japan to work on sugar plantations.

In 1964, Onizuka enrolled at the University of Colorado, where he joined the Air Force Reserve Officer Training Corps. He received both a bachelor's and a master's degree in aerospace engineering from the University of Colorado in 1969. In 1970, he went on active duty with the Air Force. NASA selected him as an astronaut in 1978 for the first team of space shuttle crew members.   James Oberg

Janet Green, Masterfile

Beautiful woodlands on the coast of Georgian Bay

Ontario

Ontario, *ahn TAIR ee OH,* has more people than any other Canadian province. More than a third of Canada's people live in Ontario. Service industries provide Ontario with its greatest source of income. Ontario's manufacturing industries produce about as much as those of the nine other provinces combined. Ontario ranks first among the Canadian provinces in farm income and in the production of metallic minerals.

Toronto is the capital of the province, and the Toronto area is Canada's leading manufacturing center. Ottawa, the capital of Canada, lies on the Ottawa River in southeastern Ontario.

Ontario has a larger area than any other Canadian province except Quebec. It is the southernmost province, but it also extends so far north that some of the ground beneath the surface is *permafrost* (permanently frozen ground).

The contributors of this article are Walter Peace, Associate Professor at the School of Geography and Earth Sciences, McMaster University; and Peter A. Baskerville, Professor Emeritus of History at the University of Victoria.

The busy factories, mills, and plants of Ontario have given it the nickname *Manufacturing Heartland of Canada.* Most industries are in the warm southern region, south of Lake Nipissing. About 95 percent of the people live there, on about 12 percent of the land area. The province's richest manufacturing section, called the Golden Horseshoe, curves around the western shores of Lake Ontario.

Ontario's major industry is manufacturing automobiles. Most of the province's automobile plants are in the Golden Horseshoe. Almost all the automobiles made in Canada come from there. Hamilton, a city in the Golden Horseshoe, is Canada's greatest iron and steel center. Nearby is Toronto, one of the chief Canadian ports on the Great Lakes. The region's varied products travel from Toronto to many parts of the world by way of the St. Lawrence Seaway.

The mines of Ontario provide about a fourth of all the nonfuel minerals produced in Canada. Deposits near Greater Sudbury yield much of the world's supply of nickel. One of the largest known uranium deposits in the world lies near Elliot Lake. Ontario is also one of North America's leading producers of gold.

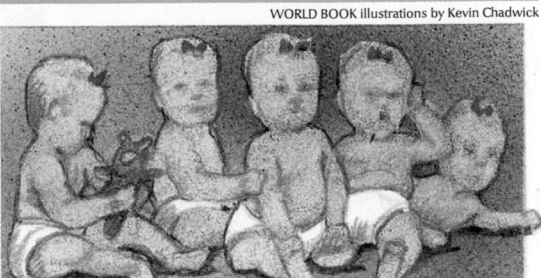
© Gary Blakeley, Shutterstock
Downtown Toronto

Interesting facts about Ontario

WORLD BOOK illustrations by Kevin Chadwick

Dionne quintuplets

The Dionne quintuplets were born in a farmhouse near Callander in 1934. They were the first quintuplets known to live more than a few days after birth. All five girls were identical. There had been only two previous cases of identical quintuplets in medical history.

Insulin, a hormone that regulates the body's use of sugar, was discovered in 1921 at the University of Toronto by Frederick G. Banting, Charles H. Best, John J. R. Macleod, and James B. Collip.

The Ambassador Bridge connecting Windsor and Detroit, Michigan, is the world's longest international suspension bridge. It has a span of 1,850 feet (564 meters).

The CN (Canadian National) Tower in Toronto is Canada's tallest freestanding structure. The tower rises 1,815 feet (553 meters) and is used for broadcasting and observation.

Ambassador Bridge

Ontario is Canada's leading producer of eggs and poultry and also leads in the production of fruits and vegetables. It provides nearly a fourth of Canada's farm products. Herds of beef and dairy cattle graze in rich pastures between Lake Huron and Lake Ontario. Tobacco grows along Lake Erie, and orchards thrive in the Niagara fruit belt. Northern Ontario has thick forests that provide wood for the pulp and paper industry. Trappers catch fur-bearing animals there, and campers hunt and fish.

The province's name came from the Iroquois Indians, who lived in the Ontario region when French explorers first arrived. The word *Ontario* may mean *beautiful lake.* Or it may mean *rocks standing high* or *near the water*—referring to Niagara Falls. These spectacular falls attract many visitors. Niagara Falls ranks among the greatest natural sources of hydroelectric power in North America.

Ontario, together with New Brunswick, Nova Scotia, and Quebec, was one of the original provinces of Canada. For the relationship of Ontario to the other provinces, see **Canada; Canada, Government of; Canada, History of.**

AP Photo
Automobile assembly plant in Oshawa

Ontario in brief

Symbols of Ontario

The provincial flag, adopted in 1965, bears the British Union Flag and the shield of Ontario. The shield has the cross of St. George, representing the province's ties with England. The three maple leaves symbolize Canada. The crest is a bear atop a wreath of green and gold. A moose and a deer support the shield. The shield was granted by royal warrant in 1868. The crest and supporters were granted in 1909.

Provincial flag

Ontario

Provincial coat of arms
Province of Ontario

Ontario (brown) ranks as the second largest province of Canada.

General information

Entered the Dominion: July 1, 1867, as one of the original four provinces.
Provincial abbreviation: ON (postal).
Provincial motto: *Ut Incepit Fidelis Sic Permanet* (Loyal She Began, Loyal She Remains).

The Provincial Parliament Buildings are in Toronto, the capital since 1867. The region had several other capitals as Upper Canada and part of the Province of Canada.

Land and climate

Area: 412,581 mi² (1,068,580 km²), including 68,491 mi² (177,390 km²) of inland water.
Elevation: *Highest*—2,275 ft (693 m) above sea level in Timiskaming District. *Lowest*—sea level.
Coastline: 752 mi (1,210 km).
Record high temperature: 108 °F (42 °C) at Biscotasing on July 20, 1919, at Atikokan on July 11 and 12, 1936, and at Fort Frances on July 13, 1936.
Record low temperature: −73 °F (−58 °C) at Iroquois Falls on Jan. 23, 1935.
Average July temperature: 66 °F (19 °C).
Average January temperature: 9 °F (−13 °C).
Average yearly precipitation: 31 in (79 cm).

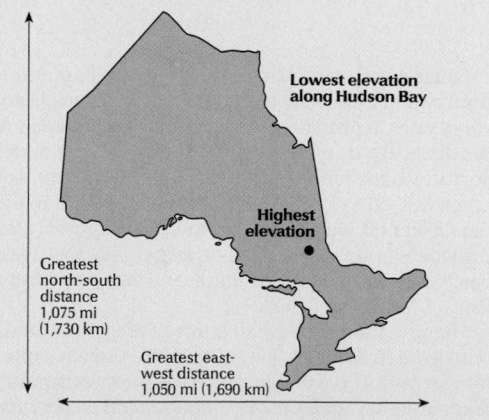

Lowest elevation along Hudson Bay

Highest elevation

Greatest north-south distance 1,075 mi (1,730 km)

Greatest east-west distance 1,050 mi (1,690 km)

Important dates

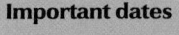

French missionaries founded Fort Sainte Marie.

Ontario became one of the original four provinces on July 1.

| 1610 | 1639 | 1763 | 1867 | 1883 |

Étienne Brulé of France became the first white person to explore the Ontario region.

Britain obtained the Ontario region from France.

The world's largest copper-nickel reserves were discovered at Sudbu

Bird
Loon

Tree
White pine

Floral emblem
White trillium

People

Population: 12,160,282 (2006 census)
Rank among the provinces: 1st
Density: 29 persons per mi² (11 per km²), provinces average 13 per mi² (5 per km²)
Distribution: 85 percent urban, 15 percent rural
Largest cities and towns*

Toronto	2,503,281
Ottawa	812,129
Mississauga	668,549
Hamilton	504,559
Brampton	433,806
London	352,395

*2006 census.
Source: Statistics Canada.

Population trend

Millions

Year	Population
2006	12,160,282
2001	11,410,046
1996	10,753,573
1991	10,084,885
1986	9,113,515
1981	8,625,107
1976	8,264,465
1971	7,703,106
1966	6,960,870
1961	6,236,092
1951	4,597,542
1941	3,787,655
1931	3,431,683
1921	2,933,662
1911	2,527,292
1901	2,182,947
1891	2,114,321
1881	1,926,922
1871	1,620,851

Source: Statistics Canada.

Economy
Chief products

Agriculture: beef and dairy cattle, chickens and eggs, corn, floriculture and nursery products, hogs, soybeans, vegetables.
Manufacturing: chemicals, electronic equipment, food and beverage products, machinery, metal products, transportation equipment.
Mining: cement, copper, gold, nickel, sand and gravel, stone.

Gross domestic product

Value of goods and services produced in 2008: $587,905,000,000.* *Services* include community, business, and personal services; finance; government; trade; and transportation and communication. *Industry* includes construction, manufacturing, mining, and utilities. *Agriculture* includes agriculture, fishing, and forestry.

*Canadian dollars.
Source: Statistics Canada.

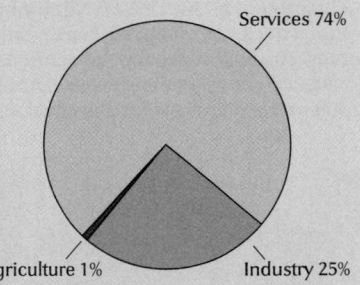

Services 74%
Agriculture 1%
Industry 25%

Government
Provincial government

Premier: term of 4 years
Members of the Legislative Assembly: 107, terms of 4 years

Federal government

Members of the House of Commons: 106
Members of the Senate: 24

Sources of information

Ontario's official website at http://www.ontario.ca provides a gateway to much information on the province's economy, government, and history.

In addition, the website at http://www.ontariotravel.net provides information on tourism in the province.

One of the world's largest uranium deposits was discovered at Elliot Lake.

The Ontario legislature passed laws to merge several cities, including Toronto, with their surrounding communities.

| 1912 | 1952 | 1972 | 1982 | 1997-1999 |

Ontario gained the territory north of the Albany River.

Ontario began a program of free medical and hospital care for the elderly and the poor.

Large gold deposits were discovered near Marathon.

Population. The 2006 Canadian census reported that Ontario had 12,160,282 people. The population of the province had increased about 6 ½ percent over the 2001 figure of 11,410,046.

The great majority of Ontarians—about 95 of every 100 people—live in 12 percent of the land area in the province. This heavily populated region, the southernmost part of Ontario, lies south of Lake Nipissing. This area includes all of Ontario's metropolitan areas except those of Greater Sudbury/Grand Sudbury and Thunder Bay.

Ontario has 15 Census Metropolitan Areas as defined by Statistics Canada. For the names and populations of these metropolitan areas, see the *Index* to the political map of Ontario.

About 85 percent of the people of Ontario live in urban areas. Ontario contains more cities with populations of 50,000 or more than any other Canadian province.

Toronto is the largest city in Ontario and in Canada. Ontario's other large cities include Brampton, Hamilton, Kitchener, London, Markham, Mississauga, Ottawa, Vaughn, and Windsor. See the list of separate articles on the cities of Ontario listed in the *Related articles* at the end of this article.

About 70 percent of the people in Ontario were born in Canada. The province also has many people born in China, India, Italy, and the United Kingdom. Many Ontarians have some English ancestry. There are also many people with Chinese, French, German, Irish, Italian, and Scottish ancestry.

Ontario has about 160,000 North American Indians. About a third of the Indians live on the province's reserves. These areas cover a total of 1 ⅔ million acres (674,000 hectares) in the province. Another 80,000 of Ontario's people have some Aboriginal ancestry.

Population density

The vast majority of Ontario's people live in the southeast part of the province, where most of the largest cities are located. The northern areas of Ontario are thinly populated.

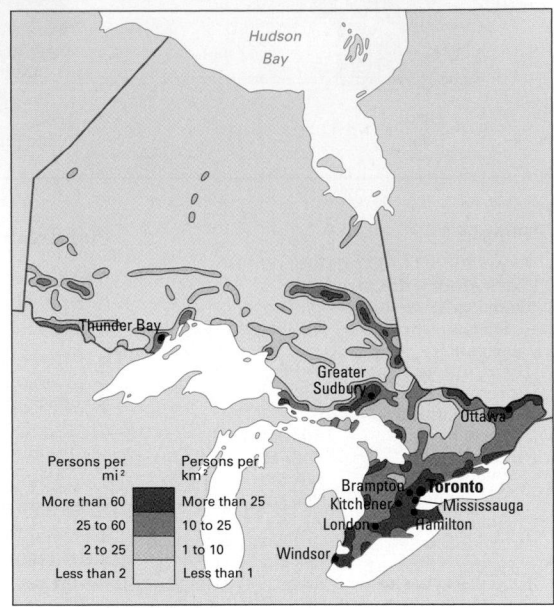

Persons per mi²	Persons per km²
More than 60	More than 25
25 to 60	10 to 25
2 to 25	1 to 10
Less than 2	Less than 1

WORLD BOOK map; based on the *National Atlas of Canada.*

John Foster, Masterfile

Indians cut firewood on an Ontario Indian reserve. About 160,000 people in Ontario are North American Indians. About a third of these people live on Indian reserves.

© Bill Brooks, Alamy

Yorkville is a fashionable area of Toronto that features art galleries, boutiques, and sidewalk cafes. The district is also known for the variety of its architecture.

Schools. The first *common* (elementary) schools in the Ontario region were established during the late 1780's. In 1807, Ontario's provincial government provided by law for a *grammar* (high) school in each of the province's eight districts. In 1816, the government provided for common schools throughout the province. A royal charter was granted in 1827 for a college in York (now Toronto). This college opened as King's College in 1843 and became the University of Toronto in 1850.

Ontario's school system took its present basic form during the 1870's. Grammar schools became known as high schools or collegiate institutes. Common schools were called *free schools.* Free schools were financed by local taxes and government grants.

Today, Ontario has public schools and Roman Catholic schools. Both types of schools are tax supported and under the jurisdiction of the Ministry of Education. Most schools teach in English, but the province also has some French-language schools. Attendance from age 6 to age 18 is required by law.

Universities and colleges

This table lists the universities and colleges in Ontario that grant bachelor's or advanced degrees and are members of the Association of Universities and Colleges of Canada.

Name	Mailing address
Algoma University	Sault Ste. Marie
Brescia University	London
Brock University	St. Catharines
Carleton University	Ottawa
Dominican University College	Ottawa
Guelph, University of	Guelph
Huron University College	London
King's University College at the University of Western Ontario	London
Lakehead University	Thunder Bay
Laurentian University of Sudbury	Sudbury
McMaster University	Hamilton
Nipissing University	North Bay
OCAD University	Toronto
Ontario, University of, Institute of Technology	Oshawa
Ottawa, University of	Ottawa
Queen's University	Kingston
Redeemer University College	Ancaster
Royal Military College of Canada	Kingston
Ryerson University	Toronto
St. Jerome's University	Waterloo
St. Michael's College, University of	Toronto
St. Paul University	Ottawa
Sudbury, University of	Sudbury
Toronto, University of	Toronto
Trent University	Peterborough
Trinity College, University of	Toronto
Victoria University	Toronto
Waterloo, University of	Waterloo
Western Ontario, University of	London
Wilfrid Laurier University	Waterloo
Windsor, University of	Windsor
York University	Toronto

Libraries. Ontario's first subscription library was established in 1800 at Niagara. By 1867, Ontario had more than 60 *mechanics' institutes,* which provided books for working people. Ontario passed Canada's first public library legislation, the Free Libraries Act, in 1882.

Library and Archives Canada, the Canada Institute for Scientific and Technical Information, the Library of Parliament, and the Supreme Court of Canada Library are in Ottawa. The Thomas Fisher Rare Book Library of the University of Toronto includes well-known collections of Canadian, English, and Italian literature. The National Gallery of Canada Library and Archives, also in Ottawa, includes an extensive collection of visual-arts literature.

Museums. The Royal Ontario Museum in Toronto has galleries containing archaeology, art, history, and natural history exhibits. The Ontario Science Centre, also in Toronto, features exhibits and demonstrations dealing with science and technology. National museums in Ottawa include the Canadian Museum of Nature, with collections covering botany, earth sciences, and vertebrate and invertebrate animals; the Canada Science and Technology Museum, with exhibits on communications, industrial technology, natural resources, and transportation; and the National Gallery of Canada, which features artworks from Canada and other parts of the world.

Fort William Historical Park in Thunder Bay is a reconstruction of a local fur-trading post of the 1800's. Sainte-Marie Among the Hurons, near Midland, is a re-creation of a fortress and headquarters for Jesuit missionaries of the 1600's. The fortress was Ontario's first European community. Ottawa's Canadian War Museum displays art, artifacts, and memorabilia representing the nation's military history.

Mike Dobel, Masterfile

University College is one of the oldest colleges of the University of Toronto and a national historic monument. The University of Toronto ranks as Canada's largest university.

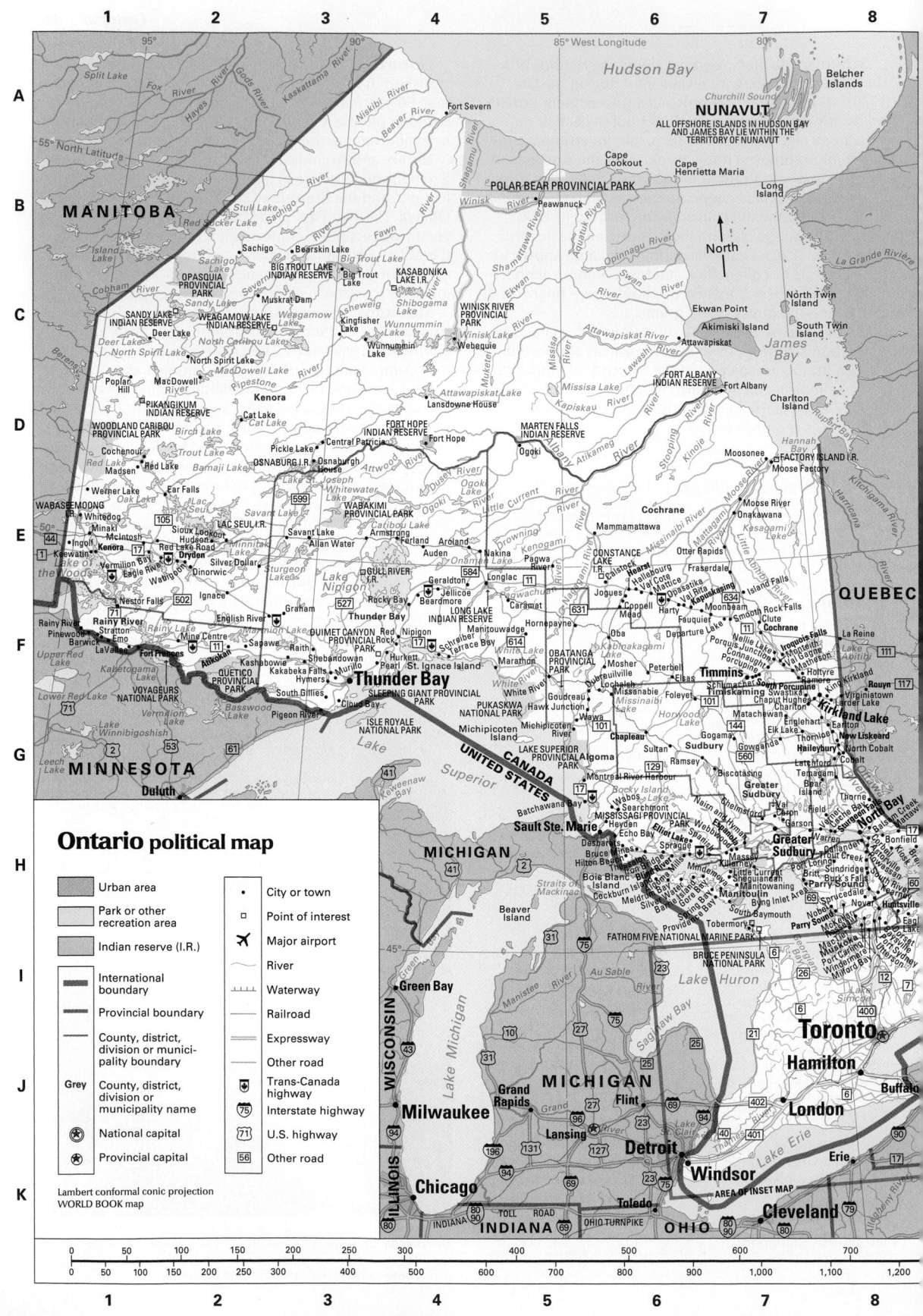

Ontario political map

Urban area	•	City or town
Park or other recreation area	□	Point of interest
Indian reserve (I.R.)	✈	Major airport
		River
International boundary		Waterway
Provincial boundary		Railroad
County, district, division or municipality boundary		Expressway
		Other road
Grey County, district, division or municipality name		Trans-Canada highway
	75	Interstate highway
⊛ National capital	71	U.S. highway
⊛ Provincial capital	56	Other road

Lambert conformal conic projection
WORLD BOOK map

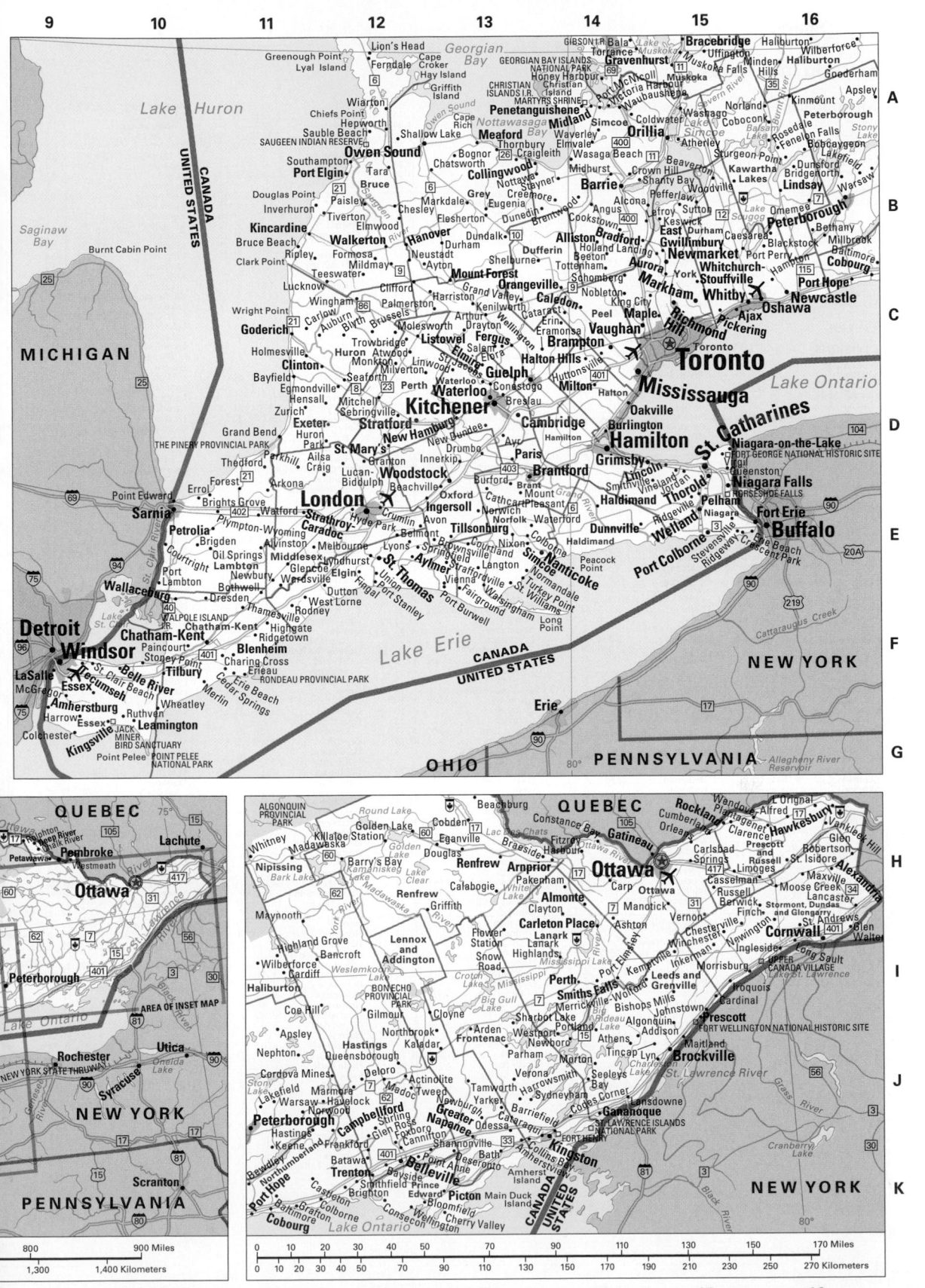

Ontario map index

Ottawa is the capital of Canada. The city is noted for its government buildings, parks, and museums. The Parliament Buildings, *shown here,* stand on three sides of a square on Parliament Hill.

© Jeremy Woodhouse, Masterfile

Mississippi
Mills ....11,734 ..H 14
Mitchell ....D 12
Molesworth ....C 12
Monkton ....C 12
Mono ....7,071 ..C 14
Montague§# .....3,595 ..J 15
Moonbeam# .....1,298 .F 7
Moose Creek ....I 16
Moosonee ......2,006 ..D 7
Morley§# ......492 .F 1
Morris-
Turnberry§** ..3,403 ..E 11
Morrisburg ....I 15
Mount Forest ....C 13
Mount Pleasant ......E 13
Mulmur§# .....3,318 ..C 14
Murillo ....F 3
Muskoka
Lakes§# ....6,467 ..I 8
Nairn and
Hyman# .....493 ..H 7
Nakina ....E 4
Nanticoke ....E 13
Neebing§** .....2,184 ..G 3
Neustadt ....B 12
New Dundee ....D 13
Newboro ....J 14
Newburgh ....J 13
Newbury ....439 ..E 11
Newcastle ....C 16
Newington ....H 16
Newmarket ...74,295 ..B 15
New Tecum-
seth§ ......27,701 ..B 14
Neyaashiining-
miing Indian
Reserve ....591 ..A 12
Niagara Falls ....82,184 ..D 15
Niagara-on-
the-Lake ....14,587 ..D 15
Nipigon# ......1,752 .F 4
Nixon ....E 13
Nobel ....H 8
Norfolk
County§ ...62,563 ..E 13
Norland ....A 16
Normandale ....E 13
North Bay ......53,966 ..H 8
North
Dundas# .....11,095 ..I 15
North
Glengarry# ..10,635 ..H 16
North
Grenville** ..14,198 ..I 15
North
Perth** ....12,254 ..D 12
Northeastern
Manitoulin
and the
Islands .....2,711 ..H 7
Norwich# ....10,481 ..E 13
Norwood ....I 11
Nottawa ....B 13
Novar ....J 13
Oakville ....165,613 ..D 14
Odessa ....J 13
Oil Springs ....717 ..E 11
Oliver
Paipoonge§** ..5,757 ..E 11

Omemee ....B 16
Opasatika# ....280 ..E 6
Orangeville ....26,925 ..C 14
Orillia ....30,259 ..A 15
Oro-
Medonte# ..20,031 ..B 14
Oshawa ......141,590 ..C 16
Otonabee-South
Monaghan§# ..6,934 ..J 11
Ottawa ......812,129 ..H 10
Owen Sound ...21,753 ..A 13
Paincourt ....F 10
Paisley ....B 12
Pakenham ....H 14
Palmerston ....C 13
Paris ....D 13
Parkhill ....D 11
Parry
Sound ......5,818 ..H 8
Pelham ......16,155 ..E 15
Pembroke ...13,930 ..H 9
Penetangui-
shene ....9,354 ..A 14
Perry§# ......2,010 ..H 7
Perth ....5,907 ..I 14
Perth East# ...12,041 ..D 12
Perth South# ...4,132 ..D 12
Petawawa ...14,651 ..H 9
Peter-
borough ...74,898 ..J 9
Petrolia .....5,222 ..E 11
Pickering ...87,838 ..C 15
Pickle Lake# ....479 ..D 3
Picton ....K 13
Pikangikum
Indian
Reserve ....D 1
Plantagenet ....H 16
Plympton-
Wyoming ...7,506 ..E 11
Point Edward ..2,019 ..E 10
Pointe Anne ....K 12
Port Burwell ....E 13
Port Carling ....I 8
Port
Colborne ..18,599 ..E 15
Port Elgin ....B 12
Port Elmsley ....I 14
Port Hope** ..16,390 ..K 11
Port Lambton ....E 10
Port Loring ....H 8
Port McNicoll ....A 14
Port Stanley ....E 12
Portland ....I 14
Powassan** ...3,309 ..H 8
Prescott .....4,180 ..I 15
Prince
Edward§ ...25,496 ..K 12
Providence
Bay ....H 7
Puslinch§# ....6,689 ..E 13
Queens-
borough ....I 14
Quinte West ...42,697 ..J 12
Rainy River .....909 .F 1
Ramara# ....9,427 ..A 15
Red Lake** ....4,526 ..D 1
Red Lake
Road ....F 2
Red Rock# ....1,063 .F 4

Renfrew ....7,846 ..H 13
Richmond ....H 15
Richmond
Hill .....162,704 ..C 15
Rideau
Lake§# ...10,350 ..E 13
Ridgetown ....F 11
Ripley ....B 11
Rodney ....F 11
Rosseau ....H 8
Russell# ....13,883 ..H 15
Ruthven ....G 10
Sables-Spanish
Rivers§# .....3,237 ..H 6
St. Andrews ....H 16
St. Catha-
rines ....131,989 ..D 15
St.-Charles** ...1,159 ..H 7
St. Clair# ...14,649 ..E 10
St. Clair Beach ....F 10
St. Isidore ....H 16
St. Jacobs ....D 13
St. Joseph# ...1,129 ..H 6
St. Mary's .....6,617 ..D 12
St. Thomas ...36,110 ..E 12
St. Williams ....E 13
Salem ....C 13
Sandy Lake
Indian
Reserve ......1,843 ..C 2
Sarnia ......71,419 ..E 10
Sauble Beach ....A 12
Saugeen
Indian
Reserve ....758 ..A 12
Saugeen
Shores ...11,720 ..B 12
Sault Ste.
Marie ....74,948 ..H 6
Schomberg ....C 14
Schreiber# ....901 .F 4
Scugog# ....21,439 ..C 15
Seaforth ....C 12
Sebringville ....D 12
Seeleys Bay ....J 14
Seguin§# ....4,276 ..H 8
Severn# ....12,030 ..A 14
Shallow Lake ....A 12
Shannonville ....K 13
Sharbot Lake ....I 13
Sheguiandah
Indian
Reserve§ ....160 ..H 7
Shelburne ....5,149 ..B 13
Simcoe ....E 13
Sioux
Lookout** ...5,183 ..E 2
Smith-
Ennismore-
Lakefield# ..17,413 ..B 16
Smithfield ....K 12
Smiths Falls ...8,777 ..I 14
Smooth Rock
Falls ....1,473 ..F 7
South
Baymouth ....H 7
South Bruce
Peninsula ...8,415 ..A 12
South
Dundas# ...10,535 ..I 15

South
Frontenac# ..18,227 ..J 13
South
Glengarry# ..12,880 ..H 16
South
Huron** ....9,982 ..D 11
South River ...1,069 ..H 8
South
Stormont# ..12,520 ..I 16
Southampton ....B 12
Southgate§# ...7,167 ..C 13
Southwold§ ...4,724 ..E 12
Spanish§ ....728 ..H 6
Spragge ....H 6
Spring Bay ....H 7
Springfield ....E 12
Springwater# ..17,456 ..B 14
Sprucedale ....H 8
Stayner ....B 14
Stirling-
Rawdon# ....4,906 ..J 12
Stone Mills# ...7,568 ..J 13
Stoney Point ....F 10
Straffordville ....E 13
Stratford ...30,461 ..D 12
Strathroy-
Caradoc# ..19,977 ..E 11
Stratton ....F 1
Sturgeon Falls ....H 8
Sudbury, see
Greater Sudbury
[/Grand Sudbury]
Sultan ....G 6
Sundridge .....942 ..H 8
Sydenham ....J 13
Tamworth ....J 13
Tara ....B 12
Tay# ....9,748 ..A 14
Tay Valley§# ...5,634 ..I 14
Tecumseh ...24,224 .F 9
Teeswater ....C 12
Temagami** .....934 ..G 7
Temiskaming
Shores§ ...10,732 ..G 8
Terrace
Bay# ....1,625 .F 4
Thames
Centre** ...13,085 ..E 12
Thamesville ....F 11
Thedford ....E 11
The Nation/
[La Nation]** ..10,643 ..H 16
Thessalon ....1,312 ..H 6
Thornbury ....A 13
Thorne ....G 8
Thornloe ......105 ..G 8
Thorold .....18,224 ..D 15
Thunder
Bay ......109,140 .F 3
Tilbury ....F 10
Tillsonburg ...14,822 ..E 13
Timmins .....42,997 .F 7
Tincap ....J 15
Tiny# ......10,784 ..A 14
Tiverton ....B 12
Toronto ...2,503,281 ..J 8
Tottenham ....B 14
Trent Hills§** ...12,247 ..J 11
Trenton ....K 12
Trout Creek ....H 8

Trowbridge# ....C 12
Turkey Point ....E 13
Tweed** .....5,614 ..J 12
Tyendinaga§# ..4,070 ..J 13
Union ....E 12
Uxbridge§# ...19,169 ..B 15
Vankleek
Hill ....H 16
Vaughan ...238,866 ..C 14
Vermilion
Bay ....E 2
Vernon ....H 15
Verona ....J 13
Victoria
Harbour ....A 14
Vienna ....E 13
Virginiatown ....G 8
Wabigoon ....E 2
Wainfleet# ....6,601 ..E 15
Walkerton ....B 12
Wallaceburg ....F 10
Walpole
Island
Indian
Reserve ....1,878 ..F 10
Walsingham ....E 13
Wardsville ....F 11
Warwick§# ....3,945 ..D 11
Wasaga
Beach ....15,029 ..A 14
Waterloo ...97,475 ..D 13
Watford ....E 11
Waverley ....A 14
Wawa ....G 5
Weagamow
Lake Indian
Reserve ....700 ..C 3
Webbwood ....H 7
Webequie
Indian
Settlement§ ......614 ..C 5
Welland ....50,331 ..E 15
Wellesley§# ...9,789 ..D 13
Wellington ....K 12
Wellington
North§# .....11,175 ..C 13
West Lorne ....E 11
West
Nipissing** ..13,410 ..H 7
Westport ......645 ..J 14
Wheatley ....G 10
Whitby ....111,184 ..C 15
Whitchurch-
Stouffville ...24,390 ..C 15
White River# .....841 .F 5
Wiarton ....A 12
Wikwemikong
Unceded
Indian
Reserve§ ...2,387 ..H 7
Wilmot§# ....17,097 ..D 13
Winchester ....I 15
Windsor ...216,473 ..K 6
Wingham ....C 12
Woodstock ...35,480 ..D 13
Woodville ....B 15
Woolwich§# ...19,658 ..D 13
Yarker# ....J 13
Zorra# .....8,125 ..E 13
Zurich ....D 11

*Type of census division. Census divisions administer services to a group of municipalities.
†This regional municipality is split into the cities of Haldimand County and Norfolk County.
‡United Counties, united for administrative purposes.
§Does not appear on map; key shows general location.

#Township.
**Municipality.
Source: 2006 census. Places without populations are unincorporated areas.

More than 100 million tourists visit Ontario every year. The province has more than 250,000 lakes and rivers, which offer a variety of vacation attractions, including fishing and boating. Ontario's forests attract campers and hunters.

The sunny, southernmost resort region of the province, along Lakes Erie and Ontario, is known as *Canada's Sun Parlor* and *Canada's Banana Belt.* Boat cruises are available to take vacationers through the Thousand Islands and other islands in Ontario waters. The Haliburton Highlands and the Kawartha and Muskoka lakes

near Toronto are famous resort areas. Low, wooded hills line their shores. The landscape becomes more rugged toward the northern and northwestern vacationlands of James Bay and Lake of the Woods. Many hunters fly in seaplanes to the far northern lakes to hunt bear, geese, moose, and a variety of other game.

Ontario is the home of two major annual drama festivals. The Stratford Shakespeare Festival, held in Stratford, features the plays of William Shakespeare. The Shaw Festival, at Niagara-on-the-Lake, presents plays by George Bernard Shaw and other dramatists of his time.

John de Visser, Masterfile

Horseshoe Falls, the largest part of Niagara Falls, near the Ontario-New York border

Places to visit

Following are brief descriptions of some of Ontario's many interesting places to visit:

Agawa Canyon, near Sault Ste. Marie, is a scenic wilderness area with waterfalls, mountains, ravines, and forests.

Art Gallery of Ontario, in Toronto, is one of the largest art museums in North America. The gallery's collections represent European, Canadian, modern, Inuit, and contemporary art.

Canadian Warplane Heritage Museum, in Mount Hope, features over 30 aircraft as well as interactive displays, simulators, a theater, and Canadian history memorabilia.

CN Tower, in downtown Toronto, stands 1,815 feet (553 meters) tall. This communication tower includes several observation decks and a rotating restaurant.

Horseshoe Falls, near the Ontario-New York border, is the largest part of Niagara Falls. It is about 2,600 feet (792 meters) wide and 167 feet (51 meters) high.

Old forts in Ontario that have been restored include Fort Erie in Fort Erie, Fort George in Niagara-on-the-Lake, Fort Henry in Kingston, Fort Malden in Amherstburg, Fort St. Joseph on St. Joseph Island, Fort Wellington in Prescott, Fort York in Toronto, and Old Fort William in Thunder Bay.

Parliament Buildings, in Ottawa, are three Gothic-style stone buildings with green copper roofs. They form Canada's seat of government. The Changing of the Guards ceremony takes

place in front of these buildings in the summer.

Royal Botanical Gardens, on the border of Burlington and Hamilton, attract many visitors from around the world. The botanical gardens were established in 1941.

Sainte-Marie Among the Hurons, near Midland, is a reconstructed Jesuit mission of the 1600's. Martyrs' Shrine, which stands nearby, honors eight missionaries who were martyred by the Iroquois.

Upper Canada Village, near Morrisburg, shows life in Ontario in the 1860's. Some of its buildings were moved from the Lake St. Lawrence area.

National parks. Ontario has five national parks—Bruce Peninsula, between Lake Huron and Georgian Bay; Georgian Bay Islands, in Georgian Bay; Point Pelee, on the Lake Erie peninsula; Pukaskwa, on the shore of Lake Superior; and St. Lawrence Islands, along the St. Lawrence River. Ontario also has about 35 national historic parks and sites and 2 national marine parks—Fathom Five in Georgian Bay and Lake Superior. For the area and main features of the national parks in Ontario, see **Canada** (National Park System).

Provincial parks. Ontario has many provincial parks. Most provide camping facilities and waterside ramps for small boats. Visit the website maintained by Ontario Parks at http://www.ontarioparks.com for helpful information on provincial parks in Ontario.

© Rommel, Masterfile

Ontario Place in Toronto

© Greg Stott, Masterfile

Agawa Canyon, near Sault Ste. Marie, between Lakes Huron and Superior

Bill Brooks, Masterfile

Thousand Islands area in the St. Lawrence River

Land and climate

The St. Lawrence Lowland is an important agricultural area. Fruits, grains, and vegetables are the chief crops grown in this fertile valley region between the Ottawa and St. Lawrence rivers.

Al Harvey, Masterfile

Land regions. Thousands of years ago, glaciers moved across Ontario, eroding and depositing materials and so helping to shape the land. Today, Ontario has four main land regions. They are, from north to south: (1) the Hudson Bay Lowland, (2) the Canadian Shield, (3) the St. Lawrence Lowland, and (4) the Great Lakes Lowland.

The Hudson Bay Lowland curves around the southern part of Hudson Bay and extends as far south as Kesagami Lake. This flat region of northern Ontario is poorly drained, and much of it is covered by *muskeg* (peat bogs). The lowland includes a narrow belt of *permafrost* (permanently frozen ground) near the Arctic.

The Canadian Shield is a vast, horseshoe-shaped region that covers almost half of Canada and part of the northern United States. This low, rocky region covers more than half of Ontario. It contains some of the oldest rocks on Earth. These rocks date from Precambrian times, which ended more than 500 million years ago. Small lakes and rivers surrounded by wooded hills attract many vacationers. The highest point in Ontario rises 2,275 feet (693 meters) in Timiskaming District.

The Canadian Shield is rich in game, minerals, and timber. Patches of clay, scattered throughout the region, were formed by deposits in ancient glacial lakes. The largest clay area, known as the clay belt, extends from the Hearst area to the Quebec border. Farmers raise a variety of crops, including grains and vegetables, in the rich clay soil. Beef and dairy cattle graze on fenced grasslands in the region. See **Canadian Shield**.

The St. Lawrence Lowland runs along the St. Lawrence River. In Ontario, it forms the tip of the wedge of land between the Ottawa and St. Lawrence rivers. Low hills rise above the fertile valleys. Farmers grow fruits,

grains, and vegetables in this region. Dairy farming is extensive there.

The Great Lakes Lowland lies along much of the Great Lakes in Canada and the United States. In Ontario, the region touches Lakes Erie, Huron, and Ontario. Great quantities of many crops are grown in the fertile gray-brown soil of the low, flat, southwestern section. The land rises gently in the northeast, where beef and dairy cattle are raised. The Niagara Escarpment, a high cliff or

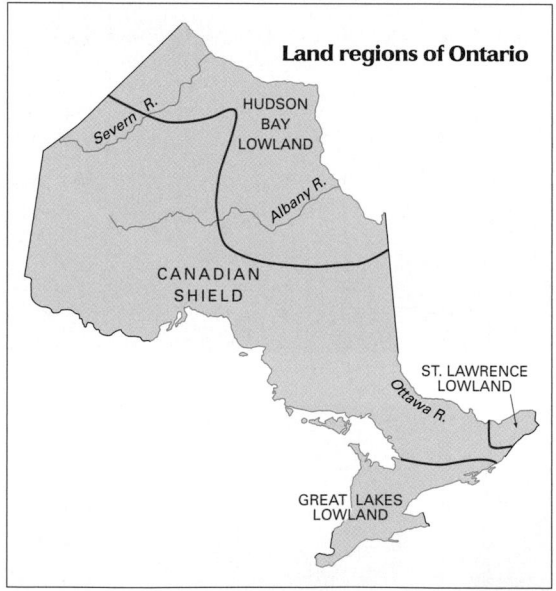

Land regions of Ontario

WORLD BOOK map

Map index

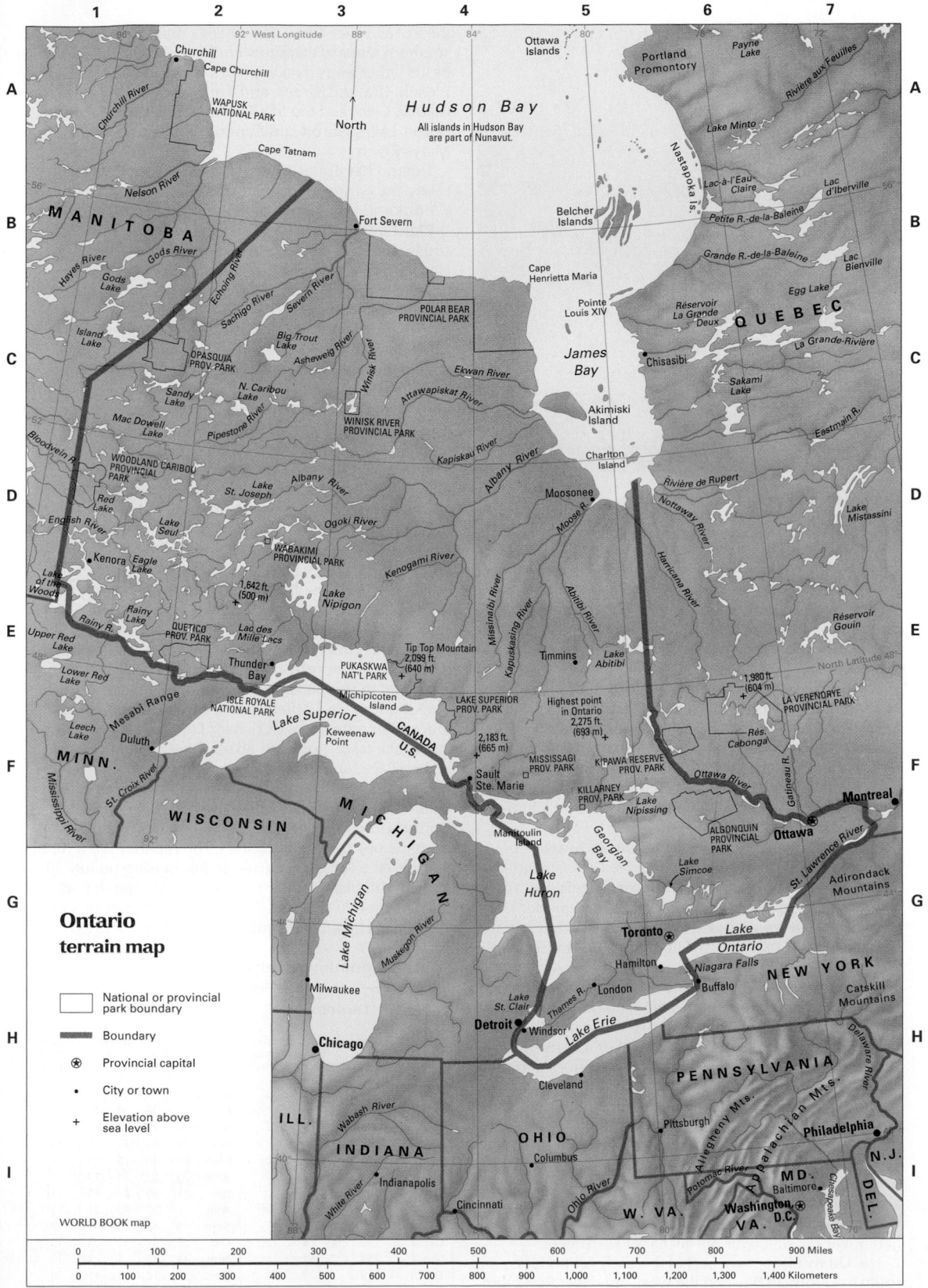

	1	2	3	4	5	6	7

A

Churchill
Cape Churchill
WAPUSK
NATIONAL PARK
Churchill River

Ottawa
Islands

Portland
Promontory

Payne
Lake

Rivière aux Feuilles

Hudson Bay
All islands in Hudson Bay
are part of Nunavut.

Lake Minto

North

B

MANITOBA

Nelson River

Cape Tatnam

Fort Severn

Belcher
Islands

Lac-à-l'Eau-
Claire

Lac
d'Iberville

Petite R.-de-la-Baleine

Grande R.-de-la-Baleine

Lac
Bienville

Hayes River
Gods River
Gods Lake
Echoing River
Sachigo River
Severn River
Island
Lake

Cape
Henrietta Maria

Pointe
Louis XIV

POLAR BEAR
PROVINCIAL PARK

Réservoir
La Grande
Deux

QUEBEC

Egg Lake

La Grande-Rivière

C

Sandy
Lake
N. Caribou
Lake
Big Trout
Lake
Asheweig River
Winisk River

Ekwan River

Attawapiskat River

*James
Bay*

Akimiski
Island

Chisasibi

Sakami
Lake

Eastmain R.

Mac Dowell
Lake
Pipestone River

OPASQUIA
PROV. PARK

WINISK RIVER
PROVINCIAL PARK

Kapiskau River

Charlton
Island

Rivière de Rupert

Lake
Mistassini

D

Bloodvein R.
WOODLAND CARIBOU
PROVINCIAL
PARK
Red
Lake
English River

Lake
St. Joseph
Albany River

Ogoki River

Albany River

Moosonee

Moose R.

Nottaway River

Harricana River

E

Kenora
Eagle
Lake
Rainy
Lake
QUETICO
PROV. PARK
Lad des
Mille Lacs

Lake
Seul

WABAKIMI
PROVINCIAL PARK

1,642 ft.
(500 m)
+

Lake
Nipigon

Kenogami River

Missinaibi River

Kapuskasing River

Timmins

Abitibi River

Lake
Abitibi

Réservoir
Gouin

1,980 ft.
(604 m)
+

LA VERENDRYE
PROVINCIAL
PARK

North Latitude 48°

Upper Red
Lake
Lower Red
Lake
Leech
Lake

Mesabi Range

Thunder
Bay

PUKASKWA
NAT'L PARK

Tip Top Mountain
2,099 ft.
(640 m)
+

LAKE SUPERIOR
PROV. PARK

Highest point
in Ontario
2,275 ft.
(693 m) +

Rés.
Cabonga

F

MINN.
Duluth
St. Croix River
Mississippi River

ISLE ROYALE
NATIONAL PARK
Michipicoten
Island
Keweenaw
Point

Lake Superior

CANADA
U.S.

2,183 ft.
(665 m)
+

Sault
Ste. Marie

MISSISSAGI
PROV. PARK

K'PAWA RESERVE
PROV. PARK

Ottawa River

Gatineau R.

Montreal

WISCONSIN

MICHIGAN

Manitoulin
Island

KILLARNEY
PROV. PARK

Lake
Nipissing

ALGONQUIN
PROVINCIAL
PARK

Ottawa

G

Lake Michigan

Muskegon River

*Lake
Huron*

Georgian
Bay

Lake
Simcoe

St. Lawrence River

Adirondack
Mountains

Toronto ⊛

Lake
Ontario

H

Milwaukee

Lake
St. Clair
Detroit
Windsor

Thames R.
London

Hamilton
Niagara Falls
Buffalo

NEW YORK

Catskill
Mountains

Chicago

Lake Erie

Cleveland

PENNSYLVANIA

Pittsburgh

Allegheny Mts.

Appalachian Mts.

Delaware River

Philadelphia

I

ILL.
Wabash River
INDIANA

White River
Indianapolis

Columbus

OHIO

Ohio River

Cincinnati

W. VA.

VA.

Pittsburgh

Potomac River

MD.
Baltimore

Washington
D.C. ⊛

Chesapeake Bay

N.J.

DEL.

WORLD BOOK map

Ontario
terrain map

▭	National or provincial park boundary
▬	Boundary
⊛	Provincial capital
•	City or town
+	Elevation above sea level

0	100	200	300	400	500	600	700	800	900 Miles

| 0 | 100 | 200 | 300 | 400 | 500 | 600 | 700 | 800 | 900 | 1,000 | 1,100 | 1,200 | 1,300 | 1,400 Kilometers |

George Hunter

Quetico Provincial Park, near Atikokan, is a large wilderness area of beautiful lakes and dense forests. Many people visit the park to enjoy camping, canoeing, and fishing.

ridge, extends 250 miles (402 kilometers) from Manitoulin Island, through Bruce Peninsula, to Niagara Falls. The escarpment forms a natural shelter for Ontario's best fruit-growing belt. Many of Canada's largest cities are in the Great Lakes Lowland.

Shoreline and coastline. Ontario's southern shores of bays, narrow inlets, and sandy beaches stretch 5,252 miles (8,452 kilometers). This shoreline, including 2,414 miles (3,885 kilometers) of offshore island shoreline, is on Lakes Erie, Huron, Ontario, and Superior. Ontario's Manitoulin Island is the world's largest inland island. It has an area of 1,067 square miles (2,765 square kilometers) in Lake Huron.

Oceangoing ships use the St. Lawrence Seaway to reach the Great Lakes ports of Ontario. These inland seaports include Hamilton, Port Colborne, Sarnia, Sault Ste. Marie, and Toronto. Thunder Bay on Lake Superior is a major Canadian grain port. Northern Ontario has a coastline of 752 miles (1,210 kilometers) on Hudson Bay and James Bay.

Rivers, waterfalls, and lakes cover a sixth of the province. A land rise separates the Ontario streams that flow into the Great Lakes from those that empty into the Ottawa River or Hudson Bay. Many lakes and rivers, some linked by canals, are important transportation routes.

The St. Lawrence River, a great natural highway for commerce, has contributed much to the growth of Ontario's economy. The river was enlarged in the 1950's to create the St. Lawrence Seaway, enabling ocean vessels to reach the Great Lakes. Hydroelectric plants on the Niagara and other rivers provide Ontario with cheap power. The mighty Horseshoe Falls are formed by the Niagara River passing over the Niagara Escarpment.

The Ottawa River was part of the early fur traders' route to Georgian Bay and the west. This river flows into

the St. Lawrence River. The Ottawa drains the part of southern Ontario that does not lie in the Great Lakes basin. Other important southern rivers include the French, Grand, Thames, and Trent. The Detroit River, Lake St. Clair, and the St. Clair River link Lakes Erie and Huron. Lakes Huron and Superior are joined by the St. Marys River.

Ontario has about 400,000 lakes. Besides the Great Lakes, the largest lakes in the province are Lake of the Woods and Lakes Abitibi, Nipigon, Nipissing, and Seul.

Plant and animal life. Ontario has about 180,000 square miles (466,000 square kilometers) of forests. Northern Ontario has huge forests of balsam, pine, spruce, and other softwoods. It also has birch and poplar. Thick forests of hardwoods such as ash, beech, elm, maple, and walnut once covered southern Ontario. Most of the timber in the south was cut in the 1800's, and the forests there now have second-growth trees.

Wildflowers are plentiful in Ontario. Trilliums and bloodroots blossom in spring. Autumn brings masses of asters and wild carrot blooms. Northern lakeside hills are thick with wild blueberry bushes in forest clearings. Shrubs and mosses grow in the far northern areas, where frost stays deep in the ground. Tamarack and spruce, which grow there, do not reach their usual height in this cold, poorly drained region.

Moose and caribou roam the wooded northlands of Ontario. Shy white-tailed deer pause to drink from streams in the Canadian Shield. People in this region often see the tracks of black bears. Fur-bearing animals such as beavers, minks, muskrats, foxes, and otters live throughout Ontario. Snowshoe hares are also plentiful in all parts of the province. Raccoons and rabbits are abundant in southern Ontario. Birds of Ontario include ducks, geese, and ruffed grouse. The haunting cries of loons pierce the air at dusk over Ontario's lakes. Brook trout, lake trout, northern pike, whitefish, and yellow pickerel are found in the lakes and rivers.

Climate. Winds from the Great Lakes give southern Ontario a milder climate than the rest of the province. Northern Ontario gets cold waves from the Arctic, or from the northwestern prairies. The record high temperature, 108 °F (42 °C), occurred in Biscotasing on July 20, 1919, in Atikokan on July 11 and 12, 1936, and in Fort Frances on July 13, 1936. The lowest temperature, −73 °F (−58 °C), occurred in Iroquois Falls on Jan. 23, 1935.

Average monthly weather

	Toronto					Ottawa			
	Temperatures			Days of rain or snow		**Temperatures**			Days of rain or snow
	°F		**°C**			**°F**		**°C**	
	High	Low	High	Low			High	Low	High	Low	
Jan.	28	12	−2	−11	15	Jan.	21	5	−6	−15	17
Feb.	30	14	−1	−10	12	Feb.	25	9	−4	−13	13
Mar.	39	23	4	−5	13	Mar.	36	19	2	−7	14
Apr.	54	34	12	1	12	Apr.	52	34	11	1	12
May	66	45	19	7	12	May	66	46	19	8	13
June	75	54	24	12	11	June	75	55	24	13	12
July	81	59	27	15	10	July	81	59	27	15	11
Aug.	79	57	26	14	11	Aug.	77	57	25	14	11
Sept.	70	50	21	10	11	Sept.	68	48	20	9	13
Oct.	57	39	14	4	12	Oct.	55	37	13	3	13
Nov.	45	30	7	−1	13	Nov.	41	27	5	−3	15
Dec.	34	19	1	−7	15	Dec.	27	12	−3	−11	18

Average January temperatures

Ontario has wide variations in wintertime temperatures. Temperatures moderate steadily from the far north to the south.

Average July temperatures

The southeast and west are the warmest areas in Ontario during the summer. The far north has the coolest temperatures.

Average yearly precipitation

The heaviest amounts of precipitation in the province fall in the southeast. The northeast is the driest section.

WORLD BOOK maps; based on the *National Atlas of Canada.*

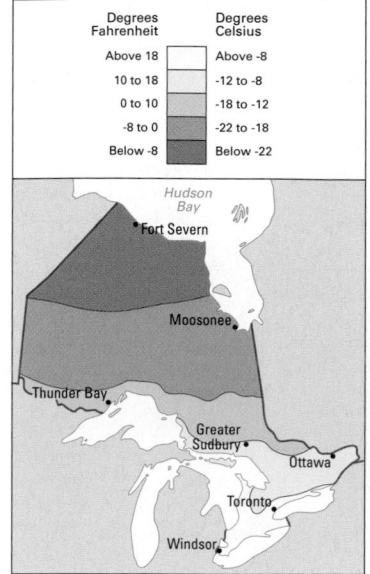

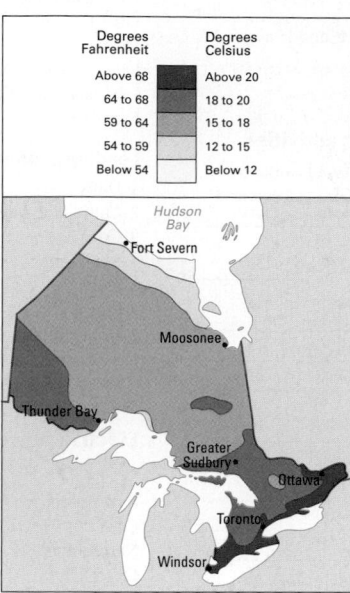

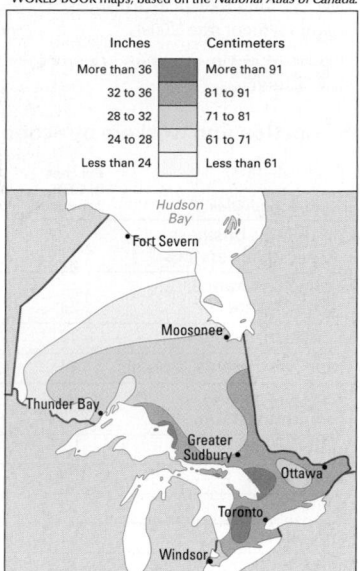

The average January temperature in southern Ontario ranges from 12 °F (–11 °C) in Ottawa to 23 °F (–5 °C) in Windsor. The average July temperature is 66 °F (19 °C) in Greater Sudbury and 73 °F (23 °C) in Windsor. The temperature in northern Ontario in January averages –9 °F (–23 °C) at Big Trout Lake and –6 °F (–21 °C) at Moosonee. The temperature in July averages 61 °F (16 °C) at Big Trout Lake and 66 °F (19 °C) at Sioux Lookout.

Ontario's average annual *precipitation* (rain, melted snow, and other moisture) ranges from 24 to 28 inches (60 to 70 centimeters) in the northern part of the province to 31 to 35 inches (80 to 90 centimeters) in the southern part. Annual snowfall in most of Ontario ranges from 48 to 105 inches (123 to 267 centimeters).

Economy

The highly developed industries of Ontario make it one of the richest economic regions of North America. Service industries make up the largest part of the province's *gross domestic product* (GDP)—the total value of goods and services produced in the province in a year. Ontario has a higher GDP than any other province. It leads the provinces in business and high-technology services and in the manufacture of high-technology and industrial products.

The economy of Ontario benefits from the province's location near key North American population centers and waterways. Ontario is close to many large U.S. cities, which provide markets for the province's goods and services. Several major U.S. corporations have large operations in Ontario. The St. Lawrence Seaway provides Ontario's Great Lakes ports with an outlet to the Atlantic Ocean. Thus, ships can travel to and from Ontario ports from any ocean port in the world.

Natural resources. The great forests and abundant wildlife of Ontario are valuable natural resources. Other important resources of the province include fertile soils, many mineral deposits, and a plentiful water supply.

Soil. The soils of the northernmost parts of Ontario are frozen the year around. The Hudson Bay Lowland's soils consist mostly of clay and marshes of moss called *muskeg.* Thin soils cover ancient rock in most of the Canadian Shield. Near the Quebec border, glacial clays and silt cover the fertile clay belts of the Cochrane and Teniskaming districts. The St. Lawrence and Great Lakes lowlands are Ontario's chief farming regions. The St. Lawrence Lowland has black loams and well-drained sands over limestone and shale. The Great Lakes Lowland has rich, sandy soils.

Minerals are found throughout central and northern Ontario in the rocks of the Canadian Shield. The Sudbury Basin, in the southern part of the shield, is the greatest single source of Ontario's mineral wealth. Much of the world's nickel comes from this district. The ores there also contain cobalt, copper, gold, platinum, and silver. Other areas in the Canadian Shield produce copper, gold, nickel, and zinc.

Service industries, taken together, account for about three-fourths of Ontario's GDP and employment. Service industries are especially important in Toronto and the other major urban areas of southern Ontario.

Toronto, the provincial capital, is the center of government activities. The city is also the nation's leading financial center. Most of Canada's largest banks, insur-

Ontario economy

General economy

Gross domestic product (GDP)* (2008) $587,905,000,000
   Rank among Canadian provinces   1st
Unemployment rate (2009)   9.0% (Canada avg: 8.3%)

*Gross domestic product is the total value of goods and services produced in a year and is
  in Canadian dollars.
Source: Statistics Canada.

Production and workers by economic activities

Economic activities	Percent of GDP produced	Employed workers	
		Number of people	Percent of total
Community, business, & personal services	23	2,262,500*	34*
Finance, insurance, & real estate	23*	472,400	7
Manufacturing	17	901,200	13
Trade, restaurants, & hotels	14	1,421,700	21
Transportation & communication	8	639,400	10
Construction	5	439,000	7
Government	5	363,500	5
Utilities	2	65,100	1
Agriculture	1†	84,500	1
Mining	1	38,100†	1†
Total	100	6,687,400	100

*Includes figures from establishments that manage other companies.
†Includes figures from forestry and fishing.
Figures are for 2008.
Source: Statistics Canada.

Agriculture

Cash receipts $10,187,135,000
   Rank among Canadian provinces   1st
Distribution   51% livestock, 49% crops
Farms   57,200
Farm acres (hectares)   13,285,900 (5,376,600)
   Rank among Canadian provinces   4th
Farmland   5% of Ontario

Leading products

1. Dairy   (ranks 2nd in Canada)
2. Cattle and calves   (ranks 3rd in Canada)
3. Corn   (ranks 1st in Canada)
4. Soybeans   (ranks 1st in Canada)
5. Hogs   (ranks 2nd in Canada)
6. Floriculture & nursery products   (ranks 1st in Canada)
7. Hens and chickens   (ranks 1st in Canada)
Other products: apples, beans, eggs, grapes, hay, turkeys,
  tobacco, vegetables, wheat.

Electric power

Nuclear   50.3%
Hydroelectric   22.0%
Coal   20.4%
Natural gas   6.7%
Other   0.6%

Agriculture figures are for 2008; electric power figures are for 2007.
Dollar amounts are in Canadian dollars.
Source: Statistics Canada.

continued on page 781

WORLD BOOK map

Economy of Ontario

This map shows the economic uses of land in Ontario and where the province's leading farm, mineral, and forest products are produced. The major urban areas (shown on the map in red) are Ontario's important manufacturing centers.

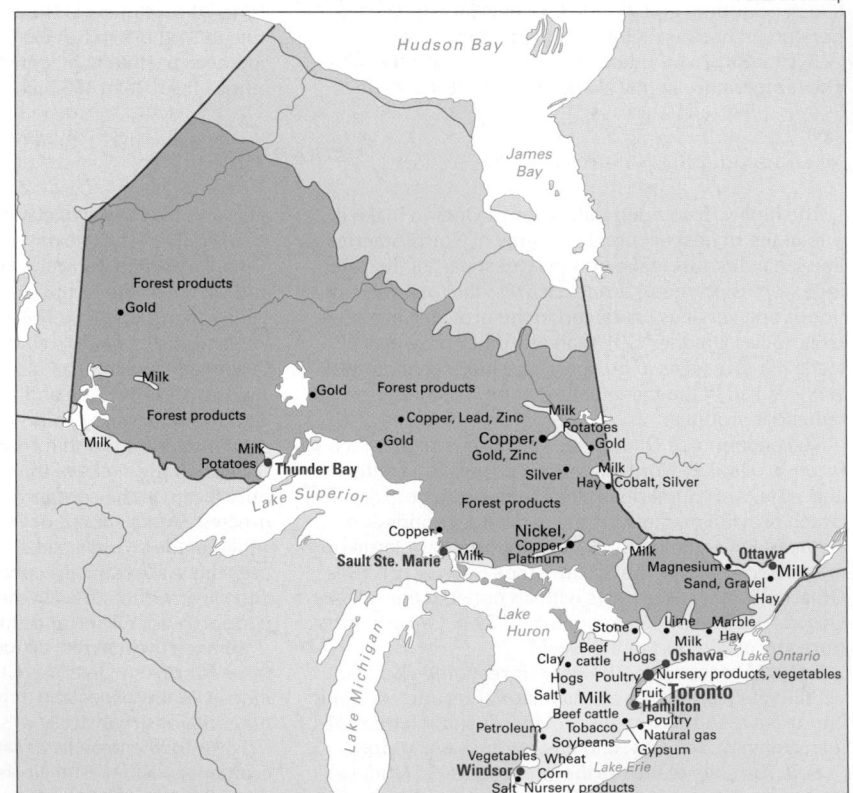

Cropland and grazing land

Fruit region

Forest land

Northern woodland

Tundra and wetland

● Manufacturing and service industry center

● Mineral deposit

Mining

Mineral production	$10,933,901,000
Rank among Canadian provinces	5th
Minerals	$10,821,382,000
Coal	*
Crude oil and crude oil equivalents	$51,464,000
Natural gas	$61,055,000

*No significant mining of this product in Ontario.

Leading products

1. Nickel	(ranks 1st in Canada)
2. Copper	(ranks 2nd in Canada)
3. Gold	(ranks 1st in Canada)
4. Stone	(ranks 1st in Canada)
5. Cement	(ranks 1st in Canada)

Other products: clay, cobalt, lime, platinum, salt, sand and gravel, silver, zinc.

Manufacturing

Value added by manufacture*	$100,934,799,000
Rank among Canadian provinces	1st

Leading products

1. Transportation equipment
2. Food and beverage products
3. Fabricated metals
4. Chemicals
5. Primary metals
6. Machinery

Other products: computer and electronic products, paper products, plastic and rubber products.

*Value added by manufacture is the increase in value of raw materials after they become finished products.

Figures are for 2007.
Dollar amounts are in Canadian dollars.
Source: Statistics Canada.

ance companies, and property developers are headquartered there. The Toronto Stock Exchange is one of the largest in North America. Many of Canada's largest hospitals and law firms are in Toronto. The city is also the home of the University of Toronto and York University, two of Ontario's largest universities.

Service industries are also important outside of Toronto. Federal government activities are based in Ottawa. Large universities at Hamilton, London, Ottawa, and Waterloo employ many people. Rapid population growth in such metropolitan areas as Kitchener, Oshawa, and Ottawa has benefited Ontario's real estate companies by increasing the demand for housing in the province. Each year, more tourists visit Ontario than any other Canadian province. Restaurants, hotels, and other service industries benefit from tourist spending.

Manufacturing is one of Ontario's most important economic activities. About half of Canada's industrial workers live in Ontario. These workers produce about half the country's manufactured products. The Toronto area ranks as Canada's leading industrial center.

The production of transportation equipment is On-

Ontario Ministry of Tourism and Recreation
Farmers harvest grapes from a field in the Niagara fruit belt, a famous fruit-growing region in southeastern Ontario. The province is Canada's leading producer of grapes.

tario's chief manufacturing industry. Automobile manufacturing is the main part of this industry. Most of Canada's automobile manufacturing takes place in Ontario. Several major automobile companies have large assembly plants in southern Ontario. Many trucks are also produced in Ontario. Automobile parts are manufactured in many cities, including Barrie, Burlington, Guelph, London, Mississauga, Toronto, and Windsor. Hamilton and Sault Ste. Marie are Ontario's major steel centers.

Chemicals, electronics, and plastic products are also important parts of Ontario's manufacturing industry. Most of Ontario's chemical products are manufactured in Sarnia and Toronto. Telecommunications and computer equipment are the leading types of electronic equipment made in Ontario. The manufacture of electronic equipment is based mainly in the Toronto and Ottawa areas. Packaging materials rank among Ontario's leading plastics products. Toronto is also the home of much of Ontario's plastics manufacturing industry.

The processing of agriculture and forest products is also important. Toronto is a major North American meatpacking center. Fruits and vegetables grown in the Great Lakes region of Canada are processed in Ontario factories. Plants in the province produce large quantities of milk and other dairy products. Ontario's mills process Canadian-grown wheat into flour and prepared baking mixes. Beer, liquor, and soft drinks are the leading beverage products. Most of Ontario's pulp and paper mills and sawmills are in the northern part of the province.

Agriculture. Ontario's farms cover about 5 percent of the province's land area. Livestock and crops each account for about half of Ontario's farm production.

Milk is the leading source of farm income. The raising of beef cattle and hogs is also important. Beef and dairy cattle graze on pastureland between the southeastern shores of Lake Huron and the lower western shores of Lake Ontario. Dairying is also important eastward along Lake Ontario and the St. Lawrence River. Farmers in southern Ontario raise large numbers of hogs.

Ontario farmers grow the feed crops they need for their livestock. The major crops include corn, hay, soybeans, and wheat. Ontario leads the provinces in the production of eggs and poultry.

Ontario is also Canada's leading producer of fruits and vegetables. Orchards and vineyards of the famous Niagara fruit belt produce apples, grapes, peaches,

Freight containers, carried piggyback on railroad flatcars, await shipment at a sprawling rail yard outside Toronto. Ontario has about a fourth of Canada's total railways. Southern Ontario has the finest railway network in Canada.

strawberries, and other small fruits. The chief vegetables grown in the province include beans, cabbage, carrots, cucumbers, mushrooms, onions, peppers, potatoes, sweet corn, and tomatoes. Tobacco, which grows along Lake Erie, is among the leading cash crops in Ontario.

Ontario also has the largest *floriculture* industry in Canada. Many growers raise flowers and vegetables indoors to protect the plants from the weather and to control the growth of the plants. Greenhouse vegetables are primarily grown in the Leamington area.

Mining. Most of Ontario's mining income comes from the production of metal ores. The province produces more metallic minerals than any other province.

Copper, gold, and nickel are among Ontario's most valuable mineral products. Gold-producing areas are scattered throughout the Canadian Shield region. The Hemlo gold field, near Marathon, is the single leading gold-producing area. The Greater Sudbury area is Canada's center of nickel production. Copper is mined in the Greater Sudbury and Timmins areas.

Other leading mined products in Ontario include cement, petroleum products, salt, sand and gravel, and stone. Ontario is Canada's leading producer of cement, salt, sand and gravel, and stone. Natural gas and petroleum have been found in southern Ontario and beneath the waters of Lake Erie. Sand and gravel are obtained primarily from pits in the southern part of the province. Granite, limestone, and marble from Ontario grace buildings around the world.

Electric power and utilities. Hydroelectric plants, nuclear power plants, and plants that burn coal or natural gas supply almost all of Ontario's electric power. Ontario and the state of New York share the water of Niagara Falls under terms of a 1910 treaty between Canada and the United States.

Transportation. Waterways have played an important part in the history of Ontario. French explorers traveled up the Ottawa River in canoes. Early canals, particu-

larly the Rideau and Trent systems, carried passengers and freight. The St. Lawrence Seaway, which was completed in 1959, brought oceangoing ships to the inland ports (see **Saint Lawrence Seaway**).

During the navigation season, from late March or early April to late December, many freighters travel between the ports of Ontario and those of the United States. Grain-carrying ships crowd the docks of Thunder Bay on Lake Superior.

Toronto Pearson International Airport, just outside Toronto, is the largest and busiest airport in Canada. A number of government, industrial, and private airlines carry passengers and supplies to distant mining and lumbering camps in the northern part of Ontario.

Ontario has about a fourth of Canada's total railways. Southern Ontario has Canada's finest railway network. Toronto is the province's chief rail center. The Canadian National Railway, the Canadian Pacific Railway, and VIA Rail are the largest railways in Ontario. The province owns the Ontario Northland Railway, whose main line runs through the clay belt and the silver-mining region to James Bay.

Thousands of miles of highways crisscross Ontario. Part of the east-west Trans-Canada Highway runs across Ontario. A 510-mile (821-kilometer) expressway stretches from Windsor to the Quebec border.

Communication. Louis Roy, a Frenchman from Quebec, published the first newspaper of the Ontario region. His paper, the *Upper Canada Gazette, or American Oracle,* first appeared in 1793 in Newark (now Niagara-on-the-Lake). York (now Toronto) became the capital of Ontario in 1797, and the *Gazette* moved there in 1798. It was published until 1849.

Today, the *Toronto Star* ranks first in circulation. Ontario's other leading dailies include *The Globe and Mail* and the *National Post* of Toronto, the *Toronto Sun,* the *Ottawa Citizen,* the *Ottawa Sun, The Hamilton Spectator, The London Free Press,* and *The Windsor Star.*

Lieutenant governor of Ontario represents the British monarch, Queen Elizabeth II, in her role as Canada's queen. The lieutenant governor is appointed by the *governor general in council,* the governor general of Canada acting with the advice and consent of the Cabinet. The position of lieutenant governor is largely honorary.

Premier is the actual head of government. Ontario, like the other provinces and Canada itself, has a parliamentary government. The premier is an elected member of the Legislative Assembly and is usually leader of the Assembly's majority party. The head of Ontario's government was called the premier until 1906, when the title was changed to prime minister. In 1972, Prime Minister William Davis changed the title back to premier.

The premier heads the Executive Council (cabinet). The Executive Council includes ministers chosen by the premier from members of the premier's party in the Assembly. Many ministers direct one or more government ministries. The Executive Council, like the premier, resigns if it loses the support of most of the Assembly.

Legislative Assembly of Ontario is a one-house legislature that makes the provincial laws. The Assembly has 107 members who are elected from 107 electoral districts called *constituencies.* The members of the Assembly serve four-year terms.

Courts. Ontario's highest court is the Court of Appeal. It consists of a chief justice, an associate chief justice, and 21 other justices.

Ontario's Superior Court of Justice hears major civil, criminal, and family cases. It has a chief justice, an associate chief justice, eight regional senior judges, and hundreds of other judges. The Superior Court also contains the Divisional Court, the Small Claims Court, and the Family Court. The Divisional Court hears reviews of provincial administrative action and some Superior Court appeals. The Small Claims Court hears minor civil cases. The Family Court hears all aspects of family law disputes. The governor general of Canada, with the advice and consent of the Cabinet, appoints the Superior Court justices, who may serve until age 75.

The Ontario Court of Justice handles provincial of-

The premiers of Ontario*

	Party	Term
John S. Macdonald	Liberal	1867-1871
Edward Blake	Liberal	1871-1872
Oliver Mowat	Liberal	1872-1896
Arthur S. Hardy	Liberal	1896-1899
George W. Ross	Liberal	1899-1905
James P. Whitney	Conservative	1905-1914
William H. Hearst	Conservative	1914-1919
Ernest C. Drury	United Farmers of Ontario	1919-1923
George H. Ferguson	Conservative	1923-1930
George S. Henry	Conservative	1930-1934
Mitchell F. Hepburn	Liberal	1934-1942
Gordon D. Conant	Liberal	1942-1943
Harry C. Nixon	Liberal	1943
George A. Drew	†Progressive Cons.	1943-1948
Thomas L. Kennedy	†Progressive Cons.	1948-1949
Leslie M. Frost	†Progressive Cons.	1949-1961
John P. Robarts	†Progressive Cons.	1961-1971
William Davis	†Progressive Cons.	1971-1985
Frank S. Miller	†Progressive Cons.	1985
David Peterson	Liberal	1985-1990
Bob Rae	New Democratic	1990-1995
Michael D. Harris	†Progressive Cons.	1995-2002
Ernie Eves	†Progressive Cons.	2002-2003
Dalton McGuinty	Liberal	2003-

*The title *prime minister* was used from 1906 to 1972.
†Progressive Conservative.

fenses and some family and young offenders cases. It has a chief justice, an associate chief justice, eight regional senior judges, a senior judge of the Family Court, and hundreds of other full-time judges. The provincial lieutenant governor in council appoints the judges, who may serve until age 65. With annual approval from the chief justice, the judges may serve until age 75.

Local government. The basic unit of local government in Ontario is the municipality. A municipality may be called a city, town, township, or village. A municipal council governs each municipality. The council makes decisions about public services and how to finance them. It consists of a leader, called a mayor or a *reeve,* and a number of elected councilors or aldermen.

© Mark Blinch, Reuters/Landov

Members of Ontario's Legislative Assembly listen to a speech in the Legislative Building in Queen's Park, Toronto. The Legislative Chamber has detailed wood carvings and elaborate plasterwork. The public can tour the Legislative Building and its grounds.

Municipal governments raise money primarily by collecting property taxes from residents of the municipality.

In some areas of the province, where it is more efficient to do so, a county, district, or regional government administers services to a group of municipalities. A *warden* heads each county council, and a *regional chair* heads each regional council. A county council consists of elected members from the constituent municipalities. The method of selecting a regional council varies. Ontario's only district government, the District Municipality of Muskoka, provides the same kinds of services that county and regional governments provide.

In northern Ontario, which is sparsely populated, District Social Service Administration Boards and Local Service Boards provide municipal services over broad geographical areas. Ontario also has a number of Consolidated Municipal Service Managers. These organizations serve to integrate the social services and community health services of separate municipalities.

Revenue. Taxes collected by the provincial government provide about 70 percent of the province's *general revenue* (income). Most of this money comes from taxes on personal and corporate income and retail sales. Other important revenue sources include taxes on gasoline and tobacco. About 20 percent of the revenue comes from the federal government.

Politics. Ontario has three major political parties—the provincial Progressive Conservative, Liberal, and New Democratic parties. The Progressive Conservative Party was formerly named the Conservative Party, and today its members are usually called simply Conservatives. Of the three parties, the New Democrats are the most left-leaning, and the Conservatives are the most right-leaning. Other provincial parties include the Communist, Family Coalition, Freedom, Green, Libertarian, and Ontario Provincial Confederation of Regions parties.

The Liberals and Conservatives have controlled Ontario's government for most of its history. But a couple of other parties have governed for isolated periods. In 1919, during an economic depression, the United Farmers of Ontario took over the government. Under the leadership of Ernest C. Drury, the party governed until 1923. The New Democrats controlled the province from 1990 to 1995. Since 2003, the Liberals have governed Ontario. Ontario citizens must be at least 18 years of age to vote in federal or provincial elections.

History

Original inhabitants. Three major Native American groups lived in what is now Ontario when European explorers first arrived. The Chippewa (also known as the Ojibwa or Anishinabe) hunted beavers and small game in the forests north and east of Lake Superior. The Huron (also called the Wendat) lived between Lake Huron and Lake Ontario. They depended mainly on cultivated crops for food. The Huron often fought with the Iroquois, who lived in several settlements south of Lake Ontario.

European exploration. The first European to explore the Ontario region was Étienne Brulé of France. Samuel de Champlain, the founder of Quebec, sent Brulé to the area in 1610. In 1613, Champlain paddled up the Ottawa River. In 1615, he journeyed farther south, into the Lake Huron area, where he joined Brulé. Brulé had been living with the Huron for a time and had adopted the Huron language and customs. Champlain found the Lake Huron region rich in fur-bearing animals. French fur traders followed his course to collect pelts. They traveled deep into the forests, accompanied by native guides. The French traded with the Native Americans, swapping guns and knives for furs. In the 1620's and 1630's, French explorers, including Brulé and Jean Nicolet, explored the Lake Superior region, Lake Michigan, and beyond.

Early settlement. French missionaries followed the fur traders into the Ontario region. In 1639, Jesuit priests built Fort Sainte Marie as the center of a group of missions among the Huron. These missions were known together as Huronia. Weakened by malnutrition and diseases that the Europeans had brought with them, the Huron became easy prey for the Iroquois. Under pressure from the Iroquois, the Jesuits and the Huron fled Huronia in 1648 and 1649.

During the 1650's and 1660's, French explorers entered the region north of Lake Superior. These explorers included Pierre Esprit Radisson and Médard Chouart, Sieur des Groseilliers. Their explorations led to the founding of a trading company called the Hudson's Bay Company in London (see **Hudson's Bay Company**).

In 1763, at the end of the French and Indian War, France gave the Ontario region to Britain (now also called the United Kingdom). By then, only a few scattered French settlements remained near what are now Kingston, Niagara Falls, and Windsor. Little further settlement took place until 1784. That year, after the American Revolution, people loyal to England began arriving from the United States. About 6,000 of these United Empire Loyalists, as they were called, came by 1785. They settled near present-day Kingston and Windsor and on the Niagara Peninsula, an isthmus that connects Ontario and New York. The Loyalists had lost their homes and wealth. The British government gave them food, clothing, land, livestock, and seed. About 4,000 other settlers also arrived from the United States.

Upper Canada. In 1791, the southern part of what is now Ontario became the colony of Upper Canada. Newark (now Niagara-on-the-Lake) was the capital. The British government appointed a lieutenant governor to govern the colony. The lieutenant governor appointed a 7-member Legislative Council and an Executive Council to advise him. The people elected a 16-member Legislative Assembly. Colonel John Graves Simcoe, the first lieutenant governor, promoted roadbuilding and expanded settlement. In 1793, Simcoe chose York (now Toronto) as the site for a new capital, and the government finished moving there in 1797.

Gradually, more settlers arrived, some in organized groups. A group of Pennsylvania Dutch, most of whom were descended from German immigrants, settled near what is now Kitchener. Many people came from the United States to acquire cheap land. Traders from the Hudson's Bay Company posts in the Far North settled

Historic Ontario

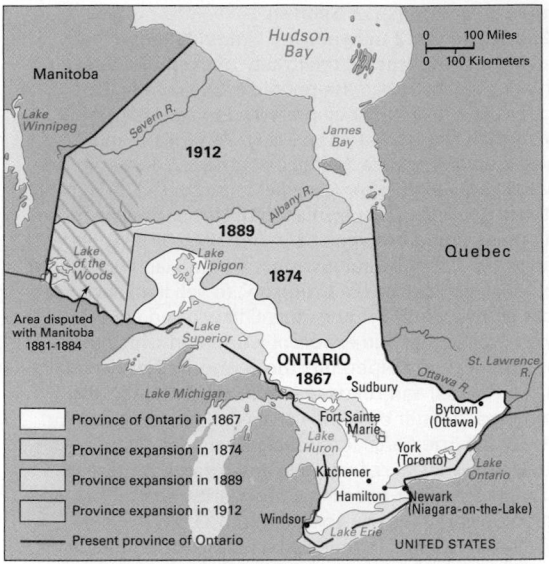

WORLD BOOK map

The Welland Ship Canal, which opened in 1829, links Lake Ontario with Lake Erie. The original canal was extended and expanded several times between 1829 and 1932.

Ontario became one of four provinces of the Dominion of Canada on July 1, 1867. The Province of Ontario expanded north and west several times until 1912, when it took its present shape.

Sir John A. Macdonald of Ontario became the first prime minister of the Dominion of Canada in 1867.

Important dates in Ontario

WORLD BOOK illustrations by Richard Bonson, The Art Agency

1610 Étienne Brulé of France became the first white person to explore the Ontario region.

1613 Samuel de Champlain of France explored the Ottawa River area.

1639 French missionaries founded Fort Sainte Marie.

1648-1649 Indians destroyed the French missions.

1763 The Ontario region became a British possession.

1791 The region became the province of Upper Canada.

1812-1814 American forces invaded Upper Canada during the War of 1812.

1837 A rebellion against British rule broke out in Upper Canada.

1867 Ontario became one of the original four provinces of the Dominion of Canada on July 1.

1883 The world's largest copper-nickel reserves were discovered at Sudbury (now part of Greater Sudbury).

1904 Ontario's automobile industry began in Windsor.

1912 Ontario gained the territory north of the Albany River.

1952 The Western world's largest uranium deposit was discovered at Elliot Lake.

1959 The St. Lawrence Seaway opened.

1964 A huge field of copper, silver, and zinc was discovered near Timmins.

1972 Ontario began a program of free medical and hospital care for the elderly and the poor.

1982 Large gold deposits were discovered at Hemlo, near Marathon.

1985 After 42 years of Progressive Conservative rule, the Liberal Party won control of the provincial government and began a five-year period of Liberal leadership.

2003 Ontario's highest court, the Court of Appeal, upheld a lower court decision to allow same-sex marriage in the province.

with their families in the southern towns. Most of these people were English or Scottish.

The War of 1812 between the United Kingdom and the United States tested the loyalty of Upper Canada's settlers. Well over half the people of the colony were former U.S. citizens. Many preferred to stay out of the war. British troops, aided by Native Americans and some Canadian militia, halted invading U.S. forces in several battles in Upper Canada.

Early growth. The population of Upper Canada more than quadrupled between 1812 and 1842. By 1851, it had reached 952,000. Private investors formed land companies, such as the Canada Company, to sell land and promote immigration. Bytown (now Ottawa) and other towns prospered. The export of wood and wheat to the United Kingdom helped fuel the economy. Canals, mills, small factories, and roads were built. The Rideau, the Trent, and the first Welland canals date from this period. In 1825, the Erie Canal linked Lakes Erie and Ontario with New York City. Many Irish immigrants, motivated by Upper Canada's economic prosperity, arrived in the region during the early and middle 1800's.

Political unrest. In the 1830's, many Upper Canadians became dissatisfied with their government. Under the colony's system of government, the people elected only the Legislative Assembly. But substantial power lay with the lieutenant governor and with the councils that he appointed to assist him. The members of these councils were often called the Family Compact and generally represented the wealthy and powerful people of the colony. The Legislative Council often blocked legislation that the Legislative Assembly had passed. Such legislation included building roads and schools and providing free land to settlers.

The Family Compact and the British government blocked political reforms that would have given the people more power. William Lyon Mackenzie, a member of the Legislative Assembly, and a group of several hundred followers rebelled in 1837. A colonial militia put down the uprising. The government arrested some of the rebels, banished some, and executed two. Mackenzie and others fled to the United States.

In 1840, the British Parliament passed the Act of Union. This act, which took effect in 1841, united Upper Canada and Lower Canada (part of present-day Quebec) into a single colony called the Province of Canada. The British hoped that the French-speaking majority in Lower Canada would be absorbed into the English-speaking majority in Upper Canada. But French- and English-speaking Reformers agreed to protect their distinct rights and also demanded more political freedom. They achieved some success in 1848, when the Province of Canada gained *responsible government.* Under responsible government, the head of government and a cabinet govern for as long as they have the support of a majority of the people's elected representatives.

Confederation. In 1864, politicians from the Province of Canada proposed a federal union of all the British colonies in eastern North America. All the colonies except Prince Edward Island and Newfoundland agreed to join the confederation. On July 1, 1867, the British North America Act created the Dominion of Canada. New Brunswick, Nova Scotia, Ontario, and Quebec became provinces in the Dominion. Ottawa was chosen as the federal capital. Sir John A. Macdonald of Ontario became the first prime minister of Canada. John S. Macdonald, no relation to him, was Ontario's first premier.

Progress as a province. Following confederation, Ontario's economy grew slowly at first. However, the development of scientific methods of agriculture and the use of machinery led to an increase in farming, and lumbering expanded in the Canadian Shield region. New railroad tracks expanded land transportation, and a network of canals opened water navigation in the province. Manufacturing increased, and the cities of Toronto and Hamilton became important business and industrial centers. Despite this slow yet substantial economic growth, many Ontarians moved to the United States for better job opportunities. In 1883, railroad construction crews found the world's richest copper-nickel deposits near Sudbury (now part of Greater Sudbury). Major mining did not begin until after 1892, when a copper company developed a practical process for separating copper and nickel.

In the early 1900's, mining and manufacturing began to increase rapidly. The city of Cobalt became a thriving mining center after a huge silver deposit was discovered nearby in 1903. Mineral exploration took place throughout the Canadian Shield. Within a few years, prospectors discovered many new deposits of gold, silver, and other minerals. The region soon became one of the world's richest mining areas.

A pulp and paper industry developed in Ontario during the early 1900's, and it soon grew to major importance. Ontario's automobile industry began in 1904, when ferryboats first carried automobile parts across the Detroit River from Detroit, Michigan, to Windsor. Windsor became an automobile assembly center. In 1906, the provincial government established the Hydro-Electric Power Commission of Ontario. This agency developed Niagara Falls and other hydroelectric sources.

By 1911, more Ontarians lived in urban than in rural communities, and more people worked in business and manufacturing than as farmers. In 1912, Ontario's northern boundary was extended from north of the Albany River to Hudson and James bays. This expansion gave the province its present area. The outbreak of World War I (1914-1918) hastened Ontario's economic development. Ontario led the provinces in the production of weapons and other military supplies. During the war, more volunteers in Canada's armed forces came from Ontario than from any other single province. In 1917, women in Ontario gained the right to vote in provincial elections.

During the 1920's, prospectors developed new mines in the northern forest regions. Many Finns, Scandinavians, and French-speaking Canadians from Quebec settled in these areas. Automobile production continued to increase. The iron and steel and the pulp and paper industries prospered. This prosperity ended with the Great Depression of the 1930's. During the Depression, Ontario experienced labor unrest. This led to an increase in labor unions during the 1940's.

The mid-1900's. World War II (1939-1945) put an end to the Great Depression in Ontario. During the war, Ontario's factories, farms, and mines increased production to help arm and feed the Allied armies. Later, hundreds of thousands of Europeans left their war-torn countries and migrated to Ontario. More than half of the 3 million people who settled in Canada between 1945 and 1970 made their homes in Ontario. The population rose from about 4 million to 7 ½ million. The largest numbers of immigrants came from Germany, Italy, the United Kingdom, south and east Asia, and the West Indies.

The war stimulated Ontario's manufacturing production, which peaked in the early 1950's. Discoveries of various minerals contributed to the economic boom. In 1952, a geologist found one of the world's largest single uranium ore deposits at Elliot Lake. In 1953, prospectors found another huge uranium deposit near Bancroft and a rich zinc-copper field at Lake Manitouwadge.

Also during the 1950's, energy companies laid pipelines to carry natural gas and oil to Ontario from western Canada. The oil, piped to Sarnia, led to the development of that city's refining industry. Ontario's iron and steel industry grew rapidly. The province also expanded hydroelectric stations at Niagara Falls and other sites.

In the 1960's, factory production doubled once more. In 1964, an American mineral company discovered a huge field of copper, silver, and zinc ores near Timmins. An open-pit mine began operating there in 1966.

Ontario's growing industries required great increases in electric power. The province looked to nuclear energy to meet its needs. In 1945, Canada's first nuclear reactor had gone into operation near Chalk River, Ontario. Laboratories there worked to find ways of developing cheap nuclear power. By 1960, the station had five experimental reactors and other research facilities, including a particle accelerator. Canada's first nuclear power station, at Rolphton, Ontario, began operating in 1962. Its success led to the development of Canada's first full-scale nuclear station, which began operating at Douglas Point, Ontario, in 1967. A nuclear plant at Pickering, Ontario, opened in 1971.

Not all Ontarians benefited equally from the prosperity of the 1950's and 1960's. Manufacturing in the north and east developed less than it did in the southeast. In 1968, the Canadian Senate reported that 13 percent of Ontarians—over 1 million people—lived in poverty.

The late 1900's. Ontario's strong economy helped Toronto emerge as Canada's leading financial center in the 1960's and 1970's. Many banks and other financial institutions, including the Toronto Stock Exchange, Canada's major stock exchange, have headquarters there.

Tourism became increasingly important to Ontario's economy during the late 1900's. The province's forests and lakes attracted growing numbers of vacationers. Historic sections of Toronto and other Ontario cities also attract visitors.

In 1972, the province passed the Ontario Health Insurance Plan. Under the plan, Ontario residents pay small or no premiums, depending on their ability to pay. The plan provides financial assistance with most hospital and physician bills up to a minimum level of care.

Canada suffered an economic downturn in the 1990's. Many people blamed a free trade agreement made between Canada and the United States in 1989. The agreement called for the elimination of tariffs and other trade barriers between the two countries. It removed government restrictions against U.S. imports, thus creating greater competition for Ontario manufacturers. The passage of the North American Free Trade Agreement

(NAFTA) in 1994 strengthened the original agreement between Canada and the United States.

Since the 1980's, many people from developing countries in Asia and from the Middle East and the West Indies have migrated to Ontario in search of better opportunities. In 1995, the United Nations declared Toronto the most culturally diverse city in the world. The city has experienced problems of racial discrimination against nonwhite immigrants.

Ontario faced a growing budget deficit during the 1980's and early 1990's. In an effort to reduce the deficit, Progressive Conservative Premier Michael D. Harris cut spending on a wide range of government programs. For example, he reduced funding for welfare, cities, health care, education, and the environment. Harris also lowered income taxes. Although the economic and social programs of the Harris government caused controversy, the Conservatives won reelection in 1999.

In 1997, Ontario's legislature voted to merge Toronto and the surrounding communities. The provincial government said the merger would reduce duplication of municipal services. The new unified City of Toronto came into being in 1998. The following year, the legislature passed a law requiring other municipalities, including Hamilton and Ottawa, to merge with surrounding communities and rural areas to form enlarged cities.

Recent developments. The municipal mergers passed in 1999 took effect at the start of 2001. That same year, under increasing pressure from dissatisfied voters, Harris announced that he would step down as premier in 2002. The Conservatives elected Ernie Eves to replace Harris. In a provincial election in 2003, the Progressive Conservatives lost control of the government to the Liberals. Dalton McGuinty, leader of the Liberal Party in Ontario, became premier.   Peter A. Baskerville and Walter Peace

Related articles in *World Book* include:

Biographies

Bowell, Sir Mackenzie	King, W. L. Mackenzie	McCrae, John
Brown, George	Lampman, Archibald	McLaughlin, Audrey M.
Callaghan, Morley	Macdonald, Sir John A.	Milne, David B.
De la Roche, Mazo		Mowat, Sir Oliver
Diefenbaker, John G.	Mackenzie, Alexander	Munro, Alice
Durham, Earl of	Mackenzie, William Lyon	Pearson, Lester Bowles
Esposito, Phil	Macphail, Agnes C.	Scott, Duncan Campbell
Fleming, Sir Sandford	Mair, Charles	Secord, Laura I.
Gould, Glenn	Massey, Vincent	Simcoe, John Graves
Hayden, Melissa	McClung, Nellie	Thomson, Tom
Johnson, Pauline		

Cities

Greater Sudbury	London	Ottawa	Thunder Bay
Hamilton	Mississauga	Sault Sainte Marie	Toronto
Kitchener	Oshawa		Windsor

History

Canada, History of	United Empire Loyalists
Rebellions of 1837	

Physical features

Canadian Shield	Georgian Bay	Lake Huron
Detroit River	Hudson Bay	Lake Ontario
Earth (picture: Precambrian rocks)	James Bay	Lake Saint Clair
	Lake Erie	Lake Superior

Manitoulin Island
Muskoka Lakes
Niagara Falls
Niagara River
Ottawa River

Rainy Lake
Saint Lawrence River
Saint Marys River
Stratford Shakespeare Festival
Thousand Islands

Other related articles

Canada (pictures)
Rideau Canal
Saint Lawrence Seaway

Soo Canals
Welland Ship Canal

Outline

I. People
  A. Population
  B. Schools
  C. Libraries
  D. Museums
II. Visitor's guide
III. Land and climate
  A. Land regions
  B. Shoreline and coastline
  C. Rivers, waterfalls, and
    lakes
  D. Plant and animal life
  E. Climate
IV. Economy
  A. Natural resources
  B. Service industries
  C. Manufacturing
  D. Agriculture
  E. Mining
  F. Electric power and utilities
  G. Transportation
  H. Communicatio
V. Government
  A. Lieutenant governor
  B. Premier
  C. Legislative Assembly
  D. Courts
  E. Local government
  F. Revenue
  G. Politics
VI. History

Additional resources

Level I
Beckett, Harry. *Ontario.* Weigl, 2008.
Ferry, Steven. *Ontario.* Lucent Bks., 2003.
Mackay, Claire. *The Toronto Story.* Rev. ed. Annick, 2002.
Rowe, Percy. *Toronto.* World Almanac Lib., 2004.

Level II
Baskerville, Peter A. *Sites of Power: A Concise History of Ontario.* Oxford, 2005.
Frost, Karolyn S. *I've Got a Home in Glory Land: A Lost Tale of the Underground Railroad.* Farrar, 2007. An archaeological find beneath an old Toronto schoolyard in 1985 helped historians discover the story of Thornton and Lucie Blackburn, who escaped from slavery and then settled in Canada.
Mays, John B. *Arrivals: Stories from the History of Ontario.* Penguin Group, 2002.
Montigny, Edgar-André, and Chambers, Lori, eds. *Ontario Since Confederation.* Univ. of Toronto Pr., 2000.

Ontario, Lake. See Lake Ontario.

Ontology. See Philosophy (Metaphysics).

Onyx, *AHN ihks,* is a term that is used loosely to apply to a banded carbonate rock and also to agate, a fine-grained variety of quartz (see **Agate**).

Ordinary onyx of quartz is black and white, green and white, or red and white, and so on. *Sardonyx* is a reddish-brown and white onyx. Onyx is hard and takes a high polish. It is widely used in the carving of cameos and intaglios. Today, jewelers refer to single-color agate as *onyx.* When they speak simply of onyx, they mean the black stone.

Onyx marble (Mexican onyx) is a variety of calcite rock found on the walls of caves. Mexican onyx shows a banding like that of agate, but much coarser. The colors of Mexican onyx range from white to green, red, and brown. Much of this soft onyx marble is cut into gemstones, colored with an aniline dye, and set in inexpensive silver jewelry. The stones are brittle and not durable. Mexican onyx is also carved into animals or other

shapes and used as a decorative stone.   John C. Butler
See also **Cameo; Gem** (picture); **Sardonyx.**

Oort cloud, *oort* or *ohrt,* is a cluster of comets, smaller objects, and perhaps even planets in the outermost region of our solar system. The Oort cloud is shaped like a slightly flattened, hollow sphere. The nearest part of the cloud may be roughly 500 billion miles (800 billion kilometers) from the sun. The farthest part may be up to 18 trillion miles (30 trillion kilometers) from the sun. The cloud may hold up to 1 trillion comets. A comet can leave the Oort cloud and enter the inner solar system when disturbed by a large gravitational force, such as the gravity of a passing star. Many objects in the cloud may have formed around other stars but were pulled away by the sun's gravity.

The Oort cloud is named for the Dutch astronomer Jan H. Oort, who in 1950 suggested that it existed. Oort based his suggestion on two characteristics of the orbits of *long-period comets*—those that take 200 years or longer to revolve once around the sun: (1) The orbits originate hundreds of billions of miles or kilometers from the sun, and (2) The orbits intersect the *ecliptic plane* at random angles. The ecliptic plane is an imaginary surface through Earth's orbit around the sun. If long-period comets intersected the plane at small angles—as do short-period comets, which complete their orbits in less than 200 years—the cloud would be disk-shaped. Short-period comets come from the Kuiper belt, a disk-shaped band of rocky objects orbiting the sun just beyond Neptune.   S. Alan Stern
See also **Comet; Kuiper belt; Solar system.**

Oostende. See Ostend.

Opal is a glassy material, some of which is valued as a gem for its flashes of color. Opal is one of the birthstones for October.

Much opal is white, gray, brown, or black. Some opal shows a brilliant flash of color, called *play of color,* on top of its background color. Opal with play of color is called *precious opal.* Opal without color play has little or no gem value, unless it is clear or brightly colored. Opal without gem value is called *common opal* or *potch.*

Opal consists of water and a mineral called *silica,* the most common ingredient in sand. Precious opal forms underground when water flows through cracks and spaces in the rocks. The water slowly evaporates, depositing tiny spheres of silica. If the spheres are the right size and in a uniform structure, they *diffract* (bend) light. Light diffraction within an opal removes some of the colors in light and strengthens others. This bending of light produces the play of color seen in gem-quality opal.

The value of an opal gemstone is mostly determined by its weight, its background color, and the color and extent of its play of color. The most valuable opals have a black body color with a vivid play of color dominated by flashes of red and violet. Opal with a dark body color is called *black opal.* The best-known source of black opal is New South Wales, Australia. Australia is also the main source of precious white opal. White opal has a white body color and usually has smaller patches of play of color that are often green, blue, red, and yellow.

Precious opal is less durable than most gems. It is relatively soft—it can be scratched with a knife—and can chip easily. In some opals, the water within dries up and the stone shrinks, causing tiny cracks. This process, called *crazing* or *checking,* lowers the value of opal.

Because the beauty of most opal lies in its color flashes, opal is rarely cut with *facets* (flat, polished surfaces). Instead, opal gemstones are cut with a curved upper surface. This style of cutting is called *cabochon cutting.* Opal with vivid body color, such as some fire opal, may be cut with facets.

Gemological Institute of America
White opal

Large opals include a Hungarian opal that weighs 21 ounces (594 grams) in the Museum of Natural History of Vienna, in Austria. The Roebling opal, found in Nevada, is a beautiful American opal. It is pitch-black with brilliant flashes of color. It weighs 18.7 ounces (530 grams) and is on display at the National Museum of Natural History in Washington, D.C. The Andamooka Desert Flame opal weighed over 15 pounds (6,800 grams) when found in Australia in 1969.   Mark A. Helper

Oparin, Alexander Ivanovich (1894-1980), was a Soviet biochemist. His theory of how life on Earth originated from chemical substances became the basis of many later scientific ideas about the origin of life. Oparin also conducted research on the chemical conversion of raw agricultural crops into such products as bread, sugar, and wine.

Oparin's theory of the origin of life rests on his assumption that the mixture of gases in Earth's early atmosphere was much different from that of today's atmosphere. The present atmosphere is about 99 percent oxygen and nitrogen. In Oparin's view, the early atmosphere was mostly ammonia, hydrogen, and methane. These gases are composed of simple molecules.

Large amounts of these gases would have dissolved in the oceans and would have received energy from sunlight, lightning, and Earth's internal heat. Oparin suggested how this energy could have caused the simple molecules to combine into more complex molecules and how the complex molecules could have formed larger and larger combinations. After several hundred million years, such combinations could have formed the first living cells.

Oparin was born on March 2, 1894, near Moscow. He graduated from Moscow State University in 1917. He first published his theory in 1924 and expanded it into a book called *The Origin of Life on Earth* (1936). From 1946 to 1980, he headed the Bahk Institute of Biochemistry in Moscow. He died on April 21, 1980.   Martin D. Saltzman

See also **Life** (Modern explanations).

OPEC. See **Organization of the Petroleum Exporting Countries.**

Open classroom. See **Alternative school** (Features).

Open-Door Policy is a term used in international relations. It means that powerful countries have equal opportunities to trade with colonial or developing countries. When countries agree to observe the Open-Door Policy in an area, they simply agree to permit their merchants and investors to trade freely there.

John Hay, United States secretary of state, started the idea of the Open Door in 1899. At that time, several Western powers had special interests in China. Each power was trying to get all the trading rights for itself.

Hay sent notes to the competing powers, asking them to maintain complete equality for all nations that wished to trade with China. The competing powers accepted Hay's proposal, and they signed treaties agreeing to observe the Open-Door Policy.   Robert J. Pranger

See also **China** (The Open-Door Policy).

Open-hearth furnace. See **Iron and steel** (The open-hearth process).

Open housing refers to the belief that people have a right to live wherever they choose and can afford to live. In the United States, the federal government and many state and local governments have laws and regulations to protect this right. Open housing laws are sometimes called *fair housing* laws or *open occupancy* laws.

The U.S. Civil Rights Act of 1968 included the first national open housing legislation of the 1900's. The act prohibits discrimination in the sale or rental of most housing in the United States on the basis of race, color, religion, or national origin. In 1974, this law was revised to prohibit discrimination on the basis of sex. In 1988, Congress added further revisions to protect people with disabilities and families with children from housing discrimination. The law applies to almost all housing in the United States. It does not apply to some owner-occupied housing; buildings with fewer than four units, such as duplexes; and single-family houses sold or rented without the aid of a broker or real estate agent.

In 1977, the Community Reinvestment Act (CRA) became law. The law was designed to force banks to lend to all members of their community regardless of race or social or economic status. This law increased bank lending for home purchase and repair in low- and moderate-income and minority neighborhoods.

In 1993, some banks began offering *subprime loans* for home purchase and repair. Subprime lending makes loans available to borrowers who have below-standard credit histories or who lack evidence of their ability to repay the loan. Risky subprime lending contributed to an economic crisis that began in 2007. See **United States, History of the** (Financial troubles).

Fair housing laws are weakly enforced in the United States. Discrimination against African Americans, immigrants, single parents, the elderly, and people with disabilities still occurs in the housing market. Countries outside the United States vary greatly in how they protect housing rights. Some countries, such as South Africa, include housing laws in their national constitutions. In other countries, lower units of government primarily establish laws regarding fair housing practices. Problems of homelessness and inadequate housing persist in many areas of the world.   Lynne M. Dearborn

Open-pit mine. See **Iron and steel** (Open-pit mining); **Mining** (Kinds of mining; picture).

Open shop is a business that employs both union and nonunion workers. It is the opposite of a *closed shop,* where only union members may be employed. In one use of the term, a union may represent the workers in an open shop if a majority of them belong to the union. But no one must be required to belong to the union in order to be hired. The term may also refer to a company in which the employer does not deal with a union. See also **Closed shop.**   Daniel Quinn Mills

Opening of the West. See **Western frontier life in America; Westward movement in America.**

Scene from a production by the Royal Opera, Covent Garden, London; Reg Wilson

Elaborate scenery and colorful crowd scenes add excitement to many operas. The spectacular "Triumphal March" shown above takes place in Act II of Giuseppe Verdi's tragic opera *Aida.*

Opera

Opera is a drama in which the characters sing, rather than speak, all or most of their lines. Opera is one of the more complex of all art forms. It combines acting, singing, orchestral music, costumes, scenery, and often ballet or some other form of dance.

In telling a story, opera uses the enormous power of music to communicate feeling and to express emotions. Singers, accompanied by an orchestra, may bring a dramatic situation to life more vividly than actors with spoken dialogue. Vocal and orchestral music can also tell an audience much about a character and his or her state of mind.

Because music expresses emotions so forcefully, most opera composers base their works on highly emotional stories. An opera, more than a spoken play, is likely to emphasize passionate scenes of anger, cruelty, jealousy, joy, love, revenge, sadness, or triumph. Music can also add excitement to scenes portraying spectacle. Some of the most stirring music in opera accompanies colorful crowd scenes, such as a coronation or a military parade.

Opera differs in several ways from other kinds of plays that have music. For example, William Shake-

speare's comedy *A Midsummer Night's Dream* has scenes that call for music. Such music is called *incidental music* because the play is dramatically complete without it. Different productions of the same play may use incidental music by different composers.

Musical comedies and operettas resemble opera, but most of them have much more dialogue than an opera has, and their music is lighter. Compositions called *oratorios* also share certain features with opera. Like an opera, an oratorio has music for soloists, chorus, and orchestra. It may also tell a story. But unlike operas, almost all oratorios are performed in a concert hall and without acting, costumes, or scenery.

Organizations called opera companies produce most operas. Most companies are *repertory theaters*—that is, they present several operas alternately during a season. The operas a company presents are called its *repertoire.*

Operas are usually performed in specially designed theaters called *opera houses.* Most opera houses seat many more people than do theaters reserved for spoken drama. An opera house also has special facilities and equipment to provide the elaborate staging required by many operas. All modern opera houses have an orchestra pit between the stage and the seats of the auditorium. From the pit, the orchestra, led by the conductor, accompanies the singers onstage.

Most opera houses built in the 1700's and 1800's, and

Thomas A. Bauman, the contributor of this article, is Professor of Music at Northwestern University.

some modern ones, have rows of boxes arranged in the auditorium. Originally, the boxes were owned by the nobility who patronized the opera and were occupied by their families and guests. Because it is difficult to get a good view of the stage from many box seats, modern opera houses rarely feature this arrangement.

Opera, as we know it today, began in Italy in the late 1500's. Through the years, Italian composers, singers, and conductors have played a leading role in the development of opera. By the end of the 1600's, opera had spread from Italy to other European countries. Today, opera can be enjoyed by people in many parts of the world.

The best-known opera companies in Europe include those that perform at the Teatro alla Scala (La Scala) in Milan, Italy; the Opera House in Rome; the Opéra de la Bastille and the Opéra-Comique in Paris; the Royal Opera House, Covent Garden, in London; the State Opera in Vienna; and the Festival Opera House in Bayreuth, Germany.

The most famous opera company in the United States is the Metropolitan Opera Association, which performs in New York City. The Boston Opera Company, the Lyric Opera of Chicago, the New York City Opera, and the San Francisco Opera Company are also famous. Other important American companies include the Greater Miami Opera, the Houston Grand Opera, the San Diego Opera, the Seattle Opera, and the Washington (D.C.) Opera. Every summer, the Santa Fe Opera Company performs in an outdoor theater in Santa Fe, New Mexico.

Opening night at the opera ranks as one of the most glamorous social events of the year. The opening-night crowd shown here mingles in the lobby of the Metropolitan Opera House.

WORLD BOOK photo

Terms used in opera

Aria, *AH ree uh,* is a vocal solo that usually expresses a character's feelings.

Bel canto refers to a style of singing that emphasizes beautiful tone and technical skill.

Coloratura is a flowery, ornamental vocal style generally used by soprano voices.

Ensemble, *ahn SAHM buhl,* is a small group of singers, usually from two to five. The music the group sings is also called an *ensemble.*

Grand opera refers to operas of the mid-1800's that emphasized spectacular stage effects, big crowd scenes, and complicated, elaborate vocal and instrumental music. The term *grand opera* also means an opera with no spoken dialogue.

Leitmotif, *LIHT moh TEEF,* is a short musical passage that identifies certain ideas, places, and characters each time they appear in the drama.

Libretto is the text of an opera.

Opera buffa, *BOOF fah,* is an Italian comic opera that deals with humorous situations and characters from everyday life.

Opera seria, *SEH ree ah,* was the leading opera form of the 1700's. It dealt primarily with historical themes from ancient times and stressed brilliant singing.

Recitative, *REHS uh tuh TEEV,* is a part of the text that provides information about the action and moves the plot forward. It is sung in a rapid, speechlike style, sometimes to orchestral accompaniment. In *simple recitative,* the accompaniment is provided by only a harpsichord or a harpsichord and cello or other bass instrument.

Score is the written or printed music for an opera, used by the conductor.

Singspiel, *ZIHNG shpeel,* is a form of German opera, usually comic, that has spoken dialogue instead of recitative. Most of the songs are simple and folklike.

Verismo, *vair EES moh,* is a style of realistic Italian opera that focuses on violent actions and emotions.

The elements of opera

An opera has two basic elements: (1) the libretto and (2) the music. The libretto, which means *little book* in Italian, consists of the words, or text, of an opera. The music, which is also called the *score,* consists of both vocal and instrumental music. To translate the libretto and music into a performance, an opera must have singers, a conductor, and an orchestra.

The libretto

To enjoy an opera fully, an operagoer should read the libretto or a summary of the action before viewing the opera. It is especially important for an audience member to read a translation of the libretto or a summary if an opera is sung in an unfamiliar language. Some public libraries have librettos. Most of them have books that contain summaries of the action in individual operas. Generally, an opera house provides a printed program that has a summary of the plot. Most opera houses in the United States provide translations on a screen above the stage.

The libretto of most operas is shorter than the text of a spoken play because it takes longer to sing a given number of words than to speak them and because some words and phrases may be repeated for emphasis. Librettos may also be shorter than the script of a spoken play because a few measures of music can often express emotions more vividly than many lines of spoken words. Because a libretto must be relatively short, the story of an opera is likely to be simpler than that of a spoken play, with fewer characters and fewer secondary plots.

Many operas have been criticized for their poor librettos. Such operas give the impression that the composer used the text merely as an excuse for the music. Many people do attend the opera mainly to hear beautiful music sung by beautiful voices. Other people, however, feel that a good opera must also be a good drama. And in fact, some librettos are excellent works of literature. These librettos include those that the Austrian poet Hugo von Hofmannsthal wrote for the operas of Richard Strauss and adaptations of Shakespeare's plays that composer-poet Arrigo Boito made for *Otello* (1887) and *Falstaff* (1893) by Giuseppe Verdi.

The definition of good drama in opera has changed over the years. Numerous subjects that were popular in operas of the 1600's, 1700's, or 1800's are now out of fashion. Yet modern operagoers can still enjoy these older operas if they learn something about the customs in drama and music that influenced their composition.

Recitative and arias. Certain parts of the libretto simply provide information for the audience. For example, one character may tell another about something that has happened. In some operas, the characters speak these portions of the text. But in many operas, including nearly all Italian operas, the characters sing them in a simple, speechlike style called *recitative.* Most recitatives are written in everyday language—that is, they do not rhyme. Recitatives were especially popular in operas of the 1700's and early 1800's.

The most emotional parts of the libretto are solo numbers called *arias.* They usually express a character's feelings or thoughts. Most arias are written in rhythmical, rhymed verse. They are also set to far more elaborate music than are recitatives. In fact, arias provide the most beautiful and dramatic music in many operas.

Spoken dialogue or recitative carries the action forward. At intervals, the action stops and the characters sing arias to express their feelings. An example of the use of recitative and aria appears in the following passage from Wolfgang Amadeus Mozart's opera *Don Giovanni.* In the passage, a character sings several lines of recitative, ending with:

> Every means must be sought to
> discover the truth ... I shall avenge her!

He then sings an aria that begins with these lines:

> My peace depends on hers; that which
> pleases her gives life to me.

The recitative above tells the audience about the character's future actions. The aria expresses his state of mind. The original Italian text for this aria was written in rhymed poetry.

Ensembles. In many operas, the libretto calls for two or more singers to engage in a musical dialogue, called an *ensemble.* The most common ensembles are duets, trios, quartets, and quintets. Some ensembles require several characters to sing at the same time and express their thoughts and feelings. They may sing the same words, showing agreement. Or they may sing different words and melodies, expressing conflict.

The music

The singers. In an opera, each role calls for a singer with a specific voice range. Opera singers are therefore classified according to the range of their voices.

The basic vocal classifications for women, from highest to lowest range, are soprano, mezzo-soprano, and contralto. Each of these classifications can be divided into more specialized groups. For example, sopranos can be divided into coloratura sopranos, lyric sopranos, and dramatic sopranos. Coloratura sopranos have a very high range and can sing with great agility. Lyric sopranos have a light, graceful voice appropriate to youthful roles. Dramatic sopranos have a rich, strong voice suited to highly emotional parts.

The chief voice classifications for men, from highest to lowest range, are tenor, baritone, and bass. Each classification can be divided into more specialized groups. For example, tenors can be divided into lyric tenors and dramatic, or heroic, tenors. A lyric tenor has a light, high voice. A dramatic tenor, often called by the German word *Heldentenor,* has a rich, powerful voice with a lower range than a lyric tenor. Such voices are needed for the heroic roles in operas by Richard Wagner. Bass voices are classified as basso cantante, basso buffo, or basso profundo. A basso cantante has the highest bass voice, with a character similar to that of a lyric tenor. A basso buffo has a deeper, flexible voice and sings comic roles. A basso profundo has an especially low voice and usually sings majestic, serious roles.

Choral singing. Most operas include choral singing as well as arias, ensembles, and recitatives. The function and importance of the chorus vary from opera to opera and even within an opera. A chorus may provide only visual background for a scene. For example, it might portray a crowd at a festival. Or a chorus may be required merely to shout an exclamation, such as "Hail to our great king!" But in some works, the chorus plays a leading part in the story and sings complicated music.

Scene from a production by the Lyric Opera of Chicago, with Regina Resnik, *left,* Joan Sutherland, *center,* and Spiro Malas (WORLD BOOK photo)

An opera ensemble is a small group of singers. The music they sing is also called an *ensemble.* A countess, her daughter, and a soldier sing a lively, comic ensemble in this scene from Act II of *The Daughter of the Regiment* by Gaetano Donizetti.

Scene from a production by the Lyric
Opera of Chicago (WORLD BOOK photo)

An opera chorus is a large group of singers who perform as a unit. Members must be able to act expressively while they sing. The chorus above portrays an excited crowd outside a bull ring in a scene from Act IV of *Carmen* by Georges Bizet.

Acting in opera. For a successful career in opera, a singer must have acting skill in addition to an outstanding voice. Most young singers who plan a career in opera take several years of acting lessons.

Opera acting presents special problems because it is difficult to act and sing at the same time. Sudden movements, walking, running, and twisted body positions may all interfere with the production of a beautiful, clear, and steady tone. For this reason, opera acting tends to be less lively and less realistic than acting in other forms of drama.

The conductor plays a key role in opera. Throughout a performance, the conductor must keep the singers and orchestra together. The beat must be clearly seen

Bruno Bartoletti conducting the orchestra of the
Lyric Opera of Chicago (WORLD BOOK photo)

The conductor sets the tempo for both the musicians in the orchestra pit and the singers onstage. He or she must keep the orchestra and vocalists together. The conductor must also adjust the *balance* (loudness) between the singers and the orchestra.

by singers far from the conductor and by musicians sitting in the dim light at the ends of the orchestra pit. Although the conductor sets the tempo, he or she must be able to react to unexpected circumstances. If a soloist begins to sing faster, for example, the conductor may have to adjust the orchestra's tempo. Because of all these special demands, opera conducting requires greater skills than does any other kind of conducting.

Some operas call for scenes in which musicians and singers perform offstage. In such instances, an assistant conductor directs the offstage music. In some modern opera houses, the assistant conductor directs the offstage music while following the conductor's beat over closed-circuit television.

The orchestra. The number and kinds of instruments in the orchestra depend on the opera being performed. The instruments needed for Italian operas composed in the late 1700's differ greatly from those needed for operas written by Wagner in the late 1800's.

The particular opera being performed also determines the orchestra's function. In most operas, the orchestra's basic job is to accompany the singers. The accompaniment may be simple, providing only enough harmonic and rhythmic background to keep the singers on pitch and in time. But the orchestra may also serve a more important role. For example, it might play music that introduces the general emotional quality of an aria before a note has been sung. The orchestra may even emphasize a passage in the text. For example, a heavily rhythmic beat might accompany the words "my heart pounds faster."

In some scenes, one or more characters may be alone a long time without singing or speaking. During that period, the orchestral music expresses their feelings. This kind of characterization through music is one of the strengths of opera and is impossible in spoken plays.

In many operas, the orchestra often repeats a melody or short theme from an earlier scene. This melody or theme, without singing or spoken words, is called a *leitmotif.* Composers repeat the leitmotif to remind listeners of some action, character, or idea previously introduced in the opera. Composers of the 1800's, notably Wagner, used the leitmotif most effectively.

Pieces of orchestral music called *interludes* are used to connect scenes. Interludes provide time for scenery changes or for new characters to enter. Interludes also may indicate shifts in the emotional atmosphere in an opera. Occasionally, orchestral music imitates the sounds of nature. In Wagner's *Siegfried,* the orchestra imitates the sounds in a forest.

Most operas begin with an orchestral overture. Some overtures merely indicate that the performance is about to begin. But others have a more important function. Some introduce the opera's principal melodies. Others set the mood for the opening scene or for the opera in general. In some older operas, the overture is uncomplicated and brief. A number of overtures of the 1800's are elaborate pieces that run 10 minutes or longer.

Musicians occasionally perform onstage in costume and participate in the action of the opera. For example, musicians may take part in such onstage activities as a military parade or a religious procession.

An opera company produces several operas in a season. In selecting each work for production, the company must consider several factors. These factors include the estimated cost of presenting the opera and whether the work will attract a large audience. Most opera companies attempt to balance their season with both comic and tragic operas. They also try to select works by a variety of composers and from different historical periods.

The people behind the scenes

During an opera performance, the audience sees only the conductor, orchestra, and performers. But an opera production also requires the skills of many other people. These people include (1) the general manager, (2) the stage director, (3) costume and set designers, (4) the members of the technical staff, and (5) the stage manager. All these specialists perform about the same work for an opera as they would for a spoken play. But opera requires that they coordinate all parts of the production with the music.

The general manager supervises the overall artistic and business policy of the opera company. This person plays a major part in choosing the repertoire and in hiring singers, conductors, and stage managers. The general manager follows each production through the planning and rehearsal stages to make sure it is progressing satisfactorily. Some companies have a music director or artistic director who controls the hiring of singers and conductors.

The stage director is responsible for the visual aspects of an opera production, just as the conductor is responsible for the music. The stage director must coordinate every action on the stage with the music. The director helps singers interpret their roles, works with the designers on ideas for costumes and sets, and helps determine the lighting. See **Theater** (The director).

The stage director faces one of the greatest challenges in handling choral scenes. The chorus should not simply stand still and look at the conductor while singing. All dramatic illusion would be lost. The director must assign all members of the chorus some activity so they will appear natural on the stage. Some operas have scenes in which the chorus takes part in vigorous action while singing. One such scene takes place near the end of Act II of Wagner's opera *The Mastersingers of Nuremberg.* A riot breaks out among a crowd of angry townspeople played by the chorus. In such scenes, the chorus must act convincingly while singing and following the conductor. The stage director has to plan choral scenes like these carefully and then rehearse the scenes frequently.

Sometimes, a stage director may create a new interpretation of an opera. Because the repertoire of opera companies consists chiefly of a few dozen works performed repeatedly, audiences may welcome a production that presents a familiar opera in a fresh way. But some directors have been criticized for taking too many liberties with an opera, for example, by setting it in a different historical period.

The designers. The story of most operas in the standard repertoire takes place before the 1900's. Therefore, the costume and set designers must generally research the particular period of the story so their designs accurately reflect the time and place of the action. In Giuseppe Verdi's *Aida,* for example, the costumes and sets should realistically portray ancient Egypt.

The costumes and sets should be designed so that the performers can move about freely. In addition, the set designer always has to consider the requirements of the music. For example, the music may allow a singer a certain amount of time to move from a door to a table and begin an aria. The designer must arrange the set so the singer can move naturally and still arrive at the table at the precise moment in the music when the aria be-

Metropolitan Opera Association, New York City (WORLD BOOK photo)

The set designer makes a scale model of a set, *foreground,* to determine how the scenery will look on the full stage. The workers in the background are painting a large backdrop for a set.

Lyric Opera of Chicago (WORLD BOOK photo)

The costume designer creates costumes suitable to an opera's time and place. These designers fit a singer with a gown for Jules Massenet's *Manon,* which is set in the 1720's in France.

Metropolitan Opera Association, New York City (WORLD BOOK photos)

Opera rehearsals involve both technicians and performers. At a lighting rehearsal, *left,* an electrician in a lighting booth works with the director onstage to create desired lighting effects. The director also rehearses the singers, *right,* to develop stage movements and interpretations of roles.

gins. The set designer may also have to plan the sets to provide space for large choral or dance scenes. See **Theater** (Scene design; Costumes and makeup).

The technical staff. Many technicians work with the stage director in planning and carrying out the visual aspects of the production. The electricians are especially important members of the technical staff. They operate the complicated lighting equipment that is used to illu-

minate parts or all of the stage and to provide atmosphere. Some stage directors rely on lighting, rather than on realistic sets, to express an opera's mood. See **Theater** (Lighting and sound).

During an opera performance, the various crews of technicians and stagehands must work quickly, quietly, and efficiently backstage. One crew changes the scenery between acts or scenes. Another crew adds the small

Lyric Opera of Chicago (WORLD BOOK photos)

The stage manager, *above,* has charge of backstage activity during an opera performance. He uses a score to follow the action onstage and watches the conductor over closed-circuit TV. He communicates with backstage technicians over a headset.

A crew of stagehands changes the scenery between acts and scenes, *right.* Another stage crew puts such objects as chairs and weapons in their proper places onstage. A third crew arranges the lights. The crews must work quickly and efficiently.

Lyric Opera of Chicago (WORLD BOOK photo)

The prompter speaks the entire libretto during a performance in case a singer forgets a line. He works in a *prompter's box* below the stage where only the singers can see him. The prompter follows the conductor over closed-circuit television.

objects, called *props,* that the performers use in the action. A third crew sets up and adjusts the lights. For changing scenery, some opera houses use revolving stages or stages that can be raised or lowered by elevator. Special technicians operate the machinery that moves these stages. See **Theater** (Changing scenery).

The stage manager has charge of all backstage activity during a performance. He or she sees that all the props needed for a scene are on the stage and in the correct place. The stage manager calls the performers from their dressing rooms at specific times so they can make their entrances on schedule. The stage manager also gives the electricians cues to change the lighting during the performance.

Preparing a production

Planning a production. After a company selects an opera, the general manager and the management staff establish the production's budget. They also choose the cast and assign a stage director and conductor to the production. Most companies employ a resident group of singers, conductors, and directors for an entire season. However, nearly all companies also hire guest singers to take the leading roles for a single production. In addition, companies frequently use guest conductors, stage directors, and designers.

In some cases, the most important consideration in selecting an opera is whether a company can hire a particular guest singer. Sometimes a company wants a certain singer so much it will let the artist choose the opera. In casting the leading parts, the opera company first of all seeks singers who have outstanding voices. But the performers should also act well and, preferably, have the physical appearance suited to the characters they are to portray.

During the early stages of a production, the key personnel hold many conferences. The stage director, for example, meets frequently with the costume and set designers. Sketches of the designs must be approved early

to allow enough time for the costumes and sets to be made. The costumes and sets may be manufactured in the opera house workshops or by outside firms. Sometimes, sets and costumes are borrowed or rented from another opera company.

Rehearsing a production. After many months of planning the production, rehearsals begin. At first, the singers, chorus, and orchestra rehearse separately in rehearsal rooms. If the opera calls for dancing, the dancers also practice by themselves.

The stage director rehearses the principal singers to work out stage movements and establish interpretations of the roles. The chorus rehearses under the direction of a chorus master. A *choreographer* (dance creator) supervises dance rehearsals. The conductor and the conductor's assistants rehearse the orchestra.

A few weeks before the opera is to open, rehearsals move from separate facilities to the main stage. These rehearsals take place with piano accompaniment only.

Meanwhile, the stage director and the chief electrician hold lighting rehearsals. In most operas, directors use elaborate lighting that is changed frequently during the performance. Lighting rehearsals develop the best ways to achieve desired effects. The rehearsals also set the timing for the various lighting changes.

As the opening nears, the orchestra rehearses with the entire cast on the main stage. Because of the central function of the music, the conductor takes charge of these rehearsals.

A few days before opening night, the performers and orchestra stage a dress rehearsal. A dress rehearsal is presented like an actual performance, with costumes, makeup, and sets. By this time, the production should move with split-second timing. The music sets the pace for the action and should not have to be sped up or slowed down to adjust to what happens onstage.

Lyric Opera of Chicago (WORLD BOOK photo)

Offstage music is required in some operas. An assistant conductor leads the musicians and singers hidden in the wings. He conducts from a score while following the beat of the conductor in the orchestra pit over closed-circuit television.

The first operas were composed and performed in the 1590's in Florence, Italy. There, a group of noblemen, musicians, and poets had become interested in the culture of ancient Greece, especially Greek drama. This group, called the *Camerata,* believed that the Greeks sang rather than spoke their tragedies. The Camerata attempted to re-create the spirit of ancient Greek tragedy in music. They took most of their subjects from Greek and Roman history and mythology. The Camerata called their compositions *dramma per musica* (drama for music) or *opera in musica* (musical work). The term *opera* comes from the shortened form of opera in musica. Jacopo Peri, a member of the Camerata, composed what is generally considered to be the first opera, *La Dafne* (1597).

Baroque opera

Opera emerged as an art form in western Europe during the Baroque period in music history. This period began about 1600 and ended about 1750. Baroque music was elaborate and emotional. Italians composed the earliest Baroque operas, and Italian-style opera dominated most of the period.

Early Baroque opera. The first Baroque operas consisted of recitatives, sung by soloists, and choral passages. A small orchestra accompanied the singers.

During the 1600's, the aria gradually emerged and developed a function separate from that of the recitative. The recitative served to carry the plot of the opera forward. The arias became pauses in the action in which characters expressed their thoughts and feelings. Singers often used arias for showing off their vocal skills rather than for dramatic expression. A common form of presentation called *simple recitative* developed in the 1600's. In it, the singers were accompanied by only a harpsichord—or by a harpsichord and cello or other bass instrument—rather than by the full orchestra.

Claudio Monteverdi, the first great composer of Baroque opera, wrote the first opera masterpiece, *Orfeo* (1607). Later, Monteverdi worked in Venice and helped make the city the center of opera by the mid-1600's. The world's first public opera house, the Teatro San Cassiano, opened in Venice in 1637.

By the late 1600's, operas were being written and performed in a number of European countries outside Italy, especially in England, France, and Germany. Italian opera was the accepted style, and many non-Italian composers wrote operas in the Italian manner and to Italian librettos.

Opera seria and opera buffa. Italian opera of the early 1700's developed into two basic types: (1) *opera seria* (serious opera) and (2) *opera buffa* (comic opera). Both types consisted of a series of recitatives and arias.

Opera seria. Composers of opera seria based their works on stories of ancient heroes and heroines. In the 1600's, similar stories had included both comic and serious characters. They had provided spectacular stage effects, such as earthquakes and floods, as well as big coronation and battle scenes. However, comic scenes and spectacle were eliminated from serious opera in the 1700's. Emphasis fell instead on the skills of the principal singers. By the 1800's, many singers were trained in a vocal style called *bel canto,* which emphasized technical skill and beauty of tone. The *da capo* aria became a major feature of opera seria. It had three parts, the third being a repetition of the first. In the repeated part, the singer was expected to add difficult passages and other *ornamentation* (additional note or notes) not included in the score.

Opera buffa began as comic skits, called *intermezzi,* performed in front of the curtain between the acts of an opera seria. The characters in opera buffa were common people, unlike the characters in opera seria. Characters in opera buffa represented the professions and

Engraving by Stefano della Bella of a scene from *The Wedding of the Gods* (1637) by Giovanni Carlo Coppola; The Newberry Library, Chicago

Opera in Italy during the 1600's called for spectacular scenery and often dealt with ancient heroes and heroines. The Italian designer Alfonso Parigi created the elaborate set shown in this engraving, for an opera seria. The engraving portrays the workshop of Vulcan, the blacksmith to the gods in Roman mythology. Parigi designed the workshop as a cave at the foot of several towering cliffs.

social classes of the time, including doctors, farmers, merchants, servants, and soldiers. The typical opera buffa dealt with humorous situations from everyday life. Many characters in opera buffa sang in *dialects* (local forms) of Italian rather than the formal Italian of opera seria. An especially successful intermezzo was *La serva padrona* (1733) by Italian composer Giovanni Pergolesi.

Italian opera seria and opera buffa were extremely popular. Hundreds of them were written, often in a short time. Most of these works were performed for one season and then forgotten. Because of the constant demand for new operas, composers used the same librettos over and over. By today's standards, many librettos have unconvincing plots and unbelievable characters. Although some operagoers complained about the weak librettos of many Italian operas, most audiences of the 1600's and early 1700's enjoyed the works, chiefly for their music.

French opera. A distinctly French style of opera appeared in the 1670's. Before that time, the French showed little interest in opera. The few operas performed in the country were written in the Italian style. Jean-Baptiste Lully, though born in Italy, established a French form of opera. In the mid-1700's, Jean-Philippe Rameau became the leading composer of French opera.

French opera composers avoided the rapid recitatives and showy arias of Italian opera. Instead they preferred expressive melodies or simple songs. The recitatives were accompanied by a full orchestra and closely followed the rhythms of the French language. Ballet played an important part in French opera during the Baroque period, as well as later.

In France, royalty became the chief patrons of opera. Lully acquired his fame at the court of King Louis XIV. The nobility in France and other countries competed with one another in maintaining large opera companies. To impress audiences with their wealth, the nobility sponsored productions noted for expensive scenic effects, such as gods riding chariots in the sky.

Classical opera

Dissatisfaction with Italian opera began to spread among operagoers during the mid-1700's. Attacks centered on the increasingly long and dramatically weak arias, which served only to glorify the singers. The reaction against Italian opera led to a series of reforms early in the Classical period. The Classical period began about 1750 and lasted about 70 years. The first important Classical opera composer was Christoph Willibald Gluck, a German. The greatest Classical composer was Wolfgang Amadeus Mozart, an Austrian.

Gluck and opera reform. Gluck believed drama and music should be unified in opera. By integrating the music with the story in *Orpheus and Eurydice* (1762) and other works, he put his beliefs into practice.

Gluck rejected unlikely plots and emphasis on showy arias. In his operas, the music served the story. Gluck simplified the action to make the stories and characters appear more natural. He also was one of the first composers to supervise all aspects of a production.

Mozart, like Gluck, felt that the music in an opera should help make the story and characters believable.

Mozart achieved this goal by carefully relating the instrumental and vocal music to the action. He showed particular skill in using music to create *characterization*—that is, to develop the personality of a character. Mozart did this in ensemble scenes and in arias.

Mozart composed operas in both Italian and German. His best-known Italian operas are *The Marriage of Figaro* (1786), *Don Giovanni* (1787), and *Così Fan Tutte* (1790). His notable German operas include *The Abduction from the Seraglio* (1782) and *The Magic Flute* (1791). Both of these works contain elements of *Singspiel* (sung play). Singspiel is a form of German opera that has spoken dialogue rather than recitative. Most stories are comic. The melodies often are simple and resemble the style of German folk and popular songs.

Opera in the 1800's

Romanticism was a movement from the late 1700's to the mid-1800's that stressed strong feelings in the arts, including opera. The typical Romantic opera had a setting in nature, a theme based on folklore or the supernatural, and colorful music. Carl Maria von Weber, a German, wrote one of the earliest and greatest Romantic operas, *Der Freischütz* (1821). The story is set in Germany's Black Forest, and most of the chief characters are simple countrypeople. The orchestra has an important part in portraying many of the sounds of nature as well as supernatural forces.

Several Italians also created a Romantic style of opera. The most successful of these composers were Vincenzo Bellini and Gaetano Donizetti. Many of their operas require voices trained in the bel canto style.

Grand opera became popular in the early 1800's, especially in France. Composers of grand opera favored heroic episodes from history, in which they could use crowd scenes, spectacular stage effects, and complicated and elaborate vocal and instrumental music. Giacomo Meyerbeer, a German, became the leading composer of French grand opera with such works as *Les Huguenots* (1836) and *Le Prophète* (1849). Gioacchino Rossini, an Italian-born composer living in France, also wrote a famous grand opera, *William Tell* (1829).

Giuseppe Verdi dominated Italian opera during the middle and late 1800's. He is still perhaps the most popular opera composer in history. Verdi's best-known works include *Rigoletto* (1851), *Il Trovatore* (1853), *La Traviata* (1853), and *Aida* (1871). All are noted for their emotional power, which is expressed through eloquent vocal music. *Aida* is also an example of grand opera.

Verdi wrote his last two operas—*Otello* (1887) and *Falstaff* (1893)—when he was in his 70's. Both works demonstrate that old age did not diminish but rather refined his genius. The operas are masterpieces of characterization through music, and they show complete fluidity of vocal and instrumental writing.

Richard Wagner was the most important German opera composer of the 1800's. Wagner believed that all the parts of an opera production—acting, costumes, drama, orchestral music, singing, and staging—should have equal value. He wrote his own librettos and, whenever possible, supervised the staging of a production. Wagner departed from tradition by making the orchestra as important as the singers. In many of Wagner's late works, instruments perform the main melodies.

As a young man, Wagner was greatly impressed by Weber's romantic opera *Der Freischütz. The Flying Dutchman* (1843), one of Wagner's early works, shows similar romantic qualities. These include the supernatural aspects of the plot and the musical representation of forces of nature, such as the wind and the sea. In *The Flying Dutchman,* Wagner first used musical themes to identify certain characters, places, or ideas each time they appear in the drama. He expanded this *leitmotif* technique greatly in his later operas. *Tristan and Isolde* (1865) and the four works called *The Ring of the Nibelung* (1876) represent his fully developed personal style.

Nationalism influenced many composers throughout Europe during the 1800's. These composers based much of their work on the folk music of their nation or region. Czech nationalism, for example, dominates the operas of Antonín Dvořák and Bedřich Smetana. *The Bartered Bride* (1866) by Smetana and *Rusalka* (1901) by Dvořák are outstanding examples of nationalistic operas. Russian composers of nationalistic operas include Modest Mussorgsky with *Boris Godunov* (1874) and Alexander Borodin with *Prince Igor* (1890).

Verismo opera. In the late 1800's, some Italian composers began to write grimly realistic operas. These *verismo* (meaning true or realistic) operas focused on violent emotions and actions. The earliest and best-known verismo operas are *Cavalleria rusticana* (1890) by Pietro Mascagni and *Pagliacci* (1892) by Ruggiero Leoncavallo, both one-act works usually performed together.

The 1900's

Giacomo Puccini was the most popular Italian opera composer of the early 1900's. His operas are noted for their melodic and sometimes sentimental music and for their theatrically effective librettos. Puccini first gained widespread attention in the 1890's with *Manon Lescaut* (1893) and *La Bohème* (1896). He followed these works with *Tosca* (1900), a verismo opera. His other notable operas include *Madama Butterfly* (1904) and *Turandot* (produced in 1926, after his death).

Richard Strauss became the most important and successful German opera composer after Wagner. Strauss wrote operas that require singers with great vocal power. He is best known for three early operas—*Salome* (1905), *Elektra* (1909), and *Der Rosenkavalier* (1911). *Salome* and *Elektra* originally caused much controversy among operagoers because of their brutal action and harsh music. *Der Rosenkavalier,* however, is entirely different in mood and theme. In this opera, Strauss and the librettist, Hugo von Hofmannsthal, created an affectionate portrait of aristocratic society in Vienna in the 1700's.

The search for new forms. After World War I (1914-1918), many composers began to search for new forms of operatic expression. Some composers included ele-

Festspiele Bayreuth, Germany

New techniques in staging have given a fresh interpretation to many older operas. At its première in 1876, Richard Wagner's opera *Siegfried* was presented in a realistic setting, *above.* A modern staging of the work eliminates the detailed scenery and achieves mood largely through lighting effects, *below.*

Wilhelm Rauh, Festspiele Bayreuth, Germany

Scene from a production by the New York City Opera, with Claramae Turner; © Beth Bergman

Bomarzo by Alberto Ginastera is one of the few modern operas to win international fame. The tragic opera concerns the tortured mental state of Duke Bomarzo, a deformed Italian nobleman. Bomarzo and his grandmother, *shown here,* sing a duet.

ments of American jazz in their operas. Ernst Křenek, an Austrian, used jazz in his opera *Jonny spielt auf* (1927). The German composer Kurt Weill wrote *The Threepenny Opera* (1928) in the style of the music heard in German *cabarets* (nightclubs).

Meanwhile, a movement called Expressionism had developed in the arts. Expressionism aimed at exploring the subconscious and became especially important in drama and painting. But Expressionist qualities also appeared in several operas. Such operas had a brooding, nightmarish atmosphere, reinforced by dissonant music and symbolic and violent actions.

Strauss's *Salome* was an early example of the Expressionist style. But Alban Berg, an Austrian composer, ranks as the leading opera composer in the movement. Berg wrote *Wozzeck* (1925), the most successful Expressionistic opera. Other operas related to Expressionism include *Duke Bluebeard's Castle* (completed 1911, first performed 1918) by the Hungarian composer Béla Bartók and *From the House of the Dead* (1930) by the Czech composer Leoš Janáček.

Some of the most successful and theatrically effective operas of the 1900's were written by the British composer Benjamin Britten. His opera *Peter Grimes* (1945) is a brooding but lyrical portrait of social alienation.

American opera. American composers wrote no important operas until the 1900's. George Gershwin wrote a highly original and popular American opera, *Porgy and Bess* (1935). The work describes life among blacks in Charleston, South Carolina, in the 1920's. *Porgy and Bess* has been acclaimed worldwide as a genuine American folk opera.

Gian Carlo Menotti became the most successful opera composer in the United States. He composed in a traditional style that shows the influence of Puccini. Menotti wrote an opera for radio, *The Old Maid and the Thief* (1939), and one for television, *Amahl and the Night*

Visitors (1951). His best-known stage operas include two tense dramas, *The Medium* (1946) and *The Consul* (1950).

Since the mid-1900's, the best operas have been written by more tradition-minded composers. They include Douglas Moore's folk-inspired *The Ballad of Baby Doe* (1956) and Virgil Thomson's *The Mother of Us All* (1947). The text for *The Mother of Us All* was written by American author Gertrude Stein.

Opera has played only a minor role in modern American experimental music. Some Americans associated with the Minimalist movement have written several important operas. The Minimalist style uses repeated short patterns of music with complex rhythmic variations but simple harmonies. Operas in this style include Phillip Glass's *Einstein on the Beach* (1975), which draws on rock music, and John Adams's *Nixon in China* (1987).

Opera today

The experimentation in opera that began after World War I continues today. Some composers have explored new dramatic and musical techniques, including the use of electronic sounds, motion pictures, and color slides. *Aniara* (1959), a science-fiction opera by the Swedish composer Karl-Birger Blomdahl, takes place in a spaceship and uses taped and electronic sounds. *Bomarzo* (1967) by the Argentine composer Alberto Ginastera also features unconventional sound effects, especially in fantastic, dreamlike scenes.

Operagoers today, however, still prefer older, traditional works. Only a few operas composed since the end of World War I receive frequent productions. But many changes have occurred in the way older operas are staged. For example, stage directors often try to create desired moods through lighting effects made possible by modern lighting equipment.

Meanwhile, artistic and economic problems trouble all major opera companies. Before the development of fast, convenient air travel, leading singers remained with one company an entire season. But jet travel enables singers to appear as guest artists in many opera houses in a season. Artists earn more money as guests, and audiences can see and hear many famous singers. However, traveling artists often follow a tight, exhausting schedule that leaves too little time for rehearsal. As a result, audiences often attend performances that show a lack of adequate preparation.

The cost of producing opera has risen steadily. Even if an opera house sells every ticket for an entire season, it cannot meet expenses. Ticket sales seldom provide more than half the income needed to operate an opera company. American companies rely on contributions from individuals, corporations, and foundations to make up losses. Many European countries, cities, and states support opera with public funds. Numerous people in the United States believe the national government or local governments should help support opera and the other arts, as governments do in Europe.

Most U.S. colleges and universities have opera workshops. They provide training and experience for young singers and also present performances for the general public. Some colleges and universities have staged revivals of worthwhile but little-known works.

Opera companies today present mainly works that were composed between the late 1700's and the early 1900's. Almost all the operas in this standard repertoire were written by Austrian, French, German, Italian, and Russian composers. This section describes some of the most popular operas in the standard repertoire. Some of the recommended books that are listed at the end of this article provide more detailed discussions of the repertoire.

Aida, a tragic opera in four acts by Giuseppe Verdi. Libretto in Italian by Verdi and Antonio Ghislanzoni. First performed in Cairo, Egypt, in 1871.

The *khedive* (ruler) of Egypt asked Verdi to write *Aida* to help celebrate the opening of the Suez Canal and the Cairo opera house. The story takes place in ancient Egypt and concerns the tragic love affair between Aida, an Ethiopian slave, and Radames, an Egyptian military officer. *Aida* is grand opera and so requires a large cast. The work has impressive crowd scenes, featuring choruses of soldiers, slaves, and priests, and an elaborate ballet. In Act I, Radames expresses his love for Aida in a beautiful aria, "Celeste Aida." Act II includes the stirring "Triumphal March," in which the Egyptian king reviews his victorious army.

Barber of Seville, The (*Il Barbiere di Siviglia*), a comic opera in two acts by Gioacchino Rossini. Libretto in Italian by Cesare Sterbini, based on the French play *The Barber of Seville* by Pierre de Beaumarchais. First performed in Rome in 1816.

The story of *The Barber of Seville* takes place in Seville, Spain, in the 1600's. This work is a good example of Italian comic opera, or *opera buffa*. The libretto has many characters and situations typical of this style. The characters include an old man called Doctor Bartolo who is interested in a beautiful and rich young woman named Rosina. He jealously watches over her but cannot prevent a dashing young nobleman (Count Almaviva) from meeting and finally marrying her. Other traditional characters include a drunken soldier, who is really the count in disguise, and an irritable housekeeper. Figaro, the barber in the opera's title, helps the count win Rosina.

In Act I, Rosina's aria "Una voce poco fa" provides opportunities for brilliant singing. Also in Act I, Figaro makes his first appearance singing a popular comic aria, "Largo al factotum," in which he boasts how clever he is. The opera also has a lively overture, which Rossini had used in two earlier operas.

Bohème, La (*The Bohemian*), a tragic opera in four acts by Giacomo Puccini. Libretto in Italian by Giuseppe Giacosa and Luigi Illica, based on the French novel *Scenes from Bohemian Life* by Henri Murger. First performed in Turin, Italy, in 1896.

Four poor but carefree young men are living a bohemian life together in an attic in Paris about 1830. They are Rodolfo, a poet; Marcello, a painter; Schaunard, a musician; and Colline, a philosopher. Mimi, a frail young girl in poor health, is their neighbor. She and Rodolfo meet and fall in love. But at the end of the opera, Mimi dies. The main secondary plot deals with a stormy love affair between Marcello and a young woman named Musetta.

Although *La Bohème* ends tragically, it has many humorous and sentimental moments. The opera also has a number of Puccini's most beloved melodies. One of these melodies is "O soave fanciulla," a love duet between Rodolfo and Mimi that ends Act I. Perhaps the opera's most familiar melody is the aria "Musetta's Waltz" in Act II.

Boris Godunov, a tragic opera in a prologue and four acts by Modest Mussorgsky. Libretto in Russian by the composer, based primarily on the Russian play *Boris Godunov* by Alexander Pushkin. First performed in St. Petersburg, Russia, in 1874.

The opera takes place in Russia and Poland from 1598 to 1605 and concerns Russian historical figures. Boris

Scene from a production by the New York City Opera; Beth Bergman

The Barber of Seville by Gioacchino Rossini is one of the most popular comic operas. Act I ends in the wild argument shown here between Doctor Bartolo, *left center,* and Count Almaviva, *right center,* who is masquerading as a drunken soldier. Don Basilio, a music teacher, and Berta, a maid, try to hold back the doctor. Figaro, a barber, and Rosina, the count's sweetheart, attempt to restrain the nobleman.

Scene from a production by the Lyric Opera of Chicago, with
Luciano Pavarotti and Ileana Cotrubas (WORLD BOOK photo)

La Bohème by Giacomo Puccini deals with a love affair between
Rodolfo, a poet, and Mimi, a young seamstress in failing health.
Near the end of Act IV, above, Rodolfo and the dying Mimi sing
a beautiful love duet in the poet's attic lodging.

Godunov, an adviser to the czar, has the czar's young
heir murdered. After the czar dies, Boris takes the
throne. But in time, his feelings of guilt cause him to
have visions of the murdered heir, and he finally collapses and dies. The "hero" of the opera is the Russian people, portrayed by the chorus. The chorus takes part in
many scenes, including an impressive coronation.

Many musicians in Mussorgsky's time considered the
music for *Boris Godunov* too harsh and crude. After
Mussorgsky's death, his friend and fellow Russian composer Nikolai Rimsky-Korsakov revised the orchestration
for the opera. Rimsky-Korsakov's version is often performed today.

Carmen, a tragic opera in four acts by Georges Bizet.
Libretto in French by Ludovic Halévy and Henri Meilhac,
based on the French story "Carmen" by Prosper
Mérimée. First performed in Paris in 1875.

The action of *Carmen* is set in and near Seville, Spain,
about 1820. Carmen is a beautiful Gypsy dedicated to a
life of unrestrained freedom. While working in a cigarette factory in Seville, she meets Don José, a soldier,
and has a love affair with him. Later, she leaves Don José
for Escamillo, a bullfighter. At the end of the opera, Don
José pleads with Carmen to return to him. After she
scornfully refuses, Don José stabs her to death in a jealous rage.

The exciting plot, colorful Spanish setting, and stirring
music have made *Carmen* one of the most popular
works in the repertoire. Many of the opera's melodies
have become almost as familiar as popular songs. They

Scene from a production by the Bolshoi Theater Company, Moscow; Novosti Press Agency, Moscow

Boris Godunov by Modest Mussorgsky is a psychological tragedy based on events in Russian history. In the prologue to the opera, *above,* Russian peasants in Moscow bow before Boris shortly after he has been crowned czar. Members of the Russian nobility stand behind him.

include Carmen's dancelike arias "Habañera" and "Seguidilla" in Act I and Don José's "Flower Song" and Escamillo's "Toreador Song" in Act II. The opera also has rousing choral and dance numbers.

Cavalleria rusticana (*Rustic Chivalry*), a tragic opera in one act by Pietro Mascagni. Libretto in Italian by Guido Menasci and Giovanni Targioni-Tozzetti, based on the Italian story and play *Cavalleria rusticana* by Giovanni Verga. First performed in Rome in 1890.

Traditionally, *Cavalleria rusticana* is performed with Ruggiero Leoncavallo's two-act opera, *Pagliacci.* The passion, realism, and violence of both works make them major examples of verismo opera.

The action in *Cavalleria rusticana* takes place in a Sicilian village in the 1800's. There, Lola, a married woman, has a love affair with Turiddu, a young soldier. The title of the opera refers to the villagers' code of honor. According to this code, Alfio, Lola's husband, must seek revenge. He challenges Turiddu to a duel and kills him.

The composer and librettists used several effective dramatic devices. Halfway through the opera, the villagers are in church, and the stage is empty. During this interval, the orchestra plays the "Intermezzo." This gentle, melodic instrumental piece provides relief from the tense, highly emotional atmosphere of the opera. In another dramatic device, Turiddu's death takes place offstage. The opera audience learns of the outcome of the duel through the horrified reactions of the villagers onstage.

Don Giovanni, a comic opera with serious elements in two acts by Wolfgang Amadeus Mozart. Libretto in Italian by Lorenzo da Ponte. First performed in Prague, Bohemia (now part of the Czech Republic), in 1787.

Mozart's opera *Don Giovanni* has become the best-known version of the legend about Don Juan, the Spanish rogue. The action takes place in and near Seville, Spain, in the 1600's. In the opening scene, Don Giovanni

Scene from a production by the Lyric Opera of Chicago, with Viorica Cortez and Lorenzo Saccomani (WORLD BOOK photo)

Carmen by Georges Bizet describes the love affairs of a beautiful Gypsy. In this scene from Act IV, Carmen sings a duet outside a bull ring with her latest lover, the bullfighter Escamillo.

(Don Juan) flees from the home of Donna Anna after trying to seduce her, and then he kills her father in a duel. Several later episodes further show Giovanni's immoral nature. At the end of the opera, the marble statue of Donna Anna's slain father visits Giovanni and urges him to abandon his sinful ways. Giovanni refuses. The scene is then enveloped in smoke and fire as he disappears into hell, dragged off by a chorus of demons.

The mixture of comic and serious qualities of *Don Giovanni* has always fascinated audiences. Leporello, Giovanni's servant, provides most of the comedy. The

Scene from a production by the New York City Opera; Beth Bergman

Don Giovanni by Wolfgang Amadeus Mozart has been praised as the greatest opera ever composed. It deals with the legendary Spanish rogue Don Juan (Don Giovanni). Act I ends with this elaborate ball in Giovanni's castle.

most serious figure is Donna Anna. In addition to many beautiful arias, *Don Giovanni* has highly dramatic recitatives and long, complicated ensembles. In one scene in Act I, three orchestras onstage perform three different dance numbers at the same time during a party given by Don Giovanni. While the three onstage orchestras play, the opera orchestra in the pit accompanies the singers.

Faust, a tragic opera in five acts by Charles Gounod. Libretto in French by Jules Barbier and Michel Carré, based on part I of the German play *Faust* by Johann Wolfgang von Goethe. First performed in Paris in 1859.

The story of *Faust* takes place in Germany in the 1500's. Faust is an old philosopher who yearns for his lost youth. Mephistopheles, the Devil, appears to Faust and grants him youth. Faust, in return, agrees that after he dies, he will serve the Devil in hell. The opera centers on the love story between the now young Faust and Marguerite, a beautiful village girl. At the end of the opera, Marguerite dies and a chorus of angels escorts her to heaven. The Devil then drags Faust down to hell.

In the 1800's, the German composers Louis Spohr and Heinrich Zöllner and the Italian composer Arrigo Boito also wrote operas based on the story of Faust and his agreement with the Devil. But Gounod's version has become the most popular. The 1859 version had spoken dialogue. Gounod substituted recitative in a production first given in 1869, and that version is performed today. In Act III, Marguerite sings the beautiful "Jewel Song." The lively "Soldiers' Chorus" in Act IV is one of the best-known choral numbers in the entire repertoire.

Lucia di Lammermoor, a tragic opera in three acts by Gaetano Donizetti. Libretto in Italian by Salvatore Cammarano, based on the Scottish novel *The Bride of Lammermoor* by Sir Walter Scott. First performed in Naples, Italy, in 1835.

Donizetti wrote *Lucia di Lammermoor* in the melodramatic style typical of Italian romantic opera of the early 1800's. The story takes place in Scotland in the late 1600's. It concerns a doomed love affair between Lucia Ashton and Edgardo di Ravenswood. Enrico Ashton, Lucia's brother, wrongfully holds Edgardo's estate. To prevent Lucia and Edgardo from marrying, Enrico tricks Lucia into wedding another man. Lucia goes insane, kills her husband, and then dies. Edgardo hears of Lucia's death and stabs himself to death.

The opera has one of the most dramatic ensembles in the repertoire, the sextet "Chi mi frena." It is sung in Act II at Lucia's wedding. But the opera is probably best known for the "Mad Scene" in Act III, in which the insane Lucia sings of an imaginary wedding between herself and Edgardo. This scene is considered one of the greatest challenges for a coloratura soprano in all opera.

Madama Butterfly, a tragic opera in three acts by Giacomo Puccini. Libretto in Italian by Giuseppe Giacosa and Luigi Illica, based on the American play *Madame Butterfly* by David Belasco, from a story by John Luther Long. First performed in Milan, Italy, in 1904.

The story of *Madama Butterfly* takes place in Nagasaki, Japan, about 1900. Cio-cio-san (Madame Butterfly) is a *geisha* (young Japanese woman trained to entertain men) who falls in love with an American naval officer, B. F. Pinkerton. They marry in a Japanese ceremony. According to Japanese law, either the husband or the wife may cancel the marriage on a month's notice. Pinkerton must leave Japan with his ship. After he has left, the young woman gives birth to his child. Three years later, Pinkerton sends a letter saying that he has married an American. Shortly after the letter arrives, Pinkerton appears with his American wife. The heartbroken Cio-cio-san agrees to give them the child. She then commits suicide.

Puccini tried to give *Madama Butterfly* an Oriental flavor by basing some of his score on Japanese music. He also included a passage from "The Star-Spangled Ban-

Scene from a production by the New York City Opera; Fred Fehl

Madama Butterfly by Giacomo Puccini describes a tragic romance between Cio-cio-san, a young Japanese woman, and B. F. Pinkerton, an American naval officer. In Act I, the young woman and her friends arrive for the marriage ceremony. Standing on a bridge in the garden, Cio-cio-san sings of her love for Pinkerton.

The Magic Flute by Wolf-gang Amadeus Mozart is a fairy-tale opera. Act II, the final act, ends with this scene in the sacred Temple of Wisdom, ruled by the high priest, Sarastro. Marc Chagall, the famous Russian-born modern artist, designed this set for a production at the Metropolitan Opera House.

Frank Dunand, the Metropolitan Opera Guild

ner" in one of Pinkerton's numbers. The opera's best-known aria is the exquisite "Un bel dì" in Act II. In it, Cio-cio-san describes the happiness she will feel when Pinkerton returns.

Magic Flute, The (*Die Zauberflöte*), a fairy-tale opera in two acts by Wolfgang Amadeus Mozart. Libretto in German by Emanuel Schikaneder. First performed in Vienna, Austria, in 1791.

Mozart and Schikaneder were both members of a secret society called the Masons, and much of *The Magic Flute* deals symbolically with Masonic beliefs and rituals. However, the opera can be enjoyed as a fairy tale about two lovers, Tamino and Pamina. The opera takes its name from a magic flute that protects Tamino from danger.

The opera has spoken dialogue instead of recitative. Some of the music resembles simple folk songs, though several of the arias are dramatic and solemn. The Queen of the Night, Pamina's mother, sings two arias that are showpieces for a coloratura soprano. The arias have very hard passages and high notes. The overture is often performed as a separate work in concerts.

Marriage of Figaro, The (*Le Nozze di Figaro*), a comic opera in four acts by Wolfgang Amadeus Mozart. Libretto in Italian by Lorenzo da Ponte, based on the French play *The Marriage of Figaro* by Pierre de Beaumarchais. First performed in Vienna in 1786.

Beaumarchais wrote *The Barber of Seville* before *The Marriage of Figaro*. Mozart selected the second play for his opera. The Italian composer Giovanni Paisiello had

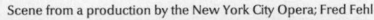

Scene from a production by the New York City Opera; Fred Fehl

Pagliacci by Ruggiero Leoncavallo is a tragedy about a company of traveling actors who stop in an Italian village to give a performance. In an aria in Act I, Canio, the leader of the company, describes the play the actors will present that night in the village.

already composed an opera based on *The Barber of Seville*. The same principal characters appear in both works. The plot of *The Marriage of Figaro* follows the action begun in *The Barber of Seville*. Mozart's opera describes the problems that develop when Figaro, servant to Count Almaviva, tries to marry Susanna, Countess Almaviva's maid. The Count wants Susanna for himself, but a final scene of multiple disguises brings him back to his wife.

Operagoers have praised *The Marriage of Figaro* for its vivid, realistic characters. Unlike many opera composers of the time, Mozart relied far more on ensembles than on arias to develop his characters.

Pagliacci (The Players), a tragic opera in a prologue and two acts by Ruggiero Leoncavallo. Libretto in Italian by the composer. First performed in Milan, Italy, in 1892.

A short verismo opera, *Pagliacci* deals with life among members of a traveling company of actors in Italy in the 1860's. The story concerns the jealousy of Canio, the leader of the players. The opera opens with a prologue sung in front of the curtain by Tonio, who plays a clown. The prologue announces the theme of the drama.

Early in Act I, Canio learns that Nedda, his wife, is unfaithful. He discovers that she is having a love affair, but he does not know the identity of the man. Canio sings one of the great tenor arias in all opera, "Vesti la giubba," which expresses his tragic fate of playing a clown while his heart is breaking. During a performance of the play, Canio learns that his wife's lover is Silvio, a peasant who lives in the village where the actors are performing. Canio then stabs Nedda and Silvio as the opera ends.

Porgy and Bess, a folk opera in three acts by George Gershwin. Libretto in English by Gershwin's brother Ira and DuBose Heyward, based on Heyward's novel *Porgy* (1925). First performed in Boston in 1935.

Gershwin's *Porgy and Bess* is one of the few American operas that has achieved worldwide fame. The opera portrays life among African Americans in Charleston, South Carolina, in the 1920's. It deals with the love of the crippled Porgy for the beautiful Bess. The story is highly dramatic and has considerable humor. In his score, Gershwin captured the flavor of the songs sung by black people of the southeastern United States.

The opera consists largely of individual songs and choral scenes, connected by recitative. Only the white characters have spoken dialogue. Some of the songs, including "Summertime," "I Got Plenty o' Nuttin'," and "It Ain't Necessarily So," have become popular hits.

Rigoletto, a tragic opera in three acts by Giuseppe Verdi. Libretto in Italian by Francesco Maria Piave, based on the French play *Le Roi s'amuse (The King Is Amused)* by Victor Hugo. First performed in Venice, Italy, in 1851.

The opera tells a story of treachery and revenge in the court of an Italian nobleman, the Duke of Mantua, in the 1500's. The chief characters include the duke; Rigoletto, a hunchback who is the duke's jester; and Gilda, Rigoletto's daughter. Through intrigue and deceit, Rigoletto's beloved daughter is murdered.

For *Rigoletto,* Verdi composed some of his most glorious melodies. In Act I, Gilda sings the beautiful aria "Caro nome," in which she expresses her love for the duke, who is disguised as a student. In Act III, the duke sings one of the most popular arias in the repertoire, "La donna è mobile." The aria is an ironic comment by the faithless duke on how changeable women are in their affections. The emotional and melodic quartet "Bella figlia dell' amore" is sung later in Act III.

Ring of the Nibelung, The (Der Ring des Nibelungen), a cycle of four operas by Richard Wagner. Libretto in German by the composer. The three main parts are

Scene from a production by the New York City Opera; Fred Fehl

Der Rosenkavalier by Richard Strauss portrays life among people of high social class in Vienna during the 1700's. Part of the story concerns a romance between Octavian, who is a young nobleman, and Sophie, who is a wealthy young girl. This photograph shows Octavian and Sophie meeting and falling in love in a scene in Act II. Octavian brings Sophie a silver rose sent by Baron Ochs. The baron—a coarse, middle-aged nobleman—intends to marry Sophie.

Die Walküre (The Valkyrie, 1870*); Siegfried* (1876); and *Die Götterdämmerung (The Twilight of the Gods,* 1876). Wagner called the fourth work, *Das Rheingold (The Rhine Gold,* 1869), the prologue to the other three. However, it is a complete opera. All four works were first performed as a cycle at the opening of the Festival Opera House in Bayreuth, Germany, in 1876.

The four operas have a continuous plot based on ancient German and Icelandic legends. The Rhine-Maidens guard a treasure of gold on the bottom of the Rhine River. Alberich, one of a group of dwarfs called Nibelungs, steals the Rhine gold and makes a ring from it. The ring gives magic powers to whoever possesses it. After the ring of the Nibelungs is stolen from Alberich, he puts a curse on it. The ring changes owners several times during the four operas.

Many gods and goddesses take part in the action, including Wotan, their chief; and Fricka, his wife. Other important characters include Brünnhilde, one of several female warriors called Valkyries; Siegmund, a mortal son of Wotan; Siegfried, Siegmund's son; and Sieglinde, Siegmund's sister. The Ring cycle deals with the decline and downfall of the gods, brought about by their greed and lust for power as represented by the ring.

***Rosenkavalier, Der** (The Cavalier of the Rose),* a partly comic, partly serious opera in three acts by Richard Strauss. Libretto in German by Hugo von Hofmannsthal. First performed in Dresden, Germany, in 1911.

Unlike most opera texts, the libretto for *Der Rosenkavalier* is an outstanding work of literature. It glamorously portrays life among the aristocracy in Vienna in the 1700's. In most productions, the sets for the first two acts are spectacular, representing luxurious Viennese palaces. The work also calls for magnificent costumes.

The opera describes the love affairs of four chief characters: Princess von Werdenberg, called the Marschallin; Octavian, a young nobleman; Sophie, a beautiful girl; and Baron Ochs, a coarse and comic country nobleman. Strauss wrote the role of Octavian to be played by a female, and a mezzo-soprano sings the part.

Strauss composed many brilliant ensemble scenes for *Der Rosenkavalier.* One of the most impressive takes place in Act I when the Marschallin receives many visitors. The composer emphasized the light-hearted Viennese quality of the opera in a number of lilting waltzes. These waltzes are sometimes performed separately in concerts.

Salome, a tragic opera in one act by Richard Strauss. Libretto in German by Hedwig Lachmann; a translation of a play in French, *Salomé,* by the Irish-born author Oscar Wilde. First performed in Dresden, Germany, in 1905.

Wilde based his play on the story of Salome in the New Testament, but he invented many details that shocked audiences of his time. In Wilde's play, Salome, a 15-year-old girl, is attracted to the religious prophet Jochanaan (John the Baptist). After Jochanaan rejects her advances, she decides to take revenge. Salome's stepfather, King Herod, asks her to dance for him and, in return, promises her anything she wishes. Salome performs the famous "Dance of the Seven Veils" and then asks Herod for Jochanaan's head on a silver dish. Herod,

Scene from a production by the Metropolitan Opera Association, with Birgit Nilsson; Frank Dunand, the Metropolitan Opera Guild

Salome by Richard Strauss is a passionate and violent opera that takes place in Palestine at the time of Christ. In the one-act opera's best-known scene, *shown here,* Salome performs the "Dance of the Seven Veils" before King Herod and his court.

though horrified, keeps his promise and has Jochanaan beheaded. Salome kisses the head of the prophet, an act that audiences of the early 1900's considered especially objectionable.

Strauss's score captures perfectly the mood of Wilde's gruesome story. The music is often violent and harsh. At other times, it is vigorous and passionate. The orchestral music especially helps create the rich Oriental atmosphere of the opera. The role of Salome is one of the most difficult in the repertoire. The performer must not only sing extremely complicated music, but she must also act and dance well. In addition, she should look young and beautiful.

Tosca, a tragic opera in three acts by Giacomo Puccini. Libretto in Italian by Giuseppe Giacosa and Luigi Illica, based on the French play *La Tosca* by Victorien Sardou. First performed in Rome in 1900.

The story of *Tosca* takes place in Rome in 1800, when the city is torn by political intrigue. The chief characters are Floria Tosca, a famous singer; Mario, a painter and Tosca's lover; and Baron Scarpia, the villainous chief of police. In the story, Cesare Angelotti, an escaped political prisoner, has fled from Scarpia. Both Tosca and Mario know Angelotti's hiding place. Much of the action concerns Scarpia's attempts to force Tosca and Mario to reveal where Angelotti is hiding. Scarpia also wants to make Tosca his mistress. Tosca kills Scarpia and then commits suicide after she watches a firing squad execute Mario.

Puccini's music powerfully expresses the passion and violence of the plot. The work also has several beautiful melodies, including Tosca's "Vissi d' arte" in Act II and Mario's "E lucevan le stelle" in Act III.

***Traviata, La** (The Wayward Woman),* a tragic opera in three acts by Giuseppe Verdi. Libretto in Italian by Francesco Maria Piave, based on the French play *The*

Scene from a production by the Santa Fe (New Mexico) Opera, with George Shirley and Maralin Niska; Santa Fe Opera

La Traviata by Giuseppe Verdi describes a tragic love affair between Alfredo and Violetta in France during the mid-1800's. In this scene from Act I, they meet for the first time at a party.

Lady of the Camellias by Alexandre Dumas the Younger. First performed in Venice, Italy, in 1853.

Although *La Traviata* failed dismally at its première, it has become one of the most frequently performed works in the repertoire. Verdi set the action in and near Paris in the mid-1800's. The opera shocked many people during the mid-1800's because Violetta, its heroine, leads an immoral life.

Unlike many earlier operas, *La Traviata* has realistic characters with complicated emotions. Their thoughts and feelings seem especially convincing because of Verdi's theatrically effective music. For example, in Act I, Violetta tries to decide whether to fall in love with Alfredo, who loves her. The music clearly reflects her indecision. In Act III, she sings one of the opera's most haunting arias, "Addio del passato," in which she bids farewell to the happy days of the past.

Trovatore, Il (The Troubadour), a tragic opera in four acts by Giuseppe Verdi. Libretto in Italian by Salvatore Cammarano, based on the Spanish play *El Trovador* by Antonio García Gutiérrez. First performed in Rome in 1853.

Like most Verdi operas, *Il Trovatore* tells a gloomy and violent story filled with passion. The action takes place in Spain in the 1400's. The principal characters include Manrico, a *troubadour* (poet-musician); Leonora, a noblewoman; Azucena, a Gypsy; and the Count di Luna. Manrico and Leonora are lovers, but the count also loves Leonora. In addition, di Luna and Manrico are brothers, though only Azucena knows it. Azucena seeks revenge against the count because his father had her mother burned at the stake. By the opera's end, Leonora has committed suicide and the count has executed Manrico. After Manrico's death, Azucena tells the count he has killed his brother, and she thus has her revenge.

Despite a frequently confusing plot, *Il Trovatore* is brilliantly effective theater. The opera also has some of

Verdi's most memorable music. In Act II, a band of Gypsies in their mountain camp sings what is perhaps the most familiar choral number in all opera, the stirring "Anvil Chorus."

Wozzeck, a tragic opera in three acts by Alban Berg. Libretto in German by the composer, based on the German play *Woyzeck* by Georg Büchner. First performed in Berlin in 1925.

Wozzeck is a private in the Austrian army about 1830. His superiors abuse and ridicule him. Even worse, Marie, the woman he loves, deceives him with another man. Driven almost insane by jealousy, Wozzeck stabs and kills Marie. Later, he throws the knife into a pond. Finally, he drowns while searching for the knife.

Much of the text for *Wozzeck* is set in an intensely emotional vocal style midway between spoken dialogue and singing. This style is known by the German term *Sprechstimme* (speaking voice). Most of the music is *atonal*—that is, it does not fall into the traditional keys.

Although *Wozzeck* is difficult to sing and play, it has been performed in many countries. Some people consider the music jarring and too hard to understand. But others feel that it powerfully expresses a great variety of emotions.   Thomas A. Bauman

Study aids

Related articles in *World Book* include:

American composers

Barber, Samuel	Hanson, Howard
Bernstein, Leonard	Menotti, Gian Carlo
Blitzstein, Marc	Moore, Douglas Stuart
Bloch, Ernest	Sessions, Roger
Copland, Aaron	Still, William Grant
Gershwin, George	Thomson, Virgil
Glass, Philip	

British composers

Britten, Benjamin	Vaughan Williams, Ralph
Delius, Frederick	Walton, Sir William
Purcell, Henry	

French composers

Berlioz, Hector	Massenet, Jules
Bizet, Georges	Milhaud, Darius
Debussy, Claude	Offenbach, Jacques
Delibes, Léo	Poulenc, Francis
Dukas, Paul	Rameau, Jean-Philippe
Fauré, Gabriel	Ravel, Maurice
Gounod, Charles	Saint-Saëns, Camille
Lully, Jean-Baptiste	

German-language composers

Bach, Johann Christian	Meyerbeer, Giacomo
Beethoven, Ludwig van	Mozart, Wolfgang Amadeus
Berg, Alban	Schoenberg, Arnold
Gluck, Christoph Willibald	Schubert, Franz
Handel, George Frideric	Strauss, Richard
Haydn, Joseph	Wagner, Richard
Hindemith, Paul	Weber, Carl Maria von
Humperdinck, Engelbert	Weill, Kurt

Italian composers

Bellini, Vincenzo	Dallapiccola, Luigi
Boito, Arrigo	Donizetti, Gaetano
Cherubini, Luigi	

Leoncavallo, Ruggiero
Mascagni, Pietro
Monteverdi, Claudio
Pergolesi, Giovanni

Puccini, Giacomo
Rossini, Gioacchino
Scarlatti, Alessandro
Verdi, Giuseppe

Russian composers

Borodin, Alexander
Glinka, Mikhail
Mussorgsky, Modest
Prokofiev, Sergei
Rimsky-Korsakov, Nikolai
Shostakovich, Dimitri
Stravinsky, Igor
Tchaikovsky, Peter Ilich

Other composers

Bartók, Béla
Dvořák, Antonín
Falla, Manuel de

Kodály, Zoltán
Smetana, Bedřich

American opera singers

Anderson, Marian
Callas, Maria
Fleming, Renée
Garden, Mary
Hayes, Roland
Horne, Marilyn
Maynor, Dorothy

Merrill, Robert
Milnes, Sherrill
Peerce, Jan
Price, Leontyne
Robeson, Paul
Sills, Beverly
Tucker, Richard

Australasian opera singers

Melba, Nellie
Sutherland, Joan

Te Kanawa, Kiri

European opera singers

Björling, Jussi
Caruso, Enrico
De los Angeles, Victoria
Domingo, Placido
Fischer-Dieskau, Dietrich
Flagstad, Kirsten

Lind, Jenny
McCormack, John
Pavarotti, Luciano
Raisa, Rosa
Tebaldi, Renata
Terfel, Bryn

Other related articles

Ballet
Classical music
Drama (Intermezzi and operas)
Intermezzo
Italy (The arts [picture])
Musical comedy

Operetta
Oratorio
Overture
Singing
Traviata, La

Outline

I. **The elements of opera**
  A. The libretto
  B. The music
II. **Producing an opera**
  A. The people behind the scenes
  B. Preparing a production
III. **The development of opera**
IV. **The opera repertoire**

Questions

Why is the libretto of most operas shorter than the text of a spoken play?
What qualities make *The Barber of Seville* an example of opera buffa?
Why is the role of Salome one of the most difficult in the repertoire?
What is the difference between recitatives and arias?
What dramatic function does the "Intermezzo" serve in *Cavalleria Rusticana?*
How does a coloratura soprano differ from a dramatic soprano?
What was the *Camerata?*
Why does opera acting tend to be less lively and less realistic than acting in other forms of drama?

Who was the most important German opera composer of the 1800's? Of the 1900's?
What is the function of a general manager in an opera company?

Additional resources

Bourne, Joyce. *Who's Who in Opera: A Guide to Opera Characters.* 1998. Reprint. Oxford, 1999.
Ganeri, Anita, and Barber, Nicola. *The Young Person's Guide to the Opera: With Music from the Great Operas on CD.* Harcourt, 2001. Younger readers.
Geras, Adèle. *The Random House Book of Opera Stories.* Random Hse., 1998. Younger readers.
Holden, Amanda, ed. *The New Penguin Opera Guide.* Penguin, 2001.
Kirk, Elise K. *American Opera.* Univ. of Ill. Pr., 2001.
Kuhn, Laura. *Baker's Dictionary of Opera.* Schirmer Bks., 2000.
Lee, M. Owen. *The Operagoer's Guide: One Hundred Stories and Commentaries.* Amadeus Pr., 2001.
Raeburn, Michael. *The Chronicle of Opera.* Thames & Hudson, 1998.
Siberell, Anne. *Bravo! Brava! A Night at the Opera: Behind the Scenes with Composers, Cast and Crew.* Oxford, 2001. Younger readers.
Somerset-Ward, Richard. *The Story of Opera.* Abrams, 1998.

Operation. See Surgery.
Operation Desert Storm. See Persian Gulf War of 1991.
Operetta is a type of musical theater that achieved its greatest popularity from the 1850's to about 1920. Different from a typical serious opera, operetta contains spoken dialogue rather than sung dialogue and fairly simple, straightforward songs rather than complex arias. Many operetta overtures consist of a medley of tunes from the show instead of a separate composition, as is the case in opera.

Operettas generally are composed in an uncomplicated and popular style. The music is easy to perform and to understand. The plots of most operettas are romantic, sentimental, or satirical. They often involve confusion over mistaken identities and have happy endings, frequently with a moral. Most operettas also feature dances and choruses.

Operettas developed from French comic opera. Several national schools of operetta developed, beginning in France. Jacques Offenbach, a German-born French composer, wrote the first masterpieces in the operetta form. Offenbach's major works include *Orpheus in the Underworld* (1858), *La Belle Hélène* (1864), and *La Périchole* (1868).

The Austrian composer Franz von Suppé was the first composer of Viennese-style operettas, beginning in the 1860's. This musical style is based on dance forms, especially the waltz. The settings are also more exotic than those of French operettas.

Johann Strauss, Jr., was the master of the Viennese school. Strauss's operetta *Die Fledermaus* (1874) is the greatest example of the school. Romantic Viennese operettas dominated the form during the early 1900's with such works as *The Merry Widow* (1905) by Franz Lehar.

English composers were greatly influenced by both French and Viennese operetta. By the 1870's, the team of Sir William Gilbert and Sir Arthur Sullivan had developed an English style in such humorous and satirical works as *H.M.S. Pinafore* (1878) and *The Mikado* (1885).

Operettas were extremely popular in the United States, with French, Viennese, and English works receiving numerous productions. By the 1890's, American composers began writing successful operettas. The principal composers included Reginald de Koven, Rudolf Friml, Victor Herbert, Sigmund Romberg, and John Philip Sousa.   Katherine K. Preston

Related articles in *World Book* include:

Friml, Rudolf	Romberg, Sigmund
Gilbert and Sullivan	Sousa, John Philip
Herbert, Victor	Straus, Oscar
Lehar, Franz	Strauss, Johann, Jr.
Offenbach, Jacques	

Ophthalmia, *ahf THAL mee uh,* is a name for severe diseases affecting the eye membranes. These diseases may be caused by infections, poisons, or injuries. For example, *ophthalmia neonatorum* is an infection of the eyes of newborn babies, usually caused by the germ that causes gonorrhea. *Sympathetic ophthalmia,* a rare condition, spreads to both eyes after a serious injury to one eye and can lead to blindness if untreated. See also **Blindness** (Diseases).   Ronald Klein

Ophthalmology, *AHF thal MAHL uh jee,* is the field of medicine involving the diagnosis and treatment of eye diseases. An *ophthalmologist* must have an M.D. degree and three to five years of specialized training in a residency program, usually in a hospital.

Most ophthalmologists limit their medical and surgical practice to the eye. They examine the eye with special equipment and check *visual acuity* (the ability of the eye to see). If a patient's visual acuity is less than normal, an ophthalmologist usually does a *refraction* to determine whether the decrease in vision can be corrected with glasses. A refraction is a check of the power of the lens and cornea of the eye relative to the size of the eye. If the patient needs glasses, the ophthalmologist usually gives the patient a prescription for them. Glasses are made by an *optician.*

If the patient's vision cannot be corrected with glasses, the ophthalmologist's examination will help detect the cause of poor vision. An ophthalmologist performs the necessary operation if an eye condition requires corrective surgery, such as the removal of *cataracts* (clouding of the lens of an eye). Ophthalmologists also may perform other types of surgery, which include surgery to correct *strabismus* (cross-eye) or other muscle imbalances of the eyes, corneal transplants, and surgery to control *glaucoma* (increase in fluid pressure in the eye).

By studying the *retina* (back layer of the eye), an ophthalmologist may discover signs of diseases of other parts of the body. For example, such diseases as diabetes, AIDS, and certain forms of anemia may cause changes in the appearance of the retina.   Ronald Klein

See also **Optometry; Surgery** (Surgical specialties).

Ophthalmoscope, *ahf THAL muh skohp,* is an optical instrument for examining the interior of the eye. Ophthalmologists and optometrists can make certain diagnoses by using the ophthalmoscope to examine abnormalities in the eye.

There are two types of ophthalmoscopes, the *direct ophthalmoscope* and the *indirect ophthalmoscope.* The direct ophthalmoscope contains a light, a prism and a mirror, and lenses. These parts are mounted in the head of the instrument, which is attached to a handle contain-

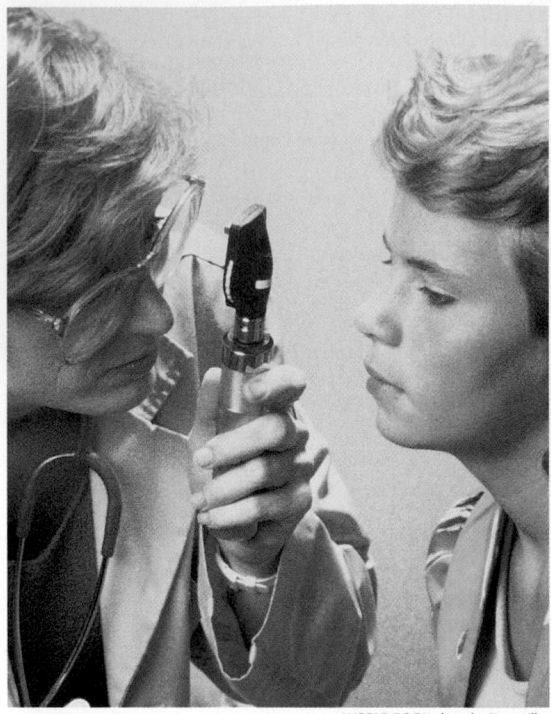

WORLD BOOK photo by Dan Miller

An ophthalmoscope is used to examine the interior of the eye. The examiner peers through a tiny hole in the ophthalmoscope while focusing light into the patient's eye.

ing a battery. The prism and mirror project the light on the back of the eye. The lenses enable the examiner to focus the light to provide a clear, magnified view of the eye's interior. The indirect ophthalmoscope consists of a light worn on the examiner's head and a lens held in front of the patient's eye. This instrument enables the examiner to see a larger area than the direct ophthalmoscope does, but with lower magnification.

The ophthalmoscope was invented by a German physicist, Hermann von Helmholtz, in 1851 (see **Helmholtz, Hermann L.**). Helmholtz's instrument consisted of a sandwich of three thin plates of glass mounted at a 45-degree angle on a handle. A light was placed to the side of the eye under examination. Some light passed through the glass plates, but some was reflected into the eye. The lighted inside of the eye was observed through the glass.   Ronald Klein

Opiate, *OH pee iht,* is any drug made from or containing opium. Opium is a dried milky substance obtained from unripened seedcases of the opium poppy plant. Morphine and codeine are opiates used for their healing properties. These drugs are *analgesics* (painkillers). Physicians prescribe them mainly for people with severe pain. Opiates also are used to help control coughing and severe diarrhea.

Continued use of opiates can reduce their healing effects and can also lead to addiction. Therefore, opiates and synthetic drugs that have the same chemical structure as opiates have been made *controlled substances* by law. This means they can be obtained lawfully only by getting a prescription from a doctor or, in some cases, by signing a register at a pharmacy. Heroin is a highly addictive opiate. Federal law totally prohibits the sale and use of heroin in the United States.   Barbara M. Bayer

Opinion poll. See Public opinion poll.

Opium is a plant product that serves as the source of several medicines, including codeine and morphine. Heroin, an illegal drug, is also made from opium. Opium and most *opioids* (drugs made from or containing opium) are used to treat severe pain but may result in addiction. The United States and many other nations restrict their manufacture, distribution, and use.

Opium is made from the juice of the opium poppy. Most opium used by U.S. drug manufacturers comes from poppies grown on farms in India. Opium farmers make cuts on the poppy flower, enabling the milky-white juice to leak out. The opium is dried into powder and formed into bricks for shipment. Drug manufacturers use products derived from raw opium to make medicines, including codeine, methadone, morphine, oxycodone, and other medicines.

Medical uses. Opium ranked as the most effective pain-relieving drug until the development of morphine in the early 1800's. Opium was also used to stop coughing and diarrhea, to ease worry, and to cause drowsiness. Opiates serve many of the same purposes today. Physicians prescribe morphine to relieve severe pain. Codeine, probably the most widely used opiate, stops coughing. The opiate paregoric controls diarrhea.

Opium addiction. The misuse of opium or of drugs made from it can lead to addiction. Opium, when first used, can give users a feeling of calm and *euphoria* (well-being). Their troubles may seem unimportant. They temporarily live in an unreal world of isolated contentment. People smoke, sniff, or eat opium for these effects. But an addict may have vivid dreams and daydreams that may be unpleasant. Addicts who want to stop taking opiates can obtain medical treatment and counseling.

Some experimental programs use a drug called methadone to help patients overcome addiction to opiates (see **Methadone**). People addicted to opium who stop using methadone abruptly experience pain and flu-like symptoms known as *withdrawal.*

History. The use of opium began at least 6,000 years ago in the Middle East. Greek and Roman physicians prescribed the drug before the time of Christ. Arabian traders took opium to China and India, probably starting in the A.D. 600's. At first, the Chinese used the drug chiefly as a medicine. European traders introduced opium smoking into China in the early 1600's. The Chinese government outlawed opium in 1729, but traders continued to exchange it for silk, porcelain, and other Chinese products. In the late 1700's, opium addiction became widespread among the Chinese. In the mid-1800's, the opium trade helped to cause two wars, known as the Anglo-Chinese Wars or the Opium Wars (1839-1842 and 1856-1860), in which the United Kingdom defeated China (see **China** [Clash with the Western powers]).

During the 1800's, people in the United States and Europe could buy laudanum, morphine, and other opiates legally and without a prescription. By 1900, at least 200,000 Americans had become addicted to opiates. The Harrison Act, a group of laws passed in 1914, greatly reduced the problem in the United States. Addiction to opiates, particularly heroin, began to increase in the late 1940's and has continued to rise ever since. Today, a number of nations and international organizations cooperate in fighting the illegal manufacture and sale of opium and opiates.   Christopher M. Herndon

See also **Codeine; Drug** (picture: Some sources of drugs); **Drug abuse; Heroin; Morphine; Poppy.**

Opium War. See China (Clash with Western powers).

Oporto. See Porto.

Opossum, *uh PAHS uhm,* is a small furry mammal of the Americas. Dozens of *species* (kinds) of opossum exist. They are *marsupials,* mammals who bear extremely undeveloped young. The female opossum carries the young in a pouch on her abdomen. Opossums are the only marsupials native to North America. They live from Ontario in Canada southward into South America. Both opossums and the possums of Australia and New Guinea are marsupials, but they are not closely related. See **Possum.**

Most opossums live in Central America and South America. Small, tree-dwelling *murine opossums* resemble mice. *Woolly opossums* have thick, soft fur. The *yapok,* or *water opossum,* is the only marsupial adapted for living in water. Its webbed feet help make it a good swimmer.

The *Virginia opossum,* also called the *common opossum* or *North American opossum,* is the only species found north of Mexico. This opossum grows about as big as a house cat. It has rough grayish-white hair, a long snout, dark eyes, and big hairless ears. A long, nearly hairless tail helps the animal grasp objects and stabilize itself while climbing. The Virginia opossum has 50 teeth, more than any other North American mammal. Its teeth and claws are sharp. Its tracks are easy to recognize from the animal's long, widely separated toes.

Opossums are born in groups of up to 25. At birth, an opossum is about as big as a kidney bean. The newborn attaches itself to one of its mother's nipples, sometimes contained in her pouch. Nourished by its mother's milk, the young opossum stays there for about two months. After leaving the nipple, the young stay near the mother

WORLD BOOK illustration by Robert Hynes

The opium poppy is a plant used to produce opium, a drug that is the source of heroin and several medicines.

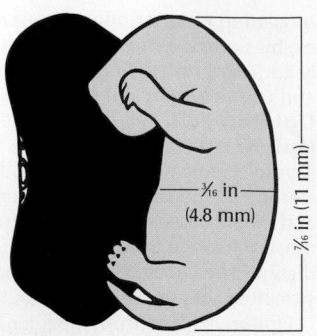

³⁄₁₆ in
(4.8 mm)

⁷⁄₁₆ in (11 mm)

A newborn opossum is about the same size as a kidney bean.

E. R. Degginger

A mother opossum carries its young on its back. Baby opossums stay in their mother's pouch for about two months after birth. They remain near her for several more weeks.

for several more weeks. When they can take care of themselves, the young go off on their own. In the wild, opossums rarely survive more than two years.

Opossums are *nocturnal,* or most active at night. They eat almost any kind of plant or animal food. When in danger, opossums sometimes enter a temporary shock-like state and appear to be dead.   Michael L. Augee

Scientific classification. Opossums make up the opossum family, Didelphidae. The scientific name for the Virginia opossum is *Didelphis marsupialis.*

See also **Animal** (picture: Animals of the temperate forests); **Mammal** (picture: Marsupials); **Marsupial**.

Oppenheimer, *AHP uhn HY muhr,* **J. Robert** (1904-1967), an American physicist, became known as the father of the atomic bomb. From 1942 to 1945, he directed the Manhattan Project, the United States government's program to build the first atomic bomb during World War II (1939-1945). Much of this work took place in Los Alamos, New Mexico.

From 1947 to 1952, Oppenheimer headed the advisory committee of the newly formed United States Atomic Energy Commission (AEC). He also advised the U.S. Department of Defense and helped write the first U.S. proposal for international control of nuclear energy.

In 1953, Oppenheimer's loyalty to the United States was questioned. The charges of disloyalty gave rise to a famous security hearing of the 1950's. Oppenheimer's initial opposition to the development of the hydrogen bomb, together with his past associations with Communists, led to an investigation in 1954 by an AEC security panel. The panel cleared Oppenheimer of all charges of disloyalty, but it denied him further access to secret information. In 1963, the AEC gave Oppenheimer its highest honor, the Enrico Fermi Award, for his contributions to theoretical physics. Many people viewed this as an effort by the government to correct a tragic mistake.

Oppenheimer was born on April 22, 1904, in New York City. He graduated from Harvard University in 1925 after three years of study. In 1927, Oppenheimer received his Ph.D. from the University of Göttingen in Ger-

many. From 1929 to 1947, Oppenheimer was on the faculty of the University of California at Berkeley, where he established a center for research in theoretical physics. During that time, he taught part of each year at the California Institute of Technology. Oppenheimer served as director of the Institute for Advanced Study in Princeton, New Jersey, from 1947 to 1966. He died on Feb. 18, 1967.

Matthew Stanley

Opposition is a term that describes the relative position of two heavenly bodies when Earth comes closest to being directly between them. At full moon, for example, the moon is in opposition to the sun. The term is most commonly used to describe positions with respect to the sun. When a *superior planet*—that is, one whose distance from the sun is greater than Earth's—is on the opposite side of Earth from the sun, it is said to be *in opposition.* For example, Mars is in opposition when Earth is directly between Mars and the sun.   Lee J. Rickard

Optic nerve. See Eye (The retina; diagram).

Optical disc. See Compact disc.

Optical fiber. See Fiber optics.

Optical illusion. As we look down a long, straight road, we see that it seems to grow narrower in the distance. Trees and telegraph poles along the road appear to grow smaller as they stretch away toward the horizon. We know that a white house looks larger than the same house painted a dark color, and that a man wearing a suit with up-and-down stripes looks thinner than he would if the stripes went crosswise. We call appearances of this kind *optical illusions* because we know that in such cases things are not the way they appear to be.

Optical illusions of the kind described above are called "normal" illusions, because every person with normal eyesight experiences them. But an optical illusion does not occur every time we are deceived by what we see. Often we make mistakes in interpreting the impressions our eye receives. For example, many people will read the sentence "he walked though the busy street," and never notice that the third word has no "r" in it. They *expect* to see "through" and therefore they *do*

Some common optical illusions

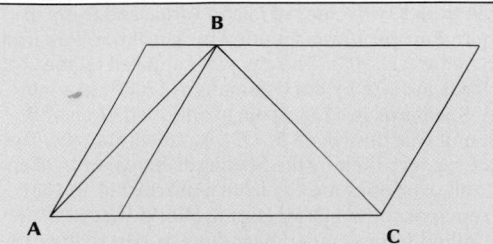

Lines A-B and B-C in the above figure are equal in length. However, line B-C appears to be longer because of the angles of the other lines in the figure.

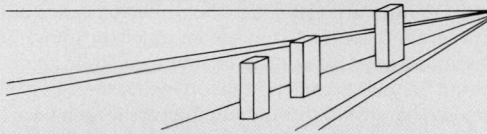

These blocks are all the same size, but the ones drawn to appear farther from the viewer seem larger. This illusion occurs because the blocks are not drawn in perspective.

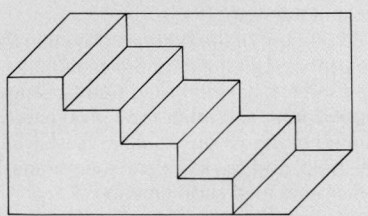

This staircase has stairs that run up from right to left. But the figure can also be seen as an upside-down staircase, with the stairs running "up" from left to right.

see "through." Such mistaken impressions are not optical illusions.   David E. Eifrig

See also **Color** (Surprising color-vision effects); **Perception** (Factors affecting perception; illustration: Perceptual effects); **Mirage.**

Optics is the branch of physics and engineering that is concerned with the properties of light. Optics deals with how light is produced, how it is transmitted, and how it can be detected, measured, and used. Light includes all the rays of the *electromagnetic spectrum.* They are gamma rays, X rays, ultraviolet light, visible light, infrared light, microwaves, and radio waves.

Many instruments operate according to the principles of optics. They include binoculars, cameras, microscopes, projectors, and telescopes. These instruments transmit and manipulate light using optical devices, such as lenses and mirrors. Visible light can be detected and measured with an instrument called a *light meter.*

The study of optics has increased the number of uses of light. For example, scientists have developed *optical fibers* that can transmit light along a twisted or curved path. Such fibers are used to carry many signals once carried by wire. Scientists have developed concentrated

light sources called *lasers* for many practical uses.

Scientists may use a *prism* or other device to divide light into a band of colors called a *spectrum.* Scientists analyze *spectra* (the plural of spectrum) with instruments called *spectrometers.*

There are three major branches of optics. *Geometrical optics* is concerned with the study of light as rays. *Physical optics* deals with the nature and behavior of light as a wave. *Quantum optics* studies the nature of light as individual particles called *photons.*

Basic principles of optics describe what light is and how it behaves. A number of reactions may occur when light strikes an object. Many of them can be described by the principles of reflection, *refraction* (the bending of light rays), and *diffraction* (the spreading of light rays). Other principles of optics include *polarization,* the lining up of light waves in certain directions; the *photoelectric effect,* the transfer of energy from light to an electric current; and *interference,* a reinforcing or canceling effect between two or more light waves.

History. The Arab scientist Alhazen is sometimes called the founder of optics. In the 1000's he wrote *Kitab al Manazir (Book of Optics),* an important book on the theory of light and its role in vision. But the steady development of modern optics did not begin until the 1600's. At that time, the Italian scientist Galileo built telescopes to observe the planets and stars. Sir Isaac Newton, an English scientist, experimented with lenses and used a prism to break sunlight into its colors. In the Netherlands, the physicist Christiaan Huygens studied polarization and later proposed a theory of light as a wave.

In the early 1800's, two physicists did much to confirm Huygens's theory—Thomas Young of England and Augustin Fresnel of France. Young formulated the principle of the interference of light. Fresnel later developed a mathematical formula that supported this principle.

During the mid-1800's, two French scientists, Armand H. L. Fizeau and Jean B. L. Foucault, made accurate measurements of the speed of light. At about the same time, the German scientists Robert Bunsen and Gustav Kirchhoff showed that chemical elements produce distinctive color bands of the spectrum. In 1864, the Scottish physicist James C. Maxwell introduced the electromagnetic theory of light. Such scientists as Albert A. Michelson of the United States, Frits Zernike of the Netherlands, and Dennis Gabor of the United Kingdom have won the Nobel Prize in physics for advances in optics.

Duncan T. Moore

Related articles in *World Book.* For more information on optics, see the article **Light** and its list of *Related articles.*

Optimist International is an association of service clubs. The vast majority of Optimist Clubs are in the United States, Canada, and the Caribbean. Membership is by invitation to business and professional people of the local community. Optimist Clubs work to develop optimism as a philosophy of life. They promote good government, respect for law, patriotism, friendship among all people, and service to youth.

Under the motto "Friend of Youth," Optimist Clubs conduct a wide range of service projects for young people. The Optimist Childhood Cancer Campaign promotes cancer research and provides assistance to children with cancer and their families. The organization sponsors three annual contests in which high school students compete for college scholarships. These contests are an essay contest, a public speaking contest, and a communication contest for people with hearing disabilities. Other programs include youth safety and youth appreciation activities, sports skills contests, and the Optimist International Junior Golf Championships.

Eleven Optimist Clubs founded Optimist International in Louisville, Kentucky, in 1919. The organization is based in St. Louis.   Critically reviewed by Optimist International

Option. See **Commodity exchange** (Options contracts).

Optometry, *ahp TAHM uh tree,* is a profession devoted to the care of vision. Optometrists give eye health and vision examinations. They diagnose vision problems that affect a person's ability to see nearby and distant objects clearly and to judge distance. Optometrists also test the ability of the eyes to work together and to change focus easily. Optometrists prescribe eyeglasses and contact lenses to correct faulty vision. In the United States, optometrists can perform minor procedures, such as removing foreign objects from the eye. They can treat some forms of glaucoma and other eye diseases with drugs. Optometrists also may recommend vision therapy to help overcome certain vision problems.

To practice optometry in the United States or Canada, a person must pass an examination for a state or a provincial license. Optometrists in the United States must have completed two or three years of preoptometry college work and graduated from a four-year school or college of optometry. Most optometry students have undergraduate degrees before entering the professional degree program. All schools and colleges of optometry award the Doctor of Optometry (O.D.) degree. Canada has similar requirements. Additional information may be obtained from the American Optometric Association.

Critically reviewed by the American Optometric Association

See also **Eye** (Care of the eye); **Ophthalmology.**

Oracle, *AWR uh kuhl,* in the ancient Greek world, was a shrine where people came to seek advice from prophets or prophetesses. They were individuals who had special powers to speak on behalf of a god. These sacred persons were believed to have the power to reveal the will of the gods and to foretell the future. The word *oracle* also refers to the prophet and prophetess, and to their prophecy.

The most important oracle was in Delphi in central Greece and was dedicated to the god Apollo. The prophetess of Delphi, often called the Pythia, sat on a large three-legged stand or tripod. In a state of ecstasy inspired by Apollo, she frequently uttered his oracles in a strange and puzzling form. The meaning of the Pythia's oracles was often so unclear that priests at the shrine interpreted them for the public.

Most oracles were dedicated to Apollo. Some were dedicated to Zeus or other gods. One famous oracle of Zeus was in a grove of oak trees in Dodona in northwestern Greece. The people believed that Zeus spoke through the rustling of the oak leaves. The priests at Dodona interpreted these rustlings. Other important oracles were in Italy, Libya, and Syria.   John Hamilton

See also **Delphi.**

Oraibi. See **Hopi Indians.**

Oral surgery. See **Dentistry.**

Oran, *oh RAN* or *aw RAHN* (pop. 705,335), is a Mediterranean seaport in Algeria. It lies about 225 miles (362

kilometers) west of Algiers. For the location of Oran, see **Algeria** (map).

Oran trades with cities of inland Africa and ports of southern Europe. It was founded by Muslim sailors from Spain in the A.D. 900's. The city was captured by the Spaniards in 1509, by the Ottomans in 1708, and again by the Spaniards in 1732. Spain abandoned Oran after much of it was destroyed in 1791 by an earthquake. The Santa Cruz fort, built by the Spaniards between 1698 and 1708, still overlooks the city from a nearby hill. In 1831, the French occupied Oran. During World War II (1939-1945), Allied forces landed near Oran as part of the campaign to drive the Axis powers from North Africa.

Kenneth J. Perkins

Orange. See **Color.**

Orange is a popular citrus fruit enjoyed throughout the world. Oranges are valued for their delicious juice and high vitamin C content. They are an excellent source of potassium. They also contain thiamine and folic acid.

About 72 million tons (65 million metric tons) of oranges are harvested throughout the world each year. Brazil is the world's leading orange-producing nation.

In the United States, more than 9 million tons (8 million metric tons) of oranges are harvested yearly. More oranges are harvested than any other fruit. Florida produces about 80 percent of the U.S. crop. California grows most of the rest.

About 80 percent of the oranges grown in the United States are processed into juice. Small amounts of oranges are used for making baked goods, candy, marmalade, soft drinks, and other food products. Most of the remaining orange crop is sold as fresh fruit. The orange peel, pulp, and *rag* (core and membranes) are used primarily as cattle feed supplements.

There are several types of oranges. The most popular is the sweet orange. Oranges vary in shape from round to oval. When ripe, the peel ranges from pink to orange to dark red in color. Oranges grow best in regions with warm summers and cool winters. The temperatures should not usually go below freezing. Freezing temperatures can damage the tree and the fruit.

The fruit and the tree

The orange is a type of berry called a *hesperidium.* The peel consists of two layers. There is a colored outer layer called the *flavedo.* Under the outer layer is a white, spongy inner layer known as the *albedo.* The flavedo contains tiny glands that hold a mixture of aromatic oils. The edible interior of the orange consists of 10 to 15 segments. The segments surround a spongy core. The segments contain many *juice sacs.* The sacs hold the juice and make up the pulp of the orange. The segments of some varieties of oranges also contain seeds. Other varieties of oranges are seedless.

The orange tree has dark green leaves. In the spring, it has beautiful, white, fragrant flowers. Orange flowers do not require pollination by bees or other animals to produce fruit. The fruits are the ovaries of the flowers. Some varieties of oranges may be harvested within 7 months after the flowers bloom. Others may remain on the tree up to 16 months. Growers plant different varieties of oranges in the same area so that mature fruit is available during most or all of the year.

Orange trees develop new branches during periods

of rapid growth called *growth flushes*. During these growth flushes, new stems, leaves, and often blossoms appear on the trees. Some of the flowers develop into fruit. The number and timing of growth flushes that occur each year vary according to the climate. There usually are two to five growth flushes per year. In climates like those of Florida and California, growth flushes do not occur during the winter. Instead, a period of vigorous growth takes place in the spring. During the spring growth flush, many flowers appear on the trees and a large number of fruits develop.

Varieties

The word *orange* commonly refers to three types of citrus fruit: sweet oranges, sour or bitter oranges, and mandarins.

Sweet oranges. Growers around the world raise more sweet oranges than any other type of citrus fruit. These oranges have a sweet flavor. They are round to oval in shape. There are four groups of sweet oranges. These are (1) common or round oranges, (2) navel oranges, (3) blood oranges, and (4) acidless oranges.

Common oranges are the most important type of sweet orange. Most oranges sold as fresh fruit are common oranges. In addition, almost all orange juice is made from common oranges. Juice from the Valencia orange, a type of common orange, makes the highest quality juice products. The Valencia is the most popular variety of orange in the world.

Navel oranges have a small secondary fruit within the bottom end of the main fruit. They are seedless and have a pleasant flavor. But they produce less juice than do common oranges. They are best eaten as fresh fruit. California produces most of the U.S. navel-orange crop.

WORLD BOOK illustration by Kate Lloyd-Jones, Linden Artists Ltd.

Oranges are popular citrus fruits that contain delicious juice and large amounts of vitamin C. In the United States, more oranges are harvested yearly than any other type of fruit.

Blood oranges have an unusual color. In other ways, they resemble common oranges. The flesh and peel of blood oranges range in color from light red to dark red. The oranges only become dark red in climates with cool night temperatures. Blood oranges are grown mostly in Mediterranean countries.

Acidless oranges have a low level of acid in their juice. Consequently, they have a bland flavor. Acidless oranges have little commercial value except in Egypt and Brazil.

Sour or bitter oranges generally are not eaten fresh because the flesh has a bitter taste. Sour oranges are widely used in making marmalade. Oils from the peel of some sour oranges and ingredients from the leaves and flowers are used in manufacturing perfume. This variety is often used as an ornamental plant.

Mandarins are a group of fruits that includes true mandarins, tangerines, and various hybrids. Examples of hybrids are tangelos and tangors. Mandarins are not really oranges. However, people often refer to them as oranges because of their orange color. Mandarins taste sweet and are generally eaten fresh. Their peel separates easily from their edible interior. See **Tangelo; Tangerine; Tangor.**

Raising oranges

Planting and caring for orange trees. Most orange trees are grown from buds in special nurseries. A small piece of stem containing a bud is cut from a tree that produces the variety of orange desired. The stem is then grafted to a seedling orange tree called a *rootstock* (see **Grafting** [Other kinds of grafting]). Rootstock varieties are selected for their ability to produce high-yielding trees. They must also adapt to the local soil and climate, and resist pests and disease. Because oranges are grown from the buds of other orange trees, each new tree is a *clone* (genetic copy). Orange trees are transplanted in groves 6 to 12 months after grafting. They start to bear fruit 2 to 4 years later. A tree may produce oranges for 50 years.

Pests and diseases. Orange trees are attacked by many pests and diseases. Scale insects suck the sap from the fruit, leaves, and twigs. Certain wasps kill these insects. To control scale insects, growers foster the growth of these wasps in orange groves. Two other sucking pests, rust mites and aphids, also damage the leaves. These pests are killed by spraying the trees with pesticides. Nematodes and weevils may attack orange roots. Some insects, such as aphids, may carry serious citrus diseases.

Diseases caused by bacteria weaken or kill orange trees. The bacterial diseases *huanglongbing* (citrus greening) and citrus canker are especially deadly. Diseases caused by viruses, such as tristeza, also are deadly. In addition, such fungal diseases as greasy spot, melanose, and sweet orange scab cause damage. Growers control diseases by using sprays, by planting trees that are resistant, by removing diseased trees, and by other methods.

Harvesting and processing. As oranges mature, the amount of sugar and juice they contain increases. At the same time, their acid content decreases. Oranges and other citrus fruit do not mature further after they have been harvested. They differ from most other fruit in this

Harvesting oranges that are to be sold as fresh fruit involves clipping the ripe fruit by hand. If the oranges are pulled from the trees roughly, they may be damaged.

At a packing house, oranges that are to be sold as fresh fruit are sorted according to grade and size. They are then packed in boxes for shipment to markets.

way. For this reason, growers pick the oranges only when the fruit contains the desired levels of juice, sugar, and acid.

If oranges are pulled from the trees roughly, they may be bruised or damaged. These damaged fruit may be easily attacked by fungal diseases that cause decay. For this reason, oranges to be sold as fresh fruit are carefully harvested from the trees by hand. They are then transported to packing houses in large bins that hold as much as 900 pounds (400 kilograms) of oranges. The oranges are then washed, dried, and graded on their appearance. Next, they are waxed with an edible coating that prevents dehydration and improves their appearance. The oranges are then sized, packed into boxes, and shipped to markets.

Some mature oranges have a partly green peel. They may be treated with ethylene gas to reduce the green color of the peel.

Oranges that are to be sold for processing can be harvested by hand or shaken off the tree using a machine. They are then transported in bulk by truck. If they are processed within a few days, few losses are suffered from bruising or decay. The juice is extracted from the fruit by machine. The juice is then heat-treated to kill microbes and to inactivate enzymes.

History

Oranges are among the oldest cultivated fruits. People have grown oranges for more than 4,000 years. Oranges probably originated in the part of Asia that now includes India, Myanmar, and southwestern China. By the A.D.

800's, Arab traders had introduced oranges into eastern Africa and the Middle East. In the 1400's, Portuguese explorers carried oranges from India to Europe. The Italian explorer Christopher Columbus brought orange seeds

Leading orange-growing countries

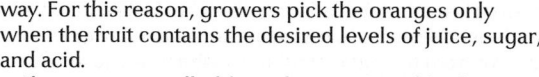

Tons of oranges produced in a year

Brazil — 20,248,000 tons (18,369,000 metric tons)
United States — 9,062,000 tons (8,221,000 metric tons)
Mexico — 4,671,000 tons (4,237,000 metric tons)
India — 4,446,000 tons (4,034,000 metric tons)
China — 3,565,000 tons (3,234,000 metric tons)
Spain — 3,492,000 tons (3,168,000 metric tons)
Indonesia — 2,761,000 tons (2,505,000 metric tons)
Iran — 2,609,000 tons (2,367,000 metric tons)
Italy — 2,598,000 tons (2,357,000 metric tons)
Egypt — 2,320,000 tons (2,104,000 metric tons)

Figures are for a three-year average, 2006-2008.
Source: FAOSTAT, Statistics Division, Food and Agriculture Organization of the UN http://www.faostat.fao.org. Data accessed in 2010.

to America in 1493. During the 1500's, European settlers planted orange trees in Florida and Brazil. The first orange groves in California were established by Spanish missionaries in the late 1700's. The major varieties of oranges grown today were selected during the 1800's and early 1900's.

The orange industry has grown rapidly since the early 1900's. At that time, oranges were rare and expensive. Many people ate them only as a treat on holidays. Today, because of improved growing methods and other factors, most people can afford oranges and orange juice throughout the year. Glenn C. Wright

Scientific classification. Sweet oranges are *Citrus sinensis.* Sour oranges are *Citrus aurantium.* Mandarins are the fruits of several species and their hybrids. True mandarins belong to the species *Citrus reticulata.*

Orange Free State is a historic region in South Africa. Before Europeans conquered the area in the 1830's, most of its inhabitants were black Africans of the Sotho group. About 1836, Boers (people of mainly Dutch ancestry) from Cape Colony settled the region. The Boers named the area the Orange Free State in 1854.

In 1899, disagreements between the Boers and the British led to the Anglo-Boer War of 1899-1902. The Boers were defeated. In 1910, the Orange Free State became one of the four provinces of the Union of South Africa (now the Republic of South Africa). In 1994, South Africa increased the number of its provinces to nine. The Orange Free State remained a province, but the province's name was changed to the Free State in 1995.

The Free State covers 49,866 square miles (129,152 square kilometers). Black Africans make up a large majority of the province's population, but white people of European descent own nearly all the land. Most of the black Africans work for white farmers or in gold and uranium mines in the northern part of the province. Bloemfontein is the capital of the Free State and the judicial capital of South Africa. Bruce Fetter

See also **Afrikaners; Anglo-Boer Wars; Bloemfontein.**

Orange Order is a Protestant organization in Northern Ireland. It seeks to keep Protestants in power in Northern Ireland and maintain Northern Ireland's union with the United Kingdom. The Orange Order was founded in 1795 by Anglican Protestant farmers in County Armagh, Ireland, in what is now the southern part of Northern Ireland. It grew out of a conflict between Protestant and Roman Catholic farmers who were bidding to become tenants on the same farmlands. The Protestants joined together to drive Catholic families out of the region.

The organization was named for William of Orange. William was the Protestant leader of the Netherlands who, in 1688, helped overthrow James II, the Catholic king of England, Scotland, and Ireland.

The Orange Order of Northern Ireland is organized into units called *lodges.* The members, called *Orangemen,* parade through Protestant and Catholic neighborhoods during the "marching season," lasting from spring to early fall. They sing and carry banners to celebrate past Protestant victories over Catholics. Paul E. Gallis

Orange River is the longest river in South Africa. It flows westward across the southern part of the African continent (see **South Africa** [terrain map]). Sandbars and shallow waters make the Orange River useless for navi-

gation. However, the river serves as an important source of hydroelectric power and provides much-needed water for irrigation projects. In some areas, the gravel of the river contains diamond deposits.

The Orange River rises in the mountains of Lesotho and flows into South Africa. It winds west and northwest for about 1,400 miles (2,300 kilometers). It empties into the South Atlantic Ocean at Alexander Bay. The upper river separates Northern Cape and Eastern Cape provinces from the Free State province. The river then flows across the plateaus of central South Africa to the town of Prieska. From Prieska to the Augrabies Falls, the river's elevation drops steadily. The lower course of the river stretches from the Augrabies Falls to the western coast, flowing through rugged desert country. The lower section separates Northern Cape province and Namibia.

Much of the Orange River is narrow, with deep gorges. A large sand bar blocks the mouth of the river and prevents passage by seagoing ships. The river has two major branches, the Vaal and Caledon rivers.

The Orange River was named in honor of the Dutch Prince of Orange in the late 1700's. Robert J. Gordon, a Dutch military commander in South Africa, chose the name. Africans who lived in the area had called the river the Gariep. During the 1860's, diamonds were discovered along the river's course. In 1962, the South African government announced a development plan for the Orange River. Since then, the government has built dams on the river to provide hydroelectric power. It has also built canals and tunnels to irrigate nearby land and to provide flood control. Hartmut S. Walter

Orange roughy. See Roughy.

Orangutan, *oh RANG u tan,* is a large, red-haired ape that lives in the tropical rain forests on the islands of Borneo and Sumatra in Southeast Asia. Larger male orangutans stand about 4 ½ feet (140 centimeters) tall and weigh about 180 pounds (80 kilograms). Mature males usually have broad cheek pads called *flanges* that jut out from the sides of the face. Females are about half as large as males. They have no cheek pads.

Orangutans are the largest tree-dwelling mammals. They are well adapted to life in the trees. An orangutan's arms are extremely long compared with its legs and upper body, reaching to its ankles when the animal stands upright. Orangutans also have long, curved fingers and toes that help them grasp branches, making them excellent climbers. They eat and sleep high in the treetops and rarely come to the ground.

Orangutans prefer to eat ripe fruits. Figs are an important part of their diet, especially at certain times of the year. When fruit is scarce, they also eat leaves, bark, and occasionally insects and meat. Like other apes, orangutans are highly intelligent. They build nests of woven branches for resting and sleeping. They also make simple tools from sticks and leaves. They use these tools as probes, sponges, and umbrellas.

Orangutans are generally less social than other apes. Adults live far apart in the forest and usually avoid one another. Males and females may spend several days together when they mate, but they soon part. Females usually produce one infant every seven to nine years. Males do not care for infants. Offspring remain with their mother for six years or more. Orangutans live about 40 years in the wild.

A male and female orangutan have different physical features. The mature male, *right,* has broad cheek pads and a large throat pouch. He is about twice as big as the female, *left,* who has no cheek pads.

Orangutans once lived throughout southern China and Southeast Asia. Today, they live on only two islands and are in danger of becoming extinct. The chief threats to orangutans include deforestation and hunting. Some local people hunt orangutans for their meat. But most hunting is of females to collect their babies for sale as pets. Laws protect the remaining orangutans and preserve their habitat. However, these laws are rarely enforced.   Andrew J. Marshall

Scientific classification. The scientific name of the Bornean orangutan is *Pongo pygmaeus.* The Sumatran orangutan is *Pongo abelli.*

See also **Ape.**

Oratorio is a dramatic vocal composition usually based on a religious story. Oratorios resemble operas. Both tell a story and are performed by solo singers, a chorus, and an orchestra. The main difference is that oratorios have no acting, costumes, or scenery. Most oratorios are presented in concert halls or in churches.

In oratorios, soloists often portray specific characters, and the chorus usually is an important element. Although there is no acting or scenery, such theatrical effects as fires and storms can be suggested by the music. Many oratorios have a narrator who introduces the story and supplies details.

Oratorios developed from musical settings of religious texts. The form as it is known today emerged in Rome in the mid-1500's. The most important period of oratorio composition was the 1600's and 1700's. The German-born composer George Frideric Handel was the greatest composer of oratorios. His *Messiah* (1742) is the most famous oratorio ever written. Amateur and professional groups, especially in the United States and the United Kingdom, still perform oratorios regularly.

Katherine K. Preston

See also **Cantata; Handel, George Frideric.**

Oratory is the art of eloquent speaking. An *orator* is a speaker who tries to persuade listeners by logical arguments and emotional appeals to their feelings. An *oration* is a speech that uses principles of *rhetoric* (the art of using words for persuasion). An oration, unlike a public speech, has a formal style and includes similes, metaphors, and other figures of speech.

Beginnings. A mass of lawsuits arose when a democracy was established in Syracuse in Sicily in 466 B.C. They were brought by former exiles whose property had been seized by the tyrants. Many claims were several years old, and documentary evidence was often lacking. The claimants needed help in presenting their cases. Corax, a Sicilian Greek, was the first to supply this help, and is considered the founder of oratory. He established a system of rules for public speaking in the 460's B.C., with the aid of his pupil Tisias.

Corax said that a speech usually should have five parts. He described these parts as (1) *proem* (introduction); (2) narrative; (3) arguments; (4) subsidiary remarks; and (5) summary.

Other early teachers of rhetoric include Protagoras, who developed the principles of debate; Gorgias, who emphasized style; Hippias, who was chiefly interested in the use of memory; and Lysias, who "showed how perfect elegance could be joined to plainness."

The study of speechmaking spread to Athens. During the 400's B.C., almost all male Athenian citizens attended the general assembly, where public policies were debated. The citizens took part in the formulation of policies and the administration of justice. In the courts, they acted as jurors. The decision in each case rested with the jury, because there were no judges. Those who brought the charges and those who defended themselves pleaded their own cases. This practice led to a study of speechmaking.

Classical orators. The first great Greek orator was Pericles. His speeches were reported by Thucydides in his famous *History of the Peloponnesian War*. Pericles's Funeral Oration is his best-known speech. The greatest Greek orator was Demosthenes. He is best known for his *Philippics*, speeches in which he attacked Philip II of Macedonia as a threat to Greek independence.

The outstanding Greek writer on rhetoric was Aristotle. He defined rhetoric as "the faculty of discovering in every case the available means of persuasion." Aristotle emphasized three methods of proof: (1) *ethical* (the influence of the speaker's personality); (2) *pathetic* (the influence of the speaker's use of emotional appeal); and (3) *logical* (the influence of the use of formal principles of reasoning in proof).

Cicero holds first place among the important early Roman orators. Authorities believe that the *Rhetorica ad Herennium* was written by Cicero about 86 B.C. It states that an orator must divide the preparation of a speech into five steps. These steps are: (1) *invention* (analysis of speech situation and audience, investigation and study of subject matter, and selection of speech materials); (2) *disposition* (the arrangement of the speech materials under what we now call introduction, discussion, and conclusion); (3) *style* (the use and grouping of words to express ideas clearly, accurately, vividly, and appropriately); (4) *memory* (methods of memorizing material); and (5) *delivery* (the oral presentation).

Book I of Cicero's *De Oratore*, written about 55 B.C., develops the theme that a great orator must be a person of great learning and that the "proper concern of an orator ... is language of power and elegance accommodated to the feelings and understandings of mankind." Book II emphasizes the importance of invention and disposition, with particular attention to court oratory. Book III deals with style and delivery.

Institutio Oratorio (The Training of an Orator), written by Quintilian about A.D. 90, was a complete manual for the training of public speakers. Even today, it is one of the most comprehensive works on training speakers.

Later orators. With the coming of Christianity, the preacher replaced the political speaker. Famous early preachers include Paul, John Chrysostom, and Augustine. Outstanding speakers for religious reform were Savonarola in the late 1400's and Martin Luther and John Calvin during the Reformation in the 1500's.

Political oratory again became important in the 1700's. During the French Revolution (1789-1799), Comte de Mirabeau spoke for the common people fighting royal authority. The United Kingdom has produced many distinguished speakers. They include Edmund Burke, Benjamin Disraeli, William Gladstone, and Winston Churchill. American orators include Patrick Henry, John C. Calhoun, Daniel Webster, Stephen A. Douglas, and William Jennings Bryan.   James M. Copeland

Related articles in *World Book* include:

Famous American orators

Adams, John Q.	Everett, Edward
Bryan, William J.	Grady, Henry W.
Clay, Henry	Hamilton, Alexander
Dickinson, Anna E.	Henry, Patrick
Dirksen, Everett M.	Kennedy, John F.
Douglas, Stephen A.	King, Martin L., Jr.
Douglass, Frederick	Lincoln, Abraham
Phillips, Wendell	Sumner, Charles
Roosevelt, Franklin D.	Webster, Daniel
Rutledge, John	

Other orators

Burke, Edmund	Mirabeau, Comte de
Chrysostom, Saint John	Pericles
Churchill, Sir Winston	Pitt, William
Cicero, Marcus Tullius	Pitt, William the Younger
Demosthenes	Quintilian
Lysias	

Orbit, in astronomy, is the path of an object whose motion is influenced by the gravitational attraction of another object. Often, *orbit* refers to the nearly circular path maintained by an object under the gravitational pull of a much larger object. The larger object is often called the *primary,* and the smaller one is the *secondary.* For example, Earth is a secondary orbiting the sun, its primary.

No secondary known to scientists orbits in a perfect circle. Instead, most orbits form a closed curve called an *ellipse.* In an elliptical orbit, the primary is not in the exact center. As a result, the distance from primary to secondary varies along the orbit. A secondary of Earth is nearest to Earth at a point called *perigee.* It is farthest at

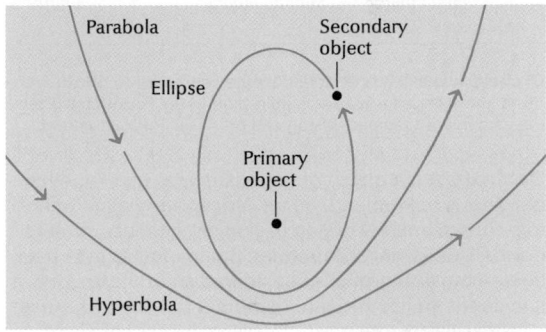

WORLD BOOK diagram

The shape of the orbit taken by a *secondary* object around a *primary* object may be an ellipse, parabola, or hyperbola, as shown here. It is determined by the speed of the secondary in relation to the speed required to escape from the primary.

apogee. For a secondary of the sun, the nearest point is called *perihelion,* and the farthest point is *aphelion.*

A secondary is often described as if orbiting a *fixed* (motionless) primary. In actuality, both objects orbit a common *center of mass,* the point where their masses would balance. If the difference in mass is great, the center of mass lies close to the primary, so the primary appears not to move. If the masses are similar, however, the objects appear to orbit a point between them.

A secondary may gain enough speed to escape the pull of its primary, called *escape velocity.* Its orbit then becomes an open curve called a *parabola.* If a secondary moves faster than escape velocity, its orbit is a broader curve, called a *hyperbola.* Spacecraft leaving Earth orbit travel a hyperbolic path.   Edward Belbruno

See also **Ellipse; Planet** (Orbits); **Satellite, Artificial** (Satellite orbits).

Orbiting observatory. See Satellite, Artificial.
Orca. See Killer whale.
Orchard. See Fruit; Horticulture.

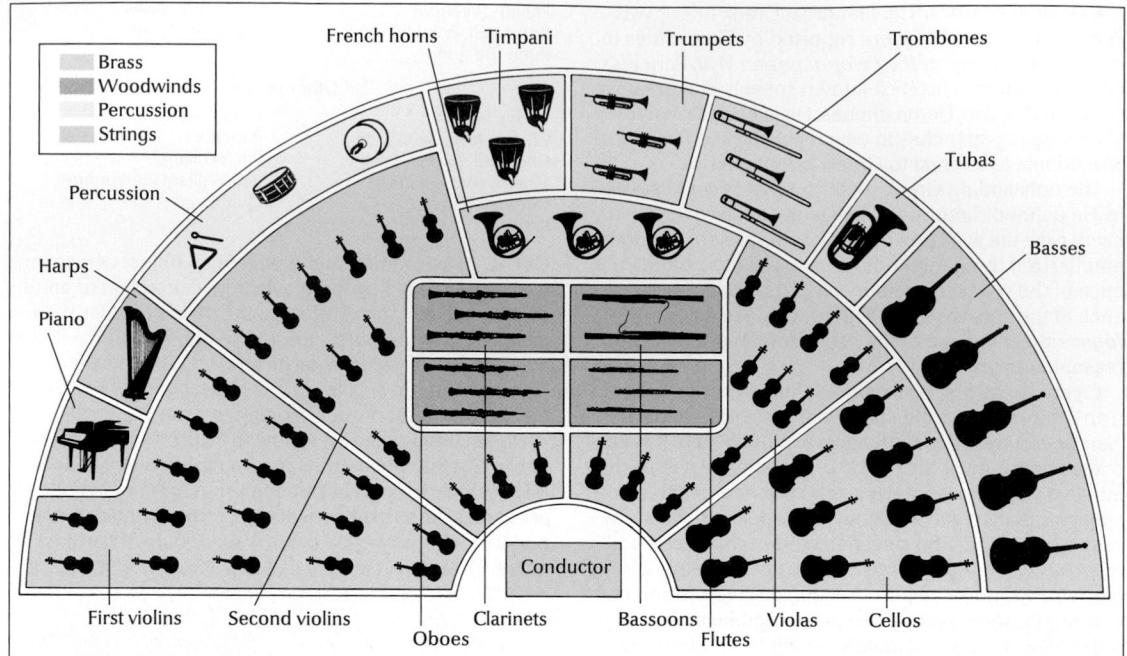

French horns | Timpani | Trumpets | Trombones

Brass
Woodwinds
Percussion
Strings

Tubas

Percussion

Basses

Harps

Piano

Conductor

First violins | Second violins | Clarinets | Bassoons | Violas | Cellos
Oboes | Flutes

WORLD BOOK illustration by Linda Kinnaman

Orchestra seating is designed by the conductor to produce a certain blend of sounds. In this diagram, the strings form a semicircle around the conductor. The woodwind instruments are arranged in the center, with the percussion and brass sections at the rear.

Orchestra is a group of musicians who play together on various instruments. Some African and Asian orchestras consist entirely of percussion instruments, such as drums, gongs, and xylophones. But in most Western nations, a musical group is considered an orchestra only if it includes violins and other stringed instruments. An orchestra differs from a band, which consists chiefly of wind and percussion instruments.

Some orchestras, called *string orchestras,* have only stringed instruments. On the other hand, *dance orchestras* resemble bands in most ways but may include a small string section. The word *orchestra* generally refers to a *symphony orchestra,* which consists mainly of stringed instruments. Symphony orchestras also have woodwind, brass, and percussion instruments, which enable them to produce a full range of musical sounds.

Symphony orchestras play all types of music, but most of them specialize in classical works. An orchestra may perform alone, or it may accompany one or more instrumental or vocal soloists or a chorus. Orchestras also accompany ballets and operas and provide background music for motion pictures and television productions.

Some symphony orchestras are made up entirely of professional musicians. Most of the world's major cities have a professional symphony, and some cities have several. They include such large, well-known orchestras as the Berlin Philharmonic, the Boston Symphony, the Chicago Symphony, the London Symphony, the New York Philharmonic, the Philadelphia Orchestra, and the Vienna Philharmonic. Many smaller communities, especially in Western countries, also have a symphony orchestra. These orchestras consist chiefly of amateur musicians. Many schools in Western countries have student orchestras.

The structure of a symphony orchestra

Orchestral music is written in the form of a *score,* which shows the notes to be played by each instrument. Most scores call for about the same kinds of instruments, and so most orchestras have a similar structure. A typical orchestra has about 20 kinds of instruments, but the number of each varies among different groups. A large orchestra may have more than 100 musicians, and small orchestras have from about 15 to 40 players. The small groups are often called *chamber orchestras.* During a performance, only the conductor follows the complete score. The printed music used by the musicians shows only their individual parts.

The musicians are divided into four main groups called *sections:* (1) the string section, (2) the woodwind section, (3) the brass section, and (4) the percussion section. The various instruments in the string, woodwind, and brass sections are pitched in different ranges, like the voices in a chorus. In the following discussion, the instruments in each of these sections are listed in order from those of the highest range to those of the lowest. Some percussion instruments are also tuned to definite pitches, but most of them have an indefinite pitch.

The string section is the heart of a symphony orchestra. It has more than half the musicians and consists of from 20 to 32 violins, 8 to 10 violas, 8 to 10 cellos, and 6 to 10 string basses. The violinists are divided into two groups of equal size. The *first violins* play the highest-pitched part in the string section, and the *second violins* play the next highest part. The leading first violinist

The Saint Paul Chamber Orchestra

Chicago Symphony Orchestra (Jim Steere)

An orchestra, also called a *symphony orchestra, above,* consists chiefly of stringed instruments. A typical symphony orchestra also includes woodwind, brass, and percussion instruments. This type of orchestra may have more than 100 musicians. A small orchestra, *top,* often called a chamber orchestra, normally has about 15 to 40 musicians.

serves as *concertmaster* of the orchestra. The concertmaster directs the other musicians in tuning their instruments and may also be the orchestra's assistant conductor.

The woodwind section consists chiefly of flutes, oboes, clarinets, and bassoons. An orchestra has from 2 to 4 of each of these instruments. The musicians in the section also play various other woodwind instruments when a score requires them to do so. For example, a flutist may switch to the piccolo, and an oboe player may double on the English horn.

The brass section consists of 2 to 5 trumpets, 2 to 8 French horns, 2 to 4 trombones, and 1 tuba.

The percussion section includes two or more *timpani,* or kettle drums; bells and cymbals; wood blocks; and a bass drum, gong, snare drum, triangle, tambourine, and xylophone.

Other instruments are added to an orchestra if a score calls for them. They include such instruments as the harp, harpsichord, organ, piano, synthesizer, and various saxophones.

The conductor directs the musicians by keeping time with the baton or with his or her hands, and by means of gestures and facial expressions. However, conductors do their most important work before a performance—and even before rehearsing a composition. In

most cases, the conductor selects the music to be played at a concert. After selecting a work, the conductor's first job is to *interpret* the music by deciding exactly how it should be played. Interpretation of a work includes such elements as tempo, tonal quality, and phrasing. After determining these features of the score, the conductor rehearses the music with the players.

During a rehearsal, the conductor asks individual musicians or sections to play various parts of the score again and again until the desired effect has been achieved. He or she strives for the correct balance among the many instruments playing at the same time and adjusts the sound to suit the acoustics of the performance hall. The finest conductors are respected not only for their musical skill but also for their ability to inspire both musicians and audiences.

Most conductors also help audition musicians who apply for positions in an orchestra. A conductor listens to the applicants perform and then recommends who should be invited to join.

Orchestra management. Most major orchestras in the United States are operated by private, nonprofit corporations called *symphony societies.* The chief concern of a symphony society is to raise funds to help support the orchestra. The board of directors of the society also acts on the conductor's recommendations regarding

Orchestras of the 1700's performed in the homes of wealthy patrons. This painting from about 1775 shows a typical orchestra of the time. The performers gather around an early keyboard instrument called a *harpsichord.*

musicians to be offered positions in the orchestra.

Most professional orchestras have a business manager to handle most of the administrative work. The business manager works out the orchestra's budget; prepares employment contracts; plans rehearsal, concert, and recording schedules; and organizes ticket sales and publicity.

History

The term *orchestra* was first used by the ancient Greeks for the front area of a stage. During the Middle Ages, *orchestra* came to mean the musicians on that part of the stage. In modern times, *orchestra* has come to mean both the musicians on stage and the seats directly in front of the stage.

Beginnings. The first orchestras were organized at the royal court of France and in Italian churches and palaces during the late 1500's and the 1600's. At first, orchestras served chiefly to accompany social dances, ballets, religious vocal music, and operas. Most of these orchestras consisted mainly of string instruments. In Germany, wind instruments were also popular. Except in France, these orchestras had no standard structure. String, wind, and percussion instruments were often mixed. The orchestra of King Louis XIII of France was the first standardized orchestra. It had 24 instruments of the violin family, divided into five sections, and 12 wind instruments. Beginning in the 1600's, most orchestras also played a bass line called a *basso continuo,* usually with a lute, harp, organ, or harpsichord.

The 1700's and 1800's. By the early 1700's, some European composers also began to write music for orchestra in its own right. These composers included Johann Sebastian Bach, Arcangelo Corelli, George Frideric Handel, and Antonio Vivaldi. Their compositions were called *concerti, concerti grossi, overtures,* and *suites.*

Orchestral works called *symphonies* first appeared as overtures or small instrumental interludes in operas about 1600. By the 1720's and 1730's Giovanni Battista Sammartini began to write independent string symphonies in Italy. In the late 1700's, Joseph Haydn and Wolfgang Mozart perfected the *classical symphony.* The clarinet became standard in the symphony orchestra in the 1790's. In the early 1800's, Ludwig van Beethoven composed the first symphonies that included trombones and voices.

During the 1800's, cities began to take over patronage of orchestras. Many orchestras were regularly engaged in accompanying operas in municipal opera houses and also played concerts on the side. A few, however, were established independently of the opera. The Gewandhaus Orchestra of Leipzig, Germany, is the oldest orchestra still playing. It was founded in 1781. The Paris Conservatory Orchestra was established in 1800, and what is now the Royal Philharmonic Society was founded in 1813.

Until the early 1800's, orchestras were small enough to perform without a conductor. The concertmaster or a keyboard player in the basso continuo served as the leader. By 1830, orchestras had grown so large that nearly all were led by a conductor. Composers Hector Berlioz and Felix Mendelssohn were among the earliest conductors. Berlioz was one of the first to conduct with a baton.

Popular types of orchestral music in the 1800's included symphonies, overtures, symphonic poems, and concertos. Orchestras also continued to accompany opera, ballet, and religious music. In the late 1800's and early 1900's, such composers as Richard Wagner, Anton Bruckner, Gustav Mahler, and Richard Strauss wrote works for orchestras of 100 or more musicians.

Modern orchestras. Since the early 1900's, there has been renewed interest in works for smaller orchestras. Some composers have added electronic instruments or reorganized the orchestra into groups to create new kinds of musical sounds. Today, most large orchestras have several conductors on their staffs.

The symphony orchestra originated in Europe, but its form has been copied throughout the world. There are now many symphony orchestras in non-European countries including Argentina, Australia, Brazil, China, Israel, Japan, and Mexico. The first orchestras in the United

Thomas D. W. Friedmann, Photo Researchers

An Indonesian orchestra includes double-ended drums and xylophonelike instruments called *gambangs.* These musicians are playing at a religious festival.

States were formed in the late 1700's. The oldest American orchestra still performing is the student orchestra at Harvard University, which was formed in 1808. Important orchestras in the United States include the New York Philharmonic (1842), the Boston Symphony Orchestra (1881), the Chicago Symphony Orchestra (1891), and the Philadelphia Orchestra (1900).

The cost of maintaining an orchestra has increased dramatically since the mid-1900's. The income from ticket sales pays only a fraction of an orchestra's expenses. Many European orchestras rely heavily on funds that they receive from government sources. In the United States, many orchestras receive additional funds from both private and public sources and from recording royalties. Organizations such as the National Endowment for the Arts, an independent federal agency, distribute funds to symphony societies. Some orchestras have sought other sources of funding in new types of programming. For example, these orchestras have provided background music for movies, radio, and videos.

John H. Baron

Related articles in *World Book* include:

Conductors

Abbado, Claudio	Masur, Kurt
Ashkenazy, Vladimir	Mehta, Zubin
Barbirolli, Sir John	Mendelssohn, Felix
Barenboim, Daniel	Mitropoulos, Dimitri
Beecham, Sir Thomas	Monteux, Pierre
Bernstein, Leonard	Ormandy, Eugene
Boulez, Pierre	Ozawa, Seiji
Caldwell, Sarah	Previn, André
Damrosch, Leopold	Rostropovich, Mstislav
Damrosch, Walter	Solti, Sir Georg
Johannes	Stokowski, Leopold
Fiedler, Arthur	Strauss, Johann, Jr.
Furtwängler, Wilhelm	Strauss, Johann, Sr.
Karajan, Herbert von	Strauss, Richard
Klemperer, Otto	Szell, George
Koussevitzky, Serge	Toscanini, Arturo
Levine, James	Wagner, Richard
Maazel, Lorin	Walter, Bruno
Mahler, Gustav	Zukerman, Pinchas

Other related articles

Band	Concerto	Symphonic poem
Chamber music	Jazz	Symphony
Classical music (Orchestral music)	Opera (The orchestra)	

Additional resources

Ganeri, Anita. *The Young Person's Guide to the Orchestra.* Harcourt, 1996. Includes compact disc. Younger readers.
Lawson, Colin, ed. *The Cambridge Companion to the Orchestra.* Cambridge, 2003.

Orchestra bells imitate the effect of authentic cast bronze bells. The two types of orchestra bells are tubular chimes and metal bars. The chimes are usually from 1 to 2 inches (2.5 to 5.1 centimeters) in diameter and vary in length with the pitch. They are hung from a metal frame, and are struck with heavy leather-headed mallets. Their sound is deep and resonant. The metal bars are of varying sizes, usually not more than ½ inch (13 millimeters) in thickness, and are arranged in rows much like the piano keyboard. They are struck with a hard mallet, and produce a ringing sound, more brilliant and higher pitched than that of the tubular, hanging chimes.

John H. Beck

See also **Glockenspiel; Xylophone.**

Orchid, *AWR kihd,* is any of an extremely large family of plants, many of which bear beautiful flowers. There are thousands of *species* (kinds) of these plants. They are widely cultivated as house, garden, and greenhouse flowers, and they also grow wild. Orchids are *perennials,* which means the plants live for at least three years.

Orchids range in size from small plants only ¼ inch (0.6 centimeter) high to vines as much as 100 feet (30 meters) long. The flowers come in all colors except black, and they may be speckled or streaked.

Wild orchids grow in all parts of the world except Antarctica. They are most abundant in regions with plentiful rainfall. Most species grow on the trunks and branches of trees, or on rocks, in warm or tropical areas. Wild orchids that live in cooler regions grow on the ground. Some species even inhabit desert regions. The Australian *underground orchids* live below the surface of the soil in order to conserve water.

Parts of orchids. Like lilies, orchids have three inner petals and three outer, petallike *sepals.* However, unlike lilies, orchids have a central petal that is usually larger and more showy than the other petals. This petal is called the *lip* or *labellum.* It may look like a cup, a scoop, a trumpet, or a bag. Among most orchids, each flower has one *stamen* (male part) and one *pistil* (female part) at its center. The stamen bears pollen grains, which usually occur in large clusters called *pollinia.* The pollen produces sperm cells, while the pistil contains egg cells. Among these orchids, the stamen and the pistil are joined, forming a *column.*

How orchids reproduce. Most orchids reproduce by *cross-pollination.* In this process, an insect, a bat, or a bird carries pollen from the stamen of one flower to the pistil of a flower of another plant. An orchid's fragrance and the size and shape of its blossoms may attract certain kinds of insects or birds. For example, many orchids look or smell like bees, attracting bees to the flowers.

After pollination occurs, sperm cells unite with egg cells in the pistil and seeds develop. Orchid seeds are so tiny that they need the help of certain types of fungi

Some kinds of orchids

As many as 20,000 species of orchids grow in most parts of the world. These beautiful flowers have a wide variety of shapes and colors. Some of the orchids shown below grow in various countries and have no common name in English. The scientific name is given for such flowers.

Jim Annan

Christmas orchid

Loren McIntyre, Woodfin Camp, Inc.

Star orchid

E. S. Ross

Corcium nigrescens

Harold Hungerford

Boat orchid

Lynn M. Stone, NAS

Epidendrum oncidioides

M. P. L. Fogden, Bruce Coleman Inc.

Scorpion orchid

C. B. Sharp, Van Cleve Photography

Moth orchid

Bill Noel Kleeman, Tom Stack & Associates

Semi-terete hybrid orchid

to begin their growth. These fungi supply the seeds with various substances needed for growth.

Kinds of orchids. Most botanists divide orchids into three groups, according to the number of stamens and the form of the column in the flower. The largest group of orchids—the vast majority of all species—have flowers with a completely joined column that typically contains one stamen. This group includes the vinelike *vanilla orchids,* which grow in Mexico and throughout the tropics. Vanilla, a flavoring in many foods and beverages, occurs naturally in these orchids (see **Vanilla**).

Species with two stamens almost completely joined in the column make up a group called *lady's-slipper orchids* (see **Lady's-slipper**). A third group consists of orchids with two or three stamens that are at most only partly joined in the column. Margaret R. Bolick

Scientific classification. Orchids make up the orchid family, Orchidaceae.

See also **Flower** (pictures: The fly orchid; Clamshell orchid); **Root** (picture: Specialized roots).

Orcus. See Pluto.

Orczy, *AWRT see,* **Baroness** (1865-1947), was a Hungarian-born English author known chiefly for her adventure-filled novels and detective stories. She also wrote several plays.

Orczy's most famous novel, *The Scarlet Pimpernel* (1905), is set during the French Revolution (1789-1799). The hero, an English aristocrat named Sir Percy Blakeney, appears to be an idle, useless person. But, as the mysterious Scarlet Pimpernel, he gallantly rescues aristocrats who have been sentenced to death. This character also appears in 12 other novels.

Orczy created several detectives in short stories. For example, the nameless Old Man in the Corner solves baffling crimes as he sits in a corner of a London tea shop, knotting and unknotting a piece of string. He appears in the story collection *The Old Man in the Corner* (1909). Another detective, Lady Molly Robertson-Kirk, one of the first female detectives, is featured in the collection *Lady Molly of Scotland Yard* (1910).

Baroness Emmuska Orczy was born on Sept. 23, 1865, in Tarnaörs, Hungary, near Jászberény. Her family moved to London when she was 15. She died on Nov. 12, 1947. David Geherin

Order is a unit of scientific classification. Living things are divided into groups called kingdoms; phyla, or divisions; classes; orders; families; genera; and species. Members of an order are more closely related than are members of a class. But members of orders are not so closely related as are members of families. See also **Classification, Scientific** (table). Theodore J. Crovello

Order in Council is a decree issued by the British Crown when a matter of great importance confronts the nation. Orders in Council get their name from the fact that they are proclaimed with the advice of the Privy Council. In 1807, the United Kingdom issued Orders in Council in answer to the French military leader Napoleon's threat to blockade the island empire. By these orders, British ships blockaded the European coast and kept neutral trading vessels from entering ports of Napoleonic Europe. See also **Continental System; Privy Council.** Arthur I. Cyr

Order of . . . See articles on orders listed under their key word, as in **Bath, Order of the.**

Ordered pair. See Algebra (Functions).

Ordinance of 1787. See Northwest Ordinance.

Ordovician Period, *AWR duh VIHSH uhn,* was a time in Earth's history that lasted from around 488 million to 444 million years ago. The period takes its name from the Ordovices, an ancient Celtic tribe that inhabited an area of Wales where rocks of this age are found. Ordovician rocks occur around the world. Examples of such rocks found near Cincinnati are noted for abundant, well-preserved fossils.

During the Ordovician Period, life flourished in Earth's oceans. Some Ordovician animals were the ancestors of common modern groups, such as clams and snails. Most of them, however, belonged to groups that are now extinct or rare. Long-extinct animals that thrived during the Ordovician Period include trilobites and graptolites. *Brachiopods* (lamp shells) and *crinoids* (sea lilies) were plentiful. Primitive jawless fish swam in the oceans. *Orthocone nautiloids* appear to have been the main predators. These sea creatures had narrow, cone-shaped shells and squidlike tentacles on their heads.

During the Ordovician Period, much of the world's land lay in the Southern Hemisphere. The land mass now known as North America lay near the equator. What is today northern Africa sat over the South Pole, with glaciers covering what is now the hot, dry Sahara.

Many creatures died off at the end of the Ordovician Period in the earliest major extinction event in Earth's history. Rapid glacier formation probably caused the extinction. The spreading ice cooled the oceans and trapped much water, lowering sea levels. P. B. Wignall

See also **Earth** (The Paleozoic Era).

Ore is a mineral or rock that contains enough metal to make it worth mining. Ore deposits often occur in cracks of rocks called *veins* and in layers known as *beds.* Ore spread thinly in rock is *disseminated ore.* Worthless minerals mixed in with ore are called *gangue.*

There are two types of ores—*native metals* and *compound ores.* In *native metals,* the valuable mineral occurs as a pure metal. It is not chemically combined with other substances. Gold, silver, platinum, and copper often occur as native metals. In *compound ores,* the valuable metal is joined to other substances, such as oxygen, sulfur, carbon, or silicon, to form chemical compounds. The ores of iron, aluminum, and tin are usually found joined with oxygen in compounds called *oxides.* Copper, lead, zinc, silver, nickel, and mercury are commonly found joined with sulfur in compounds called *sulfides.*

Metal is separated from ore in various ways. In a process called *concentration,* ore is crushed and ground so that metals separate from gangue. Metals can also be freed from ore and purified by *smelting,* in which ore is melted. Some metals can be dissolved out of ore by a process called *leaching.* In the *electrolysis* process, metals are separated by passing an electric current through a solution that contains metal atoms. See **Metallurgy** (Extractive metallurgy). Mark A. Helper

See also **Mineral; Rock.**

Oregano, *uh REHG uh noh* or *awr uh GAH noh,* is a seasoning used in many popular foods, including pizza and spaghetti sauce. Oregano commonly is prepared from the dried leaves of the wild marjoram plant. Oregano has a strong, sweet flavor.

See also **Marjoram.**

Ed Cooper, StockFile

Cannon Beach lies along the rocky Pacific coast in the northern part of Oregon. Oregon's rugged shoreline, scenic mountains, and vast evergreen forests attract millions of tourists every year.

Oregon *The Beaver State*

Oregon, a Pacific Coast state of the United States, is known for its vast forests of evergreen trees. Forests cover almost half of the state, and many Oregon cities have mills that manufacture wood products. Oregon ranks among the leading states in lumber production.

The rugged beauty of Oregon's mountains, seacoast, and forest lands attracts millions of tourists every year. Skiers delight in the heavy snowfall on the state's numerous slopes. Hunters shoot deer and elk and other game in Oregon's wooded regions. People enjoy fishing in the sparkling lakes and rivers, and in Pacific waters.

Oregon is often called the *Pacific Wonderland* because of its outstanding natural wonders. These include Crater Lake in the Cascade Mountains, the Columbia

River Gorge, Hells Canyon on the Snake River, and Oregon Caves National Monument. Mount Hood, Mount Jefferson, and other snow-covered peaks rise majestically in the Cascade Range. The Wallowas, in the northeastern part of the state, also offer spectacular mountain scenery. Steep cliffs rise along much of Oregon's waveswept coast. But parts of the coast have sandy beaches and protected harbors.

The dry lands east of the Cascade Mountains have large livestock ranches. Onions, potatoes, and other vegetables grow in irrigated areas of eastern Oregon. Wheat, Oregon's most valuable food crop, comes chiefly from the north-central area of the state. Orchard fruits, which are also primarily grown in the north-central part of the state, are world famous.

The mighty Columbia River forms most of the boundary between Oregon and Washington. Huge dams on the Columbia supply electric power for homes and industries. The dams also improve the river for shipping and provide water for irrigation.

The contributors of this article are Katrine Barber, Associate Professor of History at Portland State University, and Thomas Harvey, Professor of Geography at Portland State University.

Ed Cooper, StockFile

Vast fields of golden wheat grow in the plateau area of north-central Oregon. Wheat is one of the state's most valuable crops.

Interesting facts about Oregon

WORLD BOOK illustrations by Kevin Chadwick

Lava forest

The world's largest forest of lava-cast trees is on the slopes of Newberry Volcano in Deschutes National Forest, south of Bend. The imprint of pine bark is still visible on the insides of many casts, which were formed about 6,000 years ago when molten lava flowed into a living pine forest. The lava cooled against the tree trunks, which caught fire and burned away, leaving perfect molds. The forest covers about 4 square miles (10 square kilometers).

The first state antilitter law affecting nearly all beverage containers was passed by the Oregon legislature on July 2, 1971, and became effective on Oct. 1, 1972. The "Oregon bottle bill" outlaws pull-tab cans and requires that all beverage cans and most types of bottles be returnable for a cash refund.

The world's smallest official park is on a traffic island on S. W. Front Avenue in Portland. Mill Ends Park is 24 inches (61 centimeters) across and has a total area of 452 square inches (2,916 square centimeters). A Portland journalist, Dick Fagan, created the park on St. Patrick's Day, 1948, as a colony for leprechauns and a site for snail races. It became a city park in 1976.

World's smallest park

The Columbia River was at one time called the Oregon, or *Ouragan,* which means *hurricane* in French. Some authorities think that Oregon's name came from this historic name. Oregon is known as the *Beaver State* because the region supplied thousands of beaver skins during fur-trading days.

In the early days, Oregon meant the end of the trail for a number of pioneers. During the 1840's and 1850's, thousands of settlers traveled by covered wagon on the Oregon Trail to the fertile farmlands of the Willamette Valley.

Today, the Willamette Valley is Oregon's greatest center for trade and industry. It is also important for greenhouse and nursery products, flower bulbs, fruits, milk, seed crops, and vegetables. Most of Oregon's large cities are in the Willamette Valley. They include Portland, the largest city, and Salem, the state capital. Portland extends along both banks of the Willamette River near the place where the Willamette flows into the Columbia. It is an industrial city and a major seaport.

David Falconer, Frazier Photolibrary

Downtown Portland rises along the west bank of the Willamette River near Oregon's northern border. Portland is Oregon's largest city and the state's major center of industry and trade.

Oregon in brief

Symbols of Oregon

The state flag, adopted in 1925, bears elements of the state seal. The seal, adopted in 1859, has 33 stars around a shield to show that Oregon was the 33rd state. The seal includes an ox-drawn wagon to symbolize the settling of the region by pioneers. The reverse side of Oregon's flag, *not shown,* has an illustration of a beaver, the state animal. Oregon is the only state whose flag has a different design on the reverse side.

Oregon Secretary of State's Office
State seal

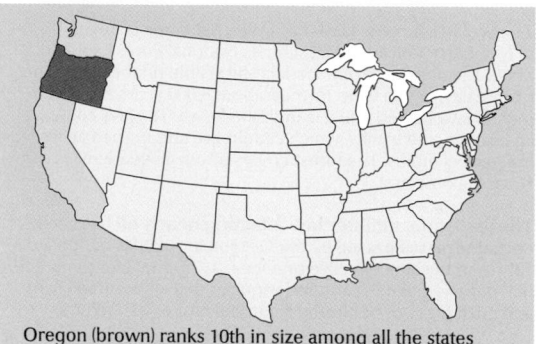

Oregon (brown) ranks 10th in size among all the states and 2nd in size among the Pacific Coast States (yellow).

General information

Statehood: Feb. 14, 1859, the 33rd state.
State abbreviations: Ore. or Oreg. (traditional); OR (postal).
State motto: *She Flies with Her Own Wings.*
State song: "Oregon, My Oregon." Words by J. A. Buchanan; music by Henry B. Murtagh.

The State Capitol is in Salem, the capital since statehood in 1859. Earlier capitals were Oregon City (1849-1851), Salem (1851-1859), and Corvallis (1855, for six months).

Land and climate

Area: 97,047 mi² (251,351 km²), including 1,050 mi² (2,720 km²) of inland water but excluding 80 mi² (207 km²) of coastal water.
Elevation: *Highest*—Mount Hood, 11,239 ft (3,426 m) above sea level. *Lowest*—sea level.
Coastline: 296 mi (476 km).
Record high temperature: 119 °F (48 °C) at Prineville on July 29, 1898, and at Pendleton on Aug. 10, 1898.
Record low temperature: –54 °F (–48 °C) at Ukiah on Feb. 9, 1933, and at Seneca on Feb. 10, 1933.
Average July temperature: 66 °F (19 °C).
Average January temperature: 32 °F (0 °C).
Average yearly precipitation: 28 in (71 cm).

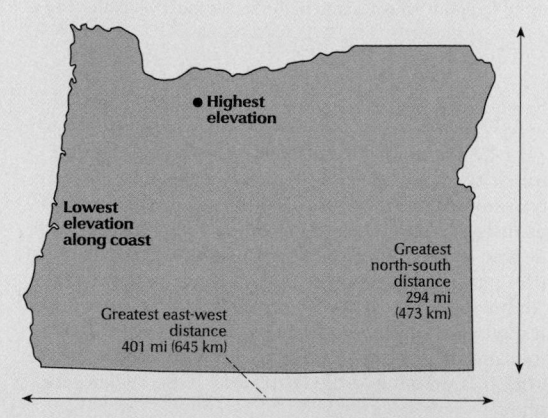

Highest elevation

Lowest elevation along coast

Greatest north-south distance 294 mi (473 km)

Greatest east-west distance 401 mi (645 km)

Important dates

John Jacob Astor's Pacific Fur Company founded Astoria.

A treaty between the United States and Spain fixed the present southern border of Oregon.

| 1792 | 1811 | 1818 | 1819 |

Robert Gray sailed into the Columbia River.

A treaty between the United States and the United Kingdom allowed citizens of both countries to occupy the Oregon region.

State bird
Western meadowlark

State flower
Oregon grape

State tree
Douglas-fir

People

Population: 3,831,074
Rank among the states: 27th
Density: 39 per mi² (15 per km²), U.S. average 85 per mi² (33 per km²)
Distribution: 79 percent urban, 21 percent rural
Largest cities in Oregon

Portland	583,776
Eugene	156,185
Salem	154,637
Gresham	105,594
Hillsboro	91,611
Beaverton	89,803

Source: 2010 census, except for distribution, which is for 2000.

Population trend

Millions

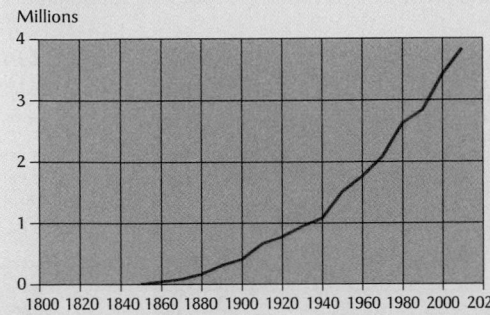

Source: U.S. Census Bureau.

Year	Population
2010	3,831,074
2000	3,421,399
1990	2,842,321
1980	2,633,105
1970	2,091,385
1960	1,768,687
1950	1,521,341
1940	1,089,684
1930	953,786
1920	783,389
1910	672,765
1900	413,536
1890	317,704
1880	174,768
1870	90,923
1860	52,465
1850	12,093

Economy

Chief products
Agriculture: beef cattle, greenhouse and nursery products, hay, milk, timber, wheat.
Manufacturing: computer and electronic products, fabricated metal products, food products, machinery, paper products, primary metal products, transportation equipment, wood products.
Mining: sand and gravel, traprock.

Gross domestic product

Value of goods and services produced in 2008: $169,479,000,000. *Services* include community, business, and personal services; finance; government; trade; and transportation and communication. *Industry* includes construction, manufacturing, mining, and utilities. *Agriculture* includes agriculture, fishing, and forestry.

Source: U.S. Bureau of Economic Analysis.

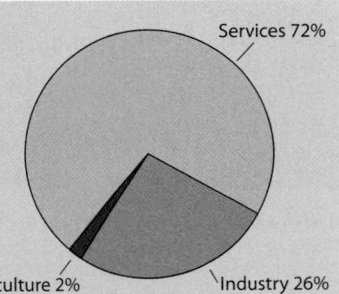

Services 72%
Agriculture 2%
Industry 26%

Government

State government

Governor: 4-year term
State senators: 30; 4-year terms
State representatives: 60; 2-year terms
Counties: 36

Federal government

United States senators: 2
United States representatives: 5
Electoral votes: 7

Sources of information

Oregon's official website at http://www.oregon.gov provides a gateway to much information on the state's government, history, and economy.

In addition, the website at http://www.traveloregon.com provides information about tourism.

A treaty between the United States and the United Kingdom fixed the international boundary at the 49th parallel.

Oregon became the 33rd state on February 14.

Bonneville Dam was completed.

| 1846 | 1848 | 1859 | 1902 | 1937 | 1982 |

Oregon became a territory.

Oregon adopted the initiative and referendum, procedures that permit voters to take a direct part in lawmaking.

Construction was completed on a second powerhouse of Bonneville Dam.

People

Population. The 2010 United States census reported that Oregon had 3,831,074 people. The state's population had increased 12 percent over the 2000 census figure, 3,421,399. According to the 2010 U.S. census, Oregon ranks 27th in population among the 50 states.

A majority of the people of Oregon live in the state's metropolitan areas (see **Metropolitan area**). For the names and populations of these areas, see the *Index* to the political map of Oregon.

Most of Oregon's large cities lie in the rich Willamette Valley in the northwestern part of the state. Portland, Oregon's largest city, is the commercial, industrial, and cultural center of the state. Portland's lovely rose gardens give it the nickname *City of Roses*.

Eugene, a trading and processing center and home of the University of Oregon, ranks as the second largest city in Oregon. Salem is the state capital. The largest cities outside the valley are Medford in the southwest and Bend in central Oregon.

Some of Oregon's people trace their ancestry to settlers who came on the Oregon Trail. Oregon's largest population groups include people of German, English, Irish, American Indian, Norwegian, French, Italian, Swedish, and Scottish descent.

Schools. Jason Lee, a Methodist missionary, established a school for Indian children in French Prairie as early as 1834. After the Oregon Territory was organized in 1848, an act provided that income from two sections (1,280 acres, or 518 hectares) of land in each township should be set aside for education. In 1849, the territorial

David Falconer, Frazier Photolibrary

A rose garden in Portland attracts flower lovers. Portland is nicknamed *City of Roses* because of its many public and private rose gardens. Roses thrive in the city's mild, moist climate.

Population density

More than half of Oregon's residents live in the Willamette Valley, in the northwestern part of the state. Thinly populated eastern Oregon is largely mountainous.

	Persons per mi²	Persons per km²
	More than 50	More than 20
	25 to 50	10 to 20
	10 to 25	4 to 10
	Less than 10	Less than 4

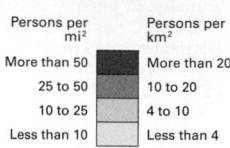

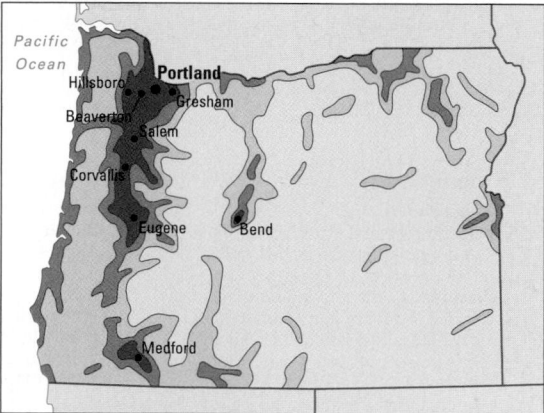

WORLD BOOK map; based on U.S. Census Bureau data

Chris Luneski

Runners in Eugene compete in the annual Butte to Butte 10-kilometer run through the city. Eugene, Oregon's second largest city, is a favorite training site for world-class athletes because of its extensive running facilities.

legislature passed laws providing for a free public school system. The first public school in Oregon opened in 1851.

Today, a State Board of Education heads Oregon's public school system. The governor appoints the seven board members, subject to approval by the state Senate. The superintendent of public instruction is elected to a four-year term. The superintendent oversees the public school system. Children from age 7 through 18 must attend school. For the number of students and teachers in Oregon, see **Education** (table).

Libraries. Oregon's first library was set up in Oregon City in 1842. The Library Association of Portland (now the Multnomah County Library) was the first to serve the public on a large scale. It began in 1864 on a membership basis and became a free public library in 1902.

Today, Oregon has public libraries and branches throughout the state. The largest library in the state is the Multnomah County Library in Portland. The Oregon State Library in Salem provides information to the state government and serves as the library for the blind.

Museums. The Portland Art Museum displays a large collection of paintings and sculpture. It features Indian art from the Northwest Coast and pre-Columbian art. The Jordan Schnitzer Museum of Art at the University of Oregon in Eugene has a large collection of Korean art. The Oregon Museum of Science and Industry in Portland features interactive exhibits representing every major branch of science. The Oregon History Museum in Portland features exhibits from every era in the state's known history. The Favell Museum in Klamath Falls has collections of Western art and Native American artifacts.

Universities and colleges

This table lists the nonprofit universities and colleges in Oregon that grant bachelor's or advanced degrees and are accredited by the Northwest Commission on Colleges and Universities.

Name	Mailing address	Name	Mailing address	Name	Mailing address
Concordia University	Portland	Oregon, University of	Eugene	Reed College	Portland
Corban University	Salem	Oregon Health &		Southern Oregon	
Eastern Oregon University	La Grande	Science University	Portland	University	Ashland
George Fox University	Newberg	Oregon Institute of		Warner Pacific College	Portland
Lewis & Clark College	Portland	Technology	Klamath	Western Oregon University	Monmouth
Linfield College	McMinnville		Falls	Western Seminary	Portland
Marylhurst University	Marylhurst	Oregon State University	Corvallis	Western States,	
Mount Angel Seminary	St. Benedict	Pacific Northwest College		University of	Portland
Multnomah University	Portland	of Art	Portland	Willamette University	Salem
National College of		Pacific University	Forest		
Natural Medicine	Portland		Grove		
Northwest Christian		Portland, University of	Portland		
University	Eugene	Portland State University	Portland		

Chris Luneski

The University of Oregon, in Eugene, was founded in 1872. The statue *Pioneer Mother* (1932), *shown here,* by the Canadian-born sculptor A. Phimister Proctor symbolizes Oregon pioneers.

Tricia Hines, West Stock

The Saturday Market in Portland features jugglers and other performers. People come to the open-air market to enjoy various forms of entertainment and to shop for arts and crafts.

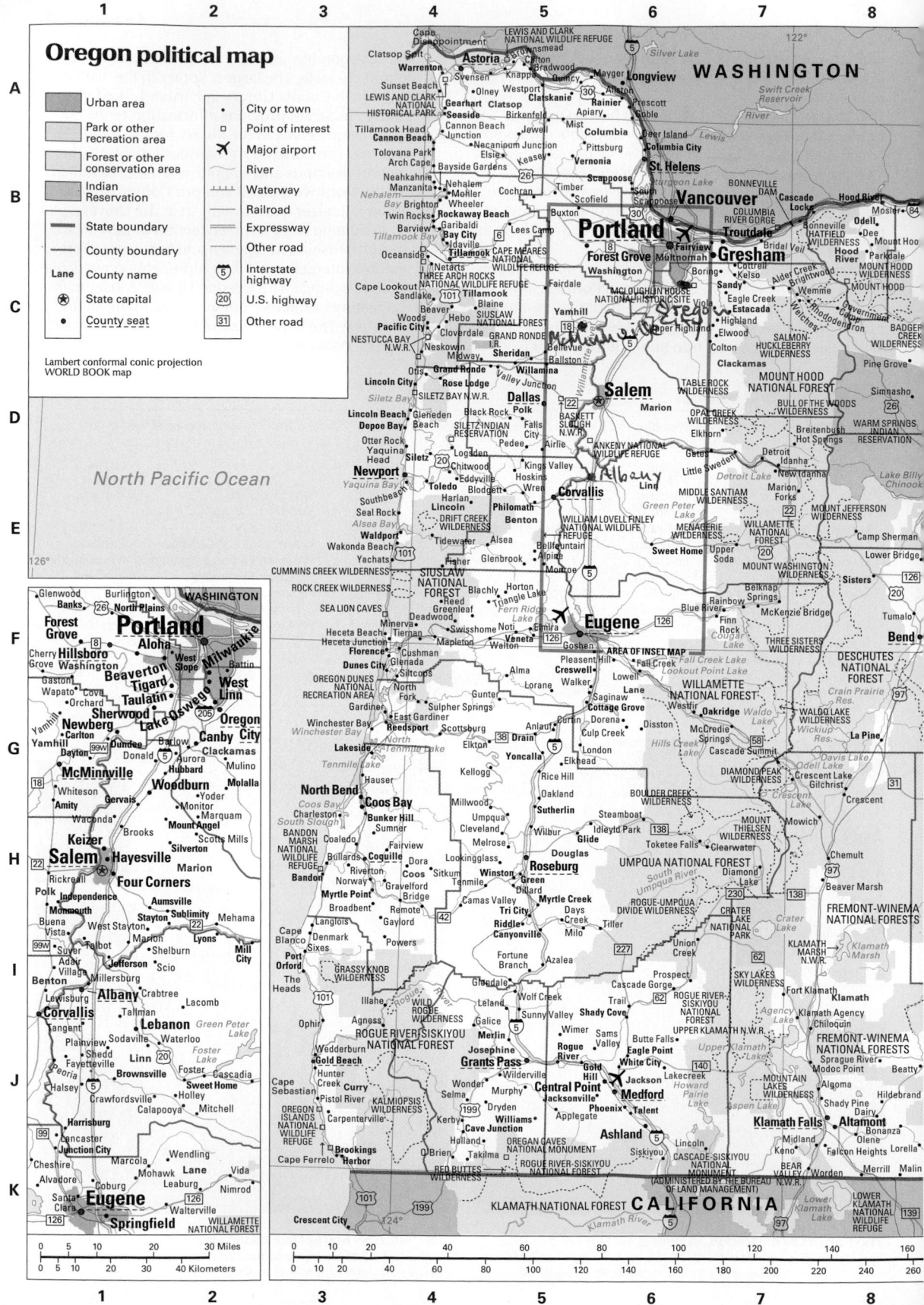

Oregon political map

Legend:
- Urban area
- Park or other recreation area
- Forest or other conservation area
- Indian Reservation
- State boundary
- County boundary
- Lane — County name
- State capital
- County seat
- City or town
- Point of interest
- Major airport
- River
- Waterway
- Railroad
- Expressway
- Other road
- 5 — Interstate highway
- 20 — U.S. highway
- 31 — Other road

Lambert conformal conic projection
WORLD BOOK map

North Pacific Ocean

WASHINGTON

CALIFORNIA

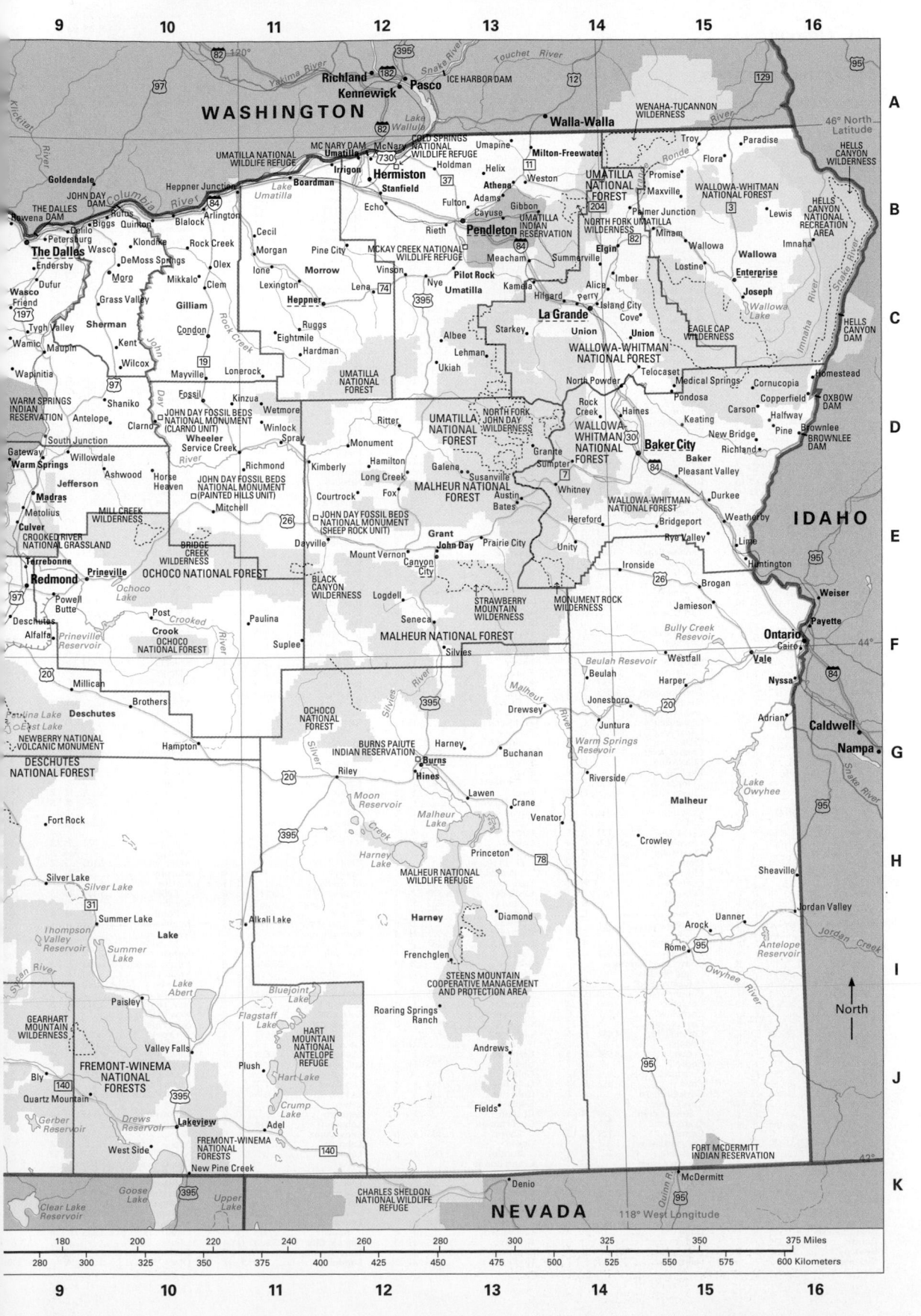

Oregon map index

*Does not appear on map; key shows general location.
†Census designated place—unincorporated, but recognized as a significant settled community by the U.S. Census Bureau.

°County seat.
Places without population figures are unincorporated areas.
Source: 2010 census.

Steve Terrill

Mount Hood, Oregon's highest peak, rises 11,239 feet (3,426 meters) above sea level. The mountain, an inactive volcano, is located about 50 miles (80 kilometers) east of Portland.

Oregon is known for its beautiful mountains and coastal scenery. Majestic snow-covered Mount Hood towers above the Cascade Range about 50 miles (80 kilometers) east of Portland. United States Highway 26 skirts Mount Hood and offers close-up views of its glacier-clad slopes. United States Highway 101 follows the Oregon coastline for about 300 miles (480 kilometers). Motorists along this route see views of white sand dunes, coastal lakes and bays, and cliffs rising above the shore.

Oregon is a recreational paradise. Deer, elk, and pronghorns roam the fields and forests. People catch salmon, steelhead, trout, and other game fish. Grouse, pheasant, quail, and other game birds are plentiful.

Slopes in the Cascade, Siskiyou, and Blue mountains offer excellent skiing. Timberline, on Mount Hood, has skiing the year around. The skiing season in most other areas begins in November and lasts through April.

One of Oregon's most famous events is the Oregon Shakespeare Festival in Ashland. Indoor plays are presented from late February through late October. Outdoor plays are presented from June through September. The "Green Show" before showtime features dancers, jugglers, and musicians dressed in costumes from Shakespeare's time.

Other leading events are the Portland Rose Festival in early June and the Pendleton Round-Up and Happy Canyon Pageant in mid-September. The Rose Festival features parades, stage events, an international rose show, auto races, and a carnival. The festival's main event is a spectacular Grand Floral Parade. The Pendleton Round-Up includes a presentation by local Indian tribes featuring a tipi camp and ceremonial dancing.

Crater Lake, deepest lake in the United States

Ed Cooper, StockFile

Places to visit

Following are brief descriptions of some of Oregon's many interesting places to visit:

Bonneville Dam, the first major dam on the Columbia River, has a series of fish ladders. In season, salmon and other fish jump up the ladders on their way upstream to spawn.

Columbia River Gorge. Here the Columbia River cuts through the Cascade Mountains. Colorful basalt cliffs line the gorge for about 60 miles (97 kilometers) between The Dalles and Troutdale. A number of waterfalls tumble into the gorge.

The Museum at Warm Springs on the Warm Springs Indian Reservation has interactive historical exhibits and collections of art and artifacts from the Confederated Tribes of Warm Springs.

National Historic Oregon Trail Interpretive Center, in Baker City, has exhibits and demonstrations that re-create some of the experience of traveling along the Oregon Trail.

Sea Lion Caves, on the Pacific Coast near Florence, house hundreds of sea lions. The animals can be seen in the caves and on nearby rocks. It is the world's largest sea cave.

National parks and forests. Crater Lake National Park, the state's only national park, lies in the Cascade Mountains in south-central Oregon. Crater Lake, 1,943 feet (592 meters) deep, rests at the top of an ancient volcano. See **Crater Lake National Park.** Ten national forests lie entirely within Oregon. They are Deschutes, Fremont, Malheur, Mount Hood, Ochoco, Siuslaw, Umpqua, Wallowa-Whitman, Willamette, and Winema. Oregon shares Umatilla National Forest with Washington, and Klamath, Rogue River, and Siskiyou national forests with California. Congress set aside dozens of areas in Oregon's national forests as national wilderness areas, to be preserved in their natural condition.

National monuments, memorials, and historic sites. Oregon Caves National Monument is in the Siskiyou Mountains. Its limestone caverns contain beautiful stone formations. John Day Fossil Beds National Monument in north-central Oregon features fossils of prehistoric animals and plants (see **John Day Fossil Beds National Monument**). Lewis and Clark National Historical Park includes Fort Clatsop, near Astoria. The fort was the site of the winter camp of Meriwether Lewis and William Clark during their expedition to the area in 1805 and 1806. McLoughlin House National Historic Site in Oregon City was built by John McLoughlin, who is often called the *Father of Oregon.* He lived there from 1847 to 1857.

State parks. Oregon has dozens of state parks. Many have camping and recreational facilities. Visit the official Web site of the Oregon Parks and Recreation Department at http://www.oregon.gov/OPRD/PARKS/index.shtml for more information.

Photri

Sea Lion Caves near Florence

David Stoecklein, West Stock

Skiing on Mount Hood

David R. Frazier

Pendleton Round-Up and Happy Canyon Pageant

© David Cooper, Oregon Shakespeare Festival

Shakespeare Festival in Ashland

Land regions. Oregon has six main land regions. They are: (1) the Coast Range, (2) the Willamette Lowland, (3) the Cascade Mountains, (4) the Klamath Mountains, (5) the Columbia Plateau, and (6) the Basin and Range Region.

The Coast Range region borders the Pacific Ocean from Washington's Chehalis Valley on the north to the Klamath Mountains of Oregon on the south. The rolling coast ranges run parallel to the shoreline. They are the lowest of Oregon's main mountain ranges, with average elevations of less than 2,000 feet (610 meters). Marys Peak, southwest of Corvallis, rises 4,097 feet (1,249 meters) and is the highest point in the region. Forests of Douglas-fir, hemlock, spruce, and other evergreen trees cover much of the area.

Several valleys in the region, such as Triangle Lake Valley, are beds of ancient lakes. Many small coastal lakes were formed when the mouths of streams sank and sand dunes dammed their waters. Along much of the coast, the land rises from the sea in sheer cliffs, some of them nearly 1,000 feet (300 meters) high. In some places, the coastal mountains rise in a series of terraces. Each terrace was once the coastline.

The Willamette Lowland is a narrow strip wedged between the Coast Range on the west and the Cascade Mountains on the east. The Willamette River and its branches flow north to the Columbia River. They drain the farm and forest lands of the Willamette Valley. Over half the state's people live in the region. Rich soil and a favorable climate make it the most important farming and industrial area in the state.

The Cascade Mountains region, a broad belt of rugged land crowned by volcanic peaks, includes some of the highest mountains in North America. Mount Hood, the highest peak in Oregon, rises 11,239 feet (3,426 meters) above sea level. Mount Jefferson is 10,497 feet (3,199 meters) high. Other beautiful peaks in the Cascade Mountains include the Three Sisters, more than 10,000 feet (3,000 meters) high, and Mount McLoughlin, 9,495 feet (2,894 meters) high.

The Klamath Mountains cover the southwestern corner of Oregon. Thick forests grow on the mountainsides and provide shelter for a variety of animals. This region also has the state's richest mineral deposits.

The Columbia Plateau, also called *the Columbia Intermontane,* covers most of eastern Oregon and extends into Washington and Idaho. Thousands of years ago, lava flowed out of cracks in the earth's crust to form the plateau. Deep canyons of the Deschutes, John Day, and other rivers cut through the plateau in north-central Oregon. The state's great wheat ranches lie there. Much of the so-called "plateau" in Oregon is actually rugged and mountainous. The Blue and Wallowa mountains rise in northeastern Oregon. Timberlands cover the Blue Mountain area. The Wallowa Mountains, cut by glaciers, provide spectacular scenery. The Snake River has carved the famous Hells Canyon on the Oregon-Idaho border. This great gorge lies between the Wallowa Mountains and Idaho's Seven Devils Mountains. Its average depth is about 5,500 feet (1,680 meters).

The Basin and Range Region covers part of southeastern Oregon and extends into California and other nearby states. In Oregon, the region consists of high basins broken by occasional steeply sloped mountains. The Cascade Range to the west cuts off moisture-bearing winds from the Pacific Ocean and makes much of the area a semidesert.

Coastline. Oregon's coastline extends 296 miles (476 kilometers) along the Pacific Ocean. Much of the shore

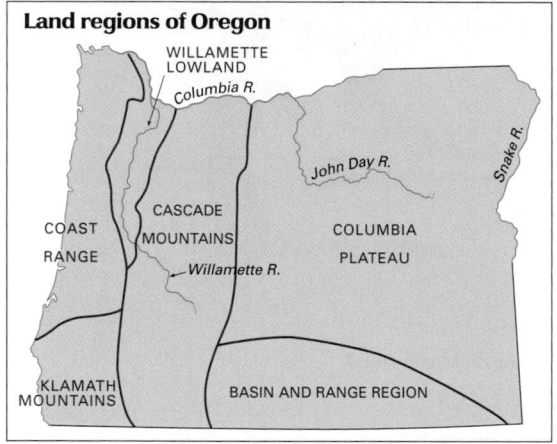

Land regions of Oregon

WORLD BOOK map

Map index

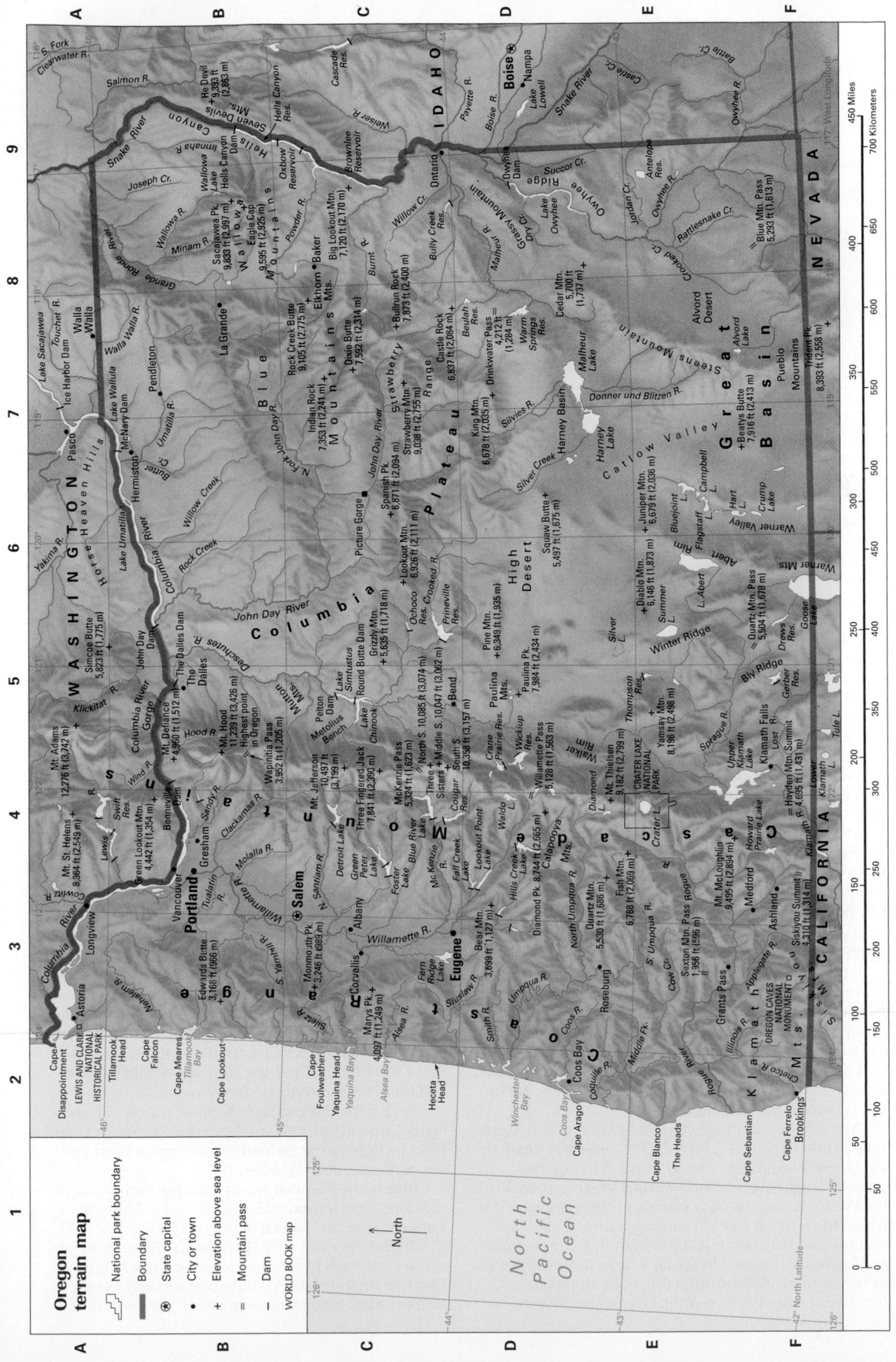

Grant Heilman

The towering Cascade Mountains include several peaks over 10,000 feet (3,000 meters) high. The Three Sisters rise in the foreground. Mount Jefferson and Mount Hood are in the distance.

is rugged, with steep cliffs rising up from the sea. But many bays and harbors have been formed where rivers from the coast ranges and Klamath Mountains flow into the sea. These bays and harbors include Tillamook, Yaquina, Alsea, Winchester, and Coos.

Rivers, waterfalls, and lakes. The mighty Columbia River flows westward to the Pacific Ocean, forming most of the border between Oregon and Washington. The Columbia drains more than half of Oregon. The Columbia and its branch, the Willamette River, form the largest system of navigable waterways in the state. The Snake River forms much of the Oregon-Idaho border. It joins the Columbia in Washington. The Snake and its branches drain the easternmost part of Oregon. The Deschutes River travels northward through central Oregon and empties into the Columbia. The John Day River rises in the Strawberry Mountains in eastern Oregon. It flows west and north to the Columbia and drains much of north-central Oregon.

Hundreds of streams in the Cascade Mountains rush down the slopes in rapids and waterfalls. Among the best known waterfalls are Benham, Pringle, Salt Creek, Steamboat, and the many falls along Silver Creek. About a dozen waterfalls, some of them over 200 feet (61 meters) high, tumble into the Columbia River Gorge. These waterfalls include Bridal Veil, Coopery, Elowah, Horsetail, Latourell, and Multnomah.

The Cascade Mountains region has many lakes. Crater Lake in the Cascades, 1,943 feet (592 meters) in depth, is the deepest lake in the United States. It lies in the *caldera* (crater) of an extinct volcano. Wallowa Lake in the Wallowa Mountains is famous for its sparkling clear water. Most of the lakes in southeastern Oregon are shallow and salty. Some evaporate during dry seasons and leave salt deposits in the lake beds. But a few, such as Harney and Malheur, are large year-round lakes. A number of small lakes near the Oregon coast were formed when deposits of soil and sand blocked the mouths of streams and kept the streams from emptying into the ocean.

Plant and animal life. Forests cover nearly half of Oregon. Softwood trees include cedars, firs, hemlocks, pines, and spruces. Hardwoods include alders, ashes, cottonwoods, junipers, madrones, maples, and willows. Many kinds of wildflowers grow in Oregon because the state has a variety of climates and elevations. Oregon is famous for its azaleas, laurels, and other flowering shrubs. The state flower, the Oregon grape, grows in most parts of the state.

Columbian black-tailed deer and Roosevelt elk live in Oregon's Cascade Mountains and coastal forests. Mule deer, Rocky Mountain elk, and bighorn sheep are found east of the Cascades. Pronghorns thrive in the southeast. A small number of mountain goats live in the Wallowa Mountains. Smaller animals that are found in Oregon include beavers, bobcats, coyotes, foxes, minks, muskrats, and river otters. Seals and sea lions live along Oregon's coast.

Every year, thousands of salmon leave the ocean and swim up Oregon's rivers to lay their eggs. They leap up low waterfalls and climb fish ladders to get around dams. Cod, halibut, herring, ling cod, sablefish, sole, and tuna live in Oregon's coastal waters.

The steelhead is perhaps the most prized of Oregon's many game fishes. Other fishes in the state's rivers and lakes include perch; striped bass; sturgeon; and cutthroat, brook, and rainbow trout.

Climate. Mild, moist winds from the Pacific Ocean give western Oregon an unusually mild climate for a state so far north. Coastal temperatures average 45 °F (7 °C) in January and 60 °F (16 °C) in July. The winds become cooler when they rise over the coast ranges. Much of their moisture condenses and falls as rain. In some coastal mountain areas, yearly *precipitation* (rain, snow, and other moisture) is more than 130 inches (330 centimeters).

In the Willamette Valley, east of the Coast Range, precipitation averages about 40 inches (100 centimeters) a year, almost all during the cool season. As the winds rise up the western slopes of the Cascade Mountains, more of their moisture falls. Precipitation in this area averages 50 to 75 inches (130 to 191 centimeters) a year.

The winds are usually dry by the time they have crossed the Cascades. Dry winds do not keep the climate mild, as moist winds do. For this reason, eastern Oregon has relatively cold winters and hot summers. In the southeast, temperatures average 27 °F (−3 °C) in January and 72 °F (22 °C) in July. Much of eastern Oregon receives only 6 to 12 inches (15 to 30 centimeters) of precipitation a year. Oregon's record low of −54 °F (−48 °C) occurred on Feb. 9, 1933, at Ukiah, and on Feb. 10, 1933, at Seneca. The highest temperature, 119 °F (48 °C), occurred at Prineville on July 29, 1898, and at Pendleton on Aug. 10, 1898.

Average monthly weather

	Portland						Medford				
	Temperatures				Days of rain or snow		Temperatures				Days of rain or snow
	°F		°C				°F		°C		
	High	Low	High	Low			High	Low	High	Low	
Jan.	46	34	8	1	19	Jan.	47	31	8	−1	14
Feb.	50	36	10	2	16	Feb.	54	33	12	1	11
Mar.	56	39	13	4	17	Mar.	58	36	14	2	12
Apr.	61	42	16	6	15	Apr.	64	39	18	4	10
May	67	48	19	9	12	May	72	44	22	7	8
June	73	52	23	11	9	June	81	50	27	10	5
July	79	57	26	14	4	July	90	55	32	13	2
Aug.	80	57	27	14	5	Aug.	90	55	32	13	2
Sept.	75	53	24	12	7	Sept.	84	48	29	9	4
Oct.	63	45	17	7	12	Oct.	70	40	21	4	7
Nov.	52	40	11	4	18	Nov.	53	35	12	2	13
Dec.	45	35	7	2	19	Dec.	45	31	7	−1	14

Average January temperatures

Moist, mild ocean winds give far western Oregon unusually mild winters for a state so far north.

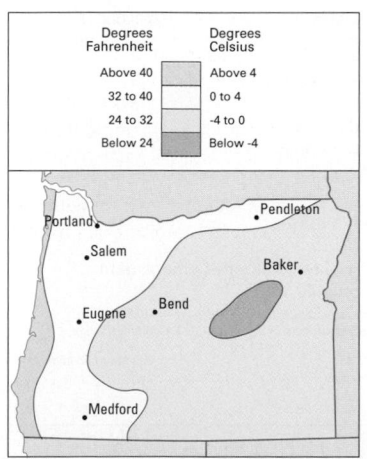

Degrees Fahrenheit	Degrees Celsius
Above 40	Above 4
32 to 40	0 to 4
24 to 32	−4 to 0
Below 24	Below −4

Average July temperatures

The state has mild summers. The western and central sections are generally cooler than the rest of Oregon.

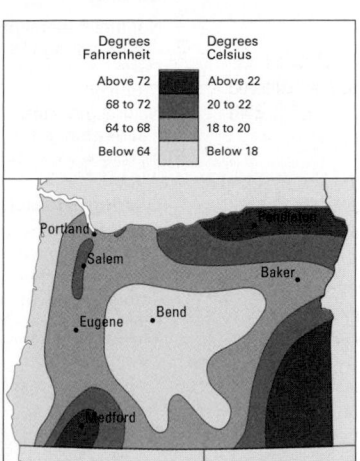

Degrees Fahrenheit	Degrees Celsius
Above 72	Above 22
68 to 72	20 to 22
64 to 68	18 to 20
Below 64	Below 18

Average yearly precipitation

There are wide differences in precipitation throughout the state. The west gets heavy rains, while the southeast is dry.

WORLD BOOK maps

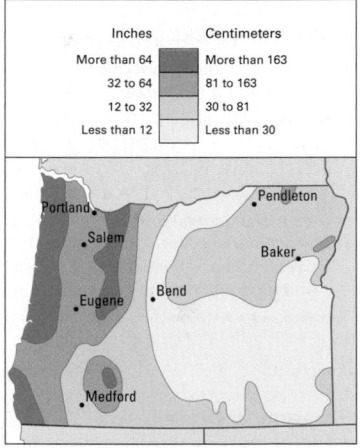

Inches	Centimeters
More than 64	More than 163
32 to 64	81 to 163
12 to 32	30 to 81
Less than 12	Less than 30

Economy

Service industries, taken together, account for most of Oregon's *gross domestic product*—the total value of all goods and services produced in the state in a year. Manufacturing is also an important industry in the state, accounting for about 20 percent of the gross domestic product. The electronic products industry became Oregon's most important manufacturing sector during the 1990's. Factories in the Portland area produce such high-technology products as computer products and digital televisions. Wood processing, formerly the leading manufacturing activity, still plays a significant role. The economies of many Oregon cities rely almost entirely on this industry.

The Cascade Mountains divide Oregon into two major economic regions. Manufacturing and service industries are concentrated in the Willamette Valley in western Oregon. Western Oregon also produces large amounts of flower bulbs, milk, seed crops, timber, and vegetables. The dry lands east of the Cascades are most important for cattle, wheat, and potato production.

Millions of tourists visit Oregon yearly. Tourism contributes billions of dollars annually to the state economy.

Natural resources. Oregon's many natural resources include vital forestlands, small deposits of many minerals, a plentiful water supply, and fertile soils.

Forests. Oregon is one of the leading states in timber production. Forests cover nearly half the state. Oregon has two forest regions: (1) the Douglas-fir region west of the Cascade Mountains, and (2) the ponderosa (western yellow) pine region east of the mountains.

Oregon economic statistics

General economy

Gross domestic product (GDP)* (2008) $169,479,000,000
   Rank among U.S. states   26th
Unemployment rate (2010)   10.6% (U.S. avg: 9.6%)

*Gross domestic product is the total value of goods and services produced in a year.
Sources: U.S. Bureau of Economic Analysis and U.S. Bureau of Labor Statistics.

Agriculture

Cash receipts $3,893,448,000
   Rank among U.S. states   27th
Distribution   77% crops, 23% livestock
Farms   38,600
Farm acres (hectares)   16,400,000 (6,640,000)
   Rank among U.S. states   17th
Farmland   26% of Oregon

Leading products

1. Greenhouse and nursery products   (ranks 4th in U.S.)
2. Cattle and calves
3. Dairy products
4. Hay   (ranks 5th in U.S.)
5. Wheat
Other products: cherries, fescue, grapes, hazelnuts, onions, pears, potatoes, ryegrass.

Manufacturing

Value added by manufacture* $36,308,309,000
   Rank among U.S. states   25th

Leading products

1. Computer and electronic products
2. Food and beverages
3. Wood products
4. Fabricated metal products
5. Machinery
Other products: chemicals, paper, primary metals, transportation equipment.

*Value added by manufacture is the increase in value of raw materials after they become finished products.

Economic production in Oregon

Economic activities	Percent of GDP* produced	Employed workers	
		Number of people	Percent of total
Finance, insurance, & real estate	21	234,300	10
Manufacturing	20	209,600	9
Community, business, & personal services	19	739,600	32
Trade, restaurants, & hotels	14	499,700	21
Government	12	295,900	13
Transportation & communication	6	113,500	5
Construction	5	140,000	6
Agriculture, forestry, & fishing	2	96,900	4
Utilities	1	5,100	*
Mining	*	5,000	*
Total	100	2,339,600	100

*Less than one-half of 1 percent.
Figures are for 2008; employment figures include full- and part-time workers.
Source: *World Book* estimates based on data from U.S. Bureau of Economic Analysis.

Mining

Nonfuel mineral production $398,000,000
   Rank among U.S. states   35th
Coal   *
Crude oil   *
Natural gas (cubic feet†)   778,000,000
   Rank among U.S. states   29th

*No significant mining of this product in Oregon.
†One cubic foot equals 0.0283 cubic meter.

Leading products

1. Crushed stone (mainly traprock)
2. Sand and gravel
Other products: cement, clays, diatomite, emery, gemstones, lime, perlite, pumice.

Figures are for 2008, except for the agricultural figures, which are for 2009.
Sources: U.S. Census Bureau, U.S. Department of Agriculture, U.S. Geological Survey.

continued on page 843

Economy of Oregon

This map shows the economic uses of land in Oregon and where the leading farm, mineral, and forest products are produced. Major manufacturing centers are shown in red.

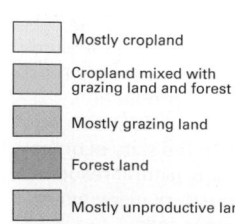

    Mostly cropland
    Cropland mixed with grazing land and forest
    Mostly grazing land
    Forest land
    Mostly unproductive land
    Urban area
 • Manufacturing center
 • Mineral deposit

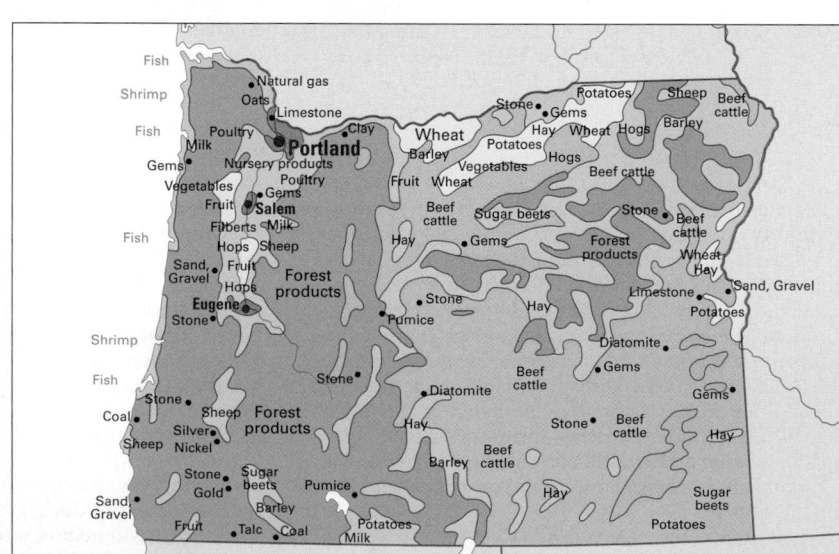

WORLD BOOK map

Fishing

| Commercial catch | $103,096,000 |
| Rank among U.S. states | 11th |

Leading catches

1. Crab	(ranks 5th in U.S.)
2. Shrimp	
3. Sablefish	(ranks 2nd in U.S.)
4. Tuna	(ranks 3rd in U.S.)

Other catches: hakes, oysters, salmon, sardines, shrimp, sole.

Electric power

Hydroelectric	57.6%
Natural gas	29.6%
Coal	6.9%
Wind	4.4%
Other	1.5%

Figures are for 2008.
Sources: U.S. Energy Information Administration, U.S. National Marine Fisheries Service.

The Douglas-fir, Oregon's state tree, provides the largest amount of timber. Ponderosa pine, western hemlock, western redcedar, Sitka spruce, and several kinds of true firs also grow in the Douglas-fir region. Some Douglas-fir trees grow in the ponderosa pine region. So do Engelmann spruce, western white pine, lodgepole pine, sugar pine, and true firs.

Minerals. Widespread deposits of crushed stone and of sand and gravel are Oregon's most important mined resources. These resources are found in almost all parts of the state.

A small natural gas field lies beneath Columbia County in the northwestern part of the state. Diatomite, which is used to make filters, is found in east-central Oregon. The state also has deposits of clays, copper, gemstones, gold, lime, pumice, and talc.

Water is one of Oregon's most important resources. Melted snow and winter rain from the mountains feed Oregon's rivers. The rivers provide unusually pure water for industry and home use. The Columbia River and its tributaries provide water for power and irrigation.

Soils. Gray-brown soils cover the Coast Range and Klamath Mountains regions. The Willamette Lowland has deep, fertile soils. Shallow soils cover most of the eastern Cascade slopes, and the Basin and Range Region. The wheat belt of north-central Oregon has rich soils good for growing crops.

Service industries produce the largest portion of Oregon's employment and gross domestic product. These services are concentrated in the state's metropolitan areas, especially in the Portland area.

Portland is the state's main financial center. Oregon Health and Science University in Portland is a center of medical research. The Port of Portland, one of the largest ports on the West Coast, handles much whole-sale trade. Its trade includes the import of foreign cars and the export of wheat.

Many hotels, restaurants, and retail trade establishments are in the Eugene, Portland, and Salem areas. State government agencies are based in Salem, Oregon's capital. Nike, a distributor of athletic shoes and other sportswear, is based in Beaverton.

Manufacturing. Computer and electronic products are Oregon's leading manufactured products. Most of these products are made in the Corvallis, Eugene, and Portland areas. Oregon's factories manufacture computer components, digital television sets, microprocessors, and oscilloscopes.

Much of Oregon's manufacturing is dedicated to processing the state's agricultural and forest products. The Portland and Salem areas are the leading food-processing areas. Frozen fruits and vegetables are the leading products of this industry. Other foods made in the state include baked goods and dairy products. Oregon is a leading state in lumber production. The state is also a major producer of particleboard, plywood, and veneer. Many parts of western Oregon have large wood-processing plants. Paper mills operate mostly in northwestern Oregon.

The Portland area is the center of production for fabricated metal products, machinery, primary metals, and transportation equipment. Fabricated metals products include machine shop products, tools, and other items. Factories produce machinery for the wood products and metalworking industries. Primary metals products include aluminum and steel. Motor homes, ships and boats, and parts for motor vehicles and the aerospace industry are important transportation products.

Agriculture. Farmland covers about a fourth of Oregon's land area. Greenhouse and nursery products are

Steve Terrill

A tulip farm near Monitor produces flower bulbs. Farmers in western Oregon also grow daffodils, gladioli, irises, lilies, and peonies for bulbs.

Steve Terrill

Loggers in a forest near Westport cut timber for Oregon's forest products industry. Wood processing is one of the state's leading manufacturing activities. Oregon ranks among the leading states in the manufacture of forest products.

the state's leading agricultural products. Northwestern Oregon is an important bulb-growing region. Farmers there grow daffodils, gladioli, irises, lilies, peonies, and tulips for bulbs.

Timber is another valuable agricultural product in Oregon. The most important timber trees are Douglas-fir and ponderosa pine. Douglas-fir trees grow mainly in the Cascade Mountains region and in smaller ranges west of the Cascades. Ponderosa pines grow primarily in the Blue Mountains of eastern Oregon. The state is a leading producer of Christmas trees.

Beef cattle and milk are also important agricultural products in Oregon. Most beef cattle are raised on ranges east of the Cascades. Northwestern Oregon has many herds of dairy cattle.

Wheat is Oregon's most valuable food crop. Most wheat grows in the plateau region of north-central Oregon. Hay is Oregon's most important feed crop. Much of the hay is grown in the southeastern part of the state.

Oregon ranks among the top states in vegetable production. Onions and potatoes are the leading vegetables. Large onion and potato crops grow on irrigated land in the eastern part of the state. Most of the state's other vegetables grow in the Willamette Valley, the state's most diverse agricultural region. These vegetables include green peas, snap beans, and sweet corn. Other western Oregon crops include hops, which are used in making beer, and hazelnuts (also called filberts). Oregon is the nation's only hazelnut producer.

Oregon is among the leading states in the production of berries, pears, and sweet cherries. North-central Oregon leads the state in apple, cherry, and pear production. Berries are grown mainly in northwestern Oregon.

Oregon farmers specialize in several crops that are not grown widely in many other states. For example, Oregon produces most of the nation's seed for crimson clover, fescue, orchardgrass, and ryegrass. Bentgrass and Kentucky bluegrass are also important products in Oregon. These crops are grown mainly in Willamette Valley counties. Oregon is also a leader in the production of peppermint oil.

Sheep are raised primarily in western Oregon. Most of the state's chickens are raised in the Willamette Val-

ley. Oregon farmers also raise goats, hogs, and minks.

Mining. Two mined products—sand and gravel and traprock—provide about two-thirds of Oregon's mining income. These products are mined in several regions of the state. Oregon is a leading state in the production of gemstones, perlite, and pumice. Other mined products include clays, diatomite, lime, and portland cement. Oregon is the only state to produce emery.

Fishing industry. Crab, sablefish, salmon, shrimp, and tuna are among the state's leading catches. Oregon ranks as a leading tuna-catching state.

Electric power and utilities. Hydroelectric plants supply over half of the state's electric power. Most of the hydroelectric power comes from dams on the Columbia River between Oregon and Washington. They include Bonneville, John Day, McNary, and The Dalles. The remaining hydroelectric power comes from dams on rivers entirely within Oregon, including the Deschutes, Rogue, and Willamette. Plants that burn coal or natural gas supply most of the rest of the power.

Transportation. From 1841 to the coming of the railroads in the 1860's, thousands of people traveled the famous Oregon Trail to Oregon (see **Oregon Trail**). Today, Oregon has an extensive system of roads and highways. Rail lines carry freight on thousands of miles of rail track in the state. Passenger trains serve several Oregon cities.

Portland International Airport is one of the major airports in the western United States. Oregon also has airports in Eugene, Hillsboro, and Medford.

Portland is a major ocean port, though it is about 100 miles (160 kilometers) inland. Oceangoing ships follow a deepened channel up the Columbia and into the Willamette River to reach Portland's harbor. Oregon's other major ports are Astoria and Coos Bay.

Communication. Oregon's first newspaper, the *Oregon Spectator,* began publication at Oregon City in 1846. It is no longer published. *The Oregonian* was established in Portland in 1850 as the *Weekly Oregonian.* The *Oregon Statesman* (now the *Statesman Journal*) appeared in Oregon City in 1851. It later moved to Salem. These two papers are still published today. Other leading newspapers in Oregon include the *Mail Tribune* of Medford and *The Register-Guard* of Eugene.

Constitution. The present state Constitution was adopted in 1857, two years before Oregon joined the Union. Constitutional amendments may be proposed by either house of the state legislature. A majority of the members of each house must approve the amendments. Voters must then approve the amendments in the next regular general election, unless the legislature orders a special election.

In addition, amendments to the Constitution of Oregon may be proposed and passed directly by the people, through their powers of *initiative and referendum* (see **Initiative and referendum**). The Constitution may also be revised by a constitutional convention. A convention may be called after a majority of legislators and voters give their approval.

Executive. Oregon voters elect the governor to a four-year term. The governor has the power to appoint members of many state boards and commissions. Other top state officials include the attorney general, commissioner of labor and industries, secretary of state, superintendent of public instruction, and treasurer. These officials are also elected to four-year terms.

Legislature is called the Legislative Assembly. It consists of a Senate of 30 members and a House of Representatives of 60 members. The state has 30 senatorial districts and 60 representative districts. Voters in each senatorial district elect one senator. Voters in each representative district elect one representative.

State senators serve four-year terms, and representatives serve two-year terms. The Assembly meets in regular session in odd-numbered years. Legislative sessions usually begin on the second Monday in January. There is no limit to a session's length.

Courts. The highest court in Oregon is the state Supreme Court. It has seven justices elected to six-year terms. The court elects one of its members to serve a six-year term as chief justice. The next highest state court is the Court of Appeals. It has 10 judges who are elected to six-year terms.

Oregon is divided into 27 judicial districts. Each judicial district has one or more circuit court judges. Voters elect the circuit court judges to six-year terms by *non-partisan* (no-party) ballot. A special Tax Court ranks with

The governors of Oregon

	Party	Term
John Whiteaker	Democratic	1859-1862
A. C. Gibbs	Republican	1862-1866
George L. Woods	Republican	1866-1870
La Fayette Grover	Democratic	1870-1877
Stephen F. Chadwick	Democratic	1877-1878
W. W. Thayer	Democratic	1878-1882
Z. F. Moody	Republican	1882-1887
Sylvester Pennoyer	Democratic-Populist	1887-1895
William Paine Lord	Republican	1895-1899
T. T. Geer	Republican	1899-1903
George E. Chamberlain	Democratic	1903-1909
Frank W. Benson	Republican	1909-1910
Jay Bowerman	Republican	1910-1911
Oswald West	Democratic	1911-1915
James Withycombe	Republican	1915-1919
Ben W. Olcott	Republican	1919-1923
Walter M. Pierce	Democratic	1923-1927
I. L. Patterson	Republican	1927-1929
A. W. Norblad	Republican	1929-1931
Julius L. Meier	Independent	1931-1935
Charles H. Martin	Democratic	1935-1939
Charles A. Sprague	Republican	1939-1943
Earl Snell	Republican	1943-1947
John H. Hall	Republican	1947-1949
Douglas McKay	Republican	1949-1952
Paul L. Patterson	Republican	1952-1956
Elmo Smith	Republican	1956-1957
Robert D. Holmes	Democratic	1957-1959
Mark O. Hatfield	Republican	1959-1967
Tom McCall	Republican	1967-1975
Robert W. Straub	Democratic	1975-1979
Victor G. Atiyeh	Republican	1979-1987
Neil Goldschmidt	Democratic	1987-1991
Barbara Roberts	Democratic	1991-1995
John Kitzhaber	Democratic	1995-2003
Ted Kulongoski	Democratic	2003-2011
John Kitzhaber	Democratic	2011-

the circuit courts. Lower courts in Oregon include district, county, justice, and municipal courts.

Local government. Oregon gives its cities and towns *home rule.* This means they have the right to choose their own form of government. Most cities with more than 5,000 people have the council-manager form of

The Oregon House of Representatives meets in the State Capitol in Salem. Each of its 60 members is elected to a two-year term.

government. Portland has a mayor and four commissioners. Most of Oregon's smaller cities have a mayor and a city council.

A 1958 amendment to the state Constitution extended home rule privileges to Oregon counties. However, only 9 of the state's 36 counties have taken action under this law. A three- or five-member board of commissioners governs most counties in Oregon. In most cases, the county commissioners are elected to four-year terms.

Revenue. Taxes account for about half of the state government's *general revenue* (income). Other sources of revenue include charges for government services and grants from the federal government. The most important source of tax revenue is a personal income tax. Other major sources of tax revenue are taxes on corporate income, motor fuels, motor vehicle licenses, and to-

bacco products. The state also receives revenue from a lottery. Oregon has no state sales tax.

Politics. The Republican Party controlled Oregon politics during most of the state's history. Many industrial workers who settled in Oregon cities after World War II (1939-1945) caused changes in the state's politics. In the mid-1950's, registered Democrats began to outnumber registered Republicans.

The legislative districts have been changed periodically, beginning in the 1960's. These actions have given more representation to urban areas, where the Democrats have their greatest strength. Since the early 1970's, both Democratic and Republican candidates have won election to the highest state offices. For Oregon's voting record in presidential elections since 1860, see **Electoral College** (table).

History

Early days. When the first white people entered the Oregon region, many American Indian tribes lived there. The Chinook lived along the lower Columbia River, where they fished for salmon. The Clackama, Kalapuya, Multnomah, and Tillamook tribes also made their homes in the northwest. The Bannock, Cayuse, Paiute, Umatilla, and a major band of the Nez Perce lived east of the Cascade Mountains. The Klamath and the Rogue lived near the present-day border with California.

Exploration and settlement. Spanish explorers sailing north from Mexico in 1543 were the first white people to see the Oregon coast. Sir Francis Drake of England may have seen Oregon's southern coast in 1579 while searching for a water route between the northern Pacific and Atlantic oceans.

In 1778, British explorer James Cook sailed to Yaquina Bay and named Cape Foulweather as he went north. In 1788, the first American ships arrived off the Oregon coast, including one led by Captain Robert Gray. In May 1792, Gray became the first to sail into the Columbia River, which he named for his ship. A few weeks later, British captain George Vancouver, who was exploring the Northwest coast, sent William Broughton, one of his lieutenants, into the Columbia. Broughton probably sailed as far as the Sandy River, east of present-day Portland, and named such landmarks as Mount Hood and Mount St. Helens. The explorers Meriwether Lewis and William Clark reached the mouth of the Columbia by land in 1805. The Lewis and Clark expedition, together with Gray's trip on the Columbia River, gave the United States a strong claim to the Oregon region.

In the early 1800's, the Oregon region stretched from Alaska, which was claimed by Russia, to California, which was claimed by Spain. It extended eastward from the Pacific Ocean to the Rocky Mountains. Russia, Spain, the United Kingdom, and the United States claimed parts of the region. Russia based its claims on Russian explorations along the northern Pacific Coast. In treaties with the United Kingdom and the United States in 1824 and 1825, Russia gave up its interests south of latitude 54° 40. In 1819, by treaty, Spain gave up its claim north of latitude 42°, Oregon's present southern boundary. The United Kingdom and the United States could not agree

on a boundary line. They signed a treaty in 1818 that permitted citizens of both countries to trade and settle in the region. The treaty was renewed in 1827.

John Jacob Astor, an American fur trader, began the white settlement of Oregon. His company, the Pacific Fur Company, set up a fur-trading post at Astoria in 1811. But the North West Company, a British fur company, gained possession of Astoria in 1813 during the War of 1812. In 1821, the company merged with the Hudson's Bay Company, another British trading firm. This firm founded Fort Vancouver (now Vancouver, Washington) in 1825. John McLoughlin guided the activities of the Hudson's Bay Company and ruled the region for about 20 years. He later became a U.S. citizen. McLoughlin played a leading part in settling the region. Today, he is known as the *father of Oregon.*

In 1834, Methodist missionaries established the first permanent American settlement in the Willamette Valley. The first large overland migration into Oregon came in 1843. That year, about 900 people traveled the Oregon Trail and settled in the Willamette Valley. Hundreds of American settlers arrived each year from then on. The increasing number of settlers put pressure on the U.S. government to settle the boundary dispute with the British. In 1844, James K. Polk based his campaign for the presidency partly on the claim that land south of latitude 54° 40 belonged to the United States (see **Fifty-Four Forty or Fight**). In 1846, President Polk signed a treaty with the United Kingdom. It fixed the 49th parallel as the chief dividing line between U.S. and British territory.

Indian treaties and conflicts. In 1847, Cayuse Indians killed the American pioneer Marcus Whitman, along with his wife and several other settlers, near present-day Walla Walla, Washington (see **Whitman, Marcus**). These killings led to the Cayuse War of 1847-1848. It also resulted in the execution in 1850 of five Indians held responsible for the killings.

The federal government began negotiating treaties with Oregon's Indians in the 1850's. In several treaties, Indians *ceded* (gave up) millions of acres of land to the United States, while reserving small reservations and off-reservation rights for themselves. The treaties did not halt conflict between Indians and settlers, however. The

Historic Oregon

Captain Robert Gray visited what is now Oregon in 1792. He sailed into the mouth of a great river that he named after his ship, the *Columbia*.

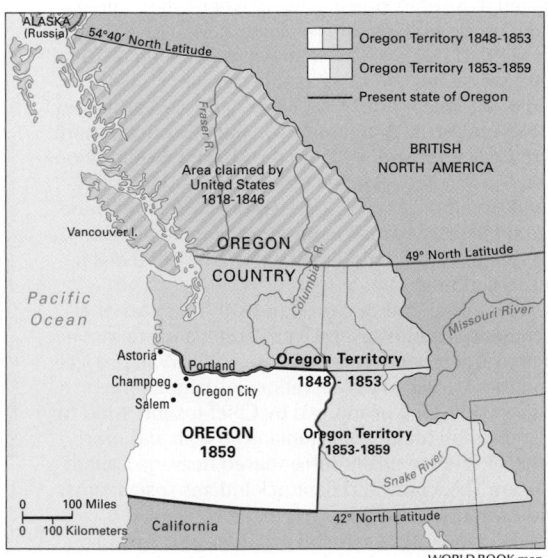

WORLD BOOK map

Oregon was part of the Oregon Country, split between the United States and the British in 1846. The Oregon Territory was created in 1848 and divided in 1853. Oregon became a state in 1859.

Settlers traveled west on the Oregon Trail from Independence, Missouri, to the Willamette Valley during the 1840's. The first large overland migration into the Oregon region came in 1843, when 900 settlers arrived.

Important dates in Oregon

WORLD BOOK illustrations by Richard Bonson, The Art Agency

1579 Sir Francis Drake possibly touched the Oregon coast.

1792 Robert Gray sailed into the Columbia River.

1805 Meriwether Lewis and William Clark reached the mouth of the Columbia.

1811 John Jacob Astor founded Astoria.

1819 A treaty between the United States and Spain fixed the present southern border of Oregon.

1843 The Willamette settlers at Champoeg organized a provisional government.

1846 A treaty made the 49th parallel the chief boundary between British and U.S. territory in the Oregon region.

1848 Oregon became a territory.

1849 Oregon City was proclaimed the territorial capital.

1850 Congress passed the Oregon Donation Land Law.

1859 Oregon became the 33rd state on February 14. Salem became the state capital.

1902 Oregon adopted the initiative and referendum.

1903 Flash floods in the Heppner area killed more than 200.

1912 The state adopted woman suffrage.

1937 Bonneville Dam was completed.

1950's McNary Dam and The Dalles Dam were built on the Columbia River.

1964 Heavy floods damaged western Oregon.

1982 Construction was completed on a second powerhouse at Bonneville Dam.

1991 Barbara Roberts became Oregon's first woman governor. She held office until 1995.

2004 Lewis and Clark National Historical Park opened near Astoria.

discovery of gold in southwest Oregon during the early 1850's led to a series of conflicts between white miners and the Rogue Indians. The resulting Rogue River Indian War ended in 1856 with the removal of the Indians to a reservation on the central coast of Oregon.

One of the major Indian wars, the Modoc War, lasted from November 1872 to June 1873. The U.S. government forced the Modoc Indians onto the Klamath Reservation. But the Modoc fled from the reservation and hid near the California border among lava beds, which provided a natural fortress. A small band of warriors kept more than a thousand U.S. soldiers at bay until the Indians finally surrendered.

The Nez Perce War occurred in 1877. That year, the government ordered several Nez Perce bands to move from their traditional lands in the beautiful Wallowa Valley and other areas to a reservation in Idaho. Some bands resisted. One group, led by Chief Joseph, tried to escape through Idaho and Montana. Joseph and more than 400 Nez Perce finally surrendered near the Canadian border. The Paiute and Bannock Indians rose against Oregon settlers in 1878, but were quickly defeated.

Provisional and territorial governments. In 1843, settlers in the Willamette Valley met at Champoeg (near present-day Newberg) and organized a provisional government. The settlers adopted a set of laws which were based on the laws of Iowa.

Oregon became a territory in 1848, and Oregon City was proclaimed the territorial capital in early 1849. The legislature moved to Salem in 1851. Oregon's northern boundary was drawn in 1853, when Congress created the Washington Territory.

The Donation Land Law of 1850 spurred territorial growth and development. This law provided that any male American citizen older than 18 who settled in Oregon before December 1850 could receive 320 acres (129 hectares) of land. His wife could also receive 320 acres of her own. To qualify for ownership, a man had to cultivate his claim for four years. From December 1850 to December 1855, a settler had to be at least 21 to receive land, and he got only 160 acres (65 hectares). A settler's wife could receive the same amount.

Progress as a state. Oregon joined the Union as the 33rd state on Feb. 14, 1859. Salem became the state capital. During the American Civil War (1861-1865), state volunteers protected eastern Oregon against Indian attacks. The attacks continued for 15 years after the war. The population increased rapidly after the war as former soldiers sought opportunities in the West. The population grew from about 52,000 in 1860 to over 300,000 by 1890. Much of this increase occurred during the 1880's after the arrival of the transcontinental railroads.

The early 1900's. In 1902, Oregon adopted the *initiative and referendum,* procedures that permit voters to take a direct part in lawmaking (see **Initiative and referendum**). In 1908, it adopted the *recall,* a procedure for removing undesirable officials from office. The use of these direct-government procedures became known as the *Oregon system*. Many states have passed initiative, referendum, and recall laws based on this system.

In 1903, Heppner, in north-central Oregon, suffered one of the worst natural disasters in the state's history. Flash floods killed about 200 people and destroyed about one-third of the town.

Oregon Historical Society

Bonneville Dam, built with federal funds, made the Columbia River navigable. The dam supplies electric power for industry. This picture shows construction on the dam in the mid-1930's.

In 1912, Oregon gave women the right to vote. Passage of the law followed a long and difficult campaign for women's rights led by Abigail Jane Scott Duniway.

During the Great Depression of the 1930's, the federal government provided money to build Bonneville Dam on the Columbia River. The dam and nearby locks supplied electric power for industry and improved the river for navigation. Owyhee Dam, which was completed in 1932, provided irrigation water for vast areas of farmland in the Owyhee and Snake river valleys.

The mid-1900's. By 1940, Oregon's population had grown to more than a million. During World War II (1939-1945), many of the state's factories produced military equipment. Portland became a major port for shipment of supplies to the Soviet Union and to U.S. armed forces in the Pacific. The city's shipyards produced cargo vessels and warships. Thousands of people from other states came to work in Oregon defense plants, and many of them settled in the state after the war.

During the 1950's, McNary and The Dalles dams were built on the Columbia River and greatly increased Oregon's supply of low-cost electric power. In 1956, pipelines brought natural gas into the state. Both developments contributed greatly to Oregon's industrial growth. Many people began to move from rural to urban areas to take manufacturing jobs.

Important changes took place in the Oregon timber industry during the 1960's. In the past, sawdust, bark, and other logging by-products had been wasted. But in the 1960's, Oregon companies began to use many of these materials to make hardboard, pulp, and other wood products. Forestry specialists discovered new uses for forest products and studied ways to conserve the state's timber reserves. The industry replanted an increasing number of trees to replace those that had been cut down.

Changes also occurred in Oregon agriculture. The state's farms became larger and more closely linked with food processing. Farmers used more and more machinery. Irrigation projects allowed farmers to grow fruits and vegetables on land that once had been too dry for any crops except grasses.

Low-cost hydroelectric power from dams on the Columbia and Willamette rivers helped Oregon's economy grow during the 1960's. Industries, including the manufacture of electrical equipment, machinery, and metals, grew in importance.

Some of the worst floods in Oregon's history hit in 1948 and 1964. They caused millions of dollars of damage, killed several people, and forced thousands from their homes.

The late 1900's. In the late 1960's, Oregon became known for its legislation to protect the environment. In 1967, Governor Tom McCall led efforts to pass the Oregon Beach Bill, which protected the state's beaches from private development. In 1971, the state legislature passed the Beverage Container Act, or "bottle bill." It required that nearly all beverage containers be returnable for a cash refund. In 1973, Oregon formed the nation's first statewide urban growth management system. The system protected the state's farm and forest lands by setting boundaries to city expansion.

Completion of a number of dams on the Columbia and Snake rivers in the early 1970's provided deepwater transportation from the mouth of the Columbia to Lewiston, Idaho. These dams also increased the hydroelectric power capacity in Oregon. The power output of Bonneville Dam, the first federal dam constructed on the Columbia River, was more than doubled in 1982 when construction of a second powerhouse was completed.

In the early 1980's, Oregon experienced its worst economic crisis since the Great Depression. A widespread decline in housing and construction led to hard times in the lumber, wood processing, and construction industries. Low prices for farm products, including wheat and dairy and livestock products, contributed to the crisis.

Improvements in Oregon's economy began in the mid-1980's and continued in the 1990's. Some of the lumber mills that had closed reopened. The electronics industry became important, though employment in trade and other service industries grew more rapidly than jobs in manufacturing. Expansion of the fruit, grass seed, nursery, nut, and wine industries also improved economic conditions.

In 1991, Barbara Roberts became Oregon's first woman governor. She served until 1995.

Katrine Barber and Thomas Harvey

Related articles in *World Book* include:

Biographies

Astor, John Jacob
Duniway, Abigail J. S.
Gray, Robert
Lee, Jason
McLoughlin, John
McNary, Charles L.
Meeker, Ezra

Miller, Joaquin
Morse, Wayne L.
Palmer, Joel
Parkman, Francis
Pauling, Linus C.
Whitman, Marcus
Whitman, Narcissa

Cities

Astoria Eugene Portland Salem

History

Fifty-Four Forty or Fight
Indian, American
Lewis and Clark expedition
Oregon Trail
Pioneer life in America

Western frontier life in America
Westward movement in America

National parks and monuments

Crater Lake National Park
John Day Fossil Beds National Monument

Physical features

Bonneville Dam
Cascade Range
Coast Ranges

Columbia River
Crater Lake
Great Basin

Owyhee Dam
Snake River
Willamette River

Outline

I. **People**
   A. Population
   B. Schools
   C. Libraries
   D. Museums
II. **Visitor's guide**
III. Land and climate
   A. Land regions
   B. Coastline
   C. Rivers, waterfalls, and lakes
   D. Plant and animal life
   E. Climate
IV. **Economy**
   A. Natural resources
   B. Service industries
   C. Manufacturing
   D. Agriculture
   E. Mining
   F. Fishing industry
   G. Electric power and utilities
   H. Transportation
   I. Communication
V. **Government**
   A. Constitution
   B. Executive
   C. Legislature
   D. Courts
   E. Local government
   F. Revenue
   G. Politics
VI. **History**

Additional resources

Level I
Hart, Joyce. *Oregon.* Benchmark Bks., 2006.
Kent, Deborah. *Oregon.* Children's Pr., 2008.
Shannon, Terry M. *Oregon.* Children's Pr., 2009.
Stefoff, Rebecca. *Oregon.* 2nd ed. Benchmark Bks., 2006.

Level II
Abbott, Carl. *Greater Portland.* Univ. of Penn. Pr., 2001.
Bishop, Ellen M. *In Search of Ancient Oregon: A Geological and Natural History.* 2003. Reprint. Timber, 2006.
Clucas, Richard A., and others, eds. *Oregon Politics and Government.* Univ. of Neb. Pr., 2005.
Peterson del Mar, David. *Oregon's Promise: An Interpretive History.* Oregon State Univ. Pr., 2003.
Robbins, William G. *Oregon.* Oregon Hist. Soc., 2005.

Oregon, University of, is a public university in Eugene, Oregon. The university has a law school and one of the oldest schools of journalism. It also operates a campus at Portland, Oregon. At Charleston, Oregon, the school offers undergraduate and graduate degrees at its Oregon Institute of Marine Biology. The university's Pine Mountain Observatory in central Oregon is an astronomical observatory and research facility. The University of Oregon has a museum of art and a museum of natural and cultural history. The university was chartered in 1872 and opened to students in 1876. Its athletic teams are called the Ducks. The university's website at http://www.uoregon.edu offers additional information.

Critically reviewed by the University of Oregon

Oregon grape is the state flower of Oregon. This wild plant, also called the Oregon holly grape, grows from western Oregon through Washington into British Columbia. Despite its names, the Oregon grape is neither a grape nor a holly. It grows to 2 feet (61 centimeters) tall and does not climb as the wild grape does. The leaves look like those of the holly, and the wood is yellow. Clusters of yellow flowers open in early summer. The berries ripen in the fall. They look like grapes or blueberries and are often used for jelly. See also **Barberry; Oregon** (picture: State flower).　Fred T. Davies, Jr.

Scientific classification. The scientific name of the Oregon grape is often given as *Mahonia aquifolium.* Some scientists classify it as *Berberis aquifolium.*

Oregon State University is a public school with its main campus in Corvallis, Oregon. It offers bachelor's, master's, and doctoral degrees. Oregon State University has a smaller campus in Bend, Oregon. The university operates an extension service and agricultural experiment stations. It also has the Hatfield Marine Science Center in Newport, Oregon. The school was founded in 1868. Its athletic teams are called the Beavers. The school's website at http://oregonstate.edu offers additional information.　Critically reviewed by Oregon State University

Oregon Territory was created after the settlement in 1846 of a boundary dispute between the United States and the United Kingdom. It included the present states of Idaho, Oregon, and Washington and part of Montana and Wyoming. Before 1846, the Oregon Country, occupied jointly by the United States and the United Kingdom, included the area south of Alaska, north of California, and west of the Rocky Mountains. The 1846 settlement gave the United States the land south of the 49th parallel, except for Vancouver Island. The Oregon Country became a territory in 1848. Oregon was admitted to the Union on Feb. 14, 1859.　Jerome O. Steffen

Oregon Trail was the longest of the great overland routes used in the westward expansion of the United States. It wound 2,000 miles (3,200 kilometers) through prairies and deserts and across mountains from Independence, Missouri, to the Pacific Northwest. More than 50,000 people used the trail between 1841 and 1860. Even today, travelers can see the deeply rutted road cut by wagon wheels along sections of the trail.

Families traveling to the Oregon region usually began their journey at Independence, near the Missouri River.

They followed a trail that ran northwest to Fort Kearny, Nebraska. Then they traveled up the Platte River and its north branch to Fort Laramie, Wyoming. From this point, they continued along the North Platte to its Sweetwater branch and crossed through South Pass in the Rocky Mountains to the Green River Valley at Fort Bridger, Wyoming. The route turned northwest to Fort Hall in the Snake River area and on to Fort Boise, Idaho. Settlers crossed the Grande Ronde Valley and the Blue Mountains to Marcus Whitman's mission at Walla Walla, Washington. Then they went down the Columbia River to Fort Vancouver and the Willamette Valley of Oregon.

Travel on the Oregon Trail was a severe test of strength and endurance. The journey in a covered wagon took six months. Settlers often had to cross flooded rivers. Indians attacked the wagon trains, and cholera and other diseases were common. Food, water, and wood were always scarce, and the travelers often encountered contaminated water holes.

Explorers and fur traders first traced the course of the Oregon Trail. In 1805, Meriwether Lewis and William Clark traveled on a western section of the route in the region of the Snake and Columbia rivers. Robert Stuart used the trail while returning from Fort Astoria. Benjamin Bonneville is credited with taking the first wagons through South Pass in the 1830's. Nathaniel J. Wyeth also led companies over the trail. John C. Frémont surveyed a portion of the route in 1842 for the United States Army.

Settlers began following the trail to Oregon in 1841. The first large group, about 900, used the trail in the "Great Migration" of 1843. In that year, a provisional government was organized. The Territory of Oregon was set up in 1848.　Phil Roberts

Related articles in *World Book* include:

Bridger, Jim
Meeker, Ezra
Palmer, Joel
Parkman, Francis

Pioneer life in America
(Crossing the plains)
Westward movement in
America (The Oregon Trail)

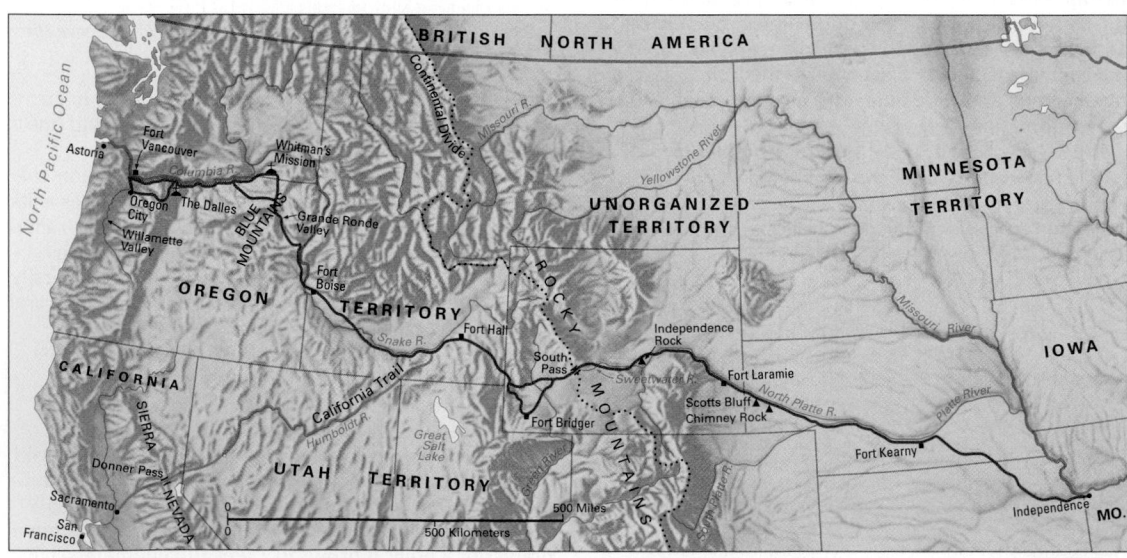

WORLD BOOK map

The Oregon Trail was the chief route to the Northwest in the mid-1800's. Thousands of pioneers traveled along the trail from Independence, Missouri, to the Pacific Northwest. Other pioneers, attracted by gold in California, turned off near Fort Hall and followed the California Trail.

O'Reilly, Leonora (1870-1927), was an American labor leader and reformer. She became well known as a lecturer and union organizer. O'Reilly strongly supported vocational training for girls.

O'Reilly was born on Feb. 16, 1870, in New York City and went to work in a shirt collar factory at the age of 11. In 1897, she helped organize a local garment workers' union. From 1902 until 1909, O'Reilly taught at the Manhattan Trade School for Girls, where she developed a strong belief in vocational education.

In 1903, O'Reilly helped establish the National Women's Trade Union League. This group promoted laws to protect the rights of women factory workers and aided the growth of women's labor unions. In 1909, O'Reilly helped lead a strike in New York City by the International Ladies' Garment Workers' Union. Thousands of workers won wage increases after the five-month strike.

O'Reilly helped found the National Association for the Advancement of Colored People (NAACP) in 1909. She also was active in the Woman Suffrage Party and the Socialist Party. She died on April 3, 1927.   Lisa Phillips

Orellana, OH ray LYAH nah, **Francisco de** (1511?-1546), a Spanish explorer, headed the first group of Europeans to navigate the entire length of the Amazon River in South America. In March 1541, he joined a Spanish expedition traveling eastward from Quito in what is now Ecuador. The expedition was led by Gonzalo Pizarro, a half brother of the Spanish explorer and conqueror Francisco Pizarro. The Spaniards soon began to starve and become sick. In December 1541, Orellana and about 55 other men set out by boat on a tributary of the Amazon River in search of food, but they never returned. Instead, they sailed to the Atlantic Ocean, which they reached in August 1542. Some historians consider Orellana a traitor for abandoning Pizarro. In 1544, Orellana was named governor of the territory he had explored. See **Amazon River** (History).   Helen Delpar

Orestes. See Electra; Iphigenia.

Orff, Carl (1895-1982), was a German composer and music educator. His major works were for the stage. They combine instrumental music, singing, and gesture and dance into a unified spectacle. Orff's music emphasizes simple, folklike melodies and harmonies that are sometimes colored with dissonance. He used instruments percussively to create a powerful rhythmic drive. Orff used Oriental and medieval scales and texts in several languages, sometimes simultaneously.

Orff's best-known compositions are three pieces he called *Trionfi (triumphs)*. The first, and most popular, *Carmina Burana (Songs of Beuron,* 1937), consists of songs set to medieval texts. He used poems by the Roman poet Catullus as texts in *Catulli Carmina (Songs of Catullus,* 1943). In *Trionfo di Afrodite (The Triumph of Aphrodite,* 1953), Orff adapted texts by Catullus and the ancient Greek writers Sappho and Euripides.

Orff was born on July 10, 1895, in Munich. In 1924, he cofounded a school of gymnastics, music, and dance in Munich. He summed up his theories on musical education for children in an important five-volume book called *Music for Children* (1930-1934, revised 1950-1954). Orff died on March 29, 1982.   Daniel T. Politoske

Organ. See Human body.

Organ is a keyboard musical instrument. There are two chief kinds of organs, *pipe organs* and *electronic or-*

gans. Most pipe organs are found in churches, concert halls, and theaters. The history of the pipe organ can be traced back to the 200's B.C. Many masterpieces of music have been composed for the pipe organ.

The electronic organ was invented in the mid-1900's. Most performers consider the pipe organ superior to the electronic organ. However, electronic organs are popular instruments in the home, and many churches also have them. The electronic organ ranks behind only the piano and the guitar as the most widely played instrument in the United States.

Both the pipe organ and the electronic organ have one or more keyboards that resemble a piano keyboard. However, the instruments produce sounds differently. A piano makes sounds by causing steel strings to vibrate. A pipe organ creates sounds by forcing air through metal or wooden tubes called *pipes.* An electronic organ produces sounds by means of electrical signals.

A pipe organ is the largest and most powerful of all musical instruments. Many pipe organs are so large that they must be built as part of the building where they are to be used. A large pipe organ can produce effects of grandeur that even a symphony orchestra cannot duplicate. It also can play delicate and refined music.

Pipe organs. A small pipe organ has only a few hundred pipes, but a large organ has more than 5,000 pipes. Most pipes are made of lead or of lead mixed with tin. Some are made of other metals or wood.

An organist creates music by combining the sounds of different *ranks* (rows) of individual pipes. Each pipe in a rank is tuned to a single pitch and produces only one musical tone. Some ranks are pitched one or two octaves higher or lower than others.

How a pipe organ works

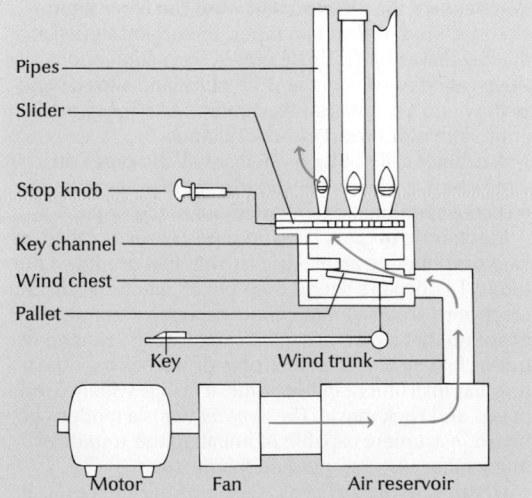

WORLD BOOK diagram by Art Grebetz

This diagram shows how wind flows through a pipe organ. An electric motor provides power for most modern organs. It operates a fan that forces wind into an air reservoir. The wind moves through a wind trunk into a wind chest. When a key is pressed, a pallet opens, and wind enters the key channel. From there, a slider, controlled by a stop knob, allows wind to flow into the pipes. As the wind passes through a pipe, it produces a note.

Most organs have two types of pipes—*flue pipes* and *reed pipes*. A flue pipe works like a simple whistle. Air enters from a hole in the bottom of the pipe and causes a column of air inside the pipe to vibrate. The vibration creates the sound. A reed pipe contains a thin brass reed that vibrates as air passes around it.

About 80 percent of the pipes in an organ are shaped like cylinders. But no two pipes of an organ look or sound exactly alike. The shape and size of the pipe determines the sound it makes. The longest pipes, which produce the lowest notes, may be more than 30 feet (9 meters) long and 1 foot (30 centimeters) in diameter. But most pipes measure less than 4 feet (1.2 meters) long. The smallest pipes, which produce the highest notes, are only 7 inches (18 centimeters) long and less than $\frac{1}{4}$ inch (6 millimeters) in diameter.

Most pipe organs have one, two, or three keyboards. A few have as many as six. The additional keyboards enable the organist to create a wide variety of musical effects. The keyboards played with the hands are called *manuals*. Large organs may have up to five manuals called, in order of importance, the *great organ; swell organ; positive,* or *choir, organ; solo organ;* and *echo organ.* Most organs also have a *pedalboard,* a keyboard played with the feet. Each keyboard—manuals and pedalboard—operates a number of ranks. Every key controls several pipes. All the ranks operated by a keyboard are arranged on a *wind chest,* a box that receives an even flow of *wind* (air) from a reservoir. An electrically powered fan fills the reservoir with wind.

A thin strip of plastic or wood called a *slider* lies under each rank of pipes on a wind chest. A slider has holes in it that match the number and size of the holes in the rank of pipes above it. A slider regulates the passage of wind into the pipes. Sliders are controlled by *stop knobs,* commonly called *stops,* near the manuals. By pulling a stop, the organist moves the slider into position beneath the pipes so that wind can enter them.

To let wind into certain pipes, the organist presses the key that controls those pipes. This action opens a valve called a *pallet* in the wind chest and allows wind to flow into a compartment called the *key channel.* Wind enters the pipes from the key channel.

A cabinet called a *case* encloses all the pipes on a wind chest. It blends the sounds of the pipes and projects this combination of sound out of the organ.

Electronic organs have no pipes. Devices called *oscillators* generate an electric current that produces the tones. The organ's sound is amplified electronically. An electronic organ cannot create the variety and richness of sound that a pipe organ can. But it costs less and requires less space. The electronic organ has become a popular instrument in the home. It also is widely used in jazz and rock music. The *synthesizer* is a modern keyboard instrument capable of imitating the sounds of many other instruments. See **Synthesizer.**

History. In the 200's B.C., Ctesibius of Alexandria, a Greek engineer, built an organ that was called a *hydraulis,* or *hydraulus.* This organ used water power to force air into the pipes. Organs that used a bellows first appeared in Byzantium (now Istanbul, Turkey) during the A.D. 100's and 200's. The major features of the modern organ were developed from the 200's to the 1500's. The keyboard was developed by the end of the 1400's.

From the 1500's to the mid-1700's, many composers wrote organ masterpieces. The greatest of these composers was Johann Sebastian Bach of Germany. Other leading organ composers included François Couperin of France and Girolamo Frescobaldi of Italy. During this period, organists accompanied singers in operas and in oratorios. Large organs were played in churches. Small organs were popular at home and at public events.

By the late 1700's, small organs had lost their popularity. Many composers believed an orchestra or a piano could provide a wider range of musical effects. By 1900, interest in the organ had declined among composers and performers. The instrument was played regularly only in churches as part of religious services.

A revival of interest in the organ began during the early 1900's. The German humanitarian Albert Schweitzer, an accomplished organist, began this revival. He gave concerts in many European cities and stimulated interest in the instrument. In 1934, Laurens Hammond, an American inventor, patented the first commercially practical electronic organ.   Dale C. Carr

Related articles in *World Book* include:

Bach, Johann Sebastian	Harmonica
Buxtehude, Dietrich	Harmonium
Franck, César	Music (picture: Keyboard in-
Hand organ	struments)

Organ donation is the process through which human organs are obtained for transplant surgery. Most organs used in transplant operations come from young, otherwise healthy patients who suffer *brain death* (a permanent end of brain function), often following a fatal head injury. Organs commonly transplanted from one person to another include the heart, kidney, liver, and lung.

Advances in organ transplant surgery and powerful drugs to prevent organ rejection have made transplants an established medical treatment for many diseases and injuries. Organ donation can save lives and restore health, and most major religions permit such donations. The supply of human organs falls far short of the demand, however. As a result, medical professionals must make difficult ethical decisions to obtain human organs and assign them to people in need of transplants.

In most countries, doctors must obtain permission to remove organs from the dead to use for transplant. In the United States and the United Kingdom, people can use donor cards or mark a space on their driver's license to give permission to donate their organs after death. In practice, however, many hospitals consult the family even if the patient has signed an organ donor card. In Australia, donor permission is required, but final approval must come from family. In some other countries, including Austria and Belgium, doctors may remove organs for transplant after death unless there is written evidence that the person does not want to be a donor. This system, called *presumed consent,* increases the supply of human organs available for transplant. But under such a system, some people who would not want to donate their organs might become donors.

Medical professionals are investigating ways to increase the supply of human organs for transplant, including increasing live donation and compensation for organ donors. More than one-third of transplanted kidneys in the United States come from live donors, because a person can donate one kidney and remain healthy. Live liver donation, where a lobe of the donor's liver is transplanted and grows into a fully functioning organ, is also becoming more common. Most living organ donors are close relatives of the recipient, but about 20 percent of live organ donations involve unrelated people.

In the United States, the National Organ Transplant Act of 1984 prohibits the exchange of organs for any kind of payment. However, lawmakers are considering legislation that allows compensation to donors to encourage more live organ donations.   Arlene J. Klotzko

See also **Transplant.**

Organic chemistry is the study of compounds that contain carbon atoms. Carbon atoms are unusual because they can form chemical bonds in many different ways, both with other carbon atoms and with other chemical elements. As a result, many kinds of carbon-containing compounds are possible. Scientists have identified several million organic compounds.

A large number of simple organic compounds are obtained from plant and animal sources. For example, petroleum and natural gas contain many hydrocarbons from the remains of organisms that lived millions of years ago. Ethanol, a kind of alcohol, is formed by the fermentation of fruits, grains, and vegetables. Other organic compounds in living matter include amino acids, sugars, and nucleic acids. Inorganic compounds, which generally do not contain carbon, occur chiefly in rocks and in minerals.

Scientists once believed that carbon-containing compounds could be obtained only from living sources. However, in 1828, the German chemist Friedrich Wöhler prepared the organic compound urea in his laboratory. Since then, scientists have found many ways of making organic compounds from both organic and inorganic materials, and many important new compounds have been prepared in the laboratory. These compounds include medicines, insecticides, and chains of molecules called *polymers* (see **Polymer**).   Marianna A. Busch

See also **Chemistry.**

Organic food is grown or raised using little or no synthetic fertilizers, pesticides, or other artificial chemicals. Instead, organic farmers try to work with natural processes to promote the health of their crops and livestock. For example, an organic farmer might apply *compost* (decaying plant material) instead of chemical fertilizer to replenish the soil. Instead of using pesticides, the farmer may rely on natural predators to control insect pests.

Although organic food does not necessarily cost more to grow or raise than other food, it is often sold at higher prices in stores. Shoppers buy organic food for various reasons. Consumers may buy organic meat and dairy products because of their concerns with the treatment of livestock on large commercial farms. Some people buy organic food because they believe modern agriculture leads to environmental and health problems.

Standards. A number of organizations regulate the labeling of organic food in a process called *certification*. The organizations include nonprofit associations, private businesses, and some governments. They inspect organic operations and make sure certain standards are followed. In the United States, for example, farmers who sell their crops as organic cannot use most pesticides and fertilizers made from chemicals or sewage. Organic

livestock must be fed chiefly organically grown feed, without medicines called antibiotics or artificial growth hormones. Packagers and distributors of organic foods must also follow certain rules.

Some foods are labeled or advertised as "all natural," "naturally raised," "free range," or similar terms. Such labels are often not as strongly regulated as the *organic* label, and in some cases may not be regulated at all.

History. Sir Albert Howard, a British scientist, became one of the first people to advance the idea of organic farming in the West. In the 1940's, he described in published accounts ideas about soil fertility and waste reuse he saw in practice in India. In 1946, his ideas inspired the formation of the Soil Association, a United Kingdom organization that promotes organic agriculture.

In the 1960's, public concern over possible environmental dangers of certain chemicals led to increased interest in organic farming. In the 1980's, low prices for regularly grown crops caused some large-scale farmers to turn to organic farming. Restaurant chefs also began to feature organically grown vegetables. Beginning in the 1990's, a wide variety of organic products became available at many supermarkets.   Julie Guthman

See also **Farm and farming** (Organic farming).

Organisation for Economic Co-operation and Development (OECD) is an association of 34 nations in Europe, North America, and the Pacific area. The organization works to promote the economic and social welfare of its members and coordinates their efforts to aid less developed countries. The OECD was established in 1961 to succeed the Organisation for European Economic Co-operation (OEEC). Seventeen European nations formed the OEEC in 1948 as a result of the Marshall Plan. Under the Marshall Plan, the United States helped Europe achieve economic recovery after World War II (1939-1945). The OECD's headquarters are in Paris. See also **International Energy Agency.**

Critically reviewed by the Organisation for Economic Co-operation and Development

Members of the OECD

Countries that became members of the OECD in 1961 do not have dates after their names. Other nations are listed with their years of admission.

Australia (1971)	Hungary (1996)	Norway
Austria	Iceland	Poland (1996)
Belgium	Ireland	Portugal
Canada	Israel (2010)	Slovakia (2000)
Chile (2010)	Italy	Slovenia (2010)
Czech Republic (1995)	Japan (1964)	Spain
Denmark	Korea, South (1996)	Sweden
Estonia (2010)	Luxembourg	Switzerland
Finland (1969)	Mexico (1994)	Turkey
France	Netherlands	United Kingdom
Germany	New Zealand (1973)	United States
Greece		

Organization for Security and Co-operation in Europe (OSCE) is an association of more than 55 countries in Europe, Asia, and North America that work to increase their security. Until 1995, it was called the Conference on Security and Co-operation in Europe (CSCE).

The OSCE's members are Russia and all the other nations of Europe, plus the United States, Canada, and the central Asian countries that were once part of the Soviet Union. Members include all countries of the North Atlantic Treaty Organization (NATO) as well as the lands that once belonged to the Warsaw Pact. NATO is a non-Communist defense alliance, and the Warsaw Pact was a Communist one. The two alliances were intense rivals during the Cold War, a period of hostility that developed between the Communist and non-Communist nations after World War II ended in 1945. The Warsaw Pact, led by the Soviet Union, dissolved in 1991.

The first CSCE conference met in 1975 in Helsinki, Finland. That conference produced the Helsinki Accords. In the accords, Western countries finally recognized Eastern European boundaries that had been set up after World War II. The accords also stimulated the formation of human rights groups that later helped overthrow many Communist governments in Eastern Europe and the Soviet Union. In 1990, a CSCE conference in Paris declared an end to the Cold War. The Paris conference also established a CSCE secretariat in Prague, in what is now the Czech Republic; and, in Warsaw, Poland, an office to monitor elections in European countries.

The Soviet Union belonged to the CSCE until 1991, when the country broke up into a number of independent states. After the breakup, Russia assumed the Soviet seat, and all the other states that had been part of the Soviet Union eventually joined the CSCE. In 1992, the CSCE acquired the authority to send peacekeeping forces to its member nations. It also agreed to oversee the negotiation of arms-control agreements between its Eastern and Western members.　　Joseph Preston Baratta

See also **Helsinki Accords.**

Organization of American States (OAS) is an association of 35 American countries. It seeks to provide for collective self-defense, regional cooperation, and the peaceful settlement of controversies. The OAS Charter sets forth the group's guiding principles. These principles include a belief in the value of international law, social justice, economic cooperation, and the equality of all people. The OAS Charter also states that an act of aggression against one American nation is regarded as an act of aggression against all the nations in the OAS.

The OAS functions through several bodies. Major policies are formed at annual sessions of the General Assembly. All member nations can attend, and each has one vote. Special Meetings of Consultation of Ministers of Foreign Affairs deal with urgent problems, especially those relating to defense or the maintenance of peace in the Americas. The Permanent Council, with headquarters in Washington, D.C., is the executive body of the OAS. Each member nation is represented. For convenience, diplomatic representatives in Washington serve as council members. The council supervises the General Secretariat, makes plans for General Assembly sessions, and oversees OAS administration. The secretary-general, the chief administrator of the OAS, is elected to a five-year term by the General Assembly. Specialized conferences promote inter-American cooperation.

The OAS had its early beginning at the First International Conference of American States, which met in Washington in 1889 and 1890. The delegates established the International Union of American Republics, with the Commercial Bureau of the American Republics as its central office. This bureau was renamed the Pan Ameri-

Members of the OAS

Countries are listed with the years they became OAS members.

Antigua and Barbuda (1981)	Dominican Republic (1949)	Peru (1952)
Argentina (1956)	Ecuador (1950)	St. Kitts and Nevis (1984)
Bahamas (1982)	El Salvador (1950)	St. Lucia (1979)
Barbados (1967)	Grenada (1975)	St. Vincent
Belize (1991)	Guatemala (1955)	and the
Bolivia (1950)	Guyana (1991)	Grenadines (1981)
Brazil (1950)	Haiti (1950)	Suriname (1977)
Canada (1990)	Honduras (1950)	Trinidad and
Chile (1953)	Jamaica (1969)	Tobago (1967)
Colombia (1951)	Mexico (1948)	United States (1951)
Costa Rica (1948)	Nicaragua (1950)	Uruguay (1955)
Cuba (1952)	Panama (1951)	Venezuela (1951)
Dominica (1979)	Paraguay (1950)	

can Union in 1910. The Pan American Union became the permanent body of the OAS when it was organized in 1948 at the ninth Pan-American Conference, held in Bogotá, Colombia. The organization's original charter became effective in December 1951. An amended charter took effect in February 1970, and the Pan American Union was renamed the General Secretariat of the OAS.

Early in 1962, the Organization of American States voted to exclude Cuba's Communist government from active membership. Cuba remained an OAS member, but its government could not participate in any of the organization's activities. In 2009, the OAS voted to readmit Cuba to active membership.

In 1965, a revolt in the Dominican Republic led the OAS to set up its first military force. Troops from six Latin American countries and the United States took part. The troops and OAS committees restored order in the Dominican Republic. In 1969, the OAS ended a five-day invasion of Honduras by troops from El Salvador.

During the late 1970's, the organization's main concern became human rights. The Inter-American Commission on Human Rights—a specialized OAS agency—interviewed political exiles and conducted on-site investigations of human-rights violations. The commission also issued reports about electoral fraud, illegal imprisonment, and torture and other acts of brutality.

The influence of the OAS began to decline during the early 1980's because of increased involvement by other international agencies in Latin American affairs. These agencies included the International Monetary Fund and the World Bank.　　George W. Grayson

See also **Pan-American conferences.**

Organization of the Petroleum Exporting Countries (OPEC) is an association of 12 countries that depend heavily on oil exports for their incomes. Its members work together to try to increase their revenue from the sale of oil on the world market. OPEC members produce about 40 percent of the world's oil and possess about 70 percent of the world's recoverable oil reserves. The members of OPEC are Algeria, Angola, Ecuador, Iran, Iraq, Kuwait, Libya, Nigeria, Qatar, Saudi Arabia, the United Arab Emirates, and Venezuela. Ecuador joined OPEC in 1973, suspended its membership from 1992 through 2007, then became a member again in 2008. Indonesia withdrew from OPEC at the end of 2008.

OPEC was founded in 1960 by Iran, Iraq, Kuwait, Saudi Arabia, and Venezuela. At that time, the petroleum industry in these countries was controlled by United States and European oil companies. These firms paid the host governments income taxes and *royalties* (shares of their profits) based on the *posted price* the companies charged for crude oil on the world market. In 1959 and 1960, oil production greatly exceeded world demand. The surplus that was thereby created prompted several of the major companies to cut the posted price and thus their payments to host governments. OPEC was founded in response to this price cut.

OPEC had little influence on oil prices during the 1960's, when production expanded to keep pace with demand. In the 1970's, however, world demand for oil began to outgrow what was available from non-OPEC sources. In 1973, OPEC stopped consulting with oil companies and decided to raise oil prices in keeping with the rate of *inflation* (the rise of all prices).

Armed conflict also contributed to rising oil prices. During the Arab-Israeli War of 1973, some Arab members of OPEC stopped or reduced oil exports to countries supporting Israel. As a result, oil prices in those countries, including the United States and other Western industrial nations, rose sharply. During the late 1970's, the Iranian revolution caused a shortage that helped OPEC increase oil prices again.

OPEC was less successful at achieving its goals in the 1980's, when the world oil supply again exceeded demand. In 1983, OPEC cut the price of its oil for the first time. Since the mid-1980's, OPEC has sought to control production by its members. However, some members have ignored the limits, causing prices to fall during certain periods. By the early 2000's, the price of oil was less easily influenced by OPEC policy. The rapid rise in oil prices that began in 2003 was largely caused by political conflict in oil-producing nations, rising global demand for oil, and speculation by investors and traders on the commodities markets.   Bob Williams

Orient is another name for the Asian countries and islands, or the East. See also **Asia; Far East.**

Oriental Exclusion Acts, a series of actions and acts approved by the United States government, restricted and prohibited Asians from entering the United States.

Chinese first came to the United States in large numbers after the discovery of gold in California in 1848. They were initially well received but met hostility as they moved into urban areas. Between 1864 and 1869, Chinese laborers were brought to the United States to help build the Central Pacific Railroad. In 1868, China and the United States signed the Burlingame Treaty to protect this immigration.

During the 1870's, however, the immigration of Chinese coincided with an economic depression, and the Chinese were made the scapegoats. Americans accused them of unfair competition in business, of lowering wages, and of immoral and unsanitary habits. In some instances, they were victims of mob violence. Despite the treaty of 1868, Congress passed the Chinese Exclusion Act of 1882. This law and an extension of it that was passed in 1892 were intended to be only temporary, but Congress made exclusion permanent in 1902.

After the Chinese were barred, Japanese immigrants began coming to the United States in increasing numbers during the late 1800's. Many of them settled on the West Coast and became farmers. Their innovative farm-

ing methods, thrift, and low living standards made them a competitive force and aroused the anger of white farmers. California petitioned Congress to extend the Chinese exclusion law to the Japanese. In 1908, a "gentlemen's agreement" between the United States and Japan provided a temporary solution. Japan agreed to stop emigration of its workers to the United States, and the United States agreed to halt discriminatory immigration laws against the Japanese (see **Gentlemen's agreement**). The Immigration Act of 1924 prohibited the entry of all Asian laborers.

During World War II (1939-1945), Congress repealed the laws against the Chinese, permitting a limited number to enter the United States each year and be eligible for citizenship. The Immigration and Nationality Act of 1952 extended the same privileges to other immigrants, including the Japanese. The national quota system was abolished in 1965.   Frank J. Coppa

See also **Asian Americans** (History of Asian immigration).

WORLD BOOK photo by Dan Miller
Origami is the Japanese art of folding paper into decorative objects. Most figures can be made without cutting or pasting.

Origami, *AWR uh GAH mee,* is the art of folding paper into decorative objects. The term is the Japanese word for *folded paper.* There are about 100 traditional origami figures. Most depict such natural forms as birds, flowers, and fish. An abstract, ceremonial form of origami, called a *noshi,* is a pleated paper ornament attached to gifts. Most origami is folded from an uncut square of paper. The most common sizes of square are 15 centimeters and 25 centimeters (6 and 10 inches). The preferred paper is thin Japanese paper called *washi.* Foil-backed wrapping paper and heavy art paper are also used.

Origami, like paper, originated in China. But the art flourished in Japan. Since the 1940's, it has reached new levels of complexity and realism.   Robert J. Lang

Orinoco River, *OHR uh NOH koh,* is the longest river in Venezuela. It is 1,284 miles (2,066 kilometers) long. The Orinoco has two known sources, both in the Parima highlands in Venezuela, near the border of Brazil. The river flows northwest to Colombia and forms the boundary between Colombia and Venezuela. Then it swings east across Venezuela. About 110 miles (177 kilometers) before it reaches the seacoast, it divides into many channels. For location, see **Venezuela** (terrain map).

Small oceangoing vessels can sail 260 miles (418 kilometers) upstream from the mouth of the Orinoco. Ships can use the river for about 500 miles (800 kilometers) above the Maipures and Atures rapids. Ciudad Bolívar is the center of the Orinoco river trade. Steamships run between Ciudad Bolívar and the island of Trinidad most of the year. Major branches of the Orinoco are the Apure, Caroní, and Meta rivers. Including its branches, the Orinoco has a navigable length of 4,300 miles (6,920 kilometers).   Gregory Knapp

Oriole, *AWR ee ohl,* in the Americas, is a group of small songbirds. In Europe, the name *oriole* is given to a group of birds that are not related to American orioles. Most of the American orioles live in or near the tropics. In Jamaica, they are known as banana birds. Three common *species* (kinds) of orioles spend the summer in southern Canada and the United States—the Baltimore oriole, Bullock's oriole, and the orchard oriole. Several other oriole species also live in the United States.

Orioles have beautifully colored feathers and loud, musical voices. They weave hanging nests and help farmers by eating insects. But in some areas, these birds may eat grapes. Some orioles are also called troupials.

Donald F. Bruning

Scientific classification. American orioles make up the genus *Icterus*. The Baltimore oriole is *Icterus galbula*. Bullock's oriole is *I. bullockii*, and the orchard oriole is *I. spurius*.

See also **Baltimore oriole; Bird** (pictures: Birds of forests and woodlands; Birds' eggs).

Orion, *aw RY uhn* or *oh RY uhn,* was a handsome and energetic hunter in Greek mythology. He was a giant who could walk through the sea and on its surface.

Orion had a troubled love life. His wife was sent to Hades after she boasted that she was more beautiful than the goddess Hera (see **Hades**). Because Orion seduced his fiancée, Merope, her father, King Oenopion, blinded him. Helios, the sun god, restored Orion's sight.

According to one myth, Artemis, the goddess of hunting, killed Orion because he tried to rape her. Another myth says that Artemis considered marrying Orion, but her jealous brother Apollo tricked her into hitting Orion with an arrow while he was swimming. In her sorrow at his death, Artemis placed Orion in the sky as a constellation. Another myth tells that Gaea, the earth, sent a scorpion to sting Orion to death.   Nancy Felson

Orion, *aw RY uhn* or *oh RY uhn,* the Hunter, is a brilliant constellation that includes two of the brightest stars in the sky. Orion is often pictured with his back turned toward us. In this view, the bright red star, Betelgeuse, marks his left shoulder. A blue-white star called Rigel marks his right foot. Two fainter stars, Bellatrix and Saiph, mark Orion's right shoulder and left foot. Orion is easily identified by a row of three stars forming his belt. A sword, made of faint stars, dangles from the belt.

Two *nebulae* (clouds of gas and dust) are in Orion. The Great Nebula, which appears in the middle of Orion's sword, is visible as a misty spot under a dark sky. The Horsehead Nebula in Orion's belt is difficult to see.

Jay M. Pasachoff

See also **Betelgeuse; Nebula** (picture); **Star** (picture: The constellation Orion).

Orizaba, *AWR uh ZAH buh* or *AW ree SAH vah,* **Pico de,** is the highest mountain in Mexico and the third highest in North America. Only Mount McKinley and Mount Logan are higher. Pico de Orizaba rises 18,410 feet (5,611 meters) above sea level. Its Aztec name, Citlaltépetl *(see tlahl TAY peht uhl),* means "mountain of the star." The mountain stands about 30 miles (48 kilometers) north of the city of Orizaba, Mexico. It is a volcano and part of Mexico's Neo-Volcanic Chain. It last erupted in the late 1600's.   John J. Winberry

See also **Mountain** (diagram: Major mountains).

Orkney Islands (pop. 19,245) are a group of islands that form part of Scotland. The islands make up a *unitary authority,* the United Kingdom's primary unit of local government. The islands are separated from Scotland's north coast by the Pentland Firth, a channel about 7 miles (11 kilometers) wide (see **Scotland** [political map]).

About 65 islands and some rocky isles make up the Orkney Islands, which have a total land area of about 377 square miles (976 square kilometers). Kirkwall and Stromness are the only towns. They lie on Mainland, the largest island. Nearly all the people are of Scandinavian or Scottish ancestry.

Rich soil and a mild climate help make agriculture the leading industry in the Orkney Islands. The chief products include cattle, cheese, eggs, and barley. Fishing is also an important economic activity. In addition, the islands have a major oil terminal that receives oil piped from wells in the North Sea.

Archaeological evidence indicates that people lived in the Orkney Islands about 5,000 years ago. Vikings from Norway ruled the islands from the A.D. 800's to the 1400's. Most of the islands' place names are of Viking origin. Scotland (now part of the United Kingdom) acquired the Orkney Islands from Norway in 1469, when Scotland's king, James III, married Princess Margaret of Norway and Denmark. The islands served as an important base for the British Navy during World War I (1914-1918) and World War II (1939-1945).   H. R. Jones

Orlando, *awr LAN doh,* Florida (pop. 238,300; met. area pop. 2,134,411), is a popular winter resort and tourist center. Orlando's warm climate has helped make it one of the fastest-growing cities in the United States. Walt Disney World Resort opened about 15 miles (24 kilometers) southwest of the city in 1971. This famous entertainment center has contributed greatly to Orlando's rapid growth. Many people, including large numbers of retired citizens, have settled in Orlando because of the mild climate. Orlando's temperature averages 60 °F (16 °C) in January and 83 °F (28 °C) in July.

Orlando, the county seat of Orange County, lies in central Florida (see **Florida** [political map]). Its museums include the Orange County Regional History Center and the Orlando Science Center, which features the Dr. Phillips CineDome, a theater that presents large-format films, planetarium shows, and laser light performances. The University of Central Florida is in Orlando. The city is also the home of the Orlando Magic of the National Basketball Association.

Orlando's chief industry is tourism, and Walt Disney World Resort is its chief employer. Other major employers include Lockheed Martin, an aerospace firm; hospitals; and supermarket and department store chains.

Seminole Indians lived in what is now Orlando before European settlers first arrived in 1837. In 1850, the settlement was named Jernigan for Aaron Jernigan, an Orange County trader. It became known as Orlando in 1857. This name probably honors Orlando Reeves, a soldier who died in a battle with the Indians.

Orlando's first major period of growth followed demands of early citrus fruit growers for better transportation for their crops. A railroad reached the city in 1881, and more planters started citrus groves during the 1890's. In the early 1900's, a real estate boom helped increase the population of Orlando and many other Florida communities. Orlando's population grew from 9,282 in 1920 to 52,367 in 1950.

The development of Walt Disney World Resort led to many construction projects in Orlando. They included apartment buildings, banks, hotels, motels, restaurants, and shopping areas. In 1972, Orlando completed a new Municipal Justice Building. A Civic Theatre (now the Orlando Repertory Theatre) opened in 1973. In 1982, Walt Disney Productions opened Epcot (Experimental Prototype Community of Tomorrow), a permanent world's fair, at Walt Disney World Resort. Another attraction there is Disney's Hollywood Studios (formerly Disney-MGM Studios), which opened in 1989. Disney's Animal Kingdom, which opened in 1998, displays hundreds of animals in re-creations of a jungle, savanna, and other habitats. Universal Studios Florida—a motion-picture and television studio and theme park—opened in Orlando in 1990. Orlando has a mayor-council form of government. Judy L. Grimsley

Orlando, *awr LAN doh,* **Vittorio Emanuele,** *veet TAW ryoh EH mah noo EE leh* (1860-1952), served as prime minister of Italy from 1917 to 1919. He took office just after the Italian Army suffered a terrible defeat at Caporetto (now in Slovenia) in World War I. His efforts to restore civilian morale and army discipline helped keep Italy in the war, on the side of the Allies, until the Allied victory in 1918. After the war, he led the Italian delegation at the Paris Peace Conference in 1919. He temporarily left the conference in protest after the Allies refused to meet Italy's claims to the port of Fiume in Yugoslavia and to former Austrian territories. His opponents in Parliament later forced him to resign as prime minister.

Orlando supported Benito Mussolini when Mussolini became prime minister of Italy in 1922. But Orlando denounced him in 1925 when Mussolini began openly to create a dictatorship. In 1946, when Italy's monarchy was abolished, Orlando helped establish the Italian republic.

Orlando was born on May 19, 1860, in Palermo. A law professor, he began his political career in the Italian Chamber of Deputies in 1897. He died on Dec. 1, 1952.

Susan A. Ashley

See also **Wilson, Woodrow** (picture: The "Big Four").

Orléans, *AWR lee uhnz* or *AWR lay AHN* (pop. 113,130; met. area pop. 269,283), is an important commercial center in north-central France. The city lies along the Loire River. For location, see **France** (political map).

Orléans is in the Loire Valley, a region that is famous for its many estates and *chateaux* (castles). The city has a number of medieval buildings—including the Gothic Cathedral of St. Croix and the University of Orléans. Orléans grows most of the commercially raised roses in France. Its many other products include automobiles, candies, clothing, computers, electric appliances, farm machinery, liqueurs, and pharmaceuticals.

Roman soldiers established a colony at the site of what is now Orléans in 52 B.C. In 1429, Joan of Arc led the French Army in saving the city from English invasion (see **Joan of Arc, Saint**). Mark Kesselman

Orléans, Battle of. See Hundred Years' War.

Ormandy, *AWR muhn dee,* **Eugene** (1899-1985), became one of the world's best-known orchestra conductors as director of the Philadelphia Orchestra. From 1936 to 1938, Ormandy shared leadership of the orchestra with Leopold Stokowski. Ormandy was the orchestra's sole music director from 1938 to 1980. His specialties were Romantic and Neoromantic music in which he emphasized fine string playing and rich orchestral tones. Under his leadership, the orchestra toured many countries and made many recordings.

Eugene Ormandy Blau was born on Nov. 18, 1899, in Budapest, Hungary. He studied the violin with Jenö Hubay, a noted Hungarian violinist. In 1921, Ormandy went to the United States to make a concert tour. Instead, he became a violinist in the orchestra of the Capitol Theater in New York City. Soon Ormandy began to conduct, and he became principal conductor of the Minneapolis Symphony Orchestra in 1931. He held this position until moving to Philadelphia. Ormandy became a U.S. citizen in 1927. He died on March 12, 1985.

Martin Bernheimer

Ornament. See Art and the arts; Clothing; Gem; Jewelry and their lists of *Related articles.*

Ornithischian. See Dinosaur (Kinds of dinosaurs).

Ornitholestes, *awr nih thuh LEHS teez,* was a small meat-eating dinosaur that lived about 150 million years ago, near the end of the Jurassic Period. Its name comes from the Greek words for *bird* and *robber.* Scientists once believed this dinosaur hunted mainly birds. *Ornitholestes* belonged to a group of dinosaurs called *coelurosaurs (see LOOR uh sawrz)* from which birds may have evolved. Coelurosaurs, in turn, belonged to a larger dinosaur group called *theropods (THUR uh podz).*

Ornitholestes had a lightly built body with hollow bones. The dinosaur was about 6 feet (1.8 meters) long but weighed only about 25 pounds (11 kilograms). It stood on two legs and was a fast runner. A long, tapered tail probably helped it balance and turn quickly. *Ornitholestes* had a long, flexible neck and a small head. Sharp teeth rimmed the front half of its long, narrow jaws.

Ornitholestes lived in fern meadows and forests in what is now the western United States. The dinosaur most likely ate lizards, small mammals, and insects. It may also have preyed on birds, birdlike dinosaurs, and flying reptiles called *pterosaurs.* Scientists first uncovered *Ornitholestes* fossils in Wyoming in 1900.

Kenneth Carpenter

Ornithology, *AWR nuh THAHL uh jee,* is the scientific study of birds. It includes the description, history, and classification of birds; and their distribution, numbers, activities, ecological importance, and economic value to people. The activities of birds that ornithologists study include mating, nesting, rearing of young, feeding, flight, navigation, migration, and communication. Photography often is used to document the activities of birds, and recordings are made of their songs.

People have valued birds throughout history because of their beauty, their interesting habits, and their importance as a source of food and clothing. Many people belong to bird clubs, and a large number of amateurs participate in ornithological research. The American Ornithologists' Union, a nonprofit educational organization, was established in 1883.   Richard E. Bonney, Jr.

See also **Audubon, John James; Audubon Society, National; Bird** (Bird study and protection).

Ornithomimus, AWR nihth uh MY muhs, was a dinosaur that resembled a modern ostrich. Its name, which means *bird mimic,* refers to the animal's birdlike appearance.

Ornithomimus measured about 10 to 13 feet (3 to 4 meters) in length and stood about 6 to 8 feet (1.8 to 2.4 meters) tall. It had a lightly built body with an elongated neck and tail; short arms; and long, strong hind legs. One of the fastest dinosaurs, *Ornithomimus* may have run as swiftly as an ostrich—30 to 40 miles (48 to 64 kilometers) per hour. It used its speed and keen eyesight to avoid *predators* (hunting animals). Its tail helped it balance during quick turns.

Ornithomimus had a toothless, beaklike mouth and probably ate eggs, insects, small animals, and fruit. The dinosaur used its long, claw-tipped fingers to uncover food on the ground or to dig for prey. It may also have stolen eggs from the nests of other dinosaurs.

Ornithomimus lived about 76 million to 65 million years ago, near the end of the Cretaceous Period. Scientists have found its remains in western North America and central Asia.   David B. Weishampel

See also **Dinosaur** (pictures: Dinosaurs and birds; When dinosaurs lived).

Ornithopod. See **Dinosaur** (Kinds of dinosaurs).

Ornithopter, AWR nuh THAHP tuhr, is a machine designed to fly by flapping its wings like a bird. People have dreamed of such a vehicle since ancient times. Some small-scale models have flown. But all attempts to build ornithopters that carry people on a regular basis have failed because materials that are light enough and strong enough have not been developed.

Ornithopters are classified in two ways. The first type relies on a person's muscles to flap the wings. The second type uses an engine to power the wings. The English philosopher Roger Bacon suggested the idea of the ornithopter about 1250.

Roger E. Bilstein

See also **Airplane** (Early experiments and ideas).

Ornithosis. See **Psittacosis.**

Oroville Dam, OHR uh vihl, is the highest dam in the United States. It rises 770 feet (235 meters) and extends 6,800 feet (2,073 meters) across the Feather River, near Oroville, California. The Oroville Dam is the chief dam of the State Water Project, which supplies irrigation water to central and southern California.

The dam is an earth-fill dam (see **Dam** [Embankment dams]). About 80 million cubic yards (61 million cubic meters) of earth materials were used in its construction. It was completed in 1968. The materials came from waste piles at nearby gold-mining operations.

The Oroville Dam forms a reservoir called Lake Oroville, which contains about 3 ½ million acre-feet (4.3 billion cubic meters) of water. Water from Lake Oroville is used to irrigate farmland as far as 650 miles (1,050 kilo-

meters) away in southern California. A hydroelectric power plant connected to the dam also uses the water. The dam also helps control floods.   Allen Soast

Detail of a fresco (1934); courtesy of the Trustees of Dartmouth College

An Orozco mural shows the god Quetzalcoatl rising above Aztec temples to arouse the Indians to improve their culture. The Aztec believed the god brought knowledge and civilization.

Orozco, oh ROHS koh, **José Clemente,** hoh SAY klay MAYN tay (1883-1949), a Mexican painter, became known for murals that use themes from Mexico's history. His style emphasizes human figures who are portrayed with strong lines, dramatic angles, and brownish colors.

Orozco was born on Nov. 23, 1883, in Zapotlán. He spent his early career drawing political and satirical cartoons. In the early 1920's, Orozco and other Mexican artists began painting frescoes on walls in public buildings (see **Fresco**). Unlike the work of fellow muralists Diego Rivera and David Siqueiros, Orozco's frescoes seldom contain political messages. Instead, his paintings express his reaction to the struggles of common people everywhere.

In the 1930's, Orozco turned to a more abstract style. Examples of this style include the murals called *Epic of New World Culture* (1932-1934) in the Dartmouth College library in Hanover, New Hampshire, and murals in public buildings in Guadalajara and Mexico City. Orozco died on Sept. 7, 1949.   Judith Berg Sobré

Orphanage. See **Children's home.**

Orpheus, AWR fee uhs or OHR fyoos, was a musician in Greek and Roman mythology. The music of his voice and lyre was so beautiful that animals, trees, and stones followed him, and rivers stopped flowing to listen. His mother was the muse Calliope, and his father was either the mortal Oeagrus or the god Apollo.

Orpheus joined the Argonauts in their quest to capture the Golden Fleece. Later, he married Eurydice. After Eurydice died, he went to the underworld to bring her back. His music charmed Hades and Persephone, the rulers of the underworld, and they granted Eurydice permission to leave. But they warned Orpheus not to look back at her on the way up to the earth. He glanced back too soon, and she disappeared. Orpheus angered some women of Thrace because he took no interest in them or in their worship of the god Dionysus, and they tore him to pieces.   Justin M. Glenn

See also **Argonauts; Eurydice.**

Orr, Bobby (1948-   ), was one of the greatest defensemen in the history of ice hockey. He revolutionized the position with his graceful skating and extraordinary ability to carry the puck up the ice without weakening his team's defense. Orr's 139 points in the 1970-1971 season remains a record for National Hockey League (NHL) defensemen. Orr is the only defenseman to have led the NHL in scoring, doing this in the 1969-1970 and 1974-1975 seasons. He won the Hart Memorial Trophy as Most Valuable Player in the NHL three seasons, from 1969-1970 through 1971-1972. He captured the James Norris Memorial Trophy as the league's best defenseman a record eight consecutive seasons, from 1967-1968 through 1974-1975.

Robert Gordon Orr was born on March 20, 1948, in Parry Sound, Ontario. He played for the Boston Bruins from 1966 to 1976. Orr signed with the Chicago Black Hawks in 1976. He retired in 1978 because of knee problems.   Larry Wigge

Orrisroot, AWR ihs ROOT, is the dried, sweet-smelling *rhizome* (underground stem) of certain irises. Orrisroot yields a waxy material containing a fragrant oil that is used to give perfumes a scent like that of violets. The oil is obtained by dissolving the waxy material in a fat or other organic substance. That substance is then removed, leaving the oil. Because of its high price, the oil has largely been replaced by synthetic substitutes. But small amounts are still used in some expensive perfumes. Orrisroot comes from irises cultivated in France, India, Italy, and Morocco. See also **Iris.**   James E. Simon

Ortega, awr TAY gah, **Daniel** (1945-   ), became president of Nicaragua in 2007. Ortega also had served as head of Nicaragua's government from 1979 to 1990.

In 1979, the Sandinista National Liberation Front, a revolutionary movement with diverse social and political origins, overthrew the government of Anastasio Somoza Debayle. Ortega was named leader of the new revolutionary government and was elected president of Nicaragua in 1984. His term as president ended in 1990, when he lost a presidential election to Violeta Barrios de Chamorro, the leader of a coalition that opposed Sandinista rule. Ortega ran for president again in 1996 and 2001, but he was defeated both times by candidates from the Liberal Constitutionalist Party.

© Jack McKigney, Picture Group
Daniel Ortega

During the 1980's, Ortega's government improved health care in rural areas, built many new schools, and reduced illiteracy. It also took control of many businesses, increased press censorship, and restricted the civil rights of its political opponents. Critics of Ortega, including the United States government, charged that he and the Sandinistas had set up a Communist dictatorship. In 1981, Nicaraguans

known as *contras* began a guerrilla war against Ortega's government. In 1988, Ortega helped negotiate a cease-fire between his government and the contras.

Nicaragua's relationship with the United States greatly influenced Ortega's national leadership from 1979 to 1990. The United States had been Nicaragua's chief trading partner and had supported the dictatorship of the Somoza family. After the Sandinistas came to power, the United States sharply reduced trade with Nicaragua and provided funds to the contras. Ortega and his party struggled to improve an economy crippled by the U.S. trade cuts, by the war against the contras, and by high government spending for health and education programs. The economic crisis and fear of continued U.S. aggression contributed to Ortega's 1990 electoral defeat.

Daniel José Ortega Saavedra was born on Nov. 11, 1945, in the town of La Libertad. During the 1960's, he became a guerrilla leader of the Sandinista opposition to the Somoza government. The government imprisoned Ortega from 1967 to 1974. After receiving military training in Cuba, he helped lead the overthrow of the Somoza government.   Francisco J. Barbosa

See also **Nicaragua** (Recent developments).

Ortega y Gasset, awr TAY guh ee gah SEHT, **José** (1883-1955), was a Spanish philosopher and essayist. He wrote *Meditations on Quixote* (1914), which anticipated themes that Existentialist philosophers made popular more than 10 years later. Ortega emphasized the idea that we are "condemned to be free," and therefore all individuals must determine their own place in history. See **Existentialism.**

Ortega cherished aristocratic values. He believed that without spiritual leadership from the top, society would be drawn down to the level of its lowest members. For Ortega, this problem was especially serious because of the decline of self-confidence that he saw in Europe and the rise of merely technical modes of thought and organization in the 1900's. He explored these ideas in his best-known book, *The Revolt of the Masses* (1930). In *The Dehumanization of Art* (1925), Ortega discussed the tendency of modern art to rid itself of human content.

Ortega was born on May 9, 1883, in Madrid. He was strongly influenced by the ideas of the German philosopher Immanuel Kant while he was studying in Germany. Ortega was professor of philosophy at Madrid University from 1910 to 1936. Because of the Spanish Civil War, he lived in exile from 1936 until 1945, when he returned to Spain. He died on Oct. 18, 1955.   Karl Ameriks

Orthodontics, AWR thuh DAHN tihks, is the branch of dentistry that prevents and corrects irregular positions of the teeth. In addition to causing poor personal appearance, irregularly positioned teeth are difficult to clean. Thus, they are more likely to decay and promote gum diseases (see **Teeth** [Periodontal diseases]). Irregularly positioned teeth also can cause chewing and speech problems and can damage the jaw.

Irregularities in the position of teeth are called *malocclusions.* Malocclusions usually arise during childhood as the teeth grow. They most commonly occur when the teeth are too large for the available jaw space. Under such conditions, the teeth become crowded and turned out of position. In some cases, one of the jawbones is larger than the other, creating either an overbite or an underbite.

Malocclusions can sometimes be prevented by the early removal of certain *deciduous teeth* (baby teeth). This process, called *serial extraction* or *guidance eruption,* relieves crowding that occurs as new teeth break through the gums. If the teeth are already out of position, orthodontists cement metal or plastic braces to the front of each tooth and connect the braces with wires. By gradually tightening the wires, they move the teeth into proper position. In some cases, a tooth is extracted so that other teeth can be moved into its place. Orthodontic treatment is sometimes combined with surgery on the jawbones to correct malocclusions.

Orthodontic treatment is typically begun when patients are 10 to 16 years old and lasts about two years. Some adults also undergo orthodontic treatment, but treatment time is generally longer. John P. Wortel

See also **Dentistry** (Orthodontics [picture]); **Teeth** (Malocclusion).

Orthodox, Eastern. See Eastern Orthodox Churches.

Orthopedics, *AWR thuh PEE dihks,* is a branch of medicine that deals with disorders of the bones and muscles and their associated tissues. The word is also spelled *orthopaedics.* Doctors who practice orthopedics are called *orthopedists* or *orthopedic surgeons.* They treat a range of problems, including fractures, injuries to tendons and ligaments, and deformities of the limbs and spine.

Orthopedists provide care for patients who range from the newborn to the elderly. Some orthopedic disorders are present at birth. Others occur during childhood because of problems of growth or in later life as a result of aging. Still others result from injury or illness. People injured in automobile accidents and athletic or recreational activities account for a large number of the patients treated by orthopedists.

In treating orthopedic disorders, orthopedists prescribe drugs, surgery, or physical therapy. For example, an orthopedist may perform surgery to correct a fracture or deformity. After the surgery, the orthopedist may apply a cast or brace and prescribe physical therapy to aid healing. An orthopedist also may perform surgery to replace an injured or arthritic joint with an artificial joint made of plastic, metal, or other materials. Joints most commonly replaced include the hip, the knee, and joints in the hands and feet. William J. Kane

Orwell, George, was the pen name of Eric Arthur Blair (1903-1950), a British novelist and social critic. Orwell became famous with his novel *1984,* which was published in 1949. The book is a frightening portrait of a *totalitarian* (government-controlled) society that punishes love, destroys privacy, and distorts truth. The novel includes the well-known statement "Big Brother Is Watching You." The grim tone of *1984* distinguishes it from Orwell's *Animal Farm* (1945), an animal fable that satirizes Communism. Orwell's familiar saying "All animals are equal, but some animals are more equal than

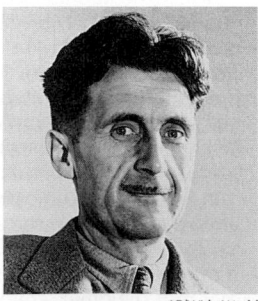

AP/Wide World
George Orwell

others" appears in *Animal Farm.*

Orwell was a unique combination of middle-class intellectual and working-class reformer. A strong autobiographical element runs through most of Orwell's writing, giving his novels and essays a sense of immediacy and conviction. Orwell's experiences living in poverty color *Down and Out in Paris and London* (1933), *A Clergyman's Daughter* (1935), and *The Road to Wigan Pier* (1937). The novels attack social injustice and range from the miseries and hypocrisies of the poor from middle-class backgrounds to the near-starvation of the slum-dweller. *Homage to Catalonia* (1938) is a nonfiction work based on Orwell's brief career as a soldier. In it, he describes his military experiences during the Spanish Civil War (1936-1939).

Orwell was born on June 25, 1903, in Bengal, India, the son of a British civil servant. He attended Eton school from 1917 to 1921 and served with the Indian Imperial Police in Burma (now Myanmar) from 1922 to 1927. He lived in poverty in England and Europe until the mid-1930's. He died on Jan. 21, 1950. Garrett Stewart

Osage Indians, *OH sayj,* once gathered food and hunted buffalo throughout a vast region of what are now Arkansas, Kansas, Missouri, and Oklahoma. The tribe also had permanent camps along the Osage River, which was named for them. The Osage lost most of their land to the United States government as a result of treaties made from 1808 to 1870. In 1872, the tribe moved to a reservation in Oklahoma and took up farming.

Oil was discovered on the Osage reservation in the late 1800's. It produced income that made the tribe extremely wealthy, and some Osage moved off the reservation. Today, the Osage preserve some aspects of their culture, including their language and religious ceremonies. Many Osage still live on the reservation, and many other Osage return in June for an annual ceremonial dance called I'n-Lon-Schka. Cherokee Cheshewalla

Osage orange, *OH sayj,* is a small- to medium-sized tree planted across the United States for hedges, ornamental purposes, and shade. It originally was found in Texas, Oklahoma, and Arkansas. The name refers to the Osage Indians of that region and to the tree's greenish-yellow fruit, which looks like an orange but is inedible. The Osage orange is sometimes called *bodark, bois d'arc, bowwood,* or *hedge apple.*

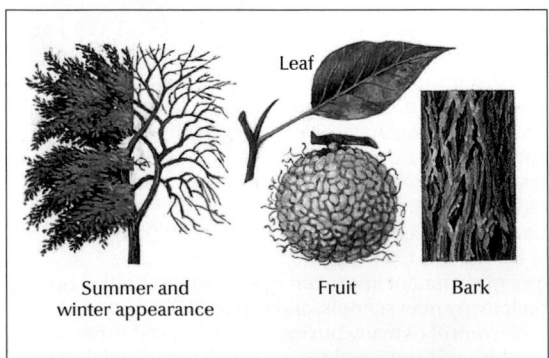

Leaf

Summer and winter appearance | Fruit | Bark

WORLD BOOK illustration by Chris Skilton
The Osage orange has greenish-yellow fruit that resembles an orange. The tree has a short trunk and crooked branches and long, pointed leaves. Its yellow wood is hard and durable.

The tree has a short trunk and crooked branches. Its long, pointed leaves are a shiny, dark green. It has thorny twigs and a milky, bitter sap. Pioneers planted Osage orange trees as a "living fence" around their farms before barbed wire came into use.

The yellow wood of the Osage orange is hard, strong, and durable. The Indians preferred it for their bows and war clubs. It makes good fence posts and was used for wagon wheels. A yellow dye can be made by boiling chips of the wood in water.   Norman L. Christensen, Jr.

Scientific classification. The Osage orange tree belongs to the mulberry family, Moraceae. It is *Maclura pomifera.*

Osaka, *oh SAH kuh* (pop. 2,628,811), is the third largest city in Japan. Only Tokyo and Yokohama have more people. Osaka, an important industrial and commercial center, lies on Osaka Bay on the southern coast of Honshu Island (see **Japan** [political map]).

Osaka covers about 80 square miles (206 square kilometers). It is sometimes called the "Venice of Japan" because of its many canals and rivers. Since the 1960's, some of these waterways have been filled and highways built over them. Downtown Osaka lies on the delta of the Yodo River. Office buildings, stores, hotels, restaurants, and entertainment centers fill this section of the city. Many shopping centers have been built underground because of a shortage of land.

Osaka has many museums, theaters, and religious shrines. Osaka Castle, built in 1584, houses a museum with historical exhibits. Bunraku Theater presents puppet shows, and Kabuki Theater offers stage performances. Osaka has several universities, including government-supported Osaka University. In 1970, Osaka was the site of Expo '70, the first world's fair to be held in Asia.

World Photo Service from Madeline Grimaldi

Osaka, Japan's third largest city, is an important commercial and cultural center. Numerous canals and rivers run through the city, which lies on the southern coast of Honshu Island.

In the past, most Osakans lived in small wooden houses. Today, many Osaka residents live in large apartment buildings. The city's population increased by more than a million during the 1950's, and this rapid growth led to shortages of land and housing. Many Osakans have moved to the suburbs to escape the city's crowded conditions, high prices, and pollution.

Osaka is famous for its good food, especially seafood. Local specialties include eel; shrimp; turtle; and *kaminabe,* a fish stew cooked in a paper pot.

Osaka is one of Japan's manufacturing centers. The city exports clothing, electrical appliances, and fabrics. The city is also a financial and trade center.

Osaka has serious traffic problems in spite of efforts to improve public transportation. Buses, a subway system, and commuter trains serve the city. High-speed trains travel between Osaka and Tokyo, a distance of about 250 miles (400 kilometers). Osaka has two airports, Kansai International Airport and Osaka Airport. Kansai International is one of the busiest airports in Asia.

Osaka was settled in ancient times. It later became Japan's major port and commercial center. Toyotomi Hideyoshi, the ruler of Japan from 1585 to 1598, encouraged merchants to move to Osaka. The government opened Osaka's port to foreign trade in 1868.

Allied bombing raids destroyed much of Osaka during World War II (1939-1945). The people rebuilt their city following the war. Osaka's population growth created a need for more housing, sewers, highways, and subways. Many of these improvements were completed during the city's preparations for Expo '70.

Kenneth B. Pyle

Osborn, Henry Fairfield (1857-1935), was an American *paleontologist* (expert on prehistoric life). He was an authority on fossil vertebrate animals and evolution. His best-known work consisted of his studies of ancient reptiles and mammals. Osborn wrote about rhinoceroses; elephants and their relatives; and *titanotheres,* large mammals that once roamed the American West. Osborn's book *From the Greeks to Darwin* (1894) discussed evolution.

Osborn served as president of the American Museum of Natural History in New York City from 1908 to 1933. Under his administration, it became one of the world's largest museums. Osborn was born on Aug. 8, 1857, in Fairfield, Connecticut, and died on Nov. 6, 1935.

Carolyn Merchant

Osborne, John (1929-1994), a British dramatist, became famous with his first important play, *Look Back in Anger* (1956). The drama deals with Jimmy Porter, an educated but poor young man. Porter lashes out at everyone around him in anger and frustration because the world no longer offers any ideals or causes he can believe in. The play was a vivid contrast to the sort of polite upper-middle-class stories and characters presented in most British plays of the time. Osborne continued the story of Jimmy Porter's life in *Dejavu* (1992).

Osborne's other early plays also criticized society. *The Entertainer* (1957) uses a run-down old comedian to symbolize the decline of the British Empire. *Luther* (1961) presents a modern interpretation of Reformation religious leader Martin Luther as a troubled rebel. *Inadmissible Evidence* (1964) portrays the breakdown of a successful lawyer as he realizes how empty his life is.

As Osborne grew older, his plays became more con-servative. He defended the way of life he had once criti-cized, and he attacked younger social critics. He also wrote an autobiography, *A Better Class of Person* (1981). John James Osborne was born on Dec. 12, 1929, in Lon-don. He died on Dec. 24, 1994.   Gerald M. Berkowitz

Osborne, Thomas Mott (1859-1926), was an Ameri-can prison reformer. In 1913, as chairman of the New York State Commission for Prison Reform, he spent a week in prison, secretly, so he could understand and help prisoners. He served as warden of Sing Sing (New York) Prison from 1914 to 1916 and of Portsmouth (New Hampshire) Naval Prison from 1917 to 1920. Osborne or-ganized the Mutual Welfare League to help prisoners rebuild their lives. He wrote *Within Prison Walls* (1914) and *Society and Prisons* (1916). Osborne was born on Sept. 23, 1859, in Auburn, New York, and died there on Oct. 20, 1926.   Robert A. Pratt

Oscan, *AHS kuhn,* was a language used by one of the earliest known peoples of Italy. It was part of the Indo-European family and was distantly related to Latin.

Oscar. See **Motion picture** (Festivals and awards).

Osceola, *AHS ee OH luh* (1804?-1838), led the Seminole Indians in Florida during the Second Seminole War (1835-1842). He fought attempts by the United States Army to move the tribe west of the Mississippi River to the Indian Territory.

Osceola was born in a Creek Indian village near the Tallapoosa River in what is now eastern Alabama. The name *Osceola,* or *Asi-Yaholo,* comes from *asi,* a drink containing caffeine; and *Yaholo,* a cry shouted by the men who served asi during tribal ceremonies. After the Creek War (1813-1814), Osceola and many Creeks re-treated to Florida and joined the Seminole.

During the 1820's, Osceola became known as a suc-cessful hunter and war leader. His warriors defeated United States troops in several battles early in the Second Seminole War. In 1837, Osceola met with U.S. troops under a flag of truce to discuss peace. But General Thomas Jesup or-dered the troops to cap-ture and imprison him. Osceola died soon after-ward—on Jan. 30, 1838—in the Fort Moultrie prison near Charleston, South Carolina.

Detail of a painting (1838) by George Catlin; National Portrait Gallery, Smithsonian Institution

Osceola

Many Americans were outraged by Jesup's trick-ery, and the Army's repu-tation fell sharply. Osceola won widespread respect. Several towns and counties were named for him.   Michael D. Green

See also **Indian wars** (Conflicts in the South).

Oscillograph. See **Oscilloscope.**

Oscilloscope, *uh SIHL uh skohp,* is an electronic in-strument used to observe one or more electrical signals. An oscilloscope displays *oscillations* (back-and-forth changes) in a signal's voltage. It shows these oscillations as wavy lines or other patterns on a video screen or dis-play. Typically, the lines form a graph showing how the voltage of the signal changes over time.

Oscilloscopes are used in such fields as industry, medicine, and scientific research. Engineers use them to test computers, radios, and other electronic equipment. Physicians use them to study electrical impulses from the brain or heart. People also use oscilloscopes to study oscillations in forms of energy other than electric current, such as light, mechanical motion, and sound. Devices called *transducers* can convert these forms of energy into an electrical signal, which can then be ob-served using an oscilloscope.

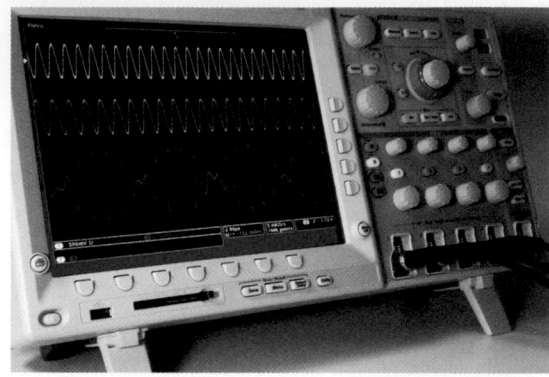

© GIPhotostock/Photo Researchers

An oscilloscope shows changes in the voltage of one or more electrical signals as wavy lines or other patterns on a screen.

Most oscilloscopes today use *digital* technology—that is, they measure the voltage of a signal at various inter-vals and convert the measurements into numerically en-coded data. A computer can process, store, and recall such data. A stored signal can usually be recalled at a faster or slower rate than that at which it was recorded. For example, a *seismic wave,* the pattern of vibration generated by an earthquake, may be recorded over half a minute and then played back in a fraction of a second. Many digital oscilloscopes use displays similar to those found in flat-screen televisions and computer monitors.

In a traditional *analog* oscilloscope, on the other hand, the screen is the front of a type of vacuum tube called a *cathode-ray tube.* Inside the tube, a device called an *electron gun* projects a beam of electrons onto a fluorescent screen. Any sideways or up-and-down movement of this beam leaves a glowing trail on the screen. A circuit called the *time base* causes the beam to move repeatedly from left to right. At the same time, the signal to be studied is fed into the oscilloscope, where it causes the electron beam to move up and down. The beam moves up and down as it passes from left to right, repeatedly tracing a pattern that represents the oscillat-ing signal.   Daniel G. Jablonski

OSHA. See **Occupational Safety and Health Adminis-tration.**

Oshawa, *AHSH uh wuh* (pop. 141,590; met. area pop. 330,594), is an important Canadian industrial city in On-tario. It is sometimes called *Canada's Motor City.* The city is the home of General Motors of Canada, the nation's largest manufacturer of motor vehicles. Oshawa lies on Lake Ontario in southeastern Ontario. For location, see **Ontario** (political map).

The Oshawa area was first settled in 1794, when Benjamin Wilson, a Vermont farmer, and his family moved there. In 1842, the community was named Oshawa, an American Indian word meaning *crossing between the waters*. The community was given this name because it lay between Lake Ontario and Lake Scugog.

In 1907, R. S. McLaughlin established the McLaughlin Motor Car Company in Oshawa. This firm produced McLaughlin-Buick automobiles. The Chevrolet Motor Car Company of Canada was established in Oshawa in 1915. The two firms united in 1918 to form General Motors of Canada. Oshawa received a city charter in 1924.

General Motors of Canada is one of Oshawa's chief employers. Other major employers include the Ontario Ministry of Finance, Oshawa's hospital, the regional school system, Durham College, and the University of Ontario Institute of Technology. Oshawa has a council-manager form of government.   Donald G. Cartwright

Osier, *OH zhuhr,* is the name of certain willows that grow as shrubs and small trees. They grow best along streams. These willows have tough, slender stems that can be used for making baskets and furniture. The common osier (also called the basket willow) and the purple osier were brought to the United States from other countries. They are cultivated for their flexible stems. In the Northeast, they have escaped from cultivation and grow wild. One dogwood is called the red-osier dogwood because its bark resembles that of some willows. It is not closely related to osiers. See also **Willow.**

Richard C. Schlesinger

Scientific classification. Osiers are in the genus *Salix.* The common osier is *Salix viminalis.* The purple osier is *S. purpurea.* The red-osier dogwood is *Cornus sericea.*

Osiris, *oh SY rihs,* an Egyptian fertility god, became the chief god of the underworld. He is generally shown as a bearded human mummy with green or black flesh. He holds a shepherd's crook and a whip and wears a conical white crown with ostrich feathers.

As son of the Earth god Geb, Osiris was regarded as a source of Earth's fertility. Egyptians sometimes compared him to the Nile River. As a popular Egyptian god, Osiris was often identified with other gods. At Busiris in the Nile Delta region, he took on the characteristics of an earlier god-king. At the burial ground at Abydos, he replaced a god of the dead.

In Egyptian royal theology, the pharaoh was a living Horus, who was the son of Osiris. After the pharaoh died, he became Osiris. Egyptian funeral practices later became more democratic, and every Egyptian expected to become an Osiris after death. Osiris was the central figure in Egypt's most popular myth (see **Mythology** [The Osiris myth]).   Robert K. Ritner

See also **Isis; Mythology** (Egyptian mythology; pictures); **Serapis; Seth.**

Osler, *OHS luhr,* **Sir William** (1849-1919), was a Canadian physician and one of the greatest medical educators. His brilliant teaching and informal and genial personality greatly influenced many of his students. Through his students, Osler influenced medicine in English-speaking countries throughout the world.

One of Osler's most notable contributions to medicine was the organization of a clinic at the Johns Hopkins Hospital in Baltimore. It became the model for modern medical education in the United States. Osler

strongly favored using "the patient for a text," and he perfected the method of teaching that encourages students to become actively involved in patient care and learn the art of medicine at the bedside.

Culver
Sir William Osler

Osler discovered the presence in the bloodstream of what later were called *disks,* or *blood platelets* (see **Blood** [Platelets]). Among his many scientific papers are important studies of the heart and research on typhoid fever, pneumonia, malaria, infant mortality, and other medical and public health problems. He also helped found the Association of American Physicians in 1886 and the National Tuberculosis Association (now the American Lung Association) in 1904.

His writings. Osler wrote *Principles and Practice of Medicine* in 1892. For many years, it was a standard textbook in the United States. In 1897, a member of John D. Rockefeller's philanthropic staff read the book and was inspired by the potential of medical research, especially in microbiology. This incident led to the founding of the Rockefeller Institute for Medical Research in 1901. Osler's humanistic essays were collected in *Aequanimitas* (1904) and *An Alabama Student* (1908).

Painting on papyrus from Dynasty XVIII (1554-late 1300's B.C.); SCALA (Art Resource)
Osiris was one of the principal ancient Egyptian gods. He ruled the underworld and is often portrayed as a mummy seated on a throne wearing the crown of Upper Egypt.

His life. Osler was born on July 12, 1849, in Bondhead, Ont., Canada. He graduated from McGill University in 1872. He served at McGill from 1875 to 1884 as a lecturer in physiology and as professor of medicine. In 1884, he became clinical professor of medicine at the University of Pennsylvania. He was appointed professor of medicine at the new Johns Hopkins University four years later. At the same time, he was made physician-in-chief to the new hospital there. Osler went to Oxford University in 1905 as regius professor of medicine, one of the most prestigious medical positions in the United Kingdom. He became a baronet in 1911. He helped organize the British medical profession during World War I to meet the war emergency.   Dale C. Smith

Oslo (pop. 512,589) is the capital and largest city of Norway. It is also the nation's chief economic, industrial, and cultural center, and one of its leading seaports. Oslo lies on the southeast coast at the head of the great Oslo Fiord. The city is about 80 miles (130 kilometers) north of the Skagerrak, an arm of the North Sea (see **Norway** [map]). From 1624 until 1925, Oslo was called Christiania in honor of King Christian IV, who planned the rebuilding of the city after a fire destroyed it.

The Oslo metropolitan area covers about 175 square miles (454 square kilometers). But over two-thirds of the metropolitan area consists of forests and lakes. These features make the city a favorite recreation center.

The Royal Palace and the Parliament Building stand along Karl Johans Gate, the main street in the central section of Oslo. City Hall, the medieval Akershus Castle, and the city's commercial district are south of Karl Johans Gate. Most of Oslo's people live in apartment buildings. The majority of Oslo's single-family homes are located in outlying areas of the city.

Oslo has Norway's oldest and largest university, an Evangelical Lutheran cathedral, and many museums. The Viking Ships Museum displays ships used by the Vikings about a thousand years ago. The Fram and Kon-Tiki museums house the *Fram,* a famous polar exploration ship; and the *Kon-Tiki,* the raft of anthropologist and adventurer Thor Heyerdahl (see **Heyerdahl, Thor**). Other museums include the Norwegian Folk Museum, Norwegian Maritime Museum, Historical Museum, and Edvard Munch Museum. About 150 works by Gustav Vigeland, one of Norway's greatest sculptors, are in Oslo's Frogner Park.

Manufacturing employs about 25 percent of Oslo's workers. Major industries include shipbuilding and the production of chemicals, machinery, metals, paper, textiles, and wood products. Banking, communications, electronics, food processing, shipping, and tourism also play important roles in the city's economy. Oslo is the hub of the Norwegian national railroad system. An international airport lies just outside the city.

Oslo was founded by King Harold Hårdråde about 1050. In 1299, Akershus Castle was built on a rocky peninsula overlooking the fiord. Fire destroyed Oslo in 1624, but the people rebuilt the city northeast of the castle. Norway was united with Denmark from 1380 to 1814, and with Sweden from 1814 to 1905. In 1905, it became independent, with Oslo as the capital. By the mid-1800's, the city had grown into a major administrative, economic, and military center. The development of shipping and industry, plus the forest and agricultural resources of southeastern Norway, soon helped give Oslo the dominant role in the nation's economy that it still has today.

M. Donald Hancock

See also **Norway** (Climate; pictures).

Dale Brown, DPI   Adeline Haaga, Tom Stack & Assoc.

Oslo is the capital and largest city of Norway. It also ranks as the country's leading seaport. Passenger ships, cargo vessels, and fishing boats dock at Oslo's busy harbor, *above left.* Many parks and gardens, such as the one shown above at the right, add to the scenic beauty of the city.

Osman I, *AHZ muhn, AHS muhn,* or *ahs MAHN* (1258?-1326?), was the founder of the Ottoman Empire, which was named after him. Osman became known as a skillful military leader and a just ruler.

Osman, who is sometimes called *Othman* or *Uthman,* was probably born near Bursa, in northwestern Anatolia (now Turkey). His father was the leader of a group of nomadic Turks. According to some historical traditions, this group settled in Anatolia in the 1200's. At first, they served as soldiers for the Seljuks, who ruled much of the region. After he succeeded his father as leader in the 1280's, Osman established a small independent state in the Sakarya Valley in northwestern Anatolia.

Osman gradually expanded Ottoman territory by conquering small neighboring states or forming alliances with them. In 1301, he defeated an army of the nearby Byzantine Empire in the Battle of Baphaeon. About 1324, Osman turned over leadership of the Ottomans to his son Orhan.   Virginia H. Aksan

Osmium, *AHZ mee uhm,* is a hard metallic element. It is one of the densest elements, with a density of 22.57 grams per cubic centimeter. Osmium is rare and expensive and is found in the same ores as platinum. Smithson Tennant, a British chemist, discovered osmium in 1804.

Osmium occurs in several large deposits spread around the world and in meteorites. Refined osmium is a fine, black powder or a hard, blue-gray mass. Osmium alloys, which resist corrosion, are used to tip penpoints and in mechanical parts. When heated in air, osmium forms *osmium tetroxide,* which vaporizes at about 100 °C. This compound can damage the eyes, skin, and lungs. It is used in certain scientific processes.

Osmium's chemical symbol is Os. The element has a boiling point of 5012 plus or minus 100 °C and a melting point of 3033 plus or minus 30 °C. Its *atomic number* (number of protons in its nucleus) is 76. Its *relative atomic mass* is 190.23. An element's relative atomic mass equals its *mass* (amount of matter) divided by $\frac{1}{12}$ of the mass of carbon 12, the most abundant form of carbon.
                    Emily Jane Rose

Osmosis, *ahz MOH sihs,* is the movement of liquid from one solution through a special membrane into a more concentrated solution. It is essential for the survival of living things. For example, plants absorb most of their water by osmosis. In animals, osmosis helps regulate the flow of water and nutrients between body fluids and cells. Industries reverse osmosis for such purposes as water purification and food preservation.

A liquid solution consists of a dissolved substance called a *solute,* and a liquid called a *solvent.* During osmosis, some of the solvent from one solution moves through microscopic holes in a membrane into another solution. The membrane is *semipermeable*—that is, it allows solvent molecules to pass through its holes, but it blocks solute molecules. The solute molecules are larger than the holes in the membrane.

In osmosis, more solvent moves into the solution with the greater concentration of solute molecules. This is mostly because, in the weaker solution, there are fewer solute molecules blocking the solvent's movement.

Solvent from the weaker solution continues to dilute the more concentrated solution until the concentrations are equal. At this point, the amount of solvent entering each solution equals the amount leaving each solution.

However, the flow of solvent will stop before the concentrations become equal if a certain pressure is exerted on the more concentrated solution. This pressure is called the *osmotic pressure.*

Experiment. Osmosis can be demonstrated by performing the following experiment. First, fasten a piece of cellophane over the bottom of a glass tube. Next, pour a solution of sugar and water into the tube. Then place the tube into a container of pure water so the levels of the water and the sugar solution are equal. After several hours, the liquid in the tube rises because of osmosis.

In this experiment, the cellophane is the semipermeable membrane. It allows water molecules to pass through but blocks sugar molecules. The sugar molecules are too large. In the tube, the sugar molecules interfere with the water molecules and prevent some wa-

An osmosis experiment

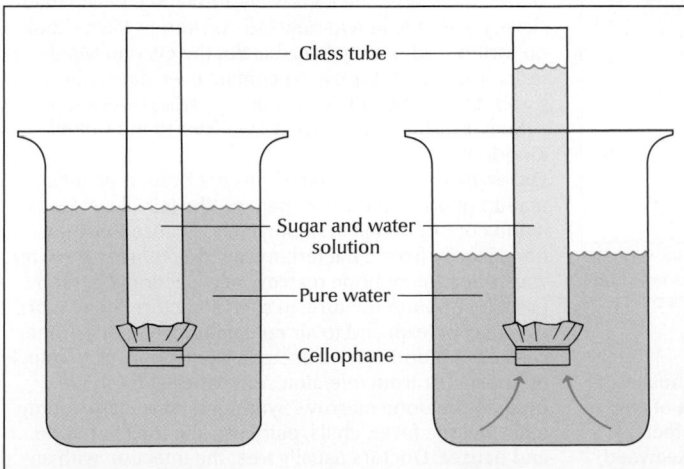

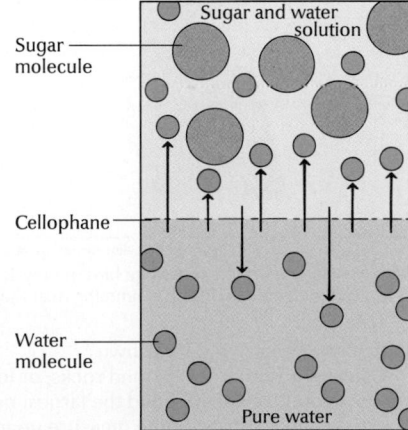

WORLD BOOK diagrams

The process of osmosis can be demonstrated in the experiment shown here. Water enters the glass tube through the cellophane, which serves as a semipermeable membrane. As the water mixes with the sugar solution, the solution rises.

Molecules of water pass through the cellophane, as shown in this diagram, but the larger sugar molecules do not. The level of the sugar solution rises because more water molecules move into the solution than out of it.

ter from moving through the membrane. As a result, more water moves into the tube than out of it.

As water moves into the tube, the sugar solution rises, thereby increasing the pressure in the tube. The solution continues to rise until the pressure that it exerts equals that of the pure water.

Reverse osmosis. Chemists use a process called *reverse osmosis* to purify water and perform other functions. In normal osmosis, water flows from fresh water into seawater when they are separated by an appropriate semipermeable membrane. But, by applying pressure to the seawater, chemists can reverse the movement of the water and produce fresh water from seawater. Some shipwreck victims have used survival kits that convert seawater into drinking water by osmosis (see **Water** [diagram: Reverse osmosis]).

Robert B. Prigo

Osprey, *AHS pree* or *AH spray,* also called *fish hawk,* is a fish-eating bird. Ospreys feed by making spectacular plunges into water from heights of 50 to 100 feet (15 to 30 meters). They hit the water feet first with a great splash and seize a fish with their long, slender claws. These birds live throughout the world along rivers, lakes, seacoasts, and bays. Ospreys in northern regions migrate to warm areas for the winter.

The osprey is about 2 feet (60 centimeters) long, with a wingspread of nearly 6 feet (1.8 meters). It is dark brown above and has some white on its head. It is white below

WORLD BOOK illustration by Trevor Boyer, Linden Artists Ltd.

The osprey is a brown-and-white bird of prey. It lives near bodies of water and feeds on fish swimming near the surface.

with a few streaks of dark brown.

Ospreys nest in trees, jagged rocks, or low bushes, or on the ground. Ospreys build the largest nests of any North American birds. Some measure up to 6 feet (1.8 meters) high. Nest-building materials include seaweed, sticks, bones, and driftwood. In North America, during April or May, ospreys usually lay three eggs. Incubation of the eggs lasts about 37 days.

Insecticides, such as DDT, and human disturbance of

the bird's habitat reduced the number of ospreys in several locations. However, conservation measures on the United States mainland helped to increase the osprey population.   Thomas G. Balgooyen

Scientific classification. The osprey's scientific name is *Pandion haliaetus.*

Ossining Correctional Facility. See Sing Sing.

Ostend, *ah STEHND* (pop. 68,594), is a Belgian city on the North Sea, about 77 miles (124 kilometers) northwest of Brussels (see **Belgium** [political map]). Ostend lies in the Dutch-speaking region of Belgium. Its name in Dutch is *Oostende.* It is an important Belgian port that conducts export-import business with many countries. The city serves as the harbor for cross-channel boats from Dover, England. Ostend fishing crews catch cod and herring. Oysters are cultivated offshore. Ostend is a fashionable summer resort. Visitors enjoy its sea walk and listen to concerts in a building called the Kursaal.

Dutch, Spanish, and French troops have fought many battles for Ostend because of its value as a port. In 1865, its fortifications were destroyed by the Belgian government, and Ostend became important for shipping. Ostend was damaged in World War I (1914-1918) and again in World War II (1939-1945).   Aristide R. Zolberg

Ostend Manifesto, *ah STEHND,* was a controversial document drafted in 1854 as part of a plan by the United States to acquire the colony of Cuba from Spain. It stated that the United States might be justified in seizing Cuba for reasons of national security if Spain refused to sell the island.

During the mid-1800's, several United States leaders wanted to annex Cuba as a new slave state. In 1854, William L. Marcy, secretary of state under President Franklin Pierce, asked three U.S. diplomats to make recommendations for the acquisition of Cuba. They were minister to Spain Pierre Soulé, minister to France John Y. Mason, and minister to the United Kingdom James Buchanan. They met at Ostend, Belgium, in October 1854. Newspapers obtained copies of the ministers' dispatch. They called it the Ostend Manifesto and published it in 1855. The implied threat to seize Cuba added to the uproar started in 1854 by the Kansas-Nebraska Act, which made slavery possible in two new U.S. territories. Pierce took no further action to gain Cuba. But the Ostend Manifesto added to the growing conflict over slavery between the North and the South.   Robert Freeman Smith

See also **Buchanan, James** (Minister to the United Kingdom).

Osteomyelitis, *AHS tee oh MY uh LY tihs,* is an inflammation of bone and *bone marrow,* the jellylike material in the core of bones. Osteomyelitis is caused by infection, usually from a bacterium called *Staphylococcus aureus.* Infection of bone marrow may occur if a person has a compound fracture. In such a fracture, bone marrow may be exposed to air containing bacteria. In other cases, the blood carries bacteria from a boil, from infected tonsils, or from infection somewhere else in the body to the bone marrow. Symptoms of acute osteomyelitis include fever, chills, pain over the infected bone, and nausea. Doctors usually treat the infection with antibiotics.   Madison B. Cole, Jr.

Osteopathic medicine, *AHS tee uh PATH ihk,* is a system of medical care based on the belief that all body systems are interrelated. Disease in one part of the body affects other parts of the body, and so the whole person must be considered in providing treatment. Osteopathic medicine emphasizes the importance of the body's *musculoskeletal system*. This system consists of the muscles and bones and their connecting tendons and ligaments.

Osteopathic medicine involves all aspects of medicine and includes various medical specialties. Osteopathic physicians use all the medical, surgical, immunological, pharmacological, psychological, and hygienic procedures of modern medicine.

The musculoskeletal system makes up 60 percent of the body's weight. Because this system is so extensive, osteopathic medicine maintains that it has especially important interrelationships with other body systems. The musculoskeletal system may be affected by many internal illnesses and, in turn, may speed or worsen the process of disease in other body systems, including the circulatory system and the nervous system. Osteopathic physicians are trained to use osteopathic manipulation of the musculoskeletal system as a diagnostic and treatment tool, when it is appropriate. Such *osteopathic manipulative treatment* (OMT) is a distinctly osteopathic approach to the problems of health and disease.

History. The founder of osteopathic medicine was Andrew Taylor Still, an American medical practitioner. Still announced the basic principles of the osteopathic system in 1874. In 1892, he organized the first osteopathic college, which was established at Kirksville, Missouri.

The first law regulating osteopathic medicine was passed in Vermont in 1896. There are now such laws in all the states, and in some of the provinces of Canada. In every state, graduates of osteopathic medical schools are eligible to be licensed as physicians and surgeons.

Careers in osteopathic medicine. To become an osteopathic physician, a person must complete four years of preprofessional training in an accredited college or university and four years of professional education in an approved osteopathic medical college. The graduate receives a Doctor of Osteopathy (D.O.) degree. There are 15 approved colleges of osteopathic medicine in the United States. After graduating, osteopathic physicians gain additional training by spending a year as an intern in an approved osteopathic hospital. The United States has about 180 osteopathic hospitals, about 130 of which offer intern training programs.

Osteopathic physicians may become certified special-ists in any of a number of medical fields. Certification programs require two to five years of additional training after internship. More than 28,000 osteopathic physicians practice in the United States. Most of them are members of the American Osteopathic Association, which has its headquarters in Chicago.

The association publishes two professional periodicals, *Journal of the American Osteopathic Association* and *D.O.* It also publishes the *American Osteopathic Association Yearbook and Directory of Osteopathic Specialists.*   Critically reviewed by the American Osteopathic Association

Additional resources

Belshaw, Chris. *Osteopathy: Is It for You?* 1990. Reprint. Element Bks., 1993.
Gevitz, Norman. *The D.O.'s: Osteopathic Medicine in America.* 2nd ed. Johns Hopkins, 2004.

Osteoporosis, *AHS tee oh puh ROH sihs,* is a condition in which bones become abnormally fragile. It is a major cause of pain and disability in older adults. People with osteoporosis have an increased risk of breaking bones throughout their bodies, especially in their wrists, spine, and hips. Breaks may result from minor falls or injuries that would not harm normal bones. Severely affected bones—especially in the spine—may collapse just from the pressure of holding up the body's own weight.

Causes. Osteoporosis occurs as a result of bone loss through a lifelong process called *remodeling* or *bone turnover*. Remodeling is the chief means by which bones repair themselves. In remodeling, certain bone cells remove worn tissue and other cells form new bone. But the amount of new bone falls short of the amount lost by a tiny fraction. As a result, bone density gradually declines after reaching a peak in early adulthood, when a person finishes growing. In osteoporosis, bone density drops below the level needed to keep bones strong and prevent them from breaking.

Many factors can trigger osteoporosis. Some people form less bone than average, due to heredity or inadequate diet. These people may develop osteoporosis as normal bone loss occurs with age. Other people begin with normal bones but have greater than usual bone loss as they grow older. Factors that can cause excessive bone loss include injury, prolonged lack of exercise, and certain hormonal, inflammatory, and digestive disorders.

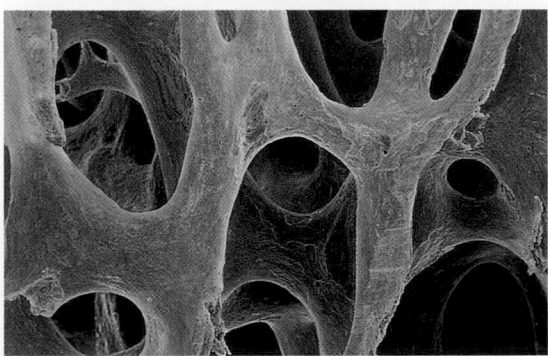

© SPL from Custom Medical

Healthy bone is strong because the tissue making up its microscopic honeycomblike structures is smooth and dense.

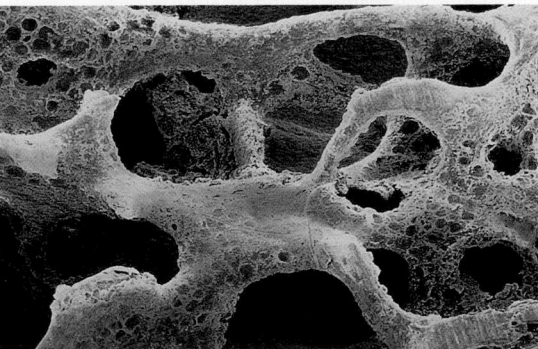

© P. Motta/SPL from Photo Researchers

Bone affected by osteoporosis is weakened by loss of bone tissue, leaving pits in its microscopic honeycomblike structure.

One common form of osteoporosis affects women who have passed *menopause,* the time when menstruation stops. Around menopause, production of the hormone estrogen decreases greatly. Lack of estrogen increases the rate of remodeling, which in turn speeds up the gradual bone loss that accompanies the process.

Prevention and treatment. People need to consume a well-balanced diet to form and maintain healthy bones. Certain minerals and vitamins, especially calcium and vitamin D, are important for bone health. Doctors recommend that everyone—especially women—eat three or more calcium-rich servings of dairy products each day. People who cannot eat dairy products can take calcium supplements. Regular exercise also helps keep bones strong.

Certain tests use X rays or sound waves to measure bone density. For people with low bone density, several treatments in addition to diet and exercise help limit further bone loss. Some women who have passed menopause can take medication called *hormone replacement therapy* to supply the body with estrogen or estrogen-like compounds. Scientists have also developed nonhormone drugs that help preserve bone in men and in women who cannot take hormones.   Robert Marcus

See also **Bone; Hormone replacement therapy; Menopause; Nutrition** (Minerals).

Osteosclerosis, *AHS tee oh sklih ROH sihs,* means hardening, thickening, and increased density of bone. It may involve part of a bone, a whole bone, or the whole skeleton. The most common form, called *marble bones* or *osteopetrosis,* is a rare inherited disease that occurs in children. In this disease, the bones become excessively dense and thick. This increased thickness fills in the space containing the bone marrow, the tissue that makes red blood cells. As a result, the child develops severe anemia. Bones affected by osteosclerosis become brittle and fracture more easily than do normal bones. Osteosclerosis may develop in part of a bone as a result of an infection or tumor.   Madison B. Cole, Jr.

Ostrava, *AW strah vah* (pop. 313,568), is one of the largest cities in the Czech Republic. It lies in the northeastern part of the country (see **Czech Republic** [map]).

Ostrava is the center of the country's largest industrial area. The city is known for its great iron and steel works and its manufacture of metal products. The region also has chemical plants, coal mines, and oil refineries. Other products of Ostrava include food products, furniture, house-building materials, and wearing apparel.

Vojtech Mastny

Ostrich is the largest living bird. It may stand nearly 8 feet (2.4 meters) tall and weigh as much as 345 pounds (156 kilograms). Ostriches live on the plains and deserts of Africa.

The ostrich is the only bird that has two toes on each foot. The rhea, which is sometimes called the *South American ostrich,* is three-toed. It is not really an ostrich. See **Rhea.**

The male ostrich has black feathers on its bulky body, with large white feathers, called *plumes,* on its wings and tail. The female ostrich has dull brown feathers on her body and white feathers on her wings. The ostrich's long, thin legs, upper neck, and small head have almost no feathers. The bare skin ranges in color from pink to blue. Thick black eyelashes surround its eyes, which

measure almost 2 inches (5 centimeters) across.

The male ostrich has an unusual voice. It can make a deep booming call. Both males and females may make deep hissing sounds when threatened.

The ostrich cannot fly, but it is known for its speed on the ground. The bird's long legs can take 15-foot (4.6-meter) steps at speeds up to 40 miles (64 kilometers) per hour. The ostrich's speed and sharp eyesight help the bird escape from *predators* (hunting animals). These predators are mainly lions, cheetahs, and people. The ostrich also kicks with its powerful legs. Its long toes, the largest of which is 7 inches (18 centimeters) long, have thick nails that serve as weapons when the bird is cornered. It may use such kicks to defend the nest. It also may pretend to be injured. In this way, it leads predators away from the nest.

The belief that the ostrich hides its head in the sand when frightened is not true. This belief probably stems from the bird's habit of rearranging the eggs in the nest with its bill. From a distance, it may appear that the ostrich's head has disappeared into the sand.

How the ostrich lives. The ostrich usually eats plants. It occasionally eats insects and other small animals. It also eats much sand and gravel to help grind food for digestion. Ostriches drink water when they find it. But they can live for long periods without drinking if the plants they eat are green and moist.

Ostriches are *polygamous*—that is, both males and females have more than one mate. Each *cock* (male) digs a shallow nest in sand, and from three to six *hens* (females) lay their eggs in the nest. Each hen lays as many

E. R. Degginger

The ostrich is the world's largest bird. Adults stand nearly 8 feet (2.4 meters) tall and may weigh up to 345 pounds (156 kilograms). The male, *shown here,* has black and white feathers.

© Giuseppe Mazza

A female ostrich stands guard over a nest of eggs. Three to six females lay their eggs in the same nest.

as 10 eggs. Each egg is almost round, nearly 6 inches (15 centimeters) in diameter, and weighs about 3 pounds (1.4 kilograms). The eggs are a dull yellow and have large pores and a thick shell.

The male sits on the eggs at night. But during the day, the *dominant* (highest-ranking) hen helps keep them warm. The eggs hatch in about six weeks. Ostriches usually do not live for more than 40 years.

Ostrich farming. Hundreds of years ago, great flocks of ostriches roamed over Africa and western Asia. Arabs in western Asia hunted ostriches for sport, and Africans took their eggs for food or killed the birds for their feathers.

© Anthony Bannister, NHPA

A baby ostrich has spotted down that blends with the ground and helps protect the bird from hunters.

In the late 1800's and early 1900's, ostrich plumes became popular as decorations on hats and clothing. Large numbers of ostriches were killed for their plumes, and the birds disappeared from Asia and much of Africa. Ostrich plumes were in great demand and were so expensive that it became highly profitable to raise ostriches in captivity. Plumes could be taken twice a year from live birds kept on ostrich farms. Ostrich farms were started in Africa, Australia, southern Europe, and the United States. But between 1914 and 1918, fashions changed, and the market for ostrich plumes dropped sharply.

Today, most ostrich farms are in South Africa and Israel, but a few operate in Europe and the United States. Ostriches are now raised for their skin, which provides fine quality leather to make gloves, shoes, and bags. Ostriches also are raised for their eggs and meat. In addition, ostriches are popular zoo animals because of their unusual appearance and usually mild disposition.

Maud Bonato

Scientific classification. The ostrich's scientific name is *Struthio camelus.* Many scientists classify the Somali ostrich as a separate species. If classified as a species, it is *S. molybdophanes.*

See also Bird (picture: The fastest bird on land).

Ostrogoths. See Goths.

Ostrovsky, Alexander. See Russian literature (Early realism).

Ostwald, *OHST vahlt,* **Wilhelm,** *VIHL hehlm* (1853-1932), a German chemist, writer, and teacher, won the 1909 Nobel Prize in chemistry. He received the award mainly for his studies in surface phenomena and speeds of chemical reactions. Ostwald wrote one of the early books on electrochemistry. His research on the oxidation of ammonia helped Germany make explosives during World War I (1914-1918). Friedrich Wilhelm Ostwald was born on Sept. 2, 1853, in Riga, Latvia. He died on April 4, 1932.   Arthur I. Miller

Ostwald process. See Nitric acid.

Oswald, Lee Harvey (1939-1963), was accused of assassinating United States President John F. Kennedy on Nov. 22, 1963, in Dallas. Two days later, while millions of television viewers looked on, Oswald was killed. He was shot to death by Dallas nightclub owner Jack Ruby, while being transferred from the city jail to the county jail in Dallas. Ruby pushed through a ring of police officers to shoot Oswald down.

The high-powered Italian rifle said to have killed the president was traced to Oswald through a Chicago mail-order firm. Oswald worked in the Texas School Book Depository, the building from which the fatal shots were fired. A worker recalled seeing Oswald carry a long narrow package into the building the morning of the assassination. Police captured Oswald, who was armed with a revolver, in a Dallas motion-picture theater about 90 minutes after the assassination.

Oswald was also charged with killing police officer J. D. Tippit. Tippit was shot to death in Dallas shortly after the president was killed. But Oswald denied killing either Tippit or the president. A presidential commission headed by Chief Justice Earl Warren investigated the case. After a 10-month investigation, the commission reported in September 1964 that Oswald, acting alone, had killed Kennedy and Tippit. However, a U.S. congressional committee later reexamined the evidence and concluded that Kennedy "was probably assassinated as a result of a conspiracy."

In 1964, a Dallas jury convicted Ruby of killing Oswald on Nov. 24, 1963. The conviction was reversed in 1966 on the grounds that the trial judge had allowed illegal testimony. A new trial was ordered, but Ruby died in 1967 before the new trial started.

Oswald was born in New Orleans on Oct. 18, 1939. Investigators said his school and military records showed emotional difficulty. Oswald dropped out of high school at 17 and joined the U.S. Marine Corps. He was discharged in 1959 and went to the Soviet Union. He tried to become a Soviet citizen but was turned down. He returned to the United States in 1962 with his Soviet-born wife, Marina. In 1963, Oswald worked as a secretary of a group that supported Cuban President Fidel Castro.

A few people believed that Oswald never returned to the United States. They maintained that a Soviet agent assumed Oswald's identity and killed Kennedy. But in 1981, Oswald's grave was opened, and medical experts identified the body as Oswald's.   Carol L. Thompson

See also **Kennedy, John F.; Warren Report**.

Oswego, New York (pop. 18,142), is the easternmost port on the Great Lakes. It lies at the point where the Oswego River empties into Lake Ontario (see **New York** [political map]). The name *Oswego* comes from an Iroquois Indian word meaning *pouring out place.* The city's factories make rolled aluminum, fabricated steel products, paper products, and processed foods. Oswego's Nine Mile Point nuclear power plant generates electric power for several Northeastern states. The city is also home to the State University of New York at Oswego.

Oswego stands on the site of a British and Dutch fur-trading post founded about 1722. The British controlled Oswego until 1796 and again during the War of 1812 (1812-1815). Oswego became a village in 1828 and a city in 1848. With the opening of the Saint Lawrence Seaway in 1959, Oswego became a major world port. It is the county seat of Oswego County and has a mayor-council form of government.   John Kenneth White

Oświęcim. See **Auschwitz**.

Othman I. See **Osman I**.

Otis, Elisha Graves (1811-1861), was an American inventor who built the first elevator with an automatic safety device. The device prevented the elevator from falling if the rope that held it broke. Otis demonstrated his elevator in 1854 in New York City by having the rope cut after he had ascended in the elevator. But his invention did not come into wide use until the rise of the skyscraper in the late 1800's. Otis was born in Halifax, Vermont, on Aug. 3, 1811. From 1830 to 1851, he held various jobs. By 1851, he was master mechanic at a firm that made bedsteads. It sent Otis to Yonkers, New York, in 1852 to supervise installation of machinery in a new factory. That year, Otis invented the safety elevator while building an elevator for the factory. He died on April 8, 1861. See also **Elevator** (picture).   Michael M. Sokal

Otis, James (1725-1783), was an American patriot and agitator against Great Britain. In 1756, he became the British king's *advocate general* (representative) on the vice-admiralty court at Boston. This court dealt with cases involving the sea and shipping. In 1760, Otis resigned his post in protest over the issuing of new *writs of assistance,* general search warrants that did not name the

Granger Collection

James Otis was one of the most forceful leaders in the American Colonies' struggle for independence from the British.

place to be searched. British authorities wanted to use the writs to catch colonists who smuggled goods into the colonies to avoid paying British taxes. Otis argued that the writs violated the British constitution and the laws of nature. In 1761, Otis became one of Boston's representatives in the Massachusetts legislature. There he proposed a meeting of representatives of all the colonies. His suggestion led to the Stamp Act Congress of 1765, in which delegates from nine colonies considered joint action against the British. In 1769, British revenue officers who resented his criticism attacked Otis. He received a head wound that eventually caused him to lose his mind. He was killed by lightning on May 23, 1783.

Otis was born in West Barnstable, Massachusetts, on Feb. 5, 1725. His sister, Mercy Otis Warren, was a writer active in the American independence movement.   Robert A. Becker

Otoscope is an instrument that doctors use to examine the eardrum. The otoscope consists of a magnifying lens and a light that is powered by a battery. The light illuminates the eardrum and the lens magnifies it. The otoscope enables the doctor to see changes in the eardrum resulting from infections and diseases.

Frank E. Musiek

WORLD BOOK photo by Dan Miller

An otoscope makes it possible for a physician to examine the eardrum of a patient.

Norm Piluke, Canada in Stock

Ottawa, the capital of Canada, lies along the Ottawa River. The Rideau Canal joins the river near the slopes of Parliament Hill. The green-roofed Parliament buildings stand atop the hill.

Ottawa, *AHT uh wuh,* Ontario, is the capital of Canada. It lies on gently rolling hills along the south bank of the Ottawa River, about 110 miles (175 kilometers) west of Montreal, Quebec. Attractive parks, stately government buildings, and scenic drives add beauty to the city. Ottawa faces the city of Gatineau, Quebec, across the Ottawa River.

In 1826, British troops founded the first settlement in the area that is now Ottawa. The soldiers had come to build the Rideau Canal, which links the Ottawa River and Lake Ontario. The town that sprang up around the construction site became known as Bytown. In 1855, the townspeople changed its name to Ottawa, adapted from the Indian word *Outaouak*. The Outaouak were an Algonquin tribe that settled and traded furs in the area.

Ottawa was a small lumbering town when Queen Victoria chose it in 1857 to be the capital of the United Province of Canada. The Dominion of Canada was established in 1867, with Ottawa as its capital. The city's layout has changed greatly through the years in keeping with Ottawa's standing as a national capital.

Metropolitan Ottawa

About 85 percent of the city of Ottawa is a rural area. The Rideau River flows through Ottawa from the south.

It plunges 37 feet (11 meters) over a cliff into the Ottawa River at the northeastern end of the city, forming the Rideau Falls. The Rideau Canal cuts through the city on its way from the Ottawa River to Lake Ontario (see **Rideau Canal**).

Parliament Hill borders the Ottawa River just west of the canal. The hill, with wooded slopes and beautiful lawns, offers a dramatic view of the heart of Ottawa. The graceful spires and green roofs of the three Parliament buildings and the Library of Parliament rise above a bluff near the river. The Peace Tower, a memorial to Canada's

Facts in brief

Population: 812,129. *Metropolitan area population*—1,130,761.

Area: 1,073 mi² (2,778 km²). *Metropolitan area*—2,207 mi² (5,716 km²).

Climate: *Average temperature*—January, 12 °F (–11 °C); July, 69 °F (21 °C). *Average annual precipitation* (rainfall, melted snow, and other forms of moisture)—37 in (94 cm). For the monthly weather in Ottawa, see **Ontario** (Climate).

Government: Council-manager. Terms—4 years for the mayor and 23 other council members.

Founded: 1826. Incorporated as a city in 1855.

war dead, rises 302 feet (92 meters) from the central Parliament building. The tower, topped by a lighted clock, houses a set of 53 bells that weigh a total of 60 tons (54 metric tons).

The areas immediately to the west and east of the Rideau Canal are the oldest parts of Ottawa. The city's chief shopping districts center around the Sparks Street Mall to the west of the canal and Byward Market and Rideau Street to the east.

Ottawa includes the urban and rural areas that, until 2001, were part of the region of Ottawa-Carleton and the municipalities of Cumberland, Gloucester, Goulbourn, Kanata, Nepean, Osgoode, Rideau, Rockcliffe Park, Vanier, and West Carleton. The Ottawa metropolitan region also includes the Outaouais, an area in western Quebec directly across the Ottawa River from Ottawa. The main city in the Outaouais is Gatineau. It consists of five former Quebec municipalities—Aylmer, Buckingham, Gatineau, Hull, and Masson-Angers—that merged in 2002.

A visitor's guide

Millions of tourists visit the Ottawa-Gatineau area yearly. They come to see Parliament in action and to view such attractions as the Peace Tower and eight locks of the Rideau Canal. Ottawa's annual festivals and fairs, its numerous museums, and the Casino du Lac-Leamy also attract many visitors to the area.

The Parliament Buildings rank as one of Ottawa's most popular tourist attractions. These four buildings form three sides of a 35-acre (14-hectare) square. They include the Centre Block, the East Block, the West Block, and the eight-sided Library of Parliament.

The Prince of Wales, who later became King Edward VII of the United Kingdom, laid the first stone of the Centre Block in 1860. The three main buildings were completed in 1865. The library was completed in 1876. Fire destroyed most of the Centre Block in 1916. The Centre Block was soon rebuilt, and it reopened in 1920.

The Centre Block includes the House of Commons, the Senate chamber, the Peace Tower, and offices of members of Parliament. The East Block includes the restored office of Sir John A. Macdonald, Canada's first prime minister. The West Block contains offices for members of Parliament and other government officials. During the summer, visitors may watch a daily changing-the-guard ceremony on Parliament Hill.

Other notable government buildings include the Royal Canadian Mint, where visitors may watch coins being made. The Library and Archives Canada building exhibits historical documents. The Supreme Court of Canada building also attracts many visitors.

Rideau Hall, also called Government House, is the official residence of Canada's governor general. It stands near the mouth of the Rideau River. Thomas McKay, a lumberman, built it in 1838. The Canadian government bought this gray limestone building in 1868 for Viscount Monck, the governor general at the time of Canadian confederation. The home of the prime minister is nearby, at 24 Sussex Drive.

The National War Memorial, at Confederation Square, honors Canadians who have served their country in times of war. It consists of bronze figures of servicemen and servicewomen marching through a granite arch. Many other monuments and statues in Ottawa also celebrate the people, events, ideals, and accomplishments of the city and of Canada.

The National Arts Centre, in the heart of Ottawa, opened in 1969. This structure houses a 2,300-seat opera and concert hall and a number of smaller performance spaces. The National Arts Centre Orchestra performs in the concert hall.

Museums. The National Gallery of Canada has Canadian and European paintings and sculpture. In addition, it regularly hosts special exhibitions of international artists. The Canadian Museum of Nature features minerals, animals, and fossils. The Canada Science and Technology Museum includes Canadian aircraft. Laurier House, the former residence of Canadian Prime Ministers Sir Wilfrid Laurier and W. L. Mackenzie King, is a historical museum. The Canadian War Museum houses the most extensive military collection in Canada. Exhibits

Malak from Shostal

The National Arts Centre stands in a landscaped area in the heart of downtown Ottawa. The facility houses several performance spaces, including a 2,300-seat opera and concert hall.

at the Canadian Museum of Civilization in Gatineau, Quebec, trace Canada's development from the time of the Vikings to the present. They illustrate the cultures of Inuit (formerly called Eskimos) and First Nations (American Indians).

Parks and recreation. The Ottawa region has hundreds of parks and playgrounds. The Ottawa Senators compete in the National Hockey League. The Central Experimental Farm and the Dow's Lake area include attractive gardens.

Annual events in Ottawa include the Canadian Tulip Festival in May. Millions of tulip bulbs bloom in parks, along roadways, and on the grounds of public buildings. The late Queen Juliana of the Netherlands sent the first bulbs to Ottawa as a gift. During World War II (1939-1945), Juliana, then a princess, lived in Ottawa while German troops occupied her country. After returning home, she sent Ottawa 100,000 tulip bulbs in gratitude for the city's hospitality and for Canada's role in freeing the Netherlands. Juliana then sent Ottawa 15,000 tulip bulbs

annually until she gave up the throne in 1980. Since 1980, the Dutch government has sent tulip bulbs to Ottawa each year for the festival.

Ottawa holds a winter festival called Winterlude in February. It features snow sculptures and ice carvings and such sports as broomball, ice skating, and dog-sled racing. The Festival Franco-Ontarien (Franco-Ontarian Festival), held in the city every June, celebrates Ontario's French Canadian culture. It includes art exhibits and folk dancing. The city's jazz, blues, folk, and chamber music festivals, held in the summer, are also popular.

People

Most Ontarians were born in Canada. Most of the rest immigrated from Asia, Western Europe, or the United States.

A majority of Ontarians have some British or French ancestry. About three-fifths of Ottawa's residents speak English as their first language. French is the first language of approximately one-seventh of the population.

City of Ottawa

Ottawa, the capital of Canada, lies on the Ottawa River in southeastern Ontario. It is an important high-technology center. The map at the right shows major points of interest in and near Ottawa.

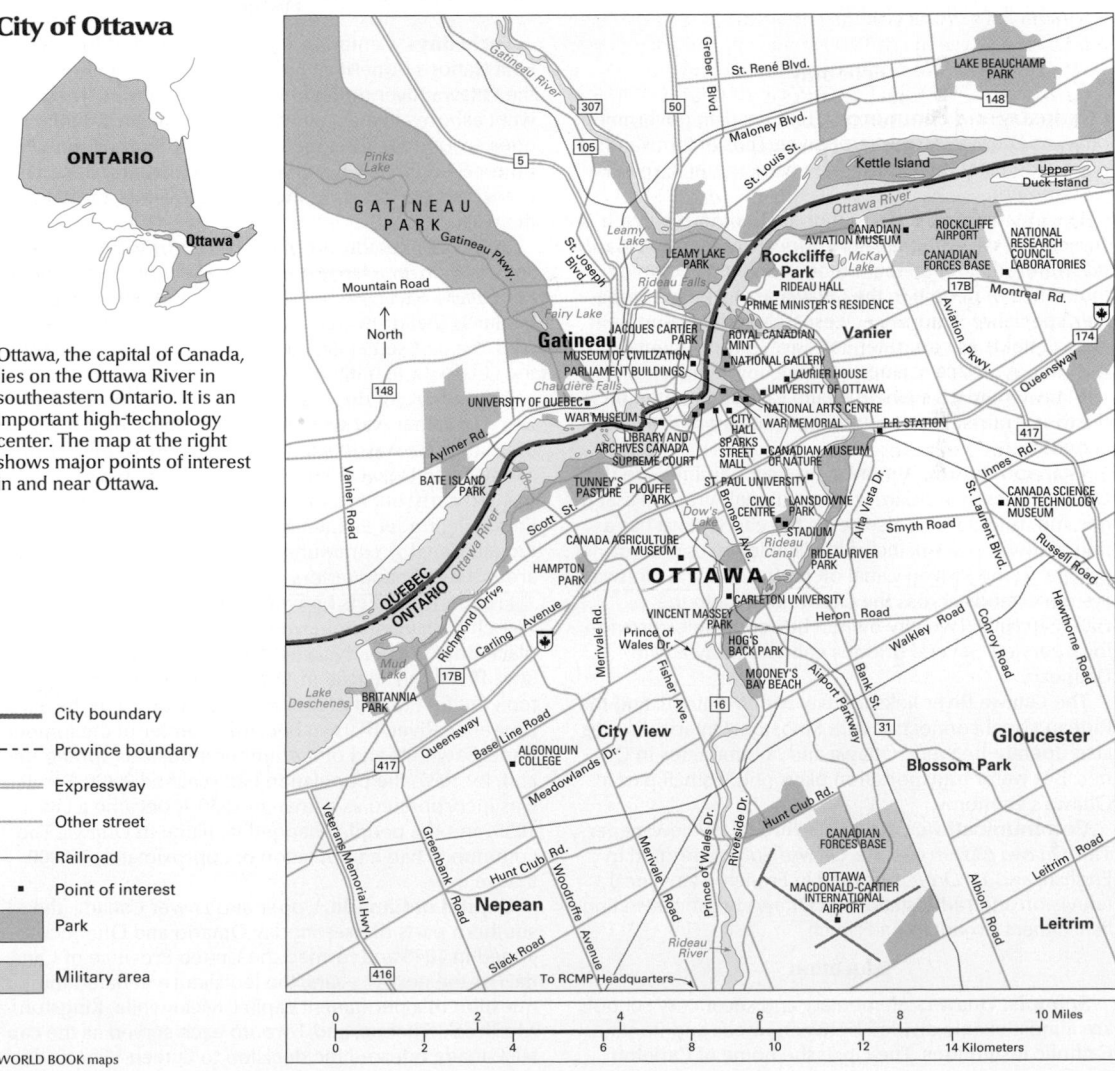

WORLD BOOK maps

Malak from Shostal

Sparks Street Mall, in downtown Ottawa, is the heart of one of the city's chief shopping districts.

Economy

Industry and commerce. The Canadian government ranks as Ottawa's largest employer. Tens of thousands of the residents of the Ottawa area work for the Canadian government.

The Ottawa area is also a high-technology center. It is sometimes called *Canada's Advanced Technology Capital.* Hundreds of high-technology companies employ thousands of people in the Ottawa area. These companies specialize in advanced research and development in such fields as computer software, environmental technology, space science, and telecommunications.

Many Ontarians work in health care and related industries. Tourism is also an important part of the local economy.

Transportation. A number of major airlines use the Ottawa Macdonald-Cartier International Airport. Passenger and freight trains also serve the city. Ottawa has a fine highway system, including scenic drives that run parallel to the Rideau Canal on both sides. The highway system extends across the Ottawa River into the Gatineau Hills. Two city-owned bus companies provide local service. Several bridges connect Ottawa with Gatineau.

The Ottawa River links the city with Montreal, and the Rideau Canal connects it with Kingston, Ontario. Ferries also operate between Ottawa and communities in Quebec. But water transportation plays only a small part in Ottawa's economy.

Communication. Ottawa has three daily newspapers. The *Ottawa Citizen* and the *Ottawa Sun* are printed in English, and *Le Droit* is printed in French. Many local television and radio stations in Ottawa broadcast in English. Others broadcast in French.

Education

Schools. Ottawa's elementary and secondary schools are almost evenly divided between public and Roman Catholic institutions. The city is the home of Carleton

University and the University of Ottawa. The University of Ottawa, founded in 1848 as the College of Bytown, offers most of its courses in both English and French. St. Paul University and the Dominican University College are also in Ottawa. The Algonquin College of Applied Arts and Technology and its French counterpart, La Cité collégiale, offer post-secondary education in various academic and professional disciplines.

Libraries. The Ottawa Public Library and the Bibliothèque Municipale de Gatineau (Municipal Library of Gatineau) have dozens of branches. Ottawa is also home to the Library of Parliament and to Library and Archives Canada.

Government

An elected city council governs Ottawa. The council includes a mayor and 23 councilors who represent districts called *wards.* The mayor and the councilors serve four-year terms. Taxes on property, sales, and businesses provide most of the revenue of the government. In addition, Ottawa receives federal and provincial grants.

History

Early days. Centuries ago, Algonquin and Iroquoian First Nations (American Indian) people traveled down the Ottawa River on hunting and trading trips. They went ashore at what is now Ottawa and carried their canoes around the Chaudière Falls. In 1613, the French explorer Samuel de Champlain passed through the area. French fur traders used the Ottawa River as a route to the west.

In 1800, Philemon Wright, a farmer from Massachusetts, took over a large tract of land on the north side of the Ottawa River. He built a sawmill and began a lumber business that grew into a thriving industry. Ira Honeywell, the first settler on the south bank, began to farm on the Ottawa side of the river in 1811.

Bytown. After the War of 1812 (1812-1815), the British feared another war with the United States. As a result, they sought a way to send gunboats and supplies from Montreal to Lake Ontario without passing near U.S. territory. To carry out this project, the British sent the Royal Engineers under Lieutenant Colonel John By to build the Rideau Canal. A community known as Bytown grew up around By's headquarters.

Frequent conflicts between Irish canal workers and French Canadian lumbermen made Bytown a stormy place during its early years. The lumber trade on the Ottawa River had started in 1806, when Philemon Wright took the first raft of processed timber down to the St. Lawrence River. Bytown became a center of the lumber trade. Sawmills and other lumber industries sprang up and, by 1837, the population had reached 2,400. Bytown was incorporated as a town in 1850. It became a city in 1855, and the people changed its name to Ottawa. The community had a population of approximately 10,000 that year.

Capital of Canada. Upper and Lower Canada (the southern parts of present-day Ontario and Quebec) joined in 1840 and formed the United Province of Canada. For the next 17 years, the legislature debated the question of a permanent capital. Meanwhile, Kingston, Montreal, Quebec, and Toronto each served as the capital. Canada referred the decision to Queen Victoria of the United Kingdom in 1857. She chose Ottawa as the capital because of its beauty and location. Ottawa lay on the boundary of what had been Upper and Lower Canada. The city was far enough from the United States to protect it from attack.

In 1867, Ottawa became the capital of the newly formed Dominion of Canada. Its population had reached 18,000. The city grew in a disorganized fashion, with numerous railroads crisscrossing through the center of town to accommodate the lumber trade. In 1896, Prime Minister Wilfrid Laurier called for a beautification program to make Ottawa the "Washington of the North." Three years later, the Ottawa Improvement Commission was formed.

The 1900's. In 1900, a great fire left nearly one-fourth of Ottawa's 60,000 people homeless. But by 1912, the city's burned-out areas had been rebuilt, and its population had reached 90,000.

The Federal District Commission replaced the Ottawa Improvement Commission in 1927. Ten years later, Prime Minister W. L. Mackenzie King appointed Jacques Gréber, the Paris city planner, to develop a plan for Ottawa. But World War II broke out in 1939 and interrupted the project. Gréber returned to France. Ottawa became the center of Canada's war effort.

After the war, Gréber returned to Canada. In 1951, Parliament accepted his plan to beautify Ottawa. The Gréber Plan brought about significant changes. Ottawa removed 32 miles (51 kilometers) of unattractive railroad tracks and relocated the railroad station to the east edge of the city. It set aside land for a belt of parks and green spaces around the capital. The commission also developed the 88,000-acre (35,600-hectare) Gatineau Park just north of Ottawa. Instead of grouping all government offices in the city's core area, the plan called for new government buildings on the outskirts of the city.

The National Capital Commission replaced the Federal District Commission in 1959. It is responsible for acquiring land for beautification purposes. It set up a national capital region of 1,800 square miles (4,660 square kilometers)—900 square miles (2,330 square kilometers) in Ontario and 900 more in Quebec. In the 1960's and 1970's, the commission created beaches and parkways within the capital region. At the same time, the area's rapidly growing computer-software and electronics industries built research facilities and factories.

In 1962, Ottawa established the Commercial and Industrial Development Corporation, later renamed the Economic Development Corporation, to promote economic growth. This government corporation created 12 industrial parks in Ottawa during the late 1960's and early 1970's. In 2001, the corporation merged with the Ottawa Centre for Research and Innovation (now the Ottawa Centre for Regional Innovation).

In 1973, the city repealed a law that had limited the height of buildings in the downtown area. As a result, taller buildings began to be constructed in Ottawa. City leaders predicted that the additional apartment dwellers and office workers in the new buildings, along with commuters from the growing suburbs, would strain Ottawa's transportation system. The provincial government announced a plan to avoid this problem by helping the city government build a new bus system. Much of the system is reserved for buses only. The plan called for

Ontario to pay 75 percent of the cost of this Transitway project. Construction of the system began in 1981, and new parts are added continually.

In 1999, the Ontario legislature passed a law to create a new, enlarged city of Ottawa. The new city came into being on Jan. 1, 2001. It includes the urban and rural areas that once comprised the Ottawa-Carleton region and the municipalities of Cumberland, Gloucester, Goulbourn, Kanata, Nepean, Osgoode, Ottawa, Rideau, Rockcliffe Park, Vanier, and West Carleton.   Serge Barbe

Ottawa, University of, or Université d'Ottawa, is a coeducational school in Ottawa, Canada. The university is supported by the province of Ontario. It was operated by the Roman Catholic Oblates of Mary Immaculate until 1965, when control was transferred to an independent board of governors. The university's administration, instruction, and research are conducted in French and English. The university has *faculties* (colleges) of arts, education, engineering, health sciences, law, management, medicine, science, and social science. In addition, there is a school of graduate studies.

The University of Ottawa was founded as the College of Bytown in 1848. It received a civil charter in 1866 and a papal charter in 1889. In 1965, its faculties of theology and canon law were grouped to form Saint Paul University, which is federated with the University of Ottawa. The university's website at http://www.uottawa.ca/ offers additional information.

Critically reviewed by the University of Ottawa

Ottawa River is the chief branch of the St. Lawrence River and one of the most important streams of Canada. Great quantities of lumber float down the Ottawa from forests in the north.

The river begins in Quebec, about 160 miles (257 kilometers) north of the city of Ottawa. For location, see **Quebec** (terrain map). It flows west to the Quebec-Ontario border and forms the border as it flows southeast. The city of Ottawa, Canada's capital, stands along the river. The river ends its 696-mile (1,120-kilometer) course north of Montreal, where it empties into the St. Lawrence River.

Rapids and falls along the river make it unnavigable for big ships. But the rapids and falls also produce valuable hydroelectric power. Chaudière Falls, north of the city of Ottawa, is the largest waterfall on the river.

Dams and slides for large logs have been built on the Ottawa to aid the lumber industry. Canals built along the river once aided shipping. But they are now used only for pleasure boats. The Rideau Canal system connects the Ottawa River with Lake Ontario. The river was an early canoe route to the interior of Canada. The French explorer Samuel de Champlain explored the river during the early 1600's.   Roger Nadeau

Otter is the name for a number of furry animals that spend much of their time in the water. Otters are expert swimmers and divers and can stay underwater for three or four minutes. The animals move awkwardly on land.

Otters live on all the continents except Australia and Antarctica. Most weigh from 10 to 30 pounds (4.5 to 14 kilograms) and grow from 3 to 4 ½ feet (0.9 to 1.4 meters) long, including the tail. The giant otter of South America may measure up to 7 feet (2 meters) long. Otters live along rivers, streams, lakes, and coastal waters, or in marshes. This article discusses otters that inhabit fresh

Hans Reinhard, Bruce Coleman Ltd.

The North American river otter lives in burrows along the banks of rivers and feeds mainly on fish and crayfish. The animal is a swift and graceful swimmer but moves awkwardly on land.

waters. For information about *sea otters,* which live in the Pacific Ocean, see the article on **Sea otter.**

Body. An otter has a small flattened head; a long, thick neck; and a thick, pointed tail. Special muscles enable the animal to close its ears and nostrils tightly to keep water out. Elastic webbing grows between the otter's toes. In most *species* (kinds) of otters, the webbing is extensive enough to help the animals swim swiftly.

Otters, like beavers and muskrats, have long coarse *guard hairs* that cover and protect the short, thick underfur. This underfur traps air and keeps the otter's skin dry. In some species, a layer of fat under the skin insulates the otter from the cold. An otter's fur varies in color from brownish-gray to dark brown when dry, and appears darker when wet.

Otters often use their paws to handle objects. They hold and play skillfully with such things as stones and small shellfish. Some African and Asian otters that have only a little webbing between their toes can use the toes like fingers. Such *clawless* and *small-clawed otters* handle food in much the same way as raccoons do. These otters feed on shellfish that live in shallow water. All otters have claws. Even the so-called clawless otter has short claws on the three middle toes of its hind feet.

The life of an otter. Otters eat crayfish, crabs, and fish. Although otters can sometimes catch such swift-swimming fish as trout, they generally capture slower fish. They also eat clams, frogs, insects, snails, snakes, and occasionally waterfowl. Otters remain active the year around. Where people hunt them, they move about more at night than during the day. The animals hunt mostly alone, but sometimes they hunt in family groups.

Otters spend much time playing. They wrestle and play and slide down steep muddy slopes in summer and down icy riverbanks in winter. Otters use a variety of sounds to communicate among themselves. All species have a warning growl. In addition, otters use various kinds of chirps, chuckles, screams, and squeals as forms of communication.

Most otters make their homes in burrows in riverbanks or under rocky ledges, or in abandoned dens of other animals. Most female otters give birth to two or three young at a time. The babies, called *cubs* or *pups,* are born blind. The young do not swim until they are several months old.

People hunt otters for their valuable and beautiful fur.

Certain species, especially the giant otter, are in danger of becoming extinct. Daniel K. Odell

Scientific classification. Otters belong to the weasel family, Mustelidae. The scientific name for the giant otter is *Pteronura brasiliensis,* and the North American river otter is *Lontra canadensis.* The Cape clawless otter is *Aonyx capensis,* the Congo clawless otter is *A. congicus,* and the Asian small-clawed otter is *Amblonyx cinereus.*

Otterhound is a breed of dog that was developed in Britain for the sport of hunting otters. It has a thick, rough coat, with an oily undercoat that enables it to stay in cold water for long periods. Its feet are slightly webbed, which helps make the dog a good swimmer. A male otterhound stands about 24 to 27 inches (61 to 69 centimeters) high at the shoulder and weighs from 75 to 115 pounds (34 to 52 kilograms). Females stand about 22 to 26 inches (56 to 66 centimeters) high and weigh 65 to 100 pounds (29 to 45 kilograms). The otterhound's color ranges from grizzled blue and white to sand, with black and tan markings. The breed probably originated in the 1300's. Its ancestry is unclear, but many breeders believe the otterhound was developed from the Vendee hound of France. Others believe it originally came from the bloodhound. Critically reviewed by the American Kennel Club

Joyce R. Wilson

The otterhound is a hardy dog and a good swimmer.

Otto I (1815-1867), was the first king of Greece after the Greeks won their independence from the Ottoman Empire (now Turkey) in 1830. France, Russia, and the United Kingdom—who had helped Greece win independence—named Otto king in 1832, and he ruled from 1832 to 1862. Otto was an unpopular ruler. He failed to move toward the realization of the "Great Idea," which sought to liberate all Greeks still under Ottoman rule in such territories as Crete, Thessaly, and Macedonia.

Otto and the Greeks were prepared to join the Russians against the Ottoman Turks in the Crimean War (1853-1856). France and the United Kingdom sent troops to Greece to prevent it. The Greeks blamed Otto for this failure and deposed him in 1862. During his reign, Otto rebuilt Athens, established the first Greek university, and refounded Sparta. Otto I was born on June 1, 1815, in Salzburg, Austria, as Otto Friedrich Ludwig, a prince of Bavaria (now part of Germany). He died on July 26, 1867.

John A. Koumoulides

See also **Greece** (Otto I).

Otto I, the Great (912-973), a German king, was the first emperor of what became known as the Holy Roman Empire. He followed his father, Henry I, as king of Germany in 936. Otto's father had actually ruled only his own duchy of Saxony, but Otto tried to rule all Germany.

In 951, Otto crossed the Alps and declared himself the king of Italy. He was forced to return to Germany when the other German princes began a series of revolts. At the same time, the Slavs in Poland and Bohemia revolted, and the Magyars, or Hungarians, invaded Germany. Otto crushed the Magyars in the battle of the Lech River in 955. The Poles and Bohemians were forced to accept his rule. Otto was able to replace most of the rebellious German princes with members of his own family. The young king of Arles, or Burgundy, also had to accept German rule. Otto then turned his attention toward Italy. He married the widow of an earlier Italian king and defeated a rival for the throne. In 961, Otto crossed the Alps to put down an uprising in Rome. For this service, Pope John XII crowned him emperor of what was later known as the Holy Roman Empire. Otto was born in Quedlinburg.   Jonathan W. Zophy

See also **Holy Roman Empire.**

Otto II (955-983), a German king, was the second emperor of what became known as the Holy Roman Empire. He succeeded his father, Otto I, also called Otto the Great, in 973. Otto II's claim to the throne was challenged by his powerful cousin Henry the Wrangler, Duke of Bavaria. But by 978, Otto had defeated Henry and had named an ally to replace Henry as duke.

Otto II defended his borders against Slavs to the east, Danes to the north, and the French to the west. Beginning in 980, Otto II tried to extend his power into southern Italy. Muslims also were seeking control of the region at that time, and they defeated Otto near Crotone in 982. Danes and Slavs in the northern part of the empire then revolted and regained lands that they had lost to Otto I.

Otto II was born in Saxony. Along with his mother, Adelaide, and his wife, the Byzantine princess Theophano, he promoted the arts and church reform. After Otto II's death, Adelaide and Theophano ruled on behalf of his infant son, Otto III.   Jonathan W. Zophy

Ottoman Empire was the most powerful empire in the world during the 1500's and 1600's. At its height, it controlled what is now Turkey and parts of northern Africa, southwestern Asia, and southeastern Europe. The empire began about 1300 and lasted until 1922. The Ottomans were nomadic Turkish tribes that migrated to the Middle East from central Asia. The term *Ottoman* comes from *Osman,* also called *Othman* or *Uthman,* the founder and first *sultan* (ruler) of the empire.

Before the arrival of the Ottomans, the Byzantine Empire had occupied parts of Asia Minor (now Turkey) and southeastern Europe for almost 1,000 years. That empire ended in 1453, when the Ottomans conquered the Byzantine capital of Constantinople (now Istanbul). They made the city their capital. By the mid-1500's, the Ottomans ruled Asia Minor, the Balkans, and parts of northern Africa and present-day Iran, Saudi Arabia, and Syria. The Ottomans were Muslims, and they spread their religion, Islam, throughout the empire.

The Ottoman Empire slowly declined only after 1700, when it was faced with the emerging powers of Europe.

When World War I began in 1914, the Ottoman Empire consisted of only Asia Minor, parts of southwestern Asia, and part of the Balkans. The Ottomans were defeated in the war, and the empire came to an end in 1922.

Ways of life

People of the Ottoman Empire, in addition to Turks, included many Arabs, Armenians, Greeks, and Slavs. The official language was Ottoman Turkish. The empire had two classes of people. The ruling class paid no taxes and included the imperial family, owners of large estates, and military and religious leaders. The rest of the people were peasants and craftworkers who did pay taxes. The sultan was responsible for protecting them against invasion and abuse by his ruling class. The profession and status of most individuals could be determined by the color and style of clothing and the size of the turban or other headdress they wore.

Almost all the women of the Ottoman Empire lived restricted lives. Islamic law permitted a man to have as many as four wives at a time. Muslim women lived most of their lives in seclusion, usually in a separate section of a household. This section was called a *harem* (see **Harem**). Some women gained power within their harem and had great influence over their husbands and sons. Muslim women also were required to wear veils in public. Many similar restrictions affected non-Muslim women as well.

Most Muslims strictly followed the rules of Islam as set down in their holy book, the Quran (see **Islam** [Teachings and practices]). However, the Ottomans allowed all religious groups to practice their own faiths. Christians and Jews made up the largest non-Muslim groups. Each religious group, including the Muslims, formed a *millet* (nation), whose leader represented its members before the government.

Cultural life. Neighborhood *mosques* (Muslim houses of worship) served as both religious and social centers for Muslims. Other millets had their own religious ceremonies and social events. The Ottomans adopted many styles of Byzantine and Persian art and literature. Major Ottoman contributions came in the fields of architecture, carpet weaving, and tile making.

Ottoman education emphasized religious studies. Beginning in the 1300's, boys attended schools in mosques. The best students went on to high schools called *medreses.* Girls began to go to elementary school in the mid-1800's. *Secular* (nonreligious) education at the high school and university levels began about the same time.

Economy. Most of the people of the Ottoman Empire worked as farmers. Grain was grown in fertile areas of Egypt, Syria, and lands surrounding the Black Sea. Craftworkers and merchants practiced their trade in the cities and towns.

The Ottoman Empire gained great wealth through trade. Some of the busiest trade routes between Asia and Europe ran through the empire. Merchandise offered in the markets of Ottoman cities included Chinese porcelains, European woolens, Persian silks, and spices from Asia.

Government. The Ottoman sultans made all important governmental decisions for the empire. The sultans appointed officials to collect taxes and to keep peace within the empire. The sultans had limited powers. For example, they needed the army's support to maintain their position. New laws required approval of the chief religious judge, the *grand mufti,* to take effect.

Until the 1630's, the oldest or favorite son succeeded to the throne upon the death of a sultan. After the 1630's, it became common for the successor to be the oldest surviving male member of the family. Some sultans removed threats to their throne by murdering potential rivals or confining princes to the royal palace.

History

The beginning of the empire. The Turkish tribes led by Osman began to expand their small territory in the northwest corner of Anatolia (now part of Turkey) during the late 1200's. In 1326, the tribes captured the city of Bursa, which had been part of the Byzantine Empire. In the late 1300's, the Ottomans formed a group of highly trained soldiers called Janissaries (see **Janissaries**).

Expansion and decline. By the mid-1400's, the Ottomans had conquered the entire Byzantine Empire except for the city of Constantinople. Ottoman troops, led by Sultan Mehmet II, captured Constantinople in 1453.

Under Mehmet II, or Mehmed II, the Ottomans also conquered much of southeastern Europe and territory near the Black Sea. They took over Syria in 1516 and Egypt in 1517. The empire reached its peak of power and wealth under Sultan Süleyman I, who ruled from 1520 to 1566. His armies conquered Hungary, northern Africa, and territory on the east coast of the Red Sea down to what is now Yemen.

In 1571, naval forces from Spain, Venice, and the Papal States of Italy almost destroyed the Ottoman fleet in the Battle of Lepanto. But the navy was rebuilt. In 1683, Austrian and Polish troops turned back an Ottoman attack on Vienna, Austria, ending the empire's expansion.

During the next 200 years, many nations won independence from Ottoman rule. Government corruption, oppressive taxation, inflation, and weak sultans also contributed to the decline of the empire.

The empire ends. In 1908, a group of Ottoman military officers called the Young Turks forced Sultan Abdülhamit II to restore the empire's Constitution, which guaranteed an elected parliamentary government. The Constitution had been adopted under Abdülhamit in 1876, but he suspended it the next year following a Russian invasion.

After World War I ended in 1918, Allied nations, including the United Kingdom and Greece, occupied the Ottoman Empire. The empire had supported Germany in the war. Mustafa Kemal, a Turkish military hero later called Kemal Atatürk, led a nationalist movement that ended the occupation in 1922. The Turkish government abolished the Ottoman Empire that year and created the Republic of Turkey in 1923.   Virginia H. Aksan

Related articles in *World Book* include:

Atatürk, Kemal	Osman I	Safavid dynasty
Mehmet II	Romania (Ottoman	Süleyman I
Muslims (The Ottoman Empire)	rule)	Turkey (History)

Ouachita River, WAHSH ih taw, begins in the Ouachita Mountains of western Arkansas and flows east and then south into Louisiana. Sometimes called the Washita, it is about 605 miles (974 kilometers) long. The Ouachita joins the Tensas River to form the Black River about 25 miles (40 kilometers) west of Natchez, Louisiana. Small barges can sail about 350 miles (563 kilometers) up the river to Camden, Arkansas. During some high water seasons, barges can go about 70 miles (110 kilometers) farther, to Arkadelphia (see **Arkansas** [physical map]; **Louisiana** [terrain map]).

The river's name was formerly spelled Washita. Another river called the Washita flows in Texas and Oklahoma.   John G. Hehr

Ouagadougou, WAH guh DOO goo (pop. 821,474), is the capital and largest city of Burkina Faso. For the location of Ouagadougou, see **Burkina Faso** (political map). The city has a modern central district and numerous churches and *mosques* (Islamic houses of worship). The palace of the Moro Naba, the chief of the country's Mossi people, is also in the city. Ouagadougou has an airport and a university. Its industries include food processing, the bottling of beverages, and the production of building supplies and textiles.

Ouagadougou was founded in about the 1100's. In the mid-1400's, it became the Moro Naba's capital. In 1896, French forces captured the city. It grew little until 1954, when a railroad connected it with Bobo Dioulasso and Côte d'Ivoire. In 1960, the independence of what is now Burkina Faso also stimulated growth.   Dennis D. Cordell

Oubangui River. See Ubangi River.

Ouija board, WEE juh or WEE jee, is a device supposed to allow people to talk with supernatural spirits and ask them questions. Two or more people gather

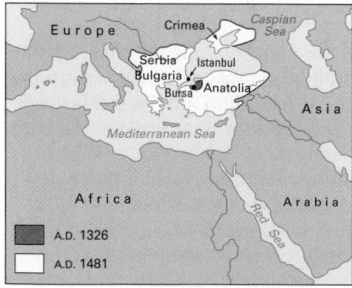

The Ottoman Empire started as a small state around Bursa in Anatolia (now Turkey). By the late 1400's, the empire had expanded into eastern Europe.

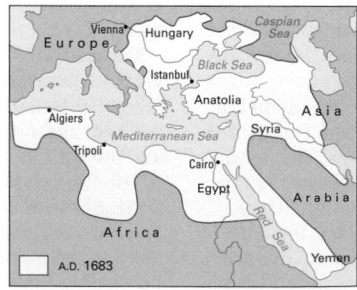

During the 1600's, it was the world's largest empire. It had its capital in Istanbul and covered parts of Eastern Europe, the Middle East, and North Africa.

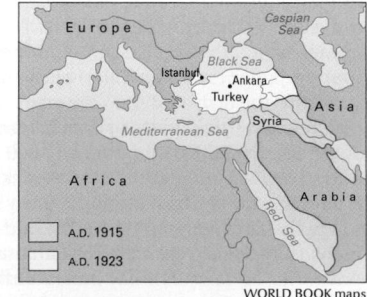

WORLD BOOK maps

The empire declined in the 1700's and 1800's and collapsed during World War I (1914-1918). Turkey was formed in 1923 from the remaining territory.

around a board with alphabet letters and numbers printed on it. They lightly place their fingers on a small three-legged pointer called a *planchette*. The pointer seems to move by itself, answering questions by pointing to "yes" or "no" on the board or by spelling out words by moving from letter to letter.

According to people who believe in the Ouija board, spirits guide the pointer. Some believers fear that users can put themselves in danger by contacting demons in this way. Others think that the motion is an illusion and that the fingers of the questioner influence the pointer. Still others use the Ouija board just as a game for fun.

The Ouija board was invented in 1892 by William Fuld, the owner of a novelty company in Baltimore. Its name comes from the French word *oui* and the German word *ja,* both of which mean *yes.*   Bill Ellis

Ounce. See Snow leopard.

Ounce is a unit of weight or volume used primarily in the United States. As a unit of weight, it is used to measure *mass* (the amount of matter in an object) or force. In commercial and everyday use, the term *weight* is understood to mean mass, and the ounce is used as a unit of mass. In science and technology, *weight* refers to the gravitational force on an object, and so the ounce is also used as a measure of that force.

In the *avoirdupois* system of weights, there are 16 ounces in a pound. As a unit of force, the avoirdupois ounce equals 0.278 newton in the metric system; as a unit of mass, 28.350 grams in the metric system. This ounce also equals 437.5 grains of mass. The *troy weight* system, used throughout the world to measure the mass of precious metals, has a heavier ounce. The troy ounce equals 31.103 grams, or 480 grains. In the troy weight system, there are 12 ounces in a pound.

As a measure of liquid volume, one *fluid ounce* equals 29.574 milliliters. There are 32 fluid ounces in a liquid quart.   Michael Dine

See also Avoirdupois; Metric system; Troy weight; Weight; Weights and measures.

Ouray. See Ute Indians.

Our Lady of Guadalupe. See Guadalupe Day.

Outback is a term that refers to the rural interior of Australia and its unique characteristics. Some people use the term *outback* to describe all thinly populated areas away from Australia's coastal cities. Others apply the term to only those areas with low rainfall. The land and climate in much of the outback are harsh and variable. Many people associate life in the outback with a sense of adventure, individualism, and isolation.

Millions of years of weathering and erosion have flattened the outback's landscapes and reduced the quality of the soil. Most mountains in the region stand less than 3,900 feet (1,200 meters) tall. Large deserts with plant-covered sand dunes stretch across much of the outback. Since the late 1800's, large areas have been used for grazing sheep and cattle. The outback also has rich mineral resources, and mining is now an important activity.

The outback is famous for its wide variety of unusual wildlife. The region's plants and animals include spinifex grass and eucalyptus and acacia trees; kangaroos and other marsupials; and large flightless birds called emus.

Less than 10 percent of Australia's people live in the outback. But many Australian Aborigines live there, usually in small, isolated communities or on livestock sta-

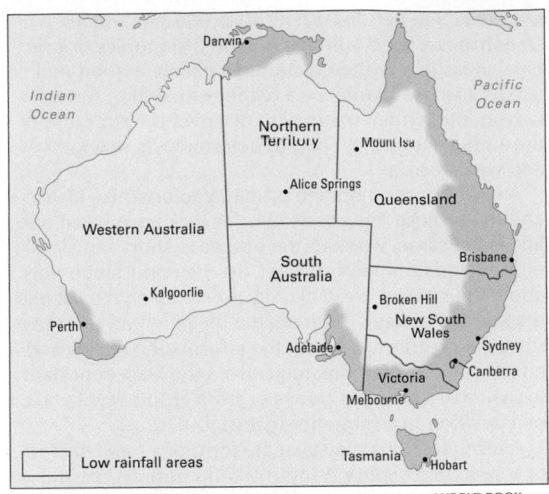

WORLD BOOK map

The Australian outback, according to some people, refers only to those areas with low rainfall, *shown here.* But others define the outback as all thinly populated parts of the continent.

tions (ranches). Outback residents lack easy access to health care and education. As a result, they generally have poorer health and fewer career opportunities than people in the cities. A special aviation service called the Royal Flying Doctor Service provides medical treatment to people in remote areas. Also, schools of the air help students in isolated regions communicate with teachers using radio, telephone, and computer equipment.

The word *outback* comes from the phrase "out in the back country." This saying was first used in the 1800's to describe Australian frontier areas where the British colonial governments had little control.   Stuart Pearson

See also Australia (Country life).

Outcault, *OWT kawlt,* **Richard Felton** (1863-1928), was an American cartoonist. He created the first comic strip that gained widespread popularity. This weekly strip, called "Hogan's Alley," first appeared in 1895 in *The New York World,* a New York City newspaper. The strip quickly became an immense success.

The main character of "Hogan's Alley," a boy named Mickey Dugan, wore a long gown that soon was colored yellow. As a result, the character became known as the Yellow Kid. In 1896, "Hogan's Alley" was renamed "The Yellow Kid." Still later that year, Outcault accepted an enormous salary from the *New York Journal* to draw the strip for it. The *World* hired another artist to draw "The Yellow Kid," and the papers began a sensational rivalry. Other newspapers called them the "Yellow Kid journals." The term *yellow journalism,* meaning a highly sensational kind of newspaper writing, was symbolized by "The Yellow Kid" comic strip. In 1898, Outcault quit drawing his most popular creation. In 1902, he created "Buster Brown," a strip about an angelic-faced boy who still had nasty intentions. "Buster Brown" was one of the most popular newspaper features of its time and a merchandising sensation, best known for Buster Brown shoes. Outcault became wealthy and retired in 1921.

Outcault was born on Jan. 14, 1863, in Lancaster, Ohio. He died on Sept. 25, 1928.   Thomas Spurgeon

See also Comics (picture).

Outlaw. See Bandit with its list of *Related articles.*

Outline is a short summary of the main topics or principal ideas of a written work or a speech. A good outline serves as a useful tool for a reader or a writer. A reader can outline written material to discover the structure of the author's argument and to determine its strengths and weaknesses.

A writer uses an outline primarily to organize ideas about a subject. The procedure for making such an outline is the same, whether the outline is short and simple or long and complicated. First, list the important points about the subject. Next, classify the items on the list into meaningful groups. Then decide on a method of organizing the groups to present the information clearly and effectively. For example, move from the least important to the most important points or from arguments in favor of a position to arguments against it.

A formal outline may take the form of a *topic outline* or a *sentence outline.* A topic outline summarizes the chief topics and subtopics of the piece in brief phrases. A sentence outline uses complete sentences for each topic and subtopic. Most formal outlines have a thesis statement that identifies the main argument or subject. The thesis statement is followed by topic headings and indented subheadings.

Here is an example of a topic outline:

Thesis statement: There are better reasons for not buying a car than for buying one.

- **I. Reasons for buying a car**
  - A. Convenience
  - B. Status
- **II. Reasons for not buying a car**
  - A. Inconvenience
    1. High cost of fuel
    2. Increasingly crowded roads
    3. Parking a growing problem
       - a. Urban areas unpredictable
       - b. Weather unpredictable
  - B. Hazards
    1. Highway systems inadequate
    2. Possibility of accidents
  - C. Poor financial investment
    1. Initial investment
       - a. High taxes
       - b. High interest rates
    2. Continuing investment
       - a. Fuel
       - b. Equipment
       - c. Maintenance
       - d. Fees to government agencies

William E. Coles, Jr.

Outrigger is a term that refers to two kinds of boating devices and to the boats that use them. In the Indian and Pacific oceans, an outrigger is a float attached to certain rowing and sailing canoes. The canoes are also called outriggers. The float is a long log that runs parallel to the boat and is linked to it by a frame. The float acts as a counterbalance, or secondary hull, to prevent the canoe from tipping over. A canoe that has two floats, one on each side, is called a *double outrigger.*

In the United States, the term *outrigger* refers to brackets that extend from the sides of certain small, narrow racing boats called *shells.* The brackets support the oars. The rowing boats that have such brackets are sometimes called outriggers.   Paul F. Johnston

See also **Catamaran.**

Outsourcing is the shifting of business operations from within an organization to a person or group outside the organization. It occurs when an organization hires a person or business to take over specific activities that the organization would otherwise perform itself. Outsourcing can help businesses by increasing *specialization*—that is, by allowing businesses to focus primarily on the activities they are best suited to perform.

Organizations of all types outsource. Manufacturing businesses, for instance, might pay other companies to provide the basic parts and materials they need. Many businesses also outsource their accounting processes, computer operations, legal services, advertising, human resources management, and customer service. Governments may hire private contractors for such functions as garbage collection, prison management, and the operation of social programs. Many families outsource their housecleaning, yard work, and other duties to specialized businesses.

Some companies outsource jobs to other countries where the work can be performed at a lower cost. This practice is sometimes called *offshoring.* Many people oppose offshoring because they believe it causes a loss of jobs in the company's home country. Supporters of offshoring, however, argue that it leads to cheaper goods and services, increased efficiency, and other economic benefits.   Price V. Fishback

Outward Bound is an international educational organization that provides challenging wilderness experiences as courses of study. These experiences are intended to contribute to the self-discovery and personal growth of the participants.

Outward Bound offers courses to anyone 12 years of age or older and in good health. Most of the courses last from 21 to 26 days and include such activities as backpacking, rock climbing, canoeing, sailing, and cross-country skiing. A small group of people take a course together. Each person, working with the others, must solve various problems in an unfamiliar wilderness environment. Outward Bound believes that dealing with these problems increases a person's self-confidence, self-awareness, and appreciation of others.

The first Outward Bound school was established in 1941 in Aberdovey, Wales, near Aberystwyth. Kurt Hahn, a German educator, founded it as a survival program for British sailors during World War II (1939-1945). The organization's first school in the United States was started in 1962 near Aspen, Colorado. Outward Bound has schools in more than 30 countries. Its U.S. headquarters are in Garrison, New York.   Outward Bound USA

Ouzel. See Dipper.

Ovarian cancer is uncontrolled multiplication of cells of the *ovaries,* a pair of female sex organs that store and release eggs. The ovaries also secrete *estrogens* and *progesterone,* the female sex hormones. Ovarian cancer occurs most often in women over the age of 60. It is more common among women in developed countries and relatively rare among women in Asia and many Third World countries. A high fat diet, early onset of menstruation, late menopause, never being pregnant, and having a close relative with the disease are factors that may increase an individual's risk of developing ovarian cancer.

In the early stages of ovarian cancer, when the chance

for successful treatment is greatest, the disease causes few or no symptoms. Also, early symptoms are often mistaken for those of other, less serious, conditions. By the time symptoms develop, the cancer is often in a more advanced stage. Early symptoms of ovarian cancer include discomfort, *bloating* (abdominal swelling), a feeling of fullness in the abdomen, and a frequent, urgent need to urinate. Loss of appetite and unusual vaginal bleeding may also occur.

If ovarian cancer is suspected, doctors may begin by performing a blood test. Cancers of the ovary may produce a protein called *CA 125,* which can be measured in the blood. Elevated levels of CA 125 occur in about 80 percent of cases of ovarian cancer. To make a definite diagnosis, however, physicians must perform a procedure called a *biopsy* in which a surgeon removes a sample of ovary tissue. Experts then examine the tissue with a microscope, looking for cancer cells. If the biopsy reveals cancer, doctors may order additional tests to determine the extent of the disease. These tests include computed tomography (CT) scans of the abdomen and pelvis, and X rays of the chest and other organs.

The treatment for ovarian cancer usually starts with surgical removal of the ovaries and nearby tissues, including the fallopian tubes and often the uterus. The patient may also receive *chemotherapy* (drugs that kill cancer cells). Chemotherapy is more effective in some cases when the drugs are pumped directly into the abdomen of the patient. Patients whose cancer has not spread have an excellent chance of being cured. Physicians often monitor the level of CA 125 in the blood of patients to detect any recurrence of the cancer.   Marc B. Garnick

Ovary, *OH vuhr ee,* is either of a pair of female sex organs that store and release eggs. The ovaries also secrete *estrogens* and *progesterone,* the female sex hormones. The human ovary is oval in shape and about the size of an unshelled walnut. One ovary is on each side of the uterus, at the base of the abdomen.

At birth, each ovary contains about 400,000 immature eggs. About 400 of these eggs will mature and be released during a woman's childbearing years. During the first half of each menstrual cycle, one of the eggs matures. The ovaries also release estrogens, which cause the lining of the uterus to thicken in preparation for pregnancy. *Ovulation* (the release of the mature egg) occurs about midway through the menstrual cycle.

After ovulation, the ovary that released the egg secretes progesterone, which maintains the uterine lining, as well as estrogens. If the egg is fertilized, a pregnancy begins. The ovary and *placenta*—an organ that develops early in pregnancy—secrete progesterone and other hormones, and the menstrual cycle stops until after the baby has been born. If the egg is not fertilized, the ovary stops producing progesterone about 14 days after ovulation. The egg and the uterine lining then pass out of the body during menstruation.

Between the ages of 45 and 55, most women stop menstruating and enter a period called *menopause.* The ovaries gradually stop functioning and shrink to about the size of a pea.   Lois Kazmier Halstead

Related articles in *World Book* include:

Menopause	Pelvic inflammatory disease
Menstruation	Progesterone
Ovarian cancer	Reproduction, Human

Oven. See Cooking (Methods; History); **Range.**

Ovenbird is a common North American bird that belongs to the family of wood-warblers, also known as New World warblers. Ovenbird may also refer to the family Furnariidae, a group of birds in Central and South America that are not related to the North American ovenbird. The North American ovenbird looks like a small thrush. It is about 6 inches (15 centimeters) long

WORLD BOOK illustration by Trevor Boyer, Linden Artists Ltd.
The ovenbird is a common North American warbler.

and has a brownish olive-green back, dull orange crown, and a white breast spotted with black. Its song sounds like the word *teacher,* repeated with increasing loudness. The ovenbird is often called the *teacher bird.*

The ovenbird nests from Oklahoma to Georgia, and north to Manitoba and Labrador. Its name comes from the shape of its nest, which looks somewhat like an old-fashioned rounded oven. The ovenbird hides its nest on the forest floor. It lays four to six white eggs, speckled with cinnamon-brown. It eats mostly insects.

Sandra L. Vehrencamp

Scientific classification. The ovenbird belongs to the wood-warbler, or New World warbler, family, Parulidae. Its scientific name is *Seiurus aurocapillus.*

See also **Warbler.**

Overeaters Anonymous is an organization for people whose eating habits disrupt their lives or threaten their health. The group uses the term *compulsive overeating* to describe many types of eating problems. For example, some members overeat regularly. Others eat too much, then starve themselves or try to eliminate the excess food from their bodies by vomiting or using laxatives. The organization has members in every weight category, from underweight to overweight.

Overeaters Anonymous considers compulsive overeating an illness that can be managed. Members follow a recovery program adapted from Alcoholics Anonymous. This program encourages personal change through applying spiritual principles to life. Members gain support for their personal commitment by attending as many meetings as they wish. At meetings, members provide one another with fellowship, caring, acceptance, and practical advice. The organization's head office is in Rio Rancho, New Mexico.

Critically reviewed by Overeaters Anonymous

Overture, *OH vuhr chur,* is an instrumental composition that introduces a longer musical work, especially an opera. Some overtures, called *concert overtures,* are always performed as independent compositions.

The first overture was written in the 1660's by the French composer Jean-Baptiste Lully. Lully opened his operas and ballets with *French overtures,* which were short pieces consisting of two sections. The first section was slow, and the second lively. The second section often ended with a brief return to the slow tempo.

In the 1690's, Alessandro Scarlatti, an Italian composer, developed the *Italian overture,* also called the *sinfonia.* It consisted of three movements, of which the first was lively and written in the sonata form (see **Sonata**). The second was slow, and the third extremely fast. The Italian overture had an important role in the development of the symphony.

Overtures were revolutionized during the 1700's by the German-born Christoph Willibald Gluck and by Wolfgang Amadeus Mozart of Austria. Gluck became the first major composer to use an overture to set the proper mood for an opera. Previously, the overture had no direct connection with the opera that followed it. Mozart continued Gluck's ideas and established the overture as a single movement. The overtures written by Mozart served as models for overtures to future operas.

During the 1800's, orchestras often performed opera overtures separately at concerts. These performances inspired composers to write concert overtures. Most of these concert overtures were short pieces that musically told a story or set a mood. Popular concert overtures include the *1812* (1880) by Peter Ilich Tchaikovsky of Russia and the *Academic Festival* (1881) by Johannes Brahms of Germany. During the 1900's, composers wrote many concert overtures for school orchestras and bands.

The concert overtures composed by Felix Mendelssohn of Germany during the 1820's and 1830's led to the development of the *symphonic poem* in the mid-1800's (see **Symphonic poem**). Another German composer, Richard Wagner, avoided the traditional overture in his operas of the mid-1800's. Instead, he used an orchestral piece called a *prelude* that led directly into the opera's first scene. Many later composers used neither an overture nor a prelude in their operas.   R. M. Longyear

Ovid, *AHV ihd* (43 B.C.-A.D. 17?), was a great Roman poet. He became best known for his witty and sophisticated love poems.

Perhaps Ovid's most famous work is the *Art of Love,* a kind of manual in verse on how to find and keep a lover. It consists of three books, two addressed to men and one to women, all written in a humorous, satirical style.

Ovid believed that the *Metamorphoses* was his greatest work. It is a narrative poem beginning with the creation of the world and ending in Ovid's time. The poem describes the adventures and love affairs of deities and heroes, with more than 200 tales from Greek and Roman legends and myths. Many of the stories involve a *metamorphosis* (transformation), such as a woman changing into a bird. For information about some of the stories, see **Narcissus; Pygmalion;** and **Pyramus and Thisbe.**

Ovid's other poems include the *Heroides (Letters of Heroines)* and the unfinished *Fasti (The Calendar).* The *Heroides* consists of 21 imaginary letters between famous women of mythology and their husbands or lovers. The *Fasti* deals with Roman religious festivals and customs and anniversaries of historical events.

Ovid was born on March 20, 43 B.C., in Sulmona, Italy. His full name was Publius Ovidius Naso. In A.D. 8, Emperor Augustus banished Ovid to an isolated fishing village on the Black Sea. Ovid wrote many poems pleading to return to Rome. But his pleas were ignored, and he died in exile.   Elaine Fantham

See also **Latin literature** (The Augustan Age).

Oviparous animal, *oh VIHP uhr uhs,* is an animal that reproduces by means of fertilized eggs that develop outside of the mother's body. In *viviparous* animals, eggs are fertilized and develop inside the parent. Most *vertebrates* (animals with backbones) are oviparous, although there are exceptions. For example, certain types of fish, sharks, lizards, and snakes, and all mammals except for the platypus and the echidna, are viviparous. See also **Viviparous animal.**   George B. Johnson

Oviraptor, *OH vuh RAP tuhr,* was a dinosaur that resembled a bird called the *cassowary.* It belonged to a group of similar animals called *oviraptorids.* They lived in what is now central Asia between 100 million and 65 million years ago.

The dinosaur grew about 6 feet (1.8 meters) long. It had a bony crest crowning the top of the head. *Oviraptor* had a beaked mouth with no teeth. A bony peg in the roof of its mouth could have served to stab or crush food. The dinosaur ran swiftly on long hind legs. It had large claws on its forelimbs.

Oviraptor was discovered in 1923. It received its name, which means *egg robber,* because the first skeleton was found atop a nest of eggs. Scientists believed it was feeding on the eggs. However, later discoveries showed that the *Oviraptor* had been a parent tending its nest. What *Oviraptor* ate is not known.

In 1993, fossil hunters found another skeleton of an oviraptorid on top of its nest. This fossil was preserved in exactly the same position as that of a modern bird. The dinosaur sat in the middle of its ring of eggs to protect them. It also may have kept them warm. This discovery suggested that dinosaurs took better care of their young than previously believed. It also strengthened the view that birds are closely related to certain meat-eating dinosaurs.   James M. Clark

Owen, Robert (1771-1858), was a Welsh-born social reformer. He tried to prove as a businessman that it was good business to think of the employees' welfare. He set up the famous New Harmony community in Indiana in 1825. Owen also pioneered in cooperative movements (see **Cooperative** [History]).

Owen was born in Newtown, Wales, on May 14, 1771. He left school when he was 9 years old and went to England to work as a cotton spinner. In 1799, Owen became part owner and the head of the New Lanark cotton mills in Scotland. The Industrial Revolution had begun, and machines were replacing home sewing and weaving. New factories were rarely built with the comfort of the workers in mind. Wages were low, and women and children were not treated with consideration.

Owen organized a model community. Instead of employing children, he built schools for them. He kept his mills in good repair and tried to take care of his laborers' needs. His successful mills impressed many visitors.

New Harmony. Owen wrote on the subject of proper social conditions and tried to interest the British government in building "villages of cooperation." He thought these villages ought to be partly agricultural and partly industrial. He made up his mind to show they could succeed. He then bought the town of Harmonie, Indiana, and renamed it New Harmony. There he attempted to create a *utopia* (perfect society).

Owen believed in equal opportunity for all. His ideas in education were influenced by Johann Pestalozzi, a Swiss educator. Owen opposed mere book learning. He believed children also could be taught "correct ideas" by surrounding them with good examples. Some people disliked the fact that he held antireligious views.

Many of New Harmony's residents eventually gave up Owen's principles. In 1827, the community failed, and Owen returned to England.

Cooperatives. Owen retired from business to concentrate on his social theories. He lived in London in 1828. There, trades unions became interested in his "villages of cooperation." In 1833, Owen helped organize the Grand National Consolidated Trades Union. It had over 500,000 members. The movement tried to reorganize industry into cooperatives. The government and manufacturers opposed it, and by 1834, the union had collapsed. Owen continued to write and agitate for government aid. Although his plans were not accepted, his ideas influenced all later cooperative movements.

Owen died in Newton on Nov. 17, 1858. His son Robert Dale Owen became a well-known social theorist.

David L. Anderson

See also **Kindergarten** (History); **New Harmony; Pestalozzi, Johann H.**

Owen, Robert Dale (1801-1877), was a social theorist and an American legislator. He worked with his father, social reformer Robert Owen, in model communities in Scotland (at New Lanark) and in the United States (at New Harmony, Indiana). He edited the New Harmony *Gazette* with Frances Wright. When the New Harmony community failed in 1827, Owen moved to New York City. He and Wright edited the *Free Enquirer* and tried to organize the Workingmen's Party in 1829 in New York.

Owen returned to Indiana in 1833. He served in the state legislature from 1836 to 1838 and in 1851 and 1852. He was a member of the U.S. House of Representatives from 1843 to 1847. He served as a minister to Naples from 1853 to 1858. Owen championed emancipation for black slaves and influenced President Abraham Lincoln's views. He was a freethinker in religion and a pioneer in advocating birth control and universal education. Owen was born on Nov. 9, 1801, in Glasgow, Scotland. He died on June 24, 1877. David L. Anderson

See also **New Harmony; Owen, Robert.**

Owen, Ruth Bryan (1885-1954), was the first American woman chosen to represent the United States in another country. She served as U.S. minister to Denmark from 1933 to 1936. The United States did not have an ambassador to Denmark at the time. The first woman to serve as a U.S. ambassador to a foreign country was Eugenie Anderson, when she became ambassador to Denmark in 1949.

Owen was born on Oct. 2, 1885, in Jacksonville, Illinois. She was the oldest daughter of the well-known statesman William Jennings Bryan. She served as a Democrat from Florida in the U.S. House of Representatives from 1929 to 1933. Owen served as alternate U.S. representative to the United Nations General Assembly in 1949. She died on July 26, 1954. Alonzo L. Hamby

Owens, Jesse (1913-1980), was an American track-and-field star. His performances during the mid-1930's in college and in the Olympic Games made him one of the most famous athletes in sports history.

Owens won four gold medals at the 1936 Summer Olympic Games in Berlin, Germany. He won the 100-meter and 200-meter races and the broad jump (now called the long jump), and he was a member of the winning American 400-meter relay team. He set Olympic records in the 200-meter race and in the broad jump. The performance of Owens, who was African American, was embarrassing to Adolf Hitler, the ruler of Germany. Hitler and his followers were hoping that German athletes would prove that the Aryans—a term they used for Germans and certain other peoples of northern Europe—were superior to all other peoples.

Owens was born on Sept. 12, 1913, in Oakville, Alabama, near Danville. His given and family name was James Cleveland Owens. His nickname, Jesse, came from his initials, J. C. He was the son of a sharecropper. At the age of 9, he moved with his family to Cleveland. Owens excelled in track and field while attending Ohio State University from 1933 to 1936. At a college meet in Ann Arbor, Michigan, in 1935, he broke three world records and tied a fourth within 45 minutes. Owens set seven world records during his career.

Owens eventually went into the public relations business. He worked in community service, especially youth work. He traveled widely, giving many speeches that supported clean living, fair play, and patriotism. Owens believed that athletic competition could help solve racial and political problems. He died on March 31, 1980.

William F. Reed

See also **Olympic Games** (picture: Jesse Owens).

Owensboro (pop. 57,265; met. area pop. 114,752), lies in western Kentucky, on the south bank of the Ohio River (see **Kentucky** [political map]). Factories there make automotive frames, chemicals, electrical goods, food products, furniture, liquor, and tobacco products. The city is the home of Brescia University and Kentucky Wesleyan College.

Owensboro was founded in the late 1790's as Yellow Banks and later renamed in honor of Colonel Abraham Owen, who died in the 1811 Battle of Tippecanoe. The city was incorporated in 1817. It is the seat of Daviess County. Owensboro's government is headed by a manager and a commission. Keith Lawrence

Owl is a type of bird that usually lives alone and hunts for food at night. Owls are *birds of prey,* or birds that kill and eat animals. Yet scientists do not consider them closely related to other birds of prey, such as falcons or hawks. Owls have long benefited people by eating mice, rats, and other animals harmful to crops.

Scientists have identified more than 200 *species* (kinds) of owls. These birds live throughout much of the world, including many oceanic islands. The smallest owl, the *elf owl,* inhabits the southwestern United States and western Mexico. It grows about 6 inches (15 centimeters) in length. The largest species, the *Eurasian eagle-owl,* grows about 28 inches (70 centimeters) long. It lives in Europe, Asia, and parts of northern Africa. In most owl species, females grow larger than males.

Owls have long symbolized wisdom. The ancient

Greeks believed the owl was sacred to Athena, their goddess of wisdom. Actually, blue jays, crows, and many other birds are probably smarter than owls.

Appearance. Every owl species has a large, broad head with a saucer-shaped ruff of feathers around the eyes. This ruff, called the *facial disk,* reflects sound to the owl's ear openings. In some species, the facial disk and the ear openings are very large. The eyes of most owls are enlarged and directed forward, unlike the eyes of most birds. For this reason, owls can watch an object with both eyes at the same time. Thus they have *binocular vision,* as have people. But unlike people, owls cannot move their eyes in their sockets. Instead, they must move their heads to watch moving objects. Owls have transparent inner eyelids that close over the eyes when the birds attack prey. These eyelids keep the eyes clean and moist and protect the eyes from getting scratched.

Owls possess short, thick bodies; strong, hooked beaks; and powerful feet with sharp claws called *talons.* Some owls have tufts of feathers on their heads that resemble ears or horns. They probably use these feathers to attract mates or to identify other owls of the same species. The long, soft, fluffy feathers of owls often make the birds seem larger than they really are. This plumage usually has dull brown or gray coloring, so the birds can blend into their habitat to avoid enemies.

Way of life. Owls generally hunt at night, though a few species hunt primarily during the day. All owls have bodies well adapted for hunting. They can fly fairly fast, and their soft feathers make little noise when in flight. Night hunters rely not only on their excellent night vision, but also on their hearing to catch prey. The birds can locate and catch mice, voles, and other small creatures in total darkness by listening to the soft noises the animals make on the ground. Most owls search for prey from a perch. Some types search while flying back and forth over fields or marshes. Once the owl spots prey, it quickly and quietly swoops down to make the catch. Occasionally, some owls may pick up animals that have been recently injured along highways.

Owls eat mostly small mammals. But they may also capture birds, reptiles, fish, crayfish, worms, and insects. The biggest owls can seize prey the size of geese or large hares. Some owls feed on many different kinds of prey. Others specialize only in certain types, such as fish from shallow waters. Like hawks, owls tear large prey into pieces when they eat it. But if the prey is small enough, they swallow it whole. They later cough up pellets of bones, fur, scales, and feathers, which they cannot digest. These pellets can be found under their nests and roosting places.

Owls rank among the most useful birds to farmers. They eat many animals that may damage crops, including mice, rabbits, rats, voles, and insects. They seldom take poultry, which are usually asleep and inside when the owls come out to hunt.

Owls do not build their own nests. Instead, many use the old nests of such birds as hawks or crows. Others may use cavities in trees, ledges in caves or cliffs, scraped-out holes in the ground, or underground burrows. Some owls nest in such man-made structures as barns, silos, or belfries. Most female owls lay 2 or 4 eggs, but some lay as few as 1 or as many as 12. The eggs are nearly round and mostly white.

In most owl species, the female incubates the eggs and keeps the nest warm. The male provides food for the female and young. After hatching, the young stay in the nest for 4 to 5 weeks. Owl parents fiercely protect their young from intruders, usually with their strong talons. Young owls remain dependent on the parents for several weeks after leaving the nest. During this time, the young must learn to fly well and to hunt for themselves.

Important owls. Scientists divide owls into two families. One family consists of the *barn owl* and its relatives. The second, and much larger, family contains all other owl species. Biologists refer to birds from the second family as *typical owls* or *true owls.*

The barn owl lives on all continents except Antarctica. It measures about 16 inches (41 centimeters) long. Sometimes called the *monkey-faced owl,* this species has a heart-shaped face, beady eyes, and amusing actions that seem like those of a monkey. Barn owls vary in color, depending on where they live. They usually nest in barns or other places built by people. They may also nest in caves or hollow trees. Barn owls often hunt in open fields. Their call consists of a long screech.

Another member of the barn owl family, the *greater sooty-owl,* lives in dense forests of New Guinea and eastern Australia. This rare species has largely blackish-brown plumage with white markings. It grows to about 20 inches (50 centimeters) in length. Its call consists of a shriek that descends in pitch and lasts about 2 seconds.

Typical owls account for most owl species. The *great horned owl* lives throughout North America and in parts of South America. It inhabits a wide variety of forests and open lands. This large owl grows about 22 inches (56 centimeters) long. Like the barn owl, it varies in color depending on location. The great horned owl gets its name from the hornlike tufts of feathers on its head. Its call features a series of hoots—*whoo, hoo-hoo, whoo, whoo.*

The Eurasian eagle-owl, the largest owl species, is a close relative of the great horned owl. It occurs throughout much of Europe and Asia and in parts of northern Africa. This species lives in a variety of habitats, but it often prefers woodlands. It has mostly brownish coloring with black markings. It also has earlike tufts of feathers on its head. The bird's call repeats a two-note hoot that descends in pitch and sounds like *boo-oh.*

Screech-owls make up a large group of small owls that live throughout the Americas. They measure about 7 to 8 inches (18 to 20 centimeters) long and possess ear tufts. Most screech-owls bear from four to six young. The *eastern screech-owl* lives in woodlands east of the Rocky Mountains, from northern Canada to Mexico. Eastern screech-owls may have reddish or grayish coloring. They like to spend the day in hollow trees and to nest there. The birds often use trees along city streets and in parks. At night, they give trembling calls and hollow whistles that run up and down the musical scale.

The *barred owl* lives in woodlands throughout much of North America. It grows a bit smaller than the great horned owl and has no ear tufts. Brownish-gray bars run horizontally across its upper breast and vertically across its lower breast and belly. The barred owl gives a series of loud hoots, the last one ending with an *ah: whoo, whoo, whoo, whoo—whoo, whoo, whoo, whoo-ah.*

Some kinds of owls

Owls have large, broad heads with saucer-shaped ruffs of feathers around the eyes. These eyes typically face forward and may possess bright yellow *irises* (colored parts). Most owls hunt at night. But some types, such as the burrowing owl, hunt primarily during the day. Owls prove helpful to people because they often eat mice, rats, and other pests.

Burrowing owl
Athene cunicularia
Found in North and
South America
Body length: About 9 inches
(23 centimeters)

Elf owl
Micrathene whitneyi
Found in the southwestern United States
and in Mexico
Body length: About 6 inches
(15 centimeters)

Leonard Lee Rue III, Monkmeyer

Russ Kinne, Photo Researchers

Snowy owl
Nyctea scandiaca
Found in the Arctic
Body length: About 23 inches
(58 centimeters)

Great horned owl
Bubo virginianus
Found in North and South America
Body length: About 22 inches
(56 centimeters)

Walker, APF

Barn owl
Tyto alba
Found on all continents except Antarctica
Body length: About 16 inches
(41 centimeters)

Laura Riley

James R. Fisher, DRK

The *spotted owl* occurs in forested mountains of the western United States and Mexico. It measures about 18 inches (46 centimeters) long and has dark brown plumage with white spots. This owl has become threatened in some areas because of habitat destruction and because a competing species, the barred owl, has gradually invaded its range. The spotted owl's call features several loud hoots: *whoo, woo-hoo, hoo.*

The *great grey owl* lives mostly in northern forests of North America, Europe, and Asia. This large owl grows about 27 inches (69 centimeters) long. Despite its size, it generally feeds on small prey. Its call consists of booming hoots that descend in pitch toward the end: *Whoo-whoo-whoo-whoo-whoo-whoo-whoo.*

The large *snowy owl* breeds in the *tundras* (cold treeless plains) of the Arctic. Adults measure about 23 inches (58 centimeters) long and have mostly white plumage with brown markings. Adult females possess more brown markings than do adult males. The snowy owl may migrate south for the winter. Its call features several rough notes and sounds somewhat like a dog's bark.

Fishing-owls are powerful birds with large, strong bills. They have generally unfeathered legs and scaly feet. They use their feet to grip fish, their main prey. All fishing-owl species live in Africa south of the Sahara. They inhabit forested areas near rivers and lakes. The most widespread species, the *Pel's fishing-owl,* grows about 24 inches (60 centimeters) long and has brownish plumage. It gives a loud two-part call: *hoo, hoo-hoo-hoo.*

The *long-eared owl* lives throughout much of North America, Europe, and Asia, and in parts of northern Africa. It nests in the forests but often hunts in meadows and fields. This species grows to about 15 inches (38 centimeters) in length. Its long ear tufts occur close together, and it has largely *buff* (dull yellow) plumage with vertical brown streaks. Its call consists of several repeated notes, each of which sound like *whoop.*

The *short-eared owl* and *burrowing owl* are among the few owls that hunt mostly during the day. The short-eared owl grows to about the size of a long-eared owl. It also has similar, though slightly darker, coloring. Its short ear tufts are hardly noticeable. Short-eared owls occur in many areas, including northern parts of North America, Europe, and Asia; southern South America; and many oceanic islands. They nest on the ground, often in prairies, meadows, and marshes. Their rapid hooting call first goes higher in pitch and then lower.

The burrowing owl typically lives in deserts and grasslands of the Americas. It has brownish plumage and grows about 9 inches (23 centimeters) long. It often nests in burrows that it steals from such mammals as prairie dogs. The owl's long legs help it walk about easily. Its song repeats the sounds *coo-whooh.*   Eric Forsman

Scientific classification. Owls belong to the barn owl family, Tytonidae, or the typical owl family, Strigidae. The scientific name for the barn owl is *Tyto alba,* and the greater sooty-owl is *T. tenebricosa.* The Eurasian eagle-owl is *Bubo bubo,* the eastern screech-owl is *Otus asio,* and the Pel's fishing-owl is *Scotopelia peli.* The barred owl is *Strix varia,* the spotted owl is *S. occidentalis,* and the great grey owl is *S. nebulosa.* The long-eared owl is *Asio otus,* and the short-eared owl is *A. flammeus.*

See also **Animal** (pictures); **Bird** (pictures: Birds of grasslands; Birds of the desert); **Bird of prey** (picture); **Spotted owl.**

Owyhee Dam, *oh WY hee* or *oh WY ee,* is one of the larger concrete arch gravity dams in the world. It lies on the Owyhee River in Oregon, about 11 miles (18 kilometers) southwest of Adrian, Oregon, near the Idaho state line. The dam is 417 feet (127 meters) high and 830 feet (253 meters) long. It forms a reservoir 52 miles (84 kilometers) long that stores water for irrigating about 16,000 acres (6,470 hectares) of land. The reservoir holds about 715,000 acre-feet (882 million cubic meters) of water. The Owyhee Dam was completed in 1932 at a cost of $6,671,000. See also **Dam.**   Larry W. Mays

Ox is a common name for a variety of cattlelike mammals, including bison, musk oxen, water buffalo, and yak. Many different kinds of animals may be called oxen, but only domestic cattle are true oxen.

In the strictest sense, oxen are domestic cattle trained to work for people. These powerful work animals serve as beasts of burden in some parts of the world. Oxen are generally male cattle that work in pairs to pull a cart or load. These males are usually *castrated*—that is, their sex glands are removed. Oxen have horns that help to hold in place the *yoke* (harness) that enables them to pull loads. Although the term *ox* refers to males, female cattle also can be used as working cattle.   Wendy C. Turner

Scientific classification. The different kinds of oxen belong to the bovid family, Bovidae. Domestic cattle are *Bos taurus.*

Related articles in *World Book* include:

Buffalo	Gaur	Musk ox	Water buffalo
Cattle	Kouprey	Takin	Yak

Oxalic acid, *ahk SAL ihk,* is a strong organic acid found in many vegetables and other plants. It occurs abundantly as its potassium salt in the sap of dock and other plants in the oxalis and rumex plant groups. It is found in grapes, rhubarb, spinach, sweet potatoes, and tomatoes. Oxalic acid is also produced in the body. It has been known since early times.

Industry uses oxalic acid in processing textiles, bleaching straw hats, and removing paint and varnish. It is widely used in chemistry as an analytical reagent. Oxalic acid forms substances called *complexes* with various metals, especially iron. For this reason, it is also used as a rust and scale remover. The acid is prepared commercially by heating sodium formate with sodium hydroxide or by bubbling carbon monoxide gas into a concentrated sodium hydroxide solution.

Oxalic acid occurs as clear, colorless crystals, soluble in water. It is highly poisonous if swallowed. Its chemical formula is $(COOH)_2 \cdot 2H_2O$, and it melts at 101.5 °C (215 °F). This formula is the dihydrate form, as shown by the two water molecules. When heated to 212 °F (100 °C), the crystals lose the water and have the formula $(COOH)_2$ (see **Hydrate**).   Roger D. Barry

See also **Acid; Oxalis.**

Oxalis, *AHK suh lihs,* is the name of a large group of plants that grow chiefly in South Africa and South America. There are hundreds of *species* (kinds) of oxalis. Many species grow as weeds. However, gardeners cultivate some species as ornamental plants and grow them in hanging baskets, window gardens, or rock gardens.

Most kinds of oxalis grow from bulbs, from rootlike *rhizomes,* or from thickened underground stems called *tubers.* They have showy flowers that may be white or a variety of pastel colors. The leaves are shaped somewhat like clover leaves. Both the leaves and flowers close up at night. The leaves taste sour because they contain *oxalic acid.* The acid is so named because it comes from the oxalis plant. The leaves of some kinds of oxalis can be used in salads. One species of oxalis is cultivated in South America for its edible tubers.

August A. De Hertogh

Scientific classification. Oxalis makes up the genus *Oxalis.*

Oxbow lake is a crescent-shaped lake that forms when a river channel is cut off from the main stream. Such a lake is created when a river changes its course to a more direct path to the sea. The river leaves deposits of earth at either end of the curve, and these deposits eventually separate it from the main stream. Many oxbow lakes are shallow. They may become filled with sediments from river floods and decayed vegetation,

Grant Heilman

An oxbow lake, *center,* was once a part of the river in the foreground. Deposits of earth have cut it off from the main stream.

and so disappear. Many oxbow lakes are found in Louisiana, Arkansas, and Mississippi along the Mississippi River and some of its slow-moving branches.

Paul R. Bierman

Oxen. See Ox.

Oxford, England (pop. 134,248), is the seat of the University of Oxford, often called Oxford University. The university, which began to develop in the 1100's, is the oldest British university (see **Oxford, University of**). The city lies between the rivers Thames and Cherwell, about 50 miles (80 kilometers) northwest of London (see **England** [political map]).

The original center of the city was probably a home for nuns that was founded in the 700's. The home was on the present site of the cathedral at Oxford University. Oxford is now an important industrial center, with automobile factories on the outskirts of the city.

Peter R. Mounfield

Oxford, University of, often called Oxford University, is the oldest university in the United Kingdom and one of the world's most famous institutions of higher learning. Oxford University started to develop during the 1100's. It is in Oxford, England, about 50 miles (80 kilometers) northwest of London.

The university consists of 38 colleges, plus several *private halls* established by various religious groups. The

colleges include All Souls, Balliol (pronounced *BAYL yuhl),* Brasenose, Christ Church, Jesus, Lady Margaret Hall, Magdalen (pronounced *MAWD lihn),* Merton, New College, Nuffield, Oriel, St. John's, Somerville, Trinity, and University.

At Oxford, each college is a corporate body distinct from the university and is governed by its own head and *fellows.* Most fellows are college instructors called *tutors,* and the rest are university professors, readers, and lecturers. Each college manages its own buildings and property, elects its own fellows, and selects and admits its own undergraduate students. The university provides some libraries, laboratories, and other facilities, but the colleges take primary responsibility for the teaching and well-being of their students.

Educational program. Each student at Oxford is assigned to a tutor, who supervises the student's course of study, primarily through *tutorials.* Tutorials are weekly meetings of one or two students with their tutor. Students may see other tutors for specialized instruction. They may also attend lectures given by university teachers. Students choose which lectures to attend on the basis of their own special interests and on the advice of their tutor.

The university, not the individual colleges, grants degrees. The first degree in the arts or sciences is the Bachelor of Arts with honors. Oxford also grants higher degrees, diplomas, and certificates in a wide variety of subjects.

The Rhodes scholarship program enables students from the United States, Canada, and many other nations to study at Oxford for a minimum of two years (see **Rhodes scholarship**). The British government grants Marshall scholarships to citizens of the United States for study at Oxford and other universities in the United Kingdom.

History. During the 1100's, a university gradually developed from a number of schools in the city of Oxford. Its development was aided by a break in relations between England and France in 1167. Hostility between the two nations prevented English students from attending the University of Paris, and many of them went to Oxford instead. The university received its first official recognition in 1214.

The three oldest Oxford colleges—University, Balliol, and Merton—date from the 1200's. Twelve more colleges were founded between 1300 and 1555. The first colleges for women were established during the late 1800's. The university did not grant degrees to women until 1920. Oxford's website at http://www.ox.ac.uk presents information about the university.   P. A. McGinley

See also **Architecture** (Gothic revival; picture); **Bodleian Library; Europe** (picture).

Oxford Movement was a revival of the Church of England that began in 1833 at the University of Oxford in England. The English clergyman John Keble preached a powerful sermon intended to show people the evils that threatened the church because of their indifference and ignorance. Keble's fellow leaders of the Oxford Movement were the English clergyman John Henry Newman and the English theologian Edward B. Pusey. Members of the Oxford Movement were also known as Tractarians.

The movement's leaders preached and wrote for a

number of years. They sought to impress the people that the church was "more than a merely human institution; that it had …a ministry ordained by Christ." They wrote a series of essays called "Tracts for the Times" (1833-1841). Many people read these essays, and the movement grew. But in 1841, Newman wrote a *tract* (pamphlet) so decidedly Catholic that the Anglican bishops condemned it. Anglicans are a group of Christians who include members of the Church of England. In 1845, Newman joined the Roman Catholic Church, and he was eventually made a cardinal. Keble and Pusey continued the work of the Oxford Movement, and new leaders took it up.

The Oxford Movement greatly influenced the Anglican world, including the Episcopal Church in the United States. It revived faith in the church as the divine society, not to be controlled by the state. It made the office of the pastor more important. The movement increased the importance of tradition and the *sacraments* (religious ceremonies). It extended the work of the church among the poor in larger cities. In general, it awakened church and laity—that is, members of the church other than the clergy—to a broader view of their power and duty.

Peter W. Williams

See also **Church of England; Newman, John Henry; Wilberforce, Samuel.**

Oxidation, *AHK suh DAY shuhn,* is a chemical reaction in which a substance loses electrons. The term originally referred to any chemical process in which a substance combines with oxygen. This definition of oxidation was formulated by chemists before they discovered that some reactions of this kind could occur without oxygen.

The electrons that are released during oxidation must be captured by another substance. Thus, oxidation is always accompanied by a reaction called *reduction,* in which a substance gains electrons. The combined transfer of electrons is often referred to as a *redox process.* See **Reduction.**

Oxidation can be shown by heating iron and sulfur together. In this case, each neutral iron atom (Fe) loses two electrons and becomes an iron ion (Fe^{2+}). The chemical equation for the oxidation of iron can be written:

$$Fe \rightarrow Fe^{2+} + 2e^-$$

The electrons released during oxidation are immediately picked up by sulfur atoms, resulting in the formation of sulfide ions (S^{2-}). These sulfide ions combine with the iron ions to form the compound iron sulfide (FeS).

The rusting of iron is a common example of the original meaning of oxidation. Iron combines with oxygen in the presence of moisture to form rust. Another example is the formation of such air pollutants as nitrogen oxides and sulfur oxides. Nitrogen oxides are produced when oxygen combines with nitrogen in hot, fuel-burning automobile engines. Sulfur oxides form when oxygen reacts with sulfur in coal-burning furnaces.

Oxidation also occurs inside the human body when food molecules combine with inhaled oxygen to slowly produce carbon dioxide, water, and energy. The combustion of natural gas and other fossil fuels is a form of rapid oxidation. Marianna A. Busch

Related articles in *World Book* include:

Antioxidant	Fire	Oxide
Combustion	Metal (What	Rust
Corrosion	metals are)	

WORLD BOOK photo by Dan Miller

Oxidation with oxygen occurs when oxygen combines with another substance. In a gas flame, *shown here,* oxygen combines rapidly with the carbon and hydrogen in methane, producing carbon dioxide gas and water vapor.

Alice Dole

Rust can result from oxidation with oxygen. Metal rusts, *shown here,* when iron combines slowly with oxygen and water.

Oxide, *AHK syd,* is a chemical compound of oxygen with some other element. Oxides are commonly formed when the elements are oxidized by oxygen in the air. For example, burning the carbon present in coal or wood gives carbon dioxide (CO_2) and carbon monoxide (CO). Burning is rapid oxidation. Carbon dioxide is also formed by slow oxidation processes in animal cells, and it is exhaled from the lungs. The rusting of iron is slow oxidation. Rust contains ferric oxide (Fe_2O_3).

Metallic oxides commonly combine with water to form basic hydroxides, while nonmetallic oxides with water form oxygen acids. The oxides of sulfur and nitrogen are used to form sulfuric and nitric acids.

Sulfur dioxide and nitrogen oxides pollute the air when given off by automobiles, by factories, and by power plants that burn coal or oil. They also mix with moisture in the air to form sulfuric and nitric acids, which fall as *acid rain* (see **Acid rain**). Acid rain damages plants, wildlife, and certain building structures.

Calcium oxide is *quicklime* (CaO). When mixed with water it forms the *slaked lime* used in whitewash and plaster. Sand, important in glassmaking, is one form of *silicon dioxide,* called silica (SiO_2). Other forms of silicon dioxide are quartz, onyx, and opal. Marianna A. Busch

See also **Nitrous oxide; Oxidation.**

Oxidizer. See **Rocket** (introduction; How rockets work; Kinds of rocket engines).

Oxycodone is a drug prescribed by physicians for the management of moderate to severe pain. It is an *opioid* drug, made from a chemical in the opium poppy called thebaine. Oxycodone was first produced in Germany in 1916. At the time, scientists were searching for a less dangerous pain reliever to replace other opium-based drugs. Taken orally, oxycodone is about twice as effective as the drug morphine in relieving pain. Like heroin and morphine, oxycodone is addictive. Laws restrict the availability of oxycodone in the United States and most other countries.

In medicine, oxycodone is used to treat severe pain due to cancer and other serious ailments. It is sold as tablets, capsules, or liquid. It is often combined in a single tablet with other pain medications, such as acetaminophen. A popular slow-release form of the drug is sold under the brand name OxyContin. Like other opioid drugs, oxycodone can cause nausea, constipation, and itching. Abruptly discontinuing the drug after prolonged use may result in *withdrawal.* Signs of withdrawal include diarrhea, sweating, anxiety, and flulike symptoms.

Oxycodone is widely abused. Drug abusers may take it by crushing tablets and "snorting" a small amount into the nose. There, it is absorbed through the nasal lining. Some users smoke crushed tablets or dissolve and inject them. Oxycodone taken in these ways reaches the brain quickly. There, it causes an intense *euphoria* (feeling of well-being). However, like other opioid drugs, oxycodone decreases breathing and can be dangerous. In the United States, abuse of oxycodone and similar prescription pain relievers is the leading cause of fatal overdoses.   Christopher M. Herndon

See also **Drug abuse** (Prescription drugs); **Opiate.**

Oxygen is a life-supporting gas. Nearly all living things need oxygen to stay alive. It combines with other chemicals in plant and animal cells to produce energy needed for life processes. Oxygen is also needed to make most fuels burn. During the burning process, it combines with the fuel in a chemical reaction. Heat is released during the burning process.

Oxygen is one of the most plentiful chemical elements on Earth. It makes up about a fifth of the volume of air. Nitrogen makes up most of the other four-fifths. Oxygen is also found in Earth's crust and in water. This oxygen is not pure but is combined with other elements. On the average, 100 pounds of Earth's crust contains about 47 pounds of oxygen. Nearly half of the weight of most rocks and minerals is oxygen. Every 100 pounds of water contains about 89 pounds of oxygen. Hydrogen makes up the other 11 pounds of water.

Chemical properties. Oxygen has an *atomic number* (number of protons in its nucleus) of 8. Its *relative atomic mass* is 15.9994. An element's relative atomic mass equals its *mass* (amount of matter) divided by $\frac{1}{12}$ of the mass of carbon 12, the most abundant form of carbon. The chemical symbol of oxygen is O.

Ordinary oxygen molecules, such as those that make up about 20 percent of the atmosphere, have two oxygen atoms bonded together. This ordinary oxygen, O_2, is colorless, odorless, and tasteless. Oxygen molecules that have three oxygen atoms make up a gas called *ozone*, O_3. Oxygen combines with many other elements, forming compounds called *oxides* (see **Oxide**).

Ordinary oxygen changes to a pale blue liquid when cooled to its boiling point. Oxygen *liquefies* (becomes a liquid) at −182.962 °C at atmospheric pressure. Oxygen liquefies at a higher temperature when the pressure is increased. At a pressure of 731.4 pounds per square inch (51 kilograms per square centimeter, or 5.043 megapascals), oxygen liquefies at −118.55 °C. These values of temperature and pressure are oxygen's *critical temperature and pressure.* It is impossible to liquefy oxygen at a higher temperature at any pressure. Liquid oxygen is magnetic. It can be held between the poles of a strong magnet. It freezes at −218.4 °C.

How oxygen supports life. Only a few kinds of living things, including certain germs, can live without *free* (chemically uncombined) oxygen, O_2. Human beings and other land animals get oxygen from the air. Fish and most other water animals obtain dissolved oxygen from water.

Free oxygen enters a person's bloodstream through the lungs. It enters a fish's bloodstream through the gills. The blood carries oxygen to the cells of the body. In the cells, oxygen combines with chemicals obtained from food. Energy produced during this process makes it possible for each cell to perform its function in the body. Carbon dioxide is produced in the cells as a waste product (see **Respiration**).

Plant cells use oxygen in much the same way that animal cells do. Plant cells also make oxygen in the process of *photosynthesis.* During this process, the cells use the energy of sunlight to make sugar from carbon dioxide and water. Oxygen is produced as a by-product. The plants release it into the atmosphere. Scientists believe that all of the air's oxygen has been formed from water by this process over billions of years.

Geologists studying ancient soil layers have observed a large increase in iron oxide compounds (rust) dating from about 2.4 billion years ago. These layers of oxygen compounds indicate the time in Earth's history when free oxygen from photosynthesis began to build up in the atmosphere. This time is known as the Great Oxidation Event. Scientists believe the Great Oxidation Event helped more complex organisms to evolve.

Other uses of oxygen. Oxygen has many uses in industry. Some steel is manufactured by the *basic oxygen process.* In this process, a stream of high-pressure oxygen blasts down on melted pig iron. The oxygen burns out impurities. Welders mix oxygen with fuel in their torches to produce a hot flame. The flame burns at a temperature of about 6000 °F (3300 °C).

Liquid oxygen, called *LOX,* is used in rockets propelled by liquid fuels. LOX combines with various fuels, including kerosene and liquid hydrogen, to produce the rocket's *thrust* (pushing force). LOX is also mixed with other fuels to make explosives for blasting.

Making oxygen. Most commercial oxygen is distilled from liquid air. During distillation, the nitrogen boils before the oxygen does, because nitrogen has a lower boiling point. As the nitrogen boils away, the liquid air is left with a greater concentration of oxygen. Commercial oxygen is stored in steel tanks at a pressure of about 2,000 pounds per square inch (140 kilograms per square centimeter, or 14 megapascals). That pressure is more than a hundred times the pressure of the atmosphere.

Small amounts of oxygen can be made by heating potassium chlorate. A little manganese dioxide added to the potassium chlorate speeds up the formation of oxygen.

History. Oxygen was discovered by two chemists working independently, Carl Scheele of Sweden and Joseph Priestley of England. Scheele's laboratory notes show that he prepared oxygen in the early 1770's by heating various compounds, including saltpeter and mercuric oxide. Scheele's experiments were not published until 1777. But Priestley had published his experiments with oxygen in 1775 and published further observations concerning the gas in 1777. He described how he prepared oxygen in 1774 by heating mercuric oxide.

Scheele called oxygen *fire air.* Priestley called it *dephlogisticated air.* In 1779, the French chemist Antoine Lavoisier named the gas *oxygen.* The word means *acid producer.* Lavoisier and others had found that oxygen is a part of several acids. Lavoisier incorrectly reasoned that oxygen is needed to make all acids. He combined the Greek words *oxys* (meaning *sharp* or *acid)* and *gignomai* (meaning *produce)* to form the French word *oxygene.* This word is *oxygen* in English.   Roger E. Summons

Related articles in *World Book* include:

Anoxia	Oxidation
Element, Chemical	Oxide
Hyperbaric oxygen therapy	Oxygen tent
Iron and steel (The basic	Ozone
oxygen process)	Welding
Liquid air	

Oxygen tent is a device that has been used in medicine for patients who require more oxygen than is normally contained in the air. Oxygen tents were once used extensively to treat oxygen deficiencies in infants and children. Physicians seldom use oxygen tents today.

Oxygen tents are made of plastic or other material through which oxygen cannot pass. Oxygen enters the tent through a hose. Some tents are dome-shaped hoods large enough to completely cover an infant. Others can cover an entire bed.

Newer methods of administering oxygen enable doctors and nurses to reach the patient more easily. Oxygen may be given through tubes inserted into the nostrils, or through a mask placed over the nose and mouth. Newborns may receive oxygen through a plexiglass hood placed over the head. Patients who have severe difficulty breathing may need machines called *respirators* (see **Respirator**). People with carbon monoxide poisoning may be placed in a *hyperbaric chamber,* an airtight compartment in which oxygen is provided at pressures greater than atmospheric pressure.   Gerald B. Merenstein

Oyster is a type of shellfish that people harvest for food and pearls. Its soft, edible body is protected inside a hard, two-piece shell. The shell is usually irregular in shape. An oyster spends all except the first few weeks of its life attached to hard surfaces on the seabed. Oysters live in relatively calm waters of mild to tropical coastal oceans. They often form large reefs.

People began eating oysters thousands of years ago. About 100 B.C., the ancient Romans raised oysters on "farms" along Italy's coast. Today, oysters are farmed along coasts of the United States, Europe, and East Asia.

Oysters—like clams, scallops, and some other shellfish—are a type of *mollusk,* a group of soft-bodied animals that have no bones. Oysters are called *bivalve* (two valve) mollusks because their shell is made up of two parts called *valves.*

There are several different groups of oysters. One group includes pearl oysters, which produce high-quality pearls. The oysters most often eaten by people are known as true oysters. They are the most abundant and well-known group. This article chiefly deals with true oysters.

The body of an oyster

Shell. The valves of an oyster's shell are held together at the hinge by an elastic *ligament.* A ligament is a band of stringy fibers. One valve is deeper, larger, and thicker than the other. This large valve is the one that the animal normally fastens to the ocean bottom.

The elastic ligament usually keeps the valves slightly apart. A strong muscle called an *adductor* closes the shell. When threatened or during long periods out of the water, oysters close their valves tightly. They can live with their shell closed for several weeks.

An oyster's shell is made of a hard, chalky material called *calcium carbonate.* The shell is produced by a skinlike organ called the *mantle,* which lines the inside of the shell. The mantle takes minerals from food the oyster eats and directly from seawater. It uses these minerals to produce the shell. Because the mantle makes shell in cycles, periods without shell growth leave a line. Shell lines can be used like the rings of a tree to estimate the age of an oyster. The shell grows as long as the oyster's body grows.

The inside of the shell is white with colored highlights. The shell of a pearl oyster is lined with a smooth, shiny substance called *mother-of-pearl.* A scar inside the shell indicates where the adductor muscle was attached.

Sometimes a piece of grit or other substance becomes caught between the mantle and the shell, irritating the mantle. The irritation stimulates the production of a pearl. Shell material is evenly laid down around the particle to stop the irritation. In this way, a pearl is formed. Pearl oysters can produce high-quality pearls and are the primary source of pearls. True oysters rarely produce pearls. When they do, the pearls are dull in color, irregular in shape, and of little value.

Body organs. An oyster, like all bivalves, does not have a head. A pair of W-shaped gills is beneath the mantle. The oyster uses its gills to breathe. Also, the gills are covered by fine, hairlike *cilia.* Water flow created by the cilia brings single-celled plantlike organisms called *phytoplankton* toward the gills. The cilia direct the food to the mouth. The food then moves into the oyster's stomach. The oyster's heart pumps blood to the parts of its body. A pair of kidneys removes wastes.

An oyster has a simple nervous system made up of a few nerve bundles and connecting nerves. An oyster does not have eyes. However, it does have two rows of sensitive *tentacles* (feelers) along the mantle edge that can sense changes in light, chemicals in the water, and water currents. Any change will cause the tentacles to *contract* (become smaller). In response, the adductor muscle quickly closes the shell against possible danger.

The life of an oyster

Many kinds of oysters are *hermaphrodites* (pronounced *hur MAF ruh dyts)*—that is, animals with both male and female reproductive organs. Certain oysters begin their life as males but later develop into females.

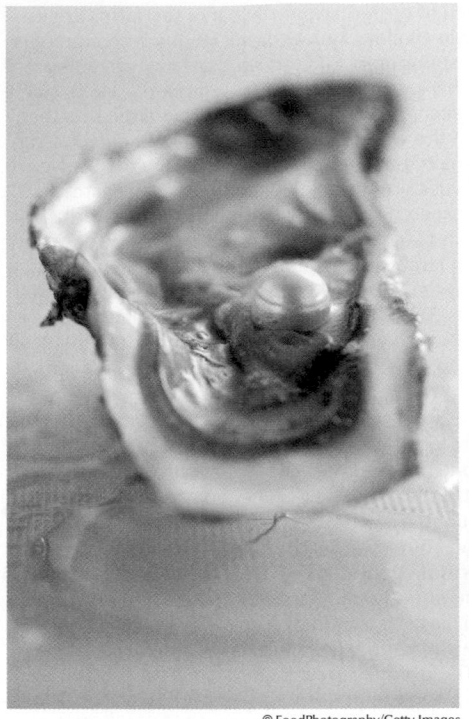

© FoodPhotography/Getty Images

A pearl oyster, *above,* is valued for the high-quality pearls it produces. A pearl forms when an oyster encloses a piece of grit or other irritant in a smooth, shiny substance called *mother-of-pearl.*

© Joy Spurr, Bruce Coleman Inc.

Oysters fasten their shells to rocks or other hard objects on the ocean bottom. Most species live in shallow coastal waters.

Other kinds alternate between male and female several times during their lives. During the female stage, oysters can produce more than 100 million eggs each year. Male oysters release sperm, which fertilize the eggs. In many oysters, the eggs are fertilized after the female releases them into the water. In others, the sperm enter the female's body to fertilize the eggs.

Young. An oyster begins life drifting as part of the mass of tiny organisms called *plankton.* An oyster larva develops from the fertilized egg. After a day, the larva is called a *veliger (VFF luh juhr).* Veligers use their cilia to move. A tiny bivalve shell is visible.

Veligers swim in the water for about two weeks. During this time, the animal continues to develop and forms a muscular "foot" that extends between the valves. The animal is now called a *pediveliger (PEHD uh VEE luh juhr).* The foot is used to test different surfaces as the oyster searches for an appropriate site to settle. An oyster usually chooses a hard surface, such as a rock or the shell of another animal. It then attaches itself permanently to the surface using cement produced by its body. Most pediveligers settle with adult oysters, and together they often form crowded *beds* (groups) in coastal waters. They sometimes form large reefs.

Young oysters lose their foot shortly after they settle. A month-old oyster is about the size of a pea. A year-old oyster is approximately 1 inch (2.5 centimeters) in diameter. Oysters usually grow at a rate of an inch per year for three or four years. After this time, their growth rate

slows. Some oysters grow as large as 14 inches (36 centimeters). Most oysters live about 6 years, but some can survive more than 20 years.

Predators. Many *predators* (hunting animals) feed on oysters. Also, diseases caused by various viruses and *protozoa* (single-celled organisms) can kill millions of oysters in a single year.

Most newly hatched oysters are eaten by predators, including fish and comb jellyfish. Once settled, even adult oysters fall prey to many animals. Starfish use their tube feet to pull at the oyster's valves, which eventually causes the shell to open slightly. The starfish then eats the soft oyster meat. Some crabs with powerful claws can crack the shells of small oysters, as can some fish with strong jaws. An oyster-drill snail uses secretions and its filelike tongue to make a hole in an oyster's shell. The snail then sucks out the oyster meat. Such birds as the oystercatcher can pry an oyster's shell apart with their strong beaks.

People are the greatest predators of oysters. They collect and eat millions of oysters each year. Overfishing and pollution have reduced the stock of oysters.

Oysters and ecosystems

Oysters may form large reefs. These reefs are made up of several generations of oysters attached one on top of another. Oyster reefs can rise above the seabed for 10 to 12 feet (3 to 4 meters). They may cover several acres or hectares. These reefs are important to many *ecosys-*

The body of an oyster

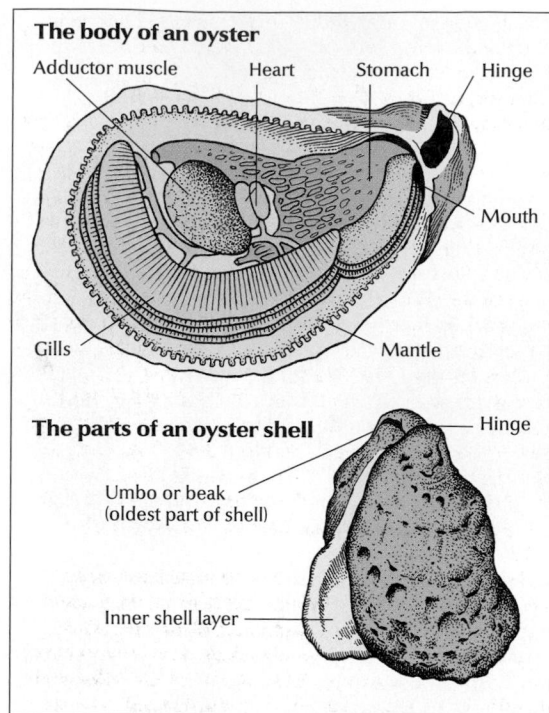

Adductor muscle Heart Stomach Hinge

Mouth

Gills Mantle

The parts of an oyster shell

Hinge

Umbo or beak
(oldest part of shell)

Inner shell layer

WORLD BOOK illustration by Tom Dolan

tems. An ecosystem includes the things that live in an area as well as their relationships with one another and their environment.

Oyster reefs were once much larger than they are today. But they have diminished as a result of human activities, including overfishing and pollution.

Oyster reefs and biodiversity. Oyster reefs provide habitat for many marine organisms. Barnacles, anemones, sea squirts, and other animals attach to the shells of living oysters. Several kinds of fish use empty oyster shells as nesting sites. Some animals hide from predators on oyster reefs. Others come to oyster reefs to feed. The result is that oyster reefs support *biodiversity*—that is, the variety of living things.

Water quality. Oysters filter large volumes of water to remove phytoplankton for food. In the process, they remove nutrients from the water. In many areas, coastal waters are polluted by excess nutrients. This pollution results mainly from human activities, especially agriculture. Water filtration by oysters and other bivalves helps to reduce this pollution. This filtration also makes the water clearer, allowing sunlight to reach greater depths. In this way, oysters improve the quality of the water for other living things.

Reef conservation and restoration. Overfishing and pollution have severely damaged many oyster reefs. As much as 85 percent of natural oyster reef habitat has been destroyed by human activities in about the last 150 years. Scientists and conservation groups are working to restore oyster reefs in many areas.

The oyster industry

Oyster farming. The popularity of oysters as food—and the threat to their natural populations—has led to

the growth of oyster farming. Most oyster farms are established in shallow, quiet coastal waters where there is a firm ocean bottom. Shifting sand or mud can cover and smother oysters. Floats mark a farmed area. Oyster farmers place old shells or tiles on the bottom or suspended in the water. These materials act as *cultch,* a surface to which the young oysters can attach themselves. In areas where oysters do not settle naturally, farmers often buy seed oysters to "plant" in the farming areas. Some oyster farmers spawn oysters and grow the veligers in tanks of seawater. Following settlement, the juvenile oysters are grown in flowing seawater for several weeks. Then, they are planted in coastal waters to finish growing. Workers harvest the crop when the oysters are 2 to 4 years old and 2 to 4 inches (5 to 10 centimeters) in diameter.

Many oysters raised for market come from commercial oyster farms. Large oyster-farming centers include those along the southwest coast of France and the west coast of the United States. China, South Korea, Japan, the United States, and France are the leading oyster-producing countries.

Oyster harvesting is heaviest during fall and winter in most regions. Farmers use long tongs to collect oysters in shallow waters. In deeper waters, they gather the oysters with *dredges,* which are nets attached to metal frames. The dredges are attached to a boat by a line and dragged along the bottom.

Oyster meat. People eat oysters fried, broiled, *scalloped* (baked in sauce), and prepared many other ways. Oysters provide a rich source of protein and several minerals and vitamins. But the U.S. Food and Drug Administration advises that people with diabetes, weakened immune systems, or other medical conditions should avoid eating raw oysters. People once believed that oysters were unsafe to eat during months without an *r* in their name—that is, from May to August. Scientists now know that oysters *spawn* (produce eggs) during the summer. Oysters are less tasty when they are spawning, but they are safe to eat.   Mark Luckenbach

Scientific classification. True oysters make up the oyster family, Ostreidae. The pearl oyster belongs to the family Pteriidae.

See also **Aquaculture; Mother-of-pearl; Pearl.**

© Walter Michot, MCT/Landov

Harvesting oysters from the bottom of Apalachicola Bay in Florida, workers fill a small boat with their catch. The oysters will be taken into port to be cleaned and packaged for market.

Oyster plant. See Salsify.

Oystercatcher is a group of coastal wading birds with chisel-shaped, orange-red bills. An oystercatcher uses its sharp bill to open the shells of such mollusks as mussels and oysters, and to pry limpets from rocks. During the breeding season, females scrape a shallow depression in the ground to use as a nest. They generally lay from two to four eggs.

The *American oystercatcher* lives on the Atlantic coast from the northern United States to Argentina and on the Pacific coast from Lower California to Chile. It has a blackish-brown upper body, white underparts, and a black head and neck. The *American black oystercatcher,*

WORLD BOOK illustration by Trevor Boyer, Linden Artists Ltd.

The oystercatcher uses its sharp, orange-red bill to open mollusks. The species shown here, the common oystercatcher, has black feathers on its upper body and white feathers below.

which is black and blackish-brown, inhabits the Pacific coast from Alaska to Lower California. The *common oystercatcher* lives in Africa, Asia, Australia, and Europe. It has black coloring above and white below. The *sooty oystercatcher* of Australia has all black feathers.

George L. Hunt, Jr.

Scientific classification. Oystercatchers make up the genus *Haematopus.* The scientific name of the American oystercatcher is *Haematopus palliatus.* The American black oystercatcher is *H. bachmani,* the common oystercatcher is *H. ostralegus,* and the sooty oystercatcher is *H. fuliginosus.*

Ozark Mountains, *OH zahrk,* are a range of hills extending from southern Illinois across Missouri and into Arkansas and Oklahoma. The Ozarks rise from 1,500 to 2,300 feet (457 to 701 meters) above sea level. Their highest peaks are the Boston Mountains of Arkansas. The Ozarks are part of the Ozark region, which also includes areas of flatland. The region covers about 40,000 square miles (100,000 square kilometers).

Timber covers the Ozark hills. Many caves lie in the areas where the hills are made of limestone. The Ozarks of southeastern Missouri contain the most important lead mines in the United States. Mines in the Ozarks also produce iron and barite. The raising of beef cattle is the most important agricultural activity over most of the region. Farmers raise dairy cattle on the Springfield Plateau in southwest Missouri. Crops grown in the Ozark region include apples, grapes, peaches, and

wheat. Tourism provides a major source of income in many parts of the region.   Dale Robert Martin

See also **Missouri** (Land regions).

Ozarks, Lake of the. See Lake of the Ozarks.

Ozawa, *oh ZAH wah,* **Seiji,** *SAY jee* (1935-   ), is one of the outstanding orchestra conductors of his time. He established his reputation with a broad range of music, including that of many modern Japanese composers.

Ozawa was born on Sept. 1, 1935, in Hoten, in northeastern China. He went to Europe in 1959 and studied with the Austrian conductor Herbert von Karajan in West Berlin. There, Leonard Bernstein, conductor of the New York Philharmonic Orchestra, observed Ozawa and named him one of the orchestra's three assistant conductors for the 1961-1962 season. Bernstein recalled him as sole assistant conductor for the 1964-1965 season. Ozawa was the Toronto Symphony's conductor from 1965 to 1969 and the San Francisco Symphony's music director from 1970 to 1976. He served as artistic and music director of the Boston Symphony from 1973 to 2002 and director of the Vienna State Opera from 2002 to 2010.   Charles H. Webb

Ozick, Cynthia (1928-   ), is an American author whose works consistently address fundamental questions of Jewish life. Ozick often incorporates Jewish myth and lore into modern circumstances in her novels, short stories, and essays. Her major themes include the shadow of the Holocaust over Jewish identity, the tensions for Jewish immigrants between heritage and *assimilation* (the act of becoming like the people of a nation), and the moral significance of storytelling.

Ozick believes "that stories ought to judge and interpret the world." The influence of the American author Henry James appears in Ozick's specific, deliberate attention to fiction as a forum for social and philosophical ideas. Ozick has written the novels *Trust* (1966), *The Cannibal Galaxy* (1983), *The Messiah of Stockholm* (1987), *The Puttermesser Papers* (1997), and *Heir to the Glimmering World* (2004). Her short fiction has been collected in *The Pagan Rabbi* (1971), *Bloodshed* (1976), *Levitation* (1982), *The Shawl* (1989), and *Dictation: A Quartet* (2008). Ozick writes about various aspects of literature in the essays collected in *Art and Ardor* (1983), *Metaphor and Memory* (1989), *What Henry James Knew* (1993), *Fame and Folly* (1996), and *The Din in the Head* (2006). A collection of autobiographical essays was published as *Quarrel & Quandary* (2000). Ozick was born on April 17, 1928, in New York City.   Arthur M. Saltzman

Ozone is a gas that is present in small amounts in Earth's atmosphere. In the *troposphere* (lowest level of the atmosphere), ozone is a pollutant. It can harm plant and animal tissues, and it can damage rubber and plastic. Ozone in the *stratosphere,* the layer above the troposphere, blocks harmful ultraviolet rays from the sun, protecting life on Earth. Every spring in the Southern Hemisphere since the late 1970's, scientists have observed a depletion of the ozone layer over Antarctica. The region of decreased ozone is called the *ozone hole.*

Ozone is related to the oxygen molecules that sustain life. An oxygen molecule has two oxygen atoms and the chemical formula O_2. An ozone molecule has three oxygen atoms and the formula O_3. Pure ozone is a pale blue gas. The word *ozone* comes from a Greek word meaning *to smell,* reflecting ozone's sharp, irritating odor.

Ozone occurs naturally through *photochemical reactions* and by *electrical discharges*. In photochemical reactions in the stratosphere, ultraviolet rays from the sun strike oxygen molecules, breaking each molecule into two oxygen atoms. The oxygen atoms combine with other oxygen molecules, forming ozone. Electrical discharges include lightning and sparks from motors. Such discharges can break up oxygen molecules, leading to ozone formation. Near Earth's surface, reactions between such gases as nitrogen oxides and hydrocarbons create ozone and other ingredients of a dangerous pollutant called *photochemical smog*.

Commercial applications of ozone include the bleaching of pulp in paper mills and the purification of water. Manufacturers produce ozone by creating electrical discharges in a machine.

Ozone's *relative molecular mass* (formerly called *molecular weight*)—that is, its amount of matter compared to that of the most common form of carbon—is 47.998. The German chemist Christian Friedrich Schönbein discovered ozone in 1840.   Linnea M. Avallone

See also **Catalysis; Environmental pollution** (Air pollution); **Ozone hole; Smog.**

Ozone hole is a region of the atmosphere over Antarctica where a protective layer of ozone gas, a form of oxygen, becomes less concentrated every spring. The ozone layer blocks harmful ultraviolet rays from the sun, protecting life on Earth.

The ozone layer is roughly 10 miles (16 kilometers) thick. The bottom of the layer is about 6 miles (10 kilometers) above the North and South poles. When the gas becomes less concentrated, those dimensions remain about the same, but the number of ozone molecules in the layer decreases. Scientists say that the layer is *depleted*.

Scientists monitoring the atmosphere over Antarctica first noticed ozone depletion in the late 1970's. In 1985, researchers led by the British atmospheric scientist

Joseph C. Farman showed that the ozone hole had grown since the 1960's. That is, over the years, the area of low concentrations of ozone had become larger. In addition, the ozone concentrations had become smaller.

A combination of cold weather and chemical activity creates an ozone hole every year. The cold weather creates ice surfaces on which certain chemical reactions can take place. The chemical activity begins when chemicals called *chlorofluorocarbons* (CFC's) break apart, creating molecules that take part in the reactions.

Most of Antarctica receives little or no sunshine from April through August, so the air becomes extremely cold. In addition, a powerful wind known as the *polar jet* prevents the cold air from mixing with warmer air to the north. As a result, ice clouds form in the ozone layer.

CFC molecules rise to the upper atmosphere, where ultraviolet rays break them up into smaller molecules. The smaller molecules, in turn, take part in chemical reactions on ice particles in the clouds. Those reactions create molecules that destroy ozone in the presence of sunlight.

Between August and October of each year, the number of ozone molecules in the ozone layer over Antarctica decreases by about two-thirds. The reactions that deplete the layer stop around the end of November—late spring in Antarctica. The polar jet also weakens, helping to return ozone concentration to normal.

Ozone depletion also occurs over the Arctic. However, depletion there is usually less severe because Arctic air is not as cold as Antarctic air.

CFC's do not occur in nature. Instead, they are industrially produced. They were once widely used as refrigerants and as propellants in aerosol spray cans. By international agreement, most countries have halted the production of CFC's. But an ozone hole occurs every year because of CFC molecules that remain in the atmosphere.   Linnea M. Avallone

See also **Aerosol; Chlorofluorocarbon; Ozone.**

NASA/Goddard Space Flight Center

The ozone hole is a region over Antarctica where ozone becomes less concentrated every spring. These maps, based on satellite observations, show changes in the hole since 1971. Low concentrations are shown in purple and blue, and high concentrations are in orange and red. The black circle in the 1971 map represents an area for which data were unavailable.